DICTIONARY

OF EARLY

CHRISTIAN

LITERATURE

DICTIONARY OF EARLY CHRISTIAN LITERATURE

Edited by
Siegmar Döpp and Wilhelm Geerlings

Translated from the German
by Matthew O'Connell

A Herder and Herder Book
The Crossroad Publishing Company
New York

The Crossroad Publishing Company
481 Eighth Avenue, New York, NY 10001

Originally published under the title *Lexikon der antiken christlichen Literatur*
©1998 by Verlag Herder Freiburg in Breisgau

Printed in the United States of America

Library of Congress Cataloging-in-Publication Data

Lexikon der antiken christlichen Literatur. English.
   Dictionary of early Christian literature / edited by Siegmar Döpp
and Wilhelm Geerlings ; translated from the German by Matthew O'Connell.
      p.   cm.
   Includes bibliographical references and index.
   "A Herder and Herder book."
   ISBN 0-8245-1805-5
   1. Christian literature, Early—Dictionaries.   I. Döpp, Siegmar.
II. Geerlings, Wilhelm, 1941– .   III. Title.
BR66.5 .L4813 2000
270.1'03—dc21
                                          00-010545

1   2   3   4   5   6   7   8   9   10   04   03   02   01   00

ET SOCIETATI GOERRESIANAE ET PRAESIDENTI EIUS
VIRO CLARISSIMO
PROFESSORI DOCTORI

PAULO MIKAT

MAXIMA CUM GRATIA SUMMAQUE REVERENTIA

Foreword

Textbooks have their history. In Germany the introductory and standard textbook for patristic studies, later known as "Altaner," began its career with the *Grundriß der Patrologie* (Outline of Patrology) of Gerhard Rauschen, a "short textbook for students and clergy." Since the third edition in 1910, this "Outline," enriched by numerous additional references, was already the standard work in patrology, which by this time had begun to move away from pure church and dogmatic history.

Starting in 1921, Josef Wittig attended to the production of several new editions, and the "Outline" appeared under the name of the editors: Rauschen-Wittig. After Wittig left the theological faculty at Breslau, he was replaced as editor by Berthold Altaner in 1931. The tradition of hyphenated names continued: Wittig-Altaner, *Grundriß der Patrologie* (Freiburg, 1931). In 1938, however, Altaner presented a newly conceived textbook which he alone had designed entitled *Patrologie*.

Altaner's three-part presentation of the individual authors and anonymous works—life, writings, teaching—remained binding for later editions. In the third part, "teaching," Altaner attempted to sketch briefly the basic ideas of individual church fathers. This provided a first entry into patrology and dogmatic history for the beginner, even if the sketches remained problematic because of their neoscholastic coloring. In the spring of 1959, Altaner handed over editorial responsibility for his handbook to Alfred Stuiber, who brought out an expanded new edition in 1960. The seventh edition appeared in 1966 under the name Altaner-Stuiber. The eighth edition, published in 1978, remained unchanged except for an appendix with bibliographical supplements.

The advantages of the proven handbook are evident: it provides a one-volume, ready reference work with the most important bibliographical information regarding text editions and secondary literature, providing the reader with a first impression of the personality and work of a given church father. From this perspective, "Altaner" was an indispensable reference work for a generation of theologians. It was intended not so much to be read in its entirety as to be a source of initial information.

The new editors have decided to break from the historical-genetic presentation of "Altaner" and to capitalize on its lexical value by transforming it into a thoroughgoing dictionary. This not only corresponds to the actual use of its predecessor, but also takes into account the contemporary academic situation. No individual researcher is in the position to survey the entire scope of early Christian literature, especially in light of the amount of new information generated by research into Middle Eastern national literatures.

The preliminary work necessary for a transition to a purely literary and genre history of Christian literature is lacking. This being the case, it seemed reasonable to the editors to include articles addressing questions of literary genre, schools, and language.

As a rule, articles on individual authors do not focus on their theological teachings. A sketch of the content of the theology of the most important authors is presented, wherein their influence on later theology is less determinative of the content than the importance they enjoyed among their contemporaries. Included (with few exceptions) are authors and writings from which works or fragments exist and who, in the widest sense, can be counted as belonging to the Christian tradition. A borderline case is the Nag Hammadi writings, which are fully represented.

The traditional dating of the patristic period has been retained with John of Damascus in the East (d. before 754 CE), and Isidore of Seville in the West (d. 636 CE), constituting the upper limits of the period.

A work such as this cannot be accomplished without a great deal of help. We therefore want first to thank the numerous scholars who wrote articles for this work.

In the area of Middle Eastern literature, Privatdozent Dr. Peter Bruns lent the project his acknowledged expertise, while Father Dr. Matthias Skeb, O.S.B., attended to the area of monastic studies. In addition to writing his own articles, Georg Röwekamp also did an excellent job of editing the work.

In addition, we want to thank those who through their technical competence made the publication of this dictionary possible. These are Sebastian Bialas, Sabine Harwardt, Richard Höffner, Jutta Kreilos, Dr. Horst Schneider, Manuel Sango, Christian Schulze, but especially Christine Boll and Dr. Bettina Windau. Last but not least, a special thanks goes to the secretary of the theological chair, Heide Rohlmann.

Further, we want to thank the Gerda-Henkel-Stiftung, the German Bishops Conference, and the Ruhr-Universität Bochum for their support in the production of this work.

Göttingen-Bochum   Siegmar Döpp
August 28, 1998   Wilhelm Geerlings
Feast of St. Augustine

Foreword to the Second Edition

Within a very short time, a second edition became necessary. It was possible only to correct obvious mistakes and printer's errors.

Göttingen-Bochum   Siegmar Döpp
January 6, 1999   Wilhelm Geerlings
Feast of the Epiphany of the Lord

History of a Textbook

G. Rauschen, *Grundriß der Patrologie mit besonderer Berücksichtigung der Dogmengeschichte.* Freiburg, 1903, [2]1906 [3]1910, [4+5]1913.

G. Rauschen-J. Wittig, *Grundriß der Patrologie mit besonderer Berücksichtigung des Lehrgehalts der Väterschriften.* Freiburg, [6+7]1921.

G. Rauschen-J. Wittig, *Grundriß der Patrologie. Die Schriften der Kirchenväter und ihr Lehrgehalt.* Freiburg, [8+9]1926.

G. Rauschen, *Patrologie. Die Schriften der Kirchenväter und ihr Lehrgehalt.* Neubearbeitet von B. Altaner. Freiburg, [10+11]1931 (= Herders Theologische Grundrisse).

B. Altaner, *Patrologie.* Freiburg, 1938 (= Herders Theologische Grundrisse).

B. Altaner, *Patrologie. Leben, Schriften und Lehre der Kirchenväter.* Freiburg, [2]1950, [3]1951, [4]1955, [5]1958, [6]1960.

B. Altaner-A. Stuiber, *Patrologie. Leben, Schriften und Lehre der Kirchenväter.* Freiburg/Basel/Vienna, [7]1966, [8]1978, [9]1980.

S. Döpp-W. Geerlings, *Lexikon der antiken christlichen Literatur.* Freiburg, 1998.

List of Authors

Balke, Klaudia, Münster
Barth, Dr. Heinz-Lothar, Bonn
Baumeister, Prof. Dr. Theofried, Mainz
Beck, Dr. Marcus, Halle
Biermann, Dr. Martin, Göttingen
Böhm, Dr. Thomas, Munich
Boll, Christine, Bochum
Breilmann, Beate, Dortmund
Broszio, Dr. Gabriele, Dortmund
Brox, Prof. Dr. Norbert, Regensburg
Bruns, PD Dr. Peter, Bochum
Bürsgens, Dr. Dr. Wolfgang, Arnsberg

Daur, Dr. Klaus, Hamburg
Delhey, Dr. Norbert, Munich
Döpp, Prof. Dr. Siegmar, Göttingen
Dümler, Bärbel, Leichlingen
Dünzl, Dr. Franz, Regensburg
Durst, Prof. Dr. Michael, Chur

Eymann OSB, P. Dr. Hugo, Beuron

Feiertag, Dr. Jean-Louis,
    Villars-sur-Glâne
Feige, Prof. Dr. Gerhard, Erfurt
Felbecker, Dr. Sabine, Bochum
Feulner, Hans-Jürgen, Tübingen
Fiedrowicz, PD Dr. Michael, Berlin
Fitschen, PD Dr. Klaus, Kiel
Fuhrer, Prof. Dr. Therese, Zurich
Fürst, Dr. Alfons, Regensburg

Gahbauer OSB, P. Dr. Dr. Ferdinand, Ettal
Geerlings, Prof. Dr. Wilhelm, Bochum
Glei, Prof. Dr. Reinhold F., Bochum

Hamm, Ulrich, Oberhausen
Hammerich, Dr. Holger, Kiel
Hanig, Dr. Roman, Munich
Hartmann, Dr. Christoph, Lahnstein
Höffner, Richard, Bochum

Hoffmann, Dr. Andreas, Lüdinghausen
Hofmann, Prof. Dr. Johannes, Eichstätt
Holthaus, Hermann, Dortmund
Hübner, Thomas, Halle

Jacobi, Prof. Dr. Rainer, Halle
Just, Volker, Herne

Kaczynski, Prof. Dr. Reiner, Munich
Kampert, Dr. Otmar, Lüdinghausen
Kamptner, M., Vienna
Kany, Dr. Roland, Mainz
Kasper, Dr. Clemens, Rüdesheim
Kessler SJ, P. Dr. Stephan Ch., St. Blasien
Kinzig, Prof. Dr. Wolfram, Bonn
Klimek, Dr. Nikolaus, Bochum
Klöckener, Prof. Dr. Martin, Fribourg
König, Prof. Dr. Hildegard, Aachen
Krampe, Prof. Dr. Christoph, Bochum
Kranemann, PD Dr. Benedikt, Trier
Kreilos, Jutta, Bochum
Kriegbaum, Prof. Dr. Bernhard, Innsbruck
Kurth, Dr. Thomas, Aachen

Lattke, Prof. Dr. Michael, Queensland
Löhr, PD Dr. Winrich, Bonn
Lößl, Dr. Josef, London

Markschies, Prof. Dr. Christoph, Jena
Marti, Prof. Dr. Heinrich, Küsnacht
Meier, Mischa, Bochum
Merkt, Dr. Andreas, Mainz
Metzler, Dr. Karin, Berlin
Müller, Dr. Hildegund, Vienna
Müller-Abels, Dr. Susanne, Sasbach
Münch-Labacher, Dr. Gudrun, Ammerbuch

Neuschäfer, Dr. Bernhard, Göttingen

Pauli OSB, Sr. Dr. Judith, Altenstadt
Pilhofer, Prof. Dr. Peter, Greifswald
Pillinger, Ao. Univ-Prof. Dr. Renate, Heinberg

Pollmann, PD Dr. Karla, St. Andrews
Prostmeier, PD Dr. Ferdinand Rupert,
    Regensburg
Prünte, Michael, Werl
Puzicha OSB, Sr. Dr. Michaela, Rietberg-
    Varensell

Reichert, PD Dr. Eckhard, Winsen/Luhe
Röwekamp, Georg, Stuttgart

Sand, Prof. Dr. Alexander, Lemberg
Schieffer, Prof. Dr. Rudolf, Munich
Schindler, Prof. Dr. Karl Heinz, Mannheim
Schmidt, Christiane, Dortmund
Schneider, Dr. Horst, Bochum
Schröder, Andreas, Essen
Schröder, Dr. Burghard, Hilchenbach-
    Allenbach
Schulz-Flügel, PD Dr. Eva, Beuron
Schulze, Christian, Bochum
Schwarte, Prof. Dr. Karl-Heinz,
    Meckenheim-Merl
Schwind, Dr. Johannes, Trier
Seeliger, Prof. Dr. Hans Reinhard, Siegen
Skeb OSB, P. Dr. Matthias, Meschede

Speyer, Prof. Dr. Wolfgang, Salzburg
Steimer, Dr. Bruno, Freiburg
Stüben, Dr. Joachim, Heist
Suchla, PD Dr. Beate Regina, Göttingen

Treu, Dr. Ursula, Berlin

Ulrich, PD Dr. Jörg, Erlangen

Vetten, Dr. Claus Peter, Bochum
Vogt, Prof. Dr. Hermann Josef, Tübingen
Volk, Dr. Robert, Scheyern
Vollenweider, Prof. Dr. Samuel, Bern

Wacht, PD Dr. Manfred, Regensburg
Weber, Dr. Dorothea, Vienna
Weigand, Prof. Dr. Rudolf, Würzburg †
Weikmann, Prof. Dr. Hans Martin, Würzburg
Wengst, Prof. Dr. Klaus, Bochum
Windau, Dr. Bettina, Bochum
Wischmeyer, Prof. Dr. Wolfgang, Vienna
Wyrwa, Prof. Dr. Dietmar, Bochum

Zelzer, Prof. Dr. Michaela, Vienna
Ziegenaus, Prof. Dr. Dr. Anton, Augsburg

General Abbreviations

acc.	according	Germ.	German
Alex.	of Alexandria, Alexandrian	Gk.	Greek
anon.	anonymous	hagiog.	hagiographical
apoc.	apocryphal	h.e.	*historia ecclesiastica,* church
Arab.	Arabic		history
Areo.	the Areopagite	hellen.	hellenistic
Arm.	Armenian	hom.	homily
b.	born	Jerus.	of Jerusalem
bibl.	biblical	L	Literature
Byz.	Byzantine, of Byzantium	Lat.	Latin
c.	century	liturg.	liturgical
ca.	circa	LXX	Septuagint
Caes.	of Caesarea	Mops.	of Mopsuestia
Carth.	of Carthage, Carthaginian	ms(s).	manuscript(s)
ch(s).	chapter(s)	Naz.	of Nazianzus
christol.	christological	NT	New Testament
chron.	chronological	Nyss.	of Nyssa
comm.	commentary	OT	Old Testament
Constant.	of Constantinople	philol.	philological
Copt.	Coptic	Pont.	of Pontus, Ponticus
cosmol.	cosmological	Ps.-	Pseudo-
d.	died	Rom.	Roman
dogm.	dogmatic	Ruf.	Rufinus (of Aquileia)
eccles.	ecclesiastical	S	source
ep.	epistle, letter	Soc.	Socrates (historian)
eschat.	eschatological	Soz.	Sozomen (historian)
Eth.	Ethiopian	Syr.	Syriac
Eus.	Eusebius (of Caesarea)	Theod.	Theodoret (of Cyrrhus)
exeget.	exegetical	theol.	theological
frag.	fragment	trans.	translation
Georg.	Georgian	W	Works

Biblical Books

Old Testament

Gen	Genesis
Exod	Exodus
Lev	Leviticus
Num	Numbers
Deut	Deuteronomy
Josh	Joshua
Judg	Judges
Ruth	Ruth
1 Sam	1 Samuel
2 Sam	2 Samuel
1 Kgs	1 Kings
2 Kgs	2 Kings
1 Chr	1 Chronicles
2 Chr	2 Chronicles
Ezra	Ezra
Neh	Nehemiah
Tob	Tobit
Jud	Judith
Esth	Esther
Job	Job
Ps(s)	Psalter, Psalms
Prov	Proverbs
Qoh	Qohelet
Song	Song of Songs
Wis	Wisdom
Sir	Sirach
Isa	Isaiah
Jer	Jeremiah
Lam	Lamentations
Bar	Baruch
Ez	Ezekiel
Dan	Daniel
Hos	Hosea
Joel	Joel
Am	Amos
Obad	Obadiah
Jonah	Jonah
Mic	Micah
Nah	Nahum
Hab	Habakkuk
Zeph	Zephaniah
Hag	Haggai
Zech	Zechariah
Mal	Malachi

New Testament

Mt	Matthew
Mk	Mark
Lk	Luke
Jn	John
Acts	Acts
Rom	Romans
1 Cor	1 Corinthians
2 Cor	2 Corinthians
Gal	Galatians
Eph	Ephesians
Phil	Philippians
Col	Colossians
1 Thess	1 Thessalonians
2 Thess	2 Thessalonians
1 Tim	1 Timothy
2 Tim	2 Timothy
Tit	Titus
Phlm	Philemon
Heb	Hebrews
Jam	James
1 Pet	1 Peter
2 Pet	2 Peter
1 Jn	1 John
2 Jn	2 John
3 Jn	3 John
Jude	Jude
Rev	Revelation

Bibliographical Abbreviations

See Schwertner, Siegfried, *Internationales Abkürzungsverzeichnis für Theologie und Grenzgebiete.* Berlin/New York, 1992.

ABD	The Anchor Bible Dictionary, ed. D. N. Freedman. 6 vols. New York, 1992.
AFFB	Anuario de filologia. Barcelona, 1975–.
ALCP	Annali del Liceo Classico "G. Garibaldi" di Palermo. Palermo, 1964–.
BanMat	Banber Matenadarani. Erevan, 1956–.
Baz.	Bazmavêp, Révue des études arméniennes. Venetik, 1843–.
CCA	Corpus Christianorum. Series Apocryphorum. Turnhout.
CCG	Corpus Christianorum. Series Graeca. Turnhout.
CCL	Corpus Christianorum. Series Latina. Turnhout.
CCM	Corpus Christianorum. Continuatio Mediaevalis. Turnhout.
CLLA/CLLA.S	K. Gamber, Codices liturgici latini antiquiores. 2 vols. Fribourg, ²1968. Supplementum, Fribourg, 1968.
CoptE	The Coptic Encyclopedia, ed. A. S. Atiya. 8 vols. New York, 1991.
DHP	Dictionnaire historique de la papauté, ed. P. Levillain. Paris, 1992.
EECh	Encyclopedia of the Early Church, ed. A. Di Berardino. 2 vols. Cambridge, 1992.
GrLat	Grammatici Latini, ed. Heinrich Keil. 8 vols. Hildesheim, 1981 = Leipzig, 1857–1880.
HLL	Handbuch der Lateinischen Literatur, ed. R. Herzog, P. L. Schmidt. Vol. 4: Die Literatur des Umbruchs von der röm. zur christl. Lit., ed. K. Sallmann. Munich, 1997 (HAW 8.4); vol. 5: Restauration und Erneuerung, ed. R. Herzog. Munich, 1989 (HAW 8.5).
HWRh	Historisches Wörterbuch der Rhetorik, ed. G. Ueding, W. Jens. 3 vols. Tübingen, 1992ff.
JECS	Journal of Early Christian Studies. Baltimore, Md. 1993–.
JStAI	Jerusalem Studies in Arabic and Islam. Jerusalem, 1979–.
MarL	Marienlexikon, ed. L. Scheffczyk and R. Bäumer, 4 vols. St. Ottilien, 1988ff.
NAMSL	Nouvelles archives des missions scientifiques et littéraires. Paris, 1891–1910; n.s. 1911–1917.
NHC	Nag Hammadi Codex/Codices.
NHL	The Nag Hammadi Library in English, ed. J. M. Robinson. Leiden, ⁴1996.
ODB	The Oxford Dictionary of Byzantium, ed. A. P. Kazhdan. 3 vols. New York/Oxford, 1991.
OOSA	Sancti Ambrosii episcopi Mediolanensis opera. Milan/Rome, 1977ff.
PAC	A. Mandouze, Prosopographie chrétienne du Bas-Empire 1: Prosopographie de l'Afrique chrétienne (303–533). Paris, 1982.
PLRE	The Prosopography of the Later Roman Empire, ed. A. H. M. Jones, J. R. Martindale, J. Morris. 3 vols. Cambridge, 1971–1992.
RANL	Rendiconti dell'Accademia Nazionale dei Lincei. Rome, 1892–.
RTStFR	Revista trimestrale di studi filosofici e religiosi. Perugia, 1920–1923.
WJA	Würzburger Jahrbücher für die Altertumswissenschaft. Würzburg, 1946–1950; n.s. 1975–.
ZAC	Zeitschrift für Antike und Christentum. Berlin, 1997–.

Abbreviations of Ancient Authors and Works

Latin: Thesaurus Linguae Latinae. Index librorum scriptorum inscriptionum ex quibus exempla afferuntur. Leipzig, 1990. For Augustine: See the abbreviations in AugL (Augustinus Lexikon) 1:26*–41*.

Greek (secular): A Greek-English Lexicon, ed. Henry George Liddell, Robert Scott, and Henry Stuart Jones/Roderick McKenzie. Oxford, 1961. Additionally, revised supplement ed. P. G. W. Glare. Oxford, 1996.

Greek (Christian): G. W. H. Lampe, A Patristic Greek Lexicon. 7th ed. Oxford, 1984.

𝒜

Aba

A., who acc. to the *Testamentum Ephraemi* (CSCO 335:66f.) was the first disciple of Ephraem, composed a commentary on the → *Diatessaron* (*diat.*), as well as a homily (*hom.*) on Job and an explanation of the Psalms. A few fragments of these works have been preserved. The second commentary on the gospel (*comm. in Ev.*) that has come down under the name of Ephraem is possibly to be attributed to A.

W: *hom.*, F. Nau: ROC 17 (1912) 69-73 [text]. — T. Lamy, S. Ephraemi opera 4:87f. [text]. — *diat.*, J. R. Harris, Diatessaron of Tatian (London, 1890), 92-94 [text]. — *comm. in Ev.*, G. A. Egan, CSCO 291/292 [Armenian text/English trans.].
L: G. J. Reinink, Neue Frgm.: OLoP 11 (1980) 117-133.

P. BRUNS

Aba I (Mar), Catholicos

A. was born into a respected pagan family of Persia and was converted as a young man from Mazdaism to the Chr. faith. He attended the theological school of Nisibis and later, in Edessa, learned Greek from a man named Thomas. While on his extensive journeys throughout the Near East, he met Cosmas, "who sailed to India" (*Indicopleustos*), in Alexandria. As Nestorian catholicos from 540 to 552 he headed the church of Persia, and in 541, after the school of Nisibis had aroused the wrath of the Persian authorities because of its philhellenism, he established a school of theology in Seleucia-Ctesiphon. After several years of imprisonment and exile and shortly before his death (552), A. finally obtained freedom for the church during the regency of one of the Chosroes princes. He carried out fundamental reforms in the Persian hierarchy, as attested by the canonical collections and numerous synodal documents. Ebedjesus (BOCV 3/1:74-81) mentions among A.'s works a translation of the OT; canons (*can.*); synodal letters; a book on the impediments to marriage and, in particular, against the practice, favored by the Persians, of marriage with sisters and daughters; various liturgical hymns; as well as the Syr. translation of the Liturgy of Nestorius, or rather Theodore (*lit.*). In christology A. follows closely his theological model → Theodore Mops., but expressly rejects the Two-Sons doctrine. In his moderate Nestorianism A. always sought for a balance with the orthodoxy of the Greek imperial church.

S: *vita*, P. Bedjan, Histoire de Jahbalaha (Paris, 1895), 206-287 [Syriac text]. — A. Scher, PO 7:154-164 [Arabic text/French trans.]. — O. Braun, Ausgewählte Akten (Kempten, 1915), 188-220 [German trans.].
W: *lit.*, P. G. Badger, Syriac Liturgies (London, 1875) [English trans.]. — idem, Nestorians 2 (London, 1852), 215-243 [English trans.]. — *can.*, E. Sachau, Syr. Rechtsbücher (Berlin, 1914), 255-258. — J. B. Chabot, Synodicon Orientale (Paris, 1902), 69-95, 318-351, 540-561 [text/French trans.].
L: A. Baumstark, Griech. u. hebr. Bibelzitate: OrChr 1 (1911) 1-19. — J. Labourt, Christianisme perse (Paris, 1904), 162-194. — P. Peeters, Recherches d'histoire 1 (Brussels, 1951), 117-163. — G. J. Reinink, Mar Aba-Quelle: ZDMG Suppl. 4 (1980) 171-174. — D. Webb, B. D. Spinks, Anaphora of Theodore: EL 104 (1990) 3-22. — W. Wolska, Topographie chrétienne (Paris, 1962), 63-85.

P. BRUNS

Abdias, Pseudo- (of Babylon)

Ever since its first printing in 1552, a collection of Acts of the apostles (I: Peter; II: Paul; III: Andrew; IV: James the Elder; V: John; VI: James the Brother of the Lord, Simon, and Jude; VII: Matthew; VIII: Bartholomew; IX: Thomas; X: Philip), also known as *Virtutes apostolorum*, has been linked with the name of Abdias of Babylon. In an appendix to the *Passio* of the apostles Simon and Jude, A. is described as a disciple of the apostles and the first bishop of Babylon, who supposedly composed these Acts in Hebrew; they were then translated into Greek and later into Latin by his disciple Eutropius. This Abdias was also identified with the Abdos mentioned in Eusebius, *h.e.* 1.13. In fact, the collection probably comes from the Irish or Frankish world and is to be dated to the 6th c.

W: J. A. Fabricius, Codex apocryphus Novi Testamenti 2 (Hamburg, 1719 = 1522) [text]. — R. A. Lipsius, M. Bonnet, Acta Apostolorum 2/1 (Leipzig, 1898), 128-216 [text]. — L. Moraldi, Apocrifi 2 (Turin, ²1986), 1431-1606 [Italian trans.]. — E. Junod, J. D. Kaestli, CCA 2:750-834 [text of the *Virtutes Johannis*].
L: R. A. Lipsius, Die apokryphen Apostelgeschichten 1:117-178; Ergänzungsband, 5-11. — T. Zahn, Wanderungen: NKZ 10 (1899) 191-218.

P. BRUNS, G. RÖWEKAMP

Abecedary

An abecedary is a poem in which the initial letters of the successive verses or stanzas follow an alphabetical order. This parastichic rather than metrical linking has its origin in prose and was introduced when the traditional metrical form ceased to be obligatory. The abecedary appears almost exclusively in wisdom poetry and hymns and as a help in memorizing. It is to be distinguished from the → acrostic, in which the initial letters of the verses or strophes form a word or a sentence.

The most important Christian abecedaries are, in chronological order: Commodian's poems, from the mid-3rd c., *De ligno vitae et mortis* (*Instructiones* 1.35; CCL 128:29f.) and *Matrones ecclesiae dei vivi* (*Instructiones* 2.15; CCL 128:54f.); the *Hymni* (*qui restant*) of → Hilary of Poitiers, which contain two abecedaries on the Trinity and baptism (2nd third of 4th c.; CSEL 65:209-14); the *Psalmus contra partem Donati* (393) of → Augustine (CSEL 51:3-15); *Hymnus* II of → Sedulius (first half of 5th c.; CSEL 10:163-68); the *ABCedarius* of → Fulgentius of Ruspe (beginning of 6th c.; CCL 91A:877-85); the *Hymnus de Leontio Episcopo* of → Venantius Fortunatus (second half of 6th c.; MGH. AA 4, 1, 19-21), as well as the poem *In Natali SS. Petri et Pauli* of Venerable Bede (beginning of 8th c.; CCL 122:428-30) and the *Analecta hymnica* 50 of Paulinus of Aquileia (second half of 8th c.; MGH.PL 1:123-49).

L: D. N. Anastasijewicz, Die paränetischen Alphabete in der griech. Lit. (Munich, 1905). — A. Dietrich, ABC-Denkmäler: RMP 56 (1901) 77-105. — F. Ermini, Il Psalmus contra partem Donati: Miscellanea Agostiniana 2 (Rome, 1931), 341-352. — W. Geerlings, Augustini Psalmus contra partem Donati: FS H.-J. Pottmeyer (Freiburg i.Br., 1994), 39-66. — K. Thraede, Abecedarius: JAC (1960) 158f.

W. GEERLINGS

Abgar, Legend of

A. was the name of several rulers of Osroene. The Abgar legend, which is connected with Abgar V Ukkāmā ("the Black"), who ruled Edessa from 4 to 7 and 13 to 50 C.E., has come down in several eastern versions. According to the oldest account, in Eusebius *h.e.* 1.13.2, the archives of Edessa contained a correspondence, in Syriac, between A., who asks for a cure, and Jesus, who promises to send a disciple after his own ascension, as well as an account of the cure of the king by the apostle Addai (Thaddeus). This account is found in an expanded form in the legend of Thaddeus, the so-called *Doctrina Addai* (→ Addai), which combines various strands of tradition: blessing of Jesus on Edessa, establishment of the hierarchy and the order of worship, the authentic image of Christ, the finding of the cross by Protonike, and the apotropaic use of the letter of Christ as a phylactery (Deut 6:4-6) (see *Pereg. Aeth.* 19.9, 16f.; Procop., *Pers.* 2.12). The entire legend is an echo of the early period of Christianity in Edessa under Abgar IX, who took severe steps against pagan superstition (Barde-

sanes, *LLR* 45). At the same time it is to be understood as a narrative defense of orthodox Christianity, which saw itself increasingly challenged by the spread of Manichaeism during the 3rd c. Even though the *Decretum Gelasianum* declares the letter of Jesus to be apocryphal, the legend of Abgar had great historical influence in the East, as can be seen from the numerous translations of it (Syr., Gr., Lat., Pers., Copt., Arab., Arm., Slav.).

W: G. Philipps, Doctrina Addai (London, 1876) [Syriac text/English trans.]. — R. A. Lipsius, M. Bonnet, Acta Apostolorum 1 (Leipzig, 1891), 273-283 [Greek text]. — C. Picard, Un texte nouveau: BCH 44 (1920) 41-69 [Greek text]. — R. Peppermüller, Griech. Papyrusfrgm.: VigChr 25 (1971) 289-301 [Greek text]. — H. P. Blok, Kopt. Abgarbriefe: AcOr 5 (1927) 238-251 [Coptic text]. — S. Giversen, Sahidic Version: AcOr 24 (1959) 71-82 [Coptic text]. — Y. Abd al-Masih, Bohairic Letter: BIFAO 45 (1947) 65-80; 54 (1954) 13-43 [Coptic text]. — R. W. Thomson, History of the Armenians (New York, 1981), 95f., 142-162 [Armenian text]. — L. Alischan, Doctrina Addai (Venice, 1868) [Armenian text/French trans.]. — H. J. W. Drijvers, Abgarsage: NTApo⁶ 1:389-395 [German trans.]. — E. N. Mescherskaya, Slavonic Versions: PalSb 23 (1971) 168-172; 26 (1978) 102-106 [Slavonic text].
L: A. Carrière, La légende d'Abgar (Paris, 1895). — E. Cerulli, L'oriente cristiano (Rome, 1964), 9-43. — A. Desreumaux, Témoins syriaques et grecs: Aug. 23 (1983) 181-186. — E. v. Dobschütz, Briefwechsel: ZWTh 43 (1900) 422-486. — idem, Christusbilder: TU 18 (1899) 102-196. — H. J. W. Drijvers, Cults and Beliefs at Edessa (Leiden, 1980). — idem, Addai u. Mani: OCA 221 (1983) 171-185. — F. Hiller, Höhleninschrift: SBA (1914) 817-828. — R. A. Lipsius, Die edessenische Abgarsage (Braunschweig, 1880). — J. B. Segal, Edessa, the Blessed City (Oxford, 1970). — L. J. Tixeront, Les origines de l'église d'Édesse (Paris, 1888).

P. BRUNS

Abibus of Doliche

Bishop A. of Doliche, a suffragan of Alexander of Hierapolis, was hunted from his office, along with Alexander, as being a Nestorian. In the Lat. version of the acts of the Synod of Ephesus there is a short letter from A. in which he complains to friendly colleagues, such as Theodoret of Cyrrhus, of the unjust treatment given him and emphasizes his determination to persevere.

W: PG 84:749f. — ACO 1, 4, 162 [text].

U. HAMM

Abraham of Beth Rabban

A. belonged to the "House of our Teacher," that is, → Narses. He headed the school of Nisibis for sixty years as Narses' successor. He composed numerous exegetical commentaries, as well as a "History of the

Schools," but nothing of these has survived. In the Chaldean Breviary there is a hymn for the night office that is attributed to him.

W: P. Bedjan, A. Kayyat, Breviarium Chaldaicum (Paris, 1886f.), 42 [text].
L: A. Vööbus, School of Nisibis (Leuven/Louvain, 1965), 134-210.

P. BRUNS

Abraham bar Dasandat

A. lived in the 8th c. and taught biblical exegesis in the Nestorian school in Basos (Persia). He was one of the most important mystics of the Persian church. Fragments of his commentary on *Marcus monachus* (BM 17270, 9th c.) have survived, as has his entire treatise on the eremitical life.

W: A. Mingana: WoodSt 7 (1934) 248-255 [text], 186-197 [English trans.].
L: H. L. Jansen, Mysticism: Numen 4 (1957) 114-126.

P. BRUNS

Abraham of Ephesus

A. was initially a monk and founded the monasteries of the Abramites in Constantinople and of the Byzantines in Jerusalem (John Moschus, *prat.* 97). Around the middle of the 6th c. (not before 553) he became bishop of Ephesus. Two homilies of his have been handed down, both seemingly addressed to monks. The *Homilia de annuntiatione* (*annunt.*) can be dated between 530 and 553. It is the oldest witness to the celebration of the feast of the Annunciation on March 25. The *Homilia de hypapante* (*occurs.*) is an exegetical sermon on the presentation of Jesus in the temple. Both sermons follow the teaching of Chalcedon and are directed against, among others, Nestorius, Eutyches, and the Origenists.

W: *annunt., occurs.*, M. Jugie, PO 16:442-454 [text/Latin trans.]. — O. Bardenhewer, Ein neuer Prediger: ZKTh 57 (1933) 426-438 [German trans.].
L: H. G. Beck, Kirche u. theol. Lit. (Munich, 1959), 214, 260, 398f. — M. Jugie, loc. cit., 429-441. — G. Morelli, A.: BSS 1:117f.

B. WINDAU

Abraham of Kashkar

As a young monk, A. (b. 503; d. Jan. 8, 588) served as a missionary among the Arab. tribes of the Syr. wilderness; he visited Scete and, finally, attended the school of Nisibis. He later withdrew to Mount Izla, where he founded its well-known monastery and reorganized the life of the Nestorian monks. He

composed several rules (*reg.*) and a hymn of praise (*hymn.*) in the Chaldean Breviary.

W: *reg.*, J. B. Chabot: RANL 7 (1898) 41-59 [text/Latin trans.]. — A. Vööbus, Syriac Documents (Stockholm, 1960), 150-162 [text/English trans.]. — *hymn.*, P. Bedjan, A. Kayyat, Breviarium Chaldaicum 2 (Paris, 1886f.), 67f. [text]. — J. Molitor, Chaldäisches Brevier (Düsseldorf, 1961), 106 [German trans.].
L: T. Hermann, Regeln: ZNW 22 (1923) 286-298. — J. van der Ploeg, Oud-Syrisch monniksleven (Leiden, 1942).

P. BRUNS

Abraham bar Lipeh

A. was one of the most important liturgists of the Persian Nestorian church. Active in Mesopotamia in the late 7th and early 8th c., he composed a commentary on the liturgy, the *Interpretatio officiorum*, which is important for our knowledge of the Nestorian liturgy.

W: R. H. Connolly, CSCO 29:161-180 [text]; CSCO 32:145-181 [Latin trans.].
L: J. Mateos, Lelya-Sapra (Rome, 1959).

P. BRUNS

Acacius of Beroea

A. was born ca. 322 and initially gave himself to the monastic life. In 378 he was ordained bishop of Beroea. There he sided with Meletius of Antioch, attempted at Rome to end the Antiochene schism, and took part in the Council of Constantinople in 381. Although he had at first been a friend of John Chrys., he became, probably for personal reasons, one of his sharpest critics. At the Synod of the Oak in 403 he was one of the judges rejected by Chrysostom. He played an increasingly important part in the controversy between Cyril Alex. and Nestorius and attempted to mediate between the parties, both before and after Ephesus (431). As a result he played a decisive role in the Union of 433.

Letters and a profession of faith have come down from A., who corresponded with Basil of Caesarea, among others; in response to his inquiry, → Epiphanius of Salamis composed his *Panarion*. Two letters to Nestorian Alexander of Hierapolis (*ep. Alex.*) deal with the agreement that was to be sought between Cyril and the Antiochene bishops; a letter to Cyril (*ep. Cyr.*) urges peace with the Nestorians. In addition, there is a letter to Maximianus of Constantinople (*ep. Maxm.*) and the profession of faith (*confessio fidei*) that was to help toward unity at Ephesus. Two further letters to Cyril are preserved only in fragments (*fr.*); of these the text preserved by → Pelagius I (*defens.* 4) is perhaps from the letter opposing the *capitula* of Cyril.

W: *ep. Alex.,* (1) ACO 1, 4, 85 [Latin text]. — (2) ACO 1, 1, 7, 146f. [Greek text]. — ACO 1, 4, 93f. [Latin text]. — *ep. Cyr.,* ACO 1, 1, 1, 99f. [Greek text]. — ACO 1, 3, 39f [Latin text]. — *ep. Maxm.,* ACO 1, 1, 7, 161f [Greek text]. — *confessio,* ACO 1, 4, 243-245. — *fr.,* J. Lebon, CSCO 93:15 [Syriac text]; CSCO 94:10f. [Latin trans.]. — PLS 4:1338f.
L: G. Bardy, A. et son rôle dans la controverse nestorienne, *RevSR* 18 (1938) 20-44. — V. Emoni, A. (6): DHGE 1:241f. — Die Geschichte des Christentums 2 (Freiburg i.Br., 1996), 451, 558, 563f., 594, 613f., 618-620. — A. Grillmeier, Jesus der Christus 1 (Freiburg i.Br., 1979), 703f. (Eng., Christ in Christian Tradition, vol. 1 [London, ²1975]).

B. WINDAU

Acacius of Caesarea

In 340 A. succeeded Eusebius as bishop of Caesarea. In christology he followed the homoiousian path of his predecessor and was the author of the formula *homoiōs kata tas graphas* ("in like manner acc. to the scriptures"), which was accepted at the joint Synod of Rimini-Seleucia in 359 and was confirmed in Constantinople in 360. He was partly responsible for the consecration of his like-minded colleague Meletius as bishop of Antioch, and he also consecrated Cyril as bishop of Jerusalem, though he later came in conflict with him. He died in 365.

Little is preserved of his numerous works, which bear the stamp of Antiochene exegesis. Jerome (*vit. ill.* 98) and Socrates (*h.e.* 2.4) mention especially exegetical titles. Fragments exist of a commentary on Romans (*fr. Rom.*), of *Quaestiones variae* (*quaest.*), and of a polemic against Marcellus of Ancyra (*fr. Marcell.*).

W: *fr. Rom.,* K. Staab, Pauluskommentare aus der griech. Kirche (Münster, 1933), 53-56. — *quaest.,* R. Devreesse, Les commentateurs de l'Octateuque et des Rois (Rome, 1959), 105-122. — Jerome, *ep.* 119.6. — *fr. Marcell.,* Epiphanius, *haer.* 72.6-10.
L: H. C. Brennecke, Studien zur Geschichte der Homöer (Thessalonica, 1988). — J. M. Lerroux, A., évêque de Césarée: StPatr 8 (1966) 82-85 (literature). — J. T. Lienhard, A.: Contra Marcellum: CrSt 10/1 (1989) 1-22.

G. RÖWEKAMP

Acacius of Constantinople

A., formerly Orphanotrophos, was patriarch of Constantinople from 471 to 491. He expanded the Constantinopolitan primacy of honor as set down in can. 28 of Chalcedon into a primacy of jurisdiction over the East. Above all, however, he played an important role in the reception of the Council of Chalcedon.

When Basiliscus the ursurper issued his *Encyclion* condemning the theol. doctrines of Chalcedon as innovations, A. arranged a public meeting between Daniel the Stylite and Basiliscus, who as a result returned to orthodoxy. On the other hand, it was A. who composed the *Henotikon*, issued by Emperor Zeno in 482, which was intended as a formula of compromise with the moderate Monophysites. Here the concept of *physis* was avoided and Chalcedon was not mentioned. In fact, Peter Mongus in Alexandria and Peter the Fuller in Antioch endorsed the formula. After the failure of an embassy to Rome, at a Roman synod A. was excommunicated by Felix III. This Acacian Schism lasted until 519, when the new emperor, Justin, withdrew the *Henotikon*. When church unity was restored, the name of A. was stricken from the diptychs.

A letter of A. to Simplicius of Rome (468-483) is preserved in which he reports on the confusion in Alexandria after the death of Timothy (*ep. Simpl.*); Zachary the Rhetor preserves a letter to Peter of Alexandria (*ep. Petri*). A letter to Peter the Fuller and one to Peter Mongus are not authentic.

W: *Henotikon,* E. Schwartz, Publizistische Sammlungen zum Acacianischen Schisma (Munich, 1934), 52-54 [text]. — A. Grillmeier, Jesus der Christus 2/1 (Freiburg i.Br., 1986), 285-287 (Eng., Christ in Christian Tradition, vol. 2/1 [London, 1987]). — *ep. Simpl.,* PL 58:46f. — E. Schwartz, loc. cit., 4f. [text]. — *ep. Petri,* Zacharias Rhetor, *h. e.* 11, E. W. Brooks, CSCO 83:235-237 [Syriac text]; CSCO 87:163f. [Latin trans.].
L: P.-T. Camelot, Ephesus u. Chalkedon (Mainz, 1986), 170-194. — W. H. C. Frend, The Rise of the Monophysite Movement (Cambridge, 1972), 143-254. — A. Grillmeier, loc. cit., 267-290. — M. Jugie, A.: DHGE 1:244-248. — A. Kazhdan, A.: ODB 43.

K. BALKE

Acacius of Melitene

Ca. 384 A. was tutor of Euthymius (377-473) and before 430 was elected bishop of Melitene in Cappadocia. This follower of Cyrillian christology took part in the Council of Ephesus as a fierce opponent of Nestorius and shared in the consecration of Maximus of Constantinople as successor to Nestorius. From 433 to 436 A. stirred up a campaign against Theodore Mops. and Diodorus of Tarsus. He died between 438 and 449.

Surviving writings: a sermon (*hom.*) delivered at the Council of Ephesus on the unity of person in the God-man and on the justification of the Theotokos title; a letter to Cyril (*ep. Cyr. Alex.*) ca. 433 (handed down in two different Lat. versions by the *Synodicon adversus tragoediam Irenaei*) in which he praises Cyril's action against the Nestorians and at the same time condemns anti-Nestorian Christians, who nevertheless see in Christ two natures that are independent in their action; a letter to Arm. Patriarch Sahak (d. 439) (*ep. Sahak*) and a letter to the Arm. Christians (*ep. Arm.*), both composed around 436 and preserved only in an Arm. translation, contain a warning against the teachings of Theodore Mops. and Nestorius.

Further letters of A. to Cyril have probably been lost; their existence, however, can be surmised on the basis of the four letters of Cyril to A. (*ep.* 40, 41, 68, 68).

W: *hom.*, PG 77:1468-1472. — ACO 1, 1, 2, 90-92 [text]. — *ep. Cyr. Alex.*, PG 84:693, 838. — ACO 1, 4, 118-119, 232 [text]. — *ep. Sahak*, J. Ismeriantz, Liber epistularum (Tiflis, 1901), 14-15 [Armenian text]. — *ep. Arm.*, J. Ismeriantz, loc. cit., 19-21 [Armenian text].
L: L. Abramowski, Der Streit um Diodor u. Theodor zwischen den beiden ephesinischen Konzilien: ZKG 67 (1955/56) 252-287. — A.-J. Festugière, Cyrille de Scythopolis. Vie de saint Euthyme (Paris, 1962), 62f., 87. — V. Inglesian, Die Beziehungen des Patriarchen Proklos v. Konstantinopel u. des Bischofs A. zu Armenien: OrChr 41 (1957) 35-50. — M. Richard, A., Proclus de Constantinople et la grande Arménie: FS L. Petit (Bucharest, 1948), 273-308, 394-336, 398-400. — U. Rouziès, A.: DHGE 1:242f. — M. Tallon, Livre des Lettres. Ier Groupe: Documents concernant les relations avec les Grecs: MUSJ 32 (1955) 1-146, 29-44. — G. Winkler, Die spätere Überlieferung der arm. Quellen zu den Ereignissen der Jahre vor bis nach dem Ephesinum: OrChr 70 (1986) 143-180.

C. SCHMIDT

Achilleus of Spoleto

A. was bishop of Spoleto during the first half of the 5th c. The only sure date we have for him is 419. During the controversy involving Boniface I and Eulalius, A. was appointed by Emperor Honorius to preside over the celebration of Easter in Rome (*Coll. Avellana, ep.* 21-32; *ep.* 22 is addressed to A.). A. is identified with an Achilles (the name probably shortened for metrical reasons) who authored four epigrams (*epigr.*) that were probably placed on the wall of the Church of St. Peter which the composer built on the Via Flaminia near Spoleto. The verses are of interest in the history of dogma, since they emphasize the primacy of Peter.

W: *epigr.*, ICUR 2,1, 113f.
L: A. Di Berardino (ed.), Patrology 4 (Westminster, Md., '1994), 318f. — A. P. Frutaz, Spes e A.: Atti del 2. Convegno Studi Umbri (Perugia 1964), 352-377. — H. Leclercq, Spolète: DACL 15:1643f. — U. Rouziès, A.: DHGE 1:314f.

B. DÜMLER

Acrostic

An acrostic results when the initial letters of the verses or stanzas of a poem form a word or sentence. If the concluding letters form a word, the term "telestic" or "mesostic" may be used. Acrostics were widely used in esoteric religious literature. In Christian literature of the late 2nd c., the following famous acrostic occurs in the → *Sibylline Oracles: Iēsous Chreistos Theou Huios Sōter Stauros* (*Orac. Sib.* 8: "Jesus Christ, Son of God, Redeemer, Cross"). This was the basis for the new acrostic: *ICHTHUS* ("fish").

Acrostics were very popular in Syr. literature (→ Ephraem the Syrian). In Latin literature this kind of play on words was practiced by Optatian, → Porphyry, → Ausonius, and → Commodian. In addition, many epitaphs took this form. In consecratory inscriptions, too (e.g., St. Agnes Outside the Walls), the name of the donor (in this case, Princess Constantina) was included in acrostic form.

The → abecedary, or alphabetic acrosticon, is a special form.

L: F. Dölger, Das Fischsymbol in frühchr. Zeit (Münster, ²1928). — A. Kurfess, J. D. Gauger, Sibyllinische Weissagungen (Darmstadt, 1998). — idem, T. Klauser, A.: RAC 1:235-238.

W. GEERLINGS

Acts of Andrew

The *A. Andr.* have not come down to us in their original Gr. form. They are first attested in Eusebius (*h.e.* 3.25.6) and rejected as "senseless and godless." Augustine and Evodius of Uzala attribute them to → Leucius; Innocent I attributes them to Xenocharides and Leontius, disciples of Andrew.

The *A. Andr.* can be reconstructed with the help (1) of the *Liber de miraculis Beati Andreae Apostoli* of → Gregory of Tours (a revision that reflects the overall structure of the *A. Andr.*, which Gregory probably had before him in a Lat. version); (2) of Copt. *Utrecht Papyrus* 1 (4th c.); (3) of the Arm. *Martyrdom of Andrew* (the concluding part is a 6th-c. revision); (4) of five Gr. recensions of the concluding section and of various excerpts in other writings.

In content the work is a biographical narrative describing the journey of Andrew from Pontus through various Gk. cities to Patras, as well as his deeds in Patras and Achaia. Theologically there is a discernible kinship with gnosis (no mention of the earthly Jesus; revelation of the divine element in the human being; ascent of the individual soul in death), with Platonism (Andrew's death resembles that of Socrates; God as beautiful and good), and with Stoic ethics. In addition there is a kinship with the *Acts of → John;* they may have also influenced the *Acts of→ Thomas* and → *Paul.*

The educated author seems to have discovered in Christianity a true philosophy. The place of composition cannot be determined; both Greece and Alexandria (because of the intellectual environment) have been suggested. The date of writing was probably 150-200; this is suggested by the unpolemical way in which the *A. Andr.* expound even heterodox ideas in christology and the quite undeveloped ecclesial structure reflected in the work.

Because of their dualism and encratite tendency, the *A. Andr.* were popular with the Manichees and the Priscillianists. Despite their condemnation by, e.g., Innocent I and the *Decretum Gelasianum,* they were passed on and widely read in revised form.

It is debated whether the *Acta Andreae et Matthiae apud anthropophagos* (BHG 1:109ff.) were originally part of the *A. Andr.* or arose independently of that work. By the 6th c. at the latest they formed part of the traditional material of the *A. Andr.*

The *Acta Petri et Andreae* (*A. Petr. et Andr.*; BHG 2:1489) are a continuation of *A. Andr.*; the *Acta Andreae et Bartholomaei,* handed down in a Copt. (BHO 57) and an Arab. (BHO 55) version, arose in dependence on that work. Only two Copt. fragments survive of the *Acta Pauli et Andreae* (*A. Paul. et Andr.*; BHO 917). See → Abdias, Pseudo-, for the *Virtutes Andreae.*

W: *A. Andr.,* J.-M. Prieur, CCA 5-6. — idem, The Acts of Andrew, Texts and Translations 33 (Atlanta, 1990). — NTApo⁶ 2:109-137 [German trans.]. — *A. Petr. et Andr.,* M. Bonnet, Acta apostolorum apocrypha 2/1 (Darmstadt, 1959 = 1891), 117-127 [text]. — M. Erbetta, Gli Apocrifi del NT 2 (Turin, 1966), 530-534 [Italian trans.]. — *A. Paul. et Andr.,* X. Jacques, Les deux fragments: Or. 38 (1969) 187-213 [text]. — idem: RSR 58 (1970) 289-296 [French trans.].
L: F. Blatt, Die lat. Bearbeitungen der Acta Andreae et Matthaei apud anthropophages (Giessen, 1930). — M. Blumenthal, Formen u. Motive in den apokryphen Apostelgeschichten, TU 48/1 (Berlin, 1933), 38-57. — F. Dvornik, The Idea of Apostolicity in Byzantium and the Legend of the Apostle Andrew, DOS 4 (Cambridge, Mass., 1958). — J. Flamion, Les Actes d'André (Leuven/Louvain, 1911). — HLL 4:396-398. — D. R. MacDonald, Odysseus's Oar and Andrew's Cross (Atlanta, 1981). — idem, J.-M. Prieur, The Apocryphal Acts of the Apostles: Semeia 38 (1986) 9-39. — NTApo⁶ 2:399-406. — P. M. Peterson, Andrew, NT.S 1 (Leuven/Louvain, 1958). — J.-M. Prieur, La figure de l'apôtre dans les A. Andr.: F. Bovon et al., Les actes apocryphes (Geneva, 1981), 121-139. — idem, Les actes apocryphes de l'apôtre André: ANRW II 25/6 (1988) 4384-4414. — G. Quispel, An Unknown Fragment of the A.

Andr.: VigChr 10 (1956) 129-148. — R. C. Rodman, A. Andr. as a rhetoric of resistance: Semeia (1997) 27-43.

G. RÖWEKAMP

Addai (*Doctrina Addai*)

A., the legendary apostle of northern Mesopotamia, appears for the first time in the Syr. → Abgar legend. Eusebius (*h.e.* 1.13; 2.1.6-8) identifies him with Thaddeus, one of the 70 disciples of the Lord. A. is one of the outstanding figures of the Christian mission in the region of Syria and Mesopotamia (→ *Chronicle of Arbela*). The *Doctrina Addai* (*doct.*), which contains the nucleus of the Abgar legend and came into existence ca. 400, describes A.'s activity. Barhadbeshabba attributes the founding of the school of Edessa to A. In its present form the *doct.*, a legendary fiction, is an important part of the defense of Edessan orthodoxy as found in → Ephraem, who in his battle against heresy appeals to A. as guarantor of apostolic orthodoxy (*CNis.* 27.11). The Antiochene and Palestinian origin of the early Christian mission in Edessa is to be regarded as the historical nucleus of the legend.

The name of A. appears occasionally in Syr. hagiography, especially in the Mari tradition. Since the Christian mission to the Parthian region came from northern Mesopotamia, A., along with his disciples Aggai and Mari, is regarded as patron of Persia and first bishop of Seleucia-Ctesiphon. The liturgical tradition ascribes to A. and Mari a eucharistic prayer which, in an expanded form, became a fixed part of the Nestorian liturgy. It contains a thanksgiving, *Sanctus,* anamnesis, intercessions, and epiclesis.

W: *doct.,* G. Philipps, Doctrine of Addai (London, 1876) [text/English trans.]. — G. Howard, Teaching of Addai (Chicago, 1981) [text/English trans.]. — P. Bedjan: AMS 1 (1925) 45-94 [text]. — J. B. Abbeloos, Historiae Mar Mari: AnBoll 4 (1885) 50-131. — *lit.,* A. Gelston, Eucharistic Prayer of A. (Oxford, 1992) [text/English trans./comm.].
L: W. Bauer, Rechtgläubigkeit u. Ketzerei (Tübingen, 1934), 6-48. — B. Botte, L'anaphore: OCP 15 (1949) 259-276. — idem, Problèmes: OrSyr 10 (1965) 89-106. — H. J. W. Drijvers, Addai and Mani: OCA 221 (1983) 171-185. — idem, Jews and Christians: JSSt 36 (1985) 88-102. — idem, Facts and Problems, SecCen 2 (1982) 175. — H. Engberding, Fürbittgebet: OrChr 41 (1957) 102-124. — W. Macomber, Oldest Known Text: OCP 32 (1966) 335-371. — R. Raabe, Geschichte des Mari (Leipzig, 1893). — A. Raës, Récit de l'institution: OCP 10 (1944) 216-226. — E. C. Ratcliffe, Original Form: JThS 30 (1928/29) 23-32. — C. Wieckwort, On Heathen Deities: JThS 25 (1923/24) 402-422.

P. BRUNS

Aeneas of Gaza

I. Life: A. (b. ca. 450; d. ca. 518) belonged to a noble house (Procop., *ep.* 82 [564 H.]); whether his parents were pagans or Christians is unknown. He received his early education in Gaza, then studied rhetoric (*ep.* 15), philosophy, and law in Alexandria. He speaks of Hierocles, a Neoplatonist, as his teacher of philosophy (*dial.* 2.9.20). He returned to Gaza and in the school there, along with Procopius and his disciple Choricius, undertook the teaching of rhetoric (*ep.* 11.13), jurisprudence (*ep.* 11; see Procop., *ep.* 82 [564 H.]), and perhaps philosophy. Thanks to his exceptional knowledge of law he seems to have been occasionally entrusted with public functions (Procop., ibid.). Journeys took him to other cities of Palestine and Syria and perhaps to Constantinople.

II. Works: Along with twenty-five mostly personal letters to friends and disciples there has survived a dialogue, *Theophrastes* (*dial.*), in the Socratic style, which can be dated to the period shortly after 484 because of the reference to the persecution of Catholics in Tipasa (66.10ff.). In the interests of apologetics and proselytism, A. compares Christian teaching with Neoplatonic philosophy. In keeping with this aim he renounces specifically Christian proofs and argues extensively from the Middle Platonic and Neoplatonic tradition, which had already been opened to Christian influences by his teacher, Hierocles. Some of his themes are the preexistence of the soul or migration of souls, the creation of the world, and the bodily resurrection.

W: *ep.*, L. M. Positano (Naples, 1962) [text/Italian trans./comm.]. — *dial.*, M. E. Colonna (Naples, 1958) [text/Italian trans./comm.].
L: N. Aujoulat, Le Théophraste d'Énée de Gaza: Koin. 10 (1986) 67-80. — idem, Le De providentia d'Hiéroclès d'Alexandrie et le Théophraste d'Énée de Gaza: VigChr 41 (1987) 55-85. — E. Gallicet, Per una rilettura del Theophrasto di Enea di Gaza e dell'Ammonio di Zacaria Scolastico 1/2: AAST. M 112 (1978) 117-135, 137-167. — T. Kobusch, Studien zur Philosophie des Hierokles v. Alexandrien (Munich, 1976). — E. Legier, Essai de biographie d'Énée de Gaza: OrChr 7 (1907) 349-369. — M. Wacht, A. als Apologet (Bonn, 1969).

M. WACHT

Aerius, Presbyter

In 355, A., an ascetic in the circle of Eustathius of Sebaste, became a priest and manager of a hospice in Pontus. Shortly afterward, he broke with Bishop Eustathius, probably because of his own radical rejection of the ecclesiastical hierarchy (Epiphanius, *haer.* 75.3.3 and 4.4). A. then gathered together some

ascetics, both men and women (the Aerians), in order to live the eremitical ideal in the wilderness.

The polemical picture of A. given by Epiphanius (*haer.* 75), on which Philastrius (*haer.* 72) and Augustine (*haer.* 53) depend, cannot be used without reservations in reconstructing A.'s main theological ideas. The most reliable source seems to be the one presupposed in Epiphanius, *haer.* 75.3.3-9, according to which A. rejected the hierarchy, the established practice of fasting, the Christian feast of Easter, and intercession for the dead; such ideas can be well explained in terms of a radically monastic setting. The motif of envy which Epiphanius brings into play is a heresiological commonplace. The connection of A. with Arianism (*haer.* 75.1.3) is due to a polemical distortion of the theology of the homoousians around Eustathius, who was probably well disposed to A.

S: Epiphanius, *haer.* 75. — Ps.-Epiphanius, *anac.* — Filastrius, *haer.* 72. — Augustine, *haer.* 53.
L: G. Bardy, Sources: Miscellanea Agostiniana 2 (Rome, 1931), 397-416. — F. W. Bautz, A.: BBKL 1:49.

J. ULRICH

Aetius of Antioch

A., born in humble circumstances in Coele-Syria ca. 313, was initially a servant, a goldsmith, and a doctor. He then received a theological education from Paulinus of Tyre and Athanasius of Anazarba, who were opponents of Nicaea, and from Leontius of Antioch. The latter ordained him a deacon ca. 351. In the following period A. took part in the Arian religious controversies. Because of his disagreements with the homoean religious policy, Constantius II exiled him in 360. In 361/362, Julian, whose tutor A. had been, brought him back and honored him (*ep.* 46). After being consecrated a bishop, A. broke with the official church. He and Eunomius organized their own ecclesiastical structure and offices. He died in 365 or 367.

The most important of his surviving works is the *Syntagmation* (*synt.*). Here he endeavors to show, in thirty-six syllogisms, that the *ousia* of God the *agennētos* must be clearly distinguished from that of the Son, and that *agennēsia* definitively describes the nature of God. According to A., God is thus beyond any causation and any bringing forth or generation. Therefore the Son, as one who has become, cannot share in the *ousia* of God but by reason of his becoming is subordinated to God. A similar line of argument can be seen in other, now fragmentary texts, e.g., in the fragment of Ps.-Didymus and in the fragment of a letter in Basil of Caesarea (*ep.*) that clearly brings out the connection between name and *ousia*.

W: *synt.*, Epiphanius, *haer.* 76.11.1-37; 76.14-54. — Ps.-Athanasius, *Trin.* 2.10. — Frgm. bei Ps.-Didymus, *Trin.* 1:10. — *ep.*, Basil, *Spir.* 2.4. — *ep. ad Mazonem*, F. Diekamp, Doctrina Patrum (Münster, 1907), 311f. — *fr. ex oratione de filio*, Ps.-Anastasius Sinaita, *monoph.*, PG 89:1181AB.

L: G. Bardy, L'Héritage littéraire d'A.: RHE 24 (1928) 809-827. — R. Barnes, D. H. Williams (eds.), Arianism after Arius (Edinburgh, 1993). — H. C. Brennecke, Homöer (Tübingen, 1988), esp. 44-59, 215f. — V. H. Drecoll, Die Entwicklung der Trinitätslehre des Basilius von Cäsarea (Göttingen, 1996), esp. 73, 113, 213, 216. — V. Grumel, Les Textes monothélites d'A.: EO 28 (1929) 156-166. — R. P. C. Hanson, The Search for the Christian Doctrine of God (Edinburgh, 1988), 598-611. — R. M. Hübner, Zur Genese der trinitarischen Formel bei Basilius von Caesarea: FS F. Kard. Wetter (St. Ottilien, 1998), 123-156, here 136-138. — T. A. Kopecek, A History of Neo-Arianism 1 (Philadelphia, 1979), 61-297. — R. Mortley, From Word to Silence 2 (Bonn, 1986), 128-135. — M. Simonetti, La crisi ariana nel IV secolo (Rome, 1975). — L. R. Wickham, The Syntagmation of A.: JThS NS 19 (1968) 532-569. — idem, A. and the Doctrine of Divine Ingeneracy: StPatr 11/2 (1972) 259-263.

T. Böhm

Agapitus, Deacon

A., a deacon of Constantinople, was the author of a document dedicated to Emperor Justinian (527) shortly after his accession: the *Ekthesis*, a "little book of exhortation," on the duties of a Christian ruler (*Capitula admonitoria*; *cap.*). The text contains seventy-two short maxims; A. makes use of models that have not come down to us, probably florilegia containing selections from, among others, Ps.-Isocrates (*Ad Dem.*; *Ad Nic.*), → Basil of Caesarea, → Gregory Naz., and → Gregory Nyss.). Emphasis is placed on the ruler's eminence (no. 8) and likeness to God (nos. 3, 21) and his responsibility before God (no. 30), which gives rise to such duties as humaneness (no. 50), charitableness (no. 19), and mercy (no. 37).

A.'s work became an element in the medieval and early modern tradition of the *Mirror of Princes*. In the East (e.g., the *Hypothekai* of Manuel II Paleologus) and the West (e.g., its reception into Erasmus's *Inst. Princ. Christ.*) it exerted an immense influence, especially since the text was also used in schools as a general manual of morality.

W: PG 86:1164-1185. — R. Riedinger (Athens, 1995) [text/German trans./comm.]. — W. Blum, BGrL 14:59-80 [German trans.]. — F. Iadevaia (Messina, 1995) [text/Italian trans./comm.]. — J. Dashian, Studien 2 (Vienna, 1901), 153-255 [Armenian text from the 7th cent.].

L: A. Bellomo, A. (Bari, 1906). — R. Frohne, A. (Tübingen, 1985). — P. Hadot, Fürstenspiegel: RAC 8:615-617. — P. Henry III, Mirror: GRBS 8 (1967) 281-308. — J. Irmscher, Bild: Klio 60 (1978) 507-509. — K. Prächter, Roman: BZ 2 (1893) 444-460. — idem, Rez. A. Bellomo, A.: BZ 17 (1908) 152-164. — I. Sevcenko, A.: RESEE 16 (1978) 3-44.

J. Ulrich

Agapitus I of Rome

A. I (May 535–April 22, 536), a nobleman highly educated in canon law, has left us seven letters (*ep.*). In these he stresses the claim of the bishop of Rome to authority, especially in questions of faith (see *ep.* 2-4). He reprimands Caesarius of Arles for having slandered him and refuses to make a contribution to his poor box (*ep.* 6f.). On a mission to Constantinople A. deposes the monophysitically minded Anthimus and consecrates Mena, a priest, as the new patriarch; he receives assurances from Justinian I regarding the maintenance of the Chalcedonian Creed.

W: PL 66:35-80. — *ep.* 1-4, O. Guenther, CSEL 35:229f., 330-347.

L: E. Caspar, Geschichte des Papsttums 2 (Tübingen, 1933), 199-228. — J. Hofmann, Der hl. Papst A. I.: OS 40 (1991) 113-132.

O. Kampert

Agathangelus

Pen name of the author of a *History of the Armenians*. The work describes the christianization of the Arm. people by Gregory the Illuminator, using much older material for the purpose, e.g., a catechism, the so-called *Doctrina Gregorii*, and the life of Mesrop by → Koriun. The history of the transmission is rather complex. Originally composed in Armenian, it very quickly had its first Gr. translation, which was then circulated in other oriental languages. The Gr. and Arab. bits that have survived represent a shorter recension, according to which Gregory also converted the Georgians and Causcasian Albanians. This recension was connected with the Council of Dwin (506); a later reworking of it in Syriac (ca. 600) has been preserved. The official Arm. version represents the longer recension. It has three parts: (1) description of radical political changes in Persia and Armenia; (2) teaching of Gregory the Illuminator; (3) conversion of the Arm. royal house and people. The second part, which shows clearly the handwriting of later catholicoi (beginning of 7th c.), is especially important for the history of dogmatic development in the Arm. church. The various recensions differ greatly on the date and circumstances of the conversion of Armenia (ca. 314).

W: G. Ter Mekerttschian, St. Kanayeanc', A. (New York, 1980 = Tiflis, 1909, Venice, 1930) [Armenian text]. — G. Lafontaine, Version grecque (Leuven/Louvain, 1973) [Greek text]. — P. Lagarde, AGWG. PH 35 (1888) 3-164 [Greek text]. — R. W. Thomson, A. History of the Armenians (New York, 1976) [Armenian text/English trans./comm.]. — idem, Teaching of S. Gregory (Cambridge, Mass., 1970) [English trans.]. — G. Garitte, Fragments: Muséon 56 (1943) 35-53 [Arabic text]. — idem, Version arabe: Muséon 63 (1950) 231-247 [Arabic text]. — idem, Passion: Muséon 75 (1962) 233-251 [Georgian text]. — idem, Vie de Grégoire: Muséon 65 (1952) 51-71 [Arabic text]. — idem, Sur la foi: Muséon 78 (1965) 119-172 [Georgian text].

L: M. v. Esbroeck, Un nouveau témoin: REArm 8 (1971) 13-167. — N. G. Garsoïan, Iranian Substratum: idem, East of Byzantium (Washington, 1982), 151-174. — G. Garitte, Documents (Rome, 1946). — A. Hultgard, Change and Continuity: T. J. Samuelian, Classical Armenian Culture (Washington, 1982), 8-26. — P. Peeters, Grégoire l'Illuminateur: AnBoll 60 (1942) 91-130. — G. Winkler, History of A.: REArm 14 (1980) 125-141.

P. BRUNS

Agathonicus of Tarsus

A. of Tarsus is the name of a fictive individual to whom some treatises of a dogmatic and apologetic kind have been attributed. These consist of seven writings that have been preserved in Coptic: *De fide*, a profession of faith; *De resurrectione*; *Disputatio cum Iustino de resurrectione*, on faith in the resurrection in response to the doubts of Justin, a Samaritan; *Dialogus cum Stratonico*, in response to the doubts of Stratonicus, a Cilician, about divine providence; *De incredulitate*; *Contra synodum Chalcedonensem*.

Views vary on the author, the original language, and the time of composition. For some, A. is an author associated with Evagrius Pont.; he composed the treatises in Greek at the beginning of the 5th c.; these were later translated into Coptic with alterations and expansions (e.g., the reshaping of the professions of faith to reflect the anthropomorphism of the White Monastery). Others think of an originally Copt. text, composed by an Egyptian Monophysite monk at the end of the 5th or beginning of the 6th c. In either case, the impression is of a series of problems being discussed among the monks of Egypt.

W: W. E. Crum, Der Papyruscod. saec. VI-VII (Strasburg, 1915) [text/German trans.].

L: A. Erhard, A.: W. E. Crum, loc. cit., 154-168. — F. Haase, Rez. W E. Crum: ThRv 15 (1916) 258-260. — H. Kraft, A.: LMA 1:203. — T. Orlandi, A.: CoptE 1:69f.

B. WINDAU

Agrestius

A. was bishop of Lugo (Galicia). Acc. to Hydatius (*chron.* 102), he opposed the choice, in 433, of two anti-Priscillianists as bishops; as an obvious result, he was suspected of Priscillianism. He took part in the Council of Orange in 441. A now fragmentary poem is attributed to him: *Versus Agresti ep. de fide ad Avitum ep.*, a kind of profession of faith that he may have composed in order to avoid being suspected of heresy.

W: PLS 5:400-401. — K. Smolak, Das Gedicht des Bischofs A. (Vienna, 1973) [text/German trans./comm.]. — A. C. Vega, Un poema inedito: BRAH 159 (1966) 203-206 [text].

L: A. Di Berardino (ed.), Patrologia 3 (Turin, 1983), 310f. — B. Löfstedt, Drei patristische Beiträge: Arctos 16 (1982) 65-72, here 65f. — A. C. Vega, loc. cit., 167-209.

B. WINDAU

Agroecius

A. was bishop of Sens in Gaul. He certainly held this office in 475, when Apollinaris Sidonius (*ep.* 7.5) invited him to take part in the election of a bishop in Bourges. He died around 487 and was first buried in St. Gervais but was later transferred to St. Pierre-le-Vif. His feast on June 13 or 15 represents the date of the transfer. A. composed a treatise *Ars de orthographia* (*gramm.*) as an addition to the book of grammarian Flavius Caper; the treatise was dedicated to Bishop Eucherius of Lyons and dates from between 434 and 450. The work deals with the differences in meaning of words that sound alike or derive from the same root or are similar in sense, as well as with the various meanings of one and the same word; it also contains rules of grammar. The work influenced → Isidore of Seville and → Venerable Bede, among others.

W: M. Pugliarello (Milan, 1978) [text/Italian trans./comm.]. — GrLat 7:113-125 [text].

L: M. Besson, A.: DHGE 1:1017f. — J.-C. Didier, A.: BSS 1:619. — M. Prou, A.: DBF 1:802f. — M. Pugliarello, loc. cit., 5-27. — M. Schanz, C. Hosius, G. Krüger, Geschichte der röm. Lit. 4/2 (Munich, 1959 = 1920), 206f.

B. WINDAU

Aithallaha of Edessa

A. was bishop of the church of Edessa from 324/325 to 345/346. In this capacity he took part in the Council of Nicaea in 325. Toward the end of his episcopate he addressed the Christians of the Persian empire in a letter *On Faith*, in which he reported on the council and defended the divinity of the Holy Spirit against the Pneumatomachians. In his theology of creation he rejects Persian dualism and defends traditional teaching on the angels and on the immortality of the human spiritual soul against Thnetopsychism. The original Syr. version of the work is lost, and it survives only in an Arm. translation.

W: J. Thorossian, A. *epistula* (Venice, 1942) [Armenian text/Latin trans.]. — P. Bruns, A.s Brief: OrChr 76 (1992) 46-73; 77 (1993) 120-136 [German trans./comm.]. L: D. D. Bundy, Letter of A.: OCA 221 (1983) 135-142. — M. G. Durand, Un document: RSPhTh 50 (1966) 615-627. — J. Thorossian, A.: Baz. 69 (1911) 559-567.

P. BRUNS

Akathistos

The Akathistos (from "not sitting [in order to sing]") is a Byzantine hymn to Mary in the form of an alphabetic → acrosticon containing twenty-four stanzas. After a proem it recalls the events of Mary's life from the annunciation to the presentation in the temple and then offers mariological reflections and meditations. The short, even-numbered stanzas end with an Alleluja; the long, odd-numbered ones end with Marian *chairetismoi* (salutations). Scholars think of → Romanus the Singer (among others) as the composer of this text, which since the 11th c. has also influenced western Marian poetry; but an earlier date has also been assigned to it.

W: G. G. Meersseman, Der Hymnos A. im Abendland, 2 vols. (Fribourg, Switzerland, 1958/60 [text of various versions]. L: E. Lucchesi Palli, A.: LCI 1:86-89. — T. Nikolaou, V. Trenner, A.: MarL 1:66-68. — K. Onasch, A.: Liturgie u. Kunst der Ostkirche (Berlin, 1993), 20f. — G. Prinzing, A.: LMA 1:250. — I. Szövérffy, A Guide to Byzantine Hymnography 1 (Brookline, Mass., 1978), 116-135. — E. Wellesz, The A. Hymn (Copenhagen, 1957).

B. KRANEMANN

Alexander of Alexandria

During his period of office as bishop of Alexandria, A. was involved in difficult controversies with the Meletians and Arius. He took part in important synods (Antioch [325] and Nicaea [325]). Only fragments of his works remain. Document 4b is perhaps from Athanasius. The *De anima et corpore* may possibly have been composed by A. Of special importance theologically is that A. stressed the equality of Father and Son, the substantial unity of both, and the eternity of the divine generation; with this last Arius strongly disagreed.

W: H.-G. Opitz, Athanasius' Werke 3/1 (Berlin, 1934). — A. v. Harnack, Geschichte der altchr. Lit. 1/1 (Leipzig, ²1958), 449-451. — *an. et corp.*, CPG 2004.

L: E. Bellini, A. e Ario (Milan, 1974). — R. P. C. Hanson, The Search for the Christian Doctrine of God (Edinburgh, 1988). — C. Pietri, C. Markschies, Theologische Diskussion zur Zeit Konstantins: Die Geschichte des Christentums 2, ed. T. Böhm et al. (Freiburg i.Br., 1996), 271-344. — W. Schneemelcher, Der Sermo "De anima et corpore": idem, Gesammelte Aufsätze (Thessalonica, 1974), 240-273. — O. Skarsaune, A Neglected Detail in the Creed of Nicaea (325): VigChr 41 (1987) 34-54. — G. C. Stead, Athanasius' Earliest Written Work: JThS 39 (1988) 76-91. — M. Vinzent, Die Entstehung des "Römischen Glaubensbekenntnisses": Tauffragen und Bekenntnis, ed. W. Kinzig et al. (Berlin/New York, 1999), 185-409.

T. BÖHM

Alexander of Apamea

A. was metropolitan of the province of Syria Secunda and a close friend of Alexander of Hierapolis, whom he accompanied to the Council of Ephesus (431). In a document preserved in the Lat. version of the synodal acts of Ephesus, a version that probably came into existence some years later, A. urgently requests the opportunity for a personal meeting and conversation.

W: PG 84:748. — ACO 1, 4, 159 [text]. L: U. Rouziès, A.: DHGE 2:191. — E. Venables, A.: DCB 1:82f.

U. HAMM

Alexander of Cyprus

A., a Cypriote monk, lived in the second half of the 6th c., in the time of Emperor Justin (527-565).

A.'s *Inventio crucis*, a treatise on the finding of the cross of Christ, provides at the same time a summary of the history of religion from the creation of the world to the time of Constantine, as well as explanations of the doctrines of the Trinity and incarnation; it ends with a tribute to the cross. The work is also preserved in a Georg. and an Old Russian translation. The *Laudatio Barnabae apostoli*, an encomium of the apostle Barnabas that is read in the Church of Barnabas in Salamis, follows Byzantine rhetoric in its form and names as sources, among others, the *Periodoi* ("Travels"), 5th-c. stories about the journeys of this apostle. A. is especially interested in the discovery of Barnabas's relics in Salamis in the time of Emperor Zeno (474-491), as confirmation that the church of Cyprus was an apostolic foundation and therefore independent.

W: *inventio crucis*, PG 87:4016-4076. — P. C. Pennachini, Discorso storico dell'invenzione della Croce del monaco A. (Grottaferata, 1913) [text]. — *laudatio Barnabae apostoli*, PG 87:4087. — ActaSS Iun. 2:436-452; 3a:431-447 [text].

L: E. Bihain, Une vie arménienne de saint Cyrille de Jérusalem: Muséon 76 (1963) 361 n. 6. — H. Delehaye, Saints de Chypre: AnBoll 26 (1907) 236f. — S. Salaville, Le moine A.: EOr 15 (1912) 134-137. — idem, A.: DHGE 2:191f.

C. SCHMIDT

Alexander of Hierapolis

A. of Hierapolis (originally Mabbug, today Manbij) in Syria was metropolitan of the Euphrates province. At the Council of Ephesus (431) he showed himself to be one of Nestorius's most decided followers and was condemned along with him and other eastern bishops. He turned against the christology of Cyril Alex. and, in particular, opposed the Union of 433. Despite his great age he was exiled to Egypt, where he died in 434/435.

About thirty letters and fragments of letters have been preserved, by far the greater number in the Lat. version of the synodal acts of Ephesus. The addressees of these writings, which deal with the Nestorian question, include, among others, → Andrew of Samosata and → Theodoret of Cyrrhus.

W: PG 84:551-864. — C. C. Torrey, Letters of Simeon the Stylite: JAOS 20 (1899) 271f. [Syriac text/English trans.]. — H. Hilgenfeld, TU 32/4 (Leipzig, 1908), 192 [text]. — ACO 1, 4 (Verzeichnis ebd. 1, 3, 1, 95-98) [text].
L: R. Devreesse, Après le concile d'Ephèse: EOr 30 (1931) 271-292. — F. Nau, A.: DHGE 2:190f. — H. Quilliet, A.: DThC 1/1, 766-769. — M. Richard, Théodoret, Jean d'Antioche et les moines d'Orient: MSR 3 (1946) 147-156.

U. HAMM

Alexander of Jerusalem

The most important information about A. of Jerusalem is in Eusebius (h.e. 6, passim). According to Eusebius, A., acknowledged to be a confessor, became bishop of Jerusalem in a marvelous manner ca. 212. There he founded a library and entrusted Origen, even before the latter's ordination as a priest, with the task of catechizing and preaching. A. died in prison during the Decian persecution. Eusebius preserves for us fragments of three letters to the communities of Antioch and Antinoe and to Origen as well as of the letter on justification on behalf of Origen (examples for lay sermons).

W: Eusebius, h. e. 6.11.3, 5f.; 6.14.8f.; 6.19.17f.
L: A. v. Harnack, Geschichte der altchr. Lit. (Leipzig, [2]1958), 1:505-507; 2/2:92f. — P. Nautin, Lettres et écrivains (Paris, 1961), 105-137. — M. J. Routh, Reliquiae Sacrae 2 (Oxford, [2]1846), 161-179.

R. HANIG

Alexander of Lycopolis

According to Photius (contra Man. 1.11), A. was bishop of Lycopolis (Assiut), but he was in fact a pagan Neoplatonist philosopher who toward the end of the 3rd c. composed a treatise Answer to the Teachings of Mani, one of the earliest sources on Manichaeism. A.'s description of the most important facts about this religion (4.23-7.25) and his report on the success of the Manichean mission in Upper Egypt (4.17; 8.12), which was the occasion for his treatise, have been confirmed in their substance by important new discoveries. Noteworthy is the curious attitude, marked by benevolent condescension, toward institutional Christianity (3.1-18; 8.21–9.4; 36.4-14) that is displayed by this witness, the only one apart from Simplicius, to the Neoplatonic objection to Mani's system, whose dualism and its consequences he combats. He treats Manichaeism as a Chr. heresy and an ill-conceived attempt to close the gaps in the "simple philosophy of Christians" in the area of doctrinal principles. There is disagreement among scholars about the special Alexandrian Neoplatonism that A. supposedly represents.

W: A. Brinkmann (Stuttgart, 1989 = Leipzig, 1895) [text]. — A. Adam, Texte zum Manichäismus (Berlin, [2]1969), 54-56 (= 4, 8-8, 4 Brinkmann) [text]. — P. W. van der Horst, J. Mansfeld, An Alexandrian Platonist against Dualism (Leiden, 1974) [text/English trans.]. — A. Villey, A. contre la doctrine de Mani (Paris, 1989) [French trans./comm.].
L: M. Dibelius, A.: RAC 1:270f. — I. Hadot, Le problème du néoplatonisme alexandrin (Paris, 1978). — P. W. van der Horst, J. Mansfeld, loc. cit. — G. Widengren (ed.), Der Manichäismus (Darmstadt, 1977), 3, 21, 57f., 69, 75, 119, 121, 488.

C. P. VETTEN

Alexandrian Synod

The Alexandrian Synod is a pseudoapostolic collection of → church orders that originated at the beginning of the 5th c. in Egypt (therefore "Alexandrian") and is divided into (synodal) canons (sinodos or senodos). Composed probably in Greek, it is preserved in Sahidic, Eth., and Arab. versions. The compilation contains, in addition to the → Apostolic Church Order, two successive texts based on the → Traditio apostolica, which offer the same material, first in an archaic version, then as a parallel to book 8 of the → Apostolic Constitutions (8.3-46).

W: W. Horner, The Statutes of the Apostles (London, 1904) [Arabic, Ethiopic text/English trans.]. — A. de Lagarde, Aegyptiaca (Osnabrück, 1972 = Göttingen, 1883), 209-291 [Sahidic text/English trans. by Horner, 295-363]. — J. and A. Perier, Les "127 canons des apôtres," PO 8/4 [Arabic text/French trans.].

11

L: B. Steimer, Vertex traditionis (Berlin, 1992), esp. 134-140 (literature).

B. Steimer

Allogenēs

Allogenēs is the title of a Copt. work (NHC 11, 3) that is also mentioned in Epiphanius, *haer.* 40.2.2. Allogenēs, "the stranger," who is frequently identified with Seth, shares with a certain Messos the revelation of a thrice-powerful God who teaches humanity the way to knowledge. This way leads at the same time to interiority and to the ascent of the light-soul among the higher aeons. The work is to be taken as witness to a completely Neoplatonic gnosis that shows no Christian influence.

W: C. W. Hedrick, NHC 11, 3 (Leiden, 1990), 173-267 [text/English trans.].
L: M. Scopello, A.: Colloque sur Nag Hammadi, ed. B. Barc (Quebec, 1981), 374-382.

P. Bruns

Amatorium canticum

The *Amatorium canticum* is a Manichean hymn of which Augustine (*Contra Faustum* 15.5f.) cites some fragments that can suggest the content of the hymn. Augustine lists some themes of the hymn, which evidently combined the lyrical features of the Song of Songs with images from the Apocalypse. It praised the most high, eternal Lord God and his kingdom of light and professed love of him. The scepter-bearing king of heaven is crowned with flowers and surrounded by the twelve aeons and flower-strewing gods. Also present are dwellers in his kingdom: other gods and throngs of angels. There are special descriptions of, once again, the radiant supreme ruler—a *rex honoris* with his angels, an armed hero, a *rex gloriosus* who moves the three wheels, fire, water, and wind—as well as of Atlas, who carries the world on his shoulders. Augustine, who refuses to give these images a mystical meaning, criticizes the presentation and the hymns to such a god.

W: A. Bruckner, Faustus v. Mileve (Basel, 1901), 77f. [text].
— I. Zycha, CSEL 25/1:425-428.
L: F. Decret, Aspects du manichéisme (Paris, 1970), 99f.

B. Windau

Ambrose of Milan

I. **Life:** A. was born in Trier, probably in 333/334 (339 is less probable; see *ep.* 49[59].3), as the child of a high-ranking family of (urban?) Roman Christians. His three siblings included an older sister, Marcellina, and a likewise older brother, Uranius Satyrus (PLRE 1:809). The Greek names *Ambrosios* = "the immortal," and *Saturos* indicate the origin of the family, but may also be taken as a reference to their level of education. Unfortunately, we do not know either the clan name (*nomen gentile*) of the family or A.'s surname (*cognomen*); his clan can at most be inferred from his kinship with the pagan rhetor and politician Q. Aurelius Symmachus (Eusebius) (*hex.* 1.32). The suspicion remains that the affiliation of A. with the *gens Aurelia*, which from time to time has been considered or even claimed as certain, is due to early medieval hagiography. Even if A. did belong to that clan, this does not tell us very much, since acc. to the *Constitutio Antoniniana* of 212 C.E. "Aurelius" was one of the most common clan names.

Only from A.'s biographer (Paulinus, *v. Ambr.* 3.1) do we know something of A.'s father, Ambrose the Elder (PLRE 1:51), who was pretorian prefect of Gaul, probably between 337 and 340/341, with his residence in Trier. After the father's death (connected perhaps with the ignominious end of the Augustus of Gaul, Constantine II, in the spring of 340), the mother and children lived in Rome; there, and previously in Trier, A. received a careful but rigorous education (*hex.* 6.38). A. says nothing about well-known contemporary teachers in Rome (such as Donatus or Marius Victorinus); in any case, the level and range of his knowledge of Greek are striking by comparison with his contemporaries. His readings and use of pagan literature reflect contemporary educational norms. As a young man (*adolescens*) (*v. Ambr.* 4.11), A. experienced the solemn profession of his sisters in the Basilica of St. Peter (Jan. 6, 353/354); in 377 A. imitated the address given by the local bishop, Liberius, on that occasion (*virg.* 3.1.1–1.14).

It is not surprising that at the end of the various stages of his education, which concluded with instruction in jurisprudence, A. entered upon a career as a civil servant. His first position was as counsellor (*advocatus*) at the court of the pretorian prefect of Illyria in Sirmium (365 at the earliest), and he became an advisor to Prefect Sextus Claudius Petronius Probus (from 368; *v. Ambr.* 5.1). Both in Rome and in Sirmium A. was already able to witness the eccles. controversies over the Nicene Creed. Probably a little later than is usually assumed, namely, between 372 and 374 (the usual assumption is 370), he attained consular rank as provincial governor of Aemilia Liguria, with his seat in Milan at the western imperial residence (*v. Ambr.* 5.2; Ruf., *h.e.*

11; Soz., *h.e.* 6.24.2; Soc., *h.e.* 4.30.2; Theod., *h.e.* 4.7). This final stage in his career as an imperial official in one of the most prominent governorships of the realm shows that had he not subsequently shifted to the eccles. hierarchy he might well have rapidly reached the highest positions in the civil government.

Under the local (Greek) bishop, Auxentius (355-374), Milan had developed into a main support of the Lat. homoeans, with the followers of Nicaea being a minority there. The various reports on the election of A. as bishop in 374 (403: Ruf., *h.e.* 11.11; 411/412: *v. Ambr.* 6.1f.; before 439: Soc., *h.e.* 4.30.1-8; after 439: Soz., *h.e.* 6.24.1-5; even 449/450: Theod., *h.e.* 4.6.5–7.6), amid their embellishments, both specifically literary and in part motivated by considerations of eccles. politics, have one thing in common: that the governor, as part of his official duties, was present for the tricky election of a bishop and after a difficult phase was unanimously elected as a compromise candidate, so to speak, but that he hesitated to accept the election and was compelled to do so by Emperor Valentinian I himself. It is difficult to come to a clear judgment on the historicity of the details reported by A.'s secretary, Paulinus (e.g., the child's voice, the flight). Possibly on Dec. 7, 374 (or Nov. 24, 373 is also maintained) A. was baptized; the choice of a catechumen or a neophyte as bishop was, of course, contrary to canon law (e.g., can. 2 of Nicaea).

A. taught and learned at the same time (*off.* 1.1.4) under the influence of Simplician, a priest (Augustine, *conf.* 8.2.3), who was a friend of Marius Victorinus. In a surprisingly single-minded and rapid way, immediately after his election as bishop, A. dedicated himself to a Neo-Nicene course of action of a Cappadocian kind, but he also retained the clergy of his predecessor in their offices: he corresponded with Basil of Caesarea (Basil, *ep.* 197, but this letter is only partially authentic) and expressed himself along Neo-Nicene lines in his writings.

A.'s eccles. politics during his first four years in office remain obscure (this holds also for the "great Illyrian Synod of Sirmium," traditionally associated with him). It is certain that after the death of Valentinian I, A. tried to win over his son Gratian (sole ruler of the West since 375) to an antihomoean eccles. policy which he introduced as anti-Arian. This attempt was aided by the first two books *de fide*; it is debated whether they belong to 378 or 380/381. It is certain that Gratian's anti-Donatist rescript (*Cod. Theod.* 16.5.5) does not represent a "retraction" of the so-called "Edict of Tolerance" (378) of

Sirmium (Soc., *h.e.* 5.2.1), which would supposedly be explained by A.'s influence over the emperor.

Clear evidence of cooperation between emperor and bishop and unambiguous measures in the service of a Neo-Nicene eccles. policy are present in 381: A. addressed three more books *de fide* to the emperor and in September 381 held a synod in Aquileia in order to break the influence of homoean bishops (chiefly Illyrian) and (following the model of an imperial judicial inquiry) to hand them over for criminal prosecution. In the winter of 382/383 A. urged the emperor to remove the statue of Victory from the Roman senate and to introduce further measures against pagan worship in the city. Around the same time, possibly with A.'s participation, a Lat. Nicene synodal document was issued in Rome (the so-called *Tomus Damasi*, or "Long letter"). In 383 Gratian finally also set aside his insignia and title as *pontifex maximus* (Soz., *h.e.* 4.36.3-5).

A few years later, A. was again involved in intense controversies with followers of homoean theology, when, before Easter 385, and after the death of Gratian (383), his mother Justina (d. 388), who was regent for Gratian's brother, Valentinian II (b. 371), demanded that the Basilica Portiana, outside the city gates, be reassigned for homoean worship. The ensuing conflicts drew great attention and are therefore documented by a whole series of sources (A., *ep.* 75[21]-77[22] and *c. Aux.* = *ep.* 75a[21a]; see Ruf., *h.e.* 11.15-16; Aug., *conf.* 9.7.15; *v. Ambr.* 15; Soc., *h.e.* 5.11; Soz., *h.e.* 7.13; Theod., *h.e.* 5.13). Acc. to the traditional chronology, the hearings in the imperial consistory in 385 collapsed because of the protest of the Nicene-minded people outside the door and because of a lack of juridical basis. After an edict of tolerance for the homoeans (*Cod. Theod.* 16.1.4) on Jan. 23, 386, before Easter the court demanded the "new basilica, the one inside the walls" (*ep.* 76[20].1). The confiscation of the Portiana (or the new?) Basilica, undertaken on Palm Sunday, March 27, 386, on behalf of the homoean confession, which now had equal legal status, had to be abandoned on Holy Thursday or Good Friday, because the community offered passive resistance by continuously occupying the church(es). In addition, A. threatened the military with excommunication. The bishop of Milan had rejected imperial arbitration, on the grounds that "the churches belong to the bishop" (*ep.* 76[20].19). But this represented only a partial victory, because the conflict with the military was repeated (others assume a single incident). A while later, a further law was issued; a new confiscation and siege of the Portiana were turned back because of a continuous occupation of the church by the community, to the accompaniment of sermons by A. (e.g., *c. Aux.* = *ep.* 75a[31a]), and communal singing. The third capitulation of the court is regarded by some as final and due to fear of a civil war; it is explained by others as provisional because of political pressure from usurper Magnus Maximus.

The discovery (*inventio*), accompanied by miracles, of the bones of martyrs Gervase and Protase gave further credit to the course of the bishop in eccles. politics (A. tells his sister of the discovery in *ep.* 77[22]; see also *v. Ambr.* 14). The transfer of the relics to beneath the altar gave rise to a tradition, still observed today, of linking the martyrs with the Eucharist: "the triumphal sacrifice . . . on the spot where Christ is offered in sacrifice" (*ep.* 77[22].13). To interpret the events as simply "an anti-Arian fiction and a move in a game of chess" is certainly inadequate; see Augustine's enthusiastic account (*conf.* 9.7.16). The ultimate success of the Neo-Nicene creed was connected with the growing influence of Emperor Theodosius in the West after his victory over Maximus in 388, or, if you will, after the death of Empress Justina that same year; it led to laws against heretics (e.g., *Cod. Theod.* 16.5.20 of May 19, 389).

There were also two incidents involving Theodosius and A. that illustrate the quick opportunism but also the profound problematic of the great bishop's self-awareness over against the monarch, as well as his inflexibility in matters theological. In December 388, Christians burned down a synagogue in Callinicum (Syria; modern Raqqa), and A. forbade the emperor to order Christians to rebuild the place of worship (revised as *ep.* 74[40]; original = *extra collationem* 1a). Although A. judged the action to have been a violation of the law and an overzealousness for the church (*ep.* 74[40].6/11), he was at the same time convinced that forms of worship that he regarded as heretical were not to be tolerated. This led him to the startling claim that he was ready to assume responsibility for that infringement: "I declare that I would burn down a synagogue . . . so that no place might exist in which Christ were denied" (74[40].8 = *ext. coll.* 1a, 8). Theodosius, however, did not abandon his policy and in 393 again forbade the destruction of synagogues (*Cod. Theod.* 16.8.8/9).

A further conflict arose when Buteric, military commander in Illyria, was killed by a mob in Thessalonica. Theodosius, a man of violent temper, ordered the people in the circus to be slaughtered, with the loss of thousands of lives (Soz., *h.e.* 7.24; Theod., *h.e.*

5.17). Exercising a degree of circumspection, A. wrote the king a sensible but clear letter (*ep. ext. coll.* 11[54]): The emperor's cruel sentence was a sin because it caused the death of many innocent persons (11[54].6/12); unless he does eccles. penance A. will no longer offer the sacrifice in his presence (13). Only after a suitable act of penance did A. again admit Theodosius to the sacrament of the altar (probably on Dec. 25, 390; Theod., *h.e.* 5.18.5). In the abundant literature on this unparalleled event there is disagreement over whether it represented a conflict over eccles. policy and a victory of the church over the state or rather a pastoral problem of church discipline.

In his person A. lived an outwardly simple life; for example, he never breakfasted (*v. Ambr.* 38.1) and did a great deal of work. He was a convinced Roman (*hereditas maiorum fides vera est*: *in psalm.* 36.19), a man who despite his friendly and kindly ways always retained a certain aristocratic dignity, as is shown not least by Augustine's accounts of him (*conf.* 5.13.23 and 24). The latter also attests to A.'s abilities as a preacher (*conf.* 5.13.25), who preached every Sunday and feastday, as well as daily during the instruction of catechumens (*myst.* 1.1). Among A.'s responsibilities was the organization of an extensive range of social services, as well as of the eccles. province.

A. died in 397 and was buried on Easter by the tomb of the martyrs Gervase and Protase. Paulinus tells us that one of the last things A. said was: "I am not afraid to die, because we have a Lord who is good" (*v. Ambr.* 45.2). His outward appearance is shown (in probably an authentic way) in a mosaic portrait made soon after his death in the Chapel of St. Victor in Ciel d'Oro, close by the bishop's tomb.

L: H. v. Campenhausen, A. als Kirchenpolitiker (Berlin, 1929). — idem, Lat. Kirchenväter (Stuttgart, [4]1978), 77-108 (Eng., The Fathers of the Latin Church [Stanford, 1969]) — P. Courcelle, A. et Calcidius: FS J. H. Waszink (Amsterdam, 1973), 45-53. — idem, Recherches sur saint A. "Vies" anciennes, culture, iconographie (Paris, 1973). — E. Dassmann, A.: TRE 2:362-386. — idem, Das Leben des hl. A. (Düsseldorf, 1967). — A. Dihle, Zum Streit um den Altar der Viktoria: FS J. H. Waszink, (Amsterdam, 1973), 81-97. — F. J. Dölger, Der erste Schreib-Unterricht in Trier nach einer Jugend-Erinnerung des Bischofs A.: AuC 3 (1932) 62-72. — F. H. Dudden, The Life and Times of St. A., 2 vols. (Oxford, 1935). — O. Faller, La data della consacrazione vescovile di sant'A.: Ambrosiana (Milan, 1942), 97-112. — B. Fischer, Ist A. wirklich in Trier geboren?: FS T. Klauser: JAC. E 11 (1984) 132-135. — T. Förster, A., Bischof v. Milan (Halle, 1884). — G. Gottlieb, A. u. Kaiser Gratian (Göttingen, 1973). — idem, Gratianus: RAC 12:718-732. — idem, Der Mailänder Kirchenstreit von 385/386: MH 42 (1985) 37-55. — G. Haendler, Wulfila u. A. (Berlin, 1961). — J. M. van Haeringen, De Valentinano II et A.: Mn. 5 (1937) 28-33, 152-158, 229-240. — R. Klein, Der Streit um den

Viktoriaaltar (Darmstadt, 1972). — F. Kolb, Der Bußakt von Milan: FS K.-D. Erdmann (Neumünster, 1980), 41-74. — A. Lenox-Conyngham, The Topography of the Basilica Conflict of A. D. 385/6 in Milan: Hist. 31 (1982) 353-363. — A. Lippold, Theodosius der Große u. seine Zeit (Munich, ²1980). — J. Matthews, Western Aristocracies and Imperial Court A. D. 364-425 (Oxford, ²1990). — Milano capitale dell'impero romano 286-402 d. c., Mostra Milano 24 gennaio-22 aprile 1990 (Milan, 1990). — C. Moreschini, A.: GK 2 (Stuttgart, 1984 = 1993), 101-123. — J.-R. Palanque, A. et l'Empire romain (Paris, 1933). — A. Paredi, S. A. e la sua età (Milan, ²1960). — M. Pavan, Sant' A. e il problema dei barbari: Romanobarbarica 3 (1978) 167-187. — H. Savon, A. de Milan (Paris, 1997).

II. Works: The Lat. edition of Flavius Josephus, *bell.* (CSEL 66), formerly attributed to A. as a youthful work, is not his.

1. *Exegetical Works:* About half of A.'s writings are exegetical in kind and originated as edited and expanded sermons on bibl. texts as recorded by stenographers. In these A. accepts, changes, and interprets especially Philo and Origen; formerly widespread prejudices regarding A.'s supposedly unimaginative plagiarization go back ultimately to the attacks of a literary rival, — Jerome (*hom. Orig. in Lucam. praef.; Didym. spir. praef.*), and do not take into account the theological concerns in A.'s "rereading." The dates of the works are to some extent quite uncertain; from here on I follow Frede (VL 1/1, 98-110).

Among the earliest writings (perhaps 378) is *De paradiso* (*parad.*), in which, e.g., the four rivers of paradise are interpreted as the four cardinal virtues (as in Philo, H *all.* 1.63). Paradise is an image of the human soul. *Parad.* is continued in *De Cain et Abel* (*Cain et Ab.*). Also to be dated early, around 375/376, is *De Tobia.* In these homilies against usury A. uses passages from Basil, *hom. in Ps.* 14.2, but formulates them very independently and with exceptionally artful rhetoric. After the catastrophic outcome of the battle of Adrianopolis (Aug. 8, 378) A. composed an interpretation of the ark as an image of human life: *De Noe* (*Noe*). Only after a lengthy interval were the two books *De Abraham* (*Abr.*; perhaps 382/383) written; perhaps these two books, though combined by A. himself, do not really belong together, since the first consists of homilies to catechumens (1.4.23-24; 1.9.89), while the second consists of homilies to the baptized (see *patr.* 1.1). This fact explains differences in content: the first book is a *moralis tractatus et simplex* (1.1.1) on the life of Abraham (down to Gen 25); the second refers *ad altiora sensum* (2.1.1) and gives an allegorical explanation but only as far as Gen 17 (is it unfinished?). The two books *De Iacob et vita beata libri duo* (*Iac.*) are dated to the beginning of

386: they take up the connection between *beata vita* and the struggle against the passions (book 1) as exemplified by the patriarchs Jacob and Eleazar and the Maccabean martyrs (book 2). The text contains a Lat. translation and arrangement of 4 Mac (1.2.1-2.7; 5.17-18; 2.10.343-12.58).

De Isaac et anima, perhaps originally directed to the neophytes in particular (*Isaac*; see 4.35), had its origin in the Easter season of 386. Here the marriage of Isaac and Rebekah is interpreted as referring to the union of Christ with the soul of the believer. Then, using the Song of Songs, A. describes the progress of the soul in four stages: after the initial union, the dangers, then the purification and the definitive attachment of the soul to the Word. There is debate as to whether A. is here describing mystical experiences, eschatological promises, or the adornment of the soul by grace. Perhaps the work was originally sermons on the Song of Songs, which only later were included in the cycle of interpretations of the patriarchs; it is likely that the commentary of → Origen on the Song of Songs, largely lost in its Gr. original, was a substantial source for A. Directly connected in time and in content is *De bono mortis* (*bon. mort.*; see 1.1), on the value of bodily death. Given its use of the *Poros* (Plenty) myth, the text is probably a witness to A.'s knowledge of Plotinus. The *Exameron libri sex* (*hex.*) of 386/387 also makes use of Basil's work of the same title on the story of creation (Jer., *ep.* 84.7); careful explanations alternate with examples and ethical applications. Along with Origen and Hippolytus, Philo and also Cicero and Virgil serve as sources. In the fall of 388 or in 389/390 A. wrote *De Ioseph* (*Ioseph*), in which he represents the patriarchs as models of chastity and an example of redemption through Christ (*Ioseph* 9.46–14.83).

Probably at the beginning of 389 (or perhaps 387 or 391) A. composed *De Helia et ieiunio* (*Hel.*), sermons on fasting with abundant bibl. examples, especially Elijah. Sermons of Basil (*hom.* l: *Hel.* 1-40, 68; *hom.* 10: *Hel.* 41-64, 67; and *hom.* 11: *Hel.* 56-58) among others, served as a model. *De Nabuthe Iezraelita* (*Nab.*) is likewise dated to 389, and uses the example of Naboth to attack greed (as did Basil, the model, in *hom.* 5 and 6). Like his model, A. takes a critical view of riches. The four sermons *De interpellatione Iob et David* (*Iob*; the sequence is reconstructed variously) are now preferably dated to 387/389 and deal with bibl. laments over the frailty of human life (with allusions to the end of Gratian's life [Aug. 25, 383] and the political fate of Valentinian II).

The *Expositio de Psalmo* 118 (*in psalm.* 118), in the

form of twenty-two sermons on each section of an → abecedary, must have originated around 389/390. Scholars suppose that in addition to a work of Origen on the psalms (CPG I:1426 II:5), a lost work of Philo and the etymology and symbolism of the letters of the Hebrew alphabet served as sources. Augustine preserves a fragment of a work *Expositio Esaiae prophetae* (Aug. *gr. et pecc. or.* 1.54) by A. that must go back to before 389 (*in Luc.* 2.56; already lost in the time of Cassiodorus: *inst.* 3).

The only work of A. on the NT, the ten books of the *Expositio Evangelii secundum Lucam* (*in Luc.*), is dated somewhat later, that is, in 390. Since in addition to Origen (*hom. in Luc.*) Eusebius (*qu. Mar.*; *qu. Steph.*) also served, especially in book 3, as a source for the homilies and their revision, the accord between the Gospels plays a large part. A. takes interpretation to mean proclamation, and understanding to mean discipleship in thought. The procedure, an extensive paraphrasing or citing of the bibl. texts, represents an effort to capture the peculiar dynamics of Christ's self-interpretation.

The final version of *De apologia prophetae David ad Theodosium Augustum* (*apol. Dav.* I) was done by A. probably in 390, the original composition dating between 383 (assassination of Gratian; see 6.27) and the publication of the commentary on Luke (see 3.38). The sins of David are compared to the support given to the homoeans by Valentinian II and his mother, Justina, and to the killing of Gratian by Magnus Maximus. The dedication to Theodosius, which is attested at an early date, may well come from A.

The *Apologia David altera* (*apol. Dav.* II) was for a long time taken to be pseudepigraphical but is now accepted as a stenographer's transcript of a sermon of A. Somewhat later (perhaps 390 or 391) came the *De patriarchis* (*patr.*), which is in fact an exegesis of Jacob's blessing (Gen 49) on the basis of the corresponding work of → Hippolytus. Among the latest exegetical works are *De fuga saeculi* (*fug. saec.*; fall of 384). Its subject is flight from the world in the form of an interpretation of the six cities of refuge in Num 35:11-15; in this approach it follows Philo (*fug.*).

The *Explanatio XII psalmorum* (*in psalm.*) was composed from 387 to 397; it is an explanation of Pss 1, 35-40, 45, 47-48, and 61, here again in "continual dependence" on Origen (thus Jer., *ep.* 112.20) and on Basil (for *in psalm.* 1). Unlike Origen, A. lays greater emphasis on the praise aspect of the Psalms and on the concrete life of the community, e.g., in the prayer of the hours (ibid., 307). A. understands psalmody to be an image "of the delight of future blessedness" (*in*

psalm. 1.1.1), and endeavors to give a continuous christological interpretation. The explanations of the framing Psalms, 1 and 61, are probably the earliest; the explanation of Ps 36 presupposes the victory of Theodosius over Eugene (Sept. 6, 394); A. dictated the incomplete explanation of Ps 43 while on his deathbed (*v. Ambr.* 42.1).

2. *Ethical Writings*: The writings of A. on ethical and ascetical questions were likewise heavily based on sermons. For his clergy the bishop wrote the three books *De officiis* (*off.*) in 388 or 389. Though the text takes Cicero's work of the same title as a guide, it is once again far more than a superficial revision of that work. The Chr. "rereading" is distinguished from its pagan model by the examples from the Bible, which at the same time serve to structure the somewhat confused work. The first book (as in Cicero) deals with the *honestum*, the second with the *utile*, and the third with a combination of the two. The work is the first independent Chr. ethics as a literary genre. Cicero's ideal figure, namely, the wise man, is replaced, acc. to Chr. custom, by the just man; the law by which justice is measured has for its content the bibl. tradition's love of God and neighbor (*off.* 1.253).

Five works are devoted to the state of virgins: *De virginibus ad Marcellinam sororem libri tres* (*virg.*) was probably written in 377 (or 378) at the sister's wish (1.3.10) and incorporates sermons (1.2.5), such as the reworked address of Liberius in 353. While the first book gives general praise of the state as such, the second is chiefly given over to models (among them Thecla and Mary), and the third contains exhortations to the sister. The short work *De viduis* (*vid.*) is likewise assigned to 377. A. exhorts widows to remain in their state and not to marry again. A defense, in sermon form, of statements critical of marriage in *virg.* (5.25f.), made its appearance as *De virginitate* (*virginit.*); A. may have written the text in 388/390; §§14-23 may have been interpolated. The work *De institutione virginis et S. Mariae virginitate perpetua ad Eusebium* (*inst. virg.*) originated at around the same time and may have been written down in 392/393. The work is an address to an Ambrosia who intended to take the veil at Easter 392; it is preceded by a dedication to her grandfather Eusebius (1.1), who is not to be identified with the bishop of Bologna; see *ep.* 26[54] and 38[55]. The real theme is in fact the perpetual virginity of Mary and the rebuttal of attacks on this doctrine by Bishop Bonosus of Sardica. The work *Exhortatio virginitatis* (*exhort. virg.*) is a sermon preached around Easter

394 for the consecration of the Basilica of St. Lawrence in Florence, which had been rebuilt by a widow named Julia. A. speaks in the person of the donor and exhorts her children to enter the state of celibacy.

3. *Systematic Writings*: A. composed three works of a more strictly theological-systematic kind. The *De fide ad Gratianum Augustum libri quinque* (*fid.*) was probably a revision, in two stages, 378 and 380, of sermons to the people with application to the monarch. The work is based on a careful reading of texts of Athanasius but also of Basil (as shown by the verbatim citation of *ep.* 52.3 in *fid.* 3.15.126). For this reason there is no vacillation between the old and the new Nicene formulas: in his theology of the Trinity A. transposes the Cappadocian form of Neo-Nicenism (retaining the *asygchytos* – *henōsis* terminology) into the traditional Lat. terminology of *substantia* and *natura* or *persona*. The arguments of (Illyrian) homoean theology with its heavy dependence on bibl. texts is rebutted with detailed arguments from the Bible.

Shortly after the completion of *fid.*, or at any rate before the end of spring 381, A. supplemented his reflections for the emperor with his *De Spiritu sancto ad Gratianum Augustum* (*spir.*), which depends on the corresponding treatise of Didymus (and, interestingly enough, not on the somewhat more demanding works of Athanasius or Basil). Again, it is primarily with passages from the Bible that the author rebuts the thesis that the Spirit is a creature and endeavors to prove the equality of the three persons.

Only a short time later, A. again supplemented these works in the treatise *De incarnationis dominicae sacramento* (*incarn.*). The first part (1.7–7.78) consists of a (revised?) sermon delivered in the Basilica Portiana, the circumstances of which can be quite accurately reconstructed (*c. Ambr.* 18: two homoean chamberlains of Gratian had asked for the answer to a question, but because of a fatal accident missed A.'s response). The preacher focuses on Apollinarism and asserts the human soul of Christ. A second part (7.78–10.116) discusses a question of Gratian— "How can the unborn and the born possess a single nature and substance?" (8.79)—and takes up the attack on homoeanism once again. The "exposition of the faith" (*ekthesis pisteōs*), to which Theodoret refers in *eran. Flor.* 2.29 as being from "St. Ambrose, Bishop of Milan," and which scholars still like to claim for A., is definitely not his.

4. *Writings on Catechesis and Church Music*: The two works *De sacramentis libri sex* (*sacr.*) and *De mysteriis*

(*myst.*) are so closely related in content and language that *myst.* has been regarded as the corrected version of the stenographic recording of *sacr.* But the independence of the two is also defended, with reference both to the annually recurring occasion for such addresses to the newly baptized and to A.'s memory. The oral character of the *myst.* may be a literary fiction. The thesis that *sacr.* was written by → Nicetas of Remesiana is completely absurd. Following convention, *sacr.* deals with baptism and the Eucharist and well as with the Our Father (5.18-30) and the ordering of daily prayer (6.11-25). In contrast, *myst.* gives only an introduction to the meaning of the two sacraments (3-42 and 43-58).

De paenitentia libri duo (*paenit.*), written after 386 but before 390 (see *in psalm.* 37.1), is directed against the Novatians and emphasizes the authority of the church to forgive sins. It is hardly surprising that Tertullian and Cyprian served A. as sources.

In Augustine (*c. Iul.* 2.14, 15, 19, 24, and 32) there are fragments of A.'s work *De sacramento regenerationis sive de philosophia*, in which he inveighs against Platonism. There has long been disagreement over the authenticity of the sermon *Explanatio symboli ad initiandos* (*symb. rec.*), to which we cannot assign a date, but today the authenticity can be taken as quite certain.

Among the writings of this kind special attention has been given to the *Hymni* (*Hymn. Ambros.* 1-14); the compelling power of his hymns was admitted by A. himself (*ep.* 75a[21a].34) and was demonstrated at an early stage. The hymns provide theol., ethical, and spiritual knowledge and guidance in a pleasing and at the same time artistic form. On the basis of early attestation the following hymns are undoubtedly authentic: 1 (*aeternae rerum conditor*, a song for early morning), 3 (*iam surgit hora tertia*, in remembrance of the hour of the crucifixion), 4 (*deus creator omnium*, an evening song), as well as 5 (*Intende qui regis Israel*, an anti-Arian Christmas song). The following are regarded as very probably authentic: 2 (*splendor paternae gloriae*, another song for early morning), 8 (*Agnes beatae virginis*), 10 (*Victor Nabor Felix pii*), and 11 (*Grates tibi*, a hymn of thanksgiving for the discovery of the relics of Sts. Gervase and Protase). Authenticity is considered possible for 6 (*amore Christi nobilis*, addressed to John the Baptist), 12 (*apostolorum passio*, to Peter and Paul), and 14 (*aeterna Christi munera*, to the martyrs). Numbers 7, 9, 13, and 16-19 are not authentic.

It is highly likely that in addition to hymns A. composed some inscriptions in verse: the epitaph for his brother Satyrus (ILCV 2165), as well as inscrip-

tions (*tituli*) for the baptistry of the churches of Thecla and of the Apostles (ILCV 1841, 1800 or 1801). It is rather unlikely that the twenty-one *tituli* for a cycle of pictures in the Basilica Ambrosiana in Milan are from A. (*tituli*; PLS 1:587-89).

Three funeral orations give evidence of A. as a sensitive pastor: *De excessu fratis Satyri libri duo* (*exc. Sat.*) contains the two orations for his brother Satyrus, who also worked as a high-ranking civil servant. Acc. to tradition, this beloved brother died on Sept. 17, 378; the first book contains the revised funeral oration, the second the *consolatio* (2.3), which was delivered a week later. When Valentinian II was assassinated on Feb. 15, 392, A. delivered a funeral oration *De obitu Valentiniani consolatio* (*obit. Valent.*) for the family. A theme of this text is the dead man's desire to be baptized by A., which supposes that it was never done (*obit. Valent.* 51-53). More reserved is the *De obitu Theodosii oratio* (*obit. Theod.*), delivered forty days after the monarch's death on March 24, 395, in the presence of Honorius, the new western Augustus, and of the military. In addition to the recall of history, as the genre required, there are some interesting emphases in the area of eccles. politics.

5. *Letters*: Very important, finally, is the collection of letters that is divided into ten books (as with prominent predecessors, e.g., Pliny the Younger); there are also some letters *extra collationem*, not intended for publication. Reports, memoranda, and letters on theol. questions predominate. The tenth book (as with Pliny) contains especially texts that document the public activity of the bishop of Milan. The letters that attest to the controversies between A. and Theodosius were not published by A., because after the latter's death A. wanted to document his own good relationship with him (as he did in the funeral oration).

III. **Importance**: A. has for a long time been underestimated. The earlier judgment on him as an eccles. politician who was essentially a borrower and not creative and was concerned with pastoral activity rather than theology has been revised at various points or is presently being revised. A.'s way of borrowing shows a man of education, sensitivity, and mastery; his attitude to philosophy and his knowledge of it have until now been misinterpreted or underestimated. While he had a praiseworthy knowledge of philosophy, his orientation to the scriptures increasingly became the standard for his theol. thought. Very important for our understanding of this development in A. is a careful

description of his profound piety. Notable is the energy with which A. took seriously and dealt with all areas of the office of bishop as understood in late antiquity. In addition, attention has been called to theol. developments in A.: in a surprisingly short time, through contact with Eastern theologians, he deepened his knowledge of trinitarian theology and developed a form of Neo-Nicene theology on the basis of traditional Lat. terminology. Among other considerations, this theology became useful for the community of Milan. The extensive bibl. citations are not added on but reflect A.'s bibl.-theol. thinking. So too, a concept of faith that is initially thought of in terms of virtue is enriched with theol. substance (e.g., *fid.* 3.17.138 and 4.1.3), and the likewise philosophically oriented concept of sin is broadened by inclusion of the themes of commandment and freedom (*parad.* 6.30; 7.35).

After a lengthy period in which the dependence of A.'s scriptural exegesis on sources was exclusively emphasized and very carefully documented, attention is now being paid to its organizing principles: among these is, e.g., the Christ-event, which continues to influence the interpretation of scripture and to which the interpreter attunes himself (*in Luc.* prol. 6). Also important is A.'s interpretation of the Song of Songs, for this reason, if no other: it is the embryonic beginning of the momentous mariological interpretation of that book (espec. *inst. virg.* 14.87 and 89). The goal of theology is worship, as becomes clear even at the literary level from prayerlike insertions into the texts.

A. is probably (along with Damasus) the theologian who played the most important role in the imposition on the West of the creed of Nicaea (325) in its Neo-Nicene interpretation (as even his rival Jerome says: *chron. a. Abr.* 2390). Not least for that reason has he been numbered, at least since the end of the 6th c., among the four western church fathers (Letter of the Milan Synod, PL 87:1261-65).

W: *Abr.*, F. Gori, OOSA 3 (Milan, 1980) [text/Italian trans./comm.]. — *apol. Dav.* I, P. Hadot, M. Cordier, SC 239. — *apol. Dav.* I/II, F. Lucidi, OOSA 5 (Milan, 1981) [text/Italian trans./comm.]. — *bon. mort.*, W. T. Wiesner: PatSt 100 (1970) [text/English trans./comm.]. — *ep., c. Aux., conc. Aquil.*, O. Faller, M. Zelzer, CSEL 82/1-3 (Vienna, 1968-1990). — G. Banterle, OOSA 19-21 (Milan, 1988) [text/Italian trans./comm.]. — *exc. Sat., obit. Valent., obit. Theod.*, G. Banterle, OOSA 18 (Milan, 1985) [text/Italian trans./comm.]. — *hex.*, G. Banterle, OOSA 1 (Milan, 1979) [text/Italian trans./comm.]. — *hex., parad., Cain et Ab., Noe, Abr., Isaac, bon. mort.*, C. Schenkl, CSEL 32/1 (New York, 1962 = Prague, 1897). — *Iac., Ioseph, patr., fug. saec., Iob, apol. Dav., Hel., Nab., Tob.*, C. Schenkl, CSEL 32/2 (Prague, 1897). — Isaac, *bon. mort., Iac.*, C. Moreschini, R. Palla, OOSA 3 (Milan, 1982) [text/Italian

trans./comm.]. — *fid.*, O. Faller, CSEL 78 (Vienna, 1962).
— C. Moreschini, OOSA 15 (Milan, 1984) [text/Italian
trans./comm.]. — *Hel., Nab., Tob.,* F. Gori, OOSA 6
(Milan, 1985) [text/Italian trans./comm.]. — *Hel.,* M. J. A.
Buck: PatSt 19 (1929) [text/English trans./comm.]. —
Hymn., J. Fontaine et al. (Paris, 1992) [text/French
trans./comm.]. — M. Simonetti, BPat 13 (Florence, 1988)
[text/Italian trans./comm.]. — *in Luc.,* M. Adriaen, CCL 14.
— G. Tissot, SC 45/52. — G. Coppa, OOSA 11/12 (Milan,
1987) [text/Italian trans./comm.]. — *Nab.,* M. McGuire:
PatSt 15 (1927) [text/English trans./comm.]. — M. G. Mara
(L'Aquila, 1975) [text/Italian trans./comm.]. — *off.,* M.
Testard: CUFr (1984/92) [text/French trans./comm.]. — G.
Banterle, OOSA 13 (Milan, ²1991) [text/Italian trans./
comm.]. — *paenit.,* R. Gryson, SC 179. — *parad., Cain et
Ab., Noe.,* P. Siniscalco, A. Pastorino, OOSA 2 (Milan,
1984) [text/Italian trans./comm.]. — *patr., fug. saec., Iob,* G.
Banterle, OOSA 4 (Milan, 1980) [text/Italian trans./
comm.]. — *in psalm.* 61.33.2, M. Petschenig, CSEL 64. —
L. F. Pizzolato, OOSA 7/8 (Milan, 1980) [text/Italian
trans./comm.]. — *in psalm.* 118, M. Petschenig, CSEL 62.
— L. F. Pizzolato, OOSA 9/10 (Milan, 1987) [text/Italian
trans./comm.]. — *sacr., myst.,* J. Schmitz, FC 3. — *spir.,
incarn.,* O. Faller, CSEL 79. — C. Moreschini, E. Bellini,
OOSA 16 (Milan, 1979) [text/Italian trans./comm.]. —
*symb. rec., sacr., myst., paenit., exc. Sat., obit. Valent., obit.
Theod.,* O. Faller, CSEL 73. — *symb. rec., sacr., myst.,
paenit.,* G. Banterle, OOSA 17 (Milan, 1982) [text/Italian
trans./comm.]. — *symb. rec.,* R. H. Connolly: TaS 10 (1952)
[text/English trans./comm.]. — *Tob.,* L. M. Zucker: PatSt
25 (1933) [text/English trans./comm.]. — *virg.,* O. Faller:
FlorPatr 31 (1933). — E. Cazzaniga: CSLP 1 (1948). — *virginit.,* E. Cazzaniga: CSLP 47 (1954). — *exhort. virg., inst.
virg., virg., virginit.,* F. Gori, 2 vols., OOSA 14/1-2 (Milan,
1989) [text/Italian trans./comm.].
L: L. Krestan, Wortindex zu den Schriften des hl. A.,
CSEL.B 4 (Wiesbaden, 1979).
Le Fonti Greche su Sant'A., ed. C. Pasini, OOSA Sus
24/1 (Milan, 1990). — Le Fonti Latine su Sant'A., ed. G.
Banterle, OOSA Sus. 24/2 (Milan, 1991). — P. F. Beatrice
et al., Cento anni di bibliografia ambrosiana (1874-1974):
SPMed 11 (1981). — Ambroise de Milan. XVIᵉ centenaire
de son élection épiscopale, éd. Y.-M. Duval (Paris, 1974)
(EAug). — Ambrosius Episcopus. Atti del Congresso inter-
nazionale, ed. G. Lazzati: SPMed 6 (1976). — Nec timeo
mori. Atti del Congresso internazionale, ed. L. F. Pizzolato,
M. Rizzi: SPMed 21 (1998).
B. Albers, Über die erste Trauerrede des hl. A. zum Tode
seines Bruders: FS A. Ehrhard (Bologna, 1921 = Amsterdam, 1969), 24-52. — G. Bartelink, Sprachliche u. stilistische Bemerkungen in A.' Schriften: WSt 13 (1979) 175-202.
— K. Baus, Das Nachwirken des Origenes in der Christus-
frömmigkeit des hl. A.: RQ 49 (1954) 21-55. — G. Bernt, A.:
"Hic est deus verus dei": Liturgie u. Dichtung, ed. H.
Becker, R. Kaczynski (St. Ottilien, 1983), 509-546. — M. M.
Beyenka, St. Augustine and the Hymns of St. A.: ABenR 8
(1957) 121-132. — M. Biermann, Die Leichenreden des A.
(Gottingen, 1995). — W. K. Bietz, Paradiesesvorstellungen
bei A. u. seinen Vorgängern, Diss. (Giessen, 1971). — J. den
Boft, A. Hilhorst (ed.), A. Lyricus (Leiden, 1993), 77-89. —
P. Brown, The Body and Society (New York, 1988). — E.
Cattaneo, La religione a Milano nell'età di Sant'A. (Milan,
1974). — R. H. Connolly, Some Disputed Works of St. A.:
DR 65 (1947) 7-20, 121-130. — P. Courcelle, Les Lettres
Grecques en Occident (Paris, 1948). — idem, Plotin et

Saint A.: RPh 76 (1950) 29-56. — L. Cracco Ruggini, A. e le
opposizioni anticattoliche fra il 383 e il 390: Aug. 14 (1974)
409-449. — M. L. Danieli, La verginità, le vergini, le vedove
(Rome, 1974). — E. Dassmann, A. u. die Märtyrer: JAC 18
(1975) 50-68. — idem, A.: AugL 1:270-285. — idem, Ecclesia vel anima: RQ 61 (1966) 126-129. — idem, Die Frömmigkeit des Kirchenvaters A. (Münster, 1965). — M. D.
Diederich, Vergil in the Works of St. A. (Washington,
1931). — A. Dihle, Gerechtigkeit: RAC 10:233-360. — R.
M. D'Izarny, La virginité selon saint A. (Lyons, 1952). — F.
J. Dölger, Zur Symbolik des altchr. Taufhauses: AuC 4
(1934) 153-187. — G. M. Dreves, A., "der Vater des
Kirchengesanges" (Freiburg i.Br., 1893). — G. L. Ellsper-
mann, The Attitude of the Early Christian Latin Writers
toward Pagan Literature (Washington, 1949). — A. Engelbrecht, Studien über den Lukaskommentar des A. (Vienna,
1903). — U. Faust, Christo Servire Libertas est (Salzburg,
1983). — A.-L. Fenger, Aspekte der Soteriologie u. Ekklesi-
ologie bei A. (Frankfurt a.M., 1981). — K. Gamber, Die
Autorschaft von De Sacramentis (Regensburg, 1967). —
idem, Nochmals zur Autorschaft von De Sacramentis:
ZKTh 91 (1969) 587-589. — T. Graumann, Christus interpres (Berlin, 1994). — R. Gryson, Melchisédech, type du
Christ, selon saint A.: RTL 10 (1979) 176-195. — idem, Le
prêtre selon saint A. (Leuven/Louvain, 1968). — P. Hadot,
Platon et Plotin dans trois sermons de s. A.: REL 34 (1956)
202-220. — H. Hagendahl, Latin Fathers and the Classics
(Göteborg 1958). — V. Hahn, Das wahre Gesetz (Münster,
1969). — L. Herrmann, A. als Trinitätstheologe (Heidelberg, 1954). — C. Hill, Classical Traditions in some Writings of St. A., Diss. (Oxford, 1979). — O. Hiltbrunner, Die
Schrift "De off. min." des hl. A.: Gym. 71 (1964) 174-189.
— F. R. M. Hitchcock, The Explanatio Symboli compared
with Rufinus and Maximus of Turin: JThS 197 (1946) 58-
59. — J. Huhn, Bewertung u. Gebrauch der hl. Schrift
durch den Kirchenvater A.: HJ 77 (1958) 387-396. — M.
Ihm, Studia Ambrosiana (Leipzig, 1890). — M. Klein,
Meletemata Ambrosiana, Diss. Phil. (Königsberg, 1927).
R. Klein, Die Sklaverei aus der Sicht der Bischöfe A. u.
Augustinus (Stuttgart, 1988). — H. Leeb, Die Psalmodie bei
A. (Vienna, 1967). — A. Lenox-Conyngham, A. and Philos-
ophy: FS C. Stead: VigChr S 19 (1993) 112-128. — idem,
Law in St. A.: StPatr 23 (1989) 149-152. — idem, The
Judgement of A. the Bishop on A. the Roman Governor:
StPatr 17 (1982) 62-65. — idem, Juristic and Religious
Aspects of the Basilica Conflict of A.D. 386: StPatr 18
(1986) 55-58. — idem, Natural and Positive Law in St. A.:
Colloquium 7 (1974) 17-29. — E. Lucchesi, L'usage de
Philon dans l'œuvre exégétique de Saint A. (Leiden, 1977).
— G. Madec, A., Athanase et l'Apollinarisme: ThH 27
(1974) 365-376. — idem, Saint A. et la Philosophie (Paris,
1974). — C. Markschies, A. u. die Trinitätstheologie
(Tübingen, 1995). — idem, War der Bischof A. ein
schlechter Theologe?: JAWG (1994) 63-66. — idem, Was
bedeutet οὐσία?: Origenes, ed. W. Geerlings, H. König
(Bonn, 1995), 59-82. — H. J. auf der Maur, Das Psalmen-
verständnis des A. (Leiden, 1977). — S. Mazzarino, Storia
Sociale del Vescovo Ambrogio (Rome, 1989). — N.
McLynn, A. (Berkeley, 1995). — idem, The "Apology" of
Palladius: JThS 42 (1991) 52-76. — M. Meslin, Les Ariens
d'Occident 335-430 (Paris, 1967). — C. Mohrmann,
Observations sur le "De Sacramentis" et le "De Mysteriis":
SPMed 6 (1976) 103-123. — H. Moretus, Les Bénédictions
des patriarches dans la littérature du IVᵉ au VIIIᵉ siècle: BLE
(1909) 398-411; (1910) 28-40, 83-100. — C. Morino,

Chiesa e Stato nella dottrina di S. A. (Rome, 1963). — D. H. Müller, Die Deutung der hebr. Buchstaben bei A.: SAWW. PH 167/2 (1911). — G. Nauroy, Exégèse et création littéraire chez A. (Paris, 1996). — idem, Le fouet et le miel. Le combat d'A. en 386: RechAug 23 (1988) 3-86. — J. E. Niederhuber, Die Eschatologie des hl. A. (Paderborn, 1907). — J. Pepin, Echos de théories gnostiques de la matière au début de l'Exaemeron: FS J. H. Waszink (Amsterdam, 1973), 259-273. — idem, Textes et doctrines de la fin de l'antiquité (Paris, 1971). — idem, Théologie cosmique et théologie chrétienne (Paris, 1964). — O. Perler, L'inscription du baptistère de Sainte-Thècle: RivAC 27 (1951) 145-166. — A. Pertusi, Le antiche traduzioni greche delle opere di S. A.: Aevum 18 (1944) 184-207. — G. Piccolo, Per lo studio della spiritualità ambrosiana: ScC 98 (1970) 32-74. — L. F. Pizzolato, La dottrina esegetica di sant'A. (Milan, 1978). — A. Portolano, La dimensione spirituale della proprietà nel "De Nabathae Jezraelita" (Naples, 1973). — D. T. Runia, Philo in Early Christian Literature (Assen, 1993). — S. Sagot, Le "Cantique des Cantiques" dans le "De Isaac": RechAug 16 (1981) 3-57. — M. Sanders, "Fons vitae Christus." Der Heilsweg des Menschen nach der Schrift De Isaac et anima des A.: MThA 42 (Altenberge, 1996). — R. A. Sauer, Studien zur Pflichtenlehre des A., Diss. (Würzburg, 1982). — H. Savon, Saint A. et saint Jérôme, lecteurs de Philon: ANRW II 21/1 (1984) 731-759. — idem, Quelques remarques sur la chronologie des œuvres de Saint A.: StPatr 10/1 (1970) 156-160. — T. Schermann, Die griech. Quellen des hl. A. (Munich, 1902). — R. Schieffer, Von Milan nach Canossa: DA 28 (1972) 333-370. — J. Schmitz, Gottesdienst im altchr. Mailand (Bonn, 1975). — K. P. Schneider, Chr. Liebesgebot und weltliche Ordnungen, Diss. (Cologne, 1975). — M. Simonetti, Innologia Ambrosiana: VSen 5 (1956). — idem, Note su antichi commenti alle Benedizioni dei Patriarchi: Annali Facoltà Lettere Cagliari 28 (1960) 1-71. — A. Solignac, Nouveaux parallèles entre saint A. et Plotin: ArPh 19 (1956) 148-156. — W. Steidle, Beobachtungen zu des A. Schrift De Officiis: VigChr (1984) 18-66. — A. Steier, Untersuchungen über die Echtheit der Hymnen des A. (Leipzig, 1903). — E. Stolz, Didymus, A., Hieronymus: ThQ 87 (1905) 371-401. — I.-S. B. Tschang, Octo beatitudines, Diss. (Bonn, 1986). — M. Testard, Étude sur la composition dans "De off. min." de saint A.: Ambroise de Milan (Paris, 1974), 155-197. — G. Toscani, Teologia della chiesa in sant'A. (Milan, 1974). -— V. R. Vasey, The Social Ideas in the Works of St. A., Diss. theol. (Rome, 1974). — G. Visonà, Lo status quaestionis della ricerca ambrosiana: Nec timeo mori, 31-71. — H. Vogels, Hymnus "splendor paternae gloriae": FS A. Knöpfler (Munich, 1907), 314-316. — A. Wacht, Privateigentum bei Cicero u. A.: JAC 25 (1982) 28-64. — A. S. Walpole, Notes on the Text of the Hymns of St. A.: JThS 9 (1908) 428-436. — C. Weyman, Beiträge zur Geschichte der chr.-lat. Poesie (Munich, 1926). — W. Wilbrand, A. u. Plato: RQ 25 (1911) 42-49. — idem, Zur Chronologie einiger Schriften des hl. A.: HJ 41 (1921) 1-19. — D. H. Williams, A. and the End of the Arian-Nicene Conflicts (Oxford, 1995). — K. Zelzer, Zur Beurteilung der Cicero-Imitatio bei A., De officiis: WSt 90 (1977) 168-191. — idem, Randbemerkungen zu Absicht u. Arbeitsweise des A. in De officiis: WSt 107/108 (1994/95) 481-493. — M. Zelzer, Die Briefbücher des heiligen A. und die Briefe extra collectionem: AÖAW. PH 112 (1975) 7-23. — eadem, Die Bedeutung Mailands für die Überlieferung der A.-briefe: StPatr 17 (1982) 55-58. — eadem, Zu Aufbau u. Absicht des

zehnten Briefbuches des A.: FS R. Hanslik: WSt. B 8 (1977) 351-362. — eadem, Zur Chronologie der Werke des A. Überblick über die Forschung: Nec timeo mori, 73-92. — eadem, Gli scritti Ambrosiani sulla verginità: ScC 135/136 (1997) 801-821.

C. MARKSCHIES

Ambrosiaster

An unknown commentator on Paul, who in the time of Damasus (366-384) composed commentaries (*comm.*) on thirteen letters of Paul (excluding Hebrews). Beginning in the early Middle Ages, his writings were handed down under the name of → Ambrose, until Erasmus proved them unauthentic. Whether the name A. was introduced by Erasmus must remain open. There is disagreement on the question of authorship; none of the hypothetical attributions thus far offered has proven acceptable. Also assigned to Ambrosiaster (A.) are the Ps.-Augustinian *Quaestiones veteris et novi testamenti* (*quaest. test.*).

Earlier scholars attributed to A. five fragments of a commentary on Matthew, but this attribution is no longer tenable (→ *Anonymi Chiliastae*).

The attribution to A. of the *Collatio legum Mosaicarum et Romanorum* is likewise improbable.

The work *De bello judaico* or *De excidio urbis Hierosolymitanae* (→ Hegesippus) is no longer attributed to A.; the two fragments *Contra Arianos* (Ps.-Hilary) and *sermo* 246 (Ps.-Augustine) are likewise to be regarded as unauthentic.

A. composed his commentaries with great care. The commentary on Romans has been handed down in three versions, that on Corinthians in at least two. The *quaest.*, which have been handed down in two collections (150 and 127 questions respectively), answer questions about the Bible and factual matters in a loose, unsystematic way. A. displays an aversion to philosophy and offers an exegesis that is rational, focused on the text, and almost completely free of allegory. He is familiar, however, with typology.

In his teaching on God A. lays great emphasis on the doctrine of the Trinity and stresses the consubstantiality of the Son against the Arians. In christology, therefore, he attacks Photinus and Marcion (*Ad Gal. arg.* 1). God created this world and humanity through Christ (*quaest. test.* 2.3). The fall of Adam led to physical death, the corruption of the body, and the beginning of sin. In his soteriology A. stresses the point that Christ has given redeemed humanity an example of the new life which human beings must, however, first lay hold of. Human justification is thus a central problem for A.

A.'s markedly juridical cast of mind leads him to a clear sympathy for Roman law and to a strong emphasis on the justice of God, along with a stress on human free will. At the same time, a definite emphasis on human sinfulness stands in contrast with this optimistic assessment of human volition. Because all descend from Adam, all have also sinned in him. A. is cited as a witness to Augustine's teaching on original sin, because he translates the *eph'hō* of Rom 5:12 as a relational *in quo*, and already has the formula: all were present in Adam *quasi in massa*. But for A. the guilt handed down from Adam is not yet the basis for human condemnation, even though he relates the *in quo* to Adam, as the Augustinian tradition does.

Because of his theological independence, the question of whether A. leads to → Pelagius or to → Augustine cannot be answered unequivocally.

A. takes a polemical attitude to paganism and dissociates himself from Judaism. Pagan cults and astrology seem to have been still very much alive in the Rome of A.'s time. For apologetic purposes, he contrasts the Chr. miracles with them.

A. betrays a remarkable knowledge of Judaism. His polemics are directed primarily against Christians who are in danger of falling back into Judaism. In regard to the law A. distinguishes between *lex divinitatis* (commandments 1-4), *lex naturalis* (5-10), and *lex factorum* (ritual prescriptions). The *lex naturalis* remains always in force, while the *lex factorum* has been abrogated. The relation between *lex* and *evangelium* is defined in good Pauline fashion.

Contemporary writers (Jerome, Augustine, Pelagius) make use of A. or argue with him. Beginning in the early Middle Ages his writings were very widespread.

W: *quaest. test.*, A. Souter, CSEL 50. — *comm.*, H. J. Vogels, CSEL 81/1-3.
L: F. Cumont, La polémique de l'A. contre les paiens: RHCR 8 (1903) 417-440. — J. Doignon, Rom 7, 16 dans l'exégèse latine ancienne: FZPhTh 29 (1982) 131-139. — W. Geerlings, Röm. Recht u. Gnadentheologie: FS L. Verheijen (Würzburg, 1987), 357-377. — idem, Das Verständnis von Gesetz im Galaterbrief des A.: FS U. Wickert (Berlin, 1997), 101-113. — O. Heggelbacher, Vom röm. zum chr. Recht (Freiburg i.Br., 1959). — idem, A. u. Maximus v. Turin: FZPhTh 41 (1994) 5-44. — C. Martini, A. (Rome, 1944). — A. Merkt, Wer war der A. ?: WiWei 59 (1996) 19-33. — W. Mundle, Die Exegese der paulinischen Briefe im Kommentar des A. (Marburg, 1919). — L. Perrone, Echi della polemica pagana sulla Bibbia negli scritti esegetici fra IV e V secolo: F. E. Consolino, Pagani e Cristiani da Giuliano l'apostata al sacco die Roma (Messina, 1995), 149-172. — A. Souter, A Study of A. (Cambridge, 1905). — J. Stüben, Das Heidentum im Spiegel von Heilsgeschichte u. Gesetz (Hamburg, 1990). — A. Stuiber, A.:

TRE 2:356f. — L. Wallach, A. u. die Libri Carolini: DA 29 (1973) 197-205.

W. GEERLINGS

Ammon of Adrianople

A. lived in the second half of the 4th c. and was bishop of Adrianople in Thrace. In 394 he took part in the Synod of Constantinople and in 399/400 in another assembly in which Eusebius of Valentinopolis accused Anthony of Ephesus of simony (Palladius, *v. Chrys.* 13). A. composed a work *De resurrectione* (*fr.*) against Origen, of which only two fragments remain.

W: *fr.* 1, ACO 1, 1, 5, 67. 7-13 [text]. — *fr.* 2, PG 4:65C-D.
L: E. Honigmann, Trois mémoires posthumes d'histoire et de géographie de l'Orient chrétien (Brussels, 1961), 38 n. 148.

C. SCHMIDT

Ammon, Bishop

Before being consecrated a bishop, A. (second half of the 4th c.) spent three years as a cenobitic monk in Pbou under the direction of Theodore of Tabennisi.

A. composed a letter to Theophilus of Alexandria (*ep.*) which gives information about his years with the cenobites as well as about the life and work of Pachomius the Elder and his successor, Theodore. A. is regarded as the most important source for the life of Pachomius.

W: ActaSS Maii 3:54-61 [text], 346-355 [Latin trans.]. — F. Halkin, S. Pachomii Vitae graecae (Brussels, 1932), 97-121 [text].
L: J. F. Goehring, The letter of A. and Pachomian Monasticism (Berlin, 1986). — A. Veilleux, La liturgie (Rome, 1968).

C. SCHMIDT

Ammonas

There is hardly any biographical information about A. (4th c.). In 356 he succeeded his teacher, Anthony (351-356), as head of a colony of monks in Pispir on the right bank of the Nile; later he was bishop of an unknown community. He died before 396.

A. wrote fourteen letters (*ep.*), initially attributed to Anthony and preserved completely only in a Syr. version. In close reliance on the *Ascensio Isaiae* (→ Isaiah) and the → *Testament of the Twelve Patriarchs*, the letters develop a special form of mysticism. A fifteenth letter is spurious. It is probable that not all of the eleven sayings attributed to A. in the → *Apophthegmata Patrum* are from him. Because of the frequency of the name A. in the Egyptian world, it is not possible clearly to identify A. as author of the other writings and sayings (*opusc.*, *fr.*) attributed to him.

W: *ep.*, M. Kmosko, PO 10:555-616 [Syriac text]. — *ep.* 1-7, F. Nau, PO 2:432-454 [Greek text]. — *ep.* 8, G. L. Mariott, Macarii Anecdota: HThS 5 (1918) 47ff. [Greek text]. — *opusc.*, F. Nau, loc. cit., 455-458 [text]. — *fr.* 1. 2, F. Nau, loc. cit., 403-423, 455-458, 484-486 [text].
L: H. Dörries, Symeon v. Mesopotamien (Berlin, 1941), 381ff. — J. C. Guy, Recherches sur la tradition grecque des Apophthegmata (Brussels, 1962). — F. Klejna, Antonius u. A. Eine Untersuchung über Herkunft u. Eigenart der ältesten Mönchsbriefe: ZKTh 62 (1938) 309-348.

C. Schmidt

Ammonius of Alexandria

A. (2nd half of 5th c.) was an Alexandrian priest and eccles. steward who in 457 cosigned an accusation by orthodox clerics, addressed to Emperor Leo, against Timothy Aelurus. A. is identified by many with the exegete A. of whom a number of catena fragments on the OT and NT have survived. Although the Origenist "A." of the 4th c. as well as a priest A. of the 6th/7th c. are also considered possible authors of the catenas, various historical references in the text suggest rather a date in the 2nd half of the 5th c. A further reason that makes it impossible to settle definitively the identity of the scholiast is the frequency of the name A. in the Egyptian world.

The individual fragments vary greatly in size, but the longer ones give an instructive impression of the exegetical method and theol. attitude of the author. The *fr. in Dan.* (*Dan.*) covers the entire Gr. book of Daniel, with special attention to the story of Susanna, and must be regarded as parts of a continuous commentary or a cycle of sermons. The *fr. in Jo.* (*Jo.*) likewise gives an almost complete commentary on the gospel of John; it takes divergent interpretations into consideration and brings out the dogmatic content. The *fr. in I Petr.* (*I Petr.*) contain an account of a conversation of the author with a teacher, Caesarius, on the preaching of Christ in the underworld.

W: PG 85:1361-1610, 1823-1826. — *Ps.*, R. Devreesse: DBS 1:1137. — *Dan.*, M. Faulhaber, Die Propheten-Catenen nach röm. Hs. (Freiburg i.Br., 1899), 185-188. — *Jo.*, J. Reuss, Johannes-Kommentare aus der griech. Kirche (Berlin, 1965), 196-358. — *Lc.*, J. Sickenberger, Titus v. Bostra. Studien zu dessen Lukashomilien (Leipzig, 1901). — *Ac.*, R. Devreesse: DBS 1:11209. — *1 Cor.*, K. Staab, Die Pauluskatenen (Rome, 1926), 249. — *1 Petr.* 3, 19-20, K. Staab, Die griech. Katenenkommentare zu den kath. Briefen: Bib. 5 (1924) 296-353, 310. — *Mt.*, J. Reuss, Der Exeget A. u. die Frgm. seines Matthäus- u. Johannes-Kommentars: Bib. 22 (1941) 13-20.
L: H. Dörrie, A., der Lehrer Plotins: Hermes 83 (1955) 439-477. — E. Elorduy, A. en las catenas: EE 44 (1969) 383-432. — J. Reuss, Der Presbyter A. u. sein Kommentar zum Johannes-Evangelium: Bib. 44 (1963) 159-170. — T. Zahn,

Der Exeget A. u. andere Ammonii: ZKG 38 (1920) 1-22, 311-336.

C. Schmidt

Ammonius, Monk

A., second half of 4th c., lived as a hermit at Canopus in Egypt and during a pilgrimage in 373-378 witnessed the slaying of forty-three monks at Raithu (Sinai Peninsula) by the Belmyans and of another forty by the Saracens. The account of A.'s martyrdom, composed in Coptic, was translated into Greek by a presbyter John from Naucratis but can be used only with great caution as a historical source.

W: F. Combefis, Illustrium Christi martyrum lecti triumphi (Paris, 1660), 88-138 [Greek text/Latin trans.]. — Acta SS Ian 2:235-249 [Latin trans.].
L: K. Heussi, Untersuchungen zu Nilus dem Asazeten (Leipzig, 1917). — S. Schiwietz, Das morgenländische Mönchtum 2 (Mainz, 1913).

C. Schmidt

Amphilochius of Iconium

I. Life: A., b. ca. 340/345, belonged to the rich Christian upper class of Cappadocia. He was a cousin of Gregory Naz.; in 360 he became a student of Libanius in Antioch and in 364/365 an orator or lawyer in Constantinople. In 370, after an (unclear) affair he wanted to become an anchorite in his native place, Diocaesarea, but in 373 Basil made him bishop of Iconium, the capital of the new province of Lycaonia. His episcopate was characterized by the struggle against Arianism and by the imposition of the Neo-Nicene christology, but also by a struggle against the Apotactites, Encratites, and Messalians. In 376, in his episcopal city, A. held a synod against the Pneumatomachians; in 381 he took part in the Council of Constantinople and became one of the guarantors of orthodoxy (see *Cod. Theod.* 16.1.3). In 383 he took part in a synod in Side against the Messalians, in 394 in the Synod of Constantinople. He died between 398 and 404.

II. Work: A. does not seem to have been an independent or original thinker; many of his works are lost (the works *De Spiritu sancto*, *De generatione domini secundum carnem*, the sermons, the letters, and a work on the *Acta Johannis*). Nevertheless, he was soon considered an authority in the church.

Preserved (transmitted by Gregory Naz.) are the so-called *Iambs to Seleucus* (*Seleuc.*), which is an introduction to a devout life and study (with a list of biblical books that is important for the history of the canon). Also preserved are the synodal letter (*ep.*

syn.) of the assembly of 376; a Syr. creed (*symb.*) that may have originated as a preliminary to the council of 381 but is certainly nothing more than a sketch; and a work *Contra haereticos* (*c. haer.*) against the radical ascetics of Cappadocia, the Apotactites and the Encratites, whom A. also called "Gemellians" (after Gemellus, a son of Simon Magus).

Preserved in Greek are nine sermons (*or.*) on the birth of Christ, the presentation of the Lord, Lazarus, the sinful woman (this homily is also attributed in part to Severian of Gabala and Chrysostom), Good Friday, Mt 26:39 (a controversy with Arians), the newly baptized (*or. de rec. bapt.*; this homily has been transmitted also in Armenian and Georgian and was also attributed to Chrysostom and Epiphanius), Zechariah, and Jn 5:30. In Syriac there is a homily on Jn 14:28, and in Coptic one on Abraham (*or. de Abr.*). In addition there is a series of to some extent important fragments (*fr*).

Spurious are a homily for the middle of the Easter period (*or. in mesopent.*), an encomium on Basil (*Enc.*), and a life of the same (*v. Bas.*), as well as a story about Basil and an unworthy priest.

W: C. Datema (CCG 3). — Rez. S. J. Voicu: Aug. 19 (1979) 359-364. — *Seleuc.*, PG 37:1577-1600. — E. Oberg, PTS 9. — *ep. syn., or., fr.*, PG 39:36-129. — *or. in Mt* 26, 39, K. Holl, A. (Darmstadt, 1969 = 1904), 91-102 [text]. — *or. de rec. bapt.*, H. Gstrein, Unedierte Texte zur Geschichte der byz. Osterpredigt, Diss. (Vienna, 1968), 111-120 [text]. — *or. de Abr.*, G. Ficker, Amphilochiana 1 (Leipzig, 1906) [German trans.]. — *or. in Joh* 14, 28, C. Moss: Muséon 43 (1930) 317-364 [Syriac text/English trans.]. — *symb.*, R. Abramowski, Das Symbol des A.: ZNW 29 (1930) 129-135. — I. Rucker, Florilegium Edessenum Anonymum, SBAW PH 1933 (Munich, 1933), 87-90 [text]. — *c. haer.*, G. Ficker, loc. cit. 21-77 [text]. — *or. in mesopent.*, C. Datema, loc. cit. 245-262. — *Enc.*, P. J. Alexander: DOP 7 (1953) 61 [Greek frags.]. — K. v. Zettersteen, Eine Homilie des A: FS E. Sachau (Berlin, 1915), 223-247 [Syriac text]. — idem: OrChr 31 (1934) 67-98 [German trans.]. — *v. Bas.*, F. Combefis, SS. Patrum Amphilochii . . . opera omnia (Paris, 1644), 155-225. — J. Wortley, An unpublished legend of an Unworthy Priest and St. Basil the Great: AnBoll 97 (1979) 363-371.
L: C. G. Bonis, The Heresies Combatted in A.'s "Regarding False Asceticism": GOTR 9 (1963) 79-96. — F. Cavallera, Les fragments d'A. dans l'Hodegos et le tome dogmatique d'Anastase le Sinaite: RHE 8 (1907) 473-497. — C. Datema, A. et Ps.-Chrysostome: JÖBG 23 (1974) 29-32. — H. R. Drobner, Bibliographia Amphilochiana: Th-Gl 77 (1987) 14-35, 179-196. — G. Ficker, loc. cit. — H. Gstrein, A. Der vierte große Kappadozier: JÖBG 15 (1966) 133-145. — K. Holl, loc. cit. — E. Oberg, Das Lehrgedicht des A.: JAC 6 (1973) 67-97. — I. Ortiz de Urbina, Mariologia: OCP 23 (1957) 186-191. — M. Richard, Le frgm. XXII d'A.: FS E. Podechard (Lyons, 45), 199-210. — L. Saltet, La théologie d'A.: BLE 1905:121-127.

G. RÖWEKAMP

Amphilochius of Side

A. was a 5th-c. bishop of the port city of Side in Pamphylia and took part in the Council of Ephesus in 431 as an opponent of Nestorius. In 449 he supported the rehabilitation of Eutyches, but changed his attitude at the Council of Chalcedon (451). A letter to Emperor Leo the Great, of which only a short fragment remains, indicates a further change of conviction and a rejection of the decisions of Chalcedon.

W: PG 77:1516; 86, 1841B. — C. R. Henry, The Chronicle of John Bishop of Nikiu (London, 1916), 110f. [English trans.].

C. SCHMIDT

Ananias of Shirak

A. (b. ca. 600, d. 670) is regarded as an important Arm. mathematician and philosopher. Catholicos Anastasius (662-667) asked him to draw up a calendar for the festal seasons. From his pen came numerous works on mathematical and astronomical subjects (*cosm.*), an autobiography (*vita*), and a chronicle, as well as some shorter theol. treatises (*tract.*). A description of the world (*geogr.*), handed down under the name of → Moses of Choren, has recently been attributed to A.

W: *cosm.*, K. Pakanean (St. Petersburg, 1877) [text]. — A. Abrahamian (Eriwan, 1944) [text]. — idem, Cosmographical works (Eriwan, 1940) [text]. — idem, Cosmology and Calendar (Eriwan, 1962) [text]. — *geogr.*, J. Saint-Martin, La géographie: Mémoires sur l'Arménie 2 (Paris, 1819), 301-394 [text/French trans.]. — A. Soukry, Géographie de Moïse de Chorène (Venice, 1881) [text/French trans.]. — R. H. Hewsen, VIIth century Geography attributed to A. (Delmar, NY, 1994) [text/English trans.]. — idem, Geography of A. (Wiesbaden, 1992) [English trans.] — *tract.*, F. Conybeare, A.'s Autobiography. Tract. on Easter: ByZ 6 (1897) 572-584 [English trans.]. — idem, A. on Christmas: Exp. 4 (1896) 321-327. — *vita*, H. Berbérian, Autobiographie d'A.: REArm 1 (1964) 189-189 [French trans.].
L: R. Hewsen, Science in VIIth century: Isis 49 (1968) 32-45. — J.-P. Mahé, Quadrivium et cursus: TMCB 10 (1987) 159-206. — N. Petri, A.: ein arm. Kosmograph: ZDMG 114 (1964) 269-288. — J. R. Russell, Dream Vision of A.: REArm 21 (1988/89) 159-170. — idem, Book of the Six Thousand: Baz. 147 (1989) 221-243.

P. BRUNS

Anastasius I of Antioch

A. was probably a native of Palestine and lived as a monk on Sinai. Initially apocrisiary (legate) in Antioch of the patriarch of Alexandria, he succeeded Domnus III as patriarch of Antioch. In 570, because of his opposition to the teaching of the Aphthartodocetes (Evagrius, *h.e.* 4.40), Emperor Justin II banished him to Jerusalem. Only in 593, at the request of Pope Gregory I, did he return to his see. He died in 598/599. During his time in office, the *Notitia Antiochena* was recorded.

What is preserved of A.'s work shows him to have been a Neo-Chalcedonian theologian who built a bridge over to Monotheletism or Monenergism. He exercised great influence by reason of his clear, almost "scholastic" expository method.

Five dogmatic orations (*or.*) have been preserved (in Latin) in which A. defends the theology of Chalcedon. Some remarks in them indicate his unpropitious circumstances. Also important are his philosophical *Definitiones* (*def.*) and a dialogue with a tritheist (*dial.*). A further address (*or. pacificatoria*) was delivered in connection with his return to Antioch.

Sermons have been handed down on the transfiguration, the annunciation (the first of the two justifies the date of the feast), Hypapante, and Easter. But they are to some extent either unpublished or controverted. Probably spurious or from a later time is the now fragmentary sermon on the three periods of fasting (*serm. de quadragesima*).

Only fragments have survived of a document on the sabbath (*sabb.*) addressed to Simeon of Bostra, from which John Damascene cites testimonies on the veneration of images; of a defense of the *Tomus Leonis* (*apol. tomi Leonis*); and of a document addressed to Gabriel, a Persian priest (*Gabr.*). The catenas contain some citations from commentaries on the NT.

The → *Doctrina Patrum* transmits some philosophical-theol. *capita*, as well as citations from a work on the energies, and a work against the *Diaitetes* of → John Philoponus.

The so-called dialogue on religion at the court of the Sasanids (→ Dialogues against the Jews) is not from A. The same is true of the explanation of the faith attributed to him (PG 89:1400-1404).

W: *or.*, PG 89:1309-1362. — J. B. Pitra, Anastasiana. Anastasiorum Antiochenorum et Sinaitorum (Rome, 1866), 60-99 [text]. — S. N. Sakkos, Ἀναστασίου . . . ἔργα (Thessalonica, 1976), 17-78 [text]. — *def.*, K. H. Uthemann: OCP 46 (1980) 306-366 [text]. — *dial.*, K. H. Uthemann: Tr. 37 (1981) 73-108 [text]. — S. N. Sakkos, loc. cit., 80-105, 107-119 [text]. — *or. pacificatoria*, J. B. Pitra, Iuris ecclesiastici graecorum historia et monumenta 2 (Rome, 1868), 251-257 [text]. — S. N. Sakkos, loc. cit., 121-124 [text]. — *serm.*, PG 89:1361-1389 [Latin text]. — *serm. de quadragesima*, PG 95:76. — *sabb.*, S. N. Sakkos, loc. cit., 140f. [text]. — *Apol. tomi Leonis*, Mansi 11:435-437; 10:1107 [text]. — S. N. Sakkos, loc. cit., 134f [text]. — *fr. in Mt*, G. Weiss, loc. cit., 123-127 [text]. — *fr. in Ioh.*, I. A.

Cramer, Catenae Graecorum Patrum 2 (Oxford, 1844), 410-412 [text]. — *fr. in Pauli epistulas et epistulas catholicas*, G. Weiss, loc. cit., 89-91 [text]. — *Gabr.*, G. Weiss, loc. cit., 128f. [text]. — S. N. Sakkos, loc. cit., 142 [text].
L: E. Chrysos, Νεώτεραι ἔρευναι περὶ Ἀναστασίων Σιναίτων: Kl. 1 (1969) 121-144. — S. Helmer, Der Neuchalkedonismus (Bonn, 1962), 223f. — E. Honigmann, Studien zur Notitia Antiochena: ByZ 25 (1925) 60-88. — R. Riedinger, ByZ 60 (1967) 339-342. — S. N. Sakkos, Περὶ Ἀναστασίων Σιναίτων (Thessalonica, 1964), 44-86. — G. Weiss, Studia Anastasiana 1. Studien zum Leben, zu den Schriften u. zur Theologie des Patriarchen A. (Munich, 1965).

C. Schmidt

Anastasius, Apocrisiary

A., a papal apocrisiary, or representative, in Constantinople, was a disciple of Maximus Conf. With the latter he was taken prisoner in Rome and accused of heresy. After condemnation, exile, and mutilation he died in 666.

One of A.'s main themes is the fate of Maximus, which he describes and interprets (*Relatio motionis, Adv. Constantinopolitanos, Acta in primo exilio*). Of theol. importance is the fact that in his defense of Maximus he appeals especially to the tradition of the fathers in behalf of two wills in Christ (e.g, letter to Theodosius of Gangra). The philosophical concepts used in christology are the subject of a letter to the monks of Askalon; thus far only the beginning and two fragments of this letter have been published. It is an open question whether A. is also to be regarded as one of the authors of the *Doctrina Patrum*.

W: *ep. ad Theodosium Gangrensem*, R. Devreesse: AnBoll 73 (1955) 10-16. — *ep. ad Mon. Ascalonitas*, PG 89:1191. — F. Diekamp, Doctrina Patrum (Münster, 1981 = 1907) 262.13, 264.4. — Cod. Vat. gr. 662. — *Acta pr. exsilio*, PG 90:136-171. — *Rel. mot.*, PG 90:109-129. — *Adv. Const.*, PG 90:201-205.
L: R. Devreesse, La Vie de S. Maxime: AnBoll 46 (1928) 5-49. — idem, La lettre d'A. sur la mort de S. Maxime: AnBoll 73 (1955) 5-16. — C. N. Tsirpanlis, Acta s. Maximi: Theol (A) 43 (1972) 106-124. — F. Winkelmann, Die Quellen zur Erforschung des monergetisch-monotheletischen Streites: Klio 69 (1987) 515-559, especially 541f., 545f.

T. Böhm

Anastasius, Monk

In ca. 618 A. became a follower of Maximus Conf. in Chrysopolis until his banishment (655-662). In 662, along with Maximus, he was publicly tortured, mutilated, and deported (d. July 24, 662). A letter to the monks of Cagliari (*ep. ad mon. Cal.*) is authentic, whereas scholars are uncertain about *fr. in Lucam* and *De festis*. On the other hand, the *Disputatio cum*

Pyrrho is probably not from A. As a follower of Maximus, A. opposed Monotheletism: Chalcedon makes it necessary to hold two wills in Christ, a divine and a human. By "will" A. understands the spiritual nature of the human being.

W: *Ep. ad mon. Cal.*, PG 90:133-136. — *fr. in Lucam*, PG 89:1285-1288. — *de festis*, Carellius: Nuova raccolta d'opusc. sc. e fil. 34 (Venice, 1780).
L: G. Bausenhart, "In allem uns gleich außer der Sünde" (Mainz, 1992), 112-121, 196-316. — J.-M. Garrigues, Le martyre de saint Maxime le Confesseur: RThom 76 (1976) 410-452.

T. BÖHM

Anastasius, Poet

A. is the name given to the author of a → kontakion for the dead that is part of the burial service for a priest in the Byz. rite. The first *dikos* (stanza) is also sung at other funerals. The identity of this A. cannot be established with certainty. In addition to → Anastasius the Sinaite (d. shortly after 700), whose homilies the kontakion closely resembles, Anastasius Quaestor, nicknamed *ho traulos* (the stammerer), has been suggested.

W: ASSSP 1 (1876) 242-249 [text]. — P. Matzerath, Die Totenfeiern der byz. Kirche (Paderborn, 1939), 118-126 [German trans.].
L: E. Bouvy, Le cantique funèbre d'A.: EOr 1 (1897/98) 262-264. — idem, Les A. du Sinai: RAug 1 (1902) 135f. — V. Bruni, I funerali di un sacerdote nel rito bizantino (Jerusalem, 1972), 175-179. — C. Emereau, A.: EOr 21 (1922) 264. — S. Petrides, Les deux mélodes du nom d'A.: ROC 6 (1901) 444-452.

U. HAMM

Anastasius I of Rome

Shortly after his election as bishop of Rome (Nov.[?] 27, 399) A. was drawn into the controversies surrounding the work of → Origen. This conflict set its mark on A.'s literary output during his time in office, although people in Rome did not have a very accurate knowledge of the controversies in the East. A. died on Dec. 14 or Dec. 19, 402. In two letters to Simplician and Venerius, bishops of Milan, A. made his own the Alexandrian church's condemnation of Origen, "in order that the people of God in the various churches may not greatly blaspheme by reading Origen" (*ep. ad Simplicianum* 1). But in a letter to John II of Jerusalem A. disapproves of a punishment for Origen's translator, Rufinus of Aquileia, who had previously sent the pope a defense of his actions (*Apologia ad Anastasium*: CCL 20:25-28). A.'s

friends, Jerome (*ep.* 95; 127.10; 130.16) and Paulinus of Nola (*ep.* 20), speak of him with great respect.

W: *ep. ad Simplicianum*, I. Hilberg, CSEL 55:157f. [text]. — *ep. ad Venerium*, PLS 1:791f. — J. van den Gheyn: RHLR 4 (1899) 5-8 [text]. — *ep. ad Joannem*, ACO 1, 5, 3f. — S. Wenzlowsky, Papstbriefe 2, BKV¹:492-505 [German trans.].
L: E. Caspar, Geschichte des Papsttums 1 (Tübingen, 1930), 285-287. — E. Clark, The origenist controversy (Princeton, 1992), 171-173. — G. de Senneville, A.: DHP 84f.

S. C. KESSLER, S.J.

Anastasius II of Rome

A., a Roman deacon, was elected bishop of Rome on Nov. 24, 496. His short term of office came at the time of the Acacian Schism and in the early years of Ostrogoth rule in Italy. A. dropped the hard-line attitude of his predecessor, Gelasius I, in the dogm. conflict with Acacius. His policy of reconciliation with the East was not accepted by the Roman clergy. This conflict led to schism after the death of A. (d. Nov. 19, 498). Six letters of a theol. kind have been handed down from A. (*ep. pontif.*). A. sent a conciliatory announcement of his election to the east Roman emperor, in which he declared his desire for the restoration of church unity (*ep.* 1). In a letter to the bishops of Gaul on the origin of the soul A. condemns generationism (*ep.* 6). His formula of faith was mistakenly attributed to → Gelasius (*ep.* 3). The congratulatory letter on the baptism of Chlodwig (*ep.* 2) is a forgery.

W: *ep. pontif.*, PLS 3:788-797. — A. Thiel, Epistulae Romanorum Pontificum Genuinae (Hildesheim, 1974 = 1868), 615-637 [text]. — S. Wenzlowsky, Papstbriefe 7, BKV¹:541-597 [German trans.].
L: E. Caspar, Geschichte des Papsttums 2 (Tübingen, 1933), 82-88. — A. Di Berardino (ed.), Patrologia 4 (Genoa, 1996), 130-132. — F. Hofmann: KonChal 2:66-70. — H. Rahner, Die gefälschten Papstbriefe (Freiburg i.Br., 1935), 67-128. — J. Richards, The popes and the papacy (London, 1979). — C. Sotinel, A.: DHP 85f.

S. C. KESSLER, S.J.

Anastasius the Sinaite

Accurate dates for the life of A. (ca. 610-701) are unknown. As a priest-monk (and abbot) in the monastery of Sinai, he took part in the theol. discussions in Egypt and Syria. In particular, he endeavored to refute the Monophysites and Monothelites. The identification of his numerous works caused great difficulty for a long time. Thus, the attribution of his most important theol. work, the *Hodegos* (*hod.*) (provided with scholia ca. 686/689), was uncertain until 1980. As a result, this work (like many others) was attributed to Patriarch Anastasius II of Antioch. In the *hod.* A. takes a position against the theol. terminology of the Monophysites. Thus he rejects the description of the unity of the two natures in Christ as a mixture (*sygkrasis*), because this removed the distinction between the two (*hod.* 13.1.21; 3.109f.). He also rejects the opinion of the Monophysites that the one nature of Christ is made up of two incomplete parts (18.2-5 and 18f.; 19.5). He describes the unity of the person of Christ in Neo-Chalcedonian terms as "union in person" *henōsis kata hypostasin* (3.3.9). A. also opposes the Gaianites, who claimed the human nature of Christ to be incorruptible (23).

The *Capita XVI contra Monophysitas* deals with the same subject. Some of the *Capita* of John of Caesarea really belong to A.

The three collections of edifying stories about monastic life (*diēgēmata psychōphelē*) have not yet been critically edited.

Among the important exegetical writings are the *Sermones in constitutionem hominis secundum imaginem Dei* (*serm. imag.*). In these A. shows that the human being, who is created in the image and likeness of God (see Gen 1:26f.), is made up of body and soul, analogously to Christ, who is a hypostatic unity of human and divine natures (2.1.42-48). The attribution of the scholia on the so-called *serm. imag.* 3 was debated for a long time. In these A. continued the themes of the first two *serm. imag.* and between 686 and 689 provided notes on the entire body of writings. As a result, *serm. imag.* 3 became a work against the Monothelites. Further sermons on various subjects have also been preserved.

The 154 *Quaestiones et responsiones* (*qu. et resp.*) of A. deal primarily with exegetical questions.

The origin of the *Disputatio adversus Judaeos*, the work *De haeresibus*, a commentary on the hexaemeron, and some other works is uncertain. In addition, A. was regarded for a long time as the author of the → *Doctrina Patrum*, which was also attributed to → Anastasius the Apocrisiary.

W: PG 89. — *hod.,* K. H. Uthemann, CCG 8. — *serm.,* K. H. Uthemann, CCG 12. — *qu. et resp.,* M. Richard, A. Guillou, Le monastère de la Theotokos au Sinai . . . Homélie inédite d'A. Sinaita sur la Transfiguration: MAH 67 (1955) 216-258 [text].
L: K. Alpers, Die Etymologiensammlung im *hod.:* JÖB 34 (1984) 55-68. — J. D. Baggarly, The Conjugated Christ (Rome, 1974). — H. G. Beck, Kirche u. theol. Lit. (Munich, 1959), 442-446. — P. Canart, Une nouvelle anthologie monastique: Muséon 75 (1962) 109-129. — E. Chrysos, Νεώτεραι ἐρευναὶ περὶ Ἀναστασίων Σιναιτῶν: Κληρονομία 1 (1969) 121-144. — G. Dahan, Paschalis Romanus.

Disputatio contra Judaeos: RechAug 11 (1976) 161-213. — R. Feraudy, L'icone de la transfiguration (Begrolles, 1978). — A. Grillmeier, Jesus der Christus 2/1 (Freiburg i.Br., 1986), 68f., 96f.; 2/4 (Freiburg i.Br., 1990), 49f. — A. Kazhdan, A.: ODB 87f. — H. Kraft, A.: LMA 1:574. — J. B. Kumpfmüller, De A. Sinaita (Würzburg, 1865). — G. Levi della Vida, Sulla versione araba di Giovanni Mosco e di Ps.-A. Sinaita: FS G. Mercati (Rome, 1946), 104-115. — M. Richard, A. le Sinaïte, L'Hodegos et le Monothélisme: idem, Opera Minora 3 (Turnhout, 1977), Nr. 63. — idem, Les véritables "Questions et réponses": ebd., Nr. 64. — S. N. Sakkos, Περὶ Ἀναστασίων Σιναιτῶν (Thessalonica, 1964). — K. H. Uthemann, Antimonophysitische Aporien des A. Sinaita: ByZ 74 (1981) 11-26. — idem, Die dem A. Sinaita zugeschriebene Synopsis De haeresibus: AHC 14 (1982) 58-82. — idem, Sprache u. Sein bei A.: StPatr 18/1 (1983), 221-231.

F. R. GAHBAUER, OSB

Anatolius of Alexandria/Laodicea

A., b. in Alexandria, founded a school of Aristotelean philosophy there in the second half of the 3rd c. On a journey to Palestine this senator was ordained an auxiliary bishop by Bishop Theotechnus of Caesarea and appointed as his successor. In 268 A. became a follower of Bishop Eusebius of Laodicea. He died after 282.

Eusebius (*h.e.* 7.32.6ff.) mentions three writings of A.: a treatise determining the date of Easter (*peri tou pascha*; *can. pasch.*), a manual of arithmetic in ten books (*arithmētikas en holois deka suggrammasin eisagōgas*; *arith.*), and a theological document (*peri ta theia*). This last seems to have been completely lost, whereas fragments of the other two have been preserved: Eusebius gives a lengthy passage from the work on Easter, and the statements cited under the name of an A. in the Pythagorean *Theologoumena arithmeticae* are regarded as fragments of the handbook on arithmetic.

A Lat. *Liber Anatoli de ratione paschali*, published by A. Bucher in 1634, which contains the passage cited by Eusebius and was initially regarded as a Lat. translation of the entire work, is a forgery.

W: *can. pasch.* (fr.), Eusebius, *h.e.* 7.32.14-19. — *arith.* (fr.), J. L. Heiberg, A. sur les dix premiers (Paris, 1901) [text]. — PG 10:209-232 (*Liber Anatoli de ratione paschali*).
L: A. Anscomb, The Paschal canon attributed to A.: EHR 10 (1895) 515-535. — V. Grumel, La date de l'équinoxe vernal dans le canon pascal d'A.: FS E. Tisserant 2 (Rome, 1964), 217-240. — B. Krusch, Studien zur chr.-mal. Chronologie 1 (Leipzig, 1880), 316-328. — T. Nicklin, The date and origin of Ps.-A. de ratione paschali: JP 28 (1901) 137-151. — A. Strobel, Ursprung u. Geschichte des frühchr. Osterkalenders (Berlin, 1977), 133-137.

C. SCHMIDT

Anatolius of Constantinople

A., b. in Alexandria and molded by Cyril of Alexandria, was ordained a deacon by the latter and appointed apocrisiary of the Alexandrian church in Constantinople. His election as patriarch of Constantinople in December 449 had been pushed by Dioscurus of Alexandria, but was confirmed by the Roman Bishop Leo I in 450 only after A.'s acceptance of the *Tomus Leonis* and his rejection of Eutyches. A. played an active part at the Council of Chalcedon as a supporter of Cyril's christology. Later on, he used the patriarchal privileges given him by can. 28 to intervene in the patriarchate of Antioch. He died July 3, 458.

There exist some letters of A. to the Roman Bishop Leo (*ep.*) and a report to Emperor Leo I (*ep. Leo. imp.*) on the situation in Egypt; a fragmentary *Encyclica ad Pascha* is attributed to him.

W: *ep.*, PL 54:854-856, 952-965, 976-984, 1082-1084. — *ep. Leo. imp.*, ACO 2, 5, 24-26 [text]. — *Encyclica ad Pascha*, PG 95:73C.
L: G. Eldarov, A.: BSS 1:1083. — M. Jugie, A.: DHGE 2:1497-1500.

C. SCHMIDT

Andrew of Caesarea

A. was archbishop of Caesarea in Cappadocia. Of his work a commentary on the Apocalypse (*Apoc.*) and five fragments on eschatological questions from a work entitled *Therapeutikē* (*therap. fr.*) have survived. Otherwise unknown is a commentary on Daniel that is attributed to an Andrew, archbishop of Caesarea in Cappadocia, in a catalogue of the patriarchal library in Constantinople, which was printed in Strasbourg in 1578. A.'s dates can only be inferred from the reconstructed date of the commentary on the Apocalypse: certainly after the explanation of the Apocalypse by → Oecumenius, and certainly before the conquest of Jerusalem by the Arabs in 638: perhaps in the first years of the 7th c., before 614.

The eclectic explanations of the Apocalypse in twenty-four books, concluding with a doxology, each book having three chapters, sometimes comment on only short parts of the text. Other explanations are frequently cited. The personal contribution of the author is to be seen in his consistent critical discussion of the commentary by Oecumenius, to which he refers in many passages, but without mentioning him by name. The visions of the Apocalypse are explained in their meaning for the present and the future and not, as in Oecumenius, for the past. A.

reads the book as primarily a prophecy of the last times. The large number of mss. of the commentary show that it had an extensive influence. Only at the end of the 9th c. did Aretas of Caesarea write a new Gr. commentary that was heavily influenced by A. A.'s commentary is, among other things, an important text-critical witness for one of the two more recent recensions of the Gr. text of the Apocalypse.

W: *Apoc.*, J. Schmid, Studien zur Geschichte des griech. Apokalypsetextes (Munich, 1955) [text]. — PG 106. — *therap. fr.*, F. Diekamp: OCA 117 (1938) 161-172 [text/comm.].
L: F. Diekamp, Das Zeitalter des Erzbischofs A.: HJ 18 (1897) 1-36. — A. Monaci Castagno, Il problema della datazione dei Commenti all'Apocalisse di Ecumenio e di A.: AAST.M 114 (1980) 223-246. — eadem, I commenti di Ecumenio e di A.: MAST.M 5/5 (1981) 303-426.

M. BIERMANN

Andrew of Crete

A., b. ca. 669 in Damascus, became a monk in the monastery of the Holy Sepulcher in Jerusalem in 678; after 680, perhaps in 685, he became a deacon in Constantinople and in ca. 692 archbishop of the island of Crete with his seat at Gortyna. In 712, like Germanus I of Constantinople, he gave his agreement to the Monothelite Synod of Constantinople under Emperor Philippicus (711-713), but after the fall of the emperor he returned to orthodoxy in 713. A. died July 4, 740.

A. was a famous poet and an outstanding orator and preacher. With his *Canones* (songs consisting usually of nine odes which differed in their stanzaic and metrical structure as well as in their melody), he founded a new genre of liturgical hymns that expanded on and led to the abandonment of the → kontakion. The following have come down: *Canon in Annae conceptionem* (*can. Ann.*), *Canon in BVM nativitatem* (*can. BVM*), *Canon in Lazarum* (*can. Laz.*), *Canon magnus* (*can. mag.*), *Canon in medium pentecosten* (*can. mesopent.*). The best known is the *can. mag.*, a 250-stanza penitential song that is still sung in the Byz. liturgy today on Thursday of the fifth week of Lent. Almost every stanza is a paraphrase of an OT poetic verse. In addition to the *Canones*, A. composed *idiomela* (*idiomela varia*; *idiomel.*). He also addressed to Agatho, a deacon, an iambic poem (*Agath.*) of 128 verses which make known his return to orthodoxy after his deviation into Monotheletism. A.'s work as orator and preacher is represented by forty-five sermons and panegyrics (*Orationes* [*or.* 1-17, 19-21]; *Homiliae variae*) in which he dealt with certain Sundays, feast-days, the deceased, and saints. He experienced the first phase of the controversy over image veneration, being a defender of such veneration, as the fragment *de sanctarum imaginum veneratione* (*imag.*) shows.

A. is important for his hymns, espec. his *Canones*, a genre continued by → Cosmas the Singer and → John Damascene, among others.

W: *or.* 1-17, 19-21, *homiliae variae, imag., can. Ann., can. BMV, can. Laz., can. mag., can. mesopent., idiomel.*, PG 97:805-1444. — *Agath.*, A. Heisenberg: ByZ 10 (1901) 508ff. [text]. — *can. mag.*, N. Nilles, Kalendarium manuale utriusque ecclesiae orientalis et occidentalis 2, I ²1897, 147-153 [text]. — P. Kilian Kirchhoff, Die Ostkirche betet 3 (Leipzig, 1936), 161-197 [German trans.]. — *Laudatio martyrum Cretensium*, B. Laourdas: Kretikà Chroniká 3 (1949) 101-117 [text].
L: G. Bardenhewer, Marienpredigten aus der Väterzeit (Munich, 1934), 118-130. — H.-G. Beck, Kirche u. theol. Lit. (Munich, ²1977), 500-502. — J. N. Birdsall, Homilies ascribed to A. in MS Halensis A 119 (text and text criticism) (Berlin, 1987). — T. Detorakis, Le vocabulaire d'A.: JÖB 36 (1986) 45-60. — M. Donnini, A. vulgo adscripta homilia in silentium s. Zachariae: Aug. 15 (1975) 201-211. — K. Krumbacher, Der hl. Georg in der griech. Überlieferung (Munich, 1911). — T. Nissen, Diatribe u. Consolatio in einer Predigt des 8. Jh.: Ph. 92 (1937) 177-198. — idem, Zum Text der Rede des A. über die Vergänglichkeit: Ph. 92 (1937) 382-385. — J. Noret, H. Gaspart, Un éloge de Jacques, le frère du Seigneur, par un ps.-A. (Toronto, 1978). — K. Treu, Ein Frgm. der Palmsonntagspredigt des A.: JÖB 14 (1965) 125-128.

B. R. SUCHLA

Andrew of Samosata

As bishop of the Syr. city of Samosata, A. (d. after 444) was a partisan of → Nestorius and a vigorous opponent of → Cyril Alex. His theologian friends → John of Antioch and → Theodoret of Cyrrhus asked A. to refute (*ref.*) the twelve anathematisms of the Alexandrian patriarch; this work has come down to us only in Cyril's response. A. did not take part in the Council of Ephesus (431), but after initial hesitation did accept the compromise formula of 433, without involving himself in a condemnation of Nestorius. His few surviving letters (*ep.*) provide a good insight into the theol. debates after Ephesus and elicited various echoes in the Syr. world (→ Rabbula [of Edessa]). A.'s christology prepared the way for the Chalcedonian concepts of *prosōpon* and *hypostasis*.

W: *ref.*, PG 76:315. — *ep.*, PG 84:649-720. — ACO 1, 1, 7, 33-65. — F. Pericoli-Ridolfini, Lettera di A.: RSO 28 (1953) 154-169 [Syriac text/Italian trans.]. — J. J. Overbeck, S. Ephraemi, Rabbulae aliorumque opera (Oxford, 1865), 220-224 [Syriac text].
L: L. Abramowski, Zum Brief des A.: OrChr 41 (1957) 51-65. — P. Evieux, A.: REByz 32 (1974) 253-300. — A.

Grillmeier, Jesus der Christus 1 (Freiburg i.Br., 1979), 700-707.

P. BRUNS

Anianus of Celeda

A. (ca. 420) was the most important translator of Chrysostom's sermons and the only one known to us by name. In two prefaces he explained his principles. He translated at least twenty-five homilies on Matthew (*hom.*) and seven panegyrics on Paul (*laud. Paul.*), but other Lat. works of Chrysostom are probably also from him. Some possible ones: *De compunctione, Quod nemo laeditur, De reparatione lapsi = Ad Theodorum lapsum, Ad neophytos, In Christi natalem diem, De Ioseph, De eleemosyna.*

Scholarly research is in a state of flux, but the peculiarities of A.'s style can be clearly grasped.

W: *hom.* 1-8, PG 58:977-1058. — *hom.* 9-25, Basler Chrysostomus-Ausgabe 1558. — *hom.* 15-18, M. G. A. Skalitzky, Diss. (Fordham University, 1968). — *laud. Paul.*, PG 50:471-514. — A. Piédagnel, SC 300. — *De compunctione*, 2 Bücher, G. Schmitz (Hannover, 1883). — *Quod nemo laeditur*, A. M. Malingrey, SE 16 (1965) 327-354. — *De reparatione lapsi*, J. Dumortier, SC 117. — *Ad neophytos*, A. Wenger, SC 50. — *In Christi natalem diem*, M. Aubineau, J. Lemarié: VetChr 22 (1985) 35-89, 259-260. — *De Ioseph*, J. P. Bouhot: FS M. Geerard 1 (Brussels, 1984), 47-56 [literal translation, 5th-c. Africa]. — *De eleemosyna*, P.-P. Verbraken: FS M. Geerad 1 (Brussels, 1984), 33-45. — *Prefaces*, PG 50:471; 58:975-978.
L: B. Altaner: HJ 61 (1941) 215-217 [= Kl. patr. Schriften, TU 83:419-423]. — H. J. Frede, Kirchenschriftsteller, (Freiburg i. Br., ⁴1995). — H. Marti, Übersetzer der Augustin-Zeit (Munich, 1974). — H. Musurillo, Versions of A.: FS J. Quasten (Münster, 1970), 452-460. — A. Primmer, Originalfassung von A.' ep. ad Orontium: FS W. Kraus: WSt.B 5 (1972) 278-289. — F. W. Schlatter, Author of the Opus Imperfectum: VigChr 42 (1988) 364-375. — A. Siegmund, Überlieferung: ABBA 5 (1949) 91-101. — W. Wenk, Zur Sammlung der 38 Hom.: WSt.B 10 (1988). — A. Wilmart, Collection des 38 hom. lat.: JThS 19 (1918) 305-327.

H. MARTI

Anianus, Chronicler

In 412 A., an Alexandrian monk, composed a chronicle of world history that has disappeared as a complete work but has been partially handed on by Gr. and Syr. chroniclers; some of these are George Syncellus, → John Malalas, Elijah of Nisibis, Michael the Syrian, and Gregory Bar-Hebraeus. Syncellus briefly describes A.'s characteristics; he also takes over A.'s determination of the birth of Christ as occurring in the year 5501 of the world, as well as March 25 as the day of creation, the incarnation, and the resurrection. Thus A.'s work, a revised version of the chronicle of → Panodorus in popular Greek, had a considerable influence. A. harmonizes his chronicle with an Easter calendar that was produced prior to him; it was based on the Alexandrian system of a 532-year cycle, in which a nineteen-year lunar and a twenty-eight-year solar cycle were combined, so that after the completion of the cycle the Easter full moon would fall on the same weekday and the same day of the month.

W: George Syncellus, ed. A. Mosshammer (Leipzig, 1984). — cf. also CPG 5537.
L: W. Adler, Time Immemorial (Washington, 1989), passim. — A. Bauer, J. Strzygowski, Alexandrinische Weltchronik (Vienna, 1905), 82-92. — E. Bratke, Zwei Frgm. aus A.: NJDTh 1 (1892) 110-154. — E. Honigmann, Le prétendu "moine Athénée" en réalité le chronographe A.: AIPh 12 (1953) 177f. — A. Jülicher, A.: PRE 1:2194. — H. Kraft, A.: LMA 1:644.

K. FITSCHEN

Anonymi Chiliastae in Mt. Fragmenta

Under this title five fragments have survived that were probably excerpts from a commentary. The first three, orate ne fiat fuga vestra hieme vel sabbato; de adventu Christi Domini; de diem [sic!] et hora nemo scit), give a traditional exegesis of Mt 24:20-44

De tribus mensuris (Mt 13:33) uses the three measures of yeast as a model of the varying acceptance of the word of God. The fragment de Petro Apostolo endeavors to justify Peter's denial (Mt 26:31-34, 69-75).

The dating of the fragments and the attribution to a particular author (→ Victorinus of Petau, → Ambrosiaster) must remain open questions.

W: PLS 1:665-670.
L: HLL 5:416. — C. Martini, De unitate auctoris commentarii Paulini: idem, Ambrosiaster (Rome, 1944), 50-64. — A. Pollastri, Nota all'interpretazione di Matteo 13, 33, Luca 13, 21 nel frammento incipit de tribus mensuris: SSR 3 (1979) 61-78. — A. Souter, Reasons for Regarding Hilarius (Ambrosiaster) as the Author of the Turner-Mercati Anecdoton: JThS 5 (1904) 608-621. — C. H. Turner, An Exegetical Fragment of the Third Century: JThS 5 (1904) 218-241.

W. GEERLINGS

Anonymus Placentinus

The account of an anonymous pilgrim from Piacenza (Anon. Plac.) was earlier known as Itinerarium Antonini Placentini (itin. Anton. Plac.). In fact, Antoninus was the name of the city's patron, under whose "guidance" the anonymous pilgrim began his journey. The account comes from the period after Justinian (the pilgrim mentions the new church of Jerusalem [542] and the destruction of Beirut [554]) and before the Persian invasion (614). He may have been familiar with the account of → Theodosius the Archdeacon. The text has come down in two versions, version B being a reworking of the text in the Carolingian period. The Vulgar Latin of the work shows more clearly than → Egeria the transition from Latin to the romance languages.

The text looks back to a journey from Constantinople via Cyprus to Syria, Palestine, Egypt, and Mesopotamia. It provides a good deal of important information on cultural history and attests to the growing importance of saints' graves and relics in pilgrimages, in contrast to the recall of salvation history that marked earlier times.

W: PL 72:899-918. — P. Geyer, CSEL 39:159-218. — P. Geyer, CCL 175:127-174. — H. Donner, Pilgerfahrt ins hl. Land (Stuttgart, 1979), 240-314 [German trans./comm.]. — J. Gildemeister, Antonini Placentini Itinerarium, (Berlin, 1899) [text/German trans.]. — C. Milani (Milan, 1977) [text/Italian trans./comm.].
L: F. Mian, L'Anonimo Piacentino al Sinai: VetChr 9 (1972) 267-301. — C. Milani, Aspetti fonetici del ms. Sang. 133: RIL 108 (1978) 335-359. — eadem, Problemi di morfologia e sintassi nell'Itin. Anton. Plac.: RIL 108 (1978) 360-416. — eadem, Per una nuova edizione del cosideto Itin. Anton. Plac.: Aevum 48 (1974) 359-366. — eadem, Un esempio di normalizzazione linguistica: la recensio altera dell' Itin. Anton. Plac.: FS S. Pugliatti (Milan, 1978), 679-703. — A. Orengo, L'Itin. Anton. Plac. e la Bibbia: SSL 25 (1985) 67-109. — H. Schmeja, "ad breve missi" beim Pilger von Piacenza: FS J. Knobloch (Innsbruck, 1985), 379-383. — G. Uggeri, La terminologia portuale romana e la documentazione dell'Itin. Anton. Plac.: SIFC 40 (1968) 225-254. — G. F. M. Vermeer, Observations sur le vocabulaire du pèlerinage chez Egérie et chez Antonin de Plaisance (Nijmegen, 1965). — J. H. Waszink, Rez. zur Ausgabe von C. Milani: VigChr 35 (1981) 440-444. — J. Wilkinson, Jerusalem Pilgrims Before the Crusades (London, 1977), 79-89.

G. RÖWEKAMP

Anonymus Sicilianus

This anonymous writer was a supporter of Pelagius and composed six documents in which he made a very strict Chr. life the norm. In his rigorism he even went beyond Pelagius; he was sometimes identified with Sixtus III because of the latter's sympathy for Pelagianism. The description of the writer as Sicilian points to the fact that Rome and Sicily were the original centers of the Pelagian movement.

W: ep. 1, PLS 1:1687-1694. — ep. 2, PLS 2:1375-1380. — de divitiis, PLS 1:1330-1418. — de malis doctoribus et operibus fidei, PLS 1:1418-1457. — de possibilitate non peccandi, PLS 1:1457-1462. — de castitate, PLS 1:1464-1505. — B. R. Rees,

The Letters of Pelagius and his Followers (Woodbridge, 1991) [English trans.].
L: J. Morris, Pelagian Literature: JThS NS 16 (1965) 26-60.

W. GEERLINGS

Anonymus Valesianus

The *Anonymus Valesianus* (*Anon Vales.*) is more correctly known as *Excerpta Valesiana*: two historiographical texts published for the first time in 1636 by H. Valois (Valesius) in connection with Ammianus. The first text (*Origo Const.*) covers the years 305 to 337 and is an excerpt from a history of the emperors that was probably written shortly after Constantine's death in 337. The author was not a Christian; a Christian later interpolated the work, drawing on → Orosius. The second text (*Theodoriciana*) covers the years 474-526. It was probably composed in the 6th c. before the end of Ostrogothic rule. Inasmuch as a tendency favorable to Theodoric is discernible in the years up to 518, whereas in what follows the author seems hostile to the Ostrogoths and Arians, there were perhaps two authors of this text, which harks back to, among others, the *Vita* of Severinus by → Eugippius.

W: J. Moreau, V. Velkov (Leipzig, ²1968) [text]. — *Origo Const.*, I. König (Trier, 1987) [text/comm.]. — C. Büchele, Ammianus Marcellinus (Stuttgart, 1854), 949-960 [German trans.]. — *Theodericiana*, W. Bracke, L'Anon. Vales. II, c. 79-96 (Bologne, 1992) [text/comm.]. — D. Coste, Prokop, Gotenkrieg (Leipzig, ²1903), 374-385 [German trans.].
L: J. Gruber, Anon. Vales.: LMA 1:675. — HLL 5:174, 195f. — M. Schanz, Geschichte der röm. Lit., 4/1 (Munich, ²1959 = ²1914), 107f.

B. WINDAU

Anonymus: Versus contra Marcum

In his *haer.* 1.15.6, Irenaeus cites eight iambic verses, an attack on Marcus Magus, by an unknown *presbytēs*, to whom other citations are probably also to be attributed.

W: Iren. *haer.* 1, pr. 2; 1.13.3; 1.15.6; 3.17.4 (cf. also *haer.* 4, pr. 2).
L: J. Daniélou, Figure et événement: FS O. Cullmann (Leiden, 1962), 282-292. — T. Zahn: FGNK 6 (1900) 53-58.

R. HANIG

Anthimus of Nicomedia

Acc. to Eusebius (*h.e.* 8.6.6; 8.13.1) Bishop A. died a martyr's death by beheading in 303 during Diocletian's persecution of Christians. This is confirmed by the letter of Pamphylus to the Antiochenes (*Chronicon Paschale* 227). The story in the *Vita SS. Inde et Domnae* (PG 116:1073-76) that during the persecution A. wrote letters of encouragement to his community from a hiding place is a legend, as is the late life of A. (PG 115:172-84). Hagiographical researchers discuss the identity of A. with an A. from the Via Salaria in Rome. A fragment *De sancta ecclesia* (*eccl. fr.*) has come down under A.'s name; because of its anti-Arian expressions it has been attributed to Marcellus of Ancyra or more recently to his disciples or to Eustathius.

W: *eccl. fr.*, G. Mercati: StT 5 (1901) 87-98.
L: R. P. C. Hanson, Date and authorship: PIA 83 (1983) 251-254. — A. v. Harnack, Geschichte der altchr. Lit. 2/2 (Leipzig, ²1958), 158-160. — M. G. Mara, "Passio Anthimi" (Rome, 1964). — M. Richard, Opuscule méconnu de Marcell d'Ancyre: MSR 6 (1949) 5-28.

B. DÜMLER

Anthimus of Trebizond

A. was bishop of Trebizond after 518 but left his see and lived as an ascetic in Constantinople; in 535 Justinian appointed him patriarch of Constantinople due to the support of Empress Theodora. As late as 532 he took part, on the orthodox side, in a dialogue on the faith with the Monophysites, but he then joined Severus of Antioch, so that in Constantinople in 536 Roman bishop Agapitus broke communion with him. Justinian immediately deposed him and a synod (May/June 536) condemned him in his absence (he had taken refuge with Theodora). Reconciled again with the emperor, A. died after 548.

Three letters (in Syriac) of A. to leading Monophysites exist: to Severus of Antioch (*ep. Sev.*) and Theodosius of Alexandria (*ep. Thds.*), in which he supports the first three councils and the *Henotikon*, and after 542 to Jacob Baradaeus (*ep. Iac.*). A. also wrote other, now lost letters to other patriarchs (ACO 3, 179, 13). There are three known fragments (*fr.*) of a *Sermo ad Iustinianum*, in which he professes Monophysitism.

W: *ep. Sev., ep. Thds.*, Zacharias Rhetor, *h. e.* 9.21, 25, E. W. Brooks, CSCO 84:141-147, 163-168 [Syriac text]; CSCO 88:96-100, 111-113 [Latin trans.]. — *ep. ad Iac.*, I. E. Rahmani, Studia Syriaca, 3 (Sarfa, 1908), 23-25 (71-72) [text/Latin trans.]. — F. Nau, Littérature canonique: RCO 14 (1909) 123f. [French trans.]. — *fr.* 1/2, Mansi 11, 440E-441C. — *fr.* 3, A. Grillmeier, Jesus der Christus, 2/2 (Freiburg i. Br., 1989), 384f. [German trans.].
L: H. G. Beck, Kirche u. theol. Lit. (Munich, 1959), 392. — A. Grillmeier, loc. cit., 192, 243, 246, 364-372, 383-385. — E. Honigmann, Patristic Studies (Rome, 1953), 185-193.

B. WINDAU

Anthologia Latina

The *Anthologia Latina*, in the strict sense, is the collection of Lat. poems that was made in North Africa, basically between 532 and 534; it was also named *Anthologia Salmasiana* after a temporary possessor of the most important ms. (Paris, BN lat. 10318). The poems belong to various genres (Virgilian centos, epithalamia, panegyrics, short erotic poems, epigrams, mythological poems, riddles). Along with a few classical and postclassical poems (Virgil, Ovid, Seneca, Martial, among others), there are chiefly poems from late antiquity (notably the *Pervigilium Veneris*) and others from as late as the time of the last Vandal kings (see the epigrams by Flavius Felix, 201-5 [numbering according to the edition of Shackleton Bailey] and the panegyric of Florentinus on King Thrasamund [371] as well as a mocking epigram on drunken barbarians [279]). Only a few of the poems have an explicitly Chr. content (79-82, 373-75: Chr. epigrams).

The most important poets (dates are mostly uncertain) are: → Luxurius (Luxorius?), who ca. mid-6th c. in North Africa wrote a Virgilian cento as well as eighty-nine poems in various meters, mostly epigrams in imitation of Martial; Pentadius wrote three poems in affected elegiac distichs (*versus echoici*; 226, 227, 259; also under his name: 260-62); there are one hundred epigramlike riddling poems, each of three hexameters, by → Symphosius (281); Reposianus wrote *De concubitu Martis et Veneris* (247, a mythological erotic poem in 182 hexameters); included is a humorous debate in verse, *Iudicium pistoris et coci* (190).

The *Anthol. Lat.* in a broader sense is a modern edition that includes various anthologies of Lat. poems.

W: F. Buecheler, A. Riese (Amsterdam, 1973 = Leipzig, ²1894-1906) (1/1 Anthologia Salmasiana). E. Lommatzsch, Suppl. (Stuttgart, 1982 = Leipzig, 1926). — D. R. Shackleton Bailey (Stuttgart, 1982).
L: A. J. Baumgartner, Untersuchungen zur Anthologie des Codex Salmasianus (Baden [Switzerland], 1981). — G. Bernt, Das lat. Epigramm im Übergang von der Spätantike zum frühen MA (Munich, 1968). — J. Gruber, Anthologie: LMA 1:695-699. — H. Happ, Luxurius (Stuttgart, 1986). — R. Keydell, Epigramm: RAC 5:539-577. — A. Mandouze, Africa C. 2. 1: RAC Suppl., 216-218. — F. Munari, Die spätlat. Epigrammatik: Ph. 102 (1958) 127-139. — M. Rosenblum, Luxorius (New York, 1961). — J. P. Schwindt, Anthologie: Der Neue Pauly 1:734-738. — V. Tandoi, A. L.: Enciclopedia Virgiliana 1:198-205.

                                                                H. MÜLLER

Anthologia Palatina

The *AP* is a collection of Gr. epigrams that derives its name from the sole surviving codex (Heidelberg, Bibl. Pal. 23; a part of it is now in Paris, BN graec. suppl. 384). It was put together ca. 980 by an unknown editor on the basis of older collections. Along with Gr. and Hellen. epigrams, the fifteen books of this thematically organized collection (the sixteenth book added in modern editions consists of further poems from the related collection of Maximus Planudes [1301]) also contain works of Byz. poets, especially of the 6th c. (Agathias, Julianus, → Paul the Silentiary, Macedonius of Thessalonica, among others), especially sepulchral epigrams, but also feasting and amatory poetry in the Hellen. tradition. Some books are devoted exclusively to Chr. poems: book 1 contains anonymous Chr. inscriptions on works of art and buildings; book 8 contains the epigrams of → Gregory Naz. (on the death of his parents and of friends, against grave robbers, against banquets in the church).

W: P. Waltz, F. Buffière (Paris, 1928ff.) [text/French trans.]. — H. Beckby, ²1965ff. [text/German trans.]. — C. Preisendanz, AP: codex Palatinus et codex Parisinus phototypice editi (Leiden, 1911).
L: R. Aubreton, La tradition manuscrite des épigrammes de l'Anthologie grecque: REA 70 (1968) 32-82. — A. Cameron, The Greek Anthology from Meleager to Planudes (Oxford, 1993). — J. Gruber, Anthologie: LMA 1:695-699. — H. Hunger, Die hochsprachliche Literatur der Byzantiner (Munich, 1978). — R. Keydell, Epigramm: RAC 5:539-577. — F. Lenzinger, Zur griech. Anthologie (Bern, 1965). — A. E. Raubitschek et al., L'épigramme grecque (Vandœuvres, 1968). — R. Reitzenstein, Epigramm: PRE 6/1:71-111. — J. P. Schwindt, Anthologie: Der Neue Pauly 1:734-738.

                                                                H. MÜLLER

Anti-Jewish Dialogue

In the course of Christianity's separation from Judaism the expression of anti-Jewish sentiments soon appeared, especially since many passages of the NT can be interpreted as anti-Jewish. A first high point came with → Melito's accusation of deicide (*pass.* 72-99). In the following period anti-Jewish polemic took various forms. Alongside legends, which played an important part in promoting resentment among large sectors of the population, the (mostly fictive) → dialogues between Christians and Jews became the most important genre. The anonymity of the later dialogues was due to their character as literature for everyday use. There was often a fluid distinction between these and simulated dialogues directed chiefly against judaizing tendencies among Chr. converts from paganism. The latter include, among others, the → *Letter of Barnabas,* the sermon *Adversus Iudaeos* (CSEL 3/3:133-44) of Ps.-→ Cyprian, which is one of the oldest surviving Lat. sermons (end of 2nd c.), and the *Altercatio Simonis et Theophili* of → Evagrius (an anti-Jewish polemicist; 4th-5th c.). In regard to all of this literature it is to be noted that the Chr. authors made hardly any efforts to obtain an authentic knowledge of Judaism. In this respect the anti-Jewish writings were radically different from the → apologies addressed to a pagan public.

The earliest surviving dialogue is that of → Justin with Trypho, a Jew; it is marked by an atmosphere of goodwill. The first work in this special genre is the *Adversus Iudaeos* of → Tertullian, but this too was occasioned by a (probably real) dialogue. In contrast to this work, in which Tertullian still speaks, to some extent, respectfully of Judaism, the distance between Jews and Christians is already discernible in Cyprian's *Ad Quirinum,* a collection of bibl. texts against the Jews.

The dialogue between Jason and Papiscus by → Ariston of Pella has not survived; this was probably a slight work, but served as a model for later dialogues. All that has survived is the preface by a 3rd-c. Lat. translator named Celsus, which is in the Ps.-Cyprianic *Ad Vigilium episcopum de judaica incredulitate* (CSEL 3/3:119-32). This is the place to mention the → *Consultationes Zacchaei et Apollonii,* which describe a dialogue between a Christian and a pagan, but in chs. 4-10 treat of Judaism in great detail. Next, along with some unpublished writings from the 4th/5th c. there are some anonymous dialogues that almost always end with the conversion of the Jewish partner. The themes and arguments are traditional (Trinity and christology with reference to the plural in Gen 1:24 among others; christological reading of the OT; replacement of Judaism by Christianity with a reference to the destruction of Judaism).

Among the writings of Athanasius there is a *Dialogus Athanasii et Zacchaei* (*Ath. et Zacch.*), which probably dates from the 4th/5th c. Also among his writings is the *Quaestiones ad Antiochum ducem* (*qu. Ant.*), which probably date from the 6th c.; no. 137 treats of how to make Jews understand that Jesus is the Messiah and not a deceiver.

Ca. 480 there appeared a work on the discussion between Bishop Gregentius and Herbanus, a Jew (*Greg. et Herb.*), which takes place in southern Arabia; for the first time the presence of a king is mentioned. The subjects are mainly the Torah, the Messiah, and thus the understanding of the OT.

A supposed dialogue on religion at the court of Sassanid King Arrinatus is reported in a novel-like work that was written ca. 500 and is also known as *Narratio Aphroditiani* (*narr.*); it has been handed down as part of the → *Narratio de rebus Persicis.* It includes the so-called *Testimonium Flavianum* (*Ant.* 18.63f.) as one of a series of (supposed) Jewish testimonies to the truth of Christianity.

The *Dialogus Timothei et Aquilae* (*Tim. et Aqu.*) documents an alleged dialogue between Timothy, a Christian, and Aquila, a Jew, in the time of Cyril Alex. It probably comes from the 5th/6th c. and not the 4th. The conversation is not unfriendly; genuine Jewish objections are voiced, though they come probably from the literary tradition and not from real dialogues with Jews. The work may depend on the dialogue between Jason and Papiscus.

An anonymous, fictitious dialogue of the 6th c. that was later attributed to John Damascene is connected with Justinian's plan for a single religion in the empire (*dial. anon.*).

The Gr. work *Doctrina Jacobi nuper baptizati* (*Doct. Jac.*) dates from 634. It is the account by a baptized Jew, Joseph, of Jacob, who is forcibly baptized but through instruction becomes a real Christian. In the Eth. version it is an account by the governor of Carthage, who carries out the forced baptism. The many citations from scripture make the work almost more a collection of testimonies. In addition, there are many correspondences with *Ath. et Zacch.*

The *Trophaea Damasci* ("Banners of Victory over the Jews of Damascus") (*troph. Dam.*) tell of a supposed four-day disputation, held in 680, between the Jews of the city and a monk from a monastery near Damascus. A *Dialogus contra Monophysitas* is probably from the same author (N. Bonwetsch: NGG 1909, 123-59).

The *Dialogus Papisci et Philonis Judaeorum cum quodam monacho* (*Papisc. et Phil.*) was probably handed down originally under a different title (the one we have suggests a scholarly Philo and Ariston of Pella, but no Philo appears). Sources of this early-8th-c. work were, among others, the *troph. Dam.* and the Ps.-Athanasian *qu. Ant.* In fact, espec. toward the end, the work becomes rather a Chr. monologue assuring Christians of the correctness of their own outlook. Given the time of origin, the work also has the veneration of images as a theme. It served as a source of the *Disputatio adversus Iudaeos* of → Ps.-Anastasius the Sinaite (PG 89:1204-81).

W: Ps.-Athanasius, *Ath. et Zacch.*, F. Conybeare (Anecdota Oxoniensia 1/8) (Oxford, 1898) [text]. — Ps.-Athanasius, *qu. Ant.*, PG 28:684-700. — *Greg. et Herb.*, PG 86:621-784.

— *narr.*, T. E. Bratke (TU 4/3) (Leipzig, 1899) [text/German trans.]. — *Tim. et Aqu.*, F. Conybeare, loc. cit. — *dial. anon.*, J. H. Declerck, CCG 30. — *Doct. Jac.*, N. Bonwetsch, AGG.NF 12/3 (Berlin, 1910) [text]. — S. Grébaut, PO 3/4; 13/1 [Ethiopic text]. — *troph. Dam.*, G. Bardy, PO 15:171-292 [text/French trans.]. — *Papisc. et Phil.*, A. C. McGiffert, Dialogue between a Christian and a Jew (New York, 1889) [text].
L: A. B. Hulen, The Dialogues with the Jews as Sources for the Early Jewish Argument against Christianity: JBL 51 (1932) 58-70. — K. Hruby, Juden u. Judentum bei den Kirchenvätern (Zurich, 1971). — H. Schreckenberg, Die chr. Adversus-Iudaeos-Texte u. ihr literarisches u. historisches Umfeld (1.-11. Jh.) (Frankfurt a.M., 1982). — A. L. Williams, Adversus Iudaeos (London, 1935). — C. W. Williamson, The "Adversus Judaeos" Tradition in Christian Theology: Encounter 39 (1978) 273-296. — O. Zöckler, Der Dialog im Dienste der Apologetik (Gütersloh, 1894).

G. RÖWEKAMP

Antimontanist, Anonymous

In *h.e.* 5.16.1–17.4, Eusebius has preserved ten fragments from the three books of an anonymous anti-Montanist document (ca. 192) that contain important information about the early history of Montanism. Ancient (→ Rhodon, → Apollinaris of Hierapolis) and modern (→ Polycrates) efforts to identify the author are incorrect or speculative.

W: R. Heine, Montanist oracles (Macon, Ga., 1989), 14-23 [text/English trans.].
L: W. Bauer, Rechtgläubigkeit und Ketzerei (Tübingen, ²1964), 136-140. — A. v. Harnack, Geschichte der altchr. Lit. (Leipzig, ⁴1958), 1:240f.; 2/1, 364-369. — A. Jensen, Gottes selbstbewußte Töchter (Freiburg i. Br., 1992), 278-285. — W. Kühnert, Anonymus: ThZ 5 (1949) 436-446. — M. Wunsche, Ausgang der urchr. Prophetie (Stuttgart, 1996), esp. 264-297.

R. HANIG

Antiochus of Ptolemais

A. was bishop of Ptolemais (Akko) and died after 407. Along with Theophilus of Alexandria, Severian of Gabala, and Acacius of Beroea, he was an enemy of John Chrys. and shared the responsibility for John's condemnation at the Synod of the Oak in 403. The works mentioned by Gennadius (*vir. ill.* 20) against greed and on the healing of a blind man are lost. Fragments of a Christmas sermon on Jan. 1 (*nativ.*) and other fragments (*fr.*) remain.

W: *nativ.*, C. Martin, Un florilège grec d'homélies christologiques des IVᵉ et Vᵉ siècles sur la nativité: Muséon 54 (1941) 34-38, 53-57 [text]. — E. Schwartz, Publizistische Sammlungen zum Acacianischen Schisma (Munich, 1934), 101, 105 [text]. — *fr.*, Severus v. Antiochien, J. Lebon, CSCO 102:236 [Latin text]. E. Schwartz, loc. cit., 101 [text].

G. RÖWEKAMP

Antiochus of the Sabas Monastery (Monk)

A., born in Ancyra, became a monk in the monastery of St. Sabas near Jerusalem. After the Persian invasion of Palestine (614) and Asia Minor, Euthalius, abbot of the monastery of Attaline near Ancyra, asked A. for a spiritual manual that would replace the lost monastic library. Ca. 620 A. wrote a letter to Eustathius (*ep. Eust.*) and composed his *Pandektēs tēs hagias graphēs*, a collection of citations from the Bible and the fathers in 180 parts (*hom.*) that dealt especially with the sins and virtues and with the duties of monks and superiors. Among them are valuable citations from Ignatius, Polycarp, Hermas, and Irenaeus and from two Ps.-Clementine letters of the 3rd c. against the practice of virgins living with celibate men. Attached to the *Pandektēs* is an *Exomologēsis* (*conf.*) in which A. bemoans the Persian invasion; at the beginning of the *Pandektēs* there is also an account of forty-four martyrs in the Kidron Valley. But A. is not identical with the monk → Strategius.

W: PG 89:1421-1856.
L: G. Bardy, A.: DSp 1:701-702. — S. Haidacher, Nilus-Exzerpte im Pandektes des A.: RBen 22 (1905) 24-250. — J. Kirchmeyer, Une source d'A., Pandectes 127-128: OCP 28 (1962) 418-421. — P. Mayerson, A.'s Homily on dreams: JJS 35 (1984) 51-56. — F. Nau, Note sur les Mss. de Paris qui renferment la notice biographique d'A.: ROC 11 (1906) 327-330. — R. Schick, The Christian Communities of Palestine (Princeton, 1995), 9-48.

G. RÖWEKAMP

Antipater of Bostra

A., bishop of Bostra (Arabia), is mentioned in a circular letter of Leo I. The Second Council of Nicaea counts him among the acknowledged teachers of the past. A. distinguished himself by a (now fragmentary) polemical work against Origen and his defenders → Eusebius and → Pamphilus of Caesarea. Only two of his many homilies have survived in their entirety; their subjects are the birth of John the Baptist and the annunciation to Mary. Two other homilies are attested, on the woman with the flow of blood and on the holy cross; four homilies on the birth of Christ have come down in Armenian. It is possible that some writings of → Hippolytus of Bostra are to be attributed to A. A.'s christology is heavily influenced by the *Henotikon*.

W: PG 85:1763-1796.
L: M. van Esbroeck, De Fide: AnBoll 102 (1984) 321-328.

P. BRUNS

Anthony of Choziba

A. (b. ca 608; d. after 640) was from earliest youth a monk in the Choziba laura near Jerusalem; he experienced the Persian invasion of Palestine, the expulsion of monks from the wilderness, and their return.

A.'s works are the following: (1) A life of his teacher, George of Choziba (*vit. Georg.*), which also describes the conversations of George and A. and is the only source for a biography of A.; it gives valuable information on topographical and historical points. (2) A collection of Marian miracles in the Choziba monastery (*mir.*), which reflects the important place given the Mother of God as the real abbess of the monastery.

W: *vit. Georg.,* C. Houze: AnBoll 7 (1988) 97-114, 336-359 [text]. — *mir.,* C. Houze, loc. cit., 360-370 [text].

C. SCHMIDT

Anthony, Hagiographer

A. lived in the second half of the 6th c. and was a disciple of Simeon Stylites (d. 459), whose life he composed in Greek (*v. Sym. Styl.*) shortly after Simeon's death. He used as his basis the account by Theodoret of Cyrrhus (*h. rel.* 26), writen ca. 444, but he continued it and described in detail Simeon's last years, death, and burial. In comparison with the Syr. life of Simeon by Simeon Bar Apollon and → Bar Chatar, A.'s life is less reliable: it greatly embellishes the reality and shows little knowledge of localities and the historical situation.

Because of the large number of surviving mss. the original version is very uncertain. The Greek was published in 1907, Lat. translations as early as 1643.

W: *v. Sym. Styl.,* H. Lietzmann, Das Leben des hl. Simeon, TU 32/4 (Leipzig, 1908), 20-78 [text/Latin trans.]. — PL 73:325-334 [Latin trans.]. — *Acta SS Ian.* 1:264-274 [Latin trans.].
L: H. Delehaye, Les saints stylites (Brussels, 1923), 2-34. — P. Peeters, St. Syméon stylite et ses premiers biographes: AnBoll 61 (1943) 29-71.

C. SCHMIDT

Anthony the Hermit

A. was born ca. 251 in Coma/Ceman in central Egypt (Soz., *h.e.* 1.13.2) and, according to the testimony of Serapion of Thmuis, died in 356. Jerome says A. reached the age of 105 (*vir. ill.* 88). The main source for the interpretation of his life is the *Vita* by Athanasius of Alexandria, which was composed immediately after A.'s death (357/358; see Augustine, *Conf.* 8.6.15). Struck by Mt 19:21, A. withdrew into the wilderness and became the "father of monasticism." Athanasius describes him as an ascetic, a wrestler with demons, and an apologist against pagans and heretics.

Jerome (*vir. ill.* 88) speaks of seven Copt. letters (*ep.*) of A. in Gr. translation, which were regarded as authentic. They have been handed down in their entirety in Georgian. The Arab. tradition has twenty letters, among them the seven genuine ones; in addition, there is the letter to Theodore on sincere repentance. The language of the first letter, an introduction for novices, differs radically from the christological and soteriological language of the others. The letters correct the picture of A. as an uneducated monk and show him to be knowledgeable about the Platonic and gnostic traditions. A. was influenced by the bibl. theology of Origen and in his turn influenced Evagrius Pont., John Cassian, Macarius of Alexandria, and Dorotheus of Gaza.

Thirty-eight sayings of the fathers under his name → *Apophthegmata Patrum* give a glimpse of his personality. They show him as a hermit who possessed the charism of discernment. The question of the authenticity of these sayings remains open.

A.'s work is important in that it points by its terminology and spirituality to the currents of his age.

Spurious works: the *Sermones XX ad filios suos* and the *Regulae.*

S: Athanasius v. Alexandrien, *Vita Antonii,* G. J. M. Bartelink, SC 400.
W: PG 40:977-1000; 65:76-88. — *ep.,* A. Louf (Bellefontaine, 1976) [French trans./comm.]. — G. Garitte, CSCO 148-149 [Latin trans.].
L: T. Baumeister, Mentalität des frühen ägyptischen Mönchtums: ZKG 88 (1977) 146-160. — H. Dörries, Vita Antonii als Geschichtsquelle: idem, Wort u. Stunde 1 (Göttingen, 1966), 145-224. — K. S. Frank, A. u. seine Briefe: FS H. Riedlinger (Stuttgart, 1998), 65-82. — A. Guillaumont, A.: CoptE 1:148-150. — B. Miller, Weisung der Väter (Trier, ³1986). — W. Myszor, A.-Briefe u. Nag-Hammadi-Texte: JAC 32 (1989) 72-88. — S. Rubenson, The letters of St. A. (Lund, 1990).

M. PUZICHA

Apelles

Little is known of the circumstances of A.'s life: he probably lived after 140, first in Rome (where he met his teacher → Marcion and became his most independent and best-known disciple), and then in Alexandria (before 160: Tertullian, *praesc.* 30.5). "After years" (ibid.) A. again taught in Rome. Since Irenaeus and Clement do not mention A., it may be that his school, which he established in Rome outside the Marcionite church, began to be more influential only at the beginning of the 3rd c. When A. on his own initiative had a disputation with Rhodon, a disciple of Tatian (probably before 180), he was already an old man (Rhodon in Eusebius, *h.e.* 5.13.6). In Tertullian's time people were still living who could remember Philumene, a prophetess and virgin in the company of A. (*praesc.* 30.7); Tertullian himself obviously never met A.

A.'s works, written perhaps only after 170, are lost except for a few fragments: following his teacher he says that philological study of the OT reveals contradictions. He published his results in at least thirty-eight books of *Syllogisms*. His work *Phanerōseis* contains revelations of the prophetess and virgin Philumene.

Acc. to the oldest surviving account of A. (by Rhodon), A. broke away from the dualism of Marcion and taught the monarchic character of the one, good God. Hope in the crucified Christ, together with good works, brought redemption (see Eusebius, *h.e.* 5.13.5). He ascribed creation to a subordinate Principle (*deuteros theos,* or something similar), and the OT to a fallen angel (Hippolytus, *haer.* 7.36). He therefore declined to give a defense (*apodeixis*) of his teaching (i.e., from the OT).

W: A. v. Harnack, Marcion. Das Evangelium vom fremden Gott, TU 45 (Darmstadt, 1960 = Leipzig, 1924), 404-420.
L: B. Aland, Marcion/Marcioniten: TRE 22:89-101, esp. 99f. — K. Greschat, A. u. Hermogenes (Leiden et al., 1999). — A. v. Harnack, De Apellis gnosi monarchica (Leipzig, 1874). — idem, Marcion, TU 45 (Darmstadt, 1960), 177-196. — idem, Sieben neue Bruchstücke der Syllogismen des A., TU 6/3 (Leipzig, 1890), 111-120. — idem, Unbeachtete u. neue Quellen zur Kenntnis des Härctikers A., TU 20 (Leipzig, 1900). — A. Jensen, Gottes selbstbewußte Töchter (Freiburg i. Br., 1992) 373-426. — G. May, A. u. die Entwicklung der markionitischen Theologie: ANRW (soon to be published). — G. Quispel, Die Reue des Schöpfers: ThZ 5 (1949) 157-158. — E. Junod, Les attitudes d'A., disciple de Marcion, à l'égard de l'Ancien Testament: Aug. 22 (1982) 113-133.

C. MARKSCHIES

Aphraates

Twenty-three demonstrations (*demonstrationes*; *dem.*) have come down under the name of "Aphraates, the Persian sage." Gennadius (*vir. ill.* 1) and the Arm. tradition erroneously identify the author with the famous Jacob of Nisibis, who as bishop of Edessa took part in the Council of Nicaea. Little is known of A.'s life and person. He describes himself as a celibate ascetic, one of the so-called "Sons of the Covenant" (18.1, 12) and was active in the western part of the Sassanid kingdom (10.9). His

Demonstrations fall into two parts (10.9): the first is from the year 337 and deals with faith (1), love (2), fasting (3), prayer (4), the Sons of the Covenant (6), penitents (7), the resurrection of the dead (8), humility (9), and pastors (10). Demonstration 5, "On Wars," is a historical interpretation, along the lines of the book of Daniel, of the Roman war against Shapur II.

The twelve demonstrations from the year 344, which form the second part of the work (22.25), display a strongly anti-Jewish attitude and deal with circumcision (11), Passover (12), the sabbath (13), admonition (14), the distinction of foods (15), the nations instead of the one people (16), the divine sonship of the Messiah (17), virginity and holiness (18), against the Jewish hope of reunification in the land of Israel (19), care of the poor (20), persecution (21), and death and the last things (22). *Dem.* 23 is a postscript from the year 345 on the blessing that has passed from Israel, the vine, to the world of the nations.

A.'s literary importance consists in that he can be claimed as the first important witness to an independent Syr. literature that did not owe its existence to translation from Greek. His power as a writer is his imaginative reproduction and reworking of traditional and especially OT-Jewish material. His main theol. sources are the OT and the gospel, which was accessible to him only in the form of the → *Diatessaron* of → Tatian. On the basis of OT and later rabbinic traditions he explicitly defends the divinity of the Messiah, the primacy of celibacy over marriage, and Chr. freedom from Jewish ritual law. His theology is marked by images and symbols and makes no use of Hellen. and philosophical concepts. The contemporary Arian controversy has left no mark on A.'s christology. In his anthropology and pneumatology there are parallels with other representatives of the Syr. world. A.'s idea of the sleep of the soul (6.14; 8.23) anticipates a characteristic of later Nestorian eschatology (→ Narses), but met with strong criticism from Arabian Bishop → George.

W: *dem.,* J. Parisot (PS 1; 2) [text/Latin trans.]. — W. Wright (London, 1869) [text]. — G. Lafontaine, La version arménienne des œuvres d'A. (Leuven/Louvain, 1977-1980) [Armenian text/Latin trans.]. — *dem.* 6, G. Garitte: BeKa 17/18 (1964) 82-87 [Georgian text]. — idem: Muséon 77 (1964) 301-366 [Georgian text/Latin trans.]. — *arab. Frgm.,* J. M. Sauget: Muséon 92 (1979) 61-69. — *dem.* 5, M. Esteves Pereira: FS Nöldeke (Giessen, 1906), 877-892 [Ethiopic text]. — T. Baarda: NTS 27 (1981) 632-640 [Ethiopic text]. — *dem.,* M. J. Pierre, SC 349/359 [French trans.]. — P. Bruns, FC 5/1-2 [German trans.]. — Selected works, J. Gwynn (Michigan, 1983 = New York, 1898), 343-

412 [English trans.]. — A. and Judaism, J. Neusner (Leiden, 1971) [English trans. 2d part of the corpus].

L: A. Adam, Grundbegriffe des Mönchtums: ZKG 65 (1953/54) 209-239. — T. Baarda, The Gospel quotations, A 1975. — E. Beck, Symbolum-Mysterium: OrChr 42 (1958) 19-40. — B. Bonifacino, Santo, Santità, Santificare: SROC 1/1 (1978) 67-78; 1/2 (1978) 17-38. — P. Bruns, Christus-bild (Bonn, 1990). — J. H. Corbett, Pauline Tradition: OCA 229 (1984) 13-32. — W. Cramer, Geist Gottes u. des Menschen (Münster, 1979). — E. J. Duncan, Baptism in the Demonstrations (Washington, 1945). — J. M. Fiey, Notule de littérature syriaque: Muséon 81 (1968) 449-454. — D. Juhl, Askese bei A. (Wiesbaden, 1996). — R. Murray, Symbols of Church and Kingdom (Cambridge, 1975). — G. Nedungatt, Authenticity (dem. 14): OCP 46 (1980) 62-88. — R. J. Owens, Genesis and Exodus citations (Leiden, 1983). — M. J. Pierre, L'âme ensommeillée: POC 32 (1982) 233-262; 33 (1983) 104-142. — F. Pericoli Ridolfini, Antropologia, escatologia: SROC 1/1 (1978) 5-17; 1/2 (1978) 5-16. — idem, Problema trinitario/cristologico: SROC 2/2 (1979) 99-125. — idem, Sacramenti: SROC 2/3 (1979) 151-171. — P. Schwen, A.s Person u. Verständnis des Christentums (Berlin, 1907 = Aalen, 1973). — R. Terzoli, Il tema della beatitudine nei padri siri (Brescia, 1972), 47-79. — I. Ortiz de Urbina, Gottheit Christi (Rome, 1933).

P. BRUNS

Apocalypse of Adam

The so-called *Apocalypse of Adam* (NHC 5, 5) contains revelations supposedly received by Adam and passed on to his son Seth. In them A. tells his son of the loss of the original splendor and knowledge of God; then heavenly spirits appear and communicate saving knowledge to the elect. An "Illuminator" (Phōstēr) is mentioned as a redeemer who descends from the highest spheres of heaven to bestow knowledge of God on humanity. The writing has nothing Christian about it and must be viewed as an example of pagan-Jewish gnosis.

W: A. Böhlig, P. Labib, *Kopt.-Gnostische Apokalypsen* (Halle, 1963) [Coptic text/German trans.]. — G. W. MacRae (Leiden, 1979) [Coptic text/English trans.]. — F. Morard (Quebec, 1981) [French trans.].
L: A. Böhlig, Zeugnis jüd.-iranischer Gnosis: idem, Mysterion u. Wahrheit (Leiden, 1968), 149-161. — C. W. Hedrick, The Apocalypse of A. (Chicago, 1980). — G. W. MacRae, Apocalypse of A.: HeyJ 6 (1965) 27-35. — F. Morard, L'Apocalypse d'A.: Gnosis and Gnosticism, ed. M. Krause (Leiden, 1977), 35-42. — idem, Polémique anti-baptismale: RSR (1977) 214-233. — W. Perkins, Function of gnostic apocalypse: CBQ 38 (1977) 382-395.

P. BRUNS

Apocryphal Writings

The Gr. word *apokryphos* probably appeared as a literary term for the first time in connection with gnostic writings. In that context it means "secret" writings that are accessible or intelligible only to a limited group of individuals. When eccles. writers adopted the word, it became in many cases a synonym for "heretical" (in Tertullian it means "false"). But since the (gnostic) writings in question were primarily works not accepted into the church's canon of sacred writings, the word came to mean, quite generally, noncanonical writings that by their title, genre, and supposed origin laid a claim to canonicity. At least in part this group includes the writings found in the Copt. gnostic library of Nag Hammadi, which reveal a world in which gnostic teachings were proposed in a Chr. framework.

In fact, for a time, until the definitive fixing of the canon, some apoc. works (such as the *Acts of* → *Paul* or the *Apocalypse of* → *Peter*) enjoyed an almost canonical status. Literary testimonies to the development of the canon are, e.g., the → *Canon Muratori*; for the condemnation of apocryphal writings see also the → *Decretum Gelasianum*. All the NT writings were mentioned for the first time in Athanasius's Easter letter of 367. The literary genres of the NT were further developed in the apoc. writings.

L: H. v. Campenhausen, Die Entstehung der Bibel (Tübingen, 1968). — J. H. Charlesworth, Research on the NT Apocrypha: ANRW II 25/5 (1988) 3919-3968. — NTApo⁶ 1-61. — L. Fabricius, Die Legende im Bilde des 1. Jt. der Kirche. Der Einfluß der Apokryphen u. Pseudepigraphen auf die altchr. u. byz. Kunst (Kassel, 1956). — W. R. Farmer, D. M. Farkasfalvy, The Formation of the NT Canon (New York, 1983). — H. Köster, J. M. Robinson, Entwicklungslinien durch die Welt des frühen Christentums (Tübingen, 1971). — M. Krause (ed.), Essays on the Nag Hammadi Texts, FS P. Labib (Leiden, 1975). — P. Vielhauer, Geschichte der ur-chr. Lit. (Berlin, 1975), 485-718 (literature). — R. McL. Wilson, Apokryphen: TRE 3:316-362. — T. Zahn, Geschichte des ntl. Kanons 1-2 (Leipzig, 1888-1892).

1. Gospels: A distinction must be made between collections of logia and stories that (like the later canonical gospels) were to serve as a standard for preaching, and texts that were composed after 200 as supplements to the canonical gospels and were intended from the outset to challenge the canonical traditions.

To the first group belong the Jewish-Chr. gospels (→ *Gospel of the Ebionites*, → *Gospel of the Hebrews*, and → *Gospel of the Nazareans*) and fragments of possibly different gospels in papyri (*Pap. Oxyrhynchos 840*, *Pap. Egerton 2*, *Pap. Oxyrhynchos 1224*, *Pap. Cairensis 10735*, the Fayyum fr., Strasbourg Copt. Pap., Freer Logion on Mk 16). Their preservation only in fragments is connected with the later rejection and destruction of these writings.

Among the supplements are the *Protevangelium of → James the Younger,* the (gnosis-influenced) *Infancy Gospel of → Thomas,* and the → *Arabic Infancy Gospel.* Here too belongs the literature on → John the Baptist and on the good thief who was discovered in the wilderness during the flight into Egypt (M. R. James, *Latin Infancy Gospels* [Cambridge, 1927], 120-26). These are not gospels in the strict sense but did have a strong influence on the liturgy and iconography.

The chief rivals of the canonical gospels were the gnostic revelatory writings. Frequently they are not gospels in the literary sense but only instructions given by the risen Jesus on the "good news" of redemption (this is so even in the → *Evangelium veritatis*). The most frequent form is the "dialogue" of Jesus and his disciples (see below).

Not preserved: the *Gospel of the Four Heavenly Regions,* attested by → Marutha of Maipherkat; the *Gospel of Perfection,* mentioned by Epiphanius (*haer.* 26.2.5); the *Gospel of the Twelve* (Apostles) and the *Gospel of* → *Basilides,* both attested by Origen (*hom.* 1 *in Luc.*); the *Memoria Apostolorum* mentioned by Turibius of Astorga (*ep. ad Idacium et Ceponium* 5); and various other gospels of the twelve apostles.

It is unclear whether the *Gospel of* → *Judas* (Irenaeus, *haer.* 1.28) and the variously named gospels of → Cerinthus, → Apelles, and → Bardesanes ever existed.

L: D. Dormeyer, H. Frankemölle, Evangelium als literarische Gattung: ANRW II 25/2 (1984) 1543-1704. — S. Gero, Apocryphal Gospels: ANRW II 25/5 (1988) 3969-3996. — E. Haenchen, Ntl. u. gnostische Evangelien: (ed.), Christentum u. Gnosis (BZNW 37), ed. W. Eltester (Berlin, 1969), 19-45. — HLL 4:380-385. — J. Jeremias, Agrapha (Göttingen, ⁴1965). — A. de Santos Otero, Los evangelios apocrifos, BAC 148 (Milan, 1984) (literature). — NTApo⁶ 1.

2. Acts/Histories of the Apostles
Unlike the canonical Acts of the Apostles, the apocryphal Acts are concerned not with the history of the church but with the destinies of the individual apostles. There is thus a similarity between them and the Hellen. novel and the philosophical aretology. At the same time, because of the growing importance of "apostolicity," they were used to propagate particular teachings and ideas. Even the gnostics made increasing use of the genre. The point of contact with the canon for these often encratitically colored documents is Acts 24:25, where justice, self-control, and judgment are said to be the content of Paul's preaching. A collection of five Acts (→ Andrew, → John,

→Paul, → Peter, → Thomas) bearing these marks played a major role among the Manichees and Priscillianists. This group of Acts later became part of Lat. collections such as that of → Abdias (Ps.-). On the whole, the Acts are better preserved than the apocryphal gospels, because they did not really compete with the canonical Acts and were therefore tolerated, as were the infancy gospels.

L: Aug. 23 (1983). — M. Blumenthal, Formen u. Motive in den apokryphen Apostelgeschichten, TU 48/1 (Berlin, 1933). — F. Bovon et al., Les Actes Apocryphes des Apôtres (Genoa, 1981) (literature). — A. Hamman, "Sitz im Leben" des actes apocryphes de NT: StPatr 8 (1966) 62-69. — HLL 4:391-405. — E. Junod, J.-D. Kaestli, L'Histoire des Actes apocryphes des Apôtres du IIIᵉ au IXᵉ siècle: le cas des Actes de Jean (Lausanne, 1982). — R. A. Lipsius, Die apokryphen Apostelgeschichten u. Apostellegenden, 3 vols. (Amsterdam, 1976 = Braunschweig, 1883-1884). — D. R. MacDonald (ed.), The Apocryphal Acts of the Apostles = Semeia 38 (1986) (literature). — P. Nagel, Die apokryphen Apostelakten in der manichäischen Lit.: Gnosis u. NT, ed. K. W. Tröger (Berlin, 1973), 149-182. — R. E. Pervo, Profit with Delight. The Literary Genre (Philadelphia, 1987). — E. Plümacher, Apokryphe Apostelakten: PRE.S 15:11-70. — R. Söder, Die apokryphen Apostelgeschichten u. die romanhafte Lit. der Antike (Stuttgart, 1969 = 1932). — C. Sturhahn, Die Christologie der ältesten apokryphen Apostelakten, Diss. (Heidelberg, 1951). — P. Vielhauer, Geschichte der urchr. Lit. (Berlin, 1975), 696-712.

3. Letters: Pseudepigraphical → letters were not rare in pagan antiquity (see → Pseudepigraphy) and originated in part in the schools of rhetoric. The Chr. apocrypha make relatively rare use of the letter form; their (narrative and dogmatic) interests were better served by gospels and histories of the apostles. In addition, many supposed letters are not letters at all but treatises (e.g., the → *Letter of Titus* and the → *Epistula Jacobi* [→ James the Younger]) or stories (e.g., the correspondence with → Abgar or parts of the Letters of Pilate [→ Pilate Literature]).

Behind the composition of letters with the names of NT persons there was often an attempt to fill in gaps in the bibl. text; this was the case with the so-called *Third Letter to the Corinthians* and the *Letter to the Laodiceans* (→ Paul).

In particular, there were supposed letters of Jesus (→ Abgar, → Sunday Letter), letters of → Pilate, a letter of all the apostles (→ *Epistula apostolorum*), letters of → Peter and → Paul, → James, → Titus, and → Barnabas.

L: N. Brox (ed.), Pseudepigraphie in der heidnischen u. jüd.-chr. Antike (Darmstadt, 1977). — P. Vielhauer, Geschichte der urchr. Lit. (Berlin, 1975), 58-70. — W. Michaelis, Die apokryphen Schriften zum NT (Bremen, 1956), 440-446.

4. Apocalypses: This genre from Jewish literature was used by Christians for their own purposes. Characteristics: the idea of the two aeons and the gaze fixed on the end of the world and the other world; in the apocryphal apocalypses, NT references to these realities became central and were imaginatively developed. The depictions were increasingly used for exhortation and the consolation of individuals.

The → *Canon Muratori* is the first to call apocryphal the *Apocalypses of* → *John* and → *Peter*. Other Chr. apocalypses were those of → Paul, the fifth and sixth books of → Esdras, parts of the *Ascension of* → *Isaiah,* and an untitled apocalypse that has been transmitted, along with the → Books of Jeu in the *Cod. Burcianus.* Apocalypses in title only are the two Apocalypses of → James.

The apocalypses that have come down under the following names: → Adam, → Asclepius, → Daniel, → Elijah, → Marsanes, → Noema, → Zechariah, → Zephaniah, and the → Second Coming of Christ are, in part, gnostic treatises.

L: F. C. Burkitt, Jewish and Christian Apocalypses (London, 1914). — F. T. Fallon, The Gnostic Apocalypses: Semeia 14 (1979) 123-158. — G. Filoramo, Apocalissi gnostiche: Aug. 23 (1983) 123-129. — M. Krause, Die lit. Gattungen der Apokalypsen von Nag Hammadi: Apocalypticism in the Mediterranean World and the Near East, ed. D. Hellholm (Uppsala, 1983), 621-637. — W. Perkins, Function of Gnostic Apocalypses: CBQ 38 (1977) 382-395. — A. Yarbro Collins, Early Christian Apocalyptic Literature: ANRW II 25/6 (1988) 4664-4771.

5. Dialogues: The genre of the dialogue (of the redeemer with his disciples), which was developed primarily by gnostics, resembles the genre of the instructional conversation and the → *Quaestiones et responsiones/Erotapokriseis.* These dialogues include the *Gospel of Mary* (→ Mary, Literature on), the *Book of Thomas the Contender* (→ Thomas, Literature on), the → *Epistula apostolorum,* the *Letter of* → *James the Younger,* the →*Dialogue of the Savior,* the → *Sophia Iesu Christi,* the → *Pistis Sophia,* the *Apocryphon of* → *John,* the *Apocalypses of* → *James and of Peter,* as well as the so-called *Letter of Peter to* → *Philip.* The *Dialogue of Jesus with the Devil (JThS* NS 6 [1955]: 49-65) does not belong in this setting.

L: H. Koester, Dialog u. Spruchüberlieferung: EvTh 39 (1979) 532-556. — P. Perkins, The Gnostic Dialogue (New York, 1980). — K. Rudolph, Der gnostische Dialog als lit. Genus: idem, Gnosis u. spätantike Religionsgeschichte, NHS 42 (Leiden, 1996), 103-122. — NTApo[6] 1:189-192.

6. Testaments: The genre of "testament" is an early Jewish literary form. But at least in the so-called → *Testaments of the Twelve Patriarchs* there are addi-

tions from the Chr. period, while the *Testament of Solomon* was also given a Chr. revision. The title → *Testament of Our Lord Jesus Christ* was given to various writings in the genre of the church order.

L: M. de Jonge, Christian Influence in the Testaments of the 12 Patriarchs: NT 4 (1960/61) 182-235.

G. RÖWEKAMP

Apollinaris of Hierapolis

Claudius A. was bishop of Hierapolis in Phrygia (Eus., *h.e.* 5.19.2) in the time of Marcus Aurelius. Eus. (*h.e.* 4.27), Jerome (*vir. ill.* 26), and Photius (*cod.* 14) attribute a number of writings to A. Among his apologetic writings: a defense addressed to Emperor Marcus Aurelius (ca. 172/175), which is probably the same as the *Peri eusebeias* mentioned by Photius; in addition, five books *Ad Graecos*; two books *De veritate*; and possibly two books *Ad Iudaeos* (poorly attested). In addition there were *grammata* of A. against the Montanists. It is possible that the fragment cited by Eus. (*h.e.* 5.19.3) belonged to such a circular letter. Finally, A. is also supposed to have written against the Severians (encratites) (Theod., *haer.* 1.21). There is disagreement about where A. is supposed to have mentioned the miracle of rain sent upon the Melitene Legion (Eus., *h.e.* 5.5.4). The only two certain fragments (*fr.*) of A. are cited by the → *Chronicon Paschale* from an otherwise unattested work *De pascha*. A. here shows himself to have been a Quartodeciman, who nonetheless rejects a date based on the gospel of Mt. Other ancient or modern attributions (e.g., A. as the Anonymous → Antimontanist) are unbelievable or purely speculative, including the attribution of catena fragments.

W: *fr.,* R. Cantalamessa, Ostern in der Alten Kirche (Bern, 1981), 46f. [text/German trans.].
L: D. Berwig, Mark Aurel u. die Christen, Diss. (Munich, 1970), 106-110. — J. A. Fischer, A. Lumpe, Synoden v. d. Anfängen bis z. Vorabend d. Nicaenums (Paderborn, 1997), 60-87. — R. M. Grant, Greek Apologists (Philadelphia, 1988), 83-90. — A. v. Harnack, Überlieferung der griech. Apologeten (Berlin, 1991 = Leipzig, 1882), 232-239. — idem, Geschichte der altchr. Lit. (Leipzig, [2]1958), 1:243-246; 2/1:358-361. — G. Laiti, Acqua e sangue: Centro Studi Sanguis Christi 3 (Rome, 1983), 931-937. — C. C. Richardson, A New Solution: JThS 24 (1973) 74-84. — A. Strobel, Ursprung u. Geschichte des Osterkalenders (Berlin, 1977), 22f.

R. HANIG

Apollinaris of Laodicea

I. Life: A. probably lived from ca. 315 to shortly before 392. Born in Syr. Laodicea, he supposedly became a lector ca. 335, while his same-named father was a priest. Throughout his life he had good relations with Athanasius Alex., who was given shelter by him in 346 on his returning from his second exile, and with Athanasius's closest friends (such as Serapion of Thmuis). For this reason A. and his father were excommunicated by Arian-minded Bishop George of Laodicea. When the latter had to resign ca. 360, the homoeans installed their fellow fighter Pelagius as successor, while the Nicaeans chose A. The "Meletian Schism," with its three rival communities, which broke out in Antioch the capital at this same time, was said to have been an even greater challenge to A. He had probably even taught there and had by his christology helped to complicate existing differences. Two monks sent by him seem to have influenced the christological passage in the Alexandrian synodal letter of 362. In order to counteract the anti-Christian policy of Julian, A., together with his father, supposedly got the idea of paraphrasing biblical themes in a classical manner. In order to prove himself orthodox, A. immediately sent the new emperor, Jovian, a detailed profession of faith.

After the death of Athanasius in 372, the controversy over the claim to his heritage in theology and eccles. policy and the settlement of the succession to the bishop of Antioch in favor of one of A.'s supporters led finally to a break between A. and Basil of Caesarea, although the two remained linked by a correspondence over many years. The occasion for the break was probably the fact that in 376 A. ordained the Antiochene priest Vitalis as bishop after the latter had first been recognized by Roman Bishop Damasus. The first condemnation of an Apollinarist came in 377 in Rome; others followed in 379 at Antioch and in 381 at Constantinople.

A.'s christology was clearly rejected only beginning in ca. 385 (e.g., in the *Antirrheticus adversus Apolinarium* of → Gregory Nyss.). Although express laws were passed against the Apollinarists in 388, this initially had little effect on their continued existence. Even in Antioch they existed as an independent community until as late as 425. But after A.'s death his disciples split into several parties.

II. Works: Most of the many writings of A. have been lost, and what has survived is mostly in fragmentary form. The following, for example, have disappeared: thirty books *Against Porphyry*, a treatise *On Truth* against Emperor Julian, and some poetic writings. A glimpse of A.'s exegetical works is given by the critically sifted fragments from the catena tradition on the Octateuch (*gen.*), the Psalms (*Ps.*), the gospels of Matthew (*Mt.*) and John (*Jn.*), as well as on the Letter

to the Romans (*Rom.*); others are still unpublished or accessible only in uncritical editions. In method his explanations reject Alexandrian allegory and are close to the Antiochene tradition. Acc. to Jerome, who in other respects liked to listen to A., these interpretations were not careful enough. Among the most important of the surviving theol. works are two letters to Basil Caes. (*ep. Bas.*), written probably ca. 360 and 363 (found in the collection of Basil's letters, nos. 362 and 364). Also the *Apoideixis* or *Demonstratio de divina incarnatione ad similitudinem hominis,* which can be quite thoroughly reconstructed from the *Antirrheticus adversus Apolinarium* of Gregory Nyss., so that its entire train of thought can be grasped. All the other writings or fragments today regarded as composed by A. have survived only because they were handed down under the names of orthodox fathers such as Gregory the Wonderworker, Athanasius, and Julius or Felix of Rome. Some of these works are: *Fides secundum partem, De unione corporis et divinitatis in Christo, De fide et incarnatione contra adversarios,* and *Ad Iovianum.* These false attributions were used by Cyril Alex. and the Monophysites to support their position and were probably given legitimacy by this use. As early as 532 many of these works were recognized as pseudepigraphical. In light of what we know today, it is very likely that A. was author of Ps.-Athanasius, *Quod unus sit Christus* and *De incarnatione dei verbi.* Quite recently, he has also been assigned three of the Easter sermons that go under the name of John Chrys., and the Ps.-Athanasian *Contra Sabellianos* (*Sabell.*). Whether the paraphrase of the Psalms after the manner of Homer goes back to A. remains doubtful.

III. Importance: A. is known primarily for his christology, which approved the formula "a single incarnate nature of the God-Logos" as a way of protecting the full divinity of the incarnate Logos and his divine-human unity. It represents the first attempt at a systematic exploration of the mystery of the incarnation and exerted considerable influence even after its rejection as heresy. The objection of opponents, that A. denies the human soul of Jesus, finds no clear confirmation in his writings.

W: H. Lietzmann, A. u. seine Schule (Hildesheim, 1970 = text ¹1904) [text]. — J. Flemming, H. Lietzmann, Apollinaristische Schriften, AGWG.PH 7/4 (Berlin, 1904) [Syr./Greek text]. — Gen., R. Devreesse, StT 201 (Rome, 1959) [text]. — Ps., E. Mühlenberg, PTS 15 (Berlin), 1975, 1-118 [text]. — Mt., J. Reuss, TU 61 (Berlin, 1957), 1-54 [text]. — Jo., J. Reuss, TU 89 (Berlin, 1966), 3-64 [text]. — Rom., K. Staab (NTA 15) (Münster, 1933), 57-82 [text]. — ep. Bas. 1-2, Y. Courtonne, Lettres 3 (Paris, 1966), 222-226 [text/French trans.]. — H. de Riedmatten: JThS NS 7

(1956) 199-210; 8 (1957) 53-70 [text]. — H. J. Vogt: ThQ 175 (1995) 46-60 [German trans./comm.]. — (Ath.), *Sabell.*, PG 28:96-121. — R. M. Hübner, Schrift des A. gegen Photin (Berlin, 1989), 12-29 [German trans.].
L: E. Cattaneo, Trois Homélies ps.-Chrysostomiennes (Paris, 1980). — F. Cavallera, Le schisme d'Antioche (Paris, 1905). — J. Dräseke, A. (Leipzig, 1892). — G. Furlani, Studi apollinaristici: Rivista trimestrale di studi filosofici e religiosi 2 (1921) 257-285; 4 (1923) 129-146. — F. R. Gahbauer, Das anthropologische Modell (Würzburg, 1984), 127-224. — G. Gentz, A.: RAC 1:520-522. — J. Golega, Der homerische Psalter (Ettal, 1960). — A. Grillmeier, Jesus der Christus 1 (Freiburg i.Br., ²1979), 480-494. — R. M. Hübner, "Gotteserkenntnis durch die Inkarnation Gottes": Kl. 4 (1972) 131-161. — idem, Soteriologie, Trinität, Christologie: FS W. Breuning (Düsseldorf, 1985), 175-196. — C. Kannengiesser, Une nouvelle interprétation: RSR 59 (1971) 27-36. — J. T. Lienhard, Ps.-Athanasius, Contra Sabellianos: Vig-Chr 40 (1986) 365-389. — E. Mühlenberg, A. (Göttingen, 1969). — idem, A.: TRE 3:362-371. — idem, A. u. die origenistische Tradition: ZNW 76 (1985) 270-283. — idem, Zur exegetischen Methode: Chr. Exegese, ed. J. van Oort, U. Wichert (Kampen, 1992), 132-147. — R. A. Norris Jr., Manhood and Christ (Oxford, 1963), 79-122. — G. L. Prestige, St. Basil and A. (London, 1956). — C. E. Raven, Apollinarism (Cambridge, 1923). — M. Richard, L'introduction du mot 'hypostase': MSR 2 (1945) 5-32, 243-270. — H. de Riedmatten, La christologie: StPatr 2 (1957) 208-234. — H. Ristow, Zwei Häretiker (Berlin, 1960), 1-110. — A. Stegmann, Die ps.-athanasianische "IVte Rede gegen die Arianer" (Tübingen, 1917). — A. Tuilier, Le sens de l'Apollinarisme: StPatr 13 (1975) 295-305. — G. Voisin, L'apollinarisme (Leuven/Louvain, 1901). — idem, La doctrine trinitaire: RHE 2 (1901) 33-55, 239-252. — E. Weigl, Die Christologie vom Tode des Athanasius bis zum Ausbruch des nestorianischen Streites (Munich, 1925). — R. Weijenborg, De autenticitate: Anton. 33 (1958) 197-240, 371-414; 34 (1959) 245-298.

G. Feige

Apollinaris Sidonius

Gaius Sollius Apollinaris Sidonius (S.) was born November 5, 430/431 in Lyons and died between 480 and 490 in Clermont-Ferrand. He was the son-in-law of Emperor Avitus and is regarded as the most important Lat. poet and prose writer of the second half of the 5th c. in Gaul. The high point of his secular career came when Emperor Anthemius gave him the office of prefect of the city (Rome) in 468. Probably a year later, he became bishop of Clermont-Ferrand and played a decisive part in organizing the (ultimately fruitless) resistance to the Visigothic occupation of the Auvergne.

Before entering the clerical state S. himself published his poems in two editions: first, the three imperial panegyrics (modelled on → Claudian) addressed to Avitus, Majorian, and Anthemius (456, 458, and 468) with their prefaces (*carm.* 1-8), then the collection of shorter poems in which he emulated the *Silvae* of Statius (*carm.* 9-24). Most of these are occasional verses, for example, the two epithalamia (10/11; 14/15) and the three letters of thanks to hosts with their somewhat lengthy descriptive and catalogue-like excursuses (22/23 and 16, which is dedicated to the well-known Bishop → Faustus of Riez). The letters, published in nine books after the model of Pliny the Younger and → Jerome, come mainly from the period after 469. They provide valuable information about political, social, and cultural conditions but also about the life of the church in 5th.-c. Gaul. For example, we learn in *ep.* 2.10 and 4.18 of the building of new churches in Lyons and Tours; in 4.25 of the election of a bishop; in 5.17 of the course of a local church feastday; in 7.6 of repressions by the Arian Visigoths.

S., whose work was highly esteemed in the Middle Ages, is a very elegant writer and was heavily influenced by pagan Rom. literature. His Chr. faith did not keep him, e.g., from using a mythological framework for many of his poems and, in them, the old "machinery of the gods." In the clash with an increasingly germanicized environment S.'s most important concern was the preservation of the Lat. language and literature. Theol. questions are raised only rarely in his work and, in any case, superficially.

W: *carm.*, *ep.*, C. Luetjohann (Berlin, 1887) [text]. — P. Mohr (Leipzig, 1895). — W. B. Anderson, 1/2 (Cambridge, 1936/65) [text/English trans.]. — A. Loyen, 1 (*carm.*), 2/3 (*ep.*) (Paris, 1960/70) [text/French trans./comm.]. — *carm.* 14/15, G. Ravenna (Bologne, 1990) [text/Italian trans./comm.]. — *carm.* 22, N. Delhey (Berlin, 1993) [text/comm.]. — *ep.*, H. Köhler, 1 (Heidelberg, 1995) [text/German trans./comm.]
L: M. Banniard, S. et la langue classique en Gaule au Ve siècle: FS Fontaine 1 (Paris, 1992), 413-427. — M. Bonjour, La patria de S.: FS Wuilleumier (Paris, 1980), 25-37. — P. G. Christiansen, J. E. Holland, Concordantia in Sidonii A. carmina (Hildesheim, 1993). — I. Gualandri, Furtiva Lectio (Milan, 1979). — R. P. C. Hanson, The Church in Fifth-Century Gaul: Evidence from S.: JEH 21 (1970) 1-10. — J. Harries, S. and the Fall of Rome (Oxford, 1994). — A. Loyen, S. et l'ésprit précieux en Gaule (Paris, 1943). — F. M. Kaufmann, Studien zu S. (Frankfurt a.M., 1995). — K.-Å. Mossberg, Studia Sidoniana (Uppsala, 1934). — M. Müller, De Apollinaris S. latinitate (Halle, 1888). — D. & R. Rebuffat, De S. à la Tombe François: Latomus 37 (1978) 88-104. — W. Schetter, Zur Publikation der Carmina minora des S.: Hermes 120 (1992) 343-363 = Kleine Schriften (Stuttgart, 1994), 236-256. — W. H. Semple, Quaestiones exegeticae Sidonianae (Cambridge, 1930). — C. E. Stevens, S. and His Age (Oxford, 1933 = Westport, Conn., 1979). — M. Zelzer, Der Brief in der Spätantike am Beispiel des S.: WSt 107/108 (1994/95) 541-551.

N. Delhey

Apollinarists, Anonymous

Although external confirmation from ancient witnesses is lacking, certain texts, mostly passing under the name of Julius or Felix of Rome, are attributed to Apollinarist circles, because they have for the most part been handed on in connection with obviously Apollinarist works and display striking similarities to them in content. One of these is the little *Encyclion*, of which, in addition to the Gr. text and Syr. version, fragments have survived in Latin, Arabic, and Armenian. Also Apollinarist in origin is the *Confessio Antiochena*, which in editions of it is described either as a profession of faith from an Antiochene synod in the time of Gallienus (254/260-268) or as a "Profession of the 318 Fathers against Paul of Samosata" and has likewise been handed down in several languages. Also to be included are two writings preserved only in a Syr. translation: the *Epistula tertia* and the treatise *De fide*, which in their present form show clear signs of Monophysite revision. Finally, there are fragments which, with one exception (*fr.* 186), come only from Syr. (*fr.* 185 and 187) or Arab. sources (*fr.* 188-91). According to what we know today, the Ps.-Athanasian *Quod unus sit Christus* and *De incarnatione dei verbi*, which had been attributed to the Anonymous Apollinarists, were very probably composed by Apollinaris himself.

W: H. Lietzmann, A. u. seine Schule (Hildesheim, 1970 = Tübingen, ¹1904), 292-322 [Greek or Latin text/German trans.]. — J. Flemming, H. Lietzmann, Apollinaristische Schriften, AGWG.PH 7,4 (Berlin, 1904) [Syriac/Greek text]. — For the Latin, Syriac, Armenian, and Arabic versions or frags., see also CPG 2:321-324.
L: H. Lietzmann, loc. cit., 158-163.

G. FEIGE

Apollonius, Antimontanist

A., a Chr. writer of Asia Minor, is known for his polemic *Adversus Cataphrygas*, composed probably ca. 196/197. It has been partially preserved (six fragments) by Eusebius, who uses it as a source for the history of Montanism, the Phrygian heresy. In this work, which probably consisted of one book containing often sharp personal attacks, A.'s purpose was to prove Montanist prophecies to be false and to make known the irresponsible lifestyle of the Montanist prophets. Acc. to Jerome (*vir. ill.* 40 and 53), Tertullian, in the seventh book of his lost work on ecstasy, turned against A. in an effort to refute his charges. A claim that A. was bishop of Ephesus (*Praedestinatus* 1.26f.) is groundless.

W: Eusebius, *h.e.* 5.18.2-11. — P. de Labriolle, Les sources de l'histoire du montanisme (Paris, 1913), 78-82 [text/French trans.].
L: A. Ferrua, A.: EC 1: 1648. — A. v. Harnack, Geschichte der altchr. Lit. (Leipzig, ²1958), 1/1, 241; 2/1, 370-380. — A. Jülicher, A.: PRE 2/1:161. — P. de Labriolle, A. 11: DHGE 3:1013f.

B. WINDAU

Apology

The apology (*apologia*), or literary defense of the Chr. faith, was able to rely on Jewish models (→ Letter of Aristeas; Philo, *Hypothetica*; Flavius Josephus, *Contra Apionem*). Apologetic tendencies are already unmistakable in many NT writings (e.g., Acts 14:11-17; 17:22-31). An early stage of the Chr. apology can be seen in the fragmentary *Kerygma Petrou* (→ Peter); Plato's *Apology of Socrates* provided a pagan literary model.

The word *apologia* was borrowed from the speech for the defense in a court. But since such a defense was hardly possible in trials of Christians, the earliest apologists followed other institutional forms beginning in the first half of the 2nd c. — Aristides, → Justin, and → Athenagoras wrote *apologiae* in the form of a petition (*libellus*) addressed to the emperor in order initially to obtain the protection of law for Christians; in addition, however, since imperial edicts for trials were published, they sought to inform the public about the true nature of Christianity in order to forestall denunciations. At the same time these writings were also circulated within the church. The apologies of → Quadratus, → Apollinaris of Hierapolis, → Melito of Sardis, and → Miltiades have not been preserved.

After a change in the law under Marcus Aurelius had made appeals to the emperor futile, the apologists turned to other literary forms (a sign that the earlier writings had not been fictitious). The genre of the apology now included the "Address to the Greeks" (→ Tatian; → Justin [Ps.]), the letter (→ Theophilus of Antioch, *Autol.*; the → Letter of Diognetus; → Tertullian, *Scap.*; → Cyprian, *Demetr.*), the lampoon (Hermias), the → protreptic or exhortation (→ Clement of Alexandria, *prot.*), the dialogue (→ Minutius Felix, *Oct.*), the fictitious speech for the defense (Tertullian, *apol.*), and the broadsheet attacking individuals (→ Origen, *Cels.*; → Methodius of Olympus, *Proph.*; → Eusebius Caes., *Hierocl.*).

Among the central themes, even of later apologetic, were the proof of the morality and loyalty of Christians; the proof of the real age of the "new" religion (the Logos at work even before the incarnation;

dependence of the Gr. philosophers on Moses), and the superior Chr. knowledge of truth due to revelation, as compared with all other insights into truth, which were darkened by error or possible in only fragmentary form. Above all, the early apologists made some use of ideas from (Middle) Platonic philosophy.

At the beginning of the 4th c. the apologies changed their character as occasional writings (despite often defensive protreptic and propagandist elements) and became systematic and aggressive disputes with pagan religion and philosophy in the "Summas" of → Arnobius the Elder (*nat.*), → Lactantius (*inst.*), and Eusebius (*p.e.*, *d.e.*). This development reached its climax in the 5th c. with → Augustine (*civ.*), → Theodoret of Cyrrhus (*affect.*), and → Cyril Alex. (*Juln.*). At the same time, an apologetic-minded historiography (→ Orosius, *hist.*) and, even earlier, a similar poetry developed (→ Commodian, *apol.*; → Prudentius, *c. Symm.*, → Ephraem the Syrian, *Hymni c. Julian.*). The familiar older forms were still used: the dialogue (→ *Consultationes Zacchaei et Apollonii*; Anonymous, *c. philos.*), the letter (→ Ambrose, *ep.* 72; 73), the attack on polytheism and mythology (→ Athanasius, *gent.*, *inc.*; → Firmicus Maternus, *err.*), and the broadsheet against individuals (→ Gregory Naz., *or.* 4; 5 against Julian). Controversy with Judaism formed a separate branch of apologetic literature (→ Anti-Jewish Dialogue). This literature as a whole attests both to the conflict of Christianity with the non-Christian world in the various phases of its history and also to the argumentative development of Chr. truth-claims (*vera religio et verissima philosophia*), whether to assert a polemic separation or to conciliate through dialogue.

L: C. Andresen, Frühkirchliche Apologetik: RGG 1:480-485. — G. Bardy, Apologetik: RAC 1:533-543. — L. W. Barnard, Apologetik 1.: TRE 3:371-411. — A. Casamassa, Gli Apologisti Greci (Rome, 1944). — H. Conzelmann, Heiden — Juden — Christen (Tübingen, 1981). — A. J. Droge, Homer or Moses? (Tübingen, 1989). — M. Fiedrowicz, Apologie und frühes Christentum (Paderborn, 1999). — J.-C. Fredouille, L'apologétique chrétienne antique, naissance d'un genre littéraire: REAug 38 (1992) 219-234. — idem, L'apologétique chrétienne antique, metamorphose d'un genre polymorphe: REAug 41 (1995) 201-216. — idem, Heiden: RAC 13:1113-1149. — W. Geerlings, Apologetik und Fundamentaltheologie in der Väterzeit: HFTh 4: 317-333. — E. J. Goodspeed, Index Apologeticus (Leiden, 1969 = 1912). — R. M. Grant, Forms and Occasions of the Greek Apologists: SMSR 52 (1986) 213-226. — idem, Greek Apologists of the Second Century (Philadelphia, 1988). — HLL 5:363-407. — R. Joly, Christianisme et Philosophie (Brussels, 1973). — W. Kinzig, Der "Sitz im Leben" der Apologie in der Alten Kirche: ZKG 100 (1989) 291-317. — J.-L. Laurin, Orientations maîtresses des

Apologistes chrétiens (Rome, 1954). — M. Pellegrino, Gli apologeti greci (Rome, 1947). — idem, Studi sull'antica apologetica (Rome, 1978 = 1947). — P. Pilhofer, Presbyteron kreitton (Tübingen, 1990). — B. Pouderon, J. Doré (ed.), Les apologistes chrétiens et la culture grecque (Paris, 1997). — A. Puech, Les apologistes grecs du IIᵉ siècle de notre ère (Paris, 1912). — M. Rizzi, Ideologia e retorica negli exordia apologetici (Milan, 1993). — G. Ruggieri (ed.), Enciclopedia di Teologia Fondamentale (Genoa, 1987), 3-219. — A. Wlosok, Chr. Apologetik gegenüber kaiserlicher Politik bis zu Konstantin: Kirchengeschichte als Missionsgeschichte 1, ed. H. Frohnes, U. W. Knorr (Munich, 1974), 147-165.

M. FIEDROWICZ

Apophthegm

In ancient rhetoric, an apophthegm (from *apophtheggomai*, "speak one's opinion plainly and forcefully") was a striking saying that made a surprising point; it was usually occasioned by a question and accompanied by brief or lengthy information about the speaker, the hearer, and the situation. An apophthegm could also be connected with a parabolic action. As a rhetorical form its purpose was to influence, instruct, or stimulate the listener or reader. Because of its narrative structure it achieved these purposes more readily than an abstract instruction, appealing as it did simultaneously to the imagination, the feelings, and the understanding.

In pagan antiquity the apophthegm stood close to the anecdote (e.g., Plutarch, *Apophth. Reg.* 177a; *Lacon.* 229d); in the NT it is used in many sayings and parabolic actions of Jesus acc. to the Synoptics.

The → *Apophthegmata Patrum*, a collection of ascetical instructional sayings, especially of the monks of the Egyptian wilderness, originated in the 5th/6th c.

L: H. Lausberg, Handbuch der literarischen Rhetorik (Stuttgart, ³1990), 536f. — R. C. Tannehill, Types and Functions of Apophthegms in the Synoptic Gospels: ANRW II 25/2 (1984) 1792-1829.

J. PAULI, OSB

Apophthegmata Patrum

The *A.P.*, *Sayings of the Fathers*, is the name given to various collections of sayings representing the wisdom of the Egyptian monks of the 4th and 5th c. The Gr. *Alphabetikon* (PG 65:71-440) originated in the first half of the 6th c., probably in Palestine. For the purpose of "being of profit to the readers" (preface) the editors brought together material that until then had been handed down orally, ordering it alphabetically by the names of the monks (Anthony to Or) and adding a small systematically arranged appendix of anonymous sayings. A collection that has come down only in Latin (books 5-6 of the → *Vitae Patrum*, PL 73:855-1022) is likewise ordered thematically. It is a translation made from the Greek by deacon Pelagius (Pelagius I, 556-561) and subdeacon John (John III, 561-574). Partial collections of the *Apophthegmata Patrum* exist in Coptic, Ethiopic, and Armenian.

In their content the *Apophthegmata Patrum* transmit the ascetical instruction of the monks of the Egyptian wilderness in the 4th/5th c., espec. at the geographical centers Scete, the Thebaid, and the Nitrian wilderness, but also in the Sinai and Palestine.

The → apophthegm arose originally as a piece of instruction connected with a situation in the monastic training of hermits; as a result of their being put in writing and circulated, the *Apophthegmata Patrum* also had a strong influence on the monasteries of East and West.

W: *Alphabetikon*, PG 65:71-440. — J. C. Guy, SC 387. — *Vitae Patrum*, PL 73:855-1022. B. Miller, Weisung der Väter. Apophth. Patr. (Freiburg i. Br., 1965 [German trans.]. — L. Regnault, Les Sentences des Pères du désert (Sablé-sur-Sarthe, 1970) [French trans.].
L: C. M. Batlle, Die Adhortationes Sanctorum Patrum (Verba Seniorum) im MA (Münster, 1972). — W. Bousset, Apophthegmata (Tübingen, 1923). — D. Burton-Christi, The Word in the Desert (New York, 1993) (literature). — J. C. Guy, loc. cit., 7-87. — idem, Théologie de la vie monastique (Ligugé, 1961). — idem, Recherches sur la tradition grecque (Brussels, ²1984 = 1962). — F. v. Lilienfeld, Mönchtum 2: TRE 23:150-193, esp. 189f (literature). — L. Regnault, Les Apophthègmes des Pères en Palestine aux Vᵉ-VIᵉ siècles: Irén. 54 (1981) 320-330. — idem, La vie quotidienne des Pères du désert en Égypte au IVᵉ siècle (Paris, 1990).

J. PAULI, OSB

Aporias, Collection of

The collection of aporias, as a literary genre, appeared in the post-Chalcedonian period (from the first half of the 6th c. on). It represented an effort to study christological statements according to the laws of Aristotelean logic and make them a tool in intra-Christian controversy. The intention was to show the conceptual incoherence and contradictoriness of dogmatic formulas.

Forerunners in this genre were the aporias of Theodoret of Cyrrhus, the *capita* and the *Syllogismi Sanctorum Patrum* of → John of Caesarea (partially transmitted in → Anastasius the Sinaite), and the *Epaporemata* (thirty *capita* against Severus) of → Leontius of Byzantium, which are partially transmitted in ch. 25 of the → *Doctrina Patrum*.

L: A. Grillmeier, Jesus der Christus 2/1 (Freiburg i. Br., 1986), 94-100. — G. Heinrici, Zur patristischen Aporienlit. (Leipzig, 1909). — K. H. Uthemann, Syllogistik im Dienst der Orthodoxie: JÖB 30 (1981) 103-112. — idem, Antimonophysitische Aporien des Anastasius Sinaita: ByZ 74 (1981) 11-26.

G. RÖWEKAMP

Apostolic Canons

The compiler of the → *Apostolic Constitutions* (*Const. App.*) ends his work with eighty-five apostolic canons (*Canones apostolorum*; *Can. App.*) (8.47), which were soon handed on independently of the *Const. App.*, but, unlike the latter, were not rejected as heretical by Council II in Trullo (692/693). The *Can. App.* consist in part of synodal canons (Antioch, 330/340) from different sources, which had perhaps been collected in an earlier *corpus canonum*.

In their content the *Can. App.* give a very general picture of cultic, disciplinary, and constitutional conditions in the communities, with the result that no concrete addressees can be envisaged. The fiction of apostolic authorship (based on the fictive setting of the *Const. App.*) and the esteem of a → Dionysius Exiguus in the West (he translated the *Can. App.* from Greek into Latin) and of a → John of Scythopolis in the East (the *Can. App.* as part of the fifty *Titloi*) ensured that the work was highly esteemed.

W: → Apostolic Constitutions.
L: J. Gaudemet, Sources du droit de l'Eglise (Paris, 1985). — E. Schwartz, Kanonessammlungen: ZSRG 56 K 25 (1936) 1-114. — B. Steimer, Vertex traditionis (Berlin, 1992), esp. 87-94.

B. STEIMER

Apostolic Church Order

Apostolic Church Order is the usual name in English of the *kanones ekklēsiastikoi tōn hagiōn apostolōn*, Lat. *Canones ecclesiastici apostolorum* (*CEA*), to which scholars have given different names (French often "Ordonnance[s] apostolique[s]"; German "Apostolische Kirchenordnung"). The Lat. abbreviation *CEA* will be used for clarity.

The *CEA* has been transmitted both separately in Greek and as a section of canonical collections (*Fragmentum Veronense*; → Alexandrian Synod; → Octateuch of Clement) in their various recensions. They consist of two main parts: an introduction with a list of the apostles (chs. 1-3) is followed by a version of the doctrine of the Two Ways (chs. 4-14), which is in turn followed by canonical norms (chs. 15-20). The

43

material of the *CEA* is divided into canons, under the apostles who appear as the speakers. The work must have been composed in Greek at the beginning of the 4th c. Since it is well attested in the various recensions of the Alexandrian Synod (the canonical collection of the Egyptian church), Egypt may be probably taken as the place of origin.

W: J. P. Arendzen, Syriac Text: JThS 3 (1902) 59-80 [Syriac text/English trans.]. — A. v. Harnack, TU 2/2 225-237 [Greek text/German trans.]. — H. Ludolf, Commentarius (Frankfurt a.M., 1691), 314-323 [Ethiopic text/Latin trans.]. — T. Schermann, Kirchenordnung (Paderborn, 1914), 12-34 [Greek text/German trans.].
L: A. Faivre, Constitution Ecclésiastique des Apôtres: RevSR 55 (1981) 31-42. — W. Kinzig, C. Markschies, M. Vinzent, Tauffragen u. Bekenntnis (Berlin, 1999). — B. Lemoine, Étude sur la notice sur l'évêque dans la CEA: QuLi 80 (1999) 5-23. — B. Steimer, Vertex traditionis (Berlin, 1992), esp. 60-71.

B. STEIMER

Apostolic Constitutions

A.C. is the name, based on the Lat. translation of the Gr. title, of the most comprehensive and best preserved → church order, and the most important for research into the discipline, ethics, liturgy, theology of office, and constitution of the early church. Discovered in the 16th c. it was edited in exemplary fashion by Francisco Torres (Venice, 1563) on the basis of three Gr. mss. Initially, the pseudepigraphical eight books of the *Diatagai tōn hagiōn apostolōn* (Lat. *Constitutiones apostolorum*; *Const. App.*), which claimed to have been written down by Clement of Rome (*dia Klēmentos*) at the apostolic council in Jerusalem, were regarded as authentic. But since the 19th c., intensive study of texts in the genre of church order has shown the *A.C.* to be a voluminous compilation of earlier church orders: (1) Books 1-6 are a greatly expanded version of the Syr. → *Didascalia*; (2) 7.1-32 is based on the → *Didache*; (3) the content of book 8 is based on the so-called → *Traditio apostolica*; (4) the work closes with eighty-five → apostolic canons. (5) To these main parts are added various materials from different sources (a collection of Jewish prayers [7.33-38]; a version of the *Gloria in excelsis* [7.46]; a treatise on the charisms [8.1-2: Hippolytus of Rome the author?]).

There are a number of reasons for saying that the work was that of a compiler-editor (as against a compilation over time), who may be the same person as the interpolator of the long recension of the letters of → Ignatius of Antioch. Connected with this is the question of the theol. orientation of the compiler-editor, which has still not been satisfactorily decided (back in 692/693 *can.* 2 of Council II in Trullo rejected the *A.C.* as heretical).

The compiler had a clear plan for his work: he actualized obsolete ordinances in his basic texts by making radical changes (espec. additions, reformulations; more rarely abbreviations or omissions), in order to give them new validity; with technical artistry he applied apostolic authorship to the entire work. Along with this literary fiction there is the frequent citation of NT passages in order to emphasize the historical closeness of the fictive framework to the NT (in 8.47, 85 the *A.C.* are included among the canonical writings). In all this the compiler-editor had in view not so much the concrete communal circumstances of a particular group of addressees as the universal order and the spread of an ideal picture of a Chr. community.

There is a broad consensus today on the time and place of composition: The *A.C.* were composed between 375 and 400 in Syria (some details suggest Antioch).

W: F. Boxler, Apostolische Constitutionen (Kempten, 1874) [German trans.]. — F. X. Funk, Constitutiones Apostolorum 1 (Turin, 1959 = Paderborn, 1905) [Greek text]. — M. Metzger, SC 320, 329, 336. — A. Roberts, J. Donaldson, Constitutions, ANFa 7:391-505 [English trans.].
L: B. Capelle, Gloria: RHE 44 (1949) 439-457. — A. Ehrhardt, Kirchenordnungen: ZSRG.R 67 (1950) 403-439. — A. Faivre, La documentation canonico-liturgique: RevSR 54 (1980) 204-215, 273-297. — D. A. Fiensy, Redaction History and the Const. App.: JQR 72 (1982) 293-302. — idem, Prayers Alleged to be Jewish (Chicago, 1985). — F. X. Funk, Const. App. (Frankfurt a.M., 1970 = Rottenburg, 1891). — idem, Apostolische Konstitutionen: ThQ 74 (1892) 396-438; 75 (1893) 105-114, 594-666. — D. Hagedorn, Hiobkommentar (Berlin, 1973). — A. v. Harnack, Lehre der zwölf Apostel (Leipzig, 1884), 244-265. — T. A. Kopecek, Neo-Arian Religion: Arianism, ed. R. C. Gregg (Philadelphia, 1985), 153-179. — J. Lebreton, La forme primitive du Gloria: RSR 13 (1923) 322-329. — M. Metzger, La théologie des Const. App.: RevSR 57 (1983) 29-49, 112-122, 169-194, 273-294. — idem, Const. App.: TRE 19:540-544. — B. Steimer, Vertex traditionis (Berlin, 1992). — E. M. Synek, Dieses Gesetz ist gut . . . Zum Gesetzesbegriff der Const. App. (Vienna, 1997). — C. H. Turner, Notes on the Const. App.: JThS 16 (1915) 54-61, 523-538; 21 (1920) 160-168; 31 (1930) 128-141. — G. Wagner, Herkunft der Const. App.: FS B. Botte (Leuven/Louvain, 1972), 525-537.

B. STEIMER

Apostolic Presbyter (in Irenaeus)

→ Irenaeus several times mentions an unnamed presbyter. More specifically, he mentions an anti-Marcionite presbyter (*haer.* 4.27.1–32.1), a group of disciples of John (2.22.5; 5.30.1; 5.33.3; but see Papias ibid., 5.33.4), and disciples of the apostles (5.5.1; 5.36.1f.; see also 3.23.3; 4.4.2; 4.41.2; 5.17.4; *dem.* 3 and Eus., *h.e.* 5.20.4). Attempts at identification (→ Papias, → Melito, → Noetus, and → Polycarp) remain speculative.

W: E. Preuschen, Antilegomena (Giessen, ²1905), 99-107, 202-209 [text/German trans.].
L: A. Benoît, Irénée (Paris, 1960), 21-25. — N. Brox, Offenbarung, Gnosis u. gnost. Mythos (Salzburg, 1966, 150-157. — P. Bacq, De l'ancienne à la nouvelle Alliance (Paris, 1978), 343-361. — A. Orbe, Hechos: Gr. 75 (1994) 37-64. — U. Swarat, Alte Kirche (Wuppertal, 1991), 232-234. — W. C. v. Unnik, Authority: FS N. A. Dahl (Oxford, 1977), 248-260. — T. Zahn: FGNK 6 (1900) 53-94.

R. HANIG

Apponius

A. composed a Lat. commentary on the Song of Songs. Nothing is known of his person. The work, dedicated to an Armenius, shows A. to have been an educated western theologian who was close to monasticism; circumstantial evidence suggests Rome as the place of composition. The commentary accepts the traditional exegesis of the Song and prolongs it in an independent way that is evident espec. in book 9 in the christological interpretation of 6:8-11: acc. to A. the Song sings there of the union of God and humanity in the person of Christ (an interpretation unique in early exegesis of the Song). In christology the position of Chalcedon is reflected here: the work was written after 450. Parallels between A.'s interpretations and the 6th-c. Lat. commentaries on the Song (→ Justus of Urgel) suggest a date after 500.

W: B. de Vregille, L. Neyrand, CCL 19. — eadem, SC 420, 421, 430. — H. König, A. Die Auslegung zum Lied der Lieder (Freiburg i. Br., 1991) [German trans./comm.].
L: B. Stubenrauch, Der hl. Geist bei A. (Rome, 1991). — P. Hamblenne, Peut-on dater A.?: RThAM 57 (1990) 5-33.

H. KÖNIG

Apringius of Beja

A. is attested as bishop of Pax Iulia (Pace, Beja, in modern Portugal) under the Visigothic kings Theudis (531-548), Agila (549-551), and Athanagildis (552-567). Around the middle of the 6th c. he wrote a *Tractatus in Apocalypsin* (*in apoc.*), of which only chs. 1.1-5.7 and 18.6-22.21 have been preserved. Beatus of Liébana did not have the lost parts when he used A.'s work for his own commentary on the Apocalypse. In the only known ms. (12th c.) the missing parts have been supplied by excerpts from the commentary of → Victorinus of Pettau, which Jerome had revised. Whether these excerpts go back to A. himself is disputed. Isidore (d. 626) praised the merits of the commentary over older efforts (Isidore, *vir. ill.* 30). Yet the *in apoc.* does not seem to have been widely circulated, since → Braulio (d. 651) made an intensive search for a copy in order that he might have it copied in turn (Braulio, *ep.* 25).

A.'s commentary, with its primarily allegorical interpretation, is an important witness for the history of exegesis of the Apocalypse.

In addition, A. composed some other works, which were no longer known even to Isidore.

W: *in apoc.*, M. Férotin (Paris, 1900) [text].
L: M. Alamo, Hacia una edición definitiva de A.: CDios 153 (1941) 399-406. — A. de Jesús da Costa, A.: Theologica 1 (1954) 72-75. — G. Kampers, Personengeschichtliche Studien (Münster, 1979), Nr. 100. — J. van Banning, Bemerkungen zur A.-Forschung: ZAC 3 (1999) 113-119. — A. C. Vega, Apringii Tractatus in Apoc. (El Escorial, 1941).

E. REICHERT

Arabic Infancy Gospel

An infancy gospel, completely transmitted only in Arabic, belongs among those → Apocrypha, which, on the one hand, spread legends about the childhood of Jesus and, on the other, supplemented the sparse details given in the canonical gospels about the public activity of Jesus. The nucleus of the document must have come from the 5th-c. Syr. world. The stories of the Magi point back to older east Syr. and Pers. influences; the miracle-filled childhood of Jesus in Egypt shows points of contact with the Copt. *Gospel of Thomas* (→ Thomas Literature). The Syr. nucleus substantially influenced the *History of the Virgin Mary*, likewise handed down in Syriac (→ Mary, Literature on) and the *Gospel of James* (→ James the Younger, Literature on), and encouraged the formation of legends in the Qurʾan. The Syriac is also the basis of the Arm. version, which includes, moreover, the entire material of the *Gospel of James* and in addition has made use of various Pers. traditions in the Magi cycle. The *Miracles of Jesus* (*mir. Iesu*), composed in Ethiopic, also took the *Arabic Infancy Gospel* as a literary model.

W: J. C. Thilo, Codex Apocryphus NT (Leipzig, 1832) [Arabic text/Latin trans.]. — P. Peeters, L'évangile de l'enfance (Paris, 1914) [Syriac, Arabic, Armenian texts/French trans.]. — M. E. Provera, Vangelo Arabo dell'infanzia (Jerusalem, 1973) [Arabic text/Italian trans.]. — *mir. Iesu*, S. Grébaut, PO 12, 4 [Ethiopic text/French trans.]. — G. Schneider, FC 18:179-195.

L: A. Z. Aescoly, Noms magiques: JA 200 (1932) 87-137. — U. Monneret de Villard, Leggende orientali sui magi (Rome, 1952). — A. M. di Nola, Evangelo arabo dell' Infanzia (Parma, 1963).

P. BRUNS

Arator

I. Life: A. was a 6th-c. Lat. poet from Liguria. Certain facts about his life are: the encouragement given by → Ennodius to this rhetor's son who was orphaned at an early age; a career as a lawyer at the Visigothic court in Ravenna; finally, the switch, probably ca. 540, to the clergy of Rome (subdeacon). A note appended (*subscriptio*) to the mss. attests to an enthusiastically received public recitation, in the Church of St. Peter in Chains, of a poem dedicated to Bishop Vigilius of Rome.

II. Work: The poem *De actibus apostolorum* (title uncertain; 2,325 hexameters in length) treat, in forty-three loosely strung together sections, of an equal number of incidents in Acts. The prose summaries that precede each section are not authentic. A. shows no interest in giving epic stature to the events, which are frequently assumed to be known. The emphasis is placed on interpretation. Points both of structure and content that are shared with popular preaching suggest that A. thought of his work as a kind of cycle of sermons on Acts. Augustine's sermons and Rufinus's translation of Origen's sermons on the Pentateuch can be shown to be exegetical sources.

The strong trinitarian and ecclesiological trend of the exegesis, which is predominantly allegorical, shows its purpose: In addition to an anti-Arianism directed against the Gothic overlords of Italy there is the propagation of the claims of the Roman church against Byzantium, based on the primacy of Peter. At a number of points there are paeans glorifying the first rulers of the church (whose importance A. stresses at the expense of Paul) and Vigilius as the present "Prince of the Church."

In his language A. takes his lead from the classics: Virgil, Lucan, and Statius and, among Chr. poets from → Sedulius, who is also his model in the treatment of the material (stringing together of individual episodes; exhortatory-didactic meditation). In the Middle Ages A. was highly esteemed as an author for school, as is attested by, among other things, the extensive transmission and excessive glossing of his work.

W: A. P. McKinlay, CSEL 72 [Rez.: J. Schwind, A.-Studien (Göttingen, 1990), 18-21]. — R. J. Schrader (Atlanta, Ga., 1987) [English trans., unreliable].
L: R. Anastasi, Dati biografici su A. in Ennodio: MSLCA 1 (1947) 145-152. — P.-A. Deproost, L'Apôtre Pierre dans une épopée du VIe siècle. L'Historia Apostolica d'A. (Paris, 1990). — idem, J.-C. Haelewyck, Le texte biblique des Actes et l'authenticité des sommaires en prose dans l'Historia apostolica d'A.: FS H. J. Frede, W. Thiele (Freiburg i. Br., 1993), 583-604. — R. Hillier, A. on the Acts of the Apostles (Oxford, 1993). — A. P. McKinlay, A. The Codices (Cambridge, Mass., 1942). — J. Schwind, loc. cit. — idem, Origenes u. A.: REAug 41 (1995) 113-129. — idem, Sprachliche u. exegetische Beobachtungen zu A. (Mainz, 1995). — K. Thraede, A.: JAC 4 (1961) 187-196 = RAC Suppl. 1:553-573.

J. SCHWIND

Arcadius of Cyprus

A. was archbishop of Constantia in Cyprus and an opponent of Monotheletism. He died ca. 640. An encomium on St. George has been handed down (*laud. Georg.*) in which the saint is invoked as helper against the Persians and Arabs. It is uncertain whether A. is also author of a life of Stylite Simeon the Younger (*v. Sym.*). John Damascene, who transmits a fragment of it (PG 94:1393-96), names A. as author; this life was cited at the Second Council of Nicaea (Mansi 13:73-80).

W: *laud. Georg.*, K. Krumbacher, Der hl. Georg in der griech. Überlieferung: ABAW 25/3 (Munich, 1911), 78-81 [text]. — *v. Sym.*, P. van den Ven, La vie ancienne de s. Syméon stylite le jeune 1, SHG 32/1 (Brussels, 1962), 1-224 [text].
L: H. G. Beck, Kirche u. theol. Lit. (Munich, 1959), 461f. — H. Delehaye, Saints Stylites (Brussels, 1923), 238-271. — J. Noret, Deux avatars du panégyrique de s. Georges par A.: AnBoll 92 (1974) 165-170.

G. RÖWEKAMP

Archaeus

A. is described as bishop of Leptis Magna (Tripolis) in the title of a fragment calling for the celebration of Easter on Sunday. The fragment, written ca. 190, is from a Lat. translation of a piece of Arab. writing, which, however, acc. to Severus of Antioch, is from a letter of Irenaeus of Lyons. Therefore the mention of A. in the title may be due to a misunderstanding of the translator, so that a bishop A. may never have existed.

W: PG 5:1489f.
L: A. Audollent, A.: DHGE 3:1528. — A. v. Harnack, Geschichte der altchr. Lit. 1 (Leipzig, ²1958), 776. — H. Jordan, Wer war A.?: ZNW 13 (1912) 157-160.

R. HÖFFNER

Archidiaconus Anonymus Romanus

Under the name of Augustine three sermons have been handed down which are attributed to an archdeacon (A.) who probably delivered them in Rome in the 5th c. These *Postulationes* or *Sermones tres de reconciliandis peccatoribus*, whose author, perhaps from North Africa, is otherwise unknown, were delivered at the rite of reconciliation on Holy Thursday, at which an archdeacon, a bishop, and some faithful asked for the reacceptance of penitent sinners. Nothing more is known about this probably quite simple rite in 5th-c. Rome.

W: F. Heylen, CCL 9:349-363.
L: A. Di Berardino (ed.), Patrologia, 3 (Turin, 1983), 536. — F. Heylen, loc. cit., 351f. — G. Morin, Sancti Augustini sermones (Rome, 1930), 723, 748.

B. WINDAU

Arians, Anonymous

"Anonymous Arians" refers to a group of unknown, probably Arian writers to whom six works in Gr. are attributed. (1) The Ps.-Athanasian *Sermo de diabolo* (*diab.*) on the trickery of the devil, composed perhaps in the first half of the 4th c. (2) A *Sermo de virginitate* (*virg.*) attributed to Basil and addressed to fathers of families, who ought to rear their daughters in the ideal of virginity. This is possibly a Gr. translation of a 4th-c. Syr. original. (3) A Ps.-Chrysostomian *Sermo in feriam secundam hebdomadae luminum et in quintum psalmum* (*in feriam secundam*), which clearly comes from the same author as (4) the *Sermo in psalmum undecimum* (*in ps. XI*). These two sermons for the octave of Easter, in which, in addition to the Psalms named, Acts 2:22-24 and 4:5-10 are also commented on, were written probably after 431. (5) The *Homilia de annuntiatione* (*annunt.*), a commentary on Lk 1:31-44. The author, who supports a relatively moderate Arianism, strongly attacks Marcellus of Ancyra. The homily was therefore delivered probably after 336, perhaps ca. 350. (6) Finally, there is the anonymous Arian historian whose work continued the history of → Eusebius down to the death of Valens. This work (*chron.*), which is preserved in fragmentary form (see espec. → *Chronicon paschale*), is given as an appendix to the church history of → Philostorgius.

W: *diab.*, F. Scheidweiler, Eine arianische Predigt: ZKG 67 (1955/56) 132-140 [text]. — *virg.*, D. Amand, M. C. Moons, Une curieuse homélie: RBen 63 (1953) 35-69 [text/French trans.]. — *in feriam secundam, in ps. XI*, J. Liébart, SC

146:56-93, 94-127. — *annunt.*, F. J. Leroy, Une homélie nouvelle: FS J. Daniélou (Paris, 1972), 343-353 [text]. — *chron.*, J. Bidez, F. Winkelmann, GCS 21:202-241.
L: D. Amand, M. C. Moons, loc. cit., 18-69, 211-238. — J. Bidez, F. Winkelmann, loc. cit., CLI-CLXIII. — M. Tetz, Eine arianische Homilie: ZKG 64 (1952) 299-307; 67 (1955/56) 5 n. 4. — A. Vööbus, Syr. Herkunft der Ps.-Basilianischen Homilie: OrChr 40 (1956) 69-77.

B. WINDAU

Aristeas, Letter of

The *Letter of Aristeas* is not a letter in the strict sense but a pseudepigraphical document (*diēgēsis*: a report or story), that is addressed by an Alexandrian Jew, Aristeas, to his brother Philocrates in Jerusalem. Among other things, it tells of the acquisition of a Hebrew text of the Pentateuch and of the activity involved in its translation into Greek. Pharaoh Ptolemy II Philadelphus (284-247 B.C.E.) supposedly asked Eleazar, high priest in Jerusalem, for seventy-two Jewish scholars (six from each of the twelve tribes of Israel) who would translate the Torah. The concluding section of the letter tells of how the translation came about: the seventy-two scholars (rounded to seventy, therefore *Septuaginta*, LXX), working on the island of Pharos, finished their task with complete unanimity in seventy-two days.

The *Letter of Aristeas* was written ca. 130-100 B.C.E. and had for its purpose to present the Jewish community of Alexandria in a positive light (see the table talk of the pharaoh with the translators). It is debated whether it intended to explain as well the origin of the entire LXX. In any case, this tradition was taken over by Christians and turned into a miraculous event (see Irenaeus, *haer.* 3.21.?f; Ps.-Justin, *or. Gr.* 13). Philo Alex. was already familiar with the idea of a concurrent inspiration of all the translators, even though the *Letter of Aristeas* reports only a collaborative effort with parts assigned to each translator (see Jerome, *Praefatio in Pentat.*). It is unclear whether Aristeas knew of earlier Gr. translations. In any case, he is an important witness to good relations between Greeks and Jews and gives testimony to the historical necessity of ensuring esteem for the LXX and therefore its authority. The work may be a forgery, but it remains an important piece of evidence for the origin of the LXX in the 3rd century B.C.E.

W: R. H. Charles, The Apocrypha and Pseudepigrapha of the OT 2 (Oxford, 1963), 83-122 (H. T. Andrews) [English trans./comm.]. — E. Kautzsch, Die Apokryphen u. Pseudepigraphen des AT 2 (Hildesheim, 1962), 1-31 (P. Wendland) [German trans.]. — N. Meisner, Der A.: Jüd. Schriften in hellenistisch-röm. Zeit 2 (Gütersloh, 1973), 35-85 [German trans./comm.]. — P. Riessler, Altjüd. Schrift-

47

tum außerhalb der Bibel (Augsburg, 1928), 193-233, 1277-1279 [German trans.]. — H. B. Swete, Introduction to the Old Testament in Greek (Cambridge, 1914), 531-606 [text/English intro.].
L: G. Delling, Bibliographie zur jüd.-hellenistischen u. intertestamentarischen Lit. (Berlin, 1969), 61-63. — O. Eissfeldt, Einleitung in das AT (Tübingen, 1956), 745-749. — M. Görg, A.: NBL 1: 167f. — H. G. Meecham, The Letter of Aristeas (Manchester, 1935). — W. Michaelis, A.: RGG3 1:596. — K. Stendahl, A.: BHH 1:127f.

A. SAND

Aristides

The work of A., the "philosopher from Athens" (Eus., *h.e.* 4.3.3), is regarded as the earliest Chr. *apologia* (*apol.*) to have come down in its entirety. Initially only fragments in Arm. were known of this *apologia* originally written in Gr. Then a Syr. version was discovered, with the help of which parts of the *Life of Barlaam and Josaphat* (→ John Damascene) could be identified as parts of the *apologia*. There is still no consensus on the reconstruction of the text in its original form. The date of the work is likewise controverted: it dates either from the reign of Hadrian (117-138: thus Eus. and the Syr. introduction to the *apol.*) or from the reign of Antoninus Pius (138-161), who is named as the addressee in the title of the Syr. version. In any case, the content suggests that A. is to be dated before → Justin Martyr.

After speaking first of God in *apol.* 1, A. (in *apol.* 2.2, acc. to the Gr. version) divides human beings acc. to their different ways of worshiping God into pagans, Jews, and Christians, with the pagans being subdivided into Chaldeans, Greeks, and Egyptians. In very prolix fashion the various pagan gods and ideas of the divine are reduced to absurdity (*apol.* 3-13), before the Jewish (14) and finally the Chr. (15-17) positions are set forth; in the process A. makes use of popular ideas from Middle Platonism. Christians are a "new people" who trace their origin to Jesus Christ. The latter is portrayed as a "divine man," even though A. reproaches the pagans for divinizing human beings. A. presents the Chr. manner of life in very great detail: not only the theory but the practice of Christians is exalted beyond any doubt. Insofar as the complex circumstances of the work's transmission allow for a judgment, one may regard it as espec. impressive in both its language and its content. The tone is one of pride, the content rather sketchy. In contrast to most of his apologist successors A. does not use the argument from prophecy or from antiquity but presents the teaching and life of Christians as something radically new.

W: *apol.*, C. Alpigiano (Florence, 1988) [text/Italian trans./comm.]. — J. Geffcken, Zwei griech. Apologeten (Leipzig, 1907) [text/comm.]. — E. J. Goodspeed, Die ältesten Apologeten (Göttingen, 1984 = 1914), 2-23 [text]. — E. Hennecke, TU 4/3 (Leipzig, 1893) [text]. — K. Julius, BKV² 12 (Kempten, 1913), 1-54 [German trans.]. — R. Seeberg (Erlangen, 1894) [text].
L: K. Aland, H.-U. Rosenbaum, Repertorium der griech. chr. Papyri 2 (Berlin, 1995), 11-16. — L. Alfonsi, La teologia della storia nell'Apologia di A.: Aug. 16 (1976) 37-40. — C. Alpigiano, L'Apologia di A. e la tradizione papiracea: CClCr 7 (1986) 333-357. — B. Altaner, A.: RAC 1:652-654. — L.W. Barnard, Apologetik 1: TRE 3:375f. — R. van den Broek, Eugnostos and A. on the ineffable god: Knowledge of God in the Greco-Roman World (Leiden, 1988), 202-218. — G. C. O'Ceallaigh, "Marcianus" A.: HThR 51 (1958) 227-254. — H. Conzelmann, Heiden — Juden — Christen (Tübingen, 1981), 263-268. — K.-G. Essig, Erwägungen zum geschichtlichen Ort der Apologie des A.: ZKG 97 (1986) 163-188. — H.-J. Oesterle, Textkritische Bemerkungen zur "Apologie" des A.: ZDMG 130 (1980) 15-23. — P. Pilhofer, Presbyteron kreitton (Tübingen, 1990), 231-234. — A. Puech, Les apologistes grecs du IIᵉ siècle de notre ère (Paris, 1912), 32-45. — W. C. v. Unnik, Die Gotteslehre bei A.: TZ 17 (1961) 166-174.

P. PILHOFER

Ariston of Pella

A., a Christian from the Decapolis, has been regarded since the time of Maximus Conf. (*schol. myst.* 1.3) as author of an → Apologia in the form of a dialogue between Papiscus, a Jew, and Jason, a Christian; until the time of Maximus the work had been anonymous, cited first probably by Celsus and faulted for its allegorical exegesis. Acc. to → Origen, the title of this now lost disputation was *Iasonos kai Papiskou antilogia peri Christou* (*Cels.* 4.52). Origen says that by means of allegory Jason proved that the messianic prophecies were fulfilled in Jesus, while Papiscus skillfully raised Jewish objections. The debate ended with Papiscus confessing Jesus to be the Son of God and with his desire to be baptized. This outcome is reported in the preface (3rd/5th c.) to the likewise lost Lat. translation of the dialogue; the preface, titled *Ad Vigilium episcopum de iudaica incredulitate*, has been preserved in Cyprian (CSEL 3/3:119-32). The description of the disputants in ch. 8 of this preface (*Iasoni Hebraei Christiani et Papisci Alexandrini Iudaei* [CSEL 3/3:128, 10]) points to Alexandria as the work's place of origin and destination. Because of Celsus's verdict on it, the dialogue must have been written before 178. The references in Eusebius and Jerome give the latest possible dates of the writing. Under the title *Altercatio Iasonis et Papisci* Jerome cites the dialogue twice (*quaest. hebr. in gen.* 1.1; *in Gal.* 3.13). This last reference shows that A. cited

Aquila's translation of Deut 21:23 (*loidoria Theou ho kremamenos*), which suggests its composition after 135. This dating is supported by Eusebius, *h.e.* 4.6.3, who mentions A. for the first time by name and claims him as source for his own account of the course and aftermath of the Bar Cochba rebellion (*Aristōn ho Pellaios historei*). Since no other work of A. is known, this event from very recent Jewish history must be taken as told with an apologetic and anti-Jewish purpose, so that the composition of the dialogue before 135 seems to be excluded. If the work was written ca. 140, as scholars think, then it is the earliest Chr. *apologia* in dialogue form aimed at Judaism, similar to the dialogue of → Justin with Trypho, although Justin did not know of A.'s work. Acc. to Maximus, *schol. myst.* 1.3, → Clement Alex. mentioned A.'s dialogue in *Hypotyposen* 6; some used to see traces of it in → Tertullian, *adv. Iud.* 13. The (independent) use of A.'s work in later Chr. dialogues *Adversus Iudaeos* is hardly demonstrable.

W: *Disputatio Iasonis et Papisci* (frgm.), J. K. T. v. Otto (Wiesbaden, 1965 = Jena, 1872), 357.
L: Artikel A.: BBKL 1:213. — J. E. Bruns, Altercatio: StT 34 (1973) 287-294. — A. v. Harnack, Geschichte der altchr. Lit. 1 (Leipzig, 1893), 92-95 (texts!). — E. Schürer, Geschichte 1 (Leipzig, 1901), 63-65. — J. Wehnert, Pella: ZKG 102 (1991) 231-255, esp. 254f.

F. R. PROSTMEIER

Arius

Relatively little is known of the life of A. He came, possibly, from Libya and was born ca. 260 or 256, being already an old man at the outbreak of the controversies in Alexandria. The only thing certain is that A. was a popular preacher in the church of Baucalis and that as a priest he opposed Alexander and Athanasius, was condemned at Nicaea, and then exiled. Other information (student of Lucian; participation in the Meletian Schism) is uncertain. He died ca. 336.

Three documents of A. are preserved: a profession of faith (Doc. 6), a letter to Eusebius of Nicomedia (Doc. 1), and a conventional letter (written along with Euzoius) to Constantine (Doc. 30). The sources permit us to say that in theology A. conceived of the connection between Father and Son as strictly relational and did so in reliance on passages of scripture. While the Father is unbegotten, immutable, etc., the Son, who can be described as god (not God), came into being before the ages, as a perfect creature, from the will of the Father, but not as one among other creatures. A special problem is raised by A.'s so-called *Thalia*, excerpts of which have been handed down by Athanasius. Despite the evidence that the *Thalia* had a popular style, a strict meter (possibly Ionic tetrameters), and remnants of an → acrosticon, there are differences in content from the documents mentioned above. Thus, the *Thalia* stresses that the Son came into being *in* time, whereas this is completely rejected in the documents. Because of these and other divergences, the question of whether, to what extent, and by whom the *Thalia* was revised was and is controverted.

W: *Thalia*, Athanasius, *Ar.* 1:5, 6, 9. Athanasius, *syn.* 15 (=Werke 2:1:231-278). — H.-G. Opitz, Urkunden zur Geschichte des arianischen Streits (Berlin, 1934/35).
L: T. Böhm, Die Christologie des A. (St. Ottilien, 1991). — R. C. Gregg, D. E. Groh, Early Arianism (Philadelphia, 1981). — R. P. C. Hanson, The Search for the Christian Doctrine of God (Edinburgh, 1988). — C. Kannengiesser, A. and Athanasius. Two Alexandrian Theologians (Hampshire, 1991). — R. Lorenz, A. judaizans? (Göttingen, 1979). — C. Markschies, ". . . et tamen non tres dii, sed unus deus . . .": Marburger Jahrbuch, Theologie 10, Trinität, ed. W. Härle, P. Preul (Marburg, 1998), 155-179. — K. Metzler, Ein Beitrag zur Rekonstruktion der "Thalia" des A.: K. Metzler, F. Simon, Ariana et Athanasiana (Opladen, 1991), 11-45. — C. Pietri, C. Markschies, Theologische Diskussion zur Zeit Konstantins: Geschichte des Christentums 2, ed. T. Böhm et al. (Freiburg i.Br., 1996), 271-344. — M. Simonetti, La crisi ariana nel IV secolo (Rome, 1975). — G. C. Stead, The Platonism of A.: JThS 15 (1964) 16 31. — idem, Arius in Modern Research: JThS 45 (1994) 24-36. — M. Vinzent, Die Entstehung des "Römischen Glaubensbekenntnisses": Tauffragen und Bekenntnis, ed. W. Kinzig et al. (Berlin/New York, 1999), 185-409. — R. Williams, Arius. Heresy and Tradition (London, 1987).

T. BÖHM

Arnobius the Elder (of Sicca)

A. was a professor of rhetoric who taught at Sicca in Proconsular Africa. During the persecution of Diocletian (303-305) he composed his seven books *Adversus nationes* (*nat.*), in the tradition of, but probably not under the direct influence of, the apologetic literature *adversus gentes*. We owe knowledge of the date and the occasion to Jerome, *vir. ill.* 79: the time of origin given there, *sub Diocletiano principe*, is confirmed by the frequent references to the anti-Christian legislation of 303-305.

The circumstances of the writing as described by Jerome, *chr. a.* 327 (a dream as occasion for A.'s conversion, and the composition of the work as pledge of faith in order to receive baptism from the bishop) ought not to be taken as historical imaginative embellishments: from a codicological examination of the acephalous archetype of the ms. tradition,

Paris BN lat. 1661 (9th c.), scholars have concluded to the loss not only of a title (*inscriptio*) but also of an extensive preface, the content of which could have been the source of Jerome's biographical data. Acc. to Jerome, the work enjoyed wide favor with the public, which after the victory of Christianity could have had more of an aesthetic interest in A.'s eloquence, praised by Jerome (*in Is.* 8 praef.), and in his rhetorical rebuttal strategies, and was ready to dispense with a systematics and orthodoxy of a textbook kind. The heterodoxies to be met with in books 1 and 2 were the occasion for the work to be condemned as "apocryphal" in the *Decretum Gelasianum* (320). This assessment explains the break in reception: Only one Carolingian ms., the Parisinus, from northern Italy, has been shown to exist, and of this again only one copy (Brussels B. Roy. 10846-47, 11th c.) is known. In the ms. tradition the *Octavius* of → Minucius Felix has been passed down as book 8 of the *adv. nat.*; given the common origin of the two authors we may accept a North African model for their transmission in antiquity. With the exception of the 17th and 18th c., when A.'s agnosticism, which was useful to Cartesianism, gave him an influence among French theologians, the work has remained an object rather of philological interest, which since early modern times (and contrary to its author's intention) has used *nat.* as a quarry of lost sources of pagan theology.

The criticism leveled ever since Jerome (*ep.* 62.2) at the loose structure that marks the work from its very beginning fails to recognize the rhetorical tactics of the *refutatio*: the starting point but not main object (as A.'s consciously *occultatio* division [*partitio*] might suggest) is the defense or *apologia* (against the objection that the rise of Christianity is responsible for all the misfortunes and misery in the world). At the center of the work is rather the offensive reversal (*retorsio*) of the charge of impiety: it is not the faith and worship of Christians but the reprehensible cult of the gods that is impious. The first half of book 1 exhausts the apologetic section of the work; the second half is given over to a christology marked by gnosticism and Platonism, in which the author has Christ himself deliver a cosmological instruction colored by Platonism. Book 2 contains a refutation of central aspects of the Neoplatonist doctrine of the soul; it attacks "new men" (*viri novi*), who are described as defenders of a syncretism that displays elements of Hermeticism, Pythagoreanism, and espec. Neoplatonism (2.13: the attack is on Porphyry). Over against this Neoplatonist teaching is set a Chr. soteriology which was at one time suspected of

Marcionism but is marked rather by docetist traits; here the authority of Plato is brought to bear on his contemporary disciples.

After this discourse, which A. himself describes as a digression, books 3-7 bring the real goal of the demonstration into view, namely, the proof of the basic impiety of traditional belief in the gods. Books 3-5 are given over to criticism of the gods (sexuality, anthropomorphism, role as protectors in 3; Rom. divinities in particular in 4; obscenity of cultic myths in 5); books 6 and 7 attack worship (temple and idols in 6; sacrificial rites in 7). In a carefully calculated arrangement in which the attack on Rom. sacrificial rites converges with an attack on an imperialism indebted to idolatry, A. reveals the real thrust and occasion for his work: disagreement with the rules on sacrifice in the fourth edict against Christians.

Varro (espec. in book 3) and Clement of Alexandria are indicated as A.'s sources for information on the sacral in antiquity. His contemporary attack is on the relevant treatises of Porphyry, with the latter's *De abstinentia* especially being envisaged (in 7). Biblical citations include NT passages derived from syncretism; A. distances himself brusquely from the OT as being a work full of fables showing an anthropomorphic image of God (3.21).

W: C. Marchesi (Turin, ²1953) [text]. — A. Reifferscheid, CSEL 4. — H. Le Bonniec (Paris, 1982) [bk. 1] [text/comm.]. — J. Alleker (Trier, 1885) [German trans.]. — G. E. McCracken, A. The Case against the Pagans, ACW 7-8 (New York, 1949) [English trans.]. — R. Laurenti (Turin, 1962) [Italian trans.]. — G. Gierlich, A. Kommentar zu den ersten beiden Büchern seines Werkes Adversus nationes, Diss. (Mainz, 1985) [comm.]. — J. M. P. van der Putten, Arnobii Adversus Nationes, 3:1-19 (Thesis) (Leiden, 1970) [text/comm.]. — G. F. Hildebrand (Halle, 1844) [text/comm.].
L: B. Amata, Problemi di Antropologia Arnobiana: Sal. 45 (1983), 775-844; 46 (1984) 15-80. — idem, Destino finale dell'uomo nell'opera di A. (III-IV sec. d. C.): Morte e immortalità nella catechesi dei Padri del III-IV secolo (BSR 66), ed. S. Felici (Rome, 1985), 47-62. — idem, La cristologia di A.: Academia Bessarionis (1986). — P. F. Beatrice, Un oracle antichrétien chez A.: FS Gribomont (Rome, 1988), 107-129. — L. Berkowitz, Index Arnobianus (Hildesheim, 1967) (Concordance). — C. Burger, Die theol. Position des Älteren A., Diss. (Heidelberg, 1970). — S. Colombo, A. Afro e i suoi sette libri Adversus Nationes: Did. 9 (1930) 1-124. — P. Courcelle, Les Sages de Porphyre et les "viri novi" d'A.: REL 31 (1953) 257-271. — idem, Anti-Christian Arguments and Christian Platonism: The Conflict Between Paganism and Christianity in the Fourth Century, ed. A. Momigliano (Oxford, 1963), 151-192. — J. Champeaux, A. lecteur de Varron (Adv. nat. III): REAug 40 (1994) 327-352. — Y. Duval, Sur la biographie et les manuscrits d'A.: Latomus 45 (1986) 69-99. — C. Elsas, Neuplatonische u. gnostische Weltablehnung in der Schule Plotins (Berlin, 1975), 41-48. — A. J. Festugière, La doctrine des "viri novi"

sur l'origine et le sort des âmes d'après A. II, 11-66: FS Lagrange (Paris, 1940), 97-132 (= idem, Hermétisme et mystique paienne [Paris, 1967], 261-312). — K. B. Francke, Die Psychologie u. Erkenntnislehre des A. Diss. (Leipzig, 1883). — F. Gabarrou, A., son œuvre (Paris, 1921). — idem, Le Latin d'A. (Paris, 1921). — H. Hagendahl, La Prose métrique d'A. Contributions à la connaissance de la prose littéraire de l'Empire: GHÅ 42 (1936) 1-265. — idem, Latin Fathers and the Classics (Göteborg, 1958), 12-47. — idem, Von Tertullian zu Cassiodor (Göteborg, 1983), 32-38. — HLL 5:365-375 (standard). — P. Krafft, Beiträge zur Wirkungsgeschichte des älteren A. (Wiesbaden, 1966). — W. Kroll, Die Zeit des Cornelius Labeo: RhM 71 (1916) 309-357. — idem, Arnobiusstudien: RhM 72 (1917) 62-112. — R. Laurenti, Il Platonismo di A.: SF 4 (1981) 3-54. — idem, Spunti di teologia arnobiana: Orph. 6 (1985) 270-303. — H. Le Bonniec, L'exploitation apologétique par A. de De natura deorum de Cicéron: Caesarodonum 19 (1984) 89-101. — E. Löfstedt, Arnobiana (Lund, 1917). — J. D. Madden, Jesus as Epicurus. A.'s Borrowings from Lucretius: CCC 2 (1981) 215-222. — P. Mastandrea, Lettori cristiani di Seneca filosofo (Brescia, 1988), 9-50. — E. Mayer, De refutationis formis quae inveniuntur in Arnobii libris 7 Adversus Nationes, Diss. (Graz, 1939). — E. R. Micka, The Problem of Divine Anger in A. and Lactantius (Washington, 1943). — E. Rapisarda, Clemente Fonte di A. (Turin, 1939). — idem, A. (Catania, 1946). — A. Röhricht, De Clemente Alexandrino Arnobii in irridendo gentilium cultu deorum auctore (Hamburg, 1893). — P. Santorelli, Parodia virgiliana in A.: Maia 41 (1989) 241-50. — W. Schmid, Christus als Naturphilosoph bei A.: FS T. Litt (Düsseldorf, 1960), 264-284. — F. Tullius, Die Quellen des A. im 4., 5. u. 6. Buch seiner Schrift Adversus Nationes (Bottrop, 1934). — M. B. Simmons, A. Religious Conflict and Competition in the Age of Diocletian (Oxford, 1995). — A. Viciano, Retorica, Filosofia y Gramatica en el Adversus Nationes de A. (Frankfurt a.M., 1993).

R. JAKOBI

Arnobius the Younger

I. Life: A. was a native of North Africa (the name is attested only there) and came to Rome, possibly as a refugee from the Vandals, between 428 and 432. He lived there as a monk until his death after 455. What we know about his life is derived exclusively from his writings.

II. Work: The following which certainly have A. as author have been preserved: Commentarii in psalmos (in psalm.), Conflictus Arnobii cum Serapione (confl.), Expositiunculae in Evangelium (expos.), and Liber ad Gregorium in Palatio constitutum (ad Greg.). There is disagreement about → Praedestinatus, which G. Morin attributes to A.

1. The commentary on the Psalms is an allegorical interpretation, and the author, as the teaching on grace shows, was a Semipelagian. The teaching on the Trinity and christology have hardly anything about them that is peculiar to A.: he accepts the unity, eternity, and eternal equality of the three divine persons; Christ as Son of God is fully God and fully man. The divine has assumed the human.

2. In the Conflictus Arnobii cum Serapione (also called: Monomachia adversus haereses diversas; confl.) is presented the record, in two books, of a debate between A. (as a representative of "the Apostolic See of Peter") and Serapion (a supporter of Monophysitism). The main subjects in book 1 are the doctrine of the Trinity and, toward the end, christology; in book 2, christology with special attention to the incarnation of Christ: Is Mary theotokos or anthrōpotokos? A supplement of trinitarian doctrine follows and a rather short contribution to the doctrine on grace. The work includes extensive citations from writings of Augustine (s. 396; ep. 177; 299), Celestine (serm.; frgm.), Cyril Alex. (ep. 1; ep. paschalis; contra Nestorium), Damasus (ep. 3 and 4), Leporius (liber emendationis), Nestorius (fr. 142-47), and Novatian (trin. 31), and was written in the time of Leo I, approximately 454.

3. The Expositiunculae in evangelium Iohannis evangelistae, Matthaei et Lucae (expos.; also Annotatiunculae Arnobii Afri in quot evangelistarum locos) are scholia on forty-eight shorter passages from the gospels.

4. The Liber ad Gregorium in Palatio constitutum (ad Greg.) was transmitted under the name of John Chrys. and was recognized by G. Morin as undoubtedly from A. It is a book of consolation, or better, a letter urging the exercise of patience, for an unhappily married nobleman who had asked for counsel and help.

5. The so-called Praedestinatus has been transmitted without an author's name and is not in the body of A.'s writings. Close links in content and language suggest that it is from A., the composer of the commentary on the Psalms. It dates from between 432 and 439. In book 1 there is a survey of ninety heresies (see Augustine, haer.); in book 2 there is a treatise on grace and predestination that is foisted on Augustine and is refuted in book 3.

6. It is not proven but is quite possible that A. was also the author of the Actus Silvestri and other legends of the saints.

W: PL 53:239-672. — confl., in psalm., expos., ad Greg., K. Daur, CCL 25, 25A. — ad. Greg., PLS 3:213-256. — expos., G. Morin, AMar 3,3 (1903) 129-151. — ad Greg., G. Morin, Études, textes, découvertes 1 (Paris, 1913), 338-439.
L: G. Bouwman, Des Julian v. Aeclanum Kommentar zu den Propheten Osea, Joel u. Amos (Rome, 1958). — H. Diepen, La pensée christologique d'A.: RThom 59 (1959) 534-564. — D. Franses, Feuardent en de patrologie, De A.-uitgave: CFN 1 (1927) 294-298. — R. Freni, Alcune osservazioni sul testo neotestamentario utilizzato nelle expos.:

Atti della Academia Peloritana dei Pericolanti (Messina, 1986), 219-234. — idem, Arnobio il Giovane fonte di Cassiodoro?: Atti della Settimana di Studi su F. M. A. Cassiodoro (Sovezia Manelli, 1986), 421-433. — B. Grundl, Über den confl., die in psalm. u. die expos.: ThQ 79 (1897) 529-568. — H. Kayser, Die Schriften des sog. A. (Gütersloh, 1912). — W. Kinzig, Rez. zu in psalm., ed. K. Daur, CCL 25, 25A: Journal of Theological Studies 43 (1992) 693-701. — W. Levison, Konstantinische Schenkung u. Silvesterlegende: StT 38 (1924) 159-247; see also: ZSRG. K (1926) 501-511. — G. Morin, Études, textes, découvertes 1 (Paris, 1913) 33f., 309-324, 340-383. — idem, L'origine africaine d'A.: RevSR 16 (1936) 177-184. — C. Piffaré, Arnobio el Joven y la christologia del confl. (Montserrat, 1988) [recension: EThL 65 (1989) 180-183]. — J. Scharnagl, Zur Textgestaltung des arnobischen confl.: WSt 38 (1916) 382-384; 42 (1921) 75ff., 152ff. — H. v. Schuberth, Der sog. praed.: TU 24/4 (1903).

K. Daur

Arsenius the Great

A. was born ca. 354 to a noble Rom. family and, after possibly having been tutor to Arcadius and Honorius, sons of Emperor Theodosius I, withdrew ca. 394 to be a monk in Scete. Except for a short stay at Canopus due to a barbarian invasion of Scete in 407, he lived in Scete until new invasions forced him to take flight again (434, Troe; 444, Canopus). He died ca. 449 in Canopus. His education and knowledge of people are attested espec. by his forty-four apophthegms (*apophth.*). The following works have also been handed down: *Doctrina et exhortatio* (*doct.*), *In nomicum tentatorem* (*tent.*), a letter (*ep.* in Georgian), fragments of works on the Psalms (*fr. in Ps.*, unpublished), the gospel of Luke (*fr. in Luc.*, unpublished), and the Acts of the Apostles (*fr. in Act.*), and an *Epigramma in prophetam David* (*epigr.*, unpublished).

W: *apophth.*, PG 65:87-108. — L. Regnault (Solesmes, 1981), 23-36 [French trans.]. — B. Miller (Trier, [3]1986), 25-40 [German trans.]. — *doct.*, S. Phirippides: EkklPh 34 (1935) 46-50. — PG 66:1617-1620. — *ep.*, G. Garitte: Muséon 68 (1955) 259-278 [text/Latin trans.]. — *fr. in Act.*, I. Cramer, Catenae 3 (Oxford, 1844), 130 [text]. — *tent.*, PG 66:1621-1626.
L: W. Bousset, Apophthegmata (Tübingen, 1969 = 1923), 63f. — K. S. Frank, A.: FS J. Gribomont (Rome, 1988,) 271-287. — C. W. Griggs, Early Egyptian Christianity (Leiden, 1990). — J. C. Guy, Apophtegmes 1, SC 387 (Paris, 1993), 74-77. — idem, La tradition grecque des "Apophthegmata Patrum" (Brussels, 1962). — I. Hausherr, Hésychasme et prière (Rome, 1966), 183-198. — H. Holze, Erfahrung u. Theologie (Göttingen, 1992). — M. v. Parys, La lettre de saint Arsène: Irén. 54 (1981) 62-86. — L. Regnault, La vie quotidienne (Paris, 1990). — idem, A.: CoptE 1:240f.

M. Skeb, OSB

Asclepius (Apocalypse)

A treatise in the *Corpus Hermeticum* bears the title *Apocalypse of Asclepius* (*Apoc. Ascl.*) and has been preserved in its entirety only in Lat. and Copt. translations. There is also the Gr. original for ch. 41. The content of the treatise is of an anthropological and soteriological kind. The human being, offshoot of the Logos and at the same time enslaved to the lusts of the material world, is able through gnosis to free himself from his fate and find his way back to his divine self.

W: A. D. Nock, A. J. Festugière, Corpus Hermeticum (Paris, 1960), 2:259-401 [Latin text/French trans.]. — B. P. Copenhaver (Cambridge, 1992) [English trans.]. — J. P. Mahé, Hermès en Haute-Égypte (Leuven/Louvain, 1978-82) [Greek/Coptic text].
L: G. Fowden, Egyptian Hermes (Cambridge, 1986). — E. Iversen, Egyptian and Hermetic Doctrine (Copenhagen, 1984). — M. Krause, Ägyptisches Gedankengut: ZDMG 123 (1969) 45-57. — J. P. Mahé, Remarques d'un latiniste: RevSR 48 (1974) 136-155.

P. Bruns

Asterius of Amasea

I. Life: The dates of A.'s birth and death are not known. He succeeded Eulalius as bishop of Amasea between 380 and 390. Acc. to his own testimony he reached old age (d. probably after 415). He mentions as his teacher a learned "Scythian," a slave, whom he must have heard in Antioch. None of A.'s contemporaries mentions him. Only in 787, at the Second Council of Nicaea, are passages from his *Homilies* 1 and 11 cited as evidence of the veneration of images. Later on, his name occurs in Theodore of Studios, Hadrian I of Rome, Patriarch Nicephorus of Constantinople, and espec. in Photius, who transmits excerpts from ten sermons (*cod.* 271) and sparse biographical data (*ad Amphil. quaest.* 312 [PG 101:1161B]).

II. Work: Thus far only sermons have come to light (sixteen complete, four fragments, references to lost ones); a complete critical edition is still lacking. The older editions do not adequately distinguish between the parts by A. and those by Asterius the Sophist, an Arian. The homilies (*hom.*) make use primarily of these genres: → panegyric (of saints, martyrs, and their relics), parenesis or exhortation, exegesis (of Lk), and → ecphrasis.

A. is a theologian highly educated in Gr. literature, rhetoric, and philosophy. Under the influence of the Cynic-Stoic popular discourse (*dialexis*), he combines the acquisitions of the "Second Sophistic" with ideas of Platonic-Aristotelean philosophy, espec. in his anthropology. He shows knowledge of medicine, pharmacology, and geography and is one of the few eccles. writers to take notice of the arts as a specific form of intellectual expression.

His sermons are witnesses primarily to pastoral theology. He takes into account his audience, which was perhaps still pagan, but without giving up his radical attack on paganism. A pedagogical and ethical purpose takes precedence over strictly theol. questions. In passing, he combats christological errors (Eunomius, Sabellius). His sermons suggest an educated urban audience who expect of him examples from and allusions to antiquity and the OT. While his attack on his Jewish contemporaries is extremely biting, showing a strikingly nuanced understanding of society, he sides with the weak, including women, and shows here a sympathy seldom noticeable elsewhere. He also defends the rights of slaves and avoids disparaging judgments on the native cultures of the north. As a result, he enriches in no small way our picture of society and culture in late antiquity.

W: *hom.* 1-14, C. Datema (Leiden, 1970). — *hom.* 15, 16, C. Datema: SE 23 (1978/79) 63-93 [text]. — *hom.* 1-9, J. G. v. Engelhardt (Erlangen, 1931) [German trans.].
L: M. Bauer, A., Diss. (Würzburg, 1911). — A. Bretz, Studien u. Texte zu A. (Leipzig, 1914). — M. Schmid, Beiträge zur Lebensgeschichte des A. u. zur philologischen Würdigung seiner Schriften, Diss. (Munich, 1910, 1911). — W. Schmid, O. Stählin, Geschichte der griech. Lit. 2/26 (Munich, 1961 = Munich, 1924), 1429-1431. — E. Skard, A. u. A. der Sophist: SO 20 (1940) 86-132. — W. Speyer, Frühes Christentum im antiken Strahlungsfeld (Tübingen, 1989), 91-99, 495. — idem, A.: RAC Suppl. 1:626-639. — V. Vaasy, The Social Ideas of A · Aug. 26 (1986) 413-436.

W. SPEYER

Asterius of Ansedunum

A. is described in *Cod. Veron.* 93 as a "disciple" of Jerome, a bishop of otherwise unknown Ansedunum, and author of a *Liber seu epistula ad Renatum monachum de fugiendo monialium colloquio et visitatione.* This is a satire, reminiscent of → Jerome (*ep.* 22; 117) and → Ps.-Cyprian (*De singularitate clericorum*) and rich in classical citations and allusions, on virginal companions of celibate men (*syneisaktoi; virgines subintroductae*). It is uncertain whether this A. is the subdeacon Asterius who is mentioned by Jerome (*ep.* 102.1) and whom Augustine later describes as a "colleague" in the episcopate.

W: *Liber ad Renatum Monachum,* S. Gennaro, CCL 85/1:3-25.

L: G. Morin, Un curieux inédit du IVe-Ve siècle: RBen 47 (1935) 101-113. — idem, À propos d'A. "episcopus Ansedunensis," disciple de S. Jérôme: RBen 57 (1945) 5-8.

J. LÖSSL

Asterius the Homilist

A. is the otherwise unknown author of a collection of thirty-one homilies on Psalms 1-15 and 18 (among them several Easter homilies), which have been preserved only in an abbreviated form under the name of John Chrys. Other fragments are found in catenas of the Psalms. The preacher, who in the past was wrongly identified with → Asterius of Amasea or → Asterius the Sophist, lived in the late 4th or early 5th c. in Antioch or its environs. Stylistically, A. clings to the ideas of Asian rhetoric. His exegesis is interspersed with juridical concepts, which suggest his earlier training. The extreme dependence on the Bible is striking (more than 1,200 citations from the Psalms alone!). There are isolated references to apoc. works (e.g., *Ascension of* → *Isaiah* 5.1-14 in 19.27 and 31.4; *4 Mac* 8:13ff. in 31.6). On the other hand, citations from or allusions to pagan authors are almost completely lacking.

Despite isolated echoes of John Chrys. A. is largely independent in his exegesis. Literal and hortatory expositions alternate with heavily christological sermons. The completely unspeculative and linguistically very stylized and ornate theology emphasizes the revelation of the divinity of Christ as the focus of the Easter event. Dogmatically important terms are largely lacking (but see the acceptance of *homoousios* in 26.3 and 27.8; the rejection of *heteroousios* in 26.3, and the condemnation of Arius and Eunomius). The numerous images and metaphors serve the spread of a popular piety. Probably due entirely to the name of Chrysostom, A. influenced espec. Leontius of Constantinople, John Damascene, Photius, and George the Monk (Hamartolos).

W: *Asterii Sophistae commentariorum in psalmos quae supersunt; accedunt aliquot homiliae anonymae,* M. Richard, SO. S 16 (Oslo, 1956) [text]. — W. Kinzig, *hom.* 31: VigChr 50 (1996) 401-415 [text/German trans./comm.]. — W. Kinzig, BGrL, 2 vols. (Stuttgart, 1997) [German trans./comm.].
L: *Index Asterianus,* E. Skard, SO. S 17 (Oslo, 1962). — M. P. Ciccarese, Un retore esegeta: A. il Sofista nell'om. 13 sul Salmo 7: ASEs 2 (1985) 59-69. — eadem, La composizione del "corpus" asteriano sui Salmi: ASEs 3 (1986) 7-42 (also attributed to the Sophist, see below). — W. Kinzig, In Search of A. (Göttingen, 1990) (literature). — idem, Erbin Kirche (Heidelberg, 1990). — idem, A. Sophista o. A. Ignotus? Eine Antwort [to K.-H. Uthemann, see below]: VigChr 45 (1991) 388-398. — idem, Bemerkungen zur Psalmexegese des A.: Chr. Exegese zwischen Nicaea u.

Chalcedon, ed. J. van Oort, U. Wickert (Kampen, 1992), 104-131. — idem, Röm. Recht u. Unrecht in der Predigt der Alten Kirche: Recht-Macht-Gerechtigkeit, ed. J. Mehlhausen (Munich, 1998), 407-437. — K.-H. Uthemann, Rez. von Kinzig, In Search of A.: VigChr 45 (1991) 194-203.

W. KINZIG

Asterius the Sophist (of Cappadocia)

I. Life: A. was born ca. 270 in Cappadocia and, until he converted to the Chr. faith before 303, was a practicing sophist; he may have belonged to the school of Lucian of Antioch. He apostatized from Christianity in the Diocletian persecution; after being reconciled he sought in vain for a bishopric.

As one of the initial thinkers in the early phase of the Arian controversy, he spread his teachings in his *Syntagmation* ("Little Treatise"), which he used for lectures while journeying, espec. in Syria. Between 325 and 335, he defended in writing the letter of Eusebius of Nicomedia to Paulinus of Tyre (Opitz, *Urk.* 8) and was on this account sharply attacked by Marcellus of Ancyra. A. probably took part in synods for the consecration of churches in Jerusalem (335) and Antioch (341). He seems to have exerted a decisive influence on the formulation of the Antiochene Creed (the so-called second formula). After that, every trace of him is lost.

II. Works: Only fragments (*fr.*) of the *Syntagmation* (title probably not original) and the defense of Eusebius are preserved. Lost are an attack on Marcellus (existence uncertain; perhaps identical with the defense) as well as numerous exegetical works (commentaries on the Psalms, the gospels, and Romans, among others). The homilies on the Ps that were attributed to him by earlier scholars belong to → Asterius the Homilist.

In his teaching on God, to which most of the surviving passages refer, A. distinguished between the nonrelational being of God (consisting above all of nonbecoming and eternity) and his relational powers exercised ad extra. This distinction leads to a distinctive but not radical subordinationism: the Son has indeed come into being (= was created), but as such he is the "unchanged image" (*aparallaktos eikōn*) of God the Father, "essentially like" to him (*kat'ousian homoios*) and, to that extent, likewise God, but in a derived sense. In his hypostasis he is indeed to be distinguished from the Father, but at the same time he is an exact image of the Father insofar as he shares in the (relational) capabilities, properties, and names of the Father. The creation of other creatures is mediated by the first creature, the Son. The other creatures participate in the Son and thus are images of the One who does not become. In this presentation older theol. concepts (espec. of Philo, Origen, and Neoplatonism) are used in an entirely independent way.

The importance of A. for the first phase of the Arian controversy must be rated as significantly greater than was previously thought. A. must have strongly influenced Arius, but also Aetius and Eunomius, and he also left deep marks, both positive and negative, on the opponents of Arius (espec. Marcellus, Athanasius, the author of Ps.-Athanasius, *Ar.* 4 [Apollinaris of Laodicea?]). In this way, he made a decisive contribution to the development of 4th-c. trinitarian doctrine. A. was a systematic thinker, perhaps *the* system builder of the Eusebians and the thinker who led up to Arius.

W: *fr.*, G. Bardy, Recherches sur saint Lucien d'Antioche et son école (Paris, 1936), 339-357 [text]. — M. Vinzent, A. Die theol. Frgm. (Leiden, 1993) [text/German trans./ comm.].
L: G. Bardy, loc. cit., 316-339. — W. Kinzig, In Search of A. (Göttingen, 1990) (literature), esp. 14-21, 125-132. — idem, "Trample upon me. . . " The Sophists A. and Hecebolius: FS G. C. Stead (Leiden, 1993), 92-111. — M. Vinzent, A. Die theol. Frgm. (Leiden, 1993) (literature). — idem, Gottes Wesen, Logos, Weisheit u. Kraft bei A. u. Markell v. Ankyra: VigChr 47 (1993) 170-191. — idem, Die Gegner im Schreiben Markells v. Ankyra an Julius v. Rom: ZKG 105 (1994) 285-328. — idem, Ps-Athanasius, Contra Arianos IV. Eine Schrift gegen A. (Leiden, 1996).

W. KINZIG

Athanasius of Alexandria

I. Life: A. was probably born ca. 295 (or 300) in Egypt (perhaps Alexandria), probably as the child of pagan parents. Reliable information comes first from the period when he entered the service of Bishop Alexander of Alexandria as a deacon and secretary (ca. 319). He accompanied the bishop to the Council of Nicaea in 325, where he already took a public stand against Arius. A. enjoyed only a short period of general education in the Hellen. canon of subjects (*egkyklios paideia*). His language is based on the Bible. His predilection for a moderate Origenism was certainly one reason for his good relations with the monks of Nitria. Philological evidence suggests the hand of the young A. in Bishop Alexander's *Henos sōmatos*. In accordance with Alexander's wishes, after his death (328) A. was elected bishop of Alexandria; since only subsequently was the agreement of all the Egyptian bishops obtained, the election was not entirely canonical. A. took over, as Alexander's heritage, the struggles with the Meletians and the Arians. His policy was to make journeys of visitation (330-334) on which he strengthened his support among the clergy and won the support of the monks. A. was perhaps the first to consecrate monks as bishops.

A. was able to prevent the restoration of the priest Arius, who had been condemned at Nicaea but whom Constantine wanted restored for the sake of church unity. He was able to defend himself successfully in 332/333 against the charges brought against him in a secular court by the Meletians (embezzlement, bribery, murder). His situation became more critical when Constantine had him called before an episcopal court in Caesarea in 334 and before an imperial synod in Tyre in 335. A. ignored the first summons; he left Tyre for Constantinople before the verdict. Having been condemned in his absence (for political disobedience, among other things), he was sent into exile in Trier: the first of several during his time in office. After Constantine's death (337), Constantius allowed the exiled bishops to return; thus A. too returned to Alexandria. He was able to remain there, however, only until 339, when he was driven out by the party of Eusebius of Nicomedia, which installed George as an alternate bishop; this time A. fled to Rome, where he found eccles.-political support, but the western church was unable to make its position (which affected A.'s status) prevail at the imperial Council of Sardica (342). Not until 346 did Constans wring permission from his brother Constantius for A. to return, but after Constans's death (350) Constantius managed to have A. condemned at the Synods of Arles (353) and Milan (355). In 356 A. eluded a nighttime arrest by bold flight during worship in the Church of St. Theonas; monks hid him in the wilderness. The death of Constantius and the reign of Julian the Apostate made it possible for A. to return to Alexandria after the murder of George.

Under A.'s leadership the Synod of Alexandria was held in that same year; there it was made easier for opponents of Nicaea to return and conflicts within the Nicene camp were resolved. But there was no settlement of the Meletian Schism in Antioch.

Even A.'s remaining time in office was not free of banishments, although these did not bring lengthy absences: the exile imposed by Julian in 362 ended with the latter's death in 363; the Arian Emperor Valens had to cancel the exile which he imposed in 365/366. A. died probably on May 2 or 3, 373. Gregory Naz. composed an encomium (or. 21; PG 35:1081-1128). The *Historia acephala* in its collection of the acts of Theodosius contains a life of A., who was soon venerated in the liturgy as the first bishop who had not died a martyr.

After A.'s death the Arian controversy was ended by the Second Ecumenical Council of Constantinople (381). In the controversy over the place of the Holy Spirit in the Trinity, church teaching ultimately accepted the teaching represented by A.

L: D. W. Arnold, The Early Episcopal Career of A. (Notre Dame, Ind., 1991). — T. D. Barnes, A. and Constantius (Cambridge, Mass., ²1994). — W. Bright, A.: DCB 1:170-203. — G. Gentz, A.: RAC 1:860-866. — K. M. Girardet, Kaisergericht und Bischofsgericht (Bonn, 1975). — D. Ritschl, A. (Zurich, 1964). — E. Schwartz, Zur Geschichte des Athanasius 1-9: idem, Gesammelte Schriften 3 (Berlin, 1959). — G. C. Stead, A.'s Earliest Written Work: JThS NS 39 (1988) 76-91. — M. Tetz, Zur Biographie des A.: ZKG 90 (1979) 304-338. — idem, A.: TRE 4:333-349.

II. Work: The state of exile in which A. spent the greater part of his forty-five years in office played a fundamental role in his writing. For this reason the usual division of his works into dogmatic and apologetic writings, with the letter and the *Life of Anthony* being separate genres, does not capture what is most important. A. took up his pen chiefly when he was cut off from his diocese and could not otherwise intervene in controversies. Thus even the dogmatic writings, in which we find genuinely theological arguments, take a position in some current dispute and display strongly polemical traits. As a result, almost all the works have the character of occasional writings.

For this reason, the most important works will be presented here in the order of their writing (an order often indeed beset with difficulties). Among them pride of place will be given to those which show clearly the theol. aspect of A.'s politics. Despite his influence on Copt. literature A. himself probably did not speak or write Coptic.

The twofold work *Contra gentes/De incarnatione Verbi* (gent.), is in the tradition of early Christian apologetics and of the traditional Alexandrian theology of Origen. It is not possible to determine whether this was a youthful work or whether during his exile in Trier A. returned to a genre in which he did not have to engage during the Arian controversy. The double work originated, therefore, either in the first years of his episcopate (328-333) or (more probably) in 335/337. In the first work A. comes out against the errors of the pagans. Idolatry and polytheism are extensively refuted and condemned; the responsibility for our personal salvation rests on our human activity, in which we must strive for the perfection of our own souls. In the second work, A. presents the history of salvation, at the center of which he places the incarnation. Because of their imperfection human beings need a divine redemption, which has become possible through the incarnation of the Logos. This is one of A.'s most widely read works. Whether the "short recension" represents a revision by A. himself is disputed.

In the *epistula encyclica* (*ep. encycl.*) of 339 A. protests against his deposition.

In the three *Orationes contra Arianos* (*Ar.*), which A. sent from Rome to Alexandria, together with an introductory letter to the monks (*ep. mon.*), we can study A.'s aggressive attitude, but we can also see how in principle he develops christology from the soteriological aspect of the incarnation of the Son of God. In the introduction (perhaps added later on) he quotes fragments of Arius from the latter's *Thalia*, sums up his teaching, and opposes to it his own interpretation of key passages of the Bible (e.g., Prov 8:22). *Ar.* 1 and 2 were probably written in 340/341, and *Ar.* 3, in which theol. distinctions are made, in 345/346. (A fourth address added later is spurious.) The second address in particular shows the influence of Marcellus of Ancyra. The work *In illud: Omnia mihi tradita sunt* (*hom. in Mt.* 11:27) belongs to the same period and the same context.

The work *De decretis Nicaeni synodi* (*decr.*) was written about 350/351. Here A. defends the expressions *ek tēs ousias* and *homoousios*; the appended material from the acts of the synod is valuable because the acts themselves are lost. The *De sententia Dionysii* (*dion.*), on Dionysius, bishop of Alexandria, whom the Arians claimed for themselves, may be an appendix to the *decr.*

The short *Epistula ad Dracontium* (*ep. Drac.*) of 354 is an important witness to A.'s understanding of his office. The power politics, which often became a burden, had its basis, acc. to A. himself, in his pastoral responsibility.

In the *Vita Antonii* (*v. Anton.*), composed during his exile in the wilderness (after 356), A. wrote the first life of a saint. It shows his esteem for the lifestyle of the hermits, which was on the rise just at that time, but probably also contains some veiled reservations against the excessive importance given to the struggle with demons. A. revises the description of Anthony's life by Serapion of Thmuis and corrects Serapion's picture by additions that ensure the christological origin of marvelous ascetical feats (→ *Vita*). A.'s work exerted a wide influence and became the model for many Lives. It made the ascetical ideal as a way of life known to a broad public in the church. The *Vita* is regarded as basically historical, but it is not free of

propaganda and apologetic. A.'s veneration for Anthony, the father of monks, made his life different from the picture given of hermits in the *Apophthegmata Patrum* and played a key role in the development of monasticism in the East: the ascetic life now came under the jurisdiction of the episcopate. A. presents Anthony as a model ascetic who thinks and acts like A. himself and is capable of fighting for the interests of his church.

Of the remaining writings on ascetical subjects, handed down chiefly in Coptic, at least the *Epistula ad virgines* (*ep. virg.*) is probably authentic. It contains what is perhaps the earliest witness to the application of the hundredfold fruit (Mt 13:8) to the life of virginity rather than to martyrdom.

The so-called *Apologia secunda* or *Apologia contra Arianos* (*apol. sec.*) of 356/357 is important because it contains numerous letters to A.

In the *Apologia ad Constantium* (*apol. Const.*) of 357 A. defends himself in a rhetorically brilliant and skillful way against the charge that he incited Constans against his brother Constantius. In the *Apologia de fuga sua* (*fug.*), which probably appeared shortly before the *apol. Const.*, A. defends himself against the charge of cowardice that was raised after his flight in 356.

In his letters to Serapion of Thmuis (*ep. Serap.*) A. took his position in the new phase of the Arian controversy; in these letters he comes out against the creatureliness of the Holy Spirit (against the so-called Tropicists) and defends the Spirit's divinity within the Trinity. Thus he applies to pneumatology what was said about the relationship of Father and Son. *Ep. Serap.* 1 dates from 357/358; that same year brought another letter to Serapion on the death of Arius in 336 (*ep. mort. Ar.*). *Ep. Serap.* 2 and 3 (357/358) probably form a single work; *ep. Serap.* 4 (358/359) consisted originally of only chs. 1-7; the remaining chapters, 8-23, formed the work *In illud: Qui dixerit verbum in filium* (Lk 12:10) (358).

The *Historia Arianorum* (*h. Ar.*) from 357/358 is preserved only in fragmentary form. It is addressed to monks and ordinary Christians. The surviving fragment describes the drastic measures taken by Emperor Constantius in 335-337; the emperor is described as "forerunner of the Antichrist." The work thus represents a first break with the imperial theology of a Eusebius. The accompanying work, a second *Epistula ad monachos* (*h. Ar. ep.*), reflects the same context.

Despite difficult conditions, the *Epistula ad episcopos Aegypti et Libyae* (*ep. Aeg. Lib.*) was addressed (before 361) to all the bishops within the jurisdiction of Alexandria and refutes the Arian theses.

In the *Epistula ad Marcellinum* (*ep. Marcell.*) A. brings out the special literary place of the Psalms in the Bible and gives pointers on the role of the Psalms in Chr. life; the background here is the monastic practice of psalmody and the ancient theory of music.

In a letter to a friend, the *Epistula ad Adelphium* (*ep. Adelph.*), A. once again paraphrases *gent.*

De synodis Arimini in Italia et Seleuciae in Isauria (*syn.*) of 361/362 is the longest of A.'s writings.

The *Tomus ad Antiochenos* (*tom.*), written by order of the Alexandrian synod of 362, deals with the Meletian Schism and sets guidelines for the further development of trinitarian theology and christology. A. accepts the Antiochene and Meletian way of speaking of three persons in God. He was now prepared to accept the Old Nicene (*homoousios* = of one substance) and the New Nicene (*homoousios* = equal in substance) interpretation of the creed as equally right. In addition, the *tom.* deals for the first time with the Nicene concepts "becoming flesh" (*sarkōsis*) and "becoming man" (*enanthrōpēsis*). A. himself had always spoken of only one hypostasis in God, and his christology was conceived acc. to the model of Word-flesh (see Apollinaris) rather than the model of Word-man. For the first time, too, he acknowledges the christological problem to be the central question of theology.

The so-called *Epistula catholica* (*ep. cath.*) is probably the remnant of a circular letter from the synods and the immediate presupposition of *tom.*; it is an important link between the Nicene Creed and the *Tomus* of the Synod of Constantinople.

Also from 362 comes the *Epistula ad Iovinianum* (*ep. Iov.*), a synodal letter to the emperor. The two *Epistulae ad Orsisium* (*ep. Ors.*) date from ca. 368. The *Epistula ad Afros* (*ep. Afr.*) to the bishops of West Africa is also a (very authoritative) synodal letter (369/370).

The *Epistula ad Epictetum* (*ep. Epict.*) to the bishop of Corinth (371/372) was a canonical text for later councils (espec. Chalcedon): in it A. takes his position on the relationship between the Logos and the flesh he has assumed.

The *Epistula ad Maximum* (*ep. Max.*) of 372, which is addressed to Maximus, a philosopher, deals once again with the christological dogma.

The *Paschal Letters* (*ep. fest.*), which to some extent range far beyond their occasion (the determination of the date of Easter and of the periods of fast), are an important theol. and hist. witness. Numerous frag-

ments of these letters in Greek have been preserved; thirteen letters from 329-348 have been preserved in their entirety in a Syr. translation. *Ep. fest.* 39, from 367, which can be reconstructed from Gr., Syr., and Copt. fragments, contains a list of the canonical books of the OT and NT and is therefore important for the history of the canon, being the first witness to the twenty-seven books of the NT.

In addition, many spurious writings have come down under the name of Athanasius (Cyril Alex. already regarded some Ps.-Athanasian material as authentic).

The so-called *Symbolum Athanasianum* (*symb.*), also called the *Quicumque* (*vult*) after its opening word(s), was attributed to A. from the 7th c. on, but in fact came from the Lat. West (5th-c. Gaul). This "creed" is rather an explanation of the creed, but because of its clear explanation of the doctrines of the Trinity and the two natures of Christ it was even used in the liturgy.

Among the writings attributed today to → Apollinaris of Laodicea and his circle are *Contra Sabellianos* (*Sabell.*), *De incarnatione Dei Verbi* and *Quod unus sit Christus*.

Today the *De incarnatione et contra Arianos*, as well as an *Expositio fidei* and the *Epistula ad Antiochenos* or *Sermo major de fide*, are attributed to Marcellus of Ancyra. *De titulis Psalmorum* is from → Hesychius of Jerusalem; the twelve-book Lat. work *De Trinitate* is from → Eusebius of Vercelli. The attribution of many sermons, letters, and ascetical works is still doubtful.

III. Basic Thought: A.'s teaching on God is linked to the Platonic and Alexandrian tradition and rejects anthropomorphic categories. In accordance with the apophatic, or negative, theology, God is described by negative categories ("immaterial," "incorporeal," "ineffable"). Whether the young Athanasius had any influence on the formulation of the Nicene Creed is uncertain; in any case, his service consisted in its defense and success, as well as in the development of the orthodox theology of the Trinity, which has remained the common foundation of almost all Chr. churches.

The Nicene Creed was the basis of his activity in eccles. politics and in theology. At the center of everything, in his mind, is the God who from the very beginning turns his face to human beings. In creation itself the coming fall and the only possible redemption of humanity are included in God's plan. The plan of creation has its fulfillment in the incarnation of Christ, since he alone, as mediator of creation, can reconcile God with his creatures. A. is unable to conceive of any permanent salvation for human beings unless human nature is effectively united with the divine nature, and he can think of no other way to this union except the incarnation and the death of the cross. Thus the soteriological dimension is primary for A.; for that reason, in ontological questions he must first and foremost defend the place of the Son against all attacks; the formula for doing so is the *homoousios* of the Nicene Creed.

The attack of his adversary Arius on the Son of God probably did not go as far as A. would have us believe; at the center of Arius's theology, as far as we can reconstruct it, was in fact not the soteriological but the cosmological aspect. Arianism defended a creator God, understood as strictly monotheistic, against all the erosions that would have resulted from the existence of a Son who was not thought of as subordinate. At the same time, the hierarchic order in his ontology fit in well both with the categories of thought in late ancient philosophy and with the hierarchy of the recently christianized Roman empire (this was likely a reason why Arianism was repeatedly successful at the imperial court). A., on the other hand, paid the price for his emphasis on soteriology and on the fact that the relationship between the Father and his equally eternal and eternally begotten Son was beyond human power to grasp. But that was not really a loss, because at the same time he safeguarded the paradoxical character of Chr. dogma over against the philosophical and rational thinking of the surrounding world. By his theology and his way of conducting his office A. made it clear that a synthesis of Hellen. philosophy and Christianity can only be had at the expense of the experience of salvation which is so fundamental for human existence and which has as its unconditional presupposition a holding fast to the unity in substance of the Logos with God.

A.'s importance as a church politician rests on his claim to a prophetic office. Interior freedom, that is, the scripture-based freedom of faith, was for him the basis of his activity in eccles. politics, and it was in its spirit that he dealt both with pagans and with Chr. authorities. This enabled him to be the first Chr. theologian to break with the Chr. imperial ideology. His commitment to the binding character of the Nicene Creed made this confession, in the version modified by the Council of Constantinople (the Nicene-Constantinopolitan Creed), the first creed of the undivided church, with *homoousios* as the central idea that still points the way for orthodox faith.

W: *Collected works*, PG 25-28. — H. G. Opitz, Athanasius Werke 2/1 u. 3/1 (Berlin, 1934-1941) [text]. — G. Papadopoulou, C. Dimitropoulou, Ἅπαντα Μεγάλου Ἀθανασίου (Athens, 1973-1976) [text/modern Greek trans.] — K. Christou, N. Sakkou, Ἀθανασίου Ἀλεχανδρείας τοῦ Μεγάλου ἅπαντα τὰ ἔργα (Thessalonica, 1973-1977) [text/modern Greek trans.]. — *gent.*, R. W. Thomson (Oxford, 1971) [text/English trans.]. — P. T Camelot, SC 18bis. — C. Kannengiesser, SC 199 [text/French trans. of *De incarnatione Verbi*]. — A. Stegmann, BKV² 31:531-676 [German trans.]. — L. Leone (Naples, 1965) [text/Italian trans.]. — *ep. encycl.*, PG 25:221-240. — H. G. Opitz, loc. cit., 169-179. — *Ar.*, PG 26:12-468. — *Ar.* 3, E. P. Meijering, 2 vols. (Amsterdam, 1996/1997) [text/German trans./comm.]. — H. G. Opitz, loc. cit., 183-230. — A. Stegmann, BKV² 13:17-387 [German trans.]. — C. J. de Vogel (Utrecht, 1949) [Dutch trans.]. — *hom. in Mt.* 11, 27, PG 25:208-220. — *ep. mon.*, PG 26:1185-1188. — G. de Jerphanion: RSR 20 (1930) 529-544 [text/Latin trans.]. — *decr.*, PG 25:416-476. — H. G. Opitz, loc. cit., 1-45. — *Dion.*, PG 25:480-521. — H. G. Opitz, loc. cit., 46-67. — *ep. Drac.*, PG 25:524-533. — *v. Anton.*, PG 26:837-976. — G. J. M. Bartelink, SC 400. — C. Mohrmann et al. (Milan, 1974) [text/Italian trans.]. — H. Merkel, BKV² 31:687-777 [German trans.]. — A. Gottfried (Graz, 1987) [German trans.]. — *ep. virg.*, L. T. Lefort, CSCO 150:73-99 [Coptic text]; CSCO 151:55-80 [French trans.]. — *apol. sec.*, PG 25:248-409. — H. Opitz, loc. cit., 87-168. — *apol. Const.*, PG 25:596-541. — J. M. Szymusiak, SC 56:88-132. — *fug.*, H. G. Opitz, loc. cit., 68-86. — J. M. Szymusiak, SC 56:133-167. — *ep. Serap.*, PG 26:529-648. — J. Lebon, SC 15. — R. B. Shapland (Leipzig, 1951) [English trans./comm.]. — G. A. Egan (Salt Lake City, 1968) [Armenian text/English trans.]. — L. Iammarrone (Padua, 1983) [Italian trans.]. — E. Cattaneo (Rome, 1986) [Italian trans.]. — J. Lippl, BKV² 13:400-497 [German trans.]. — *ep. mort. Ar.*, PG 25:685-689. — H. G. Opitz, loc. cit., 178-180. — *h. Ar., h. Ar. ep.*, PG 25:692-796. — H. G. Opitz, loc. cit., 181-230. — F. Cesana (Milan, 1979) [Italian trans.]. — *ep. Aeg. Lib.*, K. Metzler et al., A. Werke 1/1 (Berlin, 1996). — *ep. Marcell.*, PG 27:12-45. — C. Kannengiesser, P. Bright (Philadelphia, 1986) [English trans.]. — *ep. Adelph.*, PG 26:1072-1084. — *syn.*, PG 26:681-793. — H. G. Opitz, loc. cit., 231-278. — *tom.*, PG 26:796-809. — *ep. cath.*, M. Tetz: ZNW 79 (1988) 262-281 [text/comm.]. — *ep. Jov.*, PG 26:813-820. — *ep. Ors.*, PG 26:977-980. — F. Halkin, Sancti Pachomii Vitae graecae (Brussels, 1932), 91, 95f. [text]. — *ep. Afr.*, PG 26:1029-1048. — *ep. Epict.*, PG 26:1049-1069. — G. Ludwig (Jena, 1911) [text]. — J. Lippl, BKV² 13:504-517 [German trans.]. — *ep. Max.*, PG 26:1085-1089. — *ep. fest.*, PG 26:1351-1444. — W. Cureton (Leipzig, 1848) [Syriac text]. — H. Burgess (London, 1854) [English trans. of the Syriac text]. — L.-T. Lefort, CSCO 150/151 [Coptic text/French trans.]. — P. Merendino (Düsseldorf, 1965) [German trans.]. — R. Lorenz, BZNW 49 (Berlin, 1986) [Syriac text/German trans. of ten letters].

L: *Bibliographies and additional aids:* C. Butterweck, A.-Bibliographie (Opladen, 1995). — G. Müller, Lexicon Athanasianum (Berlin, 1952). L. Abramowski, Die 3. Arianerrede des A.: ZKG 102 (1991) 389-413. — B. Altaner, Augustinus u. A.: RBen 59 (1949) 82-90. — M. Aubineau, Les écrits de s. A. sur la virginité: RAM 31 (1955) 140-173. — L. W. Barnard, Studies in A.'s apol. sec. (Bern, 1992). — idem, A. and the Meletian Schism in Egypt: JEA 59 (1973) 181-189. — idem, A. and the Emperor Jovian: StPatr 21 (1989) 384-

389. — C. A. Blaising, A. Studies in the Theological contents and Structure of the Contra Arianos, Diss. (Aberdeen, 1987). — D. Brakke, A. and the Politics of Asceticism (Oxford, 1995). — J. Ceska, Die politischen Gründe der Homoousios-Lehre des A.: Die Kirche angesichts der Konstantinischen Wende, ed. G. Ruhbach (Darmstadt, 1976), 297-321. — H. Dörries, Die v. Anton. als Geschichtsquelle: idem, Wort u. Stunde 1 (Göttingen, 1966), 145-224. — S. Elm, A.'s Letter to the Virgins: Aug. 33 (1993) 171-183. — J. D. Ernest, A.: The Scope of Scripture: VigChr 47 (1993) 341-362. — G. Garitte, Le texte grec et les versions anciennes de la Vie de s. Antoine: StAns 38 (1956) 1-12. — A. Grillmeier, Jesus der Christus 1 (Freiburg i.Br., 1979), esp. 460-479 (Engl., Christ in Christian Tradition, vol. 1 [London, ²1975]). — K. Hoss, Studien über das Schrifttum u. die Theologie des A. auf Grund einer Echtheitsuntersuchung von A.' gent. (Freiburg i.Br., 1899). — C. Kannengiesser, A. (Paris, 1983). — idem, Arius and A. (Hampshire, 1991). — idem, Le mystère pascal: RSR 63 (1975) 407-442. — idem (ed.), Politique et théologie chez A., Actes du colloque de Chantilly 23-25 Sept. 1973 (Paris, 1974). — idem, A. in heutiger Sicht: ZKTh 109 (1987) 276-293. — idem, The Homiletic Festal Letters: FS W. Burghardt (New York, 1989), 73-100. — idem, Le texte court du De incarnatione athanasien: RSR 52 (1964) 589-596; 53 (1965) 77-111. — idem, Lady Wisdom's final call: the patristic recovery of Proverbs 8: FS F. W. Schlatter. (New York, 1999), 65-77. — A. Laminski, Der hl. Geist als Geist Christi u. Geist der Gläubigen (Leipzig, 1969). — G. Larentzakis, Einheit der Menschheit — Einheit der Kirche bei A. (Graz, 1978). — J. Liébaert, La doctrine christologique: MFCL 58 (1951) 19-43. — R. Lorenz, Die Christusseele im Arianischen Streit: ZKG 94 (1983) 1-51. — A. Louth, The Concept of the Soul in A.'s gent.: TU 116 (1975) 227-231. — J. R. Lyman, Christology and Cosmology. Models of Divine Activity in Origen, Eusebius and A. (Oxford, 1993). — E. P. Meijering, Zur Echtheit der 3. Rede des A. gegen die Arianer: VigChr 48 (1994) 135-156. — K. Metzler, F. Simon (ed.), Ariana et Athanasiana. Studien zu Überlieferung u. zu philologischen Problemen der Werke des A. (Opladen, 1991). — J. R. Meyer: A.'s Use of Paul in his Doctrine of Salvation: VigChr 52 (1998) 146-171. idem, A.'s Son of God Theology: RThPhAM 66 (1999) 225-253. — H.-G. Opitz, Untersuchung zur Überlieferung der Schriften des A. (Berlin, 1935). — T. Orlandi, Sull'apol. sec.: Aug. 15 (1975) 49-79. — V. Peri, La cronologia delle lettere festali di Sant'A. e la quaresima: Aevum 35 (1961) 28-86. — H. Pietras, L'unità di Dio: Rassegna di teologia 32 (1991) 558-581. — J. Roldanus, Le Christ et l'homme (Leiden, 1958). — J. Rondeau, L'Épître à Marcellinus: VigChr 22 (1968) 176-197. — W. Schneemelcher, Gesammelte Aufsätze (Thessalonica, 1974), 242-337. — H.-J. Sieben, A. über den Psalter: ThPh 48 (1973) 157-173. — G. C. Stead, Rhetorical Method in A.: VigChr 30 (1976) 121-137. — idem, A. in Modern Research: JThS 45 (1994) 24-136. — M. Tetz, A. u. die v. Anton.: ZNW 73 (1982) 1-30 — idem, Athanasiana. Gesammelte Aufsätze (Berlin, 1995). — T. F. Torrance, The Hermeneutics of St. A.: Ekklesiastikos Pharos 52/1 (1970) 446-468; 52/2-3 (1970) 89-106; 52/4 (1970) 237-249. — idem, Homoousion: EvTh 43 (1983) 16-25. — M. Vinzent, Ps.-Athanasius, Contra Arianus IV. Eine Schrift gegen Asterius v. Kappadokien, Eusebius v. Cäsarea, Markell v. Ankyra u. Photin v. Sirmium (Leiden et al., 1996). — P. Widdicombe, The Fatherhood of God from Origen to A. (Oxford, 1994).

K. METZLER

Athanasius of Anazarba

A. was a bishop in Anazarba (Cilicia II) and, after Philostorgius, a tutor of Aetius. He may not have been present at Nicaea. In his theology A. consistently follows the approach of Arius. Thus he emphasizes the point that the Son is not like the Father (e.g., in power). In *Doc.* 11 he interprets Lk 15:4 as meaning that the Son is one of a hundred sheep and was therefore created. A homily transmitted under the name of Athanasius Alex. may be from this A.

W: *ep. ad Alexandrum*, H.-G. Opitz, Urkunden zur Geschichte des arianischen Streits (Berlin, 1934/35), 18. L: D. de Bruyne, Deux lettres inconnues de Theognis l'évêque arien de Nicée: ZNW 27 (1928) 106-110. — R. P. C. Hanson, The Search for the Christian Doctrine of God (Edinburgh, 1988), 41-43. — M. Tetz, Eine arianische Homilie: ZKG 64 (1952) 299-307.

T. BÖHM

Athanasius I. Camelarius

A. was originally from Samosata on the Euphrates and in 594/595 was consecrated the non-Chalcedonian patriarch of Antioch. A. had previously been a monk and camel-driver of the monastery of Quennesre, south of Aleppo. In 609/610 during a stay in Egypt he managed a reconciliation with the Monophysites there. But his dealings in dogma with Emperor Heraclius at Hierapolis (Mabbug) in 621 were fruitless. Shortly before his death in 630/631 he established a Monophysite hierarchy in Nestorian Persia. He was a lifelong supporter of → Severus of Antioch, whose biography (*v. Sev.*) he wrote. The original of this is lost; fragments have been preserved in Coptic and the entire work in Ethiopic. In his chronicle Michael the Syrian cites passages from A.'s circular letters.

W: *vit. Sev.*, E. J. Goodspeed, W. E. Crum, PO 4:578-718 [Ethiopic-Coptic text/English trans.]. — *ep.*, J. B. Chabot, Michel le Syrien (Paris, 1900/1910), 1:400-402, 405-409 [text]; 2:394-399, 405-408 [French trans.].

P. BRUNS

Athenagoras

Nothing reliable is known about A.'s life. His name is attached to an apology titled *Legatio pro Christianis* (*leg.*) and to a treatise *De resurrectione* (*res.*), the authenticity of which is disputed. The *leg.* can for internal reasons be dated with some probability to 177. It is addressed to Marcus Aurelius and his son Commodus. It is to be doubted that A. delivered his apology to the emperors orally or at least planned to do so. In *leg.* 3, A. lists the accusations against Christians with which he deals: he treats in greatest detail the chief charge of atheism (part 1: *leg.* 4-30), because it was for this reason that Christians were persecuted. He points out the agreement between the Chr. concept of God and the best ideas of pagan philosophy. In A. we find for the first time a trinitarian conceptual framework (the Spirit as *aporrhoia* [emanation]; *koinōnia, henotēs, diairēsis* [communion, oneness, distinction] of the three persons in the Godhead, *leg.* 10, 12). The other two accusations, that Christians celebrated Thyestean meals (cannibalism) and entered into Oedipean unions (incest), are dealt with more briefly (part 2: *leg.* 31-36). At the end of the work, which is one of the best thought out of the apologies, A. speaks of an expected future harmony between empire and church (*leg.* 37). Because an apology had the character of a petition, A. almost never appeals to the Bible. He introduces no proof from prophecy and no proof from antiquity. The *praeparatio evangelica* is found, for A., not in the OT but in philosophy. As a result, he nowhere refers to Christ: in *leg.* 10 he does speak of the Son of God and of the Logos as mediator in creation, but even here he makes no mention of the incarnation!

There has been a lively debate, still unsettled, about the authenticity of *res.* It is characteristic of *res.* (and in this respect it reflects A.) that the author tries to argue from philosophy without relying on bibl. testimonies. Thus he bases the possibility of a resurrection on the idea of a new composite of soul and body. In saying this he intends to link himself with Pythagoras and Plato; he also seems familiar with the ideas of Galen; but not a word is said of the resurrection of Jesus. Yet the author of *res.* is "the father of Chr. anthropology."

W: *leg., res.,* A. Eberhard, BKV² 12 (Kempten, 1913) [German trans.]. — J. Geffcken, Zwei griech. Apologeten (Leipzig, 1907) [text/comm.]. — E. J. Goodspeed, Die ältesten Apologeten (Göttingen, 1984 = 1914), 314-358 [text]. — B. Pouderon, SC 379. — W. R. Schoedel, OECT (Oxford, 1972) [text/English trans.]. — *leg.,* M. Marcovich, PTS 31 (Berlin, 1990) [text]. — *res.,* E. Schwartz, TU 4/2 (Leipzig, 1891) [text].
L: L. W. Barnard, Apologetik 1: TRE 3:380-382. — idem, God, the Logos, the Spirit and the Trinity in the Theology of A.: Scandinavian Journal of Theology 24 (1970) 70-92. — idem, Notes on A.: Latomus 31 (1972) 413-432. — idem, A. (Paris, 1972). — idem, The Father of Christian Anthropology: ZNW 63 (1972) 254-270. — idem, The Philosophical and Biblical Background of A.: FS J. Daniélou (Paris, 1972), 3-16. — T. D. Barnes, The Embassy of A.: JThS 26 (1975) 111-114. — R. M. Grant, A. of Ps.-A.: HThR 47 (1954) 121-129. — H. E. Lona, Die dem Apologeten A. zugeschriebene Schrift De resurrectione: Sal. 52 (1990) 525-578. — P. Keseling, A.: RAC 1:881-888. — A. J. Malherbe, The Structure of A., "Supplicatio pro Christianis": VigChr 23 (1969) 1-20. — P. Pilhofer, Presbyteron kreitton (Tübingen, 1990), 261-265. — B. Pouderon, A. (Paris, 1989). — idem, "La chair et le sang": encore sur l'authenticité du traité d'A.: VigChr 44 (1990) 1-5. — A. Puech, Les apologistes grecs du IIᵉ siècle de notre ère (Paris, 1912), 172-206. — L. A. Ruprecht, A. the Christian, Pausanias the Travel Guide, and a Mysterious Corinthian Girl: HThR 85 (1992) 35-49. — W. R. Schoedel, Christian "Atheism" and the Peace of the Roman Empire: ChH 42 (1973) 309-319. — N. Zeegers-Van der Vorst, La "prénotion commune" au chapitre 5 de la Legatio d'A.: VigChr 25 (1971) 161-170.

P. PILHOFER

Athenodorus

A., the younger brother of Gregory the Wonderworker, was born ca. 215 in Neocaesarea. Our information about his life comes espec. from Eusebius (*h.e.* 6.30; 7.14 and 28; see also Jerome, *vir. ill.* 65). Along with his brother, he attended the school of Origen in Caesarea and later became bishop of Pontus. In 264/265 he took part in the first synod against Paul of Samosata. His death occurred sometime after that. His supposed martyrdom under Aurelian has no basis in the hist. sources. He composed a work *De hebraismo,* of which three fragments remain (*fr.*). Among the writings of Gregory, Suidas lists two further, otherwise unknown works of A.: *Oratio de incarnatione* and *Oratio de fide.*

W: K. Holl, Frgm. vornicänischer Kirchenväter (Leipzig, 1899), 161 [text].
L: H. Crouzel, Faut-il voir trois personnages?: Gr 60 (1979) 287-320. — M. T. Disdier, A.: DHGE 5:43f. — P. Nautin, Origène (Paris, 1977), 81, 85. — G. Lucchesi, A.: BSS 2:561f.

B. WINDAU

Atticus of Constantinople

A. was born in Sebaste (Armenia) and received a simple education in a monastery in his native place; in the course of this he came in contact, by way of Eustathius of Sebaste, with Macedonian thought. He moved to Constantinople and there, because of his prudence and character (despite rather modest gifts as a preacher), gained a reputation among the people and at the court. At the Synod of the Oak (403) he opposed John Chrys. and, when elected patriarch of the capital in 406, Chrysostom's supporters as well, but finally, after intervention from the west Roman empire, he was ready for reconciliation. A. tried, with partial success, to extend the area and sphere of influence of the patriarchate of Constantinople. His opposition to Pelagius and Celestius brought him great posthumous renown in Ephesus and Constantinople. He died in 425.

Of his works a few letters remain among the writings of other authors: a letter to Cyril Alex. (*ep. Cyr.*) and one to Alexandrian deacons Peter and Aedesius (*ep. Petr. et Aides.*), which belong to the period of controversy with John Chrys., and a further letter to presbyter Calliopius of Nicaea (*ep. Call.*), with which A. sends a gift of money for the hungry of that city. A letter to the Council of Carthage (419) (*ep. Afr.*) accompanies a Lat. translation (also preserved) of the canons of Nicaea, which he had prepared at the wish of the council. His fragmentary letter *Ad Eupsychium* (*ep. Eups. fr.*) deals with christological questions; a letter to Bishop Sahak the Great is most probably spurious.

A treatise *De fide et virginitate*, addressed to the daughters of Emperor Arcadius, in which A. speaks out against Nestorius long before Ephesus, is mentioned with praise by Gennadius (*vir. ill.* 53); the work is lost except for a few fragments. To the same thematic realm belong fragments of a christological sermon (*hom.*) which Cyril and Ephesus cite as references for orthodoxy; contrary to common claims, the title Theotokos for Mary does not occur. The homily, preserved complete in Syriac, is authentic only in its second part, which speaks of the incarnation. There are also fragments of a sermon on the Trinity in the *Doctrina patrum* (42.8).

W: PG 65:49f. (*ep. Afr.*, also PL 67:227; 67:793; 146:1132 (*ep. Call.*); 77:348-352 (*ep. Cyr.*). — *ep. Afr.*, C. Munier (CCL 149), 163. — *ep. Eups. fr.*, M. Geerard, A. van Roey: FS E. Dekkers (Brügge, 1975), 69-81 [text/partial Latin trans.]. — *hom.*, M. Brière, Une homélie inédite d'A.: ROC 9 (1933/34) 160-186 [Syriac text/French trans.]. — J. Lebon, Discours d'A. "sur la Mère de Dieu": Muséon 46 (1933) 167-202 [Syriac text]; in addition: R. Caro, La homilética Mariana Griega (Dayton, Oh., 1971), 59-75.
L: M. T. Didier, A.: DHGE 5:161-166. — A. Kazhdan, A.: ODB 1:230.

U. HAMM

Augustalis

A. was probably a bishop in Africa. Around the middle of the 3rd c. he composed the *Laterculus (paschalis)*, a hundred-year calendar for the date of Easter (213-312). He reckoned the date of Easter on the basis of an eighty-four-year cycle, which he carried back to the year 45. His work is now lost, though it was often used and extrapolated in the computational literature and was evidently highly esteemed in Africa until the end of the 4th c. References in the

Computus Carthaginensis (*Comput. Carth*) of 455, the anonymous author of which praises A. while also pointing out his mistakes (2.8), give us information on the most important dates.

A.'s continuator was Agriustia, an African from Thimida Regia, whose work *De ratione paschali*, dedicated to Quintus Julius Hilarianus, is likewise lost. Agriustia, who may have been a Donatist, drew up his calendar in 412, probably only for the period 413-497. He sharply criticized A.'s calculations (1.4; 2.9).

W: B. Krusch, Studien zur chr.-mal. Chronologie (Leipzig, 1880), 17-19 [reconstruction].
L: A. Audollent, A. 1: DHGE 5:414. — HLL 5:177f. — B. Krusch, loc. cit., 5-23, 23-30, 138, 150. — A. Strobel, Ursprung u. Geschichte des frühchr. Osterkalenders (Berlin, 1977), 137, 273f., 384f.

B. WINDAU

Augustine

I. Life: There are numerous sources for the life of A. In addition to the *Confessiones* and many remarks in his sermons and letters, the *Retractationes* and the life written by A.'s disciple → Possidius (*vita*) make possible a comprehensive biography. A. was born on Nov. 13, 354 (*beata v.* 6; *vita* 31.1) in Thagaste in the province of Numidia. The personal name Aurelius is attested by → Orosius (*apol.* 1.4). His father, Patricius, who was a pagan at the time of A.'s birth (*conf.* 9.19.37), was, though impoverished, a member of the city senate (*curia*) (*vita* 1.1). When A. was sixteen, Patricius became a catechumen (*conf.* 2.6). Unlike the father, who is described without sympathy, A.'s mother, Monica, played a decisive role in his life. At the time of his birth she was twenty-three (*conf.* 9.28), and he erects a memorial to her in the *conf.* In the description in the *conf.* A.'s closeness to or distance from his mother reflects his relationship to the church. He had a brother, Navigius (*beata v.* 6), and a sister whose name is unknown and who, after being widowed, became head of a monastery of women (*vita* 26).

A. did his basic studies in literature in Thagaste and continued them in Madaura, probably under Maximus, a pagan grammarian (*ep.* 16.1). At the age of sixteen he was compelled to interrupt his studies for lack of money, but in 370 he was able to study rhetoric in Carthage.

During these studies he became familiar with Cicero's now lost hortatory work *Hortensius*. The reading of it aroused a love of wisdom (*conf.* 3.7; *beata v.* 4; *sol.* 1.17). When he turned to the scriptures he was disappointed because, when judged by

61

Cicero's elegance, they seemed crude. The impulse given him by the *Hortensius* led him "in a short time" to join the Manichees. In a later rational justification of this step (*conf.* 3.8f.) A. gives as reasons that the Manichees seemed to him the more serious Christians, that their teaching seemed to be based on insight (*ratio*) and not simply on authority (*auctoritas*; *util. cred.* 2), and that their criticisms of the OT condemned those dubious characters the patriarchs (*conf.* 3.12f.). He was impressed not least by the seemingly radical asceticism of the Manichees. His transition to the Manichees was not unaccompanied by hope of a subsequent career (*util. cred.* 2). In addition, the rank of *auditor* among the Manichees allowed him to retain the relationship with a woman that he had entered on a short time earlier (before 371). This conversion led initially to a break with his mother, who forbade him her house.

Ca. 374 A. returned to Thagaste to teach grammar there, but the death of a friend drove him back to Carthage, where he taught rhetoric. Ca. 380/381, in Carthage, he composed a now lost work *De pulchro et apto* (*pulch.*), which dealt with aesthetic matters and, with a view to furthering his career, was dedicated to Hierius, a Roman orator (*conf.* 4.20f.). Meanwhile his enthusiasm for Manichaeism had clearly lessened; his doubts about Manichean dogma increased when ca. 383 even the much-praised Manichean Bishop Faustus admitted he was unable to resolve A.'s continuing problems (*conf.* 5.10). Disillusioned, A. left Carthage and moved to Rome (*conf.* 5.14), where he joined the Manichean community. A severe illness (*conf.* 5.16-18) led to the resolution to move once more, this time to the imperial court in Milan. There, with the help of Symmachus, pagan prefect of the city of Rome, he was to be given the position of orator. While in Milan, out of professional interest he attended the sermons of Bishop Ambrose and learned that an allegorical interpretation of the OT answered the difficulties raised by the Manichees.

Added to the allegorical method was Neoplatonic philosophy, to which he gained access by way of → Simplicianus, a priest of Milan. The discovery of this "Milanese Platonism" was one of the most important events in A.'s intellectual development. At the same time, he became acquainted with a Christianity of a Platonist type, to which he himself was to give a distinct form for Latin Christendom. In *conf.* 7.16, he notes that God appeared to him as unchangeable Light. It is debated whether he is referring there to a mystical experience (as in the incident at Ostia: *conf.* 9.23-26). He is certainly describing an experience of ascent which led him *ictu trepidantis aspectus* to God

(*conf.* 9.23). The reading of the *libri Platonicorum* inaugurated a development comparable to that initiated by the reading of the *Hortensius*. Once again he turned to the scriptures, but unlike what had happened thirteen years before, the Bible no longer seemed to him unpolished in its language, and he learned that with the help of allegory and Platonism he could now surmount all difficulties. His conversion, ca. August 15, 386, was the culmination of a process in which the influences of Paul and the Platonists, the allegorical method, and monastic models played a part. In the literary fiction of the garden scene with its "Take and read," A. portrays his experience of final conversion. The account in *conf.* 7.26f. is confirmed by the dialogue *De Academicis* (2.5), which was written in November, 386 (thirteen years before the composition of the *conf.*).

A. put an end to his lectures on rhetoric, took a leave from teaching, and withdrew to a country estate, Cassiciacum, near Milan, together with his friends, his mother, and his son Adeodatus (Aug.-Nov., 386). There he wrote the early dialogues: *Acad.*, *beata v.*, *ord.* After the school holidays he abandoned his teaching office completely and, together with Adeodatus, enrolled as candidate for baptism at Easter 387. At this same period, in order to complete the Cassiciacum dialogues, he wrote the (unfinished) *Soliloquiorum libri* and the *Disciplinarum libros*. The last-named is lost except for the section *De grammatica*. These works were begun after his baptism and completed to some extent in Africa.

A. was baptized by Ambrose during the night of Easter (April 24/25) in 387. His conversion was complete and A. resolved to return to Africa. At Ostia, the port of departure for Africa, A. and Monica had a vision in which God gave them an experience of him. Shortly afterward, Monica died of a fever (*conf.* 9.27-33). Monica's death and the invasion of Italy by Maximus, a usurper, prevented the departure, and because of the winter A. returned to Rome. During this period he composed *De moribus ecclesiae catholicae et de moribus Manichaeorum*, *De animae quantitate*, and *De libero arbitrio*. These works marked the beginning of a campaign against the Manichees. While in Rome, A. was deeply impressed (*mor.* 1.70) by the piety and discipline of the monasteries, and this strengthened his determination to live an ascetic life in Africa. The defeat of Maximus in July 388 made it once again possible to take ship, and in the fall A. returned to Thagaste by way of Carthage (*c. litt. Pet.* 3.20; *civ.* 22.8; *cur. mort.* 13). There he formed a religious group that busied itself with prayer, study, and writing (*vita* 3.2). At this time, the

De Genesi adversus Manichaeos was written, the *De musica* was completed, and the dialogue *De magistro* was put on paper. With these works A. had made a name for himself as a writer and had become an influential person in African Christianity. In 390 he wrote *De vera religione* and in it set down a comprehensive philosophy of religion against the Manichees.

On his journeys A. avoided all cities in which the bishop's seat was vacant, lest he be forced to accept the office of bishop. When he went to Hippo Regius in Jan. 391 in order to win over a friend there for monastic life in Thagaste, he also attended the liturgy. The elderly, Greek-speaking Bishop Valerius asked for the help of a priest proficient in Latin, and the community called upon A. for this office (*vita* 4). After a short period of Bible study (*ep.* 21.1-3), A. was ordained a priest and took up his priestly duties, beginning with the instruction of candidates for baptism (*s.* 216.1). In order that he might continue his monastic form of life, Valerius gave him a house and garden near the Catholic basilica (*s.* 355.1; *vita* 5.1).

While still a priest, A. began his activity in the church politics of Africa. In his letter of congratulations to the newly chosen primate, Aurelius of Carthage (392), he called for the elimination of abuses (veneration of the martyrs at their tombs) (*ep.* 22; *conf.* 6.2). Aurelius recognized what a significant person A. was and had him give the opening address at the Council of Hippo, Oct. 8, 393; this was published as *De fide et symbolo* (*retr.* 1.17). As a result of these sermons, priests were now allowed to preach occasionally.

In addition to his activity as a preacher, A.'s main task was to suppress Manichaeism by his writing. In 391/392 he wrote three treatises: *De utilitate credendi*, *De duabus animabus*, and *Acta contra Fortunatum Manichaeum*. He began 393/394 with a commentary on Genesis: *De Genesi ad litteram imperfectus* (*retr.* 1.18), and he completed his commentary on the Sermon on the Mount: *De sermone Domini in monte* (*retr.* 1.19).

As he began his pastoral work, A. became aware of Donatism and explained its origins to the people in his → abecedary *Psalmus contra partem Donati* (393). At the same time, but at a more theol. level, he wrote *Contra epistulam Donati heretici* (*retr.* 1.21) and rounded off his literary work with the treatise *Contra Adimanti Manichaei discipulum* (*retr.* 1.22). As a result of his deeper study of the Bible, he was now in a position to refute the Manichean arguments more effectively. A fruit of these studies was the commentaries on the letters of Paul to the Romans and the

Galatians, which A. wrote in 394-395. In these works we already hear the *doctor gratiae*.

At the request of Bishop Valerius and with the agreement of Megalius of Calama, primate of Numidia (*vita* 8), A. was consecrated a bishop in mid-395 while Valerius was still alive. A. realized later on that his consecration had been contrary to canon 8 of Nicaea, and he took care that his own successor, Eraclius, should be consecrated bishop only after his death (*ep.* 213.4). During this time we can see A. clearly turning his attention to the doctrine on grace when he answers questions sent him by Simplicianus of Milan, Ambrose's successor (*Ad Simplicianum*).

A.'s life as a bishop was filled with the usual duties of that office (*vita* 19.2-5). Three areas in particular made demands on the bishop of Hippo: in addition to his usual duties as pastor of a church (which included the settling of civil complaints and acting as notary for documents at the *audientia episcopalis*), there was an extensive activity as preacher, in Carthage as well as in Hippo; in addition, involvement in the conciliar activity of the African church; finally, literary activity in the struggle against heresy, which also meant an extensive correspondence. While still in the early years of his episcopate (396-397), A. wrote a further work against the Manichees, *Contra epistulam Manichaei quam vocant fundamenti*, and a general treatise on the Chr. way of life, *De agone christiano*.

Donatism now thrust its way into the foreground of his interests. But since peaceful relations could not be developed because of social tensions, the controversy shifted in an increasing measure to the civil terrain. As a result, A.'s activity in the struggle involved three activities: literary works, disputations, and the invocation of the civil powers. After a Donatist attack on Possidius (end of 403), the latter and A. resolved to appeal to *Cod. Theod.* 16.5.21 and demand the intervention of the state. As early as June 404, the Council of Carthage appealed to the imperial authorities against the heretics (*Reg. eccl. Carth. exc.* 93). Until 410 these efforts bore no fruit; on Aug. 25, 410, however, Emperor Honorius issued an edict that an assembly be convoked which would settle disputed issues in the form of a trial. This *Collatio Carthaginensis* brought together around 288 Donatist and 286 Catholic bishops on March 1 and June 8, 411, with Tribune Marcellinus presiding. As was expected, Marcellinus gave judgment in favor of the Catholics; the Donatists appealed to the emperor, who rejected their claim on Jan. 30, 412. A. took part, both through personal contacts with individual

Donatist bishops and through his writings, in the process that then began of bringing the Donatists back with the help of pressure from the state.

In the final phase of the Donatist controversy Pelagianism was already entering the field of A.'s theol. interests. This was, however, shouldered aside for a short time by the fall of Rome in 410, to which A. responded in his large-scale apology, the *De civitate Dei*.

A.'s struggle with Pelagianism had two phases. He mobilized the African church against → Pelagius and his disciple → Caelestius; in 411 the Council of Carthage condemned Caelestius, but only in 417 was Pelagius himself condemned by Innocent I. Then the rehabilitation of Pelagius by Zosimus compelled A. and the African church to enter the fray again; with the help of the court in Ravenna an imperial condemnation of Pelagius and Caelestius was obtained (April 30, 418).

From 418 until his death A. was completely occupied by the struggle against Pelagianism. Pelagius himself disappeared after his condemnation, but his place was taken for the first time by → Julian of Eclanum, an adversary who was the equal of the elderly A. But A.'s extensive writings against Julian also elicited resistance in southern France, which protested strongly against his teaching on predestination. This movement, under the leadership of John Cassian, distanced itself from A.'s thinking. The penetration of the German tribes into Italy and later into North Africa caused A. to take up the cudgels against Arianism as well as against Pelagianism (*vita* 17.1-6). On Sept. 26, 426, A. had Eraclius, a presbyter, elected as his successor, in order to give himself the freedom for a critical examination of his writings. The fruit of this revision was the *Retractationes*, which makes it possible to construct a chronology of A.'s works.

In May 429, the Vandals under Geiseric made their way into North Africa (*vita* 28.4-13). Hippo Regius was besieged for fourteen months. In the third month A. was stricken with a fever. He had the penitential Psalms placed on the wall of his sickroom; he died on Aug. 28, 430. Shortly after his death, an imperial invitation to attend the Council of Ephesus reached his residence.

S: *vita*, A. A. R. Bastiaensen, Vita di Agostino (Verona, 1975) [text/Italian trans.]. — A. von Harnack, A.' Leben (Berlin, 1930) [German trans.].
L: G. Bonner, A. (uita): AugL 1:519-550 (literature). — P. Brown, A. of Hippo (London, 1967). — H.-J. Diesner, Possidius und A. (Berlin, 1962), 350-365. — J. J. O'Donnell, A. (Boston, 1985). — C. Kirwan, A. (New York, 1989) (London, 1991). — M. Marshall, The Restless Heart (Grand Rapids, 1987). — F. van der Meer, A. der Seelsorger

(Cologne, 1958). — C. Mohrmann, Zwei frühchr. Bischofsviten: Vita Ambrosii, Vita Augustini: AÖAW. PH 112 (1975) 307-331. — O. Perler, Les voyages de saint Augustin (Paris, 1969). — G. Wills, St. A. (London, 1999).

II. Works: A.'s works were, with few exceptions, occasioned by controversy, questions put to him, and pastoral needs. It is appropriate therefore to divide the works acc. to their occasions.

W: The abbreviations of Augustine's works follow the AugL (Augustinus Lexikon) 1:26*-41*; dating and reference to the *Retractiones* are included. Augustine's writings can be found in PL 32-47. These volumes will be referred to if no critical edition exists. Augustine's writings also exist in CD format: C. Mayer (ed.), Corpus Augustinianum Gissense (CAG) (Basel, 1996).
An overview of the editions and translations of A's work is offered by W. Eckermann, A. Krümmel, Repertorium annotatum operum et translationum S. A. (Latin editions and German trans.ations) (Würzburg, 1992) and A. Keller, Translationes Patristicae Graecae et Latinae (Stuttgart, 1997), 89-151.

A. Autobiographical Literature

(a) *Confessiones* (*conf.*; between the end of 397 and 401; *retr.* 2.6). In looking back over his writings A. observes of the *conf.* that they praise God and lift up the affections to him: "They had this effect on me while I was writing them, and they have the same when I am reading them. . . . They please and continue to please many people" (*retr.* 2.6). Before his death he noted that of all his works the *conf.* had received the greatest approval (*persev.* 53).

The *conf.* have three parts. Books 1-9 tell the story of A.'s life up to his baptism. Book 10 tells of his relationship with God until the writing of the *conf.* In books 11-13 A. interprets the story of creation. Some books have a preface. Books 10 and 13 end with an epilogue. The division just given of the thirteen books raises the controverted question of the unity of the work. Seven different efforts have been made to bring out the unity: (1) the title *conf.* covers them all; (2) the theol. approach; (3) the fit between the *conf.* and A.'s life; (4) approach through the interpretation of Genesis; (5) formal characteristics of compositional technique; (6) study of the genre; (7) the *conf.* as exhortation. None of these efforts has settled the matter conclusively.

The preface of book 1 (1.1-6) can be viewed as a paradigm of the entire work: A.'s intention is to show God to be Lord of humankind and the world. For this reason, exact historical description is secondary to theol. interpretation. Turning points and important single events are noted in order to make clear through them A.'s errors and God's guidance. The tenth book describes A.'s present relationship with God by beginning with an analysis of *memoria* (10.8-26). Books 10-13 on the story of creation are introduced by a meditation on time (11.14-20). The *conf.* end with praise of the everlasting sabbath that knows no evening (13.35-38).

W: P. Knöll, CSEL 33. — L. Verheijen, CCL 27. — M. Skutella, H. Jürgens, W. Schaub (Stuttgart, ²1969) [text]. — J. Bernhart (Darmstadt, ²1960) [text/German trans.]. — M. Boulding (New York, 1997) — J. J. O'Donnell (Oxford, 1992) [text/English trans./comm.]. — A. Solignac, BAug 13/14 (Paris, 1962) [text/French trans./comm.].
L: D. Capps (ed.), The Hunger of the Heart. Reflections on the Conf. of A. (West Lafayette, 1990). — P. Courcelle, Recherches sur les conf. de saint A. (Paris, ²1968). — idem, Les conf. de St. A. dans la tradition littéraire (Paris, 1963). — U. Duchrow, Der Aufbau von A.' Schriften conf. und De Trinitate: ZThK 62 (1965) 338-367. — E. Feldmann, conf.: AugL 1:1134-1193 (literature). — K. Flasch, Was ist Zeit? (Frankfurt a.M., 1993). — G. N. Knaur, Die Ps.-zitate in den Konfessionen A.' (Göttingen, 1955). — D. V. Meconi, The incarnation and the role of participation in conf.: AugSt 29/2 (1998) 61-75. — H. de Noronha Galvao, Die existentielle Gotteserkenntnis bei A. (Einsiedeln, 1981). — R. Severson, The Conf. of St. A. An Annotated Bibliography of Modern Criticism, 1888-1995 (London, 1996). — G. Söhngen, Der Aufbau der aug. Gedächtnislehre: idem, Die Einheit in der Theologie (Munich, 1952), 63-100. — F. M. Young, Genre of the work: AugSt 30 (1999) 1-16.

(b) *Retractationes* (*retr.*; 426/427). We are in the fortunate position of having two catalogues of A.'s writings: A.'s own *retr.* and the *Indiculum* of → Possidius. After taking a sabbatical leave from his episcopal duties A. reviewed all of his writings. In the preface to the *retr.* he observes: "I intend to review my works, books, letters, and treatises with almost the strictness of a judge and to treat what offends me with as it were the pencil of a censor." A. reviewed his ninety-three books. His death kept him from a review of the letters and sermons. The *retr.* are something unique in the history of literature. They give us important information on chronology and authenticity and for the discussion of titles. In addition, they show the lines along which A.'s thinking developed.

W: P. Knöll, CSEL 36. — A. Mutzenbecher, CCL 57. — C. J. Perl (Paderborn, 1976) [text/German trans.]. — M. I. Bogan (Washington, 1968) [English trans.]. — G. Bardy, BAug 12 (Paris, 1950) [text/French trans./comm.].
L: B. Altaner, In der Studierstube des hl. A.: idem, Kleine patristische Schriften (Berlin, 1967), 3-56. — M. J. Lagrange, Les rétractations exégétiques de saint A.: Miscellanea Agostiniana 2 (Rome, 1931), 375-395. — G. Madec, Introduction aux "Révisions" et à la lecture des œuvres de saint A. (Paris, 1996).

B. Philosophical and Antipagan Writings
Both before his conversion and later on, what A.

learned was Christianity of a Platonic kind. Any other Christianity was alien to the Greek- and Latin-speaking worlds. To that extent, A.'s encounter with Neoplatonism (Plotinus; later, Porphyry to a greater extent) and his critical analysis of it are an essential component of his philosophical writings. The themes thereby set for him were the following:

(1) Debate with the skepticism of antiquity and the teaching of the ancients on happiness; knowledge of the nature of God and the soul; the immortality of the soul; the doctrine of the ideas; the hierarchical division of the created order. (2) Harking back to Varro, A. follows up the idea of a complete description of the *artes liberales* in order to make pagan education fruitful for the Chr. church. (3) After the fall of Rome (410), A. begins a debate with the pagan philosophy of history, and espec. with Porphyry, in order to show that there is only one mediator, Jesus Christ, but also in order to free Christians from the reproach of having caused the fall of Rome. *De civitate Dei* is the last great apology from the early church.

On 1: (a) *De ordine* (*ord.*; 386; *retr.* 1.3) deals with the orderly structure of the world but remains in the area of the provisional explanation provided by the *artes liberales*.

W: P. Knöll, CSEL 63:121-185. — W. M. Green, CCL 29:89-137. — J. Doignon, BAug 4/2 (Paris, 1997) [text/French trans./comm.]. — B. R. Voss, Über die Ordnung (Zurich/Munich, 1972) [German trans.].
L: K. Flasch, A. (Stuttgart, 1993).

(b) *De Academicis* (*Acad.*; 386/387; *retr.* 1.1): A. criticizes the skepticism of antiquity and maintains that because of the incarnation a way to truth is now possible.

W: P. Knöll, CSEL 63:3-81. — W. M. Green, CCL 29:3-61. — B. R. Voss, Gegen die Akademiker: Philosophische Frühdialoge (Zurich/Munich, 1972) [text/German trans.]. — R. Jolivet, BAug 4 (Paris, 1948) [text/French trans./comm.]. — M. P. Garvey (Milwaukee, Wisc., 1957) [English trans.]. — L. Nutrimento (Treviso, 1957) [Italian trans./comm.].
L: B. J. Aiggs, St. A. Against the Academicians: Tr. 7 (1949-1951) 73-93. — T. Fuhrer, A. Acad. (Berlin, 1997) (literature). — eadem, Das Kriterium der Wahrheit in A.' Acad.: VigChr 46 (1992) 257-275. — G. Madec, Pour l'interprétation de Acad. 2, 2, 5: REA 17 (1971) 322-328. — G. Pfligersdorffer, Bemerkungen zu den Prooemien von A.' Acad. 1 und De beata vita: idem, A. Praeceptori (Salzburg, 1987), 33-58. — G. Reale, A. e il Acad.: L'opera letteraria di A. tra Cassiciacum e Milano. Testi e studi 2 (Palermo, 1987), 13-30.

(c) *De beata vita* (*beata v.*; Nov. 13-15, 396; *retr.* 1.2): The supreme good which everyone seeks is identified with the enjoyment of God (*Deo perfrui* 4.34).

W: P. Knöll, CSEL 63:89-116. — W. M. Green, CCL 29:65-85. — F. Schwarz-Kirchbauer, Philosophische Frühdialoge (Zurich/Munich, 1972) [text/German trans.]. — R. A. Brown (Washington, 1944) [English trans./comm.]. — J. Doignon, BAug 4/1 (Paris, 1986) [text/French trans./comm.].
L: W. Beierwaltes, "Regio beatitudinis." Zu A.' Begriff des glücklichen Lebens (Heidelberg, 1981). — P. Courcelle, Les premières "Confessions" de saint A.: REL 21/22 (1942) 155-174.

(d) *Soliloquia* (*sol.*; 387; *retr.* 1.4): The adopted agenda, "God and the soul," points to the spiritual nature of both.

W: W. Hörmann, CSEL 89:3-98. — P. de Labriolle, BAug 5 (Paris, 1948) [text/French trans./comm.]. — H. Fuchs (Zurich, ²1986) [German trans.]. — G. Watson (Warminster, 1990) [text/English trans.].
L: H. P. Müller, A.' sol. (Basel, 1954). — H. Stirnimann, Grund u. Gründer des Alls, A.' Gebet in den Selbstgesprächen (Fribourg, Switzerland, 1992).

(e) *De immortalitate animae* (*imm. an.*; 387; *retr.* 1.5) and (f) *De animae quantitate* (*an. quant.*; 387/388; *retr.* 1.8): both writings delve further into the theme of the *sol.*

W: *imm. an.*, W. Hörmann, CSEL 89:101-128. — H. Fuchs, H. P. Müller, Die Unsterblichkeit der Seele (Zurich, ²1986) [text/German trans.]. — P. de Labriolle, BAug 5 (Paris, 1948) [text/French trans./comm.]. — G. Watson (Warminster, 1990) [text/English trans.]. — *an. quant.*, W. Hörmann, CSEL 89:131-231. — K. H. Lütcke, Die Größe der Seele (Zurich/Munich, 1973) [text/German trans.]. — R. Jolivet, BAug 4 (Paris, 1989) [text/French trans./comm.].
L: G. J. P. O'Daly, A.'s Philosophy of Mind (London, 1987). — K. H. Lütcke, *an. quant.*: AugL 1:350-356.

(g) *De libero arbitrio* (*lib. arb.*; 387-388; *retr.* 1.9): A. takes up the question of the origin of evil and its connection with free will.

W: W. M. Green, CSEL 74 = CCL 29:211-321. — W. Thimme, Vom freien Willen (Zurich, 1962) [German trans.]. — G. Madec, BAug 6 (Paris, 1976) [text/French trans./comm.]. — F. de Capitano (Milan, 1987) [text/Italian trans./comm.]. — T. Williams (Indianapolis, 1993) [English trans.].
L: G. Madec, Saint A. et la philosophie (Paris, 1996). — W. M. Neumann, Die Stellung des Gottesbeweises in A.' lib. arb. (Hildesheim/Zurich/New York, 1986). — R. J. O'Connel, lib. arb. 1, Stoicism Revisited: AugSt 1 (1970) 49-68. — L. F. Pizzolato, lib. arb., Lectio Augustini 6 (Palermo, 1990). — E. O. Springsted, Will and Order: The Moral Self in A. lib. arb.: AugSt 29/2 (1998) 77-96.

(h) *De diversis quaestionibus octoginta tribus* (*div. qu.*; 388-397; *retr.* 1.26): The work brings together theol., phil., and exeget. questions.

W: A. Mutzenbecher, CCL 44A. — C. J. Perl (Paderborn, 1972) [text/German trans.]. — J. A. Beckaert, BAug 10 (Paris, 1952) [text/French trans./comm.]. — D. L. Mosher (Washington, 1982) [English trans.].
L: G. Bardy, La littérature patristique des Quaestiones et Responsiones sur l'Écriture sainte (Paris, 1933).

(i) *De magistro* (*mag.*; 388-391; *retr.* 1.12): A. formulates a theory of learning inspired by Plato, according to which understanding is possible only with the help of Christ, the only true teacher.

W: *mag.*, G. Weigel, CSEL 77:3-55. — K.-D. Daur, CCL 29:157-203. — G. Madec, BAug 6 (Paris, 1976) [text/French trans./comm.]. — B. Jolibert (Paris, 1988) [text/French trans.]. — R. P. Russell (Washington, 1968) [English trans.]. — E. Schadel (Bamberg, 1975) [German trans./comm.]. — G. Weigel, Der Lehrer (Zurich/Munich, 1973) [German trans.].
L: A. Locher, A.' Erkenntnislehre in dem Dialog mag. und das Problem ihrer Interpretation (Tübingen, 1960). — G. Madec, Analyse du mag.: REA 21 (1975) 63-71. — R. A. Markus, St. A. on Signs: Phron. 2 (1957) 60-83.

On 2: Of the planned complete presentation of the liberal arts the only works written were (a) *De dialectica* (*dial.*; 387; *retr.* 1.6) and (b) *De musica* (*mus.*; 388-390; *retr.* 1.11).

There is disagreement on A.'s authorship of (c) *De grammatica: Regulae* (*gramm.*; 388; *retr.* 1.6).

W: *dial.*, PL 32:1409-1420. — B. Darrel-Jackson, J. Pinborg (Dordrecht/Boston, 1975) [text/English trans./comm.]. — H. Ruef, A. über Semiotik u. Sprache. Sprachtheoretische Analysen zu A.' Schrift dial. (Bern, 1981) [German trans./comm.]. — *mus.*, PL 32:1081-1194. — W. F. Jackson Knight (London, 1949) [English trans.]. — C. J. Perl (Paderborn, ³1962) [German trans.]. — G. Finaert, F. J. Thonnard, BAug 7 (Paris, 1947) [text/French trans./comm.]. — *gramm.*, PL 32:1385-1408. — GrLat 5, 496-524 [text]. — C. F. Weber, Aurelii A. Ars grammatica breviata (Marburg, 1861) [text]. — M. Bettettini (Milan, 1993) [text/Italian trans.].
L: I. Hadot, Erziehung u. Bildung bei A.: C. Mayer, K. H. Chelius, Internationales Symposion (Würzburg, 1987), 99-130. — A. Keller, Aurelius A. u. die Musik (Würzburg, 1993) (literature on *mus.*). — V. A. Law, St. A.'s gramm. Lost or Found?: RechAug 19 (1984) 155-183. — K. Sallmann, A.' Rettung der Musik u. die antike Mimesistheorie: FS H. Hörner (Heidelberg, 1990), 81-92.

On 3: (a) *De excidio urbis Romae* (*exc. urb.*; after Aug. 24, 410): A sermon delivered by A. shortly after receiving the news of the fall of Rome. The themes later discussed in *De civitate Dei* (destiny of the just; suffering and punishment) are already touched on here. There is a strong emphasis on Job as patient sufferer, a prelude to *civ.*

W: M.-V. O'Reilly, CCL 46:249-262. — eadem (Washington, 1955) [text/English trans./comm.]. — J. A. Fischer, Die Völkerwanderung im Urteil der zeitgenössischen Schriftsteller Galliens unter Einbeziehung des hl. A. (Heidelberg, 1948), 60-69 [German trans.].

L: P. Courcelle, Histoire littéraire des Grandes Invasions Germaniques (Paris, ³1964), 31-77.

(b) *De civitate Dei* (*civ.* 412-426; *retr.* 2.43): This apology, occasioned by the fall of Rome and written in defense of Christianity, seeks to show, first of all, that the pagan gods are of no use either in this life (books 1-5) or in the life to come (books 6-10). This negative first part is followed by a positive second part (books 11-22) in which the course of history is depicted as a continuous struggle between the *civitas Dei* and the *civitas diaboli*: origin (11-14), development (15-18), and end (19-22). This presentation corresponds to the Bible's view of history as a whole from its beginning (Genesis) to its appointed end (Revelation); *civitas Dei* is not the same as the visible church nor is *civitas diaboli* identical with the state. As *ecclesia ab Abel*, the *civitas Dei* is a church beyond history, while the present course of history is devalued as being a history of perdition. The destruction of the pagan gods bolsters the proof that there is only one mediator between God and humanity, Jesus Christ (against Porphyry). The philosophy of history developed in *civ.* has left its mark on the West down to the present time.

W: E. Hoffmann, CSEL 40. — B. Dombart, A. Kalb, CCL 47, 48. — eadem, J. Divjak (Stuttgart, ³1981) [text]. — W. Thimme, Vom Gottesstaat (Zurich, 1977) [German trans.]. — G. Bardy, BAug 33-37 (Paris, 1959/60) [text/French trans./comm.]. — M. Dods (New York, 1993) [English trans.]. — R. W. Dyson (Cambridge/New York, 1998) [text/English trans.].
L: E. Cavalcanti (ed.), Il civ. L'opera, l'interpretazioni, l'influsso (Rome, 1996). — D. Donnelly (ed.), The City of God. A Collection of Critical Essays (New York, 1995). — idem, E. Scherman, A.'s civ. An Annotated Bibliography of Modern Criticism, 1960-1990 (New York, 1991). — C. Horn (ed.), A.' civ., Klassiker Auslegen 11 (Berlin, 1997) (literature). — K. Löwith, Weltgeschichte u. Heilsgeschehen (Stuttgart, 1953). — G. J. P. O'Daly, civ.: AugL 1:969-1010 (literature). — J. van Oort, Jerusalem and Babylon. A Study into A.'s City of God (Leiden, 1991). — Q. P. Taylor, A. and Political Thought: A Revisionist View: Aug(L) 48 (1998) 287-303.

C. Anti-Manichean Writings

A. was a Manichee for nine years. Admittedly he was only a "hearer" (*auditor*) and did not belong to the innermost circle of Manichees, but during these formative years he received influences that had deep and lasting effects on his piety and his understanding of life. The themes of his anti-Manichean writings have as their starting point the question: Whence

comes evil? He repeatedly discusses three themes: (1) Evil is only a lack of goodness and does not have a substance of its own. (2) The OT and NT God are one and the same; the good God of the NT cannot be played off against the evil God of the OT. (3) Catholic teaching has greater credibility and consistency.

1. Anti-Manichean Commentaries on the Bible. The controversy with the Manichees was largely over the exegesis of Genesis. For this reason A. twice commented on Genesis in the years 388-399:

(a) *De Genesi adversus Manichaeos* (*Gn. adv. Man.*; 388/390; *retr.* 1.10) and

(b) *De Genesi ad litteram liber imperfectus* (*Gn. litt. imp.*; 393/394; *retr.*1.18).

W: *Gn. adv. Man.*, D. Weber, CSEL 91. — R. J. Teske, FaCh 84 (Washington, 1991), 47-141 [English trans.] — *Gn. litt. imp.*, J. Zycha, CSEL 28/1:459-503. — R. J. Teske, FaCh 84 (Washington, 1991), 145-188 [English trans.].
L: A. Allgeier, Der Einfluß des Manichäismus auf die exegetische Fragestellung bei A.: M. Grabmann, J. Mausbach, AA, FS der Görresgesellschaft (Cologne, 1930), 1 13. — M. M. Gorman, The Text of St. A.'s Gn. litt. imp.: RechAug 20 (1985) 65-86. — A. Zacher, De Genesi contra Manichaeos libri duo, Diss. (Rome, 1961).

2. Writings on the Grounds of Faith: (a) *De utilitate credendi* (*util. cred.*; 391/392; *retr.* 1.14): Investigates the act of faith, not the content of faith, and sharply contrasts faith and insight.

W: J. Zycha, CSEL 25/1:3-48. — A. Hoffmann, FC 9. — J. Pegon, G. Madec, BAug 8 (Paris, 1982) [text/French trans./comm.].
L: A. Hoffmann, A.' Schrift util. cred. (Münster, 1997).

(b) *De duabus animabus* (*duab. an.*; 391/392; *retr* 1.15): Against the erroneous teaching of the Manichees that the human being has two souls.

W: J. Zycha, CSEL 25/1:51-80. — C. J. Perl (Paderborn, 1966), 109-165 [text/German trans.]. — R. Jolivet, M. Jourjon, BAug 17 (Paris, 1961) [text/French trans./comm.].
L: C. Conturier, La structure métaphysique de l' homme d'après saint A.: AM 1:543-550. — E. L. Fortin, Christianisme et culture philosophique au Vᵉ siècle. La querelle de l'âme en Occident (Paris, 1959). — I. P. Lamelas, duab. an. XII, 17-18: Anton. 73 (1998) 733-741.

(c) *Contra Adimantum* (*c. Adim.*; 393; *retr.* 1.22): On a series of passages of scripture which the Manichees claim contradict one another. A. tries to show the harmony between the OT and the NT. The work is important for A.'s exegetical principles.

W: J. Zycha, CSEL 25/1:115-190. — R. Jolivet, M. Jourjon, BAug 17 (Paris, 1961) [text/French trans./comm.].

L: F. Decret, Adimantum Manichei discipulum (Contra-): AugL 1:90-94.

(d) *Contra epistulam Manichaei quam vocant fundamenti* (*c. ep. Man.*; 396; *retr.* 2.2): The *ep. Man.* seems to have been a "Handbook of Doctrine" that was widely circulated in North Africa. A. refutes it in order to win back his friend Honoratus, whom A. himself had led into Manichaeism.

S: E. Feldmann, Die "Epistula Fundamenti" der nordafrikanischen Manichäer (Altenberge, 1987) [text fragments/German trans./comm.].
W: J. Zycha, CSEL 25/1:193-248. — R. Jolivet, M. Jourjon, BAug 17 (Paris, 1961) [text/French trans./comm.]. — R. Stothert, NPNF 4:129-150 [English trans.].
L: E. Feldmann, Der Einfluss des Hortensius und des Manichäismus auf das Denken des jungen A. vor 373 (Münster, 1975).

(e) *Contra Faustum Manichaeum* (*c. Faust.*; 397/398; *retr.* 2.7): Faustus of Milevis (d. before 410) was a leading thinker among the North African Manichees; he was active first in Rome and then in Carthage from 393 on. A.'s meeting with Faustus (*conf.* 7.3.3) led him away from Manichaeism because of his disillusionment with Faustus's vague teachings. The lost work of → Faustus in defense of his teaching, with its radical criticism of the OT, can be reconstructed from A.'s response.

W: J. Zycha, CSEL 25/1:251-797. — R. Stothert, NPNF 4:155-345 [English trans.].
L: A. Bruckner, Faustus v. Mileve (Basel, 1901). — F. Decret, Aspects du manichéisme dans l'Afrique romaine (Paris, 1970). — P. Monceaux, Le Manichéen Faustus (Paris, 1933).

(f) *De natura boni* (*nat. b.*; 399; *retr.* 2.9): Provides a very compressed summary of A.'s arguments against the Manichean doctrine of evil and against the doctrine of the two principles.

W: J. Zycha, CSEL 25/2:855-889. — A. Noon (Washington, 1955) [text/English trans./comm.]. — B. Roland-Gosselin, BAug 1 (Paris, 1949) [text/French trans./comm.]. — G. Reale (Milan, 1995) [text/Italian trans.].

(g) *Contra Secundinum Manichaeum* (*c. Sec.*; 399; *retr.* 2.10): Secundinus, a Manichean "hearer," whom A. knew only from his books, wrote A. a letter urging him to return. A.'s answer contains the arguments he uses elsewhere, here with a certain amount of rhetoric.

W: J. Zycha, CSEL 25/2:905-947. — R. Jolivet, M. Jourjon, BAug 17 (Paris, 1961) [text/French trans./comm.].

3. Debates with Manichees: A. often engaged in public debates with theol. opponents. These were written down by stenographers and later published by A.
(a) *Acta contra Fortunatum Manichaeum* (*c. Fort.*; August 27/28, 392; *retr.* 1.16): Fortunatus, a Manichean priest whom A. acknowledges as a very successful missionary, debates with A. on the "law." A. subjects himself to his first public test as a priest of the *Catholica*.

W: J. Zycha, CSEL 25/1:83-112. — R. Jolivet, M. Jourjon, BAug 17 (Paris, 1961) [text/French trans./comm.]. — E. Rutzenhöfer: Aug. 42 (1992) 5-72 [German trans./comm.].
L: F. Decret, c. Fort.: AugL 1:53-58.

(b) *Contra Felicem Manichaeum* (*c. Fel.*; Dec. 7/12, 404; *retr.* 2.8): Discussion of the problem of free will. Felix became a convert at the end of the debate.

W: J. Zycha, CSEL 25/2:801-852. — R. Jolivet, M. Jourjon, BAug 17 (Paris, 1961) [text/French trans./comm.].
L: F. Decret, Aspects du manichéisme dans l'Afrique romaine (Paris, 1970), 74-76. — PAC 417f.

4. Writings on Way of Life: The presentation of Catholic doctrine is accompanied by the proof that the moral teaching of the Cath. church is superior to that of the Manichean sect.
De moribus ecclesiae catholicae et de moribus Manichaeorum (*mor.*; Rome, 388, completed in Thagaste, 389-390; *retr.* 1.7): That, being the supreme Good, God must be loved, that the two Testaments are in agreement; and that Chr. asceticism is superior: these are the themes of the first book, while the second treats of the doctrine of the three seals and the problem of evil.

W: *mor.*, J. B. Bauer, CSEL 90. — B. Roland-Gosselin, BAug 1 (Paris, 1949) [text/French trans./comm.]. — P. Keseling, Das Ethos der Christen (Münster, 1948) [German trans. of book 1]. — D. A. und I. J. Gallagher (Washington, 1966) [text/English trans.].
L: J. K. Coyle, A.'s mor. (Fribourg, Switzerland, 1978).

D. Anti-Donatist Literature
The controversy with Donatism meant a criticism of a pre-Constantinian ideal of holiness and of the ecclesiology connected with it. The two central themes of the anti-Donatist debate were: the validity of a sacrament despite the unworthiness of its minister, and the appeal not (as with the Donatists) to a church limited to Africa but to the universal church in which sinners and just must, like chaff and grain, remain to the end of time. The year 411, in which the Conference of Carthage condemned the Donatists, marked a shift. From that point on A. turned his

attention to individual Donatist bishops in order to urge them to obey the decree of 411.

1. Writings before 411: (a) *Psalmus contra partem Donati* (*ps. c. Don.*; 394; *retr.* 1.20): An → abecedary in which A. describes the history of the Donatist schism. The psalm was intended for communal singing and repeats like a refrain the invitation to judge rightly.

W: M. Petschenig, CSEL 51:2-15. — W. Geerlings: FS H. J. Pottmeyer (Freiburg i.Br., 1994), 39-65 [text/German trans./comm.]. — G. Finaert, Y. Congar, BAug 28 (Paris, 1963) [text/French trans./comm.]. — R. Anastasi (Padua, 1957), 44-70 [text/Italian trans./comm.].

(b) *Contra epistulam Parmeniani* (*c. ep. Parm.*; 400; *retr.* 2.17): Parmenian, successor to Donatus, had written a letter to Tyconius, a Donatist theologian who defended the universality of the church, in order to denigrate the latter's letter, which could have been profitable to the Catholics. A. was urged to comment on Parmenian's letter.

W: M. Petschenig, CSEL 51:19-141. — G. Finaert, Y. Congar, BAug 28 (Paris, 1963) [text/French trans./comm.].
L: W. Frend, The Donatist Church (Oxford, 1952). — B. Kriegbaum, Kirche der Traditoren u. Kirche der Märtyrer (Innsbruck, 1986). — P. Monceaux, Histoire littéraire de l'Afrique chrétienne 4-7 (Paris, 1912-1923).

(c) *De baptismo* (*bapt.*; 400/401; *retr.* 2.18): A.'s most fundamental anti-Donatist work, in which he refutes the thesis that only pure ministers can administer the sacraments. A. distinguishes between validity and effectiveness in the sacraments: the sacraments are valid even if the minister is unworthy, since Christ is the real bestower.

W: M. Petschenig, CSEL 51:145-375. — G. Finaert, G. Bavaud, BAug 29 (Paris, 1964) [text/French trans./comm.].
L: F. Hoffmann, Der Kirchenbegriff des hl. A. (Munich, ²1978). — J. Ratzinger, Volk u. Haus Gottes in A.' Lehre von der Kirche (Munich, 1954). — A. Schindler, bapt.: AugL 1:573-582 (literature). — W. Simonis, Ecclesia visibilis et invisibilis (Frankfurt a.M., 1970).

(d) *Contra litteras Petiliani* (*c. litt. Pet.*; 401-405; *retr.* 2.25): A.'s answer in three books to the literary production of → Petilian (*ep. ad presbyteros et diaconos*).

W: M. Petschenig, CSEL 52:3-227. — G. Finaert, B. Quinot, BAug 30 (Paris, 1967) [text/French trans./comm.]. — A. Lombardi (Opere di Sant'A. 15, 2, 1) (Rome, 1999) [text/Italian trans.].
L: G. Bavaud, Le mystère de la sainteté de l'Église: RechAug 3 (1965) 160-166. — G. Crespin, Ministère et Sainteté (Paris, 1965).

(e) *De unitate ecclesiae = Ad catholicos fratres* (*cath. fr.*; 401/402): This letter, not mentioned in the *retr.* but listed by Possidius (*Indiculum* 3) under the title *Ep. contra quos supra ad catholicos fratres*, has been regarded since the Maurists as possibly not from Augustine.

W: M. Petschenig, CSEL 52:231-322. — G. Finaert, Y. Congar, BAug 28 (Paris, 1963) [text/French trans./comm.].
L: M. Moreau, cath. fr.: AugL 1:807-815.

(f) *Ad Cresconium Grammaticum partis Donati* (*Cresc.*; 405-406; *retr.* 2.26): Cresconius, a Donatist layman, had attacked A. in the usual African fashion, in an "open letter." A.'s answer, in two series of arguments, works through Cresconius's letter and contains a harsh critique of rhetoric and dialectic.

W: M. Petschenig, CSEL 52:325-582. — G. Finaert, C. de Veer, BAug 31 (Paris, 1968) [text/French trans./comm.].
L: M. Moreau, Cresc.: AugL 2:131-137. — J. Pinborg, Das Sprachdenken der Stoa u. A.' Dialektik: CM 23 (1962) 148-177. — C. de Veer, Exploitation du schisme maximianiste par saint A.: RechAug 3 (1965) 219-237. — F. Weissengruber, A.' Wertung von Grammatik und Rhetorik im Traktat Cresc.: Hermes 105 (1977) 101-124.

(g) *De unico baptismo contra Petilianum ad Constantinum* (*un. bapt.*; 410/411; *retr.* 2.34): A succinct summary of the debate with the Donatists on theology and eccles. policy.

W: M. Petschenig, CSEL 53:3-34. — G. Finaert, C. de Veer, BAug 31 (Paris, 1968) [text/French trans./comm.].
L: G. Madec, Introduction aux "Révisions" (Turnhout, 1996), 155f.

2. Writings after 411: After the conference of 411, A.'s first effort was to compose a short version of the acts (→ Canonical Collections) in order to inform the faithful. Such acts were read during the liturgy in Lent.

(a) *Breviculus collationis contra Donatistas* (*brevic.*; 411; *retr.* 2.39): A short version of the acts of the conference of 411. The *brevic.* consists of three books, corresponding to the three days of the conference.

W: M. Petschenig, CSEL 53:39-92. — S. Lancel, CCL 149A:261-306. — G. Finaert, E. Lamirande, BAug 32 (Paris, 1965 [text/French trans./comm.].

(b) *Contra Donatistas* (*c. Don.*; 412; *retr.* 2.40): The purpose was to convey the essential arguments of the conference of 411 to a broad public: scriptural attestation of the *Catholica*; references to historical details; self-contradiction of the Donatists in regard to the schism; Marcellinus and the accusation of bribery; mingling of good and evil in the church.

W: M. Petschenig, CSEL 53:97-162. — G. Finaert, E. Lamirande, BAug 32 (Paris, 1965) [text/French trans./comm.].
L: P. Monceaux, Histoire littéraire de l'Afrique chrétienne 4-7 (Paris, 1912-1923).

(c) *De correctione Donatistarum* (*correct.*; 417; *retr.* 2.48): This work, in the form of a letter (= *ep.* 185), is A.'s answer to the question of Tribune Boniface about the difference between the Arians and the Donatists. A. stresses the legitimacy of the measures taken by the state.

W: A. Goldbacher, CSEL 57:1-44. — W. Parsons, FaCh 30 (Washington, 1955), 141-190 [English trans.].
L: J. S. Alexander, A Quotation from Terence in the correct. of St. A. (= StPatr 27) (Leuven/Louvain, 1993), 221-224. — O. Perler, J.-L. Maier, Les voyages de saint A. (Paris, 1969), 305-309.

(d) *Sermo ad Caesariensis ecclesiae plebem* (*s. Caes. eccl.*; Sept. 18, 418): a sermon without any tight structure focused on baptism and the understanding of the sacraments.

W: M. Petschenig, CSEL 53:167-178. — G. Finaert, E. Lamirande, BAug 32 (Paris, 1965) [text/French trans./comm.].

(e) *Gesta cum Emerito Donatistarum episcopo* (*Emer.*; Sept. 20, 418; *retr.* 2.51): Summary of a stenographic report of the conversation of A. and Emeritus.

W: M. Petschenig, CSEL 53:181-196. — G. Finaert, E. Lamirande, BAug 32 (Paris, 1965) [text/French trans./comm.].

(f) *Contra Gaudentium Donatistarum episcopum* (*c. Gaud.*; 419; *retr.* 2.59): Gaudentius of Thamugudi strongly resisted the civil measures taken after 411. A.'s response to the letters of Gaudentius contains important documents and treats the question of resistance and suicide.

W: M. Petschenig, CSEL 53:201-274. — G. Finaert, E. Lamirande, BAug 32 (Paris, 1965) [text/French trans./comm.].
L: P. Monceaux, Le dossier de Gaudentius: RPh 31 (1907) 111-133.

E. Anti-Pelagian Writings

A.'s preoccupation with the subject of grace was connected with his discovery of Paul, as told in the work *Ad Simplicianum*. A.'s theology of grace was thus established long before Pelagius; it only underwent development. The controversy with Pelagius and his disciple Caelestius passed through two phases. In the first, between 410 and 418, the discussion focused on questions of free will, the goodness of nature, and the role of grace in the interplay of the human will and divine grace. Pelagius's position can be summed up in the formula: "Grace is given in order that human beings may more easily do what is good." According to A., on the other hand, "Grace is given in order that human beings may be able to do it at all" (Pelagius: *ad facilius faciendum*; A.: *ad faciendum*). In the second phase of the controversy, Bishop Julian of Eclanum takes center stage. The tone now becomes harsher, the problems are discussed in greater depth. Instead of the question raised by the ascetical tradition about striving for virtue, and how grace makes this possible, the question now is whether nature is good, whether and how we are to think of original sin, and what the consequences are of that sin. Julian accuses A. of being a Manichee and denying the goodness of creation. He forces A. to define his position ever more clearly. As a result, A. becomes the "inventor" of the doctrine of original sin, which had not existed in his formulation of it before him.

1. **Writings against Pelagius and Caelestius:** (a) *De peccatorum meritis et remissione et de baptismo parvulorum ad Marcellinum* (*pecc. mer.*; 411/412; *retr.* 2.33): This first anti-Pelagian work was written after the condemnation of Caelestius by the Synod of Carthage (Oct. 411). A. emphasizes the point that redemption by Christ and unmerited divine grace are closely connected. He sees the central place of Christ the redeemer imperiled by the denial of original sin and the rejection of infant baptism. 1 Cor 4:17 is cited and will be a leitmotif for the entire anti-Pelagian debate.

W: C. F. Urba, J. Zycha, CSEL 60:3-151. — R. Habitzky (Würzburg, 1971), 55-302 [German trans./comm.].
L: G. Greshake, Gnade als konkrete Freiheit (Mainz, 1972).

(b) *De spiritu et littera* (*spir. et litt.*: 412; *retr.* 2.37): This work is closely connected with *pecc. mer.* Written, again, in answer to a query of Marcellinus, it discusses the Pauline contrast of law and grace. The law by itself is not a help to liberation but a shackle of sin. At this same time, *ep.* 145 gives a short summary of *spir. et litt.*

W: *spir. et litt.*, C. F. Urba, J. Zycha, CSEL 60:155-229. — S. Kopp (Würzburg, 1971), 303-435 [text/German trans./comm.]. — E. Kochs (Neukirchen, 1962) [German trans.]. — A. Forster (Paderborn, 1968) [German trans.]. — J. D. Burger (Neuchâtel, 1951) [text/French trans.]. — S. Iodice (Naples, 1979) [text/Italian trans.]. — *ep.* 145, A. Goldbacher, CSEL 44:266-273.

(c) *De natura et gratia* (*nat. et gr.*; 413-417; *retr.* 2.42): Ongoing clash with the explanations of Pelagius, whose work is preserved only in A.'s excerpts from it. Even the title of Pelagius's work, written between 412 and 414, has not come down to us. Appealing to 1 Cor 4:7, A. criticizes Pelagius's idea that human beings can be without sin.

W: C. F. Urba, J. Zycha, CSEL 60:233-299. — A. Maxsein (Würzburg, 1971) [text/German trans./comm.]. — G. de Plinval, J. de la Tullaye, BAug 21 (Paris, ²1994) [text/French trans./comm.].

(d) *De perfectione iustitiae hominis* (*perf. iust.*; 415/416; *retr.* 2.46): A.'s answer to the *Definitiones*, ascribed to Caelestius and preserved in a Sicilian *chartula*, acc. to which human beings can live sinlessly by their own power. Most of Caelestius's book can be reconstructed from A.'s citations of it. The three parts of A.'s work correspond to those of his opponent's. A.'s aim is to tear down the doctrine of *impeccantia* by arguing from original sin, the necessity of grace, and redemption by Christ.

W: C. F. Urba, J. Zycha, CSEL 42:3-48. — A. Fingerle (Würzburg, 1964) [text/German trans./comm.]. — G. de Plinval, J. de la Tullaye, BAug 21 (Paris, ²1994) [text/French trans./comm.].

(e) *De gestis Pelagii* (*gest. Pel.*; 417; *retr.* 2.47): Edition, with commentary, of the acts of the Synod of Diospolis, with references to the course of the Pelagian controversy.

W: C. Urba, J. Zycha, CSEL 42:51-122. — B. Altaner (Würzburg, 1964) [text/German trans./comm.]. — G. de Plinval, J. de la Tullaye, BAug 21 (Paris, ²1994) [text/French trans./comm.].

(f) *De gratia Christi et de peccato originali* (*gr. et pecc. or.*; 418; *retr.* 2.50): After the Synod of Carthage in 418, the imperial rescript, and the *Tractoria* of Zosimus, A. composed this work in response to an inquiry from Pinianus, Albina, and Melania, Roman aristocrats. It endeavors to rebut the arguments of Pelagius, who had gotten the three to accept his version of orthodoxy. The work is not a systematic presentation of the doctrine of grace but simply corrects Pelagius's views.

W: C. F. Urba, J. Zycha, CSEL 42:125-206. — J. Plagnieux, F. J. Thonnard, BAug 22 (Paris, 1975) [text/French trans./comm.].

(g) *De anima et eius origine* (*an. et or.*; 419/421; *retr.* 2.56): The work does not primarily address a Pelagian document but does stand, both in time and in content, in the setting of the anti-Pelagian contro-

versy. A. opposes the two books of a Victorinus Victor, who reports the position of a Bishop Optatus (see *ep.* 190). The content is an unsystematic, often stereotypical refutation of the idea that the soul is material in nature.

W: C. F. Urba, J. Zycha, CSEL 60:303-419. — J. Plagnieux, F. J. Thonnard, BAug 22 (Paris, 1975) [text/French trans./comm.]. — A. Maxsein, D. Morick (Würzburg, 1977) [German trans./comm.].
L: G. J. P. O'Daly, Augustine and the Origin of Souls: JAC. E 10 (1983) (= FS H. Dörrie), 184-191. — A. Zumkeller, an. et or.: AugL 1:340-350 (literature).

2. Writings against Julian: (a) *De nuptiis et concupiscentia ad Valerium* (*nupt. et conc.*; 419/421; *retr.* 2.53): In response to Julian's accusation that A. denigrates marriage and is a Manichee, A. emphasizes the point, in book 1, that marriage is good. He explains the three blessings of marriage: *fides*, *proles*, *sacramentum*. The second book gives a proof from tradition (Bible and fathers). *Ep.* 200, to Count Valerius, is a kind of preface to *nupt. et conc.* and gives the historical context.

W: *nupt. et conc.*, C. F. Urba, J. Zycha, CSEL 42:211-319. — F. J. Thounard, E. Bleuzen, A. C. de Veer, BAug 23 (Paris, 1974) [text/French trans./comm.]. — A. Fingerle, A. Zumkeller, Ehe und Begierlichkeit (Würzburg, 1977), 77-166 [German trans.]. — *ep.* 200, A. Goldbacher, CSEL 57:293-295. — R. J. Teske (New York, 1998). [English trans.].
L: G. Bonner, Libido and Concupiscentia in St. A.: StPatr 6 (1962) 303-314. — idem, Concupiscentia: AugL 1:1113-1122.

(b) *Contra duas epistulas Pelagianorum* (*c. ep. Pelag.*; 420/421; *retr.* 2.61): A work in four books for Bishop Boniface of Rome, it responds to a letter of Julian to the Romans as well as to a second letter from Julian and seventeen bishops. The two letters have not been preserved. Against the accusation of Manichaeism (first letter), A. in his first book defends the goodness of marriage and emphasizes the necessity of baptism. Books 2-4 answer Pelagian accusations by invoking Cyprian and Ambrose and criticize the five *laudes* (*creaturae*, *nuptiarum*, *legis*, *liberi arbitrii*, *sanctorum*) in which Julian had summed up his teaching (second letter).

W: C. F. Urba, J. Zycha, CSEL 60:423-570. — F. J. Thonnard, E. Blenzen, A. C. de Veer, BAug 23 (Paris, 1974) [text/French trans./comm.]. — D. Morick (Würzburg, 1977) [German trans./comm.]. — R. J. Teske (New York, 1998). [English trans.].

(c) *Contra Iulianum* (*c. Iul.*; 421-422; *retr.* 2.63): In 421 A. received Julian's letter to Turbantius and spent the winter of 421/422 in refuting it. In 1.1.3 an outline is given of the letter's train of thought. A. protests the accusation of Manichaeism, which, he says, strikes all the other fathers (book 1); he gives the proof from tradition against Julian (book 2), and refutes Julian's individual accusations (books 3-6).

W: PL 44:641-874. — M. A. Schumacher, FaCh 35 (Washington, 1957), 3-396 [English trans.]. — R. J. Teske (New York, 1998). [English trans.].
L: J. Lössl, Intellectus gratiae. Die erkenntnistheoretische u. hermeneutische Dimension der Gnadenlehre A.' (Leiden, 1997).

(d) *Contra Iulianum opus imperfectum* (*c. Iul. imp.*; 429-430): Julian had answered A.'s *nupt. et conc.* (book 2) with eight books *Ad Florum*. A copy of this last work came to A. by way of Alypius. A. refuted the first three books and was working on the fourth (*ep.* 224.2) by giving a refutation of details as he had earlier against Faustus and Petilian. He also discussed books 5 and 6, while the introduction to book 7 was begun but has been lost. A.'s answer repeats positions taken earlier and is rather tiring.

W: *c. Jul. imp.* 1-3, M. Zelzer, CSEL 85/1:3-506. — *c. Jul. imp.* 4-6, PL 45:1337-1608. — I. Volpi (Rome, 1993) [text/Italian trans.]. — R. J. Teske (New York, 1999). [English trans.].
L: J. Lössl, Intellectus gratiae (Leiden, 1997).

3. Writings against Semipelagianism:

(a) *De gratia testamenti novi ad Honoratum* (*gr. t. nov.*; 412; *retr.* 2.36): In this work, included among A.'s letters as *ep.* 140, A. deals with five interconnected questions submitted to him: How can Christ speak of his being abandoned by God (Ps 21:2), when all things have their ground in the love of God (Eph 3:18)?

W: A. Goldbacher, CSEL 44:155-234. — W. Parsons, FaCh 20 (Washington, 1953), 58-136 [English trans.].

(b) *De gratia et libero arbitrio* (*gr. et lib. arb.*; 426/427; *retr.* 2.66): A. replies to questions from the monks of Hadrumetum (ca. 120 km. distant from Carthage) who were offended by A.'s teaching on unmerited grace. A. answers by pointing out that grace does not do away with freedom and that human beings are responsible for good and for evil. The work focuses on the interplay of grace and freedom and is chiefly practical in its orientation.

W: PL 44:881-912. — S. Kopp (Würzburg, 1955) [text/German trans./comm.]. — J. Chéné, J. Pintard, BAug 24 (Paris, 1962) [text/French trans./comm.].

(c) *De correptione et gratia* (*corrept.*; 426-427; *retr.* 2.67): In the first main section (1-9) A. points out that censure has a place even in a system of grace. Conversion is the work of grace and a sign of God's justice. Therefore a falling away is sinful (10-25). In the third main section (26-31) A. discusses the question of whether Adam incurred guilt by his fall inasmuch as there was not at yet any *massa perditionis*. He shows the radical difference between the original state and the state of redemption; there is a gift of perseverance proper to each state.

W: PL 44:915-946. — S. Kopp (Würzburg, 1955) [text/German trans./comm.]. — J. Chéné, J. Pintard, BAug 24 (Paris, 1962) [text/French trans./comm.].

(d) *De praedestinatione sanctorum liber ad Prosperum et Hilarium primus* (*praed. sanct.*; 428/429): Answer to two letters from laymen, Prosper and Hilary (*ep.* 225/226), which refer to the resistance of the monks of Marseilles. The criticism of A.'s opponents was sparked espec. by A.'s treatises *corrept.* and *gr. et lib. arb.* This work explains that the beginning of faith is due to the unmerited election of God (3-16), proves this from the example of children dying before the use of reason (17-31), and offers a scriptural proof (32-42).

W: PL 44:959-992. — A. Zumkeller (Würzburg, 1955) [text/German trans./comm.]. — J. Chéné, J. Pintard, BAug 24 (Paris, 1962) [text/French trans./comm.].

(e) *De dono perseverantiae liber ad Prosperum et Hilarium secundus* (*persev.*; 428/429): Following up on *praed. sanct.* A. proves that not only initial grace but perseverance in it are gracious gifts of God.

W: PL 45:993-1034. — A. Zumkeller (Würzburg, 1955) [text/German trans./comm.]. — J. Chéné, J. Pintard, BAug 24 (Paris, 1962) [text/French trans./comm.].

F. Anti-Arian Writings:

A. acquired a fuller knowledge of Arianism only toward the end of his episcopate due to the Vandal invasion. Until then he had regarded Arianism as a dying heresy. A first controversy arose in 419, when he came upon a *Sermo Arianorum* (*ep.* 23A.3). His controversy with Arianism did not occupy any great space.

L: M. Simonetti, S. A. e gli Ariani: REAug 13 (1967) 55-84.

(a) *Contra sermonem Arianorum* (*c. s. Arian.*; 419; *retr.* 2.52): A. gives thirty-four refutations of an Arian *sermo*, a kind of profession of faith in thirty-four articles.

S: *sermo Arianorum*, PL 42:677-684.
W: PL 42:683-708. — R. J. Teske (New York, 1995). [English trans.].

(b) *Conlatio cum Maximino Arrianorum episcopo* (*conl. Max.*; 427/428; *retr.* App.): Record of a public debate in Hippo between the Visgothic Arian Bishop Maximinus and A. Book 1 contains a lengthy presentation of the Trinity by the Arians, while in book 2 A. refutes it.

W: PL 42:709-742. — R. J. Teske (New York, 1995). [English trans.].
L: R. C. Gamble, A. contra Maximinum. An Analysis of A.'s Antiarian Writings, Diss. (Basel, 1983).

(c) *Contra Maximinum Arrianum* (*c. Max.*; 427/428): After the debate with Maximinus the latter put it about that he had vanquished A. A. refers back to the debate and refutes Maximinus.

W: PL 42:743-814. — R. J. Teske (New York, 1995). [English trans.].

G. Hermeneutics and Exegesis

Making use of Tyconius's *Liber regularum* A. develops a theory of scriptural exegesis. The goal of all exegesis is *caritas*; in its method it uses the doctrine of signs (*res-signa*). Jerome's philological method is adopted, as are pagan methods (translations, rhetorical figures, state of the text). A. adds rhetorical instructions on presenting the results. He clearly emphasizes the relativity of all exegesis and calls for moving beyond the literal meaning to the figurative. A. applies this method in his own commentaries, so that allegorical and literal interpretations complement each other.

1. Hermeneutical Writings: (a) *De doctrina christiana* (*doctr. chr.*; books 1-3: 396/397; book 4: 426-427; *retr.* 2.4): A. explains his hermeneutics (book 1: *res*; book 2: *signa*; book 3: rules of interpretation; book 4: rhetorical expression). *Doctr. chr.* is more than just a manual of hermeneutics; A. develops here a theory of Chr. education.

W: W. M. Green, CSEL 80. — J. Martin, CCL 32:1-167. — M. Moreau, I. Bochet, G. Madec, BAug 11/2 (Paris, ²1997) [text/French trans./comm.]. — M. Simonetti (Milan, 1994) [text/Italian trans./comm.]. — R. P. H. Green (Oxford, 1995) [text/English trans.]. — idem (Oxford, 1997) [English trans.]. — S. Mitterer, BKV² 49 [German trans.].
L: D. W. H. Arnold, P. Bright (ed.), doctr. chr. (Notre Dame/London, 1994). — A. M. La Bonnardière, S. A. et la Bible (Paris, 1986). — K. Pollmann, doctr. chr. (Fribourg, Switzerland, 1996). — M. Pontet, L'exégèse de saint A. prédicateur (Paris, 1944). — P. Prestel, Die Rezeption der

ciceronianischen Rhetorik durch A. in doctr. chr. (Frankfurt a.M., 1992). — G. Strauss, Schriftgebrauch, Schriftauslegung und Schriftbeweis bei A. (Tübingen, 1959).

(b) *De consensu evangelistarum* (*cons. ev.*; 400; *retr.* 2.16): In four books A. tries to eliminate possible contradictions among the gospels. Divergences are painstakingly listed; A.'s method presupposes the principle that the texts are all consistent with one another.

W: J. Weihrich, CSEL 43. — S. D. F. Salmond, P. Scharf, NPNF 6:77-236 [English trans.].
L: G. Broszio, Genealogia Christi (Trier, 1994). — H. Merkel, cons. ev.: AugL 1:1228-1236.

(c) *Contra adversarium legis et prophetarum* (*c. adv. leg.*; 419-420; *retr.* 2.58): A. responds to an otherwise unknown *adversarius*, perhaps to be identified as a Marcionite or Manichee, whose work was being sold in Carthage, where it caused considerable uproar. A. refutes the rejection of the OT, stresses the goodness of the creator God (book 1), and shows that Moses and the prophets look ahead to Christ. In addition, A. discusses particular questions (patriarchs, law, devil) raised by the adversary.

W: K.-D. Daur, CCL 49:35-131. — M. P. Ciccarese (Rome, 1981), 307-390 [text/Italian comm.].
L: T. Ravenaux, A., c. adv. leg. (Würzburg, 1987).

2. Exegeses and Commentaries on the OT: (a) *De Genesi adversus Manichaeos* (see above, C.1).
(b) *De Genesi ad litteram liber imperfectus* (see above, C.1).
(c) *De Genesi ad litteram* (*Gn. litt.*; 401-414; *retr.* 2.24): The commentary deals with only the first three chapters of Genesis and shows A.'s understanding of creation. His sovereign mastery of allegorical method is impressive and in many respects was pathbreaking for the modern age.

W: J. Zycha, CSEL 28/1:3-456. — P. Agaesse, A. Solignac, BAug 48/49 (Paris, 1972) [text/French trans./comm.]. — C. J. Perl, Über den Wortlaut der Genesis, 2 vols. (Paderborn), 1961/64 [German trans.]. — R. J. Teske (Washington, 1990) [English trans.].
L: G. T. Armstrong, Die Genesis in der Alten Kirche (Tübingen, 1962). — K. Staritz, A.' Schöpfungsglaube dargelegt nach seiner Genesisauslegung (Breslau, 1931).

(d) *Enarrationes in Psalmos* (*en. Ps.*; 391-420): This interpretation of the Psalms took place primarily in preached form. *En. Ps.* 1-18 were written down before publication and not delivered; *en. Ps.* 118 was spread over a number of sermons. This is A.'s spiritually most mature and beautiful work.

W: D. E. Dekkers, I. Fraipont, CCL 38-40. — H. U. von Balthasar, Über die Psalmen (Leipzig, 1936) [German trans. (selections)]. — H. Weber, Die Auslegung der Ps (Paderborn, 1964) [German trans. (selections)]. — A. Cleveland Coxe, NPNF 8 [English trans.].
L: M. Fiedrowicz, Psalmus vox totius Christi (Freiburg i.Br., 1997).

(e) *Adnotationes in Iob* (*adn. Iob*; before 400; *retr.* 2.15): Marginal notes on A.'s text of the Bible, which were snatched from him and published. He himself expresses doubt as to whether he published the book at all.

W: J. Zycha, CSEL 28/2:509-628.
L: W. Geerlings, adn. Iob: AugL 1:100-104.

(f) *Quaestiones* (*qu.*; 419; *retr.* 2.55) and
(g) *Locutiones in Heptateuchum* (*loc.*; 419; *retr.* 2.54): Composed at the same time as books 15-16 of *civ.* (on the OT history of the *civitas Dei*). In the manner of the ancient questions-literature A. answers questions of detail in Genesis to Judges (more fully in *qu.*, more succinctly in *loc.*). Although the *retr.* lists *qu.* after *loc.*, *qu.* was probably written first.

W: *qu.*, J. Fraipont, CCL 33:1-377. — *loc.*, idem (loc. cit.), 381-465.
L: W. Rüting, Untersuchungen über A.' qu. und loc. (Paderborn, 1916). — M. A. Sánchez-Manzano, Comentario semántico de mandato en las qu.: Augustinus 37 (1992) 353-362. — W. Süss, Studien zur lat. Bibel 1 (Tartu, 1933).

(h) *De octo quaestionibus ex veteri testamento* (*qu. vet. t.*; 419; *retr.* 2.12): Contains a short introduction, three theses on the Word, and answers to five questions on the OT.

W: W. D. de Bruyne, CCL 33:469-472. — M. A. Marcos Casquero (Obras completas de San A. 27) (Madrid, 1991) [text/Spanish trans.].
L: P. Abulesz, A.' De Genesi contra Manichaeos libri duo, qu. vet. t., Diss. (Vienna, 1972).

3. Exegeses and Commentaries on the NT: (a) *De sermone domini in monte* (*s. dom. m.*; 394; *retr.* 1.19): Interpretation of Mt 5-7, artfully based on the number seven (seven stages of ascent; seven gifts of the Holy Spirit) and giving for the most part the literal sense.

W: A. Mutzenbecher, CCL 35. — A. Schmitt, A. zur Bergpredigt, St. Ottilien 1952 [German trans.]. — D. J. Kavanaugh, FaCh 11 (New York, 1951) [English trans.].
L: A. Holl, A.' Bergpredigtexegese (Vienna, 1960). — R. C. Trench, Die Erklärung der Bergpredigt aus den Schriften des hl. A. (Moers, 1904).

(b) *Expositio quarundam propositionum ex epistula apostoli ad Romanos* (*exp. prop. Rm.*; 394-395; *retr.* 1.23): Record, with minor polishing, of talks that were probably taken down also by stenographers. Thematically unified sections of Rom 1-15 are explained; the introduction deals with the relation between law and grace. History is interpreted according to a four-stage scheme (before the law, under the law, under grace, in peace).

W: J. Divjak, CSEL 84:3-52. — T. G. Ring, Die Auslegung einiger Fragen aus dem Brief an die Römer (Vienna, 1989) [text/German trans./comm.]. — M. G. Mara, A. Interprete di Paolo (Milan, 1993), 95-159 [text/Italian trans.]. — P. Fredriksen Landes (Chico, Calif., 1982) [text/English trans.].

(c) *Epistula ad Romanos inchoata expositio* (*ep. Rm. inch.*; 394-395; *retr.* 1.25): Comments on Rom 1:1-7. The largest part is a detailed exposition of Rom 1:7.

W: J. Divjak, CSEL 84:145-181. — T. G. Ring (Würzburg, 1997) [text/German trans./comm.]. — M. G. Mara, A. Interprete di Paolo (Milan, 1993), 163-209. — P. Fredriksen Landes (Chico, 1982) [text/English trans.].

(d) *Expositio epistulae ad Galatas* (*exp. Gal.*; 394-395; *retr.* 1.24): A preface explains that Gal and Rom take up the same themes: the meritoriousness of good works, the value of circumcision, and grace. A continuous commentary follows.

W: J. Divjak, CSEL 84:55-141. — T. G. Ring (Würzburg, 1997) [text/German trans./comm.].

(e) *Quaestiones Evangeliorum* (*qu. ev.*; 397-400; *retr.* 2.12): Two books in the questions-literature genre, the first dealing with passages from Mt 11:27-26:75, the second with passages chiefly from Lk.

W: A. Mutzenbecher, CCL 44B:1-118.

(f) *In epistulam Iohannis ad Parthos tractatus* (*ep. Io. tr.*; 407): Sermons preached during Easter week 407 and aimed at countering the Donatist schism.

W: PL 35:1977-2062. — P. Agaësse, SC 75. — H. M. Biedermann, Unteilbar ist die Liebe (Vienna, 1986) [German trans.]. — J. Leinenweber (San Francisco, 1989) [English trans.].
L: D. Dideberg, S. A. et la première épître de saint Jean (Paris, 1975). — A. M. La Bonnadière, Recherches de chronologie A. (Paris, 1965), 50-53.

(g) *In Iohannis evangelium tractatus* (*Io. ev. tr.*; 414-417): Sermons delivered in Hippo and written down as 124 homilies that interpret the entire gospel of John.

W: R. Willems, CCL 36. — F. M. Berrouard, BAug 71-74A (Paris, 1969-1993) [text/French trans./comm.]. — T. Specht, BKV² 8; 11; 19 [German trans.]. — J. W. Rettig, FaCh 78, 79, 88, 90, 92 (Washington, 1988-1995) [English trans.].

L: M. Comeau, S. A. Exégète du quatrième évangile (Paris, ²1930). — R. P. Hardy, Actualité de la Révélation divine (Paris, 1974). — G. Lawless, Biblical resonances in A.'s Io. ev. tr. 40, §10: Aug(L) 48 (1998) 305-329.

H. Writings on the Philosophy of Religion and on Dogma

In his writings not directly prompted by controversy or questions, A. creates a philosophy of religion and a dogmatics that are dissociated from Neoplatonism but nonetheless are vitalized by its spirit.

(a) *De vera religione* (*vera rel.*; 389-391; *retr.* 1.13): Dissociation from Platonism but also an admission that none have come so close to Christianity as the Platonists. A.'s first attempt to present a comprehensive system of Chr. philosophy/theology.

W: K.-D. Daur, CCL 32:187-260. — W. Thimme (Stuttgart, ²1983) [text/German trans.]. — J. Pégon, BAug 8 (Paris, 1951) [text/French trans./comm.]. — A. Lamacchia (Bari, 1986) [Italian trans./comm.]. — J. H. S. Burleigh (Chicago, 1959) [English trans.].

L: H. Dörries, Das Verhältnis des Neuplatonischen und Christlichen in A.' vera rel.: ZNW 13 (1924) 64-102. F. van Fleteren, vera rel., Lectio Augustini 10 (Padua, 1994).

(b) *De fide et symbolo* (*f. et symb.*; Oct. 8, 393; *retr.* 1.17): Sermon on the creed, preached at the opening of the Council of Carthage; even though still a priest A. preached to the bishops. At some points the oral original still shines through the revised book.

W: J. Zycha, CSEL 41:3-32. — J. Rivière, BAug 9 (Paris, 1947) [text/French trans./comm.] — C. J. Perl (Paderborn, 1968) [German trans.].

(c) *Ad Simplicianum* (*Simpl.*; 396-398; *retr.* 2.1): A. answers eight questions of presbyter Simplicianus, who became Ambrose's successor. The first two questions, on Rom 7:7-25a and Rom 9:10-29, are theologically the most momentous since A. here discovered the Paul of the doctrine on grace and conceived his own teaching on grace long before Pelagius.

W: A. Mutzenbecher, CCL 44:7-91. — T. G. Ring (Würzburg, 1991) [text/German trans./comm.].

(d) *De trinitate* (*trin.*; 399-419; *retr.* 2.15): A.'s intention is to show the unity of the three divine persons. In the first section scriptural testimonies to this unity (books 1-4) and philosophical definitions needed (books 5-7) are given. The second part (books 8-15)

introduces analogies between the structure of the human soul and the divine Trinity. In the history of dogma A.'s doctrine of the Trinity is described as a "doctrine of the immanent Trinity."

W: J. Mountain, CCL 50/50A. — M. Mellet, T. Camelot, P. Agaësse, J. Moingt, BAug 15/16 (Paris, 1955) [text/French trans./comm.]. — M. Schmaus, BKV² 13-14 [German trans.]. — S. McKenna, FaCh 45 (Washington, 1963) [English trans.]. — E. Hill, A. The works part 1, vol. 5 (New York, 1991) [English trans.].

L: J. Brachtendorf, ". . . prius essecogitare quam credere": a natural understanding of trinity in A.: AugSt 29/2 (1998) 35-45. — U. Duchrow, Der Aufbau von A.' Schriften Confessiones und trin.: ZThK 62 (1965) 338-367. — D. Pintaric, Sprache u. Trinität (Salzburg, 1983). — O. du Roy, L'intelligence de la foi en la Trinité selon s. A. (Paris, 1966). — A. Schindler, Wort u. Analogie in A.' Trinitätslehre (Tübingen, 1965). — M. Schmaus, Die psychologische Trinitätslehre des hl. A. (Münster, ²1967).

(e) *De fide et caritate* (*ench.*; 421-422; *retr.* 2.63): An outline addressed to Lawrence, an otherwise unknown Chr. layman, using the virtues of faith, hope, and charity as a structure. A. interprets the creed used in Hippo (*s.* 215; PL 38:1072-76) and toward the end deals succinctly with hope and charity. The *ench.* is regarded as a short summary of "popular Catholicism" and gives a good insight into A.'s thinking.

W: E. Evans, CCL 46:49-114. — J. Barbel (Düsseldorf, 1960) [text/German trans./comm.]. — J. Rivière, BAug 9 (Paris, 1947) [text/French trans./comm.]. — L. A. Arand, ACW 3 (New York, 1978) [English trans.].

L: J. Rivière, Comment diviser l'ench. de St. A.: Bulletin de littérature ecclésiastique 43 (1942) 99-115. — O. Scheel, Bemerkungen zur Bewertung des ench. A.': ZKG 24 (1903) 401-416.

(f) *De haeresibus ad Quodvultdeum* (*haer.*; 428/429). At the request of Bishop Quodvultdeus, A. draws up a list of eighty-eight heresies, following the *haer.* of → Epiphanius. In an introduction he explains the purpose of the work. For some heresies (Tertullianists, Manichees) he provides information that goes beyond the usual outlines.

W: R. vander Plaetse, C. Beukers, CCL 46:286-345. — R. J. Teske, The works of St. A. 18 (Brooklyn, 1995) [English trans.].

L: B. Altaner, A.' Methode der Quellenbenützung: idem, Kleine Patristische Schriften (Berlin, 1967), 164-173. — G. Bardy, Le haer. et ses sources: Miscellanea Agostiniana 2 (Rome, 1931), 397-416.

I. Pastoral Writings

As pastor of an urban community and correspondent with other pastors, A. not only produced writings of a systematic kind but also spoke out on matters of practical theology. These writings very frequently provide a delightful view of the everyday life of the North African church.

1. Considerations of Principle: (a) *De catechizandis rudibus* (*cat. rud.*; 399/400; *retr.* 2.14): Answer to the question of Deogratias, a Carthaginian deacon, as to how an introductory catechesis is to be arranged. In a first section (5-22) A. explains the theoretical basis of catechesis, and in the second part (23-55) presents two model catecheses. The work has had a great influence down to our time.

W: J. B. Bauer, CCL 46:121-178. — G. Madec, BAug 11/1 (Paris, 1994) [text/French trans./comm.]. — W. Steinmann, O. Wermelinger (Munich, 1985) [German trans./comm.]. — J. P. Christopher, ACW 2 (Westminster, Md., 1962) [English trans.].
L: E. Reil, A.: cat. rud. Ein religionsdidaktisches Konzept (St. Ottilien, 1989).

(b) *De fide rerum invisibilium* (*f. invis.*; 410-420): Sermon on the necessity, already evident in everyday life, of faith in things invisible. The sermon is closely connected with *util. cred.*

W: M. P. J. van den Hout, CCL 46:1-19. — C. J. Perl (Paderborn, 1968), 56-83 [text/German trans.]. — M. F. McDonald (Washington, 1950) [text/English trans./comm.]. — J. Pégon, BAug 8 (Paris, 1951) [text/French trans./comm.].

(c) *De fide et operibus* (*f. et op.*; 410-420): Answer to the question whether those divorced and remarried may be admitted to baptism. A. cites numerous passages of the Bible, espec. 1 Cor 3:11-15, in order to show the difference between dead and living faith. The church has always refused baptism to sinners who do not realize their state.

W: J. Zycha, CSEL 41:35-97. — C. J. Perl (Paderborn, 1968), 88-185 [text/German trans.]. — J. Pégon, BAug 8 (Paris, 1951) [text/French trans./comm.]. — G. J. Lombardo, ACW 48 (New York, 1988) [English trans.].

2. Occasional Writings: (a) *De mendacio* (*mend.*; 394/395; *retr.* 1.27): A.'s reflections on lying are directed first of all to the theory of knowledge (difference from error), but are also marked by his interpretation of the different presentations of the conflict between Peter and Paul (Gal 2). He examines eight different kinds of lies and their possible permissibility.

W: J. Zycha, CSEL 41:413-466. — G. Combès, BAug 2 (Paris, 1949) [text/French trans./comm.]. — E. Keseling (Würzburg, 1953) [German trans./comm.].

L: C. Natali et al., mend., Lectio Augustini 13 (Rome, 1997).
(b) *De continentia* (*cont.*; 395): A sermon, later revised, that sets down in programmatic fashion the basic principles of Chr. asceticism.

W: J. Zycha, CSEL 41:141-183. — J. Saint-Martin, BAug 3 (Paris, 1949) [text/French trans./comm.]. — E. Keseling (Würzburg, 1949) [German trans./comm.].

(c) *De agone christiano* (*agon.*; 396; *retr.* 2.3): Using the word *agōn*, borrowed from Greek, A. describes the Chr. life as a spiritual competition against the powers of this world. The struggle is made possible by the *regula fidei* (1-12) and the *praecepta vivendi* (13-32).

W: J. Zycha, CSEL 41:101-138. — B. Rohland-Gosselin, BAug 1 (Paris, 1949) [text/French trans./comm.]. — A. Habitzky, A. Zumkeller (Würzburg, 1961) [German trans./comm.].
L: A. d'Alès, Le agon.: Gr. 11 (1930) 131-145. — A. Zumkeller, agon.: AugL 1:221-227.

(d) *De opere monachorum* (*op. mon.*; 400/401; *retr.* 2.21): Against the view that asceticism consists solely in prayer and pious meditation A. asserts the thesis that manual labor is part of monastic life, preventing the entrance of slackers into monasteries. The work, composed at the request of Carthaginian Primate Aurelius, gives arguments from scripture in its first part (1-22), while the second part (23-33) takes on the opponents in a mocking and polemical fashion.

W: J. Zycha, CSEL 41:531-595. — J. Saint-Martin, BAug 3 (Paris, 1949) [text/French trans./comm.]. — R. Arbesmann (Würzburg, 1972) [German trans./comm.].
L: A. Zumkeller, Das Mönchtum des hl. A. (Vienna, ²1968).

(e) *De bono conjugali* (*b. conjug.*; 401; *retr.* 2.22): Fundamental, tradition-based considerations on marriage. With marriage in paradise as the starting point, A. defines the blessings of marriage as *proles, fides, sacramentum.*

W: J. Zycha, CSEL 41:187-230. — G. Combès, BAug 2 (Paris, 1949) [text/French trans./comm.]. — A. Maxsein (Würzburg, 1949) [German trans./comm.]. — R. Kearney, D. G. Hunter, A. The works, part 1, vol. 9 (New York, 1999) [English trans.].
L: K. E. Boresen, Subordination and Equivalence (Mainz, 1995 = 1968). — P. Brown, The Body and Society (New York, 1988). — M. Müller, Die Lehre des hl. A. von der Paradiesesehe (Regensburg, 1954).

(f) *De sancta virginitate* (*virg.*; 401; *retr.* 2.23): A. defends the intrinsic value of virginity against Jovinian and Vigilantius. In its first part the book intends to "praise [virginity] so that it may be treasured"; in its second, it aims "to instill some fear [in virgins] lest they become proud."

W: J. Zycha, CSEL 41:235-302. — J. Saint-Martin, BAug 3 (Paris, 1949) [text/French trans./comm.]. — J. Dietz (Würzburg, 1952) [German trans./comm.]. — R. Kearney, D. G. Hunter, A. The works, part 1, vol. 9 (New York, 1999) [English trans.].

(g) *De divinatione daemonum* (*divin. daem.*; 406/411; *retr.* 2.30): A work occasioned by a conversation about predicting the future: discussion of nature of demons and their prophecies (3-10), rejection of the view that demonic prophecy is good because it is permitted by God.

W: J. Zycha, CSEL 41:599-618. — G. Bardy, J. A. Beckaert, J. Bontet, BAug 10 (Paris, 1952) [text/French trans./comm.]. — K. Kühn: Aug(L) 47 (1997) 291-337 [German trans./comm.].

(h) *De utilitate ieiunii* (*util. ieiun.*; 408/412): A two-part sermon, on the nature and purpose of fasting (1-6) and on a special higher form of fasting that will lead to peace among Christians (7-13).

W: S. D. Ruegg, CCL 46:231-241. — G. Combès, BAug 2 (Paris, 1949) [text/French trans./comm.]. — R. Arbesmann (Würzburg, 1958) [German trans./comm.].
L: R. Arbesmann, Das Fasten bei den Griechen und Römern (Giessen, 1929).

(i) *De bono viduitatis* (*b. vid.*; 414): Letter to Juliana, widow of Anicius Hermogenianus Olybrius, a woman who had joined a circle of widows and young women gathered around Proba. Chs. 1-18 develop the advantage of the widowed state, whereas chs. 19-29 are an exhortation in which theol. problems are taken up with a pastoral and practical aim.

W: J. Zycha, CSEL 41:305-343. — J. Saint-Martin, BAug 3 (Paris, 1949) [text/French trans./comm.]. — A. Maxsein (Würzburg, 1952) [German trans./comm.]. — R. Kearney, D. G. Hunter, A. The works, part 1, vol. 9 (New York, 1999) [English trans.].

(j) *Contra Priscillianistas* (*c. Prisc.*; 415; *retr.* 2.44): At the request of → Orosius, A. gives his opinion on whether the soul is created from nothing, whether souls, angels, and demons have the same origin, and whether the purification process claimed by → Origen finally rescues even the devil and the damned.

W: K.-D. Daur, CCL 49:165-178.

L: J. A. Davids, De Orosio et S. A. Priscillianistarum adversariis commentatio historica et philologica (Den Haag, 1930).

(k) *De patientia* (*pat.*; 417): A revised sermon which in its first part (1-14) defines the virtue of patience as the serene endurance of evils, but with patience being distinguished from toughness. The second part (15-29) shows that patience is a gift of God's grace.

W: J. Zycha, CSEL 41:663-691. — G. Combès, BAug 2 (Paris, 1949) [text/French trans./comm.]. — J. Martin (Würzburg, 1956) [German trans./comm.]. — R. Kearney, D. G. Hunter, A. The works, part 1, vol. 9 (New York, 1999) [English trans.].

(l) *Contra mendacium* (*c. mend.*; 420; *retr.* 2.60): Against the Priscillianists, showing every kind of lie to be reprehensible.

W: J. Zycha, CSEL 41:469-528. — G. Combès, BAug 2 (Paris, 1949) [text/French trans./comm.]. — E. Keseling (Würzburg, 1953) [German trans./comm.].
L: C. Natali et al., c. mend., Lectio Augustini 13 (Rome, 1997).

(m) *De adulterinis coniugiis* (*adult. coniug.*; 421; *retr.* 2.57): A.'s answer, in two books, to two letters of Pollentius. Book 1.1-7, takes up 1 Cor 7:10f.; 1.8-13 takes up Mt 19:9. A third section deals with the disagreement between A. and Pollentius. In an appendix A. turns to the special problem of the baptism of dying catechumens. Book 2 deals with the problem of divorce from various points of view.

W: J. Zycha, CSEL 41:347-410. — G. Combès, BAug 2 (Paris, 1949) [text/French trans./comm.]. — J. Schmid (Würzburg, 1949) [German trans./comm.]. — R. Kearney, D. G. Hunter, A. The works, part 1, vol. 9 (New York, 1999) [English trans.].
L: A. M. La Bonnardière, adult. coniug.: AugL 1:116-125.

(n) *De cura pro mortuis gerenda* (*cura mort.*; 421/424; *retr.* 2.64): Answer to the question of Paulinus of Nola whether burial in the *memoriae* of the martyrs is advantageous to the souls of the dead. In the first part (1-9) the reasons are given for a reverent treatment of the dead, while the second part (10-17) is devoted to the question of appearances of the dead.

W: J. Zycha, CSEL 41:621-660. — G. Combès, BAug 2 (Paris, 1949) [text/French trans./comm.]. — G. Schlachter, R. Arbesmann (Würzburg, 1975) [German trans./comm.].

(o) *De octo Dulcitii quaestionibus* (*Dulc. qu.*; 422/425; *retr.* 2.65): Dulcitius, a brother of the Lawrence for whom A. wrote the *ench.*, submits eight questions on: (1) the punishment of Christians for postbaptismal sins; (2) the value of sacrifice for the dead; (3) 1 Thess 4:18; (4) good and evil after death; (5) God's foreknowledge; (6) 1 Kgs 28:12-19: Samuel and the soothsayer; (7) Sarah and the pharaoh; (8) God's spirit over the waters. Because of lack of time A. refers to previously published treatments of the questions or else writes something new but very tersely.

W: A. Mutzenbecher, CCL 44A:253-297. — G. Bardy, J. A. Beckaert, J. Boubet, BAug 10 (Paris, 1952) [text/French trans./comm.].

(p) *Adversus Iudaeos* (*adv. Iud.*; 429): Sermon on the theme: the Jews spring from the trunk of Abraham but have been cut off from it. The wild olive tree of the pagan peoples has been grafted on in their place. The scriptural proofs from the OT are to be proposed for their instruction.

W: PL 42:51-64. — B. Blumenkranz, Die Judenpredigt A.' (Paris, ²1973), 89-110 [German trans.].

J. Sermons

Under the title "sermons" only those collected by the Maurists or discovered later are included. Twenty-six new sermons were discovered by F. Dolbeau in 1990. The homilies on John and parts of the commentary on the Psalms were originally sermons, but were later revised for publication. The sermons are divided into sermons on the scriptures, on the seasons, on the saints, and on various subjects.

W: PL 38:39. — As yet no critical edition is available. For separate editions, compare the translation in the Augustinus Lexikon (AugL) 1:38*f. — S. Poque, SC 116 [text/French trans./comm.]. — F. Dolbeau, A. Vingt-six sermons au peuple d'Afrique (Paris, 1996) [text/comm.]. — C. Haas, A.-Postille (Tübingen, 1861) [German trans.]. — J. E. Rotelle, A. The works, part 3, 11 vol. (New York, 1990-97) [English trans.].
L: A. Kunzelmann, Die Chronologie der s. des hl. A.: Miscellanea Agostiniana 2 (Rome, 1931), 417-520. — C. Mohrmann, Die altchr. Sondersprache in den s. des hl. A. (Nijmegen, 1965 = 1932). — S. Poque, Le langage symbolique dans la prédication d'A. (Paris, 1984). — P.-P. Verbraken, Études critiques sur les s. authentiques de saint A. (Steenbrugge, 1976).

K. Letters:

The collection contains 270 letters (*ep.*). Twenty-nine new ones were discovered in 1981. The sometimes lengthy letters occasionally have the character of treatises. This is true espec. of *ep.* 54-55 = *Ad inquisitiones Ianuarii* (*inq. Ian.*); *ep.* 102 = *Quae-*

stiones expositae contra paganos numero sex (*qu. c. pag.*); *ep.* 140 = *De gratia testamenti novi ad Honoratum* (*gr. t. n.*); *ep.* 147 = *De gestis Pelagii* 52 (*gest. Pel.*); *ep.* 147 = *De videndo deo* (*vid. deo.*); *ep.* 166 = *De origine animae* (*or. an.*); *ep* 167 = *De sententia Iacobi* (*sent. Iac.*); *ep.* 174 = *De trinitate prologus* (*trin. prol.*); *ep.* 175 = *Conc. Carth. a. 416*; *ep.* 176 = *Conc. Milevit. a. 416*; *ep.* 185 = *De correctione Donatistarum* (*cor. Don.*); *ep.* 187 = *De praesentia dei ad Dardanum* (*praes. dei*; *ep.* 211.1-4 = *regula* 1 [*reg. 1*]).

The letters deal, along with personal matters, with themes of philosophy/theology and of pastoral practice. Of special interest is A.'s correspondence with Jerome.

W: *ep.* 1-29, 31-123, A. Goldbacher, CSEL 34/1-2. — *ep.* 124-184, idem, CSEL 44. — *ep.* 185-270, idem, CSEL 57. — *ep.* 215A, idem, CSEL 58:93*. — *ep.* 173A, F. Römer: WSt 84 (1971) 230-232 [text]. — *ep.* 1*-29*, J. Divjak, CSEL 88. — J. Divjak et al., BAug 46B (Paris, 1987) [text/French trans./comm.]. — W. Parsons, FaCh 12 [*ep.* 1-82]; 18 [*ep.* 83-130]; 20 [*ep.* 131-164]; 30 [*ep.* 165-203]; 32 [*ep.* 204-270]; 81 [*ep.* 1*-29*]) [English trans.]. — T. Kranzfelder, BKV¹ 7-8 [German trans. (selections)]. — A. Hoffmann, BKV² 29-30 [German trans. (selections)].
L: J. Divjak, Les lettres de saint A. découvertes par J. Divjak (Paris, 1983). — H. Ulbrich, A.' Briefe zum pelagianischen Streit, typewritten diss. (Göttingen, 1958).

L. Doubtful

(a) *De symbolo ad catechumenos* (*symb. cat.*): Sermon on the African creed, which A. also cites elsewhere in this form.

W: R. vander Plaetse, CCL 46:185-199. — R. Storf, BKV¹: A. 4:352-481 [German trans.]. — M. Liguori, FaCh 27 (Washington, 1969), 289-307 [English trans.].
L: C. Eichenseer, Das Symbolum Apostolicum beim hl. A. (St. Ottilien, 1960).

(b) *Speculum* (*spec.*): The work combines two writings. The first is a kind of introduction to the individual books of the OT (except for the historical books) and of the NT; the second is made up of 143 questions, but their organization is not clear.

W: F. Weihrich, CSEL 12:3-285, 289-700. — C. A. Page, The Mirror of Synneres (New York, 1976) [text/English trans.].

M. Lost Writings

Carmen theatricum, Carthage, 376-383 (*conf.* 4.2.3; 3.5). — *De apto et pulchro* (*pulch.*), 380-381 (*conf.* 4.15.27). — *Panegyricus de Valentiano II*, Milan, 384-386 (*conf.* 6.6.9). — *Panegyricus de Bauto*, Milan, 384-386 (*c. litt. Pet.* 3.25.30). — *Contra epistulam Donati heretici* (*c. ep. Don.*), Hippo, 393 (*retr.* 1.21).

— *Contra partem Donati* (*c. p. Don.*), Hippo, 395/396 (*retr.* 2.5). — *Contra Hilarum* (*c. Hil.*), Hippo, 404 (*retr.* 2.11). — *Contra quod attulit Centurius a donatistis* (*c. Cent.*), Hippo, 407 (*retr.* 2.19). — *Probationum et testimoniorum contra donatistas* (*prob. et test.*), Hippo, 406/407 (*retr.* 2.27). — *Contra nescioquem Donatistam* (*c. n. Don.*), Hippo 406/407 (*retr.* 2.28). — *Admonitio donatistarum de Maximianistis* (*adm.*), Hippo, 406/407 (*retr.* 2.28). — *Expositio epistulae Iacobi ad duodecim tribus* (*exp. Iac.*), Hippo, 407 (*retr.* 2.32). — *De Maximianistis contra Donatistas* (*Max.*), Hippo, 407 (*retr.* 2.35). — *Ad Emeritum episcopum Donatistarum post conlationem* (*Emer. Don.*), Hippo, 412 (*retr.* 2.46). — *De arithmetica* (*arith.*). — *De geometria* (*geom.*). — *De philosophia* (*phil.*).

III. Appreciation: No theologian has left as deep a mark on western Christianity as A. has. In him the early church, Platonic spirituality, and a Manichean mood are combined, and yet everything is given a new formulation. He was the great "reformer of piety" (A. v. Harnack) and at the same time the theologian who in his teaching on grace effected a radical break with the Jewish heritage. He set the course for western Christianity at decisive points. In ecclesiology, sacramental doctrine, theology of history, and anthropology, and not least in the doctrine of grace, Western theology has simply nuanced the positions taken by A.

Yet the gloomy solemnity of his anthropology and his Manichean mood have placed a heavy burden on the Western church.

The history of Augustinianism has yet to be written.

Catalogue of works: AugL 1:26*-41*. — G. Madec, Introduction aux "Révisions" et à le lecture des œuvres de saint A. (Paris, 1996), 159-165.
W (in alphabetical order): *Acad.*, W. M. Green, CCL 29:3-61. — *c. Adim.*, J. Zycha, CSEL 25/1:115-190. — *adm.* — *adn. Iob*, J. Zycha, CSEL 28/2:509-628. — *c. adv. leg.*, K.-D. Daur, CCL 49:35-131. — *adult. coniug.*, J. Zycha, CSEL 41:347-410. — *agon.*, J. Zycha, CSEL 41:101-138. — *an. et or.*, C. F. Urba, J. Zycha, CSEL 60:303-419. — *an. quant.*, W. Hörmann, CSEL 89:131-231. — *arith.* — *bapt.*, M. Petschenig, CSEL 51:145-375. — *beata v.*, W. M. Green, CCL 29:65-85. — *b. coniug.*, J. Zycha, CSEL 41:187-230. — *b. vid.*, J. Zycha, CSEL 41:305-343. — *brevic.*, S. Lancel, CCL 149A:261-306. — *cat. rud.*, I. B. Bauer, CCL 46:121-178. — *cath. fr.*, M. Petschenig, CSEL 52:231-322. — *c. civ.*, B. Dombart, A. Kalb, CCL 47:1-314; CCL 48:321-866. — *conf.*, L. Verheijen, CCL 27:1-273. — *conl. Max.*, PL 42:709-742. — *cons. ev.*, F. Weihrich, CSEL 43:1-418. — *cont.*, J. Zycha, CSEL 41:141-183. — *correct.*, A. Goldbacher, CSEL 57:1-44. — *corrept.*, PL 44:915-946. — *Cresc.*, M. Petschenig, CSEL 52:325-582. — *cura mort.*, J. Zycha, CSEL

41:621-659. — *dial.*, B. D. Jackson, J. Pinborg (Dordrecht, Boston, 1975), 83-120. — *disc. chr.*, R. v. Plaetse, CCL 46:207-224. — *div. qu.*, A. Mutzenbecher, CCL 44A:11-249. — *divin. daem.*, J. Zycha, CSEL 41:599-618. — *doctr. chr.*, I. Martin, CCL 32:1-167. — *c. Don.*, M. Petschenig, CSEL 53:97-162. — *duab. an.*, J. Zycha, CSEL 25/1:51-80. — *Dulc. qu.*, A. Mutzenbecher, CCL 44A:253-297. — *Emer.*, M. Petschenig, CSEL 53:181-196. — *Emer. Don.* — *en. Ps.*, D. E. Dekkers, I. Fraipont, CCL 38:1-616; CCL 39:623-1417; CCL 40:1425-2196. — *ench.*, E. Evans, CCL 46:49-114. — *ep.* 1-29, 31-123, A. Goldbacher, CSEL 34/1-2. — *ep.* 124-184A, A. Goldbacher, CSEL 44. — *ep.* 173A, F. Römer: WSt 84 (1971) 230-232. — *ep.* 185-270, A. Goldbacher, CSEL 57. — *ep.* 215A, A. Goldbacher, CSEL 58, XCIII. — *ep.* 1*-29*, J. Divjak, CSEL 88. — *c. ep. Don.* — *ep. Io. tr.*, PL 35:1977-2062. — *c. ep. Man.*, J. Zycha, CSEL 25/1:193-248. — *c. ep. Parm.*, M. Petschenig, CSEL 51:19-141. — *c. ep. Pel.*, C. F. Urba, J. Zycha, CSEL 60:423-570. — *ep. Rm. inch.*, I. Divjak, CSEL 84:145-181. — *exc. urb.*, M.-V. O'Reilly, CCL 46:249-262. — *exp. Gal.*, I. Divjak, CSEL 84:55-141. — *exp. Iac.*, A. Goldbacher, CSEL 84:3-52. — *c. Faust.*, J. Zycha, CSEL 25/1:251-797. — *c. Fel.*, J. Zycha, CSEL 25/2:801-852. — *f. et op.*, J. Zycha, CSEL 41:35-97. — *f. et symb.*, J. Zycha, CSEL 41:3-32. — *f. invis.*, M. P. J. van den Hout, CCL 46:1-19. — *c. Fort.*, J. Zycha, CSEL 25/1:83-112. — *c. Gaud.*, M. Petschenig, CSEL 53:201-274. — *geom.* — *gest. Pel.*, C. F. Urba, J. Zycha, CSEL 42:51-122. — *Gn. litt.*, J. Zycha, CSEL 28/1:3-435. — *Gn. litt. imp.*, J. Zycha, CSEL 28/1:459-503. — *Gn. adu. Man.*, PL 34:173-220. — *gramm.* (prol. — 11, 4), C. F. Weber, Marburg 1861, 7-31. — *gramm.*, GrLat 5:496-524. — *gr. et lib. arb.*, PL 44:881-912. — *gr. et pecc. or.*, C. F. Urba, J. Zycha, CSEL 42:125-206. — *gr. t. nov.*, A. Goldbacher, CSEL 44:155-234. — *haer.*, R. V. Plaetse, C. Beukers, CCL 46:(283-) 286-345. — *c. Hil.* — *imm. an.*, W. Hörmann, CSEL 89:101-128. — *inq. Ian.*, A. Goldbacher, CSEL 34/2:158-168, 169-213. — *Io. ev. tr.*, D. R. Willems, CCL 36:1-688. — *adv. Iud.*, PL 42:51-64. — *c. Iul.*, PL 44:641-874. — *c. Iul. imp.*, M. Zelzer, CSEL 85/1:3-506; PL 45:1337-1608. — *lib. arb.*, G. M. Green, CSEL 74:3-154. — *c. litt. Pet.*, M. Petschenig, CSEL 52:3-227. — *loc.*, I. Fraipont, CCL 33:381-465. — *mag.*, K.-D. Daur, CCL 29:157-203. — *Max.* — *c. Max.*, PL 42:743-814. — *mend.*, J. Zycha, CSEL 41:413-466. — *c. mend.*, J. Zycha, CSEL 41:469-528. — *mor.*, J. B. Bauer, CSEL 90:3-156. — *mus.*, PL 32:1081-1194. — *nat. b.*, J. Zycha, CSEL 25/2:855-889. — *nat. et gr.*, C. F. Urba, J. Zycha, CSEL 60:233-299. — *c. n. Don.* — *nupt. et conc.*, C. F. Urba, J. Zycha, CSEL 42:211-319. — *op. mon.*, J. Zycha, CSEL 41:531-595. — *ord.*, P. Knöll, CSEL 63:121-185. — *orig. an.*, A. Goldbacher, CSEL 44:545-585. — *pat.*, J. Zycha, CSEL 41:663-691. — *c. p. Don.* — *pecc. mer.*, C. F. Urba, J. Zycha, CSEL 60:3-151. — *perf. iust.*, C. F. Urba, J. Zycha, CSEL 42:3-48. — *persev.*, PL 45:993-1034. — *phil.* — *praed. sanct.*, PL 44:959-992. — *praes. dei*, A. Goldbacher, CSEL 57:81-119. — *c. Prisc.*, K.-D. Daur, CCL 49:165-178. — *prob. et test.* — *ps. c. Don.*, R. Anastasi (Padova, 1957), 44-70. — *pulch.* — *qu.*, I. Fraipont, CCL 33:1-377. — *qu. ev.*, A. Mutzenbecher, CCL 44B:1-118. — *qu. Mt.*, A. Mutzenbecher, CCL 44B:119-140. — *qu. c. pag.*, A. Goldbacher, CSEL 34/2:544-578. — *qu. vet. t.*, D. de Bruyne, CCL 33:469-472. — *reg.* 1-3, L. Verheijen (Paris, 1967), 105-107, 148-152, 417-437. — *retr.*, A. Mutzenbecher, CCL 57:(1-) 5-143. — *rhet.*, R. Giomini: Studi latini e italiani 4 (1990) 35-76. — *c. Sec.*, J. Zycha, CSEL 25/2:905-947. — *sent. Iac.*, A. Goldbacher, CSEL

44:586-609. — *s.* 1, 2, 4-50, C. Lambot, CCL 41. — *s.* 3, P.-P. Verbraken: RBen 84 (1974) 250. — *s.* 51, P.-P. Verbraken: RBen 91 (1981) 23-45. — *s.* 52, P.-P. Verbraken: RBen 74 (1964) 15-35. — *s.* 53, P.-P. Verbraken: RBen 104 (1994) 21-33. — *s.* 54, P.-P. Verbraken: AnBoll 100 (1982) 265-269. — *s.* 55, 61-63, 65-67, 69-70, 73-75, 77-83, 85-87, 89-96, 98-99, 102-103, 105-110, 113, 115-120, 122-125, 127-141, 143-165, 167-176, 178-183, 185-188, 190-203, 205-210, 216, 219-220, 222-223, 225-226, 228, 230, 233-234, 236, 238-245, 247-249, 251-252, 255-256, 259-260, 262, 264-282, 284-295, 297, 299-301, 303-327, 329-338, PL 38. — *s.* 341-342, 344, 346-354, 357, 359-367, 370-378, 380-386, 390-396, PL 39. — *s.* 68, 142, 189, 213, 217, 229, 263, 296, 345, D. G. Morin, Miscellanea Agostiniana. Testi e studi. 1 (Rome, 1930). — *s.* 59, 121, 211-212, 221, 227, 231-232, 237, 246, 250, 253, 257-258, S. Poque, SC 116. — *s.* 101, 104, 166, 177, 184, 261, 298, 302, 339, 355-356, 358, C. Lambot: StPM 1 (1950). — *s.* 56, P.-P. Verbraken: RBen 68 (1958) 26-40. — *s.* 57, P.-P. Verbraken: FS L. Verheijen (Würzburg, 1987), 414-424. — *s.* 58, P.-P. Verbraken: EcOra 1 (1984) 119-132. — *s.* 60, C. Lambot: RBen 58 (1948) 36-42. — *s.* 64, C. Lambot: RBen 51 (1939) 10-14. — *s.* 71, P.-P. Verbraken: RBen 75 (1965) 65-108. — *s.* 76, R. Demeulenaere: Eulogia. Mélanges offerts à A. A. R. Bastiaensen, ed. G. J. M. Bartelink, A. Hilhorst, C. H. Kneepkens (Steenbrugge/Den Haag, 1991), 56-63. — *s.* 84, R. Demeulenaere: Aevum inter utrumque. Mélanges offerts à G. Sanders, ed. M. van Uytfanghe, R. Demeulenaere (Steenbrugge/Den Haag, 1991), 71-73. — *s.* 88, P.-P. Verbraken: RBen 94 (1984) 74-101. — *s.* 97, P.-P. Verbraken: RBen 78 (1968) 216-219. — *s.* 100, R. Demeulenaere: RBen 104 (1994) 79-83. — *s.* 111, C. Lambot: RBen 57 (1947) 112-116. — *s.* 112, P.-P. Verbraken: RBen 76(1966) 44-54. — *s.* 114, P.-P. Verbraken: RBen 73 (1963) 23-28. — *s.* 126, C. Lambot: RBen 69 (1959) 183-190. — *s.* 204, P.-P. Verbraken: A.-M. la Bonnardière (ed.), Saint Augustin et la Bible (Paris, 1986), 77-79. — *s.* 214, P.-P. Verbraken: RBen 72 (1962) 14-21. — *s.* 215, P.-P. Verbraken: RBen 68 (1958) 18-25. — *s.* 218, R. Étaix: Aug. 34 (1994) 364-369. — *s.* 224, C. Lambot: RBen 79 (1969) 200-205. — *s.* 235, C. Lambot: RBen 67 (1957) 137-140. — *s.* 254, C. Lambot: RBen 79 (1969) 63-69. — *s.* 283, R. Demeulenaere: Fructus centesimus. Mélanges offerts à G. J. M. Bartelink, ed. A. A. R. Bastiaensen, A. Hilhorst, C. H. Kneepkens (Steenbrugge/Dordrecht, 1991), 110-113. — *s.* 328, C. Lambot: RBen 51 (1939) 15-20. — *s.* 343, C. Lambot: RBen 66 (1956) 28-38. — *s.* 369, C. Lambot: RBen 79 (1969) 124-128. — *s.* 379, C. Lambot: RBen 59 (1949) 62-68. — *s.* 389, C. Lambot: RBen 58 (1948) 43-52. — *c. s. Arrian.,* PL 42:683-708. — *s. Caes. eccl.,* M. Petschenig, CSEL 53:167-178. — *s. dom. m.,* A. Mutzenbecher, CCL 35:1-188. — *Simpl.,* A. Mutzenbecher, CCL 44:7-91. — *sol.,* W. Hörmann, CSEL 89:3-98. — *spec.,* F. Weihrich, CSEL 12:3-285, 289-700. — *spir. et litt.,* C. F. Urba, J. Zycha, CSEL 60:155-229. — *symb. cat.,* R. v. Plaetse, CCL 46:185-199. — *trin.,* W. J. Mountain, F. Glorie, CCL 50, 50 A:(3-)25-380, 381-535. — *vera rel.,* K.-D. Daur, CCL 32:187-260. — *vers. mens.,* M. Pellegrino, Possidio, Vita di s. Augustino, Alba 1955, 122. — *vers. Nab.,* PLS 2:356-357. — *vid. deo,* A. Goldbacher, CSEL 44:274-331. — *virg.,* J. Zycha, CSEL 41:235-302. — *un. bapt.,* M. Petschenig, CSEL 53:3-34. — *util. cred.,* J. Zycha, CSEL 25/1:3-48. — *util. ieiun.,* S. D. Ruegg, CCL 46:231-241.

L: *Chronology:* S. Zarb, Chronologia operium s. A. secundum ordinem Retractationum digesta (Rome, 1934). —

Augustinus-Zeitschriften: Aug(L) 1 (1951) ff. — Aug-St 1 (1970) ff. — Augustinus 1 (1956) ff. — REAug 1 (1955) ff. — CDios 1 (1887/1952) ff. — Aug. 1 (1960) ff. — *Bibliographien:* T. van Bavel, Répertoire Bibliographique de saint A. 1950-1960 (Steenbrugge, 1963). — C. Andresen, Bibliographia Augustiniana (Darmstadt, ²1973). — consecutively paginated bibliography: "Bulletin augustinien" in: REAug. — Anthology: R. A. Markus, A. A Collection of Critical Essays (Garden City, N.Y., 1972). — AugM. — Miscellanea Agostiniana. Testi e studi, 2 vols. (Rome, 1930/31). — *Introductory Works:* H. Chadwick, A. (Göttingen, 1987). — K. Flasch, A. Einführung in sein Denken (Stuttgart, ²1994). — C. Horn, A. (Munich, 1995). — H. I. Marrou, A. (Reinbeck, 1961).

General: P. Alfaric, L'Évolution intellectuelle de st. A. 1 (Paris, 1918). — B. Altaner, Kleine Patristische Schriften (Berlin, 1967). — R. W. Battenhouse et al., A Companion to the Study of St. A., 2 vols. (Oxford/London, 1955). — T. J. van Bavel, The anthropology of A.: LouvSt 5 (1974) 34-47. — idem, Recherches sur la Christologie de St. A. (Fribourg, Switzerland, 1954). — B. Blumenkranz, Die Judenpredigt A.' (Paris, ²1973). — G. Bonner, St. A. Life and Controversies (Philadelphia, 1964). — P. Brown, A. (London, 1967). — J. Burnaby, Amor Dei (London, ²1947). — R. J. O'Connell, St. A. Confessions (Cambridge, Mass., 1969). — P. Courcelle, Les lettres grecques en Occident. De Macrobe à Cassiodore (Paris, 1948). — idem, Recherches sur les Confessions de st. A. (Paris, ²1968). — R. Crespin, Ministère et sainteté (Paris, 1965). — F. Decret, Aspect du manichéisme dans l'Afrique romaine (Paris, 1970). — D. Dideberg, St. A. et la Ière épître de S. Jean (Paris, 1975). — E. Dinkler, Die Anthropologie A.' (Stuttgart, 1934). — U. Duchrow, Christenheit u. Weltverantwortung. Traditionsgeschichte u. systematische Struktur der Zweireichelehre (Tübingen, 1969). — idem, Sprachverständnis u. bibl. Hören bei A. (Tübingen, 1965). — C. Eichenseer, Das Symbolum Apostolicum beim hl. A. (Munich, 1960). — E. Feldmann, Der Einfluß des Hortensius u. des Manichäismus auf das Denken des jungen A. v. 373 (Münster, 1975). — E. Franz, Totus Christus (Bonn, 1956). — H. Fuchs, A. u. der antike Friedensgedanke (Berlin, ²1965). — W. Geerlings, Christus Exemplum. Studien zur Christologie und Christusverkündigung A.' (Mainz, 1978). — W. Gessel, Eucharistische Gemeinschaft bei A. (Würzburg, 1966). — J. Guitton, Le temps et l'éternité chez Plotin et St. A. (Paris, ⁴1971). — H. Hagendahl, A. and the Latin classics, 2 vols. (Göteborg, 1967). — P. Henry, Plotin et l'occident (Paris, 1934). — F. Hofmann, Der Kirchenbegriff des hl. A. in seinen Grundlagen u. seiner Entwicklung (Munich, 1978 = 1933). — K. Holl, A.' innere Entwicklung (Tübingen, 1922 = Ges. Schriften 2). — R. Holte, Béatitude et Sagesse (Paris/Worcester, Mass., 1962). — W. Kamlah, Christentum u. Geschichtlichkeit (Stuttgart, ²1951). — G. N. Knauer, Die Psalmenzitate in den Konfessionen A.' (Göttingen, 1955). — J.-M. Le Blond, Les conversions de St. A. (Paris, 1950). — R. Lorenz, Fruitio dei bei A.: ZKG 63 (1950/51) 75-132. — idem, Die Herkunft des aug. "frui deo": ZKG 64 (1952/53) 34-60, 359f. — idem, Gnade u. Erkenntnis bei A.: ZKG 75 (1964) 21-78. — K.-H. Lütcke, "Auctoritas" bei A. (Stuttgart, 1968). — G. Madec, Christus, scientia et sapientia nostra: RechAug 10 (1975) 77-85. — J.-L. Maier, L'épiscopat de l'Afrique romaine, vandale et byzantine (Rome, 1973). — idem, Les missions divines selon St. A. (Fribourg, Switzerland, 1960). — A. Mandouze, St. A. L'aventure de la raison et de la grâce (Paris, 1968). —

R. A. Markus, Saeculum. History and Society in the Theology of St. A. (London/Cambridge, 1970). — F. van der Meer, A. der Seelsorger (Cologne, ²1958). — C. Mohrmann, Die altchr. Sondersprache in den Sermones des hl. A. (Nijmegen, ²1965). — J. Norregaard, A.' Bekehrung (Tübingen, 1923). — O. Perler, J.-L. Maier, Les voyages de St. A. (Paris, 1969). — J. Ratzinger, Volk u. Haus Gottes in A.' Lehre von der Kirche (Munich, 1954). — H. Reuter, Aug. Studien (Gotha, 1967 = ²1887). — J. Rief, Der Ordo-Begriff des jungen A. (Paderborn, 1962). — O. Scheel, Die Anschauung A.' über Christi Person u. Werk (Tübingen, 1901). — A. Schindler, Wort u. Analogie in A.' Trinitätslehre (Tübingen, 1965). — K.-H. Schwarte, Die Vorgeschichte der aug. Weltalterlehre (Bonn, 1966). — G. Strauss, Schriftgebrauch, Schriftauslegung u. Schriftbeweis bei A. (Tübingen, 1959). — W. Suerbaum, Vom antiken zum frühmal. Staatsbegriff. (Münster, ³1977). — G. Verbeke, A. et le stoicisme: RechAug 1 (1958) 67-89. — O. Wermelinger, Rom u. Pelagius (Stuttgart, 1975). — W. Wieland, Offenbarung bei A. (Mainz, 1978). — A. Zumkeller, Das Mönchtum des hl. A. (Würzburg, ²1968).

W. GEERLINGS

Augustinian Rule

In the ms. tradition a full nine versions have been handed down as the Augustinian Rule. Intended for men: (1) *Praeceptum* ([*praec.*]: a Rule concerned with spirituality; oldest ms., *Parisinus lat.* 12634, 6th/7th c.); (2) *Ordo monasterii* ([*ordo*], a Rule concerned with the external order of the monastery); (3) *Praeceptum longius* (combination of 1 and 2 in some of the mss.); (4) *Regula recepta* ([*reg. rec.*] combination of the first sentence of 2 with 1; used in the monasteries since the high Middle Ages). Addressed to women: (5) *Obiurgatio* ([*obiur.*] exhortation; = Augustine, *ep.* 211.1-4); (6) *Regularis informatio* ([*reg. inf.*] primarily a formal adaption of a ms. family of 1 to monasteries of women); (7) *Epistula longior* (combination of 5 and 6); (8) *Ordo monasterii feminis datus* (adaptation of 2 to monasteries of women); (9) *Epistula longissima* (combination of 5, 8, and 6). The different variants can be traced back to three basic forms: *praec.*, *obiur.*, and *ordo*.

The only one that certainly comes from → Augustine is the *praec.*, which he wrote, possibly ca. 397, for the lay monastery of Hippo, as a substitute for his own presence after he was appointed bishop. He perhaps wrote the *obiur.* for the monastery of women there. (The *reg. inf.* dates from Augustine's time.) The *ordo* is assigned either to Italy or North Africa (from Alypius?). The *praec.* is spiritually oriented to the ideal of the first Jerusalem community (Acts 4:31-35) and to charity; at the same time it shows a contemplative tension. It is marked by a tendency to interiorization: the decisive thing is not the number

of ascetical exercises but the spirit in which they are practiced. The Augustinian Rule strongly influenced the → *Regula Magistri* and the Rule of → Benedict of Nursia, and has become the basis of over one hundred religious communities.

W: *praec., ordo, obiur., reg. inf.,* L. Verheijen, 1 (Paris, 1967) [text]. — G. Lawless (Oxford, 1987) [text/English trans.]. — *praec., reg. inf.,* T. J. v. Bavel (Würzburg, 1990) [German trans.]. — *praec.,* A. Trapè (Milan, 1971) [text/Italian trans./comm.]. — A. Sage (Paris, 1961), 10-41 [text/French trans./comm.]. — *ordo,* E. Contreras, M. E. Suarez: CuMon 22 (1987) 486-494 [Spanish trans.]. — *reg. inf.,* A. C. Vega: FS G. Mercati 2 (Rome, 1946), 47-56. — A. Sage (Paris, 1961), 43-59 [French trans.]. — *reg. rec.,* A. Trapè (Bégrolles-en-Mauges, 1993 [French trans./comm.] = Rome, 1986 [Italian trans./comm.]). — A. Zumkeller (Villanova, 1987) [English trans./comm.].
L: *Bibliographies:* C. Andresen, Bibliographia Augustiniana (Darmstadt, ²1973), 90-94. — L. Verheijen, La Règle 2 (Paris, 1967), 221-239. — idem, La Règle: Aug(L) 36 (1986) 297-303. — idem, Nouvelle approche 2 (Leuven/Louvain, 1988), 394-400.
Studies: T. J. v. Bavel, Parallèles, vocabulaire et citations bibliques: Aug(L) 9 (1959) 12-77. — idem, Evangelical inspiration: DR 93 (1975) 83-99. — G. Lawless, Monastic rule (Oxford, 1987). — R. Lorenz, Anfänge des abendländischen Mönchtums: ZKG 77 (1966) 1-61. — A. Manrique, La vida monástica (Salamanca, 1959). — idem, Nuevas aportaciones: CDios 181 (1968) 707-746. — B. de Margerie, Eucharistie et communauté: Aug(L) 41 (1991) 507-530. — Marie-Ancilla (Sœur), La Règle de saint Augustin (Paris, 1996). — A. Trapè, Regola (Rome, 1986). — L. Verheijen, La Règle, 2 vols. (Paris, 1967). — idem, État actuel des questions: Aug(L) 35 (1985) 193-263. — idem, Non sicut servi sub lege: FS A. Zumkeller (Würzburg, 1975), 76-91. — idem, Nouvelle approche, 2 vols. (Bégrolles-en-Mauges, 1980; Leuven/Louvain, 1988). — A. de Vogüé, Office choral: Aug(L) 40 (1990) 45-57. — idem, Histoire littéraire du mouvement monastique 3 (Paris, 1996), 149-246. — A. Zumkeller, Mönchtum (Würzburg, ²1968). — idem, A.: TRE 4·745-748.

M. SKEB, OSB

Aunacharius of Auxerre

A. was bishop of Auxerre ca. 567-605. The canons of a synod that he held in 585 or 592 (PL 72:761-67) are important for knowledge of the state of the church's organization. Among other things, regular synods were introduced. There is a letter (*ep.*) of A. to Stephanus, an African priest, in which he asks him to compose a life of A.'s predecessor, Germanus, and of Amator. In addition, A. is to be regarded as editor of the *Martyrologium Hieronymianum* (→ Calendar), which survives only in his version of it.

W: *ep.,* PL 72:767f.
L: H. Atsma, Klöster u. Mönchtum im Bistum Auxerre: Francia 11 (1983) 1-96. — J. Dubois, Martyrologium

81

Hieronomianum: LMA 6:357-361. — M. Heinzelmann, A.: LMA 1:1238f.

G. RÖWEKAMP

Aurasius of Toledo

A. was bishop of Toledo (603[?]-615), which, after the end of the Visigothic anticatholic reaction, became under his leadership the metropolitan see of the province of Carthage. In an *Epistula ad Froganum* (*ep.*) A. excommunicated and anathematized Froja, a Visgothic magnate who protected the Jewish community, on the grounds that he did not respect the bishop's authority and was a judaizer.

W: W. Gundlach, MGH. Ep 3:689f. — I. Gil, Miscellanea Wisigothica (Seville, 1972), 48.
L: J. Orlandis, D. Ramos-Lisson, Die Synoden auf der Iberischen Halbinsel (Paderborn, 1981).

E. REICHERT

Aurelian of Arles

A. was the second successor of Caesarius of Arles and was bishop from 546 to 551 (d. in Lyons). He composed → monastic rules for nuns and men for the monasteries he established in Arles; these rules were chiefly expansions and revisions of the corresponding rules of Caesarius. The influence of his rules can be seen in the *Regula Tarnatensis* and the rule of → Ferreolus. A short exhortation (*ep.*) to king Theudebert I (ca. 546) has also been preserved.

W: *reg. mon., reg. virg.*, PL 68:385-406. — *reg. mon.*, A. Schmidt: StMon 17 (1975) 237-256; 18 (1976) 17-54 [text/comm.]. — *ep.*, W. Gundlach, CCL 117:426-428.
L: C. de Clercq, La législation religieuse (Leuven/Louvain, 1936). — V. Desprez, Règles monastiques d'Occident (Bellefontaine, 1980). — A. de Vogüé, A.: DIP 7:1604-1607.

C. KASPER

Aurelius of Carthage

Sources at our disposal (conciliar acts, correspondence, contemporary testimonies) tell us the following about A.: ca. 382 he was a deacon of Carthage; the place and date of his birth are unknown. When Augustine returned to Africa in 388, A. was still a deacon, but in 391 he was already bishop of Carthage. His episcopal ideal reflected the figure of Cyprian; his goal was to restore the glory of the church of Carthage. Because of his position as primate, A. presided at pan-African councils and at the conference of 411. He made very skillful use of councils for his ends; it was he who inaugurated the lengthy series of synods that began on Oct. 8, 393. These not only served for the clarification of theol. and disciplinary problems, but, above all, they increased the contacts of the African provinces with one another. Conciliar activity with A. as presider extended to three areas: (a) determination of the canon of bibl. books to be read in the liturgy; (b) support of monastic life; (c) management of eccles. legislation and the dispensation of justice by the clergy.

Between 401 and 411 the struggle of the councils against Donatism was strongly promoted by A., who continued the theol. line set down by → Optatus of Milevis. In his struggle against paganism he found support in Theodosius's legislation against pagans. In addition, the council of 399 claimed the right of asylum for Chr. churches, by analogy with that of pagan temples. After 411 the fight against Pelagianism claimed most of A.'s capacity for work. From the condemnation of Pelagius's disciple, Caelestius, in 411 to the final rejection of Pelagius and the *Epistula tractoria* of Zosimus in 419, the controversy was carried on under A.'s leadership. It was not least as a result of this conciliar activity that the self-awareness of the African church grew and that the Council of Carthage in 425 forbade appeals to Rome: *ut nullus ad Romanam ecclesiam audeat appellare.*

A.'s effectiveness cannot be separated from his close relationship with Augustine, whose theol. inspiration compelled A., the eccles. politician, to take a new path. The calendar of the church of Carthage records the *depositio sancti Aurelii episcopi* on July 20, 429 (or 430). In addition to his correspondence with Augustine, A. exchanged letters with many other bishops, but these have been lost, with the exception of a letter to the bishops of the Byzacena province on the condemnation of Pelagius.

W: PL 20:1009-1014.
L: A. M. La Bonnardière, A.: AugL 1:550-566. — PAC 105-127.

W. GEERLINGS

Ausonius

Decimus Magnus Ausonius (A.) was born ca. 310 and was of noble descent on his mother's side; from 335 on he was a *grammaticus* and *rhetor* in Bordeaux, his native city, until, as a result of his successful work as teacher, Emperor Valentinian appointed him tutor of his son Gratian in Trier in 367. Ca. 370

Valentinian made him a *comes*, in 375 *quaestor sacri palatii*; under Gratian he became *praefectus praetorii* in 377 and *consul* in 379. He exerted a special influence on Gratian in the areas of policy and legislation. After Gratian's assassination (383) A. retired to his estates. The *conversio* of his famous disciple and friend, Paulinus of Nola, to the monastic life was the occasion for an exchange of letters, in which A. seeks in vain to get Paulinus to return to Gaul and to take up again the writing of traditional poetry (Ausonius, *ep.* 21, 22, 23, 24 [Green] — Paulinus, *carm.* 10 and 11). A. died ca. 394.

The private world supplies the content of A.'s body of short poems, which follow the formal techniques of the schools of rhetoric. They may be divided into three sections: (a) personal (*praefatiunculae, Ephemeris, Gratiarum actio, Orationes [Praecationes, Versus paschales], Parentalia. Epicedion, De herediolo, Protrepticus, Genethliakos, Epistulae*); (b) history of the schools (*Ordo urbium nobilium, Commemoratio professorum Burdigalensium, Periochae, Epitaphia, Fasti, Caesares, Eclogae*); (c) artistic poetry (*Technopaegnion, Cento nuptialis, Griphus, Ludus septem sapientium, Cupido cruciatur, Mosella, Bussula, Epigrammata*). Labels such as "half-Christian," "Christian in name only," and "syncretism" are not appropriate for explaining the striking "juxtaposition" of pagan and Chr. ideas in A.'s work. It is likely that the shifting of personal religion to the interior world opened up, within the sphere of the external references of explicit religion, an area that could be filled indifferently with pagan and Chr. ideas and which made possible an abstract and transcendental picture of the Chr. God.

W: R P H Green (Oxford, 1991) [text/comm.]. — H. G. Evelyn White (London, 1988, 1985 = [1]1919, 1921) [text/English trans.]. — A Pastorino (Turin, 1971) [text/Italian trans./literature]. — R. Peiper (Darmstadt, 1976 = Leipzig, [1]1876) [text]. — S. Prete (Leipzig, 1978) [text]. — C. Schenkl, MGH. AA 5/2.
L: L. J. Bolchazy, J. A. M. Sweeney, Concordantia (Hildesheim, 1982). — HLL 5:268-308 (literature). — M. J. Lossau (ed.), A. (Darmstadt, 1991) (literature). — P. de Labriolle, A.: RAC 1:1020-1023. — M. Skeb, Christo vivere (Bonn, 1997), 23-57. — K. Smolak, Moregengebet (eph. 3): La preghiera nel tardo antico (Rome, 1999), 113-126.

M. SKEB, OSB

Auspicius of Toul

A. (d. ca. 475/478) has left a letter (*ep.*)(ca. 460) to Arbogast, the imperial Comes of Trier and later (ca. 480) bishop of Chartres, which he probably wrote at the instigation of Apollinaris Sidonius, who had been asked for an explanation of spiritual writings (*ep.* 4.17). The call to a Chr. way of life and the warning against greed make the work resemble, in its content, a Chr. "Mirror of Princes." In form it is an early example of rhythmical poetry that does not follow the rules of quantity-based metrics. *Ep.* 7.10 of → Apollinaris Sidonius is addressed to A.

W: W. Gundlach, CCL 117:442-447.
L: W. Brandes, Die Ep. des A. (Wolfenbüttel, 1905) (literature). — idem, Die Ep. des A. u. die Anfänge der lat. Rhythmik: RMP 64 (1909) 57-97. — W. Meyer, Die rhythmischen Jamben des A.: NGWG 23 (1906) 192-194 (literature). — L. Jadin, A.: DHGE 5:781. — P. Viard, A.: BSS 2:626.

C. KASPER

Authentikos Logos

Authentikos Logos ("Authoritative Teaching") is the title of a Copt. work in the Nag Hammadi Codices (6, 3). It contains a treatise on the fate of the soul that has fallen into the material world. The Neoplatonic Logos doctrine and soteriology developed here point to Alexandria as the place of origin; the work was written probably toward the end of the 2nd c.

W: J. E. Ménard, L'Authentikos Logos (Leuven/Louvain, 1977) [Coptic text/French trans.]. — D. M. Parrott, NHC 5/6 (Leiden, 1979), 257-289 [text/English trans.].
L: R. van den Brock, The A. L.: VigChr 33 (1979) 260-286. — P. Chérix, Concordance NHC 6 (Leuven/Louvain, 1993).

P. BRUNS

Autobiography

Unlike biography, autobiography was not a fixed literary form in the ancient world. There were indeed autobiographies here and there and to a limited extent, but it would be more accurate to speak of autobiographical elements.

Biography presupposes the discovery of an immutable individuality and regards this as worth communicating to others because of its uniqueness. For this reason, autobiography is to be assigned to a late phase in the discovery of the self. Thus, scholars have regarded Augustine's *Confessiones* (*conf.*) as the high point of autobiographical description and have seen all other pre-Augustinian literary testimonies as simply a preparatory prehistory. The memoir literature (*Hypomnēmata* and *Commentarii*) may be regarded as a precursor.

A purely formal division arranges autobiographical testimonies as follows: (1) funerary inscriptions; (2) personal information given by writers (Prudentius); (3) apologies (Athanasius, Gregory Naz.); (4) memoirs (Martyrdom of Perpetua, visions of Hermas, Paulinus of Pella); (5) reports of interior experiences (letters of Cyprian and Jerome); (6) stories of conversion (Paul, Justin, Cyprian, Commodian, Hilary, Ps.-Clement); (7) religious histories of the soul (Augustine, Patrick). In this division, however, insufficient heed is paid to the decisive factor of inner individuality and the desire to communicate it.

Autobiographical testimonies from the early church display three elements: (1) a look back at the person's life and God's working in it as martyrdom approaches; (2) the rejection of pagan education and culture and the turning to Chr. thought; and (3) conversion to a Chr. way of life.

On 1: An early form of this autobiographical element is Paul's look back, for clearly apologetic purposes, to his conversion and the steps leading up to it (Gal 1:11-24). In the account of the martyrdom of Perpetua (→ Acts of the Martyrs) (ch. 4) this look back at her life as martyrdom approaches is mediated through visions.

On 2: On the occasion of his panegyric to Origen, → Gregory the Wonderworker discovers that a divine educative purpose has been guiding his life (*pan. Or.* 48ff.). → Cyprian praises the divine grace (*ad Donat.* 3f.) that has led him to conversion; in baptism he was led to a mountain peak and could now look back on his earlier life (chs. 5-14). → Commodian sees the course of his life in a similar way (*instr.* 1 praef. 2.16): the reading of the divine law has set him free and therefore he now wants to teach the ignorant. → Hilary of Poitiers (*trin.* 1.1-15) interprets the stages of his intellectual development as a struggle for grace and redemption. → Jerome (*ep.* 22.7) looks back at his life in the wilderness: he had been converted from a man of the city to a monk and had foresworn his old love of Cicero. The high point of this autobiographical distancing from the education of antiquity is → Gregory Naz.'s poem *De vita sua*. His surprising resignation as bishop of Constantinople was a decisive point in his life, which he had experienced, despite all setbacks, as a journey to salvation; at the end of his career he had indeed failed as a statesman of the church, but now he could devote himself to contemplation, which he loved.

On 3: Both themes—gradual way to Chr. faith and moral conversion—are brought together in the most impressive and unsurpassable way in the *Confessiones* of → Augustine. This work shows the path of Augustine's life as an exemplar of a soul's way to God. His education led his intellect to a Neoplatonic Christianity; the conversion of his will ended in an ascetic life. The effectiveness of the work is due not only to its penetrating psychological observation of the self but to its fundamental anthropological principle, that the human heart is restless and can find its rest in God alone. The following writers were unable to reach Augustine's high level. Neither → Prudentius nor → Paulinus of Pella produced a complete autobiography but are satisfied to reveal some aspects of their lives. The first autobiographical testimony from outside the empire, a testimony from the early medieval Chr. world, is the *confessio* of → Patrick of Ireland, who describes his conversion and missionary vocation in a linguistically unpolished form. In contrast, there is the literarily polished *Confessio* of Bishop → Ennodius of Pavia, although it does not reach the heights of Jerome and Augustine.

L: G. A. Benrath, A.: TRE 4:772-789. — G. Misch, Geschichte der A. (Frankfurt a.M., ³1949/50). — A. Sizoo, A.: RAC 1:1050-1055.

W. Geerlings

Auxentius of Durostorum

A., who as a child had been a pupil of Ulfila, was forced to leave his episcopal see of Durostorum in 380 after the edict of Theodosius that required the return of churches to the orthodox. Shortly thereafter (ca. 382), under the protection of Empress Justina, he was appointed bishop of the Arian community in Milan. A. struggled with Ambrose over the return of churches to the Arians.

His work *De vita et obitu Ulfilae* has been preserved, in the form of a letter, as part of the *Dissertatio Maximini contra Ambrosium*. The first part deals with the teaching of Ulfila, while the second gives the facts of his life and his profession of faith; this has led to doubts about the unity of the work. Today, however, the entire letter is taken as a eulogy and at the same time a witness to the spiritual testament of Ulfila and dated shortly after the latter's death in 383.

W: PLS 1:703-707. — R. Gryson, SC 267:236-251. — R. P. C. Hanson, Arian controversy (Edinburgh, 1988), 104-106 [English trans.].
L: Y.-M. Duval, Concile d'Aquilée de 381: RHE 76 (1981) 317-331. — M. Meslin, Ariens (Paris, 1967), 44-58, 439.

B. Dümler

Auxentius of Milan

A., a Cappadocian, became a presbyter ca. 343 under Gregory the Cappadocian and in 355, despite a deficient knowledge of Latin, was appointed bishop of Milan as successor of the exiled Dionysius. He was attacked by Eusebius of Vercelli and Hilary of Poitiers because of his Arianism; the Synod of Rimini condemned him in 359. Under pressure from Valentinian I (364) he accepted the *homoousios* and so, thanks to the emperor's favor, was able to hold out, despite condemnation by Synods of Gaul and Spain and a Roman synod (372) under Damasus. He died in 373. His Catholic successor was Ambrose, who by imperial command was supposed to let the Arian A. have a church outside the gates of Milan. In this conflict with the emperor A. coined the saying: *Imperator enim intra ecclesiam, non supra ecclesiam est.*

A letter of A. to Emperors Valentinian and Valens has been preserved in the *Contra Auxentium* of Hilary (chs. 13-15). In it A. defends himself against the charge of Arianism and accuses Hilary and Eusebius of slander: He did not know A., never taught Arian doctrines, and had from childhood always believed in the one true God and the true Son. But he avoided describing Christ as true God.

W: Hilarius, Contra Auxentium, PL 10:617f.
L: F. H. Dudden, The Life and Times of St. Ambrose 1 (Oxford, 1935), 270-276. — M. Meslin, Les Ariens d'Occident (Paris, 1967). — H. Rahner, Kirche u. Staat im frühen Christentum (Munich, 1961), 150-159. — M. Simonetti, La Crisi ariana nel IV secolo (Rome, 1975).

W. GEERLINGS

Avitus of Braga

A., a Spaniard, was a presbyter of Braga. He happened to be in Jerusalem when in Dec. 415 the Gr. presbyter → Lucian discovered the relics of Stephen at Kaphar Gamala near the city. A. acquired some pieces and wanted to have them brought to Braga. In order to give legitimacy to the relics, he translated Lucian's account of the discovery from Greek into Latin and sent it to his bishop. Two versions of this have been published (*Lucian. ep. rec.* A 50; *rec.* B 50). A. enclosed the translation with an *Epistula ad Palconium episcopum Bracarensem de reliquiis S. Stephani* (*ep. ad Palc.*). The transfer of the relics failed because Orosius, whom A. had commissioned, carried them only to Minorca (→ Severus of Minorca) and then returned to Africa.

A. was perhaps a correspondent of → Jerome (Jerome, *ep.* 79; 106; 124).

W: *Lucian. ep. rec.* A. 50, *rec.* B. 50, *ep. ad Palc.*, PL 41:807-818. — E. Vanderlinden: EtByz 4 (1946) 188-217 [text].
L: B. Altaner, A.: idem, Kleine patristische Schriften (Berlin,

1967), 450-466. — J. Martin, Die Reuelatio S. Stephani u. Verwandtes: HJ 77 (1958) 419-433.

E. REICHERT

Avitus of Vienne

Alcimus Ecdicius Avitus (A.) was from a senatorial family and ca. 490 succeeded his father, Iscius, as bishop of Vienne (Ennodius, *Vita Epiphanii* 173). Despite the close relationship that he cultivated with Rome (*ep.* 34), he lost out to Caesarius of Arles in the disagreement over the metropolitan see. He maintained contact with Gundobald, the Arian king of Burgundy, and led his son to the Catholic faith. In 517 he presided over the Synod of Epao which dealt with questions of church discipline; he died shortly afterwards.

A.'s most important literary work is his *Carminun libri sex.* The first five books, the *De spiritalis historiae gestis* (*hist.*), treat of the creation and fall of human beings, the expulsion from paradise, the flood, and crossing of the Red Sea; at each point Christ and the church are introduced as antitypes. The sixth book is a poem of consolation to his sister, Fuscia, who had been brought to a monastery after her birth and who now is dissatisfied with her way of life. In hexameters that appeal to models, some of them bibl., A. praises virginity and paints a gloomy picture of the sufferings of married women. Remaining shorter poems have been lost, acc. to the author himself (*hist.*, prol.). This remark led to the erroneous attribution to him of a series of inscriptions from various periods.

A.'s other writings are not on the same high linguistic level. His ca. thirty-four sermons (Gregory of Tours, *Franc.* 2.34) have survived primarily in fragments. In complete form we have two *Homiliae in rogationibus*, occasioned by the rogation procession introduced at Vienne by Mamertus ca. 470. An extensive collection of letters in three books (8 *ep.*) is important for the history of the church and of culture. This was a correspondence chiefly with Gallic bishops; but letters of foreign writers to A. (*ep.* 13, 16, 21, 42, 54, 68, 71, 96) among others (*ep.* 29, 47, 78, 86, 93, 94) are included. *Ep.* 53 is a forgery. Four letters deal with theol. controversies. *Ep.* 1, *Contra Arrianos*, shows his friendly efforts to effect conversions in the family of the Burgundian king. In *ep.* 2-3, *Contra Eutychianum* (512), he attacks Nestorius; in *ep.* 4, *De subitanea paenitentia* (after 500), he approves of a *poenitentia in extremis*, against → Faustus of Riez, who rejects it in light of his own ascetical background and his theol. views. Because of his good relations with the royal house and with Rome, A. was regarded as a pillar of the Catholic church and the soul of eccles. life in the kingdom of Burgundy.

W: R. Peiper, MGH. AA 6/2:1-294.
L: P. Deproost, Le poème De diluvio mundi d'A.: JAC 34 (1991) 88-104. — J. Evans, Genesis tradition (Oxford, 1968). — R. Herzog, Bibelepik der Spätantike (Munich, 1980). — G. Krüger, Die Bibeldichtung zu Ausgang des Altertums (Giessen, 1919). — D. Nodes, A.'s Doctrinal Implications (Toronto, 1981). — idem, A. Spiritalis Historiae: VigChr 38 (1984) 185-195. — idem, Subitanea paenitentia in Letters of Faustus and A.: RThAM 55 (1988) 30-41. — idem, A. and a Fifth-Century Statement of Faith: JECS 2 (1994) 71-91. — M. Roberts, Epic and Rhetorical Paraphrase (Liverpool, 1985).

C. KASPER

B

Babai of Gbilta in Tirhan

B., of Gbilta in Tirhan, east of the Tigris (8th c.), founded a number of schools for singers and visited them each year. Some responsories in the Chaldean weekday breviary are attributed to him.

W: P. Bedjan, Breviarium Chaldaicum (Paris, 1886f.), 214 [text].

P. Bruns

Babai the Great

I. Life: B., called "the Great," was born ca. 550 in Beth 'Aynata and spent his youth in Beth Zabday before becoming a teacher in Nisibis. He finally entered the great monastery of Mount Izla, where he led a monastic life under Abraham of Kashkar and Dadiso. After the death of Catholicos Gregory I, B. headed the Persian church from 608/609 to 628 while the office of catholicos was vacant. Shortly after obtaining official recognition from the emperor, he died.
II. Works: Of the eighty-three works attributed to B. by Ebedjesu, the following have survived: his major dogm. treatise *Liber de unione* (*un.*), which treats of the mysteries of the incarnation and the Eucharist; two commentaries on the *Centuries* of → Evagrius Pont. (*cent.*); two unpublished *Sermones de lege spiritali* (*leg. spir.*), handed down under the name of Marcus; also some hagiographies (*acta*) and monastic rules (*can*).
III. Basic Lines of Thought: B. was one of the most outstanding Nestorian thinkers; he systematically developed the christological approach of → Theodore Mops., but especially his doctrine on the soul. He sharply attacked such theologians as → Henana of Adiabene, who strove to reconcile a moderate Nestorianism with Chalcedonian orthodoxy. Basing himself on Theodore, B. takes as his starting point the assertion that the Logos assumed a complete human nature, including a hypostatically united spiritual soul. In his teaching on the sleep of souls B. likewise thinks in traditional terms (→ Aphraates). For him, as for Theodore, the Eucharist is an image of the heavenly body of Christ.

S: *vita*, A. Scher, PO 13:454-456.
W: *un.*, A. Vaschalde, CSCO. S 61 [text/Latin trans.]

— *cent.*, W. Frankenberg, Evagrius Ponticus: AGWG. PH (1912) 8-471 [Syriac-Greek text]. — *leg. spir.*, P. Krüger, BM 17270: OS 6 (1957) 297-299. — *can.*, J. B. Chabot, Synodicon Orientale (Paris, 1902), 562-598 [text/French trans.]. — O. Braun, Buch der Synhados (Stuttgart, 1900), 307-331 [German trans.]. — A. Vööbus, Syriac Documents (Stockholm, 1960), 176-184 [text/English trans.]. — *acta*, P. Bedjan, Histoire de Mar Jabalaha (Paris, ²1895), 416-572 [text]. — O. Braun, Ausgewählte Akten (Kempten, 1915), 221-277 [German trans.]. — AMSS 4:201-207 [text].
L: L. Abramowski, Christologie: OCA 197 (1974) 219-245. — eadem, Christologisches Problem: OCP 41 (1975) 289-343. — J. S. Assemani, BOCV 3:88-97. — A. Baumstark, Geschichte (Bonn, 1922), 137-139. — V. Grumel, Un théologien nestorien: EOr 22 (1923) 153-181, 257-280; 23 (1924) 9-34, 162-178, 257-275, 395-400. — A. Guillaumont, Sur les Messaliens: OCA 205 (1978) 257-265. — P. Krüger, Geistiges Gesetz: OrChr 44 (1960) 46-74. — idem, Primat Petri: OrChr 45 (1961) 54-69. — idem, cognitio sapientiae: StPatr 5 (1962) 377-381. — idem, Pelagianismus: OrChr 46 (1962) 77-86. — L. I. Scipioni, Ricerche sulla cristologia (Fribourg, Switzerland, 1956). — W. Wolska, Geheimnis der Taufe: OrChr 47 (1963) 98-110.

P. Bruns

Babai the Lesser (Catholicos)

B. the Lesser (d. ca. 502) was elected catholicos in 497 and guided the destinies of the Persian church from Seleucia-Ctesiphon. In that same year he convoked a synod which, following the proposals of → Barsauma of Nisibis, did away with clerical celibacy. Some canons (*can.*) of his, dealing with clerical life and church discipline, have survived.

W: J. B. Chabot, Synodicon Orientale (Paris, 1902), 62-68, 310-317 [text/French trans.]. — O. Braun, Buch der Synhados (Stuttgart, 1900), 83-92 [German trans.].

P. Bruns

Babai of Nisibis

B. was born in 563 of a family expatriated to Nisibis. At the age of twenty-two he attached himself to the monastic patriarch Abraham of Kaskar. After the latter's death in 588, B. became a recluse. He died ca. 630 but had previously founded another monastery on Mount Izla. His literary remains consist of two unpublished *Sermones* (*serm.*) on penance and some hymns of praise (*hymn.*) in the Chaldean breviary.

S: *vita*, F. Nau, Histoire: ROC 21 (1918) 161-168 [text/French trans.]. — A. Scher, PO 13:454-456 [text/French trans.].
W: *hymn.*, P. Bedjan, Breviarium Chaldaicum (Paris, 1886f.), 1:120, 183; 2:99f [text]. — J. M. Schönfelder, Fastenzeit: ThQ 48 (1866) 193f. [German trans.]. — *serm.*, Mss

Seert 109. — N. Sims-Williams, Homily on the Final Evil Hour: OCP 48 (1982) 171-176 [English trans.].

P. Bruns

Bachiarus

B. was from Galicia, which he left ca. 411 in order to live as an itinerant ascetic. Gennadius (*vir. ill.* 24) knows of some short works by B. but had himself read only the *De fide* (*fid.*). In this work, written in Rome 383/384, B. justifies his choice of an itinerant life. It is not fear of human beings but fear of God that motivates him. His way of life would (he says) make him a co-heir of Abraham. He emphatically asserts his own decency and orthodoxy. He complains that being from Galicia is enough to bring suspicion of heresy; *fid.* attests that Galicia was a province of Priscillianists.

Between 394 and 400 B. also composed *Epistula ad Ianuarium seu De lapso*, also titled *De reparatione lapsi* (*repar. laps.*). This work is important for the history of penance in Spain. There is disagreement over whether two ascetical letters (*ep.*) are to be attributed to B.

B. did not compose any other writings. The assumption that he is to be identified with Bishop Peregrinus has not been proven. Nor is there any question of his being the author of the Priscillianist Pauline Canons. Efforts to prove him the author of Ps.-Cypriana have likewise been unsuccessful.

W: *fid.*, PL 20:1019-1036. — J. Madoz: RET 1 (1940/41) 463-474 [text]. — *repar. laps.*, PL 20:1037-1062. — *ep.*, PLS 1:1035-1044.
L: J. Duhr, Le fid. de B.: RHE 24 (1928) 9f. — O. F. Fritzsche, Über B. u. Peregrinus: ZKG 17 (1897) 210-215. — A. Mundó, Estudios sobre el fid.: StMon 7 (1965) 247-303. — F. X. Murphy, Leaders of Iberian Christianity (Boston, 1962).

E. Reichert

Balai

Little is known of the circumstances of B.'s life. He was a chor bishop in the region around Aleppo. Dating of his work is possible because he composed several poems in praise of Bishop Acacius, who died in 432. B. was a very prolific writer, but most of his poems have been lost. Among the genuine writings is the poem for the dedication of a church in Qenneshrin near Aleppo (*dedic.*) and the five poems in praise of Acacius (*Acac.*). Also to be attributed to him are some prayers (*or.*) to the Mother of God and to the martyrs. Not all the poems that bear his name in the Jacobite breviary are authentic.

W: *Acac.*, J. J. Overbeck, S. Ephraemi aliorumque opera (Oxford, 1865), 251-330 [Syriac text]. — S. Landersdorfer, Syr. Dichter (Munich, 1913), 55-99 [German trans.]. — *or.*, J. J. Overbeck, loc. cit., 331-335 [Syriac text]. — *dedic.*, F. Graffin, Dédicace de l'église: ParOr 10 (1981/82) 103-122 [text/French trans.]. — K. V. Zetterstéen, Beiträge zur religiösen Dichtung B.s (Leipzig, 1902) [Syriac text/German trans./comm.].

P. Bruns

Bar Chatar

B., of whose life nothing is known, is regarded as being, along with Simon bar Apollon, the author of the life of → Simeon the Stylite.

W: AMSS 4:507-644 [Syriac text]. — H. Hilgenfeld, H. Lietzmann, Leben des hl. Simeon (Leipzig, 1908), 79-188 [German trans.].

P. Bruns

Bardesanes (Syriac: Bardesain)

I. Life: According to the *Chronicon Edessenum*, B. was born on Tamuz (July) 11, 154, in Mesopotamia. He belonged to a distinguished Parthian family and spent the first part of his life at the court of King Abgar IX the Great (179-216) in Edessa. During this time he came in contact with Bishop Abercius of Hierapolis and supported him in his fight against Marcionism (*vit. Aber.* 175). After Edessa fell to Caracalla (216), B. was in exile in Armenia for a time (Moses of Khorene 2.66). There is sure testimony (Porphyry, *Abst.* 4.17) of B.'s meeting with an Indian delegation to Emperor Heliogabalus (217-222) in 218. Acc. to Michael of Antioch (d. 1199) B. died in 222 at the age of sixty-eight.

II. Works: B. is regarded as one of the most brilliant but also most enigmatic personalities produced by early Syr. Christianity. He represented a cosmopolitan, anti-ascetical Christianity of the Edessan upper class, in which Syr. and Gr. elements combined in a harmonious synthesis. B. was equally important in the fields of cosmology, astronomy, ethnology, philosophy, politics, and even poetry. His influence, through his followers, the Bardesanites, lasted down into the 8th c.

Almost all of his extensive writings have been lost, and his teaching can now only be reconstructed in fragmentary form from later traditions and the attacks of his opponents. Only the *Book of the Laws of* the *Countries* (*LLR*), edited by his disciple Philip, has come down to us complete. This work contains, in dialogue form, B.'s views on cosmological and anthropological questions having to do with the relationship between nature, freedom, and destiny against the background of Christian and Jewish monotheism. B. shows points of contact with Stoic speculation on the elements. Important sources for B.'s views are the hymns written against him by → Ephraem and the testimonies of later Syr. fathers of the church.

A key idea in B.'s philosophy is the concept of freedom (in the sense of the freedom to choose between good and evil), which occurs in both his cosmology and his anthropology. The human body is a mingling of the elements with darkness and is thus a small image of the cosmos. Because of their spirituality human beings participate in the divine world and find their eschatological fulfillment in the return of the soul to the bridal chamber of the Light. Christ is the Word expressing the divine thought that puts order into the conflicting elements of the cosmos. His redemptive work is to have cleared the way for the human soul into the realm of heavenly light.

In the heresiological literature B. is sometimes ascribed a gospel of his own. But these testimonies are so slight that nothing can be deduced from them; the work meant is perhaps even identical with the → *Diatessaron*.

W: *LLR*, F. Nau, PS 2 [text/Latin trans.]. — idem, B. l'astrologue (Paris, 1899) [text/French trans.]. — W. Cureton, Spicilegium Syriacum (London, 1855), 1-21/1-34 [text/English trans.]. — H. J. W. Drijvers (Assen, 1965) [text/English trans.]. — H. Wiesmann, 75 Jahre Stalla Matutina, FS 1 (Feldkirch, 1931), 553-572. — G. Levi della Vida (Rome, 1921) [Italian trans.].
L: E. Beck, B. u. seine Schule bei Ephraem: Muséon 91 (1978) 271-333. — H. J. W. Drijvers, B. (Assen, 1966). — F. Haase, Zur Bardaisanschen Gnosis (Leipzig, 1910). — A. Hilgenfeld, B. der letzte Gnostiker (Leipzig, 1864). — T. Jansma, Natuur, lot en vrijheid (Wageningen, 1969). — H. Kruse, Die mythologischen Irrtümer des B.: OrChr 71 (1987) 24-52. — A. Merx, B. (Halle, 1863). — B. Rehm, B. u. die Ps.-klementinen: Ph. 93 (1938) 218-247. — H. Schaeder, B. in syr. u. griech. Überlieferung: ZKG 51 (1932) 21-74. — J. Teixidor, B. La première philosophie syriaque (Paris, 1992). — G. v. Wesendonk, B. u. Mani: AcOr 10 (1932) 336-363.

P. BRUNS

Barhadbesabba of Beth Arbaye

B., who is not to be confused with his namesake from Halwan, was active as a priest and a translator in the school of Nisibis toward the end of the 6th c. Of the many works mentioned by Ebedjesu (BO 3.1.169) the only survivor is his church history, which is a valuable source for the study of early Nestorianism. In his presentation B. depends closely on his models, → Socrates, → Theodoret of Cyrrhus, and the *Liber Heraclidis* of → Nestorius.

W: F. Nau, PO 9/23:490-631, 177-343 [text/French trans.].
L: L. Abramowski, Untersuchungen zum Liber Heraclidis (Leuven/Louvain, 1963), 33-73.

P. BRUNS

Barhadbesabba of Halwan

B. studied under Henana in the school of Nisibis toward the end of the 6th c. and was himself later in charge of instruction there. He composed a history of the founding of schools, which is important for Nestorianism. His explanation of history begins with philosophical considerations of God and the world, the differences between created substances, and human knowledge of God.

W: A. Scher, PO 4:31-97 [text/French trans.].

P. BRUNS

Barnabas, Letter of

I. Transmission and Attestation: The twenty-one chapters of the anonymous work known since Clement Alex. as the *Letter of Barnabas* (*Barn.*) are contained, in Greek, in *Cod. Sinaiticus* (ℵ, 4th c.) and in *Cod. Hierosolymitanus* 54 (H, 11th c.). A Syr. fragment (5th/6th c.) of *Barn.* 19.1f., 8; 21.1, is very close to the above. In *Cod. Vat. gr.* 859 (11th c.) Polycarp, *ep.* 1.1–9.2 is followed immediately, without any transition, by *Barn.* 5.7–21.9; this ms., with nine descendants (15th/16th c.), is witness G; its Arm. translation (12th c.) has disappeared. The Lat. translation of *Barn.* 1–17 goes back to the 2nd/3rd c.; *Pap.* PSI 757 (3rd/5th c.), containing *Barn.* 9.1-6, closely resembles it. Since the four principal witnesses (ℵ, H, G, L) often differ and yet are of comparable value, different editorial principles are possible, which lead to divergent critical editions. Acc. to Clement, who cites *Barn.* several times, and acc. to Eusebius (*h.e.* 4.14.1, explained the letter in his *Hypotyposes* 8), *Barn.* 5.9b was cited as an objection by Celsus (Origen, *Cels.* 1.63). Jerome, *adv. Pelag.* 3.2.14-16 and *in psalm.* 15.4.175-78, depends on Origen's answer. Didymus of Alexandria cites *Barn.* 19.12b (*Ps.* 40-44.4; Cod. 300, 12f.) and refers to *Barn.* 1.1a; 4.10; 18.1c; 20.1a. Echoes in, e.g., Justin, Irenaeus, Tertullian, *CEA* (→ Apostolic Church Order), and *Didascalia* point rather to thematic traditions in the christocentric interpretation of scripture; but *CEA prooem.* may have been inspired by *Barn.* 1.1. The high esteem for *Barn.* in the early church is attested first by Clement (an apostolic letter) and Origen (a Catholic letter), and lastly by א. Only since the discovery of the Lat. translation and of a ms. of witness G in the 17th c. has the text been available to the West.

II. Form and Basic Lines of Thought: Linguistic and situational consistency, along with argumentative references and cohesiveness show the literary integrity of *Barn.* Epistolary framework (1; 21), literary momentum (1.5; 4.9; 21.9), universal addressee (1.1), claim to authority (1.1 and 8; 4.9; 5.3; 6.5; 10 passim), didactic emphasis (6.5; 7.1 and 9; 9.7-9 passim), and extensive citation and interpretation of scripture show the work to be a treatise framed as a letter. The most important christological concept is *kyrios*. This enables the author to turn the paradoxical statement that the preexistent one (5.5), who is God, suffered and died, into the point of contact that renders this event the plausible fulfillment of prophecies initiated by the *kyrios* himself and the fulfillment of his own will, espec. because of its soteriological purpose (7.2). Since this concept of the *kyrios* includes the person of the historical Jesus and therefore the crucified one (7.3-11), it is constitutive for christology, ecclesiology, and soteriology. This last is the central theol. theme (*Barn.* 4–8). The question of eschatological deliverance (2.10b; 4.1) determines the choice and treatment of the individual themes. As a result, the intention of *Barn.* is to give a compendium of accepted tradition (1.5-8; 17.1) on the basis of authoritative witnesses and so to demonstrate and safeguard (1.5; 4.9; 7.2) the Chr. identity of its readers in dealing with other Christians. For this reason, *Barn.* 2–16 shows the scriptures to be a foretelling of the Chr. age (7.1; 9.7-9). Because the scriptures in their entirety prophesy Christ and Christians, there is no history of salvation prior to this locus of salvation. Israel and its institutions are to some extent polemically voided as saving realities (4.6-8; 5.7; 13f.), and the patriarchs, Moses, and David are claimed exclusively as prophets who announce Christ and Christians (4.8; 5.7; 6.8; 9.7; 11.9; 13.7). Study of the scriptures in this perspective brings that "perfect gnosis" (1.5; 6.9; 18.1), which alone makes possible divinely obedient action in faith in Jesus Christ and a participation in the eschatological salvation (i.e., reward, resurrection, and everlasting life: 8.5; 11.11; 21.1) promised and guaranteed by the Christ-event. To this grounding and interweaving of faith and praxis *Barn.* 18–20 adds a list of actions in the form of a Two-Ways teaching (see *Didascalia* 1–6; *Const. App.* 4–15).

III. Circumstances of Composition: Since *Barn.* does not stress the Bar Cochba revolt (132-135) and inasmuch as 16.3f. refers to Hadrian's building of a temple in Jerusalem (130), it is to be dated between 130 and 132. For this reason and because of the rejection of Jewish ritual and the Jewish understanding of scripture, the author cannot be the Barnabas mentioned in Gal, 1 Cor, and Acts. The use exclusively of Gr. translations of the Bible and Gr. theol. and exegetical traditions (→ Testimonies, Collections of), as well as its scholastic ambiance, the readers' situation in life and faith (4; 21.4), the attack on a fictitious Jewish facade, its early attestation in Egypt, and so on, have since early on suggested Alexandria as the place of composition and of the intended addressees. Because of literary connections, others choose an origin in Syro-Palestine or, because of a theol. affinity to the adversaries in Ignatius, *Philad.* 8.2, an origin in Asia Minor, without necessarily excluding Alexandria.

W: A. Baumstark: OrChr 2 (1912) 235-240 [Syriac text]. — F. Scorza Barcellona (Turin, 1975) [Greek text/Italian trans./comm.]. — O. v. Gebhardt, A. v. Harnack (Leipzig, 1878) [Greek/Latin text/comm.]. — J. M. Heer, Versio latina (Freiburg i.Br., 1908) [Latin/Greek text]. — R. A. Kraft: VigChr 21 (1967) 150-163 [Greek text(P)]. — A. Lindemann, H. Paulsen (Tübingen, 1992), 23-75 [Greek text/German trans.]. — J. G. Müller, Erklärung (Leipzig, 1869) [Greek text/German trans./comm.]. — P. Prigent, R. A. Kraft, SC 172. — K. Wengst, SUC 2 (Darmstadt, 1984), 101-202 [Greek text/German trans.].
L: R. Hvalvik, Scripture (Oslo, 1994). — J. Carleton Paget, Epistle of Barnabas (Tübingen, 1994). — P. Prigent, Testimonia (Paris, 1961). — F. R. Prostmeier, Überlieferung: VigChr 48 (1994) 48-64. — idem, Der Barnabasbrief, KAV 8 (Göttingen, 1999). — M. Vinzent, Ertragen und Ausharren — die Lebenslehre des Barnabasbriefes: ZNW 86 (1995) 74-93. — K. Wengst, Tradition u. Theologie (Berlin, 1971). — H. Windisch, Barn. (Tübingen, 1920).

F. R. PROSTMEIER

Barnabas, Literature about

I. Acts: The *Acta Barnabae* (*A. Barn.*) involve two competing nuclei of traditions, the Cyprian and the Roman-Milanese. The *Periodoi kai martyrion tou hagiou Barnaba tou apostolou* is a novelistic account (supposedly by John Mark) of the coming, activity, and martyrdom of Barnabas, which is assigned to Cyprus; in form it follows the Acts of the Apostles more closely than do other Acts of apostles. It makes the Cyprian church's apostolic origin and possession of an apostle's tomb decisive arguments for that church's sovereign independence from the patriarchate of Antioch. The encomium (*enc.*) of Alexander, 6th-c. monk, seeks to justify the autonomy of the Cyprian church more openly than the above pseudepigraphon (end of 5th c.) had. The principal document of the Milanese tradition, with its own eccles.-political ax to grind against Rome, is the *Datiana Historia Ecclesiae Mediolanensis* (9th/11th c.).

W: *A. Barn.*, AAAp 2, 2, 292-302 [Greek text]. — *enc.*, PG 87/3:4101-4104. — *Datiana Historia Ecclesiae*, A. Biraghi (Milan, 1848) [Latin text].
L: J. W. Busch, B.: FMSt 24 (1990) 178-197. — NTApo[5] 2:421-423. — R. Söder, Apostelgeschichten (Darmstadt, 1932). — P. Tomea, Tradizione apostolica (Milan, 1993).

II. Gospel: The *Gospel of Barnabas* (*Ev. Barn.*) was composed, in Italian, probably in the 14th c., in Italy or Syria (Damascus). Handed down in its original language and partly in a Spanish translation, it was probably written by a Marano, a Jew compelled to become a Christian but who later became a Muslim and wanted to avenge himself on the Inquisition. This work is therefore not the *Ev. Barn.* that was listed in the → *Decretum Gelasianum*, as a result of a misinterpretation of an *Ev. Barn.* mentioned in the *Acts of Barnabas* but referring to the gospel of Mt. In the present work Jesus himself, in whose place Judas, transformed by God, dies on the cross, makes a promise to Muhammad; for this reason it became an attraction for anti-Chr. Muslim apologetics. An oddity here is the deliberate connection of the work with the letter of → Barnabas, in order to make Barnabas the author of the *Ev. Barn.* and thus attest to the great antiquity of the latter.

W: L. Cirillo, M. Fremaux (Paris, 1977) [Italian text/French trans.]. — L. and L. Ragg (Oxford, 1909) [Italian text/English trans.]. — S. M. Linges (Bonndorf, 1994) [German trans.].
L: J. Bowman, Gospel of B.: Abr-n. S 30 (1992) 20-33. — M. de Epalza, Le milieu hispano-moresque de l'Évangile islamisant de B.: ISLAMOCHRISTIANA 8 (1982) 159-183. — J. Jomier, L'Évangile selon B.: MIDEO 6 (1959-1961) 137ff. — idem, Une Enigme persistante: MIDEO 14 (1980) 271-300. — NTApo[6] 1:66 n. 1b. — M. A. Rahim, Gospel of B. (Karachi, 1973). — idem, Jesus. A Prophet of Islam (Karachi, 1980). — C. Schirrmacher, Mit den Waffen des Gegners. Chr.-muslimische Kontroversen im 19. u. 20. Jh.: IKU 162 (1992). — J. Slomp, Ps.-B.: Al-Mushir 16 (1974) 106-130. — idem, Gospel in Dispute (Rome, 1978). — idem, Das Ev. Barn.: CIBEDO. T 14 (1982). — D. Sox, Gospel of B. (London, 1984).

F. R. PROSTMEIER

Barsabas of Jerusalem

A work preserved only in Georgian, *De Christo et Ecclesiis*, is attributed to a Barsabas or Barsabbaeus (B.). Acc. to Eusebius (*h.e.* 4.5.3) B. is Justus, a Jewish-Chr. bishop of Jerusalem. But the author is a Gentile Christian, who, possibly in the 2nd c. and originally in Greek, writes against the Ebionite christology of the "true prophet." The work was used in the 6th c. in the disputes between Armenians and Georgians on the correct understanding of the *Henotikon*.

W: M. van Esbroeck, PO 41:147-256 [text/French trans./comm.].

G. RÖWEKAMP

Barsanuphius and John

I. Life: Almost nothing is known of the life of the two monks Barsanuphius (B.) and John (J.). A *Vita Barsanuphii* by Evagrius (*h.e.* 4; PG 86B) has strong legendary elements. B., an Egyptian, called "the great patriarch," lived in the 6th c. as a recluse in the monastery of Seridos near Gaza. Together with his disciple and friend J., he was the real spiritual leader of that monastery as well as director of numerous individuals (monks, bishops, laypersons) from near and far in the surrounding area. This pastoral activity was mediated by an extensive correspondence, preserved in ca. 550 letters (*ep.*). The most important disciple of the two recluses was Dorotheus of Gaza. After J.'s death, B. withdrew into complete isolation in 540.

II. Works: The spiritual correspondence of B. and J., collected by an unknown editor, was first published in 1872 as *Biblos psychophelestatē*. The letters take the form of an *Erōtapokrisis* (→ *Quaestiones et responsiones*), that is, each contains the question of the petitioner and the patriarch's answer.

In their answers, B. and J. rely on the authority of scripture and the "fathers." Among the latter are Anthony, Pachomius, all the Fathers of the Desert, Isaiah of Gaza, and the Cappadocians. The instruction given by B. in particular is very close to that in the *Apophthegmata Patrum*. Measured judgment, humility, obedience, trust in the providence of God and the guidance of a spiritual father are, in his view, the cornerstones of monastic and Chr. life. Asceticism and spiritual reading that do not lead to interior remorse are rejected by B. This is also the basis of his harsh condemnation of the writings of Origen and

Evagrius (*ep.* 600); but a polemic against Origen (PG 86:891-901) has been wrongly attributed to him.

W: N. Hagiorites, Βίβλος ψυχωφελεστάτη (Volos, 1872 = ²1960; Thessalonica, 1984). — D. J. Chitty, PO 31/3 [Greek text/English trans.]. — L. Regnault, P. Lemaire, B. Outier, B. et J. de Gaza, Correspondance (Solesmes, 1971) [French trans.]. — M. F. T. Lovato, L. Mortari, B. et G., Epistolario (Rome, 1991) [Italian trans.]. — F. Neyt, SC 426, 427.

L: I. Hausherr, B.: DSp 1:1255-1262. — F. Neyt, Lettres à Dorothée dans la Correspondance de B. et J. de Gaza, Diss. (Leuven/Louvain, 1969). — idem, Un type d'autorité charismatique: Byz 44 (1974) 343-361. — L. Perrone, La Chiesa di Palestina (Brescia, 1980), 296-307. — S. Vailhé, Les lettres spirituelles de J. et de B.: EO 7 (1904) 271f. — idem, J. le Prophète et Seridos: EO 8 (1905) 154-160. — idem, Saint B.: EO 8 (1905) 14-25.

J. PAULI, OSB

Barsauma of Karka de Laden

B. lived in the middle of the 7th c. and composed two letters, preserved in Arabic, to Catholicos Ishoyahb II, in which he complains that his eccles. superiors have omitted the names of Diodorus of Tarsus, Theodore Mops., and Nestorius from the diptychs of the Mass. His literary remains included a medico-theological *Book on the Liver,* various necrologies, hymns, and prayers of thanksgiving, but of these nothing has come down to us apart from a notice in Ebedjesu.

W: A. Scher, PO 13:562-576 [Arabic text/French trans.].

P. BRUNS

Barsauma of Nisibis

B., who had been born a slave in Beth Qardu ca. 420, attended the school of the Persians in Edessa when it was led by Ibas. Being a Nestorian, he was barred from the Robber Synod of Ephesus in 449 and had to leave Edessa. He returned to his native land and became bishop of Nisibis. In this capacity he and Narses brought the school of Edessa to his episcopal city in 457 (→ School). He enjoyed the favor of the Persian King Peroz (457-484), who appointed him to a high administrative post in the region bordering on the Roman empire. He used his position in order recklessly to combat Monophysite propaganda, and he even intrigued against his own catholicos, Babaway, who anathematized him at the Synod of Seleucia-Ctesiphon. In his aversion to Monophysite monasticism and with an eye on anti-ascetic Parseeism, he argued at the Synod of Beit Lapat in 484 for the introduction of marriage for priests, thus further exacerbating the conflict with Babaway. In that same year, the latter fell victim to a conspiracy at the Persian court, and B. was at last free to have his friend from his schooldays, Acacius, installed as catholicos. With the latter's support and thanks to the favor of King Balas, B. succeeded in finally introducing Nestorianism into Persia. A further spread into Armenia failed, however, because of the opposition of the Armenian bishops, who in 491 anathematized B. at the Council of Valarsapat. Shortly afterwards, probably ca. 495, B. died. Of B.'s extensive correspondence only five letters (*ep.*) survive, four of them to Acacius. We also have the Acts (*acta*) of the Synod of Beit Lapat and a prayer for the consecration of an altar (*cons.*).

W: *ep.,* J. Chabot, Synodicon Orientale (Paris, 1902), 525-539 [text/French trans.]. — *acta,* idem, loc. cit., 621-625 [text/French trans.]. — *cons.,* Liturgia SS. Apostolorum (Urmia, 1890), 133f. [text]. — O. Braun, Buch der Synhados (Vienna, 1900), 59-83 [German trans./comm.].

L: S. Gero, B. and Persian Christianity (Leuven/Louvain, 1981). — idem, Antiaszetische Bewegung: OCA 221 (1980) 187-191. — J. Labourt, Le christianisme dans l'empire perse (Paris, 1904), 131-152. — A. Vööbus, Les messaliens et B. de Nisibe (Pinneberg, 1947).

P. BRUNS

Bartholomew, Literature about

I. Gospel: A gospel of B. is attested by Jerome (*in Matth.,* prol.), the *Decretum Gelasianum* (5.3.6), and Ps.-Dionysius (*myst.* 1.3). It is not clear, however, to which text they are referring. On the one hand, we know of the *Questions of B.,* a text with a difficult transmission history. The original version of this writing, which in its first part is a dialogue of the disciples with the risen Jesus, comes possibly from the 3rd c. Some of its themes are the *Descensus Christi* and the liberation of Adam, and, in the second, apocalyptic part, the origin of the angels, the pains of hell, and the circumstances of Mary's pregnancy and the birth of Jesus. There are connections with the literature about Pilate and the infancy gospels of Thomas and James.

Also preserved, in part, is the *Book of the Resurrection of Jesus Christ by the Apostle Bartholomew.* This comes from the 5th/7th c., but is not dependent on the *Questions.* Further Coptic fragments belong partly to this work and partly to the gospel of → Gamaliel.

W: *Questions,* A. Vassiliev, Anecdota Graeco-Byzantina 1 (Moscow, 1893), 10-23 [text]. — N. Bonwetsch, GGA 1/42 (Göttingen, 1897) [text]. — A. Wilmart, E. Tisserant: RB 10

(1913) 161-190 [text]. — U. Moricca: RB 30 (1921) 481-516; 31 (1922) 20-30 [text]. — M. R. James, The Apocryphal NT (Oxford, 1955 = 1924), 147-151, 166-186 [text/English trans.]. — NTApo⁵ 2:427-437 [German trans.]. — *Book of the Resurrection*, E. A. Wallis Budge, Coptic Apocrypha (London, 1913), 1-48, 179-215 [Coptic text/English trans.]. — *Frgm.*, E. Revillout, PO 2/2:184-195. L: A. F. L. Beeston, The Quaestiones Bartholomaei: JThS NS 25 (1974) 124-127. — F. Haase, Zur Rekonstruktion des B.-Evangeliums: ZNW 16 (1915) 93-112. — HLL 4:390f. — D. Kaestli, Où en est l'Étude de l'Évangile de B. ?: RB 95 (1988) 5-33. — J. Kroll, Gott u. Hölle (Darmstadt, 1963 = Leipzig, 1932).

II. Acts: The Gr. *Acta et martyrium Bartholomaei* have not been published. The *Acta Andreae et Bartholomaei* have come down to us in a Copt. version, which originated in dependence on the *Acta Andreae et Matthiae apud anthropophagos* (→ Andrew, Acts of) and describe the mission of B. among the Parthians. The Eth. and Arab. versions depend on this.

The original Copt. *Acta Bartholomaei* have been preserved only in the Arab. version and in the Eth. version which emerged from it. These two versions contain the *Acta* in a short form and, in addition, describe B.'s mission in the oases of Egypt (the two also use the old *Acta* of → Thomas),

The various versions of a *Passio Bartholomaei* are independent of the preceding. A Lat. *Passio*, on which the Gr. depends, describes the mission of B. in India (this tradition is possibly more original than that connecting Thomas with India; see Eus., *h.e.* 5.10). It has come down as book 8 of → Abdias (Pseudo). One striking aspect is the lack of encratitic features. The Arm. *Passio*, also known as *History of B.*, tells of B.'s martyrdom in Armenia, but it is a late compilation and goes back to Syr. and Gr. sources.

W: *Acta Andreae et Bartholomaei*, I. Guidi: Rendiconti della R. Academia dei Lincei IV 3, 2 (Rome, 1887), 117-190 [Coptic text/Italian trans.]. — E. Lucchesi, J. M. Prieur: AnBoll 96 (1978) 347-350; 98 (1980) 75-82 [Coptic text/French trans. frg.]. — A. Smith Lewis (Horae Semiticae III-IV) (London, 1904), 3:11-25 [Arabic text]. — *Acta Bartholomaei*, A. Smith Lewis, loc. cit., 3:8-79 [Arabic text]; 4:69-75 [English trans.]. — E. A. Wallis Budge, The Contendings of the Apostles (Amsterdam, 1976 = 1899-1901), 1:83-92 [Ethiopic text]; 2:76-86 [English trans.]. — *Passio Bartholomaei*, AAAp 2, 1:128-150 [Latin text]. — *Passio* (History), L. Leloir, CCA 4:479-530 [French trans.] (literature). C. Tscherakian, Acta Apocrypha Apost. (Venice, 1904), 200-211 [Armenian text]. L: M. van Esbroeck, La naissance du culte de S. B.: REArm 17 (1983) 171-195.

G. RÖWEKAMP

Baruch (Apocalypse)

In addition to the basic material of Bar in the LXX, the Syr. Bible also contains an apocalypse attributed to B. and, in an independent tradition, a last letter of B. The apocalyptic visions reflect the period after 70 C.E. and deal with the punishment of Israel, the judgment on the nations, and the coming of the Messiah. The commendableness of obedience to the law is highlighted and the special precedence of the city of Jerusalem is emphasized. In addition to the Syr. version, there is also a much different Gr. version, which describes B.'s journey through the seven heavens. The basic version must have been of Jewish origin, and Chr. additions were made later. A shorter, Old Slavic recension probably depends on this basic version.

The Eth. apocalypse of B. has come down in several recensions: a more recent one, also called *Reliqua verborum Ieremiae* (*rel. verb. Ier.*), which is close to the Syriac, and an Armenian; the later recension must have come into existence entirely in Ethiopia, since in it the disciple of the prophet communicates a revelation intended specifically for the church of that country.

W: *apoc.*, M. Kmosko, PS 1/2:1056-1207 [Syriac text/Latin trans.]. — R. H. Charles, Libri apocryphi VT (London, 1896) [English trans.]. — O. F. Fritzsche, Libri apocryphi VT (Leipzig, 1871), 654-699 [Greek text]. — *ep.*, P. de Lagarde, Libri VT apocryphi (Osnabrück, 1972 = Leipzig, 1861), 88-100. — M. Kmosko, PS 1/2:1208-1236. — E. Kautzsch, Die Apokryphen des AT 2 (Darmstadt, 1975 = Tübingen, 1921), 402-457 [German trans.]. — P. Rießler, Altjüd. Schrifttum (Freiburg i.Br., 1984 = Heidelberg, 1928), 40-113 [German trans.]. — *rel. verb. Ier.*, A. Dillmann, Chrestomathia Aethiopica (Hildesheim, 1988 = Leipzig, 1866), 1-15 [Ethiopic text]. — E. König, Rest der Worte B.s: Theol. Studien (Leipzig, 1877), 318-338 [German trans.]. — F. Prätorius, Buch B.: ZWTh 15 (1872) 230-247 [German trans.]. — J. R. Harris, Rest of the Words of B. (London, 1889) [English trans.]. — S. Yovsep'eanc', Unkanonische Bücher des AT (Venice, 1896), 349-364 [Armenian text]. L: R. Basset, Le livre de B. (Paris, 1893). — B. Biolet, Apokalypsen des Esra u. des B. (Leipzig, 1924). — A. Laato, Apoc. and the date of the end: Journal of the Study of the Pseudepigrapha 18 (1998) 39-46. — D. S. Russel, Divine Disclosure (London, 1992). — P. Sacchi, L'Apocalittica giudaica (Brescia, 1990).

P. BRUNS

Basil of Ancyra

B., who was originally a physician (Jerome, *vir. ill.* 89), had had an outstanding education. In 336 he became a bishop and successor of the deposed Marcellus of Ancyra. B. attempted to become active in eccles. politics, in part with the help of the emperors. Thus he brought about the fall of Photinus of Sirmium (351) and the intervention of Constantius II against the election of Eudoxius as bishop of Antioch; he also took part in preparing the double Synod of Rimini/Seleucia (Soz., *h.e.* 4.16) at which the homoeans were victorious. At the end of 359 his influence at the court and in his own party faded, and in Jan. 360, he was deposed at the synod in Constantinople when the misgivings of the emperor toward him increased and his influence in the homoean party further declined (Soz., *h.e.* 4.24). In 363 he tried in vain to overturn his deposition (Soc., *h.e.* 3.25). He died after 363.

B. composed or co-composed the *Ep. synodica* and profession of faith of Laodicea (together with George of Laodicea). His authorship of *De virginitate* (*virg.*) is doubtful. In distinction from the Neo-Arians, who claimed a strict division between God and the Son, B. claimed that the *ousia* of the Son is like that of the Father. B. understood *ousia* as individual substance, so that God subsists in three hypostases and three *ousiai*. B. derives the likeness of the Father and the Son in their *ousiai* from the Father–Son relationship and from the nature of the Creator–creature relationship. The relationship of Father and Son, which B. takes over from the realm of nature, leads necessarily to a likeness of the two, but, in the case of God, with the exclusion of corporeity and the capacity for passion, which are found only in creatures. The Father is the Father of an *ousia* that is like him; if this point is neglected, one ends up with only the concepts of creator and creature. The chief opponents of this theology, which influenced Hilary and Basil of Caesarea, were the Neo-Arians, but also Marcellus and the homoousians.

W: *Ep. synodica*, Epiphanius, *haer.* 73, GCS 37:268-284. — Basilii ac Georgii Laodiceni et sociorum professio, Epiphanius, *haer.* 73, GCS 37:284-295. — *virg.*, PG 30:669-809.
L: H. C. Brennecke, Studien zur Geschichte der Homöer (Tübingen, 1988). — F. Cavallera, Le De virginitate de Basile d'Ancyre: RHE 6 (1905) 5-14. — J. Gummerus, Die homöusianische Partei bis zum Tode des Konstantius (Leipzig, 1900). — P. Hadot, Marius Victorinus (Paris, 1971), 253-280. — R. P. C. Hanson, The Search for the Christian Doctrine of God (Edinburgh, 1988), 350-371. — R. M. Hübner, Zur Genese der trinitarischen Formel bei Basilius von Caesarea: FS F. Kard. Wetter (St. Ottilien, 1998), 123-156, here 138-142. — W. A. Löhr, Die Entstehung der homöischen u. homöusianischen Kirchenparteien (Bonn, 1986). — idem, A Sense of Tradition: The Homoiousian Church Party: Arianism after Arius, ed. M. R.

Barnes, D. H. Williams (Edinburgh, 1993), 81-100. — J. N. Steenson, Basil of Ancyra and the Course of Nicene Orthodoxy, Diss. (Oxford, 1983).

T. BÖHM

Basil, Archimandrite

B. was born in Antioch and lived in the first half of the 5th c., first as a hermit and then as a deacon and archimandrite in Constantinople; he played an active role in eccles. life as a follower of Cyril Alex.

Two works of B. have survived: a petition addressed by B. and Thallasius, a monk and lector, in 430 to Emperor Theodosius II (*lib. ad imp.*), which accuses Nestorius and asks for the convocation of an ecumenical council. In a similar work addressed to Patriarch Proclus of Constantinople (*lib. ad Procl.*) in 435 and preserved only in Latin, B. calls upon Proclus to issue a posthumous condemnation of Theodore Mops., whose writings had shortly before been translated into Armenian.

Liberatus (*breviar.* 10) mentions two other, now lost works: a second petition to Proclus against Theodore and a treatise against Theodore and Diodorus of Tarsus.

W: *lib. ad imp.*, PG 91:1472-1480. — ACO 1, 1, 5, 7-10. — *lib. ad Procl.*, PG 65:851-856. — ACO 4, 1, 83-85.
L: L. Abramowski, Der Streit um Diodor u. Theodor zwischen den beiden ephesischen Konzilien: ZKG 67 (1955/56) 252-287. — X. Bauer, Proklos v. Konstantinopel (Munich, 1919), 82ff. — E. Schwartz, Konzilstudien (Strasburg, 1914), 26f.

C. SCHMIDT

Basil of Caesarea

I. Life: B. was born ca. 329/330, as the eldest son of ten children, into a rich Cappadocian family of big landowners. The family of his mother, Emmelia, had a Chr. past dating from pre-Constantinian times. His grandfather died a martyr's death; his grandmother, Macrina the Elder, a pupil of Gregory the Wonderworker, who had been a student of Origen, played the decisive role in the religious education of B. and his siblings. It was from his father, Basil the Elder, a respected rhetor and advocate in Neocaesarea, that B. received his early education; after this he attended school in Caesarea, where he first met his friend, Gregory Naz. Periods of study throughout the academic world of the time brought B. in 348/349 to Constantinople, where he became a student of the famous pagan rhetor Libanius, among others, and then in 349/350 to Athens. Here he heard the Chr.

rhetor Prohaeresius, as well as Himerius; then he was active for a short time as teacher of rhetoric in his native city, Caesarea (355-356). This period ended with B.'s definitive turn to the Chr. faith, probably under the special influence of his older sister, Macrina, who in 352 had already founded a monastery in Annisi, an estate of the family on the bank of the River Iris (opposite the present-day village of Sinisa/Uluköy). B. received baptism from Bishop Dianius and took up the ecclesiastical office of a reader. Around 357 he followed the example of his mother and his brother, Naucratius, who, like Macrina, had withdrawn into solitude in Pontus. The life of asceticism and contemplation in Annisi made possible an intensive study of the scriptures. A journey to Egypt, Palestine, Syria, and Mesopotamia made B. familiar with the way of life at the monastic centers that was coming into existence at that time and with the situation of the church of his day. In 360 he accompanied Bishop Dianius to the synod in Constantinople, and ca. 364 he was ordained a priest by Dianius's successor, Eusebius. When his bishop asked his help in the struggle against the homoean Emperor Valens in Caesarea, B. left the community of monks in Annisi. He supported Eusebius, who had little knowledge of theology, in the administration of the church, organized the caritative help of the poor, reorganized the liturgy, and took up the office of preaching, in which his aim was to lead his hearers to a more convinced Christianity, espec. in social and ethical questions. B.'s involvement in eccles. politics intensified as he took part in the synods of Lampsacus (364), where he belonged to the homoousians, who accepted the creeds of Nicaea, and of Tyana (366).

In 370, after Eusebius's death, B. succeeded him as bishop of Caesarea. He effected a reorganization of the church in Cappadocia, endeavored to consolidate the followers of Nicaea, and sought communion with the churches of the West and an end of the Antiochene schism. Despite his pro-Nicene commitment, he retained the favor of the homoean Emperor Valens, who was impressed espec. by B.'s social activities, and in 372/373 commissioned him to visit the communities in Armenia. Around this time disputes arose about the organization of the church in light of the civil division of the province of Cappadocia, as well as disputes over pneumatology between the Nicaeans and the Pneumatomachians, the group gathered around Eustathius of Sebaste. B.'s efforts to win over his former teacher and thus the latter's disciples to the "great solution," i.e., unity of the basis of Nicene orthodoxy, failed, and the result was a break

with Eustathius. The subsequent propaganda claiming that B. was in contact with Apollinaris of Laodicea and that he was a Sabellian heretic and even a tritheist, brought B. into great difficulties in eccles. politics. Due in part to a somewhat lengthy illness, B. withdrew from the public eye for a year (373/374). In 375 he began anew his efforts at a union, initially by means of a journey to Pontus in order to win over the Old Nicaeans and to check the influence of Eustathius on the monks. Ties with the West were to be aided by a renewed request for a legation, but this was turned down by Damasus of Rome (and again in 377): B.'s efforts at union with Rome had no success. In Asia Minor, however, with the aid of his allies, he was able to consolidate Neo-Nicene orthodoxy, especially when the death of Valens in 378 brought about a more favorable civil situation for the followers of Nicaea. B.'s death occurred probably in the fall of 378.

L: A. D. Booth, The Chronology of Jerome's Early Years: Phoenix (Toronto) 35 (1981) 237-259. — M. M. Fox, The Life and Times of St. B. as Revealed in his Works, PatSt 57 (Washington, 1939). — P. Maraval, La date de la mort de B.: REAug 34 (1988) 25-38. — J.-R. Pouchet, La date de l'élection épiscopale de saint B. et celle de sa mort: RHE 87 (1992) 5-33.

II. Work: B. left behind an extensive literary work, which can, for the most part, be fitted into the biographical framework given. It includes a *Corpus asceticum*, ca. forty six authentic homilies, two properly dogmatic works: *Against Eunomius* (books 1-3) and *On the Holy Spirit*, and a correspondence of ca. 350 letters (*ep.*). The authenticity of *On Baptism* is not disputed; *in Jes.* 1-16, *On Virginity*, and the *Constitutiones asceticae* are all accepted as unauthentic.

W: PG 29-32. — J. v. Wendel, 6 vols. (Vienna, 1776-1778). — Sämtliche Werke der Kirchenväter 19-26, BKV¹ [German trans.].

Of the published *Corpus asceticum* of B. seven works are to be regarded as authentic. At Annisi in 359/360, together with → Gregory Naz., B. composed the so-called (1) *Regulae morales* (ta ēthika; *moral.*), which he himself speaks of as rules (*horoi*) in the proper sense. The work was a collection and thematic organization of passages of scripture, after the manner of an index, in which originally only the location of the texts was given. Only a revised version with a twofold introduction (2) *On the Judgment of God* (De iudicio Dei; *iud.*) and (3) *On Faith* (De fide; *fid.*) gave the full collection of the 1,542 verses of the NT, which in the form of eighty rules, each having sometimes several chapters, call the attention of all classes in the church to the gospel as the sole standard of Chr. life. By means of the unity to be thereby established in the following of Christ (the scriptures are addressed to all Christians) B. seeks to promote the renewal of the church, to overcome existing divisions, and to exclude extreme tendencies as being incompatible with the gospel.

The so-called (4) *Little Asceticon* from 360-370, an early form of the *Longer Rules* (*LR*) and *Shorter Rules* (*SR*), no longer exists in its original Gr. form, but only in the Lat. translation by → Rufinus of Aquileia (ca. fifty years later) and a Syr. translation that likewise dates probably from the 4th c. The text consists of eleven *Longer Rules* (= *LR* 2-10, 15-17, 19, 21-23) and 192 *Shorter Rules*. B. answers questions put by communities of ascetics and monks on spiritual and organizational matters of common life, as indeed he had already substantially done in *ep.* 22. This work, then, like the *Great Asceticon*, is indeed addressed to monks but B. does not regard it as a "Rule" in the strict sense. It is only later generations that have regarded this work, which belongs to the ancient literary genre of *Questions and Answers* (*Erōtapokrisis*), as the "Rules of Basil."

The *Great Asceticon* includes (5) the *Longer* and (6) *Shorter Rules* (*Regulae fusius/brevius tractatae*), which represent a revision and considerable expansion of the *Little Asceticon*. It dates from the period after 373. Answers 1-11 were originally longer; a post-Basilian revision divided the *LR* into 55 and the *SR*, originally 12-203, into 313 questions and answers.

Also regarded as authentic is (7) the so-called *Prologue to the Hypotyposis* (*prol.*); this takes the form of an accompanying letter, consisting mainly of citations from scripture; important mss. place it at the head of the *Corpus*. As in *jud.*, B. makes reference to the situation of the church of his age, which must expect the judgment of God because of its disunity; in addition, he announces an exposition of the orthodox creed (*fid.*) and the answers to questions asked of him by the brethren (*moral.*).

B.'s ascetical program is bound up with his efforts to reform the church. The building up of the church comes about through life acc. to the gospel and the fulfillment of the commandments by all Christians, in particular the double commandment of love of God and neighbor (*LR* 1). As the model of the first community shows, this life and fulfillment are possible only within a communal life, that is, in the brother- and sisterhood (*LR* 7); for this reason, B. gives the cenobitic way of life precedence over the eremitical.

Some mss. insert into the *Corpus asceticum ep.* 2 and 22 (both of which precede the *Asceticon* in time) and 173. In *ep.* 2 B. sketches the basic traits of an ascetical life in solitude: a life devoted entirely to meditation on scripture and ascetical formation. *Ep.* 22 no longer expounds the stricter eremitical ideal of *ep.* 2, but defines an ascetical life as a life acc. to the gospel. B. does not use any special monastic terminology. The recipients are addressed not as "monks" but as "Christians," a point that brings out more clearly the ideal shared by both ways of life. As occasion for the letter B. mentions concrete questions of those who had written to him; these he answers with citations from scripture, as in the *Regulae morales*. *Ep.* 173 is addressed to a woman ascetic named Theodora, whom B. exhorts to be faithful to the way once chosen of life acc. to the gospel.

As a result of more recent researches, the two books *On Baptism* (*bapt.*) are regarded as authentic and dated to the time before B.'s episcopate (before 370). This work is close in form and content to the *moral.* In the first book, which takes the form of three addresses, using primarily citations from scripture, B. deals with the relationship between baptism (or, as the case may be, the Eucharist) and Chr. life. Both sacraments must have an effect on a Christian's way of life; conversely, this effect is possible only through reception of the sacraments. In the second book B. answers thirteen questions on the practice of the Chr. faith and life; the questions flow from what has been expounded in general terms in book 1.

W: *Corpus asceticum*, PG 31:619-1428. — *Little Asceticon* (Rufin), PL 103:483-554. — K. Zelzer, CSEL 86. — K. S. Frank, B. Die Mönchsregeln, St. Ottilien 1981 [German trans. /comm.]. — U. Neri, M. B. Artioli, Opere Ascetiche di B. (Turin, 1980). — *prol.*, PG 31:1509-1513. — *bapt.*, J. Ducatillon, SC 357. — U. Neri, TRSR 12 [text/Italian trans./comm.].
L: K. S. Frank, Monastische Reform im Altertum. Eustathius v. Sebaste u. B.: FS E. Iserloh (Paderborn, 1980), 35-49. — D. C. Kalamakis, The prologus I to the Asceticum Parvum: Parnassos 31 (1989) 446-448. — S. Lundström, Die Überlieferung der lat. B.-regel (Stockholm, 1989). — A. Quacquarelli, Il lavoro nella regola di S. B. tradotta da Rufino: VetChr 29 (1992) 245-260. — G. Uluhogian, La traduzione manoscritta della versione armena dell' asceticon: Muséon 100 (1987) 363-375. — K. Zelzer, Die Rufinusübersetzung der B.-regel im Spiegel ihrer ältesten Hss.: FS R. Hanslik (Vienna, 1977), 341-350. — idem, Zur Überlieferung der lat. Fassung der B.-regel: TU 125 (1981) 625-635.

The ca. forty-six homilies (*hom.*), which form the most extensive part of B.'s works, attest to his activity as preacher. There are (ca. twenty-three) addresses on ethical and religious subjects, fifteen homilies on the Psalms and nine (or eleven) on the Hexaëmeron. The so-called "social" homilies (*hom.* 9; 6; 7; 8) must have been given during his time as a presbyter (368-369), and the dogmatic homilies in defense of the trinitarian faith during the early years of his episcopate (370-373).

The homilies on the Psalms do not form a separate body but always appear in the mss. along with the ethical homilies. Fifteen of the former are regarded as authentic: *hom.* on Ps. 1.1; 7.14 (a, b); 28 (a, b); 29; 32; 33; 44; 45; 48; 59; 61; 114; 115; 132. Despite the programmatic remarks on the genre of the Psalms and the benefit of psalmody, which B. prefixes to the interpretation of Ps 1:1, he does not seem to have intended a systematic exegesis of the Pss. To some extent, the homilies take up matters of social criticism (Ps 14b) and trinitarian theology (28a; 32; 33).

The nine homilies on the Hexaëmeron (*hex.*) are among the late homilies, which B. delivered probably in 378 in Caesarea. On the mornings and evenings of successive days he commented to his community on the individual works of creation acc. to Gen 1:1-25: astonishment at the beauty of the multifaceted creation should lead to praise of its creator. B. explicitly stresses his intention of explaining the literal, and not any allegorical, meaning of the scriptures (2.5; 9.1). This intention need not be taken as an attack on the Origenists, for it may have in mind an unrestrained allegorism (gnosis, astrology) and be motivated by the level of education of his hearers, among whom there were simple folk who were not prepared for the deeper, more spiritual meaning of scripture. Nevertheless, B. does make use of tropology in short parenetic passages. In his exegesis of the biblical text he makes use of the scientific knowledge of his time in the areas of geography, physics, astronomy, and zoology. Speculations in natural philosophy that contradict the creation account, which is supported by the authority of Moses, are rejected (1.8-10), as are astrological prophecies about the destiny of human beings (6.5-7) and the belief in reincarnation (8.1). Only briefly, in *hex.* 9, does B. go into the creation of the human person (Gen 1:26); there he announces (9.6) a sequel that will explain in particular the image (*eikōn*) and likeness (*homoiōsis*). There are difficulties in taking the two homilies *On the Creation of the Human Being* (*De creatione hominis*; *creat.*) as this sequel. These two homilies are found in three different versions of the text (some mss. ascribe them to → Gregory Nyss.). In his interpretation of Gen 1:26 B. borrows thoughts from Origen. While the image of God is given to the human being through creation, B. regards the likeness to God as

incomplete and says that it is to be attained fully through life as a Christian. The capacity (*dynamis*) and the will (*proairesis*) to strive thus for the good are part of the image of God.

W: *hom.*, A. Stegmann, BKV² 47:165-444 [German trans. of 20 sermons]. — *hex.*, E. Amand de Mendieta, GCS NF 2 [text/index]. — S. Giet, SC 26. — A. Stegmann, BKV² 47:8-153 [German trans.]. — J. Blomfield (Grand Rapids, Mich., 1968) [English trans.]. — M. Naldini (Rome, 1990) [Italian trans.]. — *creat.*, A. Smets, M. van Esbroek, SC 160. — H. Hörner, Auctorum incertorum — vulgo Basilii vel Gregorii Nysseni — Sermones De Creatione Hominis, Sermo De paradiso (Leipzig, 1972) [text]. — *Specific homilies:* Y. Courtonne, Homélies sur la richesse (Paris, 1935). — S. Y. Rudberg, L'Homélie de B. sur le mot "observe-toi toi-même" (Stockholm, 1962) [text].
L: E. Amand de Mendieta, S. Y. Rudberg, La tradition manuscrite directe des Neuf Homélies sur l' Hexaemeron, TU 123 (Berlin, 1980). — Y. Courtonne, S. B. et l'hellénisme (Paris, 1934). — S. R. Holman, The Hungry Body (hom. 8): JECS 7 (1999) 227-363. — R. Lim, The Politics of Interpretation in B.'s Hexaemeron: VigChr 44 (1990) 351-370. — M.-J. Rondeau, Les Commentaires Patristiques du Psautier 1, IIIᵉ-Vᵉ siècles, OCA 219 (Rome, 1982, 107-112. — S. Y. Rudberg, Notes lexicographiques sur l'Hexaemeron de B.: S.-T. Teodorsson, Greek and Latin Studies in Memory of Caius Fabricius = SGLG 54 (1990) 24-32. — L. Salvatore, Le fonti di una sezione dell' omelia De Fide di S. B.: Aug. 30 (1990) 5-19.

Some mss. and editions of the homilies include the short work, which is difficult to date, titled *How Young Men Can Derive Profit from Pagan Writings* (*Ad adolescentes*), which B. may have intended for his nephew. In it he recommends to Christians beginning their studies the "right use" (*chrēsis*) of readings from the classical pagan authors. In these readings the need is always to imitate the bees gathering pollen: to distinguish between the useful and the harmful, that is, to take from it only what is compatible with Chr. doctrine and allied to the truth (e.g., teaching on the virtues and vices). B. considers this concern with pagan authors to be an introduction to the study of sacred scripture for those not yet able to grasp the deeper, spiritual content of the Bible.

W: F. Boulenger (Paris, 1965) [text/French trans.]. — N. G. Wilson, St. B. on the value on Greek literature (Leipzig, 1975) [text]. — M. Naldini (Florence, 1984) [Italian trans.]. — A. Stegmann, BKV² 47:446-468 [German trans.]. — idem, T. Wolbergs, SKV 4 [German trans.].
L: W. F. Helleman, B.'s "Ad adolescentes": Christianity and the Classics, ed. eadem (Lanham, 1990), 31-51. — E. Lamberz, Zum Verständnis von B.' Schrift "Ad adolescentes": ZKG 90 (1979) 221-241. — M. Naldini, Paideia origeniana nella "Oratio ad adolescentes": VetChr 13 (1976) 297-318. — L. Schucan, Das Nachleben von B.' "Ad adolescentes" (Geneva, 1973).

The two dogmatic writings of B. have their place in the trinitarian theol. controversies of the 4th c.

1. *Contra Eunomium*: In response to the defense made by → Eunomius of Cyzicus (360/361), B. wrote the three books of his *Contra Eunomium* in 363/364 (see *ep.* 20), before becoming a bishop; in them he refutes the homoean theology of the Trinity (books 4-5 are not from B.). He cites each passage of his opponent's work and then reduces it to absurdity (sometimes in a very polemic manner). Book 1 refutes Eunomius's basic thesis: that not-being-begotten (*to agennēton*) is the essential property of the Father, so that the "begotten Son" (*gennētos*) cannot be identical in essence with the Father.

In book 2 B. uses Eunomius's own arguments to refute his thesis that the Son is a creature. "Generation" does not mean that at one point the Son was not; neither is the Spirit a creation of the Son. Book 3 explains how the differences in rank and sequence among the trinitarian persons does not mean a difference in substance. The divine nature of the Spirit is demonstrated by his names, "Holy Spirit" and "Paraclete," as well as by his work as attested in the OT and NT.

W: *Eun.*, B. Sesboüè, G.-M. de Durand, L. Doutreleau, SC 299, 305. — R. P. Vaggione, Eunomius. The Extant Works (Oxford, 1986) [text/English trans.].
L: M. V. Anastos, Basil's KATA EYNOMIOY: B. Christian, Humanist, Ascetic 1, ed. P. J. Fedwick (Toronto, 1981), 67-137. — D. Schmitz, Formen der Polemik bei B. in der Streitschrift Adv. Eunomium: Glotta 67 (1989) 233-242. — M. S. Troiano, I Cappadoci e la questione dell' origine dei nomi nella polemica contro Eunomio: VetChr 17 (1980) 313-346.

2. *On the Holy Spirit* (*De Spiritu Sancto*; *Spir.*): B. composed this work in the years 374-375 (see *ep.* 159) during the controversy with the Pneumatomachians. After the break with Eustathius, and in view of the libels and criticisms against his position, B. responded to a request from Amphilochius of Iconium (*Spir.* 3.3) and wrote down an explanation of his pneumatology. Of the thirty chapters, chs. 10-27 are generally regarded as a revised record, taken at the time or later of the decisive conversation between B. and Eustathius at Sebaste in June 372. B. rebuts the objections of his adversary and argues for his own position from scripture and the fathers who preceded him (*argumentum patristicum*). In the content of what he says he is dependent on Athanasius Alex. (see *ep. Serap.*). As in *Eun.*, B. avoids describing the Holy Spirit as divinity and, using the term *homoousios*, demands of his adversary that for the sake of eccles. communion he avoid the title "crea-

ture." This degree of unclarity in his own formulas is explained by B.'s contemporaries (Athanasius, Gregory Naz.) as "economy," that is, as a renunciation of the highest form of truth in respect for the intellectual capacity of those weaker in faith. B. himself, however, offers a theol. reason, namely, the difference between *kērygma*, or what must be professed publicly, and *dogma*, or what must be passed over in silence in public. In B.'s view, Chr. knowledge requires, by its nature, growth and maturity, which will be bestowed, when the time comes, by the practice of faith (see *ep.* 113; *Spir.* 79).

W: *Spir.*, B. Pruche, SC 17 bis. — H.-J. Sieben, FC 12. — M. Blum (Freiburg i.Br., 1967) [German trans.]. — A. Maignan, P. Th. Camelot (Paris, 1979) [French trans.]. — J. Blomfield (Grand Rapids, Mich., 1968) [English trans.]
L: Y. de Andia, "In lumine tuo videbimus lumen" (Ps 35, 10): FS J. Gribomont, SEAug 27 (Rome, 1988), 59-74. — H. Dörries, "De Spiritu Sancto," AAWG. PH 3, 39 (Göttingen, 1956).

Scholars generally accept 358-359 as the date for the composition of the *Philocalia* (*philoc.*) by B. and Gregory Naz.; the place, Annisi. The anthology consists of twenty-seven chapters of excerpts taken basically from the works of Origen. The chapter headings show three themes to have been the criteria for the selection: access to sacred scripture (hermeneutic, chs. 1-14), defense of the scriptures against rhetorically trained non-Christians who object to their low linguistic level (chs. 15-20), and the free self-determination of the human person in its relationship to the divine plan of salvation (chs. 21-27). Prefixed to the work are an anonymous prologue, which tries to explain some Origenist errors in the *philoc.* as interpolations, and a letter of Gregory Naz. (*ep.* 115, dated 383) to a certain Theodore, who is generally identified with Bishop Theodore of Tyana. Prologue and letter serve as evidence for the authorship of the two Cappadocians, which has been called into question on the basis of more recent analyses of *ep.* 115.

W: *philoc.* 1-20, M. Harl. SC 302. — *philoc.* 21-27, E. Junod, SC 226.
L: E. Junod, B. et Grégoire de Nazianze sont-ils les compilateurs de la Philocalie d'Origène?: FS J. Gribomont, SEAug 27 (Rome, 1988), 349-360.

The correspondence of B. (ed. Courtonne) contains 366 letters. Of these, 325 are regarded as authentic. *Ep.* 8 is assigned to Evagrius Pont.; *ep.* 10; 16; 38-45; 189; 342; and 348 (possibly 124 as well) are attributed to Gregory Naz. B.'s correspondence covers the years 357-378 and provides information on all areas of life in Asia Minor in the 4th c.: the organization of the church, as well as ascetical and monastic life (*ep.* 1; 2; 4; 7; 14; 19; 22; 23), relations between Christians and pagans, dogmatic questions (*ep.* 173; 175; 218; 262), catechesis and the spread of the faith, and the societal and social situation. The majority of B.'s correspondents were in the eastern part of the empire, but there were also important links to the West (e.g., Ambrose, *ep.* 197; Liberius, *ep.* 263). A special place belongs to the "canonical letters" 188; 199; and 217 to Amphilochius. In these B. answers current questions of law and discipline which pastoral practice raises for a bishop. The eighty-four canons have become part of the Byz. collection of laws.

W: *ep.*, Y. Courtonne, 3 vols. (Paris, 1957-1966) [text/ French trans.]. — W.-D. Hauschild, BGrL 3, 32, 37 (Stuttgart, 1973-1993) [German trans.]. — *ep.* 2, J. Grand'henry, La réponse de S. B. à S. Grègoire: Muséon 102 (1989) 321-359 [Arabic text].
L: J. Bernardi, La lettre 104 de S. B.: FS H. Crouzel = ThH 88 (1992) 7-19. — M. Bessières, La tradition manuscrite de la correspondance de s. B. (Oxford, 1923) [= JThS 21 (1920) 1-50, 289-310; 22 (1921) 105-137; 23 (1922) 337-358]. — A. Cavallin, Studien zu den Briefen des hl. B. (Lund, 1944). — P. Devos, Aspects de la correspondance de S. B. avec S. Eusèbe de Samosate et avec S. Amphiloque d'Icononium: AnBoll 110 (1992) 241-259. — P. J. Fedwick, Bibliotheca Basiliana universalis. 1. Letters, CCL (Turnhout, 1993). — B. Gain, L'Église de Cappadoce au IVᵉ siècle d'après la correspondance de B., OCA 225 (Rome, 1985). — J. Hammerstaedt, Zur Echtheit von B.-brief 38: FS J. Engemann = JAC. E 18 (1991) 416-419. — F. Van de Paverd, Die Quellen der kanonischen Briefe: OCP 38 (1972) 5-63. — R. Pouchet, B. le Grand et son univers d'amis d'après sa correspondance (Rome, 1992) (literature). — M. S. Troiano, Sulla cronologia di Ep. 52: VetChr 27 (1990) 339-367.

The measures taken by B. for church reform extend even to concrete liturgical renewals such as the structure of the church year and the organization of the festal calendar and the monastic Liturgy of the Hours. The Liturgy of Basil, which is still celebrated today in the Orthodox Church and has circulated under his name since the 6th c., goes back, in its essentials, to Basil himself.

L: H. Engberding, Das anaphorische Fürbittgebet der B.-liturgie: OrChr 47 (1963) 16-52; 49 (1965) 18-32.

III. Importance: The literary work and practical activities of Basil, who even in his lifetime was called "the Great," were in the service of striking a balance between opposed views in the theology and church of his time. In many respects his posthumous impact has been greater than his direct influence. His pneumatology prepared the ground for the agreement reached at the Council of Constantinople in 381. His manner of arguing in pneumatology and in the doctrine of creation was indeed rhetorically sophisticated but was to an even greater extent based on the Bible; Gregory Nyss. and Gregory Naz. were able to take it further in a more principled and systematic way. His homilies on the Hexaëmeron were used by Ambrose in the West, while the sociocritical works were to some extent continued by John Chrys. The teaching of Gregory Palamas on the divine energies took up B.'s axiom on the possibility of experiencing the divine activity in the world.

The humanists of the 16th c. appreciated B.'s Hellen. formation, which left its mark on his language and teaching, as they did his attitude as a mediator of ancient Gr. literature (*Ad adolescentes*). The *Corpus asceticum* was widely accepted by eastern monasticism. Above all, B.'s promotion of the cenobitic ideal allowed later reformers (Theodore of Studios, Athanasius of Athos, etc.) to hark back to his program for the communal life. It is not possible, however, to speak of a Basilian monasticism (as we do of Benedictine monasticism in the West), since the many forms of monastic life in the East do not derive from a *single* Rule. In the West the Lat. translation of the *Little Asceticon* as the *Rule of Basil* has had its own historical influence. The maxim *ora et labora*, which is attributed to Benedict of Nursia, is based on B.'s revaluation of manual labor (*LR* 37-39; *SR* 121, 143-46) in opposition to the thinking of the ancients.

L: M. Aghiorgoussis, Application of the Term "Eikon Theou" (image of God) according to Saint B.: GOTR 21 (1976) 265-288. — S. C. Alexe, S. B. et le christianisme romain: StPatr 17/3 (1983) 1049-1059. — D. Amand, L'Ascèse monastique de S. B. (Paris, 1949). — idem, Essai d'une histoire critique des éditions générales grecques et grécolatines de s. B.: RBen 52 (1940) 141-161; 53 (1941) 119-151; 54 (1942) 124-144; 56 (1944-45) 126-173. — E. Amand de Mendieta (= idem), La tradition manuscrite des œuvres de s. B.: RHE 49 (1954) 507-551. — idem, L'édition critique des homélies de B.: StPatr 7 (1966) 35-45. — idem, The Official Attitude of B. as a Christian Bishop towards Greek Philosophy and Science: The Orthodox Churches and the West (= SCH[L] 13), ed. D. Baker (Oxford, 1976), 25-49. — A. Angelo, B. (Milan, 1968). — I. Backus, Lectures humanistes de B. Traductions latines (1439-1618) (Paris, 1990). — G. Bardy, B.: DHGE 6:1111-1126. — G. J. M. Bartelink, Observations de s. B. sur la langue biblique et théologique: VigChr 17 (1963) 85-106. — E. Behr-Sigel, La femme aussi est à l'image de Dieu, S. B.: Contacts 1983, 62-70. — J. Bernardi, La prédication des Pères Cappadociens (Paris, 1968). — K. Berther, Der Mensch u. seine Verwirklichung in den Homilien des B., Diss. (Fribourg, Switzerland, 1974). — B. T. Bilaniuk, The Monk as a Pneumatophor in the Writings of St. B.: Diakonia 15 (1980) 49-63. — B. Bobrinskoy, Liturgie et ecclésiologie trinitaire de s. B.: VC 23 (1969) 1-32. — S. de Boer, B. en de "homoousie" van de Heilige Geest: NedThT 18 (1964) 362-380. — C. Burini, La "comunione" et "distribuzione dei beni" di Atti II, 44 e IV, 32-35 nelle Regole Monastiche di

B.: Ben. 28 (1981) 151-169. — R. Cadiou, Le problème des relations scolaires entre s. B. et Libanios: REG 79 (1966) 89-98. — E. Cavalcanti, Dall' etica classica all' etica cristiana: SMSR 14 (1990) 353-387. — Y. Courtonne, S. B. et l'hellénisme (Paris, 1934). — A. J. M. Davids, Hagiografie en lofrede. De encomia van Gregorius van Nazianze en Gregorius van Nyssa op B.: De heiligen Verering, ed. A. Hilhorst (Nürnberg, 1988), 151-158. — F. Decret, B. et la polémique antimanichéenne en Asie mineure: StPatr 17 (1983) 1061-1064. — H. Dehnhard, Das Problem der Abhängigkeit des B. von Plotin, PTS 3 (Berlin, 1964). — P. J. Fedwick, The Church and the Charisma of Leadership in B. (Toronto, 1978). — idem (ed.), B. Christian, Humanist, Ascetic, 2 vols. (Toronto, 1981). — idem, New Editions and Studies of the Works of B.: FS M. Naldini (Rome, 1994), 613-627. — J. Gribomont, S. B. Evangile et Eglise. Mélanges (Bellefontaine, 1984). — R. P. C. Hanson, The Search for the Christian Doctrine of God (Edinburgh, 1988). — W.-D. Hauschild, B.: TRE 5:301-313 (literature). — R. M: Hübner, Zur Genese der trinitarischen Formel: FS F: Kard. Wetter (St. Ottilien, 1998), 123-156. — K. Koschorke, Spuren der alten Liebe (Fribourg, Switzerland, 1991) (literature). — P. Luislampe, Spiritus vivificans B. (Münster, 1981). — B. Pruche, Autour du traité sur le Saint-Esprit: RSR 52 (1964) 204-232. — idem, Δόγμα et κήρυγμα dans le traité Sur le Saint-Esprit: StPatr 9 (1966) 257-262. — D. G. Robertson, Stoic and Aristotelian Notions of Substance: VigChr 52 (1998) 393-417. — L. v. Rompay, L'informateur syrien de B. à propos de Génèse 1, 2: OCP 58 (1992) 245-251. — C. Scholten, Der Chorbischof bei B.: ZKG 103 (1992) 149-173. — M. Simonetti, Genesi e sviluppo della dottrina trinitaria di B.: B. La sua età, la sua opera e il basilianesimo in Sicilia. Atti del Congresso Internazionale (Messina 3-6 XII 1979) 1 (Messina, 1983), 169-197. — R. Staats, Die basilianische Verherrlichung des hl. Geistes auf dem Konzil von Konstantinopel 381: KuD 25 (1979) 232-253. — H. F. Stander, The Application of Themes from Graeco-Roman World in Early Christian religion: St. B.: Acta Patristica et Byzantina 2 (1991) 52-67. — M. S. Troiano, Il concetto di numerazione delle ipostasi in B.: VetChr 24 (1987) 337-352. — D. F. Wright, B. in the Protestant Reformers: StPatr 17/3 (1983) 1149-1158.

J. PAULI, OSB

Basil of Seleucia

B., a native of Isauria, was bishop of the Isaurian metropolis of Seleucia from 444 on; he died after 468. During his time in office he admittedly took various sides in the christological controversy, but this was due to his search for a compromise formula. In 448, at a synod in Constantinople, he agreed to the condemnation of Eutyches. On the other hand, under pressure from Dioscurus of Alexandria, he supported the "Monophysites" in Ephesus during the Robber Council of 449, but then agreed with their condemnation at Chalcedon. His profession of faith of 448 was cleverly worded (the one Christ "is known in two natures" [ACO 2, 1, 1, 117]) and was

taken over at Chalcedon. Despite his acceptance of Cyril's unity formula, he asserted the two natures, so that one may speak of a concept of ecumenical importance—without any successful building of a bridge to the Monophysites.

B. also composed a collection of homilies (the first edition of which he saw to himself) on scriptural texts and bibl. personages. The thirty-eighth and thirty-ninth of these forty-one homilies are probably not authentic. In addition, several homilies are to be ascribed to him that circulated under the name of Athanasius. Espec. important is an Easter homily (*hom. pasch.*). A homily on Pentecost by Ps.-Chrysostom is probably also from B., as are two homilies of Ps.-Basil, which the critics initially ascribed to Proclus of Constantinople (*hom.* 1-2). Several homilies have not yet been published. The sermons show B. to have been a moderate Antiochene.

A synodal letter of 457 (*ep.*) to Emperor Leo protests against the installation of Timothy Ailurus in Alexandria.

Acc. to Photius, *cod.* 168, B. made use of the exegetical writings of Basil and John Chrys. His own texts with their dramatic style influenced in turn the kontakia of → Romanus the Singer.

A life of St. Thecla (*vit. Thec.*) has also come down under B.'s name. The monastery built over her supposed grave was near Seleucia. In fact, a priest excommunicated by B. seems to have been the author. A poetic biography of Thecla, which Photius ascribes to B., has not survived.

W: PG 85:10-618; 28, 1047-1108 [homilies of ps.-Ath.]; 64, 417-424 [homily of ps.-Chrys.]. — *hom. pasch.*, M. Aubineau, SC 187:167-277. — *hom.* 1, S. Y. Rudberg: Muséon 72 (1959) 301-322 [text]. — *hom.* 2, D. Amand: RBen 58 (1948) 223-263 [text/French trans.]. — *ep.*, ACO 2, 5, 46-50 [text]. — *vit. Thec.*, G. Dragon, Vie et miracles de s. Thècle, SHG 62 (Brussels, 1978).

L: B. Baldwin, A. M Talbot, B.: ODB 1:260. — A. Grillmeier, Jesus der Christus 2/1 (Freiburg i.Br., 1986), 240-244, 260-262 (Engl., Christ in Christian Tradition, vol. 2/1 [London, 1987]). — E. Honigmann, Theodoret of Cyrrhus and B. (The time of their death): Patristic Studies, ST 173 (Rome, 1953), 174-184. — P. Maas, Das Kontakion: BZ 19 (1810) 285-306. — B. Marx, Der homiletische Nachlaß des B.: OCP 7 (1941) 329-369. — M. Van Parijs, L'évolution de la doctrine christologique de B.: Irénikon 44 (1971) 493-514.

B. WINDAU

Basilides

B. established a school and was active probably in Alexandria (Irenaeus, *haer.* 1.24.1) during the reign of Hadrian (117-138), probably beginning in 132/133

(Eus., *chron. ad Abr.* 2148). It is unlikely that B. also taught in Persia (this claim probably reflects a heresiological cliche of → Hegemonius, *Arch.* 67.4). He composed "24 books on the gospel" (or: *Exegetica*), a kind of commentary on the gospels (Agrippa Castor in Eus., *h.e.* 4.7.7) and perhaps included a text of the gospel (Origen, *hom. in Lc.* 1.2, speaking polemically: "Gospel acc. to B."). B. may also have written odes (Origen, *enn. in Iob* 21.12). Glaukias, Peter's interpreter, is said to have been the one who handed on the tradition to him in school (Clement Alex., *str.* 7.106.4); there was possibly an appeal also to extrabibl. prophetic traditions (so Agrippa Castor).

The sources for knowledge of B. are three, each giving a distinctive picture of heresy: fragments and information in Clement Alex. (along with Origen and the *Acta Archelai*), Irenaeus of Lyons (*haer.* 1.24), and Hippolytus (*haer.* 7.20-27). In reconstructing the teaching of B. most scholars opt for a combination of the first two; a minority thinks that authentic information is to be gotten only from Clement. Even the most recent researchers argue for starting with the fragments and then making a careful analysis of the heresiological cliches peculiar to each of the other groups. Irenaeus is the origin of the standard accusation of ethical libertinism and natural determinism that have ever since been leveled at B. as at all the gnostics.

The fragments and information show initially only that B. was a theologian who was interested in science and had a philosophical training: in his school, faith, conceived in intellectualist terms, was said to be an "undemonstrable knowledge" which he had acquired through "spiritual understanding" (at least acc. to Clement, *str.* 2.10.1, with reference to the philosophical language of the schools). B. accepted a Platonizing, dualistic doctrine of the soul (*str.* 2.112.1–114.2) and used biblical exegesis to justify his adoption of a form of Platonic metempsychosis (Clement, *exc. Thdot.* 28; Origen, *comm.* 5.1 *in Rom.* 5.12-14). In the face of human suffering he tried to show the justice of God (*str.* 4.81.1–83.1). Finally, B. seems also to have favored a Platonizing cosmology; in accordance with this, a demiurge or archon was active in the creation of the world. An explicit dualism, however, is avoided.

B. has his place in the history of 2nd-c. Alexandrian theology. The title "gnostic" applies much more to the secondary accounts in Irenaeus and Hippolytus than to the authentic fragments in Clement.

W: W. Völker, Quellen zur Geschichte der chr. Gnosis: SQS NS 5 (1932) 38-56 [text]. — W. A. Löhr, B. u. seine Schule (Tübingen, 1996) [text/German trans./comm.].

L: W. Foerster, Das System des B.: NTS 9 (1962/63) 233-255. — R. M. Grant, Place de B. dans la théologie chrétienne ancienne: REAug 25 (1979) 201-216. — W. D. Hauschild, Christologie u. Humanismus bei dem "Gnostiker" B.: ZNW 68 (1977) 67-92. — M. Jufresa, B. A Path to Plotinus: VigChr 35 (1981) 1-15. — H. Langerbeck, Die Anthropologie der alexandrinischen Gnosis: idem, Aufsätze zur Gnosis: AAWG. PH 69 (1967) 38-82. — G. May, Schöpfung aus dem Nichts (Berlin, 1978). — A. Mehat, ΑΠΟΚΑΤΑΣΤΑΣΙΣ chez B.: FS H.-C. Puech (Paris, 1974), 365-373. — E. Mühlenberg, Wirklichkeitserfahrung u. Theologie bei dem Gnostiker B.: KuD 18 (1972) 161-172. — idem, B.: TRE 5:296-301. — S. Pétrement, A Separate God (London, 1991) (Paris, 1984), 336-346. — G. Quispel, L'homme gnostique. La doctrine de B.: ErJb 16 (1948) 89-139. — A. Versluis, The red thread of gnosis: Studies in Spirituality 9 (1999) 5-12.

C. MARKSCHIES

Basiliscus

B., a usurper against Emperor Zeno, and then Byz. emperor 475-476, tried by means of his *Encyclicon* to eliminate the bitter division that had affected the eastern church since the Council of Chalcedon in 451. The theol. cornerstones of this document were the acceptance solely of the creeds of Nicaea 325 and Constantinople 381 and the prohibition of the creed of Chalcedon and the *Tomus* of Leo I. But the resistance espec. of patriarch Acacius forced B. to withdraw the *Encyclion* (*Antiencyclicon*). B. was imprisoned after Zeno's reconquest of Constantinople and died in Cappadocia.

W: *Encyclicon,* Cod. Vat. gr. 1431, E. Schwartz: ABAW. PPH 30 (1927) 49-51 [text (*rec. long.*)]. — Evagrius, *h.e.* 3.4, J. Bidez, L. Parmentier (Amsterdam, ²1964), 101-104 [text (*rec. brev.*)]. — Zacharias Rhetor, *h.e.* 5.2, E. W. Brooks, CSCO 83:211-213 [text (Syriac version)]. — A. Grillmeier, Jesus der Christus 2/1 (Freiburg i.Br., 1986), 269-271 [German trans. (text of Evagrius)] (English, Christ in Christian Tradition, vol. 2/1 [London, 1987]). — *Antiencyclicon,* Cod. Vat. gr. 1431, loc. cit., 52. — Evagrius, *h.e.* 3, 7, loc. cit., 107. — Nicepherus Callistes, *h.e.* 16.7, PG 147:129.
L: P. Allen, Evagrius (Leuven/Louvain, 1981), 122-130. — A. Demandt, Spätantike (Munich, 1989), 182-189. — A. Grillmeier, loc. cit., 267-279. — J. Jarry, Hérésies: RAPH 14 (1968) 241-253. — KonChal 2:112-116. — E. Schwartz, Sammlungen: ABAW. PH 10 (1934) 185-191.

J. ULRICH

Belisarius Scholasticus

B., who probably lived ca. 500, was author of two poems in hexameters, which praise → Sedulius and his *Carmen paschale*. In each poem there are sixteen acrostic and telestic verses, whose opening and closing letters spell the two words *Sedulius antistes*. The author relies heavily on the dedication and preface of the *Carmen paschale*. In some codices the second poem is attributed to a Liberius Scholasticus, but this person is probably the same as B.

W: J. Huemer, CSEL 10:307-310. — A. Riese (ed.), Anthologia Latina 1/2 (Amsterdam, ²1964 = Leipzig, ²1906), Nr. 492, 493.
L: A. Ferrua, B.: EC 2, 1181. — M. Schanz, C. Hosius, G. Krüger, Geschichte der röm. Lit. 4/2 (Munich, ²1959), 373.

B. WINDAU

Benedict of Nursia

I. Life: The sources for the life of B. are Gregory the Great, *dial.* 2; 3; 16; 4.8ff.: texts that draw upon the miracle stories of the Bible and the hagiography of the early church and are devoted to showing B.'s spiritual journey to God, but nonetheless offer a reliable historical nucleus. Born ca. 480-490 in or near Nursia (Norcia), B. came very young to Rome and the study of the liberal arts, but soon broke off this study. He betook himself for a short time to Enfide (now Affile) and then withdrew for three years as a hermit in a cave near Subiaco. Having become famous there, he was offered the leadership of a nearby community of monks (Vicovaro?). After failing in this office, he returned to solitude at Subiaco, where numerous disciples joined him; these he divided up, twelve to each of twelve scattered mountain monasteries, while he himself remained at the main monastery with a few monks. The resentment of the local clergy (and perhaps also this new concept of monasticism) caused B. to withdraw from Subiaco. He and a few disciples settled on the top of Monte Cassino (probably with the permission and support of the state), where he destroyed the pagan shrines that were still being visited, built two oratories, and became a missionary to the nearby population. B. did not leave this place again until his death (ca. 547).

II. Work: The monastic rule (*Regula Benedicti* [*reg.*]) (→ Monastic Rule), which B. wrote at Monte Cassino for cenobites and which in its present form dates back to 550, has come down in three recensions: (1) the *Textus purus*, which goes back, via the *Normative Copy (Normalexemplar) of Aachen* (lost) commissioned by Charlemagne, to the copy of the Rule dictated by B. himself (also lost), and which is best represented by *Cod. Sangallensis* 914 (beginning of 9th c.); (2) the *Textus interpolatus* (main representatives: *Cod. Oxoniensis* Hatton 48 [ca. 700-710], *Cod. 52 Veronensis* and *Cod. Sangallensis* 916 [both

8th c.]), which originated in Rome in the 7th c. and contains "normalizations" (orthography, word forms, grammar), explanatory additions, and shortenings of the text (espec. of the Prologue: 1-39 instead of 1-50); and (3) the *Textus receptus*, a fusion of 1 and 2, from the 9th c.

In comparison with the other monastic rules of antiquity the *reg.* displays a relatively systematic organization of the material: (1) Prologue: The basic attitude of obedience. (2) The spiritual foundation (1-7): objective: rule, monastery, abbot, council (1-3); subjective: the fundamental virtues or "the spiritual craft" (4-7). (3) The internal organization of the monastery (8-52): liturgy, dormitory, faults and punishments, material possessions, order of the day. (4) Organization of relations with the outside world (53-61): guests, the poor, acceptance of new brothers, laborers. (5) Offices in the monastery (61-66). (6) Supplement by B. (67-72). (7) Epilogue (73): The *reg.* as rule for beginners.

The sources are espec. the → *Regula Magistri*, which, in a shorter recension that is close to *Cod. Parisiensis* 12205, forms the verbal model down to ch. 7 and gives the general line of thought down to ch. 66; other sources are, e.g., Pachomius, Basil, Augustine, John Cassian, the lives of the monks (e.g., the life of Pachomius and the → *Historia monachorum in Aegypto*), Cyprian, Leo the Great, and not least the Bible. It is against this background that the distinctive spiritual character of the *reg.* becomes clear, a character that can only with difficulty be reduced to the popular phrase *Ora et labora*. There is a pronounced christocentrism; a balance between obedience to the abbot as teacher in the school of the Lord's service (compare the *Regula Magistri*), brotherly love, and a feel for the individual person; the priority of the interior for the individual monk (breadth of heart, the call for joy and love) and the community (stability and enclosure), without at the same time neglecting the exterior (monastic observance, care for the necessities of life, care of the poor, hospitality); the primacy of the communal liturgy as well as the sober sense of what is really possible for human beings.

W: R. Hanslik, CSEL 75. — A. de Vogüé, J. Neufville, SC 181-186. — T. Fry (Collegeville, 1981) [text/English trans.]. — G. Holzherr (Einsiedeln, 1982) [text/German trans./comm.]. — S. Pricoco (Milan, 1995), 115-273, 307-385 [text/Italian trans./comm.]. — Salzburger Äbtekonferenz, Benediktusregel (Beuron, 1992) [text/German trans.]. — B. Steidle (Beuron, ⁴1984) [text/German trans.]. — A. de Vogüé, J. Neufville, P. Saenz (Luján, 1990) [text/Spanish trans.].
L: *Bibliographies, Periodicals, Series:* B. Jaspert, Regula

Magistri-Regula Benedicti: StMon 13 (1971) 129-171.
— idem, Ausgaben u. Übersetzungen (Hildesheim, 1983).
— ABenR. — Ben. — BenM. — BenR. — BenS. — BHB.
— CCist. — MonS. — RBen. — RBS. — StMon.
A. Böckmann, Perspektiven (Münsterschwarzach, 1986).
— A. Borias, Approche sociologique: CCist 57 (1995) 280-
307. — Centro Italiano di Studi sull' Alto Medioevo, Atti
del 7° congresso (Spoleto, 1982). — O. Hagemeyer, Entste-
hung: EuA 53 (1977) 271-282. — R. Hanslik, Sprache: RBS
1 (1972) 195-207. — H. Holze, Erfahrung u. Theologie
(Göttingen, 1992). — U. K. Jacobs, Rechtsbuch (Cologne,
1987). — B. Jaspert, RB-Regula Magistri-Kontroverse
(Hildesheim, 1975). — M. Kaczmarkowski, Textstruktur:
FS G. Sanders (Steenbrugge, 1991), 277-287. — C. Lauer,
Gnadenbegriff: RBS 13 (1984) 17-34. — A. Linage Conde,
Anthropología: Asclepio, Ma 20 (1968) 135-163. — C.
Mohrmann, Latinité: RBen 62 (1952) 108-139. — F. Renner, B.-regel: TRE 5:573-577. — E. v. Severus, Gemeinde
für die Kirche (Münster, 1981). — A. de Vogüé, La communauté et l'abbé (Brügge, 1961). — idem, B.: TRE 5:538-
549. — idem, Theol.-spiritueller Kommentar (Hildesheim,
1983). — idem, L'école du Christ: CCist 46 (1984) 3-12. —
idem, B. (Bégrolles-en-Mauges 1981). — H. J. Vogt, Lat.
Mönchtum: HKG(J) 2/2 (1975) 265-282. — G. M. Wid-
halm, Rhetorische Elemente (Hildesheim, 1974).

M. SKEB, OSB

Benedict II of Rome

B. (June 26, 684–May 8, 685), who has left us two
letters, made his goal the condemnation of Monotheletism in the West. He succeeded in having future
papal elections confirmed in Ravenna instead of in
Byzantium, as previously.

S: LP 1:363f.
W: PL 96:423f.

G. KAMPERT

Benjamin of Alexandria

B., born ca. 590, was initially a monk in the
monastery of Canopus. In 626, during the Persian
occupation, he became patriarch of Alexandria, fled
from Cyrus, the Melkite patriarch and governor, to
Upper Egypt in 631, returned to Alexandria only in
643/644 when it was under Arab control, and had the
caliph confirm him anew in his office as patriarch.
Through tenacious negotiations with the Muslim
authorities he ensured the continued existence of the
Copt. church; he died on January 1, 665.

The life of B. is praised in a fragmentary panegyric
(vita), probably from the pen of deacon and successor Agathon, and in the history of the patriarchs
(hist. patr.) by Severus ibn al-Muqaffa. Of B.'s very
many works written in Coptic, the homily of 644/645
on the marriage feast of Cana (Cana) has survived

complete in the Copt. original and in a literal Arab.
translation. Also preserved in fragmentary form are
two sermons on Shenoute (hom.). The sixteenth
Easter letter (ep. pasch.), of 643/644, against the
Arians and Apollinarists is preserved completely in
Ethiopian; Gr. fragments of the thirtieth and thirty-
first Easter letters are attested in John of Damascus.
Further Easter letters as well as the body of letters
(ep.) from 641 are considered to have disappeared
except for a few Copt. fragments. An Arab. sermon
on Theodore the Anatolian and various exegetical
treatises (B.'s answers to various questions on the OT
and NT) have not yet been published.

S: vita, C. D. G. Müller, Homilie über die Hochzeit zu Kana
(Heidelberg, 1968), 295-300 [Coptic text/German trans.].
— hist. patr., PO 1:487-518 [Arabic text/French trans.].
W: Cana, C. D. G. Müller, loc. cit., 52-285 [Coptic-Arabic
text/German trans.]. — hom., ibid., 286-294 [Coptic
text/German trans.]. — ep. pasch. 30-31, ibid., 32 [Greek
text]. — ep. pasch. 16, ibid., 302-351 [Ethiopic text/German
trans.]. — ep., E. Amélineau, Fragments coptes: JA 12
(1888) 361-410 [Coptic text/French trans.]. — G. Graf,
Geschichte 1 (Rome, 1944), 515; 2 (Rome, 1947), 313-315
[Arabic mss.].
L: H. Brakmann, Neues Blatt der vita B. s: Muséon 93
(1980) 299-309. — Die Geschichte des Christentums 4
(Freiburg i.Br., 1994), 435, 445, 451. — A. Grillmeier, Jesus
der Christus 2/4 (Freiburg i.Br., 1990) 82-88 (English,
Christ in Christian Tradition, vol. 2/4 [London, 1996]). —
A. v. Lantschoot, B. I: DHGE 7:1341f. — J. Moorhead,
Monophysite Response: Byz. 51 (1981) 579-591. — C. D. G.
Müller, loc. cit., 9-38. — idem, B.: Muséon 69 (1956) 313-
340. — idem, Stand der Forschung: ZDMG suppl. 1/2
(1969) 404-410. — idem, B.: Copt-E 2:375-377. — F.
Winkelmann, Ägypten u. Byzanz: Bysl 40 (1979) 161-182.
— idem, Stellung Ägyptens: Graeco-Coptica, ed. P. Nagel
(Halle, 1984, 11-35).

P. BRUNS, B. WINDAU

Beza of Athrib

B. was disciple and successor (466) of → Shenoute as
head of the White Monastery at Athrib. He lived
until 474. Information on his life is to be gotten only
from his works. He composed a panegyrical life of
Shenoute in which he shows his admiration for his
teacher. The life is preserved in a Bohairic translation
of the Sahidic original and was also translated into
Syriac and Arabic. Also preserved in Coptic are
numerous letters (ep.) and sermons (hom.), which
convey an idea of monastic life. B.'s works show a
familiarity with the Bible and make clear the essential
importance of Christ.

W: ep./hom., K. H. Kuhn, CSCO 157/158 [text/English
trans.]. — vita, J. Leipoldt, CSCO 41; H. Wiesmann, CSCO

103

129 [text/Latin trans.]. — F. Nau: RSEHA 8 (1900) 153-167/252-263 [Syriac text/French trans.].
L: J. David, B.: DHGE 8:1140. — A. Grillmeier, Jesus der Christus 2/4 (Freiburg i.Br., 1990), 235-241 (English, Christ in Christian Tradition, vol. 2/4 [London, 1996]). — K. H. Kuhn, A Fifth Century Egyptian Abbot I-III: JThS NS 5 (1954) 36-48, 174-187; 6 (1955) 35-48. — idem, B.: CoptE 2:378.

B. WINDAU

Boethius

I. Life: Anicius Manlius Severinus Boethius, born in Rome ca. 480, came from a high-ranking, influential, and, from the 4th c. on, Christian family. After the early death of his father, B. was taken into the home of Q. Aurelius Memmius Symmachus (consul 485), whose daughter Rusticiana he later married; there he received an excellent education. He probably received his philosophical formation from Ammonius, a Neoplatonist, in Alexandria. In his youth B. was already noted for his academic talents and won the favor of Theodoric, who made him sole consul (*consul sine collega*) in 510; in 522 B. received a special honor in that his two sons, who were still minors, were given the consulate. The high point of his career was his appointment as *magister officiorum*, the highest-ranking of Theodoric's court functionaries (probably also in 522), but this position was at the same time to become B.'s undoing.

Theodoric's situation, which was weakened by the sudden death of his successor, Eutharic (522), and of his ally, Thrasamund, king of the Vandals (523), was in danger of complete collapse when the Roman senate, which since the end of the Acacian Schism (519) had once again drawn closer to East Rome, was suspected in 523 of conspiracy with Byzantium and high treason. When letters of leading senators to Emperor Justin were intercepted and their content told to Theodoric, B. presented himself to the senate and for this reason became suspect of high treason. In this situation Theodoric thought he had to make an example of someone: B. was stripped of his offices, imprisoned, and, after a lengthy trial and despite the intervention of his father-in-law, was executed in Oct. 524 at a place called *Ager Calventianus* (near Pavia).

II. Works: B.'s entire output may be divided into four groups: writings on the quadrivium; writings on logic; theol. writings; and the *Consolatio philosophiae*, which is unique in its kind.

1. Soon after 500 B. began the publication of his first scholarly works: introductions to the disciplines of the quadrivium (B.'s own term, *arith.* 1.1). Surviving are the *De institutione arithmeticae* (*arith.*) and *De institutione musicae* (*mus.*), but the introductions to geometry and astronomy were lost (in the Middle Ages two spurious geometries were in circulation). The writings were based on corresponding Gr. compendia, but B. arranged the material in an independent form.

2. B.'s bent for the encyclopedic shows especially in the ambitious project of his youth: to translate and comment on all the writings of Plato and Aristotle and so to demonstrate the agreement between the two philosophers (*in herm. comm. sec.* 2.3). B. was able, however, to carry out his plan only (in part) for Aristotle's *Organon*: Along with translations of Porphyry's *Isagoge* (*Porph. isag.*), the *Categories* (*categ.*), the *Perihermeneias* (*herm.*), the *Prior Analytics* (*anal. pr.*) (a translation of the *Posterior Analytics* [*anal. post.*] is spurious), the *Topics* (*top. Arist.*), and the *Elenchus sophistici* (*elench. soph.*), there also exist, sometimes in two versions, commentaries on the *Isagoge* (*in Porph. comm. pr. sec.*), the *Categories* (*in categ. comm.*), and the *Perihermeneias* (*in herm. comm. pr./sec.*). Commentaries on the *Prior Analytics* and the *Topics* have been lost. B. also composed an (incompletely surviving) commentary of the *Topics* of Cicero (*in top. Cic.*), as well as five independent writings on logic: *De syllogismo categorico* (*syll. categ.*), *Introductio ad syllogismos categoricos* (*syll. categ. introd.*), *De divisione* (*divis.*), *De hypotheticis syllogismis* (*syll. hyp.*), and *De differentiis topicis* (*diff. top.*). The only work datable with certainty is *in categ. comm.*) (510, the year of B.'s consulate). The relative chronology probably followed the canonical order of the works in the *Organon*. The independent treatises came, in all likelihood, in a later phase of B.'s work.

3. The authenticity of the so-called *opuscula sacra* was long doubted, but it is assured, with one exception, by the testimony of → Cassiodorus (*Anecdoton Holderi*, p. 4, 14ff.). These *opuscula* include: *Quomodo trinitas unus Deus est ac non tres dii* (*trin.*): presents the doctrine of the Trinity, following Augustine; probably occasioned by the theopaschite controversy and dedicated to Symmachus. *Utrum pater et filius et spiritus sanctus de divinitate substantialiter predicentur* (*div.*): a short supplement to the first treatise. *Quomodo substantiae in eo quod sint bonae sint, cum non sint substantialia bona* (*subs. bon.*; also titled *De hebdomadibus*): a Neoplatonic ontology following Proclus. *De fide catholica* (*fid. cath.*): an outline of Cath. teaching on redemption; the authenticity is disputed, since it is not mentioned by Cassiodorus and contrasts notably with the abstract character of the other treatises. *Contra Eutychen et Nestorium* (*c. Eut.*): explanation of the hypo-

static union, composed at the request of the Illyrian bishops (512/513), probably the earliest of the theol. writings.

4. B.'s most famous work is the *Consolatio philosophiae* (*cons.*), which was written in 523/524 during the months of his detention (probably not an imprisonment but a lenient house arrest with access to books and permission to have visitors). Here, in five books, B. tests the validity of consoling philosophical arguments in the face of the loss of all earthly goods. The work takes the form of a dialogue between Philosophy, who comes to him as a female physician, and B. who is "ill"; as a result he is cured of his depressive lethargy. Poems in various meters (B. was also supposed to have composed poetic works when he was young, among them a *Carmen bucolicum*) alternate with sections of prose (more important in their content), the poems to divide up and summarize the steps in the argument.

In the first book Philosophy gives a diagnosis based on information from the patient; central here is the apologia or defense (*pr.* 4), a short version of the (lost) defense statement composed by B. The second book undertakes, in the diatribe style of popular philosophy, to depreciate earthly goods (riches, honor, power, fame, pleasure), with reference espec. to the fickleness of *Fortuna*. In the third book the themes are discussed at a philosophically more demanding level; at the center of the work is the great Platonic hymn (*metr.* 9), in which God as the supreme good is contrasted with false earthly happiness. The fourth book takes up the problem of theodicy, using the Platonic theory of evil as privation, and the fifth and final book is devoted to the special question of the compatibility of divine providence and the freedom of the human will, a question to which B. gives an original and convincing solution. The sober style and abrupt ending of the fifth book do not necessarily mean that the work is incomplete, but suggests rather the incorporation of an earlier draft.

The philosophical character, which is that of secular antiquity, or, to put it differently, the lack of specifically Chr. elements in the *cons.* and in the rest of B.'s work (even the *opusc. sacra* do not betray any personal convictions) inevitably lead to the question of B.'s Christianity. Evidently, his rootedness in the Platonic-Aristotelean tradition of antiquity was so deep as to leave no room for genuinely Chr. ideas, not even when there was question of giving an account of his fundamental convictions in an extreme situation. B.'s spiritual home was, and remained, ancient philosophy, not Christianity. Nonetheless, aided by his "martyr's death" under the Arian Theodoric, he became the most important link between antiquity and the Middle Ages and the precursor of Scholasticism.

W: PL 63-64. — *arith.*, *mus.*, [*geom.*], G. Friedlein (Frankfurt a.M., 1966 = Leipzig, [1]1867) [text]. — *arith.*, M. Masi (Amsterdam, 1983) [English trans./comm.]. — *mus.*, O. Paul (Hildesheim, 1973 = Leipzig, [1]1872) [German trans./comm.]. — *Porph. isag.*, *categ.*, *herm.*, *anal. pr.*, *top. Arist.*, L. Minio-Paluello (Bruges, 1961-1966) [text]. — *elench. soph.*, B. G. Dod (Leiden, 1975) [text]. — in *Porph. comm.*, S. Brandt, CSEL 48. — in *herm. comm.*, C. Meiser (Leipzig, 1877/1880) [text]. — in *top. Cic.*, J. C. Orelli, J. G. Baiter (Zurich, 1833), 270-388 [text]. — E. Stump (Ithaca, 1988) [English trans./comm.]. — *divis.*, L. Pozzi (Padua, 1969) [Italian trans./comm.]. — *syll. hyp.*, L. Obertello (Brescia, 1969) [text/Italian trans./comm.]. — *diff. top.*, D. Z. Nikitas (Athens, 1990) [text]. — E. Stump (Ithaca, 1978) [English trans./comm.]. — *opusc. sacra*, *cons.*, R. Peiper (Leipzig, 1871) [text]. — H. F. Stewart, E. K. Rand, S. J. Tester (London, 1973) [text/English trans.]. — *opusc. sacra*, M. Elsässer (Hamburg, 1988) [text/German trans./comm.]. — *cons.*, W. Weinberger, CSEL 67. — L. Bieler, CCL 94. — K. Büchner (Heidelberg, [3]1977) [text]. — J. Gruber (Berlin, 1978) [comm.]. — E. Gegenschatz, O. Gigon (Zurich, 1990 = [2]1969) [text/German trans.].

L: L. Adamo, B. e Mario Vittorino traduttori: RSF 22 (1967) 141-164. — M. Asztalos, B. as a transmitter of Greek logic: HSCP 95 (1993) 367-407. — M. Baltes, Gott, Welt, Mensch in der *cons.*: VigChr 34 (1980) 313-340. — H. M. Barrett, B. His times and work (New York, 1965 = Cambridge, [1]1940). — R. Carton, Le christianisme et l'augustinisme de B.: RevPhil 30/1 (1930) 573-659. — H. Chadwick, B. The Consolations of Music, Logic, Theology, and Philosophy (Oxford, 1981). — P. Courcelle, Les lettres grecques en Occident (Paris, [2]1948), 257-312. — idem, La cons. dans la tradition littéraire (Paris, 1967). — I. Craemer-Rueggenberg, Substanzmetaphysik in den *opusc. sacra*, Diss. (Cologne, 1969). — T. F. Curley, The *cons.* as a work of literature: AJP 108 (1987) 343-367. — C. J. De Vogel, Philosophy and Christian Faith in B.'s *cons.*: FS J. H. Waszink (Amsterdam, 1973), 357-370. — F. Di Mieri, Il arithm. di B.: SupDom 37 (1984) 179-202. — M. Fuhrmann, J. Gruber, B. (Darmstadt, 1984). — E. Gegenschatz, Zufall, Freiheit u. Notwendigkeit [on in *herm. comm.*]: Erbe, das nicht veraltet, ed. P. Neukam (Munich, 1979), 5-61. — M. Gibson, B. His Life, Thought and Influence (Oxford, 1981). — R. Glei, Dichtung u. Philosophie in der *cons.*: WJA 11 (1985) 225-238. — idem, Fiktion u. Realität in der *cons.*: WJA 22 (1998) 199-213. — P. Huber, Göttliche Vorsehung u. menschliche Freiheit in der *cons.*, Diss. (Zurich, 1976). — F. Klingner, De Boethii *cons.* (Zurich, 1966 = Berlin, [1]1921). — S. Lerer, B. and Dialogue (Princeton, 1985). — P. B. Luettringhaus, Gott, Freiheit u. Notwendigkeit in der *cons.*: Studien zur mal. Geistesgeschichte u. ihren Quellen 15, ed. A. Zimmermann (Berlin, 1982), 53-101. — M. Masi, B. and the Liberal Arts (Bern, 1981). — C. Micaelli, Dio nel pensiero di B. (Naples, 1995). — C. Morton, Marius of Avenches, the Excerpta Valesiana, and the Death of B.: Tr. 38 (1982) 107-136. — C. Mueller-Goldingen, Dichtung in der *cons.*: RMP 132 (1989) 369-395. — L. Obertello, Severino B. (2 vols.) (Geneva, 1974). — idem, Atti del Congresso internaz. di Studi Boeziani (Rome, 1981). — G. J. O'Daly, The Poetry of B. (London, 1991). — B. Pabst,

Prosimetrum (2 vols.) (Cologne, 1994). — E. Reiss, The Fall of B. and the Fiction of the cons.: CJ 77 (1981) 37-47. — idem, B. (Boston, 1982). — C. Reitz, Zum fünften Buch der cons.: WJA 16 (1990) 239-246. — H. Scheible, Gedichte in der cons. (Heidelberg, 1972). — W. Schmid, Philosophisches u. Medizinisches in der cons.: FS B. Snell (Munich, 1956), 113-144. — V. Schmidt-Kohl, Neuplatonische Seelenlehre in der cons., Meisenheim 1965. — G. Schrimpf, Axiomenschrift des B. (De hebdomadibus) (Leiden, 1966). — V. Schurr, Trinitätslehre des B. (Paderborn, 1935). — D. Shanzer, The Death of B. and the cons.: Hermes 112 (1984) 352-366. — H. Tränkle, Zum B. prozeß: FS J. H. Waszink, A 1973, 329-339. — idem, Ist die cons. zum vorgesehenen Abschluß gelangt?: VigChr 31 (1977) 148-156. — H. Usener, Anecdoton Holderi (Hildesheim, 1969 = Bonn, 1877).

R. F. GLEI

Boniface I of Rome

In 419, B., originally chosen as an antipope (Dec. 29, 418–Sept. 4, 422), reported the end of the schism to the Roman legates in Africa (*ep.* 2.791f.). In the nine surviving letters (*ep.*), among other things, he claims a Roman primacy of jurisdiction in Illyricum (*ep.* 4f., 13-15), restores the old metropolitan order in Gaul, and asks Emperor Honorius to defend the coming papal election (*ep.* 7).

W: PL 20:749-792. — S. Wenzlowsky, Briefe der Päpste, BKV¹ 15:310-368 [German trans.].
L: H. Chantraine, Schisma von 418/19: FS K. Christ (Darmstadt, 1988), 79-94. — E. Dassmann, Kirchengeschichte 2/1 (Stuttgart, 1996), 168.

O. KAMPERT

Boniface II of Rome

Designated as successor by Felix III, B. (Sept. 22, 530–Nov. 17, 532) forced reconciliation on his opponents but failed in his own attempt to determine his successor. He claimed Roman primacy of jurisdiction in Illyricum and, in the only letter to survive, confirmed the decrees of the Second Council of Orange, which condemned Semipelagianism. A letter acknowledging Roman leadership in Africa is a forgery.

W: PL 65:31-48.
L: P. Bertolini, Bonifacio II: DBI 12:133-136.

O. KAMPERT

Braulio of Saragossa

B., bishop of Saragossa (632-651), was neither primate nor metropolitan, yet after the death of Isidore of Seville he became the most influential member of the Spanish episcopate. He took part in Councils of Toledo IV (633), V (636), and VI (638); he perhaps composed, in preparation for Toledo IV (633), which was hostile to Jews, the *Confessio Iudaeorum civitatis Toletanae* of Dec. 637, which the converted Jews (*exhebraei*) of the Toledo community had to accept. He stayed away from Council of Toledo VII (646), probably in order, like many other bishops, to make clear his reservations about royal policy. Even more than King Chindaswinth, King Reccesvinth took B.'s advice. He even asked B. to revise a legal code (not described more specifically in the letter). B.'s correspondence (*ep.*) is an important source for the history of Visigothic Spain. Evidences of B.'s efforts to give Emilian, a Spanish saint, a place alongside Martin of Tours and Anthony are the *Vita Aemilinai* (*vita*) and the *Hymnus de S. Aemiliano* (*hym.*). In addition, B. edited the *Etymologiae*, which → Isidore had dedicated to him, continued Isidore's *De viris illustribus*, and made a list of all his works (*Renotatio librorum divi Isidori*).

The attribution of other works to B. is in some cases disputed, in others untenable.

W: PL 80:649-716. — *ep.*, J. Madoz (Madrid, 1941). — L. Riesco Terrero (Seville, 1975) [text/Spanish trans.]. — C. W. Barlow, FaCh 63 [English trans./comm.]. — *vita*, L. Vázquez de Parga (Madrid, 1943). — *hym.*, C. Blume, AHMA 27:125-127. — *renotatio*, PL 83:1081-1106; 81:15-17; 82:65-68.
L: C. W. Barlow, B. (Washington, 1969). — H.-J. Diesner, B.s Vita s. Aemiliani u. die frühchr. Biographie: MLJb 11 (1976) 7-12. — A. Lambert, La famille de St. B. et l'expansion de la Règle de Jean de Biclar: Universidad 10 (1933) 65-80. — B. Löfstedt, Sprachliche u. textkritische Bemerkungen zu B.s Vita s. Aemiliani: AnBoll 95 (1977) 132. — C. H. Lynch, P. Galindo, San B. (Madrid, 1950). — J. Orlandis, D. Ramos-Lisson, Die Synoden auf der Iberischen Halbinsel (Paderborn, 1981).

E. REICHERT

Breviarium in Psalmos

The *Brev.* is a compilation of commentaries on the Psalms. There are several hypotheses as to composer and time of composition. Suggestions include someone in Gaul (Faustus of Riez?) after 450; an Irishman of the 7th/8th c.; John the Deacon, of Rome, who is identified with the later → John I (523-526); and → Cassiodorus. Finally, since the *Glosa Psalmorum* is used, the time of origin is placed in the middle or second half of the 7th c. It is certain that the compiler of the commentaries on the Psalms depends on → Ambrose, → Hilary of Poitiers, and espec. → Jerome, under whose name the *Brev.* has been handed down and whose preface to the *Commentarioli* the compiler takes over.

W: PL 26:871-1346. — H. Ashworth, The Psalter Collects: BJRL 45 (1962/63) 287-304 [partial edition].
L: H. Boese, Die alte "Glosa Psalmorum" (Freiburg i.Br., 1982), 70-72, 76-82. — L. Brou, Où en est la question des "Psalter collects": StPatr 2 = TU 64 (1957) 17-20. — D. M. Cappuyns, Cassiodore: DHGE 11:1349-1408, here 1380 Nr. 9. — A. Di Berardino (ed.), Patrologia 4 (Genoa, 1996), 465. — H. J. Frede, Pelagius. Der irische Paulustext (Freiburg i.Br., 1961), 76 n. 4. — PLS 2:76-78. — M. Schanz, Geschichte der röm. Lit. 4/1 (Munich, ²1959), 466f., 483. — G. S. M. Walker, S. Columbani opera (Dublin, 1957), LXIV.

B. WINDAU

Breviarius de Hierosolyma

This work is a short description of Jerusalem for Lat. pilgrims of the 6th c. It was composed before the account by the → *Anonymus Placentinus*. The text has been transmitted in two versions, which probably go back to a common original. Version A is incomplete, but in the surviving parts it is more detailed than Version B. Both versions use a simple Late Latin; in content, the work attests to the importance of relics (sacred spear, cup of the Last Supper, etc.) and the transfer of some traditions (creation of Adam, sacrifice of Isaac) from the Temple Mount to the Church of the Sepulcher.

W: P. Geyer, CSEL 39:151-155. — R. Weber, CCL 175:105-112. H. Donner, Pilgerfahrt ins hl. Land (Stuttgart, 1979), 226-239 [German trans.].
L: Ein kurzer Bericht über Jerusalem: HlL 59 (1915) 208-211. — A. Heisenberg, Grabeskirche u. Apostelkirche (Leipzig, 1908), 111-122. — B. Kötting, Peregrinatio religiosa (Münster, ²1980), 359f. — J. Wilkinson, Christian Pilgrims in Jerusalem: PEQ 108 (1979) 75-101. — idem,

Jerusalem Pilgrims Before the Crusades (London, 1979), 59-61, 182-183. — A. Wilmart, Un nouveau témoin: RB 37 (1928) 101-106.

G. RÖWEKAMP

Bucolic

Ca. 400 some western writers attempted to put motifs and figures of Virgilian bucolic into the service of Chr. poetry. Shortly before 400, in the poem *De mortibus boum* which → Endelechius, a rhetor, composed in thirty-three asclepiadean strophes (*Anth. Lat.* 893), Tityrus, a shepherd (from Virgil, *ecl.* 1), tells his fellow shepherds how his herd was saved from an epidemic among cattle by the sign of the cross. Tityrus's account effects the conversion of the other shepherds and leads to a decision of all of them to venerate Christ. The Chr. teaching of a Tityrus (though more abstractly conceived) is also found in the Virgilian cento of a certain → Pomponius (*Anth. Lat.* 719a, probably from the 5th c.). → Paulinus of Nola goes beyond this kind of linking of bucolic and Chr. preaching: In his *Natalicia* 6 and 8 (= *carm.* 18 and 20), in which miracle stories take us into the world of small farmers and shepherds, he finds in poems on the saints an original way of making a Chr. use of bucolic. On the whole, Chr. bucolic was only a passing phenomenon in early Chr. literature.

W: Endelechius, *De mortibus boum*, D. Korzeniewski, Hirtengedichte aus spätröm. u. karolingischer Zeit (Darmstadt, 1976), 57-71, 134-137 [text/German trans./comm.].
L: T. Alimonti, Struttura, ideologia ed imitazione virgiliana nel "De mortibus boum" di Endelechio (Turin, 1976). — W. Schmid, Tityrus Christianus: RMP 96 (1953) 101-165. — idem, B.: RAC 2:786-800.

B. SCHRÖDER

C

Caelestius, a Pelagian

C. was a Roman lawyer, who joined Pelagius in Rome ca. 390. Ca. 409 he left Rome with Pelagius and went to Africa, where in 411 he was condemned in Carthage on six counts (ACO 1, 5, 1, 66). Paulinus, deacon of Milan, had accused C. of teaching that Adam was created mortal and that the sin he committed harmed him alone and not the human race that issued from him. Newborn children (C. said) were in the same condition as Adam before the fall; consequently, even unbaptized children and pagans reached heaven.

Thereafter C. appeared in Ephesus in 416 and was ordained a priest there. In 417, having returned to Rome, he made a profession of faith to Zosimus, the bishop there, that was based on that of Pelagius. He was again exiled from Rome and Italy on the basis of the *ep. tractoria* and Honorius II's decree of April 30, 418, banishing all who denied the doctrine of original sin. He appeared, finally, in Constantinople during the Nestorian controversies and in 430 was driven from there as well and his teaching was definitively condemned at Ephesus in 431 (ACO 1, 1, 7, 125-29). In the Pelagian controversy C. was on the same footing as Pelagius; at times the Pelagians even bore his name: the Caelestians. In that partnership C. had a greater interest in systematics; without C. and Julian of Eclanum there would have been no "Pelagianism."

Of his writings the three letters written to his parents before 390 (Gennadius, *vir. ill.* 45 [Richardson]) and the *Libellus appellationis* addressed to Zosimus are lost. His most important work is the *Definitiones*, in which he aims to show that it is possible for a human being to live without sin. Fragments of this work are found in Augustine (*perf. iust.* 2.1–20.43). C.'s *Libellus fidei* (417) has likewise survived only in fragments in Augustine (*gr. et pecc. or.* 2; 5; 6; 26), as has the *Libellus brevissimus,* which he composed during the trial of 411 (*pecc. mer.* 1.34.67; see *ep.* 157.3.22; 174.6) and the *Liber Caelestii* (*gest. Pel.* 13.29–18.42). In addition, there are further fragments and three uncertain attributions to C.: *Epistula Ps. Cypriani ad Turasium, Ps. Cypriani de singularitate clericorum,* and *Ps. Hieronymi de vita clericorum ad Oceanum.*

W: *Definitiones,* C. F. Urba, I. Zycha, CSEL 42:4-48. — PL 48:617-622. — A. Bruckner, Quellen zur Geschichte des pelagianischen Streites (Tübingen, 1906), 70-78 [text]. — *Libellus fidei,* C. F. Urba, I. Zycha (loc. cit.), 167-206. — PL 48:498-505 [reconstruction]. — A. Bruckner, loc. cit., 78f. [text]. — *Libellus brevissimus,* C. F. Urba, I. Zycha, CSEL 60:64. — *Liber Caelestii,* C. F. Urba, I. Zycha, CSEL 42:82-121. — A. Bruckner, loc. cit., 14-20 [text]. — O. Wermelinger, Rom u. Pelagius (Stuttgart, 1975), 297-299, 73-75 [text/German trans.].
L: G. Bonner, C.: AugL 1:693-698. — P. Brown, Pelagius and his supporters: JThS NS 19 (1968) 93-114. — A. Di Berardino (ed.), Patrologia 3 (Turin, 1983), 458f. — F. G. Nuvolone, Pélage et Pélagianisme 1: DSp 12/2:2889-2923, here 2891-2895. — G. de Plinval, Les écrits de C.: BAug 21 (1966) 592f. — idem, Le dossier C.: BAug 22 (1975) 691f. — E. Teselle, Rufinus the Syrian, C., Pelagius. Explorations: AugSt 3 (1972) 61-95.

B. WINDAU

Caesaria the Younger

C. was a niece of → Caesarius of Arles. She succeeded Caesaria the Elder as head (ca. 525-559) of the monastery of St. John which Caesarius had founded. Her surviving writings: an ascetical *Epistula* to Richilde and Radegunde, founders of monasteries (552/557), the *Dicta,* and a fragment *Constitutum,* both of the latter liturgical in content. It was at her instigation that → Cyprian of Toulon wrote, among other things, his *Vita Caesarii.*

W: A. de Vogüé, SC 345:440-499.
L: C. Lambot, L'Abbaye S. Jean: RLM 23 (1938) 169-174. — G. de Plinval, C.: DHGE 12:212f. — Y. Labande-Mailfert, Les débuts de Sainte-Croix (Poitiers, 1986), 25-116.

C. KASPER

Caesarius of Arles

I. Life: At the instigation of C.'s niece, → Caesaria the Younger (d. 559), his disciples, Bishops → Cyprian of Toulon, Firminus of Usèz, and Viventius, along with Messianus, a presbyter, and Stephen, a deacon, composed a life of C. in two books (before 549). Along with the conciliar acts and the correspondence between Rome and Arles in the first half of the 6th c., this biography is the main source for C.'s life. He was born ca. 470 of a noble family in the Burgundian city of Chalon-sur-Saône. When he was eighteen, Bishop Sylvester accepted him into the clergy of that city. Ca. 490 he joined the monastic community of Lérins under Abbot Porcarius and there filled the office of *cellarius,* but because of his great strictness he soon had to give it up (ca. 497). He went to Arles and received training from the African orator → Julian

Pomerius. A relative of C., Bishop Eonius of Arles, ordained him deacon and priest in 499 and assigned him to govern the monastery of Trinquetaille on the Rhone. In 503 the bishop appointed C. his successor. Political clashes with the Germanic peoples caused C., under the rule of Alaric II, to be banished to Bordeaux, then to be imprisoned for alleged conspiracy after the Visigoths had been defeated by the Franks and Burgundians (508), and finally, in 513, to be deported to Ravenna, where he met Theodoric, who set him free. On the way back to Arles, Bishop Symmachus of Rome gave him the pallium in Rome (514) and confirmed him, against Avitus of Vienne, as metropolitan and papal vicar for Gaul and Spain. This ended a century of conflict between Arles and Vienne over preeminence in Gaul. The Synods of Agde (506) and Vaison (529), at which C. presided, dealt with questions of church discipline; those of Carpentras (527) and Marseilles (533) with accusations against individual bishops; the Council of Orange (529) condemned the teaching on grace current in southern Gaul. Amid all his activity, C. never abandoned his monastic past. Probably toward the beginning of his time in office he established the convent of St. John for women and placed his sister Caesaria (d. 524) in charge of it. In 515 he obtained a privilege from Hormisdas, bishop of Rome, for the monastery that had been destroyed in 508 and was rebuilt in 512 near the cathedral church. He himself remained close to this convent until his death on Aug. 27, 542.

C. was the most important bishop and popular preacher of 6th-c. Gaul and distinguished himself by social involvement and pastoral ability, which found expression in his writings.

II. **Works**: 1. *Sermons* (*serm.*): This, the largest part of his production, contains ca. 240 sermons, but because of composition techniques of the 6th and 7th c. some of these are disputed, while others were attributed to him later on. In his sermons C. also used older material, which he brought together in collections (→ Eusebius Gallicanus). In the theol. direction taken therein, C. abandons the foundations of his Lérins school and in his teaching on grace follows a moderate Augustinianism. His chief concern, however, is the pastoral formation of the clergy and the moral education of the community, whose faith he sees threatened by the entry of the Germanic peoples (Chr. life, love of God and neighbor, penance, future judgment; against the popular syncretism). A great many of his sermons are on biblical texts and figures. A further part follows the annual cycle of feasts. Despite his rhetorical training, his style is geared to the capacities of his hearers and is simple, sometimes vivid and graphic.

2. *Monastic writings*: Foremost among these is the *Regula virginum* (*reg. virg.*), which has survived in the edition of 534, but its origins reach back to the founding of the convent of St. John. It is dependent on the Augustinian Rule, shows influences of → John Cassian, and contains in its *Recapitulatio* the liturgical *ordo Lirensis*. It gives information on the order of the day, which provides, in addition to vigils (*nocturna*), for a *matutina* (possibly prime), terce, sext, none, and a *duodecima*. In addition, it gives the structural elements of the prayer: in addition to psalmody, it refers to *directaneus*, *antiphonae*, *responsus*, *lectiones*, *missae*, and a *capitellum*. C. takes over thirteen hymns in all from Lérins. Despite the importance of the *reg. virg.* for the Middle Ages, it was unable, because of the all-too-concrete (and therefore all the more important to researchers) connections with the convent of St. John, to win out against the Rule of St. Benedict in female monasticism. The Rule is preceded by an ascetical letter (*ep.*) to the community. Two further letters are spurious. At the end of his life C. wrote the short *Regula monachorum* (*reg. mon.*) (534-542), a summation of his monastic experiences (dependent on the *reg. virg.*), and his *Testamentum* (*testam.*), which once again manifests his care for his monastic establishment.

3. *Various*: To be mentioned in particular are conciliar acts and direct additions to them by C.

4. *Uncertain and Spurious Writings*: These theol. and exegetical works include trinitarian–anti-Arian polemics, influenced by → Augustine and → Faustus of Riez (*De mysterio Trinitatis*; *Breviarium adversus haereticos*) and anti-Pelagian polemics (*Opusculum de gratia*), as well as a homiletic commentary on the Apocalypse that is dependent on → Victorinus of Pettau and → Tyconius. The *Quicumque* → Creed has wrongly been attributed to C.

C. was able to exert an influence after his death through his writings on female monasticism and through the Council of Orange, the decrees of which defined (Catholic) teaching on grace down to and beyond the Reformation.

W: *Opera omnia* (and *Vita*), G. Morin (Maredsous, 1953 = [1]1937) (1, *serm.*), 1942 (2) [text]. — *serm.*, idem, CCL 103f. — M. J. Delage, SC 175, 243, 330. — M. M. Mueller, FaCh 31, 47, 76 [English trans.]. — *serm.* (not contained in the collection of Morin), R. Étaix: REAug 11 (1965) 10-12; 24 (1978) 273-275. — idem: RB 75 (1965) 204-210. — idem: IP 10 (1975) 219-227. — J. Lemarié: RBen 88 (1978) 98-108. — R. Höfer: RBen 74 (1964) 44-53. — *Conciliar Acts*, C. Munier, CCL 148:192-228 [on Agde]. — C. de Clercq, CCL 148A [all others]. — *reg. virg., reg. mon., ep., testam.,*

M. Spinelli (Rome, 1981) [Italian trans./comm.]. — A. de Vogüé, SC 345.

L: C. F. Arnold, C. u. die gallische Kirche (Leipzig, 1894). — H. G. Beck, The Pastoral Care of Souls (Rome, 1950). — A. Blaise, C. d'Arles (Namur, 1962). — P. Christophe, Cassien et C. (Gembloux, 1969). — R. J. H. Collins, C.: TRE 7:531-536. — idem, C.: DIP 2:844-848. — J. Courrou, C. et les Juifs: BLE 71 (1970) 92-112. — A. Ferreiro, Literacy, Education and divine Wisdom: JEH 43 (1992) 5-16. — P. Gassmann, Der Episkopat in Gallien (Bonn, 1977). — M. Heinzelmann, Bischofsherrschaft in Gallien (Zurich, 1976). — W. Kingshirn, Charity and Power: JRSt 75 (1985) 183-204. — idem, Job in the Sermons of C: RThAM 54 (1987) 13-27. — idem, C.'s Monastery and the V. Caes: RBen 100 (1990) 441-482. — G. Konda, Discernement et malice des practiques superstiteuses (Rome, 1970). — J. Lanczkowsky, Nonnenregel des C.: EA 66 (1990) 255-281. — G. Langgärtner, Gallienpolitik der Päpste (Bonn, 1964). — idem, Der Apokalypsekommentar: ThGl 7 (1967) 210-225. — R. M. Leikam, Doctrina espiritual: EcOra 11 (1994) 153-181. — G. Morin, Le symbole d'Athanase: RBen 18 (1901) 481-493; 44 (1932) 206-219. — idem, Teridius, propagateur des Règles de C.: RSR 28 (1938) 257-263. — J. Rivière, Rédemtion chez C., BLE 44 (1944) 3-20. — L. de Seilhac, C. et la Règle d'Augustin (Rome, 1974). — B. Szarmach, C. and the Vercelli Homilies: Tr. 28 (1970) 315-323. — A. de Vogüé, La Règle de C. pour le moines: RAM 47 (1971) 369-406. — idem, Origenes de la clausura de las monjas: StSil 12 (1986)193-195.

C. KASPER

Caesarius of Nazianzus

C., the younger brother of Gregory Naz., was active as a famous scholar, physician, and high-ranking official at the imperial court (including that of Julian). He died in 369.

There has come down under the name of C., for purposes of orthodox camouflage, a rhetorically attractive (see Photius, *cod.* 210) compilation belonging to the genre of the *erōtapokrisis*; it is also called *Kephalaia*, *Peuseis*, or, wrongly, *Dialogi* (= Ps.-Caesarius [PsC]). It probably originated in Monophysite monastic circles in the middle of the 6th c. (Ps.-Dionysian concept of *theandrikos*; mention of the Lombards and Slavs) and, in the form of 228 questions and answers, sketches a summa of theol. and secular knowledge (derived espec. from Epiphanius, *anc.*; Basil, *hex.*; Gregory Nyss., *hom. opif.*; Isidore of Pelusium, Severian, *creat.*; John Chrys., *Jud.*) in order to lead "the little ship of the soul" from "the waves of heresy" into "the harbor of reason" (Prooem., 1.1ff.).

S: Gregory Naz., *or.* 7; *ep.* 7. 20. 29f.; *epitaphia*, AP 8:85-99. — Basil, *ep.* 32.
W: PG 38:851-1190. — R. Riedinger, GCS (Berlin, 1989).
L: G. Bardy, La littérature patristique des quaestiones et responsiones: RB 42 (1933) 343-346. — H. Dörrie,

Erotapokriseis: RAC 6 (1966) 342-370. — W. Hörandner, Erotapokriseis: HWRh 2, 1417-1419. — M. Kertsch, Ps.-Kaisarios als indirekter Textzeuge für Gregor v. Nazianz: JÖB 33 (1983) 17-24. — R. Riedinger, Neue Quellen zu den Erotapokriseis des PsK: JÖB 19 (1970) 152-184. — idem, PsK. Überlieferungsgeschichte u. Verfasserfrage (Munich, 1969). — U. Riedinger, Ps.-Dionysios Areopagita, PsK u. die Akoimeten: ByZ 52 (1959), 276-296. — O. Seeck, C. (3): PRE 5:1298-1300.

C. HARTMANN

Calcidius

C. was a Neoplatonic philosopher and translator of the *Timaeus* (17A-53C) into Latin. He regarded this as the principal work of Plato and wrote a commentary on it (on 31C-53C), in which he drew chiefly on older writers. Some of this commentary was passed on through Porphyry's commentary on the *Timaeus*; notable is the almost complete absence of any Lat. literature. C. also uses the commentary of Origen on Genesis, which points to his being a Christian. The addressee, Ossius, is probably not Ossius of Cordoba; neither was C. the latter's archdeacon, as has at times been suggested. The work is to be dated rather to the end of the 4th or beginning of the 5th c. C. was possibly a member of the "Milan Group." As transmitter of the Platonic tradition, C. exerted an influence via Eriugena into the 12th c.

W: J. H. Waszink (Leipzig, ²1975) [text]. — *ep. ad Ossium*, PLS 1:196f.
L: P. Courcelle, Ambroise de Milan et C.: FS J. H. Waszink (Amsterdam, 1973), 45-53. — S. Gersh, C.'s Theory of First Principles: StPatr 18/2 (1989) 85-92. — E. Mensching, Zur C.-Überlieferung: VigChr 19 (1965) 42-56. — B. W. Switalski, Des C. Kommentar zu Plato's Timaeus (Münster, 1902). — J. H. Waszink, C.: JAC 15 (1972) 236-244. — A. C. Vega, C.: Ciudad Dios 152 (1936) 145-164; 154 (1943) 219-241.

G. RÖWEKAMP

Calendar, Martyrology, Menology, Synaxarion

Calendar, from the Lat. *kalendae* (first day of month), means the division of time into days, months, and years, based on the movement of sun and moon. In the imperial church, the system of calendar of Julius Caesar (d. 44 B.C.E.) or the "Julian calendar," was used from the 4th c. on as the astronomical basis for calculating the cycle of movable Easter feasts and for the fixed liturgical year. Of course, the gospels already provided chronological data for the passion of Christ, and the early local churches recorded in writing the "heavenly birth-day" (*dies natalis*) of their martyrs, the first of these being that of Polycarp of Smyrna on (?) Feb. 23, 167 (*M. Polyc.* 21.1). Later on, Tertullian (d. after 220), Cyprian of Carthage (d. 258), and Gregory Nyss. (d. 394) attest to local church custom of keeping lists of the names and days of death of the local martyrs and bishops, with a view to their annual memorial. The oldest calendar of this type is the → *Chronograph of 354* for Rome, which takes the form of the → *Depositio episcoporum* → *Depositio martyrum*. In addition, and based on the fixed solar year, there is a Gothic fragment from ca. 400; in the 5th c. the calendar of Perpetuus of Tours (d. 491), recorded in Gregory of Tours (*Franc.* 10.31); 535/566, the Oxyrhynchus cal-endar; in 6th-c. Alexandria a Copt. calendar; in the 7th c. the calendar of Carmona; in the 7th/8th c. the calendar of Echternach; in the 8th/9th c. the calendar of Montecassino; 821/831, an Irish calendar; and 840/850 the calendar of Naples.

At a second stage of development the local church calendars included nonlocal martyrs and saints. In this more comprehensive form they are known today as martyrologies. In second place, after the start made in the Roman *depositio martyrum* came the *M. Syriacum*, which looks eastward and was probably compiled originally ca. 360/362 in Nicomedia by a Greek-speaking Arian but has come down only in a Syr. version of 411/412. Ca. 431/450 the so-called *M. Hieronymianum* came into existence in northern Italy on the basis of the first version of the calendar of Carthage (see below), of the already mentioned lists of Rome and Nicomedia, and of the lists of some Ital-ian cities; this has survived only in a version revised under Bishop → Aunacharius of Auxerre (d. 605). The calendar of Carthage, ca. 505, draws upon a list of Carthaginian martyrs and bishops (made proba-bly in the second half of the 4th c.) but includes other African and even Italian martyrs.

In the course of the continually expanding venera-tion of the saints the Lat. West saw the rise of the so-called historical martyrology, in which the inclusion of other information besides the name, date of death, and place of burial of the saints turned the entries into short sketches of their lives. In this manner Bede the Venerable (d. 735), using the *M. Hieronymi-anum*, developed the prototype of the detailed his-torical martyrology. The number of saints and the size of the text were greatly expanded in the martyr-ology of the Anonymous of Lyons at the beginning of the 9th c., the two editions by Florus of Lyons in 825 and 849, the three editions by Ado of Vienne between 855 and 875, and, in 859 (but constantly

revised between 860 and 877), the martyrology of Usuard of St. Germain des Prés, which served as the essential basis of the *M. Romanum*. Liturgical use of the martyrology has been shown for the 8th c. at the end of Mass and, from 817 on, during prime.

The same development in the Gr. East led to the so-called Menologion (Men.), by which is meant a collection of saints' lives and homilies for the feasts of the fixed liturgical year. These go back to lost col-lections of acts of the martyrs that were combined in the mid-9th c. with homiletic texts and handed down in volumes covering the entire year or a half year or even two months or one month. In the 10th c. at the latest, the homilies for the feasts of the Lord and Mary were removed and put together in the Panegy-ricon. The texts remaining in the Men. were given a thorough stylistic revision by Simeon Metaphrastes (d. ca. 1000) and, in this form, soon occupied a dom-inant place in the Byz. church. The Slav. Men. tradi-tion adopted Byz. models from the beginning.

The Synaxarion (S.), which is akin to the Men., derives its name from "Synaxis," the name custom-ary in the Gr. East since the 4th c. for the annual commemoration at a martyr's tomb. The 7th c. saw the first mention of a Synaxographi(o)n, from which the life of the martyr in question was read during such a memorial. The Synaxarion was organized in twelve monthly volumes acc. to the liturgical year and circulated nationally. Traces of systematic hagio-graphical collections of this kind were to be seen, although not until the 9th c. Originally handed on in specifically Synaxarion mss., these greatly abbre-viated lives (as distinct from the longer ones in the Men.) were taken over into the Byz. Menaion (= the proper of the saints in the Byz. Prayer of the Hours) and are read even today after the sixth ode of the Byz. morning office. Of the new textual versions of the Synaxarion the ms. family M* (from the second half of the 12th c.) has won acceptance.

W: *Depositio martyrum, Depositio episcoporum, M. Syri-acum, Kalendarium von Karthago,* H. Lietzmann, KlT 2 (Berlin, ²1911) [text/comm.]. — *Depositio martyrum, Depositio episcoporum,* R. Valentini, G. Zucchetti, Codice Topografico della Città di Roma 2 (Rome, 1942), 1-28 [text/comm.]. — *Gothic frgm.,* H. Achelis: ZNW 1 (1900) 309-373 [text/comm.]. — *Oxyrhynchus C.,* H. Delehaye: AnBoll 42 (1924) 83-99 [text/comm.]. — *Coptic C. of Alexandria,* H. Leclercq: DACL 8/1:654-657 [French trans./ comm.]. — *Carmona C.,* J. Vives: BHBB Ser. 2, 18 (1969) 112-114 [text/comm.]. — *Echternach C.,* H. A. Wilson, The Calendar of St. Willibrord (London, 1918), 24:1-49, Tafel 1-13 [text/comm.]. — *Montecassino C.,* G. Morin: RBen 25 (1908) 486-497 [text]. — *Irish C.,* H. Leclercq: DACL 8/1:647f. [text/comm.]. — *Naples C.,* H. Delehaye: AnBoll 57 (1939) 5-64 [text/comm.]. — *M. Hieronymianum,* G. B.

de Rossi, L. Duchesne: ActaSS Nov. 2,1 (1894) [text]. — H. Quentin, H. Delehaye: ActaSS Nov. 2,2 (1931) [text/comm.]. — *M. of Bede the Venerable,* PL 94:797-1148. — *M. of Ado of Vienne,* J. Dubois, G. Renaud (Paris, 1984) [text/comm.]. — *M. of Usuard of St. Germain de Prés,* J. Dubois: SHG 40 (1965) [text/comm.]. — *M. Romanum,* H. Delehaye SJ et al., Propyläum ad ActaSS Dec. (1940) [text/comm.]. — *M. of Symeon Metaphrastes,* PG 114-116. — *Byz. S.,* H. Delehaye, Propyläum ad ActaSS Nov. (1902) [text/comm.].
L: R. Aigrain, L'Hagiographie (Paris, 1953). — H. G. Beck, Kirche u. theol. Lit. (Munich, 1959), 572-575 (M. of Symeon Metaphrastes). — H. Delehaye, Saints de Thrace et de Mésie: AnBoll 31 (1912) 274-291 (Gothic frgm.). — J. Dubois, Les Martyrologes du Moyen Âge Latin (Tournai, 1978). — idem, Martyrologium, M. Hieronymianum: LMA 6:357-361. — A. Ehrhard, Überlieferung u. Bestand der hagiographischen u. homiletischen Lit. der griech. Kirche 1-3 (Berlin, 1937-1952). — C. Hannick, Menologion: LMA 6:519f. — K. Hausberger, Heilige/Heiligenverehrung: TRE 14:647-651, 659f. — J. Hofmann, Unser hl. Vater Klemens (Trier, 1992), 3f. (Byz. S.). — H. Leclercq, Kalendaria: DACL 8/1:624-667. — K. Onasch, Kunst u. Liturgie der Ostkirche in Stichworten (Vienna, 1981), 178 (comm.); 262f. (Men.); 296 (Panegyrikon); 346 (S.). — P.-J. Schuler, Kalender: LMA 5:866. — A. Stuiber, Heidnischer u. chr. Gedächtniskalender: JAC 3 (1960) 24-33.

J. HOFMANN

Callinicus

Callinicus was the author of a biography (*v. Hyp.*) of Hypatius (b. ca. 366; d. 446), the third abbot of the monastery of Rufiniane near Chalcedon and Constantinople. Since ca. 426, C., who had been a member of the monastic community and a disciple of Hypatius, soon after the latter's death wrote the life based on what he had seen. The → *Vita* shows clear borrowings from the *Vita Antonii* of → Athanasius, but is nonetheless (provided an eye is kept on the peculiarities of the literary genre) an important historical witness to the development of monastic life in the area of Constantinople.

W: *v. Hyp.,* Sem. philol. Bonnense (Leipzig, 1895) [text]. — A. J. Festugière (Paris, 1961) [French trans.]. — G. J. M. Bartelink, SC 177. — G. Capizzi (Rome, 1982) [Italian trans.].
L: G. J. M. Bartelink, Observations sur le texte: VigChr 10 (1956) 124-126. — idem, Text Parallels between the Vita Hypatii of C. and the Pseudo-Macariana: VigChr 22 (1968) 128-136. — idem, Textkritik: VigChr 26 (1972) 288-290. — E. Merendino, Noterella testuale: Orpheus 6 (1985) 153-155. — E. Wölfle, Hypatios, Diss. (Heidelberg, 1984).

M. BIERMANN

Candidus, an Arian

Two letters by a C. are transmitted among the works of Marius Victorinus. The first presents an Arian teaching based on (Neo-)Platonism; the second contains the Lat. text of the letters of → Arius and of → Eusebius of Nicomedia, which C. sent on to Marius Victorinus.

C. develops his views on the transcendent, unbegotten, and not-begetting God and the Son, the first substance and the work of the Father, in such a way that it was not recognized by western thinkers, even by Hilary and Lucifer; thus, e.g., the arguments against the consubstantiality of the Son and the Father, using the concepts *existentia, substantia,* oneness, and new kinds of *generatio,* or applying the triad of *esse, vivere,* and *intellegere* to God to mean the interrelations of a unity that differentiates itself internally. C. may therefore be a literary fiction of Marius Victorinus, in the light of whose philosophical presuppositions (especially from Porphyry) the letters are to be read.

W: Marius Victorinus, Traités théologiques sur la trinité 1, P. Henry, SC 68:106-183.
L: W. Beierwaltes, Identität u. Differenz (Frankfurt a.M., 1980), 57-74. — idem, Platonismus im Christentum (Frankfurt a.M., 1998), 29-34. — P. Hadot, Marius Victorinus. Recherches sur sa vie et ses œuvres (Paris, 1971), 272-275. — R. P. C. Hanson, The Search for the Christian Doctrine of God (Edinburgh, 1988), 532-534. — P. Nautin, C. l'Arien: L'homme devant Dieu 1: FS H. de Lubac (Paris, 1964), 309-320. — J. Ulrich, Die Anfänge der abendländischen Rezeption des Nizänums (Berlin, 1994), 244-263.

T. BÖHM

Candidus, a Valentinian

Little is known of the life of C. In about 233 Origen carried on a debate in Athens, before a large audience, with a heretic, of whom he speaks in a letter to his friends in Alexandria; in it he complained about changes made by his opponent in the stenographic record of the conversation (Ruf., *adult.* 7; Jerome, *adv. Rufin.* 2.18). Since in this context (2.19) → Rufinus of Aquileia is speaking of a (now lost) Gr. *Dialogus adversus Candidum Valentinianum* (this is the title given in Jerome, *ep.* 33.4) and since a theme in both dialogues (the redemption of the devil) is the same, this suggests an identity of the two reports. In 2.19, Rufinus says that in the dialogue C. taught the procession of the Son from the *substantia* of the Father as being a *probolē* (this corresponds to Valentinian teaching) and challenged the position that because of his evil nature the devil could not be redeemed (ibid.).

It is disputed whether this C. is the same as the author of the work *Eis to hexaēmeron* (Eus., *h.e.* 5.27; Jerome, *vir. ill.* 48; written under Septimus Severus

193-211). The educational level and scriptural learning of the Valentinians might be an argument in favor of this.

L: H. Crouzel, A Letter from Origen "to Friends in Alexandria": OCA 195 (1973) 135-150. — idem, Origen (Edinburgh, 1989), 21f. — H. Leisegang, Valentinus 1: Valentinianer: PRE 7A/2:2272f. — C. Markschies, Valentinian Gnosticism: The Nag Hammadi Library after Fifty Years, ed. J. D. Turner, A. McGuire (Leipzig, 1997), 401-438. — P. Nautin, Origène (Paris, 1977), 161-170.

C. MARKSCHES

Canonical Collections

The activity of the early church synods found written reflection in the acts of the meetings, the letters of participants, professions of faith, and canons. The condemnation of opponents found expression in anathematisms. The main results were the professions of faith and the decrees, which were handed on in the form of canons and were therefore often passed on separately from the other acts. Such collections often served practical purposes and therefore did not bring with them their historical background. The African councils had one special characteristic: it was customary to begin each session of a council with a reading of all the decrees of earlier synods in order to recall them and to ensure their continued validity by this confirmatory reading. Since the material to be read became ever more extensive and since there were numerous overlappings and repetitions, collections of conciliar decrees began to be made. These collections once again did not reflect the historical course of events but were compiled with content as the criterion, so that the reconstruction of the history of their transmission is rather complicated.

Modern editions have broken up the separate collections and attempted to establish a chronological series of the individual decrees. The authoritative edition, begun by Eduard Schwartz in 1914, of the *Acta Conciliorum Oecumenicorum* edits the separate collections for each council, so that along with content and extent, the history and tendency of each collection become clear.

W: J. A. Alberigo, Conciliorum œcumenicorum decreta (Freiburg i.Br., ³1973) = J. Wohlmuth (ed.), Die Dekrete der ökumenischen Konzilien 1 (Paderborn, 1998) (= COD 1) [text/German trans.]. — H. T. Bruns, Canones apostolorum et conciliorum (Berlin, 1839). — J. Gaudemet, Les sources du droit de l'Eglise en Occident du IIᵉ au VIIᵉ siècle (Paris, 1985) (= G). — J. Hardouin, Acta conciliorum et epistulae decretales ac constitutiones summorum pontificum (Paris, 1714-1715) (= ACED). — F. Lauchert, Die Canones der wichtigsten altkirchlichen Conzilien nebst den apostolischen Canones (Frankfurt a.M., 1961 = Freiburg i.Br., 1896) (= Lauchert). J. D. Mansi, Sacrorum conciliorum nova et amplissima collectio (Florence/Venice, 1759-1827). Reprint and continuation: L. Petit, J. B. Martin (Paris, 1899-1927) (= Mansi). — C. H. Turner, Ecclesiae Occidentalis monumenta juris antiquissima (Oxford, 1899-1939) (= EOMJA). — E. Schwartz et al., Acta Conciliorum œcumenicorum (Berlin, 1914-1984) (= ACO).

L: B. Botte, Les plus anciennes collections canoniques: OrSyr 5 (1960) 331-350. — P. Fournier, G. Le Bras, Histoire des collections canoniques en Occident depuis les Fausses Décrétales jusqu'au Décret de Gratien, 2 vols. (Paris, 1931). — F. Maassen, Geschichte der Quellen u. Literatur des canonischen Rechts im Abendlande bis zum Ausgang des Mittelalters 1 (Graz, 1956 = 1870). — G. May, Kirchenrechtsquellen (I. Katholische): TRE 19:1-8. — W. Selb, Die Kanonessammlungen der orientalischen Kirche u. das griech. Corpus canonum der Reichskirche, FS W. Plöchl (Vienna, 1967), 371-383. — A. M. Stickler, Historia iuris canonici latini 1 (Turin, 1950). — E. Schwartz, Die Kanonessammlungen der alten Reichskirche: idem, Gesammelte Schriften 4 (Berlin, 1960), 159-275.

I. Acts and Canons of the Ecumenical Councils

1. Nicaea I (215)

2. Constantinople I (380):

The actual conciliar acts of these two councils have not been preserved, but material from the acts is contained in → Athanasius, *Apologia contra Arianos*; *De decretis Nicaeni synodi*; *ep. de synodis Arimini et Seleuciae.*

W: Athanasius, *apol. sec.*, PG 25:247-410. — *decr.*, H. G. Opitz, Werke 2/1 (Berlin, 1935), 1-80. — *syn.*, PG 26:681-794.

From the archives of the Alexandrian patriarchs Theodosius, a deacon (6th c., North Africa), compiled twenty-seven different documents dealing with the Arian controversy.

W. C. H. Turner, EOMJA 1:625-671.

The church histories of → Socrates and → Sozomen make use of a now lost collection of synodal acts, beginning with Nicaea, published by Bishop → Sabinus of Heraclea between 373 and 378. The *Book of Documents of the Council of Nicaea* that was used by → Gelasius of Cyzicus is not authentic.

W: *Nicaea (Symbol u. Canones)*, COD 1:5-19. — *Constantinople (Symbol u. Canones)*, COD 1:24-35.

3. Ephesus (431):

The first council whose acts have been preserved. They have been transmitted in the following collections.

Original Gr. texts: (a) *Collectio Vaticana*; (b) *Collectio Seguierana*; (c) *Collectio Atheniensis*. The original behind the Gr. collections was probably composed by a follower of Cyril Alex. It was probably augmented in the 7th c. and several times reedited.

Collections with Lat. translations: (d) *Collectio Casinensis*; (e) *Collectio Veronensis*; (f) *Collectio Palatina*; (g) *Collectio Sichardiana*; (h) *Collectio Winteriana*. The Lat. translations seem all to have been made in connection with the Three-Chapters controversy of the 6th c. The *Collectio Casinensis* was translated by Roman deacon → Rusticus. It is the most extensive collection and makes use of a Lat. translation (*Collectio Turinensis*) made shortly before in Constantinople. The compiler of the *Collectio Veronensis* was probably in Rome, since his letters highlight Pope → Celestine I. The *Collectio Palatina* takes excerpts from → Marius Mercator and is probably the work of a Scythian monk in Constantinople. The little *Collectio Sichardiana* was made after 533. The *Collectio Winteriana* cannot be accurately dated.

W: COD 1:40-73. —(a) ACO 1, 1, 1-6. — (b) ACO 1, 1, 7. — (c) ACO 1, 1, 7. — (d) ACO 1, 1, 3f. — (e) ACO 1, 1, 2. — (f) ACO 1, 1, 6. — (g) ACO 1, 5, 245-318. — (h) ACO 1, 5, 341-381.

4. Chalcedon (451): From the Council of Chalcedon the following have been preserved in Greek: (a) three collections of letters; (b) reports on the seventeen sessions of the council. The three collections of letters supplement one another. The first two are regarded as preliminary to the council, the first having been made probably in the interests of Patriarch → Anatolius of Constantinople. The second collection contains a Gr. translation of the *Tomus Leonis* (→ Leo I).

The following have been preserved in a Lat. translation or possibly in an original Lat. form: (c) *Collectio Novariensis de re Eutychii*; (d) *Collectio Vaticana, Canones et Symbolum*; (e) Lat. translations of (a) and (b); (f) *Leonis papae I. epistularum collectio*; (g) *Collectio Sangermanensis*.

W: COD 1:77-103. — (a) ACO 2, 1, 1f. — (b) ACO 2, 1, 1-3. — (c) ACO 2, 2, 1. — (d) ACO 2, 2, 2. — (e) ACO 2, 3, 1-3. — (f) ACO 2, 3, 4. — (g) ACO 2, 3, 5. — (h) ACO 3.

5. Constantinople II (553): No acts of the Second Council of Constantinople have been preserved, except for the fourteen anathematisms and some fragments.

W: COD 1:107-123. — F. X. Murphy, P. Scherwood, Konstantinopel II u. III (Mainz, 1990), 386-388 [survey of sources and editions].

6. Constantinople III (680/681): In a *series secunda* the ACO had been continued by the Bavarian Academy of Sciences for this and the following councils.

(a) *Johannis Maxentii libelli*; (b) *Collectio cod. Novariensis* 30; (c) *Collectio cod. Parisini* 1682; (d) *Proli tomus ad Armenos*; (e) *Johannis papae II. ep. ad viros ill.*

W: COD 1:124-130. — (a) ACO 4, 2, 1. — (b) ACO 4, 2, 1. — (c) ACO 4, 2, 1. — (d) ACO 4, 2, 1. — (e) ACO 4, 2, 2.

7. Nicaea II (787): This council, which rejected the iconoclasts, had an eventful pre- and posthistory. Tarasius, patriarch of Constantinople, presided over the synod. In addition to the canons and the Horos, there are many contemporary sources to draw upon.

W: COD 1:133-156. — G. Dumeige, Nizäa II (Mainz, 1985), 339-342 [survey of sources and editions].

8. Constantinople IV (869/870): Western canonists describe this as the eighth ecumenical council, but it does not appear in any Byz. canonical collection. It has been counted among the ecumenical councils since the 11th c.

W: COD 1:160-186.

II. Collections of Local Synods
A. Eastern Collections:

1. Syntagma Canonum (Corpus Canonum orientale): A chronologically organized collection of Gr. conciliar canons; it probably originated in Antioch before 378 and was expanded after 400. This collection was available at the Council of Chalcedon (451). The *Syntagma*, which has not been preserved, was repeatedly expanded and received by the eastern churches. It was translated into Latin as *Corpus Canonum orientale*, taken over by the African church and incorporated into Lat. collections. The *Syntagma* can be reconstructed on the basis of a Syr. translation done ca. 500/501 and of the Lat. translation in the older version of the *Collectio Isidoriana* (*Cod. Monacensis* 6243; *Cod. Würzburg Mp. theol. Joh.* 146).

The original version probably contained the decrees of the following councils: Ancyra (314), Neocaesarea (314/325), Nicaea (325), Gangra (341/342), Antioch (341), Laodicea (343-380). The decrees of Chalcedon were later added to this collection.

L: Plöchl 1:274.

2. Collection of John Scholasticus: In his *Synagōgē kanonōn* John Scholasticus systematically organized fifty canons and added as an appendix a *Collectio 87 capitulorum* from the *Novellae* of Justinian. In addition he edited material from the eighty-five *Canones Apostolorum* and 224 canons from earlier collections.

The collection was compiled in Constantinople ca. 550.

L: Plöchl 1:274f.

B. Western Collections:

1. Italian Collections: (a) *Vetus Romana*: probably the oldest collection, containing the canons of Nicaea (325) and Sardica (343) and compiled under Julius I (337-352). Because of the high esteem for Nicaea the canons of Sardica were regarded as belonging to Nicaea.

L: Plöchl 1:277.

(b) *Versio Isidoriana*: This collection, completed before the Council of Chalcedon (451), is based on the *Syntagma Canonum*. It has come down in several recensions (*antiqua, vulgata, Isidoriana-Gallica*). It contains canons of Nicaea, Ancyra, Neocaesarea, Gangra, Antioch, Laodicea, Constantinople, and Carthage (419).

L: Plöchl 1:277f.

(c) *Collectio Prisca (Itala)*: A private collection of conciliar decrees of the eastern church (Nicaea, Ancyra, Neocaesarea, Gangra, Antioch, Constantinople, Chalcedon), compiled in Rome toward the end of the 5th c. Because it was used primarily in Italy, it came to be called *Itala*.

L: Plöchl 1:278.

(d) *Collections of Dionysius Exiguus*: → Dionysius Exiguus was a Scythian monk who came to Rome after 496. Various collections that were very influential in the development of canon law in subsequent centuries go back to him.
aa. The *versio prima*, compiled at the request of presbyter Lawrence, was the first effort at an independent collection and was completed between 496 and 498.
bb. The *versio secunda* was compiled before 523 because of the *confusio priscae translationis* and was the most widely used in the Roman church.
cc. Of the *versio tertia*, compiled before 523, only the preface has survived. We know only that in it the *Apostolic Canons* and the canons of Sardica and Africa were missing.

W: PL 67:39-94, 147-230. — A. Struwe. Die Canonessammlung des Dionysius Exiguus in der ersten Redaktion (Berlin, 1931).

(e) *Collectio Quesnelliana*: A private systematic collection that probably came into existence at the end of the 5th/beginning of the 6th c. in Gaul and is named after its first editor, Pasquier Quesnel (d. 1719). The collection, which the editor describes as *Codex Canonum Ecclesiae Romanae*, contains texts from Oriental and Lat. councils, papal decretals, and letters of Leo I.

W: PL 56:356-746.

(f) *Collectio Avellana*: A collection made in Rome ca. 555 and containing papal letters and constitutions of the Roman emperors.

W: O. Günther, CSEL 35.

2. African Collections: A survey and analysis of the African collections is given by C. Munier, *Concilia Africae. A. 345–A. 525* (CCL 149). The collections are these:
(a) *Breviarium Hipponense*: Contains canons from the Council of Hippo (Oct. 8, 393) down to 525.

W: C. Munier, CCL 149:23-53.

(b) *Codex Apiarii causae*: Contains the decrees of the Council of Carthage on May 25, 419, and of the Council of 424/425 against a priest Apiarius, as well as the connected letters to Roman Bishop Boniface or Caelestius.

W: C. Munier, CCL 149:102-172.

(c) *Registri Ecclesiae Carthaginiensis Excerpta*: Decrees of the councils between 393 and 419 that were kept in the archive of the church of Carthage.

W: C. Munier, CCL 149:173-247.

(d) *Breviatio Canonum*: In contrast to the above chronologically organized collections, Carthaginian deacon Fulgentius Ferrandus composed a systematic collection of the African councils on the subject of the restoration of church discipline; he did so in 546 after the Vandal invasion, at the instigation of Bishop Boniface. Eastern decrees were also included.

W: C. Munier, CCL 149:284-306.

III. Collection of Decretals
Decretals are papal letters, addressed mostly to individuals and answering questions of canon law or discipline. They were collected beginning in the 5th c. They gained influence on legal practice as a result of growing papal influence, espec. from the 12th c. on.

The letter of Siricius to Himerius of Tarragona (PL 13:1133f.) is regarded as the oldest decretal.

The bishops who played the most important legislative roles were: → Damasus, → Siricius, → Innocent I, → Leo I, → Gelasius I, → Symmachus, → Pelagius I, → Pelagius II, and → Gregory I.

It is probable that conciliar canons and decretals were originally handed down separately, but the multiplication of papal decretals soon made collections necessary.

The collection of decretals made by → Dionysius Exiguus between 498 and 514 is very important. This *Collectio Decretalium Dionysiana* contains, in chronological order, thirty-eight decretals of Roman bishops from Siricius to Anastasius. Further decretals were added later on.

L: G. Fransen, Les décrétales et les collections de décrétales (Tournai, 1972). — R. Massigli, La plus ancienne collection de décrétales: RHLR 5 (1914) 402-424. — H. van de Wouw, Dekretalen: LMA 3:655f.

W. GEERLINGS

Canon Muratori/ Muratorian Fragment

The so-called *Canon Muratori* (*C.M.*) was discovered in the 18th c. by L. A. Muratori in the Bibliotheca Ambrosiana in Milan in a collection of mss. from the 7th or 8th c. Four other fragments of the *C.M.* were found in 1897 at Monte Cassino in four mss. of the 11th and 12th c. Lacking are the beginning and probably the end of the text, which is eighty-five lines long and contains a list of the NT books. Along with the later canonical books (except for Heb, 1-2 Pet, and 3 Jn) the *Apocalypse of* → *Peter* and the *Shepherd* of → Hermas are also included, as being disputed but orthodox and to be read only in private. The letter to the Laodiceans and a letter to the Alexandrians (→ Paul, Literature about) are described as Marcionite forgeries; the Marcionite book of Psalms is also rejected. The text of the *C.M.* is from an unknown author, probably from the West (Rome?), and the time is ca. 200. The Lat. version goes back to a Gr. original.

W: A. v. Harnack: ZKG 3 (1879) 358-408, 595-599 [text/comm.]. — T. Zahn, Geschichte des ntl. Kanons 2/1 (Leipzig, 1890), 1-143 [text/comm.]. — H. Lietzmann, Das muratorische Frgm. (Berlin, 1933) [text/comm.]. — NTApo⁶ 1:28f. [German trans.]. — M. Erbetta, Gli Apocrifi del NT 1 (Turin, 1966) [Italian trans.] (literature).
L: J. Beumer, Das Fragmentum Muratori: ThPh 48 (1973) 534-550. — H. Burckhardt, Motive u. Maßstäbe der Kanonsbildung nach dem "C. M.": ThZ 30 (1974) 207-211. — E. Dassmann, Wer schuf den Kanon des NT?: JBTh 3 (1988) 275-283. — G. M. Hahnemann, The Muratorian

Frgm. (Oxford, 1992). — P. Henne, La datation du canon de Muratori: RB 100 (1993) 54-75. — J.-D. Kaestli, La place du Fragment de Muratori dans l'histoire du canon: CrSt 15 (1994) 609-634. — A. Sand, Kanon. Von den Anfängen bis zum Fragmentum Muratorianum: HDG I 3a. I (Freiburg i.Br., 1974), 60-63. — K. Stendhal, The Apocalypse of John and the Epistles of Paul in the Muratorian Frgm.: FS O. A. Piper (London, 1962), 239-245. — A. C. Sundberg, "C. M.": HThR 66 (1973) 1-41.

A. SAND

Canons of Hippolytus

This is a → church order, based on the → *Traditio apostolica* and containing thirty-eight canons from the middle of the 4th c.; it was written in Greek, probably in Egypt, but has come down only in Arabic. After being first edited by D. B. von Haneberg (Munich, 1870), it was for a long time regarded by scholars as the earliest church order; today, however, after the reconstruction of the *Traditio apostolica*, it is of rather secondary interest. The mention of the name Hippolytus in the title is not a definite help in the disputed question of the authorship of the *Traditio apostolica*.

W: P. Bradshaw (Bramcote, 1987) [English trans.]. — R. G. Coquin (Paris, 1966) [text/French trans.]. — W. Riedel, Kirchenrechtsquellen (Leipzig, 1900), 193-230 [German trans.].
L: P. Bradshaw, The Search for the Origins (London, 1992). — H. Brakmann, Alexandreia u. die Canones des Hippolyt: JAC 22 (1979) 139-149. — A. Brent, Hippolytus and the Roman Church in the Third Century (Leiden, 1995). — B. Steimer, Vertex traditionis (Berlin, 1992), 72-79.

B. STEIMER

Capriolus (Capreolus)

C. was the successor of Aurelius (d. July 20, 429/430) as metropolitan and bishop of Carthage. The time when he ascended the episcopal throne must be before April 431, since it was he who, as bishop, received the letter from Theodosius II inviting → Augustine to attend the Council of Ephesus, scheduled for June 7 of that year. C. informed the emperor of Augustine's death and dispatched his own deacon Bessula to the council. The latter carried a letter of C. (*ep. ad concilium Ephesinum*) in which the situation of the African church is described, and the council is urged to follow Catholic teaching as explained by the Apostolic See and earlier councils. The letter is a manifestation of C.'s Augustinian thinking, which also finds expression in his letter of 432 to Spanish Bishops Vitalis and Constantius (*ep. ad Vitalem et Constantium*). There is no further literary evidence of his theol. activities, although Ferrandus calls him "the remarkable teacher of the Carthaginian church." A number of comments on the Vandals may possibly be found among the works of Augustine. C. died between July 22 and 30 (acc. to the Carthaginian calendar) and certainly before 439. His successor was Quodvultdeus.

W: *ep. ad concilium Ephesinum*, PL 53:843-849 = ACO 1, 2, 64-65. — *ep. ad Vitalem et Constantinum*, PL 53:843-858 = ACO 2, 3, 3.
L: G. Bareille, C.: DThC 2/2:1693f.

W. GEERLINGS

Carmen figuratum

In a *Carmen figuratum*, a visual-aesthetic component is added to the writing as such by inserting a drawing around the (sometimes polymetric) verses or by coloring individual letters in order to highlight them. This technique, which was used in Hellenism (→ *Anthologia Palatina* 15.21-27) and was taken over in the Roman classics (Laevius, ca. 100 B.C.E.), had as its chief representative in late Lat. antiquity → Porphyry Optatianus, who in addition to poems with drawings as frames, composed "lattice poems." The emphasized letters sketch geometrical patterns, signs (*carm.* 14: monogram of Christ), or objects (*carm.* 9: palm of victory), and, at the same time, as "woven verses" (*versus intexti*), convey a paratextual statement. Along with → Venantius Fortunatus, who composed numerous *carmina figurata* with crosses (e.g., *carm.* 2.4), Optatianus was the most important model author for early medieval representatives of this type of poetry.

L: B. Bowler, The Word as Image (London, 1970) — K. P. Dencker (ed.), Text-Bilder (Cologne, 1972). — U. Ernst, "C. f." Geschichte des Figurengedichts von den antiken Ursprüngen bis zum Ausgang des MA (Cologne, 1991). — G. Pozzi, La parola dipinta (Milan, 1981).

D. WEBER

Carpocrates

According to Clement Alex. (*str.* 3.5.1-3) C. was an Alexandrian, a married man and father of a son, Epiphanes, who died young. After his early death the son was supposedly given divine honors in a temple of his own (!) on Same/Kephallenia (the best explanation is a confusion with a local hero).

An exact dating of C.'s work is difficult, but possible with the help of a catalogue of heretics by Hegesippus (in Eus., *h.e.* 4.22): before Valentinus, i.e., perhaps under Hadrian (117-138) or in the first years

of Antoninus Pius (138-161). Irenaeus also tells us of a disciple of C. named Marcellina, who was active in Rome under Bishop Anicetus (ca. 154-166). Celsus already distinguishes between Marcellinians and Carpocratians (in Origen, *Cels.* 5.62, but Origen is not familiar with any "Marcellinians"). Carpocratians existed into the 4th c.

Acc. to Irenaeus (*haer.* 1.25.1-6) the Carpocratians taught a creation by angels. Their christology is of particular interest: Joseph begot Jesus, a pure, strong soul which, because it remembered its preworldly existence (see Plato, *Phdr.* 247c), had the power to escape the affections and the angels who created the world. Believers can receive this power. Irenaeus also tells of magical practices by the Carpocratians and of a doctrine of metempsychosis. The references to revered images probably belong in the context of a cult of the muses by a philosophical group. The accusation of libertinism was simply a heresiological cliché.

W: W. Völker, Quellen zur Geschichte der chr. Gnosis: SQS NS 5 (1932) 33-38.
L: P. Boyancé, Le culte des Muses chez les Philosophes Grecs (Paris, 1937). — A. Hilgenfeld, Die Ketzergeschichte des Urchristentums (Darmstadt, 1963 = Leipzig, 1884), 397-408. — H. Kraft, Gab es einen Gnostiker Karpokrates?: ThZ 8 (1952) 434-443 (in addition, H. Chadwick, Alexandrian Christianity [London, 1954], 26-28). — A. Le Boulluec, La notion d'hérésie dans la littérature grecque aux IIᵉ-IIIᵉ siècles (Paris, 1985). — H. Liboron, Die karpokratianische Gnosis (Leipzig, 1938). — W. A. Löhr, Epiphanes' Schrift "περὶ δικαιοσύνης": FS L. Abramowski: BZNW 67 (1993) 12-29. — idem, Karpokratianisches: VigChr 49 (1995) 23-48. — S. Pétrement, A Separate God (London, 1991; Paris, 1984), 347-350. — M. Smith, Clement of Alexandria and a Secret Gospel of Mark (Cambridge, 1973), 266-278, 295-351. — H. Usener, Das Weihnachtsfest (Bonn, ²1911), 112-117.

C. MARKSCHIES

Cassiodorus

I. Life: Magnus Aurelius Cassiodorus Senator ("Senator" was a proper name, not a rank), ca. 485 to ca. 580, grew up in Scyllaceum (now Squillace) in the province of Bruttium (now Calabria), in a distinguished Chr. family that had emigrated from Syria. C.'s father, who served under Odoacer and Theodoric, arose under the latter to the rank of pretorian prefect and *patricius*. The son began his career as panegyrist of Theodoric and, when barely fifteen, was given the office of *consiliarius* for 503-506. In 506/507-511 he was *quaestor sacri palatii* and in 523 succeeded the executed Boethius as *magister officiorum*. In the meantime, he governed Lucania and Bruttium as a *corrector*, or special commissioner, and, at his own expense, commanded a contingent of Goths. In 533, during the regency of Amalasuntha, he achieved the supreme political rank, that of pretorian prefect. He held this rank also under Theodahat and Vitiges (537-540). He played the role of mediator between Goths and Romans, seeking, by changes in direction, to overcome the dualism caused by the separation of Roman administration from Gothic military leadership and by the prohibition of marriage between the two peoples.

The end of the independent Gothic state (fall of Ravenna, 540) brought a break in C.'s life: a renunciation of politics and a *conversio*: the adoption of the monastic way of life. This last found its expression in his founding of a double monastery—cenobitic and anchoritic—in Vivarium/Castellum near Scyllaceum. It possessed what was for that time a sizable spiritual and secular library (it was recently estimated to have contained ca. 120 codices; a count in the last century yield 262 individual titles, including the bibl. books); C. built this, as he did the monastery, from his own resources. Until his death at over ninety, C. resided in the monastery, but without being its abbot.

C.'s foundation was important for cultural history, because Vivarium was one of the places at the time in which the copying, emendation, and study of codices was connected with the cenobitic life. In this respect C. initially differed radically from the approximately contemporary monastic foundation of Benedict (529).

L: Art. C.: BBKL 1:953-955. — P. Courcelle, Les lettres grecques en Occident. De Macrobe à C. (Paris, ²1948), 318 ff. — A. Franz, M. Aurelius C. Senator (Breslau, 1872). — S. Grebe, Die Bibliothek Agapets: Bibliothek u. Wissenschaft 25 (1991) 36-52. — L. M. Hartmann, Geschichte Italiens im MA 1 (Hildesheim, 1969 = Leipzig, 1897). — G. H. Hörle, Mönchsu. Klerikerbildung in Italien (Frankfurt a.M., 1914). — T. Klauser, Vivarium: FS R. Boehringer (Tübingen, 1957), 337-346. — idem, War C.s Vivarium ein Kloster oder eine Hochschule?: FS J. Straub (Berlin, 1977), 413-420. — S. Krautschick, C. u. die Politik seiner Zeit, Diss. (Bonn, 1983). — B. Meyer-Flügel, Das Bild der ostgotisch-röm. Gesellschaft bei C. (Frankfurt a.M., 1991). — T. Mommsen, Ostgothische Studien: idem: GW 6 (1910) 362-484. — J. J. O'Donnell, C. (London, 1979). — E. K. Rand, Founders of the Middle Ages (Cambridge, Mass., ²1929). — L. Teutsch, C. Senator: Libri 9/3 (1959) 215-239. — A. van de Vyver, C. et son œuvre: Spec. 6 (1931) 145 ff. — idem, Les institutions de C. et sa Fondation à Vivarium: RBen 53 (1941) 59ff.

II. **Works**: C. composed works as a statesman: *Chronica* (*chron.*: a concise compilation of world history along with a list of consuls to 519); *Historia gothica* (538), in the epitome by Jordanes (551);

Variae, a collection in twelve books of royal edicts and letters of appointment, which by their idealistic descriptions served the rapprochement of Romans and Goths. He also wrote theologico-literary works, beginning around the time of his *conversio*. The first was *De anima* (*anim.*) (538), a work drawn from → Claudianus Mamertus and → Augustine and colored by Neoplatonism. The last was small but important in the view of the decay of classical Latin, the *De orthographia* (*gramm.*), written in his old age, ca. 578, and, with its instructions on the copying and emending of codices, drawn from eight ancient grammars, geared wholly to the program of the *Institutiones* (551/562; see below). In between were the *Historia ecclesiastica tripartita* (*hist.*) (after 537/540), a compilation from church historians → Socrates, → Sozomen, and → Theodoret, and the *Exposition psalmorum* (*in psalm.*), ca. 537/540-547/550, a spacious, detailed interpretation that takes into account the several senses of scripture and that is, along with the *Enarrationes psalmorum* of → Augustine, the only commentary on the entire Psalter from antiquity. *In psalm.* (like *var.* and *hist.*) was much used and zealously copied in the Middle Ages. Less numerous are the traces left by the two books *Institutiones divinarum et saecularium litterarum* (*inst.*), written ca. 551-562, the value of which, however, can hardly be exaggerated. In book 1 (*Institutio divinarum litterarum*) C. not only requires of his monks the already mentioned copying and emending of the codices of the scriptures, and the writing of commentaries on them; the interrelationship of *lectio divina*, *opus Dei*, and the study of the fathers and the councils is likewise a subject of the work so that the *inst. div.* might be comprehensively described as a kind of "bibliographical manual for novices." The same purpose is served by book 2 (*Institutio saecularium litterarum*), which is a summary of the seven liberal arts. The ideal here developed of a *saecularis eruditio* is subordinated to the ultimate goal, sketched in book 1, of the salvation of the soul; in C.'s view, all knowledge serves this goal.

The fact that both secular and theol. formation acquired a sure place in Christianity is certainly due first of all to Augustine (*De doctrina christiana*), Jerome, and others. But it is C. who can claim for himself the first attempt at a systematic transmission to Lat. monasticism of the necessary method.

W: *Addresses*, L. Traube, MGH. AA 12. — *chron.*, T. Mommsen, MGH. AA 11/2. — *Historia gothica*, T. Mommsen, MGH. AA 5/1. — *var.*, A. J. Fridh, CCL 96. — *anim.*, J. W. Halporn, CCL 96. — *in psalm.*, M. Adriaen, CCL 97-98.

— inst., R. A. B. Mynors (Oxford, ²1961). — hist., R. Hanslik, CSEL 71. — gramm., GrLat 7:145-210.

L: E. Bickel, Rez. Inst.: Gn. 14 (1938) 322-328. — F. Brunhölzl, Geschichte der lat. Lit. des MA (Munich, 1975). — A. Crocco, Il liber de anima del C.: Sapienza 25 (1972) 133-168. — U. Hahner, C.s Psalmenkommentar: MBM 13 (1973). — A. T. Heerklotz, Die Variae des C. als kulturgeschichtliche Quelle, Diss. (Heidelberg, 1926). — G. Jenal, Italia ascetica atque monastica, 2 vols., MGMA 39/2 (Stuttgart, 1995), 1:22-225; 2:644-676. — L. W. Jones, The Influence of C. on Mediaeval Culture: Spec. 20 (1945) 433-442. — P. Lehmann, Cassiodorstudien: Ph. 71 (1912) 278-299; 72 (1913) 503-517; 73 (1914-1916) 253-273; 74 (1917) 265-269. — H. Löwe, C.: RomF 60 (1947) 421-446. — F. Milkau, Zu C.: Von Büchern u. Bibliotheken, FS E. Kuhnert (Berlin, 1928). — A. Momigliano, C. and Italian Culture of his Time: PBA 41 (1955) 207-245. — F. Prinz, C. u. das Problem chr. Aufgeklärtheit in der Spätantike: HZ 254 (1992) 561-580. — R. Schlieben, Chr. Theologie u. Philosophie in der Spätantike (Berlin, 1974). — J. Schmauch, Die eschatologischen Gedankengänge C.', Diss. (Munich, 1958). — F. Weissengruber, C.s Stellung innerhalb der monastischen Profanbildung des Abendlandes: WSt 80 (1967) 202-250.

                                                    W. BÜRSGENS

Catalogue of Writers

"You urge me, Dexter, to follow the example of Tranquillus and put together a catalogue of eccles. writers, and to do for our people what he did in listing the famous men of pagan literature." At the beginning of his catalogue of writers → Jerome adduces as models not only Tranquillus (= Suetonius) but a series of Gr. and Lat. composers of biographies in the various branches of literature. The works of those writers, as is usual with everyday literature, have survived either not at all or only in fragments, but were still available to Jerome, at least for the most part. From Suetonius's work on famous personalities of Roman literature (*De viris illustribus*), of which only the section of grammarians and orators is preserved, Jerome took the additions on literary history which he made to Eusebius's chronicle when he translated it. His own compilation, which he wrote in Bethlehem at the urging of his friend Dexter and which bore the same title (*vir. ill.*) thus forms a Chr. supplement to Suetonius, but with an apologetic purpose, as he says at the end of the prologue: "Celsus, then, and Porphyry, and Julian, those dogs who rave against Christianity, are to know, and their supporters, too (who believe the church has not had philosophers, orators, and scholars), are to know how many distinguished men founded the church and built it up and adorned it. Those people must stop accusing our faith of boorish naivete and acknowledge instead their own ignorance."

Jerome lists 135 writers, from the apostles and evangelists down to Jerome himself; heretics are also included, as are Jews Philo and Josephus and the pagan philosopher Seneca (because of the apocryphal correspondence between → Paul and Seneca, which is attested for the first time in this section). In the first part he takes his material, without mentioning the fact, from the church history of Eusebius; in the second part he relies on his own knowledge and preserves a great deal of otherwise lost information. Throughout the Middle Ages the catalogue was regarded with unreserved admiration, and yet as early as 397 Augustine criticized it in a letter (*ep.* 40.9) because of its many omissions and an inadequate distinction between orthodox and heretical writers. However, the espec. meager information on Ambrose (*vir. ill.* 126) is due not to a lack of understanding of the importance of individual writers but to Jerome's personal dislike of that bishop from the Roman nobility. The catalogue was translated into Greek between the end of the 6th c. and the 9th c.

Ca. 480 → Gennadius, a presbyter of Marseilles, composed a continuation and supplement for this *catalogus scribarum*, using the same title as Jerome. The author, a man well read in Gr. and Lat. literature and a much more careful worker than Jerome, is often the only source on the just over ninety writers (to which ten were added later) and paints an impressive picture of literary activity in the 5th c.

At the beginning of the 7th c. → Isidore of Seville composed a very independent continuation that gave preference to Spanish writers. The work originally included thirty-three writers and was later expanded to forty-six in sections added by a 6th-c. African. The supplement drawn up by Bishop → Ildefonsus of Toledo was limited to Spanish bishops, half of them from Toledo.

The catalogues of Jerome and Gennadius were combined by Cassiodorus and in the Middle Ages were circulated together, almost without exception. The composing of new catalogues for literary history began only at the end of the 11th c. with Sigebert of Gembloux (ca. 1030-1112) and his *Catalogus de viris illustribus* in which he consciously followed the older compilations.

L: J. Fontaine, Ildefonse: DECA 1:1211. — C. Pietri, Gennadius: TRE 12:376-378. — S. Pricoco, Storia letteraria e storia ecclesiastica Dal "De viris illustribus" di Girolamo a Gennadio (Catania, 1979). — M. Schanz, Geschichte der röm. Lit. 4/1 (Munich, 1914), 447-449 (Jerome); 4/2 (Munich, 1920), 552-554 (Gennadius).

                                                    M. ZELZER

Catena

The Lat. technical term *catena* ("chain") has been used since the 14th c. for a special genre of originally Gr. commentaries on the Bible; they originated presumably in 6th-c. Palestine and have been linked to the name of → Procopius of Gaza. In its ideal form, this genre is a compilation of verse-by-verse comments on a bibl. book, using verbatim excerpts from individual commentaries, homilies, or other literary forms of exegetical explanation from selected church fathers; the excerpts form a continuous series and are distinguished from one another by a special organization of the scriptural text and the naming of the author being excerpted.

The external arrangement allows a distinction between two basic kinds of catenae. One is the so-called marginal catena, in which the bibl. text is placed at the center of the page (often running to the inner margin) and is given numbers or other referral signs which also accompany the excerpts located on the upper, outer, and bottom margins of the page and show their connection with a particular verse or individual word. The other is the "text catena," in which a section of bibl. text comes first and the excerpted explanations follow without being limited by page or column; referral signs are then unnecessary since only the amount of bibl. texts that precedes is explained in the excerpts.

The ms. tradition of Gr. catenae, attested in the 6th(?) c. at the earliest, but very richly from the 10th to the 16th c., documents the spread of this genre, which gathers up and preserves the patristic exeget. tradition; Syr., Arm., and Copt. catenae since the 7th c. do the same.

The value of this genre of commentary, whether specifically Chr. or patterned on pagan models of late antiquity, is shown by the way in which the catenae, with the aid of modern catena philology, makes possible the retrieval of works lost in direct transmission, and by the investigation, corroborated by source criticism, of the exegetical methods of such bibl. interpreters as → Origen, → Apollinaris of Laodicea, → Didymus the Blind, → Diodorus of Tarsus, and → Theodore Mops., among others.

L: R. Devreesse, Chaînes exégétiques grecs: DBS 1:1084-1233. — G. Dorival, Commentaires de l'écriture aux chaînes: Le monde grec ancien et la Bible, ed. C. Mondésert (Paris, 1984), 321-383. — idem, La postérité littéraire des chaînes: REByz 43 (1985) 209-226. — idem, Les chaînes exégétiques sur les Psaumes 1-3 (Leuven/Louvain, 1986, 1989, 1992). — M. Geerard, CPG 4:185-259. — U. and D. Hagedorn, Die älteren griech. K.n zum Buch Hiob 1 (Berlin, 1994). — M. Harl, Chaîne palestinienne sur le Psaume 118, SC 189 (Paris, 1972), 17-159 (Introduction). — G. Karo, H. Lietzmann, Catenarum Graecarum Catalogus (Göttingen, 1902). — H. Lietzmann, Catenen (Freiburg i.Br., 1897). — E. Mühlenberg, Psalmenkommentare aus der K.nüberlieferung 3 (Berlin, 1978). — idem, K.n: TRE 17:14-21. — A. Rahlfs, Verzeichnis der griech. Hss. des AT (Berlin, 1914). — M. Richard, Opera Minora 1-3 (Tournai, 1976/77). — K. Uthemann, Was verraten die K.n über die Exegese ihrer Zeit?: FS E. Dassmann (Münster, 1996), 284-296. — N. G. Wilson, A Chapter in the History of Scholia: CQ NS 17 (1967) 244-256. — idem, Scholars of Byzantium (London, 1983).

B. NEUSCHÄFER

Catena trium patrum

This name describes two catena commentaries (→ Commentaries) that have been shaped into homogeneous works: one on Qoh ([*cat. in Eccles.*] chiefly from → Gregory Nyss., → Gregory the Wonderworker, → Maximus Conf.), and the other on the Canticle ([*cat. in Cant.*], chiefly from Gregory the Wonderworker, → Nilus, → Cyril Alex., Maximus Conf.). The catenae probably come from the anonymous 7th-8th-c. compiler who authored the *Catena Ps.-Procopii* on Proverbs.

W: *cat. in Eccle.*, S. Lucà, CCG 11. — *cat. in Cant.*, PG 87:1756-1780; 122:537-685.
L: M. Faulhaber, Catenen (Vienna, 1902). — J. Kirchmeyer, Un commentaire: StPatr 8 (1966) 406-413.

M. SKEB, OSB

Celestine I of Rome

C., formerly a Roman deacon and from 422 on the successor of Boniface I, made it his goal to consolidate the primacy of the bishop of Rome. In the process, in 424, on the occasion of the synod against the excommunicated presbyter Apiarius, he experienced the clear resistance of the African bishops. He resolutely fought against Pelagianism and sent Germanus of Auxerre in 429 and Palladius in 431 on a mission to England and Ireland to combat Pelagianism there. In 430, after Nestorius himself had explained his teaching to the pope and after the celebration of the Roman synod, C. supported Cyril's position and gave him the authority to demand Nestorius's recantation. In 431, through his legates, he took part in the Council of Ephesus and voted for the deposition of Nestorius. C. died in 432. The vast majority of C.'s letters (*ep.*), whether addressed to Nestorius himself or to others, deal with Nestorianism and its meaning for the church. To be noted especially is *ep.* 21 to the bishops of Gaul, warning them against Semipelagianism, praising the intervention of Prosper of Aquitania and Hilary, and attacking the disparagement of Augustine.

W: *ep.*, PL 50:417-559. — ACO 1, 1, 7, 125-137; 1, 2, 5-101. L: ActaSS Apr. 1 (1737) 543-547. — G. Bardy, C.: DHGE 12:56-58. — A. M. Bernardini, S. C. (Rome, 1938). — C. Pietri, Roma Christiana (Rome, 1976), 1026-1043, 1347-1397. — L. I. Scipioni, Nestorio e il concilio di Efeso (Milan, 1974), 149-205. — O. Wermelinger, Rom u. Pelagius (Stuttgart, 1975), 244-253. — H. J. Vogt, Papst C. u. Nestorius: FS H. Tüchle (Paderborn, 1975), 85-101.

C. Schmidt

Cento

Cento ("patchwork") describes a kind of poem in which verses or parts of verses are borrowed from the poems of classical authors (in Greece, Homer; in the Lat. world, Virgil and occasionally Ovid as well) and blended to form a poem with a new content. Even in antiquity the word was correctly derived from *kontōn*, a popular form of *kentrōn*, "rags, scraps" (see Tertullian, *praescr. haer.* 39 = Isidore, *orig.* 1.39.25).

A theory of cento technique is developed by Ausonius in the letter of dedication for his *cento nuptialis*: borrowed poetic fragments, unaltered as far as possible, are assembled, being joined at the caesura. The extent of the borrowing can range from a half-verse to a verse and a half, but the takeover of two or more continuous verses was frowned on. In a successful cento the original context of the separate elements should no longer be discernible, and the resulting new poem should give the impression of originality. It is not contrary to Ausonius's aesthetic ideal of composition that recognition by the recipient is required as a condition of artistic appreciation. The aesthetic attraction of the cento as an art form, like that of the collage, is based on the alien use of the original (a use often intended as parody) and on the recipient's surprising encounter with old familiar material in a new garb.

The playful character of the cento genre suggests an origin in Hellenism, but it is not advisable to see the formulas of epic speech, the parodic citation in comedy, or the imitative *aemulatio* as early stages of the genre. This dating is indirectly confirmed by Lucan, who in *symp.* 17 tells of a grammarian, Histaeus, who at a late hour, when merry with wine, recited an utterly ridiculous poem thrown together with verses from Hesiod, Anacreon, and Pindar. In support there is a late Hellenistic or early imperial cento from Homer that is attested in an inscription (Kaibel, *Epigr. Graeca ex lapidibus collecta* 1009). The first, though anonymous, Gr. literary cento, which uses verses from Homer to describe Heracles' adventure with Cerberus, is attested by Irenaeus, *haer.* 1.9.4. For other pagan Gr. centos, see the → *Anthologia Palatina* (e.g., 9; 361; 381f.).

In Roman literature, a first short centolike creation appears already in Petronius, *sat.* 132.9. The genre seems to have enjoyed some popularity in late antiquity, as attested by the success of the tragedy *Medea* by Hosidius Geta, which is made up of verses from Virgil (see Tertullian, *praesc.* 39). The most important, usually mythological centos are in the *Anthologia Latina* 7-18 (ed. Riese); in addition there is the above-mentioned *cento nuptialis* of Ausonius, a commissioned epithalamium made up of verses from Virgil.

Probably the first Chr. Virgilian cento (ca. 700 hexameters) was written by Faltonia Betitia → Proba, in the second half of the 4th c.

The *Versus ad gratiam domini*, in 132 hexameters, by a certain → Pomponius imitates the first *Eclogue* of Virgil. In a conversation, Tityrus instructs Meliboeus in Christianity. The date must remain uncertain, but a time close to that of Proba is perhaps indicated by Isidore's linking of the names Proba and Pomponius and by the fact that the same verses from Virgil are used to describe the creation of the world.

→ Sedulius was erroneously named, by its first editor, as author of *De incarnatione verbi*, an undatable Virgilian cento which treats of the incarnation of Christ and gives a good deal of space to the description of the angel's visit to Mary. Since the only transmitting ms., *Cod. Paris.* 13047 (9th c.), describes the address of Jesus at his ascension immediately after the description of his birth, it is likely that a sizable section has been dropped.

Also anonymously transmitted (the attribution to Mavortius, a composer of centos, is based on uncertain conjecture) are the 110 hexameters of *De ecclesia* in *Cod. Salmasianus* (7th-8th c.). At the center of the work is a sermon, made up of verses from Virgil, on the incarnation, life, passion, death, resurrection, and ascension of Christ, as well as on the announcement of the final judgment; the story that forms the framework names an early Chr. church as the place of the sermon and, toward the end, gives a brief description of a sacrificial meal and of the departure of the congregation. The postscript in prose attests to the popularity of the cento, since the public recitation brings the composer the acclamation calling him "a younger Virgil!" (*Maro iunior!*). It is of interest that the composer rejects the honorary title in a four-line improvised cento on a pagan subject: The

121

fate of Marsyas is a warning against measuring him-self with Virgil, his divine(!) teacher.

To be briefly mentioned are the centos, belonging probably to the 7th/8th c., *Victorini versus de lege domini nostri Iesu Christi* and *Victorini de nativitate, vita, passione et resurrectione Domini carmen*; the composer borrows his verses from the *Carmen adversus Marcionitas* of Ps.-Tertullian (→ Poems, Anonymous).

In Greek, → Eudocia composed centos from Homer that narrate the life of Christ acc. to the NT. Acc. to John Zonaras (*ann.* 13.23), the East Roman empress was here, along with others, continuing the work of a Bishop Patricius.

Christus patiens (A. Tuiler, SC 149) has been erro-neously attributed to → Gregory Naz., but in fact is part of 12th-c. Byz. literature; a good third of its 2,610 verses is indebted to ancient models, espec. Euripides, but also Aeschylus and Lycophron.

Along with the artistic pleasure that scholars took in literary games, a decisive desire of Chr. cento com-posers must have been to take into the service of the Chr. proclamation the pagan poetry that was thought of as an inimitable model, and this not least in order to win greater attention even from the edu-cated pagan classes. Against this background, the borrowed treasures of pagan verse could serve as a precious garb for Chr. proclamation, and, on the other hand, could themselves be ennobled by this service, a motive that led Proba to see in Virgil a *Maro sine Christo christianus* (a Virgil who was Christian without Christ) (see Jerome, *ep.* 53.7).

L: D. F. Bright, Theory and Practice in the Vergilian Cento: Illinois Classical Studies 8 (1983) 79-90. — F. E. Consolino, Da Osidio Geta ad Ausonio e Proba: AeR NS 28 (1983) 133-151. — O. Crusius, C.: PRE 3/2:1929-1332. — O. Delepierre, Tableau de la littérature du centon, 2 vols. (London, 1874/75). — F. Ermini, Il centone di Proba e la poesia centonaria latina (Rome, 1909). — R. Herzog, Die Bibelepik der lat. Spätantike 1 (Munich, 1975). — H. Hunger, Der C. u. verschiedene Versspielereien: idem, Die hochsprachliche profane Lit. der Byzantiner 2 (Munich, 1978), 98-107. — W. Kirsch, Die lat. Versepik des 4. Jh. (Berlin, 1989). — F. Kunzmann, C.: HWRh 2:148-152. — R. Lamacchia, Dall'arte allusiva al centone: AeR NS 3 (1958) 193-216. — R. Lamacchia, Centoni: Enciclopedia Virgiliana 1:733-737. — M. Manitius, Geschichte der chr.-lat. Poesie (Stuttgart, 1891). — K.-H. Schelkle, C.: RAC 2:972f. — W. Schmid, C.: LAW 565f. — M. D. Usher, Pro-legomenon to the Homeric C.s: AJPh 118 (1997) 305-321.

M. BECK

Cerealis

C., bishop of Castellum Ripense in Africa, was a par-ticipant in the religious dialogue that Vandal King Huneric convoked between the Arians and the Catholics in Carthage in February 484. At this time C. had only recently become bishop (*Not. episc. Maur. Caes.* 199). Ca. 480 he composed a *Libellus contra Maximinum Arianum* in which he treated the trinitarian controversy in dialogue form. C. answered Maximinus's questions about bibl. argu-ments with a lengthy series of citations from the OT and the NT (see also Gennadius, *vir. ill.* 97 [Richard-son]).

W: PL 58:757-768.
L: A. Di Berardino (ed.), Patrologia 4 (Genoa, 1996), 21. — A. Ferrua, C.: EC 3:1314. — PAC 207. — M. Schanz, C. Hosius, G. Krüger, Geschichte der röm. Lit. 4/2 (Munich, 1959), 571.

B. WINDAU

Cerinthus (Gospel)

The life and teaching of C. were frequently misrepre-sented by his opponents. E.g., Eusebius dates his appearance in Asia Minor to the time of Trajan (98-117) and takes over the story, told first by Irenaeus (*haer.* 3.3.4), about C.'s meeting with John in the baths (*h.e.* 3.28.1; 4.14.6). Other church fathers see C. as already an opponent of Paul, Peter, and James (Hippolytus, *Capita contra Caium*; Epiphanius, *haer.* 29.4.1; Filastrius 36.4; etc.) and assert his Egyptian training (Hippolytus, *haer.* 7.7; 7.33.1; 10.21; Theodoret, *haer.* 2.3). An appearance ca. 100 can only be a guess. Most of the independent accounts of C. (in → Gaius, → Dionysius Alex.; indirectly → *Epistula apostolorum*) point to a Jewish-Chr. back-ground (creation of the world by angels; Jesus as son of Joseph; observance of the law; chiliasm; possibly rejection of Paul), while the gnostic teachings attri-buted to C. are not specific and have little credibility (dualistic image of God and a christology of separate functions acc. to Irenaeus, *haer.* 1.26.1; 3.11.1). Reports that C. had written down visions (Gaius, in Eusebius, *h.e.* 3.28.2; Theodoret, *haer.* 2.3) probably go back to claims that C. wrote John or/and the Apocalypse (Hippolytus, *Capita contra Caium*; Dionysius Alex. in Eus., *h.e.* 3.28.4; 7.25.1f.; Epipha-nius, *haer.* 51.3.6; Filastrius 60). Epiphanius (*haer.* 51.7.3) seems to presuppose a gospel by C., but the Cerinthians used a version of Mt or possibly the → Ebionite gospel (Epiph., *haer.* 28.5.1; 30.3.7; 30.14.2). As a result, no sure work of C. is known.

L: G. Bardy, C.: RB 30 (1921) 344-373. — A. Hilgenfeld, Ketzergeschichte (Darmstadt, 1966 = Leipzig, 1884), 411-421. — A. F. J. Klijn, G. J. Reinink, Patristic Evidence for Jewish-Christian Sects (Leiden, 1973). — C. Markschies,

Kerinthos: RAC (in press). — H.-C. Puech, B. Blatz: NTApo[6] 1:317. — C. Schmidt, Gespräche Jesu mit seinen Jüngern (Hildesheim, 1967 = Leipzig, 1919), 403-452. — O. Skarsaune, The Proof from Prophecy (Leipzig, 1987), 407-409. — B. G. Wright, C. apud Hippolytus: SecCen 4 (1984) 103-115. — A. Wurm, C.: ThQ 86 (1904), 20-38.

R. HANIG

Choricius of Gaza

C. was a contemporary of Justinian and a student under → Procopius of Gaza, whom he succeeded as head of the school of sophists in Gaza. From his pen came numerous, stylistically very attractive addresses and eulogies. Two outstanding ones are encomiums of Bishop Marcian of Gaza (530-550), which are very important for the history of Chr. art because of their descriptions of churches and mosaics. C. also wrote twenty-five discussions in which popular philosophical subjects are treated in diatribe form.

W: R. Förster, E. Richsteig, Choricii Gazaei opera (Stuttgart, 1972 = Leipzig, 1929) [text]. — or. 23, W. J. Stephanes, Χορικίου Συνηγορία μίμων (Athens, 1986) [text]. — C. Mango, Art of Byzantine Empire (New Jersey, 1972), 60-72 [English trans.].
L: F. M. Abel, Gaza au 6e siècle: RB 40 (1931) 5-31. — P. Friedländer, Spätantiker Gemäldezyklus (Rome, 1939). — H. Hunger, Lit. der Byzantiner (Munich, 1978), 165-176. — W. Hörander, Prosarhythmus 1 (Vienna, 1981), 76-78. — K. Malchin, De Ch. Gazaei studiis (Leipzig, 1884). — H. Maguire, St. Stephen at Gaza: DOP (1978) 319-325. — K. Seitz, Die Schule von Gaza (Heidelberg, 1892).

P. BRUNS

Chromatius of Aquileia

C. was born between 335 and 340 and from 370 on belonged to the clergy of Aquileia. In 381, as secretary to Bishop Valerian, he took part in a local synod; from 388 to 407/408 he was bishop of Aquileia. Among his friends was Jerome (ep. 7), who dedicated parts of his work to him. Rufinus dedicated to him his translation of Origen's homilies on Joshua. C. also tried to mediate between Jerome and Rufinus (Jerome, adv. Rufinum. 3.2). In addition, C. was in contact with Ambrose by letter (ep. 5). In a letter of thanks (ep. 155) John Chrys. attests to C.'s intervention for him with Emperor Honorius. Nothing remains of C.'s own letters.

A large number of his sermons have been discovered only in recent decades. Thus far we know of forty-five sermones (serm.) and sixty-one Tractatus in Matthaeum (in Matth.). The texts reflect C.'s deeply Chr. education, espec. his knowledge of the Bible and of African writers. Two groups of serm. may be distinguished: eight deal with certain themes; the other thirty-one, as well as five fragments, are homilies of verse-by-verse exegesis, with an extensive use of typology and allegory. In the serm. as a whole pastoral concerns are to the fore. C. seeks to appeal to the feelings of his listeners. He repeatedly inserts prayers into his sermons. One characteristic of them is a doxological ending.

The in Matth. have a clearly different style. They were obviously not written for the liturgy but are intensive catecheses for small groups of listeners. They are less emotional than the serm. and have rather a didactic character aimed at spiritual formation. Their exegesis seems to be influenced by the Expositio quattuor evangeliorum of Ps.-Jerome. Also attributed to C. are the Praefatio orationis dominicae (orat. domin.) from the Gelasian Sacramentary and an explanation of the Our Father in the form of a liturgical address to catechumens. The effort to make C. the composer of psalter collects and orationes matutinales is based on pure hypothesis.

W: serm. beat., in Matth., orat. domin., A. Hosté, CCL 9. — serm., in Matth., J. Lemarié, R. Étaix, CCL 9A, CCL 9A Suppl. — E. Stanula (Warsaw, 1990) [Polish trans.]. — serm., J. Lemarié, SC 154, 164. — G. Cuscito (Rome, 1979) [Italian trans./comm.]. — M. Todde, Sermoni liturgici (Rome, 1982) [text/Italian trans./comm.]. — in Matth., R. Étaix, Un tractatus inédit: RBen 91 (1981) 225-230 [text/comm.]. — G. Trettel, 2 vols. (Rome, 1984) [text/Italian trans./comm.]. — G. Banterle (Milan, 1990) [text/Italian trans./comm.].
L: C. episcopus = AnAl 34 (Udine, 1989). — V. Cian, Catechesi (Trieste, 1993). — G. Cuscito, Bilancio bibliografico-critico: Aquileia Nostra 50 (1979) 497-572. — idem, C. e l'età sua (Padua, 1980). — R. Étaix, Note cromaziane: Aquileia Nostra 53 (1982) 301-304; 55 (1984) 241-244. — R. Fabris, Metodo esegetico: FS P. Bertolla e A. Moretti (Brescia, 1983), 91-117. — K. Gamber, Codices liturgici latini antiquiores (Freiburg i.Br., [2]1968), 82. — J. Lemarié, Italie: DSp 7/2:2162-2165. — idem, Status quaestionis: RSLR 17 (1981) 64-76. — idem, Diffusion de l'œuvre: AnAl 19 (1981) 279-291. — idem, Nouveaux témoins: RBen 98 (1988) 258-271. — L. Padovese, Pensiero etico-sociale (Rome, 1983). — A. Quacquarelli, Ecclesiologia: VetChr 26 (1989) 5-22. — G. Stival, Eucaristia: SacDoc 30 (1985) 132-154. — G. Trettel, Tipologia: MSF 59 (1979) 25-79. — idem, Ricostituzione del "Corpus Chromatianum": EL 93 (1979) 234-242. — idem, Cristologia: RRFI 1 (1981) 3-86. — idem, Interventi di C. al Concilio del 381: FS C. G. Mor (Udine, 1984), 93-108. — C. Truzzi, Zeno, Gaudenzio e C. (Brescia, 1985).

B. DÜMLER

Chronicle

From its beginnings, Chr. historical writing did not adopt solely a domestic perspective that leads to the composition of church histories. Rather it incorporated both OT history (which was regarded either as a typological preliminary stage of church history or as also a basic scaffold for a history of the pre-Chr. world) as well as "secular" world history into its presentation. History was thus perceived, presented, and interpreted as a whole. Thus, from the 3rd c. on, with the classical histories of antiquity as a model, there developed alongside the genre of church history the chronicle or universal chronicle, which presented history from the bibl. creation of the world down to the present. This often took the form of a tabular, synchronic presentation of events in the Bible or church history and in world history, following the order of the Olympiads, the consuls, and OT rulers.

The almost 6000-year duration of the world was taken as a basic framework, so that, depending on the calculation, the birth of Christ came approximately in the year 5500. The completion of the model by a 1000-year kingdom was rejected in the rejection of earlier chiliastic speculations, although a periodization based on the six days of creation was undertaken (in Paul Orosius also on the four empires in Daniel). The presentation of secular history provided reference points and proof of the age and truth claims of the Chr. church, which saw itself prefigured in the events of the OT. The coming of Christ marked a decisive dividing point in the ages both for Chr. history and for world history; nevertheless history was a unit. The beginnings of this approach can be seen also in the church histories, e.g., in → Eusebius.

The most important representatives of the genre are: → Julius Africanus with his *Chronographiai*, which reached originally to 221 (or 217) and were organized synchronically acc. to bibl. and secular history (preserved only in fragments, later completed to 235). Here the pattern of 6 × 1000 years, together with the expectation of the 1000-year kingdom, is used for the first time. The proof of antiquity plays a large role—a motif that, among others, explains the care in presentation. The synchronism between the birth of Jesus and the rise of the Roman Caesars has an apologetic background and consequences for the Chr. view of world history. The next representative of the genre is → Hippolytus with a chronicle that ends in 234 and is antichiliastic; it is preserved only in Lat. revisions (→ *Excerpta Latina Barbari*, *Liber generationis*), but with its table of contents, so that it became part of the → *Chronograph of 354*, which also contains the first chronicle of the popes. Hippolytus harks back to older secular chronicles and to Chr. sources. An important structural element is the lists

of bishops, although the bishops are listed without their years of office. → Eusebius of Caesarea composed a chronicle that was later used repeatedly but has survived complete only in Armenian (it consisted of a chronographic presentation, lists of kings, and time-tables and also had items from Chr. history); it was also widely circulated in the West as a result of the completion and revision of the tabular section by → Jerome. Its structure was provided by synchronic lists of rulers into which further items (beginning with Abraham) were inserted. Jerome tried to reconstruct individual years of it. Eusebius's chronicle was often based on Julius Africanus and shared with the latter the apologetic proof of the antiquity of the Chr. religion. → Sulpicius Severus, in his world chronicle that came down to the year 400, intended to imitate the classical models of antiquity and to provide a history of the OT period along with a sketch of church history. The *Historiae adversus paganos* in seven books of Paul → Orosius (to 417), conceived of as a supplement to → Augustine's *De civitate Dei*, is meant to deepen the latter's historical apologetic by demonstrating in detail the inferiority of the pre-Chr. world. A main emphasis in it is on the history of Rome. Orosius's work became the most important history book of the Middle Ages. Augustine's work is in fact a sketch of world history in an apologetic perspective. → Prosper Tiro is largely dependent on Jerome in his world chronicle that initially came down to 433 and then was continued to 455; he also offers the beginnings of a history of dogma. → Cassiodorus in his world chronicle (to 519) also makes use of Jerome and gives chiefly a list of consuls mixed with historical notes. → Gregory of Tours is to be mentioned for the first book of his *Historia Francorum* (finished in 591) which runs from Adam to Martin of Tours. → John Malalas (*Chronographia*, preserved down to 563) was widely read in Byzantium due to the popular character of his work. → The *Chronicon Paschale* (preserved to 628) is, along with Malalas, an early example of the chronicle literature that produced a rich harvest in the Byz. period. Following an idea of Augustine, → Isidore of Seville divided his chronicle (down to 615) into six ages of the world (which do not correspond to the 6000-year pattern). Also to be mentioned are → Panodorus and → Anianus (beginning of 5th c.). The Chr. reckoning of time became the basis of chronicles only after its introduction by → Dionysius Exiguus in the 6th c.

Syr. chronicles from the Persian (Arab.) empire reflect in a special way the life of the church in a non-Chr. environment and thus the interconnection of church history and world history; most of the older ones, except for shorter ones such as the → *Chronicle of Edessa* (6th c.), have been lost but have been incorporated into later works, such as those of Elijah of Nisibis (11th c.), Michael Syrus (12th c.), and Bar-Hebraeus (13th c.).

L: W. Adler, Time Immemorial (Washington, 1989). — J. Aßfalg, Chronik Q.: LMA 2:2022f. — S. Brock, Syriac historical writing: Studies in Syriac Christianity (Norfolk, 1992), 1-30. — B. Croke, Christian Chronicles and Byzantine History, 5th-6th Centuries (Aldershot, 1992). — H. Gelzer, Sextus Julius Africanus 1/2 (Leipzig, 1880/98). — V. Grumel, Traité d'Études Byzantines, 1. La Chronologie (Paris, 1958). — L. Koep, Chronologie B.: RAC 3:48-59. — P. Meinhold, Geschichte der kirchlichen Historiographie (Freiburg i.Br., 1967). — A. Momigliano, Pagan and Christian Historiography (Oxford, 1963), 79-99. — G. Moravcsik, Byzantinoturcica 1 (Berlin, ²1958). — P. Schreiner, Chronik N.: LMA 2:2010-2013. — G. Wirth, Chronik A.: LMA 2:1955f.

K. FITSCHEN

Chronicle of Arbela

A chronicle by Syr. author Mšiḫâ-Zkhâ (ca. 550) has been preserved which deals with the beginnings of Christianity in Persia and the work of the apostle Addai. After the manner of the Acts of the Martyrs it gives biographies for the period 100-550 and derives its name from the capital of Adiabene. Its authenticity and the historicity of the accounts have been vehemently disputed on grounds both internal and external. The only surviving ms. is a modern copy of a 10th-c. codex.

W: A. Mingana, Mšiḫâ-Zkhâ (Leipzig, 1907) [text/French trans.]. — E. Sachau, Chronik von A.: APAW. PH 6 (1915) 1-94 [German trans.]. — F. Zorell, Chronica: OrChr 8 (1927) 144-204 [Latin trans.] — P. Kawerau, CSCO. S 199/200 [text/German trans.].
L: J. Aßfalg, Textüberlieferung: OrChr 50 (1966) 19-36. — J. M. Ficy, Auteur et date: OrSyr 12 (1967) 265-301. — I. Ortiz de Urbina, Il valore storico: OCP 2 (1936) 5-32. — P. Peeters, Passionaire d'Adia-bène: AnBoll 43 (1925) 261-304. — E. Sachau, Ausbreitung: APAW. PH 9 (1919) 1-80. — idem, Persis: SPAW (1916) 958-982. — W. Schwaigert, Primat: OCA 236 (1988) 393-402.

P. BRUNS

Chronicle of Edessa

This work is one of the most important sources for early Syr. Christianity. It was composed by an anonymous author, around the middle of the 6th c., using the records of his native city for the period from 133/132 B.C.E. to 540 C.E.

W: BOCV 1:388-417 [text/Latin trans.]. — I. Guidi, CSCO 1f. [text/Latin trans.]. — L. Hallier, Untersuchungen über die Chronik v. Edessa (Leipzig, 1892) [text/German trans.]. L: H. J. W. Drijvers, Cults and Beliefs at Edessa (Leiden, 1980). — R. Duval, Histoire d'Édesse (Paris, 1892). — A. F. J. Klijn, Edessa (Neukirchen, 1965). — J. B. Segal, Edessa. The "Blessed City" (Oxford, 1970). — W. Witakowski, Chronicles of Edessa: OrSuec 33/35 (1984/86) 487-498.

P. BRUNS

Chronicon Paschale

The *Chronicon Paschale* has come down as anonymous and without a title; the name comes from its editor, Du Cange, and since then has prevailed over other attempts to name it. The work is preserved in *Cod. Vat. gr.* 1941 from the 10th c. (all the other mss. depend on this one), in which the beginning, the conclusion, and a section inside (dealing with the reigns of Emperors Claudius and Nero) have been lost. It can only be surmised that the author lived in the first half of the 7th c. and belonged to the circle of → Sergius of Constantinople (610-638). The period of time described in the work connects it with a very important age of the Byz. empire, one that ended with the victory over the Persian empire and the contemporary rise of Islam.

The work is a combination of a manual for reckoning the date of Easter (an Easter chronicle) and a chronographical exposition. In its present form the section that is an Easter chronicle follows the Alexandrian method of calculation. The years of the OT patriarchs, judges, and kings, of the Roman emperors, and of the Olympiads and the consuls are set alongside the Easter cycle. The chronographical exposition is a universal chronicle (→ Chronicle) that begins with Adam and Eve (dates converted to 550 B.C.E.) and comes down to the author's own time, i.e., to 629 (the work survives only to 628). The last section, and the one that is probably the author's own work, begins with 602 and embraces the period of Emperors Phocas and Heraclius; it is historically the most valuable part. It takes into account, e.g., events in Constantinople. Information in earlier sections of the work comes from older presentations, espec. → John Malalas. The influence of the work on later Byz. chronography is a subject still to be investigated.

W: PG 92:67-1028. — M. and M. Whitby, Chronicon Paschale 284-628 AD (Liverpool, 1989) [partial English trans.].
L: J.-M. Alonso Nuñez, Chronicon Paschale: LMA 2:1953f. — J. Beaucamp, Temps et Histoire 1: Le Prologue de la Chronique Paschale: TMCB 7 (1979) 223-301. — K. Ericsson, Revising a Date in the Chronicon Paschale: JÖBG 17 (1968) 17-28. — G. Mercati, A Study of the Paschal Chronicle: Opere Minori 2 (Rome, 1937), 462-479 = JThS 7

(1906) 397-412. — idem, I Frammenti Esaplari del Chronicon Paschale: Opere Minori 3 (Rome, 1937), 46-49. — N. Oikonomidès, Correspondence between Heraclius and Kavadh-Siroe in the Paschal Chronicle: Byz. 41 (1971) 269-281. — O. Schissel, Note sur un Catalogus Codicum Chronologorum Graecorum: Byz. 9 (1934) 269-295. — E. Schwartz, Chronicon Paschale: PRE 3:2460-2477 = idem, Griech. Geschichtsschreiber (Leipzig, 1957), 291-316. — idem, Chr. und jüd. Ostertafeln (Berlin, 1905), 20-40.

K. FITSCHEN

Chronograph (of 354)

The title Chronograph of 354 goes back to its editor, T. Mommsen. The author, who was really only a compiler of separate and unrelated lists, records, and documents, is unknown. The year 354 is the date of composition of the first copy; later copiers undertook to add updating complements in individual sections. In two recensions a later copyist even added annals of the emperor as far as 539 in one case, 496 in the other.

The compilation is a manual for administrative matters in the city of Rome and can have served Chr. purposes in only a small degree. To that extent it is also evidence of religious-eccles. conditions in Rome in the middle of the 4th c. After a dedication to a Valentinus, it contains a richly decorated astronomical-astrological and civil calendar, along with a list of pagan games, days of senate meetings, and emperors' birthdays, a list of the consuls down to the year of the compilation, a list of city-prefects of Rome for 254-354, a chronicle of the city of Rome (i.e., a list of kings, dictators, and emperors down to Licinius), a description of the regions of Rome, as well as illustrations (e.g., personifications of the cities of Rome, Alexandria, Constantinople, and Trier, as well as images of the planetary gods and portraits of the emperors). At least the calendar and the illustrations were done by calligrapher Furius → Dionysius Philocalus. A world chronicle beginning with Adam and ending in the present (Chronica Horosii) is based on a Lat. version of the Chronicle of → Hippolytus, which is correspondingly continued.

For the history of Chr. literature and the church the following parts are important, all of them having their own prehistory: A Cyclus Paschalis contains a list of the Easter Sundays for 312-411; it is based on an eighty-four-year cycle. A list of the consuls has been supplemented in its second half, although imperfectly. The dates of feasts down to 354 (and in the supplement to 358) have been reconstructed; from 359 on they are calculated in advance. A calendar of memorial days, beginning with Christmas, and of the burial places of the bishops of Rome records local traditions. A similar list of martyrs' memorials that covers the period from Lucius I to Julius I (254-352) represents the first calendar of saints (→ Depositio episcoporum — Depositio martyrum). A list of the bishops of Rome with their years in office (a "list of popes" also known as Catalogus Liberianus) begins with Peter and comes down to the entry of Liberius into his office in 352; an empty heading is left for the latter's year of death and length of term. Until the 3rd c. only names and dates are given, in a sometimes faulty reconstruction; from Pontianus (231) on there are also historical notes. In its second part, this list, a forerunner of the → Liber pontificalis and probably taken from the episcopal archive, is very valuable for the history of the church in Rome.

W: T. Mommsen, MGH. AA 9:13-148 [text]. — Supplements: T. Mommsen, Ges. Schriften 7 (Berlin, 1909), 536-579 [text]. — CIL 1:12 (Berlin, 1893), 254-279 [text]. — J. Strzygowski, Die Calenderbilder des Chronographen (Berlin, 1888).
L: A. Ferrua, Epigrammata Damasiana (Rome, 1942), 21-35. — HLL 5:178-182. — M. R. Salzman, On Roman Time (Berkeley, 1990). — E. Schwartz, Chr. u. jüd. Ostertafeln (Berlin, 1905), 41-43. — O. Seeck, Chronograph vom J. 354: PRE 3/2:2477-2481. — H. Stern, Le Calendrier de 354 (Paris, 1953).

K. FITSCHEN

Chrysippus

C., from Cappadocia (b. 409; d. 479), was a priest in Jerusalem and, acc. to Cyril of Scythopolis (vit. Euthym. 40; 60), received his education in Syria; ca. 428 he came to Jerusalem with his brothers Cosmas and Gabriel and was accepted into the laura by Euthymius as its bursar. At the wish of Empress Eudocia, who was residing in Jerusalem, C. was ordained a priest in 456 and, after his brother Cosmas was raised to the see of Scythopolis (467), was made staurophylax and entrusted with the safeguarding of the fragments of the cross kept in the Church of the Sepulcher. He held this dignity until his death. Four encomia have survived from his many sermons with their splendid rhetoric; these are addressed to the Mother of God (Dei gen.), John the Baptist (Ioan. Bapt.), St. Theodore Teron (v. Thds.), and the Archangel Michael (Mich.). C.'s christology is Chalcedonian in type but seeks to mediate between it and the other approaches.

W: v. Thds., A. Sigalas: ByA 7 (1921) 1-16 [text]. — Mich., idem: EEBS 1 (1924) 295-339; 3 (1926) 85-93 [text]. — Ioan. bapt., idem: TBNGP 20 (1937) 1-122 [text]. — Dei gen., M. Jugie, PO 9:336-343.

L: R. Caro, Homiletica Mariana: MLS 3 (1971) 211-226. — C. Martin, Ch. et Hesychius: RHE 35 (1939) 54-60. — L. Perrone, La Chiesa di Palestina (Brescia, 1980), 51f., 227f. — G. Tibertius, Antithesis Eva-Maria: DT (P) 59 (1956) 71-74.

P. BRUNS

Church History

The church has been conscious from the beginning (from the Acts of the Apostles, at the latest) of having a history, nor is this denied by the eschat. expectation. But thematic reflection on this history was limited to local retrospectives in the form of acts of martyrs or lists of bishops or to practical apologetical applications, which also influenced the genre of the Chr. → Chronicle at its origins. Even the development of the principle of tradition, in, e.g., → Irenaeus or → Tertullian, did not lead to the writing of a material history of the church. This step is first taken at the beginning of the 4th c. with the involvement of → Eusebius of Caesarea, a man of hist. and theol. learning, who is, in a way, in the line of Josephus, whom he cites. Eusebius looks back at a church that has grown and been strengthened by persecution, and he interprets this in retrospect as a history of God's preservation of the church. Thus, histories of the church are always histories of salvation as well.

Eusebius, who digested a great deal of earlier material and so preserved it from oblivion, is an example of how writers of church history in antiquity cultivated a careful knowledge of the source material and a manner of presenting it that respected the facts, while at the same time they also had a theol. point of view. Generally speaking, this viewpoint is established for them in advance by the effort to describe and interpret the history of the church as part of the history of the world. This interpretation set a different task for the Roman world after → Constantine than for the Persian world, where the church was compelled to see its history as constantly under the sign of martyrdom. After the Constantinian revolution, the great doctrinal struggles within the church also influenced the picture; the writing of church history acquired a strong heresiological component.

Eusebius is the father of the genre known as church history, as he is also one of the fathers of Chr. historiography in general, for he also produced a chronicle of world history the preparation for which served him in his church history. The first edition of Eusebius's Church History appeared ca. 303 (or perhaps in 312) and contained seven books; the last edition, after 324, contained ten books. It is not this growth in itself that is important but its cause: The

Constantinian revolution brought Eusebius to a new way of looking at church history, which now, like the history of the Roman empire, culminated in Constantine. As a result, the salvation-historical conceptions at work in his plan reached an end in the lifetime of the author, now that the coming of the Logos was seen against the background of the spread of the Roman empire. Given the historical fact in the background, namely, the political victory of Christianity, the still young literary genre of church history was given a new task.

Eusebius's Church History soon reached the West through the Lat. translation and revision by → Rufinus of Aquileia in 403 and his continuation of it to the death of Emperor Theodosius I. Rufinus assigns the genre of church history a meaning of his own: Given the Visigothic invasions of Italy, his intention is to present the history of the church as a consolation in present suffering.

Eusebius was continued by → Socrates, who deals with the period from 305 to 439. Here the history of heretics (espec. the Arians), reconstructed in part from original documents, has a special, and for the genre a new, emphasis. Socrates, like others, distances himself from Eusebius's model of history as leading up to Constantine, but he himself emphasizes Theodosius I as the emperor under whom the church has been able to develop best, since the controversy that broke out among Christians after Constantine had died out in his time.

Shortly after 439, and again in Constantinople, → Sozomen composed his church history, which covers the period 324 until ca. 422 (he had planned to go to 439). Sozomen harks back to Socrates but provides a kind of supplement to the sources used by his predecessor and used additional material as well. Sozomen broadens the subject matter of the genre by including the history of monasticism and of Christianity in the Persian empire.

The church history of → Theodoret of Cyrrhus, written after 428 and published in 449/450, had a long-lasting influence on Byz. historical writing (espec. by way of Theodore, Lector). He uses the same sources that Socrates and Sozomen had; he has an even greater interest in heresies (this too put its mark on the Byz. writing of church history).

To the same period belongs the work of → Philostorgius, who lived in Constantinople and between 425 and 433 published a work firmly geared to the defense of the Eunomians. The Gr. church history of the years 450-491 by → Zachary, an orator, served as a defense of Monophysitism. This work had a greater influence in a Syr. revision and continuation than it did in the Gr. original. → Theodore, a lector, made an eclectic compilation of the church histories of Socrates, Sozomen, and Theodoret in his *Historia tripartita* of 530; he supplemented it for the period down to 527 with a church history of his own, which has survived only in fragments and the remains of a later epitome. *Historia tripartita*, based on Socrates, Sozomen, and Theodoret also describes the compilation (after 540) of excerpts in Latin from the three historians by → Cassiodorus and his assistant → Epiphanius Scholasticus. This work exerted a strong influence in the western Middle Ages.

The church histories circulated in the Syr. world were initially translations of current Gr. works. The → *Chronicle of Arbela* (after 450; authenticity disputed) adopted a rather local perspective. → John of Ephesus wrote a Syr. church history, of which only the last part (571-585) has been preserved complete. The oldest East Syr. church history is that of → Barhadbesabba of Beth Arbaye in the 6th c. The Chronicle of Seert, from the 11th c., is also important for early Syr. church history.

For the Arm. world, in which church histories gave expression to an entirely different consciousness of an independent Chr. history, mention must be made of → Faustus of Byzantium (writing in Greek), whose church history of Armenia for 344-387 has survived in an Arm. translation. → Lazarus of Pharp continued that work to 486. A history of the christianization of Armenia was composed by a pseudonymous → Agathangelus (4th c.); from the 5th c. on this was expanded in a series of redactions.

L: H. v. Campenhausen, Die Entstehung der Heilsgeschichte: Saec. 21 (1970) 189-212. — G. F. Chesnut, The First Christian Histories (Macon, Ga., ²1986). — W. Kinzig, Novitas Christiana (Göttingen, 1994). — H. Leppin, Von Constantin dem Großen zu Theodosius II. Das chr. Kaisertum bei den Kirchenhistorikern Socrates, Sozomenus u. Theodoret (Hyp. 110) (Göttingen, 1996). — P. Meinhold, Geschichte der kirchlichen Historiographie 1 (Freiburg i.Br., 1967). — R. L. P. Milburn, Auf daß erfüllt werde (Munich, 1956). — W. Nigg, Die Kirchengeschichtsschreibung (Munich, 1934). — M. Wallraff, Die Rezeption der spätantiken Kirchengeschichtswerke im 16. Jh.: L. Grane, A. Schindler, M. Wriedt, Auctoritas Patrum 2 (Mainz, 1998), 223-260. — F. Winkelmann, Rolle u. Problematik der Behandlung der KG in der byz. Historiographie: Klio 66 (1984) 257-269.

K. FITSCHEN

Church Order

The church order is a genre of early Chr. texts that deal primarily with questions of church constitution (offices in the community), worship (liturgy in the community), and discipline (moral level of the community). The genre comprises texts composed over a period of four centuries and linked together by a very complicated network of literary dependences. In addition, what have survived, as a rule, are not the original texts but later (mostly eastern) versions of an original (usually Greek) that has to be reconstructed. This reconstruction is a continuing task for researchers (after the best possible explanation was given of questions of literary history during a period at the beginning of the 20th c. that was very fruitful for church order scholarship).

The name church order is applied to twelve texts that can be divided into three groups of four texts each: (1) The first and most important group consists of four texts that present themselves as literary units independent of one another: only from this group, therefore, is it possible to derive norms for the genre (see below): the → *Didache* (end of 1st c.), the so-called → *Traditio apostolica* (beginning of 3rd c.), the → *Didascalia* (mid-3rd c.), the *Apostolic Church Order* (end of 3rd c.). (2) Literarily dependent on the *Traditio apostolica* are three special forms: the → *Canones Hippolyti* (first half of 4th c.), the *Epitome Constitutionum Apostolorum VIII* (beginning of 5th c.), the *Testamentum Domini nostri Iesu Christi* (beginning of 5th c.); to be regarded as another special form of the genre is the *Apostolic Canons* (second half of 4th c.), which, though literarily independent of the *Constitutiones Apostolorum*, were incorporated into it at 8.47. (3) Church orders in which texts of the first and/or second group are combined, are regarded as collective works; an independent literary existence can be assumed for four of these: the *Fragmentum Veronense* (second half of 4th c.), the → *Constitutiones Apostolorum* (ca. 375), the *Alexandrian Synod* (mid-5th c.), the *Octateuch of Clement* (late 5th c.).

Important stages in the history of scholarship were the discovery of the *Didache* (Bryennios, 1873), the discovery of the *Fragmentum Veronense* (Hauler, 1896/1900), the identification of the *Traditio apostolica* as a literary unit, rendering superfluous the scientific construct of an → *Egyptian Church Order* (v. d. Goltz, 1906; Schwartz, 1910; Connolly, 1916).

Formal traits of the church order genre include: use of appellative (catalogue-form parenesis, exhortation, reminder) and prescriptive forms (apodictic decrees with casuistic expansions and accompanying justifications); use of rubrical hackneyed phrases (a syntactic unit that introduces, as a quasi title, another formally independent entity); conceptual and (more rarely) material associations as formal ways of creating series. As for the communication structure of the church order, the greeting to the addressees shows great variation, this being due to the limitations of appellative and prescriptive genres. The pseudo-apostolic attribution of the church order is not primarily a constitutive element of the genre, but, as a literary device for bringing out a specific understanding of tradition and norms, does participate in the structure of legitimation proper to the genre; moreover, this device is not used in two of the four literary units (*Didache*; *Traditio apostolica*).

The authors or compilers of the texts had in mind real community situations, as numerous specific details of the ordinances prove. As a result, the sphere in which the given ordinances were valid was really the community addressed; this is not contradicted by the fact that genre claims, at the literary level, a universal application (expressed by, among other things, the pseudo-apostolic authorship); the real addressee is simply the pragmatic correlative of the universal claim. Something analogous applies to the material scope of the ordinances: tendentially, church orders claim to incorporate all areas of community life without exception into the ordered structure proper to each document, but the completeness of the ordinances is explicitly denied. For, tendentially, church orders are not directed "conservatively" to the maintenance and safeguarding of existing relationships, but also have an undeniable innovative potential that finds expression in different ways: harmonizing of divergent traditions (*Didache*), programmatic opening of the content of tradition to possible completions (*Traditio apostolica*), attainment of specific goals (*Didascalia*). Despite all this, the order set down in writing is meant as the juridical definition of an existent or intended communal practice. Precisely because they are set down in order to be spread, church orders claim for their ordinances a validity not limited in time (they seem therefore to realize, as it were, that norms can claim validity only as long as they retain a degree of social effectiveness). It is this self-understanding that gives rise to the dynamic principle that allows for actualizations and completions of the existing order. This is confirmed by a glance at the transformation of some ordinances within various stages in the history of the genre. As areas of interaction that are the occasion for textual production, activities within the community (initiation, cultic banquet, organization of classes and offices) played a dominant role in comparison with outlying areas (dissociation from "heretical" groups as well as from "pagans"). This explains why dogmatic controversies

do not, for practical purposes, become direct subjects in the church orders; the focus of the church orders is rather on initiation, cultic meal, and the organization of offices. It is in these focal points of communal existence that the church orders see the ground on which the community's unity and stability are guaranteed. The diaspora community becomes a reality at the cultic meal, which symbolizes the unity of those who have been scattered (*Didache*); in the course of time this table fellowship is accounted for "sacramentally" (*Traditio apostolica*; *Didascalia*). The communities appoint officials (not least in order that these may preside at the cultic meal) and assign certain activities to different service groups (*Didache*). These service groups develop a class consciousness and an official ethos; this becomes a hierarchical organization of office in the *Traditio apostolica*, with important consequences, whereas the *Didascalia* is interested only in propagating the monarchical episcopate (those in the other service offices appear as supernumeraries alongside the bishop) and therefore remains without lasting effect.

Beginning in the 5th c. the genre disappeared as a result of the gradual loss of realism in the composition of the church orders, the competition from synodal legislation from the 4th c. on, and the increasingly suspect use of pseudepigraphy, which made the spuriousness of the texts ever more obvious.

L: J. V. Bartlet, Church-Life and Church-Order, ed. C. J. Cadoux (Oxford, 1943). — B. Botte, Collections canoniques: OrSyr 5 (1960) 331-350. — P. F. Bradshaw, TRE 18:662-670. — F. E. Brightman, Liturgies Eastern and Western (Oxford, 1967 = Oxford, 1896). — N. Brox, SM 2:1222-1226. — idem, Formen des Anspruchs auf apostolische Kirchenverfassung: Kairos 12 (1970) 113-140. — H. v. Campenhausen, Kirchliches Amt (Tübingen, ²1963) (English, Ecclesiastical authority and spiritual power [Stanford, 1969]). — R. H. Connolly, The So Called Egyptian Church-Order (Cambridge, 1916). — G. Dix, H. Chadwick, Apostolic Tradition (London, ²1968). — A. Erhardt, KOen als Beispiele frühbyz. Interpolationen: ZSRG. R 67 (1950) 403-439. — A. Faivre, Naissance d'une hiérarchie (Paris, 1977). — idem, La documentation canonico-liturgique: RevSR 54 (1980) 204-215, 273-297. — E. v. d. Goltz, Frgm. altchr. Gemeindeordnungen: SPAW 56 (1906) 141-157. — A. Hamel, Kirchenrechtliches Schrifttum Hippolyts: ZNW 36 (1937) 238-250. — J. M. Hanssens, La liturgie d'Hippolyte (Rome, ²1965). — O. Heggelbacher, Frühchr. Kirchenrecht (Fribourg, Switzerland, 1974). — W. Kinzig, C. Markschies, M. Vinzent, Tauffragen u. Bekenntnis (Berlin et al., 1999). — A. J. Maclean, The Ancient Church Orders (Cambridge, 1910). — J. Magne, Diataxeis des saints apôtres (Paris, 1975). — A. G. Martimort, La Tradition apostolique: ACan 23 (1979) 159-173. — idem, Nouvel examen: BLE 88 (1987) 5-25. — M.

Metzger, Prétendue Tradition apostolique: EO 5 (1988) 241-259. — W. Rordorf, Traditionsbegriff (Bern, 1983). — G. Schöllgen, Die Didache als Kirchenordnung: JAC 29 (1986) 5-26. — idem, Gattung der syr. Didaskalie: OCA 229 (1987) 149-159. — idem, Abfassungszweck der Kirchenordnungen: JAC 40 (1997) 55-77. — E. Schwartz, Pseudapostolische KOen: Gesammelte Schriften 5 (Berlin, 1963), 193-273 (= Strasburg, 1910). — B. Steimer, Vertex traditionis (Berlin, 1992). — A. F. Walls, Church Order Literature: StPatr 2 (1957) 83-92. — J. Wordsworth, The Ministry of Grace (London, ²1903).

B. STEIMER

Claudianus

Poet Claudius Claudianus was born (ca. 370?) in Alexandria and lived, at least after 394, in Italy, first in Rome, then at the imperial court in Milan (395-402) and Ravenna (from 402). In 404 all traces of him disappear. Important events in the history of the time elicited from C. hexametric poems full of verve (panegyrics, invectives, epics of war). He also composed mythological epic poetry and a series of *Carmina minora* (*c. m.*). His work often features divine figures such as Rome, Victory, and Bellona, while Chr. elements are lacking; in *c. m.* 50 (*In Iacobum magistrum equitum*) there is even an attack on Christianity. No wonder, then, that Augustine calls him "an enemy of the Chr. name" (*civ.* 5.26; see Orosius 7.35.21). Among the shorter poems there is indeed to be found one that is Christian: *c. m.* 32 (*De salvatore*), a hymn in twenty-one dactylic hexameters, the authenticity of which there is no compelling reason to doubt. On the other hand, C.'s authorship of the poems *Laus Christi* (*c. m. Appendix* 19 [thirty dactylic hexameters]) and *Miracula Christi* (*c. m. App.* 20 [nine elegiac distichs]) is disputed. C. appears to have been a writer who, while embracing a pagan religious spirit, could on occasion write poems with a Chr. content.

Under the name of "Klaudianos," probably a younger writer, two poems (forming a single whole?) "To the Redeemer" have been handed down in the Greek Anthology (*AP* 1.19/20).

W: T. Birt, MGH. AA 10. — J. B. Hall (Leipzig, 1985). — M. Platnauer (Cambridge, Mass., 1963 = 1922) [text/English trans.].
L: A. Cameron, C. (Oxford, 1970). — S. Döpp, Zeitgeschichte in Dichtungen C.' (Wiesbaden, 1980). — C. Gnilka, Götter u. Dämonen in den Gedichten C.': AuA 18 (1973) 144-160. — C. Lo Cicero, I carmi cristiani di C.: Atti della Accademia di scienze, lettere e arti di Palermo, serie quarta, 36 (1976-77) 5-51. — P. L. Schmidt, Zur niederen u. höheren Kritik von C.' Carmina minora: FS J. Fontaine 1 (Paris, 1992), 643-660. — G. Turcio, Sull'epigramma Miracula Christi attribuito a C.: RivAC 5 (1929) 337-344.

— J. Vanderspoel, C., Christ and the cult of the saints: CQ NS 36 (1986) 244-255.

S. DÖPP

Claudianus Mamertus

C. M. was a Gallic philosopher and priest (b. ca. 425; d. ca. 474), in the circle of friends of Apollinaris Sidonius. He was the closest collaborator of his brother, Bishop Mamertus of Vienne. Two letters to Sapaudus, an orator (*ep. ad Sap.*), and Apollinaris Sidonius (*ep. ad Apoll.*) have come down to us, as has the work *De statu animae* (*anim.*), composed ca. 470 and directed against the teaching of → Faustus of Riez on the soul (corporality; traducianism). The work, which argues from pagan philosophers, the *ecclesiastici doctores* (espec. the Latin), and the Bible, is indebted to Porphyry's *De regressu animae* (possibly in the translation by → Marius Victorinus) and espec. → to Augustine (teaching on the categories and on memory), whose *civ.* drew C. M.'s attention to Porphyry. His influence reached via → Cassiodorus to Abelard and Alanus ab Insulis. A hymn and a lectionary of C. M. have been lost. The authorship of the *Epistula ad Constantium* (*ep. ad Const.*) is an open question.

W: *anim.*, A. Engelbrecht, CSEL 11:18-197. — *ep. ad Sap.*, ibid., 203-206. — *ep. ad Apoll.*, A. Loyen, vol. 2 (Paris, 1970), 114f. [text/French trans.]. — *ep. ad Const.*, W. H. Frere (London, 1935), 75f. [text].
L: T. Alimonti, Arcaismo: FS M. Pellegrino (Turin, 1975), 189-228. — F. Bömer, Neoplatonismus u. Neopythagoreismus (Bonn, 1936). — P. Courcelle, Lettres grecques (Paris, 1948), 223-235. — M. Cristiani, L'espace de l'âme: Eriugena, ed. W. Beierwaltes (Heidelberg, 1980), 149-163. — E. L. Fortin, Christianisme (Paris, 1959). — E. Hårleman, Latinitatis quaestiones (Uppsala, 1938). — idem, Littérature gallo-romaine: Eranos 76 (1978) 157-169. — R. Iordache, Latin scientifique: Linguistica 26 (1986) 131-147. — G. Morin, Lettre-préface: RBen 30 (1913) 228-231. — W. Schmid, C. M.: RAC 3, 169-179.

M. SKEB, OSB

Clement of Alexandria

I. Life: Titus Flavius Clemens, of whom little is known and therefore much is disputed, had his prime in Alexandria in the last decade of the 2nd c. under Commodus and Septimius Severus. Born ca. 140/150 of a pagan family, possibly in Athens, as a Christian he made extensive journeys for study to Greece, southern Italy, Syria, and Palestine (the idea that he was initiated into the mysteries is an erroneous inference, for his supposed indiscretions are simply alphabetically ordered entries from a dictionary). Finally, he attached himself to his highly esteemed teacher Pantaenus in Alexandria. From the latter C. took over, as Eusebius reliably reports, the direction of the catechetical school there (criticism of Eusebius's claim of the existence of the school proves to be less than compelling to an impartial check). In 202, however, C. once again left the city that had become his city of adoption due to its intellectual life. This was hardly connected with a desire to flee from a threatening persecution of Christians (then it would have been more sensible for him to return to Alexandria like the other clergy when the danger had passed), but rather with the fact that at that time he was already experiencing serious tensions with Bishop Demetrius. From then on he was active as a priest in Jerusalem, where the local bishop, Alexander, entrusted him with a mission to Antioch on behalf of the church (ca. 212/213). He died ca. 220. The same Alexander, in a letter to Origen (probably 231), remembers Pantaenus and C. as already deceased fathers.

II. Work: Unlike his predecessors, C. did not give only oral instruction but also engaged in a literary activity in which he used all the fine points of an up-to-date rhetorical art. Eusebius gives a list of ten titles, but in addition to a homiletic treatise only a group of three closely related writings has survived complete. The *Protrepticus* (*prot.*), which follows the genre of philosophical protreptic (→ Protreptic), is a piece of Chr. missionary and promotional literature in which, while acknowledging that philosophy has a relative truth content, the author urges the reader to separate himself from the folly and immorality of pagan belief in the gods and acknowledge the complete revelation of the Logos-Christ.

This exhortation is carried further in the *Paedagogus* (*paed.*), a work in three books that brings the reader into the area of Chr. ethics, with Christ taking the part of educator. While book 1, in a more theoretical and programmatic way, develops the fundamentals of a universal divine pedagogy, in part against gnostic views, books 2 and 3 display, in an unpedantic manner, a wealth of individual practical precepts that extend even to behavior in eating and drinking and at social gatherings, to care of the body, clothing and adornments, household goods, married life, and sexual behavior, and that end with a magnificent hymn to Christ. The subjects discussed indicate that Christianity had gained entry into the higher level of society, among the well-to-do and the educated. When in his discussion of these matters C. avoids a stark asceticism but also demands that

Christians observe proper measure and retain their interior independence of external possessions, he is borrowing his material not only from bibl. instructions but also from the literature on decency and good manners in the popular philosophy of antiquity. The thrust of his thought, however, is far removed from any idea of juridical regimentation, but derives from the idea that as the result of the renewing and liberating power of communion with God, love becomes the principle that shapes human life.

Very closely connected in subject matter is the homily treatise *Quis dives salvetur* (*q. d. s.*), a partially allegorizing interpretation of the passage on the rich young man (Mt 10:17-31). It deals with the Chr. attitude to wealth and derives the measure and purpose of wealth from the commandment of love and the need of penance.

C.'s principal work is the seven books of the *Stromata* (*str.*) (more correctly: *Stromateis*); the full title is: "Carpets of Gnostic Explanations according to the True Philosophy," and it is a difficult and enigmatic work. It has long been disputed whether it is part of a trilogy, in the form of a dogmatic instruction following upon the works of exhortation (*prot.*) and education (*paed.*). Against this view is the fact that the *str.* are anything but a systematic explanation. But there are also difficulties with the view that in the course of writing the work C. came to realize that Chr. teaching cannot be definitively set down in writing and that he therefore abandoned his original plan. As the title shows, the *str.* belong to the ancient genre of "variety literature," the miscellany; this genre allowed the writer to propose worthwhile knowledge from all conceivable fields in a multicolored combination, without any set line of thought. The title also indicates that C. consciously places the literary form of unorganized variety in the service of a "gnostic explanation according to the true philosophy." He aims at a higher knowledge of Chr. revelation, one that rests on a "gnostic," that is, an ecclesial basis and is distinct from heretical gnosis. He does this, however, in such a way that his work gives only concealed hints: he speaks the deepest insights into truth in a hidden way, expresses them in veils, and makes them clear through silence. This literary conception, which aims at an existential appropriation of the truth, cannot be adequately evaluated apart from the Platonic assumption of the weakness, in principle, of what is written and of the radical priority of orality in the personal comprehension of philosophical didactic dialogue. The *str.* do not present any dogmatic system, because this would be useless and dangerous, but they do everything to set the properly disposed reader on the way to interiorly appropriating spiritual truth by his own intellectual participation, which is supported by divine help. When the *str.* are thus understood, it is possible to see at work as an organizing principle within the overall structure a hidden leitmotif that permeates the whole and initiates the reader to true gnosis. The main themes discussed are the relation between philosophy and theology (book 1); faith, the virtues, and the last end (2); authentic continence (3); martyrdom and perfection (4); the importance of the symbolic in a bibl. hermeneutics, and the plagiarism of the Greeks (5); and a portrait of the true gnostic (6-7). The work remained incomplete, for several announced subjects are never taken up.

Book 8 of the *str.*, as well as the *Excerpta ex Theodoto* (*exc. Thdot.*), passages from the work of → Theodore, a Valentinian gnostic, and the *Eclogae propheticae*, are to be seen as, in part, collections of material used earlier or as groundwork for a continuation.

Among the lost works the most important was the *Hypotyposes* in eight books, which contained exegetical explanations of various bibl. books, namely, Gen, Ex, Pss, and of NT letters and which were possibly an introduction to some form of *didaskalia*. Apart from information on them in Eusebius, only a few fragments have survived. The comments on 1 Pet, Jude, and 1-3 Jn that have come down to us, in a Lat. translation by Eusebius, under the title of *Adumbrationes in Epistolas canonicas*, seem to be excerpts from book 7.

There also exist insignificant fragments of some other works. Whether the recently discovered fragment of a letter with some lines from a secret gospel of Mark is really authentic can hardly be decided with final certainty (→ Mark, Literature about).

III. **Importance:** The fact that C.'s importance does not lie directly in the field of material dogmatics is connected with his unconventional manner of writing. And yet it was a pioneering accomplishment for C., writing as a Cath. Christian, to have described the relationship of faith and knowledge as one of gradual completion and to have, in the process, accepted and given a new meaning to the fashionable word "gnosis." Against his pagan critics he proves that faith is by no means unreasonable; dealing with the heretical gnostics, he emphasizes the point that faith is enough for full salvation and may not be abandoned, while true gnosis, understood as a spiritually profound and interiorly grasped and experienced knowledge, rests on the foundation of faith and is the completion of

faith; to simple but hidebound believers he defends philosophical-theol. education and ensures the abiding rights of the intellectual penetration of truth. Henceforth the way is blocked to a relapse into a narrow diaspora mentality and a piety of external observance.

There is disagreement about what C. meant precisely and in detail by "gnosis" and whether he is using a narrower concept of it (allegorical interpretation of Bible, Jewish-Chr. apocalyptic and doctrine on angels, esoteric doctrines) or a broader one (God and creation as a whole). In any case, undeniably central for C. is the revelation of the transcendent God in the Logos-Christ, which in turn makes possible a contemplative soaring beyond the intelligible sphere to God, this soaring understood as an anticipation of the eschatological perfection of the face-to-face vision of God. A closer analysis of this pattern of thought shows that C. is using the concepts and categories of the Gk. philosophy of being, but also that he does not simply adapt it in an external way but that on the basis of the nearness of Christ as grasped by faith he transforms it from within into a comprehensive application of the self-humiliation of the distant ground of being, thereby revolutionizing Gk. thought. In so doing, C. continues the line followed by the apologetes who first laid the bare foundations in their effort to take the synthesis of bibl. faith and Gr. thought that had already been made by Hellen. Judaism and link it, from within, with the primitive Chr. kerygma. Moreover, his return to Philo and his allegorical interpretation of scripture helped him to attain the spiritual-contemplative heights from a new starting point. Together with Origen, who clearly accepts C.'s aims, although he never mentions him, and although he develops a really matured systematics on a much broader scholarly foundation, C. represents an early phase of Alexandrian theology. In the (as it were) unhindered experimental form of their speculative theol. thinking, both men became founders of a Chr. metaphysics.

W: *Standard critical complete edition:* O. Stählin, L. Früchtel, U. Treu, 3 vols., GCS (Berlin, ²1970, ³1972, ⁴1985). — *Register:* O. Stählin, GCS (Berlin, 1936, ²1980). — *prot., paed., q. d. s., str.,* O. Stählin, BKV² 7, 8, 17, 19, 20) [German trans.]. — *prot.,* C. Mondésert, A. Plassart, SC 22. — M. Marcovich, SVigChr 34 (Leipzig, 1995). — *prot., q. d. s.,* G. W. Butterworth, LCL 92 (London, 1919). — *paed.,* H.-I. Marrou, M. Harl, SC 70. — C. Mondésert, H.-I. Marrou, SC 108. — C. Mondésert, C. Matray, H.-I. Marrou, SC 158. — *str.,* F. J. A. Hort, J. B. Mayor (London, 1902) [text/English trans./comm.]. — A. Le Boulluec, P. Voulet, SC 278, 279, 428. — F. Overbeck (Basel, 1936) [German trans.]. — H. Chadwick, LCC 2 (London, 1954) [partial Eng. trans.]. — J. Ferguson, FaCh 85 (Washington, 1991)

[English trans.]. — *exc.*, R. P. Casey. StD 1 (London, 1934) [text/English trans./comm.]. — F. Sagnard, SC 23. — *ecl.*, C. Nardi, BPat 4 (Florence, 1985) [text/Italian trans./comm.].

L: G. Bardy, Aux origines de l'école d'Alexandrie: RSR 27 (1937) 65-90. — J. Bernhard, Apologetische Methode (Leipzig, 1968). — A. Le Boulluec, La notion d'hérésie 2 (Paris, 1985). — J. M. Brown: Faith, Knowledge, and the Law: Romans 10-11 in strom. 2: SBL. SP 134 (1998) 921-942. — T. Camelot, Foi et gnose (Paris, 1945). — H. v. Campenhausen, Kirchliches Amt u. geistliche Vollmacht (Tübingen, ²1963), 215-233 (English, Ecclesiastical authority and spiritual power [Stanford, 1969]). — idem, Entstehung der chr. Bibel (Tübingen, 1968), 337-354. — H. Chadwick, Early Christian Thought (Oxford, 1966). — idem, C.: The Cambridge History of Later Greek and Early Medieval Philosophy, ed. A. H. Armstrong (Cambridge, 1970), 168-181. — E. A. Clark, C.'s use of Aristotle (New York, 1977). — A. H. Criddle, Mar Saba Letter attributed to C.: JECS 3 (1995) 215-220. — J. Daniélou, Message évangélique et culture hellénistique (Tournai, 1961). — A. van den Hoek, C. and His Use of Philo (Leiden, 1988). — eadem, C. on Martyrdom: StPatr 26 (1993) 324-341. — eadem, Techniques of Quotation: VigChr 50 (1996) 223-243. — eadem, The "Catechetical" School of Early Christian Alexandria: HThR 90 (1997) 59-87. — eadem, Hymn to Christ the Savior: Critical Anthology of Hellenistic Prayer, ed. M. Kiley (London, 1997), 296-303. — W. Jaeger, Das frühe Christentum u. die griech. Bildung (Berlin, 1963). — D. Kinder, Conflicting Views on Women: SecCen 7 (1989/90) 213-220. — S. R. C. Lilla, C. (Oxford, 1971). — C. Markschies, "Wunderliche Mär von zwei Logoi . . .": FS L. Abramowski (Berlin, 1993), 193-219. — G. May, Christushymnus des C.: Liturgie u. Dichtung 1, ed. H. Becker, R. Kaczynski (St. Ottilien, 1983), 257-273. — idem, Platon u. die Auseinandersetzung mit den Häresien: FS H. Dörrie (Münster, 1983), 123-132. — M. Mees, Zitate aus dem NT (Bari, 1970). — A. Méhat, Étude sur les "Stromates" (Paris, 1966) (standard!). — idem, C.: TRE 8:101-113. — J. Moingt, La Gnose dans ses rapports avec la foi et la philosophie: RSR 37 (1950) 195-251, 398-421, 537-564; 38 (1951) 82-118. — C. Mondésert, C. (Paris, 1944). — R. Mortley, Connaissance religieuse et herméneutique (Leiden, 1973). — P. Nautin, Lettres et écrivains (Paris, 1961). idem, Origène (Paris, 1977). — E. F. Osborn, The Philosophy of C. (Cambridge, 1957). — idem, Ethical Patterns (Cambridge, 1976), 50-80. — idem, C. Review of Research, 1958-1982: SecCen 3 (1983) 219-244. — idem, C., Plotin et l'Un: FS C. Mondésert (Paris, 1987), 173-189. — idem, Anfänge chr. Denkens (Düsseldorf, 1987). — idem, Arguments for Faith: VigChr 48 (1994) 1-24. — M. Pohlenz, Klemens u. sein hellenisches Christentum (Geneva, 1943). — C. Riedweg, Mysterienterminologie (Berlin, 1987). — A. M. Ritter, Christentum u. Eigentum: ZKG 86 (1975) 1-25. — idem, Klemens v. Alexandrien: GK 1, ed. M. Greschat (Stuttgart, 1984), 121-133. — idem, C. and the Problem of Christian Norms: StPatr 18/3 (1989) 421-439. — K. Schmöle, Läuterung nach dem Tod u. pneumatische Auferstehung (Münster, 1974). — C. Scholten, Die alexandrinische Katechetenschule: JAC 38 (1995) 16-37. — M. Smith, C. of Alexandria and the Secret Gospel of Mark (Cambridge, Mass., 1973). — W. Völker, Der wahre Gnostiker (Leipzig, 1952). — D. Wyrwa, Chr. Platonaneignung (Berlin, 1983).

D. WYRKA

Clement of Rome

I. Life: Acc. to the so-called first *Letter of Clement* (*1 Clem.*), C. seems to have been a convert from paganism and possibly a freedman of Roman consul T. Flavius Clemens. Since the Roman buildings under the Roman titular church of St. Clement may have belonged to that consul, they may point to the original environment of C. Acc. to Irenaeus of Lyons (*haer.* 3.3.3) C. knew the apostles Peter and Paul; for Origen (*Jo.* 6.36), C. is the fellow worker of Paul named in Phil 4:3. Along with Irenaeus we may regard C. as a bishop who, as first among equals of a presbyteral college, was head of the Roman community toward the end of the first c.

There is much to be said for limiting his time of office to 91/92-100/101, the period mentioned by Eusebius (*h.e.* 3.15 and 34). The historical nucleus of C.'s legendary *passio* (BHL 1848, 5th c.) seems to be his banishment to Chersonesus under Emperor Trajan and his martyrdom (by drowning) and burial there. The details given in the → Clementine (Pseudo-) Literature are worthless.

II. Works: *1 Clem.*, a letter addressed to the community in Corinth by an anonymous writer of the Roman local church, has been unanimously attributed to C. by the fathers beginning with Dionysius of Corinth (ca. 170; see Eus., *h.e.* 4.23.11) and by the majority of modern scholars. Ca. 96 he wrote in opposition to some young people of the Corinthian community who had deposed the officials there (bishops and presbyters, but not the deacons, who are simply mentioned). With a wide range of theol. (espec. from the theology of office and of law) but also of political, cosmological, and ethical arguments, C. calls for reinstallation of the officials, peace, and concord and exhorts the rebels to do penance and to emigrate. Acc. to C., their rebellion has violated the divine order set down, as it were, in creation and in the church. For the appointment of presbyters goes back not only to an instruction of the apostles, but beyond the first disciples of the apostles, the apostles, and Christ to God himself. In addition, the presbyters were appointed with the agreement of the community and were exercising their office in a blameless manner. Consequently, their deposition was unjust and a serious sin. All in all, *1 Clem.* (following in the tradition of Roman thought on law) bears witness to the earliest Roman sense of responsibility for the entire church, but without making any specific claim to primacy. The letter was quickly accepted by the Great Church and found a place in the liturgy of some local churches and in the canonical writings. C.'s understanding of his office, for which he appeals to divine law, was for a long time at the center of the controversy on the legitimacy of canon law and early Catholicism. Finally, an extensive → Pseudo-Clementine literature sought eccles. recognition under the highly respected name of C.

S: *Passio s. Clementis*, F. X. Funk, F. Diekamp, Patres Apostolici 2 (Tübingen, [2]1913), 50-81 [Greek and Latin text]. W: A. Jaubert, SC 167. — J. A. Fischer, Die Apostolischen Väter (Munich, [7]1976), 24-107 [Greek text/German trans./comm.]. — A. Lindemann, Die Clemensbriefe (Tübingen, 1992), 23-181 [German trans./comm.]. — idem, H. Paulsen, Die Apostolischen Väter (Tübingen, 1992), 80-151 [Greek text/German trans.]. — G. Schneider, FC 15.
L: K. Beyschlag, C. u. der Frühkatholizismus (Tübingen, 1966). — B. Bowe, A Church in crisis (Minneapolis, 1988). — A. Esser, Wo fand der hl. Konstantin-Kyrill die Gebeine des hl. C. ?: Cyrillo-Methodianum, ed. M. Hellmann (Graz, 1964), 126-147. — J. Fuellenbach, Ecclesiastical Office and the Primacy of Rome. Recent Theological Discussion of 1 Clem. (Washington, 1980). — F. Guidobaldi, Il Complesso Archeologico di San Clemente: San Clemente Miscellany 2, ed. L. Dempsey (Rome, 1978), 215-303. — J. Hofmann, Unser hl. Vater Klemens (Trier, 1992). — O. Knoch, 1 Clem. über die kirchliche Verfassung im Spiegel der neueren Deutungen seit Sohm u. Harnack: ThQ 141 (1961) 385-407. — idem, Der Brief des C. u. die Eigenart des röm. Christentums: ANRW II 27/1 (1993) 3-54. — P. Lampe, Die stadtröm. Christen (Tübingen, 1987). — J. B. Lightfoot, The Apostolic Fathers 1/1-2/3 (London, [2]1889-1890). — M. Mees, Das Christusbild: EThL 60 (1990) 297-318. — F. Snopek, Klemens u. seine Reliquien (Kremsier, 1918). — G. Wartenberg, Die Kirchenverfassung: WZ(L) 37 (1988) 26-34. — B. G. Wright: Is 1Clem 50:4 a citation of 4QPs-Ezekiel?: StTDJ 31 (Leiden, 1999), 183-193.

J. HOFMANN

Clementine (Pseudo-) Literature

According to Eusebius (*h.e.* 6.25.14), Origen suggested → Clement of Rome as the possible author of Heb. In addition, numerous pseudepigrapha sought eccles. recognition under the highly respected name of C.

Three mss. give not only *1 Clem.* but an anonymous work which in two of them is titled the second letter of C. (*2 Clem.*). But this is an early Chr. homily written ca. 130/150 in Syria or Egypt; it exhorts to obedience to Christ's commandments in return for his redemptive work. Beginning with Epiphanius of Salamis (*haer.* 30.15.1f.), early Chr. literature was almost unanimous in making C. the author of two letters *Ad virgines*; for this reason, most scholars down to the end of the 19th c. regarded them as authentic. The works, which originally formed a single letter directed against the practice of celibate men

having virgin companions, is probably from the Syro-Palestinian world of the 3rd c.

The Ps.-Clem. *Homilies* (*Hom. Clem.*) and Ps.-Clem. *Recognitions* (*Clem. recogn.*), composed in Greek, claim to be the work of C. These were seen as early as Eusebius (*h.e.* 3.38.5) to be apocryphal; modern scholarship regards the *Hom. Clem.* and *Clem. recog.* as two recensions of an original written ca. 220/250 in Coele-Syria. The *Hom. Clem.* were probably written in the first half of the 4th c.

A section of introduction to these two writings has preserved a covering letter of Peter to "Bishop James" (*ep. Petr.*), a *Contestatio* (*Cont.*) with an account of the reading of the *ep. Petr.*, and a letter of C. to James (*Clem. ep.*).

The *Clem. recog.* arose independently of the *Hom. Clem.* around the mid-4th c.; they are preserved only in Rufinus's Lat. translation. Unlike the apocryphal acts of the apostles, these writings do not so much tell a story as pass on Jewish-Chr. teaching; thus they belong to the genre of the Chr. → novel.

We can assume as source of the original the *Kerygmata Petrou*, which is mentioned in *ep. Petr.* 1.2 and *Cont.* 1.1; that work must have been written at the end of the 2nd c. It sprang from a Jewish-Chr.-gnostic milieu: central to it is the preaching of the "true prophet" who brings a gnosis that is identical with the law. Connected with this is a pronounced antipaulinism. The doctrine of the "syzygies," or pairs of opposites, which determine history (Adam-Eve; Peter-Paul) is likewise already present here.

The original work contains the essential elements of the novel: C. finds no answers to his questions from philosophy, he travels to Palestine, meets Peter, and accompanies him on his journeys, during which the conflict with Simon Magus plays a central role. This version is marked by the rationalism of the age of the apologetes: a life acc. to reason makes possible redemption at the coming judgment.

The author of the *Hom. Clem.* was an Arian theologian who finds the syzygies even in the being of God.

The *Clem. recog.* owe their title to the various recognition scenes between C. and his family, which had been scattered. The author, who belonged to the Great Church, got rid of the antipaulinism and other offensive passages. Later on, however, theol. passages were inserted by the Eunomians, causing the work to be suppressed in the East. Rufinus's translation omitted these passages and thus made it possible for the work to be widely read in the West.

Among later variants of the *Hom. Clem.* and *Clem. recog.* are several epitomes: one Syr., two Arab., and two Gr. (of these one includes the *Passio* and the

Miraculum s. Clementis). They record only the narrative material of the novel. In addition, there is a quite independent version in Church Slavonic.

The *Scroll* of C., written ca. 750/760 in Egypt, contains only echoes of *Clem. recog.*

The five *Decretals of C.*, which are part of the Ps.-Isidorean Decretals (compiled in France ca. 847/852) are based largely on *Clem. recog.* and *Clem. ep.*

From the 10th c. on, West Syr. Jacobite mss. contain a formulary for Mass that is attributed to C.; it probably reached its final form only in the 7th c.

C. is described as editor of supposedly apostolic prescriptions in the → *Apostolic Church Order* (*CEA*), the → *Apostolic Constitutions* (*Cons. App.*), and the so-called *Octateuch* of C. In this last work, an author (probably → Jacob of Edessa), writing under the name of C. in 687, translated the → *Testament of our Lord Jesus Christ*, the *CEA*, and excerpts of the *Const. App.* into Syriac, organized the translation into eight books, and so created a body of law which was widespread in the pre-Chalcedonian church in the form of Syr., Copt., Eth., and Arab. recensions.

Also going under the name of C. were the Lat. *Order of Fasting for the Twelve Fridays* (and its Gr. variants) which was composed, at the earliest, in the 8th c. in the Franko-Germanic world.

The Arab. *Canons* (*can.*) of C. supposedly go back to Peter; these are instructions in morality and worship that must date to ca. 850/1060 in Egypt; dependent on them is the Arab. *Comment on the Holy Feasts* that was attributed to C.

W: *2 Clem.*, K. Wengst (Munich, 1984), 236-280 [Greek text/German trans./comm.]. — A. Lindemann (Tübingen, 1992), 197-261 [German trans./comm.]. — *ad virgines*, F. X. Funk, F. Diekamp, Patres Apostoloci 2 (Tübingen, ⁴1913), 1-49 [Latin trans.]. — H. Duensing: ZKG 53 (1950/51) 166-188 [German trans.]. — J. T. Beelen, P. Zingerle, S. C. Epistolae binae de virginitate (Leuven/Louvain, 1856) [Syriac text/Latin trans./German trans./comm.]. — *Hom. Clem., ep. Petr., Cont., Clem. ep.*, B. Rehm, J. Irmscher, F. Paschke, GCS 42) [text]. — *Clem. recogn.*, B. Rehm, F. Paschke, GCS 51 [text]. — J. Irmscher, G. Strecker: NTApo⁵ 2:439-488 [German trans. of *ep. Petr., Cont., Clem. ep.*/partial Germ. trans. of *Hom. Clem.* and *Clem. recogn.*]. — *Syr. epitome*, A. Mingana: BJRL 4 (1917/18) 66-76, 90-109 [text/English trans.]. — W. Frankenberg, TU 48/3. — *Gk. epitomes*, A. Dressel (Leipzig, ²1873), 2-233 [text]. — *2 Arab. epitomes*, M. D. Gibson: StSin 5 (1896) 14-45 [text]. — *Church Slavonic version*, P. Lavrov (Moscow, 1911), 47-108 [text]. — I. Franko: ZNW 3 (1902) 146-155 [German trans.]. — *Scroll of C.*, M. D. Gibson: StSin 8 (1901) 1-58 [text]. — *Decretals*, P. Hinschius, Decretales Ps.-Isidorianae (Leipzig, 1863), 30-66 [text]. — S. Wenzlowsky, Briefe der Päpste , BKV¹:148-175 [German trans.]. — *Mass formulary*, PG 2:605-616 [Latin trans.]. — A. Hänggi, I. Pahl, Prex Eucharistica (Fribourg, Switzerland, 1968), 298-303 [Latin trans.]. — *Octateuch*, F.

Nau, P. Ciprotti (Milan, 1967) [French trans.]. — *Order of Fasting*, G. Mercati: StT 5 (1901) 81, 240f. [Latin and Greek text]. — *can.*, P. Fahed, Kitâb al-hudâ ou Livre de la Direction (Aleppo, 1935), 249-260 [text]. — W. Riedel, Die Kirchenrechtsquellen des Patriarchats Alexandrien (Leipzig, 1900), 165-175 [German trans.]. — *Comment on the Feasts*, F. Cöln: OrChr 8 (1908) 230-277 [text/Latin trans.].

L: K. Beyschlag, Simon Magus u. die chr. Gnosis (Tübingen, 1984). — E. C. Brooks, The Clem. ep.: TU 128 (1984) 212-216. — J. S. Cha, Diamartyria and the Ordination of Jewish Christian Teachers: AJTh 13 (1999) 124-158. — A. Faivre, Les fonctions ecclésiales: RSR 50 (1976) 97-111. — W. Frankenberg, Die syr. Clementinen (Leipzig, 1937). — H. Fuchs, Die Anaphora des Patriarchen Jôhannàn I. (Münster, 1926) (West Syrian Clementine Mass formulary). — H. Fuhrmann, Vorgratianische Einwände zu Ps.-C.-Briefen: FS F. Kempf (Sigmaringen, 1983), 81-95. — idem, Ps.-Isidor, Otto v. Ostia (Urban II.): ZSRG. K 68 (1982) 52-69 (Decretals of C.). — J. Hofmann, Unser hl. Vater Klemens (Trier, 1992), 24-44. — F. S. Jones, The Ps.-Clementines. History of Research: SecCen 2 (1982) 1-33, 63-96. — L. L. Kline, The Sayings of Jesus, 1975. — G. Lüdemann, Paulus 2: Antipaulinismus im frühen Christentum (Göttingen, 1983), 228-257. — D. Marafotti, La verginità in tempi di crisi: CivCatt 140 (1989) 434-448. — F. Paschke, Die beiden griech. Klementinen-Epitomen u. ihre Anhänge (Berlin, 1966). — B. Rehm, Zur Entstehung der ps.-clementinischen Schriften: ZNW 37 (1938) 77-184. — idem, C. II: RAC 3:197-206. — A. Stötzel, Älteste Kirchengeschichte nach den Ps.-Clementinen: VigChr 36 (1982) 24 37. — G. Strecker, Judenchristentum in den Ps.-Clementinen (Berlin, ²1981). — W. Ullmann, Clem. ep. in the Ps.-Clementines: JThS NS 11 (1960) 295-317. — R. Wams, Untersuchungen zu 2 Clem., Diss. (Marburg, 1989). — J. Wehnert, Literarkritik u. Sprachanalyse: ZNW 74 (1983) 268-301.

J. HOFMANN

Codex Justinianus

The *Cod. Iust.*, in the form in which we now have it— *Cod. Iust. repetitae praelectionis* (*Cod. Iust. rep. prael.*) from 534—is a collection of imperial laws, beginning with an undated decree of Emperor Hadrian (*Cod. Iust.* 6.23.1) and ending with a decree of Justinian issued in Nov., 534.

The *Cod. Iust.* contains over 4,600 decrees, divided into twelve books. As in the *Codex Theodosianus*, the books are subdivided into titles, while the individual decrees are ordered chronologically. The second edition replaced a first of the year 529, which in turn was intended to replace the *Codices Greg., Herm.*, and *Theod.* But that first codex could not be permanent once Justinian decided to revise the plan of Theodosius's work and to codify not only the laws but also the *ius* (the writings of the jurists).

This plan seems not yet to have existed when the first edition was composed, but to have already taken firm shape by the time of the composition of the

Quinquaginta Decisiones (*L decisiones*). The latter may originally have been meant to settle the most important disputes in the use of the writings of the jurists, but by the time they were sent out between Dec. 530 and Feb. 531, they were already an important preparation for the codification of the writings of the jurists in Justinian's *Digests* of 533.

Cod. Iust. rep. prael. had for its purpose to incorporate laws passed since the first edition while work on the *Digests* was going on, laws intended in large measure to settle classical and postclassical controversies. As in the case of the first edition, another purpose was to eliminate repetitions, contradictions, and outdated material. To this end even the texts of the decrees could be changed (interpolated). The commission, headed, as the first codex had been by Tribonian, *quaestor sacri palatii*, made extensive use of this authority.

W: *Cod. Iust.*, P. Krüger (Berlin, 1877). — *Corpus iuris civilis* 2: *Cod. Iust.* 11, P. Krüger (Berlin, 1954).
L: P. Cuneo, Codice Teodosiano, Codice giustinianeo e diritto del tardo impero: Labeo 42 (1996) 208-241. — G. L. Falchi, Sulla codificazione del diritto romano (Rome, 1989), 66-80. — T. Honoré, Tribonian (London, 1978), 212-222. — F. Pringsheim, Die Entstehung des Digestenplanes: Atti del congresso internazionale romano 1 (Pavia, 1934), 451-494 = Gesammelte Abhandlungen 2 (Heidelberg, 1961), 41-72. — K.-H. Schindler, Justinians Haltung zur Klassik (Cologne, 1966). — N. van der Wal, Die Textfassung der spät-röm. Kaisergesetze: BIDR 83 (1980) 1-27. — L. Wenger, Quellen des röm. Rechts (Vienna, 1953), 569-576, 638-651.

K.-H. SCHINDLER

Codex Theodosianus

The *Cod. Theod.* of 438 is a collection of imperial decrees (edicts and other *leges generales*) from the years 312-438 (Constantine to Theodosius II). It was based on the authentic texts of the imperial laws. The laws were divided materially into books and titles and chronologically within each title. The omission of the *praefationes* and the breaking up of decrees acc. to the different regulations they contained led to numerous changes in the text (*Cod. Theod.* 1.1.6 [935]). Some simplification of the texts must also be taken into account, since contradictions were to be removed and inconsistencies were to be emended. The changes made were not primarily material. Defects in the work cannot, however, be denied (wrong information on the time and place of individual laws; mistakes in the names of emperors and official titles). In the absolutist state of the empire more than half of the decrees belong to public law (including the church law in book 16).

The *Cod. Theod.* that has come down to us no longer reflects the original plan of codification. Acc. to *Cod. Theod.* 1.1.5 (429), after a preparatory code of imperial decrees there was to be a unified code that included the writings of the jurists, but that plan did not succeed.

The *Cod. Theod.* has not come down to us complete. About half of the text depends on the *Lex Romana Visigothorum* (Gaul, 506). In addition to further fragments, a Paris ms. of the 5th or 6th c. (*Paris. 96.43*) contains books 6-8 and a Vatican ms. of the 6th c. (*Vat. reg. 886*) contains books 9-16.

W: *Cod. Theod.*, J. Gothofredus (Leipzig, 1736ff.). — *Theodosiani libri XVI*, T. Mommsen (Hildesheim, 1905). — *Cod. Theod.* (lib. I-VIII), P. Krüger (Berlin, 1923-1926).
L: B. Albanese, Sul programma legislativo esposto nel 429 da Teodosio II.: Annali del Seminario Giuridico dell'Università di Palermo 38 (1985) 253-269. — P. Cuneo, Codice Teodosiano, Codice giustinianeo e diritto del tardo impero: Labeo 42 (1996) 208-241. — G. L. Falchi, Sulla codificazione del diritto romano (Rome, 1989). — T. Honoré, The Making of the Theodosian Code: ZSRG. R 103 (1986) 133-222. — E. Volterra, Il problema del testo delle costituzioni imperiali: Atti del II Congresso Internazionale della Società Italiana di storia del diritto (Venice, 1967) (Florence, 1971), 821-1097. — N. van der Wal, Die Textfassung der spätröm. Kaisergesetze: BIDR 83 (1980) 1-27. — L. Wenger, Quellen des röm. Rechts (Vienna, 1953), 536-541.

K.-H. SCHINDLER

Collatio legum Mosaicarum et Romanarum

The *Coll. Mos.*, which dates to the 4th/5th c. C.E., compares Mosaic and Roman law. There are three mss.: the *Cod. Berolinensis* of the 9th c. and the *Codices Vercellensis* and *Vindobonensis* of the 10th c., which give as the title of the work *Lex Dei quam Dominus praecepit ad Moysen*. The name *Coll. Mos.* has been in use since the edition of H. Stephanus (1580). From this collection a book divided into sixteen titles (chapters) has come down to us. The chapters deal mostly with the responsibility, in penal and civil law, of such offenders as murderers, adulterers, sexual criminals, coiners, thieves, arsonists, and robbers. Contractual law is represented by a single title on safekeeping (*depositum*) (*Coll. Mos.* 10). The conclusion of the work deals with the law of succession (*Coll. Mos.* 16). Each title begins with a passage from the Pentateuch. This is followed by references to Roman law, which is divided into *ius* and *leges*. Cited are Gaius, Papinian, Ulpian, Paulus, and Modestinus, that is, the classical writers who were given special authority in the "Law of Citation" of 426 (*Cod.*

Theod. 1.4.1). The excerpts from the writings of the jurists are supplemented by imperial decrees.

An accurate dating of the collection is as uncertain as its authorship. Hypotheses that the author was one of the church fathers have proved to be untenable. So too the thesis that the author was of Jewish descent has been unable to win support. A date between 390 and 438 for the *Coll. Mos.* is suggested by the fact that in the section on sexual offenders (*stupratores*) a decree of 390 is given, not in the abbreviated form of the *Cod. Theod.* of 438 (9.7.6) but in its original full form (*Coll. Mos.* 5.3). A recent hypothesis interprets the fact that the *Coll. Mos.* gives May 14, 390, as the date of publication of that decree, and not Aug. 6 as in the *Cod. Theod.*, as evidence that the *Coll. Mos.* was completed in 390. The year 426 is not a sure *terminus post quem* because the law establishes only an already existing practice. But the citations from the Bible in *Coll. Mos.* show linguistic agreements with theol. writings of this period.

At the beginning of the title on thieves and their punishment (*Coll. Mos.* 7.1) the theologically educated and probably Chr. author points out that the killing of a thief in self-defense and the killing of a thief in the night without restriction were already declared licit in the Mosaic law and not first in the Law of the Twelve Tables. He emphasizes this finding with the words: "Understand, you learned men of the law, that Moses was the first to set this down, as a reading makes clear (Ex 22:2f.)." This kind of effort to prove temporal priority and a material precedence in principle is also to be seen in, e.g., the *Apologeticum* of Tertullian (*apol.* 19 and 45.3). But apologetic aims were hardly a primary concern of the author of the *Coll. Mos.* It is more likely that by his comparative presentation the author wanted to show the compatibility of Christianity and Roman law and thus contribute to the christianization of his world.

W: Fontes Iuris Romani Anteiustiniani 2, ed. J. Baviera (Florence, 1968), 541-589 [text]. — Fragmenta Vaticana, Collatio etc., ed. J. E. Spruit, K. E. M. Bongenaar, Het erfdeel van de klassieke romeinse juristen 4 (Zutphen, 1987) [text/Dutch trans.]. — Collectio librorum iuris anteiustiniani, ed. P. Krüger, T. Mommsen, G. Studemund, vol. 3 (Berlin, 1890), 107-198 [text]. — P. F. Girard, F. Senn, Textes de droit romain 1 (Paris, ⁷1967), 545-590. — M. Hyamson, Mosaicarum et Romanarum legum Collatio (Oxford, 1913). — B. Kübler, Iurisprudentiae Anteiustinianae 2/2 (Leipzig, 1927), 325-394.
L: G. Barone-Adesi, L'età della lex Dei (Naples, 1992). — P. E. Huschke, Ueber Alter u. Verfasser der Coll. Mos.: Zeitschrift für geschichtliche Rechtswissenschaft 13 (1845) 1-49. – - M. Lauria, Lex Dei: SDHI 51 (1985) 257-275. — D. Liebs, Die Jurisprudenz im spätantiken Italien (Freiburg i.Br., 1987), 162-174. — H. L. W. Nelson, Überlieferung, Aufbau u. Stil von Gai institutiones: Studia Gaiana 6, ed. M.

David et al. (Leiden, 1981), introduction 104-123. — E. J. H. Schrage, La date de la "Collatio Legum Mosaicarum et Romanarum": FS F. Wubbe (Fribourg, Switzerland, 1993), 401-417. — F. Schulz, Geschichte der röm. Rechtswissenschaft (Weimar, 1961), 394-398. — N. Smits, Mosaicarum et Romanarum legum Collatio (Haarlem, 1934). — F. Triebs, Studien zur Lex Dei (Freiburg i.Br., 1905). — E. Volterra, Coll. Mos. (Rome, 1930). — L. Wenger, Die Quellen des röm. Rechts (Vienna, 1953), 545-548.

C. KRAMPE

Columbanus the Younger

Sources for the life of C. are the *Vita Columbani* of Jonas of Bobbio, the *Vita s. Galli* of Wetti and Walafrid Strabo, as well as C.'s own writings. C. may have been born in 543 (the dating varies between 543-547 and 525-530) in the Irish kingdom of Leinster. After being educated by the *venerabilis vir Sinilis*, he entered Bangor as an adult, under Abbot Comgall, who was known for his strictness and who after initial opposition permitted C. and twelve companions to make a *peregrinatio* to Gaul. C. settled in the Vosges, founded the monasteries of Annegray, Luxeuil, and Fontaine, and, after twenty years' labor, was exiled by King Theuderic from Burgundy to Ireland in 610, along with his monks, as the result of conflicts among the Merovingians. In any case, C. succeeded in traveling via Metz and Basel to the court of the Lombard king in Milan, where he received support for founding the monastery of Bobbio. Nov. 616 is accepted as the date of his death.

Surviving are six *Epistulae* (*ep.*) (on, among other things, the date of Easter and the Three-Chapters controversy); thirteen *Instructiones* (*Sermones; instr.*) (with spiritual content from the intellectual world of the fathers and ascetics); two monastic rules, namely, the *Regula monachorum* (*reg. mon.*), which reflects the spirit of Bangor and gives religious and ascetical instructions, and the *Regula coenobialis* (*reg. coen.*), which is a monastic penitential; also the penitential, *De paenitentia* (*paen.*), for monks, the laity, and the secular clergy; this work built on the *Paenitentiale* of Vinnian and made known outside of Ireland the practice of repeatable tariff penance. The attribution to C. of the *Carmina* (*carm.*), the *Celeuma* (*Carmen navale; cel.*), and the *Oratio S. Columbani* (*orat.*) is uncertain. The "Irish-Frankish" monasticism inaugurated by C. was characterized institutionally (in the consciousness of being the real church) by independence from local bishops; it formed a "church within the church," with its own bishops. Above and beyond the general conception of monasticism in the early church that through mortification, obedience, and the carrying of the cross (Mt 10:38) monks achieved an unbloody martyrdom and in this way became conformed to Christ (Phil 2:5-8), C.'s ascetical theology had as a constitutive element the idea that life is the way to the heavenly homeland and that by their *peregrinatio,* or travels, ascetics monks gave witness to our earthly homelessness.

W: *ep., instr., reg. mon., reg. coen., paenit., cel., orat.,* G. S. M. Walker (Dublin, 1957) [text/English trans.]. — *reg. mon., reg. coen., paenit.,* A. de Vogüé (Bégrolles-en-Mauges, 1989) [French trans./comm.].
L: A. Angenendt, C.: TRE 8:159-162. — idem, Monachi Peregrini (Munich, 1972), 124-175. — R. Baltot, Mépris du monde: RevSR 35 (1961) 356-368. — L. Bieler, Classics in Celtic Ireland (Cambridge, 1971), 45-49. — J. O'Caroll, Chronology: IThQ 24 (1957) 76-95. — H. P. Clarke, M. Brennan (ed.), C. (Oxford, 1981). — P. Engelbert, Skriptorium: RBen 78 (1968) 220-260. — P. T. R. Gray, M. W. Herren, Three Chapters Controversy: JThS 45 (1994) 160-170. — H. Haupt, C.: LMA 3:65-67. — R. Howlett, Two Works: MLJb 28 (1993) 27-46. — P. C. Jacobsen, Carmina: Iren u. Europa 1, ed. H. Löwe (Stuttgart, 1982), 448-459, 465-467. — J. F. Kelly, Letter to Gregory the Great: Institutum Patristicum Augustinianum, Gregorio Magno 1 (Rome, 1991), 213-223. — Mélanges Colombaniens. Actes du Congrès international de Luxeuil 1950 (Paris, 1952). — A. Quacquarelli, Prosa d'arte: VetChr 3 (1966) 5-24. — C. Rohr, Vita Columbani: MIÖG 103 (1995) 229-264. — K. Schäferdiek, C.' Wirken im Frankenreich: Iren u. Europa 1, ed. H. Löwe (Stuttgart, 1982), 171-201. — J. W. Smit, Language and Style (Amsterdam, 1971). — C. Vogel, Pénitence tarifée: RDC 9 (1959) 341-349. — idem, "Libri Paenitentiales" (Turnhout, 1978), 66f.

M. SKEB, OSB

Commentary

The commentary as a literary genre is characterized (a) by its function (explanations of words, objects, and content of an entire book or connected parts of it, for an educated readership or for teaching in school; → Exegesis) and (b) by its form (commenting, word by word or sentence by sentence, on a text divided into lemmas, in an independent work, i.e., a *hypomnēma* or *commentarius*). It must be distinguished, espec. in patristic literature from the → scholion (which deals only with individual problems) and from other exegetical writings (→ homilies, commentaries on problems [*Quaestiones et responsiones, Erōtapokriseis*]). While systematic interpretation of texts can be traced back to the 6th c. B.C.E. in Gk. literature, the *hypomnēmata* of Alexandrian scholars of the 2nd and 1st c. B.C.E. (Aristarchus, Didymus, Theon, commenting on, among others, Homer, the canonical lyrists and tragedians, the Attic prosewriters, the Hellenistic poets) are the first to be regarded as commentaries in

the proper sense, although we have access to them only in later compilations (scholia). Beginning in the Hellen. period (espec. in the schools of Alexandria, Pergamum, and Athens), the commentary became a literary genre (partly in the form of records of oral exegesis in the schools). Beginning in the imperial age commentaries were made on philosophical (espec. Plato and Aristotle) and scientific texts (in medicine, grammar and rhetoric, law), as well as on poetry (now including Lat. poetry).

The primarily historical and grammatical commentary contained first of all (in addition to textual criticism, or *diorthōtikon*) the explanation of words and objects (*exēgētikon*; with citation of parallels and lexical, syntactic, historical, antiquarian, etc. information) and observations on style; this might be followed by a comprehensive (aesthetic, moral, philosophical, theol.) appreciation of the passage. In addition there was a type of commentary that restricted itself almost entirely to a paraphrase or interpretation of content (philosophical commentaries, Donatus, Macrobius, *somn.*). A system for dealing with texts is given in the textbook for instruction in grammar by Dionysius Thrax, a student of Aristarchus (*ars grammatica* 1; hermeneutics). Questions on a text in its entirety (often acc. to a set pattern) were discussed in a prologue (title, arrangement, scope, genre, intention, authenticity, and possibly an overall judgment on the work).

Beginning in the 2nd c. C.E., patristic exegetical literature came into existence, paralleling the development of commentary literature in the teaching of grammar and in the philosophical schools. The methods developed in the pagan tradition and the tools used in the grammatico-rhetorical and content analysis of texts, and consequently the literary form of the commentary (with prologue), were taken over into exegesis of the bibl. text (the explanatory function of the commentary). Here, too, the commentary is addressed to an educated public, including not least pagans, Jews, or heretics, against whom the content of the bibl. writings or a particular interpretation of them is defended (apologetical function). Commentaries, like homilies, often undertake a devotional and parenetic function, although this plays a secondary role in primarily historical and grammatical commentaries.

The commentary on John by → Heracleon, a gnostic (2nd c.), which Origen uses, seems not to have contained much more than explanations of words (glosses). Even the commentaries of → Hippolytus of Rome (preserved almost exclusively in fragments) do not follow strictly the system used in pagan exegesis, but for the most part give general (homily-like) interpretations, without following the text word for word. → Origen was the first of the church fathers consistently to apply pagan commentary techniques (with the emphasis on allegory) to an intended explanation of all the books of the Bible. → Jerome distinguishes among Origen's exegetical writings between commentaries in the narrower sense (*tomoi* or *volumina*) and scholia and homilies (*hom. Orig. in Ezech. praef.*; *in Is. praef.*; *in Matth. praef.*; *ep.* 33.4). Among the Gk. authors of commentaries the following are to be singled out: → Didymus the Blind, → Eusebius Caes., → Apollinaris of Laodicea, → Diodorus of Tarsus, → Theodore Mops., → Theodoret of Cyrrhus; the exegetical writings of the Cappadocians belong to a lesser degree to the category of commentaries. The greater part of the very extensive Gr. patristic commentary literature has not survived in its original form and must be reconstructed from translations or → catenae; in this process it is often impossible to distinguish between commentary, scholion, and homily.

In the Lat. West → Victorinus of Pettau is regarded as the earliest exegete, but only fragments have come down from his (scholionlike?) commentaries. The oldest surviving commentary in Chr. Lat. literature is the commentary on Matthew of → Hilary of Poitiers, which contains hardly any philological and factual explanations and may possibly consist of revised homilies. Even in the commentaries of → Ambrose and → Augustine the boundaries between homily and commentary are often blurred. On the other hand, → Jerome, a student of Donatus, who was a commentator on Virgil, closely follows, in his own commentaries, the scientific rules set down by Origen, whose commentaries Jerome partially translated. The commentaries on Paul of → Marius Victorinus also have a scientific character and often contain lengthy dogm. and phil. excursuses. → Ambrosiaster brings an interest in philosophy and a knowledge of factual matters into his commentaries on Paul. Other composers of Lat. commentaries are: → Pelagius, → Julian of Eclanum, → Apponius, → Arnobius the Younger, → Reticius of Autun, → Fortunatian of Aquileia, and → Gregory of Elvira.

From the 5th c. on, commentators on the Bible limited themselves for the most part to excerpts and compilations of existing commentaries (→ catenae). In the Middle Ages, however, and on into the Renaissance not only the bibl. writings (→ Cassiodorus; schools of the eastern Roman empire) but pagan authors and secular literature were the subjects of independent commentaries. Along with other schoolbooks (manuals, dictionaries, compendia) commentaries were the most important form of scholarly literature (often based on transcripts of lectures) and, as the sciences became specialized from the 12th c. on, were to be found in all areas of learning.

L: J. Assmann, B. Gladigow (ed.), Text u. Kommentar (Munich, 1995) (literature). — G. Bardy, Commentaires patristiques de la Bible: DBS 2:73-103. — A. Di Berardino, B. Studer, Storia della Teologia 1 (Rome, 1992), 367-371. — A. Dihle, Die griech. u. lat. Lit. der Kaiserzeit (Munich, 1989), 519-526. — G. Dorival, Des commentaires de l'Écriture aux chaînes: Le monde grec ancien et la Bible, ed. C. Mondésert (Paris, 1984), 361-386. — H. Erbse, D. Fehling, Scholien: LAW, 2723-2726. — J. Geffcken, Entstehung u. Wesen des griech. wissenschaftlichen K.'s: Hermes 67 (1932) 397-412. — R. Gryson, D. Szmatula, Les commentaires patristiques sur Isaïe: REAug 36 (1990) 3-41. — A. Gudeman, Scholien: PRE 2A/1:625-705. — I. Hadot, Les introductions aux commentaires: Les règles de l'interprétation, ed. M. Tardieu (Paris, 1987), 99-122. — E. Lamberz, Form des philosophischen K.'s: Proclus, ed. J. Pépin, H. D. Saffrey (Paris, 1987), 1-10. — B. Neuschäfer, Origenes als Philologe (Basel, 1987). — R. Pfeiffer, Geschichte der klassischen Philologie (Munich, 1978) (= History of Classical Scholarship [Oxford, 1968]). — B. Sandkühler, Die frühen Dantek.e (Munich, 1967). — C. Schäublin, Methode u. Herkunft der Antiochenischen Exegese (Cologne, 1974). — R. Schlieben, Chr. Theologie u. Philologie in der Spätantike (Berlin, 1974). — G. Scholten, Titel — Gattung — Sitz im Leben: FS E. Dassmann (Münster, 1996), 254-269. — H. Schreckenberg, Exegese I: RAC 6:1174-1194. — H. J. Sieben, Kirchenväterhomilien zum NT (Den Haag, 1991), 185-201. — P. Siniscalco, La teoria e la tecnica del commentario: ASEs 5 (1988) 225-238. — G. Zuntz, Die Aristophanes-Scholien der Papyri (Berlin, 1975) = Byz. 13 (1938) 631-690; 14 (1939) 545-613.

T. FUHRER

Commodian

Very little is known of the life of C., a poet; thus his homeland and place of activity (North Africa?) are unknown. The son of pagan parents, C. turned late to Christianity; whether, as one codex asserts, he was really an *episcopus*, cannot be decided. The 5th-c. date given for his life by H. Brewer, among others, was refuted by K. Thraede, who rightly places C.'s work in the middle of the 3rd c. As a result, C. must be regarded as one of the first Chr. poets of the Lat. West.

C. was well acquainted with ancient pagan literature, espec. Virgil; his poems contain colloquial elements and are written in verses that take the dactylic hexameter as a model but are neither purely quantitative nor purely accentual. C. composed two works that combine (apologetic) polemics and catechesis: (1) *Instructiones* (*instr.*), a collection of eighty epigrams, which, with two exceptions (1.35 and 2.15, which are abecedaries), are acrostic in form. Book 1 mocks, among others, some divine figures such as Saturn, Jupiter, and Bacchus; it also attacks judaizing pagans (espec. 1.24 and 1.37) and Jews (1.38-40). In the second book, apostates from Christianity are urged to return to the true faith, while the faithful generally or specific groups (catechumens, penitents, matrons, deacons) are exhorted to carry out their duties and fight against the vices. (2) The *Carmen apologeticum adversus Iudaeos et gentes* (*apol.*) contains 1,060 verses and was given its name by the first editor, J. B. Pitra (1852). One codex (*Philipsianus*) does not name the author, but linguistic and material correspondences with *instr.* make the attribution to C. certain. The poem begins with an explanation of the nature of God, continues with thoughts on the incarnation of God, and ends with a description of the last judgment. Jews and pagans are exhorted to conversion. In both works C. prophesies that when the world is 6,000 years old, it will end and be subjected to the judgment of God.

W: B. Dombart, CSEL 15. — J. Martin, CCL 128. — *instr.*, J. Durel (Paris, 1912) [text/French trans./comm.]. — *apol.*, J. B. Pitra, Spicilegium Solesmense 1 (Paris, 1852), 28-49. — A. Salvatore (Turin, 1977) [text/Italian trans./comm.].
L: B. Baldwin, Some Aspects of C.: Illinois Classical Studies 14 (1989) 331-346. — H. Brewer, Kommodian v. Gaza, ein arelatensischer Laiendichter aus der Mitte des fünften Jh. (Paderborn, 1906). — P. Gruszka, Kommodian u. seine sozialen Ansichten: Klio 66 (1984) 230-256. — J. Günther, Geschichtskonzeptionelles u. soziales Denken des chr.-lat. Schriftstellers Kommodian, Diss. (Leipzig, 1983) (summary in: Ethnographisch-Archäologische Zeitschrift 26 [1985] 681-687). — E. Heck, Iuppiter-Iovis bei C.: VigChr 30 (1976) 72-76. — H. A. M. Hoppenbrouwers, C., poète chrétien (Nijmegen, 1964) (Graecitas et Latinitas Christianorum Primaeva, Suppl. 2:47-88). — V. Loi, C. nella crisi teologica ed ecclesiologica del IIIo secolo: La poesia tardoantica, tra retorica, teologia e politica (Messina, 1984), 187-207. — J. Martin, Studien u. Beiträge zur Erklärung u. Zeitbestimmung C.s (Leipzig, 1913), TU 30/4:1-142). — idem, C.: Traditio 13 (1957) 1-71. — I. Opelt, Ein Baustein der Dichtungen C.': Die Disticha Pseudo-Catonis: eadem, Paradeigmata poetica christiana (Düsseldorf, 1988), 138-147. — H. Schreckenberg, Juden u. Judentum in der altkirchlichen lat. Poesie: FS H. Koch (Leiden, 1979), 81-124. — K. Thraede, Beiträge zur Datierung C.': JAC 2 (1959) 90-114.

S. Döpp

Conon of Tarsus

C. (or Konon) was bishop of Tarsus and a defender of tritheism in the second half of the 6th c. In the time of Patriarch John III he and Eugene of Seleucia

defended the tritheist position of → John Philoponus in religious disputations in Constantinople. But C., again like Eugene, opposed Philoponus's teaching on the resurrection. He formed a teaching of his own on the resurrection, which found followers among the so-called Cononites, but had already been forgotten by the end of the 6th c. Of C.'s writings only the *Epistula ad eorum asseclas* has come down in a Syr. fragment.

W: G. Furlani, Un florilegio antitriteistico in lingua siriaca: AIVS 83/2 (1923/24) 671-673 [Italian trans.].
L: H.-G. Beck, Kirche u. theol. Lit. (Munich, ²1977), 394. — A. Grillmeier, Jesus der Christus 2/4 (Freiburg i.Br., 1990, 141-144 (English, Christ in Christian Tradition, vol. 2/4 [London, 1996]). — E. Honigmann, Évêques et évêchés monophysites (Leuven/Louvain, 1951), 179-187. — A. Van Roey, Un traité cononite contre la doctrine de Jean Philopon sur la résurrection: FS M. Geerard 1 (Wetteren, 1984), 123-139.

B. R. Suchla

Consentius Balearius

At the beginning of the 5th c., C., a lay theologian, was fighting a heretical movement in the Balearic Islands (Minorca?). In the process he wrote to → Augustine for advice, asking what means were suitable and allowable in fighting heretics. C. also presented the bishop of Hippo with the results of his own theol. efforts and asked him to critique them. Of this correspondence three letters of C. (Aug., *ep.* 119, winter 410/411; Aug., *ep.* 11* *Divj.*; 12* *Divj.*) and two answers from Augustine (*ep.* 120, 205) are known. In 420 Augustine addressed a work *Contra mendacium* to C.: C. (Augustine said) should not use lies in combating heretics but rather, with the help of theol. writings, respond to their godless teachings with Chr. truth (*c. mend.* 6.11). C. cannot be said with certainty to be the author of *Liber XXI Sententiarum*.

W: *Aug. ep.* 119, A. Goldbacher, CSEL 34/2:698-704. — *ep.* 11* *Divj.*, *ep.* 12* *Divj.*, J. Divjak, CSEL 88:51-80. — Liber XXI Sententiarum, PL 40:725-732.
L: J. Amengual i Batle, Origens del cristianisme a les Balears (Palma de Mallorca, 1991). — C. Lepelley (ed.), Les lettres de St. Augustin découvertes par J. Divjak (Paris, 1983). — J. Wankenne, C.: AugL 1:1236-1239.

E. Reichert

Consolatio

In a broader sense, the literature of consolation—*consolatio*—includes writings that offer intellectual help in various adversities (Cicero, *Tusc.* 3.81); in a narrower sense, it consists of writings meant to console in a bereavement. It includes several literary genres: philosophical essays on death, in which instructions are given for the easing of sorrow; specific letters of comfort to individuals or groups on occasion of a death; comfort in poetic form as well as funeral orations which aim, among other things, to give comfort. Comfort is given by precepts (*praecepta*) and examples (*exempla*). The consoler draws upon the fund of commonplaces handed down since Hellen. times.

In contrast to the vague and disorganized pagan *consolatio,* the Chr. *consolatio* has at its disposal a genuine, powerful means of consolation, namely, the prospect of life after death (see 1 Thess 4:13) and can offer a clearly greater certainty of consolation. Everlasting life in the next world is a promise and a good to be striven for. Alongside natural commonplaces such as "Death is the natural consequence of being born," there are properly Chr. ones, such as "What does the loss of a beloved human being count for in comparison with the death of Christ?" The latter, however, do not completely replace the former but combine with them in a new synthesis. Pagan arguments are turned into Christian when the Platonic "Live in order to die" becomes the Chr. "Die in order to live." The *exempla* are taken from the Bible, sometimes as supplementary.

Unlike pagan rationalism, the Chr. *consolatio* addresses both heart and mind. The points of departure for the Chr. *consolatio* are the *De mortalitate* of → Cyprian of Carthage, in which there is a somewhat harsh warning to cease grieving, and *carm.* 31 of → Paulinus of Nola. The contribution of → Ambrose is chiefly his funeral orations (*De excessu fratris,* and others) with their tone of compassion; → Jerome composed ten great letters of consolation (espec. *ep.* 60); for → Augustine, along with *conf.* 9.12.32, see espec. *ep.* 92; 259; 263, and *serm.* 172 and 173, which are important for the funeral liturgy. The *consolatio* that was best known in the Middle Ages, Boethius's *consolatio philosophiae*, contains no specifically Chr. elements.

L: M. Biermann, Die Leichenreden des Ambrosius (Stuttgart, 1995). — R. C. Gregg, Consolation Philosophy (Philadelphia, 1975). — G. Guttilla, Tematica cristiana e pagana nell' evoluzione finale della c. di San Girolamo: ALCP 17/18 (1980/1981) 87-152. — idem, La fase iniziale della c. latina cristiana: ALCP 21/22 (1984/85) 108-215. — L. F. Pizzolato, La c. cristiana per la morte nel sec. IV: CClCr (1985) 441-474. — J. H. D. Scourfield, Consoling Heliodorus: A commentary on Jerome, Letter 60 (Oxford, 1993).

T. KURTH

Constantine of Assiut

C. was active in the second half of the 6th c. and is regarded as one of the most important literary figures in the Coptic church during the late anti-Chalcedonian phase. C. visited the holy land while a monk; at about the turn of the 6th-7th c. he was consecrated bishop of the central Egyptian city of Lycopolis (Assiut). His many writings contributed a great deal to the spiritual renewal of the church before the Arab invasion. Two Copt. poems in praise of Athanasius (*enc. in Ath.*) have come down to us, as have two others, in Coptic and Arabic, in praise of Claudius, a martyr (*enc. in Cl.*). In addition, there are unpublished Arab. homilies (*hom.*) on the fallen soul and John the martyr.

W: *enc. in Ath.,* T. Orlandi, CSCO 349f. [text/Latin trans.]. — *enc. in Cl.,* G. Godron, PO 35:4 [text/Latin trans.]. — E. Amélineau, Contes et romans 2 (Paris, 1888) [French trans. of the Arabic text]. — *hom.,* G. Graf, Geschichte 1 (Rome, 1944), 466 [Arabic mss.].
L: R. G. Coquin, K. Bishop of Asyut: SOC. C 16 (1981) 151-170 — G. Garitte, K. évêque d'Assiout: FS W. Crum (Boston, 1950), 287-304.

P. BRUNS

Constantine, Deacon

C. lived probably between 550 and 650. He was deacon and chartophylax (archivist) of Hagia Sophia in Constantinople. He composed a *Laudatio omnium martyrum* (*laud.*) from which several passages in favor of the veneration of images were read at the Council of Nicaea in 787. This speech also serves as a reading for the feast of All Saints in the Byz. liturgy.

W: PG 88:479-528.
L: H.-G. Beck, Kirche u. theol. Lit. (Munich, 1959), 399. — A. Ehrhard, Überlieferung u. Bestand (Leipzig, 1937-52), 2:17, 26, 269 and frequently.

C. BOLL

Constantine I (the Great), Emperor

C., Feb. 27, 272 (?) to May 22, 337, was raised at the court of Diocletian, where he probably received a philosophical formation. Proclaimed Caesar of the West by the army in 306, he waged an unprecedented war of conquest to reach sole leadership in 312; from 312 on he openly trusted in the help of the Chr. God. He favored Christianity from 311 on and intervened in eccles. controversies in both West (Donatism) and East (Arianism) in order to secure order.

Ca. forty letters (*ep.*) and three speeches (*or.*) have

been handed down, mainly by Eusebius (*h.e.* and *v.C.*), Athanasius, and Optatus. His opening address at the Council of Nicaea has come down in two versions in Eusebius, *v.C.* 3.12, and Gelasius of Cyzicus, *h.e.* 2.7.1-41 (from 40 on; Theodoret, *h.e.* 1.7.12). Also preserved is the *Oratio ad sanctorum coetum* (*or. s. c.*), which forms an appendix to Eusebius's *v.C.* The speeches are very different stylistically, with the *or. s. c.* especially being different from the two opening addresses. The authenticity of the speeches is often denied, but since 1954 there has been a more positive acceptance of the *or. s. c.*

The *or. s. c.* was delivered on a Good Friday or Holy Saturday (1.1); place and year are disputed. In recent literature it was dated first to 317 in Sardica, then to 321-324 in Thessalonica, or 325 in Byzantium or Antioch. In any case, a late date is more probable on internal grounds.

The *or. s. c.* was originally composed in Latin and survives only in a (bad) Gr. translation. The beginning is mutilated. It is addressed to the "greatly loved teachers [= bishops] and all my other friends" (1.1) and gives an explanation, pervaded by a strong apologetical tendency, of the monotheistic, philosophically marked convictions of the author and of his strong faith in providence. A lot of space is given to a proof from prophecy, taken from the Sibylline books and the fourth *Eclogue* of Virgil, which is here given a Chr. interpretation for the first time. The superiority of the Chr. religion is shown by the virtues of Christianity and the victories of C.; but all the credit belongs to God. The text seems untouched by the christological controversies. Numerous trains of thought are related to those of → Lactantius. The literary genre is difficult to determine. In any case, the *or. s. c.* is only a secondary source for any evaluation of C.

W: *ep.*, H. Dörries, Das Selbstzeugnis Kaiser K.s: AAWG. PH 3:34 (1954) 16-128 [comm.]. — H. Kraft, Kaiser K.s religiöse Entwicklung (Tübingen, 1955), 160-262 [German trans./comm.]. — G. C. Hansen, Eine fingierte Ansprache K.s auf dem Konzil v. Nikaia: ZAC 2 (1998) 173-198 [text/German trans./comm.]. — *or. s. c.*, I. A. Heikel, GCS 7:149-192. — idem, TU 3.36.4 (Leipzig, 1911), 64-66 [text]. — F. Winkelmann, Annotationes zu einer neuen Edition der Tricennatsreden Eusebs u. der or. s. c. in GCS: FS M. G. (Wetteren, 1984), 1-7. — J. M. Pfättisch, BKV² 9:191-272 [German trans.]. — H. Dörries, loc. cit., 129-161 [comm.]. — H. Kraft, loc. cit., 263-272 [German trans./comm.]. — *or. s. c.* 18-21, A. Kurfess, J. D. Gauger, Sibyllinische Weissagungen (Darmstadt, 1998), 230-251 [text].
L: T. D. Barnes, The Emperor C.'s Good Friday Sermon: JThS NS 27 (1976) 414-423. — idem, K. and Eusebius (Cambridge, Mass., 1981), 73-76, 271, 323-325, 403, 405. — A. Bolhuis, Vergilius' Vierde Ecloga in de Oratio C. ad sanctorum coetum, Diss. (Amsterdam, 1950). — idem, Die

Rede K.s an die Versammlung der Heiligen u. Lactantius' Divinae Institutiones: VigChr 10 (1956) 25-32. — L. Coronati, Osservazioni sulla tradizione greca della IV ecloga di Virgilio: CCLCR 5 (1984) 71-84. — D. de Decker, Le "Discours à l'Assemblée des Saints": Lactance et son temps, ed. J. Fontaine, M. Perrin (Paris, 1978), 75-89. — idem, Evocation de la Bible dans le "Discours à l'Assemblée des Saints": JSOT. S 11 (1979) 133-143. — H. A. Drake, Suggestions of Date in C.'s Oration to the Saints: AJP 106 (1985) 335-349. — idem, C. and the bishops (Baltimore, 2000). — C. T. H. R. Ehrhardt, Constantinian Documents in Gelasius of Cyzicus' Ecclesiastical History: JAC 23 (1980) 48-57. — R. P. C. Hanson, The Oratio ad sanctos attributed to the Emperor C. and the Oracle at Daphne: JThS NS 24 (1973) 505-511. — I. A. Heikel, Kritische Beiträge zu den K.-Schriften des Eusebius: TU 3.36.4 (Leipzig, 1911), 2-49. — HLL 5:59. — D. J. Ison, The Constantinian Oration to the Saints. Authorship and Background, Diss. (London, 1985). — G. Löschke, Das Syntagma des Gelasius: RM 61 (1906) 57-61. — B. Luiselli, Il profetismo Virgiliano nella cultura veterocristiana: Sandalion 6/7 (1983/84) 134-149. — S. Mazzarino, La data dell'or. s. c.: idem, Antico, tardo-antico ed èra Costantiniana 1 (Bari, 1974), 99-150. — C. Monteleone, L'egloga quarta da Virgilio a C. (Manduria, 1975). — J. Quasten, Patrology 3 (Westminster, 1986 = 1960), 324-326 [literature]. — G. Radke, Die Deutung der 4. Ekloge Vergils durch Kaiser K.: Présence de Virgile, ed. R. Chevallier (Paris, 1978), 147-159. — I. C. Skeat, Appendix to A. H. M. Jones, Notes on the Genuineness of the Constantinian Documents in Eusebius's Life of C.: JEH 5 (1954) 196-200. — A. Wlosok, Zwei Beispiele frühchr. "Vergilrezeption": 2000 Jahre Vergil, ed. V. Pöschl (Wiesbaden, 1983), 63-86 = AAAr 25 (1984) 7-41 = eadem, Res humanae — res divinae (Heidelberg, 1990), 437-459.

H. R. SEELIGER

Constantine of Laodicea

C. was *magister militiae* before becoming bishop of Laodicea after 510. In 519 Justinian I deposed and exiled this leading Monophysite because of his opposition to the Council of Chalcedon. Even in exile he took part in Monophysite gatherings. His works, preserved in Syriac, have not been published (*Ep. ad Marcum Isauricum*, *Ep. episcoporum orthodoxorum*, *Canones*).

W: F. Nau, Littérature canonique: RCO 14 (1909) 39-48 (*ep. episcoporum*); 113-115 (*canones*); 116f. (*ep. ad Marcum*); 117-119 (*canones*) [French trans.].
L: E. Honigmann, Évêques et évêchés monophysites (Leuven/Louvain, 1951), 36-38. — E. Venables, K.: DCB 1:659.

B. WINDAU

Constantius of Lyons

Between 475 and 480, in Marseilles, C., an educated cleric (b. 410/420), composed the life of Germanus of Auxerre, at the request of Bishop Patiens of Lyons; he published it at the request of Bishop Censurius of

Auxerre. The life, which was influenced by → Eucherius of Lyons, provided a model for subsequent western hagiography.

W: R. Borius, SC 112. — K. S. Frank, Frühes Mönchtum (Zurich, 1975), 2:59-96 [German trans.].
L: W. Gessel, Germanus: RQ 65 (1970) 1-14. — J. Gruber, Constantius: LMA 3, 173.

O. KAMPERT

Consultationes Zacchaei et Apollonis

The anonymous composer of this dialogue (*CZA*) (who was mistakenly identified with → Firmicus Maternus) was probably born in the second half of the 4th c. and may have been an imperial official with rhetorical training. He came from a monastic background as can be seen from the description of a monasticism under attack (3.3). In addition, his membership in the circle of friends around → Sulpicius Severus is indicated by his expectation of a proximate coming of the Antichrist (3.7-8), his criticism of the veneration paid by Christians to the images of Chr. emperors (1.28), and the information he gives about the presence of Christ's footprints on the place of the ascension and the preservation of his burial shroud (1.21). The years shortly after 410 (invasion of Italy by the Goths) may be suggested as the date of the work. The collapse of Roman military power, the extreme eschat. expectation, and the acute consciousness that monks, i.e., the elite of Christianity, were hated even by their fellow believers, was the occasion for his addressing this instructional work to all despisers of the ascetical life. Under the influence of → Lactantius and → Tertullian, he presents the Chr. religion as a law that demands both knowledge of God and righteous deeds. The *CZA* are the only dialogue from Chr.-Lat. antiquity that gives a comprehensive description of the Chr. faith in questions and answers.

W: PL 20:1071-1166. — J. L. Feiertag, W. Steinmann, SC 401, 402. — G. Morin, I. Firmici Materni CZA: FlorPatr 39 (1939) [text].
L: G. M. Colombas, Sobre el autor de las CZA: St Mon 14 (1972) 7-14. — J. L. Feiertag, Les CZA (Fribourg, Switzerland, 1990). — G. Morin, Ein zweites chr. Werk des Firmicus Maternus. Die CZA: HJ 37 (1916) 229-266. — A. Reatz, Das theol. System der CZA (Freiburg i.Br., 1920).

J. L. FEIERTAG

Contra Origenem de visione Isaiae

In 1901 A. Amelli provided the *editio princeps* of a Lat. commentary on Isa 6:1-3(7), which he had dis-covered in mss. *Casin.* 342 and 345; it had come down without title or author, and he gave it the title *Tractatus contra Origenem de visione Isaiae*. This work, the original extent and genre of which are not clear, is characterized by a determined anti-Origenism in its hermeneutico-exegetical and dogm. arguments. With continual reference to → Origen's interpretation of the vision of the seraphs (first homily on Isaiah) the author criticizes its unhistorical, that is, subjective allegorizing and rejects Origen's identification of the two seraphim with the Son and the Spirit as blasphemous subordinationism. Scholarly research into the riddle of the authorship of the text has provisionally come down in favor of → Theophilus of Alexandria and → Jerome, the latter being the Lat. translator, the former the author of the Gr. original, which was written ca. 402 and later lost.

W: A. M. Amelli, SpicCas 3/2 (Montecassino, 1901), I-XIV, 387-399 [text]. — idem, S. Hieronymi tractatus contra Origenem (Montecassino, 1901) [text]. — G. Morin, AMar 3 (1903) XVIII-XIX, 103-122 [text] (standard edition).
L: B. Altaner, Wer ist der Verfasser des Tractatus?: ThRv 42 (1943) 147-151 (= idem, Kleine patristische Schriften [Berlin, 1967], 483-488). — F. Cavallera, St. Jérôme 1 (Paris, 1922), 81-86. — L. Chavoutier, Querelle origeniste: VigChr 14 (1960) 9-14. — E. A. Clark, Origenist Controversy (Princeton, 1992), 118. — F. Diekamp, Rez. von Amelli: LitRdsch 27 (1901) 293-295. — W. Dietsche, Didymos v. Alexandrien als Verfasser der Schrift über die Seraphenvision (Freiburg i.Br., 1942). — A. Favale, Teofilo d'Alessandria (Turin, 1958), 23f. — R. Gryson, D. Szmatula, Commentaires patristiques sur Isaie: REAug 36 (1990) 32-33.

B. NEUSCHÄFER

Corippus

Roman epic poet Flavius Cresconius Corippus (C.) was a native of Africa and lived in the 6th c. After the end of the Moorish war (548) he composed the epic *Iohannis* (*Ioh.*) in praise of the imperial field marshal; its eight books are important as a hist. source and because of their Chr. use of Virgil. At the suggestion of quaestor Anastasius, to whom C. dedicated a short poem (*Anast.*), he wrote ca. 567 a panegyric in four books of Emperor Justin II (*Iust.*). We know only the titles of the three bibl. epics which C. wrote.

W: *Anast./Iust.*, A. Cameron (London, 1976) [text/comm.]. — S. Antès (Paris, 1981) [text/French trans.]. — *Iust.*, U. J. Stache (Berlin, 1976) [comm.]. — *Ioh.*, J. Diggle, F. R. D. Goodyear (Cambridge, 1970) [text]. — *Ioh.* (B. 1), M. A. Vinchesi (Naples, 1983) [text/comm.].
L: H. Hofmann, C.: VigChr 43 (1989) 361-377. — L. Krestan, K. Winkler, C.: RAC 3:424-429. — M. Lausberg, Parcere: JAC 32 (1989) 105-126.

B. BREILMANN

Cornelius of Rome

After the martyrdom of Fabian (Jan. 250) during the Decian persecution, C. was elected bishop of Rome in March 251, after Rome was without a bishop for a year. Novatian, a presbyter, who had been leading the community at the end of that year, had himself elected antibishop. This decision was probably due to C.'s lax attitude, visible even before the election, in the question of how to deal with those who had lapsed during the persecution. In the schism that followed C. was able to win out, thanks in part to support from outside, espec. from Cyprian and Dionysius Alex. In the persecution under Gallus C. was first arrested and then banished to Centumcellae (Civitavecchia). He died in exile in June 253. Cyprian already described him as a martyr. Acc. to the → *Liber pontificalis* (22) C. was a Roman by birth. Despite all his efforts, Cyprian could say in C.'s favor only that he had passed through all the eccles. offices (*ep.* 75.8). The hatred with which C. attempted to blacken Novatian in the eyes of Fabius Alex. (see Eus., *h.e.* 6.43.5-22) does not show C. in a good light. In addition to his decision in the matter of penance, his most important contribution to the history of early Christianity was the list of distressed persons in the Roman community (preserved in Eus., *h.e.* 6.43.11ff.), which allows inferences as to the size and social structure of the community. Two letters of C. to Cyprian are preserved in the latter's correspondence (*ep.* 49; 50).

W: Cyprian, *ep.* 49, 50. — Eusebius, *h.e.* 6.43.11ff.
L: G. Bardy, Corneille: DHGE 13:891-894. — M. Bévenot, Cyprian and his Recognition of C.: JThS NS 28 (1977) 346-359. — E. Caspar, Geschichte des Papsttums 1 (Tübingen, 1930), 66-70. — H. Hammerich, Taufe u. Askese (Hamburg, 1994), 143-155. — H. J. Vogt, Coetus Sanctorum (Bonn, 1968), 37-56.

H. HAMMERICH

Cosmas the Singer

C., also known as C. Melodus, C. of Jerusalem, C. Hagiopolites, and C. of Majuma, was an adoptive brother of John Damascene and thus a member of a distinguished Arab-Chr. family of Damascus. Before 700 he and his adoptive brother John were monks in the monastery of St. Sabas near Jerusalem; he became bishop of Majuma near Gaza in 735 and died shortly after 750.

Like John Damascene, C. composed idiomela and canons. The attribution of the surviving songs is uncertain, however, since the common teacher of John and C., a Sicilian monk of the same name, Cosmas (the Elder), is also supposed to have composed hymns. Among C.'s hymns: *Odae* (*od.* 1-11), *Canon in dormitionem BVM* (*can. dorm.*), *Hymni* (*hymn.* 1-7, 9-13), and *Hymnus in sabbato sancto* (*hymn.* 8). C. composed his hymns on the model of the poetry of → Andrew of Crete and → Gregory Naz., on which C. commented in the works *Index historiarum in carminibus Gregorii Nazianzeni* (*ind.*) and *Scholia in Gregorii Nazianzeni carmina* (*schol.*). His hymns were for a long time highly esteemed and in Suidas were still regarded as the summit of all Byz. canon poetry; in the 12th c. Theodore Prodromos wrote a much-noticed commentary, and even today the poems have an assured place in the Orthodox Liturgy of the Hours.

W: *od.* 1-11, PG 98:513-524. — *hymn.* 1-7, 9-13, PG 98:459-485, 489-512. — W. Christ, M. Paranikas, Anthologia Graeca Carminum Christianorum (Hildesheim, 1963 = Leipzig, 1871), 161-180, 183-204 [text]. — *can. dorm.*, W. Christ, M. Paranikas, loc. cit., 180-182 [text]. — *hymn.* 8, PG 98:485-489. — A. Papadopoulos-Kerameus, Análekta Hierosolymitikes Stachyologías 2 (St. Petersburg, 1894), 164 f. [text]. — *ind.*, *schol.*, PG 38:339-680. — Theodoros Prodromos, *comm. in C.*, H. M. Stevenson (Rome, 1888) [comm.].
L: H.-G. Beck, Kirche u. theol. Lit. (Munich, ²1977), 515f. — L. Bernhard, Syr. Rez. von Kanones des K. Hagiopolites, Diss. (Munich, 1951). — T. Detorakis, K. (Athens, 1979).

B. R. SUCHLA

Cosmas, the Traveler to India

C. (Kosmas ho Indikopleustēs) lived in the time of Justinian, came from Egypt (probably Alexandria), and may have been a Nestorian (disputed; C. was a pupil of the Nestorian Catholicos Mar Aba I). He traveled as a trader to, among other places, East Africa and Arabia and may even have reached India or the island of Taprobane (Ceylon; Sri Lanka). After his extensive journeys he lived presumably as a hermit in Alexandria or as a monk in a Sinai monastery and after 550 wrote a Chr. topography (*Christianikē Topographia*) in twelve books on the structure of the world (*top.*), which is presupposed in the work of his contemporary, → John Philoponus (*opif.*). It is possible that the cosmological content of his chief work yielded the name "Cosmas," which is attested only at a late date (initially in an 11th-c. ms.); on the other hand, Cosmas was also a well-known saint of the East. Perhaps the work was first published only anonymously as the "work of a Christian" (*Christianou logos*; see *top.*, prol. 3).

Books 1-4 of the *top.* defend the bibl. picture of the

world. The fifth book, the most extensive of the twelve, deals with questions of introduction to the Bible. These five books were the original content of the work and were dedicated to a Pamphilus of Jerusalem. Books 6-10 were added later in order to dispel misgivings of opponents about the previous books. Book 11 and book 12, which exists only in fragments, were probably taken from other works of C. C. was renowned as "traveler to India" because of the "Description of the living things and trees of India and of the island of Taprobane" in book 11. Scholars disagree on whether he was really there.

C.'s method of interpretation is Syro-Antiochene (emphasis on the literal sense, following Theodore Mops. and the school of Nisibis). As a result, C. finds the structure of the cosmos described in the Bible (espec. in the Octateuch). He defends this bibl. picture of the world and, with the help of countless bibl. citations, attacks the Ptolemaic picture, acc. to which the earth is a ball. C. represents the cosmos in the tradition of the Syro-Antiochene school as a two-story house (after the model of Moses' tent of meeting; see *top.* 2.35f.; 5.20f. with reference to Heb 8:1f., 5; 9:1f., 11f., 24). The earth is the foundation; it is flat and rectangular (see Euphorus, *fr.* 30b). The firmament (first heaven) is built on this rectangle and is a kind of false roof with straight walls. Above it in turn is the heavenly realm (second heaven) to which Christ has ascended and to which the just will follow him.

Espec. important are the many excursuses scattered throughout C.'s work, giving information important for geography and the history of culture and of religion; e.g., on the date of Christmas, baptismal rites, the canonical status of the apostolic letters, the spread of Christianity from Spain to Persia and India, trade relations of the Roman empire with Egypt, India, and China, and the sources of the Nile. C. shows himself a keen observer who carefully distinguishes the sources of his information: personal experiences, other sources, or hearsay. He has a famous description of two inscriptions on a marble stele or statue (*eikōn*; see *top.* 2.58-59) and on a marble throne (see *top.* 2.60-63) in Eth. Adulis (today Tulla) near Massaua (OGIS 1 No. 54 and 99). We receive an impression of his conscientiousness from his description of a unicorn, which, he emphasizes, he did not himself see but knew from statues he saw in an Eth. palace (see *top.* 11.6). Important for the history of art are the miniatures found in the mss. (three complete from the 9th-11th c.) as illustrations of the descriptions.

Other works of C. (a commentary on the Canticle,

a work on astronomy, and a description of the earth) are lost.

W: PG 88:51-476. — E. O. Winstedt (Cambridge, 1909) [text]. — W. Wolska-Conus, SC 141, 159, 197. — J. W. McCrindle (London, 1897) [English trans.].
L: M. Casey, The Fourth Kingdom in C. and the Syrian Tradition: RSLR 25 (1989) 385-403. — E. Frézouls, C. et l'Arabie: L'Arabe préislamique et son environnement historique et culturel. Actes du Colloque de Strasbourg 24-27 Juin 1987, ed. T. Fahd (Leiden, 1989), 441-460. — A. Grillmeier, Jesus der Christus 2/4 (Freiburg i.Br., 1990), 150-165 (English, Christ in Christian Tradition, vol. 2/4 [London, 1996]). — J. D. Madathil, Kosmas der Indienfahrer. Kaufmann, Kosmologe u. Exeget zwischen alexandrinischer u. antiochenischer Theologie (Thaur, 1996). — E. Revel-Neher, Some remarks on the iconographical sources of the Christian topography of C.: Kairos 32/33 (1990-1991) 78-97. — B. Schleissheimer, Kosmas Indikopleustes, Diss. (Munich, 1959). — J. Strzygowski, Der Bilderkreis des griech. Physiologus, des Kosmas Indikopleustes und Oktateuch (Leipzig, 1899). — H. Wada, Aus der Beschreibung der Insel Ceylon in der frühbyz. u. chinesischen Historiographie: Antikerezeption, Antikeverhältnis, Antikebegegnung in Vergangenheit und Gegenwart, ed. J. Dummer, M. Kunze (Stendal, 1983 [1989]), 129-136. — O. Wecker, Kosmas 3: PRE 11/2:1487-1490. — D. P. M. W. Weerakkody, Taprobanê: Ancient Sri Lanka as known to Greeks and Romans (Turnhout, 1997). — W. Wolska, La "Topographie Chrétienne" de C. (Paris, 1962). — eadem, La "Topographie Chrétienne" de C.: Hypothèses sur quelques Thèmes de son Illustration: REB 48 (1990) 155-191.

H. SCHNEIDER

Creed/Explanation of the Creed

Although the NT contains more or less formulaic confessions of faith in Christ (Acts 8:37; 1 Cor 12:13; Rom 10:9; Phil 2:11), as well as binitarian formulas that name the Father and the Son together (1 Cor 8:8) and some that name the Holy Spirit as well (2 Cor 13:14; 1 Cor 12:4), we cannot yet speak of a "confession of faith" as a genre proper. Such confessions arose only in the middle of the 2nd c. with the trinitarian baptismal creed that goes back to Mt 28:19. While the declarative form of confession developed primarily in catechetical instruction (*expositio, traditio, redditio symboli*), such a confession during the celebration of baptism took the form, from the outset, of a question-and-answer dialogue (*credisne? — credo*). As a result, the early confessions of faith often took an interrogatory, not a declarative, form (Justin, *apol.* 61; Irenaeus, *epid.* 3; Tertullian, *spect.* 4; *bapt.* 2; Hippolytus, *trad. ap.* 21). The three main questions regarding the three divine persons were expanded in the course of time by numerous additions, espec. in the second part by more detailed christological explanations.

The earliest attested creed is the old Roman baptismal creed, also known as the Apostles' Creed (*Symbolum apostolorum*) (Ambrose, *ep.* 42.5). This name reflects the idea that the text goes back directly to the apostles, each of whom added a statement to make up the final version (Rufinus, *symb.* 2). The summation of church teaching in this creed was therefore closely connected with the formation of the canon of scripture and with apostolic succession, which was thought to ensure the origin and purity of the faith. Irenaeus and Tertullian were already familiar with the normative concept of a *Regula veritatis sive fidei* (*kanōn tēs alētheias*), which at that time had not yet been completely formulated and was used to defend against gnosticism and modalism. The early Roman creed first appears as a continuous text in Hippolytus (*trad. ap.* 21), and its composition is probably to be dated to the second half of the 2nd c.; but in Hippolytus's time the text was not yet completely determined. Only in the first half of the 3rd c. does the early Roman creed in its Gr. original appear in a set textual form (Epiphanius, *haer.* 72.3). In addition, there was a Lat. translation, attested in Rufinus (*symb.* 2), which was accepted by the churches of the western provinces of the empire and there received small additions and changes. The *textus receptus* of the Apostles' Creed in use today goes back to a provincial descendant of the early Roman creed that is attested chiefly in the Gallican liturgical books and became obligatory as a result of Charlemagne's liturgical reform.

In contrast to the West, in which the Roman creed achieved an unchallenged dominance from the middle of the 3rd c. on, the eastern creeds show a great variety depending on the special traditions of the spiritual centers in Caesarea, Jerusalem, Antioch, and Alexandria, but they also had in common a threefold division based on Mt 28:19 and the use of typical bibl. formulas.

W: A. Hahn, G. L. Hahn, Bibliothek der Symbole (Hildesheim, 1962 = Berlin, ³1897). — H. Lietzmann, Symbole der alten Kirche (Berlin, ⁵1961). — C. P. Caspari, Quellen zur Geschichte des Taufsymbols (Brussels, 1964 = Brussels, 1866-1875). — C. H. Turner, EOMJA (Oxford, 1899-1930).
L: H. v. Campenhausen, Bekenntnis im Urchristentum: ZNW 63 (1972) 210-253. — R. P. C. Hanson, Tradition in the Early Church (London, 1962). — F. Kattenbusch, Das apostolische Symbol (Hildesheim, 1962 = Leipzig, 1894-1900). — J. N. D. Kelly, Altchr. G.e (Göttingen, ²1993). — W. Kinzig, C. Markschies, M. Vinzent, Tauffragen u. Bekenntnis. Studien zur sog. Traditio Apostolica, zu den Interrogationes de fide und zum Röm (Genf, Berlin et al., 1999). — W. Kinzig, M. Vinzent, Recent Research on the Origin of the Creed: JThS 50 (1999) 535-559. — M. T. Nadeau, Foi de l'église (Paris, 1988). — M. Simonetti, Ortodossia ed eresia: VetChr 29 (1992) 359-389. — H. E. Turner, Pattern of Christian Truth (New York, 1978). — M. Wiles, Making of Christian Doctrine (London, 1967).

The earlier synodal creeds, the first of which are attested as early as the 3rd c., arose as a result of anti-heretical additions and explanations to local baptismal creeds. They served primarily as proof of orthodoxy, since they were presented to the bishops for their signature. Taking as a basis the Syro-Palestinian baptismal creed and inserting anti-Arian elements into the second, christological article, the Council of Nicaea (325) composed the first creed binding on the entire imperial church: the Nicene Creed. In the following years this creed was vehemently contested, but in the form of the Constantinopolitan Creed (also known as the Nicene-Constantinopolitan Creed), it had a decisive influence on the history of dogma. While the Council of Nicaea confessed belief in the Holy Spirit, but without further explanation, the Council of Constantinople (381) specified the third article in regard to the Spirit being God and to his revelation in creation and salvation history. The Council of Chalcedon (451) did not formulate a new creed, but raised the Council of Constantinople, which had been less an imperial council than a local eastern synod, to the rank of an ecumenical council and accepted the "Creed of the 150 Fathers of Constantinople" as binding. Beginning in 451, the text of this creed was widely received. In the Gr. and Lat. churches it gradually replaced the traditional baptismal creeds; but even the non-Chalcedonian eccles. communities accepted this creed in its earlier Nicene form, so that it must be seen, along with the scriptures, as the basic document of undivided Christendom. Under the Monophysite patriarch Peter the Fuller of Antioch (476-488) and the likewise Monophysite-minded Patriarch Timothy of Constantinople (511-517) the Nicene Creed became part of the liturgy of the Mass in the East. Toward the end of the 6th c. the creed is detectable in the Lat. liturgy of the Spaniards, then of the Irish, and later also of the Franks, where with its addition of the *Filioque* it replaced the old Roman creed in many places.

W: G. L. Dossetti, Il simbolo di N e di C (Rome, 1967) [Greek text/Italian trans./comm.]. — A. Vööbus, New Sources for the Symbol: VigChr 26 (1972) 291-296 [Syriac text/English trans.]. — O. Braun, De Sancta Nicaena Synodo (Münster, 1898) [Syriac text]. — F. Haase, Kopt. Quellen zum Konzil von Nizäa (Paderborn, 1920) [Coptic text]. — F. Schultheß, Syr. Kanones (Berlin, 1908) [Syriac text]. — A. Vööbus, CSCO 307/317, 439/440 [Syriac text/English trans.]. — N. Akinian, R. P. Casey, Two

Armenian Creeds: HThR 25 (1931) 143-151 [Armenian text/English trans.].

L: L. Abramowski, Konzil v. Konstantinopel: ThPh 67 (1992) 481-514. — P. T. Camelot, Ephesus u. Chalcedon (Mainz, 1963). — A. de Halleux, Cyrille, Théodoret et le Filioque: RHE 74 (1979) 597-625. — H. Kaufhold, Griech.-Syr. Listen: OrChr 77 (1993) 1-96. — D. Lissón, Filioque im westgotischen Hispanien: AHC 16 (1984) 286-299. — I. Ortiz de Urbina, Nizäa u Konstantinopel (Mainz, 1964). — L. Perrone, Von Nicaea nach Chalcedon: Geschichte der Konzilien, ed. G. Alberigo (Düsseldorf, 1993), 22-134. — A. M. Ritter, Das Konzil v. Konstantinopel (Göttingen, 1965). — idem, Noch einmal: ThPh 68 (1993) 553-560. — E. Schwartz, N u. C in Chalcedon: ZNW 25 (1926) 38-88. — R. Staats, Glaubensbekenntnis von Nizäa/Konstantinopel (Darmstadt, 1996). — idem, Pontius Pilatus: ZThK 84 (1987) 493-513. — idem, Röm. Tradition: VigChr 44 (1990) 209-221.

Other creeds and explanations of the creed have survived from numerous smaller synods of the early Chr. period. It is often impossible, however, to distinguish between a creed proper and an explanation of the creed (*ekthesis pisteōs, expositio fidei sive symboli*). This is true of the many Arian creeds of the 4th c., the creeds which individual theologians, e.g., Athanasius (*ep. ad Jov.*) and Damasus (*conf. fid.*), presented as proof of their orthodoxy, and, not least, the numerous anonymous commentaries on the creed. In Italy there is an anonymous 4th-c. commentary on the creed, (*comm. in symb.*); another is attributed to Jerome (*Explanatio fidei ad Cyrillum*). Anti-Arian traits can be seen in Gallican creeds of the 4th and 5th c. that begin with *Clemens Trinitas* (*Clem. Trin.*), one of which is also known as *Confessio S. Martini* (*conf. Mart.*). Other important anonymous creeds (*symb.*) belong to the Carolingian period.

W: Athanasius, *ep. ad Jov.*, H. Lietzmann, Apollinaris v. Laodicea (Tübingen, 1904), 250-253 [Greek text]. — idem, J. Flemming, Apollinaristische Schriften (Berlin, 1904), 33f. [Syriac text]. — H. Guerrier, Symbole de s. Athanase: ROC 20 (1915-1917) 68-76, 133-141 [Ethiopic text/French trans.]. — Damasus, *conf. fid.*, C. Turner, EOMJA (Oxford, 1913), 281-296 [Latin text]. — R. Riedinger, Recensio graeca: Byz. 54 (1984) 634-637 [Greek text]. — *comm. in symb.*, C. Turner, loc. cit. (Oxford, 1913), 329-354 [text]. — *expl. fid. ad Cyr.*, C. Turner, loc. cit. (Oxford, 1913), 354-367 [text]. — *Clem. Trin.*, J. A. de Aldama, Clemens Trinitas: Gr. 14 (1933) 485-500. — *conf. Mart.*, F. Stegmüller, Trinitätssymbolum: FS A. Stohr (Mainz, 1960), 151-164 [text]. — O. Stegmüller, Martin v. Tours: RBen 76 (1966) 177-230. — *symb.*, C. Caspari, Quellen (Brussels, 1964 = 1866-75), 290-308 [text]. — J. L. Jacobi, Unbekanntes Symbol: ZKG 6 (1884) 282-290 [text]. — M. Parmentier, Jacobi's unkown Creed: Bijdr. 52 (1991) 354-378.

The creed of Toledo exerted a great influence in Spain and in the rest of the Lat. West. It exists in two versions and was originally inspired by anti-Arianism, but was then frequently revised to serve against the Priscillianists.

L: J. A. de Aldama, El símbolo Toledano (Rome, 1934). — C. García Goldáraz, El códice Lucense (Rome, 1954). — J. Madoz, Le symbole du XIe conc. de Tolède (Leuven/Louvain, 1938). — idem, El símbolo del Conc. XVI de Toledo (Madrid, 1946). — J. de Pérez, La Cristología en los Símbolos Toledanos (Rome, 1939).

The Athanasian Creed (*Symbolum Athanasianum*), known from its opening word as the *Quicumque*, comes not from Athanasius but from the Lat. West and is more an explanation of the creed than a creed proper. Because of its very pronounced teaching on the Trinity and the two natures it became greatly esteemed and was introduced into the Lat. liturgy. The attribution to Athanasius first cropped up in the 7th c.; in any case, it is not possible to point to a particular author. This creed originated in southern Gaul in the 5th c.

W: J. N. D. Kelly, Athanasian Creed (London, 1964) [text/English trans./comm.].
L: H. Brewer, Das sog. Athanasian. G. (Paderborn, 1909). — A. E. Burn, Athanasian Creed (Oxford, 1912). — V. Laurent, Quicumque et l'Église byzantine: EOr 39 (1936) 385-404. — G. Morin, L'origine du symbole: JThS 12 (1911) 161-190, 337-361; RBen 44 (1932) 207-219. — J. Stiglmayr, Quicumque u. Fulgentius: ZKTh 49 (1925) 341-357.

P. BRUNS

Cresconius, Donatist

C., a layman and *grammaticus*, was born ca. 350 in Africa and became known only through his dispute with Augustine (between 397/401 and 405/411). In Augustine's first book *Contra litteras Petiliani*, he refuted a pastoral letter of Petilian of Constantina which attacked Catholics. C. then wrote a pamphlet in the form of a letter to Augustine in which he defended the pastoral letter, taking up three subjects: baptism, the Maximianist schism, and the persecution of Donatists. Augustine learned of this work only in 405 and, to refute it, wrote his *Contra Cresconium* in four books, which preserve for us extracts from C.'s work. By and large, C. provides a typical example of a Donatist layman who possessed but little accurate theol. knowledge (e.g., of the Bible).

W: M. Petschenig, CSEL 52:323-582.
L: P. Monceaux, Histoire littéraire de l'Afrique chrétienne 6 (Brussels, 1966 = Paris, 1922), 87-110. — PAC 230-238. — M. Schanz, C. Hosius, G. Krüger, Geschichte der röm. Lit. 4/2 (Munich, 1959 = 1920), 429.

B. WINDAU

Cyprian of Carthage

I. Life: C.—Caecilius Cyprianus, also named Thascius (*ep.* 66 pr.; *Acta procons.* 3)—was probably born at the beginning of the 3rd c. and was bishop of Carthage 248/249-258. His high level of education, considerable wealth, friends in the equestrian and senatorial classes, the degree to which he was known in Carthage, and his treatment as an *honestior* at his trial all suggest that his family belonged to the leading circles of Carthage and that he was at least of the equestrian class. Acc. to Jerome (*vir. ill.* 67), after the usual rhetorical training he worked as a teacher of oratory (or an orator); he may perhaps also have aimed at a career as administrator or even have begun it. Under the influence of presbyter Caecilian he turned to Christianity in his early to mid-forties (Pontius, *Vita Cypr.* 4). After baptism and, with it, the abandonment of his previous activity as well as the distribution of a large part of his personal property, C. soon became a presbyter and in 248/249 a bishop. His quick rise seems to have been due espec. to the community (*ep.* 43.1 and 4; Pontius, *Vita Cypr.* 5), which evidently supported the influential, wealthy, and charitable convert as its *patronus*. Among the Carthaginian clergy, on the other hand, there was until 253 a noticeable opposition centered on five presbyters who had been passed over in the episcopal election.

In the fall of 249 Decius came to power and required a sacrifice to the gods by all inhabitants of the empire as a proof of loyalty. C. left Carthage, probably before the edict became known and hid in the countryside. He justified his *secessio* with the claim that as a prominent individual he would have become a danger to the entire community and, on the other hand, could from his hiding place fulfill his duties as leader of the community (*ep.* 20).

Through extensive correspondence espec. with the clergy remaining in Carthage he attempted to regulate community life and maintain his own position. In the question of how to deal with the many "fallen" Christians (*lapsi*) who had offered sacrifice or secured a certificate that they had done so and were now asking for readmission to the community, a strife arose between C. and a (large) part of the clergy and the *confessores/martyres*. In C.'s absence and contrary to his instruction, *lapsi* who had obtained a recommendation from imprisoned *martyres*, were readmitted to the Eucharist. The conflict escalated to the point of excommunicating C.'s opponents who were gathered around Felicissimus (*ep.* 42), and delayed C.'s return, which became possible when the

civil measures abated, to shortly after Easter 251. In the meantime C. strengthened his position by gaining for himself the support of African colleagues and the Roman clergy. The Romans had initially distanced themselves from C. because of his flight (*ep.* 8), but he was able to change their attitude with his justification of his behavior (*ep.* 20). Both parties were in agreement on the question of the *lapsi*. Immediately after his return C. convoked a synod of North African bishops who in principle confirmed his attitude to the *lapsi* (they agreed, however, on taking a milder, graduated approach [*ep.* 55.6ff. and 13ff.]) and formalized the excommunication of Felicissimus and his followers (*ep.* 45.4; 59.9). Thus C.'s position was strengthened. In the next year he was able to defend it against two competitors (Fortunatus of Felicissimus's party and Maximus from among the followers of Novatian).

In the spring of 251 a split also arose in Rome, where Novatian, a follower of the hard line on the question of the *lapsi*, accused the newly elected bishop, Cornelius, of unworthiness and had himself consecrated as antibishop. After checking the facts, C. supported Cornelius, because the latter had been legitimately ordained prior to Novatian and because the accusations against him were now proved (*ep.* 44; 45; 48; 55.8ff.).

In 252, at the latest, Carthage was attacked by an epidemic (plague?), the practical and pastoral consequences of which had to be tackled. In addition, there was fear of new persecutions under Emperor Gallus. In view of this, a synod in the spring of 252, with C. presiding, decided to readmit all repentant *lapsi* (*ep.* 57). But no empire-wide persecution came. The only thing certain is that Cornelius died in exile. His successor, Lucius, was likewise banished but soon returned.

In May 254 Lucius was followed by Stephen I as bishop of Rome. From the end of 254 on, a fierce controversy developed between Stephen and C. (and large sectors of the eastern church) over the validity of baptism in heretical groups and, as a result of Stephen's arguments and attitude, over the legal position of the Roman bishop in relation to his colleagues. C. again acted as leader and spokesman of the North African bishops. This is espec. clear from the acts of the synod of Sept. 1, 256 (*sent. episc. 87*) which fully confirmed C.'s position. But C. also received support from the eastern church (→ Firmilian of Caesarea in Cappadocia [*ep.* 75]). Stephen finally broke off communion with C. and the North African church, as he had previously with a large part of the eastern church (*ep.* 74.8; 75.24f.; Eus., *h.e.* 7.3-

5). The controversy ended with the death of Stephen. His successor, Sixtus, normalized relations with his episcopal colleagues.

Beginning in August 257 there was a deliberate and bloody persecution of the church under Valerian. On Aug. 30, after refusing to "acknowledge the Roman rites" (i.e., to offer sacrifice [*Acta procons* 1]) C. was banished to Curubis. However, a while later he was able to return to his garden near Carthage but under arrest. The next summer Valerian ordered the execution of all uncompromising bishops, presbyters, and deacons. Other Christians of high social standing were to be stripped of their property and then, as the case might be, executed as well. C. learned very quickly of this decree. In order to give witness to the faith in his own city, he hid again for a short time, until the proconsul had again returned to Carthage. Here he was executed by the sword on Sept. 14, 258.

L: E. W. Benson, C. (London, 1897). — M. Bévenot, C.: TRE 8:246-254. — C. A. Bobertz, Analysis of Vita Cypriani 3, 6-10: VigChr 46 (1992) 112-128. — H. v. Campenhausen, Lat. Kirchenväter (Stuttgart, ⁶1986), 37-56 (English, The Fathers of the Latin Church [Stanford, 1969]) — G. W. Clarke, Secular Profession of C.: Latomus 24 (1965) 633-638. — H. R. Drobner, Patrologie (Freiburg i.Br., 1994), 133-139. — M. M. Sage, C. (Cambridge, Mass., 1975). — H. Montgomery, The Bishop Who Fled: StPatr 21 (1989) 264-267. — C. Saumagne, Saint C. (Paris, 1975). — M.-B. v. Stritzky, Erwägungen zum Decischen Opferbefehl: RQ 81 (1986) 1-25. — A. Stuiber, C. I: RAC 3:463-466. — W. Wischmeyer, Bischof im Prozess: FS G. J. M. Bartelink (Steenbrugge, 1989), 363-371. — idem, C. Episcopus 2: FS A. A. R. Bastiaensen (Steenbrugge, 1991), 407-419.

II. Works: C.'s works include letters and treatises. The correspondence has not been completely preserved. A presumed original collection was lost as a result of selection and regroupings. The letters preserved were brought together only at a late date. The collection contains eighty-one letters in all. But of these sixteen are from other writers (8, 21, 22, 23, 24, 30, 31, 36, 42, 49, 50, 53, 75, 77, 78, 79); seven others were composed by C. in the name of several colleagues or a synod (4, 57, 61, 64, 67, 70, 72). All date from C.'s time as bishop. Except for a few letters that deal with special questions and are difficult to date (1-4, 62, 63 [against the Aquarians]), the chronology can be established with some probability. The letters reflect the important problems C. had to deal with during his time in office: (1) In the letters from the time of his flight (5-43; spring 250 to spring 251) C. gives his clergy practical and disciplinary instructions; he praises and exhorts the confessors (5-7, 10-14, 28, [31], 37), makes known the appointment of clerics (29, 38-40), and justifies his flight, espec. to Rome ([8], 9, 20). Next, the problem of the *lapsi* and the letters of peace becomes central (15-19, 21-27, 30, 32-36). The final letters of this phase have to do with the division of the Carthaginian community by Felicissimus and his followers (41-43).

(2) The main subject of C.'s letters after his return from hiding and down to Stephen's taking office in Rome (44-66; middle of 251 to spring 254) is the Novatian schism (44-55). The question of the *lapsi* remains acute and is closely connected with the schisms in Carthage and Rome. In addition, many decisions have to be made in dealing with lapsed laypersons or clerics (56, 64, 65). Even after the decision to readmit all repentant *lapsi* (57), the problem keeps coming up. (3) The letters from Stephen's time in office (67-75; 254 to late fall 256) have to do with the baptismal controversy (except for 67, 68). (4) The final letters from the period of the Valerian persecution (beginning to autumn 258) (76-81) contain, on the one hand, the exchange of letters between C. and some Christians imprisoned in the mines (76-79) and, on the other, news about the expected steps by the state (80) and C.'s reason for his final avoidance of arrest and execution (81).

In contrast to the letters, the series of treatises was rather carefully put together shortly after C.'s death. In describing C.'s pastoral activity, Pontius, *Vita Cypr* 7, refers to most of them and seems in doing so to establish the relative chronology:

1. To Donatus (*Ad Donatum*) (after his baptism, ca. 246): Probably in order to justify his conversion before society, C. contrasts the new life given him as a gift in baptism with the abuses in the public and private life of non-Chr. society. Allusions to concepts and images from profane literature and philosophy give an inkling of C.'s high level of education.

2. *On the Behavior of Virgins* (hab. virg.) (before 250): C. exhorts consecrated virgins to a truly ascetic way of life that must find expression in their outward appearance and their behavior.

3. *On the Lapsed* (laps.) (spring 251): The text that was read at the Carthaginian synod in the spring of 251 (*ep.* 54.4) probably originated in a sermon that C. preached to his community on the *lapsi* problem shortly after his return from hiding. C. praises the steadfast, espec. the confessors, and condemns those who freely sacrificed or got a certificate of compliance for themselves. He warns the clergy against readmitting the *lapsi* without a period of penance and absolution from the bishop. The *martyres* are urged to be reserved in granting letters of reconciliation. All who have been guilty must prove their lasting repentance.

4. *On the Unity of the Catholic Church* (*unit. eccl.*) (spring 251): This work, composed shortly after *laps.* and probably also read at the synod of spring 251 (*ep.* 54.4), takes up the problem of schism. In response to the divisions in Carthage and Rome C. emphasizes the principle of the unity of the church, which he derives from the church's origin in Christ, from the communion among the apostles, and from scripture. Paragraph 4 is espec. important. It has come down in two versions, both of which probably are from C. The original version (so-called Primacy Text) exalted the person of Peter as symbol of the unity of the episcopate and in doing so used the key words *primatus* and *cathedra Petri*. Probably when Stephen claimed for himself as successor of Peter a (jurisdictional) superiority over his brother bishops, C. in the second version (so-called *textus receptus*) left out the person of Peter and more strongly emphasized the equality of all the apostles and their successors.

5. *On the Lord's Prayer* (*domin. orat.*) (251/252?): In dependence on Tertullian's *De oratione*, C. interprets the Our Father allegorically and in light of its associations and brings in general considerations on prayer.

6. To *Demetrianus* (*Demetr.*) (ca. 252): A defense against the accusation that present crises (espec. epidemic, wars [death of Decius], drought, famine) have been caused by Christians and their contempt for the gods. Rather, says C., all these are God's punishment from the refusal to believe his word and for the mistreatment of Christians. In this situation the great old age and nearing end of the world are reflected.

7. *On Mortality* (*mort.*) (252/253): On occasion of the epidemic C. urges that Christians take seriously their belief in the life to come and look upon death as a deliverance from the distresses of the world. Then there will be no longer a basis for grief over the dead and for fear of one's own death.

8. *On Charity and Almsgiving* (*eleem.*) (252/253?): In connection with the epidemic C. also exhorts his community, espec. the wealthy, to increased charity. In this he sees a primary demand upon every Christian and an important means of atoning for one's sins.

9. *On the Value of Patience* (*patient.*) (spring-summer 256): On occasion of the baptismal controversy (*ep.* 73.26) C. praises patience as a Chr. virtue that has its origin in God and was practiced by Christ and the patriarchs. Only with its help can we endure the troubles of life here below and arm ourselves against sin. The work follows Tertullian's *De patientia*.

10. *On Jealousy and Envy* (*zel.*) (256): In a work on the opposite of *patient.*, C. condemns jealousy and envy as dangerous evils inspired by the devil and as the causes of, along with many other sins, the destruction of unity and peace in the church by way of heresy, division, and disobedience to the bishops.

11. To *Fortunatus* (*Fort.*) (summer/fall 257?): Probably at the beginning of the Valerian persecution (or 253?), at the request of Bishop Fortunatus, C. assembles scriptural passages on the subject of persecution. These are to be material for strengthening the faithful during persecution and preparing them for a profession of faith and martyrdom.

There is disagreement on whether C. also composed the works *To Quirinus* or *Testimonies from Scripture* (*testim.*) and *Idols are not gods* (*idol.*). The former is usually regarded as genuine and dated ca. 248/250. Like *Fort.* it provides a bibl. anthology, although a more extensive one, on three subjects: (book 1: failure of the Jews; Christians as the new people of God; book 2: Christ; book 3 [probably added later]: ethical instructions), with almost no explanations. In contrast, the majority of critics do not attribute *idol.* to C., since it is a compilation, untypical of C., from two sources (→ Minucius Felix, *Octavius*; Tertullian, *Apologeticum*). The acts of the synod of Sept. 1, 256 (*sent. episc. 87*), are also included among C.'s writings.

Certainly not authentic, in addition to some letters, prayers, and sermons, are these works: *Against the Jews* (*adv. Iud.*) (3rd c.?); *On Sinai and Zion* (*mont.*) (mid-3rd c.?); *To Bishop Vigilius on Jewish Unbelief* (*Iud. incred.*) (3rd c.?); *Calculation of the Date of Easter* (*pasch.*) (243); *In Praise of Martyrdom* (*laud. mart.*) (253?); *On Rebaptism* (*rebapt.*) (ca. 256); *To Novatian* (*ad Novat.*) (after mid-3rd c.?); *On Clerical Celibacy* (*singul. cler.*) (end of 3rd c.); *Treatise on the Hundred-, Sixty-, Thirtyfold* (*tract.*) (3rd/4th c.?); *Exhortation to Penance* (*exhort. paen.*) (4th/5th c.?); *On the Twelve Transgressions of This World* (*abus.*) (7th c.). Two works, *On Chastity* (*pudic.*) and *On Spectacles* (*spect.*), that have come down under C.'s name are usually ascribed to → Novatian. C. is also not the author (of the prose version) of the *Banquet* (*cena*), the origin of which has not yet been cleared up, nor of poems *On Sodom* (*De sodoma*) and *On Jonah* (*De Iona*), among others; whether they were written by → Cyprian the Singer (C. Gallus) is disputed.

Some mss. of the works of Cyprian include an account of his trial and execution (*Acta proconsularia*) and the *Vita Cypriani* by Deacon → Pontius.

III. Main Lines of Thought: C. is not a systematic or speculative theologian. His writings are occasioned by practical problems and current conflicts. In order to safeguard the existence of the community, he seeks peace, order, and discipline. In doing so, he argues primarily from scripture, more rarely from the church's tradition. In connection with the question of the *lapsi*, he emphasizes primarily the sole power of the bishop in matters of penance. He rejects competing claims of the *confessores/martyres*: the latter can only bring the bishop petitions or recommendations for the readmission of the lapsed; the bishop alone has authority over readmission and thus in deciding on the spiritual life (with the eschatological reservation); this is probably the most important foundation of the bishop's rule. In controversies connected with schisms C. emphasizes espec. the unity of the true church originating in Christ, and its necessity for salvation. A criterion of membership in this church is communion with the legitimately elected bishop. Anyone breaking communion with him leaves this church and thus loses all access to salvation. Even if in this situation he confesses Christ before the authorities and on that account dies, it is of no avail to him. Given this foundation, C. has to deny the validity of baptism given in schismatic groups. Since these are outside the church, they do not have the Spirit of God in them and cannot bestow Him and the purification from sin in baptism. Anyone who is baptized by heretics and wants to be accepted into a true church must first be baptized in this church. A mere imposition of hands for giving the Spirit or for the forgiveness of sins, as Stephen I requires, is not enough. In the question of the place of the Roman bishop, which arose in connection with the baptismal controversy, C. insists on the jurisdictional equality of all bishops. Their fraternal communion embodies the unity of the universal church. In order to represent this unity, Peter was the first called, but then the other apostles received the same authority. Therefore the "primacy" of Peter consists in his temporal priority and his special place of honor, but not in a legal superiority to the other apostles. Therefore Peter's successor has no authority to instruct his colleagues.

IV. Importance: After Tertullian, who influenced him materially but from whom he is clearly different in style, C. is the second great author of the African church and, if one prescinds from → Minucius Felix, of the entire Lat. church in the pre-Constantinian period. His work is of great importance, espec. for church history, as being the earliest witness of a bishop of the western church. The letters in particu-

lar mirror the practical problems of community and eccles. life and are a rich source of information on church–state relations in the mid-3rd c. and on the organization of community life: espec. the development of the eccles. offices, the liturgical life, *caritas*, the formation of structures in the diocesan and universal church, and intraecclesial conflicts. Above all, however, they make known the understanding of the episcopal office and the bases of it. Under the pressure of civil repression and intraecclesial conflict, C. endeavors to concentrate all areas of leadership in the hand of the bishop. He understands himself to be "superior" of the community, i.e., master of the clergy, with full competence in disciplinary matters, and as teacher of the community, for whose well-being he is responsible. Thus he consolidated a hierarchical community structure of the Roman type, which triumphed in the Catholic Church. The rich ms. tradition of his works and their use in church documents (e.g., in the *Decretum Gratiani*) show their great influence.

S: Pontius, *Vita Cypr.* — Jerome, *vir. ill.* 67. — Eusebius, *h.e.* 7.3-5. — *Acta procons.*, W. Hartel, CSEL 3/3:110-114. — H. Musurillo, Acts of Christian Martyrs (Oxford, 1972), 168-175 [text/English trans./comm.]. — A. A. R. Bastiaensen, G. Chiarini, Acta Cypriani: Atti e passioni dei martiri (Milan, 1987), 206-231 [text/Italian trans.].

W: *ad Donat., idol., testim., hab. virg., unit. eccl., laps., domin. orat., mort., Fort., Demetr., eleem., patient., zel., sent. episc.* 87, W. Hartel, CSEL 3/1. — *testim., Fort.,* R. Weber, CCL 3. — *laps., unit. eccl.,* M. Bévenot, CCL 3. — *ad Donat., mort., Demetr., eleem., zel.,* M. Simonetti, CCL 3A. — *domin. orat., patient.,* C. Moreschini, CCL 3A. — *ad Donat., hab. virg., laps., unit. eccl., domin. orat., Demetr., mort., eleem., patient., zel., testim.* (selections), *Fort.* (selections), *sent. episc.* 87 (selections), J. Baer, BKV² 34 (Munich, 1918) [German trans.]. — *ad Donat., hab. virg., laps., unit. eccl., domin. orat., Demetr., mort., eleem., patient., zel., Fort., Acta procons., ep.,* G. Toso (Turin, 1980) [Italian trans./comm.]. — *laps., unit. eccl.,* M. Bévenot (Oxford, 1971) [text/English trans./comm.]. — *ad Donat., patient.,* J. Molager, SC 291. — *domin. orat.,* M. Réveillaud (Paris, 1964) [text/French trans./comm.]. — *Demetr.,* E. Gallicet (Turin, 1976) [text/Italian trans./comm.]. — *hab. virg.,* A. E. Keenan (Washington, 1932) [text/English trans./comm.]. — *mort.,* M. L. Hannan (Washington, 1933) [text/English trans./comm.]. — *eleem.,* E. V. Rebenack (Washington, 1962) [text/English trans./comm.]. — *patient.,* G. E. Conway (Washington, 1957) [text/English trans./comm.]. — *ep.,* W. Hartel, CSEL 3/2. — G. F. Diercks, CCL 3B, 3C. — J. Baer, BKV² 60 (Munich, 1928) [German trans.]. — L. Bayard, 2 vols. (Paris, ²1962/61) [text/French trans.]. — G. W. Clarke, 4 vols. (New York, 1984, 1984, 1986, 1989) [English trans./comm.].

Ps.-Cyprianic Writings: *laud. mart., ad Novat., rebapt., aleat., mont., Iud. incred., adv. Iud., or., abus., singul. cler., Fort., pasch., ep., carm.,* W. Hartel, CSEL 3/3. — *aleat.,* A. Miodonski (Erlangen, 1889) [text/German trans./comm.]. — *exhort. paen.,* A. Miodonski (Cracow, 1893) [text]. — *ad*

Novat., adv. Iud., G. F. Diercks, CCL 4:137-152, 265-278. — *adv. Iud.*, D. van Damme (Fribourg, Switzerland, 1969) [text/German trans./comm.]. — *mont.*, C. Burini (Fiesole, 1994) [text/Italian trans./comm.]. — *pasch.*, A. Strobel, Texte zur Geschichte des frühchr. Osterkalenders (Münster, 1984), 43-67 [German trans./comm.]. — *rebapt.*, G. Rauschen, FlorPatr 11:42-73 [text]. — *tract.*, PLS 1:53-67. L: *Bibliographies:* REAug 32 (1986) ff. — CCL 3:11-50. — G. W. Clarke, Letters 3:128-152; 4:113-135. — J. Molager, SC 291:67-72, 178f. — BBKL 1:1180-1183. P. Bouet et al., C. Traités. Concordance, 2 vols. (Hildesheim, 1986). — A. Adolph, Theologie der Einheit der Kirche (Frankfurt a.M., 1993). — A. d'Alès, La Théologie de s. C. (Paris, 1922). — G. Alföldy, C. u. die Krise des Röm. Reiches: Historia 22 (1973) 479-501 (reprint with supplements: idem, Krise des Röm. Reiches [Stuttgart, 1989], 295-318). — P. R. Amidon, The procedure of St. C.'s synods: VigChr 37 (1983) 328-339. — A. Beck, Röm. Recht bei Tertullian u. C. (Aalen, ²1967). — P. van Beneden, Aux origines d'une terminologie sacramentelle (Leuven/Louvain, 1974). — M. Bévenot, St. C.'s De unitate 4 (Rome, 1937 = London, 1938). — idem, A Bishop is responsible to God alone: RSR 39 (1951/52) 397-415. — idem, Primatus Petro datur: JThS NS 5 (1954) 19-35. — idem, Sacrament of penance: TS 16 (1955) 175-213. — idem, Tradition of Manuscripts (Oxford, 1961). — idem, Episcopat et Primauté: EThL 42 (1966) 176-195. — idem, C. and his recognition of Cornelius: JThS NS 28 (1977) 346-359. — idem, C.'s Platform in the Rebaptism Controversy: HeyJ 19 (1978) 123-142. — idem, Sacerdos as Understood by C.: JThS NS 30 (1979) 413-429. — idem, Salus extra ecclesiam non est: FS P. Smulders (Assen, 1981), 97-105. — C. A. Bobertz, C. as patron (Yale Univ., 1988). — idem, Historical Context of C.'s unit. eccl.: JThS NS 41 (1990) 107-111. — V. Buchheit, Cypr. Don. 2: Hermes 115 (1987), 318-334. — idem, Cypr. Don. 3-4: Hermes 117 (1989) 210-226. — L. Campeau, Le texte de la primauté dans le unit. eccl.: ScEc 19 (1967) 81-110, 255-275. — H. v. Campenhausen, Kirchliches Amt (Tübingen, ²1963), 292-322 (English, Ecclesiastical authority and spiritual power [Stanford, 1969]). — S. Cavallotto, Magistero episcopale: DT(P) 91 (1988) 375-407; 92 (1989) 33-73. — J. Colson, L'évêque, lien de l'unité et de la charité (Paris, 1961). — E. Contreras, Sententiae Episcoporum 87: Aug. 27 (1987) 407-421. — A. Cuva, Publica est nobis et communis oratio: Sal. 55 (1993) 485-498. — S. Deléani, Christum sequi (Paris, 1979). — L. Duquenne, Chronologie des lettres (Brussels, 1972). — J. Ernst, C. u. das Papsttum (Mainz, 1912). — M. A. Fahey, C. and the Bible (Tübingen, 1971). — A. Faivre, Les laïcs aux origines de l'Église (Paris, 1984), 134-159. — J. A. Favazza, The construction of religion in C.: QuLi 80 (1999) 81-90. — J. A. Fischer, Konzilien zu Karthago u. Rom 251: AHC 11 (1979) 263-286. — idem, Konzil zu Karthago Mai 252: AHC 13 (1981) 1-11. — idem, Konzil zu Karthago Frühjahr 253: AHC 13 (1981) 12-26. — idem, Konzil zu Karthago Herbst 254: ZKG 93 (1982) 223-239. — idem, Konzil zu Karthago 255: AHC 14 (1982) 227-240. — idem, Konzil zu Karthago Frühjahr 256: AHC 15 (1983) 1-14. — idem, Konzil zu Karthago Spätsommer 256: AHC 16 (1984) 1-39. — P. Granfield, Episcopal elections in C.: TS 37 (1976) 41-52. — P. Grattarola, Problema dei Lapsi fra Roma e Cartagine: RSCI 38 (1984) 1-26. — R. Gryson, Les élections ecclésiastiques au IIIᵉ siècle: RHE 68 (1973) 353-404. — H. Gülzow, C. u. Novatian (Tübingen, 1975). — A. v. Harnack, Verlorene Briefe u. Actenstücke (Leipzig, 1902). — P. Hinch-

liff, C. and the unity of the Christian Church (London, 1974). — HLL 4:532-577 (literature). — S. Hübner, Kirchenbuße u. Exkommunikation bei C.: ZKTh 84 (1962) 49-84, 171-215. — H. Janssen, Kultur u. Sprache (Nijmegen, 1938). — H. Koch, C. u. der röm. Primat (Leipzig, 1910). — idem, Cyprianische Untersuchungen (Bonn, 1926). — idem, Cathedra Petri (Giessen, 1930). — J. Le Moyne, C. auteur de la rédaction brève du "De unitate" 4?: RBen 63 (1953) 70-115. — C. Markschies et al. (ed.), Geschichte des Christentums 2 (Freiburg i.Br., 1996), 29-54, 156-171. — M. Marin, Le sententiae 87 episcoporum: InvLuc 11 (1989) 329-359. — W. Marschall, Karthago u. Rom (Stuttgart, 1971), 29-41, 85-102. — P. Monceaux, Histoire littéraire de l'Afrique chrétienne 2 (Paris, 1902). — H. Montgomery, C.'s Secular Heritage: FS Rudi Thomsen (Aarhus, 1988), 214-223. — idem, Subordination or Collegiality: Greek and Latin Studies in Memory of Cajus Fabricius, ed. S.-T. Teodorsson (Göteborg, 1990), 41-54. — A. P. Orbán, "Gerecht" u. "Gerechtigkeit" bei C.: ABG 32 (1989) 103-120. — T. Osawa, Bischofseinsetzungsverfahren bei C. (Frankfurt a.M., 1983). — O. Perler, Datierung der beiden Fassungen des 4. Kap. von unit. eccl.: RQ 44 (1936) 1-44. — idem, De catholicae ecclesiae unitate 4-5: RQ 44 (1936) 151-168. — M. Poirier, Dans l'atelier d'un évêque écrivain (eleem.): REL 71 (1993) 239-250. — B. Poschmann, Sichtbarkeit der Kirche (Paderborn, 1908). — idem, Ecclesia Principalis (Breslau, 1933). — K. Rahner, Bußlehre des hl. C.: ZKTh 74 (1952) 257-276, 381-438. — T. G. Ring, Auctoritas bei Tertullian, C. u. Ambrosius (Würzburg, 1975), 93-110. — O. Ritschl, C. u. die Verfassung der Kirche (Göttingen, 1885). — C. M. Robeck, Prophecy in Carthage (Cleveland, Oh., 1992), 149-195, 217-223. — V. Saxer, Vie liturgique et quotidienne (Rome, 1969). — idem, Culture des évêques africains: RBen 94 (1984) 257-284. — J. Schrijnen, C. Mohrmann, Syntax der Briefe, 2 vols. (Nijmegen, 1936-1937). — J. H. D. Scourfield, The De mortalitate of C.: VigChr 50 (1996) 12-41. — R. Seagraves, Pascentes cum disciplina. Lexical Study of the Clergy (Fribourg, Switzerland, 1993). — M. Simonetti, Sulla paternità del idol.: Maia 3 (1950) 265-288. — W. Simonis, Ecclesia visibilis et invisibilis (Frankfurt a.M., 1970), 1-23. — J. Speigl, C. über das iudicium dei bei der Bischofseinsetzung: RQ 69 (1974) 30-45. — K. Strobel, Das Imperium Romanum im 3. Jh. (Stuttgart, 1993), 146-184. — B. Studer, Soteriologie C. s: Aug. 16 (1976) 427-456. — A. Vilela, La condition collégiale des prêtres (Paris, 1971), 253-338. — J. Vögtle, Schriften des hl. C. als Erkenntnisquelle röm. Rechts (Berlin, 1920). — H. J. Vogt, C. Hindernis für die Ökumene?: ThQ 164 (1984) 1-15. — G. S. M. Walker, Churchmanship of St. C. (London, 1968). — U. Wickert, Sacramentum unitatis (Berlin, 1971). — M. Wojtowytsch, Papsttum u. Konzile (Stuttgart, 1981), 39-57. — E. Zocca, Senectus mundi: Aug. 35 (1995) 641-677.
On the Pseudo-Cyprianic writings: P. F. Beatrice, Martirio ed ascesi nel sermone ps.-cipreaneo De centesima (= tract.): FS G. Lazzati (Milan, 1979), 3-24. — idem, Il sermone De centesima e la teologia del martirio: Aug. 19 (1979) 215-243. — J. E. Bruns, Biblical citations in Ps. C.'s mont.: VigChr 26 (1972) 112-116. — S. T. Carroll, An Early Church Sermon against Gambling: SecCen 8 (1991) 83-95. — J. Daniélou, La littérature latine avant Tertullien: REL 48 (1970) 357-375. — idem, Le traité De centesima: VigChr 25 (1971) 171-181. — HLL 4:529-532, 577-584; 5:416-418, 501-510. — W. Horbury, The Purpose of Ps.-C., adv. Iud.: StPatr 18/3 (1989) 291-317. — M. Marin, Citazioni biblici e para-

biblici nel aleat.: ASEs 5 (1988) 169-184. — P. Mattei, Tradition et notions connexes dans la querelle baptismale (*rebapt.*): La tradizione, SEAug 31 (Rome, 1990), 325-339. — idem, Extra ecclesiam nulla salus (*rebapt.*): StPatr 24 (1993) 300-305. — E. Romero-Pose, El tratado mont. y el donatismo: Gr. 63 (1982) 273-299. — A. Roncoroni, Ps.-C., De ligno crucis (= *pasch.*): RSLR 12 (1976) 380-390. — P. Sellew, Five Days of Creation? (De centesima 26): ZNW 81 (1990) 277-283.

A. HOFFMANN

Cyprian, Poet

Probably at the beginning of the 5th c. and in connection with a pre-Jerome translation of the Bible, a Chr. poet named C. (in all probability from Gaul; perhaps the addressee of *ep.* 40 of Jerome) composed a versification of the Pentateuch and the books of Josh and Judg; in part of the ms. tradition the work is also ascribed to → Juvencus. The widespread description of the work as *Heptateuchos* (*hept.*) is only partially justified, since catalogues of mss. and fragments show that it also included Kgs, Chr, Jdt, Esth, Mac, and other historical books of the OT. In general, C. follows his model quite closely, but (amid some expansions) omits those passages especially that are not suited to a transposition into verse or do not contribute to the obviously intended communication of the historical content of the books (espec. the legislative passages of Lev, Num, and Deut). He avoids both embellishment and digression, employs unusual expressions and neologisms only very rarely, and uses alliteration (quite frequently) as his sole rhetorical device; this fact should not be interpreted too exclusively as a lack of poetic power but rather, like the avoidances of introductions and mythological references, as a sign of his great reverence for the bibl. text. With the exception of some songs in lyric Phalacian hendecasyllables (e.g., the song of Moses after the crossing of the Red Sea [Ex 507-542]), C. uses the epic dactylic hexameter, and, despite all his offenses against meter and prosody, does so in a very elegant and skilled way. In addition to echoes of Chr. poets such as Juvencus and → Prudentius, the work also shows a knowledge of pagan authors (espec. Virgil, but also Ovid, → Claudian, and others).

The possibility that C. was also the author of the so-called *Cena Cypriani* (*cena*)—a prose → cento of passages from scripture in which a colorful crowd of bibl. personages are gathered in Cana for a wedding feast—has quite recently been challenged on good grounds.

W: *hept.*, PLS 3:1151-1243. — R. Peiper, CSEL 23. — J. E. B. Mayor (London, 1899) [text/comm.]. — *cena*, PLS 4:925-932. — K. Strecker, MGH. PL 4/2:872-898. — A. v. Harnack, Drei wenig beachtete Cyprianische Schriften (Leipzig, 1899) [text]. — C. Modesto, Studien zur Cena Cypriani (Tübingen, 1992) [text/trans./comm.].
L: E. Fernández Vallina, Presencia de Virgilio en C.: Helm. 33 (1982) 329-335. — A. Harnack, loc. cit. — W. Haß, Studien zum Heptateuchdichter C. (Berlin, 1912). — D. Kartschoke, Bibeldichtung (Munich, 1975), esp. 34f., 99-101. — L. Krestan, C.: RAC 3:477-481. — A. Longpré, Structure de l'hexamètre de C.: Cahiers d'études anciennes 1 (1972) 75-100. — G. Malsbary, Epic Exegesis and the Use of Vergil in the Early Biblical Poets: Florilegium 7 (1985) 55-83. — C. Modesto, loc. cit. — M. R. Petringa, I "sei giorni della creazione" nella parafrasi biblica di C.: Sileno 18 (1992) 133-156. — K. Pollmann, Der sog. Heptateuchdichter u. die Alethia des Claudius Marius Victorius: Hermes 120 (1992) 490-501. — K. Smolak, Lat. Umdichtungen des bibl. Schöpfungsberichtes: StPatr 12 (1975) 350-360.

U. HAMM

Cyprian of Toulon

C. belonged to the circle of friends and students of Caesarius of Arles; he was a bishop from 516 to his death in 549. At the request of Caesaria the Younger he joined Bishop Firminus of Uzèz and Viventius in writing the *Vita Caesarii* I (*V. Caes.*, 542/549); the second part, which deals with the miracles, was written by presbyter Messianus and deacon Stephen with C. as editor. In addition, C. wrote a letter to Maximus of Geneva (*ep.*, 524/533) in which he defends himself against the accusation of theopaschism, and a short preface to the *Five Books on the History of the Jewish War* by → Hegesippus (*praef.*).

W: *V. Caes.*, G. Morin, S. Caesarii opera omnia 2 (Maredsous, 1942) [text]. — *ep.*, W. Gundlach, MGH. Ep 3:434-436. — *praef.*, V. Ussani: ALMA 1 (1924) 22.
L: W. Berschin, Biographie (Stuttgart, 1986), 249-258. — S. Cavallin, Studien zur V. Caes. (Lund, 1934). — B. Krusch, Prolegomena ad V. Caes., MGH. SRM 3:440-456.

C. KASPER

Cyril of Alexandria

I. Life: Of the early career of C. we known for certain only that in 403 he accompanied his uncle Theophilus to the Synod of the Oak, at which John Chrys. was deposed, and that in 412 he succeeded Theophilus as bishop of Alexandria. The early years of his episcopate saw the killing of Hypatia the philosopher (415) by fanatical Christians; no direct involvement of C. could be proved.

C. then became spokesman in the controversy with Nestorius, bishop of Constantinople since 428, who in sermons had rejected the title of "Mother of God" (Theotokos) for Mary. C. first attacked Nesto-

153

rius in his Easter letter of 429. Both appealed to Celestine I of Rome who in 430 commissioned C. to depose Nestorius unless the latter recanted within ten days. C. himself called a synod, as a result of which he sent Nestorius his third letter containing twelve anathematisms. The council that Emperor Theodosius convoked in Ephesus at the request of Nestorius was opened by C. on June 22, 431, before the arrival of the eastern bishops and the Roman legates; his second letter to Nestorius was accepted as the correct interpretation of the Nicene Creed; the second letter of Nestorius was rejected, Nestorius was deposed, and the twelve anathematisms were incorporated into the acts of the council. C. declared a countercouncil of the easterners to be void. Like Nestorius he was imprisoned and released only after lengthy negotiations. The year 433 brought a unification on the basis of the Formula of Union composed by the easterners, but Nestorius was not rehabilitated.

The subsequent life of C., who strengthened the power of the Alexandrian patriarchate in controversies with the imperial governor (over his action against the Jews), was likewise marked by conflicts over his christology. C. died in 444.

L: H. v. Campenhausen, Griech. Kirchenväter (Stuttgart, 1955), 153-164 (English, The Fathers of the Greek Church [London, 1963]). — A. de Halleux, Les 12 chapitres au Concile d'Ephèse: RTL 23 (1992) 425-458. — J. Rougé, Politique de C.: CrSt 11 (1990) 485-504. — idem, Débuts de l'épiscopat de C: FS P. C. Mondésert (Paris, 1987), 339-349. — H. J. Vogt, C.: GK 2, ed. M. Greschat (Stuttgart, 1984), 227-238. — idem, Gespaltenes Konzil: TThZ 90 (1981) 89-105. — idem, Unterschiedliches Konzilsverständnis: FS L. Abramowski (Berlin, 1993), 429-451. — L. R. Wickham, C.: ThQ 178 (1998) 257-271.

II. Work: Ca. 1950 there was a fierce debate among French scholars as to whether C. began his literary activity with the two works on the Trinity and the commentary on John or whether the writings on the OT were composed before those three explicitly anti-Arian writings. With a degree of preference for the second chronology, first place is here given to the work *On Adoration in Spirit and in Truth* (*ador.*), in which in dialogue form C. discusses the relationship of Christianity to the law; using allegorical-typological exegesis of individual passages, not in their bibl. order, he explains that all the precepts of the law can be given a spiritual interpretation. This work is supplemented by the *Glaphyra* (*glaph. Gen-Deut*), which likewise interpret selected passages of the Pentateuch but this time in their order in the OT. Also preserved is a comprehensive commentary on Isaiah (*Is.*) and a commentary on the Minor Prophets (*Os.-Mal.*); a

number of fragments on other OT books, espec. the Ps (*Ps.*) are in the catenae. The two treatises written in quick succession *Thesaurus de sancta et consubstantiali Trinitate* (*thes.*) and the dialogue *De sancta et consubstantiali Trinitate* (*dial. Trin.* 1-7) are dated to 423. In the *thes.* Arian objections to the orthodox belief in the Trinity are refuted one after another, and this with heavy dependence on Athanasius, *Ar.*; the other work has for subject the divinity of the Son in dialogues 1-6 and the divinity of the Holy Spirit in dialogue 7.

On the NT: the commentary on John has been transmitted almost complete. In the preface C. already says that he intends to attend to the dogm. meaning of the text and the refutation of heretical doctrines. Since he then has in view primarily the views of Arius and does not yet mention the name and teaching of Nestorius, the work may be dated between 425 and 428. Of C.'s 156 homilies on Luke (*Lc.*) only three have come to us directly (*hom. div.* 9 and 12, this last comprising two original homilies). In the Gr. catenae on Luke, however, there are a large number of scholia. The complete work we owe to a Syr. translation. The homilies on Luke are primarily pastoral instructions but also contain attacks on the teaching of Nestorius, so that the controversy must have already been under way when they were composed. Except for a few fragments, the commentary on Matthew is lost (*fr. Mt.*); the catenae contain fragments on the NT letters (Rom, 1 Cor, 2 Cor, Heb, among others).

The series of anti-Nestorian polemics began with the five books against Nestorius, composed in early 430; without naming Nestorius C. quotes the latter's sermons and attacks passages in which Nestorius enters the lists against the title Theotokos for Mary, as well as statements which end up dividing Christ. Shortly after the beginning of the controversy C. addressed to the imperial court three works—*On the Orthodox Faith* (*Thds.*, largely identical with *De incarnatione unigeniti* [*inc. unigen.*]; *Ad Arcadiam et Marinam* [*Arcad.*]; *Ad Pulcheriam et Eudociam* [*Pulch.*]). When → Andrew of Samosata and → Theodoret of Cyrrhus were offended by the twelve anathematisms, C. answered with a defense of the latter against the eastern bishops (*apol. orient.*) and with the letter to Euoptius (*ep. Euopt.*). In the explanation of the twelve anathematisms (*expl. XII cap.*), composed during his imprisonment in Ephesus in the spring of 431, he endeavored to prove their accordance with scripture. After his return to Alexandria he justified his actions in Ephesus in a defense addressed to the emperor (*apol. Thds.*). The

Scholia de incarnatione (*schol. inc.*), written after 431, have survived complete only in Lat. and Syr. translations; we have only fragments of the Gr. original. The union with the easterners is attested in letter 39 to → John of Antioch (*ep.* 39); in it C. rejoices that peace between them has been restored, and at the end he gives the text of the Formula of Union.

The major apol. work dedicated to Theodosius II, *In Defense of the Holy Christian Religion against the Books of the Godless Julian* (*Juln.*), was written ca. 435 and is one of the main sources for reconstructing Julian's lost work *Against the Galileans*; the first ten books of C.'s work have survived complete, books 11-20 only in fragments.

The treatise *Contra Diodorum et Theodorum* (*Diod.*), composed probably ca. 438, has come down only in Gr. and Syr. excerpts; the two Antiochenes, Diodorus of Tarsus and Theodore Mops., are here posthumously regarded as fathers of Nestorianism. What is probably the last work against the Nestorian christological error is the dialogue *Quod unus sit Christus* (*Chr. un.*). The *Adversus nolentes confiteri sanctam Virginem esse Deiparam* (*deip. BVM*) is to be regarded as not authentic.

Finally, a good many homilies (*hom. div.*) have come down under C.'s name, which he supposedly delivered, in part, in Ephesus. The fourth homily, which is regarded as the most famous sermon on Mary from antiquity, is probably not C.'s. Like his predecessors, C. annually announced the date of Easter to the Egyptian church; twenty-nine such writings have come down to us from 414-442, and are described in older editions as *Homiliae paschales* (*hom. pasch.*). We have ca. one hundred letters from C.'s correspondence; some of these are addressed to C. Further letters have survived in translations, espec. into Syriac.

W: P. E. Pusey, 7 vols. (Brussels, 1965 = Oxford, 1868-1877). — E. Schwartz (ACO 1, 1-5). — *ador.*, PG 68. — *apol. orient.*, P. E. Pusey, loc. cit., 6:259-381. — ACO 1, 1, 7, 33-65. — *apol. Thds.*, P. E. Pusey, loc. cit., 7:425-456. — ACO 1, 1, 3, 75-90. — A. J. Festugière, Actes (Paris, 1982), 433-452 [French trans.]. — *Arcad.*, P. E. Pusey, loc. cit., 7:154-262. — ACO 1, 1, 5, 62-118. — *Chr. un.*, P. E. Pusey, loc. cit., 7:334-424. — G. M. de Durand, SC 97:302-515. — O. Bardenhewer, BKV² 12 (Munich, 1935), 109-204 [German trans.]. — J. A. McGuckin (New York, 1994) [English trans.]. — *deip. BMV*, ACO 1, 1, 7, 19-32. — H. Hayd (Kempten, 1879), 531-560 [German trans.]. — O. Bardenhewer, BKV² 12 (Munich, 1935), 205-236 [German trans.]. — *dial. Trin.* 1-7, C. M. de Durand, SC 231, 237, 246. — A. Cataldo (Rome, 1992) [Italian trans./comm.]. — H. Hayd (Kempten, 1879), 43-469 [German trans.]. — *Diod.*, P. E. Pusey, loc. cit., 5:492-537. — P. E. Pusey (London, 1881) [English trans.]. — *ep.*, PG 77:9-390. — ACO 1, 1. — L. R. Wickham (London, 1983) [text/English trans./comm.]. —

J. I. McEnerney, 2 vols. (Washington, 1987) [English trans.]. — J. A. McGuckin (Leiden, 1994), 245-279, 336-363 [English trans.]. — A. J. Festugière, Actes (Paris, 1982) [French trans.]. — *ep.* 4, 17, 39, 55, O. Bardenhewer, BKV² 12:81-107, 240-263 [German trans.]. — *ep. Euopt.*, P. E. Pusey, loc. cit., 6:384-497. — ACO 1, 1, 6, 107-146. — *glaph. Gen.-Dt.*, PG 69:9-678. — *fr. Reg., Ps., fr. Cant.*, PG 69:679-1294. — *Is.*, PG 70:9-1450. — *fr. Jer., fr. Bar., fr. Ezech., fr. Dan.*, PG 70:1451-1462. — *Os.-Mal.*, P. E. Pusey, loc. cit., vols. 1-2. — *fr. Mt.*, PG 72:365-474. — *Lc.*, PG 77:1009-1016, 1039-1050 [Greek text]. — PG 72:475-950 [Greek frags.]. — J. Sickenberger, TU 34/1 (Leipzig, 1909), 63-108 [Greek frags.]. — J. Reuss, TU 130 (Berlin, 1984), 54-297 [Greek frags.]. — R. P. Smith (Oxford, 1858) [Syriac text]. — R. P. Smith, 2 vols. (Oxford, 1859) [English trans.]. — *Lc. Hom.* 1-80, J. B. Chabot, CSCO 70 [Syriac text]. — R. M. Tonneau, CSCO 140 [Latin trans.]. — *Jo.*, P. E. Pusey, loc. cit., vols. 3-5. — L. Leone, 3 vols. (Rome, 1994) [Italian trans./comm.]. — *Jo.* 1-6, P. E. Pusey (Oxford, 1872) [English trans.]. — *Jo.* 6, 1-12, T. Randell (London, 1885) [English trans.]. — *Rom., 1 Cor., 2 Cor., Heb.*, P. E. Pusey, loc. cit., 5:173-440. — *Rom.*, V. Ugenti (Rome, 1991) [Italian trans./comm.]. — *expl. XII cap.*, P. E. Pusey, loc. cit., 6:240-258. — ACO 1, 1, 5, 15-25. — J. A. McGuckin (Leiden, 1994), 282-293 [English trans.]. — *hom. div.*, PG 77:981-1116. — *hom. div.* 1-2, 4-7, ACO 1, 1, 2, 92-104. — *hom. div.* 3, ACO 1, 1, 4, 14f. — *hom. div.* 4, O. Bardenhewer, Marienpredigten (Munich, 1934) [German trans.]. — *hom. pasch.*, PG 77:401-982. — *hom. pasch.* 1-6, 7-11, P. Evieux, W. H. Burns, L. Arragon et al., SC 372, 392. — *inc. unigen.*, P. E. Pusey, loc. cit., 7:11-153 [Greek/Syriac text]. — G. M. de Durand, SC 97:188-301. — H. Hayd (Kempten, 1879), 471-528 [German trans.]. — *Juln.*, PG 76:503-1064. — *Juln.* 1-2, P. Burguière, P. Evieux, SC 322. — *Nest.*, P. E. Pusey, loc. cit., 6:54-239. — ACO 1, 1, 6, 13-106. — P. E. Pusey (London, 1881) [English trans.]. — *Pulch.*, P. E. Pusey, loc. cit., 7:263-333. — ACO 1, 1, 5, 26-61. — *schol. inc.*, P. E. Pusey, loc. cit., 6:498-579 [Greek frags./Latin text]. — ACO 1, 5, 184-215 [Latin text]. 219-231 [Greek frags.]. — C. Conybeare (London, 1907), 95-143 [Armenian text] 168-214 [English trans.]. — J. A. McGuckin (Leiden, 1994), 294-335 [English trans.]. — *Thds.*, P. E. Pusey, loc. cit., 7:1-153 [Greek/Syriac text]. — ACO 1, 1, 1, 42-72. — O. Bardenhewer, BKV² 12:21-78 [German trans.]. — *thes.*, PG 75:9-656.

L: W. H. Alla, Discours pour la fête de la croix attribué à C.; OrChr 75 (1991) 166-197. — M. Aubineau, Les Catenae in Lucam de J. Reuss et C.: ByZ 80 (1987) 29-47. — G. M. de Durand, Une lettre méconnue de C.: FS P. C. Mondésert (Paris, 1987), 351-363. — E. R. Hardy, C.: TRE 8:254-260 (literature). — G. Jouassard, C.: RAC 3:499-516 (literature). — idem, L'activité littéraire de C. jusqu'à 428: FS E. Podechard (Lyons, 1945), 159-174. — idem, La date des écrits antiariens de C.: RBen 87 (1977) 172-178. — W. Kinzig, Zur Notwendigkeit einer Neuedition von C., *Juln.*: StPatr 29 (1997) 184-494. — J. Liébaert, C. et l'arianisme. Les sources du Thesaurus et des "Dialogues sur la Trinité" (Lille, 1948). — J. Quasten, Patrology 3 (Utrecht, 1960), 116-142 (literature). — A. Rücker, Die Lukas-Homilien des C. (Breslau, 1911). — A. Vööbus, Discoveries on the Commentary on Luke by C. (Stockholm, 1973). — F. Young, From Nicaea to Chalcedon (London, 1983), 240-265.

III. Basic Lines of Thought: *Exegesis*: C. interprets the Bible while conscious that all human language about God is inadequate, as he says at the beginning of his commentary on John. This is not simply an empty literary gesture, for in the course of the commentary he makes repeated references to the poverty of human language in the face of the divine mysteries (e.g., on John 13:21). A look at Origen, Alexander Alex., and C. shows that insight into the necessity of analogy is the basis of Alexandrian allegorical exegesis. C., too, uses allegory, but even in the explanation of the OT makes room for the *historia* (e.g., on Hos 1:3) and is able to say that there are matters in which a forced spiritual interpretation can destroy the usefulness of a straightforward historical understanding (on John 9:4). C. clearly distances himself from the ideas of Origen, e.g., on the pre-existence of souls. In addition to the straightforward meaning of scripture C. recognizes a higher spiritual meaning, which in his view is inseparably bound up with the saving mystery of the incarnation; for this reason C.'s exegesis has been described as "christocentric." C. is also a master of the paraphrasing and imaginative psychologizing of the scripture text that was usual in the ancient art of the commentary; his work is permeated by practical-religious exhortations and chains of dogm. arguments, with fictitious accusations and objections serving to structure the presentation. Pastoral concern for a manner of life worthy of Christians is always present, but the major part of C.'s explanations of scripture has for its purpose to defend the orthodox faith.

L: A. Dupré La Tour, La doxa du Christ: RSR 48 (1960) 521-543; 49 (1961) 68-94. — L. Fatica, I Commentari a Giovanni di Teodoro di Mopsuestia e di C. (Rome, 1988). — D. Keating, The Baptism of Jesus in C.: Pro ecclesia 8 (1999) 201-222. — A. Kerrigan, C., Interpreter of Old Testament (Rome, 1952). — idem, Objects of Literal and Spiritual Senses of the NT according to C.: TU 63 (1957) 354-374. — B. de Margerie, L'exégèse christologique de C.: NRTh 102 (1980) 400-425 (= idem, Introduction à l'histoire de l'exégèse I [Paris, 1980], 270-303). — D. Pazzini, Critica alla dottrina origenista della preesistenza delle anime: CrSt 9 (1988) 237-279. — H. J. Vogt, Exegese der Alexandriner u. der Antiochener: FS E. Dassmann, JAC. E 23 (1996) 357-369. — idem, Exegese des Theodor v. Mopsuestia: FS W. Brandmüller (Paderborn, 1997), 5-27.

Christology: The Nestorian controversy, with its climax at the Council of Ephesus, provides reference points for dating C.'s works, but it does not provide a basis for distinguishing divergent or even contradictory statements in his christology. The Alexandrian tradition, as embodied in Athanasius, was more or less his only inheritance; at least he does not seem to have known anything about the Cappadocians' reaction to Apollinarism. On the other hand, in his early

writings C. does not formulate his christological teaching by simply following Athanasius; rather he represents an independent christological concern, the very one that he later shows against Nestorius. Modern attempts to describe the relation established by C. between the divine and human in Christ in more grammatical terms acc. to a subject-attribute model and then in more philosophical-ontological terms acc. to a substance–accident model are intended to explain the undeniable asymmetry in C.'s image of Christ, which has been emphasized as C.'s "fundamental intuition."

C. never denies the real and complete humanity of Christ, but he does insist that the really existing humanity in Christ exists not by itself but in the person of the Logos; since the Logos makes the humanity its very own, all that happens to the humanity is to be predicated of the Logos (the unity of subject in Christ was recently emphasized once again as the special concern of C.). It is with this in mind that C. formulates his statements about Christ and does so in the same way through all his writings, using as his preferred model the linguistic structure in Phil 2:6f. ("Existing in the form of God . . . he emptied himself"). In the fourth anathematism against Nestorius C. sets forth with great clarity the point that all the statements of the scriptures are to be related to one and the same person of the redeemer and that Christ must not be divided into two *prosōpa* by dividing up the statements about him. This is a point that he does not retract even in the union with the easterners in 433, as has sometimes been claimed, although the uncompromising position taken in the fourth anathematism is expressed in a more nuanced way in the Formula of Union. In any case, even later on C. maintains his reservations against the concept of *physis* for the humanity of Christ and intends, as in the letter to Acacius, to speak of two *physeis* only in the conceptual realm, because, when he takes the concept seriously, he evidently understands it to mean that which exists in and for itself. Given this overall background, we must allow that he himself gave an orthodox interpretation to the Apollinarist formula "the one incarnate nature of the Logos," which he adopted at the height of the controversy and regarded as genuinely Athanasian.

L: P. Angstenberger, Der reiche u. der arme Christus (Bonn, 1997). — G. Gould, C. and the Formula of Reunion: DR 106 (1988) 235-252. — A. Grillmeier, Jesus der Christus 1 (Freiburg i.Br., ³1990), 673-686 (English, Christ in Christian Tradition, vol. 1 [London, ²1975]). — G. Jouassard, Une intuition fondamentale de C. en christologie: REByz 11 (1953) 175-186. — J. Liébaert, La doctrine christologique de C. avant la querelle nestorienne (Lille, 1951). — idem,

L'évolution de la christologie de C. à partir de la controverse nestorienne: MSR 27 (1970) 27-48. — J. D. McCoy, Philosophical Influences on Doctrine of Incarnation in Athanasius and C.: Encounter 38 (1977) 362-391. — J. A. McGuckin, C.: Christological Controversy (Leiden, 1994) (literature). — R. A. Norris, Christological Models in C.: StPatr 13 = TU 116 (1975) 255-268. — R. M. Siddals, Logic and Christology in C.: JThS 38 (1987) 341-367. — M. Simonetti, Alcune osservazioni sul monofisismo di C.: Aug. 22 (1982) 493-511. — L. J. Welch, Christology and Eucharist in the early thought of C. (London, 1994).

Soteriology: Like other eastern fathers, C. has been counted among the representatives of a physical soteriology or incarnational soteriology, for which the life and activity of Christ, and espec. his saving work on the cross, have no significance in themselves as redemptive acts. But since then a more nuanced picture has been drawn. For although the beginnings of a naturist view of salvation in C. are not to be rejected out of hand, he does maintain that the saving activity of Christ runs from the incarnation to the cross and reaches its completion only with his ascent to the Father. After everything on earth had been completed (C. explains in connection with John 16:7), the ascent to the Father was a still missing part of the plan of salvation: Since Christ took his place before God in heaven as our precursor, the separation from God caused by sin has been overcome, even though heavenly fulfillment is still only a hope for other human beings.

L: O. Blanchette, C.'s Idea of Redemption: ScEc 16 (1964) 455-480. — L. Koen, Saving Passion, Incarnational and Soteriological Thought in C.'s Commentary on John (Uppsala, 1991). — G. Münch-Labacher, Naturhaftes u. geschichtliches Denken bei C. (Bonn, 1996). — B. Studer, Soteriologie: HDG 3/2a (Freiburg i.Br., 1978), 190-200. — idem, Gott u. unsere Erlösung (Düsseldorf, 1985), 242-247.

IV. Appreciation: Because of his activity in eccles. politics as metropolitan of Alexandria and because as the latter he had great influence and wealth, he has often been described as an unscrupulous spiritual ruler who knew how to make use of these available means for his goals in power politics. This may have applied to his uncle Theophilus, but a look at C.'s activity as a whole shows a bishop who tried first and foremost to be a theologian and to make his teaching a vehicle for the faith tradition of the church. In addition, C. dug the bed for the river of later dogm. and eccles. development, and made it so deep that on the whole that river never flowed elsewhere. It could thus be shown that the formulations seen in the Chalcedonian profession of faith (451) in, e.g., its emphasis on "one and the same," hold closer to C. than to Leo I. But because of his use of the Apollinar-

ist one-nature formula C. met with rejection in the East; this in turn led to the rise, on the one hand, of the so-called Nestorian church and, on the other, of the so-called Monophysite church.

L: A. de Halleux, La définition christologique à Chalcédoine: RTL 7 (1976) 3-23, 155-170. — idem, À propos d'une lecture cyrillienne de Chalcédoine: RTL 25 (1994) 445-471.

G. MÜNCH-LABACHER

Cyril of Jerusalem

I. Life: C. was born ca. 313 in or near Jerusalem and ordained a priest ca. 343 by Maximus of Jerusalem. After Maximus's deposition or death C. became his successor in 348, being installed by Acacius of Caesarea, who hoped to find in him an Arian ally. C. soon came into conflict with Acacius, possibly because of his attempt to liberate Jerusalem from Caesarea in the realm of eccles. politics. In 358, at the instigation of Acacius, C. was banished to Tarsus on the grounds that during a famine in 350 he had alienated church property. In 359, at the Council of Seleucia, where he sided with the homoousians, he was rehabilitated and returned to his see. At the Council of Constantinople (360), which accepted the position of the homoeans, which had been rejected at Seleucia, C. was once again banished (place unclear), but in 362, under Julian, was able to return to Jerusalem. There he fought against the planned rebuilding of the temple; after Julian's death the decree of banishment was reinstated under Valens. Only in 378 was the exile able to return. At the Council of Constantinople (381) C. was a leading homoousian; probably because of his changed status, the council issued a statement in C.'s defense with reference to his consecration and his struggle against the Arians. C. died on March 18, 386 or 387 (Theod., *h.e.* 2.26; 5.9; Soz., *h.e.* 3.14; 4, nos. 5, 16, 20, 22, 25, 30; 7.7; Soc., *h.e.* 2.38 and 40; 3.20; 5.8f.; Jerome, *vir. ill.* 112).

L: G. Bardy, C.: DSp 2:2683-2687. — E. Bihain, Vie arménienne: Muséon 76 (1973) 319-348. — J. Mader, C. (Einsiedeln, 1891). — P. Nautin, Mort de C.: RHE 56 (1961) 33-35. — E. Yarnold, C.: TRE 8:261-266.

II. Works: Handed down are eighteen catecheses (*catech.*) and a procatechesis (*procatech.*), which C. delivered probably in Lent 348 (possibly while still a presbyter; see *catech.* 18.32). The procatechesis exhorts to proper preparation; the wrong kind of motivations makes baptism ineffective. *Catech.* 1-5 deal with penance, baptism, and faith; 6-18 with the articles of the (Jerusalem) profession of faith, which was given, only orally, to the candidates (at the beginning of their instruction). It is not clear how the catecheses were distributed over the period of Lent. The background of the instruction in the Chr. faith is the debate with pagans, Jews (judaizing Christians?), Samaritans, and Manichees, a debate still relevant in 4th-c. Jerusalem. C. argues primarily from the fulfillment of OT promises; his language is full of images. Theologically, the influence of the school of Alexandria is predominant and marks C.'s teaching on God, anthropology, and redemption. He avoids using *homoousios* (see *catech.* 11.14 and 18; *catech. myst.* 3.1). The catecheses embody the classic form of baptismal instruction in the time of the imperial church and are, together with the mystagogical catecheses and the report of → Egeria, the most important source on the liturgy (and to some extent the archeology) of Jerusalem in the 4th c. C. left a decisive mark on the development of the liturgy and thereby influenced the entire church.

C.'s authorship of the five mystagogical catecheses (*catech. myst.*), which followed upon the baptismal catecheses (*catech.* 18.33) is disputed. C. has been denied these catecheses on the basis of the ms. tradition (in which they are sometimes attributed to C.'s successor, → John II) and on the grounds of theol. differences; on the other hand, there are also numerous similarities. It is certain that the mystagogical catecheses come from a later period than the baptismal catecheses. They were delivered to the newly baptized during Easter week and treat of the rites of baptism, anointing, and the Eucharist, as well as the Our Father; only the experience of baptism enables the newly baptized to understand the catecheses (*catech. myst.* 1.1). "Mystagogy" aims to bring to light the inner meaning of the liturgy. In the background is the concept of *mimesis,* or imitation. The liturgy imitates (Christ's) history of salvation and thereby communicates this salvation to believers. In the Eucharist they become "one body" and "one blood" (*syssōmoi* and *synaimai*) with Christ. Bread and wine are truly changed into body and blood (*metaballesthai*) (*catech. myst.* 4.2f.). It is disputed whether the liturgy described in the *catech. myst.* had an account of institution. Along with the catecheses of → Ambrose (*de sac.*), → John Chrys. (*catech. bapt.*), and → Theodore Mops. (*hom. cat.*), the *catech. myst.* represent the classical form of mystagogy in the early church.

A homily on the man with palsy (*hom.*) is authentic; it may come from C.'s time as a presbyter. Four other fragments of homilies are unimportant. From the first year of C.'s episcopate (350 or 351) came a letter to Emperor Constantius (*ep. Const.*) occasioned by the appearance of a cross over Jerusalem. The legend of the finding of the cross is not told either here or in the catecheses. A letter, handed down only in Syriac, about the rebuilding of the temple under Julian is also regarded today as authentic.

Certainly not authentic are three homilies on the passion, the cross, and Mary Magdalene; these have survived only in Coptic. A fictitious correspondence between Augustine and C. on the miracles of Jerome (PL 22:230-326) is from the 14th c.

W: PG 33. — *procatech., catech., catech. myst., ep. Const., hom.,* W. C. Reischl, J. Rupp (Hildesheim, 1967 = Munich, 1848/60) [text/Latin trans.]. — *procatech., catech., catech. myst.,* A. A. Stephenson (Washington, 1970) [text/English trans./comm.]. — P. Häusler, BKV² 41 (Munich, 1922) [German trans.]. — *catech. myst.,* A. Piédagnel, P. Paris, SC 126. — A. Winterswyl (Freiburg i.Br., ²1959) [German trans.]. — G. Röwekamp, FC 7. — *ep. Const.,* E. Bihain: Byz 43 (1973) 264-296. — J. F. Coakley: AnBoll 102 (1984) 71-84 [Syriac text/English trans.]. — *ep.,* S. P. Brock: BSOAS 40 (1977) 267-286 [Syriac text/English trans.] — Omelie copte, A. Campagnano (Milan, 1980) [text/Italian trans./comm.]. — R. G. Coquin, G. Gordon, Un encomion copte sur Marie-Madeleine: BIFAO 90 (1990) 169-212 [text].
L: Biblia Patristica 4 (Paris, 1987). — A. Bonato, Dottrina trinitario (Rome, 1983). — P. T. Camelot, Théologie baptismale: FS J. Quasten (Münster, 1970), 2:724-729. — F. Cardman, Rhetoric of Holy Places: StPatr 17/1:18-25. — E. J. Cutrone, Saving Presence in the Mystagogical Catecheses, Diss. (University of Notre Dame, 1975). — idem, Jerusalem Anaphora: OCP 44 (1978) 52-64. — K. Deddens, Annus liturgicus? (Goes, 1975). — G. Garitte, Catéchèses en arménien: Muséon 76 (1963) 95-108. — J. H. Greenlee, Gospel text (Copenhagen, 1955). — R. C. Gregg, C. and the Arians: idem, Arianism (Philadelphia, 1985), 85-109. — G. Hellemo, Adventus Domini (Amsterdam, 1989), 146-198. — P. Jackson, Use of Scripture: TS 52 (1991) 431-450. — W. R. Jenkinson, Image and the Likeness of God in Man: EThL 4 (1964) 46-71. — J. Lebon, Arianisme: RHE 20 (1924) 181-210, 357-386. — E. Mazza, Mystagogy (New York, 1989). — A. Piédagnel, Catéchèses mystagogiques. Tradition manuscrite: StPatr 10, 141-145. — A. Renoux, Version arménienne: Muséon 85 (1972) 147-153. — idem, Les catéchèses mystagogiques dans l'organisation hierosolymitaine: Muséon 78 (1965) 355-359. — H. M. Riley, Initiation (Washington, 1974). — A. A. Stephenson, Text of the Jerusalem Creed: StPatr 3:303-313. — idem, Alexandrian Heritage: TS 15 (1954) 573-593. — idem, Lenten Catechetical Syllabus: TS 15 (1954) 103-116. — idem, C. and the Alexandrian Christian Gnosis: StPatr 1, 142-156. — idem, C.'s Trinitarian Theology: StPatr 11, 234-241. — W. J. Swaans, Catéchèses mystagogiques: Muséon 55 (1942) 1-43. — P. Wainwright, Authenticity: VigChr 40 (1986) 286-293. — H. A. Wolfson, Philosophical Implications: DOP 11 (1957) 1-19. — E. Yarnold, Authorship of the Mystagogical Catecheses: HeyJ 19 (1978) 143-161.

G. RÖWEKAMP

Cyril of Scythopolis

C. was born ca. 525 in Scythopolis (Beth-Shean), the capital of Palestina Secunda and in 543 went to Jerusalem to attend the dedication of the Nea Church. In 544 he entered the New Laura, where he remained until 555. During this period he was active primarily in the struggle against Origenism, which had gained strength in Palestine. In 557 he transferred to the great Laura of St. Sabas. There he worked until his death (ca. 558) as composer of numerous lives of monks; these, despite the overgrowth of legend, contain a great deal of source material on the Origenist controversy in Palestine and on life in the monasteries of the Judean wilderness. The following have come down: *Vita Euthymii* (d. 473), *Vita Sabae* (d. 532), *Vita Ioannis Silentiarii* (d. 558), *Vita Cyriaci* (d. 556), *Vita Theodosii* (d. 529), *Vita Theognii* (d. 522), *Vita Abramii* (d. 557).

W: *vitae*, PG 114:595-734; 115:919-944. — E. Schwartz, TU 49/2 [text/German trans.]. — A. Festugière, Les moines d'Orient 3:1/3 (Paris, 1962-63) [French trans.]. — G. Graf, Geschichte der arab. Lit. 1 (Rome, 1944), 408 [Arabic mss.]. — P. Peeters, Versions arabes: Mach. 8 (1903) 258-265; 12 (1909) 344-353 [Arabic text]. — R. M. Price, Lives of the Monks of Palestine (Kalamazoo, 1991) [English trans.].
L: R. Draguet, Palladius: RAM 25 (1949) 213-218. — G. Garitte, Version géorgienne: Muséon 75 (1962) 399-440. — idem, Mort de s. Jean: AnBoll 72 (1954) 75-84. — idem, Réminiscences de la vie d'Antoine: FS Mercati (Rome, 1957), 117-122. — J. Gill, Life of Stephen the Younger: OCP 6 (1940) 114-139. — T. Herrmann, Chronologie: ZKG 45 (1926) 318-339. — E. Stein, C. de Scythopolis: AnBoll 62 (1944) 169-186.

P. Bruns

Cyrillonas (Qûrillônâ)

There have come down under the name of C. six poems (*carm.*) in a ms. of the British Museum. Their subjects: the footwashing, crucifixion, Easter, whipping post and flogging, conversion of Zacchaeus, and the wheat. For stylistic reasons the last-named poem can be certainly attributed to C. On the other hand, C. can probably be called the author of an anonymously transmitted poem on the Holy Spirit (*spir.*). Nothing more is known of C.'s life except that he was active at the time of the war with the Huns (395/396) and was probably a native of the area around Edessa. Ephraem's influence on him is unmistakable. In addition to his accomplishments as a poet who was master of the form known as the *sogita*, a kind of dialogue, C. is also important in the history of piety, since he can be adduced as a witness to the flourishing veneration of saints and relics in the Syr. church.

In his sermonlike poems C. often takes up apocalyptic and parenetic subjects (end of the world, repentance, and judgment). His image of Christ is popular and traditional (*descensus*) and closely allied with that of other Syr. writers (→ Ephraem, → Aphraates). His conception of the Eucharist has a strongly realistic tinge.

W: *carm.*, G. Bickell, Gedichte: ZDMG 27 (1873) 566-598; 35 (1881) 531f. [Syriac text]. — S. Landersdorfer, Syr. Dichter (Munich, 1913), 3-54 [German trans.]. — R. Graffin, Deux poèmes: OrSyr 10 (1965) 307-330 [French trans.]. — C. Vona, I Carmi di Cirillona (Rome, 1963). — D. Cerbelaud, L'agneau véritable (Chevetogne, 1984) [French trans.]. — *spir.*, T. Jansma, Sur l'effusion du Saint-Esprit: OrSyr 10 (1965) 157-178 [text/French trans.].
L: I. Ortiz de Urbina, Mariologia: OCP 1 (1935) 110f.

P. Bruns

Cyrus of Alexandria

C. was initially (626) bishop of Phasis but from 631 on was patriarch of Alexandria and prefect of Egypt. In June 631, on the basis of Alexandrian Monenergism, he reached an agreement of union with the Theodosians, whose new dogmatic *kephalaia* (*cap.*) he formulated. In 639/640 he was deposed and banished by Emperor Heraclius because of his dealings with the Arabs, but was reinstated in 641 and sent back to Alexandria. He was finally obliged to surrender Alexandria to the Arabs; he died in March 642. Three letters of C. (*ep.*) to Sergius of Constantinople have also survived.

W: *cap.*, Mansi 11:564C8-568B6. — *ep.*, Mansi 10:1004E9-1005D2; 11:560D11-561D4; 11:561D5-564C7.
L: A. Alcock, C. the Makaukas: Muséon 86 (1973) 73f. — E. Amélineau, Fragments Coptes: JA 12 (1888) 372-410. — A. S. Atiya, C.: CoptE 3, 682f. — H. G. Beck, Kirche u. theol. Lit. (Munich, 1959), 292, 431f. — Die Geschichte des Christentums 4 (Freiburg i.Br., 1994), 26f., 41, 46, 48. — F. S. Pericoli Ridolfini, C.: EC 3:1734. — S. Vailhé, C.: DThC 3/2:2582f.

B. Windau

Cyrus of Edessa

C. was a teacher in the school of Nisibis in the 6th c. He later established his own school in Hirta. He completed the treatise of → Thomas of Edessa on the feasts of the liturgical year.

From his pen come six explanations (*Explanationes*) of Lent, Easter, the passion of Christ, the resurrection, the ascension, and Pentecost. These are didactic treatises on questions of liturgy and the Chr. mysteries of salvation. They are distinguished by a more thorough systematization of the material discussed by → Theodore Mops. in his catechetical homilies and are an important source for the liturgy and doctrine of the 6th-c. Nestorians.

W: W. F. Macomber, CSCO 355/356 [text/English trans.].
L: W. F. Macomber, Theological Synthesis: OCP 30 (1964) 5-38, 363-384.

P. BRUNS

Cyrus of Panopolis, Poet

Poet and prose writer Flavius Taurus Seleucus Cyrus Hierax (C.), who was born ca. 400 in Panopolis (Egypt), had a many-sided career. From 439 to 441 he was *praefectus urbis* for Constantinople and, rather exceptionally, was at the same time *praefectus praetorio Orientis*; in 441 he became consul. He completed the city walls of Constantinople and built a church in honor of Mary as Theotokos. He owed his promotion to Empress Eudocia, who was likewise a poet. Through the intrigue of pagans at the court he was indicted, lost his offices in 441, and was banished by Theodosius II. Under pressure from the emperor he allowed himself to be consecrated bishop of Cotyaeum (Phrygia) in 443. Ca. 450 he returned to Constantinople as a private individual and died there ca. 470.

C. composed espec. epics (Suidas 2776 [ed. A. Adler, vol. 3, Leipzig, 1933], 220), which were still well known in the 6th c. (Lydus, *mag.* 2.12) but today are completely lost. Since Evagrius Scholasticus (*h.e.* 1.19) aligns C. with Claudius Claudianus, these epics were probably panegyrics for members of the imperial court. Of the epigrams (*epigr.*) which the Gr. anthology puts under the name of C., 1.99 (three elegiac distichs on Daniel the Stylite), 9.136 (three elegiac distichs on C.'s banishment), and 15.9 (eight dactylic hexameters, an encomium of Theodosius II) may be taken as authentic, while the authenticity of 7.557; 9.623, 808, and 809 remains uncertain. In Cotyaeum, probably in Dec. 441, C. was compelled by the people to preach a sermon on Christmas. His *Homilia in nativitatem* (*nat.*) (handed down by Theophanes Homologetes [ca. 752 to 818]) consists of two sentences that show him a defender of orthodoxy: "Brethren, the birth of God and our Savior Jesus Christ should be honored with silence, for the Word of God was conceived in the holy Virgin solely through hearing. God be praised for ever! Amen." Acc. to a hypothesis developed by A. Cameron after P. Peeters, C. is also author of the anonymously transmitted *Passio S. Menae*, an account (modeled on Basil's homily *In Gordianum martyrem*) of the martyrdom of Menas, the most important of the saints from Egypt.

W: *epigr.*, H. Beckby, Anthologia Graeca (Munich, 1957/58) [text/German trans.]. — *nat.*, Theophanes, Chronographia A. M. 5937, C. de Boor (Leipzig, 1883). — *Passio S. Menae*, G. van Hooff: AnBoll 3 (1884) 258-270.
L: A. Cameron, The Empress and the Poet: Paganism and Politics at the Court of Theodosius II: YCS 27 (1982) 217-289. — D. J. Constantelos, Kyros Panopolites, Rebuilder of Constantinople: GRBS 12 (1971) 451-464. — T. E. Gregory, The Remarkable Christmas Homily of Kyros Panopolites: GRBS 16 (1975) 317-324. — PLRE 2:36-339. — P. Peeters, Le tréfonds oriental de l'hagiographie byzantine (Brussels, 1950), 39f.

S. DÖPP

Cyrus of Tyana

C. was bishop of Tyana. From him we have two fragments of an *Ep. ad Iulianum et Severum* (*fr.*) written perhaps between 508 and 511, in which he takes a stand against the Chalcedonian Creed. Ca. 518, however, he recanted.

W: F. Diekamp, Doctrina patrum (Münster, ²1981), 313, Nr. 35/36 [text].
L: A. Grillmeier, Jesus der Christus 2/2 (Freiburg i.Br., 1984), 263f. (English, Christ in Christian Tradition, vol. 2/2 [London, 1995]). — E. Honigmann, Évêques et évêchés monophysites (Leuven/Louvain, 1951), 113f.

B. WINDAU

D

Dadiso of Bet Qatraje

D. was a monk in the monastery of the Apostles and in those of Rabkennare and Rabban Shabor and was active in the second half of the 7th c. as a commentator on monastic-ascetic writings. Thus he composed a commentary (*comm.*) on → Isaiah, an ascetic, and on the *Paradise of the Fathers* by → Enaniso. From his pen came a *Sermo de solitudine* (*solit.*) as well as another treatise that was previously attributed to → Philoxenus of Mabbug and that has come down in Eth. and Arab. versions. The *Exhortationes ad monachos* may also be his. Also surviving is a letter (*ep.*) to Abkos on the soul's rest.

W: *solit.*, A. Mingana, Early Christian Mystics (Cambridge, 1934), 201-247, 76-143 [text/English trans.]. — *comm.*, R. Draguet, CSCO 326/327 [text/French trans.]. — N. Sims-Williams, Sogdian fragment: AM 18 (1973) 88-105. — *ep.*, A. Guillaumont, M. Albert, Lettre de D.: FS A. J. Festugière (Geneva, 1984), 235-245.
L: P. Bettiolo, Purezza di cuore: ASEs 3 (1986) 201-213.

P. BRUNS

Dalmat(i)us, Archimandrite

D. was first an officer of the guard under Theodosius I. Only in his advanced years did he, along with his son Faustus, enter the chief monastery in Constantinople; in 406 he succeeded Isaac as its head; it came to be called the monastery of Dalmatus after him. Later on, D., who was highly esteemed and was venerated as a saint after his death, became archimandrite of the monasteries of Constantinople. During the Council of Ephesus (431) he supported Cyril. To this end he finally left the monastery for the first time in forty-eight years and went to Theodosius II with a crowd of faithful and monks. In response, Theodosius summoned the followers of Cyril and Nestorius to Chalcedon for a clarificatory dialogue. D.'s involvement in the Nestorian controversy is attested by two letters to the Council of Ephesus (*ep. Eph.* 1; 2) and an address to the people of Constantinople (*apologia*; *apol.*). He died ca. 440.

W: *apol.*, ACO 1, 1, 2, 68f. [Greek text]. — ACO 1, 3, 89 [Latin text]. — *ep. Eph.* 1, ACO 1, 1, 7, X [Greek text]. — *ep. Eph.* 2, ACO 1, 1, 3, 14f. [Greek text]. — ACO 1, 3, 95f. [Latin text].
L: P. Bazoche, D.: BSS 4:428f. — A. Berger, Untersuchungen zu der Patria Konstantinupoleos (Bonn, 1988), 630. — G. Dagron, Les moines et la ville: TMCB 4 (1970) 229-276. — V. Grumel, D.: DHGE 14:27f.

B. WINDAU

Damasus I of Rome

I. Life: D. was born ca. 305, presumably in Rome, and died there on Dec. 11, 384. He was a deacon of Liberius, joined antipope Felix for a while, and then, after returning from exile, sided again with Liberius. After the latter's death (Sept. 24, 366) there was a double election and a bloody fight with many killed. After being consecrated bishop of Rome on Oct. 1, 366, D. was able, with the emperor's help, to win out against the minority candidate, Ursinus, but almost his entire pontificate was overshadowed by the hostility of the opposing party (including criminal proceedings brought by Isaac). He nevertheless managed to achieve important successes in establishing the preeminence of Rome: in 378, in addition to ensuring the support of the state in carrying out eccles. court proceedings, Gratian gave the bishop of Rome juridical supremacy over the metropolitans of the West; in the edict *Cunctos populos* (380) Theodosius II made the faith of Bishops D. and Peter (of Alexandria) the standard of orthodoxy; on the *Decretum Gelasianum*, see II, below. D. worked closely with Ambrose (struggle against Arianism; rejection of the appeal of Priscillian), Jerome (among other things, the revision of the Latin Bible), Athanasius, and his successor, Peter. D.'s intransigent attitude during the Antiochene Schism (recognition of Paulinus, rejection of Meletius) disturbed his relations with Basil, but the numerous confessions of faith and anathematisms of D. and Roman synods were partially accepted at the Synod of Antioch (379). The extensive building activity of D. in turning Rome into the Chr. capital (erection of several churches, building or adornment of martyrs' memorials) is attested by inscriptions.

II. Works: Under the name of D. various texts have come down that have to some extent a complicated history of transmission. The dating of the writings usually known as *Epistulae* (*ep.*) 1-9 is in some cases disputed. *Ep.* 1 (*Confidimus quidem*; RPR[J] 232) is the letter of a Roman synod of 371 (condemnation of Arian Bishop Auxentius of Milan; fidelity to Nicaea; rejection of the Synod of Rimini [359]). *Ep.* 2 (RPR[J], after 233) consists of three fragments (*Ea gratia, Illud sane miramur, Non nobis*), from between 375 and 377, which take positions in eastern controversies: the trinitarian (espec. the pneumatological) and the incipient christological (Apollinaris of Laodicea); the prohibition against the transfer of bishops in *Ea gratia* (see also *ep.* 4 and 5) is aimed at Meletius. *Ep.* 3 (*Per filium meum*; RPR[J] 235; 376?) to Paulinus of Antioch demands the confession of

Nicaea and the complete humanity of Christ as a condition for church communion. *Ep.* 4 (RPR[J] 235), the *Tomus* or *Fides Damasi*, also known as the twenty-four *Anathematisms*, is the document of a Roman synod at the end of 377/beginning of 378: Eight statements introduced by anathemas condemn, among others, the opponents of the *homoousios*, the Macedonians, and the Apollinarists; the ninth condemns the translation of bishops (Meletius); the next fifteen statements, beginning with *Si quis*, reject particular theol. positions of the groups named. *Ep.* 5 (*Decursis litteris*; RPR[J] 237) complains of the illegal installation of Maximus, a Cynic, as bishop of Constantinople and asks that the synod convoked there (381) see to a canonically unobjectionable election of a bishop (also includes a prohibition against translation of bishops). *Ep.* 6 (*Ad meritum*; RPR[J] 238), a short letter of recommendation, refers back to *ep.* 5 (both probably from the end of 380/beginning of 381). *Ep.* 7 (RPR[J] 234; between 371 and 381[?]), which has come down only in a Gr. translation in Theod., *h.e.* 5.10), praises the respect shown to the Apostolic See by the inquirer (a presbyter in Beirut?) and explains that a new, express condemnation of Bishop Timothy of Berytus (Beirut) is unnecessary. In *ep.* 8 (*Commentaria cum*; RPR[J] 239) and *ep.* 9 (*Dormientem te*; RPR[J] 253) D. asks (383/384?) Jerome for information on exegetical questions, which the latter gives in his *ep.* 20 and 36.

At least the nucleus of the third chapter (*Post has omnes*) of the so-called → *Decretum Gelasianum* (RPR[J] 251) must go back to the Roman synod of 382, for in response to canons 2 and 3 of Constantinople (381) it formulates the doctrine of the three Petrine sees as the basis of precedence in the church; chs. 1 and 2 seem to be later. The decretal *Ad episcopos Galliae*, an anonymously transmitted collection of Roman decrees on church discipline, is ascribed in part to → Siricius (*ep.* 10), in part to D.; the date is likewise uncertain. The synodal letter to Gratian, *Et hoc gloriae vestrae* (378; see above), was certainly not written without the input of D. Of the many poems (*carm.*) transmitted under the name of D. fifty-nine → inscriptions are genuine. In addition, *carm.* 1 and 2 are really inscriptions, for which Furius Dionysius Philocalus created a new, neoclassical script (*litterae Damasianae*). The great majority of the inscriptions are eulogies of Roman martyrs which in the tradition of the ancient Roman funeral eulogies praise the new heroes of Chr. Rome (e.g., *carm.* 15-17; 37; 40); some report on buildings undertaken by D. (e.g., *carm.* 3; 24; 57; 58), and some are simple inscriptions for

tombs (e.g., *carm.* 10-12). *Carm.* 16; 21; 25; 37 have come almost complete in the original, the others in copies or fragments. Attested, but not surviving, are further letters (RPR[J]) and writings on virginity in verse and in prose (Jerome, *ep.* 20; 22). In the course of time, a whole series of letters (e.g., further correspondence with Jerome) and poems (e.g., *De vitiis*) have been attributed to D., all of them unauthentic (see PL 13:423-42; PLS 1:323f., 568; RPR[J] +240-+250; Ferrua, *carm.* 60-77).

W: *ep.*, PL 13:347-373. — *ep.* 1-2, E. Schwartz, Sammlung des Cod. Veronensis LX: ZNW 35 (1936) 19-23 [text/comm.]. — M. Richard, La lettre Confidimus quidem: AIPh 11 (1951) 323-340 = idem, Opera minora 2 (Turnhout, 1977), nr. 35 [text/comm.]. — *ep.* 3, C. H. Turner, EOMJA 1.2.1, 295 [text]. — *ep.* 4 = Tomus/Fides Damasi = 24 Anathematismen, C. H. Turner, EOMJA 1.2.1, 283-294 [text]. — *ep.* 5-6 = Collectio Thessalonicensis 1-2, C. Silva-Tarouca, TD. T 23, 16-19 [text]. — *ep.* 7 = Theodoret, *h.e.* 5.10, L. Parmentier, F. Scheidweiler, GCS 44 [19]:295-297 [Greek text]. — A. Seider, BKV² 51:281f. [German trans.]. — *ep.* 8-9 = Hieronymus, *ep.* 19.35, I. Hilberg, CSEL 54:103f., 265-267 [text]. — *Decretum Gelasianum*, E. v. Dobschütz, TU 38/4 [text/comm.]. — C. H. Turner, EOMJA 1.1.2, 155a-158a [text]. — PL 13:374-376 [text]. — *ad episcopos Galliae* = Siricius, *ep.* 10, PL 13:1181-1194. — E. Babut, La plus ancienne décrétale (Paris, 1904), 65-87 [text/comm.]. — *Et hoc gloriae vestrae*, PL 13:575-584. — S. Wenzlowsky, Briefe der Päpste 2, BKV¹: 265-406, 460-476 [German trans.]. — *carm.*, C. Carletti, D. u. die röm. Martyrer (Rome, 1986) [text/German trans./comm.; selections]. — A. Ferrua, Epigrammata Damasiana (Rome, 1942) [text/comm.]. — E. Schäfer, Bedeutung der Epigramme des D. für die Geschichte der Heiligenverehrung (Rome, 1932) [text/German trans./comm.; selections].

L: R. Brändle, Petrus u. Paulus als nova sidera: ThZ 48 (1992) 207-217. — F. di Capua, Ritmo prosaico nelle lettere dei papi: Lat. 3 (1937) 251-273. — E. Caspar, Geschichte des Papsttums 1 (Münster, 1985 = Tübingen, 1930), 196-256, 592-599. — A. Di Berardino (ed.), Patrologia (Turin, 1983 = 1978), 260-264. — G. L. Dossetti, Simbolo di Nicea e di Constantinopoli (Rome, 1967), 94-111. — Epistolari Cristiani 2 (Rome, 1990), 22-24. — J. Fontaine, Naissance de la poésie dans l'occident chrétien (Paris, 1981), 111-125. — H. Getzeny, Stil u. Form der ältesten Papstbriefe (Günzburg, 1922), 17-22, 94-100. — P. P. Joannou, Ostkirche u. Cathedra Petri (Stuttgart, 1972), 14-19, 159-293. — H. Leclerq, D.: DACL 4/1:145-197. — C. Pietri, Roma Christiana 1 (Rome, 1976), 575-884. — G. Puglisi, Giustizia criminale e persecuzioni antieretiche: SicGym 43 (1990) 91-137. — Saecularia Damasiana, Atti del XVI centenario della morte di D. (Rome, 1986). — P. Santorelli, L'epigramma a Proietta di D. (51 F): Sicilia e Italia suburbicaria, ed. S. Pricoco, N. F. Rizzo, T. Sardella (Soveria, 1991), 327-336. — J. Speigl, Die Päpste in der Reichskirche: Das Papsttum 1, ed. M. Greschat (Stuttgart, 1985), 46-48. — R. Staats, Röm. Tradition im Symbol von 381 (NC) u. seine Entstehung auf der Synode v. Antiochien: VigChr 44 (1990) 209-221. — W. Ullmann, Gelasius I. (Stuttgart, 1981), 8, 20-34, 256-259. — G. Wesch-Klein, D. I., Vater der päpstlichen Epigraphik: FS H. Mordek (Frankfurt a.M.,

1999), 1-30. — M. Wojtowytsch, Papsttum u. Konzile (Stuttgart, 1981), 138-204, 430-437.

H. M. WEIKMANN

Damian of Alexandria

D., a Monophysite patriarch of Alexandria (578-606/607), was a native of Syria. After first living in various Egyptian monasteries, in 575 he became secretary of Peter IV, and in 578 patriarch of Alexandria. He consolidated the Monophysite church of Egypt, but was unable to achieve union with the Jacobite church of Syria. Due to a controversy with Peter of Callinicus, patriarch of Antioch, a schism arose which ended only after D.'s death in 616. Even then, however, a group of his followers (Damianites) continued in existence.

Letters and fragments of various writings of D., who was accused of Sabellianism, have survived. In two letters of 578, namely, the synodal letter (*ep. synodica*) to → Jacob Baradaeus, to whom D. introduced himself after his ordination, and a letter of consolation (*ep. consolatoria*) after Jacob's death, D. wrote attacks on Chalcedon and the *Tomus* of Leo, on tritheism and Julian of Halicarnassus. His initial friendship with → Peter of Callinicus is attested by three letters praising Peter (*ep. ad Petrum* of 581/582) that are preserved in Peter's work *Contra tritheistas*. But this friendship turned into enmity after D. in ca 586 sent Peter a work against the tritheists (probably the same as the treatise *Adversus tritheistas*), in which he criticized Peter. Fragments (*fr.*) of this and other writings (*Apologia secunda, ep. ad episcopos Orientis*) are preserved in Peter's *Adversus Damianum*. Finally, a fragment has come down of a Copt. sermon (*hom. in nat.*) which D. preached on Christmas in Alexandria.

During his patriarchate an important school of Coptic-speaking writers came into existence.

W: *ep. synodica*, J. B. Chabot, Chronique de Michel le Syrien (Brussels, 1963 = Paris, 1901/1910), 2:325-334/4, 358-363 [Syriac text/French trans.]. — W. E. Crum, Coptic Fragments: Monastery of Epiphanius, ed. H. E. Winlock (New York, 1926), 2:331-337 [Coptic text]. — *ep. consolatoria*, J. B. Chabot, loc. cit., 2:339-342/4, 368f. [text/French trans.]. — *ep. ad Petrum*, R. Y. Ebied, A. van Roey, L. R. Wickham, Peter of Callinicus. Anti-Tritheist Dossier (Leuven/Louvain, 1981), 81f./54f., 84-86/57f., 91f./62f. [Syriac text/English trans.]. — *fr.*, Petrus C., *Contra Damianum*, R. Y. Ebied, A. van Roey, L. R. Wickham, CCG 29 [Syriac text/English trans.]. — *hom. in nat.*, W. E. Crum, Theological Texts from Coptic Papyri (Oxford, 1913), 21-33 [text/English trans.]. — F. Rossi, I papiri copti 2/4 (Turin, 1887-1892), 56-79 [Coptic text].
L: R. Y. Ebied, Peter of Antioch and D.: FS A. Vööbus

(Chicago, 1977), 277-282. — A. Grillmeier, Jesus der Christus 2/4 (Freiburg i.Br., 1990), 73f., 76-82 (English, Christ in Christian Tradition, vol. 2/4 [London, 1996]). — J. Maspéro, Histoire des patriarches d'Alexandrie (Paris, 1923), 278-317. — C. D. G. Müller, D., Papst u. Patriarch v. Alexandrien: OrChr 79 (1986) 118-142. — S. Vailhé, D. 1: DTC 4/1:39f.

B. WINDAU

Daniel bar Maryam

D. was active in Syria in the mid-7th c. and, in addition to a manual on the calendar, composed a four-part history of the church that has been lost, except for a few citations from it. It seems to have been a main source for the author of the *Chronicle of Seert*.

L: E. Degen, D. Ein nestorianischer Kirchenhistoriker: OrChr 52 (1968) 45-80. — idem, Kirchengeschichte des D.: ZDMG Suppl. 1 (1969) 511-516.

P. BRUNS

Daniel of Salah

Acc. to his own testimony, D., from Salah in Mesopotamia, was the author of a three-volume commentary on the Psalms (*comm. in Ps.*) in homily form, which he composed in 541-542. This work was supplemented by a commentary on Qoh and a work on the plagues of Egypt; nothing is left of these two works but a few references.

W: *comm. in Ps.*, G. Diettrich, Eine jakobitische Einleitung in den Psalter (Giessen, 1912) [text/German trans.]. — L. Lazarus, Homilien des D.: WZKM 9 (1895) 85-108, 149-224 [text/German trans.].

P. BRUNS

David the Armenian (the Unconquered)

Under the name of a certain D. a number of translations and other works have come down, but their attribution is disputed. The name D. applies to at least two authors, the first of whom, because of his philosophical erudition, was also called "the Unconquered" and was active probably in the 5th c. The second came from the village of Hark and is clearly to be located in a later period (7th c.). Various treatises on Aristotle (*an., cat., def.*), Porphyry (*intr.*), and translations (→ Cyril Alex., → Nemesius of Emesa) are attributed to D. the philosopher. He also translated and commented on the grammar of Dionysius Thrax (*gramm.*). D. of Hark is thought to have been the author of scholia (*schol.*) on five addresses of → Gregory Naz., as well as of an anti-Nestorian homily on the cross (*cruc.*).

W: *Collected works* (Venice, 1932). — *an.*, Y. Mandian, D. Commentarius in Aristotelem (St. Petersburg, 1911). [text]. — *cat.*, S. S. Arevshatean, D. Philosophische Kategorien (Erevan, 1960) [text/Russian trans.]. — *intr.*, idem, D. Analyse zur Eisagoge des Porphyrius (Erevan, 1976) [text/Russian trans.]. — *def.*, B. Kendall, R. W. Thomson, Definitions and Divisions (Chico, Calif., 1983) [text/English trans.]. — *cat., intr., def.*, A. Busse, Commentaria in Aristotelem (Berlin, 1904) [Greek text]. — *schol.*, A. Mandian, Scholien (Marburg, 1903) [Armenian text/German trans.]. — *cruc.*, PP Mechitaristae, Coriun, David Invicti al. opera omnia (Venice, 1833) [Armenian text]. — *gramm.*, J. C. de Cirbied, Grammaire de Denis de Thrace (Paris, 1830) [Greek and Armenian text/French trans.]. — N. Adontz, Denys de Thrace (Leuven/Louvain, 1970) [Armenian text/French trans.].
L: N. Akinian, D. der Unbesiegte u. D. v. Hark: HandAm 70 (1956) 123-163, 301-320. — idem, D. v. Hark u. seine Übersetzungen: HandAm 71 (1957) 267-281. — L. G. Chatscherian, Dionysius Thrax: HandAm 101 (1987) 527-554. — F. C. Conybeare, D. the Invincible (Vienna, 1893). — idem, A Collation with the Armenian Versions of Aristoteles (Oxford, 1892). — A. K. Sanian, D. the "Invincible Philosopher" (Atlanta, 1986).

P. BRUNS

De Martyrio Maccabaeorum

A Lat. poem of 394 hexameters which the tradition has ascribed to → Hilary of Poitiers, → Hilary of Arles, and → Victorinus of Pettau. There are two versions of this little poem, which is characterized by a rather direct use of bibl. material

The *Passio Machabeorum* (H. Dörrie [Göttingen, 1938]), on the other hand, is a Lat. translation from late antiquity of 4 Maccabees (which has the same material as 2 Mac 6-7 and at one time was counted among the canonical books, but never was part of the Lat. Bible).

W: PL 50:1275-1286. — R. Peiper, CSEL 23:240-254, 255-269.
L: D. Kartschoke, Bibeldichtung (Munich, 1975), 35f., 105-111. — M. Schatkin, The Maccabean martyrs: VigChr 28 (1974) 97-113.

P. BRUNS

De Miraculis S. Stephani

This anon. work in two books on the miracles wrought by the relics of St. Stephen in Africa Proconsularis was composed ca. 424, after the relics of the first martyr, found in 415, reached Africa in 418. The work was composed at Augustine's suggestion (see *civ.* 22.8) under Bishop Evodius of Uzala. It is an early and important witness to the rapid spread of the veneration of relics.

W: PL 41:833-854. — J. Hillgarth [in preparation].
L: H. Delehaye, Les premiers libelli miraculorum: AnBoll 29 (1910) 427-434. — idem, Les recueils antiques des miracles des saints: AnBoll 43 (1925) 74-85. — V. Saxer, Morts, martyrs, reliques en Afrique (Paris, 1980), 246-254.

G. RÖWEKAMP

De monogramma Christi

The work *De monogramma* (or: *monogrammate*) *Christi* is a short treatise on the form and meaning of the monogram of Christ in its Gk. form. The monogram is made up of the three superimposed letters X, I, and S, the numerical value of which is 616, a number from which it should be possible ultimately to derive the real name of Christ. The work, found after the commentary on the Apocalypse of → Victorinus of Pettau, which Jerome edited, was attributed to Jerome, specifically either as an appendix to the commentary on the Apocalypse or an independent exegetical work on Rev 13:18. But the attribution to Jerome was rejected and the composition of the work dated to the time after Jerome.

W: PLS 2:287-291 — G. Morin, Hieronymi de monogramma: RBen 20 (1903) 232-236.
L: G. Grützmacher, Hieronymus 3 (Berlin, 1908), 238. — I. Haussleiter, CSEL 49:124 n. 4. — E. Peterson, De monogramma Christi: EC 4:1427. — M. Schanz, Geschichte der röm. Lit. 4/1 (Munich, [2]1959), 472.

B. WINDAU

De Ogdoade et Enneade

Among the gnostic-hermetic writings of Nag Hammadi (NHC 6, 6) is a cosmological treatise *The Discourse on the Eighth and the Ninth* (*Ogdo. et En.*). It deals with the eighth and ninth divine spheres, beyond the seven planets, as the place of origin of the light-soul and the place to which it returns after being delivered from the misery of matter.

W: J. P. Mahé, Hermès en Haute-Égypte (Leuven/Louvain, 1978) [Coptic text/French trans./comm.]. — K. W. Tröger: ThLZ 98 (1973) 495-503 [German trans.]. — NHL 322-327 [English trans.].
L: P. Chérix, Concordance NHC 6 (Leuven/Louvain, 1993). — C. de Santis, Gli scritti ermetici: SMSR 11 (1987) 57-65. — J. P. Mahé, Sens et composition: RevSR 48 (1974) 54-65. — idem, Voie d'immortalité: VigChr 45 (1991) 347-375. — L. Motte, Vache multicolore: Études Coptes 3 (Leuven/Louvain, 1989), 130-149.

P. BRUNS

De origine mundi

This anon., untitled Copt. treatise on the origin of the world (*orig.*), from the Nag Hammadi library (NHC 2, 5 and 13, 2), gives a gnostic reinterpretation of Gen 1-3 and offers cosmological considerations on the origin of the universe as well as on the origin and destiny of the light-soul within it. The Pistis Sophia, an ur-divinity beyond the universe, uses a demiurge to create the world, the nonrational, material part of which is governed by the archons. The work is very much a compilation; it deals critically with ancient Gk. creation myths (Hesiod), while on the other hand taking over a wealth of Hellen. material (Eros and Psyche; phoenix). Also present are Jewish-apocalyptic traditions about the divine throne-chariot (*merkabah*) and Egyptian ideas (sacred bulls and crocodiles).

W: A. Böhlig, P. Labib, Kopt.-Gnostische Schrift ohne Titel (Berlin, 1962) [Coptic text/German trans.]. — L. Painchaud, W. P. Funk, L'écrit sans titre (Leuven/Louvain, 1995) [Coptic text/French trans./comm.]. — H. G. Bethge, Vom Ursprung der Welt (Berlin, 1975) [German trans.]. B. Layton, NHC 2, 2-7; 13, 2 (Leiden, 1989), 11-134 [Coptic text/English trans.]. — NHL 170-189 [English trans.]. L: J. Mansfeld, Hesiod and Parmenides: VigChr 35 (1981) 174-182. — G. Mussies, Catalogues of Sins: Studies in Gnosticism, ed. R. van den Broek (Leiden, 1981), 315-335. — L. Painchaud, Something is rotten: Acts of V. Congress of Coptic Studies, ed. D. W. Johnson (Rome, 1993), 339-353. — idem, Redaction: Sect.en 8 (1991) 217-234. — idem, Sommaire anthropogonique: VigChr 44 (1990) 382-393. — P. Perkins, Origin of the World: VigChr 34 (1980) 36-46.

P. Bruns

Decretum Gelasianum

The so called *Decretum Gelasianum de libris recipiendis et non recipiendis* (*Decr. Gelas.*) is a work in five chapters, in which two originally independent blocks have been combined. Ch. 1 deals with the names of Christ and the Holy Spirit; ch. 2 gives a canonical list of OT and NT books, in which all twenty-seven of the NT books are found. The *Decr. Gelas.* thus documents the close of the development of the canon. Ch. 3 deals with the primacy of the Roman church. At least in these first three parts the *Decr.* mirrors Roman tradition and, in this form, may go back to → Damasus I (366-384) or to a Roman synod of 382.

Ch. 4 contains a list of recognized synods and writers, and ch. 5 a list of apocrypha and other writings to be rejected. This second block of material comes probably from the end of the 5th or beginning of the 6th c. from southern Gaul. The latest apocryphal writer mentioned is Peter of Alexandria (d. 489). The Three-Chapters controversy is not mentioned. The joining of the two blocks probably occurred at the beginning of the 6th c. Since the 7th c., the work has gone under the name of → Gelasius, bishop of Rome (492-496), who was regarded as a reformer.

W: PL 19:787-794 (chs. 1-3); 59:157-180 (chs. 4-5). — E. v. Dobschütz, TU 38/4 [Latin text/comm.]. — NTApo⁶ 1:31-33 [German trans. of part 5]. — M. Erbetta, Gli Apocrifi del NT 1 (Turin, 1966) [Italian trans.] (literature). L: H. Leclercq, Gélasien: DACL 6:722-747. — E. Schwartz, Zum Decr. Gelas.: ZNW 29 (1930) 161-168.

G. Röwekamp

Definitions, Collections of

Collections of definitions became a literary genre in the post-Chalcedonian period (beginning in the first half of the 6th c.). From that time on, knowledge of philosophical logic was regarded as indispensable in dogm. controversies. Manuals contained definitions of concepts such as *ousia*, *physis*, and *hypostasis*, but also statements on the theory of knowledge and the various degrees of being. The chief source used was the Alexandrian Aristoteleans (and, among others, → David the Armenian, a Chr. Neoplatonist).

To this genre belong the definitions in the *ep. ad Acacium philosophum* of → Ephraem of Antioch, the *Capita philosophica* of → Anastasius I of Antioch, the *Praeparatio* of Theodore of Raithu, the *Hodegos* of Anastasius Sinaita, some *Opuscula* of → Maximus Conf., the → *Doctrina Patrum* (although to some extent this was still a patristic florilegium), in which in ch. 33 a definition is given that is based on Aristotle, *cat.*, and on Porphyry's *eisag.*, on the *Institutio elementaris* and *Capita philosophica* of → John Damascene, the *Enchiridion* of → Jacob of Edessa (for the Syrians), and the works of → Michael Badoqa (for the Nestorian East Syrians).

L: H. G. Beck, Bildung u. Theologie im früh-mal. Byzanz: FS F. Dölger (Heidelberg, 1966), 69-81. — A. Grillmeier, Jesus der Christus 2/1 (Freiburg i.Br., 1986), 94-100 (English, Christ in Christian Tradition, vol. 2/1 [London, 1987]). — M. Roueché, Byzantine Philosophical Texts of the 7th Century: JÖB 23 (1974) 61-76.

G Röwekamp

Demetrius of Alexandria

We have a historically certain basic knowledge of D., patriarch of Alexandria ca. 189 to 232 (see Eus., *Chron.* for 189; *h.e.* 5.22; 6.26), mainly because of the marked part he played in the life of Origen: by having the latter teach in the Chr.-philosophical school of Alexandria (Eus., *h.e.* 6.3.3; the date 203 is disputed), he promoted the protreptico-religious instruction of the educated and at the same time strengthened the episcopal hierarchy against freelance teachers of theology. The convocation, presumably, of two Egyptian synods 231/232 and the ensuing universal acceptance (with the exception espec. of Palestine) of the condemnation there passed on Origen attest to the importance of his patriarchate in eccles. politics. Of his literary production, only the following official writings are authenticated by fairly reliable testimonies:

1. Two letters to Origen, in which he urgently calls Origen, who has been living in Rome (ca. 215) and then in Palestine (first stay, ca. 221?), to return to Alexandria and the resumption of his teaching (Eus., *h.e.* 6.14.11; 6.19.19). 2. A letter of eccles. accreditation for Origen on his journey to Greece (229/230?) (Jerome, *vir. ill.* 54; Photius, *cod.* 118 does not contradict this). 3. At least one synodal letter (see Jerome, *ep.* 33.4), probably sent to Rome, Antioch, and Jerusalem (see Eus., *h.e.* 6.8.4; Jerome, *vir. ill.* 54), in which Origen's permission to reside and teach in Alexandria is revoked, and reasons are given for the nonacceptance of his ordination to the priesthood in Caesarea (Photius, *cod.* 118; Jerome, *ep.* 33.5; for the detailed content of this/these letter[s] see Eus., *h.e.* 6.8.3-5; 6.19.17f.; 6.19.12-14; Ruf., *adult.* 7). 4. A letter on the calculation of the Easter fast and the Easter feast, supposedly sent to Victor of Rome (the date, accordingly, would be the end of the 2nd c.) as well as to Antioch, Ephesus, and Jerusalem (Eutychius Alex., annals §172; *Synax. alex.* CSCO 78, Arab. 12.64f.; *Synax. arab. jacob.*, PO 1:333f.; 3:374f.). The attribution of a catena fragment on Jer 3:18 to a work *Eis ton seismon* of D. is based on a confusion with Demetrius Calatianus.

L: A. S. Atiya, D.: CoptE 3, 891-893. — M. Chaine, Chronologie (Paris, 1925), 25-31. — J. A. Fischer, Synoden gegen Origenes: OS 28 (1979) 3-16. — C. W. Griggs, Early Egyptian Christianity (Leiden, 1990). — V. Grumel, D.: DHGE 14:198f. — A. v. Harnack, Geschichte der altchr. Lit. 1/1 (Leipzig, ²1958 = 1893), 330-332; 2/2 (Leipzig, ²1958 = 1897), 23f. — P. Nautin, Lettres et écrivains (Paris, 1961), 122-134. — idem, Origène (Paris, 1977). — J. Pitra, ASSS 2:345f. — M. Roncaglia, Histoire de l'église copte 3 (Beirut, ²1971), 20-23. — C. Scholten, Alexandrinische Katechetenschule: JAC 38 (1995) 16-37. — A. Strobel, Ursprung u. Geschichte des Osterkalenders (Berlin, 1977), 382f.

B. Neuschäfer

Depositio episcoporum—Depositio martyrum

The → *Chronograph of 354*, which was written by Furius → Dionysius Philocalus and also illustrated by him in its first sections and which has come down to us only in (secondary?) copies from the 9th to the 16th c., takes the form of a calendrical manual for the city of Rome; in its ca. fourteen to sixteen original parts it uses chiefly disparate, relevant lists. With it go the *Depositio martyrum* and *Depositio episcoporum romanorum* (*d. e.*; *d. m.*), which are organized in calendar form. These form an important complement to other official lists of state and city, in which "an absence of Christianity" has been remarked. The two *Depositiones* give, in each case, the day of the month, the name of the bishop or martyr, and his place of burial. Probably the two lists were originally on facing pages and supplemented each other (see Sixtus) and thus formed a (still two-part) *Feriale*.

In its original form the *d. e.* (like the list of city prefects) begins with Lucius I (255) and goes down to Sylvester (335/336). It was then extended to Julius I (352).

The *d. m.* likewise shows the development of a calendar of Chr. feasts for the city of Rome and is the earliest martyrology (→ Calendar) of the western church. It is of interest that it begins with the birth of Christ on Dec. 25. Because of Lent April does not show any feasts of martyrs. The Roman martyrs of the 3rd and early 4th c. predominate. In addition there are Cyprian, Perpetua, and Felicity from Africa.

Famous and much disputed among scholars, in addition to the feast of the *Cathedra Petri* on Feb. 22 (which falls on the date of the non-Chr. *caristia* feast), is the entry on June 29. Either this recognizes (according to a reading corrected in light of the *Martyrologium Hieronymianum*) a common celebration of Peter and Paul *in catacumbas* (at the later Church of the Apostles on the Via Appia, today St. Sebastian's) in addition to the veneration of Peter on the Vatican and the celebration of Paul on the Via Ostiense, and connects this celebration with the consular year 258, which has led scholars to very disputed attributions to separate communities; or else it knows only of the veneration of Peter *in catacumbas*. The omission in the *d. m.* of the *memoria* on the Vatican would point to the construction of old St. Peter's, which was still unfinished in 354. The question remains of how the finds in the excavation of Platonia are to be interpreted and what the date 258 means (connection with persecution?).

W: T. Mommsen, MGH. AA 9:70-76. — LP 1:2-12. — R. Valentini, G. Zucchetti, Codice Topografico della Città di Roma 2 (Rome, 1942), 12-28 [text].
L: G. Binder, Der Kalender des Filocalus oder der Chronograph von 354 (Meisenheim/Glan o. J., 1970/71). — A. Ferrua, Filocalo: CivCatt 80 (1939) 35-47. — J. P. Kirsch, Der stadtröm. chr. Festkalender im Altertum (Münster,

1924). — C. Pietri, Roma Christiana (Rome, 1976). — M. R. Salzmann, On Roman Time (Berkeley, 1990). — H. Stern, Le calendrier de 354 (Paris, 1953). — idem, Les calendriers Romains illustrés: ANRW II 12/2 (1981) 431-475. — J. Strzygowski, Die Calenderbilder des Chronographen (Berlin, 1888).

W. WISCHMEYER

Desiderius of Cahors

D. was born ca. 590 in Obrège (Gallia Nabonensis) of an old Gallo-Roman family; he was in the service of the Frankish kings and died in 655. Like his four brothers and sisters, he had a splendid secular and eccles. career. After being called to the law court of King Chlotar II, he soon (618) became his and Dagobert's treasurer. After the assassination of his older brother Rusticus, D. became bishop of Cahors (630), where he did a lot of building and founded a good many rural parishes. Sixteen letters (ep.) of his have survived; twenty others are addressed to him by, among others, Audoin, Eligius, and Modoald. A Vita from the 8th c. contains further documents.

W: W. Arndt, MGH. Ep 3:191-214 [text]. — D. Norberg, Ep. Sancti Desiderii, SLS 6 (Stockholm, 1961) [text].
L: L. Duchesne, Fastes épiscopaux 2:46. — G. Mathon, D.: BSS 4:580f. — H. Platelle, D.: Cath. 4:1900f. — Vie des Saints 11 (Paris, 1955), 476-484.

C. KASPER

Dexter

Nummius Aemilianus Dexter, son of Bishop Pacian of Barcelona, was proconsul in Asia Minor from 379 to 387 (CIL 2:4512) under Emperor Theodosius, in 387 comes rerum privatarum (Cod. Iust. 7.38.2), and in 395 praetorian prefect of Italy (Cod. Theod. 6.4.17 and elsewhere). Jerome, who dedicated vir. ill. to him in 392, calls him clarus ad saeculum and author of a lost omnimoda historia. D. had suggested that Jerome write the vir. ill., a collection of lives of Chr. writers, modeled on Suetonius, in order to demonstrate the intellectual power of the church (vir. ill. prol. 132; adv. Rufin. 2.23). The Chronicom Dextri is a forgery by Spanish Jesuit J. R. de la Higuera (1538-1611).

W: Chronicon, PL 31:55-572.
L: A. Jülicher, D.: PRE 5/1:297. — L. R. Fernández, San Paciano. Obras (Barcelona, 1958), 7f. — PLRE 1:151.

J. LÖSSL

Diadochus of Photice

D. became bishop of Photice in Epirus after 451 and lived until before 486. Nothing is known of his life except for remarks in → Victor of Vita and Photius and for the fact that he cosigned a letter to Emperor Leo I (ACO 2, 5; 95, 11).

D.'s main literary work is the Capita centum de perfectione spirituali (perf.), that is, an introduction to spiritual perfection, divided into chapters and intended for students; various practical and theol. themes are developed in it. In a varied sequence it deals with moderation in eating and drinking and conduct during illness, but also with the discernment of spirits, visions and illusions, teaching on prayer, and the progressive reaching of God through love. The spiritual life is a ceaseless battle. Fundamental to all this is the distinction between eikōn and homoiōsis acc. to Gen 1:26 LXX: Human beings are created as an "image" of God, and this dignity is completely restored by baptism, but they achieve the "likeness" only through ascetical and spiritual perfection (cap. 89). In cap. 76-89, in connection with baptism and while expounding his own teaching on grace, D. refutes the views of unnamed adversaries who play down the importance of baptism on the grounds that even after it two wills, one to good, one to evil, are at work in human beings. Some have identified these adversaries with the Messalians, but it is more likely that D. is here criticizing the views of → Macarius the Egyptian/Simeon. D. for his part stresses the completeness of baptism: it drives Satan from the depths of the soul (cap. 76), so that grace may work in it. Evil is only external, that is, it dwells in the flesh and is activated by human beings' deliberate acceptance of it (cap. 88). A basic theme, then, is the attainment of salvation by the free will (already in cap. 2-5). In addition, a person becomes conscious of the profound action of baptism only through his own efforts, which then lead him to perfection (cap. 77 and 85); this perfection, however, espec. in the form of apatheia, is not definitive but is constantly attacked by demons (cap. 98).

In a homily on the ascension of Christ (ascens.) D. briefly sets forth his own anti-Monophysite theology: There are two inseparable natures in one hypostasis. The "vision" (vis.), which is composed in the form of an erotapokrisis (questions and answers), has for its subject the baptism of Jesus by John, the eschat. vision of God, and the nature of the angels; it is, like cap. 36-40, skeptical of present visions. The catechesis (cat.) attributed to D. in some mss. may also be from Simeon the New Theologian.

D. is a mediator between the experience-based mystical theology of earlier fathers (→ Evagrius Pont., Macarius/Simeon) and later Gk. writers. His "reception" extended to modern times: in 1782 he was accepted into the *Philocalia*, a devotional book of the eastern church.

W: *perf., ascens., vis., cat.,* É. des Places, SC 5ter. — *perf.,* V. Messana, Diadoco. Cento considerazioni sulla fede (Rome, 1978) [Italian trans.]. — J. E. Weis-Liebersdorf (Leipzig, 1912) [text/Latin trans.].
L: P. Christou, Διάδοχος ὁ Φωτικῆς (Thessalonica, 1952). — É. des Places, D. et le Messalianisme: FS J. Quasten (Münster, 1970), 591-595. — idem, D.: DSp 3:817-834. — F. Dörr, D. u. die Messalianer (Freiburg i.Br., 1938). — H. Dörries, D. u. Symeon: idem, Wort u. Stunde 1 (Göttingen, 1966), 352-422. — E. Honigmann, Patristic Studies (Rome, 1953), 174-184. — G. Horn, Sens de l'esprit d'après D.: RAM 8 (1927) 402-419. — H. I. Marrou, D. et Victor de Vita: REA 45 (1943) 225-232. — V. Messana, D. e la cultura cristiana in Epiro nel V secolo: Aug. 19 (1979) 151-166. — T. Polyzogopoulos, Life and Writings of D.: Theol(A) 55 (1984) 772-800. — R. Reitzenstein, Historia monachorum u. Historia Lausiaca (Göttingen, 1916), 123-142. — M. Rothenhäusler, La Doctrine de la "theologia" chez D.: Irén. 14 (1937) 536-553. — idem, Zur asketischen Lehrschrift des D.: FS I. Herwegen (Münster, 1938), 86-95. — M. Viller, K. Rahner, Aszese u. Mystik (Freiburg i.Br., 1990 = 1939), 216-228. — K. Ware, D.: TRE 8:617-620.

K. FITSCHEN

Dialogue

In Chr. literature the name dialogue can apply to every work that consists largely or entirely of a conversation, that is, a discussion by at least two speakers of one or several subjects; this discussion is carried on not in a series of actions, as in a novel, short story, or drama, but solely in dialogue. As a result, the Chr. dialogue is less sharply defined than the dialogue of pagan antiquity; the style of the loose chat is seldom to be found, and a background setting or the inclusion of excursuses is rare. When an imitation of the pagan dialogue is attempted, the model is always Plato or Cicero, who were generally known through reading of them in school. The following subdivision aims to give a survey of subjects and intentions.

A conscious dependence on classical models is most likely to be found in the *philosophical-theol. dialogue:* After a brief blossoming at the end of the 3rd and beginning of the 4th c. (e.g., → Methodius of Olympus, *symp.,* modeled on Plato), at the end of the 4th c., even in pagan literature, this kind of dialogue knew a period of intense competition with the classics, reaching its high point in the works of → Gregory Nyss. and → Augustine. Gregory's *Macrinia* (*anim. et res.*), a conversation on the last things between the author and his dying sister, can be taken as a Chr. pendant to Plato's *Phaedo.* Augustine's *Acad.* contrasts with Cicero's *Academica*; in his other Cassiciacum dialogues, too, there is a scenic setting

and a carefully weighed distribution of roles—elements that slip into the background in the same author's later philosophical dialogues (*an. quant., mag., lib. arb.*). From a later period mention may be made of, e.g., the dialogues of Aeneas of Gaza, as well as Boethius's *in Porph. comm. pr.* A special place belongs to introspective dialogues, espec. Augustine's *sol.* and Boethius's *cons.*; both works were written in an existentially critical situation and show their authors in conversation with a personification (*Ratio* and *Philosophia* respectively), which makes it possible for them to cope with their problem at the intellectual level.

The subgenre of the apologetical-polemical *controversy dialogue* shows a substantially greater independence of the ancient pagan dialogue. From the beginning of Christianity this was used to refute religious positions of an adversary, whether Jew (→ Anti-Jewish Dialogue), pagan, or heretic. The earliest dialogue of this kind and, at the same time, the first Chr. dialogue of any kind came from → Ariston of Pella. The disputation between Jason, a Jewish Christian, and Papsicus, a Jew of Alexandria, ends with the conversion of the Jew and his request for baptism. Here a pattern can be seen that can be called constitutive of the controversy dialogue: The discussion does not lead the partners to a new insight that harmonizes initially divergent viewpoints; rather it is certain from the outset that the (orthodox) Christian will emerge from the struggle of the disputation as victor. Despite the widespread acceptance of usages specific to the genre in antiquity, that statement is true, at bottom, even of the dialogue of → Justin (at no point in the debate between the author and Trypho, a Jew, is there any doubt which viewpoint will prevail) and of → Minucius Felix (Caecilius, a pagan, sees himself finally compelled to retract his accusations against Christians). The very frequently occurring polemical dialogue against heretics reflects with special clarity the contemporary theol. controversies. From a literary point of view, these dialogues range from highly stylized dialogues (e.g., of → John Chrys.) to notes of disputations (e.g., → Augustine, *emer.*), from protreptic to dogm. polemics. The number of controversy dialogues that have come down as anonymous or pseudepigraphical is disproportionately large, showing that these works were taken as literature for practical use. Within the anti-heretical dialogues a special place belongs to the so-called *Adamantius Dialogue* (which Ruf. translated as supposedly composed by Origen), for in it not only are five heretics refuted one after another, but even the pagan who is appointed as arbiter is converted. A number of erroneous teachings are likewise attacked together in the → *Consultationes Zacchaei et Apollonii* (before the end of the 5th c.); this dialogue represents a straightforward controversy inasmuch as it ends with a justification of monastic life.

The *didactic dialogue* is in some respects a form halfway between the two subgenres already described, since its subjects are those of the philosophical-theol. dialogue but the distribution of roles resembles that of the controversy dialogue inasmuch as one of the partners knows the "truth" from the outset, while the other achieves full understanding only at the end. The earliest example is → Methodius, *lepr.*; the correct—that is, the allegorical—exegesis of Lev 13 is communicated in a lecture by Eubulius, which is interrupted by questions from Sistelius. A more important role is given to the "student" in Augustine's *mus.*, since he himself undertakes the discussion of details as soon as he has acquired sufficient basic knowledge. Also to be mentioned: → John Cassian, *conl.*, and → Eucherius of Lyons, *instr.* 1; these works may be regarded as halfway forms between dialogue and erotapokriseis (→ *Quaestiones et responsiones*).

The *hagiographical dialogue* is related to the didactic insofar as both are concerned to communicate knowledge without any polemical overtones. The origins of this subgenre are not to be found in the methods of the ancient schools but in various, partly nonliterary forms of accounts of the life and miracles of the saints. An influence from ancient biographies in dialogue form, such as the life of Euripides by Satyrus (ca. 219 B.C.E.), can be excluded. Three examples of this type of dialogue have survived from late Chr. antiquity: → Sulpicius Severus wrote his dialogues, which describe mainly the miracles of St Martin, as a supplement to *Mart.* → Palladius of Helenopolis had an apologetic purpose in his *V. Chrys.*, which he wrote shortly after the death of this bishop of Constantinople. The conclusion of the series comes in the *dial.* of → Gregory the Great, in which, at the request of deacon Peter, the author narrates the lives of Italian saints, among them Benedict of Nursia (book 2).

L: G. Bardy, D., Chr.: RAC 3:945-954. — M. Hoffmann, Der D. bei den chr. Schriftstellern der ersten vier Jahrhunderte (Berlin, 1966). — C. Schäublin, Konversionen in antiken D.en?: FS G. Wyss (Basel, 1985), 117-131. — P. L. Schmidt, Zur Typologie u. Literarisierung des frühchr. lat. D.s: EnAC 23 (1977) 101-180. — idem, Formtradition u. Realitätsbezug im frühchr. lat. D.: WJA NF 3 (1977), 211-223. — B. R. Voss, Der D. in der frühchr. Literatur (Munich, 1970).

D. WEBER

Dialogue of the Savior

The *Dialogue of the Savior (Dial.)* is in NHC 3, 5, and is badly damaged in parts. The work is called a dialogue; this title also serves to describe a whole genre of gnostic writings that have a similar structure (→ Apocryphal Writings). In its present form *Dial.* is probably made up of five different sources that were put together in the 2nd c. by an editor who uses the title "Savior" instead of "Lord."

As in other dialogues, the risen Savior appears, teaches the questioning disciples about the realm of light and about gnosis, and in this way communicates salvation to them. Judas, Matthew, and Mary Magdalene play special roles. The first section, probably written by the editor, speaks of the migration of the soul through the heavenly spheres; after this comes the original text, into which a gnostic creation myth has been inserted, giving instruction on the elements (darkness, light, fire, water, and wind). The original dialogue on the stages of gnosis (seeking and finding, wondering, prevailing, resting) picks up again, with an apocalyptic vision being inserted. This section on gnosis takes the form of a collection of sayings, on which the disciples comment and which the Lord explains.

W: The Facsimile Edition of the NHC. Cod. 3 (p. 120,1-147, 23) (Leiden, 1977). — S. Emmel et al., NHC 3, 5 (NHS 26) (Leiden, 1984) [text/English trans.]. — P. Claude, Le dialogue de Sauveur (Quebec, 1980) [text]. — NHL 244-255 [English trans.]. — NTApo⁶ 1:247-253 [German trans.].
L: C. H. Dodd, The Appearances of the Risen Christ: FS R. H. Lightfoot (Oxford, 1957), 9-35. — S. Emmel, A Fragment of NHC III: BASPap 17 (1980) 53-60. — H. Köster, Dialog u. Spruchüberlieferung in den gnostischen Texten von Nag Hammadi: EvTh 3 (1979) 532-556. — M. Krause, Der Dialog des Soter in Cod. III von Nag Hammadi: Gnosis and Gnosticism (NHS 8), ed. idem (Leiden, 1977), 13-34. — E. Pagels, Visions, Appearances and Apostolic Authority: FS H. Jonas (Göttingen, 1978), 415-430. — P. Perkins, The Gnostic Dialogue (New York, 1980). — K. Rudolph, Der gnostische "Dialog" als literarisches Genus: idem, Gnosis u. spätantike Religionsgeschichte, NHS 42 (Leiden, 1996), 103-122.

G. RÖWEKAMP

Diatessaron

Diatessaron (or *to dia tessarōn euaggelion*) is the name given to the harmony of the gospels prepared by → Tatian the Syrian; he probably did the work during his stay in Rome with → Justin Martyr, but certainly before his journey to the East in 172. The *Diatessaron* was probably composed originally in Syriac, but was soon translated into Greek and Latin and from there into other European languages. Numerous translations (Arm., Georg., Pers., Turk., Arab.) were made in the East, attesting to the extraordinary dissemination of the *Diatessaron*. In the early period of the Syr. church Tatian's *Diatessaron* was even regarded as canonical; it was not attacked and prohibited as heretical until the time of the aggressive Rabbula of Edessa (d. 435). But only the *textus receptus* of the → Peshitta (6th c.) finally succeeded in suppressing the older versions almost entirely. Since early Syr. mss. are lacking, the bibl. citations of Aphraates, the *Liber graduum*, and Titus of Bostra, but especially the completely surviving commentary on the *Diatessaron* by → Ephraem the Syrian (*comm. in Diat.*) have been of decisive importance for the reconstruction of the *Diatessaron*.

W: P. A. Ciasca, Tatiani evangeliorum harmonia (Rome, ²1934) [Arabic text/Latin trans.]. — A. S. Marmardji, D. de Tatien (Beirut, 1935) [Arabic text]. — C. H. Kraeling, A Greek Fragment of Tatian's D. (London, 1935) [Greek text]. — G. Messina, D. persiano (Rome, 1951) [Persian text/Italian trans.]. — D. Plooij, C. A. Phillips, A. J. Barnouw, The Liège D. (Amsterdam, 1929-1935) [Dutch text]. — V. Todesco, A. Vaccari, M. Vatasso, Il D. (Rome, 1938) [Italian text]. — A. Baumstark, J. Rathofer, Vorlage des althochdt. Tatian (Cologne, 1964). — I. Ortiz de Urbina, Vetus Evangelium Syrorum (Madrid, 1967) [Syriac text/Spanish trans.]. *comm. in Diat.*, L. Leloir, CSCO 137/145 [Armenian text/Latin trans.]. — idem (Dublin, 1963) [Syriac text/Latin trans.]. — idem, SC 121. — idem, Commentaire de l'Évangile Concordant (Leuven/Louvain, 1990) [Syriac text/French trans.]. — G. Moesinger (Venice, 1876) [Armenian text/Latin trans.].
L: M. E. Boismard, Le D.: De Tatien à Justin (Paris, 1992). — J. R. Harris, The D. of Tatian (London, 1890). — A. Hjelt, Die altsyr. Evangelienübersetzung (Leipzig, 1903). — L. Leloir, Doctrines et méthodes (Leuven/Louvain, 1961). — idem, L'évangile d'Éphrem (Leuven/Louvain, 1958). — idem, Commentaire sur le D.: RB 94 (1987) 481-518. — idem, Sermon sur la montagne: Aug. 27 (1988) 361-391. — S. Lyonnet, Les origines de la version arménienne (Rome, 1950). — J. Molitor, Tatians D.: OrChr 53 (1969) 1-88; 54 (1970) 1-75; 55 (1971) 1-61. — C. Peters, Das D. Tatians (Rome, 1939). — W. L. Petersen, Tatian's D. (Leiden, 1994). — D. Plooij, A Primitive Text of the D. (Leiden, 1923). — E. Preuschen, Untersuchung zu Tatians D. (Heidelberg, 1918). — G. Quispel, Tatian and the Gospel of Thomas (Leiden, 1975). — A. Vööbus, Gospel Text in Syriac (Leuven/Louvain, 1951). — H. J. Vogels, Die altsyr. Evangelien (Freiburg i.Br., 1911). — T. Zahn, Tatians D. (Erlangen, 1881).

P. BRUNS

Didache

The *Didache* (*Did.*) is the oldest surviving → church order; it was discovered in 1873 in Constantinople as part of Gr. *Codex Hieronymianus* 54 (ff. 76ʳ-80ᵛ;

henceforth H) and was first given a critical edition in 1883.

H supplies two titles, one after the other: a shorter one, *Didachē tōn dōdeka apostolōn*, and a longer, *Didachē kyriou dia tōn dōdeka apostolōn tois ethnesin*. Both titles must have been added to the originally anonymous compilation soon after its production, in order to claim apostolic authorship for its content.

The *Did.* can be divided into four sections: (1) ethical instruction: the doctrine of the Two Ways (chs. 1-6); (2) liturgical instruction (chs. 7-10); (3) community ordinances (chs. 11-15); and (4) eschat. instruction (ch. 16). The doctrine of the Two Ways (1) was originally a probably Jewish treatise with moral content; in the *Did.*, it is christianized by the addition of a "gospel section" (sayings from the Jesus tradition: 1.3b–2.1) and, by means of further changes, adapted to the needs of prebaptismal catechesis in the young community. In the liturgical instruction (2) specific instructions are given for baptism and the celebration of a meal (whether there is here an archaic form of the Eucharist or an *agapē* must remain an open question; → Liturgy); the ritual for baptism is expanded by specific instructions for fasting and prayer. The community ordinances (3) give, in the first part (chs. 11-13), instructions on how Christians coming to the community are to be dealt with. Among the groups envisaged are teachers (11.1f.), apostles (11.3-6), prophets (11.7-12, with criteria for distinguishing true prophets from false), and strangers (12.1f.). Rules are given for cases in which a stranger wishes to join the community (12.3-5), then for (genuine) prophets wishing to do the same (13.1); finally, the question of community support for the prophets is raised (13.3-7). In the second part of the community ordinances (chs. 14-15) various particular aspects of community life are mentioned: call for reconciliation (as condition for Sunday worship), instruction on choosing a bishop and deacon. The eschat. instruction (4) has parenetic material followed by a short apocalyptic text; this is to give force to the previous instructions and motivate obedience to them.

The *Did.* had an eventful textual history. The → *Apostolic Constitutions* used the *Did.* as source of chs. 1-32 of the seventh book and expanded it considerably. There is question, however, of the extent to which the *Did.* text used there corresponds to the text in H. Older than this adaptation of the *Did.* are three textual parallels to the version of the Two-Ways doctrine found in the *Did.*: (1) one is in *Barn.* 18-20; (2) one is a parallel recension, consisting of two Lat. mss., under the title *Doctrina apostolorum* (*Doctr.*

apost.); and (3) one is a "Moral Teaching of the Eleven Apostles" (the textual content of the Two-Ways doctrine is divided up with each apostle speaking part of it), which has been handed down in the → *Apostolic Church Order* and, independently of this, in two Gk. mss. The relation between these parallel texts has not been explained. There seems to be agreement on all sides that, in contrast to *Barn.*, the compiler of the *Did.* had before him an already rather heavily christianized version of the Two Ways doctrine; the correspondences between *Did.* and *Doctr. apost.* seem best explained by a common source.

Textual criticism can for practical purposes rely solely on H, since a Gk. papyrus fragment (1.3b-42; 2.7–3.2) from the end of the 4th c. is of no consequence for the establishment of the text; neither do the Copt. (10.3b–12.12a) and Eth. (8.1f.; 11.3–13.7) fragments (embedded in the Eth. recension of the Synodos of the Alexandrian church) play any great role. Because of its later and dubious transmission, the Georg. version cannot be used in reconstructing the text.

At one time the textual integrity of the *Did.* was asserted; it was also called into question for a time (because of a two-recension theory; interpolation hypotheses; fiction hypotheses). The common view today is once again that a compiler ("Didachist") independently edited traditions he had at hand and merged them into the version in H; however, the question of the share of tradition in the *Did.* is given various answers. Nevertheless, today, as previously, renowned scholars claim that H is the result of the work of two editors.

As for the time and place of the Didachist's redaction of the several pieces of tradition, there is agreement that the years around 100 C.E. were the time of composition and that Syria was the most likely location.

The importance of the *Did.* for patristic research consists (1) generally in the originality of its form and (2) in the community structures that appear in it (along with interesting liturg. passages [prayer over the gifts] there is espec. the effort to bring an archaic concept of the apostles, a well-defined prophetic office, and teachers as representatives of itinerant charismatics, into harmony with local functionaries [bishops and deacons]).

W: A. Adam, Herkunft der *Did.*: ZKG 68 (1957) 1-47 [German trans. of the Ethiopic frags.]. — P. Bryennios (Constantinople, 1883) [Greek text]. — G. W. Horner, Statutes (London, 1904), 54f./193f. [Ethiopic text/English trans.]. — A. Lindemann, H. Paulsen, Apostolische Väter (Tübin-

gen, 1992) [Greek text/German trans.]. — W. Rordorf, A. Tuilier, SC 248. — C. Schmidt, Kopt. *Did.*-Fragment: ZNW 24 (1925) 81-99 [Coptic text/German trans.]. — G. Schöllgen (FC 1). — K. Wengst (Darmstadt, 1984) [Greek text/German trans.].
L: R. E. Aldridge, Lost Ending: VigChr 53 (1999) 1-15. — J. P. Audet, Did. (Paris, 1958). — G. Deussen, Bischofswahl im 1Clem. und Did.: ThGl 62 (1972) 125-135. — J. A. Draper, Commentary on the Did. in the Light of the Dead Sea Scrolls (Cambridge, 1983). — idem (ed.), The Did. in Modern Research (Leiden, 1996). — idem, Resurrection and Zechariah 14, 5 in Did. Apocalypse: JECS 5 (1997) 155-179. — idem, Weber, Theissen and the "Wandering Charismatics": JECS 6 (1998) 541-576. — K. Gamber, Die "Eucharistia" der Did.: EL 101 (1987) 3-32. — S. Giet, L'énigme de la Did. (Paris, 1970). — A. de Halleux, Les ministères dans la Did.: Irén. 53 (1980) 5-29. — A. Harnack, Die Lehre der zwölf Apostel (Leipzig, 1884). — I. H. Henderson, Did. and Orality: JBL 111 (1992) 283-306. — C. N. Jefford, Presbyters in the Community of the Did.: StPatr 21 (1989) 122-128. — idem, The Sayings of Jesus in the Teaching of the Apostles (Leiden, 1989). — idem (ed.), The Did. in Context (Leiden, 1995) (16 essays on the Did. with extensive bibliography). — B. Layton, The Sources, Date and Transmission of Did. 1.3b-2.1: HThR 61 (1968) 343-383. — A. Milavec, The Pastoral Genius of the Did. (New York, 1995). — K. Niederwimmer, Wanderradikalismus im Traditionsbereich der Did.: WSt 11 (1977) 145-167. — idem, Doctr. apost.: FS F. Zerbst (Freiburg i.Br., 1979), 266-272. — idem, Did. (Göttingen, 1989) [commentary]. — G. Peradse, Georg. Überlieferung: ZNW 31 (1932) 111-116. — F. Prostmeier, Did. 7, 4 und 8, 1: FS N. Brox, Gr 1995, 55-75. — J. A. Robinson, Did.: JThS 35 (1934) 225-248. — W. Rordorf, Liturgie, foi et vie des premiers chrétiens (Paris, 1986). — idem, Die Mahlgebete in Did. 9-10: VigChr 51 (1997) 229-246. — G. Schille, Recht der Propheten und Apostel: Theol. Versuche 1, ed. P. Wätzel, G. Schille (Berlin, 1966), 84-103. — G. Schöllgen, Did. als Kirchenordnung: JAC 29 (1986) 5-26. — H. R. Seeliger, Apokalyptisches Schlußkapitel der Did.: StPatr 21 (1989) 397-408. — B. Steimer, Vertex traditionis (Berlin, 1992). — H.-A. Stempel, Der Lehrer in der Did.: VigChr 34 (1980) 209-217. — N. L. Tidwell, Did. XIV:1 revisited: VigChr 53 (1999) 197-207. — A. Tuilier, Did.: TRE 8:731-736. — idem, Liturgie dans la Did. et l'essénisme: StPatr 26 (1993) 200-210. — M. del Verme, The Did. and Judaism: StPatr 26 (1993) 113-120. — F. E. Vokes, The Riddle of the Did. (London, 1938). — A. Vööbus, Liturgical traditions (Stockholm, 1968).

B. Steimer

Didascalia

Didascalia (*Didasc.*) (from Gk. *didaskalia*, "teaching") is the name given to a voluminous → church order that is preserved complete in several mss. of a Syr. translation (therefore the work is often called "Syrian Didascalia"), in an extensive papyrus fragment of the Lat. *Codex Veronensis* 55 (about three-eighths of the Syr. text), and a Gk. revision in books 1-6 of the → *Apostolic Constitutions*, on which Arab. and Eth. recensions depend. The Syr. translation (a work of the late 4th c.) is from a Gk. original (of which few fragments survive), that must have been composed in the middle of the 3rd c. The author must have been a bishop, and Syria is the most likely place of composition.

The title of the work has not been unambiguously transmitted (the Syr. mss. have a long and a short title), but it must originally have been *Didaskalia tōn apostolōn*. Apostolic authorship was thus asserted in the very title. The work claims to be the result of the apostolic council in Jerusalem, and the unknown author endeavors to maintain this fiction by means of a pseudepigraphic style that becomes increasingly strained in the course of the work. The division of the Syr. version into chapters contributes as little to the structuring of the material, which is typical of the genre (see below), as does that of books 1-6 of the *Apostolic Constitutions*; in addition, about a third of the text consists of citations from scripture. Nonetheless a series of self-contained sections can be identified that deal with the following sets of subjects: (1) problems of everyday life (exhortations to men and women); (2) position and authority of the bishop (criteria for electing him; rules of his office; questions of his support; and, in detail, the ritual of penance); (3) worship (seating arrangements; attendance); (4) care of the poor (widows; tasks of deacons and deaconesses; orphans; warning against givers who do not live a Chr. life); (5) other subjects (e.g., martyrdom, the Easter fast, Chr. education, schism and heresy, Jewish-Chr. practices). The *Didasc.* supposes the community being addressed to have a clearly outlined hierarchy of offices and class system. The person who towers over everything and everyone is the bishop, who rules as a monarch. The *Didasc.* gives an account of his prominent position by appealing, on the one hand, to Ignatian theological ideas and, on the other, to OT traditions (bishop as Levite, high priest, Moses). The functions essential to a community (teaching, worship, discipline) are concentrated in the person of the bishop; providers of other services play minor roles (the bishop, not the clergy, stands over against the laity). The author of the *Didasc.* was therefore probably a bishop who was setting down the law in virtue of his office. But the issue is not the legitimation of his office (the authority of a bishop is not justified either dogmatically [guarantor of orthodoxy] or historically [succession]), but rather his claim to social and moral leadership. There is no doubt that what is said in the *Didasc.* displays concrete historical points of reference; its value as a source must, however, be measured by its limited communication structure and its

extraordinary episcopal orientation, acc. to which a bishop seeks to assert the particular interests of persons and less so those specific to his office.

W: H. Achelis, J. Flemming (Leipzig, 1904) [German trans.]. — R. H. Connolly (Norwich, 1969 = Oxford, 1929) [English trans.]. — F. X. Funk, *Didasc.*, vol. 1 (Turin, 1959 = Paderborn, 1905) [Latin text]. — P. A. de Lagarde, *Didasc.* syriace (Wiesbaden, 1967 = Leipzig, 1854) [Syriac text]. — F. Nau (Paris, 1912) [French trans.]. — E. Tidner (Berlin, 1963) [Latin text]. — A. Vööbus, CSCO 401f.; 407f./CSCO. S 175f.; 179f. [Syriac text/English trans.].
L: J. V. Bartlet, Greek Fragments of the Didasc.: JThS 18 (1917) 301-309. — S. Brock, M. Vasey, Liturgical Portions (Bramcote, 1982). — F. C. Burkitt, Didasc.: JThS 31 (1930) 258-265. — R. H. Connolly, The Use of the Didache in the Didasc.: JThS 24 (1923) 147-157. — J. J. C. Cox, Dominical logoi in the Didasc.: AUSS 13 (1975) 23-29. — idem, Title of the Didasc.: AUSS 13 (1975) 30-33. — A. Faivre, Documentation canonico-liturgique: RevSR 54 (1980) 204-215, 273-297. — P. Galtier, Date de la Didasc.: RHE 42 (1947) 315-351. — E. Hauler, Palimpsestübersetzung: SAWW 134 (1896) IX. — idem, Kapiteleinteilung: FS V. Jagic (Berlin, 1908), 663-669. — E. A. Knauf, Didasc.: Damaszener Mitteilungen 3 (1988) 77-82. — M. Metzger, Didasc. et Constitutions apostoliques: L'eucharistie des premiers chrétiens (Paris, 1976), 187-210. — F. Nau, Didasc.: DThC 4:743-748. — K. Rahner, Bußlehre der Didasc.: ZKTh 72 (1950) 257-281. — J. C. J. Sanders, Didasc.: FS A. Vööbus (Chicago, 1977), 47-53. — J. Schlosser, Didasc. et épîtres pastorales: RevSR 59 (1985) 81-94. — G. Schöllgen, Gattung der Didasc.: OCA 229 (1987) 149-159. — B. Steimer, Vertex traditionis (Berlin, 1992). — E. Tidner, Sprachlicher Kommentar zur Didasc. (Stockholm, 1938). — W. C. van Unnik, Significance of Moses' Law: Sparsa Collecta 3 (Leiden, 1983), 7-39. — M. Viard, Didasc. (Langres, 1906). — A. Vööbus, Nouvelles sources: RSR 64 (1976) 459-462.

B. STEIMER

Didymus the Blind

I. Life: D.'s lifetime was almost coextensive with the 4th c.; the place where he received his intellectual stamp, and where he in turn affected others, was Alexandria. He was born in 310 (see Jerome, *vir. ill.* 109) or 313 (see Palladius, *h. laus.* 4) and at the age of five or six lost his sight, without having previously learned to read and write (thus Jerome, *chron.*; GCS 47:246; Ruf., *h.e.* 11.7; Palladius, ibid.; in disagreement, Soc., *h.e.* 4.45.2; Soz., *h.e.* 3.15.2).

By listening to and constantly memorizing material communicated orally, D. gained a knowledge, astonishing to his contemporaries, in all the disciplines of the *Enkyklios Paideia* as well as of philosophy in particular. Public lectures, taken down by stenographers (*notarii*), strengthened D.'s authority as a very learned interpreter of the Bible. He became a prominent teacher. It is not possible to say in detail how his teaching activity fitted into the institutional framework of the Alexandrian catechetical school.

Contrary to the tendency observable since the middle of the 3rd c. for the teachers or leaders of the so-called Alexandrian catechetical school to be ordained priests, nothing of this is reported of D. He lived an ascetic life in a "cell" (Palladius, ibid.). Reports of D.'s meetings with Anthony the Hermit (first reported in Jerome, *ep.* 68.2) should be interpreted as a response to his ascetic tendencies. The importance of the latter is also reflected in the fact that ascetically minded young men became his best known students: Rufinus, Jerome, Palladius. D. died at the age of 85, probably in 398 (Palladius, ibid.).

II. Works: 1. Bibl. commentary bulks larger than dogm. works in the fragmentarily surviving body of writings of D., who was condemned as an Origenist for the first time in 543. Only through the discovery of the → Tura Papyri (1941) do we have a direct transmission of remains (critically edited since then) of his bibl. exegesis.

On the OT: The interpretations of Gen 1:1–17:6 (*Gen.*), Job 1:1–16:8a (*Job*), and Zech (*Zach.*) belong probably to the genre of literarily sophisticated commentary intended for the general public. The incompleteness of the commentary on Gen and Job is probably due to the history of its transmission. Only *Zach.*, produced at the request of Jerome, can be dated, with high probability, to 387. The exegesis of Pss 20:1–44:4a (LXX) (*Ps.*), which is probably from the mid-370s, and that of Qoh 1:1–12:6d, which is from the last quarter of the 4th c., represents notes from spoken lectures. On the NT: direct transmission provides only a shorter text on Jn 6:3-33 (*Jo.*), which is likewise a note from a lecture, probably to be dated to 374/375.

The other remnants of D.'s bibl. exegesis have come down only indirectly, primarily in the → catenae. On the OT: The close agreement of D.'s identified fragments on Gen and Job with the two Tura commentaries points to a common archetype. The catena fragments on Pss 1–150, as distinct from *Ps.*, may come from D.'s complete commentary on the Psalms (Jerome, *vir. ill.* 109). Perhaps the same explanation holds for the lack of agreement between *Eccl.* and the catena tradition. Insofar as their authenticity is assured, catena fragments on Ex, 1-2 Sam, Jer, Dan, Hos, Prov, and Cant, as well as excerpts from a commentary on Isaiah (John Damascene, *parall.* PG 95:1093BC and 1169BC; PG 96:525A) illustrate the scope of D.'s OT exegesis, as do his own references to a (lost) commentary on Lev and Ezek (*Zach.* 4.144; 5.170).

For the NT there are also catena fragments: on John (presumably distinct from *Jo.*), belonging to D.'s commentary on John (see Jerome, ibid.), on Rom, 1-2 Cor, and the Catholic Letters; finally there is a commentary handed down in a Lat. translation (*enarratio*). It is as yet unclear whether the catena tradition contains sure traces of D.'s commentary on Mt (see Jerome, ibid.) and on Acts, Heb, and Rev; the commentaries on Gal and Eph which Jerome mentions must be regarded as lost.

2. Of the dogm. (antiheretical) works the direct tradition has preserved an incomplete Gk. work which is from D. acc. to an excerpt probably from its now lost beginning (John Damascene, *parall.*, PG 95:1582A) and bears the title *Contra Manichaeos* (*Man.*). It deals with subjects typical of anti-Manichean literature since the 4th c. (dualism, problem of evil, etc.). Central to D.'s refutation is the denial of evil as a metaphysical principle (*archē*) that determines human nature, and the argument, instead, that evil becomes established by the deliberate decision (*proairesis*) of human beings, who, thanks to their free will and the support of divine grace, can choose the good (chs. 1, 10, 13, 15, 18).

Antiheretical theologizing is also documented in the record of a discussion between D. and an Apollinarist on the soul of Christ (*Pr.*). Among the indirectly transmitted dogmatic (antiheretical) writings is *De Spiritu Sancto* (*Spir.*), which was translated by Jerome after 385. This is D.'s most important work, inasmuch as, being complete and of undenied authenticity, it played a very effective part in the formation of doctrine on the Trinity and the Spirit. The original cannot be dated with certainty. Ambrose obviously had it before him when he wrote his *De spiritu sancto* (381). In agreement with Athanasius, D. stresses the homoousios within the Trinity, of which the Holy Spirit is a part (§§81, 145). D.'s main interest is in the bibl.-exeget. foundations of pneumatology and the doctrine of the Trinity (see §§132-230).

A fragment specifically attributed to D. from a Lat. lectionary for the feast of the Epiphany, *Sermo s. Didymi de theophaneia* (*serm.*), deals with the invisibility of the Trinity.

The following dogm. (antiheret.) works are lost: (a) mentioned by D. himself: *Dogmatum volumen* (*Dogm. vol.*), *Sectarum volumen*, *De virtutibus*, *De filio*; (b) mentioned by Jerome: *Contra Arianos libri* 2 (probably identical with *Dogm. vol.*), *Liber ad Rufinum, quare moriantur infantes*, *Hypomnēmata eis ta Peri archōn Origenous*, *De impari numero*; (c) mentioned by John Damascene: *Ad philosophum*, *De incorporeo*; (d) mentioned in the catena tradition:

De anima. Still disputed among scholars is the attribution to D. of *De Trinitate libri* 3 (*Trin.*) and *Adversus Eunomium* 4-5 (*Eun.*); but the doubts about his authorship carry more weight. Unanimously denied him are: *Adversus Arium et Sabelium*, a refutation of a Montanist, → *Contra Origenem de visione Isaiae*, and seven pseudo-Athanasian dialogues.

III. Main Lines of Thought: The extent and the weightiness of D.'s exegesis of scripture already betray his closeness to Origen. The latter's exeget. method acquires a scholasticized form in D. The bibl. text is interpreted predominantly in two stages: first acc. to the literal sense (*pros rhēton*) and then acc. to its deeper spiritual sense (*pros anagōgēn*). Reference to the "meaninglessness" of the literal sense often serves to prove the need of a figurative (anagogical) interpretation. In differing degrees the commentaries document the propaideutic and espec. the philosophical learning of D., which reaches beyond a knowledge of the Aristotelean, Platonic, and Stoic traditions to include the Sophistic and Epicurean traditions as well and makes possible controversies specifically with Porphyry.

While being a clear-cut Origenist even in his acceptance of Origen's fundamental convictions (preexistence of the soul, fall into sin before time, apocatastasis), D. takes his stand on Nicene orthodoxy in opposing the (Neo-)Arians and the Pneumatomacheans, and develops against the Apollinarists his own "Two-Natures Christology" that emphasizes the full humanity (i.e., the possession of a rational soul) of the redeemer.

D. owes his influence on the Lat. West to his characteristic combination of Origenist scriptural interpretation and an "orthodox" teaching on the Trinity.

W: PG 39. — *Gen.*, P. Nautin, SC 233, 244. — *Job* 1-4, 1, A. Henrichs, U. and D. Hagedorn, L. Koenen (Bonn, 1968-1985) [text/German trans./comm.]. — *Zach.*, L. Doutreleau, SC 83, 84, 85. — *Ps.* 1-5, L. Doutreleau, A. Gesché, M. Gronewald (Bonn, 1968-1970) [text/German trans.]. — *Ps.* 4, Suppl., M. Gronewald: ZPE 46 (1982) 97-111. — B. Kramer, Kleine Texte aus dem Turafund (Bonn, 1985), 121-135. — *Ps.*, Quaternio 9, A. Kehl (Bonn, 1964) [text/German trans./comm.]. — *Eccl.* 1-6, G. Binder et al. (Bonn, 1969-1983) [text/German trans./comm.]. — *Jo.*, B. Kramer, loc. cit., 58-103 [text/German trans./comm.]. — *Pr.*, B. Kramer, loc. cit., 107-117 [text/German trans./comm.]. — eadem: ZPE 32 (1978) 202-212. — *Spir.*, L. Doutreleau, SC 386. — *serm.*, M. Bogaert: RBen 73 (1963) 9-16. — *Trin.* 1, J. Hönscheid; *Trin.* 2, 1-7, I. Seiler (Meisenheim, 1975) [text/German trans.]. — *Eun.* 4, 5, F. X. Risch (Leiden, 1992) [German trans./comm.].
Catenae: R. Devreesse, Commentaires grecs de l'Octateuque et des Rois (Rome, 1959). — F. Petit, Catenae Graecae in Gen et Ex, 1, CCG 2. — eadem, La chaîne sur la Génèse 1/2/3 (Leuven/Louvain, 1992/93/95). — U. and D.

Hagedorn, Die älteren griech. Katenen zum Buch Hiob (Berlin, 1994). — M. Harl, La chaîne palestinienne sur Ps 118, SC 189, 190. — E. Mühlenberg, Ps-Kommentare aus der Katenenüberlieferung 1/2 (Berlin, 1975/77). — S. Leanza, Procop. Gaz. Catena in Eccl, CCG 4. — J. Reuss, Joh-Kommentar aus Katenenhss.: TU 89 (Berlin, 1966), 177-186. — K. Staab, Pauluskommentar aus Katenenhss. (Münster, ²1984). — idem, Die griech. Katenenkommentare zu den kath. Briefen: Bib. 5 (1924) 296-353. — F. Zoepfl, Didymi in canon. ep. enarratio (Münster, 1914).
L: G. Bardy, D. l'Aveugle (Paris, 1910). — P. F. Beatrice, D. et la tradition de l'allégorie: Origeniana Sexta, ed. G. Dorival, A. le Boulluec (Leiden, 1995), 579-590. — L. Béranger, Sur deux énigmes de de Trin.: RSR 51 (1963) 255-267. — W. A. Bienert, Anagoge u. Allegoria (Berlin, 1972). — idem, Rez. D. Traité du Saint-Esprit: JAC 38 (1995) 183-185. — G. Binder, Eine Polemik des Porphyrios gegen die allegorische Auslegung des AT: ZPE 3 (1968) 81-95. — idem, Heidnische Autoritäten im Eccl-Kommentar: RBPH 57 (1979) 51-56. — idem, L. Liesenborghs, Eine Zuweisung der Sentenz οὐκ ἔστιν ἀντιλέγειν an Prodikos v. Keos: Sophistik, ed. C. J. Classen (Darmstadt, 1976), 452-462. — eadem, L. Koenen, Ein neues Epikurfrgm. bei D.: ZPE 1 (1967) 38-44. — C. Bizer, Studien zu den ps.-athanasianischen Dialogen (Bonn, 1970). — B. D. Ehrman, D. the Blind and the Texts of the Gospels (Atlanta, 1986). — W. J. Gauche, D. the Blind, an Educator of the Fourth Century (Washington, 1934). — A. Gesché, La christologie du "Comm. sur les Psaumes" (Gembloux, 1962). — M. Ghattas, Die Christologie D., Diss. (Marburg, 1996). — M. Gronewald, Ein neues Protagorasfrgm.: ZPE 2 (1968) 3f. — idem, Porphyrios' Kritik an den Gleichnissen des Evangeliums: ZPE 3 (1968) 96. — D. Hagedorn, R. Merkelbach, Ein neues Frgm. aus Porphyrios "Gegen die Christen": VigChr 20 (1966) 86-90. — A. Heron, Studies in the Trinitarian Writings of D. the Blind, Diss. (Tübingen, 1972). — E. L. Heston, The Spiritual Life as Described in the Works of D. (Rome, 1938). — W. W. Klein, Die Argumentation in den griech.-chr. Antimanichaica (Wiesbaden, 1991). — B. Kramer, D.: TRE 8:741-746. — J. Leipoldt, D. (Leipzig, 1905). — M. Orphanou, Ἡ ψυχὴ καὶ τὸ σῶμα τοῦ ἀνθρώπου κατὰ Δίδυμον Ἀλεξανδρέα (τὸν τυφλόν) (Thessalonica, 1974). — E. Prinzivalli, D. e l'interpretazione dei Salmi (Rome, 1988). — M. Sanchez, El "Comentario al Eccl" de D. (Rome, 1990). — P. H. Sellew, Achilles or Christ? Porphyry and D. in Debate over Allegorical Interpretation: HThR 82 (1989) 75-100. — M. Simonetti, Lettera e allegoria nell'esegesi veterotestamentaria di D.: VetChr 20 (1983) 341-389. — idem, Didymiana: VetChr 21 (1984) 139-155. — G. I. Swensson, God's Ikon in Man's History (London, 1985). — E. Staimer, Die Schrift "De spiritu sancto" von D., Diss. (Munich, 1960). — J. Tigcheler, D. l'Aveugle et l'exégèse allégorique (Nijmegen, 1977).

B. NEUSCHÄFER

Diodorus of Tarsus

I. Life: D. was born in the first quarter of the 4th c. in Antioch or Tarsus (Cilicia) of a distinguished family (Theod., *h.e.* 4.25.4). At Athens he received a higher education in the pagan tradition (see Julian, *ep.* 90;

opposite view, Jerome, *vir. ill.* 119: "ignorance of secular literature"). He learned the bibl. sciences from Silvanus, later bishop of Tarsus, and probably also from Eusebius of Emesa (in Antioch?). In Antioch D. fought at the side of the (temporarily banned) Bishop Meletius against the Arians and was ordained a priest by him. Together with a companion, Carterius, he was head of a monastery (an *askētērion*; Soc., *h.e.* 6.3.6; Soz., *h.e.* 8.2.6), where he taught his exeget. method to his students (among them Theodore Mops., John Chrys.; see the latter's *Laus Diodori*, PG 52:761-766); together with (later Bishop) Flavian, D. introduced the antiphonal singing of the Psalms (*ek diadochēs*) (Theod., *h.e.* 2.24.9). His asceticism, his ascetic way of life, and his Chr. faith displeased Emperor Julian, who in the winter of 362/363 stayed in Antioch during his expedition against the Persians (in his *ep.* 90 he describes D. as *acutus sophista religionis agrestis*), for he evidently saw in D. a danger to his plans for the restoration of paganism. In the implementation of Valens's pro-Arian religious policy, D. and Flavian were banished from Antioch (372); Basil met D. in Getasa (Armenia) where he was staying with Meletius (*ep.* 99.3; his *ep.* 135 and 160 are addressed to D.). After the death of Valens (378) Meletius appointed him bishop of Tarsus. On the occasion of the Council of Constantinople (381) Emperor Theodosius appointed D. and Pelagius of Laodicea as guarantors of the Nicene orthodoxy of the Oriens diocese (*Cod. Theod.* 16.1.3). If one assumes that Jerome passed his negative judgment on D. only after the latter's death (*vir. ill.* 199), the date of D.'s death is to be placed before 392 or certainly before 394 (Valerius is known to have been bishop of Tarsus in that year). Ca. 438, in a (lost) polemic, Cyril Alex. accused D. and Theodore Mops. of having justified the teaching of Nestorius (*Diod.*; see *epp.* 45, 67, 69, and 71); acc. to → Victor of Tunnuna (*chron.* II, p. 193) D.'s writings were condemned as Nestorian at the Council of Constantinople, and D. was held responsible for the erroneous teaching of Theodore. The anathema against D. which Photius claims for 553 (*cod.* 18) is probably not historical.

L: L. Abramowski, D.: DHGE 14:496-504. — G. Bardy, D.: DSp 3:986-993. — R. Leconte, L'Asceterium de D.: FS A. Robert (Tournai, 1957). — J. R. Pouchet, Les rapports de Basile avec D.: Bulletin de la littérature ecclésiastique 87 (1986) 243-272. — C. Schäublin, D.: TRE 8:763-767.

II. Work: As a result of D.'s condemnation in 499 only a few fragments of his writings have survived in Nestorian anthologies (mostly Syr.) and in catenas.

Photius's judgment that D. was learned and a scholar (*cod.* 223) is confirmed by the lengthy ancient lists of his works. Named there are (a) dogm. and polemical-apologetic works against pagans (debates with, among others, Plato and Porphyry), Jews, and heretics (Arians, Manichees, against Photinus, Malchio, Sabellius, Marcellus of Ancyra). The work *Kata synousiastōn* (*synous.*), of which thirty-three fragments are preserved in a Syr. florilegium, attacks the christology of the Apollinarists.

(b) Commentaries on all the books of the OT, the gospels, Rom, and 1 Jn. Fragments have survived of a commentary on the Octateuch (*Oct.*), which took the form of a collection of problems and solutions, as well as fragments of a commentary on Romans (*Rom.*). The work *Tis diaphora theōrias kai allēgorias* evidently dealt with hermeneutical questions. D.'s authorship of the commentary on the Psalms (*Ps.*) that has been transmitted under the name of Anastasius of Nicaea is disputed (chiefly because of differences from D.'s christology in *synous.*); the exeget. method used suggests D. The work certainly contains at least parts of a corresponding commentary by D. Four works of Ps.-Justin that are close to the Antiochene school of exegesis and that Harnack regarded as D.'s come in fact from the 5th c.

(c) Of D.'s cosmological-astronomical and chronological writings, the treatise *Kata astronomōn kai astrologōn peri heimarmenēs* (*fat.*, 8 books) is preserved in excerpts by Photius (*cod.* 223). Here, with reference to Stoic and Peripatetic thought, D. opposes the determinism of pagan astrology (the power of *physis* and the human *logos*, not fate, are active in the created world) and, to some extent, proposes his own astronomical speculations. A *Chronicon*, opposing → Eusebius of Caesarea, may have dealt with questions of bibl. chronology. The title *Kata Aristotelous peri sōmatos ouraniou* attests to D.'s debate with Aristotle.

III. Main Lines of Thought: D. takes his position in dogma against the Arians, on the one hand, against whom he stresses the full divinity of Christ, and, on the other hand, against the Apollinarists, against whom he emphasizes the full humanity of Christ (Christ is also son of David; Mary is also *anthrōpotokos*). The result is a strict separation of the two (closely connected but unmingled) natures in Christ (and a Logos-Anthropos christology). This brought upon D., who was regarded in his lifetime as Nicene and orthodox, the accusation of having been, with Theodore, the originator of Nestorius's error. D. is regarded as founder of the Antiochene school of exegesis, which turned against an exclusively allegorical-mystical interpretation of scripture (this was accused of artificiality and arbitrariness) and taught a literal-historical understanding of the bibl. text (see espec. *Oct.* frag. 93: "We should esteem the historical more than the allegorical"). The OT is interpreted in Chr. and salvation-history terms with the help of typology (*theōria*). The technique used in the → commentary is in the pagan tradition (espec. of Hellen.-Alex. philology). The characteristic traits of historical and grammatical exegesis as practiced by D. are found again in the commentary on the Psalms of D.'s disciple → Theodore Mops. Also in D.'s exeget. tradition are → Theodoret of Cyrrhus, → Basil, and → John Chrys., who carries the Antiochene commentary technique over to the homily.

W: *Oct.*, J. Deconinck, Essai sur la chaîne de l'Octateuque (Paris, 1912) [text]. — R. Devreesse, Les commentateurs de l'Octateuque (Rome, 1959), 155-167 [text]. — *Catenae Graecae in Genesim et in Exodum*, F. Petit, CCG 2:15. — F. Petit, La chaîne sur la Genèse 2 (Leuven/Louvain, 1993) [text]. — *Ps.*, J. M. Olivier, CCG 6. — *Rom.*, K. Staab, Pauluskommentare aus der griech. Kirche (Münster, 1933), 83-112 [text]. — *synous.*, R. Abramowski, Der theol. Nachlaß des D.: ZNW 42 (1949) 16-69 [text/German trans./comm.]. — M. Brière, Quelques fragments syriaques de D.: ROC 30 (1946) 231-283 [text/French trans./comm.]. — *fat.*, Photius, *cod.* 223, R. Henry, 4.7-48 (Paris, 1965) [text/French trans.].
L: R. Devreesse, Les commentateurs des Psaumes (Rome, 1970), 302-311. — R. A. Greer, The Antiochene Christology: JThS 17 (1966) 327-341. — G. Rinaldi, Polemica Antiallegorista: Aug. 33 (1993) 407-430. — M.-J. Rondeau, Le "Commentaire des Psaumes": RHR 176 (1969) 5-33; 177 (1970) 5-33. — eadem, Les commentaires patristiques du Psautier 1 (Rome, 1982), 93-102. — C. Schäublin, D. gegen Porphyrios?: MH 27 (1970) 58-63. — idem, Methode u. Herkunft der Antiochenischen Exegese (Cologne, 1974). — idem, Zu D.s Schrift gegen die Astrologie: RMP 123 (1980) 51-67. — E. Schweizer, D. als Exeget: ZNW 40 (1941) 33-75. — F. A. Sullivan, Christology (Rome, 1956), 181-196.

T. Fuhrer

Diognetus, Letter to

I. Work and Author: The title *Letter to Diognetus* (*Diogn.*) comes from the heading in the one ms. (burned in 1870) of the work. The description "letter" is not justified by the formal characteristics of the work; it is therefore more appropriate to speak of the "work addressed to Diognetus." The dedication is typical: "Illustrious Diognetus" (1.1), which suggests that *Diogn.* is claiming literary merit and is looking, among the pagan public being addressed, for those whose questions to Christians must be answered (1.1). The author looks beyond apologetic arguments and is concerned above all with a positive recruitment to Christianity, so that his work may best be regarded as in the genre of → protreptic. Chs. 11-12 are an addition by another hand; it probably served to make *Diogn.*, which was intended for a pagan audience, useful for Christians as well.

The author does not give his name. Interior evidence in the work shows him to be an educated person, probably privileged socially and well connected politically, who does not seem to have been very closely tied to an ecclesial community. A date between 190 and 200 and a location in Alexandria are good possibilities.

II: Main Lines of Thought: From a theol. point of view, *Diogn.* is distinguished above all by its idea of God. The question of the nature of the Chr. God is first answered negatively by contrast with the Greeks and the Jews. The argument against the former takes the form of a brilliant attack on the images of the gods (2); the letter rejects Jewish worship as superstition; it ridicules Jewish customs (3f.). *Diogn.* shares with the Middle Platonism of the age certain decisive principles: God's lack of any need and his immutability (8.8). The OT is completely ignored. God is not the God of Israel. He is seen in a unilateral way as merciful and kind; the judgment comes into view only peripherally and affects only other people.

It is into this picture that christology is incorporated. The name "Jesus" does not appear. The name most frequently used is "Son." There is no hint that this Son was a particular human being and even a Jew who suffered a wretched end. The God who is always the same made a decision to redeem, but he shared it only with the Son, through whom he also created the world; he revealed and carried out this decision only in the sending of the Son, which took place at a predetermined point in time (8.9-11). That is how *Diogn.* explains why the God of the Christians was proclaimed only at so late a time. The principle at work here, that God is separated from history, excludes the history of God with his people Israel, while the christology accepts the earthly concreteness of the man Jesus.

Diogn. shows the influence of Paul in its understanding of the sending of the Son as an act of the God who takes pity on sinners (9.1-6) and in the formulation of the ethic derived therefrom as an imitation of the kindness Christians have experienced from God. In the explanation of these ideas, the Platonic tradition on the imitation of God and on assimilation to him in the doing of the morally good comes into play (10.4-6). Distance from the world is essentially interiorized (5f.).

W: F. X. Funk, K. Bihlmeyer, Die Apostolischen Väter 1 (Tübingen, ²1956) [text]. — A. Lindemann, H. Paulsen,

Die Apostolischen Väter (Tübingen, 1992) [text/German trans.]. — H. I. Marrou, SC 33. — H. G. Meecham, The Epistle to Diognetus (Manchester, 1949) [text/English trans./comm.]. — K. Wengst, Schriften des Urchristentums 2 (Darmstadt, 1984) [text/German trans./comm.].
L: L. W. Barnard, Enigma: idem, Studies in the Apostolic Fathers (Oxford, 1966), 165-173. — T. Baumeister, Datierung: VigChr 42 (1988) 105-111. — R. Brändle, Ethik (Zurich, 1975). — idem, Mysterium: StPatr 13 (1975) 131-137. — W. Eltester, Mysterium: ZNW 61 (1970) 278-293. — J. Geffcken, Der Brief an Diognetos: ZKG 43 (1924) 348-350. — idem, Der Brief an Diognetos (Heidelberg, 1928). — J. A. Kleist, ACW 6 (Maryland, 1948). — W. Kühnert, Sinndeutung: FS Ev.-Theol. Fakultät Wien (Munich, 1972), 35-41. — J. T. Lienhard, Christology: VigChr 24 (1970) 280-289. — A. Lindemann, Paulinische Theologie: FS C. Andresen (Göttingen, 1979), 337-350. — E. Molland, Lit.-u. dogmengeschichtliche Stellung des D.: idem, Opuscula Patristica (Oslo, 1970), 79-101. — P. Nautin, L'épître à Diognète. Révision: ANRW II 27/2. — C. M. Nielsen, The Epistle to Diognetus: AThR 52 (1970) 77-91. — F. Overbeck, Brief an Diognet: idem, Studien zur Geschichte der Alten Kirche (Darmstadt, 1965 = Schloß Chemnitz, 1875), 1-92. — S. Petrement, Valentin est-il l'auteur de l'épître à Diognète?: RHPhR 46 (1966) 34-62. — M. Rizzi, La questione dell'unità dell'Ad Diognetum (Milan, 1989). — J. Schwartz, L'épître à Diognète: RHPhR 48 (1968) 46-53. — J. J. Thierry, The Logos as Teacher: VigChr 20 (1966) 146-149. — K. Wengst, "Paulinismus" u. "Gnosis": ZKG 90 (1979) 41-62.

K. WENGST

Dionysius of Alexandria

I. Life: D. was probably born in the last decade of the 2nd c. as a pagan and child of a rich Alex. family. Acc. to his own testimony, he came to Christianity through reading various works about it. During this period of searching, he was a student of Origen and probably received baptism from Demetrius Alex. When Heraclas was elected bishop, D. took over from him the leadership of the Alexandrean catechetical school in 231/232 and also became his successor as bishop in 247/248. He avoided the Decian persecution (249-251) by flight and, like Cyprian, later on was obliged to justify himself. He was consistent in supporting the possibility of penance and reconciliation for apostate Christians, the *lapsi*, and in resisting the rigorism of a Novatian. During his episcopate the controversy with chiliasm in Egypt occurred, as did the so-called controversy of the two Dionysiuses, in which D. had to defend the orthodoxy of his trinitarian teaching against his namesake in the Roman see. D. survived the persecution under Valerian (257-260) in exile. After his return he was active in pastoral work and church politics, but as early as 263/264 had to absent himself from a synod

in Antioch for reasons of age and illness; he died in 264/265.

II. Works: D.'s works have come down almost entirely in fragments (*fr.*). Most of these are in Eus. Caes., but also in Athanasius and Basil. In addition, there are fragments in later authors and in the canonical literature; there are also fragments in Syriac and Armenian, as well as one in Latin.

By far the majority of the writings are *letters*. In the surviving remains D. shows himself to be an involved eccles. politician who takes positions on contemporary theol. controversies, but also a pastor who devotes himself to practical eccles. problems. Only a fragment of a letter to Conon survives to illustrate D.'s views on penance; here he speaks of the forgiveness of sins for the mortally ill. When the question of such a reconciliation for the *lapsi* led to a controversy with Novatian, D. tried through letters to exert a pacifying influence. He also played a mediating and unifying role in the question, which arose out of the Novatian schism, of the validity of heretical baptism, and he attempted to help settle matters between the main adversaries, Stephen I of Rome and Cyprian of Carthage. Under this heading only parts of a letter to the Roman side have survived.

Entirely different in character are the letters to Fabius of Antioch and Germanus, in which the bishop vividly describes the terrors of the Decian persecution or else gives a defense of his behavior during the hard times under that emperor and under Valerian. In his Easter letter *To Dometius and Didymus* (D. probably began the tradition of Easter letters) the period under Decius comes alive; the letters *To Hierax* and *To the Brethren in Alexandria* tell of civil war and epidemic in that city. In the second of these two letters there are clear allusions to Thucydides' description of the plague in Athens in 430 B.C.E. (Thucydides 2.47-54). A letter *To Hermannon*, which also belongs among the Easter letters, contains a highly rhetorical panegyric of Emperor Gallienus.

The preeminence of letters in D.'s work is also made clear by the fact that Eus. (*h.e.* 7.26.2) describes even the other documents of the Alexandrian as "lengthy . . . in letter form." In his *On Nature* (*Peri physeōs*) D. aims to refute the teaching of Democritus and Epicurus on atoms by contrasting divine providence (*pronoia*), in a Stoic-Chr. manner, with the blind chance (*tychē*) that reigns in that teaching. Here he brings all his rhetorical skill to bear and shows his own classical (scholastic) education by quoting Homer, Hesiod, Plato, and Democratus.

In a treatise *On the Promises*, D. uses the controversy over Egyptian chiliasm to develop his own understanding of the divine promises by a careful exegesis espec. of the Apocalypse; in the process he reaches the conclusion that the Apocalypse and John's gospel could not have had a single author. Finally, the "controversy of the two Dionysiuses" has left us, in addition to the fragment of a letter, a series of citations from the Alexandrian's *Refutation and Defense*.

Since only a commentary on Qoh is attested with certainty, the authenticity espec. of the exeget. fragments attributed to him is disputed. Probably authentic are some fragments on Qoh and exegeses of Gen 2:8f. and Lk 22:42, 45f. (these last may come from the work *On Martyrdom to Origen*, mentioned in Eus., *h.e.* 6.46.1); fragments on Job and Cant are probably spurious.

W: PG 10:1237-1344, 1577-1602. — *fr.*, C. L. Feltoe (Cambridge, 1904) [text/comm.]. — idem (London, 1918) [English trans.]. — W. A. Bienert, BGrL 2 (Stuttgart, 1972) [German trans./comm.]. — idem, Neue Frgm.: Kl. 5 (1973) 308-314 [text/comm.]. — M. v. Esbroeck, Nouveaux fragments arméniens: OCP 50 (1984) 18-42 [text/French trans.]. — S. Leanza, Due nuovi frammenti sull'Eccl.: Orph. 6 (1985) 156-161 [text/comm.]. — *Catena Haun. in Eccl.*, A. Labate (CCG 24).
L: C. Andresen, "Siegreiche Kirche": ANRW II, 23/1 (1979), 387-459. — W. A. Bienert, D. Zur Frage des Origenismus im 3. Jh. (Berlin, 1978). — idem, D. u. Origenes· StPatr 16 (1985) 219-223. — E. Boularand, D. et Arius: BLE 67 (1966) 161-169. — S. J. Bouma, D. van Alexandrië (Purmerend, 1943). — J. Burel, D. d'Alexandrie (Paris, 1910). — F. H. Colson, Two Examples of Literary and Rhetorical Criticism: JThS 25 (1924) 364-377. — J. Ernst, Stellung zur Ketzertauffrage: ZKTh 30 (1906) 38-56. — S. Leanza, Commentario sull'Ecclesiaste di D.: FS S. Pugliatti 5 (Milan, 1978), 379-429. — A. Martin, La réconciliation des lapsi en Égypte: RSLR 22 (1986) 256-269. — P. S. Miller, Studies in D. (Erlangen, 1933). — K. Müller, Grundlagen des Ketzertaufstreits: ZNW 23 (1924) 235-247. — idem, D. im Kampf mit den libyschen Sabellianern: ZNW 24 (1925) 278-285. — H.-G. Opitz, D. u. die Libyer: FS K. Lake (London, 1937), 41-53. — H. Pietras, Lettera pros Germanon: Gr. 71 (1990) 573-583. — idem, L'unità di Dio in D.: Gr. 72 (1991) 459-490. — G. Roch, Schrift des D. "Über die Natur" (Leipzig, 1882). — E. Schwartz, Eine fingierte Korrespondenz mit Paulus dem Samosatener: SBAW. PH 1927, 3. — M. Simonetti, Il problema dell'unità di Dio da Clemente a D.: RSLR 22 (1986) 439-474. — M. Sordi, D. e le vicende della persecuzione di Valeriano: FS G. Lazzati (Milan, 1980), 288-295.

U. Hamm

Dionysius the Areopagite

I. Dating and Authenticity: D. (also: Ps.-D.) is the pseudonym of an author who lived ca. 500 and wrote the Gk. works *De divinis nominibus* (*d. n.*), *De caelesti*

hierarchia (*c. h.*), *De ecclesiastica hierarchia* (*e. h.*), and *De mystica theologia* (*myst.*) (other works under D.'s name are probably fictive), as well as ten letters (*ep.* 1-10). The author's real name and dates are unknown. The writer pretends to be the Areopagite mentioned in Acts 17:34 (*d. n.* 2.11; *ep.* 7.3), to have witnessed the eclipse of the sun in Heliopolis at the death of Christ (*ep.* 7.2), and to have met with Peter and James (*d. n.* 3.2), but the name and the period are fictions. Attempts to identify him with → Severus of Antioch, → Peter the Iberian, and → Peter the Fuller, among others, are unconvincing. As a result, a dating can only be derived from within the works themselves: these works depend on the writings of Proclus, a Neoplatonist (d. 485), and are close in their christology to the *Henotikon* issued by Emperor Zeno in 482. Furthermore, D. refers to the creed which Peter the Fuller introduced into the Syro-Antiochene Mass in 482 (*e. h.* 3.7.87.24ff.). In addition, the works of D. are first mentioned ca. 518/528 in some writings of Severus of Antioch. Some guess the writer to have been close to → John of Scythopolis. This thesis has received support in recent studies acc. to which John himself and a group of scholars around him edited the works between 536 and 543/553, commented on them, prefixed an introduction, and combined them, with the preface and commentary, into a single corpus. The transmission of the writings in this corpus and the supposed closeness of the author to the apostles promoted the high reputation of the works. They were even translated into Syriac before 536, and later into Armenian, Georgian, and Church Slavonic. The first Lat. translation was made by Abbot Hilduin (827-835). John Scotus Eriugena completed a translation (852) that improved on Hilduin's and substantially determined the medieval understanding of D., espec. since Anastasius Bibliothecarius, a contemporary of Eriugena, added a Lat. translation of the scholia and combined both into the so-called *Corpus Anastasianum*. Numerous copies were made of this corpus. The translations by John Sarracenus (ca. 1160) and Robert Grosseteste (between 1240 and 1243) finally replaced Eriugena's translation in importance.

Eus., following Dionysius of Corinth, identified D., the disciple of Paul named in Acts 17:34, with the first bishop of Athens (*h.e.* 3.4.10; 4.23.3). He was followed by John of Scythopolis who, in his preface, then identified D., Paul's disciple, with both the first bishop of Athens and the writer of these works. Gregory of Tours numbered a Dionysius who suffered martyrdom in Paris as one of the seven missionary bishops who came to Gaul under Emperor Decius

(249-251) (*Franc.* 1.30). Finally, later sources identified this Dionysius with the first bishop of Paris. The second *Passio Dionysii* identified this martyr bishop of Paris with Dionysius Areo. of the Acts of the Apostles (PL 106:23-50; BHL 2178; ca. 750). It was the third *Passio Dionysii*, this one by Abbot Hilduin, that identified the Parisian martyr bishop with the Dionysius who was regarded as author of the treatises in the *Corpus Dionysiacum* (BHL 2175; 832).

Doubts about the author's closeness to the apostle were voiced as early as the 6th c. by Hypatius of Ephesus, but these were sharply rejected by John Philoponus and John of Scythopolis. The skillful interpretation of the works by John of Scythopolis (*schol.*) finally secured acceptance of their authenticity by, among others, Leontius Byz., Gregory the Great, Sophronius Jerus., and Maximus Conf. Only in the high Middle Ages did doubts spring up again, as, e.g., in Peter Abelard (PL 178:154f.). The public doubts of humanists Lorenzo Valla and Erasmus of Rotterdam influenced the Reformers in particular. Finally, the dependence of the works on the Neoplatonism of Proclus was discovered.

II. Works: D. was not interested in the christological disputes of his time between the defenders of Chalcedon (451) and the Monophysites. As a result, fruitlessness has marked scholarly discussions of whether the position of the Monophysites, who claimed the writings of D. for their christology at a dialogue between Monophysites and Chalcedonians in Constantinople in 532-533, was in fact strengthened by the writings of D. and their formulations "of a single divine-human reality" in Christ (*ep.* 4.161.9) and of "the divine formation" of Jesus (*d. n.* 2.9.133.5f.). D.'s interest was rather in the problem of truth and the theory of knowledge, i.e., the question of the knowability and knowledge of God from the ontological system present in his creation. The *d. n.*, as a Chr. interpretation and transformation of Plato's *Parmenides*, inquires into the knowability and knowledge of the *hen*, the One, which D. identifies with the one triune God. The essence of God is not knowable; knowable are only the symbolic, along with the positive (cataphatic) and negative (apophatic) names which God has revealed in his three self-communications, namely, his creation, his words in revelation, and his irradiations.

C. h. and *e. h.* describe the ontological system made known in the three self-communications of God, a system that is hierarchically structured and ordered from top to bottom (an ontology of gradations). The heavenly hierarchy is divided into nine degrees made up of three hierarchically ordered triads, each consisting of three hierarchically ordered choirs of angels. The first triad includes seraphim, cherubim, and thrones (*c. h.* 7); the second: dominions, powers, and authorities (*c. h.* 8); the third: principalities, archangels, and angels (*c. h.* 9). These nine classes mediate from the top down, in a descending series, between God and humanity. The eccles. hierarchy, being an image of the heavenly hierarchy, is likewise divided into three triads, each containing three groups. The triad of the holy sacraments consists of baptism, Eucharist, and confirmation (*e. h.* 2-4); the triad of priestly classes consists of bishops, priests, and deacons (*e. h.* 5); the triad of the three subordinate classes consists of monks (catechumens), members of the communities (energumens), and the imperfect (penitents; *e. h.* 6). With these two treatises D. was not only creator of the concept of hierarchy; he was also a systematizer who succeeded, in a convincing and lasting way, in representing and accounting for the substance of the divine order of creation. D.'s work reaches its high point in *myst.*, which gives an aporetic answer to the question of the knowableness and knowledge of the transcendent *hen*: "There is no speaking of it [the supreme cause], nor name nor knowledge of it. Darkness and light, error and truth—it is none of these" (5.150.3-5). The only way to God is that of mystical union. *Ep.* 1-10 were intended to complete the content of the several tracts.

The hypothesis that later interpolations were made in *d. n., e. h.*, and *ep.* 6-10 was refuted by the *Editio critica maior* of Göttingen (PTS 33; 36).

Non-authentic writings: *Ep.* 11 *ad Apollophanum philosophum*, in a Lat. version; *Ep. ad s. Timotheum de passione apostolorum Petri et Pauli*, in Lat., Syr., Arm., Georg,. Arab., and Eth. versions; *Ep. ad Titum*, in an Arm. version; *Narratio de vita sua*, in Syr. versions, and in Copt., Arab., Georg., and Arm. forms; *Tractatus astronomicus et meteorologicus* in a Syr. version; *Confessio fidei*, in an Arab. version.

III. Importance: D. was an innovative thinker. By means of an astute combination of Neoplatonism and Christianity he christianized Neoplatonism and incorporated it into Christianity. On the one hand, he thus deprived Neoplatonism of its power as the worldview of the richly traditional pagan competitor of Christianity; on the other, by his Chr. transformation of Platonic thought, he enabled Platonism to continue to influence Chr. thought.

D. influenced Chr. philosophy and theology down to the 20th c. The thinkers of the Scholastic period tackled his thought in a critical manner, espec. Thomas Aquinas, who cites D. ca. 1,700 times. Mystics such as Eckhart, John Tauler, Jan van Ruysbroek, John of the Cross, and John Gerson took his work as a basis. As a result, D. was among the authors of the Middle Ages and the Renaissance most frequently commented on. Numerous Syr., Gk., and Lat. commentaries, such as those of John of Scythopolis, Maximus Conf., Theodore Bar Zarudi, Iwannis of Dara, John Scotus Eriugena, Hugh of St. Victor, John Sarracenus, Bar Salibi, Robert Grosseteste, Thomas Gallus, Albert the Great, Thomas Aquinas, Thomas Hibernicus, George Pachymeres, John Gerson, Denis the Carthusian, and Marsilius Ficinus, attest to the attention paid to D.'s thought in both East and West; that thought continued to influence German idealism. If the importance of an author is to be judged by the history of his influence, then D. is one of the most important authors of the West.

W: *d. n.*, B. R. Suchla, PTS 33 [text]. — *c. h.*, *e. h.*, G. Heil, PTS 36 [text]. — *myst.*, *ep.* 1-10, A. M. Ritter, PTS 36 [text]. — *schol.*, B. R. Suchla, PTS [text; in preparation]. — *Indices Ps.-D.*, A. Van Den Daele (Leuven/Louvain, 1941). — *Thesaurus Ps.-D. Textus graecus cum translationibus latinis*, M. Nasta/CETEDOC (Turnhout, 1993). — *Dionysiaca*, P. Chevallier, 2 vols. (Bruges, 1937, 1950) [text/Latin trans.]. — *d. n.*, *c. h.*, *e. h.*, *myst.*, *ep.*, P. Rorem, Ps.-D. A Commentary on the Texts and an Introduction to their Influence (Oxford, 1993) [commentary]. — P. Rorem (London, 1987) [English trans.]. — M. de Gandillac (Paris, 1943) [French trans.]. — E. Turolla, Padua 1956 [Italian trans.]. — *c. h.*, *e. h.*, *d. n.*, *ep.* 8, J. Stiglmayr, BKV² 2; 2/2 [German trans.]. — *c. h.*, *e. h.*, G. Heil, BGrL 22 [German trans.]. — *d. n.*, B. R. Suchla, BGrL 26 [German trans.]. — *myst.*, *ep.*, A. M. Ritter, BGrL 38 [German trans.].
Unauthentic W: *ep.* 11, PG 3:1119-1122 [Latin text]. — *ep. ad s. Timotheum*, BHL 6671; BHO 966-970. — *ep. ad Titum*, BHO 642. — *Narratio de vita sua*, BHO 255.2.3. — P. Peeters, La version ibéro-arménienne de l'autobiographie de D.: AnBol 39 (1921) 293-313. — *Tractatus astronomicus et meteorologicus*, M. A. Kugener: Actes du 14e Congrès International des Orientalistes, Alger 1905 (Paris, 1907), 2:137-198 [text/French trans./comm.].
L: Y. de Andia (ed.), Actes du Colloque sur D. et sa postérité en Orient et en Occident (Paris, 1996). — H. U. v. Balthasar, Das Scholienwerk des Johannes v. Scythopolis: Schol. 15 (1940) 16-38 (improved: Kosmische Liturgie [Einsiedeln, ²1961], 644-672). — A. Becca, Il problema del male (Bologna, 1967). — H.-G. Beck, Kirche und theol. Lit. (Munich, ²1977), 376f. — G. von Bredow, Platonismus im MA (Freiburg i.Br., 1972). — B. Brons, Sekundäre Textpartien im Corpus Pseudo-Dionysiacum?: NAWG. PH 5 (1975) 99-140. — idem, Gott u. die Seienden (Göttingen, 1976). — E. Corsini, Il trattato De divinis nominibus dello Ps.-D. e i commenti neoplatonici al Parmenide, PFLUT 13/4 (Turin, 1962). — A. Dempf, Der Platonismus des Eusebius, Victorinus und Ps.-D. (Munich, 1962). — J. Durantel, S. Thomas et le Ps.-D. (Paris, 1919). — M. van Esbroeck, Peter the Iberian and D.: OCP 59 (1993) 217-227. — R. F. Hathaway, Hierarchy and the Definition of Order in the Letters of Ps.-D. (Den Haag, 1969). — J. Hochstaffl, Negative Theologie (Munich, 1976). — E. Honigmann,

Pierre l'Ibérien et les écrits du Ps.-D. (Brussels, 1952). — J.-M. Hornus, Le corpus d. en syriaque: ParOr 1 (1970) 69-93. — E. von Ivánka, Plato Christianus (Einsiedeln, 1964). — H. Koch, Proklus als Quelle des Ps.-D. in der Lehre vom Bösen: Ph. 54 (1895) 438-454. — idem, Ps.-D. in seinen Beziehungen zum Neuplatonismus und Mysterienwesen (Mainz, 1900). — A. Louth, D. (London, 1989). — B. McGinn, Die Mystik im Abendland 1 (Freiburg i.Br., 1994), 233-269. — H. Meinhardt et al., D.: LMA 3:1076-1087. — E. Moutsopoulos (ed.), Philosophie Dionysienne: Diotima 23 (1995). — W. M. Neidl, Thearchia (Regensburg, 1976). — G. O'Daly, D.: TRE 8:772-780. — W. Otten, Negative Theology A Negative Anthropology: HeyJ 40 (1999) 438-455. — U. Riedinger, Petros der Walker als Verfasser der Ps.-D. Schriften: SJP 5/6 (1961/62) 135-156. — R. Roques, L'univers dionysien. Structure hiérarchique du monde (Paris, 1954). — idem et al., D.: DSp 3:244-429. — idem, D.: RAC 3:1075-1121. — M. Schiavone, Neoplatonismo e Cristianesimo (Milan, 1963). — P. Sherwood, Sergius of Reshaina and the Syriac Versions of the Ps.-D.: SE 4 (1952) 174-184. — E. Stein, Wege der Gotteserkenntnis: Thom. (1946) 379-420. — J. Stiglmayr, Der Neuplatoniker Proclus als Vorlage des sog. D. in der Lehre vom Übel: HJ 16 (1895) 253-273, 721-748. — idem, Das Aufkommen der Ps.-Dionysischen Schriften: 4. Jahresbericht des öffentlichen Privatgymnasiums an der Stella Matutina zu Feldkirch, 1895. — W. Strothmann, Das Sakrament der Myron-Weihe in der Schrift e. h. des Ps.-D. in syr. Übersetzungen u. Kommentaren, 2 vols. (Göttingen, 1977/78). — B. R. Suchla, Die sog. Maximus-Scholien des Corpus Dionysiacum (Göttingen, 1980). — eadem, Eine Redaktion des griech. Corpus Dionysiacum A. im Umkreis des Johannes v. Skythopolis (Göttingen, 1985). — eadem, Verteidigung eines platonischen Denkmodells einer chr. Welt (Göttingen, 1995). — eadem, Überlieferungsgeschichte des Corpus Dionysiacum, PTS in Vorb. — J. Vanneste, Le mystère de dieu (Bruges, 1959). — W. Völker, Kontemplation und Ekstase (Wiesbaden, 1958). J. Williams, The Apophatic Theology of D.: DR 117 (1999) 157-172.

B. R. Suchla

Dionysius Exiguus

I. Life: D. (Exiguus was a later, self-chosen expression of humility) was born probably ca. 470 in Scythia Minor, where he also received his education from a Bishop Peter. After the death of Roman Bishop Gelasius I (d. 496), D. went to Rome, where he was presumably active for some time as a teacher. In keeping with his life as a monk and as a theologian skilled in languages, he took part in the intellectual controversies of the time, but not in a political way (e.g., in the Symmachian schism). Since he had a good command of Greek and Latin, he was able to mediate between East and West in the areas of canon law and theology. The stylistically splendid prefaces to his works bear witness that he had links with many important personages of his time, to whom he dedicated these commissioned works. Some translations (ca. 520) were probably intended to support the cause of Scythian monks in the theopaschite controversy. As his friend Cassiodorus attests, he was "an excellent man" (whether he was a priest or abbot is questionable) and a genuine "Roman," who by his "reliable translations of important documents" promoted "understanding between the eastern and western churches." D. died before 556; he certainly lived past 526, but anything more is uncertain.

L: I. Coman, Les "scythes" Jean Cassien et D.: Kl. 7 (1975) 27-46. — G. J. Dragulin, Le hieromoine D. Exiguus (env. 470-550): StTeol 37 (1985) 521-539. — F. de Marini Avanzo, Secular and Clerical Culture in D.'s Rome: Proceedings . . . Berkeley = MIC. S 7 (1985) 83-92. — H. Mordek, D. Exiguus: LMA 3:1088-1092. — W. M. Peitz, D. Exiguus-Studien, ed. H. Foerster (Berlin, 1960). — J. Rambaud-Buhot, D.: DDC 4:1131-1152. — M. Richter, D. Exiguus: TRE 9:1-4. — A. L. Tautu, Dionisie Românul (Rome, ²1967).

II. Works: 1. Canon Law: The most important works here are the collections of canons (*can.*), the occasion for which D. gives in each case in a preface (*praef.*). Because earlier translations of Gr. canons into Latin were not reliable, D., in response to requests, made a new, faithful, and stylistically good translation of the fifty → *Apostolic Canons*, the canons of the councils of Nicaea, Ancyra, Neocaesarea, Gangra, Antioch, Laodicea, Constantinople I, Sardica, and Chalcedon, to which he added thirty-three African canons. A novelty that contributed to his success was a prefixed table of contents (*tituli*) that gave a reliable account of the essential contents. A second edition with numerous changes was published probably soon after 500 and was dedicated to Bishop Stephen of Salona. Only the preface has survived of a Gk.-Lat. edition that he did at the request of Hormisdas of Rome (d. 523); D. says that he did not include the *Apostolic Canons* and the canons of Sardica and Africa, because they were not accepted everywhere. He included a detailed table of contents once again in his collection of thirty-nine decretals of the Roman bishops from Siricius (d. 399) to Anastasius II (d. 498). In these two works D. did pioneering work for future canon law. He made reliable collections of material in chronological order, distinguished clearly between canons of councils and decretals of the Roman bishop, and yet viewed them as connected sources of a system of eccles. law. The tables of items made it easy to use the contents. Although D.'s work never became an official book of church laws, it was quickly accepted, initially by John II of Rome in 534 and then down to the time when Hadrian I gave a greatly expanded version to Charlemagne in 774 (Dionysio-Hadriana). Ca. one hundred mss. of the

various (expanded) editions are known. In addition, the *Dionysiana* served as the basis for other, likewise systematic collections, e.g., of Cresconius (probably in Italy), the *Vetus Gallia*, and the *Dacheriana*. It is not possible, however, to go so far as to say, as scholars sometimes have, that the copy of D. in the papal archives was the basis for the entire canonical tradition of the early centuries and that (later) textual differences go back to variants in translation (contamination of the source).

2. Translations (from Greek): (a) hagiographical and devotional writings: *The Penance of St. Thais, Life of Pachomius, Discovery of the Head of St. John the Baptist.*

(b) Gregory of Nyssa's phil. work *The Creation of Man* (*hom. opif.*) was accurately translated despite doubts about its content.

(c) Dogmatic writings: The *Libellus de fide*, which a legation from the bishop of Rome to Constantinople received (colophon: *D. E. Romae de Graeco converti*), was translated in 497. The translation of two works of Proclus Constant. and three letters of Cyril Alex. (ACO 2, 5, 233-49 and 294-307; 4, 2, 196-205) offered arguments against the Nestorians in the West. It is doubtful whether D. himself collected the *Exempla patrum*, which served theopaschism and are found in *Cod. Novara* 30 (only here has the preface to the third edition of the collection of canons survived).

3. Chronology: D. was able to settle the disagreement over the date of Easter (525/526) because he knew the relevant Gk. writings and had translated the letter of Proterius Alex. to Leo I. In his works *De cyclo magno paschae* (*cyc.*) and *Argumenta paschalia* (*pasch.*) he decided in favor of the eastern (Cyril Alex.) reckoning of the date of Easter with its nineteen-year cycle, which he extrapolated for the years 532-626. Because in doing so he appealed to the Council of Nicaea (as he did again in his letter of 526 answering an official inquiry from the people around the Roman bishop [*ep. de ratione paschae*; *ep. pasch.*]), his results were accepted in Rome. His radical innovation, which was to count years from the birth of Christ (to which he assigned a slightly late date, 754 from the founding of Rome) and no longer, as in the East, from Emperor Diocletian, was accepted only over the course of several centuries.

W: PL 67:9-520; 73:223-282, 661-664. — PLS 4:17-22. — *praef.*, F. Glorie, CCL 85:27-81, 83-127. — *Exempla patrum*, ACO 4, 2, 74-96. — *Can.*, C. H. Turner, Ecclesiae occidentalis monumenta (Oxford, 1899-1939), passim. — A. Strewe, Die Canonessammlung des D. Exiguus in der ersten Redaktion (Berlin, 1931). — H. Wurm, Decretales selectae: Apoll. 12 (1939) 40-93. — *cyc., pasch., ep. pasch.*, B. Krusch,

Studien zur chr.-mal. Chronologie (Berlin, 1932), 63-87.
L: K. Christ, Eine unbekannte Hs. der ersten Fassung der Dionysiana: FS Leidinger (Munich, 1930), 25-36. — B. Krusch, Die Einführung des griech. Paschalritus im Abendland: NA 9 (1884) 99-169. — V. Lozito, Culti e ideologia politica negli autori cristiani (Bari, 1987), 57-72. — F. Maassen, Geschichte der Quellen u. der Lit. des canonischen Rechts (Graz, 1870 = 1956), 422-476. — H. Mordek, Kirchenrecht u. Reform im Frankenreich (Berlin, 1975), 241-249. — C. Munier, L'œuvre canonique de D.: ScEc 14 (1963) 236-250. — H. Wurm, Studien u. Texte zur Dekretalensammlung des D. (Bonn, 1936 = Amsterdam, 1964). — K. Zechiel-Eckes, Die Concordia canonum des Cresconius (Frankfurt a.M., 1992).

R. Weigand

Dionysius of Corinth

Our knowledge of D., the bishop of Corinth who was greatly revered in the early church, comes entirely from Eus. (*h.e.* 2.25.8; 3.4.10; 4.21.23, and 25; Eus. is the source for Jerome, *vir. ill.* 27 and *ep.* 70.4). D. lived ca. 170 and was one of the leading churchmen of his time; he addressed other communities in his "Catholic Letters." In *h.e.* 4.23, Eus. preserves more or less extensive information on seven such letters.

Acc. to Eus., the letters to the Lacedemonians and to the Athenians, among others, had for their subject the orthodox faith as well as peace and unity in the communities. In the second of those two letters D. described Dionysius Areo., who was converted by Paul in Acts 17:34, as having been the first bishop of Athens (also *h.e.* 3.4.10).

In a letter to the Nicomedians D. opposed the supporters of Marcion; the letter to the community of Gortyna and the other communities of Crete seems to have been prompted by similar concerns. In the letters to the community of Amastris and the other communities of Pontus and to the residents of Cnossus (Eus. speaks here of an answering letter from Pinytus of Cnossus) the leading of a Chr. life and the dispute with encratitic or Montanist tendencies seem rather certainly to have played a role. D. warned against such rigorist tendencies and exhorted to unity.

Eus. has preserved three fragments of a letter to the Romans: D. thanks the Romans for their support of other communities (4.23.10), refers to the reading of *1 Clem.* at the Sunday liturgy (4.23.11; a decisive testimony to the authorship of → Clement of Rome), and attests to the connection, of whatever kind, of Peter and Paul with Rome and Corinth (2.25.8). Attempts to see in these seven a body of letters collected by D. or someone else and thematically organized must remain simply speculative. Nevertheless,

a fourth fragment (4.23.12), which, acc. to Eusebius's introduction to it, does not certainly belong to the letter to the Romans and in which D. complains of his letters being tampered with, may be taken as reason for speaking of a collection, to which, however, a letter to an otherwise unknown Chrysophora, mentioned at the end by Eus., probably did not belong.

D.'s eloquence, praised by Jerome (*vir. ill.* 27), cannot be seen in the brief surviving fragments, which, on the contrary, do not suggest any rhetorical structuring.

W: M. J. Routh, Reliquiae Sacrae 1 (Oxford, ²1846), 175-201 [text/comm.]. — P. Nautin, Lettres et écrivains (Paris, 1961), 13-32 [with text/French trans. of the frags.]
L: G. Bardy, D.: DSp 3:449f. — P. Burchi, D.: BSS 4:638f. — A. Harnack, Die Briefsammlung des Apostels Paulus (Leipzig, 1926), 36-40. — A. Jülicher, D.: PRE 5/1:993f. — W. Kühnert, D.: FS F. Zerbst (Vienna, 1979), 273-289. — P. Nautin, loc. cit. — S. G. Papadopoulos, Δ. (Athens, 1975) (problematic).

U. Hamm

Dionysius Philocalus

Furius Dionysius Philocalus or Filocalus (D.) is as much known as writer (and editor, *titulavit*) of the → *Chronograph of 354* as he is for his activity on behalf of Damasus I (366-384) in decorating graves of the martyrs (he included his own name three times). An identification with the grammarian of the same name must remain an open question; the same for the identification with the Filocalus named in the *Anthologia latina* (120, Riese ed.). He describes his relationship with Damasus as that of a *cultor et amator* (no. 18, Ferrua). He may therefore have been a Christian. The absence of Christianity from large sections of the calendar of 354 would then be typical of the time in late Constantinian urban culture. To be emphasized is his artistic script in the formation of the so-called Philocalian letters (i.e., decorative script), which had a long posterity.

W: J. Strzygowski, Die Calenderbilder des Chronographen (Berlin, 1888).
L: T. D. Barnes, More missing names: Phoenix 27 (1973) 135-155 (esp. 148). — A. Ferrua, Filocalo: CivCatt 80 (1939) 35-47. — idem, Epigrammata Damasiana 2 (Rome, 1942). — C. M. Kaufmann, Handbuch der altchr. Epigraphik (Freiburg i.Br., 1917). — T. Mommsen, Über den Chronographen: Ges. Schriften 7 (1909 = 1850), 563-579. — C. O. Nordenfalk, Der Kalender vom Jahr 354 u. die lat. Buchmalerei des 4. Jh.: GVSH. H 5/2 (1936) 5-36. — C. Pietri, Roma Christiana (Rome, 1976). — M. R. Salzmann, On Roman Time (Berkeley, 1990).

W. Wischmeyer

Dionysius of Rome

Dionysius I of Rome (D.), 3rd c., initially a Roman presbyter, 259/260–267/268, and then successor of Bishop Sixtus II, reorganized the Roman community, which had been greatly weakened by persecution. In 262, as a result of complaints from Alex. presbyters about the Origenist type of christology represented by Dionysius Alex., D. held a synod in Rome that condemned Sabellianism and subordinationism.

The letters of D. are almost entirely lost; only a fragment (in Athanasius, *decr.* 26) has survived of a synodal letter of D. to Dionysius Alex. in which the latter is told of the decrees of the Roman synod. In a second, now lost synodal letter, mentioned by Athanasius (*Dion.* 13) D. was supposed to have told Dionysius Alex. about the complaints against him. Basil the Great (*ep.* 70) mentions a letter of consolation from D. to the community of Caesarea that was suffering from the consequences of the barbarian invasions; D. added a gift of money for the release of Chr. captives.

W: PL 5:109-116 [text]. — C. L. Feltoe, Διονυσίου Λείψανα (Cambridge, 1904), 176-182 [text].
L: L. Abramowski, D. († 268) and D. of Alexandria († 264/265) in the Arian Controversies of the Fourth Century: eadem, Formula and Context (London, 1992), n. 11. — W. A. Bienert, Das vornizänische homoousios als Ausdruck der Rechtgläubigkeit: ZKG 90 (1979) 151-175. — idem, D. v. Alexandrien (Berlin, 1978), 220f. — B. Botte, D.: DHGE 14:247f. — H. Hagemann, Die röm. Kirche und ihr Einfluß auf Disziplin u. Dogma (Freiburg i.Br., 1864), 432-453. — M. Simonetti, Ancora su homoousios: VetChr 17 (1980) 85-98. — G. C. Stead, Divine Substance (Oxford, 1977), 216-222.

C. Schmidt

Dionysius, Pseudo-, of Tell-Mahre

The Ps.-Dionysian chronicle of 774/775 makes use, along with Eusebius and the → *Chronicle of Edessa*, of a great deal of legendary material from the *Treasure Cave* (→ *Spelunca Thesaurorum*) and other apocrypha. It is not to be confused with the *Chronicle* of Jacobite Patriarch Dionysius of Tell-Mahre (818-854), which describes the years 582-842.

W: J. B. Chabot, CSCO 91, 104, 121 [Syriac text/Latin trans.].
L: P. Nagel, Grundzüge syr. Kirchengeschichtsschreibung: BBA 55 (1990) 245-259. — N. Pigulevskaya, Syriac Chronicle of PsD.: PalSb 19 (1969) 118-126. — W. Witakowski, Syriac Chronicle of Ps-D. (Uppsala, 1987).

P. Bruns

Dioscurus of Alexandria

A life that has been preserved complete only in Syriac tells of the life of D., who governed the church of Egypt as patriarch of Alexandria from 444 to 451. This former deacon of Cyril attempted to assert the importance of his see in eccles. politics over against a strengthened Constantinople; at the "Robber Synod" of Ephesus (449) he associated his opposite number, Flavian, with other diophysites. At the instigation of Leo I, D. was himself deposed at Chalcedon and sent into exile in Gangra, where he died on Sept. 4, 454.

Some letters (*ep.*) from his extensive correspondence have come down in the Syr. Acts of Ephesus II; in these D. essentially represents the christological position of his teacher, Cyril Alex., prior to the Union of 433. D. also fought against the extreme Origenists of his day. A panegyric on Macarius of Tkow (*hom. in Mac.*) and an anaphora (*an.*) that were attributed to D. are to be regarded as spurious.

S: W. E. Crum, Coptic Texts relating to D.: PSBA 25 (1903) 267-276 [Coptic text/English trans.]. — E. O. Winstedt, Some Munich Coptic Fragments: PSBA 28 (1906) 137-142 [Coptic text/English trans.]. — F. Nau, Histoire de D.: JA 10 (1903) 5-108, 241-310 [Syriac text/French trans.].
W: *ep.*, J. Fleming, Akten des Ephesinum II (Wiesbaden, 1970 = 1917), 132-157 [Syriac text/German trans.]. — K. N. Khella, Ein D.-Zitat: Probleme der kopt. Literaturwissenschaft (Halle, 1968), 187-196 [Coptic text/German trans.]. — *hom. in Mac.*, D. W. Johnson, CSCO 415f. [Coptic text/English trans.]. — *an.*, W. de Vries, Anaphorae syriacae (Rome, 1944), 267-321 [Syriac text/Latin trans.].
L: W. H. C. Frend, The Monophysite Movement (Cambridge, 1972), 25-48. — A. Grillmeier, Peste d'Origène: FS C. Mondésert (Paris, 1987), 221-237. — F. Haase, D.: KGA 6 (1908) 141-236. — J. Lebon, Le monophysisme sévérin (Leuven/Louvain, 1909), 84-93. — W. de Vries, Räubersynode: OCP 41 (1975) 357-398

P. Bruns

Discourse of Jesus to His Disciples in Galilee

This apocalyptic discourse of Jesus (*or. Iesu*) to his disciples in Galilee is a more recent text that was preceded by the Eth. → *Epistula apostolorum*. It depicts the events of the final days as communicated by Jesus after his resurrection to his disciples in Galilee.

W: L. Guerrier, S. Grébaut, PO 9/3 [Ethiopic text/French trans.]. — C. Schmidt, Gespräche Jesu (Hildesheim, 1967 = Leipzig, 1919), 48*-66* [German trans.].

P. Bruns

183

Doctrina Patrum

The *Doctrina Patrum* (*logoi hagiōn paterōn*) is an anthology of patristic testimonies on christology from the second half of the 7th c. Along with scripture, the testimony of approved fathers came to carry special weight during the christological controversies within the imperial church. → Maximus Conf., → Leontius Byz., and → Leontius Jerus. had already made similar compilations of patristic texts, on which the *Doctrina* could rely. Because of the overall compilational character of the work, there can be hardly any possibility of attributing it to an individual author; among those suggested are → Anastasius the Sinaite or → Anastasius the Monk. The special value of the *Doctrina Patrum* is that it is often the only source for lost writings of the 5th and 6th c.

W: F. Diekamp, Doctrina Patrum de incarnatione Verbi (Münster, 1981 = Münster, ¹1907).
L: J. Stigelmayr, Autorschaft der D.: ByZ 18 (1909) 14-40. — K. H. Uthemann, Anastasius v. Antiochien in D.: OCP 46 (1980) 343-366. — R. Vancourt, Stephanus Alexandrinus in D.: idem, Derniers commentateurs d'Aristoteles (Lille, 1941), 39-42.

P. BRUNS

Domitian of Ancyra

D., abbot of the Martyrius monastery near Jerusalem, was, along with Theodore Askidas, a leader of Palestinian monks and Origenists. In 576 he took part in a synod in Constantinople and afterwards remained there. Finally, ca. 537, he became archbishop of Ancyra with the support of Leontius of Byzantium, but he showed little concern for his episcopal city; instead he negotiated with the emperor in behalf of the Origenists. In a memorandum of ca. 545 to Bishop Vigilius of Rome (*Libellus ad Vigilium papam*) he likewise interceded for Origen. A passage from this memorandum is given by Facundus of Hermiane (*defens.* 4.4.15).

W: J. M. Clément, R. vander Plaetse, CCL 90A:126.
L: H. G. Beck, Kirche und theol. Lit. (Munich, 1959), 384. — A. Grillmeier, Jesus der Christus 2/2 (Freiburg i.Br., 1989), 405 (English, Christ in Christian Tradition, vol. 2/2 [London, 1995]), 435f. n. 13.

B. WINDAU

Domnus II of Antioch

D. was bishop of Antioch from 442 to 449. In the controversy over Eutyches he belonged to the Antiochene party and was deposed, along with Theodoret

of Cyrrhus and Ibas of Edessa, at the Robber Synod. Surviving are a letter to Emperor Theodosius (in Facundus of Hermiane; *ep. Theod.*); in Syriac, two letters to Dioscorus Alex. (*ep. Diosc.*), who had complained to D. about Theodoret; and fragments of a sermon (*fr.*) that D. had delivered during the synod.

W: *ep. Theod.*, J. Clément, R. vander Plaetse, CCL 90 A:244f. — *ep. Diosc.*, *fr.*, J. Flemming, Akten der ephesinischen Synode vom Jahre 449, AGWG NF 15/1 (Göttingen, 1917), 138-141, 144-147, 118f. [Syriac text/German trans.].
L: E. Schwartz, Der Prozeß des Eutyches, SBAW. PH 25/5 (Munich, 1925).

G. RÖWEKAMP

Donatus of Besançon

D., born ca. 590/597 as son of a duke, became in very early life a monk under Abbot Columbanus at Luxeuil. In 625/626 he became bishop of Besançon. He took part in the Councils of Clichy, Chalon-sur-Saône, and Rheims. He also founded the monastery of St. Paul for men, giving it a rule based on that of Columbanus; ca. 636, together with Flavia, his mother, he found the monastery of Jussa Moutier for women, in Besançon. For this foundation he drew up a *Regula ad virgines* (*Regula Donati*) in seventy-seven sections; this rule expanded the monastic rule of Columbanus by adding passages from Caesarius of Arles, the Rule of Benedict, and some additions of his own. It is preceded by a letter of dedication to the abbess and community of nuns. D., later venerated as a saint, died ca. 660 and was buried in the family burial place of St. Paul's.

W: PL 87:273-298. — A. de Vogüé: Ben. 25 (1978) 219-314 [text].
L: M. Heinzelmann, D.: LMA 3:1237f. — J. Marilier, D.: BSS 4:785f. — T. de Morembert, D. 14: DHGE 14:648f. — G. Moyse, Les origines du monachisme: BECh 131 (1973) 21-104, 369-485. — F. Renner, Die literarische Struktur der Demutsstufe: RBS 8/9 (1979/80) 13-33. — M. Schanz, C. Hosius, G. Krüger, Geschichte der röm. Lit. 4/2 (Munich, 1959), 594. — M. Zelzer, Die Regula Donati: RBS 16 (1987) 23-36.

B. WINDAU

Dorotheus of Gaza

I. Life: D. was born at the beginning of the 6th c., probably in Antioch; after a classical education he became a monk in the monastery of Abbot Seridus near Gaza. He remained for fifteen years under the spiritual guidance of the two recluses Barsanuphius and John. After the death of John and the retirement of Barsanuphius D. left the monastery of Seridus ca.

540 and established his own monastery between Gaza and Majuma.

II. Works: From this period come the seventeen *Didaskaliai* (*Diaskaliai psychōphelais diaphoroi; Dd.*) and sixteen letters, which were collected and put together by an unknown hand and are regarded as only a part of his spiritual instruction. D. deals with themes of monastic or Chr. life, drawing upon the tradition as passed on to him in Seridus's monastery, espec. upon the *Apophthegmata Patrum* and Evagrius Pont., as well as upon the Cappadocians. Basic theol. ideas are contained especially in *Dd.* 1 and 16, whereas the other homilies had a more ascetical and practical orientation (humility, conscience, fear of God, love of neighbor, necessity of spiritual guidance, lying, acquisition of the virtues, etc.). Because pride led to the violation of the command in paradise, human beings can return to their lost communion with God only by the way of humility, which the example of Christ shows to us. An essential element of this process is purification from the passions as causes of ever new sins. This purification is attained by following the commandments (obedience) and through the prayers of the saints.

D.'s method of description is comparable to those of the → *Apophthegmata* and → John Moschus. In vivid narrative style he uses examples from his own experience and the experiences of others in order to illustrate what he says. The *Life of Dositheus*, his first disciple, seems to be a summary of his teaching; it is added to the *Dd.* in most mss.

W: L. Cremaschi (Rome, 1980) [Italian trans.]. — M. Paparozzi (Rome, 1979) [comm./Italian trans.]. — J. Pauli (FC in prep.). — L. Regnault, J. de Preville, SC 92. — F. Rivas (Luján, 1990) [Spanish trans.]. — S. Schoinas, Abba Dorotheou oi katanyktikoi logoi (Volos, ²1975 = reprint of ed. of 1770). — C. Wagenaar (Bonheiden, 1986) [Dutch trans.]. — E. P. M. Wheeler, CSS 33 (Kalamazoo, Mich., 1977) [English trans.].
L: P. M. Brun, Vie de St. Dosithée: OrChr 26.2 (Rome, 1932), 89-122. — P. Canivet, D. est-il un Disciple d'Évagre?: REG 78 (1965) 336-346. — F. Neyt, Lettres à D. dans la Correspondance de Barsanuphe et Jean de Gaza, Diss. (Leuven/Louvain, 1969). — J. Pauli, Menschsein u. Menschwerden nach der geistlichen Lehre des D., Diss. (St. Ottilien, 1998). — J. M. Szymusiak, J. Leroy, D.: DSp 3:183-200. — A. Veselinowitsch, Barsanuphios ho megas, Ioannes ho prophetes kai D., Diss. (Athens, 1941).

J. PAULI, OSB

Dorotheus of Marcianopolis

D., bishop of Marcianopolis and metropolitan of Moesia II in the first half of the 5th c., was a supporter of Nestorius. He took part in the Council of Ephesus (431), where, along with the eastern bishops, he was condemned by Cyril's party. Nestorius's successor in Constantinople had D. condemned by a synod and deposed, along with Helladius of Tarsus, among others. The people, however, refused to recognize his successor, Saturninus. Paul of Emesa intervened with the emperor for D., but in vain. Emperor Theodosius finally sent D. into exile at Caesarea in Cappadocia.

From D. we have some letters in Latin (*ep. ad populum Constantinopolitanum*, after the accession of Saturninus; *ep. ad Alexandrum episc. Hierapolis et Theodoretum episc. Cyri* on a letter from Proclus; two letters to John of Antioch on a legation from Paul of Emesa), a Syr. fragment of a letter *Ad Marcianum imperatorem*, and a Syr. fragment of an *Interpretatio fidei*, which is a commentary on the Nicene Creed.

W: *ep. ad populum*, ACO 1, 4, 88. — *ep. ad Alexandrum*, ACO 1, 4, 164f. — *ep. ad Iohannem*, ACO 1, 4, 114. 144. — *ep. ad Marcianum*, F. Nau, PO 13:181 [Syriac text/French trans.]. — *Interpretatio*, J. Lebon, CSCO 101/102:95/68f. [Syriac text/Latin trans.].
L: J. Lebon, Les anciens symbols: RHE 32 (1936) 809-876, here 845. — A. v. Roey, D. 8: DHGE 14:688.

B. WINDAU

Doxology

The Chr. doxology is an expression of praise such as is common in the bibl. language of prayer and has its original *Sitz im Leben* in the liturgy. Since a doxology attributes to God aspects of his being and action, theol. reflections can be found in it (see, e.g., 1 Cor 1:3f.; Eph 1:3f.; Rev 4:8, 11; 5:9, 12, and 13). A doxology, understood in a more restricted sense as a concluding formula, is also frequently found in NT letters and prayers (see, e.g., Rom 11:36; 16:27; Phil 4:20).

In the early Chr. period these NT forms were taken over and expanded (see, e.g., *1 Clem.* 58.2; 61.3; 64; 65.2; *Did.* 9; 10). The concept *doxologia*, however, appears first in connection with gnostic formulas (see, e.g., Irenaeus, *haer.* 1.14.7; Hippolytus, *ref.* 6.48.3) but, from the 3rd c. on, also in general Chr. contexts (see Clement Alex., *q. d. s.* 42.2; Origen, *or.* 33.1, 6). In Origen the doxology is also found as one of the four sources of prayer.

Important doxological texts are the *Gloria* (the "great doxology") and the concluding doxology of the liturgy (the "little doxology"). In the little doxology the bibl. formula that had been expanded to include the Holy Spirit: "Glory to the Father through *(dia)* the Son in *(en)* the Holy Spirit" was replaced in Basil, as a result of the anti-Arian movement, by the formula already customary in Syria, which used *meta* and *syn* ("Glory . . . with the Son and with the Holy Spirit"). After protests against this usage, Basil wrote his *Spir.* The doxology is thus a witness to the development of trinitarian theology. The use of the doxology at the end of a psalm in recitation is first attested in John Cassian (*inst.* 2.8). It was expanded by a reference to eternity and (in the West) by the anti-Arian "As it was in the beginning. . . ."

L: A. Häußling: Gottesdienst der Kirche 3 (²1990), 229-232, 421. — H.-C. Schmidt-Lauber, Formeln: TRE 11:266f. — A. Stuiber, D.: RAC 4:210-226. — G. Wainwright, Doxology (London, ²1982).

G. Röwekamp

Dracontius

Blossus Emilius Dracontius (D.) was a Lat. poet of the late 5th c. The meager biog. sources identify him as a member of the provincial Roman upper class in Africa (and thus as a Catholic), who was active as a jurist (*togatus*) at the law court of the proconsul of Carthage. A poem in which he praised a foreign ruler (presumably the eastern Roman Emperor Zeno) brought him into conflict with the Vandal authorities. During an imprisonment of many years he composed two poems, the *Satisfactio* (*satisf.*) and the *De laudibus Dei* (*laud. dei*). The former is a poetic plea for clemency in which he admits his guilt before God and King Gunthamund (484-496) and appeals to mitigating circumstances. The choice of meter (elegiac distichs) places the poem in the line of Ovid's *Tristia,* which had a similar origin. D.'s chief work, the *laud. dei* (2,327 hexameters) praises the work of divine grace in the world in a very personal, epical-lyrical combination of a greatly expanded paraphrase of bibl. texts and extended meditative or hymnic praises of God. The manifestation of this grace in creation is the subject of book 1; its continuation after the fall and its full manifestation in the mission of Christ are the subject of book 2. Book 3 exhorts to love of God in return, using as arguments bibl. and pagan (espec. national Roman) examples. A deeply emotional penitential prayer of the prisoner concludes the work. With regard to the anti-Arian polemic in book 2 (vv. 98ff.): the poem must have been published only during the reign of the more tolerant King Thrasamund (496-523), to whom, evidently, D. also owed his deliverance from prison. The part of *laud. dei* on creation and the fall was widely circulated in the Middle Ages as an independent hexameron poem, in a 7th-c. revision (by → Eugene of Toledo).

In addition, D. composed a collection, titled *Romulea* (*Romul.*), of ten secular poems containing between 20 and 655 verses: short mythic epics (*Hylas, Medea, Raptus Helenae*), epithalamia, versified declamations (*Verba Herculis, Controversia de statua viri fortis, Deliberativa Achillis*), as well as two poems dedicated to a teacher, Felicianus, who was endeavoring to revive classical studies in Africa. The anonymously transmitted *Orestis tragoedia* in epic form (974 verses) is generally attributed to D. The fact that in his "Chr." poems D. makes extensive use of pagan topoi and forms of thought, while in his "pagan" poetry, although less strikingly, many religious ideas are to be found, may be taken as reflecting the mental and spiritual line of division, which ran no longer between pagans and Christians but between Cath. Romans, as representatives of the ancient culture, and the Arian "barbarians."

W: F. Vollmer, MGH. AA 14 (Berlin, 1984 = 1905). — idem (Leipzig, 1914), 1-237. — *laud. dei, satisf.,* C. Moussy, C. Camus (Paris, 1985, 1988) [text/French trans.]. — *laud. dei* 1, F. Irwin, Diss. (Philadelphia, 1942) [text/English trans./comm.]. — *laud. dei* 2, J. E. Bresnahan, Diss. (Philadelphia, 1949) [text/English trans./comm.]. — *satisf.,* M. S. Margaret, Diss. (Philadelphia, 1936) [text/English trans./comm.]. — *Romul.,* J. M. Diaz de Bustamante (Santiago de Comp., 1978).
L: I. C. Devine, A Study of the Laudes Dei of D., Diss. Columb. Univ. (New York, 1945). — J. Duvernet, D.: DHGE 14:774-781. — P. Langlois, D.: RAC 5:250-269. — C. Moussy, D. Œuvres 1 (Paris, 1985), 7-110; 2 (Paris, 1988), 143-160. — D. J. Nodes, Doctrine and Exegesis in Biblical Latin Poetry (Leeds, 1993), 45-55, 108-118. — W. Schetter, D. togatus: Hermes 117 (1989) 342-350. — idem, Zur "Satisfactio" des D.: Hermes 118 (1990) 90-117. — K. Smolak, Die Stellung der Hexamerondichtung des D. (*laud. dei* 1:118-426) innerhalb der lat. Genesispoesie: FS W. Kraus (Vienna, 1972), 381-397. — W. Speyer, Kosmische Mächte im Bibelepos des D.: Ph. 132 (1988) 275-285. — idem, Der Bibeldichter D. als Exeget des Sechstagewerkes: FS E. Dassmann, JAC. E 23 (Münster, 1996), 464-484. — F. Stella, Per una teoria dell' imitazione poetica "cristiana." Saggio di analisi sulle Laudes Dei di D.: InvLuc 7-8 (1985-86) 193-224. — idem, Fra retorica e innografia. Sul genere letterario delle Laudes Dei di D.: Ph. 132 (1988) 258-274. — F. Vollmer, D.: PRE 5/2:1635-1644. — B. Weber, Der Hylas des D. (Stuttgart, 1995) (literature).

J. Schwind

Dynamius Patricius

We know only the date of the death of D. of Marseilles: he died as *rector provinciae* in 601 (see Gregory of Tours, *Franc.* 6.7, 11; 9.11). Shortly after 585 he composed a life of Maximus, second abbot of

Lérins and later bishop of Riez (*V. Max.*). His basis was the addresses given by → Faustus of Riez about his predecessor as abbot and bishop. In addition, he used the lives of other monk-bishops from Lérins (*V. Hon.*; *V. Hil.*; and *V. Caes. Arel.*). Although he had received training in rhetoric, D. broke away from the rhetorical form of the old *sermo* and replaced the kind of address still directed to an old public with a series of miracle stories in the style of the later 6th c. In the history of literature his *V. Max.* is an important example of the shift from the style of one period to that of another. Among his writings is also a poem on Lérins (*poe.*) (ca. 580) that emphasizes the observance and revival of the *prisca regula* (→ Honoratus of Arles). The *Vita S. Martini* (PL 80:25-30) that is associated with his name is from a later period. A study of all the literature connected with D. is a desideratum.

W: *V. Max.*, S. Gennaro (Catania, 1966). — *poe.*, A. Riese, Anthologia Latina 1/2 (Leipzig, 1906), 265f., nr. 786a.
L: W. Berschin, Biographie (Stuttgart, 1986), 259f. — J. A. Fabricius, Bibliotheca Latina (Florence, 1885), 2:484. — S. Gennaro, Dinamio agiografho (Catania, 1980). — P. Riché, Éducation et culture (Paris, 1962), 230.

C. KASPER

ℰ

Easter Letters

Easter letters were an element in the practice of the bishops of Alexandria, who after Epiphany each year made known to their suffragans the date of Easter and the beginning of the period of fasting. This practice may be older than its first attestation by the Easter letters of → Dionysius in the mid-3rd c. The letters show that at that time the date of Easter was not determined in a set way. In addition, in the 4th c. there were inconsistencies in the length of the period of fasting; as a result Athanasius made a forty-day fast the rule (Quadragesima or Lent).

The letters are of interest for the history of the church chiefly because of their function as official circular letters. The bishops of Alexandria used them to advance their concerns in theology and eccles. politics; the letters also made known the appointment of new bishops. This is true especially of the Easter letters of Athanasius, which are preserved almost complete in a Syr. translation, although not in their chronol. order; espec. during the periods of Athanasius's exile the letters served an important function as "pastoral letters." Attention should be called espec. to Letter 39 of 367, since it documents the completion of the formation of the OT canon. The twenty-nine surviving Easter letters of → Cyril, composed as homilies, have for their main subject the practice of Chr. life and devotion during the period of fasting. From the early church, the letters of Dionysius (d. 264/265), Peter (d. 311), Athanasius (d. 373), Theophilus (d. 412), and Cyril (d. 444) have survived complete or in fragments.

L: A. Camplani, Le lettere festali di Atanasio di Alessandria (Rome, 1989). — L. T. Lefort, Les Lettres festales de Saint Athanase: BCLAB 39 (1953) 643-656; 41 (1955) 183-185. — idem, A propos des festales de S. Athanase: Muséon 67 (1954) 43-50. — R. Lorenz, Der zehnte Osterfestbrief des Athanasius (Berlin, 1986). — P. Merendino, Paschale Sacramentum (Münster, 1965), 1-38. — V. Peri, La Cronologia delle Lettere festali di sant'Athanasio: Aevum 35 (1961) 28-86. — J. Rist, Osterfestbriefe: LMA 6:1517. — J. Ruwet, Le Canon alexandrin des Écritures: Bib. 33 (1952) 1-29. — E. Schwartz, Zur Kirchengeschichte des 4. Jh. (I): ZNW 34 (1935) 129-137 = idem, Ges. Schriften 4 (Berlin, 1960), 1-11. — idem, Die Osterbriefe: idem, Ges. Schriften 3 (Berlin, 1959), 1-19.

K. FITSCHEN

Ebionites, Gospel of the

Epiphanius mentions and cites a Jewish-Chr. gospel used by the (heretical) sect of the Ebionites. He describes it as a distorted and shortened gospel of Mt, which the Ebionites supposedly also called "Gospel of the Hebrews" or "Hebrew Gospel" (similarly Irenaeus, *haer.* 1.26.2; 3.11.7; 3.21.1; 5.1.3). This *Gospel of the Ebionites* (*Ev. Ebion.*) is not to be identified with the → *Gospel of the Hebrews* (as a misunderstood passage in Jerome, *adv. Pelag.* 3.2, seems to suggest). It is disputed whether the *Ev. Ebion.* is identical with the heterodox *Gospel of the Twelve* mentioned by Origen (*hom. in Luc.* 1) (this work was perhaps originally titled *Gospel of the Twelve Apostles according to Matthew*).

The fragments that Epiphanius transmits from the beginning of the Gr. text (only these fragments can be regarded as belonging to the *Ev. Ebion.*) show the Synoptic character of the work, which can best be described as a harmony of the gospels (apart from Jn).

The omission of the infancy story is due to the rejection of the virgin birth; the fragments on the Baptist and the baptism of Jesus document the sect's adoptionist understanding of the divine sonship, the rejection of cult, and the vegetarianism of the Ebionites. The *Ev. Ebion.* may possibly have originated in the 2nd c. in the land east of the Jordan.

W: Epiphanius, *haer.* 30.13.2-8; 30.14.5; 30.16.4f.; 30.22.4. — A. F. J. Klijn, Jewish-Christian Gospel Tradition (Leiden, 1992), 65-77 [text/comm.]. — NTApo⁶ 1:130-142 [German trans.].
L: D. A. Bertrand, L'Évangile des Ebionites: NTS 26 (1980) 548-563. — G. Howard, The Gospel of the Ebionites: ANRW II 25/5 (1988) 4034-4053. — A. F. J. Klijn, G. J. Reinink, Patristic Evidence for Jewish-Christian Sects (Leiden, 1973), 19-43. — G. Strecker, Ebioniten: RAC 4:487-500. — P. Vielhauer, Geschichte der urchr. Lit. (Berlin, 1975), 653-655. — H. Waitz, Das Evangelium der zwölf Apostel: ZNW 13 (1912) 338-348.

G. RÖWEKAMP

Egeria

I. Life: E. is the author of a pilgrim's narrative that was discovered in 1884 by G. F. Gamurrini in Arezzo. Since the beginning and end of the account are lost, the name can be inferred only from a letter of Valerius of Bierzo (d. 691), in the versions of which, however, two forms of the name, Aetheria and Egeria, are used. The name Silvia, chosen by Gamurrini, was based on an incorrect identification of the author with a pilgrim mentioned in Palladius (*h. laus.* 55.1).

E. came from Aquitania or (more probably) from Galicia and belonged to a group of religious women, to whom the account of her journey is addressed; she had been instructed in the Bible and probably also had a little knowledge of Greek. The dating of the account (and therefore the period of E.'s life) remains uncertain. One suggested date is 381-384; the journey certainly took place toward the end of the 4th c.

II. Work: The account of the journey, which has come down only in an 11th-c. ms., is usually titled *Itinerarium Egeriae* (*Itin. Eger.*; or *Peregrinatio Aetherieae, peregr. Aeth.*), but it has only partially the traits of an → *itinerarium;* the work is rather a personal account of a journey in the form of several letters. The language is Late Latin, with a tinge of the popular speech that already suggests the transition to the romance languages.

The *Itin. Eger.* and the lost parts that can be to some extent reconstructed with the help of a medieval compilation of Peter the Deacon, *De locis sanctis* (*loc. sanct.*), yield the following course of travel: journey from Constantinople to Jerusalem; journey through Galilee and Samaria; first journey to Egypt (*loc. sanct.* C-Y, 3); second journey to Egypt and the Sinai (*loc. sanct.* Y, 4-17; *Itin. Eger.* 1-11); journey to Mt. Nebo, Karnion, Edessa, and Haran; return to Constantinople via Seleucia (*Itin. Eger.* 12-23).

The second part of the account describes the liturgy of Jerusalem, which was also characteristic of other eccles. provinces: order of prayer on weekdays and Sundays, the liturgical year with Epiphany, Lent, Holy Week, Easter, Pentecost, and the consecration of a church (*Itin. Eger.* 24-49).

The account is the first major witness to the pilgrimage devotion that developed in connection with the places established by Constantine in Jerusalem and Palestine. It gives a great deal of hist. information on buildings and traditions and clarifies the theol. conception at work in the developing liturgical year: By imitation of the bibl. events in the liturgy, which is celebrated on each occasion "at the appropriate time and place" (*Itin. Eger.* 47.5, etc.), the history of salvation is made present. The (sometimes long-winded) account itself is meant to serve the interior, "step-by-step" repetition of the experiences of the journey.

W: *Itin. Eger.*, H. Donner, Pilgerfahrt ins hl. Land (Stuttgart, 1979), 82-137 [German trans. chs. 1-23]. — A. Franceschini, R. Weber, CCL 175:29-103. — J. F. Gamurrini (Rome, 1887) [text]. — P. Geyer, CSEL 39:37-101. — E. Gianarelli (Milan, 1992) [Italian trans.]. — G. E. Gingras, ACW 38 (New York, 1970) [English trans.]. — P. Maraval, SC 296. — H. Petré, K. Vretska (Klosterneuburg, 1958) [text/German trans.]. — G. Röwekamp, FC 20. — P. Siniscalco, L. Scarampi, CTePa 48 (Rome, ²1992). — J. Wilkin-

son (London, 1981) [text/English trans./comm.]. — C. di Zoppola, A. Candelaresi (Rome, 1979) [Italian trans./comm.]. — *loc. sanct.*, R. Weber, CCL 175:93-103. — G. Röwekamp, FC 20:310-359.
L: C. Barault, Bibliographia Egeriana: HispSac 7 (1954) 203-215. — D. R. Blackman, G. G. Betts (ed.), Concordantia in Itin. Eger. (Hildesheim, 1989). — S. Janeras, Contributo alla bibliografia Egeriana: Atti del Convegno internazionale sulla Peregrinatio Egeriae (Arezzo, 1990), 355-366. — W. van Oorde, Lexicon Aetherianum (Hildesheim, 1963 = Amsterdam 1929). — W. Starowieyski, Bibliografia Egeriana: Aug. 19 (1979) 297-318. Atti del Convegno internazionale sulla Peregrinatio Egeriae (Arezzo, 1990). — C. Basevi, Vocabulario liturgico: Helm. 36 (1985) 9-38. — A. Bastiaensen, Observations sur le vocabulaire liturgique (Nijmegen, 1962). — idem, L' "Itinéraire d'E.": REAug 30 (1984) 136-144. — A. Bludau, Die Pilgerreise der Aetheria (Paderborn, 1927). — A. L. Conde, El monacato femminino entre la clausura y la pelegrinación: StMon 34 (1992) 29-40. — P. Devos, E. a Bethléem: AnBoll 86 (1968) 87-108. — idem, E. à Édesse: AnBoll 85 (1967) 381-400. — idem, La date du voyage d'E.: AnBoll 85 (1967) 165-194. — idem, Une nouvelle E.: AnBoll 101 (1983) 43-47. — idem, Egeriana 2: AnBoll 105 (1987) 415-424. — idem, Egeriana 3. AnBoll 109 (1991) 363-381. — idem, Egeriana 4: AnBoll 112 (1994) 241-254. — E. Doblhofer, Drei spätantike Reiseschilderungen: FS K. Vretska (Heidelberg, 1970), 1-22. — M. Férotin, Le véritable auteur de la "Peregrinatio Silviae": RQH 74 (1903) 367-397. — R. Klein, Die Entwicklung der chr. Palästinawallfahrt: RQ 85 (1990) 145-181. — B. Kötting, Peregrinatio Religiosa (Münster, ²1980). — E. Löfstedt, Philologischer Kommentar zur Peregrinatio Aetheriae (Darmstadt, 1970 = Uppsala, 1911). — C. Milani, I grecismi: Aevum 43 (1969) 200-234. — C. Mohrmann, E. et le Monachisme: FS E. Dekkers (Brügge, 1975), 163-180. — N. Natalucci, L'epistola del monaco Valerio: GIF 35 (1983) 3-24. — idem, E. e il monachesimo femminile: Ben. 35 (1988) 37-55. — J. Oroz-Reta, J. Del latin cristiano al látin liturgico: Latomus 48 (1989) 401-415. — H. Sivan, Holy Land Pilgrimage and Western Audiences: CQ 38 (1988) 528-535. — L. Spitzer, The Epic Style of the Pilgrim Aetheria: idem, Romanische Lit. studien 1936 1956 (Tübingen, 1959), 871-912. — R. Taft, The Liturgy of the Hours in East and West (Collegeville, Minn., 1986). — A. Vaccari, Itin. Eger.: idem, Scritti di Erudizione e di Filologia (Rome, 1958), 259-269. — V. Väänänen, Le Journal-épitre de E. (Helsinki, 1987). — G. Vermeer, Observations sur le vocabulaire du pèlerinage chez Égerie (Nijmegen, 1965). — C. Weber, E.'s Norman Homeland: HSCP 92 (1989) 437-456. — A. de Vogüé, Histoire littéraire du mouvement monastique dans l'antiquité 1 (Paris, 1993). — J. Ziegler, Die Peregrinatio Aetheriae u. das Onomastikon des Eusebius: Bib. 12 (1931) 70-84. — idem, Die Peregrinatio Aetheriae u. die hl. Schrift: Bib. 12 (1931) 162-198. — R. Zerfaß, Die Schriftlesungen im Kathedraloffizium Jerusalems (Münster, 1968).

G. RÖWEKAMP

Egyptian Church Order

Egyptian Church Order is the name which Hans Achelis (London, 1891) introduced into scholarship for a series of unidentified canons of the → Alexandrian Synod, an Egyptian → Church Order of the 5th c. The *Egyptian Church Order* is represented, in its Sahidic recension, by can. 31-62; in the Eth. recension by can. 22-48; and in the Arab. recension by can. 21-47. Since the discovery that these canons are based on the so-called → *Traditio apostolica*, the name *Egyptian Church Order* has become obsolete and has disappeared from scholarship; the question of the author of the *Traditio* has not yet been resolved.

W: G. W. Horner, *Statutes* (London, 1904).
L: H. Achelis, J. Flemming, Die ältesten Quellen des orientalischen Kirchenrechtes, 2 vols. (Leipzig, 1891). — R. H. Connolly, The So-Called Egyptian Church Order (Cambridge, 1916). — E. von der Goltz, Frgm.: SPAW 56 (1906) 141-157. — E. Schwartz, Gesammelte Schriften 5 (Berlin, 1963), 192-273. — B. Steimer, Vertex traditionis (Berlin, 1992), esp. 28-33.

B. STEIMER

Egyptians, Gospel according to the

The fragments of an *Euaggelion kata Aigyptious*, preserved in Clement Alex., all come from a dialogue between Jesus and Salome on death and sexuality. Possibly, therefore, we are dealing with a text not in the genre of gospel but with a "Dialogue of the Redeemer," of the kind beloved of the gnostics (→ Apocryphal Writings). The name probably did not arise in Egypt, nor is the document, as earlier suggested, a gospel of the Egyptian Christians converted from paganism (as opposed to the Jewish Christians, → Gospel of the Hebrews). The source is most likely to have been an encratite group close to gnosticism; there is disagreement on whether the document is already cited in *2 Clem.* 12.1f. Clement, who does not radically reject the writing, speaks especially of Julius Cassianus as one who used it; Origen, however (*hom.* 1 *in Lc.*), already shows the document to be no longer accepted by the church.

W: Clemens, *str.* 3:45, 63, 64, 66, 68, 91-93, 97, GCS 15:216f., 225-227, 238-241. — E. Klostermann, Apocrypha 2 (KlT 8) (Bonn, ³1929), 15f. [text]. —NTApo⁶ 1:174-179 [German trans.].
L: M. Hornschuh, Erwägungen zum "Evangelium der Ägypter": VigChr 18 (1964) 6-13. — P. Vielhauer, Geschichte der urchr. Lit. (Berlin, 1975), 662-665.

To be distinguished from the above is the *Sacred Book of the Great Invisible Spirit*, which has been found in two Nag Hammadi codices and is expressly described in the *explicit* as "Gospel of the Egyptians." The two manuscripts represent two independent Copt. translations of a Gr. document which from a literary point of view is not a gospel but a dogmatic treatise. The supposed author → Seth reveals therein the structure of the next world and his intervention to establish a Sethian lineage; Jesus is his manifestation. The work comes from a gnosticizing group of the 2nd-3rd c.

W: The Facsimile Edition of the NHC. Cod. 3 (Leiden, 1976), 40, 12-44, 28, 49, 1-69, 20; Cod. IV (Leiden, 1975), 55, 20-60, 30. — NHC 3, 2; 4, 2, A. Böhlig, F. Wisse (Leiden, 1975) [text/English trans.]. — J. Doresse: JA 254 (1966) 317-435 [text]; 256 (1968) 289-386 [comm.]. — J. M. Robinson (ed.), The Nag Hammadi Library in English (Leiden, ³1988), 195-205 [English trans.] — H. M. Schenke: NTS 16 (1969/70) 196-208 [German trans.].
L: A. Böhlig, Christentum u. Gnosis im Ä. von Nag Hammadi: Christentum u. Gnosis, ed. W. Eltester (Berlin, 1969), 1-18. — C. Colpe, Heidnische, jüd. u. chr. Überlieferungen in den Schriften aus Nag Hammadi: JAC 19 (1976) 127-131. — J. M. Sevrien, Le dossier baptismale séthien (Quebec, 1986), 80-144.

G. RÖWEKAMP

Ekphrasis

The Gr. term *ekphrasis*, Lat. *descriptio*, signifies every kind of formal description. In ancient literature the *ekphrasis* was widely used. The earliest definition of the concept that has come down to us comes from the rhetoric of the imperial age: "*Ekphrasis* is a description that brings the described object clearly before the eye" (Theon 2.118.6f.). The hearer must become a spectator. Consequently, vividness (*saphēneia . . . kai enargeia*, ibid. 2.119.28) is one of its most important characteristics. Theoreticians (see also Hermogenes, Aphthonius, and Nicholas of Myra) list, as possible areas for themes: persons, places, times, actions, and festivals, then also animals, plants, and works of art. In rhetoric *ekphrasis* served as a *progymnasma*, i.e., an exercise for sheer beginners. Some rhetoricians traced its origin to poetry and historiography. Examples are descriptions of shields, the earliest being that of Achilles' armor in the *Iliad* (18.476ff.); or descriptions of cities and buildings, which were customary in historical writing from Herodotus on. In fact, *ekphrasis* was an essential element of the more expansive genres: in addition to → epic and historiography, the novel and letter writing (→ Letter) may be mentioned. Furthermore, *ekphrasis* existed as an independent genre in prose and was a type of → epigram in poetry. As persons and actions became the subjects of other genres (e.g., the → Panegyric), the *ekphrasis* concentrated increasingly on the description of architecture and works of art.

In the NT *ekphrasis* does not occur as a literary device, if we prescind from the description of allegorical visions in Rev. Nor does it occur as a distinctive form in the works of the early fathers. → Clement Alex. is the first to use it, at the beginning and end of his *Protrepticus*. Following him, Chr. writers used it quite frequently for didactic purposes. The writings of Plato provided the classical model here. Also important for the allegorical interpretation of works of art was the *Cebetis tabula*, an anon. treatise from the 1st c. C.E. Chr. philosophers and poets too practiced mystical meditation on works of art with the eye of the soul, after the example of, e.g., Plotinus. Another kind of *ekphrasis* is seen in the literary description of allegorical myths: an example is given by → Lactantius, who in a poem describes the phoenix and its garden. After the manner of the ancient historians → Eus. Caes. composes numerous *ekphraseis*. He describes, among other things, a statue of Christ (*h.e.* 7.18), various churches (*h.e.* 10.4.37ff.; *v. C.* 3.26ff.; 3.41ff.; 3.50; 4.58ff. and 70ff.), Constantine's visions and dreams (*v. C.* 1.28 and 31), and an allegorical painting of the emperor (*v. C.* 3.3). The Cappadocians too wrote *ekphraseis* of places and pictures: Basil, *ep.* 14; Greg. Naz., *or.* 18.39ff.; 35.3f.; Greg. Nyss., *ep.* 25. Also worth noting is how Gregory Naz. describes the springtime in an address (*or.* 44.10f.). John Chrys. occupies a special place in the use of the *ekphrasis*. His homilies in particular yield many and varied *ekphraseis* such as are found in no other Chr. author. He even has a description of a battle (*sac.* 6.12; PG 48:689f.). His contemporary, → Asterius of Amasea, gives *ekphraseis* of the art of weaving and of frescoes, dealing in the process with bibl. and hagiog. themes (*hom.* 1; 11). → Nilus of Ancyra gives details of a planned decoration of a church (*ep.* 4.61).

Lat. authors, espec. → Ambrose, → Paulinus of Nola, and → Prudentius, made an important contribution to the series of *ekphraseis* that instruct the reader on the significance of pictures as decorations of a church. Twenty-one *tituli* have come down under the name of Ambrose; the dedicatory inscription of the Church of St. Nazarius in Milan also goes back to him (ILCV 1800). In his *ep.* 32, *carm.* 27, and *carm.* 28, Paulinus of Nola gives detailed descriptions of buildings and paintings. His poems also contain further interesting *ekphraseis* depicting the festive adornment of the Basilica of St. Felix, a cross, lamps, the tomb of Felix, the song of a nightingale, and the human eye (*carm.* 14.98-103; 19.604-94, 405-24, 456-74; 23.129-47; 21.586-91; 23.27-36, 174-83). Forty-nine *tituli* of Prudentius are captions for paint-

ings with scenes from the OT and NT. Like the previous two Lat. authors mentioned, he too uses *ekphraseis* in hagiographical writings (*perist.* 12.49-54).

Bibl. epic likewise provided room for *ekphraseis*: among the Lat. poets of the 5th/6th c. reference may be made, e.g., to → Cyprian the poet/Gallus (*exod.* 1098-1103), Claudius → Marius Victorinus (*aleth.* 2.13f.), and Alcimus Ecdicius → Avitus (*carm.* 5.477-81). In emulation of Statius and in occasional verses, → Apollinaris Sidonius composed pure *ekphraseis* and also introduced them into larger works (*carm.* 22; 15.158-84).

Finally, in the East the school of Gaza produced renowned writers of *ekphraseis*. Nonnus of Panopolis (*D.* 5.144ff.: necklace of Harmonia; *D.* 25.384ff.: shield of Dionysus) and Procopius of Gaza (painting of "Phaedra and Hippolytus," an artistic clock) produced no genuinely Chr. descriptions; the case is different with → Choricius of Gaza, who in the 6th c. described church buildings and their pictures (*laud. Marc.* 1.17ff. and 48ff.; 2.28ff.). His contemporary, John of Gaza, gives a poetic description of a picture (*kosmikos pinax*). In him and in the epigrammist Agathias (*AP*, espec. book 9) Chr. subjects are not necessarily given priority. → Procopius of Caesarea composed a famous *ekphrasis* of Hagia Sophia (*aed.* 1.1.20ff.). → Paul the Silentiary deals with the same subject in a poem of 562. Writers continued to practice this genre in the Byz. period.

L: G. Downey, E.: RAC 4:921-944. — W. Elliger, Stellung zu den Bildern (Leipzig, 1930). — idem, Zur Entstehung der altchr. Bildkunst (Leipzig, 1934). — D. P. Fowler, Narrate and Describe: JRS 81 (1991) 25-35 [Bibl.]. — P. Friedländer, Johannes v. Gaza (Leipzig, Berlin, 1912). — idem, Spätantike Gemäldezykl. in: Gaza (Vatican City, 1939). — F. Graf, E.: Die Entstehung der Gattung in der Antike: Beschreibungskunst — Kunstbeschreibung, ed. G. Boehm, H. Pfotenhauer (Munich, 1995), 143-156. — B. D. Hebert, Spätantike Beschreibung v. Kunstwerken (Graz, 1983). — G. Ravenna, L'e. poetica: Quaderni dell'Istituto di Filologia latina dell' Università di Padova 3 (1974) 1-52. — M. Roberts, The Jeweled Style (New York, 1989).

B. BREILMANN

Elegy

In the postclassical period the genre of the elegy is taken to include poetic productions in elegiac distichs that have a personal and subjective content and that by reason of their extent do not belong to the genre of the epigram. Although it must be acknowledged that in Chr. literature as well as in the pagan literature of late antiquity (see the fables of Avian, 4th c.) the external form of the elegy is used for the most varied subjects (e.g., → Sedulius, *hymn.* 1: history of salvation; → Orientius, *comm.*: leading a Chr. life; → Venantius Fortunatus, *carm.* 10.9: description of a journey), yet the classical Roman elegy was the most important model. Correspondingly, the Chr. elegy appears chiefly in Latin and in the following forms: as letter or dedication (see Catullus 65), e.g., among others, in → Apollinaris Sidonius (e.g., *carm.* 1), → Arator (*ad Flor.*; *ad Vigil.*), and Corippus (*Ioh.*, praef.); as complaint, in → Dracontius (*satisf.*), → Boethius (*cons.*, praef.) (see also Greg. Naz., *carm.* 2.1.45); and as love elegy in the Chr. adaptation of the epithalamium (e.g., → Paulinus of Nola, *carm.* 25). Elements of the last two types named are linked by Maximian (who is possibly to be dated to the early Middle Ages) with apotreptic purposes.

L: L. Alfonsi, W. Schmid, E.: RAC 4:1026-1061. — G. Catanzaro, F. Santucci (ed.), Tredici secoli di elegia latina. Atti del convegno internazionale (Assisi, 1988, 1989). — R. Herzog, Probleme der heidnisch-chr. Gattungskontinuität: EnAC 23 (1977) 373-411.

D. WEBER

Elijah, Apocalypse of

The *Apocalypse of Elijah*, transmitted in Coptic, goes back to a Jewish-Hebrew base text that is to be dated to between the 1st c. B.C.E. and the 1st c. C.E. and that originated in Egypt. All the prophecies it contains relate to Egyptian conditions. In any case, the *Apocalypse of Elijah* was much revised by Christians; in particular, passages were introduced on the incarnation of the Son of God (20.1f.) and on the appearance of the cross at the Last Judgment (32.1f.).

W: R. F. G. Steindorff, Die Apokalypse des Elias (Leipzig, 1899) [Coptic text/German trans.]. — P. Rießler, Altjüd. Schrifttum (Freiburg i.Br., 1984 = Heidelberg, 1928), 114-125 [German trans.]. — M. Buttenwieser, Die hebr. E. (Leipzig, 1897) [Hebrew text].

P. BRUNS

Elise Vardapet

E., who was given the surname Vardapet ("teacher," "archimandrite"), was one of the most important Arm. historians; he lived ca. 645 in Palestine and the Sinai and composed a *History of the Armenian War* (*hist.*). The history of the editing of this work is extremely complicated. A comparison with → Lazarus of Pharp reveals numerous anachronisms, which make it probable that it was not composed

before the Arm. revolt under Vardan II (572-580). In form and content the description of the revolt under Vardan II resembles that of the Pers.-Arm. war of 451 under Vardan I; it also contains some additions by a later hand. The work presupposes an Arm. translation of the Gk. Philo; this too suggests the Hellen. period of Arm. literature (6th-7th c.). Numerous mss. name an Elise as author not only of this hist. work but also of exegetical-homiletic writings on the OT (*comm.*), which is interpreted primarily in allegorical terms. Also attributed to him are an explanation of the Our Father, an exhortation to hermits, and homilies on events of the life of Jesus (*hom.*). Whether we are dealing here with a single author and whether this author is the historian E. are unresolved questions.

W: *Collected works* (Venice, 1859) [text]. — *hist.*, E. Ter-Minasean (Eriwan, 1957) [text]. — R. W. Thomson, E. History of Vardan (Cambridge, Mass., 1982) [English trans.]. — V. Langlois, Collections des historiens (Paris, 1869), 2:177-252 [French trans.]. — G. Garapacean, Soulèvement national de l'Arménie chrétienne (Paris, 1844) [French trans.]. — *hom.* (Jerusalem, 1836) [text]. — B. Sargisean, E. u. Zacharias über die Grablegung Christi (Venice, 1910) [text]. — F. Conybeare, Revelation of the Lord: ZNW 23 (1924) 8-17 [English trans.]. — R. W. Thomson, A Seventh Century Armenian Pilgrim: JThS 25 (1924) 232-46 [English trans.]. — S. Weber, BKV 58 [German trans.]. — L. Leloir, Homélie d'E. sur la montagne de Tabor: REArm 20 (1986/87) 175-207 [French trans.]. — *comm.*, N. Akinean (Vienna, 1924) [text]. — idem, S. Kogean, Questions et réponses (Vienna, 1928) [text/French trans.].
L: N. Akinean, Elische Vardapet u. seine Geschichte des arm. Krieges (arm.), 3 vols. (Vienna, 1932, 1936, 1953). — L. Leloir, Elische and the Bible: JSAS 5 (1990-91) 3-21. — A. Meillet, Notice: JA 80 (1902) 548-559. — M. Minassian, Remarques sur Lazare et E.: REArm 4 (1967) 37-48. — B. Outtier, Une exhortation aux moines: FS A. Guillaumont (Geneva, 1988), 97-101. — R. W. Thomson, E. History of Vardan: Classical Armenian Culture, ed. T. J. Samuelian (Philadelphia, 1982), 41-51. — idem, Vardapet in the Early Armenian Church: Muséon 75 (1962) 367-384. — S. Weber, Palästinische Ortskunde: HandAm 41 (1927) 817-826. — B. L. Zekian, E. as Witness of Ecclesiology: East of Byzantium, ed. N. G. Garsoïan (Washington, 1982), 187-197.

P. BRUNS

Elxai

E. was the leader of the Elkesaites, a Jewish-Chr. gnostic sect, the existence of which can be detected from the 3rd to the 10th c. It was probably in 101, in the southeastern Jordan, that Elxai composed the work revealed to him as an apocalypse or esoteric doctrine for the Jewish-Chr. syncretistic group known as the *Sobiai* ("Those who have bathed"). The content of the lost Gk. translation of the Aramaic original can be reconstructed by means of excerpts from it in Hippolytus (*haer.* 9.13, 15, 16, 17) and accounts in Epiphanius (*haer.* 19; 30); it offers a blend of Jewish, Chr., naturalistic pagan, gnostic, astrological, and magical elements: among other things, a second baptism and repeated immersions to ward off demons; rejection of sacrifices; invocation of the elements; astrology; prayer toward Jerusalem; teaching on the angels; rejection of some passages of the OT and NT (Pauline letters). In essential points (great importance of the law; place of the OT, rejection of sacrifices, Adam-Christ typology) a close connection can be seen between E. and the Ps.-Clementines. The lessening of the Jewish element and strengthening of the Chr. in the latter (uniqueness of baptism, discontinuation of circumcision) illustrate the evolution of the Jewish-Chr. doctrinal system.

W: A. Hilgenfeld, NT extra canonum receptum III 22 (1881), 227-240 [text]. — NTApo⁵ 2:619-623 [German trans.].
L: G. Bareille, E.: DThC 4/2:2233-2239. — W. Brandt, E. (Leipzig, 1912). — L. Cirillo, E. e gli Elchasaiti (Cosenza, 1984). — A. F. J. Klijn, R. Reinink, E. and Mani: VigChr 28 (1974) 277-289. — G. P. Luttikhuizen, The revelation of E. (Tübingen, 1985). — G. Strecker, E.: RAC 5:1171-1186. — idem, Eschaton u. Historie (Göttingen, 1979), 320-333. — H. Waitz, Der Prophet E.: FS A. v. Harnack (Leipzig, 1921), 87-104.

C. SCHMIDT

Enaniso, Monk

E. was a fellow student of the later Catholicos Patriarch Iso'yabh III at the school of Nisibis; he later became a monk on Mount Izla. On a pilgrimage to the Holy Land and to the Egyptian Scete E. came into contact with the monks there and acquired some Gk. mss. which he translated into Syriac in the mid-7th c. at the monastery of Beth'Abe. From these works he compiled various glossaries and anthologies. In particular, he compiled the so-called *Paradise of the Fathers*, a compendium of the lives of various monks from the *Historia Lausiaca* of → Palladius and from the → *Historia monachorum* ascribed to Jerome.

W: E. A. Wallis Budge, Book of Paradise 1-2 (London, 1904) [Syriac text]. — idem, Book of the Holy Fathers 1-2 (London, 1907) [English trans.]. — P. Bedjan, Acta Martyrum Sanctorum 7 (Hildesheim, 1968 = Leipzig, 1897) [Syriac text]. — J. M. Sauget, CSCO 495 [Arabic text]

P. BRUNS

Endelechius

A bucolic epic of conversion (→ Bucolic, → Epic), *De mortibus boum* (or *De virtute signi crucis*), probably composed ca. 400, has come down under the name of Severus Endelechius (E.), a Gallic orator and member of Paulinus of Nola's circle (*ep.* 28.6) (the exact dates of E.'s life are unknown). The epic has thirty-three strophes (meter: 2nd Asclepiadean) and contain numerous borrowings from Ovid, Horace, and Virgil (espec. *Georg.* 3 [cattle epidemic] and *ecl.* 1 [Tityrus and his god]). The protection of Tityrus's herd, which has been sealed with the sign of the cross against the cattle mortality all around, to which the cattle of Aegon and Bucolos have fallen victim, enables E. to make a religious application of bucolic themes. Convinced by the power of the Chr. faith Bucolos and Aegon are converted. The poem is clearly directed against the "ancient error" (v. 123) of the rural population that still closes its mind to Christianity.

W: F. Bücheler, A. Riese (ed.), Anthologia Latina 1/2 (Leipzig, 1906), 334-339 [text]. — D. Korzeniewski (Darmstadt, 1976), 58-71 [text/German trans.].
L: T. Alimonti, Struttura, ideologia ed imitazione (Turin, 1976). — F. Corsaro, De mortibus boum: Orph. 22 (1975) 3-26. — D. Korzeniewski, Hirtengedichte (Darmstadt, 1976), XII-XIII. — U. Moricca, E.: Did. NS 6 (1926) 91-94. — W. Schmid, E.: RAC 5:1-4.

M. SKEB, OSB

Ennodius

Magnus Felix Ennodius (E.) was born, probably in Arles, in 473/474 and grew up in Cisalpine Gaul. He entered the clergy of Bishop Epiphanius of Pavia, initially as a simple cleric, but between 495 and 499 he moved to Milan and Bishop Lawrence. Soon after 502 he was ordained a deacon and, in 513, bishop of Pavia. He died in 521 and was buried on July 17; his epitaph in the Church of St. Michael in Pavia has survived (CIL 5:2:6464).

E.'s numerous writings come almost entirely from the period when he was a cleric in Milan (ca. 497-513). They were transmitted in a collection in which they followed the order of their writing (see Vogel's ed.). Ever since they were edited by J. Sirmond (Paris, 1611) they have usually been divided into letters, various shorter works, lectures/speeches, and poems (see Hartel's ed.). E.'s works, strongly marked by ancient rhetoric, are a mixture of the spiritual and the secular; characteristically, the remark that he wants to give up completely his preoccupation with secular literature (*opusc.* 5 H[artel] = no. 188

V[ogel]) occurs first in the sketch of his life which he wrote in 511 after recovering from a serious illness.

Of the carefully written letters (*ep.*) 297 have survived (divided by Sirmond into nine books). In style E. follows Symmachus (ca. 345-403), the representative of pagan culture. His addressees are chiefly aristocrats such as Boethius, Liberius, and Olybrius, Symmachus the bishop of Rome, and deacon Hormisdas, as well as noble women such as Barbara and Firmina and the Euprepia sisters.

There are ten *Opuscula miscella* in prose. *Opusc.* 1 H (= no. 263 V), *Panegyricus Theodorico regi dictus*, is an encomium, probably not intended for public delivery, which praises the beneficial rule of a king who has been called by divine favor: praised, among other things, is his concern for eloquence, but E. says nothing about the king's religious policy (spring 507). *Opusc.* 2 H (= no. 49 V), *Libellus contra eos, qui contra synodum scribere praesumpserunt*, takes the side of the Roman Bishop Symmachus in the Lawrentian schism (soon after 502), in an answer to the pamphlet of Lawrence's supporters, *Adversus synodum absolutionis incongruae*. *Opusc.* 2 H (= no. 80 V), the *Vita Epiphanii episcopi Ticinensis*, was composed in 502/503 as an encomiastic life of the bishop who died in 496; it is adorned with numerous rhetorical figures. *Opusc.* 4 H (= no. 240 V), the *Vita Antonii monachi*, is a biography, written probably in 506, of a monk from Pannonia who spent the last years of his life at Lérins. *Opusc.* 5 H (= no. 438 V) is the so-called *Eucharisticum de vita sua*, in which E. speaks of the nothingness of earthly things as he looks back over his life (after 511). *Opusc.* 6 H (= no. 452 V), the so-called *Paraenesis (concinnatio) didascalica*, is a piece of metrical prose, written probably in 511, in which E. urges his friends Ambrose and Beatus to practice love of God and neighbor, to lead a life marked by the virtues of *verecundia*, *castitas*, and *fides*, and to educate themselves in grammar and rhetoric, which is the crowning part of an education. *Opusc.* 7 H (= no. 8 V), *Praeceptum de cellulanis*, advises bishops, priests, and deacons to live together with a cleric. In *Opusc.* 8 H (= no. 123 V), *Petitorium quo absolutus est Gerontius*, E. requests Roman citizenship for Agapitus, a freedman. *Opusc.* 9 H (= no. 14 V) and 10 H (= no. 81 V) are blessings of the Easter candle.

The third group of prose writings are the twenty-eight *dictiones* (lectures/speeches). *Dict.* 1-6 have a spiritual content (*dict.* 1 H [= no. 1 V]: for the anniversary of the day when Bishop Lawrence of Milan took office; *dict.* 2 H [= no. 98 V]: a speech that Bishop Honoratus of Novara was to deliver at the dedication of the Church of the Apostles; *dict.* 5 H [= no. 336 V]: a model of a speech for a bishop taking office). *Dict.* 7-13 have to do mostly with the scholastic world (*dict.* 12 H [= no. 320 V]: praise of letters, addressed to Arator, with a preface of three elegiac distichs). *Dict.* 14-28 consist mostly of model speeches for rhetorical training (*dict.* 14-23: *controversiae*; *dict.* 14-28: *dictiones ethicae* on themes from mythology, among them a speech by Thetis on the future death of her son Achilles [*dict.* 25 H = no. 220 V] and a lament of Dido at the departure of Aeneas [*dict.* 28 H = no. 466 V]).

The poems (*Carmina* [*c.*]) have been divided, since Sirmond, into two books. Book 1 contains nine longer poems, among them two descriptions of journeys (*c.* 1.1 H = no. 245 V: *Itinerarium Brigantionis castelli* in elegiac distichs; *c.* 1.2 H = no. 423 V: description of a journey down the Po in flood, in dactylic hexameters); a polymetrical epithalamium telling how Amor and Venus bring a bride to Maximus (*c.* 1.4 H = no. 388 V: *praefatio* in elegiac distichs; dactylic hexameters; sapphic stanzas; hexameters; hendecasyllabics); three panegyrics (for Bishop Epiphanius for his thirty-year anniversary as a priest [*c.* 1.9 H = no. 43 V, in dactylic hexameters with a preface in prose; ca. 496]; for politician and poet Faustus [*c.* 1.7 H = no. 26 V, polymetrical, with a prose preface]; and for Olybrius the orator [*c.* 1.8 H = no. 27 V, in elegiac distichs, also with a prose preface]); and twelve hymns imitating Ambrose, espec. for feastdays and saints venerated in Milan, usually in iambic dimeters, but in one case (*c.* 1.17 H= no. 348 V) in Alcaic verses (*c.* 1.10-21 H = no. 341-54 V). Book 2 contains 151 epigrams that are for the most part occasional verses (mostly in dactylic hexameters and elegiac distichs, but also in sapphic stanzas: epitaphs, including obituaries for Milanese bishops (*c.* 2.77-78 H = no. 195-207 V); inscriptions (e.g., *C.* 2.8 H = no. 96 V, and *c.* 2.9 H = no. 97 V); descriptions of works of art, but also erotic poems (e.g., *c.* 2.103 H = no. 233 V, on Pasiphae and the Minotaur).

E.'s work displays not only deep piety but also at every point a receptiveness to the cultural heritage from antiquity. The author has always received a good deal of attention as a witness to Chr. culture in the late 5th and early 6th c. Only in recent scholarship has his often difficult style and his delight in experimentation, which results in an astonishing variety of prose and poetic forms, begun to be adequately appreciated.

W: W. Hartel, CSEL 6. — F. Vogel, MGH. AA 7. — *opusc.* 1: B. S. Haase, M. A. Thesis (Ottawa, Ontario, 1991) [English trans./comm.]. — C. Rohr (Hannover, 1995) [text/German

trans./comm.]. — *opusc.* 3: M. Cesa (Como, 1988) [text/Italian trans./comm.]. — *opusc.* 5: M. Fertig (Passau, 1855) [partial German trans.]. — *opusc.* 6: R. A. Rallo Freni (Messina, ²1981) [text/Italian trans.].
L: C. Fini, Le fonti delle dict. di E.: AAH 30 (1982-1984) 387-393. — J. Fontaine, E.: RAC 5:398-421. — E. Galbiati, A. Poma, L. Alfonsi, Magno Felice E. (474-521) (Pavia, 1975). — F. Gastaldelli, E. di Pavia (Rome, 1973). — S. A. H. Kennel, E. and the Pagan Gods: Athenaeum 80 (1992) 236-242. — W. D. Lebek, Deklamation u. Dichtung in der "Dictio Ennodi diaconi quando de Roma abiit": FS A. Dihle (Göttingen, 1993), 264-299 (on c. 1, 6 H. = Nr. 2 V., with edition and German trans.). — S. Léglise, St. E., évêque de Pavie (Paris, 1906). — A. Lumpe, Die konzilien-geschichtliche Bedeutung des E.: AHC 1 (1969) 15-36. — F. Magani, E. (Pavia, 1886), 3:351-375 (on *ep.*). — B. Marotta Mannino, La Vita Antoni di E. fra tradizione classica e cristiana: Orpheus 10 (1989) 335-357 (on *opusc.* 4). — B. Näf, Das Zeitbewußtsein des F.: Hist. 39 (1990) 100-123. — L. Navarra, Le componenti letterarie e concettuali delle dict. di E.: Aug. 12 (1972) 465-478. — idem, E. e la "facies" storico-culturale del suo tempo (Cassino, 1974). — idem, A proposito del De navigio suo di Venanzio Fortunato in rapporto alla Mosella di Ausonio e agli Itinerari di E.: SSRel 3/1 (1979) 79-131. — P. Orth, Eine vermeintliche Sammlung von Briefen aus dem Ostgotenreich: DA 53 (1997) 555-561. — H. Peter, Der Brief in der röm. Lit. (Hildesheim, 1965 = Leipzig, 1901), 162-168 (on *ep.*). — M. R. Pizzino, L'Eucharisticum di E. di Pavia e le Confessioni di S. Agostino: Scritti in onore di S. Pugliatti 5 (Milan, 1978), 801-810 (on *opusc.* 5). — R. A. Rallo Freni, Atteggiamenti topici nel programma poetico di Magno Felice Ennodio: Scritti in onore di S. Pugliatti 5 (Milan, 1978), 833-858. — J. Relihan, Ancient Menippean Satire (Baltimore, 1993), 164-175 (and 260-270), 211-219 (and 281-284) (on *opusc.* 6, with English trans.). — W. Schetter, Die Thetisdeklamation des E.: FS J. Straub (Bonn, 1977), 395-412; also in: idem, Kaiserzeit u. Spätantike (Stuttgart, 1994), 406-424 (on dict. 25). — idem, Zu E. c. 2, 1 Hartel: Hermes 114 (1986) 500-502; also in: idem, Kaiserzeit u. Spätantike (Stuttgart, 1994), 425-427. — E. Wirbelauer, Zwei Päpste in Rom (Munich, 1993), 148-154 (on *opusc.* 2)

S. Döpp

Ephraem of Antioch (of Amida)

E. (d. ca. 545) was originally from Amida and, before becoming bishop of Antioch in 527, had a rapidly rising secular career that brought him to the position of *comes Orientis.* He was a zealous defender of the Chalcedonian Creed and sought, by means of numerous pastoral visitations and synods, espec. in 428 in Antioch, to stem the influence of the Monophysite-minded supporters of → Severus of Antioch. An Origenism that was gaining strength provided him with another theol. adversary, which he condemned at another synod in Antioch in 542, before Emperor Justinian a year later issued an edict (in which the bishop of Antioch did not fail to play a part) that cre-

ated the necessary imperial juridical conditions for getting completely rid of Origenism. Only a few fragments have survived of the many works mentioned in Photius, *cod.* 228f.; they show E.'s Neo-Chalcedonian orientation. Yet as a defender of Chalcedon he took second place behind other authors (→ Leontius Byz., → Leontius Jerus.).

W: PG 86/2:2104-2109. — S. Helmer, Neuchalkedonismus (Hildesheim, 1952), 262-265, 271f.
L: G. Downey, E. Patriarch of Antioch: ChH 7 (1938) 364-370. — A. Grillmeier, Jesus der Christus 2/1.64f.; 2/2.407f. (English, Christ in Christian Tradition, vol. 2/1 [London, 1987]). — S. Helmer, loc. cit., 185-195. — J. Lebon, E. d'Amide: FS C. Moeller (Leuven/Louvain, 1914), 197-214.

P. Bruns

Ephraem the Syrian

I. Life: E., born in or near Nisibis (Soz., *h.e.* 3.16), was, acc. to Barhadbesabba of Beth Arbaye, initially an ascetic and a student of Bishop Jacob of Nisibis, in whose school he later taught. Tradition gives him the rank of deacon (Soz., *h.e.* 3.16; Jerome, *vir. ill.* 115); he calls himself a "subordinate shepherd" (*HcHaer.* 56.10). The destruction of Nicomedia by an earthquake in 358 (Gennadius, *vir. ill.* 3.67) found an echo in E.'s work, as did the policy of restoration of paganism under Emperor Julian (361-363). After Nisibis was ceded to the Persians in 363 E. left his native city with his fellow believers and settled in Roman Edessa. His remaining ten years were filled with brisk caritative activity among the refugees. At the same time, he continued teaching in the Edessan school of exegesis and played a solid part in the growing dogm. controversies. Acc. to the *Chronicle of Edessa* E. died in 373, highly esteemed and praised even among the Greeks (Epiphanius, *haer.* 51.22.7).

E. is regarded as the classic writer of the Syrian church. He was an author of exceptional productivity and equally important as exegete, apologete, preacher, and poet. His literary remains are extensive and to be found everywhere in the thinking of the Syrian church. The genuine works were all written in Syriac and exist almost without exception in their Syr. originals, but a few have come down also in an Arm. translation. Most of the material handed down in Greek is not authentic.

II. Works: *Exegetical works:* among the authentic exeget. works are the *Commentary on Genesis* and the *Interpretation of Exodus (comm. in Gen. et Ex.).* A commentary on Qoh (*comm. in Qoh.*) and one on Jonah (*comm. in Ion.*) are also attributed to him. A commentary on the *Diatessaron (comm. in Diat.)* has survived only in fragments in Syriac, but is complete in Armenian; it certainly contains much that is authentic but has been enlarged with later material. The Arm. *Interpretation of the Gospel* (*comm. in Ev.*) that is ascribed to E. is certainly not authentic, but may well be from the pen of E.'s disciple Mar → Aba. In addition, commentaries on Acts (*comm. in Acta*) and on the letters of Paul (*comm. in ep. P.*) have survived in Armenian. The OT is interpreted both literally and typologically; the exegesis of the NT is primarily in the service of preaching.

W: *comm. in Gen. et Ex.*, R. M. Tonneau, CSCO 152/153 [Syriac text/Latin trans.]. — P. Féghali, Commentaire de l'Exode: ParOr 12 (1984/85) 91-131 [French trans.]. — *comm. in Diat.*, L. Leloir, CSCO 137/145 [Armenian text/Latin trans.]. — idem (Dublin, 1963) [Syriac text/Latin trans.]. — idem, SC 121. — *comm. in Diat.*, G. Moesinger (Venice, 1876) [Armenian text/Latin trans.]. — *comm. in Ev.*, G. A. Egan, CSCO 291/292 [Armenian text/English trans.]. — *comm. in Qoh.*, K. Deppe, Qohelet in der syr. Dichtung (Wiesbaden, 1975) [Syriac text/German trans.]. — *comm. in Ion.*, G. Garitte, Sur Jonas: REArm 6 (1969) 23-43. [Armenian text/French trans.]. — *comm. in Acta*, N. Akinian (Vienna, 1921) [Armenian text/German trans.]. — F. C. Conybeare: Beginnings of Christianity, ed. F. Jackson (London, 1926), 373-453 [English trans.]. — *comm. in ep. P.*, PP Mechitharistae, Explicatio Apostoli (Venice, 1836) [text]. — eadem, *Comm. in ep. P.* (Venice, 1893) [Latin trans.].
L: E. Beck, Syr. Kommentar zu Joh 1,1-5: OrChr 67 (1983) 1-31. — idem, Wunder am Kreuz: OrChr 77 (1993) 104-119. — idem, Sünde wider den hl. Geist: OrChr 73 (1989) 1-37. — idem, Samariterin: OrChr 74 (1990) 1-24. — idem, Sünderin: OrChr 75 (1991) 1-15. — idem, Reicher Jüngling: OrChr 76 (1992) 1-45. — F. C. Burkitt, E. Quotations from the Gospel (Cambridge, 1901). — R. A. Darling, Church from the Nations: OCA 229 (1987) 111-122. — P. Féghali, Gen 1, 1-2, 4: ParOr 13 (1986) 3-30. — idem, Influence des Targums: OCA 229 (1987) 71-82. — S. Hidal, Interpretatio Syriaca (Lund, 1974). — M. Hogan, E.'s Commentary on the Lord's Prayer: Ephrem's Theological Journal 3 (1999) 31-44. — T. Jansma, Berichtigungen zu Gen u. Ex: OrChr 56 (1972) 59-79; OrChr 58 (1974) 121-131; OCP 39 (1973) 5-28; JSSt 17 (1972) 203-212. — N. el-Khouri, Hermeneutics: OCA 229 (1987) 93-100. — A. Kowalski, Genesis: CrSt 3 (1982) 41-60. — L. Leloir, Doctrine et méthodes (Leuven/Louvain, 1961). — idem, Christologie: HandAm 75 (1961) 449-466. — A. Levene, Early Syrian Fathers on Genesis (London, 1951). — A. Merk, Kommentar zur Apg: ZKTh 48 (1924) 37-58, 226-260. — J. Molitor, Paulustext (Rome, 1938). — B. Outtier, Commentaire de l'Evangile: ParOr 1 (1970) 385-408. — P. Yousif, Formes littéraires: OCA 229 (1987) 83-92.

Dogmatic works: Among the dogm. writings in prose are the *Refutations* (*ref.*), in which E. sharply attacks Bardesanes, Marcion, and Mani. Along with the *Hymni contra haereses* (see below) they offer important evidence of the lost works of Bardesanes. E. was also an artistic writer of letters (*ep.*) with dogm. and ascet. content. Outstanding among the prose homilies is the treatise *Sermo de Domino Nostro* (*SDN*), which deals with the incarnation and redemption.

W: *ref.*, C. W. Mitchell, Prose Refutation (London, 1912-1921) [Syriac text/English trans.]. — *ep.*, E. Beck, E.'s Brief an Hypatius: OrChr 58 (1974) 76-120. — idem, Gegen eine philosophische Schrift des Bardaisan: OrChr 60 (1976) 24-68. — S. P. Brock, E.'s letter to Publius: Muséon 89 (1976) 261-305. — idem, Unpublished letter of E.: ParOr 4 (1973) 317-323. — *SDN*, E. Beck, CSCO 116/117 [Syriac text/German trans.].
L: E. Beck, E.'s Polemik gegen Mani u. die Manichäer (Leuven/Louvain, 1978). — A. Vööbus, A Letter of E. to the Mountaineers (Pinneberg, 1947).

Poetic works: Syr. versification, already cultivated by Bardesanes and his son Harmonius, reached its high point in E. He wrote metrical homilies (*memre*) which contain clauses with a fixed number of syllables, as well as didactic hymns (*madrese*), the clauses of which vary in the number and length of the syllables but whose strophes end with a responsory (*onita*) to be sung by a choir. Among the authentic works are the *Sermones de fide* (*SdF*) and the sermons in Nicomedia (*SNic*), which have come down complete only in Armenian. The many sermons contain much that is authentically E.'s, but, like the *Sermones in hebdomadam sanctam* (*SHebdS*), they were later revised. The fifteen *Hymni de paradiso* (*HdP*) are probably E.'s earliest work and clearly reflect the setting of early Syr. Christianity with its strongly Jewish-rabbinic influence. The fifty-six *Hymni contra haereses* (*HcHaer*), like the refutations in prose, struggle with the three chief Syr. heretics: Bardesanes, Marcion, and Mani. As the name implies, the *Carmina Nisibena* (*CN*) are from the period in Nisibis (before 363) and deal with, among other things, such eschat. subjects as the descent of Christ into Sheol and his victory over the forces of chaos. The eighty-seven *Hymni de fide* (*HdF*), which come from the Edessan period (after 363), are E.'s most mature theol. work and develop his teaching on the Trinity against a burgeoning Arianism. The collection of hymns ends with six meditations on the pearl (81-86), which are among the greatest creations of all Syr. poetry. The four hymns against Emperor Julian (*CIul*) deal with the period from 361 to 363, whereas the hymns on the church (*HdEccl*) with their vine symbolism and the hymns on virginity (*HdVirg*) cannot be dated with certainty. The same is true of the poetic *Hymni de nativitate* (*HdNat*) and *De epiphania* (*HdEpiph*). In them, however, the liturgical setting is just as clear as in the *Hymni de ieiunio* (*HdIeiun*) and *De paschate* (*HdPasch*). They deserve attention not only because of their espec. edifying and poetic form but also because of their christology with its extensive symbolism and deep feeling.

W: *SdF*, E. Beck, CSCO 212/213 [Syriac text/German trans.]. — *Sermones*, E. Beck, CSCO 305/306, 311/312, 320/321, 334/335 [Syriac text/German trans.]. — *Hymni et sermones*, L. Mariès, C. Mercier, PO 30 [Armenian text/Latin trans.]. — N. Akinian, E. Madrasche (Berlin, 1951) [Armenian text/German trans.]. — *Sermones*, K. Samir: OCP 39 (1973) 307-332; ParOr 4 (1973) 265-315; OrChr 58 (1974) 51-75; OCA 205 (1978) 229-242 [Arabic text] — *HdP*, E. Beck, CSCO 174/175 [Syriac text/German trans.]. — *HdP*, R. Lavenant, SC 137. — S. P. Brock, St. E. on paradise (New York, 1990) [English trans./comm.]. — *HcIul*, E. Beck, CSCO 174/175. — *SNic*, C. Renoux, PO 37 [Armenian-Syriac text/French trans.]. — *HdPasch*, E. Beck, CSCO 248/249 [Syriac text/German trans.]. — G. A. M. Rouwhorst, Hymnes pascales (Leiden, 1989). — *HdEccl*, E. Beck, CSCO 108/109 [Syriac text/German trans.]. — *HdF*, E. Beck, CSCO 154/155 [Syriac text/German trans.]. — *HcHaer*, E. Beck, CSCO 169/170 [Syriac text/German trans.]. — *HdIeiun*, E. Beck, CSCO 246/247 [Syriac text/German trans.]. — B. Outtier, Sur le jeûne et la pénitence: BeKa 31 (1974) 109-117 [Georgian text/French trans.]. — *HdNat/HdEpiph*, E. Beck, CSCO 82/83 [Syriac text/German trans.]. — *CN*, E. Beck, CSCO 92/93, 102/103 [Syriac text/German trans.]. — *HdVirg*, E. Beck, CSCO 223/224 [Syriac text/German trans.].
Doubtful and spurious: E. Beck, CSCO 322/323 [Syriac text/German trans.]. — *SHebdS*, E. Beck, CSCO 412/413 [Syriac text/German trans.]. — *Nachträge*, E. Beck, CSCO 363/364 [Syriac text/German trans.]. — B. Outtier, Sur les ruses de Satan: REArm 13 (1978/79) 165-174. [Armenian text/French trans.]. — G. Garitte, Sur la mort et le diable: Muséon 82 (1969) 123-163 [Syriac text/French trans.].
L: E. Beck, Theologie E.s in den Hymnen über den Glauben (Rome, 1949). — idem, E.s Reden über den Glauben (Rome, 1953). — idem, E.s Hymnen über das Paradies (Rome, 1951). — P. Féghali, St. Paul dans les carmina Nisibena: ParOr 9 (1979/80) 5-25. — F. Graffin, Sur la perle: OrSyr 12 (1967) 129-150. — J. Gribomont, Sur la Pâque: Melto 1-2 (1967) 147-182. — idem, Hymnes pascales: ParOr 4 (1973) 147-189, 191-246. — L. Mariès, Bénédiction de la table: OrSyr 4 (1959) 73-109, 163-192, 285-298. — C. Molenberg, Christological Names: OCA 236 (1990) 135-142. — N. Séd, Traditions juives: Muséon 81 (1968) 455-501.

III. Main Lines of Thought: It is difficult to overestimate E.'s place in early Syrian theology. His polemical works clearly show him to be a man of the Great Church and one who helped orthodoxy gain its lasting place in Syria. In opposition to dualistic systems (Marcionism, Manichaeism) he stubbornly defended the Chr. doctrine of the one creator and lord even of material creation. In his anthropology he resists both determinism and pessimism and places a high value on the freedom of the will. His teaching on sin is therefore very voluntaristic and to be understood in light of his monastic spirituality, in which fasting, penance, and prayer play a dominant role. As an ascetic withdrawn from the world, he attacks the speculation on the elements that marked Bardesanes, who was proud of his knowledge and of his elitist royal court of Edessa.

In the later Edessan period Arianism too came increasingly within E.'s ken. He fought against it with determination as being a fabrication of Hellen. philosophy and contrasted it with the knowledge of God and Christ through symbols. Gr. rationalism entangled the church in useless dogm. disputes and led ultimately to loss of unity in the faith, whereas the way of symbolic knowledge of God can unite souls. E. did not call for any abandonment of knowledge in matters of faith, but his theology is indeed to be located in a different place: the proper worship that is offered to the Son of God by the church and its faithful. The high esteem of symbol and image stems in E. from his strongly sensible starting point in his theory of knowledge and from the lack of abstraction that went with it. Generally speaking, as compared with the contemporary Cappadocians, an abstract and conceptual theology is very underdeveloped among the early Syrians. E.'s trinitarian and christological concepts are unclear and hazy, although his teaching on the Trinity, using the image of the sun and light, holds a balance between Sabellian modalism and subordinationist tritheism. The distinction and unity of name (*schma*) and person (*gnoma*) in trinitarian thought allows for differentiating between the immanent and the economic Trinity. E.'s christological terminology is likewise largely indeterminate: the mythic image of a donning of the body or of a mingling, which occurs again in sacramental theology, could later on be taken over by both Monophysites and Nestorians.

In any case, independently of later confessional boundaries, E. remains the classical poet and theologian of the Syrian church.

W: J. S. Assemani, S. E. Assemani, S. E. opera omnia 1-6 (Rome, 1732-1746) [Syriac-Greek text/Latin trans.]. — C. Emerau, S. E. Son œuvre littéraire grecque (Paris, 1921). — M. Geerard, E. Graecus: CPG 2 (1974) 366-468. — T. J. Lamy, S. E. Syri Hymni et Sermones 1-4 (Mecheln, 1882-1902) [Syriac text/Latin trans.]. — PP Mechitaristae, S. E. opera armeniace 1-4 (Venice, 1836). — J. J. Overbeck, S. E. Syri opera selecta (Oxford, 1865) [Syriac text].
L: E. Beck, E.s Psychologie u. Erkenntnislehre (Leuven/Louvain, 1980). — idem, E.s Trinitätslehre (Leuven/Louvain, 1981). — idem, Bild vom Sauerteig: OrChr 63 (1979) 1-19. — idem, Bild vom Weg: OrChr 65 (1981) 1-39. — idem, Glaube u. Gebet: OrChr 66 (1982) 15-50. — idem, Eucharistie: OrChr 38 (1954) 41-67. — idem, Taufe: OrSyr 1 (1956) 111-136. — idem, Mariologie: OrChr 40 (1956)

22-39. — idem, symbolum – mysterium: OrChr 41 (1958) 19-40. — idem, σάρξ/σῶμα bei E.: OrChr 70 (1986) 1-22. — idem, Zwei Bilder: OrChr 71 (1987) 1-23. — idem, τέχνη: OrChr 47 (1981) 295-331. — T. Bou Mansour, Liberté: ParOr 11 (1983) 89-156; 12 (1984/85) 3-89. — idem, Liberté humaine: EThL 60 (1984) 252-282. — C. Bravo, Neomática: EX 6 (1956) 198-265. — S. P. Brock, The Harp of the Spirit (London, 1975). — idem, The Luminous Eye (Kalamazoo, Mich., 1992). — idem, Christ as Light in Mary: ECR 7 (1976) 137-144. — P. Bruns, Arius hellenizans? E. u. die Neoarianer: ZKG 101 (1990) 21-57. — W. Cramer, Die Engelvorstellung bei E. (Rome, 1965). — F. Graffin, L'eucharistie: ParOr 4 (1973) 93-121. — S. H. Griffith, Eucharist als "Living Medicine": MoTh 15 (1999) 225-246. — L. Hammersberger, Mariologie (Innsbruck, 1938). — A. de Halleux, Mar E. théologien: ParOr 4 (1973) 35-54. — S. A. Harvey, Embodiment in Time and Eternity: SVTQ 43 (1999) 105-130. — N. el-Khoury, Interpretation der Welt bei E. (Mainz, 1976). — T. Koonammakkal, Ephrem and Greek Wisdom: OCA 247 (1994) 169-176. — J. Martikainen, Das Böse u. der Teufel (Abo, 1978). — idem, Gerechtigkeit u. Güte Gottes (Göttingen, 1980). — C. McCarthy, Allusions and Illusions: Scriptural Interpretation in the Fathers, ed. T. Finan (Cambridge, 1995), 143-162. — J. Melki, Bilan de l'édition critique: ParOr 11 (1983) 3-88. — R. Murray, Symbolism: ParOr 6-7 (1975/76) 1-20. — idem, Angelology: OCA 236 (1990) 143-154. — I. Ortiz de Urbina, La Vergine Maria: OCA 197 (1974) 65-104. — G. Ricciotti, S. E. Siro (Turin, 1925). — J. Teixidor, La descente aux enfers: OrSyr 6 (1961) 25-40. — idem, Muerte, cielo y Seol: OCP 27 (1961) 82-114. — A. Vööbus, Literary-critical Studies in S. E. (Stockholm, 1958). — P. Yousif, Symbolisme christologique: ParOr 8 (1977/78) 5-66. — idem, Histoire et temps: ParOr 10 (1981/82) 3-36. — XVIᵉ Centenaire de S. E.: ParOr 4 (1973).

P. BRUNS

Epic

Epic is a lengthy kind of narrative poetry in one kind of verse that we find in Greco-Roman antiquity, initially in the heroic songs of Homer. Characteristic of the epic are lofty speech with stereotyped devices (formula, comparison, repetition, etc.), a central figure or leading idea, broad descriptions by a remote narrator, and an enclosed world order as setting. For its material the epic relies chiefly on the sagas of gods and heroes; from the Hellen. age on, the history of the age or (among the Romans) the national history also supplies the subject. The most important Gr. representatives of the epic are Homer and Apollonius of Rhodes, the most important Latin representatives are Virgil, Ovid, Lucan, and Statius.

Since ancient literature did not clearly distinguish in theory or in practice between epic and other poetic genres, the concept of epic is also used in the broader sense of every more or less lengthy text in dactylic hexameters and lofty language, and therefore even of poems with a didactic or philosophical purpose (e.g.,

Hesiod, Lucretius). Only in this broader sense is it possible to speak of Chr. epic. Narrative distance here gives way to the strong personal involvement of the poet. Along with *delectatio*, edification and instruction in the faith play important roles. The narrative element still has value in the hagiographical epic. Insofar as the so-called bibl. epic is not a mere paraphrase with epiclike ornamentation (Juvencus, Cyprian the Poet of Gaul), the narrative of its model gives way to independent individual scenes that are reduced to their essentials, and these become the starting point for meditative reflections and theol. commentary (espec. Sedulius, Arator). When the hexaemeron is the subject, cosmol. explanations and hymns of praise are added. The didactic epic with its exhortations to faith and its antiheretical element follows the line of Chr. apologetics and dogmatics. Prudentius's *Psychomachia* is an allegorical epic that has no model or parallel in the ancient world. Traditional epic with its subjects from mythology and (contemporary) history is continued (and developed) in late antiquity espec. by Claudian and the poems of Corippus with their very slight Chr. coloration.

A list of the most important representatives of Chr. epic (all works are in Latin, except for that of Nonnus):

1. Bibl. epic: With NT material: Juvencus, *Evangeliorum libri IV* (ca. 330); Nonnus, *Paraphrasis evangelii Ioannei* (5th c.); Sedulius, *Carmen paschale* (ca. 430); Arator, *De actibus apostolorum* (544). With OT material: "The Poet of the Heptateuch" or "Cyprian, Poet of Gaul" (5th c.?); Claudis Marius Victor(ius), *Alethia* (first half of 5th c.); Dracontius, *De laudibus Dei* (ca. 490); Alcimus Avitus, *De spiritalis historiae gestis* (before 518).

2. Didactic epic: Commodian, *Carmen apologeticum* and *Instructiones* (3rd c.?); Prudentius, *Apotheosis*, *Hamartigenia*, and *Contra Symmachum* (published together in 405); (Ps.?)-Prosper, *De providentia divina* (416); Prosper, *De ingratis* (429/430), *Carmen adversus Marcionitas* (first half of 5th c.).

3. Allegorical (heroic) epic: Prudentius, *Psychomachia* (published 405).

4. Hagiographical epic: Paulinus of Périgueux, *Vita Martini* (460/470); Venantius Fortunatus, *Vita Martini* (shortly after 600).

L: C. Braun-Irgang, Untersuchungen zum Verhältnis von spätantiker u. mittellat. Bibelepik: FS P. Klopsch (Göppingen, 1988), 1-45. — C. Fabian, Dogma u. Dichtung. Untersuchungen zu Prudentius' Apotheosis (Frankfurt a.M., 1988). — J. Fontaine, Naissance de la poésie dans l'Occident chrétien (Paris, 1981). — R. Herzog, Die Bibelepik der lat. Spätantike 1 (Munich, 1975). — idem, Exegese-Erbauung-Delectatio. Beiträge zu einer chr. Poetik der Spätantike: Formen u. Funktionen der Allegorie, ed. W. Haug (Stuttgart, 1979), 52-69. — D. Kartschoke, Bibeldichtung. Studien zur Geschichte der epischen Bibelparaphrase von Juvencus bis Otfrid v. Weißenburg (Munich, 1975). — W. Kirsch, Die lat. Versepik des 4. Jh. (Berlin, 1989). — idem, Strukturwandel im lat. E. des 4.-6. Jh.: Ph. 123 (1979) 38-53. — J. McClure, The Biblical Epic and its Audience in Late Antiquity: Pap. Liverpool Lat. Sem. 3 (1981) 305-321. — D. J. Nodes, Doctrine and Exegesis in Biblical Latin Poetry (Leeds, 1993). — M. Roberts, Biblical Epic and Rhetorical Paraphrase in Late Antiquity (Liverpool, 1985). — K. Smolak, Lat. Umdichtungen des bibl. Schöpfungsberichtes: StPatr 12 (1971) 350-360. — C. E. Springer, The Gospel as Epic in Late Antiquity. The Paschale Carmen of Sedulius (Leiden, 1988). — K. Thraede, E.: RAC 5:983-1042. — M. Wehrli, Sacra Poesis. Bibelepik als europäische Tradition: FS F. Maurer (Stuttgart, 1963), 262-283. — C. Witke, Numen litterarum. The Old and the New in Latin Poetry from Constantine to Gregory the Great (Leiden, 1971).

J. Schwind

Epictetus of Corinth

E., bishop of Corinth ca. 369, was a contemporary of Athanasius and fought against Arianism. He questioned Athanasius regarding christol. errors that had surfaced in Corinth. Athanasius's answer, which analyzed the errors in detail and reproached E. for having allowed such errors to circulate, has been preserved not only in its Gr. original but in Latin, Syriac, and Armenian (three different versions in all), with the texts varying somewhat from one another.

W: G. Ludwig (Jena, 1911) [text]. — ACO 1, 5, 321-334 [Latin text]. — R. W. Thomson, CSCO 257/258, 73-85/55-64 [Syriac text/English trans.]. — R. P. Casey, An Armenian Version: HThR 26 (1933) 127-150 [Armenian text].
L: R. Y. Ebied, L. R. Wickman, A Note on the Syriac Version: JThS 23 (1972) 144-154. — J. Lébon, Altération doctrinal: RHE 31 (1935) 713-761. — W. M. Sinclair, E. 7: DCB 2:147. — R. W. Thomson, The Transformation of Athanasius: Muséon 78 (1965) 47-69.

B. Windau

Epigram

The literal translation of epigram is "inscription," and in this sense it is found as early as the 8th/7th c. B.C.E., initially as dedicatory inscriptions or epitaphs, later also on images of the gods and on buildings. Epigrams expressing feelings at the death of a person or at the sight of a portrait were in continuity with fictive epitaphs and dedicatory inscriptions that were hardly distinguishable from the real thing. Ulti-

mately, an epigram could express anything that moved the poet, with the result that a great variety of themes, motifs, and forms emerged, e.g., erotic and derisive epigrams. As for meters, in the elegiac distich hexameters and iambs predominated.

Chr. epigram-poetry took the existing forms of the literary epigram and filled them with a new content (more or less clearly so depending on the author). → Gregory Naz., who consciously wanted to create a Chr. poetry, limited himself almost completely to epitaphs and inscriptions warning against the violation of graves or against eccles. abuses. Later Chr. authors in the East had fewer scruples about using traditional themes and motifs, including mythological and erotic (see the cycles of Agathias Scholasticus and → Paul the Silentiary). The same phenomenon can be seen in the West in → Ausonius, → Claudian (was he a Christian?), → Apollinaris Sidonius, → Ennodius, and → Luxurius. An exclusively Chr. content (meter, language, and style were of course always determined by the rules of the genre) is to be seen in the epigrams of → Damasus I of Rome, whose praises of the martyrs are in the tradition of the ancient Roman tomb eulogies (Scipio inscriptions), → Paulinus of Nola, → Prosper Tiro of Aquitania, who used the epigram as a weapon in theol. polemics, and → Venantius Fortunatus. As is shown by the example of Damasus, almost all of whose epigrams are truly inscriptions, the usual distinction between the literary and the inscriptive epigram was pragmatic rather than based on content. For metrical inscriptions (→ Epitaph) on graves (beginning even in pre-Constantinian times) and on buildings (churches, baptistries), what was said about the Chr. literary epigram applies. Finally, there were special groups: epigrams for martyrs and the explanatory captions for pictures (*tituli*) or epigrams on images, as composed by → Prudentius and → Helpidius Rusticus, in addition to some of the already mentioned Lat. authors.

L: G. Bernt, Latein. E. im Übergang von der Spätantike zum frühen MA (Munich, 1968). — E. Degani, M. Lausberg, E.: Der Neue Pauly 3:1108-1114. — U. Ecker, Grabmal u. E., Studien zur frühgriech. Sepulkraldichtung (Stuttgart, 1990). — J. Fontaine, Naissance de la poésie dans l'occident chrétien (Paris, 1981). — HLL 5:224-236. — R. Keydell, E.: KP 2:308-310. — idem, E.: RAC 5:539-577. — M. Lausberg, Einzeldistichon, Studien zum antiken E. (Munich, 1982). — F. Munari, Spätlateinische Epigrammatik: Ph. 106 (1958) 127-139. — G. Pfohl, Das E. (Darmstadt, 1969). — idem, Bibliographie der griech. Versinschriften (Hildesheim, 1964). — P. Santorelli, L'E. a Proietta di Damaso (51 F): Sicilia e Italia suburbicaria, ed. S. Pricoco, N. F. Rizzo, T. Sardella (Soveria, 1991), 327-336.

H. M. Weikmann

Epiphanes

Reliable information on E. is probably to be found only in Clement, *str.* 3.5.1–10.1. According to him, E. was the son of Alexandria and Carpocrates, who also gave him instruction; E. was founder of the monadic gnosis from which the Carpocratians took their rise. When he died at the age of seventeen in ca. 150, he was venerated as a god in Same on Kephallenia. Clement mentions hymns (not preserved) of the admirers (*str.* 3.5.2f.; see Theod., *haer.* 1.5); he also cites some connected fragments from the "famous book" *De iustitia* (*str.* 3.6.1–8.3; 3.9.2f.) in which E. makes justice a matter of the equality of all. Injustice (acc. to E.) arose from the introduction of property rights; therefore E. also argues for communities of women and attacks legislators, which probably made it easier to accuse the Carpocratians of libertinism.

W: W. Völker, Quellen zur Geschichte der chr. Gnosis (Tübingen, 1932), 33-36 [text]. — W. Foerster, Die Gnosis 1 (Zurich, ³1995), 53-55 [German trans.].
L: A. Hilgenfeld, Ketzergeschichte (Darmstadt, 1966 = Leipzig, 1884), 402-408. — H. Kraft, Gab es Karpokrates?: ThZ 8 (1952) 434-443. — H. Leisegang, Gnosis (Stuttgart, ⁵1985), 258-262. — H. Liboron, Die karpokratianische Gnosis (Leipzig, 1938). — W. A. Löhr, Schrift: FS L. Abramowski (Berlin, 1993), 12-29. — idem, Karpokratianisches: VigChr 49 (1995) 23-48.

R. Hanig

Epiphanius, Archdeacon

E., archdeacon and syncellus (adviser) under Cyril Alex., was author of a letter to Patriarch Maximian of Constantinople (ca. 432/433 C.E.) having to do with the controversy between Nestorius and Cyril.

W: PG 84:826-829. — ACO 1, 4, 222-224.
L: P. Batiffol, Les présents de saint Cyrille à la cour de Constantinople: BALAC 1 (1911) 247-267 = Études de liturgie et d'archéologie chrétienne (Paris, 1912), 154-179. — J. W. Stanbridge, E.: DCB 2:159.

W. A. Löhr

Epiphanius of Benevento

E. took part in a Roman synod under Pope Symmachus in March 499 (Mansi 8:235) that responded to difficulties in papal elections with a synodal decree on the subject.

L: A. H. D. Acland, E.: DCB 2:157. — E. Caspar, Geschichte des Papsttums 2 (Tübingen, 1933), 88ff.

W. A. Löhr

Epiphanius of Constantinople

E. was patriarch of Constantinople from 520 to 535; after the Acacian schism he renewed ties with Rome and to this end wrote five letters to Roman Bishop Hormisdas (*ep.*). His attempt to bring Illyrium under the eccles. authority of Constantinople was rejected by Rome when, in 531, a Roman synod under Boniface II took up a complaint from Bishop Stephen of Larissa, whom E. had deposed. In theology E. supported the formula *unus de trinitate crucifixus.* Some canons (*can.*) have survived in Arabic.

W: *ep.*, O. Guenther, CSEL 35:642-645, 707-710, 741f. — PL 63:494-499, 506f., 523f.; 86:783-786. — *can.*, W. Riedel, Die Kirchenrechtsquellen des Patriarchats Alexandrien (Leipzig, 1900), 288-294 [German trans.].
L: E. Caspar, Geschichte des Papsttums (Tübingen, 1933), 2:172f., 175f., 206f. — J. Darrouzès, E.: DHGE 15:614. — G. Fedalto, Hierarchia Ecclesiastica Orientalis 1 (Padua, 1984), 4. — V. Grumel, Les Regestes des actes du Patriarcat de Constantinople 1:217-227. — Mansi 8:502-524. — W. M. Sinclair, E.: DCB 2:157f.

W. A. Löhr

Epiphanius of Salamis

I. **Life:** E. was born between 310 and 320 near Eleutheropolis (Palestine). As a young man he lived in Egypt and had close ties to monastic circles. At about the age of twenty he founded and was head of a monastery in Besanduc. In 366, he was consecrated bishop of Salamis (Cyprus), an office he held until his death in 403. He was involved in the dogm. conflicts of his time in a number of ways: he debated with Athanasius about the date of Easter (see PG 92:76C) and attacked Chr. images. In addition, he intervened in the schism that divided the church of the metropolises of Salamis and Antioch: E. favored the minority party of the Nicene Eustathians, led by Paulinus, who, in opposition to the three-hypostases theology of Meletius, a homoean who had turned Nicaean, maintained that the Nicene *homoousios* was to be interpreted in terms of a one-hypostasis theology (Basil Caes., *ep.* 258). In 382 E. and Paulinus took part in a synod convoked by Roman Bishop Damasus (Jerome, *ep.* 108.6; 127.7). Finally E. was involved in both phases of the Origenist controversy. He first came in conflict with John Jerus. and accused him of Origenism; then for a time he supported Theophilus Alex. against the Origenist monks of Nitria and John Chrys. In 402 he traveled to Constantinople and, in violation of all eccles. regulations, tried to agitate against John in the latter's own diocese. Because of local opposition he gave up and died in 403 on the sea journey back to his homeland of Cyprus. The fame of the pugnacious ascetic, who had philol. talents (he had knowledge not only of Greek but also of Syriac, Hebrew, Coptic, and Latin) and was well versed in heresies, survived his death in his native land (saint's feast: May 12). His *Panarion omnium haeresium* in particular but also his exegetical works (see below) were widely circulated and used; as a result of his reputation for orthodoxy, not only was he cited as an authority in the Byz. iconoclastic controversy, but in addition pseudonymous works such as the → *Physiologus* were attributed to him.

II. Works: The *Ancoratus* (*anc.*: "The Firmly-Anchored Man") was an antiheretical work on the fundamentals of the faith (Trinity, creed), composed in 374 and addressed to communities in Pamphylia.

The *Panarion omnium haeresium* (*haer.*) ("Chest of Medicines against All Heresies") is E.'s main work, written between 374 and 376, and is the most important and extensive heresiological encyclopedia from the early church. Citing Cant 6:8, E. presents twenty pre-Chr. (philosophical and Jewish) and sixty Chr. heresies in a chronological and systematic order. For each heresy E. first describes the teaching and, if relevant, the morals of the heretics, and then refutes them. Valuable original documents are cited verbatim. E. harks back to the writings of earlier heresiologists such as Irenaeus of Lyons and Hippolytus of Rome. E.'s *De mensuris et ponderibus* (392), which is complete only in Syriac, deals with biblical place-names, measures, and weights.

The *De XII gemmis* is dedicated to Cyprian of Tyre. The work, sent to Jerome, has survived complete only in Georgian. It interprets the twelve precious stones in the breastplate of the high priest (Ex 28:17ff., 39.10ff.).

Four works of E. against images have come down: (a) a treatise against images, ca. 394; (b) a letter to Emperor Theodosius (ca. 394) that has come down only in fragments; (c) the likewise fragmentary testament of E. to his community (before 403); and (d) a fragmentary dogmatic letter.

In addition to the *Letter to the Arabs* in *haer.* 78.2-24, the following letters of E. have survived: (a) a letter to John Jerus. (preserved in Latin as *ep.* 51 of Jerome); (b) a letter to Jerome (preserved in Latin as *ep.* 91 of Jerome); (c) a letter to Eusebius, Marcellus, Vivianus, and Carpus on the date of Passover; and (d) fragments of letters in a Syr. translation.

Finally, some catena fragments of E. have come down

W: PG 41-43. — *Anc., haer.*, K. Holl, GCS 25, 31, 37, vols. 1-3 (Berlin, 1915-1933); J. Dummer, vols. 2-3 (Berlin, [2]1980, [2]1985). — *Anc.*, C. Riggi, L'àncora della fede (Rome, 1977). — J. Leipoldt, E.' "Ancoratus" in saidischer Übersetzung: BVSGW. PH 1902:136-171 [Coptic text]. — *haer.*, F. Williams, The Panarion of E., vol. 1 (Leiden, 1987); vols. 2-3 (Leiden, 1994) [English trans.]. — C. Riggi (Rome, 1967) [text/Italian trans./comm.]. — *De mensuris et ponderibus*, P. de Lagarde, Veteris Testamenti ab Origene recensiti fragmenta apud Syros (Göttingen, 1880) [Syriac text]. — J. E. Dean, E.'s Treatise on Weights and Measures (Chicago, 1935) [Syriac text]. — E. Moutsoulas: Theol(A) 41 (1970) 618-637; 42 (1971) 473-505; 43 (1972) 309-340, 631-670; 44 (1973) 157-209 [Greek frags.]. — idem, L'œuvre "De mensuris et ponderibus" d'E. (Athens, 1971) [Greek frags./comm.]). — M.-J. van Esbroeck, CSCO 460/461 (Leuven/Louvain, 1984) [Georgian text/French trans.]. — *De XII gemmis*, R. P. Blake, H. de Vis, E. de Gemmis (London, 1934) [Georgian text/Armenian frags./Coptic text]. — *Treatise against Images*, H. G. Thümmel, Die Frühgeschichte der ostkirchlichen Bilderlehre, TU 139 (Berlin, 1992), 298-299 [frgm.], 65-67 [German trans.]. — *Letter to Theodosius*, H. G. Thümmel, loc. cit., Nr. 37, 300-302 [frgm.], 67-68 [German trans.]. — *Testament*, H. G. Thümmel, loc. cit., Nr. 38, 302 [frgm.], 69 [German trans.]. — *Dogmatic Letter*, H. G. Thümmel, loc. cit., Nr. 36, 300 [frgm.], 68 [German trans.] — *Letter to John of Jerusalem*, I. Hilberg, CSEL 54:395-412. — P. Maas: BZ 30 (1929/30) 279-286 [Greek frags.]. — H. G. Thümmel, loc. cit., Nr. 34, 297 [frgm.]. 69 [German trans.]. — *Letter to Jerome*, CSEL 55:145-146. — *Letter about the Date of Easter*, K. Holl, Ein Bruchstück aus einem bisher unbekannten Brief des E.: idem, Gesammelte Aufsätze zur Kirchengeschichte 2 (Darmstadt, 1964 = Tübingen, 1928), 204-224. — *Letterfragments*, J. Lebon, Sur quelques fragments de lettres attribuées à E.: FS G. Mercati 1 (Rome, 1946), 145-174. — idem, Severi Antiocheni Liber contra impium Grammaticum, CSCO 102:235. — I. Rucker, Florilegium Edessenum: SBAW. PH 1933, 5, Nr. 52-56, 41-44.

L: P. J. Alexander, The Iconoclastic Council of St. Sophia (815) and Its Definition (Horos): DOP 7 (1953) 35-66. — A. Camplani, E. (Ancoratus) e Gregorio di Nazianzo (Epistulae) in copto: Aug. 35 (1995) 327-347. — E. A. Clark, The Origenist Controversy (Princeton, 1992). — H. Crouzel, Encore sur Divorce et remariage selon E.: VigChr 38 (1984) 271-280. — J. Dechow, Dogma and Mysticism in Early Christianity: E. and the Legacy of Origen (Macon, Ga., 1988). — G. Deeters, E.' de XII gemmis: ZDMG 90 (1936) 209-220. — J. Dummer, Die Angaben über die gnostische Lit. bei E., haer. 26: Koptologische Studien in der DDR (WZ [H] Sonderheft) (Halle, 1965), 191-219. — idem, E., Ancor. 102, 7 u. die Sapientia Salomonis: Klio 43-45 (1965) 344-350. — idem, Ein naturwissenschaftliches Handbuch als Quelle für E.: Klio 55 (1973) 289-299. — idem, E. u. Homer: Ph. 119 (1975) 84-91. — idem, Zur E.-Ausgabe der GCS: Texte u. Textkritik, ed. idem (Berlin, 1987), 119-125. — L. A. Eldridge, The Gospel Text of E. (Salt Lake City, 1969). — P. Fraenkel, Histoire sainte et hérésie chez E.: RThPh 12 (1962) 175-191. — idem, Une réédition du panarion d'E.: RThPh 19 (1969) 111-114. — W.-D. Hauschild, E.: LMA 3:2068. — B. Hemmerdinger, E. iconoclaste: StPatr 10 (1970) 118-120. — H. Hennephof, Textus byzantii ad iconomachiam pertinentes (Leiden, 1969). — K. Holl, Die handschriftliche Überlieferung des E. (Leipzig, 1910). — idem, Die Schriften des E. gegen die Bilderverehrung: idem, Gesammelte Aufsätze zur Kirchengeschichte (Darmstadt, 1964 = Tübingen, 1928),

2:351-387. — G. Jouassard, Deux chefs de file en théologie mariale dans la seconde moitié du IVᵉ s.: E. et S. Ambroise: Gr. 42 (1961) 5-36. — R. A. Lipsius, Zur Quellenkritik des E. (Vienna, 1865). — idem, Die Quellen der ältesten Ketzergeschichte neu untersucht (Leipzig, 1875). — E. Lucchesi, Un corpus épiphanien en copte: AnBoll 99 (1981) 95-100. — M. Mees, Die antihäretische Polemik des E. u. ihr Gebrauch von Jn 4: Aug. 22 (1982) 405-425. — idem, Textverständnis u. Varianten in Kap. 5 des Johannesevangeliums bei E.: Lat. 46 (1980) 250-284. — idem, Textformen u. Interpretation von Jn 6 bei E.: Aug. 21 (1981) 339-364. — E. Moutsoulas, Der Begriff "Häresie" bei E.: StPatr 7/1 (1966) 362-371. — idem, L'œuvre d'E. "De mensuris et ponderibus" et son unité littéraire: StPatr 12 (1975) 119-122. — idem, La tradition manuscrite de l'œuvre d'E. "De mensuris et ponderibus": Texte u. Textkritik, ed. J. Dummer (Berlin, 1987), 429-440. — P. Nautin, E.: DHGE 15:617-631. — idem, Divorce et remariage chez E.: VigChr 37 (1983) 157-173. — G. Ostrogorsky, Studien zur Geschichte des byz. Bilderstreites (Breslau, 1929). — A. Pourkier, L'hérésiologie chez E. (Paris, 1992). — U. Riedinger, Die E.-Paraphrase des Ps.-Kaisarios: Miscellanea Critica, hg. v. der Deutschen Akademie der Wissenschaften zu Berlin (Leipzig, 1964), 218-239. — C. Riggi, La figura di E. nel IV secolo: StPatr 8/2 (1966) 86-107. — idem, Il termine "Hairesis" nell'accezione di E.: Sal. 29 (1967) 3-27. — idem, E. contro Mani (Rome, 1967). — idem, E. divorzista?: Sal. 33 (1971) 599-666. — idem, Comprensione umana nella Bibbia secondo E. (Panarion LIX): FS Q. Cataudella (Catania, 1972), 607-635. — idem, Διαλογή come figura sententiae nel Panarion: Aug. 14 (1974) 549-558. — idem, Nouvelle lecture du Panarion LIX, 4 (E. et le divorce): StPatr 12/1 (1975) 129-134. — idem, Catechesi escatologica dell' "Ancoratus" di E.: Aug. 18 (1978) 163-171. — idem, Questioni cristologiche in E.: La cristologia nei Padri della Chiesa. Le due culture (Quaderno 2) (Rome, 1981), 63-70. — idem, Sangue e antropologia biblica in E.: Centro Studi sanguis Christi. 2: Atti della Settimana Sangue e Antropologia Biblica nella patristica (Ro 23-28. 11. 1981), 2 (Rome, 1982), 389-411. — idem, Il comportamento pastorale di S. Basilio e di E.: Basilio di Cesarea, la sua età, la sua opera e il Basilianiesimo in Sicilia, Atti del congresso internazionale (Messina, 3.-6. 12. 1979), 1 (Messina, 1983), 155-166. — idem, Catechesi sullo Spirito Santo in E.: Spirito Santo e catechesi patristica, ed. S. Felice (Rome, 1983), 59-73. — idem, Rapporto tra battesimo e penitenza nel IV secolo (E., Haer. 59): Catechesibattesimale e riconciliazione nei Padri del IV secolo, ed. idem (Rome, 1984), 81-93. — idem, La διαλογή des Marcelliens dans le Panarion, 72: StPatr 15 (1984) 368-373. — idem, La forma del corpo risorto secondo Metodio in E. (Haer. 64): Morte e immortalità nella catechesi dei Padri del III-IV secolo, ed. idem (Rome, 1985), 75-92. — idem, Différence semantique et théologique entre μεταμέλεια et μετάνοια en E., haer. 59: StPatr 18/1 (1986) 201-206. — idem, Origene et Origeniste secondo E. (Haer. 64): Aug. 26 (1986) 115-142. — M.-J. Rondeau, A propos d'une prophétie non canonique citée par E.: RSR 55 (1967) 209-216. — I. Rucker, E.' de XII gemmis: ThRv 34 (1935) 329-335. — W. Schneemelcher, E.: RAC 5:909-927. — B. Schultze, Das Filioque bei E.: OS 35 (1986) 105-134; 36 (1987) 281-300. — M. Tetz, Zwei De fide-Frgm. des E.: ThZ 11 (1955) 466-467. — H. G. Thümmel, Die bilderfeindlichen Schriften des E.: BySl 47 (1986) 169-188. — O. Viedebantt, Quaestiones Epiphaninianae metrologicae et criticae (Leipzig, 1911). — B. M. Weischer,

Die urspr. nikänische Form des ersten Glaubenssymbols im Ankyrôtos des E.: ThPh 53 (1978) 407-414.

W. W. Löhr

Epiphanius Scholasticus

E. lived in the middle of the 6th c. in Cassiodorus's *monasterium Vivariense* near Scyllaceum in Calabria and, at Cassiodorus's suggestion, translated Gr. works into Latin.

W: *Cassiodori-Epiphanii Historia Ecclesiastica Tripartita*, W. Jakob, R. Hanslik, CSEL 71. — *Philonis Carpasii Commentarium in Canticum Canticorum. Ex antiqua versione Epiphanii Scholastici*, A. Ceresa-Gastaldo (Turin, 1979). — F. Zoepel, Didymi Alexandrini in Epistolas canonicas brevis enarratio (Münster, 1914). — *Cod. encyclius in der Collectio Sangermanensis*, ACO 2, 5, 9-98.
L: F. Brunhölzl, Geschichte der lat. Lit. des MA (Munich, 1975), 1:41f., 511f. — V. Bulhart, Zur Historia tripartita: ALMA 24 (1954) 5-17. — D. M. Cappuyns, E.: DHGE 15:631f. — R. Hanslik, Apollo Pythius Azizus u. sein Kult: VigChr (1954) 176-181. — idem, Epiphanius Scholasticus o. Cassiodor? Zur Historia ecclesiastica tripartita: Ph. 115 (1971) 107-113. — W. Jacob, Die handschriftliche Überlieferung der sog. Historia tripartita des Epiphanius-Cassiodor (Berlin, 1954). — S. Lundström, Sprachliche Bemerkungen zur Historia tripartita des Cassiodor: ALMA 23 (1953) 19-34. — A. Siegmund, Die Überlieferung der griech. chr. Lit. in der lat. Kirche bis zum 12. Jh. (Munich, 1949). — F. Weissengruber, Epiphanius Scholasticus als Übersetzer (Vienna, 1972).

W. A. Löhr

Epistula apostolorum

The *Ep. ap.* is a pseudo-apostolic circular letter of the second half of the 2nd c.; originally composed in Greek, it has survived complete in Ethiopic, partially in Coptic, and in smaller sections in Latin. The text claims to be a letter from the college of apostles, who are named, to the churches in the four regions of the world. It stresses the place of Christ as God and Son of God, goes into the incarnation, and emphasizes the miracles done by the redeemer as a boy (to match the infancy gospels). Although not entirely free of gnostic motifs, the *Ep. ap.* with its emphasis on the material reality of Christ's sufferings (9-12) and his bodily resurrection (16-30) is in fact antignostic. In its Logos christology, which suggests Asia Minor as a possible place of origin of the *Ep. ap.*, the oneness of the revelation of Son and Father is so overemphasized that no room is left for the real distinction of persons in the Trinity. For the history of dogma the section on the descent of Christ to the netherworld (27) is important, as is an early short creed (5). The description of the *agapē* and Eucharist on the night of Passover bears witness to Quartodeciman practice and again points to Asia Minor.

W: L. Guerrier, S. Grébaut, PO 9/3 [Ethiopic text/French trans.]. — C. Schmidt, I. Wajnberg, Gespräche Jesu (Hildesheim, 1967 = Leipzig, 1919) [Coptic text/German trans./comm.]. — H. Duensing, Ep. ap. (Bonn, 1925) [German trans.]. — NTApo⁶ 1:205-233 [German trans.].
L: H. Duensing, Besprechung: GGA 184 (1922) 241-252. — A. A. T. Ehrhardt, Judaeo-Christians, TU 88 (Berlin, 1964), 360-382. — M. Hornschuh, Studien zur E. a. (Berlin, 1965). — C. Schmidt, Rez.: OLZ 28 (1925) 855-859. — R. Staats, Törichte Jungfrauen: W. Eltester, Christentum u. Gnosis (Berlin, 1969), 98-115. — idem, Ogdoas als Symbol der Auferstehung: VigChr 26 (1972) 29-52.

P. BRUNS

Epistula de patria

The so-called *Epistula de patria ad Polychronium* is a letter whose authors are various clerics, among them a Francus, a Paul, and a Malerian, who are evidently in exile, perhaps because of the penetration of the German tribes into the West. They address their letter to a certain Polychronius, their bishop, who is also in exile. The writers thank Polychronius for intervening on their behalf with a Bishop Castor, who as a result has assigned them a place of refuge; they invite Polychronius to visit them at Easter and thus console them. The historical setting of the letter and the identity of the persons are uncertain. Polychronius was possibly a bishop of Verdun, and Castor a bishop of Chartres, and the letter may be from the second half of the 5th c. In addition, ca. 407 and the 6th c. have been suggested as times of writing.

W: G. Morin, Castor et Polychronius: RBen 51 (1939) 31f. [text]. — PLS 3:831f. = C. Turner, Chapters in the History of Latin MSS: JThS 30 (1929) 227-229 [text].
L: P. Courcelle, Histoire littéraire des grandes invasions (Paris, ³1964), 64 n. 1. — G. Morin, loc. cit., 31-36. — Repertorium fontium historiae medii aevi 4 (Rome, 1976), 353. — C. Turner, loc. cit.

B. WINDAU

Epistulae Austrasicae

The *Epistulae Austrasicae* is a collection of forty-eight letters written between 460 and 590 and collected, probably in Metz, shortly thereafter. The authors of the individual letters were important Franks, among them rulers and bishops (among these Germanus of Paris, Remigius of Rheims, Theodebald, Theodebert). Apart from a few on political subjects, the letters serve to ensure mutual friendship and esteem and are thus in the tradition of earlier epistolary literature. At the same time, however, most of the letters

are also of historical importance. It is possible that the compiler wanted to make a collection of models for the most varied occasions.

W: W. Gundlach, CCL 117:403-470 = MGH. Ep. 3:110-153.
L: A. Di Berardino (ed.), Patrologia 4 (Genoa, 1996), 314f. — P. Goubert, Chronologie des lettres austrasienne: Mélanges d'histoire du Moyen Âge L. Halphen (Paris, 1951), 291-295. — I. N. Wood, Letters and Letter Collections: The Culture of Christendom, ed. M. A. Mayer (London, 1993), 29-43

B. WINDAU

Epitaph

Epitaphs are either literary or monumental funerary inscriptions (often metrical). Among the former are, e.g., the *titulus* in → Jerome's *ep.* 108.33 (CSEL 55:350), that is, the hexametric *Epitaphium Paulae viduae*, which he composed for her tombstone after her death in 404. In it we learn (in the form of a unique *laudatio* of her descent and family) of, e.g., her daughter Eustochium, who had come to Bethlehem with her mother and Jerome, in order to govern the monastery founded there by her wealth.

To the same genre belong the epitaphs attributed to → Gregory Naz. (*AP* 8, H. Beckby 2:448-469), which also provide insight into the liturgy of the 4th c.; thirty-five epitaphs of → Ausonius (MGH. AA 5/2.72-80), and an epitaph of → Venantius Fortunatus (*carm.* 4, M. Reydellet, 129-163).

The epitaphs of → Damasus of Rome (366-384) (A. Ferrua, *Epigrammata Damasiana* [Rome, 1942]) have come down to us in both literary and monumental form, e.g., the poem of praise in the papal crypt of the catacombs of Callistus in Rome (*epigr.* 16 = ILCV 1986 – ICVR 4.9513).

Among the monumental epitaphs special mention must be made of the twenty-two-hexameter funerary inscription of Abercius. It consists of two pieces found at Hierapolis near Synada in Phrygian Asia Minor and displayed today in the Vatican's Museo Pio Christiano. It was composed during the lifetime of Abercius himself: he describes himself as disciple of a holy shepherd (= Christ), who, with wide-open eyes feeds his sheep and provides them with reliable knowledge (= scripture). Abercius was sent by Christ to Rome to see a kingdom, a queen in golden robes and golden shoes (= the Chr. church), and a people with a shining seal (= baptism); but he also went to Syria and Nisibis on the Euphrates. Everywhere he found brethren in the faith, and he had Paul (probably his writings) in his coach. Pistis (faith) went before him and gave him as food a great fish (=

Christ) which a pure virgin (= Mary) had caught in a great, pure well, that is, in mixed wine and bread. The author of the epitaph was probably Bishop Abercius of Hierapolis, since the text just paraphrased is found in his life by Simeon Metaphrastes (AASS Oct. 9, 485ff.). Since the text is also cited in the funerary inscription of an Alexander, datable to 216 and likewise discovered in Hierapolis, it may have originated before that date and may be the oldest Chr. monument; this explains the language, which is still heavily indebted to the pagan tradition. And yet practically the entire theology of the church at that time is set forth in these mysterious symbols.

No less important information is given in the epitaph of Pectorius of Autun (the ancient Augustodunum in Gaul) (W. Wischmeyer). It was composed, again in Greek, probably in the late 4th c. From a purely formal viewpoint, the first six verses (distichs) make a unified whole that is further consolidated by the → acrosticon, i.e., the first letter of the first five lines form the word *Ichthys* (ΙΧΘΥΣ). As a result, "immortal source" can only mean baptism and "Savior of the saints" can only mean Christ, who puts in people's hands the "honeysweet food," i.e., the Eucharist, which is again described as a fish. The language of the entire inscription is very symbolic, but it confirms the existence of communion in the hand, which is documented by Cyprian (*de lapsis* 22) and others from the mid-3rd c. on, that is, the giving of communion into the hands of the laity; a short time later, this is described in detail in Cyril Jerus., *catech. myst.* 5.21.

Of equal interest is the epitaph, in five distichs, for Turtura, who was buried *ad sanctos* (= ICVR 6018 = ILCV 2142 = CLE 2103); it appears on her probably 6th c. tomb with its magnificent fresco in the catacomb of Commodilla in Rome. In the picture an elderly woman (Turtura), who carries in her hands a scripture scroll in a white cloth, is led by the holy martyr Adauctus—and by Felix on the other side— to Christ at the center, where he is enthroned on the breast of the Mother of God. This "iconographic portrait" is matched by a moral portrait in the epitaph in two columns which Turtura's son placed there. The epitaph begins with a reflection on her name (Turtura = turtle dove) and the appropriateness of its meaning for her. But special emphasis is placed on her marital fidelity after the death of her husband, since she lived for thirty-six years as a widow.

Much less private in character is the (again metrical) funerary epitaph for deacon Severus, which is again in the catacomb of Callistus in Rome (ICVR n.s. 4.10183) and is chiseled into a marble shutter. It informs us that Severus had adorned the double chamber with arched recesses and an air shaft at the order of *PP Marcellini*. It is thus the earliest witness to the Roman bishop's title of pope and must belong to the period of office of Marcellinus (June 30, 296, to Oct. 25, 304). In addition, it attests to the administration of the catacombs by the bishop of Rome and to faith in the resurrection of the flesh, for it says that little Severa, the deacon's daughter, also rests in the tomb until the Lord shall awaken her and join her soul again to her body in spiritual glory.

In summary, it can be said that, as the few examples given show, the most important function of even the Chr. epitaph was the *laudatio*, i.e., the list of virtues, in order that these might be remembered in later time; as a result, they are an inexhaustible source for the history of the culture and ideas of their time.

L: F. J. Dölger, ΙΧΘΥΣ. Das Fischsymbol in frühchr. Zeit 3 (Münster, 1922). — H. Donner, St. Sophronius Eusebius Hieronymus. Die Pilgerfahrt der röm. Patrizierin Paula: FS G. Besch (Bremen, 1974), 20-47. — M. Guarducci, Epigrafia greca 4 (Rome, 1978), 487-494 (literature). — HLL 4:231-234. — D. Pikhaus, Portrait d'une mère par son fils. À propos de l'épitaphe de Turtura (ICVR 6018 = ILCV 2142 = CLE 2103): Studia varia bruxellensia ad orbem graecolatinum pertinentia 2 (Brussels, 1990), 153-176 (literature). — A. Quacquarelli, Morte e vita eterna negli epitaffi di Gregorio Nazianzeno: Gregorio Nazianzeno teologo e scrittore, ed. C. Moreschini, G. Menestrina (Trent, 1992), 27-42. — W. K. Wischmeyer, Die Aberkiosinschrift als Grabepigramm: JAC 23 (1980) 22-47.

R. PILLINGER

Epitome

An epitome (Lat. *breviatio, breviarium*) serves to reproduce a lengthy and in the broadest sense didactic work in a short form and so meet readers' need of information in a concise form. Depending on the author and subject, the shortening may range in kind from verbatim excerpts to a report or review in any language desired. What is omitted from the original is chiefly direct speeches, repetitions, examples, and difficult proofs; for material or linguistic reasons additions are occasionally found. The subject areas of ancient epitomes of a clearly Chr. character are limited chiefly to history (e.g., Heliconius of Byzantium, → Sozomen [both lost], → Prosper Tiro of Aquitania [*chron.*], → Jordanes [*epi.*]) and to theology (e.g., → Lactantius [*epit.*]. → [Ps.?-] Epiphanius of Salamis [*anac.*], → Eucherius of Lyons [on the *Collationes* of John Cassian; lost], and an anonymous, difficult-to-date epitome of the Pseudo-Clementine

Homilies, which was itself epitomized in turn). In addition, in late antiquity epitomes were made chiefly of medical, grammatical, and legal works (epitomes of the *Novellae* of Justinian were popular).

L: M. Fuhrmann, Das systematische Lehrbuch (Göttingen, 1960). — M. Galdi, L'E. nella letteratura latina (Naples, 1922). — I. Opelt, E.: RAC 5:944-973.

D. WEBER

Eraclius of Hippo

As a young man E. became a member of Augustine's community (Augustine, *s.* 356.7; PL 39:1577) and, before Easter of 425, a deacon. In this office he took care of the *memoria* of St. Stephen and did caritative work in Hippo. On Sept. 26, 426, he was ordained a priest and took on further tasks (among them, preaching) to relieve Augustine. Of this pastoral activity two sermons have survived which display great veneration of Augustine and show E. to have been a modest priest.

W: P. Verbraken, Les deux sermons du prêtre Eraclius d'Hippone: RBen 71 (1961) 3-21 [text].
L: PAC 357f.

W. GEERLINGS

Erechtius of Antioch in Pisidia

E., bishop of Antioch in Pisidia, has left only a fragment of a homily on Epiphany (*theoph.*; also in Syriac and Armenian), which he preached in Constantinople in the time of Patriarch Proclus (434-464) and which is cited by Timothy Aelurus. In addition, there is a Syr. homily on the birth of Christ (*nat.*) that is marked by Monophysitism or was used by the Monophysites as an argument against the doctrine of the two natures.

W: *theoph.*, PG 86/2:3321f. — *nat.*, F. Nau, PO 13:169-180 [Syriac text/French trans.].
L: A. van Roey, E.: DHGE 15:693

G. RÖWEKAMP

Ethelbert

E., born ca. 552, was king of Kent (560/565). Under the influence of his Chr. wife he gave a friendly reception to the missionaries sent in 597 by Gregory the Great and allowed them free missionary activity. Finally, after 597 (perhaps ca. 601) he himself was baptized by Augustine of Canterbury, built a number of churches, and promoted the establishment of bishoprics. After his baptism, this first Chr. king of

England (saint's feast: Feb. 24/25) published the first criminal code in England (*Praeceptiones*), which also contains directives meant to protect the church and the clergy. The attribution to E. of the *Donationes ad diversas ecclesias* is uncertain.

W: *praeceptiones*, F. Liebermann, Die Gesetze der Angelsachsen 1 (Aalen, 1960 = Halle, 1903), 3-8 [text/German trans.]. — PL 80:345-354. — D. Whitelock, English Historical Documents 1 (London, 1955), 357-359 [English trans. 1-90]. — *donationes*, PL 80:341-346.
L: E. Demougeot, Grégoire le Grand: Grégoire le Grand, ed. J. Fontaine (Paris, 1986), 191-203. — H. Dauphin, E.: DHGE 15:1156-1158. — N. Del Re, E.: BSS 5:116-118. — K. Schäferdieck, Die Grundlegung der angelsächsischen Kirche: KGMG 2/1:149-191, here 151-162.

B. WINDAU

Eubulus of Lystra

E. is regarded as the author of a treatise against the Severian bishop → Athanasius I Camelarius (d. 630/631); only two rather small fragments have come down in the *Doctrina Patrum*.

W: F. Diekamp, Doctrina Patrum (Münster, 1907), 141-148 [text].

P. BRUNS

Eucherius, Comes

Comes Eucherius (or Euclerius; E.) is reckoned among the Roman nobility of the 4th c. The attribution to him of a poem in ten hexameters is not justified; the work is more probably medieval (15th c.?). The content proves the author to have been a jurist. He asks for the intellectual illumination needed to grasp the mysteries of the law and coins a lapidary answer: *inter nebulas legum dignoscere causas*. It is unusual to find in a Chr. jurist this kind of concern to become immersed in the mass of laws that had come down from the Roman tradition, a concern that ultimately leads to a call for divine help in avoiding error. Thus the poem has more the character of a prayer.

W: PLS 1:779. — F. Bücheler, A. Riese (ed.), Anthologia Latina 1/2 (Leipzig, 1906), 268 Nr. 789.
L: M. Manitius, Geschichte der chr. lat. Poesie (Stuttgart, 1891), 317.

C. KASPER

Eucherius of Lyons

I. Life: Born ca. 380 of a senatorial family, in ca. 410 he and his family joined the community of ascetics at

Lérins. He left his sons Salonius and Veranus to be educated by Honoratus and Hilary and, later, after their appointments as bishop of Arles, to Vincent and Salvian. He himself, with his wife Galla (see Paulinus of Nola, *ep.* 3) and his daughters (Consortia and Tullia), withdrew to the nearby island of St. Marguerite (Lero). He was in contact with Rusticus, Apollinaris Sidonius, and Cassian, who dedicated the second part of his *Conlationes* to him. Before 441 (when he was a signatory of the first Synod of Orange) E. became bishop (metropolitan) of Lyons (probably 434). He died ca. 450 (Gennadius, *vir. ill.* 64; *Chronica Gallica* 134; Marcellinus: 456).

II. Works: 1. *Exegetical writings*: (a) *Instructionum ad Salonium libri duo* (*instr.*, after 428). A first book, following Jerome, Augustine, Ambrose, and Cassian, deals, among other things, with difficult questions in scripture; the second deals with ideas and objects in bibl. history, but it also explains expressions used in church life in the manner of an encyclopedia and a foreign language dictionary. (b) The *Liber formularum spiritualis intellegentiae* (*form.*) attempts (following Cassian, *conl.* 14) a metaphorical explanation of bibl. concepts acc. to the fourfold meaning; but in this ten-part work, organized acc. to areas, this exegesis is not carried through to the end. Both works provide information on the library and bibl. versions used at Lérins; in addition, they give us an idea of E.'s knowledge of Greek and Hebrew, and, since they are compendia, of efforts made by the monastic community on the island to conduct a school.

2. *Ascetical writings*: (a) *De laude eremi* (*laud. her.*) addressed to Hilary of Arles on the occasion of the latter's return from Arles, where he had followed Honoratus for his consecration as bishop. In this work, E. praises the outstanding worth of the *eremus*; a life of asceticism (i.e., on the island) is for E. the most successful form of following Christ and a guarantee of closeness to God. At the end, he describes in vivid colors the place, life, and community of Lérins; in the process, the real world slips completely into the background and does not make an appearance even as a contrast. This is the only work of E. known to Isidore of Seville (*vir. ill.* 28). (b) *De contemptu mundi et saecularis philosophiae* (*cont.*), 432 (1185 years after the foundation of Rome), is addressed to a relative, Valerian (Priscus, prefect of Gaul and relative of Emperor Avitus?). E. urges him to turn more energetically to God and to care for his soul. To this end, Valerian ought to turn his back on the world and seek security (probably not only religious but also physical and moral) on the island of Lérins. This letter shows clearly the resignation and uncertainty

of the aristocrat who, in contrast to Salvian, can see in the forcible entry of the Germans only a general decline and loss of values, which the letter describes in richly imaged language. There are fragments of letters of E. in the *Vita Honorati* (ch. 22) by → Hilary, and in the *Vita Hilarii* (ch. 7) by → Hilary of Marseilles (or Ravennius, Reverentius).

3. The *Passio Acaunensium martyrum* (*pass. Acaun.*), a report on the martyrdom of the Theban Legion, was written by E. when already a bishop, for Silvius. The work shows the changed political-religious understanding of late antiquity. Here, in comparison with older presentations, martyrdom has a new basis: it is not the refusal of all military service by Christians that leads to their being killed; acc. to E., officers are ready to obey the emperor but not kill their brothers in the faith.

All these writings, which were treasured down to modern times for their brevity (exegetical works) and their linguistic appeal (ascetical works) show the theol. involvement that was characteristic of the island monks. The confession of the martyrs echoes an old creed of southern Gaul (of interest for the orthodox doctrine of the Trinity); espec. in the exegetical works there are the first references to an explicit Semipelagianism with a Lérins stamp.

4. Lost are excerpts from the *conl.* of Cassian (Gennadius, *vir. ill.* 64), as is a treatise on the true philosophy (see PL 50:724B).

The *Epitome operum Cassiani*, the *Exhortatio*, and the *Sententia ad monachos* (PL 50:865-68, 1207-10) are not authentic. The homilies attributed to him are not his and are now contained in the collection of → Eusebius Gallicanus. Probably not E.'s is *De situ Hierosolimae vel Juda* (*sit.*), a kind of regional study of Palestine, which makes use espec. of Jerome and Flavius Josephus and was composed between the middle of the 5th and the middle of the 7th c.

W: *instr., form., laud. her., ep.*, C. Wotke, CSEL 31. — *pass. Acaun.*, B. Krusch, MGH. SRM 3:20-42. — *laus, cont., form. praef.*, C. L. Cristiani, Du mépris du monde (Paris, 1959) [French trans./comm.]. — *laus*, S. Pricoco (Catania, 1965). — *instr.*, G. Maioli: ECarm 30 (1979) 481-485; 32 (1981) 445-520. — *cont.*, S. Pricoco (Florence, 1990) [text/Italian trans./comm.]. — *sit.*, J. Fraipont, CCL 175:235-243.
L: L. Alfonsi, Il De laude eremi: Conv. 36 (1968) 361-369. — D. van Berchem, Le martyre de la légion Thébaine (Basel, 1956). — P. Courcelle, Nouveaux aspects de la culture lérinienne: REL 46 (1968) 379-409. — C. Curti, Passio Acaunensium martyrum: Convivium Dominicum (Catania, 1959), 297-327. — F. Diekamp, Epitome operum Cassiani: RQ 14 (1900) 341-355. — L. Dupraz, Les Passions de S. Maurice d'Agaune (Fribourg, Switzerland, 1961). — C. Honselmann, Bruchstücke von Auszügen aus den Werken Cassians: TG 51 (1961) 300-304. — C. M. Kasper, Theologie u. Askese (Münster, 1991). — idem, Monastischer

Lebensentwurf: RBS 18 (1994) 129-144. — G. de Montauzan, E. et l'école de Lérins: BHDL (1923) 81-96. — R. Nouailhat, Les premiers moines de Lérins (Paris, 1988). — T. O'Loughlin, The Symbol Gives Life: Scriptural Interpretation in the Fathers, ed. T. Finan (Cambridge, 1995), 221-252. — I. Opelt, Quellenstudien: Hermes 91 (1963) 476-483. — eadem, Literarische Eigenart: VigChr 22 (1968) 198-208. — G. M. Pintus, E. nella cronologia di Gennadio e Marcellino: StMed 25 (1984) 795-812. — S. Pricoco, Per una nuova edizione del De contemptu mundi (Turin, 1969). — idem, Teologia politica: Romano-Barbarica 2 (1977) 209-229. — idem, L'isola dei Santi (Rome, 1978). — idem, E.: un padre della Chiesa tra Erasmo e Tillemont: SSR 6 (1982) 323-334. — L. R. Wicham, E.: TRE 10:522-525.

C. KASPER

Euchologion ('Εὐχολόγιον)

1. With reference to the early church, euchologion is understood as a collection of various prayers (with or without some rubrics), perhaps in the form of *libelli* (= small codices containing liturgical formularies, espec. for priests in the Roman titular churches) or similar to western → sacramentaries or also as special material in → church orders. The oldest euchologia or fragments with euchological content are from Egypt (= Alexandrian liturgical family).

(a) From the Egyptian hinterland of Alexandria comes the euchologion handed down under the name of monk-bishop → Serapion of Thmuis (d. after 362); it contains thirty texts for Mass (anaphora with *Sanctus* but without *Benedictus*), Chr. initiation, ordinations, blessings, anointing of the sick, and liturgy of the dead. But this collection of prayers (Athos, ms. *Lavra* 149; 11th c.) has been revised along Arian or Pneumatomachian lines; this probably led to structural changes in, e.g., the anaphora (e.g., placing of the anaphoral intercessions after the second [Logos] epiclesis).

(b) For the sacramental liturgy we also have remains of an Alexandrian euchologion of the 5th c., contained in the special material of the Eth. recension of the so-called → *Traditio apostolica*; it contains a complete formulary for baptism, as well as formulas (and rubrics) for Mass. The presence of euchological material is probably also to be assumed in Arab. recension B (*Vat. Borg. ar.* 22) of the → *Testament of Our Lord Jesus Christ* and in parts of books 7 and 8 of the → *Apostolic Constitutions* (*Const. App.* 7.39-45; 8.29 and 35-41).

(c) The Dēr-Balyzeh papyrus (*Bodl. Gr. lit. d* 2-4 [P]; 6th-7th c.), which was discovered in 1907 in the ruins of the monastery of Apa Apollon (south of Assiut) and is preserved at Oxford, consists of fragments of three sheets and gives fragments of a

euchologion, espec. a part of the Gr. anaphora and a short confession of faith.

(d) A series of early euchological fragments from the Alexandrian Anaphora of Mark, which goes back to the 4th c., has been preserved in papyri *P. Straub. inv. gr.* 254 (4th/5th c.; Strasbourg), *P. Ryl.* 465 (6th c.; Manchester), *P. Lond. Lit.* 232 (6th/7th c.; London), and ostracon *O. Hall pl.* 12.2 (7th/8th c.; London).

(e) Further liturg. witnesses are constantly being found in papyri discoveries that give examples of the multiplicity of euchologia used at one time in the patriarchate of Alexandria. Among the oldest liturg. papyri with euchological content is *P. Würzb.* 3 (end of 3rd c.), with intercessions from the pre-Constantinian period; papyrus codex *P. Barc. inv.* 154b-157b (4th c.; Barcelona), which perhaps comes from the monastery of Pachomius and contains Gr. and Lat. texts of pagan and Chr. origin, as well as prayers for the Mass and the liturgy of the sick. The anaphora of this last codex has been identified as a Gr. version of Copt. euchological fragment *Coptica Lovan.* 27 (ca. 600). Berlin papyrus *P. Berol. inv.* 13918, written in the 5th c. and containing liturg. texts likewise provides euchological material not known from other sources (prayers after the communion of the faithful).

2. At a later period a euchologion was understood to be a comprehensive liturg. book (espec. in the Byz. and Copt. rites) with to some extent detailed rubrics for the presider at the celebration of the Eucharist, the sacraments, and blessings, and therefore comparable to the *Pontificale Romano-Germanicum* (*PRG*; ca. 950). An impression of the riches of the southern Egyptian euchologion can be gotten from the Sahidic *Great E. of the White Monastery* (11th/12th c.).

L: H. Brakmann, Neue Funde u. Forschungen: Actes du IVᵉ Congrès Copte, ed. M. Rassart (Leuven/Louvain, 1992), esp. 419-427. — A. Stuiber, Libelli Sacramentorum Romani (Bonn, 1950). — on 1. a: B. Botte, L'Eucologe de Sérapion: OrChr 48 (1964) 50-56. — B. Capelle, L'anaphore de Sérapion: Muséon 59 (1946) 425-443. — G. J. Cuming, Thmuis Revisited: TS 41 (1980) 568-575. — K. Gamber, Serapion-Anaphora: OS 16 (1967) 33-42. — M. E. Johnson, Prayers of Sarapion of Thmuis (Rome, 1995) [Greek text/English trans./comm.]. — on 1. b: H. Duensing, Der Ethiopic Text der Kirchenordnung des Hippolyt (Göttingen, 1946), 25-31, 81-127. — G. Kretschmar, Beiträge zur Geschichte der Liturgie: JLH 8 (1963) esp. 1-10, 28-30. — A. Baumstark, Ägyptische Meß- u. Taufliturgie: OrChr 1 (1901) 1-45. — R.-G. Coquin, Le Test. Dom.: ParOr 5 (1974) 165-188. — on 1. c: A. Bugnini, L'eucologio di Dêr-Balizeh: EL 65 (1951) 157-170 [Latin trans.]. — K. Gamber, Eucharistiegebet: OS 7 (1958) 48-65. — J. van Haelst, Nouvelle reconstitution: EThL 45 (1969) 444-455 [Greek text]. — C. H. Roberts, B. Capelle, An Early Euchologium (Leuven/Louvain, 1949) [Greek text/comm.]. — **on 1. d**: H. Brakmann, Bedeutung des Sinaiticus gr. 2148: JÖB 30 (1980) 240 n. 1 [literature to the editions]. — **on 1. e**: H. Brakmann, Berliner Pap. 13918: OS 36 (1987) 31-38. — K. Gamber, Teile einer Anaphora: OS 34 (1985) 178-182. — M. Krause, Ägypten II: RAC Suppl. 1:74f. (P. Barc.). — L. T. Lefort, Coptica Lovaniensia: Muséon 53 (1940) 1-66. — R. Roca-Puig, Anàfora de Barcelona (Basel, ²1996 (P. Barc.). — P. J. Sijpesteijn, K. Treu: ZPE 72 (1988) 67f. (P. Würzb.). — **on 2**: Cod. Vat. Barb. gr. 336, S. Parenti-E. Velkovska, BEL S 80 (Rome, 1995) [Greek text]. — Großes E., E. Lanne, PO 28/2 [Coptic text/French trans.].

H.-J. FEULNER

Eudocia

E. was the daughter of a pagan orator from Athens and was named Athenais until her baptism and marriage to Emperor Theodosius II (421). After the birth of a daughter, and with the rank of Augusta, she traveled to Jerusalem, where she settled after her divorce (440/443). There she built a church for the bones of Stephen, discovered in 415, and was partly responsible for the extension of the city through the walls named for her. Although she initially supported the Monophysites (despite Leo I's *ep.* 123 to her), a meeting with Simeon Stylites caused her to accept Chalcedon. She died in 460; beginning in the 6th/7th c. her life story was made into novels (e.g., by John Malalas and in the *Chronicon paschale*.).

E. was the first Byz. empress to be a writer. Large sections are preserved of her poem on the martyrdom of St. Cyprian, as is a Homeric cento (→ Cento) on NT themes. This latter work, begun and later revised by a Bishop Patricius, is an important witness to the search for a "Chr. Homer." Some verses have survived of *Laudes Antiochiae* (Soc., *h.e.* 1.20) and *Metaphrasis Octateuchi* (Photius, *cod.* 183), the latter a witness to a program of Chr. bibl. poetry that went further than in, e.g., Nonnus. E.'s early work on the victory over the Persians (Soc., *h.e.* 7.21) is lost.

W: A. Ludwich, Eudociae, Procli, L. Claudiani carminum graecorum reliquiae (Leipzig, 1897), 13-114 [text].
L: A. M. Alfieri, La tecnica compositiva: Sileno 14 (1988) 137-156. — H. G. Beck, E.: RAC 6:844-847. — A. Cameron, The Empress and the Poet: YCS 27 (1982) 217-289. — F. Gregorovius, Athenais (Leipzig, 1882). — K. Holum, Theodosian Empresses (Berkeley, 1982). — O. Seeck, E.: PRE 6:906-912.

G. RÖWEKAMP

Eudoxius of Constantinople

E., born ca. 300, was from Little Armenia and was one of the most important Arian bishops of the 4th c.

His education in Antioch was probably influenced by Lucian, as was that of Arius. E. became bishop of Germanicia (Commagene) after the Nicene bishop of Antioch had been driven out (Athanasius, *h. Ar.* 4). In 342/343 he took part in the Synod of Sardica and belonged to the delegation of eastern bishops who, in Milan in 344, presented their faith with the aid of the *Ekthesis makrostichos* (Athanasius, *syn.* 20). In 357/358 he succeeded Leontius as bishop of Antioch. In this role he spread the radically Arian, anomoean second formula of Sirmium. Attacked by the homoiousians around Basil of Ancyra, he was suspended by Emperor Constantius II but rehabilitated in 359 by the Synod of Seleucia and in 360 became bishop of Constantinople. He pulled back from the radical Arian position and broke with the anomoeans around Aetius. Because of his influence on Emperor Valens, whom he baptized in 366, he was able to guide the emperor's policy in favor of the Arians, as well as in the christianization of the Germans. He was regarded as a splendid preacher (Soz., *h.e.* 4.26.1).

Sozomen (*h.e.* 3.14.2) also considers E. one of the most important theologians and writers of his time; only a fragment of an address on the incarnation (*fr.*) has survived; its Logos/Sarx christology is very close to that of Apollinaris of Laodicea. Fragments of a commentary on Dan cannot be denied him with certainty.

W: *fr.*, F. Diekamp, Doctrina Patrum (Münster, 1981 = 1907), 64f. [text].
L: H. C. Brennecke, Studien zur Geschichte der Homöer (Tübingen, 1988). — A. Grillmeier, Jesus der Christus 1 (Freiburg i.Br., 1979), 380f. (English, Christ in Christian Tradition, vol. 1 [London, ²1975]). — M. Spanneut, E.: DHGE 15:1337-1340. — M. Tetz, E.-Frgm.: StPatr 3 (1961) 314-323.

K. METZLER

Eugene of Ancyra

E., a deacon of Ancyra in the 4th c., was a supporter of Marcellus of Ancyra. He was spokesman of an embassy sent to Athanasius to convince him of the orthodoxy of the Marcellians; the mission was successful. To this end, E., who with the embassy probably arrived at the time of a meeting of bishops in Egypt in the summer/fall of 371, handed Athanasius a profession of faith (*Expositio fidei ad Athanasium pro causa Marcelli Ancyrani*; *exp. fid.*). In it E. distinguished the Marcellians from Arianism, Sabellianism, Paulianism, and the Pneumatomachian heresy and defended them against objections from the

Apollinarists. The *exp. fid.*, which resembles a christological florilegium, is indirect evidence of the theological views of the elderly Marcellus.

W: M. Tetz, Markellianer u. Athanasios: ZNW 64 (1973) 78-84 [text].
L: A. Grillmeier, Jesus der Christus 2/1 (Freiburg i.Br., 1986), 58f. (English, Christ in Christian Tradition, vol. 2/1 [London, 1987]). — M. Tetz, loc. cit., 75-121.

B. WINDAU

Eugene of Carthage

E. was elected in 480/481 to occupy the see of Carthage, which had been vacant for twenty-four years since the death of Deogratias in 456/457. Although Vandal King Huneric had agreed with the election, he banished E. in 484 to Turris Tamalleni(?) in Africa during a persecution of Catholics. In 487 he was summoned back by Gunthamund, Huneric's successor, but ca. 498 was again banished, this time to Gaul, by Gunthamund's successor, Thrasamund. He died in 505 near Albi.

On the occasion of a meeting of all the Cath. bishops of Africa, a *Liber fidei catholicae* was composed in which E. collaborated and for which he was responsible. The work was handed on in → Victor of Vita and shows a knowledge of the → *Consultationes Zacchaei et Apollonii* as well as of the *Competentibus ad baptismum instructionis libelli* of → Nicetas of Remesiana. It stresses the unity of Father and Son against the Arians. When E. was banished in 484, he exhorted his faithful, in an *Epistola ad cives suos pro custodienda catholica* (transmitted by Gregory of Tours, *Franc.* 2.3), to remain loyal to the Cath. faith. Acc. to Gennadius (*vir. ill.* 98), E. composed a number of letters, as well as polemical works against the Arians, and petitions and defenses addressed to Huneric; these are lost. It is possible that behind the petition to Huneric in → Victor of Vita, *Hist.* 2.41-42, there is a draft by E., which Victor then worked up.

W: *liber fidei catholicae*, Victor v. Vita, *Hist.* 2.56-101. — *ep. ad cives suos*, Gregor v. Tours, *Franc.* 2.3.
L: PAC 362-365.

W. GEERLINGS

Eugene II of Toledo

E., born of a noble family, was a cleric of the church at the court of Toledo; in 640 he withdrew to Saragossa, where he served as a monk and as archdeacon under Bishop → Braulio (Ildefonsus, *vir.*

ill. 14). In 646 King Chindasvinth appointed him archbishop of Toledo. E. introduced order into the liturgy and liturgical chant. He played a leading role at councils 7-10 of Toledo (646, 653, 655, 656) and presided at the last two before his death in 657. He had a thorough knowledge of theology and ancient poetry. His volume of prose writings (among them, *De sancta Trinitate*) is lost. Apart from his poetry only fragments of three letters (*ep.*) and texts in conciliar acts have survived. At the suggestion of Chindasvinth, E. edited the *De laudibus Dei* and the *Satisfactio* of → Dracontius. E. put together a collection of his own poems (*carm.*), with a preface. The collection contains minor verse in widely varying forms and content, e.g., epitaphs, *tituli*, epigrams. His versification shows a skilled and independent artist. There is disagreement over whether E. wrote purely quantitative verse or accentual as well.

W: *carm./ep.*, F. Vollmer, MGH. AA 14:31-291 [text]. — *ep.*, Epistolario de S. Braulio, L. Riesco Terreo (Seville, 1975), 132-137, 140-147 [text]. — *Drac. laud dei./satisf.*, F. Vollmer, loc. cit., 27-131 [text]. — *Drac. satisf.*, F. Speranza (Rome, 1978) [text].
L: F. Brunhölzl, Geschichte 1 (Munich, 1975), 95-99, 522. — C. Codoñer, Poetry: Pap. of the Liverp. Lat. Sem. 3 (Arca 7 [1981]) 323-342. — H.-J. Diesner, E.: FS B. Kötting (Münster, 1980), 472-480. — D. Norberg, Carmen: MLJb 19 (1984) 63-72. — K. Reinwald, Laudes Dei (Speyer, 1913). — F. Vollmer, Gedichtslg.: NA 26 (1901) 393-409.

B. BREILMANN

Eugippius

E. was born ca. 467 (460?), probably in Ufernoricum, the son of Roman parents; he entered the monastery of Severin in Favianis (Mautern), probably after the death of the founding abbot (482). In 488, because of the barbarian invasions, the monks, along with the Roman population of Noricum, settled in Italy. During the pontificate of Gelasius (492-496) the community resettled in Castellum Lucullanum (Pizzofalcone) near Naples. There E. was elected third abbot of the community. He had an interest in theol. questions and took steps to have a well-provided library and a productive scriptorium. In the 6th c. the monastery was a center of religious culture. E. was in contact with important Chr. scholars such as Dionysius Exiguus, Fulgentius of Ruspe, Ferrandus, and Cassiodorus. During the Acacian and Lawrentian schisms he sympathized with pro-Byz. circles in the Roman senate. He died after 533.

E. won fame as biographer of St. Severinus (*Sev.*). His *Commemoratorium*, i.e., "List (of hidden objects of value)," composed in 511, deserves attention, for one reason, as a hist. source, since it supplies information about the collapse of Roman government in the Danube province. No less treasured is the literary importance of the → *Vita*, which is in the historiographical tradition. E. uses the devices of ancient artistic prose, although he deliberately adopts a simple style. The biography is preceded by a letter to Deacon → Paschasius (*ep. ad Pasch.*). After 511 E. collected the extensive *Excerpta ex operibus s. Augustini* and, in a letter to the Roman lady Proba, dedicated the work to her (*ep. ad Probam*). The collection shows a thorough knowledge of the works of → Augustine. The anthology is meant to serve those who did not have any works of the fathers in their library; it supplied a great demand. The work also plays an important role in textual criticism for editions of Augustine. In addition, before his death E. left a rule (*reg.*) for the monks of his monastery. It was for a long time thought to have been lost; it has since been identified with an anonymous compilation of rules (*Cod. Parisin. lat.* 12634).

W: *ep. ad Pasch./Sev.*, T. Mommsen, MGH. SRG 26 [text] (corrected printing: W. Bulst, Edit. Heidelberg. 10 (Heidelberg, 1948). — R. Noll (Berlin, 1963) [text/German trans./comm.] — T. Nüßlein (Stuttgart, 1986) [text/German trans.] — P. Régerat, SC 374. — *ep. ad Prob./exc. Aug.*, P. Knoell, CSEL 9/1 [text]. — *reg.*, F. Villegas, A. de Vogüé, CSEL 87 [text].
L: *Bibliography:* R. Pillinger: Mitteilungen zur chr. Archäologie 5 (1999) 93-96. — W. Berschin, Biographie 1 (Stuttgart, 1986), 174-188. — idem, Livius: Altsprachl. Unterr. 31/4 (1988) 37-46. — P.-I. Fransen, Florilèges: RBen 97 (1987) 187-194. — M. M. Gorman, Manuscript Trad. (exc. Aug.): RBen 92 (1982) 7-32. — F. Lotter, Severinus (Stuttgart, 1976). — idem, Interpr. hagiogr. Quellen: MLJb 19 (1985) 37-62. — M. Pavan, Lucullanum: FS S. Calderone (Messina, 1986), 105-125. — E. M. Ruprechtsberger, Stil u. Sprache: Röm. Österr. 4 (1976) 227-299. — D. Straub (ed.), Severin zwischen Römerzeit u. Völkerwanderung (Linz, 1982). — A. de Vogüé, Règle retrouvée?: RAM 47 (1971) 233-266. — idem, Bourgogne: RBS 16 (1987) 123-135. — F.-R. Weissengruber, Regelkompilation (Salzburg, 1989).

B. BREILMANN

Eugnostus, Letter of

In the gnostic writings of the Nag Hammadi library (NHC 3, 3; 5, 1) there is a letter of an otherwise unknown "Eugnostus the Blessed" (*ep. Eug.*) which treats of the unbegotten God and the origin of the superior cosmos through emanations from the All-One. The work contains no references to Jewish-Chr. teaching on creation; but in the → *Sophia of Jesus Christ* there is a superficial christianization of the cosmol. material in *ep. Eug.* The text was probably written in the 2nd c. in Alexandria, Egypt.

W: W. Till: TU 60 (1955) 52-55, 200-274 [Coptic text/German trans./comm.]. — J. Doresse, Secret Books of Egyptian gnostics (London, 1960), 209-213 [English trans.]. — C. Barry, Sagesse de Jésus Christ (Leuven/Louvain, 1993) [text/French trans./comm.]. — D. M. Parrott, NHC 3, 3f.; 5, 1 (Leiden, 1991) [text/English trans./comm.]. — M. Krause, Die Gnosis (Zurich, 1971), 2:32-45 [German trans.]. — NHL 220-243 [English trans.].
L: R. van den Broek, E. and Aristides: Knowledge of God, ed. idem (Leiden, 1988), 202-218. — R. Charron, Concordance NHC 3 (Leuven/Louvain, 1995). — J. Helderman, Gnostische Gottesschau: Gnosticisme, ed. J. Ries (Leuven/Louvain, 1982), 245-262. — D. M. Parrott, Eugnostos: FS A. Böhlig (Wiesbaden, 1988), 153-167. — idem, Significance: SBL. SP 107 (1971) 387-416. — B. A. Pearson, Roots of Egyptian Christianity (Philadelphia, 1986), 190-203. — C. Scholten, Sophiamythos (Münster, 1987), 240-261. — J. L. Summey, Gnosis: NT 31 (1989) 172-181. — M. Tardieu, Écrits gnostiques (Paris, 1984). — D. Trakatellis, Transcendent God of Eugnostos (Athens, 1977).

P. BRUNS

Eulogius of Alexandria

Originally a monk and priest in Antioch, E. was consecrated the (loyal to Chalcedon) patriarch of Alexandria in 580 in Constantinople. From that time on, he maintained ties with Pope Gregory I, several letters of whom to E. have been preserved. E.'s term of office was marked by controversy with Monophysitism (and with the agnoetism of Themistius). E. died in 607 or 608.

E.'s numerous works have survived only in fragments; Photius (*cod.* 182; 208; 225-27; 230; 280) lists four treatises and twelve addresses. From the *Dubitationes orthodoxi* (*dub.*) and the *Defensiones* (*def.*) it can be seen that E. regarded the *mia physis* formula as completely orthodox, but he interprets it by referring in addition to the two natures in Christ. Thus he saw himself as a follower of Cyril but also defended the *Tomus* of Leo. For this reason, Photius can describe him as a "Neo-Chalcedonian" mediating theologian. Other fragments deal with Ps 31:1f.; Lk; Jn 21:16.

W: PG 86:2937-2964. — *dub.*, Doctrina Patrum, ed. F. Diekamp (Münster, 1981 = 1907), 152-155. — *def.*, ebd. 209f., 211-213.
L: P. Goubert, Patriarches d'Antioche et d'Alexandrie: REByz 25 (1967) 71-74. — A. Grillmeier, Jesus der Christus 2/4 (Freiburg i.Br., 1990), 66-72 (English, Christ in Christian Tradition, vol. 2/4 [London, 1996]). — S. Helmer, Der Neuchalkedonismus (Bonn, 1962), 236-241. — J. Maspéro, Histoire des Patriarches d'Alexandrie (Paris, 1923).

G. RÖWEKAMP

Eunomius of Beroea

At the end of the 4th c., E., together with Polemon, belonged to the radical Apollinarists, or Synousiasts, who claimed that the divinity combined with the human body of Jesus to form a single being. A fragment of a letter of E. to Zosimus has survived in the *Doctrina patrum*.

W: Doctrina Patrum, ed. F. Diekamp (Münster, 1981 = 1907), 309, 312.
L: H. Lietzmann, Apollinaris v. Laodizea u. seine Schule (Tübingen, 1904), 153, 273-277.

G. Röwekamp

Eunomius of Cyzicus

E., a disciple of Aetius of Antioch, came from Cappadocia and was probably originally a stenographer and an orator. In 357 he was ordained a deacon by Eudoxius of Constantinople and in 360 bishop of Cyzicus. His views elicited protests from the people, so that he had to go into exile. After 362 he worked closely with Aetius and caused a break with Eudoxius and Euzoius. In 393 he was again exiled by Theodosius I, first to Moesia, then to Caesarea. He died in 394 at Dekora, near Caesarea.

Only a few of his many writings have survived. His *Apologia*, which he delivered in Constantinople (360/361), was rejected by Basil Caes. and, probably earlier, by Ps.-Basil (Apollinaris?; *Eun.* 4-5). E. answered Basil's reproaches and objections ca. 368 in his *Apologia apologiae*; excerpts from this have survived in Gregory Nyss. The *Confessio fidei* (383) gives a summary of his teaching. Except for a few fragments, nothing has survived of the writings mentioned by Photius (*cod.* 138).

In theology E. strictly separates the transcendent God from the Son. Because the *ousia* of the Son is created, it is different from the *ousia* of God. A subordination of the Son to the Father can also be seen in the manner of their operation (*energeia*), which implies a difference between Father and Son. To this twofold distinction E. adds a theory of the revelation of the names: the names give the possibility of access to the *ousia* and the *energeia*. There is disagreement about which philosophical doctrines E. is here bringing to bear.

W: The Extant Works, R. P. Vaggione (Oxford, 1987) [text/English trans.]. — Gregor v. Nyssa, *Eun.*, W. Jaeger, GNO 1-2 (Leiden, 1960).
L: L. Abramowski, E.: RAC 6:936-947. — T. Böhm, Theoria — Unendlichkeit — Aufstieg (Leiden, 1996). — E. Cavalcanti, Studi eunomiani (Rome, 1976). — V. H. Drecoll, Die

Entwicklung der Trinitätslehre des Basilius v. Cäsarea (Göttingen, 1996). — R. P. C. Hanson, The Search for the Christian Doctrine of God (Edinburgh, 1988), 611-636. — R. M. Hübner, Zur Genese der trinitarischen Formel bei Basilius von Caesarea: FS F. Kardinal Wetter (St. Ottilien, 1998), 123-156, here 150f. — T. Kobusch, Sein u. Sprache (Leiden, 1987). — T. A. Kopecek, A History of Neo-Arianism (Cambridge, Mass., 1979). — A. Meredith, Orthodoxy, Heresy and Philosophy in the Latter Half of the Fourth Century: HeyJ 15 (1975) 5-21. — B. Pottier, Dieu et le Christ selon Grégoire de Nysse (Paris, 1994). — F. X. Risch, Ps.-Basilius, Adversus Eunomium IV-V (Leiden, 1992). — K.-H. Uthemann, Die Sprache der Theologie nach E.: ZKG 104 (1993) 143-175.

T. Böhm

Euprepius of Paltus

E., bishop of Paltus in Phoenicia, is known only from a citation in → Severus of Antioch, in which he is adduced as a main witness against Messalianism. The citation, which reports the Messalian depreciation of baptism (it resembles → Theodoret, *haer.* 4.11; PG 83:429B), is from a letter of E. to Flavian (not to Paulinus) of Antioch. E. must therefore have lived at the end of the 4th c.

W: Severus, *Contra additiones Juliani*, R. Hespel, CSCO 295:34 [Syriac text]; CSCO 296:28 [French trans.].

K. Fitschen

Eusebius of Alexandria

A collection of homilies is ascribed to E. by a certain John, who claims to be E.'s secretary. In an appended life of E., John makes him the successor of Cyril Alex. (444); after seven years E. turned over the see to Alexander, whom he had converted. The life thus proves to be fiction. The author of the homogeneous collection of twenty-two Gr. homilies is therefore not to be identifiable personally; he is probably one with the author of the life. Perhaps this author (John, an orthodox cleric of Alexandria?) was using his story in order to give the homilies a special recommendation.

The homilies, which have been handed down in part under the name also of → John Chrys. and in various versions or recensions, deal with various problems and questions of religious and eccles. life (the life and redemptive activity of the Lord; moral and ascetical questions). Many claim to be answers to questions put by an Alexander. They originated probably at the end of the 5th or beginning of the 6th c. and were quickly circulated, as is attested by the many versions in other languages (Georg., Old Slav., Arm., Arab., Syr.). A Lat. version was made by the so-called Eusebius of Gaul → Eusebius Gallicanus (CCL 101/101A), who produced, however, not a translation but a quite free version of the homilies.

W: *serm.*, PG 61:733-738, 775-778; 62:721-724; 64:45-48; 86.1:313-462, 509-536. — *serm.* 15/17, E. K. Rand: MPh 2 (1904) 261-278 [Latin version]. — *serm.* 16, F. Nau: ROC 13 (1908) 414-420 [2 versions]. — G. Morin: RBen 24 (1907) 530-535 [Latin version]. — T. Zahn, Skizzen aus dem Leben der alten Kirche (Erlangen/Leipzig, 1894), 278-286; ²1898, 321-330 [German trans. of a version]. — *vita*, PG 86:1:297-309.
L: H. G. Beck, Kirche u. theol. Lit. (Munich, 1959), 400f. — J. Darrouzès, E.: DSp 4/2:1686f. — G. Lafontaine, Les homélies d' E. (Leuven/Louvain, 1966) (typescript of Diss.). — J. Leroy, F. Glorie, E., source d' Eusèbe de Gaule: SE 19 (1969/70) 33-70. — F. Nau, E. 2: DThC 5/2:1526f.

B. WINDAU

Eusebius of Caesarea

I. Life: E., born before 264/265 (*h.e.* 3.28.3 with 7.28.3), grew up in the second half of the 3rd c., a period of relative peace for the church, in the capital, Caesarea, of the province of Palestine. The city was at this time a thoroughly Hellen. "multicultural" center of commerce, culture, and learning; the population included large Jewish, pagan, Samaritan, and Chr. sectors. Since the time of Origen, Caesarea was also known for its Chr. scholarship. As a student of Pamphilus, who had been a student of Origen and whom E. esteemed highly (*h.e.* 7.32.25f.; *m.P.* 11.1f.) E. must have enjoyed a broad-based formation. At an early age he must have come in contact with such works as the collection of acts, documents, texts, and excerpts of every provenance that aimed at universality; with the building of the library of Caesarea; with the handing on of the writings of Origen; and, above all, with the intensive scholarly work being done on the bibl. text on the basis of the Hexapla. In view of E.'s early works, we may assume that even before the beginning of the Diocletian persecution E. had an important place in the circle around Pamphilus, although more accurate information is lacking, since the life of E. by Acacius, his successor in office (Soc., *h.e.* 2.4), is lost.

After the outbreak of the Diocletian persecution in 303, E. remained for the time being in Tyre and in Egypt, a decision that later repeatedly brought against him the accusation of defeatism or even of collaboration (Epiphanius, *haer.* 68.8). After the martyrdom of Pamphilus in 309 E. took over a great many of his works and duties. Ca. 314 he was consecrated bishop of Caesarea, and a little later preached at the consecration of the church of Tyre (*h.e.* 10.4).

His efforts to put church life on a firm basis after the persecution led him at a quite early point to collaborate with Constantine, the first Chr. emperor (ruler of the entire empire since 324), whose court in Nicomedia and Constantinople E. visited, before whom he delivered the address for the thirtieth anniversary of the regime (*laus Constantini* [*l. C.*] 1-10), and for whom he composed a panegyric (*vita Constantini* [*v. C.*]).

In the trinitarian controversy over the teaching of Arius E. initially but conditionally sided with the latter and tried to take a middle position between Arius and his bishop, Alexander Alex. This attitude brought him not only the accusation of twofacedness (Soc., *h.e.* 1.23) but also a provisional excommunication by the Synod of Antioch in early 325 "until the great synod meets." At the Council of Nicaea, which met in the summer of that same year, E. subscribed with great reluctance (*ep. Caes.*) and probably with an eye especially on the will of the emperor, to the Nicene Creed, which seemed to him excessively "Sabellian," and to the condemnation of Arius.

Shortly after 325, E. was accused by his episcopal colleague Eustathius of Antioch of departing from the dogm. decrees of Nicaea. In fact, in the theol. controversies of the thirties, E. inclined rather to the positions of the "Origenist mediating party" around Eusebius of Nicomedia, as they were later to be displayed in the second Antiochene formula of 341. As presider at the Council of Tyre in 335 he was just as involved in the deposition of Athanasius for violations of discipline as he was later in the dogm. condemnation of Marcellus of Ancyra, whose teaching on the Trinity E. tried to refute in detail in two works.

E. died, probably in 339 or 340 (Soc., *h.e.* 2.3-5), before the Enkainia Synod of Antioch in 341. The Syr. calendar of martyrs gives May 30 as the date of his death.

II. Works: 1. Apologetics: Of E.'s early work, the *General Elementary Introduction* in ten books, only books 6-9 have been preserved; in them he explains the messianic prophecies of the OT.

The *Praeparatio evangelica* and the *Demonstratio evangelica* (*p. e.* and *d. e.*), which, along with the history of the church, may be called E.'s main works, were planned in advance as a two-volume work in which the first part (*p. e.*) was meant to prove the radical superiority of the Jewish-Chr. tradition over the Gr. philosophers and the pagan-polytheistic religions, while the second part (*d. e.*) asks why Christians separated themselves from the Jewish religion. E. demonstrates his first claim with the help of the argument from antiquity and the evidence of moral superiority over the polytheistic religions. He answers his question in part 2 with a reference to Chr. universalism vs. Jewish particularism and with the "proof" that OT passages and prophecies all refer to Christ and were fulfilled in him. The two-part work was intended primarily as a source of arguments for Christians, with the debate with the pagans (*p. e.*) being primarily for beginners and that with the Jews (*d. e.*) for those more advanced in Christianity. E.'s purpose is pedagogical but also to supply learning and proofs. He locates himself consciously in the apologetic tradition, but, acc. to his own testimony, departs from it inasmuch he looks beyond the acceptance of individual arguments and offers a comprehensive "religio-historical" sketch that is meant to prove by a logical series of arguments that Christianity is the "correct" religion and a "new, true knowledge of God."

E.'s late apologetic work, the *Theophania* (preserved in Syr.), gives a summary, tailored to a wider readership, of the ideas and arguments developed in *p. e.* and *d. e.* (*theoph.* 5 = *d. e.* 3.3-7).

E. must have been producing a preliminary version of his two-volume apologetic work in the *Eclogae propheticae* (*ecl.*) and *De vitis prophetarum* (*proph.*), but the few remaining fragments do not permit any more detailed inferences.

Among the apologetic works is also the work against Hierocles (*Hierocl.*), in which E. attacks the comparisons made by pagans between Apollonius of Tyana and Christ in respect of their miracles.

Parts of the now-lost defense against Porphyry (Soc., *h.e.* 3.23.37) found a place in *p. e.* and *d. e.*

2. **Historiography and Imperial Theology:** E.'s historical works are wholly inspired by his basic apologetic purpose. The *Chronicle* (*chron.*) (before 303) intends (like *p. e.*) to prove the greater age (and therefore the superiority) of the Jewish religion (and therefore of Christianity) over the pagan religions. This is accomplished in an introductory outline of the history of the ancient peoples (Chaldeans, Assyrians, Hebrews, Egyptians, Greeks, Romans) and by drawing up synchronic tables of world history, which run from the birth of Abraham, dated 2105/2106 B.C.E., to 303 C.E. (to 325 in a second edition). The Gk. original is lost, but an Arm. version survives, as does a Lat. translation, addition, and continuation to 378 by → Jerome. As compared with the Chr. chroniclers who preceded him, → Hippolytus and → Julius Africanus, on whom E. falls back at many points, his work is more accurate and more critical in its overall conception and in its choice and evaluation of sources.

E.'s most important work, his *History of the Church* (*h.e.*), is the first work in the literary genre "history of the church" (*h.e.* 1.1.3) and, at the same time, shows the consistent application of E.'s apologetics to the Roman empire. In several editions between 290 and 325, in which the work grew to ten books, the *h.e.* tells the history of the Chr. church from its beginnings down to the sole rule of the first Chr. emperor, Constantine, in the year 324. The victory of Christianity in the Roman empire, which was thereby ensured, proved at the same time the legitimacy and divine origin of the Chr. religion and its superiority to other religions. Acc. to the introduction in book 1, the *h.e.* intended to provide information on successors in office and on the church's teachers and writers; on heretics; on the sufferings of the Jews (as punishment for their crime against God's Anointed); on the persecutions endured by the church, including the present Diocletian persecution (the work on the Palestinian martyrs [*m.P.*] that is added to the *h.e.* in some mss. gives forty accounts of Palestinians martyred between 303 and 311); and on the eventual gracious help of God (*h.e.* 1.1.1f.). The arrangement of this material is based on a theol. concept of salvation history (which is also located within universal history), acc. to which the Logos is bringing his church to victory with the infallible certainty of the divine plan and in a manner visible to all who believe in him. Thus the real subject of the *h.e.* is "the action of Christ, recognizable as supernatural" (1.1.7), that shapes all of history.

In E.'s understanding of history this action of Christ has an educational purpose, in accordance with which humanity was, on the one hand, warned by divine punishments (disasters, illnesses, wars) and, on the other, purified by the spread of the Jewish law, and in this way prepared morally for the coming of the redeemer. The high point of this process and a real presupposition for the appearance of the Logos was the beginning of the Roman empire, with which, therefore, the beginning of Jesus' activity on earth coincided (*h.e.* 1.2.23). In the presence of Constantine, this presupposed significance of the empire for salvation history becomes a theory that ultimately sees in the first Chr. emperor the chosen executor of God's saving deeds on earth. To this setting of an excessive salvation-historical exaltation of Constantinian (religious) policy belongs the famous description, in the panegyric on Constantine (*v.C.* 3.15), of the assembly of emperor and bishops as an image of the kingdom of Christ. Despite all the legitimate theol. reservations against such a casual introduction of Roman imperial ideology into Chr.

theology this point must be kept in mind: The discrediting of the *v.C.* in the literature espec. of an earlier time as being "thoroughly dishonest" is based on a confusion of the genre of panegyric with that of critical biography. It is not the purpose of this text to give an "objective" description of the life of the first Chr. emperor; the text is rather one of posthumous praise that follows strict rules as to form and content; this fact strips much of the work of any biog. value, but (and the same is true of the address for the thirtieth jubilee, *l. C.* 1-10) is very valuable for an analysis of the (Chr.) imperial ideology of the *imperium Romanum*.

3. **Exegesis:** In his exegetical works E. shows himself to be influenced by Origen but, at the same time, to be independent. Like Origen, he makes a fundamental distinction between a literal and a figurative sense of scripture, but he does not attend to any threefold meaning of scripture; he busies himself much more than Origen does with the literal meaning (*ecl., proph.*). He repeatedly compares the readings of the Gr. translation of the OT (→ Symmachus, → Theodotion, → Aquila [*d. e., Is.*]), but significantly less often those of the Heb. original.

E. consistently reads and interprets all passages of scripture in the light of Christ and as referring to him. Every passage has revelatory value not only for the contemporaries of its author but also for present (and future) readers. Passages are shown to be true by the fact that all the prophecies in them have been fulfilled (in Christ). This approach corresponds to the proof from history that is so dominant elsewhere in E.

Almost completely preserved are the commentaries on Isaiah (*Is.*) and the Psalms (*Ps.*); the latter was translated into Latin by → Hilary of Poitiers and → Eusebius of Vercelli. There are fragments on Dan, Lk, and Heb (*fr. Dan., Lc., Heb.*). The large fragment of the work on Easter (*pasch.*) sheds light on, among other things, E.'s teaching on the Eucharist.

The work in three books on questions of the gospel (*qu. ev.*), which is preserved in an epitome and in fragments, deals with the differences in the gospel accounts of the infancy and of the resurrection.

The synopsis of the gospels or *Evangelical Canons*, explained in a letter to Carpianus (*ep. Carp.*), recorded in ten tables the fourfold, threefold, and twofold traditions; it quickly became an indispensable aid in exegesis. These canonical tables were taken over in Syr. and Lat. mss. of the Bible.

4. **Teaching on the Trinity and Christology:** In the question of the Trinity, which amid the Arian controversy was brought to a (provisional) theol. solu-

tion at the Council of Nicaea, E. (as did initially all who were involved in the controversy) followed Origen in maintaining a qualified subordination of the Son to the Father. In order to safeguard monotheism, E., like Arius, wanted a clear distinction between the Father and the Son, but, unlike Arius, he spoke not of the Son being created by the Father but of the generation of the Son. For intratrinitarian relationships he, like Alexander, used the concepts "image" and "light from light." He subscribed to the Nicene Creed but gave his home community a quite independent (re-)interpretation of the text, among other things neutralizing the homoousios by translating it as "from the Father, not: part of the Father" (*ep. Caes.*). In the polemical writings against Marcellus (*Contra Marcellum* [*Marcell.*]; *De ecclesiastica theologia* [*e. th.*]) E. accuses him, on the one hand, of dividing up the substance of God (because of the participation of the Son in the *ousia* of the Father) and, on the other, of Modalism or Sabellianism (because of an inadequate distinction between the two); in the process he summons up for polemical purposes the genealogies of the relevant heretics, but he also exercises penetrating and subtly differentiated criticism.

In E.'s christology the conception of the three offices (*munus triplex*) of Christ, the royal, the priestly, and the prophetic, appears for the first time (*d. e.* 4.15.20). These three offices, which are geared to the salvation of humanity, are continued in the offices of the church (priest, teacher, martyr).

5. **Other Works:** E.'s *Onomasticon* of bibl. place-names (*onomast.*) is indispensable even today in questions of the topography of the Holy Land; in addition to attempts to identify location, it gives brief notices on the history of each place, in reliance on the bibl. text, Josephus, and his own experience.

In addition to the letter to his community (*ep. Caes.*) there are letters to Alexander Alex., Euphratio, and Flaccus (*ep. Alex. Al., Euphrat., Flacc.*). The question of E.'s attitude to images must remain open, since the authenticity of the letter to Constantine's sister Constantia (*ep. Constant.*) has been disputed for weighty reasons.

A work on the star of the Magi (*stell. mag.*) has been preserved in Syriac. The compilation *De mensuris et ponderibus* (*mens. et pond.*), likewise transmitted in Syriac, dates from the 6th c. at the earliest.

III. **Importance:** E.'s hope that his *h.e.* would be "very useful to historians" (1.1.6) has been more than fulfilled. E.'s rank as *the* paramount chronicler and historian of his time is unchallenged, for to him we owe not only most of our knowledge of the history of the church in the first three centuries but also the transmission of many otherwise lost texts of pagan and Jewish authors. The *h.e.*, which very soon acquired almost canonical authority, quickly led to successors; as a result, also because of his other historical and apologetical writings, E. became known as "the father of church history."

For an equally long time, the positive judgment on E.'s works as historian and chronicler has stood in contrast to the rather reserved evaluation of his theol. accomplishments. Jerome regarded him as simply a heretic (*adv. Ruf.* 2.15); Photius similarly (*cod.* 13.196). He was regarded as an Arian, an Origenist, and (because of the *ep. Constant. Aug.*) an enemy of images. This negative judgment has persisted down into the 20th c.

Changes of judgment have, however, been underway in more recent times. A more differentiated understanding of the non-Nicene texts and confessions of the 4th c. shows that the description "Arian" cannot be maintained, any more than can a negative judgment in principle on his trinitarian theology and christology. Even in the matter of E.'s reception of Origen we must not diagnose simply an imitative reproduction of the latter's thought; what we see instead, in almost all areas, is a critical, productive, and careful assimilation of it.

E.'s extreme theory of the salvation-historical coincidence of the Roman empire and the church will certainly, at this distance and from today's point of view, prove frightening, but here again the question must at least be raised of the alternatives available at that time. (A historically correct critical evaluation of E.'s imperial theology can and must therefore reach the fundamental conclusion that in the final analysis all attempts to prove God's direct action in history represent a program which is theologically not realizable.)

W: *chron.*, R. Helm, U. Treu, GCS E. 8 [Latin trans. of Jerome and Greek frags.]. — J. Karst, GCS E. 5 [German trans. of the Armenian version]. — *Is.*, J. Ziegler, GCS E. 9. — *Ps.* 37, PG 30:81-104. — *Ps.* 51-95:3, PG 23:441-1221. — *Ps.* 49, R. Devresse: RB 33 (1924) 78-81 [text]. — *Ps.* 118, M. Harl, SC 189, 190. — *d. e.*, I. A. Heikel, GCS E. 6. — W. J. Ferrar, Proof (London, 1920) [English trans.]. — *e. th.*, E. Klostermann, G. C. Hansen, GCS E. 4:60-182. — *ecl., proph.*, PG 22:1021-1262. — *ep. Carp.*, NT Graece ²⁷1993, 84*-89*. — *ep. Euphrat.*, H. G. Opitz, Athanasius Werke 3/1 (Berlin, 1934), Urk. 3. — *ep. Alex. Al.*, ibid., Urk. 7. — *ep. Caes.*, ibid., Urk. 22. — *ep. Constant. Aug.*, H. J. Geischer, Bilderstreit (Gütersloh, 1968), 15-17 [text]. — *ep. Flacc.*, E. Klostermann, G. C. Hansen, GCS E. 4:60. — *introd.*, PG 22:1021-1273. — *fr. Dan.*, PG 24:525-528. — *fr. Lc.*, PG 24:529-605. — *fr. Heb.*, PG 24:605. — *h.e.*, E. Schwartz, GCS E. 2/1-3. — G. Bardy, SC 31, 41, 55, 73. — P. Haeuser, E.: Kirchengeschichte, ed. H. Kraft (Darmstadt,

²1981) [German trans.]. — R. J. Deferrari (Washington, 1955) [English trans.]. — G. del Ton (Rome, 1964) [Italian trans.]. — *l. C.*, I. A. Heikel, GCS E. 1:195-259. — H. A. Drake (London, 1976) [English trans.]. — *Hierocl.*, E. des Places, M. Forrat, SC 333. — *Marcell.*, E. Klostermann, G. C. Hansen, GCS E. 4:1-58. — *m. P.*, E. Schwartz, GCS E. 2/2:907-950. — A. Bigelmair, BKV E. 1:273-313 [German trans.]. — G. del Ton (Rome, 1964) [Italian trans.]. — *mens. et pond.*, F. Hultsch, Metrologicorum scriptorum reliquiae 1 (Leipzig, 1864), 276-278. — *onomast.*, E. Klostermann, GCS 3/1 [Greek text/Latin trans.]. — I. Rahmani et al.: ROC 23 (1922/23) 225-276 [Syriac frgm.]. — *p. e.*, K. Mras, E. des Places, GCS E. 8. — E. des Places, J. Sirinelli, G. Schroeder, G. Favrelle, O. Zink, SC 206, 228, 262, 266, 215, 369, 292, 307, 338. — E. Gifford (Oxford, 1903) [English trans./comm.]. — *qu. ev.*, PG 22:880-1016. — G. Beyer: OrChr 12-14 (1925) 30-70; 23 (1926) 80-97; 24 (1927) 57-69 [German trans. of the Syriac version]. — *pasch.*, PG 24:693-706. — *proph.*, PG 22:1261-1272. — *stell. mag.*, W. Wright, E. on the Star: JSL 4. Ser. 9 (1866) 117-136; 10 (1867) 150-164 [text]. — *theoph. fr.*, H. Gressmann, A. Laminski, GCS E. 3/2 [Greek frags. and trans. of the Syriac version]. — *v. C.*, F. Winkelmann, GCS E. 1/1. — J. M. Pfättisch, BKV E. 1/1:1-190 [German trans.]. — L. Tartaglia (Naples, 1984) [Italian trans.].

L: P. Allen, War: StPatr 19 (1989) 3-7. — L. Allevi, Storiografica: SeC 68 (1940) 550-564. — H. W. Attridge, G. Hata (ed.), E., Christianity, and Judaism (Leiden, 1992). — G. Bardy, Théologie: RHE 50 (1935) 5-20. — L. W. Barnard, Bede and E.: Famulus Christi, ed. G. Bonner (London, 1976), 106-124. — T. D. Barnes, Composition: JThS NS 26 (1975) 412-415. — idem, Speeches: GRBS 18 (1977) 341-345. — idem, Editions: GRBS 21 (1980) 191-201. — idem, Constantine (Cambridge, Mass., 1981). — idem, Inconsistencies: JThS NS 35 (1984) 470-475. — idem, Panegyric: FS H. Chadwick (Cambridge, 1990), 94-123. — N. H. Baynes, Christian Empire: Byzantine and Other Studies (London, 1955), 168-172. — H. Berkhof, Theologie (Amsterdam, 1939). — idem, Kaiser (Zurich, 1947). — A. Bolhuis, Rede Konstantins: VigChr 10 (1956) 25-32. — F. Bovon, L'Histoire: FS O. Cullmann (Hamburg, 1967). — J. E. Bruns, Agreement: VigChr 31 (1977) 117-125. — R. Cadiou, Bibliothèque: RevSR 16 (1936) 474-483. — H. v. Campenhausen, Bekenntnis: ZNW 67 (1976) 123-139. — A. J. Carriker, Seven Unidentified Sources in h.e.: FS F. W. Schlatter (New York, 1999), 79-92. — F. Chesnut, Christian Histories (Macon, Ga., ²1986), 33-174. — T. Christensen, Appendix: CM 34 (1983) 177-209. — R. H. Conolly, h. e. 5, 28: JThS 49 (1948) 73-79. — F. E. Cranz, Kingdom: HThR 45 (1952) 47-66. — C. Curti, Commentarii in Psalmos: Aug. 13 (1973) 483-506. — J. G. Davies, Description: AJA 61 (1957) 171-173. — A. Dempf, Platonismus des E. (Munich, 1962). — idem, E. als Historiker (Munich, 1964). — A. M. Denis, P. e. 9, 17-18: JSJ 8 (1977) 42-49. — H. Doergens, Vater der Kirchengeschichte: ThGl 29 (1937) 446-448. — H. A. Drake, L. C.: Hist. 24 (1975) 345-356. — idem, E. on the True Cross: JEH 36 (1985) 1-22. — idem, Genesis of the V. C.: CP 83 (1988) 20-38. — H. Eger, Kaiser u. Kirche: ZNW 38 (1939) 97-115. — C. T. H. R. Ehrhardt, E. and Celsus: JAC 22 (1979) 40-49. — R. Farina, L'impero (Zurich, 1966). — G. Fau, Eusèbe (Paris, 1976). — G. Feige, Lehre Markells (Leipzig, 1991). — E. Ferguson, E. and Ordination: JEH 13 (1962) 139-144. — H. Fischer, Kartographie von Palästina: ZDPV 62 (1939) 169-189. — F. J. Foakes-Jackson, E. Pamphili (Cambridge, 1933). — G.

Florovsky, Iconoclastic Controversy: ChH 19 (1950) 77-96. — S. Gere, E.'s Letter to Constantia: JThS NS 32 (1981) 460-470. — K. M. Girardet, Herrscheridee: Chiron 10 (1980) 569-592. — M. Gödecke, Geschichte (Frankfurt a.M., 1987). — R. M. Grant, Lives of Origen: FS C. M. Pellegrino (Turin, 1975), 635-649. — idem, Case: StPatr 12 (1975) 413-421. — idem, Gnostic Origins: FS M. Simon (Paris, 1978), 195-205. — idem, Civilization: FS G. H. Williams (Leiden, 1979), 62-70. — idem, E. (Oxford, 1980). — H. Grégoire, L'auteur: Byz. 13 (1938) 561-583. — idem, Vision: Byz. 14 (1939) 341-351. — D. Groh, Onomasticon: StPatr 18 (1983) 29. — B. Gustafsson, Principles: StPatr 4 (1961) 429-441. — S. G. Hall, Sources: FS L. Abramowski (Tübingen, 1993), 239-263. — T. Handrick, Bild des Märtyrers: StPatr 19 (1989) 72-79. — R. P. C. Hanson, Oratio ad Sanctos: JThS NS 24 (1973) 505-511. — idem, Search (Edinburgh, 1988), 46-59, 159-171. — R. Helm, Hypothesen: SPAW. PH (1929) 371-408. — A. H. H. Jones-Skeat, Notes: JEH 5 (1954) 196-200. — W. Kinzig, Novitas Christiana (Göttingen, 1994), 517-568. — A. Kofsky, Prophecy in the Service of Polemics: CrSt 19 (1998) 1-29. — D. König-Ockenfels, Weltgeschichte: Saec. 27 (1976) 348-365. — H. J. Lawlor, Eusebiana (Amsterdam, 1973 = Oxford, ¹1912). — R. Leeb, Konstantin (Berlin, 1992), 166-176. — L. I. Levine, Cesarea under Roman Rule (Leiden, 1975), 113-134. — S. Lieberman, Martyrs: JQR 36 (1945-46) 239-253. — A. Louth, Date: JThS NS 41 (1990) 111-123. — C. Luibheid, Nicene Creed: IThQ 39 (1972) 299-305. — idem, Arian Crisis (Dublin, 1978). — A. Möhle, Jesajakommentar: ZNW 33 (1934) 87-89. — J. Moreau, Eusèbe: DHGE 15:1437-1460. — idem, E.: RAC 6:1052-1088. — A. A. Mosshammer, Chronicle (Leipzig, 1979). — K. Mras, Schluß der P. e.: WSt 66 (1953) 92f. — idem, Stellung der "Praeparatio": AÖAW. PH (1956) 209-217. — M. Müller, Überlieferung: ThStKr 105 (1933) 425-455. — T. Nolte, Eclogis Propheticis: ThQS 43 (1861) 95-109. — H. H. Oliver, Epistle to Carpianus: NT 3 (1959) 138-145. — H. G. Opitz, E.: ZNW 34 (1935) 1-19. — E. des Places, Eusèbe Commentateur (Paris, 1982). — idem, Le Contre Hiéroclès: StPatr 19 (1989) 37-42. — A. Raban, K. G. Holum (ed.), Caesarea (Leiden, 1996). — F. Ricken, Logoslehre: ThPh 42 (1967) 341-358. — idem, Rezeption: ThPh 53 (1978) 321-352. — J. Ringel, Césarée (Paris, 1975). — G. Ruhbach, Apologetik (Heidelberg, 1962). — idem, Politische Theologie: Die Kirche angesichts der Konstantinischen Wende, ed. idem (Darmstadt, 1976), 236-258. — idem, GK 1, ed. M. Greschat (Stuttgart, 1984). — M. M. Sage, Rain Miracle: HZ 36 (1987) 96-113. — J.-M. Sansterre, Naissance: Byz. 42 (1972) 131-195, 532-594. — C. Sant, OT Interpretation of E. (Rome, 1964). — K. Schäferdiek, Verfasserschaft: ZKG 91 (1980) 177-186. — F. Scheidweiler, Kirchengeschichte: ZNW 49 (1958) 123-129. — C. Schmitt, Prototyp: Die Kirche angesichts der Konstantinischen Wende, ed. G. Ruhbach (Darmstadt, 1976), 220-235. — A. Schoene, Weltchronik (Berlin, 1900). — E. Schwartz, E.: PRE 6:1370-1439 = idem, Griech. Geschichtsschreiber (Leipzig, ²1959), 495-598. — H. R. Seeliger, Kirchengeschichtsschreibung: WiWei 44 (1981) 58-72. — M. Simonetti, Commente a Isaia: RSLR 19 (1983) 1-44. — J. Sirinelli, Vues historiques (Dakar, 1961). — R. E. Somerville, Ordering Principle: VigChr 20 (1966) 91-97. — G. C. Stead, Council: JThS NS 34 (1973) 85-100. — R. H. Storch, Constantine: ChH 40 (1971) 145-155. — M. J. Suggs, Text of John: JBL 75 (1956) 137-142. — idem, Text of Matthew: NT 1 (1956) 233-245. — idem, Gospel Text:

HThR 50 (1957) 307-310. — M. Tetz, Christenvolk: Jenseitsvorstellungen in Antike u. Christentum, ed. T. Klauser (Münster, 1982), 30-46. — F. S. Thielmann, Eschatology of E.: VigChr 41 (1987) 226-237. — F. Trisoglio, Escatologia: Aug. 18 (1978) 173-182. — V. Twomey, Apostolikos Thronos (Münster, 1982). — J. Ulrich, E. u. die Juden (Berlin, 1999). — idem, HistEccl 3, 14-20: ZNW 87 (1996) 269-289. — J. W. Verghis, Apostolic Age (Chicago, 1981). — W. Völker, Tendenzen: VigChr 4 (1955) 157-180. — L. Voelkl, Kirchenbauten: RivAC 29 (1953) 49-66, 187-206. — J. Vogt, Vita: Hist. 2 (1954) 463-471. — D. S. Wallace-Hadrill, Chronicle: JThS NS 6 (1955) 248-253. — idem, Gospel Text: HThR 49 (1956) 105-114. — idem, E. (Leipzig, 1960). — idem, Testimonium Flavianum: JEH 25 (1974) 353-362. — idem, Commentary on Luke: HThR 67 (1974) 55-63. — idem, E.: TRE 10:537-543. — B. H. Warmington, Sources: SP 23 (1985) 93-98. — A. Weber, Arche (Munich, 1965). — F. Winkelmann, Authentizitätsproblem: Klio 40 (1962) 187-243. — idem, Textbezeugung (Berlin, 1962). — idem, E. (Berlin, 1991). — C. U. Wolf, Onomasticon: BA 27 (1964) 66-96. — N. Zernov, Paschal Controversy: CQR 96 (1933) 24-41. — J. Ziegler, Peregrinatio: Bib. 12 (1931) 70-84.

J. ULRICH

Eusebius of Cremona

E., born in mid-4th c. in Cremona, was initially an imperial official and a friend of Paulinus of Nola. After 385 he became a monk in Jerome's monastery at Bethlehem. In the conflict between Jerome and Rufinus, E. agitated against Rufinus and, in this connection, traveled to Rome in 398. E. seems to have remained close to Jerome until the latter's death. Whether he succeeded Jerome as head of the monastery in Bethlehem seems dubious. Jerome dedicated to E. his commentaries on Jeremiah and Matthew. Letter 49 to Cyril in the *Collectio Avellana* is attributed to E.

W: *ep.*, O. Guenther, CSEL 35/1:113-115.
L: D. Gorce, E.: DHGE 15:1460-1462. — J. Labourt, Jérôme. Lettres 3 (Paris, 1953), 239-241. — S. Rebenich, Hieronymus u. sein Kreis (Stuttgart, 1992), 231f. and passim.

B. DÜMLER

Eusebius of Dorylaeum

In 430, in Constantinople, E., a layman, an orator well versed in the law, and a man with connections at the court, attacked Bishop Nestorius and publicly demanded of him a clear confession that the only-begotten Son of God and the Son of Mary are one and the same person. He thereby gave rise to the theol. controversy that led to the Council of Ephesus (431), at which Nestorius was condemned. We know of another attack by E., who had meanwhile become bishop of Dorylaeum in Phrygia: in 448 he complained to Bishop Flavian of Constantinople about the monk Eutyches, also of Constantinople. The latter (E. said) did not hold to the doctrine that Christ has both a human and a divine nature but claims that as man his nature was solely human (something Eutyches had not maintained). A synod acknowledged the complaint to be justified; Eutyches lost his offices and was excommunicated. Thanks, however, to his influence in Constantinople, Eutyches got Emperor Theodosius II to convoke a council in Ephesus in 449, which was to deal once again with the question of Jesus' divinity. There, with Dioscurus Alex. presiding, Eutyches was vindicated; Flavian and Eusebius were to be imprisoned. E. managed to flee to Rome and Leo I. There, with the latter's support, he secured his return. The Council of Chalcedon in 451 condemned Dioscurus and completely vindicated E. All trace of E. after the council has been lost; the date of death is unknown.

W: *contestatio*, PG 84:581-83. — ACO 1, 2, 101f. — *libellus ad Flavianum et synodum*, ACO 2, 1, 1, 100f. — *ep. ad imperatores*, ACO 2, 1, 66f. — *libellus ad concilium Chalcedonense*, ACO 2, 1, 2, 8f. (204f). — *libellus appellationis ad Leonem papam*, ACO 2, 2, 1, 79-81.
L: G. Barcille, E.: DThC 5:1532-1537. — E.: DHGE 15:1462. — A. J. Festugière, Ephèse et Chalcédoine: Actes des conciles. (Paris, 1982). — KonChal 1:196 (and passim); 2:210 (and passim)

S. MÜLLER-ABELS

Eusebius of Emesa

E. was born in Edessa ca. 300. As the son of a respected family, he received a careful education; he was a student of, among others, Eusebius Caes. As a young man he continued his education in Antioch and Alexandria. In Alexandria he was offered the see after Athanasius had been driven out, but he refused. Instead, he became bishop shortly thereafter of Emesa in Phoenicia but had to give up his office because of the complaint that he had practiced astrology. Through the intervention of George of Laodicea he was able to regain his episcopal rank. He died before 359.

Only fragments (*fr.*) have come down of his various works, which are mentioned by Jerome (*vir. ill.* 91): *Adversus Iudaeos, Adversus gentes, Adversus Novatianos*, commentaries on Gal and Gen, homilies on the gospels, and a work against the Marcionites and Manichees.

In Lat. translation, twenty-two homilies (*hom.*) on dogm. questions have survived in two collections. The theology of the Trinity that E. develops there is largely in agreement with that of Eusebius Caes. In his view, the Father is unbegotten (*non natus*); the Son is the perfect image (*perfecta similitudo*) of the Father. The Son's origin is described in negative terms: *non secundum incisionem seu divisionem aut scissionem*. Contrary to Arius, E. emphasizes the generation of the Son before time and the divinity of the Father and the Son. He nevertheless subordinates the Son to the Father; the Father is *causa sui*; he has life in himself and had passed it on to the Son. The Father decrees; the Son as *anima mundi* executes. The assumption of a human form does not bring any change in the divine nature of the Son; he is subject to change only as a human being (an interpretation that is rigorously anti-Arian). The relationship of Father and Son is clearly in the foreground of E.'s thought; he deals with the Holy Spirit only marginally. In the Syro-Palestinian world E.'s subordinationism exerted a great influence in the post-Nicene controversies. In his exegetical writings E. shows that he is in the Antiochene tradition; he prefers an interpretation based on the literal sense and rejects an excessively allegorical exegesis.

A collection of sermons in Armenian also goes under E.'s name, but the individual pieces probably belong in part to an earlier author, in part to → Severian of Gabala.

W: *fr.*, E. M. Buytaert, L'héritage littéraire de E. (Leuven/Louvain, 1948) [text/French trans.]. — *hom.*, idem, SSL 26f. (Leuven/Louvain, 1953-57) [text].
L: E.-M. Buytaert, L'authenticité des 17 opuscules contenus dans le manuscrit Troyes 523 sous le nom d' E.: RHE 43 (1948) 5-89. — idem, L'héritage littéraire d'E. (Leuven/Louvain, 1949). — P. Godet, E.: DThC 5:1537-1539. — W. A. Löhr, Die Entstehung der homöischen u. homöusianischen Kirchenparteien (Bonn, 1986). — M. Simonetti, La crisi Ariana nel IV secolo (Rome, 1975), 187-198

S. MÜLLER-ABELS

Eusebius Gallicanus

This is the name given by modern scholars to a collection of sermons from southern Gaul that in the mss. has gone under the name of Eusebius of Emesa since the 7th c. The history of the origin of E. G. is extraordinarily complicated; apart from the edition by → Caesarius in the 6th c. neither author nor final editor can be discovered. Despite the critical edition, which showed the question of author or compiler to be insoluble in the present state of the mss., there has until very recently been no lack of attempts to answer that question. That → Faustus of Riez is the favorite is because much of the material undoubtedly comes from his works or harmonizes with his style and thought. But (revised) fragments can be shown to have come from the writings of Ambrose, Augustine, Cyprian, Tertullian, Zeno, and others. The collection contains seventy-six homilies (or fragments), of which the first thirty-four are arranged acc. to the liturg. year. In the second half there is a self-contained collection of ten *Sermones ad monachos*, as well as sermons on, for the most part, ascet., theol., and hagiog. subjects. Nine *Sermones extravagantes* are added on.

W: F. Glorie, CCL 101, 101 A, 101 B.
L: W. Bergmann, Sichtung der südgallischen Predigtlit. (Leipzig, 1898). — A. Engelbrecht, Schriften des Faustus (Vienna, 1889). — E. Griffe, La Collectio Gallicana: BLE 61 (1960) 27-38. — idem, Nouveau plaidoyer pour Fauste: BLE 74 (1973) 187-192. — C. M. Kasper, Theologie u. Askese (Münster, 1991), 373-385 (also references there to investigations of individual homilies). — J. Leroy, F. Glorie, Eusèbe de Gaule: SE 19 (1969) 33-70. — G. Morin, La collection gallicane: ZNW 1 (1935) 92-115.

C. KASPER

Eusebius of Heraclea

In his capacity as bishop of Heraclea in Bithynia E. subscribed to the decree deposing Patriarch Nestorius at the Council of Ephesus (431). He composed a homily against Nestorius; its Gr. original is lost, but it has come down in an Eth. translation.

W: A. Dillmann, Chrestomathia Aethiopica (Hildesheim, 1988 = Leipzig, 1941), 102f. [Ethiopic text]. — S. Grébaut, Homélie d'E.: ROC 16 (1911) 424f. [French trans.].

P. BRUNS

Eusebius of Milan

E., who was bishop of Milan ca. 449-462, took part in a Roman synod convoked by Leo I; in 451 he himself, evidently at the request of Leo, convoked a synod of the northern Italian bishops (in Milan?). After the Hun invasion of 452 he devoted himself espec. to the rebuilding of the city. Leo's letter to E. is lost, but we have the synodal letter (*ep.*), signed by nineteen other bishops, which E. sent to Leo and in which the synod, relying on the *Tomus ad Flavianum*, condemns Monophysitism. Other works that E. composed acc. to Gennadius (*vir. ill.* 34) have not survived.

W: *ep.*, PL 54:945-950.
L: C. J. Hefele, Histoire des Conciles 2/1 (Paris, 1908), 625-628. — B. Morel, E.: DHGE 15:1466.

B. DÜMLER

Eusebius of Nicomedia

Because, among other things, of a statement of Arius in a letter to E. (*Doc.* 1), the latter is described as a fellow Lucianist. It is questionable, however, whether this means he was a disciple. It is certain that E. was bishop of Berytus (Beirut). Shortly before 318, he transferred to Nicomedia, an action that drew criticism from Alexander Alex. (*Doc.* 6b; or from Athanasius acc. to Stead), because such a transfer was uncanonical. E. took several steps in favor of Arius: he led a campaign against Alexander (*Doc.* 8; 321?) and, shortly before Nicaea, held a synod in Bithynia. At the beginning of the Council of Nicaea he explained his teaching on the Son, which was declared blasphemous (Athanasius, *decr.* 3; Ambrose, *De fide* 3.15; Theod., *h.e.* 1.6). He seems nevertheless to have signed the creed of Nicaea, possibly in order to avoid being condemned. Three months after the council he had to go into exile, after he had let an explanation of his views reach Constantine. After three years he was able to return from exile after having an explanation of his views brought to Constantine. His restoration was read out at a second session of Nicaea (but this claim is strongly disputed by scholars). Beginning in 329, he obtained the deposition of a determined adversary of the Arians, Eustathius of Antioch (Theod., *h.e.* 1.20; Soc., *h.e.* 1.14; Soz., *h.e.* 2.19). When he regained the confidence of Constantine, he tried to work for the expulsion of Athanasius Alex. Arius, who had returned from exile, circulated a profession of faith (*Doc.* 30). E. demanded the same from Athanasius; the latter refused, so that with the consent of the emperor E. was able to gather a large number of eastern bishops against him. A first synod of the Eusebians (333) in Caesarea, Palestine, produced hardly any results. But in Tyre (335), under the emperor's protection, they managed to have Athanasius deposed; he had to go into exile in Trier. An offensive of E. at the Dedication Synod (Dec., 335) resulted in Arius and his followers being accepted again into communion. In 337 E. baptized Constantine (d. May 22, 337) and, from 339 to 342, he took over the education of Julian, Constantine's nephew. At the end of 338/beginning of 339, E. became bishop of Constantinople, an event made possible by the conflict between the local candidates, Paul and Macedonius (Athanasius, *apo. sec.* 6). In 339 E. presided at a council in Antioch which again deposed Athanasius. The latter fled and took refuge in Rome with Pope Julius I. A small synod rehabilitated Athanasius and Marcellus. E. died (possibly winter 341/342) before receiving the letter from

Rome that communicated the synod's decrees to the eastern bishops. This sequence of events shows how E. was involved in the politics of the imperial court, but not all his undertakings can be understood from that context (Hanson).

Only a letter to Paulinus (*Doc.* 8) and two fragments (Athanasius, *syn.* 17; Ambrose, *fid.* 3.15) have survived of E.'s writings. It is difficult to make out just how the fragment in Athanasius (the Son of God is uncreated and *homoousios* with the Father) is to be reconciled with the letter to Paulinus. For in *Doc.* 8 E. stresses the point that the one God did not become, while the Son, who did become, is not from the *ousia* of the Father and has no participation in the uncreated nature and *ousia*; rather he stands over against God as another being with his own nature and power. If he were from God as a part of or emanation from the *ousia* of God, he would himself not have undergone a becoming and would not be created. He proceeds from the will of the One who does not become (God).

W: Proclamation to the history of the Arian controversy, H. G. Opitz (Berlin, 1934/35), 3, 15-17, 42.
L: G. Bardy, Recherches sur saint Lucien d'Antioche et son école (Paris, 1936). — T. D. Barnes, Constantine and Eusebius [of Caesarea] (Cambridge, Mass., 1981). — T. Böhm, Die Christologie des Arius (St. Ottilien, 1991). — E. Boularand, L'hérésie d'Arius et la "Foi" de Nicée (Paris, 1972). — G. Dagron, Naissance d'une capitale (Paris, 1974). — R. M. Grant, Religion and Politics at the Council of Nicaea (1973). — R. C. Gregg, D. E. Groh, Early Arianism (Philadelphia, 1981). — R. P. C. Hanson, The Fate of Eustathius of Antioch: ZKG 95 (1984) 171-179. — idem, The Search for the Christian Doctrine of God (Edinburgh, 1988), esp. 27-32. — A. Lichtenstein, E. (Halle, 1903). — U. Loose, Zur Chronologie des arianischen Streites: ZKG 101 (1990) 88-92. — G. Luibhéid, The Arianism of E.: IThQ 43 (1976) 3-23. — P. Nautin, Note critique sur la lettre d'E. à Paulin de Tyr (Théodoret, *h.e.* 1.6.2): VigChr 17 (1963) 24-27. — G. C. Stead, Athanasius' Earliest Written Work: JThS 39 (1988) 76-91. — M. Vinzent, Asterius v. Kappadokien (Leiden, 1993). — D. S. Wallace-Hadrill, Christian Antioch (Cambridge, 1982). — M. Wiles, Attitudes to Arius in the Arian Controversy: Arianism after Arius, ed. M. R. Barnes, D. H. Williams (Edinburgh, 1993), 31-43. — R. Williams, Arius (London, 1987).

T. BÖHM

Eusebius of Vercelli

E., born in Sardinia, became a lector in Rome under Pope Julius. He became a friend of the future Pope Liberius and also made the acquaintance of Athanasius. In 345 E. became bishop of Vercelli. In Milan (355) he refused to consent to the condemnation of Athanasius and was therefore banished to Scythopolis in Palestine, then to Cappadocia, and finally to the

Thebaid. It was Julian's edict (361) that ended his exile. At the request of Athanasius E. took part in the Synod of Alexandria and then traveled on to Antioch, where he was unable to prevent the schism of Lucifer of Cagliari. In 363 he returned to Vercelli and devoted himself to the struggle against Arianism in northern Italy. E. was the first western bishop to found a *Coenobium*, which became so important that in subsequent years the northern Italian cities recruited their bishops from it.

Of E.'s literary production three letters (*ep.*) have survived. The first is an answer to the invitation of Constantius II to participate in the Synod of Milan. The second E. sent to his community from exile; in it he tells of the atrocities he had to suffer from Patrophilus, the Arian bishop of Scythopolis, and he again emphasizes his orthodox outlook. The authenticity of the third letter, to Gregory of Elvira, is disputed. Lost are a translation of the commentary on the Psalms by Eusebius Caes. (Jerome, *vir. ill.* 96), as well as a translation of Origen's commentary on the Psalms (Jerome, *ep.* 61, 62). The capitular library of Vercelli possesses a 4th-c. northern Italian codex of the gospels, whose pre-Jerome text may have come from E.

E.'s authorship of the Ps.-Athanasian *De trinitate* is rejected today on grounds of its rather pre-Augustinian theology. Nor is E. any longer suggested as author of the *Symbolum quicumque.*

W: *ep.* 1, 2, V. Bulhart, CCL 9:103-110. — *ep.* 3, A. Feder, CSEL 65:66. — Cod. Vercellensis, A. Gasquet, 2 vols. (Rome, 1914).
L: H. C. Brennecke, Hilarius v. Poitiers (Berlin, 1984), 172-194. — M. Capellino, Storia di E. (Rome, 1971). — E. Crovella, Biografia critica (Vercelli, 1961). — L. Dattrino, De Trinitate (Rome, 1976). — idem, Lettera al clero e al popolo: Lat. 45 (1979) 60-82. — idem, E. martire, monaco?: Aug. 24 (1984) 167-187. — idem, Cenobio: Ben. 31 (1984) 37-45. — R. P. C. Hanson, Arian controversy (Edinburgh, 1988), 507-516. — HLL 5:483-486. — E. Mazorra, Carta a Gregorio de Elvira: EE 42 (1967) 241-250. — P. Meloni: Lucifero di Cagliari ed E. di Vercelli nel giudizio di Sant'Ambrogio: FS O. P. Alberti (Cagliari, 1998), 61-72. — E. Milano, E.: IMU 30 (1987) 313-322. — L. A. Speller, Council of Milan: JThS NS 36 (1985) 157-165. — W. Tietze, Lucifer v. Calaris (Tübingen, 1976), 274-276.

B. DÜMLER

Eustathius of Antioch

I. Life: E. was born between 280 and 288 in Side (Pamphylia) (Jerome, *vir. ill.* 85); his knowledge of rhetoric and philosophy show a higher education. In 319 E. became bishop of Syr. Beroea, where he got in touch with Athanasius Alex. and was soon drawn into the Arian controversy. At the Council of Antioch (end of 324 or beginning of 325) he was, at the instigation of Bishop Ossius of Cordoba, elected bishop of Antioch. At the Council of Nicaea he supposedly presided and delivered a eulogy of Emperor Constantine (Theod., *h.e.* 1.7.10); the success of his eccles. policy against the Arians (espec. Eusebius of Nicomedia) is a hist. fact. He energetically continued the anti-Arian struggle (espec. against Eusebius Caes.), which probably led to his fall (Soz., *h.e.* 2.29; date disputed: between 326 and 331). The Arians accused him of, among other things, "tyranny," heresy (Sabellianism), sexual immorality, and insulting Helena, the queen mother, and he was banished to Thrace (Trajanopolis) by the emperor (Theod., *h.e.* 1.21.3-9; Soc., *h.e.* 1.23.8–24.4). E. died in exile (date uncertain: before 337, 343/345, or ca. 370). After his deposition, a schism arose in Antioch between his Arian successors and the Eustathians. E. was later rehabilitated and ca. 438 his bones were transferred to Antioch.

L: H. Chadwick, The Fall of E.: JThS 49 (1948) 27-35 = idem, History and Thought (Leipzig, 1982), XIII. — R. P. C. Hanson, The Fate of E.: ZKG 95 (1984) 171-179. — R. Lorenz, E.: TRE 10:543-546. — R. V. Sellers, E. and his Place in the Early History of Christian Doctrine (Cambridge, 1928). — M. Spanneut, E.: DHGE 16:13-23.

II. Works: Despite E.'s reputation for "orthodoxy" and his importance in 4th-c. eccles. politics (see the *Laus Eustathii* of → John Chrys., PG 50:597-606), of his extensive and chiefly exegetical works only one has survived: the *Kata Origenous diagnōstikos eis to tēs eggastrimythou theōrēma* or *The Witch of Endor* (*engast.*), in which, on the one hand, he attacks Origen's historical understanding of the appearance of Samuel's spirit (1 Sam 28) and, on the other, attacks Origen's allegorical exegesis. He himself comes out in favor of a hist., philologically grounded exegesis that allows typology and allegory only to a limited degree. The same work also discusses questions of christology and of the soul (against Origen's idea of the preexistence of souls). Also attested are one or two treatises *Peri psychēs* (*kata philosophōn* and *kata Areianōn*); several anti-Arian works (among them, at least eight books *Kata Areianōn*); exegetical works (including on Ps 92, the psalm titles, and Prov 8:22); homilies and letters (among the latter, to → Alexander Alex. on Melchizedek). Ninety-two fragments have survived in florilegia, doctrinal controversial literature, and catenae (*fr.*, *fr. in Ps.*, *fr. in Pr. 8:22*, *Melch.*). The authenticity of a work against Photinus (*Phot.*) (transmitted in Syr. fragments) is disputed

(the question has consequences for determining the date of E.'s death). Other works are certainly not from E.: the address to Constantine at Nicaea (*alloc.*), a commentary on the hexaemeron (*hex.*) and on Ps. 15 as well as a homily on the supper in the house of Lazarus, Mary, and Martha (*Laz.*). Sozomen (*h.e.* 2.19.7) praises E.'s artistic style (use of archaic words; reminiscences of the classics). In his writings E. holds the unity of the *dyas*, viz., God and the Son of God (the Logos); divine nature and human body (spotless temple) and soul are blended in the person of Christ. E.'s theology and christology suggest Origenist influence (linking of the human soul and the divine Logos) and also anticipate later Antiochene formulations (distinction of divine and human nature).

W: PG 18:613-794. — *engast.*, E. Klostermann, Origenes, E. u. Gregor v. Nyssa über die Hexe v. Endor (Bonn, 1912) [text]. — Origene, Eustazio, Gregorio di Nissa, La maga di Endor, M. Simonetti (Florence, 1989) [text/Italian trans./comm.]. — *fr.*, Recherches sur les Ecrits d'E., M. Spanneut (Lille, 1948) [text/comm.]. — *Catenae Graecae in Genesim*, F. Petit, CCG 15:210f., 227f. [text]. — *Melch.*, B. Altaner, Der Brief Περὶ τοῦ Μελχισεδέκ: ByZ 40 (1940) 30-47 = Kleine patristische Schriften (Berlin, 1967), 343-362 [text/comm.]. — *Phot.*, R. Lorenz, Gegen Photinus: ZNW 71 (1980) 109-128 [text/German trans.].
L: F. Scheidweiler, Zu der Schrift des E. über die Hexe von Endor: RMP 96 (1953) 319-329. — idem, Die Frgm. des E.: ByZ 48 (1955) 73-85. — M. Spanneut, E. exégète: StPatr 7 (1966) 549-559. — J. W. Trigg, E.'s Attack on Origen: JR (1995) 219-238.

T. Fuhrer

Eustathius of Berytus

E., bishop of Berytus, sided at first with Cyril and the Monophysites. In 448 he was a member of an imperial commission that was to test the accusations against Ibas of Edessa. In 449 he spoke out against the confession of faith of → Flavian of Constantinople. In 451 at Chalcedon he adopted a mediating position and acknowledged the legal validity of the creed he had previously rejected. Probably at the end of the 50s he defended a dogm. letter of Leo I against Monophysite Timothy Aelurus (*Apologia Leonis epistulae ad Timotheum Aelurum*).

W: F. Diekamp, Doctrina patrum (Münster, ²1981), 96f. [text]. — PG 85:1803f. [Latin trans.].
L: F. Diekamp, loc. cit., XLVIII. — A. Grillmeier, Jesus der Christus 2/1 (Freiburg i.Br., 1986), 114; 2/2 (Freiburg i.Br., 1989), 436 (English, Christ in Christian Tradition, vol. 2/1 [London, 1987; vol. 2/2, London, 1995]). — A. van Roey, E.: DHGE 16:23.

B. Windau

Eustathius of Epiphania

E., from Syr. Epiphania, was a Byz. chronicler who wrote a world history (*chronikē epitomē*), which, acc. to Evagrius Scholasticus (*h.e.* 5.24), was divided into two parts: the first came down to the destruction of Troy, the second (possibly identical with a twelve-book chronicle mentioned in Suidas and beginning with Aeneas) down to the twelfth year of the reign of east Roman Emperor Anastasius (therefore 502/503). Whether, as Evagrius (*h.e.* 1.19) reports, there was further work of E.'s just on the capture of Amida by the Persians (503/504) is disputed. E. died after 502 without completing his work. Among his many sources: Charax (for the sagas), Dionysius of Halicarnassus, Polybius, Arrian, and his contemporaray Zosimus (see Evagrius, *h.e.* 5.24). E.'s work is lost except for a few fragments found espec. in → John Malalas and → Evagrius Scholasticus, who praises and perhaps uses him; the work seems, however, to have been still preserved complete in 1201 in a ms. of the monastery of John on Patmos.

W: L. Dindorf, Historici Graeci minores 1 (Leipzig, 1870), 353-363 [frgs.]. — C. Müller, E.: FHG 4:138-142 [frgs.]. — J. Bidez, L. Parmentier, The Ecclesiastical History of Evagrius with the Scholia (London, 1898) [frgs.].
L: P. Allen, An Early Epitomator of Josephus: ByZ 81 (1988) 1-11. — C. Benjamin, E.: PRE 11:1450f. — M. E. Colonna, Gli storici bizantini dal IV secolo al XV secolo 1 (Naples, 1956), 44f. — G. Garitte, E.: DHGE 16:24-26. — H. Hunger, Die hochsprachliche profane Lit. der Byzantiner 1 (Munich, 1978), 323. — A. Labate, E: DECA 1:925. — P. Maas, Eine Hs. der Weltgeschichte des E.: BZ 38 (1938) 350.

C. Schulze

Eustathius, Monk (Theodoulus)

Nothing is known in detail about E.'s life. Around the middle or in the second half of the 6th c. he composed the *ep. de duabus naturis*, addressed to a Timothy Scholasticus and attacking the Monophysitism of Severus of Antioch. His purpose as defender of the dogma of Chalcedon was to bring out the contradictions in the theol. thought of Severus. Extensive citations from E.'s work make it possible to reconstruct Severus's christology. In his terminology E. is close to Leontius Byz.

W: P. Allen, CCG 19:411-447.
L: P. Allen, Greek Citations from Severus of Antioch in E.: OLP 12 (1981) 261-264. — A. Grillmeier, Jesus der Christus 2/2 (Freiburg i.Br., 1989), 277-285 (English, Christ in Christian Tradition, vol. 2/2 [London, 1995]). — KonChal 1:684f.

M. Puzicha

Eustathius of Sebaste

E., one of the important personages of the church of Asia Minor in the 4th c., was born before 300, the son of Bishop Eulalius of Sebaste. (The Bishop Eulalius of Caesarea, whom Soc. [*h.e.* 2.43.1] and Soz. [*h.e.* 4.24.9] name as his father, does not exist in the lists of bishops.) Basil describes E., with possibly a somewhat polemical intent, as a disciple of Arius in Alexandria (*ep.* 130.1; 223.3). Athanasius mentions E. among the Arian clergy to whom Eustathius of Antioch forbade admission among his own clergy (before 330; see PG 25:70). In Alexandria E. probably came in contact with Egyptian monasticism, whose ascet. ideals he practiced in a strict form in Asia Minor and sought to spread. After 330 E. was a cleric of Hermogenes in Caesarea but transferred, probably because of his ascetic manner of life, to Eusebius of Constantinople; from there he moved for similar reasons back to the region of Pontus. Even as a cleric he wore the garb of an ascetic and for this reason was excommunicated by the Synod of Neocaesarea (339?). In 340/341 the Synod of Gangra condemned the ascet. rigorism and critical attitude to the church of his disciples, who were called "Eustathians" after him. He himself took a moderate position, insofar as he did not seek a break with the official church. Ca. 356 he became bishop of Sebaste. It is hardly possible to determine exactly his influence on the ascetic and monastic life of Basil (from 357). Basil did venerate E. as a model and teacher (*ep.* 1; 223) and was his friend until the break in 373 because of the pneumatological controversies (see below). That the two men shared a monastic ideal is clear from, among other things, the fact that Sozomen attributes the *Asceticon* of Basil to E. (*h.e.* 3.14).

In eccles. politics E. was one of the leading homoousians at the Synod of Ancyra; he was able initially to win over Emperor Constantius to that synod's anti-Arian program. When the emperor decided to take the contrary position, the homoeans gained the upper hand. At the imperial Synod of Seleucia in 359 and in the negotiations in Constantinople 359/369 the homoousians were defeated, and E. agreed to the homoean doctrine of the emperor. Because of disciplinary accusations he was nonetheless removed from his office and then, together with other deposed bishops—Macedonius of Constantinople, Basil of Ancyra, and Eleusius of Cyzicus—organized resistance to the homoeans and the imperial religious policy. After the rapprochement with the homoousians in 362 (*Tomus ad Antiochenos*) E. appeared in 364 at the Synod of Lampsacus (with Basil, among others) and in 365/366 was a member of the embassy to Rome that sought the support of the West. From 367 on, E. became leader of the pneumatomachians. The efforts of Basil to win him over to the Nicene position failed. After 373 E. joined the homoeans against Basil and the Neonicenes. He is not mentioned as part of the embassy of pneumatomachians invited by Emperor Theodosius; he probably died, therefore, shortly before 381.

S: Basil, *ep.,* Y. Courtonne, Saint Basile, Lettres 1-3 (Paris, 1957-66) [Greek text/French trans.]. — W.-D. Hauschild, Basilius, Briefe 1-3 (BGrL 3, 32, 37) (Stuttgart, 1973-1993). — Socrates, *h.e.,* R. Hussey, Socratis Scholastici Ecclesiastica Historia 1-3 (Oxford, 1853). — Sozomenus, *h.e.,* J. Bidez, G. C. Hansen, GCS 50.
L: D. Amand, L'Ascèse monastique de saint Basil (Paris, 1949). — H. Dörries, De Spiritu Sancto. Der Beitrag des Basilius zum Abschluß des trinitar. Dogmas, AAWG. PH 3/39 (Göttingen, 1956). — K. S. Frank, Monastische Reform im Altertum: FS E. Iserloh (Paderborn, 1980), 35-49. — C. A. Frazee, Anatolian ascetism in the IVth cent: CHR 66 (1980) 16-33. — J. Gribomont, Le Monachisme au IVe s. en Asie Mineure: StPatr 1 (1957) 400-415. — idem, E. le Philosophe et les voyages du jeune Basile de Césarée: RHE 54 (1959) 115-124; reprinted in: Saint Basile. Evangile et Eglise, Mélanges (Bellefontaine, 1984), 107-116. — idem, E. de Sébaste: DSp 4/2:1707-1712. — idem, E. de Sébaste, DHGE 16:26-33; reprinted in: Saint Basile. Evangile et Eglise, Mélanges (Bellefontaine, 1984), 95-106. — W.-D. Hauschild, Die Pneumatomachen, Diss. (Hamburg, 1967). — idem, E.: TRE 10:547-550. — F. Loofs, E. u. die Chronologie der Basilius-Briefe (Halle, 1898). — S. Mongelli, Eustazio di Sebaste: Nicolaus 3 (1975) 455-469. — E. Schwartz, Zur KG des 4. Jh.: ZNW 34 (1935) 129-213 (= idem, Gesammelte Schriften 4 [Berlin, 1960], 1-110). — H.-J. Sieben (ed.), Basilius v. Cäsarea, Über den hl. Geist, FC 12 (Freiburg i.Br., 1993), 21-29.

J. Pauli, OSB

Eustratius of Constantinople

E. is known as author of an obituary of Bishop Eutyches of Constantinople (d. 582) (*v. Eutych.*), to whose clergy he belonged. No information about his life has come down, but he did leave a treatise *De statu animarum post mortem* (*stat. anim.*) which deals with the state of souls separated from the body, the sufferings of the deceased, and the connection of the prayers and sacrifices of the living with the forgiveness of the sins of the deceased. The chief value of the work is the number and accuracy of citations from other authors used by E., among them Ephraem the Syrian, Basil, Gregory Naz., Gregory Nyss., Methodius, Hippolytus, John Chrys., and Ps.-Dionysius. A further work, the life of St. Golindouch (*passio Golin.*) is a revision of the story of the sufferings of this Persian female martyr.

W: *v. Eutych.,* PG 86:2273-2390. — *passio Golin.,* A. Papadopoulos-Kerameus, Analekta Hierosolymitikes stachyologias (St. Petersburg, 1897). — *stat. anim.,* C. Allatius, De utriusque Ecclesiae occidentalis atque orientalis perpetua in dogmate de purgatorio consensione (Rome, 1655), 336-580 [Greek text/Latin trans.].
L: H. G. Beck, Kirche u. theol. Lit. (Munich, 1959), 410f. — J. Darrozès, E.: DSp 4:1718f. — K. Laya, E. (Leuven/Louvain, 1958). — P. Peters, Sainte Golindouch, martyre perse: AnBoll 62 (1944) 74-125.

S. Müller-Abels

Euthalius

The dates and identity of E. are disputed. He is the author of an edition of Acts (*Ac.*), the letters of Paul (*ep. Paul.*), and the Catholic Letters (*ep. cath.*); each of the three parts is preceded by an introduction, in which E. speaks about the contents of the texts, his method of editing, and the life of Paul (*praef. ep. Paul.*; partly with reference to → Eusebius Caes.). The work is dedicated to Athanasius. E. divides the NT text into sense lines (*stichēdon*) and into chapters (*kephaleia*), subdivisions (*merikai hypodiaireseis*), and (for liturgical purposes) sections of readings (*anagnōseis*); citations in Acts and the Catholic letters are identified and tabulated. E. sees the Caesarean text of → Pamphilus as the original text (PG 85:692). Although the *Corpus Euthalianum* is clearly to be attributed to a single author (see, e.g., PG 85:629), some things seem to have been added by a later hand (stichometry, details of contents and tables of contents, apparatus of variants based on a collation with Pamphilus's text). The mss. give as the author E., deacon and later bishop of *Soulkē*, so that some have wanted to identify him with Euthalius of Sulci (7th c.). But since E.'s edition had already been translated into Armenian, Syriac, and Gothic in the 5th c. and the beginning of the 6th, this identification is not possible. Since the originally pagan technique of dividing texts into *kōla, kommata,* and *kephaleia,* etc., was applied to the bibl. text by Eusebius and Jerome (praef. *Vulg. Is.*) in the 4th c. and since E. explains the method in detail, while appealing to a particular predecessor (praef. *ep. Paul.,* PG 85:708: *eis tōn sophōtatōn tis kai philochristōn paterōn hēmōn*), we may surmise that he was a grammarian of the (early?) 4th c. and perhaps from the school of Caesarea (= → Evagrius Pont.? Euzoius Caes.?).

W: *Ac., ep. Paul., ep. cath.,* PG 85:627-790.
L: G. Bardy, E.: DBS 2:1215-1218. — A. Jülicher, E.: RE 6, 1459f. — J. W. Marchand, Gothic Evidence for "Euthalian Matter": HThR 49 (1956) 159-167. — H. v. Soden, Die Schriften des NT 1/1 (Berlin, 1902), 637-682. — L. C. Willard, A Critical Study of the Euthalian Apparatus (Ann

Arbor, 1971). — G. Zuntz, E. = Euzoius?: Vig Chr 7 (1953) 16-22.

T. FUHRER

Eutherius of Tyana

The known dates in the life of E. are connected with the Council of Ephesus (431) and the negotiations for union between Cyril Alex. and the Antiochenes (432/433). As bishop of Tyana and metropolitan of Cappadocia II, he was present at the Council of Ephesus as a decided partisan, along with John of Antioch, of Nestorius; for this reason both were deposed. When John devoted himself to Cyril's efforts for peace, he brought E. with him. During the negotiations for union in 433 E. was exiled to Scythopolis (Palestine), whence he fled to Tyre (Phoenicia). The date of his death is unknown.

E.'s writings are marked by the events of 431 to 433. Twenty-one short treatises with an introduction (*confutationes quarundam propositionum* or *Antilogia* [*confut.*]) are directed against the christology of Cyril and his political tactics; the treatises have mistakenly come down under the name of → Athanasius Alex. and → Theodoret of Cyrrhus (for which reason they were preserved, as being one of the rare authentic sources for a nonorthodox teaching). E. maintained the Antiochene "division theology": it was not God but Christ who suffered (like Nestorius, E. calls his opponents "theopaschites"). His work shows rhetorical training; the arguments are marked by Nestorian rationalism.

In addition, Deacon → Rusticus has transmitted five letters translated into Latin, in which, against various opponents of Cyril's christology, E. comments on the events of 432/433 (1: to → John of Antioch; 2: to → Helladius of Tarsus; 3: to → Alexander of Hierapolis and → Theodoret of Cyrrhus; 4: to → Sixtus III; 5: to Alexander of Hierapolis).

W: *confut., ep.,* Eine Antilogie des E., M. Tetz (Berlin, 1964) [text/comm.]. — *ep.,* ACO 1, 4, 109-112, 144-148, 213-221 [text].
L: G. Ficker, E. Ein Beitrag zur Geschichte des Ephesinischen Konzils (Leipzig, 1908). — A. Van Roey, E.: DHGE 16:50f.

T. FUHRER

Eutropius, Presbyter

E., a presbyter, was a contemporary and friend of Paulinus of Nola, at whose ascetical ideal he marvels; he was a native of the Spanish-Aquitanian area in the late 4th and early 5th c. In 394/395 to 431 he wrote

three consolatory letters of an ascet. kind to Cerasia, probably a relation of Paulinus's wife, and to her sister: *De contemnenda haereditate vel De testamento Gerontii, De vera circumcisione,* and *De perfecto homine,* as well as a consolatory treatise, *De similitudine carnis peccati* (*sim. carn.*).

The first two are identical with the two letters mentioned by Gennadius (*vir. ill.* 50 [49]), which E. wrote to two sisters who had been disinherited by the their parents, because they had entered the ranks of virgins dedicated to God. All three letters, and *ep.* 6, as well as *sim. carn.,* were handed down under the name of Jerome (*ep.* 2; 6; 19) and were first cited in the adoptionist literature of the 8th c. in Spain (Agobard, Alcuin, etc.). After *sim. carn.* was rediscovered in 1911 and initially attributed to Pacian, it became possible, later on, to reestablish E.'s literary works. As one under the influence of ascet. tendencies and Gallican rhetoric, E. was able to translate the work of the great theologians into pastoral terms and administer consolation.

W: *ep.,* PL 30:45-50, 75-104, 188-210. — *sim. carn.,* PLS 1:529-556. — H. S. Eymann (Regensburg, 1985), 24-97 [text/German trans.].
L: F. Cavallera, L'héritage littéraire: RAM 24 (1948) 60-71. — idem, L'épître pseudohiéronymienne: RAM 25 (1949) 158-167. — P. Courcelle, Un nouveau traité: idem, Histoire littéraire (Paris, ³1964), 303-317. — J. Madoz, Herencia literaria: EE 16 (1942) 27-54. — A. Michel, La culture en Aquitaine. AMidi 71 (1959) 115-124. — H. Savon, Le prêtre Eutrope: RHR 199 (1982) 273-302, 381-404. — idem, Béatitudes virgiliennes: Latomus 62 (1983) 850-862

H. S. EYMANN, OSB

Eutropius of Valencia

E., abbot of the monastery of Servitanum (near Cartagena?), was from 589 bishop of Valencia, attended the Council of Toledo III (589), and died ca. 600.

His correspondence with → Licinianus of Cartagena (Isidore, *vir. ill.* 42; 45) is lost. E. addressed two surviving treatises on morality to Peter of Arcavia. In his *Epistula de octo vitiis* (*ep.* 1.l, 198) E. is concerned chiefly with sins that threaten monastic life. Correspondingly, he argues for strict discipline in monasteries in his *Epistula de districtione monachorum et ruina monasteriorum* (*ep.* 2.l, 184).

W: *ep.* 1, 2, PL 80:9-20. — M. C. Díaz y Díaz: Anecdota Wisigothica 1 (1958) 20-35.
L: J. Orlandis, D. Ramos-Lisson, Die Synoden auf der Iberischen Halbinsel (Paderborn, 1981).

E. REICHERT

Eutyches

Born ca. 370 in Constantinople, E. entered a monastery there at an early age; immediately after priestly ordination he led that monastery as archimandrite. He had close ties with Cyril, patriarch of Alexandria, and his successor, Dioscurus, and became a zealous defender of an extreme Monophysitism, which he also tried to push through at the imperial court with the help of his godchild, head chamberlain Chrysaphius. In 447/448 he was suspected by Theodoret of Cyrrhus of being an Apollinarist and was officially condemned by the permanent synod in Constantinople in 448; a year later, at the "Robber Synod" of Ephesus he was rehabilitated by his friend Dioscurus but in 451, at Chalcedon, was definitively deposed and exiled. In his occasional letters E. does not have any thought-out christology but held fast to the *mia physis* formula of the young Cyril, which however he interpreted in a very arbitrary way. Even later moderate Monophysites such as Severus of Antioch expressly distanced themselves from E.'s conception of the unity of Christ.

W: *ep.*, PG 84:854-856. — PL 54:714-717. — ACO 2, 1, 1:90-96, 152f., 177f.
L: P. T. Camelot, De Nestorius à E.: Chalkedon 1, ed. A. Grillmeier, H. Bacht (Würzburg, 1951), 213-242. — R. Draguet, La christologie d'E.: Byz. 6 (1931) 441-457. — G. May, Lehrverfahren gegen E.: AHC 21 (1989) 1-61. — W. de Vries, Konzil von Ephesus 449: OCP 41 (1975) 357-398.

P. BRUNS

Eutychius of Constantinople

E., an ordained monk and archimandrite, born 512 in Phrygia, came to Constantinople in 552 as apocrisiarius of his bishop, in order to take part in the planned council. In that same year Justinian I appointed him patriarch of Constantinople in succession to Menas (d. Aug. 21, 552). In this capacity, and as an opponent of Antiochene theology, E. presided at the fifth ecumenical council (553), which condemned the Three Chapters. E. drafted the synodal decree (Mansi 9:396-400). But when E. proceeded against the emperor's aphthartodocetism, the latter deposed him in 565 and exiled him to the monastery of Amaseia. On Oct. 3, 577 Emperor Justin II restored him to his patriarchal see, which he occupied until 582. Because of his supposedly Origenist teaching on the resurrection of the flesh, E. came in conflict with Gregory I, at that time apocrisiarius in Constantinople. Eustratius, a disciple of E., wrote a life of E. (PG 86:2273-2390) between 582 and 602.

A work titled *De differentia naturae et hypostaseos* (*diff.*) has come down in Armenian; in it E. defends Chalcedonian christology. He distinguishes strictly between *physis* and *hypostasis* in order to avoid tritheism. Also surviving are a letter of Jan. 6, 553 (*ep.*) to Vigilius of Rome on the Three Chapters, as well as some canons (*can.*) and a fragment of a sermon on the Eucharist.

W: PG 86/2:2390-2406. — *diff.*, P. Ananian, L'opusculo di E. patriarca di Constantinopoli sulla "Distinzione della natura e persona": Armeniaca. Mélanges d'études arméniennes 5 (1969) 316-382 [Armenian/Italian trans.]. — *ep., can.*, ACO 4, 1:235f., 240-245.
L: S. S. Areyšatyan, Le "Livre des êtres" et la question de l' appartenance de deux lettres dogmatiques anciennes: REArm 18 (1984) 23-32. — H. G. Beck, Kirche u. theol. Lit. (Munich, 1959), 380, 410f. — H. M. Biedermann, E.: LMA 4:124. — A. Grillmeier, Jesus der Christus 2/2 (Freiburg i.Br., 1989), 512-514; 2/4 (Freiburg i.Br., 1990), 138-141 (English, Christ in Christian Tradition, vol. 2/2 [London, 1995]; vol 2/4 [London, 1996]). — V. Grumel, Regestes 1 (Constantinople, 1932), 244-249, 260-263. — A. Kazhdan, E.: ODB 759. — L. Magi, La Sede Romana nella corrispondenza degli imperatori e patriarchi bizantini (6.-7. sec.) (Rome, 1972), 148-160.

F. R. GAHBAUER, OSB

Evagrius, Anti-Jewish Polemicist

E., a monk, is known from Gennadius (*vir. ill.* 50). He lived in the 4th/5th c. and is sometimes identified with a disciple of Martin of Tours, mentioned by Sulpicius Severus, who withdrew into solitude (*dial.* 3.1; 4.2.8). His dates are unknown. He composed an *Altercatio legis inter Simonem Iudaeum et Theophilum Christianum*, a fictional dialogue, the purpose of which was to harmonize Jewish monotheism with the Chr. dogma of the Trinity. He used as sources → Cyprian's *Testimonia (Ad Quirinum)*, → Tertullian's *Adversus Iudaeos*, and perhaps also the *Disputatio Iasonis et Papisci* of → Ariston of Pella. There are parallels in the *Tractatus Origenis* of → Gregory of Elvira (Illiberis).

W: PL 20:1165-1172. — E. Bratke, CSEL 45. — R. Demeulenaere, CCL 64:255-302.
L: E. Schulz-Flügel, Gregorius Eliberritanus (Freiburg i.Br., 1994), 256-302 (literature). — A. L. Williams, Adv. Judaeos. A Bird's-Eye View of Christian Apologia until the Renaissance (Cambridge, 1935).

C. KASPER

Evagrius of Antioch

E. was born ca. 320 and died after 394; he was possibly from a Lat. family, was married, and climbed the career ladder until 362. Then he accompanied Euse-bius of Vercelli when the latter returned to his see from exile in Palestine and remained in Italy until 372. In Antioch E. joined the Eustathians, the minor-ity in the Meletian schism, which was led by Bishop Paulinus and supported by Rome. In 376 he carried Damasus's answering letter to Basil and Meletius (PL 13:352f.). In 388 he succeeded Paulinus.

E., who introduced Jerome to monasticism in Chalcis, made the (later) Lat. translation of Athana-sius's *Vita Antonii* (Jerome, *vir. ill.* 125); because of its refined style it was to rouse interest in the monas-tic ideal even among the western Chr. upper class, and it exerted a great influence. A series of rhetorical expansions (in the Hellen. tradition) go back to E. For a time he was regarded as a possible author of → Ambrosiaster.

W: PG 26:833-976. — PL 73:125-170.
L: G. J. M. Bartelink, Einige Bemerkungen über E.' Über-setzung der Vita Antonii: RBen 82 (1972) 98-105. — G. Garitte, Le texte grec et les versions anciennes de la Vie de s. Antoine: StAns 38 (1956) 1-12. — K. S. Frank, E.: LMA 4:126. — HLL 5:537-539.

                                                        K. BALKE

Evagrius Ponticus

I. Life: E., born ca. 345 in Ibora (Pontus), was ordained a lector by Basil and a deacon (379) by Gre-gory Naz., who took him to Constantinople. In 382, E., who until then had prospects of an eccles. career, had to leave Constantinople because of a love affair. This marked the decisive turning point in his life. He traveled, via Jerusalem, where he stayed with Melania the Elder and Rufinus of Aquileia, to Egypt, where he lived first in the desert of Nitria and then at Cellae, from 383 until his death in 399. He earned his living by copying books. At Cellae, a group of educated anchorites, who occupied themselves chiefly in the reading of Origen, gathered around E. and Ammo-nius (one of the "long brothers"). But this exposed E. and his work to a steadily growing anti-Origenism; E. avoided persecution by Patriarch Theophilus Alex. only by his premature death, but his work was marked for posterity by the stain of Origenism. As a result, his writings as well as those of Origen were definitively condemned in 553.

II. Works: E.'s literary works, all of which were writ-ten after the turn in his life but are not individually datable, are taken up with ascetical-practical and theol. questions. The history of the transmission of the original Gr. writings was lastingly influenced by the anti-Origenist condemnation: many have sur-vived only in Syr. or Arm. translation; others were handed down under the name of → Nilus. Practical and ascet. questions are the subject of the *Rerum monachalium rationes* (*rer. mon.*), which give advice for beginners in the anchoritic life, and of the *Prak-tikos* (*pract.*), which gives further advice for the ascet. struggle. The counterpart to the *Praktikos* is the *Gnostikos* (*Gnost.*), for those advancing on the way to perfection. The *Antirrhetikos* (*antirrh.*) is a hand-book on the struggle against evil thoughts suggested by demons; it offers bibl. passages as weapons. A *Mirror for Nuns and Monks* (*sent. mon./sent. virg.*) is directed to cenobites.

E.'s principal theol. work is the *Kephalaia Gnostica* (*keph. gnost.*), which is preserved in two Syr. transla-tions. The work contains six centuries of ninety *kephalaia* each, to which another work of E., contain-ing sixty *kephalaia*, was added as a "supplement." The scholia of E. on the bibl. books (*schol.*) show the spirit of Origenist exegesis; they are found in parts of the catena tradition and under the name of Origen. From a collection of sixty-eight letters (*ep.*) the one transmitted as letter 8 of Basil calls for special atten-tion. E. is also very probably the author of the treatise *Ad Eulogium* (*Eulog.*), which is attributed to Nilus, of *De malignis cogitationibus* (*mal. cog.*), *De octo spi-ritibus malitiae* (*spir. mal.*), and *De oratione* (*or.*). In addition, there is a host of smaller works, fragments, and collections of sentences.

III. Main Lines of Thought: The works of E. manifest an internal system that is directed to describing a way of salvation. His writings are not conceived as instructional lectures but are intended for careful meditation on the individual *kephalaia*, the "gnostic" parts having an esoteric character and being intended only for the experienced and the initiated. The way of salvation has two phases, which in E.'s scheme are to be described as "practical" and "gnos-tic." The person must first immerse himself in the practice of asceticism and reject the world. In this phase, the main task is the struggle against the evil thoughts inspired by demons, a fight to be carried on in the monk's cell. In this way one attains to *hesychia* and then to *apatheia*, which, however, initially affects only the passions of the soul. This is the transition from the practical to the gnostic way, on which the person now strives for complete *apatheia*, since there is question now not of the purification of the soul but of the redemption of the whole person as one with the rational essence of the entire fallen creation. The person draws near to this redemption through an increasing advance toward *theōria*, that is, not the immediate vision of God but the vision of the person's own *nous* and of the formless divine light. The vision occurs in "pure prayer," which is done in contemplative absorption.

Despite his condemnation E. had a great influence on posterity, espec. in Syria. As a result, he was one of the literary fathers of the mysticism of the eastern anchorites and cenobites. His is the standard formulation of the doctrine of the eight evil thoughts ("capital sins") that are the greatest threat on the way to perfection.

W: *rer. mon.*, PG 40:1252-1264. — *pract.*, A. and C. Guillaumont, SC 170/171. — B. Sarghissian (Venice, 1907), 22-54 [Armenian text]. — *Gnost.*, A. and C. Guillaumont, SC 356. — W. Frankenberg (Berlin, 1912), 546-553 [Syriac text/griech. RückÜ]. — B. Sarghissian, loc. cit., 12-22 [Armenian text]. — *antirrh.*, W. Frankenberg, loc. cit., 472-544 [Syriac text/Greek back trans.]. — B. Sarghissian, loc. cit., 217-323 [Armenian text]. — O. Zöckler (Fr. Baethgen), E. (Munich, 1893), 104-125 [partial German trans.]. — *sent. mon./sent. virg.*, H. Greßmann, TU 39/4 [Greek text]. — *sent. mon.*, B. Sarghissian, loc. cit., 114-124 [Armenian text]. — *keph. gnost.*, A. Guillaumont, PO 28/1 [Syriac text/French trans.]. — W. Frankenberg, loc. cit., 48-422 [Syriac text/Greek back trans./comm. of Babai]. — B. Sarghissian, loc. cit., 143-216 [Armenian text]. — *schol. in prov.*, P. Géhin, SC 340. — *schol. in eccl.*, P. Géhin, SC 397. — *schol. in pss.*, PG 12:1054-1686; 27:60-545. — J. B. Pitra, Analecta sacra 2, 444-483; 3, 1-364. — *ep.*, W. Frankenberg, loc. cit., 564-619 [Syriac text/Greek back trans.]. — B. Sarghissian, loc. cit., 334-376 [Armenian text]. — Ps.-Bas., *ep.* 8, Y. Courtonne (Paris, 1957), 22-37 [Greek text/French trans.]. — *ep.*, G. Bunge (Trier, 1986) [German trans.]. — *Eulog.*, PG 79:1093-1140. — *mal. cog.*, PG 79:1200-1233. — *spir. mal.*, PG 79:1145-1164. — *or.*, PG 79:1165-1200. — I. Hausherr: OCP 5 (1939) 7-71 [Syriac and Arabic texts]. — *Other works:* PG 40:1220-1286; 79:1093-1240. — W. Frankenberg, loc. cit. [Syriac text/Greek back trans.]. — J. Muyldermans (Leuven/Louvain, 1952) [Syriac text/French trans.]. — B. Sarghissian, loc. cit. [Armenian text].
L: R. Augst, Lebensverwirklichung u. chr. Glaube (Frankfurt a.M., 1990). — H. U. v. Balthasar, Die Hiera des E.: ZKTh 63 (1939) 86-106, 181-206. — idem, Metaphysik u. Mystik des E.: ZAM 14 (1939) 31-47. — W. Bousset, Apophthegmata (Tübingen, 1923), 281-341. — G. Bunge, Evagrianische Mystik: FS A. M. Haas (Frankfurt a.M., 1999), 27-41. — I.-H. Dalmais, L'héritage évagrien dans la synthèse de S. Maxime le Confesseur: StPatr 8 (1966) 356-362. — A. Guillaumont, E.: TRE 10:565-570. — idem, Les Képhalaia Gnostica (Paris, 1962). — idem, Un philosophe au désert: RHR 181 (1972) 29-56. — idem, Évagre et les anathématismes antiorigénistes de 553: StPatr 3 (1961) 219-226. — A. and C. Guillaumont, É.: DSp 4:1731-1744. — eadem, E.: RAC 6:1088-1107. — W. Lackner, Zur profanen Bildung des E.: FS H. Gerstinger (Graz, 1967), 17-29. — J. Muyldermans, À travers la tradition manuscrite (Leuven/Louvain, 1932). — K. Rahner, Die geistliche Lehre des E.: ZAM 8 (1933) 21-38. — F. Refoulé, La christologie d'Évagre: OCP 27 (1961) 221-266. — M. Viller, K. Rahner, Aszese u. Mystik (Freiburg i.Br., 1990 = 1939), 97-109.

K. FITSCHEN

Evagrius Scholasticus

E. (b. ca. 536 in Syr. Epiphania, d. ca. 600) was a lawyer in Antioch, whence the name "Scholasticus." Later on, he worked as secretary of Antiochene Patriarch Gregory, whom he defended in Constantinople against accusations brought by Count Asterius.

After Gregory's death (593) E. composed a history of the church in six books (*h.e.*), from the Council of Ephesus in 431 to the death of Gregory. As a result, the orthodox author reports on the period of the 5th- and 6th-c. christological disputes, which were of such great interest for theology and eccles. politics; he provides important sources, which he handles in a critical way. In other respects, too, he is credible and relatively untouched by polemics. In the introduction to his *h.e.* E. regards himself as successor to other church historians: Sozomen, Theodoret, and Socrates; he used the works of Zechariah the Orator, Theodore the Lector, Eustathius of Epiphania, and Procopius of Caesarea.

In E.'s view, the emperors are the key historical figures. However, the concept of fate also plays a role in the thinking of E., who treasured Gk. culture. In the sixth book he describes the Roman-Persian war and thus shows an interest in secular history as well. His other works, some of which he mentions in his history (6.4), have not survived.

W: PG 86/2:2405-2906. — J. Bidez, L. Parmentier (Amsterdam, 1964 = 1899) [text]. — A. J. Festugière: Byz. 45 (1975) 188-471 [French trans.].
L: P. Allen, E. (Leuven/Louvain, 1981). — G. Chesnut, The First Christian Historians (Paris, 1977), esp. 206-221. — A. Grillmeier, Jesus der Christus 2/1 (Freiburg i.Br., 1986), 38f. (English, Christ in Christian Tradition, vol. 2/1 [London, 1987]). — A. de Halleux, E.: DHGE 16:1495-1498.

K. BALKE

Evangelium veritatis

A "Gospel of Truth" (*ev. ver.*) is mentioned by Irenaeus, *haer.* 3.11.9. It is not clear whether this is the same as the gnostic homily with the same opening words in the gnostic library at Nag Hammadi (NHC 12, 2). The form and content of the latter *ev. ver.* do not correspond to those of the canonical gospels; rather the work is a homily which seeks to present redemptive gnosis as the good news. The author reflects on the knowledge, brought by Jesus, of the unknown God, a knowledge that shows the world to be a mere appearance, destroys its error, and shows true believers the way to the everlasting homeland. The relatively moderate christology of the work makes it difficult to ascribe it to the Valentinian gnostics. It was composed probably in the 2nd c. in Egypt and originally in Greek. The work is important for the history of the canon because it uses the letter to the Hebrews and the Apocalypse

W: H. C. Puech, G. Quispel, W. Till (Zurich, 1956-1961) [Coptic text/German trans./comm.]. — J. E. Ménard (Paris, 1962) [Greek trans./comm.]. — idem (Leiden, 1972) [French trans./comm.]. — K. Grobel (Nashville, 1960) [English trans./comm.]. — H. M. Schenke, Herkunft des ev. ver. (Göttingen, 1959) [German trans./comm.]. — F. García Bazán: RevBib 51 (1989) 193-248 [Spanish trans./comm.].
L: S. Arai, Christologie (Leiden, 1964). — A. Böhlig, Ursprache: Gnosis 2, ed. idem (Tübingen, 1989), 373-394. — J. D. Dubois, Contexte judaïque: RThPh 24 (1974) 198-216. — A. M. Guire, Conversion and Gnosis: NT 28 (1986) 338-355. — J. Heldermann, Literatur: ANRW II 25/5, 4054-4106. — T. Orlandi, Rassegna di studi: RSLR 6 (1971) 491-501. — idem, Ev. ver. (Brescia, 1992). — E. Segelberg, Confirmation Homily: OrSuec 7 (1959) 3-42. — B. Standaert, Question du titre: VigChr 30 (1976) 138-150. — idem, Critique et Lecture: NTS 22 (1975/76) 243-275. — C. I. K. Story, Nature of Truth (Leiden, 1971). — C. M. Tuckett, Synoptic Tradition: JThS 35 (1984) 131-145.

P. Bruns

Eve, Gospel of

A gospel of Eve (probably 2nd c.) is mentioned only in Epiphanius, haer. 26.2.6, who attributes it to the gnostics. Only a fragment of this apocalyptic work, which probably took the form of a report of a vision, has survived (haer. 26.3.1). The attribution of a second fragment (26.5.1) to the same work is very dubious.

W: Epiphanius, haer. 26.3.1.
L: A. v. Harnack, Geschichte der altchr. Lit. (Leipzig, ²1958), 1:166; 2/1:539. — H. Jonas, Gnosis u. spätantiker Geist I (Göttingen, ⁴1988), 139f. — H. Leisegang, Gnosis (Stuttgart, ⁵1985), 189f. — NTApo⁶ 1:288-290.

R. Hanig

Evodius of Uzala

E. was born on about July 28, 388 in Thagaste and was thus a little younger than Augustine. He entered the civil service as an agens in rebus (an imperial courier), converted, and was baptized by Augustine (conf. 9.8.17). In Milan he was one of the group that decided to return to Africa with Augustine and there live a religious life in community. In the De animae quantitate and the De libero arbitrio, E. is a partner in dialogue and in the two works raises the question of the nature of the soul and the origin of evil. He supported Augustine on various missions and became

bishop of Uzala in Africa Proconsularis between 395 and 401. After his installation there he carried on an extensive correspondence with Augustine, of whom eight letters to him have survived (ep. 158, 160, 161, 163 are by E.). The Indiculus of Possidius mentions only three letters. The letters show that E. was interested in theol. questions, as he had been in the early dialogues. A work De fide contra Manichaeos (fid.) is attributed to him with high probability. Improbable, on the other hand, is the attribution of the → Consultationes Zacchaei et Apollonii. E. showed himself active in church affairs by his erection of a memoria in honor of St. Stephen in Hippo and his transference of the martyr's relics to a memoria in Uzala. In addition, he endeavored to promote the veneration of the martyrs (Felix, Gennadius). Between 422 and 427 he was in contact with Abbot Valentinus of Hadrumetum. It is to be assumed that he died shortly after.

W: ep., A. Goldbacher, CSEL 44:448 197, 503 506, 507 511, 520f. — G. Morin: RB 13 (1896) 481-486; 18 (1901) 241-256 [unpublished letter]. — fid., J. Zycha, CSEL 25:949-973.
L: PAC 366-373.

W. Geerlings

Excerpta Latina Barbari

This name is given to an Alexandrian revision and continuation (to 518, year of the death of Emperor Anastasius) of the universal chronicle of → Hippolytus. This anonymous work is dedicated to an unknown barbarus of Gaul. The text has come down mutilated; Scaliger discovered and edited the complete Lat. text.

W: C. Frick, vol. 1 (Leipzig, 1892), 183-371 [text]. — T. Mommsen, MGH. AA 9:272-298 [text].
L: F. Jacobi, Barbarus Scaligeri: PRE 6/6:1566-1576.

M. Skeb, OSB

Exegesis

Inasmuch as early Chr. theology took the form in very large degree of scriptural interpretation that found expression in preaching (→ Homily), literature (→ Commentary), art, and → liturgy, patristic exegesis was of fundamental importance in the development of dogma, moral theology, and spirituality. An adequate evaluation requires a distinction between temporally conditioned methods, borrowed in part from the culture of the time, and the theol. convictions that underlay the use of those methods.

Unlike modern exegesis with its historical-critical method, the patristic interpretation of scripture was not concerned primarily to understand the bibl. text as historically conditioned human words but rather to decipher its meaning as God's word for a life of faith within the church. To this end, the mystery of Christ was the hermeneutical key, and the entirety of scripture was read in light of it (see Lk 24:27). At the same time, therefore, exegesis implied a theology of history and became itself the interpretation of salvation history. The OT was looked at in the light of a twofold confrontation: against Judaism, as a comprehensive prophecy of Christ and his church (see 2 Cor 3:14-16; → Justin, *dial.*) and against → Marcion and gnosis, as a salvific divine pedagogical process that prepared the way for the NT dispensation (→ Irenaeus, *haer.* 4.13.3; 4.20.8–21.3). The reception of Jewish and Hellen. methods of interpretation and the expansion of NT reinterpretations of OT texts with the help of allegory and typology (see Gal 4:22-24; 1 Cor 10:11; Heb 8:5), when combined with the Pauline antithesis of spirit and letter (see 2 Cor 3:6), made possible a Chr. reading of the entire Bible, in which the past became revelatory of the future, the provisional of the definitive, the unique of the abiding, and the earthly of the heavenly. Although patristic exegesis, being under the influence of pagan interpretive practice, was not able always to resist the temptation of arbitrary allegorism and symbolism, we must nonetheless regard the adherence to the historical meaning of the bibl. words and the demonstration of salvation-historical correspondences as the specific element of Chr. exegesis. At the same time, however, there was a reciprocal relation between the OT and the NT. Not only was the OT read in light of the NT, but reflection on the OT prefigurations in turn helped to a deeper understanding of the NT fulfillments. Although acc. to modern terminology many interpretations can be viewed only as developments of the so-called accommodated sense, a large part of patristic exegesis leads definitely to the so-called fuller meaning (*sensus plenior*), which, while remaining in the line of the originally intended meaning, looks at the bibl. text in light of the entirety of revelation and shows the inner fullness of the literal sense that is contained in the wording. But these exeget. methods were applied not only to the OT writings but also and espec. to the interpretation of the gospels (miracles, parables) in order to make the texts relevant to later generations. Homiletic and catechetical concerns thus contributed to the development of exeget. practice. Given the danger of their misuse by heretics,

these techniques of interpretation based on the text itself had to be supplemented by external rules of interpretation, since the gnostics, too, commented on the scriptures (see, e.g., → Heracleon, *Jo.*) and added their own hermeneutical considerations (see, e.g., → Ptolemy, *ep.*). Controversies over the correct literal and allegorical interpretation of the bibl. writings led in the 2nd and 3rd c. to an emphasis on the community of faith as the only locus of a true understanding of scripture (see 2 Pet 1:20), so that apostolic tradition and the *regula fidei* became the normative exeget. criterion. Initially, given the apologetical-polemical and catechetical contexts, exegesis was limited more to individual passages of scripture, but at the end of the 2nd and beginning of the 3rd c. we find → Hippolytus producing systematic interpretations of individual bibl. books.

A leading role in E. was occupied by Alexandria, where the intellectual heritage of Philo (alleg. interpretation acc. to a blend of Hellen. philosophy and Jewish exegesis) lived on and left an unmistakeable mark on Chr. exegesis. → Clement Alex. did not produce any systematic exegesis but did leave behind an important theory of allegory (*str.* 5.19-58). The high point of Alexandrian exegesis was reached, however, in → Origen, who put his philol. studies (*Hexapla*) and hermeneutical reflections (*prin.* 4.1-3) in the service of an exegesis geared to the threefold meaning (literal, moral, mystical) of the scriptures. → Eusebius Caes. and → Didymus the Blind were strongly influenced by Origen. The spiritual and allegorical exegesis promoted by the Alexandrian school elicited not only attacks based on pagan philosophy (Celsus, Porphyry) but also, from the beginning of the 4th c., critical reactions within the church (→ Eustathius of Antioch, *engast.* 21f.); at the end of the 4th and beginning of the 5th c., the center of this criticism was the so-called Antiochene → School (→ Diodorus of Tarsus, → Theodore Mops., → Theodoret of Cyrrhus). Their distinctive interest in the literal sense led to more independent consideration of the OT; in the so-called *theōria* this exegesis remained open to a messianic-christological interpretation, but it greatly reduced the number of relevant passages. As understood by the Antiochenes, Alexandrian allegorism did away with the literal sense in order to discover hidden mysteries in inconspicuous details of the scriptures. In contrast (they said), from the historical sense of individual passages, the proper meaning of which was retained, a further prophetic meaning, one which the sacred writer already intended, was to be derived in accordance with certain criteria (analogy). But the divergent emphases in Alexandrian and Antiochene exegesis must not be exaggerated, since representatives of both tendencies (Origen, → Cyril Alex., Theodoret of Cyrrhus) took into consideration the concerns of the other school. In addition, exegetes from Palestine (→ Eusebius Caes.) and Cappadocia (→ Gregory Nyss.) gave priority in their various works now to the literal meaning, now to the allegorical.

Among Lat. authors, except for → Victorinus of Pettau at the end of the 3rd c., it was only in the second half of the 4th c. that exegesis began an extensive development in homilies and commentaries on both the OT and the NT, espec. on the letters of Paul. While the allegorical exegesis of Origen left its mark on → Hilary of Poitiers, → Ambrose, → Jerome (less strongly later on), and → Gregory the Great, others, → Marius Victorinus, → Ambrosiaster, → Pelagius, and → Julian of Eclanum gave priority to the literal meaning. → Augustine initially favored the spiritual and allegorical exegesis he had learned from Ambrose, but he gradually developed his ability to deal with the literal meaning. Acc. to his own hermeneutical statements (*doctr. chr.* 3.10.14; 3.15.23), the preference for one or other level of interpretation was subject to the norm of the agreement of the exegesis with the twofold commandment of love and the rule of faith. In the 4th c., in addition to Augustine, → Tyconius (*reg.*) offered extensive reflections on hermeneutics, as did → Hadrian (*introd.*) in the 5th c. A repertory of allegorical interpretations of bibl. expressions was compiled by → Eucherius of Lyons (*form.*) in the 5th c., and → Junius Africanus composed a handbook of introduction to the Bible (*instituta regularia divinae legis*) in the 6th c. Patristic exegesis found its final expression in the → catena, which did not represent an original exeget. accomplishment since it was a compilation from older commentaries; but by providing verbatim excerpts, it preserved much valuable material from otherwise lost writings, mostly in Greek.

L: J. v. Banning, Allegorische Schriftauslegung: ZKTh 117 (1995) 265-295. — G. Bardy, Commentaires patristiques de la Bible: DBS 2:73-103. — idem, E. patristique: DBS 4:569-591. — Biblical Interpretation in the Early Church, ed. K. Froehlich (Philadelphia, 1985). — BiPa 1-6, Suppl. (Paris, 1986-1995). — BiToTe 1-3 (Paris, 1984-1986). — M. Canévet, Bible et les Pères: NRTh 116 (1994) 48-60. — The Cambridge History of the Bible 1-2 (Cambridge, 1969-1970). — H. Chadwick, Antike Schriftauslegung (Berlin/New York, 1998). — J. Daniélou, Divers sens de l'Écriture: EThL 24 (1948) 119-126. — H. Dörrie, Methodik antiker E.: ZNW 65 (1974) 121-138. — M. Fiedrowicz, Prinzipien der Schriftauslegung in der Alten Kirche (Bern, 1998). — R. M. Grant, History of the Inter-

pretation of the Bible (New York, ²1963). — J.-N. Guinot, Typologie comme technique herméneutique: CBiPa 2 (1989) 1-34. — C. Kannengießer, Die Bibel in der frühen Kirche: Conc(D) 27 (1991) 25-30. — H. de Lubac, Allégorie chrétienne: RSR 47 (1959) 5-43. — idem, E. médiévale 1-2 (Paris, 1959-1961). — idem, Geist aus der Geschichte (Einsiedeln, 1968). — idem, Typologie et Allégorisme: RSR 34 (1947) 180-226. — B. De Margerie, Histoire de l'e. 1-4 (Paris, 1983-1990). — E. Norelli, La Bibbia nell'antichità cristiana 1 (Bologna, 1993). — G. Pelland, Histoire de l'e. ancienne: Gr. 69 (1988) 617-628. — J. Pépin, Hermeneutik: RAC 14:722-771. — A. Pollastri, F. Cocchini, Bibbia e storia nel cristianesimo latino (Rome, 1988). — H. Reventlow, Epochen der Bibelauslegung 1-2 (Munich, 1990-1994). — M.-J. Rondeau, Actualité de l'e. patristique?: Les quatre fleuves 7 (1977) 91-99. — eadem, Commentaires patristiques du Psautier 1-2 (Rome, 1982-1985). — C. Schäublin, Antiochenische E. (Cologne, 1974). — idem, Pagane Prägung der chr. E.: Chr. E. zwischen Nicaea u. Chalcedon, ed. J. v. Oort, U. Wickert (Kampen, 1992), 148-173. — G. Schöllgen (ed.), Stimuli. E. u. ihre Hermeneutik in Antike u. Christentum, FS E. Dassmann: JAC. E 23 (Münster, 1996). — H. J. Sieben, Exegesis Patrum. Saggio bibliografico (Rome, 1983). — M. Simonetti, Lettera e/o Allegoria (Rome, 1985). — B. Studer, Die patristische E.: REAug 42 (1996) 71-95. — idem, Schola christiana (Paderborn, 1998).

M. FIEDROWICZ

Exegesis de anima

Exegesis on the Soul (Ex. an.) is the title of a work in the Nag Hammadi library (NHC 2, 6) that deals with the fall and rescue of the immortal light-soul. *Ex. an.* was probably written toward the end of the 2nd or beginning of the 3rd c. in Egypt. The gnostic origin of the work is disputed; more recently scholars point to a more strongly bibl.-based theology. The recurring call to repentance and turning away from the sinful world are themes in ascet.-parenetic literature, so there is no need of appealing to a gnostic background.

W: J.-M. Sevrin (Leuven/Louvain, 1983) [Coptic text/French trans./comm.]. — B. Layton, NHC 2 (Leiden, 1989) [Coptic text/English trans.]. — M. Krause, Die Gnosis (Zurich, 1971), 2:125-135 [German trans.]. — NHL 190-198 [English trans.].
L: S. Arai, Simonianische Gnosis: Gnosis and Gnosticism, ed. M. Krause (Leiden, 1977), 185-203. — M. Krause, Sakramente: Textes de Nag Hammadi, ed. J. E. Ménard (Leiden, 1975), 47-55. — B. Layton, Soul: Muséon 91 (1978) 155-169. — P. Nagel, Septuaginta-Zitate: APF 22/23 (1974) 249-269. — M. Scopello, L'exégèse de l'âme (Leiden, 1985).

P. BRUNS

Expositio Valentiniana

A cosmol. work with a heavily gnostic soteriology is found in the Nag Hammadi library (NHC 11, 2) under the modern title *A Valentinian Exposition* (*Exp. Val.*). The poorly transmitted Copt. text offers a gnostic cosmogony, inspired by Valentinian, with speculations on the Pleroma, Sophia, and the Demiurge, and a corresponding soteriology which in its sacramental practice (baptism, anointing, Eucharist) is close to the practice of the Chr. Great Church.

W: C. W. Hedrick, NHC 11-13 (Leiden, 1990), 89-172 [Coptic text/English trans./comm.]. — J. É. Ménard, L'exposé valentinien (Leuven/Louvain, 1985) [Coptic text/French trans./comm.]. — NHL 481-489.
L: J. E. Ménard, Exposé valentinien, RevSR 58 (1984) 52-63. — idem, Termes et thèmes valentiniens: CBCo 3 (1986) 161-168. — C. Scholten, Martyrium u. Sophiamythos (Münster, 1987). — E. Thomassen, Valentinianism: Muséon 102 (1989) 225-236.

P. BRUNS

Exsultet/Praeconium paschale

The song of praise of the Easter candle and Easter night that begins the Easter Vigil is known by the first word of its introduction as the *Ex(s)ultet*; it is known in the Roman rite since 1955 as the *Praeconium paschale* (*p.p.*: Easter Praise) but earlier as *laus, carmen, benedictio,* or *consecratio cerei*. It is a genre peculiar to the western liturgies and is first attested in 384. Eight texts, dependent to some extent on one another, have survived: *p.p. Gallicanum* (end of 4th, beginning of 5th c.; also called *Vulgata*); *p.p. Ambrosianum* (5th c.); two *p.p.* of → Ennodius (d. 521); *p.p. Gelasianum* (end of 5th, beginning of 6th c.); *p.p. Beneventanum* (follows Ennodius before 981/997; also called *Vetus Itala*); the Old Spanish *p.p.* attributed to Isidore of Seville (d. 636), as well as *p.p. Escorial* (7th c.?); and a fragment in Augustine (*civ.* 15.22). These are *eucharistiae* with a prologue (originally only in *Gall.*, but then transferred to *Ambrosianum* and *Beneventanum*) in which elements of the early church's thanksgiving for the light are combined with praise of the Easter event as developed espec. in typologies. Some of the *p.p.* have the so-called Praise of the Bee, which represents, typologically, the virginal birth of Christ.

W: All texts: H. Zweck, Osterlobpreis u. Taufe (Frankfurt a.M., 1986) [text/German trans./comm.]. — H. Schmidt, Hebdomada Sancta (Rome, 1957), 2:362f., 627-650, 824-826 [text]. — *Gall.*, G. Fuchs, H. M. Weikmann, Das E. (Regensburg, 1992) [text/German trans./comm.].
L: H. Auf der Maur, Die österliche Lichtdanksagung: LJ 21 (1971) 38-52. — R. Buchwald, Osterkerze u. E.: ThPQ 80 (1927) 240-249. — B. Fischer, Ambrosius der Verfasser des E.: ALW 2 (1952) 61-74. — C. Giraudo, Questa è la notte: RdT 25 (1984) 113-131, 227-243. — H.-W. Kruft, E.-Rolle: RDK 6, 719-740.

H. M. WEIKMANN

Eznik of Kolb

E., from the village of Kolb in the Caucasus, was active in the 5th c. He was a disciple of Mesrob and, acc. to Elische and Lazarus of Pharp, was bishop of Bagevand. His most important work is the *Refutation of Errors*, also known in the tradition as *De Deo*. It has four main parts: (1) against the errors of the pagans; (2) against the religion of the Persians (Mazdaism); (3) against the religion of Gr. philosophy; (4) against the errors of Marcion. The composition is to be dated, with a good deal of certainty, to the 5th decade of the 5th c. E.'s work is a classical apologetics in which he contributes not a little to distinguishing Arm. theology from Gr. paganism in the form of philosophy and from dualisms of every kind (Parsism, Marcionism). In addition, the work is distinguished by its elegant classical Arm. language and marks the beginning of an original Arm. literature after a period of translation from Syriac and Greek. Furthermore, the work is an irreplaceable source for the knowledge of Parseeism and of some heretical movements within the church (Marcionism). Homilies (*hom.*) and a letter to Mesrob (*ep.*) are also attributed to E.

W: *De Deo*, L. Mariès, C. Mercier, PO 23/3f. [text/French trans.]. — Z. B. Tosunian, Concordantia E. episcopi (Eriwan, 1972 = Venice, 1826). — J. Schmid, Des Wardapet E. Wider die Sekten (Vienna, 1900) [German trans.]. — S. Weber, BKV[2] 57 [German trans.]. — *hom.*, J. Muyldermans, E. sententiae: Muséon 56 (1943) 102-111 [text]. — *ep.*, N. Akinean: HandAm 49 (1935) 615-617 [text].
L: N. Adontz, Grégoire l'Illuminateur et ses rapports avec E.: ROC 25 (1925/26) 309-337. — R. Ajello, A. Borghini, Il serpente: Baz. 147 (1989) 259-279. — G. Cuendet, E. et la bible: REArm 9 (1929) 13-40. — C. Dowsett, E. Refutation of the Chaldeans: REArm 6 (1969) 45-65. — R. Hewsen, E. and the Problem of Evil: ECR 3 (1971) 396-404. — L. Mariès, Le De Deo d'E. (Paris, 1924). — idem, Sur les noms et verbes d'existence chez. E.: REArm 8 (1928) 79-210. — idem, L'emploi du mot "Dieu" chez E.: REArm 9 (1929) 89-112. — M. Minasean, Traduction russe d'E.: REArm NS 9 (1972) 79-101. — idem, Un passage d'E.: Muséon 86 (1973) 341-363. — J. Rivière, Exposé marcionite de la Rédemption: RSR 1 (1921) 185-207. — L. van Rompay, E. et Théodore de Mopsueste: OLoP 15 (1984) 159-175. — S. Weber, Abfassungszeit u. Echtheit: ThQ 79 (1897) 365-398. — idem, Apologie: Kath. 17 (1898) 212-231, 311-326. — C. Williams, Marcion in E.: JThS 45 (1944) 65-73.

P. BRUNS

Ezra, Literature about

The fourth book of Ezra is a Jewish apocryphal work that deals in seven visions with the problem of theodicy. The Gr. version of a Heb. original from the period after 70 was received by Christians more than by Jews. In the Lat. translation two chapters are added at the beginning and two at the end that are lacking in eastern translations. Yet there is probably a Gr. original at the bottom. Chs. 1-2 are also known as *5 Esr.*, chs. 15-16 as *6 Esr.* Both books are works of Chr. prophecy, intended to interpret the present.

In the first part of *5 Esr.* a Jewish model may have been used but given a Chr. revision and turned into an OT-based invective against Israel (after the manner of an OT cento). In the second part, Ezra sees the church of the Gentiles on Zion. *6 Esr.* describes the collapse of the four empires (Babylon, Asia, Egypt, Syria) in dramatic images, but persecuted Christians are exhorted and consoled. While *5 Esr.* was probably written in the 2nd c. (there are similarities to the *Passio Perpetuae* and to Ps.-Cyprian, *adv. Judaeos*), *6 Esr.* can be dated only very roughly (period of persecutions in the East; 3rd c.?).

A Gr. *Apocalypsis Esdrae* (*Apoc. Esd.*) uses *4 Esr.* and the Jewish *Apocalypse of Sedrach*. Of probably Chr. origin also is the *Visio Esdrae* (*Vis. Esd.*), trans-mitted in Latin, since it, like the *Apoc. Esd.*, has a passage on the punishment of Herod.

W: *5 Esr.*, *6 Esr.*, Biblia Sacra iuxta Vulgatam Versionem, ed. R. Weber et al. (Stuttgart, 1969, 1931-1934, 1967-1974) [text]. — NTApo⁵ 2:582-590 [German trans.]. — *Apoc. Esd.*, *Vis. Esd.*, O. Wahl, PVTG 4 (Leiden, 1977) [text]. — *Vis. Esd.*, A. Riessler, Altjüd. Schrifttum (Augsburg, 1928), 350-354 [German trans.].
L: I. Andrews, Being Open to the Vision: A Study from Fourth Ezra: JLT 12 (1998) 231-241. — T. A. Bergren, Fifth Ezra (Atlanta, 1990). — M. D. Brocke, On the Jewish Origin of the "Improperia": Immanuel 7 (1977) 44-51. — H. Danielou, Le Vᵉ Esdras et la judeo-christianisme latin: FS G. Widengren (Leiden, 1972), 162-171. — HLL 4:375-377. — W. G. Kümmel, Jüd. Schriften aus hellenistisch-röm. Zeit 5/2 (Gütersloh, 1976), 85-102. — M. J. Labourt, Le Vᵉᵐᵉ livre d'Esdras: RB 17 (1909) 97-109. — G. Mercati, Note di Letteratura Biblica (Rome, 1901), 61-79. — J. M. Charlesworth, The Old Testament Pseudepigrapha 1 (London, 1983), 516-559, 561-579, 581-590. — G. N. Stanton, 5 Esr and Matthean Christianity: JThS 28 (1977) 67-83. — W. Schneemelcher, Esra: RAC 6:604-606.

G. RÖWEKAMP

F

Facundus of Hermiane

F., bishop of Hermiane in North Africa, was one of the most learned authorities on the Lat. and Gr. literature of his age. His entire literary production was in defense (*defens.*) of the Three Chapters of theologians → Theodore Mops., → Ibas of Edessa, and → Theodoret of Cyrrhus, which were condemned by Emperor Justinian in 544. His apology, composed between 546 and 548, placed him in direct opposition both to the emperor, who secured the condemnation of the Three Chapters at the Second Council of Constantinople (553), and to Bishop Vigilius of Rome, whom F. attacked for his all too accommodating attitude to secular authority. Out of fear of imperial repression F. went into hiding in the province of North Africa. From the underground he continued until his death (568) his literary feud in the form of a work against Mocianus (*Moc.*), a scholar loyal to the emperor, and of an *Epistula fidei catholicae* (*ep.*).

In his writings F. shows himself a strict Chalcedonian, who was also able to appreciate the two-nature doctrine of the Antiochene type. F. regarded the posthumous condemnation of Theodore Mops. as invalid. The first book of the *defens.* contains a detailed compendium of Lat. christology and, in its explanations of the *unus ex Trinitate* formula, made an important contribution to the trinitarian debate of the 6th c.

W: PL 67:527-878. — *defens.*, I. M. Clément, R. Vander Plaetse, CCL 90A:1-398 [text]. — *c. Moc.*, eadem, CCL 90A:399-416 [text]. — *ep.*, eadem, CCL 90A:417-434 [text]. L: P. Bruns, Zwischen Rom u. Byzanz: ZKG 106 (1995) 151-178. — E. Chrysos, Zur Datierung der Werke des F.: Kl. 1 (1969) 311-323. — idem, The Ecclesiastical Policy of Justinian (Thessalonica, 1969). — R. B. Eno, Doctrinal Authority: REAug 22 (1976) 95-113. — L. Fatica, La defensio di F.: Asp. 38 (1991) 359-374; 39 (1992) 35-55. — A. Grillmeier, Jesus der Christus 2/2 (Freiburg i.Br., 1989), 431-484 (English, Christ in Christian Tradition, vol. 2/2 [London, 1995]). — W. Pewesin, Imperium, Ecclesia universalis (Stuttgart, 1937). — A. Placanica, Facondo Ermianense e la polemica per i Tre Capitoli: Maia 43 (1991) 41-46. — R. Schieffer, Drei-Kapitel-Schisma: ZKG 87 (1976) 167-201. — idem, V. ökum. Konzil: ZSRG. K 90 (1973) 1-34. — M. Simonetti, Haereticum non facit ignorantia: Orph. NS 1 (1980) 76-105

P. BRUNS

Fastidiosus

Of F.'s dates we know only that he was alive between 522 and 533, first as a Catholic priest and monk, and then as an Arian. He composed a sermon, transmitted in the works of → Fulgentius of Ruspe, in which he defends himself against the charge of a disorderly life; in the process he plagiarizes two letters of Fulgentius against the Pelagians and the Donatists.

W: J. Fraipont, CCL 91:280-283.
L: PAC 362.

W. GEERLINGS

Fastidius, a Pelagian

F., of whose history no further details are known, was a bishop of the Britons ca. 430. He is considered to have been a disciple of Pelagius. Acc. to Gennadius (*vir. ill.* 57 [Richardson]) F. was the author of two works addressed to a certain Fatalis: *De vita christiana* and *De viduitate servanda*. But it is difficult to identify these works. Attempts to identify the first with the *Admonitio e cod. Augiensi ccxxi* or the Ps.-Augustinian *De vita christiana* (both come down among the writings of Pelagius) and to see in the second the central idea of the work of the same name by → Caesarius of Arles are unsatisfactory. Other letters and works found among the writings of Pelagius have been attributed to F., espec. the so-called *Corpus Caspari* (*Tract. Pelag.*), which contains ascetic and moral writings. But it remains uncertain whether F. defended Pelagian theses.

W: R. S. T. Haslehurst, The Works of F. (London, 1927) [text/English trans.]. — *Tract. Pelag.*, C. P. Caspari, Briefe, Abhandlungen u. Predigten (Brussels, 1964 = Christiania, 1890), 3-167 [text]. — B. R. Rees, The Letters of Pelagius and his Followers (Woodbridge, 1991), 147-298 [English trans.]. — *Admonitio*, G. Morin: RBen 46 (1934) 5-15. — *ps. Aug. vit. christ.*, PL 40:1031-1046. — Caesarius of Arles, De viduitate servanda, PL 67:1094-1098.
L: A. Di Berardino (ed.), Patrologia 3 (Turin, 1983), 441f., 446f. — R. F. Evans, Pelagius, F.: JThS 13 (1962) 72-98. — J. Kirmer, Das Eigentum des F. (St. Ottilien, 1938). — F. G. Nuvolone, Pélage et Pélagianisme: DSp 12/2:2889-2923, here 2912-2914. — G. de Plinval, F.: DHGE 16:676f. — O. Wermelinger, Neuere Forschungskontroversen: Internationales Symposium über den Stand der Augustinusforschung, ed. C. Mayer, K. H. Chelius (Würzburg, 1989), 189-217.

B. WINDAU

Faustinus

F. was a Roman presbyter in the second half of the 4th c., a supporter of Bishop Liberius, who was exiled 355-358, a follower of Ursinus, who was deposed in 367, and an antibishop to Damasus. After being banished by the latter to Eleutheropolis in Palestine in

367, he joined the party of the radically Nicene Lucifer of Cagliari.

Ca. 380, at the urging of Flacilla, wife of Emperor Theodosius I, F. wrote a defense of the Cath. doctrine of the Trinity, *De Trinitate* (*trin.*), against the Arians and, together with the Roman presbyter → Marcellinus, a petition, known as the *Libellus precum*, that was presented in Constantinople in 383/384. In it, F. defended the supporters of Lucifer as being orthodox and asked for imperial protection against Cath. attacks; this Theodosius granted in 384 in a rescript to praetorian prefect Cynegius (16.5.13). The work contains extremely important hist. data on the Luciferians. Finally, there is preserved a creed (*fid.*) of F. that was presented to Emperor Theodosius 379/381 in defense against the accusation of Sabellianism and Apollinarism.

W: *fid.*, PL 13:1050. — M. Simonetti, CCL 69:355-357. — *trin.*, PL 13:37-80. — M. Simonetti, CCL 69:287-353. — *libellus precum*, PL 13.81-107. — M. Simonetti, CCL 69:359-391. — O. Günther, CSEL 35.1:5-44.
L: G. Barbille, F.: DThC 5:2105-2107. — A. Jülicher, F.: PRE 6/2:2088-2090. — M. Simonetti, Note su F.: SE 14 (1963) 50-98.

C. SCHMIDT

Faustus (of Byzantium)

The pseudonym Faustus conceals an otherwise unknown compiler of a collection of "epic stories" (*buzandaran patmutiwnk*) that have for their content the period between Trdat the Great (330) and the year 387. Even the early Arm. tradition wrongly connected *huzand* with Byzantium, but in any case the word is part of the title and not of the author's name. The work has come down in incomplete form; only books 3-6 with the history of the christianization of Armenia down to 387 have survived. The work was later continued by → Lazarus of Pharp. We can only speculate about the content of the lost first two books; in addition to possible Gr. sources there may have been an Arm. version of the *Doctrina Addai* (→ Addai) and an early form of the hist. work of → Agathangelus. Some inconsistencies in the presentation, as well as obvious anachronisms, raise the question of a later revision in the 5th c. Although many questions of detail still await answers, the "epic stories" remain an important source for the early history of Chr. Armenia.

W: N. G. Garsoïan, The Epic Histories or History of Armenians (New York, 1984 = St. Petersburg, 1883) [text]. — idem, The Epic Histories (Cambridge, Mass., 1989) [English trans.]. — V. Langlois, Collection des historiens (Paris, 1867), 201-310 [French trans.]. — M. Lauer, Des F. Geschichte Armeniens (Cologne, 1879) [German trans.]. — M. Gevorgian, Istorija Armenii (Eriwan, 1953) [Russian trans.].
L: N. Akinean, F.: HandAm 52 (1938) 9-56, 129-172. — N. Andrikean, F.: Baz. 61 (1903) 256-264. — H. Armen, F.: Baz. 121 (1963) 23-32. — N. Biwzandac'i, Epic Histories: HandAm 97 (1983) 357-370. — F. Feydit, Un passage énigmatique: Baz. 115 (1957) 282-284. — idem, L'Histoire de F.: Baz. 116 (1958) 140-143. — idem, Solution de l'énigme du livre VI: Baz. 124 (1966) 95-97. — N. G. Garsoïan, Protecteur des pauvres: REArm 15 (1981) 21-32. — H. Gelzer, Die Anfänge der arm. Kirche: BSGW 47 (1895) 109-174. — E. Kettenhofen, Toponyme bei F.: HandAm 103 (1989) 65-80. — J. Marquart, Zur Kritik des F.: Ph. 55 (1896) 213-234. — G. Menevischean, F. Übersetzung: WZKM 3 (1889) 51-68. — P. Peeters, Persécution de Sapor: REArm 1 (1920) 15-33. — idem, La Vie de S. Basil dans F.: AnBoll 39 (1921) 65-88.

P. BRUNS

Faustus of Milevis

Only Augustine provides some information on the life of F. He was born ca. 340, in Milevis, Numidia. He was a Manichean bishop and evidently had special talents as an orator. He was active first in Rome and later in Carthage (from 383), where Augustine met him; Augustine was initially enthused about him but was later disillusioned when F. could not satisfactorily answer his questions. Ca. 383 F. was exiled. After his exile he composed *Capitula* (*cap.*), a work that is known only through Augustine's *Contra Faustum*, in which a large part of F.'s work is cited verbatim. The *cap.*, meant to serve as a weapon in dealings with Catholics, attempted to show the agreement between the Bible and Manichean belief, or, if need be, to show the Bible as mistaken; for this reason, the *cap.* firmly rejected the OT. Augustine combatted F. and his work in his *Contra Faustum* and rejected his method. F. died probably before 400, even before his refutation by Augustine.

W: P. Monceaux, Le manichéen F. (Paris, 1924) [reconstruction].
L: A Bruckner, F. (Basel, 1901). — F. Decret, Aspects du manichéisme (Paris, 1970). — A. M. La Bonnardière, F. 13: DHGE 16:729-731. — PAC 390-397.

B. WINDAU

Faustus of Riez (Reji)

F. (b. ca. 410, probably in Britain; d. ca. 495, in Riez) became a monk of Lérins after 426. While abbot there (433 to ca. 460), at the third Synod of Arles (ca. 456) he obtained, for the first time in Gaul, a legal decree of jurisdiction for the monastery against the diocese or local ordinary. The institutionalization of monasticism at Lérins, which under F.'s leadership became the most important monastery in Gaul, was largely his doing, although it is still disputed how far his influence went in the formation of rules. He followed Maximus, his predecessor as abbot, to the episcopal see of Riez.

Esteemed as a theologian, he formed the theology of all of Gaul against the predestinationism of Lucidus at the Synods of Lyons and Arles (under Bishop Leontius) (470/472; see *grat.* prol.; *ep.* 1 and 2 = recantation of Lucidus). In political negotiations (by order of Emperor Julius Nepos) with the Arian Visigothic King Euric he fell into disfavor with the Germanic rulers, probably because of his anti-Arianism (Apollinaris Sidonius, *ep.* 7.6), and was forced into exile in 477. This he spent with Bishop → Ruricius of Limoges, until he was able to return to Riez in 486.

For an understanding of his theology his express aim of combining theol. and ascet. positions is decisive. Even his early *ep.* 7 to Graecus (ca. 441; Gennadius, *vir. ill.* 86) shows his anti-Nestorian and anti-Arian viewpoint, following Augustine and Cassian, and ends with the advice to seek the *via regia* in theology and asceticism at Lérins.

At the request of the Synod of Lyons F. composed the two books *De gratia* (*grat.*), in which he takes a clear position against Pelagius but also against an extreme Augustinianism, which denied the cooperation of the human will and activity in redemption. In the background here was F.'s fear that the ascetical life might ultimately be invalidated. The clash with the Arian Visigoths led to the two books *De spiritu sancto* (*spir.*) in dialogue form (Apollinaris Sidonius, *ep.* 9.9; see Gregory, *dial.* 4.42, who ascribes them to a Paschasius) against the Arians and Semiarians (Macedonians). Connected with this are *ep.* 3 (Gennadius, *vir. ill.* 86) and 5, with their statements on the corporeality of the soul (no traducianism: in keeping with his teaching on grace, F. follows the creationism of → John Cassian); in the background is the fear that people might call into question the divine nature of Christ and of the Holy Spirit if the divine property of incorporeality were allowed to creatures. In the remaining *epp.* to Ruricius, F. takes up questions of the ascetical way of life and of the renunciation of property and lifelong penance; in the process he speaks out against Novatian and a *poenitentia in extremis* (see *gr.* 2.9; Avitus, *ep.* 4). But his *hom.*, to a greater extent even than his major works, were revised and scattered. Much of his material has

existed since the 7th c. in the collection of southern Gallic sermons of → Eusebius Gallicanus; among them are also addresses on his predecessors Honoratus and Maximus, as well as ten *Homiliae ad monachos*, which are indebted primarily to → John Cassian and → Pachomius. The collection of twenty-two *hom.* in the *Codex Durlacensis* (CSEL 21) is not only a late compilation but comes mostly from → Caesarius. The work *De ratione fidei* is certainly not authentic.

F. was undoubtedly the most important abbot and bishop of 5th c. Gaul. → Apollinaris Sidonius composed a *eucharisticon* in his honor (*Carmen* 16). But the views of this monk-theologian did not go unchallenged: his teaching on grace was opposed by → Avitus (*ep.* 4) after 500 and, after 519, by the Scythian monks under → John Maxentius and by the African monks banished to Sardinia under → Fulgentius of Ruspe (eight lost books against F.; see Isidore of Seville, *vir. ill.* 27). In 529 his teaching was condemned at the Council of Orange at the instigation of Caesarius. His statements on the corporeality of the soul were contested by → Claudianus Mamertus, *De status animae* (468). The *Decretum Gelasianum* condemned F.'s writings as *apocrypha*. He is described as a main representative of Semipelagianism.

W: *spir., grat., ep., frgm.* on *grat.*, A. Engelbrecht, CSEL 21. — *ep. ad Ruricum,* R. Demeulenaere, CCL 64:406-415. — *hom.,* F. Glorie, CCL 101, 101A, 101B. — C. M. Kasper (monastic sermons of F.): EA 67 (1991) 293-304, 368-384, 453-466; 68 (1992) 108-124, 186-194, 279-292, 369-384, 471-480 [German trans./comm.].
L: W. Bergmann, Südgallische Predigtlit. (Leipzig, 1898). — P. L. Carle, L'homélie de Pâques de F.: Div. 27 (1983) 123-154; 28 (1984) 2-24, 203-242. — R. J. H. Collins, F.: TRE 11:63-67. — M. Djuth, Initium Bonae Voluntatis: AugSt 21 (1990) 35-55. — E. Griffe, Sermons de F.: BLE 61 (1960) 27-38. — idem, Nouveau plaidoyer de F.: BLE 74 (1973) 187-192. — J. Huhn, De ratione Fidei: TQ 130 (1950) 176-183. — C. M. Kasper, Weg u. Ziel des asketischen Lebens: ThPh 63 (1988) 230-241. — idem, Der Beitrag der Mönche zur Entwicklung des Gnadenstreites: FS C. Mayer (Würzburg, 1989), 153-182. — idem, Theologie u. Askese (Münster, 1991). — J. B. Leroy, L'œuvre oratoire de F., typescript of diss. (Strasburg, 1954). — D. J. Nodes, Paenitentia in Letters of F.: RThAM 55 (1988) 30-40. — S. Pricoco, La datazione del spir.: Did. 15 (1965) 115-140. — M. Simonetti, I fonti del spir.: SicGym 29 (1976) 413-425. — idem, Il grat. di F., SSRel 1 (1977) 125-145. — idem, F. e i Macedoniani: Aug. 17 (1977) 333-354. — C. Tibiletti, Libero arbitrio e grazia in F.: Aug. 19 (1979) 259-285. — idem, La salvezza umana in F.: Orph. 1 (1980) 371-390. — A. de Vogüé, Emprunts de Colomban à F.: StMon 10 (1968) 119-123. — idem, Vie monastique à Lérins: RHE 88 (1993) 5-53. — G. Weigel, F. (Philadelphia, 1938).

C. KASPER

Felix I of Rome

F. was bishop of Rome from 268 (269?) to 273 (274?) and recognized Domnus I as bishop of Antioch (this is the only sure information about his life). A letter of his with Monophysite ideas is a forgery, just as are the Ps.-Isidorean letters, attributed to F., which deal with eccles. procedures in suspicions against clerics and with the relationship between God the Father and the Son.

S: LP 207f.
W: PL 5:135-156. — S. Wenzlowsky, Briefe der Päpste, BKV[1] 13:467-473 [German trans.].
L: P. Nautin, Félix Ier: DHGE 16:886f.

O. KAMPERT

Felix (II) of Rome

After the banishment of Liberius, Emperor Constantius II appointed F. antibishop of Rome. Liberius's return led, after bloody fighting, to the withdrawal of F. to his estate in Porto, where he died in 365. In one legend F. becomes an orthodox martyr. Ps.-Isidorean letters and decretals, attributed to F., give advice on conduct under persecution.

S: LP 1:207f.
W: P. Hinschius, Decretales (Leipzig, 1868), 484-494.
L: K. S. Frank, Lehrbuch (Paderborn, 1996), 262. — P. Nautin, F.: DHGE 16:887-889.

O. KAMPERT

Felix II of Rome

F. (March 13, 483–March 1, 492), eighteen of whose letters (ep.) have come down, communicated his election as bishop of Rome to Emperor Zeno and reported the misconduct of Patriarch Acacius of Constantinople and of Peter Mongus, the Monophysite-minded patriarch of Alexandria (ep. 1). The conflict led subsequently to the Acacian schism, a break that F. defended in the East (ep. 2.12 and 14-18). In letters F. attacked Pelagianism and took up the cause of Christians persecuted in Africa (ep. 13). Ep. 3-5, from the synod of October 484, are not authentic.

W: O. Guenther, CSEL 35:155-161, 398-439. — PL 58:889-973. — A. Thiel, Epistolae Romanorum pontificum (Hildesheim, 1974 = 1868), 222-284 [text]. — S. Wenzlowsky, Briefe der Päpste, BKV[1] 18:205-329 [German trans.].
L: P. Nautin, F.: DHGE 16:889-895.

O. KAMPERT

Felix III of Rome

Elected by order of Theodoric the Great, F. (July 12, 526–Sept. 22, 530), who has left four letters (ep.) and an edict, intervened in the controversy on grace during his externally peaceful pontificate. In the defense against Semipelagianism he supported → Caesarius of Arles with Capitula on the doctrine of grace; these rely espec. on texts of Augustine, were accepted at the Second Council of Orange (529), and put an end to the controversy. By handing over his pallium shortly before his death and by means of an edict, F. chose → Boniface II as his successor (ACO 4, 2, 96f.).

W: PL 65:11-16. — ACO 4, 2, 96f.
L: E. Caspar, Geschichte des Papsttums (Tübingen, 1933), 2:193-201.

O. KAMPERT

Ferrandus of Carthage

F., a monk and deacon of Carthage, was born in Africa and lived in the 5th/6th c. He early attached himself to Fulgentius of Ruspe and accompanied him into exile in Sardinia (508); he was a disciple of Fulgentius, perhaps his secretary. He returned with him to Byzacena after the death of Thrasamund, the Vandal ruler (523). The anonymously transmitted Vita of Fulgentius was probably by F. Twelve letters from F.'s correspondence have come down. Letters 1-5, addressed to various spiritual persons (1 and 2 to Fulgentius; 3 to Deacon Anatolius; 4 to Abbot Eugippius of Lucullanum; 5 to scholasticus Severus), deal with theol. problems (e.g., Trinity, baptism, christology, theopaschism); ep. 6 is a report on the Three-Chapters controversy for Roman deacons Anatolius and Pelagius; ep. 7 continues the letter of the (meanwhile deceased) Fulgentius to comes Reginus and sketches a picture of an ideal Chr. military commander. Letters 8-12 contain only personal communications to various addressees. F. also collected and systematically arranged the canonical decrees of numerous Gr. and African councils (Breviatio canonum). Eugippius regarded him as worthy of being Fulgentius's successor. F. died 545/546 as a man highly esteemed in the eccles. life of North Africa.

W: vita, PL 65:117-150. — G. G. Lapeyre (Paris, 1929). — A. Isola, CTP 65 (Rome, 1987). — ep. 1/2 (= Fulgentii ep. 11/13), PL 65:378-380, 392-394. — J. Fraipont, CCL 91:357-362, 383-387. — ep. 3-7, PL 67:887-908. — ep. 4, A. Mai, Scriptorum veterum nova collectio 3/2 (Rome, 1828), 169-184. — ep. 8-12, A. Reifferscheid, Anecdota Casinensia, Index scholarum Vratislavensium 1871-1872 (Breslau, n.d.), 5-7. — *Breviatio canonum*, PL 67:949-962; 88:817-830. — C. Munier, CCL 149:284-311.

L: R. B. Eno, F. and Facundus on doctrinal authority: Studia Patristica 15, ed. E. A. Livingstone (Berlin, 1984), 291-296. — A. Isola, Sulla paternità della Vita Fulgentii: VetChr 23 (1986) 63-71. — PAC 446-450. — M. Schanz, C. Hosius, G. Krüger, Geschichte der röm. Lit. 4/2 (Munich, 1959), 572-574. — M. Simonetti, F. di Cartagine nella controversia teopaschita: Fides Sacramenti, Sacramentum Fidei. Studies in Honour of Pieter Smulders, ed. H. J. Auf der Maur, et al. (Assen, 1981) 219-231. — idem, Note sulla Vita Fulgentii: AB 100 (1982) 277-289.

H. Schneider

Ferreolus of Uzès

F., bishop of Uzès, died in 581. He was probably author of a rule for monks (between 553 and 573) that was meant for a monastery named after the martyr Ferreolus. The author was undoubtedly a Gallic bishop of the second half of the 6th c. His rule contains elements of the monastic tradition of Pachomius and Basil, Cassian and Augustine, as well as that of the monks of Lérins, and accurately reflects monastic observance in Provence at this period. His direct models were the monastic rules of → Caesarius and → Aurelian, bishops of Arles. The *Regula Tarnatensis* was influenced by the *Regula Ferreoli* and may have had the same author. Letters F. supposedly wrote after the manner of → Apollinaris Sidonius (Gregory of Tours, *Franc.* 6.7) are lost.

W: PL 66:995-996. — V. Desprez: RMab 60 (1982) 117-148. L: L. R. Desalle, Règles de Césaire, F. et Regula Tarnatensis: Aug. 11 (1961) 5-26. — V. Desprez, Règles monastiques d'Occident (Bellefontaine, 1980), 287-339. — G. Holzherr, Regula F. (Einsiedeln, 1961). — P. Viard, F.: DSp 5:189-191. — A. de Vogüé, F.: DIP 7:1576-1579.

C. Casper

Fides Hieronymi

This a Lat. profession of faith (→ creed) of the 4th c. that has been ascribed not only to → Jerome but also to → Gregory of Elvira. It represents an early form of the Apostles' Creed (Apostolicum) and contains the first Lat. mention of the descent of Christ to the lower world (*descendit ad inferna*) and of the communion of saints (*sanctorum communionem*). The opening words are *credo in unum deum patrem omnipotentem*; it is not to be confused with a creed of the same title that is close to that of Toledo I.

W: G. Morin: AMar 3 (1903) 199f. [text]. — A. Wilmart: RBen 30 (1913) 274f. [text]. — V. Bulhart, CCL 69:273-275.

L: G. Morin, Un symbole inédit attribué à saint Jérôme: RBen 21 (1904) 1-9. — Fides Hieronymi: ODCC3 610.

J. Lössl

Filastrius

We are told of F. (in the sources also called Filaster, rarely Philastrius) by his successor Gaudentius (*serm.* 21) that for a long time he traveled the Roman world as a preacher, that before Ambrose's election as bishop of Milan F. fought against the Arian bishop Auxentius (355-374), then lived in Rome for a long time, and finally became bishop of Brescia. As such, he took part in the Council of Aquileia in 381. Augustine says (*ep.* 222.2) that he met F. several times in the company of Ambrose, therefore between 383 and 387. F. died on a July 18, between 387 and 397.

Handed down in its completeness is the *Diversarum hereseon liber*, which must have been composed between 380 and 390. A preface is followed by 156 chapters, of which twenty-eight describe pre-Chr. (!), the other 128 Chr. heresies. F. gives no definition of heresy and in other respects too his work is superficial. Even when writing of heresies known to him, such as Arianism, he makes numerous mistakes. He used as sources the *Panarion* of → Epiphanius of Salamis and the *Adversus haereses* of → Irenaeus. Scholars today exclude any use of the *Syntagma* of → Hippolytus. Augustine cites the work several times but does not have a high opinion of it (*haer.* 41). The language shows that the author had but little education.

W: F. Marx, CSEL 38. — F. Heylen, CCL 9. — G. Banterle (Milan, 1991) [text/Italian trans.].
L: S. Döpp, Kann modus "personales Vorbild" bedeuten?: Glotta 61 (1983) 228-233. — H. Frank, Weihnachts- u. Epiphaniezeugnis: JLW 13 (1936) 10-23. — P. C. Juret, Étude grammaticale (Erlangen, 1904). — J. Pépin, Platonisme judéo-chrétien: idem, Ex Platonicorum Persona (Amsterdam, 1977), 39-130. — D. Portarena, Doctrina scripturistica (Rome, 1946). — M. J. Rondeau, Polémiques concernant le psautier: RHR 41 (1967) 1-51. — F. Vattioni, Prima lingua: Aug. 34 (1994) 397-436.

B. Dümler

Firmicus Maternus

I. Life: Julius Firmicus Maternus Junior (F.) was from Sicily; the dates of his birth and death are unknown. While active as an advocate in Rome, he wrote *Matheseos libri 8* (*math.*) on astrology. At the time of composition F. knew little of Christianity and held a "somewhat deformed monotheism." Under the influence of the sons of Constantine the Great he became a Christian and then became a fanatical opponent of paganism in his *De errore profanarum religionum* (*err.*).

II. **Works:** The *math.* (between 334 and 337), along with the *Tetrabiblos* of Ptolemy, is the most extensive presentation of ancient teaching on the influence of the stars on human life. Apart from the *Astronomica* of Manilius and the astrological elements in the *Chronograph of 354*, the *math.* is the only surviving manual of ancient astrology in Latin. In light of its structure, which is comparable to that of the *Astronomica*, both works may have had a common Gr. source. *Err.* (between 346 and 350) is not an apology but a sharp attack on paganism. F. demands that Christianity no longer tolerate paganism but root it out. Only the end of the preface has come down; the dedication to the emperor is lost. Chs. 2-17 offer a traditional euhemeristic critique of the gods. Chs.18-27 unmask the pagan mysteries as a perverted imitation of Chr. worship and are important for knowledge of the various mysteries. The final chapters, 28-29, contain a twofold exhortation: to pagan readers that they convert, and to the emperor that he root out paganism without mercy. There is no ancient testimony to the influence of the work on the emperor, but it may have influenced his religious policy. The so-called *Consultationes Zacchaei et Apollonii* are no longer attributed to F.

W: *math.*, W. Kroll, F. Skutsch, 2 vols. (Stuttgart, 1968) [text]. — W. Kroll, F. Skutsch, K. Ziegler, 2 vols. (Leipzig, 1897/1913) [text]. — *err.*, C. A. Forbes (New York, 1970) [English trans./comm.]. — G. Heuten (Brussels, 1938) [text/French trans./comm.]. — A. Müller, BKV 14 (Munich, 1913) [German trans.]. — A. Pastorino (Florence, 1956), 1969 [text/Italian trans./comm.]. — R. Turcan (Paris, 1982) [text/French trans./comm.]. — K. Ziegler (Munich, 1953) [text/German trans.].
L: A. Bartalucci, Considerazioni: SIFC 39 (1967), 165-187. — J. B. Bauer, Zu F. err.: ErJB 57 (1959), 73-75. — P. F. Beatrice (ed.), L'intolleranza cristiana (Bologna, 1990). — F. J. Dölger, Nilwasser u. Taufwasser: AC 5 (1936) 153-187. — C. A. Forbes, F. and the Secular Arm: CJ 55 (1960) 146-150. — T. Friedrich, In Iulii F. M. err. quaestiones (Bonn, 1905). — K. Hoheisel, Das Urteil über die nichtchr. Religionen, Diss. (Bonn, 1971). — C. H. Moore, F., Diss. (Munich, 1897). — D. Morin, Ein zweites chr. Werk: HJ 37 (1916) 229-266. — A. Müller, Zur Überlieferung der Apologie des F., Diss. (Tübingen, 1908). — A. Quacquarelli, La sicilianità di F.: VetChr 25 (1988) 303-342. — A. Reatz, Das theol. System: FThSt 25 (1920) 135-146. — F. Skutsch, Ein neuer Zeuge: ARW 13 (1910) 291-305. — A. Vecchi, F. e la "Lettera agli Ebrei": Conv. 25 (1957) 641-651.

H. Holthaus

Firmilian of Caesarea

From ca. 230 to 268 F. was bishop of Caesarea in Cappadocia. Our information on his life comes mainly from Eusebius (*h.e.* 6; 7 passim). F. was one of the leading figures of the eastern church. He was in contact with Origen, whom he invited to his city and whom he himself visited in order to receive theol. instruction. There was also a correspondence between them, beginning after 238. F. fought against the Montanists of his province and was spokesman at the Synod of Antioch, which dealt with Novatian and his supporter Fabian of Antioch. In the controversy over heretical baptism between Cyprian and Stephen of Rome, F., along with most bishops of Asia Minor, sided with Cyprian. In this connection there is also a letter of F. to Cyprian in autumn 256, which is an answer to a lost letter of Cyprian and is found, in a Lat. translation, among the letters of Cyprian (*ep.* 75). In it F. approves Cyprian's attitude and attacks Stephen. Because of his position in the heretical baptism controversy F. was excommunicated by Stephen, but there was a later restoration of communion with Rome. F. presided at the first two synods of Antioch on christology and the manner of life of Paul of Samosata. He died on the way to the third synod in 268. Basil the Great says F. wrote a work called *Logoi* in which he held the same teaching on the Holy Spirit as Basil did (*spir.* 29.74). But these views of F., of which nothing else is known, are not described in detail.

W: W. Hartel, CSEL 3/2:810-827. — G. W. Clarke, ACW 47:246-276 [English trans./comm.].
L: J. Doignon, Points du vue comparés de Cyprien et F.: Aug. 22 (1982) 179-185. — Die Geschichte des Christentums 2 (Freiburg i.Br., 1996), 27, 48, 100f. — M. Girardi, Scrittura e battesimo degli eretici: VetChr 19 (1982) 37-67. — A. Harnack, Geschichte der altchr. Lit. (Leipzig, ²1958), 1/1:407-409; 2/2:102f. — G. A. Michell, F. and Eucharistic Consecration: JThS NS 5 (1954) 215-220. — P. Nautin, Lettres et écrivains (Paris, 1961), 152-156, 238f., 250. — idem, F.: DHGE 17:249-252. — idem, Origène (Paris, 1977), 173-175.

B. Windau

Firmus of Caesarea

F., bishop of Caesarea in Cappadocia, was one of the most outstanding representatives of orthodoxy at the Council of Ephesus (431). In addition, he was one of the envoys of the Cyrillian party whom Theodosius summoned to Chalcedon, along with delegates of the opposing party. In 432 F. was deposed by the eastern bishops at Tarsus but remained in his bishopric. A sermon against Nestorius, delivered probably at Ephesus, has survived in Ethiopic. In addition, forty-five short letters (*ep.*) have come down in their original Greek. They contain numerous citations of the classics and are composed in an elegant style but say little about real theol. questions.

W: *hom.,* A. Dillmann, Chrestomathia Aethiopica (Darmstadt, 1967 = Leipzig, 1866/Berlin, ²1955), 106f. [text]. — B. M. Weischer, Qerellos 4/1: Homilien u. Briefe zum Konzil von Ephesos (Wiesbaden, 1979), 134-137 [text/German trans.]. — S. Grébaut, Traduction de la version éthiopienne: ROC 15 (1910) 324f. [French trans.]. — *ep.,* PG 77:1481-1514.
L: Die Geschichte des Christentums (Freiburg i.Br., 1996), 2:610, 614. — P. Godet, F.: DThC 5/2:2554; supplements: DHGE 17:264. — E. Venables, F 10: DCB 2:524.

B. WINDAU

Flavian I of Antioch

While still a layman, F. joined Diodorus of Tarsus as leader of the Nicene party in Antioch. He was ordained a priest 362/363 and became successor to Meletius, bishop of Antioch, in 381 but was acknowledged only in 398, since the West initially joined sides with his episcopal rival Paulinus. In 383 F. presided over a council that condemned the Messalians. In 387, after the overthrow of the statues in Antioch, he led an embassy to Theodosius in Constantinople to ask for mercy on the Antiochenes. F.'s speech to Theodosius is in → John Chrys. (*stat.* 212.3), whom F. ordained a priest; but this is probably John's own work, not the original speech. F., under whom the church of Antioch won high esteem, died in 404. Apart from a sermon transmitted under Chrysostom's name, *De anathemate* (*anath.*), which contains an exhortation to love of neighbor, only fragments of sermons (*fr.*) by F. have come down in Greek and Syriac. The letters on the Messalians, which Photius (*cod.* 52) mentions, are lost.

W: *anath.,* PG 48:945-952. — Greek *fr.,* F. Cavallera, S. Eustathii ep. A. in Lazarum . . . homilia (Paris, 1905), 105-110 [text]. — *Syr. fr.,* I. Rücker, Florilegium Edessenum: SBAW. PH 1933, 5, 34 Nr. 40, 35 Nr. 41/42 [text/Greek back trans.].
L: R. Devreesse, Le patriarcat d'Antioche (Paris, 1945), 36-41, 113. — Die Geschichte des Christentums (Freiburg i.Br., 1996), 2:454, 791, 1034. — D. Gorce, F.: DHGE 17:380-386.

B. WINDAU

Flavian of Constantinople

F., a presbyter, became patriarch of Constantinople in 446 as successor to Proclus. Under his leadership a local synod condemned Eutyches the Monophysite in Nov. 448. Leo I was informed of this by F. (*ep. Leon.*) and approved the measure in his *Tomus ad Flavianum*. Eutyches for his part succeeded in getting F. deposed and banished by the "Robber Synod" of Ephesus in 449. F. died on the journey into exile (449/450) but probably not as a result of supposed ill treatment during the synod. The Council of Chalcedon (451) rehabilitated F. That council was based on the profession of faith that F. had presented to Emperor Theodosius II (*ep. Thds.*) and that mediated between the christologies of Alexandria and Antioch.

W: *ep. Leon.,* PL 54:723-732, 743-751. — *ep. Thds.,* PG 65:889-892.
L: K. Baus, HKG(J) 2/1:116-120. — H. Chadwick, The Exile and Death of F.: JThS 6 (1955) 17-34. — P. Galtier: KonChal 1 (1954) 350-353. — A. Grillmeier: KonChal 1 (1954) 195-198. — idem, Jesus der Christus (Freiburg i.Br., 1979), 1:731-737 (English, Christ in Christian Tradition, vol. 1 [London, ²1975]). — J. Liébaert, F.: DHGE 17:390-396.

R. HÖFFNER

Flavius of Chalon-sur-Saône

F. was an official of King Guntram of Burgundy. After the death of Bishop Agricola he became bishop of Châlon (Cabillonum) and took part in councils (1 and 2 of Macon, 581, 583; 3 of Lyons, 583; 2 of Valence, 585) and in the baptism at Namur of Clothar, son of Fredegund; he died in 592. To him is attributed the hymn *Versus ad mandatum in cena Domini*, which was sung after the washing of the feet (Holy Thursday) in Cluny, Besançon, Chartres, and Tours.

W: A. S. Walpole, Early Latin Hymns (Cambridge, 1922), 210ff. [text/comm.].

C. KASPER

Florilegium

Florilegium, a Lat. term imitating the Gr. *anthologion* (documented in imperial times at the earliest), has served only since the early modern age as a description of independent collections in which (ideally) verbatim excerpts (with note of their origin) are brought together, frequently acc. to thematic viewpoints, from existing works belonging to completely different genres. Anthologies of gnomic verse, primarily from Euripides and Menander and transmitted in Hellen. papyri, point to the schools as the place of origin of this kind of collection. An educational purpose (i.e., communicating morality and wisdom) was served not only by such anthologies of poets but also by collections of excerpts from prose texts read in the schools (e.g., the *Kyriai doxai* of Epicurus). The high point of pagan florilegium literature was reached in the *Eklogoi* of John Stobaeus (end of 4th, beginning of 5th c. C.E.), which were based on substantially older collections. Chr. authors such as → Clement Alex., → Origen, and → Gregory Naz. make demonstrable use of pagan anthologies of verse and gnomes. If we take as norms both the literary type of the excerpted sources and the intended or realized use of a florilegium, then the following types of Chr. florilegia may be distinguished within the genre:

1. Bibl. florilegia (*Testimonia*): From the third c. on in North Africa collections are attested of bibl. prooftexts which were arranged in *capitula* and were to be the basis of a Chr. apologetic line of argument against Jewish objections (→ Cyprian, *Ad Quirinum*) or of a polemical separation of the church from heretics (→ Ps.-Vigilius of Thapsus, *Contra Varimadum*, 5th c.). That 2nd-c. Gk. collections of testimonies are to be presupposed is only speculation.

2. Theol. florilegia: collections of excerpts from the writings of one or more church fathers. The earliest example is the *Philocalia*, drawn from the works of Origen, linked with → Basil and → Gregory Naz., but probably made in Caesarea in the first half of the 4th c. In Chr. Lat. literature this type of florilegium probably appeared first in excerpts from the works of → Augustine (→ Prosper Tiro of Aquitania, mid-5th c.; → Eugippius).

3. Dogm. florilegia: These arose in the Gr. East in connection with the pneumatological (second half of 4th c.) and christological (5th c.) controversies and were based on the fundamental supposition that the dogm. tradition of the fathers, as an actualizing interpretation of the bibl. witness, was to be used in justifying any particular doctrinal viewpoint (Basil, *Spir.* 29.71-74; Cyril Alex., *ep.* 1.4; *Arcad.* 10-18; *apol. orient.* 13-17 [drawn from this: Monophysite florilegia, see espec. Timothy Aelurus]; Theodoret, *Eranistes* [drawn from this: Diphysite florilegia]). The Monothelite (7th c.) and iconographic (8th c.) controversies elicited other florilegia of this kind. A special form of the dogm. florilegium is the → *Doctrina Patrum* of a certain Anastasius (?) (second half of 7th c.), which offers a complete doctrine of the faith in systematically organized citations from the fathers.

4. Spiritual florilegia: The starting point of these florilegia, which emphasize the ascet. orientation of patristic wisdom, is the *Sacra Parallela* of → John Damascene (?) (8th c.). The flowering of this type came in the Byz. period.

L: F. Brunhölzl, F. 2: TRE 9:219-221. — H. Chadwick, F.: RAC 7:1131-1160. — E. Dekkers, Florilèges augustiniens, AugL 40 (1990), 27-44. — F. Diekamp, Doctrina Patrum de Incarnatione Verbi (Münster, ²1981). — A. Grillmeier, Jesus der Christus 2/1 (Freiburg i.Br., ²1991), 58-89 (Eng., Christ in Christian Tradition, vol. 2/1 [London, 1987]). — P. Monat, Les testimonia bibliques de Cyprien à Lactance: La monde latin antique et la Bible, ed. J. Fontaine, C. Pietri (Paris, 1985), 499-507. — E. Mühlenberg, F. 1: TRE 9:215-219. — E. Rauner et al., F.: LMA 4:566-572. — M. Richard, Florilèges spirituels grecs: DSp 5:475-512, reprinted in: idem, Opera Minora 1 (Turnhout/Leuven, 1976), Nr. 1. — idem, Opera Minora 1-3 (Turnhout/Leuven, 1976/77). — T. Schermann, Geschichte der dogmatischen F. en vom 5.-8. Jh. (Berlin, 1904). — E. Schwartz, Codex Vaticanus gr. 1431 (Munich, 1927). — A. Sieber, F.: HWRh 3, 367-371. — C. Wachsmuth, Studien zu den griech. F.en (Osnabrück, 1971 = Berlin, 1882). — M. Tetz, Streit zwischen Orthodoxie und Häresie an der Wende des 4. zum 5. Jh.: EvTh 21 (1961) 354-368, reprinted in: idem, Athanasiana (Berlin/New York, 1995), 275-289.

B. NEUSCHÄFER

Florilegium Edessenum anonymum

The *florilegium edessenum* was probably compiled shortly after the Council of Ephesus (431) by a nameless author and is largely dependent on the florilegium *De fide ad reginas* of → Cyril Alex. The Gr. original is regarded as lost and only a 6th-c. Syr. translation has survived; the latter shows a certain closeness to → Severus of Antioch.

W: I. Rücker, F. E. syriace (Munich, 1933) [text].

P. BRUNS

Fortunatian of Aquileia

F., from Africa, was bishop of Aquileia under Constantine (Jerome, *vir. ill.* 97); he is regarded as builder of the post-theodorian North Basilica there. At the Council of Sardica he was among the defenders of Athanasius and subsequently took him in. But in the struggle between Constantius and Liberius he came down on the anhomoean side. He died before 368.

In addition to the previously known three fragments of his commentary on the gospels, one of the first exegetical works in Latin, further fragments in the form of short *expositiones* on the gospels have recently been attributed to him. There is radical disagreement, however, as to whether the formula *tituli ordinarii* in Jerome refers to an exegesis of pericopes by F. or to an Aquileian list of gospel pericopes that is the basis of the commentary on the gospels. The thesis cannot be maintained that F.'s commentary survives in the *Expositio quatuor Evangeliorum* of Ps.-Jerome.

W: A. Wilmart, B. Bischoff, CCL 9:365-370. — P. Meyvaert, New Fragments: FS B. Bischoff (Munich, 1988), 277-289 [text/comm.].
L: V. C. DeClerq, F.: DHGE 17:1182-1185. — L. Duchesne, Libère et F.: MEFR 28 (1908) 47f. — K. Gamber, Codices liturgici (Freiburg i.Br., ²1968), 79-81, 172. — HLL 5:419-421. — J. Lemarié, Italie: DSp 7:2161f.

B. DÜMLER

Fragmenta Ariana

In 1828 A. Mai published twenty-one fragments of a Bobbio palimpsest. The content of the first nineteen is Arian. The unity of style suggests that all may be from the same author. This writer opposes the views of Hilary, Phoebadius, and Ambrose but also of the Macedonians. The identification of the author with Ulfila, Auxentius, or others is disputed. The author does come from that period, probably from among the associates of Ulfila.

In content the fragments give a radically Arian theology. In a creed the author stresses the point that God the Father has no beginning and is immutable, whereas the Son acting as mediator before his descent into Mary always showed obedience to God. The ascension involved the flesh. The Spirit is neither God nor Lord, but Servant of Christ.

W: PL 13:593-628. — R. Gryson, CCL 87A:229-265.
L: P. P. Gläser, Phoebadius v. Agen, Diss. (Augsburg, 1978). — R. Gryson, Litterature Arienne Latine 1 (Leuven/Louvain, 1980) [concordance]. — M. Meslin, Les Ariens d'Occident (Paris, 1967), 113-134. — J. Ulrich, Die Anfänge der abendländischen Rezeption des Nizänums (Berlin, 1994), 136-194 (background).

T. BÖHM

Fravitas of Constantinople

F. followed Acacius (d. Nov. 28, 489) as bishop of Constantinople. Of his life we know only that he was previously a priest. His name suggests Gothic descent. Acc. to custom F. made his entrance into office known to the bishops of Rome, Felix III, and of Alexandria, Peter Mongus. The importance of this fact is that it was an effort to mediate in the Acacian schism. Acacius and Peter, a Monophysite, had agreed, with the approval of the emperor, to accept the creed of Nicaea as binding and to reject everything that went beyond it. As a result, Felix condemned F.'s predecessor for refusing to excommunicate Peter. F. knew that an excommunication of

Peter would have led to unrest in Egypt and would not have been tolerated by the emperor. He therefore asked Peter, in a letter handed down in Syriac, to make concessions to Rome; he himself asked in only a general way for a rejection of the errors condemned at Nicaea and for adherence to traditional teaching. The letter to Felix has not survived, but the latter's answer has (PL 58:971-974): the pope continued to call for the excommunication of Peter, who persisted in the condemnation of Chalcedon. But F. did not experience the failure of his effort to mediate; he died in 490, after only four months in office.

W: E. W. Brooks, CSCO 84:9-11 [text]; CSCO 88:6f. [French trans.].
L: P. Nautin, F.: DHGE 18:1128f.

S. MOLIERE-ABELS

Fredegarius

"Fredegarius" (F.) is the name first given in the 16th c. (and unconfirmed) to the author of a chronicle running from the creation of the world to 642; the first three books are a compilation from known sources, and only the fourth book (from 584), which presents Frankish-Merovingian history, has the value of a source. A distinction was earlier made between three authors, but today a single author is accepted, who wrote in barbaric Latin ca. 658/660. The work is famous for the first attestation of the saga of the Trojan descent of the Franks and for its early awareness of the Slavs. In the 8th c., the work was continued in three stages (down to 768).

W: B. Krusch, MGH. SRM 2 (Hannover, 1888), 1-193 [text]. — J. M. Wallace-Hadrill, The Fourth Book of F. with Its Continuations (London, 1960) [text/English trans.]. — A. Kusternig, H. Haupt: AQDGMA 4a (1982) 1-325 [starting with 2.53: text/German trans.].
L: W. Fritze, Untersuchungen zur frühslav. u. frühfränkischen Geschichte bis ins 7. Jh. (Frankfurt a.M., 1994). — H. Löwe, F.: RGA 9:519-521. — I. N. Wood, F.' Fables: Historiographie im frühen MA, ed. A. Scharer, G. Scheibelreiter (Vienna, 1994), 359-366.

R. SCHIEFFER

Fructuosus of Braga

F. was abbot of Dumio from 654 to 655, bishop of Braga from 656, and died before 675. After schooling in Palencia he withdrew to an estate of his family near Bierzo. There, as well as in Galicia and the Baetica region, he established several monasteries, for which he wrote rules. While the *Regula monachorum* (*reg. monach.*) goes back directly to F. and shows his inclination to eremitism, the *Regula communis* (*reg. comm.*) seems to be the joint work of some abbots who supported F.'s goals. The effect of these monastic rules on Iberian monasteries was perceptible even centuries later. Interest in F. remained great. A *Vita Fructuosi* was written; at the beginning of the 12th c. his remains were transferred to Saragossa from a monastic community he had founded between Braga and Dumio.

Along with the rules, two letters of F. have survived: one to → Braulio of Saragossa (*ep.* 1) and one to King Recceswinth (*ep.* 2). The question of the authorship of the *Hymnus de Cucuphate* and the *Pactum Fructuosi* remains open.

W: *reg. monach.*, J. Campos Ruiz, BAC 321:127-162 [text/Spanish trans.]. — *reg. commun.*, J. Campos Ruiz, BAC 321:172-208 [text/Spanish trans.]. — C. W. Barlow, FaCh 63 [English trans./comm.]. — *ep.* 1, J. Madoz, Epistolario de s. Braulio (Madrid, 1941), 186-189. — *ep.* 2, MGH. Ep 3:688f. — *Hymnus de Cucuphate*, C. Blume, AHMA 27:150-152 [text]. — *Pactum Fructuosi*, PL 87:1127. — D. de Bruyne: RBen 28 (1911) 80-86.
L: Actas do congresso de estudíos a comemoraco do XIII centenário da morte de S. F. (Braga, 1967). — M. C. Díaz y Díaz, La Vida de S. F. (Braga, 1974). — I. Herwegen, Das Pactum des hl. F. (Stuttgart, 1907). — E. A. Thompson, Two Notes on St F.: Her. 90 (1957) 59-60.

E. REICHERT

Fulgentius, the Donatist

F., the Donatist, was probably a priest and, shortly after the Conference of Carthage (411), wrote a *Libellus de baptismo*. The work has survived in the response of a disciple of Augustine. F. wrote about the one baptism and denied Catholics (in his eyes, "the new Samaritans"), espec. the *traditores*, the ability to administer this and the other sacraments. F. also cites one of the participants in the Synod of Carthage in 312, which condemned Caecilian, and thus provides the only document on that important assembly.

W: Ps.-Augustine, *Adversus Fulgentium Donatistam*, M. Petschenig, CSEL 53:289-310. — C. Lambot, L'écrit attribué à S. Augustin: RBen 58 (1948) 177-222 [text/comm.]. — *Libellus de baptismo*, P. Monceaux, Histoire littéraire de l'Afrique chrétienne 5 (Paris, 1920), 335-339 [text].
L: P. Monceaux, loc. cit. 6 (Paris, 1923), 221-232. — PAC 506f.

G. RÖWEKAMP

Fulgentius, Mythographer

Fabius Planciades, or Fabius Claudius Gordianus Fulgentius (the name in the mss.), was probably from North Africa and probably of senatorial rank, as the title *V. C.* (*vir clarissimus*) handed down with his name indicates. He wrote a number of works in the 5th/6th c.

In two works F. explains pagan myths and classical Roman poetry in a symbolic and allegorical way. In the three books of the *Mythologiae* (*myth.*) fifty sagas from the world of the pagan imagination are given a Chr. interpretation. The influence of the *myth.* can be seen espec. in the medieval *Mythographi Vaticani I et II*. F. found a congenial follower in the symbolic-allegorical interpretation of the pagan mythic world in the person of Franciscan John Ridewell (14th c.), known as *F. metaforalis*. F.'s second work, the *Expositio Virgilianae continentiae secundum philosophos moralis* (*Virg. cont.*) gives a Chr. interpretation of the *Aeneid*. The shade of Virgil appears to F. in a fictitious vision and explains to him the deeper, i.e., Chr., meaning of the *Aeneid*, which really describes the conditions of human existence (*status humanae vitae*). This Chr. interpretation of Virgil influenced espec. such medieval authors as Sigebert of Gembloux, John of Salisbury, and Bernard of Chartres. F. also produced a glossary (*Expositio sermonum antiquorum*; *serm. ant.*) in which sixty two rare words are explained. The commentary on the *Thebais* of Statius (*Super Thebaidem*; *Theb.*) continues the symbolic-allegorical interpretation of Virgil. This work is transmitted only in a medieval ms. under the name of *Sanctus F. episcopus*, and its authenticity is disputed.

In addition there is an outline of world history (*De aetatibus mundi et hominis*; *aet. mund.*). This was intended as a piece of play with grammar after the model of a poet named Xenophon: each numbered chapter lacks its corresponding letter of the alphabet. The twenty-three chapters (matching the twenty-three letters of the Roman alphabet) were to correspond to twenty-three periods of world history. Only fourteen chapters were completed. Chs. 1-9, 12, and 13 deal with bibl. episodes (from the fall of Adam to Christ and the apostles), ch. 10 with Alexander the Great, ch. 11 with the history of Rome (to Caesar), and ch. 14 with the Roman emperors (to Valentinian).

Lost are F.'s youthful verses, a *Physiologus* (not related to the well-known book of animal fables), and a commentary on the first two books of Martianus Capella. The identity of the mythographer with Bishop → Fulgentius of Ruspe is disputed.

W: *Collected works*, R. Helm (Leipzig, ²1970) (with a bibliography by J. Préaux = 1898). — L. G. Whitbread (Columbus, 1971) [English trans.]. — *Virg. cont.*, T. Agozzino, F.

Zanlucchi (Padua, 1972) [text/comm./Italian trans.]. — *Mythographi Vaticani I et II*, P. Culcsár, CCL 91c.
L: B. Baldwin, F. and His Sources: Tr 44 (1988) 37-57. — B. Bischoff, Mal. Studien (Stuttgart, ²1967), 271 n. 138. — R. Edwards, F. and the Collapse of Meaning: Helios 3 (1976) 17-35. — P. Langlois, F.: RAC 8:632-661. — idem, Les œuvres de F. le Mythographe et le problème des deux F.: JAC 7 (1964) 94-105. — H. Liebeschütz, F. metaforalis. Ein Beitrag zur Geschichte der antiken Mythologie im MA (Leipzig/Berlin, 1926). — P. Magno, Su alcune citazioni di F. riguardanti Ennio e Pacuvio: RSC 26 (1978) 451-458. — E. Pasoli, Dividias mentis conficit omnis amor (Fulg. Exp. 34): Giornale Italiano di Filologia 24 (1972) 363-371. — U. Reinhard, Das Parisurteil bei F. (myth. 2, 1), Tradition und Rezeption: Studien zu Gregor v. Nyssa und der chr. Spätantike, ed. R. Drobner, C. Klock (Leiden, 1990), 343-362. — J. C. Relihan, F. Mitologiae 1. 20-21: American Journal of Philology 109 (1988) 229f. — G. Rauner-Hafner, Die Vergilinterpretation des F.: MLJb 13 (1978) 7-49. — M. van Roy, Notes sur les mss. Wolfenbüttel, Herz. Aug. Bibl., 23-24 Gudiani Latini (= 4328-4329): Scr. 41 (1987) 127-128. — M. Schanz, C. Hosius, G. Krüger, Geschichte der röm. Lit. 4/2 (Munich, 1959), 196-205. — C. Stoecker, Alexander der Große bei F. und der Historia Alexandri Macedonis des Antidamas: VigChr 33 (1979) 55-75. — L. C. Stokes, F. and the "Expositio Virgilianae Continentiae" (Ann Arbor, Mich., 1969). — eadem, F.' Expositio Virgilianae Continentiae: Classical Folia 26 (1972) 27-63. — C. Zintzen, Zur Aeneis-Interpretation des Cristoforo Landino: MLJb 20 (1985) 193-215.

H. SCHNEIDER

Fulgentius of Ruspe

I. Life: F. was born in Telepte (Medinet el Khedima) in the Roman Byzacena province in 468 (or 462). Soon after his death his disciple → Ferrandus, a monk and deacon of the Carth. church, wrote his life. F. was from a Carth. senatorial family. His grandfather, Gordian, was banished to Italy in 439 by Geiseric, after the conquest of Carthage. After Gordian's death two of his sons returned home and recovered part of his possessions. Claudius, father of F., died early, and his education was seen to by his mother, Marina. F. learned Greek and supposedly mastered it, as he did his mother tongue. Only after instruction in Greek did he receive instruction in Lat. literature. Even as a young man he became a *procurator* (receiver of taxes). The decisive factor in his conversion to the spiritual life was the reading of Augustine's *en. Ps.* 36 (in the life by Ferrandus this incident is described with echoes from Augustine, *conf.* 8.5.12 and 8.6.15: Ponticianus's account of the two men converted at Trier). After his conversion F. always lived, like Augustine, in a monastic community (*Vita* 39). But he constantly changed monasteries either because he was forced by external circumstances (barbarian invasions) or because he wanted a stricter asceticism. Wherever he stayed for a longer period, he usually soon founded a monastery (e.g., Mididi, Ruspe, Cagliari). When he was stirred by the reading of the works of → John Cassian and the desert fathers and wanted to travel to Egypt, he did not continue his journey beyond Sicily, on the advice of Bishops Eulalius and Rufinianus, because the Egyptian monks were supposedly heretics. Instead he went to Rome in 500 in order to visit the *sacra loca martyrum*. There he met the Ostrogothic King Theodoric at his triumphal entry into the city. After returning to Africa F. led a life of retirement as a simple monk near Junca (Bordj Younga). At this time the Arian Vandal King Thrasamund (496-523) was combatting the refusal of the Catholics to obey his order not to fill episcopal sees that had become vacant. While the see of Ruspe was vacant because of Thrasamund's restrictive policy, F. became a priest and presbyter and then, at the request of the populace, was ordained a bishop by Victor, the primate. Soon after his election as bishop, F. and sixty other Cath. bishops were banished to Sardinia by order of Thrasamund. There F. became the spiritual leader of the exiled bishops. His exile was interrupted for a time (ca. 515) when he was summoned to Carthage to defend the Cath. faith before Thrasamund. But two years later, as a result of Arian influence at the court of the Vandal king, F. had to go into exile again. Only after the accession of Hilderic in 523 was F. able to return to Ruspe where he spent the remainder of his life. He died in 533 (or 527) at the age of sixty-five after a twenty-five-year episcopate.

II. Works: Acc. to Ferrandus's life the works of F. may be divided into periods: the times in Sardinian exile, and the time of each return home. The works of the first exile in Sardinia are lost. During the period of his first return, in the work *Dicta regis Trasamundi et contra ea responsiones* (*seu Contra Arianos; c. Arian.*) F. answered ten questions of Thrasamund. In the three books *Ad T(h)rasamundum regem* (*ad Tras.*) the controversy is continued. The work *Adversus Pintam* is lost. Bishop Pinta, an Arian, had tried to refute the three books addressed to Thrasamund. Only two fragments have survived of the anti-Arian work *De spiritu sancto ad Abragilam presbyterum commonitorium* (*spir.*). From the period of the second exile we have the work on the forgiveness of sins (*De remissione peccatorum ad Euthymium*; *rem. pecc.*) in two books. To this period belongs the anonymously transmitted anti-Arian *Psalmus abecedarius* (*psalm.*), which is probably to be ascribed to F.; it was conceived on the model of Augustine's *Psalmus contra partem Donati*. In the three books *Ad Monimum* (*ad Monim.*) F. answers questions of Monimus, a layman, on various theol. problems (e.g., predestination and the doctrine of the Eucharist). The seven (lost) books *Contra Faustum Reiensem* were in response to the Semipelagian work *De gratia* of → Faustus of Riez.

From the period of the second return come the ten books *Contra Fabianum* (*c. Fab. frg.*) which have been handed down in thirty-nine sometimes quite lengthy fragments. Fabian, an Arian, had published the minutes of oral negotiations with F., which contained a series of false claims. From this same period comes the treatise *Contra sermonem Fastidiosi Ariani* (*c. Fastid.*). F. refutes the sermon of → Fastidiosus, a former Cath. monk who had become an Arian priest. F. wrote a work in three books against Semipelagianism: *De veritate praedestinationis ad Iohannem presbyterum et Venerium diaconum* (*praedest.*).

This final productive period also saw the composition of the work *De fide seu de regula fidei ad Petrum* (*fid.*), which was intended as a handbook of heresies for Jerusalem pilgrims and was in two parts. In the first, Cath. teaching is comprehensively presented (Trinity, incarnation, sacraments). The second contains forty articles of faith. This work, addressed to Peter, a layman, and influenced especially by the handbook of → Gennadius of Marseilles (*Liber sive definitio ecclesiasticorum dogmatum*), is in the tradition of such Augustinian presentations of the Cath. faith as *De doctrina christiana* or the *Enchiridion de fide, spe, et caritate*. It is a kind of original "Summa" of the Cath. faith and is to be seen as an important forerunner of medieval collections of sentences (e.g., *Summa sententiarum*). Dates uncertain: the response to Scarila (*De incarnatione filii Dei et vilium animalium auctore liber unus; incarn.:* the Son alone, not all three persons of the Trinity, assumed human nature) and the anti-Arian treatise (not named in the *Vita*) *De Trinitate ad Felicem notarium* (*trin.*). In addition, there are four fragments of an anti-Pelagian work (*Fragmenta IV ex opusculis ad Eugippium presbyterum contra sermonem cuiusdam Pelagiani directis*). The authenticity of the "autobiographical" marginalia in a codex of Hilary (*Autographae notae marginales in codice Basilicano S. Hilarii de Trinitate*) is disputed.

From F.'s extensive correspondence, eighteen letters (*ep.*) (some datable) from various periods of his life have been preserved. Five of these are addressed to F. himself. Letters to Roman aristocrats or to Abbot Eugippius of Lucullanum deal with various questions of the spiritual life (e.g., *ep.* 6: *Ad Theodorum senatorem de conversione a saeculo*) or problems

of Cath. faith (e.g., *ep.* 8: *Ad Donatum de fide orthodoxa et diversis haereticorum erroribus*). Among the letters are also answers to letters of Ferrandus (e.g., *ep.* 12: *De salute Aethiopis moribundi*). In addition, there are collective letters of the Sardinian bishops in exile (*ep.* 15 and 17). Although F. must have delivered a great many sermons and was praised by the ancients (e.g., Isidore) as a preacher, only a few sermons (eight to ten) have thus far been regarded by scholars as authentic. But there still exists a great number (ca. 400-500) of sermons from late antiquity in North Africa, among which some by F. may lie hidden. Some poetic works ascribed to F. (e.g., a poem on St. Saturninus) have not yet been shown to be authentic. Finally, a series of other works has been wrongly attributed to F.

F., who was strongly influenced by Augustine (and was called a "short Augustine"), was the greatest theologian of his age. He was the Catholic Church's most important fighter against the anti-Nicene homoean creed that was defended by the Arian Germans. He tried to prove against the Arians that the Son is not created but generated; that he is of one essence with the Father; that the Holy Spirit is as much God as the Father and the Son and that he proceeds from Father and Son (*ex utroque*). He also tried to present Cath. teaching on person and nature (one God, i.e., one nature, in three persons; two natures, i.e., human and divine in the one person of Christ). In refuting Semipelagianism, he, like Faustus of Riez, showed himself a completer of the Augustinian theology of grace inasmuch as he systematized it. He shared Augustine's pessimism: without the grace of God fallen human nature is completely helpless. Acc. to F., the grace of God is absolutely necessary in order to produce anything good at all. Without it free will cannot develop. F.'s influence (along with the decrees of the Council of Orange in 529) helped to end the controversy over Augustine's teaching on predestination. As a result, F. was repeatedly cited in the predestination controversy of the Carolingian period (Gottschalk the Saxon, Hincmar of Rheims) and, later on, espec. in the Jansenist controversy of the 17th c. His works were highly esteemed in Spain. They were cited by authoritative authors of the 7th/8th c. (e.g., Isidore) and used in formulas of faith by several councils of Toledo. In other theol. questions, too, F. was often consulted. Thus, Ratramnus of Corbie and Aeneas of Paris (9th c.) used formulations of F. in documents they composed for Pope Nicholas I on the dogma of the twofold procession of the Holy Spirit. Florus of Lyons (9th c.) cited many passages of *ad Monim.* and *c. Fab.* in his compilatory

exeget. work *Duodecim patrum in epistulas Pauli.*
Depending on how Augustine was regarded in the
times after him, the reputation of F. likewise rose or
fell. The identity of F. with → Fulgentius the mythographer is disputed.

W: *Collected works,* J. Fraipont, CCL 91, 91A. — L. Kozelka,
BKV² 9 (Munich, 1934) [German trans.]. — *rem. pecc., fid.,*
M. G. Bianco, CTP 57 (Rome, 1986). — *psalm.,* A. Isola,
Salmo contro i Vandali ariani, CP 9 (Turin, 1983). — C.
Lambot: RBen 48 (1936) 221-234 [text]. — *vita Fulgentii,
fid., rem. pecc., ad Monim., ep.,* R. B. Eno, FaCh 95 (Wash-
ington, 1997) [English trans.].
L: R. J. H. Collins, F.: TRE 11:723-727. — P. Courcelle, Les
confessions de saint Augustin dans la tradition littéraire
(Paris, 1963), 221-223. — H. J. Diesner, F. als Theologe u.
Kirchenpolitiker, AzTh 1/26 (Stuttgart, 1966). — M. Djuth,
F.: The initium bonae voluntatis: AugSt 20 (1989) 39-60. —
A. Grillmeier, F. De fide ad Petrum und die Summa senten-
tiarum: idem "Mit ihm u. in ihm" (Freiburg i.Br., 1975),
637-679. — idem, Patristische Vorbilder frühscholastischer
Systematik: StPatr 6 = TU 81 (1962) 390-408. — A. Isola,
Sulla Struttura dei Sermones di F.: Quaderni dell'Istituto di
Lingua e Letteratura latina 2-3 (1980-1981) [1983] 37-47.
— M. L. W. Laistner, F. in the Carolingian Age: The Intel-
lectual Heritage of the Early Middle Ages. Selected Essays
(New York, 1957), 202-215. — P. Langlois, F.: RAC 8:632-
661. — J. McClure, Handbooks against Heresy in the West,
from the Late Fourth to the Late Sixth Centuries: JThS NS
30 (1979) 186-197. — B. Mapwar, La polémique anti-
arienne de St. F. en Afrique du Nord (Vᵉ-VIᵉ siècles) (Rome,
1988). — B. Nisters, Die Christologie des F. (Rome, 1930).
— M. Schanz, C. Hosius, G. Krüger, Geschichte der röm.
Lit. 4/2 (Munich, 1959), 575-581. — S. T. Stevens, The
Circle of Bishop F.: Tr. 38 (1982) 327-341. — A. Wilmart,
L'odyssée du manuscrit de San Pietro qui renferme les
œuvres de S. Hilaire (cod. D. 182): Classical and Medieval
Studies in Honor of E. K. Rand (New York, 1938), 293-305.

H. SCHNEIDER

G

Gaius (of Rome), Antimontanist

G. is known only from notices by other authors (Eusebius, *h.e.* 2.25.6; 3.28.1-2; 3.31.4; 6.20.1; Theodoret, *haer.* 2.3; 3.2; Photius, *cod.* 48; Jerome, *vir. ill.* 59; Pacian, *ep.* 1.2); he was active in the time of Zephyrinus (198-217). Acc. to Eusebius he was orthodox; acc. to Dionysius he was a heretic, close to the Alogi. Like the latter, G. ascribed the fourth gospel and Apoc to → Cerinthus and denied their canonicity. G. also gave testimony of the monuments to the princes of the apostles in Rome.

G. wrote a dialogue, now lost except for two fragments in Eusebius, *Adversus Proclum,* a Montanist (see Tertullian, *adv. Val.* 5.1; Ps.-Tertullian, *haer.* 7.2). Photius mentions a *Liber contra Artemonis haeresim* and the attribution of a *De universo* and *Labyrinthus* to G, but these works probably come from Hippolytus. On the Montanist question the fragments preserved by Eusebius and Dionysius bar Salibi (12th c.) say only that Proclus appealed to the daughters of Philip and thus to the prophetic tradition in Asia Minor. Hippolytus wrote his *Capitula contra Caium* and the lost *Apologia pro apocalypsi et evangelio Ioannis apostoli et evangelista* in defense of the Johannine writings.

W: *fr.,* E. Schwartz, GCS 9/1-2:176-179, 256-259, 264-267, 566f. — Dionysius bar Salibi, *In Apokalypsin,* I. Sedlacek, CSCO 53:1-2, 8-10, 19 [Syriac text]; CSCO 60 [Latin trans.].
L: G. Bardy, C.: DHGE 11:236f. — G. Barcille, C.: DThC 2/2:1309-1311. — A. Bludau, Die ersten Gegner der Johannesschriften (Freiburg i.Br., 1925), 40-73, 220-230. — H. v. Campenhausen, Die Entstehung der chr. Bibel (Tübingen, 1969) (English, The Formation of the Christian Bible [Philadelphia, 1977]). — E. Dinkler, Petrus u. Paulus in Rom: Gymn. 87 (1980) 1-37. — E. Kirschbaum, Die Gräber der Apostelfürsten (Frankfurt a.M., ³1974). — T. Klauser, Die röm. Petrustradition (Cologne, 1956), 17-21. — E. Prinzivalli, G. e gli Alogi: SSRel 5 (1981) 53-68. — J. D. Smith, G. and the Controversy over the Johannine Literature, Diss. (Yale University, 1979).

C. SCHMIDT, E. SCHULZ-FLÜGEL

Gamaliel, Gospel of

In a homily of a not otherwise known Bishop Heryaqos/Cyriacus of Bahnasa a story is told that was supposedly composed by Gamaliel (see Acts 5:34; 22:3) and is described as the "Gospel of Gamaliel." Its content is the events of Good Friday. The first part gives the "Lament of Mary" (see → Mary, Literature about); the second part is concerned primarily with Pilate, who believes in the resurrection. A number of Arab. fragments and versions have been preserved. Even the 14th c. Eth. version, which is the most complete of all and was read in the Copt. liturgy of Holy Week, is translated from an Arab. model. The original document was composed probably in the 5th/6th c. and probably in Coptic. It was written by a Christian who was hostile to Jews and was concerned primarily to demonstrate the innocence of Pilate, who was venerated as a saint in the Copt. church.

W: M. A. van den Oudenrijn, Gamaliel, SpicFri 4 (Fribourg, Switzerland, 1959) [Ethiopic text/German trans./comm.]

G. RÖWEKAMP

Gaudentius of Brescia

During a stay in Palestine G. was appointed successor of Filastrius, but it took pressure from Ambrose to make him accept. His consecration must have taken place between 387 and 397. In 406 he traveled to Constantinople as a member of a delegation for securing the reversal of the condemnation of John Chrys. The latter thanked G. in a letter (*ep.* 814) for his intervention. Rufinus of Aquileia dedicated to G. his translation of the Ps.-Clementine *Recognitiones.* Recently discovered were two fragments of a letter to G. which suggest that he intervened in the conflict between Jerome and Rufinus. G. died ca. 410.

The twenty-one *Tractatus,* primarily exegetical in content, that have come down to us articulate G.'s pastoral efforts with their emphasis on christology and their attack on pagans, Jews, Arians, and "halfway Christians." G. himself sent fifteen sermons to Benivolus, his former *magister memoriae.* Together with these, four other pieces—two sermons and two letters, one exegetical, one dogmatic—were put together as a *corpus,* perhaps by Benivolus.

W: A. Glueck, CSEL 68. — G. Banterle (Milan, 1991) [text/Italian trans.]. — S. L. Boehrer (Washington, 1965) [English trans./comm.]. — C. Truzzi, CTePa 129 (Rome, 1996) [Italian trans./comm.].
L: M. Bettelli Bergamaschi, Rapporti tra Ambrogio e G.: Ambrosius episcopus 2, ed. G. Lazzati (Milan, 1976), 151-167. — G. M. Bruni, Teologia della storia (Vicenza, 1967). — Y. M. Duval, Léon le Grand et G.: JThS 11 (1960) 82-84. — idem, "Liber Hieronymi ad Gaudentium": RBen 97 (1987) 163-186. — L. Padovese, Originalità cristiana (Rome, 1983). — F. Trisoglio, G. scrittore (Turin, 1960). — idem, Fonti: RSC 24 (1976) 50-125. — C. Truzzi, Zeno, G. e Cromazio (Brescia, 1985).

B. DÜMLER

Gaudentius, Donatist

G., b. ca. 355, was Donatist bishop of Thamagudi from 398 to 428. He was one of the seven *actores* at the conference on religion in Carthage (411) but spoke only briefly on the concept of "catholic" (*Collat. Carthag.* 3.102). He left Thamagudi after the condemnation of the Donatists but was able to return after a time and to recover at least one church. Ca. 420 the imperial tribune Dulcitius issued two edicts in which he demanded that the Donatists turn over their churches. G. threatened self-immolation, whereupon Dulcitius sent him a moderate letter to dissuade him. G. answered in two letters confirming his decision. The first contains a categorical refusal to give in; in the second, much more detailed, letter G. justifies his decision. Dulcitius then asked Augustine to respond to the letters, which he did in the first book of his *Contra Gaudentium*. G. wrote a rejoinder, which Augustine answered in a second book, from which some fragments of G.'s reply may be reconstructed. Nothing is known of the further course of these events.

W: *ep. ad Dulcitium,* P. Monceaux, Histoire littéraire de l'Afrique chrétienne 5 (Brussels, 1966 = Paris, 1920), 329-333 [reconstruction]. — *ep. ad Augustinum,* P. Monceaux, Gaudentii ad Augustinum epistulae fragmenta: RPh 31 (1907) 127-132 [reconstruction].
L: P. Monceaux, Histoire littéraire de l'Afrique chrétienne 6 (Brussels, 1966 = Paris, 1922), 191-219. — PAC 522-525. — M. Schanz, C. Hosius, G. Krüger, Geschichte der röm. Lit. 4/2 (Munich, 1959), 429.

B. WINDAU

Gelasius of Caesarea

G. was a nephew of Cyril Jerus. and from 365 the successor of Acacius as bishop of Caesarea. In his person the Nicene party held the metropolitan see of Palestine. G. died in 395.

  G.'s history of the church (*h.e.*), which survives only in fragments and is attested by Photius (*cod.* 89), was a continuation of Eusebius to 395. A reconstruction is extremely difficult. Sizable sections are preserved in two *Vitae* (BHG 1279; BHG 185), in Rufinus and Socrates, and espec. in → Gelasius of Cyzicus, whose work goes back in large measure to G. In a dogm. work, likewise preserved only in fragments (*fr.*), G. probably dealt with the main Chr. doctrines.

W: *fr.,* F. Diekamp, Analecta Patristica (Rome, 1938), 44-49 [text].
L: A. Glas, Die Kirchengeschichte des G. (Leipzig, 1914). — P. Nautin, La continuation de l'Histoire ecclésiastique d'Eusèbe: REByz 50 (1992) 163-183. — J. Schamp, The Lost

Ecclesiastical History of G.: PBR 6 (1987) 146-152. — idem, G. ou Rufin: Byz. 57 (1987) 360-390. — F. Scheidweiler, Die Bedeutung der Vita Metophanis et Alexandri: ByZ 50 (1957) 74-98. — P. van der Ven, Fragments de la recension grecque de Rufin: Muséon 33 (1915) 92-115. — idem, Encore le Rufin grec: Muséon 59 (1946) 281-294. — F. Winkelmann, Untersuchungen zur Kirchengeschichte des G. (Berlin, 1966). — idem, Charakter u. Bedeutung der Kirchengeschichte des G.: ByF 1 = FS F. J. Dölger 1 (Amsterdam, 1966), 346-385. — idem, Zu einer Edition der Frgm. der Kirchengeschichte des G.: BySl 34 (1973) 193-198. — idem, Die Quellen der Kirchengeschichte des G.: BySl 27 (1966) 104-130.

G. RÖWEKAMP

Gelasius of Cyzicus

G. was son of a priest of Cyzicus and, shortly after 476, wrote a three-volume work on church history, titled *Treatise on the Council of Nicaea.* In fact, it is a life of Constantine with special attention to the events surrounding the Council of Nicaea in 325. Whether G. saw the acts of Nicaea, as he claims in the preface, is disputed, Undisputed, however, is the compilatory character of the work, which draws on known sources (Eusebius, Rufinus, Theodoret, Socrates) and espec. on the lost church history of → Gelasius of Caesarea. It is unclear what G. owes to the book of Bishop Dalmatius of Cyzicus, which he mentions, and to a presbyter John.

W: PG 85:1191-1360. — G. Loeschcke, M. Heinemann, GCS 28. — G. C. Hansen (in prep.)
L: P. Nautin, G.: DHGE 20, 301f. — F. Scheidweiler, Die Kirchengeschichte des G.: ByZ 46 (1953) 277-301; 50 (1957) 74-98; 51 (1958) 87-99. — F. Winkelmann, Die Quellen der Kirchengeschichte des G.: BySl 27 (1966) 104-130 (literature).

G. RÖWEKAMP

Gelasius I of Rome

Almost nothing is known of the life of G., bishop of Rome from 492 to 496. Acc. to the *Liber pontificalis* he was from Africa or from an African family living in Rome. Under his predecessors Simplicius and Felix III he appears as clerk; Felix's policy in the Acacian Schism and most of his letters bear G.'s stamp. They show the Gelasian style with its mastery of language, clear line of thought, and precise juridical concepts. In addition to a theol. education G. shows a well-grounded knowledge of law. The connection of faith and law is seen also in his writings. Numerous letters (*ep.*) and six treatises have survived. Of the latter, four (*Gesta de nomine Acacii, Tomus de anathematis vinculi, De duabus naturis, De damnatione nominum Petri et Acacii*) are directed at Mono-physitism and one against Pelagianism (*Adversus Pelagianam haeresim*). The *Gesta* give a survey of the history of the controversy between Rome and Byzantium; the *De duabus naturis* also provides a collection of *testimonia*. There is a work against the Lupercalia (*Contra lupercalia*). G. does not expressly do away with this pagan rite, but he does forbid Christians to take part in it, which probably led to its abandonment.

The controversy with Emperor Anastasius I, which was important for its later effects, had to do with whether bishops were under imperial jurisdiction. Gelasius demanded a special law for bishops: the emperor cannot pass judgment on them because they are responsible for all the faithful and therefore for him as well and must give an account to God. In *ep.* 12 to Anastasius (494) G. speaks of two kinds of rule, the consecrated authority of bishops (*sacrata auctoritas pontificum*) and the power of the emperor (*regalis potestas*). Some scholars describe this distinction as the "doctrine of the two powers," others as a "division of labor." The emperor is responsible for the public weal, but only for its external framework, the *Externa* or *Humana*, while the *Interna* or *Divina* are reserved to the bishops. The eschat. orientation of these *Interna*, as well as the appeal to divine revelation, mean the subordination of the *Externa*. It is not for the emperor to determine the truths of faith (therefore G. objects to the imperial publication of the *Henotikon*), because in these matters he is a learner, not a teacher. The theologically educated bishops are competent here; their *potestas* is based on their *scientia*. In relation to them the emperor is a layman. The establishment of diverse competences in theology has repercussions in law and is the basis for a subsequent special eccles. jurisdiction.

G.'s description of the role of the bishops and espec. of the bishop of Rome can be traced back to the Roman tradition of the *pater familias*, who is responsible for the offenses of all the members. In this sense the pope is responsible for the sins of all Chr. Romans, including the emperor, whom he calls *filius*. This view also corresponds to the Rom. custom of guardianship. The idea of the Roman bishop as father of all Christians was already widespread toward the end of the 5th c.; G. seems to understand himself as also a guardian, whose responsibility it is to keep even the emperor from mistakes. Thus G. not only removes eccles. officials from civil jurisdiction but also strengthens the idea of the monarchy of the Roman bishop.

G. understands the church as *congregatio fidelium*;

salvation is to be found only within this community. The community needs qualified teachers. G.'s ideal priest must have a solid theol. education as well as modesty and a helpful attitude to the needy. G. describes the church's possessions as the possessions of the poor; here the point is not so much to give a stimulus to personal love of neighbor as to set down an objective-juridical observation. G.'s ethics were evidently marked by firm principles; he is accused of being rigorous and conservative, but he is also regarded as devout, and he loved the poor. The so-called → *Decretum Gelasianum* and the → *Gelasian Sacramentary* are not from him.

W: *ep.*, PL 59:13-116. — A. Thiel, Episcoporum Romanorum Pontificum Genuinae 1 (Hildesheim, 1974 = 1867), 284-613. — *ep.* 3, 8, 10-12, 27, 45, E. Schwartz, Publizistische Sammlungen (Munich, 1934). — *Gesta de nomine Acacii*, PL 48:928-934. — *Tomus de anathematis vinculo*, *De duabus naturis*, *De damnatione nominum Petri et Acacii*, E. Schwartz, loc. cit., 7-111. — *Adversus Pelaginam haeresim*, PL 59:116-137. — *Contra lupercalia*, G. Pomarès, SC 65.
L: Y. Congar, Doctrines christologiques et théologie de l'eucharistie: RSPhTh 66 (1982) 233-244. — M. H. Hoeflich, G. I and Roman Law: JThS NS 26 (1975) 114-119. — A. W. J. Holleman, Pope G. and the Lupercalia (Amsterdam, 1974). — B. Moreton, G.: TRE 12:273-276. — J. L. Nelson, G. I's Doctrine of Responsibility: JThS NS 18 (1967) 154-162. — G. Otranto, Note sul sacerdozio femminile nell'antichità in margine a una testimonianza di G. I: VetChr 19 (1982) 341-360. — J. Taylor, The Early Papacy at Work: G. I (492-496): JRH 8 (1974/75) 317-332. — W. Ullmann, G. I. (492-496) (Stuttgart, 1981). idem, Der Grundsatz der Arbeitsteilung bei G. I.: HJ 97/98 (1978) 41-70.

S. FELBECKER

Geminianus of Modena

G. was bishop of Modena from approximately 344 to 396. His participation in the Synod of Milan against Jovinian in 390 is documented. A recent thesis holds that the *Vita* is not from the 10th c. and dependent on that of Zeno of Verona, as previously thought, but is rather an original lying behind that of Zeno. Against this background an attempt has been made to ascribe book 1 to a treatise (*tract.*) of G. that has been handed down under the name of Zeno, and book 2 to a successor of the same name in the second quarter of the 5th c.

W: *tract.*, W. Montorsi (Modena, 1991).
L: W. Montorsi, Lunga eclissi (Modena, 1989). — J.-C. Picard, Souvenir des évêques (Rome, 1988), 633-635. — G. Pistoni, G. (Modena, 1983).

B. DÜMLER

Gennadius I of Constantinople

G., b. ca. 400 and a presbyter of Hagia Sophia, was successor of Anatolius as patriarch of Constantinople from 458 on. As an Antiochene, G. opposed the christology of Cyril and defended the decrees of Chalcedon. Relying on can. 28 of that council, he defended his patriarchal privileges against Rome. He was a close friend of Daniel the Stylite; he died in Cyprus Nov. 20, 471.

Of G.'s numerous exeget. and homilet. works, listed by Gennadius of Marseilles (*vit. ill.* 92) and Marcellinus Comes (*chron. ad a.* 470), of which his commentary on Dan deserves special mention, only fragments of the commentaries on Gen (*fr. Gen.*), Ex (*fr. Ex.*), Ps (*fr. Ps.*), the minor prophets (*fr. proph.*), and the letters of Paul (*fr. Pauli ep.*) have survived. This surviving material shows G.'s opposition to Cyril and sets him clearly apart from his exeget. predecessors in language and style. The only surviving dogm. work is the *Epistula encyclica* (*encycl.*) from a synod held by G. in Constantinople 458-459, which dealt with the problem of the buying of offices. Facundus of Hermione (*defens.* 2.4) transmits some passages of G.'s polemic against the twelve anathematisms of Cyril (430) (*adv. cap. Cyr.*). John Damascene (*parall.* 2) preserves a citation from G. on the origin of the soul; some other fragments (*fr.*) are insignificant.

W: *fr. Gen, fr. Ex.*, PG 85:1624-1666. — R. Devreesse, Les anciens commentateurs grecs de l'Octateuque et des Rois (Rome, 1959), 183-185 [text]. — *fr. Ps.*, PG 85:1666-1668. — R. Devreesse, Les anciens commentateurs grecs des Psaumes (Vatican City, 1970), 318 [text]. — *fr. proph.*, Y. M. Duval, Le livre de Jonas dans la littérature chrétienne grecque et latine 2 (Paris, 1973), 651-652 [text]. — *fr. Pauli ep.*, K. Staab, Die Pauluskommentare aus der griech. Kirche (Münster, 1933), 352-422 [text]. — *adv. cap. Cyr.*, PG 85:1621-1622. — F. Diekamp, Analecta patristica (Rome, 1938), 73-76 [text]. — *encycl.*, PG 85:1613-1621. — F. Diekamp, loc. cit., 79-81 [text]. — P. P. Joannou, Fonti 2. Fascicolo 9 (Rome, 1963), 292-299 [text]. — *fr.*, F. Diekamp, loc. cit., 77f., 83f. [text].
L: H. Delehaye, Les saints stylites (Brussels, 1923), 39f. — J. Kirchmeyer, G.: DSp 6:204f. — S. J. Voicu, G. La transmissione del frammento In Hebr. 9, 25: OCP 48 (1982) 435-437.

C. Schmidt

Gennadius of Marseilles

Acc. to the concluding chapter added by an unknown hand to his catalogue of writers (*vir. ill.* 101), G. was a presbyter of Marseilles during the pontificate of Roman Bishop Gelasius (492-496).

Notices in that work on persons living under Emperor Zeno (d. 491) make it probable that G. was active in the second half of the 5th c. In that same chapter of *vit. ill.* there is also an (incomplete; see below) list of G.'s writings. According to this list G. also wrote the works *Adversus omnes haereses* (8 B.), *Adversus Nestorium* (5 B.), *Adversus Eutychen* (10 B.), *Adversus Pelagium* (3 B.), the treatises *De mille annis* and *De Apokalypsi beati Ioannis*, and a profession of faith to Bishop Gelasius in the form of a letter. Although these writings are lost, as are G.'s translations of works of → Evagrius Pont. and → Timothy II Aelurus of Alexandria (see *vir. ill.* 11; 73) (except possibly for some fragments of *Adversus omnes haereses*, which may be additions to the *Indiculus* of Ps.-Jerome and Augustine's treatise *De haeresibus*), it is possible to determine that G.'s preferred area of work was the antiheretical-dogm. realm. To it belong also two *opuscula* which, at least under their present title, are not in the above-mentioned list but are usually ascribed to G. The *Liber* (or, in the mss., also *Definitio*) *ecclesiasticorum dogmatum* (*dogm.*), a concise list of the essential propositions of faith and a rejection of the principal heresies, belongs to G., at least in an abbreviated version of ca. 470. A close connection with the *Adversus omnes haereses* (as the latter's conclusion?) is possible. Also attributed today to G., with high probability, is the → *Statuta ecclesiae antiqua* (*Stat. eccl. ant.*), a short collection of canons, influenced espec. by the → *Apostolic Constitutions* and the eastern rite, which is important for the history of liturgy and law.

But G.'s most important surviving work is the *De viris illustribus* (*vir. ill.*), a continuation and in its first sections also a completion of Jerome's work of the same name; immediately after its publication (probably ca. 475) G.'s work was so closely associated with Jerome's that it was often transmitted as the second book of the earlier work. It originated in several stages beginning ca. 467 and was probably published only after the whole was completed. In the form in which we have it today it contains sections on 101 (or 103: Roman Bishops Zosimus and Sixtus are included with their predecessors Innocent I and Celestine) Chr. authors, of which ten, however, are not from G. but were added by an unknown hand (chs. 30, 87, 93, 95-101). The "autobiographical" chapter (see above) was probably added after the model of the corresponding section of Jerome's *vir. ill.* (ch. 135). G. follows his predecessor and model, Jerome (the very lack of a special preface tells us something), in many ways, espec. in the structure and form of the individual chapters. In many respects, however, he goes beyond Jerome, espec. because he has read most of the works reviewed.

Despite some inaccuracies G. shows himself a knowledgeable and careful scholar, whose judgment often strikes us as more objective than Jerome's (but the objectivity is achieved with a loss of verve). The bibliog. data are everywhere more generous and reliable than the biog. Both G.'s knowledge of languages, unusual in the West at this period (he knew Greek; see the translations mentioned above; he may have had some familiarity with Syriac), and the choice and presentation of authors show his interest in the eastern part of the empire. In his day, this interest was a sign of the revival of Hellen. currents in southern Gaul, and it gives the *vir. ill.* the character of a universal history of Chr. literature.

G.'s work also shows the high place he gives to the church and to ecclesiol. questions. Within this (universal) church, the church of (southern) Gaul (and espec. Massilia/Marseilles) with its close links to the monastic-ascetic way of life has outstanding importance for G. And yet the Semipelagian tendencies strong in that region have not left the clear traces which a large number of scholars seem to find in G.'s work.

W: *Stat. eccl. ant.*, PL 56:103-107, 879-889. — C. Munier (Paris, 1960) [text/investigations]. — *dogm.* revised, *vir. ill.*, PL 58:979-1000, 1059-1120. — *fr.*, PL 81:644-647. — *dogm.*, C. H. Turner: JThS 7 (1906) 78-99; 8 (1907) 103-114 [text]. — *vir. ill.*, C. A. Bernoulli (Freiburg i.Br., 1895) [text]. — E. C. Richardson (Leipzig, 1896) [text]. — W. Herding (Leipzig, 1924) [text].
L: B. Czapla, G. als Litterarhistoriker (Münster, 1898). — A. Feder, Der Semipelagianismus im Schriftstellerkatalog des G.: Schol. 2 (1927) 481-514. — idem, Die Enstehung und Veröffentlichung des gennadianischen Schriftstellerkatalogs: Schol. 8 (1933) 217-232. — idem, Zusätze des gennadianischen Schriftstellerkatalogs: loc. cit., 380-399. — D. Gorce, G.: DHGE 20:477-479. — A. Grillmeier, Patristische Vorbilder frühscholastischer Systematik: StPatr 6 (1962) 390-408. — G. Morin, Le Liber Dogmatum de G.: RBen 24 (1907) 445-455. — C. Munier, La profession du foi des Statuta ecclesiae antiqua et les écrits de G.: StPatr 3 (1961) 248-261. — idem, G.: DSp 6:205-208. — C. Pietri, G.: TRE 12:376-378. — S. Pricoco, Storia letteraria e storia ecclesiastica dal De viris illustribus di Girolamo a G. (Catania, 1979).

U. HAMM

George, Bishop of the Arabs

In 686 G. became bishop for the Arab tribes in the borderlands between Syria and Mesopotamia, and he was active there until his death (724). On his many visitations he always found time for philosophical studies. Thus he not only completed the *Hexaemeron* of → Jacob of Edessa, but also translated Aristotle's *Organon* (*org.*), *Analytics* (*anal.*), *Categories* (*cat.*), and *Hermeneutics* (*herm.*) into Syriac and accompanied them with detailed commentaries. Of his extensive correspondence the letters (*ep.*) to Jacob on the orations of → Gregory Naz. and to Isho the recluse on the immortality of the soul are important. Also attributed to G. are a homily for Palm Sunday and a commentary on the liturgies of Mass and baptism (*myst. Eccl.*) in the 8th. c. Jacobite church. Another sermon in verse deals with the life of → Severus of Antioch (*hom. in Sev.*). G. is possibly the author also of a didactic poem on the consecration of chrism (*cons. chris.*) that has come down under the name of → Jacob of Sarug.

W: *cat.*, G. Furlani, Le categorie: Memorie della Regia Accademia Nazionale dei Lincei, Classe di Scienze Morali 6/5 (1935) 1-68 [text/Italian trans.]. — *org.*, idem: SIFC 3 (1925) 305-333. — *anal.*, idem, Il procmio: RSO 18 (1939) 116-130 [text/Italian trans.]. — *herm.*, idem: Memorie della Regia Accademia Nazionale dei Lincei, Classe di Scienze Morali 6/5 (1935) 143-230; 6/6 (1937) 233-287 [text/Italian trans.]. — *ep.*, P. de Lagarde, Anecdota Syriaca (Osnabrück, 1967 = Berlin, 1858), 108-134 [text]. — V. Ryssel, G. Gedichte u. Briefe (Leipzig, 1891) [German trans.]. — *myst. Eccl.*, R. H. Connolly, H. G. Codrington, Two Commentaries of the Jacobite Liturgy (London, 3-15) [text], 11-23 [English trans.]. — F. Rillet, Sur la fête des hosanna: OrChr 74 (1990) 72-201 [text/French trans.]. — *cons. chris.*, V. Ryssel: Rendiconti della Regia Accademia Nazionale dei Lincei 4/9 (1893) 1-33 [text]. — idem, Gedichte 9f., 14-36 [German trans.]. — *hom. in Sev.*, K. E. McVey, CSCO 530/531 [text/English trans.].
L: K. Georr, Catégories d'Aristote (Beirut, 1948). — K. E. McVey, Memra on the Life of Severus (Cambridge, Mass., 1977).

P. BRUNS

George Choiroboscus

G., nicknamed "swineherd" (probably an allusion to his lowly origin), was deacon and chartophylax (archivist) in Constantinople. His lifework is to be dated to the late 7th or early 8th c. and includes lectures and commentaries on the Psalms and Canticle, which have come down to us as notes in a different hand.

W: T. Gaisford, G. dictata (Oxford, 1842) [text].
L: W. Bühler, C. Theodoridis, Johannes Damascenus u. G.: ByZ 69 (1976) 397-401. — C. Theodoridis, Hymnograph Klemens: ByZ 73 (1980) 341-345.

P. BRUNS

George Grammaticus

A "George Grammaticus" wrote, probably in the 6th c., two eulogies of the Apostle Barnabas (BHG

218a/b) which have not yet been published. He is probably not to be identified with George Grammaticus the poet, a student of the epic poet Colluthus.

L: H. G. Beck, Kirche u. theol Lit. (Munich, 1959), 400.

G. Röwekamp

George of Laodicea

G., an Arian presbyter, was driven from Alexandria ca. 320 for supporting Arius and was welcomed in Arethusa. Ca. 328 Constantine tapped him for the see of Antioch (Eus., *v. C.* 3.62) at the suggestion of the Eusebians, but instead G. became bishop of Laodicea (Athanasius, *h. Ar.* 4) ca. 330. He fought against the Niceans and Athanasius at several synods, with the result that he himself was condemned by the Synod of Sardica in 343. Ca. 346 he probably excommunicated Apollinaris of Laodicea for his fidelity to the Nicene Creed. When Antioch under Eudoxius adopted a radical Arianism, G. became a leader of the homoiousians along with Basil of Ancyra, Eustathius of Sebaste, and Silvanus of Tarsus. With Basil he composed the homoiousian memorandum of the Synod of Ancyra on the fourth formula of Sirmium; it is preserved by Epiphanius (*ep. dogm.*). Only fragments remain of other letters. Because of his acceptance of homoiousianism G. was deposed by Acacius of Caesarea at the Synod of Constantinople 359/360, and died probably soon afterward. His encomium of Eusebius of Emesa (Soc., *h.e.* 2) and a treatise against the Manichees (Epiphanius, *haer.* 66.21.3) are lost.

W: *ep. dogm.*, Epiphanius, *haer.* 73. — *ep. ad Alexandrum Alexandrinum*, Athanasius, *de syn.* 17. — *ep. ad Arianos*, ibid. — *ep. ad Macedonium*, Sozomenus, *h.e.* 14.13.
L: F. Loofs, G.: RE 6:539f. — J. N. Steensson, Basil of Ancyra and the Course of the Nicene Orthodoxy, Diss. (Oxford, 1983).

G. Röwekamp

George, a Monk

Following the example of Epiphanius, this George, a writer of the first half of the 7th c., about whom we know nothing, composed a *De haeresibus ad Epiphanium* (*haer.*), a "history of heresy" running from the Manichees and Gnostics, by way of the Origenist controversy, down to the Agnoetes. He also composed two computational works: *De quartodecimana Pascha* (*quart.*) and *De tribus circulis solis et lunae* (*trib.*).

W: *haer.*, M. Richard: REByz 28 (1970) 239-269 [text]. — *quart.*, F. Diekamp: ByZ 9 (1900) 24-32 [text]. — *trib.*, ibid., 32f. [text].

L: D. Afinogenov, The date of G. reconsidered: ByZ 92 (1999) 437-447. — F. Diekamp, G.: ByZ 9 (1900) 14-51. — V. Grumel, Chronologie (Paris, 1958), 115-157. — M. Richard, "Sur les hérésies": idem, Opera minora 3 (Turnhout, 1977), Nr. 61.

M. Skeb, OSB

George of Pisidia

The exact dates of G. are not certain. He was probably born before 600 in Antioch of Pisidia and died between 631 and 634. As deacon of Hagia Sophia he held the offices of skeuophylax and chartophylax or possibly referendarius, that is, he was an ambassador of Patriarch Sergius I (610-638) to Emperor Heraclius (610-641). In 622-623, as adviser to the emperor he took part in the campaign against the Persians.

G. is regarded as a representative of the new twelve-syllable verse. His literary activity spanned two periods. In his poems (*carm.*) of 619-630 he celebrated the military successes of his friend Emperor Heraclius. In doing so, he also gave an account of the victory over the Persians and the recovery of the holy cross (628). One poem is dedicated to Bonus the Patricius, defender of the capital. The encomia of Heraclius are considered important hist. sources for his period of government. In the second period, after 630, G. composed works on theology and morality. Of thematic interest are the poems *In humanam vitam* (*carm. vit.*) and *De vanitate vitae*. A dogm. didactic poem opposes Severus of Antioch. In the twelve-syllable verse form G. also published a lengthy *Hexaemeron*, a didactic poem on creation. Along with an exeget. commentary it contains meditations on the variety of creation and has come down also in Arm. and Old Slav. translations. G.'s numerous epigrams (*epigr.*) deal with spiritual and secular subjects. He composed a prose *Vita* of Anastasius, a martyr. The hymn → *Akathistos* is not from G.

W: PG 92:1197-1754. — *carm.*, A. Pertusi, SPB 7 (Ettal, 1960) [text]. — *carm. vit.*, L. Sternbach: Analecta graeco-latina (Cracow, 1893), 38-54 [text]. — *epigr.*, L. Sternbach: WSt 13 (1891) 1-4, 16-62; 14 (1892) 51-68 [text]. — *vit.*, A. Pertusi: AnBoll 76 (1958) 5-63 [text].
L: B. Baldwin, G.: ODB 838. — H. G. Beck, Kirche u. theol. Lit. (Munich, 1959), 448f. — G. Bianchi, Note sulla cultura a Bisanzio: RSBN 12 (1965) 137-143. — idem, Sulla cultura astronomica di G.: Aevum 40 (1966) 35-52. — M. R. Dilts, Krumbacher on G.: Byz. 35 (1965) 612. — A. R. Dyck, Michael Psellus. The Essays on Euripides and G. (Vienna, 1986). — G. Fermeglia, Studi sul testo delle due versioni dello Hexaemeron di G.: Memorie dell'Istituto Lombardo, Accademia di Scienze e Lettere, Classe di Lettere 28/2 (1964) 225-234. — D. C. Frendo, The Poetic Achievement of G.: FS R. Browning (Canberra, 1984), 159-187. — H.

Hunger, G.: LMA 4:1287f. — M. Radoševic, Sestodnev G. Piside i njegov slovenski prevod (Belgrade, 1979). — R. Romano, Teoria e prassi della versificazione: ByZ 78 (1985) 1-22. — I. Shahid, Heraclius Πιστὸς ἐν Χριστῷ βασιλεύς: DOP 34/35 (1980/81) 225-237. — P. Speck, Zufälliges zum Bellum Avaricum des G. (Munich, 1980). — L. Van Dieten, Zum Bellum Avaricum des G.: ByF 9 (1985) 149-178.

F. R. Gahbauer, OSB

George of Sykeon

G. (also called George Eleusios), whose exact dates are unknown, must have been born in the insignificant village of Algermara in Galatia toward the end of the 6th c. Since his parents had been childless, they asked the intercession of a monk, Theodore of Sykeon, and gave the child over to him shortly after its birth. The monk raised the child for twelve years until his own death in 613. When G. became abbot of the monastery founded by Theodore, he wrote a life of his deceased teacher. Although not free of hagiog. cliches, the life is nonetheless an important document for the religious and contemporary history of Asia Minor in the 7th c.

W: A. J. Festugière (Brussels, 1970) [text].
L: R. Janin, G.: BSS 12:263-265.

F. R. Gahbauer, OSB

Germanus of Constantinople

I. Life: The date of the birth of G., patriarch of Constantinople, is unknown. His father, Justinian, a patrician, held important offices under Emperor Heraclius. Since he played a part in the removal of Emperor Constans II (668), Justinian was executed by Constans's successor, Constantine IV. Probably in this context, G. was castrated, destined for the religious state, and given a place in the clergy of Hagia Sophia. In 705 he received the rank of a metropolitan of Cyzicus. In this capacity, under pressure from Byz. Emperor Anastasius II (713-715), he professed monotheletism, but distanced himself from it under Emperor Theodosius III (715-717). In 712 G. became patriarch of Constantinople. When the controversy over the veneration of images broke out under Emperor Leo III (717-741) G. sided with image veneration and therefore lost his office in 729 or 730. He took refuge near his paternal estate in Platanion. He died soon thereafter (between 730 and 733). The Vita Germani, probably by an 11th c. monk, has little hist. reliability.

S: A. Papadopulos-Kerameus, Vita Germani (Constantinople, 1884) [Greek text].

L: L. Lamza, Patriarch G. (Würzburg, 1975) [German trans. of the Vita]. — P. Plank, Der hl. G.: COst 40 (1985) 16-21.

II. Works: G.'s literary production includes many letters, homilies, and theol. treatises, and is an important source for the period of the image controversy. In letters to the spiritual fathers of the image controversy, Bishops John of Synada and Thomas of Claudiopolis, G. defends the veneration of icons. In a letter to the Armenians the patriarch explains the christology of Chalcedon to the Arm. catholicos and tries to move him toward union.

Of the many homilies that have come down under G.'s name, only one part (or. 1-9) can be shown to be authentic. Some of the homilies belong to Patriarch Germanus II of Constantinople (d. 1240). But the sermons on the annunciation, presentation of the Lord, and dormition of Mary are from G.

Several treatises are devoted to theol. questions. The treatise De haeresibus et synodis (ca. 727), dedicated to Deacon Anthimus, gives a history of heresies; it is to be noted that in composing this work G. was unable to consult any books. The work De vitae termino (vit. term.), composed in the form of a dialogue between a rationalist and an orthodox, explains the meaning and goal of human life and treats of the doctrine of God's foreknowledge and providence. Photius (cod. 233) gives a summary of the lost work De vera et legitima retributione. In order to defend Gregory Nyss. against the accusation that he held an apocatastasis, as understood by Origen, G. claimed that the Origenists had falsified the writings of Gregory. For a long time the authenticity of the Historia ecclesiastica et mystica contemplatio (contempl.), which contains an important commentary on the symbols of the Byz. liturgy and church buildings, was disputed, but the substance of it is today attributed to G.

G. is also regarded as author of numerous hymns for use in the liturgy of the hours and the eucharistic liturgy (hymn.); a thorough study of these hymns is still a desideratum. G. is no longer claimed as author of the → Akathistos.

W: PG 98:39-454. — contempl., P. Meyendorff (Crestwood, 1984) [text/English trans./comm.]. — idem, D. Sheerin (Fairfax, 1984) [English trans.]. — hymn., J. Schirò, Analecta hymnica graeca 1-13 (Rome, 1966-1983), passim [text]. — W. Christ, M. Paranikas, Anthologia Graeca carminum Christianorum (Leipzig, 1871), 98f. [text]. — or. 1-9, V. Fazzo, Omelie mariologiche (Rome, 1985) [Italian trans./comm.]. — vit. term., C. Garton, L. G. Westerink (Buffalo, 1979) [text/English trans.].
L: H. G. Beck, Kirche u. theol. Lit. (Munich, 1959), 473-475. — N. Borgia, Il commentario liturgico di S. G. patriarca (Grottaferrata, 1912). — idem, Ἐξήγησις di S. G. e la ver-

sione latina di Anastasio Bibliothecario: ReO 2 (1911) 144-156, 219-228, 286-296, 346-354. — R. Bornert, Les commentaires byzantins de la liturgie du VIIᵉ au XVᵉ siècle: AOC 9 (1966) 125-180. — F. E. Brightman, The Historia Mystagogica: JThS 9 (1918) 248-267, 387-397. — J. Darrouzés, Deux textes inédits: REByz 45 (1987) 5-13. — V. Fazzo, Agli inizi dell'iconoclasmo: FS S. Cipriani (Brescia, 1982), 809-832. — G. Dumeige, Nizäa 2 (Mainz, 1985), 83-92. — S. Eustratiades, Ἡ ἀκολουθία τοῦ μεγάλου σαββάτου: Νέα Σίων 12 (1937) 145-152, 209-226, 657-673; 13 (1938) 433-452. — S. Gero, Byzantine Iconoclasm during the reign of Leo III (Leuven/Louvain, 1973), 94-112. — V. Grumel, L'iconologie de saint G.: EOr 21 (1922) 165-175. — idem, Homélie de saint G.: REByz 16 (1958) 183-205. — A. Kazhdan, G.: ODB 846f. — W. Lackner, Ein hagiographisches Zeugnis: ByZ 38 (1968) 42-104. — C. Schönborn, L'icona di Cristo (Milan, 1988), 160-165. — H. J. Schulz, Die byz. Liturgie (Trier, ²1980), 118-130. — P. Speck, Klassizismus im 8. Jh. ?: REByz 44 (1986) 209-227. — D. Stein, Der Beginn des Byz. Bilderstreits (Munich, 1980). — idem, G.: LMA 4:1144f. — R. Taft, Liturgy of the Great Church: DOP 34/35 (1980/81) 45-75. — T. Xydes, G. als Hymnograph (Greek) (Athens, 1955).

F. R. Gahbauer, OSB

Germanus of Paris

The life and work of G. (b. end of 5th c.; d. 576) are narrated by Venantius Fortunatus (MGH.SRM 7:372-418), who mentions G.'s strict manner of life and integrity as well as some miracles. G. was ordained a priest by Agrippinus; Bishop Nectarius appointed him abbot of the monastery of St. Symphorien. King Chilperic (561-613) summoned him to Paris to be successor of Bishop Libanus and, despite this king's despotism and cruel regime, he treasured G.'s advice. G. composed a courageous letter to warlike Queen Brunhilde (ca. 534 to 613), in which he appealed to her peaceful views, her gentleness and humility. The *Expositio brevis antiquae liturgiae gallicanae* (PL 72:88-98) is not from G.; it consists of two letters that describe all the liturgical rites and usages of Gaul at the beginning of the Middle Ages as being immemorial traditions. Although large parts of the Gallican liturgy can be reconstructed from this work, elements of the Spanish (→ Isidore of Seville) and Byz. liturgies are present; these entered the Gallican liturgy at the time of the writing of the work.

W: *ep.*, W. Gundlach, CCL 117:423-426.
L: M. Becker, Neue Überlegungen: Francia 19 (1992) 50-54. — Y. Chausy, G.: Cath. 4:1885-86. — G. Mathon, G.: BSS 6:257-259. — J. Quasten, Expositio G. ascripta (Münster, 1934). — A. Wilmart, G.: DACL 6:1049-1102.

C. Kasper

Germinius of Sirmium

G., who was from Cyzicus, became bishop of Sirmium in Illyria in 351. Initially, along with → Valens and Usacius, he adopted a strict homoean position and, among other things, signed the second and fourth formulas of faith (dated creed) of Sirmium. In the mid-60s he moved away from that position and drew closer to the homoousians, as can be seen from a profession of faith (creed) of G. from 366. In a letter of Dec. 18, 366 (CSEL 65:159f.), Valens and Ursacius asked G. to withdraw his reservations, but in a letter from perhaps the winter of 366/367 G. stood by his mediating position without any decisive change in the direction of the Niceans (*Ep. ad Rufinianum, Palladium et ceteros*). In contrast, in a disagreement with an orthodox layman, Heraclianus (H.) (*Altercatio Heracliani laici cum Germinio episcopo Sirmiensi de fide synodi Nicaenae et Arimensis Arianorum*; *Altercat. Heracl.*), dated Jan. 13, 366 in Sirmium, G. appears as a strict homoean, who is clearly bested by H. in the dispute. This was possibly a piece of propaganda on the Nicene side, aimed at making G. appear an Arian heretic and poor theologian. G. died after 376, the year of his resignation.

W: *Alterc. Heracl.*, C. P. Caspari, Kirchenhistorische Anecdota 1 (Brussel, 1964 = Christiania, 1883), 133-147 [text]. — PLS 1:327, 345-350. — *ep.*, A. Feder, CSEL 65:160-164. — *Symbolum*, A. Feder, CSEL 65:47f.
L: A. Di Berardino (ed.), Patrologia 3 (Turin, 1983), 46, 49, 85f., 180. — Die Geschichte des Christentums 2 (Freiburg i.Br., 1996), 382, 382, 454. — R. P. C. Hanson, The Search for the Christian Doctrine (Edinburgh, 1988), passim. — HLL 5:445, 481, 497, 499f. — C. Markschies, Ambrosius v. Milan (Tübingen, 1995), 45-57. — M. Meslin, G.: DHGE 20:984f. — M. Simonetti, H.: DHGE 23:1339f. — idem, Osservazioni sull' "Altercatio Heracliani": VigChr 21 (1967) 39-58.

B. Windau

Gerontius

G., born ca. 395 in Jerusalem, first became a monk in his native city and then archimandrite of the cenobites in Palestine. After the death of his patroness, Melania the Younger (439), he became administrator of her monastery on the Mount of Olives. G. initially opposed Nestorius but later the Chalcedonian Creed as well, which he accused of Nestorianism. When a union was achieved in 479 with the moderate anti-Chalcedonians, G., who continued to resist along with Peter the Iberian, had to leave the Mount of Olives. He died between 480 and 485 (John Rufus, *pleroph.* 41; Cyril of Scythopolis, *v. Euthym.* 42-44).

G. wrote a life of Melania. Of the two versions the

Gr. is more likely the original than the Lat. It is historically reliable and important in the history of culture for its information on the development of Chr. asceticism.

W: R. Rampolla (Rome, 1905). — D. Gorce, SC 90. — Sanctae Melaniae iunioris vita, T. C. Papaloizos (Ann Arbor, Mich., 1979) [English trans./comm.]. — The Life of Melania, E. A. Clark (Lewiston/Toronto, 1984) [English trans./comm.]. — S. Krottenthaler, BKV² 5:445-498 [German trans.].
L: A. d'Alès, Les deux vies de la Sainte Melanie la Jeune: AnBoll 25 (1906) 401-450. — N. Moine, Melaniana: RechAug 15 (1980) 3-79. — L. Perrone, La chiesa di Palestina (Brescia, 1980), 38f., 103-139.

G. RÖWEKAMP

Gesta purgationis Felici et Caeciliani

These are the records of the case of Felix of Apthungi, who was coconsecrator of Bishop Caecilian of Carthage in 311 (Optatus, Contra Parmenianum Donatistam 1.18). At the Donatist Synod of Carthage in 312 Felix was condemned as a traditor, and the consecration of Caecilian was thereby proclaimed invalid. The Roman synod of 313 confirmed the validity of Caecilian's consecration. Constantine ordered Aelius Paulinus, the vicar of Africa, to investigate the case. The investigations carried out in Aphtungi and Carthage (314) led to the acquittal of Felix. The records of the investigation—the Gesta, or Acta purgationis—are confirmed by Optatus (1.13) and Augustine (ep. 43.6f.; 53.2-4; Cresc. 3.27 and 30f.).

W: C. Ziwsa, CSEL 26:185-216.
L: B. Kriegbaum, Kirche der Traditoren oder Kirche der Märtyrer (Innsbruck, 1986).   PAC 175f., 409f.

W. GEERLINGS

Gildas the Wise

G. (sapiens), born in Scotland ca. 500, was the first Chr. historian of Britain and the first Celtic writer in Britain who wrote in Lat. after the withdrawal of the Romans. He was active primarily in Wales and probably also made journeys to Rome and Gaul, where the founding of the monastery of St. Gildas-de-Rhuis is attributed to him; he is supposed to have been its first abbot. Another, likewise not historically verifiable, journey took him to Ireland ca. 565. He died ca. 570.

His major work is a history of Britain, De excidio et conquestu Britanniae (Brit.), written ca. 515/520 or certainly before 547. It describes the tragedy of his country when the Roman troops withdrew from it at the end of the 4th c., and the Picts, Scots, Angles, and Saxons then laid it waste. Carmina 2-26 relate the history of Britain from the beginnings to the invasions of the barbarians (beginning of 6th c.), whom Ambrose Aurelian strenuously but unsuccessfully resisted at Mons Badonicus. In carmina 27-110 G. reprimands the vices of the Bretons who, despite the disaster they have suffered, trample on justice and truth. In the process he endeavors to give bibl. examples showing how Christianity has abdicated in Britain. The first part seems to be an interpolation and comes perhaps wholly or partially from a forger ca. 700 in the circle of Aldhelm (abbot of Malmesbury and bishop of Sherborn). Brit. was a valuable source for Bede in his history of the English church. Among the certainly authentic works of G. is a penitential (poen.) and two poems (poem., lorica). These last are also attributed to Lathen, a monk of Clúain-Ferta-Molúa (d. 661). In the eleven fragments of letters (ep.) on disciplinary subjects the authenticity of 9-11 is disputed. G. writes rather laborious but careful Latin; the mingling of literary genres is typical of his time.

W: PL 69:329-392. — PLS 4:1260f. — ep., Brit., T. Mommsen, MGH. AA 13:25-85. — M. Winterbottom (London et al., 1978) [text/English trans.]. — poen., L. Bieler, The Irish Penitentials: SLH 5 (1963) 60-64. — lorica, F. J. H. Jenkinson, The Hisperica Famina (Cambridge, 1908), 50-54. — poem., K. Strecker, MGH. PL 4/2:618f.
L: F. W. Bautz, G.: BBKL 2:246f. (literature). — E. Kerlovégan, Le exc. (Paris, 1987). — M. Lapidge, G. New Approaches (Woodbridge, 1984). — T. D. O'Sullivan, The exc. of G. (Leiden, 1978). — E. A. Thompson, G. and the History of Britain: Britannia 10 (1979) 203-226.

C. KASPER

Gloria

The early Chr. hymn Gloria (also Hymnus angelicus), which is already attested in the 4th c., has come down in several versions (e.g., Greek in the Const. App. 7.47 [end of 4th c.]; in the Cod. Alexandrinus [5th c.]; oldest Lat. version in the Irish so-called Bangor Antiphonary [7th c.]). The text in the Roman liturgy is first attested in the Bobbio Missal (8th c.). This "Great Doxology" has three parts: a citation of the angel's song in Lk 2:14; praise of God; invocations of Christ. In the West the Gloria has been part of the Ordinary of the Mass since the 4th c.; in Rome until the 12th c. it was reserved to the papal liturgy (except at the Easter Vigil and at a first Mass) and has been part of Sunday Mass and feasts of the martyrs since Roman Bishop Symmachus (498-514), except in penitential seasons. In the East, following an older tradition, the *Gloria* has remained part of the morning Office.

L: C. A. B(ouman), G.: Liturgisch Woordenboek 1:868-870. — K. Falconer, G.: MGG2 3:1484-1493 (literature). — K. Gamber, Die Textgestalt des G.: Liturgie u. Dichtung, ed. H. Becker, R. Kacznyski (St. Ottilien, 1983), 1:227-256 (literature). — J. A. Jungmann, Um den Aufbau des "G. in excelsis": LJ 20 (1970) 178-188. — idem, Missarum Sollemnia (Vienna, ⁵1962), 1:446-461. — J. Magne, Carmina Christo. III: Le "G. in excelsis": EL 100 (1986) 368-390. — W. Stapelmann, Der Hymnus Angelicus (Heidelberg, 1948). — A. J. Vermeulen, G.: RAC 11:196-225.

B. KRANEMANN

Gregentius

G. was perhaps from Milan; he went later to Alexandria and lived for a time as an anchorite in Egypt. He is said to have then been sent by Justinian ca. 535 to be bishop of Safar (Taphar) in southern Arabia, the capital of the "Homerites" (*Himjar*) in Yemen and to work for the conversion of Jewish Arabs. His activity was perhaps connected with the consolidation of Christianity among the Arabs under Ethiopic rule. The extensive *Vita Gregentii*, with the many miraculous details included in the description of his life, belongs to the hagiog. tradition. The attribution of the following works to G. is probably wrong, so that scholars speak today of Ps.-G. He is supposed to have collected the *Leges Homeritarum* (*leg. Hom.*), which were initially handed down incomplete; sixty-four chapters (no. 41 is missing) formulate legal penalties for murder, adultery, homosexuality, prostitution, theft, venality, abuse of free persons, slaves, and beasts of burden, as well as for disregard of Sundays and feastdays; both OT and NT influences can be seen.

G. was also regarded as author of the *Disputatio cum Herbano Iudaeo* (*disp.*), which claims to be a continuation of the *leg. Hom.* In reality, it is a part of the *Vita Gregentii*, although in the tradition it also appears at times as an independent work.

The *disp.* reports a four-day debate between G. and the learned Herbanus, in which the Jews are supposed to have become convinced of the truth of the Chr. faith. G. emphasizes chiefly the relation of the OT prophecies to Jesus Christ and to such Chr. institutions as baptism. Dogm. questions, such as the nature of the Trinity, are also discussed. The climax of the *disp.* comes when Jesus Christ appears on a cloud, with the result that all the Jews receive baptism. G. shows Monophysite tendencies but is venerated by the Gr. orthodox.

W: *Vita Gregentii,* there is no edition of the entire text; A. Vasiliev: VV 14 (1907) 23-67 [Frgm. of historical and geographical importance/Russian trans.]. — K. Dukakes, Μέγας Συναξαριστὴς πάντων τῶν ἁγίων 12 (Athens, 1897), 484-490 [modern Greek paraphrase]. — *leg. Hom.*, PG 86:565-620. — *disp.*, PG 86:621-784.
L: A. Moberg, The Book of the Himyarites (Lund, 1924).

K. POLLMANN

Gregory of Agrigentum

G. was presumably a bishop of Agrigentum in the time of Emperor Justinian II (685-711) and the author of a commentary on Qoh in ten books. He is often identified with the G. who was bishop of Agrigentum in the second half of the 6th c. and is mentioned in some letters of Gregory the Great. But on the basis of the life of the earlier Gregory (PG 98:549-716) and of the theol. and philosophical sources of the commentary on Qoh it must be assumed that there were two different individuals belonging to different eras and cultural contexts, one Latin, the other Greek.

The commentary on Qoh looks chiefly into the literal meaning but without completely neglecting the allegorical content. The results of earlier commentaries are critically sifted. The author shows a good knowledge of exegesis and patristics as well as a comprehensive classical Gr. education and is influenced espec. by Aristotle and Gregory Naz. It is noteworthy that the text of scripture on which G. comments differs from the LXX in many passages.

W: PG 98:741-1181.
L: R. Aubert, G.: DHGE 21:1464-1467. — A. P. Christophilopulos, Πότε ἔζησεν ὁ Γρηγόριος ὁ Ἀκράγαντος: EEBS 19 (1949) 158-161. — J. L. van Dieten, Geschichte der Patriarchen von Sergios I. bis Johannes VI. (610-715) (Amsterdam, 1972), 150 n. 6. — E. Merendino, Gli inediti nella tradizione agiografica di s. G.: OCP 45 (1979) 359-372. — G. Stramondo, G. (Catania, 1952).

C. SCHMIDT

Gregory of Antioch

G.'s life and work are told in detail by his chancellor and lawyer, → Evagrius Scholasticus, in the last two books of his history of the church (*h.e.* 5 and 6; see also John Moschus, *prat.* 129f.). Born in the first quarter of the 6th c., as a young man G. became a monk and later abbot of a monastery in Jerusalem. Emperor Justin II appointed him abbot of the monastery in Pharan on Sinai, where he mediated in the dispute between Arab. Sinaites and Christians. In 570 Justin called him to succeed the deposed Anastasius I as patriarch of Antioch (at that time: Theopolis). There he proved his worth in various ecclesiastical-political and diplomatic missions: peacemaking between religious parties and Monophysite sects; rescuing church treasures from the Pers. invaders in Antioch; taking care of Chosroes II, the exiled chief king of Persia; missionary journeys in Mesopotamia in the service of Chalcedonian orthodoxy. When the Roman troops in Litarba near Antioch mutinied after a severe earthquake (589), G. pacified them with a speech and gifts. He himself fell into difficulties when he was slandered and accused by political enemies in Antioch, but he was successfully defended by Evagrius in Constantinople. Ill with gout, he resigned as patriarch in 593 and died a short time later from an overdose of medication.

Evagrius gives (verbatim?) G.'s speech to the mutinying soldiers (*exerc.*); this rhetorically elaborate speech appeals to the traditional Roman virtues, using the example of Manlius Torquatus. Also surviving is a sermon *In mulieres unguentiferas* (*mul. ung.*) on the suffering and resurrection of Christ, delivered during Easter week; it consists essentially of citations from the gospels, paraphrases, and only brief explanations of the texts. In two connected sermons on different days on the baptism of Christ, *De baptismo domini* (*bapt.* 1) and *In illa verba "hic est filius meus"* (*bapt.* 2) G. defends the creeds of Ephesus and Chalcedon against Nestorianism and Monophysitism and objects to dogm. debates over words. *Bapt.* 1 is attributed to G. only in a Lat. translation; in its Gr. version the sermon is handed down as a work of → Gregory the Wonderworker.

W: *bapt.* 1, PG 88:1865-1872 [Latin text]. — PG 10:1177-1190 [Greek text]; vgl. PG 61:761-764. — *bapt.* 2, PG 88:1871-1884; 64:33-38. — *exerc.*, Evagrius, *h.e.* 6.12 (= PG 88:884f.). — *mul. ung.*, PG 88:1848-1865.
L: P. Allen, Evagrius Scholasticus (Leuven/Louvain, 1981). — M. Aubineau, Une homélie de G.: Byz. 42 (1972) 595-597. — F. Celi, G.: DHGE 22:42-47. — P. Goubert, Patriarches d'Antioche et d'Alexandrie: REByz 25 (1967) 65-76. — S. Haidacher, Zu den Homilien des G.: ZKTh 25 (1901) 367-369.

T. FUHRER

Gregory of Elvira

I. Life: The dates of G.'s birth and death are unknown. Mentions by contemporaries yield the following information: Jerome mentions G. as still living in 393/394 (*vir. ill.* 105). He was bishop in 357/359 but had not been long in office (Faustinus, *fid.* 10.34), therefore he was over thirty, and his date of birth would have been ca. 320. We hear nothing more of him after 392/393. He was known as a strict

anti-Arian (Jerome, *chron. a. Abr.* 246.1-4) and had connections with Lucifer of Cagliari (Faustinus, *fid.* 25.90). It is very questionable whether, as has been suggested, he became leader of the Luciferians after Lucifer's death. The inference that G. did not die until after 403 because he used Rufinus's seventh homily on Gen is erroneous (see below). In any case he is listed among the participants of the Council of Toledo (400).

II. Works: In the mss. only one of G.'s works is attributed to him directly, namely, a commentary on the Song (*in cant.*), which has also been attributed sometimes to Origen, sometimes to Jerome, Ambrose, and others; in one version the *De fide* has even been attributed to Gregory Naz. G.'s authorship of the so-called *Tractatus Origenis* (Ps.-Origen, *tract.*) was long disputed (attributions to Phoebadius, Novatian, Avitus, Rufinus). It is so difficult to establish G.'s authorship because he was not a very creative writer. He made extensive use of the works of his predecessors (Tertullian, Novatian, Hilary, etc.) and probably also of florilegia of Gr. authors (Origen, Hippolytus) in Lat. translation. It is possible that the lost works of Victorinus of Pettau played a role in the transmission. In his exeget. works G. represents the allegorical interpretation of the Bible; in his *De fide* he lays special emphasis on the Nicene *homoousios*. The *Tractatus Origenis* (except for the last, on Acts 1-2) deal with OT themes, with the figures of the OT pointing ahead to Christ, his incarnation, the church, and the synagogue. *Tract.* 1 is heavily dependent on Hilary; in *tract.* 3 long passages correspond to Rufinus's seventh homily on Gen; both go back to the same Lat. original. *In cant.*, too, uses allegorical interpretation. Here G. takes over the approach of Hippolytus, who explains the text as referring historically to the love between Christ and the church and incorporates the synagogue into the history of salvation as being latently the church. At the center is the incarnation and the church as *corpus Christi*. To some extent G. uses the same sources here as in the *tract.* There are also parallels in the *De arca Noe* (*de arca*); here as in *tract* and *cant.* G. shows a liking for number symbolism. The *Sermo* on Prov 30:18-29 goes back to Hippolytus (ed. M. Richard, *Muséon* 79 [1966] 61-94); the sermon has come down in several versions, one of which is to be seen as a reworking by G. of Ps.-Ambrose, *De Salomone*. Probably from G. are the fragments *in eccl.*, *in gen.* 1, *in gen.* 2, and Ps.-Origen, *in psalm.* Certainly not from him are Ps.-Jerome, *ep.* 34 and 35, Ps.-Jerome, *fid.* and *Symb. Corp. Christi* 69.271-72. G.'s works are espec. important because of their bibl. citations, which often reflect a very old phase of the Lat. text of the Bible. G. was used by Beatus of Liébana, Gaudentius, Caesarius, Eucherius, Isidore of Seville, and the so-called *Clavis Melitonis* (→ Melito of Sardis).

W: *Opera omnia,* V. Bulhart, CCL 69:1-283 [partly from older editions]. — PLS 1:358-521 [without *De fide*]. — A. Vega: EspSag 55/56 (1957) 1-216. — *de arca,* V. Bulhart, loc. cit., 149-155. — *fid.,* M. Simonetti, CPS. L 3 (Turin, 1975). — *in cant.,* J. Fraipont: V. Bulhart, loc. cit., 167-210 [obsolete]. — E. Schulz-Flügel, AGLB 26. — *in eccl.,* V. Bulhart, loc. cit., 263. — *in gen.* 1, ibid., 159. — *in gen.* 2, ibid., 163. — Ps.-Ambrosius, *serm.* 46, ibid., 253-259. — Ps.-Origenes, *in psalm.,* ibid., 213-215. — Ps.-Origenes, *tract.,* P. Battifol, A. Wilmart (Paris, 1900). — V. Bulhart, loc. cit., 3-146.
L: T. Ayuso Marazuela, El Salterio de G.: Bib. 40 (1959) 135-159. — A. Bacala Muñoz, Sobre las citas bíblicas: RET 37 (1977) 147-151. — P. Battifol, Question des Tractatus Origenis: BLE (1905) 307-323. — F. J. Buckley, Christ and the Church according to G. (Rome, 1964). — E. C. Butler, The New Tractatus Origenis: JThS 2 (1901) 113-121. — E. Cavalcanti, L'aquila, il serpente, la nave, il giovane: SEAug 37 (1992) 187-200. — M. Didone, G. e la paternità del "De Salomone": Div. 24 (1980) 178-210, 310-323. — U. Domínguez del Val, Herencia literaria de G.: Helm. 24 (1973) 281-357. — D. Gianotti, G., interprete del Cantico: Aug. 24 (1984) 421-439. — HLL 5:408-433. — H. Koch, Zu G.s Schrifttum u. Quellen: ZKG 51 (1932) 238-272. — P. Lejay, L'héritage de G.: RBen 25 (1908) 435-457. — E. Mazorra, El patrimonio literario de G.: EE 42 (1967) 387-397. — G. Morin, Autour des "Tractatus Origenis": RBen 19 (1902) 243-245. — M. Simonetti, La doppia redazione del De fide: FS M. Pellegrino (Turin, 1975), 1022-1040. — C. Vona, I Tractatus de libris sacrarum scripturarum. Fonti e sopravvivenza medievale (Rome, 1970). — A. Wilmart, Les "Tractatus" sur le Cantique attribués a G.: BLE (1906) 233-299.

E. Schulz-Flügel

Gregory the Great

I. Life: Born ca. 540 in Rome, G. was from a prominent Roman senatorial family. He received a solid education in grammar, rhetoric, and law and in 572/573 was *praefectus urbi,* the highest position in the Roman civil administration. Soon thereafter (574/575) he resigned this office to lead a monastic life. Because of his abilities he was ordained a deacon in 579 and sent as apocrisiarius (legate) of the pope to the imperial court of Constantinople in order to represent the concerns of Italy, which was under attack by the Lombards. In 585/586, after returning to his monastic community in Rome, he was adviser to Bishop Pelagius II and, after the latter's death, was, not without an interior struggle, enthroned as his successor on Sept. 3, 590. His fourteen-year pontificate was overshadowed by the chaos of war, natural disasters, famines, as well as abuses among the clergy

(espec. in Frankish Gaul), schisms (Three-Chapters schism, Arianism), and disciplinary controversies (North Africa; patriarchate of Constantinople). But due to his abilities, this *Consul Dei* (G.'s epitaph) was able to ease material suffering in Rome and outside it by caritative measures, to restructure the administration of the church's patrimonial estates, reorganize the weakened episcopate, prepare the way for the conversion of the mostly pagan, partly Arian Lombards, counteract paganism in Sardinia, Sicily, and Corsica, and carefully promote the mission to the Anglo-Saxons. But the esteem that G. (d. March 12, 604) enjoyed espec. in the Middle Ages did not rest primarily on his hist. importance as a reform pope. He lived on in later centuries rather as teacher and preacher because of his bibl. commentaries and homilies. The life and work of G. are described, with legendary adornments, in the *Vita S. Gregorii* of an unknown English monk ca. 713, by Paul the Deacon toward the end of the 8th c., and by John the Deacon at the end of the 9th c. G.'s own works, however, along with notices in Gregory of Tours (*Franc.* 10.1) and in the *Liber pontificalis* are of greater importance.

L: E. Caspar, Geschichte des Papsttums 2 (Tübingen, 1933). — C. Dagens, G. avant son pontificat: FS J. Fontaine 1 (Paris, 1992), 143-150. — F. H. Dudden, G. the Great (New York, 1967 = London, ¹1905). — R. Gillet, G. Ier: DHGE 21:1387-1420. — R. Godding, Bibliografia di G. (1890-1989) (Rome, 1990), Nr. 29-629. — G. Jenal, G. I.: GK 11:83-99. — R. Manselli, G.: RAC 12:930-951. — R. A. Markus, G. I.: TRE 14:135-145. — idem, G. the Great and His World (Cambridge, 1997). — V. Paronetto, G. Magnus (Rome, 1985). — J. Richards, G. (Graz, 1983). — idem, G. I.: LMA 4:1663f.

II. Works: It is very likely that the incomplete commentary on Cant 1:1-8 (*in cant.*) originated during the monastic period (575-579). The notes taken of his oral addresses by the monk Claudius were later criticized by G. as inadequate, but they bear his unmistakable mark in style and content. G. follows the traditional interpretation, espec. as found in → Origen, when he explains the bride as the church and describes the individual soul in its relationship to Christ, the bridegroom. The focus is less on mystical union with God than on the way to it through seeking and desire. The work is addressed espec. to those who are advanced in the contemplative life. Direct pastoral references are lacking. During his time as apocrisiarius in Constantinople G. composed a complete exegesis of Job in the form of monastic conferences. The *Moralia in Iob* (*moral.*), which were revised and updated during his pontificate, are G.'s most extensive and important work, a summa of his theology and spirituality. Acc. to the author the work was not intended for wide circles of readers but rather presupposed a certain degree of spiritual maturity, although the focus is not on a purely monastic spirituality. In G.'s allegorical and typological interpretation the person of Job stands for the destiny of Christ and the churches, whose sufferings G. sees sketched out in the OT. Within the patristic tradition of interpretation of this OT book G.'s originality consists in the ecclesiol. interpretation; the book's powerful imagery inspires him to numerous alleg. interpretations. The stylistic elegance and poetic sensibility of not a few passages also reveal the often-underestimated linguistic power of this author of late antiquity. The *Pastoral Rule* (*past.*), composed between Sept. 590 and Feb. 591 outlines, on the one hand, G.'s principles of church government and, on the other, as a programmatic handbook for bishops, aims at reform of this eccles. office, of which a lofty assessment is given. The work is thus in the line of similar works by → Gregory Naz. (*or.* 2) and → John Chrys. (*sac.*) and belongs to the so-called pastoral trilogy of the early church. *Past.* was translated into Greek in the author's lifetime; and, because, among other things, of recommendation by several 9th c. synods, it achieved a wide circulation; in the Middle Ages it was even read as a mirror for princes. The forty homilies on the gospels (*in evang.*), delivered to the people in various Roman station churches from Nov. 590 to spring 592, are often inspired by → Augustine and illustrated with many examples from everyday life. The style is measured by the capacity of the audience and is less eloquent than that of earlier Lat. homilists. Almost everything said in each gospel pericope is interpreted allegorically and morally. *In evang.* is a precious source for knowledge of the history of the Roman liturgy. Because of ill health G. had the first twenty homilies read in his presence, but the other twenty he himself delivered. Shortly after the end of this cycle of sermons, sometime between the end of autumn 593 and spring 594, G. began to explain in twenty-two, later (601) revised, homilies (*in Ezech.*) the visions of Ezek (1:1–4:3; 40:1-47) to a small group of monks, clerics, and advanced believers. In this series G. occasionally refers to Jerome's explanation of Ezek. The allegorical-moral exegesis of the enigmatic visions constantly circles around the themes of the church's service of proclamation and of the contemplative life and the struggle to effect an internal unity between them. The Lombard invasion not only overshadowed these homilies but eventually forced an end to them. The *Dialogues* (*dial.*), named after their literary form, were composed in 593/594 and are a collection in four books of the lives of holy men of Italy. The second book consists entirely of the earliest *Vita* of → Benedict of Nursia, which was important for later hagiography. The eschat. themes discussed in the fourth book (death, purgatory, heaven, hell) left their impress on many ideas of the other world in later periods. The question of authenticity, raised anew a few years ago, has not yet been conclusively settled. Probably in the middle or later period of his pontificate G. commented on the opening chapters of 1 Sam (*in I reg.*); the stories of worthy and unworthy servants of God reflected, in G.'s typolog. interpretation, his own experiences with the bishops and priests of his time and, being geared espec. to them, were meant to serve the cause of a reform of the clergy. The substantial authenticity of this work can be assumed, but the question remains open of the extent to which G. may have revised abbot Claudius of Ravenna's record, which he felt to be inadequate, of his oral exegesis. The sober language here is unmistakably different from the empathetic style of the interpreter of Job and Ezek, though the world of ideas remains identical. A valuable testimony to the manifold activities of G. in the administrative, disciplinary, and caritative spheres is his correspondence of over eight hundred letters (*ep.*). Alongside numerous letters in the formal curial style there are personal letters that shed further new light on G. as spiritual man and pastor. Lost are the exegeses, mentioned by G. (*ep.* 12.6), of Prov, the Heptateuch, and the prophets. There is disagreement over the authenticity of some of the *Libellus responsionum* (*resp. ad Aug.*), a work addressed to Augustine of Canterbury, missionary to the Anglo-Saxons. The *Sacramentarium Gregorianum* dates from a later period (8th c.) but contains prayers that go back to G.

W: *in cant.*, P. Verbraken, CCL 144. — K. S. Frank, CMe 29:81-129 (Einsiedeln, 1987) [German trans./comm.]. — R. Bélanger, SC 314. — *moral.*, M. Adriaen, CCL 143, 143A, 143B. — *moral.* 1-2, R. Gillet, A. De Gaudemaris, SC 32bis. — *moral.* 11-14, 15-16, A. Bocognano, SC 212, 221. — *moral.* 1-8, 9-18, C. Dagens, P. Siniscalco, E. Gandolfo (Rome, 1992-1994) [text/Italian trans./comm.]. — *past.*, B. Judic, F. Rommel, C. Morel, SC 381, 382. — J. Funk, BKV² 2/4 (Munich, 1933) [German trans.]. — *in evang.*, M. Fiedrowicz, FC 28/1-2. — G. Cremascoli (Rome, 1994) [text/Italian trans./comm.]. — *in Ezech.*, M. Adriaen, CCL 142. — G. Bürke, CMe 21 (Einsiedeln, 1983) [German trans.]. — C. Morel, SC 327, 360. — V. Recchia, E. Gandolfo (Rome, 1992-1993) [text/Italian trans./comm.]. — *dial.*, A. De Vogüé, P. Antin, SC 251, 260, 265. — J. Funk, BKV² 2/3 (Munich, 1933) [German trans.]. — *in I reg.*, P. Verbraken, CCL 144. — A. De Vogüé, C. Vuillaume, SC 351, 391. — *ep.*, D. Norberg, CCL 140, 140A. — M. Feyerabend (Kempten, 1807-1809) [German trans.]. — J. Funk,

BKV[2] 2/4 (Munich, 1933) [German trans., selections]. — P. Minard, SC 370f. — *resp. ad Aug.*, P. Ewald, M. L. Hartmann, MGH. Ep 2:332-343. — Thesaurus S. Gregorii Magni, Series A: Formae (Turnhout, 1986).
L: F. Clark, Pseudo-Gregorian Dialogues (Leiden, 1987). — J. P. Coffey, G. the Great "ad populum": XL Hom. in evang., Phil. Diss. (Fordham Univ., 1988). — A. De Vogüé, Auteur du commentaire des Rois: RBen 106 (1996) 319-331. — R. Godding, Bibliografia di G. (1890-1989) (Rome, 1990), Nr. 630-1835. — S. C. Kessler, G. als Exeget. Interpretation der Ez. homilien (Innsbruck, 1996). — idem, Rätsel der Dialoge: Fälschung o. Bearbeitung?: ThPh 65 (1990) 566-578. — H. Leclerq, Lettres: DACL 8/2:2861-2867. — G. Lo Menzo Rapisarda, L'empathia di G. M. attraverso il suo epistolario: Orph. 24-25 (1977-78) 15-65. — E. Massa, Arte del linguaggio: G. M. e il suo tempo 2 (Rome, 1991), 59-104. — S. Müller, "fervorem discamus amoris." Das Hohelied u. seine Auslegung bei G. (St. Ottilien, 1990). — D. Norberg, Style personnel et style administratif dans le Registrum epistularum: G. le Grand, ed. J. Fontaine (Paris, 1986), 489-497. — G. Pfeilschifter, Authentische Ausgabe der Evangelien-Homilien. Geschichte ihrer Überlieferung (Aalen, 1970 = Munich, [1]1900). — E. Pitz, Papstreskripte (Sigmaringen, 1990). — V. Recchia, Esegesi di G. M. al Cantico dei Cantici (Turin, 1967). — idem, Memoria di Agostino nell'esegesi biblica di G.: Aug. 25 (1985) 405-434. — idem, Metodo esegetico nei Moralia: InvLuc 7-8 (1985-86) 13-62. — idem, Omelie di G. M. su Ezechiele (Bari, 1974). — S. E. Schreiner, Interpretation of Job: ABenR 39 (1988) 321-342. — H. Schwank, G. als Prediger (Hannover, 1934). — J. Speigl, Pastoralregel: RQ 88 (1993) 57-76.

III. Main Lines of Thought: G.'s writings reflect both the hist. situation and the interior development of his personality. The apocalyptic mood of that period, but also monastic spirituality, turned G. into the "teacher of longing," who tirelessly called on his hearers to turn away from the visible world to what is eternal. But his call to eccles. office caused G., who described himself as "servant of the servants of God," to discover gradually a mysticism of service, in which he sought to combine action and contemplation in the higher ideal of a *vita mixta* (*moral.* 6.37.56; 28.13.33; *past.* 2.5; *ep.* 1.24; *in evang.* 2.38.10). This is the perspective that controls the exegesis of the scriptures in commentaries and homilies, both in method and in content. The spiritual sense of scripture, with a strong emphasis on morality and mysticism, is dominant; this kind of meditation is intended to awaken the longing for heaven, without forgetting, however, responsibility for the things of earth. While G.'s desire for the contemplative life led him to discover the bridal mysticism of the Cant during the monastic phase of his life, his experience of life and suffering gave him a deep sympathy for patient Job (*moral., ep. dedic.* 5), who became for him the symbol of that age of radical change. G. wanted to use the fate of Job in order to show how all superficial ways of seeing reality must be done away with in order to see everything in the light of eternity. Even the *dial.* with their many miracle stories are intended to bear witness to God's saving action in the present with all its crises. It is true that the homilies *in evang.* were determined for G. by the liturgy, but the interpretations given in them bear the mark of contemporary events, which he viewed as confirmation of Christ's words about the approach of the kingdom of heaven (*in evang.* 1.1.1; 1.4.2; 2.38.3). There is hardly a homily that does not call for turning away from the world and preparing for the coming judgment. This is why G. chose Ezek, too, as a subject for further homilies, since he saw an analogy between the situation of Israel in exile and the distresses of his own age (*in Ezech.* 2.6.22f.). So, too, G. discovered himself in the person of the prophet, to whom, as to himself, providence had given the office of watcher (Ezek 3:17) over the people of God (*in Ezech.* 1.11.4-7). Meanwhile those in eccles. office acquired many new tasks even in the civil realm, which gave reason for concern about the primary service, which was preaching. Evidence of this concern is found espec. in *past.*, in *I reg.* and *ep.*

All of G.'s works attest to his biblically oriented spirituality. Exegesis of scripture and interpretation of history are inseparably interwoven in G. Just as, on the one hand, the hist. situation was understood in light of God's word, so too, on the other hand, this word received its ultimate fullness of meaning in the context of the church's life and of personal existence within it. The basic principle *divina eloquia cum legente crescunt* (*in Ezech.* 1.7.8) gives evidence of this understanding of scripture, as does the maxim on actualizing the bibl. word, *cotidie fieri in ecclesia* (*moral., praef.* 1; *in evang.* 2.29.4). In order to plumb this dimension of depth and actuality in the Bible, G. uses the plurality of senses of scripture (*moral., ep. dedic.* 1-4; *in Ezech.* 1.7.9f.). Here the classical principle of interpretation, *ecclesia vel anima*, which G. accepted, blurred the borderline between typological-ecclesiological and moral-individual interpretation (see *in Ezech.* 2.2.15). G.'s importance does not rest on theol. speculation and systematization, but on existential, scripture-oriented meditation on Chr. existence in the tension between time and eternity, world and God, action and contemplation. Even during his lifetime his writings were widely circulated; soon excerpted, commented on, and translated into numerous vernaculars, they became a well-used source for important medieval authors. By reason of the theol. authority of his works, G. made a decisive contribution to the establishment of the Chr. culture of the Middle Ages.

L: P. C. Bori, "Divina eloquia cum legente crescunt": ASE 2 (1985) 263-274. — P. Catry, Parole de Dieu (Bellefontaine, 1984). — F. Clark, G., Theologian of Christian Experience: ABenR 39 (1988) 261-276. — C. Dagens, G. (Paris, 1977). — idem, G. et le monde oriental: RSLR 17 (1981) 243-252. — G. R. Evans, Thought of G. (Cambridge, 1988). — M. Fiedrowicz, Kirchenverständnis G.s. (Freiburg i.Br., 1995). — J. Fontaine, Expérience spirituelle: RHSp 52 (1976) 141-153. — K. S. Frank, Actio et contemplatio: TThZ 78 (1969) 283-295. — R. Gillet, G. le Grand: DSp 6:872-910. — idem, Cento anni di ricerche: G. M. e il suo tempo 1 (Rome, 1991), 293-304. — J. Fontaine et al. (ed.), G., Colloque Chantilly 1982 (Paris, 1986). — G. M. e il suo tempo (SEAug 33-34) (Rome, 1991). — D. Hofmann, Geistige Auslegung der Schrift (Münsterschwarzach, 1968). — L. La Piana, Teologia e ministero della Parola (Palermo, 1987). — J. Leclerq, Wissenschaft u. Gottverlangen (Düsseldorf, 1965), 34-45. — F. Lieblang, Grundfragen der mystischen Theologie (Freiburg i.Br., 1934). — J. Modesto, G., Nachfolger Petri u. Universalprimat (St. Ottilien, 1989). — J. M. Petersen, "Homo omnino latinus?": Spec. 62 (1987) 529-551. — M. Stark: G.s d. Gr. Angaben zum liturgischen Gebrauch des Allelujas: EL 112 (1998) 469-478. — C. E. Straw, G. (Berkeley, 1988). — L. Weber, Moraltheologie G.s (Fribourg, Switzerland, 1947). — D. Wyrwa, Persönlicher Zugang in der Bibelauslegung: Sola scriptura, ed. H. H. Schmid et al. (Gütersloh, 1991), 262-278.

M. FIEDROWICZ

Gregory the Illuminator

G. (d. ca. 325) was the first bishop of all of Armenia and is regarded as the real organizer of Arm. Christianity. → Agathangelus the historian deals with G.'s work under King Trdat, whose house G. converted to the Chr. faith. Ca. 315 G. was consecrated a bishop in Caesarea of Cappadocia; in his last years he withdrew and left the government of the Arm. church to his son Aristaces, who also took part in the Council of Nicaea. Until the time of catholicus → Sahak the Great, the patriarchal dignity was an inheritance in G.'s family. The hymns attributed to G. are probably not from his pen; the Teaching of G. (doct. Greg.) transmitted by Agathangelus is today often attributed to → Mesrob, the inventor of the Arm. alphabet.

W: doct. Greg., K. Ter Mekerttschian, Agathangelus (Tiflis, 1914), §§ 259-715 [text]. — R. W. Thomson, The Teaching of St. Gregory (Cambridge, Mass., 1970) [English trans./comm.]. — G. Schmid, Reden u. Leben des hl. G. (Regensburg, 1872) [German trans.].
L: N. Adonts, Questionnaire de S. G. (Paris, 1927). — idem, G. et Anak le Parthe: REArm 8 (1928) 233-245. — N. Akinean, G.: HandAm 63 (1949) 3-58. — P. Ananian, La consecrazione di G.: Muséon 74 (1961) 43-73, 317-360. — M. van Esbroek, Sépultures de S. G: AnBoll 89 (1971) 387-418. — B. MacDermot, The Conversion of Armenia: REArm NS 7 (1970) 281-359. — M. Minasean, Kanones des hl. G.: Baz. 139 (1981) 57-72. — M. A. van den Oudenrijn,

Verehrung des hl. G.: HandAm 75 (1961) 477-494; 76 (1962) 23-29. — idem, Offizium des hl. G.: HandAm 77 (1963) 235-246. — P. Peeters, Grégoire l'Illuminateur: AnBoll 60 (1942) 91-130.

P. BRUNS

Gregory of Nazianzus

I. Life: The most important sources for the biography of G. are his own orations, letters, and poems (even the Vita by → Gregory the Presbyter in the 7th c. follows them to a great extent); this is true espec. of the lengthy (1,979 verses) Carmen de vita sua (carm. 2.1.11 = dvs). G. was born probably ca. 326 in Arianzus (the date is inferred from dvs 239.512f., ep. 50.8; conventional dating 329/330 acc. to the hagiog. tradition and Suidas; death ca. 390 at over seventy). He was the eldest son (siblings: Caesarius, or. 7; Gorgonia, or. 8) of a Cappadocian landowner Gregory (the elder, b. ca. 275; member of the Hypsistarian sect; 325, baptized; 329-374, bishop of Nazianzus, or. 18.5ff., dvs 51-56) and the scrupulous Christian Nonna (or. 18.7-11; dvs 57-67; ep. 7.7). The course of his studies took him from Nazianzus (or. 7.6) via Caesarea in Cappadocia (or. 43.13), Caesarea in Palestine (or. 7.6; Jerome, vir. ill. 113), and Alexandria (influence of Didymus the Blind?) to Athens (teachers of rhetoric: Himerius a pagan; Prohairesius a Christian, see Soc., h.e. 4.26; Soz., h.e. 6.17.1; friendship with Basil, see or. 43.14.24; dvs 211-26; 355, acquaintance with Julian), and perhaps, earlier, even to Antioch (as student of Libanius; see Soc., Soz., ibid.). Returning home "in his thirtieth year" (dvs 239; probably 356), he leaned first toward monastic philosophia (visit to the Pontic isolation of Basil: ep. 1-6; Basil, ep. 2.14.1; on toward the Origenist Philocalia, see ep. 6.4 and 115), but then, after his baptism (sole reference: PG 35:257B), he was ordained a priest against his wishes by his father ("we were compelled," ep. 8) and then evaded the frightening dignity by flight to Pontus (361/362). At Easter 362 he returned repentantly (or. 1) but at the same time justified his behavior in an oration (or. 2) that celebrated, with hitherto unmatched intensity, the responsibility and distinction of a strictly organized, spiritually and socially hierarchical priesthood (model for → John Chrys.'s De sacerdotio). During the following decade G. lived in retirement at Nazianzus, partly as assistant to his aging father (from this period, or. 4/5, the denunciations of Julian; or. 6: mediation in the schism at Nazianzus; or. 7/8: funeral orations for his siblings).

In 372 Basil chose him, for political reasons (division of Cappadocia by Valens), to be bishop of a miserable but strategically important place named Sasima (Basil, *ep.* 98), but G. again fled from this betrayal (*or.* 10.2; 43.59; *dvs* 386ff.; *ep* 47-50) into the hills (*dvs* 490f.); he repented and publicly justified his flight after his return (*or.* 9-11) but never entered upon his office. Instead, pressured again (*dvs* 495-525), he now officially assisted his father in the government of the Nazianzus community (*or.* 12; pastoral orations from this period: *or.* 13-17 and 19), but after the father's death categorically refused to be his successor. In 375 (after his mother's death, see *AP* 8:24-76) he withdrew for several years ("not a short time," *dvs* 511) to the monastery of Thecla in Seleucia of Isauria.

At the beginning of 379, after the enthronement of the Nicene-minded Theodosius, G. was called to be, as "speaker of the word" (*dvs* 608), leader of the small Nicene community in Constantinople, which was still entirely Arian (gathering place: the so-called Anastasia church: *dvs* 1079ff.; Soz., *h.e.* 7.5.3f.). His artistic skill (about half of the surviving orations, *or.* 20-42, are from 379-381) served orthodoxy so powerfully that the emperor himself, at his triumphal entry into the capital (Nov. 24, 380), made him its bishop (*dvs* 1311ff.). The council convoked there for 381 confirmed his investiture (*dvs* 1525: "they established me"). But after only a few weeks in office, G. failed, as successor of council president Meletius, in resolving in a balanced way the Antiochene (Meletian) schism (his oration: *dvs* 1591-1679; Theodoret, *h.e.* 5.8.6f.). When he asked to resign, neither the emperor nor the council held him back (the famous farewell oration, *or.* 42; on the whole affair see Soc., *h.e.* 5.6-8; Soz., *h.e.* 7.7.6-8). Ca. 383, after a short interval (*ep.* 138f.) in Nazianzus, he gave his definitive renunciation to that community (*ep.* 153; 182f.; *carm.* 2.1.68) and withdrew for good to his estate at Arbala in Arianzus in order to devote himself to monastic *theōria*, continued public polemics (*or.* 42.26), and, above all, his poetry, which was for the most part (*carm.* 2.1) autobiographical. Increasingly isolated (*ep.* 76.80; *or.* 43, end) and alienated from life (*ep.* 152; 164; 168; 172; *dvs* end; *carm.* 2.1.72/73; etc.), he died ca. 390, "in the thirteenth year of the rule of Theodosius" (Suida; Jerome, *vir. ill.* 117). In his will he left his property to the community of Nazianzus for the care of the poor (PG 37:389-96). He wrote his own epitaph (*carm.* 2.1.91-99).

L: G. Bellini, Bibliografia su G.: ScC 98 (1971) 165-181. — A. Benoit, Saint G. (Hildesheim, 1973 = Paris, 1876). — J. Bernardi, G. Le théologien et son temps (Paris, 1995). — F. J. Dölger, Nonna: AuC 5 (1936) 44-73. — E. Fleury, Hel-

lénisme et christianisme: G. et son temps (Paris, 1930). — P. Gallay, La vie de Saint G. (Paris, 1943). — M.-M. Hauser-Meury, Prosopographie zu den Schriften G.s (Bonn, 1960). — T. Kopecek, The Social Class of the Cappadocian fathers: ChH 42 (1973) 453-466. — J. Lercher, Die Persönlichkeit des hl. G., Diss. (Innsbruck, 1949). — F. Loofs, G.: RE 7:138-146. — G. Misch, Geschichte der Autobiographie I (Frankfurt a.M., ³1950), 612-636. — J. Mossay, G.: TRE 14:164-173. — idem, G. in Konstantinopel: Byz. 47 (1977) 223-238. — P. Nautin, La date du De vir. ill. de Jérôme . . . et de celle de G.: RHE 56 (1961) 33-35. — B. Otis, The Throne and the Mountain: CJ 56 (1961) 146-165. — J. Rousse, G.: DSp 6:932-971. — J. M. Szymusiak, Pour une chronologie des discours: VigChr 20 (1966) 183-189. — F. Trisoglio, San G. in un quarantennio di studi (1925-65): RivLas 40 (1973) 1-462 (= Turin, 1974). — idem, San G. (Genoa, 1987). — C. Ullmann, G. (Gotha, ²1867). — R. van Dam, Self-representation in the Will of G.: JThS 46 (1995) 118-148. — B. Wyss, G.: RAC 12:793-863.

II. Works: The surviving works of G. (on the numerous pseudepigrapha and forgeries see *CPG* 3059-3105) include forty-four orations (*or.* 35 is not authentic), approx. 17,000 verses and 249 letters (*ep.* 249 to Flavian is transmitted as *ep.* 1 of Gregory Nyss.). G. is above all the speaker, who became the accepted stylistic model in Byzantium (at a very early date Philostorgius 8.11; Psellus; G.'s own model was the moderate Asianist Polemon, see Jerome, *vir. ill.* 117 and his *ep.* 50.2; 52.8; scholia: *CPG* 3011-31; PG 36:738-1205). The orations served partly for remorseful self-defense (*or.* 1-3, 9-11), partly for censorious attacks (*or.* 4; 5; 20; 27-31; 33), partly for irenic mediation (6; 22; 23), but above all for panegyric celebration (addresses on the feasts of martyrs and saints: *or.* 15; 21; 24; 44; on high Chr. feastdays: *or.* 1; 44, Easter; 38, the first Christmas sermon [379/380]; 39, Epiphany [380/381]; 40, baptism; 41, Pentecost; encomia of deceased persons, *or.* 7; 8; 18; 43). To a degree not seen elsewhere, they always have a *personal* character: the mingling of the discussed (faith) content with subjective pathos is the hallmark of the Gregorian style. It is his own person that he relates to everything and most of all to Christ. Therefore the antithesis rhetor-Christian is inadequate for G. (despite *ep.* 11; 39; *or.* 27.10; 42.24; etc.): precisely because the divine *logoi* (*or.* 1.6; 7.1; 39.2) are used to praise the *Logos* (explicitly in *or.* 6.5f.; 45.30; *dvs* 608), precisely because of G.'s rhetorical Christ-mysticism, the spoken word participates no longer (as in Plato) in the outward appearance but in the truth of Christ (*alētheuein*, *dvs* 1225ff.); like silence, speech is a sacrifice to God (*or.* 6.4).

The poems (divided in the Maurist ed. into *Carmina theologica* [I], i.e., *dogmatica* [1] and *moralia* [2]; *historica* [II], i.e., *ad seipsum* [1] and *ad alios spectantia* [2]; and *epitaphia* [III]), composed almost exclusively in classical meters, represent, and not only in extent, the most important late blooming of Hellen. poetry (selection of scholia: PG 38:539-846). Making different kinds of demands but always of high value (mnemonics for school use or meditation—see *carm.* 1.1.12-27 and the catalogue of heretics in *dvs* 1146-1187—and poetry on the ascetic virtues stand side by side with the lofty didactic poetry of the *Carmina arcana* [1.1.1-5 and 7-9] and the plaintive lyricism of the group "to himself"), this poetry owes much to the following themes: control of the poet's own "excess"; the "sweetening" of didactic material; esthetic rivalry with ancient Greece; swansong and consolation in old age (*carm.* 2.1.39 *in suos versus* 34-57; compare *dvs* 6). Above all, however, G.'s aim is to replace the heretical corpus of Apollinaris (*ep.* 101.73), who, among other things, is supposed to have written Chr. dramas in the style of Euripides (Soz., *h.e.* 5.18.3f.); if these had survived, it would be easier to judge the *Christus patiens,* the authenticity and date of which are still in dispute.

Finally, as a letter writer G. is wholly in the sophistic tradition. He is the first Chr. writer to have made a collection of his own letters (*ep.* 51-55) and to have offered a stylistic theory of letter writing (*ep.* 51; ideal: brevity, clarity, elegance). It is in this ideologically neutral genre that G. best demonstrates his familiarity with the Gr. heritage (*ep.* 32; 188, "We and the Attics"!)

W: PG 35-38. — *carm.* 1:2, 1:215-732, K. Sundermann, SGKA NF 2.9 (Paderborn, 1991) [comm.]. — *carm.* 1:2, 2:1-354, F. E. Zehles, Diss. (Münster, 1987) [comm.]. — idem, M. J. Zamora, SGKA NF 2:13 (Paderborn, 1996) [comm.]. — *carm.* 1.2.8, H. M. Werhahn (Wiesbaden, 1953) [text/comm.]. — *carm.* 1.2.9, R. Palla, M. Kertsch, GrTS 10 (Graz, 1985) [text/German trans./comm.]. *carm.* 1.2.25, M. Oberhaus, SGKA NF 2:8 (Paderborn, 1991) [comm.]. — *carm.* 1.2.28, U. Beuckmann, SGKA NF 2:6 (Paderborn, 1988) [comm.]. — *carm.* 1.2.29, A. Knecht (Heidelberg, 1972) [text/German trans./comm.]. — *carm.* 2.1.11 (*dvs*), J. T. Cummings, Diss. (Princeton, 1966) [text]. — C. Jungk (Heidelberg, 1974) [text/German trans./comm.]. — *carm.* 2.1.12, B. Meier, SGKA NF 2:7 (Paderborn, 1989) [text/German trans./comm.]. — *poemata arcana,* C. Moreschini, D. A. Sykes, L. Holford-Strevens (Oxford, 1997) [text/English trans./comm.]. — *epitaphia,* H. Beckby, Anthologia Graeca 2 (book 8) (Munich, 1958) [text/German trans./comm.]. — C. Peri (Milan, 1975) [Italian trans./comm.]. — *ep.,* P. Gallay, GCS (Berlin, 1969) [text]. — M. Wittig (Stuttgart, 1981) [German trans.]. — *ep. theol.* (101f., 202), P. Gallay, SC 208. — *or.,* J. Bernardi, P. Gallay, M. Jourjon, G. Lafontaine, C. Moreschini, J. Mossay, M. Calvet-Sebasti, SC 247, 250, 270, 284, 309, 318, 358, 384, 405 (Paris, 1978-95) [text/French trans./comm., 1-12, 20-43]. — P. Haeuser, BKV 59 (Munich, 1928) [German trans., 1-20]. — P. Haeuser, M. Kertsch, G.: Reden über den Frieden. Über die Liebe zu den Armen (Munich, 1983). — T. Michels, Macht des Mysteriums (Düsseldorf, 1956) [German trans., 38-40, 41, 44, 45]. — J. Röhm, 2 vols., BKV (Kempten, 1874/77) [German trans. selections]. — T. Rufinus, ed. A. Engelbrecht, CSEL 46 [Latin trans.]. — G. Lafontaine, B. Coulie, CSCO 446 [to the Armenian trans.]. — *or.* 4/5, A. Kurmann (Basel, 1988) [comm.]. — *or. theol.* (27-31), A. J. Mason (Cambridge, 1899) [comm.]. — J. Barbel (Düsseldorf, 1963) [text/German trans./comm.]. — C. Moreschini (Rome, 1986) [Italian trans./comm.]. — F. W. Norris, L. Wickham, F. Williams, Faith Gives Fullness to Reasoning, Suppl. VigChr 13 (Leipzig, 1991) [English trans./comm.]. — *Philokalia,* E. Junod, M. Harl, SC 226, 302. — H. J. Sieben, FC 22. — J. A. Robinson (Cambridge, 1893). — *Christus patiens,* A. Tuilier, SC 149. — *Corpus Nazianzenum* 1-4, B. Coulie, G. Garitte, J. Mossay, J. Nimmo Smith, J. Grad'Henry, CCG 20, 27, 28, 34.

L: *Thesaurus S. Gregorii Naz.,* J. Mossay, B. Coulie, C. Detienne and CETEDOC, 2 vols. (Turnhout [CCG], 1990/91) [microfiche]. — Repertorium Nazianzenum, J. Mossay, B. Coulie, 1-6, SGKA NF 2:1, 5, 10-12, 14 (Paderborn, 1981-1998). — H. G. Beck, Rede als Kunstwerk u. Bekenntnis (Munich, 1977). — J. Bernardi, La prédication des Pères Cappadociens (Paris, 1968). — Biblia Patristica 5 (Paris, 1991). — Q. Cataudella, Cronologia e attribuzione del Christus patiens: Dioniso 43 (1969) 405-412. — CPG 2:3010-3125. — B. Coulie, Les richesses dans l'œuvre de G. (Leuven/Louvain, 1985). — K. Demoen, The Attitude towards Greek Poetry: Early Christian Poetry, ed. J. den Boeft (Leiden, 1993), 235-252. — H. Dörrie, Die Epiphanias-Predigt des G. (*or.* 39): Kyriakon 1 (1970) 409-423. — G. Galavaris, The illustrations of the liturgical homilies of G. (Princeton, 1969). — P. Gallay, Langue et style de G. dans sa correspondance (Paris, 1932). — N. Gertz, Die handschriftliche Überlieferung der Gedichte des G., Gruppe 1, SGKA NF 2/4 (Paderborn, 1986). — M. Guignet, S. G. et la rhétorique (Paris, 1911). — A. Hanriot-Coustet, Quel est l'auteur du discours 35?: RHPhR 71 (1991) 89-99. — W. Höllger, Die handschriftliche Überlieferung der Gedichte des G., Gruppen 20/11, SGKA NF 2:3 (Paderborn, 1985). — P. Karavites, G. and Byzantine Hymnography: JHS 113 (1993) 81-98. — G. Kennedy, Greek Rhetoric under the Christian Emperors (Princeton, 1983). — M. Kertsch, Bildersprache bei G. (GrTS 2) (Graz, 1980). — F. Lefherz, Studien zu G.: Mythologie, Überlieferung, Scholiasten, Diss. (Bonn, 1958). — A. Mayer, Psellos' Rede über den rhetorischen Charakter des G. [text/comm.]: ByZ 20 (1911) 27-100. — D. M. Meehan, Editions of G.: IThQ 18 (1951) 203-219 (esp. 215-19: bibliography for the work of Sinko, Sajdak, Przychocki, Sternbach). — C. Moreschini, Poesia e cultura in G.: Crescita dell'uomo, ed. S. Felici (Rome, 1988), 51-63. — idem, Sulla tradizione manoscritta dei carmina di G.: FS M. Gigante (Naples, 1994), 521-530. — idem, G. Menestrina (ed.), G. teologo e scrittore (Bologna, 1992) [collection]. — J. Mossay, La date de l'oration 2: Muséon 77 (1964) 175-186. — idem (ed.), Repertorium Nazianzenum 1-3, SGKA NF 2:1, 5, 10 (Paderborn, 1981-1993). — P. Nautin, L'éloge funèbre de Basile par G.: VigChr 48 (1994) 332-340. — E. Norden, Die antike Kunstprosa (Darmstadt, 1982 = Leipzig, ²1909), 562-569. — R. Palla, Ordinamento e polimetria delle poesie bibliche di G.: WSt 102 (1989) 169-185. — M. Pellegrino, La poesia di G. (Milan, 1932). — V. Pyykkö, Die griech. Mythen bei den großen Kappadokiern (Turku, 1991). — R. R. Ruether, G. (Oxford, 1969). — J. Sajdak, Die Scholiasten der Reden des G.: ByZ 30 (1929/30) 268-274. — idem, Historia critica scholiastarum et commentatorum (Cracow, 1914). — G. Swart, The Christus Patiens and Romanos the Melodist: ACl 33 (1990) 53-64. — D. A. Sykes, The poemata arcana: JThS NS 21 (1970) 32-42. — II. Symposium Nazianzenum, ed. J. Mossay, M. Sicherl, SGKA NF 2:2 (Paderborn, 1983). — F. Trisoglio, L'uomo di fronte a Dio nella tragedia greca e nel Christus patiens (Genoa, 1983). — M. Vinson, G.'s homily 36: CM 44 (1993) 255-256. — A. C. Way, P. O. Kristeller, F. E. Cranz, Catalogus translationum et commentariorum 2 (Washington, 1971), 43-192. — H. M. Werhahn, Dubia u. Spuria unter den Gedichten G.s: StPatr 7 (1966) 337-347. — B. Wyß, G.: ein griech.-chr. Dichter: MH 6 (1949) 177-210.

III. Main Lines of Thought:

In the Byz. tradition G. is, like John the evangelist, called *ho theologos*, "the theologian" without qualification (see John Damascene, PG 94:1068A; *theologikōs* = "in the manner of G.," 1237C, 1328B). While broadly developed in the so-called theol. orations (*or.* 27-31; emphasis on the unknowableness of God against the epistemological optimism of the Eunomians; distinction between *theologia* as doctrine on the being of God and *oikonomia* as doctrine on God's activity; see *or.* 45.4), the nucleus of G.'s teaching on the Trinity is carefully formulated in almost every oration during the sixties (*or.* 3.6; 6.13; 20.7-10; 32.5; 33.16f.; 37.4; 39.11; espec. 40.41-45 and 42.14-17). Conceived of as a "golden mean" (*mesotēs, or.* 20.6) between the extreme "errors" of Sabellius and Arius, this doctrine supports the Nicene *homoousia* of the divine hypostases (or *prosōpa*), Father, Son, and Spirit, whose common *ousia* manifests itself in three *idiotētēs: agennēsia, gennēsis* and (a new term coined by G. on the basis of Jn 15:26) *ekporeusis* (*or.* 39.12; 31.9; or *ekpempsis, or.* 25.16). Generally speaking, it is in the forcing of the claim of divinity for the Holy Spirit that G.'s real contribution to the development of trinitarian dogma consists (confirmation by NC 381; see *dvs* 1754). This claim, like G.'s entire teaching, is made on fundamentally soteriological grounds (*dvs* 1867; *or.* 2.28; 39.20; *ep.* 101.13f.): *theōsis*, which for G. is the goal of the entire history of salvation (*or.* 2.5; 2.22; 45.4; 29; *ep.* 178; 101.13ff.) is to be reached only through one divine Spirit and one divine Logos.

This accounts, conversely, for G.'s rejection of the christology of the (Nicene) Apollinaris (*ep.* 101f.; 202; see *or.* 29.19). Since it was a trangression of reason that hurled man into sin (*or.* 38.12), the divine Logos had to assume not only human flesh (*sarx*) but also the human *nous,* which was espec. in need of redemption (Christ is *theos anthrōpophoros*, not *sarkophoros, ep.* 102.20), "for what was not assumed was not healed" (*to gar aproslēpton atherapeuton, ep.* 101.32). Thus as in the doctrine of the Trinity there is

a single common *ousia* (nature) and three hypostases (*allos kai allos kai allos*), so in G.'s christology there are two natures (*physeis*) and a single person (*prosōpon*; see *en tēi sygkrasei, ep.* 101.21, as distinct from *sygkysis*) in the redeemer Jesus Christ (*allo kai allo, ep.* 101.20). In keeping with his theology of the economy, G.'s anthropology remains untouched by the problem raised by Augustine's teaching on grace: at the center is man's primordial *worthiness* of (not: capacity for) redemption, since he is the image of his creator; only with divine help does this worthiness emerge from the fog of the material. The fall into sin was because of haste not error. History is not meaningless suffering but a course of preparation for the goal (*or.* 38.12f.). Purification, enlightenment (baptism), and illumination (*or.* 40 passim; 39.2 and 20; 31.33; 32.15) through strict asceticism (e.g., *carm.* 1.2.1ff. on virginity) and contemplative absorption in the word mark the stages of the redemptive way, but also and not least practical *caritas. Or.* 14 (375/373) develops a pioneering theory of Chr. care of the poor and sick; it is based entirely on concepts of *eikōn* and *theōsis*: "Practice is the application of theory" (*or.* 20.12).

But both *theōria* and *praxis* have as their common source the Bible and the history of its interpretation (principle of tradition, *or.* 33.15; 40.44 *graphōn ha grammatai kai didaskōn kai memathēka*; but no *argumentum patristicum*, such as Basil is the first to use, *Spir.* 29.71ff.). Even for his contemporaries G.'s teaching became the authoritative model of orthodoxy: "it is clear that whatever is not in agreement with the faith of Gregory is not a pointer to right faith" (Rufinus in the preface to his translation of G., CCL 20:256); Augustine often appeals to him. Soz. (*h.e.* 6.27.1-6) cites G.'s letter 202 as a valid doctrinal decision (as do later councils). Erasmus (PG 35:309-16) praises his *pietas* and *facundia*. In Byzantium G. has long since joined Basil and Chrysostom as the "three hierarchs"; in the West, too, since 1568 he has been numbered with them and Athanasius as the four church doctors of the East. In 1580 Gregory XIII had his relics brought to Rome, an action symbolic of the increasing esteem for G. at the time of the Counterreformation.

L: H. Althaus, Die Heilslehre des hl. G. (Münster, 1972). — S. Bergmann, Geist, der Natur befreit (Mainz, 1995). — A.-S. Ellverson, The Dual Nature of Man. A Study in the Theological Anthropology of G. (Uppsala, 1981). — V. Harrison, Some Aspects of G. s Soteriology: GOTR 34 (1989) 11-18. — K. Holl, Amphilochius v. Ikonium in seinem Verhältnis zu den großen Kappadokiern (Tübingen, 1904). — M. Kertsch, G.s Stellung zu Theorie u. Praxis: Byzantion 44 (1974) 282-289. — U. Knoben, G.: LCI 6:1444-450. — N. B.

MacLynn, The Other Olympias. G. and the Family of Vitalianus: ZAC 2 (1998) 227-246. — E. P. Meijering, The Doctrine of the Will and the Trinity: idem, God Being History (Amsterdam, 1975), 103-113. — C. Moreschini, La persona del padre nella teologia di G.: VetChr 28 (1991) 77-102. — J. Mossay, La mort et l'au-delà dans G. (Leuven/Louvain, 1966). — B. Otis, Cappadocian Thought as a Coherent System: DOP 12 (1958) 97-124. — J. Plagnieux, Saint G. (Paris, 1951/52). — F. X. Portmann, Die göttliche Paidagogia bei G. (St. Ottilien, 1954). — F. Rudasso, La figura di Cristo in G. (Rome, 1968). — T. Spidlik, G. Introduction à l'étude de sa doctrine spirituelle (Rome, 1971). — J. M. Szymusiak, Éléments de théologie de l'homme selon G. (Rome, 1963). — G. Telepneff, Theopaschite Language in the Soteriology of G.: GOTR 32 (1987) 403-416. — T. F. Torrance, The Doctrine of the Holy Trinity in G. and John Calvin: Sobornost' 12 (1990) 7-24. — F. Trisoglio, Filone Alessandrino e l'esegesi cristiana [on G.]: ANRW II 21/1 (1984) 588-730. — D. F. Winslow, Christology and Exegesis in the Cappadocians: ChH 40 (1971) 389-396. — idem, G. and Love for the Poor: AThR 47 (1965) 348-359. — idem, The Dynamics of Salvation (Cambridge, Mass., 1979).

C. HARTMANN

Gregory of Nyssa

I. Life: G. was born between 335 and 340, the son of a large and prosperous Chr. family of Cappadocia that probably belonged to the class of the *curiales*. The course of his education was less spectacular than that of his eldest brother, Basil, whom he himself honors as "father and teacher" (e.g., *hom. opif. prol.*). His works show him however to be an educated, rhetorically trained writer with many interests. Although he was already a church lector, in about 364 he took up the career of a rhetor (energetic objections from Gregory Naz., *ep.* 11). He refers to his marriage in *virg.* 3.

G. became involved in the eccles.-political struggle over the reception of the Nicene Creed because of Basil (since 370 a bishop and metropolitan of Caesarea in Cappadocia), who in 371/372 entrusted to G. the newly created see of Nyssa in order to strengthen his own (Basil's) position. But G.'s tactics (e.g., against the Marcellians) occasionally elicited Basil's criticism. In theology the brothers opposed the dominant party, the homoeans, who therefore at two synods obtained G.'s deposition in 375/376, thus securing their position. The shift in religious policy in 378 returned G. to his office; the death of Basil (378/379) gave him the task of continuing his brother's work in writing, theology, and eccles. politics. At the synods of 379, 381, (382?) 383, and 394, G. worked for the success and continuation of the Nicene Creed, which was imposed by Emperor Theodosius (from 379 on); he accomplished this by journeys to Pontus (his surprising election as bishop of Sebaste, an office later taken over by his younger

brother, Peter), to Jerusalem, and into Arabia. The esteem in which he was held is shown by his funeral addresses for Meletius, president of the Council of Constantinople (381), and for members of the imperial house (385/386). The imperial decree confirming the synod of 381 emphasizes his authority. After 386 we have no further information about G.'s life, which may now have taken a stronger ascetic turn but remained literarily productive. His death probably occurred before the end of the century.

II. Works: 1. *Catechetical-parenetic works: De virginitate* (*virg.*), probably G.'s earliest treatise (before 378), sheds a favorable light on virginity by praising its advantages, contrasting it with marriage, and evoking models of it, but moves beyond it in the direction of a comprehensive ordering of the soul's powers.

The content of the work *De professione christiana* (*prof. chr.*) likewise points to an early stage of G.'s life and stresses the point that the name of Christ(ian) implies all the virtues and that to be a true Christian means an imitation of God. On the other hand, the treatise *De perfectione* (*perf.*), which turns the NT descriptions of Christ into stimuli to a life of ceaseless striving for perfection, must have been written rather late.

In the dialogue often extolled as the "Chr. Phaedo," *De anima et resurrectione* (*anim. et resurr.*; after 380), which presupposes the *v. Macr.*, G.'s eldest sister, Macrina, in the role of the "teacher," answers questions and objections about the immortality of the soul and the bodily resurrection; here Platonic philosophy is adapted and surpassed by the Bible.

The work *De mortuis* (*mort.*; after 380) is meant to help overcome grief in the face of death through knowledge of the true good and the comparison between earthly life and the life of heaven; it also deals with questions about the meaning of bodily existence and about the risen body.

In a sermon (*castig.*; Jan. 2, 382?) G. seeks to counter the opposition caused in his community by his sanctions against Chr. participation in pagan celebrations. Another homily (*hom. in 1 Cor.* 6.18) attacks sexual permissiveness. Social criticism marks sermons on behalf of the homeless and beggars (*paup.* 1, certainly a Lenten sermon) and lepers and against lending at interest (*usur.*).

Theol. problems arising from the death of underage children are discussed in the work *De infantibus praemature abreptis*, addressed to Hierius, who is honored with choice rhetoric (*infant.*; ca. 386); it attests to G.'s optimism regarding salvation and to his positive view of theodicy.

The *Great Catechetical Treatise* (*or. catech.*; ca. 387) is intended as a help to catechists; it gives an outline of Chr. teaching on God and his *oikonomia* (plan of salvation) (chap. 26 teaches the apocatastasis or universal reconciliation, including that of the "adversary"); the different intellectual backgrounds and possible objections of the fictive groups addressed are taken into account.

A medicinal understanding of sin and repentance can be seen in the so-called *Epistula canonica ad Letolum* (*ep. can.*), in which G. sketches a systematic "pathology" of the soul and calls for a "healing" appropriate to each case (and not only in the set seasons of penance).

The treatise *De instituto christiano* (*instit.*; after 390) deals with the abridgement of the Messalian "Great Letter" of Ps.-Macarius of Egypt/Simeon; G. accepts, while carefully correcting, its stimuli to monasticism.

2. *Dogmatic works:* In the shorter treatises written ca. 379/380, *Ad Graecos. Ex communibus notionibus* (*comm. not.*) and *De differentia essentiae et hypostaseos* (*diff. ess.*; = Basil, *ep.* 38; the authorship is disputed) as well as in the later work *Ad Ablabium. Quod non sint tres dei* (*tres dei*), G. supports the Neo-Nicene teaching on the one nature or essence and three hypostases in God and endeavors to safeguard it in a somewhat strained way. The three books *Contra Eunomium* (*Eun.*), 380-83, continue the controversy of Basil with → Eunomius of Cyzicus, leader of the anhomoeans. In addition to a defense of his brother and attacks on Eunomius and his teacher Aerius at the beginning of book 1, G. deals with his adversary's outline of trinitarian theology and its presuppositions in the philosophy of language, and then in his turn shows the inadequacy of human concepts for God. G. defines the being of God (against Eunomius) as unlimited, i.e., incomprehensible, and thus strengthens the tradition of negative theology. The *Refutatio confessionis Eunomii* (*ref. Eun.*) rejects a confession of faith that Eunomius had presented at the Synod of Constantinople (383).

An anti-Arian treatise (*hom. in 1 Cor* 15.28) of ca. 382 seeks to refute the subordinationist interpretation of the "subjection" of Christ to the Father acc. to 1 Cor 15:58 by interpreting it as referring to the "body" of Christ, the church. The work *Adversus Arium et Sabellium* (*Ar. et Sab.*) departs from that interpretation; for this reason, among others, its authenticity is disputed. Further examples of Arian argumentation are refuted in G.'s *Ad Simplicium. De fide* (*fid.*).

In the treatise *Ad Eustathium. De sancta Trinitate* (*Trin.*; ca. 380) and later in the work *Adversus Macedonianos. De spiritu sancto* (*Maced.*) G. defends the divinity of the Holy Spirit, who is distinct from the Father and the Son as a hypostasis but not in essence and activity.

Disappointment over the unsuccessful union with the Pneumatomachians marks G.'s address (*ordin.*) at a synod (381 rather than 394); a further address on the divinity of the Son and the Holy Spirit (*deit.*), attacking the Eunomians and the Pneumatomachians, is to be connected with the synod of 383, at which the various credal formulas were once again tested.

G. involved himself in the christological debate with a letter to Bishop Theophilus Alex. (*Thphl.*; after 385), in which he turns aside Apollinarist attacks and calls for support, and in the *Antirrheticus adversus Apollinarium* (*Apoll.* 386/387), from which the latter's *Explanation of the Divine Incarnation* can to some extent be reconstructed; in his refutation G. insists on the completeness of Christ's human nature, which was assumed by the Logos on earth and changed into the divine at his exaltation.

In the framework of a letter G. hands on his dialogue *Contra fatum* (*fat.*; 386) in which he combats, primarily with rational arguments, a pagan philosopher's belief in the power of the stars to control destinies.

3. *Exegetical works:* The eight homilies on the beatitudes (*beat.*) explain Mt 5:1-10 as a ladder leading to the conquest of the passions, which are vividly described, and to virtue.

In a treatise on the titles of the Pss (*Pss. titt.*) G. first presents the five parts of the Psalter as stages of an ascent to blessedness, and, in a second review, connects many Psalm titles, among other notable details, with this teleological vision.

The works dedicated to G.'s brother Peter, *De hominis opificio* (*hom. opif.*) and *Apologia in hexaemeron* (*hex.*), both written shortly after Basil's death, make reference to the latter's sermon on "the work of the six days." *Hom. opif.* is meant to complement those sermons; it deals espec. with the creation of human beings acc. to Gen 1:26f.; G. dissociates the difference of the sexes (therefore also reproduction and history) from the image of God and explains it by means of God's plan of salvation for overcoming the sin which he foresaw. Here G. defends the resurrection and rejects the preexistence of souls (→ Origen) and metempsychosis. *Hex.* discusses possible objections against Basil's exegesis; but in the process G. introduces his own emphases and, despite protestations to the contrary, also uses allegory. The emphasis is placed on the creation of the entire world by a single act of God and on the *akolouthia* (logical sequence) of its development in time. In contrast, two addresses on the creation of man (*or.* 1 and 2 *in Gen* 1:26) and one on paradise (*parad.*) are not authentic.

The eight homilies on Qoh (*hom. in Eccl.*; ca. 380) interpret Qoh 1:1–3:13 partly as instructions given by the Son of God, partly as experiences of Solomon (both in the role of the "preacher"), all of which show the nothingness of the visible world and its goods (criticism of the owning of slaves in *hom.* 4), purify souls, and, like a schoolmaster, lead them to higher wisdom and virtue.

Of the five homilies on the Lord's Prayer (*or. dom.*) the first deals with the meaning of prayer, while the others interpret the Our Father in a pronouncedly parenetic way (*hom.* 3 reaffirms the divinity of the Holy Spirit).

The letter *De engastrimytho* (*engast.*; "On the Myth of the Ventriloquist"), in addition to answering other questions, gives a detailed explanation to a Bishop Theodosius of G.'s view that it was not Samuel's soul but a demon that appeared to the woman who called up the dead at En-Dor (1 Sam 28) in order to deceive King Saul.

In a homily (*Ps.* 6) the content of Ps 6 is related to the concept of *ogdoē* in its title; it is explained as meaning the "eighth day" of the universal judgment and the consummation.

The *Vita Moysis* (*Mos.*; ca. 390) consists of a retelling of the story of Moses' life and a *theōria* (meditation, interpretation) of it; G. sees this life as a paradigm for the soul that strives for virtue, perfection, God, without ever coming to an end.

In the fifteen homilies on the Cant (*hom. in Cant.*), which are reworked sermons given ca. 394 at the request of Deaconess Olympias of Constantinople, G. interprets Cant 1:1–6:9 allegorically as referring to Christ and the soul or the church; he defends his exeget. method in the prologue. The "red thread" running through the work is the endless ascent of souls to God, who, inspired by insatiable love, leads them to the eschat. unity of all in Christ. These homilies provide mystical theology with a strong pedagogical element. The influence of → Origen is perceptible but not determinative.

4. *Festal sermons:* A series of sermons has come down on the the feasts of the church year: a sermon on the only recently introduced feast of Christmas (*nativ.*: Dec. 25, 386), which uses not only Mt 1–2 and Lk 1–2 but the *Protevangelium of James*; a sermon on the feast of Stephen (*Steph.* 1; Dec. 26, 386) that describes the martyr as an athlete and attacks the Arian-Pneumatomachian interpretation of Acts 7:56f.; a further sermon (*Steph.* 2) on the next day leads skillfully from the subject of Stephen to the feast of the apostles Peter, James, and John, whose (dogmatic) harmony is emphasized.

The eulogy of Basil (*laud. Bas.*; Jan. 1, 381) justifies placing his memorial among the feasts and sketches, chiefly through a *sugkrisis*, i.e., a comparison with (bibl.) models, the portrait of an ideal bishop of the Orthodox Church.

At the center of the sermon on the "Day of Lights" (*bapt. Chr.*; Jan. 6, 383? in Nyssa), which could also be a day for baptisms, is the sacrament of baptism rather than the subject of the feast (the baptism of Christ). On a set date before the beginning of Lent (also on Jan. 6?) G. also calls upon the catechumens to enroll among the baptizands and not to put off baptism as a result of mistaken calculation (*bapt. diff.*).

Late winter saw the feasts of Theodore the Legionary, whom G. praises in his burial church at Euchaïta in Pontus (*Thdr.*; before 376), and of the forty martyrs of Sebaste, who were espec. venerated in G.'s family and to whom he dedicates two sermons (*mart.* 2 evidently followed a sermon of Basil in Caesarea; *mart.* 1a was interrupted and continues in *mart.* 1b, and this at the martyrs' shrine in Sebaste).

Of the Easter sermons attributed to G., *res.* 2 is not authentic; *res.* 5 is disputed; *res.* 4 picks up thoughts from *res.* 1 and is probably a brief closing address at the end of the liturgy; the subject of *res.* 1 (after 386) is the triduum of the death and resurrection of Jesus in which various questions (*zētēmata, noēmata*) are raised; *res.* 3 (379; see the echoes of *hom. opif.*) defends espec. the bodily resurrection.

A short sermon is devoted mainly to the new feast of Christ's ascension (*ascens.*; 388?) but makes this reference clear only indirectly (exegesis of Ps 23; 67:19 LXX), while the homily for Pentecost (*Spir.*; 388?) is clearly based on Acts 2 and builds a proof for the divinity of the Holy Spirit from Ps 94:7-9 LXX/Heb 3:7-9.

The festal sermon for Origen's disciple → Gregory the Wonderworker/Thaumaturgus (*v. Gr. Thaum.*), who christianized Pontus (and even instructed G.'s grandmother Macrina), is less biographical than panegyrical and sings the praises espec. of Gregory's miracles. In contrast, the festal sermon on → Ephraem the Syrian (*v. Ephr.*) and the sermon *De occursu domini* (*occurs.*) for the feast of the Lord's presentation in the temple are no longer attributed to G.

5. *Biographical works:* The letter on the life of Mac-

rina, written for the monk Olympius (*v. Macr.*: shortly after 380), is a memorial to G.'s sister (espec. her death) and changes the genre of ancient biography.

The traditional *topoi* of lament, praise, and consolation, which G. christianizes as needed, characterize the funeral sermons for Bishop Meletius of Antioch, who died while presiding at the synod of 381 (*Melet.*), for Pulcheria, daughter of Emperor Theodosius (*Pulch.*; 385), and for her mother, Empress Flacilla (*Flacill.*)

6. *Letters*: A collection of thirty letters gives information about, among other things, G.'s rivalry with his metropolitan, Helladius (*ep.* 1), his critical attitude toward pilgrimages to Jerusalem (*ep.*2), G.'s life (*passim*), and the building of a church in Nyssa (*ep.* 25), and contains the only letter of his brother Peter (*ep.* 30).

Spurious: In addition to *or.* 1 and 2 *in Gen.* 1:26, *parad. Ar. et Sab.*, *res.* 2 (and 5?), *v. Ephr.*, and *occurs.* (see above), twenty-two other works are mistakenly attributed to G. (see M. Altenburger, F. Mann, in bibliog. XIIf.).

III. Main Lines of Thought: G.'s literary production reflects his role as bishop, (polemical) theologian, and spiritual teacher (also for monastic circles) and proves his membership in the Chr. elite of the post-Constantinian age. His Hellen. education, which displays mainly (Middle- and Neo-)Platonic thought but with Stoic and Aristotelean elements as well, and thus gives evidence of philosophical syncretism in a Chr. milieu, is no less consciously put in the service of theology than are his rhetorical training (influence of the so-called Second Sophistic) and his noteworthy interest in scientific (e.g., anatomical and physiological) questions. G.'s freedom in dealing with the traditions of "Gr. wisdom" (or "wisdom from outside"), which he adopts to some extent but also modifies or transcends through "divine philosophy," shows the functional value and limited importance that he allows to pagan education. Yet it cannot be denied that his works have a fundamentally Platonic character (priority of the spiritual over the material; devaluation of the body).

In controverted theol. questions of the 4th c. G. follows his brother Basil in essentials: he defends Neo-Nicene teaching on the Trinity, argues (more aggressively than Basil) for the divinity of the Holy Spirit, and takes up the controversy with Apollinaris of Laodicea at the argumentative level. As a writer, however, he emerges from the shadow of his "teacher" and develops his own rich spiritual gifts. It is espec. in the idea of the endless ascent of the soul to God (also described as *epektesis* ("stretching out toward") on the basis of Phil 3:13 or as a progressive participation in or endless approach to God, who is conceived as limitless in every respect) that G.'s contribution to mysticism or, better, mystical theology can be seen. But in his case this theology has a universal perspective and carries with it a pedagogical duty to help others to spiritual growth.

Important theol. perspectives adopted by G. (e.g., in eschatology) and his exeget. insights and methods (espec. allegorism, which is applied even to NT passages) betray the influence of Origen. The latter's theology is not, however, taken over uncritically but is corrected at characteristic points; thus G. denies trinitarian subordinationism, the preexistence of souls, and the idea that there can be aversion in God. There is an almost modern air about G.'s critique of theology, which was sharpened in the controversy with the positivism of his adversary Eunomius: God's infinity relativizes every theol. assertion; a comprehensive knowledge of the divine being is impossible. G. is thus in the tradition of negative theology (Philo Alex.; Origen), but at the same time he transcends this in his idea of the "limitless journey" to God of the human person, whose blessedness consists precisely in the fact that it does not attain an ultimate goal.

G.'s influence, which reached even into the area of the eastern languages (Syr. translations, among others), was far greater in the Byz. world (e.g., Ps.-Dionysius Areo., Maximus Conf., Gregory Palamas) than in the West, where only a few works of G. were translated into Latin (*hom. opif.* by Dionysius Exiguus in the 6th c. and John Eriugena in the 9th; *v. Gr. Thaum.* in the 8th-11th c. in southern Italy). The Union Council of Florence 1439 roused a new interest in G. in the West. In the 16th c., works of G. were printed in a Lat. translation. The first Gr.-Lat. collection of his works appeared in 1615.

W: Gregorii Nysseni Opera (= GNO), vol. 1-10/2 (Leiden, 1952ff.) [text]: *Eun.* 1, 2, W. Jaeger, GNO 1. — *Eun.* 3, *ref. Eun.*, W. Jaeger, GNO 2. — *Trin., comm. not., tres dei, fid.,* [*Ar. et Sab.,*] *Maced., Thphl., Apoll.*, F. Mueller, GNO 3/1. — *hom. in 1Cor.* 15:28, J. K. Downing. — *fat.*, J. McDonough. — *infant., engast.*, H. Hörner, GNO 3/2. — *or. catech.*, E. Mühlenberg, GNO 3/4. — *Pss. titt.*, Ps. 6, J. McDonough, *hom.* 1-8 *in Eccl.*, P. Alexander, GNO 5. — *hom.* 1-15 *in Cant.*, H. Langerbeck, GNO 6. — *v. Mos.*, H. Musurillo, GNO 7/1. — *or. dom.* 1-5, *beat.* 1-8, J. F. Callahan, GNO 7/2. — *instit., prof. Chr., perf.*, W. Jaeger, *virg.*, J. P. Cavarnos, *v. Macr.*, V. Woods Callahan, GNO 8/1. — *ep.*, G. Pasquali, GNO 8/2. — *mort.*, G. Heil, *paup.* 1, 2, A. van Heck, *usur., hom. in 1Cor.* 6, 18, *bapt. Chr., res.* 3, *res.* 1, *res.* 4, [*res.* 5,] *ascens., ordin.*, E. Gebhardt, *Melet., Pulch., Flacill.*, A. Spira, GNO 9. — *v. Gr. Thaum.*, G. Heil, *Thdr.*, J.

P. Cavarnos, *Steph.* 1, 2, *laud. Bas., mart.* 1a, 1b, 2, O. Lendle, GNO 10/1. — *bapt. diff.*, H. Polack, *deit.*, E. Rhein, *nativ.*, F. Mann, *Spir., castig.*, M. Altenburger, GNO 10/2. — *mort.*, G. Lozza, CorPat 13 (Turin, 1991) [text/Italian trans./comm.]. — *diff. ess.* (= Basil, *ep.* 38), M. Forlin Patrucco, CorPat 11 (Turin, 1983), 178-195, 407f. [text/Italian trans./comm.]. — *v. Mos.*, J. Daniélou, SC 1bis. — *hom. opif.*, J. Daniélou, SC 6. — *virg.*, M. Aubineau, SC 119. — *v. Macr.*, P. Maraval, SC 178. — *ep.*, P. Maraval, SC 363. — PG 44-46 [text; up to now not in GNO ed.]: *hex., hom. opif.*, PG 44:61-124, 125-256. — *ep. can.*, PG 45:221-236. — *anim. et res.*, PG 46:12-160. — *or. catech.*, J. Barbel, BGrL 1 (Stuttgart, 1971) [German trans./comm.]. — *prof. Chr., perf., virg.*, W. Blum, BGrL 7 (Stuttgart, 1977) [German trans./comm.]. — *diff. ess.* (= Basil, *ep.* 38), W.-D. Hauschild, BGrL 32 (Stuttgart, 1990), 83-91, 183-189 [German trans./comm.]. — *ep.*, D. Teske, BGrL 43 (Stuttgart, 1997) [German trans./comm.]. — *v. Macr., or. catech., hom. opif., anim. et res.*, H. Hayd, BKV 24 (Kempten, 1874). — *or. dom.* 1-5, *beat.* 1-8, *paup.* 1, 2, *usur., hom. in 1Cor.* 6, 18, *nativ., bapt. Chr., res.* 1-5, *ascens., ordin., laud. Bas., mart.* 1a, 1b, 2, *Thdr., v. Gr. Thaum., Melet., Pulch., Flacill.*, J. Fisch, BKV 70 (Kempten, 1880). — *or. catech., or. dom.* 1-5, *beat.* 1-8, *anim. et res.*, K. Weiß, *v. Macr.*, E. Stolz, BKV² 56 (Munich, 1927). — *hex., fat., fid., comm. not.* et al.: Sämmtliche Werke der Kirchen-Väter, vol. 39 (Kempten, 1853) [German trans.]. — *fid., Trin., tres dei, comm. not.* et al., F. Oehler, Bibliothek der Kirchenväter. Gregor v. Nyssa. vol. 2 (Leipzig, 1858) [text/German trans.]. — *Eun.* 1, *ref. Eun., Eun.* 3, *Eun.* 2 (in obsolete series), *infant.* et al., M. Day, H. C. Ogle, H. A. Wilson, NPNF 2/5 (Grand Rapids, Mich., 1954 = Oxford, 1892) [English trans.]. — *Thphl., Apoll.*, E. Bellini, Apollinare . . . su Cristo (Milan, 1978), 321-483, 543-546 [Italian trans.]. — *Trin., comm. not., tres dei, Maced., Thphl., hex.* et al., C. Moreschini, Opere di G (Turin, 1992) [Italian trans.]. — *Eun.* 1: El "Contra Eunomium I," ed. L. F. Mateo-Seco, J. L. Bastero (Pamplona, 1988) [English trans./comm.]. — *Eun.* 1:1-146, J.-A. Röder (Frankfurt a.M., 1993) [German trans./comm.]. — *comm. not.*, H. J. Vogt: ThQ 171 (1991) 204-218 [German trans./comm.]. — *engast.*, P. Maraval, CBiPa 1 (Strasburg, 1987), 283-294 [French trans.]. — *fat.*, C. McCambley: GOTR 37 (1992) 309-332 [English trans./comm.]. — *hom.* 1-15 *in Cant.*, F. Dünzl, FC 16/1-3. — *hom. in 1Cor.* 15:28, R. M. Hübner, Die Einheit des Leibes Christi (Leiden, 1974), 35-40 [partial German trans.]. — *hom.* 1-8 *in Eccl.*: Gregory of Nyssa, Homilies on Ecclesiastes, ed. S. G. Hall (Berlin, 1993) [English trans./comm.]. — *instit.*, C. Bouchet, CPF 40 (Paris, 1990), 61-100 [French trans.]. — *Pss. titt.*, R. E. Heine, OECT (Oxford, 1995) [English trans.]. — *res.* 1, 4, H. R. Drobner, G. v. Nyssa. Die drei Tage (Leiden, 1982) [German trans./comm.]. — *res.* 3, 1, 4, A. Spira, C. Klock, The Easter Sermons (Cambridge, 1981) [English trans./comm.]. — *Steph.* 1, O. Lendle, Gregorius Nyssenus. Encomium (Leiden, 1968) [text/German trans.]. — *v. Mos.*, M. Blum (Freiburg i.Br., 1963) [German trans.]. **Dubious/Spurious:** *Ar. et Sab.*, F. Mueller, GNO 3/1 (Leiden, 1958), 69-85. — *res.* 5, E. Gebhardt, GNO 9 (Leiden, 1967), 313-319. — *or.* 1, 2 *in Gen.* 1:26, *parad.*, H. Hörner, GNO Suppl. 1 (Leiden, 1972). — *res.* 2, *v. Ephr., occurs.*, PG 46:628-652, 820-849, 1152-1181. — *res.* 2, *res.* 5, *v. Ephr.*, J. Fisch, BKV 70 (Kempten, 1880). — For further inauthentic writings see M. Altenburger, F. Mann, Bibliographie XIIf. **L: (Additional aids):** A. Altenburger, F. Mann, Bibliographie (Leiden, 1988) [lit. until 1987; continuation is

planned]. — H. Drobner, Bibelindex zu den Werken G.s (Paderborn, 1988). — C. Fabricius, D. Ridings, A Concordance to G. (Göteborg, 1989). — (**Collections**): The Biographical Works, ed. A. Spira (Cambridge, 1984). — Colloquii Gregoriani III Leipzigsis Acta, ed. J. C. M. van Winden, A. van Heck (Leiden, 1976). — El "Contra Eunomium I," ed. L. F. Mateo-Seco, J. L. Bastero (Pamplona, 1988). — The Easter Sermons, ed. A. Spira, C. Klock (Cambridge, 1981). — Écriture et culture philosophique, ed. M. Harl (Leiden, 1971). — Epektasis. FS J. Daniélou (Paris, 1972), 415-548. — ΕΡΜΗΝΕΥΜΑΤΑ. FS H. Hörner (Heidelberg, 1990), 93-150. — G. v. Nyssa u. die Philosophie, ed. H. Dörrie et al. (Leiden, 1976). — Gregory of Nyssa. Homilies on Ecclesiastes, ed. S. G. Hall (Berlin, 1993). — Studien zu G. u. der chr. Spätantike, ed. H. R. Drobner, C. Klock (Leiden, 1990). — (**further lit.**): R. Albrecht, Das Leben der hl. Makrina (Göttingen, 1986). — D. L. Balás, G. v. Nyssa: TRE 14:173-181. — idem, Μετουσία θεοῦ (Rome, 1966). — H. v. Balthasar, Présence et pensée (Paris, 1942). — M. R. Barnes, Eunomius of Cyzicus and G. Two Traditions of Transcendent Causality: VigChr 52 (1998) 59-87. — K. Bjerre-Aspegren, Bräutigam, Sonne u. Mutter (Lund, 1977). — T. Böhm, Die Konzeption der Mystik bei G.: FZPhTh 41 (1994) 45-64. — idem, Theoria — Unendlichkeit — Aufstieg (Leiden, 1996). — J. A. Brooks, The New Testament Text of G. (Atlanta, 1991). — M. Canévet, Grégoire de Nysse: DSp 6:971-1011. — eadem, Grégoire de Nysse et l'herméneutique biblique (Paris, 1983). — A. Capboscq, El bien siempre mayor (Santiago de Chile, 1992). — G. Castelluccio, L'antropologia di G. (Bari, 1992). — D. Coffigny, Grégoire de Nysse (Paris, 1993). — J. Daniélou, La chronologie des œuvres: StPatr 7 (1966), 159-169. — idem, La chronologie des sermons: RevSR 29 (1955) 346-372. — idem, L'être et le temps (Leiden, 1970). — idem, Platonisme et théologie mystique (Paris, ²1954). — H. Dörrie, Gregor III: RAC 12:863-895. — F. Dünzl, Braut u. Bräutigam (hom. in Cant.) (Tübingen, 1993). — idem, Die Canticum-Exegese des G. und des Origenes: JAC 36 (1993) 94-109. — E. Ferguson, Preaching at Epiphany. G. and John Chrysostom on Baptism and the Church: ChH 66 (1997) 1-17. — G.-I. Gargano, La teoria di G. sul cantico dei cantici (Rome, 1981). — M. Girardi, Annotazioni alla esegesi di G. nel De beatitudinibus: Aug. 35 (1995) 161-182. — V. E. F. Harrison, Grace and Human Freedom (Lewiston, 1992). — M. Harl, Le déchiffrement du sens (Paris, 1993), 279-413. — M. D. Hart, Marriage, Celibacy, and the Life of Virtue (*virg.*) (Ann Arbor, Mich., 1992). — M. Heath, Echoes of Longinus in G.: VigChr 53 (1999) 395-400. — R. E. Heine, Perfection in the Virtuous Life (*v. Mos.*) (Cambridge, 1975). — R. Hübner, Die Einheit des Leibes Christi (Leiden, 1974). — E. v. Ivánka, Plato Christianus (Einsiedeln, 1964), 149-185. — W. Jaeger, G.s Lehre vom Hl. Geist (Leiden, 1966). — R. J. Kees, Die Lehre von der Oikonomia Gottes (*or. catech.*) (Leiden, 1995). — C. Klock, Untersuchungen zu Stil und Rhythmus (Frankfurt a.M., 1987). — T. A. Kopecek, The Social Class of the Cappadocian Fathers: ChH 43 (1972) 453-466. — A. Kowalski, Tempio di Dio in Cristo nella "Vita di Mosè" di G.: Ricerche teologiche 8 (1997) 401-408. — H. Langerbeck, Zur Interpretation G.s: ThLZ 82 (1957) 81-90. — A. Le Boulluec, Corporéité ou individualité: Aug. 35 (1995) 307-326. — C. W. Macleod, Allegory and Mysticism in Origen and G.: JThS 22 (1971) 362-379. — G. May, Die Chronologie des Lebens u. der Werke des G.: Écriture et culture philosophique, ed. M. Harl (Leiden, 1971), 51-66.

— idem, G. v. Nyssa: KlTh 1, ed. H. Fries, G. Kretschmar (Munich, 1981), 91-103. — idem, G. in der Kirchenpolitik seiner Zeit: JÖB 15 (1966) 105-132. — H. M. Meissner, Rhetorik u. Theologie (*anim. et res.*) (Frankfurt a.M., 1991). — A. Meredith, Origen's De Principiis and G.'s Oratio Catechetica: HeyJ 36 (1995) 1-14. — H. Merki, Ὁμοίωσις θεῷ (Fribourg, Switzerland, 1952). — E. D. Moutsoulas (Athens, 1997). — E. Mühlenberg, G. v. Nyssa: GK 2, ed. M. Greschat (Stuttgart, 1984), 49-62. — idem, Die Sprache der religiösen Erfahrung bei G.: Religiöse Erfahrung, ed. W. Haug, D. Mieth (Munich, 1992), 63-73. — idem, Die Unendlichkeit Gottes bei G. (Göttingen, 1966). — R. A. Norris, The Soul Takes Flight: G. and the Song of Songs: AThR 80 (1998) 517-532. — M. Parmentier, Syriac Translations of G.: OLoP 20 (1989) 143-193. — E. Peroli, G. and the Neoplatonic Doctrine of the Soul: VigChr (1997) 117-139. — A. Placida, La presenza di Origene nelle Omelie sul Cantico dei Cantici di G.: VetChr 34 (1997) 33-49. — B. Pottier, Dieu et le Christ selon G. (Brussels, 1994). — R. Schwager, Der wunderbare Tausch. Zur "physischen" Erlösungslehre G. s: ZKTh 104 (1982) 1-24. — A. Siclari, L'antropologia teologica di G. (Parma, 1989). — R. Staats, G. v. Nyssa u. die Messalianer (Berlin, 1968). — D. F. Stramara, G.'s Terminology for Trinitarian Perichoresis: VigChr 52 (1998) 257-263. — M.-B. von Stritzky, Zum Problem der Erkenntnis (Münster, 1973). — J. Ulrich: Wallfrahrt u. Wallfahrtskritik: ZAC 3 (1999) 87-96. — W. Völker, G. v. Nyssa als Mystiker (Wiesbaden, 1955). — G. Zachhuber, G. und das Schisma von Antiochien: ThPh 72 (1997) 481-496. — P. Zemp, Die Grundlagen heilsgeschichtlichen Denkens bei G. (Munich, 1970).

F. DÜNZL

Gregory, Presbyter

Two works have come down under the name of Presbyter Gregory (G.). It is usually assumed that there were two different authors, probably from Caesarea in Cappadocia. The first composed a biography of Gregory Naz. in the 6th/7th c. (*v. Gr. Naz.*), which Simeon Metaphrastes incorporated into his Menologion. In the 9th c. at the latest, the second author wrote a eulogy of the fathers of Nicaea and Constantine (*or.*). But there has as yet been no conclusive study of whether there was really only a single author. In one codex, the *De ieiunio* of Ps.-Chrysostom is likewise attributed to a Presbyter Gregory.

W: *or.*, PG 11:420-440. — J. Compernass, Gregorios Lobrede (Bonn, 1908), 17-31 [text]. — *v. Gr. Naz.*, PG 35:244-304.
L: H. G. Beck, Kirche u. theol. Lit. (Munich, 1959), 459, 545f. — J. Compernass, G. (Bonn, 1907). — J. Mossay, Grégoire de Cesarée: DHGE 21, 1491f. — S. J. Voicu, Rifacimenti pseudocrisostomici: Aug. 16 (1976) 499-504, here 503.

B. WINDAU

Gregory of Tours

I. Life: G., born on Nov. 30, probably in 538 in the Auvergne, belonged to a family of the Gallic-Roman senatorial nobility; he boasts of numerous bishops among his forebears and relatives. After a spiritual and literary formation in Clermont and Lyons, he became a deacon in 563 at the latest and from 573 on was bishop of Tours, where he was very active as pastor and builder, both in the administration of the church, as supreme representative of the city of St. Martin, and in dealings with the estranged Frankish (local) kings. This activity is mirrored in his writings. He died on Nov. 17, 594.

II. Works: The best known is *Historiarum libri X* (*Franc.*) (not: *Historia Francorum*), which is by far our most important source for Frankish history of the 5th/6th c. Work on this history occupied G. throughout his episcopate and is based where possible on earlier approaches. In keeping with a conception of the history of salvation, the work runs from the creation of the world to notice of the end, which G. regards as near because of the evils of his age. The first book takes the reader to the death of St. Martin (397) and follows, in addition to the Bible, current presentations of late antiquity. From book 2 on, which contains an account of Clodwig's baptism, Gaul and the Franks increasingly take center stage; the situation regarding sources is unclear. The first four books (down to 575) end with an epilogue, which is to be understood as a provisional end to the work. From book 5 on, G. organizes sixteen years of contemporary history, which he has experienced, acc. to his own impressions and oral accounts. The use of memoirs is as unmistakable as is G.'s love of episodes turned into dramas, but we must not overlook the fact that primarily moral and parenetic goals guided him in the choice of material and in the composition, as did the quest for typolog. connections with the bibl. people of Israel and its kings and for signs of the end-time. The civic organization of political life was of less interest to him than the *ecclesia*, which he understands in theol. terms and into which the *res publica* is as it were absorbed. Much space is given to the immediate intervention of God and the saints in earthly events.

In a list of his works at the end of *Franc.* (10.31) G. says he also composed "seven books on miracles and one on the life of the fathers." These are usually combined as eight books and contain *Liber in gloria martyrum* (bibl. miracles and early Chr. saints), *Liber de passione et virtutibus sancti Iuliani martyris* (venerated in Brioude/Auvergne), *Libri I-IV de virtutibus sancti Martini episcopi* (*Mart:* continuation of → Paulinus of Périgueux), *Liber vitae patrum* (*vit. patr.*; twenty saintly bishops, mostly from the Auvergne or Touraine), and *Liber in gloria confessorum* (further Gallic saints). Written models can be assumed only to a limited extent. In general, it is characteristic of G.'s hagiography that the gifts and testing of the saints during their earthly lives are given far less attention than their miraculous activity after death, espec. when this activity was closer in time and space to G.'s field of vision. His aim frequently is to spread the word about certain places of worship; his talent as a realistic narrator gives a large number of details that are informative for the history of the liturgy, culture, and society. The list mentioned earlier names as further works a treatise on the course of the stars (*De cursu stellarum ratio*; *stell.*), which is an aid in the astronomical determination of the times for prayer, but in it the author also speaks of the ancient wonders of the world and the saving deeds of God; also a commentary on the Psalms, of which only a few fragments have survived. Apart from the list, there is good reason for attributing to G. a *Liber de miraculis Andreae apostoli*, and a Lat. version of the eastern legend of the seven sleepers (*Passio VII dormientium apud Ephysum*). A work on the Mass texts of → Apollinaris Sidonius, mentioned in *Franc.* 2.22, has disappeared. The *Passio Iuliani martyris* and the *Passio sive miracula sancti Thomae apostoli* (*Thom*) must be considered not authentic.

III. Importance: Although G. draws on the patristic heritage to a greater degree than is usually claimed, he nevertheless remains the representative of an essentially changed, even early medieval religiosity. This replaced speculative reflection with the elementary conviction of the omnipotence of God and the power of saints in the struggle with the devil and demons, as compared with the ambivalent behavior of human beings. To this degree the borderline between historiography and hagiography was blurred for G. As a writer, he no longer followed classical models but, for the sake of being better understood, adopted a *sermo rusticus* based on the Latin of the Bible and of everyday eccles. life. Both *Franc.* and the works on miracles had a wide and persistent echo in the Middle Ages.

W: *Franc.*, B. Krusch, W. Levison, MGH. SRM 1/1² (Hannover, 1937-1951) [text]. — R. Buchner: AQDGMA 1-2 (1955-1956) [text/German trans.]. — *miracula et opera minora*, B. Krusch, MGH. SRM 1/2 (Hannover, 1885) [text]. — *vit. patr.*, S. Rose (Platina, Calif., 1988) [English trans.]. — *gloria martyrum*, R. v. Dam (Liverpool, 1988) [English trans.]. L: W. Berschin, Biographie u. Epochenstil 1 (Stuttgart, 1986), 288-304. — A. H. B. Breukelaar, Historiography and Episcopal Authority in Sixth-Century Gaul (Göttingen, 1994). — W. Goffart, The Narrators of Barbarian History (Princeton, 1988), 112-234. — M. Heinzelmann, G., "Zehn Bücher Geschichte" (Darmstadt, 1994). — G. de Nie, Views from a Many-Windowed Tower (Amsterdam, 1987). — J. Verdon, G. (Le Cateau, 1989). — idem, G., évêque de Tours: RMab 61 (1988) 339-354. — B. K. Vollmann, G.: RAC 12:895-930. — M. Weidemann, Kulturgeschichte der Merowingerzeit 1-2 (Mainz, 1982). — K. Zelzer, Zur Sprache der Franc.: StPatr 18/4 (1989) 207-211.

R. SCHIEFFER

Gregory the Wonderworker

I. Life: G. was born between 210 and 213 and was originally named Theodore; he came from a prominent pagan family of Neocaesarea in Asia Minor. The name Gregory may have been his baptismal name. After the death of his father, when G. was fourteen, the latter began to be interested in Christianity. His mother saw to it that he had a thorough education; he learned Latin, rhetoric, and Roman law. Along with his brother Athenodorus he was supposed to complete a legal training at Berytus (Beirut). On their way there G. and his brother were accompanied by their sister on her way to Caesarea in Palestine, where her husband was on the governor's staff of advisers. In Caesarea G. met Origen, whose fascinating personality made so deep an impression on him that he and his brother joined Origen's students. G. remained five years in Caesarea. When his brother returned to Pontus in 238, G. delivered a panegyric on Origen before a large but select audience. After his return, Phaidimus of Amaseia consecrated G. the bishop of a small Chr. community in his native city, Neocaesarea. In a letter (*ep* 2) Origen encouraged him to continue his theol. studies and reading of the Bible. During the Decian persecution in 250 G. fled to the mountains along with a part of his community. As bishop, G. engaged in so successful a missionary activity that finally all the inhabitants of Pontus could be said to be Christians. Also attested is his participation in the first Synod of Antioch ca. 264. It is difficult to separate truth from poetry in the accounts of his miracles, but in any case G. must have been an extraordinarily charismatic personality. He died in the time of Emperor Aurelian (270-275).

The most important source for G.'s life is his panegyric on Origen. In addition to Eusebius (*h.e.* 6.30; 7.28 with the addition by Rufinus), Jerome (*vir. ill.* 65), and details in Basil the Great, there are various *Vitae* (the most important is by Gregory Nyss.), but these focus on the legendary wonderworking of the Thaumaturgus.

In the memory of Chr. communities G. lived on chiefly as wonderworker and saintly protector against demons. His name was introduced into old and new formulas of exorcism in order to lend these greater power. Exorcisms are attributed to G. in the Byz. liturgy.

II. **Works:** In the panegyric on Origen (*pan. Or.*) G. sees divine providence at work in the complicated events leading to his meeting with Origen in Caesarea. This speech of thanks and farewell gives valuable information on Origen's dealings with his students and his program of studies. In addition to the study of the natural sciences, all the ancient poets and philosophers were read and explained, except for the atheists. Dialectical abilities were trained *more socratico* in penetrating discussions. Ethical instruction aimed not only at the four cardinal virtues and self-knowledge in accordance with the Delphic oracle's "know thyself" (*gnōthi seauton*) but also at the specifically Chr. virtues of patience (*hypomonē*, i.e., of the martyrs) and piety (*eusebeia*, "the mother of all virtues"). Theology was the high point in the course of studies. Origen proved an expositor of genius in bibl. exegesis. The panegyric is an eloquent testimony to the extraordinarily close and friendly relationship between student and master. G. describes Origen as the paradigm of the wise man (*paradeigma sophou*). G. thought of his stay with Origen in Caesarea as "paradise" (to use the language of the panegyric). When he had to say farewell, he felt like a second Adam being expelled from the garden.

Acc. to the account in Gregory Nyss., the *Confessio fidei* (*symb.*) was given to G. in a supernatural appearance of the Mother of God along with St. John, before he entered on his episcopal office. G. immediately wrote down this creed, which deals with the three divine persons individually and with the Trinity as a whole. The autograph was still in Neocaesarea in the time of Gregory Nyss.

In the so-called *Canonical Letter* (*ep. can.*) G. gives an unknown bishop advice on how to deal with Christians who in 258, during the invasions of the Goths and Boranes into Pontus and Bithynia, had been forced to act against their Chr. faith or to take up the cause of the invaders. The letter is an important witness to church discipline. The work on Qoh (*Eccl.*) is a paraphrase of the bibl. book.

Surviving only in Syriac is the apologetic work addressed to Theopompus (*Theopomp.*). In the manner of a Platonic dialogue, the work discusses the pagan idea of the inability of God to suffer. The suffering of the Son of God (G. says) is voluntary and is at the same time a victory over suffering and death; therefore the pagan axiom about God's inability to suffer is left untouched.

Also transmitted under G.'s name are some works regarded by scholars as not authentic (e.g., addresses on Mary). The authenticity of the panegyric, the confession of faith, and the work on God's inability to suffer has been doubted by some scholars, but it is generally accepted. Still disputed is the authenticity of the dialogue on consubstantiality addressed to Philagrius (*ep. Philagr.*) and the short treatise on the soul addressed to Tatian (*anim.*). The debate with Ailianus (see Basil, *ep.* 210.5) and some letters are lost.

W: *pan. Or.*, PG 10:1049-1104. — P. Koetschau, SQS 9 (Freiburg i.Br., 1894) [text]. — H. Crouzel, SC 148. — P. Guyot, R. Klein, FC 24 [with *ep.* 2 of Origen]. — E. Marotta, TePa 40 (Rome, 1983) [Italian trans.]. — *ep. can.*, PG 10:1020-1048. — P. P. Ioannu (Rome, 1963) [text/French trans.]. — K. M. Phouskas (Athens, 1978) [text]. — *Eccl.*, PG 10:988-1017. — J. Jarick (Atlanta, 1990) [text/comm.]. — S. D. F. Salmond, ANFa 6:9-17 [English trans.]. — *symb.*, PG 46:912f. — C. P. Caspari, Alte u. neue Quellen zur Geschichte des Taufsymbols (Christiania, 1879) [text]. — ACO 3, 3, 1-13. — *Theopomp.*, P. Lagarde, Analecta Syriaca (Osnabrück, 1967 = Berlin, 1858), 46-64 [Syriac text]. — J. B. Pitra, Analecta Sacra 4 (Paris, 1883), 103-120 [text], 363-376 [Latin trans.]. — V. Ryssel (Leipzig, 1880), 71-93 [German trans.]. — *anim.*, PG 10:1137-1145. — V. Ryssel: RMP 51 (1896) 1-9 [German trans.]. — P. Lagarde, loc. cit., 31-46 [Syriac text]. — G. Furlani: JAOS 35 (1919) 297-317 [Italian trans.]. — *ep. Philagr.*, PG 46:1101-1108. — *fr. syriaca de resurrectione, de fide et incarnatione*, P. Lagarde, loc. cit., 64-67 [Syriac text].
L: L. Abramowski, Das Bekenntnis des G. bei Gregor v. Nyssa u. das Problem seiner Echtheit: ZKG 87 (1976) 145-166. — eadem, Die Schrift G.s des Lehrers "Ad Theopompum" u. Philoxenus v. Mabbug: ZKG 89 (1978) 273-290. — A. Brinkmann, G. des Thaumaturgen Panegyricus auf Origenes: RMP 56 (1901) 55-76. — H. Crouzel, Faut-il voir trois personnes en Grégoire le Thaumaturge?: Gr. 60 (1979) 287-319. — idem, G.: DSp 6:1014-1020. — idem, G. I: RAC 12:779-793. — idem, L'école d'Origène à Cesarée: BLE 71 (1970) 15-27. — idem, Le "Remerciement à Origène" de saint G.: ScEc 16 (1964) 59-91. — A. Drage, Der kanonische Brief des G.: JPTh 7 (1981) 102-126. — P. Koetschau, Zur Lebensgeschichte G.s: ZWTH 41 (1898) 211-250. — L. S. MacCoull, G.'s Vision Re-envisioned: RHE 94 (1999) 5-14. — E. Marotta, I riflessi biblici nell'orazione ad Origene di G.: VetChr 10 (1973) 59-77. — P. Nautin, G.: DHGE 22, 39-42. — idem, Lettres et écrivains chrétiens des IIe et IIIe siècles (Paris, 1961). — V. Ryssel, G. Sein Leben u. seine Schriften (Leipzig, 1890). — M. Simonetti, Una nuova ipotesi su G.: RSLR 24 (1988) 17-41. — idem, Gregorio Nazianzeno o G. Taumaturgo?: RIL. L 86 (1953) 101-117. — idem, Ancora sulla lettera ad Evagrio: RCCM 4 (1962) 371-374. — M. Slusser, G.: TRE 14:188-191. — W. Telfer, The Cultus of St. G.: HThR 29 (1936) 225-344.

H. SCHNEIDER

H

Hadrian, Exegete

H. was author of an *Eisagōgē eis tas theias graphas* (*introd.*). From the indirect tradition in Cassiodorus (*inst. div.* 1.10) and Photius (*cod.* 2) we infer that the transmitted text is only part of the original and that H. was active in the first half of the 5th c. This introduction is the first of its kind and name. It investigates primarily the peculiarities of the Heb. language, such as images and rhetorical figures (*Idiōmata tēs dianoias, tēs lexeōs, tēs syntheseōs*). H. gives general principles of exegesis that show the author to be an Antiochene. Whether he is the same as the addressee of three letters of Nilus (PG 79:225, 437, and 516) is uncertain.

W: PG 98:1273-1312. — F. Gössling, Adrians Ἐισαγωγὴ εἰς τὰς θείας γραφάς (Berlin, 1887) [text/German trans./comm.].
L: G. Mercati, Pro Adriano: RB 11 (1914) 246-255. — K. T. Schäfer, Eisagoge: RAC 4:900f. — K. F. Schlüren, Zu Adrianos: JPTh 13 (1887) 136-159.

G. RÖWEKAMP

Harmonius

Little is known of H. Acc. to Soz. (*h.e.* 3.16.5-7) he was a son of Bardesanes and highly educated; acc. to Theodoret (*haer.* 1.22) he was educated in Athens. These notices show that H. was born at the end of the 2nd c., probably in Edessa.

Soz. (ibid.) says that H. composed the first Syr. hymns and melodies. Since Ephraem tells us that H.'s father Bardesanes did this, H. may have collected, edited, and supplemented his father's poems. Acc. to Soz., the hymns were to some extent marked by H.'s teaching; he, it is said, added to his father's views the positions of Gr. philosophers on "the soul, the becoming and decay of the body, and rebirth." Since these melodies were still used in the 4th c. because of their beauty, → Ephraem supposedly composed new verses for them (same in Theodoret, *h.e.* 4.29.2; *haer.* 1.22).

W: F. Nau, Une biographie inédite de Bardesane (Paris, 1897), 7. — E. Beck, CSCO 169/170:202-204/181-184 [Syriac text/German trans.].
L: A. Baumstark, Geschichte der syr. Lit. (Berlin, 1968 = Bonn, 1922), 14. — E. Beck, Bardaisan u. seine Schule bei Ephraem: Muséon 91 (1978) 271-333. — H. J. W. Drijvers, Bardaisan of Edessa (Assen, 1966), 180-183. — G.

Hölscher, Syr. Verskunst (Leipzig, 1932), 1-8. — J. Teixidor, Bardesane d'Édesse (Paris, 1992).

C. MARKSCHIES

Hebrews, Gospel of the

The chief witnesses for a (Gr.) *Gospel of the Hebrews* (*Ev. Hebr.*) are Clement, Origen, and Jerome. The surviving fragments are from an account of the baptism of Jesus and from the story of the temptations (with a rapture of Jesus on Tabor); they contain various logia and a resurrection appearance to James, brother of the Lord, who is also present at the last meal. Despite similarities, no use of the canonical gospels can be proved but rather a proximity to sapiential and gnostic ideas as well as to the *Gospel of Thomas* and the Ps.-Clementines. The prominence given to James and the (Semitic) idea of Jesus as Son of the Spirit, who is identified with the Mother of Jesus (see the Coptic *Letter of James*), point to the Jewish-Chr. milieu in Egypt as the place of origin, while the attestation in Clement points to the first half of the 2nd c. as the time of composition.

W: Clemens, *str.* 5.14.96; Origen, *comm. in Jo.* 2.12; Jerome, *in Eph.* 5.4; *vir. ill.* 3.2; *in Is.* 11.1ff.; *in Ez.* 18.7. — NTApo⁶ 1:146f. [German trans.].
L: G. Bardy, S. Jérome et l'evangile: MSR 3 (1946) 5-36. — S. P. Brock, A New Testimonium: NTS 18 (1971) 220-222. — R. v. d. Broek, Der Bericht des kopt. Kyrillos v. Jerusalem über das Ev. Hebr.: idem, Studies in Gnosis and Alexandrian Christianity (Leiden, 1996), 142-156. — L. Goppelt, Christentum u. Judentum im 1. u. 2. Jh. (Gütersloh, 1954). — A. F. J. Klijn, Das Hebräer- u. das Nazoräerevangelium: ANRW II 25/5 (1988) 3997-4033. — R. N. Longenecker, Christology of Early Jewish Christianity (London, 1970). — D. Luhrmann, Das Bruchstück aus dem Ev. Hebr. bei Didymus v. Alexandrien: NT 29 (1987) 265-279. — G. Quispel, The Gospel of Thomas and the Gospel of the Hebrews: NTS 12 (1965/66) 371-382. — A. Schmidtke, Zum Ev. Hebr.: ZNW 35 (1936) 24-44. — H. J. Schoeps, Theologie des Judenchristentums (Tübingen, 1949). — P. Vielhauer, Geschichte der urchr. Lit. (Berlin, 1975), 656-661. — H. Waitz, Untersuchungen: ZNW 36 (1937) 60-81.

G. RÖWEKAMP, P. BRUNS

Hegemonius

Acc. to a secure tradition H. was the name of the author of an anti-Manichean polemic written before 350: the so-called *Acta Archaelai* (*Arch.*), which give an account of a fictional disputation between Mani, founder of Manichaeism, and Catholic Bishop Archelaus; the debate had a novellistic setting. Of what is very probably the Gr. original only fragments remain (espec. in Epiphanius, *haer.* 66); the work is complete only in a 4th c. Lat. translation that shows itself to be rather faithful where comparison with the original is possible, but also uncertain to some extent and defective because of the translator's linguistic deficiencies. There are also Copt. citations and terse retellings in Greek and Arab.

The bishop intends, by means of this debate, to protect a rich and charitable Christian named Marcellus against the influence of Mani; he triumphs so completely (15-42) that his adversary flees and his disciple Trubo, who previously acted as a messenger and gave a lecture on the Manichean doctrinal system (7-13), becomes a deacon (43). When informed in a letter from a presbyter named Diodorus of further trouble caused by the departed Mani (44f.), Archelaus first gives advice in writing (45-51) but then engages again in a debate and is again victorious (54-60[65]). The *Arch.* is of value espec. because of its information about Manichaeism. H. was evidently able, at least to some extent, to make use of authentic documents. Literarily, on the other hand, this work is of little importance. Espec. in view of Mani's pitiable role, there was no real debate.

The catalogue of heretics (*haer.*) that follows upon the *Arch.* in an important Lat. ms. from the last decades of the 4th c. is certainly not from H.

W: PG 10:1429-1524. — *Arch.*, M. J. Routh, Reliquiae Sacrae 5 (Oxford, ²1848), 1-206 [text/comm.]. — S. Salmond, The Works of Gregory Thaumaturgus (Edinburgh, 1871), 267-429 [English trans.]. — H. J. Polotsky, Kopt. Zitate: Muséon 45 (1932) 18-20. — *Arch., haer.*, C. H. Beeson (Leipzig, 1906) [Greek/Latin text]. — *haer.*, A. Hoste, CCL 9:325-329.
L: G. Bareille, H.: DThC 6/2:2113-2116. — G. C. Hansen, Zu den Evangelienzitaten: StPatr 7 (1963) 473-485. — W. Klein, Die Argumentation in den griech.-chr. Antimanichaica (Wiesbaden, 1991), 21-24. — S. N. C. Lieu, Fact and Fiction in the Acta Archelai: Manichaean Studies, ed. P. Bryder (Lund, 1988), 69-88. — H. v. Zittwitz, Acta disputationis Archelai et Manetis untersucht: ZHTh 43 (1873) 467-528.

U. HAMM

Hegesippus

H. came from the East (Syria?) and was perhaps a Jewish Christian, whose mother tongue was probably Greek. Ca. 160 (under Anicetus, ca. 154-166) he undertook a journey by way of Corinth to Rome, where he tracked down the unadulterated apostolic tradition. Ca. 180 H. wrote a work in five books of which only fragments remain in the church history of → Eusebius and in excerpts from → Philip of Side (TU 5/2, 169 no. 3) and from Stephen Gobarus, a tritheist (in Photius, *cod.* 222; 288b). On the basis of

the term used by Eusebius and Stephen Gobarus, the work is usually cited as *Hypomnemata*. But this word is neither a title nor a genre, meaning little more than "notes" or "books." Although the work (espec. the fifth book) does contain information on the history of the church, it was not, contrary to Jerome's view (based on inferences), a history of the church from the crucifixion of Jesus to H.'s own time, but instead served to ensure and safeguard the apostolic tradition against gnostic and other heresies.

Disputed is H.'s statement (in Eus., *h.e.* 4.22.3): "When I came to Rome, I drew up a succession (*diadochēn epoiēsamen*) down to Anicetus." Recent scholarship tends to the view that H. neither made a formal list of the bishops nor inserted such a list into his work but rather became convinced of the reliable transmission of apostolic tradition on the basis of the unbroken succession of bishops of Rome. The suggestion that *diatribēn* be read for *diadochēn* is an arbitrary conjecture. The fragments of H. contain information that is valuable, even if to some extent distorted by legend, regarding the martyrdom of James, brother of the Lord, the choice of Simeon as bishop of Jerusalem, the relatives of Jesus, etc., which are drawn from early Palestinian tradition and tradition independent of the NT.

W: *Collection of the frags.*, T. Zahn, Forschungen zur Geschichte des ntl. Kanons 6 (Leipzig, 1900), 228-249. — E. Preuschen, Antilegomena (Giessen, ²1905), 107-113 [text], 210-216 [German trans.]. — H. J. Lawlor, Eusebiana (Amsterdam, 1973 = Oxford, 1912), 98-107.
L: L. Abramowski, Διαδοχή u. ὀρθὸς λόγος bei H.: ZKG 87 (1976) 321-327. — N. Backmund, H.: DHGE 23:772f. — G. Bareille, H.: DThC 6/2:2116-2120. — W. Bautz, H.: BBKL 2:649f. — K. Beyschlag, Das Jakobusmartyrium u. seine Verwandten in der früh-chr. Lit.: ZNW 56 (1965) 149-177. — L. Bieler, Adamnan u. H.: WSt 69 (1956) 344-349. — G. G. Blum, Tradition u. Sukzession (Berlin, 1963), 78-90. — T. Camelot, H.: Cath. 5 (1963) 568f. — H. v. Campenhausen, Kirchliches Amt u. geistliche Vollmacht (Tübingen, ²1963), 179-185 (English, Ecclesiastical Authority and Spiritual Power [Stanford, 1969]). — E. Caspar, Die älteste röm. Bischofsliste (Berlin, 1926), 233-237. — M. Durst, H.: MarL 3:91-93. — idem, H.s "Hypomnemata" — Titel o. Gattungsbezeichnung: RQ 84 (1989) 299-330. — B. Gustafsson, H.'s Sources and his Reliability: TU 78 (1961) 227-232. — T. Halton, H. in Eusebius: StPatr 17/2 (1982) 688-693. — idem, H.: TRE 14:560-562. — L. Hermann, La famille du Christ d'après H.: RUB 42 (1936/37) 387-394. — N. Hyldahl, H.s Hypomnemata: StTh 14 (1960) 70-113. — A. M. Javierre, El "diadochen epoiesamen" de H. y la primera lista papal: Sal. 21 (1959) 237-253. — H. Kemler, H.s röm. Bischofsliste: VigChr 25 (1971) 182-196. — H. Lietzmann, H. nr. 7: PRE 7/2, 2611f. — A. Lumpe, Zum H.-Problem: ByF 3 (1968) 165-167. — K. Mras, Die H.-Frage: AAWW 95 (1958) 143-153. — C. Papadopoulos, The Martyrdom of Saint James: DVEM 11/2 (1982) 41-46. — W. Telfer, Was H. a Jew?: HThR 53 (1960) 143-153. — E. W.

Turner, The Pattern of Christian Truth (London, 1954), 379-386. — E. Zuckschwerdt, Das Naziräat des Herrenbruders Jakobus nach H.: ZNW 68 (1977) 246-287.

M. Durst

Hegesippus, Pseudo- (*De bello judaico*)

Under the name of Hegesippus (H.) (from Lat. Iosippus for Gr. *Iōsipos*) has been transmitted a Lat. translation of the Gr. work on the Jewish war (*bell.*) by Josephus Flavius. This is a free translation (*stilo curato*) of the 4th or 5th c. that is not the same as the translation attributed to Rufinus. The text, unlike the original, is divided into five books, not seven. One chapter (3.2), on the encounter between Peter and Simon Magus, is a Chr. addition. The author probably belonged to the sphere of Ambrose; Jerome speaks of a → Dexter (*vir. ill.* 132). Even the later Heb. version of the *bell.* is dependent on this Lat. reworking.

The preface (by → Cyprian of Toulon) mentions rewritings of the books of Samuel and Kings and a work on the Maccabees (*Res gestae Macchabaeorum*) by the same author. But it is possible that these were works of Josephus and not of H. The *Passio ss. Macchabaeorum*, an early Lat. translation of the apocryphal 4 Mac, which was already attributed to Josephus by Eusebius (*h.e.* 3.10), is not from H.

W: PL 15:2061-2310. — V. Ussani, CSEL 66.
L: H. Dörrie, Passio ss. Machabaeorum (Göttingen, 1938), 42f. — W. F. Dwyer, The vocabulary of H. (Washington, 1931). — J. P. McCormick, A study of the nominal syntax and of indirect discourse in H. (Washington, 1935). — K. Mras, Die H.-Frage: AAWW 95 (1958) 143-153. — O. Scholz, Die H.-Ambrosiusfrage, Diss. (Breslau, 1913).

G. Röwekamp

Helladius of Tarsus

H., a disciple of Theodosius of Antioch, led a monastic life before becoming metropolitan of Tarsus. In 431 he was among the bishops who protested the condemnation of Nestorius at Ephesus. He also took part in the countercouncil of John of Antioch and continued to support Nestorius. After being deposed by the new patriarch of Constantinople, H. initially opposed utterly the Agreement of Union of 433. But as he found himself increasingly isolated, he finally joined Proclus, the orthodox bishop of Constantinople. He convoked a synod of the bishops of Cilicia and then sent Theodosius and Valentinian a letter in which he stated his unreserved acceptance of Ephesus, communion with Cyril, and the condemnation of the followers of Nestorius. In a subsequent letter

to Nestorius he made his excuses for seeing himself as finally forced to acceptance of the Union agreement. In addition to these letters there are six others accepted as from H.: four to Alexander of Hierapolis, one to Alexander, Theodoret, and others, and one to Meletius Mops. All the letters have survived in the Lat. translation of → Rusticus.

W: *ep. ad Alexandrum*, ACO 1, 4, 105, 142, 143f., 183. — *ep. ad Alexandrum, Theodoretum e. a.*, ACO 1, 4, 158f. — *ep. ad Meletium*, ACO 1, 4, 169. — *ep. ad Theodosium*, ACO 1, 4, 204f. — *ep. ad Nestorium*, ACO 1, 4, 205.
L: R. Aubert, H. 5: DHGE 23, 920-922.

B. Windau

Helpidius Rusticus (Poet)

Various identities have been suggested for poet Helpidius Rusticus (H.; the most probable form of the name): (1) a Deacon (H)Elpidius, frequently mentioned in → Ennodius, perhaps the same as the personal physician of Theodoric the Great; (2) a signer of several Ravenna mss. whose name was Flavius Rusticius (H)Elpidius Domnulus (probably belonging ca. 500 to the highly respected family of the Flavii Rusticii), who gives as his title *vir clarissimus et spectabilis comes consistorialis*; (3) a Gallic poet named Domnulus, mentioned by → Apollonius Sidonius. If one is forced to choose one of these possibilities, the better arguments suggest (3), possibly in combination with (2). Because of this uncertainty and lack of evidence from the works themselves, H. can be dated only generally to the second half of the 5th or first half of the 6th c.

Surviving are two shorter poems: the *Historiarum testamenti veteris et novi tristicha* (*hist. testam.*) is a collection of twenty-four hexametric three-line stanzas with bibl. content. Eight pairs of thematically associated scenes from the OT and NT (1-16; e.g., 7-8: tower of Babel/miracle of tongues on Pentecost) are followed by eight descriptions of NT events, all from the earthly (miracle) activity of Jesus (17-24). The *Dittochaeum* of Prudentius obviously served as a model; it must remain uncertain, however, whether the three-line stanzas were intended, like the four-liners of → Prudentius, as explanations of real images.

More ambitious both poetically and in content is the *Carmen De Iesu Christi beneficiis* (*benef.*) in 149 hexameters. After an introductory prayer or rather a petition for help in his manner of life and for acceptance of the poem (1-49), the poem describes the benefits bestowed on the human race by Jesus in his incarnation and earthly work, which culminated in his death on the cross (50-132). The way is thereby opened for human beings to an—expansively imagined (see 138-48)—better world, and hope is given which makes possible an attitude of peaceful trust in God even in the present life (133-49). On the whole, the *carmen* has a strongly hymnic character, although after the opening prayer apostrophes to and proclamations of Christ occur repeatedly in the description of the *beneficia*. H. sees his own modest song as sharply contrasting with the artful poetry of pagan poets, which is indeed sweetly enticing but empty of content (espec. 38-44), an attitude reflecting the earlier views of a → Tertullian or an → Arnobius the Elder rather than those of 4th and 5th c. poets (→ Juvencus, → Sedulius). But the quite successful verse structure, the elevated, though occasionally contrived and even seemingly shadowy language, and the extensive use of rhetorical stylistic devices make it clear that H. was not without claims to artistry. It is hardly possible to show the influence of classical models on his poems; on the other hand, there are contacts with Juvencus, Dracontius, and especially the *Carmen paschale* of → Sedulius.

W: PL 62:543-548. — *benef.,* W. Brandes, Programm (Braunschweig, 1890) [text/comm.]. — *benef., hist. testam.,* D. H. Groen (Groningen, 1942) [text/Dutch trans./comm.]. — F. Corsaro: MSLCA 3 (1951) 22-44 [Italian trans.]. — idem (Catania, 1955) [text/Italian trans./comm./investigations].
L: L. Alfonsi, Su una fonte del Carmen de Christi Iesu beneficiis di H.: RFIC 34 (1956) 173-178. — idem, Note ad H.: VigChr 10 (1956) 33-42. — S. Cavallin, Le poète Domnulus: SE 7 (1955) 49-66. — F. Corsaro, Questioni biografiche su H.: MSLCA 3 (1951) 7-21. — D. Kartschoke, Bibeldichtung (Munich, 1975), esp. 40f., 11-114. — M. Schanz, C. Hosius, G. Krüger, Geschichte der röm Lit., 4/2 (Munich, 1920), 389-391.

U. HAMM

Helvidius

H., a Roman layman, was probably a follower of Arian Bishop Auxentius of Milan (Gennadius, *vir. ill.* 32). Ca. 380 he got into a dispute with a monk, Carterius (or Cantherius), who had written a work on the superiority of monastic life to marriage (Bonosius, → Jovinian) and in the process had defended the perpetual virginity of Mary (*virginitas post partum*). H. appealed to bibl. statements about the "brothers and sisters of Jesus" in order to hold the opposite view, and he maintained the superiority of marriage over monastic forms of life. In 383 → Jerome refuted him in a biting attack, *Adversus Helvidium*, in which he showed not only the meager dogmatic content of H.'s now lost work but also its stylistic poverty.

W: *fr.,* Jerome, *adv. Helv.,* PL 23:193-216.
L: F. Cavallera, Saint Jérôme 1 (Leuven/Louvain, 1922), 94-100. — G. Jouassard, La personnalité d'H.: FS Saunier (Lyons, 1944), 139-156. — I. Opelt, Hieronymus' Streitschriften (Heidelberg, 1973), 28-36. — J. N. D. Kelly, Jerome (London, 1975), 104, 107, 110. — D. G. Hunter, H.: JECS 1 (1993) 47-71.

J. LÖSSL

Henana of Adiabene

H. was originally from the province of Adiabene in the western part of the Persian empire. In the time of Abraham of Beth Rabban (509-569) H. attended the school of Nisibis, but, under pressure from the local bishop, Paul, was compelled to leave it because of the pro-Chalcedonian tendency of his christology. But H. returned in 572 and became head of the school; he was active there until his death in 610.

Acc. to Ebedjesu's list of writers (BOCV 1:81-84) H. wrote a number of commentaries (on Gen, Ps, Job, Prov, Qoh, Cant, the minor prophets, Mk, and the Pauline letters). Also mentioned are commentaries on the creed and the mysteries of the church, and homilies on Palm Sunday, Friday of Pentecost week, the finding of the cross, and Lent. Of these works only the last two homilies (*hom.*) have come down complete; of the many commentaries only fragments have survived in citations by the great commentator Isodad of Merw.

In his christology H. came close to the Chalcedonian position on the hypostatic union, inasmuch as he taught one prosōpon, one hypostasis (→), and two natures. Consequently he also accepted without reservation the title of Theotokos for Mary. As a result, he opposed → Babai the Great, who represented the classic Nestorian position of two hypostases. In exegesis, too, H. departed from the prevailing Nestorian tradition by allowing not only the literal sense but also the allegorical method of the Alexandrians. H.'s reputation suffered among the Nestorians, not only because of his christology but also because of his open sympathy for Origen, who became accessible to him through Evagrius Pont.

W: *hom.,* A. Scher, PO 7:53-87 [text/French trans.].
L: W. de Vries, Syr.-nestorianische Haltung zu Chalcedon: A. Grillmeier, H. Bacht, Konzil v. Chalkedon (Würzburg, 1951), 603-635.

P. BRUNS

Henaniso I

H. was elected catholicus in 685/686 and held this office until 692/693, when some of his suffragans forced him to resign. He then withdrew to a monastery near Nineveh, where he died of the plague in 699/700. He composed various works on law and commentaries on the gospels of the church year; these have not yet been published.

W: E. Sachau, Syr. Rechtsbücher (Berlin, 1914), 2:1-49, 101-106 [English trans./comm.].
L: A. Baumstark, Geschichte (Bonn, 1922), 209.

P. BRUNS

Henaniso, Monk

H. was born in Hirta in the Roman-Mesopotamian borderland and was active in the first half of the 7th c. He belonged to a prominent Arab. family and together with George, monk and later martyr, reached the Persian court in 612. There he preached the gospel and founded a monastery in Darad near Beth Garmai. He became known through a fragmentarally preserved anti-Chalcedonian polemic against deviants in his own ranks, espec. → Henana of Adiabene.

W: L. Abramowski, A. E. Goodman, Nestorian Collection (Cambridge, 1972), 1:170-179 [Syriac text]; 2, XLIV-XLVI [German trans.].
L: A. Baumstark, Geschichte (Bonn, 1922), 134.

P. BRUNS

Heracleon

H. was, along with Theodotus (and perhaps Ptolemy), one of the chief representatives of "Valentinian" gnosis (thus Clement Alex., *str.* 4.71.1). On his dates (second half of 2nd c.?) and circumstances almost nothing is known. Whether he was a direct disciple of Valentinus (thus Origen, with reservations: *Jo.* 2.14.100) remains uncertain. We know that his own disciples were in Alexandria in the time of Origen (Hippolytus, *haer.* 6.35.6; Origen, *Jo.* 20.20.170).

In his commentary on John (itself fragmentary) Origen preserves forty-eight fragments of a commentary on John by H. Whether these were titled *Hypomnēmata* (memorabilia) remains uncertain, since the content is rather that of a traditional commentary: H. evidently explained the text verse by verse acc. to the usual philol. method of antiquity. In particular, there are explanations of subjects (*historikon*), some of which go deeply into philology and thus presuppose the explanation of words (*glōssēmatikon*) and grammatical-rhetorical exegesis (*technikon*), although such passages are rarely transmitted

by Origen. H. is the first writer known to have written a continuous exegesis of a NT book; like Origen, he explains the text at both the historical and the symbolic levels.

It is not possible to reconstruct from H.'s fragments a complete system of Valentinian teaching, but the classic Valentinian themes do emerge: the supreme God and the demiurge or creator, side by side (frag. 1/40); the pessimistic view of creation (frag. 1); a savior helps individual depraved persons who acknowledge him (frag. 22), while the others perish (frag. 33/46). It is debated whether H. taught a division of human beings into classes, determined at creation and insuperable. It is clear, however, that H.'s exegesis of scripture does not present a fundamental attitude reflecting a truly syncretistic and non-Chr. gnosis but shows rather an honest effort to grasp the bibl. text, even if against the background of a platonizing cosmology and anthropology and on a Jewish-Hellen. basis.

W: W. Völker, Quellen zur Geschichte der chr. Gnosis: SQS. NF 5 (1932) 63-86 [text]. — W. Foerster, Die Gnosis 1 (^{2}1995), 214-240 [German trans.].
L: B. Aland, Erwählungstheologie u. Menschenklassenlehre: Gnosis and Gnosticism (Leiden, 1977), 148-181. — C. Bammel, H.: TRE 15:54-57. — C. Blanc, Le Commentaire de Héracléon sur Jean 4 et 6: Aug. 15 (1975) 81-124. — Y. Janssens, H. Commentaire sur l'Évangile selon Jean: Muséon 72 (1959) 101-152, 277-299. — E. Mühlenberg, Wieviel Erlösungen kennt der Gnostiker H.?: ZNW 66 (1975) 170-193. — E. H. Pagels, The Johannine Gospel in Gnostic Exegesis: SBL. MS 17 (1973). — J.-M. Poffet, La Méthode exégétique d'H. et d'Origène (Fribourg, Switzerland, 1985). — M. Simonetti, Eracleone e Origene: VetChr 3 (1966) 111-141; 4 (1967) 23-64. — H. Strutwolf, Gnosis als System (Göttingen, 1993).

C. MARKSCHIES

Heraclian

H. was bishop of Chalcedon after June 4, 536 and died before May 5, 553. He is probably identical with the H. who between 520 and 535 was a priest at Hagia Sophia in Constantinople and syncellus of Patriarch Epiphanius. He took part in two diplomatic missions to Rome (520 and 535) and appears as a participant in the dialogue on the faith in 532 between the representatives of Chalcedonian christology, to whom H. belonged, and supporters of Severus of Antioch. Two works of H. are known but are lost except for fragments. Photius (*cod.* 85; 231; *Contra Manichaeos* 1.11) mentions a work *Contra Manichaeos* in twenty books, composed perhaps after 527; he praises its style and philosophical content. A few words of this work have survived in → Maximus Conf. (*opusc.*, PG 91:125CD). In addition, there is a treatise *Ad Soterichum (fr.)*, the metropolitan of Caesarea, written perhaps ca. 537, in which H. defends the orthodox Chalcedonian christology.

W: *fr.*, F. Diekamp, Doctrina patrum (Münster, ²1981), 42f., 134, 207f., 216f. [text]. — *contra Manichaeos*, PG 91:125 CD.
L: H. G. Beck, Kirche u. theol. Lit. (Munich, 1959), 372. — E. Honigmann, Patristic Studies (Vatican City, 1953), 205-216. — A. Grillmeier, Jesus der Christus 2/2 (Freiburg i.Br., 1984), 262-265 (English, Christ in Christian Tradition, vol. 2/2 [London, 1995]). — L. Magi, La sede romana (Rome, 1972), 68, 90, 92, 118.

B. WINDAU

Heraclidas of Nyssa

Very little is known of 5th c. Cappadocian bishop H. of Nyssa; he is mentioned only in Photius, *cod.* 52 (PG 103:89C). He is regarded as author of the following two works. First, he is supposed to be the author of *recensio B* of the *h. Laus.* of → Palladius. This revision, which alters and expands the *h. Laus.* is from the 5th c. and is preserved in a large number of mss.

H. is also supposed to be the author of the anonymously transmitted *Vita Olympiadis* (*V. Olymp.*), which is also from the 5th c. and describes the life of Deaconess Olympias (d. 408 in Nicomedia), a member of a wealthy family and a supporter of → John Chrys., on whose account she had to go into exile where she died. This biography shows similarities with the corresponding *Vita* in *recensio B* of the *h. Laus.*, which are missing in → Palladius of Helenopolis; yet H., primarily a compiler of little originality, was fundamentally influenced by Palladius.

W: *h. Laus.* (*recensio B*), Fronto Ducaeus, Bibliothecae veterum patrum 2 (Paris, 1624), 894-1053. — *V. Olymp.*, H. Delehaye: AnBoll 15 (1896) 400-423. — A.-M. Malingrey, SC 13bis:406-448.
L: E. Honigmann, Heraclidas of Nyssa: Patristic Studies, ed. idem (Rome, 1953), 104-122 (J. Daniélou agrees in his review [RSR 44, 1956, 596f.] that the question has not been completely resolved).

K. POLLMANN

Heraclitus, an Antignostic

In *h.e.* 5.27 (on which Jerome, *vir. ill.* 46 depends) Eusebius mentions H., along with five other "ecclesiastical" writers, and has him the author of a lost work *On the Apostles*. It is pure speculation that H. was here opposing a gnostic reception of Paul. Even Eusebius's dating to the period ca. 180-210 is uncertain.

L: W. Bauer, Rechtgläubigkeit u. Ketzerei (Tübingen, ²1964), 150-153, 160f. — A. v. Harnack, Geschichte der altchr. Lit. (Leipzig, ²1958), 1:758f.; 2/1:701.

R. HANIG

Heretics, Catalogues of

Catalogues or collections of heretics are the literary, systematizing expression of a new heresiological expertise that was first formed and passed on in certain Chr. schools of the 2nd c. In form they are close to ancient philosophical historiography (which was often incorporated into heresiological collections, e.g., in → Hippolytus of Rome), which fell into two literary genres: works *peri haireseōn*, that is, presentations of the opinions of various philosophical schools, and *Diadoxai tōn philosophōn*, i.e., in which the philosophers were arranged in the succession in which they taught, and biog. and anecdotal material was given. An important difference from philosophical doxography was the sharply polemical orientation of the catalogues of heretics. These could be transmitted independently or as part of a larger antiheretical treatise. Furthermore, they could be limited to a brief but polemical portrait of the heretic or complement this with a more or less detailed refutation. The catalogues of heretics construct a sequence of heretics, whose origin is placed increasingly far back in pre-Christian or early Chr. times and who are organized acc. to variable categories. In this way, knowledge of heresies staked a universal claim. The doxological description of individual heresies reduces their teaching to a heresiolog. portrait. The biog. notices on the heretics denounce their ethics. Later catalogues of heretics continue earlier ones, with variations in doxographical presentation and polemical method. An analysis of heresiolog. doxography, espec. of its underlying dialectical and rhetorical stucture, is a scholarly desideratum. In their short, schematic form the later catalogues of heretics in particular were in the service of ecclesial practice: knowledge of heresies was to facilitate the identification and classification of heretics and lead the latter to proper behavior on their readmission to the civilly privileged, orthodox Great Church.

The oldest, nonsurviving Syntagma (ca. 150 C.E.) against heresies came from → Justin Martyr and was directed mainly against Marcion. → Irenaeus of Lyons followed in ca. 180 with his extensive and quickly disseminated work Adversus omnes haereses (*haer.*); book 1 of this work refutes in detail the outline of the history of salvation given by the Valentinian school. In showing its genealogy in 1.23-28,

Irenaeus gives a catalogue of heretics from Simon Magus to Marcion and Tatian. → Hippolytus of Rome (d. 225), himself the head of a school in Rome, composed a syntagma against all heresies, one that presumably tightened up and continued Irenaeus's catalogue (lost; can be reconstructed from the catalogues of heretics of Ps.→ Tertullian [3rd c.; author unknown] and → Epiphanius of Salamis) as well as a *Refutatio omnium haeresium* (ten books; book 1.4-10 survives), in which he goes beyond the syntagma with independent new material and emphasizes the dependence of the heresies on pagan philosophy and astrology. Hippolytus's heresiology is marked by an effort to formulate knowledge of heresies in encyclopedic fashion. In this respect he is followed, in 374-77, by → Epiphanius of Salamis with his monumental *Panarion* (medicine cabinet) against all heresies (eighty heresies including Jewish sects and pagan schools of philosophy; basic treatment of each heresy: presentation of teaching; refutation): here the knowledge of heresies is treated after the model of a handbook of natural science on snake poisons. Each heresy corresponds to a different snake, and its refutation is the antidote supplied by the heresiological therapist. Epiphanius supplies valuable original sources but also draws heavily on Irenaeus and Hippolytus's syntagma. Epiphanius's work was also disseminated in an abridgment by an unknown hand (*Anakephalaiosis*; end of 4th/beginning of 5th c.). Directly or indirectly dependent on Epiphanius are, presumably, → Filastrius of Brescia (c. 397) and certainly Augustine, *De haeresibus* (428). Dependent on Augustine in turn is the anonymous → *Praedestinatus* (composed 432-440), which in its book 1 reviews ninety heresies. The short catalogue of Ps.→ Hegemonius was evidently compiled at the end of the 4th c. (CCL 9:327-29). At the end of the 5th c. → Gennadius of Marseilles wrote eight books, now lost, *Adversus omnes haereses*.

In the East, in the 5th c., → Theodoret wrote *Haereticarum fabularum Compendium* (heresies down to Eutyches). From the 5th c. on, heresiology reflects the fragmentation of the old Chr. world after the Council of Chalcedon (451): e.g., → Barhadbsabba writes from the Nestorian viewpoint (history of the church: PO 23/2:186-99). The Monophysite viewpoint is represented by, e.g., → Philoxenus of Mabbug (PO 13:248-51). A pro-Chalcedonian outlook is represented by, e.g., the 6th c. → Liberatus (560/566: *Breviarium causae Nestorianorum et Eutychianorum*), → Theodore of Raithu (F. Diekamp, *Analecta patristica* [OCA 117] 185-222) and the unknown author of the *De sectis* (PG 86:1193-1268);

in the 7th c., → Timothy of Constantinople (*De receptione haereticorum*: PG 86:12-68), → Sophronius Jerus. (634-638) (PG 87:3148-3200), monk and presbyter → George, and by a work *De haeresibus*, which can be dated ca. 692-695 and whose origin is unknown (J. B. Pitra, *Iuris ecclesiastici Graecorum historia et monumenta* [Rome, 1868], 2:257-71). 8th c. heresiologists: → Germanus of Constantinople (d. 727) (*De haeresibus et synodis*: PG 98:40-88) and → John Damascene (d. before 754) (*De haeresibus*: B. Kotter, *Die Schriften des Johannes v. Damascus* 4, PTS 22 [Berlin, 1981], 1-67; J. expands the *Anakephalaiosis* of Ps.-Epiphanius by twenty to a total of one hundred heresies).

L: B. Altaner, Augustinus u. Epiphanius v. Salamis: idem, Kleine Patristische Schriften, TU 83 (Berlin, 1967), 286-296. — M. Aubineau, Un recueil "de haeresibus": Sion College, Cod. Graecus 6: REG 80 (1967) 425-429. — G. Bardy, L'Indiculus de Haeresibus du Pseudo-Jérôme: RSR 19 (1929) 385-405. — idem, Le "De haeresibus" et ses sources: Miscellanea Agostiniana 2 (Rome, 1931), 397-416. — W. Bauer, Rechtgläubigkeit u. Ketzerei im ältesten Christentum (Tübingen, ²1964). — N. Brox, Häresie: RAC 13:248-297. — Eresia ed Eresiologia nella Chiesa Antica: Aug. 15 (1985). — J. Fellermayer, Tradition u. Sukzession im Lichte des rom.-antiken Erbdenkens (Munich, 1979), 131-213. — J. Gouillard, L'hérésie dans l'empire byzantin des origines au XIIᵉ siècle: idem, La vie religieuse à Byzance (London, 1981), Nr. 1. — A. Grillmeier, Jesus der Christus 2/1 (Freiburg i.Br., 1986), 89-94 (English, Christ in Christian Tradition, vol. 2/1 [London, 1987]). — A. Hilgenfeld, Die Ketzergeschichte des Urchristentums (Hildesheim, 1966 = Leipzig, 1884). — A. Le Boulluec, La notion d'hérésie dans la littérature grecque aux IIᵉ-IIIᵉ siècles (Paris, 1985). — S. N. C. Lieu, An Early Byzantine Formula for the Renunciation of Manichaeism: JAC 26 (1983) 152-218. — R. A. Lipsius, Zur Quellenkritik des Epiphanius (Vienna, 1865). — idem, Die Quellen der ältesten Ketzergeschichte neu untersucht (Leipzig, 1875). — J. McClure, Handbooks against Heresy in the West: JThS 30 (1979) 186-197. — J. Mansfeld, Heresiography in Context. Hippolytus' Elenchos as a Source for Greek Philosophy (Leipzig, 1992). — J. Mejer, Diogenes Laertios (Wiesbaden, 1978). — L. G. Müller, The "De haeresibus" of St. Augustine (Washington, 1956). — A. Pourkier, L'hérésiologie chez Épiphane de Salamine (Paris, 1992). — A. Schindler, Häresie 2. Kirchengeschichtlich: TRE 14:318-341. — R. W. Thomson, An Armenian List of Heresies: JThS 16 (1965) 358-367. — K.-H. Uthemann, Die dem Anastasios Sinaites zugeschriebene Synopsis de haeresibus et synodis: AHC 14 (1982) 58-94.

W. A. Löhr

Hermas (*Shepherd of Hermas*)

I. Life: It is not possible to reconstruct a biography of H., a Roman Christian (b. ca. 100). But elements of one can be cautiously extracted from the autobiographically formulated data in the *Pastor Hermae*

(*PH*). The *PH* gives the following personal details, all of which are not likely to be fictitious: H. was a slave, bought in Rome, then freed, and became a Christian. He was very unhappy with himself and his family, possessed some land, and came in conflict with the social obligations involved in business and possessions. He was evidently a small businessman with the mentality of one. Origen (*comm. in Rom.* 10:31) and Eusebius (*h.e.* 3.3.6) are aware of the untenable opinion that the H. of *PH* was identical with the Hermas in Rom 16:14. Likewise, the information in the *Canon Muratori*, lines 73-77 (still in the 2nd c.), that H. wrote the *PH* in the time of Roman Bishop Pius (dated to 140-155) and was the latter's brother, is a fiction, since in the time of H. the monarchical episcopate had not yet been established in the Roman church.

II. Work: H. left behind, from the period ca. 140, a unique, quite extensive work in Greek. The title *The Shepherd* alludes to the fact that in the lengthy second part of the work the *angelus interpres* appears as revealer in the garb of a shepherd. The book is made up in complicated fashion of several parts, but it has a single author. The concluding chapters have come down only in Latin. A book of visions (*vis.* 1-5) comes first, followed by twelve commandments (*Mandata/mand.*) and ten parables (*Similitudines/sim.*). But H. continually moves out of these genres. The *PH* claims to be in many of its elements an apocalypse, but it is in fact a book of allegories. The main themes are expressed in allegories (the church as a woman and/or a tower; the members of the church as stones or vines; the law of God as a tree and, at the same time, the Son of God as this tree or as a rock and as the door of the tower). The central theme of the *PH* is the possibility of penance for postbaptismal sins. H. adopts a reforming middle position: against the rigorists he maintains that there is still penance for sins after baptism; against current practice, that it can only be had once. We are left in the dark regarding by what authority and jurisdiction H. makes this serious intervention in the penitential practice of the (a) community in Rome. In any case, he does not derive authority from the revelatory experiences he claims to have had. Nevertheless, the most plausible explanation is that H. falls into the category of visionaries and thereby has authority.

There is much that is unconventional in the theology of the *PH*: H. does not have the names Jesus, Christ, and Logos in his vocabulary; christology and pneumatology undergo very strange variations; there is no mention of cross and resurrection. Yet the *Canon Muratori* recommended reading *PH* for edification; the book remained popular from Irenaeus down into the Middle Ages because of its (social) ethics. In the early church, however, there are few citations from the popular and attractive allegories or the parables, images, and apocalyptic prospects, or even from the curious popular motifs in *vis.* 1.1.1-2, but there are surprisingly frequent citations of *mand.* 1.1, with its monotheistic confession. H. cites no one (sole exception: *vis.* 2.3.4) but is under many pagan and Jewish influences. H.'s world is a world of virtues and vices, good and evil spirits, God and angels, visions, forces and drives, dread and consolation, morality, sin and eroticism (for this last: *vis.* 1.1.1-2; *sim.* 9.10.6–11.8).

In some regions the popularity of the *PH* may have led to its being regarded as canonical. From the literary viewpoint and in its content the *PH* is unique in early Chr. literature, but it mirrors the world of its author and addressees.

W: PH., M. Whittaker, GCS 48[2]. — R. Joly, SC 53[3]. — A. Vezzoni, Il Pastore di Erma, Versione Palatina (Florence, 1994) [Latin text/Italian trans.]. — A. Carlini, Pap. Bodmer XXXVIII. Erma: Il Pastore (Ia-IIIa visione) (Cologne, 1991) [text]. — F. Zeller, BKV[2] 35 [German trans.]. — M. Dibelius, HNT suppl. vol. 4 (Tübingen, 1923) [German trans./comm.]. — N. Brox, KAV 7 (Göttingen, 1991) [German trans./comm.]. — M. Leutzsch, SUC 3 (Darmstadt, 1998), 107-497 [text/German trans./comm.].
L: N. Brox, Der Hirt des H. (Göttingen, 1991). — F. X. Funk, Die Einheit des Hirten des H.: ThQ 81 (1899) 321-360. — S. Giet, H. et les Pasteurs (Paris, 1963). — J. Goldhahn-Müller, Die Grenze der Gemeinde (Göttingen, 1989). — A. Hilhorst, Sémitismes et latinismes dans le Pasteur d'H. (Nijmegen, 1976). — idem, H.: RAC 14:632-701. — R. Joly, Le milieu complexe du "Pasteur d'H.": ANRW II 27/1 (1993) 524-551. — P. Lampe, Die stadtröm. Christen (Tübingen, [2]1989). — M. Leutzsch, Die Wahrnehmung sozialer Wirklichkeit im "Hirten des H." (Göttingen, 1989). — C. Osiek, The Shepherd of H. in Context: Acta Patristica et Byzantina 8 (1997) 115-134. — L. Pernveden, The Concept of the Church in the Shepherd of H. (Lund, 1966). — E. Peterson, Frühkirche, Judentum u. Gnosis (Rome, 1959). — B. Poschmann, Paenitentia secunda (Bonn, 1940). — R. Staats, Hauptsünden: RAC 13:734-770. — idem, H.: TRE 15:100-108. — D. Völter, Die Visionen des H., die Sibylle u. Clemens v. Rom (Berlin, 1900). — M. Whittaker, H., Shepherd of: NCE 6 (1967) 1074f.

N. BROX

Hermias

Ca. 200, H., an otherwise unknown philosopher and satirist, wrote a short lampoon, *Irrisio* (*irr.*), for Christians, in which with the aid of various forms of direct and ironic criticism he made fun of the mutually contradictory opinions of the pagan philosophers. He mentions, among other, Anaxagoras, Parmenides, Anaximenes, Empedocles, Protagoras, Thales, Anaximander, Archelaus, Plato, Aristotle, Pherecydes, Leucippus, Democritus, Epicurus, Carneades, Clitomachus, and Pythagoras. Not mentioned are the philosophers of Middle and Neo-Platonism, which may be taken as an important clue to the early date of the work. Bibl. reminiscences (1 Cor 3:19 and Isa 40:12 LXX) show that H. may have been a Christian. He must have had direct access to Plato and Aristotle. For the other philosophers he probably made use of early doxographical manuals. Among H.'s models are Aetius (*Placita*), Lucian of Samosata (*Hermotimus, Ikaromenippus, Vitarum auctio*), and possibly → Tatian (*Oratio*).

W: R. P. C. Hanson, SC 388. — J. Leitl, A. di Pauli, BKV² 14 (Munich, 1913), 111-122 [German trans.]. — G. A. Rizzo (Siena, 1929) [Italian trans.]. — L. Torraca (Padua, 1961), 429-435, 480-482 [partial Italian trans.].
L: L. Alfonsi, Ermia (Brescia, 1947). — R. Bauckham, Fall of the Angels: VigChr 39 (1985) 313-330. — F. W. M. Hitchcock, Skit on Greek philosophy: Theology 32 (1936) 98-106. — J. F. Kindstrand, Date and Character: VigChr 34 (1980) 341-357. — A. Puech, Apologistes (Paris, 1912), 279-283. — A. di Pauli von Treuheim, irr. (Paderborn, 1907). — idem, irr.: ThQ 90 (1908) 523-531. — J. H. Waszink, H.: RAC 14:808-815.

M. SKEB, OSB

Hermogenes

Little is known of the precise circumstances of H.'s life, but in any case he must have lived around the turn of the 2nd to the 3rd c. Since Theophilus of Antioch wrote against him (*The Heresy of Hermogenes Answered;* Eusebius, *h.e.* 4.24) and Clement knew him, he may have resided in the East for a time. On the other hand, he was in Carthage between 203 and 213, but such moves between the two halves of the empire were not unusual. In Carthage, Tertullian wrote a now lost work against him, *De censu animae adv. Hermog.*, and (ca. 204/205) the surviving *Adv. Hermog.* Also important are the report in Hippolytus (*haer.* 8.17.1-4) and the notice in Clement Alex. (*ecl.* 56).

H. seems to have composed a work on the eternity of the world.

Acc. to the reports in the heresiologies H. was a painter by profession (Tertullian, *adv. Hermog.* 1.2— whether he was a "proper Gr. artist" must obviously remain an open question). He taught, in the Platonic tradition, the eternity of matter (1.3–9.2) and reduced evil to matter (9.3). In christology he fol-

lowed the majority church but taught that Christ left his body behind in the sun (Hippolytus, *haer.* 8.17.3f. = Clement, *ecl.* 56.2)—probably a straight exegesis of Ps 18:5c. It is improbable that H. denied the resurrection; Ps.-Ambrose's *De anima* is a *reductio ad absurdum* of H.'s position, claiming that he said the soul consists of matter.

W: Tertullian, *adv. Hermog.,* J. H. Waszink (Utrecht, 1956) [text]. — E. Kroymann, CCL 1:397-435 = CSEL 47:126-176. — Clemens, *ecl.,* C. Nardi (Florence, 1985) [text/Italian trans./comm.].
L: F. Bolgiani, Sullo scritto perduto di Teofilo d'Antiochia "Contro Hermogene": FS G. Lazzati (Milan, 1979), 77-118. — K. Greschat, Apelles u. H. (Leiden et al., 1999). — G. May, H. Ein frühchr. Theologe zwischen Platonismus u. Gnosis: StPatr 15 (1984) 461-473. — idem, Schöpfung aus dem Nichts: AKG 48 (1978) 142-149. — A. Orbe, Hacia la primera teología de la procesión del Verbo = Estudios Valentinianos 1/1 (AnGr 99) (Rome, 1958), 270-280. — E. Pfuhl, H. 26: PRE 8/1:878.

C. MARKSCHIES

Hesychius, Abbot of the Monastery of the Burning Bush

H., also called H. the Sinaite, was abbot of the Burning Bush monastery on the Sinai peninsula, probably in the 7th/8th c.

He composed the ascetical work *Ad Theodolum de temperantia et virtute*, which was earlier attributed to H. of Jerusalem and survives only in two 13th c. recensions. The *recensio longior* is divided into two hundred didactic sayings, of which the *recensio brevior*, which is divided into twenty-four chapters, contains only about a half. The dependence of the two recensions on each other and the structure of the original cannot be clearly determined. The sentences underscore the lofty significance of *nēpsis* (sobriety, temperance) as condition for an ideal spiritual life and develop the various stages of this virtue, in reliance on earlier ascetical teachings of, among others, Evagrius Pont. and John Climacus.

W: PG 93:1479-1544 (1). — M. Waegemann, Les 24 chapitres "De temperantia et virtute" d'H. Edition critique: SE 22 (1974/75), 195-285 (2) [text].
L: J. Kirchmeyer, H.: DSp 7/1:408-410. — W. Völker, Die beiden Centurien "De temperantia et virtute" des H.: Scala Paradisi (Wiesbaden, 1968).

C. SCHMIDT

Hesychius of Alexandria, Exegete

Acc. to Jerome (*praef. in Paral., praef. in Evv., adv. Ruf.* 2.27), an Alexandrian exegete named H. revised the text of the LXX and the NT ca. 300. This recension, which Jerome criticizes (*ep. ad Damasum*), cannot be connected with a surviving version of the LXX or with the Egyptian text of the gospels. The *Decretum Gelasianum* mentions it and, probably following Jerome, describes it as apocryphal. It is unclear whether H. is to be identified with the bishop of the same name who died under Diocletian (Eus., *h.e.* 8.13.7) or with one of the bishops who protested against Meletius (PG 10:1565-68).

L: Septuaginta XIV, ed. J. Ziegler (Göttingen, 1939), 22f. — Septuaginta, ed. A. Rahlfs (Stuttgart, 1935, 1979), XXXI. — G. Dorival et al., La Bible grecque des Septante (Paris, 1988), 172. — S. Jellicoe, The Hesychian Recension Reconsidered: JBL 82 (1963) 409-418. — F. G. Kenyon, H. and the Text of the NT: FS M.-J. Lagrange (Paris, 1940), 245-250. — A. Vaccari, The Hesychian Recension of the Septuagint: Bib. 46 (1965) 60-66.

G. RÖWEKAMP

Hesychius of Alexandria, Lexicographer

In the lexicon of the probably pagan, 5th/6th c. writer H., which is transmitted only in a 15th c. ms., there are numerous glosses on Chr. writers as well. The interpolations that are of interest for early Chr. literature (glosses on Homer, Euripides, the LXX, and Gregory Naz.) come first of all from the so-called Cyril Glossary and the early Byz. *Lexeis tēs Oktateuchou.* More recent additions (further glosses on the LXX, Epiphanius, and Roman law) come from, among other sources, an onomasticon of the Bible and a collection of proverbs.

W: K. Latte, H. Alexandrini Lexicon 1-2 (Copenhagen, 1953, 1966) [text]. — M. Schmidt (Amsterdam, 1966 = 1858-1868) [text].
L: H. Erbse, Rez. zu Latte: ByZ 48 (1955) 130-138; 61 (1968) 71-77. — H. Hunger, Die hochsprachliche-profane Lit. der Byzantiner 1 (Munich, 1978), 35f., 56 (literature).

G. RÖWEKAMP

Hesychius of Castabala

In a short letter contained in the Lat. version of the acts of the Council of Ephesus (431), H., bishop of Castabala in Cilicia, tells Meletius Mops. of H.'s and his fellow bishops' (once again benevolent) attitude to John of Antioch.

W: PG 84:720f. — ACO 1, 4, 177f. [text].
L: R. Aubert, H.: DHGE 24:297f. — W. M. Sinclair, H.: DCB 3:9f.

U. HAMM

Hesychius of Jerusalem

I. Life: Acc. to Theophanes (*chron.*, PG 108:228 and 241-44), H., a priest and exegete, was active in Jerusalem in 412. Cyril of Scythopolis (*v. Euthym.* 16) mentions him as a *didaskalos* in Jerusalem in 429 and praises him as a "theologian." Acc. to Pelagius (*In defensione trium capitulorum* 2) he welcomed the fugitive Eutyches and wrote against the Council of Chalcedon. Despite H.'s sympathies for Alexandrian theology, the lack of remains of his works and the testimony of the orthodox Cyril of Scythopolis speak against the truth of Pelagius's claims. Acc. to the *Menologion* of Basil, H. explained the entire Bible. He died after 451. A pilgrim's report from the 6th c. (*Anon. Plac.* 27) speaks of his grave being located before the gates of Jerusalem.

II. Works: Of the commentaries on the Bible these have survived: the commentary on Lev (*comm. Lev.*), a commentary on Job in the form of twenty-four homilies surviving only in Arm. (*comm. Iob*), an *Epitome de prophetis* (*epit. proph.*), the *Capita XII prophetarum* (*cap. XII proph.*), an *Interpretatio Isaiae* (*Is.*) assembled from catenas, an *Interpretatio in prophetas minores,* of which only a few fragments have been published, and a *Collectio difficultatum et solutionum* (*coll.*). The Psalms are the subject of *De titulis psalmorum* (*Ps. tit.*; transmitted as a work of Athanasius) and of the short (*comm. b. Ps.*) and long (*comm. m. Ps.*; transmitted as a work of Chrysostom) commentaries on the Psalms. In addition, there is a commentary on the thirteen canticles of the OT and NT (*od.*) as well as various fragments.

H.'s homiletic work consists above all of twenty-one feastday homilies (*hom. fest.*). Authentic are those on the Presentation of the Lord, Lent, Easter, Mary, Lazarus, Peter and Paul, Andrew, Anthony, Stephen, James and David, and Procopius of Persis. The eulogies of all the martyrs and of John the Baptist are dubious. The homilies on Palm Sunday, Luke, and Longinus are not authentic. In addition, there are homilies, in Georgian, on the raising of the dead (*hom. res.*) and the Presentation of the Lord (*hom. Hyp.*), and a homily, in Armenian, on John the Baptist (*hom. Joh.*). A fragment from H.'s history of the church, expressing opposition to Theodore Mops., was read at the Council of Constantinople (ACO 4, 1 90-92).

Not authentic: *Narratio de Abraam* and *De prophetarum vita et obitu recensio "Hesychiana."* The work *De temperantia et virtute* is by → Hesychius, abbot of the Burning Bush Monastery.

III. Importance: H. is a brilliant stylist; his work is full of antitheses and metaphors. As an exegete, he explains the Bible by the Bible. In christology, which is a focus of his works, he argues against Nestorius, without, however, accepting the formulas of Cyril Alex. (see espec. the Easter homilies). The homilies are exemplary in disclosing the liturgical and kerygmatic life in the first half of the 5th c. They came into existence at the same time as the Arm. lectionary of Jerusalem and help with the reconstruction of the Jerusalem calendar of feasts, espec. the first Marian feasts. The clear statements on original sin are to be understood against the background of the controversy about Pelagius, in which H. evidently did not share the viewpoint of John Jerus.

W: *comm. Lev.*, PG 93:787-1180 [Latin text]. — *comm. Iob*, C. Mercier, C. Renoux, PO 42 [Armenian text/French trans.]. — *epit. proph.*, PG 93:1340-1344. — *cap. XII proph.*, PG 93:1345-1369. — *Is.*, M. Faulhaber (Freiburg i.Br., 1900) [text]. — *coll.*, PG 93:1392-1448. — *Ps. tit.*, PG 27:649-1344. — *comm. b. Ps.*, V. Jagic, Supplementum Psalterii Bononiensis (Vienna, 1917) [text]. — *comm. m. Ps.*, R. Devreesse: RB 33 (1924) 512-521 (on Ps 37) [text]. — PG 55:711-784 (on Ps 77-79). — R. Mennes, H. (Gent, 1971) (on Ps 100, 102) [text]. — PG 93:1180-1340 (frgs. of Ps 100-107, 118). — *od.*, V. Jagic, loc. cit. — *hom. fest.*, M. Aubineau, SHG 59 (Brussels, 1978/80) [text/French trans.]. — M. Aubineau, Homélies pascales, SC 187. — *hom. res.*, M. van Esbroeck: Muséon 87 (1974) 1-21 [Georgian text]. — *hom. Hyp.*, G. Garitte: Muséon 84 (1971) 353-372 [Georgian text]. — *hom. Joh.*, A. Renoux, M. Aubineau: AnBoll 99 (1981) 45-63 [Armenian text/French trans./comm.].
L: M. Aubineau, Index verborum homiliarum festalium H. (Hildesheim, 1983). — idem, "H. redivivus": FZPhTh 27 (1980) 253-270. — idem, Textes nouveaux d'H.: StPatr 17/1 (1982) 345-350. — idem, Chrysostome, Severien, Proclus, H. et alii. Inventaire des manuscrits, textes inédits, traductions, études (London, 1988). — J. Chocheyras, Fin des terres et fin des temps: The Use and Abuse of Eschatology, ed. W. Verbeke (Leuven/Louvain, 1988), 72-81. — M. P. Ciccarese, Simbolismo antropologico degli animali: ASEs 7 (1990) 529-567. — M. R. James, The Testament of Abraham (Cambridge, 1892), 77-104. — K. Jüssen, Die dogmatischen Anschauungen des H., 2 vols. (Münster, 1931/34). — J. Kirchmeyer, H.: DSp 7:399-408. — S. Leanza, Uno scoliaste del V secolo: H.: ASEs 8 (1991) 519-523. — C. Renoux, Document nouveau sur la liturgie de Jérusalem: MD 139 (1979) 139-164. — idem, Église de Sion dans les homélies sur Job d'H.: REArm 18 (1984) 135-146. — J. Reuss, Studien zur Lk-Erklärung des Presbyters H.: Bib. 59 (1978) 562-571. — H. Savon, Les Homélies festales d'H.: RHR 197 (1980) 429-450. — T. Schermann, Prophetarum vitae fabulosae (Leipzig, 1907), 98-104. — A. Vaccari, Esichio e il suo "Commentarius in Leviticum": idem, Scritti di erudizione e di filologia 1 (Rome, 1952), 165-206. — S. Vailhé, Date de la mort d'H.: EOr 9 (1906) 219-220.

G. RÖWEKAMP

Hesychius of Miletus

H., called *Illustris* and born in Miletus, was a pagan chronicler and historian of literature in Byzantium (d. after 582).

H.'s works are divided into two main parts: a history of the world (*hist.*) that runs from Assyrian King Belos to the beginnings of Justinian's reign (527-565) (only fragments survive); and a lost work on the history of literature, *Onomatologos ē Pinax tōn en paideia onomatōn*, a collection of biographies of the best-known Hellen. writers. The second work was probably edited in the 9th c., supplemented with the lives of Chr. writers, and, in this form, used in the library (*cod.* 69) and lexicon of Photius and in Suidas.

The fragment *in Christi natalem* (*fr.*) that used to be attributed to Hesychius Jerus. is demonstrably from H.'s history of the world.

W: *hist.*, F. Jacoby, Die Fragmente der griech. Historiker, Nr. 390. — *onomatologus*, J. Flach (Leipzig, 1882) [text]. — *fr.*, PG 93:1449. — PG 92:1057.
L: T. Schermann, Die Geschichte der dogmatischen Florilegien vom 5.-8. Jh. (Leipzig, 1904), 98-100. — H. Schultz, H.: PRE 8/2:1922-1927. — W. Spoerri, H.: KP 2:1121f.

C. SCHMIDT

Hieracas of Leontopolis

H. (end of 3rd/beginning of 4th c.) was one of the founders of monastic life in Egypt. He was praised for his virtue and education (Epiphanius, *haer.* 67.1). In Alexandria he came in conflict espec. with Peter, who accused him of teaching Origenist ideas on the preexistence of souls and on resurrection in a spiritual body. At the same time, H. supposedly maintained that celibacy ought to be obligatory for all Christians. The accusation suggests a strict asceticism (Epiphanius, *haer.* 67.3). In trinitarian doctrine H. supposedly held strange views, espec. on the Holy Spirit (Epiphanius, *haer.* 67.3 and 7). Even Arius attacked H.'s conception of the Trinity (Doc. 6). It is said of H. that he spoke Greek and Coptic (Epiphanius, *haer.* 67.3); Copts, too, then, must have belonged to his area of influence.

W: Epiphanius, *haer.* 67, GCS 37:132-140.
L: T. Böhm, Die Christologie des Arius (St. Ottilien, 1991), 40. — R. P. C. Hanson, The Search for the Christian Doctrine of God (Edinburgh, 1988), 7, 479. — P. Nautin, École Pratique des Hautes Études, Vème section, Annuaire 84 (1975/76) 312-314. — R. Williams, Arius (London, 1987), 41.

T. BÖHM

Hilarianus, Quintus Julius

H. was probably a bishop in North Africa, a chronographer, and a supporter of chiliasm in the second half of the 4th c.

Two of H.'s exactly datable writings are based on an early work that he himself revised and which was organized thematically, *De ratione paschae numeroque annorum mundi*. The two works are the treatise *De ratione paschae et mensis* (*pasch.*), finished on Mar. 5, 397, which is a collection of various theories on the computation of Easter, and the treatise *De cursu temporum* (*curs. temp.*), finished on Mar. 14, 397, which dates the creation of the world on Mar. 25, Christ's birth to the second year B.C.E., and the end of the world to the year 470 after Christ's birth, and ends with a detailed description of the apoc. struggle with the Antichrist and of the one-thousand-year worldwide sabbath.

W: *pasch.*, PL 13:1105-1114. — *curs. temp.*, PL 13:1097. — C. Frick, Chronica minora (Leipzig, 1892), 153-174 [text]. L: H. Gelzer, Sextus Julius Africanus u. die byz. Chronographie 2/1 (Leipzig, 1885), 121-130. — B. Kötting, Endzeitprognosen zwischen Lactantius u. Augustinus: HJ 77 (1958) 129f. — B. Krusch, Studien zur chr.-mal. Chronologie (Leipzig, 1880), 24. — E. Schwartz, Chr. u. jüd. Ostertafeln (Berlin, 1905), 59f.

C. SCHMIDT

Hilary of Arles

H., born in 401, was one of the first generation of educated noblemen who left a decisive mark on the monasticism of Lérins. Scholars infer that he was from northern Gaul because of his blood relationship with Honoratus, the founder of that community. His sister's marriage made him brother-in-law of Lupus and Vincent, both of Lérins (*V. Lupi* 1). Acc. to his own testimony in his *Vita Honorati* (*V. Hon.* 23-24), Honoratus had, laboriously and lovingly, compelled him to enter Lérins. H. followed him again to Arles when the latter became bishop there, but he soon returned to the island. → Eucherius of Lyons, whose sons H. instructed, praises this step in a work dedicated to H.: *De laude eremi* (see also Apollinaris Sidonius, *carm.* 16). In 429/430, at the deathbed of Honoratus (*V. Hil.* 9), H. was chosen bishop of Arles. He was a man pastorally and socially involved, did not shun manual labor (Gennadius, *vir. ill.* 70), founded a school for clerics in Arles (*V. Hil.* 7), and carried on an intensive (conciliar) work (Riez 439; Orange 441; Vaison 442; Arles 443, Besançon 444), that was aimed at, among other things, the establishment of the vicariate in Arles,

something for which the foundations had already been laid under Roman Bishop Zosimus. Because of repeated interferences in the jurisdictions of other bishops, Leo I (445) summoned H. to Rome and corrected him. H. died 449 in Arles.

Gennadius mentions this work of H: the *Vita Honorati* (430/431), a biography in the form of an address of consolation and praise. This work was the first in a series of rhetorical lives of Gallic bishops and is an important source for early Lérins. Gennadius also mentions *aliqua et parva* but says nothing more about them. The life of H. (*V. Hil.*) 14, the main source for his life (by Ravennius, → Reverentius, → Honoratus of Marseilles?), lists among H.'s works: (a) *homiliae* (*hom.*), (b) *Symboli expositio* (*symb.*), (c) *Epistolae* (*ep.*), and (d) *Versus fontis ardentis* (*fo.*). Of the homilies, which outnumbered those of Augustine (ibid.), only a single authentic one has survived with some certainty (→ Eusebius Gallicanus, 66: *De natale s. Genesii*, which in turn goes back to a *Passio s. Genesii Arelatensis*, supposedly composed by H.). The *Explanatio symboli* attributed to him is likewise not surely his. Of the letters only one to Eucherius (after 434) and of the *fo.* only four lines have come down to us. Despite the rhetorical praise of his literary abilities by otherwise unknown contemporaries (citations in Gennadius and *V. Hil.* 14), these works, which even in the list in the *V. Hil.* are not treated as significant, hardly permit the inference that H. left behind more extensive theol. or exeget. writings, which should be attributed to him by reason of their theol. implications (*Carmen de Providentia Dei*, → Prosper Tiro of Aquitaine; *De Evangelio* [*ev.*]; *In Genesim ad Leonem papam* [*gen.*]; and *Tractatus in septem ep. canonicas* [*tract.*]).

A reading of the authentic works, however, and also of those attributed to him shows that both literarily and theologically H. fitted in with the first men of Lérins and left a mark on the image of a monasticism that in its own interests expounded currently debated aspects of the doctrine on grace and the Trinity.

W: *Passio/hom.*, S. Cavallin: Er. 43 (1945) 150-175 [text/comm.]. — *hom.*, F. Glorie, CCL 101A:648-654. — *V. Hon.*, S. Cavallin (Lund, 1952). — D. Valentin, SC 235. — M. Labrousse (Bellefontaine, 1995) [French trans./comm.]. — *symb.*, K. Künstle, Eine Bibliothek der Symbole (Mainz, 1900), 173-175. — *ep.*, C. Wotke, CSEL 31:198f. — *fo.*, A. Riese, Anthologia Latina 1/2 (Leipzig, 1906), Nr. 487. — *ev.*, R. Peiper, CSEL 23:270-274. — *gen.*, ibid., 231-239. — *tract.*, R. E. McNally, CCL 108B:53-124.
L: B. Axelson, Marginalia in vitas Honorati et H.: VigChr 10 (1956) 459-471. — W. Berschin, Biographie (Stuttgart, 1986), 242-249. — F. Blatt, La latinité et la vie de Honorat: Er. 45 (1950) 67-88. — J. P. Bouhout, Le texte de V. Hon.:

REAug 28 (1982) 133-147. — E. Contreras, V. Hon. y la Regla de los Cuatro Padres: StMon 32 (1990) 341-365. — F. E. Consolino, Fra biographia e confessio: Orph. 2 (1981) 170-182. — G. Gallo, Uno scritto filo-pelagiano attribuibile a Ilario: Aevum 51 (1977) 333-448. — P. Gassmann, Der Episkopat in Gallien (Bonn, 1977). — M. Heinzelmann, Bischofsherrschaft in Gallien (Zurich, 1976). — C. M. Kasper, Theologie u. Askese (Münster, 1991). — B. Kolon, Die V. Hil. (Paderborn, 1925). — G. Langgärtner, Gallien-politik der Päpste (Bonn, 1964). — M. Marcovich, De Providentia Dei (New York, 1989). — M. P. McHugh, The Carmen De Providentia Dei (Washington, 1964). — S. Pricoco, Sermo de V. Hon.: Annuario dell'Istituto Magistrato Turino Colonno 1968 (Catania, 1969), 175-182. — idem, Modelli di santità a Lerino: SicGym 27 (1974) 54-88. — J. P. Weiss, Étude du mot gratia dans V. Hon.: Aug. 24 (1984) 265-280.

C. KASPER

Hilary, Deacon (A Luciferian)

H., a Roman deacon, accompanied Lucifer of Cagliari as legates of Liberius to the imperial court and to the Synod of Milan (355). H., who supported Lucifer, was more radical than the latter. Like Lucifer, he sharply attacked → Hilary of Poitiers (see apol. resp. Vbis) because of the middle position between homoousians and homoiousians, which the latter took in his De synodis. Acc. to Jerome (c. Lucif. 21.26f.), H. in his (now lost) Libelli de haereticis rebaptizandis demanded the rebaptism of repentant Arians but was alone in this view. When Jerome wrote ca. 382 (or 379), H. was already dead. The identification of H. with → Ambrosiaster (on the basis of Augustine, c. ep. Pel. 4.4 7) is untenable.

L: H. C. Brennecke, Hilarius v. Poitiers u. die Bischofsopposition gegen Constantius II. (Berlin, 1984), 150-153, 182f., 192, 212. — Y. M. Duval, S. Jérôme devant le baptême des hérétiques: REAug 14 (1968) 145-180. — M. R. Green, The Supporters of Antipope Ursinus: JThS 22 (1971) 531-538. — G. Grützmacher, Hieronymus 1 (Aalen, 1986 = Leipzig, 1901), 59, 204. — J. N. D. Kelly, Jerome (London, 1975), 62-64. — G. Krüger, Lucifer, Bischof v. Calaris (Hildesheim, 1969 = Leipzig, 1886), 61, 71, 88f. — P. Smulders, Two Passages of Hilary's Apologetica responsa rediscovered: Bijdr. 39 (1978) 234-243.

M. DURST

Hilary Gallus

H., a layman who came perhaps from Africa, sent a letter (428/429) to → Augustine (Aug., ep. 226). In it he reports, as does his friend → Prosper Tiro of Aquitaine (Aug., ep. 225), on the resistance of the Semipelagians in Marseilles and southern Gaul to Augustine's teaching on grace, and he asks for support. Augustine immediately answered with his De

praedestinatione sanctorum and De dono perseverantiae. Ca. 431/432 H. and Prosper tried to get Celestine I of Rome to issue a decree against these anti-Augustine trends. Celestine's answer (ep. 21) was rather reserved. There is nothing to prove an identification of H. with the writer (Hilary of Syracuse) of Augustine's ep. 156, who turned to Augustine in 414, likewise in connection with the teaching of Pelagius.

W: A. Goldbacher, CSEL 57:468-481.
L: Die Geschichte des Christentums 2 (Freiburg i.Br., 1996), 535. — C. M. Kasper, Der Beitrag der Mönche: FS C. P. Mayer (Würzburg, 1989), 153-182. — M. Schanz, C. Hosius, G. Krüger, Geschichte der röm. Lit. 4/2 (Munich, 1959 = 1920), 435, 492f. — O. Wermelinger, Rom u. Pelagius (Stuttgart, 1975), 244-249.

B. WINDAU

Hilary, Poet

H., a Gallic poet (dated to ca. mid-5th c.) of whose life nothing further is known, is regarded as the composer of some hexametric poems. In Genesim ad Leonem papam (gen.) narrates the creation, fall, and flood in 198 verses. The poet tries for a lofty, dramatic style while dealing very freely with the bibl. material; there are numerous borrowings from Ovid but also from Virgil, Lucretius, and Horace. The fragment De evangelio (evang.) takes the birth of Christ and the adoration of the wise men as the starting point for strongly worded praise. Both works have come down under the name of → Hilary of Poitiers. Whether the somewhat longer poem → De martyrio Maccabaeorum, a treatment of the story of the martyrdom of seven brothers in 2 Mac 7, which has come down in two versions, is also to be attributed to H. is dubious given important stylistic differences. It is possible that the figure of H. the poet is a construct of modern scholarship and that all three works are from different unknown authors.

W: Macc., gen., PL 50:1275-1286 or 1287-1292. — gen., Macc. (both versions), evang., R. Peiper, CSEL 23:231-239, 240-269, 270-274 [text].
L: L. Brésard, Rez. G. Gallo, Uno scritto filo-pelagiano (Aevum 51 [1977] 333-348): REAug 24 (1978) 365, Nr. 146. — P.-A. Deproost, H. (5): DHGE 24:449f. — A. L. Feder, Studien zu H. v. Poitiers 3 (Vienna, 1912), 68. — D. Kartschoke, Bibeldichtung (Munich, 1975), 38f., 41, 90-93, 105-111. — M. Manitius, Geschichte der chr.-lat. Poesie (Stuttgart, 1891), 102-105, 189-192. — R. Peiper, CSEL 23:XXVIII-XXIX. — M. Schanz, Geschichte der röm. Lit. 4/1 (Munich, 1959 = Munich, ²1914), 228. — K. Smolak, Lat. Umdichtungen des bibl. Schöpfungsberichtes: StPatr 12 (1975) 350-360.

M. MEIER

Hilary of Poitiers

I. Life: H. was from a distinguished pagan family and was born, probably in Arles, ca. 315. His writings show him familiar with the philosophical and rhetor. education of his time. The search for truth and knowledge of God seems to have led him to the study of the scriptures and to the Chr. faith (a stylized literary description in *Trin.* 1.1-14). Some time after his baptism, which he received as an adult, H. became the presumably first bishop of Poitiers ca. 350. It was only on the eve of his exile, which probably came after the Synod of Milan (355), that H. became acquainted with the Nicene Creed, which he recognized as being in agreement with the scriptures (*syn.* 91) and whose defender he was to become. During the Arian controversy, H., in cooperation with other Gallic bishops, excommunicated Saturninus of Arles, the leading Arian (homoean) bishop and representative of the pro-Arian imperial religious policy in Gaul. On a false accusation (which connected him perhaps with the unsuccessful usurpation of Silvanus in 355) H. was cited before a synod presided over by Saturninus at Biterrae (Béziers) in the spring of 356; he was deposed and exiled by Constantius to Asia Minor (Phrygia), where he became familiar with currents in eastern theology. During his exile, in which he had relative freedom of movement, and despite his deposition, H. remained in full communion with his fellow Gallic bishops, whom he kept informed, through letters and writings, of the eccles. situation in the eastern part of the Roman empire. The goal of his efforts was the defeat of Arianism and the victory of the Nicene Creed. At the Synod of Seleucia in Isauria (359) H. took the side of the homoiousian minority and traveled with their ambassadors to Constantinople where in the winter of 359/360 he sought in vain for an audience with the emperor. Whether on his own or at the command of the emperor, he traveled from there back to Gaul. With H. as reference, the Synod of Paris (360/361?) renewed the excommunication of Saturninus and excommunicated the Arian (homoean) spokesmen for the Synod of Rimini (359). In 364/365, at a gathering of bishops in Milan, H., together with Eusebius of Vercelli, sought in vain for the deposition of that city's homoean bishop, Auxentius, who remained in office until his death (373). H. died at Poitiers in 367 or 368. He was married and had a daughter, but the *Epistula ad Abram filiam*, which has come down under his name, is not authentic.

II. Works (see Jerome, *vir. ill.* 100): **a. Exegetical works:** (1) The *Commentarius in Matthaeum* (in *Matth.*) is H.'s earliest work (353/355). It shows no profound knowledge of Arianism and no direct influence of eastern theology. Its main sources are the writings of → Tertullian, → Cyprian, and → Novatian. There is a continuous exegesis of the text of the gospels (with deliberate omissions), and the deeper, spiritual (allegorical and typological) meaning is tracked down. (2) Of the *Tractatus super psalmos* (in *psalm.*), which perhaps originally covered all the psalms, only the interpretations of fifty-eight psalms have survived (Pss 1f., 9, 13f., 51-69, 91, 118-150). This work may have been based on homilies. In addition to the Lat. Bible, H. makes use of the LXX and Gr. commentaries. Espec. demonstrable is the influence of Origen. Correspondingly, but without neglecting the literal sense, H. makes fruitful use of the method sketched in the *instructio psalmorum* (using allegorical and typological interpretation) for understanding of the saving event in Christ. (3) Only in 1887 was the two-volume, but incompletely preserved, *Tractatus mysteriorum* (*tr. myst.*) discovered. This work, written ca. 365 and usually identified with the *Liber mysteriorum* mentioned by Jerome, explains OT figures typologically by reference to Christ and the church. (4) Only *Fragmenta minora* (*fr.*) remain of the *Tractatus in Iob* and an exegesis of the Pauline letters (?). There is no trace of a commentary on the Canticle, which Jerome mentions without having seen.

b. Dogmatic works: (5) H.'s most important dogm. work is the twelve books of the *De Trinitate* (*trin.*; another title: *De fide, adversus Arianos*), composed 356/359. After a preface (1.1-14) and an overview of the entire work (1.20-36), books 1-3 give a positive explanation of the doctrine of Father, Son, and Holy Spirit. These books were composed as a separate work while H. was still in Gaul or at the beginning of his exile and were later incorporated into the larger work. In books 4-12 H. discusses Arian theology and exegesis but also the views of → Marcellus of Ancyra and → Photinus of Sirmium, and, with constant appeal to the scriptures, sets forth orthodox teaching on the divinity of Christ. The work ends with a prayer. (6) To the request of Gallic and British bishops for information and explanation of the decrees on the faith by eastern bishops H. replied in the winter of 358/359 in the letter *Epistula de synodis* (*syn.*). In the first part (chs. 1-65) he gives them a Lat. translation of the synodal decrees normative for the homoiousians (except for the second, heret. formula of Sirmium 357), together with a commentary showing these to be orthodox, and (in ch. 64) he formulates his own confession of faith. In the second part (chs. 66-91), in which he consults also the homoiousians around Basil of Ancyra, he tries to mediate between them and the western homoousians but rejects an incorrect interpretation of *homoousios* while also showing the possibility of an orthodox interpretation of *homoiousios*; he warns against a formal condemnation of the *homoousios* and urges the acceptance of a correctly understood *homoousios*. H.'s attempt to mediate met with unyielding criticism from → Lucifer of Cagliari and Roman Deacon → Hilary. H. responded (after 360) with his so-called *Apologetica ad reprehensores libri de synodis responsa* (*apol. resp.*), marginal notes on the censured passages in a copy of the work sent to Lucifer.

c. Historical and polemical works: (7) The *Liber adversus Valentem et Ursacium*, a polemical edition of documents with H.'s commentary, can be only partially reconstructed from excerpts, which were completely removed from their context, in the *Collectio antiariana Parisina* (*col. antiar. Par.*) The work, which was intended to unmask the machinations of the Arians, was composed in two parts, in 356 (or 357) and ca. 360, which (perhaps after H.'s death) were supplemented with a few documents and combined into a single work (the so-called *Opus historicum*). To the first part belongs also the separately circulated *Liber I ad Constantium* (*ad Const. 1*), a work addressed to Constantius II, with a commentary from II., by the western partial Synod of Sardica (353). (8) In a petition submitted in the winter of 359/360, (*Liber II*) *Ad Constantium* (*ad Const. 2*), H. asked the emperor for an audience to discuss his case and the question of faith, in which he appealed to the baptismal creed as norm. (9) When the audience was refused, H. wrote the pamphlet *Contra Constantium* (*c. Cons.*), which, however, he probably published only after the emperor's death. (10) In *Contra Auxentium* (*c. Aux.*), a letter addressed to the western bishops faithful to Nicaea, H. told of the unsuccession action taken in Milan in 364/365 and warned against Auxentius as the Antichrist. The documents appended by H. (record of the investigation of Auxentius and of his confession of faith) are lost. The letter of Auxentius that is added at the end (chs. 13-15), with its confession of faith addressed to the emperor, is a secondary appendage, intended to replace the lost documents. (11) The work *Ad praefectum Sallustium sive contra Dioscorum*, which Jerome praises (*ep.* 70.5.3) and which was written in the context of Julian's measures for the restoration of paganism, has disappeared. Likewise lost are letters to the bishops of Gaul and to Lucifer of Cagliari.

d. Hymns: (12) H. was the first Chr. hymn writer of the Lat. West. His now lost *Liber hymnorum* (*hymn.*) included three incompletely surviving hymns first published in 1877: *Ante saecula qui manes* and *Fefellit saevam* (two abecedaries [→ Abecedary] on the Trinity and Baptism), and *Adae carnis gloriosae*, a song on Christ, the new Adam, and his victory over the devil. These hymns were in the Lat. poetic tradition and, following a Gr. model, came to be used in the liturgy. It is doubtful whether the hymn *Hymnum dicat turba fratrum* is from H. All other hymns attributed to H. in the mss. are not authentic.

III. Importance and Influence: H.'s importance is not limited to his steadfast struggle on behalf of the Nicene Creed; he was also a theologian and exegete of superior rank. During his exile he made himself familiar to a high degree with the sometimes difficult theol. questions of the easterners; he made eastern theology intelligible to the Lat. West and thus paved the way for the later merger of the Nicenes and the homoiousians. It was not least because of his involvement that Gaul and the Latin West remained faithful to Nicaea. The Synod of Paris attested to his high authority in matters of the faith. Because of his reputation Martin of Tours visited him, had H. ordain him an exorcist, and set up his monk's cell in Ligugé near Poitiers ca. 360. Jerome, who, like → John Cassian, gives H. the title of confessor, and → Cassiodorus recommend the reading of H.'s works. Many Lat. church fathers and Visigothic synods use or cite them. → Augustine several times calls upon H. as a witness to his teaching on original sin; → Facundus of Hermiana appeals to him in the Three-Chapters controversy. Pius IX made H. a doctor of the church in 1851.

W: PL 9-10. — PLS 1:241-286. — *in Matth.*, J. Doignon, SC 254, 258. — *in psalm.*, A. Zingerle, CSEL 22. — J. Doignon, CCL 61. — *in psalm.* 118, M. Milhau, SC 344, 347. — *in psalm.* 150, A. Wilmart: RBen 43 (1931) 277-283. — *tr. myst.*, J.-P. Brisson, SC 19bis. — *tr. myst., coll. antiar. Par., ad Const., hymn., fr., spuria*, A. Feder, CSEL 65. — *trin.*, P. Smulders, CCL 62, 62A. — *apol. resp.* Ibis u. Vbis, P. Smulders: Bijdr. 39 (1978) 234-243. — *c. Const.*, A. Rocher, SC 334. — *trin.*, J. Fisch, BKV 56 [German trans.]. — A. Antweiler, BKV² 2. Reihe 5-6 [German trans.]. — *syn., trin., in psalm.* 1, 53, 130, E. W. Watson, L. Pullan et al., NPNF 2:9 (Buffalo, 1898 = 1973) [English trans.]. — *trin.*, S. McKenna, FaCh 25 (New York, 1954) [English trans.]. — A. Blaise (Namur, 1964) [French trans.]. — A. Martin, L. Brésard, 3 vols. (Paris, 1981) [French trans.]. — G. Tezzo (Turin, 1971) [Italian trans.].
L: T. D. Barnes, H. on his Exile: VigChr 46 (1992) 129-140. — G. Bardy, Un humaniste chrétien: RHEF 27 (1941) 5-25. — F. W. Bautz, H.: BBKL 2:835-840. — C. F. A. Borchardt, H.'s Role in the Arian Struggle (Den Haag, 1966). — E. Boularand, La conversion de s. H.: BLE 62 (1961) 81-104.

— H. C. Brennecke, H. u. die Bischofsopposition gegen Konstantius II. (Berlin, 1984). — idem, H: TRE 15:315-322. — P. C. Burns, The Christology in H.'s Commentary on Mt. (Rome, 1981). — M. F. Buttell, The Rhetoric of St. H. (Washington, 1933). — A. Charlier, L'Église corps du Christ chez s. H.: EThL 41 (1965) 451-477. — J. Doignon, H.: RAC 15:139-165. — idem, H. avant l'exil (Paris, 1971). — idem, Hypothèse sur le contenue du Contra Dioscorum d'H.: TU 92 (1966) 170-177. — idem, Les plebes de la Narbonnaise et la communion d'H. durant la crise arienne du VIe siècle: REA 80 (1978) 95-107. — M. Durst, Die Eschatologie des H. (Bonn, 1987). — idem, H.: MarL 3, 187-190. — idem, Nizäa als "autoritative Tradition" bei H.: FS E. Dassmann (JAC. E 23) (Münster, 1996), 406-422. — J. E. Emmenegger, The Functions of Faith and Reason in the Theology of H. (Washington, 1947). — A. L. Feder, Studien zu H. 1-3 (Vienna, 1910-1912). — A. Fierro, Sobre la gloria en s. H. (Rome, 1964). — M. Figura, Das Kirchenverständnis des H. (Freiburg i.Br., 1984). — J. Fontaine, L'origine de l'hymnodie chrétienne latine: MD 161 (1985) 33-74. — P. Galtier, H., le premier Docteur de l'Église latine (Paris, 1960). — K. Gamber, Der Liber mysteriorum des H.: TU 80 (1962) 40-49. — N. J. Gastaldi, H. exégeta del salterio (Paris, 1969). — É. Goffinet, L'utilisation d'Origène dans le commentaire des Psaumes de s. H. (Leuven/Louvain, 1965). — HLL 5:447-480 (literature). — J. W. Jacobs, The Western Roots of the Christology of St. H.: TU 116 (1975) 198-203. — C. Kaiser, The Development of the Johannine Motifs in H.'s Doctrine of the Trinity: SJTh 29 (1976) 237-247. — C. Kannengiesser, H.: DSp 7:466-499. — R. J. Kinnavey, The Vocabulary of H. (Washington, 1935). — E.-R. Labande (ed.), H., évêque et docteur (Paris, 1968). — idem (ed.), H. et son temps (Paris, 1968). — L. F. Ladaría, Adán y Cristo en los Tractatus super psalmos de H.: Gr. 73 (1992) 97-122. — idem, La cristología de H. (Rome, 1989). — idem, El Espiritu Santo en s. H. (Madrid, 1977). — idem, trin. X 20: un precedente de la teología agustiniana del pecado original?: Coram deo (1997) 245-261. — P. Lazzaro, Fede e grazia in H. (Reggio di Calabria, 1956). — X. Le Bachelet, H.: DThC 6:2388-2462. — H. Lindemann, Des hl. H. Liber mysteriorum (Münster, 1905). — P. Löffler, Die Trinitätslehre des Bischofs H. zwischen Ost u. West: ZKG 71 (1960) 26-36. — J. M. McDermott, H.: The Infinite Nature of God: VigChr 27 (1973) 172-202. — L. Malunowicz, De voce sacramenti apud s. H. (Lublin, 1947). — A. Martinez Sierra, La prueba escriturística de los Arrianos segun H. (Madrid, 1965). — E. P. Meijering, H. on the Trinity (Leiden, 1982). — C. Moreschini, Il linguaggio teologico di H.: ScC 103 (1975) 339-375. — I. Opelt, H. als Polemiker: VigChr 27 (1973) 203-217. — A. Orazzo, La salvezza in H. (Naples, 1986). — G. Pelland, La subiectio du Christ chez s. H.: Gr. 64 (1983) 423-452. — idem, Le thème biblique du Règne chez. s. H.: Gr. 60 (1979) 639-674. — M. Pellegrino, La poesia di s. H.: VigChr 1 (1947) 201-226. — A. Penamaría de Llano, La salvación por la fe (Burgos, 1981). — M. Schiktanz, Die H.-Frgm. (Breslau, 1905). — M. Simonetti, Note sul commento a Mt. di H.: VetChr 1 (1964) 35-64. — idem, Note sulla struttura e la cronologia del De trinitate di H.: SUr 39 (1965) 274-300. — idem, H. e Novaziano: RCCM 7 (1965) 1034-1047. — P. Smulders, La doctrine trinitaire de s. H. (Rome, 1944). — idem, H.: GK 1 (Stuttgart, 1984), 250-266. — idem, H. als exegeet van Mattheüs: Bijdr. 44 (1985) 59-81. — idem, H.'s Preface to his Opus historicum (Leiden, 1995). — T. F. Torrance, Hermeneutics according to H.: AbSal 6 (1975) 37-96. — M. Weedman, Martyrdom and docetism in trin.: AugSt 30 (1999) 21-41. — P. T. Wild, The Divinisation of Man according to H. (Mundelein, Ill., 1950). — D. H. Williams, A Reassessment of the Early Career and Exile of H.: JEH 42 (1991) 202-217. — A. Wilmart, Le De mysteriis de s. H. au Mont-Cassin: RBen 27 (1910) 12-21. — idem, L'Ad Constantium Liber primus de s. H. et les Fragments historiques: RBen 24 (1907) 149-179, 291-317. — idem, Les Fragments historiques et le synode de Béziers de 356: RBen 25 (1908) 225-229.

M. Durst

Hilary of Rome

During his peaceful pontificate H. (Nov. 19, 461–Feb. 29, 468), among other things, took steps against the Arian community of Rome. His thirteen surviving letters (*ep.*) deal mainly with matters of church discipline in Gaul and Spain. As a deacon, H. composed two letters in which he reports on the Synod of Ephesus (449) (*ep.* 1) and commissions Victor of Aquitaine to determine the correct date of Easter (*ep.* 2). He sent notices of his election to metropolitan Leontius of Arles (*ep.* 4; 6), whom he later called to task for not reporting events in Gaul to Rome (*ep.* 7; 9). On the grounds that the judgment of the bishop of Rome should be authoritative in more important questions that could not be settled at provincial synods (*ep.* 8), H. intervened in jurisdictional disagreements, protecting the right of metropolitans (*ep.* 8-12, 15-17). In a lost letter he supposedly confirmed the doctrinal decision of → Leo I in the theol. controversy in the East. Some decrees on questions of canon law are forgeries.

W: A. Thiel, Epistolae Romanorum pontificum (Braunsberg, 1868), 126-174. — *ep.* 11, W. Gundlach, MGH. Ep 3:29f. — P. Hinschius, Decretales (Leipzig, 1863), 630-632. — S. Wenzlowsky, Briefe der Päpste, BKV^1 18:11-98 [German trans.].
L: E. Caspar, Geschichte des Papsttums (Tübingen, 1933), 2:10-14. — B. Cignitti, Ilaro: BSS 7:737-753. — K. S. Frank, H.: LMA 5:8.

O. Kampert

Himerius of Tarragona

H., bishop of Saragossa (from ?), is known to have been elderly in 385. He did not take part in the antipriscillianist Synod of Saragossa in 380. Because the Spanish bishops were in disagreement on many disciplinary issues, H. wrote to → Damasus. His (lost) query can only be reconstructed from the response of Damasus's successor → Siricius on Feb. 10, 385. The issues raised were the authority of the Roman bishop, baptism (espec. heretical baptism), the rigoristic Span. penitential practice, and clerical celibacy. H.'s letter is also important for the history of the feast of Christmas.

W: Siricius, *ep.* 1.
L: J. Orlandis, D. Ramos-Lisson, Die Synoden auf der Iberischen Halbinsel (Paderborn, 1981).

R. REICHERT

Hippolytus

I. Life: H., also called Hippolytus of Rome (Hippolytus Romanus), was a 3rd-c. writer, possibly born as early as before 170 in Asia Minor or Alexandria and a Roman presbyter ca. 189-198 under Victor I and Zephyrinus. The hypothesis that H. was active in Alexandria as a presbyter and a supporter of the Novatians could not prevail. Under Zephyrinus in Rome, H. came in conflict with Callistus because the latter, in H.'s view, was promoting modalism, monarchianism, or patripassionism. When Callistus was elected bishop of Rome in 217, H. and his supporters were condemned as ditheists, worshippers of two Gods. It is unclear whether H. then allowed himself to be elected antipope in a small Roman community. The controversy over modalism to which H. gave rise continued under Urban I (222-230) and Pontianus (230-235), until Emperor Maximinus Thrax in 235 finally exiled H. to Sardinia, where he died that same year.

II. Works: Although both Eusebius (*h.e.* 6.22) and Jerome (*vir. ill.* 61) give lists of H.'s writings and although in H.'s cemetery on the Via Tiburtina a statue was discovered in 1881 on which the titles of some of his works are inscribed, the attribution of the numerous works that go under H.'s name is still problematic and disputed. In 1947 P. Nautin suggested that the name H. covers two authors, a "Josipe" (Josippus or Josepus), a presbyter in Rome and an antipope, and an eastern bishop named H. This hypothesis elicited strong opposition. Loi finally modified Nautin's hypothesis: the name H. covers two authors of the same name. One, a Roman presbyter and author, would be author of the *Refutatio omnium haeresium* (*haer.*), *Chronicon, fr. ex libro de paschate, Canon paschalis, Syntagma, fr. de resurrectione et incorruptione, Contra Gaium, Homilia in Psalmos, fr. in Gen., fr. in Pr.* (*fr.* 1-29.54 in Pr.), as well as the → *Traditio apostolica* (*trad. ap.*). The other, an eastern bishop, would be author of *Contra haeresim Noeti* (*Noet.*), *Demonstratio de Christo et antichristo* (*antichr.*), *Commentarii in Dan.* (*Dan.*), *fr. in Canticum canticorum* (*Cant.*), *De David et Goliath, De benedictione Jacobi* (*ben. Jac.*), *Canticum Mosis*

(*cant. Mos.*), as well as *fr. in Is.* Frickel and others opposed Loi's explanation: *Noet.*, they said, is certainly not authentic, but all the other works belong to H. of Rome. Scholten (503f.) added further serious objections that compel us to maintain (provisionally) the oneness of authorship. Yet precisely *Noet.* shows that even amid the supposition of unity there are disputed efforts at attribution. There the following list of works is offered only with reservations:

Authentic writings: (1) Exegetical works: *fr. in Canticum canticorum* (*Cant.*); *Demonstratio de Christo et antichristo* (*antichr.*); *Commentarii in Danielem* (*Dan.*); *Benedictiones Isaac et Jacobi* (*ben. Jac.*); *Benedictiones Moysis; De David et Goliath; fr. in Gen.; fr. arabica XXVII in Pentateuchum; In Num. 22-24* (or: *De benedictione Balaam*); *In Deut.* (or: *Canticum Mosis; cant. Mos.*); *In Iud.; In Ruth; fr. in I Reg.; In I Reg., quae de Helcana et Samuele; In II. Reg.; Argumentum syriace; Homilia in Psalmos; In Ps.; Commentarii/fr. in Pr.; fr. in Eccl.; fr. in Is.; fr. in Ez.; fr. in Mt. 24.15-34; fr. in Mt. 25.24; fr. in Jo.; fr. in Apocalypsim* (*Capita contra Gaium; apologia*). (2) Chronographical works: *Chronicon Paschale; Canon paschalis; Chronicon.* (3) Polemical works: *Refutatio omnium haeresium* (*haer.;* also *philosophoumena*); *Contra haeresim Noeti* (*Noet.*).; *Demonstratio adversus Judaeos* (*Jud.*).; *fr. de universo* (*Adversus Graecos; Graec.*). (4) Various writings: *fr. epistulae ad reginam* (*ep. reg.; De resurrectione ad Mammaeam imperatricem*); *fr. de resurrectione et incorruptione.*

Uncertain works: (1) Exegetical works: *De coturnicibus et de manna; fr. de Apocalypsi; Narratio de virgine Corinthiaca.* (2) Polemical works: *Syntagma contra haereses; Contra Artemonem* (*Parvus labyrinthus; Artem.*). (3) Various writings: *sermo in sancta Theophania; Homilia in s. Pascha; Traditio apostolica* (*trad. ap.*).

Inauthentic works: *fr. in I Reg. 28.11ff.* (*de engastrimytho*); *Introductio in Ps.; Index apostolorum et discipulorum* (*De LXX discipulis*); *Index apostolorum ex Hippolyto, Dorotheo et Epiphanio; Homilia in quatriduanum Lazarum; fr. de Trinitate; De fide; fr. de fide; Parabola de serpente; Forma promissionis; Oratio de consummatione mundi; Contra Beronem et Heliconem haereticos; Constitutiones per Hippolytum* (also: *Epitome libri VIII Constitutionum apostolorum*); → *Canones Hippolyti* (*can.*); → *Canon Muratori.*

In his voluminous production, many works of which have been lost or transmitted only in fragments, H. is close to the apologetes in his thinking. Among his early works are *Cant.* and *antichr.*, an exeget.-eschat. work written ca. 200, that describes the person of the Antichrist, his distinguishing marks, and the events of the end-time. Under the impress of the persecution of Christians by Septimius Severus, between 200 and 204 H. wrote his *Dan.*, a commentary on Dan in four books, which includes the deuterocanonical passages; H. follows the Gr. translation of Theodotion, and his is the oldest surviving commentary on the Bible. In *Dan.* H., who proposes an antichiliastic theology of history, interpreted the Susanna story allegorically (referring to Christ and the church; the giving of the exact dates of the birth and death of Jesus in 4.23 seems to be an early interpolation). *In Ps.* may have been written before 214/218. H. could have written the *trad. ap.* in Rome ca. 215; it is, among other things, a witness to the liturg. tradition before Constantine. It has a special place among the transmitted church orders because it represents the first attempt to provide a set organization for the life of the community. The definitive hierarchization of the community can be seen in the separation of clergy (bishop, presbyter, deacon) from the laity as well as in the sacralization of office, which withdraws office holders from the community. In addition, *trad. ap.* provides a description of the early Roman liturgy, along with liturgical texts (ordination prayers for bishop, presbyter, and deacon; the Eucharistic Prayer, and prayers for the blessing of oil, cheese, and olives). H. also deals with offices and services in the community and gives rules for the acceptance of new community members as well as numerous particular regulations.

In *Noet.* H. fights against Antiochene currents of modalism that had representatives in Rome, and in *Artem.*, against adoptionist trends. The work *Graec.*, which was evidently written before 222 and of which John Damascene preserves fragments, was directed against the Middle Platonism of Albinus. The fragments with their discussion of the Platonic conception of an interim state and the other life confirm that the work was apologetic and polemical in character. The same character can be seen in *Haer.*, written probably after 222. *Haer.* is an antiheretical work in ten books of which only books 1 and 4-10 have survived (the concluding chapters 11 and 12 of the *Letter to Diognetus* are sometimes taken as the conclusion of the work; but possibly they are also part of H.'s treatise on Easter). *Haer.* aims to show that heretics are closer to pagan philosophy than to Chr. revelation: Book 1 gives a summary of Gk. philosophy; book 4 takes up astronomy and magic; books 5-9 describe thirty-three gnostic systems. Book 10, in addition to an epitome of the philosophers (6f.) and one of the heretics (9-29), gives a summary of "cor-

rect" Chr. teaching (32-34). H.'s sources are undoubtedly first-rate and, in part, documented only by him (e.g., some fragments of Empedocles, Heraclitus, Basilides, and Valentinus); his information is therefore to some extent uniquely valuable (e.g., his division of Valentinianism into schools). The work *Syntagma contra haereses*, which describes thirty-two heresies, of which the last is that of Noetus, must have been written before *haer.*, since it is used as a source in the latter.

Like apologetes Justin, Athenagoras, Theophilus, and Tertullian, H. conceived of the Word as subordinate to the Father: the Logos appears first in time and in the manner that the Father willed. If the Father had so willed, he could have turned a human being into God. This ditheistic position elicited the opposition of Roman Bishop Callistus, to whom H., a conservative, was also uncompromisingly opposed in the area of ethical principles: While Callistus liberally allowed marriages (not recognized by the state) of free persons with slaves, H. regarded marital relations between free and slave as concubinage; while Callistus facilitated the reacceptance of serious sinners into the church, H. called for greater strictness. In his view, the church, as continuation of the redemptive work of Christ, had to be a church of the pure and holy; the activity of officials depended therefore on their personal holiness.

III. **Importance:** H.'s controversy with Callistus provides valuable insights into the social tasks and disciplinary activity of the Roman church in the 3rd c. He was one of the last Roman writers in Greek, a language which in the West, as a result of Latinization, was quickly forgotten but in the East was widespread. Thus his works were soon translated into Syriac, Coptic, Armenian, Georgian, and Arabic. By his attempt to be one of the first to produce a continuous commentary on the OT, he had a special influence on Origen, who heard him preach (probably in Rome) in 212. His *Syntagma* and *haer.* also influenced Epiphanius (who mentions H. by name in his *haer.* 31.38.3) and Theodoret of Cyrrhus.

W: PG 10. — G. N. Bonwetsch, GCS 1/1, H. Achelis, GCS 1/2, P. Wendland, GCS 26, A. Bauer, R. Helm, GCS 36, GCS² 46. — *Cant.*, G. N. Bonwetsch, TU 23/2 [German trans./comm.]. — *antichr.*, V. Gröne, BKV¹ [German trans.]. — *Dan.*, M. Lefèvre, G. Bardy, SC 14. — *ben. Jac.*, M. Brière, L. Mariès, B. C. Mercier, PO 27/1-2:2-115 [text/French trans./comm.]. — *Deut.* 33, M. Brière, L. Mariès, B. C. Mercier, PO 27/1-2:116-199 [text/French trans.]. — M. Richard: Muséon 86 (1973) 264 = Opera Minora 1 (Turnhout, 1976), Nr. 4 [text]. — *cant. Mos.*, G. H. Ettlinger, Theodoret of Cyrus (Oxford, 1975), 155f. [text]. — *fr. in I Reg.*, G. H. Ettlinger, loc. cit., 99, 155 [text]. — *In I Reg., quae de Helcana et Samuele*, J. Lebon, CSCO 102

[French trans.]. — *Homilia in Psalmos*, P. Nautin, Le dossier d'H. et de Méliton (Paris, 1953) [text]. — *fr. in Pr.*, M. Richard: Muséon 78 (1965) 257-290; 79 (1966) 61-94; 80 (1967) 327-364, = Op. Min. 1, 17; additions and corrections: Op. Min. 1, 8. 11, also: Op. Min. 3 (Turnhout, 1977), Nr. 84; review: P. Géhin: Byz. 49 (1979) 188-198, [text/comm.]. — *fr. in Is.*, G. H. Ettlinger, loc. cit., 99, 26-31 [text]. — *fr. in Mt.* 24.15-34, P. Bellet: Sef. 6 (1946) 355-361 [Coptic text]. — F. J. Caubet Iturbe: StT 254 (1969) 209-215 [Arabic text]; 255 (1970) 222-228 [Spanish trans.]. — *fr. in Mt.* 25.24, G. H. Ettlinger, loc. cit., 155:4-13 [text]. — *fr. in Jo.* 19.33-34, G. H. Ettlinger, loc. cit., 231:1-3, 4-10, 11-14 [text]. — *haer.*, M. Marcovich, PTS 25 [text]. — J. Legge (London, 1921) [English trans.]. — A. Siouville, 2 vols. (Paris, 1928) [French trans.]. — K. Preysing, BKV² 40 [German trans.]. — *Noët.*, E. Schwartz, Zwei Predigten H.s, SBAW. PPH 1936, 3 [text]. — P. Nautin, H. Contre les hérésies (fragment) (Paris, 1949) [text/comm.]. — R. Butterworth (London, 1977) [text/English trans.]. — *Jud.*, E. Schwartz, loc. cit. [text]. — *Graec.*, K. Holl, Fragmente vornizänischer Kirchenväter, TU 20/2 [text]. — *ep. reg.*, G. H. Ettlinger, loc. cit., 155:15-19; 230:21-25, 27-31 [text]. — M. Richard: SO 38 (1963) 79f. = Op. Min. 1, 5. — idem: StPatr 12 (1975) 51-70 = Op. Min. 1, 11, 69 [text]. — *Syntagma contra haereses*, P. Nautin, loc. cit. [text]. — *Artem.*, E. Schwartz, GCS 9:1 [text]. — *Homilia in S. Pascha*, R. Cantalamessa, L'omelia "In s. Pascha" dello Ps.-I. di Roma (Milan, 1967) [comm.]. — *trad. ap.*, B. Botte, LQF 39 (Münster, ⁵1989) [Latin text/French trans.]. — B. Botte, SC 11bis. — G. Dix (London, ²1968) [Latin/Greek text/English trans.]. — R. Tateo (Turin, 1972) [Italian trans./comm.]. — W. Geerlings, FC 1 [Latin/Greek text/German trans./comm.].

Not authentic W: *Constitutiones per H.*, F. X. Funk, Didascalia et Constitutiones Apostolorum 2 (Turin, 1962), 72-96 (= Paderborn, 1905) [text]. — *can.*, H. Achelis, TU 6/4 [Latin trans.]. — R.-G. Coquin, PO 31:273-444 [Arabic text/French trans.].

L: Ricerche su Ippolito: SEAug 13 (1977) pass. — Nuove ricerche su I.: SEAug 30 (1989) pass. — P. F. Bradshaw, Kirchenordnungen I: TRE 18:662-670. — A. Brent, H. and the Roman Church (Leiden, 1995). — B. Capelle, H. de Rome: RThAM 17 (1950) 145 174. — G. Chappuzeau, Die Auslegung des Hl durch H.: JAC 19 (1976) 45-81. — A. Faivre, Naissance d'une hiérarchie (Paris, 1977). — J. Frickel, Contradizione nelle opere e nella persona di I. di Roma: SEAug 13 (1977) 137-149. — idem, Das Dunkel um H. (Graz, 1988). — idem, Der Antinoëtbericht des Epiphanius als Korrektiv für den Text von H.s Noët.: Comp. 35 (1990) 39-53. — idem, H.s Schrift Noët.: ein Pseudo-H.: Logos., FS. L. Abramowski: BZNW 67 (1993) 87-123. — W. Geerlings, FC 1, 143-208. — M. Guarducci, La statua di "Sant'I.": SEAug 13 (1977) 17-30. — A. Hamel, Die Kirche bei H. (Gütersloh, 1951). — J. M. Hanssens, La liturgie d'H.: OCA 155 (1959, ²1965) 283-340. — idem, H. de Rome fut-il Novatianiste?: AHP 3 (1965) 7-29. — idem, La liturgie d'H. (Rome, 1970). — W. Kinzig, C. Markschies, M. Vinzent, Tauffragen u. Bekenntnis (Berlin et al., 1999). — K. Koschorke, H.s Ketzerbekämpfung (Göttingen, 1975). — V. Loi, La problematica storico-letteraria su I. di Roma: SEAug 13 (1977) 9-16. — idem, L'identità letteraria di I. di Roma: SEAug 13 (1977) 67-88. — M. Marcovich, H. v. Rom: TRE 15:381-387. — A. G. Martimort, Nouvel examen de la "Tradition Apostolique" d'H.: BLE 88 (1987) 5-25. — idem Encore H. et la "Tradition Apostolique": BLE 92

(1991) 133-137. — P. Nautin, H. et Josipe (Paris, 1947). — idem, Le dossier d'H. et de Méliton dans les florilèges dogmatiques et chez les historiens modernes (Paris, 1953). — idem, Lettres et écrivains chrétiens des IIᵉ et IIIᵉ siècles (Paris, 1961). — idem, L'homélie d'H. sur le psautier et les œuvres de Josipe: RHR 179 (1969) 137-179. — C. Osborne, Rethinking Early Greek Philosophy: H. of Rome and the Presocratics (Ithaca, N.Y., 1987). — D. L. Powell, The Schism of H.: StPatr 12 (1975) 449-456. — M. Richard, Comput et chronographie chez s. H: MSR 5 (1948) 294-308; 7 (1950) 237-268; 8 (1951) 19-50; 10 (1953) 13-52. 145-180. — idem, Dernières remarques sur s. H. et le soi-disant Josipe: RSR 43 (1955) 379-394. — idem, H. R.: DSp 7:531-571. — idem, Opera Minora 1 (Turnhout, 1976), Nr. 10-20. — C. Scholten, H. II (v. Rom): RAC 15:492-551. — G. Visona, Pseudo I. In sanctum Pascha (Milan, 1988). — A. Zani, La cristologia di I. (Brescia, 1984).

B. R. Suchla

Hippolytus of Bostra

The Arm. *Seal of the Faith*, an anti-Chalcedonian florilegium of the 7th or 8th c., mentions a H. of Bostra as author of a treatise on the Trinity (*trin.*). Both the Arm. and the Syr. traditions identified this H. with the bishop of Bostra because of a misinterpretation of Eusebius, *h.e.* 6.20. An exact dating of *trin.* is hardly possible. One hypothesis assigns an early date and brings this otherwise unknown H. into the same period of time as his Roman namesake, at the beginning of the 3rd c. Another hypothesis locates the work in the 4th c., where it would have its place in the course of the post-Nicene debate on the Trinity.

W: L. M. Froidevaux, Questions et Réponses: RSR 50 (1962) 32-73 [Armenian text/French trans.].
L: S. P. Brock, Some New Syriac Texts: Muséon 94 (1981) 177-200. — C. Renoux, H. de Bostra?: Muséon 92 (1979) 133-158. — A. Vardanean, Severian u. H.: HandAm 26 (1912) 153-159

P. Bruns

Historia Monachorum in Aegypto

The *Hist. mon.* is an account, composed in 394 by an unknown deacon of Jerusalem and addressed to the monastic communities of Melania the Elder and Rufinus (who translated it from Greek in 403f.), of a journey to the monks of the Egyptian wilderness. In the ms. tradition the hagiog. stories of the *Hist. mon.* are mingled with those of the *Historia Lausiaca* of → Palladius of Helenopolis. Individual monks are treated with very widely differing degrees of fullness and with emphasis on various types (wonderworkers, ascetics, storytellers, exhorters).

W: A. J. Festugière (Brussels, 1971) [Greek text/French trans./comm.]. — L. Eberle (Kalamazoo, Mich., 1977)

[English trans.]. — N. Russel, B. Ward (London, 1981) [English trans.]. — K. S. Frank (Düsseldorf, 1965) [German trans.]. — M. Paparozzi (Milan, 1981) [Italian trans.]. — E. Schulz-Flügel (Berlin, 1990) [Latin trans.(Rufinus)].
L: P. Devos, Les nombres: AnBoll 92 (1974) 97-108. — A. J. Festugière, Le problème littéraire: Hermes 83 (1955) 257-284. — R. Reitzenstein, Hist. mon. (Göttingen, 1916). — G. Trettel, Hist. mon.: Accademia Card. Bessarione, Rufino di Concordia, vol. 1 (Udine, 1987), 215-226. — B. Ward, Signs and wonders: St-Patr 17 (1982) 539-542.

M. SKEB, OSB

Homily

The homily, rooted in the explanation of the scriptures at the Jewish divine service, is, in the strict sense, the address that follows upon the liturg. reading of bibl. texts. The word *homilia* was originally used to describe the familiar conversation between philosophers and their students; in its Latinized form it came into use in the West via Jerome and Rufinus. Largely synonymous in meaning were the Gr. *logos* and the Lat. *tractatus* (→ Tractate), but the latter gradually took second place to *sermo*.

From apostolic times the Chr. self-consciousness developed and was expressed through comment on the word of God; for this self-consciousness, the mystery of Christ became the key to any interpretation of the scriptures. The Sunday celebration of the Eucharist and the liturgy of the word during the week became the place for the homily, which interpreted the gospel as well as the OT and NT readings. Only after the 3rd c. do we have testimonies to the homily, often in the form of continuous commentaries (following the *lectio continua*) in which the methods of ancient gram. interpretation of texts but also of rabbinical interpretation were fundamental. Not only exeget. techniques but also ancient rhetoric, together with elements of the popular philosophical diatribe, shaped the form of the homily, which often made lively contact with the hearers, whose reactions were attentively noted. Along with the exeget. homily, other, more thematic forms of proclamation developed (sermons on the feasts of the church year; sermons on the saints; catecheses; eulogies of the deceased). From earliest times the bishop was the primary preacher. Then priests also preached, initially in the East, then in the West (Synod of Vaison, 529). Beginning in the 5th c., homiliaries (collections of homilies) were compiled as, among other things, helps to preachers.

L: M. Banniard, Viva voce. Communication écrite et communication orale du IVe au IXe siècle en Occident latin (Paris, 1992). — W. Ehlers, Homilia: ThesLL 6/3:2870f. —

R. Étaix, Homéliaires patristiques latins (Paris, 1994). — A. Hammann, Dogmatik u. Verkündigung in der Väterzeit: ThGl 61 (1971) 109-140, 202-231. — D. G. Hunter (ed.), Preaching in the Patristic Age (New York, 1989). — W. Kinzig, The Greek Christian Writers: Handbook of Classical Rhetoric in the Hellenistic Period 330 B. C.–A. D. 400, ed. S. E. Porter (Leiden et al., 1997), 633-670. — J. Longère, Prédication médiévale (Paris, 1983), 24-35. — A. Olivar, Objet de l'homilétique patristique: MD 177 (1989) 19-33. — idem, Predicación cristiana antigua (Barcelona, 1991). — M. Sachot, H.: RAC 16:148-175. — J. B. Schneyer, Geschichte der kath. Predigt (Freiburg i.Br., 1968), 41-95. — W. Schütz, Geschichte der chr. Predigt (Berlin, 1972), 8-23. — H. J. Sieben, Kirchenväterhomilien zum NT (Steenbrugge, 1991).

M. FIEDROWICZ

Honoratus Antoninus

Ca. 437 H., bishop of Constantina in Numidia, wrote a letter to an Arcadius, a Span. Catholic who had been banished to Africa by Vandal King Genseric, who wanted to introduce the Arian faith (*Ep. consolatoria ad Arcadium*). It is a letter of comfort, in which Arcadius is urged to hold fast to the true faith and to be patient, and martyrdom (which he did eventually suffer) is set before him as a meritorious end of life.

W: PL 50:567-570. — T. Ruinart, Historia persecutionis Vandalica (Paris, 1699), 433-439 [text].
L: PAC 75, 89f. — M. Schanz, C. Hosius, G. Krüger, Geschichte der röm. Lit. 4/2 (Munich, 1959 = 1920), 572.

B. WINDAU

Honoratus of Arles

Born ca. 365 of a consular family in northern Gaul, H. founded on the island of Lérins (ca. 410) what was originally a loose community of hermits. Previously he undertook a journey to Egypt; whether he reached his destination is uncertain; the shaping of his monasticism acc. to Asia Minor and Pachomian models may be the result of H.'s knowledge of monastic literature. He was ordained a priest by Bishop Leontius of Fréjus. In 426 he became bishop of Arles. → Hilary of Arles, who wrote his life (*V. Hon.*), praises his addresses on the Trinity. H. died on Jan. 16, 430.

There is no ms. witness to any works he left behind. Quite recently there has been a growing assumption that in the form of a Rule he created a tradition that determined the development of monasticism. Sermons on him in → Eusebius Gallicanus (35 and 72; by → Faustus of Riez?) give some clues about him. Under discussion are sections of the

Regula quattuor patrum and the *Secunda regula patrum*, which regulate only the most necessary course of events in the developing community life.

S: *V. Hon.*, D. Valentin, SC 235. — M. Labrousse, Saint Honorat (Bellefontaine, 1995) [French trans./comm.].
W: *Regulae Patrum*, A. de Vogüé, SC 297. — M. Puzicha, Die Regeln der Väter (Münsterschwarzach, 1990) [text/ German trans./comm.].
L: M. Carrias, Vie monastique et règle de Lérins: RHEF 74 (1988) 185-195. — C. M. Kasper, Theologie u. Askese (Münster, 1991). — S. Pricoco, L'isola dei santi (Rome, 1978). — A. de Vogüé, La vie monastique à Lérins: RHE 88 (1993) 5-53. — J. P. Weiss, H. — héros antique et saint: Aug. 24 (1984) 265-280.

C. KASPER

Honoratus of Marseilles

Acc. to the continuator of Gennadius (*vir. ill.* 100), Bishop H. was a skilled preacher and zealous opponent of *haereticorum perversitas* (probably the Pelagians) and also composed the *Vita Hilarii episcopi Arelatensis* (*V. Hil.*: 477/496). Acc., however, to a remark added in the ms. the work was by Hilary's successor, → Reverentius (Ravennius). The authorship remains uncertain. H. died after 492. The *V. Hil.* is one of a series of biographies of bishops of southern Gaul. The structure and themes reflect the rhetorical panegyric of the ancient scholastic tradition. In its content it is dependent on the *V. Hon.* of Hilary but adds valuable material on the conflict over the vicariate in Arles.

W: *V. Hil.*, S. Cavallin (Lund, 1952) [text/comm.].
L: W. Berschin, Biographie (Stuttgart, 1986), 245-249. — S. Cavallin, Hagiographes arlésiens: Er. 46 (1948) 133-157. — idem, Lobrede des Hilarius: FS P. Lehmann (Berlin, 1950), 83-93. — M. Corti, Osservazioni nella vita di S. Ilario. RIL 73 (1939) 202-212. — L. Hakanson, Vita Hilarii: VigChr 31 (1977) 55-59. — B. Kolon, Die Vita H. (Paderborn, 1925).

C. KASPER

Honorius I

H. was from a prosperous family of the Compagna and was elected pope in 625. He saw himself as in the line of Gregory I and, with the help of his private fortune, engaged in significant building activity. He promoted the mission in England and put an end to the Three-Chapters schism in Istria and Venetia. A series of letters has survived but not all are authentic. Only a Gr. translation exists of the important letters 4 and 5 (see below).

The position taken by H. on the question of one will in Christ was important. With the aid of the formula maintaining a single "energy" in Christ, Patri-arch Sergius of Constantinople had reached an agreement with the Monophysite Alexandrians. After a protest from Sophronius Jerus., it was agreed that such expressions be avoided. When Sergius asked H. for his view and spoke not of a single energy but a single will, H. in his answer accepted this formula. He stuck to his position even after receiving Sophronius's synodal letter (*ep.* 5). Thereupon Emperor Heraclius published the *Ecthesis* composed by → Sergius of Constantinople. It was only after H.'s death that, under the influence of Maximus Conf., the doctrine of the two wills and energies developed and became a dogma at the Council of Constantinople 680/681. In this connection all "monotheletes" and "monenergetes" were condemned, including H. While this fact was soon suppressed in the West, it remained known in the East. It has been debated since the 15th c. as the "Honorius question" and played an important role in the debate over the dogma of infallibility in 1870.

W: PL 80:467-494, 601-607. — W. Gundlach, MGH. Ep 3:694-696. — ACO 2, 2, 2, 535-537 [Greek text of *ep.* 3-5)]. — G. Kreuzer, Die H.-frage im MA u. in der Neuzeit (Stuttgart, 1975), 32-53 [Greek text/German trans./ comm.].
L: P. Conte, Nota su una recente appendice sulla questione di Onorio: RSCI 37 (1983) 173-182. — F. Carcione, Enérgheia, Thélema e Theokínetos nella letteratura di Sergio a Papa Onorio: OCP 51 (1985) 263-276. — G. Kremer, H.: LMA 5:119f. — G. Kreuzer, loc. cit. (literature). — G. Schwaiger, H.: TRE 15:566-568. — A. Thanner, Papst H. (St. Ottilien, 1989) (literature). — F. Winkelmann, Die Quellen zur Erforschung des monenergetisch-monotheletischen Streites: Klio 69 (1987) 515-559. — E. Zocca, Una possibile derivazione Gregoriana per il "monotelismo" di Onorio: Aug. 33 (1993) 519-575.

G. RÖWEKAMP

Honorius Scholasticus

H. has left a poetic letter in fourteen distichs, written probably in the mid-6th c. and addressed to a Bishop Jordanes, who is not to be identified with the author of the history of the Goths (*Rescriptum Honorii scholastici contra epistulas Senecae ad Iordanem episcopum*). The author is a recently converted Christian, perhaps not yet baptized, who asks Jordanes for further instruction in Chr. doctrine. H. compares Jordanes with Seneca and himself with Lucilius; despite indirect praise, he disparages Seneca's letters to Lucilius because Seneca did not have Chr. enlightenment.

W: A. Riese (ed.), Anthologia Latina 1/2 (Amsterdam, ²1964 = Leipzig, ²1906), Nr. 666.
L: P. Faider, Études sur Sénèque (Gand, 1921). — W. Kroll,

291

H. 6: PRE. S 3:1159f. — O. Plasberg, Zum Senecagedicht des H.: RMP NF 54 (1899) 144-149. — E. Thomas, Zum Senecagedicht des H.: RMP NF 54 (1899) 313-316. — M. Schanz, C. Hosius, G. Krüger, Geschichte der röm. Lit. 4/2 (Munich, 1959 = 1920), 118, 269, 312.

B. WINDAU

Hormisdas of Rome

H., a southern Italian aristocrat, was elected bishop of Rome on July 20, 514, as having been the trusted collaborator of his predecessor Symmachus. In office, he cleared away the remnants of the Laurentian schism. Together with Justin I and Justinian, he ended the conflict with the eastern church over Acacius (519). He was able, for a short time, to achieve a theoretical acknowledgment of the teaching authority of the bishop of Rome, independently of the emperor. H. died in Rome on Aug. 6, 513.

Like most of the Roman bishops of his age, H. did not produce any literary work of his own but did leave behind official documents and letters. There are ca. 150 letters (*ep.*) from and to H., the majority in the *Collectio Avellana* (→ Canonical collections). H.'s formula of union (*Libellus Hormisdae*), which ended the thirty-five-year schism between the eastern and western churches, had to be signed by all who desired to be in *communio* with the Roman bishop (*Avell.* 116b). The formula includes not only the acceptance of Chalcedonian christology but also an unambiguous recognition of the claims of Rome as the apostolic see that had always kept the Cath. faith intact. The union achieved was again endangered by imperial support for the theopaschite formula (*Avell.* 187), which H. rejected as not Chalcedonian and misleading (*Avell.* 231; 236).

W: *ep.*, A. Thiel, Epistulae Romanorum Pontificum Genuinae (Hildesheim, 1974 = 1868), 741-1006 [text]. — nearly all the letters are better edited in Collectio Avellana, *ep.* 105-243, O. Günther, CSEL 35: 495-742.
L: A. Di Berardino (ed.), Patrologia 4 (Genoa, 1996), 134-137. — A. Grillmeier, Jesus der Christus 2/1 (Freiburg i.Br., 1986), 351-358 (English, Christ in Christian Tradition, vol. 2/1 [London, 1987]). — R. Haacke, Die Glaubensformel des Papstes H. (Rome, 1939). — J. Meyendorff, Imperial Unity and Christian Division (New York, 1989), 211-221. — A. Quacquarelli, Papa Ormisda al vescovo Possessore: VetChr 30 (1993) 5-15. — J. Richards, The Popes and the Papacy (London, 1979), 100-112. — J. Speigl, Formula Iustiniani: OS 44 (1995) 105-134.

S. C. KESSLER, SJ

Horsiesi

From ca. 320 on, H., who had been born ca. 305 of unknown descent, was one of the first disciples of

Pachomius and a witness to the first years of cenobitic life at Tabennisi. After the death of Pachomius and the early death of his successor, Petronius, H. became the third head of the monastic group in 346. During a crisis that was caused by the increased prosperity of the monastery and threatened to split the group, H. gave the leadership to Theodore of Tabennisi, but without ever formally abdicating it, and took it back after Theodore's death. He died around 380/390. His works include: fragmentary *Catecheses* (*catech.*; Copt.), *Excerpta* (*exc.*; Copt.), *Monita* (*mon.*; Copt.; a kind of commentary on the rule of Pachomius), two letters (*ep.* 1f.; Copt.), and two further letters, discovered in 1972 (*ep.* 3f.; Copt.; unpublished), occasioned by the annual assembly of the Pachomians at Easter. Espec. important is the *Liber Orsiesii* (*Orsies. doctr.*), which Jerome translated from Greek into Latin in 404; the Copt. original and the Gr. "intermediate stage" are lost. The work is H.'s spiritual testament and exhorts the monks, in Bible-based language, to remain true to the heritage of Pachomius, espec. in the matter of poverty. The *Libellus de sex cogitationibus sanctorum* (*lib. cog.*) is not from H.

W: *catech., exc., mon., ep.* 1f., L. T. Lefort, CSCO 159f. [Coptic text/French trans.]. — *catech., ep.* 1-4, *exc.*, A. Veilleux, vol. 3 (Kalamazoo, Mich., 1982), 135-152, 153-168, 169f. [English trans.]. — *ep.* 3f., A. de Vogüé: StMon 28 (1986) 7-50 [French trans./comm.]. — *Orsies. doctr.*, A. Boon (Leuven/Louvain, 1932), 109-147 [Latin text]. — H. Bacht (Würzburg, 1972), 1:58-189 [Latin text/German trans./comm.]. — P. Deseille (Bellefontaine, 1968) [French trans.]. — M. de Elizalde: Cuadernos Monasticos 4f. (1967) 173-244 [Spanish trans./comm.]. — *lib. cog.*, PG 40:895f.
L: H. Bacht, Vermächtnis 1 (Würzburg, 1972), 9-55, 191-264, 267-278 (bibliography). — T. Baumeister, Mentalität: ZKG 88 (1977) 145-160. — M. Krause, K. Hoheisel, Aegypten II: RAC. Suppl. 1 (1985) 83. — F. Ruppert, Gehorsam (Münsterschwarzach, 1971). — A. Veilleux, Pachomian Koinonia, 3 vols. (Kalamazoo, Mich., 1980-82). — idem, Horsiesios: CoptE 4:1257f.

M. SKEB, OSB

Hydatius of Aquae Flaviae

H. was born ca. 394 in the *Lemica civitas* (probably near the present-day Xinzo da Limia, Portugal) and in early youth (ca. 406) made a pilgrimage to the Holy Land, where he met Jerome, among others. A bishop from 427 on (probably in Aquae Flaviae, today Chaves, Portugal), he seems to have devoted himself, in church matters, chiefly to the struggle against the Priscillianists, and, in the political realm, to the struggle against the Suebi, whose prisoner he was for three months in 460. He died ca. 470.

H. composed, in Latin, an important continuation of Jerome's chronicle for the years 379-468 (*chron.*). Using a chronol. framework based on the Olympiads and the reigns of the emperors, but occasionally also on the Span. *aera*-computation of time, he records the most important events of each year, initially in concise form but from 455 on in great detail. The work shows a clear pro-Roman and antibarbarian tendency; the focus of interest is the Span. provinces, espec. Galicia. This provincial outlook is one reason for H.'s pessimistic vision of history. He has no positive development to set over against the terrible state of affairs under the Vandals and Suebi, such as, e.g., Prosper Tiro of Aquitania sees in the growth of eccles. power amid the contemporary decline of the secular power. H. seems to have expected an imminent end of the world. In such a situation the preservation of the true faith was of the greatest importance to H., so that the increasingly tough attitude that the *chron.* shows toward the Priscillianists and other heretics becomes understandable.

The sources of the *chron.* were, among other things, letters of contemporaries (e.g., → Leo I the Great), the chronicle of → Sulpicius Severus, and the *Consularia Constantinopolitana* (*Consul. Const.,* a list of Roman consuls from 509 B.C.E. to 468 C.E., at times with extended additions). After 428 H. writes from his own experience. His contribution to the concluding section of the *Consularia* (often called *Fasti Hydatiani*) is disputed.

H.'s language shows an effort to use classical diction, but the influence of the Latin of late antiquity and espec. the language of Chr. writers is often evident.

W: PL 74:701-750; 51:873-914. — *chron.*, T. Mommsen, Chronica Minora 2 (Berlin, 1894), 1-36 [text]. — J. Campos (Salamanca, 1984) [text/Spanish trans./comm.]. — A. Tranoy, SC 218f. — *Consul. Const.,* Mommsen, loc. cit. 1 (Berlin, 1892), 197-247 [text]. — *chron., Consul. Const.,* W. Burgess (Oxford, 1993) [text/English trans.].
L: C. Cardelle de Hartmann, Philologische Studien zur Chronik des H. (Stuttgart, 1994). — C. Courtois, Auteurs et scribes: Byz. 21 (1951) 23-54. — C. Molé, Uno storico del v secolo: SicGym 27 (1974) 279-351; 28 (1975) 58-139. — S. Muhlberger, The Fifth-Century Chroniclers (Leeds, 1990). — P. Nautin, Introduction d'H.: RHT 14/15 (1984/85) 143-153. — S. Teillet, Des Goths à la nation gothique (Paris, 1984), 207-254. — E. A. Thompson, The End of Roman Spain: NMS 20 (1976) 3-28; 21 (1977) 3-31; 22 (1978) 3-22; 23 (1979) 1-21. — C. Torres Rodríguez, H., el primer cronista español: RABM 62 (1956) 755-794.

U. HAMM

Hyginus of Cordoba

H., bishop of Cordoba, played an important role in the controversy over → Priscillian, for in a (lost) letter to Hydatius of Merida, metropolitan of Lusitania, he pointed to → Instantius and Salvian as the first Priscillianists (Sulpicius Severus, *chron.* 2.47.3). H. then persecuted the new sect, whose leaders tried to prove their orthodoxy in debates and confessions of faith. H. was convinced and turned from enemy to supporter of Priscillian. He did not even take part in the antipriscillianist Synod of Saragossa (380), evidently thinking it impossible to defend himself.

L: H. Chadwick, Priscillian (Oxford, 1976). — J. Orlandis, D. Ramos-Lisson, Die Synoden auf der Iberischen Halbinsel (Paderborn, 1981).

E. REICHERT

Hymenaeus of Jerusalem

H. was bishop of Jerusalem and took part in the synods of 264 and 268 against Paul of Samosata. He was the first signer of the letter of six bishops to Paul that was written at the end of the synod of 264. Maximus Conf. (*prol. operum S. Dionysii Areopagitae*; PG 4:20) says that Eusebius in his *h.e.* fails to mention some writers, espec. Palestinian, H. among them, several of whose works he, Maximus, had read.

W: G. Bardy, Paul de Samosate (Louvain, 1929), 13-19 [text]. — Mansi 1:1033-1040.
L: G. Bardy, loc. cit., 9-34.

G. RÖWEKAMP

Hymn

Not every poem described in antiquity as a hymn is a hymn, and many a poem not expressly called a hymn is in fact a hymn. This is the dilemma faced in study of the genre: What makes a hymn a hymn? The attempts of the ancient theoreticians of rhetoric such as Theon and Menandros to define hymn as praise of God in contrast to an encomium, which is praise of human beings (*Rhetores* 2.209.22-28; 3.331.15-20, Spendel), are as imprecise as Augustine's influential definition of a hymn as praise, praise of God, praise of God with song (*en. Ps.* 72.1; 148.17). Even for the liturg. hymn this definition is much too narrow, if we think of Marian songs and praises of the martyrs. As for the literary hymn, Augustine's definition does not apply at all, because the musical element is lacking.

In early antiquity—Chr. and non-Chr., Jewish and

gnostic—a hymn was defined primarily by its content (praise or glorification of gods, God, divine messengers, persons, objects). The hymn thus belonged to a collective genre, under which many forms of poetry, songs, and psalms (→ Psalm) could be subsumed. As for its form or forms, only minimal criteria were applied at first: it must have poetic language or elevated artistic prose. Further characteristics were to be seen in each case: salutation proper to prayer, greeting of God, chiasm, use of relative clauses or predicates. Paeans, dithyrambs, prose odes, parthenaia, and hyporchemata could be regarded as special forms of hymn.

After the NT hymnic texts, which are in the tradition of the Psalms, after the *Odes* of → Solomon, the gnostic → *Pistis Sophia*, the unique case of the anapestic hymn to Christ in → Clement Alex. (*paed.* 3, end), and the classically structured stanzaic songs of → Hilary of Poiters, something entirely new began in the Chr. sphere with the hymn of → Ambrose. The novelty consisted espec. in the fact that these literary strophes of Ambrose, so often imitated later, eight of which form an easily sung hymn, are composed in each case of four acatalectic iambic dimeters.

L: W. Bulst, Hymni Latini (Heidelberg, 1956). — W. Christ, M. Paranikas, Anthologia Graeca (Hildesheim, 1963 = Leipzig, 1871). — F. Crüsemann, Studien zur Formgeschichte (Neukirchen, 1969). — R. Deichgräber, Gotteshymnus (Göttingen, 1967). — G. Delling, ὕμνος κτλ.: ThWNT 8:492-506. — H. Follieri, Initia, 5 vols. (Rome, 1960-1966). — M. Hengel, H. u. Christologie: FS K. H. Rengstorf (Leiden, 1980), 1-23. — idem, Christuslied: FS J. Ratzinger (St. Ottilien, 1987), 357-404. — A. Kehl, Beiträge: JAC 15 (1972) 92-119. — G. Kennel, Frühchr. Hymnen (Neukirchen, 1995). — J. Kroll, Hymnodik (Darmstadt, 1968). — M. Lattke, H. (Fribourg, Switzerland, 1991). — H. Leclercq, Hymnes: DACL 6/2:2826-2928. — J. W. McKinnon, Music (Cambridge, 1987). — E. Norden, Kunstprosa (Darmstadt, ⁷1974 = ²1909) (supplements: ³1915). — idem, Theos (Darmstadt, ⁴1956 = Leipzig, 1913). — G. Schille, Frühchr. Hymnen (Berlin, 1965). — B. Stäblein, H.: MGG 6 (1957) 993-1018. — K. Thraede, H. 1: RAC 16:915-946. — A. S. Walpole, Latin Hymns (Hildesheim, 1966 = Cambridge, 1922). — P. G. Walsh, Hymnen 1: TRE 15:756-762. — T. Wolbergs, Gedichte (Meisenheim, 1971). — R. Wünsch, H.: PRE 9/1:140-183. — K. Ziegler, H.: KP 2:1268-1271.

M. LATTKE

Hypatius of Ephesus

H., orthodox archbishop of Ephesus, was a confidant of Emperor Justinian in 531-536. At a conference on the faith in Constantinople, the so-called *Collatio cum Severianis*, where he acted as spokesman for the orthodox bishops and the supporters of strict Chal-

cedonian christology, he rejected the writings of → Dionysius the Areopagite as a forgery of the Severians, who claimed these writings as favoring their Monophysite christology. A year later, 533, H., along with Demetrius, bishop of Philippi, journeyed to John II in Rome, by commission of the emperor, in order to obtain episcopal recognition of the theopaschite formula (*unus ex trinitate passus*) in → Justinian's decree on the faith, a formula challenged by some of the Acoemetae, and to obtain also condemnation of its deniers (*Ep. ad Iohannem II papam*). As spokesman for all in attendance, H. appeared at the synod held in Constantinople from May 2 to June 4, 536 against Anthimus, a Severian; the synod ended with an anathema on Severus of Antioch, Peter of Apamea, and Zooras. At the beginning of 540 H. was a member of a special commission set up by Emperor Justinian that met in Gaza, Palestine, to deal with some Severians. He died between 541 and 552.

An inscription found during excavations in Ephesus in 1904 contains a decree of H. on the obligation of Chr. burial (*Decretum de mortuis sepeliendis*). It appears from some catenas that H. wrote commentaries on the Psalms (*fr. in Ps.* 77), the twelve minor prophets (*fr. Os.-Zach.*), and Luke (*fr. Lc.*). In addition, he composed a likewise fragmentary work *Quaestiones miscellaneae* (*fr.*), in which he answered questions of Julian of Atramytion concerning, among other things, the veneration of images.

W: *Decretum de mortuis sepeliendis, fr., fr. in Ps.* 77, *fr. Os.-Zach., fr. Lc.*, F. Diekamp: OCA 117 (1938) 126, 127-129, 129f., 130-151, 151-153 [text].
L: H.-G. Beck, Kirche u. theol. Lit. (Munich, ²1977), 303, 372, 376. — F. Diekamp, Analecta patristica = OCA 117 (1938) 109-125. — S. Gero, H. on the Cult of Images: FS M. Smith 2 (Leiden, 1975), 203-216. — J. Gouillard, H. ou du Pseudo-Denys à Théodore Studite: REByz 19 (1961) 63-75. — A. Grillmeier, Jesus der Christus 2/2 (Freiburg i.Br., 1989), 242-262, 356f. (English, Christ in Christian Tradition, vol. 2/2 [London, 1995]). — E. Schwartz, ACO 3, 178-180, 182; 4, 2, 16-84, 169-184. — H.-G. Thümmel, H. u. Julianos v. Adramytion zur Bilderfrage: BySl 44 (1983) 161-170.

B. R. SUCHLA

Hyperechius

There has come down under the name of H. an *Exhortation to Ascetics*, which also appears among the works of Ephraem the Syrian (Assemani G. 2.356ᵇ-364ᶜ). It contains 160 sentences in the form of a parenetic alphabet (→ Abecedary) dealing with the basic themes of monastic asceticism; it may have taken as a model the gnomic alphabet of → Evagrius Pont. (see PG 40:1268f.). Eight items are also found in the alphabetic collection of the → *Apophthegmata Patrum* (PG 65:429-32). H. is therefore considered to have been an Egyptian monk living in the 4th/5th c.

W: PG 79:1473-1489. — L. Cremaschi, Iperechio, Stefano di Thebe, Zozima (Magnano, 1992) [Italian trans.]. — P. Tirot et al., Enseignements des Pères du Désert (Hyperéchios et al.) (Bellefontaine, 1991) [French trans.].
L: V. Grumel, H.: DTC 5:1144. — J. M. Sauget, Iperechio: BSS 7:863f. — K. Rahner, M. Viller, Aszese u. Mystik der Väterzeit (Freiburg i.Br., 1989 = 1939), 177.

J. PELE, OSB

Hypostasis archonton

The *Hypostasis of the Archons* is the title of a Copt. treatise in the Nag Hammadi Library (NHC 2, 4). It contains the instructions of a gnostic teacher on primitive history, espec. the genesis of the archons, as well as Adam and Eve and the building of Noah's ark. This is followed by the revelation of an angel to Norea, the wife of Seth. The work is part of the world of Sethian gnosis and is probably to be dated to the end of the 2nd/beginning of the 3rd c.

W: B. Barc, M. Roberge (Leuven/Louvain, 1980) [text/French trans./comm.]. — R. A. Bullard (Berlin, 1970) [Coptic text/trans./comm.]. — B. Layton: HThR 67 (1974) 351-425 [Coptic text/English trans./comm.]. — J. Leipoldt, H. M. Schenke, Kopt.-gnost. Schriften (Hamburg, 1960), 69-78 [German trans.]. — P. Nagel, Das Wesen der Archonten (Halle, 1970) [Coptic text/German trans./comm.]. — NHL 161-169 [English trans.].
L: F. T. Fallon, Enthronement of Sabaoth (Leiden, 1978). — I. S. Gilhus, Nature of Archons (Wiesbaden, 1985). — M. Krause, Zur Hypostase: Enchoria 2 (1972) 1-20. — R. Kasser, Hypostasis: RThPh 22 (1972) 168-202. — M. Tardieu, Trois mythes gnostiques (Paris, 1974).

P. BRUNS

Hypsiphrone

H. is a fragmentary gnostic work in the Nag Hammadi library (NHC 11, 4), written in Sahidic Coptic. It deals with the descent of H., "the High-minded One," from the upper virginal world into defilement by the material cosmos, and with the heavenly revelations thereby given.

W: J. D. Turner: NHS 28 (1990) 269-279 [Coptic text/English trans.]. — NHL 501f. [English trans.].
L: C. Colpe, H.: JAC 17 (1974) 115f.

P. BRUNS

I

Ibas of Edessa

I. followed Rabbula on the episcopal throne of Edessa in 435. He distinguished himself as translator of the works of → Theodore Mops., → Diodorus of Tarsus, and → Nestorius from Greek into Syriac. As a zealous supporter of traditional Antiochene christology he tried to turn back the growing influence of the extreme Cyrillians but was unsuccessful. Intriguing monks accused I. of misuse of church money and forced his deposition at the Robber Synod of Ephesus in 449. But I. was rehabilitated two years later at Chalcedon and retained the episcopal throne of Edessa thenceforth until his death in 457. In 433 he wrote his famous letter to Persian Bishop Mari (*ep.*) in which he declared his opposition to → Cyril Alex. The Syr. original of the letter is lost, but it survives in a Gr. translation. The letter was a subject of the Three-Chapters dispute and was rejected at Constantinople in 553. In his list of writers (BOCV 3/1:85f.) Ebedjesu attributes to I. a commentary on Prov and various hymns and homilies.

W: *ep.*, ACO 2, 1, 3, 32-34; 2, 3, 3, 39-43 [Latin-Greek text]. — E. Flemming: AGWG 15 (1917) 48-52 [Syriac text].
L: A. de Alès, Lettre d'I.: RSR 22 (1932) 5-25. — R. Devreesse, La querelle de Trois-Chapitre: RevSR 11 (1931) 543-565. — idem, Essai sur Théodore (Rome, 1948), 125-152. — M. van Esbroeck, Who is Mari: JThS 38 (1987) 129-135. — E. R. Hayes, L'école d'Édesse (Paris, 1930).

P. BRUNS

Ignatius of Antioch

The judgment on the letters that go under the name of I. determines the answer to the question of who I. was. Polycarp (*ep.* 13) seems to be the earliest witness to collections of I.'s literary works in Philadelphia, Smyrna, and Syria (Antioch) and, at the same time, to his rank and reputation. Eusebius, *h.e.* 3.36.3-15, lists seven letters that I., whom he knew to be bishop of Antioch on the Orontes (*Rom.* 2.2), dictated at two stopping places on his deportation to Rome and in expectation of dying in the arena at the claws of wild animals (*Rom.* 4; 5.2). Therefore, *Eph., Magn., Trall.,* and *Rom.* were written in Smyrna, *Philad., Smyrn.,* and *Polyc.* in Troas.
I. Transmission of the Letters: We no longer have the first collections in their original form, but the three recensions and collections that we do have go back to the 4th c.

The so-called longer recension includes, in addition to the seven listed by Eusebius (but which differ in wording from the citations in him and early fathers), six more: a petition addressed to I. by Maria of Cassobola, followed by I.'s answer (*Mar.*), letters from I. to the communities in Tarsus, Philippi, and Antioch, and one to Deacon Hero of Antioch.

In the 17th c. shorter, simpler versions of the seven letters named by Eusebius were discovered, which are closer in wording to the citations from I. by early fathers; this body of seven is therefore regarded as original. Since the longer recension is found with the letters not mentioned by Eusebius, the shorter body of seven must have been revised by the same person who composed the other six forgeries collected under I.'s name. There is much to suggest that this writer was the compiler of the *Const. App.* (→ *Apostolic Constitutions*), but this connection is not certain.

The other letters in the *recensio longior*, but without *Phil.*, are attached to the shorter recension of the letters with addressees in Asia Minor; *Rom.*, which was inserted into the *Martyrium Ignatii Antiocheni* (*M. Ign. Ant.*) (*CPG* 1036) completes the collection. A considerably shorter Syr., monastically motivated recension from the 4th c. consists of excerpts from *Eph., Rom.,* and *Polyc.* Zahn and Lightfoot proved that in the mixed collection of letters only the seven named by Eusebius go back to I. The single Gr. witness to this recension of the seven with addressees in Asia Minor is *Cod. Florent. Laur. plut.* 57.7 (G, 11th c.); *Rom.*, which is lacking in this ms., the end of which is defective, is best preserved in the *M. Ign. Ant.* of *Cod. Bibl. Parisinus* 1451 (G¹, 10th c.). For this reason the careful and complete Lat. translation (L, 13th c.) of the *collectio mixta* is very valuable; also important are the sometimes only fragmentary translations into Syriac, Armenian, Arabic, and Coptic.
II. Authenticity of the Letters: Since the discovery of the *Corpus Ignatianum* and the publication of the *editio longior* (Lat. 1498, without the petition from Maria of Cassobola, Lat. 1536, Gr. 1557) doubts about the origin and authenticity of the letters have characterized Ignatian scholarship. This skepticism has been fed, down to our day, by the complicated textual history, in which textual criticism was soon interwoven with theol. questions and was affected or sometimes even guided by confessional choices, and which increasingly became a vehicle for a literary criticism not always free of presuppositions regard-

ing content. Also working against the originality and authenticity of the body of seven from the mixed collection were the self-portrait of the author, the situation (specific descriptions of opponents; the pyramidal triad of offices, and their theol. justification), the methodical composition, and, in general, the entire character of the letters, as well the distinctive picture in *Rom.*, tensions between Polycarp *ep.* 9 and 13, linguistic references, e.g., to → Hermas, *Martyrium Polycarpi* (*M. Polyc.*, → Marcion, author of the *Martyrdom of Polycarp*), Noetus, and the theol. terminology which is from a later time and close to gnosticism; furthermore, the fact that *Smyrn.* does not mention Polycarp and that Polycarp in his letter does not depict himself as a (monarchical) *episkopos*. With the acceptance of the letters as forgeries goes the late dating.

(Acc. to Weijenborg preference should be given to the long version, compiled by → Evagrius Pont. in the mid-4th c., from which the half way version arose through abridgment, probably at the end of the 4th c.; no collection comes from I. himself. Acc. to Rius-Camps, I., who did not know Polycarp of Smyrna and was not *episkopos* of Antioch but rather *episkopos* of the Syr. church [*Rom.* 2.2], composed *Magn.*, *Trall.*, *Eph.*, and *Rom.* between 80 and 100. In the mid-3rd c. someone, presumably the bishop of Philadelphia, who did not know of *Rom.*, forged the letters from Troas and edited *Magn.*, *Trall.*, and *Eph.* Acc. to Joly, someone, presumably Marcion of Smyrna, shortly after the martyrdom of Polycarp, between 165 and 168, wrote the seven letters under the pseudonym I., finding the name in Polycarp [*ep.* 13], I. never existed.)

Later, the references in Polycarp [*ep.* 9 and 13] to I. were interpreted as the work of the same forger, or else Polycarp, *ep.*, was dated to the middle of the 2nd c. But the hypothesis of authenticity is in many respects preferable because the extent and range of the consequences for the history of the church and of theology seem clearly slighter if the authenticity of the letters is accepted than if pseudepigraphy or simply a later date are the option (because of Polycarp, *ep.*, whose writing he will not put before 140/150, Heussi dates the half-way collection to the middle of the 2nd c.; Kraft locates I.'s martyrdom under Hadrian and therefore dates the letters to this later time). Authenticity accepted, the seven letters are the only reliable prosopographical source. If, in addition, we trust what Eusebius says in his chronicle (GCS 20:216) and in *h.e.* 3.22 about I.'s martyrdom, the seven letters give important insights into the history of the church and of theology at the beginning of

the 2nd c., espec. in Asia Minor, but also in Antioch and Rome.

III. Contents of the Seven Letters: Gratitude for love shown, exhortation to unity in the community, and rejection of erroneous teaching mark the five letters to communities in Asia Minor. The monarchic constitution of the community ensures unity and orthodoxy. At the news of the end of the pogrom in Antioch, which reaches I. in Troas, he asks in gratitude that messengers be sent to his home community. He sends Polycarp instructions on the conduct of his office. *Rom.* stands apart. Here I. makes himself known to a community he praises highly (*Rom.*, praescr.) and asks, among other things, that it not hinder his following of Christ in martyrdom.

IV. Basic Theological Ideas: A correct understanding of Jesus Christ, martyrdom imminent and longed for (*Rom.*), and ecclesial unity (*henōsis*) are the main themes. It is in light of these that the writer speaks of conditions for the life and faith of the communities and espec. their endangerment by other Christians, as well as the organization of the communities under a hierarchic triad of offices. Christology, which takes on its character in functional connection with these factual questions, marks I.'s entire theological thought and its soteriological scope. The salvific significance of Jesus, whose divinity (*Eph.* 7.2; 19.3; 20.3) but also distinction from (and subordination to) God the Father I. professes (*Eph.* 3.2; *Magn.* 2; 13.2; *Trall.* 3.1; *Philad.* 7.2; *Smyrn.* 8.1), has its basis in his humanity (*alēthōs*). The Christ event in its entirety is relevant to salvation, but the emphasis is laid on the passion as soteriological when I. interprets his own martyrdom. In opposition to the soteriological deficiencies of (probably) docetist christologies, I., using Johannine terminology, stresses the incarnation of the preexistent divine Logos. In his profession of the salvific importance of the birth, suffering, and resurrection of Christ I. is countering Jewish tendencies which, by insisting on the high place and salvific importance of scripture (*Philad.* 8; *Magn.* 8) and tradition, remove Christ as center of faith and Chr. life. Since both forms of opposition affect unity in faith, they blend together in I.'s polemic. For this reason, too, the position of these adversaries is hardly to be identified with theologies combated elsewhere. The hierarchical triad of offices (*episkopos*, *presbyteroi*, *diakonoi*) with their important competences and functions, which serves the unity of the community in faith, worship, and action under the leadership of the monarchical *episkopos*, has its roots in structures of the economy of salvation, and is justified by the comparison with

God, Jesus Christ, and the apostolic college, appears to be an existing but not uncontroversial institution (in Syria and Asia Minor). For this reason and because the genesis as well as the modes of participation and succession in this structure that is centered on a single *episkopos* are not mentioned, I.'s outline of it may be an anticipation, motivated by theology and the situation, of a stage in the history of the church that was only beginning. *Rom.* does not presuppose a monarchical *episkopos* in the Roman community; nor does Polycarp, *ep.*, attest to its existence.

W: *ep. vii genuinae*, J. A. Fischer, SUC 1 (Munich, ⁹1986), 109-225 [text/German trans.]. — P. T. Camelot (Paris, ²1969) [text/French trans.]. — J. B. Lightfoot (London, ²1889 = Grand Rapids, Mich., 1984) [text/English trans.]. — A. Lindemann, H. Paulsen (Tübingen, 1992), 176-241 [text/German trans.]. — *ep. interpolatae et ep. suppositiciae*, F. X. Funk, F. Diekamp (Tübingen, ²1906), 83-268. — *additional inauthentic works*, CPG 1028-1030; 1035.
L: C. P. H. Bammel, Problems: JThS NS 33 (1982) 62-97. — U. Bleyenberg, "in einem Leib seiner Kirche": TThZ 104 (1995) 106-124. — C. T. Brown, The Gospel and I. (New York, 1999). — N. Collmar, I.: BBKL 2:1251-1255. — J. Calloud, Les lettres d'I.: de la langue à la lettre: Les lettres dans la Bible et dans la littérature (Paris, 1999), 209-231. — M. D. Goulder, "Docetists": VigChr 53 (1999) 16-30. — K. Heussi, Petrustradition (Tübingen, 1955). — D. L. Hoffman, I. and Early Anti-Docetic Realism in Eucharist: FiHi 30 (1998) 74-88. — R. M. Hübner, Noët: MThZ 40 (1989) 279-312. — idem, Thesen zur Echtheit u. Datierung der sieben Briefe des I.: ZAC 1 (1997) 44-72. — R. Joly, Le dossier (Brussels, 1979). — H. Kraft, Kirchenväter 5 (Munich, 1966). — A. Lindemann, Antwort: ZAC 1 (1997) 185-194. — H. E. Lona, ΣΑΡΞ: ZKTh 108 (1986) 383-408. — C. Munier, Où en est la question d'Ignace d'Antioche: ANRW II 27/1 (1992) 359-484. — K.-W. Niebuhr, "Judentum" u. "Christentum" bei Paulus und I.: ZNW 85 (1994) 218-233. — H. Paulsen, Studien (Göttingen, 1978). — idem, Briefe des I. (Tübingen, 1985). — J. Rius-Camps, Authentic Letters (Rome, 1979). — idem, Indicios de una redacción muy temprana de las cartas auténticas de Ignacio (ca. 70-90 d. C.): Aug. 34 (1995) 199-214. — W. R. Schoedel, I. (Munich, 1990). — idem, Polycarp of Smyrna and I.: ANRW II 27/1 (1992) 272-358. — G. Schöllgen, Monepiskopat: ZNW 77 (1986) 146-151. — idem, Ignatianen: ZAC 2 (1998) 16-25. — R. Staats, Begründung des Romprimats: ZThK 73 (1976) 461-470. — C. Trevett, Ignatius of Antioch (Lewiston, N.Y., 1992). — C. Uhrig, Einheit (Altenberge, 1988). — L. Wehr, Arznei (Münster, 1987). — R. Weijenborg, Les lettres (Leiden, 1969). — T. Zahn, I. (Gotha, 1873).

F. R. PROSTMEIER

Ildephonsus of Toledo

I., b. ca. 607, a monk and then abbot of the monastery of Agalí near Toledo, took part in Councils VIII (653) and IX (655) of Toledo. From 657 to his death (667) he was successor of Eugene as bishop of Toledo; it is noteworthy that during his time in office no synod was held.

I. organized his writings in four groups. The first includes theol. works; to the second belongs a *Liber epistolarum*. The third group contains *Missae*, *Hymni*, and *Sermones*, and the fourth *Epitaphia* and *Epigrammata* (Julian, *vita Ildef.*, PL 96:44A). Only the writings of the first group have been preserved. In them I. shows himself to be an outstanding representative of Span. theology during its flowering in the 7th c.; all the more to be lamented, then, are the great losses, since they hinder any appreciation of his work as a whole.

Closely connected with the decision of Toledo X, on Dec. 18, 656, to establish a Marian feast is I.'s treatise *De virginitate perpetua beatae Mariae* (*virg.*) in which he defends the church's mariology against the views of heretics Jovinian and Helvidius, which Jerome and Augustine had opposed in their day, and of the Jews. I. was the most important mariologist of the Visigothic church; even the christological statements of Toledo XI (675) owe their mariological connections to I. It seems reasonable, therefore, but hardly justified, to see in him the author also of some *Orationes de B. Maria Virgine* in the *Orationale Visigothicum* and of a *Sermo in diem S. Mariae*.

In addition, I. dealt with other important theol. subjects. In the treatise *De cognitione baptismi* (*bapt.*), which is based on an earlier work of → Justinian of Valencia, he describes the way human beings travel to the grace of a rebirth in which they are consecrated to God. The moral and ascetical treatise *De itinere deserti* (*itin.*) interprets the wandering of the Israelite people in the wilderness in order to show how, after baptism (the crossing of the Red Sea), human beings pass through the wilderness of earthly life to eternal life (the promised land). In his work *De virorum illustrium scriptis* I. intended to continue Chr. literary history after the model of → Jerome, → Gennadius, and → Isidore of Seville, but his accomplishment fell short of those of his predecessors. In his presentation I. gives a one-sided preference to the bishops of Toledo and tries in this way to reinforce the status of the see of Toledo, which had become the metropolitan see of the Carthaginian province only in 610. In general, with one exception he describes only individuals who were born in Spain and most of whom left no writings behind. In I.'s view it was the services of these *viri illustres* to the church that was the most important thing.

A connection is occasionally made between I. and

the *Homiliae Toletanae*, but the question of authorship is still an open one.

W: PL 96:51-330. — *virg., bapt., itin.*, V. Blanco García, J. Campos (Madrid, 1971).
L: A. Braegelmann, The Life and Writings of Saint I. (Washington, 1942). — J. M. Canal, San I. Historia y Leyenda: EphMar 17 (1967) 437-462. — G. von Dzialowski, Isidor und I. als Literarhistoriker (Münster, 1898). — J. Fontaine, El »De viris illustribus« de S. I.: AnTol 3 (1970) 59-96. — B. de Gaiffier, Les Vies de S. I.: AnBoll 94 (1976) 235-244. — I. Lobo, Notas histórico-criticas entorno al´ "De cognitione baptismi" de S. I.: RET 27 (1967) 139-158. — J. Madoz, San I. (Madrid, 1943). — R. Maloy, The Sermonary of St. I. of Toledo, 2 vols. (New York, 1971). — J. Orlandis, D. Ramos-Lisson, Die Synoden auf der Iberischen Halbinsel (Paderborn, 1981). — A. C. Vega, De Patrología española. San I.: BRAH 165 (1969) 35-107.

E. REICHERT

Innocent of Maronia

I., bishop of Maronia, was one of the orthodox participants in the conference on the faith held in Constantinople in 552 between the orthodox and the Severians. From him we have a comprehensive report on the conference, in a Lat. translation and in the form of a letter (*ep. ad Thomam presbyterum Thessalonicensem de collatione cum Severianis habita*), which may have been written for the episcopal embassy sent to the bishop of Rome by Emperor Justinian. A second work of I., likewise preserved in Lat., was probably also taken to Rome by the ambassadors: *De his qui unum ex trinitate vel unam subsistentiam seu personam dominum nostrum Iesum Christum dubitant confiteri*, a treatise on events after the condemnation of Nestorius and on the theopaschite question.

W: *ep.*, ACO 4, 2, 169-184. — *de his*, ACO 4, 2, 68-74.
L: H. G. Beck, Kirche u. theol. Lit. (Munich, 1959), 376. — A. Grillmeier, Jesus der Christus 2/2 (Freiburg i.Br., 1984), 244-259, 355, 433f. (English, Christ in Christian Tradition, vol. 2/2 [London, 1995]). — J. Speigel, Das Religionsgespräch: AHC 16 (1984) 264-285.

B. WINDAU

Innocent I of Rome

I., bishop of Rome from Dec. 21, 402 to March 12, 417, was probably the son of his predecessor → Anastasius I. He endeavored to expand the position of the Roman see and to impose the primacy on the entire church. In a letter to Bishops Decentius of Gubbio, Victricius of Rouen, and Exuperius of Toulouse, he demanded that *causae maiores* be handled and decided in Rome. He therefore claimed

supreme teaching authority in the struggle against heretics. For the same reason he felt called upon to confirm the decisions of the two African synods against Pelagius and Caelestius. In church politics he played an active part in establishing the papal vicariate of Thessalonica, thus strengthening the rights of the metropolitan there against the influence of Constantinople. As a result Illyria became more closely tied to Rome. I. had no success in his intervention on behalf of the deposed → John Chrys.; this led to a temporary break with the patriarch of Constantinople.

Thirty-six letters of I. have been preserved, which reflect the state of church teaching. He took a position on all questions raised: validity of heretical baptism (*ep.* 2); penance and reconciliation (*ep.* 6; 25); determination of the canon of scripture and the apocrypha (*ep.* 13). *Ep.* 29 is important for knowledge of the primatial consciousness, since in it I. intervenes in the Pelagian controversy (29.1 says of the Roman see: "from which the episcopate itself and the entire authority associated with it have proceeded"). The letters show a self-aware and politically active bishop.

W: PL 20.463-638. — LP 1:220-224. — *Coll. Avellana*, O. Guenther, CSEL 35:92-98. — R. Cabié, La lettre du pape I. à Décentius de Gubbio (Leuven/Louvain, 1973) [text/French trans./comm.]. — S. Wenzlowsky, Die Briefe der Päpste 3, BKV¹.7-223 [German trans.].
L: W. Marschall, Karthago u. Rom (Stuttgart, 1971). — O. Wermelinger, Rom u. Pelagius (Stuttgart, 1975), 116-133.

W. GEERLINGS

Instantius

I., a bishop (in Lusitania?), belonged to Priscillian's inner circle. He may have presented his *Liber de fide et apocryphis* (*tract.* 3) to the antipriscillianist Synod of Saragossa (380). After his condemnation he sought to justify himself with his *Liber ad Damasum episcopum* (*tract.* 2), but only with the help of the emperor did he regain his episcopal see. With his *Liber apologeticus* (*tract.* 1) he tried in vain to influence the Synod of Bordeaux (384), which again accused him and finally exiled him.

In addition to these three treatises, seven homilies and a prayer may be mentioned: *Tractatus paschae* (*tract.* 4), *Tractatus genesis* (*tract.* 5), *Tractatus exodi* (*tract.* 6), *Tractatus psalmi I* (*tract.* 7), *Tractatus Psalmi III* (*tract.* 8), *Tractatus Psalmi XIV* (*tract.* 9), *Tractatus Psalmi LIX* (*tract.* 10), *Benedictio super fideles* (*tract.* 11).

The anonymously transmitted treatises have been

claimed not only for I. but also for → Priscillian or some other of his disciples.

W: G. Schepß, CSEL 18.
L: H. Chadwick, Priscillian (Oxford, 1976).

E. REICHERT

Interpretatio gnoseos

The Interpretation of Knowledge (int. gnos.) is the title of a badly damaged work in the Copt. Nag Hammadi Library (NHC 11, 1). It deals chiefly with the teaching and passion of Christ, with special attention to the unity of the church. At the center of theol. interest is the interpretation of Mt as well as the Body of Christ ecclesiology of the Pauline letters. Int. gnos. shows parallels with Valentinian gnosis (→ Evangelium veritatis) and the gnostic teaching on Sophia. The work's christology is strongly docetist in tendency; the suffering of Christ is regarded as merely external; the material world with its emotions is entirely downgraded. Int. gnos. probably originated toward the end of the 2nd c. or at the beginning of the 3rd in Alexandrian Egypt.

W: C. W. Hedrick, NHC 11-13 (Leiden, 1990), 21-88 [Coptic text/French trans./comm.]. — NHL 472-480 [English trans.].
L: K. Koschorke, Gnostische Gemeindeordnung: ZThK 76 (1979) 30-60.

P. BRUNS

Invective

Invective, the genre of defamatory writing already documented in both the prose and poetry of Gr. and Roman classical literature, is directed in Chr. literature no longer only against political or personal enemies who are to be belittled by accusations (e.g., of sexual faults, laziness, stupidity, etc.) but also and espec. against religious adversaries (pagans, heretics). Consequently, elements of invective are to be found in every kind of polemical writing (e.g., Gregory Naz.'s speeches against Julian; Prudentius, c. Symm., in a clash with the poetic invectives of Claudian) but with special frequency in apologiae (e.g., Tatian, orat.) and antiheretical works (e.g., those of Jerome). The so-called Carmen contra paganos (adversus Nicomachum), written 393/394, attacks the pagan conception of the gods in 122 hexameters and disparages Nicomachus, a committed pagan (the man was Virius Nicomachus Flavianus), who had died shortly before. The Carmen ad quendam senatorem, written possibly by the same author but

handed down among the works of Cyprian, shows vividly in eighty-five hexameters how the addressee, a former consul, is making himself an object of ridicule by his renewed practice of pagan cults; it urges him to return to Christianity. Many elements of an invective kind likewise mark the Carmen adversus Marcionitas of Ps.-Tertullian (five books; first half of 5th c.), which accuses heretics of blindness (1.115, etc.), madness (1.71, etc.), and even criminality (e.g., 3.286).

W: carm. c. pag., PLS 1:780-784. — D. R. Shakleton Bailey, Anthologia Latina 1/1 (Stuttgart, 1982, 17-23). — carm. ad senat., R. Peiper, CSEL 23:227-230. — A. Riese, Anthologia Latina 1/2 (Leipzig, ²1906), 163-166. — carm. adv. Marc., K. Pollmann (Göttingen, 1991) [text/German trans./comm.]. — R. Willems, CCL 2:1417-1454.
L: C. J. Classen, Satire, the Elusive Genre: SO 63 (1988) 95-121. — S. Koster, Die I. in der griech. und röm. Literatur (Meisenheim, 1980). — I. Opelt, Hieronymus' Streitschriften (Heidelberg, 1973). — eadem, Die lat. Schimpfwörter (Heidelberg, 1965). — eadem, Die Polemik in der chr. Literatur von Tertullian bis Augustinus (Heidelberg, 1980). — W. Süss, Der Heilige Hieronymus und die Formen seiner Polemik: Gießener Beitr. zur deutschen Philologie 60 (1938) 217-229. — D. S. Wiesen, St. Jerome as a Satirist (Ithaca, 1964).

D. WEBER

Ioca monachorum

Ioca monachorum is a collective name for a group of anonymous texts, probably based on a Gr. original, in the genre of → Quaestiones et responsiones. Among the texts of monastic origin that were popular in the Middle Ages are (1) Altercatio Adriani et Epicteti (alterc.; 6th/7th c.); three untitled works whose incipits are (2) Quod tempore adnunciavit Gabrihel archangelus (quod tempore), (3) Quid primo ex Deo processit? (quid primo), and (4) De principio mundi usque ad diluvium quot anni fuerunt? (de princ.); (5) Ioca monachorum (ioc.); (6) Enigmata interrogativa (enig.); (7) Interrogationes quedam mirabiles (interrog.); (8) Chronica S. Gironimi presbyteri, with its first part De plasmationem Adam (cron./de plasm.) (7th/8th c.). These texts were widely circulated throughout Europe in various recensions.

W: alterc., de princ., enig., interrog., quid primo, W. Suchier (Tübingen, 1955) [text/comm.]. — chron. /de plasm., C. Munier: RBen 104 (1994) 106-122 [text/comm.]. — quod tempore, G. Baesecke (Halle, 1933), 7f. [text]. — ioc., E. A. Lowe (London, 1920), 2:5-7[text].
L: F. Brunhölzl, Geschichte 1 (Munich, 1975), 147f., 527f. — H. Leclercq, Joca monachorum: DACL 7:2569-2572.

M. SKEB, OSB

Irenaeus of Harpasus

I. was the Monophysite bishop of Harpasus (Caria) ca. 500. A fragment of a work against the Council of Chalcedon is preserved in the *Doctrina Patrum*.

W: Doctrina Patrum, ed. F. Diekamp (Münster, 1981 = 1907), 312 [text].
L: E. Honigmann, Évêques et évêchés (Leuven/Louvain, 1951), 124f.

G. RÖWEKAMP

Irenaeus of Lyons

I. **Life:** Born in Asia Minor in the first half of the 2nd c., I. in his early youth (*haer*. 3.3.4) saw the very elderly Bishop Polycarp of Smyrna (d. 156). After settling in the western part of the empire, probably because of some eccles. commission, and now a presbyter of the Lyons community, ca. 177 he traveled to Rome to Bishop Eleutherus (ca. 174-189) with a letter of recommendation regarding imprisoned Christians of Vienne and Lyons; the letter urged a more tolerant attitude to the Montanists. After his return I. became successor to Bishop Pothinus of Lyons, who had died a martyr's death under Marcus Aurelius (161-180) along with the Christians mentioned above. During his episcopate I. seems to have made it his duty to impress Christianity not only on the members of his Greek-speaking community but also on the native Celts, although acc. to *haer*. 1, *praef*. 3, he spent most of his time struggling with their "barbarian dialect." Despite his own complete agreement with Roman practice, during the controversy over the date of Easter, I. wrote a letter to Roman Bishop → Victor I in which he asked emphatically for a more conciliatory attitude toward the Quartodecimans (located chiefly in Asia Minor→) and in this way declared peace between the local churches to be the main priority. In other areas, too, he clearly acted as a conciliator and thus honored his name in the view of Eusebius, *h.e.* 5.24.18, who calls him a true "peacemaker" (*eirēnopoios*). I. died probably ca. 200 in unknown circumstances. The concrete information given first in Jerome, *in Is*. 17.64.4f., lacks any historical basis.

II. **Works:** I.'s principal work is the *Examination and Refutation of Falsely Named "Knowledge"* (*Elegchos kai anatropē tēs pseudōnymou gnōseōs*), which is usually called by its short Lat. name *Adversus haereses* (*haer*.) (thus Jerome, *vir. ill.* 35, following Eusebius, *h.e.* 2.13.5; etc.). The Gr. original has been preserved in only fragmentary form. Most of these fragments are found in citations by later eccles. writers, espec.

Hippolytus, Eusebius, Epiphanius, and John Damascene; large parts of book 5 are found in a Jena papyrus. The work has come down complete only in a very literal Lat. translation that goes back to the 4th c.; there are also Arm. and Syr. fragments.

The only reference point for dating the work is the mention of the current Roman bishop, Eleutherus, in *haer*. 3.3.3, during whose episcopate (ca. 174-189) the work seems to have been written, with several starts, over a number of years. Because of the danger, which I. felt to be acute, of a confusion of gnosis with Christianity, he attacks the gnostics in this work. In the two stages of examination (*elegchos/detectio*) by means of a careful, evaluative description and of active refutation (*anatropē/eversio*) he demonstrates the untenableness of this teaching to an unidentified addressee who seems likewise to have been leader of a community (see 1 *praef*. 2). He thus provides a tool for turning the danger away. Information on I.'s method is given both in the *praefationes* of the individual books (1 *praef*. serves also as a preface to the entire work) and in transitional remarks that serve to subdivide the text (e.g., 1.9.5; 1.11.1; etc.).

In accordance with his plan, in book 1 I. gives an explanation of gnostic teaching and its difficult mythology, referring to the system developed by → Ptolemy, which was in turn a branch (*apanthisma*, 1 *praef*. 2) of the school of → Valentinus (1-9). In I.'s view, Christianity shows itself clearly superior by reason of its worldwide unity and uniformity (10) and precisely in this respect stands in contrast to the many varieties of gnosis and to the contradictions, immanent to the system, that are already visible within the individual branches; these contradictions are then described in greater detail for the Valentinian school (11-22). At the end of the description, I. surveys the rise of gnosis; this survey goes beyond the early period proper and for reasons that cannot be accurately determined includes nongnostic groups such as the Ebionites and Nicolaites (23.1–31.2). Even though the very description of this absurd system already amounts to its *eversio*, I. turns in what follows, i.e., from book 2 on, to its refutation (31.3f.).

The refutation takes the form of a serial discussion of Valentinian doctrines that is only roughly structured and contains many repetitions because of the need of many returns to the material in book 1. The doctrines refuted are those of the Pleroma and the creator (1-11), the aeons (12-19), the recurring speculation about numbers (20-28), and the ideas of the last things and the demiurge (29f.). Although the other heretics, too, are thereby refuted (31.1), chs. 31-35 contain supplementary material on the other gnostic schools. This *eversio*, which takes the form chiefly of arguments from reason and logic, is followed by a far more appropriate refutation, the basis of which is the positive proof (*probatio = apodeixis*) from sacred scripture (35.4).

After detailed exposition of the nature of the church as the place of truth, a nature based on the principles of apostolicity and succession (3.1-5), the positive proof is laid down in the remaining chapters of book 3 and in books 4 and 5. The focal points of theol. content here are the doctrines of the one true God and his Christ (book 3), the unity of the divine *oikonomia* (book 4), and the redemption of the human creature in its *sarx* (book 5; see below).

In his discussion of gnosis I. uses caricature, which is espec. evident in book 1, i.e, in the expository part of the work where he describes the complicated gnostic mythology. The opposite of these extravagant constructs is in each case the unified, unmistakable teaching of the church. In his exposition I. displays a comprehensive and detailed knowledge of gnostic groups and their ideas; in fact he seems often to want to prove precisely that he has this knowledge. He also shows himself to have a detailed familiarity with the scriptures of both testaments and of the church's tradition, and he is at ease with the ranking scholarship of his time. Key terms in I.'s theology, such as *oikonomia* and *anakephalaiōsis* (see below), had their origin in Gr. grammar and rhetoric; his familiarity with pagan poetry is clear when, e.g., a Homeric cento is used to illustrate the gnostic way of interpreting scripture (1.9.4).

There is no agreed answer to the question of I.'s sources. In addition to → Polycarp, → Papias, → Ignatius, → Clement of Rome, and → Justin Martyr, whom I. demonstrably uses, we must think here also of → Theophilus of Antioch. The only thing certain is that for all his originality I. was able to rely at many points on the work of predecessors, espec. since *haer.* was not the first antignostic work ever written but is only the oldest one preserved. Clear, on the other hand, is the immense influence that the *haer.* had, in many ways, on numerous early church writers such as → Clement Alex., → Athanasius, and → Augustine.

After *haer.* had for a long time been the only complete known work of I., in 1904, in a 13th c. ms., an Arm. translation was discovered of what had previously been known only by its title (Eus., *h.e.* 5.26): the *Demonstration of the Apostolic Preaching (Epideixis tou apostolikou kērygmatos)* (*epid.*). The addressee of the work is an otherwise unknown Marcian, probably a baptized Christian, who is to be informed in "a few sentences" (99) about the "preaching of the truth" (1); that is, in principle, about what I. has already expounded in much greater detail in (the therefore earlier) *haer.* In fact, all the theol. affirmations of *epid.* are already in *haer.*, espec. in books 3-5 (this is the weightiest argument, along with stylistic similarities, for the attribution of the work to I.). The degree of abridgment, however, does not always show the same proportions as the materials in the principal work. In a very simple structure, I. follows the order given to him in the *oikonomia* or divine plan of salvation (see below); espec. beginning in ch. 43 he uses OT texts to ensure the christological content of the NT. In so doing, he very likely follows older models that can no longer be ascertained with certainty. It is likewise not possible to determine unequivocally the genre of the *epid.*: "catechesis" or "apologia"? But, given the almost complete lack of polemic elements, it should rather be thought of as a catechetical work.

Only fragments (*fr.*) or even just the titles of other works have been preserved. Thus we have extended passages of the above-mentioned letter to Victor I (*ep. Vict.*) on the occasion of the Easter controversy (Eus., *h.e.* 5.23.3; 5.24.12-17), as well as a short Syr. piece of a "Letter to the Alexandrians" that belongs in the same context. From the struggle against gnosticism come (Eus., *h.e.* 5.20.4-8) parts of a letter addressed to a Roman presbyter Florinus who was leaning toward the teaching of Valentinus, and dealing with *The Absolute Rule (of God)* or that God is not the author of evil. To the same subject area belongs a letter known only by its title and addressed to a certain Blastus, as well as a Syr. fragment addressed to Victor I, warning him against Florinus. The latter broke away from the church, occasioning a treatise (*spoudasma*) of I. titled *On the Number Eight*, whose closing words, preserved by Eusebius (5.20.2), are of interest for the history of books in antiquity. We know only the titles of a treatise "against the Greeks," *On Knowledge*, and of a book of "addresses on various subjects" (Eus., *h.e.* 5.26), probably a collection of sermons, which would then be the oldest known to us.

It is uncertain whether I. ever wrote the work against Marcion that is promised in *haer.* 1.27.4 and 3.12.12; the same holds for his authorship of the fragments, transmitted in Maximus the Confessor (PG 91:276) and in a miscellaneous ms. of Paris, of a work *On the Faith* addressed to Deacon Demetrius of Vienne. Furthermore, the words in which Jerome (*vir. ill.* 9) seems to refer to a commentary on Rev are to be referred rather to the eschat. remarks in *haer.* 5.

Certainly not from I. are works *On the Nature of the Universe* and *On the Holy Trinity*, short sentences of which are cited in the *Sacra Parallela*. Other scattered fragments in Greek, Syriac, and Armenian are either very probably or certainly not authentic. The so-called Pfaff Fragments, discovered in the 18th c. by C. M. Pfaff, were unmasked as forgeries of the "discoverer."

III. Basic Lines of Thought: The theol. thought of I., which hardly differs in its dogmatic principles from that of others in the 2nd c., is wholly determined by the struggle against gnosticism or, in other words, by the essential difference between this heresy and the teaching of Christianity. It is precisely in the establishment of the foundations needed for this struggle that I. achieves his greatest originality and his long-term importance for subsequent theology.

So unshakably clear is the truth of the Chr. faith to I. that he can have only a complete lack of appreciation for gnostic teaching and espec. its mythology: reason already shows its foolishness. In addition, there are the sacred scriptures of the OT and NT, the firm canonical parameters of which I. already knows; these writings form a complete and fully sufficient body of truth which heretics try mistakenly to abridge or expand. The proof from authentic tradition is a third criterion of truth for I., who, like the church of his age, already knows of periods within Chr. history, speaks of "intermediate times" (*haer.* 3.4.3), and consequently thinks of himself as belonging to a late period. This truth was given in the beginning to the apostles and has continued in a direct line in the churches they founded, among which—at least for a leader of Gallic Christians—the church of Rome has a special rank as *primus inter pares* (*haer.* 3.3.2). These three pillars—tradition, sacred scripture, and rational insight or, rather, faith—constitute a realm of truth that does not exist as such but is available only in the pillars themselves; this realm of truth I. calls *kanōn tēs alētheias* (*regula veritatis*, canon of truth).

A plan of salvation for human beings (the divine *oikonomia*) thus becomes discernible. That which the gnostics with their dualist vision think they see as a chaos, hostile to God and created by a demiurge, proves to be something entirely opposite: an order of salvation, established by the one God and creator and developing gradually with an irresistible dynamism; in this order the incarnation of Jesus Christ matches the disobedience of Adam with an *anakephalaiōsis* (*recapitulatio*), a "re-establishment" starting at the decisive point. Through the incarnation and the sending of the Spirit, human beings, who are still on the journey and only conditionally capable of salvation, are brought closer to their God and led to their goal, the resurrection of body, soul, *pneuma*, that is, to participation in the divine Spirit.

I. opts for a moderate chiliasm, which he regards as orthodox, even while acknowledging the orthodoxy of nonchiliasts, and he recognizes a stay of the soul in the lower world until the definitive, complete resurrection.

In practical questions such as episcopal authority, the organization of the church, and a moral way of life, his thought is clearly influenced by ideas of order prevalent in the Roman worldwide empire.

W: PG 7:433-1118. — *haer.*, A. Rousseau, L. Doutreleau, B. Hemmerdinger, C. Mercier, SC 263f., 293f., 210f., 100, 152f.). — *haer.* 4f., E. Ter-Minassiantz (Leipzig, 1910) [Armenian text]. — H. Lietzmann, Der Jenaer I.-Pap.: NGWG. PH 1912:292-320 [text/Latin trans./comm.]. — II. Jordan, Arm. Frgm. (Leipzig, 1913) [text/German trans./comm.]. — A. Strobel, Ein Katenenfrgm. mit *haer.* 5.24.2f.. ZKG 68 (1957) 139-143 [text/comm.]. — M. Richard, B. Hemmerdinger, Trois nouveaux fragments grecs (*haer.*): ZNW 53 (1962) 252-255 [text/comm.]. — C. Renoux, Nouveaux fragments arméniens (*haer.*, *epid.*), PO 39/1 [text/Latin trans./comm.]. — A. de Santos Otero, Dos capítulos inéditos del original griego de haer.: EM 41 (1973) 479-489 [text/comm.]. — *haer.*, *epid.*, E. Klebba, S. Weber, BKV² 3f. [German trans.]. — *epid.*, *haer.* 1-4, N. Brox, FC 8/1-4. — *haer.*, *epid.*, *fr.*, E. Bellini (Milan, 1981) [Italian trans./comm.]. — *haer.*, A. Rousseau (Paris, ²1985) [French trans.]. — *haer.* (*arm.*), L. Froidevaux, G. Bayan: ROC 9 (1933/34) 315-377; 10 (1935/36) 47-169, 285-340 [French trans.]. — *haer.* 5, A. Orbe (Madrid, 1985/87) [comm.] — *epid.*, J. Barthoulot, S. Voicou, A. G. Hamman (Paris, 1977) [French trans./comm.]. — E. Peretto (Rome, 1981) [Italian trans.]. — J. N. Sparks (Brookline, Mass., 1987) [English trans.]. — E. Romero Pose (Madrid, 1992) [Spanish trans.]. — A. Rousseau, SC 406. — J. P. Smith (Westminster, N.Y., 1952) [English trans./comm.]. — K. Ter-Mekerttschian, E. Ter-Minassiantz (Leipzig, 1907) [text/German trans.]. — K. Ter-Mekerttschian, S. G. Wilson, J. Barthoulot, J. Tixeront, PO 12/5 [text/French, English trans./comm.]. — *fr.*, C. Martin, I. et son correspondant le diacre Démètre de Vienne: RHE 38 (1942) 143-152 [text/comm.]. — M. Richard, Le traité d'I. au Diacre Démétrius: FS F. Dölger (Heidelberg, 1966), 431-440 [text/comm.].

L: *Additional aids*: B. Reynders, Lexique comparé (*haer.*), CSCO 141/2. — idem, Vocabulaire de la *epid.* et des *fr.* (Chevetogne, 1958).
B. Aland, Fides u. Subiectio: FS C. Andresen (Göttingen, 1969), 9-28. — A. d'Alès, La doctrine eucharistique d'I.: RSR 13 (1923) 24-46. — Y. de Andia, Homo vivens (Paris, 1986). — eadem, I., théologien de l'unité: NRTh 109 (1987) 31-48. — eadem, L'actualité d'I.: BStSul 13 (1987), 107-120. — A. N. Andritsopoulos, The Doctrine of Recapitulation, Diss. (Michigan, 1970). — P. Bacq, De l'ancienne à la nouvelle alliance selon I. (Paris, 1987). — D. L. Balás, Use and Interpretation of Paul in haer.: SecCen 9 (1992) 27-39. — M. Balwierz, The Holy Spirit and the Church (Rome, 1980). — A. Bengsch, Heilsgeschichte u. Heilswissen (Leipzig, 1957). — A. Benoît, I. (Paris, 1960). — G. Bentivegna,

Economia di salvezza e creazione (Rome, 1973). — R. Berthouzoz, Liberté et grâce (Fribourg, Switzerland, 1980). — J. Birrer, Der Mensch als Medium u. Adressat der Schöpfungsoffenbarung (Bern, 1989). — G. N. Bonwetsch, Die Theologie des I. (Gütersloh, 1925). — N. Brox, Juden u. Heiden bei I.: MThZ 16 (1965) 89-106. — idem, Offenbarung, Gnosis u. gnostischer Mythos bei I. (Salzburg, 1966). — idem, Tendenzen und Parteilichkeiten im Osterfeststreit: ZKG 83 (1972) 291-324. — idem, Rom und "jede Kirche": AHC 7 (1975) 42-78. — idem, I.: GK 1/1 (1984), 82-96. — idem, I.: RAC 18:820-854. — H. v. Campenhausen, Ostertermin o. Osterfasten?: VigChr 28 (1974) 114-138. — J. C. Capodanno, Rhetorical Examination of haer. (Ann Arbor, Mich., 1995). — A. M. Clerici, La storia della salvezza in I.: RSLR 10 (1974) 3-41. — M. A. Donovan, I. in Recent Scholarship: SecCen 4 (1984) 219-241. — F. Dünzl, Spuren theol. "Aufklärung" bei I.: FS N. Brox (Graz, 1995), 77-117. — A. Ebneter, Die "Glaubensregel" als ökumenisches Regulativ: FS H. Stirnimann (Fribourg, Switzerland, 1980), 588-608. — P. Evieux, La Théologie de l'accoutumance chez I.: RSR 55 (1967) 5-54. — = J. Fantino, L'homme image de Dieu chez I. (Paris, 1986). — idem, La théologie d'I. (Paris, 1994). — J. Friesen, Influence of Confessional Bias (Ann Arbor, 1980). — N. Gendle, I. as a Mystical Theologian: Thom. 39 (1975) 185-197. — J. I. González Faus, Carne de Dios (Barcelona, 1969). — R. M. Grant, I. and Hellenistic Culture: HThR 42 (1949) 41-51. — idem, I. (London, 1997) [partial English trans. haer.]. — M. Guerra Gómez, Análisis filológico de haer. 3, 3, 2b: ScrTh 14 (1982) 9-57. — A. v. Harnack, Fälschungen Pfaff's (Leipzig, 1900). — J. D. Hernando, I. and the Apostolic Fathers (Madison, 1990). — F. R. M. Hitchcock, I. (Cambridge, 1914). — A. Houssiau, La christologie d'I. (Leuven/Louvain, 1955). — H.-J. Jaschke, Der Hl. Geist (Münster, 1976). — idem, I. (Rome, 1980). — idem, I.: TRE 16:258-268. — G. Joppich, Salus carnis (Münsterschwarzach, ²1967). — J. Jossa, Regno di Dio e Chiesa (Naples, 1970). — B. Kereszty, The Unity of the Church: SecCen 4 (1984) 202-218. — B. Kraft, Die Evangelienzitate des I. (Freiburg i.Br., 1924). — E. Lanne, L'Eglise de Rome (haer. 3.3.2): Irén. 49 (1976) 275-322. — H. Lassiat, Promotion de l'homme en Jésus d'après I. (Paris, 1974). — J. Lawson, The Biblical Theology of I. (London, 1948). — G. Leroux, Mythe et mystère du péché originel (Montreal, 1967). — F. Loofs, Theophilus v. Antiochien (Leipzig, 1930). — S. Lundström, Studien zur lat. I.-Übersetzung (Lund, 1943). — idem, Neue Studien zur lat. I.-Übers. (Lund, 1948). — idem, Die Überlieferung der lat. I.-Übers. (Uppsala, 1985). — E. P. Meijering, I.'s Relation to Philosophy: FS I. H. Waszink (Amsterdam, 1973), 221-232. — L. Menville, Marie, mère de vie (Venasque, 1986). — D. Minns, I. (London, 1994). — J. T. Nielsen, Adam and Christ in the Theology of I. (Assen, 1968). — R. Noormann, I. als Paulusinterpret (Tübingen, 1994). — J. Novelli, Paix, justice, intégrité de la création: Irén. 64 (1991) 5-42. — J. Ochagvía, Visibile patris filius (Rome, 1964). — A. Orbe, Antropología de I. (Madrid, 1969). — idem, Parábolas evangélicas en I. (2 vols.) (Madrid, 1972). — idem, I. y la doctrina de la reconciliación: Gr. 61 (1980) 5-50. — idem, Visión del Padre e incorruptela según I.: Gr. 64 (1983) 199-241. — idem, Espiritualidad de I. (Rome, 1989). — E. Osborn, Recapitulation and the Beginning of Christian Humour: The Idea of Salvation, ed. D. W. Dockrill, R. G. Tanner (Auckland, 1988), 64-76. — E. Peretto, Criteri di ortodossia e di eresia nella epid.: Aug. 25 (1985) 645-666. —

M. Richard, La lettre d'I. au Pape Victor: ZNW 56 (1965) 260-282. — L. N. Rivera, Unity and Truth (New Haven, 1970). — D. R. Ruppe, God, Spirit, and Human Being (New York, 1988). — E. Scharl, Recapitulatio mundi (Freiburg i.Br., 1941). — R. Schwager, Der Gott des AT u. der Gott des Gekreuzigten, in: ZKTh 102 (1980) 289-313. — C. R. Smith, Chiliasm and Recapitulation in the Theology of I.: VigChr 48 (1994) 313-331. — T. L. Tiessen, I. on the Salvation of the Unevangelized (Metuchen, 1993). — Y. Torisu, Gott u. Welt (Nettetal, 1991). — K. M. Tortorelli, Some Methods of Interpretation in I.: VetChr 27 (1990) 123-132. — R. Tremblay, La manifestation et la vision de Dieu selon I. (Münster, 1978). — idem, I. (Rome, 1979). — D. Unger, The Holy Eucharist according to I.: Laur. 20 (1979) 103-164. — W. C. van Unnik, The Authority of the Presbyters in I.: FS N. A. Dahl (Oslo, 1977), 248-260. — G. Vallée, A Study in Antignostic Polemics (Waterloo, 1981). — H. J. Vogt, Die Geltung des AT bei I.: ThQ 160 (1980) 17-28. — M. Widmann, I. u. seine theol. Väter: ZThK 54 (1957) 156-173. — R. L. Wilken, The Homeric Cento in haer. 1, 4, 9: VigChr 21 (1967) 25-33. — G. Wingren, Man and the Incarnation (Edinburgh, 1959). — H. Ziegler, I. (Berlin, 1871).

U. Hamm

Irenaeus of Tyre

As an imperial *comes* and a friend of Nestorius, I. tried to serve as mediator in the controversies surrounding the patriarch in Constantinople. In 435 he, like Nestorius, was banished and went to Petra (edict in PG 84:802f.; ACO 1, 4, 203). Between 443 and 446 he was elected bishop of Tyre, despite his second marriage (Theodoret, *ep.* 91: *digamos*) and banishment. He accepted the Union of 433 and was consecrated by Domnus II of Antioch. At the instigation of Patriarch Dioscurus of Alexandria, I. was reduced to the lay state on Feb. 17, 448 and banished once again, this time to his (unknown) native city. He died ca. 450.

Of I.'s works a letter (*ep.*) to the eastern bishops on his mission to Constantinople during the period after the Council of Ephesus has been preserved. During his first exile I. composed the so-called *Tragoedia* (*trag.*) on the first phase of the Nestorian controversy (probably using the acts of the Council of Ephesus). (This work was translated into Syriac by Ebedjesus but is not preserved in that form.) It was attacked in the *Synodicon adversus Irenaei Tragoediam*, which cites large sections of *trag.* The *Synodicon* in turn served as the basis of the *Collatio Casiniensis* (216 of the 236 items of the *Collatio* are from the *Synodicon*), which was translated into Latin by Deacon → Rusticus. The latter gave these items an opposite meaning in order to show the injustice of the condemnation of the Three Chapters.

W: *trag.,* Collatio Casiniensis, PG 84:551-862 = ACO 1, 4.
— *ep.,* PG 84:613-616 = ACO 1, 5, 135f.

G. Röwekamp

Isaac of Amida

I. the Younger of Amida was supposedly a disciple of Ephraem, but more probable chronologically is the information that he received his theol. formation from Ephraem's disciple Zenobius (BOCV 1:214f.). As a young man, I. visited Rome and there witnessed the secular games of 404, which he praised in poems of which nothing is preserved except for a notice in → Ps.-Dionysius of Tell-Mahre, *chron. lib.* 1 (8th c.). I. was often confused with his more famous namesake → Isaac of Antioch and with the Nestorian mystic → Isaac of Nineveh. Acc. to a statement of → Jacob of Edessa, I. was imprisoned in Constantinople after his return to the East and later on, after his release, was active as a presbyter in his native city. It was probably during this time in Constantinople that he wrote his homily on the "royal city" (*hom.*). On chronol. grounds he is often identified with the Isaac mentioned in Gennadius (*vir. ill.* 66), who in 459 wrote a homily on the devastation of Antioch by an earthquake and who died around 461. I. is also supposed to have written against Nestorius and Eutyches. But only a thorough literary-critical and stylistic study of all the works handed down under the name of I. can lead to a more accurate definition of his literary production.

W: *hom.,* P. Bedjan, Homiliae S. I. (Paris, 1903) [Syriac text]. — C. Moss, I. Homily on the Royal City: ZS 7 (1929) 295-306 [Syriac text]; 8 (1930) 61-72 [English trans.].
L: F. Graffin, I. et Isaac d'Antioche: DSp 7:2010f.

P. Bruns

Isaac of Antioch

Under the name of I. have come down numerous metrical discourses (*memre*), which were catalogued for the first time, although incompletely, by Jacobite Patriarch John bar Susan (d. 1073). The sixty-seven *memre* published under the name of I. cannot be attributed with certainty to a single I. But the divergent information in the Syr. tradition and the different dogmatic views expressed in the few christol. treatises ascribed to I. suggest a plurality of authors. Acc. to information in → Jacob of Edessa (7th c.) the homonym I. conceals at least three authors of the same name: → Isaac of Amida, → Isaac of Edessa, and finally the present I., who is also called "the Great." Of the three authors I. was the most produc-

tive and the most important. He came originally from Edessa, was active in Antioch under Emperor Zeno and Peter the Fuller (468-488), and intervened actively on the Monophysite side in the dogm. controversies of his time. For chronol. and dogm. reasons, however, it is difficult to identify him with the Isaac mentioned in Gennadius (*vir. ill.* 66), who supposedly composed several works against the Nestorians and the Monophysites (!) and a lament over the destruction of Antioch by an earthquake (none of these works have been preserved). Throughout his life I. remained a convinced Monophysite; he composed the still-existing poem about the peculiar talking bird who was able to recite the Trisagion with a theopaschite addition. I.'s homilies (*hom.*) are written in a seven-syllable meter, often lack unity, and wander, and are concerned substantially with practical questions of asceticism. The principal dogm. subjects are the incarnation (the one nature of Christ) and the Trinity.

W: *hom.,* P. Bedjan (Paris, 1903) [Syriac text]. — G. Bickell (Leipzig, 1873-1877) [Syriac text/Latin trans.]. — S. Kazan, I. Homily against the Jews: OrChr 45 (1961) 30-53; 46 (1962) 87-97; 47 (1963) 89-97; 49 (1965) 57-78 [Syriac text/English trans./comm.]. — S. Landersdorfer, Syr. Dichter (Kempten, 1913), 101-248 [German trans.]. — G. Furlani, Tre discorsi di I. sulla fede: Rivista Trimestrale dei Scienze Filosofiche e Religiose 4 (1923) 257-287 [Italian trans.]. — P. Krüger, Über den Glauben: OS 1 (1952) 46-54. — P. Feghali, L'hymne sur l'incarnation: ParOr 11 (1983) 201-222.
L: S. Brock, Published homilies of I.: JSSt 32 (1987) 279-313. — A. Klugkist, Pagane Bräuche: OCA 197 (1974) 353-369. — P. Krüger, Mariologie: OS 1 (1952) 123-131. — idem, Gehenna u. Scheol: OS 2 (1953) 270-279.

P. Bruns

Isaac of Edessa

I.'s period of activity is located by → Jacob of Edessa under Bishops Paulus (d. 512) and Asclepius (d. 522). Under the former he was still a Monophysite, while under the latter he changed to the "Chalcedonian heresy." His literary remains have been completely merged with those of → Isaac of Antioch. He is probably the author of two complete homilies (*hom.*) handed down under the name of the other Isaac, which hold a strongly Antiochene-type two-nature doctrine, and of some fragments of homilies.

W: *hom.,* G. Bickell (Geneva, 1873-1877), 1:3-25, 33-53 [Syriac text/Latin trans.].

P. Bruns

Isaac Judaeus

I., a converted Jew, appears in connection with the disputes between Damasus of Rome and Urbinus. He initiated proceedings against Damasus (374), but they were dismissed and he was banished to Spain. Before 378 he returned to Judaism. Gennadius (*vir. ill.* 26 [Richardson]) attributes to him a work on the Trinity and the incarnation; the latter has been identified with the *Fides Isaatis* (*fides*) which may be a part of the work mentioned by Gennadius. An *Expositio fidei catholicae* (*expositio*) also seems to be his work. In the *fides* the three divine persons are said to have one and the same nature, while each person has special properties. Christ combines divine and human natures in his person. The arguments are possibly directed against Priscillianists. Because of conceptual and stylistic similarities I. was identified with → Ambrosiaster as author of the commentary on Paul and of the *Quaestiones veteris et novi testamentum*, but this attribution was disputed and also rejected. Yet in connection with this identification numerous other anonymous or pseudonymous works were also attributed to I.: *Tractatus contra Arianos*, *Lex Dei sive Mosaicarum et Romanarum legum collatio*, *Hegesippus sive de bello Iudaico*, *Quae gesta sunt inter Liberum et Felicem episcopos*, *De concordia Matthaei et Lucae in genealogia Christi*, *Epistula ps. Hilarii ad Abram*, and *Fragmentum in Matthaeum*.

W: *fides*, A. Hoste, CCL 9:331-343. — H. Zeuschner, Studien zur Fides Isaatis: KGA 8 (1909) 110-128 [text/German trans.]. — *expositio*, A. Hoste, CCL 9:345-348.
L: G. Bareille, E. Mangenot, I.: DThC 8/1:1-8. — A. Di Berardino (ed.), Patrologia 3 (Turin, 1983), 169-172, 175f., 260. — C. Martini, Ambrosiaster (Rome, 1944), 154-159. — C. Mras, CSEL 66/2:XXXII-XXXVII. — G. Morin, L'Ambrosiaster et le juif converti I.: RHLR 4 (1899) 97-121. — idem, Deux fragments d'un Traité contre les Ariens: RBen 20 (1903) 125-131. — PLS 1:654f. — M. Schanz, Geschichte der röm. Lit. 4/1 (Munich, ²1959 = ²1914), 355-358. — O. Scholz, Die Hegesippus — Ambrosius Frage: KGA 8 (1909) 149-195. — W. Schwierholz, Hilarii in epistola ad Romanos librum I: KGA 8 (1909) 57-96. — J. Wittig, Der Ambrosiaster u. Hilarius (Breslau, 1906). — idem, Filastrius, Gaudentius u. Ambrosiaster: KGA 8 (1909) 1-56. — idem, Papst Damasus I. (Rome, 1902). — H. Zeuschner, loc. cit., 97-148.

B. WINDAU

Isaac of Nineveh

I. came from Beit Qatraye and was consecrated bishop of Nineveh by Catholicos George I (658-680). As a man of mystical interiority he refused the agitation and demands connected with the office and finally, after only five months, renounced his see

entirely and withdrew into the solitude of the Persian wilderness of Susiana. Last of all, he became a monk in the monastery of Rabban Shabbor. Because his name is the same as that of other authors (→ Isaac of Antioch, → Isaac of Amida, → Isaac of Edessa) it is not always possible to determine with certainty what works are his. Of his many religious writings the volumes *On the Spiritual Life* (*tract.*) have been published in part. In any case, the incarnation, cross, resurrection of the flesh, and the binding eccles. and dogm. nature of faith play but a subordinate role. The foremost goal of his mysticism is to determine the relationship between the individual spiritual soul and the divine All/One. Along with the classical Syr. ascetical tradition, a great deal of Neoplatonic and Stoic thought comes to the fore in his writings. In the subsequent period, as the many translations attest, I.'s undogmatic theology could be accepted by Monophysites, Greeks, Latins, and even Muslims.

W: *tract.*, PG 86:811-886. — P. Bedjan, De perfectione religiosa (Paris, 1909) [Syriac text]. — A. J. Wensinck, Mystic Treatises (Amsterdam, 1923) [English trans.]. — G. Bickell, Ausgewählte Schriften (Kempten, 1874), 273-408 [German trans.]. — S. Brock, CSCO 554/555 [Syriac text/English trans.]. — P. Sbath, Traités religieux (Cairo, 1934) [Arabic text]. — N. Theotokis, I. Spezieris, I. Syrou Askitiki (Thessalonica, 1977 = Athens, 1895) [Greek text]. — J. Touraille, I. Œuvres spirituelles (Paris, 1981) [French trans.]. — P. Bettiolo, I. Discorsi spirituali (Bose, 1985) [Italian trans.].
L: S. P. Brock, Spirituality: Sob. 7/2 (1975) 79-89. — J. B. Chabot, De I. vita (Paris, 1892). — K. Deppe, Logoi asketikoi: P. de Lagarde u. die syr. Kirchengeschichte (Göttingen, 1968), 35-57. — E. Khalife-Hachem, Prière pure: FS G. Khouri-Sarkis (Leuven/Louvain, 1969), 157-173. — D. A. Lichter, Tears and contemplation: Diak. 11 (1976) 239-258. — P. T. Mascia, Gift of Tears: Diak. 14 (1979) 255-265. — I. Ortiz de Urbina, I.: DSp 7:2041-2054. — J. Popovits, Gnoseologie: Theol(A) 38 (1967) 206-225, 386-407. — A. Vööbus, Neue Schriften: OS 21 (1972) 309-312.

P. BRUNS

Isaiah (Ascension of Isaiah)

The pre-Chr. work *Martyrdom of Isaiah*, which is possibly to be linked to Qumran and is attested in Heb 11:37, forms the first part (1-5) of the early Chr. *Ascension of Isaiah* (*Ascens. Is.*). Since in it there is a reference to, among others, Beliar, "the prince of wickedness, who rules this world," a Chr. apocalypse (3.13–4.18) dealing with Christ and the Antichrist (Beliar/Nero) may have been inserted into this part. The second, Chr. part (6-11) contains the "vision of Isaiah," who passes through the seven heavens and points ahead to the coming redemption. A separate insertion with docetic tendencies (11.2-22) has to do with Joseph and Mary and with the birth and crucifixion of the Messiah. The complete work is preserved only in Ethiopic; it may be surmised that the Chr. sections came from Chr.-gnostic circles in Egypt, perhaps ca. 150. Beginning in the 3rd c. (the time when the whole was put together?), the *Ascens. Is.* was used by groups increasingly persecuted as heretical (Hieracas, Arian, Manichees, Messalians). The Lat. version of *Ascens. Is.* 6-11 (*Visio Isaiae*) probably goes back to the Gr. text and later played an important role among the Cathars.

W: P. Bettiolo, E. Norelli, CCA 7-8. — R. H. Charles, The Ascension of Isaiah (London, 1900) [Ethiopic text/Greek and Latin frags./Latin and English trans.]. — J. K. L. Gieseler, Vetus translatio latina Visionis Isaiae (Göttingen, 1832) [Latin text]. — E. Tisserant, Ascension d'Isaie (Paris, 1909) [Latin and French trans. of the Ethiopic text]. — A. Dupont-Sommer, M. Philonenko, La Bible: écrits intertestamentaires (Paris, 1987), 1017-1033 [French trans.]. — J. H. Charlesworth, The Old Testament Pseudepigrapha (London, 1985), 2:143-176 [English trans.]. — NTApo⁵ 2:549-562 [German trans.]. — M. Erbetta, Gli Apocrifi del NT 3 (Turin, 1981, 175-208) [Italian trans.] (literature). — M. Knibb, Martyrdom and Ascension of Isaiah: J. H. Charlesworth, The Old Testament Pseudepigrapha (London, 1985), 2:143-176 [English trans.].
L: A. Acerbi, Serra lignea (Rome, 1984). — idem, L'Ascens. Is. (Milan, 1989). — V. Burch, Material for the Interpretation: JThS 21 (1920) 249-265. — A. Caquot, Bref commentaire: Semitica 23 (1973) 65-93. — D. Flusser, The Apocryphal Book of Ascens. Is. and the Dead Sea Sect: IEJ 3 (1953) 30-47. — O. v. Gebhardt, Die Ascens. Is. als Heiligenlegende: ZWTh 21 (1878) 341-353. — A. K. Helmbold, Gnostic Elements in the Ascens. Is.: NTS 18 (1971/72) 222-227. — E. Norelli, L'Ascens. Is. come apocrifo cristiano: ANRW II 25/6 (1988) 4751. — M. Pesce (ed.), Isaia, Atti del Convegno di Roma, 9.-10. 4. 1981 (Brescia, 1983). — A. Renoux, Note sur l'Ascens. Is.: Cristianesimo nella storia 2 (1981) 367-370 — J. M. Schmidt, Die jüd. Apokalyptik (Neukirchen, 1969).

G. RÖWEKAMP

Isaiah, Ascetic (of Gaza/of Scete)

I. **Life:** In the first half of the 5th c. the Egyptian monk I. (of Gaza) first took up residence in Scete in the time of the first generation of desert fathers (Poimen, Anub, Paphnutius, Sisoes, Or). With his disciple Peter he moved from there to Palestine (452/453) and settled as a recluse at Beit Daltha near Gaza. He was in close contact with Peter the Iberian in Thawatha (beginning in the fall of 485). During the first years of the *Henotikon* both were advisers to the opponents of Chalcedon in Egypt. For reasons of health I. avoided an invitation to Constantinople. He died on Aug. 11, 491.
II. **Works:** The *Asceticon* handed down under the name of I. was probably put together only after his

death by Peter, his disciple and successor. The Gr. version (first published by Augustinos, Jerusalem, 1911) has twenty-nine chapters: addresses to young monks on basic themes of monastic life (renunciation of the world, love, virtues, humility, etc.) and on external behavior. I. passes on to his hearers the thought of the desert fathers. The *Asceticon* shows no Monophysite tendencies.

The Syr. edition of Draguet (1968) also contains an *Antirrhetikon* and a small collection of sayings.

W: S. Schoinas, Τοῦ ὁσίου πατρὸς ἡμῶν ἀββᾶ Ἡσαίου λόγοι κθ (Volos, ²1962) [text]. — PG 40:1105-1206. — N. Hagiorites, Philokalia ton hieron neptikon (Athens, ⁵1982), 1:30-38 [Greek text]. — Abbé Isaïe. Recueil Ascétique (Bellefontaine, 1970) [French trans.].
L: D. J. Chitty, Abba Isaiah: JThS 22 (1971) 47-72. — R. Draguet, Les cinq récensions de l'Ascéticon syriaque d'abba Isaïe, CSCO 289/290, 293/294 (Leuven/Louvain, 1968). — F. Neyt, Citations "isaïennes" chez Barsanuphe et Jean de Gaza: Muséon 84 (1971) 65-92. — L. Perrone, La chiesa di Palestina (Brescia, 1980), 268-295. — L. Regnault, Isaïe de Scété: DSp 7:2083-2095. — idem, Isaïe de Scété ou de Gaza?: RAM 46 (1970) 33-44. — S. Vailhé, Un mystique monophysite, le moine Isaïe: EO 9 (1906) 81-91.

J. PAULI, OSB

Ishobokht of Rev-Ardashir

Little is known of I.'s person and life. He received episcopal consecration from Catholicos Henaniso (I [686-693] or II [694-701]). He is regarded as the most important Nestorian canonist, whose primary work was to put secular Persian law at the service of the Chr. community. He composed six books of jurisprudence in Middle Persian (Pahlevi), which Catholicos → Timothy I (780-823) had translated into the official Syr. language of the church. I. dealt extensively with questions of Persian marriage law (he fought zealously against the custom of marriage between close relatives), but also with Aristotelean logic and mathematical calculations of probability. His references to Islam, which was expanding, are rather few.

W: E. Sachau, Syr. Rechtsbücher (Berlin, 1914), 1-201 [text/German trans.].
L: J. de Menasce, Some Pahlavi words in I.: FS J. M. Unvala (Bombay, 1964), 6-11. — N. Pigulevskaya, Sammlung syr. Rechtsurkunden: IOK 24 (1959) 219f.

P. BRUNS

Iso'Yabh I, Catholicos

I. was originally from Bet-Arabaye and headed the school of Nisibis from 569-571; he left it to become bishop of Arzon. In 581/582 he was elected catholicos. He left behind thirty-one canons of a synod which he held in Seleucia-Ctesiphon in 585/586; in them he approved the writings of → Theodore Mops. These canons, which have been preserved in a letter to Bishop James, are also valuable for the history of the liturgy. Also preserved are a treatise on the Trisagion (*trish.*) and a confession of faith (*symb.*).

W: *can.*, F. Graffin: ROC 4 (1899) 247-262 [Syriac text/French trans.]. — J. B. Chabot, Synodicon Orientale (Paris, 1902), 130-165, 166-192 [text/French trans.]. — O. Braun, Buch Synhados (Vienna, 1900), 191-236, 237-272 [German trans.]. — *trish.*, G. Furlani: RSO 7 (1916-18) 687-715 [text/Italian trans.]. — *symb.*, J. B. Chabot, loc. cit., 192-196 [text/French trans.]. — O. Braun, loc. cit., 272-297.

P. BRUNS

Iso'Yabh II, Catholicos

I., born in Gedala, Mesopotamia, studied at first in Nisibis but left the school because of conflicts with the rector → Henana, and settled in Balad, where he was consecrated bishop. In 628 he became catholicos and guided the destinies of the Persian church. In this capacity he, along with other bishops, traveled to Berea where he met with Emperor Heraclius for a dialogue on religion. There he presented a confession of faith which, because its Nestorianism was mild, was benevolently accepted by the orthodox Chalcedonians. When the Arabs invaded, I. sought refuge in Karka de Bet-Selok, where he died ca. 644. He composed numerous commentaries and menologies, which have been lost. Preserved in an Arab. translation are some letters to Bishop → Barsauma of Karka de Laden (*ep.*) in which he justifies himself for reconciling with the Chalcedonians, as well as the creed of Union addressed to Emperor Heraclius (*symb.*)

W: *symb.*, G. Gismondi, Nestorianorum commentaria (Rome, 1907), 2:53f. [text], 31 [Latin trans.]. — *ep.*, A. Scher, PO 13:576-579 [Arabic text/French trans.]. — L. R. M. Sako, Lettre christologique (Rome, 1983) [text/French trans./comm.].
L: L. R. M. Sako, I.'s syro-oriental terminology: COri 5 (1984) 134-141.

P. BRUNS

Iso'Yabh III, Catholicos

I., son of wealthy Persian parents, came from near Kuplana in the Adiabene. After completing his studies in Nisibis, he was entrusted by Catholicos → Iso'Yabh II with leadership of the see of Nineveh-Mosul and, shortly thereafter, became metropolitan of the eccles. province of Arbela. Around 650 he was consecrated catholicos, but only a little later was driven from Seleucia-Ctesiphon by the Muslims. He

found refuge in the monastery of Bet-Abe, where he composed his liturgical and pastoral writings. But the resistance of the monks there prevented him from establishing in the monastery a school modeled on Nisibis. Therefore, a few months before his death in 657/658, an embittered I. moved back to his old native place. In addition to the pastoral letters (*ep.*) I. also wrote a biography of Isosabran the martyr (*vit.*).

W: *ep.*, R. Duval, CSCO 10/11 [text/Latin trans.]. — *vit.*, J. B. Chabot, Biographie: NAMSL 7 (1907) 485-584 [text/French trans.]. — G. Graf, Geschichte (Rome, 1947), 2:134 [Arabic trans.].
L: J. M. Fiey, I. le Grand: OCP 35 (1969) 305-333; 36 (1970) 5-46.

P. BRUNS

Isidore, Gnostic

I. was the son and disciple of Basilides (Hippolytus, *haer.* 7.20.1; Clement Alex., *str.* 6.53.2; Theodoret, *haer.* 1.4) and presumably taught in Egypt in the second half of the 2nd c. Only fragments of his writings are preserved in Clement, who does not, however, always distinguish carefully between citations from Basilides, I., and those "around Basilides" (*str.* 2.113.4–114.1; 3.2.2–3.2; 6.53.3-5; see also 2.10.1 and 3; 2.27.2; 2.36.1; 2.112.1; 3.1.1–2.1). In *De anima adhaerente* I. says of the soul that the rational soul (*logistikon*) must gain the upper hand over the "adventitious soul" (*prosphyēs psychē*), which is responsible for evil desires (*str.* 2.113.4–114.1).

A nuanced ethical argumentation that excludes libertinism is shown in the fragment on 1 Cor 7:9 from I.'s *Ethica* (*str.* 3.2.2–3.2; a work probably identical with the *Paraineseis* mentioned in Epiphanius, *haer.* 32.4.1). In the *Explanationes prophetae Pachor* (at least two books) I. claims that the Gr. philosophers took their teaching from the prophets. Also mentioned is a *Prophecy of Ham* (*str.* 6.53.3-5).

W: W. Völker, Quellen zur Geschichte der chr. Gnosis (Tübingen, 1932), 41-44 [text]. — W. Foerster, Die Gnosis 1 (Zurich, ³1995), 105-110 [German trans.].
L: A. v. Harnack, Geschichte der altchr. Lit. (Leipzig, ²1958), 1:157-161; 2/1:291, 537. — P. J. G. A. Hendrix, De Alexandrijnsche Haeresiarch Basilides (Paris, 1926), 85-92. — A. Hilgenfeld, Ketzergeschichte (Darmstadt, 1966 = Leipzig, 1884), 213-218. — H. Leisegang, Gnosis (Stuttgart, ⁵1985), 209-212. — W. A. Löhr, Basilides (Tübingen, 1996). — K. Rudolph, Gnosis (Göttingen, ³1990), 277f., 337.

R. HANIG

Isidore of Pelusium

I. Life: Knowledge of the life of I. is to be gotten almost entirely from his letters. Born probably in

Pelusium in the eastern Nile delta, he would have received his higher education in Alexandria. In Pelusium he had an official function as teacher of rhetoric and was active later as a priest under Bishop Ammonius. He came in conflict with the latter's successor, Eusebius, because of corruption in the clergy and withdrew to the nearby wilderness where as a monk he lived an ascetic life but was also active in (eccles.) politics. He was still alive at the time of the events having to do with the Council of Ephesus (431) and Cyril Alex.'s negotiations for union with the Antiochenes. Acc. to biog. testimonies I. lived to a great age. His date of birth can therefore be placed after the middle of the 4th c. Doubts about I.'s historicity are hardly justifiable.

L: P. Evieux, I. de Péluse (Paris, 1995). — C. M. Fouskas, I. of Pelusium (Athens, 1970). — U. Riedinger, Flavius Josephus u. Klemens v. Alexandria: ByZ 57 (1964) 15-25. — A. M. Ritter, I.: DSp 7:2097-2103.

II. Works: The mss. give us a body of two thousand letters (doublets not counted), partially in a set (probably originally numbered) sequence (no. 1378 is missing). The archetype was a collection that must have originated in the monastery of the Acoimetae in Constantinople at the beginning of the 6th c. Since → Severus of Antioch (c. imp. gram. 3.39; CSCO 102:182-82) reports the existence of almost three thousand letters, we must assume a larger orig. correspondence, the authorship of which scholars have assigned to a circle of monks around I. Parts of the corpus have been transmitted in smaller collections, florilegia, collections of apophthegmata, and catenae; in the 6th c., Deacon → Rusticus translated forty-nine letters into Latin. Since individual letters are certainly not complete or, to some extent, contain lengthy verbatim citations from other writers (espec. Demosthenes, Clement Alex., Gregory Naz., and John Chrys.), some have suspected that the letters are a complete forgery, but the historically and locally circumscribed range of persons and subjects speaks clearly against this hypothesis. Two or three longer treatises, of which both I. and Severus speak, have not been preserved, unless they are to be identified with letters.

The collection contains 489 letters to prosopographically distinguishable persons (Emperor Theodosius II, officials in the imperial administration, local politicians of Pelusium, bishops, clerics, monks, private persons). It attests to an extensive involvement in (eccles.-) political events (espec. in Pelusium), with I. rather frequently criticizing abuses (espec. involving Cyril Alex.). I. had a comprehen-

sive education in pagan culture and literature (knowledge of Homer, Plato, Aristotle, Demosthenes; wide knowledge of manuals), which, in the tradition of the Cappadocians and of John Chrys., whom he venerated, he sought to place entirely at the service of Chr. instruction and monastic philosophy (see, e.g., ep 1.1). As an exegete I. was close to the Antiochene school: he advises against allegory (ep. 4.117), which, however, he himself uses rather frequently. He himself engages in no theol. speculations, but his statements reflect contemporary christological discussion. He declares himself in favor of the Nicene conception of the divinity of Christ (espec. ep. 4.99) and emphasizes the unity of Christ in whom duo physeis exist without confusion (ep. 1.23; 1.202; 1.323; 1.405), thus anticipating to some extent the results of the Council of Chalcedon. But for the most part the letters deal with general moral or practico-theol. questions. Because of his clear style (his declared model was Demosthenes) Photius lists him, along with Libanius, Basil, and Gregory Naz., as a model of epistolary style.

W: PG 78. — P. Evieux, SC 422. — ep: 1:43; 1:51; 1:192f.; 1:453; 2:47; 2:49; 3:95; 3:180; 3:296, Catenae Graecae in Genesim, F. Petit, CCG 15.
L: B. Altaner, Zu den Epp. III 154 u. III 253: ByZ 42 (1942) 91-100 = idem, Kleine patristische Schriften (Berlin, 1967), 363-374. — G. J. M. Bartelink, Observations stylistiques et linguistiques: VigChr 18 (1964) 163-180. — L. Bayer, I.'s klassische Bildung (Paderborn, 1915). — P. Evieux, I. de Péluse (Paris, 1995). — R. Maisano, Esegesi veterotestamentaria: Koin. 4 (1980) 39-75. — G. Redl, I. als Sophist: ZKG 10 (1928) 325-332. — A. Schmid, Die Christologie (Fribourg, Switzerland, 1948). — M. Smith, The Manuscript Tradition: HThR 47 (1954) 205-210.

T. FUHRER

Isidore of Seville

I. Life: Information of the origin and life of I. is owed chiefly to references in his work vir. ill. (to his brother, Leander of Seville) and in the Renotatio Isidori of his disciple, → Braulio of Saragossa.

I. was born ca. 560 as the youngest child of Span.-Roman family; the Gr. names of I. and his brother may point to a North African or Byz. origin. The family had to leave the province of Carthaginiensis Nova in 554 when the country was occupied by Byz. troops which Visigothic King Athanagild called upon for support during a civil war.

After the father's death the eldest brother, Leander, undertook the education of his siblings, Fulgentius, Florina, and I. I. received a comprehensive secular and spiritual formation, probably in the episcopal school of Seville, where Leander was bishop from 584 on.

I. followed his brother in this office in 600/601. After experiencing the unification of Spain under King Leovigild and the conversion of the Arian Visigoths to Catholicism (Toledo III, 589), he devoted himself in collaboration with Kings Sisebut (612-621) and Suintila (621-631), to the reorganization of the church and the educational system in Spain. It was during this period of episcopal activity that I. produced all of his writings, which draw primarily on Ambrose, Jerome, Augustine, and Gregory the Great. In 619 he presided at the provincial Synod of Seville (rejection of Monophysitism) and through his writings (espec. *sent.* and *diff.*) decisively influenced the decrees of Toledo IV (633), which pointed the way for the organization and canonical-liturgical practice of the Span. church. I. died in 636.

II. Works: The attribution of many works to I. is still disputed. The *Renotatio* of Braulio names those that are certainly from I., although the titles are not always unambiguous. In addition, a dating is not always possible. The writings may be divided into didactic, exeget., dogm., and canonical, although I. is concerned primarily with a comprehensive vision of the world in which no distinction in principle is made between natural science and theology.

1. Didactic writings: I.'s major work, *Etymologiae*, or *Origines* (*orig.*), in twenty volumes, was given its definitive present form by Braulio. The work deals not only with the seven *artes liberales* but also with medicine, jurisprudence, political science, zoology, cosmology, and human activities (war and play, clothing, agriculture, eating and drinking). The work owes to him its basic conviction that the origin of a word is the key to understanding of it (1.20.1: *etymologia est origo verborum*) and that the word expresses the essence of the thing.

De natura rerum (*nat.*) describes and explains natural events (among others, the course of the planets in the firmament, the solstice, eclipses of sun and moon, thunder, earthquakes, weather, etc.), as well as chronology. The work *De ordine creaturarum* likewise has its place in this context.

The *De differentiis verborum* (*diff.*), possibly I.'s earliest work, lists same-sounding words with different meanings and different words with the same meaning.

2. Exegetical writings: The *Quaestiones de veteri et novo Testamento* (*quaest. test.*) deal with the Pentateuch, Josh, Judg, 1-2 Sam, Kgs, Ezra, Mac. Here citations chiefly from older authorities (beginning with Origen) are given; only Gen is discussed verse by

verse. The section on Gen was possibly a separate commentary to which other material was added later.

De ortu et obitu patriarcharum (*ort. et obit.*) describes the life and death of sixty-four OT personages and brings out their typological meaning. Lives of twenty-two NT figures follow.

The *Prooemia* to bibl. writings give introductions and short lists of contents. The *Liber numerorum* (*num.*) on bibl. numbers and their symbolism was foundational for medieval number symbolism.

The attribution of *Allegoriae* (*alleg*) to I. is uncertain, but the way in which the work speaks of bibl. personages and their typological meaning corresponds to I.'s way of proceeding.

3. Dogmatic writings: The work *De fide catholica contra Judaeos* (*fid. cath.*) may originally have been a collection of OT testimonies that point typologically to NT events; in any case, the work was baneful politically and in its influence. (One of Alcuin's associates produced, among other things, one of the first translations into Old High German.) The *Isaiae testimonia* is probably a cento from the *fid. cath.*

The *Sententiae* (*sent.*) is a kind of manual of dogmatics, spirituality, and ethics for Visigothic society. It is based primarily on Augustine and on the *Moralia in Iob* of Gregory the Great.

De haeresibus (*haaer.*) offers little more than extracts from Augustine's work of the same title and from Jerome's *Indiculus de haeresibus*.

The *Synonyma* (*synon.*), subtitled *Lamentatio animae peccatricis*, is a very personal late work which constantly uses similar words with the same meaning to describe the experience of sin and conversion in a dialogue between the person and reason. The popular style had a strong influence on later Span. literature.

The *De trinitate* (PLS 4:1807-15) is a cento from I.'s works.

4. Historical writings: The *Historia Gothorum* or *De origene Getarum* (*Goth.*), from ca. 624, has great documentary value and tells of those who ruled Spain from the 4th c. on. The Visigoths are here described as the true successors of Rome; the preceding *laus Hispaniae*, with all its literary topoi, describes Spain as an earthly paradise and served later on as an ideological justification of the Reconquista. An appendix deals also with the Vandals and Suebi.

The *Chronica* (*chron.*) continue the work of Eusebius to 615 but are heavily dependent on → John of Biclaro.

The *De viribus illustribus* (*vir. ill.*) picks up Jerome's work of the same name and supplements it chiefly with 6th-7th c. writers of Spain and North Africa. It was later continued by → Ildefonsus of Toledo.

5. *Canonical writings*: *De ecclesiasticis officiis* (*eccl. off.*) explains eccles. concepts and discusses degrees of importance in the clergy and the sacraments. Following Ambrose, the concept of *officium* is here applied to eccles. offices and to the liturgy. The work gives an important insight into eccles. administration.

The *Regula monachorum* (*reg. monach.*), written probably ca. 616-619, is based essentially on Basil and Benedict.

The *ep. ad Masonem* and *ep. ad Leudefredum* deal with questions of penance but are not from I. (The genuine letters of I. are short and addressed to Braulio.)

To what extent the (lost) canonical *Collectio Hispana* goes back to I. is unclear. The editors of the Ps.-Isidorean decretals (→ Canonical collections) give as the supposed author an Isidore Mercator, but in fact the decretals draw heavily on the *Hispana* collection.

III. Importance: Precisely because of its encyclopedic form I.'s work passed on to the Middle Ages a large part of ancient culture and also the concept of the *artes liberales*. (I. himself knew much about these things only from manuals.) I. turned pagan literature into legitimate material which one would do better to read than the Chr. heretics. In the years before 711 (conquest of the Visigothic kingdom by the Arabs), Spain, which for a while was the cultural leader of the West, experienced an "Isidorean renaissance." During the following period I.'s style was more imitated in Spain than his substance. The *Etymologiae*, however, became a "fundamental book for the Middle Ages." Eugene II of Toledo put parts of it into verse; the Carolingian exegetes, Thomas Aquinas, and even Roger Bacon, an empiricist, refer to it. Only with the direct reception of antiquity in the Renaissance did the importance of I., whom Braulio called *doctor egregius*, dwindle.

W: PL 81-84. — *orig.*, W. M. Lindsay, 2 vols. (Oxford, 1985 = 1911) [text]. — J. Fontaine et al. (Paris, 1981ff.) [text/French trans.]. — *nat.*, J. Fontaine (Bordeaux, 1960) [text/French trans.]. — *diff.*, C. Codoñer (Paris, 1992) [text/Spanish trans./comm.]. — *ord. creat.*, M. C. Díaz y Díaz (Santiago, 1972) [text]. — *quaest. test.*, R. E. McNally, CCL 108. — *ort. et obit.*, C. Chaparro Gómez (Paris, 1985) [text/Spanish trans.]. — *praef. test.*, D. de Bruyne, Prefaces de la Bible latin (Namur, 1920), passim [text]. — *in num.*, R. E. McNally, Diss. (Munich, 1957). — *alleg.*, PL 83:97-130. — *fid. cath.*, PL 83:449-538. — *sent.*, I. Roca Mella, BAC 321 (Madrid, 1971), 213-525 [text/Spanish trans.]. — *haer.*, A. C. de Vega (Escorial, ²1940) [text]. — *synon.*, PL 83:827-868. — *Goth.*, T. Mommsen, MGH. AA 11:267-303. — G. Donini, G. B. Ford (Leiden, 1970) [English trans.]. — C. Rodriguez Alonso (León, 1975) [text/Spanish trans./comm.]. — A. Heine (Essen, 1986) [German trans.]. — *chron.*, T. Mommsen, MGH. AA 11:425-488. — *vir. ill.*,

C. Codoñer (Salamanca, 1964) [text]. — *eccl. off.*, C. Lawson, CCL 113. — idem (Madrid, 1982) [Spanish trans.]. — *reg. monach.*, J. Campos Ruiz, BAC 321 (Madrid, 1971), 77-125 [text/Spanish trans.]. — *ep.*, G. B. Ford (Amsterdam, ²1970) [text/English trans.].

L: *Bibliographies:* B. Altaner: Miscellanea Isidoriana (Rome, 1936), 1-32. — W. Haubrichs: ZDP 94 (1974) 1-15. — J. Hillgarth: Isidoriana (Leon, 1960), 11-74. — idem: StMed 24 (1983) 817-905.
Anthologies: Isidoriana, ed. M. C. Díaz y Díaz (Leon, 1960). — Miscellanea Isidoriana (Rome, 1936).
A. Borst, Das Bild der Geschichte in der Enzyklopädie des I.: DA 22 (1966) 1-62. — A. Carpin, L'eucaristia in I. (Bologna, 1993). — idem, Il sacramento dell'ordine (Bologna, 1985), 7-74. — R. J. H. Collins, Early Medieval Spain (London, 1983). — E. R. Curtius, Europäische Lit. u. lat. MA (Munich, ¹¹1993). — H.-J. Diesner, I. u. seine Zeit (Stuttgart, 1973). — idem, I. u. das westgotische Spanien (Trier, 1978). — J. Fontaine, I.: DSp 7:2104-2116 (literature). — idem, I. et la culture classique, 2 vols. (Paris, ²1983). — idem, Cohérence et originalité de l'etymologie isidorienne: FS E. Elorduy (Bilbao, 1978), 89-106. — idem, Isidorus Varro christianus?: FS M. C. Díaz y Díaz (Madrid, 1982), 89-106. — idem, Traditions et actualité chez I. (London, 1988) (collection of essays). — idem, I.: RAC 15:675-680. — J. Madoz, San I. (León, 1960). — F. J. Lozano Sebastián, San I., teología del pecado y la conversión (Burgos, 1976). — idem, San I. y la filosofía clásica (León, 1982). — G. Martínez Díez, La coleccion canónica Hispana I (Madrid, 1966). — S. Merino Martin, Sistematización de la Iglesia: RevAg 29 (1988) 3-40. — R. E. McNally, Isidoriana: TS 20 (1959) 432-442. — P. J. Mullins, The Spiritual Life according to Saint I. (Washington, 1940). — C. Munier, Saint I., est-il l'auteur de L'Hispana chronologique?: SE 17 (1966) 230-241. — J. Pérez de Urbel, San I. Leben, sein Werk u. seine Zeit (Cologne, 1962). — I. Quiles, San I. (Madrid, ²1965). — D. Ramos-Lissón, Doctrina soteriologica: GAKGS 31 (1984) 1-23. — M. Reydellet, La royauté dans la litterature latine (Rome, 1981). — R. E. Reynolds, The "Isidorian" Epistula ad Leudefredum: MS 41 (1979) 252-330. — W. Schweikard, "Etymologia est origo vocabulorum." Zum Verständnis der Etymologiedefinition: Historiographica linguistica 12 (1985) 1-25. — P. Séjourné, Saint I. Son rôle dans l'histoire du droit canonique (Paris, 1929).

G. RÖWEKAMP

Itinerarium

The literary genre known as the itinerarium corresponds to the Gr. *periplous* (account of a coasting voyage) and in Roman times meant a "travel guide," which primarily gave information about road systems and distances between places. Such guides served, among other things, in preparing military expeditions; also in circulation were *Itineraria adnotata* (guides with commentary) and *Itineraria picta* (guides with maps) (see, ca. 400, Vegetius, *De re militari* 3.6). The title itinerarium is first attested ca. 340 in the *I. Alexandri*, a description of Alexander's expedition with advice from Constantius II on the Persian war.

The first preserved itinerariums are from the late period of the empire; older works in the genre (practical handbooks), which is probably just as old as road systems themselves, are lost. The oldest transmitted literary work is the *Itineraria Antonini Augusti*, which was written probably in the first years of the reign of Domitian, following a model from the time of Caracalla. An itinerarium in the form of a map is the *Tabula Peutingeriana*, which is in a ms. of the 12th-13th c. and is probably a copy of a map from ca. 365. The *Cosmographia* of the Anonymous author of Ravenna (7th c.) is based on a similar map.

In the Chr. world the itinerarium was used as a topographical aid. At the same time, the itinerarium as a genre was undergoing change. In hagiog. contexts the information on routes for journeys was taken over but was subordinated to the spiritual way of life (as in some *carmina* of Paulinus of Nola and Venantius Fortunatus, in Prudentius, *perist.*, and Jerome, *ep.* 108).

The properly Chr. itinerariums arose in connection with pilgrimages. They fall, first of all, into the category of *Itineraria adnotata*; information on routes is accompanied by brief references to sights worth seeing (thus the *I. Burdigalense* of 333). In the course of time, information on distances increasingly took second place to descriptions and personal experiences (already the case in the *I. Egeriae*, end of 4th c.). This may possibly be connected with the increasing organization of pilgrimages. In fact, Chr. itinerariums came into existence only in the western part of the empire and in connection with pilgrimages to/via Rome and Palestine. As "descriptions of a journey" they served not only for preparing and carrying out real journeys but also making them repeatable through a book.

The East produced no itinerariums; what were produced there, in imitation of ancient works, were rather geographical works such as the ethnography of → Cosmas the Traveler to India/Indicopleustes, or liturgical books (rituals, calendars) in which information about the holy places was included. Only beginning in the 9th c. do guides for pilgrims appear in the East.

For Palestine the following itinerariums are to be mentioned: (1) The → *I. Burdigalense* (333), in which an anonymous pilgrim describes the way from Bordeaux to Jerusalem. At the end there are references to local (chiefly Jewish) traditions and to the buildings of Constantine. (2) The itinerarium of → Egeria from the end of the 4th c., a not completely preserved account in letter form of a three-year journey through Palestine, Egypt, the Sinai, Syria, and Mesopotamia, which also gives information about the Jerusalem liturgy. (3) The description *De situ terrae sanctae* of → Theodosius the Archdeacon from between 518 and 530, in which the North African author made use of very diverse sources. (4) The → *Breviarius de Hierosolyma*, a kind of "short guide" for pilgrims, from the period ca. 550. (5) The account of a journey through the Near East by the → Anonymus Placentinus (Anonymous of Piacenza), from ca. 570, which because of the writer's invocation of St. Antoninus was for a long time called *I. Antonini*. (6) The letter *De situ Hierosolymae*, which has come down under the name of → Eucherius of Lyons (ca. 443-449) but probably dates from a later time and is a short treatise on Palestine, based on older literature. (7) The account given by Irish Abbot Adomnanus (ca. 679-688) of a journey of Gallic Bishop Arculf, which the latter took before 683/684 (i.e., after the Arab conquest) and on which he used the earlier writings of Jerome, among others.

For Rome the following writings may be mentioned, which consist in large measure of lists of the martyrs' tombs (CCL 175): (1) The itinerarium of priest John (written in the time of Gregory I [590-604]), which was connected with the search for holy oils from the tombs of the martyrs. (2) The register of *Cymiteria totius Romanae urbis*, which, however, despite its title lists only seventeen catacombs. (3) The *Notitiae ecclesiarum urbis Romae* (composed 625-649) lists the tombs of the martyrs acc. to their location on the arterial roads of Rome. The sole reference to a church within the city is a later addition. (4) *De locis sanctis martyrum quae sunt foris civitatis Romae* (composed 635-645) adds the names of twenty-one city churches to the preceding list. (5) The itinerarium of Malmesbury (between 648 and 682). (6) The itinerarium of Eisiedeln (8th c.) contains a series of epigraphical and historical references to the history of Rome.

L: G. Bardy, Pèlerinages a Rome vers la fin du IVe siècle: AnBoll 67 (1949) 224-235. — A. Elter, Itinerarstudien (Bonn, 1908). — J. Heurgon, La fixation des noms de lieux en latin d'après les itinéraires routiers: RPh 26 (1952) 169-178. — HLL 5:94-97. — R. Klein, Entwicklung der chr. Palästinawallfahrt: RQ 85 (1990) 145-181. — B. Kötting, Peregrinatio religiosa (Münster, ²1980). — idem, Ecclesia Peregrinans (Münster, 1988). — J. W. Kubitschek, Itinerarstudien (Vienna, 1919). — idem, Itinerarien: PRE 9/2:2308-2363. — A. Külzer, Studien zu Pilgerführern und Reisebeschreibungen (Frankfurt a.M., 1994). — H. Leclercq, Itinéraires: DACL 7/2:1841-1922. — P. Maraval, Lieux saints et pèlerinages d'Orient (Paris, 1985). — K. Miller, Itineraria Romana (Stuttgart, 1916). — E. Olshausen, Einführung in die Historische Geographie der Alten Welt (Darmstadt, 1991), 87-90. — J. Reumann, The

"Itinerary" as a Form in Classical Literature and the Acts of the Apostles: FS J. A. Fitzmyer (New York, 1989), 335-357. — J. Richard, Les récits de voyages et de pèlerinages (Turnhout, 1981). — T. Teixidor, Geographie du voyageur au Proche-Orient ancien: Aula Orientalis 7 (1989) 105-115. — J. Wilkinson, Christian Pilgrims in Jerusalem: PEQ 108 (1979) 75-101. — idem, Jerusalem Pilgrims before the Crusades (London, 1977).

G. RÖWEKAMP

Itinerarium Burdigalense

The *Itinerarium Burdigalense* (*itin. Burdig.*), the oldest account of a pilgrim's journey to Palestine, has to do, on the one hand, with an actual journey from Bordeaux to Jerusalem in 333; on the other hand, it uses an impersonal language throughout and, like an authentic → *Itinerarium*, lists first distances, stations for changing horses (*mutationes*), and places to sleep (*mansiones*). References to sights worth seeing in Palestine make it an *Itinerarium adnotatum*, in this case a handbook for pilgrims. The reference to the journey of 333 seems to be a note by a contemporary user. Discrepancies in distances given are owing to copyist's mistakes in the three preserved mss., only one of which is complete.

The route of the journey is by way of southern France, northern Italy (Milan), the Balkans, Asia Minor, and Syria. At the border of Palestine (Sarepta near Sidon) the references to places commemorating the Bible begin. Primarily because Chr. topography was as yet rather undeveloped, the references are mostly to OT and Jewish local traditions. Chr. places are limited to Jerusalem and its environs. Mentioned are the Constantinian edifices at the tomb of Jesus, on Mount Olivet, in Bethlehem and Hebron. Some references are to secular history (e.g., the birthplace of Alexander, the tomb of Euripides). The way home leads (after a sea journey from Caesarea to Heraclea) by way of the Balkans, southern Italy, Rome to Milan.

W: PL 8:784-796. — P. Geyer, CSEL 39:3-33. — P. Geyer, O. Cuntz, CCL 175:1-26. — O. Cuntz, Itineraria Romana 1 (Leipzig, 1929), 86-102 [text]. — H. Donner, Pilgerfahrt ins hl. Land (Stuttgart, 1979), 36-68 [German trans./comm.]. — O. Cuntz, O. Wirth, Itineraria Antonini Augusti et Burdigalense (Stuttgart, 1990 = 1929) [text]. — J. Wilkinson, Egeria's travels to the Holy Land (Jerusalem, ²1981), 153-163 [English trans./comm.].
L: R. Eckardt, Das Jerusalem des Pilgers v. Bordeaux: ZDPV 29 (1906) 72-92. — R. Gelsomino, L'Itin. Burd. e la Puglia: VetChr 3 (1966) 161-208. — R. Hartmann, Die Palästinaroute des Itin. Burd.: ZDPV 33 (1910) 169-188. — HLL 5:97-99. — P. Maraval, Le temps du pèlerin (IVᵉ-VIIᵉ s.): Le temps chrétien de la fin de l'Antiquité au Moyen Age, ed. J. M. Leroux (Paris, 1984), 479-488. — C. Milani, Strutture formali nell'Itin. Burd.: Aevum 57 (1983) 99-108. — C. Mommert, Das Jerusalem des Pilgers v. Bordeaux: ZDPV 29 (1906) 177-193.

G. RÖWEKAMP

J

Jacob Baradaeus

A life attributed to a certain John of Asia (→ John of Ephesus is probably meant) tells us what we know of the life of J. (d. 578), who was nicknamed "Burdânâ" (Gr.: Baradaius), "the tattered one," an allusion to his monk's habit. J. entered the monastery of Mount Pesilta (Izla) and was sent to Constantinople in 527/528 in order to represent the Severian cause. He gained the favor of Empress Theodora who cleverly blocked the religious policy of her husband, Justinian, and sided secretly with the Monophysite party. J. remained in an influential position at the court until 542/543 and used it to bring Severian-minded theologians to important episcopal sees. At the urging of Arab client princes he himself was consecrated bishop of the Arabs in 544 and on his journeys of visitation installed a Monophysite hierarchy throughout the entire East; these became known as "Jacobites." J. died in 578 on a pastoral journey aimed at uniting the Monophysites of Egypt and Syria. Of his extensive correspondence there exist some letters (*ep.*) translated from Greek. Also attributed to J. is an anaphora and a confession of faith (*symb.*), as well as a homily on the annunciation to Mary, all preserved in Arab. and Eth. translation. Their authenticity is strongly suspect.

S: *vita*, J. P. Land, Anecdota Syriaca 2 (Osnabrück, 1989 = Leiden, 1862), 364-383 [text]. — E. Brooks, PO 19:228-273 [text/English trans.]. — W. G. van Douwenland, Ioannis Ephesini Commentarii (Amsterdam, 1889), 203-215 [Latin trans.]. — M. A. Kugener, Translatio corporis J.: ROC 7 (1902) 186-217 [text].
W: *ep.*, H. G. Kleyn, J. de Stichter der syr. Kerk (Leiden, 1882), 164-194 [text]. — *symb.*, idem, loc. cit., 121-163 [Arabic text/Dutch trans.]. — K. H. Cornill, J. symbolum: ZDMG 30 (1876) 417-466 [Ethiopic text].
L: D. D. Bundy, J. State of Research: Muséon 91 (1978) 45-85. — H. G. Kleyn, loc. cit. — A. Vööbus, Neue Funde: OS 23 (1974) 37-39.

P. BRUNS

Jacob of Edessa

I. Life: J., later bishop of Edessa, was one of the greatest scholars produced by the Syr. church. As a man of letters, he was equally important in the fields of natural science, exegesis and textual criticism, canon law, and liturgical poetry. He was born ca. 633 not far from Antioch and pursued his basic studies in biblical theology at the monastery of Quennesrin. He acquired his knowledge of philosophy from → John Philiponus in Alexandria, where he devoted himself espec. to the physics of Aristotle. In 684 he returned to Edessa, where he was consecrated bishop. As bishop he laid great emphasis on clerical discipline, which he endeavored to control by means of his canons. Because his rigorism and impetuous temperament made him many enemies among the native clergy, he finally resigned his see after four years of ceaseless conflicts and withdrew with some of his disciples to a monastery near Samosata. A short time later he moved to another monastery near Antioch, where he worked for twelve years as an exegete. But even there he fell out with the community and moved to Tell 'Adda on Mt. Berakat. Here he revised the Syr. version of the OT to make it depend more strongly on the LXX. Finally, at the urging of his diocesans, he returned to his old see for a few months. But he insisted on ending his life at Tell 'Adda, where he died on June 3, 708.

II. Works: Only a few letters from J.'s extensive correspondence have thus far been published.

Canonical writings: Some of J.'s letters contain canonical regulations on the Eucharist and the eccles. community. *Canones* (*can.*) and a polemic work, *On Church Disciplines: Against Despisers of the Canons* (*disc.*), have also come down under J.'s name.

Exegetical writings: J. composed a number of scholia on the OT (*schol.*), some of which have also come under the name of → Ephraem the Syrian. But J.'s main work was the composition of the OT → Peshitta, which was purified on the basis of the Gr. hexapla and the Samaritan Pentateuch; this work is of incalculable value for the history of the bibl. text. J.'s extensive knowledge of the natural sciences made their way into his *Hexaemeron* (*hex.*).

Liturgical writings and didactic poems: J. set great value on the cultivation of liturgical song. Thus he edited the collection of liturgical songs (*carm.*) that had been made by → Paul of Edessa and that in its nucleus goes back to → Severus of Antioch; to it he added a series of his own poems. In addition, J. composed didactic poems of a philosophical kind (*fid.*). Also attributed to him are a recension of the Anaphora of James, as well as rituals for baptism (*bapt.*) and marriage and, finally, hymns (*hymn*) for the weekday breviary that have not yet been critically edited.

Chronicles: J. is regarded as the author of an incompletely preserved *Chronicle* (*chron.*) of events to the year 691/692. For the period down to the 4th c.

he relied on Eusebius's *History of the Church*. After J.'s death, a disciple continued the work to 710.

Philological writings: J.'s textual studies of the OT required a profound knowledge of Syr. grammar and style. The bishop of Edessa is regarded as founder of a Syr. Masora, which with the help of Gr. letters and diacritical marks established the vocalization of the bibl. text. Only fragments of both treatises (*tract.*) are preserved.

Philosophical writings: J. composed a philosophical handbook (*ench.*) which is of importance for the history of the concepts and meanings of Gr. terms (*ousia, hypostasis, physis, prosōpon*) that played a role in the christological controversy.

Translations: J. not only translated the homilies of → Severus of Antioch from Greek into Syriac but is also said to have translated the *Categories* of Aristotle, the visions of Zosimus, a monk, and the orations of → Gregory Naz. He also translated a Gr. collection of the canons of the Council of Carthage (256) having to do with heretical baptism and the apocryphal → *Testament of Our Lord Jesus Christ*.

III. **Main Lines of Thought**: Because of his exceptional linguistic gifts and outstanding knowledge of the Bible, J. has, not without justice, been called the Syr. Jerome, whom he also greatly resembled in his unstable character. J. is regarded as having maintained a moderate Monophysitism of a Severian kind. He consistently refused to support a radical aphthartodocetism of the type represented by → Julian of Halicarnassus. In his opposition to the Chalcedonian Creed he was more moderate than in his treatment of the Nestorians. His numerous works on biblical theology and the liturgy won J. the sympathy of many Melkites of the East, who preserved his memory in the Arab. tradition.

W: *ep.*, R. Schröter, Zwei Briefe J.': ZDMG 24 (1870) 261-300 [text/German trans.]. — W. Wright, Two letters: JSL 4 (1858) 258-82 [text/English trans.]. — F. Nau, Lettres de J.: ROC 5 (1900) 583-596; 6 (1901) 115-131, 512-531; 10 (1905) 197-208, 258-282 [text/French trans.]. — G. Phillips, A letter of J. (London, 1869) [text/English trans.]. — P. Martin, J. E. epistula (Paris, 1869) [text/Latin trans.]. — *can.*, P. de Lagarde, Reliquiae iuris ecclesiastici (Leipzig, 1856), 117-134 [text]. — C. Kayser, Canones des J. (Leipzig, 1886) [German trans.]. — F. Nau, Ancienne littérature canonistique syriaque 2 (Paris, 1906), 38-75 [French trans.]. — A. Vööbus, Syriac and Arabic Documents (Stockholm, 1960), 93-96 [text/English trans.]. — *disc.*, T. Lamy, De Syrorum fide et disciplina in re eucharistica (Leuven/Louvain, 1859), 98-171 [text/Latin trans.]. — *schol.*, G. Phillips, Scholia on the Old Testament (London, 1864) [text/English trans.]. — J. B. Chabot, A. Vaschalde, CSCO 92/97 [text/Latin trans.]. — *hex.*, J. Y. Çiçek, Sechstagewerk (Glane, 1985) [text]. — *carm.*, E. W. Brooks, PO 6/7:1-179/593-802 [text/English trans.]. — *fid.*, M. Ugolini, J. de

fide (Rome, 1888) [text/Latin trans.]. — *hymn.*, A. Baumstark, Festbrevier (Paderborn, 1910), 45-47 [German trans.]. — *bapt.*, J. Marquess of Bute, Blessing of the Waters (London, 1901), 79-100 [English trans.]. — *chron.*, E. W. Brooks, I. Guidi, J.-B. Chabot, CSCO 5/6 [text/Latin trans.]. — idem, Chronological Canon: ZDMG 53 (1899) 261-311 [English trans.]. — *tract.*, W. Wright, Catalogue (London, 1870/72), 1169-1173. — G. Phillips, Letter of J. (London, 1869), 14-24 [text/English trans.]. — *ench.*, G. Furlani, J.: RANL 6/4 (1928) 222-249 [text]. — idem, J.: SMSR 1 (1925) 262-282 [Italian trans.].
Translations: M. Brière, PO 12:70-76; 22:78-83; 23:84-90; 25:91-98, 104, 112; 26:113-119 [text/French trans.]. — M. A. Kugener, E. Triffaux, PO 16:763-866 [text/French trans.]. — I. Guidi, PO 22:99-103 [text/French trans.].
L: W. Baars, Bruchstück aus syr. Bibelrevision: VT 18 (1968) 548-555. — A. Baumstark, Überlieferung u. Bezeugung des Testamentum: RQ 14 (1900) 1-45. — idem, Geschichte (Bonn, 1922), 248-256 (Syr. mss.). — S. P. Brock, J. Discourse on the Myron: OrChr 63 (1979) 20-36. — M. Cook, Epistle of J.: idem, Early Muslim Dogma (Cambridge, 1981), 145-52. — F. X. Funk, Testament (Mainz, 1901). — G. Graf, Geschichte 2 (Rome, 1947), 454-456. — F. Graffin, La catéchèse de Sévère d'Antioche: OrSyr 5 (1960) 47-54. — idem, J. réviseur de Sévère d'Antioche: OCA 205 (1978) 243-255. — A. Hjelt, Études sur l'Hexaémeron (Helsinki, 1892). — E. J. Revell, The Grammar of J.: ParOr 3 (1972) 365-374. — K. E. Rignell, Letter from J. to John the Stylite (Lund, 1979). — L. Schlimme, Lehre des J. vom Fall des Teufels: OrChr 61 (1977) 41 58. — S. Schüler, Übersetzung der Categorien (Berlin, 1897). — A. Vööbus, New Cycles of Canons and Resolutions: OCP 34 (1968) 412-419.

P. BRUNS

Jacob of Sarug

J. was born ca. 451 at Curta on the Euphrates and studied ca. 466 at the school of Edessa. In 502-503 he was a chorbishop in Hawra and in 518/519 became bishop of Batne/Sarug; he died two years later. He was an exceptionally prolific poet; over 700 *memre* or metrical homilies (*hom*), mostly in twelve-syllable lines, are attributed to him, all of which are not certainly authentic. Outstanding among his prose works are not only the sermons on the feasts of the church (*fest.*) but also a collection of forty-three letters (*ep.*), which are instructive for his theology and biography. J.'s christology is located at the intersection of Hellenistic-Alexandrian (→ Cyril Alex.) and Semitic-Syr. piety (→ Ephraem the Syrian). When required to take sides in the dogm. struggles of his time, J. opted for a moderate Monophysitism of a Severian kind, but his reserved temperament was averse of any controversy. As a poet he was consciously indebted to Ephraem; as Ephraem fought Arianism, so J. fought rationalism in theology by continuing the early Syr. tradition of a christology of images and symbols, and he passionately warned against reducing the mystery of the incarnation to a purely con-

315

ceptual abstraction. At a time that called for increasingly precise concepts in christology, J.'s concern for a christology of symbols was controversial even among his own supporters. In addition to his activity as poet and theologian, J. is said to have been the translator of → Evagrius Pont. The themes of his countless homilies are very varied. In his commentaries (*comm.*) on the OT, J. deals espec. with creation, the place of the patriarchs and prophets in the history of salvation, and the symbols and types that prefigure the coming Messiah. In his NT exegesis J. focuses espec. on the incarnation and on the parables and symbols of Christ (→ Aphraates). J.'s distinctive mariology presupposes a profound knowledge of the apocryphal literature and the various legends.

W: *hom.*, P. Bedjan (Paris, 1905-1910) [text]. — J. Overbeck (Oxford, 1865), 382-408 [text]. — M. Albert, PO 38/1 [text/French trans.]. — idem, Sur la synagogue: OrSyr 7 (1962) 143-162 [French trans.]. — S. Landersdorfer, Syr. Dichter (Kempten, 1913), 251-431 [German trans.]. — G. Bickell, Gedichte (Kempten, 1874), 195-227 [German trans.]. — F. Graffin, Vision de Jacob à Béthel: OrSyr 5 (1960) 225-246 [French trans.]. — idem, Sur les deux oiseaux: OrSyr 6 (1961) 51-66 [French trans.]. — E. Khalifé-Hachem, Sur l'amour: ParOr 1 (1970) 281-300 [French trans.]. — P. Krüger, Zwei Hymnen: OrChr 56 (1972) 80-111, 112-149 [German trans.]. — C. Moss, On the Spectacles: Muséon 48 (1935) 87-112 [English trans.]. — P. Mouterde, Deux homélies inédites: MFOB 26 (1944-46) 1-37 [French trans.]. — J. van der Ploeg, Réception de la sainte communion: StT 233 (1964) 395-418 [French trans.]. — W. Strothmann, Drei Gedichte (Göttingen, 1976) [text/German trans.]. — C. Vona, Omelie mariologiche di G. (Rome, 1953) [Italian trans.]. — M. Wurmbrand, La mort d'Aaron: OrSyr 6 (1961) 255-278. — idem, Homélies: OrSyr 8 (1958) 343-394 [Ethiopic trans.]. — *ep.*, G. Olinder, CSCO. S 57 [text]. — idem, Letters of J. (Lund, 1937) [English trans./comm.]. — M. Albert, Lettre sur la foi: OrSyr 12 (1967) 491-504 [French trans.]. — idem, Lettre au prêtre Jean: FS G. Khouri-Sarkis (Leuven/Louvain, 1969), 115-120 [French trans.]. — idem, Une lettre spirituelle: ParOr 3 (1972) 65-74 [French trans.]. — *festa*, F. Rilliet, PO 43/4 [text/French trans.]. — *comm.*, W. Strothmann, J.: Der Prophet Hosea (Göttingen, 1976) [text/German trans.]. — T. Jansma, L'hexaémeron de J.: OrSyr 4 (1959) 3-43, 129-162, 253-285. — K. Alwan CSCO. S 214f. [text/French trans.].
L: J. B. Abbeloos, De vita et scriptis J. (Leuven/Louvain, 1867). — F. Graffin, Thème de la perle: OrSyr 12 (1967) 355-370. — G. van Groningen, Did Christ die physically?: VR 15 (1970) 1-16. — M. Guinan, Purgatory in J.: OCA 197 (1974) 541-550. — T. Jansma, Credo of J.: NAKG 44 (1960) 18-36. — idem, Encore le Credo de J.: OrSyr 10 (1965) 75-88, 193-236, 331-370, 475-510. — idem, Christologie: Muséon 78 (1965) 5-46. — P. Krüger, Problem der Rechtgläubigkeit: OS 5 (1956) 158-176, 225-242. — idem, Einheit in Christus: OS 8 (1959) 184-201. — idem, Caractère monophysite: OrSyr 6 (1961) 301-308. — idem, Kirchliche Zugehörigkeit des J.: OS 13 (1964) 15-32. — idem, Über

den Glauben: OS 23 (1974) 188-196. — P. Martin, Un évêque poète: RSE 4/3 (1876) 309-352, 385-419. — P. Peeters, J. S. monophysite?: AnBoll 66 (1948) 134-199. — F. Rilliet, Rhétorique: OCA 229 (1987) 289-296. — A. van Roey, Sainteté de Marie: EThL 31 (1955) 46-63. — B. M. B. Sony, Méthode exégétique de J.: ParOr 9 (1979/80) 67-103. — J. Thekeparampil, Malkizedeq: OCA 247 (1994) 121-134. — A. Vööbus, Handschriftliche Überlieferung 1-4 (Leuven/Louvain, 1973-1980).

P. BRUNS

James (the Elder), Literature about

There are no surviving Gr. Acts of James the Elder (on his death see Acts 12:1); only Copt. fragments are preserved of the *Acta Jacobi Zebedaei* (*Praedicatio* and *Martyrium*). A Lat. *passio* of the 6th c. has been passed down as the 4th book of → (Ps.-) Abdias and corresponds in part to the Arm. *Historia Jacobi* (BHO 419). As the basis for the veneration of James at Santiago, the *Passio* was inserted into the medieval *Liber S. Jacobi*.

W: *Acta Jacobi Zebedaei (Praedicatio et martyrium)*, I. Guidi, Frammenti copti: AAL. R ser. 4, vol. 3/1 (1887) 54-60 [Coptic text]. — idem: GSAI 2 (1888) 15-20 [Italian trans.]. — Historia Jacobi, L. Leloir, CCA 3:267-288 [French trans.].

G. RÖWEKAMP

James (the Younger), Literature about

In the apocryphal literature J. almost always refers to the "brother of the Lord" and leader of the Jerusalem community (see Acts 12:17; on his death see also Josephus, *AJ* 20.9.1). According to the *Protevangelium*, James was the child of a first marriage of Joseph, an idea attacked by Jerome, for whom James was a cousin of Jesus. Espec. in gnostic texts J. is the recipient and mediator of special revelations. The source for all (late) Acts is Hegesippus in Eusebius, *h.e.* 2.23. → (Ps.-) Abdias also transmits a *Passio*. In the → (*Ps.-*) *Clementines* J. is described as *episkopos episkopōn*.

L: K. Beyschlag, Das J.-Martyrium: ZNW 56 (1965) 149-178. — C. Gianotto, La letteratura attribuita a Giacomo a Nag Hammadi: Aug. 23 (1983) 111-121. — W. Pratscher, Der Herrenbruder J. u. die J.-Tradition (Göttingen, 1987). — R. Voorst, The Ascents of James. History of a Jewish-Christian Community (Atlanta, 1989).

1. **Pseudepigraphical writings:** Traces have thus far been found only in the Irish world of an *Evangelium nomine Jacobi apocryphum* that is mentioned in the *Decretum Gelasianum* (5.33).

Under the (modern) title of *Protevangelium of James* has been preserved a work which originally was probably titled *Birth of Mary* (in the subtitle, in the oldest preserved ms., Pap. Bodmer 5, it is also called *Apocalypse of James*). But even this Gr. papyrus of the 3rd-4th c. gives an expanded version of a (likewise Gr.) original version into which in turn still earlier passages were inserted. The author claims to be J., the brother of the Lord, but seems in fact to be a converted pagan (lack of familiarity with Jewish customs). The work, which was probably already known to Clement Alex., was possibly composed in the second half of the 2nd c. in Egypt. It presupposes the infancy stories of the gospels, but the formation of the canon has not yet been completed. In its genre it is not a gospel but a garland of legends in glorification of Mary, a garland that leads into the NT history. The story (using OT motifs) tells, among other things, of the miraculous birth of Mary as daughter of Anna and Joachim, her childhood in the temple, her being entrusted to Joseph, the annunciation as she was making a curtain for the temple, her defense against the charge of unchastity, the preservation of her virginity even during the birth of Jesus (including the story of the unbelieving midwife). An appendix tells of the death of Zechariah (see Mt 23:35), who is identified with the father of the Baptist.

Numerous, espec. eastern (Syr., Georg., Arm., Arab., Copt., Eth.) translations quickly appeared, as did similar writings. In the West the *Protev.* was condemned in the *Decretum Gelasianum*; the legendary material was circulated in the form of the gospel of → (Ps.-) Matthew. The *Protev.* was extremely influential in mariology (virginity understood biologically; miraculous birth of Mary), the history of piety (high appreciation of virginity), and Chr. art.

W: C. v. Tischendorf, Evangelia apocrypha (Hildesheim, 1966 = Leipzig, ²1876), 1-50 [text]. — M. Testuz, PapyBod 5 (Geneva, 1958) [text/French trans.]. — E. de Strycker, La forme la plus ancienne du Protévangile de Jacques, SHG 33 (Brussels, 1961) [text/French trans./comm.]. — E. de Strycker, Une ancienne version latine: AnBoll 83 (1965) 365-402 [text]. — idem, Une ancienne version latine: AnBoll 83 (1965) 365-402 [text]. — A. de Santos Otero, Los evangelios apocrifos, BAC 148 (Munich, ⁸1993), 136-170 [text/Spanish trans.]. — M. R. James, The Apocryphal NT (Oxford, 1955 = 1924), 38-49 [English trans.]. — M. Erbetta, Gli Apocrifi del NT 1 (Turin, 1966), 7-43 [Italian trans.]. — NTApo⁶ 1:338-349 [German trans.]. — G. Schneider, FC 18:96-145.
L: E. Amman, Le Protev. et ses remaniements latins (Paris, 1910). — E. Cothenet, Le Protévangile: ANRW II 25/6 (1988) 4252-4269. — E. Fuchs, Konkordanz zum Protev. (Linz, 1978). — E. Lucchesi, "Martyre" de Zacharie: Muséon 101 (1988) 65-76. — L. M. Peretto, Influsso del Protovangelo di Giacomo nei secoli II-IV: Mar. 19 (1957) 59-78. — H. R. Smid, Protev. A Commentary (Assen,

1965). — P. A. van Stempvoort, The Protev.: StEv 3/2 (Berlin, 1964), 410-426. — E. de Strycker, Die griech. Hss. des Protev.: Griech. Kodikologie, ed. D. Harlfinger (Darmstadt, 1980), 577-612. — idem, Le Protévangile: StEv 3/2 (Berlin, 1964), 339-359. — R. Warns, Apokryphe Erzählung von der Hebamme Salome: Studien zur spätantiken u. frühchr. Kunst u. Kultur des Orients, ed. G. Koch (Wiesbaden, 1982), 56-71. — S. Voicu, Notes sur l'histoire du texte de l'Histoire de l'Enfance de Jésus: Apocrypha 2 (Tournai, 1991), 119-132.

In a letter to a Quadratus that is preserved in Syriac and Armenian, J. asks what Emperor Tiberius intends to do, after receiving a supposed report from Pilate, against the Jews who crucified Jesus.

W: I. E. Rahmani, Studia Syriaca 1 (Scharfeh, 1904), 1f. [Syriac text/Latin trans.]. — J. Daschean: Azgayin Matenadaran 20 (Vienna, 1896), 386-391 [Armenian text]. — P. Vetter: Lit. Rdsch 22 (1896) 259f [German trans. of the Armenian text].
L: R. van den Broek, Der Brief des J. an Quadratus: FS A. F. J. Klijn (Kampen, 1988), 56-65.

The apocryphal *Letter of James* (*Ep. Jac.*), also known as *The Apocryphon of James*, is found as a Copt. ms. in NHC 1 (*Cod. Jung.*) and is not mentioned anywhere else in early Chr. literature. The work was originally in Greek and addressed to a "Son of Cerinthus." The letter form, in which the author claims to be J. and depicts his ascent in vision, is a secondary framework for a gnostic didactic work. There are similarities to the teaching of → Cerinthus (see Irenaeus, *haer.* 1.25f.). The esoteric teaching in the form of a revelation to J. and Peter on the day of the ascension, 550 days after Easter, has to do with these disciples being "filled" and in this way achieving present salvation and surpassing Jesus. There is an exhortation to faith, knowledge, martyrdom, and contempt for all that is corporeal-psychic (even in Jesus). The distant God does not himself intervene, nor is he influenced by prayers. The *Ep. Jac.*, which came from Egypt or Syria/Palestine, was written perhaps at the end of the 1st or beginning of the 2nd c. and thus documents early Chr. thinking that took place alongside the later canonized tradition. The → *Epistula apostolorum* deals with themes of the *Ep. Jac.* (though to some extent with a different interpretation), but there is no literary dependence.

W: The Facsimile Edition of the NHC. Cod. I (Leiden, 1977), 5-20. — H. W. Attridge, NHC I (NHS 22f.) (Leiden, 1985) [text/English trans.]. — M. Malinine (Zurich, 1968) [text/French trans.]. — D. Kirchner, TU 136 (Berlin, 1989) [text/German trans.]. — H.-M. Schenke, Der J.-Brief aus dem Cod. Jung: OLZ 66 (1971) 117-130 [German trans.]. — J. M. Robinson (ed.), The Nag Hammadi Library in English (Leiden, ³1988), 29-36 [English trans.]. — D. Rouleau, BCNH Section Textes (Quebec, 1987) [text]. — NTApo⁶ 1:238-244 [German trans.].

L: R. v. d. Broek, Text and Testimony: FS A. F. J. Klijn (Kampen, 1988), 56-65. — J. Brown, A religio-historical Study of the Relations between Jewish, Gnostic and Catholic Christianity, Diss. (Brown University, 1972). — R. Cameron, Sayings Traditions in the Apocryphon of James, HThS 34 (Philadelphia, 1984). — idem, Seeing is not Believing: Forum 4/1 (1988) 47-57. — C. Colpe, Heidnische, jüd. u. chr. Überlieferung in den Schriften aus Nag Hammadi VII: JAC 21 (1978) 125-146. — B. Dehandschutter, L'Ep. Jac.: ANRW II 25/6 (1988) 4529-4550. — C. Gianotto, La letteratura apocrifa attribuita a Giacomo a Nag Hammadi: Aug. 23 (1983) 111-121. — E. Haenchen, Lit. zum Cod. Jung: ThR 30 (1964) 39-82. — C. W. Hedrick, Kingdom Sayings and Parables of Jesus in the ApocrJoh: NTS 29 (1983) 1-4. — J. Helderman, Anapausis: Nag Hammadi and Gnosis, ed. R. McL. Wilson (Leiden, 1978), 34-43. — Y. Janssens, Traits de la Passion: Muséon 88 (1975) 97-101. — K. Kipgen, Gnosticism in Early Christianity, Diss. (Oxford, 1975). — D. Kirchner, Ep. Jac. (Berlin, 1977). — idem, Zum Menschenbild: Studien zum Menschenbild, ed. P. Nagel (Halle, 1979), 139-145. — H. Koester, Dialog u. Spruchüberlieferung: EvTh 39 (1979) 532-556. — idem, Überlieferung u. Geschichte der frühchr. Evangelienlit.: ANRW II 25/2 (1984) 1463-1542. — P. Perkins, Johannine Traditions: JBL 101 (1982) 403-414. — H.-C. Puech, G. Quispel, W. C. v. Unnik, The Jung Cod. (London, 1955). — D. Rouleau, Les paraboles du royaume des cieux dans l'Ep. Jac.: Colloque international sur les textes de Nag Hammadi (22-25 août 1978), ed. B. Barc (Quebec, 1981), 181-189. — H. M. Schenke, Der J.-Brief aus dem Cod. Jung: OLZ 66 (1971) 117-130. — J.-M. Sevrin, Écriture et traditions dans l'Apocryphon de J.: Écritures et traditions dans la litterature copte, ed. J.-E. Ménard (Leuven/Louvain, 1983), 73-85. — W. C. v. Unnik, The Origin: VigChr 10 (1956) 149-156. — J. van der Vliet, Spirit and Prophecy in the Ep. Jac.: VigChr 44 (1990) 25-53. — J. Zandee, Trekken in een apokryphe Brief van J.: NedThT 17 (1963) 401-422.

2. Apocalypses: Two apocalypses of James are likewise not attested in early Chr. literature; they are to be found only in the, to some extent, poorly preserved NHC 5 from the 4th c.

The Copt. *First Apocalypse of James* (*1 Apoc. Jac.*) is probably a translation of an original Gr. work that was composed at the end of the 2nd c., at the earliest, and possibly in eastern Syria. This last is suggested by the role of Addai, who is here sent to Edessa by James, thus possibly reflecting a historical link between East Syrian Christianity and Palestine. *1 Apoc. Jac.* is not strictly an apocalypse but rather a "revelation" of Jesus to J., who is here the brother of Jesus only in a spiritual sense. The revelation takes the form of a gnostic-style dialogue; the first part takes place before the passion, the second after the resurrection on "Mount Gangela." The subject is the deliverance of the gnostic from earthly existence. In order that this may be successful, J. gives the "passwords" for the ascent (these correspond to those of the Valentinian groups in Irenaeus, *Haer.* 1.21.5, and

Epiphanius, *haer.* 36.3.1-6); the ascent already begins in earthly suffering.

The second *Apocalypse* (*2 Apoc. Jac.*), likewise transmitted in Coptic, is more difficult to situate. The part played by J. suggests Syria/Palestine as the place of origin. The content is an account sent by a priest to the father of J. regarding "an address which James the Just delivered in Jerusalem." In it J. cites two addresses of the risen Christ to him, his brother, in which a twofold christology (Jesus is at the same time a stranger) is developed. As a speaker, Jesus is portrayed (see *Ps.-Clementines* 1.73.2; Epiphanius, *haer.* 30.16; Hegesippus in Eus., *h.e.* 2.23) as the prototype of the gnostic and a quasi-mythical mediator of redemption. An appendix describes the martyrdom and deathbed of J. in the form of a gnostic psalm of ascent.

In a Ps.-Chrysostomic sermon preserved in Coptic, J. is credited with a further apocalypse that describes the ascension of J. and of the apostles, who honor → John the Baptist in the third heaven.

W: *1 Apoc. Jac.*; *2 Apoc. Jac.*, The Facsimile Edition of the NHC. Cod. V (Leiden, 1975), 32-52, 52-73. — D. M. Parrot (ed.), NHC V, 2-5 and VI (Leiden, 1979), 65-103, 105-149 [text/English trans.]. — A. Böhlig, P. Labib, Kopt. gnostische Apokalypsen: WZ(H) Sonderband (1963) 29-55, 56-85 [text/German trans.]. — A. Veilleux (Quebec, 1986) [text]. — J. M. Robinson (ed.), The Nag Hammadi Library in English (Leiden, ³1988), 242-248, 249-255 [English trans.]. — R. Kasser, Bibliothèque gnostique VI: RThPh 101 (1968) 163-186. — M. Erbetta, Gli Apocrifi del NT 3 (Turin, 1981), 333-340, 341-347. — NTApo⁶ 1:258-264, 269-275 [German trans.]. — *2 Apoc. Jac.*, W. P. Funk, TU 119 (Berlin, 1976) [text/comm.].
L: A. Böhlig, Mysterion u. Wahrheit (Leiden, 1968), 102-111. — idem, Zum Martyrium des J.: NT 5 (1962) 207-213. — S. K. Brown, Jewish and Gnostic Elements in 2 Apoc. Jac.: NT 17 (1975) 225-237. — W. P. Funk, Die 2. Apokalypse des J.: ThLZ 97 (1972) 947-950. — C. Gianotto, La letteratura apocrifa attribuita a Giacomo: Aug. 23 (1983) 111-121. — R. Kasser, Textes gnostiques: Muséon 78 (1965) 71-98, 299-312. — K. Koschorke, Die Polemik der Gnostiker (Leiden, 1978), 196-198. — idem, Rez. zu Funk: ThLZ 105 (1980) 43-46. — H.-M. Schenke, Rez. zu Böhlig/Labib: OLZ 61 (1966) 23-34. — idem, Exegetische Probleme der 2 Apoc. Jac.: Probleme der kopt. Literatur, Wissenschaftliche Berichte der Universität Halle (1968/1) 109-114. — W. R. Schoedel, Scripture and the 72 heavens in 1 Apoc. Jac.: NT 12 (1970) 118-129. — idem, A Gnostic Interpretation of the Fall of Jerusalem: NT 33 (1991) 153-178. — K.-W. Tröger, Die Passion Jesu Christi (Berlin, 1978), 194-207, 235-243.

G. RÖWEKAMP

Jeu, Books of

The *Book of the Great kata mystērion logos*, from the *Cod. Brucianus* (discovered in Thebes in 1769 and containing a further, untitled apoc. work) is identical with the *Two Books of Jeu* twice mentioned in the → *Pistis Sophia*. The work comes probably from the 3rd c. and was probably composed originally in Greek but has been preserved only in Coptic. It is a gnostic gospel that transmits its teaching in the form of conversations of Jesus with his disciples. The esoteric teaching has to do with the emergence of the true son, Jeu (*Ieou*), from the bosom of the father, the emanations from this son, the three baptisms (water, fire, spirit), and the ascent through the eons of the soul thus purified. There are links to the *Apocryphon of John* (→ John, Literature about).

W: C. Schmidt, Gnostische Schriften, TU 8/1-2 [text]. — idem, V. MacDermot, The Books of Jeu and the Untitled Text, NHS 13 (Leiden, 1978) [text/English trans.]. — idem, H.-M. Schenke, Kopt.-gnostische Schriften, GCS 45 [13] (Berlin, ⁴1981), 257-329 [German trans.]. — F. Lamplough, Gnosis of the Light (Leipzig, 1918) [text/comm. on the untitled work].
L: C. Colpe, Heidnische, jüd. u. chr. Überlieferungen in den Schriften aus Nag Hammadi: JAC 25 (1982) 65-101. — C. Schmidt, Gnostische Schriften in kopt. Sprache (Leipzig, 1892). — idem, Die "Beiden Bücher des Jeu" in ihrem Verhältnis zur Pistis Sophia untersucht: ZWTh 37 (1894) 555-585.

G. Röwekamp

Jerome

I. Life: Sophronius Eusebius Hieronymus (J.) was born ca. 347 (thus modern scholarship against → Prosper of Aquitania, *chron.* I, p. 451, 1032: 331) in Stridon in Dalmatia (precise location unclear). He belonged to an affluent Chr. family (*vir. ill.* 135; *ep.* 82.2); we know of a sister and a younger brother, Paulinianus. H. spent the first half of his life in major cities of late antiquity: study and baptism in Rome (*ep.* 15.1; 16.2); conversion to the monastic way of life in Trier; contacts in Aquileia with ascetic-minded Christians; priestly ordination in Antioch by Paulinus, a Eustathian (367/368-373/374); 380-382 in Constantinople; 382-388 in Rome as secretary of Damasus (*ep.* 123.9) and *spiritus rector* of an ascetical group of noblewomen (Marcella, Paula, Blesilla, Asella, Lea, and others). After a failed withdrawal to the wilderness of Chalcis (375-378) and a flight from Rome (*ep.* 45) and after a *peregrinatio* through Palestine and Egypt in 386 with Paula and her daughter Eustochium (see *ep.* 46), J. established monasteries of men and women, with an attached inn for pilgrims, in Bethlehem, remaining as their head and leading the life of an ascetic and a scholar until his death on Sept. 30, 419 (Prosper, *chron.* I, p. 469, 1274: 420).

L: P. Antin, Essai sur Saint Jérôme (Paris, 1951). — A. D. Booth, The date of Jerome's birth: Phoe. 33 (1979) 346-353. — idem, The chronology of Jerome's early years: Phoe. 35 (1981) 237-259. — F. Cavallera, Saint Jérôme, 2 vols. (Leuven/Louvain, 1922). — I. Fodor, Le lieu d'origine de S. Jérôme: RHE 81 (1986) 498-500. — G. Grützmacher, H., 3 vols. (Aalen, 1986 = Leipzig, 1901-1908). — J. N. D. Kelly, Jerome (London, 1975). — S. Rebenich, H. u. sein Kreis (Stuttgart, 1992) (further literature, ibid., 10 n. 9).

I: Works: The foundations of J.'s manysided literary productivity were, first of all, a high-quality education (grammar under Aelius Donatus; rhetoric from an unknown teacher): J. wrote excellent Latin, and the genres, forms, and motifs of classical Roman literature, with citations from it and echoes of it, are present to a high degree in all his works (justification in *ep.* 70); second, an extensive library of pagan and Chr. works which he built up (*ep.* 5.2; 10.3; 36.1) beginning in his days as a student (*ep.* 22.30); third, knowledge of languages (*vir trilinguis*: see *adv. Rufin.* 3.6): in addition to an actively acquired mastery of Greek in Antioch, he had a less well-developed knowledge of Hebrew (*ep.* 125.12) and some Syriac (*ep.* 17.2); fourth, excellent relations (*amicitiae*) with Roman aristocrats (espec. Pammachius, a friend from student days), who supported J. financially and saw to the dissemination of his works.

A fixed basis for the chronology is the list of the works of Chr. writers, *De viris inlustribus* (392/393) in which J. imitated Suetonius: the works listed in *vir. ill.* 135 (see *ep.* 47.3) were composed before 393. The earliest work is the account, written probably in Aquileia, of the miraculous rescue of a Chr. woman of Vercelli (*ep.* 1). J.'s interest in historiography can be seen in his translation and revision of the chronological tables in → Eusebius's chronicle (ca. 380), which he continued for the years 327-378.

J. promoted a radically ascetical way of life. Competing with → Athanasius's *Vita Antonii*, he wrote three highly imaginative novels about monks, which were translated into Greek: *Vita Hilarionis* (*vita Hilar.*), *Vita Malchi*, and *Vita Pauli* (before 393). The last-named, composed probably in Chalcis, made J. known as a writer. Quite a number of letters attest to his ascetical ideal (in addition to *ep.* 22, see 14; 24; 38; 43f.; 51; 54; 55.4f.; 79; 107; 117f.; 122f.; 125; 128; 130; 145; 147; Epitaphs: 23; 39; 60; 66; 75; 77; 108; 127), which he militantly defended: in 383 against → Helvidius's De Mariae virginitate perpetua, which J. saw as a model of ascetical virginity (*virg. Mar.*); in 393 against Jovinian (*adv. Iovin.*), in which J.'s depreciation of marriage as compared with celibacy did more harm than good to the promotion of monasticism, so that Pammachius tried to hinder the dissemination of the work (*ep.* 48-50). Finally, in a renewal of this controversy (expanded to include among other things the veneration of relics) against Vigilantius (*ep.* 61), in 404 J. translated a Gr. version of Copt. Pachomiana: the Rule of → Pachomius (*reg. Pachom.*), eleven of his letters (*ep. Pachom.*), a letter of → Theodore Mops. (*ep. Theod.*), and the spiritual testament of → Horsiesi (*Orsies. doctr.*).

In the East J. acquired a knowledge of exegesis and theology. He names as his teachers (*ep.* 50.1; 84.3; *adv. Rufin.* 1.13) → Apollinaris of Laodicea (in Antioch), → Gregory Naz. (in Constantinople), and → Didymus the Blind (during a short stay in Alexandria), whose *De Spiritu Sancto* he translated (*Didym. spir.*; completed 387). But he learned more from the books of → Origen (list of works: *ep.* 33.4), of which he translated (c. 380/381) nine homilies *in Is.*, fourteen *in Ier.*, fourteen *in Ezech.*, and, in Rome, two *in Cant.* and (392) thirty-nine *in Luc.*

In Rome J. revised the Lat. text of the four gospels in light of the Greek and emended the translation of the Psalter in light of the LXX (= *Psalterium Romanum*?). Of the revision begun in Bethlehem of Job, Chron, Pss, and the Solomonic books of Prov, Eccl, and Cant in light of the Hexaplaric LXX, the revisions of Job (*interp. Iob*) and the psalms (= *Psalterium Gallicanum* in the Vg) have survived; of the *interp. par.* and *Salom.*, only the prefaces. Beginning in 391, J. went back consistently to the original text as normative for a reliable edition (see *ep.* 106) and worked until 405/406 on the books of the Heb. canon acc. to the *veritas Hebraica* and those of Tob and Jdt according to the Aramaic; the deuterocanonical books were revised acc. to Theodotion, Esth acc. to the LXX.

For the NT J. composed commentaries, drawn entirely from Origen, on four letters of Paul (in quick succession during the summer of 386: *in Philem.*, *in Gal.*, *in Eph.*, *in Tit.*), as well as glosses *in Matth.* (398), and reviewed the commentary on the Apocalypse of → Victorinus of Pettau (*Victorin. Poetov. in apoc.*). For the OT he made a first attempt (probably 374/375) with a lost commentary on Obad (*in Abd. prol.*). The earliest surviving work of exegesis (381) is on Isa 6:1-9 (*ep.* 18A and B). After the first commentary ca. 388-389 (*in eccles.*) he worked on aids for scholarly interpretation: 389-391 he translated an etymological lexicon of bibl. proper names (*nom. hebr.*) and → Eusebius's *Onomasticon of Biblical Place Names* (*sit. et nom.*) and busied himself with problems of the Heb. text of Gen (*quaest. hebr. in Gen.*). During the following period, in addition to *Commentarioli* on the Psalms (*in psalm.*; before 393),

he concentrated on the prophetic books. In three starts he commented on the minor prophets (*in proph. min.*): Nah, Mi, Zeph, Hag, Hab (393), Jon, and Obad (396), and finally Zech, Mal, Hos, Joel, and Am (406). Next came the large commentaries *in Dan.* (407), *in Is.* (408-410), *in Ezech.* (410-414), and *in Ier.* (to Jer 31; 414-416). Numerous letters in which he discussed exegetical problems document the carefully cultivated reputation he sought as an exegete (*ep.* 19-21; 25f.; 28-30; 34-37; 45; 55.1-3; 59; 64f.; 72-74; 78; 119-21; 129; 140).

There is disagreement over whether J.'s sermons on the Pss, of which two series exist (*tract. in psalm* 1 and 2) are translations or independent works that show dependence on Origen. Also regarded as authentic are homilies on Mark (*tract. in Marc.*) and twelve short addresses on various occasions and subjects: on bibl. texts (Mt 18:7-9; Lk 16:19-31; Jn 1:1-14), feasts of the church year (Christmas, Epiphany, Lent, Easter Vigil, on Ps 41 to the newly baptized, two Easter sermons); on obedience and *De persecutione Christianorum,* in which J. says that ascetics are constantly "persecuted" by the world and must "persevere" (*tract. varii*). Of two sermons on Isa 1:1-6 and 6:1-7 (*tract. in Is.*) the second is a translation of an anonymous anti-Origenist work (→ *Contra Originem de visione Isaiae*).

J. had little bent for speculative theology. In the trinitarian debates connected with the Antiochene schism he held fast to the old Nicene equivalence of *ousia* and *hypostasis* and rejected the formula, later canonized, of "one *ousia*, three *hypostases*"; after a (vain) appeal to Damasus, he fled Chalcis and the quarrelling (*ep.* 15-17). The question of what to do with repentant Arian bishops and the validity of Arian baptism are discussed in the debate between Helladius, a supporter of the rigoristic → Lucifer of Cagliari, and an orthodox believer, the *Altercatio Luciferiani et Orthodoxi* (*c. Lucif.*; before 393). Baptism and the episcopal office are the subjects of *ep.* 146; *ep.* 41 is against the Montanists.

In the Origenist controversy J. fell back on the (completely un-Origenist) distinction between Origen as pioneering exegete and Origen as suspect dogmatic theologian; he hoped in this way to rescue Origen's scholarly foundations (*ep.* 62; 83f.). Siding with anti-Origenists → Epiphanius of Salamis (*ep.* 91) and → Theophilus Alex. (*ep.* 63; 86-89; 99; see 97; also 95: Anastasius of Rome to Simplicianus of Milan), whose anti-Origenist Easter letters he translated (*ep.* 96; 98; 100; other translations: 90: Theophilus to Epiphanius; 92f.: synodal letters; 94: Dionysius of Lidda to Theophilus; fragments survive of Theophilus's lampoon of → John Chrys., which J. translated: *ep.* 133f.; Facundus, *defens.* 6.5.23), J. wrote invectives against John Jerus. (*c. Ioh.*; 396-397; see *ep.* 82) and his own schooldays' friend, → Rufinus of Aquileia (*ep.* 80 = Rufinus's *praef.* to his translation of the first two books of Origen's *De principiis*, in which he refers to J. as an authority; *ep.* 81: J.'s conciliatory response, suppressed meanwhile by Roman friends; finally, *adv. Rufin.*: 401, books 1 and 2 against Rufinus's defense against J.; 402, book 3, really a reply to a lost letter of Rufinus). Only fragments are known of the literal translation of the *De principiis* (not disseminated by Pammachus) which J. prepared in 398/399 to offset Rufinus's (surviving) translation, in which the translator smooths over what is dogmatically offensive. The turmoil caused by J.'s translation of a letter of Epiphanius to John (*ep.* 51) led him to the first theory of translation in antiquity.

Not in an unpolemical way, yet objectively in great measure, J. entered the debate with Pelagius from 414 on, in *ep.* 133 to Ctesiphon, a Pelagian, and in an anti-Pelagian dialogue (415) between the orthodox Atticus and Critobulus, a Pelagian (*adv. Pelag.*); this dialogue seeks to resemble in its form a Socratic-Platonic dialogue (*adv. Pelag., prol.* 1). As an ascetic J. was interested only in the practical aspects of Pelagian soteriology; for the rest he followed → Augustine (*adv. Pelag.* 3.17-19), although J. the monk was closer to the spirituality of Pelagius the monk than to the teaching of Augustine on grace, which was always foreign to him.

J.'s correspondence (*ep.*), of which he himself published parts (*vir. ill.* 135), is a rich source for the history of culture and is a mirror of his activity. Here, translations and attacks stand side by side with ascetical and exegetical treatises. Elements of satire, to which J. had a pronounced inclination (see *ep.* 117.1), are not lacking (*ep.* 40). *Ep.* 2-13, 31ff., 68, 71, 76 are letters of friendship. Only *ep.* 53, 58, and 85 survive from the correspondence with → Paulinus of Nola; the recently discovered *ep. Divj.* of Augustine testify to contacts with Aurelius of Carthage. The only "real" correspondence is the lively exchange of letters with Augustine (394/395-419). Their bitter disagreement over the interpretation of Gal 2:11-14 and over J.'s method of returning to the original languages in his translations of the Bible broke off without resolution in 405 (*ep.* 56, 67, 101-5, 110-12, 115f.); but beginning in 415 (prehistory: *ep.* 126) the two men put aside theol. differences and made an alliance, sought by Augustine, against Pelagius (*ep.* 131f., 134, 141-43, 144 = Augustine, *ep.* 202A; on this see Aug., *ep. Divj.* 19).

During an attack in the summer/fall of 416 the monasteries in Bethlehem were set afire (*ep.* 135-37). The commentary on Jer remained incomplete. From J.'s last years, which were marked by old age and illness (*ep.* 154.3), only some short anti-Pelagian notes have survived (*ep.* 138f., 151-54). The epitaph for Paul (*ep.* 108.33) is the only verse of J. that has been handed down.

While Ps.-Jerome, *ep.* 18 (on the Easter candle), 21, 22, and 26-29 (homilies) are authentic, Jerome, *ep.* 149, is not; the same for *ep.* 150, the Lat. translation of → Procopius of Gaza, and *ep.* 81, to an Egyptian named Jerome. *Ep.* 148 of J., as well as Ps.-Jerome *ep.* 1.16 (the so-called *Libellus fidei* which Pelagius sent to → Innocent I of Rome), and 41 (possibly also 3f., 7, 13, 32f.) belong to Pelagius. The so-called → *Fides Hieronymi* of 381 is not from J. Ps.-Jerome *ep.* 9, an influential treatise *De assumptione sanctae Mariae virginis*, and 50, *De nativitate sanctae Mariae*, are by Paschase Radbert (9th c.). Among the numerous *spuria* (CPL 623a:42) belong also the → *Breviarium in psalmos*; the expression *peccatum originale* found here (50.7) was not coined by J. but goes back to Augustine, *Simp.* 1.1.10f.

III. **Importance**: J., the man of letters, combined asceticism and scholarship in his life and activity. His ascetical ideal, shaped by the military virtues (watching, fasting, sexual abstinence) looked to withdrawal from cities into solitude and to a radical severing of worldly ties. His novels about monks became the basis of Lat. hagiography. The Pachomiana made their way into various monastic rules. As a scholar, J. concentrated on the safeguarding and explanation of the text of the Bible; textual criticism, philology, and factual knowledge were more important to him than theol. interpretation. From his revision, at took initially refused (*ep.* 27; *praef.* to the translations), of the Lat. text of the Bible in light of the original texts came the Lat. Bible in common use from the 7th c. on (→ Vulgate). In his translations and commentaries he handed on to the West the fruits of Gr. and espec. of Origenist exegesis. The importance of J. as writer, monk, and bibl. scholar is his extensive communication of Gr. spirituality and theology to Lat. Christendom.

W: PL 22-30; PLS 2:18-328. — *chron.*, R. Helm, GCS 473. — *in Dan.*, F. Glorie, CCL 75A. — *Didym. spir.*, L. Doutreleau, SC 386. — *in eccles.*, M. Adriaen, CCL 72:247-361. — *in Eph.*, PL 26:439-554. — *ep.*, I. Hilberg, 3 vol., CSEL 54-56. — L. Schade, BKV² 15:85-194, 298-302, 55, 56 [German trans., selections]. — C. C. Mierow, T. Comerford Lawler, ACW 33 (Westminster, 1963) [English trans./comm.: *ep.* 1-22]. — J. Labourt, 8 vols. (Paris, 1949-1963) [text/French trans.]. — L. Schade, J. B. Bauer, SKV 2 (Munich, 1983)

[German trans./comm.: *ep.* 14; 22; 52; 107; 125]. — *ep.* 1; 60; 107, J. H. D. Scourfield (Oxford, 1983) [comm.]. — *ep.* 57, G. Bartelink (Leiden, 1980) [comm.]. — *ep.* 108, J. W. Smit, L. Canali (1975), 145-237, 319-369 [text/Italian trans./comm.]. — *ep. mutuae Hieronymus et Aug.*, J. Schmid, FlorPatr 22 (Bonn, 1930) [text]. — C. White (Lewiston et al., 1990) [English trans.]. — (Ps.-)Jerome, *ep. 18 ad Praesidium*, G. Morin: BALAC 3 (1913) 51-60 [text]. — *ep. ad Sophronium*, M. van Esbroeck: Revue de Kartuélologie 35 (1977) 127-131 [text]. — *Aug. ep. Divj. 27 ad Aurelium Carthaginiensem*, J. Divjak, CSEL 88:130-133. — idem, Y.-M. Duval, BAug 46B:394-401, 560-568 (Paris, 1987) [text/French trans./comm.]. — *in Ezech.*, F. Glorie, CCL 75. — *in Gal.*, PL 26:307-438. — *hom. Orig. in cant.*, W. A. Baehrens, GCS 33:26-60. — O. Rousseau, SC 372. — *hom. Orig. in Ezech.*, W. A. Baehrens, GCS 33:318-454. — M. Borret, SC 352. — *hom. Orig. in Ier.*, PL 25:585-692. — W. A. Baehrens, GCS 33:290-317. — P. Nautin, SC 238:300-367). — *hom. Orig. in Is.*, W. A. Baehrens, GCS 33:242-289. — *hom. Orig. in Luc.*, M. Rauer, GCS 492:1-222. — H. Crouzel, F. Fournier, P. Périchon, SC 87. — H.-J. Sieben, 2 vols., FC 4. — *in Ier.*, S. Reiter, CSEL 59; CCL 74. — *c. Ioh.*, PL 23:355-396. — W. H. Fremantle, NPNF 6 (Grand Rapids, 1983 = 1892), 424-447 [English trans.]. — *adv. Iovin.*, PL 23:211-338. — E. Bickel (Leipzig, 1915), 382-420 [text: 1:41-49; 2:5-14]. — W. H. Fremantle, NPNF 6 (Grand Rapids, 1983), 346-416 [English trans.]. — *in Is.*, M. Adriaen, CCL 73, 73A:1-799. — R. Gryson et al., 3 vols. (Freiburg i.Br., 1990-1996) [text: 1-11]. — *c. Lucif.*, PL 23:155-182. — W. H. Fremantle, loc. cit., 319-334 [English trans.]. — *in Matth.*, D. Hurst, M. Adriaen, CCL 77. — É. Bonnard, SC 242, 259. — *nom. hebr.*, P. de Lagarde, CCL 72:57-161. — *adv. Pelag.*, C. Moreschini, CCL 80. — L. Schade, BKV² 15:324-497 [German trans.]. — *in Philem.*, PL 26:599-618. — *in proph. min.*, M. Adriaen, CCL 76, 76A. — *in Ion.*, Y.-M. Duval, SC 323. — T. M. Hegedus, Diss. (Waterloo, Ont., 1991) [English trans./comm.]. — N. Pavia (Rome, 1992) [Italian trans./comm.]. — *in psalm.*, G. Morin, CCL 72:163-245. — *quaest. hebr. in gen.*, P. de Lagarde, CCL 72:1-56. — C. T. R. Hayward (Oxford, 1995) [English trans./comm.]. — *reg. Pachom., ep. Pachom., ep. Theod., Orsies. doctr.*, A. Boon (Leuven/Louvain, 1932) [text]. — *reg. Pachom., Orsies. doctr.*, P. B. Albers, FlorPatr 16 (Bonn, 1923) [text]. — *adv. Rufin.*, P. Lardet, CCL 79. — idem, SC 303. — idem (Leiden, 1993) [comm.]. — *sit. et nom.*, E. Klostermann, GCS 11/1. — *in Tit.*, PL 26:555-600. — *tract. (varii)*, G. Morin, B. Capelle, J. Fraipont, CCL 78:501-559. — L. Schade, BKV² 15:210-218 [German trans.: *tract. de nativitate Domini*]. — M. L. Ewald, FaCh 57 (Washington, 1966), 193-264 [English trans.]. — *tract. in Is.* 1.1-6, G. Morin, CCL 73A:801-809. — Y.-M. Duval ?S H. J. Frede, W. Thiele (Freiburg i.Br., 1993), 422-482 [text/comm.]. — *tract. in Is.* 6.1-7, G. Morin: AMar 3/3 (1903) 103-122 [text]. — L. Schade, BKV² 15:225-249 [German trans.]. — *tract. in Marc.*, G. Morin, CCL 78:449-500. — M. L. Ewald, loc. cit., 119-192 [English trans.]. — M.-H. Stébé (Paris, 1986), 23-100 [French trans.]. — *tract. in psalm.* 1.2, G. Morin, CCL 78:1-352, 353-446. — L. Schade, BKV² 15:202-209, 218-225 [German trans.: Ps 1.95; 2.91]. — M. L. Ewald, FaCh 48 (Washington, 1964) [English trans.]. — eadem, FaCh 57 (Washington, 1966), 1-117 [English trans.]. — *tract. fr.*, CPL 607, 607a. — *Victorin. Poetov. in apoc.*, J. Haußleiter, CSEL 49:11-154. — *c. Vigil.*, PL 23:339-352. — L. Schade, BKV² 15:303-323 [German trans.]. — *virg. Mar.*, PL 23:183-206. — L. Schade, BKV²

15:253-292 [German trans.]. — *vir. ill.*, E. C. Richardson (Leipzig, 1896), 1-56 [text]. — C. A. Bernoulli (Frankfurt a.M., 1968 = Freiburg i.Br., 1895), 1-57 [text]. — G. Herding (Leipzig, 1924) [text]. — A. Ceresa-Gastaldo (Florence, 1988) [text/Italian trans./comm.]. — *vita Hilar., vita Malchi, vita Pauli*, PL 23:17-60. — M. Fuhrmann (Zurich, 1983) [German trans.]. — *vita Hilar.*, A. A. R. Bastiaensen, C. Moreschini (1975), 69-143, 291-317 [text/Italian trans./comm.]. — *vita Malchi*, C. C. Mierow: FS J. A. Kleist (St. Louis, 1946), 31-60 [text]. — *vita Pauli*, R. Degorski (Rome, 1987) [text]. — I. S. Kozik (Mount Vernon, 1968) [text/comm.]. — E. Camisani (Turin, 1971), 219-235 [Italian trans./comm.]. — P. C. Hoelle (Ohio, 1953) [comm.]. — *Vulg., praef. Vulg., psalt. sec. Hebr.* (with *praef.*), *interpr. Iob praef., interpr. par. praef., interpr. Salom. praef.*, Monachi s. Benedicti commissionis Pontificiae, 18 vols. (Rome, 1926-1995) [text: OT]. — I. Wordsworth, H. J. White, H. F. D. Sparks (Oxford, 1889-1954) [text: NT]. — R. Weber, R. Gryson (Stuttgart, 1994) [text]. — *interpr. Iob* (sec. LXX), PL 29:61-114. — Ps.-Jerome, *ep.*, PL 30:13-308. — *ep.* 9, A. Ripberger, CCM 56C:97-172. — idem (Fribourg, Switzerland, 1962) [text/comm.]. — *brev. in psalm.*, PL 26:821-1270. — Codices: B. Lambert, Bibliotheca Hieronymiana Manuscripta, 7 vols. (Steenbrugge, 1969-1972).

L: *Bibliographies:* P. Antin, CCL 72:IX-LIX. — G. Sanders, M. v. Uytfanghe, CC Lingua Patrum 1:71-76. — A. Vaccari, Scritti II (Rome, 1958), 83-146. — Miscellanea Geronimiana (Rome, 1920). — F. X. Murphy (ed.), A monument to St. Jerome (New York, 1952). — Y.-M. Duval (ed.), Jérôme entre l'occident et l'orient (Paris, 1988).
N. Adkin, Some features of Jerome's compositional technique: Ph. 136 (1992) 234-255. — P. Antin, Recueil sur s. Jérôme (Brussels, 1968). — E. P. Arns, La technique du livre (Paris, 1953). — A. A. R. Bastiaensen, Jérôme hagiographe: Hagiographies 1, ed. G. Philippart (Tournhout, 1994), 97-123. — D. Brown, Vir trilinguis (Kampen, 1992). — E. A. Clark, The Origenist Controversy (Princeton, 1992). — P. Courcelle, Paulin de Nole et saint Jérôme: REL 25 (1947) 250-280. — idem, Les lettres grecques en occident (Paris, 1948), 37-115. — M. Dulaey, Jérôme "éditeur" du Commentaire sur l'Apocalypse de Victorin de Poetovio: REAug 37 (1991) 199-236. — Y.-M. Duval, S. Jérôme devant le baptême des hérétiques: REAug 14 (1968) 145-180. — idem, Sur les insinuations de Jérôme contre Jean de Jérusalem: RHE 65 (1970) 353-374. — idem, Le Livre de Jonas dans la littérature chrétienne, 2 vols. (Paris, 1973). — idem, Pélage est-il le censeur inconnu de l'Adversus Iovinianum à Rome en 393?: RHE 75 (1980) 525-557. — idem, Jérôme et Origène avant la querelle origéniste: Aug. 24 (1984) 471-494. — B. Feichtinger, Der Traum des H.: VigChr 45 (1991) 54-77. — eadem, Konsolationstopik in "Sitz im Leben": JAC 38 (1995) 75-90. — eadem, Apostolae apostolorum (Frankfurt a.M., 1995). — A. Fürst, Veritas Latina: REAug 40 (1994) 105-126. — idem, Zur Vielfalt altkirchlicher Soteriologie: FS N. Brox (Graz, 1995), 119-185. — idem, H. über die heilsame Täuschung: ZAC 2 (1998) 97-112. — idem, Augustins Briefwechsel mit H. (Münster, 1999). — R. Gryson, D. Szmatula, Les commentaires patristiques sur Isaïe d'Origène à Jérôme: REAug 36 (1990) 3-41. — H. Hagendahl, Latin Fathers and the Classics (Göteborg, 1958), 91-328. — idem, Jerome and the Latin Classics: VigChr 28 (1974) 216-227. — R. Hennings, Der Briefwechsel zwischen Augustinus u. H. (Leiden,

1994). — P. Jay, S. Jérôme et le triple sens de l'écriture: REAug 26 (1980) 214-227. — idem, L'exégèse de s. Jérôme (Paris, 1985). — J. Lößl, Satire, Fiction and Reference to Reality in Jerome's ep. 117: VigChr 52 (1998) 172-192. — P. C. Miller, Jerome's Centaur: JECS 4 (1996) 209-233. — P. Nautin, Études de chronologie hiéronymienne: REAug 18 (1972) 209-218; 19 (1973) 69-86. 213-239; 20 (1974) 251-284. — idem, L'activité littéraire de Jérôme de 387 à 392: RThPh 115 (1983) 247-259. — idem, La liste des œuvres de Jérôme dans le "De viris inlustribus": Orph. 5 (1984) 319-334. — W. A. Oldfather (ed.), Studies in the Text Tradition of St. Jerome's Vitae Patrum (Urbana, 1943). — I. Opelt, H.' Streitschriften (Heidelberg, 1973). — eadem, Des H. Heiligenbiographien: RQ 74 (1979) 145-177. — F. Overbeck, Aus dem Briefwechsel des Augustinus mit H.: Werke u. Nachlaß 2 (Stuttgart, 1994), 335-377 = HZ 42 (1879) 222-259. — V. Peri, Omelie origeniane sui salmi (Rome, 1980). — S. Rebenich, Der hl. H. u. die Geschichte: RQ 87 (1992) 29-46. — idem, Jerome: VigChr 47 (1993) 50-77. — E. F. Rice, S. Jerome in the Renaissance (Baltimore/London, 1985). — A. de Vogüé, La "Vita Pauli" de Jérôme: FS A. A. R. Bastiaensen (Steenbrugge, 1991), 395-406. idem, Histoire littéraire du mouvement monastique dans l'antiquité, 2 vols. (Paris, 1991/93). — D. S. Wiesen, St. Jerome as a Satirist (Ithaca, 1964).

A. FÜRST

Jerome of Jerusalem

Under the name of J. of Jerusalem (or: Hieronymus Graecus) some fragments have come down of a seemingly quite lengthy anti-Jewish work that took as its model Justin's dialogue with Trypho. Because of the surviving fragments on the Trinity the work is given the title *Dialogue on the Trinity* (*Trin.*).

A fragment on the cross (*cruc.*), transmitted by John Damascene, probably belongs to the above work; it deals with the subject of veneration of images with reference to the veneration of the ark of the covenant. Espec. interesting is a fragment on baptism (*bapt.*), which, because of its conception of the experiential grace of baptism, has been linked with Messalianism, but also with Simeon the New Theologian. Some fragments on the Pss (*fr.*) are also to be attributed to J. J. was possibly a Jerusalem theologian of the 7th/8th c., who, like Stephen of Bostra, belonged to the anti-Jewish movement that arose in connection with the advance of the Persians and Arabs.

W: *Trin., bapt., cruc.*, PG 40:848-865; 94:1409. — *cruc.*, Die Schriften des Johannes v. Damaskos 3, B. Kotter, PTS 17 (Berlin, 1973), 194. — *fr.*, Fragmenta in Psalmos, G. Morin, Anecdota Maredsolana 3/3 (Maredsoli, 1903).
L: P. Batiffol, Jérôme de Jérusalem d'après un document inédit: RQH 39 (1886) 148. — J. Darrouzès, Jérôme le Grec: DSp 8:919. — I. Hausherr, Les grands courants de la spiritualité orientale: OCP 1 (1935) 126-128. — K. Rahner, Ein messalianisches Frgm. über die Taufe: ZKTh 61 (1937) 258-

271. — J. Waldis, Hieronymi graeca in Psalmos fragmenta untersucht u. auf ihre Herkunft geprüft, ATA 1/3 (Münster, 1908.

G. RÖWEKAMP

Jobius, Apollinarist

J. (4th c.) was a disciple of Apollinaris of Laodicea and belonged to a moderate group that denied and anathematized the doctrine of the *homoousia* of the body with the divinity. J. was opposed to the more radical Apollinarist, Timothy (PG 86/2:1954A). → Leontius Byz. (*Apoll.*) preserves a confession of faith of J. which appeals for support to Valentinus, an Apollinarist, whose treatise Leontius cites. In his *Symbolum*, drawn up probably on the occasion of a synod, J. professes a Diphysite position. This creed is of interest as documenting the positions of an Apollinarist group.

W: C. P. Caspari, Alte u. neue Quellen zur Geschichte des Taufsymbols (Brussels, 1964 – Christiania, 1879), 24 [text]. — H. Lietzmann, Apollinaris v. Laodicea (Hildesheim, 1970 = Tübingen, 1904), 286f. [text]. — PG 86/2:951 or 3320.
L: E. Ammann, Job 2: DThC 8/2:1486. — H. Lietzmann, loc. cit., 157.

B. WINDAU

Jobius, Monk

Nothing is known of the person of J., a monk and Byz. theologian of the 6th c. (perhaps ca. 530). From Photius (*cod.* 222) we know of two works of J. While Photius simply mentions an otherwise lost work against Severus of Antioch, he gives the contents in detail, along with some excerpts, from a treatise *De verbo incarnato* in nine books. In this work J., who thought in Chalcedonian terms, raised the general question *Cur deus homo?* He discusses, among other subjects, the problem of why the Son became flesh and denies a relation between the Son and the Holy Spirit. This work, further fragments of which are transmitted in catenas, had a strong influence on Photius; along with praise the latter criticizes J., who in his opinion was better at posing problems than at answering them.

W: PG 103:736-829. — R. Henry, Photius, Bibliothèque 3 (Paris, 1962), 152-227 [text/French trans.]. — PG 86/2:3313-3320.
L: E. Ammann, Job 3: DThC 8/2:1486f. — H. G. Beck, Kirche u. theol. Lit. (Munich, 1959), 383. — A. Grillmeier, Jesus der Christus 2/2 (Freiburg i.Br., 1989), 268f. (English, Christ in Christian Tradition, vol. 2/2 [London, 1995]). —

J. Slipyi, Die Trinitätslehre des Photios: ZKTh 45 (1921) 66-95, here 81-87.

B. WINDAU

John, Literature about

1. Pseudepigraphical writings: The so-called *Apocryphon of John* (*Apoc. Jo.*) is a gnostic revelatory work that has come down in four Nag Hammadi mss. (and two different long recensions) and has only secondarily been recast as a conversation of the risen Jesus with J. on Mt. Olivet. At the end of the longer and earlier recension of this very important gnostic work there is a hymn which is older than the work and sums up the gnostic mystery of redemption using the language of the bibl. account of creation. The dating of the orig. Gr. work shifts from between the first half of the 2nd c. and the 3rd c. A part of it may have already been assessed by Irenaeus.

W: The Facsimile Edition of the NHC. Cod. II (Leiden, 1974). — Cod. III (Leiden, 1976). — Cod. IV (Leiden, 1975). — M. Waldstein, F. Wisse, The Apocr. Jo. Synopsis of NHC II, 1; III, 1; IV, 1 with BG 8502, 2, NHS 33 (Leiden, 1995) [text/English trans.]. — M. Krause, P. Labib, Die drei Versionen des Apocr. Jo., ADAI 1 (Wiesbaden, 1962) [text]. — J. M. Robinson (ed.), The Nag Hammadi Library in English (Leiden, ³1988), 98-116 [English trans.]. — M. Tardieu, Écrits gnostiques. Cod. de Berlin (Paris, 1984) [French trans./comm.]. — S. Giversen (Copenhagen, 1963) [text/English trans./comm.].
L: S. Avai, Zur Christologie des Apocr. Jo.: NTS 15 (1969) 302-318. — R. v. d. Broek, The Creation of Adam's Psychic Body: idem, Studies in Gnosticism, NHS 39 (Leiden, 1996), 67-85. — S. Giversen, The Apocryphon of John and Genesis: StTh 17 (1963) 60-67. — Y. Janssens, L'Apocr. Jo.: Muséon 83 (1970) 157-165; 85 (1971) 43-64, 403-432. — R. Kasser, Le livre secret de Jean: RThPh 14 (1964) 140-150; 15 (1965) 129-155, 163-181. — M. Krause, Literaturkritische Untersuchung des Apocr. Jo. (Münster, 1965). — A. Logan, The Development of Gnostic Theology, Diss. (St. Andrews, 1980). — T. Onuki, Gnosis und Stoa (Freiburg i.Br., 1989). — G. Quispel, The Demiurge in the Apocr. Jo.: Nag Hammadi and Gnosis, NHS 14, ed. R. McL. Wilson (Leiden, 1978). — H. M. Schenke, Das lit. Problem des Apocr. Jo.: ZRGG 14 (1962) 57-63. — idem, Die Spitze des dem Apocr. Jo. und der Sophia Jesu Christi zugrunde liegenden gnostischen Systems: ibid. 352-361. — M. Waldstein, The mission of Jesus in John, Diss. (Harvard, 1990).

Fragments of a *Conversation of John with Jesus* are preserved in a ms. of the 4th/5th c.; the age of the work is unclear. It is clearly gnostic in character (many parallels in the Nag Hammadi writings). It deals with revelations by the risen Christ, which are passed on by J.; there are thus similarities with the *Apocryphon of John* (see above), but no dependence.

W: W. E. Crum, Coptic Anecdota: JThS 44 (1943) 176-182 [text/comm.]. — P. E. Kahle, Bala'izah 1 (London, 1954), 473-477 [text/English trans./comm.].

2. Acts: The earliest reference to *Acta Johannis* (*A. Jo.*) are found at the end of the 3rd c. in the Manichean Psalmbook (→ Psalm). Eusebius (*h.e.* 3.25.6) lists it among heretical apocryphal works; in a special work, now lost, Amphilochius of Iconium criticized the *A. Jo.* In the West, too, the work is first attested as part of a Manichean collection of apocryphal Acts of the Apostles (Augustine, *Io. ev. Jo.* 124.2). The *Acta* are echoed in the Priscillianists; the repeated condemnation of the Manichean collection led to its being preserved only in fragments.

Large sections of these *Acta* were passed down as an expansion of the later *Acta Johannis* of Ps.-Prochorus (see below) (*A. Jo.* 18-36, 37-55, 58-86, 106-15) (*A. Jo.* 56f.). Also transmitted independently is the so-called *Metastasis*, the account of the death of J. (*A. Jo.* 106-15) and of J.'s preaching of the gospel in Ephesus (*A. Jo.* 87-105). In addition, there are some partly iconoclastic fragments that were read at the council of 787 (*A. Jo.* 27f., 93f., 97), as well as fragments of Lat. translations to be found in the Letter of → Titus or the *Virtutes Johannis* (see below). Eastern translations exist only of the *Metastasis*.

After an introduction by → Leucius, the narrator and companion of J., to whom the *A. Jo.* are often attributed, the text, using either the We or the I form, tells of J.'s journey to Miletus and Ephesus and of his first stay there, inclusive of the destruction of the temple of Artemis. This part contains the section (which does not correspond to Jn) on J.'s preaching of the gospel, with the heterodox passages, of great interest for the history of religion and theology, on the many forms of Christ (*A. Jo.* 88-93), the hymn of Christ (94-96), and the revelation of the mystery of the cross (97-102). These older sections bear the gnostic stamp (an only seeming crucifixion; distinction between the earthly and the heavenly Jesus) and thus attempt, by means of a gnostically revised Johannine theology, to place the Ephesine Johannine tradition in opposition to the Great Church. After a journey of J. through the communities of Revelation, the *A. Jo.* tell in the *Metastasis* of a final liturgy of J. (with celebration of the Eucharist) and his death at Ephesus.

Eastern Syria is a likely place of origin for *A. Jo.* (this is certain for 97-102); the setting shows the mark of an interest in philosophy and of a literary formation (the form and style of the ancient → Novel seem to be not unknown). The community seems not to have a strong set of offices nor to repress women. A possible time of composition is the end of the 2nd or beginning of the 3rd c.

W: E. Junod, J.-D. Kaestli, CCA 1.2 [text/French trans./comm.] (literature). — NTApo⁵ 2:155-190. — W.

Michaelis, Die Apokryphen zum NT (Bremen, [3]1963), 222-268 [selected German trans.]. — M. R. James, The Apocryphal NT (Oxford, 1955 = 1924), 228-270 [English trans.]. — A.-J. Festugière, Les actes apocryphes de Jean et de Thomas, COr 6 (Geneva, 1983), 9-37 [French trans.]. — M. Erbetta, Gli Apocrifi del NT 2 (Turin, 1966), 29-67 [Italian trans.].
L: J. Bremmer (ed.), The Apocryphal A. Jo. (Kampen, 1995). — D. R. Cartlidge, Transfigurations of Metamorphosis Traditions: Semeia 38 (1986) 53-66. — A. Dewey, The Hymn in the A. Jo.: Semeia 38 (1986) 67-80. — HLL 4:398-400. — E. Junod, J.-D. Kaestli, Les traits caracteristiques: RThPh 26 (1976) 125-145. — eadem, L'Histoire des Actes apocryphes (Lausanne, 1982). — eadem, Le dossier des A. Jo.: ANRW II 25/6 (1988) 4293-4362. — K. Schäferdiek, Herkunft u. Interesse der alten A. Jo.: ZNW 74 (1983) 247-267. — idem, Johannesakten: RAC 18:564-595. — G. Sirker-Wicklaus, Untersuchungen zur Struktur, zur theol. Tendenz u. zum kirchengeschichtlichen Hintergrung der A. Jo., Diss. (Bonn, 1988).

The *Acta Johannis* of Ps.-Prochorus, the supplements of which contain parts of the *A. Jo.*, presuppose the latter, but otherwise have little to do with it. This 5th c. work seemingly represents a largely independent creation of the author; the story is located chiefly on Patmos and betrays no interest in dogma or any ascetical-encratitic interest (common elsewhere). Numerous translations show how popular the work was. The Syr. *Historia Johannis* (BHO 468) is similar in its material. The *Passio Johannis* of Melito of Laodicea is from the 5th c. *Virtutes Johannis*, a Lat. work going under the name of → Abdias (Ps.), is a revised version of the *Passio* and comes from Gaul at the end of the 6th c.

W: *Acta Johannis*, T. Zahn (Hildesheim, 1975 = Erlangen, 1880). — M. Erbetta, Gli Apocrifi del NT 2 (Turin, 1966), 71-110 [Italian trans.]. — *Historia Johannis*, E. Junod, J.-D. Kaestli, CCA 2:718-749. — W. Wright, Apocryphal Acts (Amsterdam, 1968 = London, 1871), 3-65 [text/English trans.]. — *Virtutes Johannis*, ibid., 799-834 [text/English trans.]. — *Passio*, PG 5:1239-1250. — J.-D. Kaestli, CCA 3:111-123.
L: R. H. Conolly, The Original Language of the Syriac Acts of John: JThS 8 (1906/07) 249-261. — NTApo[5] 2:385-391. — K. Schäferdiek, Die Passio Johannis u. die Virtutes Johannis: AnBoll 103 (1985) 367-382.

G. RÖWEKAMP

John Aegeates

This Monophysite author of the 5th c. is not, as is often suggested without good reason, identical with the Monophysite historian John of Cilicia. Two Syr. fragments are preserved of a letter to Theodoret of Cyrrhus, who answers him and defends Chalcedon. These fragments are transmitted in the *Contra*

impium Grammaticum of → Severus of Antioch, the original of which is lost.

W: F. Nau, PO 13:188f. [text/French trans.].
L: M. Richard, La lettre de Theodoret à Jean d'Égées: idem, Opera minora 2 (Tournai, 1977), 48.

G. RÖWEKAMP

John the Almsgiver

Born ca. 555 in Amathus on Cyprus as the son of well-to-do parents in the second half of the 6th c., J. received an education befitting his social rank but had to abandon his worldly career. After the death of his wife and children he renounced his possessions and devoted himself to a spiritual way of life and works of brotherly love. From 612 on he was Melkite patriarch of Alexandria and stood out as a defender of the Chalcedonian Creed and espec. as an organizer of caritative works. On Nov. 11/12 of 617/618 J. died on Cyprus, to which he had withdrawn before the Persian invasion of Egypt. He left behind only (in fragmentary form) a life of St. Tychon, a bishop of Amathus (*v. Tych.*). A lamentation over the conquest of Jerusalem by the Persians is lost.

W: H. Usener, vol. 1 (Leipzig, 1907), 111-149 [text].
L: J. L. v. Dieten, Geschichte der Patriarchen (Amsterdam, 1972), 25f. — E. Honigmann, Patristic Studies (Rome, 1953), 229f. — J. Maspéro, Histoire des Patriarches (Paris, 1923), 326-329, 351f. — C. D. G. Müller, Johannes der Almosengeber: BBKL 3:251-253. — J.-M. Sauget, M. C. Celletti, Giovanni l'Elemosiniere: BSS 6:750-756. — D. Stiernon, Jean l'aumônier: DSp 8:267-269.

M. SKEB, OSB

John III of Alexandria

J., also known as "the Merciful," was originally a monk. Under the Arab rule of Egypt and with the support of Emir Abd-al-Aziz, he was consecrated patriarch of the Copts of Alexandria in 677. He strengthened the Copt. position against the Chalcedonians, helped the poor, and restored church buildings such as the Church of St. Mark in Alexandria. He died in 686. J. has left two (possibly fictitious) disputations. One, with presbyter Theodore, deals with questions of bibl. exegesis (*quaest.*) in the form of an erotapokrisis; it is preserved in a Sahidic version. The second disputation (*disp.*), with a Jew and a Chalcedonian, is transmitted in Bohairic and Arabic. There is disagreement over the attribution to J. of an encomium (in Coptic) on St. Menas (*pan.*) that consists of five parts and deals with the legend of the saint and the fate of his relics; it also calls for visits to the holy places.

W: *quaest.*, A. van Lantschoot, Les Questions de Théodore (Rome, 1957) [Sahidic text/Arabic /Ethiopic recension]. — *disp.*, H. G. Evelyn White, The Monasteries of the Wâdi 'n-Natrûn 1 (New York, 1936), 171-175 [frag.]. — *pan.*, J. Drescher, Apa Mena (Cairo, 1946) [Coptic text].
L: C. D. G. Müller, J.: CoptE 4:1337f.

B. WINDAU

John of Antioch

J. was probably born in Antioch in the second half of the 4th c. He received his education, along with Nestorius and Theodore Mops., in the monastery of Euprepius near Antioch and was elected bishop in 428. Our knowledge of his activities until his death in 441/442 comes from his extensive correspondence. Numerous letters are preserved. Even before the Council of Ephesus (summer, 431), he urged Nestorius in a letter (*ep. Nest.*) to accept the title of *Theotokos* for Mary. On the other hand, he pressed Andrew of Samosata and Theodoret of Cyrrhus to reject Cyril's condemnation of Nestorius. Leading ca. forty eastern colleagues, J. reached Ephesus two days after Cyril and saw himself faced with a fait accompli: Cyril had highhandedly opened the council and condemned Nestorius. J. then gathered his entourage, rejected the condemnation, and condemned Cyril in turn. The Roman delegation, which arrived two weeks late, strengthened the Alexandrian side, but even with the intervention of Emperor Theodosius II, an agreement could not be reached that approved the two condemnations. In a letter to the emperor J. accepted the title *Theotokos* and set forth his christology in formulas that corresponded in essence to the future Union of 433. The council, however, ended in Sept. 431 without an agreement. In the following months J. and Cyril, with Acacius of Berea as intermediary, sought a reconciliation. Finally, in 433, a formula was found that would be taken over in a similar form by Chalcedon, but J. was unable to get all his bishops to sign it.

Numerous letters of J. (*ep.*) are connected with this controversy; the letters of the eastern synods (*ep. syn.*) also go under J.'s name.

W: *ep. Nest.*, PG 77:1449-1457. — ACO 1, 1, 1, 93-96. — *ep., ep. syn.*, PG 83:1440-1466; 84:607-877.
L: A. Grillmeier, Jesus der Christus 2/2 (Frankfurt a.M., 1989), 431-484 (and additional places) (English, Christ in Christian Tradition, vol. 2/2 [London, 1995]). — KonChal 1:160 (et al.); 2:193-203 (et al.). — L. I. Scipioni, Nestorio e il concilio di Efeso (Milan, 1974), 195-299. — R. V. Sellers, The Council of Chalcedon (London, 1953), 6-34.

S. MÜLLER-ABELS

John of Apamea

J., who is perhaps identical with "John the Hermit," was active in the first half of the 6th c. Acc. to Babai the Great, J. composed a number of letters (*ep.*), a dialogue on the soul (*dial.*), a treatise on perfection (*perf.*), another on baptism (*bapt.*), and a commentary on Qoh, which has recently been attributed to → Theodore Mops. J.'s literary remains are difficult to define since in the tradition there are confusions with → John of Lycopolis. J. had an extensive knowledge of medicine and is also regarded as one of the most important mystics of the eastern church. In his ascetical thought his threefold division of the human person into body, soul, and spirit corresponds to the three stages of pure prayer, with the final stage preparing for the vision of God. In his teaching on God J. distinguishes between the invisible nature of God and his visible glory, which can be seen by mystics in ecstasy.

W: *dial.*, S. Dedering (Leipzig, 1936) [text/German trans.]. — I. Hausherr, Jean le Solitaire (Rome, 1939) [French trans.]. — *ep.*, L. G. Rignell (Lund, 1941) [text/German trans.]. — S. P. Brock, The Syriac Fathers on Prayer (Kalamazoo, Mich., 1987), 77-100 [English trans.]. — *perf., bapt.*, L. G. Rignell (Lund, 1960) [text/German trans.]. — W. Strothmann, J. v. Apamea (Berlin, 1972) [text/German trans.]. — R. Lavenant, SC 311.
L: P. Bettiolo, Sulla Preghiera: Muséon 94 (1981) 75-89. — R. Beulay, La lumière sans forme (Chevetogne, 1987), 95-125. — S. P. Brock, J. on Prayer: JThS 30 (1979) 84-101. — A. de Halleux, Christologie: Muséon 94 (1981) 5-36. — P. Harb, Doctrine spirituelle: ParOr 2 (1971) 225-260. — I. Hausherr, Un grand auteur spirituel: OCP 14 (1948) 3-42. — T. Jansma, Neue Schriften: BiOr 31 (1974) 42-52. — R. Lavenant, Le problème de J.: OCP 46 (1980) 367-390. — J. Martikainen, J. u. die Entwicklung der Syriac textheologie: OCA 229 (1987) 257-263. — W. Strothmann, Buch Koh: G. Wießner, Erkenntnisse u. Meinungen (Göttingen, 1973), 189-238.

P. BRUNS

John bar Aphtonia

An anonymous *Vita* gives us a good idea of the life of J. Born ca. 475 as son of an Edessene rhetor and of Aphtonia, J. became a monk in the monastery of Thomas near Seleucia-Ctesiphon in 490. In 518 Emperor Justin decreed the expulsion of all Monophysite monks from that monastery, but they returned ten years later with J. leading them as archimandrite. But ca. 530 J. had to leave this monastery for good, and he founded the monastery of Quennesrin on the Euphrates, opposite Europos; important individuals later emerged from this monastery. J. laid special emphasis on his disciples knowing

Greek. He himself visited Constantinople after 531 in order to make some gains for the Monophysite side, but no union with the Chalcedonians resulted. He died in 537.

J. composed a commentary on the Canticle (*comm. in cant.*), of which only fragments in catenas survive. He is also regarded as the author of various hymns, which were added to the collection of → Severus of Antioch.

S: *vita*, F. Nau: ROC 7 (1902) 97-135 [text/French trans.]. W: *comm. in cant.*, P. Krüger: OrChr 51 (1967) 78-96 [text/German trans.]. — R. Köbert, Syr. Frgm.: Bib. 48 (1967) 111-114. L: A. Baumstark, Geschichte (Bonn, 1922), 180f. (Syriac mss.). — A. Vööbus, Severus v. Antiochien u. J.: OS 24 (1975) 333-337.

P. BRUNS

John the Baptist, Literature about

Stories of the childhood of J. are found in works on the martyrdom of his father, Zechariah, who is often identified with the prophet named in Mt 23:25, as well as in various infancy gospels (→ Apocryphal Writings).

L: A. Berendts, Studien über Zacharias-Apokryphen u. Zacharias-Legenden (Leipzig, 1895), — idem, Die hs. Überlieferung der Zacharias- u. J.-Apokryphen, TU 11/3 (Leipzig, 1904). — H. v. Campenhausen, Das Martyrium des Zacharias: HJ 77 (1957) 383-386.

In addition to various late *Passiones*, a *Vita* (with *Passio*) by a Mark has been preserved. A further work, titled *Vita et miracula*, is mentioned in a homily, transmitted in Syriac, of Ps.- → Serapion of Thmuis. A Copt. encomium is attributed to → Theodosius Alex. Finally, in a Copt. homily of Ps.-Chrysostom there is an encomium called *Gloria praecursoris* or *Apocalypse of James, Brother of the Lord*, in which the author claims to have found in a church of Jerusalem a book of James in which he tells of an ascension of Jesus and his disciples, during which they venerate J. in the third heaven.

W: *Vita*, F. Nau, PO 4:526-541 [text/French trans.]. — *Vita et miracula*, A. Mingana, A New Life of John the Baptist, WoodSt 1 (Cambridge, 1927), 234-287 [text/English trans.]. — *Encomium*, K. H. Kuhn, CSCO 268f. [Coptic text/English trans.]. — idem, Three Further Fragments: Muséon 88 (1975) 103-112 [Coptic text/English trans.]. — *Gloria praecursoris*, E. A. Wallis Budge, Coptic Apocrypha (London, 1913) [text/English trans.]. — W. C. Till, J. in der kopt. Lit.: MDAI. K 16 (1958) 322-332 [German trans.].

G. RÖWEKAMP

John of Berytus

Little is known of the life of J., bishop of Berytus, and that little is from the *Vita* of Severus of Antioch by Zacharias Scholasticus (PO 2:66, 69, 73, 78). J. was evidently a supporter of the Chalcedonian Creed and was active in the struggle against magic and the conjuring up of the dead. The years of his episcopate cannot be exactly determined, but he was a bishop between 474 and 491. He was personally acquainted with Severus of Antioch and Zacharias. In addition, he collaborated with Rabbula of Samosata in the founding of a monastery. A short sermon of his (*Homilia in resurrectionem salvatoris*) is preserved.

W: M. Aubineau, SC 187:296-304. L: M. Aubineau, loc. cit., 281-294.

B. WINDAU

John of Biclaro

J., a Goth, was born ca. 540 in Lusitania; he was raised a Catholic in Constantinople, and at the age of seventeen he returned to his native land, where he came in conflict with the Arian rulers. After 586 he founded the monastery of Biclaro and, acc. to Isidore, *vir. ill.* 34.63, composed a monastic rule for it. He became bishop of Gerona before 614 and died ca. 621.

J. composed a continuation of the universal chronicle of → Victor of Tunnuna for the years 567-590. Its focus is on Byzantium (treaty of Maurice with the Persians), but it is also an important witness to the unification of Spain under Leovigild, the conversion of the Visigoths to Catholicism, and the third Council of Toledo (589)

W: PL 72:863-870. — T. Mommsen, MGH. AA 11:211-222. — J. Campos, Juan de Biclaro (Madrid, 1969) [text/comm.]. L: P. Alvarez Rubiano, La cronica de J.: Analecta Sacra Tarracon 16 (1943) 7-44. — J. N. Hillgarth, Historiography in Visigothic Spain: La storiografia altomedievale (Spoleto, 1970), 266-271. — A. C. Vega, De patrología espanola: BRAH 164 (1969) 13-74. — A. de Vogüé, De Trithème: SE 23 (1978/79) 217-224 [on Monastic Rule].

G. RÖWEKAMP

John of Caesarea, Grammarian

Whether J. the Grammarian was of Cappadocian or Palestinian origin is unclear. He may have taken part in the Neo-Chalcedonian Synod of Alexandretta (between 514 and 518) and may have written the synodal letter to Emperor Anastasius. J. is known only through his principal work, *Defense of the Council of Chalcedon*, which was written ca. 515. The work can to a great extent be reconstructed with the help of Severus of Antioch, who in his reply *Contra impium Grammaticum* cites forty-four sections of the *Defense*, and of some fragments that are attributed to Eulogius of Alexandria in the *Doctrina Patrum*. J. is the first representative of Neo-Chalcedonianism. For the first time, he uses the concepts of *ousia* and *hypostasis*, which the Cappadocians applied to trinitarian theology, in order to describe the unity of the two "natures" in the "person" of Christ. At the same time, he tried, in vain, to achieve a balance between Antiochene and Alexandrian theology, by taking as his starting point the principle that various formulas combine to express the truth: thus he accepted both the theopaschite formula *unus ex trinitate passus est* and the anathematisms of Cyril, the Formula of Union of 433, the *Tomus Leonis*, and the conciliar decree of 451. Also attributed to J. today are two other anti-Monophysite texts, two anti-Manichean homilies, a debate with a Manichee, and two exegetical fragments on Jn 8:44 and 20:18. Of the anti-Monophysite *Capitula XVII contra acephalos* (*cap.*) *cap.* 12-17 are by Anastasius the Sinaite.

W: M. Richard, CCG 1:6-46.
L: A. de Halleux, Le "synode néochalkedonien" d'Alexandrette (ca. 515) et l' "Apologie pour Chalkedoine" de J.: RHE 72 (1977) 593-600. — S. Helmer, Der Neuchalkedonismus, Diss. (Bonn, 1962). — C. Moeller, Trois fragments grecs de l'apologie de J.: RHE 46 (1951) 683-688. — idem, Nephalius d'Alexandrie: RHE 40 (1944f) 73-140. — M. Richard, Le Néo-chalcedonisme: MSR 3 (1946) 156-161. — K. H. Uthemann, Antimonophysitische Aporien des Anastasios Sinaites: ByZ 74 (1981) 11-26. — S. Vailhé, Jean le Khozbite et Jean de Césarée: EO 6 (1903) 107-113.

G. RÖWEKAMP

John II of Cappadocia

The dates of J.'s birth and death in Cappadocia are unknown. He was initially syncellus of the (anti-Chalcedonian) Patriarch Timothy I of Constantinople (511-518). After the latter's death J. was patriarch from April 518 to Feb. 520. Under Emperor Anastasius (491-518) he condemned the Chalcedonian Creed but changed his mind in favor of Chalcedon at the Synod of Constantinople (July 518) under the new Emperor Justin I (518-527) and at the urging of the monks. Beginning in Sept. 518 J. wrote letters to Hormisdas of Rome that were intended to lead to the ending of the Acacian schism. Negotiations between Sept. 518 and March 519 were followed on March 28, 519 by the signing of the formula of faith composed by Hormisdas and by the ending of the schism that had existed between Rome and Byzantium since 484. In a further letter to Hormisdas (March 28, 519) J. condemned Acacius and accepted the *Tomus Leonis*. J. died in 520. In his surviving letters we find the title "Ecumenical Patriarch" used for the first time as a salutation for the bishop of Constantinople.

S: Theophanes, *Chronographia* (1:164-166 de Boor).
W: Mansi 8:436f., 451f., 457f., 1066f. — ACO 3, 76f. — PL 63:443-445, 449f. 480f. [under the letters of Hormisdas]. — O. Guenther, CSEL 35:591-640 [letters to Hormisdas].
L: M. V. Anastas, The Emperor Justin I. 's Role in the Restauration of Chalcedonian Doctrine, 518-519: Byz(T) 13 (1985) 127-139. — H. G. Beck, Geschichte der orthodoxen Kirche (Göttingen, 1980), 17-19. — A.-V. Grumel, Regestes 1/1 (Constantinople, 1932), Nr. 206-216. — KonChal 2:84-92, 681-686. — T. Nikolaou, J.: BBKL 3:431-433. — G. Prinzing, J.: LMA 5:548 (literature). — E. Schwartz, Zur Kirchenpolitik Justinians, SBAW. PH 2 (Munich, 1940), 33-37. — idem, Ges. Schriften 4 (Berlin, 1960), 276-328. — B. Stephanidis, Ἐκκλησιαστικὴ Ἱστορία (Athens, ²1959), 230-232, 291f. — A. A. Vasiliev, Justin the First (Cambridge, Mass., 1950), 68-82.

F. R. GAHBAUER, OSB

John of Carpathus

J. was a probably a bishop of Carpathus, an island between Crete and Rhodes. He lived between the 5th and 7th c. He was often identified with the J. who was a subscriber to the conciliar acts of 680.

J. composed doctrinal instructions and exhortations, divided into short sentences and addressed to monks; there is no original teaching but a close dependence on Maximus Conf. and Evagrius Pont. His first collection, *Capitula hortatoria ad monachos in India* (*cap. hort.*), which numbered one hundred acc. to J. but of which only ninety-seven are preserved, gives concrete advice for implementing the monastic ideal in the everyday life of the monastery. Ch. 96 was later published as an independent work. The second collection, *Capita theologica et gnostica* (*cap. theol.*), handed down in eighty-six sections, gives advice for overcoming sin and purifying the soul by asceticism and contemplation. Demonstrably not from J., though originally attributed to him, are *Narrationes variae de viris anachoretarum* (stories of the Egyptian monks, also known as *Gerontika* or *Paterika*) and the *Florilegium de sacra eucharistia et de communione*, as well as the *Capita moralia*, of which Elias Ekdikos has been shown to be the author.

W: *cap. hort.*, PG 85:1837-1860. — *cap. theol.*, PG 85:811-826. — D. Ossieur, Diss. (Geneva, 1973) [text].
L: H.-G. Beck, Kirche u. theol. Lit. (Munich, 1959), 817. —

M. T. Disdier, J.: EO 31 (1932) 284-303. — L. Petit, J.: DThC 8:753f. — D. Stiernon, J.: DSp 8:589-592.

C. SCHMIDT

John Cassian

I. Life: C. was born ca. 360 in the Dubrudsha area (Gennadius, *vir. ill.*: *natione Scythica*) the son of an affluent Chr. family; he received a classical education and spoke fluent Greek and Latin. After he and Germanus entered a monastery in Bethlehem (378-380), the two received permission to journey, for spiritual studies, to the anchorites of Egypt, among whom Evagrius Pont. exerted great influence at that time. In 399, because of the Origenist controversy, C. and Germanus, like many monks, left Egypt and went to Constantinople where John Chrys. ordained C. a deacon against his wishes; C. and Germanus then took charge of the cathedral treasure. After the downfall of Chrys. (404), C. carried a letter in defense of him to Innocent I in Rome, where he won over the later pope, Leo I, and lost Germanus through death. C. was ordained a priest there. From Rome he went to Marseilles and founded the monasteries of St. Victor for monks and St. Salvator for nuns. C. died after 432.

II. Works: During his time at St. Victor's C. composed three works: (1) between 419 and 426, he wrote and dedicated to Bishop Castor of Apt (Provence), who requested it, the *Institutiones* (*conl.* 9.1; 11 *praef.*: *instituta coenobiorum*) (*inst.*), which in many mss. has come down in two parts (*inst.* 1-4 and 5-12). With the intention of drawing a picture of monasticism in Palestine and Egypt, *inst.* 1-4 deal with particular questions of external life (e.g., monastic garb, nocturnal prayer, psalmody), while *inst.* 5-12, following Evagrius Pont., deal with the eight principal sins (gluttony, sexual offenses, avarice, anger, sadness, antipathy, vanity, arrogance). (2) In their structure, the twenty-four *Conlationes* (*conl.*) (*conl.* 1-10 *praef.*: *conlationes patrum*) follow the stages of C.'s stay in Egypt; they take the form, familiar from the → *Apophthegmata patrum* and the rules of Basil (→ Basil of Caesarea; → Monastic Rule), of → *Quaestiones et responsiones* and contain the spiritual teachings of the desert monks, which, however, C. does not give verbatim but in his own words. The work is divided into three parts (*conl.* 1-10, 11-17, 18-24) which were successively composed and independently circulated from 425-429; they do not form a systematic whole but do give a complete treatment of monastic perfection. *Conl.* 1-10 are intended for Bishop Leontius of Fréjus and Hella-dius, later bishop of Arles; *conl.* 11-17 for Honoratus of Lérins and Eucherius, later bishop of Lyons; *conl.* 18-24 for abbots Jovinian, Minervius, Leontius, and Theodore on the island of Hyères. (3) *De incarnatione contra Nestorium* (*c. Nest.*), composed at the beginning of the Nestorian controversy, is the sole attempt at refuting Nestorius in the Lat. church.

III. Main lines of thought: In the *inst.* and *conl.* C. sets forth the earliest "teaching" on monastic life in the Lat. language. Apart from *inst.* 1-4, which are intended for cenobites, C. follows the distinction of Evagrius Pont. between the monk as *praktikos* and the monk as *gnōstikos* and describes both kinds of work for monks at the various stages on a spiritual journey, independently of whether they are cenobites or anchorites. This spiritual journey begins with the stages of *scientia actualis*, which aims at purity of heart and consists in knowledge of the vices, the ways in which they arise and are overcome, and in the gradual conquest itself. As a result, the monk possesses peace (*tranquillitas*) and God's freely given gift of the virtues. The *scientia actualis*, which is the highest stage cenobites can reach, is the basis for the *scientia spiritualis*, which anchorites alone can reach and which is the true goal of monastic life: the "unceasing" prayer (contemplation), which signifies the union of the human being with God through love after the model of the intratrinitarian unity and love. The love of God that graciously works in human beings forms them into the *imago* and *similitudo Dei*. While the monk living on the lower steps of the *scientia actualis* is still busied with meditation on his faults, he attains in the course of his ascent to the control of his thoughts, the primary goal of which is to fill his mind with better thoughts by memorizing and meditating on the Bible. Depending on the degree of their moral perfection, monks assimilate the words and images of sacred scripture and understand them in their existential meaning.

Conl. 13 became important in the history of dogma because here, in contrast to Augustine and Prosper Tiro of Aquitania, C. sets forth a teaching on grace that would later be regarded as "Semipelagian"; for this reason, it was condemned in the *Decretum Gelasianum*. C.'s influence on monasticism can be seen in, among other things, the monastic organization of Lérins and in → Eucherius of Lyons. → Benedict of Nursia (*reg.* 42; 73) regards *inst.* and *conl.* as obligatory monastic reading, and C.'s works accompanied the spread of Benedictine monasticism.

W: *inst.*, *conl.*, *c. Nest.*, M. Petschenig, CSEL 13, 17. — A. Abt, K. Kohlhund, BKV[1] [German trans.]. — C. S. Gibson (Grand Rapids, 1982) [partial English trans./comm.]. —

conl., E. Pichery, SC 42, 54, 64. — O. Lari (Rome, 1966) [Italian trans.]. — O. Chadwick, C. Luibhéid (New York, 1985) [partial English trans.]. — *inst.*, J.-C. Guy, SC 109. — I. Vanbrabant (Bonheiden/Brugge, 1984) [Dutch trans.]. — *c. Nest.*, L. Dattrino (Rome, 1991) [Italian trans.]. — *inst., conl.*, G. and T. Sartory, 3 vols. (Freiburg i.Br., 1981/82/84) [partial German trans.].
L: D. Burton-Christie, Scripture, self-knowledge and contemplation: StPatr 15 (1993) 339-345. — R. Byrne, Goals of monastic life: CiSt 22 (1987) 3-16. — O. Chadwick, John Cassian (Cambridge, ²1968). — idem, C.: TRE 7:650-657. — L. Christiani, Spiritualité du désert, 2 vols. (Saint-Wandrille, 1946 = ²1991). — V. Codina, Aspecto cristológico (Rome, 1966). — T. Damian, Birthplace: PBR 9 (1990) 149-170. — J. Fleming, C.'s disagreement with Augustine concerning the ethics of falsehood: AugSt 29/2 (1998) 19-24. — C. Folsom, Anger, dejection and acedia: ABenR 35 (1984) 219-248. — K. S. Frank, C. über C.: RQ 90 (1995) 183-197. — idem, Schriftauslegung: FS E. Dassmann (Münster, 1996), 435-443. — E. Griffe, Historien du monachisme égyptien?: StPatr 8 (1966) 363-372. — A. Hoch, Natur und Gnade (Freiburg i.Br., 1895). — H. Holze, Erfahrung und Theologie (Göttingen, 1992). — S. Kinsella, Covetousness and Renunciation in inst. VII: StMon 40 (1998) 203-212. — J. Leroy, Cénobitisme: RAM 43 (1967) 121-158. — idem, Préfaces: RAM 42 (1966) 157-180. — D. J. MacQueen, Grace and free will: RechTh 44 (1977) 5-28. — S. Marsili, Evagrio Pontico (Rome, 1936). — É. Rebillard, Controverse pélagienne: REAug 40 (1994) 197-210. — K. E. Russell, The Unanswered Question in C.'s Second Conference: EeT 29 (1998) 291-302. — E. Schwartz, Konzilsstudien 1 (Strasburg, 1914). — M. Sheridan, Spiritual Progress: Spiritual Progress, ed. J. Driscoll, M. Sheridan (Rome, 1994), 101-125. — T. Sternberg, Westliche Diakonien in Ägypten: JAC 31 (1988) 173-209. — G. Summa, Geistliche Unterscheidung (Würzburg, 1992). — Thesaurus Patrum Latinorum 3: Thesaurus Iohannis Cassiani. Series A: Formae, ed. CETEDOC (Tournai, 1992). — M.-A. Vannier, De incarnatione: StPatr 24 (1993) 345-354. — idem, Jean Chrysostome: RevSR 69 (1995) 453-462. — A. de Vogüé, Monachisme et l'Église: Théologie et la vie monastique (Paris, 1961), 213-240. — idem, Sources: StMon 27 (1985) 241-311. — R. H. Weaver, Access to Scripture: Experiencing the text: Interp. 52 (1998) 367-379. — H. O. Weber, Außerpachomianische Mönchstradition (Münster, 1960). — L. Wrzol, Psychologie: DT 32 (1918) 181-214, 425-456; 34 (1920) 70-96; 36 (1922) 269-294; 37 (1923) 385-404; 38 (1924) 84-91. — K. Zelzer, Südgallier: WSt 104 (1991) 161-168.

M. Skeb, OSB

John of Cellae

As a member and leader of the Monophysite church of Alexandria, J. became, ca. 565, the Monophysite bishop of Cellae (Kellia) in Egypt. Ca. 567 he wrote an *Anathema*, preserved only in Syriac, against the collected works of → John Philoponus. In addition, J. composed a letter, again preserved only in Syriac, to Longinus, bishop of Nubia, by whose efforts Theodore, a monk of Syr. descent, was consecrated patriarch of the Monophysite church of Alexandria

in 575. But since the Egyptians refused to recognize the new patriarch, and although J. assured Longinus of his complete loyalty, in that same year J. and two Syr. bishops consecrated Peter as antipatriarch of Alexandria.

W: *Anathema*, I.-B. Chabot, CSCO 17:160f. [text]; CSCO 103:111f. [Latin trans.]. — *ep. ad Longinum*, I.-B. Chabot, CSCO 17:277f. [text]; CSCO 103:194f. [Latin trans.].
L: A. Grillmeier, Jesus der Christus 2/4 (Freiburg i.Br., 1990), 72, 135f. (English, Christ in Christian Tradition, vol. 2/4 [London, 1996]). — E. Honigmann, Évêques et évêchés monophysites (Leuven/Louvain, 1951), 175, 183, 226f., 232f. — J. Maspero, Histoire des patriarches d'Alexandrie (518-616) (Paris, 1923), 236f.

B. R. Suchla

John Chrysostom

I. **Life:** J., who because of his oratorical gifts has been known since the 5th/6th c. as "Chrysostom" ("Golden Mouth"), was born, probably in 349, in Antioch of Syria; he had one older sister. His father, Secundus, a Roman officer stationed in Antioch, died before J. was two years of age. His mother, Anthusa, raised him in the purely Gr. manner, as befitted her own heritage, and provided him with a comprehensive intellectual formation. Throughout his life his only language was Greek. He devoted himself to the study of rhetoric and was probably also a student of the Antiochene sophist and orator Libanius, who was hostile to Christianity.

In July 367 J. completed his studies and turned to the group around Bishop Meletius (360-381), who that same year had returned from his second exile. J. received baptism from him at Easter 368. For the next three years J. was in close contact with Meletius, with Diodorus, later bishop of Tarsus, and with Flavian, later successor of Meletius. He visited, perhaps in company with his friend Theodore Mops., the monastery of Diodorus and Carterius, where he became familiar with the historical and grammatical exegesis of the Antiochene school, heard lectures on theology and spirituality, and probably concelebrated the liturgy. Even before bishop Meletius was banned from his see the third time, he appointed J. an anagnostes (reader) in 371. Probably in 372, J. withdrew to the mountains near his native city and for a full six years led an ascetical life of great privation, first for four years under the direction of an old Syr. monk, then for two years as a hermit in a cave, where he learned the sacred scriptures by heart.

In 378 Bishop Meletius was able to return to his see after the death of Arian Emperor Valens. J. also returned from the mountains to Antioch at this time, after sustaining serious harm to his health; he took up his service as reader and in 380/381 was ordained a deacon by Bishop Meletius, before the latter journeyed to the second ecumenical Council of Constantinople. Meletius's successor, Flavian, ordained J. a priest at the beginning of 386.

After the death of Bishop Nectarius of Constantinople (Sept. 27, 297), Emperor Arcadius appointed J. as his successor. Without knowing of his appointment, J. was led by a ruse to the capital city and then consecrated a bishop on Feb. 26, 398, by his later adversary, Theophilus Alex. He immediately set about an interior renewal of his see: his first concern was the manner of life of the clergy; he opposed the practice of *virgines subintroductae* and demanded of his clergy a simple way of life, for which he himself provided a model. He did not take part in the social life of the court and the city. Instead, he devoted himself to the study of sacred scripture and to caritative works. He used any surplus funds to support the poor and establish hospitals and shelters for strangers, the direction of which he entrusted to priests and in which he provided doctors, cooks, and orderlies. He also urged the laity to renounce excessive wealth and to care for the needy. He also devoted his care to monks and virgins, widows and deaconesses, from whom he required an exemplary way of life corresponding to their state. He was espec. concerned about liturg. celebrations and, in this connection, with nocturnal liturgies and processions; he also cared for the liturgical needs of the Gothic part of the population. As bishop of the imperial capital, J. could not avoid taking a stand even in civic matters and intervening in political events. In this area he was unsuccessful, for he was not a prince of the church who acted with diplomatic skill, but a spiritual man bound to honesty and sincerity. It cannot be denied, however, that he was to some extent naive.

A drastic change came for J. in 402. He had received at Constantinople, and demanded a fair trial for, the four "Long Brothers" and their companions, about fifty Egyptian monks in all, who had been accused of Origenism and excommunicated and persecuted by their bishop, Theophilus Alex. The emperor agreed with Theophilus's request and invited him to Constantinople, that he might justify his behavior before an eccles. court with J. presiding. Theophilus first sought in vain to have Bishop Epiphanius of Salamis accuse J. himself of Origenism. Only in August 403 did Theophilus himself come to Constantinople. There, for the success of his plans he managed to win over J.'s enemies, namely, the clergy of Constantinople who did not agree with

the reform measures, the outside bishops who thought J.'s personal asceticism and exhortations to morality went too far, and the women of high society, including Empress Eudoxia, who felt insulted by Chrysostom's exhortations to modesty. Theophilus had put together a series of flimsy and even obviously false charges against J. The latter was unwilling to pass judgment on Theophilus, as the emperor asked at the request of the monks, but was willing only to explain the issues in a dialogue. He had gathered forty bishops loyal to him in order to debate with Theophilus, but the latter had journeyed to Constantinople with the declared purpose of having J. deposed. Therefore he was not ready to submit to a synod. Instead, he gathered thirty-six bishops on an estate known as "The Oak," outside the gates of Constantinople; in the autumn of 403 these bishops condemned J. in his absence and removed him from office ("Synod of the Oak"); the imperial court agreed with the verdict.

Against the will of the majority of his community J. was led into exile and taken to the other side of the Bosporus. When, on the next day, "a misfortune" occurred "in the imperial bedroom" (Palladius, *dial.* 9), possibly a miscarriage, the empress interpreted this as a sign from heaven and had J. called back. After a triumphal entry into Constantinople J. called for a new, nonpartisan synod; before this could be held, he again spoke up undismayed for his rights and those of his church. At the urging of some bishops hostile to J., Emperor Arcadius called on J., before Easter 404, to leave his community. The bishop did not obey this instruction. He had to celebrate the Easter liturgy with baptism in the Baths of Constantius; it ended with a bloodbath. On June 9, 404, the emperor signed the definitive decree of banishment. J. was taken to Cucusa in Cappadocia and in the following year to the not far distant border fortress of Arabissus, while his supporters in Constantinople were subjected to serious harassment. J. kept his links with them alive through letters. This roused new suspicions in his enemies, and it was therefore decreed that he be banished to Pityus on the eastern shore of the Black Sea. On the way there he died on Sept. 14, 407, at Comana in Pontus as a result of the strains and privations imposed on him. "God be praised for everything. Amen" were supposedly his final words. In 412, at the demand of Innocent I of Rome (402-417), to whom J. had appealed, he was rehabilitated. In 418 his bones were transferred in a triumphal procession to Constantinople; since May 1, 1626, they have rested in the choir chapel of St. Peter's in Rome.

S: Palladius, *dial.* — Photius, *cod.* 59. — Socrates, *h.e.* 6.2-23; 7.25, 45. — Sozomenus, *h.e.* 8.2-24, 26-28. — Theodoret, *h.e.* 5.27-36.

L: C. Baur, J. u. seine Zeit, 2 vols. (Munich, 1929f.). — R. E. Carter, Chronology: Tr. 18 (1962) 357-364. — J. Dumortier, Valeur historique de Palladius: MSR 8 (1951) 51-56. — G. H. Ettlinger, Date of St. John Chrysostom's birth: Tr. 16 (1933) 373-381. — A.-J. Festugière, Antioche paienne et chrétienne (Paris, 1959). — H. Lietzmann, J.: TU 67 (1958) 326-347. — A.-M. Malingrey, La nuit de Pâques 404 à Constantinople: Mélanges de la Bibliothèque de la Sorbonne 8 (1988) 61-69. — A. Naegele, Chrysostomos u. Libanios: Chrysostomica (Rome, 1908), 81-142. — J. H. Newman, Saint Chrysostom: idem, Historical Sketches 2 (1917), 217-302. German: Historische Skizzen, trans. T. Haecker (Munich, 1948), 9-103. — F. van Ommeslaeghe, Chrysostomica. La nuit de Pâques 404: AnBoll 110 (1992) 123-133. — idem, J. en conflit avec l'impératrice Eudoxie: AnBoll 97 (1979) 131-159. — idem, J. et le peuple de Constantinople: AnBoll 99 (1981) 329-349. — idem, Que vaut le témoignage de Pallade sur le procès de saint J. ?: AnBoll 95 (1977) 389-414. — P. Stockmeier, J.: GK 2, ed. M. Greschat (Stuttgart, 1984), 125-144. — A. Wenger, J.: DSp 8:331-355.

II. Works: No Gr. father of the church has left behind such an extensive body of work as J. Seventeen treatises, over seven hundred certainly authentic sermons, and four commentaries on books of the scriptures, as well as 241 letters have come down from him. For most of these works it is not possible to date the composition to a particular year or, for the sermons, to a particular day.

1. Treatises: Since anyone not yet ordained a priest was forbidden to preach, J. could publish only other works until that point. In fact, his ascetical treatises belong for the most part to that period. The books dealing with monasticism and addressed to monks may have been written even before his ordination as deacon: the *Comparison between King and Monk* (*comp.*), *Against the Enemies of Monks* (*oppugn.*) in defense of the Antiochene monks and hermits, the treatise and letter *To the Fallen Theodore* (*Thdr.* 1-2), the consolation in three books to the monk Stagirius, who was suffering from epilepsy (*Stag.* 1-3), and the two books on *Compunction of Heart* to two monks, Demetrius (*compunct.*) and Stelechius (*compumct.* 2).

Probably from J.'s time as deacon come the works *On Virginity* (*virg.*), the consolation *To a Young Widow* (*vid.* 1), and the work *That No Man Should Marry Twice* (*vid.* 2), and, very probably, the dialogue *On Priesthood* (*sac.*), which was J.'s best-known work even in his own lifetime (Jerome, *vir. ill.* 129). This work can be regarded as an influential source for the later, ever more widespread, onesidedly cultic understanding of the priestly office. In it J. presents

the priestly dignity partly in a way that inevitably promoted the position of power of eccles. officials during the age of the state-church but is today felt to be importunate and seen as oppressive. The composition of the two works against *virgines subintroductae* (*subintr.* and *fem. reg.*) are today ascribed to this period rather than to the time in Constantinople, where Palladius locates them. It was probably not until he became a priest that J. composed the two apologetic works *On St. Babylas, against Julian and the Pagans* (*pan. Bab.* 2) and *Against Jews and Pagans: That Christ is God* (*Jud. et gent.*), as well as the work *On Pride and the Education of Children* (*educ. lib.*), which in all likelihood was written between the tenth and eleventh homilies on the Letter to the Ephesians and was originally a draft of sermons. This last-named work is considered to be the sole coherent treatment of early Chr. private education and the oldest self-contained teaching on Chr. education. To the period of exile in Cucusa and Arabissus belong the two works of consolation, *That No One is Harmed Except by Himself* (*laed.*) and *The Providence of God* (*scand.*), which was the final message to his community, written in the last year of his life.

2. Sermons: Sermons make up by far the largest part of J.'s writings, He delivered his first sermon on the day of his priestly ordination. In it he explained his conception of his office: he wanted, above all, to proclaim the word of God and intended definitively to devote himself to this for the sake of the community and out of love for it. But at the same time he understood his service as preacher to be a sacrifice to God; he intended his first sermon to be a "first-fruits" offering to God, who had given him a mouth for speaking (*ordin.* 1). The sermons delivered during his eighteen years of priestly and episcopal activity consist chiefly of homilies, but they also include thematic series of sermons, addresses on particular occasions, and catecheses. The homilies generally provide continuous exegeses of entire books of scripture, but there are also homilies on single verses. The explanations of Job, fifty-eight Psalms, Isa 1:1–8:10, and Gal can be counted among the series of homilies.

(a) Homilies, commentaries, explanations: J.'s style of preaching did not change throughout his life. For this reason, it is not possible to say of many homilies where they were preached.

Generally assigned to Antioch are the nine sermons of which eight were delivered in Lent of 386, and the sixty-seven homilies on Gen (*serm. in Gen.* and *hom. in Gen.*); the ninety homilies on Mt (*hom. in Mt.*), which are especially important for their content; the eighty-eight homilies on Jn (*hom. in Jo.*); the thirty-two homilies on Rom (*hom. in Rom.*), which, ever since Isidore of Pelusium (*ep.* 5.32), have been regarded as exegetically J.'s best work; the forty-four homilies on 1 Cor (*hom. in 1 Cor.*), the only ones of which J. himself says that he delivered them in Antioch; the thirty homilies on 2 Cor (*hom. in 2 Cor.*); the commentary on Gal (*comm. in Gal.*), which with high probability originated as homilies; the eighteen homilies on 1 Tim and the ten on 2 Tim (*hom. in 1 Tim.* and *hom. in 2 Tim.*); the six homilies on Tit (*hom. in Tit.*); and the twenty-four homilies on Eph (*hom. in Eph.*). Also delivered in Antioch were a number of homilies on single verses of the NT books.

To the Constantinopolitan period are assigned the fifteen homilies on Phil (*hom. in Phil.*) and the twelve on Col (*hom. in Col.*); the fifty-five homilies on Acts (*hom. in Ac.*), in which not much care is given to the form; the eleven homilies on 1 Thess and the five on 2 Thess (*hom. in 1 Thess.* and *hom. in 2 Thess.*); the three on Phlm (*hom. in Phlm.*); and the thirty-four on Heb (*hom in Heb.*), which appeared only after the author's death. It is not possible to say when the explanations of Job (*exp. in Job*), Pss 4-12, 43-49, 108-17, 119-50 (*exp. in Ps.*), and Isa 1:1–8:10 (*Is. interp.*) were composed. The explanation of Ps 41 is clearly to be described as a homily (*hom in Ps.* 41).

J. represents the historical and grammatical exegesis of the Antiochene school, but because of his lack of theol. originality and because his preaching is in the service primarily of Chr. living, he has no especially important place in that school. Nonetheless, his extensive life's work attests to a critical kind of interpretation that takes seriously the literal sense above all else. Espec. important is the idea, always in the background and repeatedly finding expression, of the condescension of God; this idea is at the same time an important key to this church father's thinking. This divine condescension did not end with the formulation of revelation in writing but is constantly renewed, espec. when the words of scripture, in which God's Word itself is present to dialogue with human beings, are read and explained in the liturgy. Although J. regards the explanation of God's word as the primary task of the interpreter, he rarely limits himself solely to the explanation of scripture. It is precisely a characteristic of his homilies that they do not simply explain scripture but almost always end with a statement on some question of Chr. life.

(b) Sermons: Several cycles of sermons have been preserved from the Antiochene period. The best known are the twenty-two "Homilies on the Statues" (*stat.* as well as *catech.* 1), which he delivered during Lent, 387. A large sector of the population, angered by the emperor's new taxes, had overthrown statues of Theodosius and his family that were set up in Antioch. The city authorities had already begun punishing the malefactors and had sent reporters to the emperor. While the elderly Bishop Flavian was traveling to Constantinople in order to ward off further punishments, J., his presbyter, took advantage of Lent to move the people to penance and conversion by means of his "Homilies on the Statues." Flavian succeeded in mollifying Theodosius; the feast of Easter could now be celebrated in peace and with gratitude. Other cycles of sermons are the twelve against the Anomoeans (*incomprehens.*; *anom.*) and the eight against the Jews or the judaizing Christians of his community (*Jud.*), as well as the nine on penance (*poenit.*). Also belonging to the Antiochene period are the sermons on the major feasts of the Lord in the church year (*nativ.*; *bapt.*; *prod. Jud.* 1-3; *cruc.* 1-2; *res. Chr.*; *ascens.*; *pent.* 1-2); twenty-seven in honor of the saints, the best known being the seven on St. Paul (*laud. Paul.*); the sermons on OT figures: five on Hannah (*Anna*), three on David and Saul (*David*), one on Elijah and the widow (*El. et vid.*). Twenty-two sermons were connected with political events in Constantinople that affected J. personally (*Eutrop.* 1-2; *Saturn.*; *a exil.* 1-2; *p. redit.* 1-2; *dimiss. Chan.*; *hom. div.*).

(c) Catecheses: Eleven catecheses have been preserved from the time when J. was a presbyter of the church of Antioch: four from 388 (*catech.* 2/1-2/4), seven from a year between 389 and 397 (*catech.* 3/1-3/7). Some of these were in the preparation for the incorporation of members into the church during the Easter Vigil; others were mystagogical catecheses delivered during Easter week. The four homilies on the beginning of Acts (*hom.* 1-4 *in Ac. princ.*), which contain sections addressed to the newly baptized, were delivered during Easter week 388 in place of mystagogical catecheses.

3. Letters: 241 letters have come down under J.'s name (*ep.* 1-236, 242; *ep. carc.*; *ep. Eud.*; *ep. Innoc* 1; *ep. Innoc.* 2). All of the letters were written from exile except for the first letter to Innocent I of Rome, which J. composed in Constantinople after Easter 404 before being banished a second time, and the letter to the empress (*ep. Eud.*), who had expropriated a piece of property. A special treasure is the seventeen letters of consolation to Deaconess Olympias (*ep.* 1-17), between whom and the bishop there was a profound spiritual friendship.

4. Dubious and inauthentic works: Many insignificant writers who wanted to ensure circulation and influence for their works published these under the name of J. In most cases the forgeries are easily recognizable. The best-known example is probably the *Catechetical Address of John Chrysostom* (PG 59:721-24) which is read annually at the Byz. Easter Vigil but is certainly not his. Of the formulary for the "Liturgy of Chrysostom," which is celebrated on all but ten days of the year in the Byz. rite, it seems that far more goes back to J.'s time than had long been thought, although he is not the direct author of that liturgy in its present form.

III. Main Lines of Thought: J. is regarded as a church father who did not make any important contribution to the development of the church's teaching on faith. Since he was not an espec. independent theol. thinker, he was not interested in a systematic, theoretical presentation and speculative analysis of theol. questions. As a result, he did not leave behind any important dogm. treatise, although he lived in an age of great creedal struggles. As an up-to-date preacher of God's word, however, his genius surpasses that of any other father of the Gr. church. He may therefore be regarded as an espec. reliable witness for the stage of dogm. development reached at that time. On the other hand, it must be remembered that it was not his duty as a preacher to inform his community of the full scope and detail of theol. problems. Acc. to himself, he "often chose not to discuss speculative questions, because the people were incapable of following such discussions; and even if they could, they would not end up with anything firm and sure" (*hom.* 4 [3] *in Jo.*). He saw it as his task in preaching to give his communities the clearest possible answers to questions of faith that concerned them. He regarded this preaching as the central element in his pastoral activity (not without some reason did people blame him for his reserve outside the liturgy, a reserve interpreted as arrogance [Palladius, *dial.* 19]). Moreover, since he carried out his duty of preaching at the liturgy of various communities, he regarded the liturgy as the center of community life. Yet, just as J. was not known as a dogmatic innovator in Antioch and Constantinople, neither did he act as a real reformer of the community liturgy. Apart from the introduction or revival of nocturnal vigils in Constantinople, he did not undertake any major changes in the liturgy. It was only ca. 1000 that the authority of his name was attached to the formulary most frequently used in the Byz. Eucharist. Much more important to J. was the task of making known to his communities the meaning and function of the liturgy and its elements; this he did in preaching that did not lack for originality. In this way he created the interior conditions for forming and shaping the life of the communities with the liturgy and, above all, the preached word of God as its center. Only those who act acc. to God's word in everyday life (J.'s focus here was on obedience to the chief commandment of Jesus through loving attention to the poor) can turn their entire lives into a liturgy and teach their fellow Christians by their example. A community that endeavors to do this will also influence its pagan environment and even become a model for other communities and for later generations.

W: PG 47-64. — *a exil.* 1, M. Schmitz, BKV[1] J. 3 [German trans.]. — *anom.* 7-12, A.-M. Malingrey, SC 396. — *ascens.*, M. Schmitz, BKV[1] J. 3 [German trans.]. — *bapt.*, M. Schmitz, BKV[1] J. 3 [German trans.]. — *catech.*, R. Kaczynski, FC 6/1-2. — P. W. Harkins (London, 1963) [English trans.]. — *catech.* 2/1-2/3, A. Piédagnel, L. Doutreleau, SC 366. — *catech.* 2/2-2/4, A. Papadopoulos-Kerameus (Leipzig, 1975) [text]. — *catech.* 2/4-3/7, A. Wenger, SC 50bis. — *educ. lib.*, B. K. Exarchos, Das Wort der Antike 4 (Munich, 1958) [text/comm.]. — A.-M. Malingrey, SC 188. — J. Glagla (Paderborn, 1968) [German trans./comm.]. — M. Gärtner (Cologne, 1985) [German trans./comm.]. — *eleem.*, M. Schmitz, BKV[1] J. 3 [German trans.]. — *ep.* 1-17, A.-M. Malingrey, SC 13bis. — *ep. Innoc.* 1, idem, SC 342. — *ep.* 1-17, *ep. Innoc.* 1-2, M. Schmitz, BKV[1] J. 3 [German trans.]. — *ep.*, R. Callegari (Milan, 1976) [Italian trans./comm.]. — *Eutrop.* 1, M. Schmitz, BKV[1] J. 3 [German trans.]. — *hom.* 1-67 in Gen., M. zu Sachsen (Paderborn, 1913) [German trans.]. — *serm.* 1-9 in Gen., idem (Paderborn, 1914) [German trans.]. — *exp. in Job*, H. Sorlin, L. Neyrand, SC 346; 348. — *Is. interp.*, J. Dumortier, A. Liefooghe, SC 304. — *hom.* 1-6 in Is. 6.1, idem, SC 277. — *hom.* 1-90 in Mt., C. Baur, BKV[2] J. 1-4 [German trans.]. — *hom.* 1-88 in Jo., F. Knors (Paderborn, 1862) [German trans.]. — *hom.* 1-32 in Rom., J. Jatsch, BKV[2] J. 5-6 [German trans.]. — *hom.* 1-44 in 1 Cor., J. C. Mitterrutzner, BKV[1] J. 5 [German trans.]. — *hom.* 1-30 in 2 Cor., A. Hartl, BKV[1] J. 6 [German trans.]. — *comm. in Gal.*, W. Stoderl, BKV[2] J. 8 [German trans.]. — *hom.* 1-24 in Eph., idem, BKV[2] J. 8 [German trans.]. — *hom.* 1-15 in Phil., idem, BKV[2] J. 7 [German trans.]. — *hom.* 1-12 in Col., idem, BKV[2] J. 7 [German trans.]. — *hom.* 1-11 in 1 Thess., B. Sepp, BKV[1] J. 8 [German trans.]. — *hom.* 1-5 in 2 Thess., idem, BKV[1] J. 8 [German trans.]. — *hom.* 1-18 in 1 Tim., J. Wimmer, BKV[1] J. 9 [German trans.]. — *hom.* 1-10 in 2 Tim., idem, BKV[1] J. 9 [German trans.]. — *hom.* 1-6 in Tit., idem, BKV[1] J. 9 [German trans.]. — *hom.* 1-3 in Philm., idem, BKV[1] J. 9 [German trans.]. — *hom.* 1-34 in Heb., J. C. Mitterrutzner, BKV[1] J. 10 [German trans.]. — *incomprehens.*, F. Cavallera, J. Danielou, R. Flacelière, SC 28bis. — *kal.*, M. Schmitz, BKV[1] J. 3 [German trans.]. — *laed.*, A. M. Malingrey, SC 103. — *laud. Paul.*, A. Piédagnel, SC 300. — M. Schmitz, BKV[1] J. 3 [German trans.]. — *Laz.* 6, M. Schmitz, BKV[1] J. 3 [German trans.]. — *nativ.*, M. Schmitz, BKV[1] J. 3 [German trans.]. — *ordin.*, A.-M. Malingrey, SC 272. — M. Schmitz, BKV[1] J. 3 [German trans.]. — *p. redit* 1, M. Schmitz, BKV[1] J. 3 [German trans.]. — *pan. Bab.* 2, M. A. Schatkin, C. Blanc, B. Grillet, SC 362. — *pan. mart.* 3, M. Schmitz, BKV[1] J. 3 [German trans.]. — *pent.* 1-2, M. Schmitz, BKV[1] J. 3 [German trans.]. — *poenit.* 1-9, J. C. Mitterrutzner, BKV[1] J. 1 [German trans.]. — *prod. Jud.* 2, M. Schmitz, BKV[1] J. 3 [German trans.]. — *res. mort.*, M.

Schmitz, BKV[1] J. 3 [German trans.]. — *sac.* 1-6, A.-M. Malingrey, SC 272. — A. Naegle, BKV[2] J. 4 [German trans./comm.]. — *scand.,* A.-M. Malingrey, SC 79. — *stat.* 1-21, J. C. Mitterrutzner, BKV[1] J. 2 [German trans.]. — *Thdr.* 1-2, J. Dumortier, SC 117. — *Thdr.* 1, J. Rupp, BKV[1] J. 1 [German trans.]. — *vid.* 1-2, B. Grillet, G. H. Ettlinger, SC 138. — *virg.,* H. Musurillo, B. Grillet, SC 125. — J. C. Mitterrutzner, BKV[1] J. 1 [German trans.]. — A. Wenger, A son retour d'Asie: REByz 19 (1961) 110-123 [text/French trans./comm.]. — A. Wenger, Sur l'épiphanie: REByz 29 (1971) 117-135 [text/French trans./comm.]. — S. Haidacher, Drei uneditierte Chrysostomustexte einer Baseler Hs.: ZKTh 30 (1906) 572-582; 31 (1907) 141-171. 347-360 [text/comm.]. — Codices chrysostomici graeci 1-5, ed. M. Aubineau, R. E. Carter, W. Lackner (Paris, 1968-1983). — Repertorium pseudochrysostomicum, ed. J. A. de Aldama (Paris, 1965). — M. van Esbroek, Une homélie arménienne sur la Dormition attribuée à Chrysostome: OrChr 74 (1990) 199-233. — K.-H. Uthemann, Die ps.-chrysostomische Predigt CPG 4701: OCP 59 (1993) 5-62 [text/comm.]. — Homiliae pseudo-chrysostomicae 1, K.-H. Uthemann, R. F. Regtuit, J. M. Tevel (Tournai, 1994) [text].

L: A. C. de Albornoz, J. y su influencia social (Madrid, 1934). — P.-G. Alves de Sousa, El sacerdocio ministerial en "De sacerdotio" (Pamplona, 1975). — idem, El sacerdocio permanente en "De sacerdotio": TeSa 5 (1973) 1-29. — E. Amand de Mendieta, Un thème socratique et stoicien dans J.: Byz. 36 (1966) 353-381. — T. E. Ameringer, Stylistic influence of the Second Sophistic on the panegyrical sermons (Washington, 1921). — P. Andres, Missionsgedanke (Bottrop, 1935). — D. Attwater, J. Pastor and Preacher (London, 1959). — I. Auf der Maur, Mönchtum u. Glaubensverkündigung (Fribourg, Switzerland, 1959). — C. Baur, Kanon des J.: ThQ 105 (1924) 258-271. — idem, J. dans l'histoire littéraire (Leuven/Louvain, 1907). — S. Bezdeki, Chrysostomus et Plato: Ephemeris Dacoromana 1 (1923), 291-337. — M. v. Bonsdorff, Predigttätigkeit des J. (Helsingfors, 1922). — G. Bosio, Preghiera ed Eucaristia: Seminarium 21 (1969) 654-678. — E. Boularand, La venue de l'homme à la foi (Rome, 1939). — idem, Le sacerdoce mystère de crainte et de l'amour: BLE 72 (1971) 3-36. — R. Brändle, Matth. 25, 31-46 im Werk des J. (Tübingen, 1979). — idem, Synergismus als Phänomen der Frömmigkeitsgeschichte: Gnadenwahl u. Entscheidungsfreiheit, ed. F. v. Lilienfeld, E. Mühlenberg (Erlangen, 1980), 69-89, 113-121. — D. C. Burger, Bibliography of the Scholarship on the Life and Work (Evanston, 1964). — R. Burnish, Baptismal preparation: FS R. E. O. White (Sheffield, 1999), 379-401. — Chrysostomica, ed. Comitato per il XVo centenario della sua morte (Rome, 1908). — E. A. Clark, Jerome, Chrysostom, and friends, SWR 2 (New York/Toronto, 1979). — J. et Augustin: Actes du Colloque de Chantilly, 22-24 septembre 1974, ed. C. Kannengiesser (Paris, 1975). — G. Colombo, L'Eucaristia come sacramento di unità, Diss. Gregoriana (Rome, 1959). — J. Coman, Le rapport de la justification et de la charité: TU 103 (1968) 248-271. — C. Corsato, Dottrina battesimale: StPat 23 (1976) 270-296. — L. Daloz, Le travail selon s. J. (Paris, 1959). — A. Dannassis, J. Pädagogisch-psychologisch Ideen (Bonn, 1971). — H. Degen, Die Tropen der Vergleichung, Diss. (Fribourg, Switzerland, 1921). — H. Dörries, Erneuerung des kirchlichen Amts: Bleibendes im Wandel der Kirchengeschichte, ed. B. Moeller, G. Ruhbach (Tübingen, 1973), 1-46. — F.-X. Druet, Langage, images et visages de la mort (Namur,

1990). — A. Dupleix, Théologie et expérience du sacerdoce, Diss. masch. (Rome, 1987). — H. Eising, Schriftgebrauch u. Schriftverständis in den Matthäus-Homilien: OrChr 48 (1964) 84-106. — C. Fabricius, Zu den Jugendschriften (Lund, 1962). — T. M. Finn, The Liturgy of Baptism (Washington, 1967). — G. Fittkau, Der Begriff des Mysteriums (Bonn, 1953). — J. Förster, Die Exegese des vierten Evangeliums, Diss. masch. (Berlin, 1951). — M. J. G. Fouyas, The social message, Diss. (Manchester, 1962). — M. Gärtner, Familienerziehung in der Alten Kirche (Cologne, 1985). — J. Goffinet, Péché et corps mystique: REcL 45 (1958) 3-17, 65-87. — A. González Blanco, Sexualidad y matrimonio: ScrVict 25 (1978) 42-66. — P. Gorday, Principles of Patristic Exegesis (New York, 1983). — J. Gülden, Religiöse u. liturgische Erneuerung: ThJb(L) 3 (1960) 305-334. — S. Haidacher, Die Lehre über die Schriftinspiration (Salzburg, 1897). — M. Haidenthaller, J. Nachweis der Gottheit Christi (Linz, 1951). — F. Halkin, Douze récits byzantins sur Chrysostome (Brussels, 1977). — T. Harjunpaa, St. J. in the light of his Catechetical and Baptismal Homilies: LuthQ 29 (1977) 167-195. — C. Hay, St. J. and the integrity of the human nature of Christ: FrS 19 (1959) 298-317. — W. Jaeger, Die Sklaverei bei J., Diss. (Kiel, 1974). — R. Kaczynski, Wort Gottes in Liturgie u. Alltag (Freiburg i.Br., 1974). — M. Kertsch, Exempla chrysostomica (Graz, 1995). — P. Klasvogt, Leben zur Verherrlichung Gottes (Bonn, 1992). — G. Kupp, Die Stellung des J. zum weltlichen Leben (Münster, 1905). — J. Korbacher, Außerhalb der Kirche kein Heil? (Munich, 1963). — B. Kosecki, La pérennité des actes sauveurs du Christ: Lat. 46 (1980) 285-319. — J. Knupp, Mystagogieverständnis (Munich, 1995). — M. E. Lawrenz, The Christology of J. (Ann Arbor, 1989). — J. Lécuyer, Le sacerdoce céleste du Christ: NRTh 72 (1950) 561-579. — idem, Saint J. et le diaconat: FS B. Botte (Leuven/Louvain, 1972), 295-310. — idem, Saint Pierre dans l'enseignement de Chrysostome: Gr. 49 (1968) 113-133. — F. Leduc, Gérer l'agressivité et la colère: POC 38 (1988) 31-63. — idem, L'eschatologie: POC 19 (1969) 109-134. — idem, Péché et conversion: POC 26 (1976) 34-58; 27 (1977) 15-42; 28 (1978) 44-84. — idem, Penthos et larmes: POC 41 (1991) 220-257. — P. E. Legrand, Saint J. (Paris, 1924). — J.-M. Leroux, Monachisme et communauté chrétienne d'après saint J.: Théologie de la vie monastique (Paris, 1961), 143-190 — J. H. W. G. Liebeschuetz, Barbarians and Bishops (Oxford, 1990). — M. Lochbrunner, Über das Priestertum (Bonn, 1993). — W. A. Maat, A Rhetorical Study of De sacerdotio (Washington, 1944). — F. Marinelli, La carta del prete (Rome, 1986). — W. Mayer, Women in C.'s circle: VigChr 53 (1999) 265-288. — A. de Mendieta, Un thème socratique et stoicien: Byz. 36 (1966) 353-381. — A. Merzagora, S. Paolo nella prospettiva di S. Giovanni Crisostomo (Rome, 1963). — L. Meyer, Perfection chrétienne et vie solitaire: RAM 14 (1933) 232-262. — idem, Saint J. maître de perfection chrétienne (Paris, 1933). — C. Militello, Donna e chiesa (Palermo, 1987). — A. Monaci Castagno, Paeideia classica ed esercizio pastorale: RSLR 26 (1990) 429-459. — J.-P. Mondet, Le Sacerdoce dans le Commentaire sur l'Épître aux Hébreux, Diss. masch. (Leuven/Louvain, 1986). — A. Moulard, J. (Paris, 1949). — idem, Le défenseur du mariage et l'apôtre de la virginité (Paris, 1923). — A. Naegle, Die Eucharistielehre (Freiburg i.Br., 1900). — T. Nikolaou, Der Neid bei J. (Bonn, 1969). — F. Norman, Neue Existenz, Freiheit u. Gnade: ThGl 70 (1980) 250-283. — E. Nowak, Le chrétien devant la souffrance

(Paris, 1972). — L. J. Ohleyer, The Pauline Formula Induere Christum, Diss. Cath. Univ. America (Washington, 1921). — R. Otto, Das ganz Andere (Gotha [4]1929), 1-10. — O. Pasquato, Carne, croce, sangue e condiscendenza divina: Atti della Settimana Sangue e antropologia nella letteratura cristiana, ed. Centro Studi Sanguis Christi (Rome, 1983), 1267-1300. — idem, Catechesi ecclesiologica nella cura pastorale: Ecclesiologia e catechesi patristica, ed. S. Felici (Rome, 1982), 123-172. — idem, Eredità giudaica e famiglia cristiana: Lat. 54 (1988) 58-91. — idem, Gli spettacoli in S. Giovanni Crisostomo (Rome, 1976). — idem, Pastorale familiare: Sal. 51 (1989) 3-46. — F. van de Paverd, Anaphoral intercessions, epiclesis and communion-rites: OCP 49 (1983) 303-339. — idem, Zur Geschichte der Meßliturgie (Rome, 1970). — O. Plassmann, Das Almosen bei Chrysostomos (Münster, 1961). — K. Prümm, Der Abschnitt über die Doxa des Apostolats 2Kor 3,1-4,6: Bib. 30 (1949) 161-196, 377-499. — P. Rancillac, L'église, manifestation de l'esprit (Beyrouth, 1970). — P. Rentinck, La cura pastorale in Antiochia (Rome, 1970). — F. I. Rigolot, Note sull'anafora antiochena: Atti della Settimana Sangue e antropologia nella letteratura cristiana, ed. Centro Studi Sanguis Christi (Rome, 1983), 1449-1471. — H. M. Riley, Christian initiation (Washington, 1974). — A. M. Ritter, Charisma im Verständnis des J. (Göttingen, 1972). — idem, Erwägungen zum Antisemitismus in der Alten Kirche: Bleibendes im Wandel der Kirchengeschichte, ed. B. Moeller (Tübingen, 1973), 71-91. — J. Roldanus, Le chrétien — étranger au monde: SE 30 (1987-1988) 231-251. — A. K. Ruf, Sünde u. Sündenvergebung, Diss. masch. (Freiburg i.Br., 1959). — D. Sartore, Il mistero del battesimo: Lat. 50 (1984) 358-395. — J. A. Sawhill, The Use of the Athletic Metaphors, Diss. (Princeton, 1928). — C. Scaglione, Tra rigore e condiscendenza: Per foramen acus, ed. G. Visona et al. (Milan, 1986), 329-360. — V. Schmitt, Die Verheißung der Eucharistie bei Cyrillus v. Jerusalem u. J. (Würzburg, 1903). — J. Seidlmayer, Die Pädagogik des J. (Münster, 1926). — A. Sifoniou, Les fondements juridiques de l'aumône et de la charité: RDC 14 (1964) 241-269. — M. Simon, La polémique anti-juive de S. J.: AIPh 4 (1936) 403-421. — M. Soffray, Recherches sur la syntaxe de s. J. (Paris, 1939). — J. M. Soto Rábanos, El matrimonio in fieri en la doctrina de S. Ambrosio y S. J. (Rome, 1976). — P. Stockmeier, Theologie u. Kult des Kreuzes (Trier, 1966). — W. Stoellger, Das Marienbild des J. Diss. masch. (Heidelberg, 1973). — A. Stötzel, Kirche als "neue Gesellschaft" (Münster, 1984). — Symposion, ed. P. C. Christou (Thessalonica, 1973). — G. J. Theocharides, Zur Geschichte des byz. Profantheaters (Thessalonica, 1940). — F.-J. Thonnard, Chrysostome et Augustin dans la controverse pélagienne: REByz 25 (1967) 189-218. — K. Tsouros, La dottrina sul matrimonio: Asp. 21 (1974) 5-46. — B. H. Vandenberghe, La théologie du travail: RET 16 (1956) 475-495. — idem, Saint J. et la parole de Dieu (Paris, 1961). — S. Verosta, J. Staatsphilosoph u. Geschichtstheologe (Graz, 1960). — A. Wenger, La tradition des œuvres: REByz 14 (1956) 5-47. — R. L. Wilken, J. and the Jews (Berkeley, 1983). — S. Zincone, Richezza et povertà nelle omilie (L'Aquila, 1973). — idem, Commento alla Lettera ai Galati (L'Aquila, 1980). — T. N. Zissis, Man and World in the History of Salvation (Thessalonica, 1971). — M. Zitnik, Θεὸς πιλάνϑρωπος bei J.: OCP 41 (1975) 76-118. — idem, Das Sein des Menschen zu Gott: OCP 42 (1976) 368-401; 43 (1977) 18-40.

R. KACZYNSKI

John Climacus

I. Life: J., nicknamed "Scholasticus," is generally called "Climacus" (*ho tēs klimakos*) because of his principal work (see below). He lived probably between 575 and 650. Daniel of Raithu composed a short *Vita* (PG 88:596-608). Acc. to this, J. became a monk in the Sinai at sixteen, the first four years there as disciple of abbot Martyrius, and then spent forty years as a hermit in the Wadi Tlah, 8 km. from the present-day monastery of St. Catherine. The somewhat lengthy stay in some monasteries near Alexandria, which J. himself mentions (PG 88:776B), can be presumed to have occurred during this period. Afterward J. became abbot of the monastery in the Sinai.

II. Works: At the request of Abbot John of Raithu (PG 88:624f.) J. composed his *Ladder* (*klimax*; *scala paradisi*) with its thirty steps of the spiritual ascent. In the work the image of Jacob's ladder (Gen 28) is combined with the thirty years of the hidden life of Jesus. J. provides a (nonsystematic) synthesis of the monastic spirituality of the previous centuries. He gives as explicit sources John Cassian, Evagrius Pont., and Gregory Naz.; he also depends on Basil, Gregory Nyss., Didachus of Photice, and espec. on the → *Apophthegmata Patrum* and the monasticism of Gaza (Isaias, Barsanuphius, and Dorotheus).

The *Ladder* is written for monks. Following the ascent sketched by Evagrius, it describes, after the renunciation of the world (steps 1-3), the basic monastic attitudes to be cultivated (steps 4-7: obedience, conversion, remembrance of death, penitential sorrow), as well as the wrong attitudes and the vices to be overcome (steps 9-10, 12-18, 20-23: grudges, slander, lying, aversions, appetite for food, sexual license, avarice, laziness, insensitivity, blasphemy, pride, desire of glory). After these have been overcome, it is possible to attain to gentleness (simplicity), humility, and the gift of discernment (steps 24-26). After the process of asceticism and purification (*praktikē*), in the final four steps (27-30: peace of heart, prayer, freedom from passion, love) J. comes to the realm of mysticism (*theōria*). Here he brings out the goal of monastic life: union with God in prayer and love. As has been intimated already in the individual steps (9: silence; 14: psalmody), this goal is more easily reached by hermits than by cenobites. Union with God makes it possible then to speak of him (*theologia*).

Attached to the *Ladder* is the short work, *To Shepherds*, a mirror of abbots, containing fifteen short chapters. J. describes an abbot as a guide of souls after the example of the Good Shepherd, who with wise discernment exercises the offices of physician, teacher, and pilot for those entrusted to him.

The *Ladder* is one of the works that had the greatest influence on eastern monasticism. It is especially important in hesychasm for the development of the Jesus-prayer, which J. was one of the first to recommend expressly (step 15; PG 88:889D and frequently). There is as yet no critical edition. The *editio princeps* by M. Rader, SJ (PG 88:583-1163) is defective. Rader's edition also contains scholia, i.e., short commentaries by later authors on particular sections of the *Ladder*.

The mss. tradition is very extensive in Greek and the eastern languages (Syriac, Arabic, Armenian, Georgian). After reaching Russia in the hesychast movement, the *Ladder* was first translated into Church Slavonic in the 12th c. It began its influence on the West with the 13th c. Lat. translation by Angelo Clareno.

Iconography represents a special thread in the history of the *Ladder*'s influence. Illuminated mss. go back to the 10th c. In addition to miniatures for the individual steps, there were also icons and frescoes representing the *Ladder* in its entirety.

W: *Ladder, To Shepherds*, PG 88:581-1210. — *Ladder*, P. Deseille (Bellefontaine, 1978) [French trans.]. — F. Handwercher (Landshut, 1834); anonymous reprint 1874; reprint 1987 by R. F. Kastner. — Sophronius Eremites 1883, (Athens, 1979) [Greek text]. — Archimandrit Ignatios, Parakletoskloster ([3]1986) [Greek text/modern Greek trans.]. — C. Luibheid, N. Russell (New York, 1982) [English trans.]. — C. Riggi (Rome, 1989) [Italian trans.]. — I. G. Almodi, M. Mattei (Zamora, 1990) [Spanish trans.]. — M. del C. Saenz, L. C. del Conzález (Buenos Aires, 1988/89) [Spanish trans.].
L: J. Chryssavgis, The Sources of St. John Climacus: OS 37 (1988) 3 13. — idem, Katanyxis: Compunction as the Context for the Theology of Tears in St. John Climacus: Kl. 17 (1985) 131-136. — idem, Oboediences and the Spiritual Father: Theol. 58 (1987) 551-571. — idem, The Jesus Prayer in the Ladder of St. John Climacus: OS 35 (1986) 30-33. — idem, St. John Climacus and the Monk's Ascetic Struggle: Tjurunga 34 (1988) 3-17. — idem, The Sources of St. John Climacus: OS 37 (1988) 3-13. — G. Couilleau, S. Jean Climaque: DSp 9/1:369-389. — J. Gribomont, La "Scala Paradisi": StMon 2 (1960) 345-358. — I. Hausherr, La théologie du monachisme chez saint Jean Climaque: Théologie de la vie monastique (Paris, 1961), 385-410. — E. v. Ivanka, Aufstieg und Wende: JÖB 19 (1979) 141-152. — G. Kaster, Joh. Klimakus (Climax) vom Sinai (Scholastikus): LCI 7, 140-144. — R. T. Lawrence, The Three-Fold Structure of the Ladder of Divine Ascent: St. Vladimir's Theological Quarterly 32 (1988) 101-118. — J. Pauli, Peri Xeniteias. Über das Fremdsein. Die dritte Stufe der Leiter des J.: Studia Monastica 41 (1999) 35-52. — K. Rahner, M. Viller, Aszese u. Mystik der Väterzeit (Freiburg i.Br., 1989 = 1939), 155-164. — W. Völker, Scala paradisi (Wiesbaden, 1968). — C. Yannaras, Eros divin et éros humain (Athens, 1971).

J. PAULI, OSB

John III of Constantinople

J. III Scholasticus (b. ca. 510-15) belonged to the family of a priest from Seremis near Antioch. He worked as a lawyer (*scholastikos*), received priestly ordination from Patriarch Domnus II of Antioch (545-559), and was sent by the latter to Constantinople as his apocrisiarius (messenger) ca. 550. In Jan. 565 Emperor Justinian appointed him successor of the deposed Eutychius as patriarch of Constantinople. J. persecuted the anti-Chalcedonians and led the church of Constantinople until 577, when Eutychius was restored to his office. Modern scholarship no longer identifies J. with → John Malalas.

The following canonical collections go back to J.: (1) *Synagōgē kanonōn ekklēsiastikōn* in fifty titles (*nomoc.*). It took over the canons of various councils and synods as well as the *Apostolic Canons* and canons from *ep.* 11 and 111 of Basil. The collection later served as basis for the Nomokanon of Methodius. It was translated into Slavonic toward the end of the 9th c. (2) The *Collectio 87 capitum* (*coll. cap.*) is a collection of excerpts from the *Novellae* of Justinian that touch on church affairs. J. revised both works ca. 570. The *katēchētikos logos*, which was composed ca. 567/568, is a sermon that goes back to J.; it was attacked by John Philoponus and has not been preserved.

W: *nomoc.*, V. N. Beneševic, J. Scholastici synagoga L titulorum, Tom. 1: ABAW NF 14 (Munich, 1937, [2]1972) [text]. — *coll. cap.*, I. B. Pitra, JEGH 1 (Rome, 1868), 385-405 [text].
L: H. G. Beck, Kirche u. theol. Lit. (Munich, 1959), 422f. — A.-V. Grumel, Regestes 1 (Constantinople, 1932), Nr. 250-259. — J. Haury, Johannes Malalas, identisch mit Patriarch J. ?: ByZ 9 (1900) 337-356. — A. Kazhdan, J.; ODB 1047. — E. Schwartz, Die Kanonessammlung des J.: SBAW. PH 6 (1933) 3-6. — S. Troianos, J.: LMA 5:548f. — P. van den Ven, L'accession de J. au siège patriarcal: Byz. 35 (1965) 320-352.

F. R. GAHBAUER, OSB

John IV of Constantinople

J. (b. between 500 and 530; d. Sept. 2, 595) was originally a manufacturer of coins. He became a deacon and the treasurer of the patriarch of Constantinople and finally, on April 5/6, 582, became himself patriarch; he held this office until his death. Because of his strict ascetical way of life he became known as "Nesteutes" (*Ieiunator*, "Faster"). He came in conflict with Pelagius II and Gregory I because of the title "Ecumenical Patriarch," since the popes saw in this an expression of a quest for primacy over the entire church.

The following works have come down under J.'s name. The *Kanonarion* is a treatise on penance (*canonar.*). In the *Didascalia Patrum* an *Akolouthia kai Taxis* for confession, along with an address to the penitent (*poenit.*), is ascribed to J. In its original form, the *Kanōnikon* (*can.*) with fifty-one canons probably goes back to the regulations of Basil on penance but is the work of later compilers. All these works are dated to the period between the end of the 8th c. and the 10th c.; the author of the *canonar.* was probably an otherwise unknown monk and deacon named John.

In addition, a sermon to those making confession has come down under J.'s name but is probably from Chrysostom. The Ps.-Chrysostomic sermon on Susanna (PG 56:584-89) has come down under J.'s name in the Copt. tradition. An address on penance, continence, and virginity may be authentic (*poen. con. virg.*); a work on baptism, addressed to Leander of Seville, has disappeared.

W: *canonar.*, J. Morinus, Commentarius historicus de disciplina paenitentiae (Paris, 1651) [text]. — *poenit., serm., poenit. cont. virg.*, PG 88:1889-1978. — *can.*, I. B. Pitra, Spicilegium Solesmense 4 (Paris, 1858), 429-435 [text].
L: H. G. Beck, Kirche u. theol. Lit. (Munich, 1959), 423-425. — E. Herman, Il più antico penitenziale greco: OCP 19 (1953) 70-127. — A. Kazhdan, J.: ODB 1049. — D. Stiernon, J.: DSp 8:586-589. — N. A. Zaozerskij, A. S. Chachanov, Nomokanon Joanna Postnika (Russian), (Moscow, 1902).

F. P. GAHBAUER, OSB

John VI of Constantinople

J., a deacon and librarian, was installed as patriarch in 712 after the deposition of Cyrus, who was orthodox, by Emperor Philippicus, who once again favored Monotheletism. But in 713, after the fall of Philippicus, J. crowned the latter's successor, Anastasius II, who ceased support of Monotheletism. J. remained patriarch until the year of his death, 715; it is unclear whether he was deposed before his death. A synodal letter to Pope Constantine (708-715) is preserved in which J. justifies his acceptance of the patriarchate and stresses the fact that he had confessed his orthodoxy in the presence of Roman apocrisiaries.

W: PG 96:1416-1433.

G. RÖWEKAMP

John of Dalyata

J. was active in the first half of the 8th c. as a hermit in the vicinity of Dalyata. He was a convinced Nestorian, but his spiritual works also won him some fame among the Jacobites. His letters (*ep.*) and mystical treatises (*hom.*), as well as his *Hundred Sayings* (*cent.*) suggest a degree of closeness to the thought of Evagrius and Origen. Because J. became suspect of Sabellianism and Messalianism in regard to the vision of God, his works were solemnly condemned by the Nestorian Catholicos-Patriarch → Timothy I (Catholicos) ca. 786. In the ms. tradition it is very difficult to distinguish the works of J. from those of → Joseph the Seer and → Isaac of Nineveh and from those of → John bar Penkaye. Arab and Ethiopian translators later gave J. the nickname "Saba," "The Old Man."

W: *ep., hom., cent.*, R. Beulay, PO 39/3:253-538 [text/French trans.]. — G. Graf, Geschichte 1 (Rome, 1944), 434-436 (Arabic mss.).
L: R. Beulay, J. et la lettre 15: ParOr 2 (1971) 261-279. — idem, Un mystique: Carmel 3 (1977) 190-201. — idem, La lumière sans forme (Chevetogne, 1987). — idem, Enseignement spirituel (Paris, 1990). — G. G. Blum, Die ekstatischen Konfessionen des J.: Syr. Christentum weltweit, ed. M. Tamcke, W. Schwaigert, E. Schlarb (Münster, 1995), 202-219. — B. E. Colless, Le mystère de J.: OrSyr 12 (1967) 515-523. — idem, Biographies of John Saba: ParOr 3 (1972) 45-64. — idem, Mysticism of J.: OCP 39 (1973) 83-102. — P. Sherwood, J. Sur la fuite du monde: OrSyr 1 (1956) 305-313. — A. Vööbus, Entdeckung wichtiger Urkunden: ZDMG 125 (1975) 267-269.

P. BRUNS

John Damascene

I. Life: J., born ca. 650 in Damascus, belonged to the distinguished family of the Mansûr, which had for generations held offices, espec. in the financial administration of the state. His father, Sargûn ibn Mansûr, was finance minister under Caliph Muawija I (660-680). After an extensive education J. probably worked with his father and was also writing. Like his father, J. seems to have more or less unwillingly withdrawn because of the growing hostility to Christians that set in under Abd el-Malik (685-705). A sentence in the acts of Nicaea II compares J.'s vocation with that of Matthew the tax collector. With his adoptive brother Cosmas (later bishop of Majuma near Gaza), J. withdrew, possibly even before 700, to the monastery of Mar Saba near Jerusalem, where his reputation as a scholar and poet had preceded him. Patriarch John V of Jerusalem (706-735), from whom J., acc. to a rare reference to himself, received his theol. formation (*trisag.* 26.13-15), ordained him a priest against his wishes and then repeatedly called on him for important tasks, espec. in the iconographic controversy that agitated the Byz. empire from 726/727 on. Some of J.'s works were written at the request of various other bishops. J. also preached in Jerusalem. Toward the end of his life he supposedly revised his writings, a claim that seems to be confirmed at least by the ms. tradition of his great work, *Fountain of Knowledge* (*Pēgē gnōseōs*). He worked on to the alleged old age of 104 and died on Dec. 4 of an unknown year (749 is not tenable); he was buried at Mar Saba. The iconoclast Synod of Hiereia (754) spoke of him as dead and anathematized him; in this setting Emperor Constantine V turned J.'s Arab. family name into a curse borrowed from Hebrew: *Manzēros*, "bastard." J. was rehabilitated by Nicaea II (787) and described as praiseworthy. There is much that is legendary in the 10th and 11th c. *Vitae* preserved in Arabic and Greek.

S: ACO 13, 357B. — *Vitae*, PG 94:429-504. — Theophanes, *chron.* (417, 16-21 de Boor).
L: H.-G. Beck, Kirche u. theol. Lit. (Munich, 1959), 476-486. — H. M. Biedermann, L. Hödl, J.: LMA 5:566-568. — B. Flusin, Une vie de St Jean Damascène: Traduction et traducteurs au Moyen Âge, éd. G. Contamine (Paris, 1989), 51-61. — G. Garitte, La vie de St. Étienne le Sabeite: AnBoll 77 (1959) 332-369. — C. Hannick, J.: EdM 7:586-591. — J. M. Hoeck, Stand u. Aufgaben der Damaskenos-Forschung: OCP 17 (1951) 5-60. — A. Kallis, Handapparat z. J.-Studium: OS 16 (1967) 200-213. — A. Kazhdan, S. Gero, Kosmas of Jerusalem: ByZ 82 (1989) 122-132. — B. Kotter, J.: TRE 17:127-132. — J. Nasrallah, St. Jean de Damas (Harissa, 1950). — B. Studer, Jean Damascène: DSp 8:452-466. — K.-H. Uthemann, J.: BBKL 3:331-336.

II. Works: J.'s writings encompass the entire range of theology in his day.

1. His principal dogmatic work is the *Pēgē gnōseōs* (*Fountain of Knowledge*). In the dedicatory epistle to his adoptive brother, Cosmas, the author explains the principles of this tripartite work on which he had already been working in earlier years: (1) in the philosophical chapters, which are also titled *Dialectic* (*dialect.*), J. intends to set forth the best of pagan philosophy and, in substance, offers a patristically filtered summary of the *Eisagogē* of Porphyry, the Neoplatonist; (2) in the book on false doctrines (*haer.*) J. summarizes one hundred heresies still abroad in his day; he takes the first eighty from the *Anakephalaiosis* ascribed to Epiphanius and discusses the remaining twenty (which include Islam) apparently from his own knowledge; (3) the one hundred chapters on orthodox faith (*f. o.*) carefully explain church teaching: God and creation, anthropology, christology, mariology, veneration of saints and images, soteriology, and eschatology; toward the end particular questions are taken up. This *Expositio fidei*

follows the structure of book 5 of the *Epitome* of → Theodoret of Cyrrhus, and makes use of ideas from, among others, Gregory Naz., the *Doctrina Patrum*, Ps.-Cyril, Eulogius of Alexandria, and Nemesius of Emesa. In the West, in the mid-13th c., the work was divided into four books, following the model of the *Sententiae* of Peter Lombard, and was often named *Sententiae Damasceni*. Each of these three parts of the *Fountain* was twice revised by the author, the second revision being the fullest. Various chapters of the *Expositio fidei* exist in the mss. as seemingly independent, specialized works of J.

Shorter dogm.-polemical works are the elementary introduction to dogma (*inst. el.*), which one of J.'s listeners wrote down and dedicated to a Bishop John of Laodicea; a confession of faith titled *Little Book on Rightmindedness* (*rect. sent.*); and, above all, various disputes with all the heresies still alive or revived, in which many problems addressed in *f. o.* are handled with substantially greater depth and clarity. There are two works against the Nestorians (*fid. Nest., haer. Nest.*), three against the Monophysites (*nat.; Jacob.; trisag.*), one against the Monotheletes (*volunt.*), and one in dialogue form against the Manichees (*Man.* 1). The debate, aimed at Islam, between a Saracen and a Christian (*disp.*), may have been written by a disciple, Theodore Abu Qurra, based on a lecture of J.

J. became the classic theologian of the veneration of images through his three well-known addresses to the scorners of sacred images (*imag.* 1-3); these were hardly written before 730 and possibly only after 741, when he could write them without danger outside the Byz. empire.

2. In the area of morality and asceticism there is a work on fasting (*jej.*) but above all the third book of the *Sacra Parallela* (*parall.*), a colossal florilegium (books 1 and 2, on God and man, exist only in an abridgment). Not authentic are the works on the virtues and vices (*virt.*) and on the eight spirits of wickedness (*spir. nequ.*).

3. J.'s only exegetical work is a commentary on the letters of Paul (*Rom.-Philm.*), which the author describes as an excerpt from the corresponding commentaries of John Chrys., although this is only partially the case.

4. Genuine works in the field of hagiography are the encomium of St. Barbara (*hom.* 12), the encomium of John Chrys. (*hom.* 11), and the *Passio* of St. Artemius (*Artem.*). The question of J.'s authorship of the *Edifying Story of Barlaam and Josaphat* (*B. J.*), which is part of world literature, was in recent decades usually resolved in favor of Georgian Abbot

Euthymius of Mt. Athos (d. 1028), but now J.'s authorship has again become more likely; this work took over, among other things, parts of the Buddha legend, various parables from India, and the Gr. original of the *Apology* of → Aristides, now lost except for two papyrus fragments. The primary unresolved question today is whether *B. J.* is a work of J., suggested directly or indirectly by the Georgian *Balavariani*, or of another, exceptionally well-read monk, John of Mar Saba, of the 8th-9th c. The hagiog. texts *On St. Anastasia* (*Anast.*) and *On the Prophet Elijah* (*El.*), first published in 1988, are not authentic.

5. In the area of homiletics a great deal has been amassed under the name of J. The following homilies are authentic: *On the Birth of Christ* (*nativ. dom.*), with its incorporated religious dialogue at the court of the Sassanids; *On the Withered Fig Tree and the Parable of the Vineyard* (*hom. 2*); *On Holy Saturday* (*hom. 4*), and *On the Transfiguration of the Lord* (*hom. 1*); as well as the three sermons, regarded as a work of J.'s old age, *On the Dormition of the Mother of God* (*hom. 8-10*). Doubts exist about the sermons on the Presentation of the Lord (*hypap.*). Not authentic, finally, are the text on the birthday of the Mother of God (*hom. 6*), the homily on Palm Sunday (*palm.*), and the homily on those who have fallen asleep in faith (*fid. dorm.*).

6. Largely still unclarified is the extent of J.'s poetic work, espec. his share of the *Oktoechos*, which as a whole is of later origin. Certainly authentic are the so-called iambic *Canons* for Christmas, Epiphany, and Pentecost (*carm. theog., carm. theoph., carm. pent.*) and those for Easter, the Sunday after Easter, Ascension, and the Transfiguration (*carm. pasch., carm. antipasch., carm. assumpt. Chr., carm. transfig.*).

J.'s programmatic statement, that he intends to say nothing of his own, has often led to his being viewed as an industrious and well-read but ultimately uncreative imitator and compiler. He is, in fact, important chiefly for his systematic synthesis of the orthodox faith; although he had to choose among the many post-Chalcedonian developments and opinions, he was able with astonishing certainty to find the orthodox middle ground, so that he may be regarded as the clearest representative of a consistently developed Chalcedonian christology. As such, he is the last teacher acknowledged by both the eastern and the western church. The address, repeatedly asserted to be the work of J., to the iconoclastic Emperor Constantine V (*Const.*), as well as a further work against the iconoclasts (*icon.*), are from a monk, John of Jerusalem, who was active ca. 770.

W: PG 94-96. — *inst. el., dialect.*, B. Kotter, PTS 7 (Berlin, 1969) [text/comm.]. — *dialect.*, G. Richter, BGrL 15 [German trans./comm.]. — *f. o.*, B. Kotter, PTS 12 (Berlin, 1973) [text/comm.]. — D. Stiefenhofer, BKV² 44 (Munich, 1923) [German trans.]. — *imag.* 1-3, B. Kotter, PTS 17 (Berlin, 1975) [text/comm.]. — V. Fazzo, CTePa 36 [Italian trans.]. — A.-L. Darras-Worms, C. Schönborn, M.-H. Congourdeau, CPF 57 [French trans./comm.]. — G. Feige, W. Hradsky (Leipzig, 1994) [German trans.]. — *haer., fid. Nest., haer. Nest., nat., Jacob., trisag., volunt., Man. 1, disp.*, B. Kotter, PTS 22 (Berlin, 1981) [text/comm.]. — *disp.*, R. Le Coz, SC 383. — *Anast., Artem., El., hom. 1, hom. 2, hom. 4, hom. 6, hom. 8-12, hypap., nativ. dom., palm.*, B. Kotter, PTS 29 (Berlin, 1988) [text/comm.]. — *hom. 6, hom. 8-10*, P. Voulet, SC 80. — *hom. 1-2, hom. 4, hom. 6, hom. 8-10*, M. Spinelli, CTePa 25 [Italian trans.]. — *B. J.*, AGCR 4 (Paris, 1832 = Hildesheim, 1962), 1-365 [text] = PG 96:857-1246 [text/Latin trans.] = G. R. Woodward, H. Mattingly, LCL 34 [text/English trans./comm.] (since 1967 comm. by D. M. Lang for the homilies of Abbot Euthymios) = P. S. Papaeuangelu (Thessalonica, 1991) [text/modern Greek trans./comm.]. — S. Kechagioglu (Athens, 1884) [text]. — J. Martínez Gázquez (Madrid, 1997) [Latin trans. of 1048/comm.]. — F. Liebrecht (Münster, 1847) [German trans.]. — L. Burchard (Munich, 1924) [German trans.]. — S. Ronchey, P. Cesaretti (Milan, 1980) [Italian trans./comm.] (uncertain authorship). — P. Bádenas de la Peña (Madrid, 1993) [Spanish trans./comm.]. — *carm. pasch.*, F. Gahbauer: SMGB 106 (1995) 133-174 [text/German trans./comm.].
L: W. J. Aerts, Überlegungen zu Sprache u. Zeit der Abfassung v. B. J.: Die Begegnung des Westens mit dem Osten, ed. O. Engels, P. Schreiner (Sigmaringen, 1993), 357-364. — T. Bräm, Barlaam et Josaphat: DPA 2:63-83. — F. R. Gahbauer, Anthropologie des J.: ThPh 69 (1994) 1-21. — E. Jammers, Die jamb. Kanones des J.: idem, Schrift, Ordnung, Gestalt (Bern, 1969), 195-256. — A. Kazhdan, Where, when and by whom was B. J. not written: FS G. Wirth (Amsterdam, 1988), 1187-1209. — O. Knorr, Zur Überlieferungsgeschichte von haer.: ByZ 91 (1998) 59-69. — B. Kotter, Überlieferung der Pege Gnoseos (Ettal, 1959). — H. Menges, Bilderlehre des J. (Münster, 1938). — T. Nikolaou, Ikonenverehrung nach J.: OS 25 (1976) 138-165. — G. Richter, Dialektik des J. (Ettal, 1964). — K. Rozemond, La Christologie de J. (Ettal, 1959). — D. Sahas, Arab character of Christian disputation with Islam: Religionsgespräche im MA, ed. B. Lewis, F. Niewöhner (Wiesbaden, 1992), 185-205. — B. Studer, Theol. Arbeitsweise des J. (Ettal, 1956). — H. G. Thümmel, Entstehungsgeschichte der Pege Gnoseos: BySl 42 (1981) 20-30. — R. Volk, Urtext u. Modifikationen bei B. J.: ByZ 86/87 (1993/94) 442-461. — idem, Symeon Metaphrastes — ein Benutzer von B. J.: RSBN n. s. 33 (1996) 67-180. — O. Wahl, Prophetenzitate der parall. (Munich, 1965). — idem, Sir-Text der parall. (Würzburg, 1974). — idem, Weish-Text der parall.: Sal. 42 (1980) 559-566. — idem, Spru. Koh-Text der parall. (Würzburg, 1985).

R. VOLK

John the Deacon

J. lived in Rome after 554. He is perhaps to be identified with → John III of Rome. Several works have come down under his name. The *Expositum in Hep-*

tateuchum (expos.) is a florilegium that preserves otherwise lost fragments and gives knowledge, presumably, of the scholia of → Victor of Capua. Also ascribed to J. is the revision, by Ps.-Jerome, of the Pelagian commentary on Paul (comm.). Less probable is the attribution of the Lat. translation of the sixth book of the → Vitae patrum, the Ep. ad Senarium virum illustrem, and the Collectanea in quattuor evangelia.

W: expos., J. Pitra, SpicSol 1 (Paris, 1852), LV-LXIV, 278-301 [frags.]. — comm., PL 30:645-902. — A. Souter (Cambridge, 1931).
L: A. Di Berardino (ed.), Patrologia 4 (Genoa, 1996), 146f. — G. Morin, Jean Diacre et le ps.-Jérôme sur L'épître de S. Paul: RBen 27 (1910) 113-117. — M. Schanz, C. Hosius, G. Krüger, Geschichte der röm. Lit. 4/2 (Munich, 1920), 595f.

W. GEERLINGS

John Diacrinomenus

J.'s nickname, derived from diakrinesthai (to separate oneself), already points to a rejection of the Chalcedonian Creed. Probably between 512 and 518, he composed a History of the Church (ekklēsiastikē historia) in ten books, of which the first five (acc. to Photius, cod. 41) dealt, in a Monophysite perspective, with the period from the Nestorian controversy (ca. 429) down to the expulsion of Peter the Fuller from Antioch (ca. 476). Large sections of the work must have dealt with the reign of Anastasius I (491-518). A fragment of the work is preserved in the acts of the seventh ecumenical council; other fragments are in the Byz. historians (→ Theodore the Lector seems already to have gladly used J.) or in an epitome of church history based on them. On the basis of the few remaining fragments, Photius's description of J.'s language as "clear and elegant" (tēn phrasin supōs kai anthēros) can be accepted only within limits.

W: G. C. Hansen, Theodoros Anagnostes (Berlin, 1971), 152-157 [text/comm.]. — E. Miller, Fragments inédits de Théodore le Lecteur et de Jean d'Égée: RAr 26 (1873) 273-288, 396-403 [partial text/French trans. of frag.]
L: A. Jülicher, J.: PRE 9/2:1806. — E. Miller, loc. cit. — PLRE 2:606.

U. HAMM, M. MEIER

John the Egyptian

J. was from Gaza. He was initially a monk in an Egyptian monastery and was ordained bishop of Hephaistos by Theodosius Alex. in 534. He was deposed in 536 as a Monophysite and sent into exile in Constantinople, along with Theodosius. From

there, however, he undertook three journeys, to Lydia and Cilicia among other places, on which he ordained Monophysite priests and brought news of other exiled bishops. In Rhodes he met → John of Ephesus, who accompanied him on his third journey, probably in 541, and later composed a biography of him (hist. beat. 25). An unpublished letter of J. from Cyprus to the archimandrites of the East is extant.

W: F. Nau, Littérature canonique: ROC 14 (1909) 48f. [French trans.].
L: E. Honigmann, Évêques et évêchés monophysites (Leuven/Louvain, 1951), 165-167.

B. WINDAU

John of Ephesus

J., born 507 near Amida, entered the monastery of Maro the Stylite while still young; a year later he moved to a monastery near Amida, where he was ordained a deacon in 529. Because of his Monophysite leanings, he was expelled from the monastery by the forceful Patriarch → Ephraem of Antioch, but thanks to Justinian's wife Theodora he was able to establish good relations with the court in Constantinople and finally, at the emperor's order, was given the pastoral care of some localities near Ephesus. By establishing monastic communities he was able to strengthen Christianity in these areas and convert the pagan remnants. Under Emperor Justin II he lost the favor of the court and was arrested. He died as a Monophysite martyr in 586.

J. is regarded as an outstanding historian among the Syrians. He had an equal mastery of Greek and Syriac. Only the historical works in Syriac have survived. The Historia beatorum orientalium (hist. beat.) deals in an edifying manner with the history of the monastery of St. John near Amida. His history of the church (h.e.) was written during the period of persecution. The first part describes events down to the Robber Synod of 449, the second the period to 575 and the remaining ten years until J.'s death.

W: hist. beat., J. P. N. Land, Anecdota Syriaca 2 (Osnabrück, 1989 = Leiden, 1868), 1-288 [text]. — E. W. Brooks, PO 17/1; 18/4; 19/2 [text/English trans.]. — W. van Douwen, J. P. N. Land, Ioannis Ephesini commentarii (Amsterdam, 1889) [Latin trans.]. — h.e., E. W. Brooks, CSCO 105f. [text/Latin trans.]. — W. Cureton, Third part (Oxford, 1853). — J. M. Schönfelder, Kirchengeschichte des J. (Munich, 1862) [German trans.].
L: P. Allen, New date: OLoP 10 (1979) 251-254. — idem, "Justinianic plague": Byz. 49 (1979) 5-20. — S. E. Ashbrook, Ascetism: BMGS 6 (1980) 1-11. — idem, Physicians and Ascetics: DOP 38 (1984) 87-93. — idem, Politisation of

the Byzantine Saint: S. Hackel, Byzantine Saint (London, 1981), 37-42. — idem, Ascetism and Society (Berkeley, 1990). — P. Brown, Eastern and Western Christendom: SCH(L) 13 (1976) 1-24. — J. J. van Ginkel, J. A Monophysite Historian, Diss. (Groningen, 1995). — J. P. N. Land, Gedenkschriften van een Monophysit (Amsterdam, 1888). — P. Plank, Mimesis Christu: P. Hauptmann, Studien zur ostkirchlichen Spiritualität (Munich, 1981), 167-182. — N. Nebes, Satzanschluß: FS J. Aßfalg (Wiesbaden, 1990), 254-268.

P. BRUNS

John of Euboea

J., a younger contemporary of John Damascene, was first a monk, then later bishop either of Euroia near Damascus or of the see of the same name in Epirotus (but not on the island of Euboea). There have come down from him three homilies in a lively and popular style: a sermon on the conception of Mary (*concept. BVM*) that prepares the way for the doctrine of the Immaculate Conception; a sermon on the Holy Innocents (*innoc.*) that dates from 744 and describes the killing of the children; and a sermon on the raising of Lazarus (*Laz.*). A Christmas sermon ascribed to J., a *passio* of St. Paraskeue, and an encomium of St. Anastasia seem to belong rather to J.'s contemporary John Damascene. J. died after 744.

W: *concept. BMV*, PG 96:1460-1500. — *innoc.*, PG 96:1501-1508. — *Laz.*, F. Dölger: AnBoll 68 (1950) 19-26 [text].
L: H.-G. Beck, Kirche und theol. Lit. (Munich, ²1977), 483f., 502f. — F. Dölger, Iohannes v. Euboia: AnBoll 68 (1950) 5-26.

B. R. SUCHLA

John II of Jerusalem

J. was a monk before becoming successor to Cyril as bishop of Jerusalem in 387. Epiphanius of Salamis and Jerome (*ep.* 51) accused him of Origenism and thus gave rise to the first Origenist controversy in Palestine. J. defended himself in a letter to Theophilus of Antioch and in 394 excommunicated Jerome, who then wrote his *Contra Joannem Hierosolymitanum* (PL 23:371-412). In this work he accused J. of having accumulated great wealth from the numerous pilgrims and also tried to depict him as a secret Arian. The Council of Diospolis/Lydda in 415, with J. presiding, declared Pelagius, whom J. had taken in, to be orthodox. J. died in 417. Only fragments remain of J.'s letter of defense, which took the form of a confession of faith. The *Mystagogical Catecheses* that have come down under the name of Cyril Jerus. are probably J.'s. In recent years, parts of his extensive body of sermons (*hom.*) have been rediscovered, often among the works of Ps.-Chrysostom. Important, among others, is the sermon for the dedication of a church, which was delivered, it is thought, at the dedication of Hagia Zion in 397. A Lat. commentary on the gospels (ms. 427 Rheims) goes under J.'s name.

W: *apol.*, E. Bihain, La profession de foi "Sanctae et adorandae trinitatis" de 415: Byz. [Greek text/Armenian text] (in preparation). — *hom.*, M. van Esbroeck, Nathanael dans une homélie géorgienne sur les Archanges: AnBoll 89 (1971) 155-176 [Georgian text/Latin trans.]. — idem, Une homélie sur l'église: Muséon 86 (1973) 283-304 [Armenian text/Latin trans.]. — idem, Une homelie arménienne sur la dormition attribuée a Chrysostome: OrChr 74 (1990) 199-233 [Armenian text/French trans.]. — C. Renoux, Une homélie sur Luc 2, 21: Muséon 101 (1988) 27-95 [text/French trans./comm.].
L: Y. M. Duval, Sur les insinuations de Jérôme contre J.: de l'arianisme à l'origénisme: RHE 65 (1970) 353-374. — M. v. Esbroeck, J.: AnBoll 102 (1984) 99-134. — A. Guillaumont, Les Kephalaia Gnostica d'Évagre le Pontique et l'Histoire de l'Origénisme (Paris, 1962), 87-95. — F. J. Leroy, Ps.-Chrysostomica: J.: StPatr 10 (1970), 131-136. — P. Nautin, La lettre de Theophile d'Alexandrie à l'Église de Jérusalem et la réponse de J.: RHE 69 (1974) 365-394. — D. Stiernon, J.: DSp 8:565-574. — S. J. Voicu, Giovanni e Ps.-Crisostomo: Euntes docete 24 (1971) 66-111.

G. RÖWEKAMP

John IV of Jerusalem

J. was first an Acoemete monk in Jerusalem and then patriarch of Jerusalem 574-594. A letter of his (in Armenian) to Abas, catholicos of Albania in the Caucasus, is preserved. In it he opposes Monophysitism, the theopaschite addition to the Trisagion, and the Aphthartodocetism of Julian of Halicarnassus, and appeals to the primacy and orthodoxy of Rome.

W: K. Ter-Mekerttschian: Ararat 29 (1896) 252-256 [text]. — A. Vardanian, Des J. Brief an den albanischen Katholikos Abas: OrChr NS 2 (1912) 64-77 [Latin trans.].
L: S. Salaville, Un témoignage oriental en faveur de la primauté et de infaillabilité du pape au VIᵉ siècle: EO 13 (1910) 171f.

G. RÖWEKAMP

John bar Kursos

We are informed of the life of J. by two *Vitae*. One is from the pen of his companion Elias, the other from the history of → John of Ephesus. Born ca. 482 in Kallinikon on the Euphrates, J. followed a military career before becoming a monk. In 519 → Jacob of Sarug consecrated J. bishop of Tella, but two years later J. was forced to vacate his see when Emperor

Justin I, in cooperation for the orthodox patriarch → Ephraem of Antioch, moved forcefully against the Monophysites. At first, J. was able to avoid attack, but in 533 he was arrested and thrown into prison, where he died in 538. His literary works, preserved in Syriac, contain canons and liturgical instructions (*can.*), as well as answers (*resp.*) to questions on the Eucharist and, finally, a commentary on the Trisagion (*tris.*) and a confession of faith.

S: *vita*, H. G. Kleyn, Het Leven van J. (Leiden, 1882) [text/trans.]. — E. W. Brooks, PO 18:513-526 [text/English trans.].

W: *can.*, C. Kuberczyk, Canones J. (Leipzig, 1901) [text/Latin trans.]. — F. Nau, Canons et résolutions canoniques (Paris, 1906), 8-19 [French trans.]. — *resp.*, T. Lamy, Dissertatio de Syrorum fide (Leuven/Louvain, 1859), 62-97 [text/Latin trans.]. — *tris.*, H. I. Grigorios, V. Poggi, Il commento al Trisagio: OCP 52 (1986) 202-210.

P. Bruns

John of Lycopolis

A series of partly unpublished Syr. treatises dealing with questions of the ascetical life have come down under the pseudonym John of Lycopolis, a contemporary of Emperor Theodosius. Some of these can with considerable certainty be assigned to → John of Apamea; others are from authors also named John. We are told of J.'s life in a *Vita*, which, except for a few Copt. fragments, has been lost.

S: *Vita*, P. Devos, Fragments coptes: AnBoll 87 (1969) 417-440. — idem, J. et l'empereur Marcien: AnBoll 94 (1976) 303-316 [text/French trans.].

W: A. Baumstark, Geschichte (Bonn, 1922), 89-91 (Syriac mss.). — G. Graf, Geschichte 1 (Rome, 1944), 394f. (Arabic mss.). — S. Dedering, J. Ein Dialog über die Seele (Uppsala, 1936) [text/German trans.].

L: I. Hausherr, Mystique syrienne: OCP 4 (1938) 497-520. — idem, Un grand auteur spirituel: OCP 14 (1948) 3-42. — A. J. Wensinck, Syriac Mystic Literature (Amsterdam, 1923).

P. Bruns

John Malalas

J. composed the earliest (almost) completely preserved Byz. universal chronicle (*Chronographia*; *chron.*). Hardly anything is known of his person: born ca. 490, he was probably from Antioch and may have lived from the mid-30s of the 6th c. on in Constantinople, where he died during the reign of Justin II (564-578). The nickname Malalas (from Syr. *malal*, rhetor, scholasticus, or even lawyer) points to a sound education; J. may have worked in the high-level legal administration of the empire (as *comes Orientis?*). He is not to be identified with John Scholasticus, patriarch of Constantinople, despite earlier assumptions.

J.'s *Chronicle* in eighteen books covered the period from Adam to the death of Justinian (565); it is not possible to decide definitively whether the work came down to 574. Books 1-6 cover bibl. history, into which J. inserted historical or possibly mythological traditions of the Greeks and traditions of the ancient East. To this are added the period of the Roman kings (book 7: it is striking that the Roman republic is almost completely ignored), Alexander the Great, and the Hellen. states (book 8). Books 9-12 cover the principate from Augustus to Diocletian; 13 and 14 cover from Constantine to Leo II (474). After this, a book is devoted to each emperor (15: Zeno; 16: Anastasius; 17: Justin I; 18: Justinian).

It is noteworthy that down to 532 Antioch is at the center of the work, while thereafter the situation in Constantinople is the focus of attention, a fact that suggests the author's change of residence. Not too much should be made of the supposed discrepancy between the first part with its Monophysite leanings (written ca. 533) and the orthodox second part or, as it may be, the second edition of the work (completed down to 565 or possibly to 574), the author of which is certainly the same J., as shown by stylistic characteristics. J. was not a theologian but was interested in theol. questions; he was not a Monophysite but, while in Antioch, was inevitably influenced by Monophysite tendencies. He was uncritically loyal to Justinian.

The work proves to be a colorful compilation of wide-ranging, often contradictory and false information; glaring anachronisms, resulting from reading present circumstances back into the past, are not infrequent. Contrary to the judgment of earlier scholars, this finding is not proof of J.'s naivete and ignorance; on the one hand, it is to be explained by the universal chronicle genre and, on the other, it reflects the general level of contemporary dealing with the past. In order to appeal to a broader readership, J. did not, as was customary, write in a standard Greek based on classic Attic but in an idiom closer to the spoken Greek of the 6th c., one, however, that contained elements of the standard language.

The question of sources is a difficult one: for the early period J. probably used earlier bibl. chronicles and many ancient mythographers; he also went back to now lost historiographical works, to chronicles of the cities of Antioch and Constantinople, as well as to laws, decrees, and letters. From time to time, he identifies his sources; beginning with Zeno, he relies chiefly on oral accounts. J.'s work was extremely popular and influential in Byzantium; from the late 6th c. on he was used by historians and chronographers (→ Evagrius Scholasticus, → John of Ephesus, the author of the → *Chronicon Paschale*) and was later on translated as a whole or in parts into a number of languages, among which the translation into Church Slavonic (11th c.) is important. Since the Gr. text has come down only with abridgements and even then not completely (book 1, the beginning of book 2, the years 217-253, and the end from 563 on are missing), citations in later authors and the translations must be used in reconstructing the text.

W: L. Dindorf (Bonn, 1831) [text]. — E. Jeffreys et al. (Melbourne, 1986) [English trans.].
L: E. Bikerman, Les Maccabées de J.: Byz. 21 (1951) 63-83. — J. B. Bury, J.: Text of the Cod. Ba.: ByZ 6 (1897) 219-230. — E. Chernousov, Études sur J.: Byz. 3 (1926) 65-72. — R. E. G. Downey, References to Inscriptions in the Chronicle of J.: TPAPA 66 (1935) 55-72. — idem, Seleucid Chronology in Malalas: AJA 42 (1938) 106-120. — idem, Imperial Building Records in Malalas: ByZ 38 (1938) 1-15. — A.-J. Festugière, Notabilia dans J. I: RPh 52 (1978) 221-241. — idem, Notabilia dans J. II: RPh 53 (1979) 227-237. — J.-M. Fiey, Les chroniqueurs syriaques avaient-ils le sens critique?: ParOr 12 (1984/85) 253-264. — H. Gelzer, Sextus Julius Africanus und die byz. Chronographie (Leipzig, 1885 = New York, 1970). — J. Haury, J. identisch mit dem Patriarchen Johannes Scholastikos?: ByZ 9 (1900) 337-356. — P. Helms, Syntaktische Untersuchungen zu J.: Helikon 11/2 (1971/72) 309-388. — E. Hörling, Mythos und Pistis (Lund, 1980). — H. Hunger, Die hochsprachliche profane Literatur der Byzantiner I (Munich, 1978), 319-326. — L. Jeep, Die Lücken in der Chronik des J.: RMP 36 (1881) 351-361. — E. M. Jeffreys, J.'s Use of the Past, in: Reading the Past in late Antiquity, ed. G. W. Clarke et al. (Canberra, 1990), 121-146. — E. M. Jeffreys et al. (ed.), Studies in John Malalas (Sydney, 1990) (lit.!). — E. Patzig, Der angebliche Monophysitismus des J.: ByZ 7 (1898) 111-128. — idem, Von J. zu Homer: ByZ 28 (1928) 1-11. — S. W. Reinert, Greek Myth in J.'s Account on Ancient History before the Trojan War (Los Angeles, 1981). — A. Schenk v. Stauffenberg, Die röm. Kaisergeschichte bei J. (Stuttgart, 1931) [with text B. 9-12]. — O. Schissel v. Fleschenberg, Die psycho-ethische Charakteristik in den Porträts des J.: Studien zur vergl. Lit.-Gesch. 9 (1909) 428-433. — R. D. Scott, J. and Justinian's Codification: Byzantine Papers, ed. E. M. Jeffreys et al. (Canberra, 1981), 12-31. — idem, J., The Secret History, and Justinian's Propaganda, in: DOP 39 (1985) 99-109. — idem, Malalas' View of the Classical Past, in: Reading the Past in Late Antiquity, ed. G. W. Clarke et al. (Canberra, 1990), 147-164. — W. Weber, Studien zur Chronik des J.: FS A. Deissmann (Tübingen, 1927), 20-66. — K. Weierholt, Studien zum Sprachgebrauch des J. (Oslo, 1963). — J. A. Wyatt, The History of Troy in the Chronicle of J. (Berkeley, 1976).

U. HAMM, M. MEIER

John Mandakuni

The Arm. tradition counts J. among the "holy translators" and liturgical reformers. He led the Arm. church as catholicos from 478 to 490 and exerted a decisive influence on clerical discipline through his canons (*can.*). In addition to liturgical prayers, twenty-five homilies (*hom.*) and circular letters (*ep.*) on moral and ascet. questions are attributed to him. An accurate distinction between his works and those of other authors of the same name is extremely difficult, espec. since the ms. tradition is often vague in its attributions.

W: *hom.* (Venice, 1860) [text]. — N. Covakan, *hom. de mart.*: Zion 28 (1963) 48f. [text]. — G. Ter-Mekerttschian, Die Überlieferung des J.: Ararat (1903), 562-575, 662-672, 774-784. — J. Blatz, S. Weber, BKV² 583:31-269 [German trans.]. — J. Schmid, Hl. Reden des J. (Regensburg, 1871) [German trans.]. — F. Feydit, hom. sur les charmes: FS J. Dauvillier (Toulouse, 1979), 293-306. — *can.*, V. Hakobian, 2 vols. (Eriwan, 1964-1971). — *ep.*, Book of Letters (Tiflis, 1901), 29-40, 239f. [text]. — M. Tallon, Livres des lettres (Beirut, 1955), 78-138.
L: N. Akinean, J. Katholikos: HandAm 85 (1971) 132-162, 385-398. — G. Hakobian, J.: Edschmiazin (1971), 31-36. — H. Wojtowicz, J.: StSan 2 (1981) 440-453.

P. BRUNS

John Maxentius

J., a supporter of Augustine's teaching on grace, was leader of a Scythian delegation (519/520) to Constantinople and Rome, asking that the theopaschite formula *Unus ex Trinitate carne passus est* be added to the Chalcedonian Creed for the sake of a clear distinction from Nestorianism and Monophysitism. Despite a number of letters, among them J.'s *Ep. ad legatos sedis apostolicae*, the monks were unsuccessful, and Hormisdas of Rome even found open fault with their actions in a letter to Bishop Possessor. The theopaschite formula did, however, become part of the Chalcedonian and imperial faith in 533.

J.'s work, composed in Latin, consists of several shorter treatises, letters, and two lengthier works. The first is the *Dialogus contra Nestorium*, in which J. emphasizes the indispensableness of the theopaschite formula in order to block any Nestorian interpretation of the Chalcedonian Creed; it is noteworthy that the dialogue, unlike similar works, does not end with the conversion of the opponent but breaks off because the viewpoints are irreconcilable. The second work is the *Responsio adversus epistulam Hormisdas*, J.'s response to Hormisdas's letter to Possessor, which J. condemns as a possible forgery by one of his adversaries.

J. is often identified with → John of Tomi.

W: PG 86:75-158. — ACO 4, 2, 3-10 [text]. — F. Glorie, CCL 85A:5-153.
L: B. Altaner, Zum Schrifttum der "skythischen" (gotischen) Mönche: TU 83 (1967) 489-506. — W. C. Bark, J. and the Collectio Palatina: HThR 36 (1943) 93-107. — W. Elert, Die theopaschitische Formel: ThLZ 75 (1950) 195-206. — KonChal 2, 797-805. — G. Morin, Le temoignage perdu de Jean évêque de Tomi: JThS 7 (1906) 74-77.

C. Schmidt

John Moschus

I. Life: J., nicknamed "Moschus" or "Eukratas," was born between 540 and 550 in Damascus or in Aigai in Cilicia. At a very young age he entered the convent of St. Theodosius near Jerusalem and from there withdrew for six years to the laura of Phara. After 578, by commission of his monastery, he undertook, probably with his disciple and friend Sophronius (patriarch of Jerusalem 634-638), an extended journey to the monastic settlements of Egypt. On the way back, both remained for ten years in the monastery of the Acliotes in the Sinai. On returning to Jerusalem the two men were present at the installation of Patriarch Amos (602). They then visited the lauras of Palestine but left the country after the assassination of Emperor Mauritius; their departure was also occasioned by the threatening Persian invasion. After a short stay in Syria and Cilicia, they remained for twelve years in Alexandria. During this time they made a second journey to the monasteries on the Nile. After the Persian capture of Jerusalem (614) J. and Sophronius turned west. J. died in Rome in 619 or 628. Sophronius was able to take his body back to the monastery of St. Theodosius for burial.

II. Works: J. left behind, as the fruit of his travels, the Meadow (Ho leimōn, Pratum spirituale), a collection of accounts of events and stories illustrating the variety of monasticism in his time. The work may have been given its final form by Sophronius, to whom it is dedicated. Like the Apophthegmata, the Meadow is intended to edify by the examples of virtue of holy monks. All areas of asceticism are represented. The only theol. motif is the christology of Chalcedon, which J. strongly defends, not however by arguments but by reporting miracles and private revelations that promoted orthodoxy.

While the Meadow enjoyed ever greater popularity in the East, it first became known in the West through the translation by A. Traversari (1423; printed 1558).

Also attributed to J. and Sophronius is the Vita of John Eleemon, whom they knew from their time in Alexandria.

W: PG 87/3:2847-3116. — PL 74:119-240. — S. Feldhohn (Düsseldorf, 1957) [partial German trans.]. — R. Maisoni (Naples, 1982) [Italian trans.]. — C. Metsios (Thessalonica, 1987) [Greek text/modern Greek trans.]. — P. Pattenden, The Text of the Pratum spirituale: JThS NS 26 (1975) 38-54. — M.-J. Rouët de Journel, SC 12. — T. Nissen: ByZ 38 (1938) 351-376 [12 additional chaps.]. — H. Usener, Der hl. Tychon (Leipzig, 1907), 91-93 [= text of the anonymous Vita of J.].
L: H. Chadwick, John Moschus and his Friend Sophronius the Sophist: JThS 25 (1974) 41-74. — D.-C. Hesseling, Morceaux choisis du Pré spirituel de Jean Moschus (Paris, 1931). — E. Mioni, Jean Moschus: DSp 8/1:632-640. — C. Pasini, Il monachesimo nel Prato di Giovanni Mosco e i suoi aspetti popolari: VetChr 22 (1985) 331-379. — P. Pattenden, J., TRE 17:140-144 (literature).

J. Pauli, OSB

John of Naples (Mediocris)

J., called Mediocris, was bishop of Naples for twenty years (ca. 533/535 to 553/555). A collection of thirty-one (or thirty) Lat. sermons, handed down under the name of → John Chrys., was at one time attributed to him, but this attribution was later dropped; the author now seems to be Ps.-Chrysostom Latinus. The Sermones may have been composed in Africa or southern Italy in about the second half of the 6th c. The only thing certain is that the author, who comments on, among other things, passages from the OT and from Mt, depends on Augustine and cites Prosper Tiro of Aquitania.

W: PLS 4:741-834.
L: Archivio biografico italiano 1:487, 72. — J.-P. Bouchot, La collection homilétique: REAug 16 (1970) 139-146. — A. Di Berardino (ed.), Patrologia 4 (Genoa, 1996), 235f. — A. H. Dyke Acland, J. 258: DCB 3:384. — B. Fischer, Rez. zu CPL (Dekkers): ThLZ 7 (1952) 287-289, here 288. — M. Lambert, Édition d'une collection latine: REAug 15 (1969) 255-258. — J. F. Leroy, Vingt deux homélies: RBen 104 (1994) 123-147. — G. Morin, Études sur une série de discours: RBen 11 (1894) 385-402. — idem, Un essai autocritique: RBen 12 (1895) 385-402, here 390f.

B. Windau

John of Nikiu

J. was bishop of Nikiu in Egypt and was active in the second half of the 7th c. He composed a universal history, probably in Greek, that has come down to us only in an Eth. translation. It begins with primitive history and tells of events in the times of the Greeks and Romans, with special emphasis on Egypt. J.'s chronicle is an important source for the period of the Persian and Arab. conquest of Egypt.

W: H. Zotenberg, Chronique de Jean de Nikiu (Paris, 1913) [Ethiopic text/French trans.]. — R. H. Charles, Chronicle

of John (London, 1916) [English trans.]. — G. Graf, Geschichte 1 (Rome, 1944), 470-472 (Arabic mss.).
L: F. Altheim, Geschichte der Hunnen 2 (Berlin, 1960), 40-46.

P. Bruns

John of Paralos

J. was active in Egypt toward the end of the 6th or beginning of the 7th c. and composed numerous spiritual works in Coptic. After his formation as a monk in the monastery of Macarius in Scete, he was consecrated bishop of Paralos in the Nile delta. Only fragments of his many homilies have survived; in them he attacks the use of certain apocryphal writings.

W: A. van Lantschoot, Fragments: FS G. Mercati (Rome, 1946), 296-326.

P. Bruns

John bar Penkaye

J. was from Penek near Bet Zabdai and was active there in the 7th c. as monk and spiritual writer. Of his many writings a universal history in fifteen chapters has been preserved which describes events down to 686. It is an important contemporary source for the period of the Muslim conquerors. Also preserved is a seven-syllabic Memre on fear of God, in which the author bemoans in lively language the decay of monastic disciplines.

W: A. Mingana, Sources Syriaques 1 (Leipzig, 1907), 1-171, 172-197 [text/French trans.]. — J. de Mesnace: BSOAS 9 (1937/38) 587-601 [text/French trans.].
L: M. Albert, Une centurie de J.: FS Guillaumont (Geneva, 1988), 143-151. — S. P. Brock, North Mesopotamia: JStAI 9 (1987) 51-75. — T. Jansma, Projet d'édition: OrSyr 7 (1963) 87-106. — P. G. Sfair, Il nome e l'epoca: Bess. 31 (1915) 135-138. — H. Suermann, Das arab. Reich: FS C. D. G. Müller (Cologne, 1987), 59-71.

P. Bruns

John Philoponus

J. (also: J. Grammaticus) was a 6th c. Chr. thinker living in Alexandria. He was given his nickname either because of his industriousness or because he belonged to the Chr. community of the Philoponoi. He was a disciple of Neoplatonic philosopher Ammonius Hermeiou and author of grammatical writings on accent, commentaries on Aristotle, works on arithmetic, and treatises on systematic theology. He died after 570.

In his philosophical works, which must have been written before 553, J. shows himself a critic of Neoplatonic thought, which led to attacks on Simplicius; in particular he was a determined adversary of Proclus the Neoplatonist. Thus after 543/553 he wrote a commentary (comm.) that took for its subject the literary connection between → Dionysius the Areopagite and Proclus: it was not Dionysius, the disciple of the Apostle, who "stole" from pagan Proclus, but vice versa. As the convinced supporter of Severus of Antioch, J. sharply rejected the doubts raised by → Hypatius of Ephesus regarding the association of this Dionysius with the Apostle. J.'s treatises Contra Aristotelem and De aeternitate mundi contra Proclum (Proc.) were directed against, among other things, the doctrine of the eternity of the cosmos.

In his theol. works, which must have been written after 553, J. opposed the Roman primacy, was a Monophysite tritheist and founder of a teaching on the resurrection that was condemned as heresy in 680/681. In his De opificio mundi (opif.) he commented on the bibl. account of creation with the help of the ancient philosophy of nature. For some of his contemporaries he set forth a tritheism that he defended with Aristotelean logic in his principal work, Diaeetes (or: Arbiter; arb.), which is preserved only fragmentarily in the original but is complete in a Syr. translation, and in his De trinitate, which is preserved only in fragments (fr.). This tritheism was defended by Bishops → Conon of Tarsus and Eugene of Seleucia, while → Anastasius I of Antioch, for instance, wrote against J.'s tritheism in a work (PG 89:1283-84) that was later cited by → Maximus Conf.

Next to → Dionysius the Areopagite and → John of Scythopolis, J. was the most important thinker of the 6th c. His works influenced Byz. and Arab. philosophy as well as thinking in the natural sciences in the Middle Ages and early modern period.

W: fr., A. van Roey, Les fragments trithéistes de J.: OLoP 11 (1980) 135-163. — idem, Fragments antiariens de J.: OLoP 10 (1979) 237-250. — comm., B. R. Suchla, NAWG. PH (1995), 1, 12, 19-20 [text]. — Procl., H. Rabe (Hildesheim, 1963 = Leipzig, 1899) [text]. — opif., G. Reichardt (Leipzig, 1897) [text]. — C. Scholten, FC 23/1-3. — libellus de paschate, C. Walter (Jena, 1899) [text]. — arb., A. Sanda, Opuscula monophysitica 1 (Beirut, 1930), 3-48, 35-88 [Syriac text/French trans.]. — Epitome libri diaetetis, A. Sanda, loc. cit., 49-62, 89-103 [Syriac text/French trans.]. — Dubiorum quorundam in Diaetete solutio duplex, A. Sanda, loc. cit., 63-80, 104-125 [Syriac text/French trans.]. — ep. ad Iustinianum, A. Sanda, loc. cit., 123-130, 172-180 [Syriac text/French trans.]. — Tractatus de totalitate et partibus ad Sergium presbyterum, A. Sanda, loc. cit., 81-94, 126-129

[Syriac text/French trans.]. — *Tomi quattuor contra synodum quartam*, J.-B. Chabot, Chronique de Michel le Syrien, Bl² (1963), 2:92-121 [French trans.], 4:218-238 [Syriac text]. — *Commentaria in Aristotelem Graeca*, H. Diels, 13:1-17 (Berlin, 1882-1909) [text]. — *Comm. in De anima Aristotelis*, G. Verbeke, CLCAG 3 [text]. — W. Böhm, J. (Munich, 1967) [German trans./comm.].
L: H.-G. Beck, Kirche u. theol. Lit. (Munich, ²1977), 391f. — E. Evrard, Les convictions religieuses de J. et la date de son commentaire aux "Météorologiques": BCLAB 5, 39 (1953) 299-357. — G. Furlani, Sei scritti antitriteistici, PO 14/4:675-766. — A. Grillmeier, Jesus der Christus 2/1 (Freiburg i.Br., 1986), 77-79; 2/2 (Freiburg i.Br., 1989), 516-520; 2/4 (Freiburg i.Br., 1990), 109-149 (English, Christ in Christian Tradition [London, 1987-96]). — T. Hermann, J. als Monophysit: ZNW 29 (1930) 209-264. — H. Martin, J. et la controverse trithéite du VIᵉ siècle: StPatr 5 (1962) 519-525. — C. Scholten, FC 23/1:7-66 — idem, Antike Naturphilosophie u. chr. Kosmologie in der Schrift "de opificio mundi" des J., PTS 45 (Berlin, 1996). — R. Sorabji (ed.), J. and the Rejection of Aristotelian Science (London/Ithaca, 1986). — idem, J.: TRE 17:144-150. — B. R. Suchla, Verteidigung eines platonischen Denkmodells einer chr. Welt (Göttingen, 1995).

B. R. SUCHLA

John I of Rome

After his election as bishop of Rome (Aug. 13, 523), J., already elderly, was caught in the political tensions between Justin and Theodoric. As a deacon, J. had submitted to → Symmachus of Rome during the Laurentian schism (see Symmachus's *ep.* 8) and was a friend of Boethius, who dedicated three theol. treatises to him. Under pressure from Theodoric, J. had to approach the imperial government in Constantinople and ask for the withdrawal of anti-Arian measures. After his return, he was detained in Ravenna by Theodoric and died of exhaustion on May 18, 526. J.'s authentic letters are lost. In the period before his episcopate, J. is supposed to have written, under the name of → John the Deacon, the *Epistula ad Senarium*, which is important for the liturgy of baptism.

W: PL 59:399-408.
L: A. Di Berardino (ed.), Patrologia 4 (Genoa, 1996), 137f. — P. Goubert, Autour du voyage à Byzance du pape S. Jean I.: OCP 24 (1958) 339-352. — L. Magi, La sede romana nella corrispondenza degli imperatori e patriarchi bizantini (Rome, 1972), 101-103. — J. Richards, The Popes and the Papacy (London, 1979), 109-113.

S. C. KESSLER, SJ

John II of Rome

After a period when there was no pope and of confusion about resolving the succession, Mercurius, a Roman presbyter, was elected bishop of Rome as a compromise candidate on Jan. 2, 533. Since he was named after a pagan divinity, he became the first Roman bishop to take the name of his predecessor, → John I, who was venerated as a martyr. J. attempted to follow a policy of balance between the Goths and Byzantium. He died on May 8, 535.

From J.'s episcopate five letters have been preserved on theol. questions in dispute between the eastern and western churches (*ep. pontif.*). J. formally accepted a decree issued by Emperor Justinian that included the theopaschite formula of faith which → Hormisdas had rejected as being open to misunderstanding.

W: *ep. pontif.* 2, O. Günther, CSEL 35:320-328. — *ep. pontif.* 3, ACO 4, 2, 206-210. — *ep. pontif.* 4-6, C. de Clercq, CCL 148A:86-89.
L: M. V. Anastos, Justinian's Despotic Control over the Church as Illustrated by His Edict on Theopaschite Formula and His Letter to Pope John II in 533: FS G. Ostrogorsky 2 (Belgrade, 1964), 1-11. — A. Di Berardino (ed.), Patrologia 4 (Genoa, 1996), 141f. — L. Magi, La sede romana nella corrispondenza degli imperatori e patriarchi bizantini (Rome, 1972), 109-118.

S. C. KESSLER, SJ

John III of Rome

J. had to wait over four months, between his election as bishop of Rome and his consecration on July 17, 561, for imperial confirmation. Not only dependence on Byzantium but the Lombards, who controlled large parts of Italy from 568 on, played a decisive role in J.'s pontificate. In the Three-Chapters controversy, he managed to reconcile some separated churches of northern Italy. He died in Rome in 574.

Only one letter (*ep.*) has survived from his pontificate; it deals with the privileges of the church of Ravenna. The other letters attributed to him (PL 72:13-18) are not authentic. It had traditionally been assumed that J. is identical with → John the Deacon, who perhaps, together with → Pelagius I, translated parts of the → *Apophthegmata Patrum* (*Vitae patr.*). In addition, J. probably compiled an unpublished catena of interpretations of the Heptateuch (*Expositum in Heptateuchum*), which has come down in fragments.

W: *ep.*, P. Ewald, MGH. Ep 1:230 [text]. — *Vitae patr.*, PL 73:993-1062. — *Expositum in Heptateuchum*, J. Pitra, Spic-Sol 1 (Paris, 1852), LV-LXIV, 278-301 [text in frags.].
L: O. Bertolini, Roma e i Longobardi (Rome, 1972). — G. Haendler, Das Papsttum unter gotischer u. byz. Herrschaft: Das Papsttum 1, ed. M. Greschat (Stuttgart, 1985), 71-82. — C. Sotinel, J.: DHP 929f.

S. C. KESSLER, SJ

John IV of Rome

After his election on Dec. 24, 640, but before imperial confirmation and his consecration, J., acting as bishop elect of Rome, *servans locum sanctae sedis apostolicae*, sent a letter answering questions from Irish bishops and clerics regarding the date of Easter and Pelagianism. This letter is transmitted in Bede's history of the church. In 641, in Rome, J. held a synod that condemned Monotheletism. In a letter to Emperor Constantine II or to his successor, Heraclius, which is preserved only in a Lat. back-translation from Greek, J. defended the orthodoxy of → Honorius I against misunderstandings and attacks by Patriarch Pyrrhus I of Constantinople (*Apol. pro Honorio Papa*). After a short episcopate J. died in Rome on Oct. 12, 642.

W: *Apol. pro Honorio Papa*, PL 80:602-607. — *ep. ad episcopos et presbyteros Scottiae*, Beda, *h.e.* 2.19 (G. Spitzbart [ed.], Kirchengeschichte des englischen Volkes [Darmstadt, 1982], 196-199) [text/trans.].
L: H. H. Anton, Von der byz. Vorherrschaft zum Bund mit den Franken: Das Papsttum 1, ed. M. Greschat (Stuttgart, 1985), 100-114. — D. Ó Cróinín, Pelagianism in Ireland and the papal letter of 640: Spec. 60 (1985) 505-516. — L. Magi, La sede romana nella corrispondenza degli imperatori e patriarchi bizantini (Rome, 1972), 206-212. — C. Sotinel, J.: DHP 930.

S. C. KESSLER, SJ

John Rufus

After studying law in Berytus, J., an Arab from southern Palestine (perhaps Ascalon), was ordained a presbyter by Peter the Fuller, the first anti-Chalcedonian patriarch of Antioch, and became the latter's syncellus. J. had to leave Antioch along with Peter and, after the death of Peter the Iberian in 488, was consecrated the latter's successor as bishop of Maluma near Gaza. During the period when Severus of Antioch was in office (512-518), J. wrote his *Plērophorai* (*pleroph.*). Though written in Greek, this work is preserved only in two Syr. recensions. This work in eighty-nine chapters does not primarily give the dogm. arguments of the anti-Chalcedonians (successful under Severus) but intends to show, with the help of numerous accounts of visions and miracles, that the Council of Chalcedon was simply an act of revenge by the Nestorians who had been defeated in 431. This widely read and popular work was also used by many later Monophysite historians of the church. J. is also the author of an account of the death of Theodosius Jerus. (*v. Theod.*). Probably not from J. himself but from his circle is the *Vita* of Peter

the Iberian (*v. Petr.*), an important witness to the eccles. situation in Palestine at the beginning of the 6th c.; it also gives information on the topography of Jerusalem.

W: *pleroph.*, F. Nau, PO 8 [Syriac text /French trans.]. — T. Orlandi, Kopt. Papyri theol. Inhalts: MPSW 23 (1974) 110-120 [Coptic frags.]. — *v. Theod.*, E. W. Brooks, CSCO 7:21-27 [Syriac text]; CSCO 8:15-19 [Latin trans.]. — *v. Petr.*, R. Raabe, Petrus der Iberer (Leipzig, 1895) [text/German trans./comm.].
L: M. v. Esbroeck, Peter the Iberian and Dionysius the Areopagite: OCP 59 (1993) 217-227. — E. Honigmann, Pierre l'Ibérien et les écrits du Ps.-Denys l'Aréopagite: MAB. L 47:3 (1952) 52-55. — D. M. Lang, Peter the Iberian and his Biographers: JEH 2 (1951) 158-168 [also P. Devos: AnBoll (1952) 385-388]. — T. Orlandi, Un frammento delle Pleroforie in copto: SROC 2 (1979) 3-12. — E. Schwartz, J., ein monophysitischer Schriftsteller, SHAW. PH (Heidelberg, 1912).

G. RÖWEKAMP

John of Scythopolis

J. (also John Scholasticus), a contemporary of John of Caesarea, was bishop of Scythopolis in Palestine between 536 and 553. He was a widely educated thinker, most of whose works are nonetheless lost. We have fragments of a defense of the Council of Chalcedon (*apol.*) that was evidently composed before 518 and had at least ten books, as well as of a work *Contra Severum* (*fr.*) that must have been written about 527 against Severus of Antioch, a Monophysite. Between 536 and 542-553 J. or the scholars in his circle edited the works of → Dionysius the Areopagite; J. himself commented on them, wrote a preface for them, and combined preface, works, and commentary into a corpus. It was principally the transmission of the Areopagite's writings in this corpus (along with the author's supposed closeness to the Apostle) that promoted great esteem for the works, for in his preface and commentary J. refuted the accusation that the Areopagite's writings were works of pagan philosophy, and his ordering of the writings within the corpus was already producing an interpretation of them.

In his explanations of the Areopagite's works, explanations which, on the one hand, legitimated the acceptance of Platonic philosophy while emphasizing its Chr. transformation and, on the other, were based on a linking of the Platonic and Aristotelean traditions, J. shows himself to be a thinker concerned with reconciliation and balance. The same search for reconciliation can also be seen in the fragments of the above-mentioned writings. In *fr.* and *apol.*, therefore, he is to be seen as a Neo-Chalcedonian theologian who takes a middle ground between Monophysitism and Diphysitism.

W: *fr.*, ACO 10, 1107f.; 11, 437-440 [text]. — F. Diekamp, Doctrina Patrum (Münster, 1981 = 1907), 85f. [text]. — *apol.*, J. Lebon, CSCO 94:202-204 [Syriac trans.]. — *Scholia in Corpus Dionysiacum Areopagiticum*, PG 4. — New edition (= Editio princeps), B. R. Suchla, PTS, in preparation, expected in 1999.
L: H. U. v. Balthasar, Das Scholienwerk des J.: Schol. 15 (1940) 16-38. — idem, Kosmische Liturgie (Einsiedeln, ²1961), 644-672. — H.-G. Beck, Kirche u. theol. Lit. (Munich, ²1977), 376f. — A. Grillmeier, Jesus der Christus 2/2 (Freiburg i.Br., 1989), 252f. (English, Christ in Christian Tradition, vol. 2/2 [London, 1995]). — S. Helmer, Der Neuchalkedonismus (Bonn, 1962), 176-184. — R. Henry, Photius. Bibliothèque 2 (Paris, 1960), 48, 74-78. — B. R. Suchla, Die sogenannten Maximus-Scholien des Corpus Dionysiacum Areopagiticum (Göttingen, 1980). — eadem, Die Überlieferung des Prologs des J. zum griech. Corpus Dionysiacum Areopagiticum (Göttingen, 1984). — eadem, Eine Redaktion des griech. Corpus Dionysiacum Areopagiticum im Umkreis des J. (Göttingen, 1985). — eadem, Verteidigung eines platonischen Denkmodells einer chr. Welt (Göttingen, 1995).

R. SUCHLA

John of Shmun

J. lived in the second half of the 6th c. in the time of Alexandrian Patriarch Damian. J. was first a monk, then bishop of Shmun (Hermopolis Magna) in central Egypt. His works were entirely geared to the renewal of Copt. literature, which at that time was becoming increasingly conscious of its national character. J. composed an encomium of Mark the evangelist (*Marc.*), the national saint of Egypt, and another on the equally popular monastic father, Anthony (*Ant.*).

W: *Marc.*, T. Orlandi, Encomio di Marco: StCopt 3 (1968) 1-52 [text/Italian trans.]. — *Ant.*, G. Garitte, Panégyrique de Saint Antoine: OCP 9 (1943) 100-134, 330-365 [text/French trans.].

P. BRUNS

John I of Thessalonica

J. became archbishop of Thessalonica ca. 590/600. Ca. 618 he encouraged the city's inhabitants to defend themselves against the Avars and Slavs. After he had, as was believed, preserved the city from an earthquake by his prayers, he died ca. 620. He was evidently a popular preacher, a collection of whose sermons existed in all likelihood. Preserved are a homily on the women at the tomb (the chrism-bearers, *mul. ung.*) or, more accurately, a concordance of

the gospel accounts of the resurrection, and a homily or possibly a pastoral letter on the introduction of the feast of the assumption of Mary in his city (*dorm. BVM*); but probably only the preface and conclusion are from J. A homily in defense of images is preserved only in fragments (*fr.*); another on the beheading of John the Baptist has not been published. In addition to a prayer to (*prec.*) and an encomium of St. Demetrius (*laud. Dem.*), J.'s most important work was a first collection of the miracles of St. Demetrius, compiled soon after 610; this work was continued later on.

W: *mul. ung.*, PG 59:635-644 [partial ed.]. — F. Combefis, Novum auctarium 1 (Paris, 1648), 791-822 [text]. — *dorm. BMV*, M. Jugie, PO 19:344-438. — D. Wilmart, Analecta Regiensia (Vatican City, 1933), 323-357 [Latin version]. — F. Halkin, Une légende byzantine: REByz 11 (1953) 156-164 [epitome]. — *fr.*, Mansi 13:164B-165C. — *prec.*, PG 116:1341AB. — *laud. Dem.*, A. Philippidis-Braat, L'enkomion de S. Demetrius: TMCB 8 (1981) 397-414 [text]. — *mir. Dem.*, P. Lemerle (Paris, 1979), 1:74-179; 2:27-81 [text/comm.].
L: H. G. Beck, Kirche u. theol. Lit. (Munich, 1959), 458. — P. Lemerle, loc. cit. — D. Stiernon, Jean 214: DSp 8:778-780.

B. WINDAU

John of Tomi

Nothing is known of the person of J., a monk and bishop of Tomi in Thrace in the 5th/6th c. At the end of the *Collectio Palatina* he is named as author of *Sermones* against the Nestorians and Eutychians, but the *Sermones* are lost. A work of J.'s, *De duabus haeresibus Nestorianorum et Eutychianistarum*, known from a fragment found elsewhere, is probably the same as the *Sermones*. J. attests in clear language to his orthodox faith.

W: G. Morin, Le temoignage perdu de Jean: JThS 7 (1906) 74-77 [text]. — F. Glorie, CCL 85A:234-239.
L: H. G. Beck, Kirche u. theol. Lit (Munich, 1959), 375 n. 2.

B. WINDAU

Jordanes

J. is the name of a 6th c. Roman historian of Gothic origin (*Get.* 60.316), who is perhaps to be identified with Bishop Jordanes of Croton and who in 551 composed two works in faulty Latin: a summary of world history (*De summa temporum vel origine actibusque gentis Sae* [*Rom.*]) and a history of the Goths (*De origine actibusque Getarum* [*Get.*]). Apart from borrowings from Orosius, Rufinus, and others, this second work is mainly "a meager and hurried" excerpt from the lost *History of the Goths* (*Historia Gothica*) of → Cassiodorus. While the *Rom.* of 551 is hardly more than some genealogies of rulers and lists of consuls compiled from Florus, Ammianus Marcellinus, and others, the *Get.*, finished by Cassiodorus in 533 and brought up to 551 by himself (and perhaps by J.) is a compilation (making free use of sources) of a compilation. The *Get.* aims to show the equality of the Gothic race to the Romans and, in order to show the antiquity of the Goths, identifies them with the Getes and Scythians and to some extent with the Huns (*Get.* 6.44). The ulterior purpose of the *Get.* in both Cassiodorus and J., is to propagate racial harmony between Rome/Byzantium (*gens Anicia*) and the Goths (race of the Amals): *originem Gothicam historiam fecit esse Romanam*. The updating probably represents an effort to make Emperor Justinian amenable to the idea of two races as he was preparing (551) for his expedition for the reconquest of Italy and the destruction of the Goths. The *Historia Gothica* of Cassiodorus is the first and only work of a Roman on a people who mastered Rome.

W: T. Mommsen, MGH. AA 1.
L: D. R. Bradley, The Composition of the Get.: Er. 64 (1966) 67-79. — idem, In altum laxare vela compulsus. The "Get." of J.: Hermes 121 (1993) 211-236. — idem, Manuscript Evidence for the Text of the "Get." of J.: Hermes 123 (1995) 346-362, 490-501. — F. Brunhölzl, Geschichte der lat. Lit. des MA 1 (Munich, 1975), 29f. — G. Dragon, L. Marin, Discours utopique et récit des origines, 1. Une lecture de Cassiodore-J.: 361-368. Annales (1971) 230-237. — P. Heather, Cassiodorus and the Rise of the Amals: JRS 79 (1989) 103-128. — A. Kappelmacher, Iordanis: PRE 9/2:1908-1929. — A. Momigliano, Cassiodorus and Italian Culture of His Time: PBA (1955) 207-245. — H. Usener, Anecdoton Holderi (Hildesheim, 1969 = Bonn, 1877). — L. Várady, J.-Studien: Chiron 6 (1976) 441-487. — F. Werner, Die Latinität der Get. des J. Diss. (Halle, 1908). — E. Wölfflin, Zur Latinität des J.: ALLG 11 (1900).

W. BÜRSGENS

Joseph of Arimathea, Literature about

The Gr. *Narratio Iosephi de Arimathaea* is part of the → Pilate Literature and is a compilation from the *Acts of Pilate*, the *Anaphora*, and the *Paradosis*.

W: C. Tischendorf, Evangelia apocrypha (Hildesheim, 1987 = Leipzig, ²1876), 459-470. — A. Santos Otero, Los evangelios apocrifos (Madrid, ⁶1988), 495-506 [Greek text/Spanish trans.].

This work is not to be confused with the Georg. *Narratio Iosephi de Arimathaea*, which has two parts.

The first is again connected with the Pilate Literature, while the second is an account of the church of Diospolis/Lydda, which, because it possessed images of Mary, was preserved. The Gr. and Lat. versions of this tale go back to the Georg. version.

W: N. Marr, Teksty i razyskanja po armjano-gruzinskoj filologii 2 (Petersburg, 1900), 25-72 [Georgian text]. — T. Kluge, Die apokryphe Erzählung des J.: OrChr NS 4 (1914) 24-38 [German trans.]. — M. v. Esbroeck, L'histoire de l'église de Lydda: Bedi Kartlisa 35 (1977) 108-131 [French trans.]. — E. v. Dobschütz, Christusbilder, TU 18 (Leipzig, 1899), 219**f., 234**-266** [Greek text]. — B. Pez, T. F. Crane, Liber de miraculis (Ithaca, 1925), 1:23f. [Latin text].

G. RÖWEKAMP

Joseph the Carpenter, History of

The *History of Joseph the Carpenter* was composed in Greek, in Egypt, ca. 400, but is preserved in fragments in Sahidic, Bohairic, and Lat. translations, as well as complete in various Arab. versions. The work was influenced by the → *Arabic Infancy Gospel*, the canonical gospels, and the *Gospel of James* (→ James the Younger, Literature about) and depicts events before the birth of Jesus, his miraculous birth, and his early childhood. In addition, it contains an account of the last days, death, and burial of the foster father of Jesus. The work is extremely important for Chr. hagiography and for an understanding of eastern popular devotion.

W: P. de Lagarde, Aegyptiaca (Osnabrück, 1972 = Göttingen, 1883), 1-37 [Coptic text]. — E. Revillout, Apocryphes coptes du NT (Paris, 1876). — A. Battista, B. Bagatti, Historia Iosephi fabri lignarii (Jerusalem, 1978) [Arabic text/Italian trans.]. — G. Wallin, Historia Josephi arabice (Leipzig, 1722) [Arabic text/Latin trans.]. — G. Graf, Geschichte 1 (Rome, 1944), 234-236 [Arabic mss.]. — C. Peeters, C. Michel, Evangiles Apocryphes 1 (Paris, 1911), 192-245 [French trans.]. — J. C. Thilo, Codex Apocryphus NT (Leipzig, 1832), 1-61 [Coptic-Arabic text/Latin trans.]. — F. Robinson, Coptical Apocryphal Gospels (Cambridge, 1896), 130-159, 220-235 [Coptic text/English trans./comm.]. — L. Stern: ZWTh 26 (1883) 270-294 [German trans.]. — G. Schneider, FC 18:271-283 [Latin trans./German trans. (selections)].
L: H. Engberding, G.: OrChr 37 (1953) 56-88. — G. Giamberardini, S. Giuseppe nella tradizione copta: SOC. C 2 (1966) 4-291. — G. Klameth, Herkunft der apokryphen G.: Angelos 3 (1928-30) 6-31. — L.-T. Lefort, L'histoire de Joseph: Muséon 66 (1953) 201-223. — S. Morenz, G. von Joseph (Berlin, 1951).

P. BRUNS

Joseph the Seer (Hazzaya)

J., who in the tradition is also called Ebedjesu (Abdiso), lived in the second half of the 7th c. He was a Persian by origin and, when a prisoner of war, had his freedom bought for him by a Christian named Cyriacus. After being freed, he led a strict penitential life as a monk and was head of several monasteries, Along with → Isaac of Nineveh, J. is regarded as one of the most important mystics of the Syr. church. He composed a series of spiritual treatises (*tract.*), few of which, however, have survived, while others have not been published. In his mystical letters (*ep.*) J. accepts the trichotomist anthropology of John of Apamea and teaches the mortification of the bodily members at the lowest level, the mastery of the passions at the second level, in order finally to liberate the spiritual powers at the third and highest level of the person.

J. was accused of Messalianism and Origenism: that he taught the preexistence of souls and, in mystical enthusiasm, accepted the thesis that even in this life human beings can see God with their bodily eyes. His radical spiritualization led him to a complete rejection of ritual, cultic prayer, and of the manual work customary in monastic circles.

W: *tract.*, A. Mingana, Early Christian Mystics (Cambridge, 1934), 256-279 [text/English trans.]. — A. Baumstark, Geschichte (Bonn, 1922), 222f. [Syriac mss.]. — *ep.*, R. Beulay, PO 45/2 [Syriac text/French trans.]. — G. Bunge, Briefe über das geistliche Leben (Trier, 1982) [German trans.].
L: R. Beulay, Des centuries de J. Hazzaya retrouvées: ParOr 3 (1972) 5-44. — idem, La lumière sans forme (Chevetogne, 1987). — A. Guillaumont, Sources de la doctrine de J.: OrSyr 3 (1958) 3-25. — A. Scher, J. Hazzaya écrivain syriaque: RSO 3 (1910) 54-63. — E. J. Sherry, The Life and Words of J.: W. S. Mc Cullough, Seed of Wisdom (Toronto, 1964), 78-91.

P. BRUNS

Joshua the Stylite

J. was a priest in the monastery of Zuqnin near Amida and is considered the author of a richly detailed chronicle that was written probably in the winter of 506/507 and describes the period from 495/496 to Nov. 28, 506.

W: W. Wright, Chronicle of J. (Amsterdam, 1968 = Cambridge, 1882) [text/English trans./comm.].
L: S. P. Brock, Syriac Historical Writing: idem, Studies in Syriac Christianity (Hampshire, 1992), 1-30. — F. Gelzer, J. u. die kirchlichen Parteien: ByZ 1 (1892) 34-49. — F. Haase, Chronik des J.: OrChr NS 9 (1920) 62-73. — H. Leclainche, Crises économiques à Edesse: Le Miral 16 (1980) 89-100. — G. M. Lee, Three Notes: Muséon 85 (1972) 523f. — O. Nicholson, From Lactantius to J.: M. J. Chiat, Medieval Mediterranean (Minnesota, 1988/89), 11-18. — A. N. Palmer, Who Wrote the Chronicle of J. ?: FS J. Assfalg (Wiesbaden, 1990), 272-284.

P. BRUNS

Jovinian

Though originally an ascetic, J. came to Rome (from Milan?) ca. 385 and sought followers for his anti-ascetical teaching. Acc. to the surviving fragments (chiefly in Jerome) and his adversaries, J. taught, among other things, the equal value of marriage and celibacy, the equal value of fasting and thankful eating, the same heavenly reward for all who preserve their baptism, and the impossibility of sinning on the part of those who receive baptism with complete faith. He supposedly denied the virginity of Mary during and after the birth of Jesus. In 390 J. was condemned in Milan and Rome; in 398 Emperor Honorius banished him to a Dalmatian island, where he died before 406. In 393 Jerome wrote his *Adversus Jovinianum* against him, and Augustine his *De bono coniugali* and *De sancta virginitate*.

W: Jerome, *Adv. Jovin.* 2, W. Haller, TU 17/2 (Leipzig, 1897), 1-31 [text].
L: D. G. Hunter, Resistance to the Virginal Ideal in the Late Fourth-Century Rome: TS 48 (1987) 45-64. — G. J. Nolan, Jerome and J. (Washington, 1956). — A. Rayez, J.: DSp 8:1469f. — F. Valli, Gioviniano. Esame delle fonte e dei frammenti (Urbino, 1954).

G. RÖWEKAMP

Judas, Gospel of

Irenaeus (*haer.* 1.31.1) speaks of a *Gospel of Judas* (ca. 150-180), which Epiphanius, *haer.* 38.1.5, and Theodoret, *haer.* 1.15, ascribe to the Cainites, and which may have contained a gnostically reinterpreted account of the passion. Fragments are known only from other accounts of the same type (Iren., *haer.* 1.31.2; Epiph., *haer.* 38.2.4; see Ps.-Tertullian, *haer.* 2.5f.).

W: *Iren. haer.* 1.31.1f. — *Epiph. haer.* 38.2.4. — W. Foerster, Die Gnosis 1 (Zurich, [3]1995), 57-59 [German trans.].
L: H.-J. Klauck, Judas (Freiburg i.Br., 1987), 19-21. — H.-C. Puech, B. Blatz: NTApo[6] 1:30f.

R. HANIG

Julian, Apollinarist

After the split among the Apollinarists, J., along with Eunomius of Berea in Thrace, belonged to the extreme wing of Polemon. At least this is suggested by the only surviving fragment of his *Ep. ad Polemonem*. In it, he follows Polemon's idea of a single will and activity of the incarnate Logos, although he nuances it insofar as he describes the one being and one nature

351

of Christ as composed of "movable and immovable, active and passive." This is approximately the same view expressed in a letter to him from his teacher → Apollinaris of Laodicea (*fr.* 150-52).

W: *ep.*, H. Lietzmann, Apolinaris und seine Schule (Hildesheim, 1970 = Tübingen, 1904), 277 [text]. — F. Diekamp, Doctrina Patrum (Münster, 1907), 308.

G. Feige

Julian, Arian

J. is the author of a commentary on Job (*Job*) that used to be attributed to → Julian of Halicarnassus. The name Julian, which does not occur in the direct transmission of the commentary, is known from catena fragments and from a prologue to our commentary. J. was an Arian, probably a follower of Aetius and Eunomius. *Job* was written probably between 357 and 365 in Syria and, more specifically, in Antioch. Two other works are attributed to J.: the → *Apostolic Constitutions* and the Ps.-Ignatian writings, which show a great similarity to *Job* in theol. questions, dogm. terminology, general style, and characteristic topoi. These were probably written after the commentary. J. may have concealed himself behind the names of the apostles and the pseudonym Ignatius when he and his like-minded friends were put on the defensive or persecuted.

W: *Ijob*, D. Hagedorn (Berlin, 1973). — *Const. App.*, F. X. Funk, Didascalia et Constitutiones Apostolorum, 2 vols. (Paderborn, 1905). — *Pseudoignat.*, J. B. Lightfoot, The Apostolic Fathers 3/2 (London, ²1885).
L: R. Draguet, Un commentaire grec arien sur Job: RHE 20 (1924) 38-65. — D. Hagedorn, loc. cit., XXIII-LXXXVIII.

B. Windau

Julian of Eclanum

I. Life: J. (ca. 385-450) was born toward the end of the 4th c. as son of the southern Italian Bishop Memorius and his wife Juliana. In 403, when a lector, J. married Titia, the daughter of Bishop Aemilius of Benevento. On this occasion, → Paulinus of Nola dedicated his *carm.* 25 to him. J. received a classical education in rhetoric. At the request of J.'s father, Memorius, Augustine sent a partial copy of his *De musica* (Augustine, *ep.* 110); in addition, he asked for a visit from J. who had meanwhile become a deacon. J. came only as far as Carthage and there met Augustine's friend Honoratus. In 416/417 J. became bishop of Eclanum (south of Benevento). In 418 he and a

group of Ital. and Sicil. bishops refused to subscribe to the *Ep. tractoria* of → Zosimus of Rome, in which Pelagianism was condemned. An imperial edict of June 9, 419, threatened with punishment anyone who did not proceed against the Pelagians (Augustine, *ep.* 201.1f.). For this reason, Patriarch Atticus of Constantinople expelled a group of Pelagians (Caelestinus, *ep.* 13.1; PL 50:469). Despite an appeal to Count Valerius in Ravenna and their expectation that a council would be called, J. and his fellow combatants were deposed and exiled. In 419/420 he and his colleagues were banished from Italy and found refuge in 421 with Theodore Mops., who had himself taken the side of the Pelagians. Here in exile J. seems to have occupied himself with exegesis, since his commentaries on the Bible are espec. indebted to Theodore's method of interpretation. J.'s persevering efforts to regain his episcopal see were unsuccessful. In 418 he appealed to Valerian and made his claim known in his treatises *Ad Turbantium* (419) and *Ad Florum* (421). In 428/429 Marius Mercator foiled efforts on J.'s behalf that were supported by Emperor Theodosius II and Patriarch Nestorius: he convinced the emperor that the Pelagians were heretics, and he secured their banishment from Constantinople. J.'s fate was sealed when the Council of Ephesus condemned Pelagianism as a heresy. Efforts at a reconciliation under Sixtus III and Leo I were defeated by J. himself, since he was unwilling to change his views (Prosper Tiro, *chron.*, year 439). Acc. to a lost work of → Fulgentius of Ruspe (*Contra Faustum*; see PL 48:296ff.), J. seems to have found a shelter in southern Italy, where he visited Faustus of Lérins. After that he seems to have been a teacher in Sicily before dying before 455.

II. Works: (a) J.'s commentaries are indebted to the Antiochene method of interpreting scripture; thanks to his knowledge of Greek, he was able to make an intensive study of that method. He supported a historical approach but made some room for typology. His clear Lat. style enabled him to present his thoughts pleasingly and accurately. The following works are preserved: a Lat. translation of the *Expositio in psalmos* (*epit. in ps.*) of → Theodore Mops.; an abbreviated commentary on *Job* (*in Job*); an incomplete commentary on the minor prophets Hosea, Joel, and Amos (*in Os., in Ioel, in Am.* are attributed to J). Fragments of *In canticum* and *De bono constantiae* are transmitted in Bede.

(b) While Pelagius and Caelestinus defended their orthodoxy, J. realized that attack was far more effective than defense, and therefore he cast doubt on Augustine's orthodoxy. The controversy between these two defined the years 418-421. J.'s main accusation against Augustine was Manichaeism. Acc. to J., it was this that made Augustine locate evil in nature and desire and not in the will; as a result, as in Manichaeism, creation and marriage in particular were condemned. Also (acc. to J.) desire is not evil in itself but only in excess. J. endeavored to defend the justice of God and the goodness of creation. Whoever uses free will properly can (he says) attain to the good. This is true of every human being, even pagans, and therefore everyone must be exhorted to it. Thus even grace cannot be in conflict with personal freedom. Reason takes priority over the scriptures and eccles. authority. J.'s extensive rhetorical training enabled him to define and argue with clarity. Without his intellectual efforts, Pelagianism would have lacked any systematic coherence, as Augustine himself conceded. J. forced Augustine to define his teaching ever more precisely and thus brought to light the fatal consequences of Augustine's position. In J. Augustine had his only evenly matched opponent. Their different backgrounds, experience, and opposing philosophical starting points (Augustine: the Platonists; J.: the Aristoteleans) made mutual understanding almost impossible. In spite of this, J.'s writings show a clear concern for ethics and religion.

Because of the condemnation of Pelagianism, the anti-Augustinian and defensive writings of J. have survived only in fragments and in citations by → Augustine, → Marius Mercator, and Bede.

A few lines of J.'s letter to Valerius (*ep. ad Valerium*) are preserved in Augustine's *nupt. et conc.* In the summer of 419 J. replied to *nupt. et conc.* with his *Ad Turbantium* (*ad Turb.*), which can to a great extent be reconstructed from Augustine's *c. Iul.*, *nupt. et conc.* 2, and *c. Iul. imp.* Marius Mercator's *Commonitorium* preserves J.'s letter to Zosimus (*ep. ad Zosimum*), as well as a public debate in Rome (*Dicta in quadam disputatione publica*; *dict.*). An anonymous *Libellus fidei* is probably the second part of a letter to Zosimus. In Augustine's *c. duas ep. Pelagianorum* two letters of J. are preserved, one to the Roman church after the death of Zosimus, a second to Rufus of Thessalonica (*ep. ad Rufum*). J.'s work *Ad Florum* (421) is to a large degree preserved in Augustine's *c. Iul. imp.*

W: *commentarius in Canticum canticorum*, L. de Coninck, M. J. d'Hont, CCL 88:398-401. — *de bono Constantiae*, 401f. — *dict.*, ibid., 336. — *ep. ad Romanos*, ibid., 396-398. — *ep. ad Rufum*, ibid., 336-340. — *ep. ad Valerium*, ibid., 335. — *ep. ad Zosimum*, ibid., 335f. — *in Iob*, ibid., 3-109. — *in Os.*, *in Ioel*, *in Am.*, ibid., 115-329. — *ad Turb.*, ibid., 340-396. — A. Bruckner (Berlin, 1910 = Aalen, 1973). — *epit. in psalm.*, L. de Coninck, M. J. d'Hont, CCL 88A.

— *ad Florum*, Augustine, *c. Iul. imp.*, M. Zelzer, CSEL 85/1:3-506.
L: P. L. Barcliff, In Controversy with Saint Augustine. J. on the Nature of Sin: RThAM 58 (1991) 5-20. — J. Baxter, Notes on the Latin of J.: ALMA 21 (1949) 5-54. — G. Bouwmann, Des J. Kommentar zu den Propheten Osee, Joel und Amos (Rome, 1958). — P. Brown, Sexuality and Society in the Fifth Century A. D. Augustine and J.: Tria Corda. Scritti in onore di Arnaldo Momigliano, ed. E. Gatta (Como, 1983), 49-70. — idem, Die Keuschheit der Engel (Munich, 1991). — A. Bruckner, J. (Leipzig, 1897). — G. de Plinval, J. devant la Bible: RSR 47 (1959) 345-366. — J. Lössl, Intellectus gratiae. Die Erkenntnistheoretische und hermeneutische Dimension der Gnadenlehre Augustins v. Hippo=SVigChr 38 (Leiden, 1997) (literature). — idem, Birthplace: REAug 44 (1998) 223-239. — F. J. Thonnard, L'aristotelisme de J. et de Saint Augustin: REAug 11 (1965) 296-304.

W. GEERLINGS

Julian of Halicarnassus

J. was a Monophysite bishop of Halicarnassus in the first quarter of the 6th c. He died, probably in 527, in Egypt where he sought refuge after the accession of Justin I (518), since the latter was trying to push through the decrees of Chalcedon. J. was known as an adversary of Severus of Antioch who, like J., lived in exile in Alexandria; their disagreement had to do with the question of the transitoriness of the body of Jesus. During the controversy with Severus J. composed several works that can be partially reconstructed from anti-Julian texts (preserved in Syriac): (1) the *Tomus*, in which he presents his ideas to Severus; (2) supplements to this explanation; (3) a defense; (4) a work *Adversus blasphemias Severi*; (5) a work *Disputatio adversus Achillem et Victorem Nestorianos*. In addition, there are fragments of three letters to Severus on dogm. subjects.

The background of the controversy was J.'s idea that since Christ was sinless his body could not be affected by the consequences of sin, namely, death and transitoriness. In contrast, Severus insisted that Christ was indeed perfect in his divine nature but that his human body responded in ways proper to his human nature. The sin of Adam (he said) is not inherited as a bodily mark; but Adam was created as a mortal and therefore transitory human being. Severus thus attributes immortality to the body of Christ only beginning with the resurrection. J.'s teaching on the *aphtharsia* of the body of Christ demonstrably found supporters in Syria, Mesopotamia, and Armenia down into the 8th c.; they were called Julianists, Aphthartodocetists, or Gaianists (after Gaianus, a friend of J. who was for a short time bishop of Alexandria).

W: R. Draguet, J. et sa controverse avec Sévère d'Antioche (Leuven/Louvain, 1924) [Syriac text/Greek reverse trans.]. — *ep.*, R. Hespel, La polémique antijulianiste, CSCO 244:206-209 [text]; CSCO 245:159-162 [French trans.].
L: R. Draguet, J.: DThC 8:1931-1940. — H. Grondijs, L'iconographie byzantine du crucifié mort sur la croix (Brussels, 1941). — E. Honigmann, Évêques et évêchés (Leuven/Louvain, 1951), 125-131. — M. Jugie, Gaianité: DThC 6:1002-1022.

S. MÜLLER-ABELS

Julian Pomerius

P. was from Mauretania and toward the end of the 5th c. went to southern Gaul, where he was ordained a priest. He settled in Arles as a teacher of rhetoric and around 497/498 taught Caesarius of Arles (Gennadius, *vir. ill.* 99). Further information about his life is lacking. He composed his writings at the beginning of the 6th c.; the only one preserved complete is the *De vita contemplativa* (*Pomer.*), which at one time was ascribed to → Prosper Tiro of Aquitania. This edifying doctrinal treatise in three books answers, at varying lengths, ten questions of a Bishop Julian (*capitula; prol.* 3).

Book 1, devoted to the contemplative life, describes its characteristics (1.1-11: *capitulum* 1), defines it in distinction from the active life (1.12: 2), and explains how even a priest busy in the church can achieve contemplation (1.13-25: 3). Book 2, which is devoted to the active life, calls for a nuanced dealing with sinners in the church, depending on the motive and gravity of the sin (2.1-19: 4), brands as serious sin the unjustified claim to the church's gifts to society (2.19f.: 5), praises detachment from earthly possessions as the perfection of continence (2.12-15: 6), and stresses the point that continence (*abstinentia*) must be practiced by body *and* by spirit, with Jesus Christ the redeemer as model (2.17-24: 7). Book 3 contains teaching on the virtues and vices. True virtues are distinguished from false (3.1: 8), *superbia/cupiditas* is said to be the root of all the vices (3.2-17: 9), and the four cardinal virtues are described (3.18-34: 10).

Despite dependence on Augustine, Jerome, and others, the work is independent in its conception and presentation and was influential down into the Middle Ages. Of P.'s *De natura animae et qualitate eius* in eight books (Isidore, *vir. ill.* 25) only a few traces are left in Julian of Toledo (*Prognosticorum futuri saeculi libri tres*).

W: *Pomer.*, PL 59:415-520 (a new edition is a *desideratum*). — M. J. Suelzer, ACW 4 (Westminster, Md., 1947) [English trans.]. — M. Spinelli, CTP 64 (Rome, 1987) [Italian trans.].
L: J. P. Bouhot, Un pseudo-témoin du De natura animae: REAug 23 (1977) 113-121. — J. Devisse, L'influence de J. Pomère sur les clercs carolingiens: RHEF 56 (1970) 285-295. — A. Roncoroni, Su plausus e gemitus nella predicazione cristiana da Gerolamo a Cesario: Sileno 2 (1976) 303-315. — M. Spinelli, Il sacerdos docens nel De vita contemplativa: Crescita dell'uomo nella catachesi dei Padri, ed. F. Sergio (Rome, 1988), 287-300. — C. Tibiletti, La teologia della grazia in Giuliano Pomerio: Aug. 25 (1985) 489-506.

K. POLLMANN

Julius Africanus

I. **Life**: Born in Jerusalem ca. 160, (Sextus) Julius Africanus (J. A.) is usually regarded in the literature as the first Chr. chronographer. Only a few facts are known about the life of this writer, whose chief interest was not at all in theol. questions but was of a general scientific kind. He was a respected, widely traveled man, who in 195 took part in the expedition of Septimius Severus against the Osrhoenes. He visited the court of Edessa and was in contact there with Cardesanes the Syr. gnostic. Before 221 he attended Origen's school for catechumens in Alexandria and the lectures of Origen's assistant, Heraclas. J. A. presumably made friends with Origen himself. In the service of Emperor Alexander Severus he established the library of the Pantheon in Rome. As ambassador of Vespasian's colony of veterans at Emmaus-Nicopolis, where he lived until his death in 240, J. A. tried in 222 (224) to use his influence with the emperor to obtain municipal rights for the military city. On this occasion J. A. presumably met Hippolytus in Rome.

II. **Works**: Only fragments remain of the five books of the *Chronography* (*Chronographiae*). This earliest Chr. universal chronicle begins with the creation of the world and comes down to 217 or 221 C.E. The basis for the synchronic presentation is the historical data of the Bible, as well as chronographical information of Jewish and pagan origin (Justus of Tiberias, list of the Olympiads). Eusebius in his church history makes use of the *Chronography*, and Hippolytus corrected his chronicle presumably with the help of J. A.'s work.

Likewise preserved only in fragments are the *Embroideries* (*Cesti*), originally in twenty-four books. This work, dedicated to Alexander Severus, contains information on questions in the natural sciences, medicine, warfare, and magic.

Preserved complete and transmitted along with the answer is a letter to Origen. Here J. A. challenges the authenticity of the Susanna episode in the Heb.

book of Daniel. Fragments of a letter to an otherwise unknown recipient named Aristides are handed down in large measure in Eusebius (*h.e.* 1.17). Here J. A. explains the differences between the genealogies of Mt and Lk with the aid of the law of the levirate in Deut 25:5ff.

W: *Chronographiae* (*fr.*), PG 10:63-94. — M. J. Routh, Reliquiae sacrae 2 (Oxford, 1846), 238-308 [text/Latin trans.]. — *Cesti* (*fr.*), J. R. Vieillefond, Les "Cestes" de J. A. (Florence, 1970) [text/French trans./comm.]. — *ep.*, W. Reichardt, Die Briefe des S. J. A. an Aristides u. Origenes (Leipzig, 1909) [text/comm.]. — *ep. ad Aristidem*, PG 10:52-64. — M. J. Routh, loc. cit. 2:228-237. — *ep. ad Origenem*, PG 11:41-48. — M. J. Routh, loc. cit. 2:225-228.
L: E. Amann, J. A.: DThC 8:1921-1925. — W. Bauer, Rechtgläubigkeit (Tübingen, ²1964), 162-167. — E. H. Blakeney, A letter to Origenes on the story of Susanna: Theol. 29 (1934) 164-169. — H. Gelzer, S. J. A. u. die byz. Chronographie, 1/2 (Leipzig, 1880/98). — J. Granger, J. A. and the Western Text: JThSt 35 (1934) 361-368. — idem, J. A. and the Library of the Pantheon: JThSt 35 (1934) 157-161. — A. v. Harnack, Handbuch der altchr. Lit. 1/2 (Berlin, 1921), 507-513. — W. Kroll, J. Sickenberger, J. A.: PRE 10:116-125. — F. Spitta, Der Brief des J. A. an Aristides (Halle, 1877). — O. Stählin, Geschichte der griech. Lit. 2 (Munich, ⁶1924), 1346-1348. — F. C. R. Thee, J. A. and the Early Christian View of Magic (Tübingen, 1984).

G. BROSZIO

Julius Cassian

J., a leading encratite, was active in the second half of the 2nd c., probably ca. 170, presumably in Alexandria. Clement Alex. names him twice, each time with Tatian. In *str.* 1.101.2, he mentions J.'s *Exegetica* (at least two books); in the first book J. apparently spoke of the greater antiquity of "Hebrew philosophy" as compared with all other wisdom. We may suppose that J. derived his encratite teaching exegetically from the Heb. Torah. In the second passage, *str.* 3.91–102.2, Clement deals in detail with J.'s encratism by citing four fragments of the work *On Continence or Living as a Eunuch* and referring to others. In the first citation J. explains that the conclusion may not be drawn from the existence of human genitalia that intercourse is allowed by God, for it is forbidden by Mt 19:12 and Isa 56:3. In the next fragment J. has recourse to the idea that the Savior has recreated us and liberated us from error and from community established via the sexual, shameful members. It is not grammatically clear whether Clement intends to say in this context that J. (or Tatian?) came from the school of Valentinus. In the next fragment J. refers, as Clement notes, to the dialogue between Jesus and Salome on the overcoming of sexuality, a dialogue from the *Gospel of the Egyptians*.

In the final citation, begetting and being begotten, which is under the control of the earthly, is contrasted with the heavenly transformation of the encratites. A protological grounding of encratitism seems to be the point of the note that J. derived generation (*genesis*) from Eve's deception by the serpent in accordance with 2 Cor 11:3 and that he applied the garments of skin in Gen 3:21 to human bodies. Clement's judgment is that J. followed too closely the Platonic doctrine of the fall of preexistent souls into the world of bodies. In addition, Clement accuses him of being responsible, by reason of his hostility to material creation, for the docetism that links him with Marcion and Valentinus.

Eusebius and Jerome took over what Clement says about J.'s *Exegetica;* but J. did not produce an independent work on chronography, as Jerome believes, although Jerome may have had further information at hand (from lost works of Origen?).

W: *Frgm.*, O. Stählin, L. Früchtel, U. Treu, GCS Clemens Alexandrinus 2 (Berlin, ⁴1985).
L: F. Bolgiani, La tradizione eresiologica sull'encratismo: Atti e Memorie dell'Accademia delle Scienze di Torino 96 (1961/62) 537-664. — A. Le Boulluec, La notion d'hérésie 2 (Paris, 1985), 297f., 340-350. — H. Chadwick, Enkrateia: RAC 5.343-365. — A. v. Harnack, Geschichte der altchr. Lit. 1 (Leipzig, ²1958), 201f., 491; 2/1:535. — G. Sfameni Gasparo, Protologia ed encratismo: Aug. 22 (1982) 75-89. — N. Walter, Der angebliche Chronograph J.: FS E. Klostermann (Berlin, 1961), 177-192 (older literature).

D. WYRWA

Julius of Rome

In the (eccles.-)political and theological struggles after Nicaea, J., bishop of Rome 337-352, sought to reverse the decrees of deposition issued in the eastern part of the empire against → Athanasius and → Marcellus, who fled into exile in Rome in 339. In 340/341 a Roman synod under J. determined the innocence of both men. In his *ep.* 1 (Athanasius, *apol. sec.* 21-35) to the bishops of the East J. gave a detailed account of the grounds for this decision and claimed Rome's right to act as the court of arbitration (*apol. sec.* 33.3-5), a claim not accepted in the East. Nonetheless, the right to serve as court of appeal for review of regional synodal judgments (a right that emerged from the canons of the western Synod of Sardica 343 [C. H. Ryrner, *EOMJA* 1/2:452-86]) represented an important stage on the way to the legal establishment of the Roman claim to primacy.

Ep. 2 (Athan., *apol. sec.* 52f.) of 346 is a letter of congratulations to the community of Alexandria for the return of Athanasius from exile to his see. The

Liber pontificalis 36 reports the reorganization of the episcopal chancery and the building of two Roman churches (S. Maria in Trastevere and the Basilica of Julian — SS. Apostoli) under J.

W: *ep.* 1, Ath., *apol. sec.* 21-35, Athanasius Werke 2/1, ed. H.-G. Opitz (Berlin, 1938), 102-113 [text]. — *ep.* 2, Ath., *apol. sec.* 52f., ibid., 132f. [text].
L: L. W. Barnard, Council (Sofia, 1983), 26-37, 109-118. — idem, Pope J.: RThAM 38 (1971) 69-79. — W. Gessel, Bewußtsein: FS H. Tüchle (Paderborn, 1975), 63-74. — K. M. Girardet, Kaisergericht (Bonn, 1975), 88-105. — R. P. C. Hanson, Search (Edinburgh, 1988), 267-273, 284-314. — H. Hess, Canons (Oxford, 1958), 110-127. — C. Pietri, Roma (Rome, 1976), 187-237. — A. Raddatz, Kaisertum (Berlin, 1963), 33-36. — H. J. Sieben, Konzilsidee (Paderborn, 1979), 359-362. — J. Ulrich, Anfänge (Berlin, 1994), 32-35.

J. ULRICH

Junilius Africanus

J., also called Junillus, came originally from North Africa and, at the urging of → Primasius, edited, while quaestor of the imperial palace in Constantinople, a Gr. work of Persian → Paul of Nisibis under the title *Instituta regularia divinae legis*. This is an introduction to study of the Bible that faithfully follows the views of → Theodore Mops. and sets great value on the literal meaning of the scriptures.

W: PL 68:15-42 [text]. — H. Kihn, Theodor u. J. (Freiburg i.Br., 1888), 465-528 [text].
L: H. Kihn, loc. cit. — E. Stein, Datierung: BAB. L 23 (1937) 165-190.

P. BRUNS

Justin the Gnostic

Our only information on J. comes from Hippolytus (*haer.* 5.23-27; 10.15), who says nothing about origin or dates. Acc. to him, J. practiced a strict discipline of secrecy and used both Gr. myths and his own writings for instruction. Hippolytus's knowledge is probably based solely on the work *Baruch*, which was presumably available to him only in excerpts. That work (at least two books) gave an unconventional story of creation, the eruption of evil, and the process of redemption. The driving forces in this process were three unbegotten principles (*treis archai tōn holōn agennētoi*; 5.26.1), namely: the Good which is totally removed from anything cosmic; next, the father Elohim, who is coresponsible for the eruption of evil but who by sending his angel Baruch makes redemption possible; and, finally, Edem, who embodies the earth or the psyche and promotes evil

through a wicked angel. Human beings as possessors of pneuma and psyche are stamped with this opposition. The possibility of their turning to the Good, that is, their redemption, in the form of a flight from this wicked world, is modeled by Jesus, who, though as son of Joseph he is a mere man, is the first to break out of the spell of evil. The adoption of the story of Jesus, the use of other NT traditions (Lk, 1 Cor, Gal, possibly Jn), and the borrowing from the world of the Gr. sagas and from astrology—all these for the most part pay no attention to the original meaning.

W: Hippolyt, *haer.* 5.23.1-27.6; 10.15. — W. Völker, Quellen zur Geschichte d. chr. Gnosis (Tübingen, 1932), 27-33 [text]. — W. Foerster, Die Gnosis 1 (Zurich, ³1990), 65-79 [German trans.].
L: R. van den Broek, Edem: VigChr 27 (1973) 35-45. — E. Haenchen, Das Buch Baruch: idem, Gott u. Mensch (Tübingen, 1965), 299-334. — H. Jonas, Gnosis u. spätantiker Geist 1 (Göttingen, ⁴1988), 335-341. — H. Leisegang, Gnosis (Stuttgart, ⁵1985), 156-168. — M. Marcovich, Studies in Graeco-Roman Religions and Gnosticism (Leiden, 1988), 93-119. — J. Montserrat-Torrents, Philosophie: StPatr 18/1 (1989) 253-261. — M. Olender, Éléments: FS M. J. Vermaseren 2 (Leiden, 1978), 874-897. — A. Orbe, La cristología: EE 47 (1972) 437-457. — M. Simonetti, Note sul libro di Baruch: VetChr 6 (1969) 71-89.

R. HANIG

Justin Martyr

I. Life: As sources for the life of J., even Eusebius had available only a few biographically helpful passages in the authentic writings of the apologete. J. came from the Roman colony of Flavia Neapolis (now Nablus) in the province of Syria Palestina. From the names of his father and grandfather, Priscus and Baccheius (1 *apol.* 1), scholars usually infer a Roman or Gr. descent. But J.'s style and manner of thinking show hardly any traces of a formal Hellen. education; he describes himself as a "Samaritan" (*Samareus*: *dial.* 120.3), and in fact some "Samaritanisms" indicate a certain cultural connection with Samaria, although not membership in the community that worshiped on Gerizim (as Epiphanius claims, *haer.* 2, independently of the other traditions), since J. was not circumcised (*dial.* 28.2) and counted himself a pagan (*dial.* 41.3). As a follower of contemporary, so-called Middle Platonism, he accepted Christianity but did not therefore put off his philosopher's garb (*dial.* 1.12). The *Acta Iustini et sodalium* (→ *Martyrs, Acts*), which Eusebius did not know of, note that J. twice stayed in Rome. We may think that the first part of his *Apology* was written during the first stay and that his absence is reflected in the setting of the dialogue with Trypho the Jew. J.'s activity as teacher, reported in the *Acta*, seems to belong in the period of his second stay in Rome. His school produced Tatian, who later turned heretic but who mentions his teacher with praise (*orat.* 18.2f.; 19.1). Eusebius attributes J.'s death as a martyr directly to the hostile machinations of Cynic philosopher Crescens (*h.e.* 4.16). In his *Chronicle* (year 2168 = Jerome, 2170), Eusebius gives the year of death as the fifteenth year of Antoninus Pius (138-161), but this contradicts his statement (*h.e.* 4.16.1; 4.18.2) that J. addressed his second apology to Emperors Marcus Aurelius and L. Verus. Furthermore, in the *Acta* it is *praefectus urbi* (Q. Iunius) Rusticus (PIR² I 814) who conducts the interrogations during J.'s trial; but Rusticus held this office under Marcus Aurelius ca. 162-168.

L: G. A. Bisbee, The Acts of J. A Form-Critical Study: Sec-Cen 3 (1983) 129-156. — A. G. Hamman, Chronologie de la vie et des œuvres de J.: Aug. 35 (1995) 231-240. — W. Hüttl, Antoninus Pius I (Prague, 1931). — P. Lampe, Die stadtröm. Christen (Tübingen, 1987). — U. Neymeyr, Die chr. Lehrer (Leiden, 1989). — P. R. Weis, Samaritanisms: JThS 1:45 (1944) 199-205.

II. Works: Eusebius (*h.e.* 4.18.1-6) gives the following list of J.'s writings: (a) *Apology* to Emperor Antoninus Pius and his sons; (b) a second *Apology* to his successor Antoninus Verus (= Marcus Aurelius); (c) *Answer to the Greeks* (= pagans), espec. on the nature of demons; (d) *Elenchus* (refutation, against the pagans); (e) *The Sovereignty of God*; (f) *The Harpist* (*Psaltes*); (g) *Scholikon* (lecture) on the soul; (h) a dialogue in answer to the Jews. We ought to believe that Eusebius had read these works under J.'s name, since the *Syntagma against All Heresies* and the *Syntagma against Marcion*, the titles of which he knew only from J. himself (*h.e.* 4.11.10: 1 *apol.* 26.8) and from Irenaeus (*h.e.* 4.18.9: *haer.* 4.6.2), are not in his list. Of the eight works listed, b, c, f, and g are completely lost, while in place of d and e have been suggested the *Cohortatio ad Graecos* (*coh. gr.*), which has recently been attributed to → Marcellus of Ancyra, and the treatise *De monarchia* (*monarch.*), a collection of testimonies to the oneness of God, but from Gr. poetic literature, whereas acc. to Eusebius J.'s collection also contained bibl. material. This last probably represented a by-work that resulted from the apologetic writings, as 1 *apol* 20.5 suggests. Under c and g we may think of systematic developments of subjects touched only in passing in the surviving works: psychology (*dial.* 4-6; 1 *apol.* 18) and demonology (1 *apol.* 5; 2 *apol.* 5). Traces of the lost work against heresies appear espec. in 1 *apol.* 26; 56; 58. The *Syntagma,* which perhaps contained the

work against Marcion, was used by Irenaeus and through him influenced later antiheretical literature.

The tendency to amplify the work of the apologete and martyr by means of falsely attributed writings soon paid little attention to Eusebius's list. In the *parall.* of John Damascene, which also contains some passages from the authentic writings, under J.'s name a treatise *De resurrectione* is cited almost in its completeness; *Cod. gr.* IX (burned in 1870) of the Strasbourg city library has J. as author of the Letter to → Diognetus, as well as of a short *Oratio ad Graecos* (*or. Gr.*), which goes under the name of another writer in a Syr. ms.; the famous Arethas Codex (*Paris. gr.* 451), which is an anthology of early Chr. literature, assigns to J. an ethical instruction in letter form, the *Ep. ad Zenam et Serenum*; finally, *Cod. Paris. gr.* 450, from the year 1363, an edition of the "Collected Works" of J. and the sole direct transmitter of the authentic works, adds to the majority of the works just mentioned a further treatise on the bodily resurrection that is elsewhere attributed to → Athenagoras. The *Expositio rectae fidei* and the *Quaestiones et responsiones ad orthodoxos* (*qu. et resp.*) belong also certainly to Theodoret of Cyrrhus, while Harnack wanted to assign to → Diodorus of Tarsus all three of the collections of questions transmitted under J.'s name, along with the *Refutation of Some Doctrinal Statements of Aristotle.*

W: CorpAp III-V. — *fr., fr. res.,* K. Holl, Frgm. vornizänischer Kirchenväter aus den Sacra Parallela (Leipzig, 1899) [text]. — *coh. Gr., monarch., or. Gr.,* M. Marcovich (Berlin, 1990) [text]. — *coh. Gr., C.* Riedweg, Ps.-J. (Markell v. Ankyra?) (Basel, 1994) [text]. — *qu. et resp.,* A. Papadopulos-Kerameus, Theodoret (Leipzig, 1975 = 1895) [text].
L: P. Beskow, En judisk missionsskrift: KIIÅ 4 (1993) 49-62 [on *coh. Gr.*]. — U. Amadino, Il fascino della poesia: Ben. 39 (1992) 291-295 [on *monarch.*]. — F. X. Funk, Kirchengeschichtliche Untersuchungen 3 (Paderborn, 1907), 323-350 (against A. v. Harnack). — A. v. Harnack, Diodor v. Tarsus, TU 6/4 (Leipzig, 1901). — H. Lona, Ps.-J. s res. u. die altchr. Auferstehungsapologetik: Sal. 51 (1989) 691-768.

The *Apology* (*apol.*), which was written after the *Syntagma*, can be dated rather exactly: The term of office of (L. Munatius) Felix (PIR² M 723), who is mentioned in 1 *apol.* 29.2f. as *praefectus Aegypto*, is attested by papyri as between 150 and 154; (Q. Lollius) Urbicus (PIR² L 237), described in 2 *apol* 2 as judge at a trial of Christians, was *praefectus urbi* 146-160; in 1 *apol.* 46.1 it is said, obviously following the Lukan chronology, that Christ had been born 150 years earlier. From these indications the year 150 is the *terminus ad quem.* 2 *apol.* 2 is missing in almost all the mss. and is preserved in one of Eusebius's many citations; the chapter on the Cynic Crescens comes in the mss. before 2 *apol.* 9, whereas most editors, relying on an unclear remark of Eusebius (*h.e.* 4.17.14), place it after 2 *apol.* 2. The famous rescript of Hadrian (1 *apol.* 68.5-10), which J. cites in its original Lat. version, is transmitted only in a Gr. translation made by Eusebius (*h.e.* 4.8.8). No satisfactory explanation has as yet been found for why Eusebius attributes passages from 1 *apol.* to 2 *apol.* and from 2 *apol.* to 1 *apol.* Perhaps the second was simply a new edition of 1 with negligible changes. But the 2 *apol.* that we have is not at all identical with such a second apology. For one thing, 1 *apol.* 1 is satisfied with an address to the authorities in the form of a petition; 2 *apol.*, however, begins almost immediately with the past history of a trial of Christians. In addition, 2 *apol.* cannot possibly have been published as an independent work because in it J. repeatedly and explicitly refers to 1 *apol.* But, even though 2 *apol.* (14f.), unlike 1 *apol.*, has a formal conclusion, it has not thus far been convincingly shown that the two were parts of a planned whole. It seems rather that in introducing 2 *apol.* 1-13 J. was reacting to two actual events, the trial of Ptolemaeus and the criticism of Crescens, and took this occasion to state more precisely his earlier views on, among other things, demonology, eschatology, and the doctrine of the Logos (this last in the theory of the *Logos spermatikos*).

A critique, based on the comparison with Athenagoras, of J.'s digressive manner of presentation fails to take into account that J. had set himself an almost impossible task. Along with public opinion, which accused Christians of incest and cannibalism, and along with the state, which tolerated the most esoteric religions and philosophies but persecuted Christianity, J. faced another enemy, for us largely anonymous, namely, anti-Christian journalism. This regarded Christianity as a young and therefore inferior religion, its founder as a charlatan, and demanded proof of the reasonableness of the faith. J. parries with a proof, comprehensive but with many presuppositions, from the prophets for the divinity of Christ (1 *apol.* 30-53) and here proves himself to be "the most Christian" of the Chr. apologetes of the 2nd c., a man who "is not ashamed of the scandal of the cross" (Jerome, *vir. ill.* 23).

A further characteristic of J.'s apologetics is the important role of demons. These enemies of the Logos, the divine Reason incarnated in Jesus Christ, blind the minds of officials and lead them astray into irrational proceedings against Christians; they have brought into the world the founders of heresies,

whose supporters are harming the reputation of true Christians; they have passed themselves off to humanity as gods and, knowing the messianic prophecies of the old covenant, have inserted anticipations of the Christ event into classical mythology in order to defame Christianity as a mere imitation of what is supposedly older. Against the accusation of plagiarism J. has two more arrows in his quiver. The philosophers copied their most important ideas in cosmology from Moses (proof from antiquity). When Chr. and pagan values resemble each other, the Logos-Christ is at work, who before his incarnation worked not only in the prophets but also in the philosophers, though admittedly only seminally, as the *Logos Spermatikos*, as the many self-contradictions of the philosophers show.

J. often did not succeed in distinguishing clearly these many themes and types of argument. There is another reason for the weakness of his presentation that we will readily pardon: where others made polished attacks, J. explained and gave arguments. A redaction-critical study could absolve him of responsibility for the-all-too-numerous digressions and repetitions.

Dialogue with Trypho the Jew (*dial.*). This too has not been transmitted in its completeness. It lacks its preface with the dedication to Marcus Pompeius, who is apostrophized at the end (141.5), and the information (given in Eus., *h.e.* 4.18.6) that the dialogue took place in Ephesus. After 74.3 there is a gap, in which, among other things, mention was made of the conversation being interrupted by night.

In *dial.* 2.1–8.3 J. describes how, after being disillusioned by Stoicism, Peripateticism, and Phythagoreanism, he turned to Platonism. He thought he was nearing its goal when a mysterious old man pointed out some internal contradictions in Plato and recommended to the uncertain seeker the revelation given by the prophets, which is exalted beyond all proof because inspired by God. The literary convention of the "philosophical journey" (*dial.* 2.3-6) and the figure of the "venerable bearer of revelation," as well as the comparatively elegant presentation raise doubts about the biographical reliability of this much discussed passage; but this much at least may be taken from it, that in J.'s judgment Platonism surpassed all other philosophical schools and in his view was closest to Christianity. The passage prepares protreptically for the method subsequently used of finding truth through exegesis of an extensive collection of testimonies to the divine sonship of Jesus Christ.

The object of the not infrequently cutting but in the end conciliatory controversy with Trypho is not only the christological interpretation of scripture but also the literal meaning (e.g., Isa 7:14), whenever the other side is accused of changing the canonically accepted text to falsify the meaning. For J. is the first to attribute the Gr. text not only of the Pentateuch but also of the prophetical books, including Pss, to the work of the legendary seventy-two translators (Septuagint). Remarkably, most of the readings rejected by J. have entered the LXX tradition; his departures from the LXX text of the minor prophets are justified by the discovery at Naḥal Ḥever. The citations from the gospels, from what J. calls the "memoirs of the apostles" (*apomnēmoneumata tōn apostolōn*), come perhaps from a harmony of the gospel such as the *Diatessaron* of → Tatian.

III. **Main Lines of Thought:** The disputed christological interpretation of the OT theophanies and the creation story in *dial.* (52: Gen 1:26, *poiēsamen*) is due to J.'s Platonically influenced understanding of God as transcendent. He therefore links transcendence and providence with the help of the angels, to whom the subheavenly realm is entrusted (2 *apol.* 5). He is the first eccles. writer who draws a parallel between the myth of the origin of the world in Plato's *Timaeus* and the bibl. account of creation; as a result, the Logos-Christ takes the place of the world-soul of the Platonic system (1 *apol.* 59f.). J. justifies (*dial.* 61.1) the idea that the preexistent Christ, instead of the transcendent God, comes in contact with the world and takes on various functions, by asserting that the Son "serves the will of the Father and is begotten of (*apo*) the Father by an act of the will." This subordinationism should also be understood as a reaction to the modalist christology of Marcion. J. describes the procession of the Son from the Father (*dial.* 61.2; 128.3) in a noteworthy anticipation of the Neoplatonic principle of emanation.

As a Platonist, J. was convinced of the unlimited freedom of the human will as being necessary to justify punishment after death. But the idea of retribution also led to his rejection of Platonic psychology, since in the latter an immortal soul is necessarily without beginning and is therefore free of the passions. J.'s faith in the one-thousand-year reign of the Messiah before the general resurrection (chiliasm) is because of his high regard for Rev, to the canonization of which he must have indirectly contributed (*dial.* 81.4; see Eus., *h.e.* 4.18.8).

IV. **Importance:** The honorary title "Philosopher and Martyr," which was to remain J.'s permanently, was given him by Tertullian (*adv. Valent.* 5). Traces of use of the surviving authentic works are hardly to be found before Eusebius; between John Damascene

and 1363, the date of the Paris ms., they are nonexistent. One exception is perhaps J.'s well-known description of the early Chr. baptismal and Sunday liturgies (1 *apol.* 65-67), an important source for the history of the liturgy, that was handed down separately in some late collections of texts. Apart from this, J.'s prestige since early Byz. times was owing to his reputation as a fighter of heresy and a martyr. His subsequent influence is impressively clear from the immense scholarly literature; scholars are interested primarily in the biblicism and philosophical distinctiveness of this first Chr. Platonist.

W: *apol., dial.,* E. J. Goodspeed, Die ältesten Apologeten (Göttingen, 1984 = 1914), 24-265 [exact copy of the manuscripts with the most necessary changes]. — *apol.,* M. Marcovich (Berlin, 1994) [first real critical edition]. — C. Munier (Fribourg, Switzerland, 1995) [text/French trans.]. — G. Rauschen, BKV² 12 [German trans.]. — H. Veil (Strasburg, 1894) [best German trans./comm.]. — C. P. Vetten, FC [text/trans. in preparation]. — *dial.,* G. Archambault, TDEHC 8:11 (Paris, 1909) [text/French trans.]. — P. Haeuser, BKV² 33 [German trans.]. — A. Lukyn Williams (London, 1930) [English trans.]. — K. Thieme, Kirche u. Synagoge, Olten 1945 [trans. of selections].

L: *Bibliographies:* A. Davids (Nijmegen, 1983) [thematic bibliog. 1923-1973]. — E. R. Goodenough, The Theology of J. (Amsterdam, 1968 = Jena, 1923), 295-320. — C. Munier, L'Apologie de St. J. (Fribourg, Switzerland, 1994), IX-XXV [alphabetical bibliog., esp. on *apol.*]. — O. Skarsaune, The Proof from Prophecy (Leiden, 1987), 473-487 [esp. on *dial.*]. — B. Wildermut: BBKL 3:890-895 [chronological bibliog. 1886-1986].

C. Andresen, J. u. der mittlere Platonismus: ZNW 44 (1952-1953) 157-195 = C. Zintzen (ed.), Der Mittelplatonismus (Darmstadt, 1981), 319-358 [standard work]. — A. Bellinzoni, The sayings of Jesus in the writings of J. (Leiden, 1967). — M.-É Boismard, A. Lamouille, Le Diatessaron: de Tatien à J. (Paris, 1992). — H. Dörrie, Der Platonismus in der Antike 2 (Stuttgart, 1990), 198-202, 488-493; 3 (Stuttgart, 1993), 100-102, 364-367. — M. J. Edwards, Platonic Schooling of J.: JThS NS 42 (1991) 17-34. — idem, J.'s Logos and the Word of God: JECS 3 (1995) 261-280. — E. Ferguson, J. and the Liturgy: RestQ 36 (1994) 267-278. — J. Geffken, Zwei griech. Apologeten (Leipzig, 1907), 97-104. — G. Girgenti, Giustino Martire: RFNS 82 (1990) 214-255. — M. D. Goulder, A poor man's christology: NTS 45 (1999) 332-348. — R. M. Grant, A Woman of Rome: ChH 54 (1985) 461-472 [on 2 *apol.* 2.1-9]. — S. Heid, Frühjüd. Messianologie: JBTh 8 (1993) 219-238. — M. Hengel, Die Septuaginta als "chr. Schriftensammlung": Die Septuaginta zwischen Judentum u. Christentum, ed. M. Hengel, A. M. Schwemer (Tübingen, 1994), 182-284. — R. Holte, Logos Spermatikos: StTh 12 (1958) 109-168. — W. Horbury, Jewish-Christian Relations in Barnabas and J.: Jews and Christians, ed. J. D. G. Dunn (Tübingen, 1992), 315-345. — P. Katz, J.'s Old Testament Quotations and the Greek Dodekapropheton Scroll (1957): Studies in the Septuagint, ed. S. Jellicoe, M. Orlinsky (New York, 1974), 530-540. — W. Kinzig, Der "Sitz im Leben" der Apologien in der alten Kirche: ZKG 100 (1989) 291-317 [form]. — H. J. Krämer,

Der Ursprung der Geistesmetaphysik (Amsterdam, 1964), 322 n. 486 [important reference to Justin's anticipation of emanationist teaching]. — M. Marcovich, Patristic Textual Criticism 1 (Atlanta, 1994). — G. May, Schöpfung aus dem Nichts (Berlin, 1976). — H. Meyer, Keimkräfte (Bonn, 1914), 80-93. — C. Nahm, The Debate on the "Platonism" of J.: SecCen 9 (1992) 129-151. — W. L. Petersen, Tatian's Dependence upon J.'s ΑΠΟΜΝΗΜΟΝΕΥΜΑΤΑ: NTS 36 (1990) 512-534. — J. W. Pryor, J. and the Fourth Gospel: SecCen 9 (1992) 153-169. — P. Pilhofer, Πρεσβύτερον κρεῖττον (Tübingen, 1990) [proof of age]. — J. Salzmann, Lehren u. Ermahnen (Tübingen, 1994), 235-257 [liturgy of the word]. — W. Schmid, Inversionsphänomen (1975): idem, Ausgewählte philologische Schriften (Berlin, 1984), 338-364 [1 ap-2 ap]. — B. Studer, Der apologetische Ansatz zur Logos-Christologie J. s: FS C. Andresen (Göttingen, 1979), 435-448. — R. A. Werline, The transformation of Pauline arguments in dial.: HThR 92 (1999) 79-93.

C. P. Vetten

Justinian I

I. Life: J., b. 482, was brought to the Byz. court as a youngster by his uncle, the later Emperor Justin I; there he was a student under Agapetus, a deacon of Hagia Sophia. In 521 he was made consul. Before 525 he married Theodora, a woman of lowly descent, who nonetheless quickly acquired considerable influence at the court. In 527 J. ascended the throne of Byzantium and held it until his death in 565.

II. Works: Evidently supported by Bishop Theodore Askidas, a man of great influence at the court, J. emerged not only as a lawgiver but as a theol. writer. Preserved are twenty-one letters (ep.); prominent among them are the ep. to Bishop Hormisdas of Rome in Sept. 520, and the letter to Bishop John II of Rome in June 533, in both of which J. pushed for the acceptance of the theopaschite formula (unus ex trinitate passus). The acceptance of it and the condemnation of its opponents came in 533, when some Acoemetes challenged the use of the formula in a 527 decree of J. on the faith, and Hypatius, orthodox archbishop of Ephesus and J.'s close friend, along with Demetrius, bishop of Philippi, traveled to Bishop John II in Rome and personally presented J.'s letter to him. Also preserved are four dogm. works: a Constitutio contra Severum etc. (Sev.) of 536, addressed to Bishop Menas of Constantinople; a treatise Contra Monophysitas (monoph.) of 542/543; the Confessio rectae fidei (conf.) of 551/553 with thirteen anathemas (conf. anath. 1-13); and a typos (edict) against Theodore of Mops. (typ. Thdr. Mops.); as well as edicts, decrees, digests, and institutes.

In all his works J. shows himself a trained, independent-minded, Neo-Chalcedonian theologian, who wrote espec. against the Monophysites (Sev., monoph.), as well as against the person and teaching of Theodore Mops. (typ. Thdr. Mops.) and of Origen (Edictum contra Originem [Or.] of 543; letter to the Holy Synod in 553 [ep. ad synodum de Origine; typ. Thdr. Mops.]). He purposefully intervened in the dogm. controversies of his time and wanted to decide them. In fact, because of the political power that came from his role as protector of the church and from the legal powers given to him by the Codex Iustinianus (cod.) of 534 and the supplementary Novellae (nov.) of 535 to 564, he was able not only to win acceptance of the theopaschite formula in 533 but also to call a council and secure the condemnation of Origenism and of the "Three Chapters" (i.e., [1] of the person and teaching of → Theodore Mops.; [2] of some writings of → Theodoret of Cyrrhus; and [3] of the letter of Bishop → Ibas of Edessa to Maris). It is unclear whether shortly before his death J. accepted aphthartodocetism. Also uncertain is whether he composed the Troparion Monogenes.

III. Importance: J. was defender of a politicized Christianity that was meant to bring about the ideological unification of the state. He therefore ruthlessly persecuted heretics and apostates, Jews and pagans; he forcibly christianized philosophy and in 529 closed the Academy of Athens, which was the center of pagan thought. In addition, he kept the eccles. hierarchy dependent on himself and directed all eccles. affairs. Thus in nov. 123 he divided the imperial church into the five patriarchates of Rome, Constantinople, Alexandria, Antioch, and Jerusalem, thereby legitimizing an existing state of affairs. The forcible christianization of thought, which meant the end of the ancient educational system, and the closing of the Athenian Academy marked the end of antiquity and the beginning of the Chr. Middle Ages. But J.'s influence extended far beyond the Middle Ages: his magnificent legislative system (cod., nov., Digesta, Institutiones), which was originally intended only to strengthen the unity of the state, continued, via the 12th c. school of Bologna, to be the basis of law down into modern times.

W: A. Letters: a. 9 ep. ad Hormisdam papam, PL 63:430-510. — O. Guenther, CSEL 35:592f., 614, 644-646, 648f., 655f., 659f. — b. 5 ep. ante synodum Constantinopolitanam (536) scriptae: ep. ad Constantinopolitanos, P. Krueger, Corpus Iuris Civilis 2: Codex Iustinianus 1, 1, 6 (Berlin, 1915), 7f. [text]. — ep. ad Epiphanium Constantinopolitanum, loc. cit., 1, 1, 7, 8-10 [text]. — ep. ad Iohannem II papam, PL 66:14-17. — O. Guenther, CSEL 35:322-325. — 2 ep. ad Agapetum papam, idem, CSEL 35:338-340, 344-347. — c. 7 ep. dogmaticae ad synodum Constantinopolit.: ep. ad Zoilum,

PG 86:1145-1150. — *ep. ad synodum de Theodoro Mop-suesteno*, PL 69:30-37. — ACO 4, 1, 8-14. — *ep. ad Iohan-nem episcopum Iustinopolis*, PL 69:119. — ACO 4, 1, 117. — *ep. ad Cosmam episcopum Mopsuestiae*, PL 69:119-120. — ACO 4, 1, 117f. — *ep. contra tria capitula*, PG 86:1041-1095. — PL 69:275-327. — E. Schwartz, SBAW. PPH 1939 (Milan, ²1973), 47-69 [text]. — *ep. ad synodum de Origine*, PG 86:989-993; 110:780-784. — *ep. ad synodum de Vigilii nomine a diptychis auferendo*, ACO 4, 1, 201-202. — B. Dogmatic writings: *Constitutio contra Anthimum, Sev., Petrum, Zooram*, PG 86:1095-1104. — PL 72:976-984. — ACO 3, 119-123. — *monoph.*, PG 86:1104-1146. — E. Schwartz, SBAW. PPH 1939 (Milan, ²1973), 7-43 [text]. — *conf., conf. anath.* 1-13, *typ. Thdr. Mops.*, PG 86:993-1035. — PL 69:225-267. — E. Schwartz, SBAW. PPH 1939 (Milan, ²1973), 72-111 [text]. — *in damnationem trium capitulorum*, E. Schwartz, Zur Kirchenpolitik Justinians, SBAW. PPH 1940, 2 (Munich, 1940), 73-81 [text]. — C. Edicts, decrees, digests, institutes, and novellae: a. *Or.*, PG 86:945-993. — PL 69:177-225. — ACO 3, 189-214. — PG 86:1149-1152 [text]. — F. Diekamp, Doctrina Patrum (Münster, 1981 = 1907), 134 [text]. — b. *Corpus Iuris Civilis* (*cod., Institutiones, Digesta, nov.*), T. Mommsen, P. Krüger, R. Schöll, G. Kroll, 3 vols. (Berlin, 1908-1912) [text].
Not Authentic W: *Troparium Monogenes*, W. Christ, M. Paranikas, Anthologia graeca carminum christianorum (Hildesheim, 1963 = Leipzig, 1871), 52 [text].

L: C. Andresen, Antike u. Christentum: TRE 1:50-99. — H.-G. Beck, Kirche u. theol. Lit. (Munich, ²1977), 285-287, 376-378 and others. — J. Breck, The Troparion Mono-genes: SVTQ 26 (1982) 203-228. — S. Brock, The conversa-tions with the Syrian Orthodox under Justinian (532): OCP 47 (1981) 87-121. — M. A. Cassetti, Giustiniano e la sua legislazione in materia ecclesiastica (Rome, 1958). — A. Demandt, Die Spätantike (Munich, 1989), 195-210. — M. van Esbroeck, La lettre de l'empereur Justinien sur l'An-nonciation et la Noël en 561: AnBoll 86 (1968) 356-362; 87 (1969) 442-444. — P. Gray, J.: TRE 17:478-486. — A. Grillmeier, Jesus der Christus 2/2 (Freiburg i.Br., 1989), 329-498 (English, Christ in Christian Tradition, vol. 2/2 [London, 1995]). — V. Grumel, L'auteur et la date de com-position du tropaire M.: EOr 22 (1923) 398-418. — S. Helmer, Der Neuchalkedonismus (Bonn, 1962). — C. Hohenlohe, Einfluß des Christentums auf das Corpus iuris civilis (Vienna, 1937). — H. Hunger, Kaiser J. I. (527-565) (Vienna, 1965). — G. Ostrogorsky, Geschichte des byz. Staates (Munich, 1940, ³1963) = History of the Byzantine State (Oxford, ²1968), Sonderausgabe 1965, new printing, 1980, 57-72, 103-118. — E. Schwartz, Zur Kirchenpolitik Justinians (Munich, 1940). — B. R. Suchla, Verteidigung eines platonischen Denkmodells einer chr. Welt (Göttin-gen, 1995), 10-18. — K. H. Uthemann: J. als Kirchenpoli-tiker u. Theologe: Aug. 39 (1999) 5-83.

B. R. SUCHLA

Justinian of Valencia

J., bishop of Valencia, took part in the Synods of Lérida (546) and Valencia (546). In his (lost) writ-ings J. evidently dealt primarily with questions of everyday church life. Isidore of Seville (*vir. ill.* 33)

says that J. wrote a *Liber responsionum ad quendam Rusticum de interrogatis quaestionibus*. In the first part he answered questions on the Holy Spirit; in the second he attacked the Bonosians; and in the third he spoke of rebaptism. (Was J. thinking of the conver-sion of Arians to the Cath. confession?) The fourth part had for its subject the difference between the baptism of John and the baptism of Christ, and the fifth the problem of the invisibility of both Father and Son. The *Liber* is completely lost.

On the other hand, the *De cognitione baptismi* of → Ildephonsus makes it possible to reconstruct a treatise of J. on baptism which handed on the text of the baptismal creed of the Visigothic Span. church.

W: Ildefons, *De cognitione baptismi*, PL 96.
L: C. P. Caspari, Quellen zur Geschichte des Taufsymbols 2 (Christiania, 1869), 290-300. — A. Helfferich, Der west-gothische Arianismus (Berlin, 1860). — G. Kampers, Per-sonengeschichtliche Studien (Münster, 1979), Nr. 68.

E. REICHERT

Justus of Toledo

J., a contemporary of Isidore of Seville, has tradition-ally been regarded as author of *De aenigmatibus Salomonis*, but this work is to be ascribed rather to Taio of Saragossa (651-683).

W: A. C. Vega: EspSag 56 (1957) 308-419 [text].

E. REICHERT

Justus of Urgel

J. came from Valencia (*serm.*) and was bishop of Urgel. He is mentioned by Isidore (*cir. ill.* 33; 34) as brother of Nebridius, Elpidius, and Justinianus, all of whom were active during the reign of Theudis (531-548). J. took part in the Synods of Toledo (527), Lérida, and Valencia (546), obviously as already an elderly man. There is no information on him after 546.

Only two works are known and preserved: a ser-mon on Vincent, a martyr (*serm.*), and an *Expositio in Cantica Canticorum* (*in cant.*). J. dedicated this second work to Deacon Justus (*ep. ad Iust.*) and, in a second letter, to Metropolitan Sergius of Tarragona. J. stresses the point that he chose the Vulgate as the text of his commentary and that he strove for brevity (*in cant., prol.*; see also Isidore, *vir. ill.* 34). In addi-tion, he used, without quoting them verbatim, Gre-gory of Elvira, Jerome, and Epiphanius Scholasticus. J.'s commentary was used by → Gregory the Great and obviously also by → Apponius. J. avoids the traditional eccles.-historical interpretation and the application to the soul's relationship with Christ; instead he interprets the text as referring primarily to the church of his times with its states and members. His concern is with the priesthood, but espec. with the martyrs and ascetics. In his view, the church had its origin more in the passion than in the incarnation. It is unclear whether he alludes to contemporary persecutions and, if so, to which ones (*in cant.* 41; 107-16).

W: *ep. ad Iust., in cant.*, PL 67:961-994. — *ep. ad Serg., ep. ad Iust., in cant.* (partial), E. Felipe Fernández: Revista española de estudios bíblicos 1 (1926) 1-28 (copy of ms. Madrid, B. N. 13. 086). — *in cant. prol., ep. ad Iust., serm.*, PLS 4:235-238.
L: R. Étaix, Note sur le "De aenigmatibus Salomonis": MSR 15 (1958) 137-142, here 138f.

E. Schulz-Flügel

Juvenal of Jerusalem

J. was bishop of Jerusalem from 422 on. He succeeded in having the Council of Chalcedon recognize Jerusalem as a patriarchate, after claiming since 431, on the basis of apoc. documents (see Leo, *ep.* 119.4; ACO 1, 1, 3), that Antioch was subject to Jerusalem. Initially a supporter of Cyril and Dioscurus, he switched to the line of the council in 451 and thereby provoked controversies and the election of an anti-bishop in Jerusalem, which in the end, however, remained Chalcedonian. J. introduced the feast of Christmas in Jerusalem on Dec. 25; he died in 458. Preserved are letters to Celestine, bishop of Rome (*ep. Cael.*) and to the presbyters and archimandrites of Palestine (*ep. presb.*), as well as a homily delivered in Ephesus (*hom. Eph.*). A homily on the presentation (*hom. Hyp.*) may also be his.

W: *ep. Cael.*, ACO 1, 1, 7, 124f. — *ep. presb.*, ACO 2, 5, 9. — *hom. Eph.*, E. Littmann, Chrestomathia Aethiopica (Hildesheim, 1988 = Leipzig, 1866), 100-102 [text]. — S. Grébaut, Traduction d'une homélie de J.: ROC 15 (1910) 440f. [French trans.]. — B. U. Wischer, Qêrellos 4 (Wiesbaden, 1979), 35f., 82-85 [Ethiopic text/German trans.]. — *hom. Hyp.*, PG 33:1188-1204.
L: R. Devreesse, Les anciens évêches de Palestine: FS Lagrange (Paris, 1940), 217-227. — E. Honigmann, J.: DOP 5 (1950) 209-279. — R. Laurentin, Bulletin sur la Vierge Marie: RSPhTh 52 (1968) 542. — L. Perrone, I vescovi palestinensi ai concili cristologici: AHC 10 (1978) 16-52.

G. Röwekamp

Juvencus

Gaius Vettius Aquilinus Juvencus (J.), a Chr. poet, came from a distinguished Span. family and was a presbyter in the time of Constantine (*evang.* 4.806ff.). Jerome attests to a lost work, in hexameters, on the sacraments.

Ca. 330 J. composed a bibl. epic, which in the mss. bears the title *Evangeliorum liber I-IIII* (*evang.*) (because of the extra verses, of questionable authenticity, the ms. tradition deserves special attention). Each book contains ca. eight hundred metrically correct hexameters in the style of Virgil. There is a preface to the entire work that is devoted espec. to the idea of literary fame and merit and, in a conscious comparison, calls attention to the gulf separating antiquity (Homer, Virgil) and Christianity. Poetry and literature are thus given a specifically Chr. motivation. The ensuing four poems are written as independent compositions, although J. essentially follows Mt in giving a poetic shape to the story of Jesus' life. He takes the infancy story (1.1-306) from both Lk and Mt. Three rather lengthy sections follow from the gospel of Jn.

J. read the gospels in an early Lat. translation but occasionally used the Gr. original and presumably also a commentary on the Bible or earlier theol. and exeget. traditions. The transitions between the books look less to content than to formal criteria; they look to the fact that there are four gospels and they are adorned with ecphrases of day and night. The handling of the NT text often seems cramped and literal (see Jerome, *vir. ill.* 84: *IV evangelia hexametris versibus paene ad verbum transferens*), while Sedulius, in his emulation of J., follows the NT text much less closely. But J. does also alter and change perspectives, establish emphases (e.g., direct speech is used only for main personages), interpret or explain within modest limits, characterize persons and their feelings from the perspective of author and reader and against a changed background, and "set the scene" for their coming and going. He occasionally creates scenes in an independent manner.

Scholars at the present time are beginning to bring to light, through detailed comparison with the bibl. passage in each case, the precise methods used in taking over each passage by means of *paraphrasis, breviatio,* and *amplificatio*. In this last, J. not only links bibl.-Chr. language, including its Gr. loanwords, with the traditional vocabulary of the Roman epic poets (espec. Virgil, Statius, Lucan, Ovid.; see espec. the epithets for the gods); he also makes conscious use of epic motifs (e.g., the calming of a storm at sea). This procedure had a missionary purpose. Pagan images are given a Chr. use, their content is deepened, they are cleansed of "disruptive" details, and thus are elevated entirely to the spiritual realm. As far as tendencies and leitmotifs in the content are concerned, scholars have studied, among other things, antisemitic tendencies in descriptions of the Jews.

J.'s work was meant to replace Virgil's; it had numerous imitators and readers (e.g., Prudentius, Proba, Paulinus of Nola, Orosius, and Venantius Fortunatus). Its importance in the history of literature is that it inaugurated a series of bibl. epics reaching down to Klopstock. It therefore found a rather early place in the canon of bibl. epics of late antiquity and was read and admired down to the end of the Middle Ages.

W: PL 19:9-346. — J. Huemer, CSEL 24. — K. Marold (Leipzig, 1886) [text]. — A. Knappitsch (Graz, 1910-1913) [text/German trans./comm.].
L: E. Borrell, J. Evangeliorum concordantiae secundum J. Huemer editionem (Barcelona, 1990). — eadem, J. index verborum et alia instrumenta lexica (Barcelona, 1990). — J. Cornu, Beiträge zur lat. Metrik: SBW 159/3 (1908) 1-81. — M. Flieger, Interpretationen zum Bibeldichter J. (literature) (Stuttgart, 1993). — P. Flury, Zur Dichtersprache des J.: FS

W. Ehlers (Munich, 1968), 38-47. — C. Gnilka, Interpretation frühchr. Lit.: Impulse für die lat. Lektüre, ed. H. Krefeld (Frankfurt a.M., 1979), 138-180. — N. Hansson, Textkritisches zu J. Mit vollständigem Index verborum (Lund, 1950). — J. T. Hatfield, A study of J. (Bonn, 1890). — R. Herzog, Bibelepik (Munich, 1975), 52-157. — HLL 5:331-336. — D. Kartschoke, Bibeldichtung (Munich, 1975). — H. H. Kievits, Ad I. evangeliorum librum primum commentarius exegeticus, Diss. (Groningen, 1940). — W. Kirsch, Die lat. Versepik des 4. Jh. (East Berlin, 1989). — P. G. van der Nat, Die Praefatio der Evangelienparaphrase des I.: Romanitas et Christianitas, ed. W. den Boer et al. (Amsterdam, 1973), 249-257. — H. Nestler, Studien über die Messiade des I. (Passau, 1910). — I. Opelt, Die Szenerie bei I.: VC 29 (1975) 191-207. — J.-M. Poinsotte, I. et Israël (Paris, 1979). — C. Ratkowitsch, Vergils Seesturm bei I. u. Sedulius: JAC 29 (1986) 40-58. — M. J. Roberts, Biblical Epic (Liverpool, 1985). — E. Vivona, De I. poetae amplificationibus (Palermo, 1913). — M. Wacht, Concordantia in J. Evangeliorum libros (Hildesheim, 1990). — H. Widmann, De Gaio Vettio I. carminis evangelici poeta et Vergili imitatore (Breslau, 1905). — J. de Wit, Ad I. evangeliorum librum secundum commentarius exegeticus, Diss. (Groningen, 1947).

M. Prünte

𝒦

Kontakion

The term *kontakion,* "little rod," is documented from the 9th c. on. It is the name given to the Byz. genre of a sung sermon in verse that originated in the late 5th c. The kontakion poets themselves had no set terminology but called their works, e.g., → Hymn, → Psalm, → Epic, poem, praise, song, or prayer (*hymnos, psalmos, epos, poiēma, ainos, ōdē, deēsis*). The name kontakion may have been given to these poems because at a time when other liturg. texts were collected in a codex, these poems were still being written separately on a scroll that was wound around a little rod (*kontos*). The collection of the separate hymns and their compilation in codexes, so-called kontakaria, began, at the earliest, in the second half of the 7th c. Kontakia were initially (5th-6th c.) sung in the church during the agrypnia or vigil for a layperson. Only later on were they used in the orthros or matins of monks. In illustration of the reading, the kontakion used all the themes that early Byz. → Homilies used in prose: e.g., the bibl. passages of the Christmas, Easter, and Pentecost cycles, bibl. figures, martyrs, and saints. The genre is singled out by its narrative, epic character. Kontakia are, among other things, given dramatic form through dialogue and have their effect espec. through vivid images, bold metaphors, and living portraits of the acting persons. Accentual meter came into Gr. poetry by way of the kontakion. Its verses are built up on the principles of isosyllables and homotony: what is decisive is no longer the length of the individual syllables but their equality in number and the sameness of the position of the main accents in the verse. Sermons in song form consist mostly of eighteen to twenty-four metrically identical strophes (*oikoi*), introduced by a prooemium (*koukoulion*) in a different meter. The initial letters of the strophes form an acrosticon. The last line of the prooemium introduces the refrain (*ephymion*) with which all the following strophes end. The musical accompaniment has not been preserved. At the beginning of the kontakion, a model stanza, the hirmos (*heirmos*), gives the melody and the complex metrical structure for the kukulion and the strophes.

Three kinds of hymn are distinguished: the *idiomelon* had its own, as yet unknown, meter. For a *proshomoion* the melody of another kontakion is used. In the *semi-idiomelon* only the prooemium has a new melody.

The origins of the kontakion were in the Syro-Palestinian world. Syr. genres gave essential impulses: the *memra,* a narrative sermon in verse; the *madrasa,* a homily using the acrosticon and refrain; the *sogita,* a sermon in dialogue form. The work in particular of → Ephraem the Syrian exerted an important influence. Of course, the Gr. homilies of the 3rd and 4th c. and contemporary preaching practice also provided important stimuli. The oldest surviving kontakion is the *Threnos Adam,* the work of an anonymous author of the late 5th or early 6th c. To this period belongs also the work of → Anastasius (poet), whose name alone we know, and this from the acrosticon of his song of lament. This kontakion, like the → Akathistos, is still used today in the liturgy of the Greek Orthodox Church. The genre reached its highpoint in → Romanus the Singer ca. the mid-6th c., who, under the influence of Syr. poetry, brought the kontakion in koine to its perfection. Romanus is the most famous of the early singers and the only one whose biography we know. About one hundred kontakia have come down under his name. His authorship of the Akathistos is questionable. Other composers of kontakia, contemporaries of Romanus, are known only by name: Cyriacus and perhaps Domitius. In the 7th c. lived singers Stephen, Gregory of Syracuse, Cosmas (not to be confused with Cosmas of Maiuma), and perhaps the anonymous poet who signed himself *Hamartolus* (sinner).

W: Contacarium Ashburnhamense, ed. C. Høeg (Copenhagen, 1956).
L: H.-I. Dalmais, Tropaire, K., Canon: FS W. Dürig (St. Ottilien, 1983), 421-434. — J. Grosdidier de Matons, Romanos (Paris, 1977), 3-156. — idem, Aux origines de l'hymnographie byzantine: FS W. Dürig (St. Ottilien, 1983), 435-463. — C. Hannick, Metrik des K.: FS H. Hunger (Vienna, 1984), 107-119. — P. Maas, Das K.: ByZ 19 (1910) 285-306. — K. Mitsakis, Ὑμνογραφία 1 (Thessalonica, 1971), 171-353 — W. L. Petersen, Diatessaron (Leuven/Louvain, 1985 (esp. 3-19). — L. van Rompay, R. Poète syrien: Early Christian Poetry, ed. J. den Boeft, A. Hilhorst (Leiden, 1993), 283-296. — E. Wellesz, Byzantine Music (Oxford, ²1961).

B. Breilmann

Koriun

K. is considered to have been a disciple of → Mesrob, the inventor of the Arm. alphabet. K. wrote a biography of his teacher a few years after the latter's death in 440. K.'s precise dates are not known. Together with other disciples of Mesrob and on the latter's behalf, K. visited Constantinople and translated Gr. eccles. writers into Armenian.

W: M. Abelean, Koriun. Leben des Maschtotz (New York, 1985 = Eriwan, 1941) [text]. — N. Akinean, Koriun. Lebensgeschichte des hl. Maschtotz (Vienna, 1950) [text]. — B. Norehad, Life of Mashtotz (New York, 1964) [English trans.]. — B. Welte, K. Lebensbeschreibung des hl. Mesrop (Tübingen, 1841) [German trans.]. — V. Inglisian, Leben des hl. Maschtotz (Düsseldorf, 1913) [German trans.]. — S. Weber, BKV² 57:181-233 [German trans.]. — G. Winkler, K.s Biographie des Mesrop (Rome, 1994) [German trans./comm.].

L: H. Adjarian, Les sources de la biographie (Paris, 1909). — C. E. Cox, Purpose of K.'s Life: FS L. G. Lewis (Abilene, 1981), 303-311. — A. S. Mat'evosean, K.s Geschichte des Mesrop (Venice, 1990). — H. J. Nersoyan, Why and When of Armenian Alphabet: JSAS 2 (1985/86) 51-71. — P. Peeters, L'origine de l'alphabet arménien: REArm 9 (1929) 203-237. — A. Terian, K. Life as an Ecomium: JSAS 3 (1987) 1-14.

P. Bruns

L

Lactantius

I. Life: L. Caecilius Firmianus Lactantius (L.) was born in Africa ca. 250; he died probably in 325. One of his teachers was Arnobius. Between 290 and 300, he was summoned to Nicomedia by Diocletian to teach Lat. rhetoric; at the court he made the acquaintance of Constantine, the later emperor, and experienced the beginning of Diocletian's persecution of Christians (303). At that time he gave up his teaching activity (whether voluntarily or not is uncertain) and began to devote himself as a writer to the new religion, which he had probably already come to know in Africa. L. spent the period of persecution near Nicomedia; after Galerius's Edict of Tolerance (311) and the so-called Edict of Milan (313) he returned to the city; ca. 314/315 Constantine brought him to Trier as teacher of Crispus. Some influence of L. on the policy and legislation of Constantine is conceivable.

II. Works: Writings of L. before 303 have not survived (a *Symposium* and a poem in hexameters on the journey to Nicomedia; see Jerome, *vir. ill.* 80). The surviving works all have a Chr. orientation and (except for the poem on the phoenix) are prose writings in various genres.

(1) *De opificio Dei* (*opif.*): composed in 303/304 and emulating Cicero, this is a cryptochristian (because of the persecution) treatise on the human being as a successful work of God that is obliged to venerate its creator.

(2) *Divinae institutiones* (*inst.*): published in a first version between 304 and 311, expanded beginning in 324 by speeches of the emperor and dualistic additions, and in this version published perhaps only after L.'s death. This is L.'s chief work: in keeping with situations that had changed since the 2nd c., L. seeks to present the Chr. faith with two purposes: an apologetic, which is to show the hostility and persecution of the Chr. religion to be unjustified, and a protreptic, which is to present Chr. doctrine as the sole way to salvation: rejection of polytheism, worship of the gods and philosophy, espec. Stoic, ethics (books 1-3), interpretation of Chr. revelation as wisdom guaranteed by the incarnate Son of God and as basis of true divine worship (book 4), defense of the Chr. way of life as effective justice (*pietas*) and true worship of God (books 5-6), and a description of Chr. ideas of the endtime and the other world that is

chiliastic in tendency (book 7). In taking into account the higher intellectual level of anti-Chr. apologetics, L. opens a new phase of Lat. apologetics by making the literary and philosophical standards of the opposition the starting point of his own explanations: literarily by a stylistic imitation of Cicero and by an impartial use of the non-Christian classics; philosophically by an effort to synthesize Platonic-Stoic teaching, gnosticism, and Chr. revelation. L. allows only the divine revelation in Christ to be the source of the knowledge of God and of the way of salvation proper to the true religion, since God is not accessible to the probings of the human mind. In an analogy with the Roman *pater familias*, L. sees God as *pater et dominus*: as caring "father" and punishing "master." L. the theologian (as Jerome already complains, *ep.* 58.10.2) was less up-to-date than L. the apologete: his use of the Bible is overlaid by his acceptance of nonbibl. and nonchr. ideas; he is antiquated espec. in christology; he has no doctrine of the Trinity; his eschatology is burdened by apocalyptic elements.

(3) *Epitome divinarum institutionum* (*epi.*): a summary of the principal work, whose apologetic purpose, basic conception, and themes are retained, not in a condensed summary but in a new abridged version with a somewhat altered arrangement, an often tighter argumentation, and at all points a Lat. translation of Gr. citations. Time of composition after 314, probably between the first and second editions of *inst.*

(4) *De ira Dei* (*ira*): a defense of the bibl. picture of an angry and, in his anger, justly punishing God, in response to the philosophical (Epicurean and Stoic) idea of an unmoved divinity who acts always with imperturbable love. The aim is to show fear of God as the origin of all religion.

(5) *De mortibus persecutorum* (*mort. pers.*): a politically inspired meditation on persecutions of Christians down to 313. Doubts about the authenticity of the work are not tenable; the time of composition can be narrowed down to the period from the end of 313 to the summer of 316. The topicality of the work is clear even from the arrangement: chs. 2-6 are allotted to Nero, Domitian, Decius, Valerian, and Aurelian; chs. 7-49 to the years, which L. himself experienced, from Diocletian to Maximinus Daia (7-16: Diocletian persecution; 17-23: abdication of Diocletian and rule of Galerius; 24-30: beginning of the reign of Constantine and the usurpation of Maxentius; 31-35: edict of toleration and death of Galerius; 36-40: persecutions under Maximinus; 41-42: death of Diocletian; 43-49: victory of Constantine over

Maxentius and fall of Maxentius). The guiding idea is that all the emperors who persecuted Christians were punished by God and died a dreadful death. At the center is the contrast between persecutors Diocletian, Galerius, and Maximinus, on the one hand, and Constantine and his father Constantius, on the other. A strong attack on Galerius, whom L. sees as Constantine's real enemy, serves the pro-Constantinian tendency. Despite all its partisanship *mort. pers.* is a very important historical source.

(6) *De ave Phoenice* (*Phoen.*), a poem of eighty-five distichs, written probably between 303 and 311, on the phoenix, a marvelous bird who appears first in Herodotus 2.37 and, in a Chr. interpretation, in *1 Clem.* 25f. The traditional story line is kept, but new motifs are added. In L.'s version, the bird flies to Syria every thousand years and burns to death in its nest on a tall palm tree; from the ashes emerges a worm, from this a butterfly who picks up the bones remaining from the old body, places them on the altar of the sun in Heliopolis of Egypt, and then returns to its homeland. The debated Chr. line taken by the poem is sure: it could be read by nonchr. readers as an artistic continuation of a traditional theme, but L. gives Chr. readers clear allusions to the symbolic meaning: the resurrection and everlasting life of the dead. In this way doubts of the authenticity of the poem are likewise shown to be groundless. The high literary rank of the poem was matched by the influence it soon began to exercise.

W: *opif.*, S. Brandt, CSEL 27/1:3-64. — M. Perrin, SC 213, 214. — A. Knappitsch, BKV² 36:221-284 [German trans.]. — *inst.*, S. Brandt, CSEL 19. — 1: P. Monat, SC 326. — 2: P. Monat, SC 327. — 4: P. Monat, SC 377. — 5: P. Monat, SC 204, 205 — M. F. McDonald (Washington, 1964) [English trans.]. — E. Sánchez Salor, 2 vols. (Madrid, 1990) [Spanish trans.]. — *epit.*, S. Brandt, CSEL 19:675-761. — E. Heck, A. Wlosok (Stuttgart, 1994) [text]. — M. Perrin, SC 335. — A. Hartl, BKV² 36:129-218 [German trans.]. — *ira*, S. Brandt, CSEL 27:67-132. — H. Kraft, A. Wlosok (Darmstadt, 1957); ²1971 [text/German trans./comm.]. — C. Ingremeau, SC 289. — A. Hartl, BKV² 36:67-126 [German trans.]. — *mort. pers.*, S. Brandt, G. Laubmann, CSEL 27/2:171-238. — J. Moreau, SC 39. — F. Corsaro (Catania, 1970) [text/Italian trans.]. — J. L. Creed (Oxford, 1984) [text/English trans./comm.]. — A. Hartl, BKV² 36:3-63 [German trans.]. — *Phoen.*, S. Brandt, CSEL 27/1:135-147. — M. Fitzpatrick (Philadelphia, 1933) [text/English trans./comm.].
L: M. v. Albrecht, Geschichte der röm. Lit. (Munich, ²1994), 1263-1276. — T. D. Barnes, L. and Constantine: JRS 63 (1973) 29-46. — A. Bender, Die natürliche Gottes-erkenntnis bei L. (Bern, 1983). — V. Buchheit, Cicero inspiratus — Vergilius propheta? Zur Wertung paganer Autoren bei L.: Hermes 118 (1990) 357-372. — A. S. Christensen, Lactantius the Historian (Copenhagen, 1980). — J. Fontaine, M. Perrin (ed.), Lactance et son temps (Paris, 1978). — E. Heck, Die dualistischen Zusätze und die

Kaiseranreden bei L. (Heidelberg, 1972). — idem, MH ΘΕOMAXEIN oder: Die Bestrafung des Gottesverächters (Frankfurt a.M., 1987). — idem, L. und die Klassiker: Ph. 132 (1988) 160-179. — HLL 5:375-404. — V. Loi, Lattanzio nella storia del linguaggio e del pensiero teologico pre-niceno (Zurich, 1970). — R. M. Ogilvie, The Library of Lactantius (Oxford, 1978). — E. Papisarda, Il carme De ave Phoenice di Lattanzio (Catania, 1946, ³1959). — M. Perrin, L'homme antique et chrétien. L'anthropologie de Lactance (Paris, 1981). — R. Pichon, Lactance (Paris, 1901). — S. Prete, Der geschichtliche Hintergrund zu den Werken des L.: Gym. 63 (1956) 365-382, 486-509. — P. A. Roots, The opif. The workmanship of God and Lactantius: CQ 37 (1987) 455-486. — G. Runchina, Polemica filosofica e dottrinale nel De ira Dei di Lattanzio: AFLB 6 (1987) 159-181. — J. Speigl, Zum Kirchenbegriff des L.: RQ 65 (1970) 15-28. — M. Walla, Der Vogel Phoenix in der antiken Literatur und der Dichtung des L. (Vienna, 1969). — A. Wlosok, Zur Gottesvorstellung bei L.: FS O. Regenbogen (Heidelberg, 1956), 129-147. — eadem, L. und die philosophische Gnosis (Heidelberg, 1960). — eadem, Die Anfänge chr. Poesie lat. Sprache: Laktanzens Gedicht über den Vogel Phoenix: Dialog Schule-Wissenschaft 16 (1982) 129-167. — eadem, Zur lat. Apologetik der constantinischen Zeit: Gym. 96 (1989) 133-148. — eadem, Wie der Phoenix singt: FS V. Pöschl (Frankfurt a.M., 1990), 209-222. — eadem, L.: TRE 20.370-374.

K. H. Schwarte

Languages

I. Greek

There was originally a range of local dialects in the Greek tongue. These made their appearance in literature only to a limited degree and were mainly the following: Ionic, Attic, Aeolic, and Doric. Ionic and Attic are closely related, and it was on the basis of an Ionicized Attic that a single language for writing and everyday life developed during the Hellen. and Roman periods: it was called "Koine." In the course of general language development Koine acquired some traits that distinguished it from Attic prose (change of sounds; disappearance of diphthongs; morphology; neologisms; vocabulary; increase in composite words; syntax: a greater degree of parataxis).

To begin with, Koine gradually replaced the various dialects. It became the language of the chancery under the Macedonian kings and then a worldwide language in the Roman empire. It became the common lingua franca in the eastern part of the empire and thus was very important for the spread of Christianity. The retreat of the Gr. language to its present-day area of use corresponds to the loss of territory by the Byz. empire.

In the western half of the empire the rule that higher posts in administration and in the military could be held only by Roman citizens meant auto-

367

matically that the educated classes spoke two languages. This tradition ended only when Caracalla in his *Constitutio Antoniniana* extended Roman citizenship to all inhabitants of the realm.

The composers of the NT bibl. writings wrote in the ordinary language of their day, Koine. Early Chr. literature belongs, linguistically and developmentally, to the spoken language of the people, which had its start during the Hellen. age. Within this framework there were great differences. The letter to the Hebrews, e.g., is closer to artistic Attic prose than are the other NT writings. Luke is closer to the ordinary language of the educated classes, i.e., he write an elevated Koine.

These varied findings apply also to patristic literature. Like the NT letters, the literary witnesses that make their appearance in the first half of the 2nd c. are community regulations, moral instructions, liturg. prayers. The linguistic and literary level of these texts is not very sophisticated and, in keeping with their purpose, are close to the language of everyday life. Occasionally, however, they display Latinisms which may have entered the language through oral contacts. More frequent are pronounced Semitisms. This is due to the fact that the writers were very familiar with the LXX, for the LXX, being translation Greek, contained many Semitisms reminiscent of the Hebrew original. The fact that the OT in the form of the LXX was part of the Chr. liturgy provided Chr. writers with many points of reference. Thus a variety of forms of expression can be cited. *1 Clem.* uses a variety of expressions from literary language; the letter to Diognetus reaches a high level of artistic prose. Clement Alex. is such a master of prose style that he can disregard the rules of a strict Atticism. Synesius of Cyrene endeavors to write a pure Attic Greek in his letters, while his hymns are composed in the Doric dialect.

It can be said, in general, that Chr. literature strove for a less strict Atticism. Because of their preaching, some writers show a greater closeness to the language of the ordinary people.

L: R. Browning, Von der Koine bis zu den Anfängen des modernen Griech.: Einleitung in die griech. Philologie, ed. H. G. Nesselrath (Stuttgart/Leipzig, 1997), 156-168. — A. Dihle, Die griech. u. lat. Literatur der Kaiserzeit (Munich, 1989). — J. Hammerstaedt, Geschichte der griech. Lit.: 4 Spätantike: Einleitung in die griech. Philologie, ed. H. G. Nesselrath (Stuttgart/Leipzig, 1997), 294-315. — G. W. H. Lampe, A Patristic Greek Lexicon (Oxford, 1961). — E. Mühlenberg/J. van Oort (ed.), Predigt in der Alten Kirche (Kampen, 1994). — E. Schwyzer, Griech. Grammatik 1 (Munich, ²1953), 45-137.

II. Latin

Because of its origin and missionary method the early church used Greek everywhere, even in Italy, for its liturgy and preaching. Thus the first theol. writers of the Lat. West (Justin, Irenaeus and Hippolytus of Rome) wrote in Greek. Only as the Gr. majority in the Roman community dwindled did people need Lat. translations of the Bible, as well as sermons, instructions, and theol. literature in Latin. Lat. translations of the Bible can certainly be assumed to have existed in Rome as early as the second half of the 2nd c., since the Lat. translation of *1 Clem.* cites a contemporary Lat. Bible. In Africa, around 200, Tertullian cites a Lat. Bible available to him. The earliest document of Lat. Christianity is the Acts of the Scillitan Martyrs, which report a trial that took place in Carthage on July 14, 180. Typically enough, the document is from North Africa, where the majority of the Latin-speaking people of the West lived.

For a long time it was disputed whether Tertullian or Minucius Felix was the first Lat. Chr. writer. Today, priority seems to have belonged to Tertullian. It was also he who, along with the *Vetus Latina* and the Vulgate, contributed most to the development of Chr. Latin, since he created ca. 1,000 new words. And yet Tertullian cannot be called the creator of Chr. Latin. No single person can be called the origin of Chr. Latin, for its creation was rather a process that went on within Late Latin. For missionary reasons, Chr. Latin depended very much on the ordinary speech of simple people. In addition, a great many words were borrowed from Greek in order to form theol. concepts, since Lat. terms were handicapped by their use in pagan religion and would have had to be filled with a new conceptual content if they were to be usable in Chr. theology. On the other hand, the new Chr. Latin was not an "early Christian specialized language" (J. Schrijnen, C. Mohrmann), but an independent branch of Late Latin. Early Chr. Latin thus arose in a conscious process of "dealing with the ancient culture" (C. Gnilka). Dependence on classical pagan literature, to which there was no alternative, led to *topoi* of "disapproving adaptation" (Jerome, *ep.* 22) but finally—after being both interrupted and promoted by Julian's education laws—to the development of Chr. Latin's own literary forms, e.g., the bibl. epic.

The process of adaptation and reorganization was not, however, completed in the first two centuries, since, because the cultural gradient ran from east to west and because of the overpowering presence of Gr. theology, there was a continual work of translation from Greek into Latin. The converse of this process is rarely to be observed.

Espec. in the area of conciliar discussion this process of translation and assimilation went on into the 8th c.

Acc. to Ambrosiaster, *quaest. vet.* 109.20f. (CSEL 50:268), it was ca. 380 that the Lat. church moved from Greek to Latin in worship and thus cut itself off from a common liturg. language.

L: Bibliography: G. Sanders, M. van Uytfanghe, Bibliographie signalétique du latin des chrétiens, CCLingua Patrum 1 (Tournai, 1989).
G. Bardy, La question des langues dans l'église ancienne (Paris, 1948). — A. Blaise, Manuel du latin chrétien (Strasburg, 1955). — idem, H. Chirat, Dictionaire latin-français des auteurs chrétiens (Tournai, ²1962). — E. Dekkers, Les traductions grecques des écrits patristiques latins: SE 5 (1953) 193-233 (Latin and Greek trans.). — L. J. Engels, H. Hofmann (ed.), Spätantike, Neues Handbuch der Literaturwissenschaft 4 (Wiesbaden, 1997). — E. A. Fisher, Greek translations of Latin literature in the fourth century A. D.: YCS 27 (1982) 173-215 (Latin and Greek trans.).
M. Fuhrmann (ed.), Christianisme et formes littéraires (Geneva, 1977). — C. Gnilka, Chresis. Die Methode der Kirchenväter im Umgang mit der antiken Kultur, 2 vols. (Basel, 1984/1993). — T. Klauser, Der Übergang der röm. Kirche von der griech. zur lat. Liturgiesprache: idem, Gesammelte Arbeiten (Münster, 1974), 184-194. — H. Marti, Übersetzer der Augustin-Zeit (Munich, 1974). — C. Mohrmann, Le latin des chrétiens, 4 vols. (Rome, 1958ff.). — P. E. Satterthwaite, The Latin Church Fathers: S. E. Porter, Handbook of Classical Rhetoric in the Hellenistic Period 330 B.C.–A.D. 400 (Leiden, 1997), 671-694. — J. Schrijnen, Charakteristik des altchr. Latein (Nijmegen, 1932). — B. Studer, Schola christiana (Paderborn, 1998).

W. GEERLINGS

III. Oriental

In close connection with Gr. literature, which was espec. rich, various national Chr. literatures developed within the Roman empire and even outside it. First of all, there was literature translated from Gr.: the scriptures, and also liturgical, canonical, and exegetico-homiletic works were translated into the languages of the various countries. But in addition, the Syrians, Copts, Ethiopians, Armenians, and Georgians soon developed their own literatures.

L: M. Albert, Christianismes orientaux (Paris, 1993). — J. Assfalg, P. Krüger, KWCO (Wiesbaden, 1975). — G. Bardy, La question des langues (Paris, 1948). — C. Brockelmann, Geschichte der chr. Lit. (Leipzig, 1972 = Leipzig, ²1909).

1. Ethiopian Literature

Ethiopian literature of the patristic age dates from the period of the Aksumite empire (4th-7th c.) and consists, in addition to a few inscriptions, primarily of translations from Greek. In addition to the scrip-

tures, these translations were chiefly of the apocrypha (*Shepherd of Hermas, Enoch*), which enjoyed canonical status in the Eth. church. In addition, there were translations of → Cyril Alex., with the result that at an early date the christology of the Ethiopians took a slight Monophysite tinge; also translated were the → *Physiologus* and some monastic writings (→ Pachomius, → Anthony). From its first written witnesses in the 4th c. down its golden age in the 16th c., Ethiopian literature was composed in Old Ethiopian, also known as Ge'ez. This language had been brought to Ethiopia in pre-Christian times by Semites migrating from southern Arabia. Old Ethiopian therefore is closely related to southern Arabic as far as sounds and many words are concerned. At about the beginning of the 11th c., Ge'ez gradually died out as an everyday language but has remained into modern times as the language of theology and scholarship.

Mss.: M. Chaîne, Catalogue 1-2 (Paris, 1912-1913). — A. Dillmann, Verzeichnis (Berlin, 1878). — idem, Catalogue (London, 1847). — E. Grébaut, Catalogue (Paris, 1938). — idem, E. Tisserant, Codices aethiopici (Rome, 1935-36). — E. Hammerschmidt, V. Six, Äth. Handschriften 1-2 (Wiesbaden, 1982-1989). — O. Löfgren, Katalog (Stockholm, 1974). — S. Strelcyn, Catalogue (Paris, 1954). — idem, Catalogue (London, 1978). — idem, Catalogue (Rome, 1976). — W. Wright, Catalogue (London, 1877). — H. Zotenberg, Catalogue (Paris, 1877).
L: R. Beylot, Langue et littératures éthiopiennes: Christianismes orientaux, ed. M. Albert (Paris, 1993), 219-260. — E. Cerulli, Letteratura etiopica (Florence, ³1968). — A. Dillmann, Lexicon Linguae Aethiopicae (New York, 1970 = Leipzig, 1865). — idem, J. Bachmann, Anthologia Aethiopica (Hildesheim, 1988 = Leipzig, 1866). — idem, Grammatik (Graz 1959 = Leipzig, ²1899). — J. Drewes, Inscriptions de l'Éthiopie antique (Leiden, 1962). — S. Grébaut, Supplément (Paris, 1952). — I. Guidi, Letteratura etiopica (Rome, 1932). — E. Littmann, Sabäische u. altabessinische Inschriften (Berlin, 1913). — idem, Äth. Inschriften (Berlin, 1950). — D. H. Müller, Epigraphische Denkmäler (Vienna, 1894). — F. Praetorius, Grammatik (New York, 1955 = Leipzig, 1886). — E. Ullendorff, The Ethiopians (London, ³1973).

2. Armenian Literature:

Armenian literature began immediately after the invention of the Arm. alphabet at the beginning of the 5th c. Until that point, the Armenians used Greek or Syriac as the language of literature and liturgy. The first half of the 5th c., the so-called golden age, saw the first translations from Syriac and Greek: the Bible, liturg. texts, and the most important works of the Syr. and Gr. fathers were translated into Armenian; some original creations also appeared. The second phase, or "silver age," which ran from the second half of the 5th c. to the first half of the 7th, was marked by assiduous translation from Greek, with the result that, espec. in the so-called Hel-lenophile School toward the end of the 6th c., Arm. was almost slavishly assimilated to Gr. The early patristic period was followed by a new flowering during Arm. independence in the kingdom of the Bagratides (885-1045) and during the period of the crusades in the kingdom of Little Armenia (1080-1375); classical Armenian, however, was replaced by the popular language of the time, known as "Middle Armenian."

Armenian literature begins with the translation of the Bible, which was based on both the Gr. original and Syr. translations. There was also the translation of a series of OT-Jewish and NT apocrypha. The relevant liturg. texts, such as anaphoras, were early translated from Greek. In addition, the Hellenophile School translated the most important Syr. and Gr. fathers (→ Aphraates, → Ephraem the Syrian, → Basil, → Gregory Nyss., → Gregory Naz., → Eusebius Caes., → John Chrys.), but also some philosophers (Aristotle, Plato, Porphyry). Original Armenian literature was begun by → Eznik of Kolb; homilies were composed by → John Mandakuni and → Mambre Verzanol. Hagiography began with the *Vitae* of → Mesrob and → Gregory the Illuminator. Historical writing was promoted by → Faustus (of Byzantium), → Lazarus of Pharp, → Elise Vardapet, and → Moses of Khorene.

Mss: J. Aßfalg, J. Molitor, Arm. Hss (Würzburg, 1962). — N. Bogharian, Grand Catalogue I-V (Jerusalem, 1966-1972). — O. Eganian, Erevan I-II (Erivan, 1965-1970). — B. Sargisean, Venedig. San Lazaro I-III (Venice, 1914-1966). — Y. Taschean, H. Oskian, Katalog I-II (Vienna, 1895-1963). — E. Tisserant, Codices Armeni (Rome, 1927). L: E. Finck, Geschichte der arm. L.: Geschichte, ed. C. Brockelmann (Leipzig, 1972), 75-130. — V. Inglisian, arm. L.: HO 1:7 (Leiden, 1963), 156-250. — C. Renoux, Langue et littératures arm.: Christianismes orientaux, ed. M. Albert (Paris, 1993), 107-166. — A. Sarkissian, Brief introduction (Bergenfeld, ²1974). — H. Thorossian, Histoire de la littérature arm. (Paris, 1951).

Armenian is a separate branch of the Indo-European languages. Its vocabulary includes many borrowed words, espec. from Persian; but many words for things sacred are borrowed from Syriac. The stock of sounds closely resembles that of the southern Caucasian languages. A native literature became possible only after the invention of the Arm. alphabet, which tradition ascribes to St. → Mesrob (Mastoc'). Arm. script is an original, independent creation that exactly fits the sounds of the language. The dialect of Ayrarat is regarded as having been the basis of the written language used in the 5th c. for monastic and eccles. inscriptions and for the literature then beginning. As early as the second half of the 5th c., the first elements of the popular language made their way in; this language was to develop further into Middle Armenian (in the silver age). It is chiefly the early works (till the mid-7th c.) that are important for the patristic period.

L: D. van Damme, Short Classical Armenian Grammar (Göttingen, 1974). — D. Froundjian, Arm.-Dt. Wörterbuch (Hildesheim, 1987). — H. Hübschmann, Arm. Grammatik (Hildesheim, 1962 = Leipzig, 1987). — H. Jensen, Altarm. Grammatik (Heidelberg, 1959). — idem, Altarm. Chrestomathie (Heidelberg, 1964). — A. Meillet, Altarm. Elementarbuch (Heidelberg, 1913). — idem, Grammaire comparée (Hildesheim, 1971 = Vienna, ²1936). — M. Minassian, Grammaire descriptive (Geneva, 1996). — I. Miskgian, Manuale Lexicon Arm.-Latinum (Leuven/Louvain, 1966 = Rome, 1887). — R. Schmitt, Grammatik (Innsbruck, 1981). — G. R. Solta, Stellung der arm. Sprache (Vienna, 1960). — R. W. Thomson, Introduction (Delmar, ²1989).

3. Georgian Literature

Georg. Chr. literature began during the 5th c. after the invention of its script, which acc.to Arm. tradition goes back to St. → Mesrob. Until the 7th c. this literature was very much under Arm. and Syr. influence. During the Neo-Chalcedonian controversies the Georgians sided with the Diphysites and in opposition to the Syrians and Armenians. With the expansion of monasticism in the 7th c. a national Georgian literature gained strength, although later it came more under Gr. influence. From the beginning, translations played a dominant role in Georg. literature. In addition to the translation of the Bible, there were translations espec. of the apocrypha, liturg. texts, commentaries on the Bible, and relevant patristic writings; translations of the latter were very numerous by the 11th c. and included, to some extent, authors very rarely or poorly translated into other languages. Independent creations in Georg. literature were primarily in the field of hagiography, espec. martyria.

Mss: J. Assfalg, Georg. Handschriften (Wiesbaden, 1963). — G. Garitte, Catalogue du Sinaï (Leuven/Louvain, 1956). — E. Metreveli, Description des manuscripts (Tiflis, 1987). — E. Nikoladze, Description des manuscrits I-II (Tiflis, 1953-1964). L: G. Deeters, Georg. Literatur: HO 1:7 (Leiden, 1963), 129-156. — D. M. Lang, Landmarks in Georgian Literature (London, 1966). — B. Outtier, Langue et littérature georg.: Christianismes orientaux, ed. M. Albert (Paris, 1993), 261-296. — M. Tarchnischvili, J. Assfalg, Geschichte der kirchl. georg. Literatur (Rome, 1955).

From the 5th c. on, Old Georgian became the language of literature, inasmuch as after the invention of the Georg. script it was used most in inscriptions, leading to the loss of the older, preclassical language. The classical Old Georgian language was used down to about the 13th c., before being replaced by the Neo-Georgian still spoken today.

L: H. Fähnrich, Grammatik der altgeorg. Sprache (Hamburg, 1994). — J. Molitor, Altgeorg. Glossar (Rome, 1952). — idem, Glossarium Ibericum in epp. S. Pauli (Leuven/Louvain, 1976). — idem, Glossarium Ibericum in IV Evv. (Leuven/Louvain, 1962-1965). — idem, Glossarium Latinum-Ibericum-Graecum (Leuven/Louvain, 1967). — K. Tschenkeli, Einführung (Zurich, 1958). — idem, Georg.-dt. Wörterbuch (Zurich, 1965-1974). — F. Zorell, Grammatik (Rome, 1978 = 1930).

4. Coptic Literature:

Apart from the remnants of magical papyri, Coptic literature owed its development and blossoming chiefly to Chr. monasticism of Egyptian origin. At the beginning there were the hermits of Scete and the Nitrian wilderness who gathered around Abbot Anthony (d. 356). Their sayings (apophthegmata) were first handed down orally but then written down in Greek and afterwards translated back into Coptic. In any case, this use of two languages is one of the notable characteristics of Egyptian Christianity. All the important patriarchs, beginning with Athanasius the Great, who led the Egypt. church from 328 to 373, used Greek when they wanted to be heard outside Egypt, while the Copt. language was mainly used for the sake of the native population. The actual founders of Coptic literature are regarded as having been the monastic Patriarch → Pachomius (d. ca. 346) and archimandrite Shenoute of Atripe (d. ca. 466), who moulded the elevated written language by his sermons, catecheses, and letters.

Even greater than the influence of classical monasticism on nascent Coptic literature was that of the many translations from Greek. The translation of the Bible was, of course, the first step, but here the many dialectal variations cause scholars no small problems. In addition, many apocrypha found a place in the Copt. canon. Liturg. texts, lives of saints, legends of martyrs, and sermons of every kind were borrowed from Greek and enriched with Copt. material.

Also worth mentioning is Copt. magical literature, which came in part from Greek, as well as the extensive gnostic-Manichean library of Nag Hammadi, which was translated into Coptic at an early date.

After the invasion of Islam, Coptic continued to be the literary and eccles. language of Chr. Egypt, but beginning in the 8th c. it was increasingly replaced by Arabic, until after the millennium even Chr. theologians made almost exclusive use of the new language.

The *Triadon* in praise of monastic life, from 1322, seems to have been the last more important work of Coptic literature.

Mss: W. E. Crum, Catalog of John Rylands Library (Manchester, 1909). — idem, Catalog of British Museum (London, 1905). — W. Pleyte, P. A. A Boeser, Manuscripts coptes (Leiden, 1897). — A. Mingarelli, Aegyptiorum codicum reliquiae (Bologna, 1785). — H. Munier, Manuscripts Coptes (Cairo, 1916). — W. H. Worrell, Freer collection (New York, 1923). — idem, Michigan collection (Ann Arbor, Mich., 1942). — idem, Ägyptische Urkunden (Berlin, 1904/05). — G. Zoëga, Catalogus codicum Copticorum (Hildesheim, 1973 = Rome, 1810).
L: R. G. Coquin, Langue et littérature coptes: Christianismes orientaux, ed. M. Albert (Paris, 1993), 167-217. — M. Krause, Kopt. L., in: Lexikon der Ägyptologie 3:694-728. — J. Leipoldt, Geschichte der kopt. L.: Geschichte der chr. Literaturen des Orients, ed. C. Brockelmann et al. (Leipzig, 1979 = Leipzig, ²1909), 131-183. — T. Orlandi, Elementi di lingua e letteratura copta (Milan, 1970). — idem, La patrologia copta: Complementi interdisciplinari di Patrologia, ed. A. Quacquarelli (Rome, 1989), 457-502. — idem, Patristica copta e greca: VetChr 10 (1973) 327-341. — idem, Coptic Literature: Roots of Egyptian Christianity, ed. B. A. Pearson (Philadelphia, 1986), 51-81. — idem, Traduzioni dal greco: Graeco-coptica, ed. P. Nagel (Halle, 1984), 181-203. — C. H. Roberts, Manuscript, Early Christian Egypt (Oxford, 1979). — G. Steindorff, Anfänge: FS W. E. Crum (Boston, 1950), 189-214.

Coptic is the literary language of the Chr. Egyptians and represents the most recent form taken by the Egyptian language. It received its characteristic shape in the first Chr. centuries after the translation of the Bible into the popular Egyptian of that time. As a written language, Coptic replaced the previous literary language, demotic, once it developed its own script with the help of the current Gr. alphabet and the addition of six other signs from demotic; paleographically, this script follows closely the ductus of Gr. uncial script. As a result of the lasting dominance of Greek, espec. in the northern parts of the country, Coptic is very much permeated by words borrowed from Greek; nor is the syntax entirely free of Gr. influence, espec. in translations, whereas in original literary creations the Egypt. character is more dominant. Copt. has two main dialects: Sahidic or Saïdic (from Arab. sa'îd = highland) and Bohairic in Lower Egypt (from Arab. buhaira = land by the sea). Since the 5th c. Sahidic has been the literary and standard language of all Upper Egypt, after having replaced older dialects (Akmimic, Subakmimic, or Assiutic). It was in competition until the 8th c. with Faiyumic, a dialect of the Faiyum, a land of oases west of the Nile valley, which is used primarily in private records. Bohairic is the language of the northern Egyptians, probably the dialect of Alexandria and northwestern Lower Egypt, including the Nitrian wilderness. In the course of time, the monasteries of the Wâdi n-Natrûn brought this dialect to such a pitch that it became then the eccles. and standard language of Lower Egypt. Although Bohairic, along with the other dialects, was replaced by Arabic as the everyday language in the 11th c., it has remained to the present day the *lingua sacra* of the Copt. liturgy.

L: K. Abel, Kopt. Untersuchungen (Berlin, 1970 = Berlin, 1876). — J. Cerny, Coptic etymological dictionary (Cambridge, 1976). — W. E. Crum, Coptic dictionary (Oxford, 1990 = Oxford, 1939). — idem, R. Kasser, Complements au dictionnaire copte (Cairo, 1964). — W. Kosack, Lehrbuch des Kopt. (Graz, 1974). — T. O. Lambdin, Introduction to Sahidic Coptic (Macon, Ga., 1983). — H. J. Polotsky, Grundlagen des kopt. Satzbaus, 2 vols. (Atlanta, 1987-1990). — A. Shisha-Halevy, Coptic grammatical categories (Rome, 1986). — idem, Coptical grammatical chrestomathy (Leuven/Louvain, 1988). — G. Steindorff, Kopt. Grammatik (Hildesheim, 1979 = Berlin, 1930). — idem, Kurzer Abriß (Hildesheim, 1980 = Berlin, 1921). — idem, Lehrbuch (Amsterdam, 1981 = Chicago, 1951). — K. Stern, Kopt. Grammatik (Leipzig, 1971 = Leipzig, 1880). — W. C. Till, Kopt. Dialektgrammatik (Munich, 1961). — idem, Kopt. Grammatik (Leipzig, ⁶1986). — J. Vergote, Grammaire copte. 2 vols. (Leuven/Louvain, 1973-1983). — W. Westendorf, Kopt. Wörterbuch (Heidelberg, 1965-1977).

5: Syriac Literature

Syr. literature includes the body of writings which were composed in East Aramaic, the everyday language of Mesopotamia and its surroundings (Edessa dialect). With a few exceptions, only the works of Chr. authors have survived in that language. In addition to the Bible, which was translated into Syriac (→ Peshitta) at a very early date, and the translation of some apocrypha, an independent Chr. literature flowered as early as the 3rd c. but more fully in the 4th, that did not owe its existence to translations from Greek (→ Bardesanes, → Aphraates, → Ephraem). The Persian Acts of the Martyrs give valuable information on the history of the church. Important information on the early period comes from the → Chronicle of Edessa as well as from the → Chronicle of Arbela, though the authenticity of the latter is disputed. → John of Ephesus (d. ca. 586) is regarded as the earliest Syr. chronicler known to us; also of considerable hist. value are the chronicles of → Joshua the Stylite (6th c.), → Jacob of Edessa (d. 708), and → Dionysius of Tellmahre. Scholarly Syr. theology has taken the form chiefly of metrical hymns (→ Ephraem, → Cyrillonas, Balai, → Jacob of Sarug, → Isaac of Antioch). Except in the area of christology, no major dogmatic treatises were composed in the early period (→ Philoxenus of Mabbug,

→ Severus of Antioch, → Babai the Great). From the very beginning, the exeget. work of Syr. theologians was marked by an intense effort to gain a correct understanding of the Bible in light of the tradition. To this end, Aphraates and Ephraem followed the model of Jewish rabbinical exegesis; the latter commented extensively on the books of the OT (Gen, Ex) and NT (→ *Diatessaron*, letters of Paul) and thus introduced the commentary genre into Syr. literature. Syr. exegesis did not reach its golden age until the Middle Ages with Ishodad of Merw, Dionysius bar Salibi, and Barhebraeus, who systematized the teachings of their ancient predecessors. Secular scientific knowledge made its way into the commentaries on the hexaemeron of Jacob of Edessa and Moses bar Kepha, while other authors such as Anthony of Tagrit (d. 825) showed an interest in rhetoric. → Sergius of Ris'ayna (d. 536) acquired a knowledge of medicine by way of his numerous translations of Aristotle; from early times (Bardesanes) the Syrians had endeavored to translate, above all, the Gr. fathers and philosophers, with the result that they preserved numerous works of which the original is lost. Syr. translators also passed on ancient philosophy and secular science to Islam; one such was the well-known Nestorian physician and scholar Hunaim ibn Ishaq (9th c.).

Mss: J. S. Assemani, BOCV (Hildesheim, 1975 = Rome, 1719-1728). — J. Assfalg, Syr. Hss. (Wiesbaden, 1963). — F. Briquel-Chatonnet, Manuscrits syriaques (Paris, 1997). — M. Goshen-Gottstein (Ann Arbor, Mich., 1979). — A. van Lantschoot, Inventaire (Rome, 1965). — A. Mingana, Catalogue of Mingana Collection (Cambridge, 1933-1939). — E. Sachau, Handschriftenverzeichnisse (Berlin, 1899). — A. Smith-Lewis, Catalogue of Syriac Mss on Mt. Sinai (London, 1894). — W. Wright, Catalogue of Syriac Mss (Cambridge, 1901). — idem, Catalogue of Syriac Mss (London, 1870-1872). — H. Zotenberg, Catalogues (Paris, 1874).
L: M. Albert, Langue et littérature syriaques: Christianismes orienteaux, ed. M. Albert (Paris, 1993), 297-375. — A. Baumstark, Geschichte der syr. Literatur (Berlin, 1968 = Bonn, 1922). — J. B. Chabot, Littérature syriaque (Paris, 1934). — R. Duval, La littérature syriaque (Amsterdam, 1970 = Paris, ³1907). — I. Ortiz de Urbina, Patrologia Syriaca (Rome, ²1965). — W. Wright, Short History of Syriac Literature (Amsterdam, 1966 = London, 1894).

Syriac is closely related to Mandean and to the Aramaic of the Babylonian Talmud; it was in the form of the dialect of Edessa that it acquired its normative status as an eccles. language. As a result of the christological controversies of the 4th and 5th c., it split into East Syrian and West Syrian dialects, which are distinguished chiefly in articulation and shifts of accent.

L: C. Brockelmann, Syr. Grammatik (Leipzig, [8]1981). — idem, Lexicon Syriacum (Hildesheim, 1966 = Halle, 1928). — T. Nöldeke, Syr. Grammatik (Darmstadt = Leipzig, 1898). — R. Payne-Smith, Thesaurus Syriacus (Hildesheim, 1981 = Oxford, 1879-1901). — J. P. Margoliouth, Supplement to the Thesaurus (Hildesheim, 1981 = Oxford, 1927). — eadem, Syriac Dictionary (Oxford, 1985 = Oxford, 1903).

P. BRUNS

Laurentius Mellifluus

L. was given his nickname by Sigebert of Gembloux (d. 1112) (PL 160:572C) because of his eloquence. L. was bishop either of Novae (Lower Moesia; today Sistov, Bulgaria) or of Novara (Italy) and probably the 5th c. author of the treatises *De paenitentia* (also known as *De duobus temporibus*) (*paen.*) and *De eleemosyna* (*eleem.*). His work *De muliere Chananaea* (*Chan.*) is a free translation of the Gr. homily *eis tēn epilysin tēs Chananaias*, which is probably from → John Chrys. (PG 52:449-60). The theology of penance that L. develops espec. in *paen.* is noteworthy: his starting point is the two ages, one from Adam to Christ, the second embracing the entire following period; before their baptism all human beings still belong to the first age, in which every sin is forgiven by God (*remissio publica*), whereas those belonging to the second age, i.e., all the baptized, must themselves see to the forgiveness of their sins (*remissio privata*) through penance (*poenitudo*) ("In that age, the gift of God; in this, the labor of human beings; in that age, baptism; in this, penance" [89]), and this without the need of a priest, since through baptism human beings are given the capacity for self-knowledge and penance.

W: *paen.*, PL 66:89-105. — *eleem.*, PL 66:105-116. — *Chan.*, PL 66:116-124.
L: G. Morin, L'évêque Laurent de "Novae": RSPhTh 26 (1937) 307-317. — M. Perotti, Sanctus Laurentius, "Mellifluus," terzo vescovo di Novara: Novarien 1 (1967) 21-74. — M. Schanz, C. Hosius, G. Krüger, Geschichte der röm. Lit 4/2 (Munich, 1959 = Munich, [1]1920), 596. — A. Solignac, L.: DSp 9:402-404. — A. Wilmart, La traduction des 38 homélies de saint Jean Chrysostome: JThS 19 (1917/18) 305-327, esp. 318.

M. MEIER

Lazarus of Pharp

L. was from a distinguished family and from youth was a close friend of prince Vahan Mamikonian, who commanded the united troops of Armenia. By Vahan's commission L. composed a history of Arme-

nia that continued the work of → Faustus (of Byzantium) and covered the years 385-485. L. is the only source for this important period, during which Armenia had to assert itself in a long war of religion against the invading Persians until it achieved a certain independence under Vahan in 485. Because L. was so heavily influenced by the Arm. language of the people, he belongs among the writers of the "silver age" (450-572).

W: G. Ter-Mekerttschian, S. Malkhasian, L. Geschichte der Armenier (New York, 1985 = Tiflis, 1904) [text]. — G. Sargsean, Die Vision des hl. S. (Venice, 1932) [text]. — S. Ghesarian, Histoire d'Arménie: V. Langlois, Collections 2 (Paris, 1869), 253-368 [French trans.]. — R. W. Thomson, History of L. (Atlanta, 1991) [English trans.].
L: N. Akinean, Die Vision des hl. Sahak (Vienna, 1948). — idem, Vardan bei L. (Vienna, 1951). — idem, L.: HandAm 86 (1972) 1-22, 141-154, 257-272, 385-414; 87 (1973) 1-23, 129-154, 257-286. — C. Dowsett, Newly discovered fragments: Muséon 89 (1976) 97-122. — P. Esapalean, Agathangelus u. L.: HandAm 49 (1935) 571-596; 50 (1936) 22-40, 185-195, 338-349. — G. Garitte, La Vision de Sahak: Muséon 71 (1958) 255-278. — A. S. Margaryan, Konkordanz zu L. (Eriwan, 1972). — M. Minassian, Remarques sur L. et Elisée: REArm 4 (1967) 37-48. — P. Muradian, L.: BanMat 11 (1973) 7-32. — C. Sanspeur, Fragment de L.: REArm 10 (1973/74) 83-109. — idem, L'Armenie au temps de Peroz: REArm 11 (1975/76) 83-172. — idem, Tradition textuelle: REArm 12 (1977) 85-99. — idem, Fragment de Leningrad: HandAm 94 (1980) 13-22.

P. BRUNS

Leander of Seville

L. was born before 549 of a distinguished family in Cartagena (Sicily). He became head of the family after his father's death and devoted himself espec. to the education of his younger brother, Isidore, who was also his successor as bishop of Seville. In 580 he stayed in Constantinople where he became a friend of → Gregory the Great. At L.'s request Gregory composed his commentary on Job (*Moralia in Iob*) and dedicated it to him. L. was bishop of Seville from 579 to 601. With him presiding, the third Synod of Toledo (589) received the Arian Visigothic King Reccared into the Cath. Church. The address of L. on this occasion is preserved: *De triumpho ecclesiae ob conversionem Gothorum* (*hom.*). For his sister L. wrote a monastic rule (*reg.*) that has come down in several versions. His letters as well as two anti-Arian works are lost. We know of them from his brother Isidore's mention of them (*vir. ill.* 28). The *Liber orationum psalmographus* was also attributed to L.

W: *reg.*, PL 72:873-894. — PLS 4:1421-1449. — J. Campos, I. Roca, Santos Padres Españoles 2 (Madrid, 1971) [text].

— J. Velásquez Arena (Madrid, 1979) [Spanish trans./comm.]. — *hom.*, PL 72:893-898; 84:360-364. — J. Fontaine, La homilia de San L. ante el Concilio III de Toledo: Concilio III de Toledo, XIV Centenario (Toledo, 1991), 349-370. — *liber psalmographus*, J. Pinell (Barcelona/Madrid, 1972) [text].
L: D. Ramos-Lisson, Die Synoden der iberischen Halbinsel (Paderborn/Munich, 1981), 116f. — L. Navarra, L. (Rome, 1986). — K. Schäferdieck, Die Kirche im Reich der Westgoten (Berlin, 1967).

W. GEERLINGS

Lectionary

1. Typology: To be distinguished by their content: the bibl., patristic lectionary (known as the homiliary/sermoniary) and the hagiographical (passionary/legendary); these were to some extent combined in accord with the liturg. use of the lectionary in the Mass and in the liturgy of the hours (Office).
2: Lectionaries for Mass: The beginnings of the system of bibl. pericopes for Mass (two or three readings in most liturg. families) are attested for the 4th c. (e.g., the sermons of Cyril Jerus. and Augustine presuppose an organized set of readings) but may go further back. Subsequently, the organization of the gospel readings and that of the nongospel scripture readings developed independently in successive but coexisting stages down to the Middle Ages. Initially, marginal notes in bibl. codexes signaled the liturgical use of a given passage. Meanwhile, lists of pericopes were compiled (*capitula[re] lectionum/evangeliorum*) that gave the readings acc. to their liturgical succession and were often bound into Bibles (earliest example is from the 6th c.). The lectionary in the strict sense became a reality when the full texts of the readings were given in their liturg. order. The main types were the Comes/Epistolary (nongospel readings) and the Evangeli[st]ary (oldest fragment from the end of the 5th or beginning of the 6th c.); more rare were lectionaries of the OT texts. With the rise of the complete missal the bibl. lectionaries for Mass were gradually phased out in the early Middle Ages.

The reading of the Acts of the Martyrs at Mass is documented first for North Africa (possibly the 3rd c., certainly by the end of the 4th), but did not have a long life (except in the hagiog. reading of the Office). The same is true of the patristic reading, which occurred at Mass as the preacher's text (see Council of Vaison 529, can. 2; Caesarius of Arles).
3. Lectionaries for the Office: For the bibl. reading (in the form of *lectio continua*) at vigils a complete Bible was mostly used, supplemented by marginal notes or lists of pericopes (see *Ordo rom.* 14; 6th/7th

c.), while short readings were sometimes proclaimed from memory (*RegBen.* 9.12f.); from the 9th c. on they were collected in separate codexes or a Collectary.

The use of a patristic reading in the Office (see, e.g., at the beginning of the 5th c., the *Decr. Gelas.* 8-10 Dobschütz; *RegBen* 9.8) led to the widespread lectionary-types the homiliary and sermonary. But for the Office people sometimes turned directly to codexes containing patristic texts.

The hagiog. reading is met first in non-Roman liturgies (Gallic monastic rules of the 6th c.); in Rome, only in the 9th c. in the legendary and passionary. Some 10th c. mss. combine all the readings for the Office into a single Office lectionary. Like the lectionaries for Mass, lectionaries for the Office fell out of use with the rise of the complete missal.

L: S. Beissel, Entstehung der Perikopen des röm. Meßbuches (Freiburg i.Br., 1907 = Rome, 1967). — A. Chavasse, La liturgie de la ville de Rome du Vᵉ au VIIIᵉ s. (Rome, 1993). — K. Gamber, CLLA/CLLA. S. — T. Klauser, Das röm. Capitulare Evangeliorum (Münster, 1935). — G. Kunze, Die gottesdienstliche Schriftlesung (Göttingen, 1947). — A.-G. Martimort, Les lectures liturgiques et leurs livres (Tournai, 1992) (with classification and catalogue of the mss.; lit.). — E. Palazzo, Histoire des livres liturgiques. Le Moyen Âge (Paris, 1993). — E. Ranke, Das kirchliche Perikopensystem aus den ältesten Urkunden der röm. Liturgie (Berlin, 1847). — C. Vogel, Medieval Liturgy (Washington, 1986).

M. KLÖCKENER

Leo of Bourges

L. was bishop of Biturgia (Bourges) in the mid-5th c. After taking part in the Council of Angers (Oct. 4, 453) he joined Bishops Victurius (Le Mans/Cenomannis) and Eustochius (Tours/Turones) in composing a letter to Bishops Sarmatio, Cariato, and Desiderius and to all priests "who are within the third province," in which clerics were forbidden to appeal to a secular court.

W: PL 54:1239-1240 (among the letters of Leo I, *ep.*). — C. Munier, CCL 148:136.
L: L. Duchesne, Fastes épiscopaux 2:244-245. — E. Griffe, La Gaule chrétienne 2 (Paris, 1966), 142.

C. KASPER

Leo I the Great

I. Life: L. was born in Tuscany toward the end of the 4th c. but became an inhabitant of Rome at an early age; he soon drew the attention of the Roman clergy and received influential positions. He is probably to be identified with Leo the Roman acolyte whom Augustine mentions in 418 as bringing a written message to Carthage. By ca. 430 he already had the leading role of the archdeacon who induced John Cassian to engage in the literary struggle against Nestorius, who got the bishop of Rome to act energetically against the Pelagian Julian of Eclanum, and whose mediation was used by no less a personage than Cyril Alex. After the death of Sixtus, while L. was occupied with a diplomatic mission in Gaul, he was elected, *in absentia*, as the new pope. His ordination took place on Sept. 29, 440.

L. immediately tackled the duties of his new office by linking the Italian bishops more closely to Rome and giving them instructions on discipline. Two conflicts in particular marked his first years in office. He took personal charge of the persecution of the Manichees who had fled to Italy and Rome before the storms of the barbarian invasions. In summer 445 he succeeded at last in having Valentinian III reinstate the old laws against the Manichees. The struggle continued however, espec. in Spain where Priscillianism, which was regarded as a version of Manichaeism, flared up. Second, L. opposed the claims of Hilary of Arles to be primate of Gaul, but he did not allow a full break to occur. Here again, in the summer of 445 he secured an imperial rescript that confirmed his decision and declared the decrees of the bishop of Rome to be legally binding.

Toward the end of 448, archimandrite Eutyches, who had been condemned by a local Synod of Constantinople and who had previously complained to L. about recent Nestorian machinations, wrote to the Roman bishop to secure his rehabilitation. From that point on, the christological question raised by the Eutychian controversy became the dominant theme of L.'s pontificate. It must be regarded as a major event in eccles. politics and the history of dogma that L. himself took the initiative in this doctrinal question and set down the western two-nature teaching in a solemn doctrinal letter, the *Tomus* addressed to Flavian (*ep.* 28, June 449). When, after a shift in imperial church policy under the new ruling couple, Pulcheria and Marcian, the council met at Chalcedon in Oct. 451, L.'s *Tomus* was read, along with two doctrinal letters of Cyril, to applause and acclamation, and substantial passages of it found their way into the definition of faith, the Chalcedonian Creed that was drawn up by a committee. On the other hand, L. never accepted can. 28 of the council, which raised the status of Constantinople in eccles. politics and placed it on the same level as Rome.

At the same time, as the political instability of the western Roman empire increased dramatically, L. increasingly became the real possessor of civil authority. When the Huns invaded Italy in 452, L. and an imperial delegation met Attila at Mantua and persuaded him to withdraw. After the assassination of Valentinian III the Vandals landed at Ostia and again L. went out in person to meet them. He was unable to prevent the plundering of Rome, but he did at least avoid looting and killing. During this turbulent period from March 455 to June 457, L.'s correspondence ceased, but after the accession of eastern Emperor Leo in Feb. 457 L. became active again and defended Chalcedon in, among other things, a second dogm. letter to the emperor with an extensive appendix of patristic testimonies (*ep.* 165, Aug. 458). He also experienced the satisfaction of seeing the Monophysite patriarch of Alexandria banished, as he had demanded. L. died on Nov. 10, 461.

II. Works: The total number of letters (*ep.*) preserved in various collections runs to 173, of which thirty are letters addressed to L. Among his own letters is a series of decretals, but by far the greater number have to do with the christological controversies, for which they are a source of the highest value since they have usually been handed down with reliable dates. Not authentic are *ep.* 43 and, with very high probability, *ep.* 120; the skepticism of some scholars regarding twenty other letters has not been justified.

We also have from L. ninety-seven *tractatus* or sermons (*tract.*). From an *incipit* notice in some mss. it may be inferred that there were originally two collections made by L. himself. The earlier collection contained fifty-nine sermons from the years 440-445. Here the sermons were in their temporal sequence, corresponding to the church's calendar of feasts and beginning with L.'s address at his ordination. The second collection contained sermons from L.'s later time in office, along with some second versions. The origin of the nucleus of this collection can be pinpointed to 454, with some final expansions in 457/458. The organizing principle was the same as in the first collection. On the basis of this information it is possible to give an exact date for most of the *tract.* and to place them accurately in their historical context.

III. Importance: A classical style of brilliant conciseness and carefully formulated structure characterizes L., who regarded himself as bound by the entire tradition of the church (he never viewed the Chalcedonian Creed as a victory over the East), just as, having had a gripping experience of the grace of God, he made the heritage of Augustine his own. He did not simply reproduce Augustine's theology but, while in no way weakening it, applied it in a new perspective, inasmuch as (as his rejection of allegory shows) he brought spiritual transcendence down into the incarnational "hereness" of the Christ who is present in the liturgical-sacramental activity of the church. In addition, by fusing the late-ancient but christianized idea of Rome with his consciousness of the primacy of Peter's representative, he brought Roman centralism to a first complete stage in which it offered protection and support to the church in the remaining imperial provinces of the West amid the tempests of the age.

W: PL 54-56. — *ep.*, C. Silva-Tarouca, TD. T 9, 15, 20, 23 (Rome, 1932, 1934f., 1937). — ACO 2, 2, 1; 2, 3; 2, 4. — O. Guenther, CSEL 35:117-124. — W. Grundlach, MGH. Ep 3:15-22. — S. Wenzlowsky, Briefe der Päpste 4-5, BKV[1] [German trans.]. — E. Hunt, FaCh 34 (Washington, 1957, 1963) [English trans.]. — *tract.*, A. Chavasse, CCL 138, 138A. — J. Leclercq, R. Dolle, SC 22. — R. Dolle, SC 49, 74, 200. — T. Steeger, BKV[2] 54, 55 [German trans.]. — J. P. Freeland, A. J. Lonway, FaCh 93 (Washington, 1995) [English trans.].
L: H. Arens, Christologische Sprache (Freiburg i.Br., 1982). — C. Bartnik, L'interprétation de la crise de l'empire: RHE 63 (1968) 745-784. — W. Blümer, Rerum Eloquentia (Frankfurt a.M., 1991). — E. Caspar, Geschichte des Papsttums 1 (Tübingen, 1930). — F. J. Dölger, Inschrift im Baptisterium: AuC 2 (1930) 252-257. — R. Dolle, Les idées morales: MSR 15 (1958) 49-84. — Y.-M. Duval, Quelques emprunts à Saint Augustin: MSR 15 (1958) 85-94. — C. Folsom, Mysterium fidei and L.: EO 15 (1998) 289-302. — J. Gaidioz, Prosper et le Tome à Flavian: RevSR 23 (1949) 270-301. — J. Gaillard, Noël, memoria ou mystère?: MD 59 (1959) 37-59. — A. Grillmeier, Jesus der Christus 1 (Freiburg i.Br., 1979) (English, Christ in Christian Tradition, vol. 1 [London, [2]1975]). — A. de Halleux, La définition christologique à Chalcédoine: RTL 7 (1976), 3-23, 155-170. — P. Hervé de l'Incarnation, La grâce dans l'œuvre de L.: RThAM 22 (1955) 16-55, 193-212. — M. Herz, Sacrum Commercium (Munich, 1958). — D. R. Holeton, The sacramental language: EL 92 (1978) 115-165. — S. O. Horn, Petrou Kathedra (Paderborn, 1982). — G. Hudon, La perfection chrétienne (Paris, 1959). — idem, Les présupposés "sacramentels" de L.: EeT 10 (1972) 323-341. — idem, L.: DSp 9:597-611. — idem, L'église dans la pensée de L.: EeT 14 (1983) 305-336. — idem, Le concept d'"assumptio" dans l'ecclésiologie: StPatr 18/1 (1989) 155-162. — T. Jalland, The life and the times of L. (Leipzig, 1941). — N. W. James, L. and Prosper: JThS 44 (1993) 554-584. — J. P. Jossua, Le Salut (Paris, 1968). — H. M. Klinkenberg, Papsttum u. Reichskirche bei L.: ZSRG. K 38 (1952) 37-112. — C. Lepelley, L. et la cité romaine: RevSR 35 (1961) 130-150. — H. Lietzmann, L. I.: PRE 12/2:1962-1973). — L. J. McGovern, The Ecclesiology of L. (Rome, 1957/Münster, 1958). — P. McShane, La Romanitas et L. (Tournai, 1979). — H. Rahner, L., der Papst des Konzils: KonChal 1:323-339. — H.-J. Sieben, Die Konzilsidee der Alten Kirche (Paderborn, 1979). — M. B. de Soos, Le mystère liturgique (Paderborn, [2]1971). — P. Stockmeier, Beurteilung der kaiserlichen Religionspolitik (Munich, 1959). — idem, L.: GK 11, ed. M. Greschat (Stuttgart, 1985), 56-70. — idem,

Universalis Ecclesia. L. u. der Osten: FS G. Kretschmar (Stuttgart, 1987), 83-91. — B. Studer, "Consubstantialis Patri, Consubstantialis Matri": REAug 18 (1972) 87-115. — idem, Einflüsse der Exegese Augustins: FS M. Pellegrino (Turin, 1975), 915-930. — idem, L. u. der Primat des röm. Bischofs: FS H. Stirnimann (Freiburg i.Br., 1980), 617-630. — idem, Una persona in Christo. Ein augustinisches Thema bei L.: Aug. 25 (1985) 453-487. — idem, L.: TRE 20:737-741. — A. Tuilier, Le primat de Rome et la collégialité de l'épiscopat: NDid 15 (1965) 53-67. — W. Ullmann, Papal Primacy: JThS 11 (1960) 25-51. — R. Weijenborg, L. u. Nestorius: Aug. 16 (1976) 353-398. — D. Wyrwa, Drei Etappen: Rezeption der Formel von Chalkedon, ed. J. van Oort, J. Roldanus (Kampen, 1997).

D. WYRWA

Leo of Sens

L., bishop of Senonas (Sens), took part in the second and third Councils of Orleans (533; 538). In a letter to Childebert he objected to the establishment of a see of Melun. He is also identified with a Leo who, with Bishops Heraclius of Paris and Theodosius of Auxerre, came out in favor of a more severe punishment of a guilty cleric, Claudius. All that has survived is the negative answer of Remigius of Rheims.

W: PL 68:11. — W. Gundlach, CCL 117:489-491 = MGH. Ep 3:437-438.
L: J. Hubert, La liste épiscopale de Sens (Paris, 1946). — P. Viard, G.: BSS 7:1227-1228.

C. KASPER

Leontius of Arabissus

Nothing is known about the person of L., bishop of Arabissus. We know only of two homilies, one of which, on creation and the raising of Lazarus, is preserved in excerpts by Photius (*cod.* 272). The second sermon, on Lazarus Saturday, has not yet been published.

W: PG 104:224-230. — R. Henry, Photius, Bibliothèque 8 (Paris, 1977), 100-106 [text/French trans.].
L: H. G. Beck, Kirche und theol. Lit. (Munich, 1959), 506.

B. WINDAU

Leontius of Arles

L. was bishop of Arles (462-491?) and there (473) and in Lyons (475) presided over synods against the predestinationism of Lucidus. In 474 he and other bishops of southern Gaul negotiated a peace with the Visigothic King Euric. At his request, Ennodius of Pavia wrote the life of Antoninus of Lérins. L.'s letters to Hilarius of Rome are not preserved.

S: *Concilia Galliae*, C. Munier, CCL 148:159f.
L: J. Douerin, Fauste de Riez, Diss. (Paris, 1973). — K. Schäferdiek, Kirche in Reichen der Westgoten (Berlin, 1967).

C. KASPER

Leontius the Armenian

L., a priest and historian, is regarded as author of a *History of Muhammad, His Caliphs, and Their Conquest of Armenia*. Using eyewitness accounts, L.'s history describes events of ca. 770 and must probably have been written shortly after that. It is of particular hist. interest as the earliest Arm. source on the Arab. invasion.

W: G. Schahnarazian, History of the Armenians (Paris, 1857) [text]. — K. Ezean, L. History (St. Petersburg, 1887) [text]. — G. Schahnarazian, Histoire des guerres (Paris, 1856) [French trans.]. — Z. Arzoumanian, History of L. (Philadelphia, 1982) [English trans.].
L: N. Akinean, L.: HandAm 43 (1929) 330-348, 458-472, 593-619, 705-718. — L. Alisan, Ill. L.: Baz. 109 (1951) 235-243, 325-330; 110 (1952) 20-26, 78-86. — E. Filler, Quaestiones de Leontii Armenii Historia (Leipzig, 1903). — S. Gero, Byzantine Iconoclasm (Leuven/Louvain, 1973), 153-171. — A. Jeffrey, Correspondence between Umar II and Leo III: HThR 37 (1944) 269-332.

P. BRUNS

Leontius, Biographer (Roman Abbot)

Abbot L. of the Roman monastery of St. Sabas wrote a life of bishop and exegete → Gregory of Agrigentum (end of 6th or second half of 7th c.). Since some time seems to have passed between the death of the saint and the writing of the work (no accurate dates are given), the biography, which contains legendary embellishments and yet on the whole gives an impression of reliability, must be from the 8th c. It formed the basis of a second, unpublished life of Gregory by an Abbot Marcus of the same monastery.

W: PG 98:549-716.
L: H.-G. Beck, Kirche u. theol. Lit. (Munich, ²1977), 466. — G. Stramondo, Elementi storici e fantastici nella biografia di s. Gregorio d'Agrigento: SBNE 7 (1953) 207.

U. HAMM

Leontius of Byzantium

I. Life: For a long time there was no clarity about the person of L. Today, his identification with the Palestinian monk of whom Cyril of Scythopolis speaks in his *Vita Sabae* seems certain. L. is not to be identified with Leontius of Jerusalem or with the Leontius of the theopaschite controversy.

Born before 500, L. was one of the (Origenist) monks of Palestine who in 520 accompanied the ousted Nonnus on his return to the New Laura. In 530 he traveled to Constantinople with the elderly Sabas, who was representing the monks. Acc. to his own testimony, in his youth he belonged to a group of "sham Chalcedonians" who followed Theodore Mops. and Diodorus of Tarsus, but by a "grace from above" he was converted to a new outlook. From 531 on, he was leader of an Origenist-Chalcedonian party in the capital, debated with the Monophysites, and in 532 took part in a dialogue between the opponents (Severians) and defenders of Chalcedon, while in 536 he attended the synod against Patriarch Anthimus. In 537 he returned to Palestine but later, probably after the condemnation of the Origenists in 543, went back to Constantinople, where he died that same year.

II. Works: The *Contra Nestorianos et Eutychianos* (*Nest. et Eut.*) has three parts. The first defends Chalcedon against the extremes of Nestorianism and Monophysitism, with the real opponents being the Severians. Here L. uses the anthropological model of soul and body for christology in order to show that in the hypostatic union the properties of the several natures are preserved. He opposes the *mia physis* formula because in his view only the Diphysite interpretation of the *henōsis kata hypostatēn* ensures the possibility of the Chalcedonian *communicatio idiomatum*. The second part of the work is a dialogue against the aphthartodocetists; the third seeks to prove Theodore Mops. to be the father of Nestorianism.

The so-called *Epilysis* (*Epil.*) is an answer to criticism of the first part of *Nest. et Eut.* The thirty chapters against Severus (*Epap.*) is a collection of aporias.

The work *Adversus fraudes Apollinistarum* (*Apoll.*), which contains many Apollinarist texts, is probably an authentic work of L. In a meditation based on the Bible and the economy of salvation L. here develops a picture of Christ in light of the basic principles of Chalcedon.

In his writings L. uses Aristotelean logic (substance and accidents and, among the latter, quality and relation). In the past L. was regarded as founder of Neo-Chalcedonianism and a systematic thinker who introduced a new phase of speculation with his concept of "enhypostasis." This view cannot be maintained in this form. Rather, L. fails to grasp the problem in the Monophysite distinction between essence and nature. Nevertheless he was the first one,

377

after 527, to accept the challenge which Severian-Julianist christology posed for the teaching of Chalcedon. L.'s theol. achievement consisted in his extensive appeal to the body-soul analogy, in which the dissimilarity between the Logos and the spiritual soul was espec. emphasized while at the same time the traditional two-nature teaching of Chalcedon was maintained. The debate with the Severians compelled L. to reflect espec. on such properties of the humanity of Christ as imperishability and participation in the omniscience of the Logos and on the concrete relationship between createdness and uncreatedness.

W: PG 86:1273-1385, 1901-1945. — B. E. Daley, CCG in preparation.
L: B. Altaner, Der griech. Mönch L. u. L. der skythische Mönch: ThQ 127 (1947) 147-165. — B. E. Daley, The Origenism of L.: JThS 27 (1976) 333-369. — D. B. Evans, L.: TRE 21:5-10. — idem, L. (Washington, 1970). — A. Grillmeier, Jesus der Christus 2/2 (Freiburg i.Br., 1989), 190-241 (English, Christ in Christian Tradition, vol. 2/2 [London, 1995]). — idem, Die anthropologisch-christologische Sprache des L. u. ihre Beziehung zu den Symmikta Zetemata des Neuplatonikers Porphyrius: FS H. Hörner (Heidelberg, 1990), 61-72. — F. Loofs, L. u. die gleichnamigen Schriftsteller der griech. Kirche (Leipzig, 1887). — N. J. Montafakis, Christology and its philosophical complexities: History of Philosophy Quarterly 10 (1993) 99-119. — S. Otto, Person u. Subsistenz (Munich, 1968). — L. Perrone, La chiesa di Palestina (Brescia, 1980). — idem, Il "Dialogo contro gli aftartodeceti" di L.: CrSt 1 (1980) 411-443. — S. Rees, The Literary Activity of L: JThS 19 (1968) 229-242. — H. Stickelberger, Substanz u. Akzidens bei L.: ThZ 36 (1980) 153-161. — D. Stiernon, L.: DSp 9:651-660. — A. Tuilier, Remarques sur les fraudes des Apollinaristes: Texte u. Textkritik, ed. J. Dummer (Berlin, 1987), 581-590. — J. H. I. Watt, The Authenticity of the Writings Ascribed to L.: StPatr 7 (1966) 321-336.

G. RÖWEKAMP

Leontius of Constantinople

L., a presbyter and homilist, was active in Constantinople, probably ca. the mid-6th c. (in the time of Patriarch Eutychius). Contrary to what was earlier assumed by some, he is not identical with Leontius of Byzantium or Leontius of Jerusalem.

To be attributed to him with certainty are eleven homilies (one on John the Baptist, two on Palm Sunday, three on Job, one on Good Friday, two on Easter, one on the middle of the Pentecost season, and one on Pentecost). There is disagreement on the extent to which other homilies (espec. those of Ps.-Chrysostom) are to attributed to him. Very probably he was author of a sermon on the birth of Christ, one on Pentecost, and one on the transfiguration. (In the

ms. tradition there are also overlappings with presbyter → Leontius of Jerusalem.)

The sermons are to some extent influenced by predecessors (among others, Proclus of Constantinople and Ps.-Asterius the Sophist), but L. was not simply a compiler.

W: C. Datema, P. Allen, CCG 17. — M. Aubineau, SC 187 [text/French trans. of both Easter homilies].
L: C. Datema, P. Allen, L. — a compiler?: JÖB 29 (1980) 18-20. — eadem, L., author of ps. Chrysostom, In Ps. 92, CPG 4548?: VigChr 40 (1986) 169-182. — C. Datema, When did L. preach?: VigChr 35 (1981) 346-351. — J. Noiret, Thesaurus (Turnhout, 1992). — M. Sachot, Les homélies de L.: RSR 51 (1977) 234-245. — idem, L'homélie ps.-chrysostomienne sur la transfiguration CPG 4724 (Frankfurt a.M., 1981). — D. Stiernon, L.: DSp 9:660-662.

G. RÖWEKAMP

Leontius of Jerusalem

L., one of the educated monks who in the course of their ascetical-theol. formation also acquired secular philosophical knowledge and played a part in the christological controversies of the 6th c., is not to be identified with → Leontius of Byzantium, as is still occasionally maintained. This L., who probably came from Palestine, composed his works between 536/538 (the exile and death of Severus of Antioch) and 544 (start of the Three-Chapters controversy), probably in Constantinople.

The work Contra Monophysitas (monoph.) consists of sixty-three capita or aporias and a collection of testimonies, all set within the framework of questions and answers (erotapokriseis). Both parts were probably originally appendixes of a lost work against the Severians. L.'s Adversus Nestorianos (Nest.) originally had eight books. They are espec. valuable because long passages of original Nestorian texts are cited. Unfortunately book 8 is lost, in which L. criticized what he regarded as defective terminology for the unity of Christ.

L.'s theol. merit is found in his reflective distinction between union of natures and union of hypostases, by means of which he removed the obscurities in both the 4th c. Apollinarist synthesis of natures and the Severian doctrine of one nature. Against the Nestorians L. emphasizes the point that in the incarnation the Logos did not acquire an additional hypostasis but only a human nature which he united hypostatically with the divine nature. L.'s language is marked by a high degree of conceptual precision that led to numerous neologisms (synhypostanai, enhypostanai) for appropriately describing the subsistence-in and the subsistence-with of divinity and humanity in Christ.

W: PG 86:1769-1900. — P. T. R. Gray, CCG in preparation. L: L. Abramowski, Ein nestorianischer Traktat bei L.: 3. Symposium Syriacum 1980, OCA 221 (Rome, 1983), 43-55. — A. Basdekis, Die Christologie des L., Diss. (Münster, 1974). — P. T. R. Gray, The Defence of Chalcedon in the East (Leiden, 1979). — idem, An Anonymous Severian Monophysite of the Mid-Sixth Century: PBR 1 (1982) 117-126. — idem, L.'s Case for a "Synthetic" Union in Christ: StPatr 18/1 (1985) 151-154. — A. Grillmeier, Jesus der Christus 2/2 (Freiburg i.Br., 1989), 286-328 (English, Christ in Christian Tradition, vol. 2/2 [London, 1995]). — S. Helmer, Der Neuchalkedonismus (Bonn, 1962). — C. Moeller, Textes "monophysites" de L.: EThL 27 (1951) 467-482. — S. Rees, The Literary Activity of L. of Byzantium: JThS 19 (1968) 229-242. — M. Richard, L. de Jérusalem et L. de Byzance: MSR 1 (1944) 35-88. — J. H. I. Watt, The Authenticity of the Writings Ascribed to L. of Byzantium: StPatr 7 (1966) 321-336. — K. P. Wesche, The Christology: SVTQ 31 (1987) 65-95.

G. RÖWEKAMP

Leontius of Jerusalem, Presbyter

Under the name of a presbyter L. of Jerusalem some sermons have come down that in some cases are also attributed to Chrysostom. This L. is possibly the same as a monk in the Jerusalem monastery "of the Byzantines," who is mentioned in a ms. of a sermon on the middle of the Pentecost season (by → Leontius of Constantinople) and who was identified with the latter because of his origin.

L. was certainly the author of a sermon for the fourth Sunday of Lent on the Samaritan woman (hom. in Joh. 4) who changed "from prostitute to apostle," and a sermon for the fourth or fifth Sunday of Lent on the story of the merciful Samaritan (hom. in Lc. 10:25-37), which is applied allegorically to Christ and fallen Adam. Possibly L.'s are a sermon on Palm Sunday (PG 61:715-20) and one on Pentecost.

W: hom. in Joh 4, PG 59:535-542. — hom. in Lc 10:25-37, PG 62:755-758. L: A. Erhard, Überlieferung u. Bestand der hagiographischen u. homiletischen Lit. der griech. Kirche (Leipzig, 1937-1953). — D. Stiernon, L.: DSp 9:662f.

G. RÖWEKAMP

Leontius of Neapolis

L. (b. ca. 590, d. ca. 650), was bishop of Neapolis/Naplus on Cyprus; the sources are silent on other aspects of his life. Between 641 and 648 he composed the Life (→ Vita) of → John the Almsgiver (v. Jo. Eleem.), in which he uses the lives of John by → John

Moschus and → Sophronius; a life of Simeon of Emesa (v. Sym.) in which he presents this monk as a fool (salos) for Christ; a life of Spyridon, the Cyprian national saint (v. Spyr.), which is still preserved in the revision by Simeon Metaphrastes. Also preserved are two sermons—the Sermo in Symeonem (Lk 2:22-35) (serm. in Sym.) and the Sermon in mediam Pentecosten (serm. in med. Pent.)—and five fragments of works against the Jews (c. Iud.) which, among other things, refute Jewish objections to the Chr. veneration of images.

W: v. Jo. Eleem., H. Gelzer (Freiburg i.Br., 1893), 1-103 [rec. brevior; rec. media; text]. — A. J. Festugière, L. Rydén (Paris, 1974), 343-437 [rec. longior, text/comm.]. — v. Sym., A.-J. Festugière, L. Rydén (Paris, 1974), 55-104 [text/comm.]. — II. Lietzmann (Jena, 1911), 63-81 [partial German trans.]. — v. Spyr., P. van den Ven (Leuven/Louvain, 1953), 104-128 [text]. — serm. in Sym., PG 93:1565-1581. — serm. in med. Pent., PG 93:1581-1597. — c. Iud., PG 93:1597-1609; 130:295f. — B. Kotter, Iohannes v. Damaskus (Berlin, 1975), 156-159, 178-181. L: N. H. Baynes, Icons: HThS 44 (1951) 93-106. — V. Déroche, Contre les Juifs: BCH 110 (1986) 655-669. — idem, Léontios de Néapolis (Uppsala, 1995). — H. Gelzer, Volksschriftsteller: HZ 61 (1889) 1-38. — idem, Leben des hl. Joannes (Freiburg i.Br., 1893). — N. Gendle, Defender of holy images: StPatr 18 (1985) 135-139. — L. Rydén, Bemerkungen (Uppsala, 1970).

M. SKEB, OSB

Leontius Scholasticus

A Leontius (L.) is author of the work De sectis (sect.), which was written between 581 and 607, probably in Constantinople. This L. is not the same as → L. of Byzantium, to whom this work was long attributed, nor is the Abbot Theodore named in the title and on the basis of whose lectures L. writes identical with Theodore of Raithu. The work itself, of which a Georg. version exists, deals with the concepts of ousia, physis, hypostasis, and prosōpon, and with the history of salvation; it also describes and refutes various heresies. The emphasis is on the defense of Chalcedon, and the work is marked by a sense of hist. developments. Its "old Chalcedonian" character is seen in its sympathy for Theodore Mops., its emphasis on the two-natures formula, and its rejection of the body-soul analogy as found in L. of Byzantium.

W: PG 86:1193-1268. L: M. v. Esbroeck, La date et l'auteur du sect.: FS A. Van Roey (Leuven/Louvain, 1985), 415-424. — A. Grillmeier, Jesus der Christus 2/2 (Freiburg i.Br., 1989), 514-523 (English, Christ in Christian Tradition, vol. 2/2 [London, 1995]). — S. Rees, The sect.: JThS 40 (1939) 346-360. — M. Richard, Le traité sect.: RHE 35 (1939) 695-723. — idem, ΑΠΟ ΦΩΝΗΣ: Byz. 20 (1950) 191-222. — J. Speigl, Der

Autor der Schrift sect.: AHC 2 (1970) 207-230. — M. Waegemann, The Text Tradition of sect.: AnCl 45 (1976) 190-196. — idem, The OT Canon: AnCl 50 (1981) 813-818.

G. RÖWEKAMP

Leporius

In order not to say anything unworthy about God, this Gallic monk, in a (lost) letter of ca. 415, rejected the communication of idioms and denied that God himself was born of Mary and suffered on the cross. Rather, he said, "a complete human being was born with God." Episcopal censures of this theory, which John Cassian, *c. Nest.*, later interpreted on grounds of Pelagianism as a form of pre-Nestorianism, drove L. to North Africa, where Augustine persuaded him to a more proper christology. In a *Libellus emendationis*, composed probably by L. in the middle of 418, L. acknowledges both "substances," flesh and Word, in one and the same person who is inseparably God and man, without such a "mingling" producing a change or diminution of God. Thus what was God's passes over to the man, and conversely; the Word *personally*, and not *naturally* together with the Father and the Spirit, became flesh. The *Lib.*, which left traces in the christology of the 5th c. (espec. → Leo I), was signed by, among others, L. and African bishops and was sent by the latter as a covering letter to the Gallic bishops, in which L.'s turn to orthodox belief was confirmed and his reacceptance urged (Aug., *ep.* 219). Ca. 430 L. was living in Africa (John Cassian, *c. Nest.* 1.4). Perhaps he was the Leporius who was responsible for a number of buildings in Hippo Regius ca. 425/426 (Aug., *ep.* 213.1; *serm.* 356.10).

W: *Lib.*, R. Demeulenaere, CCL 64:95-123. — Ergänzung: F. Gori: Aug. 34 (1994) 201-206.
L: E. Amann, L.: DThC 9:434-440. — F. de Beer, Une tessère d'orthodoxie: REAug 10 (1964) 145-185. — A. Chavasse, L. et le livre X du "De Trinitate": RBen 74 (1964) 316-318. — F. Gori, "De Trinitate" X pseudoatanasiano nel Lib.: Aug. 31 (1991) 361-386. — A. Grillmeier, Jesus der Christus 1 (Freiburg i.Br., 1979), 661-665 (English, Christ in Christian Tradition, vol. 1 [London, ²1975]). — J.-L. Maier, La date de la rétractation de L.: REAug 11 (1965) 39-42. — B. Morel, Invloed van L. op Cassianus: Bijdr. 21 (1960) 31-52. — PAC 634f. — A. Trapè, Nestorianismo prenestoriano: CDios 155 (1943) 45-67.

R. KANY

Leucius (Carinus)

There was a tradition in Asia Minor of the 2nd/3rd c. about L., a disciple of John. Epiphanius (*haer.* 51.6.7-9) names him, along with John, as an opponent of Cerinthus. A L. is also named as author of the

Manichean collection *Journeys*, of five apocryphal Acts of Apostles (Peter, John, Andrew, Thomas, Paul), which were probably composed in the last third of the 3rd c. Witnesses to it are Faustus of Milevis (Aug., *c. Faust.* 30.4), Filastrius of Brescia (*de haer.* 88.6), and also Photius (*cod.* 114), acc. to whom L. was named, in addition, Charinos. L. the author may have originally been connected with the *Acts of John* (→ John, Literature about) (thus Innocent I, *ep.* 6.7; Turibius of Astorga, *ep. ad Idac. et Cepon.* 5; Melito of Laodicea, *Passio Johannis*). The identification of the disciple of John with L. the author occurs first in Ps.-Melito (*De transitu Mariae*, prol.) in the 5th/6th c. The Acts of → Pilate gives the names Leucius and Carinus to the sons of Simon who were delivered from Hades.

L: NTApo⁵ 2:81-93 (literature).

G. RÖWEKAMP

Libellus fidei

The *Libellus fidei* was directed against measures taken following upon the *Epistula tractoria* of Pope Zosimus in 418 and the corresponding condemnation of Pelagius and Caelestius by Emperor Honorius. The author suggested by some was Julian of Eclanum and a group of bishops around him who directed their protest to Zosimus himself. The initial occurring in the opening address of *Libellus* is interpreted as a Z. On the other hand, some bishops of the eccles. province of Venetia, perhaps with support from Dalmatia and western Illyria, are regarded as the authors, who addressed their work to their metropolitan, Augustine of Aquileia (408-434). In this second hypothesis the initial is interpreted as an A.

W: PL 48:506-526 [text/comm.].
L: G. Cuscito, Cristianesimo (Trieste, 1977), 193f. — O. Wermelinger, Rom u. Pelagius (Stuttgart, 1975), 220-226.

B. DÜMLER

Liber diurnus

The *Liber diurnus* or *Liber diurnus Romanorum pontificum* was a collection of formularies used in the papal chancery from ca. the 6th/7th c. to the 10th/11th c. for legal acts, e.g., the production of papal charters. In this connection the question is debated whether the three mss. transmitted under the title *Liber diurnus* (these are copies) were really used as working mss. in the papal chancery. Some are of the opinion that the mss. did indeed come from the sphere of the Roman curia but that neither they nor their exemplars were really a *Liber diurnus*; they served perhaps as school books and collections of canonical sources. But recent investigation seems to show that the transmitted *Liberi* were in the 7th/8th c. actually used in the papal chancery.

W: H. Förster (Bern, 1958) [text].
L: H. H. Anton, Der L. d. in angeblichen u. verfälschten Papstprivilegien: Fälschungen im MA 3 (Hannover, 1988), 115-142. — A. Di Berardino (ed.), Patrologia 4 (Genoa, 1996), 147f. — H. Leclerq, L. d.: DACL 9/1:243-344. — L. Santifaller, L. d. (Stuttgart, 1976).

B. WINDAU

Liber genealogus

The *Liber genealogus* is a chronology by an unknown North African chronicler. The work, composed at the beginning of the 5th c., is preserved in four slightly differing versions: the *Codices Taurinensis* (*De generationibus*; *Origo generis humani*), *Lucensis* (*Genealogiae*), *Sangallensis*, and *Florentinus* (*Liber genealogus*). The author used a Lat. translation of the *Chronicle* of → Hippolytus. In calculating the number of generations given in the OT, this chronology goes beyond almost all known chronicles. The genealogies of Jesus in Mt and Lk are also taken into account.

W: *Chronica minora*, C. Frick (Leipzig, 1892), 2-27, 133-152 [text]. — P. de Lagarde, Septuaginta Studien 2 (Göttingen, 1892), 5-41 [text]. — T. Mommsen, MGH. AA 9:160 196.
L: T. Mommsen, op. cit., 154-160. — W. Speyer, Genealogie: RAC 6, 1246-1247.

G. BROSZIO

Liber generationis mundi

The *Liber generationis mundi* is a universal chronicle of → Hippolytus. The work covered the period from Adam to 234 C.E. but consisted mainly of the OT generations. The Gr. original is preserved only in fragments (*Cod. Matr.* 4701). A revision and expansion of the chronicle has come down in the Lat. translation of a 5th c. African chronicler in the → *Excerpta latina Barbari*.

More widespread than Hippolytus's original work was a quite early reorganization of it. The text of this second version can be reconstructed from the translations of two Lat. chronographers: the *Liber generationis I*, known from 460 on, and the *Liber generationis II*, translated before 334 and preserved in the → *Chronograph of 354*.

W: *Chronica minora*, C. Frick (Leipzig, 1892). — T. Mommsen, MGH. AA 9:78-140. — *Chronicon*, R. Helm, GCS 46 [36] (Berlin, 1955).

L: A. v. Harnack, Handbuch der altchr. Lit. 1/2 (Berlin, 1921), 626-627. — W. Speyer, Genealogie: RAC 6:1246f.

G. BROSZIO

Liber graduum

Behind the title *Liber graduum* lies a collection of thirty treatises in Syriac that deal with the individual stages of Chr. perfection and contain exhortations to an ascetical life. The anonymous author probably wrote in the second half of the 4th c. or at the beginning of the 5th c. and was a native of the Mesopotamian region. His expositions of Chr. asceticism closely reflect the views of earlier Syr. authors such as Ephraem and Aphraates. He also shares the latter's views on pneumatology: The human being consists of body and spirit-soul, which the consoler Spirit then joins as a third component. The *Liber graduum* also presupposes a knowledge of the widely varying Jewish and Chr. traditions and legends about Adam (→ *Spelunca Thesaurorum*). Adam in his original body, which was still free of all perverse desires, was raised to a spiritual sphere beyond the earthly, and through his intense life of prayer was in contact with the immaterial world of the angels. It was original sin that gave concupiscence its power, weakened human nature, and made necessary the divine law that introduces order. Christ, the new Adam, brought the pure heavenly knowledge that kills all lusts and makes possible a life of grace, continence, and continual prayer (Messalianism).

W: PS 2:1306-1360 [Syriac text/Latin trans./comm.].
L: P. Bäss, LG — ein messalianisches Buch?: XVII. Dt. Orientalistentag, ed. W. Voigt (Wiesbaden, 1969), 2:368-374. — A. Baker, Gospel of Thomas and LG: NTS 12 (1965/66) 49-55. — J. Gribomont, Philoxène et le messalianisme: OrSyr 2 (1957) 419-432. — A. Guillaumont, Situation du LG: OCA 197 (1974) 311-322. — I. Hausherr, Quanam aetate: OCP 1 (1935) 495-502. — idem, L'erreur fondamentale: OCP 1 (1935) 328-360. — D. Juhl, Askese im LG (Wiesbaden, 1996). — A. Kemmer, Charisma maximum (Leuven/Louvain, 1938), 52-91. — A. Kowalski, Perfezione e giustizia (Rome, 1989). — R. Terzoli, Il tema della beatitudine (Brescia, 1972), 149-177. — A. Vööbus, LG: FS J. Kopp (Stockholm, 1954), 108-128. idem, History of Ascetism (Leuven/Louvain, 1958), 178-184, 190-197.

P. BRUNS

Liber monstrorum de diversis generibus

This work, written possibly in Ireland in the 7th/8th c., is a kind of manual describing fabulous beings of Gr.-Roman mythology (human beings, monsters of land and sea, serpents); the author and addressees are unknown, and a basic skepticism pervades the presentation.

W: C. Bologna (Milan, 1977) [text]. — F. Porsia (Bari, 1976) [text].
L: S. Backx, Date: Latomus 3 (1939) 61. — F. Brunhölzl, Liber monstrorum: LMA 5:1946. — M. Lapidge, Liber monstrorum: StMed NS 23 (1982) 151-192. — B. Löfstedt, Notizen: Orph. 11 (1990) 117.

M. Skeb, OSB

Liber pontificalis

Duchesne gave the name *Liber pontificalis* to a collection of notes on the bishops of Rome which were put together in several strata and redactions and whose transmission history is very complex. The actual *Liber pontificalis* begins with Peter and ends with Stephen V (885-886). Its first part survives in a second edition (probably made under Vigilius, 537-555), but from it a first can be inferred. Behind the latter in turn lay the so-called *Catalogus Liberianus*, a list of popes down to Liberius, in the *Chronograph of 354*. The separately transmitted *Catalogus Felicianus* may be regarded as an excerpt from the first edition, the *Catalogus Cononianus* as an excerpt from the second edition. The ensuing lives in the second part of the *Liber pontificalis* were written largely by contemporaries. Prefixed to the *Liber pontificalis* is an apocryphal exchange of letters between Jerome and Damasus in which the former asks the bishop of Rome for the composition of a history of the popes.

After a pause in the 10th and 11th c., in which only short catalogues of popes were compiled, the actual *Liber pontificalis* was given a continuation in several versions down to the time of Martin V (d. 1431). The lengthy period of time covered by the *Liber pontificalis* resulted in a number of texts, all of which, however, display a parallel structure: the name, origin, and length of pontificate of each pope are followed by details of disciplinary and liturg. decrees, churches built or furnished, ordinations of bishops and clerics, contemporary events, place and date of the pope's burial, and the period elapsing until a new pope was elected. The language of the *Liber pontificalis* is clear and unadorned. The anonymous compilers are to be looked for in the administration, probably in the *scrinium* or even in the *vestiarium* of the Lateran. Because of the great deal of information it supplied for liturg. history, topography, and archeology the *LP* served for a long time simply as a source; more recently, as a *sui generis* text, it has increasingly become a subject of patristic and early medieval research.

W: L. Duchesne, C. Vogel, 3 vols. (Paris, 1955/57) [text/comm.]. — T. Mommsen, MGH. GPR 1. — J. M. March (Barcelona, 1925) (textual variants).
L: O. Bertolini, Lib. pontif.: SSAM 17/1 (1970) 387-455. — O. Capitani, Pontificato romano da Teodoro I a Martino I: Atti del 28 Convegno storico internazionale, ed. E. Menestò et al. (Spoleto, 1992), 69-83. — E. Caspar, Papsttum 2 (Tübingen, 1933), 314-320. — H. Geertmann, Edifici ecclesiastici (Groningen, 1975). — idem, Fonte archeologica: FS U. M. Fasola (Vatican City, 1989), 347-361. — P. Jeffery, Introduction of Psalmody: ALW 26 (1984) 147-165. — H. Leclerq, Lib. pontif.: DACL 9:354-360. — F. Mosino, Grecismi: BBGG 37 (1983) 61-73. — T. F. X. Noble, New Look at the Lib. pontif.: AHP 23 (1985) 347-358. — L. Reekmans, Constructions des papes: FS G. Sanders (Steenbergen, 1991), 355-366. — C. Vogel, Lib. pontif.: Monseigneur Duchesne et son temps, ed. École Française de Rome (Rome, 1975), 99-140.

B. Dümler

Liberatus

L., deacon (Liberatus Carthaginiensis, diaconus), was archdeacon of the church of Carthage in the mid-6th c.; in 534 and 535 he stayed in Rome as a member of an embassy and in Constantinople as companion of Bishop Reparatus in connection with the Three-Chapters controversy. L. was an uncompromising opponent of Bishop Vigilius of Rome and, after the latter's death (555), wrote a *Breviarium causae Nestorianorum et Eutychianorum*, a short history of heresies from Nestorius to 533. The purpose of this work, written between 560 and 566, was to defend the Three Chapters and prove that in condemning them Justinian had made a wrong decision. L. used valuable sources: he attests to the Lat. version of the *Henotikon* of → Zeno (ACO 2, 5, 127-29), reports on the Origenist disputes under Justinian (ACO 2, 5, 138-40) and on the activities of Bishop Theodore Askidas, Justinian's theol. adviser (ACO 2, 5, 140f.), and attests to the Lat. version of a letter of → Proclus of Constantinople to John of Antioch (ACO 2, 5, 111).

W: *Breviarium causae Nestorianorum et Eutychianorum*, PL 68:969-1050. — ACO 2, 5 (Collectio Sangermanensis), 98-141.
L: A. Grillmeier, Jesus der Christus 2/1 (Freiburg i.Br., 1986), 327-328; 2/2 (Freiburg i.Br., 1989), 407f.; 2/4 (Freiburg i.Br., 1990), 36f., et al. (English, Christ in Christian Tradition [London, 1987-97]). — G. Krüger, L.: RE3 11:449f.

B. R. Suchla

Liberius of Rome

When L., a Roman deacon, became successor of Julius I on May 17, 352, he found on his desk a letter of eastern bishops calling for the condemnation of Athanasius. He then appealed to Constantius II to call a council. The emperor then had Athanasius condemned at a synod in Arles in 353, and L. again appealed to the emperor in 354 and asked for an imperial council, which met in Milan. There Eusebius of Vercelli and Lucifer of Cagliari, who were legates of L., and Dionysius of Milan were exiled for their refusal to subscribe to a condemnation of Athanasius. L.'s subscription was demanded. When he too refused, he was brought to the court in Milan and exiled to Berea in Thrace (355/356—357/358). Three letters from this period are ascribed to L., but their authenticity is strongly disputed: acc. to these letters he subscribed to a formula of faith—the first (351), second (357), or third (358) of Sirmium?—and proclaimed his communion with Athanasius. What is certain is that L. must have returned to Rome, where he had to share his office with Felix II, who had meanwhile been installed. Felix was, however, driven out. L. was not represented at the double Synod of Seleucia-Rimini in 359. He died on Sept 24, 366.

Thirteen letters from the controversy over Athanasius have survived, among them the letter of 354 to Constantius in which L. calls for an ecum. council, three letters of 355 to Eusebius of Vercelli in which he urges the latter's participation in the Council of Milan, and, from the time after that council, a letter of consolation to his exiled fellow fighters. The disputed letters from exile must be dated to 357: two to the eastern bishops, one to Arian Bishops Ursacius, Valens, and Germinius, and one to Vincent with the request that he get the emperor to allow L.'s return. To the period after the exile belong the composition of a letter to the Cath. bishops of Italy in which L. defends the rebels of Rimini; also a letter to the Cath. bishops of the East (364) in which L. thanks them for holding fast to the *fides Nicaena*. Ambrose himself is suggested as author of the *Oratio in natale domini* (*or.*) (Ambrose, *virg.* 3.1-3), which L. is supposed to have delivered at the *velatio* of Marcellina, Ambrose's sister. In the West L. developed a rather negative reputation because of his weakness in exile and on the basis of the formation of confused legends. Three Copt. texts have come down under L.'s name: an *Oratio consolatoria de morte Athanasii* (*orat. cons.*), which should rather be assigned to → Damasus, and two fragments of a Lenten sermon (*serm.*) that attest to the esteem for L. in Egypt.

W: *ep.*, G. Hartel, CSEL 14:320f., 327-331. — A. Feder, CSEL 65:89-93, 155-157, 164-173. — W. Jakob, R. Hanslik, CSEL 71:423-426. — G. F. Diercks, CCL 8:311-316. — V. Bulhart, CCL 9:121-124. — S. Wenzlowsky, BKV[1], Papstbriefe 2:197-264 (Kempten, 1876) [German trans.]. — *orat.*, O. Faller (Bonn, 1933), 63-66. — I. Cazzaniga (Turin, 1948), 57f. — Ps-Liber., *orat. cons.*, F. Wisse: Muséon 103 (1990) 43-65 [text/English trans./comm.]. — Ps-Liber., *serm.*, T. Lefort: Muséon 12 (1911) 1-22.

L: H. C. Brennecke, Hilarius v. Poitiers (Berlin, 1984), 147-195, 265-301. — E. Caspar, Papsttum 1 (Tübingen, 1930), 169-195, 588-592. — J. Doignon, Formulation juridique: La tradizione, ed. W. Rordorf et al. (Rome, 1990), 383-387. — idem, Impietas de l'empereur: StPatr 24 (1991) 70-74. — G. Fernandez, Letter Pro deifico timore: Arianism, ed. R. C. Gregg (Philadelphia, 1985). — M. Goemans, Exil: FS C. Mohrmann (Utrecht, 1963), 184-189. — A.-G. Hamman, Études patristiques (Paris, 1991), 235-242. — R. P. C. Hanson, Arian controversy (Edinburgh, 1988), 329-341, 358-362 et al. — J. Hermann, Streitgespräch zwischen Konstantius u. L.: FS H. Liermann (Erlangen, 1964), 77-86. — HLL 5:510-516. — R. Klein, Constantius II. (Darmstadt, 1977), 137-144. — W. A. Löhr, Homöische u. homöusianische Kirchenparteien (Bonn, 1986), 58f. — V. Monachino, Primato nella controversia ariana: MHP 21 (1959) 46-58. — C. Pietri, Roma Christiana 2 (Rome, 1976), 25-28, 237-268. — M. Simonetti, Crisi ariana (Rome, 1975), 216-243, 395-397 et al. — W. Tietze, Lucifer v. Calaris (Tübingen, 1976), 265-273. — G. N. Verrando, L. Felice: RSCI 35 (1981) 91-125.

B. DÜMLER

Licentius

Born in Thagaste as son of Romanianus, L. was a friend and disciple of Augustine and the father of Alypius. In 386, despite his youthful age, he belonged to the circle at Cassiciacum in which Augustine discussed philosophical questions. He stayed for a while in Rome with the intention of pursuing the *cursus honorum*. Along with Augustine he converted to Christianity (the date of his baptism is unknown); Paulinus of Nola (*ep.* 8) and Augustine (*ep.* 26) urged him to lead an ascetical life. L. also tried his hand as a poet. Among the works of Augustine is a poem of 154 hexameters in which L. speaks of the difficulties of reading Varro and of critical problems of the day.

W: A. Goldbacher, CSEL 34/1:89-95. — D. Shanzer: REAug 27 (1991) 110-143 [text].

L: G. Bardy, Un élève de saint Augustin: AThA 14 (1954) 55-79. — U. Pizzani, Carmen Licentii: Helmantica 44 (1993) 497-515. — PLRE 2:682. — D. Romano, Licenzio poeta: Nuovo Didaskaleion 11 (1961) 1-22. — M. Zelzner, De carmine Licentii (Arnsberg, 1915).

M. SKEB, OSB

Licinianus of Carthagena

L., bishop of Carthagena who died ca. 603 and was the most important bishop of Byz. Spain, composed a great many letters (Isidore, *vir. ill.* 42) of which only three, from the years 590-600, have been preserved. The first (*ep.* 1) is a letter of thanks to Gregory I, who had sent L. his *Regula pastoralis*. In the second letter, to Epiphanius (*ep.* 2), L. and his fellow writer → Severus of Malaga explain that angels and the human soul are necessarily spiritual and incorporeal. The third letter (*ep.* 3) faults Bishop Vincent of Ibiza for his credulity: Vincent had come upon a letter from heaven, *De die dominica*, supposedly written by Jesus himself; L., however, has examined the style and the teaching of the letter and come to the conclusion that it contained *nec sermo elegans nec doctrina sana* (PL 72:699f.): it is a forgery; therefore he has torn up the forged "Sunday Letter," and Vincent should do the same in the presence of all the people.

W: *ep.,* PL 72:689-700. — J. Madoz, Liciniano de Cartagena y sus cartas (Madrid, 1948) [text/comm.].
L: W. Speyer, Die literarische Fälschung (Munich, 1971).

E. REICHERT

Linus of Rome

The *Liber pontificalis* reports that L. was from Etruria; Irenaeus (*haer.* 3.3.3) and Eusebius (*h.e.* 3.2; 3.4.8) identify him with the Linus mentioned in 2 Tim 4:21. The sources agree in naming him the first successor of Peter. The dates given for his pontificate vary between 64 and 81. The *Martyrium beati Petri Apostoli a Lino conscriptum*, a Lat. version of an excerpt from the Gr. *Acts of Peter*, is today dated to the 6th c.

W: *mart. Petri,* A. H. Salonius (Helsingfors, 1926). — M. Erbetta, Apocrifi 2 (Casale, 1966), 170-177 [Italian trans.]. L: E. Sauser, E.: BBKL 5:98-100. — G. Salmon, L.: DCB 3:726-729. — G. N. Verrando, Collocazione cronologica degli apocrifi Atti di Pietro: VetChr 20 (1983) 391-426.

B. DÜMLER

Liturgy

1. "Early Chr. liturgy" signifies, in a narrower sense, the orders of Mass in the eastern churches; in the broader sense, it refers to firmly structured liturgical orders of every kind. The earliest references to and texts of the Chr. liturgy are found in the NT (e.g., Acts 6:6; 13:3; 1 Tim 4:14 [ordination]; 1 Cor 11:23-34 [Eucharist]; Acts 8:38; 19:5f., etc. [baptism]; Jas 5:14 [anointing of the sick]; 1 Cor 16:20-24; Phil 2:6-11). Liturgical regulations and as yet nonbinding formularies are first handed on in early → Church Orders, in the *Didache* (*Did.* 7–10; 14: baptism, fasting, prayer, celebration of a meal) and espec. in the

so-called *Traditio apostolica* attributed to Hippolytus of Rome (*trad. ap.*: eucharistic prayer, ordinations, initiation, blessings, times of prayer). In a detailed description of the early Chr. eucharistic celebration (with baptism) → Justin Martyr (1 *apol.* 61; 65-67) already reflects the essential structure of all later liturgies. In the course of the anti-Arian movement many forms of prayer changed: thus the widely used prayer to the "Father *through* (*dia*) the Son *in* (*en*) the Holy Spirit (e.g., Clement Alex, *q. d. s.* 42.20; Origen, *or.* 33.1 and 6) became the formula "the Father *and* (*kai*) the Son *and* (*kai*) the Holy Spirit" (e.g., Basil, *Spir.* 29.73; the evening hymn *Phos hilaron*). In addition, many prayers were addressed directly to Jesus Christ and no longer to the Father.

The eastern position in prayer was very early adopted in the liturgy and led from the outset to an eastern orientation of the church buildings gradually erected from the 3rd c. on; a distinction must be made here between the orientation of the entrance and that of the apse.

The codification of the several liturgies from the 4th c. on was connected primarily with the formation of the patriarchates (Rome, Alexandria, Antioch, Constantinople) and the confessional divisions of the Chr. East (rise of liturg. families: Alexandrian and Antiochene [with West Syr. and East Syr. types]). The method of comparative liturg. science (A. Baumstark) made it possible to bring out, for Chr. antiquity, a number of regularities important in liturg. history.

2. (a) The most liturgically fruitful region of the early church was Syria and Asia Minor. In addition to the apocryphal *Acts of the Apostles* (→ Thomas, Literature about, → John, Literature about, → Peter, Literature about) of the 2nd-3rd c., which despite encratitic and gnostic influences on them, document a liturg. practice widespread among Syr. Christians, the most important sources are the Syr. → *Didascalia* (*Didasc.*, 3rd c.) and the → *Testament of Our Lord Jesus Christ* (*T. Dom.*, 5th c.) as well as, in particular, the → *Apostolic Constitutions* (*Const. app.*, ca. 400). The last-named contains rich liturg. material and, in the eighth book, a detailed formulary for Mass, the so-called Clementine Liturgy, in which the eucharistic prayer of the *Traditio apostolica* is reworked (*Const. app.* 8.11.7–15.11).

From the Antiochene world comes the Syr. "Anaphora of the Twelve Apostles" and thus the basis of the liturgy of Chrysostom and possibly also that of the liturgy of Basil, the oldest form of which is preserved in the Egypt. (and Arm.) tradition; also the liturgy on which → Theodore Mops. comments in

Liturgies in Christian Antiquity

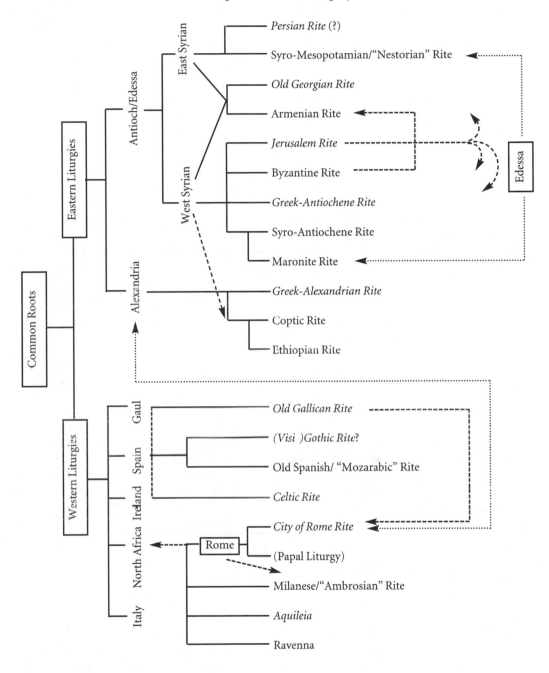

Names in Italics: Rites that disappeared in antiquity or early Middle Ages

——————— Dependence

------▶ Influence

···········▶ Influence suspected

his catechetical homilies (*hom. catech.*). After the Monophysite schism ca. 800, anaphoras were composed in Syriac. The Maronite liturgy, which originally resembled the East Syr. type (e.g., in its Anaphora of Peter IIIa [šarar]), increasingly came to resemble the Syro-Antiochene liturgy.

(b) The Jerusalem order of Mass was the origin of the liturgy of James, the earliest witness to which is the mystagogical catecheses usually attributed to → Cyril Jerus. (*catech. myst.* 5 [*catech.* 19-23]; mid-4th c.), and which influenced many other liturgies. In Syriac it became the normal liturgy of the "Jacobites." Lectionaries in an ancient Arm. translation (*Lect. Hieros. arm.*; mid-5th c.) and in Georgian (*Lect. Hieros. iber.*; 5th-8th c.), together with the pilgrimage account of Egeria (*Itin. Eger.* 24-47; end of 4th c.), make it possible to reconstruct the Jerusalem calendar of feasts, which influenced all the liturgies of the East and West.

(c) The nucleus of the East Syr. (Syro-Mesopotamian) liturgy of the Apostles (or liturgy of the Apostles Addai and Mari) goes back to the pre-Nicene period and at the beginning probably did not have an account of institution (see the earliest mss.). Later on it was reshaped by secondary, more heavily Gr.-influenced formularies that were named after → Nestorius and → Theodore Mops. Because of the isolation forced upon the Mesopotamian church for political reasons beginning in the 5th c., its liturgy has retained many ancient Semitic traits. In addition, there may even have been a Persian liturgy in the province of Persia (e.g., fragments of liturg. Pahlevi psalter [5th c.]).

(d) In the Byz. church the liturgy of the city of Constantinople gradually predominated; since the 10th c. this has been attributed to → John Chrys. (d. 407), and in its basic content, it, like the liturgy of Basil, goes back to the 4th/5th c. Alongside it there arose in the 6th c. the so-called liturgy of the Presanctified, which is traced back to Gregory the Great and had its origin in Syria.

(e) The Arm. (and Old Georg. [before the 9th c.]) liturgy originated in the tension between the native tradition and strong influences from Jerusalem, Persia, and Byzantium. By the beginning of the 5th c. the older form of the liturgy of Basil had been translated from Greek into Armenian (see the anaphora fragment in the *Buzandaran Patmutiwnk* [*lib.* 5.28l; ca. 425] of → Faustus of Byzantium).

(f) The history of the Alexandrian liturgy of Mark (in its Copt. form it is named after Cyril Alex.) can, espec. with the aid of papyrus fragments, be followed quite closely (e.g., *P. Strasb. inv. Gr.* 254 [4th/5th c.];

P. Ryl. 465 [6th c.]; → Euchologion). Since it was the normal liturgy of Egypt, the euch. prayer of → (Ps.-)Serapion of Thmuis (*euch.*; end of 4th c.) was already dependent on it. Later, it was marginalized by the liturgy of Basil, alongside which, espec. among the Monophysites, other formularies of Syro-Antiochene origin, such as the liturgy of Gregory, became widespread. Probably the earliest witnesses to the Eth. liturgy are the Anaphora of the Apostles (= expanded version of the euch. prayer of the *trad. ap.*) and the "Anaphora of Our Lord Jesus Christ" (see *T. Dom.*).

3. (a) The Lat. liturgies of the West are discernible almost exclusively only from the 5th/6th c. on. Latin as a liturg. language is first documented for North Africa (references in → Tertullian, → Cyprian of Carthage, and → Augustine). For the rest, a distinction can be made between the liturgy of the city of Rome and the non-Roman Lat. liturgies, which are much closer to those of the East. All the Lat. liturgies have in common that most of the prayers of the euch. celebration vary acc. to the rhythm of the liturg. year.

(b) In Rome, from the mid-4th c. at the latest, the liturgy was celebrated in Latin and no longer in Greek. Important are the papal stational liturgies which, as in other episcopal cities, were celebrated in certain presbyteral titular churches in turn. The Roman canon of the Mass goes back to the mid-4th c.; anaphoral intercessions are documented as early as under → Innocent I. The liturgy of the city of Rome (and the papal liturgy, which had taken over many elements of Byz. court ceremonial) was codified in the Roman → Sacramentaries: the *Veronense* (*Ve*), *Gelasianum Vetus* (*GeV*), and *Gregorianum-Hadrianum* (*GrH*). The course of the liturgy (= rubrics) can be derived espec. from the early medieval *Ordines Romani* (*OR*). From the 7th c. on, the Roman liturgy became normative in England, with its Roman missionaries, and in France under the Carolingians.

(c) Of the non-Roman Lat. liturgies the liturgy of Milan (later called the Ambrosian) is closest to the Roman and was increasingly assimilated to it. It can first be discerned in the baptismal catecheses of → Ambrose (*sacr.*, *myst.*). Other churches of Italy, e.g., Ravenna and Aquileia, seem to have developed their own liturgies.

(d) The remaining non-Roman Lat. liturg. world included the Old Spanish or Mozarabic (→ Isidore of Seville, *eccl. off.*), the Old Gallic (*Missale Gothicum*, *Missale Gallicanum Vetus*), and Celtic liturgies (*Stowe Missal*). Only a fragment of a calendar (5th/6th c.) in Gothic remains of a possible (Visi-)

Gothic liturgy of an Arian kind. The earliest known description of the course of the Old Gallic euch. celebration is in the letters of → (Ps.-) Germanus of Paris (d. 576; *Expos. antiqu. liturg. gallicanae*).

S: C. A. Swainson, Greek Liturgies (Hildesheim, 1971 = London, 1884). — J. Assemani, Cod. Liturgicus, 13 vols. (Farnborough, 1968-1969 = Rome, ¹1749-1766). — E. Renaudot, Liturgiarum orientalium collectio, 2 vols. (Farnborough 1970 = Frankfurt, ²1847). — F. E. Brightman, Liturgies Eastern and Western (Oxford, 1965 = 1896). — A. Hänggi, I. Pahl, Prex eucharistica (Fribourg, Switzerland, ²1968). — M. Andrieu, Ordines Romani, 5 vols. (Leuven/Louvain, 1931-1961). — E. Martène, De antiquis ecclesiae ritibus, 4 vols. (Hildesheim, 1967-1969 = Antwerp, 1736-1738).
L: A. Baumstark, Vom geschichtlichen Werden der L. (Freiburg i.Br., ¹⁻⁵1923). — idem, Liturgie Comparée (Chevetogne, ³1953) (literature). — H.-G. Beck, Kirche u. theol. Lit. (Munich, ²1977), 233-246 (literature). — J. A. Jungmann, L. der chr. Fruhzeit (Fribourg, Switzerland, 1967). — A. A. King, Liturgies of the Past (London, 1959). — idem, Liturgies of the Primatial Sees (London, 1957). — G. Kretschmar, Abendmahlsfeier I. TRE 1:232-278 (literature). — H. B. Meyer, Eucharistie (Regensburg, 1989), 73-169 (literature)
on 1: G. Delling, Gottesdienst im NT (Berlin, 1952). — F. J. Dölger, Sol Salutis (Münster, ³1972). — F. Hahn, Der urchr. Gottesdienst: JLH 12 (1967) 1-44. — J. M. Hanssens, Liturgie d'Hippolyte (Rome, 1970). — J. A. Jungmann, Stellung Christi im liturgischen Gebet (Münster, ²1962). — E. Peterson, Frühkirche (Freiburg i.Br., 1959), 1-35, 97-106, 146-182. — C. Vogel, Anaphores eucharistiques préconstantiniennes: FS A. G. Hamman (Rome, 1980), 401-410.
on 2. a: H. Engberding, Basileiosliturgie (Münster, 1931). — idem, Die syr. Anaphora der zwölf Apostel: OrChr 34 (1937) 213-247. — M. Hayek, Liturgie maronite (Tours, 1964). — R. Kaczynski, Wort Gottes in L. u. Alltag der Gemeinden des Johannes Chrysostomus (Freiburg i.Br., 1974). — H. Kruse, Geist-Epiklesen der Syriac texthomasakten: OrChr 69 (1985) 33-53. — W. F. Macomber, Maronite and Chaldean Versions: OCP 37 (1971) 55-84. — F. van de Paverd, Geschichte der Meß-L. in Antiocheia (Rome, 1970). — idem, Anaphoral Intercession: OCP 49 (1983) 303-339. — A. Raes, Anaphorae Syriacae (Rome, 1939ff.) [Syriac text/Latin trans.]. — F. J. Reine, Liturgy of the Myst. Catech. of Theodor of Mopsuestia (Washington, 1942). — G. Winkler, Beobachtungen zur frühen Epiklese: OrChr 80 (1996) 177-200. — on 2. b: J. F. Baldovin, Liturgy in Ancient Jerusalem (Bramcote, 1989). — *Liturgy of James*, B.-C. Mercier, PO 26/2 [Greek text/Latin trans.]. — G. Kretschmar, Jerusalemer L.: JLH 2 (1956) 22-46. — *Lect. Hieros. arm.*, A. Renoux, PO 35/1; 36/2 [Armenian text/French trans./comm.]. — *Lect. Hieros. iber.*, M. Tarchnišvili (CSCO. I 9-10, 13-14) [Georgian text/Latin trans.]. — A. Renoux, L'organisation liturgique hiérosolymitaine: Muséon 78 (1965) 335-355. — A. Tarby, Prière eucharistique (Paris, 1972). — R. Zerfaß, Schriftlesung (Münster, 1968). — on 2. c: R. J. Galvin, Addai and Mari Revisited: EL 87 (1973) 383-414. — A. Gelston, Eucharistic Prayer of Addai and Mari (Oxford, 1992) [Syriac text/English trans./comm.]. — W. F. Macomber, Oldest Known Text: OCP 32 (1966) 334-371 [Syriac text/Latin trans.]. — S. Naduthadam, Anaphore de Mar Nestorius, Diss. (Paris,

1992) [Syriac text/French trans./comm.]. — B. D. Spinks, Anaphora of Nestorius: OCP 62 (1996) 273-294. — J. Vadakkel, Anaphora of Theodor of Mopsuestia, Kottayam 1989 [Syriac text/English trans./comm.]. — on 2. d: H.-J. Feulner, Präsanktifikaten-L.: LMA 7:152f. — G. Khouri-Sarkis, Origine syrienne de l'anaphore byzantine: OrSyr 7 (1962) 3-68. — R. F. Taft, Évolution historique: POC 22 (1972) 241-287; 24 (1974) 3-33, 105-138; 25 (1975) 274-300. — idem, Authenticity: OCP 56 (1990) 5-51. — idem, Byzantine Rite (Collegeville, Minn., 1992), 22-41 (literature). — G. Wagner, Ursprung der Chrysostomus-L. (Münster, 1973). — G. Winkler, Interzessionen der Chrysostomusanaphora: OCP 36 (1970) 301-336; 37 (1971) 333-383. — eadem, Randbemerkungen zu den Interzessionen: OS 20 (1971) 55-61. — on 2. e: G. Paradze, Vorbyz. L. Georgiens: Muséon 42 (1929) 90-99. — A. (C.) Renoux, L'anaphore arménienne: Eucharisties d'Orient et d'Occident 2 (Paris, 1970), 83-108. — idem, Liturgie arm. et liturgie hiérosolymitaine: Liturgie de l'Église particulière (Rome, 1976), 275-288. — A. Wade, Oldest Iadgari: OCP 50 (1984) 451-456. — G. Winkler, Das arm. Initiationsrituale (Rome, 1982). — eadem, Zur Geschichte des arm. Gottesdienstes: OrChr 58 (1974) 154-172. — on 2. f: H. Brakmann, Die Kopten: A. Gerhards, Die kopt. Kirche, ed. idem (Stuttgart, 1994), esp. 12-20 (literature). — G. J. Cuming, Liturgy of St. Mark (Rome, 1990) [Greek text/comm.]. — A. Gerhards, Griech. Gregorios-anaphora (Münster, 1984) [Greek text/German trans./comm.]. — E. Hammerschmidt, Ethiopic Anaphoras (Stuttgart, ²1987). — idem, Kopt. Gregoriosanaphora (Berlin, 1957) [Coptic text/German trans./comm.]. — M. E. Johnson, Prayers of Sarapion of Thmuis (Rome, 1995) [Greek text/English trans./comm.].
on 3. a: F. Cabrol, II. Afrique: DACL 1:591-657. — M. Klöckener, Hochgebet bei Augustinus: FS C. P. Mayer (Würzburg, 1989), 461-495 (literature). — W. Roetzer, Augustinus' Schriften als liturgie-geschichtliche Quelle (Munich, 1930). — V. Saxer, Vie liturgique et quotidienne à Carthage (Rome, ²1984). — E. Schweitzer, L. in Nordafrika: ALW 12 (1970) 69-84. — A. Zwinggi, Wortgottesdienst bei Augustinus: LJ 20 (1970) 92-113, 250-253. — on 3. b: B. Botte, Canon Missae: RAC 2, 842-845. — A. Chavasse, La liturgie de la ville de Rome (Rome, 1993). — K. Gamber, Missa Romensis (Regensburg, 1970). — T. Klauser, Übergang der röm. Kirche von der griech. zur lat. L. sprache: FS G. Mercati 1 (Vatican City, 1946), 467-482. — H. B. Meyer, Eucharistie (Regensburg, 1989), 167-171, 173-196 (literature). — G. G. Willis, Essays in Early Roman Liturgy (London, 1964). — idem, Further Essays (London, 1968). — on 3. c: F. Cabrol, II. Aquilée: DACL 1:2683-2691. — H. Leclercq, Ravenne V. Liturgie: DACL 14:2086f. — H. Leeb, Psalmodie bei Ambrosius (Vienna, 1967). — P. Lejay, Ambrosien (Rit): DACL 1:1373-1442. — J. Schmitz, Gottesdienst im altchr. Milan (Cologne, 1975). — on 3. d: F. Cabrol, Mozarabe (La Liturgie): DACL 12:390-491. — M. Dietz, Gebetsklänge aus Altspanien (Bonn, 1947). — K. Gamber, L. der Goten: OS 10 (1961) 109-135. — L. Gougaud, Celtique (Liturgies): DACL 2:2969-3032. — H. Leclercq, Gallicane (Liturgie): DACL 6:473-593. — M. Metzger, Les Sacramentaires (Turnhout, 1994). — H. B. Meyer, Eucharistie (Regensburg, 1989), 154-161 (literature). — W. S. Porter, The Gallican Rite (London, 1958). — D. N. Power, Celtic Liturgy: StLi 27 (1997) 1-32 (literature). — J. Quasten, Oriental Influence: Tr. 1 (1943) 55-78. — J. B. Thibaut, L'ancienne liturgie gallicane (Paris, 1929). — G.

F. Warner, Stowe Missal, 2 vols. (Suffolk, 1989 = London, 1906-1915) [Latin text/comm.]. — F. E. Warren, Liturgy and Ritual of the Celtic Church (Suffolk, ²1987).

H.-J. FEULNER

Longinus

L. was a Monophysite priest of Alexandria before Empress Theodora appointed him in 545 as the first bishop of Nubia, which had been christianized at the beginning of the 6th c. But after Theodora's death (548) Patriarch Theodosius Alex., a man old and infirm, prevented L.'s consecration and appointed him to be his own successor. In 566, after the death of Theodosius, L. was consecrated bishop of Nubia at Constantinople but was prevented from leaving the city. He was involved in the struggle against the tritheists. In 568 he was charged with hindering church unity and imprisoned. In 569 he was able to flee and reach his diocese. In 575, after being appointed by the clergy of Alexandria to see that the orphaned patriarchal see was filled, L., with the assistance of Paul of Antioch, consecrated Syr. archimandrite Theodore as patriarch, but the Alexandrians refused him and replaced him with Peter, who in his turn deposed Paul of Antioch. In 576/577, amid great dangers, L. tried in vain to rehabilitate Paul. In 577 he returned to Nubia but was accused of heresy by Damian, the new patriarch of Alexandria; L. did productive missionary work in other regions and by means of the ruler, whom he had brought to Christianity, secured the rehabilitation of Theodore as patriarch of Alexandria. L. died after 580.

From L., whose detailed life was written by John of Ephesus (*h.e.* 4), there have survived three Syr. fragments of letters (to Syr. archimandrites, to John of Bet Hanina, and to Paul of Antioch) concerning the rehabilitation of Paul. There is also a declaration, signed by L. among others, of some Constantinopolitan presbyters who accepted the Monophysite treatise of Theodosius of Alexandria and condemned its opponents.

W: I.-B. Chabot, CSCO 17:84-86, 241-244 [Syriac text]; CSCO 103:58f., 168-170 [French trans.].
L: E. Honigmann, Évêques et évêchés (Leuven/Louvain, 1951).

C. SCHMIDT

Lucian of Antioch

Information on L. comes, with few exceptions, from the hagiog. tradition. Sure references to his life come from Eusebius (*h.e.* 8.13.2; 9.6): during the persecution of Maximinus Daia this ascetic and theol. educated priest was brought to Nicomedia; there he was questioned in the presence of the emperor and suffered martyrdom (Jan. 7, 312). That L. delivered a defense on that occasion is probably a commonplace.

Little of L.'s works have survived. Jerome mentions several *Libelli de fide* and letters (*vir. ill.* 77). On the basis of Eusebius's remark that L. defended himself before the emperor, Rufinus included in his translation an apologetic text that is probably not from L. (*or. apol.*). The only writings of L. that have survived are a fragment of a letter (*fr.*) and an interpretation of Job 2:9f. (*in Job*) that probably came from a homily and is preserved in a homoean commentary on Job.

L. is often said to have been the founder of Antiochene exegesis by making a literal interpretation of the scriptures. But the sources (espec. Eusebius and Philostorgius) do not say this. The formation of a school in Antioch began only with Diodorus and Theodore.

An influential theory, based on various sources (Arius [Doc. 1]; Alexander Alex. [Doc. 14]; Marius Victorinus [*adv. Arium* 1.43]; Epiphanius [*anc.* 33.4]; and Philostorgius [*h.e.* 2.3; 14.3.15]), maintained that L. was a precursor of Arius; it included a literal exegesis that does not in fact provably represent Arius. In almost a vicious circle, the theorists seek to derive from Arius and other "Lucianists" a doctrine of L. that they then apply as a means of determining the views of Arius. But the theory of an influence of L. on Arius must be abandoned. In addition, there are clear differences between Arius and the other Lucianists and among the latter themselves, so that an attempt to reconstruct the teaching of L. must fail.

Finally, the *Ekthesis* of the Antiochene Enkainia synod (341) is regarded as a confession of L. that either goes back directly to L. and uses a baptismal creed of L., or at least can be traced back to L. through literary criticism. Against this theory is the fact that in the pre-Arian period there were no local baptismal creeds. In addition, the *Ekthesis* seems in many respects to resemble the theology of Asterius the Sophist and thus to be Nicene. It is uncertain whether the document came from the circle of Eusebius of Nicomedia, which used Asterian theology and traditional elements. A linking of the *Ekthesis* to L. could have served to give the work a theol. legitimacy in homoiousian circles.

Not least, a effort has been made to discover a Lucianic recension of the LXX and the NT Koine, which formed the basis of the *textus receptus*. But, for one thing, the criteria are unclear for determining how this recension could have been made by L. (the relationship to the Hexapla is also unclear). For another, what is regarded as typical of L. can be seen prior to L. (Philo, Josephus, Clement Alex., papyri of the 1st and 2nd c., etc.). The effort to find a Lucianic recension must be regarded as a failure.

W: *or. apol.*, Rufin, *h.e.* 9.6.3. — *fr.*, PG 92:689B. — *in Job* 2,9-10, D. Hagedorn, PTS 14:30.21-33.15.
L: K. Aland, Der Text des NT (Stuttgart, 1982). — G. Bardy, Recherches sur saint L. et son école (Paris, 1936). — T. Böhm, Die Christologie des Arius (St. Ottilien, 1991). — H. C. Brennecke, L.: TRE 21:474-479. — idem, L. in der Geschichte des Arianischen Streites: Logos. FS L. Abramowski (Berlin, 1993), 170-192. — J. R. Busto Saiz, The biblical text of Malachias Monachus to the book of Wisdom: La Septuaginta en la investigación contemporánea, ed. N. F. Marcos (Madrid, 1985), 257-269. — H. Dörrie, Zur Geschichte der Septuaginta im Jh. Konstantins: ZNW 39 (1940/41) 57-110. — A. Hahn, Bibliothek der Symbole u. Glaubensregeln der alten Kirche (Hildesheim, 1962) (reprint). — R. P. C. Hanson, The Search for the Christian Doctrine of God (Edinburgh, 1988), 79-84. — P. de Lagarde, Librorum Veteris Testamenti canonicorum pars prior graece (Göttingen, 1883). — W. Löhr, Die Entstehung der homöischen u. homöusianischen Kirchenparteien (Bologna, 1986). — R. Lorenz, Arius judaizans? (Göttingen, 1979). — B. M. Metzger, The Lucianic Recension of the Greek Bible: idem, Chapters in the History of the NT Textual Criticism (Leiden, 1964), 1-41. — T. E. Pollard, The Origin of Arianism: JThS 9 (1958) 103-111. — M. Simonetti, La crisi ariana nel IV secolo (Rome, 1975). — M. Spanneut, La Bible d'Eustathe d'Antioche — Contribution à l'histoire de la "version Lucianique": StPatr 4 (1961) 171-190. — E. Tov, Lucian and Proto-Lucian: Qumran and the History of the Biblical Text, ed. F. M. Cross, S. Talmon (Cambridge, 1975), 293-305. — D. S. Wallace-Hadrill, Christian Antioch (Cambridge, 1982). — R. Williams, Arius. Heresy and Tradition (London, 1987).

T. BÖHM

Lucian of Caphargamala

L., a presbyter of Caphargamala (near Diospolis/ Lydda), with the help of a vision of Gamaliel, discovered the supposed grave of Stephen in 415; the discovery was made public at a Synod of Diospolis being held at that same time by John II of Jerusalem. The bones were placed in the church of Zion until a church dedicated to Stephen was built in the northern part of the city. At the request of → Avitus of Braga L. composed an account of the discovery in the form of a letter. Avitus made a Lat. translation of the letter which has come down in two versions and was soon translated in turn into Syriac, Armenian, Georgian, and Ethiopic. Jerome mentions it (*vir. ill.* 2.46); the *Decretum Gelasianum* rejects it as apocryphal; it

nonetheless had considerable influence on medieval *inventio* literature.

W: PL 41:805-818. — N. Franco: ReO (1914) 293-307 [Greek text]. — E. Vanderlinden: REByz 4 (1946) 178-217 [Latin text].
L: B. Altaner, Avitus v. Braga: ZKG 60 (1941) 456-468. — M. Heinzelmann, Translationsberichte (Tournai, 1979). — J. Martin, Die Revelatio S. Stephani u. Verwandtes: HJ 77 (1958) = FS B. Altaner, 419-433.

G. RÖWEKAMP

Lucidus

L., a presbyter, appears only in the controversy on grace in southern Gaul: ca. 473 a synod was held in Arles, with Metropolitan Leontius presiding, in order to proceed against the predestinationism that had developed out of the views of the later Augustine. L., who evidently maintained this teaching, was obliged to renounce it. *Ep.* 1 of → Faustus of Riez, who was likewise condemned by the bishops of southern Gaul for both Pelagian and predestinationist errors, and the preface of the same writer's *De gratia*, report on the affair. At a second synod in Lyons (474) L. recanted his opinion (among the letters of Faustus, *ep.* 2) and accepted the southern Gallic conciliationist teaching that goes under the name of Semipelagianism.

W: *ep.*, A. Engelbrecht, CSEL 21:165-168.
L: J. Douerin, Fauste de Riez, Diss. (Paris, 1973), 188-220. — M. Simonetti, Il De gratia di Fausto di Riez: SSRel 1 (1977) 125-145. — C. Tibiletti, Libero arbitrio e grazi in Fausto: Aug. 19 (1979) 259-285. — idem, La salvezza umana in Fausto: Orph. 1 (1980) 371-390.

C. KASPER

Lucifer of Cagliari

I. Life: L., a radical Nicene theologian, first comes on the scene in 354/355 as bishop of Calaris (modern Cagliari) in Sardinia. Liberius of Rome sent him as an ambassador to the imperial court and to the Synod of Milan (355), at which, despite massive imperial pressure, L. steadfastly refused to condemn the absent Athanasius and was therefore sent off to the East. Three of his four places of exile are known: Germanicia in the Commagene (in the see of Bishop Eudoxius), Eleutheropolis in Palestine, and the Thebaid in Egypt. After the amnesty issued by Julian the Apostate in 362, L. went to Antioch, where he consecrated Paulinus, a presbyter, to be bishop of the Nicene group, because he did not acknowledge the orthodoxy of Bishop Meletius, who was still in exile. He thereby frustrated the efforts of Athanasius and the Synod of Alexandria (362), at which L. was represented by two deacons, to secure a merger of the Meletians and Eustathians; he thus contributed in a decisive way to prolonging the Antiochene schism. After returning to Calaris by way of Naples and Rome, L. persevered in his rigid refusal to be in eccles. communion with the former Arians and the bishops who accepted them. He died in schism in the year 370, acc. to the *Chronicle* of Jerome.

II. Works: L. was active espec. as a polemicist and pamphleteer. His five polemics addressed to Constantius II were composed in exile: (1) *De non conveniendo cum haereticis* (*non conv.*, 355/356) uses many passages of scripture to prove the need of separating from the Arians. (2) *De regibus apostaticis* (*reg. apost.*, 356) uses examples of apostate kings of the OT to give notice to Constantius II that God would punish him for his behavior. (3) The two-book *De Athanasio* (*quia absentem nemo debet iudicare nec damnare*) (*Athan.*, 358) castigates as unjust the condemnation of Athanasius issued in Milan without first hearing the defendant, and they prove from scripture that Constantius's behavior violates the commandments of God. (4) In *De non parcendo in Deum delinquentibus* (*non parc.*, 359) L. rejects the emperor's complaint of his, L.'s, impudence by telling him that as a heretic he deserves no reverence. (5) *Moriendum esse pro Dei filio* (*moriend.*, 360/361) reminds Constantius of his acts of violence and proclaims his own readiness for martyrdom.

(6) *Epistulae* (*ep.*): *Ep.* 7, addressed to Eusebius of Vercelli in 355, asks him to continue his fight against Arianism (at the Synod of Milan). In a correspondence (*ep.* 1f.; 359-361) with Florentius, *Magister officiorum*, L. admits that he has sent a codex to the emperor (probably of his polemical writings). Some letters are lost, among them a correspondence with → Hilary of Poitiers in which L. sharply attacks him for his attempt, in his *De synodis*, to mediate between the homoousians and the homoiousians. (7) The *Fides sancti Luciferi*, probably an excerpt from the *Fides* of the Luciferian presbyter → Faustinus, is probably not authentic.

III. Importance: Since L., in a deliberate rejection of the educational ideal of late antiquity, makes use of the language of the people, he is an important source for knowledge of the popular Latin of late antiquity. His extensive citations of scriptural passages also make him an important witness to the early Lat. text of the Bible. The theol. contribution of a man who had no interest in speculation is extremely small. His

rigid, formalistic allegiance to the Nicene Creed made it impossible for him to come to an agreement in theol. questions that was geared to the demands of the time. He and his supporters brought about the so-called (not thoroughly organized) Luciferian schism, whose leaders, after L.'s death, were → Gregory of Elvira, Heraclidas of Oxyrhynchos, and Ephesius of Rome. Presbyters → Faustinus and → Marcellinus, by means of their *Libellus precum*, won imperial recognition of the group as orthodox, but the movement soon became unimportant.

W: W. Hartel, CSEL 13. — G. F. Diercks, CCL 8. — *moriend.*, G. Ceretti (Pisa, 1940) [text/comm.]. — L. Ferreres: AST 53/54 (1983) 1-100 [text/comm.]. — idem, SLBar 5 (Barcelona, 1982) [text/comm.]. — *reg. apost.*, J. Avilés: AST 49/50 (1976/77) 345-437. — idem, SLBar 4 (Barcelona, 1979). — *reg. apost., moriend.*, V. Ugenti, (Studi latini e greci 1, Quaderni dell'Istituto di Filol. class. Univ. di Lecce (Lecce, 1980) [text/Italian trans.]. — *non conv.*, A. Piras (Rome, 1992) [text/Italian trans./comm.]. — *fides*, A. Saba: FS P. Ubaldi (Milan, 1937), 109-116.

L: E. Amann, L.: DThC 9:1032-1044. — J. Avilés, L. Ferreres, Algunos elementos de retorica en L.: Actas del V congreso español de estudios clásicos (Madrid, 1978), 331-336. — G. Castelli, L. e il suo atteggiamento di fronte alla cultura classica: RSC 16 (1968) 219-223. — idem, Studio sulla lingua e lo stile di L.: AAST. M 105 (1971) 123-247. — idem, Lettura di L., moriend. IX: CClCr 10 (1989) 439-479. — A. M. Coleman, The Biblical Text of L., 3 vols. (Welwyn, 1927 and Oxford, 1946/47). — G. F. Diercks, Enige bijzonderheden van het taleigen van L.: FS J. C. F. Nuchelmans (Weesp, 1985), 75-82. — L. Ferreres, Las fuentes de L. en su moriend.: AFFB 3 (1977) 101-115. — idem, Reminiscencias luciferianas en el Commonitorium de Vincente de Lérins: AFFB 15 (1992) 19-24. — A. Figus, L'enigma di L. (Cagliari, 1973). — F. Flammini, Osservazioni critiche sul moriend. di L.: RCCM 4 (1962) 304-334. — K. M. Girardet, Kaiser Konstantius II. als "Episcopus episcoporum" u. das Herrscherbild des kirchlichen Widerstandes: Hist. 26 (1977) 95-128. — W. Hartel, L. u. sein Latein: ALLG 3 (1886) 1-58. — HLL 5:486-491 (literature). — P. Juvanon du Vachat, Recherches sur le schisme de L. (Paris, 1961). — G. Krüger, L. u. das Schisma der Luciferianer (Hildesheim, 1969 = Leipzig, 1886). — J. Liébaert, L.: Cath. 7 (1975) 1250f. — H. Lietzmann, L. nr. 2: PRE 13/2:1615f. — S. Longosz, Inwektywa Luziferiusza z Calaris (The Invective of L.): RTK 19 (1972) 181-193. — P. M. Marcello, La posizione di L. nelle lotte antiariane del IV secolo (Lodi, 1940). — P. Meloni, L. di Cagliari ed Eusebio di vercelli nel giudizio di Sant'Ambrogio: FS O. P. Alberti (Cagliari, 1998), 61-72. — A. Merk, L. u. seine Vorlagen in der Schrift moriend.: ThQ 94 (1912) 1-32. — I. Opelt, Formen der Polemik bei L.: VigChr 26 (1972) 200-226. — A. Piras, Sul latino di L.: VetChr 29 (1992) 315-343. — F. Piva, L. contro l'imperatore Costanzo (Trient, 1928). — M. Simonetti, Appunti per una storia dello scisma luciferiano: Atti del convegno di studi religiosi sardi (Padua, 1963), 67-81. — idem, La Fides Faustini e la Fides Luciferi: SE 14 (1963) 92-98. — W. Tietze, L. u. die Kirchenpolitik Konstantius' II., Diss. (Tübingen, 1976). — G. Thörnell, Studia Luciferiana (Uppsala, 1934). — M. M. Todde, Peccato e prassi penitenziale secondo L. (Vicenza, 1965). — H. J. Vogels, Lk.-Zitate u. Joh.-Zitate bei L.: ThQ 103 (1922) 23-37, 183-200. — C. Zeda, La teologia trinitaria di L.: DT(P) 52 (1949) 276-329.

M. Durst

Lucius of Alexandria

L. was consecrated bishop of Alexandria in 367 by Arian bishops, but when he arrived in Alexandria, he was unable to assert himself for more than two days against Athanasius. He was driven from Egypt but returned to Alexandria after the death of Athanasius in 373. There, under the Emperor Valens, a friend of the Arians, he prevailed against the orthodox Peter II, who fled to Rome. L. took strict measures against the orthodox, espec. monks. In 378 Peter returned, and L. renounced the see. He went to Constantinople to Arian Bishop Demophilus and accompanied him into exile in 380. Acc. to Jerome (*vir. ill.* 118) L. composed annual Easter letters and writings on various problems. A fragment of his treatise on Easter (*fr. pasch.*) has survived in which he deals with the "God in flesh" formula: it means, he says, that only the Word and the flesh, not the soul, are linked.

W: F. Diekamp, Doctrina Patrum (Münster, ²1981), 65.
L: W. Bright, L. 11: DCB 3:753f. — Die Geschichte des Christentums 2 (Freiburg i.Br., 1996), 434, 474, 1020. — W. D. Hauschild, Handbuch der Kirchen- und Dogmengeschichte 1 (Gütersloh, 1995), 161.

B. Windau

Lucius I of Rome

Very little is known of the life of L., bishop of Rome 253/254 (feastday: March 4). After his accession he was immediately banished by Emperor Gallus but was soon able to return under Emperor Valerianus. His martyrdom is a legend. Nothing has survived of his letters on the treatment of the *lapsi*, in which he argues for a milder penitential practice and which Cyprian (*ep.* 68.8) mentions. The letter (*ep.*) to the bishops of Gaul and Spain that is attributed to him is certainly apocryphal. Also attributed to him is a decree (*decr.*) against the cohabitation of a priest and an *extranea femina*. For this reason, he also seems a possible author of the Ps.-Cyprianic *De singularitate clericorum* (*singul. cler.*), acc. to which priests are to choose a life of celibacy.

W: *ep. /decr.*, PL 1007-1016. — *singul. cler.*, W. v. Hartel, CSEL 3/3:173-220.
L: A. Amore, L.: BSS 8:286f. — HLL 5:501-505. — H. Koch, Cyprianische Untersuchungen (Bonn, 1926), 426-472.

B. Windau

Luculentius

L. is the otherwise unknown author of short commentaries (homilies?), which survive only in fragments, on Mt 6:24; Lk 24:36-47; Jn 1:29; Rom 12:1, 6, and 16; 13:8; 1 Cor 1:4; Eph 3:13; 4:1, 23; 5:15; 6:10; Gal 5:25; 6:10; Phil 1:6; Col 1:9; 3:12; Tit 2:11; Heb 1:1; 1 Pet 5:6. The primarily literal exegesis echoes Jerome and (with qualifications) Augustine (and even Pelagius).

At an earlier time, possibly anti-Donatist and anti-Arian allusions suggested 5th c. Africa or perhaps 6th c. Italy, as the place of origin. Recent scholars have dated the texts to Italy of the Carolingian period (9th/10th c.).

W/L: PL 72:803-860. — A. Müller, L. *hom. in Gal* 5, 25-6, 10: ThQ 93 (1911) 206-222 [text]. — V. Bulhart, Textkritische Studien zu L.: WSt 59 (1941) 158f. — W. Affeldt, L. Frgm. eines Kommentars Rom-Hebr: Tr. 13 (1957) 388. — J. Lemarié, Deux fragments d'homéliaires (Lc 24, 36-47): REAug 25 (1979) 97-101 [text]. — idem, La collection carolingienne de L.: SE 27 (1984) 221-371 [text].

J. Lössl

Luke, Literature about

There have probably never been any "Acts of Luke" in the strict sense nor is any *Passio* found in the Gr. or Lat. worlds, since it was supposed that L. met a natural death. Oriental versions of a *Passio Lucae* (BHO 567-69) (two Copt. versions, an Arab., an Eth., and a Syr.) tell of L.'s martyrdom in Rome under Nero. The work presupposes a knowledge of the *Martyrium Petri*, the *Martyrium Pauli*, and the *Acta Pilati*.

W: I. Balestri, H. Hyvernat, CSCO. C 6:1-8 [Coptic text]; CSCO. C 15:1-6 [Latin trans.]. — II. G. Evelyn White, The Monasteries of the Wadi'n Natrun 1 (New York, 1926), 47-50 [Coptic text]. — A. Smith Lewis, Horae Semiticae (London, 1903), 3:130-133 [Arabic text]; 4:152-156 [English trans.]. — E. A. Wallis Budge, The Contendings of the Apostles (London, 1899-1901), 1:119-121 [Ethiopic text]; 2:115-117 [English trans.]. — F. Nau, Martyre: ROC 3 (1898) 41f., 151-167 [Syriac text/French trans.].

G. Röwekamp

Luxurius

In the *Salmasiana* collection of the *Anthologia Latina*, a collection connected with the kingdom of the Vandals, a good deal of room is given to Luxurius (or Luxorius, Lusorius) the grammarian. His epigrams show that he lived during the reign of Hilderic (523-530) and was a Christian (*Anth. Lat.* 345.13) but gave very little literary testimony to this fact. An entire book of eighty-nine youthful poems was accepted into the collection. Acc. to the introductory poem the book was dedicated to Faustus the Grammarian. The epigrams, mostly in hexameters, deal with matters of everyday life but scornfully and with graphic eroticism. Epigrams on sculptures and a more Chr. epitaph for a four-year-old child are on a higher level. Also preserved are a Virgilian cento and an epigram on Hilderic. The collection may also have contained a book of poems on mythological subjects.

That L. was active as a grammarian is shown by a citation from a glossary that presents him as author of a work on orthography (*Anth. Lat.* 950.1-4).

W: A. Riese (ed.), Anthologia Latina 1/1 (Leipzig, ²1884). — H. Happ, L. (Stuttgart, 1986 = Diss. Tübingen, 1958) [text/comm.].
L: M. Fuhrmann, L.: KP 3:796. — M. Schanz, C. Hosius, G. Krüger, Geschichte der röm. Lit. 4/2 (Munich, 1971 = Munich, 1920), 73f.

W. GEERLINGS

M

Macarius of Alexandria

M. (d. ca. 390) was originally an itinerant trader but later became a hermit in the wilderness of Nitria and Scete; he engaged in a lively exchange of ideas with the Origenists and Evagrius Pont. He is considered to be the author of various practical-ascetical writings (*Visio de sorte animarum*, apophthegmata, homilies, letters, rules) which the tradition has often confused with those of the more important mystic → Macarius the Egyptian/Simeon.

W: PG 34:263f., 385-392, 967-990. — A. v. Lantschoot, Révélations de Macaire . . . sur le sort de l'âme après la mort: Muséon 63 (1950) 159-189 [Syriac text]. — A. Wilmart, Epistula Macarii: RAM 1 (1920) 58-83 [Latin text]. — W. Strothmann, Erste Homilie des M.: GOF. S 24 (1983) 99-108 [Syriac text].
L: G. Bunge, Évagre le Pontique et les deux Macaire: Irén. 56 (1983) 215-227. — A. Guillaumont, Problème de deux M.: Irén. 48 (1975) 41-59.

P. BRUNS, U. HAMM

Macarius of Antioch

M., patriarch of Antioch ca. 650 to 681, appeared at the third Council of Constantinople as leader of the Monotheletes. He was deposed there and banished to Rome, where he died in 685.

The surviving writings of M. are all found in the acts of that council. Preserved complete is a confession of faith of M. (*symb.*), which uses as sources the confession of faith of Gregory the Wonderworker/Thaumaturgus (cited in his *Vita* by Gregory Nyss.) and the creed of 381. There are also excerpts (*exc.*) from a three-volume collection of patristic testimonia that were meant as witnesses to Monotheletism. An examination showed, however, that the citations were either distorted or did not prove the point. Finally, four other writings of M. were discussed, of which the Acts contain fragments (*fr.*): a *prosphonetikos logos* to the emperor, a work of an African presbyter and monk named Luke, a work not further described, and a work sent to the emperor.

W: *symb.*, Mansi 11:349-360. — *exc.*, Mansi 11:359-388. — *fr.*, Mansi 11:511-525.
L: H. C. Beck, Kirche u. theol. Lit. (Munich, 1959), 433. — Die Geschichte des Christentums 4 (Freiburg i.Br., 1994), 45f., 400. — R. Riedinger, Das Bekenntnis des Gregor Thaumaturgos: ZKG 92 (1981) 311-314. — J. Rissberger,

Das Glaubensbekenntnis des Patriarchen M. (Offenbach, 1940).

B. WINDAU

Macarius the Egyptian/Simeon

The name Macarius/Simeon is explained by an awkwardness arising from the history of transmission: In the Byz., Syr., and Arab. ms. tradition there are works that supposedly had for author a Macarius (and M. the Egyptian is meant); a small number of the mss., however, ascribe them also to a Simeon (also: "of Mesopotamia"). Now the author was undoubtedly not Macarius the Egyptian; his name may have replaced the real author's erased name in order to protect the works against suspicions of heresy. This solution can be made probable if, as has been customary since 1920, the author is linked with Messalianism, on the grounds that a collection of sentences from his writings (the *Asceticon*) was condemned as Messalian in 431 at Ephesus (ACO 1, 1, 7, 117f.). In fact, however, only some of these sentences are to be found verbatim in the author, thus showing that an intermediate step must be assumed between him and Messalianism. If the author's name was replaced by that of Macarius, then "Simeon" may have been the original author; the name is difficult to identify prosopographically. Internal evidence suggests that the author belonged to the period 360-390 and to the hinterland of Antioch. A surer indication of date is the dependence of the treatise *De instituto Christiano* of → Gregory Nyss. on the *Epistola magna* of "Macarius."

The transmission of the work split into several strands. The collections give the material (mainly didactic addresses, erotapokriseis, and letters) in differing arrangements, each with its own peculiarities. The most extensive are the Byz. collections that were put together in the period of the flowering of mysticism beginning in the 10th c. In the modern period the fifty spiritual homilies (*hom.* 1-50; Collection II) were for a long time the only ones known; in addition there are seven "homilies" (*hom.* 51-57). Only quite recently did the sixty-four *logoi* (Collection I) become known, with the *Epistola magna* at their head; the same is true of the forty-three "New homilies" (Collection III), which have not yet been published completely. The *Opuscula* in PG 34 are excerpts from the works as transmitted in the Byz. period. The very comprehensive Syr. tradition is the one that can be followed back the furthest; the Arab. tradition is also highly valuable. Some items have come down under the name of → Ephraem the Syrian.

The author and his vivid language strongly influenced Syr. and Byz. mysticism down to the controversy over hesychasm; in addition, his fifty spiritual homilies are one of the most widely read works of edification in modern times. He offers mystical meditations, descriptions of spiritual experiences, and practical instructions that are utterances of the moment and follow no system, and yet as a whole seek to point the way to perfection. At the same time, they check the enthusiasm of some followers who must in fact have had connections with Messalianism. The struggle against the evil that has its roots in the person and is strongly experienced in the process of interior purification is meant to lead one on the way to perfection, the climax of which is the experience of the Spirit *en aisthēsei kai plērophoria*. What goes on within the soul—i.e., the experience of evil, the struggle against it, and the way to perfection—is described in many images that seek also to describe the supreme feeling of union with God (the Spirit, Christ). An important role is played by prayer as the locus both of the struggle and of absorption; in prayer the participation in the Spirit is also experienced. Prayer is thus the most important of all ascetical virtues. Only with difficulty does the author manage not to describe baptism—in which the Spirit comes to indwell—almost exclusively as a mere pledge. Since, in the course of a general theol. sublimation, all human and ecclesial reality is interpreted spiritually and seen simply as a preliminary stage of truly spiritual reality, all efforts in asceticism, devotion, and even secular things have only a provisional significance. But since the spiritual ideal is reserved to only a few, those addressed are viewed as pneumatics (spirituals) who make up the true church and already experience in their souls the eschatological glory in, for example, an encounter with the heavenly bridegroom. At the same time, they are constantly called to do battle with Satan, because there is no definitive perfection in the here and now.

W: *hom.* 1-50, H. Dörries, E. Klostermann, M. Kroeger, PTS 4 [text]. — D. Stiefenhofer, BKV^2 10 (Munich, 1913) [German trans.]. — *hom.* 51-57, G. L. Marriott (Cambridge, Mass., 1918) [text]. — 64 *Logoi*, H. Berthold, GCS no series number [text]. — *ep. magna*, R. Staats (Göttingen, 1984) [text]. — *New homilies*, E. Klostermann, H. Berthold, TU 72 [text]. — *New homilies* (selections), V. Desprez, SC 275. — *Syriac translation*, W. Strothmann, GOF. S 21 (Wiesbaden, 1981) [Syriac text/German trans.]. — *Arabic translation*, W. Strothmann, Makarios/Symeon, Das arab. Sondergut, GOF. S 11 (Wiesbaden, 1975) [German trans.]. — *Georgian translation*, G. A. Ninua (Tiflis, 1982) [text]. — *Writings under the name of Ephraem*, W. Strothmann, GOF. S 22 (Wiesbaden, 1981) [Greek text].
L: A. Baker, Ps.-Macarius and the Gospel of Thomas:

VigChr 18 (1964) 215-225. — E. Benz, Die protestantische Thebais (Wiesbaden, 1963). — R. Beulay, La lumière sans forme (Chevetogne, 1987), 35-94. — H.-V. Beyer, Die Lichtlehre der Mönche: JÖB 31/2 (1981) 473-512. — M. Canévet, V. Desprez, Macaire 8. (Ps.-Macaire): DSp 10:27-43. — J. Darrouzès, Notes sur les Homélies du Ps.-Macaire: Muséon 67 (1954) 297-309. — A. J. M. Davids, Der Große Brief des M.: FS A. Rohracher (Salzburg, 1969), 78-90. — H. Dörries, Die Messalianer im Zeugnis ihrer Bestreiter: Saec. 21 (1970) 213-226. — idem, Diadochus u. Symeon: idem, Wort u. Stunde 1 (Göttingen, 1966), 352-422. — idem, Die Theologie des Makarios/Symeon (Göttingen, 1978). — idem, Symeon v. Mesopotamien (Leipzig, 1941). — idem, Urteil und Verurteilung. Kirche u. Messalianer: idem, Wort u. Stunde 1 (Göttingen, 1966), 334-351. — O. Hesse, Makarios: TRE 21:730-735. — E. Klostermann, Symeon u. M. (Berlin, 1943). — J. Meyendorff, Messalianism or Antimessalianism: FS J. Quasten (Münster, 1970), 585-590. — G. Quispel, M., das Thomasevangelium u. das Lied von der Perle (Leiden, 1967). — R. Staats, Gregor v. Nyssa u. die Messalianer (Berlin, 1968). — C. Stewart, Working the Earth of the Heart (Oxford, 1991). — W. Strothmann, Die arab. Makariustradition (Göttingen, 1934). — idem, M. u. die Makariosschriften in der syr. Lit.: OrChr 54 (1970) 96-105. — L. Villecourt, La Date et l'Origine des "Homélies Spirituelles": CRAI (1920) 250-258. — W. Völker, Neue Urkunden des Messalianismus?: ThLZ 68 (1943) 129-136. — A. Vööbus, On the Historical Importance of the Legacy of Ps.-Macarius (Stockholm, 1972).

K. FITSCHEN

Macarius II of Hierapolis

Only a letter of M., bishop of Hierapolis 563-575, to an Arm. catholicos is preserved.

W: V. Hakobian, Kanonagirk' Hayoc' (Eriwan, 1971), 216-229 [Armenian text].

G. RÖWEKAMP

Macarius of Magnesia

M., from Magnesia (in Caria or Lydia), author of the work *Apokritikos ē Monogenēs pros Hellēnas* (*apoc.*), is perhaps identical with a like-named bishop of Magnesia who, acc. to Photius (*cod.* 59), accused Bishop Heraclides of Origenist tendencies at the Synod of the Oak in 403. Information about the author must depend entirely on the interpretation of his work.

Of the work's original five books only the larger part of the second, the whole of the third and fourth, and a fragment of the fifth have been preserved. Information on the content of the first book is given in an overview of the whole that has been handed down, along with a list of the titles of the chapters in books 1-3. Most scholars date the work to the late 4th or early 5th c. In a fictitious dialogue M. refutes a pagan critic who finds inconsistencies in the NT. Scholars have produced various hypotheses as to the source of the pagan criticism: the confident identification of the source as a 4th-c. excerpt from Porphyry's work *Against the Christians* has been replaced by more recent hypotheses, such as that M. himself made independent use of Porphyry's work and did not take over objections mechanically or that he had before him a Neoplatonic-style work of ca. 370, compiled in the atmosphere of the 4th-c. pagan reaction. Some scholars have seen in the language of M.'s replies the rhetorical style of that time. In fact, the author does not get involved in the positivistic kind of criticism that depends on the literal sense of the NT; his arguments, which are in good measure supported by an allegorical explanation of scripture, are based on the hermeneutical presupposition that the scriptures must be read as a whole. M.'s work, independently of a definitive dating and its place in the history of dogma, is a witness to pagan criticism of Christianity and the state of intrachristian theol. discussion in the late 4th c.

The fragments of homilies on Gen (*fr.*) that have come down under M.'s name are, except for one, not authentic.

W: *apocr.*, C. Blondel, P. Foucart (Paris, 1876) [text]. — T. W. Crafer (London, 1919) [English trans.]. — F. Corsaro (Catania, 1968) [text/Italian trans. of "Objections"]. — G. Mercati: StT 95 (1941) 49-74 [chs. I-III superscriptions]. — R. Waelkens (Leuven/Louvain, 1974), 303-305 [frag. of bk. 5/French trans.]. — *fr.*, J. B. Pitra (Rome, 1888), 34-35 [text/Latin trans.].
L: G. Bardy, M.: DThC 9, 1456-1459. — F. Corsaro, L'apocritico e le sacre scritture: NDid 7 (1957) 1-24. — idem, Dottrina eucaristica: Convivium Dominicum (Catania, 1959), 67-86. — idem, Reazione pagana e l'apocritico: Quaderni Catanesi 6 (1984) 173-195. — R. Goulet, Porphyre et M.: StPatr 15 (1984) 448-452. — idem, La théologie de M.: MSR 34 (1977) 45-69; 145-180. — A. v. Harnack, Kritik des NT (Leipzig, 1911). — J. Palm, Textkritisches zum Apokritikos des M. (Lund, 1961). — G. Schalkhausser, Schriften des M. (Leipzig, 1907). — R. Waelkens, "Economie" dans l'apocriticos (Leuven/Louvain, 1974).

M. BIERMANN

Macarius of Tkow

Acc. to Copt. tradition, M. was bishop of Tkow in Upper Egypt and in this capacity accompanied Dioscurus to Chalcedon and supported him there against his theol. opponents; the life of M. (*vita M.*) is attributed to Dioscurus. Throughout his life M. remained a stubborn opponent of the Chalcedonian Creed and had to pay for his rejection of the *Tomus Leonis* with flight and finally with death. Of M.'s

work a Copt. homily (*hom.*) on archangel Michael has survived.

S: *vita M.*, D. W. Johnson, CSCO 415f. [text/English trans.].
W: *hom.*, G. Lafontaine, Homélie sur St. Michel: Muséon 92 (1979) 301-320.

P. BRUNS

Macrobius

Following Encolpius and preceding Lucianus, M. was bishop of the Donatist community of Rome (344/347–366/367). He was the fourth to hold that office. Acc. to Optatus (2.4) he was active in Rome in 366/367. He was very probably the author of the *Passio Maximiniani et Isaak*, which he wrote in order to strengthen his Donatist brothers in the faith during the persecution of Macarius (347/348). He himself left Carthage at that time and went to Rome. It is less certain (Gennadius, *vir. ill.* 5) that M. was author of the treatise *Ad confessores et virgines*. A. von Harnack tried to identify that work with the Ps.-Cyprianic *De singularitate clericorum*.

W: *passio*, PL 8:767ff.
L: A. v. Harnack, Der Pseudocyprianische Traktat de singularitate clericorum (Leipzig, 1903). — P. Monceaux, Histoire littéraire 3 (Brussels, 1966 = Paris, 1905), 542. — W. H. C. Frend, The Donatist Church (Oxford, 1952), 186f. — PAC 662.

W. GEERLINGS

Malchion, Presbyter

Acc. to Eusebius (*h.e.* 7.29.1f.; 7.30.1-71) and Jerome (*vir. ill.* 71), who depends on him, M. was a presbyter and head of a school of rhetoric in Antioch. At the second Council of Antioch (268) he is said to have uncovered the errors of Paul of Samosata and to have been author of a letter sent to Dionysius of Rome and Maximus Alex. in the council's name. In contrast to Paul of Samasata M. is said to have represented rather a christology of union, that is, a natural union of Logos and flesh: The Logos is in the human being as the soul is in the body. There are still strong doubts about the tradition of a dialogue between M. and Paul (*fr.*). This work seems to have been edited under Apollinarist influence.

W: *fr.*, H. de Riedmatten, Les actes du procès de Paul de Samosate (Fribourg, Switzerland, 1952), 136-158.
L: G. Bardy, Paul de Samosate. Étude historique (Leuven/Louvain, 1929). — P. Bruns, Den Menschen mit dem Himmel verbinden (Leuven/Louvain, 1995), 224f., 228f. — R. M. Hübner, Die Hauptquelle des Epiphanius (haer. 65) über Paulus v. Samosata: ZKG 90 (1979) 201-

220. — M. Richard, M. et Paul de Samosate. Le témoignage d'Eusèbe de Césarée: idem, Opera minora 2 (Tournai, 1977), Nr. 25. — H. de Riedmatten, op. cit.

T. Böhm

Mambre Vercanol

Acc. to Arm. tradition, M. was a brother of Moses of Khorene and a member of a group of translators. He composed a lost history of Armenia (*hist.*) and homilies (*hom.*).

W: *hist.*, PP Mechitaristae, Koriun magistri, M. aliorumque opera (Venice, 1833) [text]; *hom.* (Venice, 1894) [text]. — S. Weber, BKV² 58:3-27 [German trans.].
L: N. Andrikean, M.: Baz. 62 (1904) 298-304, 352-358.

P. Bruns

Mani, Gospel of

The Manichees made use of the canonical gospels but also of a work resembling the *Diatessaron* of → Tatian and of various Chr. and gnostic gospels such as those of → Peter, → Philip, and → Thomas. They may also have had a "Gospel of the 12 Apostles," of which Theodore Abu Qurra speaks.

But the actual gospel of Mani (M.) (b. 216; d. 274 or 277) is the so-called living gospel named in many catalogues of writings (e.g., *Acta Archelai* 62.6; Cyril Jerus., *catech.* 6.22; Epiphanius, *haer.* 66.2.9). It is one of the seven canonical works of M. (the others, being "non-Christian," are not to be discussed here) and possesses, in its *Ardhang*, an illustrated appendix. Preserved are two fragments (M 172; M 17) from Turfan and a fragment in the Mani codex of Cologna (CMC), which, in a biography of M., cites from the prologue of the gospel of M. On the basis of these fragments it is clear that from the literary viewpoint the work is not a gospel but a doctrinal piece containing the "lifegiving message" of M., who understands himself to have "become from the Father" and to be proclaimer of the truth that he saw with the Father.

W: *M* 172; *M* 17, APAW. PH 1904, Anhang, Abh. II, 100-103, 25-27 [text]. — CMC, L. Koenen, C. Roemer, Der Kölner Mani-Kodex (PapyCol 14) (Cologne, 1988) [text/German trans.]. — NTApo⁶ 1:325-329 [German trans.].
L: K. Rudolph, Gnosis u. spätantike Religionsgeschichte (NHS 42) (Leiden, 1996), 655-685. — W. Sundermann, Chr. Evangelientexte: MIOF 14 (1968) 386-405.

G. Röwekamp

Marcellinus, Comes

M., an Illyrian, was chancellor of the later Emperor Justinian I (a close relationship remained even after the latter's accession) and subsequently became a priest.

As a continuation of the works of → Eusebius Caes. and → Jerome, he composed, in Latin, a chronicle of the years 379-518 (*chron.*), which he himself expanded in a second edition to include 519-534 (*terminus post quem* for his death) (*chron.* II). An unknown writer continued the work down to 548 (*auct. chron.* II). The presentation, which uses as a framework the east Roman consuls and the indiction calculation based on fifteen-year taxation periods, is limited, as M. says in the short preface (almost exclusively), to the eastern part of the empire with Constantinople as focal point. Along with the most important polit. events, the significant eccles. events are also concisely recorded, the strictly orthodox position of the author being clear from what he says of the Nestorians and other heretics. He seems in addition to have set some hopes on the reconquest, begun by Justinian, of the lost provinces of the West.

For sources, M. makes extensive use chiefly of → Orosius and → Gennadius of Marseilles, to the point of verbatim similarities. The chronicle nonetheless has a quite high value, espec. for the history of east Rome.

Acc. to statements of Cassiodorus (*inst.* 1.17.1; 1.25.1) M. composed at least one other work in which, among other things, he dealt with Constantinople and Jerusalem from a historical and topographical viewpoint.

W: PL 51:913-948. — T. Mommsen, Chronica Minora 2 (Berlin, 1894), 37-108 [text]. — M. Gusso, Index Marcellinianus (Hildesheim, 1996). — B. Croke, M. on Dara: Phoe. 38 (1984) 77-88 [frags. from *De Temporum Qualitatibus et Positionibus Locorum*].
L: M. Baldwin, M.: ODB 2:1296. — B. Croke, The Manufacture of a Turning Point: Chiron 13 (1983) 81-119. — A. Demandt, Die Spätantike (Munich, 1989), 23. — O. Holger-Egger, Die Chronik des M.: NA 2 (1877) 49-109. — PLRE 2:710f. — M. Schanz, C. Hosius, G. Krüger, Geschichte der röm. Lit. 4/2 (Munich, 1920), 110-112. — S. Teillet, Des Goths à la nation gothique (Paris, 1984), 257-270.

U. Hamm

Marcellinus, Presbyter (Luciferian)

M., a Luciferian presbyter in Rome, is known only as co-author of a petition addressed to the emperor in Constantinople in 383/384: *De confessione verae fidei et ostentatione sacrae communionis* (so-called *Libellus precum*) of → Faustinus (Gennadius, *vir. ill.* 16), which sought to win recognition of Luciferian orthodoxy and imperial protection from attacks by the Catholics. Although Isidore of Seville (*vir. ill.* 14) attributes the work to M. alone, the latter's literary contribution is regarded as small. Theodosius responded to the petition in 384 with a rescript to Cynegius, *praefectus praetorio*.

W: *Libellus precum* with rescript of Theodosius: O. Günther, CSEL 35/1:5-46. — O. Günther, M. Simonetti, CCL 69:359-392.
L: W. Enßlin, M. nr. 36: PRE 14/2:1449. — M. R. Green, The Supporters of Antipope Ursinus: JThS 22 (1971) 531-538. — G. Krüger, Lucifer, Bischof v. Calaris u. das Schisma der Luciferianer (Hildesheim, 1969 = Leipzig, 1886), 62f., 77-88.

M. DURST

Marcellus of Ancyra

I. Life: Born probably ca. 280, M., already a bishop, is mentioned for the first time in connection with the Synod of Ancyra in 314. At the Council of Nicaea 325, and afterwards, he engaged zealously in the struggle against Arius and the Eusebians. A book opposing them and handed to Emperor Constantine in person led, between 330 and 337, to his condemnation and banishment by a synod of Constantinople and then to the writing of two anti-Marcellian works by Eusebius Caes. (*Contra Marcellum* and *De ecclesiastica theologia*). After Constantine's death in 337 M. was able to return to his see but was soon deposed again and betook himself, with Athanasius, to Rome. There, despite written intervention from the Eusebians, he was rehabilitated by a synod in 341. Before that, in order to prove his orthodoxy, he had sent Bishop Julius of Rome a letter containing his profession of faith. The papal decision was not accepted in the East. Instead, M. was several times condemned: 341 at the synod held in connection with the dedication of the Great Church; 342 or 343 at the eastern partial Synod of Sardica (while the western part sided with him); 344, together with his follower Photinus of Sirmium, in the so-called *Ekthesis makrostichos*; and finally even after his death by the Council of Constantinople in 381. In this situation M. probably continued to seek contact with Bishop Liberius of Rome. He died in Ancyra in 374.

II. Works: Only 128 fragments (*fr.*) remain, mostly from the writings of opponent Eusebius Caes., of M.'s once comprehensive "book," written before 337, that was destroyed by synodal order and whose title is unknown. Although the form of the text is not without problems, the fragments nonetheless give a reliable basis for inferring M.'s position and possibly even attributing some pseudonymous works to him. In these fragments M. attacks the Eusebians, espec. Asterius the Sophist, and in the process develops his own theol. conception. Apart from the fragments there is only one other text transmitted under M.'s name: the brief but complete *Epistula ad Iulium* (*ep. Iul.*), written probably in 340/341 and to be found in Epiphanius (*haer.* 72.2f.). Part of its quite personal explanation of M.'s convictions regarding the faith is a form of the early Roman creed.

Over the course of time since 1949, some other texts have been attributed to M.: the fragmentary *De sancta ecclesia* (*eccl. fr.*) that goes under the name of → Athimus of Nicomedia; the Ps.-Athanasian *Sermo maior de fide* = *Epistula ad Antiochenos* (*serm. fid.*); *Contra theopaschitas* = *Epistula ad Liberium* (*theopasch.*); *Expositio fidei* (*exp. fid.*); and *De incarnatione dei verbi et contra Arianos* (*inc. et c. Ar.*). But opinions on these works are at times sharply divided. There is thus far a general acceptance only of *eccl. fr.*; some reservations have already been voiced regarding *theopasch*. Meanwhile there is discussion of still other possible Marcelliana.

III. Importance: Against the ideas of a plurality of hypostases and a subordinate Logos in the Origenist tradition M. stresses the oneness of God in a single person or hypostasis and the indivisibility of the divine unit despite its expansion into a triad. Although he was defamed, on the basis of his monarchistic-sounding conception, as a "new Sabellius" or supporter of Paul of Samosata or of the Jews, he was directly or indirectly given a positive reception by many theologians (e.g., Athanasius and Gregory Nyss.) in the anti-Arian dispute. In addition, he seems to have given important stimuli to the development of christology and to "political theology." After having long had the reputation of being one of the more important theologians of the 4th c., M. has very recently become a subject of intense scholarship.

W: *fr., ep. Iul.*, E. Klostermann, G. C. Hansen, GCS 14 (Berlin, ³1991), 185-215 [text]. — M. Vinzent, Die Frgm., 1997 [text/German trans./comm.]. — W. Gericke, Marcell (Halle, 1940), 192-247 [German trans.]. — *fr.*, K. Seibt, Theologie des Markell (Berlin, 1994), 249-459 [German trans./comm.]. — Anthimus, *eccl. fr.*, G. Mercati: StT 5 (1901) 95-98 [text]. — Athanasius, *serm. fid.*, E. Schwartz: SBAW. PPH 1924, 6 [text]. — H. Nordberg, Athanasiana 1 (Helsinki, 1962), 57-71 [text]. — *theopasch.*, M. Tetz: ZKG 83 (1972) 145-191 [text/comm.]. — *exp. fid.*, H. Nordberg, op. cit., 49-56 [text]. — *inc. et c. Ar.*, PG 26:984-1028.
L: G. Feige, Lehre Markells (Leipzig, 1991). — idem, Konzil v. Nizäa: FS 600 Jahre Univ. Erfurt (Leipzig, 1992), 277-296. — W. Gericke, op. cit. — R. C. P. Hanson, Authorship: PIA

83, C, 9, (1983) 251-254. — A. Heron, Ps.-Athanasian Dialogues: JThS 24 (1973) 101-122. — R. M. Hübner, Einheit des Leibes Christi bei Gregor v. Nyssa (Leiden, 1974). — idem, Soteriologie, Trinität, Christologie: FS W. Breuning (Düsseldorf, 1985), 175-196. — idem, Schrift des Apolinarius gegen Photin (Berlin, 1989). — W. Kinzig, C. Markschies, M. Vinzent, Tauffragen u. Bekenntnis (Berlin et al., 1999). — J. T. Lienhard, Research: TS 43 (1982) 486-503. — idem, Contra Marcellum (Freiburg i.Br., 1986). — A. Logan, Polemics: StPatr 19 (1989) 189-197. — F. Loofs, Trinitätslehre Marcell's: SPAW. PH (1902) 764-781. — idem, M.: RE 12:259-265. — idem, Paulus v. Samosata, TU 44/5 (Leipzig, 1924). — T. E. Pollard, M.: FS J. Daniélou (Paris, 1972), 187-196. — G. M. Rapisarda, La questione: NDid 23 (1973) 23-54. — M. Richard, Un opuscule: MSR 6 (1949) 5-28. — C. Riedweg, Ps.-Justin (M. ?), Ad Graecos de vera religione (Basel, 1994). — F. Scheidweiler, Verfasser?: ByZ 47 (1954) 333-357. — idem, Paul v. Samosata : ZNW 46 (1955) 116-129. — idem, M.: ibid., 202-214. — K. Seibt, M.: TRE 22:83-89. — idem, op. cit. — M. Simonetti, Su alcune opere: RSLR 9 (1973) 313-319. — idem, Ancora sulla paternità: VetChr 11 (1974) 333-343. — M. Tetz, Theologie I-III: ZKG 75 (1964) 217-270; 79 (1968) 3-42; 83 (1972) 145-194. — idem, Orthodoxie: ZNW 66 (1975) 194-222. — M. Vinzent, Gegner: ZKG 105 (1994) 285-328. — idem, Gottes Wesen, Logos, Weisheit und Kraft bei Asterius v. Kappadokien u. M.: VigChr 47 (1993) 170-191. — T. Zahn, M. (Gotha, 1867).

G. FEIGE

Marcian, Monk

Acc. to Theodoret, *h.e.* 25, an ascetic named M. was active in the Syro-Antiochene area between 361 and 378. He produced primarily ascetical-practical works that have come down to us in Greek and Syriac. The treatise in Greek on faith is to be attributed rather to the author of the same name who is mentioned in Zacharias Rhetor, *h.e.* 3.3, who was probably from Bethlehem, and lived 410-492.

W: J. Lebon, Le Moine M. (Leuven/Louvain, 1968) [text/French trans.]. — I. A. Khalifé, Traductions arabes: MUSJ 28 (1949/50) 115-125.
L: J. Kirchmeyer, M. v. Bethlehem: TU 80 (1962) 341-359. — A. van Roey, Remarques sur le moine Marcien: TU 115 (1975) 160-177.

P. BRUNS

Marcion, Author of the *Martyrdom of Polycarp*

Acc. to the *Martyrium Polycarpi* (*M. Polyc.*) 20.1, a M. is the author of the work in the form of a letter from the community of Smyrna to the community of Philomelium and the entire church (see *M. Polyc.*, praescr.). The work exhorts to an evangelical attitude to martyrdom and a suitable remembrance of the

martyrs (→ Martyrs, Acts of). If *M. Polyc.* 19 is the original end of the letter, then M. has his place only in 20f. and in the epilogue of the history of reception attested by the Moscow ms.

W: A. Lindemann, H. Paulsen, Apostolische Väter (Tübingen, 1992) [text/German trans.].
L: G. Buschmann, M. Polyc. (Berlin, 1994). — B. Dehandschutter, The M. Polyc., A Century of Research: ANRW II 27/1 (1993) 485-522.

H. KÖNIG

Marcion of Sinope

Our knowledge of M. comes solely from anti-Marcionite literature and must therefore be reconstructed with attention to the polemical purpose, the tradition of antiheretical commonplaces, and the literary characteristics of each source. The most important early witnesses are Justin, Irenaeus, Tertullian, Clement Alex., and Origen. The most comprehensive effort at reconstruction is that of A. von Harnack who permanently shaped the image of M. in the 19th c. but whose understanding of M. has since been thought to be in need of revision.

Little that is certain about M.'s person and life can be gotten from the anti-Marcionite sources: he came from Sinope in Pontus, was a *nauclerus*, i.e., a ship owner or overseas trader (Tertullian, *praescr.* 30.1; *adv. Marc.* 1.18.4), who joined the Roman Chr. community ca. 140 but broke away from it in 144 (Tertullian, *praescr.* 30.2; *adv. Marc.* 1.19.2). M. then began his own missionary activity, which was successful with many (Justin, *1 apol.* 26.5; 58.1f.). Marcionites are attested in the West down into the 4th c.; in the East into the 5th (e.g., Theodoret, *ep.* 81).

The chief witness to M.'s work and teaching is Tertullian. He had M.'s gospel before him as he composed his *Adversus Marcionem* (1.19.4), as he did a letter from M.'s hand (1.1.6; 4.4). M.'s Bible, of which Justin still knew nothing (*1 apol.* 26.5; 58.1; *dial.* 35.5f.) but of which Irenaeus spoke critically (*haer.* 1.27.2), included the gospel of Luke and ten letters of Paul (excluding the pastoral letters and Heb). M. purified these texts of all Judaizing statements, using the usual methods of ancient textual criticism. He described the hermeneutical basis for his procedure in the *Antitheses,* which take as the starting point the Pauline opposition of law and gospel and explain that in addition to the OT creator God, who is just but also author of all evil (Iren., *haer.* 1.27.2; Clement, *str.* 2.32.1), there is an alien God of pure goodness, who reveals himself, suddenly and unannounced, through his Christ (Tert., *adv.*

Marc. 3.20.2f.). The OT, the laws, and the manifestation of the creator God's will (Tert., *adv. Marc.* 4.1) are thus the revelation solely of the demiurge and know nothing of the alien, good God. That is all without meaning for faith in the good God (Iren., *haer.* 1.27.2). M.'s excisions from the NT text (Pauline letters and Luke) are to be interpreted against this background, as is his barring of an alleg.-typological exegesis of the OT that points to Christ and his revelation (Tert. *adv. Marc.* 5.18.10; Origen, *comm. in Mt.* 15.3; *comm. in Roman* 2.13). Only through Christ is the true nature of the law and sin discovered. While the law in the world of the creator God can be regarded as right, good, and even holy, since it forbids evil, which the good God likewise does not will (Tert., *adv. Marc.* 1.27.1), it is nonetheless unmasked by the revelation of the alien, true God as being essentially seductive (5.13.14) insofar as it leads human beings, out of fear (Tert., *adv. Marc.* 1.27.3) of threatened punishments, to please the creator God by obeying his commandments (Iren., *haer.* 1.27.3). Sin is therefore less a transgressing of the commandments than a fearful fixation on the creator God and his threat of judgment, all of which is excluded by the redemption which the alien God bestows out of pure love and mercy and effects through the suffering and death of Christ. This is confirmed by M.'s interpretation of Christ's descent into the lower world: there the unjust of the OT hasten to meet him, while the just persevere in their expectation of the demiurge and his redemption (Tert., *adv. Marc.* 4.9.13f.; Iren., *haer.* 1.27.3). Those therefore who received the revelation of the good, alien God must turn away completely from the demiurge and his evil creation. For this reason M. urges upon the baptized a radical asceticism and complete sexual continence: they are not to place themselves in the service of the creator (Clem., *str.* 3.12; 3.105.1).

M. posed a considerable danger to the church of the 2nd c., as can be judged from the violent reaction to him (Clem., *str.* 3.25.2: M. "the colossus who fights against God"). But his appearance on the scene also compelled the theologians of the time to reflect on the foundations and content of the Chr. faith. Even though M. did not create the idea and reality of a Chr. Bible but rather by his own Bible attested to the complex development of the NT text, the fact is that in the debate with M. (and with gnosticism) about the authority of the OT and its connection with the message of Christ as well as about the normative character of the Christ tradition the NT canon was advanced and criteria were developed that were to guarantee the truth of the tradition (Iren., *haer.* 3.1.1; 3.2.1; 1.10.3; 2.27.1; etc.)

While the idea of the good God being foreign to the world seems to be peculiar to the teaching of Marcion (Tert., *adv. Marc.* 1.23; the same motif in Clem., *str.* 2.74f.), there are observable contacts with gnostic ideas of the inferiority of the demiurge and his creation as well as of the sudden onset of redemption, which puts an end to the lack of knowledge of the true God (Clem., *str.* 2.36.1); but the dualism of the Marcionite image of God is not the same as in gnostic approaches. In addition, M.'s teaching is ungnostic in its lack of any mythological-cosmological speculation. Particular aspects of M.'s doctrine show contact with philosophical traditions; thus the assessment of the law as not divine when seen from the viewpoint of the alien God and fear of the demiurge as motivation for keeping the commandments are similarly attested ever since the Sophistic enlightenment; the lack of any connection between the good God and evil (to put it in Marcionite terms) and the alienation of the good God from the defective world of the demiurge are reminiscent of Epicurus; the idea of the *apatheia* of the good God has a Stoic coloring in Tertullian's report (*adv. Marc.* 2.24). In any case, the tension between, on the one hand, the basic principle of philosophical thought about God since Plato, namely, that God is not the author of evil, and, on the other, the vitally anthropomorphic picture of God in the OT must have led to M.'s theology of the two Gods. The fact then that M.'s adversaries repeatedly link him with philosophy (Iren., *haer.* 3.24.2: Epicurus; Tert., *adv Marc.* 1.25.3, etc.: Epicurus; 5.19.7, etc.: the Stoa; Clem. *str.* 3.12-21: Plato) should not automatically be taken as an antiheretical commonplace, acc. to which heresy is faith corrupted by philosophy (e.g., Tert., *praescr.* 7) but may have come from the perception of these similarities.

W: A. v. Harnack, Marcion. Das Evangelium vom Fremden Gott, 1923 (Darmstadt, 1960ff. = Leipzig, ²1924) [Marcionite citations and references in patristic literature].
L: B. Aland, M. /Marcioniten: TRE 22:89-101 (literature). — J. Delobel, The Lord's prayer in the textual tradition. A critique of recent theories and their view on M.'s role: The New Testament in early christianity, ed. J. M. Sevrin (Leuven/Louvain, 1989), 293-309. — C. Giannotto, Gli gnostici e M. La risposta di Ireneo: La Bibbia nell'Antichità Cristiana, ed. E. Norelli (Bologna, 1993), 235-274. — W. Kinzig, The Title of the New Testament in the Second and Third Centuries: JThS 45 (1994) 519-544. — G. May, M. nel suo tempo: CrSt 14 (1993) 205-220. — E. Norelli, Note sulla soteriologia di M.: Aug. 35 (1995) 218-306. — idem, M. lettore dell'epistola ai Romani: CrSt 15 (1994) 635-675. — A. Orbe, En torno al modalismo de M.: Gr. 71 (1990) 43-

65. — idem, Marcionitica: Aug. 31 (1991) 195-244. — idem, Hacia la doctrina marcionita de la redención: Gr. 74 (1993) 45-74. — G. Quispel, M. and the text of the NT: VigChr 52 (1998) 349-360. — H. Räisänen, M. and the origin of Christian anti-Judaism: Temenos 33 (1997) 121-135. — U. Schmid, M. u. sein Apostolos (Berlin, 1995). — M. Vinzent, Christ's Resurrection: the Pauline Basis of Marcion's Teaching: StPatr 31 (1997) 225-233.

H. KÖNIG

Marius of Avenches

M., born ca. 530 in Burgundy, was bishop of Avenches beginning in 574; he moved his episcopal seat to Lausanne and died in 594. He composed a continuation of the universal chronicle of Prosper Tiro of Aquitania for the years 455-481. M., who was proud of his Roman descent, expressed his satisfaction at the reconquest of Italy and North Africa; otherwise his work gives information primarily about the Franks, Burgundians, Goths, and Lombards.

W: PL 72:793-802. — T. Mommsen, MGH. AA 11:232-239 [text]. — J. Favrod (Lausanne, 1991) [text/French trans.]. L: W. Eltester, M.: PRE 14:1822f.

G. RÖWEKAMP

Marius Claudius Victorius

M., who died between 425 and 450, was a rhetor in Marseilles. He was author of a hexametric poem, *Alethia*, in three books; it is introduced by a prayer (*aleth. praef.*) that is a kind of confession of faith. Since Gennadius (*vir. ill.* 61 [Richardson]) speaks of a fourth book, a fourth book may have been lost. The *aleth.*, written ca. 425, is a didactic bibl. epic that was probably intended for the instruction of youth. It ranges from the story of creation to the destruction of Sodom and Gomorrah. M. depends on numerous models (Virgil, Ovid, espec. Lucretius; Prudentius, Paulinus of Nola, espec. Ambrose's *hex.*); he does not simply paraphrase the bibl. text in verse form but rearranges it, adds explanations, introduces excursuses, and thus shows the bibl. epic to have a certain independence from the scriptures. The work, in which philosophical and espec. Platonic elements are also found, serves to justify God's punishing interventions. Also attributed to M. is the poem *De nativitate, vita, passione et resurrectione Iesu Christi* (*vit. dom.*).

W: *aleth. praef., aleth.*, P. F. Hovingh, CCL 128:116-193. — C. Schenkl, CSEL 16/1:337-498. — P. F. Hovingh, M., Alethia (Groningen, 1955) [French trans./commentary on the precatio and 1.1-170]. — A. Staat, De cultuurbeschouwing (Amsterdam, 1952) [commentary on 2.1-

202]. — *vit. dom.*, A. Mai, CAVC 5 (Rome, 1833), 382-385 [text].
L: A. Di Berardino (ed.), Patrologia 3 (Turin, 1983), 301-304. — R. Herzog, Bibelepik 1 (Munich, 1975), LIVf. — H. H. Homey, Studien zur Alethia (Bonn, 1972). — G. Malsbary, Epic exegesis: Florilegium 7 (1985) 55-83. — I. Opelt, Trinitätstheologie in der Alethia: eadem, Paradeigmata poetica Christiana (Düsseldorf, 1988), 106-112. — M. Schanz, C. Hosius, G. Krüger, Geschichte der röm. Lit 4/2 (Munich, 1959 = 1920), 363-365.

B. WINDAU

Marius Mercator

We have only a few biog. details for M. He was born probably in Africa and lived, presumably as a layman, in a Lat. monastery in Thrace. This disciple of Augustine, supporter of Cyril, and determined adversary of Pelagianism and Nestorianism died after 431.

M.'s entire work is an adamant attack on the teachings of Pelagius and Nestorius. He does not offer an original theology but takes that of Augustine and Cyril as his guide and provides some important evidence for the history of Nestorianism and the Pelagian controversies. In 418, along with two accompanying letters, M. sent Augustine two now lost anti-Pelagian works, directed espec. against Julian of Eclanum (Aug., *ep.* 293). In 429-431, for the instruction of his Latin-speaking monastic brothers, M. composed short treatises of his own and prepared numerous translations from Greek.

1. Writings against Pelagianism: the *Commonitorium super nomine Caelestii*, a memorandum addressed to the church of Constantinople and Emperor Theodosius II, composed in Gr. in 429, and surviving only in M.'s own Lat. translation, presents the teachings of Caelestius, Pelagius, and Julian and describes their condemnation. The Lat. *Commonitorium adversum haeresim Pelagii*, from the period after 429, uses Augustine's *Opus imperfectum contra Iulianum* and citations from Julian's *Ad Florum* and *Ad Turbantium* to attack the latter's rejection of the doctrine of original sin. Other works: the translation of four anti-Pelagian sermons of Nestorius and of a letter of Nestorius to Caelestius.

2. Writings against Nestorianism: The *Refutatio symboli Theodori Mopsuesteni*, a translation and refutation of Theodore's profession of faith; the *Comparatio dogmatum Pauli Samosateni et Nestorii*, 429, which points out the similarities between the teachings of Nestorius and those of Paul of Samosata, Marcellus of Ancyra, Photinus, and Theodore; the translation of: five sermons of Nestorius on the

Theotokos title, an exchange of letters between Cyril and Nestorius, and excerpts of Cyril from the writings of Nestorius.

After 533, a Scythian monk assembled M.'s writings, along with writings of Cyril and excerpts from works of Diodorus of Tarsus, Theodore Mops., and Theodoret, in the co-called *Collectio Ρalatina* (→ Canonical Collections).

W: PL 48. — ACO 1, 5, 5-70 [text].
L: E. Amann, M.: DThC 9/2:2481-2486. — W. Eltester, M.: PRE 14/2:1831-1835. — S. Prete, M. polimista antipelagiano (Turin, 1958). — idem, M., Commonitoria (Bologna, 1959). — idem, M. I memoriali antipelagiani (Siena, 1960). — O. Wermelinger, M.: DSp 10:610-615.

C. Schmidt

Marius Victorinus

I. Life: C. Marius Victorinus (M.) was born in Africa between 281 and 291. In 354 this celebrated *rhetor urbis Romae*, who had been accepted into the senatorial class, was honored with a statue in the Forum of Trajan. His acceptance of the Chr. faith (ca. 356) made a strong impression on Augustine. M. died ca. 365, after laying down his offices because of an edict of Emperor Julian in 363 (Aug., *conf.* 8; Jerome, *cir. ill.* 101).

II. Works: M.'s works on philosophy and the *artes liberales*, which were probably composed before his baptism, exerted an immense influence either directly or through intermediaries (Boethius, Cassiodorus, Isidore): the *Ars Grammatica* (*gramm.*), the commentary on Cicero's *De inventione* (*rhet.*), the translation of Porphyry's *Isagoge* (see Boethius: CSEL 48:1-132), the *De definitionibus* (*defin.*), *De syllogismis hypotheticis* (*syll.*), and *In Topica Ciceronis* (*top. Cic.*). In these writings on the trivium (grammar, rhetoric, dialectic) M. laid the literary foundations of the Middle Ages. The *libri Platonicorum* brought Plotinus and espec. Porphyry to the West. These "substantial books" provided the natural theology that opened the way to faith for Augustine (see *conf.* 7.9.13; *civ.* 8.12; *Acad.* 2.1.5); because of them M. has also been called the "inaugurator" of a Platonic Christianity.

Beginning in 359, M. defended the consubstantiality of the Son and the Spirit in nine works (*Ad Candidum Arianum* [*Adv. Arrium*], *De homoousio recipiendo* [*homoous.*], *De generatione divini Verbi* [*gen. div. verb.*]) and three hymns (Candidus the Arian is regarded as a literary fiction). In shedding light on the Trinity, this first great metaphysician in the Lat. language harked back not to Plotinus's sub-

ordinationist henocentrism but to Porphyry, who identified the One with Being and developed a coordinated Triad: God includes the phases of the One-Being who reposes in himself, the outgoing movement, and the return to himself through knowledge. In the process, M. makes extensive use of the NT and also discusses hermeneutical questions, such as the justification of using the term *homoousios*. These "obscure" (Jerome) books, composed *more dialectico* and intelligible only to the educated, are a splendid defense of faith in the Trinity. Because the philosophical works have been lost it is only the writings on the Trinity that give evidence of M.'s great merits in the area of Lat. conceptual language. M. left his mark on western thought through a great many new terms such as *ens, existentia, subsistentia,* and *intelligibilis*.

Of the commentaries on Paul (after 363) those on Eph, Gal, and Phil (*in Eph., Gal., Phil.*) have survived. In simple language M. explains justification by faith and the mystery of Christ. Along with Neoplatonic influences (preexistence of the soul, depreciation of the body) there is the striking influence of the Marcionite prologues which M. used uncritically (anti-Judaism, primacy of Paul and of revelation as understood in Gal 1:1ff.!).

The *Liber ad Iustinum manichaeum, De verbis scripturae,* and *De physicis* (PL 8:999-1014, 1295-1210) are not from M.

W: *gramm.,* J. Mariotti (Florence, 1967) [text]. — *rhet.,* C. Halm, Rhetores Latini Minores (Leipzig, 1863), 153-304 [text]. — *defin.,* T. Stangl, Tulliana et Mario-Victoriniana (Munich, 1888) [text]. — P. Hadot, M. (Paris, 1971), 331-362 [text]. — *syll.,* P. Hadot, op. cit., 323ff. [text summary] *top. Cic.,* P. Hadot, op. cit., 313ff [summary] — *Adv. Arrium, homous., gen. div. verb., hymn.,* P. Henry, P. Hadot, CSEL 83/1. — P. Henry, P. Hadot, SC 68f. — P. Hadot, K. Brenke, Chr. Platonismus (Zurich, 1967) [German trans.]. — *in Eph., Gal., Phil.,* F. Gori, CSEL 83/2.
L: W. Erdt, M., der erste lat. Pauluskommentator (Frankfurt a.M., 1980). — P. Hadot, Porphyre et Victorinus (Paris, 1968). — idem, M. (Paris, 1971). — HLL 5:342-354. — K. T. Schäfer, M. u. die marcionitischen Prologe: RBen 80 (1970) 7-16. — A. Ziegenaus, Die trinitarische Ausprägung der göttlichen Seinsfülle nach M. (Munich, 1972).

A. Ziegenaus

Mark, Literature about

In a 17th c. ms., discovered in 1958, from the Mar Sabas monastery near Jerusalem, there are excerpts from a supposed letter of Clement Alex. to a certain Theodore, in which he speaks of a "more spiritual" version of the gospel of Mark and cites a section of it, which would come between Mk 10:34 and 10:35.

This "secret gospel of Mark" was probably not an original Aramaic version of Mk (even from the 1st c.), as the discoverer thought but an expansion of it by telling the story of Lazarus in the style of Mk.

W: M. Smith, Clement of Alexandria and the Secret Gospel of Mark (Cambridge, Mass., 1973 = Auf der Suche nach dem historischen Jesus [Freiburg i.Br., 1974]). — O. Stählin, U. Treu, Clemens Alexandrinus 4, GCS (Berlin, ²1980), XVIIf. — NTApo⁶ 1:89-92 [German trans.] (literature).
L: S. Levin, The Early History of Christianity in Light of the Secret Gospel of Mark: ANRW II 25/6 (1988) 4270-4292.

Of the *Acts of Mark* (M.) two Gk. texts have been published which go back to a common original. Paulinus of Nola (*carm.* 19.84-86) speaks of an early Lat. version. The texts describe the missionary activity of M. in Egypt, Libya, and the Pentapolis, with the focus on his activity in Alexandria, which is also mentioned by Eusebius, *h.e.* 2.16. The martyrdom of M. is connected with controversies over the temple of Serapis. The list of M.'s disciples agrees to a great extent with the list of bishops in Eusebius (ibid.). In addition, there is a work titled *Acta et miracula*.

W: PG 115:164-169. — ActaSS April III, XLVI-XLVII [Greek text]; 347-349 [Latin text]. — *Acta et miracula*, F. Halkin, Actes inédits: AnBoll 87 (1969) 343-371 [Greek text].
L: A. D. Callahan, The Acts of St. Mark, Diss. (Harvard, 1991). — NTApo⁵ 2:417-420.

P. Bruns [G. Röwekamp]

Mark, Deacon

Deacon M. is regarded as author of the *Vita* of Porphyry of Gaza (395-420). The *Vita* has come down in Gr., Syr., and Georg. recensions, which to some extent differ considerably from one another. The work presupposes the *Historia religiosa* of → Theodoret of Cyrrhus as its literary model, so that it cannot have been composed before the mid-5th c.

W: PG 65:1211-1262. — H. Grégoire, M.-A. Kugener, Vie de Porphyre (Paris, 1930) [Syriac-Greek text/French trans.]. — P. Peeters, La Vie géorgienne: AnBoll 59 (1941) 65-216 [Georgian text/Latin trans.]. — G. Rohde (Berlin, 1927) [German trans.]. — C. Carta, Vita di s. Porfirio (Jerusalem, 1971) [Italian trans.].
L: M. Abel, M. Diacre (Paris, 1919). — J. Rougé, Tempête et littérature: NDid 12 (1962) 55-69. — J. Zellinger, Die Proömien: Ph. 85 (1930) 209-221.

P. Bruns

Mark Diadochus

A certain M. is given as author of the *Sermo contra Arianos*. This work issued from Nicene circles of the 4th c. and defended the substantial identity of Father and Son. An accurate linking of the work with a known author of this name is hardly possible, but the identification with → Diadochus of Photice, an ascetic active of the 5th c., is excluded.

W: PG 65:1149-1165.

P. Bruns

Mark, Gnostic

Irenaeus (*haer.* 1.13-21) tells in detail of the eastern (Asia Minor) Valentinian school of Mark (espec. of his number speculation). He transmits some liturgical formulas of M. and his followers (1.13.2f. and 6; 1.21.2-5). Apocryphal writings are attested in 1.20.1.

W: Irenaeus, *haer.* 1.13-21.
L: C. and A. Faivre, La place des femmes: RevSR 71 (1997) 310-328. — J. M. Joncas, Eucharist: QuLi 71 (1990) 99-111. — H. Leisegang, Gnosis (Stuttgart, ⁵1985), 326-349. — D. H. Tripp, Sequence: SecCen 8 (1991) 157-162.

R. Hanig

Mark, Hermit

There is a lack of clarity regarding the person and activity of M., known as "Hermit" or "Monk." Possibilities are an addressee of → Severus of Antioch (ca. 518) or a monk of Ephesus (d. ca. 390). Other traditions (Palladius, *h. Laus.* 18; Soz., *h.e.* 6.29) link M. with the circle of → Macarius the Egyptian/Simeon and with → Evagrius Pont. M. is named (Photius, *cod.* 200) as author of eight spiritual treatises (*tract.*) that have come down in Greek, Syriac, and Arabic. A book in Syriac on the stages of the spiritual life is denied to M. and attributed to → John of Lycopolis. In any case, an accurate delimitation of his literary works, which have thus far not been critically examined and edited, runs into considerable difficulties since at an early stage there was a mixup with other writers of the same name (→ Mark Diadochus, → Mark, Deacon, and → Marcian, Monk). Also to be studied is the question of the extent to which a vision of a certain "Mark of Mount Tamarqâ" on the state of souls after death is from the pen of M.

The two main treatises, on the "spiritual law" and against "justification by works," reveal M. as a high-ranking ascetical writer who offers, in century form, sentences and mnemonics on theol. and spiritual questions. On the one hand, M. criticizes a pneumatic monasticism that denies the necessity of baptism for salvation, but on the other his own views suggest the Messalianist tendencies of Marcarius/ Simeon and, together with the writings of Evagrius, had a not inconsiderable influence on Syro-Nestorian mysticism. In christology M. expressly accepts the hypostatic union and teaches the communication of idioms against the Nestorians.

W: PG 65:893-1140. — O. Hesse, BGrL 19 (Stuttgart, 1985) [German trans.]. — Philokalia ton hieron neptikon (Athens, 1982), 1:96-141 [Greek text]. — A. Baumstark, Geschichte (Bonn, 1922), 91f., 138 [Syriac mss.]. — G. Graf, Geschichte 1 (Rome, 1944), 400f. [Arabic mss.].
L: H. Chadwick, Identity and date of Mark the Monk: ECR 4 (1972) 125-130. — G. M. de Durand, Études sur Marc le moine: BLE 85 (1984) 259-278; 86 (1985) 5-23; 87 (1986) 163-188. — A. Grillmeier, M. e l'origenismo: CrSt 1 (1980) 9-58. — O. Hesse, M. u. Simeon v. Mesopotamien (Göttingen, 1973). — idem, M. u. De Melchisedech: OrChr 51 (1967) 72-77. — idem, M. in der syr. Literatur: ZDMG Suppl. 1 (1969) 450-457. — idem, Christologie des M.: W. Strothmann et al., P. de Lagarde u. die syr. Kirchengeschichte (Göttingen, 1968), 90-101. — P. Krüger, Zum theol. Menschenbild: OrChr 44 (1960) 46-74. — J. Kunze, M. (Leipzig, 1895). — K. T. Ware, Ascetic Writings of Mark the Hermit, Diss. (Oxford, 1965). — idem, Sacrament of Baptism: StPatr 10 (1970) 441-452.

P. BRUNS, J. PAULI, OSB

Mark, Poet

M. was author of a poem in praise of Benedict of Nursia (d. 547) in thirty-three elegiac distichs (*Carmen de S. Benedicto*). Its date is uncertain. The poem was written after Benedict's death (see v. 56f.), but M. is first mentioned by Paul the Deacon (second half of 8th c.) (*Hist. Lang.* 1.26). It is also unclear whether M. was a monk and knew Benedict personally. His poem, which is marked by clear, pleasing language and formal elegance, shows a knowledge of, among other, Propertius, Virgil, Ovid, and Statius. It tells of Benedict's miracles and gives an account espec. of his monastery at Montecassino, giving in the process aspects of the foundation legend that are not in the *Dialogi* of Gregory the Great. The verses, written in the form of a prayer to Benedict, climax with a wish that he intercede for the author.

W: PL 80:183-186. — S. Rocca: Romanobarbarica 3 (1978) 335-363 [text/comm.].
L: H. S. Brechter, Marcus Poeta von Monte Cassino: Benedictus, der Vater des Abendlandes, ed. H. S. Brechter (Munich, 1947), 341-459. — M. Galdi, Il carme di Marco Poeta e l'apoteosi di San Benedetto (Naples, 1929). — M. Manitius, Geschichte der chr.-lat. Poesie (Stuttgart, 1891), 388-390.

M. MEIER

Maro of Edessa

M. was a priest of Edessa and a scribe in the Persian school there. He was regarded as a supporter of Ibas and because of his Nestorian tendencies met with increasing difficulties. He composed a work against Severus of Antioch, of which a fragment has been preserved by → Anastasius the Sinaite.

W: PG 89:293-296.
L: A. Baumstark, Geschichte (Bonn, 1922), 104f. — H. G. Beck, Kirche u. theol. Lit. (Munich, 1959), 383.

P. BRUNS

Marsanes

Marsanes (Mars.) is the title of a Copt. apocalypse in the much-damaged Cod. 10 of the Nag Hammadi library (NHC 10, 1). Epiphanius, *haer.* 40.7.6, says of the "Archontic" gnostics that they venerated a prophet, Marsanios, who supposedly experienced a three-day journey through the heavens. The apocalypse dates probably from the end of the 2nd or beginning of the 3rd c. and goes back to a lost Gr. original. It shows connections chiefly with Sethian gnosis but otherwise sticks to Platonic ontology and concepts.

W: B. A. Pearson, NHC IX and X (Leiden, 1981), 229-347 [Coptic text/English trans./comm.]. — NHL 460-471 [English trans.].
L: C. Colpe, Heidnische u. jüd. Überlieferung: JAC 23 (1980) 124-127. — B. A. Pearson, Theurgie: Neoplatonism and Gnosticism, ed. R. T. Wallis (New York, 1992), 253-275. — idem, Gnosticism as Platonism: HThR 77 (1984) 55-72. — G. Wewers, Wort "Gott": Kairos 24 (1982) 207-219.

P. BRUNS

Martin of Braga

M., b. ca. 515 in Pannonia, dying in 580, became a monk while on a pilgrimage to Palestine. In 550 he went to Galicia where he established a monastery at Dumio. When Dumio became an episcopal see, M. became its bishop. As such he took part in the first Council of Braga (561), and he presided over the second (572). Under the protection of King Chararic (550-559), who became a Catholic at that time, he did missionary work among the Arian Suebi. He is supposed to have written a *Regula fidei et sanctae religionis* for his converts (Isidore, *vir. ill.* 35).

M. composed treatises on various questions, as well as sermons, letters, and poems. His writings on moral philosophy, *De ira (ira)* and *Formula vitae honestae* (*form. vit.*), attest to the continuing influence of Seneca. M. dealt with themes of monastic ethics in three connected shorter works: *Pro repellenda iactantia* (*iact.*), *De superbia* (*superb.*), and *Exhortatio humilitatis* (*humil.*). His translation of the *Sententiae patrum Aegyptiorum* (*sent. patr.*) from Greek into Latin likewise shows his close links to monasticism (see → Paschasius of Dumio). At the request of Bishop Polemius of Astorga M. composed the pastoral instruction *De correctione rusticorum* (*corr.*), which showed how to warn rural communities effectively against idolatry and the excesses connected with it. A short canonical collection, the *Capitula Martini*, also served practical purposes. Important for the history of the Span. liturgy of baptism is the *Epistola ad Bonifatium de trina mersione* (*trin. mers.*). M. is here seeking to gain acceptance for a triple immersion acc. to the Roman custom, apart from consideration of the fact that the single immersion to which he is objecting could be given an Arian interpretation. The authenticity of *De pascha* is disputed. If it is from M., then its purpose is to justify Easter being dated between March 22 and April 12. Three poems of M. are preserved: *In basilica* (*in bas.*), *In refectorio* (*refect.*), and the *Epitaphium* (*epitaph.*) which M. wrote for his own tomb. His letters are lost except for one to Reccared, which M. may have written. He cannot be shown to be the author of the apocryphal correspondence between Seneca and → Paul and of the so-called → *Opus imperfectum in Matthaeum*. The attempt to ascribe the *Symbolum Quicumque* to M. must be regarded as a failure. Nor was M. the author of *S. Martini trinae unitatis et unius trinitatis confessio*, *De paupertate*, and *De moribus*.

W: C. W. Barlow (New Haven, 1950) [text]. — C. W. Barlow, FaCh 62 [English trans./comm.]. — *corr.*, M. Naldini (Fiesole, 1991).
L: P. Francoer, The relationship in thought and language between L. Aen. Seneca and M., Diss. (Univ. of Michigan, 1944). — S. McKenna, Paganism and pagan survivals in Spain (Washington, 1938). — J. Orlandis, D. Ramos-Lisson, Die Synoden auf der Iberischen Halbinsel (Paderborn, 1981). — K. Schäferdieck, Die Kirche in den Reichen der Westgoten und Suewen (Berlin, 1967).

E. Reichert

Martin I of Rome

M., b. in Rodi (Umbria), a Roman deacon and apocrisiarius, became pope in July 649 (without imperial confirmation). In Oct. 649 he inaugurated the Lateran synod which his predecessor, Theodore I, had convoked; it condemned the *Ekthesis* of Heraclius and the *Typos* of Constans I and anathematized Sergius, Pyrrhus I, and Paul II, all of Constantinople. On June 17, 653, M. was arrested and condemned to death in Constantinople for conspiring with Olympius, at that time exarch of Ravenna (theol. differences were explicitly excluded as a cause); but after the intervention of Paul II M. was banished to the Chersonnesus (Crimea), where he died on Sept. 16, 655.

A fragment of a letter and seventeen complete letters (*ep.*) have survived, among them a circular letter calling for assent to the decrees of the Lateran synod, a letter to Amandus of Maastricht, one to Constans II, and four letters from exile to Theodore Spudaeus, in which M. complains of his calamity and his disappointment with his friends. In addition, there is a fragment of a dogmatic decree (*decr.*). Five other decrees and two privileges (*priv.*) are today regarded as not authentic.

W: *ep., decr.,* Mansi 10:790-1188. — *ep., priv.,* PL 87:119-212. — *ep.* 2, B. Krusch, MGH. SRM 5:452-456.
L: S. Consentino, Dissidenza religiosa e insubordinazione militare: RSCI 48 (1994) 496-512. — P. Conte, Chiesa e primato (Milan, 1971), 388-390, 442-454, 543f. — E. Menestò, M. I Papa. Atti del 28 Convegno storico internazionale (Spoleto, 1992). — R. Riedinger, Lateransynode: Maximus Confessor, ed. F. Heinzer, C. Schönborn (Fribourg, Switzerland, 1982), 111-121.

B. Dümler

Martyrius (Sahdona)

M., Sahdona in Syriac, was from Halmon in Beth Nuhadra and as a youth entered the monastery of Beth Abe on Mt Izla. M. was appointed bishop of Mahoze/Arewan in Beth Garmai between 635 and 640. A few years later he was deposed because of his deviant doctrinal views and fled to the West. Thanks to influential friends he was able to return, but under Catholicos Ishoyabh III (d. 658) he was again banished, this time for good. He settled in Edessa where he composed his ascetical writings on the spiritual life and on the discernment of spirits and carried on an extensive correspondence.

M. was a disciple of Henana of Adiabene and was critical of the reigning theology of the Nestorian schools. He fought against the formula, customary among Nestorians, of the two hypostases in Christ and endeavored to ground the unity of the redeemer in Monothelete or Monoergistic terms. He should not be regarded without qualification as a pioneer of Neo-Chalcedonianism; the conflict at his time was rather one within Nestorianism over the correct interpretation of the theol. heritage, espec. that of

Theodore Mops. In the process M. came increasingly into conflict with the hierarchy and with theologians such as Babai the Great, who contributed most to the formation of a strictly Nestorian system in christology.

W: P. Bedjan (Paris, 1902) [text]. — A. de Halleux, CSCO 201, 215, 253, 255 [text/French trans.]. — idem, G. Garitte, Sermon géorgien: Muséon 69 (1956) 243-313 [Georgian text].
L: S. P. Brock, Further fragment: Muséon 81 (1968) 139-154. — H. Goussen, M. Leben u. Werke (Leipzig, 1897). — A. de Halleux, Christologie: OCP 23 (1957) 5-32. — idem, Vie mouvementée: OCP 24 (1958) 93-128. — idem, Nouveau fragment: Muséon 73 (1960) 33-38. — idem, Chapitre retrouvé: Muséon 88 (1975) 253-295. — L. Leloir, La pensée monastique: OCA 197 (1974) 105-134. — B. Outtier, Martius ou M. ?: REGC 1 (1985) 225f. — N. Pigulewskaja, Ende der Hs.: OrChr 23 (1927) 293-309. — W. de Vries, Syr.-nestorianische Haltung: A. Grillmeier, H. Bacht, Konzil von Chalkedon (Würzburg, 1952), 603-635. — L. Wehbé, Textes bibliques: Melto 5 (1969) 61-112.

P. BRUNS

Martyrius of Antioch

M., a Chalcedonian, became bishop of Antioch in 459. In 470/471 he was deposed by Monophysite Peter the Fuller and fled to Gennadius of Constantinople. After regaining his see again for a short time, he finally resigned.

Two works are attributed to M. A panegyric on John Chrys. (pan.) was delivered, at the end of 407 or beginning of 408, shortly after John's death, to his supporters in Constantinople. But this work, composed in order to praise the dead man and console his supporters, was not from M. A second work going under M.'s name is the Quaestiones et responsiones (quaest.), of which fragments remain.

W: pan., F. van Ommeslaeghe, De lijkrede voor Joh. Chrys. (Leuven/Louvain, 1974), 43-142. — PG 47:43-52 [partial edition]. — quaest., A. Mai, NPB 2 (Rome, 1844), 552 [text].
L: M. Aubineau, La vie inedite de Chrysostome: AnBoll 94 (1976) 394. — F. van Ommeslaeghe, La valeur historique de la vie de Joh. Chrys.: StPatr 12 (1975) 478-483. — idem, Que vaut le temoignage de Pallade: AnBoll 95 (1977) 389-413. — idem, Jean Chrys. et le peuple de Constantinople: AnBoll 99 (1981) 329-349. — E. Venables, M. 2: DCB 3:858.

B. WINDAU

Martyrius of Jerusalem

M. was a monk in Egypt; in 451, being a Chalcedonian, he fled to the wilderness of Judea. As patriarch of Jerusalem (478-486) he reached a compromise with many anti-Chalcedonians; only extreme opponents such as Gerontius and Peter the Iberian were excluded. M.'s address of reconciliation and his letter to Peter Mongus, patriarch of Alexandria, are preserved by Zacharias Rhetor.

W: Zacharias Rhetor, h.e., E. W. Brooks, CSCO 83:237f. [Syriac text]; CSCO 87:164 [Latin trans.].
L: L. Perrone, La chiesa di Palestina (Brescia, 1980), 127-151.

G. RÖWEKAMP

Martyrs, Acts of the

The concept of "Acts of the Martyrs" is a recent one. It was introduced by Caesar Baronius during his work on the revision of the Martyrologium Romanum (1580-1583) with a reference to its use by Paulinus (vit. Cypr. 11) and became customary as a result of the publication of Ruinart's Acta sincera (1689[1]). The Acts of the Martyrs are part of the larger realm of early Chr. literature on the martyrs, within which they are distinguished from the Passiones (P.) or Martyria (M.) as a shorter form that is essentially limited to being the transcript of a trial. In contrast to the so-called Acts (A.) the P. and M. give various forms of hist. reports (often in the form of eyewitness accounts), tales of visions and miracles, speeches and dialogues, and rhetorical, encomiastic sections in combinations of various kinds; here the record of the trial is not necessarily the focus of attention. The entire range of this literature shows a great variety in formal structure but is for the most part written in everyday language and is full of bibl. reminiscences. In a large number of texts (varying acc. to locality) the liturgical reading on the martyr's commemoration day is to be presupposed as the Sitz im Leben.

Alongside these Acts, beginning in the 4th c., there arose more sprawling stories of the martyrs ("legends of the martyrs") as the third and most detailed form of the genre. M. and P. were written as late as the 7th c. (P. Afrae is the latest example). Characteristics of their form appear in other, stylistically different literary genres such as the sermon and the panegyric (e.g., Gregory Nyss., Steph.; John Chrys., pan. Ign., etc.) and the late, apocryphal acts of the apostles (e.g., A. Petr. [acta Vercellenses] 30-41, and A. Paul.). These legends of the martyrs are to be distinguished from early Chr. biographies (lives of monks and bishops; → Vita), although even here there are overlaps in individual forms.

Earlier efforts at systematization were determined primarily by the question of hist. authenticity, but

405

after a long period of work, espec. on literary criticism, several efforts have been made at the present time to control the literary material with the aid of form-criticism:

1. A division of the texts into (a) letters on martyrdom (*M. Polyc.*; *M. Lugd.*); (b) dramatic forms (*M. Just.*; *P. Scill.*; *A. Carp.*; *P. Maximil.*; *A. Marcell.*; *P. Crispin.*); (c) dramatic narratives (*P. Cypr.*; *P. Fructuos.*; *M. Apollon.*); and (d) narratives (*P. Perp.*; *P. Mar. Iac.*; *P. Montan.*).

2. A distinction between (a) *P.* in the form of acts (e.g., *P. Scill.*; *A. Carp.*; *P. Max.*; *P. Cypr. rec. I*; *P. Maximil.*; *A. Eupli*; *P. Crispin.*; *P. Afrae*; this type is espec. frequent in North Africa); (b) *Acta disputationis* (*Altercationes*; "*Interrogationes*") (e.g., *A. Acac.*; *Gesta apud Zenophilum*); (c) *P.* in commentary form (named after Caesar's *Commentarii*) with heavily autobiographical elements (*P. Perp.*; *P. Montan.*; *P. Mar. Iac.*); (d) rhetorical *P.* (Pontius, *vit. Cypr.*; Eucherius, *Acaun.*; the so-called Acts of the Donatist martyrs); (e) narrative *P.* of a bibl. character (e.g., *P. Fructuos.*; *P. Claud. Ast.*; *P. Iren. Sirm.*); (f) theatrical and dramatic stories of the martyrs (e.g., *P. Agnetis*; *P. Caecil.*; *P. Laurentii*; this genre was at home espec. in Rome) and (g) novelistic passions of the apostles (e.g., apocryphal acts of Peter) and novels about the apostles (e.g., *A. Thom.*). These observations are based almost entirely on Lat. texts.

3. A careful study of ancient records of interrogations (*Commentarii*), which are preserved on papyri, has yielded form-critical categories for the question of the authentic records behind the dialogues preserved in the *M.* Thus there is no context for the dialogue at the interrogation in *M. Polyc.*; in *M. Ign. Ant.* and possibly in *M. Just.* there is the use or revision of an original *Commentarius*. Generally speaking, only a thorough and detailed study can answer the question whether in a particular case there is question of a *Commentarius* that has been reworked by a redactor.

4. Efforts have also been made, while bracketing questions of authenticity, to sketch a history of the genres *M.* and *P.* At the beginning (a) there were *P.* in letter form which brought new elements into a primitive Chr. literary form (*M. Polyc.*; *M. Lugd.*); the interrogation was now only one element among others and had no exceptional status. The letter on the martyrdom was a mixed genre that included elements of several forms (letter, narrative, argumentation, patronal miracle, dialogue). It was composed for parenetic purposes and had a pragmatic character as identificational-parenetic, as commending an exemplar, finding fault and correcting, consoling and edifying, i.e., the same essential character that its literary predecessor, the Jewish stories of exemplars, had (espec. 2 Mac 6:18-31 and 4 Mac 5:1–6:30: martyrdom of Eleazar; 2 Mac 7:1-42 and 4 Mac 8:1-17, 16: martyrdom of the seven brothers). Only at a secondary stage and at the same time as the dialogue, which was taken over from pagan literature, did there arise in early Chr. literature (b) the *M.* (the *Acta* form) which with its special emphasis on speech and response showed a form similar to the dialogue; both had apologetic aims; they were directed at those outside but at the same time served to strengthen the faith of Christians. As in the dialogue, so in the interrogations there can often be seen the arrangement acc. to themes that is typical of apologetics, as well as autobiog. elements, rhetorical questions, the declaration of respect for civil authority, and the proof from miracles. A closer form-critical analysis shows that individual texts display various elements bringing them close to the early letters on martyrdom (e.g., recension A of the *A. Just.*, Greek *A. Carp.*) and that successive versions manifest a development toward more clearly apologetic aims. (c) The stories of martyrs may be distinguished as a third stage in the development; these frequently serve as cult aetiologies (account of the burial, etc.; admittedly, this is already present in *M. Polyc.* 18). Given this starting point, genre analysis is closely connected with the history of development.

5. In view of the difficult efforts to define more closely the genres of hagiog. texts it has been noted that these texts by and large are preceded by a "hagiog. discourse" that supports the various hagiog. genres. Some traits of this discourse: While the writers increasingly stylize and color the picture, their intention is to convey pure truth. At the same time as they give information, they seek to present in an appealing way ideal types from whose exemplary thinking and acting the hearer or reader will receive moral instruction and be spiritually edified. In this process biblicism is probably the most important means of shaping the account. The hero of the story is seen as a chosen one of God, with whom he has a special relationship; the hero often has miraculous powers at his disposal. Elements of the hagiog. discourse can be observed in biographies, the encomium, the → panegyric, the funeral discourse, the apocryphal acts of the apostles, the → novel or novella, and the miracle story, and they are already constant features of the *M.* and the *P.*

On the basis of form-critical criteria it is likely that in the future an increasing number of interrogations in the *M.* and *P.* will prove to be revised or even fictional than has hitherto been assumed. It also seems important that, above and beyond questions of the historical source value of the *M.* and *P.*, the entire group of texts that make up the literature on the martyrs be seen as a literary testimony to the piety and mentality of early Christianity and as reading material that gradually eliminated themes of pagan mythology and replaced them, in a slow process that involved numerous shaping factors, with idealized or heroicized types of individual Christians. In this development the texts served very different purposes: parenesis, doxology, concern for worship and liturgy, and the strengthening of the eccles. community by identification with the martyrs. Not to be underestimated is the fact that these texts repeatedly made even persons of the lower classes the subject of literature: women, slaves, lower military ranks, clerks of the court, actors, and so on.

A **Selection of Important Texts** in the order in which the martyrdoms depicted are dated, not in the order of the writing of the works, a subject which has often not been studied or is uncertain.

1. Martyrdom of Ptolemy and Lucius (*M. Ptol. Luc.*) = → Justin Martyr, 2 *apol.* 2: an almost contemporary account of an accusation made out of marital jealousy, the trial, and the condemnation of Ptolemy, a Chr. teacher, by the Roman city prefect Q. Lollius Urbicus, which was the occasion for the writing of the second part of Justin's *apol.* (ca. 160).

2. Letter on the martyrdom of Polycarp (*M. Polyc.*): an account of the martyrdom, composed by an author named → Marcion (ch. 20) for the community of Philomelius in the form of a letter with a number of citations at the end. Today after detailed discussion of the redaction history, which had its origin in the double tradition, the letter is generally regarded as forming a unity (chs. 1-20). The account is shaped by strong echoes of the passion of Jesus. The prayer put on the lips of the martyr is important for the history of early Chr. (eucharistic) prayers.

3. The Acts of Justus and his companions (*M. Just.*): an account, in three recensions, of the interrogation and execution of Justin the apologete, together with five men and a woman, ca. 165, under prefect Q. Iunius Rusticus.

4. Acts of Carpus, Papylus, and Agathonice (*A. Carp.*): an account, known only since 1881, of the interrogation and execution of Bishop Carpus, Papylus a deacon, and Agathonice, who was zealous for martyrdom, in Pergamum; the event took place, acc. to Eusebius (*h.e.* 4.15.48), under Marcus Aurelius, but acc. to the more recent Lat. recension, under Decius. Epic version published 1940.

5. Letter of the communities of Lyons and Vienne

(*M. Lugd.*) = Eusebius, *h.e.* 5.1.3–2.8, to communities in Asia and Phrygia on pogroms against Christians, trials, and executions in Lyons (177). A great deal of space is given to the theme of apostasy from the faith in situations of persecution.

6. Acts of the martyrs of Scilli (*P. Scill.*): the earliest Chr. work in Latin; in strict transcript form it describes the interrogation, confession, and condemnation of a group of Christians by proconsul Saturninus in Carthage on July 17, 180.

7. Acts of Apollonius (*A. Apollon.*): in its surviving Gr. and Arm. forms this is a late text with a strongly apologetic content, in which a Roman martyrdom of 182/185 is transposed to Alexandria.

8. Passion of Perpetua and Felicity (*P. Perp.*): an extraordinary text from the literary viewpoint; in it a compiler, whose Latin closely resembles that of Tertullian, has incorporated autobiographical prison notes of a noblewoman, Vibia Perpetua (chs. 3-10) and of Saturus (chs. 11-13), which have a heavily visionary and apocalyptic content. The execution took place in Carthage in 202 or 203. The Gr. version is secondary.

9. Martyrdom of Pionius (*M. Pion.*): Contrary to the impression given in Eusebius (*h.e.* 4.15.46f.), the martyr is to be dated not shortly after Polycarp but to the 3rd c. (Decius?). The text, known since 1896, is lengthy, strongly anti-Jewish, permeated by many rhetorical and narrative elements, and belongs to a later time (age of Diocletian?). Stylistic echoes of 2 and 5 (above).

10. Acts of Acacius (*A. Acacii*): Record of the interrogation of Acacius, very interesting from the literary viewpoint but of very dubious historicity; the work with its apologetic and even humorous character was composed for presentation to Emperor Decius, who after reading it reprieved the man who had been accused because of his faith.

11. Acts of Maximus (*P. Max.*): interrogation of Maximus during the Decian(?) persecution, in classical transcript form; the historicity is doubted. Sometimes literal correspondences to the (inauthentic?) acts of Peter, Andrew, Paul, and Dionisia in the Decian persecution.

12. Proconsular acts of Cyprian (*P. Cypr. rec.* I): a clearly tripartite text by different authors (edited by → Pontius?), consisting of a transcript, with commentary, of a trial ending with a death sentence and martyrdom in 258; somewhat later there was prefixed to this a completely formal record of an interrogation in 257 by proconsul Paternus that led to banishment.

13. Passion of Marianus and James (*P. Mar. Iac.*):

impressive North African story of martyrdom (259 in Cirta) told from the viewpoint of someone close to the martyrs, with strong echoes of 8 (autobiographical elements, visions). Historicity doubtful.

14. Passion of Montanus, Lucius, and their companions (*P. Montan.*): a two-part text consisting of a letter from martyrs imprisoned in Carthage in 259 and containing an account of their visions; it continued with an account of their martyrdoms with the emphasis on that of Flavian, who is named as the one who commissioned the entire work. The author remains anonymous (Pontius?).

15. Passion of Fructuosus and his two deacons (*P. Fructuos.*): a text deliberately written in a simple style and telling of the humility of Bishop Fructuosus of Tarragona, executed in 259. There is an introductory section giving the record and an appended account of the martyrdom.

16. Acts of Maximilian (*P. Maximil.*): a text in transcript form with two short appendixes on the words of the executed man who had refused military service and on the beginnings of his cult.

17. Acts of Marcellus (*A. Marcell.*): this text, known in three recensions, is marked by considerable difficulties of textual criticism. An account, with two records of interrogations, of Marcellus, a centurion, by procurator Fortunatus and (vice-)prefect Agricolanus in Tangiers (North Africa) or León (Galicia) in 298, after the centurion had refused further military duty.

18. Acts of Claudius, Asterius, and their companions (*P. Claud. Ast.*): five successive interrogations of individuals by governor Lysias in Aegaea (Cilicia) in 303; the accounts are striking for their description of tortures, to which two women have already succumbed during the proceedings.

19. Passion of Sebastian (*P. Seb.*): example of a Roman text on a martyrdom of 286/287 or 303; it is a late text, since liturgical use of such a text was originally not customary in Rome. Many miraculous elements, several attempts at killing (arrows, clubs); low assessment therefore of its historicity. The author was possibly → Arnobius the Younger.

20. Martyrdom of Dasius (*M. Das.*): an account, in very simple Greek, of the martyrdom of Dasius, a soldier, during the Diocletian persecution (in Durostorum, Bulgaria?), after his refusal to collaborate in the pagan New Year's festival. The text, which clearly serves the rejection of pagan cults, is marked by an interior monologue of Dasius and an interrogation in the form more of dialogue than of a record. It is to be dated after 325.

21. Martyrdom of Agape, Irene, Chionia, and others (*P. Agap.*): an account, consisting of three records of interrogations, of the martyrdom of Agathon and a group of six women in Salonica, from the time of the Diocletian edicts (303/304), to which is prefixed a theol.-biog. chapter.

22. Acts of Eupl(i)us (*A. Eupl.*): unlike the Gr. recension, the Lat. contains the two interrogations of Eupl(i)us in Catania during the Diocletian persecution; but it has been revised (with a Donatist tendency?) to emphasize the anti-*traditor* motive of a man who voluntarily seeks martyrdom.

23. Acts of Irenaeus of Sirmium (*P. Iren. Sirm.*) and acts of Pollio of Cibali (*A. Polyc. Cib.*): two texts in transcript form describing martyrdoms in Pannonia in the time of Diocletian; they are related by the reference of the second to the first and display a tendency to interweave local traditions. The Gr. recension of the acts of Irenaeus is more panegyrical and later in time. The acts of Pollio display strong apologetic elements (explanation of Chr. teaching on virtue).

24. Acts of Crispina (*P. Crispin.*): a record in dialogue style of a trial in 304 before North African proconsul Annius Annulinus, who is known from the Constantinian period; the martyr's profession of faith is cited.

25. Passion of Saturninus, Dativus, Felix, and their companions (martyrs of Abitene) (*P. M. Abit.*): a passion from the beginning of the 5th c. (?), reworked by Donatists, epic in breadth, and clearly rhetorical; in it a sizable group of Christians, in contrast to their bishop who had handed over the sacred writings, profess their faith before proconsul Anullinus during the Diocletian persecution.

26. Acts of Phileas (*A. Phileae*): a text whose authenticity was earlier frequently disputed and which was regarded as a catechetical text; it tells, in a curious mixture of record and dialogue, of the interrogation at the fifth examination of Bishop Phileas of Thmuis by Claudius Culcianus, prefect of Egypt, in 306. Since 1984 three recensions have been available, not directly connected but dependent on a common archetype (the official record of the court?): *Pap. Chester Beatty* XV (to be dated ca. 310-350), *Pap. Bodmer* XX (ca. 320-350), and the Lat. recension (end of 5th c.).

27. Testament of the forty martyrs of Sebaste (*M. Seb. test.*): an appendix (to historically dubious acts) in the form of a letter from prison by forty soldier-martyrs in the time of Licinius; in it they ask that after being burned they receive a common burial; then comes a parenetic section and, at the end, a lengthy list of greetings.

28. Eusebius, *De martyribus Palaestinae* (Eus., *m. P.*):

A chronologically ordered collection of martyrdoms in Caesarea and Palestine, in two recensions: the shorter is an appendix in Eus., *h.e.* (E. Schwartz, GCS 9/2:907-50), the longer is a more edifying version preserved only in Syriac. Either the booklet was originally part of *h.e.* 8 and was published separately after 313, or it was an independent work from before 313, which on the one hand was shortened and appended to the third edition of *h.e.*, and, on the other, was again separated and published in an expanded form.

29. Syrian texts of martyrdoms: In many of the Syro-Persian martyrdoms a Hellen. influence can be seen in the presentation, but not in many others; this makes them of interest as material for comparison.

30. Coptic texts: The Copt. legends of martyrdom are characterized by the many attempts, initially unsuccessful, to put the martyrs to death; thus the idea of the indestructible life of the saints becomes a special trait of the Copt. "hagiographical discourse."

W (collections): B: A. A. R. Bastiaensen, A. Hilhorst, G. A. A. Kortekaas et al. (ed.), Atti e passioni dei martiri (Vicenza, 1987) [text/Italian trans./comm.]. — **BKV:** G. Rauschen, Echte alte M., BKV² 14:289-369 [German trans.]. — E. le Blant, Les actes des martyrs. Suppl. aux Acta sincera de D. Ruinart (Paris, 1882) [text]. — **D:** H. J. Dahm, Lat. M. u. Märtyrerbriefe (Münster, 1986) [text/comm.]. — **G:** K. Gamber, Sie gaben Zeugnis (Regensburg, 1982) [German trans.]. — **GK:** P. Guyot, R. Klein (ed.), Das frühe Christentum 1 (Darmstadt, 1993) [text/German comm.]. — **Hg:** O. Hagemeyer, Ich bin Christ (Düsseldorf, 1961) [German trans./comm.]. — **Hm:** A. Hamman, Das Heldentum der frühen Martyrer (Aschaffenburg, 1958) [German trans.: paraphrase on the text]. — **K:** R. Knopf, G. Krüger, G. Ruhbach, Ausgewählte M. (Tübingen, 1965) [text]. — **L:** G. Lanata, Gli atti dei martiri come documenti processuali (Milan, 1973) [text]. — **Lz:** G. Lazzati, Gli sviluppi della letteratura sui martiri nei primi quattro secoli. Con appendice di testi (Turin, 1956). — **M:** H. Musurillo, The Acts of the Christian Martyrs (Oxford, 1972 = 1979) [text/English trans.]. — **Ra:** H. Rahner, Die M. des 2. Jh. (Freiburg i.Br., ²1954) [German trans.]. — **Rn:** G. Rauschen, Monumenta minora saeculi secundi (Bonn, ²1914) [text]. — **Ru:** T. Ruinart, Acta martyrum (Regensburg, ⁵1859) [text]. — Echte u. ausgewählte Acten der ersten Märtirer nach . . . T. Ruinart, 6 vols. (Vienna, 1832-34) [German trans.]. — **S:** A. Schwerd, Lat. M. (Munich, 1960) [text/German trans./comm.].

Individual writings: the abbreviations refer to the collections: 1. *M. Ptol. Luc.,* E. J. Goodspeed, Die ältesten Apologeten (Göttingen, 1884-1914), 78-80 [text]. — K, M [text]; Hm, Ra [translation]. — **2.** *M. Polyc.,* A. Lindemann, H. Paulsen, Die Apostolischen Väter (Tübingen, 1992), 258-285 [text/German trans.]. — B, K, L, Lz, M [text]; BKV, G, GK, Hm, Ra [translation]. — **3.** *M. Just.,* P. Franchi de'Cavalieri, Note agiografiche 6: StT 33 (1920 = 1973) 5-17 (recension A, with corrections in Lz 120f.) [text]. — B, K, L, M, Rn (recension B) [text]; BKV, G, Hm, Ra [translation]. — **4.** *A. Carp.,* A. v. Harnack, Die Akte des Karpus, des Papylus u. der Agathonike: TU 3/3-4 (Leipzig, 1888), 433-466 [text of the Greek recension]. — P. Franchi de'Cavalieri, op. cit., 3-45 [text of the Latin recension]. — H. Delehaye, Les actes des martyrs de Pergame: AnBoll 58 (1940) 142-176 [text]. — B, K, L, Lz, M, Rn [text]; BKV, G, GK, Hm, Ra [translation]. — **5.** *M. Lugd.,* E. Schwartz, GCS 9/1:402-432. — B, K, L, Lz, M [text]; G, Ra [translation]. — **6.** *P. Scill.,* F. Ruggiero, Atti dei martiri Scilitani: AAL. M 9, 1, 2 (1991) [text/Italian trans./comm.]. — B, D, K, L, Lz, M, Rn, S [text]; BKV, G, GK, Hg, Hm, Ra [translation]. — **7.** *M. Apollon.,* E. T. Klette, Der Process u. die Acta S. Apollonii, TU 15/2 (Leipzig, 1897) [text]. — K, L, Lz, M, Rn [text]; BKV, G, Hm, Ra [translation]. — **8.** *P. Perp.,* J. Amat, SC 417. — J. A. Robinson, The Passion of S. Perpetua (Cambridge, 1891) [text]. — P. Franchi de'Cavalieri, La P. Perp. (Rome, 1896) = idem, Scritti agiografici 1: StT 221 (1962) 41-155 (with addenda) [text]. — C. I. M. I. van Beek, P. Perp. (Nijmegen, 1936); ed. minor: FlorPatr 43 (1938) [text]. — G. Lazzati, Note critiche al testo della P. Perp.: Aevum 30 (1956) 30-35. — O. Hagemeyer, Die Passion der hl. Perpetua u. Felicitas (Klosterneuburg, 1938) [German trans./comm.]. — B, D, K, L, Lz, M, S [text]; BKV, G, GK, Hg, Hm [translation]. — **9.** *M. Pion.,* O. v. Gebhardt, Das Martyrium des hl. Pionius: Archiv für slav. Philologie 18 (1896) 156-171. — B, K, L, M, [text]; BKV, G, Hm [translation]. — **10.** *A. Acac.,* J. Weber, De actis S. Acacii (Borna, 1913) [text]; additionally, H. Delehaye: AnBoll 33 (1914) 346f. and F. Halkin: ibid. 72 (1954) 27. — K [text]; G [German trans.]. — **11.** *P. Max.,* K, S [text]; Hm [translation]. — **12.** *P. Cypr. rec.* 1, W. Hartel, CSEL 3/3:CX-CXIV [text]. — R. Reitzenstein, Die Nachrichten über den Tod Cyprians: SHAW. PH 1913, 14. Abh. [text]. — idem, Bemerkungen zur Märtyrerlit. 2: Nachträge zu den Akten Cyprians: NGWG. PH 1919, 177-219. — B, K, L, Lz, M [text]; BKV, Hm [translation]. — **13.** *P. Mar. Iac.,* P. Franchi de'Cavalieri, Passio SS. Mariani et Iacobi: StT 3 (1900 = 1972). — K, L, Lz, M [text]; G, Hg, Hm, [translation]. — **14.** *P. Montan.,* P. Franchi de'Cavalieri, Gli atti dei SS. Montano, Lucio e compagni: RQ. S (1898) = idem, Scritti 1:199-292 [text]. — idem, Nuove osservazioni critiche e esegetiche sul testo della P. Montan.: idem, Note agiografiche 3: StT 22 (1909 = 1966) 1-31. — K, L, Lz, M [text]; G, Hg, Hm [translation]. — **15.** *P. Fructuos.,* P. Franchi de'Cavalieri, Gli atti di S. Fruttuoso di Tarragona: idem, Note agiografiche 8: StT 65 (1935 = 1981) 129-199. — K, L, Lz, M, S [text]; G, Hm [translation]. — **16.** *P. Maximil.,* P. Siniscalco, Massimiliano, un obiettore di cosienza del tardo impero (Turin, 1974) [text]; additionally, F. Dolbeau: AnBoll 94 (1976) 422-425. — idem, Biblia e letteratura cristiana d'Africa nella P. Maximil.: FS M. Pellegrino (Turin, 1975), 595-613. — E. di Lorenzo, Gli A. Maximil. (Naples, 1975) [text/Italian trans./comm.]. — B, K, L, Lz, M [text]; G, GK, Hm [translation]. — **17.** *A. Marcell.,* H. Delehaye, Les actes de S. Marcel le centurion: AnBoll 41 (1923) 257-287 [text recension M and N], danach K, M, S [text]; Lz, L [recension of the Spanish mss.]; Hm [translation]. — **18.** *P. Claud. Ast.,* P. Franchi de'Cavalieri, Note agiografiche 5: StT 27 (1915 = 1973) 107-118. — K [text]; G, Hm [German trans.]. — **19.** *P. Seb.,* ActaSS Jan. 2, 629-642 = PL 17:1021-1058. — **20.** *M. Das.,* F. Cumont, Les actes de S. Dasius: AnBoll 16 (1897) 11-15 [text]. — R. Pillinger, Das Martyrium des hl. Dasius: SÖAW. PH 517 (1988) [text/German trans./comm.]. — K, M [text]. — **21.** *P. Agap.,* P. Franchi de'Cavalieri, Il testo greco originale degli Atti delle SS. Agape, Irene e Chione: idem, Nuove note agiografiche: StT 9 (1902 = 1973) 1-19. — K, L, M [text]; G, Hm [Trans. of chaps. 3-7]. — **22.** *A. Eupl.*, P. Franchi de'-Cavalieri, S. Euplo: idem, Note agiografiche 7: StT 49 (1928 = 1977) 1-54. 239f. [text of the Greek recension]. — K, L [text of the Greek recension]; M [text of the Greek and Latin recensions according to Ru]; Hm [trans. of the Latin recension]. — **23.** *P. Iren. Sirm.*, K, M [text]; G, Hm [translation]. — A. Polyc. Cib., ActaSS Apr. 3, 572f. = Ru 435f. [text]. — Hm [translation]. — **24.** *P. Crispin.*, P. Franchi de'Cavalieri, Osservazioni sopra gli atti di S. Crispina: idem, Nuove note agiografiche: StT 9 (1902 = 1973) 21-35 [text]. — J.-L. Maier, Le dossier du donatisme 1: TU 134 (Berlin, 1987), 105-112 [text/French trans.]. — M. Fuhrmann, D. Liebs (ed.), Exempla iuris romani (Munich, 1988), 180-187, 217 [text]. — K, L, Lz, M, S [text]; Hm [translation]. — **25.** *P. M. Abit.*, PL 8:689-703. — P. Franchi de'Cavalieri, La "passio" dei martiri Abitinensi: idem, Note agiografiche 8: StT 65 (1935 = 1981) 3-71; additionally, H. Delehaye: AnBoll 54 (1936) 293-296 [text]. — J.-L. Maier, Le Dossier du donatisme 1:57-92 [text/French trans.]; Hm [German trans.]. — **26.** *A. Phileae*, A. Pietersma, The Acts of Phileas, Bishop of Thmuis (Geneva, 1984) [text/English trans./comm.]. — K [Latin text]; M [Latin text and Pap. Bod.]; B [Latin text, Pap. Bod. and Pap. Ch. B.]; Hm [trans. of the Latin text]. — **27.** *M. Seb. test.*, P. Franchi de'Cavalieri, I ss. Quaranta martiri di Sebastia: idem, Note agiografiche 7: StT 49 (1928 = 1977) 155-184. — B, K, M [text]; G, Hm [translation]. — **28.** *Eus., m. P.*, W. Cureton, History of the Martyrs of Palaestine by Eusebius (London, 1861) = P. Bedjan, AMSS 1 (Paris, 1890 = Hildesheim, 1968), 202-276 [text/English trans.]. — H. Delehaye, De martyribus Palaestinae longioris libelli fragmenta: AnBoll 16 (1897) 113-139 [Greek frags.]. — B. Violet, Die palaestinischen Märtyrer des Eusebius, TU 14/4 (Berlin, 1896) [German trans. of the Syriac recension]. — A. Biglmair, BKV² 9:273-313 [German trans. of the Greek recension]. — **29.** *Pers. Martyrien*, P. Bedjan, AMSS, 7 vols. (Paris, 1890-97 = Hildesheim, 1968) [text]. — O. Braun, Ausgewählte Akten pers. Märtyrer, BKV² 22 [German trans.] — Hm [translation]. — **30.** *Coptic Martyrs*, I. Balestri, H. Hyvernat, Acta martyrum, CSCO 43, 44, 86, 125 [text]. — E. A. W. Budge, Coptic martyrdoms (London, 1914) [text/English trans.]. — W. Till, Kopt. Heiligen- u. Martyrerlegenden (Rome, 1935/36) [text/German trans.]. — P. Van Minnen, The earliest Account of a Martyrdom in coptic: AnBoll 113 (1995) 13-38.

L: General (the numbers of texts specifically treated are in parentheses): T. D. Barnes, Pre-Decian Acta Martyrum: JThS 19 (1968) 509-531. — idem, Early Christianity and the Roman Empire (London, 1984), Nr. I (1-9). — T. Baumeister, Die Anfänge der Theologie des Martyriums (Münster, 1980) (esp. 2). — idem, Genese u. Entfaltung der altkirchlichen Theologie des Martyriums (Bern, 1991) (esp. 2, 5, 8, 28). — W. Berschin, Biographie u. Epochenstil im lat. MA 1 (Stuttgart, 1986). — G. A. Bisbee, Pre-Decian Acts of Martyrs and Commentarii (Philadelphia, 1988) (esp. 2, 3). — J. den Boeft, J. Bremmer, Notiunculae martyrologicae I: VigChr 35 (1981) 43-56 (3, 6, 12, 15, 17, 20); II: 36 (1982) 383-402 (4, 8, 16, 20); III: 39 (1985) 110-130 (2, 9); IV: 45 (1991) 105-122 (2-6); V: 49 (1995) 146-164 (2, 5, 6, 20). — G. W. Bowersock, Martyrdom and Rome (Cambridge, 1995) (esp. 2, 5, 9). — G. Buschmann, Martyrium Polycarpi. Eine formkritische Studie (Berlin, 1994); additionally, H. R. Seeliger: ThRev 93 (1997) 24-26. — C. Butterweck, "Martyriumssucht" in der Alten Kirche? (Tübingen, 1995), 193-

201 (1, 4, 12, 13, 16, 17, 22, 28). — M. de Certeau, Hagiographie: Encyclopaedia universalis 11:160-165. — H. Delehaye, Les légendes hagiographiques (Brussels, 1973 = ⁴1955) (¹1905 = German: Die hagiographischen Legenden (Kempten, 1907). — idem, Les passions des martyrs et les genres littéraires (Brussels, ²1966) (esp. 2-10, 12-16, 20, 21, 24, 25, 27). — B. de Gaiffier, La lecture des actes des martyrs dans la prière liturgique en Occident: AnBoll 72 (1954) 134-166. — J. Geffcken, Die Stenographie in den Akten der Märtyrer: Archiv für Stenographie 57 (1906) 81-89. — A. Hamman, La confession de la foi dans les premiers actes des martyrs: FS J. Daniélou (Paris, 1972), 99-105. — A. v. Harnack, Das urspr. Motiv der Abfassung von Märtyrer- u. Heilungsakten: SPAW 1910, 106-125. — W. Hellmann, Die Wertschätzung des Martyriums als eines Rechtfertigungsmittels, Diss. (Breslau, 1912). — K. Holl, Die Vorstellung vom Märtyrer u. die M. in ihrer geschichtlichen Entwicklung: NJKA 33 (1914) 521-556 = idem, Gesammelte Aufsätze zur Kirchengeschichte 2 (Darmstadt, 1964 = Tübingen, 1928), 68-102. — G. Lanata, Gli atti dei martiri come documenti processuali (Milan, 1973) (esp. 2-9, 10, 16f., 21f., 26). — G. Lazatti, Gli sviluppi (Lz) (Turin, 1956), 1-93. — H. Musurillo, Acta martyrum et sanctorum: EdM 1:66-73. — H. Niedermeyer, Über antike Protokoll-Lit. (Göttingen, 1918). — O. Perler, Das vierte Makkabäerbuch, Ignatius v. Antiochien u. die ältesten Martyrerberichte: RivAC 25 (1949) 47-72. — A. Prießnig, Die biographischen Formen der griech. Heiligenlegenden, Diss. (Munich, 1922), 91-98. — V. Saxer, Afrique latine: Hagiographies 1, ed. G. Philippart (Turnhout, 1994), 25-95 (esp. 6, 8, 12, 13, 16, 17, 23, 24). — idem, Bible et hagiographie (Brussels, ²1966) (esp. 2-9, 12, 21, 22, 25). — idem, Zweck u. Ursprung der hagiographischen Lit. in Nordafrika: TThZ 93 (1984) 65-74. = idem, Pères saints et culte chrétien (Aldershot, 1994), Nr XIII. — M. Simonetti, Studi agiografici (Rome, 1955) (4, 9, 11, 23, 26). — M. Van Uytfanghe, Heiligenverehrung II: RAC 14:150-183. — idem, Platonisme et eschatologie chrétienne 1: les actes et passions sincères: FS G. J. M. Bartelink (Steenbrugge, 1989), 343-362. — idem, Platonisme et eschatologie chrétienne 2: les passions tardives: Antiquité tardive et christianisme ancien (Paris, 1992), 69-95. — idem, L'hagiographie: un "genre" chrétien ou antique tardive?: AnBoll 111 (1993) 135-188.

Particular studies: on 1: P. Lampe, Die stadtröm. Christen (Tübingen, ²1989), 200-203. — **on 2:** G. Buschmann, Das Martyrium des Polykarp (Göttingen, 1998). — B. Dehandschutter, Martyrium Polycarpi. Een literair-kritische studie (Leuven/Louvain, 1979). — idem, The Martyrium Polycarpi: a Century of Research: ANRW II 27/1 (1993) 485-522. — A. Lallemand, Le parfum des martyrs dans les Actes des martyrs de Lyon et le martyre de Polycarpe: StPatr 16 (1985) 186-192. — G. Lazzati, Nota su Eusebio epitomatore di Atti dei martiri: FS A. Calderini, R. Paribeni 1 (Milan, 1956), 377-384. — S. Ronchey, Indagine sul martirio di San Policarpo (Rome, 1990) (literature). — V. Saxer, L'authenticité du "martyre de Polycarpe": Bilan de 25 ans de critique: MEFRA 94 (1982) 979-1001. — **on 3:** G. A. Bisbee, The Acts of Justin Martyr: SecCen 3 (1983) 128-157. — R. Freudenberger, Die Acta Justini als historisches Dokument: FS W. v. Loewenich (Witten, 1968), 24-31. — G. Lazzati, Gli atti di S. Giustino martire: Aevum 27 (1953) 473-497. — **on 4:** F. Halkin, Une nouvelle passion des martyrs de Pergame: FS T. Klauser (Münster, 1964), 150-154. — H. Lietzmann, Die älteste Gestalt der P. Carp.: TU 67 (1958) 239-250. — **on 5:** S. J. Croteau, M. Aurelius and the Accidental Martyrs of Lyons, Diss. (Univ. of Missouri, Columbia, 1992). — D. Farkasfalvy, Christological Content and Its Biblical Basis in the Letter of the Martyrs of Gaul: SecCen 9 (1992) 5-25. — P. Keresztes, Das Christenmassaker von Lugdunum im Jahre 177: Historia 16 (1967) 75-86 = R. Klein (ed.), Marc Aurel (Darmstadt, 1979), 261-278. — H. Kraft, Die Lyoner Märtyrer u. der Montanismus: FS B. Kötting (Münster, 1980), 250-266. — P. de Labriolle, Le style de la lettre des chrétiens de Lyon: BALAC 3 (1913) 198f. — Les martyrs de Lyon (177). Colloque international du CNRS No. 575 (Paris, 1978). — C. Saumagne, M. Meslin, De la légalité du procès de Lyon de l'année 177: ANRW II 23/1 (1979) 316-339. — W. A. Löhr, Der Brief der Gemeinden von Lyon u. Vienne: FS W. Schneemelcher (Stuttgart, 1989), 135-149. — **on 6:** G. Bonner, The Scillitan Saints and the Pauline Epistles: JEH 7 (1956) 141-146. — F. Corsaro, Note sugli "Acta Martyrum Scillitanorum": NDid 6 (1956) 5-51. — R. Freudenberger, Die Akten der Scilitanischen Märtyrer als historisches Dokument: WSt NF 7 (1973) 196-215. — H. A. Gärtner, Die Acta Scillitanorum in literarischer Interpretation: WSt NF 23 (1989) 149-167. — R. Hanslick, Secretarium u. tribunal in den Acta Martyrum Scillitanorum: FS C. Mohrmann (Utrecht, 1963), 165f. — H. Karpp, Die Zahl der Scilitanischen Märtyrer: VigChr 15 (1961) 165-172. — F. Ruggiero, Il problema del numero dei martiri scillitani: CrSt 9 (1988) 135-152. — A. Wlosok, Die chr. Aufzeichnungen über das Verhör der Märtyrer von Scili: eadem, Rom u. die Christen (Stuttgart, 1970), 40-48. — **on 7:** R. Freudenberger, Die Überlieferung vom Martyrium des röm. Christen Apollonius: ZNW 60 (1969) 111-130. — J. Geffcken, Die Acta Apollonii: NGWG. PH 1904, 262-284. — E. Griffe, Les actes du martyr Apollonius et les problèmes de la base juridique des persécutions: BLE 53 (1952) 65-76. — A. v. Harnack, Der Process des Christen Apollonius: SPAW 1893, 721-746. — T. Mommsen, Der Prozeß des Christen Apollonius unter Commodus: SPAW 1894, 497-503. — H. Paulsen, Erwägungen zu den Acta Apollonii 14-22: ZNW 66 (1975) 117-126. — M. zu Sachsen, Der hl. Märtyrer Apollonius v. Rom (Mainz, 1903). V. Saxer, M. Apoll.: RPARA 55/56 (1982-84) 265-298. — idem, L'apologie au Sénat du martyr romain Apollonius: MEFRA 96 (1984) 1017-1038. — J. Schwartz, Autour des Acta S. Apollonii: RHPhR 50 (1970) 257-261. — **on 8:** J. Amat, L'authenticité des songes de la Passion de Perpétue et de Felicité: Aug. 29 (1989) 177-191. — A. A. R. Bastiaensen, Heft Perpetua haar dagboek in het Latijn of in het Grieks geschreven?: De Heiligenverering in de eerste eeuwen van het christendom, ed. A. Hilhorst (Nijmegen, 1988), 130-135. — R. Braun, Tertullien est-il le rédacteur de la P. Perp.?: REL 33 (1955) 79-81. — idem, Nouvelles observations linguistiques sur le rédacteur de la P. Perp.: VigChr 33 (1979) 105-177. — J. Campos, El autor de la P. Perp.: Helm. 10 (1959) 357-381. — E. Corsini, Proposte per una lettura della P. Perp.: FS M. Pellegrino (Turin, 1975), 481-541. — F. J. Dölger, Die Fingerringszene der P. Perp.: Verhandlungen der Versammlung dt. Philologen 54 (1923) 140-155. — idem, Gladiatorenblut u. Märtyrerblut: VBW 3 (1923/24) 196-214. — idem, Antike Parallelen zum leidenden Dinocrates: AuC 2 (1930 = 1974) 1-40. — idem, Der Kampf mit dem Ägypter in der Perpetua-Vision: AuC 3 (1932 = 1975) 177-188. — idem, Herrin u. Tochter in der P. Perp.: AuC 5 (1936 = 1976) 296. — R. Freudenberger, Probleme röm. Religionspolitik in Nordafrika nach der P. Perp.: Helikon 13/14 (1973/74) 174-183. — A. Fridh, Le Problème de la passion des saintes Perpétue et Félicité (Stockholm,

1968). — P. Habermehl, Perpetua u. der Ägypter, TU 140 (Berlin, 1992) (literature). — J. W. Halporn, Literary History and Generic Expectations in the Passio and Acta Perpetuae: VigChr 45 (1991) 223-241. — A. Jensen, Gottes selbstbewußte Töchter (Freiburg i.Br., 1992), 200-232. — A. Kessler, Der Angriff auf die Augen Perpetuas: FS D. van Damme (Fribourg, Switzerland, 1994), 191-201. — P. de Labriolle, Tertullien, auteur du prologue et de la conclusion de la passion de Perpétue et Félicité: BALAC 3 (1913) 126-132. — V. Lomanto, Rapporti fra la P. Perp. e "Passiones" africane: FS M. Pellegrino (Turin, 1975), 566-586. — C. Mertens, Les premiers martyrs et leurs rêves: RHE 81 (1986) 5-46. — M. Meslin, Vases sacrés et boissons d'éternité dans les visions des martyrs africains: FS J. Daniélou (Paris, 1972), 139-153. — A. P. Orbán, The Afterlife in the visions of the P. Perp.: FS G. J. M. Bartelink (Dordrecht, 1989), 269-277. — R. Petraglio, Lingua latina e mentalità biblica nella P. Perp. (Brescia, 1976). — idem, Des influences de l'Apocalypse dans la P. Perp. 11-13: L'apocalypse de Jean. Traditions exégétiques et iconographiques (Geneva, 1979), 15-29. — A. Pettersen, Perpetua, Prisoner of Conscience: VigChr 41 (1987) 139-153. — L. F. Pizzolato, Note alla P. Perp.: VigChr 34 (1980) 105-119. — J. Quasten, A Coptic Counterpart of a Vision in the Acts of Perpetua and Felicitas: Byz. 15 (1940/41) 1-9. — idem, Mutter u. Kind in der P. Perp.: HJ 72 (1953) 50-55. — L. Robert, Une vision de Perpétue martyre à Carthage en 203: CRAI 1982, 228-276. — E. Rupprecht, Bemerkungen zur P. Perp.: RMP 90 (1941) 177-192. — B. D. Shaw, The Passion of Perpetua: PaP 139 (1993) 3-45. — W. Shewring, Prose Rhythm in the P. Perp.: JThS 30 (1929) 56f. — M. Testard, La Passion des saintes Perpétue et Félicité: BAGB 1991, 56-75. — E. Zocca, Un passo controverso della P. Perp. IV, 9: SMSR 50 = NF 8 (1984) 147-154. — **on 9:** S. Gero, Jewish Polemic in the M. Pion.: JJS 39 (1978) 164-168. — H. Grégoire, P. Orgels, J. Moreau, Les martyres de Pionios et de Polycarpe: BAB. L 47 (1961) 72-83. — A. Hilhorst, L'Ancien testament dans la polémique du martyr Pionius: Aug. 22 (1982) 91-96. — G. Kehnscherper, Apokalyptische Redewendungen in der griech. Passio des Presbyters Pionios: StPatr 12 (1975) 96-103. — L. Robert, Le martyre de Pionios (Washington, 1994); additionally, P. Devos: AnBoll 113 (1995) 180-184. — L. Wohleb, Die Überlieferung des Pionios-Martyriums: RQ 37 (1929) 173-177. — **on 12:** R. Freudenberger, Romanas caerimonias recognoscere: FS D. Daube (Oxford, 1978), 238-254. — F. Heberlein, Eine philologische Anmerkung zu "Romanas caerimonias recognosceri" (Acta Cypriani 1): FS P. Klopsch (Göppingen, 1988), 83-100. — E. L. Hummel, The Concept of Martyrdom according to St. Cyprian (Washington, 1946). — W. Wischmeyer, Der Bischof im Prozeß: Cyprian als episcopus, patronus, advocatus u. martyr vor dem Proconsul: FS F. J. M. Bartelink (Dordrecht, 1989), 363-371. — idem, Cyprianus episcopus 2: FS A. A. R. Bastiaensen (Den Haag, 1991), 407-419. — **on 16:** H. Delehaye, Réfractaire et martyr: idem, Mélange d'hagiographie grecque et latine (Brussels, 1966), 375-378. — F. J. Dölger, Sacramentum militiae: AuC 2 (1930 = 1974) 268-280. — J. Helgeland, Christians and the Roman Army: ANRW II 23/1 (1979) 777-780. — HLL 5:520f. — P. Siniscalco, Biblia e letteratura cristiana d'Africa nella P. Maximil.: FS M. Pellegrino (Turin, 1975), 595-613. — **on 17:** A. Bonilauri, Gli "Acta Marcelli": Did. 9 (1930) 1-27. — F. Dolbeau, À propos du texte de la P. Marcell.: AnBoll 90 (1972) 329-335. — B. de Gaiffier, L' "elogium" dans la Passion de S. Marcel: ALMA 16 (1942)

127-136. — idem, S. Marcel de Tanger ou de Léon?: AnBoll 61 (1943) 116-139. — idem, Un nouveau témoin de la passion de S. Marcel: AST 43 (1970) 93-96. — J. Helgeland, op. cit., 780-783. — G. Lanata, Gli atti del processo contro il centurione Marcello: Byz. 42 (1972) 509-522. — F. Masai, Pour une édition critique des actes du centurion Marcel: Byz. 35 (1965) 277-290. — W. Seston, À propos de la P. Marcell.: FS M. Goguel (Neuchâtel, 1950), 239-246. — **on 19**: R. Gerhardt, Über die Akten des hl. Anthimus u. des hl. Sebastianus, Diss. (Jena, 1916). — G. Helgeland, op. cit., 827f. — S. Minocchi, Il martirio di San Sebastiano: Nuova antologia di lettere, scienze ed arte 154 (1911) 440-451. — B. Pesci, Il culto di San Sebastiano a Roma nell'antichità e nel medioevo: Anton. 20 (1945) 177-200. — **on 20**: R. Pillinger (Vienna, 1998). — I. Rochow, Die Passio des hl. Dasius: BBA 44 (1973) 235-247. — S. Weinstock, Saturnalien u. Neujahresfest in den M.: FS T. Klauser (Münster, 1964), 391-400. — **on 22**: F. Corsaro, Studi sui documenti agiografici intorno al martirio di S. Euplo: Orph. 4 (1957) 33-62. — **on 24**: G. Castelli, Osservazioni sulla lingua della P. Crisp.: FS M. Pellegrino (Turin, 1975), 587-594. — HLL 5:526f. — P. Monceaux, Les "actes" de Sainte Crispine: FS G. Boissier (Paris, 1903), 383-389. — K. Rosen, Passio S. Crispinae: JAC 40 (1997) 106-125. — **on 25**: HLL 5:527f. — **on 26**: A. M. Emmert, S. R. Pichering, The Importance of P. Bodmer XX: Prudentia 7 (1975) 95-103. — E. A. Jugde, The trial of bishop Phileas: NDIEC 2 (1982) 185-191. — J. R. Knipfing, The Date of the Acts of Phileas and Philoromus: HThR 16 (1923) 198-203. — G. Lanata, Note al papiro Bodmer XX: Museum philologicum Londiniense 2 (1977) 207-226. — C. H. Roberts, The Apology of Phileas: JThS 18 (1967) 437f. — E. G. Turner, A Passage in the "Apologia" of Phileas: JThS 17 (1966) 404f. — **on 27**: D. P. Buckle, The Forty Martyrs of Sebaste: BJRL 6 (1921) 352-360. — H. Delehaye, The Forty Martyrs of Sebaste: ACQR 24 (1899) 161-171. — **on 28**: H. Emonds, Zweite Auflage im Altertum (Leipzig, 1941), 41-44. — A. Halmel, Die palästinensischen Märtyrer des Eusebius v. Cäsarea in ihrer zweifachen Form (Essen, 1898). — R. Laqueur, Eusebius als Historiker seiner Zeit (Berlin, 1929). — H. J. Lawlor, The chronology of Eusebius "Martyrs of Palestine": Her. 25 (1908) 177-201 = idem, Eusebiana (Oxford, 1912 = Amsterdam, 1973), 179-210. — **on 29**: J. Rist, Die Christenverfolgung im spätantiken Sassanidenreich: OrChr 80 (1996) 17-42. — G. Wiessner, Zur Märtyrerüberlieferung aus der Christenverfolgung Schapurs II: AAWG. PH 67 (1967). — **on 30**: T. Baumeister, Martyr invictus (Münster, 1972). — idem, Fortschritte in der ägyptischen Hagiographie: FS M. Krause (Wiesbaden, 1995), 9-14. — J. Horn, Studien zu den Märtyrern im nördlichen Oberägypten, 2 vols. (Wiesbaden, 1986-92).

H. R. Seeliger

Maruta of Maiferqat

Various *Vitae* tell of the life of M., bishop of Maiferqat. He studied medicine and, following in his father's steps, undertook a political career at the Persian royal court, but soon moved into a monastic form of life. In the time of Emperor Theodosius I, he headed the diocese of Maiferqat in the Roman-Persian frontier zone. During the reign of the Persian Emperor Yezdegerd I (399-420) M. was a member of

various delegations to the court of the East Roman emperor. He used his influence over the Persian emperor to improve the general situation of the Persian church. In 403 he intervened in the West at the Synod of the Oak in behalf of his friend John Chrys. In 410 he held a synod in Seleucia-Ctesiphon, at which the decrees of Nicaea were accepted and comprehensive powers were given to the catholicos-patriarch of the Persian capital. In 417-419 M. once again traveled to Constantinople on a mission; he died shortly afterward.

It is not easy to distinguish M.'s literary work from that of his namesake, Maruta of Tagrit. Certainly authentic are a treatise against heresies (*c. haer.*), an explanation of Gr. words borrowed by Syriac (*expl.*), and a homily on White Sunday (the first Sunday after Easter) (*hom. in Dom.*). In addition, M. must have arranged for the translation of the canons of Nicaea, but these exist only in a considerably expanded recension. M. promoted veneration of the martyrs in the Persian church and saw to the publication of their corresponding acts. The Chaldean breviary attributes various liturg. hymns to M., while the Arm. tradition also ascribes three homilies to him.

S: *vita*, R. Marcus, Armenian Life of M.: HThR 25 (1932) 47-73 [Armenian text/English trans.]. — J. Noret, La Vie grecque: AnBoll 91 (1973) 77-103 [Greek text/French trans.].
W: *c. haer.*, F. Nau, PO 22:180-199 [text/French trans.]. — J. E. Rahmani, Studia Syriaca 4 (Sharfa, 1909), 76-80, 98-103 [text/Latin trans.]. — O. Braun, De Sancta Nicaena Synodo (Münster, 1898), 27f., 46-50 [German trans.]. — *expl.*, O. Braun, op. cit., 39f., 56-58 [text/German trans.]. — *hom. in Dom.*, M. Kmosko: OrChr 3 (1903) 384-415 [text/German trans.].
L: L. Ter-Petrossian, Recueil des Passions: AnBoll 97 (1979) 129f.

P. Bruns

Maruta of Tagrit

The *Vita* of M. was composed by his successor, Denha (d. 660). M. was from the Persian village of Shurzaq and as a young man studied at the monastery of Samuel. He continued his studies in the Byz. empire and returned to the Persian kingdom in 605, where he taught theology in the monastery of Mar Mattai. In 628/629 Monophysite Patriarch Athanasius I consecrated him "maphrian" or organizer, with the task of setting up an anti-Nestorian hierarchy in Persia. M. resided in Tagrit and had twelve suffragan bishops under him. He composed for the patriarch a short account of the spread of Nestorianism in Persia (*rel.*) and also composed a homily on the blessing of water on the feast of the Epiphany (*hom.*). A eucharistic prayer (*anaph.*) is also attributed to him.

S: *vita*, F. Nau, PO 3:61-96 [text/French trans.].
W: *rel.*, J. B. Chabot, Chronique de Michel le Syrien (Paris, 1900/1910), 1:424-429 [text]; 2:435-440 [French trans.]. — *hom.*, S. P. Brock, Blessing of the Water: OrChr 66 (1982) 51-74 [text/English trans.]. — *anaph.*, E. Renaudot, Liturgiarum Orientalium Collectio 2 (London, 1847), 260-268 [text/Latin trans.].
L: M. Kmosko, M.: OrChr 3 (1903) 386-388.

P. BRUNS

Mary, Literature about

(a) *De Transitu B.M.V.* The title *Transitus* (*trans.*) or *Dormitio Mariae* is used of a series of works in various languages (Greek, Latin, Coptic, Arabic, Ethiopic) that describe the death and bodily assumption of Mary into heaven. Various individuals are given as authors: John the evangelist, → Melito of Sardis, and Evodius of Antioch. The two oldest Gr. redactions are from the 5th c. and reflect Marian piety after the Council of Ephesus. Their nucleus probably goes back to a still earlier version from the end of the 4th c. The basic story is expanded and adapted acc. to cultural and linguistic milieu. The two Copt. versions, which are attributed to → Theodosius Alex., develop in narrative form the christology and mariology of Severus of Antioch and argue against both Chalcedon on the one hand and the extreme Monophysites on the other (→ Julian of Halicarnassus). The Ethiopians divide the *trans.* into several phases, in which the mother of God communicates special heavenly revelations to the apostles between her falling asleep and her final assumption.

W: *trans.*, M. Haibach-Heinisch, Neuer Transitus des Ps.-Melito (Rome, 1962) [Greek text/German trans./comm.]. — A. Wilmart, L'ancien récit lat. de l'Assumption: ST 59 (1933) 323-362 [Latin text]. — V. Arras, CSCO 342f., 351f. [Ethiopic text/Latin trans.]. — A. Smith-Lewis, Apocrypha syriaca (London, 1902) [Syriac text/English trans.]. — A. van Lantschoot, L'assomption chez les Coptes: Gr. 27 (1946) 493-526 [Coptic text/French trans.]. — M. van Esbroeck, Apocryphes: AnBoll 90 (1972) 363-369; 91 (1973) 55-75; 93 (1974) 125-163 [Georgian text/Latin trans.]. — idem, L'Histoire euthymiaque: ParOr 6/7 (1975/76) 479-491 [Arabic text/French trans.]. — idem, Homélie arménienne: OrChr 74 (1990) 199-233 [Armenian text/French trans.]. — C. Donahue, Testament of Mary (New York, 1942) [Gallic-Latin text/English trans./comm.]. — G. Graf, Geschichte 1 (Rome, 1944), 249-251 [Arabic mss.].

L: B. Capelle, Les anciens récits: RThAM 12 (1940) 209-235. — M. Jugie, La mort et l'assomption de la S. Vierge (Rome, 1944). — M. van Esbroeck, Aux origines de la Dormition (Norfolk, 1995). — J. Rivière, Le transitus latin: RThAM 8 (1936) 5-23. — A. Wenger, L'assomption dans la tradition byzantine (Paris, 1954).

(b) *Lamentatio Mariae.* The "Lament of Mary" is preserved complete in Arabic and fragmentarily in an Eth. homily attributed to a Cyriacus of Bahnasa. In it Mary laments the loss of her Son, who appears to her as risen Lord on Easter morning. The work, richly adorned with legendary ingredients, was probably composed ca. 500 in Egypt and goes back to a Gr. original.

W: A. Mingana, Lament of the Virgin: BJRL 12 (1928) 459-488, 427-458 [Arabic text/English trans.].

(c) *Historia B.M.V.* The nucleus of the *History of the Blessed Virgin Mary*, which is preserved in Syriac, Armenian, and Arabic, goes back to the apocryphal *Gospel of James*, the *Infancy Story of Thomas*, the *Arabic Infancy Gospel*, and the *trans.*, and was composed in 5th c. Syria. The conception, birth, childhood, annunciation, death, and assumption into heaven are described. Miracles worked by the Mother of God and the child Jesus are loosely connected with the story. The author's purpose is to bring out, in a popular form, the significance of the Virgin Mary and her miraculous power for Chr. devotion.

W: E. A. W. Budge, History of the Blessed Virgin Mary (London, 1899), 1:3-153; 2:3-168 [Syriac text/English trans.]. — G. Graf, Geschichte 1 (Rome, 1944), 246f. [Arabic mss.].
L: M. Gordillo, Mariologia orientalis (Rome, 1954). — S. Müller, Mariä Empfängnis in syr. und arm. Überlieferung: Schol. 9 (1934) 161-201. — idem, Mariä Empfängnis in der kopt. und äth. Kirche (Rome, 1934).

(d) *Descent of Mary.* Acc. to Epiphanius (*haer.* 26.12.1), the *Genna Marias* (*genna Marias*) or *Descent of Mary*, is a work of the Sethians. In it the assassination of Zechariah, father of the Baptist, in the Jerusalem temple is described. The work, which is lost except for this fragment, dates probably from the 2nd c. The relationship of the *generatio Mariae* mentioned in Augustine (*c. Faustum* 23.9) to the *Genna* is unclear.

W: Epiphanius, *haer.* 26.12.1-4. — NTApo[6] 1:316 [German trans.].

P. BRUNS

Mary Magdalene, The Gospel of

Mary Magdalene (M.) frequently plays an important role in gnostic literature (→ *Pistis Sophia*). At least a part of a gospel acc. to M. (*Ev. Mar.*) is contained, in a Copt. translation, in *Pap. Berol.* 8502 (which also contains the → *Sophia Jesu Christi*). Fragments of it (in the Gr. original) are in *Pap.* 463 *John Rylands* and *Pap. Oxyrh.* 3525. The work is gnostic in character and comes from the 2nd c.

It has two parts: The first is a dialogue of Jesus (described as "redeemer" and "blessed") with his disciples on the destiny of matter and the nature of sin. At the end, M. appears and consoles the disciples after the departure of Jesus. In the second part, at the request of Peter, M. communicates the revelations she in particular has been given by the redeemer who "loved her more than the other women." In these, she tells of a vision of the path of the soul (similarities with the *Apocryphon* of → John and the gospel of → Eve). Only this section properly deserves the name *Ev. Mar.*

W: *Pap. Berol.*, Die gnostischen Schriften des kopt. Pap. Berol. 8502, ed. W. C. Till, TU 60:2. Aufl. H.-M. Schenke (Berlin, 1972), 24-32, 62-79 [text/German trans.]. — G. W. MacRae, R. McL. Wilson, The Gospel according to Mary: NHC V, 2-5; VII with *Pap. Berol.* 8502, 1 and 4, ed. D. M. Parrott (Leiden, 1979), 453-471 [text/English trans.]. — A. Pasquier, BCNH Section Textes 10 (Quebec, 1983) [text]. — *Pap.* 463 *John Rylands*, C. H. Roberts, Catalogue of the Greek and Latin Papyri III (Manchester, 1938), 18-23. — *Pap.* 463 *John Rylands*, *Pap. Oxyrh.* 3525, D. Lührmann, Die griech. Frgm. des *Ev. Mar.*: NT 30 (1988) 321-339 [text]. — NTApo⁶ 1:313-315 [German trans.].
L: E. A. de Boer, M. en haer Evangelie: Gnosis, ed. G. Quispel (Utrecht, 1988), 85-98. — E. Lucchesi, Évangile selon Marie ou Évangile selon Marie Madeleine: AnBoll 103 (1985) 366. — D. Lühmann, Die griech. Frgm. des Ev. Mar.: NT 30 (1988) 321-338. — A. Marjanen, The Woman Jesus Loved, NHS 40 (Leiden, 1996), esp. 94-121 (literature). — R. McL. Wilson, Gnosis and the NT (Philadelphia, 1988), 101-103. — A. Pasquier, L'eschatologie dans l'Évangile selon Marie: Colloque international sur les Textes de Nag Hammadi, ed. B. Barc (Quebec, 1981), 390-404. — G. Quispel, Das Hebräerevangelium im gnostischen Ev. Mar.: VigChr 11 (1957) 139-144. — C. Schmidt, Ein vorirenäisches gnostisches Originalwerk in kopt. Sprache: SPAW 1896, 839-847. — idem, Pistis Sophia (Leipzig, 1925), LXXXIII-XC.

G. RÖWEKAMP

Matthew, Literature about

The Lat. gospel of Ps.-Matthew was written either in the 5th c. or not until the 8th/9th c. but was regarded as a translation by Jerome of the supposed original Heb. version of Mt. Because of this work, the legends in the *Protevangelium* of → James the Younger and in other old texts were spread abroad in the West under the authority of the man who had protested against its contents on theol. grounds (e.g., children of a first marriage of Joseph)! (see also → *Ebionites, Gospel of the*). A derivative of this work is the *De nativitate Mariae*.

W: C. v. Tischendorff, Evangelia apocrypha (Hildesheim, 1987 = ²1876), 51-111 [text].
L: M. Berthold, Zur Datierung: WSt 102 (1989) 247-249. — J. Gijsel, Die unmittelbare Textüberlieferung, VVAW. W 43, 1981, Nr. 96 (Brussels, 1981).

A *Martyrium Matthaei* takes motifs from the *Acta Andreae et Matthaei* (→ *Andrew, Acts of*) (mission to the country of the cannibals) and from the *Vita Petri slavica* (→ *Peter, Literature about*) (stay of M. in the wilderness; appearance of Jesus as a child), and then tells of the martyrdom of Matthew. The *Acta Matthaei in Kahenat* is a Copt. reworking that has survived only in Arabic. A Lat. *Passio Matthaei*, handed down as book 7 of → (Ps.-) Abdias, is independent of the preceding, but does have the assignment of Ethiopia to Matthew, which is mentioned in Rufinus (*h.e.* 3.1; 10.9).

W: *Martyrium Matthaei*, AAAp 2/1:217-262 [Greek text/Latin text]. — M. Erbetta, Gli Apocrifi del NT 2 (Turin, 1966), 511-517 [Italian trans.]. — *Acta Matthaei in Kahenat*, A. Smith Lewis (Horae Semiticae) (London, 1903), 3:83-94 [Arabic text]; 4:100-112 [English trans.]. — *Passio Matthaei*, G. Talamo Atenolfi, I testi medioevali degli Atti di S. Matteo (Rome, 1958) [text/Italian trans.]. — M. Erbetta, op. cit., 519-526 [Italian trans.].
L: F. Bovon et al., Die apokryphen Apostelakten (Geneva, 1981), 233-239. — HLL 4:401f. — R. A. Lipsius, Die apokrypen Apostelgeschichten (Amsterdam, 1976 = 1883f.), 1:147-149, 166-168; 2/2:134-141. — NTApo⁵ 2:414-417.

G. RÖWEKAMP

Matthias, Gospel of

A gospel according to M. is first attested in the list of heterodox works in Origen (*hom.* 1 *in Luc.*) and Eusebius (*h.e.* 3.25.6). Clement Alex. transmits some fragments of the so-called *Traditions of Matthias* (*paradoseis*). This work, composed probably at the beginning of the 2nd c. in Egypt, does not have a pronounced gnostic character. It is disputed whether the *Traditions* are identical with the "secret tradition of M." mentioned by Clement (*str.* 7.17.108.1) and Hippolytus (*haer.* 7.20.1) and/or with the *Gospel of M.* The reference in the *Pistis Sophia* (44.19–45.19) to Thomas, Philip, and Matthias being commissioned by Jesus to write a gospel may signify that the *Gospel of M.*, like those of Thomas and Philip, contains "traditions" and "secret traditions" of Jesus. (On the *Acta Andreae et Matthiae* see → Andrew, Acts of.)

W: Clemens Alex., *str.* 2.9.45.4; 3.4.26.3; 7.13.82.1. — NTApo⁶ 1:306-308 [German trans./comm.].

G. Röwekamp

Maximian of Anazarba

M. was metropolitan of the province of Cilicia II and in 431 protested against the premature opening of the Council of Ephesus by Cyril. He took part in the synod presided over by John of Antioch which excommunicated Cyril but subsequently joined Alexander of Hierapolis in opposition to the union for which John was striving. A synod was held in Anazarba, with M. presiding, which again condemned Cyril. His name is not found, however, among the bishops exiled in 433 as opponents of the union; he had either agreed to the union or died before the decree went into effect.

The *Synodicon* of Rusticus contains three letters of M. to Alexander (*ep.*) on the position of John, the apostasy of John of Germanicia and Andrew of Samosata, and the question of whether Alexander would carry out the decrees of Anazarba. Also preserved are the decree of the Synod of Anazarba and the synod's letter to John (*syn.*).

W: *ep.*, ACO 1, 4, 104f., 140-142. — PG 84:675, 721-724. — *syn.*, ACO 1, 4, 142f. 179f. — PG 84:773f. 724f.

G. Röwekamp

Maximian of Ravenna

M. (498-556) came to Constantinople as deacon of the community of Pula; there Justinian appointed him bishop of Ravenna in 546. In Ravenna M. met with strong resistance, but he was able to surmount this through his generous promotion of church architecture. In Istria and Aquileia M. labored throughout the Three-Chapters controversy for the maintenance of orthodoxy. The *Liber pontificalis ecclesiae Ravennatis* (*Lib. pont.*) says that M. composed a chronicle, published a translation of the Bible, put together a → sacramentary (that is from time to time held to be the original of the *Sacramentarium Leonianum* or the *Sacramentarium Gelasianum*), and published a collection of sermons in twelve books. Nothing remains of M.'s works except for two citations (*Lib. pont.* 78 and 81).

W: *Lib. pont.*, PL 106:608-610. — M. Pierpaoli (Ravenna, 1988) [Italian trans.]. — C. Nauerth, FC 21.
L: G. Bovini, Opera di M. a Ravenna: AnAl 2 (1972) 147-165. — A. Chavasse, L'œuvre littéraire de M.: EL 74 (1960) 115-120. — G. Cuscito, Cristianesimo antico ad Aquileia e in Istria (Trieste, 1977), 286f. — M. Mazzotti, M. di Pola: Pagine istriane 1, 3. ser. 4 (1950) 14-21.

B. Dümler

Maximinus, Bishop of the Goths

In the margins of fol. 298ʳ-311ᵛ of *Cod. lat.* 8907 in the Bibliothèque Nationale (Paris) there is a partial transcript of the acts of the Synod of Aquileia 381 and a letter of → Auxentius of Durostorum (principal source on → Ulfila), both with a commentary by a Bishop Maximinus (M.); on fol. 349ʳ (to be dated to the mid-5th c.) and in the same hand there is a notice citing the → *Codex Theodosianus*, which was promulgated in 438 (on fol. 336ʳ-349ʳ are fragments from → Palladius of Rathiaria). In both cases these must be either an autograph of the bishop or something directly dictated by him. Reasons of theology and language strongly suggest the identity of the author of this *Dissertatio* (*diss.*) with the M., who, perhaps as a military bishop (but without necessarily being himself a Goth), went to North Africa with the Gothic army of Sigisvult and ca. 428 appeared in Hippo Regius in a debate with Augustine, provoked by Eraclius, on questions of trinitarian theology, during which M. appealed to the "homoean" Synod of Rimini (359). For M., God the Father is the only unbegotten God; the Son, on the other hand, is the *Deus universae creaturae*, e.g., a God of the second rank; the Holy Spirit is not God. The record of the debate, to which Augustine added a work of his own against M., shows M. to be a biblicist who adopts the subordinationist trend of the so-called Arian fragments of Bobbio (CCL 87:229-65), the → *Sermo Arrianorum*, and the work *C. hereticos* of *Cod. Veron.* 51 (CCL 87:142-45), among whose progenitors was → Ulfila. Perhaps M. is to be identified with M. the leader of the "Arians" in Palermo 440 (Hydatius 120 [SC 218:136]) or even with the M. against whom → Cerealis wrote before 480 (PL 58:757-68). M. would then have been born in the 390s. Very dubious is the attribution to M. of the partly homoean sermons and treatises in *Cod. Veron.* 51 (CCL 87:3-145; see PLS 1:728-63); the attribution of the → *Opus imperfectum in Matth.* and other works is to be rejected as groundless.

W: *diss.*, R. Gryson, CCL 87:149-171, 195f. — idem, SC 267:204-263, 324-327 (review: Y. M. Duval: RHE 26 [1981] 317-331). — Augustine, *coll. c. Maximin.*, PL 42:709-814.

— R. Gryson, Littérature arienne Latine 1 (Louvain-la-Neuve, 1980) [concordance to the dissertatio and Augustine coll. c. Maximin. (with corrected ext)].

L: H. C. Brennecke, M.: BBKL 5:1082-1084. — R. C. Gamble, Augustinus contra Maximinum (Ann Arbor, Mich., 1985). — R. Gryson, Citations scripturaires: RBen 88 (1978) 45-80. — idem, Composition des "scolies": RHT 14/5 (1984/85) 369-375. — idem, L. Gilissen, Les scolies ariennes du Paris. lat. 8907 (Turnhout, 1980). — C. P. Hammond Bammel, Paris MS. Lat. 8907: JThS 31 (1980) 391-402 (additionally, R. Gryson, L. Gilissen, Paléographie et critique littéraire: Scr. 35 [1981] 334-340). — L. J. van der Lof, [M. u.] Wandalen: ZNW 64 (1973) 146-151. — M. Meslin, Les ariens d'Occident (335-430) (Paris, 1967) (additionally, P. Nautin: RHR 89 [1970] 70-89). — M. Simonetti, S. Agostino e gli Ariani: REAug 13 (1967) 55-84. — idem, Arianesimo latino: StMed 3/8 (1967) 663-744. — W. A. Sumruld, Augustine and the Arians (Selinsgrove, Pa., 1994). — R. J. Teske, Augustine, M. and imagination: Aug(L) 43 (1993) 27-41. — R. Vander Plaetse, A. Schindler, Conlatio cum M.: AugL 1:1209-1218. Zu den Texten des 51: B. Capelle, Un homiliaire de M.: RBen 34 (1922) 81-108. — G. M. Vian, Predicazione ed esegesi nell'arianesimo latino: ASEs 11 (1994) 533-544.

R. KANY

Maximus, African Bishop

The otherwise unknown Bishop M. wrote in 412 to Alexandrian Patriarch Theophilus in behalf of religious women who, accompanied by his nephew, had fled to Egypt ahead of the barbarian invasions. It remains uncertain whether he is the same as the subscriber to the Catholic synod of 416 or as a correspondent of Augustine whom Possidius mentions.

W: PLS 1:1092-1095. — G. Morin: Revue Charlemagne 2 (1912) 89-104 [text].
L: P. Courcelle, Histoire des grandes invasions germaniques (Paris, ²1964), 62-64. — PAC 737.

G. RÖWEKAMP

Maximus, Antignostic

Acc. to Eusebius (*h.e.* 5.27) a M. composed a work *De materia* ca. 180-210. The fragment from this that is cited in *p.e.* 7.22.1-64 is also found in → Methodius (*arbitr.* 5.1–12.8), with whom M. may have been confused as he is in *De recta in deum fide* (→ Origen), whose author he is considered to have been (but, if so, then ca. 250).

W: Eusebius, *p.e.* 7.22.1-64.
L: T. D. Barnes, Methodius, M., and Valentinus: JThS 30 (1979) 47-55. — W. Bauer, Rechtgläubigkeit u. Ketzerei (Tübingen, ²1964), 150-153, 160f. — A. v. Harnack, Geschichte der altchr. Lit. 1 (Leipzig, ²1958), 786f.

R. HANIG

Maximus the Confessor

I. Life: M. lived from ca. 580 to 662. It is uncertain whether, as his Syr. *Vita* says, he came from Palestine or whether, as the Gr. sources claim, he was born the son of a distinguished Byz. family. It is certain that in 626 he fled to North Africa from the invading Persians and Arabs and there became increasingly involved in the struggle against Monophysitism, then Monoenergism, and finally Monotheletism. In 638 he attacked the formula that in Christ there are two natures and a single will, and in 645 he succeeded in having several African synods reject Monotheletism. In 648 he resisted a *Typos* of the emperor that forbade any discussion of the energies and wills of Christ and in 649, at the Lateran synod convoked in Rome by Pope Martin I (649-653), secured the condemnation of Monoenergism and Monotheletism as heresies. Four years later, in 653, M. and Martin I were taken prisoner by the emperor and hauled off to Byzantium, from which M. was banished to Bizya in Thrace in 655 for high treason. Since he stood stubbornly by his position (therefore: M. the "Confessor"), in 662 he with his disciple Anastasius and the Roman apocrisiarius Anastasius were banished by a synod to Kazika on the Black Sea, but only after he and his two companions had their tongues cut out and their right hands cut off. M. died in exile in 662, but a few years later, 680/681, was rehabilitated at the third Council of Constantinople.

L: PG 90:67-172. — PG 91:287-354. — R. Brakke, Ad S. M. Vitam. Studie van de biografische documenten en de levensbeschrijvingen betreffende M. (ca. 580-662) (Leuven/Louvain, 1980). — S. Brock, An Early Syriac Life of M.: AnBoll 91 (1973) 299-346. — R. Devreesse, La vie de s. M. et ses recensions: AnBoll 46 (1928) 5-49. — R. Devreesse, La lettre d'Anastase l'apocrisiaire sur la mort de S. M.: AnBoll 73 (1955) 5-16. — J. M. Garrigues, Le martyre de s. M.: RThom 76 (1976) 410-452. — W. Lackner, Zu Quellen u. Datierung der M. vita: AnBoll 85 (1967) 285-316. — R. Riedinger, Concilium Lateranense a. 649 celebratum, ACO 2, 1 (Berlin, 1984). — C. N. Tsirpanlis, Acta S. M.: Theol(A) 43 (1972) 106-124.

II. Works: M. has left us seventy-four longer and shorter theol. treatises, fifty letters, commentaries on Aristotle and → Dionysius the Areopagite, catena commentaries, and numerous fragments. His theol. treatises may be divided into the following groups: 1. *Dogm.-polemical treatises* primarily against the Monophysites, Monoenergists, and Monotheletes. In particular, there are twenty-seven *Opuscula theologica et polemica* (*opusc.*), among which the *Variae definitiones* against the Monophysites and the short work *Adversus eos qui dicunt dicendam unam Christi* *operationem* against the Monoenergists are outstanding for their conciseness. Among the writings against the Monotheletes are the *De duabus unius Christi nostri voluntatibus* and the *Disputatio cum Pyrrho* (*Pyrr.*), a debate held in Carthage in July 645 between M. and → Pyrrhus, patriarch of Constantinople 638-641 and 654 and a zealous supporter of Monotheletism. M. was a well-read scholar who had outstanding sources at his disposal: within the *opusc.* M. transmits a work of → Anastasius I against the tritheism of → John Philoponus (*Tomus dogmaticus ad Marinum presbyterum*).

2. *Ascetico-mystical treatises*, among them the two works, written before 630, *Liber asceticus* (*ascet.*) and *Capita de caritate* (*carit.*), which contain four centuries, i.e., four times almost a hundred ascetical-mystical sentences based on citations from the fathers, and the *Capita gnostica* (*cap.*), written ca. 630-634, which contain two hundred sentences influenced by Origen.

3. *Liturgical treatises*, among them the *Mystagogia* (*myst.*), which is an interpretation of the liturgy based on the *De ecclesiastica hierarchia* of Dionysius Areo., and the *Computus ecclesiasticus* (*comput.*) in which the seasons of the church year are calculated and other chronological questions are discussed.

4. *Exegetical works*, among them one of M.'s most important writings, the *Quaestiones ad Thalassium* (*qu. Thal.*) from the years 630/633. The addressee of these sixty-five questions and answers is → Thalassius, a Libyan monk and friend of M. The earlier (ca. 626) *Quaestiones et dubia* (*qu. dub.*) contains seventy-nine questions and answers, chiefly on bibl. problems. The explanation of Ps 59 (*exp. Ps 59*) and the commentary on the Our Father (*or. dom.*) must have been written between 626 and 630. The *Ambigua ad Thomam* and the *Ambigua ad Iohannem*, written between 628 and 634, comment on passages of → Gregory Nyss. and Dionysius Areo. The fifth *Ambiguum* is a commentary on Letter 4 of Dionysius; for this reason John Scotus Eriugena described the *Ambigua* as *Scolia*. This name explains the erroneous attribution to M. of scholia (*schol.*) that belong for the most part to John of Scythopolis (PG 4:15-576).

5. *Letters* (*ep.*), which not only constitute short theol. treatises but are also extremely valuable for judgments on the history of the time. The attribution to M. of a life of Mary is uncertain. The following are regarded as not authentic: five hundred *Diversa capita theologica et oeconomica*; two hundred *Capita alia*; hymns.

III. **Importance:** M., who succeeded in making a convincing synthesis of Chr. and pagan thought, was the most important Gr. thinker of the 7th c. His work has its roots in the writings of Origen, Gregory Naz., Gregory Nyss., Evagrius Pont., and Dionysius Areo. and is also indebted to the works of Aristotle. M.'s importance is due to his christological treatises, which emphasize the two intact natures of Christ, a complete human and a complete divine nature. The completeness of the two natures means that there are in Christ two wills, two potentialities for action, and two actions. Willing and the capacity for willing belong to the nature; choice, i.e., the direction of the will or willing this or that belongs to the person. Proper to Christ's human nature is only the willing; his willing this or that is determined solely by the Logos who guides the human will by his divine will and thus excludes error and sin from the human will.

W: *qu. Thal.*, PG 90:244-785. — C. Laga, C. Steel, CCG 7. 22. — *qu. dub.*, PG 90:785-856. — J. H. Declerck, CCG 10. — *exp. Ps 59*, PG 90:856-872. — P. van Deun, CCG 23.1-23. — *or. dom.*, PG 90:872-909. — P. van Deun, CCG 23:25-73. — *ascet.*, PG 90:912-956. — *carit.*, PG 90:960-1080. — A. Ceresa-Gastaldo, Verba seniorum, collana di testi e studi patristici NS 3 (Rome, 1963) [text/Italian trans./comm.]. — *cap. 1-5*, PG 90:1084-1177. — *qu. Theop.*, PG 90:1393-1400. — *opusc.*, PG 91:9-285. — *Pyrr.*, PG 91:288-353. — M. Doucet (Montreal, 1980) [text/French trans./comm.]. — *ep.*, PG 91:364-649. — P. Canart, La deuxième lettre à Thomas de s. M.: Byz. 34 (1964) 415-445 [text]. — *myst.*, PG 91:657-717. — *Ambigua ad Thomam*, PG 91:1032-1060. — *Ambigua ad Iohannem*, E. Jeauneau, CCG 18. — *comput.*, PG 19:1217-1280. — *schol.*, B. R. Suchla, PTS, in preparation.
Uncertain attribution: Life of Mary, M. Van Esbroeck, CSCO. I 21-22 [Georgian text/French trans.].
Not authentic: *cap. al.*, PG 90:1177-1461. — *Opusculum de anima*, PG 91:353-361. — *Loci communes*, PG 91:721-1017. — *Hymni*, PG 91:1417-1424. — *Fragmentum ex opere LXIII dubiorum*. — *Definitiones in Isagogen Porphyrii et in Categorias Aristotelis*.
L: H. U. v. Balthasar, Die "Gnostischen Centurien" des M. (Freiburg i.Br., 1941). — idem, Kosmische Liturgie (Einsiedeln, ²1961). — H.-G. Beck, Kirche u. theol. Lit. (Munich, ²1977), 432, 436-442. — V. Croce, Tradizione e ricerca. Il metodo teologico di S. M. (Milan, 1974). — C. De Vocht, M.: TRE 22:298-304. — J. M. Garrigues, M. La charité (Paris, 1976). — M. L. Gatti, M. Saggio di bibliografia generale (Milan, 1987). — F. Heinzer, Gottes Sohn als Mensch (Fribourg, Switzerland, 1980). — idem, C. Schönborn, M. Actes du Symposion sur M., Fribourg, 2-5-Septembre 1980 (Fribourg, Switzerland, 1982). — A. Riou, Le monde et l'église selon M. (Paris, 1973). — P. Sherwood, An Annotated Date-List of the Works of M. (Rome, 1952). — idem, The Earlier Ambigua of St. M. and his Refutation of Origenism (Rome, 1955). — idem, Survey of Recent Work on St. M.: Tr. 20 (1964) 428-437. — B. R. Suchla, Die sogenannten M.-Scholien des Corpus Dionysiacum Areopag. (Göttingen, 1980). — eadem, Die Überlieferung des Prologs des Johannes v. Skythopolis zum griech. Corpus Dionysiacum (Göttingen, 1984). — eadem, Eine Redaktion

des griech. Corpus Dionysiacum im Umkreis des Johannes v. Skythopolis (Göttingen, 1985). — eadem, Verteidigung eines platonischen Denkmodells einer chr. Welt (Göttingen, 1995). — L. Thunberg, Microcosm and Mediator (Uppsala, 1965). — idem, Man and the Cosmos, Crestwood (New York, 1985). — M. Viller, K. Rahner, Aszese u. Mystik in der Väterzeit (Freiburg i.Br., 1989 = 1939), 239-244. — W. Völker, M. als Meister des geistlichen Lebens (Wiesbaden, 1965).

B. R. Suchla

Maximus of Saragossa

M., bishop of Saragossa, d. 619/620, took part in the Councils of Barcelona (599) and Egara (614). His poems and prose writings (Isidore, *vir. ill.* 46) are lost. Excerpts from his *Chronica Caesaraugustana* (*Chron. Caesaraug.*) are perhaps preserved in marginal notes in the histories of → Isidore of Seville. The chronicle (PL 80:617) that goes under M.'s name is a 16th c. forgery.

W: *Chron. Caesaraug.*, T. Mommsen, MGH. AA 11:222f. L: J. Orlandis, D. Ramos-Lisson, Die Synoden auf der Iberischen Halbinsel (Paderborn, 1981).

E. Reichert

Maximus I of Turin

M., d. between 408 and 423 (Gennadius, *vir. ill.* 41), was probably the first bishop of Turin. His sermons, which were transmitted to the Middle Ages under the names of Ambrose and Augustine, were in the 18th c. confused with the work of authors of the same or similar name, espec. with the sermons of → Maximus II of Turin, with whom he was for a long time identified.

The surviving sermons, over one hundred of them, give the impression of an up-to-date and zealous pastor who had to deal with the typical problems of a rural community of the young imperial church: he preaches against idolatry in the countryside, feigned Christianity, laxism, corrupt clerics, Arians, social injustices, lack of courage in the face of the Germanic invasions. He seeks to christianize the Turin area espec. by appeals to the religious sense of responsibility of the rich and powerful. His sermons, which constantly allude to the mysteries of initiation, contain important testimonies to hagiog. traditions and the festal content of Christmas, Epiphany, and Pentecost. His theology combines typical Roman patterns of thought with constant appeals to the Bible and a christocentric message. His most important source is the commentary of → Ambrose on Lk, but uses its ideas very creatively. The sermons of M.

were popular in late antiquity, the Middle Ages, and early modern times because of their clarity and vividness.

W: *serm.*, A. Mutzenbecher, CCL 23. — additionally: R. Étaix: RBen 97 (1987) 40. — B. Ramsey, ACW 50 [English trans./comm.]. — G. Banterle, SASA 4 [Italian trans.]. L: L. Cervellin, Rassegna bibliografica su M.: Sal. 54 (1992) 555-565 (literature until 1991). — idem, "Per scriptura secretum": op. cit., 763-773. — idem, Chiesa — Popolo di Dio: op. cit. 55 (1993) 657-662. — M. Mariani Puerari, Per un' ermeneutica dei tempi: ScC 119 (1991) 60-94, 476-513. — eadem, La fisionomia delle feste: EL 106 (1992) 205-235, 381-406. — A. Merkt, M. (Leiden, 1997). — M. Modemann, Die Taufe in den Predigten des hl. M. (Frankfurt a.M., 1995). — V. Zangara, I "mandata" divini: ASEs 9 (1992) 493-518. — eadem, Intorno alla collectio antiqua: REAug 40 (1994) 435-451.

A. Merkt

Maximus II of Turin

M. was a mid-5th c. bishop of Turin. He took part in the Synods of Milan 451 and Rome 465. On Oct. 18, probably of 453, in the presence of Bishop Eusebius he delivered the sermon *In reparatione* (*serm. in reparatione*) on occasion of the rededication of the cathedral of Milan after it had been damaged by the Huns; in it M., using the book of Job, interprets the disaster of the Hun invasion as a punishment but also as an impulse to a better life of grace. There is some likelihood that M. also wrote ca. ninety other sermons (*serm.*) in the Milanese ms., *Bibl. Ambr.* c. 98 *inf.* (CLA III:322) and in the homiliary of Paul the Deacon. These sermons are almost exclusively on the liturgical seasons: Christmas, Epiphany, Ash Wednesday, the Sundays of Lent, the *traditio symboli*, Easter, Ascension, Pentecost, and the feasts of saints Cyprian, Peter and Paul, Lawrence, John the Baptist, the Maccabees, Agnes, and "All the Martyrs."

The value of these sermons as models, owing to their understandable and vivid language, as well as the fact that they were confused with those of → Maximus I, ensured their being handed on.

W: *serm.*, PL 57 passim (on the attribution of particular sermons, see H. J. Frede, Kirchenschriftsteller [Freiburg i.Br., ⁴1995], 628-642). — V. Zangara (critical edition in preparation). — *serm. Mur* 1-6, PLS 3:373-379. — *serm. Mur* 7: L. A. Muratori, Anecdota 4 (Padua, 1713), 84-88. — *serm. in reparatione*, F. Dell'Oro: ArAmb 32 (1977) 297-301. — *serm. Mu* 104; 109, A. Mutzenbecher, CCL 23:412, 425. — *serm. Et* 1-3, R. Étaix: RBen 97 (1987) 30-36. — *serm.* 75B, F. Negri: Aevum 64 (1990) 266f. — *hom. Ben* 45, R. Étaix, Homéliaires patristiques (Paris, 1994), 556-558. L: R. Étaix, Trois nouveaux sermons: RBen 97 (1987) 28-41. — idem, Homéliaires patristiques (Paris, 1994), 539-558. — idem, Catéchèse inédite sur Ephpheta: REAug 42 (1996)

65-70. — F. Dell'Oro, Il discorso "In reparatione ecclesiae": ArAmb 32 (1977) 268-301. — C. Pasini, M.: DCA 4:2110-2112.

A. MERKT

Melchizedek

Under the name *Melchizedek* (*Melch.*) there is a poorly transmitted work of completely christianized Sethian gnosticism in the Copt. library of Nag Hammadi (NHC 9, 1). Because of his parentless origin, the title character symbolizes the bringer of redemptive knowledge who is fully other-worldly and supraterrestial in his origin and passing away, and whose manifestation is the Christ, the Logos and high priest. There are also parallels to fragments of an apocryphal dialogue between → John and Jesus.

W: B. A. Pearson, NHC IX (Leiden, 1981) [Coptic text/English trans./comm.]. — NHL 438-444 [English trans.].
L: C. Gianotto, Melch. e la sua tipologia (Brescia, 1984). — J. Helderman, Melch.: Actes du IVᵉ Congrès Copte, ed. M. Rassart Debergh (Leuven/Louvain, 1992), 402-415. — idem, Melch. Wirkung: BEThL 86 (1989) 335-362. — F. L. Horten, Melchizedek Tradition (London, 1976). — H. M. Schenke, Melch.: AT-Frühjudentum-Gnosis, ed. K. W. Tröger (Gütersloh, 1980), 111-136. — H. Stork, Melchisedekianer (Leipzig, 1928). — G. Wuttke, Melchisedech (Giessen, 1927).

P. BRUNS

Meletius of Antioch

M., born in Armenia, was, along with John Chrys. and Theodore Mops., a student of Antiochene exegete Diodorus of Tarsus. Initially bishop of Arm. Sebaste, in 360, at the urging of Acacius of Berea, he became bishop of Antioch, the church of which had been divided since 330 by disputes between two Nicene groups and the Arians. M. soon won over the populace of Antioch, but after a Nicene sermon of M. on Prov 8:22 (*hom.*), Constantius II brought about his deposition and banishment. M. returned in 362 under Julian; this marked the beginning of the Meletian schism, since Lucifer of Cagliari had meanwhile consecrated a presbyter, Paulinus, as bishop of one Nicene group (the Eustathians). Two further banishments under Emperor Valens heightened M.'s reputation, but he was not recognized by Alexandria and Rome. Because of the opposition between Constantinople/Antioch and Alexandria, he was chosen to preside over the Council of Constantinople. He died, however, in May 381. Gregory Nyss. (PG 46:852-64) and John Chrys. (PG 50:515-20) delivered funeral addresses. (The Meletian schism did not end until 413.)

In addition to the sermon there is preserved a synodal letter to Emperor Jovinian (*ep. syn.*) in 363, in which an interpretation of the *homoousios* is given that was meant to make possible a reconciliation between the Meletians and the Paulinians. There is also a letter to Ital. and Gallic bishops (*ep.*), but this is possibly to be ascribed to Basil.

W: *hom.*, Epiphanius, *haer.* 73.29-33. — *ep. syn.*, Socrates, *h.e.* 3.25. — Sozomenus, *h.e.* 6.4. — *ep.*, Basil, *ep.* 92.
L: W. A. Jurgens, A letter of M.: HThR 53 (1960) 251-260. — I. Ortiz de Urbina, Nizäa u. Konstantinopel (Mainz, 1964), 179-186. — M. Richard, Saint Basile et la mission du diacre Sabinus: AnBoll 67 (1949) 178-202. — H. J. Vogt, M.: LMA 6:493.

K. BALKE

Melito of Sardis

M. lived in the second half of the 2nd c. and was venerated by many as a prophet (Jerome, *vir. ill.* 24). Eusebius mentions him as bishop of the Lydian city of Sardis (*h.e.* 5.24.2-8) who traveled to Jerusalem to gain certainty about the canon of the OT; Eusebius lists many writings of M. (*h.e.* 4.26.1-4). Fragments (*fr.*) survive of: a petition addressed to Marcus Aurelius (where for the first time there is a call for cooperation between church and Roman empire for the good of humanity; see *h.e.* 4.26.7); excerpts from a work on the law and the prophets (with the earliest list of the books of the OT: *h.e.* 4.26.13f.); *The Lord's Day*; two books on *The Easter Festival*; *The Incarnation* (against Marcion); on the devil and on the Apocalypse of John; on the passion; on baptism; on soul and body; on faith. Nothing remains of his writings on the church, creation, prophecy (against the Montanists), hospitality, and the incorporeality of God. There do exist some fragments, but it is not certain to which works they belong. There survives only a homily on Easter (*pass.*), which was probably delivered between 160 and 170, after M.'s visit to Palestine, and is transmitted in two papyri (*ChesterBeatty*; *Bodmer* XIII). Some remaining lacunae in the text have been filled in by the discovery of a Lat. translation.

The homily is written in the best Asiatic artistic prose (with chiasms, antitheses, paradoxes, alliterations, etc.). The discovery of the work (1940) decisively changed the picture of the development of early Chr. literature because it had previously been assumed that classical rhetoric was revived only in the 4th c. In content, the sermon is a witness to the

"Quartodeciman" celebration of Easter on 14 Nisan, a date determined in relation to the Jewish Passover. Accordingly, the homily develops as follows: (1) A hymnic prologue with reference to the reading of Ex 12 (1-10). (2) The OT Passover (11-34). (3) The OT preparation for the Chr. Passover (35-65). (4) The NT Passover (66-105). The typological approach to the OT with the emphasis on the fall and the fulfillment of OT types by Christ is similar to Irenaeus's conception of salvation history. Connected with this is an anti-Jewish attitude that climaxes in a lengthy speech against Israel in which the accusation of "deicide" occurs for the first time (72-99). The resurrection of Christ is viewed as an apotheosis and is celebrated in a closing hymn. The homily indirectly attests to a local tradition regarding the identification of Golgotha: Christ is said to have been crucified "in the middle of the city" (72; 94), which contradicts the NT witness but corresponds to the later position of the hill of Golgotha in 2nd c. Jerusalem.

M.'s name was given to a work on the passing of Mary (*De transitu Mariae*; → Mary, Literature about), which comes from the 5th c. at the earliest, and to the *Clavis scripturae* (J. Pitra, *Analecta sacra* 2 [Tusculum, 1884] 6-127), a work on number symbolism that draws on Augustine, Gregory I, and Eucherius of Lyons and was probably composed in 7th c. Spain.

W: *pass., fr.,* O. Perler, SC 123. — S. G. Hall, OECT (Oxford, 1979) [text/English trans.]. — *pass.,* J. Blank (Freiburg i.Br., 1963) [German trans.]. — J. Ibanez Ibanez, F. Mendoza Ruiz, BTeo 11 (Pamplona, 1975) [text/Spanish trans.]. — *fr.,* O. Perler, Ein Hymnus zur Ostervigil von M.? (Papyrus Bodmer XIII) (Fribourg, Switzerland, 1960). — M. v. Esbroeck, Nouveaux fragments de M. dans une homélie georgienne: AnBoll 90 (1972) 63-99. — M. Richard, Temoins grecs des fragments XIII et XV de M.: Muséon 85 (1972) 309-336. — I. Rucker, Florilegium Edessenum Anonymum (Munich, 1933), 5:12-16, 55-60. L: *Bibliographies:* H. Drobner, 15 Jahre Forschung zu M. (1965-1980): VigChr 36 (1982) 313-333. — M. Frenschkowski, M.: BBKL 5:1219-1223. — R. M. Mainka, M. Eine bibliographische Übersicht: Clar. 5 (1965) 225-255. I. Angerstorfer, M. u. das Judentum, Diss. (Regensburg, 1985). — R. Cantalamessa, Une christologie antignostique: RSR 37 (1963) 1-26. — H. Chadwick, A Latin Epitome of Melito's Homily on the Pascha: JThS NS 11 (1960) 76-82. — L. Cohick, M.'s pass. and its "Israel": HThR 91 (1998) 351-372. — J. Daniélou, Figure et événement chez M.: FS O. Cullmann (Leiden, 1962), 282-292. — H. Drobner, Der Aufbau der Paschapredigt M.s: ThGl 80 (1990) 205-207. — W. Huber, Passa u. Ostern (Berlin, 1969). — R. M. Hübner, M. u. Noet v. Smyrna: FS W. Schneemelcher (Stuttgart, 1989), 219-240. — G. Kretschmar, Chr. Passa im 2. Jh.: RSR 60 (1972) 287-323. — B. Lohse, Das Passafest der Quartodezimianer (Gütersloh, 1953). — A. M. Manis, M.: Hermeneutic and context: GOTR 32 (1987) 387-402. — H. J. auf der Maur, M.' "Über das Pascha" (Vienna, 1988). —

P. Nautin, M.: DSp 10:979-990. — idem, Le dossier d'Hippolyte et de M. (Paris, 1953). — F. W. Norris, M. 's Motivation: AThR 68 (1986) 16-26. — O. Perler, Recherches sur le "Peri Pascha" de M.: RSR 51 (1963) 407-421. — E. Peterson, Ps.-Cyprian, Adv. Iudaeos u. M.: VigChr 6 (1952) 33-43. — W. Schneemelcher, Heilsgeschichte u. Imperium: Kl. 5 (1973) 257-275. — idem, Der Sermo De anima et corpore: FS G. Dehn (Neukirchen, 1957), 119-143. — F. Trisoglio, Dalla Pasqua ebraica a quella cristiana in M.: Aug. 28 (1988) 151-185. — D. F. Winslow, The Polemical Christology of M.: StPatr 17/2 (1982) 765-776.

G. RÖWEKAMP

Memnon of Ephesus

M. (St.; feastday Dec. 16) was bishop of Ephesus from ca. 428 to 440. He played an important part in the council held in his city. He supported Cyril and was from the beginning an opponent of the patriarch of Constantinople; he denied use of the churches to him, to John of Antioch, and to other Orientals. As a result, some sessions of the council were held in the episcopal palace. The anticouncil of the Orientals deposed M. and Cyril, but M. continued to keep the churches closed, and there were some riots. Complaints were made to Theodosius, and the latter confirmed the deposition of M. and Cyril, but finally both were confirmed again in their offices. Two letters of M. have come down. He addressed one during the Council of Ephesus to the clergy of Constantinople (*ep. ad clerum*) and in it described the sufferings of the orthodox bishops. The second he wrote, together with Cyril, to the Council of Ephesus after he had been deposed (*ep. ad Concilium*). A further letter, to Nestorius, is possibly to be ascribed to him.

W: *ep. ad clerum,* ACO 1, 1, 3, 46f. — ACO 1, 3, 115f. [Latin text]. — *ep. ad Concilium,* ACO 1, 1, 3, 16f. — ACO 1, 2, 75f. esp. 1, 3, 99f. [Latin text].
L: W. Enßlin, M. 7: PRE 15/1:654. — Die Geschichte des Christentums 2 (Freiburg i.Br., 1996), 601, 608-617. — E. Honigmann, Trois mémoires posthumes (Brussels, 1961), 74-80. — R. Janin, M.: BSS 9:315f.

B. WINDAU

Memoria Apostolorum

A work titled *Memoria Apostolorum* is mentioned by Turibius of Astorga in a letter to Bishops Idacius and Ceponius (*ep. ad Id.* 5) as being part of the apocryphal literature common to the Manichees and Priscillianists. The *Memoria Apostolorum* is also cited by Paul → Orosius in his *Commonitorium de errore Priscillianistarum* (ch. 2). In its genre it is a gospel and does not contain any account of the apostles, although it claims apostolic authority for itself. It gives a gnostic-dualistic teaching of the eternity of hell, from which the "Archon of the world" came.

W: G. Schepss, CSEL 18:154. — G. Mercati, Note di letteratura (Rome, 1901), 136 [Latin text]. — NtlA 1:301-303 [German trans.].

P. Bruns

Merobaudes

I. Life: Flavius Merobaudes (M.: the name points to German ancestry), senator, army commander, and Lat. poet, was born in Spain (Baetica) of a distinguished family. In 435, for his achievements as soldier and poet, he was honored with a statue in the Forum of Trajan, Rome; the inscription has been preserved (CIL VI 1724 = ILS 2950: *vir spectabilis, comes sacri consistorii*). After 435 he received the title of *patricius* and, in 443, as *magister utriusque militiae*, fought sucessfully against the Bagaudae in the province of Tarracona. CIL VI 31983 is perhaps his tombstone. He is possibly to be identified with the M., a *patricius*, who gave some pieces of property to the monastery in Mataniacum.

II. Works: Most of the works preserved today were first discovered in 1823 by Niebuhr in a palimpsest (*Sangall.* 908). Previously, only the poem De Christo (*Christ.*) in hexameters had been known; this was a rhetorical hymnlike discourse on the nature of Christ. In addition to some short occasional poems (1 + 2: poems on baptism; 3: an ecphrasis of a park; 4: a birthday poem for a son of Aetius), Niebuhr's discovery brought to light espec. fragments of a panegyrical *gratiarum actio* (between 443 and 446; probably for the bestowal of the title *patricius*), and of a panegyric in hexameters for the third consulate of Aetius in 446 (*poet.*). As in the shorter poems, so here in particular M. shows himself to be in the tradition of Claudian, as can already be seen in the structure of *poet.*, which evidently closely follows Claudian's *in Rufin.* In his works as court poet of the powerful army commander Aetius and of the west Roman imperial house, M. proves himself to be, again like Claudian, a follower of the court poet Stilicho. His poems are significant examples of the Chr.-pagan cultural mingling of the 5th c.; pagan-antique and Chr. elements are fused here in a unique unity.

W: *Christ.*, Pl. 53:789f.; 61:971-974. — *Fl. Merobaudis reliquiae*, F. Vollmer, MGH. AA 14 (Munich, 1984 = Berlin, ¹1905) [text]. — F. M. Clover, Flavius M. (Philadelphia, 1971) [text/English trans./comm.].
L: T. D. Barnes, M. on the Imperial Family: Phoe. 28 (1974) 314-319. — F. M. Clover, Toward an Understanding of M.'s Panegyric I: Hist. 20 (1971) 354-367. — A. Fo, Note a

Merobaude: Romanobarbarica 6 (1981/82) 101-128. — S. Gennaro Da Claudiano a Merobaude (Catania, 1959). — T. A. Janson, A Concordance to the Latin Panegyrics (Hildesheim, 1979). — A. Loyen, L'œuvre de Flavius M.: REA 74 (1972) 153-174. — T. Olajos, M. (3): PRE. S 12:863-866. — M. Mazza, Merobaude: La poesia tardoantica. Atti del V corso della scuola superiore di archeologia e civiltà medievali presso il centro di cultura scientifica E. Majorana, Messina 379-430. — S. I. Oost, Some Problems in the History of Galla Placidia: CP 60 (1965) 1-10. — PLRE 2:756-758. — W. Schetter, Zu M. Paneg. 63-68: Hermes 120 (1992) 120-123. — G. Zecchini, Aezio (Rome, 1983).

M. Meier

Mesrob (Mastoc')

We are well informed about the life of M. (b. 360; d. 440), who is also called Mastoc' in the earliest sources, by his *Vita* written by his disciple → Koriun. M. enjoyed an exceptional Gr. education and after a short administrative activity became monk, priest, missionary, and finally chorbishop. At the urging of Catholicos → Sahak the Great and Arm. King Vramshapuh (401-408/409), M. created the Arm. alphabet and himself took a lively part in the work of translation that soon began. On good grounds there is ascribed to him an early catechism, the so-called *Teaching of Gregory the Illuminator* (*doct. Greg.*), which has been handed down by → Agathangelus. Probably not authentic is a collection of twenty-three spiritual songs (*hymn.*). Some liturg. books (Ritual, Pontifical) also bear his name.

W: Rituale M. (Jerusalem, 1933) [text]. — F. C. Conybeare, Rituale Armenorum (Oxford, 1905) [English trans.]. — Pontificale M. (Valarschapat, 1876) [text]. — doct. Greg., K. Ter Mekerttschian, Agathangelus (Tiflis, 1914), §§ 259-715 [text]. — R. W. Thomson, The Teaching of St. Gregory (Cambridge, Mass., 1970) [English trans./comm.]. — hymn., N. T'ahmizean: BanMat 7 (1964) 161-208 [text].
L: N. Akinean, Lebensbild des M.: HandAm 49 (1935) 505-550. — idem, Homilienfrgm. gegen die Zauberer: HandAm 72 (1958) 379-389. — A. S. Arevschatan, L'évolution littéraire et musicale du rituel: REArm 20 (1986/87) 153-166. — A. Mnac'akaean, M.: BanMat 7 (1964) 125-159.

P. Bruns

Methodius of Olympus

I. Life: Acc. to Jerome (*vir. ill.* 83) and Socrates (*h.e.* 6.13), M. was bishop of Olympus in Lycia and later of Tyre and died a martyr in Chalcis during the Decian persecution. In reality, M. was probably an itinerant teacher; he was an educated man and familiar with the Gr. classics. He was a chiliast and an anti-Origenist but was at the same time strongly influenced by Origen's allegorism. In his anthropology

421

and christology he was influenced by Irenaeus of Lyons and philosophically by Aristotle, the Stoics, and Plato. He died probably in 311.

II. Works: Of M.'s numerous works, written chiefly in dialogue form, only the *Symposion seu convivium virginum* (*symp.*) has come down complete in its original language. Other works, *De libero arbitrio* (*arbitr.*), *De resurrectione mortuorum* (*res.*), *De lepra* (*lepr.*), *De creatis* (*creat.*; probably identical with the *Xenon* mentioned by Soc., *h.e.* 6.13), *fr. in Job*, *Contra Porphyrium de cruce* (*Porph.*), and *Sermo de martyribus* have reached us only in fragments, supplemented by a sometimes very abbreviated Slavic version of the 11th c.

The *symp.*, written in an elegant style and modeled on Plato's *Symposium*, gives a comprehensive introduction to various areas of Chr. doctrine and attests to M.'s vision of a completion of Platonism by Christianity. Ten virgins, taking part in a banquet in the garden of Virtue, each starting from a citation of scripture, praise not Eros but Parthenia as the perfect ideal of Chr. life (though marriage is not rejected). The divine image in human beings is restored by chastity/virginity; the body then obeys the soul. At the end of the work, Thecla sings a marriage hymn in 24 strophes to Christ the bridegroom (an archetype of virginity: *archiparthenos*) and his bride the church.

The dialogue *arbitr.* between two Valentinians or Platonists and a defender of orthodoxy stresses the free will of the human being as the origin of evil and denies, against dualism, the existence of two opposed first principles as well as the creation of evil by God.

The work *res.*, which is against Origen, is a dialogue between a physician Aglaophon and Proclus of Miletus, on the one hand, and Eubulius (probably M. himself) and Memmian, on the other, over the nature of the body after death. Aglaophon and Proclus hold the view of Origen on the resurrection of human beings in new, spiritual bodies, but are refuted by Eubulius/Methodius and Memmian on the basis of scripture. With the aid of the doctrine of the risen body, which is in material continuity with the earlier body because God's creation exists forever, they combat Origen's teaching on the preexistence of souls, the fall into sin before time began, and God's purpose for the world and human corporeality. Following Irenaeus, they interpret redemption as the completion of creation.

The dialogue *lepr.* between Eubulius/Methodius and Sistelius gives an allegorical interpretation of the regulations for purification from leprosy in Lev 13.

The treatise *creat.*, which is known only from a summary by Photius (*cod.* 234), opposes a dualistic

interpretation of Mt 7:6 and Origen's teaching on the eternity of the world.

The works preserved exclusively in Slavonic include the treatise *De vita*, an exhortation of a Neoplatonic kind to be satisfied with the existence granted by God and to hope for the gifts of eschat. salvation; the treatise *De cibis*, in which, after describing the attacks made on him because of *symp.* and *res.* as examples of the persecution of the just, M. gives an allegorical interpretation of Jewish alimentary laws and of the purification sacrifice mentioned in Num 19; the work *De sanguisuga*, an allegorical interpretation, requested by Eustachius, of Prov 30:15ff.; 24:50ff., and Ps 18:2.

Completely lost: the work *De corpore,* which M. announces in *De sanguisuga* 10.4; the anti-Origenist treatise on the witch of Endor, which is mentioned in *res.* 3.12.4, and by Jerome; and commentaries on Gen and Cant. Clearly not authentic are the homilies *De Symeone et Anna* (*Sym et Ann.*), *In ramos palmarum,* and *In ascensionem,* as well as the apocalypse *Revelationes S. Methodii,* which was popular in the Middle Ages.

W: PG 18:28-408. — N. Bonwetsch (Leipzig, 1917) [with a German trans. of the *arbitr.* and *res.*]. — *symp.*, M. Pellegrino, L'Inno del Simposio di S. Metodio Martire (Turin, 1958) [text/Italian trans./comm.]. — H. Musurillo, SC 95. — L. Fendt, BKV² 2 [German trans.]. — W. Christ, M. Paranikas, Anthologia graeca carminum christianorum (Hildesheim, 1963 = Leipzig, 1871), 33-37 [text/German trans. of the *Hymnus*]. — H. Musurillo, ACW 27 (Washington, 1958) [English trans./comm.]. — *arbitr.*, A. Vaillant, PO 22/5. — *arbitr., creat., fr. in Job, fr. mart., lepr., res., De sanguisuga,* N. Bonwetsch (Erlangen, 1891) [Greek frags./German trans. of Slavic text].

L: E. Amann, M.: DThC 10/2:1606-1614. — H. T. D. Barnes, M., Maximus and Valentinus: JThS NS 30 (1979) 47-55. — G. N. Bonwetsch, Die Theologie der M. (Berlin, 1903). — V. Buchheit, Studien zu M. (Berlin, 1958). — idem, Das Symposion des M. arianisch interpoliert?: TU 125 (1981) 109-114. — H. Crouzel, Les critiques adressées par M. et ses contemporains à la doctrine origénienne du corps ressuscité: Gr. 53 (1972) 679-716. — F. Diekamp, Über den Bischofssitz des hl. Märtyrers M.: ThQ 109 (1928) 285-308. — J. Farges, Les idées morales et religieuses de M. (Paris, 1929). — M. Hoffmann, Der Dialog bei den chr. Schriftstellern der ersten vier Jh.: TU 96 (1966) 67-83, 109-130. — G. Lazzati, La tecnica dialogica nel Simposio di M.: FS P. Ubaldi (Milan, 1937), 117-224. — S. Lucà, Un nuovo testimonio del banchetto: OCP 50 (1984) 446-450. — M. Margheritis, L'influenza di Platone sul pensiero e sull'arte di M.: FS P. Ubaldi (Milan, 1937), 401-412. — H. A. Musurillo, M.: DSp 10:1109-1117. — L. G. Patterson, The Anti-Origenist Theology of M., Diss. (Columbia Univ., 1958). — idem, M., Origen and the Arian Dispute: StPatr 17 (1982) 912-923. — idem, Who Are the Opponents in M.'s res. ?: StPatr 19 (1989) 221-229. — F. de Paverd, Paenitentia secunda in M.: Aug. 18 (1978) 459-485. — K. Quensell, Die wahre Stellung u. Tätigkeit des fälschlich sog.

Bischofs M. (Heidelberg, 1952). — C. Riggi, Teologia della storia nel Simposio di M.: Aug. 16 (1976) 61-84. — C. Tibiletti, L'ambiente culturale cristiano reflesso nel Simposio de M.: Verginità e matrimonio (Rome, 1983), 99-133. — R. Williams, M.: TRE 22:680-684. — T. Zahn, Über den Bischofssitz des M.: ZKG 8 (1886) 15-20. — A. Zeoli, S. M. Il banchetto delle dieci vergini (Florence, 1952).

J. Pauli, OSB, C. Schmidt

Michael Badoqa (Malphana)

M., called Badoqa (examiner) or also Malphana (teacher), was a disciple of Henana of Adiabene at the school of Nisibis and left there because of opposition to his teacher. He was active at the end of the 6th and beginning of the 7th c. and is regarded as author of a still unpublished work containing questions on the biblical text, a work influential among later Nestorians. Tradition also ascribes to him a festal treatise on the memorial of the Blessed Virgin that was celebrated after Christmas, as well as a polemical work against the Jacobites. Finally, some fragments are preserved of a dogm. treatise (*tract.*) in which M. argues against the title of Theotokos and against talk of a physical or hypostatic union.

W: *quaest.*, A. Baumstark, Geschichte (Bonn, 1922), 129 (mss.). — *tract.*, L. Abramowski, A. E. Goodman, Nestorian Collection (Cambridge, 1972), 1:105-113 [Syriac text]; 2:61-67 [English trans.].
L: A. Baumstark, De causis festorum: OrChr 1 (1901) 333f.

P. Bruns

Miltiades

M., a Gr. apologete of the 2nd c., was from Asia Minor (Jerome, *vir. ill.* 39) and was trained in rhetoric (Tertullian, *adv. Valent.* 5.1: *ecclesiarum sophista*); nothing more is known of his life. All of his writings are lost.

He wrote against Valentinian gnosticism (Tert., ibid.) and against the Montanists, attacking among other things the ecstatic prophesying customary among the Montanists (Eus., *h.e.* 5.17.1: "a prophet should not babble in a state of ecstasy"). He also composed two apologetic works, each in two books, against the (pagan) Greeks and the Jews (Eus., *h.e.* 5.17.5), and a defense of the Chr. way of life ("philosophy") against the rulers of this world ("the cosmic archons," Eus., ibid). This formulation is from 1 Cor 2:6-8; i.e., M. was offering divine and Chr. wisdom to the transitory possessors of earthly power. By "rulers" may be meant the reigning emperors (most likely, Marcus Aurelius and Commodus, 176-179) or the governors of the provinces. If the second be the

case, then the *Apologeticum* of → Tertullian served as a model. In Eus., *h.e.* 5.28.1, in a specific appeal to the earlier Chr. tradition, M. is named along with other orthodox representatives (→ Justin, → Tatian, → Clement) who wrote against the pagans and heresies of their age and described Jesus Christ as God.

L: R. M. Grant, The chronology of the Greek apologists: VigChr 9 (1955) 25-33. — idem, Five apologists and Marcus Aurelius: VigChr 42 (1988) 1-17.

K. Pollmann

Minucius Felix

Very little is known of the person and life of Marcus Minucius Felix (M.), and this little is mostly from his work *Octavius* (*Oct.*), in which the persons, in contrast to the scenery and the dialogue, are probably historical. M. was born a pagan, probably in North Africa, converted to Christianity, and became a lawyer in Rome. The *Oct.* is dated to between 197 (→ Tertullian, *apol.*) and 250 (→ Cyprian, → Novatian). Aspects of the content suggest a date in the second half of the 3rd c. The attribution to M. of *De fato/Contra mathematicos* by Jerome (*vir. ill.* 58 and *ep.* 70.5) is doubted.

The *Oct.* is a dialogue between a pagan, Caecilius Natalis (C.), who attacks Christianity, and a Christian, Octavius Januarius (O.), who defends it. A framework story encloses the two speeches, between which there is only a short dialogue (14-15) on the power of language (see Plato, *Phd.*). An obituary of O., who has since died, is followed by a description of the situation, which leads to a philosophical debate in which M. is to be the arbiter (1-4). He need not exercise his function, however, since C. announces his conversion (39-40). The speeches: C. begins with a confession of being in principle a skeptic. It is impossible (he says) to establish definitive truths, espec. for uneducated Christians; the chance character of events shows that there is no divine providence (5). Therefore people ought to practice the traditional religion, since the proper veneration of the gods is a condition for the success of the Roman empire (6-7). C. then sharply attacks Christians, their teachings and way of life, espec. their belief in the resurrection; he sees the pathetic, unfortunate life of Christians on earth as proof that their God is powerless (8–12.6). Summary: a new plea for skepticism (12.7-13). For O., knowledge of the truth is naturally available to all human beings; the cosmic order presupposes a divine providence. To this is added a proof of the one God that is in agreement with the philosophers (16–20.1). Pagan religion with its gods, who are shown to be merely mortal human beings, is ridiculed. Rome's greatness (O. says) has depended from the beginning on unpunished crimes; demons lurk behind the gods and the persecution of Christians (20.2-27). The accusations against Christians are rejected, mostly by a *retorsio criminis*; belief in the resurrection is supported by the philosophers. The nothingness of things earthly is contrasted with the certainty of a reward in the next life (28–38.4). Summary: Christians have found the truth for which the philosophers have been seeking (38.5-7).

The *Oct.*, which was handed down as the eighth book of the *nat.* of → Arnobius, marks the beginning of a new phase of Lat. apologetics. M. addresses an educated pagan public and for this reason does not present the content of a specifically Chr. faith. Instead, following espec. Cicero and Seneca, and using the classical dialogue form and rhetorically polished language, he endeavors to attack the pagans through their own sources (*Oct.* 39). An artistic structure and recurring key ideas (*veritas/error*, *lux/tenebrae*, *religio/superstitio*) ensure the unity of the work. The purpose of it is to refute the accusations against Christians and to prove the superiority of Chr. doctrine and the Chr. way of life. The *Oct.* is thus both a defense and a work of recruitment.

W: K. Halm, CSEL 2. — B. Kytzler (Stuttgart, ²1992) [text]. — B. Kytzler (Darmstadt, 1993 = Munich, 1965) [text/German trans.]. — E. Heck (Tübingen, 1981) [German trans.]. — G. W. Clarke, ACW 39 (New York, 1974) [English trans./comm.]. — J. Beaujeu (Paris, ⁷1974) [text/French trans./comm.]. — F. Solinas (Milan, 1992) [text/Italian trans./comm.]. — M. A. Naia de Silva (Lisbon, 1990) [text/Portuguese trans./comm.]. — *Concordance*, B. Kytzler, D. Najock (Hildesheim, 1991).
L: E. Ahlborn, Naturvorgänge als Auferstehungsgleichnis: WSt 103 (1990) 123-137. — B. Aland, Christentum, Bildung u. röm. Oberschicht: FS H. Dörrie (Münster, 1983), 11-30. — M. v. Albrecht, M. as a Christian Humanist: Illinois Classical Studies 12 (1987) 157-168. — C. Bammel, Die 1. lat. Rede gegen die Christen: ZKG 104 (1993) 295-311. — C. Becker, Der Oct. des M. (Munich, 1967). — V. Buchheit, Die Wahrheit im Heilsplan Gottes bei M.: VigChr 39 (1985) 105-109. — P. Ferrarino, Il problema artistico e cronologico dell'Oct.: idem, Scritti scelti (Florence, 1986), 222-273. — H. v. Geisau, M.: PRE. S 11:952-1002. — E. Heck, M. u. der röm. Staat: VigChr 38 (1984) 154-164. — HLL 4:512-519. — C. Ingremeau, M. et ses sources: REAug 45 (1999) 3-20. — P. G. van der Nat, Voraussetzungen der chr. lat. Literatur: Christianisme et formes littéraires de l'antiquité tardive en occident (Geneva, 1976), 191-234. — S. Pezzella, Cristianesimo e paganesimo romano, Bari 1972). — G. Quispel, African Christianity before M. and Tertullian: FS H. L. W. Nelson (Utrecht, 1982), 257-335. — M. Rizzi, Amicitia e veritas: il prologo dell' Oct.: Aevum antiquum 3 (1990) 245-268. — H. G. Rötzer, Chr. Apologetik u. heidnische Bildungstradition: FS W. Naumann

(Darmstadt, 1981), 33-48. — C. Schäublin, Konversionen in antiken Dialogen?: FS B. Wyss (Basel, 1985), 117-131. — C. Tibiletti, Il problema della priorità Tertulliano-M.: FS R. Braun (Paris, 1990), 2, 23-34. — I. Vecchiotti, La filosofia politica di M. (Urbino, 1973).

B. WINDAU

Modestus, Anti-Marcionite

Acc. to Eusebius (*h.e.* 4.21; 4.25), in the time perhaps of Marcus Aurelius (or Commodus) M. composed a work against → Marcion, of which, however, nothing remains. Worth noting is the information in Jerome (*vir. ill.* 32) that other works were going under M.'s name but were regarded as not authentic.

L: A. v. Harnack, Geschichte der altchr. Lit. 1 (Leipzig, ²1958), 759; 2/1:701. — idem, Marcion (Darmstadt, 1996 = Leipzig, ²1924), 317*f.

R. HANIG

Modestus of Jerusalem

In 614, during the period of the Persian invasion, M. was abbot of the monastery of Theodosius near Bethlehem. After Patriarch Zacharias had been abducted, M. carried out his duties, which he then took over officially in 631 after Zacharias's death. After the destruction of numerous churches M. reorganized the liturgical life of Jerusalem. He died in 633/634 on a journey to Emperor Heraclius. Photius transmits fragments of two homilies, on the women bringing spices to the tomb and on the presentation of the Lord. A third completely surviving homily on the Dormition of Mary (PG 86/2:3277-3312) is probably from another writer of the 7th/8th c. A letter to an Abbot Cumitas (*ep.*) is preserved in Armenian; remnants of a commentary on the Pss are found in catenas.

W: *fr.*, Photius, *cod.* 275. — *ep.*, F. Macler, Histoire d'Héraclius (Paris), 104:70-73 [French trans.].
L: R. Devreesse, Les Anciens commentateurs grecs des Psaumes (Rome, 1970), 324. — G. Garitte, La sépulture de M.: Muséon 73 (1960) 127-133. — idem, Le calendrier palestino-géorgien (Brussels, 1958). — M. Jugie, La mort et l'assomption de la sainte Vierge (Rome, 1944), 139-150. — idem, Deux homélies patristiques pseudépigraphes: EO 39 (1940-1942) 283-289.

G. RÖWEKAMP

Monastic Rule

Among the various genres of monastic literature (→ Apophthegmata, → Letter, → Treatise, → *Vita*, and → Dialogue), the name "monastic rule" is given to writings that are addressed to a particular group of monks or nuns (cenobites) with the purpose of setting down binding norms for the ordering of life in common. Treatises or letters to individuals, conciliar canons, descriptive texts, or parenetic-didactic works for monks/nuns are not monastic rules in the strict sense, even if they are sometimes described as a *regula* or something similar. The "prehistory" of monastic rules includes unwritten forms of discipline followed by female ascetics in the communities of the first centuries, and the obligations of male ascetics to give an account to the bishop; the first writings (→ *Didache*, Ps.-Clement, *De virginitate*, [Ps.-] Athanasius, *Syntagma ad monachos*, *De virginitate*) against threats to the ascetic ideal of virginity and poverty; the *Vita Antonii* of → Athanasius of Alexandria, with its parenetic concern; and the → *Apophthegmata Patrum*. Like monasticism itself, so the first monastic rules were composed in the East: the Rule of → Pachomius in Egypt, which survives complete in Jerome's Lat. translation, and the *Asceticon* of → Basil in Cappadocia. The further development of monastic life led in the East to the *Typika*, monastic foundation documents and books of regulations based on the rule of Basil. Only in the western church did the genre of monastic rule reach its full development and find expression, amid great terminological variation, as *regula*, *praecepta*, *instituta*, *leges*, *monita*, and *statuta*. It is in Jerome (*c. Joh.* 40) that *regula* for the first time signifies monastic legislation (but in the plural, *regulae*, referring to particular precepts). It is in the *Regula Patrum Secunda* (427) that *regula* (in the singular) first signifies an entire work that is normative for the monastic life of a community; in the course of time this use became firmly established in monastic literature, but as late as Gregory the Great it was not used exclusively. In addition, *regula* frequently expresses the authority of the abbot. The genre monastic rule was held together by a complicated network of literary dependencies that took shape over the course of eight generations through the progressive reuse of authoritative material for Rules and gave this genre a strongly conservative character (see the genealogical tree in Vogüé, *Règles monastiques* 14).

1. Ca. 400: Rule of → Pachomius (404; Egypt) (*reg.*); Augustine, *Praeceptum* (397; Hippo) and *Ordo monasterii* (ca. 395; by Alypius [?] for the monks of Thagaste) (*reg.*) (→ Augustinian Rule); the *Asceticon* of → Basil (397; Cappadocia; translated by → Rufinus for the monks of Pinetum) (*ascet.*) and (perhaps dependent on Aug., *reg.*, and Basil *ascet.*); the *Regula Quattuor Patrum* (Serapion, the two Macariuses, → Paphnutius; 400-410; Lérins; with a recension II:

535-540; Italy) (*patr.* I). These rules represent the "mother rules" of western monasticism.

2. Ca. 425: *Regula Secunda Patrum* (427; Lérins) (*patr.* II), a continuation of *patr.* I by a Deacon Vigilius.

3. Ca. 500: *Regula Macarii* by abbot Porcarius of Lérins (*Macar.*); *Regula Pachomii brevis* (an alternative: second generation; Italy) (*Pacbr.*), a shorter version and adaptation of Pachomius, *reg.*

4. 500-550: *Regula Orientalis* (Lérins) (*orient.*), consisting primarily of excerpts from the rule of Pachomius; → Caesarius of Arles, *Regula virginum* (512-534; Arles) (*reg. virg.*), *Regula monachorum* (534-542) (*reg. mon.*); → *Regula Magistri* (500-550; central Italy) (*mag.*); *Regula Eugippii* (530-535; Naples) (*reg.*) (→ Eugippius); *Regula Patrum Tertia* (535/Council of Clermont) (*patr.* III).

5. 530-560: Rule of → Benedict of Nursia (Monte Cassino) (*reg.*); → Aurelian of Arles, *Regula ad monachos*, *Regula ad virgines* (547-551; Arles) (*reg. mon.*, *reg. virg.*).

6. 550-600: *Regula Tarnatensis* (550-575; southern Gaul) (*Tarnat.*); *Regula Ferrioli* (553-573; Feréolac) (→ Ferreolus of Uzès) (*reg.*); *Regula Pauli et Stephani* (ca. 550; central Italy) (*Paul. Steph.*).

7. 601-625: → Columbanus the Younger, *Regula monachorum*, *Regula coenobialis* 1-9 (before 615; Luxeuil, Bobbio) (*reg. mon.*, *reg. coen.*); → Isidore of Seville, *Regula monachorum* (615-619) (*reg. monach.*).

8. 625-700: → Fructuosus of Braga, *Regula Complutensis* (ca. 640; Complutum) (*reg.*); *Regula communis* (665-680; Galicia) (*reg. comm.*), a revision of Fructuosus, *reg.*; the so-called *Regula Cassiani* (ca. 650; Spain) (*reg. Cas.*), an abbreviated version of → John Cassian, *Institutiones* 1-4 (ca. 425) (*inst.*), *Regula consensoria* (650-700; Spain) (*cons.*); → Donatus of Besançon, *Regula ad Virgines* (626-658; Jussanmoutier) (*reg. virg.*); also from the Irish-Frankish world: the *Regula Waldeberti* (629-670; Faremoutier) (*reg. Wal.*), the *Regula cuiusdam Patris* (Gaul) (*reg. cui.*); the *Regula Columbani* [?] *ad virgines* (excerpt from Columbanus the Younger, *Regula coenobialis* (*reg. Col. virg.*), and the fragment of rule known as *Psallendo* (northern France) (*Psal.*).

With a few exceptions these rules found a place in the *Codex Regularum* of Benedict of Aniane, which supplies the only text for many of the rules. A constant in the content of monastic rule as a genre is the continual reference to scripture which, with hardly any variation in the choice of texts and in their interpretation, is called upon for the explanation of basic monastic themes: humility, obedience, love, and patience; also: fasting, vigils, renunciation of property, work, silence, *ruminatio*, prayer. The composers of monastic rules make this general framework more concrete in relation to the situation of the time and personal concerns. The first decades of the 6th c. were a decisive point in the development of the content of the monastic rules, because now the formalities of acceptance into a monastery were organized, the common dormitory was introduced, as was a detailed *Ordo officii*, while a diversification of the daily routine depended on the seasons of the year. From the formal viewpoint the monastic rules showed considerable differences among themselves in extent, structure, purpose (source of information ↔ norm to be followed; foundational document ↔ later "course corrections"), addressee (single monastery, several monasteries, known or unknown monasteries), author (individual, synod, anonymous), and state of the documentary tradition (fragment, florilegium, complete work, recension). In terms of the history of the genre, the (western) monastic rules, depending on their type, are related to the → Canonical Collections or to the (fictitiously) oral *Quaestiones et responsiones*. The *Typika* of the Chr. East likewise show a link to these other genres. In any case, a comprehensive genre-historical treatment of the monastic rules that satisfies contemporary philological requirements is still a desideratum of historical study.

W: see also → Augustine, Rule of, → Aurelian of Arles, → Basil of Cäsarea, → Benedict of Nursia, → Caesarius of Arles, → John Cassian, → Columbanus the Y., → Donatus of Besançon, → Eugippius, → Ferreolus of Uzès, → Fructuosus of Braga, → Isidor of Seville, → Regula Magistri, → Pachomius. — *reg. Cas.*, H. Ledoyen: RBen 94 (1984) 154-194 [text]. — *reg. Col. virg.*, O. Sebass: ZKG 16 (1896) 465-470 [text]. — *reg. comm.*, J. Campos Ruiz, I. Rocca Melia (Madrid, 1971), 172-211 [text/Spanish trans./comm.]. — *cons.*, PL 87:1111-1130. — *reg. cui.*, P. W. Hümpfner, L. Verheijen, Règle de st. Augustin 2 (Paris, 1967), 7-9 [text]. — PL 32:1447-1450. — *reg. cui.*, F. Villegas: RHSp 49 (1973) 3-35. 135-144 [text]. — PL 66:987-994. — *Donat. reg. virg.*, A. de Vogüé: Ben. 25 (1978) 219-313 [text]. — *Macar.*, A. de Vogüé, SC 297:372-388. — H. Styblo: WSt 76 (1963) 124-158 [text]. — PL 103:447-452. — *Pacbr.*, A. Boon (Leuven/Louvain, 1932), 3-74 [critical apparatus] [text]. — PL 50:271-302. — *Paul. Steph.*, J. E. Villanova (Montserrat, 1959). — *Psal.*, F. Masai: Scr. 2 (1948) 215-220 [text]. — D. de Bruyne: RBen 35 (1923) 126-128. — *Tarnat.*, F. Villegas: RBen 84 (1974) 7-65 [text]. — *reg. Wal.*, PL 88:1053-1070. — *patr. I, patr. II, Macar., orient., patr. III*, II, A. de Vogüé, SC 297f. — *patr. I, patr. II, Macar., orient., patr. III*, C. V. Fränklin, I. Havener, J. A. Francis (Collegeville, Minn., 1982) [English trans.]. — M. Puzicha (Münsterschwarzach, 1990) [text/German trans./comm.]. — Monk of Mount Savior, A. de Vogüé: MonS 12 (1976) 249-263 [English trans./comm.]. — *patr. I, patr. II, Macar., orient., patr. III*, Bened. *reg.*, S. Pricoco (Milan, 1995), 3-113, 277-306 [text/Italian trans./comm.]. — Aug., *reg., patr. I, patr. II,*

Macar., orient., patr. III, Caes. *reg. mon. /reg. virg.*, Aurelian, *reg. mon. /reg. virg.*, Tarnat., Ferreol., *reg.*, Paul. Steph., V. Desprez (Begrolles-en-Mauges, 1980) [French trans.]. — Isid. *reg. monach.*, Fructuos. *reg.*, J. Campos Ruiz, I. Rocca Melia (Madrid, 1971), 90-125, 137-162 [text/Spanish trans./comm.].

L: A. Adam, Grundbegriffe des Mönchtums: ZKG 65 (1953f) 209-239. — idem, Monachos-Gedanke: FS E. Benz (Leiden, 1967), 209-239. — M. E. Bouillet, "Codex regularum" de saint Benoît d'Aniane: RBen 75 (1963) 345-349. — J.-M. Clément, Lexique, 2 vols. (Steenbrugge, 1978). — C. De Clerk, Législation religieuse (Leuven/Louvain, 1936). — K. S. Frank, Fiktive Mündlichkeit: StPatr 25 (1993) 356-375. — J. Gribomont, Generi letterari: Koinonia <Neapel> 10 (1986) 7-28. — A. Guillaumont, Origines du monachisme chrétien (Bégrolles-en-Mauges, 1979). — I. Herwegen, Väterspruch und Mönchsregel (Münster, ²1977). — Il monachesimo orientale. Atti del convegno di Studi Orientali, 9-12 aprile 1958 (Rome, 1958). — C. Joest, Bibelstellenkonkordanz (Steenbrugge, 1994). — K. Krumbacher, Geschichte der byz. Lit. 1 (Munich, ²1887 = New York, 1958), 314-319. — F. v. Lilienfeld, Mönchtum II: TRE 23:150-193. — R. Lorenz, Anfänge des abendländischen Mönchtums: ZKG 77 (1966) 1-61. — T. P. McLaughlin, Droit monastique (Ligué, 1935). — P. Miquel, Lexique du desert (Bégrolles-en-Mauges, 1986). — A. Mundo, Penisola iberica (Spoleto, 1957), 72-108. — idem, Synodes abbatiaux: StAns 44 (1959) 107-125. — idem, Tradizione codicologica: Atti del 7° Congresso internazionale di studi sull'alto medioevo (Spoleto, 1982), 477-520. — D. v. d. Nahmer, Schultermini in Klosterregeln: RBS 12 (1983) 143-185. — S. Pricoco, Cenobio di Lerino (Rome, 1978). — A. Schmidt, Mönchsregel des Aurelian v. Arles: StMon 18 (1976) 17-54. — E. v. Severus, Benedikt v. Aniane: TRE 5:535-538. — G. Turbessi, Antiche regole monastiche: RBS 1 (1972) 57-90. — L. Ueding, Kanones von Chalzedon: KonChal 2 (1953) 569-676. — A. de Vogüé, "Sub regula vel abbate": CCist 33 (1971) 209-241. — idem, Vie des Pères du Jura: RAM 47 (1971) 121-127. — idem, Règle de Césaire d'Arles: RAM 47 (1971) 369-406. — idem, Regula Orientalis: MonS 13 (1982) 39-45. — idem, J. Gribomont, Regola: DIP 7 (1983) 1411-1434. — idem, Saint Benoît en son temps: idem, Recueil d'articles (Hildesheim, 1984), 490-514. — idem, Règles cénobitiques: ibid., 748-763. — idem, Méditation: ibid., 807-820. — idem, Règles monastiques anciennes (400-700) (Turnhout, 1985).

M. SKEB, OSB

Monoimus, Gnostic

Hippolytus (*haer.* 8.15.1; see 8.12-15; 10.17) gives a fragment of a letter of Monoimus, a Chr.-gnostic Arab (ca. 200), that deals with the dialectic of unity and multiplicity.

W: Hippolytus, *haer.* 8.15.1.
L: C. Colpe, Gnosis: RAC 11:617f. — M. Marcovich, Studies in Graeco-Roman Religions and Gnosticism (Leiden, 1988), 134-143.

R. HANIG

Montanus

The data from antiquity on the chronology of →
Montanus's (M.) emergence as a prophet differ
(Epiphanius of Salamis: 156/157; Eus. Caes.: shortly
after 170). Since in about 177, during the persecution
in Lyons and Vienne, Christians there already had
some knowledge of the movement that had arisen in
Phrygia, it is reasonable to date its beginnings to the
60s of the 2nd c., despite the greater reliability of
Eusebius as a historian. The earliest source (anonymous and hostile to M.), which Eusebius cites extensively in *h.e.* 5.16-17, reports that M. had just become
a Christian when he began to act as a prophet in the
village of Ardabau in the borderlands of Phrygia and
Mysia. He quickly won a following in Phrygia,
including two women, Maximilla and Priscilla
(Prisca), who likewise prophesied. The movement
gave itself the name "Prophecy" or "New Prophecy";
opponents spoke of the heresy of the Phrygians or
heresy in the Phrygian manner and, beginning in the
4th c., of the Montanists. A once rich Montanist literature was suppressed and has disappeared, apart
from writings of Tertullian from the period when he
belonged to the New Prophecy. These writings of
Tertullian are sources for the second generation of
the prophetic movement, but he, like M.'s Catholic
adversaries, cites statements of the early prophets
which he attributes to the action of the Spirit of God.
One such statement, attributed to M. and cited in
Epiphanius, *haer.* 48.4.1, runs: "Man is like a lyre,
and I [= the divine Spirit] hover [over him] like a
plectrum [the instrument for plucking the strings].
Man sleeps, but I keep watch. See, it is the Lord who
disconcerts the hearts of men and gives them [differ-
ent] hearts." It is hardly possible to deny the expectation of the imminent end in original Montanism.
This explains without difficulty the various elements
of flight from the world (the dissolution of marriages
and in Tertullian the rejection of a second marriage
after a partner's death; fasting; desire for martyrdom
and, in Tertullian, rejection of flight from persecution). Even original Montanism developed forms of
organization, with a common treasury. The history
of the independent church ended in the 6th c. under
Emperor Justinian as a result of persecution in the
Phrygian heartland. By way of Tertullian, Montanism influenced North African sacramental theology and ecclesiology (Donatism).

S: P. de Labriolle, Les sources de l'histoire du montanisme
(Fribourg, Switzerland, 1913) [text/French trans.]. — D. N.
Bonwetsch, Texte zur Geschichte des Montanismus (Bonn,

1914) [text]. — R. E. Heine, The Montanist Oracles and
Testimonia (Macon, Ga., 1989) [text/English trans.].
L: K. Aland, Kirchengeschichtliche Entwürfe (Gütersloh,
1960), 105-148, 149-164. — T. Baumeister, Montanismus
u. Gnostizismus: TThZ 87 (1978) 44-60. — F. Blanchetière,
Le montanisme originel: RevSR 52 (1978) 118-134; 53
(1979) 1-22. — W. H. C. Frend, Montanismus: TRE
23:271-279. — C. Markschies, Wo lag Pepuza?: JAC 37
(1994) 7-28. — A. Stewart-Stykes, The original condemnation of Asian Montanism: JEH 50 (1999) 1-22. — A. Strobel, Das hl. Land der Montanisten (Berlin, 1980). — C.
Trevett, Montanism (Cambridge, 1996).

T. BAUMEISTER

Montanus of Toledo

M., bishop of Toledo 522-531, presided at the second
Council of Toledo (531). An appendix to its Acts
preserves two letters (*ep.* 1, 2) of M.: one to the
church of Palencia and one to Turibius (of Toledo?).
In both M. stresses episcopal authority.

W: *ep.* 1, 2, PL 65:51-58; 84:338-342.
L: J. Orlandis, D. Ramos-Lisson, Die Synoden auf der
Iberischen Halbinsel (Paderborn, 1981).

E. REICHERT

Moses of Khorene

M. (Moyses Xorenac'i) with his *History of Armenia*
(*hist.*) is one of the best known but also most controversial Arm. writers. Acc. to tradition he was from
Khorene and, acc. to what he himself says (*hist.* 3.62),
was one of the scholars commissioned by Sahak and
Mesrob to get an advanced education in Gr. philosophy. His history consists of three parts and embraces
the time from Adam to the death of Sahak and Mesrob. The epilogue is a lament in which the author
bemoans the loss of the kingship of the Arsacid
dynasty. Numerous anachronisms and stylistic peculiarities as well as the use of later sources (→ Procopius, → Socrates, etc.) raise doubts about the early
time of composition assigned to the work. In its present form the work is from the 8th or 9th c, but this
does not exclude the possibility that some substantially older material was revised. The tradition also
ascribes to M. a work on geography, which, however,
is probably from → Ananias of Sirak; M. is also supposed to have written a work on rhetoric and various
homilies.

W: Collected works (Venice, 1843, 1865) [text]. — *hist.*, M.
Abelean, S. Yarutiunean, History of the Armenians (New
York, 1981 = Tiflis, 1913) [text]. — A. B. Sargsean, History
(Eriwan, 1991) [text]. — R. W. Thomson, M. History of the
Armenians (Cambridge, Mass., 1978) [English trans.]. —
V. Langlois, Collections 2 (Paris, 1869), 45-176 [French
trans.]. — J.-P. Mahé, Histoire de l'Arménie (Paris, 1993)

[French trans.]. — M. Lauer, M. Geschichte Großarmeniens (Regensburg, 1869) [German trans.].
L: M. Abelean, M. Geschichte der Armenier (Edschmiazin, 1901). — N. Adonts, Sur la date: EtByz 11 (1936) 97-110. — N. Akinean, Leontius: HandAm 43 (1929) 330-348, 458-472, 593-619, 705-718. — idem, Abfassungszeit: WZKM 37 (1930) 204-217. — H. Armen, M. u. Elische (Jerusalem, 1951). — A. Baumgartner, Das zweite Buch des M. (Leipzig, 1885). — F. Conybeare, Version of Josephus: JThS 9 (1908) 577-583. — T. Dasnabedian, L'histoire de l'icône: HandAm 107 (1993) 149-166. — E. Gulbenkian, Narrative: Muséon 86 (1973) 365-375. — idem, Conversion of Trdat: Muséon 90 (1977) 49-62. — idem, Veiled Allusions: HandAm 106 (1992) 1-13. — F. Haase, Abfassungszeit: OrChr 11 (1923) 77-90. — H. Lewy, Date and Purpose: Byz. 11 (1936) 81-96. — J. Marquart, Genealogie: Cau. 6 (1930) 10-77. — M. Thierry, B. Outtier, Histoire des saintes: Syr. 67 (1990) 695-733. — C. Toumanoff, Date of M.: HandAm 75 (1961) 467-76. — B. L. Zekiyan, L'idéologie nationale: HandAm 101 (1987) 471-485. — idem, Ellenismo, Hebraismo in M.: Aug. 28 (1988) 381-390.

P. BRUNS

Musaeus of Marseilles

Acc. to Gennadius (*vir. ill.* 79), M., a presbyter who died between 456 and 461, composed a lectionary (*Lect.*), a responsorial (*Resp.*), a sacramentary (*Sacr.*), and a collection of homilies, all at the request of his bishop, Venerius, and the latter's successor, Eustasius. Two fragments of the *Resp.* are preserved in a Paris ms. (BN, Nouv. Acq. 1628). The identification of the *Lect.* in a Wolfenbüttel ms. (*cod. Weisenburgensis* 76) and of the *Sacr.* in a Milanese palimpsest (*Bibl. Ambr. cod.* M 12 *sup.*) is disputed.

W: *Resp.*, A. Morin: RBen 22 (1905) 329-356 [text/comm.]. — *Lect.*, A. Dold (Beuron, 1936). — *Sacr.*, A. Dold (Beuron, 1952).
L: A. DiBerardino (ed.), Patrology 4 (Westminster, Md., ⁷1994), 526. — K. Gamber, Lektionar u. Sakramentar: RBen 49 (1959) 198-215. — C. Vogel, Sources de l'histoire du culte (Turin, 1975), 259f.

B. DÜMLER

Musanus

Acc. to Eusebius (*h.e.* 4.21; 4.28; depending on him, Jerome, *vir. ill.* 31; Theodoret, *haer.* 1.21), in ca. 180-210 M. composed a lost "very penetrating book" against the Encratites, in which he may have described → Tatian as their originator.

L: W. Bauer, Rechtgläubigkeit u. Ketzerei (Tübingen, ²1964), 160. — A. v. Harnack, Geschichte der altchr. Lit. 1 (Leipzig, ²1958), 760; 2/1:701.

R. HANIG

N

Naassenes, Psalm of the

The Naassenes, also called Ophites in Greek, are considered to have been a gnostic group in whose teaching and worship the serpent of paradise (Heb. נחש, Gr. *ophis*) was greatly revered as bringer of knowledge. → Hippolytus (*haer.* 5.6-28) reports on a work of this sect (*sermo Naassenorum*) which gives an ophitic interpretation of a hymn to Attis. The hymn speaks of a sexless archetypal human being from which the soul of Adam separated and fell into a body tormented by sins; yet through continence the basis can be established for the reception of heavenly gnosis. This myth is given a Chr. garb in the *Naassene Psalm* (*ps.*) that is likewise cited in *haer.* 5.10.2, acc. to which the soul is like a shy hind in the labyrinth of the world until Christ bestows true knowledge on it.

W: *sermo*, Hippolytus, *haer.* 5.6-8. — *ps.*, Hippolytus, *haer.* 5.10.2. — W. Völker, Quellen zur Geschichte der chr. Gnosis (Tübingen, 1932), 11-27 [text].
L: W. Foerster, Die Naassener: Studi di Storia religiosa, ed. U. Bianchi (Messina, 1968), 19-33. — J. Frickel, Hellenistische Erlösung in chr. Deutung, die gnost. Naassenerschrift (Leiden, 1984) — A. Hönig, Die Naassener (Berlin, 1889). — A. Kehl, Beiträge zum Verständnis einiger gnostischer und frühchr. Psalmen und Hymnen: JAC 15 (1972) 95-101. — H. Leisegang, Gnosis (Stuttgart, 1985 = Leipzig, 1924), 111-185.

P. BRUNS

Narratio de rebus Armeniae

An anonymous history, the so-called *Narratio de rebus Armeniae*, was composed ca. 700 and tells, in a pro-Chalcedonian spirit, the history of the Arm. church from Gregory the Illuminator to the union with the Byzantines under Patriarch Sahak III Jorapor (678-705). The anonymous work has been ascribed to this Sahak and also to Nerses Bakur, the catholicos of Causcasian Albania. Originally composed in Armenian, the work has survived only in a Gr. translation of the 11th-13th c.

W: PG 132:1237-1258. — G. Garitte, CSCO 132 [text/comm.].
L: H. Bartikyan, N.: BanMat 6 (1962) 457-470. — G. Garitte, Un nouveau manuscrit: Muséon 1 (1958) 241-254.

P. BRUNS

Narratio de rebus Persicis

This story, which was written by an anonymous author at the Persian court under King Arrinatus, is a novel of conversion, at the center of which is a dialogue on religion between Christians, Greeks, Jews, and Persian magicians. The Gr. religion is seen in a very positive light because its gods foretold the birth of the Son of God from a virginal mother. The magicians, who represent the Persian religion, are forced to bend before the miraculous powers of the Chr. Bishop Castelaeus, while the Jewish community is rebuked for its lack of belief in the Messiah. The story must have been written in the second half of the 5th c. or at the beginning of the 6th, in Hellen. circles. It brings together a variety of narrative materials, such as the oracle of the wise woman Cassandra from the *Christian History* (written ca. 430) of → Philip of Side, and legends of Syro-Persian magicians. The more likely place of origin of the work is Syria, but Asia Minor is not excluded.

W: PG 10:97-108. — A. Vassiliev, Anecdota Graeco-Byzantina 1 (Moscow, 1893), 73-125 [text]. — A. Wirth, Orientalische Chroniken (Frankfurt a.M., 1894), 143-210 [text]. — E. Bartke, Das sog. Religionsgespräch (Leipzig, 1899) [German trans.].
L: E. Honigmann, Philippus of Side (Rome, 1953), 82-91. — U. Monneret de Villard, Le leggende orientali sui Magi evangelici (Rome, 1952), 107-111.

P. BRUNS

Narses of Edessa

I. Life: Narses, Syr. Narsai, was born, acc. to the testimony of Barhadbeshabba and the chronicle of Sert, ca. 399 in the village of Ain Dulbe near the Tigris. He spent his youth with his uncle in a monastery near Kfar-Mari; after his studies he was active there as a teacher, but later he resettled in Edessa in order to study theology. After the death of his uncle, N. himself was elected abbot of the monastery of Kfar-Mari but soon left it again in 435 in order to continue his studies in Mopsuestia under Theodore's successor, Theodulus. In 437 he became head of the school of theology in Edessa. Together with his friend and later Bishop Ibas, he translated the works of → Theodore Mops. and → Diodorus of Tarsus into Syriac. After the deposition of Ibas in 457, N. was driven from Edessa by Nonnus because of his Nestorianism, and he sought refuge outside the Roman empire in Persian Nisibis, whither he was soon followed by Barsauma and all the scholars of the Edessene school.

He headed this school as a respected teacher for 40 years until shortly before his death (502).

II. Works: N. was an ascetic who possessed outstanding intellectual capabilities and lent his pen to the Nestorian movement. His literary activity extended to the realm of exegesis, in which he largely followed the Antiochene tradition; his main interest here was the doctrine of creation. 360 homilies (*hom.*) of a liturgical-pastoral kind are attributed to him; a number of them found a place in the Chaldean breviary. In christology N. was an energetic opponent of → Jacob of Sarug and a zealous defender of his three teachers, Diodorus, Theodore, and Nestorius.

From the very beginning of his studies N. was under the spell of the Antiochene tradition of Diodorus, Theodore, and even Nestorius, whose disciple he always considered himself to be. In christology N. defends Diphysitism, although he, like Theodore, rejected the Two-Sons theory. The unity of Christ was established monotheletically by the one will of Christ and, in the theology of revelation, by the single prosopon. N. was also reserved in regard to the communication of idioms, which led him to reject the Ephesine title of Theotokos. Nevertheless, closely following Ephraem, he developed an important Marian typology (Mary–New Eve).

S: *vita*, F. Nau, PO 9:588-615 [text/French trans.]. — A. Scher, PO 4/7:381-387/114-117 [text/French trans.].
W: *hom.*, A. Mingana (Mossul, 1905) [text]. — F. Feldmann, Syr. Wechsellieder des N. (Leipzig, 1896) [German trans.]. — R. M. Connolly, Liturgical Homilies (Cambridge, 1909) [English trans.]. — F. D. McLeod, PO 40 [text/English trans.]. — P. Gignoux, PO 34/3-4 [French trans.]. — A. Allgeier, Über die Seele: ARW 21 (1922) 360-396 [German trans.]. — P. Brouwers, Sur le baptême: MUS 41/3 (1965) 179-207 [French trans.]. — E. K. Delly, Hom. 23: Div. 3 (1959) 514-533 [English trans.]. — P. Gignoux, Sur le baptême et l'eucharistie: LetChr(P) 7 (1963) 195-247 [French trans.]. — idem, Création d'Adam: OrSyr 7 (1962) 307-336 [French trans.]. — idem, Création du monde: OrSyr 7 (1962) 477-506 [French trans.]. — idem, Sur le commencement: OrSyr 8 (1963) 227-250 [French trans.]. — A. Guillaumont, Sur le baptême: OrSyr 1 (1956) 189-207 [French trans.]. — P. Krüger, Sur les martyrs: OrSyr 3 (1958) 299-316 [French trans.]. — F. Martin, Sur les trois docteurs: JA 14/15 (1899-1900) 446-492 [French trans.]. — P. M. Wolff, Begräbnisgesänge: OrChr 12-14 (1925) 1-29 [French trans.].
L: J. B. Chabot, N. le docteur: JA 6 (1905) 157-177. — J. Frishman, Homily for the Palm Festival: OCA 229 (1984) 217-230. — P. Gignoux, Doctrines eschatologiques de N.: OrSyr 11 (1966) 321-353, 461-488; 12 (1967) 23-54. — T. Jansma, Sur la pensée de N.: OrSyr 11 (1966) 147-168, 265, 290, 393-429. — idem, N. and Ephrem: ParOr 1 (1970) 49-68. — P. Krüger, Über die Engel: OS 1 (1952) 283-296. — idem, Bild der Gottesmutter: OS 2 (1953) 110-120. — idem, Le sommeil des âmes: OrSyr 4 (1959) 193-210. — W. F. Macomber, Metrical homilies: OCP 39 (1973) 275-306.

— K. McVey, Forensic Rhetoric: OCA 221 (1983) 87-96. — R. Nelz, Theol. Schulen (Bonn, 1916), 77-110. — A. Vööbus, History of the School of Nisibis (Leuven/Louvain, 1965).

P. BRUNS

Navigatio Brendani

The adventure-filled North Atlantic voyage of Irish Abbot Brendan in search of the promised land was one of the most popular medieval entertaining stories and was translated into many vernaculars. Its wide circulation is connected with the fact that the story, brought by the Irish to the continent, was placed in the service of the 9th c. monastic renewal. Exact hist. and geog. data show that the adventures linked to Brendan, a renowned 6th c. seafarer, are based ultimately on real occurrences (volcanic eruption off Iceland, icebergs, fog banks near the promised land), despite the fact that they are interwoven with saga motifs. It follows that before the 9th c. the Irish reached not only Iceland and Greenland but even North America and that the Vikings, regarded as the discovers of the northern route, in fact followed the Irish whom they had driven out.

W: C. Selmer (Notre Dame, 1959) [text]. — I. Orlandi (Milan, 1968). — M. Zelzer, FC [in preparation].
L: T. Severin, The Brendan Voyage (New York, 1986 = 1978) (German: Tausend Jahre vor Kolumbus [Hamburg, 1979]). — M. Zelzer, Zur Navigatio S. Brendani: Wiener Humanistische Blätter 31 (1989) 66-87. — F. Brunhölzl, Geschichte der lat. Lit. des MA 2 (Munich, 1992), 524-528.

M. ZELZER

Nazareans, Gospel of the

The *Gospel of the Nazareans* was probably composed in the first half of the 2nd c. in Jewish-Chr. circles in Coelesyria (possibly in the area around Berea). In the 4th c. it was probably in the library of Caesarea and used by the Nazareans. It was presumably a gospel of the synoptic type and was a continuation of Mt or at least used the same traditions as Mt. Composed originally in Aramaic or Syriac, it was also translated into Gr. In addition to various testimonies, about twenty fragments have been preserved in medieval sources as well as in Origen, Eusebius, and espec. Jerome, who, however, several times describes it as the Gospel of the → Hebrews and, surely incorrectly, claims to have translated it from Hebrew. The problem of attribution raised by such mistaken information is made all the greater by the question whether the *Ioudaikon* several times cited in five mss. of the gospels can be identified with the *Gospel of the Nazareans*.

W: A. F. J. Klijn, Jewish-Christian Gospel Tradition (Leiden, 1992) [text/English trans./comm.]. — NTApo⁶ 1:128-138 [German trans.].
L: A. F. J. Klijn, Das Hebräer- u. das N.: ANRW II 25/5 (1988) 3997-4033. — idem, G. J. Reinink, Patristic Evidence for Jewish-Christian Sects (Leiden, 1973). — W.-D. Köhler, Die Rezeption des Mt (Tübingen, 1987), 288-300. — S. C. Mimouni, Les Nazoréens: RB 105 (1998) 208-262. — T. C. G. Thornton, Jerome and the Hebrew Gospel: StPatr 28 (1993) 118-122.

R. HANIG

Nectarius of Constantinople

N., born in Tarsus, was initially a senator and city praetor in Constantinople; in 381, during the Council of Constantinople, though still unbaptized, he became the episcopal successor of Gregory Naz. and, in accordance with can. 3 of that council, the first patriarch of Constantinople. Despite his lack of theol. training, N. successfully played a part in eccles. politics and actively influenced important dogm. and canonical decrees: among other things, in 383, he presided at a debate on the faith, called for by Emperor Theodosius, between the several dogm. options, a debate which the emperor ended, after violent controversy, by accepting a homoousian confession submitted by N. N. was often accused of a pro-Novatian attitude (Soz., *h.e.* 7.12; Soc., *h.e.* 5.10). He died in 397.

Preserved is a homily of N. on the martyr Theodore (d. 306) (*Thdr.*), which was earlier attributed to his successor, John Chrys. Also preserved in Armenian, but not published, is an encomium of St. Stephen.

W: *Thdr.*, PG 39.1021-1840.
L: R. P. C. Hanson, The Search for the Christian Doctrine of God (Edinburgh, 1988). — K. Holl, Enthusiasmus u. Bußgewalt beim griech. Mönchtum (Leipzig, 1898). — J. Kunze, Das nicänisch-konstantinopolitanische Symbol (Leipzig, 1898). — G. Rauschen, Jahrbücher der chr. Kirche unter dem Kaiser Theodosius (Freiburg i.Br., 1897). — idem, Eucharistie u. Bußsakrament in den ersten sechs Jh. (Freiburg i.Br., 1912). — A. M. Ritter, Das Konzil von Konstantinopel (381) u. sein Symbol (Göttingen, 1965).

C. SCHMIDT

Nemesius

N., bishop of Emesa (now Homs, Syria), is said in some mss. to be the author of the earliest surviving systematic anthropology, *Peri physeōs anthrōpou* (*De natura hominis*; *nat. hom.*), which was composed ca.

400. N. is otherwise unknown, unless he is to be identified with a correspondent of Gregory Naz. (*ep.* 198-201; *carm.* 2.2.7).

In forty-two chapters N. deals with the physiology and psychology of the human being and with the most important subjects of ethics (pathology, doctrine of the will and of fate); he does so mainly in the manner of the doxographical manuals, from which he takes the relevant utterances of the ancient Gr. philosophers. Other sources are espec. Galen and Porphyry, Philo and Chr. exegesis of Gen. Acc. to N., the sensibly perceptible and intelligible realms of creation are combined in the human being, who is thus a world in miniature (microcosm, *nat. hom.* 64) and because of this peculiarity bears witness to the unity of creation and thus to the unity of the creator (39) against dualistic speculations. N. feels so deeply indebted to (Neo-)Platonism that he approves the theory of the transmigration of souls. *Nat. hom.* was used by Byz. authors from John Damascene on and was translated into the major oriental languages. Two medieval translations made the work known to scholasticism, but as the work of → Gregory Nyss. The value of N. for a reconstruction of the cosmology of Poseidonius is disputed.

W: C. F. Matthaei (Halle, 1802 = Hildesheim, 1967) [text/Latin trans.] (the *nat. hom.* is cited acc. to the pages of this edition) = PG 40:504-817. — K. Burkhard, N. Alfanus (Leipzig, 1917) [medieval-Latin trans.]. — G. Verbeke, J. R. Moncho, Burgundio v. Pisa, CLCAG. S 1 (Leiden, 1975) [medieval-Latin trans.]. — M. Morani (Leipzig, 1987) [text with apparatus of sources and testimonies; lit. on N.'s sources and on the early trans.]. — idem (Salerno, 1982) [Italian trans.]. — E. Orth, Maria-Mariental 1925 [German trans.]. — W. Telfer, LCC 4 (London, 1955), 201-455 [English trans./comm.].
L: H. Dörrie, Porphyrios' Symmikta Zetemata (Munich, 1959). — W. Jaeger, N. (Berlin, 1914). — A. Kallis, Der Mensch im Kosmos (Münster, 1978) (literature). — K. Reinhardt, N.: PRE 22/1:773-778. — A. Siclari, L'antropologia di N. nella critica moderna: Aevum 47 (1973) 477-497. — W. Telfer, The Birth of Christian Anthropology: JThS 13 (1962) 347-354. — W. Theiler, Poseidonios (Berlin, 1982), 1:XI, 227-233; 2:188-192. — M. Zonta, Nemesiana Syriaca: JSSt 36 (1991) 223-258.

C. P. VETTEN

Nephalius

N., abbot of an Egyptian monastery, was initially an extreme Monophysite, took part in 482 in an anti-Chalcedonian rebellion of three hundred monks, led by Theodore of Antioch, against the *Henotikon* of Emperor Zeno, and was opposed espec. to Peter Mongus. N. was excommunicated by Peter and protested in vain to the emperor, but he nevertheless sided with Peter by the summer of 487 at the latest. In 507 N. was the ringleader of a violent mutiny against Monophysite monks, i.e., the Palestinian supporters of Severus of Antioch. Now a representative of the Chalcedonian decrees, N. defended the Two-Nature doctrine in a dialogue on the faith in Palestine. This *Apologia* (*synēgoria*) is lost, but N.'s line of argument can be reconstructed with the help of the fragmentarily preserved *Orationes ad Nephalium* of his adversary, Severus of Antioch. N. uses patristic testimonies; his theology is heavily dependent on John Grammaticus, with support from Aristotle's teaching on categories and the ideals of Cyril Alex.

W: Severus of Antioch, *Orationes ad Nephalium*, J. Lebon, CSCO 119/120:1-69/1-50 [Syriac text/French trans.].
L: S. Helmer, Der Neuchalkedonismus (Bonn, 1962), 151-159. — J. Lebon, Le monophysisme sévérien (Leuven/Louvain, 1909), 33 n. 3, 43 n. 4. — C. Moeller, Un représentant de la Christologie néocalcédonienne: RHE 40 (1944/45) 73-140.

C. Schmidt

Nestorius

I. Life: N., b. after 381, received his upbringing and education in Antioch; as his theology clearly shows, this education was heavily influenced by the Diodorus of Tarsus and Theodore Mops., the heads of the Antiochene school. After N.'s ordination, it was primarily his outstanding reputation as a preacher that caused Emperor Theodosius II to call him to the episcopal see of the capital in 428. While the struggle against heretical groups was a focal point of his episcopate, his own orthodoxy was called into question in the controversy over describing Mary as "Mother of God" (*Theotokos*). N. rejected the title, at least in its full meaning, and from 429 on had Cyril Alex. as a bitter enemy. At the Council of Ephesus, on June 22, 431, Cyril pushed through the condemnation and deposition of N., and this stood despite all the protests and countermeasures of the Orientals. The deposed bishop was finally banished by the emperor in the fall of 435, and his writings were ordered to be destroyed. He died ca. 451 at the Great Oasis (Upper Egypt).

II. Works: Because of the condemnation and prohibition of his writings, N.'s extensive body of work is very largely lost.

Thus of more than sixty-two *sermons* (*hom.*) only four have survived complete, and this under the name of → John Chrys. Three deal with the temptations of Christ, the fourth with Heb 3:1. Large sec-

tions of two homilies have survived, as has the exhortation to → Proclus of Constantinople, in which N. responds to a sermon of the latter on the *Theotokos*. There are also more or less lengthy fragments of twenty-nine other homilies.

Of N.'s correspondence ten *letters* (*ep.*) have survived complete, the main content of which, owing probably, among other things, to the manner of transmission, is the defense of his position. In addition, in the first two of the three letters to Celestine I, as well as in the letter of encouragement to Caelestius, there is a certain sympathy for representatives of Pelagianism; the reason for this, however, seems to be less an agreement on substance than what N. felt was a similarity of destinies. The remaining letters reflect various stages of the controversy around N.

A polemic in dialogue form, the *Theopaschites*, is the first of the *apologetic writings*. The title as well as the few remnants show N.'s main accusation against his opponents (Cyril?): in their christology they make the divinity subject to suffering. Of the *Tragoedia*, too, which was N.'s first major defense (probably written during the first period in exile), only fragments have survived, but these can be supplemented by citations in the church history of → Barhadbeshabba (though these are problematic from the viewpoint of literary criticism). The fragments suggest that in this work N. probably gave his view of events until the beginning of his exile. The *Liber Heraclidis* (*Heracl.*), a Syr. translation of which was rediscovered toward the end of the 19th c., was a continuation and to some extent a repetition of the *Tragoedia*; but, in the version found, this work shows a whole series of interpolations (e.g., the theol. introduction in dialogue form and some parts of the conclusion). The Syr. title *Tegurta* (commerce) is based on an erroneous interpretation of the Gr. *pragmateia* (treatise); the person named "Heraclides" is otherwise unknown. The parts of the defense that are certainly authentic contain a rejection of the accusations raised by Cyril at Ephesus, as well as a description of individual problems and events down to the Robber Synod of 449. The state of mind of the condemned and exiled bishop also emerges clearly here in a mixture of resignation and angry denunciation of the treatment he has received.

The so-called *Twelve Counteranathemas* against Cyril, which are ascribed to N., can with a great deal of certainty be assigned to a later time.

W: F. Loofs, Nestoriana (Halle, 1905). — *Heracl.*, P. Bedjan (Paris, 1910) [Syriac text]. — F. Nau (Paris, 1910) [French trans.]. — G. R. Driver, L. Hodgson (Oxford, 1925) [English trans.]. — *ep.*, ACO 1, 1, 1. — J. Lebon, Fragments syri-

aques: Muséon 36 (1923) 47-65 [text/Latin trans./comm.].
— H. F. Stander, Another Nestorian hom. of ascension of Christ: Acta Patristica et Byzantina 7 (1996) 105-116 [text/English trans./comm.].

L: L. Abramowski, Untersuchungen zum lit. Nachlaß des N. (Bonn, 1956). — eadem, Untersuchungen zum Liber Heraclidis (Leuven/Louvain, 1963). — R. Abramowski, Zur Tragödie des N.: ZKG 47 (1928) 305-324. — E. Amann, L'affaire de N. vue de Rome: RevSR 23 (1949) 5-37, 207-244; 24 (1950) 28-52, 235-265. — M. V. Anastos, N. was Orthodox: DOP 16 (1962) 117-140. — R. Arnou, Nestorianisme et Néoplatonisme: Gr. 17 (1936) 116-131. — G. S. Bebis, "The Apology" of N.: StPatr 11 (1972) 107-112. — J. F. Bethune-Baker, N. and His Teaching (Cambridge, 1908). — T. Camelot, De N. à Euthychès: Das Konzil von Chalkedon 1, ed. A. Grillmeier (Würzburg, 1962), 213-242. — A. Grillmeier, Zum Stand der N.-Forschung: ThPh 41 (1966) 401-410. — idem, Jesus der Christus 1 (Freiburg i.Br., ²1982), 642-691 (English, Christ in Christian Tradition, vol. 1 [London, ²1975]). — L. Hodgson, Metaphysics of N.: JThS 19 (1918) 46-55. — M. Jugie, N. et la controverse nestorienne (Paris, 1912). — M. Lamberigts, Les évêques pélagiens dédoses, N. et Ephèse: Aug(L) 35 (1985) 264-280. — F. Loofs, N. in the History of Christian Doctrine (Cambridge, 1914). — F. Nau, Saint Cyrille et N.: ROC 15 (1910) 365-391. — J. J. O'Keefe, Christology of N. (Münster, 1987). — G. Podskalsky, N.: GK 2/2 (1984), 215-225. — H. Ristow, ΠΡΟΣΩΠΟΝ in der Theologie des N.: BBA 5 (1957) 218-236. — L. I. Scipioni, Ricerce sulla cristologia del "Libro di Eraclide" (Fribourg, Switzerland, 1956). — idem, N. e il concilio di Efeso (Milan, 1974), in addition: R. Weijenborg: Anton. 51 (1976) 293-301; G. Jouassard: RHE 74 (1979) 346-348. — H. E. W. Turner, N. Reconsidered: StPatr 13 (1975) 306-321.

U. HAMM

Nicetas of Remesiana

Little is known of the life of N. (Nicetas is a latinization of Nikētēs): acc. to Gennadius (vir. ill. 22) he was bishop of Romantiana (= Remesiana, today Bela Palanka, 20 km. east of Nis); acc. to the testimony of his friend Paulinus of Nola, he was a missionary among the Scythians, Getes, Dacians, and Besses in Dacia. The only sure dates are those of two stays with Paulinus in 398 and 402 (poem of Paulinus on N.'s departure for Dacia: carm. 17.195ff.). The place and date of his death (certainly after 414) have not been handed down.

Among his writings are a short treatise on the titles of Christ, De diversis appellationibus (appell.), as well as an instruction of candidates for baptism in six books, Competentibus ad baptismum instructionis libelli VI (instr.), of which only books 3, De ratione fidei, and 5, De symbolo, have survived. (The hypothetical new edition of Gamber also contains the sermons De spiritu sancto, De cognitione Dei, De figuratione animae, De praedestinatione Dei, De oratione et eleemosyna, and the six sermons De sacramentis, which are usually ascribed to Ambrose and here form book 6 of the inst. Gamber gives liturg. and stylistic arguments for his choice.)

Also preserved are two liturg. treatises, De vigiliis (vigil.), in which he justifies prayer during the nights from Friday to Saturday and Saturday to Sunday, and De psalmodiae bono (psalm.), a defense of psalmody. Psalmody is based on the authority of scripture. Singing has a spiritual as well as a practical and pedagogical function. To the fore is the unity of the community, which reflects the unity of the divine Trinity. In contrast to the singing in tragedy, which N. (like some dialogues of Plato) rejects as dissonant, liturg. singing, which joins that of the angels and saints, should express the harmony of heaven and the wisdom of Christ.

It is uncertain whether N. was the author of a lost work De agni paschalis victima; he was probably neither author nor redactor of the → Te Deum. Paulinus says that N. also wrote hymns. The work mentioned by Gennadius, Ad lapsam virginem, is perhaps identical with the Ps.-Ambrosian De lapsu Susannae (Sus.), but not, as used to be assumed, with the Ep. ad virginem lapsam (virg. laps.).

In intr. 5 there appears for the first time the concept of communio sanctorum, which is central to N.'s ecclesiology (an ecclesiology influenced by Cyril Jerus.). Against heresies he defends the unity of the church as the unity of the body of Christ; any deviation in faith means a violation of unity. N.'s theology is anti-Arian; he stresses the Nicene Creed and the divinity of the Holy Spirit. The style of his writings reflects their practical purpose, the instruction of candidates for baptism. N. uses a simple, clear language with many citations from scripture. He is a pastor, not a theologian.

W: appell., instr., PL 52:863-876. — A. E. Burn (Cambridge, 1905), 1-54 [text]. — instr., K. Gamber (Regensburg, 1964-1969) [text]. — vigil., C. Turner: JThS 22 (1921) 306-320. — psalm., PLS 3:191-199. — C. Turner: JThS 24 (1923) 225-252. — Sus., E. Cazzaniga (Turin, 1948) [text]. — K. Gamber (Regensburg, 1969) [text with a concordance to the writings of N.]. — virg. laps., PLS 3:199-202 — A. E. Burn, op. cit., 131-136.
L: V. Buchheit, Sieg auf dem Meer der Welt (Paul. Nol., carm. 17.105ff.): Hermes 109 (1981) 235-247. — K. Gamber, Die Autorschaft von De Sacramentis (Regensburg, 1967). — idem, Fragen zu Person u. Werk des Bischofs N.: RQ 62 (1967) 222-231. — idem, Ist N. der Verfasser des ps.-ambrosianischen Sermo "De Spiritu Sancto"?: OS 11 (1962) 204-206. — idem, Ist N. der Verfasser von De sacramentis?: OS 7 (1958) 153-172. — idem, N. als Katechet u. Hymnendichter: idem, Sacramentorum (Regensburg, 1984), 121-136. — idem, Nochmals zur Frage der Autorschaft von De Sacramentis: ZKTh 91 (1969) 587-589. — idem, Nochmals zur Schrift "Ad competentes" des N.: OS 13 (1964) 192-202.

— idem, Die 6 Bücher "Ad competentes" des N.: OS 9 (1969) 123-173. — idem, Die Taufkatechesen des Bischofs N.: HlD 25 (1971) 27-29. — W. Kirsch, Paulinus v. Nola u. N.: From Late Antiquity to Early Byzantium. Proceedings of the Byzantinological Symposium in the 16th International Eirene Conference, ed. V. Vavrinek (Prague, 1985), 189-193. — V. Messana, Quelques remarques sur la liturgie du chant selon N.: EL 102 (1988) 138-144. — C. Riggi, Pregare all'unisono secondo N.: StPatr 23 (1989) 162-170. — J. Schmitz, Zum Autor der Schrift "De Sacramentis": ZKTh 91 (1969) 59-69. — Z. Senjak, N. Chr. Unterweisung u. chr. Leben im spätantiken Denken (Freiburg i.Br., 1976).

S. FELBECKER

Nicholas of Ancyra

N. probably lived in the 5th or 6th c. He is also described as N. the Presbyter. Catenas show that he was the author of commentaries on Joel (*comm. Ioel*) and Amos (*comm. Am.*). Also ascribed to him are a commentary on Jonah (*comm. Ion.*) and 1 Cor (*comm. 1 Cor.*), perhaps also a commentary on the Psalms (*comm. Ps.*).

N. is possibly the same as the ascetic N. of Ancyra, whose question Mark the Hermit answers in his *Pros Nicolaon* (PG 65:1027-50) and who answers in turn with a very devout letter of thanks (*Nic.*).

W: *comm. Ioel, comm. Am.*, J. A. Cramer, Catenae graecorum patrum in V. T. 3 (Oxford, 1838), 35, 37, 38, 124 [text]. — *comm. Ion.*, Y. M. Duval, Le livre de Jonas dans la littérature chrétienne grecque et latine (Paris, 1973), 454-456, 663-665 [text]. — *comm. 1 Cor.*, K. Staab, Die Pauluskatenen nach den hs. Quellen untersucht (Rome, 1926), 15-17 [text]. — *comm. Ps.*, cf. G. Karo, I. Lietzmann, Catenarum graecorum catalogus (Göttingen, 1902), 35 [text]. — *Nic.*, PG 65:1051-1054.
L: W. Enslin, N.: PRE 17:361.

N. KLIMEK

Nilus of Ancyra

N. was a disciple of John Chrys.; he was earlier called N. of Sinai on the basis of an identification with the narrator of the *Narrationes de caede monachorum in monte Sinai* (*narr.*). N., a cenobite, was head of a monastery and novice master in Ancyra and an esteemed spiritual adviser of, among others, Gainas, leader of the Goths. He died ca. 430.

The body of work ascribed to N. is divided into letters, ethical writings, and writings on monasticism; but the question of authorship has not yet been definitively answered, except for a few treatises. Some of N.'s letters (*ep.*) (1,061 letters in four books) have to do with the exegesis of passages of scripture; a few dogm. letters show N.'s rejection of Arianism and his approval of the *Theotokos* title. But the domi-

nant subject is the striving for perfection after the model of Christ (*philosophein kata Christon*) by means of contemplation and asceticism.

The moral treatise on Lk 22:36 (*serm.*) interprets the passage allegorically as giving the ideal of the soldier of Christ whose weapons are the Chr. virtues and the word of God.

Among N.'s works on the monastic life are the encomium *In Albianum oratio* (*Alb.*) of Albianus, a hermit from Ancyra; the work *De monachorum praestantia* (*praest.*), a comparison of ascetical life in a monastery and in the world; the treatise *De monastica exercitatione* (*logos askētikos*) (*exerc.*), which in its first part sets forth the original idea of monasticism and in the second gives practical instructions for everyday monastic life; the treatise *Ad Magnam diaconissam Ancyrae de voluntaria paupertate* (*Magn.*) distinguishes three different stages of poverty and correlates monasticism with the middle stage (*mesē aktēmosyne*); the short instruction *De magistris et discipulis* (*magistr.*), addressed to novicemasters and novices in the form of sayings and gnomes.

References in other writers and a great many fragments handed down under the name of N. point to other, lost writings. However, an unambiguous attribution to N. is not possible, and a confusion with the author of the *narr.* or with some other N. cannot be excluded.

The authorship of *Peristeria* (*ad Agathium monachum*; *perist.*) is unclear. A commentary on the Canticle, of disputed authenticity, is unpublished; in the catenas are remnants of a commentary on the Psalms.

The *De oratione, De octo spiritibus malitiae*, and *Ad Eulogium*, at one time ascribed to N., are from → Evagrius Pont. (346-399). The *Epicteti Enchiridion* (ed. J. Schweighäuser, Leipzig, 1800) is likewise not from N.

W: *narr., ep., serm., praest., exerc., Magn., magistr., perist., Alb.*, PG 79:81-1093. — *magistr.*, P. van den Ven, Un opuscule inédit attribué à S. Nil: FS G. Kurth 1 (Lüttich, 1908), 73-81 [text].
L: A. Baumstark, Geschichte der syr. Lit. (Bonn, 1922), 91 nn. 4-13 [for the Syriac Opuscula]. — P. Bettiolo, La Sententiae di N.: CrSt 1 (1980) 155-184. — R. Browning, Le commentaire de s. N. sur le Cantique des Cantiques: REB 24 (1966) 107-114. — A. Cameron, The Authenticity of the Letters of St. N.: GRBS 17 (1976) 181-196. — V. Christides, Once again the "Narrationes" of N. Sinaiticus: Byz. 43 (1973) 39-50. — F. Conca, Per una edizione critica di [Nilo] "Narrationes": Acme 31/1 (1978) 37-57. — F. Degenhart, De hl. N. Sinaita (Münster, 1915). — M. T. Disdier, N.: DSp 11:345-354. — J. Gribomonz, La tradition manuscrite de s. N.: StMon 11 (1969) 231-267. — J. Henninger, Ist der sog. N.-Bericht eine brauchbare religions-

geschichtliche Quelle?: Anthr. 50 (1955) 81-148. — K. Heussi, Untersuchungen zu N. dem Asketen (Leipzig, 1917). — idem, Das N.-problem (Leipzig, 1921). — H. Ringshausen, Zur Verfasserschaft u. Chronologie der dem N. Ancyranus zugeschriebenen Werke (Frankfurt a.M., 1967). — A. Sovic, De N. monachi commentario in Canticum Canticorum reconstruendo: Bib. 2 (1921) 45-52. — V. Warnach, Theologie des Gebetes: FS T. Michels (1963), 65-90.

C. Schmidt

Noëma

Noëma (*The Concept of Our Great Power*) is the title of an apocalyptic work in the Nag Hammadi library (NHC 6, 4) that primarily describes the events of the end. It depicts the return of the light-soul to the heavenly Pleroma.

W: D. M. Parrott, NHC V and VI (Leiden, 1979), 291-323 [Coptic text/English trans./comm.]. — P. Cherix, Concept (Fribourg, Switzerland, 1982) [Coptic text/French trans./text]. — K. M. Fischer, Gedanke: ThLZ 98 (1973) 169-176 [German trans.]. — NHL 311-317 [English trans.]. L: P. Cherix, Concordance NHC VI (Leuven/Louvain, 1993).

P. Bruns

Noetus of Smyrna

Since the work *Contra Noetum* in its present form is probably from the 4th c., Hippolytus alone (*haer.* 9.7.1; 9.10.8-12; 10.27.1f.) provides useful information about Noetus of Smyrna. He may be using as his source an Easter homily (ca. 160-170?) that contained an anti-Valentinian, monarchian rule of faith with numerous references to the traditions of Asia Minor.

W: Hippolytus, *haer.* 9.7.1; 9.10.8-12; 10.27.1f. L: J. A. Fischer; A. Lumpe, Synoden v. d. Anfängen bis z. Vorabend des Nicaenums (Paderborn, 1997), 88-95. — J. Frickel, Contra Noetum: FS L. Abramowski (Berlin, 1993), 87-123. — R. M. Hübner, Melito und N.: FS W. Schneemelcher (Stuttgart, 1989), 219-240. — idem, Glaubensregel: MThZ 40 (1989) 279-311. — idem, Antivalentinianischer Charakter: FS L. Abramowski (Berlin, 1993), 57-86. — A. Pourkier, L'hérésiologie chez Épiphane (Paris, 1992), 115-146. — M. Simonetti, Tra N., Ippolito e Melitone: RSLR 31 (1995) 393-414.

R. Hanig

Nonnus of Panopolis

The time, place, and setting of epic poet N. from Panopolis in Upper Egypt are to be inferred almost exclusively from his works. It is above all the specific character of his metrics (rigorous hexametric technique; attention to word accent) that points to the middle or second half of the 5th c. He is hardly to be identified with Nonnus, bishop of Edessa.

The forty-eight books of the *Dionysiaca* (*D.*), written in Alexandria (1.13), tell in very full form the story of the god Dionysos, beginning with his prehistory and birth; the main part tells of his journey to India and return and culminates in his ascent to heaven. This not quite complete but most extensive piece of Gr. verse anywhere sums up not only the entire epic tradition (espec. the Dionysos cycles) but also uses novelistic, hymnic, learnedly allegorical, and magical-astrological materials. Despite the dependence on Homer, the work is permeated by the overflowing figure of Dionysos: its *poikilia* or intricate ornamentation, reminiscent of baroque, finds expression, in, e.g., the profusion of epic interludes and the pathos of Asianist rhetoric. In a mythical exaggeration of the expedition of Alexander, Dionysos conquers the world and brings it the blessing of his gift, wine, doing so amid exuberant ecstasy but also amid bloody violence.

The paraphrase of John (*Metabolē*; *par. Jo.*) in twenty-one cantos is almost certainly from the same author and displays the same style (profusion of epithets; contrast and ecphrasis; variation and ornamentation, clever use of bibl. language in an unfamiliar way). Noteworthy is the strong interest in the Nicene consubstantiality of the Son with the Father. The exaltation of Mary as "Mother of God" (*Theētokos* [*sic!*]) points to the age of the Nestorian controversies.

The juxtaposition of the pagan *D.* and the Chr. *par. Jo.* has given rise to the "Nonnian Question." The chronological relation between the two cannot be determined with certainty, although overlappings can be clearly seen (e.g., miracle of wine, healing of blind, redemptive figure). More probable than the hypothesis of the conversion to Christianity of the pagan author of *D.* is the assumption of a (widespread!) coexistence of a learned acceptance of inherited pagan tradition, on the one hand, with Chr. faith, on the other.

W: *D.*, R. Keydell (Berlin, 1959) [text]. — F. Vian et al., CUFr (Paris, 1976ff.) [text/French trans.]. — W. Peek (ed.), Lexikon (Berlin, 1968-1975). — *par. Jo.*, A. Scheindler, BiTeu (Leipzig, 1881) [text]. — E. Livrea (Naples, 1989) [book 18, text/Italian trans./comm.]. — D. Accorintti (Pisa, 1996) [book 20, text/Italian trans./comm.]. — *D.*, *par. Jo.*, D. Ebener (Berlin, 1985) [German trans.]. L: B. Abel-Wilmanns, Erzähllaufbau (Frankfurt a.M., 1977). — H. Bogner, Religion: Ph. 89 (1934) 320-333. — P. Chuvin, Paganisme et christianisme: BAGB 1986, 387-396. — idem, Mythologie et géographie (Clermont, 1991). — W.

435

Fauth, Eidos poikilon (Göttingen, 1981). — P. Friedländer, Chronologie (1912): idem, Studien zur antiken Literatur (Berlin, 1969), 250-263. — D. Gigli Piccardi, Metafora e poetica (Florence, 1985). — J. Golega, Evangeliendichtung (Breslau, 1930). — N. Hopkinson (ed.), Studies (Cambridge, 1994). — G. D'Ippolito, Studi Nonniani (Palermo, 1964). — R. Keydell, N.: PRE 17/1:904-920. — idem, Kleine Schriften (Leipzig, 1982), 392-585. — E. Livrea, Il poeta ed il vescovo: Prometheus 13 (1987) 97-123. — R. F. Newbold, Creativity: CIA 12 (1993) 89-110. — W. Peek, Beiträge: ADAW.S (1969), 1-52. — K. Smolak, Metabole: JÖB 34 (1984) 1-14. — K. Thraede, Epos: RAC 5:1001-1003. — D. Willers, Dionysos u. Christus: MH 49 (1992) 141-151.

S. Vollenweider

Norea

Norea or *Ode on Norea* or *The Thought of Norea* is the suggested title of an untitled work in the Nag Hammadi library (NHC 9, 2). It belongs to the Sethian type of gnosis. Norea, a daughter of Eve, is the bearer of revelation; in union with the preexistent Sophia, she appears as antagonist of the wicked demiurge.

W: B. A. Pearson, NHC IX and X (Leiden, 1981), 87-99 [Coptic text/English trans./comm.]. — B. Barc, M. Roberge, L'Hypostase des Archontes, suivi de N. (Leuven/Louvain, 1980) [Coptic text/French trans./comm.]. — NHL 445-447 [English trans.].
L: K. L. King, Book of N., Daughter of Eve: Feminist Commentary, ed. E. Schüssler Fiorenza (New York, 1994), 66-85.

P. Bruns

Notitia dignitatum

The *Notitia dignitatum omnium, tam civilium quam militarium* (*Not. dign.*) is a handbook for the private use of Roman authorities in late antiquity. It is divided into two parts, one for the East and one for the West, and lists the upper civil and military offices acc. to the ranking of the officials. The *Not. dign.* provides information about the divisions of the empire (prefectures, dioceses, provinces) and the deployment of army units and authorities. In addition, it describes the insignia of officials and the divisions of the army and gives an allegorical description of the provinces, weapons, etc. The *primicerius notariorum* needed the *Not. dign.* in order to draw up documents for appointments; the work had therefore to be repeatedly edited and updated. The surviving copy of the *Not. dign.* was composed between 425 and 430 and is an important source for the administrative and military history of late antiquity.

W: E. Böcking (Bonn, 1839-1853) [text]. — O. Seeck (Berlin, 1876) [text].

L: A. Lippold, Not. dign.: KP 4:166f. — P. Lot, La Not. dign.: REA 38 (1936) 285-328. — A. Pabst, Not. dign.: LMA 6:1286f. (literature).

W. Geerlings

Notitia Galliarum

The *Notitia Galliarum* or *Notitia provinciarum et civitatum Galliarum* (*Not. Gall.*) is a list of the seventeen provinces of Gaul (it agrees with the list in the → *Notitia dignitatum*), along with 115 *civitates*, seven *castra*, and one *portus*. The *Not. Gall.*, the original text of which was expanded through interpolations, was composed during the second half of the 4th c. and the first half of the 5th (386-450 or 367-407). It is useful as a source for the organizational structure of the church in Gaul, since the provinces, capitals, and cities were to a great extent the same as the provinces of the church and the sees of metropolitans and bishops. There is not as yet full clarity on whether the list was originally drawn up for administrative purposes and only later taken over for use in the church or whether it belonged to the church from the outset.

W: T. Mommsen, MGH. AA 9:584-612 = CCL 175:381-406.
L: P. M. Duval, La Gaule jusqu'aù milieu du Vᵉ siècle (Paris, 1971), 681f. — E. Griffe, La Gaule chrétienne à l'époque romaine 2 (Paris, ²1966), 11-125. — J. Harries, Church and State in the Not. Gall.: JRS 68 (1978) 226-243. — H. Mordek, Not. Gall.: LMA 6:1287. — A. L. F. Rivet, Gallia Narbonensis (London, 1988), 98-100. — M. Schanz, C. Hosius, G. Krüger, Geschichte der röm. Lit. 4/2 (Munich, 1959 = 1920), 130.

B. Windau

Notitia provinciarum et civitatum Africae

The *Notitia provinciarum et civitatum Africae sive nomina episcoporum vel sedium illius regionis* (*Not. episc.*) is a list of the Cath. bishops who assembled in Carthage in 484 by order of Vandal King Huneric. The list follows the division into provinces and shows the following episcopal sees: Africa Proconsularia, 54; Numidia, 125; Byzacena, 115; Mauretania Caesariensis, 123 (three of them vacant); Mauretania Sitifensis, 42; Tripolitana, 5; Sardinia, 8; 471 sees in all are listed.

W: PL 58:269-276. — C. Halm, MGH. AA 3/1:63-71. — M. Petschenig, CSEL 7:117-134.
L: R. Haensch, Capita provinciarum (Mainz, 1997). — C. Lepelley, Les cités de l'Afrique romaine au Bas-Empire, 2 vols. (Paris, 1979, 1981).

W. Geerlings

Novatian

I. Life: N., b. probably in Rome, was ordained a priest by Roman Bishop Fabian against the objections of the Roman clergy that he had been baptized when in danger of death (*clinicus*) and had not been confirmed (Eus., *h.e.* 6.43.13-17). In 250/251, after Fabian's death and while the see was vacant, N. played an important role in leading the church. In 250, by commission of the Roman clergy, he wrote three letters (*ep.*) to Cyprian on dealing with the Christians who had fallen away (*lapsi*) during the Decian persecution; the letters agreed with Cyprian's moderate attitude. Disappointed in his hope of the episcopate, N. changed his viewpoint on the *lapsi* after the election of Cornelius, sharply criticizing the latter's leniency, and had himself consecrated antibishop of Rome by three southern Ital. bishops (Eus., *h.e.* 8.43.8f.). In 251 N. and his supporters were suspended by a Roman synod of sixty bishops. He spent some years away from Rome, probably during the persecution of Gallus and Volusian or Valerian; the claim that he died during the persecution under Valerian (beginning in mid-257) (Soc., *h.e.* 4.28) is not clearly provable. Supporters of N.'s position could be found down into the 7th c.

II. Works: Of the works of N. listed by Jerome (*vir. ill.* 70; *ep.* 36), representing the first works composed in Lat. by a Roman theologian, only two have survived: the treatise *De trinitate* (*trin.*), found among the works of Tertullian, and the circular letter *De cibis iudaicis* (*cib. Iud.*), which is the same as the *De mundis atque immundis animalibus*, mentioned in the *trin.* The reason for the acceptance of *trin.* among Tertullian's works was probably the similarity to several titles of the African writer, and to a certain likeness in content. In its first part (1-8), *Trin.*, an apologetic explanation (composed ca. 240) of the *regula fidei* regarding the Trinity, defends God the Father as creator of the world against the teachings of the gnostics; in its second part (9-28) it defends the unity of godhead and humanity in Jesus Christ, the true Son of the creator, and his distinction from the Father against Marcionites, adoptionists, and modalists; in the third part (29) it explains the responsibility of the Spirit for the church and, in the fourth (30-31) the connection between the true godhead of the Son and the oneness of God. The work, which in its terminology is strongly influenced by Tertullian, reflects the still quite undeveloped christology and pneumatology of the 3rd c., which regarded the Father as a personal unity completely independent of the Son and gave the Spirit the role solely of a source

of virtues that is bestowed on human beings in baptism.

Cib. Iud., a pastoral letter to the Novatian community in Rome, probably during a time of persecution, deals with the freedom of Christians from the Jewish dietary laws but also exhorts them to moderation and prohibits the eating of flesh sacrificed to the gods. The treatise shows various echoes of the Stoic doctrines of Seneca.

Two treatises handed down in mss. of Cyprian and counted by Jerome (*ep.* 10) as probably belonging among the *Epistulae Novatiani*, namely, the *De spectaculis* (*spect.*) and the *De bono pudicitiae* (*pud.*), are likewise works of doctrine and exhortation addressed from a distance to the Roman community. The *spect.*, like Tertullian's work of the same title, warns against attending the theater because of its decadent morals and close connection with pagan belief in the gods and, in contrast, offers the spectacle of nature of God's creation and the stories of scripture as an amusement suited to Christians. *Pud.* exhorts to virginity and to continence and fidelity in marriage. Other *ep.*, as well as the treatises *De pascha*, *De circumcisione*, *De sacerdotio*, *De oratione*, *De instantia*, and *De attalo* are lost, while the *Adv. Iudaeos* is probably not authentic.

W: PL 3:911-1000. — PL 4:779-851. — R. DeSimons, FaCh 67 [English trans.]. — *trin.*, H. Weyer (Düsseldorf, 1962) [text/German trans./comm.]. — V. Loi, CPS 2 [text/Italian trans./comm.]. — *cib. Iud.*, G. Landgraf, C. Weymann: Archiv für lat. Lexikographie 11 (Leipzig, 1898), 221-249 [text]. — *spect., pud.*, W. Hartel, CSEL 3/3a.13-25. — *spect.*, A. Boulanger (Paris, 1933), 99-112 [text]. — *ep.*, Cyprian, *ep.* 30, 31, 36, W. Hartel, CSEL 3/2:549-564, 572-579.
L: E. Amann, N. et Novatianisme: DThC 11/1:816-849. — H. Gülzow, Cyprian und N. (Tübingen, 1975). — H. Koch, N.: PRE 17:1138-1156. — B. Melin, Studia in Corpus Cyprianeum (Uppsala, 1946). — R. J. De Simone, The Treatise of N. on the Trinity (Rome, 1970). — idem, N.: DSp 11:479-483. — idem, Again the Kenosis of Phil. 2, 6-11: N., Trin. 22: Aug. 32 (1992) 91-104. — H. J. Vogt, Coetus Sanctorum (Bonn, 1968). — M. Wallraff, Geschichte des Novatianismus seit dem 4. Jh. im Osten: ZAC 1 (1997) 251-279. — idem, Socrates Scholasticus on the History of Novatianism: StPatr 29 (1997) 170-177. — idem, Markianos — ein prominenter Konvertit vom Novatianismus zur Orthodoxie: VigChr 52 (1998) 1-29.

C. Schmidt

Novatus Catholicus

Nothing certain is known about N. He lived ca. 450-530 and came perhaps from Italy but possibly from Africa. A work of N., *Sententia de humilitate et oboedientia et de calcanda superbia*, is preserved which in 112 short sentences exhorts to mercy, obedience, and humility. The work is an address of a bishop or priest to monks. It must have been composed before the *Regula Eugippi* (530-535) because it is contained in the latter without the author being named. By and large, it shows the influence of the gospels and Paul.

W: F. Villegas, Les sentences pour les moines de N.: RBen 86 (1976) 49-74 [text]. — F. Villegas, A. de Vogüé, CSEL 87:66-74. — A. de Vogüé, Thoughts of N.: MonS 12 (1976) 264-270 [English trans.].
L: A. Solignac, N.: DSp 11:477f. — A. de Vogüé, Novati sententia: DIP 6, 441f.

B. WINDAU

Novel/Novelistic Literature

In the late Hellen. and early imperial periods, pagan Gr. and Roman literature saw the development of a form of narrative prose to which the modern age has given the name of novel (N. [= pagan N.]). Examples: Ninus-N. (2nd or 1st c. B.C.E.); Chariton, *Chaireas and Callirhoe* (1st c. C.E.); Petronius, *Satyrica* (1st c.); Xenophon, *Ephesiaca* (2nd. c.); Apuleius, *Metamorphoses* (2nd c.); Achilleus Tatius, *Leucippe and Cleitophon* (ca. 180); Heliodorus, *Aithiopica* (3rd c.). The fictional element predominates, but the novel can also include hist. figures and events. An important characteristic is a plot rich in adventures and including long journeys and frequent changes of scene; if love between two partners plays a role, the many temptations against fidelity are gladly emphasized. Motifs and scenes typical of the novel are also seen in Jewish and espec. in Chr. literature. An important task still to be done in the interpretation of individual works is to determine how significant the motivational correspondences to the novel are; what level of each text displays the similarities, and whether there is in fact an imitation of the novel type or of particular novels. Despite all that they have in common, there remains this essential distinction: novels aim primarily at the pleasure (*delectatio*) of the readers, while Jewish and Chr. narratives aim to edify them (*aedificatio*).

Which writings are important representatives of "novelistic" literature? A novelistic garb is to be seen in the numerous versions of the *History of Wise Ahikar*, the oldest surviving version of which (Aramaic) dates to the 5th c. B.C.E. Individual traits of the novel are to be seen in the narrative books of the OT: Esth (ca. 300 B.C.E.), Tobit (2nd c. B.C.E.), and Jud (2nd/1st c. B.C.E.). The same holds for the Letter of

→ Aristeas, an account of the origin of the Septuagint, written between 150 and 100 B.C.E. The work of Artapanus, *On the Jews* (2nd c. B.C.E.) can be described as a historical novel (fragments in Eus., *h.e.* 9.8.23 and 27). Novelistic traits also mark the telling of the biblical story by Ps.-Philo, a Jew; it was composed soon after 70 C.E. and has survived in a Latin translation. An unknown Jewish author (1st c. B.C.E.? 1st c. C.E.?) composed the story of *Joseph and Aseneth*, which is preserved in Greek and in numerous translations (Syriac, Armenian, and Latin among others). The story tells of Joseph's first meeting with Aseneth, the very beautiful daughter of priest Pentephres of Heliopolis; her conversion from Egypt. polytheism to Jewish monotheism; the threat to Aseneth from the pharaoh's son; and finally the marriage of the two protagonists. The chief personages are perhaps to be understood allegorically: Joseph as the heavenly messenger, Aseneth as the converted community. Whether the presentation shows specifically Chr. traits is disputed; in any case, before being forgotten for a long time in the modern era, the story evidently found readers among Christians, who felt themselves drawn by the dramatically described turning of Aseneth to the one God.

How close do the Synoptic gospels come to the novel? Admittedly, a number of motifs typical of the novel play a role in them (see Luke's description of Jesus' last journey to Jerusalem, 9:51—19:10; the description of a shipwreck, Acts 27f.). On the whole, however, the gospels can hardly be understood as "novelistic biographies," for in them, unlike in the novel, an eschat. conception is always linked with the narrative of past events. Something similar holds for Acts, for in it the point is not to tell the story of a possible but fictitious activity but to present events in a salvation-historical perspective and specifically events that form the foundation of the Chr. faith.

The situation is different in literary productions of a later time. Many traits of the novel are to be seen in, e.g., the Gk. apocryphal Acts of the apostles, among them, the *Acta Petri* (ca. 180-190; → Peter, Literature about); the *Acta Pauli* → Paul, Literature about), of which the *Acta Pauli et Theclae* (→ Thecla, Acts of) are an important part (end of 2nd c.); the *Acta Thomae* (→ Thomas, Literature about); *Acta Andreae* (→ Andrew, Acts of). Thus in the *Acta Pauli* a relevant example is the description of Thecla's enthusiasm for Paul's teaching, a description that carries erotic undertones; Thecla's unreserved preservation of chastity; the separation of the main personages; and their almost miraculous rescue from persecution.

The influence of the apocryphal Acts of the apostles can be seen in the 3rd-c. story *The Life and Conduct of the Holy Women Xanthippe, Polyxena, and Rebecca*; 1-21 tells of Xanthippe's conversion by Paul; 22-42 tell, among other things, of the abduction of Xanthippe's younger, pretty sister Polyxena and of a shipwreck of the brigands.

The description "novelistic" can also be applied to the so-called *Pseudo-Clementines* (*Ps.-Clem.*) (4th c.), which have been preserved in two versions, the Gk. *Homiliai* and the *Recognitiones* (there is a Lat. translation by → Rufinus of Aquileia). Clement, leader of the Roman community in the 1st c., tells, in the first person, what he experienced as companion of Peter and what the fate was of his parents (Faustus and Mattidia) and other family members. Typical novelistic motifs are, e.g., the separation of the married couple; the slandering of Mattidia by a scorned lover; and the final recognition of the spouses (*anagnorismos, recognitio*). On the other hand, the pervasive theol. thrust of the work is alien to the novel; this shows itself espec. in the disputation conducted by Faustus and his sons over the significance of astrology for human life and in the author's attack on polytheism.

In the passion literature, too, there are elements such as are found in the novel. This is true espec. of the *Diegmata* (*Narrationes* [*narr.*]) that have come down under the name of Nilus (→ Nilus of Ancyra), a writer of the 4th/5th c., but were probably not composed by him. In this work an elderly hermit tells of how he and his son Theodulus renounced the world and joined the monks in the Sinai. Bands of robbers inflicted a bloodbath there one day; Theodulus was captured but managed to escape and finally find his father, who had preserved his life.

Finally, similarities to the novel can be seen in the Gr. → *Narratio de rebus Persicis* (*Pers.*), from the 5th or 6th c., which tells of the events "that took place in Persia after the birth of Christ, our Lord and Redeemer"; at the center of the story is a dialogue on religion among Christians, Greeks, Jews, and a Persian magus, which ends with the intellectual victory of Christianity.

In Lat. literature mention is to be made of the *Historia Apollonii regis Tyri* (*Apoll.*), a story handed down in many versions, in which, among other things, the king's daughter, Tarisa, is described as the embodiment of sexual continence: while held prisoner in a brothel, she induces men for many years to desist from their lust. *Redactio A*, which is from the 5th or 6th c., displays Chr. traits as well as pagan: not only the ancient gods but the one God is

repeatedly invoked, and it is an angel who brings the hero an important message in a dream. Over the centuries the Chr. element was intensified, whereas it was probably absent from the original version (3rd c.).

W: *Ahiqar*, E. Sachau, Aramäische Papyrus u. Ostraka aus einer jüd. Militärkolonie zu Elephantine (Leipzig, 1973 = 1911). — F. C. Conybeare, J. R. Harris, A. S. Lewis (ed.), The story of Ahikar (London, [2]1913) [includes Aramaic/Syriac/Arabic/Armenian/Ethiopic text]. — *Letter of Aristeas*, M. Hadas (New York, 1931) [text/English trans.]. — *Artapanos*, F. Jacoby, Frgm. der griech. Historiker 3, C Nr. 726 (Leipzig, 1958), 680-686 [text]. — *Ps.-Philo*, G. Kisch, Pseudo-Philo's Liber antiquitatum biblicarum (Indiana, 1949) [text]. — *Joseph et Aseneth*, M. Philonenko (Leiden, 1968) [text/French trans./comm.]. — P. Riessler, Altjüd. Schrifttum (Heidelberg, 1966 – 1928), 497-538 [German trans.]. — *Xanthippe, Polyxena and Rebecca*, M. R. James (ed.), Apocrypha Anecdota 2 (Cambridge, 1893), 59-85 [text]. — A. Menzies: Ante-Nicene Fathers 9 (New York, 1896), 205-217 [English trans.]. — *narr.*, PG 79:583-694. — F. Conca (Leipzig, 1983) [text]. — *Pers.*, A. Vassiliev, Anecdota Graeco-Byzantina 1 (Moscow, 1893), 73-125 [text]. — A. Wirth, Aus orientalischen Chroniken (Frankfurt a.M., 1894), 143-210 [text]. — T. E. Bratke, Das sog. Religionsgespräch am Hof der Sasaniden (Leipzig, 1899) [text/comm.]. — *Apoll.*, F. P. Waiblinger (Munich, 1978) [text/German trans.]. — D. Tsitsikli (Königstein, 1981) [text]. — G. A. A. Kortekaas (Groningen, 1984) [text]. — G. Schmeling (Leipzig, 1988) [text].

L: K. Berger, Hellenistische Gattungen im NT: ANRW II 25/2 (1984) 1031-1432, 1831-1885. — F. Bovon (ed.), Les actes apocryphes des apôtres (Geneva, 1981). — C. Burchard, Untersuchungen zu Joseph u. Aseneth (Tübingen, 1965). — J. H. Charlesworth, The Pseudepigrapha and modern research (Chico, 1981). — L. Delehaye, Les passions des martyrs et les genres littéraires (Brussels, [2]1966). — D. R. Edwards, The New Testament and the ancient romance: The Petronian Society Newsletter 17 (1987) 9-14. — T. Holtz, Chr. Interpolationen in "Joseph und Aseneth": NTS 14 (1967-1968) 482-497. — N. Holzberg, Historie als Fiktion — Fiktion als Historie: FS H. H. Schmitt (Stuttgart, 1995), 93-101. — R. Kany, Der Lukanische Bericht von Tod u. Auferstehung Jesu aus der Sicht eines hellenistischen Romanlesers: NT 28 (1986) 75-90. — H. Köster, Einführung in das NT (Berlin, 1980). — E(dgar) Mayer, Die Reiseerzählung des Lukas (Frankfurt a.M., 1996). — J. Perkins, The apocryphal Acts of Peter: Arethusa 25 (1992) 445-457. — R. E. Pervo, Profit with Delight: The Literary Genre of the Acts of the Apostles (Philadelphia, 1987). — idem, Early Christian Fiction, Greek Fiction, ed. J. R. Morgan, R. Stoneman (London, 1994), 239-254. — idem, The Ancient Novel Becomes Christian: The Novel in the Ancient World, ed. G. Schmeling (Leiden, 1996), 685-711. — T. Pickford, Apollonius of Tyre as Greek Myth and Christian Mystery: NP 59 (1975) 599-609. — E. Plümacher, Apokryphe Apostelakten: PRE. S 15:11-70. — P. Pokorný, Die Romfahrt des Paulus u. der antike R.: ZNTW 64 (1973) 233-244. — S. M. Praeder, Luke-Acts and the Ancient Novel: SBL. SPS 20 (1981) 269-292. — B. Rehm, Clemens Romanus II: RAC 3:197-206. — M. Reiser, Der Alexanderroman u. das Mk: Markus-Philologie, ed. H. Cancik (Tübingen, 1984), 131-163. — S. P. Schierling, M. J. Schierling, The Influence of the Ancient Romances on Acts of the Apostles: ClB 54 (1978) 81-88. — G. Schmeling, Historia Apollonii: The Novel in the Ancient World, ed. idem (Leiden, 1996), 517-551. — R. Söder, Die apokryphen Apostelgeschichten u. die romanhafte Literatur der Antike (Darmstadt, 1969 = 1932). — S. West, Joseph and Asenath: CQ NS 24 (=68) (1974) 70-81.

S. Döpp

O

(ed.), HOK (Düsseldorf, ²1989), 73f., 89f. — R. F. Taft, N. P. Ševcenko, O.: ODB 1520.

F. R. GAHBAUER, OSB

Octateuch of Clement

The *Octateuch of Clement* (*OctClem.*), which is probably the latest pseudoapostolic collection (divided into canons) of → Church Orders, originated at the end of the 5th c.; probably composed originally in Greek, it survives in a Syr. and Arab. version in eight books (perhaps as a substitute for the → *Apostolic Constitutions*). The compilation includes: → the *Testament of Our Lord Jesus Christ*, → the *Apostolic Church Order*, → the *Apostolic Canons*, and texts based on the → *Traditio apostolica*. In the titles and subscriptions of the individual books, *OctClem.* claims as its compiler/author the apostolic authority of → Clement of Rome (as the *Apostolic Constitutions* had already done).

W: P. A. de Lagarde, Reliquiae (Leipzig, 1856) [Syriac text/Greek trans.]. — F. Nau, La version syriaque de l'octateuque de Clément, new ed. P. Ciprotti (Milan, 1967) [Syriac text/French trans.].
L: B. Steimer, Vertex traditionis (Berlin, 1992), esp. 141-148 (literature).

B. STEIMER

Octoechos

The *O.* (*Oktoēchos*), the book of the eight tones, is a liturg. book of the Byz. rite that contains the Propers of the liturgy of the hours and the Eucharist, except for the texts of Lent and the Easter season, which have their own books: the *Triodion* and the *Pentekostarion*. Apart from Lent and the Easter season the church year is divided into eight-week cycles, each having its own tone for recitation. The period covered by the *Octoechos* begins with All Saints' day (= Sunday after Pentecost) and ends with the beginning of the *Triodion* in the time preceding Lent. The *Octoechos* is also known as the *Parakletike*. → John Damascene contributed a great deal to the emergence of the *Octoechos* but was not its author.

W: Dimanche, office selon les huit tons, O. (Chevetogne, 1968). — S. Heitz, Das Gebet der Orthodoxen Kirche (Düsseldorf, 1981) [German trans.]. — K. Kirchhoff, J. Madey, Es preise die Schöpfung den Herrn (Münster, 1979) [German trans.]. — A. v. Maltzew, O. o. Parakletike, 2 vols. (Berlin, 1903f.).
L: A. Cody, The Early History of the O.: Syria and Armenia, ed. N. G. Garsoian et al. (Washington, 1982), 89-113. — S. Hausammann, S. Heitz, Mysterium der Anbetung (Cologne, 1986), 781. — W. Nyssen, H. J. Schulz, P. Wiertz

Oecumenius

O. composed the earliest surviving Gr. commentary on the Apocalypse of Jn (*apoc.*), but he is not the same as the like-named 10th c. bishop of Trikka in Thessaly. There have been objections to his identification as a secular dignitary, rhetor, and, under the title of *comes Oecumenius*, correspondent of Monophysite Patriarch Severus of Antioch in the first half of the 6th c.; there are good arguments for dating the commentary to the last years of the 6th c. Information on the person of the author can be derived only from interpretation of his work. The commentary, in twelve books, shows an effort to prove both apostolic authority and logical coherence for the Apocalypse. The visions are interpreted, for the most part, allegorically as referring to the past, present, and future of the history of salvation.

Various commentaries on parts of the NT that were handed down under O.'s name (PG 118) prove to be an anonymous catena that contains only isolated citations from scholia of O. on the homilies of → John Chrys. on Paul.

W: *apoc.*, M. de Groote (Leuven/Louvain, 1999) [text]. — H. C. Hoskier (Ann Arbor, Mich., 1928) [text]. — PG 119. — *Rom. Heb.*, K. Staab (Münster, 1933), 423-469 [text].
L: R. Devreesse, Chaînes exégétiques grecques: DBS 1 (1928) 1211-1214, 1228-1231. — F. Diekamp, Neuaufgefundener Kommentar des Oe. zur Apokalypse: SPAW. PH 43 (1901) 1054-1056. — A. Monaci Castagno, Datazione dei Commenti all' Apocalisse di Ecumenio e di Andrea di Cesarea: AAST. M 114 (1980) 223-246. — eadem, I commenti di Ecumenio e di Andrea di Cesarea: MAST. M 5/5 (1981) 303-426. — J. Schmid, Die griech. Apokalypsekommentare: BZ 19 (1931) 228-256. — idem, Oe. der Apokalypsen-Ausleger u. Oe. der Bischof v. Trikka: BNGJ 14 (1937/38) 322-330. — idem, Der Apokalypse-Text des Oe.: Bib. 40 (1959) 935-942. — A. Spitaler, J. Schmid, Zur Klärung des Oe.-problems: OrChr 31 (1934) 208-218.

M. BIERMANN

Olympiadorus

O. was a deacon in Alexandria (he is not to be confused with the Neoplatonic philosopher O. who was living in Alexandria at the same period). He was probably ordained under Patriarch John III Niciotas (505-516/517) and composed numerous moralizing commentaries on the sapiential and prophetic books. Fragments on Job, Qoh, Jer, Lam, and Bar have sur-

441

vived in catenas. Ps.- → Anastasius the Sinaite, who esteemed O., has preserved a fragment of the latter's work *Contra Severum Antiochenum* (*c. Sev.*). A fragment on Lk 6:23 and another on Prov (PG 93:469-78, 780) have been wrongly attributed to O.

W: PG 31:13-780. — *c. Sev.*, PG 89:1189.
L: H. G. Beck, Kirche u. theol. Lit. (Munich, 1959), 416. — M. Faulhaber, Hld-, Spr- u. Koh-Katenen (Vienna, 1902). — idem, Die Prophetenkatenen (Freiburg i.Br., 1899).

G. Röwekamp

Onomasticon

The genre onomastican is concerned with the correct names for things. The genre derives its own name from *onomastikē technē* (Plato, *Crat.* 423d, 425a). Efforts along this line are found in the Sophists and the Stoics, but onomasticon as title of a type of work is first attested in Democritus. There were onomastica for various subject areas; a pure form of the genre is seldom found. Among Chr. authors of antiquity Isidore in particular has lists that are dependent on ancient onomastica (*orig.* 11-20). Explanations of words and names often appear in the form of glosses. Even the Chr. *Onomastica sacra* are a special form of glosses, with their explanations of the names of bibl. persons and places. The earliest example of a Chr. onomasticon is the work translated by Jerome, *Liber interpretationis hebraicorum nominum*, which goes back to works of Philo on the proper names of the OT and of Origen on those of the NT. In the translation the key words are ordered according to bibl. books. The most important work is the onomasticon of bibl. names by → Eusebius, which was translated and expanded by Jerome. One source among others was an onomasticon titled *hoi topoi* (*Onomast.* 48.11).

L: A. Baumstark, Geschichte der syr. Lit. (Bonn, 1922), 260. — C. Wendel, O.: PRE 35:507-516. — J. Wilkinson, L'apport de Saint Jérome à la topographie: RB 81 (1974) 245-257. — F. Wutz, Onomastica sacra, TU 3/11 (Leipzig, 1914f.).

G. Röwekamp

Optatus of Milevis

The person of O. is hidden behind his work. An African by birth (Jerome, *vir. ill.* 110), he probably became a Christian only as an adult (Aug., *doctr. christ.* 2.41.61, suggests this). Between 364 and 367 (acc. to Jerome), when bishop of Milevis, O. wrote a work in six books against Parmenian, the Donatist bishop of Carthage (*c. Parmen.*). Accordingly, its present form in seven books, which with but a single exception is attested by the ms. tradition, represents a second edition. Generally speaking, the authenticity of the final book is not disputed today; on the other hand, the authenticity of some passages, found only in a single, now lost ms., is doubtful.

The work, which has come down without a title, was an answer to a lost work of Parmenian in which the latter attacked the Cath. Church on both hist. and theol. grounds. After the Donatist schism had torn apart the African church over a half century before and a merely superficial forced union had been established in 347, the division had again broken out beginning in 361. The pressure of these circumstances explains why for the first time a Cath. writer should justify the church's theol. position.

After a preview of his work, O. refutes the Donatist objection that the schism had been caused by the Cath. surrender of the scriptures during the Diocletian persecution; that guilt lay rather on the first Donatists (book 1). The *Catholica* is shown to be the one true church of Christ by its exclusive possession of its bridal dowry, espec. the *cathedra Petri*, with which only the Catholics of Africa are united; contrary claims of the schismatics are refuted precisely by their most recent acts of terrorism (2). It was Donatist violence, and not the Catholics, that led the state in 347 to use military force (3). Book 4 is devoted to correcting Parmenian's exegesis of some OT passages. The theology of baptism is the focus of book 5: the efficacy of baptism comes first of all from the action of God, but the faith of the baptizand is also decisive; the condition of the minister of baptism is quite secondary, contrary to the church-centered baptismal theology of Donatism, which was a heritage from Cyprian. For this reason, provided the Trinity has been invoked in the act, any rebaptism on passing from one church to the other is not allowed. O. then describes the atrocities connected with the return of once exiled Donatist bishops and the reestablishment of their ecclesial community under Julian the Apostate (6). The final book represents an obviously later appendix, which perhaps was intended simply as a collection of material for later inclusion in the text of the first six books; a large part of the book is given over to a renewed call for the Donatists to return to unity with the *Catholica*.

In his hist. argument for the beginning of the schism, O. relies, often rather unsuccessfully, on the collection of documents available to him; for the later period he relies on what has come to his attention (mostly from Numidia). His theol. merit is

442

owing to his eccles. distinction between heresy and schism and in his paving the way for the concept of *ex opere operato* in sacramental theology. In both respects he became Augustine's precursor in anti Donatist polemics.

The ascription of five *sermones* to O. is disputed.

W: C. Ziwsa, CSEL 26. — M. Labrousse, SC 412f. — O. R. Vassall-Phillips (London, 1917) [English trans.]. — L. Dattrino (Rome, 1988) [Italian trans.]. — M. Labrousse (Paris, 1995f.) [French trans.].
L: S. Blomgren, Eine Echtheitsfrage bei O. (Stockholm, 1959). — G. A. Cecconi, Elemosina e propaganda. Un'analisi della "Macariana persecutio" nel III libro di O.: REAug 36 (1990) 42-66. — A. C. De Veer, A propos de l'authenticité du livre VII d'O.: REAug 7 (1961) 389-391. — A. Di Berardino (ed.), Patrologia 3 (Casale, 1978), 116. — B. Kriegbaum, Zwischen den Synoden von Rom u. Arles. Die donatistische Supplik bei O.: AHP 28 (1990) 23-61. — C. Mazzucco, O. in un secolo di studi (Bologna, 1993) (literature). — J. A. Merdinger, Rome and the African Church in the Time of Augustine (New Haven, 1997), 50-60. — P. M. Mihalic, Constructive Confrontation. The Approach of O. the African Towards the Donatists, Diss. (Rome, 1982). — P. Monceaux, Histoire littéraire de l'Afrique chrétienne 5 (Paris, 1920). — C. Moreschini, E. Norelli, Storia della letteratura cristiana antica greca e latina 2/1 (Brescia, 1996), 347f. — PAC 795-797. — J. Ratzinger, Volk u. Haus Gottes in Augustins Lehre von der Kirche (Munich, 1954), 102-123. — W. Simonis, Ecclesia visibilis et invisibilis (Frankfurt a.M., 1970), 43-49. — L. Vischer, Basilius der Große, Diss. (Basel, 1953), 72-85.

B. KRIEGBAUM, SJ

Opus imperfectum in Matthaeum

The *Opus imperfectum in Matthaeum* is a fragmentary, anonymous commentary in homily form on Mt 1-8, 10-13, and 19-25; it was earlier attributed to John Chrys. In the 16th c. Erasmus refuted the thesis of Chrys.'s authorship and identified the author as a moderate Arian, a member of a small Arian community, whose persecution by Catholics he denounces. The allegorical exegesis, based on a pre-Jerome translation, shows a profound knowledge of the scriptures, original reflections, and a pessimistic, rigorist view of life. The author of the *Opus imperfectum in Mattahaum*, which was written in the 5th c., was probably a Lat.-speaking (but familiar with Greek) Arian presbyter or bishop in the vicinity of Constantinople, and not Maximinus, the disciple of Ulfila and a Gothic bishop in the Danube province. There is no evidence for the suggestion that *Opus imperfectum in Matthaeum* is a translation by → Martin of Braga (d. 580) of a text of Arian presbyter Timothy of Constantinople.

W: PG 56:611-946. — J. van Banning, CCL 87 B.

L: R. Etaix, Fragments inédits de l'O.: RBen 84 (1974) 271-300. — F. Mali, Das O. und sein Verhältnis zu Mt-Kommentaren von Origenes u. Hieronymus (Innsbruck, 1991). — F. Paas, Das O. (Tübingen, 1907). — J. Stiglmayr, Das O.: ZKTh 34 (1910) 1-38, 473-499. — F. Wotke, O.: PRE 18/1:824-826.

C. SCHMIDT

Orientius

O. is the name given himself by the author, in the next to last verse, of a moral sermon in elegiac distichs and titled *Commonitorium* (*comm.*) (like the prose work of → Vincent of Lérins). The *terminus post quem*, 406/407, which emerges from an allusion to the invasion of Gaul by the Germanic tribes (*comm.* 2.165-84), as well as biog. hints in three passages of the *comm.* (1.8, 611f.; 2.417), point to the author as being Orientius, bishop of Auch (Gascony), who supposedly conducted the negotiations of Visigothic King Theodoric I with the Romans in order to avert the threatened siege of Toulouse.

The *comm.* contains two books of 618 and 418 verses respectively. At the outset O. reminds his reader that the only purpose of earthly life is the attainment of everlasting life. From this he infers the necessity of keeping the commandments of love of God and neighbor and avoiding the capital sins, the description of which forms the centerpiece of the poem. The first book takes up sexual sins, envy, and avarice, the second, vanity, lying, and gluttony (1.321-592; 2.13-84). Graphic descriptions of the pain of hell and of the last judgment lend emphasis to the warnings (1.257-314; 2.263-392).

Despite its rhetorical cast (conditioned by the genre), O.'s style has a simplicity which, along with a somewhat satirical realism, makes it espec. vivid. Without indulging in extensive theol. considerations, O. does clearly distinguish himself from Pelagians and Arians by his clear acceptance of the church's teaching on grace and the Trinity (1.25; 1.39ff.; 2.403ff.).

The title *comm.*, which is missing in the mss., is attested by the medieval historian Sigbert of Gembloux. The authenticity of the shorter poems (*carm. app.*) attached to the *comm.* in one ms. is disputed. Only the last two prayers in iambic trimeters are explicitly assigned to O. (*comm. app.* 4). Of the others, the first is a short poem on the birth of Christ, the second is a list of fifty-three symbolic names of Christ; the third has three parts, each with its own title: *De trinitate, Explanatio nominum domini* (explanation of the names in *carm. app.* 2), and *Laudatio* (*Christi.*).

W: *comm., carm. app.*, R. Ellis, CSEL 16:191-261. — C. A. Rapisarda (Catania, 1958) [text]. — *comm.*, idem, ibid. ([1]1960, [2]1970) [text/Italian trans.]. — M. D. Tobin (Washington, 1945) [text/English trans./comm.]. — *comm., carm. app.* 4, L. Bellanger, Le poème d'O. (Paris, 1903), XIIIff., 293ff. [text/French trans.].

L: L. Bellanger, op. cit. — M. G. Bianco, Il comm. di O.: AFLF(M) 20 (1987) 33-86. — G. Brugnoli, L'oltretomba di O.: Orph. 4 (1957) 131-137. — R. Ellis, The comm. of O. (Oxford, 1903). — A. Hudson-Williams, O. and Lactantius: VigChr 3 (1949) 237-243. — M. G. Lagarrigue, O. et les poètes aquitains de son temps (Compte rendu de la séance du groupe Strasbourgeois du 29. 3. 1980): REL 58 (1980) 19-22. — C. A. Rapisarda, Linguaggio biblico e motivi elegiaci nel Commonitorium di O.: La poesia cristiana latina in distici elegiaci, ed. G. Catanzaro, F. Santucci (Assisi, 1993), 167-190. — F. Sciuto, Tertulliano in O.: Convivium Dominicum. Studi sull'Eucarestia nei Padri della Chiesa, ed. Centro di Studi sull'Antico Cristianesimo (Catania, 1959), 415-422. — idem, Ancora su Tertulliano e O.: MSLCA 9 (1959) 25-32. — F. Sgarlata, Nota orienziana: Helikon 9/10 (1969/70) 695-697. — D. R. Shackleton Bailey, Emendations of the comm.: CP 72 (1977) 130-133. — K. Smolak, Poetische Ausdrücke im sog. ersten Gebet des O.: WSt 87 (1974) 188-200. — V. Tandoi, Noterelle orienziane: Vichiana 13 (1984) 199-210. — C. Weyman, Zu O.: Beiträge zur Geschichte der chr.-lat. Poesie (Munich, 1926), 137-140.

N. Delhey

Origen

I. Life: O., of whom Eusebius speaks extensively in *h.e.* 6, was born in Alexandria ca. 185. His father, Leonidas, who died a martyr, made him familiar with the scriptures at an early age; later on, he probably often cited the scriptures from memory, as little alterations suggest. He gave up his profession as a teacher of grammar (literature) in order to instruct pagans desirous of converting. In order to be able to answer their philosophical questions, he studied philosophy with Platonist Ammonius Saccas. Despite the distance he kept from philosophy, he found in Platonism many ideas that seemed to be in agreement with the sacred scriptures. His reputation as a teacher of Christianity grew to such an extent that he had to divide his hearers into groups and entrust the introductory phase to Heraclas. It was probably out of his work as teacher and by putting together, one after the other, two different presentations of the entire teaching of the faith that his work *Peri archōn* (*De principiis*) arose. The presentation with its claim to sure knowledge and the attempt to answer hitherto open questions may have aroused the mistrust of Bishop Demetrius, who had entrusted him with the instruction of catechumens. When the bishop of Caesarea invited O. to preach and even ordained him a presbyter, Demetrius held two synods in opposi-

tion to O. ca. 230 and excluded him from his community. The bishop of Caesarea, however, appointed O. to preach regularly on all the books of scripture, but O. does not seem to have carried out this commission to the end; at least, in Eusebius's time, there were no sermons of O. on all the books of the Bible. In Caesarea a school of disciples developed around O., which → Gregory the Wonderworker describes in his panegyric (*pan. Or.*); but O. also traveled to, among other places, Rome, where he heard Hippolytus, and to Athens, where he acquired a Gr. translation of the OT. During the persecution of Decius he was so severely tortured that he died as a result, probably in 253.

L: Bibliographies: BiPa III O. (Paris, 1980). — U. Berner, O. (Darmstadt, 1981). — H. Crouzel, Bibliographie critique d'O. (Steenbrugge, 1971; Suppl. 1, 1982; Suppl. 2, 1996). — idem, Chronique origénienne: BLE (regularly). — idem, Current Theology. The Literature on O. 1970-1988: TS 49 (1988) 499-516.

H. Crouzel, O. (Paris, 1985). — J. Daniélou, J. O. (Paris, 1948). — J. A. Fischer, Die alexandrinischen Synoden gegen O.: OS 28 (1979) 3-16. — W. Geerlings, H. König (ed.), O. Vir ecclesiasticus (Bonn, 1995). — C. Kannengießer, W. L. Petersen (ed.), O. His World and His Legacy (Notre Dame, Ind., 1986). — S. Leanza, O.: La Bibbia nell'Antichità . . . Cristiana 1, ed. E. Norelli (Bologna, 1993), 377-407. — L. Lies, Zum derzeitigen Stand der O.-forschung (part 1): ZKTh 115 (1993) 37-62. — P. Nautin, O. Vie et œuvre (Paris, 1977). — B. Neuschäfer, O. als Philologe (Basel, 1987). — Origeniana (Colloquium Montserat 1973) (Bari, 1975). — Origeniana 2 (Coll. Bari 1977) (Rome, 1980). — Origeniana 3 (Coll. Manchester 1981) (Rome, 1985). — Origeniana 4 (Coll. Innsbruck 1985) (Innsbruck, 1987). — Origeniana 5 (Coll. Boston 1989) (Leuven/Louvain, 1992). — Origeniana 6. O. et la Bible (Coll. Chantilly 1993) (Leuven/Louvain, 1995). — Origeniana 7 (Coll. Marburg) (Leuven/Louvain, 1999). — F. Ledegang, O. Een experimenteel theoloog uit de derde eeuw (Kampen, 1995). — P. Ossandón, P. Rodríguez, El método de O.: TyV 33 (1992) 185-191. — L. Perrone, "Quaestiones et responsiones" in O.: CrSt 15 (1994) 1-50. — C. Scholten, Die alexandrinische Katechetenschule: JAC 38 (1995) 16-37. — J. C. Smith, The Ancient Wisdom of O. (Lewisburg, 1992). — J. W. Trigg, O., the Bible and Philosophy (London, 1985). — H. J. Vogt, O.: Handbook of Patristic Exegesis, ed. C. and P. Kannengiesser (Leiden, in press).

II. Works: Eusebius gives a list of O.'s works in *h.e.* 6.24; 6.32; 6.36; from the list given by Jerome in his *ep.* 33 to Paula, we can judge how many of the great commentaries (*tomoi*), homilies, and so-called scholia or excerpts (short notices) have since been lost. Because a great deal was later on deliberately destroyed, the transmission of some works is very impoverished.

Excerpts from various writings are preserved in the *Philocalia* (*philoc.*), an anthology from O.'s works, which → Basil and → Gregory Naz. put together, supposedly in 358/359.

W: Complete works, C. de la Rue, 4 vols. (Paris, 1733-1759 = PG 11-17). — C. H. E. Lommatzsch, 25 vols. (Berlin, 1831-1848). — GCS 12 vols. — H. U. v. Balthasar, O., Geist u. Feuer (Salzburg, ³1991) [selected German trans.]. — *philoc.* 1-20 (inspiration of scripture), M. Harl, SC 302. — *philoc.* 21-27 (free will), É. Junod, SC 226.
L: E. Junod, Basile de Césarée et Grégoire de Nazianze sont ils les compilateurs de la Philocalie d'O. ?: FS J. Gribomont = SEAug 27 (1988) 349-360.

1. *Hexapla*: The *Hexapla*, i.e., the "sixfold (form of the OT text)", which O. had ordered prepared as a working tool, contained the text of the LXX, which was used in the church's liturgy, the more recent translations of Aquila, Symmachus, and Theodotion, and a fifth and a sixth translation discovered by O. himself. O. wanted by this means to help those knowing no Hebrew to grasp the differences between the LXX and the Heb. text. In the complete four-volume Bible which he himself edited, he inserted the sections not found in the LXX (marking them with an asterisk), while also marking with an obelisk the sections found only in the LXX. In this way Chr. theologians could see which texts they could appeal to in discussion with the Jews.

W: Hexaplorum quae supersunt I-II, ed. F. Field (Oxford, 1875 = Hildesheim, ²1964).
L: C. P. Bammel, Die Hexapla des O.: Aug. 28 (1988) 125-149. — D. Barthélemy, O. et le texte de l'Ancien Testament: FS J. Daniélou (Paris, 1972), 247-261. — G. Dorival, L'apport des chaines exégétiques grecques à une réédition des Hexaples d'O.: RHT 4 (1974) 45-74.

2. *Exegetical works*: The earliest preserved exegetical work of O. is probably a commentary on a series of Psalms, which he approached only with great hesitation (PG 12:1076C); he later exegeted the entire Psalter.

He was urged to comment on Jn (*Jo.*) by his friend Ambrose, whom he had converted from gnosticism to Catholicism, the purpose being to refute the explanation of Heracleon, a gnostic. But this commentary seems to have reached only to Jn 8:50; in any case, O. does not cite the commentary beyond book 20.38.358. He himself seems not to have gotten beyond Jn 13:13; this is the last verse he explains in book 32 (there were no further books). Even among the 141 fragments on John only two deal with a text later than Jn 13:13, namely Jn 17:20 and 20:24. The nine books on *Jo.* that have survived are found in only two mss.; as a result the damaged sections have to be filled in by conjecture. In 1904 E. Klostermann

suggested numerous improvements to the still normative critical edition of *Jo.* by E. Preuschen (1903). In the Festschrift for A. Pincherle (1967) E. Corsini justified the decisions made in his Ital. translation (1968). The text and translation which C. Blanc presented in SC (largely in agreement with Preuschen's text) were criticized by P. Nautin. E. Corsini (1995) had reservations about Nautin's suggestions.

E. Klostermann corrected about six hundred places in the text of his edition (GCS) of the Gr. books 10-17 (preserved in only two or three mss.) of O.'s commentary on Matthew (*comm. in Mt.*); he did so with the help of the old Lat. translation, which is preserved from book 11.9 on, i.e., from Mt 16:13 to 27:66; in 1955 E. Früchtel rejected almost all these corrections. Klostermann defended them once again in 1964. The first German translation of the Matthew commentary likewise did without most of these corrections, on the grounds that the old Lat. text had not simply been translated in a mechanical fashion, as Klostermann thought, thus making a backtranslation possible, but in fact served its own monastic and spiritual interests.

A commentary on Lk is also attributed to O. but has not survived; it may be the source of the fragments from the catenas that are published as an appendix to the homilies on Luke. On the other hand, O. did not exegete Mt as such. Fairly lengthy fragments of commentaries on Pss, Rom, 1 Cor, and Eph (*comm. in Rom.*, *1 Cor.*, *Eph.*) have survived in catenas, but only scant remnants have been preserved of the great commentary on Gen (*comm. in Gen.*). The authenticity of the notes on the Apocalypse (*Apoc.*) is disputed.

The original fifteen books of the *comm. in Rom.* were abridged to ten books in Latin by Rufinus. The latter also translated the explanation of Pss 36–38 in the form of nine homilies because it "deals in an entirely moral way . . . with the improvement of life" (*Orig. in psalm.*). Perhaps the sermons of Jerome on the Pss are not only inspired by O., but are hardly revised translations of his homilies.

On the homilies delivered at Caesarea only those on Jer survive in Greek, those on the Pentateuch, Jos, and Judg, Song, Pss, and Lk (*hom. in Gen.*, *Lev.*, *Jos.*, *Jud.*, *1 Sam.*, *Cant.*, *Lc.*) in a Lat. translation. Otherwise only fragments have come down.

W: *Jo.*, E. Preuschen, GCS 10. — E. Corsini (Turin, 1968) [Italian trans.]. — C. Blanc, SC 120, 157, 222, 290, 385. — R. Gögler (Einsiedeln, 1959) [selected German trans./comm.]. — *comm. in Mt.*, E. Klostermann, GCS 40. — R. Girod (Paris, 1970) (books 10-11) [text/French trans./comm.]. — H. J. Vogt (Stuttgart, 1983, 1990, 1993)

[German trans./comm.]. — *comm. in Rom.*, A. Ramsbotham: JThS 13 (1912) 209-224, 357-368; 14 (1913) 10-22 [text]. — C. P. Hammond Bammel (Freiburg i.Br., 1990) [text]. — T. Heither, FC 2/1-5. — *comm. in 1 Cor.*, C. Jenkins: JThS 9 (1908) 231-247, 353-372, 500-514; 10 (1911) 29-51 [text]; additionally, C. H. Turner: JTS 10 (1911) 270-276. — *comm. in Eph.*, J. A. F. Gregg: JTS 3 (1902) 233-244, 398-420, 554-576 [text]. — *comm. in Gen.*, P. Sanz, Bruchstücke: MPSW 4 (1946) 87-104 [text/comm.]. — P. Glaue, Bruchstück: MPSG 2 (1928) 435 [text/German trans./comm.]. — *Apoc.* 1-27, C. J. Diobouniotis, A. v. Harnack, TU 38 (Berlin, 1911), 21-44 [text]; additionally, C. H. Turner: JThS 13 (1912) 386-397 [text]. — *Apoc.* 28-38, C. H. Turner: JThS 25 (1923) 125 [text]. — *hom. in Ps.* 36-38, E. Prinzivalli et al., SC 411. — G. Coppa, 74 omelie sul libro dei salmi. O., Gerolamo (Milan, 1993) [Italian trans./comm.]. — *hom. in Jer.*, P. Husson, P. Nautin, SC 232, 238. — E. Schadel (Stuttgart, 1980) [German trans./comm.]. — *hom. in Gen.*, H. de Lubac, L. Doutreleau, SC 7. — *hom. in Lev.*, M. Bonet, SC 286f. — *hom. in Num.*, L. Doutreleau, SC 415. — *hom. in Jos.*, A. Jaubert, SC 71. — *hom. in Jud.*, P. Messié, SC 389. — *hom. in 1 Sam.*, P. Nautin, SC 328. — *hom. in Lc.*, H. J. Sieben, FC 4/1-2. — *fr. hom.*, P. Sanz, Bruchstücke: MPSW 4 (1946), 104-110 [text/comm.].

L: C. P. Bammel, Der Römerbrieftext des Rufin u. seine O.-Übersetzung (Freiburg i.Br., 1985). — G. Bendinelli, Un confronto. I commentari a Matteo di O. e Ilario di Poitiers: DT 96 (1993, 3) 214-237. — E. Corsini, In margine a una traduzione dell'in Ioannem di O.: FS A. Pincherle, SMSR 38 (Rome, 1967), 146-169. — idem, O. Commento al Vangelo di Giovanni: Aug. 35 (1995) 183-195. — H. Crouzel, Un fragment du Commentaire sur la Genèse d'O. et la création de la matière à partir du néant: FS U. Bianchi (Rome, 1994), 417-425. — B. D. Ehrmann, G. D. Fee, M. W. Holmes, The Text of the Fourth Gospel in the Writings of O. (Atlanta, 1992). — E. Früchtel, Nachträge zu Bd. 10, 11, 12/1, GCS 12/2 (Berlin, 1955), 53-79. — E. Klostermann, O.' Joh-Kommentar: GGA 166 (1904) 265-282. — idem, Epilog zu O.-Kommentar zum Mt: SDAW. S (1964), Nr. 4. — P. Koetschau, Textkritik des Joh-Kommentars, TU 12/2 (Berlin, 1905), 76ff. — F. Mali, Das "Opus imperfectum in Matthaeum" u. sein Verhältnis zu den Mt-Kommentaren von O. u. Hieronymus (Innsbruck, 1991). — K. McNamee, O. in the Papyri: ClF 27 (1973) 28-53. — P. Nautin, Notes critiques sur l'In Iohannem d'O.: REG 85 (1972) 155-177; RPh 49 (1975) 202-216; 55 (1981) 273-284; 59 (1985) 63-75. — V. Peri, Omelie origeniane sui salmi. Identificazione del testo latino (Rome, 1980).

The papyri found at Tura in Egypt in 1941 yielded a large section of the *comm. in Rom.* that had hitherto been known only in the abridged translation by Rufinus; it also yielded two other works: the record of a discussion between O. and Bishop Heraclides on the Father and the Son and the soul (*dial.*) and a partially mutilated treatise on the feast of Easter (*pascha*).

W: *comm. in Rom.* 3.5-5.7, J. Scherer (Cairo, 1957) [text/French trans./comm.]. — *dial.*, J. Scherer (Cairo, 1949) [text]. — J. Scherer, SC 67. — E. Früchtel, BGrL 5 (Stuttgart, 1974) [German trans./comm.]. — *pascha*, O.

Guéraud, P. Nautin (Paris, 1979) [text/French trans./comm.]. — B. Witte (Altenberge, 1993) [text/German trans./comm.].

3. *De principiis*: The *De principiis* (*princ.*) deals with the fundamental realities of the faith, therefore mainly with the three divine persons. *Princ.* 4.13 is a discourse on the scriptures, their inspiration and exegesis, that is contained in Greek in the *Philocalia*. The text in its entirety exists only in the Lat. translation of Rufinus, who emended offensive passages, which he regarded as forgeries. In his critical edition P. Koetschau (1913) inserted into the Lat. text fragments in Greek which are found in, e.g., Gregory Nyss. and the anti-Origenist anathemas of the synod of 553. Such passages may, however, have been shortened or falsified, and in any case are out of place in Rufinus's text. In the introduction to his own translation M. Simonetti (1968) suggested a convincing division of the text and gave the fragments, but only in the footnotes. In SC the double tradition, that is, Gr. and Lat. espec. in book 4, are printed in parallel with the translation. The traditional division of the text is maintained, but the translation is structured in two cycles with three and nine treatises respectively, and a summary.

W: *princ.*, P. Koetschau, GCS 22 [text]. — H. Crouzel, SC 252, 253, 268, 269, 312. — H. Karpp, H. Görgemanns (Darmstadt, 1976) [text/German trans./comm.]. — G. W. Butterworth (London, 1936) [English trans./comm.]. — M. Simonetti (Turin, 1968) [Italian trans.]; in addition: H. J. Vogt: ThRv 66 (1970) 294-296.

L: R. M. Berchmann, The peri archon. O.'s apodeixis euaggelike (Providence, R.I., 1984). — R. Calonne, Le libre arbitre selon le Traité des Principes d'O.: BLE 89 (1988) 243-262. — H. Crouzel, Qu'a voulu faire O. en composant le Traité des Principes?: BLE 76 (1975) 161-186, 241-260. — J. Dillon, Imagery of Light in the First Chapter of O.'s Peri Archon (1988): idem, The Golden Chain, CStS 333 (London, 1990), Nr. 22. — L. Lies, O.' "Peri archon" (Darmstadt, 1992). — B. Studer, Die Bedeutung der Auferstehung Jesu in PA des O.: Dominus Salvator, ed. idem (Rome, 1992), 213-250. — idem, Zur Frage der dogmatischen Terminologie in der Latin trans. von O.' princ.: FS J. Daniélou (1972), 403-414. — A. Meis Wörmer, El problema del mal en O. Significado teologico del tiempo (princ. 31, 124) (Santiago, 1988). — A. Meredith, O. 's princ. and Gregory of Nyssa's "Oratio Catechetica": HeyJ 36 (1995) 1-14.

4. *Contra Celsum*: As in the case of *princ.*, a special place belongs to the eight books answering the pagan philosopher Celsus (*Cels.*), who attacked Christianity in the 2nd c. It was Ambrose again who urged O. to this refutation (*praef.* 1). O. is afraid that by such a "defense" he may weaken the persuasiveness of the words and deeds of Jesus (3), but he undertakes the work for the sake of those whose faith is wavering

(4). He cites Celsus verbatim, from the objection that Christians are forming illegal assemblies (1.1) to his exhortation to them that they take a full part in military service and politics (8.73-75); as a result it is possible partially to reconstruct Celsus's work. Since Celsus also attacked the Jews, while on the other hand making broad use of Jewish attacks on Christianity, O. first defends Judaism and then refutes its attacks (e.g., 1.26ff.), stressing the point that the OT already bears witness to Christ; on the other hand, one finds a witness to the OT only when one believes in Christ. Because Celsus had denied that the Bible could be allegorized (something he regarded as a characteristic of literature generally), O. had to show that "as a true writer" Moses "everywhere cultivated the double meaning of expressions" (1.18). Despite this, the entire Bible also has in mind "the throng of simple folk" with whom "the Greek poets did not bother" (4.50). But when one interprets the Bible allegorically, that is, discovers in it "hints of philosophy" (5.58), one generalizes the content of concrete stories; just as when Jesus stoops to an individual sick person, he shows that he intends to heal all.

W: *Cels.*, M. Borret, SC 132, 136, 147, 150, 227. — P. Koetschau, BKV² 52f. [German trans.]. — H. Chadwick (Cambridge, 1965) [English trans./comm.].
L: D. Caliandro, Il Logos e l'uomo nella visione cosmica di O. nel Contra Celso (Rome, 1987). — M. Fédou, Christianisme et religions paiennes dans le Contre Celse d'O. (Paris, 1988). — R. J. Hauck, The More Divine Proof (Atlanta, 1989). — L. Lies, Vom Christentum zu Christus nach O., Cels.: ZKTh 112 (1990) 150-177. — F. Mosetto, I miracoli evangelici nel dibattito tra Celso e O. (Rome, 1986). — C. Reemts, Auseinandersetzung zwischen Celsus u. O. im Horizont der Postmoderne: EuA 75 (1999) 5-12. — H. J. Vogt, The Later Exegesis of O.: FS J. Gribomont (SEA 27) (Stuttgart, 1988), 583-591. — idem, Die Exegese des O. in Cels.: StPatr 21 (1989) 356-373.

5. *Other Works*: O.'s piety also finds expression in his *Exhortation to Martyrdom* (*mart.*), which is addressed to his patron, Ambrose, as is the detailed treatise *On Prayer* (*or.*), which deals first with basic questions such as the providence of God and human freedom, then with the Our Father, and finally with the place, posture, and time of Chr. prayer. (Liturgical) prayer should be addressed to the Father; all prayer should be primarily "praise of God," "through Christ, who is also praised, in the Holy Spirit, who is also glorified" (33.1).

Only fragments exist of the letters and of the *Stromateis* of O.

W: *or.*, *mart.*, P. Koetschau, BKV² 48 [German trans./comm.]. — *dial.*, *mart.*, E. Früchtel, BGrL 5 (Stuttgart, 1974) [German trans./comm.].

L: P. Dyckhoff, Das kosmische Gebet. Einübung nach O. (Munich, 1994). — W. Gessel, Die Theologie des Gebetes nach or. von O. (Paderborn, 1975).

III. Basic Lines of Thought: 1. *On exegesis*: O. expresses as follows the gnostic view that he attacks in *Jo.*: "There are those who [they claim] are by nature children of God; only because of their natural relationship with God are they capable of receiving the word of God" (20.33.287). Refutation of gnosticism also appears in the *comm. in Mt.* Even in passages where one would not expect it, O. attacks the "fairy tales about natures" which God supposedly created different; to say otherwise would be unjustly to blame the creator. In addition, the example of Judas, who repented of his sin (Mt 27:3-10) proves that the saying about the good fruit of the good tree and the bad fruit of the bad tree (Mt 7:18) should not be interpreted as referring to three different natures, i.e., classes of human beings, as the gnostics claim: "It is not our nature that is the source of misdeeds, but the person's own free decision, which does evil" (*comm. in Mt.* 10.11).

O. emphasizes this point (*princ.* 4.2.1): it is because the Jews appeal to the wording of the scripture that the majority of the Jews rejected the Savior, and it is because the gnostics base themselves again on a literally understood bibl. text that they claim a distinction must be made between, on the one hand, the perfect God and Father of Jesus Christ and, on the other, the inferior creator of the world and God of the OT. O. is therefore convinced that the true meaning of the entire Bible, which the Spirit (*princ.* 4.2.7) or the Logos (4.2.9) intends to reveal, is to be sought and found behind the wording. In fact, he even reckons with three stages in the meaning of scripture, which he compares with the flesh, soul, and spirit of the human being and which are meant to build up respectively the simpler people, those a little advanced, and finally the perfect (*princ.* 4.2.4). But O. gives no convincing scriptural argument for this threefold division; probably for this reason he then speaks (*princ.* 4.2.79) only of two intentions of the revealing Spirit and, correspondingly, of two levels in what the scriptures say; that is how he operates in his later exegetical works, espec. in the commentary on Mt. But he holds fast to the necessity of allegorism, and he explains in his commentary on the Song of Songs that everything can be translated from the visible into the invisible because divine wisdom intends to lead us from earthly things to heavenly. This principle, he says, is valid not only for creation but also for the Bible and not only for the OT but the gospel as well.

O. thus stands in a tradition of interpretation that was developed for the exegesis of Homer and was later applied to the Bible by Jewish scholars in Alexandria and espec. by Philo; in both cases offensive material was to be removed; to a great extent, however, the similarity was only formal. In Philo's view, since nature loves to conceal itself (*De fuga* 32.179; *De mutatione nominum* 8.60; *De somniis* 1.2.6), physiology is identical with allegorism, which brings the nature of things to light (*De providentia* 2.40) for the few initiates (*De Abrahamo* 29.147). Thus the horizon within which Philo interprets is that which science and philosophy have made known about human beings and the world. O. decisively rejects such physiology: you may give whatever physiological explanation you wish of the falling sickness of the lunatic in Mt 17:14ff., but you will not thus grasp the meaning of the miraculous cure and of the account of it (*comm. in Mt.* 13.6). It is faith in the saving incarnation of the Son of God that is for O. the background and horizon of all exegesis, even of the OT.

L: A. F. Castellano, La exegesis de O. y de Heracleón en el Libro VI del "Commentario a Juan": TyV 31 (1990) 309-320. — idem, L'esegesi di O. e di Eracleone alle testimonianze del battista (Rome, 1991). — F. Cocchini, Aspetti del Paolinismo Origeniano: Aug. 31 (1991) 245-276. — idem, Il Paolo di O. (Rome, 1992). — R. Gögler, Zur Theologie des bibl. Wortes bei O. (Düsseldorf, 1963). — R. C. P. Hanson, Allegory and Event (London, 1959). — T. Heither, Begegnung am Brunnen: EuA 69 (1993) 5-18. — eadem, Translatio religionis (Cologne, 1990). — eadem, Mystikverständnis im Hld-Kommentar: EuA 74 (1998) 478-494. — H. Karpp, Kirchliche u. außerkirchliche Motive im hermeneutischen Traktat des O., princ. 4, 13: FS T. Klauser (Münster, 1984), 194-212. — W. Kinzig, Röm. Recht u. Unrecht in der Predigt der Alten Kirche: Recht-Macht-Gerechtigkeit, ed. J. Mehlhausen (Munich, 1998), 407-437. — L. Lies, Zur Exegese des O.: ThRv 88 (1992) 89-96. — H. de Lubac, Histoire et esprit (Paris, 1950 = German: H. U. v. Balthasar, Geist aus der Geschichte [with an introduction] [Einsiedeln, 1968]). — idem, "Du hast mich betrogen, Herr!" Der O.-Kommentar über Jeremia 20, 7 (Einsiedeln, 1984). — F. Manns, Une tradition juive dans les commentaires du Cantique: Anton. 65 (1990) 3-22. — M. Mees, Joh 6 bei O.: Lat. 48 (1982) 179-208; Laur. 25 (1984) 78-130. — idem, Joh 5 bei O.: Lat. 49 (1983) 25-55, 247-256. — idem, 2 Co 6, 1-10 u. die Auferstehung der Toten nach O. u. Methodius: Lat. 51 (1985) 153-163. — H. Strutwolf, Gnosis als System. Zur Rezeption der valentinianischen Gnosis bei O. (Göttingen, 1993). — J. A. Trumbower, O.'s Exegesis of John 8,19-53: VigChr 43 (1989) 138-154. — H. J. Vogt, Beobachtungen zum Joh-Kommentar des O.: ThQ 170 (1990) 191-208. — idem, Die Lehre des O. von der Inspiration der hl. Schrift (princ. u. Cels): ThQ 170 (1990) 97-103.

2. *Doctrine of the Trinity*: O. set the course for later trinitarian theology inasmuch as in his early com-

mentary on John (*Jo.* 2.10.75) he already speaks of Father, Son, and Holy Spirit as "three hypostases." After explaining (beginning in 1.28.200) that the various names of Christ are various ways of considering (*epinoiai*) one and the same Christ (see also 1.31.223; 1.35.259), he sharply attacks those who want to understand the distinction of Father and Son as simply between *epinoiai* instead of between *hypostases* (10.37.246); Father and Son are indeed one in substance, but not one acc. to number.

O. finds the eternal intradivine generation of the Son to be adequately described in the scriptures, e.g., in Ps 2:7: "You are my Son; this day I have begotten you." In God this "today" is always, "for God has no evening nor, I think, does he have a morning" (*Jo.* 1.29.204). O. gains the same insight from Prov 8:25 (LXX): "Before all the hills he begets me," because the text does not say that before all the hills he *has* begotten me (the past), but "he begets me," i.e., in the divine present which knows no before or after (*hom. in Jer.* 9.4). But O. thinks of the three divine hypostases not as statically juxtaposed but as dynamically interrelated; of the Son he says, e.g.: "Because he is with God he remains always God; this would not be true if he were not with God; nor would he remain God if he did not abide in the unwearying vision of the depths of the Father" (*Jo.* 2.2.17).

L: J. Dillon, O.'s Doctrine of the Trinity and Some Later Neoplatonic Theories: idem, The Golden Chain (CStS 333) (London, 1990), Nr. 21. — K. Doi, "Pathos" u. "Apatheia" bei O.: ThZ 54 (1998) 228-240. — J. Hammerstaedt, Der trinitarische Gebrauch des Hypostasisbegriffs bei O.: JAC 34 (1991) 12-20. — K. McDonnell, Does O. have a Trinitarian Doctrine of the Holy Spirit?: Gr. 75 (1994) 5-35. — A. Orbe, O. y los Monarquianos: Gr. 72 (1991) 39-72. — H. Ziebritzki, Hl. Geist u. Weltseele. Das Problem der dritten Hypostase bei O., Plotin u. ihren Vorläufern (Tübingen, 1994).

3. *Anthropology. Preexistence of souls*: The claim, which O. attributes to the schools of Marcion, Valentinian, and Basilides, that different souls have different natures (*princ.* 2.9.5), causes O. to inquire into the origin of souls. Since God is described by the Bible as good and just, he may not be accused of any unequal dealing with his creatures at the very beginning (2.9.6; also 1.8.1ff.). Distinctions among spiritual creatures must therefore be due to their own sins and merits. This conclusion, which is demanded by concern for the justice of God, is also found attested in the scripture; when, e.g., Paul (Rom 9:13) cites Mal 1:2f.: "Jacob I have loved, Esau I have hated," but nonetheless assures us that there is no injustice in God, one must conclude that Jacob was lovable

because of the merits of his earlier life, whereas Esau was hateful (*princ.* 2.9.7; see 1.7.4). Appealing also to the parable of the vineyard workers (Mt. 20:1-16), O. always holds fast to this "mysterious teaching" (*comm. in Mt.* 15.34.36), which many found offensive but which is completely different from the transmigration of souls.

L: C. P. Bammel, Adam in O.: FS H. Chadwick (Cambridge, 1989), 62-93. — H. S. Benjamins, Eingeordnete Freiheit. Freiheit u. Vorsehung bei O. (Leiden, 1994). — R. Calonne, Le libre arbitre dans le traité des Principes d'O.: BLE 89 (1988) 243-262. — H. Crouzel, Théologie de l'image de Dieu chez O. (Paris, 1956). — J. Dupuis, L'esprit de l'homme. Étude sur l'anthropologie religieuse d'O. (Paris, 1967). — M. Edwards, O. no gnostic: JThS 43 (1992) 23-37. — P. van der Eijk, O.' Verteidigung des freien Willens: VigChr 42 (1988) 339-351. — M. Hauke, Heilsverlust in Adam. Irenäus — O. — Kappadozier (Paderborn, 1993). — A. Scott, O. and the Life of the Stars (Oxford, 1991). — G. Sfameni Gasparro, O. Studi di Antropologia e di storia della tradizione (Rome, 1984). — P. Tavardon, La doctrine de la création selon O. dans la mouvance platonicienne: ETR 65 (1990) 59-76. — G. Watson, Souls and Bodies in O.'s Peri Archon: IThQ 55 (1989) 173-192.

4. *Christology:* The soul of Jesus, too, exists "from the beginning of creation"; it was always inseparable from the Logos of God and in its totality (*tota*) has taken the Logos wholly (*totum*) into itself so that it became with him one spirit in the full sense (*principaliter unus spiritus*); in this union of the preexistent soul with the Logos, O. sees realized in the fullest sense the saying of the apostle that whoever is united with the Lord is one spirit with him (1 Cor 6:17) (e.g., *comm. in Mt.* 15.24; 18.8). Indeed, the incarnation of the Son of God took place through the mediation of the soul, since "the nature of God" cannot be united "with the body apart from some medium" (*princ.* 2.6.3); therefore the Son of God comes in a human body along with the preexistent soul. Since this soul, too, has the heavenly Jerusalem as its mother, O. is able to interpret the statement that "a man will leave father and mother and cling to his wife" (Gen 2:24; Mt 19:5) as referring to the incarnation: the Son of God left God, his Father, and the heavenly Jerusalem, his mother, and clung to his fallen wife, i.e., "the church, which is his body" (thus *comm. in Mt.* 14.17; *hom in Jer.* 10.7). Thus there is a clear internal connection between christology, soteriology, and ecclesiology.

L: H. Crouzel, La christologie d'O. selon son Commentaire sur le Cantique des Cantiques: FS J. Betz (Düsseldorf, 1984), 421-438. — M. Fédou, La sagesse et le monde. Essai sur la christologie d'O. (Paris, 1995). — I. Golden, O. and Mariology: GOTR 36 (1991) 141-154. — M. Harl, O. et la fonction révélatrice du Verbe incarné (Paris, 1958). — J. Letellier, Le Logos chez O.: RSPhTh 75 (1991) 587-612. — R. Lyman, Christology and Cosmology. Models of Divine Activity in O., Eusebius, and Athanasius (Oxford, 1993). — A. Meis-Wörmer, La preeminencia de Jesús: TyV 33 (1992) 65-88. — R. Roukema, O.' visie op de Rechtvaardiging volgens zijn Commentar op Romeinen: GThT 89 (1989) 94-105. — J. M. Rowe, O.'s Doctrine of Subordination (Bern, 1987). — J. W. Trigg, The Angel of Great Counsel: JThS 42 (1991) 35-51. — H. J. Vogt, Ein-Geist-Sein (1 Kor 6, 17b) in der Christologie des O.: TThZ 93 (1984) 251-265.

5. *Church, Sacraments, Piety:* Since O. is in many passages very critical of eccles. officials and since in his view the real being of the church is not of the visible order, scholars have tried to find in him the theory of an internal hierarchy. But when, as, e.g., in *comm. in Rom* 9.2, O. interprets the comparison of the oneness of the body and the multiplicity of the members (Rom 12:4f.) in such a way as to describe Christians who distinguish themselves in study and learning as the eye of the body, those who hear God as the ear of the body, those who preach as its tongue, those who work as its hands, and those who visit the sick as its feet, and so on, he is speaking of externally perceptible activities and characteristics and precisely not of an interior, secret hierarchy.

O. does not attest to a strict succession of charismatic teachers; in his view the church is led by its officials, although their manner of life is not always blameless nor are their judgments always accurate. The reality of the church is found in those who draw near to God through knowledge and good works; all of O.'s works, even the major commentaries, are in the service of these two goals. O. finds the interior closeness to Christ expressed as expectation in the Song of Songs.

L: J. Alviar, Klesis. The Theology of the Christian Vocation according to O. (Dublin, 1993). — F. Cocchini, L'esegesi origeniana di Rom 1, 14: SMSR 54 (1988) 71-80. — H. Crouzel, "Ecclesiasticus" dans l'œuvre d'O.: FS V. Saxer (Rome, 1992), 147-162. — idem, Le thème du mariage mystique chez O. et ses sources: StMiss 26 (1977) 37-58. — idem, O.: D. S. 11 (1982) 933-962. — J. Dillon, Aisthesis Noete. A Doctrine of Spiritual Senses in O. and in Plotinus: idem, The Golden Chain, CStS 333 (London, 1990), Nr. 19. — G. A. Galluccio, L' "ut unum sint" (Gv 17, 20-26): Nicolaus 20 (1993) 25-102. — T. Heither, "Gotteserfahrung" in der Theologie des O.: EuA 68 (1992) 265-277. — L. Lies, O.' Eucharistielehre im Streit der Konfessionen (Innsbruck, 1985). — K. Nasilowski, De potestatis sacerdotalis apud Origenem distinctione: Apoll. 58 (1985) 629-699. — T. Schäfer, Das Priester-Bild im Leben u. Werk des O. (Frankfurt a.M., 1977). — R. Thomas, Nisi cognoveris te . . . Observationes in Origenis de cognitione sui doctrinam (Rome, 1993). — H. J. Vogt, Das Kirchenverständnis des O. (Cologne, 1974). — idem, Zum Bischofsamt in der frühen Kirche: ThQ 162 (1982) 221-236; esp. 228-233. — idem,

Die Witwe als Bild der Seele in der Exegese des O.: ThQ 165 (1985) 105-118.

6. *Apocatastasis pantōn*: O. raises the question of the restoration of all things in his *princ.* (*restitutio omnium*: 2.3.5). Since the subjection of the Son to the Father (1 Cor 15:28) is to be understood as good and salutary, the same must be true of the subjection of the enemies, that is, it must signify their rescue and restoration (3.5.7). O. expects that "after infinitely long ages" (3.6.6), "all rational souls" will be restored to a state of perfection (ibid.; see 3.6.9). O. probably asked himself from time to time whether even the evil spirits, espec. the devil, will be able at the end to regain their original state of closeness to God, but he never claimed this; rather, in a letter to his friends, from which both Rufinus (*adult.* 7) and Jerome (*adv. Rufin.* 2.18) cite the decisive passages, he deliberately defended himself against this misrepresentation. The idea nonetheless remained associated with his name, probably because it was thought to follow necessarily from the original equality of all spiritual creatures. In any case, in a letter to the fifth ecumenical council of 553, Justinian anathematized, in first place, "the fabricated preexistence of soul and its *consequence*, the fantastic restoration."

But the simple restoration of the original state is not for O. the ultimate goal of the history of salvation. Jesus (he says) performed his first miracle not in Capernaum but in Cana, because the Lord came as a physician only because of man's incurable illness, but his real activity looks to the joy of God's festive banquet (*Jo.* 10.12.66); the end will therefore transcend the beginning. For this reason, O. himself contradicted the mistaken idea that spiritual beings restored to their original dignity could fall again (*Jo.* 10.42.292ff.); an eternal recurrence is incompatible with free will (*Cels.* 4.67); a new fall is impossible because creatures will have experienced the love of God and thereby have been made steadfast in love (*comm. in Roman* 5.10).

L: E. dal Covolo, Appunti di escatologia origeniana: Sal. 41 (1989) 769-784. — H. Crouzel, Les fins dernières selon O. (Hampshire, 1990).

IV. **Controversies about Origen:** In his lifetime O. had to defend himself against many accusations. Ca. 300, → Methodius of Olympus in his treatise on the resurrection, remnants of which are preserved in Epiphanius, *haer.* 19, sharply attacked O.'s eschatology and allegorical interpretation of scripture. In a treatise on Saul's visit to the witch of Endor, →

Eustathius of Antioch attacked the interpretation which O. had given in his sermon on 1 Sam 28 and had suggested in *hom in Jer.* 18, in *Jo.* 20.293; 28.148f., and in *comm. in Mt.* 15.35. Here O. also defended the freedom of will of deceased human beings: Samuel, he says, freely decided to prophesy to Saul. Eustathius's chief objection to O. was that the latter did not attempt a definitive interpretation but allowed for a continuing process of ever better understanding. This "searching theology" evidently stirred in Eustathius a "horror of ambiguity."

In Caesarea, → Pamphilus, a priest who died a martyr during the persecution of Maximinus, composed, with the help of the later Bishop Eusebius, a defense of O. in five books, to which Eusebius added a sixth; only the first book has survived in the translation by Rufinus. Pamphilus lists nine current accusations against O., e.g., the doctrine of the transmigration of souls, and refutes them all from O.'s own works. Pamphilus himself does not accept all of O.'s ideas, but he does accept his theol. and exeget. methods and thus establishes an Origenism of a positive kind. But the concept of Origenism is usually understood as something negative and applied to theologians who hardened and exaggerated ideas of O. and thus contradicted the orthodoxy of their times, as, e.g., Evagrius Pont., whose authorship of explanations of the Psalms, ascribed to O., has been restored only in the 20th c. It was Evagrius more than O. who influenced the Origenist monks; it was the attack on the latter by Theophilus Alex. that started the Origenist controversy ca. 400. In the 6th c. Emperor Justinian reacted to the squabbles among monks, of whom some were extreme Origenists, by having statements ascribed to O. condemned by a synod preparatory to the fifth ecumenical council.

L: H. U. v. Balthasar, Die Hiera des Evagrius: ZKTh 63 (1939) 86-106, 181-206. — E. A. Clark, Elite Networks and Heresy Accusations. Towards a Social Description of the Origenist Controversy: Semeia 56 (1992) 79-117. — F. R. Diekamp, Die origenistischen Streitigkeiten im 6. Jh. (Münster, ²1989). — E. A. Junod, L'Apologie pour O. de Pamphile et la naissance de l'origénisme: StPatr 26 (1993) 267-286. — P. Lardet, L'Apologie de Jérôme contre Rufin (Leiden, 1993). — L'Origenismo. Apologie e polemiche intorno a Origene: Aug. 26 (1986). — D. Pazzini, La critica di Cirillo Alessandrino alla dottrina origenista della preesistenza delle anime: CrSt 9 (1988) 237-280. — E. Prinzivalli, *ΨΥΧΑΣ ΕΞ ΑΙΔΟΥ ΜΕΤΑΠΕΜΠΕΣΘΑΙ.* Una proposta di letteratura della polemica di Eustazio con O.: Aug. 35 (1995) 679-696. — M.-J. Rondeau, Le commentaire sur les psaumes d'Évagre le Pontique: OCP 26 (1960) 307-348. — J. W. Trigg, Eustathius of Antioch's Attack on O.: JR (1995) 219-238. — H. J. Vogt, Warum wurde O. zum Häretiker erklärt?: Origeniana 4 (1987) 78-99, 100-111.

Even western church fathers (Hilary, Ambrose, Augustine) learned allegorism from O. and passed it on to the Middle Ages. It was probably in circles around Cassiodorus (d. ca. 580) that the Lat. translation of the commentary on Mt was made; in the Middle Ages the section from Mt 22:34 to 27:66 (for which the Gr. text was lost) was divided into 145 segments of varying length and described as *Commentariorum Series*. Paschase Radbert (d. before 860) agrees almost word for word with O. in many passages of his own twelve-book commentary on Mt (PL 120:31-994), but he does not mention O. The homiliary compiled for Charlemagne by Paul the Deacon contains some sermons ascribed to O. The humanists paid renewed attention to O.; he seems even to have influenced the iconography of the Sistine Chapel; in the Reformation period scholars sought to derive arguments from him. Modern Origenist scholarship began with the *Origeniana* of P. D. Huet (d. 1721), which are printed in PG 17:633-1284.

L: H. Crouzel, Une controverse sur O. à la Renaissance (Paris, 1977). — J. F. Dechow, Dogma and Mysticism in Early Christianity. Epiphanius of Cyprus and the Legacy of O. (Macon, Ga., 1988). — A. Godin, Erasme, lecteur d'O. (Geneva, 1982). — V. Grossi, La presenza in filigrana di O. nell' ultimo Agostino (426-430): Aug. 30 (1990) 423-440. — H. König, "Vestigia antiquorum magistrorum sequi." Wie liest Apponius O. ?: ThQ 170 (1990) 129-136. — L. Lies, O.' Eucharistielehre im Streit der Konfessionen (Innsbruck, 1985). — idem, O. u. die Eucharistiekontroverse zwischen Paschasius Radbertus u. Ratramnus: ZKTh 101 (1979) 414-426. — E. Prinzivalli, Per un'indagine sull'esegesi del pensiero origeniano nel IV secolo: ASEs 11 (1994) 433-460. — M. Schär, Das Nachleben des O. im Zeitalter des Humanismus (Basel, 1979). — J. Schwind, O. und der Dichter Arator: REAug 41 (1995) 113-130. — G. Sfameni Gasparro, Agostino di fronto alla "eterodossia" di O.; Aug(L) 40 (1990) 219-243. — E. Wind, The Revival of O.: FS B. da Costa Greene (Princeton, 1954), 412-424.

H. J. VOGT

Orosius

I. Life: O. (the first name "Paul" is not attested with certainty) was in all probability from Bracara (today Braga, Portugal). As a young presbyter, for reasons not certain (invasions of the Visigoths and Vandals?) he left his native place and reached Africa in 414. There he made such a good impression on Augustine in his episcopal city, Hippo, that the latter sent him as his messenger to Jerome with some important works (among them, *De origine animae* and *De sententia Jacobi*)—no small manifestation of confidence. In July 415 he appeared at the Jerusalem synod against Pelagius and got into a heated controversy with John, the local bishop. In 416 he returned

to Africa with, among other things, the *Dialogus adversus Pelagianos* of → Jerome (he journeyed by way of the Span. island of Minorca, bringing there some relics of Stephen, the protomartyr, that were preserved in Palestine); until 417 he played an important role at many provincial synods as the chief authority regarding the treatment given Pelagius in the eastern part of the empire and as an informant for Augustine in the Pelagian controversy. From 418 on (the latest date for the completion of the *Historiae*; see below) we have no further information about him.

II. Works: We possess three works of O. During his first stay in Africa he addressed his *Commonitorium de errore Priscillianistarum et Origenistarum* (*comm.*) to Augustine. In the form of a letter it provides information on the state of the church in the author's homeland where, in his view, supporters of Priscillian but also representatives of an orthodox interpretation of Origen were a greater threat to the true faith than the "most bloodthirsty enemies" (*comm.* 1). Despite the element of information this short work is less a *commonitorium* (= adviser, memorandum) than a *consultatio* (= petition for advice), which elicited Augustine's *Ad Orosium contra Priscillianistas et Origenistas*.

During O.'s stay in Palestine he wrote his *Liber apologeticus* (*apol.*), a defense, addressed to a broader public, in which, using a fictitious (eccles.) court situation (the addresses are the clergy of Jerusalem), O. defends himself against accusations made by Bishop John in connection with the Pelagian question. Here he attempts, on the grounds of mistranslation (O. himself spoke no Greek) and mishearings, to refute the decisive "charge": that he had blasphemed by claiming that even with God's help human beings could not be without sin (7.2). He adds, with a clear reference to the crucifixion of Christ and the stoning of Stephen, that Jerusalem has always been a bad place for fearless Christians (8; 9). From this section of primarily self-justification O. moves on to a presentation and refutation of Pelagian teaching, which occupies the major part of the work (11-33). The work is characterized by a biting attack in which Pelagius appears as, among other things, a reviver of Priscillianism and Origenism.

The *Historiae adversus paganos* (*hist.*) in seven books, written in 416-417/418, is the first Chr. universal history; O. says that he wrote it on instructions from Augustine (1 *prol.* 1-3.8; 7.43.19f.). The work covers the time from the flood to 417 C.E. and endeavors espec. to give parallel presentations of Gr. and Roman history. The principal sources are, above all, Justin, the *Periochae* from Livy, Florus, Eutropius, perhaps Suetonius and Caesar's *Commentarii*, as well as Eusebius's *Chronicle* (in Jerome's translation) and his church history (in Rufinus's translation). Occasionally O. names source writers without having read them. As a historical source the *hist.* are important primarily for the period after 378. O.'s purpose in writing the *hist.* was similar to that of Augustine in his *civ.*: to refute the pagan objection that neglect of the old gods was responsible for the many misfortunes of the present age (e.g., Alaric's conquest of Rome in 410). Given this intention, the work is a historical supplement to Augustine's *civ.* O. tries to show that even and espec. before Christianity human history was plagued by immense suffering. Large sections of the presentation consist, therefore, in lists of catastrophes and calamities (1 *prol.* 10), which O. is able to describe with great vividness and not without exaggeration. Only since the beginning of the *christiana tempora* has a steady improvement been noticeable. In the process O., a man of the empire, lays heavy stress on the synchronism of the birth of Christ and the reign of Augustus: It was the *pax Romana* established by Augustus that created the political setting for the spread of Christianity (6.22.5f.; 7.1f.). As a result, when seen in light of the widespread teaching (which O. accepts) of the four world empires (acc. to O.: Assyrians, Macedonians, Carthaginians, Romans; see 2.1.4), the Roman empire acquires a significance in the history of salvation.

The synthesis of Romanism and Christianity provides the condition for a gradual improvement of relationships which O. sees, espec. in his glorification of the present in contrast to the pre-Chr. period, which is painted in the darkest colors. It is true that O.'s thinking, like that of Augustine, looks ultimately to the next world, but he also acknowledges and stresses a steady progress in the course of earthly history. In this respect he departs from the theology of his teacher, and in this fact we may suspect the reason for Augustine's strange silence about O.'s *hist.*, which he evidently felt gave too optimistic an interpretation of this world's history. Nonetheless it was the *hist.* of O. that considerably influenced medieval thought on history.

W: PL 31:663-1216. — *comm.*, G. Schepß, CSEL 18:149-157. — K.-D. Daur, CCL 49:157-163. — Concordances to *comm.*: CC Instrumenta Lexicologica Latina Ser. A 29. — *apol.*, *hist.*, C. Zangemeister, CSEL 5; editio minor of *hist.* (Leipzig, 1889). — *apol.*, R. M. Gover (New York, 1969) [English trans./comm.]. — *hist.*, I. W. Raymond (New York, 1936) [English trans.]. — R. J. Deferrari (Washington, 1964) [English trans.]. — A. Lippold, A. Bartalucci, G.

Chiarini, 2 vols. (Milan, 1976) [text/Italian trans./comm.]. — E. Gallego-Blanco (Barcelona, 1983) [Spanish trans./comm.]. — A. Lippold, C. Andresen, 2 vols. (Zurich, 1985/86) [German trans./comm.]. — M.-P. Arnaud-Lindet, 3 vols. (Paris, 1990f.) [text/French trans./comm.]. L: J. M. Alonso-Núñez, Die Auslegung der Geschichte bei O.: WSt 106 (1993) 197-213. — R. Ampio, La concezione orosiana della storia: CClCr 9 (1988) 217-236. — A. Bartalucci, Lingua e stile in O.: SCO 25 (1976) 213-253. — L. de Coninck, O. on the Virtues of His Narrative: AncSoc 21 (1990) 45-57. — E. Corsini, Introduzione alle "Storie" di O. (Turin, 1968). — J. A. Davids, De O. et sancto Augustino priscillianistarum adversariis commentatio historica et philologica (Den Haag, 1930). — H.-J. Diesner, O. u. Augustinus: AAH 11 (1963) 89-102. — F. Fabbrini, O. uno storico (Rome, 1979). — G. Fink, Recherches bibliographiques sur O.: RABM 58 (1952) 271-322. — H.-W. Goetz, Die Geschichtstheologie des O. (Darmstadt, 1980). — idem, O. u. die Barbaren: Hist. 29 (1980) 356-376. — T. M. Green, Zosimus, O. and their Tradition (New York, 1974). — H. Hagendahl, O. u. Iustinus (Göteborg, 1941). — A. G. Hamman, O. et le pélagianisme: BrAug 21 (1967) 346-355. — R. Herzog, O. oder die Formulierung eines Fortschrittskonzepts aus der Erfahrung des Niedergangs: Niedergang, ed. R. Koselleck et al. (Stuttgart, 1988), 79-102. — G. Hingst, Zu offenen Quellenfragen bei O. (Vienna, 1973). — Y. Janvier, La géographie d'O. (Paris, 1982). — H. Kaletsch, Zur "babylonischen Chronologie" bei O.: FS A. Lippold (Würzburg, 1993), 447-472. — S. Karrer, Der Gallische Krieg bei O. (Zurich, 1969). — D. Koch-Peters, Ansichten des O. zur Geschichte seiner Zeit (Frankfurt a.M., 1984). — B. Lacroix, O. et ses idées (Montreal, 1965). — A. Lippold, Rom u. die Barbaren in der Beurteilung des O. (Erlangen, 1952). — idem, O., chr. Apologet u. röm. Bürger: Ph. 113 (1969) 92-105. — idem, Griech.-makedonische Geschichte bei O.: Chiron 1 (1971) 437-455. — F. Martelli, Reazione antiagostiniana nelle Historiae di O. ?: Rivista storica di antichità 12 (1982) 217-239. — A. Mehl, O. über die Amnestie des Kaisers Claudius: RMP 121 (1978) 185-194. — T. E. Mommsen, Aponius and O. on the Significance of the Epiphany: Medieval and Renaissance Studies, ed. E. F. Rice (New York, 1966), 299-324. — idem, O. and Augustine, ibid, 325-348. — F. Paschoud, Roma aeterna (Neuchâtel, 1967), 276-292. — J. Schnitzer, O. e Pelagio: Rel. (1937) 336-343. — K. A. Schöndorf, Die Geschichtstheologie des O. (Munich, 1952). — W. Suerbaum, Vom antiken zum frühmal. Staatsbegriff (Münster, ²1970). — J. Svennung, Orosiana (Uppsala, 1922). — S. Tanz, O. im Spannungsfeld zwischen Eusebius u. Augustin: Klio 65 (1983) 337-346. — C. Torres Rodríguez, O. (La Coruña, 1985).

U. HAMM, M. MEIER

Ossius of Cordoba

O., born ca. 256, was bishop of Cordoba from 300 on, a confessor during the Diocletian persecution, and an adviser of Constantine. In order to restore peace to the empire, Constantine chose O. to bring his letter to Arius and Alexander Alex. (Doc. 17). Whether O. had anything to do with the content of the letter is disputed. Constantine, and possibly O. as well, initially thought the conflict in Alexandria to be a minor matter, but after Alexander had enlightened him on its real scope, O. probably made the latter's judgment his own. At the beginning of 325 he held the chairmanship in Antioch. O. seems during this period to have accepted the theology of Alexander (i.e., the theology of the image). At Nicaea (325) O. presided as the imperial adviser, but the extent to which he had any part in drawing up the confession of faith is unclear (there are differences, e.g., in the views of Athanasius, *h. Ar.* 42, and Basil, *ep.* 81). Whether the *homoousios* was inserted on O.'s advice, as Constantine supposedly demanded (Doc. 22.7), is disputed. After Nicaea O. is not perceptibly to the fore again until Sardica, whose confession of faith O. supported; he evidently viewed this creed as an authentic interpretation of Nicaea (Phoebadius, *C. Ar.* 28.2). In any case, O.'s part in composing the confession of faith is an open question (in this setting also belongs the letter written by O., together with Protogenes, to Julius, which was meant to give plausibility to the drawing up of a new creed). We hear nothing of O. again until 355. His letter to Constantius (356) emphasizes the separation between civil and eccles. authority. The context suggests that the emphasis on the church's freedom was because the emperor favored the other side. The resulting exile of O. and the pressure brought to bear on him to subscribe to a homoean creed of Sirmium (357) have recently been called into question. On the whole, it does not seem possible to derive a unified theol. vision of O. from the surviving sources.

W: *ep. ad Julium,* EOMJA I 2:644. — *ep. ad Constantium,* Athanasius, *h. Ar.* 44.

L: L. Abramowski, Die Synode von Antiochien u. ihr Symbol: ZKG 86 (1975) 356-366. — H. Chadwick, O. of Cordoba and the Presidency of the Council of Antioch in 325: JThS 9 (1958) 292-304. — V. C. de Clercq, O. of Cordova. A Contribution to the History of the Constantinian Period (Washington, 1954). — K. M. Girardet, Kaiser Konstantius II. als "Episcopus Episcoporum" u. das Herrscherbild des kirchlichen Widerstandes: Hist. 26 (1977) 95-128. — R. P. C. Hanson, The Search for the Christian Doctrine of God (Edinburgh, 1988). — R. Klein, Constantius II. u. die chr. Kirche (Darmstadt, 1977). — J. Ulrich, Die Anfänge der abendländischen Rezeption des Nizänums (Berlin/New York, 1994), 111-135. — idem, Einige Bemerkungen zum angeblichen Exil des O.: ZKG 105 (1994) 143-155.

T. Böhm

P

Pacatus

The person of P. eludes our grasp. He is to be identified either with the Aquitanian rhetor Latinus Dra-
panius Pacatus, who lived in the 4th/5th c., or with
the apologist and author of the treatise *Contra Porphyrium* (*Por.*), fragments of which were preserved,
by way of Victor, bishop of Capua (d. 554), in the
catenas of → John the Deacon (PL 68:359; PG
5:1025-1238). In the latter's catena on the gospels a
further five fragments are preserved, as well as some
in fragments of a catena on Mt and in the catena on
the Heptateuch. Acc. to another thesis, P. was a personal friend of Paulinus of Nola. In 431 Uranius, a
presbyter of Nola and himself a disciple of Paulinus,
wrote a letter to P.: *Ep. de obitu Paulini ad Pacatum*
(PL 53:859-66). Acc. to this letter P. intended to
compose a life of Paulinus in verse (ch. 1: "Let us
turn now to the material at your disposal for writing
his life in verse"). In the final analysis, the person of
P. is left in the dark; the only thing certain is that he
lived before 500; his time and place are undeter-
mined.

W: *Por.*, F. X. Funk, F. Diekamp, Pacati (Ps.-Polycarpi
Smyrnensis) Contra Porphyrium: Patres Apostolici 2
(Tübingen, 1913), 397-400.
L: W. Bährens, P.: Hermes 56 (1921) 443-445. — A. v. Har-
nack: SPAW (1921) 266-384. — J. F. Matthews, Gallic Sup-
porters of Theodosius: Latomus 30 (1971) 1073-1099. — J.
B. Pitra, P.: SpicSol 1 (1852) LVIII-LLIX, 281-282.

C. KASPER

Pachomius

P. was born in Upper Egypt ca. 292 as the child of
pagan parents and was converted while a soldier; he
was baptized in 313 and, drawn initially by the ideal
of service to the brethren, entered the community of
Chenoboskion, but turned ultimately to the school
of Palamon the hermit. After seven years he settled in
the abandoned village of Tabennesi, where disciples
joined him. After negative experiences and to some
extent against the resistance of the community he
began to establish regulations for discipline in common life and for poverty that were inspired by the
spirit of mutual service and were binding on all alike.
P. thus became the inaugurator of cenobitic monasticism. Athanasius Alex. was his constant patron. The
vigor of his disciples rescued P. from a condemnation by a synod of the local episcopate in Latopolis
(345). At his death in 347 (or 346) over five thousand
monks lived in the nine monasteries he had founded;
he served as their "abbot general." The writings, part
of them gnostic, that were found at Nag Hammadi
probably were from among the books of the Pachomians. Shortly after P.'s death, the monks, aided by
the reminiscences of P.'s successor, → Theodore of
Tabennesi, and by materials already gathered, began
to write the *Vita Pachomii*, of which there were many
Copt. recensions and which is also found in Gr., Lat.
(by Dionysius Exiguus), and Arab. translations
(these to some extent dependent on each other). An
important source for the biography of P. and also the
material basis for most of the Gr. lives of P. is the
Paralipomena, a collection of stories about P. and
Theodore of Tabennesi. The rules that P. set down
for his monastic communities in light of what their
situations required (we must not think yet of a fixed
monastic rule) have not been preserved. "Pachomian" (but not coming from P. himself) describes
the Copt., four-part collection of individual regulations from the Pachomian monastery of Metanoia
(Canopus), which → Jerome had before him in a
fragmentarily preserved Gr. translation when he
made his own translation into Latin and which is
preserved complete in that language: the *Regula*
(*reg.*). The "Rule of the angels" (→ Palladius of Helenopolis, *h. laus.* 32.1-7) and the Eth. versions of the
rule in some mss. have no value for study of the
Pachomian Rule. A central place in the Rule belongs
to the work of obedience, which (like all other regulations) is in the service of maintaining common life
and is binding even on superiors. The spiritual standard for everything that goes on in the monastery is
the sacred scriptures. The *Catecheses* (*catech.*) which
P. gave his monks likewise show a profound knowledge of scripture. Eleven letters (*ep.*) have also come
down from P. in Coptic, Greek, and a Lat. translation
by Jerome; they deal primarily with spiritual subjects,
and their cryptic language, a kind of "secret language," makes a spiritual use of the letters of the
Copt. alphabet. Also attributed to P. are some of the
→ *Apophthegmata Patrum* (*apophth.*). The *Monita
Sancti Pachomii* (*mon.*) are not authentic.

S: *vitae*, A. N. Athanassakis (n.p., 1975) [Greek text/English
trans.]. — H. v. Cranenburg (Brussels, 1969) [Latin text (of
Dionysius Exiguus)]. — F. Halkin, A.-J. Festugière
(Geneva, 1982), 11-72 [Greek text]. — L. T. Lefort, CSCO
89, 99f. [Coptic text]. — idem, CSCO 107 [Latin text]. — F.
Moscatelli (Padua, 1981) [Italian trans./comm.]. — A.
Veilleux, vol. 1 (Kalamazoo, Mich., 1980) [English trans.].
— idem, Abbaye de Bellefontaine (Bégrolles-en-Mauges,
1984) [French trans.]. — *vitae, paralipomena*, F. Halkin

(Brussels, 1932) [Greek text]. — *paralipomena*, E. A. W. Budge (London, 1904) (mistakenly referred to as the Rule of Pachomius) [English trans.]. — idem (Oxford, 1934), 373-416 [English trans.]. — F. Halkin, A.-J. Festugière (Geneva, 1982), 73-98, 123-145 [Greek text/French trans.]. W: *catech., ep.*, A. Veilleux, 2 (Kalamazoo, 1981f.), 141-195; 3:13-83 [French trans./comm.]. — *reg.*, L. T. Lefort, CSCO 159/160:30-36/30-37 [text/French trans. (frags.)]. — idem: Muséon 37 (1924) 1-28 [Greek and French trans. (frags.)]. — A. Boon (Leuven/Louvain, 1932), 169-182 [Greek trans. (frags.)]. — idem (Leuven/Louvain, 1932), 13-74 [Latin trans.]. — H. Bacht, 2 (Würzburg, 1983) [Latin trans./German trans./comm.]. — *catech.*, L. T. Lefort, CSCO 159/160:1-30/1-30) [text/French trans.]. — *ep.*, H. Quecke (Regensburg, 1975) [text/Greek trans.]. — idem, FS E. de Strycker (Antwerp/Utrecht, 1973), 655-663 [German trans.]. — A. Boon (Leuven/Louvain, 1932), 77-101 [Latin trans.]. — *apophth.*, PG 65:151, 303-306. — B. Miller (Trier, ³1986), 75, 196 [German trans.]. — *mon.*, A. Boon (Leuven/Louvain, 1932), 151f. [text].
L: H. Bacht, Vermächtnis 2 (Würzburg, 1983). — idem, Christusgemeinschaft: FS J. Betz (Düsseldorf, 1984), 444-455. — T. Baumeister, Mentalität: ZKG 88 (1977) 145-160. — idem, Forschungsstand: MThZ 40 (1989) 313-321. — E. Brunner-Traut, Kopten (Cologne, ²1994). — H. Chadwick, Idea of Sanctity: idem, History and Thought (London, 1982), 11-24. — J. E. Goehring, Heresy: Muséon 95 (1982) 241-262. — idem, New Frontiers: Egyptian Christianity, ed. A. Pearson Birger, J. E. Goehring (Philadelphia, 1986), 236-257. — G. Gould, Independent Monastic Community: SCH 23 (1986) 15-24. — H. Holze, Schrifterfahrung und Christuserkenntnis: ThZ 49 (1993) 54-65. — C. Joest, Abraham als Glaubensvorbild: ZNW 90 (1999) 98-122. — idem, Sinn der Armut: GuL 66 (1993) 249-271. — idem, Ursprüngliche Inspiration: EuA 67 (1991) 35-50. — T. G. Kardong, Monastic Practices: StMon 32 (1990) 59-78. — R. Lorenz, Chronologie: ZNW 80 (1989) 280-283. — I. Opelt, Dekodierungsversuch der P. briefe: FS J. Gribomont (Rome, 1988), 453-461. — eadem, Diktion: FS A. A. R. Bastiaensen (Steenbrugge, 1991), 249-253. — P. Rousseau, Community (Berkeley, 1985). — F. Ruppert, Gehorsam (Munsterschwarzach, 1971). — C. Scholten, Nag-Hammadi-Texte: JAC 31 (1988) 144-172. — W. Skudlarek (ed.), Continuing Quest for God (Collegeville, Minn., 1982). — A. Veilleux, Liturgie (Rome, 1968). — idem, Renoncement, CCist 43 (1981) 56-74. — idem, Monachisme et gnose: CCist 46 (1984) 239-258. — idem, Monasticism and Gnosis: Egyptian Christianity, ed. A. Pearson Birger, J. E. Goehring (Philadelphia, 1986), 271-306. — idem, P.: CoptE 6, 1859-1864.

M. SKEB, OSB

Pacian

P., bishop of Barcelona, who died before 392 (Jerome, *vir. ill.* 102), engaged in a controversy with an otherwise unknown → Sympronianus on the subject of Priscillianism. From the correspondence three *Ep. ad Sympronianum* have survived.

In the first letter P. coins the formula: "Christian is my name, Catholic my surname" (*ep.* 1.4). The sec-

ond letter is about the person of Novatian. In the third letter P. refutes a treatise on Novatianism which Sympronianus had sent him. Since P. almost always cites verbatim, the treatise can be reconstructed almost in its entirety.

In his *Paraenesis sive exhortatorius libellus ad paenitentiam* (*paraen.*) P. took up questions of penance; the work is important for the history of penance. The *Sermo de baptismo* (*bapt.*) speaks of human renewal and purification through faith and baptism. In a (lost) invective, *Cervulus* ("Little Stag"), P. railed against pagan survivals, espec. the mad doings on New Year's Day.

Two other works have been wrongly attributed to P.: *Ad Iustinum Manichaeum* and *De similitudine carnis peccati*.

W: C. Granado, C. Épitalon, M. Lestienne, SC 410. — L. Rubio Fernández (Barcelona, 1958) [text/Spanish trans.]. — *paraen.*, A. Anglada Anfruns (Valencia, 1983).
L: J. Borleffs, Zwei neue Schriften P.'?: Mn. 3/7 (1938/39) 180-192. — A. Gruber, Studien zu P., Diss. (Munich, 1901). — R. Kauer, Studien zu P. (Vienna, 1902). — P. Mattei, La figure de Novatien chez P. de Barcelone: Aug. 38 (1998) 355-370. — idem, Note sur l'influence de Cyrien dans un texte de P.: RTL 30 (1999) 180-194.

E. REICHERT

Palladius of Helenopolis

Most of the biog. details about P. must be gathered from his own works. He was born in Galatia in 363 or 364, was a disciple of Evagrius Pont., lived as a monk in Egypt from about 386 to 397, became bishop of Hellenopolis in Bithynia in 400, and of Aspuna in Galatia in 417, and died before 431.

In the *Historia Lausiaca* (*h. Laus.*; also titled *Lives of the Holy Fathers* and *Paradise*), which P. composed in 419/420 and dedicated to Lausus, a high official of Theodosius II, he describes in summary form (partly following the course of his own life, the manner of life of seventy-one ascetic men and women, some of whom he met personally on his journeys through Egypt and the Near East. He probably did not use Gr. or Copt. sources in the proper sense of the term. His purpose is the moral edification of the reader, since by his description of these ascetics for Christ's sake he wants to spur others to strive for the same kind of perfect virtue. The *h. Laus.* contains, among other things, descriptions of the lives of → Didymus the Blind, → Pachomius, Evagrius Pont., Melania the Elder, Olympias, Melania the Younger, and Pammachus. Anthony is not included, but the *Vita Antonii* of Athanasius is the literary model for the work. By and large, there is no noticeable idealizing tendency or theory of ascetical theology. P. also expressly includes descriptions of ascetics whose vanity caused their fall but who were able to return to the right path. Some characteristic traits are the accounts of miracles, the emphasis on excessive bodily asceticism, the marked individualism, the rule of silence, and the rejection of higher education by the ascetics. P.'s work contributed substantially to making known the ascetical ideal and is an important source on the beginnings, spread, and organization of ascetical monasticism as well as on its spiritual level. It enjoyed immense popularity, and there exist not only numerous recensions of the Gr. original (one by → Heraclidas of Nyssa), but also Lat., Syr., Copt., Arm., Georg., Arab., Eth., and Slav. translations, with new discoveries being constantly made. The many alterations in the text in the course of its transmission (interpolations, inclusion of content similar to that of another text, the → *Historia monachorum in Aegypto*) make it difficult to reconstruct the original form of the text.

The second, equally important source work composed by P. is his *Dialogus de vita S. Ioannis Chrysostomi* (*v. Chrys.*), whom P. knew personally and esteemed. In its form the work is in the tradition of Plato's *Phaedo* and was written probably in 408. In it a bishop not otherwise described relates the life of John Chrys. as a strong defense against his enemies; it also convinced Theodore, a Roman deacon, who is his partner in the dialogue.

Probably only the first part of *De gentibus Indiae et Bragmanibus* (*gent. Ind.*; an abridged Lat. translation titled *De moribus Brachmanorum* was at one time attributed to → Ambrose) was composed by P., after 408 or 412, as an appendix to *h. Laus* (*gent. Ind.* 1.1). It documents relations between the Chr. Roman empire and the Far East and contains, among other things, Christianized elements from the Romance of Alexander.

W: *h. Laus.*, C. Butler, 2 vols. (Cambridge, 1898/1904) [text]. — G. J. M. Bartelink, M. Barchiesi (Milan, 1974) [text/Italian trans.]. — L. Leloir et al. (Paris, 1981) [French trans.]. — R. T. Meyer, ACW 34 (Westminster, 1965) [English trans.]. — D. Schuetz (Freiburg i.Br., 1987) [text/German trans.]. — J. Laager (Zurich, 1987) [text/German trans.]. — *v. Chrys.*, P. R. Coleman-Norton (Cambridge, 1928). — A.-M. Malingrey, SC 341, 342. — R. T. Meyer, ACW 45 (New York, 1985) [text/English trans.]. — L. Schlaepfer (Düsseldorf, 1966) [text/German trans.]. — *gent. Ind.*, W. Berghoff (Meisenheim am Glan, 1967) [text]. — G. Desantis (Rome, 1992) [Italian trans.]. — T. Pritchard: CM 44 (1993) 109-139 [text of the Latin trans.].
L: D. F. Buck, The structure of the Lausiac history: Byz. 46 (1976) 292-307. — G. Bunge, Palladiana 1: Introduction aux fragments coptes de l'Histoire Lausiaque: StMon 32

(1990) 79-129. — J. D. M. Derrett, The History of "Palladius on the Races of India and the Brahmans": CM 21 (1960) 64-99. — G. M. De Durand, Evagre le Pontique et le Dialogue sur la vie de saint Jean Chrysostome: BLE 77 (1976) 191-206. — J. Gribomont, Le vieux corpus monastique du Vatican. Syr. 123: Muséon 100 (1987) 131-141. — S. Linnér, Syntaktische u. lexikalische Studien zur Historia Lausiaca des Palladios, Diss. (Uppsala, 1943). — E. Magheri Cataluccio, Il Lausiakon di Palladio tra semiotica e storia (Rome, 1984). — R. T. Meyer, Palladius as Biographer and Autobiographer: StPatr 17/1 (1982) 66-71. — C. Muckensturm-Poulle, Les Brahmanes de Palladios: Topoi Orient-Occident 3 (1993) 535-545. — R. Stoneman, Who are the Brahmans?: CQ 44 (1994) 500-510. — C. Vinassa, La donna nella Storia Lausiaca di P.: Quaderni del Dipartimento di Filologia, Linguistica e Tradizione Classica (To) 4 (1995) 173-192. — K. Vogt, La moniale folle du monastère des Tabennésiotes: SO 62 (1987) 95-108 (on *h. Laus.* 34). — A. De Vogüé, Palladiana 2: La version copte de l'Histoire Lausiaque: StMon 32 (1990) 323-339. — W. H. Willis, K. Maresch, The Encounter of Alexander with the Brahmans: ZPE 74 (1988) 59-83 (on part 2 of *gent. Ind.*).

K. POLLMANN

Palladius of Rathiaria

P., bishop of Rathiaria in Illyria 346-381, was deposed at the Ambrose-controlled Synod of Aquileia (autumn 381) for heresy dangerous to the state. P. then composed an attack on the first two books of Ambrose's *De fide* (*C. Ambr.*) and an extensive defense (*Apol.*) that has survived in fragments in a single ms. As a theologian P. is located entirely within homoean teaching on the Trinity (legally prohibited since *Cod. Theod.* 16.1.2 of Feb. 28, 380): Father and Son act *similiter* (fol. 336^r.8), but they are not *similis* in their substance. P. rejects the (Neo-) Nicene concept of *homoousia* because it supposedly offends against the *proprietates personarum* (fol. 336^v.50). Ambrose's polemic unjustly connects P. with the Anhomoeans Eunomius and Aetius and with Arius.

W: *C. Ambr.*, *Apol.*, R. Gryson, SC 267:264-324. — idem, CCL 87:172-195.
L: Y.-M. Duval, Présentation: RHE 76 (1981) 317-331. — R. Gryson, op. cit., 83-97. — R. P. C. Hanson, Search (Edinburgh, 1988), 562-579, 595f., 667-669. — C. Markschies, Ambrosius (Tübingen, 1995), 124-133. — N. McLynn, Apology: JThS 42 (1991) 52-76. — M. Meslin, Ariens (Paris, 1967), 85-92. — H. J. Sieben, Konzilsidee (Paderborn, 1979), 485-487.

J. ULRICH

Palladius of Suedri

The written request of P., an ascetic concerned with theology, that → Epiphanius of Salamis would explain questions of pneumatology that were being controverted in P.'s home community of Suedri (in the region of Pamphylia in Asia Minor) elicited from the Cypriote bishop his *Ancoratus* ("The Firmly Anchored Man").

W: PG 43:13-16. — K. Holl, GCS 25:3f.
L: C. Riggi, Epifanio (Rome, 1977), 35-37.

W. A. Löhr

Pamphilus of Caesarea

P., born in Berytus (Beirut), studied in Alexandria in the school of Pierius. In Caesarea of Palestine he enlarged the library set up by Origen. He was ordained a priest by Bishop Agapius but was arrested in 307 under governor Urbanus. While in prison, he, along with his disciple Eusebius of Caesarea (who acc. to P. called himself Eusebius Pamphilou), wrote a defense of Origen. Under Emperor Maximinus Daia, P. was beheaded on Feb. 16, 310, by order of governor Firminian (Eus., *h.e.* 7.32.25; 8.13.6; *m. P.* 7.4-6; 11.2-3; 14), Eusebius's biography of P. in three books is lost.

The defense of Origen originally contained six books, of which the first five were jointly composed by P. and Eusebius. P.'s introductory letter is addressed to the confessors condemned to labor in the mines. Book 1 assembles passages from Origen (espec. from *De principiis*) that are intended to prove his orthodoxy against the accusations of the anti-Origenists in the first Origenist controversy. The passages have to with the Trinity, the incarnation, the conception of scripture, the resurrection, punishment of sinners, the doctrine of the soul, and the transmigration of souls. Only this first book has survived in the translation by Rufinus (together with the latter's work on *The Falsification of the Books of Origen*). Even though the original text contained primarily harmless passages, Rufinus toned down suspect features (e.g., subordinationist tendencies) in view of the changed situation since the Council of Nicaea; Jerome blamed him for this (*adv. Ruf.* 2.15; 3.12). Books 2-5 presumably dealt with the life and writings of Origen. After P.'s death Eusebius collected in a sixth book P.'s letters on the orthodoxy of Origen (Eus., *h.e.* 6.36.3f.). Jerome claimed (*adv. Ruf.* 1.8; *ep.* 84.11) that the apology had been composed entirely by (Arian) Eusebius and that the latter had simply wanted to give it the martyr's authority. In fact, Jerome, an anti-Origenist, seemed to be challenging the authorship of the orthodox martyr P., something which even Photius, an opponent of Ori-

gen, attests (*cod.* 118). The second defense described by Photius (*cod.* 117) is not the same as that of P. but was written in the context of the Origenist controversies at the end of the 4th c. Ca. 460 → Antipater of Bostra composed a *Refutatio* of the "Apology of Eusebius," but only fragments of this have been preserved (PG 85:1791-94; 86/2:2045-53, 2077; 96:468 and 488-511).

W: PG 17:521-616.
L: W. A. Bienert, Die älteste Apologie für Origenes?: Origeniana Quarta, ed. L. Lies (Innsbruck, 1987), 123-127. — E. Hoffmann-Aleith, P.: PRE 18/2:349. — E. Junod, L'Apologie pour Origène par P.: Origeniana Quinta, ed. R. Daly (Oxford, 1993), 519-527. — idem, L'auteur de l'Apologie pour Origène: FS H. Crouzel (Paris, 1992), 165-179. — idem, Origène vu par P.: Origeniana Quarta, ed. L. Lies (Innsbruck, 1987), 128-135. — P. Nautin, Origène (Paris, 1977), 99-153. — A. Reymond, "Apologie pour Origène": Un état de la question: Origeniana Quarta, ed. L. Lies (Innsbruck, 1987), 136-145. — R. Williams, Damnosa haereditas: FS L. Abramowski (Berlin, 1993), 151-169.

G. Röwekamp

Pamphilus of Jerusalem (Theologian)

A P. of Jerusalem (not to be confused with the like-named friend of Cosmas the Traveler to India or with the anti-Chalcedonian 5th-c. deacon) wrote against the Monophysitism of Severus of Antioch. In his major work, *Kephalaia diaphorōn lysis* (*sol.*), which has once again been attributed to him with the help of the *Doctrina Patrum* and which is to be dated between 560 and 630, P. used Leontius of Byzantium and the *Confessio rectae fidei* of Justinian. The work, which belongs to the genre of → *Quaestiones et responsiones*, was originally published under the title of *Panoplia*. Also under P.'s name is an encomium (*enc.*) of the Roman martyr Soteria, who was also venerated in Jerusalem.

W: *sol., enc.,* H. Declerck, P. Allen, CCG 19. — *enc.,* P. Franchi de Cavalieri, Hagiographica = StT 19 (Rome, 1908), 113-120 [text].
L: A. Grillmeier, "O Kyriakos anthropos": Traditio 33 (1977) 1-63. — J. P. Junglas, Leontius (Paderborn, 1906). — L. Perrone, La chiesa di Palestina (Brescia, 1980), 28-38. — M. Richard, P.: Muséon 90 (1977) 277-280. — idem, Léonce et P.: RSPhTh 27 (1938) 27-52.

G. Röwekamp

Panegyric

"I was preparing to deliver my eulogy of the emperor in which it was impossible not to lie, with the lies bringing the favor of the well-informed." The art of the showpiece address as practiced by Gorgias and

Isocrates in classical Greece found an echo in speeches lauding emperors and high-ranking officials; the delivery of such speeches was among the tasks of the young Augustine, who had been called to teach rhetoric in the imperial city of Milan and who in the passage just cited refers to an undelivered speech in the presence of Emperor Valentinian II in 385 and speaks elsewhere of a similar speech in honor of Bauto, a statesman. It was the task of instruction in rhetoric to provide future statesmen with the basic model and the devices that would make such speeches linguistic and stylistic works of art. In his panegyric of Constantius II (or. 1; 356/357) the future Emperor Julian carefully observed the rules set down by rhetorician Menander in his chapter on *Basilikos logos*.

Under the title of *Panegyrici latini* there has come down from late antiquity a collection of models in which Pliny's panegyric of Trajan, the classic example of the genre, is followed by three laudatory addresses of outstanding orators: that of Pacatus in honor of Emperor Theodosius (389), that of Mamertinus in honor of Julian (362), and that of Nazarius in honor of Constantine (312), as well as eight shorter panegyrics delivered at the end of the 3rd and beginning of the 4th c. in the imperial city of Trier and in Autun. These various addresses, turned into rhetorical exemplars by removal of names, give an insight into the renowned instruction in rhetoric in Gaul. This tradition was cultivated until the end of Roman antiquity; at the beginning of the 7th c. Isidore says: "The panegyric is an unbridled and frivolous type of address in praise of kings, in the composition of which men are flattered by numerous lies" (*orig.* 6.8.7). Once the pagan instructional system disappeared, a lack of interest meant that hardly anything of that tradition was preserved. Lost is the panegyric, praised by Jerome and mentioned by Gennadius, of Paulinus of Nola in praise of Theodosius's victory over tyrants Maximus and Eugene (394/395) in which the speaker showed the emperor more as a servant of Christ than as a ruler (see Paulinus, *ep.* 28.3; Jerome, *ep.* 58.8; Gennadius, *vir. ill.* 49). The only panegyrics preserved are those of Ausonius on Gratian (379), Flavius → Merobaudes on Aetius (437), and → Ennodius on Theodoric (506/507), and fragments of panegyrics by orators Symmachus (4th c.) and Cassiodorus (6th c.).

Whereas the Middle Ages showed little interest in the *Panegyrici latini* collection of models, a collection of poems, known as *Panegyricus Constantini*, by Publilius Optatianus → Porfyrius (d. before 335) was given an unexpectedly warm reception in the insular and Carolingian worlds where its affected use of letters and verse was imitated.

Following the Gr. tradition (of which however nothing is preserved), → Claudian, the Lat. poet from Alexandria, combined historical epic and praise of rulers in his poetic panegyrics of the consulates of Emperor Honorius (396, 398, and 404) and the Vandal Stilicho (400) and of the consuls for the years 395 and 399. In his unfinished *laus Serenae* for the daughter of Honorius and wife of Stilicho he composed the first Lat. panegyric in honor of a woman; that had already been done in Gr. by the future Emperor Julian in honor of Eusebia, the wife of Constantius II (or. 3; 356/357). Following Claudian's model, poetic panegyrics of rulers were composed by → Apollinaris Sidonius (for Avitus, Majoran, and Anthemius; 5th c.), Merobaudes (446 for Aetius), → Priscian (512 for Anastasius), and → Corippus (for Justin, soon after 564).

In the 4th c., Christians applied the rhetorical tradition of the *basilikos logos* to the martyrs and thus created the new genre of the panegyrical sermon on the martyrs, a genre practiced espec. by the great Cappadocians. In Basil's address on Mamas (PG 31:589-600) there is a statement of principle on the pagan model of Christian panegyric. It was also the Cappadocians who used the genre for other saints as well. The term panegyric can thus be used in a broader sense for praise in any form, for the *encomium* or *laudatio/laus*.

L: HLL 5:161-172. — T. Payr, Enkomion: RAC 5:332-343. — K. Ziegler, P.: PRE 36:559-581.

M. ZELZER

Panodorus

P., like → Anianus the chronicler who used his work, was an Egyptian monk who between 395 and 408 composed a universal chronicle that begins with creation (the birth of Christ is assigned the year 5493). It is preserved only in remnants by George Syncellus, who praises the accuracy of the work. P.'s principal source was → Julius Africanus; in addition he was interested in sources for Egyptian and Babylonian history, the contents of which he fits into the chronology of the OT. He also goes back to Eusebius's chronicle, the dates of which, however, he criticizes in an exacting way, espec. since he brushes Eusebius off as an Arian. On the whole, the work is a late antique synthesis of Chr. and pagan historiography and culture.

W: Georgios Synkellos, ed. A. Mosshammer (Leipzig, 1984).

L: W. Adler, Berossus, Manetho and 1 Enoch in the World Chronicle of P.: HThR 76 (1983) 419-442. — idem, Time Immemorial (Washington, 1989), 72-105. — A. Bauer, J. Strzygowski, Eine alexandrinische Weltchronik (Vienna, 1905), 83f. — H. Gelzer, Sextus Julius Africanus 2/1 (Leipzig, 1885), 189-204. — O. Seel, P.: PRE 18/2:632-635.

K. FITSCHEN

Paphnutius

P. is the name of two Egyptian monks of the 4th c.: a P. Cephalas (possibly identical with P. Babal), and a P. without a surname. To the first of the two is attributed (but without certainty) some of the → *Apophthegmata Patrum* (*apophth.*), to the second the *Vita* of Onuphrius, a monk of the desert (*vit. Onu.*).

W: *apophth.*, PG 65:377-380. — L. Regnault (Solesmes, 1981), 270-272 [French trans.]. — B. Miller (Trier, ³1986), 256-259 [German trans.]. — *vit. Onu.*, E. A. Budge (London, 1914), 205-224, 455-473 [Coptic text/English trans.]. L: A. Guillaumont, P. of Scetis: CoptE 7:1884.

M. SKEB, OSB

Papias of Hierapolis

P. was bishop of his native city Hierapolis in Phrygia (Eus., *h.e.* 3.36.2; 1.15.2), which is also mentioned in Rev 3:14-22. There the Chr. faith had been preached by Epaphras, a fellow worker of Paul (see Col 4:12f.). Acc. to a later legend, P. died a martyr's death. Irenaeus describes him as an *archaios anēr* (*haer.* 5.33.4). Eusebius for his part describes P. as "man of small intelligence" (*smikros ōn ton noun*: *h.e.* 3.39.13). He had a great influence on later theologians (e.g., Irenaeus, Hippolytus of Rome, Victorinus of Pettau) because of his work, written ca. 130/140, but preserved only in fragments, titled *The Sayings of the Lord Explained in Five Books* (*Logiōn kyriakōn exēgēseōs syggrammata pente*). From the citations and excerpts in, e.g., Irenaeus and Eusebius it seems that P. was not interested in a commentary on the sayings of Jesus but in a collection of older reports on the words and deeds of Jesus, along with interpretive information. Probably the most important fragment is an introduction to the gospels of Mk and Mt (Eus., *h.e.* 3.39.15f.). P. here justifies the gospel of Mk, which he expressly ascribes to "Mark, who had been Peter's interpreter"; this gospel, he says, is careful and reliable in its representation of the "instructions" of Peter; any defects in literary skill (*taxis*) are owing to the apostle's unpretentious way of thinking. It is in connection with this that the reference to the gospel of Mt is to be read; its author is said to have compiled "the sayings of Jesus in the Hebrew language." What is probably meant is that the gospel of Mt is written in a Semitic-Jewish idiom; acc. to the final sentence of the fragment each evangelist presented his reflections (*hermeneuein*) acc. to his linguistic abilities. Only because of Origen was the assumption made that there was originally a Hebrew gospel of Mt. It cannot be said with certainty on the basis of P.'s testimony that he also knew the gospel of Luke, Acts, and the Pauline letters; it may be suspected but not said with certainty that an anti-Marcionite reaction or antignostic motives were the reason for his silence about them.

W: K. Bihlmeyer, Die Apostolischen Väter (Tübingen, ²1956), 133-140. — E. Preuschen, Antilegomena (Giessen, ²1905), 91-99, 195-202 [text/German trans.]. — U. Körtner, SUC 3 (Darmstadt, 1998), 3-103 [text/German trans./comm.].
L: H. J. Körtner, P. (Göttingen, 1983). — W. G. Kümmel, Einleitung in das NT (Heidelberg, 1973). — J. Kürzinger, Das P.-zeugnis u. die Erstgestalt des Mt: BZ 4 (1960) 19-38. — idem, P. u. die Evangelien des NT (Regensburg, 1983). — B. M. Metzger, The Canon of the NT (Oxford, 1987), 51-56. — (A. Wikenhauser), J. Schmid, Einleitung in das NT (Freiburg i.Br., 1973).

A. SAND

Parmenian

P. (b. after 362; d. before 393) was the successor of Donatus as bishop of Carthage (Aug., *retr.* 2.43.1); he was probably of non-African descent (Optatus 1.5) and may have migrated to Africa as a result of measures taken by Emperor Julian (Optatus, *c. Parm.* 2.17). Despite the drawback of not being an African, P. soon played so central a role in Donatism that the Donatists were sometimes called "Parmenians" (Aug., *haer.* 41); his rise was due to pastoral skill, his rhetorical gifts, and his many writings.

P. must have died before the Council of Cebarsussi (June 24, 393), since this council mentions Primianus as bishop of Carthage.

P.'s writings are lost, but citations in → Optatus and → Augustine show the basic lines of his theol. thought. These correspond to the traditional Donatist themes: baptism is paralleled with the flood, baptism in the Jordan, and circumcision; sacraments given by an unworthy minister are invalid (Optatus, *c. Parm.* 1.5). In his ecclesiology P. emphasized the unity of the church, defended the exclusion of heretics, and referred to the sinful failure of the Cath. Church in the *traditio*.

P. is important in the history of theology because of his controversy with → Tyconius. The lost letter addressed to Tyconius (Aug., *c. ep.Parm.* 1.1) forced

Augustine to a detailed examination of the arguments of P. and, along with the theses of Tyconius, caused him to develop his own ecclesiology. Acc. to Augustine's report, P. told Tyconius that the latter's presentation of Donatist history needed revision; that only the church of Africa was the true and pure church; and that Tyconius should give up the idea of a universal church. It was with these truths in mind that Tyconius should interpret the scriptures. P. also reproached Tyconius for his references to the impure and the *traditores* in the Donatists' own ranks. Tyconius (P. said) showed a certain inconsistency; he was therefore urged to do away with this and remain a Donatist.

W: Optatus, *c. Parm.*, C. Ziwsa, CSEL 26. — Augustine, *c. ep. Parm.*, M. Petschenig, CSEL 51:19-141.
L: PAC 816-821.

W. GEERLINGS

Parthemius

P. (the name also appears as Parthenius) was a priest of Carthage in the 5th or 6th c. A letter of his to a *comes* Sigisteus has survived (*Parthemii presbyteri rescriptum ad Sigisteum*; *rescr.*); it is an answer to a letter from Sigisteus, a Vandal (PLS 3:447f.). The letter, which praises Sigisteus, begins in prose and ends with a poetic *conclusio* in twelve hexameters and a distich.

W: *rescr.*, A. Reifferscheid, Anecdota Casinensia (Breslau, 1871), 4 [text]. — *conclusio*, M. G. Bianco, I versi di P.: Disiecti membra poetae. Studi di poesia latina in frammenti, ed. V. Tandoi, 3 (Foggia, 1988), 243-275 [text/comm.]. — A. Riese (ed.), Anthologia Latina 1/2 (Amsterdam, ²1964 = Leipzig, ²1906), Nr. 763a.
L: M. G. Bianco, Uno scambio di epistole: AFLF(M) 21 (1988) 399-431. — A. Di Berardino (ed.), Patrologia 4 (Genoa, 1996), 48. — M. Schanz, C. Hosius, G. Krüger, Geschichte der röm. Lit. 4/2 (Munich, 1959 = 1920), 324.

B. WINDAU

Parthenius

Concerning P., a presbyter and archimandrite in Constantinople, only a little information can be derived from his 5th.-c. letter to the Nestorian-minded metropolitan → Alexander of Hierapolis (*Ep. Parthenii presbyteri et archimandritae ad deo amicissimum episcopum Alexandrum*). It deals evidently with a letter that Alexander sent to Theodoret for his instruction (Rusticus Deacon, *syn.* 152). In his letter, which is also preserved in Latin by Rusticus (*syn.* 153), P. shows his esteem for Nestorius. The P.

for or against whom → Gennadius I of Constantinople composed a work (Leontius and John, *sacr.*; PG 86/2:2044) may be identical with our P.

W: PG 84:767f. — ACO 1, 4, 175f. [Latin text].
L: G. T. Stokes, P. 3: DCB 4:194.

B. WINDAU

Pascentius

P., an African and a *comes* at the imperial court, gained notoriety through his controversy with Augustine (between 404 and 411). The public debate on the creed to which P. had challenged Augustine and which took place in Carthage was reflected in an exchange of letters. Augustine responded with two letters to a campaign begun by P. in which he boasted of having bested Augustine (*ep.* 238-39); P. answered with a single letter (Aug., *ep.* 240). An apocryphal document (*Altercatio cum Pascentio Ariano*), which depicts a new debate between the two men and was wrongly attributed to Augustine, dates probably from the 5th or 6th c.

W: *ep.*, A. Goldbacher, CSEL 42:559f. — *altercatio*, PL 33:1156-1162.
L: A. Di Berardino (ed.), Patrologia 3 (Turin, 1983), 381. — PAC 1070-1075. — M. Schanz, C. Hosius, G. Krüger, Geschichte der röm. Lit. 4/2 (Munich, 1959 =1920), 570.

B. WINDAU

Paschasius of Dumium

In 550-555 P., a deacon and monk in Dumium, at the wish of his abbot (Martin of Braga) translated into Latin a Gr. collection of sayings of the fathers, which the abbot had probably brought from the East to Spain. Various titles are used for this translation: *Verba seniorum, Geronticon,* or *Liber geronticon de octo principalibus vitiis.* The collection of apophthegmata, organized acc. to virtues (and vices), was partly integrated into the *Vitae patrum* (PL 73:1025-66). The extent to which P. may have used existing Lat. translations will emerge only when the relationship of his work to similar collections has been adequately clarified.

It cannot be regarded as proved that P. also wrote a life of St. Thais (PL 73:661-64). The *De spiritu sancto* earlier attributed to P. is from → Faustus of Riez.

W: PL 73:1025-1066. — J. G. Freire (Coimbra, 1971) [text]. — Commonitiones Sanctorum Patrum (Coimbra, 1974) [text/comm.]. — C. W. Barlow, FaCh 62 [English trans./comm.].

L: J. G. Freire, A verso latina por Pascásio de Dume dos Apophthegmata Patrum (Coimbra, 1971).

E. REICHERT

Paschasius of Rome

P. was a deacon in Rome. During the Laurentian schism he sided with the antibishop Lawrence against Symmachus. He died ca. 514 and after his death was venerated as a saint. Gregory the Great, who passed a favorable judgment on him despite his siding with Lawrence (Gregory attributed this to P.'s ignorance), attributes to him a work *De spiritu sancto* (*dial.* 4.40), which is however lost. A surviving work with the same title, which was identified as P.'s work, is from → Faustus of Riez. All we have from P. is a letter (*ep.*) of 513 to Abbot → Eugippius. P. is answering a letter of Eugippius, who sent P. his *Vita* of St. Severinus and asked him to review and correct it. P. courteously declines to do so and simply praises Eugippius's work.

W: P. Knöll, CSEL 9/2:68-70. — R. Noll (Berlin, 1963), 46-49 [text/German trans.]. — P. Régerat, SC 374:156-161.
L: A. Amore, P.: BSS 10:347. — HKG(J) 2/2:198f. — M. Schanz, C. Hosius, G. Krüger, Geschichte der röm. Lit. 4/2 (Munich, 1959 = 1920), 542, 587

B. WINDAU

Pastor

P. was a 5th-c. bishop, perhaps in Galicia (Palencia?). There is disagreement on whether P. is to be identified with the Bishop Pastor consecrated in 433 (Hydatius, *chron.* 2.22). Acc. to Gennadius (*vir. ill.* 77), P. wrote a *Libellus in modum symboli* (*libell.*), in which he distinguished between prevailing church teaching and heretical views and attacked the supporters of Priscillian by name. The work, thought to have been lost, is preserved in the acts of the first Synod of Toledo (400 or 405) (a longer version of the so-called *Symbolum Toletanum* I, before 447?). The *libell.* is important for the study of anti-Priscillianism.

W: I. A. de Adama, El símbolo Toledano I (Rome, 1934), 30-37 [text]. — DH 95-98 [text/German trans.].
L: H. Chadwick, Priscillian (Oxford, 1976). — K. Künstle, Antipriscilliana (Freiburg i.Br., 1905). — G. Morin, P. et Syagrius: RBen 10 (1893) 385-394.

E. REICHERT

Paterius

P., 6th/7th c., was a Roman notary and *secundericus* of Gregory the Great (John the Deacon, *Vita Gregorii*

2.11). He wanted to collect the explanations of chosen passages of scripture that were scattered throughout Gregory's writings, espec. the *Moralia*, and organize them acc. to their bibl. sequence. Of what were probably originally three parts (two for the OT, one for the NT) only the *Liber testimoniorum veteris testamenti* down to the Song of Songs has survived. The two following parts (PL 79:917-1136) are not from P. but are a continuation from the 12th c.; this continuation is not the same as that of someone named Bruno, whose preface is preserved (PL 79:681-84).

W: PL 79:683-916.
L: R. Étaix, Le Liber Testimoniorum de P.: RSR 32 (1958) 66-78. — F. Wotke, Paterios 2: PRE 18/4:2159f.

B. WINDAU

Patrick

P., born ca. 389 with the name Sucat in Bannavem Tabernicae (Roman Britain), was dragged off to Ireland by pirates ca. 405. In 411 he escaped and returned to Britain. He became a disciple of Germanus of Auxerre and in 432 was consecrated by him as successor of Palladius, the first bishop of Ireland. His episcopal seat was Armagh in the province of Ulster. In 457 P. passed his office on to his successor Benignus; he died in 461/492 (?). P.'s chief service was the evangelization of the still pagan parts of Ireland (espec. the west), the building up of the eccles. organization, and the closer linking of the Irish church to Rome.

P.'s principal work, the *Confessions* (*conf.*), composed ca. 461, is intended, like the *Confessions* of Augustine, as an account of his life and faith in response to his enemies and, again like Augustine, stresses the unconditional dependence of human beings on the grace of God (a clear separation of himself from Irish Pelagianism). In his *Ep. ad milites Corotici* (*ep. ad C.*), written shortly before, P. criticizes the killing and abduction of Irish Christians by Coroticus, a Chr. Scottish chieftain, and threatens him with excommunication. Other works originally attributed to P.—*Ep. ad episcopos in Campo* (*ep. ad episc.*), *Dicta Patricii* (*dict.*), and *Synodus episcoporum* (*syn.*)—are probably not his. The author of the *Hymnus S. Patricii* (*hymn.*), an encomium written in P.'s lifetime, was probably P.'s nephew and episcopal coadjutor, Secundinus.

W: *ep. ad C.*, PL 53:813. — L. Bieler, Liber epistolarum S. Patricii: CM 11 (1950) 91-102 [text]. — N. J. D. White, Liber S. Patricii: Proceedings of the Royal Irish Academy,

Section C, 25 (1904/05) 542-552 [text/English trans.]. — *conf.*, PL 53:801. — L. Bieler, op. cit., 56-91 [text]. — N. J. D. White, op. cit., 201-326 [text/English trans.]. — *hymn.*, PL 53:837. — PL 72:590 [text]. — L. Bieler: Proceedings of the Royal Irish Academy 55 (1953), 117-127 [text]. — *syn.*, PL 53:823 [text]. — A. W. Haddan, W. Stubbs, Councils and Ecclesiastical Documents relating to Great Britain and Ireland 2/2 (Oxford, 1878), 328-331 [text]. — *ep. ad episc.*, P. Grosjean: AB 62 (1944) 44 [text]. — L. Bieler, Liber epistolarum, 104 [text]. — *dict.* 3a, E. Hogan, Vita S. Patricii (Brussels, 1886), 57 [text]. — L. Bieler, Liber epistolarum, 105 [text].
L: E. Amann, P.: DThC 11/2, 2297-2301. — L. Bieler, The life and legend of St. P. (Dublin, 1949). — M. O'Carroll, P.: DSp 12/1:477-483. — R. P. C. Hanson, St. P. (Oxford, 1968). — C. E. Stancliffe, Kings and Conversions: FMSt 14 (1980) 59-94. — C. Thomas, Christianity in Roman Britain to AD 500 (London, 1981), esp. 295-346.

C. Schmidt

Paul, Literature about

The genuine writings of P. played an important role as "chief authority" for the gnostic understanding of Christianity in various groups in the early church. Despite this, relatively few specifically gnostic writings have come down under the name of Paul.

L: E. Dassmann, Der Stachel im Fleisch (Münster, 1979). — H. F. Weiss, P. u. die Häretiker. Zum P.-Verständnis in der Gnosis: Christentum u. Gnosis, ed. W. Eltester (Berlin, 1969), 116-128.

1. Pseudepigraphical writings: A supposed letter of P. to the Laodiceans (*Laod.*) has come down only in Latin. This is a rather arbitrary collection of citations from P.; the letter was intended to fill a gap in the Pauline corpus that is suggested by Col 4:16. It is unclear whether the letter is identical with the *Laod.* condemned in the *Canon Muratori*, along with the (lost) letter of the Alexandrians, as Marcionite forgeries; it is unclear espec. because our letter shows no Marcionite tendencies. Acc. to Tertullian, *adv. Marc.* 5.11.17, the Marcionites gave the name *Laod.* to Eph. In light of all this the time (2nd-4th c.) and place (the West) of origin can only be conjectured. (On the so-called 3 Cor, see below.)

W: A. v. Harnack, Apocrypha IV (KlT 12) (Berlin, ²1931) [text]. — NTApo⁵ 2:43f. [German trans.]. — M. Erbetta, Gli Apocrifi del NT 3 (Turin, 1981), 63-67 [Italian trans.].
L: R. Y. Ebied, A Triglot Volume of the Laod: Bib. 47 (1966) 243-255. — A. v. Harnack, Marcion (Darmstadt, 1960 = ²1924), 124*-149*. — HLL 4:414f. — K. Pink, Die ps.-paulinischen Briefe: Bib. 6 (1925) 179-192. — G. Quispel, De Laod: NedThT 5 (1950) 43-46. — L. Vouaux, Les actes de Paul (Paris, 1913), 315-326.

A supposed secret correspondence between P. and Seneca is first attested by Jerome (*vir. ill.* 12; see also Aug., *ep.* 153.14) and was considered authentic down into the 15th c. The content of the fourteen letters is philosophical and of little theol. importance; they contain primarily manifestations of friendship. Seneca finds fault with the style of P.'s letters. The eleventh letter is espec. notable, concerning as it does the burning of Rome and the persecution of Christians, with the author drawing on an unknown source. This letter is possibly later than the other letters, which were written in the 4th c. The collection may possibly be an exercise in the schools of rhetoric; there is perhaps a connection with the attempt to link Seneca to Judaism by means of a fictive letter of high priest Anna against idolatry (Ps.- → Seneca).

W: PLS 1:673-678. — C. W. Barlow, Epistolae Senecae, PMAAR 10 (Rome, 1938). — L. Barlow (Rome, 1983) [text/English trans.]. — L. Bocciolini Palagi, BPat (Florence, 1985) [text/comm.]. — NTApo⁵ 2:44-50 [German trans.].
L: HLL 5:404-407. — A. Fürst, Pseudepigraphie und Apostolizität im apokryphen Briefwechsel zwischen Seneca und Paulus: JAC 41 (1998) 77-117. — A. Kurfess, Der Brand Roms u. die Christenverfolgung im Jahre 64 n. Chr.: Mn. 3. Ser. 6 (1938) 261-272. — idem, Zu dem apokryphen Briefwechsel: Aevum 26 (1952) 42-48. — H. Leclercq, Sénèque et P.: DACL 15/1:1193-1198. — A. Momigliano, La Leggenda del cristianesimo di Seneca: RSIt 62 (1950) 325-344. — L. D. Reynolds, The Medieval Tradition of Seneca's Letters (Leiden, 1965). — J. N. Sevenster, P. and Seneca (Leiden, 1971). — W. Trillitzsch, Seneca im lit. Urteil der Antike 1 (Amsterdam, 1971), 170-185.

The so-called *Prayer of the Apostle Paul* is found in NHC 1, 1, and is a gnostic psalm of ascents that shows similarities with the Manichean psalms and the deathbed prayer in *2 Apoc. Jac.* There may be connections with the Valentinian school; it is not possible to date the *Prayer* more precisely than to the period from the second half of the 2nd c. to the end of the 3rd c.

W: H. W. Attridge, NHC 1 (Leiden, 1985), 5-11 [text/English trans./comm.].
L: R. Kasser, Oratio Pauli: Tractatus Tripartita II et III (Bern, 1975).

2. Acts: *Acta Pauli* (*A. Paul.*) are first attested in Tertullian (*bapt.* 17), who describes them as "forged." Hippolytus and Origen seem to use them without hesitation; in Eusebius (*h.e.* 3.3.5) they are, as is the *Shepherd* of Hermas, not canonical but also not rejected as heretical. Jerome, on the other hand, describes them as apocryphal (*vir. ill.* 7); for this reason and because of their use by the Manichees they were increasingly rejected.

The *A. Paul.* have unfortunately not reached us complete; the most important textual witnesses are a Gr. papyrus of Hamburg (PH), written ca. 300, and a Copt. papyrus of Heidelberg (PHeid) from the 6th c. With the help of the surviving passages one may hypothesize that the *A. Paul.* described a single journey of Paul from Damascus (conversion), via Asia Minor, Syria, Ephesus (with the incident of the baptized wolf), Asia Minor again, and Greece, to Rome. In many places, acc. to the *A. Paul.*, Paul found an existing Chr. community, making it clear that the conception in Acts is lacking in the narrative *A. Paul.* Whether the author knew Acts is disputed. It is more likely that he did know (the not yet canonical) Acts but that his work shows no literary dependence on Acts.

Three sets of material in the *A. Paul.* have their own transmission history. (1) The → (*Acts of*) *Thecla* (conversion of Thecla in Iconium, her self-baptism and sermon). On the one hand, older material is here being used; on the other, the new acts were soon handed on independently. (2) The so-called third letter to the Corinthians, which P. supposedly wrote from Philippi, after a letter (likewise transmitted) asking about an error had reached him. This material was accepted into Arm. Bibles and into the commentaries of Ephraem on Paul (preserved in Armenian). In some mss. (e.g., PHeid) it is handed down, with an introduction and transitional report, as part of the *A. Paul.* As for its content, 3 Cor summarily and apodictically rejects the error; only in the question of the resurrection is it more understanding and vivid. (3) The Lat. *Martyrium Pauli apostoli a Lino conscripto* (BHL 2:6570) represents a revision of the concluding section of *A. Paul.*, but in the form of an imitation of the *Passio Pauli brevior* (BHG 2:1451f.; BHL 2:6571).

The *A. Paul.* are of no special theol. interest, except for the promotion of continence which, acc.to *A. Paul.*, is attractive to many women as a form of autonomy. On the whole, in the *A. Paul.* the person of Paul is made productive for popular piety. Controversy with Judaism is completely lacking Eccles. offices play no role; the emphasis is on the Spirit and its effects. The Eucharist is celebrated with water and bread. This setting has at least similarities with Montanism, but the *A. Paul.* need not be attributed to that movement. On the basis of Tertullian's witness, the period shortly before 200 is to be assumed as the time of composition; Asia Minor is the place of origin.

W: AAAp 1:23-44 [text], 104-117 (*Martyrium Pauli*), 235-272 (*ActTh*) [text]. — C. Schmidt, A. Paul. aus der Heidelberger kopt. Papyrushs. Nr 1 (Hildesheim, 1965 = ²1905)

[Coptic text]. — idem, Πράξεις Παύλου. Nach dem PH (Glückstadt, 1936) [Greek text]. — NTApo⁵ 2:214-243 [German trans.]. — L. Vouaux (Paris, 1913) [Greek text/French trans.].
L: F. Bovon et al., Les Actes Apocryphes des Apôtres (Geneva, 1981), 71-93, 109-119, 141-158. — P. Devos, Actes de Thomas et Actes de Paul: AnBoll 69 (1951) 119-130. — H. J. W. Drijvers, Der getaufte Löwe: Akten des C.-Schmidt-Kolloquiums (Halle, 1988). — HLL 4:394-396. — R. Kasser, A. Paul.: RHPhR 40 (1960) 45-57. — A. F. J. Klijn, The Apocryphal Correspondence: VigChr 17 (1963) 2-23. — D. R. MacDonald, The Legend and the Apostle (Philadelphia, 1983). — J. Rohde, Studia Evangelica 5, TU 103 (Berlin, 1968), 303-310. — W. Rordorf, Die neronische Christenverfolgung: NTS 28 (1981) 365-374. — idem, In welchem Verhältnis stehen die apokryphen A. Paul. zur kanonischen Apg?: FS F. J. Klijn (Kampen, 1988), 225-241. — idem, Nochmals A. Paul. u. Pastoralbriefe: FS E. Earle Ellis (Grand Rapids, Mich., 1987), 319-327. — idem, Was wissen wir über Plan u. Absicht der A. Paul. ?: FS W. Schneemelcher (Geneva, 1989), 71-82. — W. Schneemelcher, Gesammelte Aufsätze (Thessalonica, 1974), 154-181, 182-203, 204-222, 223-239. — L. Vouaux, Les actes de Paul (Paris, 1913).

The so-called *Acta Petri et Pauli* (BHG 1490) were composed as a Gr. base model, probably in connection with the Roman effort to link the two apostles (a tendency perceptible by the 4th c. at the latest) (see also *Decretum Gelasianum* 3.2). These *Acts* also represent a rejection of the earlier, mutually independent Peter and Paul traditions. In chs. 1-21 they describe P.'s journey from Malta to Rome, then the conflict of the apostles with Simon Magus and Nero, and their subsequent martyrdom. These *Acta* are also preserved in Armenian and Georgian.

To be distinguished from these *Acta* is the *Passio* handed down in Lat. (BHL 2:6659; there attributed to a Marcellus); this work omits in particular the description of P.'s journey, but there are other differences as well.

W: *Acta*, AAAp 1 [text]. — L. Leloir, CCA 3:7-34 [French trans. of the Armenian text]. — *Passio*, R. A. Lipsius, op. cit., 119-177 [text]. — L. Leloir, CCA 3:37-54 [French trans. of the Armenian text].
L: NTApo⁵ 2:395-399.

3. Apocalypses: An *Apocalypse of Paul* is first attested by Augustine (*Io. ev. tr.* 98.8), who makes use of it; in *Decretum Gelasianum* 5.5.1 it appears among the rejected apocrypha. The original Gr. text has survived only in an abridged form; only the Lat. version is complete. Other important witnesses are the Syr., Arm., and Copt. transmissions of a text that is much changed but does not differ much in content.

The discovery of the work in Tarsus in 388 is described in a piece of literary fiction; this may indicate the time of composition. The text describes the journey of P. though the heavens (2 Cor 12:2-4) and depicts espec. the lot of the deceased in paradise and hell (among other things, the interruption of the punishments of hell on Sundays; punishment of murderers before the eyes of their victims). In the process, the work borrows from ancient traditions (Tartarus, Lake Acherusia, ferryman) but also uses early Jewish sources (apocalypses of Zephaniah and Elijah), as well as the *Apocalypse of* → *Peter*. The text transmitted many of these images to the Middle Ages (Dante).

W: *Visio sancti Pauli*, T. Silverstein, StD 4 (London, 1935), 219-229 [Latin text] (literature). — C. v. Tischendorf, Apocalypses apocryphae (Hildesheim, 1966 = 1866), 34-69 [Greek text]. — Apocalypsis Pauli syriace, G. Ricciotti (Or. 2) (Rome, 1933), 1-24, 120-149 [Syriac text/Latin trans.]. — E. A. Wallis Budge, Miscelleaneous Coptic Texts (New York, 1975 = Leipzig, 1915). — NTApo⁵ 2:647-675 [German trans.]. — M. Erbetta, Gli Apocrifi del NT 3 (Turin, 1981), 353-386 [Italian trans.].
L: R. P. Casey, The Apocalypse of Paul: JThS 34 (1933) 1-32. — E. Dassmann, P. in der "Visio sancti Pauli": JAC 9 (1982) 117-128. — A. di P. Healey, The Vision of St. Paul, Diss. (Toronto, 1973). — A. Olivar, "Liber infernalis" o "Visio Pauli": SE 18 (1967/68) 550-554. — F. Secret, La "Revelacion de San Pablo": Sefarad 28/1 (1968) 45-67. — T. Silverstein, Did Dante know the Vision of Paul?: Harvard Studies and Notes in Philology and Literature 19 (1937) 231-247.

To be distinguished from the preceding is the Copt.-gnostic *Apocalypse of Paul* (*Apoc. Paul*) from Nag Hammadi (NHC 5, 2). It is unclear whether this is identical with the heavenly journey of Paul mentioned by Epiphanius (*haer.* 38.2.5). Here again the work is probably a Copt. version of a Gr. original that was written between the 2nd and 4th c.

The work gives a free depiction of the rapture of P. that is described in 2 Cor 12:2-4, along with revelations on the eschatology of individuals. The rapture is inserted into P.'s journey from Damascus to Jerusalem. During the ascent to the tenth heaven there is in the fourth heaven a *descensus ad inferos* and in the seventh an encounter with the Ancient One of Dan 7:9f., who is identified with the gnostic demiurge.

W: The Facsimile Edition of the NHC. Cod. V (Leiden, 1975), 25-32. — D. M. Parrott (ed.), NHC V, 2-5 and VI (Leiden, 1979), 47-63 [text/English trans.]. — A. Böhlig, P. Labib, Kopt.-gnostische Apokalypsen: WZ(H) Sonderband (1963) 15-26, 34-54 [text/German trans.]. — Review: H.-M. Schenke: OLZ 61 (1966) 23-34. — J. M. Robinson (ed.), The Nag Hammadi Library in English (Leiden, ³1988), 239-241 [English trans.]. — NTApo⁵ 2:630-633.
L: R. Kasser, Textes gnostiques: Muséon 78 (1965) 76-78,

300. — H.-J. Klauck, Die Himmelfahrt des P.: idem, Gemeinde, Amt und Sakrament (Würzburg, 1989), 391-429. — K. Koschorke, P. in den Nag Hammadi-Texten: ZThK 78 (1981) 177-205. — G. W. MacRae, The Judgement Scene in the Coptic Apocalypse of P.: Studies in the Testament of Abraham, ed. G. W. E. Nickelsburg (Missoula, 1976), 285-288.

G. Röwekamp

Paul of Antioch

P. was born ca. 500 in Alexandria. He was the syncellus of the Monophysite Patriarch Theodosius of Constantinople; in 564 he was secretly consecrated patriarch of Antioch. He represented a moderate Severian position and it was assumed that he could harmonize the positions of the Syrians and the Egyptians. After disputes over his succession as patriarch of Antioch he withdrew in 566 among the Ghassanids of al-Harith ibn Jabalah. In 567/568 he took part in the debates between Jacobites and tritheists and himself fought against the latter. In 571 he made a rather forced rapprochement with the Chalcedonians, in which connection he was arrested in Constantinople and in the end was able to escape but only as discredited. He found refuge among the successors of al-Harith and only in 575 was able to return to Syria. He supported Theodore as candidate for the see of Alexandria, but the latter was defeated. Peter IV of Alexandria then deposed P. A new schism threatened, but P. finally withdrew from his see to Constantinople, perhaps in 577. He died there in 581.

Some writings of P. are preserved in Syriac: a letter, after his consecration as patriarch, to Theodosius Alex. (*ep. synodica ad Theodosium Alexandrinum*); after 571, letters and a defense aimed at justifying his behavior (*ep. ad Iacobum et Theodorum*; *ep. ad Iacobum Baradaeum*; *apol.*); in 575 a letter to Theodore whom he supported in Alexandria (*ep. synodica ad Theodorum patriarchum Alexandriae*). There is an unpublished note on the tritheist question.

W: I. B. Chabot, CSCO 17/103 [text/Latin trans.]: *ep. syn. ad Theodos. Alex.*, 98-114/68-79. — *ep. ad Iacob. et Theod.*, 177-179/123-125. — *ep ad Iacob.*, 293/205 [frags.]. — *apol.*, 237f., 283f., 293/166, 198f., 205. — *ep. syn. ad. Theod. patr.*, 308-334/215-233.
L: A. S. Atiya, Paul the Black: CoptE 6, 1922f. — E. W. Brooks, The Patriarch P. and the Alexandrine Schisma: ByZ 30 (1930) 468-476. — W. H. C. Frend, The Rise of the Monophysite Movement (Cambridge, 1972), 291, 321-328. — E. Honigmann, Évêques et évêchés monophysites (Leuven/Louvain, 1951), 195-205. — T. Hermann, Monophysitica: ZNW 32 (1933) 277-293, here 286.

B. Windau

Paul of Aphrodisias

From 558 on P. was the Monophysite metropolitan of Aphrodisias. At the beginning of the persecution of Monophysites in 571 he was captured and made a prisoner in Constantinople. He was finally compelled to recant his profession of Monophysitism. This recantation, which he was forced to sign, was ascribed to P. as his own work (*Libellus*; → John of Ephesus, *h.e.* 2.43). After returning to Aphrodisias P. was first deposed and then consecrated again as the orthodox metropolitan. He died before 576/577.

W: E. W. Brooks, CSCO 105/106:110/80f. [text/Latin trans.].
L: E. Honigmann, Évêques et évêchés monophysites (Leuven/Louvain, 1951), 218f.

B. WINDAU

Paul of Concordia

P., who was born presumably between 270 and 275, was monk in a monastery near Concordia, and died probably shortly after 377. Jerome (*ep.* 5.2; *vir. ill.* 53) says that he was very well read and had a special esteem for Tertullian and Cyprian, with whose *notarius* he had become acquainted as a young man in Rome. *Ep.* 10 *Ad Paulum senem Concordiae* documents the importance of P.'s library. His answering letter is lost. P. probably wrote the inscription for his sister Heraclia who died in Rome in the mid-4th c.

W: ICUR NS 2, n. 5342.
L: P. Zovatto, P.: AnAl 5 (1974) 165-180.

B. DÜMLER

Paul of Edessa

To P., who was consecrated bishop of Edessa ca. 602, the Syrian church owes a series of antiphonaries (*antiph.*), which he translated from Gr. and reorganized. With this editorial activity P. decisively anticipated the reorganization of the liturgy under Jacob of Edessa. Also from P. are translations and commentaries on → Gregory Naz. (*Greg. Naz.*).

W: *antiph.*, E. W. Brooks, PO 6:1-169 [text/English trans.]. — *Greg. Naz.*, R. L. Bensly, W. E. Barnes, Fourth Book of Maccabees (Cambridge, 1895), 27-34, 55-74 [text/English trans.].
L: A. Baumstark, Festbrevier u. Kirchenjahr (Paderborn, 1908). — B. Coulie, Corpus Nazianzenum 1. Versiones orientales (Turnhout, 1988). — A. de Halleux, Commentaires syriaques: Muséon 98 (1985) 103-147. — T. Hermann, P. u. das alexandrinische Schisma: ZNW 27 (1928) 263-304. —

A. van Roey, H. Moors, Discours de s. Grégoire: OLoP 4 (1973) 121-133; 5 (1974) 79-126.

P. BRUNS

Paul of Emesa

P. was bishop of Emesa on the Orontes after 410, participated in the Council of Ephesus in 431, and was sent by John of Antioch to Cyril Alex. as peace negotiator. He played an active part in ending the conflict between the two men, and in 433 carried to Antioch the letter *Laetentur coeli* of Cyril that was the key to the union of 433. P. died between 433 and 445.

The preserved works of P.: two short sermons *De nativitate Domini* and a fragment of a sermon *De pace*, all three delivered in Alexandria (*hom.* 1-3); a book in letter form addressed to Cyril (*ep.*); a letter to army general Anatolius in a Lat. translation (*ep. ad Anatolium*); a fragment on Lk 23:33 (*fr. in Luc.*).

W: *hom.* 1-3, PG 77:1433-1444. — ACO 1, 1, 4, 9-14. — ACO 1, 1, 7, 173-174. — *ep.*, PG 77:165f. ACO 1, 1, 4, 6-7. — *ep. ad Anatolium*, PG 84:720f. — ACO 1, 4, 139f. — *fr. in Luc.*, A. Mai, SVNC 9 (Rome, 1837), 713 [text].
L: R. Caro, La homilética mariana griega en el siglo V (Dayton, 1972), 199-203, 205.

C. SCHMIDT

Paul Helladicus

P. was a hesychast at Elusa in Idumea. He composed, probably in 526, an encomiastic *Vita* of St. Theognius of Bethelia (*v. Thgn.*), which later served → Cyril of Scythopolis as a model. Also from P. is a treatise in letter form (*ep.*) on sexual license.

W: *v. Thgn.*, J. van den Gheyn, Acta sancti Theognii: AnBoll 10 (1891) 78-113 [text]. — *ep.*, V. Lundström, Anecdota Byzantina (Uppsala/Leipzig, 1902), 17-23 [text].
L: H. G. Beck, Kirche u. theol. Lit. (Munich, 1959), 406.

B. WINDAU

Paul II of Constantinople

P. (d. Dec. 27, 653) was administrator of Hagia Sophia and on Oct. 1, 641, succeeded Pyrrhus as bishop of Constantinople. In the synodal letter of 642 to Pope → Theodore he explained the agreement of his faith with that of Theodore. Pyrrhus had recanted Monotheletism in Rome in 645, but meanwhile P., in response to a petition, composed a Monotheletist creed. To this, Theodore responded in 647 by deposing P. In 648 P. secured an imperial edict, the so-called *Typos*, that simply forbade any further discussion of the wills of Christ. In 649 the

Lateran synod under Martin I anathematized P., and the 6th ecumenical council seconded this judgment. Of P.'s works only the second letter to Theodore survives, in which, with references to Athanasius, Cyril, Sergius, and Honorius, P. deduces the one will from the one person of Christ. Lost are the first letter to Theodore, the letter to the emperor that caused him to promulgate the *Typos,* a call to the Armenians for union (Sebeos, *Patmowt'iwn i Herakln* 33), a collection of letters and three *Tomoi* with addresses given in the presence of Constans II.

W: PL 87:91-99.
L: P. Conte, Chiesa e Primato (Milan, 1971). — A. Fliche, V. Martin, Histoire 5 (Paris, 1947), 165-168. — V. Grumel, Regestes (Paris, 1972), 227-229. — C. J. Hefele, H. Leclerq, Histoire des conciles 3/1 (Hildesheim, 1973 = Paris, 1909), 398-400, 426-433, 459. — L. Magi, La sede Romana (Rome, 1972), 212-223. — F. X. Seppelt, Geschichte der Päpste 2 (Munich, ²1955), 59-66, 74. — J. L. D. van Dieten, Geschichte der Patriarchen (Amsterdam, 1972), 76-103.

B. DÜMLER

Paul of Merida

P., a deacon in Merida, was long regarded as author of the anonymous *Vitae sanctorum Patrum Emeritensium* (7th c.?). This assumption cannot, however, be adequately justified. The work is not trustworthy in all its parts; only with caution can it be used as a source for the history of Merida.

W: PL 80:115-164. — J. N. Garvin (Washington, 1946).
L: K. Schäferdieck, Die Kirche in den Reichen der Westgoten u. Suewen (Berlin, 1967).

E. REICHERT

Paul of Nisibis (Paul the Persian)

P. was one of the great Nestorian exegetes and theologians. Under Mar Aba he headed a school in the Adiabene for thirty years; in ca. 551 he was consecrated bishop of Nisibis and led this diocese until his death in 571. In 532/533 he appeared before Emperor Justinian I as defender of the Nestorian causes in a dialogue on religion. P. is certainly identical with the Paul of Persia who in 527, again at the urging of the emperor, engaged in a disputation with Photius, a Manichee (*disp.*). P. composed an introduction to the Bible under the title *Instituta regularia divinae legis* (*inst.*), which was translated into Lat. by → Junilius Africanus. This manual contains a unique summary of the dogma of the → school of Nisibis and of the exegetical methods of → Theodore Mops.

W: *inst.,* H. Kihn, Theodor v. Mopsuestia (Fribourg, Switzerland, 1880) [Latin text]. — *disp.,* PG 88:529-574.
L: A. Guillaumont, Un colloque: CRAI 71 (1970) 201-207. — idem, Justinien et l'Église de Perse: DOP 23-27 (1969-70) 39-66. — D. Gutas, P. and Aristotle's Philosophy: Islam 60 (1983) 231-267. — G. Mercati, Per la vita di P.: StT 5 (1901) 180-206. — A. Vööbus, School of Nisibis (Leuven/Louvain, 1965), 170-172.

P. BRUNS

Paul of Samosata

P., a man of lowly birth, became ca. 258 the successor of Demetrianus as bishop of Antioch (Eus., *h.e.* 7.27.1); he was perhaps not in fact a *procurator ducenarius* (*h.e.* 7.30.8). No complete writings of P. have survived. He was accused of teaching (like the heretic Artemas) that Christ is "from below," i.e., a man like other men (*h.e.* 7.30.11). Several synods were held, among them two large synods in Antioch ca. 264 and 268, at which P. was condemned. Eusebius knows of a letter of Dionysius Alex. to the synod of 264 (*h.e.* 7.27.2; see 7.30.3), and he cites from the synodal letter of 268 (7.30.2-17), but only glances at the theol. objections against P. At the second synod P. was refuted in a disputation with Malchion, a presbyter and head of a local school of rhetoric (7.29.2). The stenographic record of this disputation still existed in Eusebius's time. Domnus, son of P.'s predecessor, Demetrianus, became P.'s successor. When P. and his supporters refuse to lift their control of the church buildings, a decree of Emperor Aurelian was secured against him (7.30.18-19).

The historical-dogm. profile of P. that can be reconstructed today depends very substantially on the reception of the judgment of the Antiochene synod in the theol. debates of the 4th-6th c. In the 4th c. the "heresy" of P. was not consistently distinguished from those of Sabellius and Marcellus of Ancyra. In the context of the discussion of the Nicene *homoousios,* the condemnation of P. by the Antiochene synod was interpreted by the homoiousians in 368 as supposedly a condemnation of the *homoousios.* This suggests a posthumous heresiological construct. Fragments and notes on which the stenographic record of the synod may have been based were handed on by various writers in the context of the christological controversies of the 5th and 6th c. (e.g., Eusebius of Dorylaeum, Timothy Aelurus, Severus of Antioch). Here the teaching of P. is presented in such a way as to make him deny the incarnation of the Logos (Sophia) in the full sense and speak instead of an indwelling of Sophia in the man Jesus; this indwelling was something greater than the sapiential inspiration of the prophets. The question of the authenticity of these fragments (a question important for the history of christology in the 3rd c.) has not yet been finally answered. Also unresolved is the authenticity of the so-called Letter of the Six Bishops, a document that claims to have been composed by the synod against P. and that, if authentic, would permit inferences as to the teaching of P.

S: *Letter of the Six Bishops,* G. Bardy, P, SSL 4 (Leuven/Louvain, ²1929). — F. Loofs, P. Eine Untersuchung zur altkirchlichen Lit. u. Dogmengeschichte, TU 3. Reihe 14, 5 (Leipzig, 1924). — E. Schwartz, Eine fingierte Korrespondenz mit P.: SBAW. PPH 1927, 3 (1927).
W: H. de Riedmatten, Les Actes de P.: Par. 6 (1952). — J. H. Declerck, Deux nouvaux fragments: Byz. 54 (1984) 116-140.
L: G. Bardy, op. cit. — H. C. Brennecke, Zum Prozess gegen P.: ZNW 75 (1984) 270-290. — J. Burke, Eusebius on P.: Kl. 7 (1975) 8-20. — J. A. Fischer, Die antiochenischen Synoden gegen P: AHC 18 (1986) 9-30. — R. M. Hübner, Die Hauptquelle des Epiphanius (Panarion, haer. 65) über P.: ZKG 90 (1979) 201-220. — F. Loofs, op. cit. — F. Millar, P., Zenobia and Aurelian: JRS 61 (1971) 1-17. — P. Nautin, Le procès de Paul d'Antioche, dit de Samosate: AEPHE. R 88 (1979/80) 355-357. — F. W. Norris, P. Procurator Ducenarius: JThS 35 (1984) 50-70. — L. Perrone, L'enigma di Paolo di Samosata: CrSt 13 (1992) 253-327. — M. Richard, Malchion et P.: EThL 35 (1959) 325-338 = idem, Opera Minora 2 (Leuven/Louvain, 1977), Nr. 25. — J. Rist, Paul v. Samosata u. Zenobia: RQ 92 (1997) 145-161. — R. L. Sample, The Messiah as Prophet: The Christology of P., Diss. (Northwestern University, 1977). — idem, The Christology of the Council of Antioch (268 C.E.) Reconsidered: ChH 48 (1979) 18-26. — E. Schwartz, op. cit. — M. Simonetti, Per la Rivalutazione di Alcune Testimonianze su P.: RSLR 24 (1988) 177-210. — G. C. Stead, Marcel Richard on Malchion and P.: FS L. Abramowski (Berlin, 1993), 140-150.

W. A. Löhr

Paul the Silentiary

At the court of Justinian (527-565) P. was *primicerius* of the *silentarii.* He was a friend of historian and poet Agathias (*hist.* 5.9) and wrote his own poetry during the heyday of Hellen. epigrammatic verse, espec. as practiced in court circles; this verse followed traditional thematic and linguistic models and in its metrics, which aimed at perfection, took Nonnus as a guide. P. stands out among these conventional versifiers by his ability to combine these complicated traditional handicaps with an astonishing originality.

His eighty epigrams (*epigr.*) are chiefly erotic but deal also with mythological, epideictic, and funereal themes and for this reason provide a treasury of cultural and sociohistorical information.

His two ecphrases, in particular, are of interest for the history of art. The *Description of Hagia Sophia* (*Ecphrasis tou vaou tēs hagias Sophias; Soph.*) consists of 887 hexameters, which are preceded by two introductions of 134 iambic trimeters, one addressed to Emperor Justinian, the other to Patriarch Eutychius. The description was written for the reconsecration of the main Justinian church of Constantinople after it had been considerably damaged by an earthquake in 558; it was read by P. himself in the presence of the emperor and the patriarch during the reconsecration celebration on Dec. 24, 562. After praising the emperor and the patriarch, P. expresses his consternation at the destruction and his joy at the new and more perfect reconstruction. He then gives a detailed description of all parts of the church from the atrium to the apse, with emphasis espec. on the decoration. The description of the ambo (*Ecphrasis tou ambōnos; ambo.*), which consists of 275 hexameters with twenty-nine introductory iambic trimeters, was read a few days later, probably on Jan. 6, 563. It describes the ambo that was placed in the center, under the dome of the rebuilt church. Both poems are of immense importance for our reconstruction of Justinian's monuments.

The authenticity of the poem on the Pythian baths (*Eis ta en puthiois thermu; In thermas pythicas*) is disputed.

W: *epigr.,* G. Viansino (Turin, 1963) [text/Italian trans./comm.]. — *ambo./Soph.,* P. Friedländer: Johannes v. Gaza (Hildesheim, 1969 = Leipzig, 1912), 225-310 [text/comm.]. — C. A. Mango: Art of the Byzantine Empire (New Jersey, 1972), 80-96 [English trans.].
L: B. Baldwin, An Unnoticed Quotation in the Suda: Museum Philologum Londiniense 6 (1984) 7. — C. Caiazzo, L'esametro: JÖB 32/33 (1982) 335-343. — C. Corbato, Poesia (Trieste, 1951). — G. Guidorizzi, A. P. 5, 250: RIL 112 (1978) 280-285. — A. Saija, Considerazioni linguistiche: Atti dell' Accademia Peloritana dei Pericolanti. Classe di Lettere, Filosofia e Belle Arti 60 (1984) 105-110. — M. Whitby, Eutychius: FS J. Bramble (Bristol, 1987), 297-308. — eadem, Occasion of P.'s Ekphrasis of S. Sophia: CQ 35 (1985) 215-228. — eadem, Ceremony in the Mid-sixth century Constantinople: Hist. 36 (1987) 462-488. — J. C. Yardley, P., Ovid and Propertius: CQ 30 (1980) 239-243. — G. Zanetto, Imitatio e variatio negli epigrammi erotici: Prometheus 11 (1985) 258-270.

B. Dümler

Paul of Tella

To P., bishop of Tella, is attributed the Syr. translation of a baptismal ritual described by → Severus of Antioch. At the bidding of Antiochene Patriarch Anastasius I, P. and some collaborators, among them his deacon → Thomas of Heraclea, undertook a new translation of the OT based on the Syrohexapla of

→ Origen; he completed it in the years 615-617 (*hex.*). It survives also in an Arab. version.

W: *hex.*, P. de Lagarde, Veteris Testamenti ab Origene recensiti fragmenta (Göttingen, 1880-1892) [text]. — J. Gwynn, Remnants of the later Syr. Versions (London, 1909) [text]. — R. J. V. Hiebert, The "Syrohexaplaric" Psalter (Atlanta, 1989) [text]. — Book of Isaiah, A. Vööbus, CSCO 449 [text]. — Pentateuch, A. Vööbus, CSCO 369 [text]. — W. Baars, New Syro-hexaplaric texts (Leiden, 1968) [text].
L: S. P. Brock, The Bible in the Syriac Tradition (Kottayam, 1989). — C. T. Fritsch, Treatment of the Hexaplaric Signs: JBL 72 (1953) 169-181. — M. H. Gottstein, Cambridger Syrohexapla-Hs.: Muséon 67 (1954) 291-297. — idem, Neue Frgm.: Bib. 37 (1956) 162-183. — A. de Halleux, Glanures syro-hexaplaires: Muséon 99 (1986) 251-290. — J. M. Vosté, Les citations syrohexaplaires: Bib. 26 (1945) 12-36. — A. Vööbus, Discoveries of Manuscript Sources (Stockholm, 1970). — idem, The Hexapla and Syro-Hexapla (Stockholm, 1971).

P. BRUNS

Paulinus of Biterrae

P., bishop of Biterrae ca. 400-419, was possibly the author of the poem *Epigramma* (*De perversis suae aetatis moribus*) written in hexameters ca. 407-409. Here, in a conversation in a monastery, Abbot Thesbon, an unnamed monk, and Salmon, a visitor, complain that the country is being ravaged by vices, in a devastation worse than that wrought by the Vandals.

W: C. Schenkl, CSEL 26/1:503-508.
L: A. Gallico, Nuova edizione: SSRel 6 (1982) 163-172. — R. P. H. Green, Tityrus lugens: StPatr 15 (1984) 75-78. — E. Griffe, Epigramma Paulini: REAug 2 (1956) 186-194. — K. Smolak, Textkritik: WSt 102 (1989) 206-212.

M. SKEB, OSB

Paulinus of Bordeaux

P. was a contemporary of Faustus of Riez and possibly the same person as the author, mentioned by Gennadius of Marseilles (*vir. ill.* 58), of works on penance, the beginning of Lent, Easter, obedience, and the newly baptized. Only a fragment remains of a work *De paenitentia* (*paenit.*). The attribution to P. of *Tractatus duo de initio quadragesimae* (*tract.*) and *ep.* 4 (*ep.*) of Faustus of Riez is uncertain.

W: *paenit.*, PL 58:875f. — *tract.*, A. Mai (Rome, 1940), 309-313 [text]. — *ep.*, A. Engelbrecht, CSEL 21:181-183.
L: B. Poschmann, Kirchenbuße (Munich, 1928), 128f. n. 4.

M. SKEB, OSB

Paulinus of Milan

P., b. perhaps ca. 370 in Florence, d. ca. 428/429, entered the service of Ambrose of Milan as a *notarius* in 394 at the earliest. Simplician appointed him (not before 405) as administrator of Milanese possessions in Africa. There, at the suggestion of Augustine, he composed the *Vita Ambrosii* (*vita. Ambr.*) (in 412 or 422). P. must be the same as Paulinus the Deacon, who took part in a synod against Caelestius in Carthage in 411 or 412 (Aug., *gr. et pecc. or.* 2.3.8; *c. ep. Pelag.* 2.6), for which he had previously composed a *Libellus* listing the errors of Caelestius (Aug., *gest. Pelag.* 11.3; Marius Mercator, *Cael.* 1). After being summoned to Rome by Zosimus, P. composed a second *Libellus adversus Caelestium Zosimo episcopo datus* (*adv. Cael.*) on Nov. 6, 417.

The *vita Ambr.*, modeled acc. to the author (*praef.*) on the *Vita Antonii* of Athanasius, the *Vita Pauli Thebaei* of Jerome, and the *Vita S. Martini* of Sulpicius Severus, follows the chronology of Ambrose's life. Despite some gaps and errors, numerous miracle stories, and its eulogistic character, the historical value of the life is recognized today. Its literary quality is rather small. The first *Libellus* against Caelestius has been lost, but the second, for Zosimus, is preserved. P. refuses to appear before a Roman court; he points out the errors of Pelagius and Caelestius and calls for their condemnation. The work *De benedictionibus patriarcharum*, which was published under P.'s name, is from the 9th c.

W: *adv. Cael.*, O. Günther, CSEL 35/1:108-111. — J. Chapman, Early Papacy (New York, 1928), 166-169 [English trans.]. — *vita Ambr.*, M. Pellegrino (Rome, 1961) [text/Italian trans./comm.]. — A. Bastiaensen (Verona, 1975) [text/Italian trans./comm.]. — E. Lamirande (Paris, 1983) [French trans./comm.]. — I. Opelt (Düsseldorf, 1967) [German trans.]. — M. Simonetti (Rome, 1977) [Italian trans.]. — J. A. Lacy (Washington, 1952) [English trans.].
L: L. Alfonsi, Struttura della Vita Ambrosii: RIL 103 (1969) 784-798. — G. Castelli, Lingua (Turin, 1967). — E. Lamirande, Datation de la Vita Ambrosii: REAug 27 (1981) 44-55. — idem, Vita Ambrosii (Paris/Tournai/Montreal, 1983). — J.-R. Palanque, Vita Ambrosii: RevSR 4 (1924) 26-42, 401-420. — A. Paredi, P.: SE 14 (1963) 206-230. — M. Pellegrino, Biografo di S. Ambrogio: ScC 79 (1951) 151-162. — L. Cracco Ruggini, Vita Ambrosii: At. 41 (1963) 98-110. — A. Solignac, P.: DSp 12/1:589-592. — O. Wermelinger, Rom u. Pelagius (Stuttgart, 1975), 8-19, 146-158. — A. Wilmart, Bénédictions de Jacob: RBen 32 (1920) 57-63.

B. DÜMLER

Paulinus of Nola

I. **Life:** Meropius Pontius Paulinus (P.) was b. ca. 355 in Aquitania. His family belonged to the Roman senatorial aristocracy and possessed extensive estates in Campania (Fundi), Spain (Ebromagus), and Aquitania. P. had a brother whose violent death endangered P. and his possessions. Both father and mother died as Christians, but we must not assume that they gave P. a Chr. education. He received his scholastic formation in Bordeaux, from, among others, Ausonius, rhetorician and poet, with whom he maintained close ties in later years. Ausonius probably also sponsored P.'s political career.

In 378 P. was, in all probability, *consul suffectus*, but the consulate had no visible impact on his personal development. On the other hand, the period he spent as curile magistrate (governor?) in Campania had far-reaching consequences. When at the very beginning of his time in office, he attended the feast of St. Felix in Nola on Jan. 14, 381, he was deeply impressed by the miracles at the saint's tomb. After that, he withdrew from politics and may have practiced the profession of lawyer.

It was probably on his journey home from Campania to Aquitania that P. first met Ambrose in Milan. On that journey P. also met Martin of Tours in Vienne. In about 385 P. traveled to Spain and there married the wealthy Therasia. Between 385 and 389, after receiving instruction from a presbyter Amandus, P. was baptized in Bordeaux by Bishop Delphinus. But baptism was not for him the starting point of a new life. It was rather his conversion to monasticism that he regarded as the birth of his soul. The decisive events were the violent death of his brother in 390 and the rescue from the dangers threatening P. in this connection.

In 389 (before the death of his brother) P. traveled to Spain. During 393 P. began to sell his own and his wife's properties. On Christmas day 395, at the urging of the faithful, P. was ordained a priest in Barcelona by Bishop Lampius. His conversion to monasticism received a severely critical response in Rome and led to a break with → Ausonius. The monastic life that P. and Therasia led in Nola was by no means marked by a consistent seclusion. Occasional poems (espec. *Carmina natalicia* or birthday poems for the feast of St. Felix on Jan. 14), an extensive correspondence, the building, renovating, and decoration of the pilgrimage shrine in Nola (between 400 and 405), and an annual journey to Rome for the feast of the apostles Peter and Paul, as well as, of course, the welcoming of the crowds of pilgrims that came to the tomb of St. Felix, and of other travelers—all these were part of P.'s everyday life. Melania the Elder, Nicetas of Remesiana, and Melania the Younger were among his guests. It cannot be said

with certainty when Therasia died, but it is likely to have been between 408 and 415. Between 404 and 415 P. became bishop of Nola; he died probably on June 22, 431, as the result of a pulmonary infection.

L: A. D. Booth, Sur la date de la naissance: Écho du Monde 26 (1982) 56-64. — J. Desmulliez, Études chronologiques 393-397: RechAug 20 (1985) 35-64. — P. Fabre, L'amitié chrétienne (Paris, 1949), 7-51. — D. Korol, Wandmalereien aus den Grabbauten in Cimitile, Nola, JAC. E 13 (Münster, 1987). — J. T. Lienhard, Early Western Monasticism (Cologne, 1977), 22-32. — P. Nautin, Date de la mort: Aug. 18 (1978) 547-550. — D. E. Trout, The Dates of the Ordination of P. and of His Departure for Nola: REAug 37 (1991) 237-260.

II. Works: The works listed by von Hartel in the appendixes of his editions are not authentic. The authenticity of letters 46 and 47 to Rufinus of Aquileia is not completely certain; the authorship of letter 48, a fragment, is unclear. *Carm.* 4 is by → Paulinus of Pella; *carm.* 5 must be ascribed to → Ausonius; *carm.* 32, the so-called *Carmen ultimum*, is likewise not authentic and is attributed to an otherwise unidentified poet Anthony or Jovius, the addressee of *ep.* 16 and *carm.* 22. The *Obitus Baebiani* (*carm.* 33) is perhaps inauthentic rather than genuine. The inscriptions published as *carm.* 30 are not from P.

Of the surviving letters (*ep.*) thirteen are addressed to → Sulpicius Severus, six to Amandus, five to Delphinus, four to Augustine, and one each to Alypius, Romanianus, Macarius, to Florentius and Alethius, to Sebastian, and to Eucherius and Galla. Rufinus of Aquileia is possibly the addressee of two letters, as are Victricius of Rouen, Crispinianus, Sanctus, and Amandus. Three are addressed to Aper and his wife, Amanda. A *Consolatio* in letter form is intended for Pammachius, a *Protrepticus* in letter form for Jovius; letter 34 is a sermon, sent along with letter 33 to Alethius. Letters to P. from → Augustine (*ep.* 27; 31; 42; 45; 80; 95; 149; 186), → Ausonius (*ep.* 21; 22; 23; 24), → Jerome (*ep.* 53; 58; 85), and Emperor Honorius (*Collectio Avellana*, *ep.* 25) have been preserved. The occasion for the letters is often unimportant; they offer bibl.-spiritual instruction or engage in wide-ranging associations of images, the latter being taken from the Bible or rural life.

Among the poems (*carm.*) of P., *carm.* 1, 2, and 3 (two letters to Gestidius and a fragmentary versification of Suetonius's *De regibus*) are from the years before P.'s baptism and are marked by the lifestyle of the Gallo-Roman senatorial aristocracy: exchange of little gifts and literary works, literary activity, cultivation of friendly relations. The earliest Chr. works are the bibl. epics (*carm.* 6: John the Baptist; 7: Ps 1; 8: Ps

2; 9: Ps 137); here the thinking is clearly influenced by P.'s baptism. Of his four letters in verse, two are addressed to Ausonius (*carm.* 10; 11) and justify P.'s monastic *conversio; carm.* 24 is addressed to Cytherius and exhorts him to educate his son for the monastic life; *carm.* 22 is a *Protrepticus* in letter form for Jovius and belongs with *ep.* 16. The larger part of the body of verse consists of the fourteen *Natalicia* which P. composed annually, beginning in 395, for the feast of St. Felix, thus adapting the classical *genethliakon* to the needs of Chr. veneration of the saints. The body of poems also contains an *Epithalamium* for Julian and Titia (*carm.* 25), a *Consolatio* for Pneumatius and Fidelis (*carm.* 31), and a *Propempticon* for Nicetas of Remesiana (*carm.* 17).

Other preserved works of P.: an → Epitaph for Cynegius (*epi. Cyn.*), one of his disciples, found in Cimitile; two fragments (*fr.*) of lost works of P., preserved by later writers. The panegyric for Theodosius I (*ep.* 28.6; Jerome, *ep.* 58.8) is lost; nothing is known of a planned work *Contra gentes*, to which Augustine alludes (*ep.* 31.8). The attempt to prove P. the author of a "Primitive Gelasian Sacramentary" (→ Sacramentary) must be regarded as a failure.

III. Main Lines of Thought: P.'s personality was marked by an exceptional need for friendly exchanges and a great power of drawing people, which made it possible for him, e.g., to be friends at the same time with persons at odds with each other (Augustine/Pelagius; for a time Jerome/Rufinus). The prevailing theol. and spiritual focus of his thought is Christ, for whose sake he renounced the world in his monastic *conversio*. The new direction also affected P.'s thoughts on literary theory, for, in the sense that he would now be giving back to Christ his linguistic gifts, Christ was now to be the real content of his literary activity, which would meet the need of communicating salvation and (saving) truth. P. sets this "monastic" theory of literature in the larger context of the theology of the saving activity of Christ (with its stages of incarnation, grace given in baptism, monastic *conversio*, and the eschaton, a theology developed with the help of the idea of a *commercium*); this saving activity demands the radical directing of one's whole life to Christ. The strikingly frequent christological references, in metaphors and concepts, are explicable as concretizations of that basic outlook. The emphasis on the divinity of Christ suggests an anti-Arian tendency.

W: *carm.*, W. Hartel, CSEL 30. — A. Ruggiero (Rome, 1990) [Italian trans.]. — idem, 2 vols. (Rome, 1996) [text/Italian trans./comm.]. — P. G. Walsh, ACW 40 [English trans./comm.]. — *ep.*, W. Hartel, CSEL 29. — P. G. Walsh, ACW 35f. [English trans./comm.]. — G. Santaniello, 2 vols. (Marigliano, 1992) [text/Italian trans./comm.]. — M. Skeb, FC 25:1-3. — *epit., Cyn.*, E. Diehl, ILCV 2:216f. [text]. — *fr.*, B. Dombart, A. Kalb, CCL 47:12. — L. Traube, MGH. PL 3:292 [text].

L: Academia Cardinalis Bessarionis (ed.), Atti del Convegno. XXXI cinquantenario della morte di S. P. (431-1981). Nola, 20-21 marzo 1982 (Rome, 1984). — E.-C. Babut, P. et le Priscillianisme (Paris, 1909). — K. Burkhard, Geburtstagsgedicht (Zurich, 1991), 156-160. — A. Castagnol, Le sénateur Volusien: REA 58 (1956) 241-253. — P. Courcelle, Un nouveau poème de Paulin de Pella: VC 1 (1947) 101-113. — P. Fabre, Chronologie (Paris, 1948). — idem, La suscription des lettres: REL 26 (1948) 56-58. — idem, Les citations dans la correspondance: idem, Mélanges 1945 (Paris, 1946), 17-38. — J. Fontaine, Antike u. chr. Werte: Askese u. Mönchtum, ed. K. S. Frank (Darmstadt, 1975), 281-324. — W. H. C. Frend, Last Century of the Western Empire: JRS 59 (1969) 1-11. — idem, The Two Worlds of P.: Latin Literature of the Fourth Century, ed. E. Binns (London, 1974), 100-133. — K. Gamber, Das kampanische Meßbuch: SE 12 (1961) 5-111. — R. P. H. Green, The Poetry of P. (Brussels, 1971). — G. Guttilla, Panegyricus: Koin. 14 (1990) 139-154. — idem, Aemulatio artistica: Orph. 15 (1994) 320-342. — R. Helm, P. 9: PRE 18/2:2331-2351. — C. Ianicelli, Rassegna: Centro di Studi e Documentazione su P., Disce Paulinum (Nola, 1997), 279-321. — H. Junod-Ammerbauer, Poète chrétien: REAug 21 (1975) 13-54. — W. Kirsch, P. u. Nicetas v. Remesiana. Literaturauffassung: From Late Antiquity to Early Byzantium, ed. V. Vavrinek (Prague, 1985), 189-193. — idem, Poetologie u. Poetik: MLJb 20 (1985) 103-111. — K. Kohlwes, Chr. Dichtung u. stilistische Form (Bonn, 1979). — S. Leanza, P.: TRE 26:129-133. — T. Lehmann, Sviluppo: Boreas 13 (1990) 75-93. — idem, Inschriftensammlung: ZPE 91 (1992) 243-281. — J. T. Lienhard, Some Fragments of P.: Latomus 36 (1977) 438f. — idem, Literary Tradition: FS E. A. Quain (New York, 1976), 35-45. — idem, P. and Augustine: Aug(L) 40 (1990) 279-296. — C. Magazzù, Dieci anni di studi su P.: BStL 18 (1988) 84-103. — C. Morelli, Poema ultima: Lati. 10 (1962) 208-214 (*carm.* 32). — I. Morelli, Doctrina christologica. (Naples, 1945). — S. Mratschek, Struktur u. Edition der "Natalicia": ZPE 114 (1996) 165-172. — A. P. Muys, Briefwisseling P. — Augustinus (Hilversum, 1941). — J. M. Poinsotte, Antonius: REL 60 (1982) 298-312. — S. Prete, Umanesimo cristiano (Bologna, 1964). — P. Reinelt, Briefe (Breslau, 1903). — F. G. Sirna, Poema ultimum: Aevum 35 (1961) 87-107 (*carm.* 32). — M. Skeb, Christo vivere (Bonn, 1997). — H. Sivan, P. on Teodosius I.: Latin Literature, ed. C. Deroux, 7 (Brussels, 1994), 577-594. — A. de Vogüé, Histoire littéraire 1/4 (Paris, 1997), 157-251. — P. G. Walsh, Conflict of Ideologies: FS J. Quasten (Münster, 1970), 565-571. — idem, Textual Notes on the "Epistulae": Orph. 13 (1966) 153-158 — W. S. Watt, Notes on the Poems: VigChr 52 (1998) 371-381. — C. Weyman, Der zweite Brief an Crispinianus: HJ 16 (1895) 92-99.

M. Skeb, OSB

Paulinus of Pella

Information about P.'s life is to be gotten only indirectly and exclusively from his *Eucharisticos* (*euch.*), a poetic autobiography in Latin. P. was born in Pella in 376 as son of the *vicarius* of Macedonia and nephew of Ausonius; there is disagreement on whether his father was Hesperius, son of Ausonius, or Thalassius, Ausonius's son-in-law. The family came to Bordeaux in 379 by way of Carthage and Rome. P., who had been raised speaking Greek, found Latin difficult to learn. At about the age of twenty he married; he fathered a daughter and two sons. He devoted himself to the management of the estate that came to him through the marriage. After the German invasion of Gaul in 406 P. was given the office of *comes largitionum privatarum* by Attalus. In 414 Bordeaux was destroyed and P. lost his property; he then went to Bazas. With the help of Goar, king of the Alans, P. forced the departure of the Goths. After many misfortunes P. became a *conversus* at the age of forty-five. He went to Marseilles but finally returned to Bordeaux, where he wrote the *euch.* at the age of eighty-three.

The year 459 is to be inferred as the date of composition of P.'s autobiography, which is handed down in the *Cod. Bernensis* 317 under the title *Eucharisticos Deo sub ephemeridis meae textu*. The text itself does not name an author but gives sufficient indications to distinguish it from the work of other Paulinuses. The work, in 616 hexameters with a prose *praefatio*, is entirely in the tradition of the autobiography of antiquity. But the "story of conversion" hardly fits in with the "deeds" of traditional autobiography and for this reason represents an expansion of the genre. In addition, the intention in setting down the content of Chr. autobiography has changed: the primary purpose is not to remain in the memory of human beings; P. intends to describe the fortunes and misfortunes of his life in order to console himself and to thank and praise God (*praef.* 2 and 4). P. thus follows the *Confessions* of → Augustine in intention and content.

The language and style correspond largely to what we find in Late Latin generally. P. often uses Gr. words, rhetorical terms, and specifically Pauline concepts. The syntax is characterized by extremely long sentences and numerous anacoloutha. By lengthening or shortening syllables and an excessive use of hiatus, he forces the words to fit the meter. Incomplete or hypermetric verses, on the other hand, are probably to be blamed on copyists. On the whole, there are various literary and espec. Virgilian reminiscences. In the history of culture the *euch.* is important for its documentation of hist. events; in fact it is the only source for the negotiations with the Alans. In a very personal way it provides information on the life of the Gallic nobility of that age. Not least is it a witness to the inculturation of Christianity in the society of late antiquity.

In addition, there can be attributed to P. an *Oratio* (*orat.*) in 19 hexameters that was for a long time counted among the works of Paulinus of Nola but is closely related to *euch.* in language and content. It is also very dependent on the *Oratio matutina* of Ausonius. The content of the prayer for a happy and unobtrusive death, when read against the background of P.'s biography, suggests a date between 399 and 407.

W: *euch.*, W. Brandes, CSEL 16/1:263-334. — H. G. Evelyn White, Ausonius (London, 1961), 293-351 [text/English trans.]. — A. Marcone (Florence, 1995) [text/Italian trans./comm.]. — J. Rocafort, Un type gallo-romain (Paris, 1896), appendix [French trans.]. — J. Vogt: FS F. Vittinghoff (Cologne/Vienna, 1980), 527-572 [German trans.]. — *euch., orat.*, C. Moussy, SC 209. — *orat.*, W. Hartel, CSEL 30:3.

L: A. Brun, Un poète à Marseille: Bulletin trimestriel de la société de statistique d'histoire de Marseille 2 (1922) 22-32. — C. Caeymaex, Caractère et poème: MB 1 (1897) 186-199. — idem, Métrique: MB 1 (1897) 308-317. — idem, Style: MB 2 (1898) 161-167. — N. K. Chadwick, Poetry and Letters in Early Christian Gaul (London, 1955), 123-126. — P. Courcelle, Nouveau poème. VC 1 (1947) 101-113. — idem, Confessions (Paris, 1963), 208-211. — L. Dévogel, Latinité et style: RUB 3 (1897/98) 443-451, 515-539. — J. Duboul, P. le pénitent: Actes de l'Académie imperiale des Sciences, Belles Lettres et Arts de Bordeaux 22 (1860) 97-139. — E. Griffe, Pénitence: BLE 59 (1958) 170-175. — idem, P. le Pénitent: BLE 76 (1975) 121-125. — C. Johnston, P. of Pella: HT 25 (1975) 761-769. — A. Longrè, Particularités prosodiques et métriques: Cahiers d'Études Anciennes 2 (1973) 89-112. — G. Malsbary, Virgilian Elements: FS A Bastiaensen (Steenbrugge, 1991), 175-182. — G. Misch, Geschichte der Autobiographie 1/2 (Frankfurt a.M., ⁴1974), 684-689. — C. Moussy, Poème de grâces et prière, SC 209 (Paris, 1974). — C. Müller, Observationes grammaticae (Berlin, 1932). — D. Nardo, Eco terenziana in P.: AMAP 86 (1973/74) 121-123. — L. Niedermeier, Antike poetische Autobiographie (Munich, 1919). — A. Quacquarelli, Gregorio di Nazianzo e P. Tra biografia e autobiografia: idem, Retorica e sue istituzioni interdisciplinari (Rome, 1995), 125-142. — J. Rocafort, De Paulini Pellaei vita et carmine (Bordeaux, 1890). — K. F. Stroheker, Senatorischer Adel (Darmstadt, 1970), 202f. — P. Tordeur, Concordance (Brussels, 1973).

B. DÜMLER

Paulinus of Périgueux (Petricordia)

Little is known of P.'s life. He was born in the early years of the 5th c. It is rather unlikely that he was bishop of Périgueux. His most important work is an epic about Martin of Tours, *De vita S. Martini* (*Mart.*), containing six books and written in three stages ca. 470. *Mart.* 1-3 is an epic reworking of the

Vita Martini of → Sulpicius Severus. *Mart.* 4f. have their model in the *Dialogi* of Sulpicius. *Mart.* 6 is a poetic version of stories about miracles at the tomb of St. Martin, which Bishop Perpetuus of Tours had composed in prose and sent to P. with a request that he turn them into verse. The *Praefatio ad carmina minora* is P.'s answering letter to Perpetuus. Also because of Perpetuus's initiative are the twenty-five hexameters that were intended for the new Basilica of St. Martin in Tours and are contained in the mss. under the title *De orantibus*. P.'s poem *De visitatione nepotuli sui* tells of a miracle of Martin for the nephew of P. and his wife.

W: M. Petschenig, CSEL 16/1:1-190.
L: M. Brooke, Interpretatio christiana: FS J. Bramble (Bristol, 1987), 285-295. — A. H. Chase, Metrical Lives: HSCP 43 (1932) 51-76. — F. Châtillon, Vita Martini: RMÂL 23 (1976) 5-12. — R. v. Dam, Perpetuus: Francia 16 (1986) 567-573. — J. Drevon, De vita et scriptis (Agen. 1889). — J. Fontaine, Hagiographie et politique: RHEF 62 (1975) 113-140. — A. Huber, Poetische Bearbeitung (Kempten, 1901). — G. H. Malsbary, Epic Hagiography (Toronto, 1988).

M. Skeb, OSB

Paulinus of Tyre

P. was a supporter of Arius from ca. 320 on and the addressee of the *Ep. ad Paulinum Tyrium* of → Eusebius of Nicomedia. At the urging of Constantine he signed the anti-Arian Nicene formula of faith but then supported the anti-Nicene reaction. In 327 he succeeded Eustathius as bishop of Antioch. He died shortly afterwards. The only surviving work of P. is a fragment of his *Ep. ad Alexandrum Alexandrinum.*

W: H. G. Opitz, Athanasius Werke 3/1 (Berlin, 1934), 17f. [text].
L: M. Simonetti, La crisi ariana (Rome, 1975), 31-35. — J. Wilkinson, P.'s Temple at Tyre: JÖB 32 (1982) 553-561.

M. Skeb, OSB

Pelagius

I. Life: P. (b. 350-360, d. 418-431) was a lay Christian, probably from Britain, who appeared in Rome ca. 380, was a teacher there to devout ascetical circles of distinguished Roman bourgeois, and was highly respected. After he and → Caelestius his supporter had fled to North Africa ahead of Alaric and then stayed in Palestine, P. became the chief personage in the Pelagian controversy. In 411 a Council of Carthage condemned six propositions of Caelestius, espec. those on infant baptism and the sin of Adam. In 411/412 Augustine began the controversy at the

literary level, with Jerome joining in in 413. In 415, at Augustine's inspiration, a new complaint was made against which P. defended himself so skillfully at the Synod of Diospolis that he was declared orthodox. In contrast, two North African councils condemned P. and Caelestius in 416. Innocent I of Rome agreed with these judgments in 417, but his successor Zosimus, rendered uncertain by the accused themselves and by other intercessions, remained a waverer and even rehabilitated P. In 418 Emperor Honorius intervened in favor of the North Africans, and the Council of Carthage issued nine anti-Pelagian canons. Zosimus of Rome yielded and in a circular letter, the *Epistola tractoria*, excommunicated P. and Caelestius. P. died probably in Egypt. In 431 the Council of Ephesus condemned the Pelagians, Julian of Eclanum in particular.

II. Works: Given the state of the sources it is difficult to determine the genuine works of P. Much is preserved only in fragments in other sources or under other names; the attribution is often disputed. Among the certainly authentic, completely preserved, or reconstructed works are the *Expositiones XIII epistolarum Pauli* (ca. 405; *exp.*) and the *Epistola ad Demetriadem* (413/414; *Dem.*)

The *exp.* give a picture of P.'s theology before 411 and are therefore of the greatest importance. The commentary belongs to the time of the so-called Pauline renaissance in the Lat. church. P.'s exegesis, influenced by the Antiochene school, is historical and focused on the literal sense: it avoids allegory, prefers typology, and intends to edify (in the positive sense of this term). The bibl. passages are divided into short segments and given a brief but substantial exegesis, often in the form of alternatives ("multiple choice exegesis"). In this respect, P. pointed the way and provided a form for the Middle Ages, espec. the Irish.

Dem. contains the Pelagian position in a nutshell; Augustine (*ep.* 150) and Jerome (*ep.* 130) subsequently published letters to the convert Demetrias. Another work of P., *De fide trinitatis*, has survived only in fragments.

III. Basic Lines of Thought: The hist. situation of the young state-church must be taken into account in any just judgment on P.: in an age when Christianity was spreading to the masses without schism (Donatism) P. sought to make strict moral standards a reality. Many of the views represented by him or his supporters could be accepted in broad circles or at least tolerated. P. stood within the broad current of a syncretistic popular philosophy that fed on Stoicism and had become acclimatized in Christianity since the 2nd c. Indispensable to an understanding of P. is the christianized idea of *paideia* (redemption as a historical process of salutary education), which had long had a place in Gr. theology. It can be shown for example that P. had a knowledge of Origen (or Rufinus of Aquileia), Rufinus the Syrian, Ambrosiaster, and another commentator on Paul (VL 8).

P.'s interest was in morality. In view of moral laxity and heretical currents (Manichees, Jovinians), morals seemed to him in need of reform and enlightenment. For this reason he insisted that his concern was "to bring to light the power and makeup of human nature" (*Dem.* 2). In saying this, he belonged (as originator?) to a heavily lay movement, orthodox in many respects, that was focused not on particular doctrinal propositions but rather on a specific area of concern.

P.'s starting point was Christ as the representative of moral obligations assigned by God. This anthropological horizon starts from the grace of creation in the form of conscience (see *Dem.* 4), the law, and free will. P. rejects sin as being in any way natural and, since it is an accident in relation to nature, he makes human beings responsible for it (*exp.* Rom 7:17): the divine likeness enables them to recognize what is right in the light of the natural law, the law of Moses, and the gospel, to do what is right by the power of free will, and so to earn salvation (the inalienable "ability to do"). By acting in this way, human beings become aware of their duty to bring the divine likeness to completion in themselves by means of their natural abilities (*exp.* Col 3:10). This explains P.'s preference for a terminology that expresses the perception and activity of creatures and his high esteem for experiential created reality. This reality is characterized by the unity of the orders of creation and redemption and of the OT and the NT. There can be no original sin in the sense that Adam sinned as an example and prototype (*exp.* Rom 5:12). But, acc. to P., sin can become a habitual thing that makes sinlessness almost impossible in real life. Adam constructed a powerful historical anti-image that led to a distortion of the grace of creation (*exp.* Rom 8:21). A universal "habit of sinning" (*exp.* Rom 7:23; Gal 4:4; Eph 2:3; *Dem.* 8) led, because of God's saving care of us, to the Mosaic law as a reminder of the natural law and finally to the gospel, which goes beyond the Mosaic law (*exp.* 2 Cor 3:7, 10). In P.'s view, then, grace resides in the area of interchange between natural endowment, environment, and a providence that strengthens human beings with helps given to all but does not determine their actions. P. is compelled therefore to conceive of predestination as foreknowledge (*exp.* Rom 8:29f.) in order not to endanger free will and responsibility.

The heart of the gospel is baptism for the forgiveness of sins "through faith alone" (faith understood as deliberate consent, *exp.* 1 Cor 1:1). For their part, those thus baptized must hold fast to this baptismal grace and even improve it by their good works (*exp.* Rom 3:28). Espec. helpful to this end are the life and teaching of Christ (*exp.* Rom 3:20; 6:14). In referring to baptism P. is thinking chiefly of adult baptism as a decisive turning point in the person's life. In such a perspective it is hardly possible to make sense of infant baptism for the forgiveness of sins. Christ is also a lawgiver, insofar as he is stricter than the earlier stages of the law (*exp.* Rom 7:25; Gal 3:24). The emphasis on Christ as the embodiment of the unity of teaching and action, an emphasis conditioned by P.'s ethical-pastoral concern, causes the expiatory aspect of Christ's work to become secondary but not to disappear. In addition, Christ is an eschatological prototype in reference to the resurrection (*exp.* Rom 1:4). The action of the Spirit remains vague: He dwells in believers, stimulates hope (*exp.* Rom 5:5), and thus is a gracious help, like the law and moral example. Grace and the reading of scripture are thought of as the way to awareness of the required behavior: "Show the fruit of reading and prayer!" (*Dem.* 23). Preaching and exhortation are meant to lead to the divinely willed use of freedom and to the perfecting of the image of God with means that already are a part of the image. After Christ, the church is the locus of this process (*exp.* 1 Tim 3:15). An apostle such as Paul is a model of the following of Christ in the church (*exp.* Rom 1:1; 16:25): Like the prophetic books of the OT, his letters give explanations of the law and are examples for the community (*exp.* argumentum).

P.'s theology with its broad concept of grace always looks even at the OT in the perspective of a salvation-historical universality. But P. is only partly just to Paul (e.g., in his understanding of the law). There is not lacking a tension between the (moderate) ascetical tone of P.'s theology and the goodness of nature. And yet P.'s theology may not be reduced to a shallow moralism, for behind it are serious concerns in the theology of the community (efficacy of grace!) that still occupy the church today and become ever anew the starting point for critical questions. On the other hand, the theonomic structure of P.'s teaching on grace forbids us to see him as a precursor of modern thought on autonomy.

W: *exp.*, A. Souter (Cambridge, 1926) [text/not completely correct]. — T. de Bruyne (Oxford, 1993) [English trans.].

— *Dem.*, PL 30:15-45; 33:1099-1120. — M. K. C. Krabbe (Washington, 1965) [text/English trans.]. — G. Greshake, W. Geerlings, Quellen geistlichen Lebens (Mainz, 1980), 141-178 [German trans.]. — B. R. Rees, P. (Woodbridge, 1991), 29-70 [English trans.]. — *De fide trinitatis*, PL 39:2198-2200. — PLS 1:1544-1560.

Doubtful writings: *Eclogae ex divinis scripturis*, Jerome, *Dialogi* 1:25-32, PL 23:519-526. — Augustine, *De gestis*, passim, CSEL 42:52-107. — T. de Bruyn (1993), 55-154 [English trans.]. — *Ad Livaniam*, Marius Mercator, *Commonitorium*, ACO 1, 5, 1, 69-70. — O. Wermelinger: FZPhTh 1979, 352f. [text/German trans.]. — *De natura*, Augustine, *De natura et gratia*, passim, CSEL 60:231-299; (cf. PL 48:599-606). — *Dicta in ecclesiastico iudicio Palaestino*, Augustine, *De gestis*, passim, CSEL 42:52-118. — O. Wermelinger, Rom u. P. (Stuttgart, 1975), 295-299. — *Chartula defensionis*, Augustine, *De gestis* 32.57-34.58, CSEL 42:111-113. — *Ad amicum suum*, Augustine, *De gestis* 30.54, CSEL 42:107. — *Pro (de) libero arbitrio*, Augustine, *De gratia Christi*, passim PL 48:611-613. — PLS 1:1539-1543. — *Epistola purgationis*, Augustine, *De gratia Christi*, passim, CSEL 42:150-181. — *Libellus fidei*, PL 39:2181-2183. — PL 45:1716-1718. — PL 48:488-491. — *De vita Christiana*, PL 40:1031-1046. — PL 50:383-402. — B. R. Rees, P. (Woodbridge, 1991), 105-126 [English trans.]. — *Ad viduam*, Augustine, *De gestis* 6.16, CSEL 42:68. — Jerome, *Dialogi* 3.16, PL 23:586. — *Ad Celantiam*, Paulinus v. Nola, *ep.*, CSEL 29:436-459. — CSEL 56:329-356. — *De scientia divinae legis*, PL 30:105-116. — B. R. Rees, P. (Woodbridge, 1991), 88-104 [English trans.]. — *Ad Claudiam (laus virginitatis)*, PL 30:163-175. — PL 103:671-684. — B. R. Rees, P. (Woodbridge, 1991), 71-87 [English trans.]. — *De induratione*, PLS 1:1506-1539.

L: L. W. Barnard, P. and Early Syrian Christianity: RThAM 35 (1968) 193-196. — P. Battifol, St. Augustine, P. et le siège apostolique: RB 15 (1918) 5-58. — T. Bohlin, Die Theologie des P. u. ihre Genesis (Uppsala, 1957). — G. Bonner, How Pelagian Was P.?: StPatr 9 (1966) 350-358. — idem, Rufinus of Syria and African Pelagianism: AugSt 1 (1970) 31-47. — idem, Augustine and Modern Research on Pelagianism (Villanova, 1972). — idem, P.: TRE 26:176-185 (literature). — U. Borse, Der Kol-Text des P. (Bonn, 1966). — P. R. Brown, P. and His Supporters: JThS 19 (1968) 93-114. — T. de Bruyne, P.'s Interpretation of Rom 5, 12-21: TJT 4 (1988) 30-42. — idem, P.'s Commentary on St. Paul's Epistle to the Romans (Oxford, 1993). — E. Buonaiuti, P. e l'Ambrosiastro: RicRel 4 (1928) 1-17. — J. B. Bury, The Origins of P.: Her. 13 (1904) 26-35. — A. Cameron, Celestial Consulates: JThS 19 (1968) 213-215. — C.-P. Caspari, Briefe, Abhandlungen u. Predigten (Brussels, 1964 = ¹1890). — J. Comeliau, A propos de la prière de P.: RHE 31 (1935) 77-89. — D. Dumville, Evidence for the British Transmission of P.: CMCS 10 (1985) 39-52. — Y. M. Duval, P. est-il le censeur inconnu de l'Adversus Iovinianum à Rome en 393?: RHE 75 (1980) 525-557. — H. H. Esser, Das Paulusverständnis des P. (Bonn, 1961). — idem, Thesen u. Anmerkungen zum exegetischen Paulusverständnis des P.: FS K. Kupisch (Munich, 1963), 27-42. — R. F. Evans, P., Fastidius and the Pseudo-Augustinian De Vita Christiana: JThS 13 (1962) 72-98. — idem, P.'s Veracity at the Synod of Diospolis: Studies in Medieval Culture, ed. J. Sommerfeld (Kalamazoo, Mich., 1964), 21-30. — idem, P. (London, 1968). — idem, Four Letters of P. (London, 1968). — J. Ferguson, P. (New York, 1978 = Cambridge, 1956). — E. Florkowski, Soteriologia Pelagiusza (Cracow, 1949). — H.

J. Frede, P. (Freiburg i.Br., 1961). — idem, Eine neue Hs. des Pauluskommentars von P.: RBen 73 (1963) 307-311. — C. García-Allen, P. and Christian Initiation (Ann Arbor, Mich., 1979). — idem, Was P. Influenced by Chromatius of Aquileia?: StPatr 17 (1982) 1251-1257. — G. Greshake, Gnade als konkrete Freiheit (Mainz, 1972). — V. Grossi, Il battesimo e la polemica pelagiana: Aug. 9 (1969) 30-61. — A. Guzzo, Agostino contro P. (Turin, 1958). — H. Jonas, Augustinus u. das paulinische Freiheitsproblem (Göttingen, ²1965). — J. Jäntsch, Führt der Ambrosiaster zu Augustinus oder P.?: Schol. 9 (1934) 92-99. — J. F. Kelly, P., Pelagianism and the Early Christian Irish: Mediaevalia 4 (1978) 99-124. — I. Kirmer, Das Eigentum des Fastidius im pelagianischen Schrifttum (St. Ottilien, 1938). — U. Koch, P. e la lettera agli Ebrei: Rel. 11 (1935) 21-30. — J. H. Koopmanns, Augustine's First Contact with P.: VC 8 (1954) 149-153. — W. Liebeschütz, Did the Pelagian Movement Have Social Aims?: Hist. 12 (1963) 227-241. — idem, Pelagian Evidence on the Last Period of Roman Britain: Latomus 26 (1967) 436-437. — W. A. Löhr: De natura: Rekonstruktion u. Analyse: RechAug 31 (1999) 235-294. — F. Loofs, P.: RE 15:747-774; 24:310-312. — J. R. Lucas, P. and St. Augustine: JThS 22 (1971) 73-85. — R. A. Markus, Pelagianism: JEH 37, 2 (1986) 191-204. — idem, The legacy of P.: The Making of Orthodoxy, ed. R. D. Williams (Cambridge, 1989), 214-234. — P. Marti, Die Auslegungsgrundsätze des P.: SThU 32 (1962) 167-175. — idem, P. u. seine Zeit: SThU 33 (1963) 129-134. — idem, Zur Ethik des P.: SThU 33 (1963) 129-134. — G. Morin, Le Vita Christiana de l'évêque breton Fastidius et le livre de P. Ad Viduam: RBen 15 (1898) 481-493. — idem, P. ou Fastidius?: RBen 5 (1904) 258-264. — idem, Fastidius ad Fatalem: RBen 46 (1934) 3-17. — J. N. L. Myres, P. and the End of Roman Rule in Britain: JRS 50 (1960) 21-36. — M. F. Nicholson, Celtic Theology: An Introduction to Celtic Christianity, ed. J. P. Mackey (Edinburgh, 1989), 386-413. — F. G. Nuvolone, A. Solignac, P. et pélagianisme: DSp 12B:2889-2942. — W. W. Phibbs, The Heresiarch. P. or Augustine?: AThR 62 (1980) 124-133. — B. Piault, Autour de la controverse pélagienne: RSR 44 (1956) 481-514. — R. Pirenne, La morale de P. (Rome, 1961). — G. de Plinval, Recherches sur l'œuvre littéraire de P.: RPh 60 (1934) 9-42. — idem, P. (Lausanne, 1943). — idem, Essaie sur le style et la langue de P. (Fribourg, Switzerland, 1947). — idem, Points de vues récents sur la théologie de P.: RSR 46 (1958) 227-236. — S. Prete, P. ed il pelagianesimo (Brescia, 1961). — B. R. Rees, P. (Woodbridge, 1988). — idem, The Letters of P. and His Followers (Woodbridge, 1991). — J. Rivière, Hétérodoxie des pélagiens en fait de rédemption?: RHE 41 (1946) 5-43. — A. P. F. Sell, Augustine versus P.: CTJ 12 (1977) 117-143. — A. J. Smith, The Latin Sources of the Commentary of P.: JThS 19 (1918) 162-230; 20 (1919) 55-65. — idem, The Commentary of P. on "Romans" Compared with That of Origen-Rufinus: JThS 20 (1919) 127-177. — idem, P. and Augustine: JThS 31 (1929/30) 21-35. — A. Souter, P.'s Doctrine in Relation to his Early Life: Exp. 1 (1915) 180-182. — idem, P.'s Expositions of Thirteen Epistles of St. Paul (Cambridge, 1922). — E. TeSelle, Rufinus the Syrian, Caelestius, P.: AugSt 3 (1972) 61-95. — A. Trapè, Verso la riabilitazione dei pelagianesimo?: Aug. 3 (1963) 482-516. — H. Ulbrich, Augustins Briefe zur entscheidenden Phase des pelagianischen Streites: REAug 9 (1963) 51-75, 235-258. — H. Vogels, Der P.-kommentar: ThRv 25 (1926) 121-126. — A. Wayens, Un chrétien nommé P. (Brussels/Jena, 1971). — O. Wermelinger, Rom u. P. (Stuttgart, 1975). — idem,

Das P.-dossier in der Tractoria: FZPhTh 26 (1979) 336-368. — M. Winterbottom, Pelagiana: JThS 38 (1987) 106-119. — D. F. Wright, P. the Twice-born: ChM 82 (1972) 6-15. — H. Zimmer, P. in Irland (Berlin, 1901). — A. Zumkeller, Neuinterpretation o. Verzeichnung der Gnadenlehre des P. u. seines Gegners Augustinus?: AugSt 5 (1974) 209-226.

J. Stüben

Pelagius I of Rome

Before being raised to the post of bishop of Rome (April 16, 555), P., a Roman nobleman, distinguished himself as deacon and as emissary of the Roman bishop to Constantinople. He became an adviser of Emperor Justinian who, under P.'s influence, condemned Origen (543). While still a deacon, P., together with the later bishop of Rome, → John III, made a Lat. translation of maxims of monastic wisdom from the → *Apophthegmata Patrum* (*Vitae patr.*). During the Three-Chapters controversy he initially opposed the imperial condemnation of the Antiochene theologians. The first treatise of his predecessor, Vigilius, in defense of the Three Chapters (*Constitutum*) is principally P.'s work. P. consolidated his theol. views against the fickle Vigilius in his work *In defensione trium capitulorum* (*defens.*), which was written in 554 and has come down in mutilated form; in it P. harked back to → Facundus of Hermiane. But after 555, in order to win the favor of the emperor, P. changed his position and agreed to the condemnation of the Three Chapters; the emperor rewarded him and sent him back to Rome as its bishop. In many of his approximately one hundred letters (*ep. pontif.*), P. attempted with little success to overcome northern Italian opposition to the condemnation of the Three Chapters. P.'s literary works bear the tragic mark of the theol. and political dependence of the papacy on Justinian. This immaturity lasted until P.'s death on March 3, 561.

W: *Vitae patr.*, PL 73:855-988. — *defens.*, PLS 4:1313-1369. — *Constitutum*, Avell. 83, O. Guenther, CSEL 35:230-320. — *ep. pontif.*, P. M. Gassó, C. M. Batlle, Pelagii I Papae epistulae (Montserrat, 1956), 1-228 [text]. — PLS 4:1284-1312. L: L. Abramowski, Die Zitate in der Schrift De defens.: VigChr 10 (1956) 160-193. — E. Caspar, Geschichte des Papsttums 2 (Tübingen, 1933), 286-305. — A. Di Berardino (ed.), Patrologia 4 (Genoa, 1996), 144-146. — J. Richards, The Popes and the Papacy (London, 1979).

S. C. Kessler, SJ

Pelagius II of Rome

During the siege of Rome by the Lombards P. was elected bishop of Rome. Because of the political situation he was consecrated in August, 579, without the prescribed imperial confirmation. Since the emperor was unable, because of the Persian wars, to give any political or military help to Italy in its distress, P. became the first bishop of Rome to turn to the Franks, in Oct. 580. In a letter to his later successor, → Gregory I, at that time a deacon who was an ambassador in Constantinople, P. describes the wretched condition of Italy in order to urge the emperor to act (*ep. ad Gregorium diaconum*). Of the surviving letters, three letters to the bishops of Istria are important, but *ep.* 3 is to be ascribed to Gregory I. The letters are conciliatory in tone and impressive for their theol. content (*ep. ad episcopos Istriae*). The efforts to end the schism with the northern Italian churches was unsuccessful. P. died on Feb. 7/8, 590, in a plague caused by the flooding of the Tiber.

W: *ep. 2 ad Aunarium Autussiodurensem*, W. Gundlach, MGH. Ep 3:448-450 [text]. — *ep. ad Gregorium diaconum*, L. M. Hartmann, MGH. Ep 2:440f. [text]. — *ep. 3 ad episcopos Istriae*, idem, MGH. Ep 2:442-467. — ACO 4, 2, 105-132. L: E. Caspar, Geschichte des Papsttums 2 (Tübingen, 1933), 352-374. — J. N. D. Kelly, P.: The Oxford Dictionary of Popes (Oxford, 1986), 65. — L. Magi, La sede romana nella corrispondenza degli imperatori e patriarchi bizantini (Rome, 1972), 162-165. — P. Meyvaert, A Letter of P. Composed by Gregory the Great: Gregory the Great, ed. J. C. Caradini (University of Notre Dame, 1995), 94-116. — J. Richards, The Popes and the Papacy (London, 1979). — C. Sotinel, P.: DHP 1296f.

S. C. Kessler, SJ

Peshitta

The *Peshitta* or *versio simplex*, as distinguished from the Syr. *Hexapla* that goes back to Origen, is regarded as the most important and most widespread Syr. translation of the Bible. The OT seems to have been translated directly from the Hebrew and contains the entire Masoretic canon except for Chron, Ezra, Neh, and Esth. There is no unity on the question of the Jewish or Jewish-Chr. origin of the *Peshitta*. The closeness to the Targums (Onkelos) suggests rather a Jewish origin, but in some recensions, influences of the LXX can also be seen. The *Peshitta* is not the work of a single author during a single period but must have taken shape slowly and by stages. Thus the Psalms are translated in close dependence on the original, while the Pentateuch, Ezek, Prov, and Judg are free paraphrases and resemble Targums. Some recensions betray a knowledge of earlier translations such as the → *Diatessaron*, but also of the old Syr. four gospels, the use of which → Rabbula made obligatory in Edessa.

475

W: A. S. Lewis, The Old Syriac Gospels (London, 1910). —
P. Institute, Genesis, Exodus (Leiden, 1977). — eadem,
Leviticus, Numbers, Deuteronomy, Josua (Leiden, 1991).
— eadem, Judges, Samuel (Leiden, 1978). — eadem, Book
of Psalms (Leiden, 1980). — eadem, Kings (Leiden, 1976).
— eadem, Proverbs, Wisdom of Solomon, Ecclesiastes,
Song of Songs (Leiden, 1979). — eadem, Isaiah (Leiden,
1987). — eadem, Ezekiel (Leiden, 1985). — eadem,
Dodekapropheton, Daniel (Leiden, 1980). — eadem, Apoc-
alypse of Baruch, 4 Esdras (Leiden, 1973). — eadem, Canti-
cles or Odes, Prayer of Manasseh, Apocryphal Psalm
(Leiden, 1972). — B. Aland, Die Großen Kath. Briefe
(Berlin, 1986). — eadem, Die paulinischen Briefe (Berlin,
1991).
L: P. B. Dirksen, Book of Judges (Leiden, 1972). — J. A.
Emerton, Old Testament P. Manuscripts (Leiden, 1961). —
A. Gelston, P. of the Twelve Prophets (Oxford, 1987). — M.
D. Koster, P. of Exodus (Assen, 1977). — Y. Maori, P. Ver-
sion of the Pentateuch (Jerusalem, 1975). — A. Vööbus,
Pesitta and Targumim (Stockholm, 1956). — M. M. Win-
ter, Concordance (Leiden, 1976).

P. Bruns

Peter, Literature about

The figure of P. plays a considerable role in apocryphal literature. He and his disciple Mark are linked
with Egypt. As a result, the literature on Peter reflects
various eccles. controversies about the correct tradition of Chr. doctrine (on this see also the → [Ps.-]
Clementines).

L: T. Baumeister, Die Rolle des P. in gnostischen Texten: T.
Orlandi, F. Wisse, Acts of the 2nd International Congress of
Coptic Studies (Rome, 1985), 3-12. — K. Berger, Unfehlbare Offenbarung, P. in der gnostischen u. apokalyptischen
Offenbarungslit.: FS F. Mussner (Freiburg i.Br., 1981), 261-
326. — T. Smith, Petrine Controversies in Early Christianity (Tübingen, 1985).

1. Pseudepigraphical works: A *Gospel of P.* (*Ev. Petr.*)
is mentioned by Origen (*comm. in Mt.* 10.17) and is
attested by Eusebius as not accepted (*h.e.* 3.3.2;
3.25.6). The citation given in *h.e.* 6.12.3-6 from the
work of Serapion of Antioch on the *Ev. Petr.* is
important: Serapion had discovered the work in the
community of Rhossus and had at first accepted it
but then rejected it because of its Docetist elements.
In 1886/1887 an 8th/9th c. Gr. fragment was discovered in a monk's tomb at Akhmin, Upper Egypt (also
found: the *Apocalypse of P.* and Greek *Enoch*). The
fragment describes events from the condemnation
by Pilate to Easter and was identified, probably correctly, with the *Ev. Petr.* The writer of the parchment
knew only this portion of the text; no other fragments have thus far been clearly identified. The relation of *Ev. Petr.* to the canonical gospels is disputed;
the work, composed at the beginning or middle of
the 2nd c. (in Syria?), is probably witness to a devel-

opment that ran parallel to the traditions in the
canonical gospels and then became gnostic. Characteristic is the strong OT cast of the presentation
(using espec. Isa and Ps), together with an anti-
Jewish tendency (similarities with Melito, *pass.*).

W: O. v. Gebhardt, Das Evangelium u. die Apokalypse des
P. (Leipzig, 1893) [Greek facsimile text]. — E. Kloster-
mann, Apocrypha 1 (KlT 3) (Bonn, ³1933) [text]. — M. G.
Mara, SC 201. — A. Fuchs, Das *Ev. Petr.*, StNTU 12 (Linz,
1978). — NTApo⁶ 1:185-188 [German trans.]. — M.
Erbetta, Gli Apocrifi del NT 1 (Turin, 1966), 135-145 [Ital-
ian trans.].
L: N. Brox, Doketismus: ZKG 95 (1984) 301-314. — J. D.
Crossan, The Gospel of Peter and the Canonical Gospels:
Forum 1 (1998) 7-51. — J. Denker, Die theolo-
giegeschichtliche Stellung des Ev. Petr. (Frankfurt a.M.,
1975). — A. J. Dewey, The Passion Narrative of the Gospel
of Peter: Forum 1 (1998) 53-69. — M. Dibelius, Die atl.
Motive in der Leipzigsgeschichte des P.- u. des Joh: idem,
Botschaft u. Geschichte 1 (Tübingen, 1953), 221-247. — A.
v. Harnack, Bruchstücke des Evangeliums u. der Apoka-
lypse des P., TU 9/2 (Leipzig, ²1893). — B. A. Johnson, The
Gospel of Peter: StPatr 16 (1985) 170-174. — E. Junod,
Eusèbe de Césarée, Sérapion d'Antioche et l'Évangile de
Pierre: RSLR 24 (1988) 3-16. — H. Köster, Überlieferung u.
Geschichte der frühchr. Evangelienlit.: ANRW II 25/2
(1984) 1463-1542. — J. W. McCant, The Gospel of Peter:
NTS 30 (1984) 258-273. — O. Perler, L'Évangile de Pierre
et Méliton: RB 71 (1964) 584-590. — P. Pilhofer, Justin u.
das Ev. Petr.: ZNW 81 (1990) 60-78. — L. Vaganay, L'É-
vangile de Pierre (Paris, 1930). — T. Zahn, Das Ev. Petr.
(Leipzig, 1893).

Fragments of a *Kerygma Petri* (*Keryg. Petr.*) are to
be found in Clement Alex., who regards them as
authentic. The work seems to have been a summary
of the (apostolic) preaching of P. and to date from
the first half of the 2nd c. It is probably not the same
as the *Doctrina Petri* or *Didascalia Petrou* mentioned
in Origen (*princ.*, praef.) and Gregory Naz. (*ep.* 20.2).
Origen, who documents the use of the *Keryg. Petr.* by
Heracleon (*Jo.* 13.17), already regards the apostolic
origin of the work as no longer certain; to Eusebius
(*h.e.* 2.3.2) it is apocryphal. The themes of the fragment (Chr. monotheism, the claim to the OT, Christians as a third race, exhortation) show that the work
marks a transition from NT/early Chr. preaching to
apologetic literature.

A letter of P. to Clement (*ep.*), supposedly written
by Jesus, is preserved in connection with the Arab.
Canones of Clement. (On this and on an apocryphal
letter of P. to James and on the so-called *Kerygmata
Petrou*, → [Ps.-] Clementines; on the so-called letter
of P. to Philip, → Philip, Literature about.)

W: *Keryg. Petr.*, E. v. Dobschütz, TU 11/1 (Leipzig, 1893).
— E. Klostermann, Apocrypha 1 (KlT 3) (Bonn, 1933), 13-
16 [text]. — M. G. Mara, Il Keryg. Petr.: FS A. Pincherle

(Rome, 1967), 314-342 [text]. — NTApo⁶ 2:38-41 [German trans.]. — M. R. James, The Apocryphal NT (Oxford, 1955 = 1924), 16-18 [English trans.]. — *ep.*, P. Fahed, Kitab al-Huda (Aleppo, 1935) [Arabic text]. — W. Riedel, Die Kirchenrechtsquellen des Patriarchats Alexandrien (Leipzig, 1900), 166-175 [German trans.].

L: P. Nautin, Les citations de la Predication de Pierre: JThS NS 25 (1974) 98-105. — H. Paulsen, Das Keryg. Petr. u. die urchr. Apologetik: ZKG 88 (1977) 1-37. — G. Quispel, R. M. Grant, Note on the Petrine Apocrypha: VigChr 6 (1952) 31f. — J. N. Reagan, The Preaching of Peter (Chicago, 1923). — W. Rordorf, Christus als Logos u. Nomos: FS C. Andresen (Göttingen, 1979), 424-434.

2. Acts: The *Acts of Peter* (*A. Petr.*) are possibly already attested by Origen, who at least knows of similar traditions, and certainly by *Didasc.* 6.7-9 and Eusebius (*h.e.* 3.3.2), who rejects them as uncanonical. In the West they were known to Augustine. Numerous oriental versions have come down. The relationship of the *A. Petr.* to the → (Ps.-) Clementines, which also describe the life of Peter, is not clear; it is at least possible that the author of the original version of the latter (ca. 260) knew the *A. Petr.* The *Acts of Peter* have come down in the form of the *Actus Vercellenses* (a Lat. ms. of Vercelli). It can be inferred that the beginning of the work (stay of P. in Jerusalem, first conflict with Simon Magus) is missing. What remains is the account of Paul's journey to Spain, the arrival of P., the restoration of the community devastated by Simon, the struggle with Simon, and the martyrdom of P. This *Martyrium* (4th c.) was later also handed down independently (some Gr. versions have survived).

The *Martyrium Petri a Lino conscripto* is a later Roman revision that followed the Gr. version but incorporated local Roman traditions; the address of P. before his crucifixion is important.

The *A. Petr.* can be supplemented by the story of P.'s daughter (it belongs to the lost opening section and is preserved in Coptic) and, on the basis of a reference in Augustine, *c. Adim.* 17, the story of a gardener's daughter that is also found in the apocryphal letter of → Titus. In its content, despite the emphasis on the conflict with Simon Magus, the *A. Petr.* are concerned not with Simonian gnosis but with the general war between God and the devil. The work, done within the church, intends to complement the Acts of the Apostles, but, given its popular character, it shows, on its periphery, gnostic, docetic, and encratitic ideas. The Gr. original was probably written after the *Acts of John*, which probably influenced the *A. Petr.*, and before the *Acts of Paul*, i.e., before 190. A further *Passio* is given by → Hegesippus in his version of the *Bellum Judaicum* 3.2.

W: AAAp 1:1-22. 45-103 [text]. — L. Vouaux (Paris, 1922) [text/French trans./comm.]. — C. Schmidt, Die alten P.-Akten, TU 24/1 (Leipzig, 1903), 3-7 [Coptic text]. — The NHC. Cod. V, 2-5, NHS 11 (Leiden, 1979), 473-493 [Coptic text/English trans.]. — L. Leloir, Martyre de Pierre, CCA 3:64-76 [French trans. of the Armenian version of Martyrium]. — NTApo⁵ 2:256-289. — M. Erbetta, Gli Apocrifi del NT 2 (Turin, 1966), 170-177 [Italian trans. of Martyrium].

L: A. Baumstark, Die P.- u. Paulusacten in der lit. Überlieferung der syr. Kirche (Leipzig, 1902). — C. Erbes, Ursprung u. Umfang: ZKG 32 (1911) 497-530. — A. Ferreiro, Simon Magus, Dogs, and Simon Peter: FS J. B. Russell (Leiden, 1998), 45-89. — G. Ficker, Die P.-Akten (1903). — J. Flamion, Les actes apocryphes de Pierre: RHE 9 (1908) 233-254, 465-490; 10 (1909) 5-29, 215-277; 11 (1910) 5-28, 223-256, 447-470, 675-692; 12 (1911) 209-230, 437-450. — R. Hanig, Petrusakten: StPatr (1996). — HLL 4:392-394. — B. McNeil, A Liturgical Source in A. Petr. 38: VigChr 33 (1979) 342-346. — G. Poupon, Les "Actes de Pierre" et leur remaniement: ANRW II 25/6 (1988) 4363-4383. — C. Schmidt, Studien zu den alten P.-Akten: ZKG 43 (1924) 321-348; 45 (1927) 481-513. — idem, Zur Datierung: ZNW 29 (1930) 150-155. — R. F. Stoops, Patronage in the Acts of Peter: Semeia 38 (1986) 91-100. — G. Stuhlfauth, Die apokryphen P.-Geschichten in der altchr. Kunst (Berlin, 1925). — C. H. Turner, The Latin Acts of Peter: JThSt 32 (1931) 119-133.

The *Acts of Peter and the Twelve Apostles*, which have come down only in the Copt. Nag Hammadi library, go back to a Gr. original and, probably wrongly, are regarded by many as the beginning of the *A. Petr.* In fact, the text is one that is difficult to assign to a genre (possibly a compilation from three base texts), and its title is secondary. Worth noting is the remarkable relationship between reality and vision (its allegorical character has been described as "surrealistic"). Its content concerns the heavenly assignment to mission; the focal places are two cities that symbolize heaven and the world. A being named Lithargoel, who is a manifestation of Jesus, plays an important role.

The work is possibly from the 2nd/3rd c. and from a specific group of a Jewish-Chr. kind; the emphasis on poverty and asceticism suggests the world of Syr. itinerant prophets. Later on, the work became of interest for gnosticism.

W: The Facsimile Edition of the NHC. Cod. VI (Leiden, 1972), 5-16. — M. Krause, Gnostische u. hermetische Schriften aus Cod. II u. Cod. VI, ADAI. K 2 (Glückstadt, 1971), 107-121 [text]. — D. M. Parrott (ed.), NHC V, 2-5 and VI (Leiden, 1979), 179-229 [text]. — J. M. Robinson (ed.), The Nag Hammadi Library in English (Leiden, ³1988), 265-270 [English trans.]. — H. M. Schenke, "Die Taten des Petrus und der 12 Apostel": ThLZ 98 (1973) 13-19 [German trans.].

L: A. Guillaumont, De nouveaux Actes apocryphes: RHR 196 (1979) 141-152. — M. Krause, Die P.-Akten: FS A.

Böhlig (Leiden, 1972), 36-58. — J. Kubinska, L'ange Litakskuel en Nubie: Muséon 89 (1976) 451-455. — S. J. Patterson, Sources, Redaction and Tendenz: VigChr 45 (1991) 1-17. — H. M. Schenke, review of Parrott: OLZ 79 (1984) 460-464. — J. Sell, Simon Peter's Confession: NT 21 (1979) 344-356.

The so-called *Acta Petri et Pauli* (*A. Petr. et Paul.*) (BHG 1490) probably arose, in the form of a basic Gr. text, in connection with the Roman attempt (perceptible from the 4th c. at the latest) to link the two apostles together (see also *Decretum Gelasianum* 3.2). The work also indicates a rejection of the earlier independent Peter and Paul traditions. In chs. 1-21, the *Acts* describe (with later additions) the journey of Paul from Malta to Rome, then the controversy between the apostles and Simon Magus, and finally their martyrdom. These *Acts* are also preserved in Armenian and Georgian.

To be distinguished from the preceding is the longer Lat. *Passio Petri et Pauli* (*Pass. Petr. et Paul.*) (BHL 2:6659; there ascribed to a Marcellus), chiefly by leaving out Paul's journey, but there are other differences as well.

W: *A. Petr. et Paul.*, R. A. Lipsius, Acta apostolorum apocrypha 1 (Darmstadt, 1959 = 1891), 178-222 [text]. — L. Leloir, CCA 3:7-34 [French trans. of the Armenian text]. — *Pass. Petr. et Paul.*, R. A. Lipsius, op. cit., 119-177 [text]. — L. Leloir, CCA 3:37-54 [French trans. of the Armenian text].
L: NTApo⁵ 2:395-399. — L. Vouaux, Les actes de Pierre (Paris, 1922), 160-178.

The *Doctrina Simonis Kepha in urbe Roma* (BHO 936) is a Syr. legend about Peter along with other narrative material, in which dogmatic statements of a post-Nicene type are found. The work was probably not composed until the 5th/6th c. The *Vita Petri* handed down in Slavic (there is also an unpublished Gr. version [BHG 2:1485f.]) may likewise have been composed in 5th/6th c. Syria; it shares only the external framework with the other literature on Peter and displays many peculiar features, which however also appear in other Acts (P.'s five-year stay in the wilderness, journey by ship to Rome with Jesus/Michael as helmsman, appearance of Jesus as a child who is later sold to P. as a slave).

W: *Doctrina*, W. Cureton, Ancient Syrian Documents (London, 1864) [Syriac text/English trans.]. — I. Franko, Beiträge aus dem Kirchenslav.: ZNW 3 (1902) 315-333 [German trans.]. — *Vita*, A. S. Arkhnangelskij: Bolletino della sezione di Lingua e letteratura russa 4 (1898) 112-118 [text]. — E. Follieri, L'originale greco: AnBoll 74 (1956) 115-130 [text].
L: A. Baumstark, Die P.- und Paulusacten in der lit. Überlieferung der syr. Kirche (Leipzig, 1902), 38-40. — P. Peeters, Notes sur la légende des apôtres S. Pierre et S. Paul: AnBoll 21 (1902) 121-140.

3. Apocalypses: The first allusion to a revelation given to Peter is found in Theophilus Alex. (*Autol.* 2.19). Clement Alex. regarded it as a sacred writing (Eus., *h.e.* 6.14.1). Eusebius himself regards it as a fake, and later on, even though it long enjoyed high esteem, it was suppressed.

A Gr. fragment of it was first discovered at Akhmin, along with fragments of the *Ev. Petr.*, but this contained only about a half of the text given in the subsequently discovered Eth. translation. The text has been altered in the course of its transmission (Copt. and Georg. forms) but probably provides the original content.

The work gives a speech of Jesus, delivered on Mt. Olivet, on the end of the world, in which, among other things, he interprets the parable of the fig tree (with allusions to Bar Kochba?). Unlike earlier apocalypses, this one describes the lot of the damned out of pastoral concern; for the first time, the text also harks back to Gr. and Egypt. ideas.

The main concepts are those of *revelatio* and *traditio*, the handing on of revelation to P. (who also acquires an eschat. significance) and, through him, to Clement. Both the emphasis on the figure of P. and the Egypt. motifs point to Egypt as the place of origin; the use of *4 Esd* and 2 Pet, an allusion to Bar Kochba, and the place of this apocalypse in early Chr. literature point to the years ca. 135 as the time of composition.

W: O. v. Gebhardt, Das Evangelium u. die Apokalypse des P. (Leipzig, 1893) [Greek facsimile text]. — E. Preuschen, Antilegomena (Giessen, ²1905), 84-88, 188-192 [Greek text/German trans.]. — S. Grébaut, Littérature éthiopienne ps. clémentine: ROC 12 (1907) 139-151; 15 (1910) 198-214, 307-323, 425-439 [Ethiopic text/French trans.]. — H. Duensing, Ein Stücke der urchr. P.-Apokalypse enthaltender Traktat: ZNW 14 (1913) 65-78 [German trans./comm.]. — M. R. James, The Apocryphal NT (Oxford, 1955 = 1924), 505-524 [English trans.]. — M. Erbetta, Gli Apocrifi del NT 3 (Turin, 1981), 209-233 [Italian trans.]. — NTApo⁵ 2:566-578 [German trans. of the Greek and Ethiopic text].
L: R. J. Bauckham, The Apocalypse of Peter: ANRW II 25/6 (1988) 4712-4750 (literature). — K. Berger, Unfehlbare Offenbarung, P. in der gnostischen u. apokalyptischen Offenbarungslit.: FS F. Mussner (Freiburg i.Br., 1981), 261-326. — A. v. Harnack, Bruchstücke des Evangeliums u. der Apokalypse des P., TU 9 (Leipzig, 1893). — idem, Die P.-Apokalypse in der abendländischen Kirche, TU 13 (Leipzig, 1895). — M. R. James, A New Text of the Apocalypse of Peter: JThS 12 (1911) 35-56, 362-383, 573-583. — K. Prümm, De genuino apocalypsis Petri textu: Bib. 10 (1929) 62-80. — G. Quispel, R. M. Grant, Note on the Petrine

Apocrypha: VigChr 6 (1952) 31f. — F. Spitta, Die P.-Apokalypse: ZNW 12 (1911) 237-242.

To be distinguished from the preceding is the Copt. gnostic *Apocalypse of Peter* (*Apoc. Petr.*) that is transmitted in NHC 7, 3. During Holy Week the true nature of Jesus (in the gnostic sense) is revealed to P. through visions and auditions, in order that he may pull through the experience of the passion. In the middle sections, persons and opinions from the early history of the church are assessed; this serves to console and strengthen in the present conflicts. The opponents here described were probably not to be looked for only in the Great Church; there is reference rather to various (including gnostic) groups. In opposition to these, the conventiclelike group, with its Jewish-Chr. tendencies, in which the *Apoc Petr.* originated, sets forth its own gnostic christology. The work must have been written at the end of the 2nd or beginning of the 3rd c., perhaps in Syria/Palestine.

W: The Facsimile Edition of the NHC, Cod. VII (Leiden, 1972). — M. Krause, V. Girgis: F. Altheim, R. Stiehl (ed.), Christentum am Roten Meer 2 (Berlin, 1973), 152-179, 200-229 [text/German trans.]. — J. A. Brashler, The Coptic Apoc. Petr., Diss. (Claremont Graduate School, 1977) [text/comm.]. — H. Havelaar, The Coptic Apoc. Petr., Diss. (Groningen, 1993) [text/English trans./comm./essays]. — A. Werner, Die Apoc. Petr.: ThLZ 99 (1974) 575-584 [German trans.]. — J. M. Robinson (ed.), The Nag Hammadi Library in English (Leiden, ³1988), 339-345 [English trans.]. — S. K. Brown, G. W. Griggs, The Apoc. Petr.: Brigham Young University Studies 15 (1974/75) 131-145 [English trans./comm.].
L: A. Böhlig, Zur Apoc. Petr.: GöMisz 8 (1973) 11-13. — A. Guillaumont, Textes de Nag Hammadi: Annuaire du Collège de France 80 (1980) 471-473. — D. Hellholm, "Revelation-Schema" and Its Adaption in Apoc. Petr.: SEA 63 (1998) 233-248. — K. Koschorke, Die Polemik der Gnostiker (NHS 12) (Leiden, 1978). — M. Krause, Die P.-Akten: FS A. Böhlig (Leiden, 1972), 36-58. — P. Perkins, Peter in Gnostic Revelation: SBL Annual Meeting, Seminar Papers 2 (Cambridge, 1974), 1-13. — H. M. Schenke, Bemerkungen zur Apoc. Petr.: FS P. Labib (Leiden, 1975), 277-285.

G. RÖWEKAMP

Peter I of Alexandria

P. was elected bishop of Alexandria in 300 after having been head of the school there. He was imprisoned during the Diocletian persecution but freed ca. 306 by Galerius and his Edict of Tolerance. In 311, in the course of the persecution of Maximinus Daia, he was again imprisoned and finally beheaded.

During the time of persecution P. was involved in difficult conflicts with Melitius of Lycopolis. Melitius did not share P.'s moderate attitude toward the *lapsi*,

those who had sacrificed to pagans gods and then wanted to return to the church. The question was evidently not whether or not the *lapsi* should be taken back; the conflict was over the question of how much time must pass before they were taken back and what status they were then to have. When the break with P. came, Melitius replaced imprisoned bishops with his own supporters (Epiph., *haer.* 68.3). Finally, P. condemned Melitius and had him deposed by a council (during his own two periods of imprisonment); this elicited the opposition of Arius, who had been ordained by P.

Several letters (*ep.*) of P. have survived that deal with the question of the *lapsi* (the so-called canonical letter [*ep. can.*], which is possibly a festal letter or a circular letter after Easter or a treatise on penance) or with the persecutions or the Melitian schism. In addition to homilies (*hom.*) on riches and on Epiphany (to this group belongs the fragmentary *Didascalia* in homiletic form) some theol. works have also been preserved and transmitted in Greek, Latin, and Syriac. In the work *On the Divinity and Humanity of Christ* (*deit.*) P. identifies the Logos with the Son; the Logos became incarnate in order to rescue humanity. In the work *De anima* (*an.*) P. opposes the Platonic theory of a preexistence of souls as accepted by Origen. In *On the Resurrection* (*res.*; an Easter homily?) P. attacks the teaching of Origen that after their ascent to heaven human bodies will have a spiritual *conditio*.

P.'s opposition to Origen led to a strong anti-Origenist trend in Alexandria that affected even exegetical methods. In fact, it must have been simply a controversy over already discussed Origenist views.

W: *ep. can.*, P. A. de Lagarde, Reliquiae Iuris Eccl. Antiqu. (Leipzig, 1856), 63-73, 99-117. — *ep.*, W. E. Crum, Texts Attributed to Peter of Alexandria: JThS 4 (1902/3) 387-397. — J. Barns, H. Chadwick, A Letter Ascribed to Peter of Alexandria: JThS 24 (1973) 443-455. — *hom.*, J. M. Heer, Ein neues Frgm. der Didaskalie des Martyrerbischofs P.: OrChr 2 (1902) 344-351. — *deit.*, PG 18:509-512, 521-522. — AS 4:187-189, 194-195. — M. Richard: Muséon 86 (1973) 268f. — *an.*, PG 18:520-521. — M. Richard: Muséon 86 (1973) 268f. — PG 86:961B. — AS 4:193-194. — ACO 3, 197. — W. Bienert: Kl. 5 (1973) 311-312. — *res.*, M. Richard: Muséon 86 (1973) 267-269. — AS 4:189-193. — *De pascha*, PG 18:512B-520B.
L: W. A. Bienert, Dionysius v. Alexandrien (Berlin, 1978). — C. W. Griggs, Early Egyptian Christianity (Leiden, 1990), esp. 117-120. — R. P. C. Hanson, The Search for the Christian Doctrine of God (Edinburgh, 1988), 3f., 62. — C. Markschies, ". . . et tamen non tres dii, sed unus deus . . .": Marburger Jahrbuch, Theologie 10, Trinität, ed. W. Härle, R. Preul (Marburg, 1998), 155-179, here 168. — T. Orlandi, La raccolta copta delle lettere attribuite a Pietro Alesandrino: AnBoll 93 (1975) 127-132. — L. B. Radford, Three

Teachers of Alexandria: Theognostus, Pierius and P. (Cambridge, 1908). — M. Richard, P. et l'unique hypostase du Christ: idem, Opera minora (Tournai, 1977), Nr. 26. — M. Simonetti, Le origini dell'arianesimo: RSLR 7 (1971) 317-330. — T. Vivian, St. P., Bishop and Martyr (Philadelphia, 1988). — R. Williams, Arius and the Melitian Schism: JThS 37 (1986) 35-52.

T. BÖHM

Peter II of Alexandria

P., a presbyter of Alexandria who had already been designated Athanasius's successor, was imprisoned by Valens. In P.'s place the Emperor appointed Lucius, an Arian. P. escaped and sought refuge in Rome (373-378) with Pope Damasus; there he took the side of Paulinus in the Antiochene schism. In 379 he returned to Alexandria, and in 380, in Constantinople, he tried to have Maximus replace Gregory Naz. in the anti-Arian community.

P.'s few remaining writings show that he confessed the full humanity of Jesus Christ and two persons in Christ.

W: *ep. encyclica*, Theodoret, *h.e.* 4.22, F. Scheidweiler, GCS 44:249-260. — *ep. ad episc. Aeg.*, PG 33:1291f. — *hom. in Pascha*, M. Richard, Quelques nouveaux fragments des Pères anténicéens et nicéens: SO 38 (1963) 80f.
L: C. W. Griggs, Early Egyptian Christianity (Leiden, 1990), 181-183, 185. — A. Grillmeier, Jesus der Christus 1 (Freiburg i.Br., ³1990), 533f. (English, Christ in Christian Tradition, vol. 1 [London, ²1975]). — P. Maraval, Alexandrien und Ägypten: Die Geschichte des Christentums 2, ed. T. Böhm et al. (Freiburg i.Br., 1996), 1007-1029, esp. 1020f.

T. BÖHM

Peter III (Mongus) of Alexandria

After the death of Timothy Aelurus, P. was elected bishop by the anti-Chalcedonian party (477-490). Acacius of Constantinople and Gelasius of Rome refused to recognize him. After some difficulties in Alexandria, Acacius convinced Emperor Zeno to send a letter offering mediation to Alexandria (*Henotikon*). P. and Acacius were reconciled. Severus of Antioch reproached P. for saying he was theologically satisfied with the *Henotikon*. While P. elsewhere rejected the Chalcedonian Creed, he approved of it in a letter to Acacius (*ep. Acac.*; Evagrius is the only source). P. may be ranked as a moderate Monophysite who condemned Chalcedon but supported the compromise in the *Henotikon*.

W: *ep. Acac.*, J. Bidez, L. Parmentier, The h.e. of Evagrius (Amsterdam, ²1964), 115f. — *ep. ad Frauitam*, E. W. Brooks, CSCO 84:11-14 [Syriac text/Latin trans.]. — *allocutio*, E. W. Brooks, CSCO 83:226f. [Syriac text/Latin trans.].

L: W. H. C. Frend, The Rise of the Monophysite Movement (Cambridge, 1972), 174-183. — A. Grillmeier, Jesus der Christus 2/4 (Freiburg i.Br., 1990), 38-40 (English, Christ in Christian Tradition, vol. 2/4 [London, 1996]). — C. Haas, Patriarch and People: P. and Episcopal Leadership: JECS 1 (1993) 297-316. — D. W. Winkler, Kopt. Kirche u. Reichskirche (Innsbruck, 1997), 122-135.

T. BÖHM

Peter of Callinicus

P., a Monophysite, was first a monk but became successor of Paul as patriarch of Antioch in 581. As such, he was involved in christological disputes with Patriarch → Damian Alex. in 587. He died in 591 in the monastery of Gubba Barraja, northwest of Antioch.

The works of P. survive in a Syr. version that cannot be said beyond doubt to be the original. They include a pentasyllabic hymn on the crucifixion of Christ (*hymn.*), a four-volume treatise against Patriarch Damian (*c. Dam.*), and treatises against the tritheists (*c. Trith.*). Unpublished are a letter to the bishops of the Mesopotamian East, a treatise against archimandrite John Barbûr, and an anaphora.

W: *hymn.*, R. Y. Ebied, L. R. Wickham, The Discourse of Mar P. on the Crucifixion: JThS 26 (1975) 23-27 [text]. — *c. Dam.*, R. Y. Ebied, A. van Roey, L. R. Wickham, CCG 29, 32, 35 [Syriac text/English trans.]. — *c. Trith.*, eadem, P. Anti Tritheist dossier (Leuven/Louvain, 1981) [Syriac text/ English trans.].
L: R. Y. Ebied, P. of Antioch and Damian of Alexandria: FS A. Vööbus (Chicago, 1977), 277-282. — E. Honigmann, Évêques et évêchés (Leuven/Louvain, 1951), 270. — A. van Roey, L'œuvre littéraire de P.: Orient chrétien, Actes du XXIXe congrès international des Orientalistes (Paris, 1975), 64-68. — idem, Une controverse christologique sous le patriarcat de P.: Symp. Syriacum 1976 (Rome, 1978).

C. SCHMIDT

Peter Chrysologus

Despite what is said in the *Liber pontificalis* of Agnellus, (Severian?) Peter (P.) was born not in Forum Cornelii (Imola) but in Classis, the port city of Ravenna, at the end of the 4th c., perhaps ca. 380. By 431 at the latest he was bishop of Ravenna, and in 431 became metropolitan when Ravenna became a metropolitan see. Acc. to the *Vita Germani* of Constantius of Lyons, P. was present at the death of Germanus of Auxerre in Ravenna on July 31, 448. P. did not die on Dec. 3 or in Imola, as Agnellus says on the basis of a confusion, but on July 31, probably in 451 or, in any case, before 458 (*ep.* 166). The surname "Chrysologus" is first attested by Agnellus.

168 of the 176 sermons (*serm.*) in the 8th c. *Collec-*

tio Feliciana are today regarded as P.'s. In addition, a further thirty-nine *serm.* are ascribed to him, of which fifteen are regarded as authentic. The *serm.* attest to the trained speaker, who uses antithesis in particular (to the point that whole sermons have an antithetic structure) and what amounts to a dialogue. They are made vivid by their often maximlike sentences.

For the most part the sermons are homilies on the gospels, Psalms, and letters of Paul. The homilies are given structure by a continual harking back to the bibl. text, which is interpreted in the Alexandrian manner.

Other sermons comment on the baptismal creed (56-62) and the Our Father (67-72). Important for the history of the liturgy are the sermons on the saints' feasts (86-92; 127; 129; 133; 134; 135; 137; 154; 157; 173), Christmas, Epiphany, Lent, and Pentecost (7-9; 11-13; 142-49; 156-60) as well on the consecration of bishops (130; 165). Other liturgical themes are penance (46), the Eucharist (33f.), and the discipline of secrecy (56; 59; 61). On the whole the sermons give a complete sketch of the liturgical year.

Echoing the theology of the Council of Ephesus, the sermons take anti-Arian, anti-Nestorian, and even anti-Eutychian positions (e.g., in 57-60). But P. also attacks paganism and Judaism (5; 30; 36; 75-82; 100, 170). Because of their allusions to, e.g., trade (60; 62), seafaring (7bis), farming (7), administration of justice (8), the military (14), and medicine (44) the *serm.* are not least an important source for the cultural history of the city of Ravenna as an imperial residence, an important commercial harbor, and an agricultural center in the first half of the 5th c. In P.'s works there is also transmitted a letter to Eutyches (composed after June 17, 449), who had appealed to P. after being condemned by Flavian. P. takes a clear position against Monophysitism (see also *serm.* 57; 61; 145) and refers Eutyches to the bishop of Rome as primate (see also *serm.* 84; 154). The authenticity of the so-called *Rotulus* of Ravenna, a collection of forty prayers, is disputed. It is clear that the *Rotulus* was compiled and edited in the 7th c. and that older texts were included. If the latter do not go back to P. as their composer, their content is certainly inspired by him, and they also depend literarily on him to some extent. In addition, a stylistic comparison shows P. to be the author of the *Expositio symboli* (*symb.*) of Cividale, whereas the *Benedictio fontis* on Holy Saturday has been wrongly ascribed to him.

W: *serm.*, A. Olivar, CCL 24, 24A, 24B. — idem, 3 vols. (Barcelona, 1985/87/90) [text/Catalan trans.]. — A. Pasini, 2 vols. (Siena, 1953) [Italian trans.]. — M. Spinelli (Rome, 1978) [Italian trans.]. — G. Böhmer, BKV² 43 (Kempten, 1923) [German trans.]. — M. Held, BKV¹ (Kempten, 1874) [German trans.]. — W. Schmidt (Vienna, 1958) [German trans.]. — *ep.*, A. Olivar (Montserrat, 1962), 87-94. — PL 54:739-744. — *Rotulus*, P. Siffrin: L. C. Mohlberg, Sacramentarium Veronense (Rome, 1956), Beigabe 1:173-178, 202f. — H. Franke, Wartende Kirche (Paderborn, 1937) [German trans.]. — *exp.*, A. Olivar, CCL 24:354f.
L: A. Benelli, Vita: In verbis verum amare. Miscellanea dell'Istituto di Filologia latina e medioevale dell'Università di Bologna, ed. P. Serra Zanetti (Florence, 1980), 63-79. — R. Benericetti, Il Cristo nei Sermoni di P. (Cesena, 1995). — S. Benz, Rotulus (Münster, 1967). — idem, Rotulus: ALW 13 (1971) 213-220. — G. Cortesi, P.: FR 4. ser. 127-130 (1984/85) 117-132. — K. Gamber, Rotulus: ALW 5 (1958) 354-361. — H. Januel, Commentationes philologicae, 2 vols. (Regensburg, 1905/06). — R. Ladino, Iniciación (Rome, 1969). — idem, Iniciación: Laur. 9 (1968) 395-438. — G. Lucchesi, Studi sui santi: Atti dei convegni di Cesena e di Ravenna 1 (Cesena, 1969), 51-80. — R. H. McGlynn, Incarnation (Mundelein, 1956). — A. Olivar, Principis exegètics: FS B. Ubach (Montserrat, 1953), 413-437. — idem, Clavis: SE 6 (1954) 327-342. — idem, P. autor de la bendición de las fuentes bautismales: EL 71 (1957) 280-292. — idem, Expositio symboli: SE 12 (1961) 294-312. — idem, Rotulus. ALW 11 (1969) 40-58. idem, Textüberlieferung: Texte u. Textkritik, ed. J. Dummer (Berlin, 1987), 469-487. — idem, Zur krit. Ausgabe: FS A. A. R. Bastiaensen (Steenbrügge, 1991), 223-236. — idem, Exordes des sermons: RBen 104 (1994) 88-105. — E. Paganotto, Cura pastorale a Ravenna (Rome, 1969). — G. Sessa, Dottrina cristologica (Pozzuoli, 1946). — F. Sottocornola, Anno liturgico (Cesena, 1973). — J. Speigl, Auferstehung der Toten: JAC E 9 (1982) 140-153. — M. Spinelli, Invasioni barbariche: VetChr 16 (1979) 87-93. — idem, Digiuno: VetChr 18 (1981) 143-156. — idem, Sangue, martirio e redenzione: Atti della settimana Sangue e Antropologia Biblica nella patristica 2 (Rome, 1982), 529-546. — idem, Simbologia ecclesiologica: ibid., 547-562.

B. DÜMLER

Peter, Deacon

After Scythian monks had sought vainly to win from Rome approval of the theopaschite formula *unus de trinitate passus est* as part of Neo-Chalcedonianism, an embassy, looking for support, went with a letter of deacon P. and other subscribers (*ep.*) to the African bishops whose spiritual leader was → Fulgentius of Ruspe and who had been banished to Sardinia by the Vandals. *Ep.* is to a great extent a revision of the → *Libellus fidei* of → John Maxentius that was to be given to the Roman legate in Constantinople. By interpreting the union in Christ as a *compositio*, the letter sought to avoid both the Nestorian separation and the Eutychian commingling. The two united natures yield only "the one incarnate nature of the Logos" (*ep.* 3). Probably under the influence of → John Cassian, P.'s christology (*ep.* 1-13) is bound up with his teaching on grace and his disagreements with the teachings of → Faustus of Riez in the latter area (*ep.* 14-28). In the name of the African bishops, Fulgentius of Ruspe confirmed the teaching of the Scythian monks in his *ep.* 17 and contributed to changing the Roman attitude to Alexandrian theology. The theology set forth in P.'s *ep.* was canonized in 553 at the fifth ecumenical council.

P. is not the same person as the Roman Deacon Peter who was a collaborator of → Gregory I and probably the opposite number in his *Dialogues*; this Peter died 605 in Rome.

W: *ep.*, Fulg. Rusp., *ep.* 16, J. Fraipont, CCL 91:551-562. — F. Glorie, CCL 85A:157-172.
L: E. Amann, P. Diacre: DThC 12/2:1928f. — A. Grillmeier, Vorbereitung des MA. s: Konzil v. Chalkedon 2, ed. A. Grillmeier, H. Bacht (Würzburg, 1953), 791-839, esp. 799f. — idem, Jesus der Christus 2/2 (Freiburg i.Br., 1989), 343-355 (English, Christ in Christian Tradition, vol. 2/2 [London, 1995]). — P. Langlois, Fulgentius: RAC 8:632-661, esp. 643f. — V. Schurr, Trinitätslehre des Boethius (Paderborn, 1935), 159f.
On the Roman Deacon P.: A. De Vogüé, Introduction Dialogues, SC 251:44f. — M. v. Uytfanghe, Sceptiscisme doctrinal: Grégoire le Grand, Colloque Chantilly 1982, ed. J. Fontaine et al. (Paris, 1986), 315-324.

M. FIEDROWICZ

Peter the Fuller

P., called the Fuller after his origin, is regarded as one of the most enigmatic characters of the Monophysite movement. Little is known of his life. In 469 he received episcopal consecration in Syr. Seleucia and in 471, thanks to his good connections with the *magister militum per Orientem*, the later Emperor Zeno, whose efforts at dogmatic unity (*Henotikon*) he always supported, was advanced to the position of patriarch of Antioch. This office he held until his death in 488 but with long periods of exile (472-475, 477-485). During his first period in office he intervened in the liturgical life of the church by introducing various novelties. Among those with the most serious consequences was the expansion of the traditional trisagion, widely used in Antioch, by the addition of: "who was crucified for us," which P., like the theopaschites, referred not to the incarnate Logos but to the entire Trinity. This interpretation was the subject of lively controversies in the 6th c., as can be seen from the fake correspondence in the *Collectio Sabbaitica*. In addition, the custom of reciting the creed (→ Symbol) during Mass probably goes back to a decree of P. in 476. A rite for the consecration of chrism and for the blessing of water on Epiphany also had P. for their author. P. cannot, however, be

made the author of the *Corpus Areopagiticum*, which gives the consecration of chrism a sacramental character. Both, however, probably do reflect the piety of the East Syrian world in which the various anointings were highly valued. Part of P.'s extensive correspondence (*ep.*) is a Syr. synodal letter to Monophysite Patriarch → Peter Mongus, and a series of Gr. doctrinal letters.

W: *ep.*, E. W. Brooks, CSCO 83/87:233-235/161f. [Syriac text/Latin trans.]. — ACO 3, 6-25, 217-231; E. Schwartz, Publizistische Sammlungen (Munich, 1934), 182f., 192f., 287-300 [Greek text].
L: A. Grillmeier, Jesus der Christus 2/2 (Freiburg i.Br., 1989), 267-277 (English, Christ in Christian Tradition, vol. 2/2 [London, 1995]). — E. Honigmann, Évêques et évêchés monophysites (Leuven/Louvain, 1951). — U. Riedinger, Ps.-Dionysius Areopagites: ByZ 52 (1959) 276-296. — W. Strothmann, Das Sakrament der Myronweihe (Wiesbaden, 1978).

P. BRUNS

Peter of Jerusalem

P. was patriarch of Jerusalem 514-552 and involved in the controversy over Chalcedon and Origen. As an anti-Origenist he came under pressure in Palestine, where Origenism was in favor, and was replaced by Macarius in 552. Surviving are a Christmas sermon (*hom.*) in which Chalcedonian christology is defended, and a fragment on fasting (*fr.*).

W: *hom.*, I. Abulazde, Mravalthavi (Tiflis, 1944), 307-316. — *fr.*, PG 95:76B.
L: M. v. Esbroeck, Les plus anciens homéliaires géorgiens (Leuven/Louvain, 1975), 154, 188, 303-304. — idem, L'homélie de P. et la fin de l'origenisme palestinien en 551: OCP 51 (1985) 33-59. — L. Perrone, La chiesa di Palestina (Brescia, 1980), 200-214.

G. RÖWEKAMP

Peter of Laodicea

Four commentaries on the gospels were at one time ascribed to P, but the commentary on Mt that was wrongly attributed to him is identical with that of → Victor of Antioch; the commentary on Lk is in fact a catena containing texts of → Severus of Antioch and → Cyril Alex, and even the commentary on Jn is an anonymous catena. The anonymously transmitted 7th c. work on the gospel of Mt is likewise not a commentary by a single author but a catena, the compiler of which was a Peter, acc. to an 11th c. ms. Scholia in this catena are attributed to him by three mss. of the 12th-14th c.

W: *Catena on Mt.*, C. F. G. Heinrici, Des P. Erklärung des Mt-Evangeliums (Leipzig, 1908) [Greek text]. — PG 82/2:3321-3336 [Greek text frags.].
L: H.-G. Beck, Kirche u. theol. Lit. (Munich, 1959), 468f. — C. F. G. Heinrici, Aus der Hinterlassenschaft des P. (Leipzig, 1905), 99-120. — M. Rauer, Der dem P. zugeschriebene Lk-Kommentar (Münster, 1920). — J. Reuss, Mt-, Mk- u. Joh-Katenen (Münster, 1941). — J. Sickenberger, Über die dem P. zugeschriebenen Evangelienkommentare: ThQ 86 (1904) 10-19.

R. HÖFFNER

Peter of Trajanopolis

P., bishop of Trajanopolis, took part in the Council of Ephesus in 431 and supported the Nestorian-minded John of Antioch. For this reason he and John and other supporters were condemned by the synod (ACO 1, 1, 3, 25 and 26). After his condemnation P. composed a short *Libellus poenitentiae* (*poenit.*) in which he professed the orthodox position. P. also helped compose some letters, a *Contestatio ad Cyrillum et Iuvenalem*, and a *Sententia synodi orientalium Ephesenae*.

W: *poenit.*, ACO 1, 1, 7, 139.
L: ACO 4, 3, 1, 406. — W. Enßlin, P. 63: PRE 19/2:1327.

B. WINDAU

Petilian

P. (b. after 354; d. before 419/422) was a catechumen of the Catholic Church but was forcibly baptized by the Donatists (Aug., *c. litt. Pet.* 3.16). He was a *vir clarissimus*, a brilliant lawyer, and towered over his fellow Donatist bishops when it came to learning and eloquence (ibid., 2.92). The date of his episcopal consecration must have been after April 24, 394, since he was not listed among the participants in the Donatist Synod of Bagai on that date. It is certain that shortly after that he was bishop of Constantina (Cirte) in Numidia (Aug., *ep.* 53.1; CSEL 34:153). He was one of the most effective spokesmen for his party at the conference of Carthage in 411. Little is known of his pastoral activities.

P.'s lost letters can be partially reconstructed from Augustine's reply. His letter *ad presbyteros et diaconos* came into Augustine's hands (probably incomplete). The latter answered in great haste (= *c. litt. Pet.* 1). After the entire letter became available to him, he composed a detailed refutation in which he followed P.'s line of argument (= ibid., 2). Three classic matters are discussed (as reported by Augustine): baptism, schism, persecution. The arguments offered are the traditional ones, but in addition P. lays special emphasis on the virtues of peaceableness and patience that characterized the Donatists. P. responded to Augustine's *c. litt. Pet.* 1 with a work that Augustine describes as *litterae* in *c. litt. Pet.* 3.1. Augustine was incensed by the claim of Donatist virtues and by P.'s reply and wrote an angry pamphlet *Ad cath. de secta Don.* (= *c. litt. Pet.* 3) for a wider public. To the detailed analysis in *c. litt. Pet.* 2, P. answered in a further reply (Aug., *retr.* 2.51), in which he accuses the bishop of Hippo of lying, after having earlier accused him of Manichaeism (*c. litt. Pet.* 3.16).

No further mention of P. is found until 419/422 (Aug., *c. Gaud.* 1.37; CSEL 53:247).

W: Augustine, *c. litt. Pet.*, M. Petschenig, CSEL 52:3-227.
L: S. Lancel, SC 194:221-238. — PAC 855-868.

W. GEERLINGS

Petronius of Bologna

P. was bishop of Bologna from 431/432 until probably 450 and is not to be identified either with the one-time *praefectus praetorio Galliarum* (402-409) mentioned by Gennadius (*vir. ill.* 41) and Eucherius (*ep. ad Val.*) or with his son of the same name. Under P.'s name Gennadius speaks of the *Vitae patrum Aegypti monachorum*, which is undoubtedly not from P., and of a treatise *De ordinatione episcopi*. Morin ascribes two sermons (*serm.*) to P., one of which has come down under the title *Sermo Petronii Episcopi Veronensis in Natale Sancti Zenonis*; the second which follows upon it, *Item sermo cuius supra in die ordinationis vel natale episcopi*, must, in light of its stylistic similarity, belong to the same author. Morin identifies this work with the treatise mentioned by Gennadius. No decision has as yet been reached as to whether the author of both *serm.* is P. or a Bishop Petronius of Verona (beginning of 5th c.). The text itself seems to speak against a Veronese authorship (*serm.* 3-6), while the lack of any cult of St. Zeno in Bologna, among other things, speaks against a Bolognese authorship. But the history of the text's transmission favors rather a Veronese authorship.

W: *serm.*, G. Morin: RBen 14 (1897) 3-8 = PLS 3:141-143. — E. Lodi: FS G. Lercaro (Rome, 1967), 296-301 [text/Italian trans.].
L: F. Dolbeau, Une ancienne édition et un manuscrit oublié: RBen 96 (1986) 27-29. — F. Filippini, Petronio di Bologna (Bologna, 1948). — F. Lanzoni, Petronio di Bologna (Rome, 1907). — E. Lodi, Due omilie: FS G. Lercaro (Rome, 1967), 263-301. — G. G. Meersemann et al., Orazionale dell'arcidiacono Pacifico (Fribourg, Switzer-

land, 1974), 131-134. — C. Truzzi, Zeno, Gaudenzio e Cromazio (Brescia, 1985), 95-97.

B. Dümler

Philip, Disciple of Jerome

P., d. 455/456, is mentioned by Gennadius (*vir. ill.* 63) as author of sixty-three (mostly lost) letters and of a commentary on Job (surviving in two versions). This commentary is regarded as an important witness to the transmission of the Vulgate and to the reception of Origen by (Ps.-) Jerome.

W: PL 23:1407-1470; 26:619-802.
L: J. Bauer, Corpora orbiculata. Eine verschollene Origenes-exegese bei Ps.-Hieronymus: ZKTh 82 (1960) 333-341, esp. 334. — I. Fransen, Le commentaire au livre de Job du Petre Philippe (Lyons, 1949). — A. Wilmart, Analecta Reginensia (Vatican City, 1933), 316-322.

J. Lössl

Philip, Literature about

The man who dialogues with Jesus in Jn (6:5-7; 12:21f.) and the apostle/deacon Philip (Ph.) in Acts (6:5; 8:5-13, 24-40; 21:8f.) were identified with each other by the end of the 1st c. and linked to Hierapolis in Phrygia (see Papias in Eus., *h.e.* 3.39.8; 3.31.3).

1. Gospel: A *Gospel of Philip* (*Ev. Phil.*) is attested by Epiphanius (*haer.* 26.13.2f.), who also cites it and connects it with Egyptian gnostics, and by Timothy (PG 86/1:21C) and Leontius of Byzantium (PG 86/1:1213C), both of whom connect it with the Manichees as well (as they do the *Ev. Thom.*). There is disagreement as to whether the *Ev. Phil.* in NHC 2 is the same as the above work, since the citation given by Epiphanius is not found in the NHC text. The *Gospel* is in fact a florilegium. The individual excerpts, which deal primarily with ethics and the sacraments (baptism, anointing, Eucharist, redemption, mystery of the bridal chamber) (the extent is somewhat disputed), possibly come all from a single work. It was the users who turned the florilegium into a *Gospel according to Philip*, Philip being the only apostle named, and named once. The work could have been composed in the 2nd c. in eastern Syria; it shows connections with Valentinian ideas (the savior as bridegroom of the inferior Sophia), was used in Valentinian communities, and because of its many other bits of tradition, provides important and interesting insights into Chr.-gnostic theology of the 2nd c. (among other things, its own theory of apostolic succession).

W: The Facsimile Edition of the NHC. Cod. II (Leiden, 1976), 63-98. — B. Layton, W. W. Isenberg, NHC II, 2-7

(Leiden, 1985) [text/English trans./comm.]. — L'Evangile selon Ph., J.-É. Ménard (Strasburg, 1967) [text/comm.]. — C. J. de Catanzaro, The Gospel according to Ph.: JThS NS 13 (1962) 35-71. — W. C. Till, Das Ev. Phil., PTS 2 (Berlin, 1963) [text]. — J. M. Robinson (ed.), The Nag Hammadi Library in English (Leiden, ³1988), 131-151 [English trans.]. — R. Kasser, Bibliothèque gnostique 8/9: RThPh 20 (1970) 12-35, 82-106 [French trans.]. — W. Foerster (ed.), Die Gnosis 2 (Zurich, 1971), 92-124, 163-166 [German trans.]. — B. Layton, The Gnostic Scriptures (London, 1987), 325-353 [English trans.]. — H.-M. Schenke, Das Ev. Phil.: ThLZ 84 (1959) 1-26 [German trans.]. — J. Leipoldt, H.-M. Schenke, Kopt.-gnostische Schriften (Hamburg, 1960), 31-65, 81f. [German trans.]. — NTApo⁶ 1:155-173 [German trans.].
L: G. L. Borchert, An Analysis of the Literary Arrangement and Theological View in the Gnostic Gospel of Ph., Diss. (Princeton, 1966). — J. J. Buckley, Conceptual Models and Polemical Issues: ANRW II 25/5 (1988) 4167-4194. — A. D. DeConick, Entering God's Presence: Sacramentalism in the Gospel of Ph.: SBL. SP 134 (1998) 483-523. — A. H. C. van Eijk, The Gospel of Ph. and Clement of Alexandria: VigChr 25 (1971) 94-120. — H.-G. Gaffron, Studien zum kopt. Ev. Phil., Diss. (Bonn, 1969). — R. M. Grant, The Mystery of Marriage: VigChr 15 (1961) 129-140. — W. W. Isenberg, The Coptic Gospel According to Ph., Diss. (Chicago, 1968). — Y. Janssens, L'Évangile selon Ph.: Muséon 81 (1968) 79-133. — R. Kasser, L'Évangile selon Ph.: ibid., 407-414. — K. Koschorke, Die Namen im Ev. Phil.: ZNW 64 (1973) 307-322. — R. McL. Wilson, The Gospel of Ph. (New York, 1962). — idem, the NT in the Nag Hammadi Gospel of Ph.: NTS 9 (1962/63) 291-294. — J. Ménard, Das Ev. Phil. u. der Gnostizismus: Christentum u. Gnosis, ed. W. Eltester (Berlin, 1969), 46-55. — K. Niederwimmer, Die Freiheit des Gnostikers: FS G. Stählin (Wuppertal, 1970), 361-374. — E. Segelberg, Sacramental System: Numen 7 (1960) 189-200. — idem, The Antiochene Background: BSAC 18 (1965/66) 205-223. — idem, The Gospel of Ph. and the NT: FS R. McL. Wilson (Edinburgh, 1983), 204-212. — J.-M. Sevrin, Les noces spirituelles: Muséon 77 (1974) 143-193. — G. Sfameni Gasparro, Il "Vangelo secondo Filippo": ANRW II 25/5 (1988) 4107-4166. — W. J. Stroud, The Problem of Dating the Chenoboskion Gospel of Ph., Diss. (Iliff, 1971). — idem, Ritual in the Chenoboskion Gospel of Ph.: Colloque internationale sur les textes de Nag Hammadi, ed. B. Barc (Quebec, 1981), 267-278. — M. L. Turner, The Gospel according to Ph., NHS 38 (Leiden, 1996). — M. A. Williams, Realized Eschatology: Restoration Quarterly 14 (1971) 1-17. — W. C. v. Unnik, Three Notes: NTS 19 (1964) 465-469.

2. Acts: The *Acts of Philip* (*A. Phil.*) that have come down to us are a compilation of fifteen different sections. The connecting element, espec. in sections 1-7, is encratism. Sections 8-15 give the *Acta Philippi* in Hierapolis, with a report on his crucifixion; the description of the place as the "City of the Snake" refers to the clash with the Asia Minor cult of Cybele. Since the encratites were widespread in Phrygia (Epiphanius, *haer.* 47) and a sect of this kind was condemned by the Synod of Gangra in 342 (Mansi 2:1097-1100), the origin of the *Acta Philippi* has been

connected with those circles. The suggestion that sections 8-15 represent a Messalian reworking of earlier *Acta* is probably untenable. Early translations (Armenian, Georgian) of this second part have survived. The first attestation of the work in the West is in the *Decretum Gelasianum*. The later Syr. *Historia Philippi* (BHO 972) and the Copt. *Acta Philippi et Petri*, which are preserved complete only in Arabic and Ethiopic (BHO 977; 982; BHO 978; 983), have only a few points in common with the *A. Phil.* The Lat. *Vita Philippi* transmitted in → Abdias (Ps.-) draws for the most part on the canonical scriptures and Eusebius.

W: AAAp 2, 2, 1-98 [text]. — B. Bouvier, F. Bovon (Geneva, 1989) [text missing in Bonnet]. — M. Erbetta, Gli Apocrifi del NT 2 (Turin, 1966), 457-485, 489f. [Italian trans.]. — M. R. James, The Apocryphal NT (Oxford, 1955 = 1924) [English trans.].
L: K. Berger, Jüd.-hellenistische Missionslit.: Kairos 17 (1975) 2329-248. — F. Bovon, Les Actes de Ph.: ANRW II 25/6 (1988) 4431-4527. — L. Moraldi, Apocrifi del NT 2 (Turin, 1971), 1625-1631. — E. Peterson, Die Häretiker der A. Phil.: ZNW 31 (1932) 97-111. — T. Zahn, Forschungen zur Geschichte des ntl. Kanons 6 (Leipzig, 1900), 18-24, 158-175.

3. Letter to Philip: The so-called Letter of Peter to Philip makes up the second and final part of NHC 8. The letter cited at the beginning (132.12–133.8) has given its name to the entire work, which apart from that letter is structured as a dialogue of Jesus with his disciples. The history of the origin of this complex work is probably as follows: In the beginning there was a prior form of *A. Phil.*; in order to explain and surmount an actual threatening situation a doctrinal conversation with a mythological section (135.8–136.15), containing a Sethian form of the Sophia myth, was introduced (134.19–138.3). In addition, a Chr.-gnostic history of the apostles was introduced that connects the passion of Jesus with the suffering of the author (the emphasis on Peter in this section suggests that it was a form of the *Acts of Peter*) (139.9–140.1). Abridgments at the beginning and end turned the work into a kind of epitome which, after being translated from Gr. into Copt., was received into NHC 8. The text, which has for its theme the sufferings of the disciples and their surmounting of it and therefore also stresses the importance of the earthly Jesus and his passion, is not authentically gnostic but does have gnostic passages. The basic questions asked in the didactic dialogue (134.20–135.2) resemble the classical questions in Clem. Alex., *exc Thdot.* 117.4-17. A possible time of origin was from the end of the 2nd to the middle of the 3rd c.

W: The Facsimile Edition of the NHC. Cod. VIII (Leiden, 1976). — J. H. Sieber, NHC VIII, NHS 31 (Leiden, 1991) [text]. — J. É. Menard (Quebec, 1977) [text]. — J. M. Robinson (ed.), The Nag Hammadi Library in English (Leiden, ³1988), 394-398 [English trans.]. — H. G. Bethge: ThLZ 103 (1978) 161-170 [German trans.]. — idem, "Der Brief des Petrus an Ph.," Diss. (Berlin, 1984) [text/German trans./comm.]). — M. W. Meyer (Chicago, 1981) [text/English trans./comm.]. — NTApo⁶ 1:280-284 [German trans.].
L: K. Koschorke, Eine gnostische Pfingstpredigt: ZThK 74 (1977) 323-343. — idem, Eine gnostische Paraphrase des johanneischen Prologs: VigChr 33 (1979) 383-392. — R. McL. Wilson (ed.), Nag Hammadi and Gnosis (Leiden, 1978), 96-102, 103-107. — K. W. Tröger, Die Passion Jesu Christi, Diss. (Berlin, 1977), 144-166.

G. RÖWEKAMP

Philip of Side

P. was a disciple of Rhodo in Side and was ordained a priest in Constantinople by John Chrys. Later (from 426 on) he was three times a candidate for the office of patriarch (Soc., *h.e.* 7.26f.).

Acc. to Socrates, P. responded to Emperor Julian's work *Against the Galileans*. Between 434 and 439 he composed a history of the world and the church that ran from creation to 426. The verbose and not very stylish work is preserved only in fragments and excerpts, of which some, nonetheless, are valuable (on Papias, the Alexandrian school of catechists). Photius (*cod.* 35) in his time still knew two-thirds of the original thirty-six books.

W: A. Wirth, Aus orientalischen Quellen (Frankfurt a.M., 1894), 280ff. — C. de Boor, Neue Frgm.: TU 5/2 (1898) 165-184. — G. C. Hansen, Theodoros Anagnostes, GCS 160.
L: E. Honigmann, Ph. and his "Christian History": PatSt (1953) 82-91. — H. Opitz, Ph.: PRE 19:2350f.

G. RÖWEKAMP

Philo of Carpasia

A commentary on the Cant (*Cant.*) from the 4th/5th c. is attributed to a Bishop P. by the Gr. mss. and by Cosmas Indicopleutes (*top.* 10.56). The assignment of P. to the episcopal see of Carpasia in Cyprus (indications in *v. Epiph.* 49 and Jerome, *ep.* 51.2) or to the Aegean island of Carpathos is uncertain. The commentary is not preserved in its original form; the Gr. text in PG 40 and the catena fragments in → Procopius of Gaza and Ps.- → Eusebius, go back to an abridged version; the work was translated into Latin by Epiphanius Scholasticus at Cassiodorus's suggestion; here the author is understood to be → Epiphanius of Salamis. The allegorical interpretation of the Cant follows earlier exegetes in dealing with individual motifs, but it also offers some original explanations; on the whole, the work is rather unsophisticated. → Cosmas Indicopleustes (*top.* 10.59) also cites a sentence from P.'s (lost) commentary on the Hexaemeron. The *Ep. ad Eucarpium* (falsely attributed to Basil, among others, as his *ep.* 42) is hardly a work of P.'s.

W: *Cant.*, PG 40:27-154. — A. Ceresa-Gastaldo, CorPat 6 (Turin, 1979) [Latin text/Italian trans./comm.].
L: A. Ceresa-Gastaldo, L'esegesi biblica di Filone: FS M. Pellegrino (Turin, 1975), 79-87. — idem, Philon de Carpasia: DSp 12/1:1374-1377. — F. Ohly, Hohelied-Studien (Wiesbaden, 1958), 53f. — W. Riedel, Die Auslegung des Hohenliedes (Leipzig, 1898), 75-79. — L. Welsersheimb, Das Kirchenbild: ZKTh 70 (1948) 436-440.

F. Dünzl

Philo, Historian

Anastasius Sinaita twice cites the church history of a certain P. The latter is not to be identified with → Philo of Carpasia. Nothing more can be said about the work except that it was composed after the 4th and before the 7th c.; the citations have to do with Peter Alex. and an excommunicated priest who died a martyr.

L/W: G. Mercati, Un preteso scritto di san Pietro vescovo d'Allessandria e martire sulla bestemmia e Filone l'istoriografo: idem, Opere Minori 2, StT 77 (Rome, 1937), 426-439 [text].

G. Röwekamp

Philocalia

The name *Philocalia*, whose etymology is uncertain, appears first as the name of an anthology of texts of Origen that Basil and Gregory Naz. compiled (358/359). Ever since Macarius of Corinth and Nicodemus Hagiorites published a collection of patristic texts in Venice in 1782 under the same name, the word *philocalia* has usually been understood as "love of virtue." With excerpts under the name of Anthony the Great down to Gregory of Thessalonica (= Palamas), this second *Philocalia* seeks to lead its readers to a life of union with God, the purification of their interior selves (asceticism), and the practice of the Jesus prayer (Hesychasm). By way of the translation into Church Slavonic, published by Paisij Velichkovskij in 1793 under the title *Dobrotojubie*, the work exerted a lasting influence on the spirituality of monks and laity in 19th c. Russia.

W: N. Hagiorites, Philokalia ton hieron neptikon (Athens, ⁵1982), 5 vols. [Greek text]. — B. Bobrinskoy (ed.), Ph. (Bégrolles-en-Mauges, 1979ff.) [French trans.]. — K. Dahme, Byz. Mystik, 2 vols. (Salzburg, 1989, 1995) [partial German trans.] (literature).
L: T. Spidlik, K. Ware et al., Amore del Bello, Studi sulla Filocalia (Magnano, 1991). — A.-E. N. Tachiaos, De la Ph. au Dobrotoljubie: Cyrillomethodianum 5 (1981) 208-213. — K. Ware, Philocalie: DSp 12/1:1336-1352.

J. Pauli, OSB

Philostorgius

Ca. 388, on a journey to Constantinople, P., b. ca. 368 in Borissos (Cappadocia), had a formative meeting with Eunomius of Cyzicus, leader of the moderately Arian Eunomians, to whom P. belonged. He lived on in Constantinople, journeyed to Palestine and Antioch, and died after 425.

Between 425 and 433 P. composed a history of the church (*h.e.*), which he conceived as a continuation of Eusebius's chronicle and which paid great attention to secular history; it covered the period from the beginning of the Arian controversies (ca. 315) to 425. The text is lost and can be reconstructed only from fragments and excerpts in Photius (*cod.* 40), in the *Artemii Passio* of John of Rhodes, *Suidas*, the anonymous *Vita Constantini*, and the *Thesaurus orthodoxae fidei* of Nicetas Acominatus. The clearly Eunomian work seeks to condemn Athanasius and his supporters, to glorify Eunomius and his teacher, Aetius of Antioch, as new prophets, and to represent Arianism as true teaching. The widespread reception of this work, which in other respects was strongly condemned by non-Arian authors, is owing to its detailed accounts of, among other things, Aetius, Eunomius, Asterius of Cappadocia, Theophilus Indus, and Ulfila, and of Arian writings. All these point to P.'s rich collection of sources.

The two other writings of P., mentioned in his church history, are also lost: a defense of Christianity against Porphyry and an encomium of Eunomius.

W: *h.e.*, PG 65:459-638. — F. Winkelmann, GCS 21 [text/comm.].
L: P. Batiffol, Fragmente der Kirchengeschichte des Ph.: RQ 3 (1889) 252-289. — idem, Un historiographe anonyme arien du IVᵉ: RQ 9 (1895) 57-97. — G. Fritz, Ph.: DThC 12/2:1495-1498. — G. Geutz, Ph.: PRE 20/1:119-122. — G. Moravcsik, Byzantinoturcica 1. Die byz. Quellen der Geschichte der Türkvölker (Berlin, ²1958), 473-75.

C. Schmidt

Philoxenus of Mabbug

I. Life: P., also known to Syrians as "Xenaias," was born in the mid-5th c. in Taal in the province of Beit

486

Garmai (Persia). Ca. 460 P. took up his studies in the famous Persian school of Edessa, when Bishop Nonnus was repressing Nestorianism. Despite the abiding Persian influence, P. was a Monophysite and remained one until his death. Peter the Fuller, patriarch of Antioch, installed P. as bishop of Mabbug (Hierapolis), where he resided unchallenged from 485 to 499. When the orthodox Flavian took over the see of Antioch, P. came increasingly in conflict with the strengthened Chalcedonian restoration. As a result of numerous intrigues in Constantinople he secured the deposition of his unpopular superior, brought his like-minded friend Severus to power, and in addition was able to win the see of Jerusalem to the Monophysite party; in 518, however, under the strict Emperor Justin I, who was faithful to Chalcedon, P. had to admit defeat and leave his see. A few years later he died in exile, honored by all the Jacobites of the East as a confessor.

II. Works: P. wrote extensively. His close collaboration with his chorbishop Polycarp produced the well-known translation of the NT (including the Cath. letters and Rev) and the Pss into Syriac (the so-called *Philoxiana* [*Phil.*]). Only fragments exist of P.'s commentaries (*comm.*) on Mt, Lk, and Jn.

P., together with his friend Severus of Antioch, is regarded as the great Monophysite dogmatic theologian. From his pen came the ten addresses (*diss.*) against Habib, in which he defends the incarnation of the divine Logos against Nestorians and Chalcedonians; he also wrote important treatises on the Trinity (*tract.*).

Outstanding among his practical and ascetical writings are thirteen homilies (*hom.*) that contain a detailed doctrine of the virtues and are probably to be dated between 485 and 490.

In addition, P. kept up an extensive correspondence. His body of letters includes sixteen longer ones (*ep.*) on asceticism and dogma. Espec. important is the letter to Stephen bar Sudayle, in which he attacks Origen's teaching on the apocatastasis.

Some monastic regulations (*can.*) are also attributed to P., but their literary authenticity is disputed.

III. Basic Lines of Thought: P. is inseparable from the theology and piety of the Syr. church. He is important equally as dogm. theologian, poet, and exegete. As a theologian using Syriac, P. presupposed the dogma of the Trinity and endeavored to establish the incarnation of the divine Logos using the traditional *mia physis* teaching of → Cyril Alex. and to help it be victorious in the West Syrian world. His letters and homilies show him not only to be a representative of the Alexandrian tradition but also to have a profound

knowledge of the Syr. poetry of → Ephraem, on whose works he drew and whose spiritual heritage he was able to use in an independent way.

S: *vita*, A. de Halleux, CSCO. S 100/101 [text/French trans.].
W: *Phil.*, J. Gwynn, Apocalypse of St. John (Dublin, 1907) [text/comm.]. — idem, Remnants of the Syriac Bible (London, 1909) [text/comm.]. — *comm. in Io.*, A. de Halleux, CSCO. S 165/166 [text/French trans.]. — *comm. in Mt. et Lc.*, J. W. Watt, CSCO. S 171/172 [text/English trans.]. — *tract.*, A. Vaschalde, CSCO. S 9/10 [text/Latin trans.]. — *diss.* 1/2, M. Brière, F. Graffin (Paris, 1920) [text/Latin trans.]. — *diss.* 3-5, M. Brière, F. Graffin, PO 38/3 [text/Latin trans.]. — *diss.* 6-8, eadem, PO 39/4 [text/French trans.]. — *diss.* 9/10, eadem, PO 40/2 [text/French trans.]. — *indices*, PO 41. — *hom.*, W. Budge, Discourses of Ph. 1-2 (London, 1894) [text/English trans.]. — E. Lemoine, SC 44 [French trans.]. — *ep.*, A. Vaschalde, Three letters (Rome, 1902) [text/English trans./comm.]. — A. de Halleux, CSCO. S 98/99 [text/French trans.]. — R. Lavenant, PO 30/5 [text/French trans.]. — J. Lebon, Ad reclusos: Muséon 43 (1930) 17-84, 149-220 [text/French trans.]. — G. Olinder, Letter of Ph. to a Novice (Göteborg, 1941) [text/English trans.]. — idem, Letter of Ph. to a Friend (Göteborg, 1950) [text/English trans.]. — idem, An einen Archimandriten: AUG 56 (1950) 1-63. — F. Graffin, Ad monachum: OrSyr 5 (1960) 183-196 [French trans.]. — M. Albert, A un Juif converti: OrSyr 6 (1961) 41-50 [French trans.]. — A. Tanghe, De inhabitatione Spiritus: Muséon 73 (1960) 39-72 [French trans.]. — T. Jansma, To Abraham and Orestes: Muséon 87 (1974) 79-86 [English trans.]. — A. L. Frothingham, Stephan bar Sudaili (Leipzig, 1888), 28-48 [text/English trans.]. — *can.*, A. Vööbus, Syriac Documents (Stockholm, 1960), 51-59 [text/English trans.].
L: E. Beck, Ph. u. Ephräm: OrChr 46 (1962) 61-76. — E. Bergsträsser, Monophysitismus u. Paulus-tradition (Erlangen, 1953). — D. J. Fox, The Matthew-Luke Commentary (Missoula, 1979). — F. Graffin, Florilège patristique: OCA 197 (1974) 267-290. — J. Gribomont, L'écho du messalianisme: OrSyr 2 (1957) 419-433. — S. Grill, Das NT nach dem Syriac Text (Munich, 1955). — A. de Halleux, Ph. La vie, ses écrits (Leuven/Louvain, 1963). — idem, Biographie expurgée de Ph.: OLoP 6/7 (1975/76) 253-266. — idem, Monophysitismus: ThPh 53 (1978) 353-366. — idem, Philoxénienne du symbole: OCA 205 (1978) 295-315. — idem, Commentaires: Muséon 93 (1980) 5-35. — P. Harb, Apatheia: ParOr 5 (1974) 227-241. — I. Hausherr, Contemplation et sainteté: RAM 14 (1933) 171-195. — J. Lebon, Christologie: Das Konzil v. Chalkedon 1, ed. A. Grillmeier (Würzburg, ⁵1979), 425-580. — E. Lemoine, Spiritualité de Ph.: OrSyr 2 (1957) 351-367. — J. Martikainen, Gerechtigkeit u. Güte Gottes (Wiesbaden, 1981). — A. Vööbus, Gospel Text in Syriac (Leuven/Louvain, 1951). — idem, Early Versions of the NT (Stockholm, 1954). — J. W. Watt, Ph. and Evagrius: OrChr 64 (1980) 65-81.

P. BRUNS

Phoebadius of Agen

P. was bishop of Agen from 356/357 until after 392 (Jerome, *vir. ill.* 108). In his only surviving treatise,

Contra Arrianos (*C. Ar.*), he attacks the theol. explanation given by the homoeans of Sirmium (Hilary, *syn.* 11). Relying on Hilary and Tertullian, he defends the creed of Nicaea (325), but interprets it in light of the "western" *Ecthesis* of Sardica (342), which was better known in the West at that time; that is, he proposes a strict one-hypostasis doctrine but tries to safeguard this from misinterpretations by distinguishing between the trinitarian persons (*unam substantiam–duas personas*, *C. Ar.* 14.3). On the basis of *C. Ar.*, a Gallic synod of 358 took a stand against the homoeans; in 359, however, at the Synod of Rimini, P. vainly opposed the acceptance of the homoiousian formula of Nike (Theodoret, *h.e.* 2.21.3-7). His importance consists primarily in that in the *C. Ar.* we have an authentic example of one of the earliest surviving attempts to secure reception of the Nicene Creed in the Latin West.

W: *C. Ar.*, R. Demeulenaere, CCL 64. — J. Ulrich, FC in preparation. — A. Durengues: Revue de l'Agenais 53 (1926) 339-371 [text/French trans.]. — J. Dräseke (Wandsbek, 1910) [German trans.].
L: H. C. Brennecke, Homöer (Tübingen, 1988), 34-37. — J. Dräseke, Schrift: ZKWL 10 (1889) 335-343, 391-407. — idem, Ph.: ZWTh 33 (1890) 78-98. — E. Griffe, Gaule (Paris, ²1964), 173-192, 257-259. — P. P. Gläser, Ph. (Augsburg, 1978). — R. P. C. Hanson, Search (Edinburgh, 1988), 516-519. — J. Ulrich, Anfänge (Berlin, 1994), 159-194.

J. Ulrich

Phos hilaron

The *Phos hilaron* (Gr.: "Cheerful light") is one of the earliest surviving Chr. hymns; it goes back to the 2nd or 3rd c., and Basil speaks of it as already old (Spir. 29.73). The hymn is a song of praise using the motif of light. Its original setting was the evening ritual of lamplighting. The *Phos hilaron* was influenced by the Jerusalem tradition of the liturgy of the Hours. In its first strophe it praises the immortal Father and the heavenly Son; in strophe 2 it sings the praise of the Trinity; it ends in strophe 3 with praise of the Son, who gave life. Scholars see a single author at work in the two christological sections. The middle section, at least in its genre, must go back to the NT-apostolic period.

L: F. J. Dölger, Lumen Christi: AuC 5 (1936) 1-43, here 11-26. — J. Madey, Ph.: MarL 5, 208. — K. Onasch, Ph.: Liturgie u. Kunst der Ostkirche (Berlin, 1993), 16. — P. Plank, Ph. Christushymnus u. Lichtdanksagung der frühen Christenheit (Würzburg, 1985) (typescript of Habil.). — A. Tripolitis, ΠΩΣ ΙΛΑΡΟΝ. Ancient Hymn and Modern Enigma: VigChr 24 (1970) 189-196.

B. Kranemann

Photinus of Constantinople

P. of Constantinople, who was *presbyter et defensor sanctissimae magnae ecclesiae*, was author of a *Vita Iohannis Ieiunatoris* (*fr.*) a biography of John Nesteutes, patriarch of Constantinople (589-595). The *Vita* of John, who because he assumed the title of ecumenical patriarch came in conflict with Pelagius II and Gregory the Great but was supported by Emperor Maurice, is preserved in fragmentary form in the acts of the second Council of Nicaea (787). It tells of a miracle or expulsion of a demon worked with the aid of a picture of the Mother of God. The work was composed soon after John's death, certainly after the death of Emperor Maurice (602) and probably after that of Emperor Phocas (610), both of whom are mentioned, the former as a martyr, the latter as a tyrant.

W: Mansi 13:80-85.
L: H. G. Beck, Kirche u. theol. Lit. (Munich, 1959), 459.

B. Windau

Photius

Ph. (b. 810 or 820, d. between 891 and 893/894), the son of prominent parents, was first an imperial official and a teacher of philosophy, mathematics, and theology. In 858 he became patriarch of Constantinople as successor of the deposed Ignatius. But since the followers of Ignatius spoke against him to Pope Nicholas I, he was deposed by a Roman synod (863), whereupon Ph. excommunicated the pope (867). The Synod of Constantinople (869/870) condemned and deposed Ph.; Emperor Basil was attempting in this way to win the favor of the pope. Only after the death of Ignatius, which ended the Photian schism, did Ph. once again mount the patriarchal throne. In 886 Emperor Leo VI forced the withdrawal of Ph., who spent his last years in a monastery.

Ph. is regarded as one of the most important Byz. churchmen and scholars. His principal theol. work is the *Address on the Mystagogy of the Holy Spirit*. The authenticity of the work against the Latins—*Against Those Who Claim Rome to Be the First See*—is disputed. Outstanding among the exeget. works is the *Amphilochia* (*Amph.*), a collection of questions and answers addressed to a metropolitan Amphilochius. Ph. composed the preface to the *Eisagōgē*, the introduction to the collection of legislation by Emperor Leo VI; also numerous homilies (*hom.*) and letters (*ep.*). Ph.'s *Library* (*cod.*) is a collection of descriptions and excerpts from 386 early Chr. and early Byz.

authors, whose writings are to some extent handed down only here.

W: PG 101-104. — *cod.*, R. Henry, Bibliothèque (Paris, 1959-1991). — *hom.*, B. Laourdas (Thessalonica, 1959). — idem, P. Lemerle, Ph., Récit de la Réapparition: TMCB 4 (1970) 99-183 [text/French trans.]. — C. Mango (Washington, 1958) [English trans.]. — *ep., Amph.,* L. G. Westerink (Leipzig, 1983-1988).
L: H. G. Beck, Kirche u. theol. Lit. (Munich, 1959), 520-527. — G. D. Dragas, Towards a Complete Bibliographia Photiana: Patrologia Graeca 101, Ph. (Athens, 1991), 123-236. — F. Dvornik, The Photian Schism (Cambridge, 1970 = 1948). — F. R. Gahbauer, Ph., Patriarch von Konstantinopel (Paris, in press). — A. Kazhdan, P.: ODB 1669f. — P. Lemerle, L'Histoire des Pauliciens: TMCB 5 (1973) 31-47. — C. Theodoridis (ed.), Ph. Patriarchae Lexicon (Berlin, 1982). — F. Tinnefeld, P.: LMA 6:2109f. — D. S. White, Patriarch Ph. (Brookline, Mass., 1981).

Γ. R. Gahbauer, OSB

Physiologus

The *Physiologus* is a book, composed in Greek and written ca. 200 in Alexandria, that originally contained forty-eight short stories (on forty-two animals, two plants, four stones). Almost every story begins: "The *Physiologus* says of . . . ," followed by a description of the being's *physis* (special character) and finally by a Chr. interpretation. It is not possible to determine exactly the natural-history sources used.

There were certainly three versions at quite different times: in addition to the first, the so-called second, Byz. version (5th/6th c.), and the third under the name of Basil (10th/11th c.).

The *Physiologus* was translated into all the Chr. languages at an early date. Even before the Islamic conquest it was translated from Syriac into Arabic; after 385 there were several Lat. translations, which were translated in turn into all the European languages. In the Romance languages the so-called bestiaries developed out of the Chr. work: the *Physiologus* became a book of animals (already in Isidore of Seville, *orig.* 12) and at times lost its Chr. aspect.

Many of the stories quickly became common literary possessions: the wolf, which on the third day brings its stillborn cub to life by breathing on it; the unicorn, which can be captured only by a virgin; the phoenix, which burns to death and rises from the ashes after three days; the pelican, which feeds (originally: brings to life) its young with its own blood. The iconographic and literary use of *Physiologus*-motifs continued into the early modern age in Europe.

The *Physiologus* is simple, sometimes awkward, in style. It cites only the Bible, the OT more often than

the NT. It has no "theology" but does make theol. statements: the incarnation of Christ, his death, and his resurrection on the third day are important to it. Seemingly, the only heresy it attacks is docetism. The community and its Chr. life are very important to the work. Dangers from outside are mentioned but not described.

The *Decretum Gelasianum* calls the work heretical. The reason is probably the time of the work's origin: ca. 200 things could still be said unguardedly that were later offensive.

W: PG 41:518-538. — F. Sbordone, Ph. (Hildesheim, [2]1991 = Milan, 1936) [text]. — O. Seel (Zurich, 1984) [German trans./comm.]. — U. Treu (Berlin, [2]1987) [German trans.].
L: K. Alpers, Untersuchungen zum griech. Ph. u. den Kyraniden: VB 6 (1986) 13-87. — F. Lauchert, Die Geschichte des Ph. (Geneva, 1974 = Strasburg, 1889). — N. Henkel, Studien zum Ph. im MA (Tübingen, 1976). — D. Kaimakis, Der Ph. nach der 1. Redaktion (Meisenheim, 1974). — A. Karnejew, Der Ph. der Moskauer Synodal-Bibliothek (Munich, 1964 = 1894). — D. Offermanns, Der Ph. nach den Hss. G u. M (Meisenheim, 1966). — A. Scott, The Date of the Ph.: VigChr 52 (1998) 430-441. — J. Strzygowsky, Der Bilderkreis des griech. Ph. (Leipzig, 1899).

U. Treu

Pierius

P., an Alexandrian presbyter (end of 3rd c.), was head of the school there. His writings, especially the homilies, were widely circulated. He fled to Rome, either because of the Diocletian persecution or because of disagreements with Peter I of Alexandria. Photius cites only a few fragments—on Lk and from an Easter homily (*cod.* 119)—from P.'s extensive works. Two other fragments (*fr.*) are preserved in Philip of Side. Photius also says that P. taught two *ousiai* or natures in God (*cod.* 119); how true this is is disputed.

W: *fr.*, Philippus v. Side, C. de Boor, TU 5/2. — PG 10:243f.
L: A. Grillmeier, Jesus der Christus 1 (Freiburg i.Br., [3]1990), 294, 302 (English, Christ in Christian Tradition, vol. 1 [London, [2]1975]). — L. B. Radford, Three Teachers of Alexandria: Theognostus, P. and Peter (Cambridge, 1908). — T. Vivian, St. Peter of Alexandria (Philadelphia, 1988), 12, 111, 114-116.

T. Böhm

Pilate, Literature about

Justin (*apol.* 1.35 and 48) is the first to speak of so-called *Acta Pilati* (*A. Pil.*). Tertullian (*apol.* 5.21) mentions a letter of Pilate (P.) to Tiberius that reports in such detail on the miracles of Jesus as to make Tertullian believe he was a Christian at heart. Eusebius, on the contrary, attests (*h.e.* 1.9; 9.5.1) to pagan *A. Pil.* that were hostile to Christians and composed under Emperor Maximinus. Epiphanius (*haer.* 50.1) reports details of the *A. Pil.* that correspond to the earliest transmitted version (425). It is no longer possible to determine with certainty how far this version goes back to traditions already in circulation in the time of Justin.

In the surviving text Ananias, a Christian, relates that he has received from Nicodemus the record, in Hebrew, of the trial of Jesus and has translated this into Greek (hence from the early Middle Ages on the entire work was also known as the gospel of Nicodemus). In addition to the actual record of the trial, the text contains accounts of the crucifixion and burial, as well as of subsequent negotiations in the Sanhedrin that are supposed to show the reality of the resurrection (1-16). This section has also come down in Lat., Copt., Syr., and Arm. translations.

In a more recent version an originally independent piece on the "descent of Christ into hell" (*Descensus*) has been inserted. The story claims to be a report by Simeon (Lk 2:25) and his sons (who were raised up after the crucifixion; see Mt 27:52) and experienced the encounter of Christ with Satan/Hades (17-27). This second section became espec. important for piety and iconography and was the most widely circulated apocryphon in the Middle Ages. In the earliest version of the *Descensus* the sons of Simeon are named Leucius and Carinus (→ Leucius Carinus), and at the end of the story the Jews reveal to P., behind closed doors, that the 5,500 years until the Messiah have now been fulfilled. After this, P. writes his letter to Claudius (the above mentioned, originally Gr. version, is passed down in the *Acta Petri et Pauli* [→ Peter, → Paul, Literature about]). A later Lat. version begins with the added story of three Galilean rabbis who experienced the ascension of Jesus. In the 6th c., the *Somnium Neronis* was added to the work; this is a bibl. cento on the destruction of Jerusalem (E. v. Dobschütz, *JThS* 16 [1914/15] 1-27). A letter of P. to Claudius is contained in the *Acta Petri et Pauli*; it is possibly identical with the original Gr. letter mentioned by Tertullian (see above).

W: C. v. Tischendorf, Evangelia apocrypha (Hildesheim, 1987 = ²1876), 210-332 [text]. — A. de Santos Otero, Los evangelios apocrifos (Madrid, ⁶1988), 396-449 [text/Spanish trans.]. — G. Philippart, Les fragments palimpsestes de l'Évangile de Nicodème: AnBoll 107 (1989) 171-188 [Latin text]. — NTApo⁶ 1:399-422 [German trans.]. — I. E. Rahmani, Studia Syriaca 2 (Sarpha, 1908) [Syriac text]. — A. Revillout, PO 9:2 [Coptic text]. — F. C. Conybeare, SBEc 4 (Oxford, 1896) [Greek and Latin trans. of the Armenian

text]. — H. C. Kim, The Gospel of Nicodemus, TMLT 2 (Toronto, 1973) [text].

In later literature about P. are found the so-called *Anaphora* (corresponds in content to the letter to Claudius but is independent and not written before the 5th c.) and the *Paradosis*. This last describes the handing over and death of P., who has become a Christian. The same tendency can be seen in the Copt. *Martyrium Pilati* and in the gospel of → Gamaliel. In an exchange of letters between P. and Herod (*Pil. et Her.*) P. tells of meeting (with his wife, Paula, and Longinus) the risen Christ in Galilee; a very remorseful Herod tells of the punishments that befell his family after the condemnation of the Baptist and the mocking of Jesus.

On the other hand, in the letter of Tiberius to P. (*Tib.*; not before the 5th c.), the emperor, who has been informed by Mary Magdalene, condemns P. and the Jewish leaders to death. So too in the *Mors Pilati*, the *Cura sanitatis Tiberii*, and the medieval *Vindicta Salvatoris*, which tell of the healing of Tiberius, P. is judged and imprisoned, exiled, or compelled to commit suicide; yet he is venerated as a saint in the Copt. church.

W: *Anaphora*, G. F. Abbott: JThS 4 (1903) 83-86 [text]. — *Anaphora, Paradosis*, C. v. Tischendorf, op. cit., 443-455. — *Martyrium Pilati*, M. A. van den Oudenrijn, Gamaliel (Fribourg, Switzerland, 1959), 112-180 [Ethiopic text/German trans./comm.]. — A. Mingana, WoodSt 2 (Cambridge, 1928), 241-333 [Arabic text/English trans.]. — *Pil. et Her.*, M. R. James, Apocrypha anecdota 2 (Cambridge, 1897), 65-75 [Greek text/English trans.]. — W. Wright, Contributions to the Apocryphal Literature of the NT (London, 1865), 12-24 [Syriac text/English trans.]. — I. E. Rahmani, Studia Syriaca 2 (Scharfeh, 1908), 15-19, 32-37 [Syriac text/Latin trans.]. — *Tib.*, M. R. James, op. cit., 77-81, 156f. [text/partial English trans.]. — *Mors Pilati, Cura sanitatis Tiberii, Vindicta Salvatoris*, C. v. Tischendorf, op. cit., 456-458, 471-486 [text].
L: S. P. Brock, A Fragment of the A. Pil. in Christian Palestinian Aramaic: JThS 22 (1971) 157f. — E. Cerulli, Tiberius and P. in Ethiopian Tradition: PBA 59 (1973) 141-158. — E. v. Dobschütz, Der Process Jesu nach den A. Pil.: ZNW 3 (1902) 89-114. — M. Geerard, Marie Madeleine, dénonciatrice de Pilate: SE 31 (1989-90) 139-148. — HLL 4:387-390. — J. Kroll, Gott u. Hölle (Darmstadt, 1963 = 1932). — R. A. Lipsius, Die P.-Akten (Kiel, 1871). — W. Speyer, Neue P.-Apokryphen: VigChr 32 (1978) 53-59.

G. RÖWEKAMP

Pinytus of Cnossus

In one of his letters → Dionysius of Corinth exhorts Bishop Pinytus of Cnossus not to be too strict in questions of the life of virtue. The latter, however, in a lost response to Dionysius (acc. to Eus., *h.e.*

4.23.7f.) held fast to the necessity of shifting from "spiritual milk" to "more solid food." Although Eusebius stresses P.'s orthodoxy and his intellectual and pastoral gifts, we must assume disagreements on this in Crete, during which P. and at least Philip of Gortyna came in conflict.

L: W. Bauer, Rechtgläubigkeit u. Ketzerei (Tübingen, ²1964), 79f., 129-131, 169-171. — A. v. Harnack, Briefsammlung des Paulus (Leipzig, 1926), 36-40. — W. Kühnert, Dionysius: FS F. Zerbst (Vienna, 1979), 273-289. — P. Nautin, Lettres et écrivains (Paris, 1961), 20-24.

R. HANIG

Pionius

P. is the name of a martyr of Smyrna during the Decian persecution; Eusebius (*h.e.* 4.15.46f.) connects him with the martyrdom of → Polycarp. His was the name of the author of a 4th c. *Vita Polycarpi*, which survives only in fragments; this was part of a *Corpus Polycarpianum*, which included the *Martyrium Polycarpi*, possibly the letters of Polycarp, and a lost work containing revelations of Polycarp.

W: F. X. Funk, F. Diekamp, Patres Apostolici 2 (Tübingen, ³1913).
L: H. R. Seeliger, Pionius: BBKL 7:619-621.

H. KÖNIG

Pisenthius of Kepht

We are informed of the life of P. by two Copt. *Vitae* and by the original archives in the monastery of St. Epiphanius near Thebes. P. was active toward the end of the 6th and beginning of the 7th c.; in early youth he entered the monastery of Apa Phoebammon near Thebes and was later consecrated bishop of Kepht by Patriarch Damian. His most important work is probably his encomium of St. Onuphrius (*Hon.*). Only a few fragments of his extensive correspondence have survived.

S: *vita*, E. A. T. Wallis Budge, Coptic Apocrypha (London, 1913), 75-127, 258-334 [text/English trans.]. — E. De Lacy O'Leary, PO 22:313-488 [Arabic text/English trans.].
W: *Hon.*, W. E. Crum, P.: ROC 20 (1915-1917) 38-67 [text/English trans.]. — *ep.*, E. Revillot, Extraits de la correspondence: RdE 9 (1900) 133-177; 10 (1902) 34-47; 14 (1914) 22-32 [text/French trans.].
L: G. G. Abd-el Sayed, Untersuchungen zu den Texten des Pesyntheus (Bonn, 1984). — M. Krause, P.: RdE 24 (1972) 101-107.

P. BRUNS

Pistis Sophia

The *Cod. Askewianus*, which contains the Copt. work *Pistis Sophia*, has been known since the 18th c. The ms. has four parts, of which the first three are the three books of *Pistis Sophia*, which were probably originally called "Books of the Redeemer." The title later given to the second book became the title of the entire work. It is to be interpreted, with the help of the → *Sophia Jesu Christi* (NHC 3, 106, 16-23), as a description of the redeemer's "consort" (*syzygos*), who is named Pistis and Sophia. The work was probably written in Greek in Egypt between 250 and 300. It is not possible to identify parts of *Pistis Sophia* with the *Gospel of* → *Philip* or the questions of Mary (→ Mary, Literature about); a Valentinian authorship is also rejected today.

The formal setting of the work is the instruction given by the risen Christ at the end of eleven years spent with the disciples. Of the forty-six questions asked by the disciples, thirty-nine come from Mary Magdalene. After his journey through the aeons, Jesus tells, among other things, of the fate of Sophia, who has fallen from the thirteenth aeon into matter and whom he has brought back from isolation and sorrow. A further theme is the mystery of the light; since Jesus enlightens the interior light-person, the disciples, too, can to some extent give explanations. The document that follows (part 4 of the codex) is likewise a gnostic gospel from the end of the 3rd c. that deals in dialogue form with gnostic "metanoia."

W: M. G. Schwartze, J. H. Petermann (Berlin, 1851/53) [text/Latin trans.]. — C. Schmidt, Coptica 2 (Copenhagen, ²1954) [text]. C. Schmidt, V. MacDermot, NHS 9 (Leiden, 1978) [text/English trans.]. — C. Schmidt, H.-M. Schenke, GCS 45 [13] (Berlin, ⁴1981), 1-254 [German trans.]. — E. Amélineau (Milan, 1975 = 1895) [French trans.]. NTApo⁶ 2:290-297 [German selected trans.].
L: F. C. Burkitt, PS and the Coptic Language: JThS 27 (1925/26) 148-157. — J. Carmignac, Le genre litteraire de péshèr dans la PS: RQ 4 (1963/64) 497-522. — A. Kragerud, Die Hymnen der PS (Oslo, 1967). — M. Lattke, The Gnostic Interpretation of the Odes of Salomon in the PS: BSAC 24 (1979/82) 69-84. — H. Ludin Jansen, Gnostic Interpretation in PS: FS H. Ludin Jansen (Trondheim, 1985), 145-150. — W. C. v. Unnik, Die Zahl der vollkommenen Seelen in der PS: FS O. Michel (Leiden, 1963), 467-477. — G. Widengren, Die Hymnen der PS: FS C. J. Bleeker (Leiden, 1969), 269-281. — C. Schmidt, Die Urschrift der PS: ZNW 24 (1925) 218-240. — D. Visieux, La PS et la Gnose (Puisseaux, 1988).

G. RÖWEKAMP

Poems, Anonymous

The poems included under this heading have in common only that their authors are unknown or were, in the process of transmission (mostly beginning in the Middle Ages), assigned to other, authoritative eccles. writers; to some extent they are still cited under those names (perhaps with a prefixed "Pseudo-"). → Lactantius's authorship of *De ave phoenice*, which used to be questioned by some, is now regarded as certain. The *Obitus Baebiani* (*carm.* 33) is probably not by → Paulinus of Nola.

As a rule, there is also uncertainty about the time and place of the writing of these poems. An imperative need in scholarship is a critical appraisal of these works from the viewpoints of philology, history of motifs, theology, and literature; only very recently has this challenge been taken up again with some energy. General characteristics of these poems are their practice of poetically adapting bibl. passages while taking over and often even continuing the dogm. and exeget. tradition; the wide range of genres covered (from pamphlet to didactic poem and epic). They are written predominantly in hexameters (more or less observing classic meters and prosody). In length they range from a bare hundred verses to over five thousand. Here are some prominent examples.

The mss. give no comprehensive title to the paraphrase of the Heptateuch (*hept.*), but give as its author a Cyprian of whom nothing more is known (pseudepigraphy cannot be excluded). In its sequence of narrated deeds this epic *Carmen perpetuum* of over five thousand verses essentially follows the chronology of its bibl. model; extensive repetitions are avoided, and legal prescriptions and genealogies, in particular, are summarized in the paraphrase. There is no allegory and little typology; knowledge of classical models (Catullus, Horace, etc.) is evident, but the form is by and large not strongly classical. The *terminus post quem* for the time of origin is → Claudian; imitation by → Marius Claudius Victorius cannot be shown with certainty.

The *Carmen adversus Marcionitas* (earlier: *Marcionem*; *carm. adv. Marc.*), a didactic poem in five books (5.1-18: internal prologue), attacks positions of the Marcionites (1.141-44), i.e., docetism, rejection of the OT, denial of the sameness of the OT and NT God. The composer was not → Tertullian but an anonymous writer whose native place is difficult to identify; the time of composition can be limited to ca. 420-450. For proof of the unity of the OT and NT the author uses numerous, sometimes complicated, typologies, espec. in connection with Heb and Rev. To be noted is the fact that universal history, from the beginning of the world to the final judgment, is the setting of the poem.

The classically styled epyllia *Carmen de Sodoma* (*carm. de Sod.*; 167 hexameters) and *Carmen de Iona* (*carm. de Iona*; 105 hexameters) depict two opposed OT divine judgments, the former with a negative, the latter with a positive outcome. At the end there is a typological reference to the Chr. final judgment. The same poet probably composed both texts, not before 400. The *Carmen de Pascha seu de ligno crucis* (*carm. de Pasch*) in sixty-nine hexameters was likewise written ca. 400 at the earliest; in the form of an ecphrasis (v. 1: *est locus*) it describes the tree of paradise as a type of the cross and as a ladder to heaven for the saints. Ca. 500 an anonymous Christian, probably in Africa, wrote the four-hundred-hexameter-long epyllion-like *Carmen de resurrectione ad Flavium Felicem* (*carm de resurr.*), which has for its subject proof of the resurrection of the dead (102-36) as well as the final judgment on the good (186-268) and the wicked (269-355). Frequently to be found are stylistic imitations of Virgil but also of Chr. poets, and verse endings close to rhyme.

In the *Carmen ad quendam senatorem* (*carm. ad Senat.*; end of 4th c.) an anonymous Christian wrote eighty-five hexameters against the absurdity of the pagan cults of Cybele (6-20) and Isis (21-34), the occasion being the apostasy of the previously Chr. addressees (1-5; 35-50). This poetic pamphlet uses to some extent satirical elements from Horace and espec. Juvenal. The *Carmen contra paganos* (*carm. c. pag.*) is from the same period and reflects the same outlook; in 122 classical hexameters, imitating Virgil to some extent, the work attacks alien religions in a biting, polemical manner. In content it is in the tradition of the apologia.

The earliest datable Chr.-Lat. poem, the *Laudes Domini* (*laud. dom.*; 317-26) in 148 hexameters, answers the question of the delay of the judgment on the world with the argument that miracles presently occurring are to be integrated into the history of salvation and that the end of the world is not far off. This work, which takes the form chiefly of a prayer of praise, is thoroughly rhetorical and classical in meter and language (imitation of Virgil, Lucretius, Horace, Ovid).

The reception given to these poems has been only partially studied, although in the Carolingian Renaissance poetic paraphrases of the Bible were readily cited instead of the bibl. text itself. In ms. *Vatic. Regin.* 582 (9th/10th c.) there are two connected centos of the *carm. adv. Marc.* There is disagreement over whether the *carm. de Iona* influenced the Middle English poem *Patience*. The *carm. de pascha* was very popular in the 15th c. (almost twenty mss.) since it suited the taste of the time with its rich typology and allegorizing.

W: *hept.*, R. Peiper, CSEL 23:1-211. — *carm. adv. Marc.*, K. Pollmann (Göttingen, 1991) [text/German trans./comm.]. — *carm. de Sod./Iona*, R. Peiper, CSEL 23:212-226. — L. Morisi, Versus de Sodoma (Bologna, 1993) [text/Italian trans./comm.]. — *carm. de pascha*, J. Schwind: FS F. J. Ronig (Trier, 1989), 379-402 [text/German trans./comm.]. — *carm. de resurr.*, J. H. Waszink: FlorPatr. S 1 (1937) 47-116. — *carm. ad senat.*, R. Peiper, CSEL 23:227-230. — *carm. c. pag.*, D. R. Shackleton Bailey, Anthologia Latina 1/1 (Stuttgart, 1982), 17-23. — C. Markschies, "Leben wir nicht alle unter dem selben Sternenzelt?": Die Heiden, ed. R. Feldmeier, U. Heckel (Tübingen, 1994), 325-377 [text/German trans./comm.]. — *laud. dom.*, P. van der Weijden, Diss. (Amsterdam, 1967) [text/Dutch trans./comm.].
L: R. B. Begley, The Carmen ad quendam senatorem, Diss. (microfilm) (Ann Arbor, 1984). — F. Cairns, Latin Sources and Analogues of the M. E. Patience: SNP 59 (1987) 7-18. — L. Cracco Ruggini, Il paganesimo romano tra religione e politica: AANL. M ser. 8, 23, 1 (1979) 124-130 (*carm. ad senat.*). — S. Döpp, Baebianus und Apra zu Paul. Nol. (?) c. 33: FS K. Thraede (Münster, 1995), 66-74. — J. Fontaine, Naissance de la Poésie dans l'Occident Chrétien (Paris, 1981). — R. Herzog, Die Bibelepik der lat. Spätantike 1 (Munich, 1975). — R. Hexter, The Metamorphosis of Sodom. The Ps.-Cyprian De Sodoma as an Ovidian Episode: Tr. 44 (1988) 1-35. — S. Isetta, Carmen ad Flavium Felicem. Problemi di attribuzione e reminiscenze classiche: VetChr 20 (1983) 111-140. — D. Kartschoke, Bibeldichtung (Munich, 1975). — D. M. Kriel, Sodoma in Fifth Century Biblical Epic: ACl 34 (1991) 7-20. — D. J. Nodes, Doctrine and Exegesis in Biblical Latin Poetry (Leeds, 1993). — M. Petringa, I "sei giorni della creazione" nella parafrasi biblica di Cipriano poeta: Sileno 18 (1992) 133-156. — K. Pollmann, Der sog. Heptateuchdichter und die "Alethia" des Claudius Marius Victorius: Hermes 121 (1993) 1-12. — G. Puglisi, I Rapt<or>um tractatus e le stragi capitoline del 384: SicGym 42 (1989) 47-74 (on) *carm. c. pag.* 26. — M. Roberts, Biblical Epic and Rhetorical Paraphrase in Late Antiquity (Liverpool, 1985). — idem, The Jewelled Style (London, 1989). — A. Traina, La figlia del vento (Carmen de Iona 29): RFIC 118 (1990) 200-202

K. POLLMANN

Polemius Silvius

P., who is to be identified with Silvius, the friend of Hilary of Arles (*Vita Hilarii* 14), composed ca. 448/449 a work titled *Laterculus* (*chron.*), which he dedicated to Eucherius of Lyons. The work contains, first of all, a calendar that revises the Roman tradition and introduces Chr. elements. To the calendar are added various lists: Roman emperors from Caesar to Theodosius II/Valentinian II; provinces of the Roman empire (compare → *Notitia dignitatum*); all the animals; sections of the city of Rome; history from the flood onward; onomatopoeic verbs for the voices of animals and the noises of inanimate things; mea-

sures and weights. These additions have their background in the catalogues and lists used in the schools of antiquity (see → Ausonius) and show, by their relationship to prior and subsequent literature, the continuity in the educational materials of antiquity.

W: T. Mommsen, MGH. AA 9:518-551. — *Sections of the City of Rome*, R. Valentini, G. Zucchetti, Codice topografico della città di Roma 1 (Rome, 1940), 294-301, 308-310 [text].
L: R. W. Burges, Principes cum tyrannis: CQ 43 (1993) 491-500. — E. S. Dulabahn, Studies on the Laterculus of P., Diss. (Bryn Mawr College, 1987). — M. Schanz, C. Hosius, G. Krüger, Geschichte der röm. Lit. 4/2 (Munich, 1959 = 1920), 130. — K. Ziegler, P.: PRE 21/1:1260-1263. — idem, P.: KP 4:969.

B. WINDAU

Polemon

After the split among the Apollinarists, a Polemon (or Pelemius) appears as leader (without any title) of the most extreme group, whose supporters are also called "Polemians" by Theodoret (*haer.* 4.8f.). He attacked not only the Great Church with its doctrine of the two natures but also his former like-minded colleagues, such as Timothy of Berytus, who were prepared to make christological compromises. Five fragments (*fr.*) of his works have survived. They are from an *Antirrheticus* attacking the orthodox fathers, from a polemic *Contra Timotheum*, from an *Ep. ad Timotheum* (there were at least six of these), and from an *Ep. ad Iulium*.

W: *fr.* 173-177, H. Lietzmann, Apollinaris u. seine Schule (Hildesheim, 1970 = Tübingen, ¹1904), 274-276 [text]. — *fr.* 174, E. Schwartz, Drei dogmatische Schriften Iustinians, ABAW. PH NF 18 (Munich, 1939), 17, 19-27 [text]. — F. Diekamp, Doctrina Patrum (Münster, 1907), 60f. — *fr.* 176f., F. Diekamp, op. cit., 308f.

G. FEIGE

Polychronius of Apamea

P., brother of the most important Antiochene theologian, → Theodore Mops., was bishop of Apamea in Syria until his death ca. 430 and composed commentaries on various OT books (Ezek, Dan, and Job). He is possibly the author also of a commentary on Jer (*comm. in Jer.*) that survives in catenas. His exegesis, which aims at the literal sense, shows a profound knowledge of history and chronology. In agreement with his brother Theodore, P. connects the messianic promises with specific events of OT history but not with the coming of Christ. But in

493

contrast to his brother, he maintains the canonicity of the book of Job.

W: PG 31:13-470. — *comm. in Jer.*, PG 64:739-1038.
L: O. Bardenhewer, P., Bruder Theodors v. Mopsuestia (Freiburg i.Br., 1879). — U. Bertini, La catena greca in Giobbe: Bib. 4 (1923) 129-142. — L. Dennefeld, Der atl. Kanon der antiochenischen Schule (Freiburg i.Br., 1909), 61-67. — L. Dieu, Le commentaire sur Jérémie: RHE 14 (1913) 685-701. — M. Faulhaber, Propheten-Catenen (Freiburg i.Br., 1899). — A. Vaccari, Un commento da Giobbe (Rome, 1915). — C. Weimann, Hiobkommentar: ThRv 15 (1916) 241-248.

P. BRUNS

Polycarp of Smyrna

I. Life: Our first information about P. comes from the letters of Ignatius, one of which is addressed to P., while another calls P. "bishop of Smyrna" (*Magn.* 15). Irenaeus gives details of P.'s life in letters cited by Eusebius (*h.e.* 5.20.6; 5.24,. 14ff.) as well as in *haer.* 3.3.4. According to Irenaeus P. was in contact with the apostles, who taught him and appointed him bishop of Smyrna. In the time of Roman Bishop Anicetus (ca. 150) P. journeyed to Rome in order to settle disagreements regarding the celebration of Easter. Since Anicetus and P. both felt bound by local tradition, they did not come to an agreement, but neither did they break communion. After 150 P. suffered martyrdom when he was, by his own testimony, eighty-six years of age. This fact is given in the *Martyrium Polycarpi* (→ Marcion), the earliest example of Chr. literature on martyrdom. The date of P.'s death (*M. Polyc.* 21) is still disputed by scholars; the most likely date seems to have been Feb. 23, 167.

II. Works: Irenaeus is the first to speak of P.'s *Letter to the Philippians*. The Gr. text of this letter has survived only in fragments, but it can be reconstructed from citations in Eusebius and from a Lat. version. The occasion for the letter was a request from the community of Philippi for the sending of a letter to them and for a copy of the letters of Ignatius. Since 1.1 and 9.1f. seem to presume the martyrdom of Ignatius, while 13 sounds as if Ignatius were still alive, the unity of text becomes questionable. Some saw in 13-14 a short letter accompanying the letters of Ignatius when these were sent to Philippi and composed while Ignatius was still on the way to Rome; 1-12 was taken as a later letter (datable to ca. 135 because of its anti-Marcionite tendencies). But the signs pointing to a division of the letter are not so clear that the question can be definitively answered. The central theme of the letter, determined by the request of the addressees (3.1), is justice. The case of

presbyter Valens (11) may have occasioned the request. Justice has its point of departure in the knowledge of deliverance through grace; it comes from faith in the risen Lord, the judge of the living and the dead, and consists in obedience to the Lord's commandments (2.2). The emphasis here is on the idea of forgiveness, as can be seen from the scripture citations in 2.2f. P. is describing a Chr. justice that must characterize the ethical behavior of all groups in the community and that must in a case of conflict (Valens) prove itself through patience and a readiness to forgive (11-12). Examples of this attitude, even in extreme cases, are Ignatius and the apostles. The letter makes it clear that P. "always taught what he had learned from the apostles and what the church hands on and what alone is the truth" (Irenaeus, *haer.* 3.3.4): P. speaks with and by means of the NT; he cites the *Corpus Paulinum* extensively (striking closeness to the Pastoral Letters in exhortation and antiheretical polemic), and cites in addition Mt, Lk, Acts, 1 Jn, and 1 Pet. P. also makes use of the letter of → Clement of Rome, which is here cited in the literature for the first time. Whether one prefers to see P. as a representative of "primitive catholicism" or as "builder" of a "semantic universe," P. bears witness, in any case, to the efforts of the early church to establish its identity. The fact that he opposes a "piety of preservation" to the syncretist tendencies of his time does not indeed prove him to be an original theologian; but the "piety of preservation" was to be in the following period the basis for more original theol. approaches.

W: A. Lindemann, H. Paulsen, Die Apostolischen Väter (Tübingen, 1992) [text/German trans.]. — J. A. Fischer, Die Apostolischen Väter (Darmstadt, ⁹1986) [text/German trans./comm.]. — J. B. Bauer, Die Polykarpbriefe: KAV 5 (1995) [German trans./comm.; pp. 75-85 index of text and extensive literature].
L: P. Devos, Notatio in Vita S. P.: AnBoll 10 (1992) 260-262. — M. Frenschkowski, P.: BBKL 7, 809-815 (literature). — W. Rebell, Ntl. Apokryphen u. Apostolische Väter (Munich, 1992), 225-229. — A. M. Ritter, De P. à Clément: aux origines d'Alexandrie chrétienne: Alexandrina. FS Mondesert (Paris, 1987), 151-172. — W. R. Schoedel, P. and Ignatius of Antioch: ANRW II 27/1 (1993) 272-358.

H. KÖNIG

Polycrates of Ephesus

Along with the other bishops of Asia Minor during the dispute over the date of Easter, P., bishop of Ephesus ca. 195, held fast to Quartodeciman practice, which he defended in a letter to Bishop → Victor I of Rome. The two surviving fragments of this letter contain important details of the history of Christianity in Asia Minor.

W: Eusebius, *h.e.* 3.31.3; 5.24.2-8 .
L: R. Bauckham, Papias and P.: JThS 44 (1993) 24-69. — J. A. Fischer, A. Lumpe, Synoden v. d. Anfängen bis z. Vorabend d. Nicaenums (Paderborn, 1997), 60-89. — W. Kühnert, Anonymus: ThZ 5 (1949) 436-446. — B. Lemoine, La controverse pascale: QuLi 73 (1992) 223-231. — M. J. Routh, Reliquiae Sacrae 2 (Oxford, ²1846), 11-36. — A. Strobel, Ursprung und Geschichte des Osterkalenders (Berlin, 1977), 22-36.

R. HANIG

Pomponius

P. was author of a Virgilian → cento in 132 hexameters: *Versus ad gratiam domini*. Using the first *Eclogue* of Virgil as a model, P. writes of a Christian named Tityrus and a pagan named Meliboeus. At the latter's request during a conversation, Tityrus gives an introduction to Christianity. Among other subjects, he speaks of creation, God's omnipotence, the immortality of the soul, and the sinfulness of human beings, but breaks off in mid-verse when speaking of redemption. This fact and a comparison with the conclusion of his model suggests a fragmentary transmission. The date for P. is uncertain. He is perhaps to be assigned to the 5th c., since he is named, along with Proba, by Isidore of Seville (*orig.* 1.39.26) and uses the same verse of his model as Proba does in describing the creation of the world.

W: C. Schenkl, CSEL 16/1:609-615. — A. Riese (ed.), Anthologia Latina 1/2 (Amsterdam, ²1964), Nr. 719a.
L: A. Di Berardino (ed.), Patrologia 3 (Turin, 1983), 258. — W. Enßlin, P. 98: PRE 21/2:1354. — M. L. Ricci, Note al centone Versus ad gratiam Domini: Annali della Facoltà di Magistero dell'Università di Bari 1974-1975, 1975-1976 [1977], 103-121. — M. Schanz, Geschichte der röm. Lit. 4/1 (Munich, ²1959), 220f.

B. WINDAU

Pontianus

African Bishop P. (his see cannot be accurately determined) took part in the Synod of Iunca in 523 and, together with his colleague Restitutus, brought a synodal letter to Boniface of Carthage. From his pen we have a very short *Ep. ad Iustinianum imperatorem de tribus capitulis*, which, on the one hand, probably goes back to 544/545, but on the other already rejects the condemnation of the Three Chapters, using to this end arguments adduced during the Three-Chapters controversy, such as the danger of unintentionally but harmfully promoting the Monophysites. It is

disputed whether P. expanded the *De viris illustribus* of → Gennadius of Marseilles into a work later used by → Isidore of Seville.

W: PL 67:995-998.
L: E. Amann, P.: DThC 12/2:407. — W. Enßlin, P.: PRE 22/1:25f. — W. Smidt, Ein altes Hs. frgm. der Viri illustres Isidors v. Sevilla: NA 44 (1922) 123-135.

U. HAMM

Pontianus of Rome

P., the legitimate bishop of Rome, 230-235, in opposition to Hippolytus, held a synod in 231 or 232 against → Origen; he probably communicated its decrees in a lost letter to his colleague, → Demetrius Alex. In 235 both of the Roman bishops were banished under Maximinus Thrax to Sardinia, where they died in the same year. In his lifetime P. renounced his office (Sept. 28, 235) and so ended the schism.

L: R. Aubert, RHE 55 (1960) 1168 (on Bellucci). — A. Bellucci, I martiri cristiani "damnati ad metalla" nella Spagna e nella Sardegna: Asp. 5 (1958) 25-46, 125-155; 6 (1959) 152-188. — W. Enßlin, P.: PRE 22/1:25.

U. HAMM

Pontius, Deacon

Only from a notice in Jerome (*vir. ill.* 68) do we know the name and status of the man who composed the biography of → Cyprian of Carthage (*Vita Cypr.*). P. was a deacon in 3rd-c. Carthage. He went into exile in Curubis along with Bishop Cyprian in 257 and witnessed the latter's execution in 258. With a knowledge of the proconsular record he wrote the *Vita et passio Cypriani* shortly after the bishop's death. He wanted to erect a memorial to the martyred bishop that would give later times a model to imitate. In hagiographical literature this document stands out for its rhetorical form. P. follows the classical instructions for an encomium but also gives the eulogy new characteristics that would become typical of later Chr. biographies. The life of Cyprian is not inferior to the *Passio Perpetuae* in literary merit, but its value as a historical source is lesser.

W: *vita Cypr.*, M. Pellegrino (Alba, 1955) [text/Italian trans.]. — A. A. R. Bastiaensen, Vite dei Santi 3, 4-48, 249-279 (Milan, 1975) [text/Italian trans./comm.] (bibl.). — J. Baer, BKV² 34 (Kempten, 1918), 1-32 [German trans.].
L: J. Aronen, Indebtedness to Passio Perpetuae: VigChr 38 (1984) 67-76. — W. Berschin, Biographie 1 (Stuttgart, 1986), 57-65. — G. Filoramo, Aspetto di religione popolare: Aug. 21 (1981) 91-98.

B. BREILMANN

Porfyrius

Poet Publilius Optatianus Porfyrius (P.) was probably born between 260 and 270 (in Africa?) and was originally a pagan; we do not know for sure when he converted to Christianity. For some years (probably until 325) he lived in exile; in 329 and 333 he held the office of *praefectus urbi* in Rome.

His work (*carm.*), written in various meters, has come down under the title *Panegyricus Constantini*. In it he brought over into Latin the genre known as the "figured poem" (→ *Carmen figuratum*), which was espec. popular in Hellen. poetry. P. went beyond his Gr. models and developed the *Carmen cancellatum* (the "lattice" or "grid" poem) in which, in a block of characters formed of hexameter lines, colored letters forming a pattern stand out. In addition to poems with non-Christian content (e.g., *carm.* 26 [altar of the muses] and 27 [Pan's pipe]) the collection also contains truly Chr. material. Thus a monogram of Christ appears in *carm.* 8 and 14, with the addition of the word *Iesus* in *carm.* 8. In *carm.* 16 the block of text is surrounded by four columns of letters, of which the first forms a Lat. text and the other three a Gr. text. Espec. artful is *carm.* 19: a ship whose mast consists of a monogram of Christ; on it are inscribed a Gr. hexameter and the beginning of a Gr. pentameter that is continued on the rudder. Finally, *carm.* 24 is a hymn to Christ in thirty-five dactylic hexameters.

W: E. Kluge (Leipzig, 1926) [text]. — G. Polara, 2 vols. (Turin, 1973) [text/Latin comm.].
L: J. Adler, U. Ernst, Text als Figur (Weinheim, ²1988). — G. Chmiel, Untersuchungen zu P., Diss. (Munich, 1930). — U. Ernst, Zahl u. Maß in den Figurengedichten der Antike u. des FrühMA: Mensura, ed. A. Zimmermann (Berlin, 1984), 310-332. — HLL 5:237-239. — E. Kluge, P. u. sein Werk, Diss. (Munich, 1920).

S. Döpp

Possessor

P. (484-520), Cath. bishop of Zabensis (Algeria), gave his support in Constantinople to the efforts of Roman Bishop Hormisdas to win acceptance of Chalcedon. He sent a *Libellus de confessione rectae fidei* to Hormisdas, who thanked him in a letter of April 3, 517 (*Collectio Avellana* 131). In combatting Faustus of Riez he sent his deacon Justin to Rome with a *Relatio* that arrived on July 18, 520, and was answered by Hormisdas on Aug. 13, 520. Hormisdas confirmed that Faustus could not claim the authority of the fathers for his views and that he should instead consult Augustine's works on grace. P. seems to have been accused by John Maxentius (*Responsio ad ep. Hormisdae*, ACO 4, 2, 46-62) of being inclined to Nestorianism.

W: *Relatio* (= Collectio Avellana 230), O. Guenther, CSEL 35/2:695f. — *ep. Hormisdae* (= Collectio Avellana 131), idem, op. cit., 552f.
L: PAC 889.

W. Geerlings

Possidius of Calama

P. was bishop of Calama in Numidia. From 390/391 on he belonged to Augustine's circle of friends and was a member of the monastic community in Hippo. In 397 he was consecrated bishop of Calama, probably as the immediate successor of Megalius, primate of Numidia. During his time in office P. endeavored to maintain close contact with Augustine and to seek his advice in all important matters. He served Augustine in carrying letters (to Paulinus of Nola: Aug., *ep.* 105; to Bishop Memorius, father of Julian of Eclanum: *ep.* 101; to Nectarius: *ep.* 104) and took an active part in all the important African synods. In 416, during the struggle against Pelagius, P. and four other African bishops wrote an official letter to Innocent I (Aug., *ep.* 176; Innocent's answer, *ep.* 183) and repeated their intervention a year later.

Between 415 and 426/427 P. had the relics of St. Stephen transferred to Calama. In 430 he witnessed the Vandal invasion of Numidia (*vita Aug.* 28); most of the episcopal sees were destroyed and P. fled with other bishops to Hippo. During this stay he drew up a list of the books, sermons, and letters of Augustine (known as *Indiculus, Indiculum,* or *Elenchus*) that were to be found in the archive of the church of Hippo at that time.

P. probably composed his *Vita Augustini* (*vita Aug.*) before the capture of Hippo. He portrays Augustine as a model bishop and at the same time bears witness to his own forty-year friendship with him. The *Vita* describes the several stages of Augustine's life and is impressive for its description of his everyday life. Augustine is deliberately presented as a contemporary. Unlike the *Vitae,* which in the tradition of the *Vita Antonii* present the saint as a battler against demons and as a miracle worker, as *vir Dei,* there is none of this in the *vita Aug.*

W: *vita Aug.,* A. A. R. Bastiaensen, Vita di Cipriano, Vita di Ambrogio, Vita di Agostino (Verona, 1975), 339-451 [text/comm.]. — H. T. Weiskotten (Princeton, 1919) [text/ English trans./comm.]. — A. von Harnack (Berlin, 1930) [German trans./comm.]. — *elenchus,* Operum S. Augustini elenchus, ed. A. Wilmart: Miscellanea Agostiniana 2 (Rome, 1931), 149-233.

L: A. Bastiaensen, The Inaccuracies in the Vita Augustini of P.: StPatr 6 (1985) 480-486. — W. Berschin, Biographie u. Epochenstil im lat. MA 1 (Stuttgart, 1986), 226-235. — S. Dagemark, P.'s Idealised Description of St. Augustine's Death: Aug. 58 (1997) 719-741. — PAC 890-896. — B. Stoll, Die vita Aug. des P. als hagiographischer Text: ZKG 102 (1991) 1-13. — E. Zocca, La figura del santo vescovo in Africa da Ponzia a P.: Aug. 58 (1997) 469-492.

W. GEERLINGS

Potamius of Lisbon

P. was bishop of Lisbon from ca. 350 to ca. 360. He took part in the trinitarian debate of the fifties, initially as proponent of a one-hypostasis doctrine (thus in his letter to Athanasius [*ep. ad Athan.*], a letter to be dated before 357 because of its lack of any reference to the real Nicene Creed); from 357 on, however, he joined in the dogmatically rather neutral efforts of the homoeans to achieve a balance (Father and Son are *similis*; rejection of the disputed term *substantia* in connection with the Trinity). Acc. to Hilary (*syn.* 3.11) P. was co-author of the second homoean formula of Sirmium, and acc. to Phoebadius (*C. Ar.* 5.1) P. sent out a theol. circular letter (not preserved) in support of this formula. The reason for his change of mind may have been a concern for the unity of the church (see → Ossius of Cordoba). The accusation of bribery against Luciferians Faustinus and Marcellus (*Libellus precum* 32; 41) is a hereniological commonplace.

The homilies *De Lazaro* and *De Mart. Isaiae Proph.* show P. as a popular preacher. The authorship of the *Ep. de substantia Patris* is disputed (differences of style); because of the reference to the consubstantiality of the Spirit, the work seems to belong to a later time and would therefore not be attributable to P.

W: *ep. ad Athan.*, A. Wilmart: RBen 30 (1913) 280-283 [text]. — *de Lazaro*, A. Wilmart: JThS 19 (1918) 298-304 [text]. — *de Mart. Isaiae Proph.*, PL 8:1415f. — *ep. de Subst. Patris*, PLS 1:202-216. — *Opuscula omnia Potamii*, A. C. Vega (Escorial, 1934) [text].
L: U. Dominguez del Val, P.: CDios 172 (1959) 237-259. — R. P. C. Hanson, Search (Edinburgh, 1988), 526-528. — J. Madoz, P.: RET 7 (1947) 79-109. — M. Meslin, Ariens (Paris, 1967), 31-34. — A. Montes Moreira, P. (Leuven/Louvain, 1969). — idem, Textos: Itin. 13 (1967) 457-463. — idem, Retour: Did(L) 5 (1975) 303-354. — A. Wilmart, Lettre: RBen 30 (1913) 257-279.

J. ULRICH

Praedestinatus

The *Praedestinatus* is anonymous work in three books, written between 432 and 440. Using Augus-

tine's *De haeresibus*, it describes ninety heresies, that of the predestinationists being regarded as the last and worst of them (book 1). There follows, under the name of Augustine, an overdrawn description of his teaching of grace and predestination (book 2), which is then attacked (book 3). Because of a material and linguistic affinity with the commentary on the Pss of → Arnobius the Younger, the latter has been suggested as the author, but → Julian of Eclanum has also been mentioned.

W: PL 53:579-692. — PLS 3:213-256.
L: M. Abel, Le Praedestinatus, Thèse (Leuven/Louvain, 1968). — idem, Le Praedestinatus et le pélagianisme: RTA (1968) 5-25. — G. Bouwmann, Des Julian v. Aeclanum Kommentar zu den Propheten Joel, Osse, Joel und Amos (Rome, 1958), 17-19. — H. v. Schubert, Der sog. Praedestinatus (Leipzig, 1903).

W. GEERLINGS

Praxeas

Information about P. comes almost exclusively from → Tertullian in his polemic *Adversus Praxean* (see also Ps.-Tertullian, *haer.* 8.4). Acc. to him, P., a confessor from Asia Minor, slandered the Montanists in Rome (presumably in the time of Victor I) and thwarted the bishops' letters seeking peace. At the same time, P. was (supposedly) the first to introduce there the monarchian (modalist) doctrine. All other data supplied by Tertullian are ambiguous. Thus it remains unclear, e.g., whether P. himself or only his teaching was being refuted in Carthage at the beginning of the 3rd c. (Tert., *adv. Prax.* 1.6, mentions a written retractation); who the real adversary of Tertullian was in the subsequently revived dispute; and whether several phases of the dispute are to be distinguished (see *adv. Prax.* 27.1). Above all, there has been no agreed explanation of how what Tertullian says of P. is to be reconciled with what is said by Hippolytus about Noetus, Epigonus, and Cleomenes. In this context, efforts at identification with Callistus, Epigonus, or → Irenaeus are not satisfactory.

L: R. Cantalamessa, P.: ScC 90 (1962) 28-50. — M. Decker, Monarchianer, Diss. (Hamburg, 1987), 165-182. — E. Evans, Tertullian's Treatise (London, 1948). — G. Esser, P. (Bonn, 1910). — H. Hagemann, Röm. Kirche (Freiburg i.Br., 1864), 206-257. — A. v. Harnack, Geschichte der altchr. Lit. 1 (Leipzig, ²1958), 597f. — idem, Lehrbuch der Dogmengeschichte 1 (Tübingen, 1990 = Tübingen, ⁴1909), 741-750. — S. G. Hall, P. and Irenaeus: StPatr 14 (1976) 145-147. — A. Hilgenfeld, Ketzergeschichte (Darmstadt, 1966 = Leipzig, 1884), 618-622. — T. L. Verhoeven, Tertullianus' Adversus Praxean (Amsterdam, 1948).

R. HANIG

Praylius of Jerusalem

P. was bishop of Jerusalem 417-422 as successor of John II. He may possibly be the author of the section on virginity in the homily *De laudibus Mariae*, which is usually attributed to → Proclus of Constantinople.

W: PG 65:721-733.
L: R. Laurentin, Bulletin sur la Vierge Marie: RSPhTh 52 (1968) 545.

G. Röwekamp

Precatio hermetica

The *Hermetic Prayer*, also known as *The Prayer of Thanksgiving*, has come down in the Copt. Nag Hammadi library (NHC 6, 7) and corresponds to the already known prayer in the Papyrus Mimaut (*pap.*), which is contained in Latin in the forty-first chapter of the hermetic treatise of Ps.-Apuleius (*Ps.-Apul.*). It conveys the thanksgiving of the redeemed soul, which, thanks to heavenly teachers, has found the way back to its divine self and has gradually achieved knowledge of the invisible divinity.

W: *Prec. herm.*, D. M. Parrott, NHC V, 2-5 and VI (Leiden, 1979), 328f. [Coptic text/English trans.]. — J. M. Robinson, The Nag Hammadi Library in English (Leiden, ³1988), 298f. [English trans.]. — K. W. Tröger, NHC VI, 6f.: ThLZ 98 (1973) 495-503 [German trans.]. — Ps.-Apul., A. D. Nock, Hermetica (Paris, 1960), 259-401 [Latin text/French trans.]. — *pap.*, K. Preisendanz, Pap. Gr. Mag. 3 (Stuttgart, 1973/74), 591 [Greek text]. — NHL 328f. [English trans.].
L: P. Chérix, Concordance (Leuven/Louvain, 1993). — M. Krause, P. Labib, Gnostische Schriften (Glückstadt, 1971). — J. P. Mahé, La prière d'actions de grâces: ZPE 13 (1974) 40-60.

P. Bruns

Primasius of Hadrumetum

P. was bishop of Hadrumetum (today Sousse, Tunisia) between 550 and 560. He was one of the few African bishops to agree with the condemnation of the Three Chapters. From his pen comes a commentary on the Apocalypse that is based on Augustine and Tyconius and is important for its borrowing from the (lost) work of the latter. The Apocalypse is interpreted allegorically as referring to the history of the church; the anti-Roman tendencies in the Apocalypse are eliminated. A work of P., *De haeresibus*, is lost; the commentary of Pelagius on the letters of Paul sometimes went under P.'s name.

W: A. W. Adams, CCL 92.
L: G. Kretschmar, Die Offb. Die Geschichte ihrer Auslegung (Stuttgart, 1985), 111f. — K. Steinhauser, The Apc-Com-

mentary of Tyconius (1987), 69-89. — H. J. Vogels, Untersuchungen zur Geschichte der lat. Apk-Übersetzungen (1920).

G. Röwekamp

Priscian

P. was the last important Lat. grammarian. He was born in Caesarea of Mauretania, was a student of Theoctistus, and was professor of grammar in Constantinople under Emperor Anastasius (491-518). His principal work was the *Institutio de arte grammatica* (*inst.*) in eighteen books, in which he undertook an explanation of all of grammar, along with syntax. This work was widespread in the Middle Ages, which used the first sixteen books as P. *maior* and books 17-18 as P. *minor*. For scholastic purposes he composed his *Institutio de nomine et pronomine et verbo* (*nom.*), which was an abbreviated version of books 6-13 of the *inst.*, in the form of rules, and his *Partitiones* (*part.*), in which, in question-and-answer form, he gives a metrical and grammatical analysis of the opening verses of each of the twelve books of Virgil's *Aeneid*. He dedicated three shorter works (before 525) to Symmachus: *De figuris numerorum* (*fig. num.*) on Roman signs for numbers, coins, and words for numbers; *De metris fabularum Terenti* (*metr.*), on the verse character of dramatic iambs and trochees; and *Praeexercitamina rhetorica* (*rhet.*), a translation of the *Progymnasmata* of Hermogenes. We possess only a later revision of another work, *De accentibus* (*acc.*), the authenticity of which is disputed. P. also composed two poems: a panegyric on Emperor Anastasius (*Anast.* before 518) and the *Perihegesis* (*periheg.*), a translation of the didactic poem of the same name by Dionysius Periegetes.

W: *inst.*, GrLat 2-3:1-384. — *nom.*, M. Passalacqua (Urbino, 1992) [text]. — *part.*, GrLat 3:459-515. — *fig. num.*, M. Passalacqua, P. Caesariensis opuscula 1 (Rome, 1987) [text]. — *metr.*, GrLat 3:418-429. — *rhet.*, C. Halm, Rhetores latini minores (Leipzig, 1863), 551-560. — GrLat 3:430-440. — *acc.*, GrLat 3:519-528. — *Anast.*, E. Baehrens, Poetae latini minores 5 (Leipzig, 1883), 264-274. — A. Chauvot, Procope de Gaza, Priscien de Césarée, Panégyriques (Bonn, 1986), 56-68 [text/French trans./comm.]. — *periheg.*, P. van de Woestijne (Brügge, 1953).
L: G. Ballaira, P. e i suoi amici (Turin, 1989). — idem, Per il catalogo dei codici di P. (Turin, 1982). — P. A. Coyne, P.'s De laude Anastasii, Diss. (McMaster Univ., Hamilton, Ont., 1988). — M. Gibson, Milestones in the Study of P.: Viator 23 (1992) 17-33. — R. Helm, P. 1: PRE 22/2:2328-2346. — M. Passalacqua, I codici di P. (Rome, 1978). — M. Schanz, C. Hosius, G. Krüger, Geschichte der röm. Lit. 4/2 (Munich, 1959 = 1920), 221-238. — P. L. Schmidt, P.: KP 4:1141f.

B. Windau

Priscillian

1. Life: P., born ca. 345 in Spain, became bishop of Avila in 380 and was executed in Trier in 385. He was born of a wealthy family, received a rhetorical training, and was baptized only as an adult; he became the leader of a rigoristic ascetical movement of laymen, clerics, and women that arose independently of (Egyptian) monasticism and was widespread espec. in Portugal. Its chief opponents (from 379 on) were Bishops Hydatius of Emerita and Ithacius of Ossonoba. Hydatius excommunicated P. and his supporters for gnostic heresy and evidently won the agreement of the Synod of Saragossa (Oct. 380). When P. was consecrated bishop of Avila at the end of 380, Hydatius obtained from Gratian an edict against Priscillianist bishops; their sees were taken from them, and they were threatened with exile. A journey that P. undertook to Rome and Milan seeking redress proved fruitless, since Damasus and Ambrose refused communion with him; meanwhile, Gratian withdrew his edict in 382. The complaint that Bishop Ithacius lodged against P. with Maximus the usurper (since 383) was passed on to a synod convoked in Bordeaux in 384 to handle the matter; P. appealed to the imperial court of justice and, in the course of a civil criminal trial and against the wishes of Bishop Martin of Tours, was convicted, along with six of his supporters, of Manichaeism and the practice of magic (*maleficium*) and executed (Jan. 385). Veneration of P. and Priscillianism itself were thereby given new life in Spain; evidence of a long-term influence is the Spanish synods between 400 and 572.

II. Works: The following have come down under P.'s name: (1) *Canones in Pauli apostoli ep. a Peregrino episcopo emendati* (*can.*): an outline of Pauline theology in ninety statements (*canones*) that rely closely on the fourteen letters of Paul and are supported by pericopes; the degree of redactional involvement by Peregrinus is disputed. (2) Fragments of letters (*ep.*) transmitted in → Orosius (*comm.* 2): evidence for P.'s teaching on the soul, probably reliable in its content. (3) Anonymously transmitted: the *Tractatus XI* (*tract.*), which were discovered by G. Schepss in 1885 in a Würzburg ms. of the 5th/6th c. and attributed to P. under this title: *tract.* 1-3 are writings in P.'s defense (*Liber apologeticus, Liber ad Damasum episcopum, De fide et de apocryphis*), 4-10 are sermons, and 11 a prayer of blessings. Priscillianist Bishop Instantius has been suggested as author instead of P. Others ascribe 4, 6, 9, and 10 to a Priscillianist writer of the period after 386, 8 and 11 to a second author, 5 and 7 to a third, while P. is acknowledged as author only of 2 and 3. Recent scholarship has tended to the idea of a single author; the problem calls for further discussion.

It is not possible to distinguish P.'s teaching from the Priscillianism handed down in other sources (*De trinitate fidei catholicae* [ed. Morin 1913 = PLS 2:1487-1507]; Sulpicius Severus, *chron.* and *dial.*; Orosius, *comm.*; Augustine, *c. Prisc.*, *c. mend.*, and *ep.* 237; Leo I, *ep.* 15). This means that there is also no way of judging with certainty the orthodoxy of the historical P. What can be achieved is a distinction between genuine Priscillianist writings and anti-Priscillianist doxographies; in this light, P. was neither a magician nor a Manichee but rather the proponent of an ascetical Christ-centered piety, the gnostic-dualist origins of which he was unable to transcend and bring into accord with the Bible and the church.

W: *can.*, G. Schepss, CSEL 18:110-147 = PLS 2:1391-1413. — *ep.*, Orosius, *comm.* 2, G. Schepss, CSEL 18:153, 11-18 — *tract.*, G. Schepss, CSEL 18:3-106 = PLS 2:1413-1483 (with emendations).
L: E.-C. Babut, P. et le priscillianisme (Paris, 1909). — K. Baus: HKG(J) 2/1:134-142. — A. Breukelaar, Priscillianus: BBKL 7:952-956. — V. Burrus, The Making of a Heretic (Berkeley, 1995). — H. Chadwick, P. of Avila (Oxford, 1976). — M. V. Escribano, Iglesia y estado en el certamen priscillianista (Zragosa, 1988). — A. Ferreiro, Simon Magus and P. in the Commonitorium of Vincent of Lérins: VigChr 49 (1995) 180-188. — idem, P. and Nicolaitism: VigChr 52 (1998) 382-392. — J. Fontaine, P.: TRE 27:449-454. — K. M. Girardet, Trier 385: Chiron 4 (1974) 577-608. — J. Martin, P. oder Instantius: HJ 47 (1927) 237-251. — G. Morin, Pro Instantio: RBen 30 (1913) 153-173. — W. Schatz, Studien zur Geschichte u. Vorstellungswelt des frühen abendländischen Mönchtums, typescript of diss. (Freiburg i.Br., 1957). — P. Stockmeier, Das Schwert im Dienste der Kirche: FS A. Thomas (Trier, 1967), 415-428. — R. Van Dam, Leadership and Community in Late Antique Gaul (Berkeley, 1985). — B. Vollmann, Studien zum Priszillianismus (St. Ottilien, 1965). — idem, Priscillianus: PRE. S 14:485-559.

K. H. Schwarte

Proba

Faltonia Betitia (probably not Anicia Faltonia) Proba (P.), an aristocratic Roman lady (b. ca. 320, d. ?), was author of a lost historical epic (*cento* 1-8), probably about the war between Constantius and Maxentius. Probably after 384 (priority of the *Carmen contra paganos*), she composed a bibl. → cento, in ca. seven hundred hexameters, of verses from Virgil (except for vv. 1-23). In her sketch of the history of salvation, which is guided by the Virgilian interpretation of history, the creation and gradual loss of paradise down to the flood is followed by the redemptive work of Christ. The cento, which is meant as a Chr. exegesis of Virgil (v. 23: *Vergilium cecinisse loquar pia munera Christi*), is able often only to allude to the bibl. passages; it sets up numerous relationships by means of the Virgilian setting which it often and consciously evokes; this means that the work assumes a knowledge both of the classical text and the content of the Bible. Despite withering criticism by Jerome (*ep.* 53.7), P. with her technique of *abbreviatio* and *amplificatio* and her use of the OT probably had a greater influence than Juvencus on the development of the bibl. epic (→ Epic).

W: C. Schenkl, CSEL 16. — E. A. Clark, D. F. Hatch, The Golden Bough (Ann Arbor, Mich., 1981) [text/English trans./comm.].
L: M. R. Cacioli, Adattamenti semantici e sintattici: SIFC 41 (1969) 188-246. — F. Ermini, Il centone di P. (Rome, 1909). — R. P. H. Green, P.'s Cento: CQ 45 (1995) 551-563. — idem, P.'s Introduction to Her Cento: CQ 47 (1997) 548-559. — R. Herzog, Bibelepik (Munich, 1975). — W. Kirsch, Lat. Versepik (Berlin, 1989). — F. Kunzmann, Cento: HWRh 148-152. — S. Kyriakidis, Eve and Mary: MD 29 (1992) 121-153. — I. Opelt, Christus: JAC 7 (1964) 106-116. — Z. Pavlovskis, Semiotics: Vergilius 35 (1989) 70-84. — D. Shanzer, Carmen contra paganos and P.: REAug 32 (1986) 232-248.

T. HÜBNER

Proclus of Constantinople

P. was consecrated bishop of Cyzicus in 426, but was not accepted by his episcopal city. In 424 he became patriarch of Constantinople (as second follower of Nestorius). He died in 446.

Sermons and letters have come down from P., but the attribution of the sermons that have come down under his name is extremely uncertain. Thirty-seven sermons (*hom.*) are regarded as certain, among them a sermon on Mary that is regarded as the most famous Marian sermon of antiquity. P. delivered it on March 25, 431, in the presence of Nestorius, who vehemently attacked P.'s formulations, which took a middle ground between Alex. and Antiochene christology (ACO 1, 5, 37-39). P.'s mediating and conciliatory sermons were widely circulated and translated at an early date into Syriac, Armenian, Coptic, Arabic, Ethiopic, Latin, Church Slavonic, and Georgian. In their style they follow Hippolytus and John Chrys., but the attempt to ascribe to P. more than eighty sermons among the *spuria* of Chrysostom must be regarded as a failure. Along with the sermons eight letters (*ep.*) have been handed down in which P. again seeks to mediate between the Anti-

ochenes and the Alexandrians. Thus in his letter to the Arm. episcopate (*Tomus ad Armenianos; Arm.*) in 425, he tried to pacify the Arm. church, which was disturbed by the controversy over Theodore Mops., who had died in 428. P.'s confession of faith, given in this letter, in the two natures in Christ and a single hypostasis (= person) of the incarnate Logos (a confession based on → Cyril Alex.) was approved by the Council of Chalcedon in 451. In a letter to deacon Maximus he urged moderation in the controversy over Theodore Mops. for the sake of peace in the church (*nihil ad confusionem vel tumultum ecclesiarum pacem habentium agi*).

P. coined the famous theopaschite formula *Unus e trinitate passus* (*Arm.; ep.* 4, *ad Iohannem Antiochenum*), which was subsequently strongly controverted and was accepted only under John II of Rome (533-535). There is disagreement as to whether P. introduced the Trisagion into the liturgy. It is possible that this story regarding the Trisagion was intended to claim the origin of the Trisagion for Constantinople rather than Antioch. It is also unclear whether P. was composer of the Anaphora of Gregory.

The ascription of the following is uncertain: *In s. baptisma; In Lucam; De transfiguratione*; three sermons *De nativitate; In annuntiatione beatissimae dei genitricis; In Iohannem Baptistam; In s. Stephanum; Tractatus de fide*. Certainly not authentic: *Laudatio s. Nicolai; Dialysis de oratione dominica; De XXIV senioribus*. The fragment *De traditione divinae missae*, handed down under P.'s name, is a forgery.

W: *hom.*, PG 31:1713-1721; 59:681-688; 62:727-730; 65:680-850. — ACO 1, 1, 1, 103-107. — M. Aubineau, SC 187:181-186. — F. J. Leroy, L'homilétique de P. (Rome, 1967), 174-212, 223-256, 298-324 [text]. — S. Y. Rudberg, L'homélie pseudo-basilienne consolatoria ad aegrotum: Muséon 72 (1959) 301-322 [text]. — D. Amand: RBen 58 (1948) 223-263 [text]. — *Arm.*, PG 65:856-873. — ACO 4, 2, 187-195. — *ep. ad Iohannem Antiochenum*, PG 65:873-877. — ACO 4, 1, 140-143. — F. Diekamp, Doctrina Patrum (Münster, ²1981), 48. — J. M. Clément, R. Vander Plaetse, CCL 90 A:231. — *ep. ad Maximum diaconum*, PG 65:879-880. — J. M. Clément, R. Vander Plaetse, op. cit., 232-233. — *ep. ad Domnum Antiochenum*, PG 65:881-884. — ACO 2, 1, 3, 67f. (426f.). — *ep. synodica*, PG 65:885f. — ACO 1, 4, 173f. — *ep. uniformis ad singulos Occidentis episcopos*, ACO 4, 2, 65-68.
L: M. Aubineau, Bilan d'une enquête sur les homélies de P.: REG 85 (1972) 572-596. — J. H. Barkhuizen, Aspects of Style and Imagery in hom.: Acta Patristica et Byzantina 9 (1998) 1-22. — F. X. Bauer, P. (Munich, 1919). — A. Gerhards, Die griech. Gregorios-anaphora (Münster, 1984). — A. Grillmeier, Jesus der Christus 1 (Freiburg i.Br., ²1982), 727-731; 2/1 (Freiburg i.Br., 1986), 64, 73, 75; 2/2 (Freiburg i.Br., 1989), 268-275, 334-338, 433-435; 2/4 (Freiburg i.Br., 1990), 247 (English, Christ in Christian Tradition [London,

1975-96]). — V. Inglisian, Die Beziehungen des Patriarchen P. u. des Bischofs Akakios v. Melitene zu Armenien: OrChr 41 (1957) 35-50. — F. J. Leroy, P., "de traditione divinae Missae": OCP 28 (1962) 288-299. — idem, L'homilétique de P. (Rome, 1967). — A. Lumpe, Die Epistola Uniformis des P.: AHC 3 (1971) 1-20. — C. Martin, Hippolyte de Rome et P.: RHE 33 (1937) 255-276. — idem, Un florilège grec d'homélies christologiques: Muséon 54 (1941) 44-48. — B. Marx, Procliana (Münster, 1940). — M. Richard, P. et le théopaschisme: RHE 38 (1942) 323-331 = Opera minora 2 (Turnhout, 1977), Nr. 52. — idem, L'introduction du mot Hypostase dans la théologie de l'Incarnation: MSR 2 (1945) 5-32, 243-270 = Opera minora 2 (Turnhout, 1977), Nr. 42. — J. M. Sauget, Une homélie de P. sur l'Ascension de Notre-Seigneur: Muséon 82 (1969) 5-33. — E. Schwartz, Konzilstudien (Strasburg, 1914), 18-53. — A. Solignac, P.: DSp 12:2374-2381.

B. R. Suchla

Proclus, Montanist

P. was a leading member of the Montanists in Rome at the end of the 2nd c. (Ps.-Tertullian, *haer.* 7.2; Eus., *h.e.* 2.25.6; Jerome, *vir. ill.* 59; Theod., *haer.* 3.2; Photius, *cod.* 48). Gaius, an anti-Montanist, wrote a dialogue against him in which P. appeals to the tomb of the prophetess daughters of Philip in Hierapolis (acc. to Eus., *h.e.* 3.31.4; see Pacian, *ep.* 1.2). P. probably claimed apostolic tradition or even succession for the Montanists. Tertullian attests (*adv. Val.* 5.1) to literary and specifically anti-Valentinian activity by a Proculus, whom he praises highly and who is probably identical with P. (see also Tert., *Scap.* 4.5).

W: Eus., *h.e.* 3.31.4.
L: A. v. Harnack, Geschichte der altchr. Lit. 1 (Leipzig, ²1958), 600f.; 2/2:206. — P. Lampe, Die stadtröm. Christen (Tübingen, ²1989), 284f.

R. Hanig

Procopius of Caesarea

I. Life: Acc. to his own statements P. came from Caesarea. The few certain dates of his life are to be gotten from his works; his birth is to be dated ca. 500. After juridical training and activity P. became *consiliarius* of Belisarius in the spring of 527 and took part in the latter's campaigns, first until 536 in Africa, then, beginning in 537, on a special strategic mission in southern Italy. From 540 on P. resided chiefly in Constantinople, where he collected material for his books. Nothing is known of his last years or the date of his death (after 555).
II. Works: P.'s main work *Bella* deals with the struggles of East Rome in the East, North Africa, and Italy until 553. The *Anekdota* (*Anek.*) were composed ca. 550 and contain the scandalous story of the Byz.

imperial couple Justinian and Theodora. In it P. does not conceal his dislike of the emperor and his lavish lifestyle. It is possible that the work circulated anonymously in opposition circles among the military and the senate; only in the 10th c. does it seem to have become known to a wider public. The late work *Aedificia*, composed probably between 553 and 555, has entirely the character of a panegyric and describes in geographical order the monuments built by Justinian.

Connected as he was outwardly and interiorly with the patrician class, P. shows great sympathy for commander Belisarius's desire to restore the external greatness of the empire. In his historical works elements of pagan style and the central concept of *Tychē* compete with Chr. faith in the divine governance of the world. P.'s demonology contains Jewish-Chr. elements; his theology of history gives the emperor anti-Chr. traits. Yet in the ruler's building policy P. sees the embodiment of the idea of the Chr. kingdom, although he finds fault with the emperor's extravagant expenditures.

W: J. Haury, G. Wirth, P. Caesariensis opera omnia (Leipzig, 1962-1964 = Leipzig, 1905-1913) [text]. — O. Veh (Munich, 1961-1970) [text/German trans.].
L: R. Browning, Justinian and Theodora (London, 1971). — A. Cameron, Procopius and the Sixth Century (London, 1985), 113-133. — F. Dahn, P. Ein Beitrag zur Historiographie der Völkerwanderung (Berlin, 1865). — I. A. Evans, Procopius (New York, 1972). — J. Meyendorff, Justinian, the Empire and the Church: DOP 22 (1968) 43-60. — B. Rubin, P. v. Cäsarea (Stuttgart, 1954). — idem, Das Zeitalter Justinians (Berlin, 1960), 173-226, 430-473. — idem, Antichrist: ZDMG 110 (1960) 55-63. — W. Schubart, Justinian u. Theodora (Munich, 1943). — O. Veh, Zur Geschichtsschreibung u. Weltauffassung des P. 1-3 (Bayreuth, 1951-1953).

P. Bruns

Procopius of Gaza

P., b. ca. 465, and probably brother of Zacharias Rhetor, received his early education in Gaza and did further studies in Alexandria; even as a young man he was already a rhetor in his native city. He died at aged sixty-two or sixty-three, therefore ca. 530, after having already lost his wife and children. He composed a good many commentaries in the form of catenas. A catena on the Octateuch exists in two versions; only the shorter version has been directly transmitted. Also from P. are catenas on Kgs, Chr, Song, and Isa. The authenticity of a catena on Prov is disputed. P.'s 163 letters (*ep.*) and his speeches (*declam.*) are as important for his biography as is the funeral oration (*or. fun.*) given by his student → Choricius, which is entirely in the style of the pagan panegyrics of antiquity. P. himself composed a panegyric on Emperor Anastasius (*Anast.*). Of some importance for the history of art is his description of a cycle of paintings (*ekphrasis eikonos*) in Gaza (*descr.*).

S: *or. fun.*, R. Förster, E. Richtsteig, Choricii Gazaei opera (Stuttgart, 1972 = Leipzig, 1929), 109-128 [text].
W: PG 87:1-1220. — *Anast.*, C. Kempen, P. encomium in Anastasium imperatorem (n.p., 1918) [text]. — A. Chavot (Bonn, 1986) [text/French trans./comm.]. — descr., P. Friedländer, Spätantiker Gemäldezyklus (Rome, 1939) [text]. — *ep., declam.*, A. Garzya, R. J. Loenertz, P. G. epistolae et declamationes (Ettal, 1963) [text]. — *Eccl.*, S. Leanza, CCG 4.
L: H. Diels, Über die von P. beschriebene Kunstuhr (Berlin, 1917). — L. Eisenhofer, P. v. Gaza (Freiburg i.Br., 1897). — E. Lindl, Die Oktateuch des P. (n.p., 1902). — E. Montmasson, L'homme créé à l'image de Dieu: EO 14 (1911) 334-339; 15 (1912) 154-162. — K. Seitz, Die Schule von Gaza (Heidelberg, 1892).

P. BRUNS

Prologue (to Books of the Bible)

Bibl. prologues, usually known as *argumenta*, are informative, although not always accurate, introductions to individual books (of OT or NT) or groups of books; they also serve as presentations and characterizations of the author or the translator. In the course of time they were added to many (Lat.) mss. The models for these prologues were, among others, that by the grandson of Jesus son of Sirach (prologue to Sir) and the prologues to the gospel of Luke (1:1-4) and Acts (1:1-3). Some of the relatively short prologues that have survived go back to the 2nd c.

One group of prologues to the gospels are known as the "Anti-Marcionite prologues," although the existence of the tendency is questioned today. In any case, the prologue to Mt is lost and those for Mk and Jn have come down only in Lat. They were probably composed in the 4th c. at the earliest.

Related to that group are the so-called Monarchianist prologues, which are usually attached to the gospels in the transmission of the Vulgate. They probably come from the end of the 4th c. and have their closest parallels in the ambiance of Priscillian or his movement.

Seven (short) prologues for the letters of Paul (Gal, 1 Cor, Rom, 1 Thess, Col, Phil, Phlm)—described in part as "Marcionite"—probably had their origin in Syria (at the same time as the Western Text), were translated into Latin in the 3rd c., and were later revised. The prologues to the OT books were the work espec. of Jerome (espec. important in the prologue *galeatus* to Sam and Kgs); the prologues to the NT books are largely excerpts from the Gr. fathers (Irenaeus, John Chrys., and others).

L: D. de Bruyne, Les plus anciens Prologues des Évangiles: RB 40 (1928) 193-214. — A. v. Harnack, Die ältesten Evangelienprologe, SPAW. PH 24 (Berlin, 1928). — HLL 4:349f. — H. Lietzmann, Synopse der drei ersten Evangelien (Tübingen, 1950), VIIIf. — J. Regul, Die antimarcionitischen Evangelienprologe (Freiburg i.Br., 1969) [with text]. — M. E. Schild, Abendländische Bibelvorreden bis zur Lutherbibel, Diss. (Heidelberg, 1964). — H. v. Soden, Die Schriften des NT 1/1 (Göttingen, 1911), 301-376. [with the text of the Greek prologue to the NT].

A. SAND

Propemptikon

A *propemptikon* is an occasional poem that "escorts" a person going away (*propempein*, "to accompany"). Its characteristics are, generally, praise of the departing person, complaint of the person remaining behind, a change of mood as the writer prays for a good journey under the protection of the gods, a description of the route for the journey, and a hope that they will think of each other and see each other again. Although individual verses of this kind are found in epic, drama, lyric, and epigram, the pagan-Greek *propemptikon* proper appears first in the Hellen. period (e.g., Theocritus 7.52-89). Important pagan-Latin *propemptika* are: Propertius 1.6; 1.8; Tibullus, 1.3; Ovid, *am.* 2.11; Horace, *epod.* 1.10; *carm.* 1.3; 1.14; 3.27; Statius, *silv.* 3.2 (the most extensive). The best known Chr.-Lat. *propemptikon* that has come down is Paulinus of Nola, *carm.* 17, addressed to Bishop Nicetas of Remesiana. With its tendency to spiritualization, to a transcendent extrapolation of the real event, this poem expands the scope of the pagan *propemptikon* in both content and form. *Carm.* 2.5 of Sedulius Scottus can be regarded as the most important Carolingian *propemptikon*. The element of petition for (one's own) successful journey and return finally became an independent entity in the genre of Chr. prayer for a journey (Gregory Naz., *Enodia Kōnstantinoupoleōs*; Gildas, *Oratio rythmica*; Paulinus of Nola, *carm.* 12) and took liturgical form in the Middle Ages. The prose form, the *propemptikē lalia*, seems to have appeared first in the Chr. era. The theory developed for the prose form (Menander Rhetor 2.395.1–399.10) is also of importance for the *propemptikon*.

L: F. Cairns, Generic Composition in Greek and Roman Poetry (Edinburgh, 1972), 3-16. — R. P. H. Green, The

Poetry of Paulinus of Nola. A Study of His Latinity: CollLat 120 (1971) 34f. — F. Jäger, Das antike Propemptikon u. das 17. Gedicht des Paulinus v. Nola, Diss. (Munich, 1913).

V. JUST

Prophetiae

The work first published in 1897 under the title *Prophetiae ex omnibus libris collectae* contains a short treatise on the seven kinds of prophecy, a list of prophets (from Adam to Zechariah) and prophetesses (from Miriam to Mary, Elizabeth, and Anna), together with the subjects of their predictions, NT prophecies, and a condemnation of Montanism. The anon. work was composed in Africa between 305 and 325 and is important for the Old Latin African text of the Bible. It is disputed whether or not the author was a Donatist.

W: PLS 1:177-180, 1738-1741.
L: HLL 5:418. — T. Zahn, Ein Kompendium der bibl. Prophetie. FS A. Hauck (Leipzig, 1916), 52-63.

G. RÖWEKAMP

Prosper Tiro of Aquitania

I. Life: P. spent his life as a lay monk in Marseilles and ca. 428, together with his friend → Hilary (Gallus), told Augustine of the opposition to his teaching on grace (Augustine, *ep.* 225). → Augustine gave his answer in his *praed. sanct.* and *persev.* After Augustine's death, P. traveled with Hilary to Rome and Celestine I in order to work for the condemnation of the Pelagians. The letter that Celestine wrote spoke of the general esteem for Augustine but did not issue a decision against his opponents. In 440 P. entered the service of Leo I and became a worker in the Roman chancery where he drafted documents against the Monophysites (Gennadius, *vir. ill.* 84; *ep.* 28 *ad Flavianum*). P. died after 455.

Until about 432 P. was a defender of strict Augustinianism. Afterward he adopted a more moderate attitude and, contrary to Augustine, represented no longer the latter's view of the limited will of God for salvation but the position that through the grace given to all human beings all are also called to salvation. Nature and grace work harmoniously together, just as the free will, the "initial grace," and the "gift of perseverance" all work together.

II. Works: In his first period as a writer, which was devoted entirely to the defense of the Augustinian teaching on grace, P. composed his *Carmen de ingratis* in 1,002 hexameters; he had already formu-

lated its basic thought in a letter to Rufinus. This first work was followed between 431 and 434 by four other treatises. *De gratia Dei et libero arbitrio contra collatorem* (*c. coll.*) is directed against → John Cassian, while under the title *Pro Augustino responsiones ad excerpta Genuensium* (*resp. ad Gen.*) three separate works are directed against → Vincent of Lérins, two Genoese priests, and the "Objections of Gallic Slanderers." P.'s second period as author was devoted still to the spread of Augustinian thought but without including his rigorous teaching on grace. Two collections of testimonies (*Liber sententiarum ex Augustini operibus delibatarum* [*sent.*] and *Epigrammata ex sententiis Augustini* [*epigr.*]), as well as an *Expositio in psalmos 100-150*, excerpted from Augustine's *en. Ps.*, served this purpose.

In the work *De vocatione omnium gentium* (*vocat. gent.*), which is with high probability to be ascribed to P., the latter explicitly teaches God's universal saving will.

Down to the year 412, P.'s *Epitome chronicorum* (universal chronicle from creation to 455 C.E.) is largely an excerpt from Jerome's chronicle. From 412 on, the *chron.* contains independent information.

The following works are attributed to P.: *Anathematismi et fidei catholicae professio* (*anath.*), a *Confessio* (*conf.*), and a *Chronica Gallica* (*chron. Gall.*). Despite its Semipelagian elements, the *Carmen de providentia dei* (*carm. de prov.*) is ascribed to P. by a few scholars; it was written ca. 416, when P. thought entirely as Augustine did.

W: *ep. ad Rufinum*, PL 51:77-90. — *carm. de ingrat.*, C. T. Huegelmeyer, PatSt 95 (Washington, 1967) [text/English trans./comm.]. — *Epigrammata in obtrectatorem Augustini*, PL 51:149-152. — *Epitaphium Nestorianae et Pelagianae haereseon*, PL 51:153f. — *Pro Augustino reponsiones ad capitula obiectionem Gallorum calumniantium*, PL 51:155-174. — *resp. ad Gen.*, PL 51:187-202. — *c. coll.*, PL 51:215-276. — *in psalm.*, P. Callens, CCL 68A:3-211. — *sent.*, M. Gastaldo, CCL 68A:221-252, 257-365. — *epigr.*, PL 51:497-532. — *Praeteritorum sedis apostolicae episcoporum auctoritates de gratia dei*, PL 51:205-212. — *vocat. gent.*, PL 51:647-722. — P. de Letter, ACW 14 [English trans.]. — *chron.*, T. Mommsen, MGH. AA 9:385-485. — *Appendices ad chron.*, ibid., 486-497 [not by P., later additions].
Inauthentic W: *anath.*, PL 65:23-26. — *conf.*, PL 51:607-610. — *chron. Gall.*, T. Mommsen, MGH. AA 9:629-666. — *carm. de prov.*, PL 51:617-638. — T. P. McHugh (Washington, 1964) [text/English trans./comm.].
L: C. Bartelink, L'universalisme de l'histoire du salut dans le De vocatione: RHE 68 (1973) 731-758. — M. G. Church, The Law of Begging: P. at the End of the Day: Worship 73 (1999) 442-453. — R. Lorenz, Der Augustinismus P. s: ZKG 73 (1962) 217-252. — M. Marcovich, P. (Leiden, 1989). — G. de Plinval, P. interprète de s. Augustin: RechAug 1 (1958) 339-355.

W. GEERLINGS

Protennoia trimorphe

Trimorphic Protennoia is the title of a Sethian work in the Copt. Nag Hammadi library (NHC 13, 1). It contains three revelatory discourses of the goddess Protennoia on her threefold parousia in the world. Only a very little of the Logos speculation of Protennoia can be shown to be clearly Chr.; noteworthy is the third discourse with its striking parallels to 1 Jn.

W: Y. Janssens (Leuven/Louvain, 1978) [Coptic text/French trans./comm.]. — G. Schenke (Berlin, 1984) [Coptic text/ German trans./comm.]. — C. W. Hedrick, NHC XI, XII, XIII (Leiden, 1990) [English trans.]. — NHL 511-522 [English trans.].
L: C. A. Evans, Gnostic and Hermetic Parallels: JSNT. S 89 (1993) 47-76. — J. Helderman, "In ihren Zelten" zu Joh 1, 14: Miscellanea Neotestamentica, ed. T. Baarda (Leiden, 1978), 181-211. — Y. Janssens, Fourth Gospel: FS R. McL. Wilson (Edinburgh, 1983), 229-244. — P. H. Poirier, Descensus: Muséon 96 (1983) 193-204. — J. M. Robinson, Sethians: Sethian Gnosticism, ed. B. Layton (1981), 643-662.

P. BRUNS

Proterius of Alexandria

In 451, against the will of the people, P. was elected as (faithful to Chalcedon) patriarch of Alexandria in place of Dioscurus, who had been deposed at Chalcedon; only with difficulty was he able to hold out against the Monophysite majority. In 456 he deposed Timothy Aelurus and Peter Mongus; on March 28, 457, he was murdered, after the death of Emperor Marcion, who had supported him. Timothy became his successor. Surviving is a letter to Leo I in about 454, in which he demonstrates his orthodoxy by accepting the *Tomus Leonis* and represents the Alexandrian position on the date of Easter, which Rome accepted for the sake of peace.

W: Leo I, PL 54:1084-1094 = Dionysius Exiguus, PL 67:507-514.
L: KonChal 2:22-25. — B. Krusch, Studien zur chr. mal. Chronologie (Leipzig, 1880), 269-278. — J. Maspéro, Histoire des Patriarches d'Alexandrie (Paris, 1923), 44f.

G. RÖWEKAMP

Protreptic

Protreptic (*protreptikos logos, adhortatio, cohortatio, exhortatio, hortatio,* exhortatory discourse, invitation, recruitment) is a rhetorical and literary concept; it meant originally the invitation to study philosophy (Sophistic, Socraticism, Aristotle), then to study one of three (Epictetus, *Dissertationes* 2.26.4;

3.23.33) or four (Seneca, *ep.* 95.65; Clement Alex., *paed.* 1.1.1f.) traditional kinds of philosophizing; later it came to mean recruitment to an involvement in a discipline or a subject, and recruitment to an activity. Thus Galen recruited for involvement in medicine, while Themistius encouraged people to study rhetoric.

Protreptic had its place both as a section of persuasion in a document and as an independent literary genre of persuasion. As a section of a work it is close to exhortation and advocacy; as an independent genre it is close to the → apology or defense. Just as the apology was used on the one hand for the argumentative refutation of attacks and, on the other, for the persuasive drawing of people to the side that had been attacked and was now defended, so protreptic included advice both pro and con. The division of protreptic into a probative and a dissuasive part seems therefore to have been typical of the genre. On the other hand, the form of protreptic was variable: in addition to the letter (e.g., in Seneca) there was the dialogue (e.g., in Plato) and the address (e.g., Clement Alex., *prot.*, or Basil Caes., *leg. lib. gent.*).

In Chr. literature protreptic served as exhortation in Chr. matters. Clement Alex. exhorted to conversion to the Chr. faith; → Origen, *mart.*, went further and exhorted to martyrdom.

L: E. R. Curtius, Europäische Literatur (Bern, [10]1984). — A. Festugière, Les trois P. de Platon (Paris, 1973). — K. Gaiser, P.: HWP 7:1540f. — M. D. Jordan, Ancient philosophic P.: Rhetorica 4 (1986) 309-333.

B. R. SUCHLA

Proverbia Graecorum

This is the title (given only in a later accompanying letter) of a work that was probably compiled in 8th-c. Ireland and contains 6th-c. material. It is a collection of aphorisms supposedly translated from Greek into Latin. The largest part (seventy-four proverbs) has been transmitted in the *Excerpta* of Sedulius Scottus (mid-9th c.); fragments are also found in, among others, the *Norman Anonymous* and in Cathulf.

W: PLS 4:1263-1267. — D. Simpson: Traditio 43 (1987) 1-22 [text/comm.].

G. RÖWEKAMP

Prudentius

I. **Life:** Aurelius Prudentius Clemens (P.), a lay theologian, is regarded as the most important poet of late Chr. antiquity; he was born in 348 in Spain, probably in Calagurris. The most important source for his biography is the poetic preface (*praef.*) that P. placed at the head of a collection of his poems in 404 (he also added an epilogue). In it he speaks of his activity as a lawyer, his office as provincial administrator, and his work as one of the highest ranking officials in the chancery of the imperial court at Milan, where he lived for probably twenty years (ca. 384-404). It is uncertain whether he returned to his homeland after retiring from politics. On the other hand, it is certain that during his stay in Italy he made a pilgrimage to Forum Cornelii (Imola) and at least once visited Rome for a lengthy stay.

II. Works: P. also speaks of his poetic works in *praef.*: Looking back at his life thus far, he says that he wants henceforth to work for his salvation through poems that praise God. The works to which he thus alludes are the ones brought together in the collection, with the exception of the *Tituli historiarum* (*tit.*). P. began to write poetry probably during the 380s, obviously without winning any great attention in the beginning; at least he is not named in the catalogue of Chr. writers that Jerome drew up in 392.

The *Cathemerinon liber* (*cath.*, "Book of Poems for the Hours of the Day") contains twelve literary (i.e., not meant for liturgical use) hymns for important sectors of the day, but also of the year: (1) *Ad galli cantum* is a song of praise reminiscent of Ambrose's hymn *Aeterne rerum conditor*: the voice of Christ is hidden in the cock's cry in the early morning; (2) *Matutinus* celebrates Christ as the true light; (3) in *Ante cibum* P. describes how individual foods are acquired and extols vegetables as suitable for Christians; (4) *Post cibum* describes, among other things, how Daniel in the lion's den was fed by Habbakuk; (5) *Ad incensum lucernae*, after describing OT manifestations in fire, praises Christ as giver of all light; (6) *Ante somnium* describes visions granted to the soul in sleep; (7) in *Ieiunantium* P. discusses the usefulness of fasting and gives, e.g., Elijah, the inhabitants of Nineveh, and Christ as examples; (8) *Post ieiunium* is meant for the ninth hour, the time when fasting ends; (9) *Omnis horae* is a praise of the redeemer; (10) *Ad exsequias defuncti*, a requiem song, bears witness to the certainty of the resurrection; (11) *VIII Kal. Ianuarias*, a Christmas hymn, glorifies the incarnation of Christ; (12) *Epiphaniae* sings of Christ as the star that outshines all else.

The *Apotheosis* (*apoth.*, "Proof of God") consists of a *Hymnus de trinitate*, a *Praefatio* (a lament over the dangers of heresy), and 1,084 dactylic hexameters; while rejecting heretical ideas (of the monarchian Patripassionists, Sabellians, Jews, Ebionites, docetist Manichees), P. defends the orthodox doctrine of the Trinity with passionate earnestness.

Also belonging to the antiheretical branch of hexametric, didactic poetry is the *Hamartigenia* (*ham.*; *ham. praef.*: Cain as type of Marcion): starting from the concept of God as the absolutely supreme being and from the unity of the three divine persons, P. combats the dualism of Marcion and explains the "emergence of sin" (the title) by the fact that a fallen angel, acting in the service of hell, led human beings astray. For the misery that thereby entered the world, man, endowed by God with free will, bears sole responsibility.

The first purely allegorical hexametric poem of the ancient world is the *Psychomachia* (*psych.*; *psych. praef.*: Abraham represents "the first way of faith"). Following the ancient tradition of epic descriptions of battles, P. here has the virtues and vices, each personified, struggling for the human soul. One by one, usually supported by helpers, the following pairs come on the scene: Chr. Faith (*Fides*)/Idolatry (*veterum Cultura deorum*); Chastity (*virgo Pudicitia*)/Unchastity (*Sodomita Libido*); Patience (*Patientia*)/Anger (*Ira*); Humility (*Mens humilis*)/Pride (*Superbia*); Moderation (*Sobrietas*)/Hedonism (*Luxuria*); Greed (*Avaritia*) (which is able to disguise itself as frugality [*Virtus Frugi*])/Charity (*Operatio*); Harmony (*Concordia*)/Discord (*Discordia*), this last "with the nickname 'Heresy.'" An address by *Fides* crowns the victory of *Concordia*. At the end the poet thanks Christ for coming to the help of human beings as they waver between turning to God and yielding to the vices. The dramatic presentation avoids any kind of schematism.

When Symmachus submitted a petition (*rel.* 3) to the imperial court in 384, asking that the altar of Victory be again set up in the Curia, P., following upon Ambrose's *ep.* 17 and 18, answered with his *Contra Symmachum* (*c. Symm.*). In book 1 (*Praefatio* to Paul), following the line of early Chr. apologetics, he describes the historical development of the cult of the gods in Rome; in book 2 (*Praefatio* to Peter) he replies to the individual arguments of *rel.* 3. For all his admiration of Symmachus's rhetorical skill, P. insists forcefully on dissociating himself from the man's Neoplatonically influenced religious ideas. Yet despite the satirical mocking of the heathen gods, P. gives the pre-Christian history of Rome its due: By attaining control of the world the city prepared the ground for the spread of Christianity as the religion of love. This work in its entirety was probably composed in 402/403; it is sometimes hypothesized that the composition was immediately preceded by a new intervention of Symmachus in the matter of the altar to Victory.

In his *Peristephanon* (*perist.*, "On Crowns") P. makes praise of the martyrs the subject of literary hymns; the work consists of fourteen poems in various meters. (1) On the Spanish brothers Emeterius and Chelidonius, who preferred the service of Christ to the service of the emperor. (2) On the Roman martyr Lawrence (written in Spain). The introduction contains an apostrophe of Rome: formerly the mother of temples, but now consecrated to Christ, she triumphs, under Lawrence's egis, over barbarian worship; while she once vanquished proud kings, she now imposes her authority over the images of the gods. (3) On Eulalia of Merida, who confessed her Chr. faith and scorned the gods Isis, Apollo, and Venus. (4) On eighteen martyrs of Saragossa. (5) On Deacon Vincent of Valencia. (6) On Bishop Fructuosus of Tarragona and his two deacons, Augurius and Eulogius. (7) On Quirinus, bishop of the Pannonian city of Siscia. (8) Introducing the second half of the book, an inscription for a place in Calahorra where martyrs suffered death and which is now a baptistery. (9) On Cassian, the stenographer of Imola, who was slain by his students. (10) On Deacon Romanus, who suffered martyrdom in Syrian Antioch (large parts consist of a discourse of the martyr against pagan polytheism). (11) On Hippolytus, who was torn apart by horses; poem addressed to Bishop Valerian of Calahorra. (12) On the apostles Peter and Paul, whose tombs in Rome are described on the occasion of a commemoration. (13) On Cyprian, the African doctor of the church. (14) On Agnes, whose chastity won victory through martyrdom.

Finally, there is a contribution in the genre of the epigram: the *Tituli historiarum* or so-called *Dittochaeum*, a collection of forty-eight hexametric tetrastichs, which deal in equal parts with themes from the OT and NT and, at least fictively, are intended as inscriptions for a cycle of pictures in a church.

A simple listing of the works already shows what important subjects P. deals with: praise of God; explanation of the dogma of the Trinity; struggle against heresy; description of the division within the human soul; antipagan polemics (apologetics); and iconography. It also shows what a variety of literary genres he is master of: lyric (hymn; praise of martyrs, and in both cases with an exceptional variety of meters), epic-didactic (argumentative as well as allegorical hexameters), and epigrammatic. The ancient pagan heritage (Lucretius, Virgil, Horace, Ovid) is given a "proper use" (*usus iustus*) by P. through spir-

itualization, as, e.g., when Virgil (*Aen.* 1.278f.) is applied to the eternity of the kingdom of God in *c. Symm.* 1.541-43. P. even moves beyond what had been accomplished by his Chr. predecessors. P.'s strongest influence was probably through his contribution to the veneration of the martyrs (*perist.*) and the creation of the allegorical poem in hexameters.

In recent years, access to P.'s work has been decisively advanced by interpretation and individual commentaries.

W: Collected works, J. Bergman, CSEL 61. — M. Lavarenne, 4 vols. (Paris, 1948/1963) [text/French trans.]. — H. J. Thomson, 2 vols. (London, 1962 = 1949/1953) [text/English trans.]. — M. P. Cunningham, CCL 126. — A. Ortega, I. Rodriguez (Madrid, 1981) [text/Spanish trans./comm.]. — *cath.*, E. Bossi (Bologna, 1970) [text/Italian trans./comm.]. — M. M. van Assendelft, Sol ecce surgit deus (Groningen, 1976) [text/comm. on *cath.* 1; 2; 5; 6]. — *apoth.*, C. Brockhaus, P. in seiner Bedeutung fü. die Kirche seiner Zeit (Leipzig, 1872), 306-335 [German trans.]. — K. Smolak, Diss. (Vienna, 1968) [comm. on *hymn.*, *praef.* and *apoth.* 1-216). — *ham.*, R. Palla (Pisa, 1981) [text/Italian trans./comm.]. — *psych.*, U. Engelmann (Basel, 1959) [text/German trans.]. — *tit.*, R. Pillinger (Vienna, 1980) [text/German trans./comm.].

L: A. A. R. Bastiaensen, P. in Recent Literary Criticism: Early Christian Poetry, ed. J. den Boeft, A. Hilhorst (Leiden, 1993), 101-134. — P. F. Beatrice, L'allegoria nella psych. di Prudenzio: StPat 18 (1971) 25-73. — V. Buchheit, Resurrectio carnis bei P.: VigChr 40 (1986) 261-285 (on *cath.* 3.186-205). — idem, Göttlicher Heilsplan bei P.: VigChr 44 (1990) 222-241. — J.-L. Charlet, L'apport de la poésie latine chrétienne à la mutation de l'épopée antique: BAGB (1980), 207-217. — idem, La création poétique dans le *cath.* de Prudence (Paris, 1982). — idem, Prudence et la Bible: RechAug 18 (1983) 3-149. — C. Davis-Weyer, Komposition u. Szenenwahl im Dittochaeum des P.: FS F. W. Deichmann (Bonn, 1986), 19-29. — S. Döpp, Vergilische Elemente in P.' c. Symm.: Hermes 116 (1988) 337-342. — idem, Die Blütezeit lat. Literatur in der Spätantike: Ph 132 (1988) 19-52. — idem, P.' Gedicht c. Symm. in der religiösen Auseinandersetzung seiner Zeit: Religiöse Kommunikation – Formen u. Praxis vor der Neuzeit, ed. G. Binder, K. Ehlich (Trier, 1997), 271-300. — W. Evenepoel, Die fünfte Hymne des Liber cath. des P.: WSt NF 12 (1978) 232-248. — idem, Explanatory and Literary Notes on P.' Hymnus ante somnum: RBPH 56 (1978) 55-70 (on *cath.* 6). — idem, Le martyr dans le Liber perist. de Prudence: SE 36 (1996) 5-35. — C. Fabian, Dogma u. Dichtung (Frankfurt a.M., 1988) (on *apoth.*). — J. Fontaine, Naissance de la poésie dans l'occident chrétien (Paris, 1981). — C. Gnilka, Studien zur Psychomachie des P. (Wiesbaden, 1963). — idem, Interpretation frühchr. Literatur: Impulse für die lat. Lektüre (Frankfurt a.M., 1979), 138-180. — idem, Die Natursymbolik in den Tagesliedern des P.: FS B. Kötting (Münster, 1980), 411-446. — idem, Exegetische Bemerkungen zu P.' ham.: Hermes 111 (1983) 338-362. — idem, Kritische Bemerkungen zu P.' ham.: Hermes 112 (1984) 333-352. — idem, Zur praef. des P.: FS F. della Corte 4 (Urbino, 1987), 231-251. — idem, Satura tragica: WSt 103 (1990) 145-177 (on *c. Symm.*). — idem, P. über die Statue der Victoria im Senat: FMSt 25 (1991) 1-44 (on *c.*

Symm.). — idem, Der Gabenzug der Städte bei der Ankunft des Herrn: FS K. Hauck (Berlin, 1994), 25-67 (on *perist.* 4.1-76). — K. R. Haworth, Deified virtues, demonic vices and descriptive allegory in P.' psych. (Amsterdam, 1980). — R. Henke, Studien zum Romanushymnus des P. (Frankfurt a.M., 1983) (on *perist.* 10). — idem, Der Romanushymnus des P.: JAC 29 (1986) 59-65 (on *perist.* 10). — R. Herzog, Die allegorische Dichtkunst des P. (Munich, 1966). — H.-R. Jauss, Form u. Auffassung der Allegorie in der Tradition der psych.: FS W. Bulst (Heidelberg, 1960), 179-206. — C. Micaelli, Consolazione cristiana e motivi didascalici nel decimo inno del cath. di Prudenzio: VetChr 24 (1987) 293-314. — idem, Problemi esegetici dell'inno XI del cath. di Prudenzio: SCO 35 (1985) 171-184. — G. Nugent, Allegory and poetics (Frankfurt a.M., 1985) (on *psych.*). — L. Padovese, La cristologia di Aurelio Clemente Prudenzio (Rome, 1980). — A. M. Palmer, P. on the Martyrs (Oxford, 1989) (on *perist.*). — M. Roberts, Poetry and Cult of the Martyrs (Ann Arbor, Mich., 1993) (on *perist.*). — R. M. Taddei, A Stylistic and Structural Study of P.'s ham., Diss. (Bryn Mawr, 1981). — J. F. Petruccione, P.'s Use of Martyrological Topoi in perist. (Ann Arbor, Mich., 1985). — idem, P.'s Portrait of St. Cyprian: REAug 36 (1990) 225-241 (on *perist.* 13). — idem, The Persecutor's Envy and the Rise of the Martyr Cult: VigChr 45 (1991) 327-346 (on *perist.* 1 and 4). — L. Rivero García, La poesía di Prudencio (Extremadura, 1996) (comprehensive treatment). — W. Schetter, P., perist. 8: Hermes 110 (1992) 110-117 (also in: idem, Kaiserzeit u. Spätantike [Stuttgart, 1994], 205-212). — A. R. Springer, P.: Pilgrim and Poet, Diss. (Madison, 1984) (on *cath.*). — K. Thraede, Studien zu Sprache u. Stil des P. (Göttingen, 1965). — idem, Auferstehung der Toten im Hymnus ante cibum des P.: JAC. E 9 (1982) 68-78 (on *cath.* 3). — idem, Hymnus I: RAC 16:915-946.

S. DÖPP

Psalm

I. Canonical and Other Jewish Psalms: The poetic book of 150 Psalms, which Philo always called "hymns," is the foundation of Chr. hymnody (→ Hymn). It consists of a variety of genres or groups of forms. The LXX contains the apocryphal, Ps.-Davidic Ps 151, while Pss 151-55 have been preserved in Syriac, and Pss 151, 154-55 in Hebrew. Then, too, the Prayer of Manasseh, which later became no. 12 among the Odes of the LXX, could be described as a penitential psalm or an individual lament. In their form, the eighteen (originally Hebrew) Psalms of Solomon, part of the LXX, and the forty-two Odes of → Solomon (which are linked with the others in their tradition-history) are close to the canonical Psalms. The same is true of the songs of praise from Qumran, although the *parallelismus membrorum* of these *Hodayot* is not carried through as strictly as in the hymns of the Psalter.

II. Christian and Gnostic Psalms: From the very beginning the Psalter was the prayerbook and hymnal of Jewish, gnostic, and Hellen. Roman Christians.

It is possible, however, that at a very early point new and specifically Chr. psalms were composed (see 1 Cor 14:26; Col 3:16; Eph 5:19).

A cosmological *psalmos* in seven lines by Valentinus has survived. It is a well-documented fact that this gnostic, regarded as the founder of Valentinianism, wrote poetry (see Tertullian, *carn.* 17.1; 20.3). Acc. to line 80 of the *Canon Muratori*, → Basilides the gnostic composed a *novum psalmorum librum Marcioni*, which has not survived. The main work of → Bardesanes, a book of 150 z^e*mîratha* or *madhrashê*, has likewise not survived but is attested by Ephraem (*c. haer.* 1.17.3; 53.5.1-3). We do have, however, a *psalmos* of the Naassenes/Ophites (→ Naassenes, Psalm of the), consisting of seven "I"-sayings of the gnostic Jesus.

In the 4th c. C.E., when psalmody was already hymnody (though not all hymnody was psalmody), new hymns (Eus., *h.e.* 5.28), and not only those of Paul of Samosata, were forbidden (Synod of Laodicea, *can.* 59). It is known that the Arians composed psalms or hymns (Soc., *h.e.* 6.8; Philostorgius, *h.e.* 2.2; 3.14). The prohibition against the composition of new psalms was hardly observed strictly. For, on the one hand, the composition of Chr. hymns underwent a flowering that began, at the latest, with Hilary and Ambrose, whose nonbibl. *hymni in laudem Dei* were later authorized (Synod of Toledo IV, *can.* 13). On the other hand, now and again new psalms were composed and circulated in Greek and Latin.

Thus, for example, from perhaps as early as the 3rd c., there is a *psalmus abecedarius* (thus the title in *Pap. Barc. Inv.* 149b), which must be regarded as the earliest example thus far known of this genre. In → Methodius of Olympus, between Logos 11 and the end, there is an alphabetic acrosticon with the title *psalmos*. → Augustine shows himself a poet in his anti-Donatist psalm, a declaratory, polemical abecedary against enemies who sang their own psalms. Among the works of the Gallic poet Drepanius Florus are three psalms: *psalmus* 22, 25, and 27. African → Fulgentius of Ruspe, in his anti-Arian *psalmus abecedarius*, imitates the structure of the lines in Augustine's anti-Donatist psalm. The *psalmus abecedarius* (twenty-three Ambrosian stanzas) of → Venantius Fortunatus is a battle song.

The second part of the Cop. Manichean *Psalmbook*, a collection of liturg. poetry of Syr. origin, translated from Greek, contains, in addition to the "Sanctuary [*bēma*] Psalms," the so-called Jesus Psalms, two groups of psalms from Heraclides, Sarakoton Psalms, Thomas Psalms, and a group of untitled psalms. This very heterogeneous collection probably does not contain the two "psalms" of Mani that are occasionally mentioned along with his "prayers."

In → Romanus the Singer, the concept "psalm" appears as one of the musicological and poetic synonyms that include *ainos, epos, hymnos,* and others in his acrostic kontakia.

W: BHS, *Psalmi* (Stuttgart, 1967/77), 1087-1226 [text]. — *LXX, Psalmi cum Odis,* ed. A. Rahlfs (Göttingen, ³1979 [text] = 1931). — *LXX, PsSal, Septuaginta,* ed. A. Rahlfs (Stuttgart, 1935), 471-489 [text]. — *Qumran, 1QH,* Texte, ed. E. Lohse (Darmstadt, ⁴1986 = ¹1964), 109-175 [text/German trans.]. — *11QPsᵃ,* Psalms Scroll, ed. J. A. Sanders (Oxford, 1965) [text/English trans.]. — *Syr. Psalmen,* ed. W. Baars: OTSy 4, 6 (Leiden, 1972) [text]. — M. Noth, Fünf Pss.: ZAW 48 = NF 7 (1930) 1-23 [text/German trans.]. — Augustine, *Anti-Donatist Psalms,* Hymni, ed. W. Bulst (Heidelberg, 1956), 139-146 [text]. — Drepanius Florus, *Psalmi et hymni,* PL 61:1081-1090 [text]. — Fulgentius, *Psalmus abecedarius,* Hymni, ed. W. Bulst (Heidelberg, 1956), 147-155 [text]. — Hippolytus, *Psalm of Valentinus,* ref. 6.37.6-7, ed. M. Marcovich [text]. — Hippolytus, *Naassene Psalm, haer.* 5.6.4-10.2, ed. M. Marcovich [text]. — *Manichaean Psalm-Book,* ed. C. R. C. Allberry (Stuttgart, 1938) [text/English trans.]. — G. Wurst, Corpus Fontium Manichaeorum. Series Coptica 1 (Tournai, 1996) [text of the Bema-Pss.]. — Methodius, *Ps.,* ed. H. Musurillo, V.-H. Debidour, SC 95:310-321. — *Pap. Barc. Inv.* 149b-153, ed. R. Roca-Puig (Barcelona, 1965) [text]. — Romanus the Singer, *Hymnes,* ed. J. Grosdidier de Matons, 5 vols. (Paris, 1964/1981), SC 99, 110, 114, 128, 283. — Venantius Fortunatus, *Psalmus abecedarius,* Hymni, ed. W. Bulst (Heidelberg, 1956), 156-158 [text].
L: J. H. Charlesworth, Prayer of Manasseh: OTP 2 (1985) 625-637. — idem, J. A. Sanders, More Psalms: OTP 2 (1985) 609-624. — H. J. W. Drijvers, Bardaisan (Assen, 1966). — K. Galling, Pss.: RGG 5:672-684. — H. Gunkel, J. Begrich, Einleitung in die Pss. (Göttingen, ⁴1985). — S. Holm-Nielsen, Hodayot (Aarhus, 1960). — idem, PsSal: JSHRZ 4, 2 (1977) 49-112. — H.-J. Kraus, Pss. (Neukirchen, ³1966 = ¹1961, ⁴1972, ⁵1978) (changed). — M. Lattke, Hymnus (Fribourg, Switzerland, 1991). — P. Nagel, Thomaspsalmen (Berlin, 1980). — J. Limburg, Psalms: ABD 5:522-536. — P. H. A. Neumann, Pss.-forschung (Düsseldorf, 1976). — E. Oßwald, Gebet Manasses: JSHRZ 4, 1 (1974) 15-27. — W. Speyer, Psalmus abecedarius (on R. Roca-Puig): JAC 10 (1967) 211-216. — W. G. E. Watson, Hebrew Poetry (Sheffield, 1984). — A. S. van der Woude, Syr. Pss.: JSHRZ 4/1 (1974) 29-47. — R. B. Wright, Psalms of Solomon: OTP 2 (1985) 639-670.

M. LATTKE

See also → Hymn

Psalmus responsorius

The *Psalmus responsorius* found in an Egypt. papyrus of the 4th c. is at the beginning of the Lat. tradition of the Chr. rhythmical → abecedary. Surviving are twelve stanzas of varying lengths (down to the letter M); the remaining stanzas are missing. With its prefixed *Hypopsalma,* it was intended for alternating voices in the liturgy. The *Psalmus responsorius,* which perhaps originated in 3rd c. Africa Proconsularis, celebrates the deeds of Christ, using chiefly Mt, Jn, and the *Protevangelium* of → James the Younger.

W: M. Naldini: RSLR 4 (1968) 155-157 [text]. — E. Peretto: Mar. 39 (1967) 258-260 [text]. — R. Roca Puig (Basel, ²1965) [text/Catalan trans./comm.].
L: A. Di Berardino (ed.), Patrologia 3 (Turin, 1983), 320f. — HLL 5:220, 328f.

B. WINDAU

Pseudepigraphy

Incorrect names of authors occur in primitive and early Chr. literature no less than in contemporary Gr., Roman, and Jewish literature. When the information is deliberately incorrect, we may speak of literary forgery. But false attributions do not represent a deliberate deception in every case; they can also occur through error, confusion, and anonymity. In any case, it is a fact that in very many instances, beginning with the books of the biblical canon, Chr. authors, deliberately and using very simple or even sophisticated literary devices, put "false" writings into circulation. Modern scholars find proof of this to be often difficult and uncertain in individual cases, but the phenomenon of pseudonymous or pseudepigraphical literature belongs (even in the Bible) to the range of literary possibilities available to writers at that time, depending on the subject of their work. The question of (moral) assessment, as well as the psychology of forgery, is extremely difficult. W. Speyer suggests that a distinction must be made between forgery, free pseudepigraphical inventiveness, and "genuine religious pseudepigraphy," in order to distinguish the trivial from "genuinely" inspired experience.

In late antiquity, people had a demonstrable concept of intellectual property. To this Christians could with little effort link a justification by good intention, and good intention is at work in many pseudonymous writings. People attached a false author's name to a work in order to win for it the reputation attaching to an authority from the (normative) past (Greeks, for example, chose Plato or Pythagoras, while Christians chose Paul, Clement, or Augustine). In the realm of Chr. literature, primary authority belonged to the apostles and the teachers of earlier times, so that there was an espec. large number of pseudoapostolic attributions in the early Chr. period. Apostolic origin was claimed not only for letters, treatises, etc., but also for liturgies, church orders, and creeds.

Pseudepigraphy was practiced in various literary genres (e.g., gospel, apocalypse, church order, homily, letter, treatise), but in Christianity, despite the frequency of the practice for various purposes and despite its wide acceptance, it was problematic and, as forgery, was by no means taken for granted. In the early church, as already in ancient literature, there was a critique of authenticity and the rejection of forged writings, but at the same time there was an indifference to and a great gullibility for the phenomenon of forgery. A single and unique document from the early Christian period, namely, the ninth letter of → Salvian of Marseilles in the 5th c., divulges the reflections of an honest forger on the literary technique of pseudepigraphy, as well as on the psychology of this practice and on its justification, yet Salvian did not confess that he was the author (which he was) of his pseudonymous four books *Ad Ecclesiam*. As a rule, pseudepigraphy was certainly practiced more thoughtlessly than in this impressive and conscientious example.

L: P. Aray, Forgery as an Instrument of Progress: ByZ 81 (1988) 284-289. — H. R. Balz, Anonymität u. Pseudepigraphie im Urchristentum: ZThK 66 (1969) 403-436. — E. J. Bickermann, Faux littéraires dans l'antiquité classique: RFIC 101 (1973) 22-41. — N. Brox, Falsche Verfasserangaben (Stuttgart, 1975). — idem (ed.), Pseudepigraphie in der heidnischen u. jüd.-chr. Antike (Darmstadt, 1977). — idem, Zum Problemstand in der Erforschung der altchr. P.: Kairos NF 15 (1973) 10-23. — J. S. Candlish, On the Moral Character of Pseudonymous Books: Exp. 4/4 (1891) 91-107, 262-279. — H. Y. Gamble, Books and Readers in the Early Church (New Haven, 1995). — A. Gudeman, Literary Frauds Among the Greeks: FS II. Drisler (New York, 1894), 52-74. — A. E. Haefner, A Unique Source of Ancient Pseudonymity: AThR 16 (1934) 8-15. — M. Hengel, Anonymität, P. u. "Literarische Fälschung" in der jüd.-hellenistischen Lit.: Entretiens sur l'Antiquité Classique. Pseudepigrapha 1 (Vandoevres, 1971), 229-329. — G. Jachmann, Gefälschte Daten: Klio 35 (1942) 60-88. — F. W. Lenz, Über die Problematik der Echtheitskritik: Altertum 8 (1962) 218-228. — D. G. Meade, Pseudonymity and Canon (Tübingen, 1986). — B. M. Metzger, Literary Forgeries and Canonical Pseudepigrapha: JBL 91 (1972) 3-24. — C. W. Müller, Die neuplaton. Aristoteleskommentatoren über die Ursachen der Pseudepigraphie: RMP 112 (1969) 120-126. — P. Pokorný, Das theol. Problem der ntl. Pseudepigraphie: EvTh 44 (1984) 486-496. — M. Rist, Pseudepigraphy and the Early Christians: FS A. P. Wikgren (Leiden, 1972), 75-91. — W. Speyer, Fälschung, literarische: RAC 7:236-277. — idem, Die literarische Fälschung im heidnischen u. chr. Altertum (Munich, 1971). — idem, Religiöse Pseudepigraphie u. literarische Fälschung im Altertum: JAC 8/9 (1965/66) 88-125. — K. Vretska, Zur Methode der Echtheitskritik: WSt 10 (1957) 306-321.

N. Brox

Ptolemy, Gnostic

P. was a Chr. teacher and exegete who lived in Rome around the middle of the 2nd c. Like Heracleon, he was student of Valentinus. His exact relationship with Valentinus is unclear. The statement in Tertullian, *haer.* 2.4, is probably little more than a heresiological cliche, but perhaps there were parallels between teacher and student in christology (compare Clement Alex., *str.* 3.102.3 with Irenaeus, *haer.* 1.6.1; Clement Alex., *Exc. Thdot.* 59.4; Tertullian, *De carne Christi* 10-11; Hippolytus, *haer.* 6.35.5-6).

The following works of P. have been preserved: (1) the letter to Flora (*ep. ad Floram*), transmitted in Epiphanius of Salamis, *haer.* 33.3-8; it is an introduction to the OT, discussing in letter form the question of who was the author of the OT law. Various sections and authors of the law are distinguished: (a) the pure law of God, which is in turn to be divided in (aa) the decalogue, (bb) the law of talion, which has been abolished, and (cc) laws of worship, which after Christ's coming are to be interpreted symbolically; (b) the law of Moses; and (c) the law of the Jewish elders. The author of the law is neither the supreme, absolutely simple and good God, nor the devil, but rather the second just God, the maker of this world.

(2) The speculative sketch of the history of salvation acc. to the Ptolemeans, transmitted in the "Great Notice" in Irenaeus, *haer.* 1.1-9; it is not now possible, however, to distinguish between what goes back to Ptolemy himself and what to his disciples. The sketch is a Chr. treatise *De principiis* with a hermeneutic function and presupposes intensive exeget. work by the school of Valentinian. The exegeses cited by Irenaeus show that P. and his disciples were capable of methodical exegesis, as can be seen in, e.g., the textually accurate citation of the NT. Acc. to P. the visible world came into existence out of the fall of the youngest Aeon, Sophia, who wanted to know the infinity of the fatherly abyss. The history of salvation consists in this: in bringing the particles of the Pneuma, which have fallen into the visible world and constitute the personal core of true Christians and pneumatics, back into the transcendent world of the Pleroma, and this through the action of the Son of God, who is at work in various hypostases. The goal is the gnosis of the fatherly abyss, which is mediated to us in an explicitly christological way; only in this way can the final state of salvation be reached.

W: *ep. ad Floram*, Epiphanius, *haer.* 33.3-8. — G. Quispel, Ptolémée. Lettre à Flora, SC 24bis. — W. Foerster, Die Gnosis 1 (Zurich, 1969), 204-213 [German trans.]. — K. Fröhlich, Biblical Interpretation in the Early Church

(Philadelphia, 1984), 37-43 [English trans.]. — Irenaeus, *haer.* 1.1-9.

L: B. Aland, Die Rezeption des ntl. Textes in den ersten Jh.: J.-M. Sevrin (ed.) The NT in Early Christianity: BEThL 86 (1989) 1-38. — F. T. Fallon, The Law in Philo and Ptolemy. A Note on the Letter to Flora: VigChr 30 (1976) 45-51. — W. Foerster, Die Grundzüge der ptolemäischen Gnosis: NTS 6 (1959/60) 16-31. — A. v. Harnack, Analecta zur ältesten Geschichte des Christentums in Rom, TU 28/2 (Leipzig, 1905), 3-5. — A. Hilgenfeld, Die Ketzergeschichte des Urchristentums (Hildesheim, 1966 = Leipzig, 1884), 345-368. — P. Lampe, Die stadtröm. Christen in den ersten beiden Jh. (WUNT 18) (Tübingen, ²1989). — A. Le Boulluec, La notion d'hérésie dans la littérature grecque 1: EAug (1985) 203-209. — R. A. Lipsius, Ptolemaeus (1): DCB 4:514-517. — W. A. Löhr, La doctrine de Dieu dans la Lettre à Flora de Ptolémée: RHPhR 75/2 (1995) 177-191. — idem, Das Gesetz bei Markion, den Gnostikern u. den Manichäern: FS E. Dassmann (Münster, 1996), 77-95. — B. Lohse, Melito v. Sardes u. der Brief des P. an Flora: FS J. Jeremias (Göttingen, 1970), 179-188. — G. Lüdemann, Zur Geschichte des ältesten Christentums in Rom. 1. Valentin u. Marcion, 2. P. u. Valentin: ZNW 70 (1979) 86-114. — S. Pétrement, Le Dieu séparé. Les origines du gnosticisme (Paris, 1984), 505ff. — F.-M. Sagnard, La gnose valentinienne et le témoignage de S. Irénée (Paris, 1947).

W. A. LÖHR

Pyrrhus I of Constantinople

Shortly after taking office as patriarch of Constantinople on Dec. 20, 638, P. convoked a synod that was intended to enforce a universal acceptance of the *Ekthesis* of Heraclius. Under political pressure P. resigned on Sept. 29, 641, and withdrew to a monastery in Africa. After a debate with → Maximus Conf. in 645 he abjured Monotheletism in Rome, but only temporarily. After the death of Paul II, P. returned to the see of Constantinople from Jan. 1 to June 3, 654. The anathema issued by the Synod of the Lateran (649) was repeated by the 6th ecumenical council. Of P.'s works the debate with Maximus (*disp.*) has been preserved. Fragments exist of a *Tomus dogmaticus* (*tom.*), the synodal decree of 639 (*decr.*), and a letter to John IV of Rome (*ep.*).

W: *disp.*, PG 91:287-354. — M. Doucet (Montreal, 1972) [text/French trans./comm.]. — A. Ceresa-Gastaldo, Umanità e divinità di Cristo (Rome, 1979), 99-156 [Italian trans./comm.]. — *tom.*, Mansi 10:988; 11:572. — *decr.*, Mansi 10:1001-1004. — *ep.*, Mansi 10:1125; 11:581.
L: P. Conte, Chiesa e Primato (Milan, 1971). — V. Grumel, Regestes (Paris, 1972), 223-226. — L. Magi, La sede Romana (Rome, 1972), 205-215. — J. L. D. van Dieten, Geschichte der Patriarchen (Amsterdam, 1972), 57-75. 104f.

B. DÜMLER

Q

Quadratus

Quadratus (*Kodratos*) is considered to have been the earliest Chr. apologete. We are informed about him solely by Eusebius; all other information is borrowed or inferred from Eusebius.

Thus, Jerome's identification (*vir. ill.* 19 and *ep.* 70.4) of Q. with the bishop of Athens under Marcus Aurelius (see Eus., *h.e.* 4.23.3) is probably owing to an unreliable combination of points taken from Eusebius. Nor has the apologete anything to do with the martyr of the same name; on the other hand, an identification with the prophet Q. of Asia Minor (see Eus., *h.e.* 3.37.1; 5.17.2ff.) is not excluded, since Eusebius presents both as contemporaries and disciples of the apostles. Acc. to Eusebius (*chron. ad a. Abra.* 2140 [124 C.E.] and *h.e.* 4.3.1f.), as a result of pagan hostility, Q. sent Emperor Hadrian a defense of the Chr. religion. Only a single fragment has been preserved. It speaks of the miracles of Christ; Q. stresses the fact that some of those healed or raised from the dead were still alive in his time. The fragment allows no conclusions as to the character of the work as a whole; various efforts to identify the work with surviving early Chr. writings must be regarded as failures or remain hypothetical, such as, e.g., the attempt to find the defense in the letter to Diognetus.

W: Eusebius, *h.e.* 4.3.2.
L: P. Andriessen, L'Apologie de Qu.: RThAM 13 (1946) 5-39, 125-149; 14 (1947) 121-156; VigChr 1 (1947) 129-136. — A. v. Harnack, Die Überlieferung der griech. Apologeten 1/1-2 (Leipzig, 1882), 100-109. — idem, Geschichte der altchr. Lit. 1:95f; 2/1, 269-271 (Leipzig, ²1958). — R. Harris, The Apology of Qu.: ET 32 (1921) 147-160. — T. Zahn, Qu. der Prophet u. Apologet: FGNK 6 (1900) 41-43.

M. BECK

Quaestiones et responsiones

Quaestiones et responsiones ("Questions and Answers") is the Lat. name for the literary genre, taken over from pagan antiquity, of the *Zetemata* (*Zētēmata kai lyseis, Erōtapokriseis, Erōtēseis kai apokriseis*), which is a commentary on a problem in the form of questions and answers. Hellen. philology used this kind of exposition espec. in explaining the Homeric epics. A first example of the use of the genre in exegesis is Philo's explanation of Genesis. As a subordinate literary form, *Questions and Answers* appears in the commentaries of Origen and Clement Alex., as well as in the homilies of John Chrys.

The *Questions and Answers* developed as an independent literary form in Chr. literature beginning in the 4th c., espec. in OT and NT exegesis. Ca. 315 → Eusebius Caes. composed the first complex *Questions and Answers*. He himself gave the name *Zētēmata kai lyseis* (*d.e.* 7.3.18) to this work that was composed as a response to questions from a young cleric named Stephen.

In the ensuing period questions of dogma and controversial theology also found their way into the questions-and-answers form. At the same time, the form became increasingly an aid in teaching. Thus ca. the middle of the 4th c. Basil Caes. developed the monastic rule in question-and answer-form out of the old apophthegmata or pastoral advice to individuals.

At the beginning of the 5th c., with the *Instructionum ad Salonium libri* of → Eucherius of Lyons, the *Questions and Answers* was developed for use in the communication of vocabulary in schoolbooks. As many questions as possible were to be answered in the briefest possible form by appeal to acknowledged eccles. authorities.

Catalogue:

Greeks: Eusebius Caes., *Qu. ad Stephanum et ad Marinum* (after 313). — Acacius Caes., *Quaestiones variae.* — Eusebius of Emesa, *Qu. in Vetus Testamentum.* — Ps.-Justin, *Qu. ad orthodoxos* (Diodorus of Tarsus: before 394; Theodoret of Cyrrhus: ca. 450). — Hesychius Jerus., *Collectio difficultatum et solutionum.* — Theodoret of Cyrrhus, *Qu. in loca difficilia scripturae sacrae.* — Ps.-Caesarius, *Qu.* — Ps.-Athanasius, *Qu. ad Antiochum ducem.* — Maximus Conf., *Qu. ad Thalassium; Qu. et dubia.* — Anastasius Sinaita, *Qu.*

Latins: Ambrosiaster (= Ps.-Augustine), *Qu. veteris et novi testamenti* (366/384?). — Jerome, *ep.* 36 *ad Damasum; ep.* 120 *ad Hedibiam; ep.* 121 *ad Algasiam.* — Augustine, *De diversis quaestionibus* 83 (388/396); *De diversis questionibus ad Simplicianum* (396); *Quaestionum evangeliorum libri* (397/400); *Quaestionum in Heptateuchum libri* (419); *De octo questionibus ex veteri Testamento* (419); *De octo Dulcitii questionibus* (422/425); *Contra secundam Iuliani responsionem opus imperfectum* (429/430). — Eucherius, *Instructionum ad Salonium libri* (before 434). — Salonius, *Expositio mystica in parabolas Salomonis et in Ecclesiasten.* — Junilius, *Instituta regularia divinae legis.* — Ps.-Isidore of Seville, *Qu. de veteri et novo testamento.*

Ascetical Writings: Basil Caes., *Asceticon magnum;*

Regulae brevius tractatae; *Regulae fusius tractatae* (after 370). — John Cassian, *Conlationes* 24 (425/429).

L: G. Bardy, La littérature patristique des "Qu." sur l'Écriture sainte: RB 41 (1932) 210-236; 42 (1933) 14-30. — H. Dörrie, H. Dörries, Erotapokriseis: RAC 6:342-370. — G. Heinrici, Zur patristischen Aporienlit. (Leipzig, 1909), 843-860. — H. Jordan, Geschichte der altchr. Lit. (Leipzig, 1911), 409-411.

G. Broszio

Quodvultdeus

Q. was a disciple and friend of Augustine and ca. 437 became bishop of Carthage. On being driven out by Geiseric in 439, he went to Campania, where he died ca. 453. Q. is possibly the same person as the Carthaginian deacon who urged Augustine to compose his *haer*.

Among the letters of Augustine are two of Q. (*ep.* 221; 223). From him come also thirteen Ps.-Augustinian sermons (*serm.*) and the work of Ps.-Prosper, *De promissionibus et praedicationibus dei* (*prom.*). The latter work, written probably while Q. was in exile in Naples between 445 and 451, follows Augustine in its theology of history and is heavily typological.

W: *prom.*, R. Braun, SC 101f. — A. V. Nazzaro (Rome, 1989) [Italian trans./comm.]. — *prom.*, *serm.*, R. Braun, CCL 60.
L: D. Fransen, Die Werke des hl. Qu. (Munich, 1920). — A. Kappelmacher, Echte u. unechte Predigten Augustins: WSt 49 (1931) 89-102. — L. G. Müller, The haer. of St. Augustine (Washington, 1956). — PAC 947-949. — W. Strobl, Notitiolae Quodvultdeanae: VigChr 52 (1998) 193-203.

G. Röwekamp

R

Rabbula

R., b. in Quennesrin near Aleppo, was the son of a pagan priest and a Chr. mother. With the help of Abraham, a recluse, he found his way to the faith, became a monk and later bishop of Edessa, where he resided 412-435. In this position he continued the work of → Ephraem against heretics by canonical means and led Bardesanites, Arians, Marcionites, Manichees, and Messalians back to the church. He rendered great service by reorganizing his diocese as a whole and monasticism in particular, to which he remained faithful even as bishop. After the Council of Ephesus 431 he supported Cyril Alex., whose christology he imposed on his episcopal city against the opposition of the traditional Antiochenes (burning of the works of Theodore Mops.). Opposition among the clergy was led at that time by Ibas, head of the Persian school in Edessa. R. had an outstanding knowledge of two languages and was thereby predestined to be a translator. By commission of Cyril Alex., he translated the latter's *De recta fide* into Syriac. He also tried to make a new Syr. translation of the NT that would be acceptable in Edessa in place of the → *Diatessaron*.

Surviving are R.'s *Canones* (*can.*) for clerics and monks; of his letters written in Greek (*ep.*) there exist in a Syr. translation those addressed to Cyril, Andrew of Samosata, and Gemellinus, as well as a homily delivered in Constantinople (*hom.*). Of particular historical value for the eccles. life of the time is the Syr. *Vita* written by a contemporary. The literary authenticity of the poems (*carm.*) that have come down under R.'s name is disputed.

S: *vita*, J. J. Overbeck, S. Ephraemi Syri, Rabbulae . . . (Oxford, 1965), 159-209. — G. Bickell, Ausgewählte Schriften (Kempten, 1874), 143-225 [German trans.]. — F. Nau, La vie de R.: RHR 103 (1931) 97-135 [French trans.]. W: *can.*, J. J. Overbeck, op. cit., 210-221 [Syriac text]. — A. Vööbus, Syriac and Arabic Documents (Stockholm, 1960), 24-50, 78-86 [Syriac text/English trans.]. — P. Bruns, Kanones des R.: FS H. Heinemann (Essen, 1995), 471-480 [German trans./comm.]. — J. Mounayer, Les canones de R.: OCP 20 (1954) 406-415 [French trans.]. — *ep.*, J. J. Overbeck, op. cit., 222-244. — F. Pericoli-Ridolfini, Lettera di Andrea di Samosata: RSO 28 (1953) 154-169 [Syriac text/Italian trans.]. — *hom.*, J. J. Overbeck, op. cit., 239-244 [text]. — G. Bickell, op. cit., 238-243 [German trans.]. — *carm.*, J. J. Overbeck, op. cit., 245-248 [text]. — G. Bickell, op. cit., 259-271 [German trans., incomplete]. L: L. Abramowski, Zum Brief des Andreas: OrChr 41 (1957)

51-65. — T. J. Baarda, Gospel Text in R.: VigChr 14 (1960) 102-127. — G. G. Blum, R. v. Edessa (Leuven/Louvain, 1969). — P. Bruns, R. Dichter u. Theologe: VII. Symposium Syriacum 1996 (Rome, 1998). — F. Nau, Les canones de R. (Paris, 1907). — P. Peeters, La vie de R.: RSR 18 (1928) 187-203. — A. Vööbus, La vie d'Alexandre (Pinneberg, 1948). — idem, Text of NT in R. (Pinneberg, 1947). — idem, History of the Gospel Text (Leuven/Louvain, 1951).

P. BRUNS

Reginus

R. was bishop of Constantia/Salamis in Cyprus and took part in the Council of Ephesus (431). Together with Zeno of Kurion and Evagrius of Soli he composed a *Libellus* in which the patriarchate of Antioch was accused of having offended against the autonomy of Cyprus. A *sermo* that has come down also in Eth. urges the deposition of Nestorius.

W: *Libellus*, ACO 1, 1, 7, 118f. [Greek text]. — ACO 1, 5, 357f. [Latin text]. — *sermo*, ACO 1, 1, 2, 70f. [Greek text]. — ACO 1, 3, 168f. [Latin text].

G. RÖWEKAMP

Regula Magistri

The composition of the *Regula Magistri* (*mag.*) by an unknown author took place (probably) in the first half of the 6th c. in the vicinity of Rome or in Campania (other hypotheses: Lérins; monasteries in the Jura). The text displays redactional discontinuities. The *actus militiae cordis* (1-10), which are basic explanations of the ascetical life, preexisted the Magister. For the second part of the *mag.* (11ff.), i.e., the *ordo monasterii* (external organization of the monastery), there was probably a model which the Magister extensively revised and gradually expanded acc. to the needs of everyday monastic life. The *mag.* is the principal source of the Rule of → Benedict of Nursia, with wide stretches of which it is in agreement (espec. *mag.* 1-10; *reg.* 1-7). Acc. to the Magister, monastic life and Chr. life have the same foundation, namely, baptism, and the same goal, namely, eternal life. The uncompromising nature of the decision for Christ distinguishes Christians in the monastery from Christians in the world. The *mag.* intends by means of a careful organization to help preserve the newly affirmed baptismal promises. Redemption comes through education: The rigorous commitment to the idea of "the monastery as a school (*schola*)" allows the monastery to be seen as an educational institution and, despite the cenobitic way of life, emphasizes the relationship between the individual monk and the abbot as teacher.

W: A. de Vogüé, SC 105f. — K. S. Frank (St. Ottilien, 1989) [German trans.]. — L. Eberle (Kalamazoo, Mich., 1977) [English trans.].
L: (see also → Benedict of Nursia) *Bibliographies, Periodicals, and Serials:* B. Jaspert, Regula Magistri — Regula Benedicti: StMon 13 (1971) 129-171. — G. Sanders, M. v. Uytfanghe, Bibliographie signalétique (Turnhout, 1989), 100f. — ABenR. — Ben. — BenM. — Benedictine Review. — Benedictine Studies. — Bulletin d'histoire bénédictine. — CCist. — Monastic Studies. — RBen. — RBS. — StMon. — *Studies:* M. J. Cappuyns, Lexique (Steenbrugge, 1964). — J.-M. Clément, J. Neuville, D. Demeslay, Règle du Maître, vol. 3 Concordance verbale, SC 107 (Paris, 1965). — P. B. Corbett, The Latin (Leuven/Louvain, 1958). — M. Dunn, Mastering Benedict: EHR 105 (1990) 567- 4; 107 (1992) 104-111. — L. Eberle, C. Philippi (ed.), Rule of the Master (Kalamazoo, Mich., 1977). — K. S. Frank, Klosteranlage: RBS 6f. (1977f.) 27-46. — idem, Ascetism and Style: ABenR 31 (1980) 88-107. — idem, Anthropologie: StPatr 17 (1982) 477-490. — idem, Magisterregel (St. Ottilien, 1989), 1-64. — R. Hanslik, Sprache: RBS 1 (1972) 195-207. — B. Jaspert, Regula Benedicti — mag.-Kontroverse (Hildesheim, ²1977). — E. Manning, Rapports: RBS 1 (1972) 99-110. — F. Masai, Les documents: RBS 1 (1972) 111-151. — B. Steidle (ed.), Regula Magistri — Regula Benedicti (Rome, 1959). — A. de Vogüé, A reply to Marilyn Dunn: EHR 107 (1992) 95-103. — idem, Le Maître (Hildesheim, 1984), 19-333.

M. Skeb, OSB

Remigius of Rheims

R., apostle of the Franks, lived from 459 to 533. He has left a metrical work on the consecration of a chalice (*cal.*) in which he professes the real presence of Christ in the Eucharist. Four letters have also been preserved: to Clodevic, whom he baptized on Dec. 25, 496/506, he addressed a letter of condolence on the death of his sister, and a "mirror for kings"; there is also a letter (512) to three Gallic bishops whose reproaches he had drawn for his excessive leniency toward Claudius, a cleric, and another to Bishop Falko of Maastricht, who had claimed jurisdiction over Mouzon, a locality belonging to the diocese of Rheims. Before his death R. composed a testament (*test.*), the shorter version of which is authentic. His sermons (Sidonius, *ep.* 9) are lost.

W: *cal., ep., test.,* B. Krusch, CCL 117:473-478, 404-413.
L: H. H. Anton, R.: BBKL 8:19-21. — A. H. M. Jones, The authenticity of the test.: RBAHA 35 (1957) 356-376. — A. Paillard-Prache, R. Eglise de pèlerinage: MSADM 76 (1959) 61-87. — K. Schäferdiek, R. Kirchenmann einer Umbruchszeit: ZKG 4 (1983) 256-278. — G. Sperduti, Il papa Ormisda e R.: Lazio 22 (1986) 202-204.

C. Kasper

Reticius of Autun

R. was (incorrectly) regarded in the Middle Ages as the first bishop of Autun. He took part in the Synods of Rome (313) and Arles (314) at which Donatism was condemned. He wrote a commentary on the Song (*comm.*), of which Jerome did not think highly (*ep.* 37; *ep.* 3), and a work against the Novatians (*c. Nov.*). Only fragments of these writings have survived. R. died ca. 334; Gregory of Tours has left an effusive obituary of him (*glor. conf.* 74).

W: *comm.,* Petrus Berengarius, PL 178:1864. — *c. Novat.,* Augustine, *c. Iul.* 1.3.7.
L: E. Griffe, La Gaule chrétienne à l'époque romaine (Paris, ²1964), 188-190. — P. Lehmann, Cassiodorstudien 5: idem, Erforschung des MA 2 (Stuttgart, 1959), 66-81, esp. 71f.

G. Röwekamp

Reverentius

The anonymously transmitted *Vita* of → Hilary of Arles was said by some mss. to have been composed by an otherwise unknown Reverentius. Acc. to an interpolated section of → Gennadius (*vir. ill.* 99) he might be identical with → Honoratus of Marseilles.

W: PL 50:1219-1246. — S. Cavallin, Vitae s. Honorati et Hilarii (Lund, 1972).
L: B. Axelson, In vitas Honorati et Hilarii marginalia critica: VigChr 10 (1956) 157-159. — B. Kolon, Die Vita Sancti Hilarii (Paderborn, 1925).

U. Hamm

Rhodo

R., student of Tatian from Asia Minor, composed an anti-Marcionite work ca. 180-190; three important fragments of it are preserved (Eus., *h.e.* 5.13.2-7). Eusebius also mentions a commentary on the Hexaemeron that may have been written against → Apelles (*h.e.* 5.13.8). We do not known whether R. completed a planned *Book of Solutions* for Tatian's *Book of Problems*.

W: Eus., *h.e.* 5.13.2-7.
L: A. v. Harnack, Rh. und Apelles: FS A. Hauck (Leipzig, 1916), 39-51. — idem, Marcion (Darmstadt, 1996 = Leipzig, ²1924), 180-188. — P. Lampe, Die stadtröm. Christen (Tübingen, ²1989), 250f., 350f. — U. Neymeyr, Die chr. Lehrer (Leiden, 1989), 35f., 186.

R. Hanig

Romanus of Rhosus

R. was bishop of Rhosus, located north of Antioch, and a contemporary of Severus of Antioch, whom he strongly attacked in writing. Of R.'s main work, *The Ladders*, only a few sparse citations have survived. Severus of Antioch, during his time in Constantinople (503-511), studied this work carefully and wrote a refutation. R. composed another work against the theopaschites (= Monophysites), which Severus strongly criticizes in his letters. Acc. to Severus, R. was condemned at a synod in Antioch at the beginning of the 6th c. and at another in Alexandria in 518. In his christology R. stays close the traditional Antiochene two-nature doctrine; his teaching on sin shows contacts with Nestorius and Theodore Mops.

W: R. Duval, PO 26/29:375-379/222f. — CPG 3:7117-7121 (unedited).
L: S. P. Brock, Some New Letters of Severus: TU 115 (1975) 22f. — R. Draguet, Julien d'Halicarnasse (Leuven/Louvain, 1924), 80f. — E. Honigmann, Évêques monophysites (Leuven/Louvain, 1951), 82f.

P. Bruns

Romanus the Singer

I. **Life:** Romanus *ho melōdos*, "the singer," was born in 485 in Emesa (Syria) and was probably descended from a Jewish family. Notices in the Menaia and calendars give details of the life of this Byz. hymnographer, whose memorial as a saint the Orthodox Church celebrates on Oct. 1. R. was initially a deacon at the Church of the Resurrection in Berytus (Beirut). Then, in the time of Emperor Anastasius I (491-518) he went to Constantinople and the Marian church in the Cyrus quarter where legend says he received the gift of poetic composition from the Mother of God. He achieved great fame through his spiritual hymns (→ Hymn), which he composed in Hellen. Greek. These works are marked by simple and profound piety. His christology may be described as "popular Monophysitism." This "Christian Pindar" died after 555.
II. **Works:** R. left behind an extensive body of work. There have come down to us about a hundred kontakia (→ Kontakion), as the sung metrical → homilies were called beginning in the 9th c. The authenticity of some is disputed. It is doubtful whether the → *Akathistos* goes back to R. The hymns were composed for the principal feasts of the church year and for many days during Lent and the Easter season. They frequently deal with the life and activity of Christ, but also with bibl. figures, the martyrs, and the saints. There is disagreement about the Greek or Semitic origin of the kontakion, which clearly differs from ancient poetry by reason of its accentual met-

rics and new structures. The influence of Syr. poetry, however, is undeniable. R. did not invent the kontakion, but he did bring it to its fullest form. His hymns contain many echoes of the works of → Ephraem the Syrian. They are characterized by gripping images, bold metaphors, antitheses, the coining of maxims, and a vivid dramatization of the material. R. was familiar with Gr. rhetoric and poetry, but he did not have any special esteem for classical pagan culture, as the Cappadocians still did and as was usual in his time. Yet he maintained the newly revived great tradition of Gr. poetry.

W: *cant.*, N. B. Tomadakis, vols. 1-4 (Athens, 1952-1961) [text]. — *cant.*, P. Maas, C. A. Trypanis, *cant. genuina* (Oxford, 1963) [text]; *cant. dubia* (Berlin, 1970) [text]. — J. Grosdidier de Matons, SC 99, 110, 114, 128, 283. — G. H. Bultmann (Zurich, 1960) [German trans. (selections)]. — M. Carpenter, 2 vols. (Columbia, 1970/73) [English trans. (selections)].
L: A. J. H. Barkhuizen, Essay (cant. 24 M/T): ByZ 79 (1986) 17-28, 268-281. — idem, Narrative Apostrophy: ACl 29 (1986) 19-27. — idem, Association: Hell. 39 (1988) 62-77. — idem, R. and the composition of his hymns: Hell. 40 (1989) 62-77. — idem, Kontakion 10: ACl 33 (1990) 33-52. — idem, Enkomium of Joseph: JÖB 40 (1990) 91-106. — idem, "New Song": Hell. 42 (1991-92) 157-162. — P. L. Gatier, Séisme, (datation): JS (1983) 229-238. — C. Hannick, Metrik des Kontakion: FS H. Hunger (Vienna, 1984). — H. Hunger, R. u. sein Publikum: JÖB 34 (1984) 15-42. — W. L. Petersen, Diatessaron and Ephrem Syrus as Sources (Leuven/Louvain, 1985). — L. v. Rompay, R. poète syrien: Early Christian Poetry, ed. J. den Boeft, A. Hilhorst (Leiden, 1993), 283-296. — G. Swart, Christus patiens (dating): ACl 33 (1990) 53-64.

B. Breilmann

Rufinus of Aquileia

I. **Life:** Tyrannius Rufinus (R.) was born ca. 345 in Concordia near Aquileia and from ca. 358 to 368 received the usual education in grammar and rhetoric in Rome. Jerome was one of his friends during that time. After returning to Aquileia he entered a monastery there and was baptized ca. 371/372. From 373 to 380 he lived in Egypt in order to learn from the monks of the Nitrian wilderness and Palestine. Guided by Didymus the Blind and Gregory Naz., he devoted himself for six years to the scriptures and Origen. In 381 he founded a monastery for men near the monastery for women that Melania the Elder had founded a short time before on Mount Olivet; he lived in this monastery until 397. Between 390 and 394 R. was ordained a priest by Bishop John II of Jerusalem. When the Origenist controversies broke out (393), R. (along with John) refused to reject the works of Origen and thus aroused the enmity of Jerome, who had meanwhile been living in Bethlehem. The conflict, publicly settled at Easter, 397, broke out again when R. returned to Rome that same year and translated into Latin Pamphilus of Caesarea's defense of Origen. R. added to this work, in the form of a prologue, his own declaration of Origen's "orthodoxy," and, as an epilogue, his work *De adulteratione librorum Origenis* (*apol. Orig.*), in which he said that the unorthodox passages in Origen were later forgeries. In 398 he translated into Latin Origen's *De principiis* (*Orig. princ.*), while at the same time "cleansing" it of seemingly unorthodox passages. Jerome, himself a translator of Origen, felt the claims of Origenism and wrote his own translation of the *De principiis* that claimed to be literal; he too added a polemical letter (*ep.* 84). R., who had been in Aquileia since 399, answered at the end of 400 with an *Apologia ad Anastasium* (*apol. ad Anas.*), the bishop of Rome, and, in about the spring of 401, an *Apologia contra Hieronymum* (*apol. adv. Hier.*). To further attacks by Jerome and his supporters R. answered in 407 with his (lost) *Rescripta ad Orientem*. R. fled to Italy and Rome (possibly in 403) before the invading Goths, and there to a monastery near Terracina, whence he withdrew to Sicily after the conquest of Rome in 410. He died in Messina at the end of 411 or the beginning of 412.

II. Works: Apart from the already named works, which are closely connected with his biography, R. has left us numerous translations, the dates of which are not certain. He translated Origen's homilies on Jos (400), Judg and Ps 36-38 (401), Gen, Ex, Lev (403-405), Num (408-410) and 1 Kgs (1 Sam) 1, 2 (ca. 410), as well as his commentaries on Rom (405f.) and the Song (ca. 410). The translation, planned 410f., of Origen's homilies on Deut was not done. Of the works of Basil, R. translated the *Asceticon parvum* (*Basil. reg.*) (397), eight homilies (*Basil. hom.*), and *De ieiunio* 1 and 2 (*Basil. ieiun.*) (398f.). In 398f. R. translated some of the *Orationes* of → Gregory Naz. (*Greg. Naz. or.*); in ca. 401 he produced a translation of the *Historia ecclesiastica* of → Eusebius of Caesarea, which R. continued down to the death of Theodosius I in 398 (*hist.*), and in 403f. the → *Historia monachorum in Aegypto* (*hist. mon.*). At this same period he translated, along with other works of Evagrius Pont., the latter's *Sententiae ad monachos* and *Sententiae ad virginem* (*Evagr. sent.*). A less critical judgment can be seen in the mistakes he made in connection with the translation of three works: he translated (398f.) Adamantius's *De recta in deum fide* (*Adamant.*) as a work of Origen; he regarded (400)

the *Sexti sententiae* (*sent. Sext.*) as the work of Roman Bishop → Sixtus II; he translated Ps.-Clement, *Ep. ad Iacobum* (*ep. Clement.*) (398) and *Recognitiones* (*Clement.*) (407) under the impression that they were works of → Clement of Rome. R. prefixed his own *Prologi/Praefationes* to many of his translations. Among the nonindependent works of R., the *Excerpta II de libro Hieronymi presbyteri ad Gaudentium* (*exc.*) is also to be mentioned (→ Gaudentius of Brescia). R. was also the author of (in addition to lost letters to → Proba) a letter to Jerome (401), fragments of which are preserved in Jerome's *adv. Rufin.* (*Hier. adv. Rufin.*) and a *Commentarius in Symbolum apostolorum* (*symb.*) (400) (→ Creed/Explanation of the Creed). R.'s chief work, *De benedictionibus patriarcharum* (*patr.*) (407f.) is an allegorical explanation of Jacob's blessing (Gen 49). Not from R.: the *Libellus de fide* (*libell. de fid.*), the *Liber de fide* (*lib. de fid.*), and the *Dicta de fide catholica* (*dicta*). R.'s importance for Chr. literature consists in his activity as translator at a time of decreasing knowledge of the Gr. language. Origen's theology is still chiefly available only in R.'s translations. R. did not undertake a philologically accurate translation of the original; his translations are to be regarded rather as sophisticated "popularizations." But, given his claim to convey truthful information, it is problematic to limit his interest to immediately practical goals ("edification").

W: For the works of Origen that have been transmitted only in the translation of Rufinus, see → Origen.
Adamant., V. Buchheit (Munich, 1966) [text]. — *apol. ad Anast.*, M. Simonetti, CCL 20:25-28. — *apol. adv. Hier.*, M. Simonetti, CCL 20:27-123. — *apol. Orig.*, PG 17:541-616. — *Basil. reg.*, K. Zelzer, CSEL 86. — *Basil. hom.*, PG 31:1723-1794. — *Basil. ieiun.*, H. Marti (Leiden, 1989) [text/German trans./comm.]. — *Clement.*, B. Rehm, F. Paschke, GCS 51:3-371. — *ep. Clement.*, B. Rehm, F. Paschke, GCS 51:375-387. — *Evagr. sent.*, PL 40:1277-1286. — J. Leclerq: Scr. 5 (1951) 195-213 [text]. — A. Wilmart: RBen 28 (1911) 143-153 [text]. — *Greg. Naz. orat.*, A. Engelbrecht, CSEL 46. — *exc.*, Y.-M. Duval: RBen 97 (1987) 163-186 [text]. — P. Meyvaert: RBen 96 (1986) 203-218 [text]. — *Hier. adv. Rufin.*, P. Lardet, CCL 79:252-256. — *hist.*, T. Mommsen, GCS 9:1f. — *hist. Mon.*, E. Schulz-Flügel (Berlin, 1990) [text]. — *patr.*, M. Simonetti, CCL 20:183-228. — M. Simonetti, H. Rochais, P. Antin, SC 140. — *praef.*, M. Simonetti, CCL 20:231-285. — *sent. Sext.*, H. Chadwick (Cambridge, 1959), 9-63 [text]. — *symb.*, H. Brüll, BKV¹ [German trans.]. — M. Simonetti, CCL 20:125-182. — idem (Rome, 1978) [Italian trans./comm.]. — *libell. de fid.*, ACO 1, 5, 4f. [text]. — *lib. de fid.*, M. W. Miller (Washington, 1964), 52-144 [text]. — *dicta*, M. Simonetti: Rivista di cultura classica e medioevale 2 (1960) 307f. [text].
L: Accademia Card. Bessarione, Atti del Convegno Internazionale di Studi. R. di Concordia e il suo tempo, 2 vols.

(Udine, 1987). — Centro di Antichità Altoadriatiche Aquileia, Storia ed esegesi (Udine, 1992). — P.-M. Bogaert, Sentences de Sexte: RBen 82 (1972) 26-46. — E. C. Brooks, Translation Techniques: StPatr 17/1 (1982) 357-364. — V. Buchheit, Adversus haereticos (Munich, 1966). — T. Christensen, Historia ecclesiastica (Copenhagen, 1989). — F. E. Consolino, Prefazioni: Origeniana Quinta, ed. R. J. Daly (Leuven/Louvain, 1992), 92-98. — G. Fedalto, R. di Concordia (Rome, 1990). — C. P. Hammond-Bammel, Last Ten Years: JThS NS 28 (1977) 372-429. — eadem, Römerbrieftext (Freiburg i.Br., 1985). — eadem, Kirchengeschichte Eusebs: FS H. J. Frede, W. Thiele, 2 (Freiburg i.Br., 1993), 483-513. — É. Junod, Apologie pour Origène: FS H. Crouzel (Paris, 1992), 165-179. — H. Marti, Übersetzer der Augustin-Zeit (Munich, 1974). — idem, St. Basil's Sermon on Fasting: StPatr 16 (1985) 418-422. — idem, Übersetzen philosophischer Texte: Rencontres de cultures, ed. J. Hamesse, M. Fattori (Cassino, 1990), 23-45. — F. X. Murphy, Life and Works (Washington, 1945). — N. Pace, "De principiis" (Florence, 1990). — E. Schulz-Flügel, Historia monachorum (Berlin, 1990). — F. Thelamon, M. C. Budischovsky, Histoire sainte: REAug 25 (1979) 184-191. — F. Thelamon, Païens et chrétiens (Paris, 1981). — idem, R. d'Aquilée: DSp 13:1107 1117. — M. Wagner, Translator (Washington, 1945). — F. Winkelmann, Übersetzungstheorie u.-methode: FS J. Quasten 2 (Munster, 1970), 532-547.

M. SKEB, OSB

Rufinus the Syrian

R. the Syrian lived in Rome from 399 on, in the house of a certain Pammachius (Marius Mercator, *Commonitorium in haeresim Pelagii*, praef.) and by his ideas influenced both Pelagius and Caelestius, who while in Carthage 411 appealed to R.

R. is possibly to be identified with the R. who was a disciple of Jerome, lived in the latter's monastery in Bethlehem, collaborated in the translation of the letters of Paul, and carried Jerome's *ep.* 81 and 84 to Rome.

R. is probably also identical with the R. from Palestine who after 412 composed the *Liber de fide* (*lib.*) in which the divinity of the Son and the Spirit is defended and in which the "Pelagian" doctrine on the creation and redemption of the human being is also found. The author knows the writings of the Cappadocians and Antiochene anthropology. → Augustine attacks this work in *De pecc. merit.* The *Libellus de fide* (*libell.*), a collection of twelve anathematisms, is probably from the same author.

W: *lib.*, PL 21:1123-1154. — M. W. Miller (Washington, 1964) [text/English trans./comm.]. — *libell.*, PL 48:451-488.
L: B. Altaner, Der lib.: ThQ 130 (1950) 432-449. — G. Bonner, R. and African Pelagianism: AugSt 1 (1970) 31-47. — F. Nuvolone, A. Solignac, Pélage et Pélagianisme: DSp 12:2890f. — F. Refoulé, Datation: REAug 10 (1963) 41-49. — E. TeSelle, R.: AugSt 3 (1972) 61-95.

G. RÖWEKAMP

Rufus of Shotep

R. was active toward the end of the 6th and beginning of the 7th c. and is known as the author of an extensive Copt. commentary on the NT. Under Patriarch Damian (578-604) he was consecrated bishop of Shotep (Hypsele) in Upper Egypt and contributed by his exeget. works to boost the stature of Copt. literature against the dominant Gr. literature. His still unpublished commentaries on Mt and Lk are clearly in the allegorizing tradition of the Alexandrians, but at the same time they do not neglect philological work on the text. Against the dualism of the Manichees and Marcionites R. defends the unity of the two testaments.

L: G. Garitte, Rufus évêque de Sotep: Muséon 69 (1956) 11-33.

P. BRUNS

Ruricius of Limoges

The life of R. can be reconstructed from his correspondence (two books with eighteen and sixty-four letters respectively, *ep.*). About ten years after his marriage to Iberia (Apollinaris Sidonius wrote the wedding song, *carm.* 11), he decided in 477, under the influence of Faustus of Riez, to take up an ascetical life and was later bishop of Limoges until his death (485-507). His grandson, Ruricius II, succeeded him in that see (Venantius composed the epitaph of the two Ruriciuses, *carm.* 4.5). Apart from a few personal letters, he composed primarily rhetorical letters of courtesy or recommendation, which (apart from *ep.* 2.34) do not mirror historical or dogmatic events. Fourteen letters to R. are preserved, eight of them from Faustus.

W: R. Demeulenaere, CCL 64:313-394.
L: A. Engelbrecht, Titulaturen bei R. (Vienna, 1892). — idem, CSEL 21, Praef. 64-74. — H. Hagendahl, Correspondance (Göteborg, 1952). — B. Krusch, MGH. AA 8, Praef. 62-74. — A. Loyen, Sidoine Apollinaire (Paris, 1943), 169-173.

C. KASPER

Rusticius, Deacon

Because of the Three-Chapters controversy, R., a Roman deacon, lived in Constantinople with his uncle, Vigilius of Rome, from 547 on. Initially he supported his uncle, but when on April 11, 548, in his *Iudicatum* Vigilius officially rejected the Three Chapters, R. dissociated himself from his uncle and, after his return to Rome, led the opposition in the college of deacons; as a result, Vigilius excommunicated him in 550. Together with North African Abbot Felix, R., in a lost polemical work, attacked the condemnation of the Three Chapters by the second Council of Constantinople; as a result, both men were banished to the Thebaid. Ca. 565 R. found temporary shelter in the monastery of the Acoimetes in Constantinople and there revised the Lat. translation of the conciliar texts of Ephesus and Chalcedon; he added important material to them in his *Synodicon* (*syn.*). He composed the *Contra Acephalos disputatio* (*disp.*) against the Monophysites. A *Sermo de definitionibus*, mentioned in *disp.*, is regarded as lost. R. shows himself quite familiar with the philosophy of → Boethius but does not use the latter's concept of person (*individua et rationalis natura*) in christology because of a possible Monophysite misunderstanding of it; he harks back to the trinitarian terminology of the Cappadocians and to the christology of → Leontius Byz.

W: *disp.*, PL 67:1167-1254. — *syn.*, ACO 1, 3f.; 2, 3, 1-3. — PLS 4:545-597.
L: A. Grillmeier, Jesus der Christus 2/1 (Freiburg i.Br., 1986), 145f.; 2/2 (Freiburg i.Br., 1989), 431-484 (English, Christ in Christian Tradition, vol. 2/1-2 [London, 1987-95]). — M. Simonetti, La disputatio contra Acephalos: Aug. 21 (1981) 259-289. — E. Wojtacha, Subsistenz bei R.: ZKTh 82 (1960) 212-217.

P. BRUNS

Rusticus, Poet

To a poet named R. are attributed some *Carmina* in distichs (*carm.*) that betray a knowledge of Augustine's *De trinitate*. Nothing more is known of R.'s life; in the transmission he is often confused with the poet → Helpidius Rusticus, the composer of a *Carmen* about Christ and about the history of the two testaments. R. is possibly identical also with the composer of a letter of thanks to Bishop Eucherius of Lyons (*ep.*).

W: *carm.*, A. Wilmart, Miscellanea Agostiniana (Rome, 1931), 271f. — *ep.*, PLS 2:46f.
L: S. Cavallin, Le Poète Domnulus: SE 7 (1955) 49-66.

P. BRUNS

Rusticus, Presbyter

Only a letter of thanks to a friend in Lyons has survived of the work of R., a 5th c. presbyter. Nothing more is known of R.'s life, but he is evidently the R. mentioned by → Apollinaris Sidonius in his *ep.* 2.11. Another possible identification is with the Rusticus of Bordeaux mentioned by Sidonius (*ep.* 8.11.3); less likely is an identification with Rusticus of Narbonne.

W: PL 58:489f. — C. Wotke, CSEL 31:198f. — PLS 3:46f.

P. BRUNS

S

Sabinus

Ca. 367/368, for eccles.-political and polemical purposes, S., bishop of Heraclea in Thrace, made a now lost collection of the synodal acts of the councils involved in the Arian controversy, with a connecting text; the collection can be partially reconstructed from → Socrates (*h.e.*) and → Sozomen (*h.e.*). The tendency of the collection was anti-Nicene and homoiousian and urged a consensus on the basis of the second Antiochene formula of 341 (Athanasius, *syn.* 23; Soc., *h.e.* 2.10.10-18 = S.).

W: Socrates, *h.e.*, GCS NF 1. — Sozomenus, *h.e.*, GCS NF 4. L: P. Battifol, S.: ByZ 7 (1898) 265-284. — H. C. Brennecke, Homöer (Tübingen, 1988), 40-53. — F. Geppert, Quellen (Leipzig, 1898), 89-98. — W. D. Hauschild, Synodalaktensammlung: VigChr 24 (1970) 105-126. — W. A. Löhr, Beobachtungen: ZKG 98 (1987) 386-391. — G. Schoo, Quellen (Berlin, 1911).

J. ULRICH

Sacramentary

1. Origin and Characteristics: The sacramentary as a liturg. book emerged at the end of the transition from spontaneous liturg. prayer to the use of existing texts and finally to the obligatory use of these. *Sacramentarium, Sacramentorum liber,* and similar terms appear in the titles of books and in other sources beginning in late antiquity, sometimes in connection with the names of popes (Gelasius, Gregory, and in modern times also Leo) in order to underscore their authoritative character.

Whereas the Christians of the first two centuries freely formulated liturg. prayers while following some basic structures and using some constant textual elements (see Justin, *1 Apol.* 65.3; 67.5), the early 3rd c. brought the beginnings of written formulas in the "model texts" of the *Traditio apostolica* for the Eucharist and ordinations. At the turn from the 4th to the 5th c., owing to the increasing regulation introduced by the North African councils, this shift to written texts entered a new phase, the result of which was the fixing of the texts of important liturg. prayers, and their official eccles. approval. This procedure, which became obligatory in North Africa, may also have influenced other liturg. families.

During that era there also arose liturg. *libelli* in which euchological texts (presidential prayers), usu-ally for the feasts and festal seasons or for special occasions, were collected for liturg. use (attributions of a *sacramentorum volumen*, probably a collection of *libelli*, to, e.g., Voconius of Castellum and → Musaeus of Marseilles, both of whom died ca. 460). Out of these works of compilation the sacramentary emerged in the 6th/7th c. as the book for the part to be played by the presiding celebrant. It contained the euchological texts of the Mass and to some extent of other liturgical celebrations and was supplemented by the books with the parts for other liturg. ministers: espec. by the → lectionary, the order of the rite (*Ordines*), and (beginning in the 8th c.) the chant books (Gradual/Antiphonary). The codices of the sacramentary were continually made more complete (in a notably systematic way during the Carolingian period) and better organized for liturg. use.

The most important types of sacramentary are to be distinguished by origin and special character: Roman (i.e., the city), Roman-Frankish, the Old Gallican and the Celtic, the Milanese and the Old Spanish sacramentaries. In addition, there was a series of mixed types. Despite the largely identical basic content within individual liturg. families and groups of sacramentaries, each codex was unique, because it was adapted to the local church area and the conditions of its use (papal, episcopal, parochial, monastic liturgies) and subject to changes in the liturgy, in devotion, and mentality. The (plenary) missal, which combined the texts from all the liturg. books needed for the Mass, definitively replaced the separate books in the 12th/13th c.

2. Important Sacramentaries and Groups of Sacramentaries: (a) *Veronense* or *Leonianum* (CLLA 601; CLLA.S 294/95). The earliest predecessor of the sacramentary, but still not a sacramentary in the strict sense (*Cod. Verona, Bibl. Capit.* 85[80]; ca. 600/625), is a collection, made privately in the second half of the 6th c., of *libelli* of liturg. prayers that were originally composed or used in the Lateran by the popes and adapted for their own use by presbyters in other Roman churches. Many of the texts go back to the 5th c. The original ordering of the texts in forty-three groups of formularies according to the months (Jan. to the first half of April), with individual feasts of the Lord, numerous feasts of saints, Masses for other occasions, and many formularies not clearly assignable but not without significance for the major liturg. seasons, show the "collective character" of the ms. The formularies are complete in varying degrees, usually with an opening prayer, a prayer over the gifts, a preface, a closing prayer, and a prayer of blessing.

(b) *Gelasianum vetus* or "Old Gelasian" (CLLA 610; CLLA.S 301/2): The *S. Gelasianum vetus (Cod. Vat. Reg. lat.* 316 and Paris, Bibl. Nat. 7139, ff. 41-56) is a "presbyteral" sacramentary composed for a Roman titular church ca. the middle of the 7th c.; it makes use of older sources and is divided into three books (Temporal; Sanctoral; various prayers and the Canon Missae). The only witness, written in the mid-8th c. in Chelles (northern France), displays numerous Frankish revisions; its predecessor must have reached Gaul from Rome at the end of the 7th c. The Mass formularies have five parts as a rule (two *Orationes*, *Secreta*, *Postcommunionem*, and prayer of blessing *Ad populum*), less frequently with a preface and changing inserts for the canon.

(c) *Eighth-century Gelasian* ("Young Gelasian," "Frankish Gelasian") (CLLA 801-98; CLLA.S 368-406): The group known as *Eighth-century Gelasians*, marked by extensive correspondences among them, came into existence in France in the course of Pippin's liturgical reform, which aimed at unification in the monastic houses; it became widely circulated. The archetype was composed ca. 760-770, probably in Flavigny, using the Gregorian and Gelasian traditions and enriching them with Frankish material. The Temporal and Sanctoral are intermingled; the Mass formularies are usually structured as in the Old Gelasian. The most important codex of this group, the *S. Gellonense* (790/800) contains, along with the S. proper, episcopal blessings, supplementary *Orationes*, the baptismal liturgy, and a section of a Pontifical.

(d) *Gregorian Sacramentaries (CLLA 701-96; CLLA.S 327-67)*: The Gregorian type of sacramentary presumably originated under Honorius I (625-638) for the papal liturgy. Beginning in about 650 it developed into three types that differed in the ordering of the material and in completeness. The Mass formularies as a rule had three presidential prayers (*Oratio*, *Super oblata*, and *Ad completa* or *Ad complendum*).

Type I of this group is known through the *Hadrianum*, which Pope Hadrian I sent to Aachen at the wish of Charlemagne (784/791); there it served during the Carolingian liturg. reform in France as the normative exemplar for further copies (best witness: *Cod. Cambrai* 184, ca. 811/812). Because of numerous lacunae and the inadequacy of this purely papal liturg. book for the liturgy in France, Benedict of Aniane (earlier scholars: Alcuin) supplemented it (810/815), more than doubling its size (*Supplementum Anianense*).

Type II survives solely in the *Paduense* (Padua, *Bibl. Capit. Cod.* D 47; mid-9th c.) and is a version

revised ca. 659/681 for a presbyteral church, with later additions.

Type III, *Cod. Trient.*, Castel del Buon Consiglio (without signature; written ca. 825 for Arno of Salzburg), goes back to a pre-Hadrianic version of ca. 685 but is supplemented by further material, e.g., from the *Eighth-century Gelasians,* the *Suppl. Anianense*, and Alcuin's votive Masses.

The *Hadrianum* with the *Suppl. Anianense* was initially the most common type of sacramentary in France from the mid-9th c. on but was mingled with the *Eighth-century Gelasians*, so that the Gregorian-Gelasian mixed type came to be dominant. A new interest in complex liturg. collections and, in addition, changes in devotion and in understanding of the Mass led from the mid-10th c. on to a considerable increase in votive Masses and Masses for the deceased; *apologiae* as a new kind of prayer were introduced (see espec. the Fulda and St. Gall sacramentaries of the 10th/11th c.), until in the early Middle Ages the sacramentary was displaced by the plenary missal.

(e) *Old Gallican and Celtic Sacramentaries* (CLLA 101-125, 201-229; CLLA.S 130-139, 153-169): The known Old Gallican sources, which to some extent had already undergone Roman influence (despite the title *Missale* their content ranges them with the sacramentaries), are all from the 6th-8th c. and have little in common. The choice of formularies, their structure, the manner of praying (theol. emphases, style, language) are essentially different from those of the Roman(-Frankish) tradition and reflect the Old Gallican liturgy, which disappeared with the Romanization under the Carolingians.

(f) *Milanese (Ambrosian) Sacramentaries* (CLLA 501-535; CLLA.S 259-570): The sacramentaries that have come down (all from after 800) arose as a result of the Carolingian reform, which also affected the Milanese liturgy. The greatest number of them hold fast to the pre-Carolingian Milanese liturgy but also incorporate elements of the Roman sacramentary tradition.

(g) *Old Spanish (Mozarabic) Sacramentaries* (CLLA 301-303; CLLA.S 194-198): The Toledo *Liber Missarum* (ca. 1100) is the only complete surviving sacramentary of the Old Spanish liturgy (which was related to the Old Gallican liturgy); it was given its characteristic texts chiefly by the great 7th-c. bishops (espec. → Isidore of Seville and → Ildefonsus of Toledo). Other euchological texts of this tradition are preserved in the *Missale Mixtum* (Toledo, 1500; reprinted PL 85).

(f) *Sacramentarium triplex* (CLLA 535; CLLA.S 270):

This codex, dating to ca. 1010, represents a unique attempt at St. Gall to produce a "scholarly concordance of sacramentaries," in which the formularies for individual days, feasts, and seasons are put together from the Milanese, Gregorian, and Gelasian euchologies.

W: *S. Veronense*, L. C. Mohlberg (Rome, 1956, ³1978) (facsimile ed. F. Sauer [Graz, 1960]).
Liber sacramentorum Romanae Aeclesiae ordinis anni circuli (S. Gelasianum), L. C. Mohlberg (Rome, ³1981, 1960) (facsimile [Rome, 1975]). — A. Chavasse, Textes liturgiques de l'Église de Rome. Le cycle liturgique romain annuel selon le sacramentaire du Vat. Reg. 316 (Paris, 1997) [partial trans.].
Eighth-century Gelasian: K. Mohlberg, Das fränkische Sacr. Gelasianum in alamannischer Überlieferung (Cod. Sangall. No. 348) (Münster, ³1971, 1918). — A. Dold, L. Eizenhöfer, Das Prager S. (Beuron, 1949). — K. Gamber, Das S. von Monza (Beuron, 1957). — *Sacr. Rhenaugiense*, A. Hänggi, A. Schönherr (Fribourg, Switzerland, 1970). — *Liber sacramentorum Gellonensis*, A. Dumas, J. Deshusses, CCL 159-159A. — *Liber sacramentorum Augustodunensis* [Autun], O. Heiming, CCL 159B. — *Liber sacramentorum Engolismensis* [Angoulême], P. Saint-Roch, CCL 159C.
Gregorian Sacramentaries: H. Lietzmann, Das Sacr. Gregorianum nach dem Aachener Urexemplar (Münster, ⁴1968 = 1921) (*Hadrianum*). — K. Mohlberg, Die älteste erreichbare Gestalt des Liber Sacramentorum anni circuli der röm. Kirche (Münster, 1927) (*Paduense*). — J. Deshusses, Le Sacramentaire Grégorien, 1 (Fribourg, Switzerland, ³1992), 2 (Fribourg, Switzerland, ²1988), 3 (Fribourg, Switzerland, 1982) (*Hadrianum, Suppl. Anianense, Paduense*, other texts) (literature). — J. Décréaux, Le Sacramentaire de Marmoutier, 2 vols. (Rome, 1985). — *Monumenta liturgica Ecclesiae Tridentinae saec. XIII antiquiora* 2A/2B/3: F. Dell'Oro, H. Rogger, Fontes liturgici. Libri Sacramentorum (Trient, 1985-1988).
Old Gallican and Celtic Sacramentaries: E. A. Lowe, The Bobbio Missal (London, 1991 = 1920/24). — *Missale Francorum*, L. C. Mohlberg (Rome, 1957). — *Missale Gallicanum vetus*, L. C. Mohlberg (Rome, 1958). — *Missale Gothicum*, L. C. Mohlberg (Rome, 1961). — G. F. Warner, The Stowe Missal (London, 1989 = 1906/15) (sole Celtic sacramentary; end of 8th c.; part Gallic, part Roman influence).
Milanese (Ambrosian) Sacramentaries: A. Paredi, Il Sacramentario di Ariberto: FS E. Bernareggi (Bergamo, 1958), 329-488. — *Sacr. Bergomense*, A. Paredi (Bergamo, 1962). — In addition: F. Combaluzier, Sacramentaires de Bergame et d'Ariberto. Table des matières, index des formules (Steenbrugge, 1962). — O. Heiming, Das ambrosianische S. von Biasca (Münster, 1969). — J. Frei, Das ambrosianische S. D 3-3 aus dem mailändischen Metropolitankapitel (Münster, 1974).
Old Spanish Sacramentaries: J. Janini, Liber Missarum de Toledo y libros místicos, 2 vols. (Toledo, 1982f.) (earlier ed.: M. Férotin [Paris, 1912]).
Triplex Sacramentary: O. Heiming (Münster, 1968).
Corpus orationum, B. Coppieters 't Wallant, CCL 160-160I. — *Corpus praefationum*, E. Moeller, CCL 161-161D. — *Corpus benedictionum pontificalium*, E. Moeller, CCL 162-162C.
L: A. Bouley, From Freedom to Formula (Washington, 1981). — E. Bourque, Étude sur les sacramentaires romains, 3 vols. (Rome/Quebec, 1948-1958). — A. Chavasse, Le Sacramentaire Gélasien, Vaticanus Reginensis 316 (Paris, 1958). — idem, Le Sacramentaire dans le groupe dit "Gélasiens du VIIIe siècle," 2 vols. (Steenbrugge, 1984). — idem, La liturgie de la ville de Rome du Ve au VIIIe siècle (Rome, 1993). — J. Deshusses, Les sacramentaires: ALW 24 (1982) 19-46. — idem, B. Darragon, Concordances et tableaux pour l'étude des grands sacramentaires, 6 vols. (Fribourg, Switzerland, 1982f.). — K. Gamber, Codices liturgici latini antiquiores, 2 vols. (Fribourg, Switzerland, ²1968); Supplementum (Fribourg, Switzerland, 1988) (fundamental, despite numerous hypothetical and disproven attributions). — M. Klöckener, Das eucharistische Hochgebet bei Augustinus: FS C. P. Mayer (Würzburg, 1989), 461-495 (esp. 465-478). — idem, Sakramentarstudien zwischen Fortschritt u. Sackgasse: ALW 32 (1990) 207-230. — idem, Sakramentar: LMA 7:1273-1275. — M. Metzger, Les sacramentaires (Tournai, 1994). — E. Palazzo, Le moyen âge (Paris, 1993) (literature). — idem, Les sacramentaires de Fulda (Münster, 1994). — C. Vogel, Medieval Liturgy (Washington, 1986), 61-134 (literature).

M. KLÖCKENER

Sahak the Great

S., called "the Great," led the Arm. church as its catholicos 387-439. → Koriun, a historian, describes S.'s work as translator. Of his extensive correspondence an exchange of letters (*ep.*) with Proclus of Constantinople and Acacius of Melitene survives. Also attributed to him are some Canons (*can.*). In addition, → Lazarus of Parpi in his chronicle sets down a vision of S. (*vis.*).

W: *ep.*, Book of Letters (Tiflis, 1901), 9-18 [text]. — *vis.*, G. Sargsean (Venice, 1932) [text]. — *can.*, N. Akinean, S. canones (Vienna, 1950) [text]. — idem, Arm. Kanonsammlung (Vienna, 1950) [German trans.].
L: F. C. Conybeare, Armenian canons of S.: AJT 2 (1898) 828-848. — P. Vardanian, Briefwechsel zwischen Proclus u. S.: WZKM 27 (1913) 415-441.

P. BRUNS

Salonius

S., son of Eucherius of Lyons, was born ca. 400. At Lérins he and his brother Veranus received a comprehensive spiritual and theol. education from Honoratus, Hilary, Salvian, and Vincent. Eucherius dedicated his exeget. works to S., and Salvian one volume of his letters and his work *De gubernatione Dei*; in a letter to S., Salvian explains why he composed his *Ad ecclesiam* under a pseudonym. As bishop, S. took part in the Synods of Orange (441) and Vaison (442). Ca. 450, he, along with his brother, now bishop of Vence, and Ceretius of Grenoble, thanked Leo I for sending them his *Tomus ad Flavianum.* S. seems to have died soon afterward.

None of the exeget. works attributed to him are his. Only in 1532 were the anonymous commentaries *In Ecclesiasten* (*Eccl.*) and *In Parabolas Salomonis* (*Prv.*) published under his name. In the mss. behind the present edition an attribution is found only in the most recent. Some of the mss. also contain the exeget. works *De evangelio Johannis* (*Jo.*) and *De evangelio Matthaei* (*Mt*). Using internal arguments the editor assigned all the writings to a single author. But since Jerome is used in *Eccl.* and *Mt.* and Augustine in *Jo.*, whereas in *Prv.* Gregory the Great and Bede are also used (in the other works, possibly Alcuin and Rhabanus Maurus), the unknown author can have composed the works only between 800 and 1000.

None of the works systematically explains a bibl. book. As in the works of Eucherius, individual verses are singled out and discussed in the form of fictitious questions and answers (between S. and Veranus), sometimes taking up other passages of scripture in a simple, unadorned style; the exegesis is predominantly allegorical.

W: *Eccl., Prv.,* C. Curti, S. Commentarii in Parabolas et in Eccl. (Catania, 1964). — *Jo., Mt.,* idem, S. De Ev. Jo., de Ev. Mt. (Turin, 1968).
L: M. Besson, Un évêque exégète de Genève: AnzSG (1902-1905) 252-265. — C. Curti, Vienna, Nationalbibliothek Lat. 807: Orph. 11 (1964) 167-184. — idem, Osservazioni sul testo di S.: FS C. Sgroi (Turin, 1965), 549-559. — V. I. J. Flint, The True Author of the Salonii Commentarii: RThAM 37 (1970) 174-186. — J. P. Weiss, L'authenticité de l'œuvre de S. de Genève: StPatr 10 (1970) 161-167. — idem, Essai de datation du Commentaire sur les Proverbes attribué abusivement à S.: SE 19 (1969-1970) 77-114. — idem, Les sources du Commentaire sur Eccl. du Ps.-Salonius: StPatr 12 (1975 178-183.

C. KASPER

Salvian of Marseilles

I. Life: S. lived ca. 400 to ca. 480. His place of birth is not handed down. His native land was (North) Gaul; he fled from there to the south ahead of the barbarians. As a contemporary witness of the invasions, he experienced one of the four destructions of the city of Trier. He had relatives in Cologne; his family belonged to the upper class. We do not know what his profession was. Ca. 420 he married Palladia; their daughter was named Auspiciola. S. involved himself in the social distress and misery of the time. Ca. 425 he and his wife underwent a second conversion, to a strict asceticism, which meant, above all, a renunciation of marriage; this was a contemporary philosophical and Chr. ideal, in keeping with which S. also

felt tied henceforth to the monastic community of Lérins. In S.'s circles, then, there were two Chr. states, that of "Christians in the world" and that of "holy" men and women, such as S. and his wife, who had undergone a second conversion or, as the case might be, had made a vow of asceticism. Ca. 440 S. became a presbyter of the church of Marseilles.

II. Works: In nine letters and two passionate but stylistically wearisome admonitions titled *God's Governance of the World* (*gub.*) and *Four Books of Timothy to the Church* (*eccl.*), S. interpreted the catastrophe of the age of invasions as God's already unfolding judgment on a sinful people (instead of as a scandalous divine neglect of the world); in addition, he set forth his very harsh criticism of society. The striking thing about S. as a person was his rigorous asceticism, which he made the starting point for a comprehensive social criticism. He issued a radical challenge to the standards prevailing in the social structures of church and society in 5th c. Gaul, seeing them as unjust and hypocritical. He denounced the state's brutal system of taxation and expropriation and the authorities' ruthless practice of burdening the poor. He condemned existing conditions as consequences of social and individual sin, which could be seen at work in the preferential treatment of some and the discrimination, oppression, and unjust treatment of other groups. He exonerated these marginalized groups (barbarians, rebels, slaves, prostitutes, heretics) by comparing them, always in a favorable way, with the corrupt Roman nobility, to which S. himself may have belonged. He saw society as universally obsessed by greed, which led to socially intolerable laws of inheritance (people retained possession for themselves even beyond death, i.e., in the person of their heirs) and to a preoccupation with wealth and property. Acc. to S., wealth is a loan that may be recalled and brings the obligation to socially responsible action. It is also part of one's social duty to help the impoverished gain their rights. S. is scandalized by the fact that the clergy is silent in the face of all this and thereby fails in its duty. In his polemic, S. is an implacable moralist, and his documentation of injustices turns his work into a scandal sheet. On the other hand, S. strengthened people's self-interest when he recommended that they generously use their stored-up money to care for their own salvation, which is not otherwise to be secured. This kind of preaching, as S. confirms in his own case, makes the presbyter uncomfortable. For all its great historical successes the church is open to strong criticism from the viewpoint of social morality. S. sketches a christology of help to the poor: Christ suffers in the many who are needy.

The differentiation of Christians into two classes plays an important role in S.'s writings. On the basis of it he develops a comprehensive nomenclature. The *saeculares* (the "mundane") are found alongside the *religiosi* (the "holy"or "devout"); or, on the one hand there are the *religionem* or *continentiam professi*, the *monachi*, the *Deo* (or *Christo*) *dediti*, the *paenitentes atque conversi*, etc., and, on the other, the *mundiales*, the *mundi amatrices*, the *peccatores homines*, etc.

Because of the explosive power with which criticism of the church is linked to criticism of society, *eccl.* is presented as a pseudepigraphical work with "Timothy" as its supposed author. When asked about this by Salonius, his bishop, S. answered with his ninth letter, a document unique in the history of ancient pseudepigraphical literature, explaining in detail the technique, psychology, and aim of this kind of (well-intentioned) manipulation; he did not, however, admit to being the actual author.

W: *gub.*, F. Pauly, CSEL 8. — G. Lagarrigue, SC 220. — A. Mayer, BKV² 11 [German trans.]. — *eccl.*, F. Pauly, CSEL 8. — G. Lagarrigue, SC 176. — A. Mayer, BKV² 11 [German trans.]. — N. Brox, SKV 3 [German trans.]. — *ep.*, F. Pauly, CSEL 8. — G. Lagarrigue, SC 176. — A. Mayer, BKV² 11 [German trans.]. — N. Brox, SKV 3 [German trans.].
L: J. Badewien, Geschichtstheologie u. Sozialkritik im Werk S.' v. Marseille (Göttingen, 1980). — N. Brox, Quis ille auctor?: VigChr 40 (1986) 55-65. — E. F. Bruck, Kirchenväter u. soziales Erbrecht (Berlin, 1956). — N. K. Chadwick, Poetry and Letters in Early Christian Gaul (London, 1955). — P. Courcelle, Histoire littéraire des grandes invasions germaniques (Paris, ³1964). — A. Demandt, Der Fall Roms (Munich, 1984). — H. Fischer, Die Schrift des S. v. Marseille "An die Kirche" (Bern, 1976). — E. Griffe, Sancti et conversi au temps de Paulin de Nole et de Salvien: idem, La Gaule chrétienne à l'époque romaine 3 (Paris, 1965), 128-142. — A. G. Hamman, L'actualité de Salvien de Marseille: Aug. 17 (1977) 381-393. — P. Lebeau, Hérésie et providence selon Salvien: NRTh 85 (1963) 160-175. — R. Nürnberg, Askese als sozialer Impuls (Bonn, 1988). — G. W. Olsen, Reform after the Pattern of the Primitive Church: CHR 68 (1982) 1-12. — A. Schaefer, Römer u. Germanen bei Salvian (Breslau, 1930). — D. Schmitz, Die Bildersprache in den Werken des S. v. Marseille: Orph. NS 12 (1991) 492-509.

N. BROX

Scholion

As a diminutive of *scholē* ("lecture" in instruction) the word *scholion* originally meant a short (oral or written?) "treatment" (Cicero, *Att.* 16.7.3), then later

an explanatory "note" on a particular problem in a text, an explanation of a word (acc. to Isidore of Seville, *orig.* 1.30.1f. and 6.8.1, but to be distinguished from a *glossa*) or the construction of a sentence, etc. (see Galen 18.2; Epictetus 3.21.6). The distinction from more detailed comments on a text in a → commentary consists partly in length and detail, but partly, too, in the fact that scholia are for the most part simply excerpts from commentaries or else notes from a lecture (*scholia apo phōnēs*). Scholion is often used as a synonym of "commentary." On the other hand, Jerome makes a clear distinction when he divides the exeget. writings of Origen into scholia (also *sēmeiōseis* = "notes"), commentaries, and → homilies (*hom. Orig. in Ezech.* praef,; see *ep.* 33.4; *in Matth.* 26 praef.).

As a literary form the scholion probably developed out of the text-critical signs, textual variants, and explanations of words written on the margins of a text by pagan philologists. Only beginning in the 4th c. were scholia again written as marginal scholia. The scholia of pagan philology became parts, almost in their entirety, of later compilations; so too did many scholia of the patristic exeget. literature become parts of → catenas, with the result that fragments surviving in this form cannot, for the most part, be assigned with certainty to the genre of the scholion.

The *Hypotyposes* of Clement Alex. are considered to be scholia. Jerome lists seven scholia of → Origen (*ep.* 33.4; Rufinus lists others, *Orig. in num.* praef.; Origen, *philoc.* 27); only fragments have survived. "Scholia" describes → Jerome's *in psalm.* and Augustine's *en. Ps.* 1-32, his *exp. prop. Rm.* and his *loc.*; the textual explanations of → Athanasius (Ps.-) and those of Evagrius Pont. on the Pss, of → Polychronius on Ezek, → Julian of Eclanum (?) on Job, → Arnobius the Younger on the NT, and → Hesychius Jerus.'s marginal comments on several books of the OT. → Cyril Alex. wrote a scholion *peri enanthrōpōseōs* (not related to a particular text).

L: G. Bardy, Commentaires patristiques de la Bible: DBS 2:73-103. — G. Dorival, Des commentaires de l'Écriture aux chaînes: Le monde grec ancien et la Bible, ed. C. Mondésert (Paris, 1984), 361-386. — H. Erbse, D. Fehling, S.: LAW 2723-2726. — A. Gudeman, S.: PRE 2A/1:625-205. — B. Neuschäfer, Origenes als Philologe (Basel, 1987). — R. Pfeiffer, Geschichte der klassischen Philologie (Munich, 1978 = History of Classical Scholarship [Oxford, 1968]). — J. Schmid, S.: RGG 5:1498f. — N. Wilson, A Chapter in the History of S.: CQ 17 (1967) 244-256. — G. Zuntz, Die Aristophanes-S. der Papyri (Berlin, 1975 = Byz. 13 [1938] 631-690; 14 [1939] 545-613).

T. FUHRER

School

The early Chr. theol. schools were not for the most part permanent institutions authorized by the local bishop but private undertakings by individual teachers who gathered students and hearers, e.g., Justin in Rome, and his disciple Tatian. A specifically Chr. school offering a general education did not exist in antiquity; elementary instruction as well as training in grammar and the branches of rhetoric were given by pagan teachers. Knowledge of the faith was conveyed in so-called schools for catechists, of which the Alexandrian school, as early as the beginning of the 3rd c., was certainly the most notable. Further institutions then quickly developed in the centers of eastern Christianity; in the course of time these made their mark on the intellectual landscape and promoted discussion with the culture and philosophy of their environment. The most important Chr. schools arose in Alexandria, Antioch, Edessa, and Nisibis.

L: G. Bardy, L'église et l'enseignement: RevSR 12 (1932) 1-28. — W. Jaeger, Das frühe Christentum u. die griech. Bildung (Berlin, 1963). — R. Nelz, Die theol. Schulen der morgenländischen Kirchen (Bonn, 1916). — U. Neymeyr, Die chr. Lehrer im 2. Jh. (Amsterdam, 1989). — A. Quacquarelli, Scuola e cultura dei primi secoli cristiani (Brescia, 1974).

Alexandria: The first Chr. teacher known by name, Pantaenus of Sicily, appeared on the scene here ca. 180. → Clement worked along with him and in his *Protrepticus* sought to win over the educated pagan world. He was followed by → Origen, to whom in 217 Bishop Demetrius entrusted charge of the instruction of catechumens. But Origen soon left elementary catechesis to his disciple Heraclas in order to devote himself to higher studies, as he had done previously as a private teacher. Ca. 230 there was a final break with the local bishop, and Origen continued his teaching activity in Caesarea (Palestine). Here a considerable Chr. library came into existence, which was expanded by → Pamphilus, a presbyter, and was later eagerly used by → Eusebius. The Alexandrian tradition exerted an influence beyond Caesarea on the leading men of Cappadocia: → Basil Caes., → Gregory Nyss., and → Gregory Naz., who endeavored to combine the Alexandrian spirit with that of Asia Minor and Antioch. After Origen's departure from Alexandria in 230 the school sank back to its former level as an elementary school for catechists. In a broad sense, important theologians such as → Dionysius, → Athanasius, and → Didymus, as well as → Cyril can be reckoned as belonging to the Alexandrian school inasmuch as they took over characteristic tendencies of Clement and Origen and developed them further.

In the explanation of scripture, the Alexandrian school, under the influence of Clement and Origen, used the allegorical method, which had for a long time been applied by Gr. philosophers to the exegesis of myths and poets (Homer) and by Jewish scholars such as Philo to the explanation of the OT. Starting from the basic idea that Christianity is the true gnosis, the historical literal sense of the Bible was neglected in favor of the allegorical and moral senses; this trend found expression to some extent in christology. In contrast to the "Antiochenes," who thought of the integrity of the human nature and of the concrete assumed man, the Alexandrians emphasized more strongly the union of natures in Christ.

L: G. Bardy, Aux origines d'École d'Alexandrie: RSR 27 (1937) 65-90. — W. Bousset, Jüd.-chr. Schulbetrieb in Alexandria u. Rom (Göttingen, 1915). — P. Brezzi, La gnosi cristiana (Rome, 1950). — M. Hornschuh, Das Leben des Origenes u. die Entstehung der alexandrinischen Schule: ZKG 71 (1960) 1-25, 193-214. — A. Knauber, Das Anliegen des Origenes: MThZ 19 (1968) 281-203. — C. Scholten, Die alexandrinische Katechetenschule: JAC 38 (1995) 16-37.

Antioch: The Antiochene school of exegetes likewise appeared in the 3rd c. and, in pronounced contrast to the allegorizing and spiritualizing method of the Alexandrians, emphasized the literal and historical meaning of the scriptures. This school was characterized by a certain sobriety and methodological rigor that was interested less in the deeper speculative and mystical sense than in historical facts. In christology the Antiochenes showed a strong concern for bringing out the transcendence of the divine Logos, with the result that it sharply rejected the idea of a synthesis of the divine and human natures in the incarnation. Predecessors of the classic Antiochene school may be seen in → Theophilus (d. 186) and in presbyter Lucius of Samosata, who, together with Dorotheus, worked as a teacher in Antioch beginning in 260 and had many students. The school's period of glory began with → Diodorus of Tarsus and continued under his disciples → John Chrys. and → Theodore Mops. → Nestorius, too, received his training here. The Antiochene view in christology was represented by → Theodoret of Cyrrhus and → Andrew of Samosata against Cyril. But with the triumph of Cyrillian mariology and christology at Ephesus (431) the star of the Antiochene school began to set. Its light was completely extinguished at the 5th ecumenical council (Constantinople), which decreed the condemnation of Theodore Mops. The Antiochene spirit in exegesis and christology remained at work in individual Syr. authors (→ Isaac of Antioch/Edessa) and had a decisive influence on the schools of Edessa and Nisibis.

L: G. Bardy, Recherches sur Lucien d'A. et son école (Paris, 1936). — C. Schäublin, Methode u. Herkunft der antiochenischen Exegese (Bonn, 1974). — P. Ternant, La theoria d'Antioche: Bib. 34 (1953) 135-158, 354-383, 456-486. — A. Vaccari, La teoria esegetica: Bib. 15 (1934) 93-101.

Edessa: The school of Edessa can be traced back, in its basic traits, to the teaching activity of → Bardesanes toward the end of the 2nd and beginning of the 3rd c. In the mid-3rd c. a certain Macarius was active there and was one of the teachers of Lucian of Samosata, later bishop of Antioch. Under the influence of → Ephraem the Syrian and others driven from Persia, the school took on a new life as the "Persian School" (365 on), but this spirit was severely dampened in the 5th c. by Bishop → Rabbula of Edessa. Bishop → Ibas (d. 457) and Narses, head of the school, sought in vain to give the christology of Theodore Mops. and Nestorius a home in the school. After the death of Bishop Ibas in 457, hierarchical support for Nestorianism collapsed and in 489 so did secular support because of the pro-Monophysite eccles. policy of Emperor Zeno. Narses, head of the school, had to leave the city and settled for good in Nisibis. From then on, theol. instruction was limited to the monastic schools already promoted by Rabbula and was characterized by a strict orthodoxy of the Cyrillian kind. Grammatical instruction emphasized primarily the techniques of translation; as early as the 4th c. numerous works of Gk. writers were translated into Syriac in Edessa: the Ps.-Clementine *Recognitiones*, the writings of → Titus of Bostra against the Manichees, the *Theophania* and Palestinian martyrology of → Eusebius. In the 5th c. it was primarily the writings of the Antiochene school, of Diodorus of Tarsus and Theodore Mops., that were translated into Syriac. In conjunction with Ibas, two teachers, Cumas and Probus, also translated works of Aristotle. In the 5th c., at least eight bishops emerged from the Edessan school of scholars, among them Acacius, patriarch and catholicos of Seleucia-Ctesiphon, who taught in Edessa until 465 and then occupied the episcopal throne of the Persian capital for twenty years. → Joshua the Stylite, too, seems to have had contacts with the Edessan schools, which at that time, however, were solidly under Monophysite control.

L: A. Baumstark, Aristoteles bei den Syrern (Aalen, 1975 = Leipzig, 1900). — S. P. Brock, Greek into Syriac: idem, Syriac perspectives (Hampshire, 1984), 1-17. — idem, Aspects of Translation Technique: idem, op. cit., 69-87. — idem, Syriac Attitudes to Greek Learning: idem, op. cit., 17-34. — idem, Syriac Translation Technique: idem, Studies in Syriac Christianity (Hampshire, 1992), 1-14. — H. J. W. Drijvers, Cults and Beliefs (Leiden, 1980). — R. Duval, Histoire d'Édesse (Paris, 1892). — E. R. Hayes, L'École d'Édesse (Paris, 1930). — A. F. J. Klijn, Edessa (Neukirchen, 1965). — H. R. Nelz, Theol. Schulen (Bonn, 1916), 53-76. — J. B. Segal, Edessa. The "Blessed" City (Oxford, 1970).

Nisibis: In the 4th c. the school of Nisibis already enjoyed a good reputation owing to the extensive teaching activity of → Ephraem the Syrian, who taught there until the fall of the city in 363. In 389 the school was established anew by Narses, who had been driven from Edessa, and quickly became very famous. Apart from → Henana of Adiabene, a dissident, the school represented a more or less strict Nestorianism. → Babai the Great, in particular, has come down in history as the classic representative of that thinking. In addition, numerous bishops and catholicoi did their studies here, among them Mar → Aba; three patriarchs, Ishoyabh I-III, Simeon of Bet Arsam, Sabriso, and Sahdona (→ Martyrius). In 465 Catholicos Acacius founded an offshoot Nisibean school in the capital, Seleucia-Ctesiphon, and further subsidiaries in Arbela and Bet Sajade and on Mount Isla. Because of the statutes that have been preserved (in → Junilius Africanus) we are well informed about studies in Nisibis. There was a three-year course of elementary studies. The first year was taken up with various readings and with copying of the *Corpus Paulinum* and the Pentateuch, as well as with an introduction to eccles. chant. In the second year the Psalms, prophets, and liturgical hymns were added, and in the third the gospels and the rest of the NT as well as the odes of Ephraem and Narses, the national poets. A supplementary course included exegetical lectures and also lectures on philosophy (Aristotle) and medicine. The high point was a scholarly biblical theology following the method of Theodore Mops. After the removal of the school of Nestorian theology in Seleucia-Ctesiphon in 541 and after the new establishment of another academy in Baghdad (830) necessitated by the Islamic conquest, the school of Nisibis lost its importance in the 9th c.

L: J. M. Fiey, Nisibe, métropole syriaque (Leuven/Louvain, 1977). — N. El-Khoury, Schule von Nisibis: OrChr 59 (1975) 121-129. — R. Macina, Cassiodore et l'École de Nisibe: Muséon 95 (1982) 131-166. — idem, L'homme à l'école de Dieu: POC 32 (1982) 86-124, 263-301; 33 (1983) 39-103. — H. R. Nelz, Theol. Schulen (Bonn, 1916), 77-110. — C. Renoux, Nisibe, face aux Perses: HandAm 90 (1976) 511-520. — A. van Selms, Nisibis, the Oldest University (Cape Town, 1966). — A. Vööbus, Statutes of the School of Nisibis (Stockholm, 1962). — idem, History of the School of Nisibis (Leuven/Louvain, 1965). — M. Wolska, Cosmas et l'école de Nisibe: Topographie chrétienne (Paris, 1962), 63-84.

P. BRUNS

Second Coming of Christ

The existing Eth. text of this apocryphon goes back to an Arab. model, which in turn goes back to the Gr. *Apocalypse of* → *Peter;* it probably originated toward the end of the 2nd or beginning of the 3rd c. It describes the eschat. distress preceding the parousia of Christ, the resurrection of the flesh, and the final judgment with the joys it brings to the chosen and the eternal sufferings it brings to the damned.

W: S. Grébaut, L'apocalypse: ROC 15 (1910) 198-214, 307-323, 425-439 [Ethiopic text/French trans.].

P. BRUNS

Secundinus

1. S., a Gallic poet, a friend of Apollinaris Sidonius, who addresses his *ep* 5.8 to him and speaks of him there as author of hexametric poems (epithalamia and court poetry, probably in honor of Visigothic King Theodoric II [453-466]) and satirical hendecasyllabics. An inscription in a church of Lyons, consecrated between 469 and 471, is also from S. (Sid., *ep.* 2.10.3). His works have not been preserved. For chronological reasons, his identification with S. (2), presumed in early research, is excluded.

L: M. Manitius, Geschichte der chr.-lat. Poesie (Stuttgart, 1891), 221, 238f. — W. Schetter, Der gallische Dichter S.: Ph. 108 (1964) 153-156.

2. S. (d. 447/448), probably of Gallic origin, went as a missionary to Ireland in 439, in order (as a bishop?) to support Patrick. Later tradition made him a son of Patrick's sister. Probably in the saint's lifetime S. wrote a hymn in his honor; it is probably the earliest surviving Lat. hymn that originated in Ireland (*Hymnum Sancti Patricii Magister Scotorum*). This work, in which Patrick's activity is praised, is an → abecedary based on the number of syllables and written in unpretentious, often defective Latin; it marks the beginning of the legend of Patrick. In the Middle Ages S. was locally venerated as a saint ("St. Sechnall").

W: PL 53:837-840. — L. Bieler, The Hymn of S.: Proceedings of the Royal Irish Academy 55 (1952) 117-127 [text/comm.]. — C. Blume, AHMA 51 (Leipzig, 1908), 340-346 [text].

L: L. Bieler, Studies on the Life and Legend of St. Patrick (London, 1986). — idem, St. Patrick and the Coming of Christianity (Dublin, 1967). — idem, St. Secundinus and Armagh: SeArm 2 (1956) 21-27. — G. F. Hamilton, In St. Patrick's Praise (Dublin, ²1920). — J. F. Kenney, The Sources for the Early History of Ireland (New York, 1966 = ¹1929), 258-260. — E. MacNeill, The Hymn of S.: IHS 2 (1940) 129-153. — M. Manitius, Geschichte der chr.-lat. Poesie (Stuttgart, 1891), 238-241. — D. Norberg, Le début de l'hymnologie latine en l'honneur des saints: Arctos 5 (1967) 115-125, esp. 118f.

M. MEIER

Secundinus, a Manichee

S., a Manichean *auditor*, sent a letter to Augustine between 398 and 406, probably from Rome, in which he attempts to bring his earlier comrade in faith back to the church of Mani and to answer Augustine's criticisms of the Manichees. The occasion for the letter was S.'s reading of anti-Manichean writings or passages of Augustine, obviously from the *Conf.* S. writes in a respectful but at times very sharp tone. He accuses Augustine of having left the Manichees out of worry (about disadvantages) and careerism; he denies Augustine any real insight into the teaching of Mani. The letter touches on a series of central topics in Manichean teaching and confirms the great importance of the bibl. elements in Manichean thought. But S. also introduces new emphases, e.g., by restricting the rational claims of Mani. The letter has come down together with Augustine's answer (*c. Sec.*), which the saint regarded as his best anti-Manichean work (Augustine, *retr.* 2.10).

W: J. Zycha, CSEL 25/2:893-901. — R. Jolivet, M. Jourjon, BAug 17 (Paris, 1961), 510-525 [text/French trans./ comm.].
L: P. Courcelle, Recherches sur les confessions (Paris, ²1968), 236-238. — F. Decret, L'Afrique manichéenne 1 (Paris, 1978), 141-157. — idem, Manichéisme en Afrique et à Rome: Aug. 34 (1994) 5-40 = idem, Essais (Rome, 1995), 209-240. — C. P. Mayer, Antimanichäische Schriften Augustins: Aug. 14 (1974) 305-308. — J. Stroux, Augustinus u. Cicero's Hortensius: FS R. Reitzenstein (Leipzig, 1931), 106-118.

A. HOFFMANN

Secundus of Trent

S. was born ca. 547, was a monk from 565 on, perhaps in Val di Non, and died 612 in Trent. In 589 he came in contact with the Lombard court in Pavia and became one of the protagonists in the Three-Chapters controversy. His lost *De Longobardis gestis historiola* (Paul the Deacon, *Hist. Longobard.* 4.41) served Paul as a source and has several times been reconstructed from his work. A twelve-line fragment, clearly the work of S., has been preserved, but there is disagreement about whether it belongs to the *Historiola*.

W: *fr.*, E. Quaresima: StTrent. SS 31 (1952) 72-76 [text/Italian trans./comm.].
L: G. P. Bognetti, Fonti di Paolo Diacono: Miscellanea di Studi Muratoriani (Modena, 1951), 357-381. — K. Gardiner, Paul the Deacon and S.: History and Historians in Late Antiquity, ed. B. Croke, A. M. Emmett (Sydney, 1983), 147-153.

B. DÜMLER

Sedatus

S. was bishop of Nîmes ca. 500. In 506 he took part in the Gallican Synod of Agde (Mansi 8:337B) and in 507 in the Synod of Toulouse. S. has left three letters to a friend, Bishop Ruricius of Limoges (*ep.*), as well as homilies (*Sermo de natale Domini*, two *Sermones in nativitate Domini*) in which his pastoral concern is clear. The first homily is also found as *Sermo* 109 among the *Sermones* of → Caesarius of Arles; there may also be fragments from S. in Caesarius (*serm.* 56; 57; 193; 194). Another letter of S. (*Ep. Sedati episcopi ad consolacionem et terrorem peccatorum*) has not yet been published. The attribution of Ps.-Augustinian *Sermones* 117 and 136.1-3, as well as of another letter (*Consolatio et monitio peccatoribus*) is uncertain.

W: *ep.*, R. Demeulenaere, CCL 64:400, 401, 403f. — *sermo de natale*, A. Wilmart, Une homélie de S.: RBen 35 (1923) 12-14 [text]. — *sermones in nativitate*, P.-P. Verbraken, Sermons jumeaux de S.: RBen 88 (1978) 87-89, 89-91 [text]. — *consolatio*, M. G. Bianco: FS R. Iacoangeli (Rome, 1992), 287-303 [text/comm.].
L: A. Di Berardino (ed.), Patrologia 4 (Genoa, 1996), 300. — J. Keune, S. â. 2: PRE 2A/1:1020. — P.-P. Verbraken, op. cit., 81-91. — A. Wilmart, op. cit., 5-16.

B. WINDAU

Sedulius

Neither the origin nor the exact life span of S. (5th c.) are certain; information given in the subscriptions in some mss. is uncertain. As he himself says in the lengthy prose letter in which he dedicated his *Paschale carmen* (*carm. pasch.*) to a presbyter Macedonius, he engaged in secular studies before turning to Chr. poetry.

The *carm. pasch.*, whose title refers to 1 Cor 5:7, is in five books and is introduced by a preface in eight elegiac distichs. The poem is addressed not only to Chr. readers but to pagans as well in an effort to smooth the way of the latter to the faith through the delight (*blandimentum*) of poetry. Book 1, which serves as the foundation for the entire poem, narrates the wonders of the triune God that are reported in the OT, with the sacrifice of Isaac being presented as a type of the sacrificial death of Christ and the crossing of the Red Sea as a type of baptism. After an attack on Arius and Sabellius as deniers of the Trinity, there is a reference to the birth of Christ. Books 2-5 (the number of books corresponds to the gospels) are devoted to the life and the salvific and miraculous deeds of Christ. Book 2 describes the life of Jesus from his birth to the choice of the disciples and ends with an explanation of the seven petitions in the Our Father of the Sermon on the Mount; book 3 narrates the saving deeds of Jesus from the miracle of the wine to the cure of the lunatic, and book 4 those from the cure of a blind man to the raising of Lazarus. Finally, the fifth deals with the saving history of Jesus from his entrance into Jerusalem to his passion and ascension; among the exeget. additions are verses on the symbolism of the cross (5.182-95). In the 9th c. Remigius of Auxerre provided explanations for the *carm. pasch.*, which is regarded as the most successful bibl. poem of late antiquity. S. himself later wrote a prose version on the same subject, likewise in five books: the *Paschale opus* (*op. pasch.*). As he says in his short dedicatory letter, he was persuaded to this prose work by Macedonius. S. understood the prose work to be, as it were, a second, improved edition of the poem; both versions are similar in subject and arrangement but differ in style and manner of expression. Unlike the *carm. pasch.*, the *op. pasch.* cites extensively from the OT (Psalms) and NT, and, above all, the exegesis of the bibl. texts is greatly expanded. The prose version did not, however, displace the *carm. pasch.* The side-by-side existence of the two works became a model for the medieval *opus geminatum*.

In addition to these two works S. composed two shorter poems ("hymns"). The first, consisting of fifty-five elegiac distichs, deals with the saving events of the OT and NT. In the second, which consists of twenty-three stanzas of four iambic dimeters each and takes the form of an → abecedary, S. praises Christ, working through his life and works from the annunciation to the ascension. In the 9th c. Remigius commented on this poem, too.

W: *Collected works*, PL 19:433-794. — I. Huemer, CSEL 10; 316-359: Remigius. — F. Corsaro (Catania, 1956) [Italian trans.]. — *carm. pasch.*, R. A. Swanson: CJ 52 (1957) 289-297 [English trans. of bk. 1]. — N. Scheps, Diss. Amsterdam (Delft, 1938) [text/Dutch trans./comm on bk. 1/2]. — M. Mazzega (Basel, 1996) [text/comm. on bk. 3]. — P. W.

A. T. van der Laan, Diss. Leiden (Oud-Beijerland, 1990) [text/Dutch trans./comm. on bk. 4].

L: S. Costanza, Da Giovenco a Sedulio: CClCr 6 (1985) 253-286. — M. Donnini, Alcune osservazioni sul programma poetico di S.: RSC 26 (1978) 426-436. — A. Grillo, La presenza di Virgilio in S. poeta parafrastico: Présence de Virgile, ed. R. Chevallier (Paris, 1978), 185-194. — R. Herzog, Die Bibelepik der lat. Spätantike 1 (Munich, 1975), XLIf., LII-LIV. — D. Kartschoke, Bibeldichtung (Munich, 1975), 41-45, 64-68, 87-90. — P. W. A. T. van der Laan, Imitation créative dans le carm. pasch. de S.: Early Christian Poetry, ed. J. den Boeft, A. Hilhorst (Leiden, 1993), 135-166. — G. Moretti Pieri, Sulle fonti evangeliche di S.: AMAT 34, NS 20 (Florence, 1969), 125-243. — I. Opelt, Die Szenerie bei S.: JAC 19 (1976) 109-119 (= eadem, Paradeigmata Poetica Christiana [Düsseldorf, 1988], 63-75). — C. D. Small, Rhetoric and exegesis in S.'s carm. pasch.: CM 37 (1986) 223-244. — C. P. E. Springer, S.'s "A solis ortus cardine," the Hymn and Its Tradition: EL 101 (1987) 69-75. — idem, The Gospel as Epic in Late Antiquity (Leiden, 1988).

S. DÖPP

Seneca, Pseudo-
(De superbia et idolis)

Probably toward the end of the 4th c. there appeared in Rome an antipagan prose work that praises the omnipotence of the one God; the work was discovered by B. Bischoff in Cologne and published in 1984 under the title Ep. Anne ad Senecam de superbia et idolis; Bischoff supposed that the fictitious letter writer was a high priest named Anna. J. Divjak, however, maintains that the Jewish origin of the text is by no means certain: the name Anna could have been due to a mistaken reading of a subscription Ep. Annei Senecae; in addition, the work is not really a letter but a sermon (sermo) against polytheism. Finally, A. Hilhorst considers the work to be a piece of Chr. literature. The establishment of the text is not yet complete.

W: B. Bischoff, Anecdota novissima (Stuttgart, 1984), 1-9 [text]. — A. Hilhorst: Eulogia. FS A. R. Bastiaensen (Steenbrugge, 1991), 147-161 [text/comm.]. — W. Wischmeyer: Juden u. Christen in der Antike, ed. J. van Amersfoort-J. van Oort (Kampen, 1990), 72-93 [German trans.].

L: L. Cracco Ruggini, La lettera di Anna a Seneca nella Roma pagana e cristiana del IV secolo: Aug. 28 (1988) 301-325. — M. Deufert, Zum Text des "Anna"-Briefes: WJA 17 (1991) 249f. — HLL 5:407. — A. Momigliano, The new letter by "Anna" to "Seneca" (Ms. 17 archepiscopal library in Cologne): At. 63 (1985) 217-220.

S. DÖPP

Serapion of Antioch

S. was bishop of Antioch ca. 190-209. Fragments have survived of his anti-Montanist Ep. ad Caricum et Pontium (Eus., h.e. 5.19.2f.) and from a letter to the community of Rhossus, near Antioch (Eus., h.e. 6.12.3-6), in which he warns against the Gospel of Peter (→ Peter, Literature about). His other writings are lost (h.e. 6.12.1)

W: Eusebius, h.e. 5.19.2f.; 6.12.3-6.
L: W. Bauer, Rechtgläubigkeit u. Ketzerei (Tübingen, ²1964), 22-24, 146f. — J. A. Fischer, A. Lumpe, Synoden v. d. Anfängen bis z. Vorabend des Nicaenums (Paderborn, 1997), 23-59. — A. v. Harnack, Geschichte der altchr. Lit. 1:503f.; 2/2:132f. — E. Junod, Observations: Suppl. 133 (1980) 195-213. — M. J. Routh, Reliquiae Sacrae 1 (Oxford, ²1846), 449-462.

R. HANIG

Serapion of Thmuis

I. Life: S., born at the end of the 3rd c., lived ca. 320 as an ascetic, probably in the eastern region of the Nile delta. Ca. 330 he was consecrated a bishop. He was in close contact with Anthony and Athanasius. S., who is regarded as a representative of Athanasian eccles. policy and who also aligned his theology with that of Athanasius, was entrusted by the latter with seeing to the establishment of Lent and with the struggle against the Meletians in Egypt. In 353 S. traveled, by commission of Athanasius, to the imperial court at Milan. He died after 362.

II. Works: At the beginning of the second quarter of the 4th c. S. composed his Adversus Manichaeos (Man.), which is regarded as the earliest Chr. treatise against the Manichees. The work displays training in logic and dialectic as well as a knowledge of exegesis; it is addressed to Christians who have been exposed to Manichean preachers. Also authentic is a letter of 356 to the disciples of Anthony (ep. Anton. disc.). S. addresses anchorites who were close to Anthony or at least very familiar with his teaching; he asks for their intercession that God may intervene against the Arians. Also genuine is a letter to Bishop Eudoxius (ep. Eudox.). Only unimportant fragments remain of other letters, an address on virginity, and other writings. The attribution to S. of catena fragments on Gen is disputed.

Also handed down under the name of S. is a → euchologion that contains thirty prayers, among them an anaphora that is important in the history of theology (→ Liturgy). In this work S. probably compiled the liturg. heritage of his episcopal city.

Regarded as not authentic: the Ep. ad Monachos (ep. mon.), a doctrinal letter on the Father and the Son, from the second half of the 3rd c. (patr. et fil.); the Vita Macarii Scetensis (8th c.), published in Coptic and Syriac; the Vita Psoi, preserved in Arab., and the *Vitae* of John the Baptist and Anthony, which survive only in Syriac.

W: *Man., ep. Eudox.,* PG 40:900-925. — *ep. Anton. disc.,* R. Draguet: Muséon 64 (1951) 1-25 [text]. — *euch.,* F. X. Funk, Didascalia et Constitutiones Apostolorum (Paderborn, 1905), 2, 158-195 [text/Latin trans.]. — G. Wobbermin, TU 17/3b [text]. — M. E. Johnson, Prayers of S. (Rome, 1995) [text/English trans./comm.]. — R. Storf, BKV² 5:135-157 [German trans.]. — *patr. et fil.,* G. Wobbermin, op. cit.
L: G. Bardy, S.: DThC 14/2:1908-1912. — B. Botte, L'Eucologe de S.: OrChr 48 (1964) 50-56. — C. J. Cuming, Thmuis Revisited: TS 41 (1980) 568-575. — H. Dörrie, S.: PRE. S 8:1260-1267. — K. Fitschen, S. Echte u. unechte Schriften sowie Zeugnisse des Athanasius et al., PTS 37 (Berlin, 1992). — M. E. Johnson, Baptismal Rite and Anphora in the Prayers of S.: Worship 73 (1999) 140-168. — B. D. Spinks, S. and Baptismal Practice in Early Egypt: Worship 72 (1998) 255-270

B. KRANEMANN

Sergia

S. was the abbess of the monastery of Olympias in Constantinople and a contemporary of Patriarch Sergius (612-638). She wrote a report on the inquiry into and translation of the bones of Olympias, to whom John Chrys. had written several letters from his exile (SC 13bis); the report exists in a single ms. S. used oral and written sources for the life and miracles of Olympias, among them a *Vita* that was perhaps written by → Heraclidas Nyss. (BHG 1374f.).

W: H. Delehaye: AnBoll 15 (1896) 400-423; 16 (1897) 44-51. — J. Bousquet: ROC 12 (1907) 255-268 [French trans.].

G. RÖWEKAMP

Sergius Amphiator

Acc. to John of Ephesus (*h.e.* 4.41), in the winter of 579/580 S., acting as master of ceremonies and sacristan (*amphiator*) in charge of vestments, took part in a secret nocturnal consecration of the Syrian Monophysite patriarch in the church of St. Cassian in Antioch; but he and the consecrators were discovered and had to flee. A short time later, he was consecrated metropolitan bishop of Edessa by the Syrian Patriarch Damian of Alexandria; there he worked in secret for the Monophysites. Later Syr. hagiography identifies S. with a certain S. the Armenian, a bishop of Edessa, who together with his brother John was involved in a theol. dispute with Peter of Callinicus in 590. S. produced some as yet unpublished Syr. *Canones.*

W: F. Nau, Littérature canonique syriaque: ROC 14 (1909) 127f. [French trans.]. — A. Baumstark, Geschichte der syr. Lit. (Bonn, 1922), 263 [Syriac mss.].
L: E. Honigmann, Évêques et évêchés (Leuven/Louvain, 1951), 241-243.

P. BRUNS

Sergius of Constantinople

S., of Syr. origin, was patriarch of Constantinople 610-638 and served, along with Theodore of Pharan and Cyrus of Phasis, as adviser to Emperor Heraclius in achieving a politically necessary agreement with the dissident Monophysites, and in 633 reached union with them by means of a Monoenergetic compromise (*mia theandrikē energeia*), which he weakened in the *Psephos* of 633 because of the strong protest of → Sophronius of Jerusalem. His preparatory theol. work formed the basis for the *Ekthesis* of 638, which spoke still of one will in Christ. This was understood, in a latently Monophysitic way, as a natural power and not a moral unity in the activity of Christ. As a result, the *Ekthesis* became the starting point of the Monotheletism controversy. The letter (*ep.*) in which S. tried to justify his action was approved by Pope Honorius; this led to the condemnation of both men by the sixth ecumenical council (Constantinople). The → *Akathistos* hymn is occasionally attributed to S.

W: *Psephos,* ACO 11 533. — *Ekthesis,* Mansi 10:991 [text]. — ACO 2, 1, 156-162. *ep.,* ACO 11, 529-537.
L: F. Carcione, Energia nella lettera di S.: OCP 51 (1985) 263-276. — J. L. van Dieten, Geschichte der Patriarchen von S. bis Johannes VI (Amsterdam, 1972). — W. Elert, Der Ausgang der altkirchlichen Christologie (Berlin, 1957). — V. Grumel, Histoire du monothélisme: EOr 27 (1928) 6-16, 257-277; 28 (1929) 19-34, 158-166, 272-282; 29 (1930) 16-28. — C. Head, Justinian II of Byzantium (Madison, 1972). — F. Winkelmann, Ekthesis: Klio 69 (1987) 526f.

P. BRUNS

Sergius of Cyprus

S. was archbishop of Cyprus in the first half of the 7th c. He has left a letter of 642 to Pope Theodore (642-649) that was read at the Lateran synod of 649, at which Martin I (649-653/655) rejected Monotheletism.

W: Mansi 10:913B-916E.
L: J. L. van Dieten, Geschichte der Patriarchen Sergios I. bis Johannes VI. (610-715) (Amsterdam, 1972), 82f.

G. RÖWEKAMP

Sergius, Grammarian

Practically nothing is known of the life of S., a grammarian. His identifying epithet points to an extensive literary formation. He is regarded as the adversary of Antiochene Patriarch → Severus, with whom in 515-520 he exchanged a sometimes rather vehement correspondence (*ep.*) on some christological questions. In his letters S. adopts the radically Monophysite viewpoint of → Eutyches, while taking over traditional Apollinarist views and justifying them from Aristotle's teaching on mixtures. He teaches without compromise the one nature, the one essence, and the one hypostasis of Christ and their properties after the incarnation.

W: *ep.*, CSCO 119:70-73, 96-103, 145-157, 177-187 [Syriac text]; CSCO 120:51-53, 71-76, 110-120, 136-143 [Latin trans.].
L: J. Lebon, Le Monophysisme sévérien (Leuven/Louvain, 1909), 163-172. — I. R. Torrance, Christology after Chalcedon (Norwich, 1988).

P. BRUNS

Sergius of Ris'ayna

I. Life: We know nothing of the birth and death dates or the birthplace of S., who was originally a Monophysite. He studied philosophy and medicine in Alexandria and even after priestly ordination exercised the profession of "senior doctor" (*archiatros*) in Ris'ayna (Theodosiopolis). In connection with his scientific and philosophical studies he maintained contacts with Chalcedonian and Nestorian scholars, to the annoyance of his bishop, Ascolius. When an open break between the two came ca. 520, S. went to Antioch, where he complained about his bishop to the Chalcedonian patriarch, Ephraem. Since his own Monophysitism was really only verbal, his conversion to Chalcedonian orthodoxy was a mere formality. In 526 he traveled to Rome on a diplomatic mission for the patriarch of Antioch; in Rome he was able to get Bishop Agapitus to travel with him to Byzantium in order to mediate in the christological controversies. S. died there in 536.
II. Works: S. translated various works of Aristotle and Ps.-Dionysius into Syriac and added an introductory commentary: *Ps.-Dionysiaca* (*Dion.*), *De mundo* (*mund.*), *De universo* (*univ.*), *De genere et specie* (*gen.*), *De categoriis* (*cat.*), *Introductio Porphyrii* (*int. Porph.*), *De anima* (*an.*), *De partibus sermonis* (*part.*), *De affirmatione et negatione* (*aff.*), *De mixtione pharmacorum* (*mixt.*), *De influxu lunae* (*infl.*). Most of them have not yet been published. S. wrote a

work in seven books on the logic of Aristotle (*org.*). Also attributed to him is a treatise (*tract.*) on the spiritual life.

In the area of Gr.-Syr. translation literature S. was a leading figure, as was acknowledged even by later Arab. witnesses. S. explained his teaching on christology in a lost treatise on the faith; he also summed this up in the prologue to *Dion*. His main interest was in ascetical-mystical questions, which he tied into a strongly Origenist philosophy.

W: *tract.*, P. Sherwood, Mimro de S. sur la vie spirituelle: OrSyr 5 (1960) 433-59; 6 (1961) 95-115, 121-156 [Syriac text/French trans.]. — *mund.*, P. de Lagarde, Analecta Syriaca (Osnabrück, 1967 = Berlin, 1858), 134-158 [Syriac text]. — *univ.*, G. Furlani: RTStFR 4 (1923) 1-22 [Italian trans.]. — *gen.*, idem: SIFC 3/4 (1925) 305-333 [Italian trans.]. — *cat.*, idem: RTStFR 3 (1922) 135-172 [Italian trans.]. — *mixt.*, A. Merx: ZDMG 39 (1885) 273-305 [Syriac text/Arabic trans.]. — E. Sachau, Inedita Syriaca (Hildesheim, 1968 = Halle, 1870), 88-97 [Syriac text]. — *infl.*, idem, op. cit., 101-126 [Syriac text].
L: A. Baumstark, Lucubrationes syro-graecae (Leipzig, 1894). — A. Freimann, Die Isagoge des Porphyrius in syr. Übersetzung (Berlin, 1897). — H. Hugonnard-Roche, Versions syriaques des Catégories: JA 275 (1987) 205-222. — eadem, Aux origines de l'exégèse orientale: JA 277 (1989) 1-17. — eadem, Tradition syro-arabe de la logique, in: Traduction et Traducteurs au Moyen-Âge (Paris, 1989), 3-14. — eadem, L'Organon: DPA 1 (1989) 502-528.

P. BRUNS

Sergius the Stylite

S. was active in the 6th c. not far from Emesa in Syria and composed a polemical treatise (*disp.*) against the Jews, which to a great extent is based on Flavius Josephus.

W: *disp.*, A. P. Hayman, CSCO 338/339 [text/English trans.].

P. BRUNS

Sermo Arrianorum

The *Sermo Arrianorum* (*serm. Arrian.*), an anonymous outline of subordinationist theology in the manner of → Ulfila, was sent to Augustine from Vicus Juliani (not far from Hippo Regius). Augustine transcribes it, unabridged, at the beginning of his refutation (*c. s. Arrian.*; PL 42:683-708), which he composed in the fall of 419 (Aug., *ep.* 23A*.3).

W: PL 42:677-684.
L: M. Meslin, Les Ariens d'Occident (Paris, 1967), 129-134 (additionally, P. Nautin: RHR 177 [1970] 70-89). — M. Simonetti, S. Agostino e gli Ariani: REAug 13 (1967) 55-84.

R. KANY

Seth

The *Second Treatise of the Great Seth* is a treatise in the Nag Hammadi library (NHC 7, 2) that has close links to Sethian gnosis. It contains an address of the gnostic Christ in which the most notable element is a docetist christology. It remains unclear, however, whether the author of this treatise is to be looked for in the circle of the "Sethians" mentioned in Hippolytus, *haer.* 5.19.1–22:1. The Nag Hammadi texts assigned to Seth (→ *The Hypostasis of the Archons,* → Adam, → *Allogenes,* → *Marsanes,* → *Norea,* → *Zostrianos*) all show an essentially judaizing trend, in which the figure of Seth as redeemer or as Jesus is seen as a manifestation of this OT archetypal figure. Seth takes the place of the murdered Abel and symbolizes the lineage of the just, from which the redeemer is to emerge. Consequently, all gnostics are seen as descendants of Seth and, in virtue of special revelation and knowledge, set themselves apart from the rest of this world's people.

W: L. Painchaud, Deuxième traité du Grand Seth (Leuven/Louvain, 1982) [Coptic text/French trans./comm.]. — B. A. Pearson, NHC VII (Leiden, 1996) [Coptic text/English trans./comm.]. — H. G. Bethge, Zweiter Logos des großen Seth: ThLZ 100 (1975) 97-110 [German trans./comm.]. — M. Krause, Zweiter Logos des großen Seth: Christentum am Roten Meer, ed. F. Altheim (Berlin, 1973), 106-151 [Coptic text/German trans.]. — NHL 362-371 [English trans.].
L: H. G. Bethge, Anthropologie u. Soteriologie: Studien zum Menschenbild, ed. P. Nagel (Halle, 1979). — A. F. J. Klijn, Seth in Jewish, Christian and Gnostic Literature (Leiden, 1977). — B. Layton, Sethian Gnosticism (Leiden, 1981). — L. Painchaud, Polémique anti-ecclésiale: Colloque international, ed. B. Barc (Leuven/Louvain, 1981), 340-351. idem, Deuxième Traité: LTP 36 (1980) 229-237. — K. W. Tröger, Christologie: FS P. Labib (Leiden, 1975), 268-276.

The *Three Steles of Seth* (*Stel. Seth*) is another independent treatise in the Nag Hammadi library (NHC 7, 5) and contains a tripartite hymn to Adamas, Barbelo, and the preexistent redeemer. *Stel. Seth* presupposes a preexistent dualism of good and evil, the spiritual and the material world, with a strong Jewish element (redemptive role of Seth); it is difficult to distinguish this group from the so-called Barbelo gnostics mentioned in Epiphanius, *haer.* 1.4.3; 25.2.4. In the background are OT conceptions of divine wisdom or of an Egypt.-Hellen. mother goddess (Isis), who functions as a feminine complement to the triad of aeons.

The *Stel. Seth* is also called *Apocalypse of Dositheus*; this description is connected with the leader of heretics whom Eusebius mentions in *h.e.* 4.22.5 and

who, acc. to him, disturbed the peace of the church in the 1st c. as leader of a gnostic Jewish sect.

W: P. Claude (Leuven/Louvain, 1983) [Coptic text/French trans./comm.]. — M. Krause, V. Girgis, Drei Stelen: Christentum am Roten Meer, ed. F. Altheim (Berlin, 1973), 180-199 [German trans.]. — M. Tardieu: RSPhTh 57 (1973) 545-575 [French trans./comm.]. — K. Wekel: ThLZ 100 (1975) 571-580 [German trans.]. — B. A. Pearson, NHC VII (Leiden, 1996) [Coptic text/English trans./comm.]. — NHL 396-401 [English trans.].
L: A. Böhlig, Pluralismus: FS P. Labib (Leiden, 1975), 19-34. — J. M. Robinson, Gnostics of Plotinus: Colloquium on Gnosticism, ed. G. Widengren (Leiden, 1977), 132-142.

P. BRUNS

Severian of Gabala

I. **Life:** Little is known of the life of S., bishop of Gabala (Syria). Ca. 400 this gifted orator became a celebrated preacher at the court of Constantinople. Before John Chrys. departed for Ephesus (401) he left S. to govern the church of Constantinople as his representative, but S. used his position for his own intrigues against the absent Chrysostom. After John's return, there was an open break between the two men, and at the Synod of the Oak (403) S. joined the patriarch's opponents. Acc. to Gennadius (*vir. ill.* 21), S. died ca. 408.

II. **Works:** The determination of S.'s literary remains faces numerous difficulties. After the condemnation of Severus of Antioch in the 6th c., S.'s homilies were in many cases handed down under the name of his opponent, John Chrys. In addition, there has been a complicated history of influences within oriental literature. In general, fourteen homilies in Greek are ascribed to S., eight in Armenian, and one in Ethiopic (*hom.*). Fragments remain of, among other things, a commentary on the letters of Paul (*Rom.-Heb.*) and a work on calculating the date of the resurrection (*comput.*).

S. favors Genesis as the source of material for his homilies. His literal exegesis is probably of Antiochene origin. He occasionally shows a good knowledge of Hebrew and Aramaic, as well as a strong inclination to attacks on Jews and heretics. His anthropology and cosmology reflect in many ways the intellectual world of the early Syrians (→ Ephraem).

W: *hom.,* PG 56:429-500. — J. Zellinger, Genesishomilien des Bischofs S. (Münster, 1916) [text/German trans.]. — M. Awgerean, S. Gabalorum episcopi homiliae (Venice, 1827) [Armenian text/Latin trans.]. — A. Wenger, Homélie inédite: REByz 25 (1967) 219-234 [Greek text]. — Y. Torosian, S. episcopi Gabalorum homilia IX: Baz. 95 (1935) 4-11 [Armenian text]. — M. van Esbroeck, Deux homélies de Sévérien: BeKa 36 (1978) 71-91 [Georgian text]. — B. M.

Weischer, Qerellos 4/3 (Wiesbaden, 1980), 19-67 [Ethiopic text/German trans.]. — C. Moss, De nativitate: BSOAS 12 (1948) 555-566. — *Rom.-Heb.*, K. Staab, Pauluskommentare (Münster, 1933), 213-351 [Greek text]. — *comput.*, H. R. Drobner, S. Die Berechnung der Auferweckung des Herrn nach drei Tagen: ThGl 78 (1988) 305-317 [text/German trans./comm.].
L: H. D. Altendorf, Untersuchungen zu S. (Tübingen, 1957). — H. J. Lehmann, Per Piscatores (Arhus, 1975), 273-367. — B. Marx, Spuria Chryosostomi: OCP 5 (1939) 281-367. — J. Zellinger, Studien zu S. (Münster, 1926).

P. BRUNS

Severinus of Cologne

The earliest mention of S. is in Gregory of Tours (*De virtutibus S. Martini* 1.4: MGH.SRM 1:590): he is supposed to have predicted the death of Martin of Tours (d. 397). If this is so, S. lived in the second half of the 4th c. and died ca. 400. He followed Euphrates as the third bishop of Cologne. He is said to have built the chapter house and Church of Sts. Cornelius and Cyprian; these have borne his name since the 9th c. A *Vita* and *Translatio* from that period have little hist. value. A series of short statements on the faith, *Doctrina de sapientia*, comes from a Severinus, but it is not clear whether this is the same S.

W: PL 74:845-848. — J. Schlecht, Doctrina XII Apostolorum (Freiburg i.Br., 1901), 127-129.
L: E. Ewig, Zur Geschichte u. Kunst im Erzbistum Köln (Düsseldorf, 1960), 17-19. — I. van Hacke, S.: ActaSS 10 (1861) 50-64. — W. Levison, Entwicklung der Legende S.': BoJ 118 (1909) 34-58. — H. Rode, S. in Köln (Cologne, 1951). — E. Sauser, S.: BBKL 10:1507-1510.

C. KASPER

Severus of Antioch

I. **Life:** Three *Vitae* inform us about the life of S.: those by → Athanasius I Camelarius, John of Bet Aphtonia, and — Zacharias Rhetor. In addition, there is a homily of → George, bishop of the Arabs. S. was born in Sozopolis in Pisidia and studied in Alexandria and Beirut, where he converted to a strict ascetical life. He received baptism in 488 and withdrew to a monastery near Maiuma/Gaza, where he was immersed in an intellectual atmosphere that was entirely permeated by the Monophysitism of Peter the Iberian. Ca. 509 he betook himself to Constantinople where the issuance of the imperial *Henotikon* created an atmosphere favorable to his christological ideas. As a result of the imperial policy of reconciliation with the Monophysites S. was able to take over the patriarchal throne of Antioch in 512. But with the accession of the orthodox Justin I in 518 S. had to flee

to Egypt, where he continued the fight against Chalcedon and some Monophysite dissidents by literary means. In 535 S. was again invited to a dialogue on religion in Constantinople, but in 536, because of pressure from Agapetus of Rome and his delegation, he was finally banished. S. died two years later in exile in Egypt.

S: M. A. Kugener, PO 2/1. 3 [Syriac text/French trans.]. — E. J. Goodspeed, W. E. Crum (Tournai, 1981 = Paris, 1907) [Ethiopic-Coptic text/English trans.]. — A. Vööbus, Memra de Giwargis sur S.: Muséon 84 (1971) 433-436. — idem, Memra of Giwargi: JSSt 18 (1973) 235-237. — T. Orlandi, Un codice copto: Muséon 81 (1968) 351-405 [Coptic text/Italian trans.].
L: M. Brière, PO 29/1:7-72. — D. O'Leary, S.'s Stay in Egypt: Aeg. 32 (1952/53) 425-436. — V. Poggi, S. alla Scuola di Beirut: M. Pavan, L'Eredità classica nelle lingue orientali (Rome, 1986), 57-71.

II. **Works:** Because of S.'s condemnation his very extensive literary remains have survived almost exclusively in Syr. translations.

Ca. 508 S. composed a polemical work against Nephalius, a Neo-Chalcedonian theologian (*Or. ad Neph.*). During the period in Constantinople (508-511) he wrote his *Philalethes* (*Phil.*), in which he defends the Monophysite character of Cyril's theology against a Chalcedonian florilegium. But S.'s principal work is the *Liber contra impium grammaticum* (*c. imp. gram.*) with its over one thousand citations from the fathers, by means of which he prepared to refute a defense of the Chalcedonian Creed by → John of Caesarea. After 518 he entered zealously into the attack on the Aphthartodocetism of → Julian of Halicarnassus (*ref. Iul.*). Between 512 and 518, as patriarch of Antioch, S. delivered over a hundred homilies which are important for the history of the liturgy and have survived only in a Syr. translation. His extensive correspondence (*ep.*) during his Egyptian exile (518-535) deals primarily with controverted questions within the Monophysite confession. Among S.'s opponents were the extreme Aphthartodocetists Sergius the Grammarian (*c. Serg. gram.*) and Julian of Halicarnassus. Numerous hymns of S. have come down in the → Octoechos, the customary hymnal of the Gr. church; the Syrians also attribute an anaphora to him (*anaph.*).

III. **Basic Lines of Thought:** In his christology S. represents a moderate Monophysitism which, despite his attacks on the Chalcedonian Creed and the *Tomus Leonis*, was closer to the latter than to the extreme positions of the Aphthartodocetists. His point of departure is the formula favored by Cyril: "the single nature of the incarnate God-Logos," which he uses very rigidly as an argument from tradition against the Chalcedonian Creed. S. understands *physis* to be concrete, individual, and subsisting and, in this sense, identical with *hypostasis*. Nevertheless, in contrast to Sergius and Julian, he maintains the integrity and specific properties of the redeemer's human nature. Materially and in terminology, S.'s christology remains at the level of discussion before the Union of 433, when he rejects any idea of unity "in two natures" as "Nestorianism." Like the Neo-Chalcedonians S. strongly emphasizes the unity of the acting subject in Christ, which he sees as based in the one hypostasis of the God-Logos.

W: *Or. ad Neph.*, J. Lebon, CSCO 119/120 [Syriac text/Latin trans.]. — *Phil.*, R. Hespel, CSCO 133/134 [Syriac text/French trans.]. — *c. imp. gram.*, J. Lebon, CSCO 93/94, 101/102, 111/112 [Syriac text/Latin trans.]. — *ref. Iul.*, R. Hespel, CSCO 244/245, 295/296, 301/302, 318/319 [Syriac text/French trans.]. — A. Šanda, Antijulianistica (Beirut, 1931) [Syriac text]. — *hom.*, R. Duval, PO 4/1. — M. Brière, PO 8/2; 12/1; 20/2; 23/1; 25/1, 4; 26/3; 29/1; 35/3. — M. A. Kugener, E. Triffaux, PO 16/5. — I. Guidi, PO 22/2 [Syriac text/French trans.]. — *ep.*, E. W. Brooks, PO 12/2; 14/1 [Syriac text/English trans.]. — idem, Selected Letters of S. (London, 1902-1904). — *c. Serg. gram.*, J. Lebon, CSCO 119/120 [Syriac text/Latin trans.]. — I. R. Torrance, Letters between S. and Sergius: AbSal 9 (1978) 9-99. — *hymni*, E. W. Brooks, PO 6/1; 7/5 [Syriac text/English trans.]. — *anaph.*, H. W. Codrington, S. Anaphora (Rome, 1939) [Syriac text/Latin trans.].

L: A. Baumstark, Geschichte (Bonn, 1922), 160. — S. P. Brock, Some New Letters of S.: TU 115 (1975) 17-24. — R. Chesnut, Three Monophysite Christologies (Oxford, 1976). — R. Draguet, Julien d'Halicarnasse et sa controverse avec S. (Leuven/Louvain, 1924). — W. H. C. Frend, Rise of the Monophysite Movement (Cambridge, 1972). — G. Graf, Geschichte der chr.-arab. Lit. (Rome, 1944), 418-420. — F. Graffin, La catéchèse de S.: OrSyr 5 (1960) 47-54. — idem, La vie à Antioche: GOF. S 17 (1978) 115-130. — A. Grillmeier, Jesus der Christus 2/2 (Freiburg i.Br., 1989), 20-185 (English, Christ in Christian Tradition, vol. 2/2 [London, 1995]). — J. Lebon, Le monophysisme sévérien (Leuven/Louvain, 1909). — idem, La christologie du monophysisme syrien: Das Konzil v. Chalkedon 1, ed. A. Grillmeier (Würzburg, 1951-1954), 425-580. — L. Perrone, Il dialogo contro gli aftartodoceti: CrSt 1 (1980) 411-442. — V. C. Samuel, Council of Chalcedon and the Christology of S. (Yale Univ., 1957). — idem, Christology of S.: AbSal 4 (1973) 126-190. — idem, Further Studies: EkklPh 58 (1976) 270-301. — J. Tabet, La vigile cathédrale: Melto 4 (1968) 5-12. — I. R. Torrance, Christology after Chalcedon (Norwich, 1988). — idem, Theological Introduction to the Letters of S.: EkTh 3 (1982) 283-321; 4 (1983) 537-571; 5 (1984) 453-481. — W. de Vries, Eschatologie des S.: OCP 23 (1957) 354-380. — K. Weber, Oktoëchos-Forschung (Leipzig, 1937). — N. A. Zambolotsky, Christology of S.: EkklPh 58 (1976) 375-386.

P. BRUNS

Severus of Malaga

S. was bishop of Malaga ca. 578-602. He was involved in the anti-Arian struggle and ca. 580 composed a work *Correctorium* against Bishop Vincent of Saragossa, who had gone over to Arianism. He wrote for his sister a treatise *Anulus* on virginity. Neither work has been preserved. Together with his friend → Licinian of Cartagena he wrote, probably after 582, a letter to a Deacon Epiphanius, in which he defends the spirituality and incorporeality of the angels and the human soul.

W: J. Madoz, Liciniano de Cartagena (Madrid, 1948), 97-124 [text]. — PL 72:691-700.
L: A. Di Berardino (ed.), Patrologia 4 (Genoa, 1996), 71. — J. Mandoz, op. cit., 9-79. — J. Novo de Vega, S.: DHEE 4:2446.

B. WINDAU

Severus of Milevis

S. was bishop of Milevis in Numidia from ca. 395 to 426. He was a close friend of Augustine, as can be seen from his letter to Augustine (in Augustine's correspondence, *ep.* 109). In it S. praises the works of Augustine, who answers in his letter 110. S. also corresponded with Paulinus of Nola and had good relations with the civil authorities. In 411 he traveled to the Conference of Carthage but was prevented by ill health from taking part in it. His name is also among the signers of the letter of the Council of Milevis (416) (Aug., *ep.* 176). S. created a controversy by appointing his successor only in the presence of the clergy, without informing the laity; it was peacefully settled by Augustine. S. died on Sept. 26, 426.

W: A. Goldbacher, CSEL 34/2:634-638.
L: PAC 1070-1075.

B. WINDAU

Severus of Minorca

Orosius had left behind on Minorca the relics of Stephen, which Avitus had commissioned him to bring to Braga. On Minorca they worked miracles, which S., the bishop of the place, reported (418) in his *Ep. ad omnem Ecclesiam* (*Sev. Minor. l.* 760). While the finding of the tomb at Kephar Gamala near Jerusalem had been accompanied by miracles, this letter, whose authenticity is not undisputed, claims that 540 Jews were converted by them in a period of eight days. Also from the 5th c. is the Ps.-Augustinian work *De altercatione Ecclesiae et Synagogae* (*alterc. l.* 599), which has been linked to S. but is not his.

W: *Sev. Minor. l.* 760, G. Seguí-Vidal, La carta encíclica del obispo Severo (Rome, 1937), 149-185 [Spanish trans./comm.]. — *alterc.*, G. Seguí-Vidal (Palma de Mallorca, 1955), 33-57.
L: B. Hambenne, Lettre-encyclique de S., Mémoire de licence (Leuven/Louvain, 1984). — L.-J Wankenne, B. Hambenne, La lettre-encyclique de S.: RBen 97 (1987) 13-27.

E. REICHERT

Severus of Synnada

S. was bishop of Synnada in Phrygia salutaris. He took part in the Council of Ephesus (431) and, at the first session, signed the decree deposing Nestorius (Mansi 4:1224c). He has left a short homily, in Ethiopic, on the events concerning Nestorius at the council; it may have been delivered on July 5, 431.

W: A. Dillmann, additions and corrections by E. Littmann, Chrestomathia Aethiopica (Darmstadt, 1967 = Leipzig, 1866/Berlin, ²1950), 99f. [text]. — S. Euringer, Übersetzung der Homilien des Cyrillus v. Alexandrien: Or. NS 12 (1943) 113-145, here 127-130 [German trans.].

B. WINDAU

Sextus (*Sententiae Sexti*)

The *Sententiae Sexti*, a Gr. collection of ethical and ascetical maxims, are among the few examples of early Chr. proverbial wisdom and occupy an important place in the history of asceticism and spiritual direction. Many of the maxims remind us of the intellectual world of Clement Alex. and *The Teachings of Silvanus* (NHC 7, 4). Several give expression to an encratism and rigorism suggestive of Alexandria in the 2nd c. In the so-called *Pythagorean Sentences* (*sent. Pythag.*), the *Sentences of Clitarchus* (*sent. Clitarch.*), and citations in Porphyry's *Ad Marcellam* there are variants of a pagan collection of maxims colored by Neo-Pythagoreanism and Stoicism, which the Chr. adapter ("Sextus") made the basis of his collection. Origen already refers to the *Sextou gnōmai* (*comm. in Mt.* 15.3), mentions the popularity of the work among Christians (*Cels.* 8.30), and calls the author "wise and a believer" (*hom.* 1.11 in *Ezech.*). In the 4th century the *Sentences* were regarded as the work of Roman bishop and martyr Sixtus II. Complete or partial translations into Arabic, Armenian, Ethiopic, Georgian, Coptic, Latin, and Syriac have come down. Rufinus's version (ca. 399) circulated in Lat. monasticism and was much read as late as the Middle Ages. Pelagius referred to some of the *Sentences*, espec. no. 36 (Lat.) on the divinely given freedom that makes likeness to God

possible for those who live without sin. In response to the Pelagians Jerome claims that the *Sentences* were the work of a pagan philosopher, and as a result they were excluded as apocryphal by the → *Decretum Gelasianum* (5.4.11). But Chadwick sees no convincing reason for distrusting the pre-Jerome tradition and thinks it conceivable that ca. 180-210, while still a young man, Sixtus II could have partly composed the *Sententiae Sexti* himself and partly collected them from other sources and revised them.

W: *sent. Sext.*, H. Chadwick, The Sentences of Sextus, TaS NS 5 (Cambridge, 1959) [text/Latin trans. Rufinus/comm./text of *sent. Pythag.*, *sent. Clitarch.*]. — R. A. Edwards, R. A. Wild, The Sentences of Sextus (Chico, 1981) [text/English trans.]. — NTApo2:625-643 [partial German trans.].
L: R. van den Broek, Niet-gnostisch christendom in Alexandrië: NedThT 33 (1979) 287-299. — G. Delling, Hellenisierung des Christentums: FS E. Klostermann, TU 77 (Berlin, 1961), 208-241. — R. F. Evans, Pelagius (New York, 1968), 43-65. — R. Kany, Die gottgeschenkte Freiheit bei Porphyrius, S. u. Pelagius: FS H.-J. Vogt (Beirut, 1992), 153-170 (Lit.; index of the editions of the Lat. and oriental trans. of *sent Sext.*, 159f). — P.-H. Poirier, Les Sentences de Sexte, NHS 12, 1 (Quebec, 1983) (index of the editions of the Lat. and oriental trans. of *sent Sext.*, 13-17). — F. Wisse, Problem der gnostischen Ethik: A. Böhlig, F. Wisse, Zum Hellenismus in den Schriften von Nag Hammadi (Wiesbaden, 1975), 55-86.

R. KANY

Sextus, an Antignostic

Acc. to Eusebius (*h.e.* 5.27; dependent on him, Jerome, *vir. ill.* 50), an otherwise unknown "ecclesiastical" writer Sextus composed ca. 180-210 (uncertain) a possibly antignostic work *De resurrectione*, of which nothing has survived.

L: W. Bauer, Rechtgläubigkeit u. Ketzerei (Tübingen, ²1964), 150-153, 160f. — A. v. Harnack, Geschichte der altchr. Lit. 1 (Leipzig, ²1958), 758f; 2/1:701.

R. HANIG

Shem

The Paraphrase of Shem (*par. Sem.*) is a Copt.-gnostic treatise in the Nag Hammadi library (NHC 7, 1) that gives an allegorical interpretation of the first chapters of Gen. The work offers an entirely gnostic anthropogony and anthropology, describing the initial cosmic catastrophe, the fall of the pleromatic sparks into the material world, and the re-ascent of the fallen souls. The soteriology, too, is thoroughly permeated by gnosticism; the redeemer's crucifixion and suffering are merely external and in a semblance of a body and are therefore irrelevant to redemption, as in docetism.

W: B. A. Pearson, NHC VII (Leiden, 1996) [Coptic text/English trans./comm.]. — M. Krause, Par. Sem.: Christentum am Roten Meer 2, ed. F. Altheim (Berlin, 1973), 2-105 [German trans.]. — NHL 339-361 [English trans.].
L: R. Charron, Concordance du codex VII (Leuven/Louvain, 1992). — C. Colpe, Heidnische und jüd. Überlieferung: JAC 16 (1973) 106-126. — R. Kasser, Fragments de la Genèse: Muséon 85 (1972) 65-89. — M. Roberge, Anthropogonie: Muséon 99 (1986) 229-248. — idem, Chute et remontée: Coptic Studies, ed. W. Godlewski (Warsaw, 1990), 355-363. — idem, Crucifixion: Actes de IVe Congrès Copte 2, ed. M. Rassart-Debergh (Leuven/Louvain, 1992), 381-387. — idem, Le rôle du Noûs: Colloque international, ed. B. Barc (Leuven/Louvain, 1981), 328f. — J. M. Sevrin, Par. Sem: Muséon 88 (1975) 69-96. — M. Tardieu, Naissance du ciel: Congrès de l'ACFEF, ed. F. Blanquart (Paris, 1987), 409-425.

P. BRUNS

Shenoute of Atripe

Sh. (Sinuthios) was archimandrite of the so-called White Monastery (also known as Sh.'s monastery) near Sohag on the western bank of the Nile, opposite Achmim in Upper Egypt; the church built ca. 440 under his leadership is still preserved. The dates of his life must be learned chiefly from his writings. According to the latter, as a young man Sh. entered his uncle's monastery, which he himself led as abbot from ca. 385 on, after the uncle's death and a short term in office by the uncle's successor. In 431 he took part in the Council of Ephesus, along with Cyril Alex. He died probably on July 1, 465.

His extensive writings in Sahidic were collected in parchment codices in the monastery library and copied there. Along with the remains of the library, parts of these codices survived into modern times, often as single sheets and in fragmentary form, in numerous collections in Cairo, Europe, and North America. The first efforts at a complete edition proved premature, since the full range of what had been preserved could not yet be gauged at the beginning of the 20th c. The preconditions for such an edition have recently been satisfied, since with the help of photography the codices in questions have been reconstructed as far as possible. It has turned out that the original holdings of the White Monastery included nine volumes of canons, the chronological order among which perhaps had its origin in Sh. himself; these were writings containing regulations for monastic life in the communities that Sh. governed, some convents of women among them. In addition, there were eight codices of Logoi: sermons and literary letters on, e.g., christology and other broad subjects. The real correspondence (letters by and to Sh.) was probably registered separately. The main importance of all these writings consists in the fact that they are works in the original Coptic and not in translation, like a great part of early Copt. literature. Sh. left a strong imprint on the theology and piety of the Copt. church; he is important for the history of the monastic movement. Earlier judgments on Sh. have to be partially corrected. For example, he held a christology that was formulated against, among others, the Egyptian disciples of Origen (Contra Origenistas); his piety was thus by no means unconnected with Christ, as was earlier assumed.

W: J. Leipoldt, W. E. Crum, H. Wiesmann, CSCO 41/129; 42/96; 73/108 [text/Latin trans.]. — E. C. Amélineau, Œuvres de Sch. 1/2 (Paris, 1907-1914) [text/French trans.]. — D. W. Young, Coptic Manuscripts from the White Monastery: Works of Sh. 1/2 (Vienna, 1993) [text/English trans.]. — Contra Origenistas, T. Orlandi (Rome, 1985) [text/Italian trans.].
L: Bibliography: P. J. Frandsen, E. Richter-Aerøe: FS H. J. Polotsky (East Gloucester, Mass., 1981), 147-176. S. Emmel, Sh.'s Literary Corpus: Acts of the 5th International Congress of Coptic Studies 2/1, ed. D. W. Johnson (Rome, 1993), 153-162. — idem, Sh.'s Literary Corpus, Diss. (Yale Univ., 1993) (publication in CSCO anticipated). — idem, Editing Sh.: Problems and Prospects: Akten des 6. Internationalen Koptologenkongresses Münster 1996 (in press). — A. Grillmeier, Jesus der Christus 2/4 (Freiburg i.Br., 1990), 170-241 (English, Christ in Christian Tradition, vol. 2/4 [London, 1996]). — J. Horn, Märtyrerverehrung u. Märtyrerlegende im Werk des Sch. (Wiesbaden, 1986). — J. Leipoldt, Sch. (Leipzig, 1903). — J. Timbie, The State of Research on the Career of Sh.: The Roots of Egyptian Christianity, ed. B. A. Pearson, J. E. Goehring (Philadelphia, 1986), 258-270.

T. BAUMEISTER

Shubhalemaran

S. was metropolitan of Karka de Bet Selok from 609 to 628 and active in the late 6th and early 7th c. Because of his attacks on Gabriel, the Monophysite court physician, Chosroes II sent him into exile. S. composed a variety of short edifying works. Along with letters there is a collection of ascetical sentences and a so-called Book of Parts, a kind of teaching on the virtues. The works have not yet been published.

L: D. J. Lane, Sh.'s Book of Gifts: OCA 229 (1987) 411-417. — idem, The Creed of Sh.: OCA 236 (1990) 155-162. — G. Troupeau, Une page retrouvée du "Livre des Parties": OCA 205 (1978) 57-61.

P. BRUNS

Sibylline Oracles

In Hellenistic diaspora Judaism (from the 3rd c. B.C.E. on) and subsequently Christians sought to use the authority of the Sibyl, a pagan seeress, for their own purposes of religious propaganda and apologetics.

Heraclitus, *fr.* 92 (Diels; ca. 500 B.C.E.), Aristophanes, *Pax* 1095.1116 (421 B.C.E.), and Plato, *Phdr.* 244b, *Thg.* 124d (4th c. B.C.E.) speak only of one sibyl (originally of oriental origin, in all probability). Later witnesses, however, speak of several sibyls. Acc. to Varro's list from the 1st c. B.C.E. (in Lactantius, *inst.* 1.6.7), which was taken over in Chr. tradition, there were ten sibyls. Well-known sibyls were those of Erythrai and Marpessus in Asia Minor and, in the West, the sibyls of Cumae (see also → Tiburtine Oracle).

Jewish and Chr. writers maintained the ancient pagan picture of an extremely old mythic prophetess. She communicated her prophecies of the future, which she received in a prophetic ecstasy (not in response to questions) through inspiration of a god (but the Jewish-Chr. God instead of Apollo). Hist. events of the past were often represented as future in order to increase the credibility of the prophecies by harking back to undeniable hist. facts (*vaticinia ex eventu*). In order to establish the connection with venerable sibylline poetry, the pagan and bibl. traditions were interwoven, and older utterances were revised and adapted to new demands. The traditional style of the oracles was maintained (hexameters; enigmatic modes of expression; leaps from one idea to another).

Until 1817 only eight books were known of a Jewish-Chr. collection that goes back to the 6th c. C.E. A. Mai's discovery added four books (books 11-14; the extensive eighth book was, in one strand of the tradition, divided into three parts and numbered as books 8-10). While books 1-5 and 11-14 are primarily of Jewish origin (partly mixed with Chr. elements; time of origin: about the 2nd c. B.C.E. to the 3rd/4th c. C.E.), books 6-8 are substantially Chr. (from 2nd c. C.E.). The sixth book has only twenty-eight verses and contains a hymn to Christ and the cross; the seventh (162 vv.; preserved in fragments) is influenced by gnosticism and combines some disparate pieces of Chr. sibylline poetry. The eighth book of five hundred vv. is the most important and most cited by the fathers, and likewise contains some loosely connected sibylline texts on various subjects (e.g., threats against godless Rome; apocalyptic visions of the destruction of the world and divine punishment at the end of time; praise of God's omnipotence and of the incarnate Logos). Prominent here is well-known acrostic (vv. 217-50: description of Christ's second coming at the universal judgment): ΙΗΣΟΤΣ ΧΡΕΙΣΤΟΣ (*sic!*) ΘΕΟΤ ΤΙΟΣ ΣΩΤΗΡ ΣΤΑΤΡΟΣ, which was cited by Constantine, *or. s. c.* 18, and Augustine *civ.* 18.23 (in an older Lat. translation, without the ΣΤΑΤΡΟΣ stanza). Augustine also calls attention to a further acrostic that emerged from the first: ΙΧΘΤΣ, which likewise has a symbolic reference to Christ.

The divinely legitimated authority of the sibyls was alleged by many Chr. writers (espec. Lactantius). The influence of the *Oracula Sibyllina* extends through the Middle Ages to the Renaissance (*Dies irae*, Dante, Calderón, Giotto, Michelangelo, Raphael).

W: J. Geffcken, GCS 8. — A. Kurfess, J. D. Gauger (Darmstadt, 1998) [text/German trans./comm.]. — A. Rzach (Vienna, 1891) [text]. — V. Nikiprowetzky, La troisième Sibylle (Paris, 1970) [text/French trans. of bk. 3]. — D. S. Potter, Prophecy and History in the Crisis of the Roman Empire (Oxford, 1990) [text/English trans./comm. on bk. 13]. — NTApo⁵ 2:591-619 [German trans. of bks. 6-8]. — J.-D. Gauger, Sibyllinische Weissagungen (Düsseldorf, 1998) [text/German trans.]. — H. Merkel, Jüd. Schriften aus hellenistisch. röm. Zeit 5, Apokalypsen, ed. H. Lichtenberger et al.: Sibyllinen (Gütersloh, 1998), 1042-1140 [comm./German trans. of bks. 3-5]. — Theosophorum Graecorum Fragmenta, ed. H. Erbse (Stuttgart/Leipzig, 1995).
L: B. Altaner, Augustinus u. die ntl. Apokryphen: idem, Kleine patristische Schriften, ed. G. Glockmann (Berlin, 1967), 204-215. — J. B. Bauer, Die Gottesmutter in den Oracula Sibyllina: Mar. 18 (1956) 118-124. — B. Bischoff, Die lat. Übersetzungen u. Bearbeitungen aus den Oracula Sibyllina: Mélanges J. de Ghellinck 1: Antiquité = ML. H 13 (1951) 121-147. — W. Bulst, Eine anglo-lat. Übersetzung aus dem Griech. um 700: Lat. MA, SAH Suppl. 3 (Heidelberg, 1984), 57-63. — J. J. Collins, The Development of the Sibylline Tradition: ANRW II 20/1 (1987) 421-459. — F. Dölger, ΙΧΘΤΣ 1 (Rome, 1910), 52-68. — J. Engemann, Sibyllen: LMA 7:1832. — J. Geffcken, Komposition u. Entstehungszeit der Oracula Sibyllina: TU 23/1 (1923). — E. Kautzsch, Die Apokryphen u. Pseudepigraphen des AT (Tübingen, 1900), 177-217. — A. Kurfess, Kaiser Konstantin u. die Erythräische Sibylle: ZRGG 3 (1951) 353-357. — idem, Dies Irae: HJ 77 (1958) 328-338. — A. Momigliano, Dalla Sibilla pagana alla Sibilla cristiana: ASNSP 17 (1987) 407-428. — J.-M. Nieto Ibáñez, El hexámetro de los Oráculos sibillinos (Amsterdam, 1992). — G. L. Potestà, Sibyllinische Bücher: LMA 7, 1832f. — K. Prümm, Das Prophetenamt der Sibyllen in kirchlicher Literatur: Schol. 4 (1929) 54-77, 221-246, 498-553. — A. Rzach, Sibyllen: PRE 2A:2073-2103. — idem, Sibyllinische Orakel: op. cit., 2103-2183. — S. A. Redmond, The Date of the Fourth Sibylline Oracle: SecCen 7 (1990) 129-149. — B. Teyssèdre, Les représentations de la fin des temps dans le chant V des Oracles sibyllins: Apokrypha 1 (1990) 147-165. — B. Thompson, Patristic Use of the Sibylline Oracles: RR 16 (1951) 115-136. — M. J. Wolf, Sibyllen u. Sibyllinen: AKuG 24 (1935) 312-325.

H. SCHNEIDER

Silvanus

A Copt. treatise in the Nag Hammadi library (NHC 7, 4) contains the teachings of a certain S. It contains a hortatory address with sapiential teachings of Jewish-Egypt. provenance and a gnostic anthropology and christology. Redemption takes place through the acquisition of a liberating knowledge that is brought by Christ the redeemer and enables those living an enslaved existence to free themselves from the bondage of the material through asceticism and mortification and to make the journey home to the divine pleroma.

W: Y. Janssens, Les leçon de S., NHC VII, 4 (Leuven/Louvain, 1983) [Coptic text/French trans./comm.]. — J. Zandee (Leiden, 1991) [Coptic text/English trans./comm.]. — W. P. Funk: ThLZ 100 (1975) 7-23 [German trans.]. — NHL 379-395 [English trans.].
L: R. van den Broek, S. en de Griekse traditie: NedThT 42 (1988) 126-133. — idem, Theology: VigChr 40 (1986) 1-23. — Y. Janssens, Leçons de S. et le monachisme: Colloque international, ed. B. Barc (Leuven/Louvain, 1981). — M. L. Peel, Descensus ad inferos: Numen 26 (1979) 23-49. — W. R. Schoedel, Jewish Wisdom: Aspects of Wisdom, ed. R. L. Wilken (London, 1975), 169-199. — J. Zandee, Teachings of S. and Clement of Alexandria (Leiden, 1977). — idem, Origène et S.: LTP 46 (1990) 369-382. — idem, Teachings of S. and Jewish Christianity: FS. G. Quispel (Leiden, 1981), 498-584.

P. BRUNS

Silvester I of Rome

No authentic letters of S. (314-335) have survived. Acc. to the legend about Constantine that went under S.'s name, S. healed Constantine of leprosy by baptizing him when he was a persecutor of Christians, and was therefore given authority over the city of Rome. The legend was widespread in the Middle Ages and became the basis for the Constantinian Donation. In addition, the primacy of the Roman church was supposedly established at that time. The *Actus Silvestri*, which were attributed to S. and explain the basics of the faith in dialogue form, were not composed until the 5th c. by an unknown author.

W: B. Mombritius, Sanctuarium 2 (Paris, 1910), 280 [text]. — F. Combefis, Martyrum triumphi (Paris, 1660), 253-264 [text]. — W. Levison, Konstantinische Schenkung u. S. legende: Misc. Ehrle 2 (Rome, 1924), 177-180 (406-408) [two *prologi*].
L: H. Fuhrmann, Konstantinische Schenkung u. S.-legende in neuer Sicht: DA 15 (1959) 523-540. — N. Huyghebaert, Une légende de fondation: MÂ 85 (1979) 177-209. — W. Levison, op. cit., 159-247. — W. Pohlkamp, Tradition u.

Topographie: Papst S. u. der Drache vom Forum Romanum: RQ 78 (1983) 1-100.

J. KREILOS

Simeon of Bet Arsam

S. was a zealous Monophysite who recruited for his confession in Persian-Nestorian territory and was able to win over Persian magicians as well as Nestorians. Because of his special contributions in interconfessional debate, the patriarch consecrated him bishop of Bet Arsam in Mesopotamia. Numerous journeys on which he spread Monophysite teaching led him to the Arab. borderlands and finally to Constantinople, where he died before 548. In Hirta, in 524, S. wrote a letter to a certain Simeon of Gabbula (*ep. ad Sim.*), in which he told of the martyrdom of Aretas (Harith) and his companions in Yemenite Nagran under the Jewish King Du Nuwas. In a later ms. there is another, anon. telling of these events (*narr. an.*). In a second letter, addressed to an anonymous person (*ep. ad an.*), S. bemoans the nestorianization of Persia by Barsauma.

W: *ep. ad Sim.*, J. S. Assemani, BOCV 1:364-379 [text/Latin trans.]. — AMSS 1:372-397 [text]. — J. P. Land, Anecdota Syriaca 3 (Leiden, 1870), 235-242 [text]. — *narr. an.*, G. Knös, Chrestomathia Syriaca (Göttingen, 1807), 37-54 [text]. — *ep. ad an.*, J. S. Assemani, BOCV 1:346-358 [text/Latin trans.].
L: A. Moberg, The Book of the Himyarites (Lund, 1924). — S. Uhlig, Nestorianisierung Persiens: OrChr 72 (1988) 68-81.

P. BRUNS

Simeon of Edessa

The only thing known of the life of S. is that he was head of a hospice in Edessa and composed a commentary on Gen (*comm. in Gen.*) and another on Dan (*comm. in Dan.*).

W: *comm. in Gen.*, Brit. Mus. Add. 17189. — *comm. in Dan.*, Brit. Mus. Add. 12172. — A. K. Fenz, Daniel-Memra des Simeon (Heiligenkreuz, 1980) [German trans.].
L: R. Köbert, Zur Daniel-Abhandlung: Bib. 63 (1982) 63-78.

P. BRUNS

Simeon Stylites

S. was born ca. 390 in the village of Sis near Nicopolis as the son of propertied parents; he initially entered the monastery of Eusebonas near Teleda but was obliged to leave it quite soon because of his extreme asceticism. He moved then to Telnesrin near Antioch, where he withdrew to the top of a column, with the columns becoming increasingly higher. From there he carried on an extensive correspondence as spiritual adviser until his death in 459. Though he had little education he intervened, in favor of Chalcedon, in the dogmatic controversies of his time. S.'s life is reported in three quite independent sources: ch. 26 of the *Historia religiosa* of Theodoret of Cyrrhus, a Syr. *Vita* by Simeon bar Apollon and → Bar Chatar, and finally a Gr. *Vita* by a certain Anthony. The hymn of Jacob of Sarug on S. has little value as a source. The correspondence of S. and Cosmas (*ep.*) is preserved in its Syr. original. Three other letters on Monophysitism have been shown to be later forgeries that replaced the correspondence that showed fidelity to Chalcedon.

S: *vita*, S. E. Assemani, Acta Sanctorum 2 (Rome, 1748), 268-398 [Syriac text/Latin trans.]. — P. Bedjan, AMSS 4:507-44 [Syriac text]. — H. Hilgenfeld, H. Lietzmann, Leben des hl. S. (Leipzig, 1908), 79-188 [Syriac-Greek text/German trans.]. — G. Garitte, CSCO 171f. [Georgian text/French trans.]. — H. G. Blersch, Säule im Weltgeviert (Trier, 1978), 123-152 [German trans.].
W: *ep.*, C. Torrey, Letter of S.: JAOS 20 (1863) 252-276 [text/English trans.]. — H. Hilgenfeld, H. Lietzmann, op. cit., 188-191.
L: E. Benz, S. u. Andreas Salos: Kyrios 3 (1938) 1-55. — H. G. Blersch, op. cit. — M. Chaine, La vie et les miracles de S. (Cairo, 1948). — H. Delehaye, Les Saints Stylites (Brussels, 1928). — A. Festugière, Antioche païenne (Paris, 1959), 357-370. — D. T. M. Frankfurter, Stylites: VigChr 44 (1990) 168-198. — H. Lietzmann, Leben des hl. S. (Leipzig, 1908). — J. Nasrallah, L'orthodoxie: ParOr 2 (1971) 345-364. — P. Peeters, S. et ses biographes: AnBoll 61 (1943) 29-72. — I. Peña, Les stylites syriens (Milan, 1975). — G. R. H. Wright, Heritage of Stylites: AJBA 3 (1970) 82-107. — idem, S.'s Ancestors: AJBA 1 (1986) 41-49.

P. BRUNS

Simon the Canaanite, Literature about

In the Copt. tradition the apostle Simon named in Mt 10:4 is not connected (as in the West) with Judas Thaddaeus (→ Thaddaeus, Acts of). He is identified rather with Simon, son of Cleopas and successor to James as bishop of Jerusalem (see Hegesippus in Eus., h.e. 3.32.1-2). The *Acts of Simon* (A. *Sim.*) tell of S.'s activity in Samaria and Jerusalem and of his crucifixion under Trajan. The *Acts* have come down complete only in Arabic and Ethiopic The legend of S. and the virgin Theonoe (*Theon.*) is a local continuation of the *Acts*, intended to link S. with Egypt.

In the Lat. tradition, in which S. is identified with Judas Thaddaeus, Persia-Babylonia is taken as the location of S.'s activity. Joint *Acts* are handed down in the sixth book of → (Ps.-) Abdias.

W: A. *Sim.*, A. Smith Lewis (Horae Semiticae) (London, 1903), 3:96-100 [Arabic text]; 4:115-119 [English trans.]. — E. A. Wallis Budge, The Contendings of the Apostles (Amsterdam, 1976 = 1899-1901), 1:67-72 [Ethiopic text]; 2:58-64 [English trans.]. — *Theon.*, F. Morard, La légende copte de S. et Théonoé: Langues orientales anciennes (in press). L: NTApo[5] 2:435f.

G. RÖWEKAMP

Simon Magus

The Simon described in Acts 8:9-24 as primarily a magician makes his appearance again in Justin (*1 apol.* 26.2f.; *dial.* 120.6) as a gnostic and, beginning with Irenaeus (*haer.* 1.23.1-4; see Hippolytus, *haer.* 4.51.3-14; 6.7-20; 10.12), as the father of all heresies. Whether S. was originally a Samaritan schismatic, a gnostic, or a *Theios aner* is disputed. Writings of the Simonian gnostics are attested several times (see Eus., *h.e.* 2.13.7; Ps.-Clement, *recog.* 2.38.4; *Const. App.* 6.16.2), but only paraphrased fragments of the *Great Revelation* (2nd c.) have survived. Some Nag Hammadi writings, → *Exegesis on the Soul*, → *Thunder, Perfect Mind*, and → *Authoritative Teaching* may show links with Simonianism.

W: Hippolytus, *haer.* 6.9-20.
L: L. Abramowski, Drei christologische Untersuchungen (Berlin, 1981), 18-62. — S. Arai, Authentikos Logos u. Bronté: Gnosis and Gnosticism, ed. M. Krause (Leiden, 1981), 3-15. — K. Berger, Propaganda: FS D. Georgi (Leiden, 1994), 313-317. — K. Beyschlag, S. Magus u. die chr. Gnosis (Tübingen, 1974). — A. Ferreiro, S., Dogs, and Simon Peter: FS J. B. Russell (Leiden, 1998), 45-89. — J. Frickel, Apophasis Megale (Rome, 1968). — idem, Neue Textausgabe: WSt 6 (1972) 162-184. — F. Heintz, S. "Le Magicien" (Paris, 1997). — G. Lüdemann, Untersuchungen (Göttingen, 1975). — idem, Beginning: NTS 33 (1987) 420-427. — S. Pétrement, Separate God (London, 1991), 233-246. — K. Rudolph, S.: ThR 42 (1977) 279-359. — idem, Gnosis (Göttingen,[3]1990), 315-319.

R. HANIG

Simon of Taibutheh

S., a physician and monk, was active in Mesopotamia under Catholicos Henaniso (d. 699/700) and is regarded as one of the most important mystics of the Persian-Nestorian church. He derived his title ("of his grace") either from the title of a lost work on medicine or, more probably, from his monastic gifts (thus Barhebraeus, *chr. eccl.* 2.139). In addition to a work on the art of healing, ascetical works are attributed to him on *Way of Life* and on *The Christening of the Monks' Cell*; these are not yet completely pub-

lished. In his mysticism S. takes up the older traditions of Evagrius Pont., Ps.-Macarius, John of
Apamea (the hermit), and Ps.-Dionysius and works
them up into a theory of the Three Altars, which correspond to his trichotomist anthropology (body,
soul, spirit) and symbolize the ascent of the mystic
from external, fleshly works to union with the divine.
As a physician, S. was interested espec. in the inter-
actions between the bodily organs and the immortal
spiritual soul.

W: A. Baumstark, Geschichte (Bonn, 1922), 209f. [Syriac
mss.]. — A. Mingana, Early Christian Mystics (Cambridge,
1934) [Syriac text/English trans.]. — A. Rücker, Aus dem
mystischen Schrifttum: Morgenland 28 (1936) 38-54 [Ger-
man trans.].
L: R. Beulay, La lumière sans forme (Chevetogne, 1987),
103-105, 202-206.

P. BRUNS

Simplicius of Rome

When S. entered his office as bishop of Rome (March
3, 468), the end of the western Roman empire was at
hand: in 472 the barbarians conquered Rome for the
third time, and in 476 Odoacer, the Arian ruler of the
Germans, had himself proclaimed king. In this
desperate political situation S. defended the claims of
the church interiorly by his literary works and exteri-
orly by his building program and skillful organization. He died on March 10, 493.

Twenty-one letters or synodal documents have
come down from the second half of S.'s pontificate
(ep. pontif.). With the exception of three, these were
occasioned by the Monophysite confusion in the
East. In his letters S. shows a determination moder-
ated by diplomatic prudence and leniency. Against
the emperor S. stresses the permanent validity of the
decrees of the Roman bishop on the faith (ep. 3.5).

W: ep. pontif., O. Günther, CSEL 35:124-155 (14 letters
from Avell.). — E. Schwartz, Sammlungen zum Acacianischen Schisma: ABAW 10 (1934) (4 letters). — A. Thiel,
Epistulae Romanorum Pontificum Genuinae (Hildesheim,
1974 = 1868), 175-214 (21 letters) [text]. — S. Wenzlowsky,
Papstbriefe 6, BKV[1] [German trans.].
L: E. Caspar, Geschichte des Papsttums 2 (Tübingen, 1933),
10-25. — A. Di Berardino (ed.), Patrologia 4 (Genoa, 1996),
124f. — W. C. H. Frend, The Rise of the Monophysite
Movement (Cambridge, [2]1979), 173-183. — J. N. D. Kelly,
S.: The Oxford Dictionary of Popes (Oxford, 1986), 45f.

S. C. KESSLER, SJ

Siricius

S. succeeded Damasus I as bishop of Rome 384-399.
His letters (ep.), which manifest the growing claim of

the Roman bishops to jurisdiction over the western
church and take the form of a papal decretal for the
first time, make it clear that S. continued, in both
content and form, the start made by Damasus on a
comprehensive legislation. Of the letters published
under S.'s name in PL, the following are authentic:
ep. 1 to Bishop Himerius of Tarragona, an answer to
fifteen questions on church discipline (among others, the date of baptism, clerical discipline); ep. 4 to
Bishop Anysius of Thessalonica against the teaching
of Bonosus of Sardica, who did not accept the permanent virginity of Mary; ep. 5 to the bishops of
North Africa, who were bound by the nine canons of
the Roman synod of 386; ep. 6 to the bishops of central and southern Gaul, a "decree" about admission
to the episcopal office with a reference to the "solici-
tude for all the churches" that is incumbent on the
Roman bishop; and ep. 7, a circular letter against
Jovinian and his teaching on the equal value of marriage and virginity. Uncertain is the attribution of ep.
9 (→ Ambrose?) and 10 (→ Damasus?), as well as of
some liturg. formulas. Not from S.: ep. 2 (Emperor
Valentinian II), ep. 3 (Maximus the usurper), and ep.
8 (Council of Aquileia 381). S.'s abilities were in the
area of eccles. administration. Theologically, literarily, and spiritually he was overshadowed by his contemporary Ambrose.

W: PL 13:1131-1196. — ep. 4, C. Silva-Tarrouca (Rome,
1937), 19 [text]. — ep. 5, C. Munier, CCL 149:59-63. — ep.
7, M. Zelzer, CSEL 82/3:296-301. — ep. 9 (De Bonoso), M.
Zelzer, CSEL 83/3:7-10. — ep. 10, M. Zelzer, CSEL
82/3:316-325.
L: J. A. de Aldama, "De Bonoso": Mar. 25 (1963) 1-22. — K.
Baus, Von Miltiades bis Leo I.: HKG(J) 2/1:254-278. — E.
Caspar, Papsttum 1 (Tübingen, 1930), 257-267. — J.
Gaudemet, L'église dans l'empire romain (Paris, 1958),
220-226. 439. — idem, Droit de l'église (Paris, 1985), 57-64.
— H. Getzeny, Stil u. Form (Tübingen, 1922). — J. Janini,
Sacramentario Leoniano (Valencia, 1958) (liturgical for-
mulas). — M. Maccarone, Principato papale (Spoleto,
1960), 633-742. — C. Pietri, Roma Christiana (Rome,
1976), 888-909. — J. Speigl, Bischofseinsetzungen: FS H.
Tuechle (Munich, 1975), 43-61.

M. SKEB, OSB

Sixtus II of Rome

No writings have survived from S. (August [?] 257—
Aug. 6, 278), who was beheaded during Valerian's
persecution of Christians. It is probable, however,
that he adopted conciliatory positions on the validity
of heretical baptism and thus improved the tense
relationship between Rome and the bishops of North
Africa and Asia Minor. The Ps.-Isidorean Decretals
contain communications on procedures against
accused bishops, to the effect that the final judgment

is left to the Roman bishop. Because, among other things, of the similarity of names, Rufinus of Aquileia wrongly names S. as author in his translation of the *Sentences of Sextus* (ca. 400).

W: PL 5:83-100. — P. Hinschius, Decretales (Leipzig, 1863), 189-194. — S. Wenzlowsky, Briefe der Päpste, BKV¹ 13:412-424 [German trans.]. — H. Chadwick, The Sentences of Sextus (Cambridge, 1959) [Greek and Latin text/comm.].
L: A. Lippold, Xystos II: PRE 9A/2:2183f. — F. X. Seppelt, Aufstieg des Papsttums (Leipzig, 1931), 62f.

O. KAMPERT

Sixtus III of Rome

S. (July 31, 432—Aug. 19, 440) initially, when a priest, sided with Pelagius but then attacked Pelagianism and therefore did not reinstate Julian of Eclanum as a bishop; S. has left eight letters. He defended his primacy of jurisdiction over Illyria against, among others, Proclus of Constantinople, in whose vicariate he did not intervene (*ep.* 7-10; see *ACO* 1, 1, 7, 143). In the East he continued the policies of Celestine I: Cyril Alex. was to keep the way open for all Nestorians, espec. John of Antioch, to return if they recognized the decrees of the Council of Ephesus (*ep.* 1f.). Cyril and the Antiochenes reached a formula of union in 433 (*ep.* 5f.), which not all bishops supported (see *ep.* 4). The treatises *De divitiis*, *De malis doctoribus*, and *De castitate* were wrongly ascribed to S., as was a letter in which S. absolved himself of an accusation of unchastity supposedly made against him in 435. The "Symmachian Forgeries" (→ Symmachus of Rome) include *Gesta de Xysti purgatione et Polychronii Jerosylymitani episcopi accusatione*, in which nobles slander S. and accuse Polychronius, bishop of Jerusalem, of simony at a synod convoked by S.

W: PL 50:583-618. — *ep.*, ACO 1, 1, 7, 143-145 (*ep.* 1f.); 1, 2, 107-110 (*ep.* 5f.); 1, 4, 145-148 (*ep.* 4). — P. Hinschius, Decretales (Leipzig, 1863), 561-565. — S. Wenzlowsky, Briefe der Päpste, BKV¹ 15:538-628 [German trans.]. — Gesta de Xysti, P. Coustant, Epistolae Romanorum Pontificum 1 (Paris, 1721), Appendix 117-124.
L: E. Caspar, Geschichte des Papsttums (Tübingen, 1930-1933), 1:381f., 416-422; 2:108f. — A. Lippold, Xystos III.: PRE 9A/2:2184-2188. — V. Monachin, Sisto III: BSS 11:1262-1264. — G. Zecchini, I "Gesta de Xysti purgatione": RSCI 34 (1980) 60-74.

O. KAMPERT

Socrates

I. Life: S. (b. after 381; d. after 439) lived in Constantinople as a scholasticus (lawyer) and composed a history of the church (*h.e.*). He says that Helladius and Ammonius, two grammarians who had fled Alexandria in 390, were his teachers (*h.e.* 5.16.9). From homoean presbyter Timothy he learned exegesis and the theology of Origen, whom he esteemed highly (*h.e.* 7.6.6). He knew the elderly Novatian presbyter Auxanon and venerated him as an ascetic (*h.e.* 1.13.2). From other sources, too, he gained a good knowledge of the Novatians, but this does not justify the inference, which goes back to Nicephorus Callistus, that S. was himself a member of the sect. No further details of his life are known.

II. Work: The *h.e.* of S. was a work commissioned by Theodore, an otherwise unknown cleric (7.48.7). It covers events of the period from the abdication of Diocletian (305) to the seventeenth consulate of Theodosius II (439) and is conceived as a continuation of the *h.e.* of → Eusebius of Caesarea (1.1.1-3). S.'s main sources are Euesbius's *v.C.*, → Rufinus, → Gelasius of Caesarea, texts of → Athanasius, the collection of synodal acts by → Sabinus of Caesarea, the *Breviarium* of Eutropius, the *Chronicle of Constantinople*, and numerous other individual sources, as well as oral accounts (Auxanon, Eudaimon) and, in the last two books, S.'s own experience.

The special character of S.'s presentation consists of a notably critical attitude toward the sources used (an attitude forced upon him, to some extent, by the one who commissioned the work). Thus he questions the hist. value of the encomium genre (with an eye on the *v.C.*: *h.e.* 1.18.14); he revises his own presentation after being told of doubts (*h.e.* 2, proem) about the value of the information used in his first edition from Rufinus, his main source (which, in part, he transcribes verbatim). S. prefers to give charters and other documents verbatim rather than report what they say. He compares sources critically and hunts out contradictions.

The books of the *h.e.* follow the reigns of the emperors (1: Constantine; 2: Constantius II; 3: Julian/Jovian; 4: Valentinian/Valens; 5: Theodosius I; 6: Arcadius; 7: Theodosius II). Within this grid the dates of office of important bishops and synodal decrees are included, a practice which acc. to S. ensures completeness and avoids onesidedness, but, more importantly, should make clear the connections and reciprocal influences of political and eccles. events (*h.e.* 5, proem).

In his theol. tendency S. is a rather "liberal" representative of eccles. orthodoxy, although he does not have any great understanding of detailed dogm. differences (*h.e.* 1.18.15f.; 5, proem 2f.). In his style S. values clarity and simplicity, which suggests that the work was intended for a somewhat broad readership. Even today the *h.e.* of S. is one of the most important sources for reconstructing the political and eccles. history of the 4th and early 5th c., espec. the Arian controversy, the controversy over Origen, the beginnings of the christological controversy, and the early history of Chr. monasticism. Its historical value is in many respects to be set relatively higher than that of contemporary or slightly later parallel enterprises, although from the viewpoint of method the careful dissection and separate critical evaluation of the building blocks remain indispensable and, as recent works show, fruitful for the hist. reconstruction and for the understanding of S.'s text. S. was imitated espec. by → Sozomen, → Theodoret, → Gelasius of Cyzicus, and → John of Antioch, and extensively used as a source in their presentation of eccles. or world history. As late as the 14th c., Nicephorus Callistus took over large sections of S. into his own presentation. There are ancient translations of S.'s *h.e.* into Old Armenian and Syriac. A Lat. translation of parts of the work was made in the 6th c. under the direction of → Cassiodorus as a section of the *h.e. tripartita* (put together from S., Sozomen, and Theodoret) by the monk → Epiphanius Scholasticus (see → Theodore, Lector).

W: *h.e.*, G. C. Hansen, GCS NF 1. — R. Hussey, 3 vols. (Oxford, 1853) [text]. — PG 67:28-842. — M. Ter Mowsesean (Valarsapat, 1897) [Old Armenian version]. — A. C. Zenos, NPNF 2/2:1-178 [English trans.]. — Cassiodorus, *hist.*, W Jacob, R. Hanslik, CSEL 71.
L: P. Allen, War: StPatr 19 (1989) 3-8. — T. D. Barnes, Athanasius and Constantius (Cambridge, Mass., 1993), 200-215. — G. Bardy, S.: DThC 14:2334-2336. — E. Bihain, Source: Byz. 32 (1962) 81-91. — G. F. Chesnut, Kairos: ChH 44 (1975) 161-166. — idem, Christian Histories (Macon, Ga., ²1986), 175-198. — F. C. Conybeare, Emendations: JP 33 (1914) 208-237. — idem, Collation: JP 34 (1915) 47-77. — G. Downey, Perspective: GRBS 6 (1965) 59-63. — W. Eltester, S.: PRE 3A, 893-901. — A. Ferrarini, Tradizioni orali: StPat 28 (1981) 29-54. — F. Geppert, Quellen (Leipzig, 1898). — G. Gentz, K. Aland, Quellen: ZNW 42 (1949) 104-141. — R. C. Hink, Stellung des Verbums (Vienna, 1957). — F. J. F. Jackson, History of Church History (Cambridge, 1939), 73-82. — L. Jeep, Quellenuntersuchungen (Leipzig, 1884). — G. C. Hansen, Einleitung zur GCS Edition (Berlin, 1995), IX-LX. — idem, Prosarhythmus: BySl 26 (1965) 82-93. — W.-D. Hauschild, Synodalaktensammlung: VigChr 24 (1970) 105-126. — P. Heather, Crossing: GRBS 17 (1986) 289-318. — G. Loeschke, S.: RE3 18, 481-486. — M. Mazza, Teoria: La storiografia ecclesiastica della tarda antichità (Messina, 1980), 335-389. — G. Moravcsik, Byzantinoturcica 1 (Berlin, ²1958), 508-510. — P. Nautin, Continuation: REByz 50 (1992) 163-183. — P. Périchon, Édition: RSR 53 (1965) 112-120. — M. Wallraff, Kirchenhistoriker S. (Göttingen, 1997). — idem, Das Zeugnis des Kirchenhistorikers S. zur Textkritik von 1 Joh 4, 3: ZNW 88 (1997) 145-148. — F.

Winkelmann, Charakter: ByF 1 (1966) 346-385. — idem, Untersuchungen, SDAW. S (1965), 3 (Berlin, 1966). — idem, Kirchengeschichtswerke, BySl 37 (1976) 172-175.

J. ULRICH

Solomon

I. Odes (Od.): Of the forty-two Ps.-Solomonic, richly imaged poems, which are also called hymns, songs, or psalms in the literature, there have survived: one Gr. *ōdē* (11), five Copt. citations (described with the foreign word *ōdē*) in the gnostic *Pistis Sophia* (1; 5.1-11; 6.8-18; 22; 25), a Lat. citation from *Od.* 19 in Lactantius (19.6-7), and forty Syr. *zᵉmîrathâ* in two incomplete mss. (3-42 and 17-42, in each case with the Jewish-apocryphal *Psalms of Solomon* (*Pss. Sal.*). The concept *zᵉmîrtâ* is also found in the *Od.* themselves (14.7; 26.2 and 3; 36.2; 40.3).

In addition to petitions, doxologies, and hymnic and didactic forms, the dominant elements are testimonies to salvation and expressions of confident hope in salvation, all more or less permeated by a gnostic-dualistic mythology. On the one hand, there are forms in which "I," sometimes "We," speak as redeemed or, as the case may be, redeeming person (or group of persons), and, on the other, forms in which "I," but never "We," speak as inviting, redeeming, creating, choosing, challenging, sent, revealing, or promising person. But the most characteristic of these forms are the ones in which the speaker(s) combine both aspects, espec. in the person of the redeemed redeemer or redeeming redeemed.

This redeemer, also called Lord and Son, appears as Christ/Messiah (9.3; 17.16; 24.1; 29.6; 39.11; 41.3; 41.15) but never under the name of Jesus. Theol. concepts such as Spirit, God, Lord, Supreme Being, and Father are as frequent as is the mention of the blessings of salvation: knowledge, joy, grace, holiness, life, light, love, rest, immortality, truth, and word.

In content, the *Od.*, which draw on the OT and show similarities with the Qumran writings, suggest the world of John and the letters of Ignatius. In two lists of canonical books (Ps.-Athanasius and Nicephorus) they are mentioned, together with the 18 *Pss. Sal.*, as doubtfully authentic OT books. The time of composition can be assigned to the first quarter of the 2nd c. C.E.. The original language was Greek or/and Syriac.

W: *Od.*, R. Harris, A. Mingana (Manchester, 1916/20) [text/English trans.]. — M. Lattke, vol. 1/1a (Fribourg, Switzerland, 1979/80) [text/German trans.]. — idem, FC 19

541

[German trans.]. — *Od.* 11, M. Testuz, PapyBod X-XII (Geneva, 1959) [text/French trans.].

L: L. Abramowski, Sprache: OrChr 68 (1984) 80-90. — J. H. Charlesworth, Od.: OTP 2 (1985) 725-771. — M. Franzmann, Od. (Fribourg, Switzerland, 1991). — M. Lattke, Od., vol. 2/3 (Fribourg, Switzerland, 1979/86). — idem, Messias-Stellen: FS F. Hahn (Göttingen, 1991), 429-445. — idem, Dating: Antichthon 27 (1993) 45-59.

II. Testament (*Test.*):

Ca. fifteen Gr. mss. preserve various versions of this mixture of teaching on demons and angels, magic, and medicine; the work calls itself *diathēkē* (title; 15.41; 26.8). Just as the miraculously tamed demons had been forced to help in the building of the temple, Ps.-Solomon, who has fallen away from God, speaks here in the first person, and now lives apart from the *doxa* of God (26.7), nevertheless praises this God from beginning to end of his work.

This syncretism, which was popular down to the early Middle Ages, has an OT-Jewish basis and a few Chr. echoes (15.10; 17.4; 22.20; 23.4). But probably the author himself, and not just a reviser, was a Greek-speaking Christian of from the 1st to the 3rd c. The place of origin may have been Palestine or Egypt, or perhaps Asia Minor or even Babylonia.

W: *Test.*, F. A. Bornemann: ZHTh 14/3 (1844) 9-56 [German trans. by Fleck]. — F. C. Conybeare: JQR 11 (1898) 1-45 [English trans. by Fleck]. — A. Delatte: Anecdota Atheniensia 36 (1927) 211-227 [text, ms. Bibliothèque Nationale 2011]. — D. C. Duling: OTP 1 (1983) 960-987 [English trans.]. — F. F. Fleck, Anecdota sacra (Leipzig, 1837), 113-140 = PG 122:1315-1358 [text, ms. P. McCown/ Latin trans.]. — C. C. McCown, UNT 9 (Leipzig, 1922) [text]. — P. Riessler, Altjüd. Schrifttum (Heidelberg, ²1966 = 1928), 1251-1262 [trans. selections]. — *Test.* 18, 34-40, K. Preisendanz: Eos 48 (1956) 161-167 [text, Vienna Pap.-frags. G 330].
L: J. H. Charlesworth, Pseudepigrapha and Modern Research (Missoula, 1976), 197-202. — D. C. Duling, OTP 1 (1983) 935-959. — B. M. Metzger, Test.: BHH 3 (1966) 1653. — K. Preisendanz, Salomo: PRE. S 8:660-704, esp. 684-690.

M. LATTKE

Sophia Jesu Christi

This work, preserved in *NHC* III, is a secondary revision of the so-called Letter of → Eugnostus; it turns the latter work on the philosophy of religion into a dialogue of Jesus with his disciples. The work is handed down in *Pap. Berol.* 8502 as well as in *NHC* III, 4.

W: The Facsimile Edition of the NHC. Cod. III (p. 90, 14-119, 18) (Leiden, 1976). — W. C. Till, Die gnostischen Schriften des kopt. Pap. Berol. 8502, TU 60 (Berlin, ²1972),

194-295 [text/German trans./comm.]. — C. Barry (Quebec, 1993) [text]. — NHL 220-243 [English trans.].
L: C. Barry, Anthropogonie gnostique et typologie paulinienne: Muséon 107 (1994) 283-297. — idem, La dynamique de l'histoire: Muséon 105 (1992) 265-273. — P. Perkins, The Soteriology of Sophia of Jesus Christ: The Society of Biblical Literature (107th Annual Meeting 28-31 Oct. 1971) (Atlanta, 1971), 165-181.

G. RÖWEKAMP

Sophronius of Jerusalem

I. Life:

S., patriarch of Jerusalem, is the same person as Sophronius Sophistes, the friend of John Moschus. Born ca. 550 in Damascus and educated there as a rhetor, S. went to Palestine ca. 580 and became a monk in the monastery of Theodosius. Together with John, a fellow monk, he undertook journeys to the Sinai, Egypt, and Italy. On the way he made the acquaintance of Maximus Conf. After his return he fought against the union, in 633, of Patriarch Cyrus of Alexandria with Sergius of Constantinople on the basis of the Monoenergetic formula, *mia theandrikē energeia*. In Constantinople, he managed to see to it that people there would speak in the future of neither one nor two energies. In 634, after the see had been vacant for three years, he was elected, when over 80, successor of Modestus as patriarch of Jerusalem. In a synodal letter written immediately after the election (and sent also to Honorius of Rome), S. avoided the concept of energy but claimed the independence of the two natures. In so doing, he indirectly occasioned the turn of Monoenergists to the formula *hen thelēma* (*Ekthesis* of Sergius), which S. likewise rejected. In 638 S. surrendered Jerusalem to the Arab conquerors; he died a few months later.

II. Works:

Dogmatically important works are the synodal letter to Sergius (*ep. syn.*), a letter to Arcadius of Cyprus (*ep. Arcad.*) in which he demonstrates the incompatibility of Monoenergism with Chalcedon, and a lost florilegium against Monotheletism. Important, above all, are the twenty-three Anacreontic odes (*carm.*), which are in the line of Gregory Naz., Synesius of Cyrene, and John of Gaza. With a mastery of his art he links the Chr. hymnic style with the ancient meter. *Carm.* 19 and 20 are espec. important for the topography of Jerusalem after the Persian invasion of 614. Two idiomela (*idiom.*) and some epigrams (*epigr.*) have also survived. The authentic, dogmatically rich homilies (*hom.*) are on the birth of Christ, the annunciation, the exaltation of the cross, Peter and Paul, the presentation, John the Baptist, and epiphany. A sermon on Palm Sunday, attributed to → Eulogius of Alexandria, is probably from S.

Together with John Moschus, S. composed a *Vita* of John the Almsgiver, which is preserved in fragments (*v. Jo. Eleem.*). S.'s encomium of John the Theologian has likewise survived only in fragments. The *Praises* (*laud.*) of Sts. Cyril and John (Alexandrian martyrs under Diocletian) is preserved, as is the *Narratio miraculorum* (*mir. Cyr. et Jo.*); the *Vita* (PG 87:3677-89) and the *Passio* (PG 87:3689-96) are not authentic, nor is a *Vita* of Mary of Egypt (PG 87:3697-3726) circulated under S.'s name; the story of this great penitent (similarity to Mary Magdalene) exerted a great influence in the history of piety. The commentary on the liturgy supposedly written by S. (PG 87:3201-3384) is from the 12th c. at the earliest.

W: *ep. syn.*, PG 87:3148-3200. — *ep. Arcad.*, B. Albert, C. v. Schönborn, PO 39/2 (Tournai, 1978) [Syriac text/French trans./comm.]. — *v. Jo. Eleem.*, H. Gelzer, Leontios v. Neapolis, Leben des hl. Johannes (Freiburg i.Br., 1893), 108-112. — *carm.*, M. Gigante, S. Anacreontica (Rome, 1957 [text/Italian trans.]. — H. Donner, Die anakreontischen Gedichte Nr. 19 und Nr. 20 des Patriarchen S., SAH 10 (Heidelberg, 1981). — *idiom.*, PG 87:4005-4009. — W. Christ, M. Paranikas, Anthologia graeca carminum christianorum (Leipzig, 1871), 96f. — *hom.*, PG 87:3201-3364; 77:1049-1072. — H. Usener, Rede auf die Geburt Christi: RMP 41 (1886) 500-516 [text]. — B. Steidle, Weihnachtspredigt: BenM 20 (1938) 417-428 [German trans.]. — H. Usener, Sophronii de praesentatione Domini sermo: Universitätsprogramm (Bonn, 1889), 8-18. — *epigr., laud., mir. Cyr. et Jo.*, PG 87:3421-3424, 3380-3421, 3424-3676.
L: A. Cameron, The Epigrams of S.: CQ 33 (1983) 284-292. — H. Chadwick, John Moschus and His Friend S.: JThS 25 (1975) 41-74. — G. Cosma, De oeconomia incarnationis secundum S. (Rome, 1940). — J. Duffy, The Miracles of Cyrus and John: Illinois Classical Studies 12 (1987) 169-177. — idem, Observations on S. Miracles of Cyrus and John: JThS 35 (1984) 71-90. — K. Kunze, Studien zur Legende der hl. Maria Aegyptiaca im dt. Sprachgebiet (Berlin, 1969). — T. Nissen, De ss. Cyri et Iohannis vitae formis: AnBoll 57 (1939) 65-71. — idem, Medizin u. Magie bei S.: BZ 39 (1939) 349-381. — P. Parente, Uso e significato del termine Θεοκίνητος nella controversia monoteletica: REByz 11 (1953) 241-251. — R. Riedinger, Die Nachkommen der ep. syn.: RöHM 26 (1984) 91-106. — C. v. Schönborn, S. (Paris, 1972). — H. Straubinger, Die Lehre des Patriarchen S. über die Trinität, die Inkarnation und die Person Christi: Katholik 87 (1907) 1:81-109, 175-189, 251-265. — S. Vailhé, S. le Sophiste et S. le Patriarche: ROC 7 (1902) 360-385. — G. Zuretti, S.: Didaskal. NS 4 (1926) 19-68.

G. Röwekamp

Sortes Sangallenses

The *Sortes Sangallenses* is an anonymous text so named because it is preserved in Palimpsest 908 of St. Gall. The origin of the ms. is disputed: the discoverer attributes it to Bobbio in northern Italy because of a supposed connection with that place; the editors argue for 4th c. Gaul. The *Sortes Sangallenses* consist of answers of an oracle to questions of a Chr. kind. Some of the questions are lost; the remaining ones are on subjects of everyday social and moral life, on manners of life and health, on love, home, and family, friendship and enmity, hope and fear; they deal with matters of house and possessions, choice of profession and various undertakings such as journeys and returns, as well as financial, professional, and economic cares and burdens.

W: A. Dold, R. Meister, K. Mras, Die Orakelsprüche: SAW 225, 4-5 (1948-1951) 21-72. — A. Kurfess, Zu den S. S.: SAW 5 (1953) 143-146 [emendations].
L: E. Schönbauer, Die S. S. als Erkenntnisquelle des röm. u. germanischen Rechts: AAWW 90 (1953) 23-24. — R. Weister, L. Krestan, Die Orakelsprüche: SAW 225, 5 (1951) 8-20.

C. Kasper

Soter of Rome

Acc. to the list of bishops of Rome, S. was bishop after Anicetus and before Eleutherus (ca. 166-174). An unpreserved letter to the community of Corinth is attested (Eus., *h.e.* 4.23.11). In the Middle Ages some letters and decrees were foisted onto S. (Ps.-Isidore, Gratian).

L: C. Burini, Epistolari cristiani 1 (Rome, 1990), 115. — P. Lampe, Die stadtröm. Christen (Tübingen, ²1989), 333, 338-343. — P. Nautin, Lettres et écrivains (Paris, 1961), 14f., 26-31, 44f. — T. Zahn: FGNK 5 (1893) 43-54.

R. Hanig

Sozomen

I. Life: S., the dates of whose birth and death are unknown, came from Bethelea near Gaza, where his grandfather had already been a member of the Chr. community in the mid-4th c. and had won renown for his interpretation of the scriptures (*h.e.* 5.14-17). Even during his early training S. was in contact with monastic circles. After 425 he worked as a scholasticus (lawyer) in Constantinople. There, between 443 and 450 he composed his history of the church, his only surviving work, since the epitome mentioned in *h.e.* 1.1.12 has been lost.

II. Work: The *h.e.* in nine books is consciously in the historiographical tradition of → Eusebius of Caesarea and intends to continue his work: whereas Eus. dealt with events from the ascension of Christ to the death of Licinius (*h.e.* 1.1.12), the *h.e.* of S. is devoted to the period from 323/324 (third consulate of Crispus and Constantine) to 439 (seventeenth consulate of Theodosius II (to whom the work is dedicated) (*h.e.*, Dedication 19f.). It is thus (without this being admitted) in competition with the *h.e.* of → Socrates, which was composed a little earlier and is used by S. not only materially but in the arrangement of the material (Soz., *h.e.* 7 corresponds to Soc., *h.e.* 5). S.'s presentation is thus an effort to outdo his unacknowledged predecessor both in completeness of content and in stylistic quality (in the line of classical Gr. historiography) (Photius, *cod.* 30).

In addition to using Socrates, S. draws espec. on → Rufinus, *h.e.* (without naming him but to some extent using him more than Socrates had); → Eus. Caes., *h.e.* and *v.C.*; → Athanasius, *apol. sec., v. Anton.*, and other texts; Zosimus and → Olympiodorus (who has survived only in fragments); the (lost) collection of synodal acts by → Sabinus; extracts from → Gregory Naz., Libanius, → Apollinaris of Laodicea; various stories of monks and accounts of martyrdom from the Persian world. For his own time and acc. to his own account, S. falls back on statements of eyewitnesses. In addition, his presentation repeatedly shows Palestinian local coloring.

Despite what is announced about the arrangement, the *h.e.* of S. does not in fact come down to 439 but only to 421/422 (peace with the Persians). In addition, the last book gives the impression, in comparison with the others, of being unrevised, and *h.e.* 9.17 ends rather abruptly. The reason is probably that S. died before his work was complete. Other theories suppose a later mutilation of the tradition and/or a politically motivated polishing by imperial censors.

S. is, in tendency, a rather liberal representative of eccles. orthodoxy (*h.e.* 1.1.15) and does not assign any great importance to dogm. matters (*h.e.* 3.15.10; 6.27.7). In his judgments he follows in the steps of his predecessor Socrates, except that unlike Soc. S. sides with Chrysostom in the controversy about him (*h.e.* 8). In comparison with Soc., S.'s *h.e.* gives the impression of being more anecdotal and full of legends. It describes the history of the imperial church in laudatory and triumphalist terms. The significance of the work is that it is an important supplement to Socrates' history; to it we owe many sources for the 4th c. history of councils and for the political history of the early 5th c., as well as a great deal of material on Chr. monasticism in the eastern world. A Lat. translation of parts of the work was made in the 6th c. under the direction of → Cassiodorus as a section of the *h.e. tripartita* (put together from S., Socrates, and Theodoret) by the monk → Epiphanius Scholasticus (→ Theodore, Lector).

W: *h.e.*, J. Bidez, G. C. Hansen, GCS NF 4. — C. D. Hartranft, NPNF 2/2:181-427 [English trans.]. — *h.e.* 1-4, B. Grillet, G. Sabbah, SC 306, 418. — Cassiodorus, *hist.*, W. Jacob, R. Hanslik, CSEL 71.
L: P. Allen, War: StPatr 19 (1989) 3-8. — G. Bardy, S.: DThC 14, 2465-2471. — P. Battifol, S.: ByZ 7 (1898) 265-284. — G. F. Chesnut, Christian Histories (Macon, ²1986), 199-207. — G. Downey, Perspective: GRBS 6 (1965) 57-70. — W. Eltester, S.: PRE 3A:1240-1248. — F. Geppert, Quellen (Leipzig, 1898). — G. C. Hansen, Einleitung zur GCS Edition (Berlin, ²1995), IX-LXVII. — idem, Prosarhythmus: BySl 26 (1965) 82-93. — L. Jeep, Quellenuntersuchungen (Leipzig, 1884). — G. Loeschke, S: RE3 18:541-547. — G. Moravcsik, Byzantinoturcica 1 (Berlin, ²1958), 510-512. — A. Primmer, S.: Gn. 39 (1967) 350-358. — J. Rosenstein, Untersuchungen: FDG 1 (1862) 58-72. — G. Schoo, Quellen (Berlin, 1911). — F. Winkelmann, Kirchengeschichtswerke: BySl 37 (1976) 175-177.

J. ULRICH

Spelunca Thesaurorum/ Cave of Treasures

The book *Cave of Treasures* tells the legend of a cave in which Adam hid a treasure of gold, frankincense, and myrrh that was intended for the later wise men from the East (see Mt 2:11), and which also served the remaining pre-flood patriarchs as their final resting place. The cycle of legends in the *Spelunca Thesaurorum* is closely connected with the Jerusalem tradition concerning Golgotha, the hill of crucifixion, as the center of the world. After the flood the treasure was buried under Golgotha along with the bones of Adam, which at the crucifixion came alive again when the blood of the redeemer flowed down on them. The *Spelunca Thesaurorum* combines various eastern legends of Adam (*Testamentum Adae, Vita Adae et Evae, Pugna Adae*) and Jewish apocrypha (*Apocalypsis Mosae, Book of Enoch*) into a garland of stories and probably took its final form in 6th-c. Mesopotamia. The work had an immense influence on popular piety (legends of the three kings) and was known and loved by both Nestorians and Jacobites. The *Spelunca Thesaurorum* has come down in two Syr. versions and was translated at an early date into various oriental languages.

W: C. Bezold (Amsterdam, 1981 = Leipzig, 1883-1888) [Syriac-Arabic text/German trans.]. — E. A. Wallis Budge (London, 1927) [English trans.]. — S. Min Ri, CSCO 486/487 [Syriac text/French trans.]. — Z. Avalichvili, La version géorgienne: ROC 26 (1927/28) 381-395. — H. Poirier, Une version copte: Or. 52 (1983) 415-423. — A. Battista, B. Bagatti (Jerusalem, 1979) [Arabic text/Italian trans.].
L: B. Bagatti, Qualche chiarificazioni: ED 32 (1979) 277-284. — A. Götze, Nachwirkung der Schatzhöhle: ZS 3

(1925) 33-71, 158-177. — U. Monneret de Villard, Leggende orientali sui Magi (Rome, 1952). — S. Min Ri, Problème d'analyse littéraire: OCA 229 (1987). — idem, Testament d'Adam: OCA 236 (1990) 111-122.

P. BRUNS

Statuta Ecclesiae Antiqua

The *Statuta Ecclesiae Antiqua* came into existence in the period after the barbarian invasions (442-506) in the area covered by the Roman province of Gallia Narbonensis (Provence) into which the Arian Visigoths had moved as a result of Constantine's settlement policy. The *Statuta Ecclesiae Antiqua,* modeled on monastic rules, is an anonymous compilation of ordinances for the strengthening of the church's structures and the exclusion of heresy. In the course of textual transmission it spread quickly in France, Spain, and Italy because of its mistaken attribution to the "fourth Council of Carthage." Using the → *Didache,* the → *Apostolic Constitutions,* and conciliar decrees (Orange, Vaison 441/442 down to Agde 506), and espec. the works of → Gennadius of Marseilles (who probably commissioned the work or was its author), western and eastern traditions are combined by the editor in the three sections of the work: (1) Examination for the episcopate: here the requirements for consecration are set before the candidates for sees; the questions have to do not only with character and faith but with practical dealings with communities. (2) Eighty-nine disciplinary canons, in an unorganized sequence, aim at strengthening the eccles. system of offices (proepiscopal/propresbyteral and antidiaconal attitude; other ministries; laity) in the daily, liturg., and sacramental life of the community. A strict separation from noncatholics (penal canons, excommunication) takes precedence over the missionary task of the church but emphasizes moral and caritative activity within the church. (3) Thirteen canons depict in detail the hierarchy of eccles. offices and ministries in the form of prescriptions for ordinations.

W: Gennadius, Liber ecclesiasticorum dogmatum, PL 58, 83. — *De viris inlustribus,* A. Bernoulli (Frankfurt a.M., 1968 = Leipzig, ¹1895). — *De haeresibus,* PL 42. — *ep. de fide,* C. Caspari (Paris, 1963).
L: C. Munier, Les SEA (Paris, 1960).

A. SCHRÖDER

Stephen, Acts of

Acts of the first martyr, Stephen, which expand on the account in Acts 6-7, are preserved only in Coptic and Arabic. In 415, presbyter → Lucian of Caphargamala composed an account of the finding of the bones of Stephen.

W: Y. Abd al-Masih, A Coptic Apocryphon: Muséon 70 (1957) 329-347 [Coptic text]. — idem, A. Khater, An arabic Apocryphon: SOC. C 13 (1968/69) 161-198 [Arabic text].

G. ROWEKAMP

Stephen of Bostra

S. of Bostra lived probably at the end of the 7th and beginning of the 8th c. It is uncertain whether he was bishop of the city in Arabia. John Damascene is the first to cite his work against the Jews (*Logos kata tōn Ioudaiōn*) in which he takes up, among other things, Jewish "iconoclasm." Together with → Jerome of Jerusalem, S. was a representative of the anti-Judaism that reached a new high point in connection with the Jewish reaction to the advance of the Persians and Arabs in the 7th c.

W: G. Mercati: ThQ 77 (1895) 663-668 (= idem, Opere minori 1, ST 76 [Rome, 1937], 202-206).
L: H. G. Beck, Kirche u. theol. Lit. (Munich, 1959), 297, 332, 447.

G. RÖWEKAMP

Stephen Gobarus

Monophysite author S. G., a supporter of the "tritheism" of John Philoponus, lived probably in the 6th c. He composed a florilegium (possibly titled *Theognosta*) on fifty-two questions on theol., anthropological, and cosmological subjects, on which Photius (*cod.* 532) reports in detail. Following the *Sic et non* method, official teaching and deviant views are brought together on each question.

W: PG 103:1092-1105. — Photius, *cod.* 232.
L: G. Bardy, Le florilège d'Étienne Gobar: REByz 5 (1947) 5-30; 7 (1949) 51f. — A. v. Harnack, The "sic et non" of St.: HThR 16 (1932) 205-234.

G. RÖWEKAMP

Stephen of Larissa

S. was successor to Proclus as bishop of Larissa in Thessaly in the time of Justinian I. After being deposed and imprisoned on canonical grounds by Epiphanius of Constantinople (520-535), S. appealed in two letters for the support of the bishop of Rome. He did so on the grounds of Roman sovereignty over western Illyricum acc. to canon 28 of the Council of

Chalcedon, and the role of the bishop of Thessalonica as papal vicar. Theodosius, a suffragan bishop of Larissa, presented these letters and twenty-seven documents on the vicarial function of the bishop of Thessalonica to a synod held in Rome in 521 with the pope presiding. The synod did not decide on S.'s case, but it did emphasize again Roman jurisdiction over western Illyricum.

W: PL 65:34-42. — C. Silva Tarouca, Epistularum Romanorum Pontificum ad Vicarios per Illyricum aliosque episcopos collectio Thessalonicensis (Rome, 1937), 2-16 [text].

C. SCHMIDT

Stephen I of Rome

S. became bishop of Rome (May 12 or 28, 254) between two waves of persecution. His externally peaceful pontificate was shaken by an intrachurch conflict over the validity of baptisms administered by heretics. In the controversy with his main opponent, → Cyprian of Carthage, S. played a decisive role in the development of the papacy. His correspondence from the period of the heretical baptism controversy has come down only in fragmentary and indirect form in the collection of Cyprian's letters (*ep.* 74; 75). Against Cyprian S. took the Roman view, which excludes any rebaptism, "since nothing new is to be introduced that has not been handed down" (*ep.* 74.1). The result was a break that was healed only after S.'s death (Aug. 2, 257). Other writings are forgeries.

W: Cyprian, *ep.*, W. Hartel, CSEL 3/2. — G. F. Diercks, CCL 3A. — J. Baer, BKV² 60:357-392 [German trans.].
L: J. Ernst, Papst S. u. der Ketzertaufstreit (Mainz, 1905). — S. Hall, St. and the One Baptism: StPatr 17 (1982) 796-798. — H. Kirchner, Der Ketzertaufstreit zwischen Karthago u. Rom: ZKG 81 (1970) 290-307. — J. Srutwa, The Gospel of Mt 16, 16-19 as an Argument of Pope S. for the Roman Primacy: ACra 27 (1995) 323-328.

S. C. KESSLER, SJ

Stephen bar Sudayle

S. was active toward the end of the 5th and beginning of the 6th c. as a monk in the neighborhood of Edessa, where he died ca. 550. He lived in Egypt for a time and became familiar with the Origenist thought of Evagrius Pont., whose writings he translated into Syriac and to the further spread of which he contributed. His teaching on the consubstantiality of all things with the supreme nature, on universal reconciliation, and on a millennialist eschatology brought

strong opposition from notable Syr. scholars (Philoxenus of Mabbug, Jacob of Sarug). S. composed a work on the "hidden mysteries of the house of God," which, under the title "Book of St. Hierotheus," was fruitful for mysticism and shows many parallels with Ps.-Dionysius. S. also composed commentaries on the Pss that have thus far not been published.

W: F. S. Marsh, Book of Holy Hierotheos (Amsterdam, 1979 = London, 1927) [text/English trans./comm.].
L: A. L. Frothingham Jr., Stephen bar Sudaili. The Syrian Mystic (Amsterdam, 1981 = Leiden, 1886). — G. Furlani, Un manoscritto Beirutino: RSO 11 (1926) 103-107. — I. Hausherr, L'influence du "Livre de s. Hiérothée": OrChr 30 (1933) 176-211. — T. Jansma, Philoxenus' Letter concerning St.: Muséon 87 (1974) 79-86. — G. Widengren, Researches in Syrian Mysticism: Numen 8 (1961) 161-198.

P. BRUNS

Strategius

S. was a monk in the monastery of St. Sabas near Jerusalem and after 614 composed an account of the Persian invasion; it survives complete only in Georgian and Arabic. The information on destruction in and near Jerusalem is not substantiated by archeology. This S. is not the same person as the S. mentioned by John Moschus nor as → Antiochius, another monk of the St. Sabas monastery, who likewise wrote about the Persian invasion. In the Arab. version, S. is called Eustratius.

W: PG 86:3228-3233, 3236-3268 [Greek frags. under Modestus of Jerusalem]. — G. Garitte, CSCO 202/203 [Georgian text/French trans.]. — idem, CSCO 340/341; CSCO 347/348 [Arabic text/French trans.]. — F. Conybeare, Antiochus Strategos' Account of the Sack of Jerusalem in A.D. 614: EHR 25 (1910) 502-517 [English trans.].
L: G. Graf, Die Einnahme Jerusalems durch die Perser 614: HlL 67 (1923) 19-29. — J. T. Milik, La topographie de Jérusalem à la fin de l'Époque byzantine: MUSJ 27 (1961) 125-189. — P. Peeters, La Prise de Jérusalem par les Perses: Récherches d'histoire et de philologie orientale 1 (Brussels, 1951), 78-116.

G. RÖWEKAMP

Successus of Diocaesarea

S. was bishop of Diocaesarea in Isauria and died ca. 440. Fragments survive of his correspondence (*ep.*) with Cyril Alex. in connection with the controversy over the Union creed of 433. In addition, there are fragments on Gen 4:7b and 22:56-9 (*fr.*) in a catena on Genesis.

W: *ep.*, ACO 1, 1, 6, 158-161 [Greek text]. — ACO 1, 5, 299-302 [Latin trans.]. — A. van den Roey, Deux fragments inédits des lettres de Succensus: Muséon 55 (1942) 87-92.

— *fr.*, R. Devreesse, Les Anciens Commentateurs grecs de l'Octateuque et des Rois (ST 201) (Rome, 1959), 180.

G. RÖWEKAMP

Sulpicius Severus

I. Life: S., who was b. ca. 363 in Aquitania and d. ca. 420, came from the wealthy provincial nobility and, after studying rhetoric in Bordeaux, worked as a lawyer. After the death of his wife, and under the influence of his friend Paulinus of Nola and with the support of Bishop Martin of Tours, he renounced his inherited property in 394 and turned to an ascetic way of life. It is unlikely that he was ordained a priest (despite Gennadius, *vir. ill.* 19). In 399 S. established a monastic organization in Primuliacum (a place not further identifiable in Périgord), where he spent the rest of his life. His writings were composed between 395 and 404; the claim that in his later years S. punished himself by silence for a temporary turn to Pelagianism is an invention of Gennadius.

II. Works: 1. *Vita sancti Martini* (*Mart.*), 396, a life of Bishop Martin of Tours in the tradition of ancient (Suetonius) and Chr. biography (espec. Athanasius, *v. Anton.*), most of it composed during Martin's lifetime. The *Vita* shows S. to be an aristocrat educated in literature and a man who zealously champions the ideals of monastic asceticism and defends the bishop, whom he honors as a model, against contemporary criticism. The *Vita* is the best source for the life of St. Martin (despite chronol. problems and edifying miracle stories). **2.** Three *Epistolae* (*ep.*), 397-398 the only letters that have come down (with supplements to the *Vita*) from S.'s extensive correspondence: (1) *Ad Eusebium* (defense of Martin's miraculous powers), (2) *Ad Aurelium Diaconum* (obituary), (3) *Ad Bassulam* (on Martin's death and burial). **3.** *Dialogi* (*dial.*), 403/404. A supplement to *Mart.* in the form of a two-day dialogue. There was originally probably a single dialogue which the tradition then divided into three parts. The form of the early Chr. dialogue, which S. expanded by including an account of a journey, made it possible to compare eastern monasticism in a vivid way with western monasticism as stamped by Martin and to paint a picture of the saint by means of a varied series of "miracle" stories told by Martin's disciple Gallus. **4.** *Chronica* (*chron.*), two books containing a calendar from creation to the year 400 C.E.; this is S.'s most important work and was completed in 404. Book 1 runs from creation to the Babylonian exile, book 2 from that point to the present. The connecting thread in the chronology is the biblical story down to John Hyrcanus (*chron.* 2.26); this is followed (without falling back on a millennialist computation,

[2.27.5]) by Jewish history to the death of Herod (2.27), the persecutions of Christians and the Constantinian revolution (2.28-34), the Arian controversy (2.35-45, focused on Hilary of Poitiers), and Priscillianism (2.46-51). It is clear that (after the composition of 2.27) S. weakened the originally apocalyptic intention of his *chron.* (calculation of the end time; the idea of *Nero redivivus* remains). The story of Priscillian links *chron.* to the writings on Martin and is a primary source, while S.'s use of sources (OT, the continuation of, among others, Flavius Josephus, Tacitus, Eusebius) is a virtuoso Chr. example of the epitome type of historical writing that prevailed at the end of the 4th c.

W: *Mart.*, C. Halm, CSEL 1:109-135. — J. Fontaine, SC 133-135. — C. Mohrmann, J. W. Smit, L. Canali, in: Vite dei Santi dal III al VI secolo 4, ed. C. Mohrmann, o. O (Milan, 1975), IX-XXX, 1-67, 241-290 [text/Italian trans./comm.]. — P. Bihlmeyer, BKV² 20:17-53 [German trans.]. — B. M. Peebles, FaCh 7:101-140. — *ep.*, C. Halm, CSEL 1:138-151. — J. Fontaine, SC 133:317-345. — P. Bihlmeyer, BKV² 20:54-69 [German trans.]. — B. M. Peebles, FaCh 7:141-160. — *dial.*, C. Halm, CSEL 1:152-216. — P. Bihlmeyer, BKV² 20:70-147 [German trans.]. — B. M. Peebles, FaCh 7:161-251. — *chron.*, C. Halm, CSEL 1:3-105. — A. Lavertujon, La chronique de Sulpice Sévère, 2 vols. (Paris, 1896, 1899) [text/French trans./comm.]. — A. Roberts, NPNF 2. ser. 11:71-122 [English trans.].
L: J. Bernays, Ueber die Chronik des S.: Gesammelte Schriften 2 (Berlin, 1885 = Hildesheim, 1971), 81-200. — S. Dagemark, Prayer: la preghiera nel tardo antico (Rome, 1999), 361-388. — F. Ghizzoni, S. (Rome, 1983). — R. Klein, Die Praefatio der Martinsvita des S.: Antike u. Unterricht 31/4 (1988) 5-32. — S. Prete, I Cronica di S. (Vatican City, 1955). — C. Stancliffe, St. Martin and His Hagiographer. History and Miracle in S. (Oxford, 1983). — G. K. van Andel, The Christian Concept of History in the Chronicle of S. (Amsterdam, 1976). — S. Weber, Die Chronik des S. (Trier, 1997).

K. H. SCHWARTE

Sunday Letter

The so-called *Sunday Letter*, which has come down in various languages (Greek, Armenian, Syriac, Arabic, Ethiopic, Latin), is a letter of Christ, supposedly sent from heaven, on the sanctification of Sunday. The Arabic is probably the oldest surviving version. The work was probably written between 451 and 453 under antipatriarch Theodosius in Jerusalem.

W: M. Bittner, DÖAW. PH 51 (Vienna, 1905), 1-233 [Greek, Armenian, Syriac, Arabic, Ethiopic text]. — G. Graf: ZS 6 (1928) 10-23 [Arabic text of Cod. Monac. arab. 1067]. — H. Delehaye, Un exemplaire de la lettre tombée du ciel: RSR 18 (1928) 164-169 [Latin text].
L: M. v. Esbroeck, La lettre sur le dimanche: AnBoll 107 (1989) 267-284.

G. RÖWEKAMP

Syagrius

The otherwise unknown S. composed (mid-4th c.?) an anti-Arian work *De fide*, which is regarded as lost. But the account in Gennadius (*vir. ill.* 66) matches so exactly the *Regulae definitionum prolatae contra haereticos* (*reg.*) of Ps.-Jerome that the latter work is probably the *De fide*. The *reg.* is important for the history of Arianism. On the other hand, it can hardly be called upon as a witness to Priscillianist teaching on the Trinity, since the work contains no sure reference to Priscillianism. Furthermore, it is difficult to identify S. with the Bishop Syagrius consecrated in 433 (Hydatius, *chron.* 2.22), so that any link to Spain, much less Galicia, remains uncertain.

A work titled *De fide et symbolo fidei* in seven books is lost; on linguistic grounds Gennadius does not assign all the books to S. In a ms. of Rheims, *reg.* is followed by seven treatises on the creed; it is possible that these are the writings mentioned by Gennadius. But the question of authorship remains open.

W: K. Künstle, Antipriscilliana (Freiburg i.Br., 1905), 142-159 [text]. — PLS 3:132-140.
L: C. P. Caspari, Alte u. neue Quellen (Christiania, 1879), 186-195. — H. Chadwick, Priscillian (Oxford, 1976). — K. Künstle, Antipriscilliana (Freiburg i.Br., 1905). — G. Morin, Pastor et S.: RBen 10 (1893) 385-394.

E. Reichert

Symmachus, Exegete

In the second half of the 5th c. an otherwise unknown exegete named S. composed an explanation of Prov, of which 357 fragments are contained in the catena in *Cod. Vat. gr.* 1802. He is also considered to be the author of a commentary on the Song (*comm. in Cant.*), of which the explanation of Song 6:9-8:14 survives in a Syr. translation. S. cultivated chiefly the allegorical and moral senses and interpreted the work on ascetical lines.

W: *comm. in Cant.*, C. van den Eynde, La version syriaque du commentaire de Grégoire de Nysse sur le cantique des cantiques (Leuven/Louvain, 1939), 77-89, 104-116 [Syriac text/French trans.].
L: M. Faulhaber, Hohelied-Proverbien u. Predigercatenen (Vienna, 1902), 90-94. — G. Mercati, Pro Symmacho (Rome, 1941), 91-93. — M. Richard, Fragments du commentaire de S. Hippolyte: Muséon 78 (1965) 286f.

P. Bruns

Symmachus of Rome

Deacon S., from Sardinia, was elected bishop on Nov. 22, 498, by the majority of the Roman clergy, who were dissatisfied with the conciliatory policy of Anastasius II toward the eastern church during the Acacian schism. The minority party, friendly toward Byzantium, elected archpriest Lawrence as antipope. This double election led to conflict in Rome that was like a civil war; King Theodoric was called upon to mediate and, beginning in 506, decided definitively for S., who died on July 19, 514.

S.'s literary work reflects his disputed position as Roman bishop during the Laurentian and Acacian schisms. Surviving are twenty-four letters (*ep. pontif.*) having to do with the theol. conflict around Acacius, jurisdictional disputes between Arles and Vienne, and synodal decrees. The so-called Symmachian Forgeries/Documents came into being in order to justify papal claims; they tried to prove that the pope cannot be judged by anyone.

W: *ep. pontif.*, A. Thiel, Epistulae Romanorum Pontificum Genuinae (Hildesheim, 1974 = 1868), 641-734 [text]. — T. Mommsen, Acta Synhodorum, MGH. AA 12:399-455 [text]. — A new edition of the "Symmachianischen Documenta" by Wirbelauer is in preparation, MGH. GPR 2.
L: J. D. Alchermes, Petrine Politics: Pope S. and the Rotunda of St. Andrew: CHR 81 (1995) 1-40. — A. Di Berardino (ed.), Patrologia 4 (Genoa, 1996), 132-134. — A. Grillmeier, Jesus der Christus 2/1 (Freiburg i.Br., 1986), 349-351 (English, Christ in Christian Tradition, vol. 2/1 [London, 1987]). — P. A. B. Llewellyn, The Church during the Laurentian Schism: ChH 45 (1976) 417-427. — J. Richards, The Popes and the Papacy in the Early Middle Ages (London, 1979), 69-99. — C. Sotinel, S.: DHP 609-1611. — E. Wirbelauer, Der Konflikt zwischen Laurentius u. S. (Munich, 1993). — S. Vacca, Prima sedes a nemine iudicatur (Rome, 1993), 33-78.

S. C. Kessler, SJ

Symmachus, Translator

S. lived in the second half of the 2nd c. and made a Gr. translation of the OT, which Origen made part of his Hexapla. Acc. to Eusebius (*h.e.* 6.17) and Jerome (*vir. ill.* 54), S. was an Ebionite; acc. to Epiphanius (*mens.* 54), he was a Samaritan who went over to Judaism. Eusebius also mentions writings in which S. supported Ebionite views while appealing to a gospel of Matthew; a woman named Juliana supposedly got them from S. and gave them to Origen (see also Palladius, *h. Laus.* 147). S.'s method of translating primarily the meaning was very much esteemed by Jerome.

W: → Origen.
L: S. P. Brock, Bibelübersetzungen 1/2: TRE 6:169. — A. v. Harnack, Geschichte der altchr. Lit. 1/1 (Leipzig, ²1958), 209-212. — J. Lust, A Lexicon of S.'s Translation of the

Psalms: EThL 73 (1997) 87-92. — H. J. Schoeps, Aus frühchr. Zeit (Tübingen, 1950), 82-119.

K. BALKE

Symphosius

S., who also appears as Symposius and whose existence is from time to time completely doubted, is considered the author (perhaps from Africa) of a collection of a hundred riddling poems (*Centum epigrammata tristicha aenigmata*) that are preceded by a poetic preface and to which further riddles, not from S., are added. The work, whose subjects are from natural history and everyday life, was at one time attributed to Lactantius, since the name S. was wrongly identified with Lactantius's lost *Symposium*. The date given to the work varies widely; it was written perhaps between 360/370 and 398. More importantly, down to the Carolingian period it was much used and imitated, espec. by the Anglo-Saxons. In 1540 Joachim Camerarius translated it into Greek.

W: D. R. Shackleton Bailey (ed.), Anthologia Latina 1/1 (Stuttgart, 1982), Nr. 281. — F. Glorie, CCL 133A:621-723 [text/English trans.]. — R. T. Ohl (Philadelphia, 1928) [text/English trans./comm.].
L: HLL 5:249-252. — M. J. Muños Jiménez, Algunos aspectos de los Aenigmatos: EM 55 (1987) 307-312. — Z. Pavlovski, The Riddler's Microcosm: CM 39 (1988) 219-251. — PLRE 2:1047.

B. WINDAU

Sympronianus

No details are known of the person and life of S. His writings are lost, among them at least two letters to → Pacian of Barcelona, the content of which can be inferred only approximately from the adversarial writings of Pacian. Acc. to Pacian, S. held the view that penance is impossible after baptism and that the church cannot forgive mortal sins. A treatise on Novatianism, which S. attached to a letter, can be extensively reconstructed from the mostly verbatim citations in the third letter of Pacian.

W/L: → Pacian. L. Wohleb, Ges. Aufsätze zur Kulturgesch. Spaniens 1 (Münster, 1930), 25-35.

E. REICHERT

Synesius of Cyrene

I. **Life:** B. ca. 370 in Cyrene as the child of a prominent and long established family, S. studied in Alexandria under Hypatia, the Neoplatonic philosopher. From 399 to 402 (or: 397-400), as emissary of Cyrenaica in Constantinople, he conveyed, evidently with success, a petition for tax reduction. After his return he spent a literarily fruitful year in Alexandria (marriage 403/404) and on his estate in Cyrene, but as a man of rank he also took part in political affairs and, from 405 on, espec. in the defense against invasions by nomadic tribes. The community of Ptolemais in 410 (or 411; alternative proposal: as early as 406) elected him its bishop, and, despite his publicly stated reservations (*ep.* 105), Patriarch Theophilus Alex. in 411 (or 412) ordained him metropolitan of the Pentapolis. Affairs of office, more intense efforts to defend the province, controversy with prefect Andronicus culminating in the latter's excommunication (*ep.* 41/42), and espec. the deaths of his children and the loss of many friendships overshadowed the remainder of his life (d. ca. 413).

II. **Works:** S. wrote a really literary Greek in which he constantly harked back to the classical authors. In contrast to his *Hymns* (and to *catast.* and *hom.*), his prose works contain no Chr. language.

1. The *Address on Kingship* (*regn.*) is a mirror for princes. S. probably submitted his encomium in the presence of Emperor Arcadius (*stephanōtikos logos*) to a radical revision later on.

2. The novel-like *Egyptian Tales* (*provid.*), which were also written in Constantinople in two stages, represent the Gothic crisis in Constantinople (399/400) in the allegorical form of an Egypt. myth (Osiris and Typhos), which the reader had to decipher. A centerpiece of the work is the farewell address of the royal father on divine providence and the problem of its discontinuity (1.9-11); an intervention of the gods is first prophesied (1.18) and then (while retaining the element of mystery) narrated (2.1ff.).

3. In Constantinople S. gave his patron Paeonius a planisphere, accompanied by a letter of praise and instruction (*astrolab.* = *De dono astrolabii*).

4. The jocular *Praise of Baldness* (*calv.*), written in the sophistic manner, was perhaps an early work and a counterpart to Dion of Prusa's *Praise of Hair*: baldness is deemed worthy of the divine.

5. Soon after his return from Constantinople S., "inspired by God" (*ep.* 154), composed a philosophical treatise "on dreams" (*insomm.*). The art of interpreting dreams is praised for its accessibility and given a basis in Neoplatonic psychology (conception of pneuma).

6. At about the same time (Alexandria, 403/404) S. wrote his *Dion* (or: "on life acc. to his model"), a combination of proptreptic and biography (a monograph on Dion of Prusa and an autobiography). S.

defends his humanistic ideal of integrating rhetoric and philosophy; he takes a position against both Chr. (uneducated monks) and pagan despisers of a graduated, comprehensive literary education.

7. From S.'s time as bishop two public addresses are preserved (*catast.* 1-2, the second probably in the form of an open letter), which were occasioned by the nomadic invasions. *Ep.* 41 is also an address. In addition, there are two fragmentary Easter sermons (*hom.* 1-2), the second addressed to the newly baptized (with a possible doubtful appendix).

8. Nine *Hymns* (*hymn.*) in old-fashioned meters and doricizing Greek have come down, which attest to an impressive vision of Neoplatonic philosophy and Chr. faith. Their main subjects are the ascent to the divine, the self-unfolding of the divine Triad, the beauty and harmony of the cosmos, the descent and ascent of the Son of God and the soul, and a prayer for spiritual and earthly blessings. *Hymns* 9 and 1 have no explicit Chr. tonality, but 2, 5, and 4 as well, take up Chr. ideas, while 3 and espec. 6-8 are to be called hymns to Christ (6: Epiphany; 8: Ascension). Most of the hymns were probably written in the period between the journey to Constantinople and episcopal office; their relative chronology cannot be determined with certainty.

9. Finally S. has left 156 letters (*ep.*). espec. to private individuals as well as to his brother Euoptius (*ep.* 5; 105) and to Hypatia (154; 16), but also, for example, to Theophilus Alex. (66-69; 90) and to priests (4; 11; see 41/42). The letters cover almost the entire period of S.'s life that is known to us, but espec. 405-407 and the late years 410/411-413. The Byz. Middle Ages treasured them greatly as models of letterwriting.

Not from S. is *hymn.* 10. *Ep.* 157-59 are not authentic. An alchemistic commentary on Ps.-Democritus in dialogue form is pseudepigraphical.

III. S. and Christianity: It does not seem that S. *converted* from a strongly traditional paganism to Christianity. On the other hand, it is an open question whether before his years as bishop S. showed an increasing tendency to express himself more strongly in Chr. ways of thought and language. Perhaps he grew up in a Chr. family (Cyrenaica was already heavily Christianized in the 4th/5th c.). He probably received baptism well before his election as bishop (despite Evagrius Scholasticus, *h.e.* 1.15), perhaps as a result of his marriage, which was blessed by Theophilus (*ep.* 105). It was mainly his sense of political responsibility that led him to episcopal office; he expressly formulated his reservations in an open letter (*ep.* 105): his remaining married, his conviction

of the preexistence of souls and the eternity of the world, as well as his symbolic interpretation of the resurrection. S. continued to follow a Neoplatonism heavily influenced by Porphyry (and had a high regard for the Chaldean oracles). Yet as a bishop he took a decisive position against the Eunomians (*ep.* 4). Hellenism and Christianity formed a tension-filled unity in S.

W: *opera omnia*, A. Garzya (Turin, 1989) [text/Italian trans.]. — N. Terzaghi (Rome, 1944) [text: opuscula]; ²1949 [text/comm.: hymn.]. — *ep.*, A. Garzya (Rome, 1979) [text]. — A. FitzGerald (Leipzig, 1926/30) [English trans.]. — *hymn.*, C. Lacombrade, CUFr (Paris, 1978) [text/French trans./comm.]. — A. Dell'Era (Rome, 1968) [text/Italian trans.]. — J. Gruber, H. Strohm, BKAW 2, NF 82 (Heidelberg, 1991) [text/German trans./comm.]. — *regn.*, C. Lacombrade (Paris, 1951) [French trans.]. — J. G. Krabinger (Munich, 1825) [German trans.]. — *calv.*, idem (Stuttgart, 1834) [German trans.]. — *provid.*, idem (Sulzbach, 1835) [German trans.]. — S. Nicolosi (Padua, 1959) [Italian trans./comm.]. — *insomn.*, W. Lang (Tübingen, 1926 = Würzburg, 1979) [German trans./comm.]. — D. Susanetti (Bari, 1992) [text/Italian trans./comm.]. — *Dion*, K. Treu, SQAW 5 (Berlin, 1959) [text/German trans.]. — idem, TU 71 (Berlin, 1958) [comm.]. — *astrolab.*, G. Stramondo (Catania, 1964) [text/Italian trans./comm.]. — *astrolab., catast., ep.* (selections), J. Vogt, Begegnung mit S. (Darmstadt, 1985) [German trans.].
L: G. Albert, Goten (Paderborn, 1984), 23-85. — D. T. Barnes, S. in Constantinople: GRBS 26 (1985) 93-112. — idem, When Did S. Become Bishop of Ptolemais?: GRBS 26 (1985) 325-329. — J. H. Barkhuizen, S., hymn. 8: Early Christian Poetry, ed. J. den Boeft (Leiden, 1993), 263-271. — J. Bregman, S. (Berkeley, 1982). — A. Cameron, S. and Late Roman Cyrenaica: Journal of Roman Archaeology 5 (1992) 419-430. — idem, J. Long, Barbarians and Politics (Berkeley, 1993) (*prov.* [English trans./comm.]). — E. Cavalcanti, Studi Eunomiani (Rome, 1976), 106-128. — J. Coman, Converti véritable?: Aug. 27 (1987) 237-245. — W. Cramer, Zweigewaltenlehre: RQ 72 (1977) 43-56. — A. Dihle, Gewissensentscheidung: FS C. Colpe (Würzburg, 1990), 324-329. — S. Elm, Isis' Loss: ZAC 1 (1997) 96-115. — H. A. Gärtner, Königtum: FS A. Dihle (Göttingen, 1993), 105-121. — A. Garzya, Dion: JÖB 22 (1973) 1-14. — W. Fritz, Briefe (Leipzig, 1898). — E. Gallicet, Inni: CClCr 4 (1983) 409-418. — G. Grützmacher, S. (Leipzig, 1913). — W. Hagl, Arcadius (Stuttgart, 1997). — I. Hermelin, Briefe (Uppsala, 1934). — R. Keydell, Kleine Schriften (Leipzig, 1982), 377-390, 677-679. — C. Lacombrade, S. (Paris, 1951). — idem, Hypatia: RAC 16:956-967. — M. Lattke, Hymnus (Göttingen, 1991), 294-296. — W. Liebeschuetz, Municipal Politics: Byz. 55 (1985) 146-164. — idem, Bishop: Byz. 56 (1986) 180-195. — idem, Barbarians and Bishops (Oxford, 1990), 228-235, 253-272. — H.-I. Marrou, La "conversion" de S.: REG 65 (1952) 474-484. — idem, S. and Alexandrian Neoplatonism: Conflict between Paganism and Christianity, ed. A. Momigliano (Oxford, 1963), 126-150. — A. Piñero Sáenz, La imagen del filósofo: CFC 9 (1975) 133-200. — H. Rahn, Literatur u. Leben: FS H. Hörner (Heidelberg, 1990), 231-255 (*Dion*). — B.-A. Roos, S. (Lund, 1991). — D. Roques, S. et la Cyrénaïque du Bas-Empire (Paris, 1987). — idem, Études sur la Corre-

spondance (Brussels, 1989). — L. de Salvo, Sinesio e l'amministrazione: La Cirenaica in età antica, ed. E. Catanni, S. M. Marengo (Pisa, 1998), 161-175. — O. Seeck, Studien zu S.: Ph. 52 (1894) 442-483. — H. Seng, Untersuchungen zum Vokabular u. zur Metrik in den Hymnen des S. (Frankfurt a.M., 1996). — K. Smolak, Himmelfahrt: JÖB 20 (1971) 7-30. — H. Strohm, Hymnendichtung: Hermes 93 (1965) 47-54. — W. Theiler, Forschungen zum Neuplatonismus (Berlin, 1966), 252-301. — K. Thraede, Hymnus I: RAC 16, 934. — F. Tinnefeld, Philosophie: FS W. Schmid (Bonn, 1975), 139-179. — idem, Chronologie: Klio 74 (1992) 547-549. — S. Vollenweider, Neuplatonische u. chr. Theologie bei S. (Göttingen, 1985). — idem, Bischofsamt: StPatr 18 (1986) 233-237. — U. v. Wilamowitz, Kleine Schriften 2 (Berlin, 1941), 163-191.

S. VOLLENWEIDER

T

Tabula Paschalis Petrocoriensis

A marble Easter table from Périgueux contains a list of ninety-one dates (month and day) for Easter; the end is lost; acc. to the brief heading, when one comes to the end of the list, one is to start from the beginning again. The origin of the table is disputed, as is the chronol. reference of the cycle: it probably begins in 631. The manner of reckoning probably depends on that of Dionysius Exiguus.

W: A. Mai: SVNC 5 (1831) 69 [text].
L: É. le Blant, Nouveau recueil (Paris, 1892), Nr. 280. — A. Cordoliani, La table pascale: CCMéd 4 (1961) 57-60. — B. Krusch, Die Einführung des griech. Paschalritus: NA 9 (1884) 129-141.

K. Fitschen

Tatian the Syrian

I. Life: Acc. to himself, T. came from the land of the Assyrians (*orat.* 42), that is, from the northern Mesopotamian-Syrian area, studied philosophy, and finally went to Rome, where he became a Christian and a student of Justin. After the latter's martyrdom, T. separated himself from the Roman community and returned to his old country, where he was active as an encratite, rejecting marriage and the eating of meat and wine (Irenaeus, *haer.* 1.28). Acc. to Epiphanius (*haer.* 46.1), he carried his encratism so far as to replace the wine with water during the Mass.

II. Works: Of T.'s numerous works only two survive: the *Address to the Greeks* (*Logos pros Hellēnas*), written in Greek ca. 165, and the → *Diatessaron*, which has come down in numerous eastern translations. The former is less a defense of Christianity than it is a promotional work addressed to educated Greeks and preaching a turn from worldly wisdom to the supposedly barbarian philosophy of Christianity.

T. derives his proof of Christianity from the great age of the divine writings, on which even the pagan philosophers themselves had drawn. On the one hand, he combats Gr. philosophy, which has split into schools, but, on the other, in his teaching on the Logos, he remains indebted to popular Stoic philosophy and Middle Platonism. He conducts a passionate attack on Gr. culture (mythology, poetry, rhetoric, art) and several times refers to his own eastern background. In his Chr. anthropology, pneumatology plays an important role, inasmuch as the divine Spirit joins the human body-soul unity as a third element and elevates it above the purely natural sphere.

W: PG 6:803-888. — E. Schwartz, T. oratio ad Graecos (Leipzig, 1888) [text]. — M. Whittaker, T. Oratio ad Graecos (Oxford, 1982) [text/English trans.]. — E. J. Goodspeed, Die ältesten Apologeten (Göttingen, 1914), 266-305 [text]. — R. C. Kukula, BKV² 12 [German trans.]. — A. Puech, Recherches sur le Discours aux Grecs de T. (Paris, 1903) [French trans.]. — S. di Cristina (Rome, 1991) [Italian trans.].
L: L. W. Barnard, The Heresy of T.: ABla 26 (1978) 181-193. — S. di Cristina, L'idea di dynamis: Aug. 17 (1977) 485-504. — M. Elze, T. u. seine Theologie (Göttingen, 1960). — R. M. Grant, The Date of T. s oratio: HThR 46 (1953) 99-101. — idem, Heresy of T.: JThS 5 (1954) 62-68. — idem, T.'s Theological Method: HThR 51 (1958) 123-128. — idem, T. and the Bible: StPatr 1 (1957) 297-308. — R. Hanig, T. u. Justin: VigChr 53 (1999) 31-73. — R. C. Kukula, T.s sog. Apologie (Leipzig, 1900). — A. Orbe, A propósito de Gen. 1,3 en la exégesis de T.: Gr. 42 (1961) 401-443. — W. L. Petersen, T. Dependence upon Justin: NTS 36 (1990) 512-534. — R. F. Shedinger, Did T. Use the Old Testament Peshitta?: NT 41 (1999) 265-279. — C. W. Steuer, Die Gottes- u. Logoslehre (Jena, 1892). — P. Yousif, Patrimonio culturale: M. Pavan et al., L'Eredità (Rome, 1986), 73-95.

P. Bruns

Te Deum

The *Te Deum* is a festive song of praise and thanksgiving in the western liturgy; acc. to a medieval Gallo-Spanish legend, Augustine and Ambrose sang alternative verses of it at the former's baptism (whence the name "Ambrosian Song of Praise"). The authorship cannot be determined; worth mentioning among the numerous writers to whom it has been attributed are Hilary of Poitiers, who might have made use of old eastern Trishagion texts, and Nicetas of Remesiana, who supposedly reworked an earlier version from the 2nd c. The hymn originated in the Gallo-Spanish world. The symmetrical structure of the twenty-nine pairs of verses, as well as the trimembered pattern of address with anaclesis (invocation), anamnesis, and epiclesis, are evidence of the unity of the text. Even the trinitarian doxology is probably part of the original. The psalm verses are attached, which corresponds to early eccles. usage. The oldest text is found in the Bangor Antiphonary. The structure and content, which reflect the text's origin in the Jewish *berakah*, suggest a closeness to the eucharistic prayer. The original setting of the hymn is the Easter liturgy; the versicles of the *Capitella per psalmos* may have been used in a playing of roles in dialogue. The earliest witness to its liturgical use is the Rule of

Caesarius of Arles, acc. to which the *Te Deum* and *Gloria* were sung at the morning office on Sundays. Acc. to Cyprian, the hymn had already spread throughout the world. The *Regula Benedicti* prescribes it for vigils (chs. 11; 14) and lauds (ch. 12) on Sundays and saints' feastdays. Outside the prayer of the Hours it was used during the translation of relics and in other processions, then also as a conclusion of synods, the consecration of abbots and kings, enthronements, and finally at all civic celebrations as an expression of the order of things as divinely given. Misuse of the hymn reached its climax during the Reformation (*Te Lutherum damnamus*) and in National Socialism (see the expansion in the Evangelical Military Hymnal: "Loyal to the Führer, the People, and the Realm").

W: M. Frost: JThS 34 (1933) 250-257. — idem, JThS 39 (1938) 388-391. — idem, 43 (1942) 59-68, 192-197.
L: A. de Almeida Matos, Algunas piezas litúrgicas y su conexión con el "Te Deum": AST 55/56 (1982/83) 293-315. — C. Alzati, A. Majo (ed.), Studi Ambrosiani. FS P. Borella (Milan, 1982). — J. Brinktrine, Eine auffallende Lesart in der mozarabischen Rezension des Te Deum: EL 64 (1950) 349-351. — K. Gamber, Das "Te Deum" u. sein Autor: RB 74 (1964) 318-321. — A. A. Häußling, review, Zak: ALW 25 (1983) 65f. — A. Heinz, Ein "Te Deum" gegen die frz. Revolution: AMRhKG 43 (1991) 389-393. — J. Hennig, Die Chöre der Heiligen: ALW 8/2 (1964) 436-456. — A. Janssens, Les structures symmétriques du Te Deum: QLP 47 (1966) 36-46. — E. Kähler, Studien zum Te Deum u. zur Geschichte des 24. Psalms in der Alten Kirche (Göttingen, 1958). — P. C. Langeveld, Te Deum: Liturgisch Woordenboek 2649-2652. — J. Magne, "Carmina Christo" 2. Le "Te Deum": EL 100 (1986) 113-137. — R. Maringer, Der Ambrosianische Lobgesang: Liturgie u. Dichtung 1, ed. H. Becker, R. Kaczynski (St. Ottilien, 1983), 275-301. — E. Werner, Das Te Deum u. seine Hintergründe: JLH 25 (1981) 69-82. — S. Zak, Das Tedeum als Huldigungsgesang: HJ 102 (1982) 1-32. — A. Zirkel, "Die du erlöst mit kostbarem Blut": KlBl 72 (1992) 193.

S. FELBECKER

Tertullian

I. Life: The first Lat. Chr. writer, Q. Septimius Florens Tertullianus (T.), was active in Carthage around the turn from the 2nd to the 3rd c. Nothing is reliably known about his life. Earlier claimed facts came mostly from Jerome (*vir. ill.* 53), who himself, however, had no precise knowledge of T., and partly from hasty inferences from T.'s own works.

It may be assumed that he lived ca. 160-220; his productive period was ca. 196-214. Jerome speaks of T.'s father as being *centurio proconsularis*, but this claim is due to a corruption of the text. The only

thing sure is that T. grew up in a pagan environment, received a comprehensive education, and became a Christian before 197. Identification with a lawyer of the same name is not to be simply excluded but is rather improbable. T.'s knowledge of law is probably part of his general education. It is probable, but not demonstrable, that T. received this education outside of Carthage, e.g., in Rome. He commanded two languages and composed works in Greek. His unconventional use of the Lat. language makes his works, to some extent, difficult to understand. He devoted his works exclusively to Chr. subjects, initially in the interests of the Great Church, but, from ca. 206/207 on, increasingly under the influence of Montanism.

Of his private life we know only that his circumstances were good and that he was married to a Christian. Scholars have tried to infer a great deal about his character from his works, but the mention of, e.g., youthful excesses, is to be considered rather a literary commonplace. An objective examination does not justify T.'s often claimed misogyny; his attitude to women reflects the outlook of the time and is to some extent more positive than the latter. A preference for ascetical ideas emerges even in the first works but grows stronger under Montanist influence. His entire life's work is marked by a basically polemical attitude, initially toward pagans, then toward Chr. heresies, and finally toward the enemies of Montanism within the Great Church. In his polemics he gives priority to juridical arguments and does not shrink from personal defamation of his opponents. Augustine's remark (*haer.* 86) that in his later years T. formed his own party, the "Tertullianists," has hardly any hist. value. After his last works, ca. 212/214, we hear nothing more of him; even the year of his death is unknown.

II. Works: In the few years from 196 to 214 T. produced a sizable body of works, of which thirty-one have been preserved; others are lost. His writings are either apologetic in character or deal with particular aspects of Chr. life. He composed no exeget. works, and dogm. questions are treated not separately but in the setting of attacks on his opponents. Several attempts have been made to establish a chronology of the works (survey in T. D. Barnes, 30-56), but allusions to events of the time and cross references within the works do not yield final certainty. On the other hand, the few fixed points of reference and the sparse data about his life do yield a sequence of works as a mirror of his intellectual development. The following periods of works and areas of interest may be distinguished:

1. *Writings after His Conversion (196-198)*:

a. Controversies with Pagans and Jews: *Ad nationes* (*nat.*; 197), a defense of Christianity and at the same time a condemnation of Roman moral and religious depravity. — *Adversus Iudaeos* (*adv. Iud.*; 197); the authenticity is doubtful at least of one part and of the bibl. citations. The first section raises the question of the validity of the Jewish law and its fulfillment by the new lawgiver, Christ. The second part (partly from *adv. Marc.* 3) proves the messiahship of Christ. — *Apologeticum* (*apol.*; 197). T. intends to make known the true nature of Christianity in order that people may not judge it in ignorance and unjustly. Christians are depicted as model citizens and followers of a revealed faith, not of a philosophical school. — *De testimonio animae* (*test. anim.*; 198). The human soul is naturally Chr.; Chr. truth imposes itself by its own power on human beings, without need of philosophical instruction.

b. Christian Behavior in a Pagan Environment: *De idololatria* (*idol.*; 196). In order to keep themselves from idolatry, Christians must avoid all activities, trades, and arts that are connected directly or indirectly with worship of the gods. — *Ad martyres* (*mart.*; 197). T. urges persecuted and imprisoned Christians to perseverance and martyrdom. — *De spectaculis* (*spect.*; between 197 and 202). Separation from pagans involves espec. an avoidance of games in all their forms. — *De cultu feminarum* (*cult. fem.*; 197-201). In the two books on women's adornments and finery T. condemns every artificial alteration of the human body, which is God's creation, as a use of diabolical inventions and practices.

2. *Writings on the Life of Christians in the Church (198-203)*:

De baptismo (*bapt.*; between 198 and 203). T. stresses the necessity of baptism for the forgiveness of sins and sets down regulations and customs for the administration and reception of baptism. The baptizand must be a grown, adult human being. Heretical baptism is rejected. — *De oratione* (*orat.*; between 198 and 204). The Lord's Prayer is explained as a *breviarium totius evangelii*; remarks on prayer generally and its effectiveness follow. — *De paenitentia* (*paenit.*; 203/204) deals with the church's practice of penance. T. knows a first penance before baptism and a (one-time) second penance after baptism in the case of serious sin (murder, idolatry, sexual offenses). Sin affects the entire person and has its origin in the will. — *De patientia* (*patient.*; 204). Patience (in the sense of perseverance) is praised as the foundation of all the virtues. God, as Father and Son, is the model of patience; the whole of earthly life

is a test of patience. — *Ad uxorem* (*uxor.*; between 198 and 203). In these two books addressed to his wife T. takes up the question of the permissibility of a second marriage. The latter is indeed not commendable, but neither is it forbidden, provided the second partner is a Christian. T. sketches a positive picture of Chr. marriage, although not without encratitic elements.

3. *Writings in Controversy with Heretical Ideas; Turn to Montanism (203-211)*:

a: General Challenge to All Heresies: *De praescriptione haereticorum* (*praescr.*; 203). With the juridical objection that by way of apostolic tradition the Great Church has gained sole legitimate possession of Chr. truth, any claim of other Chr. groups to the truth is denied in principle. The standard is the *regula fidei* based on apostolicity; every departure from it is heresy.

b: Controversy with Individual Heretics: *Adversus Hermogenem* (*adv. Hermog.*; 204/205). T. attacks the gnostic theory of creation from eternal and uncreated matter. — *De carne Christi* (*carn.*; 206) attacks, among others, Marcion, Apelles, and Valentinus and their docetist christology. As a man, Christ was born and died with flesh capable of suffering. In fact, the real birth meant that though Mary had conceived virginally, she did not give birth virginally. — *Adversus Valentinianos* (*adv. Val.*; 206/207). In a spirit of irony T. ridicules the genealogies of the Valentinians and the secret knowledge claimed by the gnostics; at the same time, he discusses such concepts as *forma* and *persona*. — *Adversus Marcionem* (*adv. Marc.*; 207/208). This version of the five books against Marcion was preceded by two others. The subjects of the individual books: against the separation of the "good God" from the creator God of the OT (1); defense of the one God as creator and as, at the same time, a good, because just, God (2); proof that the Christ of the NT is the Messiah of the old covenant (3); critique of Marcion's gospel and its selective character (4); criticism of Marcion's Apostles Creed (5). — *De anima* (*anim.*; 210). In this "theological handbook of psychology" T. rejects gnostic and philosophical doctrines of the soul. The soul's substance has its own kind of *corporalitas*; it is one of the three natures of the human being (along with *spiritus* and *caro*). The individual soul comes into being through generation (traducianism); in the process original sin is also transmitted. — *Adversus Praxean* (*adv. Prax.*; 210/211). T. contrasts the Chr. doctrine of the Trinity with the Patripassionism of Praxeas. Despite his emphasis on the equality of the three persons, T.'s understanding of the Trinity is marked by a certain subordinationism. The Trinity is defined by means of the common nature, the unity of substance, and the distinction of persons. — *De resurrectione mortuorum* (*resurr.*; 211). The resurrection of the dead, that is, the substantial identity of the risen body with the earthly body, is, acc. to T., "the hope of Christians." In response to gnostic ideas, T. brings rationally accessible proofs of the "complete restoration." In addition, many proofs from scripture are adduced. — *De scorpiace* (*scorp.*; 211/212). T. defends the moral value of martyrdom against gnostic views.

4: *Writings in Defense of Montanism (208-214)*:

De corona militum (*coron.*; 208). The separation of Christians from the pagan environment is taken up once again, but from the Montanist point of view, and is made even more rigorous. T. forbids Christians to perform military service, along with all its regulations and customs, as being idolatrous. — *De fuga in persecutione* (*fug.*; 208/209). As a Montanist, T. demands (in contrast to his *patient.* and *uxor.*) that Christians stand firm in persecution, and he forbids flight. — *De virginibus velandis* (*virg. vel.*; 209). Using as an example the veil worn by all adult women, T. opposes all privileges of eccles. states (in this case, female ascetics); asceticism is not a meritorious act but a grace. — *De pudicitia* (*pudic.*; 210). In this Montanist counterpart to *paenit.* T. maintains that the bishop cannot forgive serious sins such as sexual offenses; as a result, he touches on the question of the power to bind and loose. He distinguishes between forgivable and unforgivable sins. — *De ieiunio* (*ieiun.*; 210/211). T. defends the stricter fasts practiced by the Montanist community and accuses the Great Church of laxity and hedonism. — *De exhortatione castitatis* (*castit.*; 212). In contrast to the limited acceptance of a second marriage in *uxor.*, T. now rejects it as "prostitution." Even a first marriage, while not condemned, is depreciated in contrast to continence. — *De monogamia* (*monog.*; 214). A single marriage is called for as the only possible position for (Montanist) Christians between a heretical rejection of marriage as such and the unlimited allowance of second marriages in the Great Church. — *Ad Scapulam* (*Scap.*; 212?). Here, in urgent circumstances, T. takes up once more the subject of the persecution of Christians and he warns Scapula, a persecutor, of the inescapable wrath of God.

It is not possible to situate the work *De pallio* (*pall.*), which speaks in autobiographical form of a shift from the toga to the *pallium*, the philosopher's cloak. The authenticity of the work has recently been debated.

T. uses as sources both non-Chr. and Chr. authors such as Seneca (*patient.*), Varro (*nat.; idol.; spect.*), Soranus of Ephesus (*anim.*), Irenaeus (*praescr.; adv. Val.*), and Theophilus of Antioch (*adv. Hermog.*). T.'s influence was initially considerable, but it waned because of his Montanist views. He was used (and named) by Cyprian, Lactantius, Lucifer of Cagliari, the so-called Ambrosiaster, Optatus of Milevis, Hilary of Poitiers, Rufinus, Augustine (critically), and espec. Jerome, then later by Isidore of Seville. In the East T. became known through Eusebius's translation of the *Apologeticum*.

T. himself mentions the following, now lost, works: *De spe fidelium, De paradiso, Adversus Appelleiacos, De censu animae adversus Hermogenem, De fato.* Jerome also mentions *De Aaron vestibus, De exstasi, Ad amicum philosophum.* In addition, the following are contained under T.'s name in the so-called *Corpus Agobardinum: De carne et anima, De animae summissione, De superstitione saeculi.* Also lost are the Gr. versions of *bapt., spect.,* and *virg. vel.* Among the doubtful works, in addition to *Iud.* (at least in part) and perhaps *pall.*, there is the edition of the *Passio ss. Perpetuae et Felicitatis* (→ Martyrs, Acts of the). Not from T.: *De execrandis gentium diis, Adversus omnes haereses* (→ Zephyrinus of Rome), *Carmen adversus Marcionitas* (→ Poems, Anonymous). At times the following have been attributed to T.: *De Iona propheta, De Sodoma, De cibis Iudaicis, De iudicio Domini,* and Novatian, *De Trinitate.*

III. **Basic Lines of Thought:** The claims of T.'s importance for Chr. Latin are met nowadays with greater reserve. It is true that some Chr. terms are attested in him for the first time (see below), but on the whole his unconventional style was not imitated. T. had no influence on the Latin of the Bible translations. His at times *ad hoc* translations of Greek texts remain isolated; where T. relied on translations that may have been available, no concrete text type is recognizable.

It is in keeping with works motivated primarily by apologetic concerns that T. did not develop any coherent theology but explained particular subjects as needed in his controversies with paganism and heresies. A fundamental attitude derived from Stoic philosophy influenced his arguments against the speculative ideas of gnostic heresies and against the decline in moral standards and against the religious customs of his time. Christians, he says, are the better citizens by reason of their superior ethic and morality and therefore do not deserve persecution. T.'s attitude to civic authority is positive in principle, whereas he has a more nuanced attitude toward classical education, philosophy, and science: These are not the way to knowledge of ultimate truths, since truth is mediated by revelation. Human beings, as images of God, are, of course, rational beings and as such open to rational arguments from nature and logic; the insights thus gained serve as preparation for the reception of revelation. For this reason T. uses the instruments of human knowledge insofar as they are not inventions of the devil and therefore idolatrous. From his theory of knowledge T. derives the principle that the norm of Chr. truth is the acceptance of the *regula fidei*, that is, the content of the creed, which comes directly from revelation by way of apostolic tradition, whereas scripture and its interpretation are open to human and demonic interpolation.

T. set the direction for the terminology of western trinitarian doctrine: in opposition to the Monarchian Patripassionism of Praxeas, T. defines the Trinity as identical in essence and substance but distinct as persons. T. departed from the common view in his to some extent misleading formulations in the matter of a divine *corporalitas*, the traducianist origin of the soul, and the question of Mary's *virginitas in partu*. T.'s turn to Montanism, however, did not seem to have any impact on his dogmatic theory, apart from the idea of a continuation of prophecy by the Paraclete. On the other hand, T. did think of *disciplina* as subject to development; but the idea of a progress of the divine *oikonomia* was already a matter of special interest to T. in his Cath. period.

W: *Opera omnia*, B. Rhenanus (Basel, ¹1521) [text]. — F. Oehler (Leipzig, 1851-1854) [text]. — H. Kellner (Königsberg, 1882) [German trans.]. — E. Dekkers et al., CCL 1-2. — *anim.*, A. Reifferscheid, G. Wissowa, CSEL 20:298-396. — J. H. Waszink (Munich, 1980) [text/German trans./comm.]. — *apol.*, H. Hoppe, CSEL 69. — J. P. Waltzing (Paris, 1961 = 1929) [comm.]. — C. Becker (Munich, ²1961) [text/German trans./comm.]. — G. Esser, BKV² 24:33-182 [German trans.]. — *bapt.*, R. F. Refoulé, M. Drouzy, SC 35. — E. Evans (London, 1964) [text/English trans./comm.]. — A. Reifferscheid, G. Wissowa, CSEL 20:201-218. — A. Souter (London, 1919) [English trans./comm.]. — G. Esser, BKV² 7:274-299 [German trans.]. — *carn.*, J.-P. Mahé, SC 216-217. — A. Kroymann, CSEL 70:189-250. — *castit.*, C. Moreschini, C. Fredouille, SC 319. — A. Kroymann, CSEL 70:125-152. — G. Esser, BKV² 7:324-346 [German trans.]. — H. V. Friedrich (Stuttgart, 1990) [text/German trans.]. — *coron.*, A. Kroymann, CSEL 70:153-188. — J. Fontaine (Paris, 1964) [text/French trans.]. — F. Ruggiero, Classici greci e latini (Milan, 1992) [text/Italian trans./Latin comm.]. — G. Esser, BKV² 24:230-263 [German trans.]. — *cult. fem.*, M. Turcan, SC 173. — A. Kroymann, CSEL 70:59-95. — S. Isetta (Florence, 1986) [text/Italian trans./comm.]. — G. Esser, BKV² 7:175-202 [German trans.]. — *fug.*, V. Bulhart, CSEL 76:17-43. — J. J. Thierry (Hilversum, 1941)

[text/Dutch trans./comm.]. — *adv. Hermog.*, A. Kroymann, CSEL 47:126-176. — J. H. Waszink, ACW 24 (Westminster, 1956) [English trans.]. — *idol.*, J. H. Waszink, SVigChr 1 (Leiden, 1987) [text/English trans./comm.]. — A. Reifferscheid, G. Wissowa, CSEL 20:30-58. — G. Esser, BKV² 7:137-174 [German trans.]. — *ieiun.*, A. Reifferscheid, G. Wissowa, CSEL 20:274-297. — G. Esser, BKV² 24:519-559 [German trans.]. — *adv. Iud.*, A. Kroymann, CSEL 70:251-331. — H. Tränkle, Hermes. E 15 (Wiesbaden, 1964) [text/comm.]. — G. Esser, BKV² 7:300-323 [German trans.]. — *adv. Marc.*, R. Braun, SC 365, 368, 399. — C. Moreschini, TDSA 35 (Milan, 1971) [text]. — A. Kroymann, CSEL 47:290-650. — E. Evans (Oxford, 1972) [text/English trans.]. — *mart.*, P. Borleffs, CSEL 76:1-8. — A. Quacquarelli, OP 2 (Rome, 1963). — G. Esser, BKV² 7:215-223 [German trans.]. — *monog.*, P. Mattei, SC 343. — P. Borleffs, CSEL 76:44-78. — W. P. LeSaint, ACW 13 (Westminster, 1951) [English trans.]. — R. Uglione, CorPat 15 (Turin, 1993) [text/Italian trans./comm.]. — G. Esser, BKV² 24:473-518 [German trans.]. — *nat.*, A. Reifferscheid, G. Wissowa, CSEL 20:59-133. — A. Schneider, BHRom (Geneva, 1968) [text/French trans./comm.]. — *orat.*, E. Evans (London, 1953) [text/English trans./comm.]. — G. F. Diercks, StPM 4 (Antwerp, 1956) [text]. — A. Reifferscheid, G. Wissowa, CSEL 20:180-200. — P. A. Gramaglia (Rome, 1984) [text/Italian trans./comm.]. — G. Esser, BKV² 7:247-273 [German trans.]. — *paen.*, C. Munier, SC 316. — P. Borleffs, CSEL 76:140-170. — W. P. LeSaint, ACW 28 (Westminster, 1959) [English trans.]. — G. Esser, BKV² 7:224-246 [German trans.]. — *pall.*, V. Bulhart, CSEL 76:104-128. — S. Costanza, CStCl 3 (Naples, 1968) [text/Italian trans./comm.]. — A. Gerlo (Wetteren, 1941) [text/Dutch trans./comm.]. — G. Esser, BKV² 7:11-33 [German trans.]. — *patient.*, J.-C. Fredouille, SC 310. — A. Kroymann, CSEL 47:1-24. — G. Esser, BKV² 7:34-59 [German trans.]. — *praescr.*, R. F. Refoulé, P. de Labriolle, SC 46. — A. Kroymann, CSEL 70:1-58. — G. Esser, BKV² 24:303-354 [German trans.]. — *adv. Prax.*, E. Evans (London, 1948) [text/English trans./comm.]. — A. Kroymann, CSEL 47:227-289. — G. Scarpat, CorPat 12 (Turin, ²1985) [text/Italian trans.]. — A. Souter (London, 1920) [English trans.]. — *pudic.*, C. Micaelli, C. Munier, SC 394-395. — A. Kroymann, G. Wissowa, CSEL 20:219-273. — W. P. LeSaint, ACW 28 (Westminster, 1959) [English trans.]. — G. Esser, BKV² 24:375-472 [German trans.]. — *resurr.*, A. Kroymann, CSEL 47:25-125. — E. Evans (London, 1960) [text/English trans./comm.]. — A. Souter (London, 1922) [English trans./comm.]. — *Scap.*, V. Bulhart, CSEL 76:9-16. — G. Esser, BKV² 24:264-274 [German trans.]. — *scorp.*, A. Reifferscheid, G. Wissowa, CSEL 20:144-179. — G. Azzali Bernadelli (Florence, 1990) [text/Italian trans./comm.]. — G. Esser, BKV² 24:183-229 [German trans.]. — *spect.*, M. Turcan, SC 332. — A. Kroymann, CSEL 20:1-29. — T. R. Glover (London, 1960) [text/English trans./comm.]. — E. Castorina (Florence, 1961) [text/Italian trans./comm.]. — G. Esser, BKV² 7:101-136 [German trans.]. — *test. anim.*, A. Kroymann, G. Wissowa, CSEL 20:134-143. — J. H. Waszink (Munich, 1980) [German trans./comm.]. — C. Tibiletti (Florence, 1984) [text/Italian trans./comm.]. — G. Esser, BKV² 7:203-214 [German trans.]. — *uxor.*, C. Munier, SC 227. — A. Kroymann, CSEL 70:96-124. — W. P. LeSaint, ACW 13 (Westminster, 1951) [English trans.]. — G. Esser, BKV² 7:60-84 [German trans.]. — *adv. Val.*, J. C. Fredouille, SC 280-281. — A. Kroymann, CSEL 47:177-212. — *virg. vel.*, G. F. Diercks, StPM 4 (1956) [text]. — V.

Bulhart, CSEL 76:79-103. — P. Mattei, E. Schulz-Flügel, SC 424. — E. Schulz-Flügel, FC in preparation.

L: *Bibliographies:* CCL 1:X-XXV. — P. Siniscalco, Recenti studi su T.: RSLR 14 (1978) 396-405. — Studia Tertullianea. — *Concordance:* G. Claesson, Index Tertullianeus, 3 vols. (Paris, 1974f.).
K. Adam, Der Kirchenbegriff (Paderborn, 1907). — A. D'Alès, La théologie (Paris, 1905). — C. Andresen, "Ubi tres ecclesia est, licet laici": FS G. Krause (Berlin, 1982). — R. H. Ayers, Language, Logic, Reason (Hildesheim, 1979). — C. Aziza, T. et le judaisme (Paris, 1977). — T. D. Barnes, T. (Oxford, ²1985). — A. Beck, Röm. Recht bei T. u. Cyprian (Aalen, 1967 = 1930). — H. Brandt. T. s Ethik (Gütersloh, 1929). — R. Braun, Approches de T. (Paris, 1992). — idem, Deus Christianorum. Recherches sur le vocabulaire doctrinal (Paris, ²1977). — idem, T. et le montanisme: RSLR 21 (1985) 245-257. — F. F. Church, Sex and Salvation: HThR 68 (1976) 83-101. — J. J. Clabeaux, A Lost Edition of the Letters of Paul (Washington, 1989) [on the presumably Marcion texts by Tertullian]. — J. Daniélou, La littérature latine avant T.: REL 48 (1970) 357-375. — F. De Pauw, La justification des traditions non écrits: EThL 19 (1942) 5-46. — A. Dihle, T.s Lehre vom zweifachen Willen Gottes: FS K. Thraede (Münster, 1995), 61-65. — G. D. Dunn, T. and Rebekah: VigChr 52 (1998) 119-145. — A. Felber, Schöpfung u. Sündenfall: FS J. B. Bauer (Graz, 1987). — J.-C. Fredouille, Sur la genèse et la composition du cult.: Vita Latina 121 (1991) 37-42. — idem, T. et la conversion de la culture antique (Paris, 1972). — idem, T. et l'Empire: RechAug 19 (1984) 111-131. — W. H. C. Frend, Martyrdom and Persecution (Oxford, 1965). — idem, T.e gli Ebrei: RSLR 4 (1968) 3-10. — W. M. Gessel, Der Ternar Glaubensregel, Tradition u. Sukzession: FS J. Stimpfle (St. Ottilien, 1991), 139-154. — P. A. Gramaglia, Note sul pudic.: RSLR 31 (1995) 235-258. — R. P. Hanson, Notes on T.'s Interpretation of Scripture: JThS NS 12 (1961) 273-279. — W. v. Hartel, Patristische Studien 1-4: SÖAW. PII 120 (1890) 2., 6. and 14. Heft. — A. Hauck, T.s Leben u. Schriften (Erlangen, 1877). — G. Hébert, T.: une philosophie de l'histoire: FS J. Moingt (Paris, 1993), 413-423. — B. Hilberath, Anmerkungen zum Personbegriff in Adv. Prax.: StPatr 21 (1989) 250-253. — H. Hoppe, Beiträge zur Sprache u. Kritik T.s (Lund, 1932). — idem, De sermone Tertullianeo quaestiones selectae (Marburg, 1897). — idem, Syntax u. Stil (Leipzig, 1903). — J.-M. Hornus, "It is not lawful for me to fight." Early Christian Attitudes towards War (Scottdale, Pa., 1980). — H. Karpp, Schrift u. Geist (Gütersloh, 1955). — idem, Sorans vier Bücher Peri psyches u. T.s Schrift anim.: ZNTW 33 (1934) 31-47. — L. S. Kirkpatrick, Baptism, Scripture and the Problem of the Christian Sinner: IBSt 17 (1995) 75-85. — J. Klein, T., chr. Bewußtsein u. sittliche Forderungen (Hildesheim, 1975 = 1940). — R. Klein, T. u. das röm. Reich (Heidelberg, 1968). — N. Kokkinos, The Relative Chronology of the Nativity in T.: Studies in Memory of R. Summers (Macon, Ga., 1998), 119-131. — E. Kroymann, Zur Überlieferung des T.-Textes: RhM 68 (1913) 128f. — P. de Labriolle, T. a-t-il connu une version latine de la Bible?: BALAC 4 (1914) 210-213. — A. Labhardt, T. et la philosophie: MH 7 (1950) 159-180. — A. Lamirande, T. misogyne?: ScEs 39 (1987) 5-25. — E. Löfstedt, Zur Sprache T. s (Lund, 1920). — J. Lortz, T. als Apologet (Münster, 1927). — idem, Vernunft u. Offenbarung: Kath. 93 (1913) 124-140. — P. Mattei, Adam posséda-t-il l'Esprit?: REA 29 (1983) 27-38. — E. Meijering, T.

contra Marcion (Leiden, 1977). — C. Micaelli, Ricerche sulla fortuna: Orph. 6 (1985) 118-135. — J. R. Michaels, Almsgiving and the Kingdom within: T. on Luke 17:21: CBQ 60 (1998) 475-483. — C. Mohrmann, Jerôme et Augustin sur T.: VigChr 5 (1951) 111f. — J. Moingt, Théologie trinitaire (Paris, 1966-1969). — V. Morel, Le développement de la disciplina: RHE 35 (1939) 243-265. — idem, Disciplina: RHE 40 (1944/45) 5-46. — C. Moreschini, T. tra Stoicismo et Platonismo: FS C. Andresen (Göttingen, 1979), 367-379. — B. Nisters, T. (Münster, 1950). — T. P. O'Malley, T. and the Bible (Nijmegen, 1967). — I. Opelt, Die Polemik in der chr. Lit. (Heidelberg, 1980). — E. Osborn, The Subtlety of T.: VigChr 52 (1998) 361-370. — S. Otto, Natura u. dispositio (Munich, 1960). — P. Petitmengin, Errata tertullianea: FS R. Braun 2 (Nizza, 1991), 35-46. — B. Poschmann, Paenitentia secunda (Bonn, 1940). — D. Powell, Tertullianists and Cataphrygians: VigChr 29 (1975) 33-54. — A. Quacquarelli, La persecuzione secondo T.: Gr. 31 (1950) 562-589. — G. Quispel, "Anima naturaliter christiana": ErJb 18 (1950) 173f. — K. Rahner, Die Bußlehre T. s: FS K. Adam (Düsseldorf, 1952), 139-167. — C. Rambaux, T. face aux morales des trois premiers siècles (Paris, 1979). — R. Roberts, The Theology of T. (London, 1924). — W. Rordorf, T. s Beurteilung des Soldatenstandes: VigChr 23 (1969) 105-141. — U. Schmid, Marcion u. sein Apostolos (Berlin, 1995). — P. Schoonenberg, Eine Diskussion über den trinitarischen Personbegriff: ZThK 111 (1989) 129-162. — E. Schulz-Flügel, T. u. das "zweite Geschlecht": REA 42 (1996) 3-19. — R. D. Sider, Ancient Rhetoric and the Art of T. (Oxford, 1971). — idem, Approaches to T.: JECS 2 (1982) 228-260. — idem, Credo quia absurdum?: ClW 73 (1980) 417-419. — P. Siniscalco, Il motivo razionale della resurrezione: AAST 95 (1960/61) 195-221. — J. Speigl, Herkommen u. Fortschritt im Christentum: FS B. Kötting (Münster, 1980), 165-178. — J. K. Stirnimann, Die praescriptio T. s (Freiburg i.Br., 1949). — G. C. Stead, Divine Substance: HThS NS 14 (1963) 46-66. — G. G. Stroumsa, From Repentance to Penance in paen.: Transformations of the Inner Self in Ancient Religions (Leiden, 1999), 167-178. — S. Teeuwen, Sprachlicher Bedeutungswandel (Paderborn, 1926). — H.-W. Thönnes, Caelestia recogita, et terrena despicies: altkirchliche Apologetik (Frankfurt a.M., 1994). — G. Thörnell, Studia Tertullianea 1-4 (Uppsala, 1918-1926). — C. Tibiletti, Natura e salvezza in T.: Aug. 23 (1983) 383-397. — S. Toki, De pallio. Das Autorenproblem: Journal of Classical Studies 34 (1986) 93-103 [Engl. summary, 154]. — A. Viciano, Cristo Salvador (Pamplona, 1986). — J. M. Vis, T.' De pallio tegen de achtergrond van zijn overige werken (Nijmegen, 1949). — K. H. Wirth, Der Verdienstbegriff (Leipzig, 1892).

E. SCHULZ-FLÜGEL

Testament of Our Lord Jesus Christ

The *Testament of Our Lord Jesus Christ* (*Testamentum Domini*) is probably the latest and therefore the last individual work that in conception, content, and pretended origin belongs to the genre of early Chr. → church orders. It originated in the 5th c., probably in the Syrian world; its original language is Greek. The work, which is known in Syr. (later also Arab.

[unpublished] and Eth.) recensions, was discovered in 1869 by Paul de Lagarde but published only in 1899 by Ignatius E. Rahmani.

The *Testamentum Domini*, which must have first circulated as an independent work, forms a prelude to the → *Octateuch* of Clement, a point suggested by the work's extreme claim of authorship: the risen Christ appears to the apostles (and three women) and in a conversation with them sets forth his "testament," i.e., regulations typical of the church order genre. In their content, the regulations of the *Testamentum Domini* are based on the → *Traditio apostolica*, so that they can be used in the reconstruction of this early church order. The church order proper is preceded by an apocalypse; this is probably due to the character of the "testament" genre, in which apocalyptic elements are always part of the teaching.

W: R. Beylot (Leuven/Louvain, 1984) [Ethiopic text/French trans.]. — J. Cooper, A. J. Maclean (Edinburgh, 1902) [English trans.]. — I. E. Rahmani (Hildesheim, 1968 = Mainz, 1899) [Syriac text/Latin trans.]. — G. Sperry-White (Bramcote, 1991) [English trans.]. — A. Vööbus, CSCO 367/368:1-50/27-64 [Syriac text/English trans.].
L: R. G. Coquin, T. Dom.: ParOr 5 (1974) 165-188. — F. X. Funk, Testament (Mainz, 1901). — G. Sperry-White, Daily Prayer in the T. Dom. (Notre Dame, 1993). — B. Steimer, Vertex traditionis (Berlin, 1992), esp. 95-105.

B. STEIMER

Testaments of the Twelve Patriarchs

The name *Testaments of the Twelve Patriarchs* is given to a pseudepigraphical work (*test. XII patr.*) that is modeled on the testament of Jacob, the progenitor of the twelve tribes (Gen 49). Like their father, Jacob, before them, his twelve sons, before dying, address their descendants and give them their final ordinances in the form of a testament. These legacies are related to the life experience of each tribal leader, make midrashlike additions to the narrative core, and end with prophecies about future history. The *Testaments* are preserved complete in Greek; also important are the Arm. and Old Slav. translations. The *Testamentum Naphtali* also survives in Hebrew, but in its present form the work has been heavily revised. The Arm. version in particular shows numerous Chr. interpolations.

W: R. H. Charles, Greek Versions (Oxford, 1908) [Greek text/English trans.]. — N. Tichonravov, Pamjatniki otrecennoj russkoj literatury (London, 1973 = SPB 1863), 96-233 [Slavic text]. — E. Kautzsch, Die Apokryphen des AT 2 (Darmstadt, 1975 = Tübingen, 1921), 458-506 [German trans.]. — P. Rießler, Altjüd. Schrifttum (Freiburg i.Br., 1984 = Heidelberg, 1928), 1149-1262 [German trans.]. — J.

Becker (Gütersloh, 1974) [German trans./comm.]. — M. de Jonge (Leiden, ²1970) [text/English trans./comm.]. — M. E. Stone, Testament of Levi (Jerusalem, 1969) [Armenian text/English trans./comm.]. — idem, Armenian Version of Joseph (Missoula, 1975) [Armenian text/English trans.].
L: J. Becker, Entstehungsgeschichte (Leiden, 1970). — C. Burchard, Arm. Überlieferung: BZNW 36 (1969) 1-29. — F. C. Conybeare, Jewish Authorship: JQR 5 (1895) 375-398. — idem, Collation of T.: JQR 8 (1896) 260-268, 471-485. — A. Hultgård, L'eschatologie des T. (Uppsala, 1982). — E. Preuschen, Arm. Übersetzung: ZNW 1 (1900) 106-140. — H. D. Singerland, T. of the Twelve Patriarchs (Missoula, 1977). — M. E. Stone, Armenian Apocrypha (Jerusalem, 1982). — idem, Analytical Index of Armenian Apocrypha (Jerusalem, 1982). — idem, Epitome: REArm 20 (1986/87) 69-107. — idem, Selected Studies (Leiden, 1991). — J. Thomas, Studien zu den T. (Berlin, 1969).

P. BRUNS

Testimonies, Collections of

The "collection of testimonies" genre is a Chr. adaptation of the florilegia or excerpt literature. The term refers to a collection of citations from the OT (with preference given to the Pentateuch, psalms, and prophets) that are organized acc. to themes and given appropriate titles but contain no commentary by the compiler. The existence of systematically organized collections of testimonies cannot be proved with certainty, but it is very likely that the earliest Chr. writers, espec. those coming from paganism and lacking a bibl. education, derived their knowledge of the OT from anthologies and not from complete Bibles. Traces of the use of collections of testimonies are to be found throughout early Chr. literature, including the NT (Mt, Jn, Paul, Acts), in, e.g., the letter of Barnabas, Justin, Irenaeus, Clement Alex., Tertullian, and Cyprian, among others. The following criteria allow the inference that collections of testimonies are being used: combinations of always the same bibl. citations on the same subject or on common key concepts; the same textual variations recurring in authors who are independent of one another, variations that differ from all known OT traditions and must therefore go back to a common source, i.e., a collection of testimonies; always the same wrong attributions (e.g., Isaiah instead of Jeremiah); series of citations used by several independent writers. The origin and characteristics of collections of testimonies cannot be completely explained. There may have been collections of testimonies that were private aids to memory and more or less accidentally became public, and there may have been collections deliberately made and intended all along for publication. The latter case is suggested by the choice of bibl. passages, which on the one hand concentrates on texts useful in anti-Jewish controversy and on messianic passages having to do with the person of Christ and his passion and resurrections, or, on the other hand, on particular key ideas of Christianity (e.g., "rock"). The textual variants are probably not due to copyists' errors but to interpretive changes that were deliberately made for the purpose of the collections and that made it easier to connect the texts with Christ. In other words, we are dealing not with compilations pure and simple but with an early form of bibl. exegesis that resembles to some extent the rabbinical midrashim (commentaries on the Bible that contain either a series of citations, each with an interpretation, or simply interpretive paraphrases of the OT texts); this form of Chr. exegesis perhaps developed in imitation of the midrashim. The first preserved collection of testimonies in Latin is → Cyprian's *Testimoniorum libri tres ad Quirinum*, which gave the genre its name. Inasmuch as the title "testimonies" may not have come from the author himself, it is questionable whether the work can be taken as a typical example of the genre and therefore serve for the reconstruction of similar earlier collections. Books 1 and 2 bring together texts showing an anti Jewish tendency; book 3 has the character of a manual on the most important questions of practical Chr. ethics. Cyprian makes independent use of his models, supplements them with citations from the NT, and revises them acc. to the version of the Bible he was currently using. No comparable work in this genre has come down in Gr. literature. We have two pre-Chr. examples of testimonies in two fragments among the Qumran texts: a midrash (4QFlor) and a collection of messianic texts (4QTest).

L: J. P. Audet, L'hypothèse des Testimonia: RB 70 (1963) 381-405. — H. Chadwick, Florilegium: RAC 7:1131-1160. — J. Daniélou, Christos Kyrios: RSR 39 (1951) 338-352. — idem, Études d'exégèse judéo-chrétienne (Les Testimonia) (Paris, 1966). — idem, Les origines de l'Épiphanie et les Testimonia: RSR 52 (1964) 538-553. — idem, La vision des ossements desséchés (Ezech 37, 1-14) dans les Testimonia: RSR 53 (1965) 220-233. — idem, Un Testimonium sur la vigne dans Barnabé XII, 1: RSR 50 (1962) 389-399. — C. H. Dodd, According to Scriptures (London, 1952). — E. Earle Ellis, The Old Testament in Early Christianity (Tübingen, 1991). — J. R. Harris, Testimonies, 2 vols. (Cambridge, 1916-1920). — N. J. Hommes, Het Testimoniaboek (Amsterdam, 1935). — P. Monat, Les testimonia bibliques de Cyprien à Lactance: Le monde latin antique et la Bible, ed. J. Fontaine, C. Pietri (Paris, 1985), 499-507. — P. Prigent, Quelques testimonia messianiques: ThZ 15 (1959) 419-430. — idem, Les Testimonia dans le christianisme primitif (Paris, 1961). — idem, Justin et l'Ancien Testament (Paris, 1964). — V. Saxer, La Bible chez les Pères latins du IIIᵉ siècle: Le monde latin antique et la Bible, ed. J. Fontaine, C.

Pietri (Paris, 1985), 339-369. — O. Skarsaune, From Books to Testimonies: Imm. 24-25 (1990) 207-219.

M. KAMPTNER

Testimonium veritatis

The Testimony of Truth is a Coptic gnostic homily in the Nag Hammadi library (NHC 9, 3). *Testimony of Truth* attacks various gnostic factions but also polemicizes against the Great Church and, in particular, the belief in creation. In its form, the work uses many elements of Jewish haggadah. There are also links to Valentinian gnosticism.

W: B. A. Pearson, NHC IX and X (Leiden, 1981) [Coptic text/English trans.]. — C. Gianotto (Brescia, 1990) [Italian trans.]. — K. Koschorke: ZNW 69 (1978) 91-117 [German trans.]. — NHL 448-459 [English trans.].
L: J. D. Kaestli, Relecture polémique: FV 80 (1981) 48-62. — K. Koschorke, Polemik der Gnostiker: Gnosis und Gnosticism, ed. M. Krause (Leiden, 1977), 43-49. — J. P. Mahé, ὁμολογία: Écritures et traditions, ed. J. É. Ménard (Leuven/Louvain, 1983), 126-139. — B. A. Pearson, Jewish Haggadic Traditions, FS G. Widengren (Leiden, 1972), 457-470.

P. BRUNS

Thaddeus, Acts of

The Thaddeus (Th.) in Mk 3:18 and Mt 10:3 is usually identified with the apostle Judas named in Lk 6:16. In the western tradition his destiny is linked with that of → Simon the Canaanite; in the East, however, there is a special *Acts* of Th. The point of departure for the *Acts* is the reports of Eusebius and of the *Doctrina Addai* on the beginnings of Christianity in Edessa, where Th. is identified with → Addai. The Eddessan image of Christ plays a role in the *Acts*. For this reason, they may have originated after 544, when the image turned up during a Persian siege of the city.

The Copt. *Acts* (BHO 1141) is a translation of the *Acta Petri et Andreae* (→ *Andrew, Acts of*), with Th. replacing Andrew.

W: AAAp 1:273-278. — M. Erbetta, Gli Apocrifi del NT (Turin, 1966), 2:577f. [Italian trans.].
L: M. v. Esbroeck, Le roi Sanatrouk et l'apôtre Thaddée: REArm 9 (1973) 141-283. — R. A. Lipsius, Die apokryphen Apostelgeschichten 2/2 (Amsterdam, 1976 = 1884), 178-200. — NTApo⁵ 2:436f.

G. RÖWEKAMP

Thalassius

Thalassius (Th. Abbot) was abbot of a North African monastery ca. 650 and a friend of Maximus Conf., who dedicated his sixty-five *Quaestiones ad Thalassium* to him in 630/633 and, until ca. 639, wrote him five letters, two of which have been preserved (PG 91:445-49 and 616-17). Th. composed a collection of proverbs in four centuries (*cent.*) *On Love, Continence, and the Direction of Souls*; the collection was translated at an early date into Arabic and Georgian. It consists of loosely connected apophthegmatic aphorisms that were influenced by → Evagrius Pont. and → Dionysius Areo.; the initial letters of the aphorisms also form sentences. Th. urges harmony between body and spirit; this, he says, is not a distant ideal but a goal attainable by everyone.

W: PG 91:1427-1470.
L: H.-G. Beck, Kirche u. theol. Lit. (Munich, ²1977), 355-356, 450. — M. T. Disdier, Le témoignage spirituel de Th.: EtByz 2 (1944) 79-118. — M. van Parys, Un maître spirituel oublié: Th.: Irén. 52 (1979) 214-240. — A. Solignac, Th.: DSp 15:323-326. — M. Viller, K. Rahner, Aszese u. Mystik in der Väterzeit (Freiburg i.Br., 1989), 244f.

B. R. SUCHLA

Thecla, Acts of

It is unclear whether the *Acts of Thecla* (Th.) were originally composed as a separate work. The *Acta Pauli et Theclae* (*A. Paul. et Thecl.*) were originally handed down as part of the *Acts* of → Paul, which were composed at the end of the 2nd c. In them older traditions were certainly used, since Th. is clearly the main figure of the part dealing with her.

The text tells of Paul's preaching of "God's word on continence and resurrection" in Iconium (it includes beatitudes for the continent). When Th. refuses marriage with various men, she is condemned to death, baptizes herself during a struggle with a beast, and later on (at Paul's command) preaches in the house of Queen Tryphaena, in Iconium and Seleucia, where she dies and is buried. The hist. background of the figure of Th. remains unknown; the decisive point is the importance of the work in the history of theology. Tertullian (*bapt.* 17) tells of women who appealed to the *A. Paul. et Thecl.* for authority to baptize and preach, but he points out the abdication of the presbyter in Asia Minor who had been shown to be the author of the forged work.

The *A. Paul. et Thecl.* were soon separated from the *Acta Pauli* and handed down independently. There exist at least four translations, a Lat. and three eastern (Syr., Eth., Arm.), that are independent of each other. This independent "book called the Acts of Paul and Thecla" is rejected by the *Decretum Gelasianum*. Traditions about Th. live on in → Basil of Seleucia's *De vita ac miraculis Theclae*.

W: AAAp 1:235-269 [Greek text]. — O. v. Gebhardt, Die lat. Versionen der ActTh, TU 7/2 (Berlin, 1902) [Latin trans.]. — NTApo⁵ 2:216-224 [German trans.]. — A. Jensen, Th. — die Apostolin (Freiburg i.Br., 1995) [German trans./comm.]. — J. N. Bremmer (Kampen, 1996) [English trans.].
L: R. Albrecht, Das Leben der hl. Makrina (Göttingen, 1986). — V. Burrus, Chastity as Autonomy (Lewiston, N.Y., 1987) (review: Semeia 38 [1986] 101-135). — S. L. Davies, The Revolt of the Widows (Southern Illinois University, 1980). — J. Festugière, Les erigènes de s. Thècle: CRAI (1968) 52-63. — D. R. MacDonald (ed.), The Apocryphal Acts of the Apostles: Semeia 38 (1986) 101-135, 139-149, 151-159. — W. Rordorf, Saint Thècle: Aug. 24 (1984) 73-81. — idem, Tradition et composition: ThZ 41 (1985) 272-283.

G. RÖWEKAMP

Themistius, Deacon in Alexandria

Th., who is not to be confused with the philosopher of the same name, was the founder of Agnoetism, a moderate form of Monophysitism, that starts from the idea that in the one nature there are nonetheless two modes of willing and knowing. It also assumes, therefore, that the man Christ was limited in his knowledge. Th. defends this approach (basing himself on Jn 11:34 and Mk 13:32) against a *Tomus* (surviving only in fragments) of Patriarch Theodosius (535-566) that was addressed to Empress Theodora (*Theod.*) and responded to the attacks of Colluthus (*Coll.*). Other fragments are insignificant. Eulogius Alex. and Gregory I attacked the teachings of Th., who acc. to Photius, *cod.* 23, also wrote against the teaching of John Philoponus on the resurrection.

W: *Theod.*, Mansi 11:440. — *Coll.*, Mansi 10:1117 (= PG 91:172C), 981 (= Doctrina Patrum, ed. F. Diekamp [Münster, 1981 = 1907], 314, XL, XLI). — *fr.*, Mansi 10:981, 1120f., 1176.
L: H.-G. Beck, Kirche u. theol. Lit. (Munich, 1959), 391, 393. — T. Hermann, Monophysitica: ZNW 32 (1933) 287-293.

G. RÖWEKAMP

Theodore of Alexandria

Th. came from Syria and was abbot of the Egypt. monastery at Rhamnis. In 575, against his will, he was consecrated Monophysite (anti-)patriarch of Alexandria by Paul of Antioch. He did not leave his monastery, however, and remained patriarch only until the death of Paul in 582. A synodal letter to Paul is preserved in Syriac.

W: I.-B. Chabot, CSCO 17:298-308 [text]; CSCO 103:208-215 [Latin trans.].
L: E. Honigmann, Évêques et évêchés (Leuven/Louvain,

1951), 200-204 et al. — J. Maspéro, Histoire des Patriarches d'Alexandrie (Paris, 1923).

G. RÖWEKAMP

Theodore bar Koni (Kewani)

Th., b. in Kaskar, appeared toward the end of the 8th c. as an important Nestorian teacher and apologete. To his brother John he dedicated a scholion covering twelve treatises (*memre*) and containing remarks of great value on Chaldean, Greek, and Persian paganism. Th. combines the explanation of difficult bibl. passages with questions of logic, grammar, and speculative theology. The first five treatises deal with the OT, 6 is devoted to logic, 7-8 to the NT. Treatises 9-11 refute various heresies, among them Arianism and Monophysitism; 10 contains a catechismlike summary of the Chr. faith that attacks Islam and a judaizing variation on older heresies. Th. is an important indirect witness to many an early Chr. heresy (→ Bardesanes).

W: A. Scher, CSCO 55, 69 [text]. — R. Hespel, R. Draguet, CSCO 431/432, 448, 464/465 [text/French trans.]. — M. Levin, Die Scholien (Berlin, 1905) [German trans.]. — P. Pognon, Inscriptions mandaïtes (Paris, 1899), 105-138 [French trans. of tract. 11].
L: A. Baumstark, Griech. Philosophen: OrChr 5 (1905) 1-25. — E. Benveniste, Th. sur le zoroastrisme: MO 21 (1932) 170-215. — L. Brade, Untersuchungen zum Scholienbuch des Th. (Göttingen, 1975). — idem, Prologe in den Paulusbriefexegesen: OrChr 60 (1976) 162-171. — E. G. Clarke, Selected Questions of Isho bar Nun (Leiden, 1962). — G. Furlani, La filosofia:GSAI 1 (1926) 250-296. — S. Gero, Ophite gnosticism: OCA 229 (1987) 265-274. — S. H. Griffith, Chapter ten of Th.: OCP 47 (1981) 158-188. — idem, A Nestorian summa contra gentiles. N. Garsoian, East of Byzantium (Washington, 1982), 53-72. — V. M. Kugener, F. Cumont, La cosmogonie manichéenne (Brussels, 1908).

P. BRUNS

Theodore of Bostra

Th., a monk from Arabia, was (with Jacob Baradaeus) one of the two bishops who in 542, at the request of the Ghassanid Prince Harith, were sent to Mesopotamia and Syria by Monophysite Patriarch Theodosius Alex. Th. was given Bostra, the metropolitan city of the province of Arabia II, as his episcopal see, but he resided in the Golan. Together with Jacob, he ensured the continued life of the Monophysite-Jacobite church after the death of Severus of Antioch.

Surviving is a letter that Th. wrote from Constantinople in 564 to Paul of Antioch, whose election as bishop he advocated. In addition, he and Jacob Baradaeus wrote two letters, one to monks, against tritheism, the other to Paul on the subject of persecution by the orthodox.

W: I. B. Chabot, CSCO 17:94-96, 165f., 179f. [text]; CSCO 103:65f., 115f., 125f. [Latin trans.].
L: E. Honigmann, Évêques et évêchés (Leuven/Louvain, 1951), 157-160, 163f.

G. RÖWEKAMP

Theodore of Constantinople

Th. was a deacon, a rhetor, and the synodicarius of Paul II, patriarch of Constantinople (641-654). He authored two questions or aporias which he presented to the adversaries of Monotheletism and which, along with the answers or solutions addressed by → Maximus Conf. to a presbyter Marinus (PG 91:217-28), have been handed down among the works of Maximus (*qu. Max.*) The first question has to do with the *voluntas* and *ignorantia Christi*; in his response Maximus shows the contradiction in the aporia. The second question has to do with the term *naturales voluntates,* which Th. claims was not used by the church fathers; Maximus, however, shows that the fathers did use it.

W: PG 91:216f.
L: H. G. Beck, Kirche u. theol. Lit. (Munich, 1959), 433.

B. WINDAU

Theodore of Copros

Th. was a Monophysite deacon in Copros near Alexandria and was active in the second half of the 6th c. Acc. to John of Ephesus, *h.e.* 4.9, Th., together with presbyter → Theodosius Alex., composed a letter to Bishop Longinus of Nubia, asking him to come to Mareotis in order to consecrate a Jacobite patriarch for the church of Alexandria, which had been without a bishop for nine years. Only a fragment of Th.'s letter (*ep.*) is preserved.

W: *ep.,* J. B. Chabot, CSCO 17:273f.; CSCO 103:191 [text/Latin trans.]. — A. van Roey, P. Allen, Monophysite Texts of the 6th Cent. (Leuven/Louvain, 1994) [text/English trans.].
L: E. Honigmann, Évêques et évêchés monophysites (Leuven/Louvain, 1951), 226f.

P. BRUNS

Theodore of Heraclea

As bishop of Heraclea (formerly Perinth, in Thrace), Th. attended the Council of Tyre (355) as a semi-

Arian on the side of Eusebius of Nicomedia and against Athanasius. After the death of Eusebius (341) he, along with Narcissus of Neronias, took a leading position in eastern politics (among other things, as a member of a delegation of eastern bishops to the imperial court in Trier), and was excommunicated by the western bishops when he boycotted the Council of Sardica (342) and took part in the Countersynod of Philippopolis. His participation in the Synod of Sirmium (351) is attested. He died before the end of 355.

Theodoret of Cyrrhus praises Th. as a "very learned interpreter of the gospels" (*h.e.* 2.3.8: *ellogimos de diapherontōs*), while Jerome praises his clear style and literal interpretation (*vir. ill.* 90: *apertus sermo* and *historica intellegentia*; see praef. *in Matth.*; praef. *in Gal.*; *ep.* 112.20; 119.2). The catena fragments of Th.'s commentaries on Isa (*Isa.*), Pss (*Pss.*), Mt (*fr. Mt.*), and Jn (*fr. Jo.*, partly in a Gothic translation), among others (Lk, Acts, 1 Cor), show traits of the Antiochene school of exegetes (sober hist. interpretation; use of typology, metaphor, rarely allegory) and of the (Arian) Logos-flesh christology.

W: *Isa.*, PG 18:1307-1378. — *Pss.*, R. Devreesse, Les commentateurs des Psaumes (Rome, 1970), 328. — *fr. Luc.*, J. Reuß, Lk-Kommentare (Berlin, 1984), 11 [text]. — *fr. Mt.*, idem, Mt-Kommentare (Berlin, 1957), 55-95 [text]. — *fr. Jo.*, idem, Joh-Kommentare (Berlin, 1966), 65-178 [text]. — *fr. Act.*, J. A. Cramer, CGPNT 3 (Hildesheim, 1967 = Oxford, 1838), 145 [text]. — *fr. 1 Cor.*, Jerome, *ep.* 119.2 [text].
L: M. Faulhaber, Die Propheten-Catenen (Freiburg i.Br., 1899), 61-63. — M.-J. Rondeau, Les commentaires patristiques du Psautier 1 (Rome, 1982), 75f. — K. Schäferdiek, T. Kirchenpolitiker u. Exeget: FS J. Straub (Berlin, 1982), 393-410. — idem, Johanneskommentar: ZDA 110 (1981) 175-193 (= idem, Schwellenzeit [Berlin, 1996], 51-68, 69-87).

T. FUHRER

Theodore, Lector

Th. was a lector (*anagnōstēs*) at Hagia Sophia in Constantinople in the first half of the 6th c. Ca. 530, at the request of an unnamed bishop of Gangra in Paphlagonia, he combined the church histories of → Socrates, → Sozomen, and → Theodoret into a single work, later called the *Historia tripartita* (*h.tr.*), in four books, of which the first two have been preserved in a Venetian codex (*Cod. Marc.* 344) (not yet printed). It can be seen that Th. handled his models with great freedom, undertook both stylistic and dogmatic corrections, and introduced material of his own.

More important are the surviving remains of a second work, an independent continuation of the *h.tr.* to the time of Justin I (518-527), with the title *History of the Church* (*h.e.*). To judge by the fragments, political events were given attention only insofar as they had an impact on eccles. politics. The presentation is decisively influenced by Th.'s own eccles. and dogm. position (openly Chalcedonian, in opposition to Emperor Anastasius I and Timothy of Constantinople). The presentation also shows a major limitation of interest to the capital, as it seems to have been in the period before Justinian I strove to renew the empire. There is little to be said about Th.'s sources; he can be shown to have used, in addition to conciliar acts and other documents, other histories of the church (e.g., John Diacrinomenus). Further information about the entire *h.tr.* and *h.e.* is given in the corresponding sections of an epitome of church history (*e.*) of the 7th/8th c.

W: PG 86/1:165-228. — *h. tr., h.e., e.*, G. C. Hansen (Berlin, 1971) [text/comm.].
L: J. Bidez, La tradition manuscrite de Sozomène et la Tripartite de T. (Leipzig, 1908). — H.-G. Opitz, T.: PRE 5A/2:1869-1881.

U. HAMM

Theodore, Monk

Photius (*cod.* 108) tells of a work of Th., an Alex. monk and supporter of Patriarch Theodosius (535-566), against the agnoetism of Themistius. Photius praises the skillfulness of this *Confutatio brevis*, of which parts are preserved in Syriac but have not yet been published. After a response from Themistius, Th. answered in a three-volume work which Photius also mentions but which is entirely lost.

L: T. Hermann, Monophysitica: ZNW 32 (1933) 287-293.

G. RÖWEKAMP

Theodore of Mopsuestia

I. Life: Th., b. ca. 350 in Antioch, was from a wealthy family, who provided the young man with an excellent education under the pagan rhetor Libanius. There Th. came to know John Chrys., with whom he entered, at the age of twenty, into the Antiochene monastery of Diodorus of Tarsus; there, not without an interior crisis, he completed his theol. studies. After his studies Th. received priestly ordination from Bishop Flavian, whose Neo-Nicene wing he strengthened during the Meletian schism. After a short stay in Tarsus Th. became bishop of Mopsuestia in Cilicia in 392/393. During his thirty-nine-year episcopate (Theodoret, *h.e.* 5.40) Th. not only composed numerous commentaries and dogm. works but also made a decisive contribution to the settlement of the Pneumatomachian controversy in Asia Minor. In 394 Th. served as mediator in church matters at a provincial synod in Constantinople; in 420 he intervened in the Pelagian controversy, initially in favor of Julian of Eclanum, but he did not hesitate later on to condemn him as a heretic. Th. died in 428, before the outbreak of the Nestorian controversy.

L: L. Abramowski, Der Streit um Diodor u. Th.: ZKG 67 (1955/56) 262-293. — B. E. Carter, Chrysostom's Ad Theodorum lapsum: VigChr 16 (1962) 87-101. — R. Devrcesse, Essai sur Th. (Rome, 1948). — J. Dumortier, L'ancienne tradition latine de l'Ad Theodorum: StPatr 7 (1966) 178-183. — idem, La tradition manuscrite des traités à Théodore: ByZ 51 (1958) 66-72; 52 (1959) 265-275. — C. Fabricius, Adressat u. Titel der Schriften an Th.: CM 20 (1959) 68-97. — G. Jouassard, Ad Theodorum Lapsum: HJ 77 (1958) 140-150. — O. F. Fritzsche, De Th. Mopouestoni vita scriptis (Halle, 1834 = PG 66:1-104). — F. A. Sullivan, Some Reactions to Devreesse's New Study of Th.: TS 12 (1951) 179-201. — E. Wang, Th. et les origines du pélagianisme (Paris, 1961).

II. Works: Th. was an exceptionally prolific writer, as attested by the catalogue of Ebedjesu (BOCV 3, 1, 30-35) and the *Chronicle of Seert* (PO 5:289-91). He is regarded as the most important exegete of the Antiochene school and, with Nestorius, the most important theologian of the Persian church. His posthumous condemnation during the Three-Chapters controversy in 533 led to the almost complete destruction of his dogm. writings, which by that point had long since been translated into Syriac. Sizable parts of his exegetical works have come down either in the Gr. original or in Lat. translation.

Exegetical Works: The catenas make it possible to reconstruct the commentary on the Pss (*Ps.*) for Pss 1-80; other smaller fragments are available in an early Lat. translation. The commentary on the Minor Prophets (*Os.-Mal.*) is the only work that has survived complete in the original Gr. text. There are fragments on Gen (*Gen.*) as well as a Syr. translation of the commentary on Qoh (*Eccl.*). Th. commented on all the gospels, but only the commentary on Jn has survived complete in a Syr. translation; there are also numerous fragments in Gr. catenas. There are also considerable Gr. fragments on Mt. Th. commented on the entire *Corpus Paulinum* (*comm. in epp. Pauli*); the commentary is preserved in Greek and Latin.

Dogmatic Works: Except for a few Gr. fragments, Th.'s chief work, *De incarnatione* (*fr. inc.*), is

regarded as lost, ever since the single Syr. ms. in the library at Seert was lost in the confusion of the Kurdish rebellion of 1905. A few frags. still exist of the anti-Arian polemic against Eunomius (*c. Eun.*); the *Disputatio cum Macedonianis* (*disp. c. Mac.*), which Th. conducted in 392 in Anazarbus (Asia Minor), has come down complete in Syriac.

Practical Works: Nothing but a few fragments remain of Th.'s ascetical works *De sacerdotio* and *De perfectione morum*. The catechetical homilies (*hom. cat.*), the Syr. translation of which was discovered at the beginning of the 20th c., are of incalculable value for the history of the liturgy and for knowledge of Th.'s theology. The catecheses explain the creed (1-10), the Lord's Prayer (11), baptism (12-14), and finally the Eucharist (15/16) and come from Th.'s time as presbyter in Antioch before 392. An *Anaphora* handed down under Th.'s name is to be regarded as not authentic.

III. Basic Lines of Thought: Th. was regarded during his lifetime as an orthodox bishop but during the Nestorian controversy was denounced as a christological heretic by Cyril Alex. In Th. the Two-Nature teaching reached its interim high point. He is regarded as a classical representative of a symmetrical christology in which the two natures, or modes of existence, the divine and the human, are in perfect correspondence. The assumed man corresponds to the assuming Logos, while the moral progress of the Son of man corresponds to the gracing action of the Son of God, the two being connected by a perfect synergy. The unifying factor is given in the *prosopon* of the redeemer, but the unity is to be understood more as a result of the unification of the two natures and less as an ontologically definable reality in the sense of a hypostatic union. Th.'s chief merit is his struggle against Arianism and Apollinarism; he is one of the few 4th c. theologians who took an appropriate approach to the problem of the soul of Christ. His pneumatology, guided by the unbroken baptismal practice of the church, made an essential contribution to the completion of trinitarian dogma, inasmuch as, when applied at the ontological level, it extended the Nicene *homoousios* objectively to the divinity of the Spirit.

W: PG 66 (incomplete). — E. Sachau, Th. M. fragmenta syriaca (Leipzig, 1869) [Syriac text/Latin trans.]. — *Ps.*, R. Devreesse, Le commentaire de Th. sur les Psaumes (Rome, 1939) [Greek text]. — L. van Rompay, CSCO 435/436 [Syriac text/French trans.]. — L. de Conninck, CCL 88a [Latin text]. — *Gen.*, R. Tonneau, Interpretation de la Genèse: Muséon 66 (1953) 45-64 [text]. — E. Sachau, fr. 1-21 [Syriac text]. — T. Jansma, Interprétation du livre de la Genèse: Muséon 75 (1962) 63-92 [Syriac text]. — *Os.-Mal.*, H. N.

Sprenger, Th. Commentarius in XII prophetas (Wiesbaden, 1977) [Greek text]. — *Eccl.*, W. Strothmann, Das syr. Fragment des Ecclesiastes-Kommentar (Wiesbaden, 1988) [Syriac text]. — idem, Syr. Katenen (Wiesbaden, 1988) [Syriac text]. — *Jo.*, R. Devreesse, Essai sur Th. (Rome, 1948), 288-420 [Greek text]. — J. M. Vosté, CSCO 115/116 [Syriac text/Latin trans.]. — *Mt.*, J. Reuss, Mt-Kommentare aus der griech. Kirche (Berlin, 1957), 96-150 [Greek text]. — *comm. in epp. Pauli*, K. Staab, Pauluskommentare aus der griech. Kirche (Münster, ²1984), 113-212 [Greek text]. — H. B. Swete, Th. in epistolas B. Pauli Commentarii (Cambridge, 1880-1882) [Greek/Latin text]. — *fr. inc.*, idem, Commentarii 2 (Cambridge, 1882), 289-340 [Greek text]. — *disp. c. Mac.*, F. Nau, PO 9:637-677 [Syriac text/French trans.]. — *hom. cat.*, A. Mingana, Commentary of Th. of M. (Cambridge, 1932f.) [Syriac text/English trans.]. — R. Tonneau, R. Devreesse, Homélies catéchétiques (Rome, 1949) [Syriac text/French trans.]. — A. Rücker, Ritus baptismi et missae (Münster, 1933) [Latin trans.]. — P. Bruns, FC 17/1-2.
L: L. Abramowski, Zur Theologie des Th.: ZKG 72 (1961) 262-293. — R. Abramowski, Neue Schriften Th. s: ZNW 34 (1934) 66-84. — E. Amann, La doctrine christologique de Th.: RevSR 14 (1934) 161-190. — idem, Un nouvel ouvrage de Th.: RevSr 20 (1940) 491-528. — M. Anastos, The immutability of Christ: DOP 6 (1951) 125-160. — R. Arnou, Nestorianisme et Néoplatonisme: Gr. 17 (1936) 116-131. — E. Bihain, Le Contre Eunome de Th.: Muséon 75 (1962) 331-355. — P. Bruns, Den Menschen mit dem Himmel verbinden (Leuven/Louvain, 1995). — A. Cañizares Llovera, El catecumenato según T.: EMerced 32 (1976) 147-193. — T. A. Curtin, Baptismal Liturgy of Th. (Washington, 1971). — R. Devreesse, La méthode exégétique: RB 53 (1946) 207-241. — H. M. Diepen, L'Assumptus Homo à Chalcédoine: RThom 51 (1951) 573-608. — L. Fatica, I Commentari a Giovanni di T. e di Cirillo (Rome, 1988). — G. Ferraro, L'ora di Cristo e della Chiesa: Aug. 15 (1975) 275-307. — P. Galtier, Th.: Sa vraie pensée sur l'Incarnation: RSR 45 (1957) 161-186, 338-360. — R. A. Greer, Th. of M., Exegete and Theologian (London, 1961). — H. Kihn, Th. u. Junilius Africanus als Exegeten (Freiburg i.Br., 1880). — G. Koch, Die Heilsverwirklichung bei Th. (Munich, 1965). — J. Lécuyer, Sacerdoce chrétien: RSR 36 (1949) 481-516. — E. Mazza, La formula battesimale: EL 104 (1990) 23-34. — idem, La struttura dell'Anafora: EL 102 (1988) 147-183. — J. McKenzie, Annotations on the Christology of Th.: TS 19 (1958) 345-373. — idem, Commentary of Th. on John 1,46-51: TS 14 (1959) 73-84. — K. McNamara, Th. and the Nestorian Heresy: IThQ 19 (1952) 254-278; 20 (1953) 172-191. — J. McWilliam Dewart, The Theology of Grace (Washington, 1971). — eadem, The Notion of Person Underlying the Christology of Th.: StPatr 12 (1975/76) 199-207. — R. Norris, Manhood and Christ. A Study in the Christology of Th. (Oxford, 1963). — I. Oñatibia, Sobre la penitencia eclesiástica: FS J. Quasten (Münster, 1970), 427-440. — idem, La vida cristiana: ScrVict 1 (1954) 100-133. — L. Pirot, L'œuvre exégétique de Th. (Rome, 1913). — F. J. Reine, Eucharistic Doctrine and Liturgy (Washington, 1942). — K. Schäferdiek, Johannesverständnis des Th. (Bonn, 1958). — C. Schäublin, Methode u. Herkunft der Antiochenischen Exegese (Bonn, 1974), 84-155. — M. Simonetti, Note sull'esegesi veterotestamentaria di T.: VetChr 14 (1977) 69-102. — B. D. Spinks, The East Syrian Anaphora of Th.: EL 103 (1989) 441-455. — idem, D. Webb, The Anaphora of Th.: EL 104 (1990) 3-

22. — F. A. Sullivan, Christology of Th. (Rome, 1956). — A. Vaccari, Commento di T. ai Salmi: Misc. G. Mercati (Rome, 1946), 175-198. — idem, La θεωρία: Bib. 1 (1920) 3-36. — R. P. Vaggione, Fragments of Th. Contra Eunomium: JThS 31 (1980) 403-470. — J. M. Vosté, La chronologie de l'activité littéraire de Th.: RB 34 (1925) 54-81. — idem, De versione syriaca operum Th.: OCP 8 (1942) 477-481. — W. de Vries, Der "Nestorianismus" Th. s: OCP 7 (1941) 91-148. — idem, Das eschatologische Heil bei Th.: OCP 24 (1958) 309-338. — U. Wickert, Studien zu den Pauluskommentaren des Th. (Berlin, 1962). — A. Ziegenaus, Das Menschenbild des Th. (Munich, 1963).

P. BRUNS

Theodore of Paphos

Th. was bishop of Paphos on Cyprus around the middle of the 7th c. He has left an encomiastic speech in commemoration of St. Spiridon; he delivered it on Dec. 12, 655, in the church at Trimithus before the assembled bishops. Spiridon had been bishop of Trimithus in the 4th c. and was greatly honored on Cyprus as a prophet and wonderworker. Th. used as a source a (lost) life of the saint that was attributed to a Triphyllius; it was in iambic verse, dated from the end of the 5th c., and was also used by → Leontius of Naples for his *Vita* of St. Spiridon. Th.'s panegyric was used in turn by Simeon Metaphrastes and two other anonymous *Vitae*.

W: P. van den Ven, La légende de S. Spiridon (Leuven/Louvain, 1953), 1-103.
L: H. G. Beck, Kirche u. theol. Lit. (Munich, 1959), 456 n. 1, 463. — J.-M. Sauget, Spiridone: BSS 11:1354-1356.

B. WINDAU

Theodore of Petra

Th. was a disciple of coenobiarch Theodosius (d. 529) in the latter's monastery at Bethlehem. Th. composed a rhetorically elegant address on Theodosius that was delivered on the first anniversary of his death, on Jan. 11, 530, and, with minor changes, was published as his *Vita* after 547 (death of Patriarch Peter of Jerusalem). Th. himself later became bishop of Petra in Arabia. The *Vita* served Cyril of Scythopolis as a model for his life of Theodosius.

W: H. Usener, Der hl. Theodosius (Leipzig, 1890), 3-101 [text]. — A. J. Festugière, Les moines d'Orient 3/3 (Paris, 1963), 103-160 [French trans.].
L: K. Krumbacher, Studien zu den Legenden des hl. Theodosius, SAM 1892 (Munich, 1892), 220-279. — F. Speziale, Confronto tra le due biografie di Teodosio (Palermo, 1904).

G. RÖWEKAMP

Theodore of Philae

Th., a Monophysite bishop of Philae 525-578, played an important role in the Jacobite church of Egypt. Together with Julian, he was active in the conversion of the Nubians and, when Julian left the Nubians, Th. took over the task of caring for them. Th. remained among the new converts until 551, but evidently continued in this task until the coming of Bishop Longinus to Nubia in 569. A *Mandatum ad Longinum* is preserved in fragmentary form and in Syr. In it Th. authorized Longinus to attend, in his name, the consecration of a Jacobite patriarch for Alexandria, since he himself did not want to accompany Longinus.

W: I.-B. Chabot, CSCO 17/103:274f./192 [text/Latin trans.].
L: A. Grillmeier, Jesus der Christus 2/4 (Freiburg i.Br., 1990), 273-276 (English, Christ in Christian Tradition, vol. 2/4 [London, 1996]). — E. Honigmann, Évêques et évêchés monophysites (Leuven/Louvain, 1951), 175. — J. Maspéro, T.: RHR 59 (1909) 299-317.

B. WINDAU

Theodore of Raithu/Pharan

Th. was a monk and priest in a monastic settlement in Raithu (southwest of the Sinai peninsula) and author of a propaideutic work titled *Proparaskeuē* or *Praeparatio (praep.)*. The work consists of two parts, a heresiological and a dialectical, which have also been handed down separately. The second part offers philosophical information that endeavors, in a Neo-Chalcedonian fashion, to reconcile the statements of Chalcedon with Cyril. It is possible that the work was composed between 580 and 620 as a commentary on the dogm. treatises of → Anastasius I of Antioch.

Th. is to be identified, with considerable certainty, with the Theodore who at the end of the 6th and beginning of the 7th c. was bishop of Pharan, which was near Raithu. The latter was the first important representative of Monoenergism. When asked by Sergius of Constantinople for an opinion of the *mia-energeia* formula, he defended it in his letter to Sergius of Arsinoe and in his commentary on some testimonies of the fathers. Fragments are preserved in the acts of the sixth ecumenical council, which condemned Th. along with Sergius. Th. thus becomes an important witness to the bridge leading from Neo-Chalcedonianism to Monoenergism. He died certainly before 649, probably before 638.

Perhaps this Th. also composed the work, which Photius had read (*cod.* 1), on the genuineness of the Ps.-Dionysian writings. The work on the Trinity that is sometimes attributed to Th. is in fact an excerpt from book 5 of the *Fabulae haereticorum* of → Theodoret.

W: *praep.*, F. Diekamp, Analecta Patristica (Rome), 138, 173-227 [text]. — *fr.*, Mansi 11:568f., 572.
L: W. Elert, Die theopaschitische Formel: ThLZ 75 (1950) 195-206. — idem, Th. v. Pharan u. Th. v. Raithu: ThLZ 76 (1951) 67-76. — idem, Der Ausgang der altkirchlichen Christologie (Berlin, 1957). — M. Richard, Th.: DThC 15:282-284.

G. RÖWEKAMP

Theodore of Rome

Theodore I (Th.), b. in Jerusalem, succeeded John IV as pope (642-649) and defended Roman primacy over the other local churches. As an opponent of Monotheletism, he called in 643 for the retroactive canonical deposition of Monothelite Patriarch Pyrrhus I, who had been replaced by Paul II. In 645/646 Th. again recognized Pyrrhus, who had returned from Africa with Maximus Conf. and had abjured Monotheletism and the *Ecthesis*; Pyrrhus was hoping for Th.'s support in being reinstated as patriarch of Constantinople, but in 646/647 Th. again suspended him (as he did Paul in 648/649) because of his public profession of Monotheletism.

The two surviving letters of Th. are the one that his embassy brought to Paul and the one to the bishops who had participated in Paul's consecration, with its request to remove Paul's name from the diptychs.

W: PL 129:577-584. — PL 87:75-82.
L: O. Bertoloni, Roma di fronte a Bisanzio e ai Longobardi (Bologna, 1941), 327-337 — P. Conte, Chiesa e Primato nelle lettre dei Papi del secolo VII (Milan, 1971), 433-442. — G. Ladner, Die Bildnisse der östlichen Päpste des 7. u. 8. Jh.: Atti del V Congresso Internazionale di Studi Bizantini 2 (Rome, 1940), 169-182. — L. Magi, La sede romana (Rome, 1972), 212-221. — A. N. Stratos, Il Patriarca Pirro: Byz(T) 8 (1976) 9-19.

C. SCHMIDT

Theodore of Scythopolis

Th. was a Palestinian monk and active in the first half of the 6th c. He was head of the New Laura, an important center of the Origenism of that day, before becoming staurophylax, or guardian, of the holy cross, and then metropolitan of Scythopolis, a post which he acquired thanks to the influential Theodore Ascidas. Th. was drawn by the strict religious policy of Emperor Justinian I into the first Origenist controversy in 543. He avoided a definitive condemnation in 553 by means of his *Libellus de erroribus*

Origenianis in which he broke sharply from his own Origenist past and emphatically rejected a radical interpretation of the Apocalypse (restoration of the devil and demons and the annihilation of what is corporeal, of persons, and of every distinction in the name of the divine All-and-One).

W: PG 86:232-236.
L: F. Diekamp, Die origenistischen Streitigkeiten (Münster, 1899). — A. Grillmeier, Jesus der Christus 2/2 (Freiburg i.Br., 1989), 424-430 (English, Christ in Christian Tradition, vol. 2/2 [London, 1995]). — J. Irmscher, Teodoro Scitopolitano: Aug. 26 (1986) 185-190.

P. Bruns

Theodore Spudaeus

Th., dates of birth and death unknown, was a monk in the monastery of the Spoudaioi, who had settlements in Jerusalem and Constantinople; he was a friend of Pope Martin I (649-655) and of Anastasius the apocrisiarius. For this reason, in his *Hypomnesticon* (*hyp.*; probably ca. 668/669) he described the sufferings that Martin I and Anastasius had to endure in the Monotheletism controversy under Emperor Constans II (641-668). Anastasius the Librarian (9th c.) translated the *hyp.* into Latin. It is not certain that Th. also composed the *Commemoratio* (*com.*; written possibly in 654), which reports on the fate of Martin I until his death. The text has come down only in the Lat. translation by Anastasius the Librarian.

W: *hyp.*, R. Devreesse, Le Texte grec de l'Hypomnesticum de T.: AnBoll 53 (1935) 49-80. — PG 90:193-202 [Latin trans.]. — *com.*, PL 129:591-604.
L: H. G. Beck, Kirche u. theol. Lit. (Munich, 1959), 462f.

F. R. Gahbauer, OSB

Theodore Syncellus

In the 7th c. Th. was a presbyter and syncellus in Hagia Sophia, Constantinople. In 626 he took part in a peace-seeking mission from Emperor Heraclius to Adrianople and the khan of the Avars. Two works of Th. have been handed down. One deals with the *Inventio et depositio vestis in Blachernis* (*inv.*); it tells of the translation of the clothing of the Mother of God from Jerusalem to the church of Blachernae in Constantinople. The work was read on July 2 of a year between 620 and 625. Th.'s second work is a homily on the siege of Constantinople by the Avars and was delivered on the feast of the Deliverance from the Avars, in August 626 (*De obsidione Constantinopolitana sub Heraclio imperatore*; *obs.*); it is an important hist. document.

W: *inv.*, F. Combefis, Novum Auctarium 2 (Paris, 1648), 751-786 [text]. — C. Loparev: Vizantijskij Vremmenik 2 (1895) 592-612 [pars posterior]. — *obs.*, L. Sternbach, Analecta Avarica (Cracow, 1900), 2-24/24-27 [text/varia lectio]. — F. Makk (Szeged, 1975) [text = reprint, Sternbach/French trans./comm.].
L: H. G. Beck, Kirche u. theol. Lit. (Munich, 1959), 545. — J. L. van Dieten, Geschichte der Patriarchen (Amsterdam, 1977), 114-121, 174-178. — A. Wenger, L'assomption de la T. S. Vierge (Paris, 1955), 11-138.

B. Windau

Theodore of Tabennisi

Born ca. 314 in Upper Egypt, Th. joined Pachomius at the age of fourteen. From 350 until his death (368), as Horsiesi's representative, he guided the association of Pachomian monasteries with great skill in a time of crisis. Of Th.'s works there have been preserved the remnants of three *Catecheses* (*catech.* [Copt.]), fragments (*fr.* [Copt.]), an Easter letter *Ep. ad omnia monasteria de pascha* (*de pascha* [Lat. translation by → Jerome]), and the *Ep. ad monachos Nitriotas* (*ad monach.* [Greek]). Ca. 1972, two further Copt. mss. were discovered, including an *Ep. remissionis* ("Letter of remission,"; *ep. remiss.*) occasioned by the annual autumn meeting of the Pachomians.

W: *catech., fr.*, L. T. Lefort, CSCO 159f. [text/French trans.]. — *de pascha*, A. Boon (Leuven/Louvain, 1932), 105f. [Latin trans.]. — *ad monach.*, F. Halkin (Brussels, 1932), 118 [text]. — *ep. rem.*, H. Quecke: Or. 44 (1975) 426-433 [text]. — A. Veilleux, vol. 3 (Kalamazoo, Mich., 1982), 127-131 [English trans.]. — A. de Vogüé: StMon 28 (1986) 7-50 [French trans./comm.].
L: H. Bacht, Christusgemeinschaft: FS J. Betz (Düsseldorf, 1984), 444-455. — T. Baumeister, Mentalität: ZKG 88 (1977) 145-160. — M. Krause, Erlaßbrief: FS H. J. Polotsky (East Gloucester, 1981), 220-238. — M. Krause, K. Hoheisel, Aegypten II: RAC. Suppl. 1:83. — B. Steidle, Der heilige Abt Th.: EuA 44 (1968) 91-103. — idem, Osterbrief: ibid., 104-119. — A. Veilleux, T.: CoptE 7:2239f.

M. Skeb, OSB

Theodore of Trimithus

Of Bishop Th. of Trimithus in Cyprus we know only that he attended the sixth ecumenical council in Constantinople as representative of Epiphanius II, archbishop of Cyprus; he spoke at the fourteenth session, on April 5, 681, and took a position against Monotheletism (Mansi 7:1019). The only work of Th. that has come down is a short one *On the Life, Banishment, and Distresses of John Chrysostom* (*De vita et exsilio et afflictionibus beatissimi Joannis Chrysostomi, Archiepiscopi Constantinopolitani*).

Although Th. used the description of Chrysostom's life by → Palladius of Helenopolis, his work cannot stand the test of a historical-critical examination, even though it gives the appearance of being based on a study of the sources. To some extent the work is more of a novel and a witness to the formation of legends that had begun long before the 250th anniversary of John's death.

W: PG 47:51-88.
L: C. Baur, Chrysostomus u. seine Zeit 1 (Munich, 1929), XX.

R. Kaczynski

Theodoret of Cyrrhus

I. **Life:** Th., b. ca. 393 in Antioch, d. ca. 466, received his religious and theol. education in monasteries of that city. It is less probable, however, that Theodore Mops. was his teacher and Nestorius and John of Antioch his fellow students, even though there is an unmistakable closeness of thought among all these writers. In 423 Th. became bishop of the little city of Cyrrhus, east of Antioch, where in addition to his spiritual duties of preaching, he tried to improve the appearance of the city with bricks and mortar. Deeply rooted as he was in the thought of the Antiochene school, in 431 he published two works attacking Cyril Alex. and the Council of Ephesus at which he himself had been a presider. In 434 Th. gave his official approval to the compromise formula of 433, to the final form of which he had contributed not a little; but he did not end his personal friendship with Nestorius. The teaching of Eutyches found in Th. its sharpest critic. For this reason he was deposed at the so-called Robber Synod but, on appealing to Leo I at Chalcedon (451), was solemnly rehabilitated, after he had previously, with a heavy heart, brought himself to a formal condemnation of Nestorius's error. A hundred years later, the fifth ecumenical Council of Constantinople (553) condemned Th.'s works against Cyril and Ephesus, as well as some of his letters and sermons, as among the Three Chapters. Roman Bishop Vigilius agreed with the verdict, with some reservations, in his *constitutio*.

L: Y. Azéma, Th. de Cyr d'après sa correspondance (Paris, 1952). — K. Günther, Th. u. die Kämpfe der orientalischen Kirche (Aschaffenburg, 1913). — E. Honigmann, Th. and Basil. Time of Their death: StT 173 (1953) 243-248. — J. Schulte, Th. als Apologet (Vienna, 1904).

II. **Works:** Th. was among the most prolific writers of the Gr. church and was equally important in all literary fields. In 450 his body of work already contained thirty-five titles (*ep.* 116; 145). He had studied the classics and always sought to rival educated pagans in the area of literature. Such stylists as Photius (*cod.* 203) praise his pure Attic style.

Dogmatic writings: Th.'s chief work, which is as it were a summa of his christological thought, is the *Eranistes* (*eran.*), a polemic against Eutyches that is espec. valuable for its many testimonies. The *Expositio rectae confessionis* (*rect. conf.*) and the *Quaestiones et responsiones ad orthodoxos* (*quaest.*) have come down under the name of Justin. There are fragmentary remains of the refutation of Cyril's twelve anathematisms (431; *repr.*), of the five books (*Pentalogus*) against Cyril and Ephesus (*pental.*), and of the defense of Diodorus and Theodore (*Diod.*). In addition, Th. wrote, before 431, a work handed down under Cyril's name on trinitarian theology (*trin.*) and on the incarnation of God (*inc.*) which is preserved in two parts with separate titles. There is also from his pen an anonymous treatise on Jesus Christ. Other writings against the Eunomians, Pneumatomachians, Apollinarists, Marcionites, and Origen, as well as a *Liber mysticus* and the *Libri de virginitate*, are regarded as lost.

Apologetic Writings: Th. wrote an important apology against paganism under the title *Cure for Greek Illnesses* (*affect.*). In twelve books he provides Chr. answers to each pagan objection. He goes in great detail into basic questions of philosophy and theology, citing over a hundred pagan authors. Also apologetic in character are the ten addresses on divine providence (*provid.*) which he delivered in Antioch from 435 to 437. The first five have to do with natural knowledge of God, the others with various ethical questions and the soteriological aspect of the incarnation.

Exegetical Writings: Th. must be accounted, along with → Theodore Mops., as the leading exegete of the Antiochene school and the most important interpreter of Chr. antiquity. His numerous exegetical works are outstanding in both content and form. The foundation of his exegesis is grammatical and hist. interpretation, which does not, however, exclude a moderate use of typology and allegory. Th. composed complete commentaries on the Psalms (*Ps.*), the Song (*Cant.*), all the prophets (*proph.*), and the Pauline corpus; he also produced treatises (*qu.*) on the Octateuch and the other hist. books of the OT. Of his sermons only little remnants have survived.

Letters: Ca. 230 letters have survived of Th.'s extensive correspondence, and they form one of the most important sources for 5th c. history; outstanding are the fourteen festal letters, most of them sent to friends and acquaintances after eccles. feastdays.

Historical Works: Th. wrote three hist. works: a history of the church (*h.e.*) covering the period from 325 to 428, the work being apologetic and antiheretical in tendency and showing numerous parallels to → Socrates and → Sozomen (see → Theodore, Lector); a monastic history (*h.rel.*) describing the life of ascetics near Antioch and Cyrrhus; finally, a history of heretics (*haer.*), a compendium of heretical views down to Eutyches that is of considerable value for the history of dogma.

W: PG 80-84. — *eran.*, G. H. Ettlinger, Eranistes (Oxford, 1975) [text]. — *rect. conf.*, J. C. T. Otto, CAC IV (Jena, 1881). — *quaest.*, idem, CAC V (Jena, 1881). — A. v. Harnack, Diodor v. Tarsus (Leipzig, 1901), 61-160 [German trans.]. — *Diod.*, L. Abramowski, Streit um Diodor u. Theodor: ZKG 67 (1955/56) 252-287 [Latin frags.]. — *pental.*, E. Schwartz, Zur Schriftstellerei Th. s: SBAW. PPH 52/1 (1922) 32-40 [text]. — M. Richard, Les citations de Th.: RB 43 (1934) 78-86 [text]. — *Trin., inc.*, PG 75:1147-1190, 1419-1478. — *affect.*, J. Raeder (Leiden, 1904) [text]. — N. Festa, Terapia dei morbi pagani (Florence, 1930) [text/Italian trans.]. — R. P. Canivet, SC 57. — K. Gutberlet, BKV² 50 [German trans.]. — *provid.*, Y. Azéma, Th. Discours sur la providence (Paris, 1954) [French trans.]. — G. M. Schuler, BKV¹ 25-199 [German trans.]. — *Ps.*, R. Devreesse, Anciens commentateurs grecs: RB 44 (1935) 167-170. — A. Möhle, Th. Kommentar zu Jesaja (Berlin, 1932). — *epp. Paul.*, PG 82:35-878. — *ep.*, J. Sakkelion, Τοῦ μακαριωτάτου Θ. ἐπιστολαί (Athens, 1885) [text]. — Y. Azéma, SC 40, 98, 111, 429. — A. Seider, BKV² 51 [German trans.]. — *h.e.*, L. Parmentier, F. Scheidweiler, GCS 44 [text]. — B. Jackson, NPNF 3:1-348 [English trans.]. — A. Seider, BKV² 51 [German trans.]. — *h. rel.*, H. Lietzmann, Leben des hl. Simeon: TU 32 (1908) 1-18 [text extract]. — G. Gutberlet, BKV² 50 [German trans.]. — A. Hamman, Vie des Pères du Désert (Paris, 1962), 109-284 [French trans.].
L: J. R. Asmus, Th. s Therapeutik: ByZ 3 (1894) 116-145. — M. Aubineau, Les 318 serviteurs d'Abraham: RHE 41 (1966) 5-43. — Y. Azéma, Th. après sa correspondance (Paris, 1952). — idem, Chronologie: REG 67 (1954) 82-94. — G. Bardy, Littérature patristique: RB 42 (1933) 211-229, 219-225. — A. Bertram, Th.s doctrina christologica (Hildesheim, 1883). — M. Brok, La date du commentaire sur le psautier: RHE 44 (1949) 552-556. — idem, Date of Th.s exposition: JThS NS 2 (1951) 178-183. — idem, Lettres Festales: VigChr 5 (1951) 103-110. — idem, De waarde van de curatio: StC 27 (1952) 201-212. — L. Canet, Th. in Danielem: MAH 34 (1914) 97-200. — P. Canivet, Sur la date: RSR 36 (1949) 585-593. — idem, Histoire d'une entreprise (Paris, 1957). — idem, Th. et le messalianisme: RMab 51 (1961) 26-34. — idem, Περὶ ἀγάπης: TU 92 (1966) 143-158. — idem, Le monachisme syrien (Paris, 1977). — O. Cullmann, Étude sur le κατέχων: RHPhR 16 (1936) 210-245. — J. Darrouzès, Un recueil épistolaire: REB 14 (1956) 87-121. — H. Diepen, J. Daniélou, Th. et le dogme d'Éphèse: RSR 44 (1956) 243-248. — A. Ehrhard, Die Cyrill zugeschriebene Schrift über die Menschwerdung (Tübingen, 1888). — A. J. Festugière, Antioche païenne (Paris, 1959), 241-388. — F. X. Funk, Ps-Justin u. Diodor: idem, Kirchengeschichtliche Abhandlungen (Paderborn, 1907), 323-350. — W. Göber, Quaestiones rythmicae

(Halle, 1926). — A. Grillmeier, Jesus der Christus 1 (Freiburg i.Br., 1979), 602-700 (English, Christ in Christian Tradition, vol. 1 [London, ²1975]). — J. Gross, La divinisation du chrétien (Paris, 1938), 273-320. — A. Güldenpennig, Kirchengeschichte des Th. (Halle, 1889). — K. Jüssen, Christologie des Th.: ThGl 27 (1935) 438-452. — C. E. Hill, A Spiritual Director from Antioch: Pacifica 12 (1999) 181-191. — J. Lebon, Restitutions: RHE 26 (1930) 523-550. — K. McNamara, Th. and the Unity of Person: IThQ 22 (1955) 313-328. — P. C. da Mazzarino, La dottrina di T. (Rome, 1941). — N. del Molar, Una empresa apologética: EstFr 60 (1959) 411-434. — E. Montmasson, L'homme créé à l'image de Dieu: EO 14 (1911) 334-339; 15 (1912) 154-162. — P. Peeters, Syméon Stylite: AnBoll 61 (1943) 29-72. — M. Richard, L'activité littéraire: RSPhTh 24 (1935) 83-106. — idem, Notes sur l'évolution doctrinale: RSPhTh 25 (1936) 459-481. — idem, La lettre de Th. à Jean d'Égée: RSPhTh 2 (1941/42) 415-423. — idem, Th., Jean d'Antioche: MSR 3 (1946) 147-156. — W. Riedel, Auslegung des Hld (Leipzig, 1898). — L. Saltet, Les sources de l'eraniste: RHE 6 (1905) 289-303, 513-536, 741-754. — S. Schiwietz, Morgenländisches Mönchtum (Vienna, 1938), 238-258. — J. Schulte, Th. als Apologet (Vienna, 1904). — E. Schwartz, Zur Schriftstellerei Th. s: SBAW. PPH 52,1 (1922) 30-40. — R. V. Sellers, Ps-Justin's expositio: JThS 46 (1945) 145-160. — F. A. Specht, Exegetischer Standpunkt (Munich, 1871). — J. L. Stewardson, Christology of Th., Diss. (Evanston, 1972).

P. Bruns

Theodosius of Alexandria

Th., a disciple of anti-Chalcedonian theologian Severus of Antioch, was elected successor of Timothy III in 535. This election was challenged by Gaianus, but with the help of Empress Theodora it was confirmed. Emperor Justinian called Th. to Constantinople (536) in order to win him over to the Chalcedonian side. Th. refused and was imprisoned until his death (566). In his writings against Chalcedon (*fr.*) Th. appealed not only to the major councils but above all to Cyril, the *Henotikon* of Zeno, which he interpreted as a condemnation of Chalcedon, and to many fathers (including Apollinarist texts). Some homilies (*hom.*) are preserved in Coptic.

W: *fr.*, W. Wolska-Connus, SC 197:301, 303. — F. Diekamp, Doctrina patrum (Münster, 1981 = 1907), 314. — I. B. Chabot, CSCO 17:5-11, 34-84, 86-90, 96-98, 114-124, 132-143 [text]. — E. W. Brooks, CSCO 87:158-163, 168-173 [text]. — *hom.*, K. H. Kuhn, CSCO 268, 269 [text]. — idem: Muséon 88 (1975) 103-112. — E. A. W. Budge, Miscellaneous Coptic Texts in the Dialect of Upper Egypt (London, 1915), 312-431. — M. Chaîne: ROC 29 (1933/34) 273-313 [text/French trans.].
L: M. van Esbroeck, La date et l'auteur du De Sectis attribué à Léonce de Byzance: After Chalcedon, ed. C. Laga et al. (Leuven/Louvain, 1985), 415-424. — W. H. C. Frend, The Rise of the Monophysite Movement (Cambridge, 1972). — A. Grillmeier, Jesus der Christus 2/4 (Freiburg i.Br., 1990),

53-59 (English, Christ in Christian Tradition, vol. 2/4 [London, 1996]).

T. Böhm

Theodosius, Archdeacon

Two of twelve mss. name an (arch-) deacon Th. as author of a work titled *De situ terrae sanctae*. The author probably came from North Africa (he speaks of an Arian monastery as *religionis Vandalorum*, see 14) and wrote before 531.

The work, which lacks unity of style and content, was composed from numerous sources; it cannot be judged with certainty how extensive the redactor's work was. In terms of genre, the following parts may be distinguished: itinerarium, pilgrim's account, lists of cities, excerpts from the Bible, stories, lists of provinces. Attempts to identify individual sources remain uncertain. In its present form, the work describes the holy places of Palestine, starting with Jerusalem, as well as parts of Syria, Egypt, Armenia, and Mesopotamia. Despite numerous errors, the work provides a great deal of otherwise unattested detailed information and legends and is one of the earliest witnesses to various traditions regarding Palestinian saints (Elizabeth and George among others). Many scholars also identify Th. with the compiler of the Theodosian collection of acts and canons (→ Canonical Collections).

W: P. Geyer, CSEL 39:135-150. — P. Geyer, CCL 175:113-125. — H. Donner, Pilgerfahrt ins hl. Land (Stuttgart, 1979), 190-225 [German trans.].
L: A. Di Berardino (ed.), Patrologia 4 (Genoa, 1996), 508f. — D. Günzburg, L'Itinéraire de Th.: RCHL 16 (1882) 221-223. — B. Kötting, Peregrinatio religiosa (Münster, ²1980), 360f. — J. Wilkinson, Jerusalem Pilgrims before the Crusades (London, 1977), 5f., 63-71, 184-192.

G. Röwekamp

Theodosius of Jerusalem

Under the name of Th., bishop of Jerusalem, an encomium of George the martyr has been handed down in Coptic. Th. is possibly the same as the Monophysite monk and antipatriarch of 453.

W: E. A. W. Budge, The Martyrdom and Miracles of St. George, Oriental Text Series 1 (London, 1888), 38-44, 236-241 [text/English trans.].

G. Röwekamp

Theodosius, Presbyter in Alexandria

Th. was a Monophysite priest in Alexandria and lived in the second half of the 6th c. Together with Theodore of Copros, he saw to the reoccupation of Jacobite episcopal sees by suitable Monophysite candidates. Th. is regarded as co-author of a letter to the Nubian Bishop Longinus, formerly a priest in Alexandria, exhorting him to communion with Theodore of Philae. Th. is also regarded as author of several theol. treatises (*tract.*).

W: *ep.*, I. B. Chabot, CSCO 17:272-273. — *tract.*, A. van Roey, P. Allen, Monophysite Texts of the 6th cent. (Leuven/Louvain, 1994) [text].
L: A. Grillmeier, Jesus der Christus 2/4 (Freiburg i.Br., 1990), 63, 72 (English, Christ in Christian Tradition, vol. 2/4 [London, 1996]).

T. Böhm, P. Bruns

Theodotion

Th.'s life and work cannot be discussed separately: tradition ascribes texts from two sources to a revision of the LXX by Th.: (1) a Gr. translation of the book of Daniel that has survived complete and since the 3rd c. has superseded the LXX in eccles. use and in the mss. (although even previously, in citations by the church fathers, what is more frequently found is a textually stable, i.e., literarily established blending of LXX and Th.); (2) the fragments of this revision that are preserved in the Hexapla of → Origen (not from the sixth column but from the quite extensive material for correcting the LXX in the fifth column *sub asterisco*).

Scholars have connected this revision with a 1st c. recension of the LXX, the so-called *kaige* or Palestinian recension (the dating is affected by the fact that such "Theodotionist" readings are found in, e.g., the Gr. scroll of the prophets from Naḥal Ḥever, and possibly also in the NT, in *Barn.*, *1 Clem.* and Hermas). On this basis, some wanted to identify Th. with Jonathan ben 'Uzziel, a disciple of Hillel who lived in the 1st c., but this suggestion received less acceptance. Even the attribution of the Dan text to Th. is disputed but has also received confirmation from more recent arguments.

The reports in the church fathers are only partially in agreement with these findings: acc. to Irenaeus, Th. was a Jewish proselyte from Ephesus (*haer.* 3.21.1); improbable, on the other hand, is the idea that he came from Pontus and that before his conversion under Commodus (180-192) he had been a supporter of Marcion; acc. to Epiphanius, Th.'s translation of the OT was guided by the LXX (*mens.* 17 [Syr. text, col. 55d/56a]). It is also unlikely that Th. was an Ebionite (thus Jerome, *vir. ill.* 54.6).

The character of Th.'s revision has been described

thus (among other ways): "Changes in detail without a revision of the basic nature of the LXX" and "Hebraization."

W: cf. → Origen, Hexapla.
L: D. Barthélemy, Les devanciers d'Aquila (Leiden, 1963). — R. Bodenmann, Naissance d'une Exégèse (Tübingen, 1986). — S. P. Brock, Bibelübersetzungen 1: TRE 6:163-172. — idem, A Classified Bibliography of the Septuagint (Leiden, 1973). — C. Dogniez, Bibliography of the Septuagint (1970-1993) (Leiden, 1995). — G. Dorival, M. Harl, O. Munnich, La Bible Grecque des Septante (Paris, 1988), 151-157. — K. Koch, Die Herkunft der Proto-Theodotion-Übersetzung des Danielbuches: VT 23 (1973) 362-365. — A. Rahlfs, Ueber Theodotion-Lesarten im NT u. Aquila-Lesarten bei Justin: ZNW 20 (1921) 182-199. — A. Schmitt, Stammt der sog. "Th"-Text bei Daniel wirklich von Th.? (Göttingen, 1966). — E. Würthwein, Der Text des AT (Stuttgart, ⁵1988).

C. MARKSCHIES

Theodotus of Ancyra

I. Life: As bishop of Ancyra, Th. was initially a supporter of Nestorius, but at the Council of Ephesus (431) he changed his position and fought against John of Antioch. The latter excommunicated him on the spot and renewed the penalty at a provincial synod in Tarsus (432). Th. died before 446 after having his successor consecrated by Patriarch Proclus of Constantinople.
II. Works: The following come from Th.'s pen: three books (extant in Syr.) against Nestorius (*c. Nest.*) that have not yet been edited; an explanation of the Nicene Creed (*exp. symb. Nic.*), which is also aimed against the supporters of Nestorius; a fragmentary letter to Vitalis (*ep. ad Vit.*); and several Gr. homilies (*hom.*) on the birth of Christ and the Mother of God, which were in part delivered in Ephesus and are also preserved in Eth. A further homily on the baptism of the Lord (*bapt. Dom.*) cannot be assigned to Th. with certainty; an encomium on St. George in Copt. (*enc. in Georg.*) is also attributed to Th.

The fathers of the second Council of Nicaea (787) thought of Th. as a comrade-in-arms of Cyril; he was a zealous defender of the traditional Theotokos title and in his homilies praised the lasting virginity of the Mother of God in an effusive panegyrical style. In christology Th. was decisive in confessing the oneness of Christ *in* two natures and in objecting strongly to the Two-Sons doctrine attributed to the Antiochenes, although he himself did not adopt a specific terminology pointing to the hypostatic union.

W: *c. Nest.*, A. Baumstark, Geschichte (Bonn, 1922), 161 [Syriac mss.]. — *exp. symb. Nic.*, PG 77:1313-1348. — *hom.*,

PG 77:1349-1432. — ACO 1, 1, 2, 71-73. — M. Aubineau, Nativité du Seigneur: OCP 26 (1960) 221-250 [Greek text/French trans.]. — B. M. Weischer, Qêrellos 4/1. Homilien u. Briefe (Wiesbaden, 1979), 42-53, 122-133, 179-191 [Ethiopic text/German trans.]. — A. Baumstark, op. cit., 262 [Syriac ms]. — *ep. ad Vit.*, PG 84:814. — *bapt. Dom.*, M. Aubineau: FS J. A. Aldama (Granada, 1969), 6-30 [Greek text/French trans.]. — *enc. in Georg.*, E. A. W. Budge, Martyrdom of St. George (London, 1888), 83-172, 274-331 [Coptic text/English trans.].
L: L. Cignelli, Maria Nuova Eva (Assisi, 1966), 157-201.

P. BRUNS

Theodotus of Antioch

Th. was successor of Alexander as bishop of Antioch 420/421-429. He vindicated John Chrys. and brought the Apollinarists back to the church. At a synod in Antioch under his presidency (420/421; Mansi 4:296B) Pelagius was condemned and driven from Antioch. Th., whom his contemporaries evidently esteemed highly (Theodoret, *h.e.* 5.38), has left two fragments: *Ad Heraclidem* (*fr.*), against the Apollinarists, and *Ad Cononem presbyterum Ephesinum* (*Con.*).

W: *fr.*, F. Diekamp, Doctrina patrum (Münster, ²1981), 34, Nr. 7 [text]. — *Con.*, M. Gitlbauer, Die Überreste griech. Tachygraphie (Vienna, 1878), 81 [text].
L: Die Geschichte des Christentums 2 (Freiburg i.Br., 1996), 541. — E. Venables, T.: DCB 4:983f.

B. WINDAU

Theodotus of Byzantium

Th., a worker in leather, came to Rome from Byzantium at the end of the 2nd c. He rejected the divinity of Christ (eight supposed proofs in → Epiphanius of Salamis) and was excommunicated by Bishop Victor (Hippolytus, *haer.* 7.35; 10.23; Ps.-Tertullian, *haer.* 8.2; Epiphanius, *haer.* 54). In the time of Zephyrinus, Th.'s disciples, who had erroneous christologies, supposedly set up an antibishop named Vitalis. These disciples or a third generation of so-called dynamist Monarchians are said to have occupied themselves with ancient logic and with text-critical work on the Bible, but references to works of their own are vague (Hipp., *haer.* 7.36.1; 10.24; Eusebius, *h.e.* 5.28; Novatian, *trin.*, passim; Ps.-Tert., *haer.* 8.3; Epiph., *haer.* 55).

W: Epiphanius, *haer.* 54.1.9-6.1.
L: M. Decker, Monarchianer, Diss. (Hamburg, 1987), 66-130. — B. D. Ehrman, Theodotians: StPatr 25 (1993) 46-51. — R. Hanig, Petrusakten: StPatr 31 (1997) 112-120. — A. v. Harnack, Lehrbuch der Dogmengeschichte 1 (Tübingen, 1990 = Tübingen, ⁴1909), 708-716. — P. Lampe, Die

stadtröm. Christen (Tübingen, ²1989), 290-294. — W. A. Löhr, Theodotus: ZNW 87 (1996) 101-125. — H. Schöne, Einbruch: FS F. J. Dölger (Münster, 1939), 252-265.

R. HANIG

Theodotus, a Valentinian

Almost nothing is known of the life and works of Th., a "Valentinian" gnostic. But → Clement Alex. quotes from his writings, and these passages are preserved (under the probably later title of *Excerpta ex Theodoto* [*exc. Thdt.*] in *Cod. Laur.* V, 3, fol. 358ʳ). Therefore the indication in the title that Th. was a contemporary of Valentinus is to be accepted with reservations. The title does not at all support an identification of Th. with Theodas, a disciple of Paul. This is reason for dating Th. to the 2nd c.

Along with Clement's observations, the *exc. Thdt.* contain very varied Valentinian materials that can be divided into four groups: §§ 1-28, §§ 29-42, §§ 43-65 (these are related to the report by the disciples of Ptolemy in Irenaeus, *haer.* 1.1-8), as well as §§ 66-86. In §§ 22, 26, 30, and 35 texts are explicitly attributed to Th. Using great caution, one can conclude from these materials that Th. held a Platonizing concept of God (30.1) and taught the Valentinian Pleroma and Aeons (35.1), a demiurge as inferior creator (38.2 [?]), a split into redemptive personages (22.7; 26.1; 32.2), and a predestination of human beings by classes (41.1) or by the zodiac (25.2). Th. seems to have belonged to the "eastern school" of Valentinianism.

The well-known questions (*exc. Thdt.* 78.2: "Who were we? What have we become? Into what have we been thrown? Whither are we hastening? By what are we set free? What is birth? What is rebirth?") are not gnostic (in contrast to the answers given) nor do they belong to the material excerpted from Th.

W: Clement, *exc. Thdt.*, F. Sagnard, SC 23. — R. P. C. Casey, StD 1 (London, 1934) [text/English trans./comm.]. — W. Foerster, Die Gnosis 1 (²1995), 193-204, 287-302 [German trans.].
L: A.-J. Festugière, Notes sur les extraits de Th. de Clément d'Alexandrie: idem, Études d'Histoire et de Philologie (Paris, 1975), 161-175. — W. Foerster, Von Valentin zu Herakleon (Giessen, 1928). — C. Markschies, Valentinian Gnosticism: The Nag Hammadi Library after Fifty Years, ed. J. D. Turner, A. M. McGuire (Leiden, 1997), 401-438. — A. Orbe, A propósito de exc. ex Thdt. 54, 2: Gr. 41 (1960) 481-485. — idem, La trinidad maléfica: Gr. 49 (1968) 726-761. — F.-M. M. Sagnard, La Gnose Valentinienne et le témoignage de Saint Irénée (Paris, 1947). — T. Zahn, Geschichte des ntl. Kanons 2/2 (Hildesheim, 1975 = Erlangen, 1892).

C. MARKSCHIES

Theodulus

Th., who seems to have been a Nestorian, was a presbyter in Coelesyria. He may have been a student of Theodore Mops.; he died during the reign of Emperor Zeno (474-491). Gennadius (*vir ill.* 92 [Richardson]) attributes to him a work *De consonantia Novi et Veteris Testamenti* (*fr.*) against the Manichees or Marcionites, of which two fragments are preserved. In addition, there are fragments of exeget. works: (1) *Fragmenta 2 in Iudices* (*Iud.*); (2) *Fragmentum in Isaiam* (*Is.*); (3) *Fragmentum in Ps* 73:4.5 (*Ps.*; a treatise on the Psalms and their appropriate use); (4) *Fragmentum in ep. ad Romanos* 9:11 (*Rom.*).

W: *fr.*, F. Diekamp, Doctrina patrum (Münster, ²1981), 315, Nr. 44/45 [text]. — Mansi 10:1122C. — *Iud.*, R. Devreesse, Les anciens commentateurs de l'octateuque (Vatican City, 1959), 185 [text]. — *Is.*, C. van den Eynde, CSCO 229/230:20/25 [text/French trans.]. — idem, CSCO 303/304:21, 54, 62/27 nn. 3, 68, 78 [text/French trans.]. — *Ps.*, J. B. Pitra, Analecta sacra 3 (Westmead, 1966 = Venice, 1883), 470 [text]. — *Rom.*, K. Staab, Pauluskommentare (Münster, 1933), 97f. [text].
L: A. Baumstark, Geschichte der syr. Lit. (Bonn, 1922), 118. — R. Devreesse, Les anciens commentateurs des psaumes (Vatican City, 1970), 328. — E. Peterson, T.: EC 11, (1947). — K. Staab, Die Pauluskatenen (Rome, 1926), 41 n. 1.

B. WINDAU

Theognis of Nicaea

Th., a student of Lucian of Antioch and bishop of Nicaea, was, with Eusebius of Nicomedia, one of the leading supporters of Arius and, like Eusebius, refused to subscribe to the council's decree at Nicaea (325). Since both men continued to protect Arian presbyters and perhaps even Arius himself, they were deposed by Constantine and banished to Gaul. From that time in exile has come a "letter of repentance" (*metanoias biblion*; *ep.*), the authenticity of which is disputed and which is probably the remnant of a letter to the emperor from a provincial synod in Bithynia, but probably not a letter to a second Synod of Nicaea (327). In it the exiled men profess their orthodoxy and ask for reconciliation, as had already been granted to Arius. The petition was granted; both men were able to return from exile to their episcopal secs. Th. subsequently attacked Athanasius with great determination and played a decisive role in his condemnation and first banishment by the Council of Tyre (335). Th. probably died before the Council of Sardica (342). Apart from the "letter of repentance," three fragments of two of his letters are preserved (*fr.*).

W: *ep.*, H. G. Opitz, Athanasius Werke 3/1 (Berlin, 1934), 65f. (Urkunde 31) [Greek text]. — W. Jacob, R. Hanslik, CSEL 71/1:111f. [Latin trans.]. — *fr.*, D. de Bruyne, Deux lettres inconnues de Th.: ZNW 27 (1928) 106-110 [Latin text/comm.].
L: W. Enßlin, Th. (5): PRE 5A/2:1984f. — R. P. C. Hanson, The Search for the Christian Doctrine (Edinburgh, 1988), 172-178. — K. Müller, Zu der Eingabe der Bischöfe Euseb v. Nikomedien u. Th. an die (zweite) Syndode v. Nicaea (327): ZNW 24 (1925) 290-292. — C. u. L. Piétri, Die Geschichte des Christentums 2 (Freiburg i.Br., 1996), 87, 304, 312, 317, 322, 326, 335-339. — R. Williams, Arius (London, 1987), 71-74.

R. Höffner

Theognius of Jerusalem

Th., b. 425 in Cappadocia, came to Jerusalem ca. 455, took over the leadership of the monastery of Gethsemani, spent some years in the wilderness of Judah, and, in his old age, became bishop of Betelea near Gaza. After his death in 522, Paul Helladicus composed an encomium of him (AnBoll 10 [1891] 78-113), which served as the basis of the *Vita* by Cyril of Scythopolis (TU 49/2). Th. probably wrote a sermon for Palm Sunday which reflects the triumph of the Chalcedonians in Jerusalem.

W: J. Noret, Une homélie inédite sur les Rameaux par T. (vers 460?): AnBoll 89 (1971) 113-142.
L: I. v. d. Gheyn, Th., évêque de Bételie: RQH 50 (1891) 559-567. — L. Perrone, La chiesa di Palestina (Brescia, 1980), 97, 111, 228.

G. Röwekamp

Theognostus

From 248/249 to 282 Th. was head of the Alexandrian school for catechists. Photius tells (*cod.* 106) of an extensive work, influenced by Origen and titled *Hypotypōses* (outlines/sketches, *hypot.*). Acc. to Photius, this was a systematic summary of the doctrines of the Chr. faith in seven books. Only four fragments and one uncertain piece (*fr. incertum*) have survived.

Acc. to Photius's report, Th. dealt in book 1 with the Father as creator of the world and attacked the doctrine of the coeternity of the world. In book 2 he set forth a subordinationist teaching acc. to which the Son is a necessary creature (*krisma*) of the Father and rules only over the world endowed with reason. Book 3 gives reasons for belief in the existence of the Holy Spirit. Acc. to book 4, spirits and demons possess bodies of subtle material. In books 5 and 6, Th. tries to prove the possibility of the incarnation of the Son. The seventh and last book (perhaps a later addition) deals once again with the creative activity of the

Father and, acc. to Photius, gives a more orthodox teaching than that in books 1-6.

W: *hypot.*, PG 10:240f. — A. Harnack, TU 24/3 (Leipzig, 1903), 73-92 [text/German trans./comm.]. — *fr. incertum*, J. A. Munitiz, A Fragment Attributed to Th.: JThS 30 (1979) 56-66 [text/English trans./comm.].
L: G. Anesi, La notizia di Fozio Sulle Hypotyposeis di Th.: Aug. 21 (1981) 491-516. — L. W. Barnard, The Antecedents of Arius: VigChr 24 (1970) 172-188, esp. 179-182. — F. Diekamp, Ein neues Frgm. aus den Hypotyposen des Alexandriners Th.: ThQ 84 (1902) 481-494. — A. Grillmeier, Jesus der Christus 1 (Freiburg i.Br., 1979), 290-294 (English, Christ in Christian Tradition, vol. 1 [London, ²1975]). — R. P. C. Hanson, The Search for the Christian Doctrine (Edinburgh, 1988), 77-79, 188. — L. B. Radford, Three Teachers of Alexandria (Cambridge, 1908), 1-43.

R. Höffner

Theonas of Alexandria

Th., who succeeded Maximus on the episcopal throne of Alexandria (281/282 to ca. 300), summoned Achillas to the school for catechists and ordained Peter I and Pierius (Eus., *h.e.* 7.32.30). The letter to Lucian, *praepositus cubiculi* and a man highly esteemed by Diocletian (PG 10:1567-74), may be from Theonas of Cyzicus.

W: M. J. Routh, Reliquiae Sacrae 3 (Oxford, 1846), 439-445.
L: C. W. Griggs, Early Egyptian Christianity (Leiden, 1990), 97. — T. Vivian, St. Peter of Alexandria (Philadelphia, 1988), 10-13, 56-57, 64, 75, 80-82.

T. Böhm

Theophilus of Alexandria

Th., patriarch of Alexandria (385-412) and uncle of his successor, Cyril, did not leave behind a distinguished reputation, although in fact it was chiefly his enemies who passed on information about him (espec. Palladius, *Dialogus de vita Joh. Chrysostomi*; Socrates, Sozomen). He was esteemed by Theodoret and Leo I, among others. His primary political goal was to protect the claim to priority of the patriarchal see of Alexandria over that of Constantinople. In his zeal to wipe out the remnants of pagan culture, he destroyed the Serapeum library of Alexandria in 391. Under pressure from the monasteries he became an opponent of Origen and persecuted the latter's defenders, among them the so-called four Long Brothers. At the Synod of the Oak (403) he secured the deposition and banishment of John Chrys.

Only fragments (*fr.*) have survived of Th.'s works. In addition, a homily by Th. (*In mysticam coenam*) has come down in Cyril. Three Easter letters, a synodal letter, and letters to Epiphanius and Jerome are among the correspondence of the last-named.

W: *fr.*, PG 65:29-68. — Briefe u. Osterfestbriefe, Jerome, *ep.* 87, 89, 90, 92, 96, 98, 100. — *in mysticam coenam*, Cyril, *hom. div.* 10 PG 77:1016-1029. — *liber enormis* (against John Chrysostom), Jerome, *ep.* 113; Facundus of Hermiane, *In defensionem trium capitulorum* 6, 5.
L: H. Crouzel, Th.: DSp 15:524-530. — A. Favale, Teofilo (Turin, 1958). — G. Lazzati, Teofilo (Milan, 1936). — M. Richard, Écrits de Th.: Muséon 52 (1939) 22-50. — idem, Th.: DThC 15:523-530.

G. MÜNCH-LABACHER

Theophilus of Antioch

For the life of Th. we are dependent essentially on the information he himself provides in his (only surviving) work *Ad Autolycum* (*Autol.*): from 2.24 scholars have inferred that Th. was born in Mesopotamia; acc. to a remark in 1.14 we may assume that he became a Chr. as an adult. Acc. to Eusebius, Th. became bishop of Antioch in 169. Since Th. mentions in book 3 (28) the death of Marcus Aurelius (d. 180), that book must have been written later on. This means that his work was composed at around the same period as those of Tatian and Athenagoras. The *Autol.* may have been intended as simply a preparation for a more extensive work on the doctrines of the faith. The arrangement of the first book is so confused that scholars have suggested a different sequence of the individual chapters. Th. evidently put together apologetic materials intended for other purposes and did so only after a fashion. Consequently, a unified thematic cannot be discerned. The main part of book 2 (11-32) consists of an interpretation of the opening chapters of Gen. In addition, philosophers (2.4), poets (2.5-6), and historians (2.7) are attacked. This secondary theme is then developed in book 3: here Th. is the first Chr. writer to speak of the Greeks stealing from the sacred scriptures (3.1.14; 3.2.37). The second part of book 3 (16-30) is given over to a chronological confirmation of the proof from antiquity. Th. makes use here of, among other, Josephus, *Contra Apionem*, from which he takes many details. He offers a chronology reaching from Adam to the recently deceased Emperor Marcus Aurelius and in the process coordinates the bibl. data with Roman and Persian chronology. This section was a pioneering effort at a Chr. chronology.

Nowhere in his work does Th. speak of Christ. In his view, the first chapters of Gen already contain a summa of all Chr. knowledge. Critics have therefore appropriately spoken of a "Christianity without Christ." Unlike → Justin, Th., along with his contemporary → Tatian, places Chr. teaching in strict opposition to philosophy. The Gr. philosophers did not grasp even parts of the truth but were inspired by demons (2.8) and went astray; truth is to be found only among Christians (2.33). Eusebius describes the three books of *Autol.* as "rudimentary treatises" (*h.e.* 4.24.1), which was not meant as a compliment.

W: G. Bardy, J. Sender, SC 20. — R. M. Grant, OECT (Oxford, 1970) [text/English trans.]. — J. Leitl, A. di Pauli, BKV² 14 (Kempten, 1913) [German trans.]. — M. Marcovich, PTS 44 (Berlin, 1995) [text]. — J. C. T. Otto, CorpAp 8 (Jena, 1861) [text/German trans./comm.].
L: L. W. Barnard, Apologetik 1: TRE 3:382f. — J. Bentivegna, A Christianity without Christ by Th.: StPatr 13 (1976) 107-130. — F. Bolgiani, L'ascesi di Noé. A proposito di Th., Autol., 3, 19: FS M. Pellegrino (Turin, 1975), 295-333. — H. Conzelmann, Heiden — Juden — Christen (Tübingen, 1981), 296-298. — A. J. Droge, Homer or Moses? (Tübingen, 1989), 102-123. — J. Geffcken, Zwei griech. Apologeten (Leipzig, 1907), 250-252. — R. M. Grant, The Bible of Th.: JBL 66 (1947) 173-196. — idem, Jesus after the Gospels (Louisville, 1990). — A. v. Harnack, Lehrbuch der Dogmengeschichte 1 (Darmstadt, 1980 = Tübingen, ⁴1909), 518f. — W. Kinzig, Novitas Christiana (Gottingen, 1994), 378-383. — P. Nautin, Ciel, pneuma et lumière chez Th.: VigChr 27 (1973) 165-171. — P. Pilhofer, Presbyteron kreitton (Tübingen, 1990), 266-273. — A. Puech, Les apologistes grecs du IIᵉ siècle de notre ère (Paris, 1912), 207-227. — M. Simonetti, La sacra Scrittura in Teofilo d'Antiochia: FS J. Daniélou (Paris, 1972), 197-207. — N. Zeegers-Van der Vorst, Les citations du Nouveau Testament dans les Livres à Autolycos de Th.: StPatr 12 (1975) 371-382. — eadem, Notes sur quelques aspects judaïsants du Logos chez Th.: Actes de la XIIᵉ Conférence internationale d'Études classiques Eirene (Bucharest, 1975), 69-87. — eadem, La création de l'homme (Gn 1, 26) chez Th.: VigChr 30 (1976) 258-267. — eadem, Satan, Ève et le serpent chez Th.: VigChr 35 (1981) 152-169.

P. PILHOFER

Theophilus of Caesarea

Th. was bishop of Caesarea in Palestine in the time of Roman Bishop Victor I (189-196). Together with Narcissus of Jerusalem, he joined in the controversy over the date of Easter at a synod and opted for the "apostolic custom" of celebrating Easter on a Sunday. The circular letter of the synod (*ep.*) was sent to Rome as well and is informative on the exchange of letters between Chr. communities. The *Acts* of the synod that go under Th.'s name are not authentic and originate in a later controversy over the date of Easter (perhaps 6th/7th c. in Britain).

W: *ep.*, Eusebius, *h.e.* 5.22.25. — *Acts*, B. Krusch, Studien zur chr.-mal. Chronologie (Leipzig, 1880), 306-310 [text/comm.].

L: B. Lohse, Das Passahfest der Quartadezimaner (Gütersloh, 1953). — P. Nautin, Lettres et écrivains chrétiens de IIe et IIIe siècles (Paris, 1961), 85-89.

G. Röwekamp

Theophylact Simocatta

Th., an official born in Egypt and whose exact dates of birth and death are unknown, composed under Emperor Heraclius (610-641) a hist. work dealing with the period 581-602. In his *Dialogos peri diaphorōn physikōn aporēmatōn* (*dial.*) he took up questions of natural science. Th.'s body of writings also includes eighty-four letters (*ep.*) and a work on predetermination, *horoi zōēs*.

W: *hist.*, P. Wirth (Leipzig, 1972) [text]. — C. De Boor (Leipzig, 1887) [text]. — I. Bekker, CSHB (Bonn, 1834) [text]. — M. Whitby (Oxford, 1986) [English trans./comm.]. — *horoi*, C. Garton, L. G. Westerink, T. On Predestined Terms of Life (Buffalo, 1979) [text/English trans.]. — *dial.*, *ep.*, J. F. Boissonade, Quaestiones physicae et Epistolae (Paris, 1835) [text].
L: H. W. Haussig, Th.' Exkurs: Byz. 23 (1953) 275-462.

F. R. Gahbauer, OSB

Theotechnus of Livia

Th. was bishop of Livia, east of the Jordan (Tell er-Ram), in the 6th/7th c. Extant is a sermon for Aug. 15, which is regarded as the earliest witness to the doctrine of the bodily assumption of Mary into heaven and which contains numerous elements that show up in later Byz. sermons.

W: A. Wenger, L'Assomption de la très sainte Vierge dans la tradition byzantine du VIe au Xe siècle (Paris, 1955), 96-110, 272-291.
L: A. Wenger, Etudes sur la S. Vierge: Maria 5, ed. H. du Manoir (Paris, 1958), 936-938. — G. Söll, Storia de dogmi mariani (Rome, 1981), 192-196.

G. Röwekamp

Theotimus, a Valentinian

Tertullian (*adv. Val.* 4.3) mentions a Valentinian named Theotimus who had devoted a great deal of attention to the *imagines* of the law. We may therefore think of a work of allegorical interpretations of the OT, but nothing further is known of it.

L: W. Bauer, Rechtgläubigkeit u. Ketzerei (Tübingen, ²1964), 52. — A. v. Harnack, Geschichte der altchr. Lit. 1 (Leipzig, ²1958), 177; 2/1:294, 541.

R. Hanig

Thomas, Literature about

The *Acts of Thomas* (*A. Thom.*), with their strongly encratitic tendency (→ Tatian), were composed, originally in Syriac, in the first half of the 3rd c. The Syr. version we have today dates probably from the 4th c. and gives a text that has been purged to accord with the Great Church and shows an anti-Manichean and anti-Marcionite tendency. The older Gr. version, on the other hand, is not entirely free of gnosticizing influences. The Eth. legend of Thomas in the apocryphal collection *Struggles of the Apostles* is based on a shorter Gr. revision of the narrative material in *A. Thom.* The numerous oriental versions (Coptic, Armenian, Arabic) show the wide circulation of the work in the Near East. The *A. Thom.* belong among the apocrypha that the Manichees introduced into their canon while rejecting Luke's Acts of the Apostles. But the *A. Thom.* were very popular even in orthodox circles, as the Lat. tradition shows. They display many parallels in thought to the Syr. philosopher → Bardesanes.

The *Acts* tell, in the form of a novel, of the legendary proselytizing and wonderworking activity of the apostle Thomas and of his death as a martyr in northwest India. Scattered through the *A. Thom.* are numerous liturgical texts, sermons, and hymns which were of great importance for the history of piety in the Syr. church. Interesting from the viewpoint of religious history are the Wedding Hymn (6f.) and the Hymn of the Pearl (108-13) as evidences of a christianized gnosis that was given expression in a variety of symbols. In addition, Indian, Iranian, and Manichean motifs make the *A. Thom.* highly valuable for the history of religions.

The *A. Thom.* contain the first mention of the martyrdom of Judas Thomas (*M. Thom.*), which was otherwise handed down separately and spoke of the transfer of the apostle's bones to the West, that is, to Edessa. This tradition was known to → Ephraem the Syrian (*Carmina Nisibena* 42) and to → Egeria the pilgrim, who visited Edessa ca. 384 (*Peregr. Aeth* 17.1; 19.3).

W: *A. Thom.*, R. A. Lipsius, M. Bonnet, AAAp 2, 2, 99-288. [Greek text]. — M. Bonnet (Leipzig, 1883), 96-160 [Latin text]. — K. Zelzer, Lat. Th.-akten (Berlin, 1978) [Latin text/comm.]. — W. Wright, Apocryphal Acts (London, 1871), 1:171-333 [Syriac text]; 2:146-298 [English trans.]. — P. Bedjan, AMSS 3:3-167 [Syriac text]. — A. F. J. Klijn (Leiden, 1962) [Greek text/comm.]. — NTApo⁶ 2:289-367 [German trans.]. — C. Tcherakian, Apocrypha Apostolorum (Venice, 1904), 401-436 [Armenian text]. — L. Leloir, CCA 4:531-646 [French trans. according to the Armenian text]. — M. R. James, Apocrypha anecdota (Cambridge, 1897), 27-45 [Greek

text]. — A. W. Budge, Contendings of Apostles (London, 1899), 1:358-381; 2:335-384 [Ethiopic text/English trans.]. — M. van Esbroeck: Par Or 14 (1957) 11-77 [Arabic text]. — *M. Thom.*, G. Garitte, Passion arménienne: Muséon 84 (1971) 171-195 [Armenian text/French trans.]. — idem, Le martyre géorgien: Muséon 83 (1970) 497-532 [Georgian text/Latin trans.]. — P. H. Poirier, La version copte (Brussels, 1984) [Coptic text].
L: A. Adam, Psalmen des Th. (Berlin, 1959). — G. Bornkamm, Mythos u. Legende (Göttingen, 1933). — P. Devos, Égérie à Édesse: AnBoll 85 (1967) 381-400. — H. Kruse, Brautlied: OCP 50 (1984) 291-330. — idem, Return of Prodigal: Or. 47 (1978) 163-214. — M. Lipinski, Konkordanz (Bonn, 1987). — J. E. Ménard, Chant de la Perle: RevSR 42 (1968) 289-325. — P. H. Poirier, L'hymne de la perle (Paris, 1981). — R. Söder, Apokryphe Apostelgeschichten (Würzburg, 1932). — C. L. Stuhrhahn, Christologie (Heidelberg, 1952), 51-89, 102-127. — G. Widengren, Mesopotamian Elements (Uppsala, 1946).

The *Book of Thomas the Athlete* (*Lib. Thom.*), which has come down only in Coptic, is likewise from the Syr. world and was originally composed in Greek, probably toward the end of the 2nd or beginning of the 3rd c. In its literary character, the *Lib. Thom.* resembles the *Sophia Jesu Christi* and can be regarded as a Platonizing Hellen.-Jewish work on wisdom. In content the *Lib. Thom.* is an exhortation, its purpose the spread of an ascetical way of life.

W: R. Kuntzmann, Livre de Th. (Leiden, 1986) [text/French trans./comm.]. — H. M. Schenke, Das Thomas-Buch (Berlin, 1989) [text/German trans./comm.]. — idem, NTApo⁵ 1:192-204 [German trans./comm.]. — J. D. Turner, Book of Th. the Contender (Missoula, 1975) [text/English trans./comm.]. — B. Layton, Nag Hammadi Codex II, 7 (Leiden, 1989) [text/English trans./comm.].
L: R. Kuntzmann, L'identification: B. Barc, Nag Hammadi (Quebec, 1981), 279-287. — H. M. Schenke, Exegetische Probleme: OLZ 70 (1975) 5-13. — idem, Enthaltsamkeit. U. Bianchi, Tradizione dell' Encrateia (Rome, 1985), 263-291. — J. D. Turner, Syrian Judas Th.: FS A. Böhlig (Leiden, 1972), 109-119.

The *Gospel of Thomas* (*Ev. Thom.*) probably originated in eastern Syria around the middle of the 2nd c., although the sayings brought together in it may well date back to the 1st c. The radical encratism, the transmission under the name of Didymus Judas Thomas, and its closeness to other works (*A. Thom.*, → *Liber graduum*) make a Syr. origin likely, even though the collection of sayings has come down complete only in Coptic. The work consists of 114 sayings (*logia*) that follow one another without any connecting narrative text and in different ways show a strong gnostic influence. Redemption takes place primarily through knowledge; the Christ of this gospel seems completely without ties to history; his heavenly form is known only to the elect. The world

is judged negatively; the body is regarded as incapable of salvation. The opposition between world/body/death, on the one side, and heaven/knowledge/life, on the other, defines the individualist soteriology of the *Ev. Thom.*, which lacks any element of community and ecclesiology.

W: M. Fieger (Münster, 1991) [text/German trans./comm.]. — J. Leipoldt (Berlin, 1967) [text/German trans.]. — J. E. Ménard (Leiden, 1975) [French trans./comm.]. — A. Guillaumont (Leiden, ²1976) [text/English trans.]. — NTApo⁶ 1:93-113 [German trans.].
L: J. M. Asgeirson, Arguments and Audience(s) in the Gospel of Th.: SBL. SP 134 (1998) 325-342. — B. Ehlers, Ev. Thom. aus Edessa?: NT 12 (1970) 284-317. — A. F. J. Klijn, Altsyr. Christentum: VigChr 15 (1961) 146-159. — idem, Single One: JBL 81 (1962) 271-278. — idem, Christianity in Edessa: NT 14 (1972) 70-77. — J. E. Ménard, Milieu syriaque: RevSR 42 (1968) 261-266. — G. Quispel, Tatian and the Gospel of Th. (Leiden, 1975). V. K. Robbins, Enthymemic Texture in the Gospel of Thomas: SBL. SP 134 (1998) 343-366. — R. Trevijano Etcheverría, La antropología del Evangelio de Tomás: Coram Deo. memorial J. L. Ruiz de la Peña. (Salamanca, 1997), 209-229.

An *Infancy Story of Thomas* (*Ev. inf. Thom.*) has come down in very different versions in Latin, Greek, and various oriental languages. It tells, in fairy-tale form, very ingenuous stories of spectacular wonders worked by the boy Jesus between his fifth and twelfth years. As for the dating of the work, a citation of it in Irenaeus (*haer.* 1.13.1) gives a sure *terminus ante quem* toward the end of the 2nd c. Its origin in gentile Christianity is assured since the work betrays no knowledge of Judaism. A docetist tendency, which is usually found in apocryphal infancy gospels, shows here as well. Since the child Jesus must not grow further in wisdom (Lk 2:51) but, like a bizarre performer, embarrasses all human teachers, he acts like a gnostic revealer and during his childhood already possesses the fullness of divine wisdom. Many of the traditions encountered in the *Ev. inf. Thom.* live on in the → *Arabic Infancy Gospel* and in the *History of* → *Joseph the Carpenter*.

W: C. Tischendorf, Evangelia apocrypha (Leipzig, ²1876), 140-163 [Greek text]; 164-180 [Latin text]. — A. Delatte, Anecdota Atheniensia 1 (Paris, 1927), 264-271 [Greek text]. — E. A. W. Budge, History of the Blessed Virgin Mary (London, 1899), 1:217-222 [Syriac text]. — G. Garitte, Fragment géorgien: RHE 51 (1956) 513-520 [Georgian text/Latin trans.]. — S. Grébaut, PO 12/4:625-642 [Ethiopic text/French trans.]. — P. Peeters, L'évangile de l'enfance (Paris, 1914) [French trans./comm.].-NTApo⁶ 1:349-360 [German trans.]. — G. Schneider, FC 18:147-171 [Greek text/German trans.].
L: V. Arras, L'évangile de Th.: AnBoll 93 (1975) 133-146. — A. Fuchs, Konkordanz zum Th.-Ev (Linz, 1978). — S. Gero, Infancy Gospel of Th.: NT 13 (1971) 46-80. — S. Grébaut,

L'évangile de Th.: ROC 16 (1911) 255-265, 356-367. — A. de Santos Otero, Kirchenslav. Evangelium des Th. (Berlin, 1967).

The original Gr. text of the *Apocalypse of Thomas* (*Apoc. Thom.*), which is rejected in the *Decretum Gelasianum*, is lost, but the work is preserved in two Lat. versions. The older, shorter version was expanded into a longer version in the 5th c. by prefacing it with an introduction; the older version probably originated in gnostic-Manichean circles. In dependence on the *Apocalypse of John*, the *Apoc. Thom.* describes the signs during the seven days before the end.

W: E. Hauler, Neue Bruchstücke: WSt 30 (1908) 308-340 [Latin text]. — M. R. James, Revelatio Th.: JThS 11 (1910) 288-320 [Latin text]. — idem, Apocryphal NT (Cambridge, 1924), 555-562 [English trans.]. — P. Bihlmeyer, Text non interpolé: RBen 28 (1911) 270-282 [Latin text].
L: A. Y. Collins, Apocalyptic Literature: ANRW II 25/6 (1988) 4464-4771.

P. BRUNS

Thomas of Edessa

Th. of Edessa was active in the first half of the 6th c. and was a disciple and successor of Aba I. He composed various liturg. treatises that were completed by → Cyrus of Edessa. Preserved are a treatise on the birth of Christ (*nat.*) and, in fragmentary form, another on the Epiphany.

W: *nat.*, S. J. Carr, Th. de nativitate D. N. I. C. (Rome, 1898) [text/Latin trans.]. — *epiph.*, G. Diettrich, Fragmente: NGWG 16 (1909) 196-202 [text].
L: A. Baumstark, "De causis festorum": OrChr 1 (1901) 324f. — W. Macomber, Th. and Cyrus: CSCO 356 (1974) VII-X. — W. Wolska, La topographie chrétienne de Cosmas Indicopleustes (Paris, 1962), 72-85.

P. BRUNS

Thomas of Heraclea

Th., b. in Heraclea, first studied Greek in the monastery of Quennesrin, but then moved to the convent of Taril and was later elected bishop of Hierapolis (Mabbug). In 602 Emperor Maurice expelled him because of his Monophysite tendencies; Th. fled to Egypt, where he took part in the negotiations between the Antiochene and Alexandrian patriarchs in 609/610. In 615/616 he, along with → Paul of Tella and other theologians, revised the translation of the NT and the OT Hexapla at the bidding of Patriarch Athanasius I of Alexandria. The basis for their revi-

sion was the translation by → Philoxenus. An anaphora attributed to Th. is probably not authentic.

W: *Bible translations*, G. H. Bernstein, Das hl. Evangelium des Iohannes (Leipzig, 1853) [text]. — J. H. Hall, Syrian Epistles (Baltimore, 1886) [text]. — A. Vööbus, CSCO 400 [text]. — *anaph.*, E. Renaudot, Liturgiarum orientalum collectio 2 (Paris, 1716), 383-388.
L: B. Aland, Philoxenianisch-Harklensische Übersetzungstradition: Muséon 94 (1981) 321-383. — G. H. Bernstein, De Charklensi N. T. translatione (Berlin, ²1854). — S. P. Brock, Resolution of the Philoxenian/Harclean Problem: FS B. M. Metzger (Oxford, 1981), 325-343. — S. Grill, Das NT nach dem syr. Text (Munich, 1955). — P. Harb, Harklensische Übersetzung: ZDMG Suppl. 4 (1980) 156f. — idem, Neue Hss.-funde: OrChr 64 (1980) 36-47. — A. Hilgenfeld, Die versio Heraclea u. Apg: ZWTh 43 (1900) 401-422. — W. Strothmann, Evangelien-Hss.: FS J. Aßfalg (Wiesbaden, 1990), 367-375. — A. Vööbus, Gospel Texts in Syriac 1-2 (Leuven/Louvain, 1951-1987). — idem, Early Version of the NT (Stockholm, 1954). — G. Zuntz, Ancestry of the Harclean (London, 1945). — idem, Études harcléennes: RB 57 (1950) 550-582.

P. BRUNS

Tiburtine Oracles

An anonymous author, one very familiar with Heliopolis-Baalbek, revised and expanded (probably ca. 503/504) a now lost Gr. version (probably of the 4th c.) of the *Explanatio somni* of the Tiburtine Sibyls. The discovery of this early Byz. text was made known by S. G. Mercato in 1949. The nucleus of the prophecies of the Tiburtine Sibyls (→ Sibylline Oracle) is the explanation of a dream that one hundred Roman judges had. The dream is interpreted as an apocalyptic prevision of future world history. Better known than this Gr. version of the *Explanatio somni* is the medieval Lat. version, the content of which is far different.

W: *explanatio Somni*, P. J. Alexander, The Oracle of Baalbek: The Tiburtine Sibyl in Greek Dress (Washington, D.C., 1967) [Greek text/comm./English trans.]. — E. Sackur, Sibyllinische Texte u. Forschungen (Halle, 1898), 177-189 [Latin text/comm.].
L: P. F. Beatrice, Das Orakel v. Baalbek u. die sog. Sibyllentheosophie, RQ 92 (1997) 177-187. — B. McGinn, "Teste David cum Sibylla": FS J. Mundy (Oxford, 1985), 7-36.

H. SCHNEIDER

Timothy, Acts of

There is preserved a *Passio*, supposedly of Paul's disciple Timothy, that links the addressees of the letter to Timothy with Ephesus and John. Timothy's martyrdom was supposed to have taken place in Ephesus, and there his tomb was pointed out. The *Passio* takes the form of a letter to the church of Asia (see the letter of the Smyrna community on the martyrdom of Polycarp) and comes from the 5th c.

W: H. Usener, Acta S. Timothei: Bonner Universitätsprogramm 1877, 7-13 [text].
L: H. Delehaye, Melanges d'hagiographie grecque et latine (Brussels, 1966), 408-415. — J. Keil, Zum Martyrium: JÖAI 29 (1934) 82-92.

G. Röwekamp

Timothy I of Alexandria

T. was consecrated bishop of Alexandria in 381 as successor to his brother, Peter II. He seems to have come late to the Council of Constantinople, and there successfully opposed the election of Gregory Naz. as bishop of Constantinople. It is possible that T. presided over the council for a few days. In any case, he was unable to prevent the bishop of Constantinople being given second place behind the bishop of Rome. T. supported and promoted the monastic orders; he died ca. 385.

T. composed *Responsa canonica* or *Responsiones canonicae* (*resp.*), which set down canonical and moral regulations in question-and-answer form. These were handed down in the canonical collections of the Gr. church. *Resp.* 1-15 are authentic; the attribution of the remainder is uncertain; in addition, versions in other languages are known. T. also wrote a sycophantic letter to Diodorus of Tarsus (*ep.*) that is preserved in the Lat. translation of → Facundus of Hermiane (*defens.* 4.2). Sozomen's attribution (*h.e.* 6.26) of (lost) biographies of monks to T. is probably erroneous; their author is more likely archdeacon T. of Alexandria. Other works are also ascribed to T., among them a report on the miraculous deeds of St. Menas (*Miracula S. Menae*; *mir.*), but the authorship is uncertain.

W: *resp.*, PG 33:1296-1308. — P. P. Ioannou, Fonti 2: Les canons des pères grecs (Rome, 1963), 240-258 [text]. — I. B. Pitra, Iuris ecclesiastici graecorum historia et monumenta 1 (Rome, 1864), 630-645 [text]. — F. Nau, Littérature canonique: ROC 14 (1909) 35-37 [French trans. of a Syriac version]. — W. E. Crum, Der Papyruscodex s. VI-VII (Strasburg, 1915), 103f. [German trans. of a Coptic version]. — *ep.*, J.-M. Clément, R. vander Plaetse, CCL 90A:110. — *mir.*, I. Pomjalovskij, Zitie prepodobnago (Petersburg, 1900), 62-89 [text].
L: A. S. Atiya, T.: CoptE 7:2263. — W. Bright, T. 7: DCB 4:1029f.

B. Windau

Timothy II of Alexandria (Aelurus)

T., a presbyter in the time of Bishop Dioscurus, accompanied the latter to Ephesus (449). Together with Peter Mongus he organized the Monophysite opposition in Egypt. After the death of Proterius he became bishop and took a position against Chalcedon and the *Tomus* of Leo. Under pressure from Aspar, Emperor Leo I was compelled to drive T. from Alexandria (459/460). Leo was probably persuaded that T. was teaching a pure Eutychianism or even Manichaeism. T. was forced to go into exile in Paphlagonia, then in Crimea. In 475 he was called back to Alexandria when the pro-Monophysite usurper Basiliscus ascended the throne. In Constantinople the emperor made him welcome, but Patriarch Acacius did not. T. took part in the pro-Monophysite Council of Ephesus and then returned to Alexandria. He died in 477.

Several works of T. against Chalcedon have been handed down: a refutation of the council preserved in Armenian (there is also a shorter Syr. version) as well as shorter works against Chalcedon and the *Tomus Leonis* (the Syr. text has not been published). Some letters (*ep.*) give a picture of a T. less concerned with the controversies over Chalcedon. The presbyter stood for a moderate Monophysitism, like that of Severus of Antioch later on. T. reserves the concept of nature (Syr.: *kyana*) to the God-Logos and not to the humanity of the incarnate Logos, although he holds fast to the completeness of Christ's humanity. The human reality of Christ is expressed for T. solely by the concept *sesarkōmenē*. T. develops this theology in reliance on texts of Apollinaris (espec. *Ad Jovianum*). The divine nature remains separate from the humanity in the incarnation. It is thus possible to speak of the suffering of Christ on the cross, without the Logos being affected by this suffering.

W: K. Ter-Mekerttschian, E. Ter-Minassiantz, T.', des Patriarchen v. Alexandrien, Widerlegung der auf der Synode zu Chalcedon festgesetzten Lehre (Leipzig, 1908) [Armenian text]. — F. Nau, PO 13:202-218 [Syriac text]. — *ep.*, R. Y. Ebied, L. R. Wickham, A Collection of Unpublished Letters of T.: JThS 21 (1970) 333-346. — F. Nau, PO 13:218-239, 241-247. — E. W. Brooks, CSCO 83:175-178, 186-201. — *liber historiarum* (fr.), F. Nau, PO 8:83-85. — *sermo*, A. van Lantschoot: Muséon 47 (1934) 13-56.
L: L. Abramowski, Ein Text des Johannes Chrysostomus: After Chalcedon, ed. C. Laga et al. (Leuven/Louvain, 1985), 1-10. — R. Y. Ebied, L. R. Wickham, op. cit., 321-369. — eadem, T.: After Chalcedon, ed. C. Laga et al. (Leuven/Louvain, 1985), 115-166. — A. Grillmeier, Jesus der Christus 2/4 (Freiburg i.Br., 1990), 7-35 (English, Christ in Christian Tradition, vol. 2/4 [London, 1996]). — J. Lebon, La christologie de T.: RHE 9 (1908) 677-702. — F. Nau, Sur la christologie de T.: ROC 14 (1909) 99-103. — D. W. Winkler, Kopt. Kirche u. Reichskirche 1:1997, 110-119.

T. Böhm

Timothy IV (III) of Alexandria

T. IV (III) was Monophysite patriarch of Alexandria 517-535. He opposed the Chalcedonian Creed and the *Tomus* of Leo the Great to Flavian. Because of support from Empress Theodora, T. was untouched by the measures taken against Gr. heretics and welcomed the deported Monophysites to Egypt. The controversies between Severus and Julian of Halicarnassus, which broke out during T.'s time in office, reached their climax after his death. From T.'s pen there are (1) a homily on Jn 4:6 (*hom.*; partly in Cosmas Indicopleustes, *top.*; complete in Syriac) and (2) fragments of six other homilies preserved in Cosmas (*fr.*). Dubious or erroneous is the attribution to T. of a *Liturgia* (*lit.*), an *Ordo baptismatis* (*ord.*), and a fragment *ex dialogo cum Calonymo* (*dial.*).

W: *hom.*, PG 86/1:265-268 [Greek text and Latin trans. of the Syriac text]. — *fr.*, W. Wolska-Conus, SC 197:307-313. — *lit.*, A. Rücker, ASy 1/1 (Rome, 1939), 3-47. — *or.*, S. P. Brock: Muséon 83 (1970) 367-431 [Syriac text/comm.]. — *dial.*, PG 86/1:276BC.
L: W. H. C. Frend, The Rise of the Monophysite Movement (Cambridge, 1972), 257, 269f. — E. R. Hardy, T. III.: CoptE 7:2268. — A. Nagl, T. 25: PRE 6A/2:1357f.

B. WINDAU

Timothy of Antioch

A sermon on the cross and transfiguration of the Lord is ascribed to an otherwise unknown T. of Antioch (probably first half of 6th c.).

W: PG 86/1:256-265.
L: B. Capelle, Les homélies liturgiques du prétendu Timothée de Jérusalem: EL 63 (1949) 5-26.

U. HAMM

Timothy of Berytus, Apollinarist

Along with Vitalis, Bishop T. of Berytus was one of the intimate disciples of Apollinaris of Laodicea and one of those close in position to the Great Church. Thus, e.g., in Rome in 362, he was able, with a recommendation from Athanasius, to obtain an *Ep. canonica* for his teacher. Not only, however, was he opposed by the extremists of his own school (espec. Polemon), but he was also condemned during his second stay in Rome in 377. But before and afterwards T. was supposed to have taken steps against Paulinus, Epiphanius, and Diodorus, as well as against Peter Alex. and Basil. More of his writings have come down than from the other Apollinarists: an *Ep. ad Homonium episcopum* (*ep. Homon.*), a frag-

ment of a *Catechesis* (*cat.*), and one of a *Historia ecclesiastica* containing the text of a letter of Athanasius to Jovian (*h.e.*), as well as an *Ep. ad Prosdocium* (*ep. Prosd.*), which was initially handed down as a work of Julius of Rome.

W: *ep. Homon.*, *fr.* 181 (*cat.*), *fr.* 182 (*h.e.*), *ep. Prosd.* (*fr.* 183f.), H. Lietzmann, Apollinaris u. seine Schule (Hildesheim, 1970 = Tübingen, ¹1904), 277-286 [text]. — *ep. Prosd.*, J. Flemming, H. Lietzmann, Apollinaristische Schriften (Berlin, 1904), 39-41 [Syriac text]. — K. Ter-Mekerttschian, E. Ter-Minassiantz, Widerlegung (Leipzig, 1908), 262-264 [Armenian text].
L: G. Voisin, L'apollinarisme (Leuven/Louvain, 1901), 112f.

G. FEIGE

Timothy I, Catholicos

T. was first a monk, then bishop of Beit Bagas, before finally being elected catholicos in 780; he died on Jan. 9, 823, at the age of ninety-four. He enjoyed the favor of the caliphs and was able to win privileges for the Nestorian church. Under his rule it was possible to launch missions in India and China and among the Turks and Yemenites. Four new eccles. provinces were established and, under T.'s supervision, canons on eccles. discipline and Nestorian doctrine (*can.*) were adopted at synods in 790/791 and 804. From his pen come about two hundred letters dealing chiefly with questions of philosophy, biblical study, and canon law, as well as a disputation with Caliph al-Mahdi (*disp.*), a kind of catechism in question-and-answer form. The sources also mention lost treatises on the feasts of the Lord and a likewise lost commentary on Gregory Naz., the Gr. theologian whom T. esteemed most.

W: *can.*, O. Braun, OrChr 2 (1902) 283-311 [text/German trans.]. — E. Sachau, Syr. Rechtsbücher 2 (Berlin, 1908), 53-117 [text/German trans.]. — J. B. Chabot, Synodicon Orientale (Paris, 1902), 599-608 [text/French trans.]. — *ep.*, O. Braun, CSCO 74/75 [text/Latin trans.]. — H. P. J. Cheikho, Lettre à Serge (Rome, 1983) [text/French trans./comm.]. — T. Darmo, Letters of Patriarch T. (Trichur, 1982) [English trans.]. — R. J. Bidawid, StT 187:1*-47* [text], 89-125 [Latin trans.]. — *disp.*, A. Mingana, WoodSt 2:1-62 [text/English trans.]. — L. Cheikho, Mach. 19 (1921) 359-374, 408-418 [Arabic trans.]. — R. Caspar, Les versions arabes: Islamo-christiana 3 (1977) 107-175 [Arabic trans.].
L: R. J. Bidawid, Les lettres du patriarche T. (Rome, 1956). — O. Braun, T.: OrChr 1 (1901) 138-152. — H. P. J. Cheikho, Dialectique du langage de Dieu (Rome, 1983). — T. R. Hurst, Epistle-Treatise: OCA 229 (1987) 367-382. — W. Labourt, De T. Nestorianorum patriarcha (Paris, 1904). — P. Petitmengin, ep. 47: FS A. J. Festugière (Geneva, 1984), 247-262.

P. BRUNS

Timothy of Constantinople

T., probably a presbyter at Sancta Sophia in Constantinople, composed (ca. 600) the work *De receptione haereticorum*, a survey and categorization of heret. and schismatic movements through the history of the church. His main source was probably the record of a synod held in Side ca. 390, which also contained personal statements of heretics.

W: PG 86:12-74. — V. Benesevic, Syntagma 14 titulorum sine scholiis secundum versionem paleo-slovenicam, adiecto textu graeco (St. Petersburg, 1906/07), 707-738 [text].
L: J. Meyendorff, Le Christ dans la théologie byzantine (Paris, 1969), 163-167. — J. Pargoire, L'Eglise byzantine de 527 à 847 (Paris, ³1923), 135.

C. SCHMIDT

Timothy of Jerusalem

T. is a not certainly identifiable or perhaps even fictitious author who is to be dated to the 6th-8th c. The name may possibly be a pseudonym of → Leontius of Constantinople. Under the name of T. there have come down a sermon on Simeon (*Sym.*) in Greek and Georgian and a sermon on the presentation (*occ.*) preserved only in Georgian. T. was probably the author also of the sermon on the cross and transfiguration (*cruc.*) that has been transmitted under the name of a → Timothy of Antioch, as well as of three Ps.-Athanasian sermons on the birth of John the Baptist (*nativ. Jo. Bapt.*; sometimes also attributed to → Proclus of Constantinople), on Mary (*descr. BVM*), and on the man born blind (*caec.*). A passage in *Sym.* (PG 86:245CD) is regarded by many as an early witness to the bodily assumption of Mary into heaven.

W: *Sym.*, PG 86:237-252. — *occ.*, M. de la Bigne, Maxima bibliotheca veterum Patrum (Lyons, 1677), 1214-1216 [Latin trans.]. — *cruc.*, PG 86:256-265. — *nativ. Jo. Bapt.*, *descr. BMV, caec.*, PG 28:905-914, 943-958, 1001-1024.
L: B. Capelle, Les homélies liturgiques du prétendu T.: EL 63 (1949) 5-26. — R. Caro, La Homilética Mariana griega en el Siglo V (Dayton, 1971). — M. v. Esbroeck, Les plus anciennes homéliaires georgiennes (Leuven/Louvain, 1975), 74, 126, 141, 224. — M. Jugie, La mort et la assomption de la S. Vierge (Rome, 1944). — M. Sachot, L'homélie ps.-chrysostomienne sur la transfiguration CPG 4724, BHG 1975 (Frankfurt a.M., 1981).

G. RÖWEKAMP

Titus, Letter of

In the *Martyrium Pauli*, Paul's disciple T. is seen as the fellow disciple and companion of Luke. In con-

trast to the NT letter to T., this letter, handed down in Latin and discovered in 1896 in an 8th-c. ms., is supposedly written by T. The "inspired" ascetical work on chastity is addressed to *spadones* and *virgines* and attacks, among other things, the practice of virgins living with celibate men. The letter contains many citations from scripture and shows similarities to, among others, Ps.-Cyprian, *singul. cler.* and Jerome, *ep.* 117. In addition, there are citations from many apocrypha, espec. acts of apostles (most of these likewise ascetical in character) and some apocalypses. Conceptual and thematic affinities suggest that the work originated in Priscillianist circles in 5th c. Spain. Whether there was a Gr. model is disputed.

W: D. de Bruyne: RBen 37 (1925) 47-72 = PLS 2:1522-1542 [text]. — NTApo⁵ 2:52-70 [German trans.].
L: V. Bulhart, Nochmals Textkritisches: RBen 62 (1952) 297-299. — F. Halkin, La légende crétoise de St. Tite: AnBoll 79 (1961) 241-256. — A. v. Harnack, Der apokryphe Brief des Paulusschülers T.: SPAW 17 (1925) 180-213. — H. Koch, Zu Ps.-T.: ZNW 32 (1933) 131-144. — A. de Santos Otero, Der apokryphe T.-Brief: ZKG 74 (1963) 1-14. — G. Sfameni Gasparro, L'Epistula Titi: ANRW II 25/6 (1988) 4551-4664.

G. RÖWEKAMP

Titus of Bostra

T. was a 4th-c. bishop of Bostra, capital of the province of Arabia. In 362 he came into conflict with Julian the Apostate (Sozomen, *h.e.* 5.15; Julian, *ep.* 52). In 363 he took part in the Synod of Antioch and subscribed to the synodal letter to Emperor Jovian, which accepted the Nicene *homoousios* but with a homoiousian interpretation (Socrates, *h.e.* 3.25; 6.4). T. died under Emperor Valens (364-368) (Jerome, *vir. ill.* 102).

The work *Contra Manichaeos* (*Man.*) in four books was composed after 363; it survives in Greek only to book 3.7 but is complete in a Syr. translation. The first two books refute the Manichean picture of God and the world and give the contrasting Chr. teaching, while book 3, in response to the Manichean rejection of the OT, emphasizes its divine origin and agreement with the NT. The fourth book shows how the Manichees misinterpreted specific NT passages. Along with valuable citations from Manichean writings T. gives a detailed explanation of Cath. doctrine, e.g., on the Trinity and the virginal birth.

The *Commentarii in Lucam* (*fr. Lc.*), a commentary on almost the whole of Luke in the form of homilies and preserved in catenas, explains the scripture after the manner of the Antiochene school. The *Fragmenta in Danielem* (*fr. Dan.*) are taken from that commentary and do not go back to a special commentary on Dan. Among T.'s other writings (Jerome, *vir. ill.* 102) is the *Sermo in epiphaniam* (*serm.*) of which a few fragments in Syr. remain; the sermon *Oratio in ramos palmarum*, originally attributed to him, is not his.

W: *Man.*, PG 18:1069-1264. — P. de Lagarde, Titi Bostreni quae ex opere contra Manichaeos edito in codice Hamburgensi servata sunt graece (Berlin, 1859) [text]. — P. Nagel, Neues griech. Material zu T.: SB F. 2 (Berlin, 1973), 285-350 [text]. — *fr. Lc.*, J. Sickenberger, T. Studien zu dessen Lukashomilien (Leipzig, 1901), 140-245. — *fr. Dan.*, J. Sickenberger, op. cit., 246-248 [text]. — *serm.*, I. Rucker, Florilegium Edessenum anonymum: SBAW (1933), 5, 82-87 [text].
L: E. Amann, T.: DThC 15/1:1143f. — A. Baumstark, Der Text der Mani-Zitate in der syr. Übersetzung des T.: OrChr ser. 3, 6 (1931), 23-42. — idem, Die syr. Übersetzung des T. und das "Diatessaron": Bib. 16 (1935) 257-299. — R. P. Casey, T.: PRE 2/6:1586-1591. — A. Solignac, T.: DSp 15:999-1006.

C. SCHMIDT

Tonitruus, mens perfecta

An independent treatise in the Nag Hammadi library (NHC 6, 2) carries the enigmatic title *The Thunder, Perfect Mind* (*bront.*). It consists of a monologue by a universal goddess who embraces all contradictions and is diversely perceived by human beings. *Bront.* contains parallels both to bibl. teaching on wisdom and to Hellen.-Egypt. conceptions of Isis. There is, however, no unified mythological context and no continuous narrative thread.

W: P. H. Poirier, W. P. Funk (Leuven/Louvain, 1995) [Coptic text/French trans./comm.]. — H. G. Bethge, Nebront: ThLZ 98 (1973) 97-104 [German trans.]. — R. Unger, Sprachliche Struktur: OrChr 59 (1975) 78-107 [German trans.]. — NHL 295-303 [English trans.].
L: B. Layton, L'énigme du Tonnerre, RThPh 119 (1987) 261-280. — P. C. Miller, In Praise of Nonsense: World Spirituality, ed. A. H. Armstrong (New York, 1986), 481-505. — P. H. Poirier, Juifs et grecs: ScEs 46 (1994) 293-307. — G. Quispel, Jewish Gnosis: Les textes de Nag Hammadi, ed. J. É. Ménard (Leiden, 1975), 82-122. — J. J. Sell, Jesus: NT 23 (1981) 173-192. — M. Tardieu, Titre: Muséon 87 (1974) 523-530; 88 (1975) 365-369.

P. BRUNS

Tractatus tripartitus

The Tripartite Tractate (*tract. trip.*), also called *Treatise on the Three Natures*, is in Coptic (NHC 1, 5) and its language is difficult. It contains a strange gnostic doctrine of the Trinity (Father, Son, and preexistent church), as well as a cosmogony with an allegorical

interpretation of the story of paradise, acc. to which history follows a course from the stage of materiality via the Jewish religion to a pure spirituality; the redeemer divides humankind into three natures, the pneumatic, the psychic, and the hylic. The author is probably to be looked for among the followers of → Heracleon, the gnostic.

W: E. Thomassen, L. Painchaud (Leuven/Louvain, 1989) [Coptic text/French trans./comm.]. — R. Kasser, *tract. trip.* I-III (Bern, 1973-1975) [German trans./comm.]. — NHL 58-103 [English trans.].
L: A. Böhlig, Gottesbegriff: FS C. Andresen (Göttingen, 1979). — F. García Bazán, El Nombre: RevBib 50 (1988) 233-261. — J. P. Kenney, Platonism: Neoplatonism and Gnosticism, ed. R. T. Wallis (New York, 1992), 187-206. — H. C. Puech, G. Quispel, Codex Jung: VigChr 8 (1954) 1-51; 9 (1955) 65-102. — M. Simonetti, Eracleone: RSLR 28 (1992) 3-33. — E. Thomassen, Transcendent World: VigChr 34 (1980) 358-375.

P. BRUNS

Traditio apostolica

Traditio apostolica is the name usually given in scholarship and instruction to the best known and most important of the early Chr. → church orders, although we do not have the work either in its original form or under its original title. Also hypothetical is the attribution of the presently available, untitled reconstruction of the text to → Hippolytus of Rome.
I. The "Discovery" of the *Traditio apostolica*: H. Achelis gave the arbitrary name "Egyptian Church Order" to a series of canons (which he did not identify), handed down in Coptic, Ethiopic, and Arabic, of the → Alexandrian synod (*SinAlex.*), a collection of early Chr. church orders from 5th-c. Egypt. The fact that no one knew the original model for these canons was all the more regrettable in that numerous texts in the genre of church orders showed great similarities of content with these canons. Thus there are correspondences with (1) the → *Canones Hippolyti* (*can. Hipp.*), handed down in Arabic, and (2) the Syr. *Testament of Our Lord Jesus Christ* (*T. Dom.*). Among these parallel texts may be included parts of collections that bring together several church orders: (a) the → *Apostolic Constitutions* in Gr. (*Const. App.*; book 8.3-46 contains a parallel text); (b) a Gr. revision of passages from *Const. App.* 8, known to scholars under the title of *Epitome Constitutionum Apostolorum*; (c) the Lat. *Fragmentum Veronense* (*Frg. Ver.*) (third part); (d) individual books of the → *Octateuch of Clement* (*OctClem.*), which has come down in Arabic and Syriac. The "discovery" of the *Traditio apostolica* made it possible to identify the

model for these parallel texts. Eduard von der Goltz was the first scholar (1906) to identify these canons as fragments of the *apostolikē paradosis* (*traditio apostolica*) of Hippolytus of Rome. Goltz's conjectures were confirmed by more wide-ranging investigations that made it possible to incorporate the various parallel texts into a stemma or genealogy that left no doubt about the existence of relationships of dependence among the various parallel texts: *Traditio apostolica* (Gr. original ca. 215), incorporated, along with the Syr. → *Didascalia* (*Didasc.*) and the → *Apostolic Church Order*, into (lost) Gr. collections (beginning in 300), *can. Hipp.* (mid-4th c.), Lat. translation of a Gr. collection (*Frg. Ver.*, after 350); inclusion of recensions of the *Traditio apostolica* in (later) oriental collections (*Const. App.*, *SinAlex*, *OctClem*).

The skepticism originally voiced here and there about the authorship of Hippolytus of Rome has been expressed more plainly in contemporary scholarship.

II. Identification of Title and Author: Until the 16th c. patristic and Chr. literature knew of no work titled *Traditio apostolica*. Supporters of Hippolytus's authorship rely chiefly on two arguments: (1) They find the title of this church order in a list of writings engraved on the pedestal of the so-called statue of Hippolytus (discovered 1551 in Rome, now in the Vatican library); in the list is a title [Α]ΠΟΣΤΟΛΙΚΗ ΠΑΡΑΔΟΣΙΣ. (2) The name of Hippolytus shows up at significant points in some of the above-mentioned parallel texts: (a) in the *Inscriptio* of the Arab. *can. Hipp.*; (b) in the *Inscriptio* of the fifth book of the Arab. version of the *OctClem*; and, finally, (c) in the *Inscriptio* of the second part of the Gr. *Ep.*; this last text is of special interest, because the *Ep.* is not simply a faithful excerpt from book 8 of the *Const. App.*, but revises the *Const. App.*'s revision of the *Traditio apostolica* in light of an older (Gr.) version of the *Traditio apostolica*. It is no accident (the supporters claim) that the name of Hippolytus always shows up where the text identified as *apostolikē paradosis* makes its appearance within a parallel version.

The arguments of those who contest the authorship of Hippolytus have to do (1) with the doubtful witness value of the list of writings on the statue of Hippolytus. (2) Nowhere in the parallel texts does the title *apostolikē paradosis* appear; the inscriptions always speak of *diataxeis* (*Ep.*; Gr. fragment Ms. Ochrid 86 [ed. M. Richard] containing a text parallel to *Traditio apostolica* 36 [numbering of chs. acc. to the reconstruction of the text by B. Botte, LQF 39]) or *horoi* (Gr. translation of the Arab. *Inscriptio* of the

can.). (3) The mention of *dia Hippolytou* in the parallel texts may be interpreted as a way of claiming an apostolic origin for the instructions; this "technique" is current in other writings of the genre and a parallel can also be seen in *dia Klēmentos* (*Didasc.*, *Cons. App.*, *OctClem*, and frequently). It is possible in this connection to cite passages in early Chr. literature in which Hippolytus is called upon as a guarantor of apostolicity: Theodoret, *ep.* 145; Palladius, *h. Laus.* 146; Cyril of Scythopolis, *v. Euthym.*, and frequently. (4) A further argument comes from the compilational character of the work, which makes irrelevent the question of a single author; existing discontinuities, repetitions, contradictions, the unsystematic presentation of the material, etc., are not to be explained solely by maintaining that the issue in the *Traditio apostolica* is to reconstruct a text on the basis of various textual witnesses; all these factors may be evidence of a dynamic growth in the material of an open-ended church order.

III. Content of the *Traditio apostolica*: A prologue (ch. 1) and a epilogue (ch. 43) frame a comprehensive collection of regulations that can be structured only with difficulty. (a) Part I (*Traditio apostolica* 2-14) deals with matters of clerical interest, regulations for consecrations and ordinations, but also lay ministries (states) in the community. This section includes a series of ordination prayers (bishop, 3; presbyter, 7; deacon, 8), blessings or thanksgivings (over oil, 5; cheese and olives, 6), and more general regulations of varying length and having to do with confessors (9), widows (10), lectors (11), virgins (12), subdeacons (13), and those who claim to have the gift of healing (14). (b) The second part (15-21) gives well organized regulations for the catechumenate (15-19) and baptism (20/21). (c) The third section contains varied (rather disparate) regulations for the reception of communion (22), fasting (23), ministry to the sick (24), the blessings of lamps (25), the agape(?) (26-29), treatment of widows (30), blessing of fruits (31/32), fasting before reception of the Eucharist (33/36), prayer (35/41), reverent handling of the eucharistic gifts (37/38), deacons (34/39), and sign of the cross (42).

IV. The Community of the *Traditio apostolica*: The *Traditio apostolica* is familiar with a series of institutionalized intracommunity ministries that, with their hierarchical organization, attest to the division of the community into clergy and laity. The theol. constant in evaluating the various ministries is the gift of the Spirit, which for the clerical offices takes the liturg. and institutional form of the communication of Spirit in ordination (described as a laying on of hands/*cheirotonia* as distinct from the installation/ *institutio* of the lay ministries). The groups of clerics (bishops, presbyters, deacons), each with its specific communication of the Spirit, occupy the leadership offices, the crown of these being the office of bishop. The position of authority of the clerical office is justified with the help of a thus-structured "theology of gradated charisms" with its fine distinctions; the faithful are subordinated to this clerical office, although they have received the gift of the Spirit in baptism and for that reason have, as orthodox believers, a share in "perfect grace" (prologue). In the *Traditio apostolica*, then, the hierarchization of offices and the permanence of the ordered states of life are based on the liturgy (in the rites of ordination and installation) and given theol. legitimation (in the prayers of consecration and blessing); in the process, the consolidation of the offices of leadership, which have cut their roots in the common activity of the community, is left in the background.

Since it is an anonymous compilation, the *Traditio apostolica* does not manifest the pseudoapostolic style. Instead, the established order is judged to be the *vertex traditionis* (prologue) and "apostolic tradition" (epilogue), the material authenticity of which needs to be continually ascertained and actualized in the present. It is true that all the faithful have the ability to know how this is to be done, but it remains the duty of the leaders of the church to hand on and preserve the tradition.

V. Addressees: The *Traditio apostolica* speaks often of "the church" and usually means by this, first and foremost, the community of baptized Christians. In this sense, the work is addressed to the universal church as the community of orthodox believers (prologue). If one wanted to go further and conjecture as to the concrete community relationships reflected in the *Traditio apostolica*, one might suspect a large urban community as addressee of the regulations (see the list of trades and professions in ch. 16, acc. to which admission to the catechumenate is regulated in doubtful cases). Other passages, however, suggest the exact opposite (individual regulations point to a rural environment; also, e.g., there is never a word about a large number of [eucharistic] communities and their interaction, such as would be taken for granted in an urban situation).

VI. Period of Origin: The organization of offices and states, the stage of development of the rites of initiation and espec. of the catechumenate, the archaic form of the Eucharist (ordination and baptismal Eucharists), and the agape (the concept is lacking in the *Traditio apostolica*; ch. 27 speaks of "the Lord's supper") all suggest that a large number of the regulations came into being at the end of the 2nd c.

VII. The Exceptional Importance of the *Traditio apostolica*: The fact that the *Traditio apostolica* is the early Chr. document most often cited in the documents of Vatican II is witness to the considerable importance assigned to this work today. For liturg. scholarship it is by far the most important source from the early church. But it must be kept in mind that the *Traditio apostolica* is a work "discovered" a bare hundred years ago and that its organizational content was soon integrated into canonical collections. For this reason, it can be used only conditionally for study of an entire period of the history of early Chr. communities; more than ever, the *Traditio apostolica* leaves questions unanswered.

W: H. Achelis, J. Flemming, TU 6/4. — B. Botte, LQF 39 (Münster, ⁵1989) (currently standard text reconstruction). — B. Botte, SC 11, 11bis. — M. Cotone, The Apostolic Tradition [English trans. of the Botte text]. — G. Dix, The Treatise on the Apostolic Tradition (1937) (London, ²1968) [division (oriental) text witnesses/English trans.]. — H. Duensing, Der aeth. Text (Göttingen, 1946) [Ethiopic text/ German trans.]. — W. Geerlings, FC 1 [reconstruction of the text according to Botte/German trans.]. — E. Hauler, Fragmenta Veronensia (Leipzig, 1900) [Latin text]. — E. Jungklaus, Die Gemeinde Hippolyts (Leipzig, 1928) [German trans.]. — A. M. Schneider, Stimmen aus der Frühzeit (Cologne, 1948) [German trans.]. — E. Tidner, TU 75 [Latin text]. — W. Till, J. Leipoldt, TU 58 [Coptic text/German trans.].

Vgl. W: → Alexandrian Synod, → Canons of Hippolytus, → Octateuch of Clement.

L: J. V. Bartlet, Church-Life and Church-Order, ed. C. J. Cadoux (Oxford, 1943). — G. G. Blum, Apostolische Tradition u. Sukzession bei Hippolyt: ZNW 55 (1964) 95-110. — B. Botte, Le texte de la trad. ap.: RThAM 22 (1955) 161-172. — idem, A propos de la trad. ap.: RThAM 33 (1966) 177-186. — P. F. Bradshaw, TRE 18:662-670. — A. Brent, Hippolytus and the Roman Church (Leiden, 1995). — F. E. Brightman, Liturgies Eastern and Western (Oxford, 1967 = 1896). — R. H. Connolly, The So-Called Egyptian Church-Order (Cambridge, 1916). — H. Elfers, Die Kirchenordnung Hippolyts (Paderborn, 1938). — H. Engberding, Das angebliche Dokument röm. Liturgie: FS L. C. Mohlberg 1 (Rome, 1948), 47-71. — A. Faivre, Naissance d'une hiérarchie (Paris, 1977). — idem, La documentation canonico-liturgique: RevSR 54 (1980) 204-215, 273-297. — A. Gelston, A Note on the Text of the Apostolic Tradition: JThS 39 (1988) 112-117. — E. von der Goltz, Fragmente altchr. Gemeindeordnungen: SPAW 56 (1906) 141-157. — M. Guarducci, Statua di Sant' Ippolito: SEAug 30 (1989) 61-74. — A. Hamel, Kirchenrechtliches Schrifttum Hippolyts: ZNW 36 (1937) 238-250. — J. M. Hanssens, La liturgie d'Hippolyte (Rome, ²1965). — idem, Documents et études (Rome, 1970). — E. Jungklaus, Gemeinde Hippolyts (Leipzig, 1928). — G. Kretschmar, Ordination im frühen Christentum: FZPhTh 22 (1975) 35-69. — idem, La liturgie ancienne: MD 149 (1982) 57-90. — K. Küppers,

Eucharistie- und Bischofsweihegebet: ALW 29 (1987) 19-30. — J. Lecuyer, Episcopat et presbytérat: RSR 41 (1953) 30-50. — J. Magne, La prétendue Tradition Apostolique: OS 14 (1965) 35-67. — idem, Diataxeis des saints apôtres (Paris, 1975). — idem, En finir avec la "Tradition": BLE 89 (1988) 5-22. — C. Markschies, Wer schrieb die sog. TA?: Tauffragen u. Bekenntnis (Berlin/New York, 1999), 1-74. — A. G. Martimort, La Tradition apostolique: ACan 23 (1979) 159-173. — idem, Nouvel examen: BLE 88 (1987) 5-25. — M. Metzger, Prétendue Tradition apostolique: EO 5 (1988) 241-259. — idem, Enquêtes autour la "trad. ap.": EO 9 (1992) 7-36. — P. Nautin, Hippolyte et Josipe (Paris, 1947). — E. C. Ratcliff, Apostolic Tradition: StPatr 8 (1966) 266-270. — M. Richard, Florilège du Cod. Ochrid: idem, Opera minora 1 (Turnhout, 1976), Nr. 6. — K. Richter, Bischofsordination: ALW 17 (1975) 7-58. — W. Riedel, Kirchenrechtsquellen (Leipzig, 1900). — W. Rordorf, L'ordination de l'évêque: QLP 55 (1974) 137-150. — A. Rose, La prière de consécration pour l'ordination épiscopale: MD 98 (1969) 127-142. — E. Schwartz, Pseudoapostolische KO: idem, Gesammelte Schriften 5 (Berlin, 1963), 193-273 = (Strasburg, 1910). — H. R. Seeliger, Käse beim eucharistischen Mahl: FS T. Schneider (Mainz, 1995), 195-207. — C. Scholten, Hippolytus II. v. Rom (VI. trad. ap.): RAC 15:524-530. — M. Simonetti, Una nuova proposta su Ippolito: Aug. 36 (1996) 13-46. — J. E. Stam, Episcopacy in the Apostolic Tradition (Basel, 1969). — idem, Charismatic Theology: FS M. C. Tenney (Grand Rapids, 1975), 267-276. — B. Steimer, Vertex traditionis (Berlin, 1992). — A. Stewart-Sykes: Integrity of Ordination Rites: Aug. 39 (1999) 97-127. — A. F. Walls, The Latin Version: StPatr 2 (1961) 83-92.

B. STEIMER

Translation

The ancient Roman world was to a large extent bilingual. From the beginnings of Roman literature there was a great deal of translation and adaptation, without attention to any distinction between *interpretatio* and *aemulatio* (comedy; Catullus; Cicero). The administration, too, had to translate, into both languages. By the 2nd c., Christians had to translate their sacred scriptures into Lat., espec. for the less educated (first evidence: Scillitan martyrs, 180). The achievements in linguistic innovation were immense. Toward the end of the 4th c. bilingualism could no longer be assumed, even among the educated. Great translators/adapters such as → Ambrose, → Jerome, and → Rufinus of Aquileia made Gr. theology from Alexandria and Cappadocia accessible to their (sometimes aristocratic) readers. Ca. 420, → Anianus of Celeda, a Pelagian, translated many sermons of Chrysostom.

Practice was accompanied by discussion of theory, both in the "classical" tradition and also in connection with the theol. controversy surrounding Origen. The translation theories of a Jerome were, however, not unified (*sensus de senso* or *verbum de verbo*, espec.

in the Bible: *ep.* 57.5.2) and were applied pragmatically.

The following alphabetical list is limited to complete works (thus "plagiarisms" like those of Ambrose are not included). Also excluded are the canonical texts of the Bible, conciliar decrees, and material that is questionable or undated.

1. *Acta Archelai* by a Hegemonius: an anti-Manichean polemic (end of 4th c.; *Act. Archel.*). The list of heretics at the end is not a translation.

2. Anianus of Celeda, Pelagian translator of homilies of Chrysostom (ca. 420).

3. Avitus of Braga translated (415/416) a letter of Lucian on the discovery of the relics of Stephen, in two recensions (Avit. Brac., *Lucian. ep.*).

4. *Letter of Barnabas* (translation before Cyprian? *Barn.*).

5. *Basiliana*: → Eustathius (no. 9) and → Rufinus (no. 28).

6. Sermon *De ascetica disciplina* = *Admonitio ad monachos* (5th/6th c.? Basil, *ascet. disc.*).

7. Letter of Clement of Rome to the Corinthians (3rd or 4th c.; *1 Clem.*).

8. Cyril, seventeenth Easter letter (before 450; Cyril, *hom. pasch.*).

9. Eustathius, homilies of Basil on the Hexaemeron, ca. 400.

10. Evagrius of Antioch, revision of Athanasius's life of Anthony (ca. 370; Evagr., *vita Anton.*).

11. Evagrius Pont., 137 sentences *Ad monachos* and 56 *ad virginem*, each in two recensions, one of them by Rufinus (Evag. Pont., *sent. mon./virg.*).

12. Firmilian of Caesarea (ca. 268), letter to Cyprian (Firmil., *Cypr. ep.*).

13. Hegesippus, revision of the *Bellum Iudaicum* of Flavius Josephus, end of 4th c. (Heges.).

14. *Shepherd* of Hermas, *versio Palatina* ca. 400 (Herm., *Pal.*) and *versio vulgata*, 2nd c. (*vulg.*).

15-21. Jerome:

15. Didymus the Blind. *On the Holy Spirit* (Didym., *spir.*); Greek lost, 387.

16. Several *Epistulae* of Jerome are translations: *ep.* 51, 87, 89-94, 96, 98, 200, 223; *ep.* 124 (to Avitus) gives information on Jerome's lost translation of Origen's *Peri archōn*.

17. *Chronicle* of Eusebius (Eus., *chron.*), 381, translation, revision, continuation.

18. *On Place Names* of Eusebius (Eus., *sit. et nom.*), revision of 390.

19. *Pachomiana*, translated 404 from Greek; includes twelve letters (*ep. Pachom.*) and the Rule (*reg. Pachom.*) of Pachomius the monk, a letter of Theodore (*ep. Theod.*), and the book of → Horsiesi (*Orsies. doctr.*).

20. Sermons of Origen (*hom. Orig.*): *in cant.* 2 (Gr. text lost), Rome, 383; *in Ezech.* 14 (Gr. lost), 378/379; *In Ier.* 14 (Gr.: 12); *in Is.* 9 (Gr. lost), 378/379; *in Luc.* 39 (Gr. = fragmentary), 392.

21. *Hebrew Names* (*nom. hebr.*), revision of 390; Jerome thought the work to be from Philo.

22. Ignatius of Antioch, *Letter to the Romans* (Ign., *Rom. Colbert*), ca. 400.

23. Irenaeus, five books *Against Heresies* (Iren., *haer.*), 3rd or 4th c.

24. Julian of Eclanum, Commentary of Theodore Mops. on the Psalms (to some extent a free rendering), before 418 (Julian, *in psalm.*).

25. *Origeniana*: → Jerome, → Rufinus (no. 28); in addition, the commentary on Mt, translated by an Arian in the second or third quarter of the 5th c. (begins with book 12; Orig., *comm. in Mt.*; *comm. ser. in Mt.*).

26. *Passiones*: of Andrew (longer version, 5th/6th c.; *Andr. long.*); of George (recension a, probably 5th c.; *Georg. rec. a*); of Paul (longer version, 5th/6th c.; *Paul.*); of Peter (revision of 4th or 6th c.; *Petr.*); of Phileas, bishop of Thmuis (revision, end of 5th c., northern Italy; *Act. Phileae*); of Polycarp (3rd c.; *Polycarp.*); of Thecla (4th c.; *Thecl.*).

27. *Philoniana*: the 4th c. saw the translation of Philo of Alexandria, *Quaestiones in genesim* (Philo, *quaest. in gen.*) and *De vita contemplativa* (*vita contempl.*) and of Ps.-Philo, the sixty-five chapters (Greek lost) of the *Antiquitates* (Ps.-Philo, *antiq.*).

28. Rufinus of Aquileia, five books *Against Heretics* by "Adamantus" (probably Origen; *Adamant.*), after 400; ten sermons of Basil (Basil, *hom.*), ca. 400 and Basil's *Regula*, 397 (praef. 2 is also a translation; Basil. *reg.*); Clement of Rome's "recognitions" novel in ten books (*Clement.*), 406, and a letter (*ep. Clement.*), 405 or earlier; Eusebius, *History of the Church* in nine books with a continuation by Rufinus (two books; Eus., *h.e.*), 402/403; Gregory Naz., nine sermons (Greg. Naz., *orat.*); Origen's commentary on Rom, ten books (out of fifteen; Orig., *in Rom.*), 405/406, and on the Song (*in cant.*), three books, 410, 108 sermons on the Heptateuch (*Hept.*), 403-404 (but *in num.* not until 410), probably a sermon on 1 Kgs (*in I reg.*), nine sermons on Psalms 36-38 (*in psalm.*), 398, and in that same year the notorious dogmatics, *De principiis* (*princ.*), four books; Pamphilus, the "defense" of Origen (Gr. lost) (Pamph., *apol. Orig.*), 397 (praef. 2 is also a translation); Sextus, 451 sentences (*sent. Sexti*), ca. 400; and the anonymous *Historia monachorum* (*hist. mon.*), thirty-three chapters, 404. Rufinus was the most important translator of theol. works from the East; he defends his method in numerous prologues.

29. Ps.-Rufinus, *Bellum Iudaicum* of Flavius Josephus, 4th/5th c. (Ps.-Rufin., *Ios. bell. Iud.*).

30. Anonymous, *Vita Antonii* by Athanasius (?), before 360 (therefore before Evagrius [no. 10], *Vita Anton.*).

W: on **1.** *Act. Archel.*, PG 18:1069-1264. — C. H. Beeson, GCS 16 [with Greek frags.]. — on **3.** Avit. Brac., *Lucian. ep.*, PL 41:807-818. — E. Vanderlinden: REByz 4 (1946) 178-217 [2 versions, accompanying letter]. — N. Franco: ReO 8 (1914) 293-307 [Greek text]. — on **4.** *Barn.*, J. M. Heer (Freiburg i.Br., 1908) [Greek/Latin text]. — R. A. Kraft, P. Prigent, SC 172 [Greek text]. — on **6.** Basil, *ascet. disc.*, A. Wilmart: RBen 27 (1910) 226-233. — PG 31:648-652 [Greek text]. — on **7.** *1 Clem.*, C. T. Schäfer: FlorPatr 44 (1941) [Greek/Latin text]. — A. Jaubert, SC 167. — on **8.** Cyril, *hom. pasch.*, PG 77:768-790 [also Greek text]. — F. Gori, Arnobii iunioris Conflictus (Turin, 1993), 186-206. — J. Scharnagl (Vienna, 1909) [Greek text]. — on **9.** Eustathius, PL 53:867-966. — E. Amand de Mendieta, S. Y. Rudberg, TU 66 (Berlin, 1958) [text]. — PG 29:4-208. — S. Giet, SC 26 [Greek text]. — M. Naldini (Milan, 1990) [Greek text/Italian trans./comm.]. — E. Amand de Mendieta, S. Y. Rudberg, GCS NF 2 [Greek text/subject index]. — on **10.** Evagr., *vita Ant.*, PG 26:833-976. — PL 73:125-170. — G. Bartelink, SC 400 [Greek text]. — on **11.** Evagr. Pont., *sent. mon./virg., rec.* H, PL 20:1181-1188. — PG 40:1277-1286. — H. Gressmann, TU 39/4 (Leipzig, 1913), 146-165 [Greek text]. — *sent. mon. rec.* A, J. Leclercq: Scr. 5 (1951) 204-213. — *sent. virg. rec.* W, A. Wilmart: RBen 28 (1911) 148-151. — on **12.** Firmil., *Cypr. ep.* 75, W. Hartel, CSEL 3/2:810-827. — G. W. Clarke, ACW 47:246-276 [English trans./comm.]. — on **13.** Heges., V. Ussani, CSEL 66/1-2. — B. Niese, Ios. 6 (Berlin, ²1955 = 1894) [Greek text]. — on **14.** Herm., *Pal.*, O. de Gebhardt, A. Harnack, T. Zahn, 3 (Leipzig, 1877). — A. Vezzoni, Il pastore di Erma, Versione Palatina (Florence, 1994) [Latin text/Italian trans.]. — *vulg.*, A. Hilgenfeld (Leipzig, 1873). — M. Whittacker, GCS 48 [Greek text]. — on **15.** Jer., *Didym., spir.*, PL 23:101-154. — PG 39:1031-1086. — L. Doutreleau, SC 386. — on **17.** Eus., *chron.*, R. Helm, GCS 47 [Greek/Latin text]. — on **18.** Eus., *sit. et nom.*, PL 23:859-928. — P. de Lagarde, Onomastica sacra (Göttingen, ²1887), 117-190. — E. Klostermann, GCS 11/1 [with Greek text]. — on **19.** "Pachomiana," A. Boon, Pachomiana lat. (Leuven/Louvain, 1932). — H. Quecke, Die Briefe Pachoms (Regensburg, 1975) [Greek text]. — on **20.** *hom. Orig., in cant.*, PL 23:1117-1144. — W. A. Baehrens, GCS 33:26-60. — O. Rousseau, SC 37bis. — *in Ezech.*, PL 23:691-786. — W. A. Baehrens, GCS 33:318-454. — *in Is.*, PL 24:901-935. — W. A. Baehrens, GCS 33:242-289. — *in Ier.*, PL 25:583-692. — W. A. Baehrens, GCS 33:290-317. — E. Klostermann, P. Nautin, GCS 6 [Greek text]. — P. Husson, P. Nautin, SC 238:300-366. — *in Luc.*, PL 26:219-306. — M. Rauer, GCS 49 [Greek text/Latin text]. — H. J. Sieben, FC 4/1-2 [text/trans./Greek frags.]. — on **21.** *nom. hebr.*, P. de Lagarde, CCL 72:57-161. — on **22.** Ign., *Rom. Colbert.*, J. Mallet, A. Thibaut (Paris, 1984), 285-287. — F. X. Funk, K. Bihlmeyer (Tübingen, ³1970), 96-101 [Greek text]. — P. T. Camelot, SC 410:94-119. — on **23.** Iren., *haer.*, A. Stieren 1 (Leipzig, 1853). — W. W. Harvey (Cambridge, 1857). — A. Rousseau, L. Doutreleau, B.

Hemmerdinger, C. Mercier, SC 264, 294, 211, 100, 153 [text/French trans./Greek frags./comm. in accompanying vols.]. N. Brox, FC 8/1bis [Greek text/Latin text/German trans.]. — on **24**. Julian, *in psalm.*, R. Devreesse, ST 93 (Rome, 1939 [text/also Greek]. — L. De Coninck, CCL 88A. — on **25**. Orig., *comm. in Mt.; comm. ser. in Mt.*, E. Benz, E. Klostermann, GCS 40 [also Greek text]. — E. Benz, E. Klostermann, U. Treu, GCS 38. — on **26**. *Andr. long,* M. Bonnet 1 (Darmstadt, 1959 = 1898), 1-37 [Greek text/Latin text]. — *Georg. rec. a,* W. Arndt (Leipzig, 1874), 49-70. — K. Krumbacher (Munich, 1911), 1-40 [Greek text]. — *Ignat. Colbert.,* J. Mallet, A. Thibaut (Paris, 1984), 283-289. — F. X. Funk, F. Diekamp (Tübingen, 1913), 363-382 [Greek text]. — *Paul.,* R. A. Lipsius 1 (Darmstadt, 1959 = 1891), 23-44, 104-117 [Greek text/Latin text]. — *Petr.,* R. A. Lipsius 1 (Leipzig, 1891 = Darmstadt, 1959), 1-22. — *Phileae,* F. Halkin: AnBoll 81 (1963) 12-29 [also Greek text]. — G. A. A. Kortekaas et al., Atti e passioni dei martiri (Vicenza, 1987), 247-337 [Latin/Greek text/Italian trans.], 498-581 [comm.]. — *Polycarp.,* T. Zahn 2 (Leipzig, ³1876), 133-167 [Greek/Latin text]. — B. Dehandschutter (Leuven/Louvain, 1979) [Greek text]. — P. A. Orban et al., Atti e passioni dei martiri (Vicenza, 1987), 4-30 [Greek text], 371-383 [comm.]. — *Thecl.,* O. de Gebhardt, TU 22/2 (Leipzig, 1902) — R. A. Lipsius 1 (Darmstadt, 1959 = 1891), 235-269 [Greek text]. — on **27**. Philo, *quaest. in gen.,* F. Petit, TU 113-114 (Berlin, 1973) [with Greek frags.; cf. Codices manuscripti 9, 1983, 164-172]. — *vita contempl.,* L. Cohn, S. Reiter (Philon 6) (Berlin, 1915), XVIII-XXIX, 46-57 [Greek text]. — Ps.-Philo, *antiq.,* J. Sichardus (Basel, 1527). — G. Kisch (Notre Dame, Ind., 1949). — D. J. Harrington, C. Perrot, SC 229-230. — H. Jacobson, vols. 1-2 (Leiden, 1996) [Latin text/English trans./comm.]. — C. Dietzfelbringer, JSHRZ 2:89-271 [German trans.]. — on **28**. Rufinis, *Prologues,* M. Simonetti, CCL 20. — *Adamant.,* W. H. van de Sande Bakhuizen, GCS 4. — V. Buchheit (Munich, 1966). — Basil, *hom.* 1-8, PG 31:1723-1794. — PG 29, 31 [Greek text]. — *hom.* 2, S. Y. Rudberg (Stockholm, 1962) [Greek text]. — *hom.* 9-10, H. Marti (Leiden, 1989) [Greek text/Latin text]. — Basil., *reg.,* PL 103:485-554. — PG 31:901-1305 [similar Greek text]. — K. Zelzer, CSEL 86. — *Clement,* B. Rehm, GCS 51:6-371 [with Greek frags.; parts of the trans. are not authentic: 3.2.1-11.12, possibly 10.65a-72.5]. — *ep. Clement.,* B. Rehm, GCS 51:375-387. — B. Rehm, GCS 42:5-22 [Greek text]. — Eus., *h.e.,* T. Mommsen, GCS 9/1-2. — E. Schwartz, GCS 9:1-2 [Greek text]. — Greg. Naz., *orat.,* A. Engelbrecht, CSEL 46. — PG 35-36, Nr. 2, 6, 16-17, 26-27, 38-39, 41 [Greek text]. — Orig., *in Rom.,* PG 14:831-1294. — C. P. Hammond Bammel (Freiburg i.Br., 1990/1997) (vols. 1-6). — *in cant.,* W. A. Baehrens, GCS 33:61-241 [with Greek frags.]. — L. Brésard, H. Crouzel, M. Borret, SC 375f. — *Hept.,* W. A. Baehrens, GCS 29f.; 16 *hom. in gen.,* H. de Lubac, L. Doutreleau, SC 7bis; 13 *in exod.,* M. Borret, SC 321; 16 *in lev.,* M. Borret, SC 286-287; 28 *in num.,* L. Doutreleau, SC 415; 9 *in iud.,* P. Messié et al., SC 389; 26 *in Ios.,* A. Jaubert, SC 71. — *in I reg.,* PG 12:995-1012. — W. A. Baehrens, GCS 33:1-25. — P. + M.-T. Nautin, SC 328, 94-152 (cf. 35-49). — *in psalm.,* PG 12:1319-1410. — E. Prinzivalli, Omelie sui Salmi (Florence, 1991) [with Greek frags.]. — eadem, SC 411. — *princ.,* P. Koetschau, GCS 22. — H. Görgemanns, H. Karpp (Darmstadt, ²1985). — H. Crouzel, M. Simonetti, SC 252-253, 268-269, 312. — Pamph., *apol. Orig.,* PG 17:539-632. — *sent. Sext.,* H. Chadwick (Cambridge, 1959) [Greek/Latin text]. — *hist. mon.,* PL 21:387-462. — E.

Schulz-Flügel (Berlin, 1990). — A.-J. Festugière (Brussels, 1971) [Greek text]. — on **29**. Ps.-Rufinus, *Ios. bell. Iud.,* editions from 1470 to 1524. — B. Niese (Ios. 6) (Berlin, ²1955 = 1894) [Greek text]. — on **30**. *v. Anton.,* A. Wilmart: RBen 31 (1914-1919) 167-171. — H. Hoppenbrouwers (Nijmegen, 1960). — G. Bartelink (Milan, 1974) [text/comm./Italian trans.]. — PG 26:837-976 [Greek text]. L: H. Marti, Übersetzer der Augustin-Zeit (Munich, 1974). — C. Mohrmann, Études sur le latin des chrétiens, vols. 1-4 (Rome, 1958, ²1961-1977). — A. Seele, Röm. Übersetzer (Darmstadt, 1995). — F. Winkelmann, Aussagen des Rufinus u. des Hieronymus: FS J. Quasten (Münster, 1970), 532-547.-on **4**.: HLL 4:415. — on **5**.: P. J. Fedwick, Translations before 1400: Basilius of Caesarea (Toronto, 1981), 455-473. — on **7**.: C. Mohrmann, Origine de la latinité chrétienne: VigChr 3 (1949) 67-106 (= eadem, Études 3:67-106). — M. Simonetti, Sulla datazione: RFIC 116 (1988) 203-211. — F. Tailliez, Vulgarisme: NP 35 (1951) 46-50. — on **9**.: B. Altaner, Eustathius: ZNW 39 (1940) 161-170 [=Kl. patr. Schriften (Berlin, 1967), 437-447]. — P. J. Fedwick, op. cit. — H. Marti, Das Übersetzen philosophischer Texte: Rencontres de cultures, ed. J. Hamesse (Leuven/Louvain, 1990), 33-35. — on **10**.: G. Bartelink, Bemerkungen: RBen 82 (1972) 98-105. — idem, Quelques gloses: Mn. 26 (1973) 265-272. — idem, Grécismes: Mn. 30 (1977) 388-422. — HLL 5:537-539. — L. T. Lorić, Spiritual Terminology (Nijmegen, 1955). — B. R. Voss, Bemerkungen: VigChr 21 (1967) 93-102. — idem, Hagiographie u. Historiographie: FMSt 4 (1970) 53-69. — on **12**.: G. W. Clarke: op. cit. (literature). — on **13**.: A. A. Bell, Josephus, Judaism and Christianity (Detroit, 1987), 349-361. — J. P. Callu, Datation: Bonner Hist. Aug.-Coll., ed. J. Straub (Bonn, 1987), 117-142. — U. Winter, Zwei Neuerwerbungen: Zeitschrift für Buchkunst u. Bibliophilie 111 (1988) 31-39. — on **14**.: A. Carlini, Due estratti: SCO 35 (1985) 311-312. — I. Mazzini, Pastore di Erma: CCC 2 (1981) 45-86. — idem, Il codice Urbinate 486: Prometheus 6 (1980) 181-188. — A. Vezzoni, Un testimone: SCO 37 (1987) 241-265. — HLL 4:414. — on **15**.: B. Altaner, Augustinus u. Didymus: VigChr 5 (1951) 116-120 [= Kl patr. Schriften (Berlin, 1967), 297-301]. — L. Doutreleau, De spiritu sancto: RSR 51 (1963) 383-406. — idem, Parisinus lat. 2364: SE 18 (1967/68) 372-384. — idem, Tradition manuscrite: FS J. Quasten 1 (Münster, 1970), 352-389. — P. Nautin, Jérôme et Damase: FZPhTh 30 (1983) 331-334. — E. Stolz, Didymus, Ambrosius, Hieronymus: ThQ 87 (1905) 371-401. — on **16**.: H. Crouzel, Jérôme (Paris, 1988), 153-161. — on **17**.: G. Brugnoli, Curiosissimus excerptor: Gerolamo (Genoa, 1989), 23-43. — A. A. Mosshammer, Two Fragments: RMP 124 (1981) 66-80. — on **19**.: I. Opelt, Diktion: FS A. Bastiaensen (Den Haag, 1991), 243-253. — on **20**.: G. Lomiento, L'esegesi origeniana (Bari, 1966). — idem, Omelie su Jeremie: VetChr 10 (1973) 243-262. — P. Nautin, Note: REAug 22 (1976) 78-81. — idem, Jérôme (Paris, 1988), 27-39. — V. Peri, I passi sulla trinità: StPatr 6 (1962) 155-180. — idem, 9. Jes-Homilie: RBen 95 (1985) 7-10. — on **21**.: C. T. R. Hayward, Hebrew Questions (Oxford, 1995), 18. — H. Jacobson, Nonnulla onomastica: JThS 43 (1992) 117. — A. Kamesar, Jerome (Oxford, 1993), 104. — F. X. Wutz, Onomastica Sacra, TU 41 (Leipzig, 1914). — on **23**.: B. Altaner, Augustinus u. Irenäus: ThQ 129 (1949) 162-172 [= Kl. patr. Schriften (Berlin, 1967), 194-203]. — M. L. Arduini, Ireneo medievale: StMed 21 (1980) 269-299. — R. Doutreleau, Salmaticensis 202: Orph. 2 (1981) 131-156. — B. Hemmerdinger, Mésaventures d'un philologue: JThS 17 (1966)

308-326. — E. Köstermann, Hss. des Irenäus: ZNW 36 (1937) 1-34. — H. Koch, Tertullianisches: ThStKr 101 (1929) 462-469. — G. M. Lee, Note: VigChr 25 (1971) 29-30. — S. Lundström, Studien (Lund, 1943). — idem, Neue Studien (Lund, 1948). — idem, Observations critiques (Lund, 1969). — idem, Die Überlieferung (Uppsala, 1985). — B. Reynders, Lexique comparée, vols. 1-2 (Leuven/Louvain, 1954). — on 24.: V. Bulhart, Kritische Studien: WSt 59 (1941) 134-145. — on 25.: H. J. Vogt, Ergänzungen: ThQ 160 (1980) 207-212. — on 27.: B. Altaner, Augustinus u. Philo: ZKTh 65 (1941), 81-90 [= Kl. patr. Schriften (Berlin, 1967), 181-193]. — HLL 4:369f. — on 28.: Rufino di Concordia e il suo tempo: Antichità altoadriatiche 31/1-2 (Udine, 1987). — H. Crouzel, Les doxologies: Aug. 20 (1980) 95-107. — C. P. Hammond Bammel, Rufinus' life: JThS 28 (1977) 372-429. — F. Merlo, J. Gribomont, Il salterio (Rome, 1972). — M. Schär, Nachleben des Origenes (Basel, 1979). — M. M. Wagner, Rufinus the Translator (Washington, 1945). — *Adamant.:* V. Buchheit, Rufinus als Fälscher: ByZ 51 (1958) 314-328. — Basil, *hom.:* M. Huglo, Anciennes versions: RBen 64 (1954) 129-132. — Basil, *reg.:* J. Gribomont, Histoire du texte (Leuven/Louvain, 1953). — S. Lundström, Überlieferung der lat. Basiliusregel (Stockholm, 1989). — K. Zelzer, Überlieferungsgeschichtliche Untersuchungen, TU 125 (Berlin, 1981), 625-635. — *Clement:* O. Cullmann, Le problème littéraire (Paris, 1930). — H. Drijvers, Adam: FS C. Colpe (Würzburg, 1990), 314-323. — W. L. Petersen, Aphrahat: Vig Chr 46 (1992) 241-256. — G. Strecker, Pseudoklementinen 3, Konkordanz 1, GCS (Berlin, 1986) (Wortregister). — F. Tosolini, Paolo nelle Pseudoclementine: Aug. 26 (1986) 369-400. — *ep. Clement.:* G. Strecker, op. cit. — W. Ullman, Significance: JThS 11 (1960) 295-317. — Eus., *h.e.:* T. Christensen, h.e. 8-9: Historisk-filosofiske Meddelelser 58 (Copenhagen, 1989). — P. Courcelle, Jugements sur les empereurs: REA 71 (1969) 100-130. — L. Dattrino, Conversione secondo la h.e.: Aug. 27 (1987) 247-280. — L. Neyrand, Passion des martyrs de Lyon (Paris, 1978), 289-298. — J. E. L. Oulton, Rufinus' Translation: JThS 30 (1929) 150-174. — M. Pucci, Remarks: RSA 11 (1981) 123-128. — F. Thélamon, Payens et chrétiens (Paris, 1981). — G. W. Trompf, Logic of Retribution: JEH 43 (1992) 351-371. — M. Villain, Histoire ecclésiastique: RSR 33 (1946) 164-210. — P. Wynn, Victor Vitensis: CM 41 (1990) 187-198. — Greg. Naz., *orat.:* A. F. Memoli, Fedeltà: Aevum 43 (1969) 459-484. — A. C. Way, Catalogus translationum et commentariorum (ed. P. O. Kristeller), 2 u. 3 (Washington, 1971 and 1976), 127-139; 420. — Orig., *in Rom.:* H. Chadwick, Tura Pap.: JThS 10 (1959) 10-42. — C. P. Hammond Bammel, Scriptoria: JThS 30 (1979) 430-462. — eadem, Der Römerbrieftext (Freiburg i.Br., 1985). — *in lev.:* P. C. Porta, Omelia sul Lev 5, 1: Orph. 13 (1992) 52-76 (on 5, 1). — *in num.:* I. Linderski, An emendation: HSCP 85 (1981) 213-215 (on 17, 2). — A. Méhat, Notes: Texte & Textkritik 1 (1987) 411-416. — *in psalm.:* V. Peri, Omelie Origeniane (Rome, 1980). — *princ.:* R. G. Babcock, Marginalia: Yale University Library Gazette 64 (1989) 83-85. — N. Pace, Ricerche (Florence, 1990). — J. Rius-Camp, Localisation: VigChr 41 (1987) 209-225. — G. Sfameni Gasparro, Peri archon: Aug. 26 (1986) 191-205. — B. Studer, Dogmatische Terminologie: FS J. Daniélou (Paris, 1972), 403-414. — *sent. Sext.:* P.-M. Bogaert, Préface de Rufin: RBen 82 (1972) 26-46. — J. Bouffartigue, Études de littérature ancienne (Paris, 1979), 81-95. — A. Carlini, Vel enchiridion vel anulus: FS C. G. Mor (Udine, 1984), 109-118. — H. Marti,

Übersetzer der Augustin-Zeit (Munich, 1974), 228. — **on 30.:** A. Aragosti, v. Anton. 7, 5-6: MD 1 (1978) 223-227. — T. D. Barnes, Angel of Light: JThS 37 (1986) 353-368 [original Coptic]. — G. Bartelink, Observations: RB 81 (1971) 92-95. — idem, Patientia sine ira: Mn. 25 (1972) 190-192 [double trans.]. — idem, Lesarten: RHT 11 (1981) 397-413 [mss.]. — M. G. Bianco, Gli intenti: SSR 5 (1981) 223-250. — G. Garitte, Un témoin important (Brussels, 1939). — H. Hoppenbrouwers,Technique de la tradition: FS C. Mohrmann (Utrecht, 1973), 80-95. — A. Louth, Athanasius: JThS 39 (1988) 504-509 (authorship question). — C. Mohrmann, Note: StAns 38 (1956) 35-44. — F. S. Pericoli Ridolfini, Vita Martini e Vita Antonii: FS A. Pincherle: SMSR 38 (1967) 420-433. — V. Tandoi, Sul testo: SIFC 50 (1978) 161-190. — **on later translations** → Boethius II. 2; → Dionysius Exiguus; → Epiphanius Scholasticus; → Eusebius of Emesa; → Liber generationis mundi; → Rusticus, Deacon; → Languages; → Theodore of Mopsuestia; → Thomas, Literature about; → Ulfila.

H. MARTI

Treatise

Tractatus ("treatise") is the term used in classical Latin for the oral or written discussion of a subject or matter of special interest. In the works of Tertullian a *tractatus* is a treatment in diatribe style that is quite close to dialogue and polemic, but from the 3rd c. on, the terms *tractare* and *tractatus* were generally used in Chr. Latin to mean "preach" and "sermon." To Cyprian, Novatian, and Optatus of Milevis *tractatus* meant the proclamation of the word and the kind of public teaching that was reserved to the bishop. While in the 3rd c. the great number of bibl. treatises were predominantly dogmatic, ethical-ascetic, and eccles.-practical in content, in the works of Hilary of Poitiers the treatise developed along the lines of a sermonlike commentary. From the 4th c. on, however, treatise functioned generally as a Lat. translation of the Gr. term → homily. In contrast to the written explanation of the word of God in the form of *sermones*, treatise here meant an actual sermon with bibl. content.

L: G. Bardy, Tractare, tractatus: RSR 33 (1946), 211-235. — H. Jordan, Geschichte der altchr. Lit. (Leipzig, 1911), 308-345.

G. BROSZIO

Trifolius

From T., a priest, comes a letter written ca. 520 to a senator Faustus, who had asked him about the teaching of a Scythian monk named John, who had just come from Constantinople to Rome. Faustus's question was whether the formula "One of the Trinity has suffered" was orthodox. T.'s answer was negative, and he justified it by appealing to the four ecumenical councils. The letter is thus the earliest witness to the theopaschite controversy in the West.

W: F. Glorie, CCL 85:137-141.

G. RÖWEKAMP

Trojanus of Saintes

T. was bishop of Saintes (Santonae) at the beginning of the 5th c. He died probably in 432. Gregory of Tours mentions him in a letter (MGH. Ep. 3:437). A letter (ep.) of T. himself to Bishop Eumerius of Nantes on the understanding of baptism is first mentioned at the second Council of Orleans in 533.

W: ep., W. Gundlach, CCL 117:489.
L: Y. H. Albanes, V. Chavalier, GCN 2 (Montbéliard, 1907), 117-119. — P. Viard, T.: BSS 12:678-679.

C. KASPER

Tura Papyri

913 codex sheets and two individual sheets (= 1,830 sides) containing works of → Origen (93 fol.) and Didymus the Blind (820 fol.) form the surviving content (92 fol. are still lost) of a papyrus discovery made in the summer of 1941 in a tunnel of a quarry cave above the village of Tura (ca. 12 km. south of Cairo). The papyri, which were parts of eight codices, come probably from the Origenist-leaning monastery of Arsenius which was built above the cave in the 5th/6th c. We do not know when and why the writings of the two Alexandrians were stored in the cave. The outlawing of Origenism from the mid-6th c. on can hardly be the reason; the dating of the papyri, 6th/7th c., is against it. The publication of the Tura discovery is almost complete: the transmission of Origen's works has been notably expanded, espec. by Peri Pascha 1 and 2 and the Dialogus cum Heraclide; the transmission of Didymus's works has been exceptionally enriched, espec. by Gen., Zach., Job, Eccl., and Ps.

L: K. Aland, H.-U. Rosenbaum, Repertorium der griech. chr. Papyri 2 (Berlin, 1995). — L. Doutreleau, Que savonsnous aujourd'hui des papyrus de Toura?: RSR 43 (1955) 161-176. — O. Guéraud, Note préliminaire: RHR 131 (1946) 85-108. — idem, P. Nautin, Origène, Sur la Pâque (Paris, 1979), 15-21. — L. Koenen, L. Müller-Wiener, Zu den Papyri aus dem Arsenioskloster: ZPE 2 (1968) 40-63. — L. Koenen, L. Doutreleau, Nouvel Inventaire: RSR 55 (1967) 547-564.

B. NEUSCHÄFER

Turibius of Astorga

T., bishop of Astorga after 444 (?), combatted the Manichees and wrote against the followers of Priscillian. Extant is his Ep. ad Idacium et Ceponium episcopos (ep.). Lost is a sheaf of writings sent to → Leo I (a commonitorium, a Libellus, and an ep. familiaris), the content of which is known from Leo's answering letter (ep. 15).

W: ep., PL 54:693-695.
L: H. Chadwick, Priscillian (Oxford, 1976).

E. REICHERT

Tyconius

Little is known about T., who was from North Africa (ca. 330-390). He was originally a Donatist, but he was excommunicated by the Donatists ca. 380 when, in contrast to Donatism, he took as his point of departure the one true Chr. church that was not limited to Africa and so to the Donatists. He continued, however, to feel himself interiorly a Donatist and therefore refused to move into the Cath. camp (see Gennadius, vir. ill. 18).

T.'s most important work is his Liber Regularum (reg.), written ca. 383, in which, insofar as the state of the transmission allows us to understand it, he set down the first Chr. hermeneutics, that is, the first unified systematic theory of scriptural exegesis in an independent work. T. explains that the entire content of sacred scripture can be grasped by a system (ratio) of seven essential points ("rules") which must therefore guide every interpretation (reg. 1.1-17 Burkitt [B.]): (1) De Domino et corpore eius; (2) De Domini corpore bipertito; (3) De promissis et lege; (4) De specie et genere; (5) De temporibus; (6) De recapitulatione; (7) De diabolo et eius corpore. The seven rules can be thematically divided, broadly, into two sections: theol. rules (1-3; 7) and grammatical-rhetorical rules (4-6).

The theol. rules say that (1) when the Bible speaks of Christ, it can be referring either to the eternal Logos or to the earthly church; (2) the body of Christ contains wheat and chaff (acc. to Mt 13:24ff.); therefore bibl. statements on the subject must be distinguished as to whether they relate to the true or the false members of the church; (3) OT and NT both must be interpreted within the field of tensions between law and promise; (7) the devil's body is likewise in two parts: it consists of the false members of the body of Christ and of everyone outside the body of Christ. The theol. rules have a strong eccles. orientation and incorporate both typology and allegorism;

rule 7 also deals with the question of theodicy. One aim is the harmonization of inconsistent passages of the Bible as well as the explanation of difficult passages. The same holds for the grammatical-rhetorical rules: (4) in the Bible a statement made by a particular person can be taken as a generalization (in *reg.* 31.13-15 B, the *species* Solomon stands for the *genus* church); (5) bibl. numbers are often symbolic; (6) many bibl. statements are repeatedly fulfilled, many only in the end time.

T.'s commentary on the Apocalypse (*in apoc.*) is preserved only incomplete; it has to be reconstructed from the Turin and Budapest fragments and from testimonies in → Primasius, → Caesarius, Bede, and Beatus of Liebana; no conclusive results have yet been achieved. The commentary puts the theories of the *reg.* into practice: Using spiritual interpretation, T. emphasizes the christocentric ecclesiology and eschatology of the Apocalypse but rejects a chiliastic interpretation.

Two lost works of T. (only the titles are known) deal with intra-Donatist controversies: *De bello intestino* and *Expositiones diversarum causarum.*

In general, the great and often underappreciated originality of T. needs to be emphasized; he was one of the first to make the exeget. principles of the Antiochene school known in the West. The *in apoc.* and *reg.* were read far into the Middle Ages; this was owing especially to → Augustine's positive reception of the *reg.* in his *doctr. chr.* 3.30-37.

W: *reg.*, F. C. Burkitt (Nendeln, 1967 = Cambridge, 1894) [text]. — D. L. Anderson, Diss. (Louisville [microfilm], 1973) [English trans./comm.]. — W. S. Babcock (Atlanta, 1989) [text/English trans.]. — L. and D. Leoni (Bologna, 1997) [Italian trans.]. — *in apoc.*, F. Lo Bue (Cambridge, 1963) [text].
L: J. S. Alexander, Some Observations on T.'s Definition of the Church, StPatr 18/4 (1990) 115-119. — P. Bright, The Book of Rules of T. (Notre Dame, 1988). — M. Dulaey, La sixième règle de T. et son résumé dans le De Doctrina Christiana: REAug 35 (1989) 83-103. — eadem, T.: DSp 15:1349-1356. — P. Frederiksen, Apocalypse and Redemption in Early Christianity: From John of Patmos to Augustine of Hippo: VigChr 45 (1991) 151-183. — T. Hahn, T.-Studien (Aalen, 1971 = Leipzig, 1900). — C. Kannengiesser, P. Bright, A Conflict of Christian Hermeneutics in Roman Africa (Berkeley, 1989). — C. Mandolfo, Le Regole di Ticonio e le Quaestiones et responsiones di Eucherio di Lione: ASEs 8 (1991) 535-546. — K. Pollmann, La genesi dell'ermeneutica nell'Africa del secolo IV, in: Cristianesimo e Specificità. . . . XXII Incontro di studiosi dell'antichità cristiana (Rome, 1994), 137-145. — eadem, Doctrina Christiana (Fribourg, Switzerland, 1996). — H. D. Rauh, Das Bild des Antichrist im MA: Von T. zum dt. Symbolismus (Münster, 1973). — K. B. Steinhauser, The Apocalypse Commentary of T. (Frankfurt a.M., 1987). — M. A. Tilley, Bible in Christian North Africa. The Donatist World (Minneapolis, 1997).

K. Pollmann

U

Ulfila

U. (Gothic: "little wolf"; Gr.: *Oulphilas/Ourphilas*; Lat.: Ulfila) was a descendant of Cappadocian grandparents or great-grandparents who had been carried off by the Goths; he was born, by 311 at the latest, in the Tervingian area of Gothic territory, to the north of the Lower Danube. Between 332 and 337 he traveled in a Gothic embassy to Constantinople. When he was thirty, Eusebius of Nicomedia and other bishops consecrated him bishop of the Christians in Gothic territory, perhaps ca. 336 or at the synod held in Antioch on occasion of the dedication of the Great Church in 341, and for a mission to the Goths which the emperor planned. In the course of a Gothic persecution of Christians in 348, occasioned probably by anti-Roman sentiment, U. and many refugees crossed the Danube to the mountainous region of Moesia around Nicopolis; thereafter he was active there as bishop of the Goths. Perhaps even after the emigration U. carried on a mission among the Transdanubian Goths and shared the responsibility for the acceptance of homoean Christianity by the Tervingians who, under Fritigern, streamed into the Roman empire in great numbers from 376 on. In 360 U. took part in the Synod of Constantinople. He supported the homoean theology of Constantinople until his death, which overtook him in June 383 during the synod in Constantinople. U. confessed Christ as a God subordinate to the Father, and the Spirit as a nondivine servant subordinated to the Son.

The many *tractatus* and *interpretationes* which U. composed (acc. to his disciple → Auxentius) in Gothic, Latin, and Greek seem to be lost, although the *Skeireins*, fragments of a Gothic translation of a commentary on Jn by → Theodore of Heraclea, may go back to him. Ever since Philostorgius, U. has been regarded as the inventor of Gothic script and the author of the very literal Gothic translation of the Bible from Greek, although he hardly did this work alone. The full extent of this translation (acc. to Philostorgius it lacked only 1-2 Cor) and its precise original wording are disputed, since apart from somewhat more than half of the gospels and two-thirds of the Pauline letters only fragments of Neh are extant, and, with the exception of a few somewhat older sheets, only 6th c. mss. are preserved, which provide a text which was probably revised in Ostrogothic Italy (thus the *Cod. argenteus*, Uppsala). U. established the conditions for the mission (incorrectly described as "Arian") among the Ostrogoths, Gepids, Vandals, and other Germanic groups.

W: *fid.* (confession), transmission of Auxentius in Maximinus *diss.* fol. 308ʳ, 2-35, R. Gryson, CCL 87:166. — *Bible translation:* W. Streitberg, Die gotische Bibel (Heidelberg, ⁶1971) (with Gothic-Greek-German dictionary). — F. Haffner, P. Scardigli, Unum redivivum folium: P. Scardigli, Die Goten (Munich, 1973), 302-380 (supplement). — W. Griepentrog, Synopse der gotischen Evangelientexte (Munich, 1988). — F. de Tollenaere, R. Jones, Word-Indices (Leiden, 1976). — *Skeireins,* W. H. Bennett, The Gothic Commentary on the Gospel of John (New York, 1960) [text/English trans./comm.].
L: G. W. S. Friedrichsen, The Gothic Version of the Gospels (Oxford, 1926). — idem, The Gothic Version of the Epistles (Oxford, 1939). — W. Griepentrog, Zur Text- u. Überlieferungsgeschichte der gotischen Evangelientexte (Innsbruck, 1990). — R. Gryson, SC 267, Introduction. — G. Haendler, W. u. Ambrosius (Berlin, 1961). — idem, W · GK 2, ed. M. Greschat (Stuttgart, 1984), 63-74. — G. Kaufmann, Quellen zur Geschichte Ulfilas: ZDA 27 (1883) 193-261. — A. Lippold, Ulfila: PRE 9A/1:512-531. — B. Metzger, The Early Versions of the NT (Oxford, 1977), 375-393. — K. Schäferdiek, W.: ZKG 90 (1979) 252-292. — idem, Zeit u. Umstände: Hist. 28 (1979) 90-97. — idem, "Skeireins" u. Theodor v. Herakleia: ZDA 110 (1981) 175-193. — idem, Gotisches Christentum: FS E. Stutz (Heidelberg, 1992), 19-50. — K. D. Schmidt, Die Bekehrung der Germanen 1 (Gottingen, 1939). — E. Stutz, Gotische Literaturdenkmäler (Stuttgart, 1966). — eadem, Das NT in gotischer Sprache: K. Aland, Die alten Übersetzungen des NT (Berlin, 1972), 375-402. — E. A. Thompson, The Visigoths in the Time of Ulfila (Oxford, 1966). — H. Wolfram, Geschichte der Goten (Munich, ³1990), 84-94.

R. KANY

Uranius

U. was an otherwise unknown disciple of Paulinus of Nola. In 431 he wrote a letter on the death of his teacher, *Epistula de obitu Paulini* (*ep.*), to a certain Pacatus, who wanted to compose a *Vita Paulini* in verse.

W: PL 53:859-866.
L: P. M. Duval, La Gaule (Paris, 1971), 700f. — A. Pastorino, De obitu: Aug. 24 (1984) 115-141.

M. SKEB, OSB

$\mathcal{V}$

Valens of Mursa

V., together with his constant companion Ursacius (U.) of Singidunum, appears for the first time in 335 as an opponent of Athanasius at the Synod of Tarsus. He maintained his position until 347. Then, as the situation in the West became increasingly difficult and V. and U. were increasingly isolated, they changed their attitude and wrote, on the one hand, a letter to Julius of Rome, in which they recanted their previous behavior and anathematized Arius and his supporters, and, on the other, a letter to Athanasius in which they declared their communion with him. From 351 on, however, V. and U., who had close links with Emperor Constantius, returned to their previous policy and were the most important representatives of the homoeans in the West. They played a leading role at the Council of Sirmium in 357. In 359 both were initially excommunicated at the Council of Rimini but later managed to have their views prevail against the anti-Arian minority. After the death of Constantius V. and U. were restrained by the anti-Arian reaction but were able to keep their sees. In 366 they got into a dispute with → Germinius of Sirmium, in the course of which V. and U., with two others, addressed a letter of Dec. 18, 366, to Germinius, probably in response to his profession of faith, which took the formula of Rimini as its basis. U. died after 371. V. died probably between 371 and 378/380. In addition to the three letters mentioned, four others are attributed to V. and U.

W: A. Feder, CSEL 65: *ep. ad Iulium*, 143f. [Latin/Greek text]. — *ep. ad Athanasium*, 145 [Latin/Greek text]. — *ep. ad Germinium*, 159f.
L: Die Geschichte des Christentums 2 (Freiburg i.Br., 1996), 335, 368-389, 418. — P. Glorieux, Hilaire et Libère: MSR 1 (1944) 7-84, here 29f. — R. P. C. Hanson, The Search for the Christian Doctrine (Edinburgh, 1988), passim. — C. Markschies, Ambrosius v. Milan (Tübingen, 1995), 46-50. — M. Meslin, Les Ariens d'occident (Paris, 1967), 71-84. — M. Simonetti, La crisi ariana (Rome, 1975).

B. WINDAU

Valentinians, Anonymous

A whole series of certainly "Valentinian" texts and doxographical reports on Valentinians have been handed down anonymously and may be assigned only with caution to particular individuals: (1) Irenaeus, *haer.* 1.1.1–8.1 (school of Ptolemy, not Ptolemy himself); 2) Irenaeus, *haer.* 1.11.1 (a text combining various elements; not Valentinus); (3) Irenaeus, *haer.* 1.11.3: "another, evidently one of their teachers," which may allow an attribution to Heracleon; (4) Tertullian, *carn.* 15.3: *quidam ex Valentini fatiuncula* (possible attribution to Alexander); (5) the so-called Valentinian doctrinal letter in Epiphanius, *haer.* 31.5.2–6.10; (6) Clement Alex., *exc. Thdt.*, contains extracts from at least two other Valentinian texts; (7) Origen, *ep.* (the unknown "heretic" could have been → Candidus, the Valentinian). Also belonging, perhaps, to this body of material is (8) Hippolytus, *haer.* 6.37.8 (a Valentinian [?] commentary on Valentinus, frag. 8).

L: O. Dibelius, Studien zur Geschichte der Valentinianer 2: ZNW 9 (1908) 329-340. — A. v. Harnack, Zur Quellenkritik (Leipzig, 1873), 62f. — A. Hilgenfeld, Die Ketzergeschichte des Urchristentums (Darmstadt, 1963 = Leipzig, 1884), 312-316, 461-522. — C. Markschies, Valentinian Gnosticism: 50th Anniversary of the Discovery of the Nag-Hammadi-Texts, ed. A. M. McGuire (New York, 1996). — idem, Valentinus Gnosticus?: WUNT 65 (1992). — C. Scholten, Martyrium u. Sophiamythos im Gnostizismus: JAC. E 14 (1987). — M. Tardieu, Codex de Berlin: Sources Gnostiques et Manichéennes 1 (Paris, 1984).

C. MARKSCHIES

Valentinus

It is certain that V., a theologian of great literary and rhetorical gifts, was teaching in Rome in the mid-2nd c. without any opposition (!). He came to the capital perhaps before 140 (or possibly as early as 130) and was active there for at least fifteen years (Irenaeus, *haer.* 3.4.3). Tertullian claims that V. departed from "the authentic rule of faith" when, contrary to his expectations, he was not elected to an eccles. office (*adv. Val.* 4.1f.). Finally, Epiphanius mentions an Egypt. place of birth and an education in Alexandria (*haer.* 31.2.3). He locates V.'s apostasy from the true faith in Cyprus, where V. happened to be at some time before 161 (31.7.2). These bits of information (from Egypt. and Cypriote local traditions?) may be trustworthy.

V. wrote letters to private individuals (frags. 1, 2, 3), published sermons (frags. 4, 6), and composed hymns (frag. 8; Tertullian, *carn.* 17.1; Origen, *enarr. in Job* 21.12). Neither the *Gospel of Truth* (NHC 1, 3; 12, 2) nor the *Letter to Diognetus* nor the letter to Rheginos (*Treatise on the Resurrection*, NHC 1, 4) is from V.

Just as in the case of the tradition regarding (e.g.) → Basilides, so too, in expounding the teaching of V., one must distinguish between the authentic fragments and the later heresiological reports on V. (espec. Irenaeus, *haer.* 1.11.1). Reports on the Valentinians should obviously not be used at all, not even their least common denominators. Tertullian (*adv. Val.* 4.2) already speaks of distinctions between V. and his followers.

Acc. to the fragments, V. taught a defective creation of human beings by angels, with the supreme God making good the defects (Clement Alex., *str.* 2.36.2-4; 4.89.6–90.1). Among the effects produced by the supreme God is the well-ordered cosmos (Hippolytus, *haer.* 6.37.7). V. taught an encratite but not a docetist christology (*str.* 3.59.3). His broad conception of revelation allowed him to accept even nonbibl. commonplaces (*str.* 6.52.4).

The differences between this picture of V. and that of "Valentinian gnosticism" are striking: evidently, an extensive revision of the teaching of V. (from whom his disciple → Ptolemy did not greatly differ acc. to the evidence of the *ep. ad Floram* [Epiphanius, *haer.* 33.3-8]) by the Roman gnostics of the "School of Ptolemy," who (acc. to Iren., *haer.* 1, praef. 2) called themselves "disciples of V." (their teaching: Iren., *haer.* 1.1-8). A reason for this shift may have been the disagreement of the "School of Ptolemy" with the teaching of Marcion, but this is simply a hypothesis that would need further investigation.

W: W. Völker, Quellen zur Geschichte der chr. Gnosis: SQS NS 5 (1932) 57-60. — C. Markschies, Valentinus Gnosticus?: WUNT 65 (1992) 11-290 [text/German trans./comm.].
L: W. Foerster, Von V. zu Herakleon: BZNW 7 (1928). — A. Hilgenfeld, Der Gnostiker V. u. seine Schriften: ZWTh 23 (1880) 280 300. — J. Holzhausen, Der Mythos vom Menschen im hellenistischen Ägypten· Theoph. 33 (1994) 80-164 (additionally, A. Böhlig, C. Markschies, Gnosis u. Manichäismus: BZNW 72 [1994] 90-96). — B. Layton (ed.), The Rediscovery of Gnosticism 1 (Leiden, 1980). — G. Lüdemann, Zur Geschichte des ältesten Christentums in Rom: ZNW 70 (1979) 86-114. — A. M. McGuire, V. and the "Gnostike Hairesis," Diss. (Yale, 1983). — A. Orbe, Estudios Valentinianos 1-5: AnGr 99; 100; 65; 133; 158; 83 (Rome, 1955-1966). — E. Preuschen, V. Gnostiker: RE 20, 395-417. — G. Quispel, The Original Doctrine of V.: VigChr 1 (1947) 43-73. — F.-M. M. Sagnard, La Gnose Valentinienne et le témoignage de Saint Irénée (Paris, 1947). — H. Strutwolf, Gnosis als System (Göttingen, 1993).

C. MARKSCHIES

Valentinus, an Apollinarist

Apart from the *Capita apologiae* (*apol.*), which were preserved by → Leontius Byz., nothing is known by or about V. In his polemic V. seeks to rebut the accusation that he and his Apollinarist supporters claim the body (of Christ) to be identical in nature with

God. To this end he first strings together some passages from Apollinaris and then attacks the teaching of Timothy of Berytus and his followers, as well as their common teacher, Polemon. The fact that Timothy and Polemon have meanwhile become adversaries is unimportant to V.: in his opinion both have abandoned the position of Apollinaris. He himself regards the body of the incarnate Word as a shell and identical in nature with that of other human beings.

W: *apol.*, H. Lietzmann, Apollinaris u. seine Schule (Hildesheim, 1970 = Tübingen, ¹1904), 287-291 [text].
L: G. Voisin, L'apollinarisme (Leuven/Louvain, 1901), 112f.

G. FEIGE

Valerian of Calahorra

V. was bishop of Calahorra at the beginning of the 5th c. and composed a Cath. profession of faith (*Fides*).

W: PLS 1:1045.
L: J. Madoz, V., escritor del siglo v: HispSac 3 (1950) 131-137.

E. REICHERT

Valerian of Cimiez

V. was bishop of Cimiez 439-460. Occasional references to him in synodal acts between 439 and 459 and in letters of Leo do not reveal anything definite about his life and works. It is not possible to decide whether he is the same V. as the relative to whom → Eucherius of Lyons dedicated his letter *De contemptu mundi* and whether before taking office he was a monk of Lérins. The latter is suggested by his love of the monastic virtues, which can be seen in his writings, among which is an ascetical *Epistula ad monachos* (*ep.*), which, however, may also be from a monk named V. Twenty homilies of V. have come down in which he speaks, in the language of a trained rhetorician, about the goal and way of Chr. life. The homilies also contain valuable data on the contemporary history of Gaul. In all his writings there are clear traces of the teaching on grace that characterized southern Gaul.

W: PL 52:691-756.
L: R. W. Mathisen, Petronius, Hilarius and V.: Hist. 30 (1981) 106-112. — R. Nürnberg, Askese als sozialer Impuls (Bologna, 1988). — C. Tibiletti, V. e la teologia: Aug. 22 (1982) 513-532. — J. P. Weiss, Les Églises de Nice et de Cimiez: AFLN 2 (1967) 35-47. — idem, V. et Valère de Nice: SE 21 (1972/73) 109-146. — ders, La personnalité de V.: AFLN 11 (1979) 141-162. — idem, Dominus et Servus chez V.: ibid. 35 (1979) 298-301.

C. KASPER

Valerius of Bierzo

V. (d. 695), abbot of the monastery of Bierzo in northwestern Spain, excerpted a series of ascetical and hagiog. works. In addition, he composed almost twenty works of his own, most of them shorter ascetical and edifying treatises and poems, whose long lines are reminiscent of rhythmical prose; these works give an insight into the religious situation in monastic communities of the northwestern Iberian peninsula toward the end of the 7th c. The *Epistula de beatissimae Aetheriae (s. Egeriae) laude* is important for the history of Chr. literature; it hands on the names of→ Egeria, who had composed a diary of her travels to the holy places of Palestine.

There is disagreement as to whether V. also composed *De novae vitae institutione* and *De perfectis monachis* and compiled excerpts from → Sulpicius Severus and the → *Vitae Patrum*.

The *Vita S. Frontoni* and *Vita S. Fructuosi* are certainly not from V.

W: *tractatus*, R. Fernández Pousa (Madrid, 1942). — M. C. Díaz y Díaz, Anecdota Wisigothica 1 (Salamanca, 1958). — *ep. de beatissimae Aetheriae (s. Egeriae) laude*, M. C. Díaz y Díaz, SC 296:321-348.
L: C. M. Aherne, V., an Ascetic of the late Visigothic Period (Washington, 1949).

E. REICHERT

Venantius Fortunatus

I. **Life:** V. Honorius Clementianus Fortunatus, b. between 530 and 540 in Valdobbiadene near Treviso, died soon after 600 in Poitiers. After studying grammar and rhetoric in Ravenna, he went to Gaul in 565, where in 566, at the Austrasian court in Metz, he wrote the epithalamium for the marriage of King Sigibert and the Visigothic Princess Brunhilde (*carm.* 6.1). Speculations that the journey was for political reasons are not supported by any source. V. himself gives as the reason a pilgrimage to the tomb of St. Martin in Tours (*Mart.* 1.44). Perhaps he calculated that the Merovingian realm would also offer better opportunities for a career as a poet. In any case, V. won there the friendship of many secular and eccles. dignitaries, espec. → Gregory of Tours and Radegunde, first wife of deceased King Clothar and foundress of the convent of the Holy Cross in Poitiers. She and the first abbess, Agnes, whom she installed, induced V. to settle in Poitiers in 567 or 568 in order to help the monastery administratively and in diplomatic matters. Gregory ordained him a priest, probably ca. 576, and consecrated him bishop of Poitiers ca. 600.

II. **Works:** V. wrote over 250 poems, the greater part of which have come down in a corpus of eleven books; the compilation of these was largely V.'s own work (*carm.*). The majority are homages to bishops or secular potentates, usually in the form of friendly letters or addresses for their feasts; there are also official panegyrics for the royal Merovingian household (e.g., *carm.* 6.1a; 9.1). The only completely homogeneous book is the fourth, which contains only epitaphs. There is disagreement about the extent to which this is real or fictitious epigraphy (e.g., funeral orations). The same is true of the many poems on churches and estates, of which only a few could have been real *tituli* of buildings. Among these occasional poems the following works with religious content stand out clearly: the Easter poem (*carm.* 3.9), addressed to Felix of Nantes, in which V. describes the resurrection as an event that transforms the whole of nature, and the two hymns on the cross, *Pange lingua gloriosi* (2.2) and *Vexilla regis prodeunt* (2.6), which were written on occasion of the coming of the relics of the cross to Poitiers (569) and were taken into the Roman breviary. V. also devoted three figural poems, so-called *Carmina cancellata*, to the mystery of the cross; the first of these contains a remarkable outline of the history of salvation (2.4; 2.5; 5.6).

To the collection of poems belong nine prose letters with pretentious diction, an explanation of the Our Father, and another (based on → Rufinus of Aquileia) of the creed (*expos. orat./symb.*).

Handed down apart from the corpus there are a praise of Mary (*laud. mar.*); a group of thirty-two poems (*carm. app.*) that begins with the well-known elegy *De excidio Thuringiae*; and two letters written in Radegunde's name. The majority of the poems are notes to Radegunde and Agnes (10-31).

V.'s longest poem is his epic in four books, *De vita Martini* (*Mart.*), written in 574/575. It transposes the prose of → Sulpicius Severus into 2,243 hexameters in which V. tries to outdo his predecessor → Paulinus of Périgueux. V. also composed seven lives of saints in prose (*vita Radeg.*, etc.), those of Sts. Radegunde, Severinus, Albinus, Paternus, Marcellus, Germanus of Paris, and Hilary of Poitiers. To this last is also devoted the work *De virtutibus Hilarii episcopi Pictaviensis* (*virt. Hil.*).

Some other lives of saints and poems have been foisted on V., others wrongly attributed to him, among them the Christmas hymn *Agnoscat omne saeculum*, two Marian poems (*Ave stella maris* and, likewise accepted into the breviary, *Quem terra, pontus, aethera*), as well as another *carmen figuratum* in the form of a cross (Ps.-V., *vita Med.*, etc.; *carm. app.* 2-11). The epitaphs for Bishops Nicetius of Lyons (CE 1387) and Marius of Avenches (Inscr. christ. LaBlant, no. 441) are in all likelihood not from V.

V. has been described as the last Lat. poet of antiquity and the first of the Middle Ages. Pointers to the Middle Ages are, e.g., the lack of mythological themes in the secular poetry (the appearance of Venus and Cupido in the epithalamium, *carm.* 6, is called for by the genre) and the mysticism and veneration of Mary in the sacred poetry. On the other hand, despite some symptoms of decline, the language and verse forms (usually the elegiac distich) are those of old Roman poetry. V. exerted a strong influence on the poets of the Middle Ages, espec. those of the Carolingian period.

W: *carm., expos. orat., expos. symb., laud. Mar., Mart.,* F. Leo (Berlin, 1881) [text]. — *carm.,* M. Reydellet, 1 (1-4), 2 (5-8) (Paris, 1994/1998) [text/French trans./comm.]. — *carm.,* M. C. Nisard (Paris, 1887) [French trans.]. — B. J. Rogers, Rutgers Univ. (New Brunswick, N.J., 1969) [English trans./comm. (microfilm)]. — *carm.* 2.1, 2.2, 2.6, 3.9 (*Ps. Ven. Fort.*) *carm. app.* 4, 7, 8, A. S. Walpole, Early Latin Hymns (Cambridge, 1922 = Hildesheim, 1966), 164-200 [text/comm.]. — *carm.* 3.9, 5.3, 8.7, 8.10, 9.1, *carm. app.* 31, J. W. George, V. (Oxford, 1992), 188-207 [text/English trans.]. — *carm.* 3.13, 4.16 et al., eadem, V.: Personal and Political Poems (Liverpool, 1995) [English trans./comm.]. — *carm.* 4.26, P. Santorelli (Naples, 1994) [text/Italian trans./comm.]. — *carm.* 6.5, K. Steinmann (Zurich, 1975) [text/German trans./comm.]. — *vitae,* B. Krusch (Berlin, 1885) [text]. — *vitae Sev.,* B. Krusch, W. Levison (Berlin, 1919), 219-224, 372-418. — *Mart.,* S. Quesnel (Paris, 1996) [text/French trans.]. — S. Tamburri (Naples, 1991) [Italian trans./comm.].
L: H. Ammerbauer, Studien Zur Vita Martini (Vienna, 1966). — S. Blomgren, Studia Fortunatiana 1-2 (Uppsala, 1933/34). — idem, De duobus epitaphiis episcoporum: Er. 39 (1941) 82-99. — idem, V. cum elogiis collocatus: Er. 71 (1973) 95-111. — B. Brennan, Bishop and Community in the Poetry of V. (Melbourne, 1983). — idem, The Career of V.: Tr. 41 (1985) 49-78. — M. I. Campanale, Il "de virginitate" di V. (carm. 8, 3), un epitalamio mistico: InvLuc 2 (1980) 75-128. — A. H. Chase, The Metrical Lives of S. Martin: HSCP 43 (1932) 51-76. — E. Clerici, Note sulla lingua di V.: RIL L 104 (1970) 219-251. — R. Collins, Form, Sprache u. Publikum der Prosabiographien des V.: ZKG 92 (1981) 26-38. — F. Dagianti, Studio sintattico delle "opera poetica" di V. (Veroli, 1921). — H. Elss, Untersuchung über Stil u. Sprache des V. (Heidelberg, 1907). — U. Ernst, Carmen figuratum (Cologne, 1991), 149-157. — C. H. Kneepkens, On Hymn Pange lingua: FS G. J. M. Bartelink (Steenbrugge, 1989), 193-205. — R. Koebner, V. (Leipzig, 1915). — Y. Labande-Mailfert, Les débuts de Sainte-Croix: MSAO ser. 4, 19 (1986) 21-116. — K. Langosch, Profile des lat. MA (Darmstadt, 1965), 49-79. — F. Leo, Der Gelegenheitsdichter V.: Mittellat. Dichtung, ed. K. Langosch (Darmstadt, 1969), 57-90. — A. Meneghetti, La latinità di V.: Did 5 (1916) 195-298; 6 (1917) 1-166. — W. Meyer, Der Gelegenheitsdichter V. (Berlin, 1901). — C. M. Nisard, Le

poète V. (Paris, 1890). — L. Pietri, V. et ses commanditaires: SAM 39 (1992) 729-758. — S. Quesnel, La Vita Martini: FS Marache (Rennes, 1992), 393-407. — J. Šašel, Il viaggio di V.: AnAl 19 (1981) 359-375. — J. Szövérffy, V. and the Earliest Hymns to the Holy Cross: ClF 20 (1966) 107-122. — D. Tardi, V. (Paris, 1927). — B. Termite, T. Ragusa (ed.), V. tra Italia e Francia, Atti del convegno Valdobbiadene/Treviso 17. — 19. 5. 1990 (Treviso, 1993).

N. DELHEY

Verba seniorum

This is the Lat. title of the *Rhemata* or → *Apophthegmata Patrum*. In a narrower sense it applies to the thematically organized collection of sayings of the desert fathers, which we have in four books of the *Vitae Patrum* (3, erroneously attributed to Rufinus; 5-6, translation by Pelagius and John; 7, translation by → Paschasius of Dumio).

L: C. M. Batlle, Die Adhortationes Sanctorum Patrum (Verba Seniorum) im MA (Münster, 1972). — A. Solignac, Verba Seniorum: DSp 16:383-392.

J. PAULI, OSB

Verecundus of Junca

V. was active in the first half of the 6th c. as bishop of Junca in the North African Byzacena province and played an important part in the Three-Chapters controversy. As an opponent of the imperial religious policy, he was summoned to Constantinople in 551 but was able to flee to Chalcedon, where he died in 552. He composed *Commentarii super cantica ecclesiastica* (*in cant.*) in which he gave an allegorical interpretation of nine OT canticles. His *Carmen de satisfactione paenitentiae* (*satisfact.*) consists of 212 dactylic hexameters and describes the interior anguish of a contrite soul. He is possibly the author also of a collection of excerpts from the conciliar decrees of Chalcedon.

W: PLS 4:39-234. — R. Demeulenaere, CCL 93. — *in cant.,* J. B. Pitra, Spicilegium Solesmense (Paris, 1858). — *satisfact.,* M. G. Bianco, Carmen de paenitentia (Naples, 1984) [Latin text].
L: M. G. Bianco, V. un poeta ancora trascurato: Disiecti membra poetae, ed. V. Tandoi (Foggia, 1984), 216-231. — L. Brou, Études sur les Collectes du Psautier: SE 6 (1954) 73-95. — E. Kullendorff, Textkritische Beiträge zu V. (Lund, 1943). — C. Magazzù, Tecnica esegetica nei Commentarii super cantica di V. (Messina, 1983). — O. Rousseau, La plus ancienne liste de cantiques: RSR 35 (1948) 120-129. — H. Schneider, Die altlat. bibl. Cantica (Beuron, 1938).

P. BRUNS

Vetus Latina

Vetus latina, or "old Latin (version)," is the collective name given to the translations (therefore sometimes also *Veteres Latinae*) of the Bible that were in circulation in fragmentary form between 175 and 400 and used chiefly in the liturgy. Because Christians of the west (North Africa, Italy, Spain, Gaul) knew Greek only incompletely or not at all, more or less lengthy sections of the LXX and the Gr. NT were translated into Lat. for use in the liturgy and for missionary purposes. Evidence of these translations is found as early as Tertullian, although he also translated texts himself (*adv. Marc.* 2.9.1f.), and then espec. in Cyprian of Carthage, who ca. 240 cites almost a ninth of the Gr. NT. There can be no question of a single form of the *Vetus latina*, or even of an "African" form; there is no complete ms. of the old Lat. text. Acc. to the witness of Jerome, there were in the 4th c. almost as many different forms of Lat. Bibles as there were mss. known at the time.

The Latin of the *Vetus latina* is a "language in motion," a mixture of popular elements and Chr. everyday language that also adopted special forms from Hebrew and Greek.

A special form of the *Vetus latina* is a translation used espec. in a section of Italy and described in a (disputed) passage of Augustine (*doctr. chr.* 2.15) as *interpretatio (Itala)*. It is to be dated later than the *Vetus latina;* just which translation is being referred to is not explained. At one time the term *Itala* was also used to describe the many Lat. translations of the Bible that were in circulation; since the term was not suitable for that purpose, it was later replaced by *Vetus latina* or *Praevulgata*.

W: Vetus Latina. Die Reste der altlat. Bibel (Freiburg i.Br., 1951ff.).
L: P. M. Bogaert, La Bible latine des origines au moyen âge: RTL 19 (1988) 137-159. — O. Eissfeldt, Einleitung in das AT (Tübingen, ²1956), 870f. — HLL 4:352-367. — A. Jülicher (ed.), Itala 1: Mt (Berlin, 1938); 2: Mk (Berlin, 1940); 3: Lk (Berlin, 1954). — W. Michaelis, Einleitung in das NT (Bern, ³1961) (with supplementary booklet). — (A. Wikenhauser), J. Schmid, Einleitung in das NT (Freiburg i.Br., ⁶1973), 105-124. — R. Smend, Bibel: BHH 1:242f. — F. Stummer, Einführung in die lat. Bibel (Paderborn, 1928). — H. J. Vogels, Handbuch der Textkritik des NT (Bonn, ²1955), 78-110, 152-220.

A. SAND

Victor

V. appears between 523 and 533 as the author (not further placeable) of a letter to → Fulgentius of Ruspe, in which he asks the latter to send him his work against Fastidiosus the Arian (*c. Fastif.*). Fulgentius addresses his answer to his *carissime fili Victor*.

W: Fulgentii episcopi Ruspensis opera, J. Fraipont, CCL 91:277-280.
L: PAC 1183.

W. GEERLINGS

Victor of Antioch

V., a presbyter, is named in seventeen mss. as author of a commentary on Mark (*Mc.*) (other mss. name → Origen or → Cyril Alex.). The work is in fact a catena (with an introduction but without lemmas) that is drawn chiefly from the homilies on Matthew of → John Chrys. (and from, among others, Origen, *comm. in Mt.*; Cyril Alex., *Lc.*; → Titus of Bostra, *fr. Lc.*). Its composition is to be dated to the 6th c. Since there were only a few exeget. works on Mk, this one was often used and has therefore come down in many mss.

V. was a compiler to whom hardly any ideas of his own can be ascribed. He may be the same as the presbyter Victor who is cited in various catenas. There are 159 references to this V. in the catena on Jer, and some in those on Deut, Judg, Kgs, Lam, Dan, Prov, Pss, and Lk. Nothing is known about his person.

W: *Mc.*, J. A. Cramer, CGPNT 1 (Hildesheim, 1967 = Oxford, 1840), 259-447 [text]. — *Deut., Jud., Kgs.*, R. Devreesse, Les commentateurs de l'Octateuque (Rome, 1959), 181 [text]. — *Jer., Lam.*, M. Faulhaber, Die Propheten-Catenen (Freiburg i.Br., 1899), 107-110, 113 [text]. — *Dan., Lk.*, A. Mai, SVNC 1 (Rome, 1825), 2:177; 3:35; op. cit. 9 (Rome, 1837), 633-693 passim [text].
L: G. Bardy, V.: DThC 15/2:2872-2874. — J. Reuß, Mt-, Mk- u. Joh-Katenen (Münster, 1941), 136-141. — H. Smith, The Sources of V. s Commentary on Mark: JThS 19 (1917/18) 350-370.

T. FUHRER

Victor of Aquitania

V. composed the *Cursus paschalis* (*pasch.*), an Easter table extending from the year 28 to 559, with 560 being a signal to begin another 532-year cycle. The occasion for the work was a disagreement between Rome and Alexandria on the date of Easter; the one who commissioned the work was Hilary, future bishop of Rome. The letter of dedication to Leo the Great explains the difficulty in calculating the date of Easter. The table contains a numbering of the annual Easters from 28 on, a list of consuls down to the year of composition, 457 (later extended), the weekday and phase of the moon on each Jan. 1. The mathematical treatise *Calculus* (*calc.*) attributed to Venerable Bede is likewise from V.; V.'s authorship of the *Prologus paschae* (*praef. pasch.*) can at most be suspected (PLS 3:380).

W: *pasch.*, T. Mommsen, Chronica Minora 1 (Berlin, 1892), 677-735 [text]. — *pasch.*, B. Krusch, Studien zur chr.-mal. Chronologie (Berlin, 1938), 16-52 = PLS 3:381-426 [text]. — *calc.*, PL 90:677-680. — G. Friedlein (Rome, 1872). — *praef. pasch.*, PLS 3:427-441 [text].
L: T. Mommsen, op. cit., 667-676. — E. Schwartz, Chr. u. jüd. Ostertafeln (Berlin, 1905), 73-81.

K. FITSCHEN

Victor of Capua

The period of office and date of death of V., bishop of Capua (541-554), are attested by the preserved inscription from his tomb (CIL 10:4503). He is known to have commissioned and corrected a copy of the Lat. NT text (the so-called *Cod. Fuldensis* of 546/547) that contains the *Diatessaron* of → Tatian transposed into the text of the Vulgate (PL 68:255-358). In a preface to the edition (*harm. evang. praef.*) V. tells of the discovery and identification of Tatian's harmony of the gospels (on the basis of Eusebius, *h.e.* 4.29.6). The text also contains the oldest version of the apocryphal (Lat.) letter of → Paul to the Laodiceans. V.'s edition was the model for the Old High German and Ital. translations of the *Diatessaron* and thus had a continuing strong influence. Venerable Bede cites a work *De pascha* on the calculations of the date of Easter (*temp. rat.* 51). In addition, there are seventeen other fragments as well as traces of a work on the symbolic meaning of the measurements of the ark of Noah (*Reticulus seu de arca Noe*), of a work *Capitula de resurrectione domini*, as well as citations from the Gr. fathers on exegetical matters, which medieval authors put together from V.'s writings (*Scholia veterum patrum*). But the attribution of these fragments (*fr. Spicil. Solesm.*) to V. or to the above-named writings is to some extent questionable.

W: *harm. evang. praef.*, PL 68:251-256. — *Cod. Fuldensis* (= Bonifatianus 1), E. Ranke (Marburg, 1868), 1-3. — *fr. Spicil. Solesm.*, J. B. Pitra, SpicSol 1 (Paris, 1852), LIV, LIX, LXII, LXIV, 265-289, 296-301 [text]. — J. B. Pitra, ASSSP 5/1 (Paris, 1888), 163-165.
L: G. Bardy, V.: DThC 15/2:2874-2876. — V. Bolgiani, V. e il "Diatessaron" (Turin, 1962). — B. Fischer, Bibelausgaben des frühen MAs: La Bibbia nell'alto medioevo (Spoleto, 1963), 545-557. — idem, Lat. Bibelhss. im frühen MA (Freiburg i.Br., 1985), 57-66. — idem, Beiträge zur Geschichte der lat. Bibeltexte (Freiburg i.Br., 1986), 217-219.

T. FUHRER

Victor of Cartenna

V. (429-477), Cath. bishop of Cartenna in the province of Mauretania Caesariensis, is named by Gennadius (*vir. ill.* 78) as author of a now-lost work *Contra Arianos*, which was dedicated to the Vandal King Geiseric. Also attributed to him are the treatises *De paenitentia* (Ps.-Ambrose) and *De consolatione in adversis* (Ps.-Basil). A collection of *Sermones* has also been lost.

W: Ps.-Ambrose, *De paenitentia*, PL 17:971-1004. — Ps.-Basil, *De consolatione*, PG 31:1687-1704.
L: F. Görres, Der echte u. der falsche V.: ZWTh 49 (1906) 484-494. — PAC 1175. — M. Schanz, C. Hosius, G. Krüger, Geschichte der röm. Lit. 4/2 (Munich, 1959), 572.

W. GEERLINGS

Victor I of Rome

Roman Bishop V. (ca. 189-198), who together with a Roman synod stood up for the Lord's practice, excommunicated the Quartodecimans (of Asia Minor or Rome) in the course of a controversy over the date of Easter (Eusebius, *h.e.* 5.23f.). Writings of V. in this connection have not been preserved. Also lost are the presumed circular letter on the excommunication of → Theodore Byz. (Eus., *h.e.* 5.28; 6.9) and a list of exiled Christians (Hippolytus, *haer.* 9.12.10). V. may have rescinded letters of peace given to the Montanists (see Tertullian, *adv. Prax.* 1.5). Further early attributions (see Jerome, *vir. ill.* 34) are not trustworthy. In the Middle Ages some letters and a decree were foisted on V.

L: C. Burini, Epistolari cristiani 1 (Rome, 1990), 119f. — H. v. Campenhausen, Ostertermin o. Osterfasten: idem, Urchr. u. Altkirchliches (Tübingen, 1979), 300-330. — E. dal Covolo, Letteratura cristiana: RSLR 27 (1991) 213-221. — J. A. Fischer A. Lumpe, Synoden v. d. Anfängen bis z. Vorabend d. Nicaenums (Paderborn, 1997), 60-87. — P. Lampe, Die stadtröm. Christen (Tübingen, ²1989), 323-341. — P. Nautin, Lettres et écrivains (Paris, 1961), 65-91.

R. HANIG

Victor of Tunnuna

V. was an African bishop of a city that cannot be further identified (Isidore, *vir. ill.* 49f.; *chron.* 1). Because of his opposition to the condemnation of the Three Chapters, he was banished to Egypt by Justinian (555). In 564/565, even though he still refused to agree with the condemnation, he was allowed to return to a monastery in Constantinople, where he died in 566.

V. is author of a universal chronicle (*chron.*), of which only the second part (years 444-566) is preserved. The attribution to V. of the Ps.-Ambrosian treatise *De paenitentia* is no longer maintained; the work is attributed rather to → Victor of Cartenna.

W: *chron.*, T. Mommsen, MGH. AA 11:163-206. — PL 68:941-962. — A. Placanica, Per verba 4 (Florence, 1997) [text/Italian trans.].
L: M. Schanz, C. Hosius, G. Krüger, Geschichte der röm. Literatur 4/2 (Munich, 1971), 112f.

W. GEERLINGS

Victor of Vita

V. was bishop of a city that cannot now be precisely identified in the Byzacena province (480/481-484). There is great disagreement about the person of V. since the ms. tradition of his work gives no information. In the → *Notitia provinciarum* he is listed as a participant in the Council of Carthage 418. He is author of the *Historia persecutionis Africanae provinciae temporum Geiserici et Hunerici regis Vandalorum* (*Hist.*), in which he describes the oppression of Catholics under Vandal rule. As a member of the Carthaginian clergy, he accompanied the exiles to Sardinia in 482/483, even though he himself had not been condemned. He kept in close contact with the bishop of Carthage, at whose urging the *Hist.* was probably written. The work is dedicated to a Diadochus (of Photice?). Book 1 deals with the reign of Geiseric from its beginnings (429) until his death (477). Book 2 has to do with the rule of Huneric (477) and discusses the Council of Carthage in 484. It also contains the *Liber fidei catholicae*, in which four Cath. bishops explain Cath. teaching to the Arians. Book 3 tells of events from February 484 to the fall of that year, when Huneric died. The work closes with a sharp attack on the barbarians and a prayer for God's help.

The *hist.* was written in Carthage during the persecution after Huneric's death and is therefore to be dated to 488 or 489. It has high value as a source, since it contains various documents, including among others the three edicts of Huneric against the Catholics (2.3f.; 2.39; 3.3-14). The author largely avoids polemics and tries to give an objective presentation, although he does not hide his own views.

The prologue and the story of the suffering of seven monks martyred under Huneric may not be V.'s work, since their somewhat bombastic language is in striking contrast to the markedly objective style of the rest of the work.

W: M. Petschenig, CSEL 7. — C. Halm, MGH. AA 3/1. — M. Zink, Bischof V.s Geschichte der Glaubensverfolgung im Lande Afrika (Bamberg, 1883) [German trans.]. — S. Costanza (Rome, 1981) [Italian trans.].
L: S. Costanza, V. e la Hist.: VetChr 17 (1980) 229-268. — C. Courtois, V. (Algier, 1954). — idem, Les Vandales et l'Afrique (Algier, 1955 = Aalen, 1964). — PAC 1175f. — W. E. Fahey, History, Community, and Suffering in V.: FS F. W. Schlatter (New York, 1999), 225-241. — A. Pastorino, Osservazioni sulla Hist.: La storiografia nella tarda antichità = Atti Convegno di Erie (Messina, 1980), 45-112. — R. Pitkäranta, Studien zum Latein des V. (Helsinki, 1978).

W. GEERLINGS

Victorinus of Pettau

V. (V. Poetovionensis) was the first Lat. exegete. He was b. ca. 230, was bishop of Poetovio/Pettau (in the province of Upper Pannonia; today Ptuj in Slovenia), and died, probably in 304, as a martyr in the Diocletian persecution. The obviously accurate report that he had a better command of Greek than of Latin does not tell against an origin in Pannonia, which was influenced by Gr. culture.

V. is author of the earliest Chr. explanations of the Bible in Latin. Not preserved, but for the most part also mentioned by others, are the commentaries on Gen, Ex, Lev, Isa, Ezek, Hab, Qoh, and Song which Jerome lists as V.'s in *vir. ill.* 74, as well as the commentary on Mt attested by Jerome (*prol. hom. Orig. in Luc.* [GCS 49/2]; *in Matth. Prol.*) and Cassiodorus (*inst. div.* 1.7.1).

Preserved are:

1. *Commentarius in apocalypsin* (*in apoc.*), composed soon after the Valerian persecution, therefore ca. 260. The original version was published 1895/1916; known earlier and transmitted in older mss. is the revision (in language and content) of the original that Jerome undertook ca. 400 (additions from → Tyconius and replacement of the chiliastic with a spiritualizing interpretation of the thousand-year reign [Rev 20]). Two later versions of Jerome's recension differ chiefly in the text of Rev that is used.
2. *De fabrica mundi* (*fabr. mund.*), a typological interpretation, based on number symbolism, of the week of creation, with a chiliadic interpretation of the days of creation and a chiliastic interpretation of the sabbath that ended creation.
3. *Adversum omnes haereses* (*haer.*). This work, listed by Jerome (*vir. ill.* 74) as from V., is to be identified with the treatise of the same name that is sometimes ascribed to Tertullian.
4. *De decem virginibus* (*de decem virg.*), an explanation of the parable of the ten virgins (Mt 25:1-13); of questionable authenticity.

V.'s exegesis was based on Gr. models, → Hippolytus and espec. → Origen. It would be a mistake to regard chiliasm, which V. took over from → Papias and → Irenaeus, as the focal point of his theology. More important is his continuing influence as founder of the Lat. reception of Origen.

W: *in apoc.*, J. Haussleiter, CSEL 49:16-154 = PLS 1:103-172. — M. Dulaey, SC 423. — R. E. Wallis, ANL 18:394-433. — ANF 7:344-360. — *fabr. mund.*, J. Haussleiter, CSEL 49:3-9. — R. E. Wallis, ANL 18:388-393. — ANF 7:341-343. — *haer.*, A. Kroymann, CSEL 47:213-226 = CCL 2:1401-1410. — *de decem virg.*, A. Wilmart: BALAC 1 (1911) 35-38 = PLS 1:172-174.
L: C. Curti, Il regno millenario in V: Aug. 18 (1978) 419-433. — M. Dulaey, V. premier exégète latin, 2 vols. (Paris, 1993). — eadem, Jérôme "éditeur" du commentaire sur l'Apocalypse de V.: REAug 37 (1991) 199-236. — J. Fischer, Die Einheit der beiden Testamente bei Laktanz, V. u. deren Quellen: MThZ 1 (1950) 96-101. — J. Haussleiter, Der chiliastische Schlußabschnitt im echten Apokalypsenkommentar des Bischofs V · ThLBl 16 (1895) 193-199. — idem, Beiträge zur Würdigung der Offenbarung des Johannes u. ihres ältesten lat. Auslegers V. (Greifswald, 1901). — HLL 5:410-415. — G. Kretschmar, Die Offenbarung des Johannes (Stuttgart, 1986). — J. Quasten, Patrology 2 (Westminster, Md., 1953), 411-413. — K. H. Schwarte, Die Vorgeschichte der augustinischen Weltalterlehre (Bonn, 1966), 220-226. — E. Schwartz, Zwei Predigten Hippolyts: SBAW 3 (1936) 38-45.

K. H. SCHWARTE

Victorinus, Poet

In a ms. of the 9th/10th c. two centos that probably belong together are handed down under the name of a V. The first, *De lege Domini* (*leg. dom.*), takes up bibl. events down to Ezra; the second, *De nativitate vita passione et resurrectione Domini* (*vita dom.*), tells the story of Christ from his birth to his resurrection. Neither work is very ambitious in language, form, or content. The larger part of the 322 hexameters (in total) is taken more or less verbatim from Ps.-Tertullian, *Carmen adversus Marcionitas* (probably first half of the 5th c.; → Poems, Anonymous); there are also demonstrable borrowings from other works, e.g., the poem *De evangelio*, which is attributed to Hilary, a Gallic poet. V. may himself have been a Gaul, since the rest of the ms. contains only Gallic poems. V.'s dates are uncertain; possibly 5th-8th c. It must also remain uncertain whether the author of these two works can be identified with a Bishop V. named by Isidore, *vir. ill.* 8, as author of short poems against the Manichees and Marcionites. Earlier scholarship ascribed to yet another poet named V. two short hexametric poems, *De Iesu Christo deo et homine* (*Christ.*) and the Ps.-Cyprianic *De pascha*

(also known as *De ligno crucis* and *De cruce*; *pasch.*), but both the dating and authorship of these poems remain unclear.

W: *Christ., vita dom., leg. dom.*, PLS 3:1135-1139, 1139-1142, 1142-1147. — *vita dom.*, A. Mai, Victorini [. . .] carmen, Auctores Classici 5 (Rome, 1833), 382-386 [text]. — *leg. dom.*, A. Oxé, Versus Victorini, Gymn.-Progr. (Krefeld, 1894) [text]. — *pasch.*, PL 2:1171-1174. — G. Hartel, CSEL 3/3:305-308. — A. Roncoroni: RSLR 12 (1976) 380-390 [text/comm.]. — J. Schwind: Ars et Ecclesia, ed. H.-W. Stork, C. Gerhardt, A. Thomas (Trier, 1989), 379-402 [text/German trans./comm.].
L: W. Brandes, Zwei Victoringedichte des Vatic. Regin. 582 u. das carmen adversus Marcionitas: WSt 12 (1890) 310-316. — J. Fontaine, Naissance de la poésie dans l'occident chrétien (Paris, 1981), 278f. — J. Haußleiter, Die Commentare des V., Tichonius u. Hieronymus zur Apokalypse: ZKWL 7 (1886) 239-257. — D. Kartschoke, Bibeldichtung (Munich, 1975), 40, 111-114. — M. Manitius, Geschichte der chr.-lat. Poesie (Stuttgart, 1891), 115-119, 477-479. — K. Pollmann, Das carmen adversus Marcionitas (Göttingen, 1991), 13, 20-22. — M. Schanz, Geschichte der röm. Lit. 4/1 (Munich, 1959 = Munich, [2]1914), 159.

M. MEIER

Victricius of Rouen

V., who is known from → Paulinus of Nola (*ep.* 18; 37), → Sulpicius Severus (*dial.* 3.2), and → Innocent I (*ep.* 2), was b. ca. 340. On the occasion of his *conversio* (360-363), he paid a penalty for abandoning military service. After priestly ordination and missionary activity (among the Nervi and Morini) he became bishop of Rouen between 380 and 386 and, soon after 386, met Martin of Tours and Paulinus of Nola. In 396 the fight against Arianism took him to Britain; in 403 he went to Rome in order to defend himself against the accusation of Apollinarism and to make inquiries about questions of discipline. His only surviving work, *De laude sanctorum* (*laud.*), contains a "theology of relics."

W: J. Mulders, J. Demeulenaere, CCL 64:69-93. — R. Herval (Paris, 1966), 108-153 [text/French trans.]. *laud.*, G. Clark: see at 376-399 [English trans.].
L: P. Andrieu-Guitrancourt, Rouen: ACan 14 (1970) 1-23. — G. Clark, V., Praising the Saints: JECS 7 (1999) 365-399. — J. Fontaine, Origines: Monachisme en Normandie, ed. L. Musset (Paris, 1982), 9-29. — École Française de Rome, Fonctions des saints (Rome, 1991). — E. Griffe, Gaule chrétienne 3 (Paris, 1965), 226-230. — N. Gussone, Adventus: FMSt 10 (1976) 125-133. — R. Herval, Origines (Paris, 1966), 25-28. — Instrumenta Lexicologica A, Fasc. 28, ed. CETEDOC (Turnhout, 1985). — J. Mulders, V.: Bijdr. 17 (1956) 1-25; 18 (1957) 19-40. 270-289. — D. Norberg, Le latin: REAug 34 (1988) 39-46.

M. SKEB, OSB

Vigilius of Rome

V. was bishop of Rome from 537 to 555. Despite an oral promise, V. defied the imperial house in Constantinople and held fast to the decrees of the Council of Chalcedon and the formulations in the *Tomus* of his predecessor, Leo I. By condemning the Three Chapters in 543/544 Justinian I sought to win back the recalcitrant Monophysites and summoned the pope to Constantinople in order to compel his agreement. This the pope gave in the *Iudicatum* of April 11, 548, but the massive protest of the North African bishops forced him to withdraw his decision. In the first *Constitutum* of May 14, 553, V. directly opposed both the emperor and the fifth ecumenical Council of Constantinople, which decreed the condemnation of the Three Chapters on June 2, 553. As a result, V. was banned from the imperial synod, but by signing a second *Constitutum* was able to win release from house arrest. On the way back to Rome he died in Syracuse, after a large part of the Lat. episcopate had rejected communion with him. V. has left twenty-six letters (*ep.*) and records (*acta*), all of them having to do with the Three-Chapters controversy.

W: *ep.,* PL 69:15-114. — *acta,* PL 69:143-178. — PLS 4:1249-1252.
L: F. Carcione, V. nelle controversie cristologiche: SROC 10 (1987) 37-51; 11 (1988) 11-32. — G. Every, Was V. a Victim or an Ally of Justinian: HeyJ 20 (1979) 257-266. — A. Placanica, De epistola V. supposita: Lati. 38 (1990) 25-33. — R. Schieffer, Eine übersehene Fiktion aus dem Dreikapitelstreit: ZKG 101 (1990) 80-87. — C. Sotinel, Arator, un poète au service de la politique de V.: MEFRA 101 (1989) 805-820. — idem, Autorité pontificale et pouvoir impérial: MEFRA 104 (1992) 439-463. — J. Speigl, Leo quem V. condemnavit: FS G. Schwaiger (St. Ottilien, 1990), 1-15. — J. Straub, Die Verurteilung der Drei Kapitel durch V.: Kl. 2 (1970) 347-375. — E. Zettl, Die Bestätigung des 5. Ökumenischen Konzils durch V. (Bonn, 1974).

P. BRUNS

Vigilius of Thapsus

V. was bishop of Thapsus (modern Ras Dimas near Mahdia, Tunisia) and one of the Cath. participants in the religious dialogue of 484 in Carthage under Huneric. Nothing else is known of his life.

Among the genuine writings of V. is the dialogue against Arians, Sabellians, and Photians (*c. Arian.*) in three books. Only the section in which a Catholic debates with an Arian on the Trinity has survived. Also probably authentic is a short work on the same subject against Felician (*c. Felic.*). V. takes up the christological question in a work against Eutyches (*c. Eutych.*); the two anti-Chalcedonian works which he

attacks in these last two works are possibly from Timothy Aelurus. Lost are works against Marebadus and Palladius of Rathiaria, mentioned in *c. Arian.*, as well as a commentary on the Apocalypse, which Cassiodorus, *inst.* 9, ascribes to a V.

Wrongly attributed to V. are, among others, the Ps.-Athanasian *De trinitate* (→ Eusebius of Vercelli) and a Ps.-Augustinian *Contra Varimadum* (*c. Varimad.*).

W: *c. Arian., c. Eutych.,* PL 62:94-238. — *c. Felic.,* PL 42:1157-1172. — *c. Varimad.,* B. Schwank, CCL 90.
L: R. Eno, How original is V.: Aug. 30 (1990) 63-74. — G. Ficker, Studien zu V. (Leipzig, 1897). — B. Schwank, Zur Neuausgabe: SE 12 (1961) 112-196. — M. Simonetti, Letteratura antimonofisita d'Occidente: Aug. 18 (1978) 505-522.

G. RÖWEKAMP

Vigilius of Trent

V. was third bishop of Trent from ca. 385 (Ambrose, *ep.* 17) to 405. The legend-filled 6th-c. *Vita* makes him a martyr, presumably on the basis of the *Martyrium* of monks Sisinnius, Martyrius, and Alexander, whom V. sent as missionaries to the Val di Non. The two letters of V. (*ep.*) to Simplician and John Chrys. tell of their deaths.

W: *ep.,* E. Menestò: I martiri della Val di Non e la reazione pagana alla fine del IV secolo, ed. A. Quacquarelli, I. Rogger (Trent, 1985), 151-170.
L: A. Costa, S. Vigilio (Trent, 1975). — J.-C. Picard, Souvenir des évêques (Rome, 1988), 665f. — I. Rogger, Contrasto di opinioni: I Martiri della Val di Non (op. cit.), 135-148.

B. DÜMLER

Vincent of Lérins

V., a priest-monk in the monastery on the island off Cannes, died before 450. In 434, using the pseudonym "Peregrinus," he composed an *Adversum haereticos* (Gennadius, *vir. ill.* 64), which he himself described as a *Commonitorium*; under this title the work became very important in the church from the 16th c. on. V. learned his language and style from the classical writers, and in this work developed a model for attacks on heresy; in particular, he himself attacked trinitarian and christological errors, espec. those of Nestorius. In the process, he described as Catholic whatever "has been believed everywhere, always, and by all" (*comm.* 2) on the basis of scripture and tradition; the three criteria are to be taken alternatively, not cumulatively. Development is limited to a deeper, unbroken understanding of the content of the faith (*comm.* 23.4) and is comparable to the maturation of a human being or a seed. The second book, on the Council of Ephesus, survives only in a table of contents by V. Semipelagianism, though it had found a home in Lérins, can hardly be detected in this author; it certainly did not mark his dogmatics. V. rejected a radical predestinationism. His supposed opposition to Augustine has become improbable ever since V.'s authorship of the *Obiectiones Vincentianae*, known only through Prosper's answer, has become disputed and since Madoz discovered the *Excerpta* (*exc.*) in which V., as announced in *comm.* 16, defends the Catholic doctrine of the Trinity and the incarnation and does so with extracts from Augustine.

W: *comm.*, *exc.*, R. Demeulenaere, CCL 64. — *comm.*, G. Rauschen (Bonn, 1906) [text with notes]. — G. Rauschen,, BKV² 20 [German trans.]. — U. Uhl (Siegen, 1972 = Kempten, 1870) [German trans.].
I: F. Griffe, Pro V.: BLE 62 (1961) 26-31. — K. J. Hefele, V. u. sein comm.: idem, Beiträge zur Kirchengeschichte 1 (Tübingen, 1864), 145-174. — H. Kremser, Die Bedeutung des V. für die röm.-kath. Wertung der Trad. (Hamburg, 1959). — E. Krursel, Traditio catholica u. profectus fidei bei V.: UnaVoceKorrespondenz 24 (1994) 67-79. — J. Madoz, Cultura humanística de s. V., RSR 39 (1951/52) 461-471. — idem, Excerpta V. (Madrid, 1940). — W. O'Connor, St. Vincent of L. and St. Augustine (Rome, 1964).

H.-L. BARTH

Vita

The history of Chr. biographical literature begins with the gospels. NT scholarship, in its critique of life-of-Jesus research during the past century, did indeed emphasize the uniqueness of the gospels and think that their specific character as preaching made them for the most part an independent genre created by Mark and alien to their Jewish and Gr.-Roman world. Recently, however, voices have been increasingly raised to ask, with good arguments, for a new and more nuanced approach to the question of genre. Ancient biography must be understood as a very complex genre that was capable of development and had many subtypes, while being itself part of the larger world of hist. literature in which more or less strong rhetorical influences, e.g., of the encomium (address of praise; → Panegyric) were at work. The gospels fit very nicely into the genre of Gr.-Roman *Vitae*. Special note must be taken of the relationship with the biographical sections of the Heb. Bible and the LXX as well as with the relevant literature of Hellen. Judaism. Looking beyond the limits of the canon, the noncanonical literature on Jesus can be

viewed in a similar way. The canonical Acts of the Apostles, on the other hand, is a hist. work in the style of comprehensive, universal hist. description with biog. sections, whereas the fictitious, noncanonical Acts of the apostles that were composed from the 2nd c. on in emulation of canonical Acts (→ Apocryphal Writings) and the → Clementines, Pseudo-), belong to the novelistic literature of the ancient world; in some ways they resemble the lives of the philosophers written during the imperial age.

In his *History of the Church* → Eusebius of Caesarea took as his model Luke's hist. work (gospels and Acts) and the hist. writings of Jewish author Flavius Josephus. He had available in Caesarea the treasures of what was the best Chr. library of the age, the one started by Origen and considerably expanded by presbyter Pamphilus. Here researchers, like the Alex. literary scholars of the Serapeion, had at hand a catalogue of authors, with short biographies of each, organized acc. to a strict pattern and with details of their works; Eusebius appended this catalogue to his lost *Vita* of his teacher, Pamphilus, who died a martyr in 310. Relying on this catalogue, he composed the notices, in chronol. order, of the lives and works of eccles. writers in the course of his history. Origen, whom he and Pamphilus defended in a work of which only a little remains, became the main subject of book 6 of the history. This section may be read on its own and compared with the contemporary *Vitae* of non-Chr. philosophers. In 393, → Jerome, at Bethlehem, used the relevant information in Eusebius's history in order to write, at the request of a friend who referred to Suetonius's *De viris illustribus*, a Chr. counterpart to that work on Roman writers. Jerome's chronologically organized, bio-bibliographical lexicon, which in some biographies followed a factual order, as Suetonius had, was circulated under the same title as Suetonius's work and was later continued by → Gennadius of Marseilles, → Isidore of Seville, and → Ildefonsus of Toledo. Eusebius also wrote the *Vita Constantini*, an encomiastic biography with emphasis on the emperor's actions on behalf of Christians; the work contains numerous documents, which suggests that the author of this posthumously published work also intended to continue his history of the church.

The series of *Vitae* of saints, which became very influential as veneration of the saints became increasingly important and which made a profound impression on piety in the church, began with the *Vita Cypriani*, which was authored by Carthaginian Deacon → Pontius, acc. to Jerome (*vir. ill.* 68). Without names being mentioned, it is clear that this *Vita*,

599

composed after 258 with a knowledge of the Acts of Cyprian's martyrdom, was written in competition with the *Passio* of Perpetua and Felicity, which was composed in Carthage, shortly after their deaths (203), for public reading during the liturgy (→ Martyrs, Acts of the). The composer of the *Vita Cypriani* uses the language of Chr. martyrdom, including the borrowed words *martyr* and *martyrium*, which came into Chr. Latin from Greek; by his emphasis, right at the beginning, on Cyprian as a *testis Dei gloriosus* he shows that he understands the original meaning of the two terms. He is not satisfied, however, to describe a death that is glorious because of his conviction of Cyprian's saintliness; he also wants to use the rhetorical devices of the encomium to shed a proper light on the exemplary episcopal activity of Cyprian the martyr, *qui et sine martyrio habuit quae doceret* (1.2).

The *Vita Cypriani*, which Jerome correctly describes as *vita et passio*, points out a way in which people in the church could have come directly to the veneration of holy bishops and the writing of their *Vitae*, even though till now no one had traveled this way. In time of persecution the title of martyr was the sole basis for liturgical veneration; then men and women from the monastic world entered into the inheritance of the martyrs; it was only at this point that veneration as saints was extended to individual bishops.

Within this development, the *Vita Antonii* of → Athanasius of Alexandria was very influential. Quite disparate attempts to show a non-Christian *Vita* as model for the life of the Egypt. hermit have been unsuccessful. Perhaps Athanasius knew Porphyry's *Vita Plotini*; he probably drew on a *Vita* of Pythagoras now and then. It is probably more to the point, however, that he had in mind the kind of contemporary lives of the philosophers that always described the spiritual journey of a philosopher until he discovered his real task in life, and then his carrying out of it; he probably realized that in philosophical circles an ascetic way of life was highly esteemed. The first part of the *Vita Antonii* is shaped by the model of a supernatural ascent; the struggles with demons may well be taken over from the earlier thematic of martyrdom as a victory over the devil, espec. since Anthony is described as a martyr in desire and his asceticism as a spiritual martyrdom (46-47). The many references to the Bible play a key role, e.g., to the stories of the prophet Elijah, as do the references to christology and soteriology and their importance for the image of the martyr; the two addresses reflect the parenetic intention of the *Vita* as a whole, which

is to make Anthony a model of Chr. and eccles. monasticism.

The influence of the *Vita Antonii* on Egypt. monasticism can be seen espec. in the Sahidic translation. The present state of research makes it difficult to decide whether and to what extent the *Vita Antonii* gave rise to the biog. writings on Pachomius (d. 346/347) and his first successors. In any case, the Copt. Pachomius tradition specifically mentions Anthony, and the *Vita prima graeca Pachomii* expressly refers to the *Vita* by Athanasius, to which it is heavily indebted. The *Vita Antonii* was translated into all the languages of the Chr. East; its influence in the western part of the Roman empire is attested by, among other things, two early Lat. translations: an older, literal one and the artistic one, published before 375, by → Evagrius of Antioch, host to Jerome during the latter's stay there. It was probably in the wastes of Chalcis, not far from Antioch, where Jerome tried the eremitical life for himself, that he wrote the *Vita Pauli* as a counterpart and complement of the *Vita Antonii*, two scenes in a fairy-tale and paradisal world, with the intention of showing his earlier hero, Paul, outdoing Anthony. Then, in Bethlehem ca. 390, he composed his *Vita Malchi*, which is rather an *exemplum* of chastity with elements from the Hellen. novel, and his *Vita* of the Palestinian monk Hilarion (again following the *Vita Antonii*), which continued to influence Palestine later on, as can be seen from the 6th-c. *Vitae* by → Cyril of Scythopolis of other monastic fathers of this region. Jerome, who gives a lot of space to the wonderworking activity of Hilarion, was at the same time the author of letters of consolation on the deaths of many women in his circle of ascetical friends; the best known is *ep.* 108 on the death of Paula (d. 404), addressed to her daughter Eustochium. These letters, a christianized form of the ancient *consolatio* and the *laudatio funebris* are, of course, not *Vitae* in the strict sense, but they must be mentioned for the sake of a correct picture of Jerome's hagiography.

→ Sulpicius Severus, whose *Vita Martini* placed him in the tradition of the Lat. translation of the *Vita Antonii* by Evagrius and of Roman historiography, wrote a whole file of material about his saint, with the addition of three letters and dialogues, the aim of the latter being to exalt the Gallic monk-bishop over the Egypt. monks. The author was interested in the kind of monk who remained true to himself even as a bishop; he thus opened the door that led in the Lat. West to the liturgical veneration of individual bishops. The historical situation in Gaul, where many outstanding bishops came from monasticism, was the reason why the ideal of the holy monk-bishop was widely received and marked the form taken by many Gallic *Vitae*. It is all the more striking, therefore, that the *Vita Ambrosii* of Milanese Deacon → Paulinus, composed in perhaps 412/413 at the instigation of Augustine in North Africa, names at its beginning the *Vitae* of Paul, Anthony, and Martin, along with their authors, but then puts in the foreground the conduct of Ambrose in his office as a bishop whose holiness is given a monastic basis but not independently of that conduct. The *Vita Augustini*, written shortly after Augustine's death (430) by Possidius of Calama, a man from Augustine's monastic school, depicts in a manner reminiscent of Suetonius the distinction between the bishop's private and public lives, between the monastic teacher and the writer, although this last aspect is underscored by the addition to the *Vita* of a catalogue of writings (*indiculum*).

In the Gr. East, the change in the ideal of holiness in the 4th c. can be easily studied in the writings of → Gregory Nyss. On the feasts of the martyrs Gregory preached on witnesses who shed their blood; in the *Vita Macrinae* of his sister, he gave a picture of the life of an outstanding representative of monasticism in Asia Minor; other sermons, which were to some extent developed into *Vitae*, spread the new ideal of the saintly bishop (*Vita Gregorii Thaumaturgi*, sermons on Meletius of Antioch and on Gregory's brother Basil of Caesarea). As a result of this development, almost every region of the early church had its *Vitae*. By way of an extension of the picture thus far described, a reference must be made to the series of rhetorical *Vitae* of the bishops of Arles (Honoratus, Hilary, Caesarius), to → Venantius Fortunatus and his *Vitae* of subsequent Gallic bishops and his description of the life of Radegunde, daughter of a Thuringian king. The *Commonitorium vitae s. Severini* describes some episodes in the energetic activity of the prophetic monk by the Danube, whose bones were finally brought to Naples, where hagiographer → Eugippius was active. For Constantinople reference may be made to → Palladius of Helenopolis, *Dialogus de vita s. Ioannis Chrysostomi*, and to → Callinicus, *Vita Hypatii*; for Syria, to Gr. and Syr. lives of the stylites, Simeon the Elder and Simeon the Younger; for Palestine, to → Gerontion, *Vita Melaniae Iunioris*; and for North Africa, to Ferrandus of Carthage, *Vita episcopi Fulgentii de Ruspe*, which, like other North African biographies of bishops, gets by without miracles.

The picture is to be completed by works containing collections of short biographies: → Timothy I of Alexandria, → *Historia monachorum in Aegypto*, which originated in a pilgrimage to the Egypt. monks; → Palladius of Helenopolis, *Historia Lausiaca*, with its attention to many women; → Theodoret of Cyrrhus, *Historia religiosa* on Syr. ascetics, both men and women; John Moschus, *Pratum spirituale*; → Gregory I, *Dialogi*, with its life of Benedict of Nursia and its many stories of Italian monks; → Gregory of Tours, *Liber vitae patrum,* on Gallic saints of the 4th to the 6th c. Series of lives of bishops were collected by, e.g., the Roman church in the → *Liber pontificalis* and by the Alex. church in the history of the patriarchs that has come down in Arabic. Compilers put together collections containing large numbers of *Vitae.* The most famous collection in the East is that which Simeon Metaphrastes (d. ca. 1000) made for liturg. use; it led to the suppression of older collections. In the West men in monasteries collected, in different forms, → *Vitae Patrum* (*Vitas Patrum*), usually translations from the Gr., but also including holy women and the *Vitae* and relevant letters of Jerome. The collections of → Apophthegmata (*Verba seniorum*), which were usually included, might in particular cases contain biog. notices, but they do not belong in the genre of the *Vita* in the strict sense of the term.

W: *Vitae patrum,* PL 73-74. — BHG mit Novum Auctarium (1984). — BHL mit Novum Supplementum (1986) — BHO. — G. Bardy, Biographies spirituelles — 1. Antiquité chrétienne: DSp 1:1624-1634. — Vite dei Santi 1-4, ed. C. Mohrmann (Milan, 1974-1975) [text/Italian trans./comm.].
I.: L'agiografia latina nei secoli IV-VII: Aug. 24/1-2 (1984). — R. Aigrain, L'hagiographie (Paris, 1953). — D. E. Aune, The New Testament in Its Literary Environment (Philadelphia, 1987). — T. D. Barnes, Panegyric, History and Hagiography in Eusebius' Life of Constantine: FS H. Chadwick (Cambridge, 1989), 94-123. — G. J. M. Bartelink, Die lit. Gattung der Vita Antonii: VigChr 36 (1982) 38-62. — T. Baumeister, Heiligenverehrung 1: RAC 14, 96-150. — idem, Der hl. Bischof: StPatr 18/3 (1989) 275-282. — K. Berger, Hellenistische Gattungen im NT: ANRW II 25/2 (1984) 1031-1432. — W. Berschin, Biographie u. Epochenstil im lat. MA 1-2 (Stuttgart, 1986-1988). — R. Blum, Die Literaturverzeichnung im Altertum u. MA (Frankfurt a.M., 1983). — R. A. Burridge, What Are the Gospels? A Comparison with Graeco-Roman Biography (Cambridge, 1992). — A. Ceresa-Gastaldo (ed.), Biografia e agiografia nella letteratura cristiana antica e medievale (Trient, 1990). — Connaissance des Pères de l'Église Nr. 56 (1994): Les vies de saints (therein: S. Deléani, La Vita Cypriani, 9-13). — P. Cox, Biography in Late Antiquity (Berkeley, 1983). — D. M. Deliyannis, A Biblical Model for Serial Biography: RBen 107 (1997) 15-23. — A. de Vogüé, Histoire littéraire du mouvement monastique dans l'antiquité 1-2 (Paris, 1991-1993). — D. Frickenschmidt, Evangelium als Biographie (Tübingen, 1997). — Gerolamo e la biografia letteraria (Genoa, 1989). — H. Görgemanns, W. Berschin, Biogra-

phie: Der Neue Pauly 2:682-689. — T. J. Heffernan, Sacred Biography (New York, 1988). — D. Hoster, Die Form der frühesten lat. Heiligenv. von der V. Cypriani bis zur V. Ambrosii u. ihr Heiligenideal, Diss. (Cologne, 1963). — H. Kech, Hagiographie als chr. Unterhaltungsliteratur (Göppingen, 1977). — G. Luck, Die Form der suetonischen Biographie u. die frühen Heiligenviten: FS T. Klauser (Münster, 1964), 230-241. — C. Ludwig, Sonderformen byz. Hagiographie u. ihr lit. Vorbild (Frankfurt a.M., 1997). — E. Mühlenberg, Les débuts de la biographie chrétienne: RThPh 122 (1990) 517-529. — T. Payr, Enkomion: RAC 5, 332-343. — G. Philippart (ed.), Hagiographies 1 (Tournai, 1994) (esp.: V. Saxer, Afrique latine, 25-95; A. A. R. Bastiaensen, Jérôme hagiographe, 97-123). — J. Roldanus, Die Vita Antonii als Spiegel der Theologie des Athanasius u. ihr Weiterwirken im 5. Jh.: ThPh 58 (1983) 194-216. — E. Schulz-Flügel, Zur Entstehung der Corpora Vitae Patrum: StPatr 20 (1989) 289-300. — A. M. Schwemer, Vitae Prophetarum (Gütersloh, 1997). — A. Spira (ed.), The Biographical Works of Gregory of Nyssa (Cambridge, Mass., 1984). — M. van Uytfanghe, Heiligenverehrung 2 (Hagiographie): RAC 14:150-183. — D. v. der Nahmer, Die lat. Heiligenvita (Darmstadt, 1994). — B. R. Voss, Berührungen von Hagiographie u. Historiographie in der Spätantike: FMSt 4 (1970) 53-69.

T. BAUMEISTER

Vitae Patrum

Vitae Patrum (originally *Vitas Patrum*) is the name given, in the 6th c. at the latest, to a Lat. collection of lives of eastern monks. It includes (1) descriptions of the lives of the monastic fathers (*Vita Antonii, Pauli, Hilarionis*), as well as of converted female sinners (*Vita Mariae Aegypticae*); (2) collections of apophthegmata; (3) accounts of the journeys and experiences of eastern monks (*Historia Monachorum*; *Historia Lausiaca*). In the Middle Ages *Vitae* from the western tradition were introduced, beginning with Gallic monasticism (fathers of the Jura; Martin; Hilary), as was the *Pratum spirituale* of → John Moschus.

W: PL 73/74.
L: C. M. Batlle, Die Adhortationes Sanctorum Patrum (Verba Seniorum) im MA (Münster, 1972). — W. Berschin, Biographie u. Epochenstil 1 (Stuttgart, 1986). — E. Schulz-Flügel, Zur Entstehung der Corpora Vitae Patrum: StPatr 20 (1989) 289-300. — A. Solignac, Vitae Patrum: DSp 16:1029-1035.

J. PAULI, OSB

Vitalis, Apollinarist

V., along with Timothy, was one of those Apollinarists who were close in outlook to the Great Church. After Damasus of Rome had accepted him, Apollinaris consecrated him bishop of Antioch in 376. His only surviving work is a little fragment on christol-

ogy, which may possibly come from the profession of faith he made to Damasus (*De fide*).

W: *fr.*, H. Lietzmann, Apollinaris u. seine Schule (Hildesheim, 1970 = Tübingen, [1]1904), 273 [text] — ACO 1,1,5. 67f.
L: F. Diekamp, Das Glaubensbekenntnis des apollinaristischen Bischofs V.: ThQ 86 (1904) 497-511.

G. FEIGE

Viventiolus

V., originally a monk in Condat, was bishop of Lyons 514-524 and an important personage at councils in the kingdom of Burgundy. His letter to the bishops of the eccles. province of Lyons is preserved in which he invites them to the Synod of Epao in 517 (*ep.*). Among the letters of Avitus of Vienne is one from V. to Avitus (*Alc. Avit. ep.*).

W: *ep.*, PL 67:993. — C. de Clercq, CCL 148A:23f. — *Alc. Avit. ep.*, PL 59:272.
L: A. Coville, Recherches sur l'histoire de Lyon (Paris, 1928), 308-316. — P. Riché, V.: MÂ 63 (1957) 425-428.

G. RÖWEKAMP

Vulgate

Vulgate is today the name of the official Lat. translation of the Bible. The translation goes back in large measure to the activity of Jerome the translator. By commission of Roman Bishop Damasus, Jerome began translating the gospels in 383 (whether he also translated other books of the NT is uncertain) and then turned espec. to the books of the OT. Probably between 390 and 405/406 he had translated most of the OT from the Heb. original (except for Bar, Wis, Sir, 1-2 Mac).

Only after considerable difficulties, which lasted into the 8th c., did his translation carry the day under the title of *(editio) vulgata*, a title which, however, had previously been given to the LXX and the → *Vetus Latina*. Until the 13th c., Old Latin texts were in use alongside the Vulgate and even made their way to some extent into mss. of the Vulgate. Efforts to restore a correct Vulgate text had only temporary success.

At the desire of Charlemagne, Alcuin (ca. 730-804) revised the Vulgate and eliminated many of the Old Latin texts that had found their way into it. He was also responsible for replacing the *iuxta Hebraeos* translation of the Psalms with the Old Latin translation that Jerome corrected, after 386, acc. to the Hexapla of Origen.

This revision became the most important source

of the text that became normative, from the 13th c. on, at the University of Paris. On April 8, 1546, the Council of Trent decreed that the *vetus et vulgata editio* was to be authentic (reliable, probative) in matters of faith and morals, but the council did not prohibit further study of the original text. The possibility was also left open of still establishing a reliable text of the Vulgate. None of the revisions made toward the end of the 16th c. satisfied this requirement. Only in 1954, with the publication of Rev, was a new edition of the NT completed that met the desired standards. In 1907 Pius X entrusted the Benedictine Order with the revision of the Vulgate OT. The work of a Vulgate commission established for this purpose is being continued today at the abbey of St. Jerome in Rome.

W: Biblia sacra iuxta vulgatam versionem, ed. R. Weber et al. (Stuttgart, ³1983).
L: O. Eissfeldt, Einleitung in das AT (Tübingen, ²1956), 872f. — B. Fischer, Der Vulgatatext des NT: ZNW 46 (1955) 178-196. — (A. Wikenhauser), J. Schmid, Einleitung in das NT (Freiburg i.Br., ⁶1973), 105-124. — R. Smend, Bibel: BHH 1:242f. — H. J. Vogels, Vulgatastudien, NTA 14:2-3 (Munich, 1928). — idem, Handbuch der Textkritik des NT (Bonn, ²1955), 78-110, 152-220.

A. SAND

Z

Zachariah, Apocalypse of

An *Apocalypse of Zachariah* is thought to be a source of the *Protoevangelium* of → James and of later legends about Z. and his son, John the Baptist. Only a few Copt. fragments of the work have been preserved; they come from the 3rd/4th c. and contain apocryphal reports of the childhood of the Baptist and the slaying of his father, Z.

W: H. Wall, Childhood of John the Baptist: RdE 8 (1951) 207-214 [text/English trans.].
L: A. Berendts, Studien über Z.-Apokryphen (Leipzig, 1895). — idem, Handschriftliche Überlieferung (Leipzig, 1904).

P. BRUNS

Zacharias of Jerusalem

Z. was patriarch of Jerusalem from 609 on and, during the Sassanid invasion in 614, was taken off to Persia, where he died ca. 628. From there he wrote a letter of consolation which his successor Modestus carried back and which has come down in various versions.

W: PG 86:3228-3233. — G. Garitte, CSCO 202/203:70-76/46-50 [Georgian text/Latin trans.]. — idem, CSCO 340/341:49-53/33-35 [Arabic text/Latin trans.].
L: G. Graf, Die Einnahme Jerusalems durch die Perser 614: HlL 67 (1923) 19-29. — J.-M. Sauget, Z.: BSS 12:1451-1453.

G. RÖWEKAMP

Zacharias Rhetor

Z., whom Dionysius bar Salibi identifies with Zacharias Scholasticus, was born ca. 465 in Maiuma. He studied in Alexandria (under the sophist Ammonius, among others) and in Berytus. This friend of Severus, the later patriarch of Antioch, worked as a rhetor in Constantinople and filled some higher civil offices. After 512, the former Monophysite professed Neo-Chalcedonianism, became bishop of Mytilene on Lesbos after 527, and died before 553. Z.'s works include biographies, a history of the church, and apologetic writings. Among the biog. works are a *Vita* of Severus of Antioch until the year 512 (*vit. Sev.*), written 512-518 and preserved only in a Syr. translation; a *Vita* of Peter the Iberian (*vit. Petri*) of which only a Syr. fragment survives; a *Vita*, again preserved only in a Syr. translation, of Egyptian ascetic Isaias (*Vit. Is.*) who lived in Palestine; and a lost *Vita* of Bishop Theodore of Antinoai. The so-called *History of the Church* (*h.e.*) was composed after 492, probably in Greek, at the behest of Eupraxius, an imperial official, but it survives only in a Syr. translation as books 3-6 of the comprehensive church history of an unknown monk from Amida in Armenia; these books cover the years 450-491. Z.'s work is not based on sources but conveys only his personal experiences. → Evagrius Scholasticus used it as the basis of books 2-3 of his church history. Among Z.'s apologetic works are the dialogue *De mundi opificio contra philosophos disputatio* (*opif.*) between Z. and a student of Ammonius on the createdness and finiteness of the world; and the *Disputatio contra Manichaeos* (*disp.*) in seven chapters, written in 527 as a refutation of a Manichean work.

W: *h.e.*, PG 85:1145-1178. — E. W. Brooks, CSCO 83f., 87f. [text/Latin trans.]. — K. Ahrens, G. Krüger (Leipzig, 1899) [German trans.]. — *opif.*, PG 85:1012-1144. — M. Minniti Colonna (Naples, 1973) [text/Italian trans./comm.]. — *disp.*, M. Richard, CCG 1:33f. — *vit. Sev.*, M. A. Kugener, PO 2:7-115 [text]. — *vit. Is.*, E. W. Brooks, CSCO 7/8:1-16, 3-10 [text/Latin trans.]. — *vit. Petri*, E. W. Brooks, CSCO 7/8:18/1 [text/Latin trans.].
L: P. Allen, Z.: JThS 31 (1980) 471-488. — G. Bardy, Z.: DThC 15/2:3676-3680. — W. Bauer, Aufsätze u. kleine Schriften (Tübingen, 1967), 210-228. — S. P. Brock, Syriac historical writing: idem, Studies in Syriac Christianity (Hampshire, 1992), 1-30. — A. Guillaumont, Un nouveau texte: AnBoll 68 (1949) 350-360. — E. Honigmann, Patristic Studies (Rome, 1953), 194-204. — M. A. Kugener, Z.: ROC 5 (1900) 201-214, 461-480. — B. Tatakis, La philosophie byzantine (Paris, 1949), 34-37. — K. Wengenast, Z.: PRE 9A/2:2212-2217.

C. SCHMIDT

Zeno, Emperor

An Isaurian by birth and the son-in-law of Emperor Leo I, Z. (b. 426) first became *magister militum per Orientem*. As emperor (474-475 and 476-491), Z. had first to survive the conspiracy that brought Basiliscus to the throne (475-476). In August 476 Z. returned to power. He persuaded Theodoric to attack Odoacer in Italy. He attempted to make peace with the Monophysites by means of the *Henotikon*, a compromise formula drawn up by Patriarch Acacius in 482, but neither the Monophysites nor the orthodox were satisfied with it. The result of the failed attempt at union was the Acacian Schism (481-519) between Byzantium and Rome.

L: T. E. Gregory, Z.: ODB 2223. — A. Kramalude, Οἱ μεταβολὲς στὴν πολιτικὴ τοῦ Ζήνωνα: Symmeikta 6

(1985) 79-90. — D. Pingree, Political horoscopes: DOP 30 (1976) 133-150.

F. R. GAHBAUER, OSB

Zeno of Verona

Acc. to local tradition Z. was the eighth bishop of Verona, between 360 and 380. The earliest source of information on him is *ep.* 5.1 of Ambrose (after 380), which attests to an already deceased Bishop Z. At the beginning of the 5th c. Petronius of Bologna (or Verona) delivered a sermon in Verona on occasion of the *dies natalis* of Z. The legends begin in *dial.* 3.19 of Gregory of Tours.

Eleven mss., the oldest from the 8th c., attribute to Z. the earliest Lat. collection of sermons: ninety-three *tractatus* with only thirty complete sermons, the remainder being short outlines or drafts of sermons. After Z.'s death these were published for liturg. use in the territory of Verona. (On doubts about Z.'s authorship see → Geminianus of Modena.) The contents are homilies explaining chiefly OT texts, exhortations on virtues and vices, and texts explaining the baptismal and Easter liturgies. In refuting Arianism and Photinianism Z. deals with questions of trinitarian theology and christology in accord with Nicaea but in an archaizing way. In addition, he shows a deep interest in mariology. Information on the history of religions can be derived from the attacks on pagans and Jews. In their form, the tractates follow the ancient diatribe and take over the structure of epideictic oratory. Hitherto, indications of a possible African origin of Z. have been seen in an Asianism of the Apuleian type, numerous echoes of Tertullian, Cyprian, and Lactantius, and the introduction of the *Passio* of the Mauretanian martyr Arcadius into the body of sermons (*tract.* 1.39).

W: PL 11:9-760. — G. B. Giuliari (Verona, 1900) [text/comm.]. — B. Löfstedt, CCL 22. — G. Ederle, 4 vols. (Verona, 1955-60) [text/Italian trans.]. — G. Banterle (Milan, 1987) [text/Italian trans.]. — A. Bigelmaier, BKV² 2. Reihe, 10 (Munich, 1934) [German trans.].
L: A. Bigelmaier, Z. (Münster, 1904). — HLL 5:421-425. — R. Kampling, Juden: Kairos 26 (1984) 16-27. — B. M. Löfstedt, D. W. Packard, Concordance (New York, 1975). — L. Padovese, Pensiero etico-sociale (Rome, 1983). — L. Palanca, Prose Rhythm and Gorgianic Figures (Washington, 1970). — G. Sgreva, Teologia (Vicenza, 1989). — C. Truzzi, Z., Gaudenzio e Cromazio (Brescia, 1985). — idem, Liturgia: StPatr 27 (1980) 539-564. — O. Vincentini, Morale: StPatr 19 (1982) 241-284. — F. E. Vokes, Apuleius and Africa: TU 93 (1966) 130-134.

B. DÜMLER

Zephaniah, Apocalypse of

The *Apocalypse of Zephaniah* is regarded as a pseudepigraphical Jewish work with lengthy Chr. expansions, espec. in the surviving Copt. version. It probably comes from the first c. C.E. and teaches the difference between the special and general judgment of souls after death.

W: R. F. G. Steindorff, Die Apokalypse des Elias (Leipzig, 1899) [Coptic text/German trans.]. — P. Rießler, Altjüd. Schrifttum (Heidelberg, 1928), 168-177 [German trans.].

P. BRUNS

Zephyrinus of Rome

Z. was successor of Victor I as bishop of Rome (198/199-217). Hippolytus (*haer.* 9.11f.) accused him of being a supporter of Modalism under the influence of his archdeacon and later successor, Callistus, and of favoring the Monarchian doctrine of the Logos as seen in Patripassionism.

Z. or one of his clerics is credited with the Ps.-Tertullian treatise *Adversus omnes haereses*, which Victorinus of Pettau translated into Latin and which was later revised along anti-Origenist lines.

W: A. Kroymann, CSEL 47:213-226. — idem, CCL 2:1399-1410. — R. F. Refoulé, P. de Labriolle, SC 46.
L: E. Amann, Z.: DThC 15/2:3690f.

C. SCHMIDT

Zosimas

Born in Sinde near Tyre of Phoenicia, Z. was initially a monk in that area and ca. 520 founded his own monastery in Sindenai near Caesarea Maritima. He is probably not to be identified with Zosimas the Cilician (PG 87:3033A), who lived in Palestine at about the same time and later became bishop of Cairo. Z. has left some sayings (*Alloquia*) addressed to monks.

W: PG 78:1680-1700. — K. Chrestou, Kephalaia ophelima, Philokalia ton neptikon kai asketikon 12 (Thessalonica, 1981), 123-199 [Greek text/modern Greek trans.].
L: L. Regnault, Les Apophthegmes des Pères en Palestine aux Vᵉ-VIᵉ siècles: Irén. 54 (1981) 320-330. — A. Solignac, Zosime: DSp 16:1658. — S. Vailhé, Saint Dorothée et saint Zosime: EO 4 (1901) 359-363.

J. PAULI, OSB

Zosimus, Historian

Of Z. we know only that for a time he held the office of an *advocatus fisci*, a legal expert in the imperial finance administration, and held the title of *comes*.

His *New History* (*Historia nea*) in six books comes probably from the period around 500. The presentation, which starts with what is hardly more than a list of emperors but then becomes increasingly detailed, covers the period from the reign of Augustus to shortly before the capture of Rome by Alaric in the summer of 410. This abrupt ending, as well as the limited extent of book 6, suggests that the work remained incomplete. Z.'s chief sources were probably Eunapius of Sardis and → Olympiodorus.

Acc. to 1.57.1, Z. intends to complete Polybius, who in the second c. B.C.E. described the rise of the Roman world empire by describing its rapid decline. In his view, the reason for the decline was chiefly the neglect of the old Roman gods in favor of Chr. monotheism. The earthly image of this heavenly monarchy, namely, the reign of the emperors since Constantine, was condemned to collapse espec. because of the size of the realm (1.5.3f.). Z. thus clearly opposes the Chr. theology of history hinted at in → Eusebius of Caesarea. Because of this pagan viewpoint the *New History* becomes very important for the history of culture, but Z.'s accomplishments as a historian are modest. His language is simple and almost free of rhetorical adornment, but it is by no means always clear.

W: F. Paschoud (Paris, 1971-89) [text/French trans./comm.]. — R. T. Ridley (Sydney, 1982) [English trans./comm.]. — O. Veh, S. Rebenich (Stuttgart, 1990) [German trans./comm.].
L: A. E. Baker, Eunapius and Z. (Providence, 1987). — H. Cichocka, La prose rythmique de Z.: JÖB 32/3 (1982) 345-354. — eadem, Periodenkonstruktion bei Z.: JÖB 35 (1985) 93-112. — eadem, Z.' Account of Christianity: SicGym 43 (1990) 171-183. — K.-H. Leven, Zur Polemik des Z.: FS I. Opelt (Frankfurt a.M., 1988), 177-197. — F. Paschoud, Z.: PRE 10/2:795-841. — idem, Cinq études sur Z. (Paris, 1975). — idem, Z. et la fin de l'ouvrage historique d'Eunape: Orph. 6 (1985) 44-61. — idem, Z. et Constantin: MH 54 (1997) 9-28. — Z. Petre, La pensée historique de Z.: Studii Clasice 7 (1965) 263-272. — R. T. Ridley, Z. the Historian: ByZ 65 (1972) 277-302. — D. Scavone, Z. and His Historical Models: GRBS 11 (1970) 57-67.

U. HAMM

Zosimus of Rome

From Z., a Greek, who was bishop of Rome 417-418, there have come down fifteen letters (*ep.*) that docu-

ment, above all, his undiplomatic actions in the controversy with the Gallic bishops over the appointment of Patroclus of Arles as metropolitan and his equally clumsy behavior toward the African church in two other instances. After having rehabilitated Pelagius and Caelestius, he was forced, under pressure from the Africans, officially to condemn Pelagius in the *Epistula tractoria*. Equally unsuccessful were his instructions after the appeal from Apiarius across the sea. In the course of these controversies Z. formulated for the first time the claim to a papal *primatus iurisdictionis* (*ep*. 12.1).

W: *ep.*, PL 20:649-686, 693-695, 703f. — PLS 1:797. — S. Wenzlowsky, BKV[1] Papstbriefe 3:225-306 [German trans.]. L: E. Caspar, Papsttum 1 (Tübingen, 1930), 344-360. — D. Frye, Early Fifth-Century Gaul: JEH 42 (1991) 349-361. — E. Griffe, Gaule chrétienne 2 (Paris, 1966), 147-152, 198-200. — W. Marschall, Karthago u. Rom (Stuttgart, 1971), 150-159, 166-173. — C. Pietri, Roma Christiana 2 (Rome, 1976), 933-948, 1000-1021, 1222-1254, 1472-1480. — O. Wermelinger, Tractoria: FZPhTh 26 (1979) 336-368. — idem, Rom u. Pelagius (Stuttgart, 1975), 134-218.

B. DÜMLER

Zostrianos

Zostrianos is the title of a much-mutilated treatise in the Coptic gnostic Nag Hammadi library (NHC 8, 1) that describes a heavenly journey and offers the usual gnostic anthropology without Chr. additions. The human body is regarded as a prison of the soul, bringing only suffering and grief to the soul. The high god, a thrice-powerful, invisible spirit, is regarded as the source of all that is good; in its flight from the world the soul relies on the knowledge revealed by angels to Z. and → Seth.

W: J. H. Sieber, NHC VIII (Leiden, 1991), 7-225 [Coptic text/English trans./comm.]. — NHL 402-430 [English trans.].
L: L. Abramowski, NHC 8, 1: JAC. E 10 (1983) 1-10. — C. Colpe, Heidnische und jüd. Überlieferung: JAC 20 (1977) 149-170. — M. Scopello, Zostr. and Enoch: VigChr 34 (1980) 376-385. — J. H. Sieber, Barbelo Aeon: Sethian Gnosticism, ed. B. Layton (Leiden, 1981), 788-795.

P. BRUNS

Index of Names